Oxford Dictionary of National Biography

IN ASSOCIATION WITH

The British Academy

From the earliest times to the year 2000

Edited by

H. C. G. Matthew

and

Brian Harrison

Volume 32

Knox–Lear

OXFORD
UNIVERSITY PRESS

OXFORD
UNIVERSITY PRESS

Great Clarendon Street, Oxford OX2 6DP

Oxford University Press is a department of the University of Oxford.
It furthers the University's objective of excellence in research, scholarship,
and education by publishing worldwide in

Oxford New York

Auckland Bangkok Buenos Aires Cape Town
Chennai Dar es Salaam Delhi Hong Kong Istanbul Karachi
Kolkata Kuala Lumpur Madrid Melbourne Mexico City Mumbai Nairobi
São Paulo Shanghai Taipei Tokyo Toronto

Oxford is a registered trade mark of Oxford University Press
in the UK and in certain other countries

Published in the United States
by Oxford University Press Inc., New York

British Library Cataloguing in Publication Data
Data available

Library of Congress Cataloging in Publication Data
Data available: for details see volume 1, p. iv

ISBN 0-19-861382-2 (this volume)
ISBN 0-19-861411-X (set of sixty volumes)

Text captured by Alliance Phototypesetters, Pondicherry
Illustrations reproduced and archived by
Alliance Graphics Ltd, UK
Typeset in OUP Swift by Interactive Sciences Limited, Gloucester
Printed in Great Britain on acid-free paper by
Butler and Tanner Ltd,
Frome, Somerset

LIST OF ABBREVIATIONS

1 *General abbreviations*

AB	bachelor of arts
ABC	Australian Broadcasting Corporation
ABC TV	ABC Television
act.	active
A$	Australian dollar
AD	*anno domini*
AFC	Air Force Cross
AIDS	acquired immune deficiency syndrome
AK	Alaska
AL	Alabama
A level	advanced level [examination]
ALS	associate of the Linnean Society
AM	master of arts
AMICE	associate member of the Institution of Civil Engineers
ANZAC	Australian and New Zealand Army Corps
appx *pl.* appxs	appendix(es)
AR	Arkansas
ARA	associate of the Royal Academy
ARCA	associate of the Royal College of Art
ARCM	associate of the Royal College of Music
ARCO	associate of the Royal College of Organists
ARIBA	associate of the Royal Institute of British Architects
ARP	air-raid precautions
ARRC	associate of the Royal Red Cross
ARSA	associate of the Royal Scottish Academy
art.	article / item
ASC	Army Service Corps
Asch	Austrian Schilling
ASDIC	Antisubmarine Detection Investigation Committee
ATS	Auxiliary Territorial Service
ATV	Associated Television
Aug	August
AZ	Arizona
b.	born
BA	bachelor of arts
BA (Admin.)	bachelor of arts (administration)
BAFTA	British Academy of Film and Television Arts
BAO	bachelor of arts in obstetrics
bap.	baptized
BBC	British Broadcasting Corporation / Company
BC	before Christ
BCE	before the common (*or* Christian) era
BCE	bachelor of civil engineering
BCG	bacillus of Calmette and Guérin [inoculation against tuberculosis]
BCh	bachelor of surgery
BChir	bachelor of surgery
BCL	bachelor of civil law

BCnL	bachelor of canon law
BCom	bachelor of commerce
BD	bachelor of divinity
BEd	bachelor of education
BEng	bachelor of engineering
bk *pl.* bks	book(s)
BL	bachelor of law / letters / literature
BLitt	bachelor of letters
BM	bachelor of medicine
BMus	bachelor of music
BP	before present
BP	British Petroleum
Bros.	Brothers
BS	(1) bachelor of science; (2) bachelor of surgery; (3) British standard
BSc	bachelor of science
BSc (Econ.)	bachelor of science (economics)
BSc (Eng.)	bachelor of science (engineering)
bt	baronet
BTh	bachelor of theology
bur.	buried
C.	command [identifier for published parliamentary papers]
c.	*circa*
c.	*capitulum pl. capitula:* chapter(s)
CA	California
Cantab.	Cantabrigiensis
cap.	*capitulum pl. capitula:* chapter(s)
CB	companion of the Bath
CBE	commander of the Order of the British Empire
CBS	Columbia Broadcasting System
cc	cubic centimetres
C$	Canadian dollar
CD	compact disc
Cd	command [identifier for published parliamentary papers]
CE	Common (*or* Christian) Era
cent.	century
cf.	compare
CH	Companion of Honour
chap.	chapter
ChB	bachelor of surgery
CI	Imperial Order of the Crown of India
CIA	Central Intelligence Agency
CID	Criminal Investigation Department
CIE	companion of the Order of the Indian Empire
Cie	Compagnie
CLit	companion of literature
CM	master of surgery
cm	centimetre(s)

Cmd	command [identifier for published parliamentary papers]
CMG	companion of the Order of St Michael and St George
Cmnd	command [identifier for published parliamentary papers]
CO	Colorado
Co.	company
co.	county
col. *pl.* cols.	column(s)
Corp.	corporation
CSE	certificate of secondary education
CSI	companion of the Order of the Star of India
CT	Connecticut
CVO	commander of the Royal Victorian Order
cwt	hundredweight
$	(American) dollar
d.	(1) penny (pence); (2) died
DBE	dame commander of the Order of the British Empire
DCH	diploma in child health
DCh	doctor of surgery
DCL	doctor of civil law
DCnL	doctor of canon law
DCVO	dame commander of the Royal Victorian Order
DD	doctor of divinity
DE	Delaware
Dec	December
dem.	demolished
DEng	doctor of engineering
des.	destroyed
DFC	Distinguished Flying Cross
DipEd	diploma in education
DipPsych	diploma in psychiatry
diss.	dissertation
DL	deputy lieutenant
DLitt	doctor of letters
DLittCelt	doctor of Celtic letters
DM	(1) Deutschmark; (2) doctor of medicine; (3) doctor of musical arts
DMus	doctor of music
DNA	dioxyribonucleic acid
doc.	document
DOL	doctor of oriental learning
DPH	diploma in public health
DPhil	doctor of philosophy
DPM	diploma in psychological medicine
DSC	Distinguished Service Cross
DSc	doctor of science
DSc (Econ.)	doctor of science (economics)
DSc (Eng.)	doctor of science (engineering)
DSM	Distinguished Service Medal
DSO	companion of the Distinguished Service Order
DSocSc	doctor of social science
DTech	doctor of technology
DTh	doctor of theology
DTM	diploma in tropical medicine
DTMH	diploma in tropical medicine and hygiene
DU	doctor of the university
DUniv	doctor of the university
dwt	pennyweight
EC	European Community
ed. *pl.* eds.	edited / edited by / editor(s)
Edin.	Edinburgh

edn	edition
EEC	European Economic Community
EFTA	European Free Trade Association
EICS	East India Company Service
EMI	Electrical and Musical Industries (Ltd)
Eng.	English
enl.	enlarged
ENSA	Entertainments National Service Association
ep. *pl.* epp.	*epistola(e)*
ESP	extra-sensory perception
esp.	especially
esq.	esquire
est.	estimate / estimated
EU	European Union
ex	sold by (*lit.* out of)
excl.	excludes / excluding
exh.	exhibited
exh. cat.	exhibition catalogue
f. *pl.* ff.	following [pages]
FA	Football Association
FACP	fellow of the American College of Physicians
facs.	facsimile
FANY	First Aid Nursing Yeomanry
FBA	fellow of the British Academy
FBI	Federation of British Industries
FCS	fellow of the Chemical Society
Feb	February
FEng	fellow of the Fellowship of Engineering
FFCM	fellow of the Faculty of Community Medicine
FGS	fellow of the Geological Society
fig.	figure
FIMechE	fellow of the Institution of Mechanical Engineers
FL	Florida
fl.	*floruit*
FLS	fellow of the Linnean Society
FM	frequency modulation
fol. *pl.* fols.	folio(s)
Fr	French francs
Fr.	French
FRAeS	fellow of the Royal Aeronautical Society
FRAI	fellow of the Royal Anthropological Institute
FRAM	fellow of the Royal Academy of Music
FRAS	(1) fellow of the Royal Asiatic Society; (2) fellow of the Royal Astronomical Society
FRCM	fellow of the Royal College of Music
FRCO	fellow of the Royal College of Organists
FRCOG	fellow of the Royal College of Obstetricians and Gynaecologists
FRCP(C)	fellow of the Royal College of Physicians of Canada
FRCP (Edin.)	fellow of the Royal College of Physicians of Edinburgh
FRCP (Lond.)	fellow of the Royal College of Physicians of London
FRCPath	fellow of the Royal College of Pathologists
FRCPsych	fellow of the Royal College of Psychiatrists
FRCS	fellow of the Royal College of Surgeons
FRGS	fellow of the Royal Geographical Society
FRIBA	fellow of the Royal Institute of British Architects
FRICS	fellow of the Royal Institute of Chartered Surveyors
FRS	fellow of the Royal Society
FRSA	fellow of the Royal Society of Arts

FRSCM	fellow of the Royal School of Church Music		ISO	companion of the Imperial Service Order
FRSE	fellow of the Royal Society of Edinburgh		It.	Italian
FRSL	fellow of the Royal Society of Literature		ITA	Independent Television Authority
FSA	fellow of the Society of Antiquaries		ITV	Independent Television
ft	foot *pl.* feet		Jan	January
FTCL	fellow of Trinity College of Music, London		JP	justice of the peace
ft-lb per min.	foot-pounds per minute [unit of horsepower]		jun.	junior
FZS	fellow of the Zoological Society		KB	knight of the Order of the Bath
GA	Georgia		KBE	knight commander of the Order of the British Empire
GBE	knight or dame grand cross of the Order of the British Empire		KC	king's counsel
GCB	knight grand cross of the Order of the Bath		kcal	kilocalorie
GCE	general certificate of education		KCB	knight commander of the Order of the Bath
GCH	knight grand cross of the Royal Guelphic Order		KCH	knight commander of the Royal Guelphic Order
GCHQ	government communications headquarters		KCIE	knight commander of the Order of the Indian Empire
GCIE	knight grand commander of the Order of the Indian Empire		KCMG	knight commander of the Order of St Michael and St George
GCMG	knight or dame grand cross of the Order of St Michael and St George		KCSI	knight commander of the Order of the Star of India
GCSE	general certificate of secondary education		KCVO	knight commander of the Royal Victorian Order
GCSI	knight grand commander of the Order of the Star of India		keV	kilo-electron-volt
GCStJ	bailiff or dame grand cross of the order of St John of Jerusalem		KG	knight of the Order of the Garter
			KGB	[Soviet committee of state security]
GCVO	knight or dame grand cross of the Royal Victorian Order		KH	knight of the Royal Guelphic Order
GEC	General Electric Company		KLM	Koninklijke Luchtvaart Maatschappij (Royal Dutch Air Lines)
Ger.	German		km	kilometre(s)
GI	government (*or* general) issue		KP	knight of the Order of St Patrick
GMT	Greenwich mean time		KS	Kansas
GP	general practitioner		KT	knight of the Order of the Thistle
GPU	[Soviet special police unit]		kt	knight
GSO	general staff officer		KY	Kentucky
Heb.	Hebrew		£	pound(s) sterling
HEICS	Honourable East India Company Service		£E	Egyptian pound
HI	Hawaii		L	lira *pl.* lire
HIV	human immunodeficiency virus		l. *pl.* ll.	line(s)
HK$	Hong Kong dollar		LA	Lousiana
HM	his / her majesty('s)		LAA	light anti-aircraft
HMAS	his / her majesty's Australian ship		LAH	licentiate of the Apothecaries' Hall, Dublin
HMNZS	his / her majesty's New Zealand ship		Lat.	Latin
HMS	his / her majesty's ship		lb	pound(s), unit of weight
HMSO	His / Her Majesty's Stationery Office		LDS	licence in dental surgery
HMV	His Master's Voice		*lit.*	literally
Hon.	Honourable		LittB	bachelor of letters
hp	horsepower		LittD	doctor of letters
hr	hour(s)		LKQCPI	licentiate of the King and Queen's College of Physicians, Ireland
HRH	his / her royal highness		LLA	lady literate in arts
HTV	Harlech Television		LLB	bachelor of laws
IA	Iowa		LLD	doctor of laws
ibid.	*ibidem*: in the same place		LLM	master of laws
ICI	Imperial Chemical Industries (Ltd)		LM	licentiate in midwifery
ID	Idaho		LP	long-playing record
IL	Illinois		LRAM	licentiate of the Royal Academy of Music
illus.	illustration		LRCP	licentiate of the Royal College of Physicians
illustr.	illustrated		LRCPS (Glasgow)	licentiate of the Royal College of Physicians and Surgeons of Glasgow
IN	Indiana		LRCS	licentiate of the Royal College of Surgeons
in.	inch(es)		LSA	licentiate of the Society of Apothecaries
Inc.	Incorporated		LSD	lysergic acid diethylamide
incl.	includes / including		LVO	lieutenant of the Royal Victorian Order
IOU	I owe you		M. *pl.* MM.	Monsieur *pl.* Messieurs
IQ	intelligence quotient		m	metre(s)
Ir£	Irish pound			
IRA	Irish Republican Army			

m. *pl.* mm.	membrane(s)		ND	North Dakota
MA	(1) Massachusetts; (2) master of arts		n.d.	no date
MAI	master of engineering		NE	Nebraska
MB	bachelor of medicine		*nem. con.*	*nemine contradicente*: unanimously
MBA	master of business administration		new ser.	new series
MBE	member of the Order of the British Empire		NH	New Hampshire
MC	Military Cross		NHS	National Health Service
MCC	Marylebone Cricket Club		NJ	New Jersey
MCh	master of surgery		NKVD	[Soviet people's commissariat for internal affairs]
MChir	master of surgery		NM	New Mexico
MCom	master of commerce		nm	nanometre(s)
MD	(1) doctor of medicine; (2) Maryland		no. *pl.* nos.	number(s)
MDMA	methylenedioxymethamphetamine		Nov	November
ME	Maine		n.p.	no place [of publication]
MEd	master of education		NS	new style
MEng	master of engineering		NV	Nevada
MEP	member of the European parliament		NY	New York
MG	Morris Garages		NZBS	New Zealand Broadcasting Service
MGM	Metro-Goldwyn-Mayer		OBE	officer of the Order of the British Empire
Mgr	Monsignor		obit.	obituary
MI	(1) Michigan; (2) military intelligence		Oct	October
MI1c	[secret intelligence department]		OCTU	officer cadets training unit
MI5	[military intelligence department]		OECD	Organization for Economic Co-operation and Development
MI6	[secret intelligence department]		OEEC	Organization for European Economic Co-operation
MI9	[secret escape service]			
MICE	member of the Institution of Civil Engineers		OFM	order of Friars Minor [Franciscans]
MIEE	member of the Institution of Electrical Engineers		OFMCap	Ordine Frati Minori Cappucini: member of the Capuchin order
min.	minute(s)		OH	Ohio
Mk	mark		OK	Oklahoma
ML	(1) licentiate of medicine; (2) master of laws		O level	ordinary level [examination]
MLitt	master of letters		OM	Order of Merit
Mlle	Mademoiselle		OP	order of Preachers [Dominicans]
mm	millimetre(s)		op. *pl.* opp.	opus *pl.* opera
Mme	Madame		OPEC	Organization of Petroleum Exporting Countries
MN	Minnesota		OR	Oregon
MO	Missouri		orig.	original
MOH	medical officer of health		OS	old style
MP	member of parliament		OSB	Order of St Benedict
m.p.h.	miles per hour		OTC	Officers' Training Corps
MPhil	master of philosophy		OWS	Old Watercolour Society
MRCP	member of the Royal College of Physicians		Oxon.	Oxoniensis
MRCS	member of the Royal College of Surgeons		p. *pl.* pp.	page(s)
MRCVS	member of the Royal College of Veterinary Surgeons		PA	Pennsylvania
MRIA	member of the Royal Irish Academy		p.a.	per annum
MS	(1) master of science; (2) Mississippi		para.	paragraph
MS *pl.* MSS	manuscript(s)		PAYE	pay as you earn
MSc	master of science		pbk *pl.* pbks	paperback(s)
MSc (Econ.)	master of science (economics)		*per.*	[during the] period
MT	Montana		PhD	doctor of philosophy
MusB	bachelor of music		pl.	(1) plate(s); (2) plural
MusBac	bachelor of music		priv. coll.	private collection
MusD	doctor of music		pt *pl.* pts	part(s)
MV	motor vessel		pubd	published
MVO	member of the Royal Victorian Order		PVC	polyvinyl chloride
n. *pl.* nn.	note(s)		q. *pl.* qq.	(1) question(s); (2) quire(s)
NAAFI	Navy, Army, and Air Force Institutes		QC	queen's counsel
NASA	National Aeronautics and Space Administration		R	rand
NATO	North Atlantic Treaty Organization		R.	Rex / Regina
NBC	National Broadcasting Corporation		*r*	recto
NC	North Carolina		r.	reigned / ruled
NCO	non-commissioned officer		RA	Royal Academy / Royal Academician

RAC	Royal Automobile Club		Skr	Swedish krona
RAF	Royal Air Force		Span.	Spanish
RAFVR	Royal Air Force Volunteer Reserve		SPCK	Society for Promoting Christian Knowledge
RAM	[member of the] Royal Academy of Music		SS	(1) Santissimi; (2) Schutzstaffel; (3) steam ship
RAMC	Royal Army Medical Corps		STB	bachelor of theology
RCA	Royal College of Art		STD	doctor of theology
RCNC	Royal Corps of Naval Constructors		STM	master of theology
RCOG	Royal College of Obstetricians and Gynaecologists		STP	doctor of theology
			supp.	supposedly
RDI	royal designer for industry		suppl. *pl.* suppls.	supplement(s)
RE	Royal Engineers		s.v.	*sub verbo / sub voce*: under the word / heading
repr. *pl.* reprs.	reprint(s) / reprinted		SY	steam yacht
repro.	reproduced		TA	Territorial Army
rev.	revised / revised by / reviser / revision		TASS	[Soviet news agency]
Revd	Reverend		TB	tuberculosis (*lit.* tubercle bacillus)
RHA	Royal Hibernian Academy		TD	(1) *teachtaí dála* (member of the Dáil); (2) territorial decoration
RI	(1) Rhode Island; (2) Royal Institute of Painters in Water-Colours			
			TN	Tennessee
RIBA	Royal Institute of British Architects		TNT	trinitrotoluene
RIN	Royal Indian Navy		trans.	translated / translated by / translation / translator
RM	Reichsmark			
RMS	Royal Mail steamer		TT	tourist trophy
RN	Royal Navy		TUC	Trades Union Congress
RNA	ribonucleic acid		TX	Texas
RNAS	Royal Naval Air Service		U-boat	*Unterseeboot*: submarine
RNR	Royal Naval Reserve		Ufa	Universum-Film AG
RNVR	Royal Naval Volunteer Reserve		UMIST	University of Manchester Institute of Science and Technology
RO	Record Office			
r.p.m.	revolutions per minute		UN	United Nations
RRS	royal research ship		UNESCO	United Nations Educational, Scientific, and Cultural Organization
Rs	rupees			
RSA	(1) Royal Scottish Academician; (2) Royal Society of Arts		UNICEF	United Nations International Children's Emergency Fund
RSPCA	Royal Society for the Prevention of Cruelty to Animals		unpubd	unpublished
			USS	United States ship
Rt Hon.	Right Honourable		UT	Utah
Rt Revd	Right Reverend		*v*	verso
RUC	Royal Ulster Constabulary		v.	versus
Russ.	Russian		VA	Virginia
RWS	Royal Watercolour Society		VAD	Voluntary Aid Detachment
S4C	Sianel Pedwar Cymru		VC	Victoria Cross
s.	shilling(s)		VE-day	victory in Europe day
s.a.	*sub anno*: under the year		Ven.	Venerable
SABC	South African Broadcasting Corporation		VJ-day	victory over Japan day
SAS	Special Air Service		vol. *pl.* vols.	volume(s)
SC	South Carolina		VT	Vermont
ScD	doctor of science		WA	Washington [state]
S$	Singapore dollar		WAAC	Women's Auxiliary Army Corps
SD	South Dakota		WAAF	Women's Auxiliary Air Force
sec.	second(s)		WEA	Workers' Educational Association
sel.	selected		WHO	World Health Organization
sen.	senior		WI	Wisconsin
Sept	September		WRAF	Women's Royal Air Force
ser.	series		WRNS	Women's Royal Naval Service
SHAPE	supreme headquarters allied powers, Europe		WV	West Virginia
SIDRO	Société Internationale d'Énergie Hydro-Électrique		WVS	Women's Voluntary Service
			WY	Wyoming
sig. *pl.* sigs.	signature(s)		¥	yen
sing.	singular		YMCA	Young Men's Christian Association
SIS	Secret Intelligence Service		YWCA	Young Women's Christian Association
SJ	Society of Jesus			

2 Institution abbreviations

All Souls Oxf.	All Souls College, Oxford
AM Oxf.	Ashmolean Museum, Oxford
Balliol Oxf.	Balliol College, Oxford
BBC WAC	BBC Written Archives Centre, Reading
Beds. & Luton ARS	Bedfordshire and Luton Archives and Record Service, Bedford
Berks. RO	Berkshire Record Office, Reading
BFI	British Film Institute, London
BFI NFTVA	British Film Institute, London, National Film and Television Archive
BGS	British Geological Survey, Keyworth, Nottingham
Birm. CA	Birmingham Central Library, Birmingham City Archives
Birm. CL	Birmingham Central Library
BL	British Library, London
BL NSA	British Library, London, National Sound Archive
BL OIOC	British Library, London, Oriental and India Office Collections
BLPES	London School of Economics and Political Science, British Library of Political and Economic Science
BM	British Museum, London
Bodl. Oxf.	Bodleian Library, Oxford
Bodl. RH	Bodleian Library of Commonwealth and African Studies at Rhodes House, Oxford
Borth. Inst.	Borthwick Institute of Historical Research, University of York
Boston PL	Boston Public Library, Massachusetts
Bristol RO	Bristol Record Office
Bucks. RLSS	Buckinghamshire Records and Local Studies Service, Aylesbury
CAC Cam.	Churchill College, Cambridge, Churchill Archives Centre
Cambs. AS	Cambridgeshire Archive Service
CCC Cam.	Corpus Christi College, Cambridge
CCC Oxf.	Corpus Christi College, Oxford
Ches. & Chester ALSS	Cheshire and Chester Archives and Local Studies Service
Christ Church Oxf.	Christ Church, Oxford
Christies	Christies, London
City Westm. AC	City of Westminster Archives Centre, London
CKS	Centre for Kentish Studies, Maidstone
CLRO	Corporation of London Records Office
Coll. Arms	College of Arms, London
Col. U.	Columbia University, New York
Cornwall RO	Cornwall Record Office, Truro
Courtauld Inst.	Courtauld Institute of Art, London
CUL	Cambridge University Library
Cumbria AS	Cumbria Archive Service
Derbys. RO	Derbyshire Record Office, Matlock
Devon RO	Devon Record Office, Exeter
Dorset RO	Dorset Record Office, Dorchester
Duke U.	Duke University, Durham, North Carolina
Duke U., Perkins L.	Duke University, Durham, North Carolina, William R. Perkins Library
Durham Cath. CL	Durham Cathedral, chapter library
Durham RO	Durham Record Office
DWL	Dr Williams's Library, London
Essex RO	Essex Record Office
E. Sussex RO	East Sussex Record Office, Lewes
Eton	Eton College, Berkshire
FM Cam.	Fitzwilliam Museum, Cambridge
Folger	Folger Shakespeare Library, Washington, DC
Garr. Club	Garrick Club, London
Girton Cam.	Girton College, Cambridge
GL	Guildhall Library, London
Glos. RO	Gloucestershire Record Office, Gloucester
Gon. & Caius Cam.	Gonville and Caius College, Cambridge
Gov. Art Coll.	Government Art Collection
GS Lond.	Geological Society of London
Hants. RO	Hampshire Record Office, Winchester
Harris Man. Oxf.	Harris Manchester College, Oxford
Harvard TC	Harvard Theatre Collection, Harvard University, Cambridge, Massachusetts, Nathan Marsh Pusey Library
Harvard U.	Harvard University, Cambridge, Massachusetts
Harvard U., Houghton L.	Harvard University, Cambridge, Massachusetts, Houghton Library
Herefs. RO	Herefordshire Record Office, Hereford
Herts. ALS	Hertfordshire Archives and Local Studies, Hertford
Hist. Soc. Penn.	Historical Society of Pennsylvania, Philadelphia
HLRO	House of Lords Record Office, London
Hult. Arch.	Hulton Archive, London and New York
Hunt. L.	Huntington Library, San Marino, California
ICL	Imperial College, London
Inst. CE	Institution of Civil Engineers, London
Inst. EE	Institution of Electrical Engineers, London
IWM	Imperial War Museum, London
IWM FVA	Imperial War Museum, London, Film and Video Archive
IWM SA	Imperial War Museum, London, Sound Archive
JRL	John Rylands University Library of Manchester
King's AC Cam.	King's College Archives Centre, Cambridge
King's Cam.	King's College, Cambridge
King's Lond.	King's College, London
King's Lond., Liddell Hart C.	King's College, London, Liddell Hart Centre for Military Archives
Lancs. RO	Lancashire Record Office, Preston
L. Cong.	Library of Congress, Washington, DC
Leics. RO	Leicestershire, Leicester, and Rutland Record Office, Leicester
Lincs. Arch.	Lincolnshire Archives, Lincoln
Linn. Soc.	Linnean Society of London
LMA	London Metropolitan Archives
LPL	Lambeth Palace, London
Lpool RO	Liverpool Record Office and Local Studies Service
LUL	London University Library
Magd. Cam.	Magdalene College, Cambridge
Magd. Oxf.	Magdalen College, Oxford
Man. City Gall.	Manchester City Galleries
Man. CL	Manchester Central Library
Mass. Hist. Soc.	Massachusetts Historical Society, Boston
Merton Oxf.	Merton College, Oxford
MHS Oxf.	Museum of the History of Science, Oxford
Mitchell L., Glas.	Mitchell Library, Glasgow
Mitchell L., NSW	State Library of New South Wales, Sydney, Mitchell Library
Morgan L.	Pierpont Morgan Library, New York
NA Canada	National Archives of Canada, Ottawa
NA Ire.	National Archives of Ireland, Dublin
NAM	National Army Museum, London
NA Scot.	National Archives of Scotland, Edinburgh
News Int. RO	News International Record Office, London
NG Ire.	National Gallery of Ireland, Dublin

NG Scot.	National Gallery of Scotland, Edinburgh
NHM	Natural History Museum, London
NL Aus.	National Library of Australia, Canberra
NL Ire.	National Library of Ireland, Dublin
NL NZ	National Library of New Zealand, Wellington
NL NZ, Turnbull L.	National Library of New Zealand, Wellington, Alexander Turnbull Library
NL Scot.	National Library of Scotland, Edinburgh
NL Wales	National Library of Wales, Aberystwyth
NMG Wales	National Museum and Gallery of Wales, Cardiff
NMM	National Maritime Museum, London
Norfolk RO	Norfolk Record Office, Norwich
Northants. RO	Northamptonshire Record Office, Northampton
Northumbd RO	Northumberland Record Office
Notts. Arch.	Nottinghamshire Archives, Nottingham
NPG	National Portrait Gallery, London
NRA	National Archives, London, Historical Manuscripts Commission, National Register of Archives
Nuffield Oxf.	Nuffield College, Oxford
N. Yorks. CRO	North Yorkshire County Record Office, Northallerton
NYPL	New York Public Library
Oxf. UA	Oxford University Archives
Oxf. U. Mus. NH	Oxford University Museum of Natural History
Oxon. RO	Oxfordshire Record Office, Oxford
Pembroke Cam.	Pembroke College, Cambridge
PRO	National Archives, London, Public Record Office
PRO NIre.	Public Record Office for Northern Ireland, Belfast
Pusey Oxf.	Pusey House, Oxford
RA	Royal Academy of Arts, London
Ransom HRC	Harry Ransom Humanities Research Center, University of Texas, Austin
RAS	Royal Astronomical Society, London
RBG Kew	Royal Botanic Gardens, Kew, London
RCP Lond.	Royal College of Physicians of London
RCS Eng.	Royal College of Surgeons of England, London
RGS	Royal Geographical Society, London
RIBA	Royal Institute of British Architects, London
RIBA BAL	Royal Institute of British Architects, London, British Architectural Library
Royal Arch.	Royal Archives, Windsor Castle, Berkshire [by gracious permission of her majesty the queen]
Royal Irish Acad.	Royal Irish Academy, Dublin
Royal Scot. Acad.	Royal Scottish Academy, Edinburgh
RS	Royal Society, London
RSA	Royal Society of Arts, London
RS Friends, Lond.	Religious Society of Friends, London
St Ant. Oxf.	St Antony's College, Oxford
St John Cam.	St John's College, Cambridge
S. Antiquaries, Lond.	Society of Antiquaries of London
Sci. Mus.	Science Museum, London
Scot. NPG	Scottish National Portrait Gallery, Edinburgh
Scott Polar RI	University of Cambridge, Scott Polar Research Institute
Sheff. Arch.	Sheffield Archives
Shrops. RRC	Shropshire Records and Research Centre, Shrewsbury
SOAS	School of Oriental and African Studies, London
Som. ARS	Somerset Archive and Record Service, Taunton
Staffs. RO	Staffordshire Record Office, Stafford
Suffolk RO	Suffolk Record Office
Surrey HC	Surrey History Centre, Woking
TCD	Trinity College, Dublin
Trinity Cam.	Trinity College, Cambridge
U. Aberdeen	University of Aberdeen
U. Birm.	University of Birmingham
U. Birm. L.	University of Birmingham Library
U. Cal.	University of California
U. Cam.	University of Cambridge
UCL	University College, London
U. Durham	University of Durham
U. Durham L.	University of Durham Library
U. Edin.	University of Edinburgh
U. Edin., New Coll.	University of Edinburgh, New College
U. Edin., New Coll. L.	University of Edinburgh, New College Library
U. Edin. L.	University of Edinburgh Library
U. Glas.	University of Glasgow
U. Glas. L.	University of Glasgow Library
U. Hull	University of Hull
U. Hull, Brynmor Jones L.	University of Hull, Brynmor Jones Library
U. Leeds	University of Leeds
U. Leeds, Brotherton L.	University of Leeds, Brotherton Library
U. Lond.	University of London
U. Lpool	University of Liverpool
U. Lpool L.	University of Liverpool Library
U. Mich.	University of Michigan, Ann Arbor
U. Mich., Clements L.	University of Michigan, Ann Arbor, William L. Clements Library
U. Newcastle	University of Newcastle upon Tyne
U. Newcastle, Robinson L.	University of Newcastle upon Tyne, Robinson Library
U. Nott.	University of Nottingham
U. Nott. L.	University of Nottingham Library
U. Oxf.	University of Oxford
U. Reading	University of Reading
U. Reading L.	University of Reading Library
U. St Andr.	University of St Andrews
U. St Andr. L.	University of St Andrews Library
U. Southampton	University of Southampton
U. Southampton L.	University of Southampton Library
U. Sussex	University of Sussex, Brighton
U. Texas	University of Texas, Austin
U. Wales	University of Wales
U. Warwick Mod. RC	University of Warwick, Coventry, Modern Records Centre
V&A	Victoria and Albert Museum, London
V&A NAL	Victoria and Albert Museum, London, National Art Library
Warks. CRO	Warwickshire County Record Office, Warwick
Wellcome L.	Wellcome Library for the History and Understanding of Medicine, London
Westm. DA	Westminster Diocesan Archives, London
Wilts. & Swindon RO	Wiltshire and Swindon Record Office, Trowbridge
Worcs. RO	Worcestershire Record Office, Worcester
W. Sussex RO	West Sussex Record Office, Chichester
W. Yorks. AS	West Yorkshire Archive Service
Yale U.	Yale University, New Haven, Connecticut
Yale U., Beinecke L.	Yale University, New Haven, Connecticut, Beinecke Rare Book and Manuscript Library
Yale U. CBA	Yale University, New Haven, Connecticut, Yale Center for British Art

3 Bibliographic abbreviations

Adams, *Drama*	W. D. Adams, *A dictionary of the drama*, 1: *A–G* (1904); 2: *H–Z* (1956) [vol. 2 microfilm only]
AFM	J O'Donovan, ed. and trans., *Annala rioghachta Eireann / Annals of the kingdom of Ireland by the four masters*, 7 vols. (1848–51); 2nd edn (1856); 3rd edn (1990)
Allibone, *Dict.*	S. A. Allibone, *A critical dictionary of English literature and British and American authors*, 3 vols. (1859–71); suppl. by J. F. Kirk, 2 vols. (1891)
ANB	J. A. Garraty and M. C. Carnes, eds., *American national biography*, 24 vols. (1999)
Anderson, *Scot. nat.*	W. Anderson, *The Scottish nation, or, The surnames, families, literature, honours, and biographical history of the people of Scotland*, 3 vols. (1859–63)
Ann. mon.	H. R. Luard, ed., *Annales monastici*, 5 vols., Rolls Series, 36 (1864–9)
Ann. Ulster	S. Mac Airt and G. Mac Niocaill, eds., *Annals of Ulster (to AD 1131)* (1983)
APC	*Acts of the privy council of England*, new ser., 46 vols. (1890–1964)
APS	*The acts of the parliaments of Scotland*, 12 vols. in 13 (1814–75)
Arber, *Regs. Stationers*	F. Arber, ed., *A transcript of the registers of the Company of Stationers of London, 1554–1640 AD*, 5 vols. (1875–94)
ArchR	*Architectural Review*
ASC	D. Whitelock, D. C. Douglas, and S. I. Tucker, ed. and trans., *The Anglo-Saxon Chronicle: a revised translation* (1961)
AS chart.	P. H. Sawyer, *Anglo-Saxon charters: an annotated list and bibliography*, Royal Historical Society Guides and Handbooks (1968)
AusDB	D. Pike and others, eds., *Australian dictionary of biography*, 16 vols. (1966–2002)
Baker, *Serjeants*	J. H. Baker, *The order of serjeants at law*, SeldS, suppl. ser., 5 (1984)
Bale, *Cat.*	J. Bale, *Scriptorum illustrium Maioris Brytannie, quam nunc Angliam et Scotiam vocant: catalogus*, 2 vols. in 1 (Basel, 1557–9); facs. edn (1971)
Bale, *Index*	J. Bale, *Index Britanniae scriptorum*, ed. R. L. Poole and M. Bateson (1902); facs. edn (1990)
BBCS	*Bulletin of the Board of Celtic Studies*
BDMBR	J. O. Baylen and N. J. Gossman, eds., *Biographical dictionary of modern British radicals*, 3 vols. in 4 (1979–88)
Bede, *Hist. eccl.*	*Bede's Ecclesiastical history of the English people*, ed. and trans. B. Colgrave and R. A. B. Mynors, OMT (1969); repr. (1991)
Bénézit, *Dict.*	E. Bénézit, *Dictionnaire critique et documentaire des peintres, sculpteurs, dessinateurs et graveurs*, 3 vols. (Paris, 1911–23); new edn, 8 vols. (1948–66), repr. (1966); 3rd edn, rev. and enl., 10 vols. (1976); 4th edn, 14 vols. (1999)
BIHR	*Bulletin of the Institute of Historical Research*
Birch, *Seals*	W. de Birch, *Catalogue of seals in the department of manuscripts in the British Museum*, 6 vols. (1887–1900)
Bishop Burnet's History	*Bishop Burnet's History of his own time*, ed. M. J. Routh, 2nd edn, 6 vols. (1833)
Blackwood	*Blackwood's [Edinburgh] Magazine*, 328 vols. (1817–1980)
Blain, Clements & Grundy, *Feminist comp.*	V. Blain, P. Clements, and I. Grundy, eds., *The feminist companion to literature in English* (1990)
BL cat.	*The British Library general catalogue of printed books* [in 360 vols. with suppls., also CD-ROM and online]
BMJ	*British Medical Journal*
Boase & Courtney, *Bibl. Corn.*	G. C. Boase and W. P. Courtney, *Bibliotheca Cornubiensis: a catalogue of the writings … of Cornishmen*, 3 vols. (1874–82)
Boase, *Mod. Eng. biog.*	F. Boase, *Modern English biography: containing many thousand concise memoirs of persons who have died since the year 1850*, 6 vols. (privately printed, Truro, 1892–1921); repr. (1965)
Boswell, *Life*	*Boswell's Life of Johnson: together with Journal of a tour to the Hebrides and Johnson's Diary of a journey into north Wales*, ed. G. B. Hill, enl. edn, rev. L. F. Powell, 6 vols. (1934–50); 2nd edn (1964); repr. (1971)
Brown & Stratton, *Brit. mus.*	J. D. Brown and S. S. Stratton, *British musical biography* (1897)
Bryan, *Painters*	M. Bryan, *A biographical and critical dictionary of painters and engravers*, 2 vols. (1816); new edn, ed. G. Stanley (1849); new edn, ed. R. E. Graves and W. Armstrong, 2 vols. (1886–9); [4th edn], ed. G. C. Williamson, 5 vols. (1903–5) [various reprs.]
Burke, *Gen. GB*	J. Burke, *A genealogical and heraldic history of the commoners of Great Britain and Ireland*, 4 vols. (1833–8); new edn as *A genealogical and heraldic dictionary of the landed gentry of Great Britain and Ireland*, 3 vols. [1843–9] [many later edns]
Burke, *Gen. Ire.*	J. B. Burke, *A genealogical and heraldic history of the landed gentry of Ireland* (1899); 2nd edn (1904); 3rd edn (1912); 4th edn (1958); 5th edn as *Burke's Irish family records* (1976)
Burke, *Peerage*	J. Burke, *A general [later edns A genealogical] and heraldic dictionary of the peerage and baronetage of the United Kingdom* [later edns *the British empire*] (1829–)
Burney, *Hist. mus.*	C. Burney, *A general history of music, from the earliest ages to the present period*, 4 vols. (1776–89)
Burtchaell & Sadleir, *Alum. Dubl.*	G. D. Burtchaell and T. U. Sadleir, *Alumni Dublinenses: a register of the students, graduates, and provosts of Trinity College* (1924); [2nd edn], with suppl., in 2 pts (1935)
Calamy rev.	A. G. Matthews, *Calamy revised* (1934); repr. (1988)
CCI	*Calendar of confirmations and inventories granted and given up in the several commissariots of Scotland* (1876–)
CCIR	*Calendar of the close rolls preserved in the Public Record Office*, 47 vols. (1892–1963)
CDS	J. Bain, ed., *Calendar of documents relating to Scotland*, 4 vols., PRO (1881–8); suppl. vol. 5, ed. G. G. Simpson and J. D. Galbraith [1986]
CEPR letters	W. H. Bliss, C. Johnson, and J. Twemlow, eds., *Calendar of entries in the papal registers relating to Great Britain and Ireland: papal letters* (1893–)
CGPLA	*Calendars of the grants of probate and letters of administration* [in 4 ser.: England & Wales, Northern Ireland, Ireland, and Éire]
Chambers, *Scots.*	R. Chambers, ed., *A biographical dictionary of eminent Scotsmen*, 4 vols. (1832–5)
Chancery records	chancery records pubd by the PRO
Chancery records (RC)	chancery records pubd by the Record Commissions

CIPM	*Calendar of inquisitions post mortem*, [20 vols.], PRO (1904–); also *Henry VII*, 3 vols. (1898–1955)
Clarendon, *Hist. rebellion*	E. Hyde, earl of Clarendon, *The history of the rebellion and civil wars in England*, 6 vols. (1888); repr. (1958) and (1992)
Cobbett, *Parl. hist.*	W. Cobbett and J. Wright, eds., *Cobbett's Parliamentary history of England*, 36 vols. (1806–1820)
Colvin, *Archs.*	H. Colvin, *A biographical dictionary of British architects, 1600–1840*, 3rd edn (1995)
Cooper, *Ath. Cantab.*	C. H. Cooper and T. Cooper, *Athenae Cantabrigienses*, 3 vols. (1858–1913); repr. (1967)
CPR	*Calendar of the patent rolls preserved in the Public Record Office* (1891–)
Crockford	*Crockford's Clerical Directory*
CS	Camden Society
CSP	*Calendar of state papers* [in 11 ser.: *domestic, Scotland, Scottish series, Ireland, colonial, Commonwealth, foreign, Spain* [at Simancas], *Rome, Milan*, and *Venice*]
CYS	Canterbury and York Society
DAB	*Dictionary of American biography*, 21 vols. (1928–36), repr. in 11 vols. (1964); 10 suppls. (1944–96)
DBB	D. J. Jeremy, ed., *Dictionary of business biography*, 5 vols. (1984–6)
DCB	G. W. Brown and others, *Dictionary of Canadian biography*, [14 vols.] (1966–)
Debrett's Peerage	*Debrett's Peerage* (1803–) [sometimes *Debrett's Illustrated peerage*]
Desmond, *Botanists*	R. Desmond, *Dictionary of British and Irish botanists and horticulturists* (1977); rev. edn (1994)
Dir. Brit. archs.	A. Felstead, J. Franklin, and L. Pinfield, eds., *Directory of British architects, 1834–1900* (1993); 2nd edn, ed. A. Brodie and others, 2 vols. (2001)
DLB	J. M. Bellamy and J. Saville, eds., *Dictionary of labour biography*, [10 vols.] (1972–)
DLitB	Dictionary of Literary Biography
DNB	*Dictionary of national biography*, 63 vols. (1885–1900), suppl., 3 vols. (1901); repr. in 22 vols. (1908–9); 10 further suppls. (1912–96); *Missing persons* (1993)
DNZB	W. H. Oliver and C. Orange, eds., *The dictionary of New Zealand biography*, 5 vols. (1990–2000)
DSAB	W. J. de Kock and others, eds., *Dictionary of South African biography*, 5 vols. (1968–87)
DSB	C. C. Gillispie and F. L. Holmes, eds., *Dictionary of scientific biography*, 16 vols. (1970–80); repr. in 8 vols. (1981); 2 vol. suppl. (1990)
DSBB	A. Slaven and S. Checkland, eds., *Dictionary of Scottish business biography, 1860–1960*, 2 vols. (1986–90)
DSCHT	N. M. de S. Cameron and others, eds., *Dictionary of Scottish church history and theology* (1993)
Dugdale, *Monasticon*	W. Dugdale, *Monasticon Anglicanum*, 3 vols. (1655–72); 2nd edn, 3 vols. (1661–82); new edn, ed. J. Caley, J. Ellis, and B. Bandinel, 6 vols. in 8 pts (1817–30); repr. (1846) and (1970)
DWB	J. E. Lloyd and others, eds., *Dictionary of Welsh biography down to 1940* (1959) [Eng. trans. of *Y bywgraffiadur Cymreig hyd 1940*, 2nd edn (1954)]
EdinR	*Edinburgh Review, or, Critical Journal*
EETS	Early English Text Society
Emden, *Cam.*	A. B. Emden, *A biographical register of the University of Cambridge to 1500* (1963)
Emden, *Oxf.*	A. B. Emden, *A biographical register of the University of Oxford to AD 1500*, 3 vols. (1957–9); also *A biographical register of the University of Oxford, AD 1501 to 1540* (1974)
EngHR	*English Historical Review*
Engraved Brit. ports.	F. M. O'Donoghue and H. M. Hake, *Catalogue of engraved British portraits preserved in the department of prints and drawings in the British Museum*, 6 vols. (1908–25)
ER	The English Reports, 178 vols. (1900–32)
ESTC	*English short title catalogue, 1475–1800* [CD-ROM and online]
Evelyn, *Diary*	*The diary of John Evelyn*, ed. E. S. De Beer, 6 vols. (1955); repr. (2000)
Farington, *Diary*	*The diary of Joseph Farington*, ed. K. Garlick and others, 17 vols. (1978–98)
Fasti Angl. (Hardy)	J. Le Neve, *Fasti ecclesiae Anglicanae*, ed. T. D. Hardy, 3 vols. (1854)
Fasti Angl., 1066–1300	[J. Le Neve], *Fasti ecclesiae Anglicanae, 1066–1300*, ed. D. E. Greenway and J. S. Barrow, [8 vols.] (1968–)
Fasti Angl., 1300–1541	[J. Le Neve], *Fasti ecclesiae Anglicanae, 1300–1541*, 12 vols. (1962–7)
Fasti Angl., 1541–1857	[J. Le Neve], *Fasti ecclesiae Anglicanae, 1541–1857*, ed. J. M. Horn, D. M. Smith, and D. S. Bailey, [9 vols.] (1969–)
Fasti Scot.	H. Scott, *Fasti ecclesiae Scoticanae*, 3 vols. in 6 (1871); new edn, [11 vols.] (1915–)
FO List	*Foreign Office List*
Fortescue, *Brit. army*	J. W. Fortescue, *A history of the British army*, 13 vols. (1899–1930)
Foss, *Judges*	E. Foss, *The judges of England*, 9 vols. (1848–64); repr. (1966)
Foster, *Alum. Oxon.*	J. Foster, ed., *Alumni Oxonienses: the members of the University of Oxford, 1715–1886*, 4 vols. (1887–8); later edn (1891); also *Alumni Oxonienses … 1500–1714*, 4 vols. (1891–2); 8 vol. repr. (1968) and (2000)
Fuller, *Worthies*	T. Fuller, *The history of the worthies of England*, 4 pts (1662); new edn, 2 vols., ed. J. Nichols (1811); new edn, 3 vols., ed. P. A. Nuttall (1840); repr. (1965)
GEC, *Baronetage*	G. E. Cokayne, *Complete baronetage*, 6 vols. (1900–09); repr. (1983) [microprint]
GEC, *Peerage*	G. E. C. [G. E. Cokayne], *The complete peerage of England, Scotland, Ireland, Great Britain, and the United Kingdom*, 8 vols. (1887–98); new edn, ed. V. Gibbs and others, 14 vols. in 15 (1910–98); microprint repr. (1982) and (1987)
Genest, *Eng. stage*	J. Genest, *Some account of the English stage from the Restoration in 1660 to 1830*, 10 vols. (1832); repr. [New York, 1965]
Gillow, *Lit. biog. hist.*	J. Gillow, *A literary and biographical history or bibliographical dictionary of the English Catholics, from the breach with Rome, in 1534, to the present time*, 5 vols. [1885–1902]; repr. (1961); repr. with preface by C. Gillow (1999)
Gir. Camb. opera	*Giraldi Cambrensis opera*, ed. J. S. Brewer, J. F. Dimock, and G. F. Warner, 8 vols., Rolls Series, 21 (1861–91)
GJ	*Geographical Journal*

Gladstone, *Diaries* — *The Gladstone diaries: with cabinet minutes and prime-ministerial correspondence*, ed. M. R. D. Foot and H. C. G. Matthew, 14 vols. (1968–94)

GM — *Gentleman's Magazine*

Graves, *Artists* — A. Graves, ed., *A dictionary of artists who have exhibited works in the principal London exhibitions of oil paintings from 1760 to 1880* (1884); new edn (1895); 3rd edn (1901); facs. edn (1969); repr. [1970], (1973), and (1984)

Graves, *Brit. Inst.* — A. Graves, *The British Institution, 1806–1867: a complete dictionary of contributors and their work from the foundation of the institution* (1875); facs. edn (1908); repr. (1969)

Graves, *RA exhibitors* — A. Graves, *The Royal Academy of Arts: a complete dictionary of contributors and their work from its foundation in 1769 to 1904*, 8 vols. (1905–6); repr. in 4 vols. (1970) and (1972)

Graves, *Soc. Artists* — A. Graves, *The Society of Artists of Great Britain, 1760–1791, the Free Society of Artists, 1761–1783: a complete dictionary* (1907); facs. edn (1969)

Greaves & Zaller, *BDBR* — R. L. Greaves and R. Zaller, eds., *Biographical dictionary of British radicals in the seventeenth century*, 3 vols. (1982–4)

Grove, *Dict. mus.* — G. Grove, ed., *A dictionary of music and musicians*, 5 vols. (1878–90); 2nd edn, ed. J. A. Fuller Maitland (1904–10); 3rd edn, ed. H. C. Colles (1927); 4th edn with suppl. (1940); 5th edn, ed. E. Blom, 9 vols. (1954); suppl. (1961) [see also *New Grove*]

Hall, *Dramatic ports.* — L. A. Hall, *Catalogue of dramatic portraits in the theatre collection of the Harvard College library*, 4 vols. (1930–34)

Hansard — *Hansard's parliamentary debates*, ser. 1–5 (1803–)

Highfill, Burnim & Langhans, *BDA* — P. H. Highfill, K. A. Burnim, and E. A. Langhans, *A biographical dictionary of actors, actresses, musicians, dancers, managers, and other stage personnel in London, 1660–1800*, 16 vols. (1973–93)

Hist. U. Oxf. — T. H. Aston, ed., *The history of the University of Oxford*, 8 vols. (1984–2000) [1: *The early Oxford schools*, ed. J. I. Catto (1984); 2: *Late medieval Oxford*, ed. J. I. Catto and R. Evans (1992); 3: *The collegiate university*, ed. J. McConica (1986); 4: *Seventeenth-century Oxford*, ed. N. Tyacke (1997); 5: *The eighteenth century*, ed. L. S. Sutherland and L. G. Mitchell (1986); 6–7: *Nineteenth-century Oxford*, ed. M. G. Brock and M. C. Curthoys (1997–2000); 8: *The twentieth century*, ed. B. Harrison (2000)]

HJ — *Historical Journal*

HMC — Historical Manuscripts Commission

Holdsworth, *Eng. law* — W. S. Holdsworth, *A history of English law*, ed. A. L. Goodhart and H. L. Hanbury, 17 vols. (1903–72)

HoP, *Commons* — *The history of parliament: the House of Commons* [1386–1421, ed. J. S. Roskell, L. Clark, and C. Rawcliffe, 4 vols. (1992); 1509–1558, ed. S. T. Bindoff, 3 vols. (1982); 1558–1603, ed. P. W. Hasler, 3 vols. (1981); 1660–1690, ed. B. D. Henning, 3 vols. (1983); 1690–1715, ed. D. W. Hayton, E. Cruickshanks, and S. Handley, 5 vols. (2002); 1715–1754, ed. R. Sedgwick, 2 vols. (1970); 1754–1790, ed. L. Namier and J. Brooke, 3 vols. (1964), repr. (1985); 1790–1820, ed. R. G. Thorne, 5 vols. (1986); in draft (used with permission): 1422–1504, 1604–1629, 1640–1660, and 1820–1832]

IGI — *International Genealogical Index*, Church of Jesus Christ of the Latterday Saints

ILN — *Illustrated London News*

IMC — Irish Manuscripts Commission

Irving, *Scots.* — J. Irving, ed., *The book of Scotsmen eminent for achievements in arms and arts, church and state, law, legislation and literature, commerce, science, travel and philanthropy* (1881)

JCS — *Journal of the Chemical Society*

JHC — *Journals of the House of Commons*

JHL — *Journals of the House of Lords*

John of Worcester, *Chron.* — *The chronicle of John of Worcester*, ed. R. R. Darlington and P. McGurk, trans. J. Bray and P. McGurk, 3 vols., OMT (1995–) [vol. 1 forthcoming]

Keeler, *Long Parliament* — M. F. Keeler, *The Long Parliament, 1640–1641: a biographical study of its members* (1954)

Kelly, *Handbk* — *The upper ten thousand: an alphabetical list of all members of noble families*, 3 vols. (1875–7); continued as *Kelly's handbook of the upper ten thousand for 1878* [1879], 2 vols. (1878–9); continued as *Kelly's handbook to the titled, landed and official classes*, 94 vols. (1880–1973)

LondG — *London Gazette*

LP Henry VIII — J. S. Brewer, J. Gairdner, and R. H. Brodie, eds., *Letters and papers, foreign and domestic, of the reign of Henry VIII*, 23 vols. in 38 (1862–1932); repr. (1965)

Mallalieu, *Watercolour artists* — H. L. Mallalieu, *The dictionary of British watercolour artists up to 1820*, 3 vols. (1976–90); vol. 1, 2nd edn (1986)

Memoirs FRS — *Biographical Memoirs of Fellows of the Royal Society*

MGH — Monumenta Germaniae Historica

MT — *Musical Times*

Munk, *Roll* — W. Munk, *The roll of the Royal College of Physicians of London*, 2 vols. (1861); 2nd edn, 3 vols. (1878)

N&Q — *Notes and Queries*

New Grove — S. Sadie, ed., *The new Grove dictionary of music and musicians*, 20 vols. (1980); 2nd edn, 29 vols. (2001) [also online edn; see also Grove, *Dict. mus.*]

Nichols, *Illustrations* — J. Nichols and J. B. Nichols, *Illustrations of the literary history of the eighteenth century*, 8 vols. (1817–58)

Nichols, *Lit. anecdotes* — J. Nichols, *Literary anecdotes of the eighteenth century*, 9 vols. (1812–16); facs. edn (1966)

Obits. FRS — *Obituary Notices of Fellows of the Royal Society*

O'Byrne, *Naval biog. dict.* — W. R. O'Byrne, *A naval biographical dictionary* (1849); repr. (1990); [2nd edn], 2 vols. (1861)

OHS — Oxford Historical Society

Old Westminsters — *The record of Old Westminsters*, 1–2, ed. G. F. R. Barker and A. H. Stenning (1928); suppl. 1, ed. J. B. Whitmore and G. R. Y. Radcliffe [1938]; 3, ed. J. B. Whitmore, G. R. Y. Radcliffe, and D. C. Simpson (1963); suppl. 2, ed. F. E. Pagan (1978); 4, ed. F. E. Pagan and H. E. Pagan (1992)

OMT — Oxford Medieval Texts

Ordericus Vitalis, *Eccl. hist.* — *The ecclesiastical history of Orderic Vitalis*, ed. and trans. M. Chibnall, 6 vols., OMT (1969–80); repr. (1990)

Paris, *Chron.* — *Matthaei Parisiensis, monachi sancti Albani, chronica majora*, ed. H. R. Luard, Rolls Series, 7 vols. (1872–83)

Parl. papers — *Parliamentary papers* (1801–)

PBA — *Proceedings of the British Academy*

Pepys, *Diary* — *The diary of Samuel Pepys*, ed. R. Latham and W. Matthews, 11 vols. (1970–83); repr. (1995) and (2000)

Pevsner — N. Pevsner and others, Buildings of England series

PICE — *Proceedings of the Institution of Civil Engineers*

Pipe rolls — *The great roll of the pipe for . . .*, PRSoc. (1884–)

PRO — Public Record Office

PRS — *Proceedings of the Royal Society of London*

PRSoc. — Pipe Roll Society

PTRS — *Philosophical Transactions of the Royal Society*

QR — *Quarterly Review*

RC — Record Commissions

Redgrave, *Artists* — S. Redgrave, *A dictionary of artists of the English school* (1874); rev. edn (1878); repr. (1970)

Reg. Oxf. — C. W. Boase and A. Clark, eds., *Register of the University of Oxford*, 5 vols., OHS, 1, 10–12, 14 (1885–9)

Reg. PCS — J. H. Burton and others, eds., *The register of the privy council of Scotland*, 1st ser., 14 vols. (1877–98); 2nd ser., 8 vols. (1899–1908); 3rd ser., [16 vols.] (1908–70)

Reg. RAN — H. W. C. Davis and others, eds., *Regesta regum Anglo-Normannorum, 1066–1154*, 4 vols. (1913–69)

RIBA Journal — *Journal of the Royal Institute of British Architects* [later *RIBA Journal*]

RotP — J. Strachey, ed., *Rotuli parliamentorum ut et petitiones, et placita in parliamento*, 6 vols. (1767–77)

RotS — D. Macpherson, J. Caley, and W. Illingworth, eds., *Rotuli Scotiae in Turri Londinensi et in domo capitulari Westmonasteriensi asservati*, 2 vols., RC, 14 (1814–19)

RS — Record(s) Society

Rymer, *Foedera* — T. Rymer and R. Sanderson, eds., *Foedera, conventiones, literae et cuiuscunque generis acta publica inter reges Angliae et alios quosvis imperatores, reges, pontifices, principes, vel communitates*, 20 vols. (1704–35); 2nd edn, 20 vols. (1726–35); 3rd edn, 10 vols. (1739–45), facs. edn (1967); new edn, ed. A. Clarke, J. Caley, and F. Holbrooke, 4 vols., RC, 50 (1816–30)

Sainty, *Judges* — J. Sainty, ed., *The judges of England, 1272–1990*, SeldS, suppl. ser., 10 (1993)

Sainty, *King's counsel* — J. Sainty, ed., *A list of English law officers and king's counsel*, SeldS, suppl. ser., 7 (1987)

SCH — Studies in Church History

Scots peerage — J. B. Paul, ed. *The Scots peerage, founded on Wood's edition of Sir Robert Douglas's Peerage of Scotland, containing an historical and genealogical account of the nobility of that kingdom*, 9 vols. (1904–14)

SeldS — Selden Society

SHR — *Scottish Historical Review*

State trials — T. B. Howell and T. J. Howell, eds., *Cobbett's Complete collection of state trials*, 34 vols. (1809–28)

STC, 1475–1640 — A. W. Pollard, G. R. Redgrave, and others, eds., *A short-title catalogue of . . . English books . . . 1475–1640* (1926); 2nd edn, ed. W. A. Jackson, F. S. Ferguson, and K. F. Pantzer, 3 vols. (1976–91) [see also Wing, *STC*]

STS — Scottish Text Society

SurtS — Surtees Society

Symeon of Durham, *Opera* — *Symeonis monachi opera omnia*, ed. T. Arnold, 2 vols., Rolls Series, 75 (1882–5); repr. (1965)

Tanner, *Bibl. Brit.-Hib.* — T. Tanner, *Bibliotheca Britannico-Hibernica*, ed. D. Wilkins (1748); repr. (1963)

Thieme & Becker, *Allgemeines Lexikon* — U. Thieme, F. Becker, and H. Vollmer, eds., *Allgemeines Lexikon der bildenden Künstler von der Antike bis zur Gegenwart*, 37 vols. (Leipzig, 1907–50); repr. (1961–5), (1983), and (1992)

Thurloe, *State papers* — *A collection of the state papers of John Thurloe*, ed. T. Birch, 7 vols. (1742)

TLS — *Times Literary Supplement*

Tout, *Admin. hist.* — T. F. Tout, *Chapters in the administrative history of mediaeval England: the wardrobe, the chamber, and the small seals*, 6 vols. (1920–33); repr. (1967)

TRHS — *Transactions of the Royal Historical Society*

VCH — H. A. Doubleday and others, eds., *The Victoria history of the counties of England*, [88 vols.] (1900–)

Venn, *Alum. Cant.* — J. Venn and J. A. Venn, *Alumni Cantabrigienses: a biographical list of all known students, graduates, and holders of office at the University of Cambridge, from the earliest times to 1900*, 10 vols. (1922–54); repr. in 2 vols. (1974–8)

Vertue, *Note books* — [G. Vertue], *Note books*, ed. K. Esdaile, earl of Ilchester, and H. M. Hake, 6 vols., Walpole Society, 18, 20, 22, 24, 26, 30 (1930–55)

VF — *Vanity Fair*

Walford, *County families* — E. Walford, *The county families of the United Kingdom, or, Royal manual of the titled and untitled aristocracy of Great Britain and Ireland* (1860)

Walker rev. — A. G. Matthews, *Walker revised: being a revision of John Walker's Sufferings of the clergy during the grand rebellion, 1642–60* (1948); repr. (1988)

Walpole, *Corr.* — *The Yale edition of Horace Walpole's correspondence*, ed. W. S. Lewis, 48 vols. (1937–83)

Ward, *Men of the reign* — T. H. Ward, ed., *Men of the reign: a biographical dictionary of eminent persons of British and colonial birth who have died during the reign of Queen Victoria* (1885); repr. (Graz, 1968)

Waterhouse, *18c painters* — E. Waterhouse, *The dictionary of 18th century painters in oils and crayons* (1981); repr. as *British 18th century painters in oils and crayons* (1991), vol. 2 of *Dictionary of British art*

Watt, *Bibl. Brit.* — R. Watt, *Bibliotheca Britannica, or, A general index to British and foreign literature*, 4 vols. (1824) [many reprs.]

Wellesley index — W. E. Houghton, ed., *The Wellesley index to Victorian periodicals, 1824–1900*, 5 vols. (1966–89); new edn (1999) [CD-ROM]

Wing, *STC* — D. Wing, ed., *Short-title catalogue of . . . English books . . . 1641–1700*, 3 vols. (1945–51); 2nd edn (1972–88); rev. and enl. edn, ed. J. J. Morrison, C. W. Nelson, and M. Seccombe, 4 vols. (1994–8) [see also *STC, 1475–1640*]

Wisden — *John Wisden's Cricketer's Almanack*

Wood, *Ath. Oxon.* — A. Wood, *Athenae Oxonienses . . . to which are added the Fasti*, 2 vols. (1691–2); 2nd edn (1721); new edn, 4 vols., ed. P. Bliss (1813–20); repr. (1967) and (1969)

Wood, *Vic. painters* — C. Wood, *Dictionary of Victorian painters* (1971); 2nd edn (1978); 3rd edn as *Victorian painters*, 2 vols. (1995), vol. 4 of *Dictionary of British art*

WW — *Who's who* (1849–)

WWBMP — M. Stenton and S. Lees, eds., *Who's who of British members of parliament*, 4 vols. (1976–81)

WWW — *Who was who* (1929–)

Knox, Alexander (1757–1831), theological writer, was born in Londonderry, in the north of Ireland, on 17 March 1757, the son of Alexander Knox (*d.* 1770), a man of independent property and a leading member of the corporation of Londonderry, who was descended from the Scottish family to which the celebrated reformer John Knox belonged. His mother, whose name is unknown, died in 1792. Knox's lifelong poor health prevented him from passing through a regular course of school education, but his later writings and reputation for learning attest to his thorough grounding through extensive reading at an early age in the classics and divinity, as well as general literature.

Debt to Methodism A seminal influence on Knox's early religious development and later life was his boyhood and youthful contact with the founder of Methodism, John Wesley, who had enlisted his parents into one of his societies in Londonderry in 1765, during the course of his tenth visit to Ireland. Wesley wrote twenty letters between 1776 and 1785 to the young Alexander Knox (addressed as 'My Dear Alleck') that were full of religious and practical advice. Knox was an intelligent but very delicate youth. From his earliest years he 'had been afflicted with attacks of epilepsy, attended by depression of spirits of the most painful character' (*Thirty Years' Correspondence*, 2.24). Wesley convinced him of the providential nature of his afflictions as designed 'to balance the natural petulance of youth' (1 April 1777; ibid., 25). Knox was for a time a member of one of Wesley's societies, but a growing spiritual independence caused him to withdraw before the age of twenty. He remained an admirer of Wesley's original system, arguing that 'never, elsewhere, except in the Apostles themselves, and in the sacred books they have left, were the true foundation, and the sublime superstructure of Christianity, so effectually united' (to Joseph Butterworth, 25 Sept 1807; *Remains*, 1.74). Likewise, to his friend John Jebb, Knox insisted that in 'John Wesley's views of Christian Perfection, are combined, in substance, all the sublime morality of the Greek Fathers, the spirituality of the mystics, and the divine philosophy of our favourite platonists' (19 July 1804; *Thirty Years' Correspondence*, 1.143). Knox insisted, however, that it was to his mother rather than to John Wesley that he owed his early religious education and 'whatever I have gained of true peace' (to Mr Butterworth, 25 Sept 1807; *Remains*, 1.70). He found that the 'methods of Methodist piety were so much pointed to present effects, to the producing something new, that they seemed, when at all resorted to, to disturb my animal spirits too much'. A Sunday spent worshipping with the Methodists in Liverpool in 1802, on account of the dryness of Anglican pulpit discourse in the locality, convinced him 'that a quieter, more equable, more gradual course, was the one indicated for me to walk in' (ibid., 71). In the same letter he made clear that 'I never called Mr. Wesley, Rabbi' (ibid.).

Knox's lifelong personal devotion to Wesley's memory, his abiding sense of Wesley's providential role in recalling the contemporary church to an emphasis on holiness of life, and the importance of emotion in religion, however,

Alexander Knox (1757–1831), by Henry Weekes and Henry Adlard, pubd 1834 (after Sir Francis Legatt Chantrey)

were only partially offset by his own later, independent thinking on the primitive church and a high-church emphasis on apostolic order and authority. To the end Knox defended Wesley against a variety of different critics. In 1802 he published a defence of Wesley against a Calvinistic clergyman, John Walker, fellow of Trinity College, Dublin, who had published *Expostulatory Address to the Members of the Methodist Society in Ireland*. Knox's published remarks on this publication elicited a 'defence' from Walker. In 1822 he composed a defence of Wesley against Robert Southey's life of him as *Remarks on the Life and Character of John Wesley*; Southey himself was so impressed with Knox's defence that he decided that any new edition of his own biography of Wesley should carry it as an appendix. Moreover Knox kept up his Methodist connections, befriending and becoming the patron of the young Adam Clarke, a Methodist preacher who became a notable Orientalist. He also attended the annual Methodist conference in Ireland as late as 1807.

Public life Knox became active in political life during the 1790s. He was a friend of moderate parliamentary reform at the beginning of that decade, and remained an advocate of Roman Catholic emancipation and of a moderate endowment of the Irish Catholic priesthood. However, alarmed by events in France and at the proceedings of the United Irishmen (with which he had some early connections) and by the unrest and subsequent rising of 1798, he moved in a more conservative political direction. In 1798 he was appointed private secretary to the chief secretary for Ireland, Robert Stewart, Lord Castlereagh. His political skills as an administrator in this post were underpinned by a profound historical understanding of the philosophical principles of government and the peculiar conditions of Ireland, and were reflected in his *Essays on the political circumstances of Ireland during the administration of Lord Camden;*

with an appendix containing thoughts on the will of the people (1799), which was written at intervals between 1795 and 1797 and originally intended as papers 'for insertion in newspapers, or for circulation in the form of handbills'.

Knox's public career was cut short in August 1799, when, as he later recalled, 'I was obliged from nervous disposition to leave Ireland' (Baird Evans, 24). He had the highest respect for Lord Castlereagh, whom he praised as 'the honestest and perhaps the ablest statesman that has been in Ireland for a century' (*Remains*, 4.31), and Castlereagh reciprocated his regard. As late as 1811 Castlereagh was pressing Knox, unsuccessfully, to write the history of the Union so as to confront 'the demons of the present day' (ibid., 539). Castlereagh had urged Knox not to resign, and later urged him to accept an offer to represent his native city, Londonderry, in the United Kingdom parliament. Knox was not dissuaded from his original intention and entirely abandoned public life. Some far-fetched reasons, relating to apparent blemishes in his private life, have been adduced for his decision. The literalness of Knox's own admissions in a fragmentary diary (only part of which survives: see *Remains*, 4.41–5, 55–61), wherein he upbraided himself for having involved himself in scenes of dissipation from early manhood until about 1797, has been questioned by G. T. Stokes. Knox has been the subject of gross, racy, and unreliable anecdotes from hostile sources, perhaps originating in disapproval of his changing political allegiances in the 1790s. For example, William Fitzpatrick, who sneeringly referred to Knox as having 'made himself useful as a scribe during the reign of terror', alleged that Knox underwent an act of bodily self-mutilation prompted by 'the madness and illegality of' an unrequited passion for the beautiful young wife of the chief secretary, Robert Peel (Fitzpatrick). This story is discredited by the fact that Peel only assumed the post in 1812 and was unmarried at the time when Knox is supposed to have fallen for his wife.

Religious retirement Whatever the truth in respect of disorder in Knox's private life it can be safely assumed that it was his overriding theological interests and craving for solitude that lay at the root of his decision to retire. As his evangelical friend Hannah More noted, 'Having been a grand instrument in accomplishing the great work of the Union, he turned his back upon politics and politicians, and lives in a religious retirement' (H. More to W. Wilberforce, 24 Sept 1804, Bodl. Oxf., Wilberforce MS d. 15, fol. 71). Knox lived the last thirty years of his life in retirement, either at Bellevue, Delgany, outside Dublin, at the residence of the La Touche, a Huguenot banking family, or in his own bachelor quarters at 46 Dawson Street, Dublin. His life was one almost of a hermit, interrupted only by occasional visits to the country homes of friends. He was always plagued by a melancholy and at times neurotic temperament. None the less, in view of reports both of his brilliance as a conversationalist and of his being a gentleman of refined and exquisite taste, the image of an eccentric recluse and invalid requires modification. Moreover, it is significant that his health notably improved on his retirement and that after 1803 his epileptic fits disappeared and his state of nervousness diminished.

High-churchmanship It was during the long, later years of his retirement that Knox emerged as a profoundly original religious thinker, earning the sobriquet 'the sage of Bellevue', while his friend J. S. Harford called him 'the Plato of Bellevue'. One of the most formative personal contacts of his life after that of John Wesley was his close friendship with John Jebb, bishop of Limerick from 1823, whom he first met when Jebb was at Londonderry School. The names of Knox and Jebb became inextricably linked as representatives of a theological school. Knox used his close contacts with Charles Agar, archbishop of Dublin (1801–9), and Charles Brodrick, archbishop of Cashel (1801–22), to smooth the clerical career of the young Jebb. The two friends toured England together in the summer of 1809.

Knox's theological position has been the subject of discussion, most notably by G. T. Stokes and Yngve Brilioth. Although he was influenced by the Methodist system and maintained close contacts with the so-called Claphamite evangelicals—notably Hannah More and William Wilberforce—Knox was a high-churchman of sorts but kept his distance from the 'high and dry' contemporary variant of high-churchmanship. Knox, like Jebb, was distinctly high-church in his teaching on the sacraments, insisting on the reality of the efficacy of sacramental grace in both baptism and the eucharist, as exemplified in his *On the Doctrine Respecting Baptism Held by the Church of England* (1820) and in *An Enquiry on Grounds of Scripture and Reason into the Use and Import of the Eucharistic Symbols* (1824). Knox defended the English Reformation on Catholic grounds, regarding it as a restoration of the early church as a court of appeal. He identified much more with the eucharistic doctrine of Nicholas Ridley than that of Thomas Cranmer. He took a high-church line in asserting that the catholicity of the Church of England was based on its unbroken episcopate and on the merits of the Book of Common Prayer. For Knox the main strength of the Anglican liturgy lay in its apparent mediation of the piety of the early church. One of the abiding themes of his thought was gratitude for what he regarded as the providential escape of the Church of England from various attempts, whether from the direction of Geneva or Rome, to despoil her of her liturgical and apostolical inheritance. Those eighteenth-century establishment figures who went astray into Arianism or Socinianism or in the direction of dissent—such as Samuel Clarke, Benjamin Hoadly, and Theophilus Lindsey—did so, he argued, because they 'seem never to have been capable of feeling the peculiar excellencies of our liturgical forms' (*Remains*, 1.98). His view of Anglican catholicity was also rooted, as he showed in a letter, 'On the fathers of the Christian church and on Catholic tradition' (ibid., 277–313), in his application of the celebrated dictum of St Vincent of Lerins—*quod ubique, quod semper, quod eadem*—as the doctrinal standard of the Church of England. Newman's later idea of the *via media* found expression in Knox's words to Jebb in a letter of 1813: 'What perverse influence the nickname of Protestant has had upon our Church ... It will perhaps be at length discovered, that there is a *medium* between the two extremes' (*Thirty Years' Correspondence*, 2.122).

Knox aligned himself with high-churchmanship and against evangelicalism in his understanding of the doctrine of justification. In opposition to Joseph Milner and other Anglican evangelical exponents he wrote 'Letter to Mr Parken on justification', in which, like Wesley, he criticized the 'forensic' doctrine of justification. In contrast Knox defined justification as the acquisition of a condition of inward or interior—and not merely outward or formal—righteousness, and identified baptism with justification. He sought to read this interpretation of justification as a moral change into the articles and homilies of the Church of England. At the same time Knox was sensitive to evangelical charges of formalism against high-churchmen. He reacted strongly against sterile forms of the establishmentarian high-churchmanship of his day. In a memorable passage in a letter to a friend he made clear his position:

> Now, I am a Churchman in grain—not a Tory Churchman, for that is a disease in the Church, not its constitutional turn; nor yet a Whig Churchman, for they do not value enough the distinguishing features of our Establishment. But, if I may use the term, I am a primitive Churchman. (*Remains*, 4.206–7)

Evangelicalism This outlook brought Knox closer to Anglican evangelicals as well as to Methodists. In a letter of 1816, 'On the situation and prospects of the established church', Knox condemned the spirit in which 'the present champions for what they think high church orthodoxy, are combating their "Evangelical" opponents', lamenting that in this quarter 'inward religion is little less than systematically exploded' (ibid., 1.58). Thus when during the so-called Blagdon controversy over Sunday schools, in 1802, Hannah More endured the obloquy of some high-churchmen Knox privately defended her as 'one of the most truly evangelical divines of this whole age' (Roberts, 3.161). Knox even went so far as to claim: 'Hannah More and I are substantially of the same school, that is, we both make it our object to pass through the form of Godliness to the power thereof' (*Remains*, 4.174–5). More reciprocated Knox's compliments, regarding him as 'the most intellectual and spiritual man I ever knew' (H. More to W. Wilberforce, 24 Sept 1804; Bodl. Oxf., Wilberforce MS d. 15, fol. 75). Knox's closeness to More was also revealed by the close hand that he had in her publication *Hints towards Forming the Character of a Young Princess* (1805). He was friendly towards, but kept a critical distance from, the leading high-church faction in the church, the so-called Hackney phalanx. He admired individuals in that group but disliked what he regarded as their rigidity and narrowness, even claiming in 1816 that the 'old high church race is died out' (A. Knox, 'On the situation and prospects of the established church', 1816, in *Remains*, 1.54).

Knox and Jebb certainly parted company with most contemporary high-churchmen in their regard not only for evangelicalism and some puritan worthies such as Richard Baxter but also for the more religious strain in the latitudinarian tradition, as exemplified by Sir Matthew Hale, lord chief justice in Charles II's reign, and notably the whig historian Gilbert Burnet, bishop of Salisbury under William III. In his preface to Jebb's edition of *Lives, Characters, and an Address to Posterity by Gilbert Burnet, Late Bishop of Sarum* (1833) Knox approved Hale's tenderness towards nonconformists on the ground that it proceeded from 'puritanic presuppositions' rather than 'latitudinarian indifference' (p. lii). Knox's high regard for Burnet and historic latitudinarianism puzzled his Anglican evangelical friends as well as stricter high-churchmen. Hannah More, bemused by a present that Knox left her to give to William Wilberforce—Burnet's *Lives*, 'of which he is very fond'—observed:

> His chief delight is in contemplation and inward religion; but he is not in all points in our way. He is of the Platonic Christian school, a disciple of Cudworth, Lucas, Whichcote, Scougal, Worthington, and Joseph Mede. In our disputes, however, I tell him that while Leighton and Baxter are his favourites, we shall not quarrel much. (H. More to W. Wilberforce, 24 Sept 1804, Bodl. Oxf., Wilberforce MS d. 15, fols. 70–71)

After Jeremy Taylor, Knox's favourite spiritual authors were Henry Scougal (*Life of God in the Soul of Man*), John Worthington (*On Resignation*), and Richard Lucas (*Inquiry after Happiness*). Knox's influence on the Claphamite circle of Anglican evangelicals was such, however, that Henry Thornton privately conceded to Hannah More that evangelicals like themselves had much to learn from the 'manliness and sublimity' exhibited in the religion of Knox and Jebb but 'which we lamentably want' (H. Thornton to H. More, 9 Sept 1809 CUL, Add. 1/L4, fols. 104–5). Some Irish evangelicals on the other hand were less tolerant of Knox's departure from accepted evangelical doctrinal norms than their English Claphamite counterparts.

Roman Catholicism Knox's attitude to the Roman Catholic church and the question of reunion was also distinctive and the subject of controversy. Anglican evangelical friends, whom he strove to persuade into supporting Catholic emancipation, could be taken aback by his conversational championing of aspects of Roman Catholic teaching and by his eirenicism towards the Church of Rome. In a work defending the idea of Catholic emancipation Knox urged his protestant contemporaries to recognize the debt that the Church of England owed to the Roman Catholic church as 'having been the instrument of so much good to us' in terms of liturgical and devotional treasures (A. Knox, *An Answer to the Rt Hon. P. Duigenan's Two Great Arguments Against the Full Enfranchisement of the Irish Roman Catholics*, 1810, 41). Like Wesley, Knox was an avid reader of Roman Catholic devotional writers such as Thomas à Kempis, M. De Renty, and François de Sales, even complaining in a letter to Hannah More in December 1806 that protestantism was deficient in producing saints and saintliness. On the other hand Knox regarded his espousal of the Vincentian rule as the strongest barrier possible against the claims of the Roman Catholic church, which he regarded as being a 'mental yoke' enslaving the individual conscience. He responded respectfully and cordially, but in the negative, to the plan for reunion of the churches put forward by the Roman Catholic controversialist James Doyle, bishop of Kildare and Leighlin, in 1824. In a letter to Thomas Newenham, in which he recorded his conviction on the impossibility of any such union unless the Church of Rome parted 'with its essence', Knox none the less asserted in favour of the Roman Catholic church:

> I neither join in the charge of idolatry with which it is so customary to brand her; nor do I censure her tenets on many points which she has been condemned by Protestant controversialists. In many of these instances, I humbly think there is more truth on her side than on theirs. (A. Knox, *Letters on the Re-Union of the Churches of England and Rome*, [1824], 28–9)

Death Knox, who never married, died in Dublin on 17 January 1831. A major treatise on the epistles to the Romans and Hebrews on which he had laboured fitfully since 1817 remained uncompleted. Some of his evangelical friends, including the Revd Thomas Kelly, claimed that in his very last years and on his deathbed he abandoned what they regarded as the erroneous points in his theories, had a conversion experience, and embraced doctrinal evangelicalism. The claim, propagated in an article in the evangelical *Christian Observer* in August 1836, was publicly rejected by others of Knox's friends, such as James Hornby, and by a reviewer in the high-church *British Critic* in 1838, while Bishop Jebb's nephew John Jebb considered it based on 'the most profound ignorance of that venerable person's character' (J. Jebb to J. Hornby, 2 Oct 1836; TCD, MS 6398, letter 53). A monument to Knox was erected, at some time after his death, in St Ann's Church, Dublin, where he used to worship. A stained-glass window dedicated to his memory was erected in the same church in the early 1860s.

Reputation Knox has been claimed as a religious prophet and as 'a Christian Socrates' whose influence was as disturbing to protestant divinity as 'a comet upon the orbit of our globe' (*Remains*, 1). He has been compared to Samuel Taylor Coleridge as an original religious thinker and credited with anticipating Coleridge's famous distinction between the reason and the understanding. More controversially he has been viewed as a bridge between Wesley and Newman. There was enough in Knox's theological principles and teaching to give some credence to Stokes's contention that Knox, along with his friend Jebb, was a harbinger of the Oxford Movement. James Hornby, who edited the four volumes of Knox's *Remains* (1834–7), was the first to make this claim, arguing that there was no catholic doctrine for which the authors of *Tracts for the Times* were then contending that Knox had 'not been fighting over, and winning solid ground for, during the whole of the present century' (Hornby to Newman, 31 March 1840; *The Letters and Diaries of J. H. Newman*, ed. C. S. Dessau and others, 31 vols., 1973–7, 7.288). Certainly Knox's high doctrine of the Christian priesthood and apostolic succession, together with his advanced sacramental teaching,

marks him out as a genuine precursor of the Tractarians. His view of justification as an 'imparted' rather than 'imputed' source of 'righteousness' also closely foreshadowed Newman's position in his *Lectures on Justification* (1838). Building on the evidence of these similarities Stokes famously asserted that 'Wesley begat Knox, and Knox begat Jebb, and Jebb begat Rose and Pusey and Newman' (Stokes, 190).

Stokes, however, overstated his case in making Knox the fount or origin of the Oxford Movement, and in his estimate of the extent of Wesley's influence transmitted by Knox on Newman (who in fact had a low opinion of Wesley). Newman conceded that Knox had played a part in the broader preparation of the ground that enabled the Oxford Movement to take root in the 1830s: 'Could we see the scheme of things as angels see it, I fancy we should find he has his place in the growth and restoration (so be it) of Church principles' (Newman to S. Rickards, 9 Feb 1835; J. H. Newman, *Letters and diaries*, 5.27). Stokes, however, overlooked Newman's and especially Keble's reservations about Knox's teaching. Newman, while conceding to Robert Wilberforce in June 1838 that he had 'read very little' of Knox, remarked that he 'seems to say dangerous things … I should be unwilling to think him more than an eclectic, though that is bad enough. Froude did not like him. I think his works on the Eucharist have done much good' (D. Newsome, *The Parting of Friends*, 2nd edn, 1993, 197). Taking his cue from Froude's criticisms, Newman later hardened his attitude against Knox, telling the editor of Knox's *Remains* bluntly:

> I deliberately formed the opinion from the various works of his which I read, that he did not hold the Apostolical Succession in the sense in which Mr Froude held it; and that he entertained opinions less strict and definite than the Catholic Church teaches. (Newman to Hornby, 13 April 1840, J. H. Newman, *Letters and diaries*, 7.303)

E. B. Pusey's biographer H. P. Liddon drew attention to 'the slight use' that the Oxford school made of Knox's writings, explaining that:

> the Tractarians felt that they could not claim him as a whole; and they were certainly not indebted to him for anything which they knew of Catholic antiquity or Catholic truth. But they did occasionally use him as being a witness in dark times, to portions of the truth which they were reasserting; and in this sense he may be described as a precursor of the Oxford revival. (Liddon, 262)

Similarly Dean Church immediately challenged Stokes's argument as being built upon insufficient material. Church concluded: 'The Oxford men found their doctrines where Wesley in his younger days found them, and where Knox found them afterwards, but quite certainly they did not find them through Knox or Wesley' (*The Guardian*, 7 Sept 1887).

The mature Tractarian estimate of Knox can be compared to that of the young W. E. Gladstone before he had quite abandoned the traces of his own early evangelicalism. Gladstone's development from a youthful evangelicalism to a high-church position was influenced by his reading of Knox's religious writings, but initially his view of Knox was ambivalent. In a private memorandum composed on 24 May 1835 he praised the way in which Knox had 'in the first place vindicated, one may almost hope for ever, against the outrages of the scoffer and the saturnine contempt of formalism, the great and essential doctrine of an inward and vital religion'. However, as well as criticizing Knox's 'denial of a forensic justification' Gladstone found Knox's religion to be too 'individualised', recognizing 'no brotherhood'. 'There are few temperaments,' he concluded, 'which could afford to adopt this isolated method of religion, without serious perhaps fatal detriment' (Gladstone papers, BL, Add. MS 44724). Despite Gladstone's misgivings Knox has proved a seminal religious thinker of the period.   PETER B. NOCKLES

Sources *Thirty years correspondence between John Jebb and Alexander Knox*, ed. C. Forster, 2 vols. (1834–7) • *Remains of Alexander Knox*, ed. J. J. Hornby, 4 vols. (1834–7) • G. T. Stokes, 'Alexander Knox and the Oxford Movement', *Contemporary Review*, 52 (1887), 184–205 • W. J. Fitzpatrick, *The Sham Squire and the informers of 1798* (1866), 245 • *The Guardian* (7 Sept 1887) • J. Baird Evans, *Three hermits: short studies in Christian antiquity, Methodism and Tractarianism* (1956) • H. P. Liddon, *Life of Edward Bouverie Pusey*, 4th edn, 1 (1894), 260–62 • C. H. Crookshank, *History of Methodism in Ireland*, 3 vols. (1885–8), vol. 1, p. 235 • Y. Briloth, *Anglican revival* (1925), chap. 4; appx 1 • '*Remains* of Alexander Knox', *British Critic*, 23 (Jan 1838) • Gladstone papers, BL, Add. MS 44724, fols. 73–5; MS 44725 • J. T. A. Gunstone, 'Alexander Knox, 1757–1831', *Church Quarterly Review*, 157 (1956), 463–75 • H. More, letters, U. Cal., Los Angeles, William Andrews Clark Memorial Library • copy of a letter of Alexander Knox on Catholic emancipation, [n.d.], Bodl. Oxf., MS Wilberforce c. 52, fols. 77–82 • W. Roberts, *Memoirs of the life and correspondence of Mrs Hannah More*, 2nd edn, 4 vols. (1834), 3.161 • *DNB*

Archives BL, Gladstone papers, Add. MS 44724, fols. 73–5 • BL, corresp. with J. Jebb, Add. MSS 41163–41166 • PRO NIre., corresp. with Castlereagh • TCD, letters to Joseph Cooper Walker

Likenesses H. Weekes and H. Adlard, stipple, pubd 1834 (after bust by F. L. Chantrey), NPG [*see illus.*]

Knox, Alexander Andrew (1818–1891), journalist and police magistrate, the second son of George Knox, a landowner in Jamaica, was born in London on 5 February 1818. He was educated at Blundell's School, Tiverton, and went with a scholarship to Trinity College, Cambridge (BA 1844, MA 1847). He was called to the bar as member of Lincoln's Inn in 1844.

Knox began his journalistic career at the *Morning Chronicle*, but in 1846 he became a writer of leading articles on the staff of *The Times*. He continued to write for that paper until 1860, when he accepted Sir George Cornewall Lewis's offer of the office of police magistrate at Worship Street. In 1862 he was transferred to the Marlborough Street court, and remained there until 1878, when a stroke forced him to retire. On three occasions he received the special thanks of the Home Office for his magisterial services.

A noted conversationalist, Knox spent much of his life in the company of intellectuals. In 1842 he travelled in Italy with Shelley, his wife, Mary, and Robert Leslie Ellis, where they met Edward John Trelawny, a friend of Byron and Shelley. Knox was a frequent guest of Dr John Ayrton Paris, at whose house in London he met leading men of science, including Michael Faraday, Sir Benjamin Collins Brodie, and Charles Babbage. Among his other friends

were Sir James Brooke, Admiral Sherard Osborn, Alexander William Kinglake, Sir Spencer St John, Thomas Mozley, and Marianne North. Knox published *The New Playground, or, Wanderings in Algeria* (1881). Besides his work on *The Times* he contributed articles to the *Edinburgh Review*, *Blackwood's Edinburgh Magazine*, and many other periodicals.

In 1857 Knox married Susan Toten, daughter of James Armstrong, of the Bengal civil service. He died at his home, 125 Victoria Street, London, on 5 October 1891; he was survived by his wife.

C. A. H. CROSSE, *rev.* JOSEPH COOHILL

Sources Mrs A. Crosse [C. A. H. Crosse], 'Alexander Knox and his friends', *Temple Bar*, 94 (1892), 495–517 • [S. Morison and others], *The history of The Times*, 2 (1939), 133 • Venn, *Alum. Cant.*

Wealth at death £7,616 2s. 6d.: probate, 29 Oct 1891, CGPLA Eng. & Wales

Knox, Andrew (d. 1633), bishop of Raphoe, was born in Renfrewshire, the second son of John Knox of Ranfurly in Kilbarchan parish. Educated at Glasgow University under the regime of Andrew Melville, he graduated MA in 1579, and after continuing his theological studies in the college was appointed minister of Lochwinnoch, Renfrewshire, in 1581, and then minister of nearby Paisley in 1585. He married his cousin Elizabeth, daughter of William Knox of Silvieland; the couple had two daughters and three sons, Thomas, James, and George.

Knox came to James VI's notice in 1592 when he discovered on the isle of Cumbrae in the Firth of Clyde George Kerr, a Roman Catholic, bound for Spain with certain papers, the 'Spanish blanks', signed by the conservative northern earls. When Kerr was interrogated the earls were implicated in a proposed Spanish invasion of Scotland. The next year Knox was appointed by the general assembly of the kirk to visit the presbyteries of Ayrshire and was assigned the task of persuading the master of Eglinton to accept Andrew Boyd as minister of Eaglesham, Renfrewshire. In 1597 Knox was made a commissioner to seek out Jesuits, seminary priests, and others suspected of plotting with the king of Spain. He subsequently received parliamentary commendation for his efforts and a pardon for his part in the accidental drowning, in the course of these duties, of Hew Barclay of Ladyland. In 1598 he was selected as one of the assembly's representatives to discuss with James VI a scheme of endowment for the ministry; from 1600 he was active in securing recruits to fill vacancies in the ministry; and in 1602 he was charged by the assembly with visiting the churches of Argyll. However, he seems to have been combative and quick-tempered. Disputes with neighbours went as far as the law courts, where on one occasion Knox struck his opponent, George Stewart, a Paisley burgess. On 4 October 1604 the presbytery is said to have suspended him and required him to do public penance in his church.

None the less, memory of Knox's earlier service to the crown seems to have prevailed, and it played some part in his promotion by the king in February 1605 to the bishopric of the Isles. In this capacity Knox proved a tireless servant of royal policy in the Hebrides. Amid much pomp he was one of the bishops who rode 'betwixt the erles and the lords, two and two, clothed in silke and velvet, with their foote mantles' (Calderwood, 6.943) to the parliament of 1606, which approved the royal supremacy, exacted an oath of allegiance, and affirmed the restitution of the estate of bishops. Knox visited his diocese that year with his authority thus enhanced and further proclaimed in a new seal which depicted a bishop in an open boat, holding a book in his left hand and gesturing over the side with his right. In January 1607 Knox was appointed constant moderator of the presbytery of the Isles. In the meantime he attempted to retain his charge in Paisley, but he eventually resigned and was relieved of it on 12 November 1607.

In spring 1608 Knox was appointed to a new royal commission to the Isles, headed by Andrew Stewart, third Lord Ochiltree. As part of a government programme aimed at curbing clan power, demilitarizing highland and island society, and obtaining rents allegedly due to the crown, it was to negotiate with the chiefs of Islay and Mull. By the autumn Ochiltree had assembled a military expedition. On arrival in the Hebrides he captured several chiefs (by tricking them into coming on board ship to hear a sermon by the bishop) and took the castles of Dunyvaig and Duart. Knox, who reported to the king that the chiefs, now carried off to prison in the lowlands, had 'ane servill feir of the executioun of your majesteis justle conceawit wrath aganis tham' (Goodare, 36), favoured an amicable settlement. In spring 1609 he went to court to confer with the king, and by June had persuaded him to change from a policy of dispossession of defiant chiefs to one of conciliation. Fortified with a new commission from the crown, Knox returned to the isles. Ignoring key instructions to conduct a survey of royal property, he called Hebridean chiefs to a court on Iona, in which nine of them agreed to regulations subsequently known as the statutes of Iona. This attempt to 'civilize' men sometimes regarded in other parts of Scotland as barbarians aimed to advance the reformed church within their territories and promote law, order, and acceptance of acts of the Scottish parliament. It also reflected government policies of discouraging Gaelic culture. Ministers' salaries, sabbath observance, and church repairs were negotiated, along with the education, in English and in the lowlands, of the eldest sons of leading islanders. At the same time limitations were placed on chiefs' military retinues and on clan hospitality.

Knox soon returned to Edinburgh, and on 28 September appeared at the privy council. There has been some debate about the impact and importance of the statutes, but they clearly represented a significant manifestation of the Scottish government's stance and a benchmark for future action. Knox's action in 'reducing … the ignorant and wicked people of our Isles to the acknowledgement of God and obedience of the King's Majesty' (Canny, 198) was itself acknowledged by the council, and it seems to have been his experience in the Hebrides which led the king to reward him on 6–7 May 1610 with nomination to the bishopric of Raphoe in Donegal, Ulster. Consecrated probably

between 23 January and 24 February 1611, Knox held the two bishoprics conjointly for the next seven years.

The king's brief to Knox in Raphoe was that 'by his pains and travails the ignorant multitude within that diocese may be reclaimed from their superstition and popish opinions' (Laing, 1.427–8). In a memorandum subsequently passed by James to the lord deputy of Ireland, Sir Arthur Chichester, Knox 'suggested that the episcopate should be given extraordinary powers to suppress catholicism, including the right to arrest catholic priests' (Moody and others, 3.209). On visiting his Irish diocese in 1611 he prepared a report on the state of religion there which led the king to instruct the archbishop of Armagh to summon a meeting of bishops in his province to reform abuses. At that date Chichester considered Knox to be a 'good bishop for that part of the kingdom, and zealously affected to reform the errors and abuses of the priests and people', who had 'done much more good in church government in the short time of his being among them than his predecessor all his time' (CSP Ire., 1611–14).

In August 1618 Knox resigned as bishop of the Isles and by the following year he was granted Irish letters of denization. He was succeeded by his eldest son, Thomas, who since his graduation from Glasgow University in 1608 and a period in London seeking preferment had served as a minister on Tiree and had assisted his father in administering his turbulent Scottish diocese. Temporarily taken hostage when the MacDonalds of Islay seized Dunyvaig Castle in 1614, Thomas had been rewarded by the crown with lands in Ulster; provided to the Isles on 24 February 1619, he served until some time between 1 November 1627 and 3 April 1628, and continued to apply his father's policies. The elder Knox died on 17 March 1633.

JAMES KIRK

Sources T. Thomson, ed., *Acts and proceedings of the general assemblies of the Kirk of Scotland*, 3 pts, Bannatyne Club, 81 (1839–45) · D. Calderwood, *The history of the Kirk of Scotland*, ed. T. Thomson and D. Laing, 8 vols., Wodrow Society, 7 (1842–9) · *Reg. PCS*, 1st ser. · *CSP Scot.* · D. Laing, ed., *Original letters relating to the ecclesiastical affairs of Scotland* (1851) · R. Wodrow, *Collections upon the lives of the reformers*, 2 vols. (1834–48) · *CSP Ire., 1611–14* · C. Innes, ed., *Munimenta alme Universitatis Glasguensis / Records of the University of Glasgow from its foundation till 1727*, 4 vols., Maitland Club, 72 (1854) · J. Durkan and J. Kirk, *The University of Glasgow, 1451–1577* (1977) · D. E. R. Watt, ed., *Fasti ecclesiae Scoticanae medii aevi ad annum 1638*, [2nd edn], Scottish RS, new ser., 1 (1969) · J. B. Craven, *Records of the dioceses of Argyll and the isles* (1907) · J. Kirk, *Patterns of reform: continuity and change in the Reformation kirk* (1989) · J. Goodare, 'The statutes of Iona in context', *SHR*, 77 (1998), 31–57 · E. B. Fryde and others, eds., *Handbook of British chronology*, 3rd edn, Royal Historical Society Guides and Handbooks, 2 (1986) · J. H. Ohlmeyer, '"Civilizinge of those rude partes": colonization within Britain and Ireland, 1580s–1640s', *The Oxford history of the British empire*, ed. N. Canny, 1 (1998), 124–47 · N. Canny, *Making Ireland British, 1580–1650* (2001) · T. W. Moody and others, eds., *A new history of Ireland*, 3: *Early modern Ireland, 1534–1691* (1976); repr. with corrections (1991) · *DNB*

Knox, Archibald (1864–1933), designer and watercolour painter, was born on 9 April 1864, the fourth son of the seven children of Robert William Knox, marine engineer, and his wife, Ann, at Cronkborne, Tromode, Braddan, Isle of Man. His parents came from Scotland to the Isle of Man, where his father founded a reasonably successful marine engineering business. He was educated at Douglas grammar school where he was encouraged to take an interest in the Celtic sculptures of the island (then being studied by P. M. C. Kermode) which were much to influence Knox's designs. He trained at Douglas School of Art (1878–84), where he was student teacher until 1888. In 1892 he seems to have been working in the studio of M. H. Baillie Scott, the architect, who was then based in Douglas. In 1897 he left the island to teach in London, which he did off and on until 1912.

It was during this period (perhaps through Baillie Scott) that Knox started working in commercial design. He apparently worked with Christopher Dresser and also with the Silver Studio, where his first works, which were based on Celtic motifs, seem to have been wallpapers for the exclusive Glasgow firm Wylie and Lochhead. The Silver Studio sold five of Knox's textile designs to the London firm of Liberty, and it was thus that he made the contacts which allowed him to embark on his major design work. Based on his long-time interest in Celtic ornament, Knox developed a series of designs for the embellishment of metalwork which became immediately popular. Until 1912, either through the Silver Studio or by direct commission, he was responsible for most of the designs in Liberty's *Cymric* and *Tudric* ranges—perhaps as many as 5000 (major collections in the Victoria and Albert Museum, London, and the Silver Studio collections, University of Middlesex). Since Liberty insisted on anonymity from its designers Knox's full output is not known. (He also designed carpets and pottery.) Liberty continued to sell his designs until the 1930s. From 1904 he taught at Kingston School of Art, but was forced to resign in 1912 after the examiners complained about the style and product of his teaching. A number of his students resigned with him and founded the Knox Guild of Craft and Design, which continued as a design studio until 1939. He tried to make a new career in the United States, but failed and returned to teaching in the Isle of Man.

Knox's designs take a central place in British art nouveau. His Liberty designs drew not only on his study of British Celtic motifs, but also on his interpretation of the continental versions of this style. The swirling interlace and stylized plant motifs which formed his stock-in-trade became popular again in the late twentieth century and his reputation burgeoned. While he understood the manufacturing process of the pewter and silver objects which he designed, he was always much happier with pen or pencil. Liberty was responsible for putting the designs out to be manufactured with firms such as W. H. Haseler of Birmingham; his work is thus perhaps unjustifiably criticized as lacking the finish of his continental contemporaries, who often worked more closely with the manufacturers. Examples of his designs applied to textiles and metalwork may be found in the Victoria and Albert Museum and the British Museum, London, and in the Manx Museum, Isle of Man.

After his retreat to the Isle of Man, Knox continued to work. Perhaps the most remarkable products of these years were his monumental designs for tombstones (including that of Arthur Lasenby Liberty himself) and war memorials. The war memorial in the village of Onchan, Isle of Man, is particularly worthy of mention, and his biggest funerary monument, that to the novelist Hall Caine in Maughold churchyard, Isle of Man (although finished after his death by Winifred Tuckfield, one of the original members of the Knox guild), is both remarkable and original, being a tall, flat monolith, of fine concrete, with the lettering and figures (which are taken from the novelist's books) cast in low relief. The lettering on these monuments was his own—elaborately Celticized art nouveau. Sometimes, however, his lettering became so exaggerated as to be virtually unreadable—as in his painted manuscript, *The Deer Cry* (1916, Manx Museum, Isle of Man). An inspired watercolourist (a major collection is in the Manx Museum), particularly of Manx landscapes and buildings, he was particularly adept in his treatment of stone and whitewashed walls which he tackled with a confidence seen in few twentieth-century artists in this medium, although interestingly he has been compared with Charles Rennie Mackintosh. He rarely signed his paintings as they were done for his own enjoyment.

Knox was a shy and sensitive man, much admired by his students and by the schoolchildren he later taught in Douglas, although he had a terrible temper. Dapper, with a pointed beard, he appears to have made little money, but from time to time had family support. He never married. He died suddenly of heart failure at his home in Athol Street, Douglas, on 22 February 1933 and was buried in Braddan new cemetery, Isle of Man, with a headstone carved in Knox's own style by Thomas Quayle.

DAVID M. WILSON

Sources S. A. Martin, ed., *Archibald Knox* (1995) · A. J. Tilbrook, *The designs of Archibald Knox for Liberty and Co.* (1987)
Archives City Westm. AC, Liberty collection · Liberty, London, archive, Liberty designs · Manx Museum, Douglas, Isle of Man, letters and papers · Middlesex University, Silver Studio collection, designs · V&A, designs
Likenesses photographs, Manx Museum, Douglas, Isle of Man

Knox, (Alfred) Dillwyn (1884–1943), classical scholar and cryptographer, was born on 23 July 1884 in Oxford, the fourth of six children (four sons and two daughters) of the Revd Edmund Arbuthnott *Knox (1847–1937), a tutor at Merton College (later bishop of Manchester), and his first wife, Ellen Penelope (d. 1892), daughter of Thomas Valpy *French, bishop of Lahore. By any standards his family was remarkable, with the evangelical father and Dillwyn's three brothers: Edmund George Valpy *Knox (Evoe), for seventeen years editor of *Punch*, Wilfred Lawrence *Knox, an Anglo-Catholic priest, and Ronald Arbuthnott *Knox, Roman Catholic priest and translator of the Bible. Three years after the death of Ellen Knox in 1892 Edmund Knox remarried. Dilly, as he was called, went to Summer Fields School, Oxford, at the age of eleven and after a year was first in his election to Eton College. He went to King's College, Cambridge, in 1903 as a scholar. He obtained a first class in part one (1906) and a second (division one) in part two (1907) of the classical tripos. A friend of Lytton Strachey and J. Maynard Keynes, he was not an Apostle himself, although his name was put forward for election to the society. He was greatly influenced by Walter Headlam and inspired by his great love and knowledge of Greek literature.

When Knox became a fellow of King's in 1909, he inherited the then deceased Headlam's work on Herodas and applied himself to the fragmentary texts of the Herodas papyri in the British Museum. The inconsequential and bawdy mimes proved difficult to unravel but Knox was determined to succeed, exercising on them the scholarship combined with inspired guesswork which was to be his forte in his future career. Like his brothers, he was addicted to puzzles and a devotee of Charles L. Dodgson (Lewis Carroll). The sort of question he was apt to ask, 'Which way does a clock go round?', was pure Carroll.

Soon after the First World War broke out Knox was asked to join ID 25, the department of naval intelligence known as Room 40, as a cryptographer. By 1917 he had succeeded in breaking much of the German admirals' flag code, detecting, with his ear for metre, lines of poetry in the repeated bigrams of a message, which provided a crib. Instead of returning to Cambridge, he decided to continue working in Room 40, renamed the Government Code and Cypher School. On 21 July 1920 he married his former secretary, Olive Margaret Rickman (b. 1884), daughter of Lieutenant-Colonel Roddam John Roddam; they had two sons. He finally managed to get the Headlam–Knox Herodas published in 1922. Following German intervention in Spain he solved the Spanish military code and collaborated with the French on Italian naval codes used in Abyssinia.

Immediately before Hitler's invasion of Poland, Knox went with A. G. Denniston, the head of the Government Code and Cypher School, to a secret base at Pyry, where he was shown a reconstruction of the Enigma cipher machine, which was used by the Germans. The Polish replica moved the breaking of Enigma on from a theoretical exercise to a practical one and Knox always gave the Poles credit for the part they played. His own section, Intelligence Services Knox (ISK), which worked in 'the cottage' at Bletchley Park, achieved some notable cryptographic successes, including breaking the Italian naval code which enabled the Matapan signals to be read in March 1941. Although absorbed to the point of stuffing his pipe with sandwiches when obsessed with puzzle-solving, it would be wrong to see Knox's code-breaking as a detached intellectual exercise. It was he who insisted that, in order not to compromise Ultra (the breaking of the German high command codes), there should be an immediate press release that aerial reconnaissance had made possible the important naval victory off Cape Matapan in southern Greece (1941). Although ill with cancer, he worked tirelessly on breaking the Abwehr (a German secret service) traffic. A typical short cut was the successful assumption that some indicators set up by the operators in the four machine windows were not random but girls' names or four-letter dirty German words.

Knox worked from his bed to the last, only getting up and dressing in order to receive the CMG (1943) from the palace emissary appropriately. He died on 27 February 1943 at his home, Courns Wood House, Hughenden, near High Wycombe, Buckinghamshire.

MAVIS BATEY, rev.

Sources P. Fitzgerald, *The Knox brothers* (1977) · personal knowledge (1993) · private information (2004) · Burke, *Gen. GB* (1937) [Roddam of Roddam] · *CGPLA Eng. & Wales* (1943) · R. Erskine and M. Smith, eds., *Action this day* (2001)
Likenesses G. Spencer, drawing, priv. coll.
Wealth at death £6678 15s. 1d.: probate, 5 May 1943, *CGPLA Eng. & Wales*

Knox, Edmund Arbuthnott (1847–1937), bishop of Manchester, was born at Bangalore, India, on 6 December 1847, the second son and second child of the four sons and four daughters of George Francis Knox (1814–1891) and his wife, Frances Mary Anne, elder daughter of Thomas Forbes Reynolds MD of Wallington, Surrey. The eldest son was Sir George Edward *Knox. The father was one of the last chaplains in the East India Company's service, returning to England in 1855 and becoming a secretary of the Church Missionary Society in 1858. Although the connection with India remained a close one throughout Edmund Knox's early years, his own work lay entirely in England.

Knox was initially educated at home before going on to St Paul's School (1857–65), and had a distinguished career from 1865 as a scholar of Corpus Christi College, Oxford, and later as fellow (1868), dean (1872), tutor (1875), and chaplain (1879) of Merton College, Oxford, posts which he held until 1885. His academic ability was shown by his first classes in classical moderations (1867), *literae humaniores* (1868), and in jurisprudence and modern history (1869), and his versatility as a scholar by his election to the Boden Sanskrit scholarship (1867). His intellectual aptitude was matched by his pragmatism and his strong call to evangelism and pastoral work. He was considered one of the most effective disciplinarians of his day as dean of Merton, and in his year of office as proctor earned the inevitable nickname, Hard Knox. However, his firm belief in discipline, as proctor and later as a father and diocesan bishop, did not in any way conflict with his sense of spiritual responsibility for those under his pastoral care.

Ordained deacon in 1870 and priest in 1872, it was in 1884 that Knox's career began in earnest with his appointment as rector of Kibworth Beauchamp, near Leicester. Seven years later, in 1891, he was appointed vicar of Aston, Birmingham, where his skills as an administrator showed themselves fully. In 1878 he had married Ellen Penelope (b. 1854), eldest daughter of Thomas Valpy *French, bishop of Lahore. Her death in 1892 left him with a family of two daughters and four sons, Edmund George Valpy *Knox (1881–1971), afterwards editor of *Punch*, (Alfred) Dillwyn *Knox (1884–1943), cryptographer, Wilfred Lawrence *Knox (1886–1950), Anglo-Catholic priest, and Ronald Arbuthnott *Knox (1888–1957), Catholic chaplain at Oxford University and translator of the Bible. In 1895 he married Ethel Mary, eldest daughter of Canon Horace

Edmund Arbuthnott Knox (1847–1937), by unknown photographer

of Manchester, but kept in touch with theological developments and church affairs. He was a determined opponent of the revised prayer book (rejected by parliament in 1927 and 1928) and gave his views of Anglo-Catholic errors in *The Tractarian Movement, 1833–1845* (1933). His *Reminiscences of an Octogenarian, 1847–1934* (1935) cast many illuminating sidelights upon nearly a century of the history of the Church of England. He was in his ninetieth year when he died at 18 Beckenham Grove, Shortlands, on 16 January 1937, survived by his second wife. He was buried on 19 January at Elmers End cemetery, Beckenham.

STEPHEN GREGORY

Sources E. A. Knox, *Reminiscences of an octogenarian* [1935] · M. L. Loane, 'Edmund Arbuthnott Knox, 1847–1937', *Makers of our heritage: a study of four evangelical leaders* (1967), 99–143 · J. S. Reynolds, *The evangelicals at Oxford, 1735–1871: a record of an unchronicled movement* (1953) · Crockford (1937) · *The Times* (18 Jan 1937) · *The Times* (20 Jan 1937) · *Manchester Guardian* (18 Jan 1937) · P. Fitzgerald, *The Knox brothers* (1977) · E. Waugh, *Ronald Knox* (1959) · *DNB* · *CGPLA Eng. & Wales* (1937)

Archives NRA, priv. coll., corresp. and papers · Taylor Garrett, solicitors, London, corresp. | Lancs. RO, letters to T. H. Floyd · LPL, letters to Frank Tilt · priv. coll., earl of Oxford and Asquith family corresp.

Likenesses photograph, c.1903, NPG · A. T. Nowell, portrait, 1911; in possession of Old Rectory Club, Church House, 90 Deansgate, Manchester, 1949 · W. Stoneman, photograph, 1917, NPG · photograph, 1920, repro. in Knox, *Reminiscences of an octogenarian* · photograph, NPG [*see illus.*] · Rotary photograph, postcard, NPG

Wealth at death £8052 13s. 8d.: probate, 27 Feb 1937, *CGPLA Eng. & Wales*

Newton, vicar of Redditch, to whose quiet support he owed much both in Birmingham and in Manchester. For twelve years he exercised a wide influence in Birmingham, becoming in 1894 suffragan bishop of Coventry and archdeacon of Birmingham, and in 1895 rector of St Philip's Church (afterwards Cathedral) in Birmingham, where he laid effective foundations for the new diocesan see of Birmingham.

In 1903 Knox was appointed bishop of Manchester and was quickly recognized as the *de facto* leader of the evangelical party within the Anglican church. He took a prominent part especially in the controversies over both the church schools in the 1906 Education Act and the Church of England Assembly (Powers) Act (1919), commonly called the Enabling Act which he criticized vigorously. He was adamant that pastoral and evangelistic work should not be neglected, however, and personally founded an annual mission to holidaymakers at Blackpool. Several of his charges, including *Sacrifice or Sacrament?* (1914) and *On What Authority?* (1922), which dealt mainly with evangelical doctrines, were published, but his greatest strength was in organization rather than theological controversy. It was said of him by a Manchester layman that he was worth any six business men on a committee. Yet throughout his career he was always a pastor and always found time for personal and individual work.

Knox retired in 1920 and spent a long old age at the house at Shortlands, Kent, bought for him by the diocese

Knox, Edmund George Valpy [*pseud.* Evoe] (1881–1971), writer and magazine editor, was born in Oxford on 10 May 1881, the second child and eldest son in the family of two daughters and four sons of Edmund Arbuthnott *Knox (1847–1937), a fellow of Merton College, Oxford, and later bishop of Manchester, and his wife, Ellen Penelope French (1854–1892), daughter of Thomas Valpy *French (1825–1891), later bishop of Lahore. His father later remarried; his stepmother was Ethel Newton. Knox won a scholarship to Rugby School in 1896, and then in 1900 went to his father's old college, Corpus Christi, Oxford, with every expectation that he would likewise distinguish himself there as a scholar. However, he obtained a second class in classical honour moderations in 1902 and left without taking his degree.

The four Knox brothers were in their different ways remarkable. Dillwyn (or Dilly) *Knox was a classical scholar, mathematician, and fellow of King's College, Cambridge, who in both world wars distinguished himself as a cryptographer; Wilfred *Knox was an Anglican priest, biblical scholar, and an authority on the Apostle Paul; and Ronald *Knox translated the Bible and became a Roman Catholic and a monsignor.

Lacking the clerical or scholarly leanings of his brothers, Edmund Knox spent a year teaching at North Manchester preparatory school. There he decided to become a writer and, after several attempts, finally got a poem printed in *Punch* in 1905. In the autumn of 1906 he moved to London, determined to pursue a career in journalism, and he made a precarious living as a freelance contributor to *Punch*, the *Evening Standard*, and *The Tribune*. After a year he gained his first job as sub-editor on the *Pall Mall Magazine*, where he had responsibilities for commissioning fiction. In 1908 he met Christina Frances Hicks (1886–1935), the daughter of Edward Lee *Hicks, appointed bishop of Lincoln in 1910. Hicks, a committed suffragette, was reading English at Somerville College, Oxford, and before long the couple were engaged. Their marriage was delayed until 20 September 1912, to permit her to take her degree and to allow Knox time to improve his prospects. The couple had a son and a daughter, who became well known, under her married name, as the novelist Penelope *Fitzgerald (1916–2000).

In 1911 Knox published a volume of poems, *The Brazen Lyre*, which set the tone for his later collections of comic verse, yet did not anticipate the popularity of his later writings. He began to consolidate his working relationship with Sir Owen Seaman, editor of *Punch* from 1906 to 1932, contributing more regularly to the magazine and often deputizing in the office when the regular staff were sick or on holiday. To distinguish himself from another well-known *Punch* journalist, E. V. Lucas, he adopted the pen-name Evoe, meaning 'a cry of rejoicing uttered by the followers of the wine-god'.

At the outbreak of the First World War, Knox joined the Territorial Army, and by Christmas was a second lieutenant in the Lincolnshire regiment. He was first sent to Ireland, and then in 1917 to France. Although Seaman had invited him to send light-hearted articles to *Punch* from the front line, Knox found the realities of trench warfare incompatible with his brand of comic writing, and so failed to contribute for four years. In September 1917 he was wounded at Passchendaele. After being demobilized in April 1919 he worked for eighteen months at the Ministry of Labour in order to support his wife and small children, and moved with his family to Balcolme, Sussex.

In 1920 Knox was invited to join the table of *Punch*—the weekly gatherings to decide the subject of the issue's cartoon—and a year later he was admitted to the salaried staff and moved with his family back to Hampstead, London. In 1931 he edited an anthology of comic verse for the Phoenix Library. He was a skilful parodist, whose work drew comparisons with that of Charles Stuart Calverley and J. K. Stephen. In 1932 he took over the editorship of *Punch* from Seaman, who had retired. He was a quiet modernizer, and over several years he tactfully shortened the pictorial jokes and weeded out the mass of explanatory material in brackets which Seaman had inserted with the fear that his readers might miss the point. Knox's gentle innovations tightened up the magazine without doing violence to its middlebrow respectability. He saw *Punch* as a national institution, and colleagues remarked that 'working with him was a little like helping to edit the *Journal of Hellenic Studies*' (Price, 255). His own political views, once Liberal, had become Churchillian tory, and during the thirties, when many on the right favoured appeasement, he was a vociferous critic of Hitler and Mussolini.

However, under Knox's leadership, *Punch* became much less directly political. His dislike of public relations and the limelight meant that he was reluctant to meet people in his official capacity, and his belief in 'choosing good men and giving them their heads' (ibid., 254) made him an aloof, distant editor, loath to criticize or praise.

In 1935 Knox's wife died and on 2 October 1937 he married Mary Eleanor Jessy *Shepard (1909–2000), daughter of Ernest Howard *Shepard, A. A. Milne's illustrator and a *Punch* artist; the couple had no children. In 1943 Knox was awarded the honorary degree of MA at Oxford, and in 1951 he gave the Leslie Stephen lecture at Cambridge; his title was 'The mechanism of satire'. During his later years he took a lively interest in local affairs in Hampstead, and during the Second World War displayed an eccentric form of courage in wandering about London where the bombs fell thickest with a bottle of whisky in his pocket, looking for people who needed it. Although for the greater part of his life an agnostic, he gradually drifted back into the Church of England. Knox died at his home, 110 Frognal, Hampstead, on 2 January 1971. Three years later *In my Old Days*, a selection of his verse, was published.

KATHERINE MULLIN

Sources *DNB* · *The Times* (4 Jan 1971) · P. Fitzgerald, *The Knox brothers* (1977) · R. G. G. Price, *A history of Punch* (1957) · *WWW* · P. A. Hunt, *Corpus Christi College biographical register*, ed. N. A. Flanagan (1988)
Archives BL, corresp. with Society of Authors, Add. MS 63280
Likenesses H. Coster, photographs, 1933, NPG · photographs, repro. in Fitzgerald, *The Knox brothers*
Wealth at death £7686: administration, 4 Feb 1971, *CGPLA Eng. & Wales*

Knox, Edward Albert Cromwell [Teddy] (1897–1974), comedian, was born on 12 July 1897 in Newcastle upon Tyne, one of four sons and two daughters of George Thomas Cromwell Knox, a variety performer and extempore actor who went by the stage name George Thomas Cromwell. Knox performed and toured from early childhood in a family juggling and balancing act. By the time he was thirteen, after the family had been abandoned by his mother, he was juggling in music-hall with his brothers as The Cromwells. Following the example of the great Paul Cinquevalli, Knox developed a diabolo act and styled himself as Chinko. At fourteen he began work as a research assistant for his brother-in-law, the music-hall writer turned novelist Sax Rohmer, assisting him in the research for *Dr Fu Manchu* (1913).

With the outbreak of the First World War, Knox enlisted, joining the field artillery in 1914. He was wounded in the shoulder and invalided out of the service in 1915. During a period of wartime poverty he established an unsuccessful double act with trick-cyclist Minnie Kaufmann—Chinko and Kaufmann. In 1919 he met the acrobatic comedian Jimmy *Nervo in a Charing Cross milk bar, and in spite of some initial difficulties with his injuries formed with him a successful physical-comedy double act. From their first appearance in 1919 the two quickly gained a reputation as elegant and agile burlesquers and as excellent slapstick pantomime comedians (by the end of their careers he and Nervo estimated that they had broken some 60,000 eggs over each other's heads). They appeared in several revues, including *Fantastic Frolics* and *The Whirl of the World*, and in the United States featured in 1923 in the *Ziegfeld Follies* and on tour on the Orpheum circuit.

Their *Young Bloods of Variety* (1925) saw them experiment with a free-wheeling anarchic style, in which they played on-stage practical jokes on other acts on the bill and engaged in what were then new forms of audience participation. Their success was recognized in 1925 when they were invited to perform at that year's royal variety performance. The format they had devised in *Young Bloods of Variety*, which was followed up in shows such as *Blue Bloods of Variety* and *Chelsea Follies*, was the keystone of what would become the characteristic comedy of the *Crazy Gang, the group they would help found in 1931.

It was as a member of the gang that Knox became best known, appearing with them in a succession of popular variety shows and revues at the London Palladium before the war, and in a series of record-breaking revues after the war at the Victoria Palace. Knox was an innovative and witty physical comedian and a gifted mimic. He was by reputation the best character-actor of the gang, and was noted for being able to move his sketch characters beyond simple caricature. On 6 September 1934 he married Clarice Mabel Tate, *née* Dally (stage name Clarice Mayne; *d.* 1966), a variety performer and principal boy who had made her reputation as a glamorous doll-like singer with her first husband, the song-writer and pianist James Tate.

After a wartime hiatus in the Crazy Gang's activities, during which Knox and Nervo worked their double act in variety and with the Entertainments National Service Association at home and abroad, Knox performed continually with the group in revue and in its many royal variety performances until its farewell performance at the Victoria Palace in May 1962. During the later years of the gang's existence he suffered from the debilitating Dupuytren's disease which caused a claw-like contraction of the fingers. After the death of his first wife in 1966 he married Betty Reeves, the daughter of the Crazy Gang's former agent Horace Reeves. He died, one month after his second wife, of prostate cancer on 1 December 1974 at South Hams Hospital, Kingsbridge, Devon.

DAVID GOLDIE

Sources M. Owen, *The Crazy Gang: a personal reminiscence* (1986) · J. Fisher, *Funny way to be a hero* (1973) · R. Wilmot, *Kindly leave the stage!* (1985) · *The Times* (4 Dec 1974) · R. Busby, *British music hall: an illustrated who's who from 1850 to the present day* (1976) · R. Hudd, *Roy Hudd's cavalcade of variety acts* (1997) · I. Bevan, *Top of the bill* (1952) · B. Green, ed., *The last empires: a music hall companion* (1986) · CGPLA Eng. & Wales (1975) · General Register Office for England [birth] · m. cert. [first marriage] · d. cert.
Archives FILM BFI NFTVA, performance footage | SOUND BL NSA, documentary recording · BL NSA, performance recordings
Likenesses C. Beaton, group portrait, photograph, NPG; *see illus. in* Crazy Gang (*act.* 1931–1962)
Wealth at death £8857: administration, 18 March 1975, CGPLA Eng. & Wales

Knox, Sir Geoffrey George (1884–1958), diplomatist, was born in Double Bay, New South Wales, Australia, on 11 March 1884, the fourth child of George Knox (*d.* 1888), barrister, of Sydney, and his wife, Jane de Brixton, *née* Price. He was the grandson of Sir Edward Knox (1819–1901), who emigrated from Denmark (via London) to Sydney in 1839 and became a successful sugar refiner and banker. After his father's death Knox was brought to England by his mother and educated at Malvern College. He was one of five candidates admitted to the Levant consular service in February 1906. Among the other entrants was Reader Bullard. As part of his training Knox spent two years (1906–8) at Trinity College, Cambridge, studying languages.

Knox's first postings were in Persia, at a time of great Anglo-Russian rivalry. He became acting consul at Kermanshah in 1910, and in the following year he served in the same capacity at Shiraz. In May 1912 he was promoted to vice-consul at Cairo. During the First World War he was sent to be acting consul-general at Salonika, in 1915, after the British occupation of the city, and he subsequently served at Cavalla in 1915–16. He was granted a temporary honorary commission as a lieutenant in the Royal Naval Volunteer Reserve, served with the Aegean squadron, and was mentioned in dispatches. He returned to consular work in September 1918, and was employed at Bucharest from May 1919. In August 1920 he was transferred to the diplomatic service and posted to Constantinople as second secretary, where he earned a reputation for efficiency as head of chancery. While serving there he and a colleague, Nevile Henderson, survived without injury an automobile accident in which their car went into the Bosphorus. He was promoted first secretary in January 1923. In December that year he was transferred to Berlin. He returned to Turkey as acting counsellor in March 1926. His lungs were badly affected from living in the old wooden chalet which then served as the British embassy in the new capital city of Ankara. As a result he was unemployed from August 1928 to March 1930. He returned briefly to work at the Foreign Office from April to December 1930, but the London fog badly affected his lungs and he was again unemployed for six months until he was transferred to Madrid as counsellor of embassy in July 1931.

In April 1932 Knox was seconded to be chairman of the Saar governing commission, with the rank of minister-plenipotentiary. As chairman he also served as the territory's minister of the interior and foreign affairs. The rise to power in 1933 of the Nazi party in Germany greatly raised the level of tension in the Saar as it approached the plebiscite on its future scheduled for 1935. As Knox became the target of constant Nazi abuse the problem of his safety gave London great concern, though he himself worried about it not at all. During 1934 he was confronted by increasingly hostile Nazi broadcasts and by the detention in Germany of Saar residents. He was concerned that there were Nazi sympathizers among the local police and, deeming them unreliable, he moved decisively to recruit additional police locally and from abroad. He was able to obtain the support of Anthony Eden, the parliamentary under-secretary at the Foreign Office, which led to the dispatch of a multinational force under League of Nations auspices. This ensured a peaceful run-up to the plebiscite and a smooth transition subsequent to a vote in favour of reunion with Germany. Knox enjoyed powerful cars and would often drive from the Saar to the League of Nations at Geneva in a single day. His work in the Saar had been demanding, and was carried out in difficult circumstances. He gained the respect of Anthony Eden, who viewed him as a diplomat of great courage.

In October 1935 Knox was appointed minister to Hungary, where he warned of the dangerous trends in German policy. His health, however, was again in danger of collapse and he completed his career in a more temperate climate, as ambassador to Brazil, from November 1939 to September 1941. He retired to California in January 1942 before moving to Tobago, but did not lose interest in foreign policy; in the same year he published *The Last Peace and the Next*. A collector of rare books, first editions, and high-powered cars, an admirer of Gibbon and Voltaire, he enjoyed both a philosophical attitude and a satirical sense of humour. He was noted for being amazingly well read, seemingly having devoured every kind of literature, ancient and modern, English, French, or Italian.

Knox was a man of strong views and a pronounced realist. Pugnacious in character, he was no compromiser and, fully conscious of his abilities, took few pains to endear himself to his superiors. For his friends he had a warm smile and an infectious laugh, and he enjoyed happy relations with his foreign diplomatic colleagues. He was fond of the good things in life and had the means to ensure their enjoyment. As a result he was sometimes, and generally unjustly, accused of neglecting the less agreeable tasks performed by diplomats. Sir David Scott wrote:

> a measure alike of his professional abilities and his powers of persistence [was] that, in spite of considerable opposition in the Foreign Office, he succeeded in making for himself such a successful career and avoided being sent not only to posts ruled out by his frail health but also to those which his fastidious temperament regarded as uncongenial or unworthy. (*DNB*)

Knox was appointed CMG (1929) and KCMG (1935). He was also a chevalier of the Greek order of the Redeemer. He died at his home in Carnbee Island ward, Tobago, on 6 April 1958. He was unmarried.   ERIK GOLDSTEIN

Sources St Ant. Oxf., Middle East Centre, Sir Andrew Ryan MSS · Bodl. Oxf., MSS Sir Horace Rumbold · Bodl. Oxf., MSS Lord Simon · D. Kelly, *The ruling few, or, The human background to diplomacy* (1952) · W. Selby, *Diplomatic twilight, 1930–1940* (1953) · N. Henderson, *Water under the bridges* (1945) · *The Times* (10 April 1958) · A. Eden, earl of Avon, *The Eden memoirs*, 1: *Facing the dictators* (1962) · A. G. Lowndes, 'Sir Edward Knox', *AusDB*, 5.38–9 · S. Wambaugh, *The Saar plebiscite* (1940) · *WWW, 1951–60* · Burke, *Peerage* · *FO List* · *CGPLA Eng. & Wales* (1959)
Archives JRL, letters to *Manchester Guardian* | FILM BFI NFTVA, news footage
Wealth at death £93,792 4s. 9d. in England: Tobagan probate sealed in England, 26 Jan 1959, *CGPLA Eng. & Wales*

Knox, Sir George Edward (1845–1922), judge in India, was born at Pantheon Road, Madras on 14 November 1845, the eldest child of George Francis Knox (1814–1891), an East India Company chaplain and afterwards secretary of the Church Missionary Society, and his wife, Frances Mary Anne, daughter of Thomas Forbes Reynolds MD of Wallington, Surrey. His younger brother, Edmund Arbuthnott *Knox, was bishop of Manchester from 1903 to 1921.

Knox was educated at Merchant Taylors' School from 1856 until 1862, where in addition to the usual classical training he acquired the rudiments of Hebrew. In 1863, attending evening classes at University College, London, he gained a first prize in Sanskrit. In 1864 he passed the open examination for the Indian Civil Service and for his probationary year continued with his Sanskrit studies at University College. He proceeded to India in the autumn of 1865 and was almost the last civil servant to be posted for further study to Fort William College, Calcutta, where eighteen months later he passed another round of examinations in Hindi, Urdu, and Sanskrit. Urdu he spoke and read throughout his career with fluency and ease. He also acquired a knowledge of Persian and learned Arabic sufficiently well to be able to consult the classical authorities of Islamic law in the original texts. Such linguistic breadth marked him out as extremely rare among Indian civil servants.

In 1867 Knox was posted to Meerut as assistant magistrate and collector. In the following year, on 5 August 1868, he married Katharine Anne Louise (b. 1848/9), second daughter of Major William Loch of the 1st Bombay lancers, with whom he had five sons and two daughters.

In 1877 Knox joined the judicial department as judge of the small causes court at Allahabad. His legal reputation was already well established with the publication in 1873 of *The Criminal Law of the Bengal Presidency* (2 vols.), which he followed with *A Digest of Civil Procedure, Prevalent in British India* (1877) and *The Procedure of Mofussil Small Cause Courts* (1878). By 1879 he was regularly officiating as a district and sessions judge and in 1885 he was appointed legal remembrancer to the government of the North-Western Provinces and Oudh, a post which carried with it a seat in the local legislature. In 1890 he became a puisne judge of the Allahabad high court, and, as at the time of his appointment there was no retirement age for high court judges, he continued on the bench for over thirty years until his death in 1922, acting as chief justice on no fewer than thirteen occasions. He was knighted in 1906, and was made ISO in 1915 and CSI in 1917.

Long before his death Knox had become an almost legendary figure; in an unprecedented fifty-six years of service he had taken only one day's furlough and both a son and a grandson had joined him on the active list of service in the North-Western Provinces. His prodigious energy, coupled with his independence of official translators and accumulated legal experience, rendered him a formidably competent judge. Nevertheless, his long tenure of office appears to have been due not only to merit but also, as suggested by his obituary in *The Times*, to the fact that no one dared broach the subject of retirement to him. For all his vigour, there was something 'not altogether dignified', *The Times* further observed, in 'the spectacle of a man in the latter half of his eighth decade of life doing judicial work in the heat of the Indian plains' (22 July 1922).

Knox was a devout evangelical and rigid Sabbatarian. With his wife, Katharine, he supported numerous charitable and missionary endeavours in India, especially those involving the domiciled Anglo-Indian community. He served for two years as vice-chancellor of Allahabad University and was honoured by the university with an LLD.

After a short bout of ill health Knox died on 20 July 1922 at Braemar, Naini Tal, in the United Provinces. He was buried in the Kaladhungi Road section of St John's cemetery, Naini Tal, on the following day.

S. V. FitzGerald, rev. Katherine Prior

Sources History of services of gazetted officers in the civil department attached to the United Provinces (1915) · ecclesiastical records, BL OIOC · The Times (22 July 1922), 9 · The Times (25 July 1922), 1 · Mrs E. P. Hart, ed., Merchant Taylors' School register, 1561–1934, 2 vols. (1936) · University of London, The historical record (1836–1926), 2nd edn (1926)
Archives CUL, corresp. with Lord Hardinge

Knox, Henry (1750–1806), revolutionary army officer and politician in America, was born on 25 July 1750 at Sea Street, Boston, Massachusetts, the seventh of ten sons of William Knox (1712–1762), shipmaster and wharf owner, and his wife, Mary Campbell (d. 1771), daughter of Robert Campbell. Until the age of twelve he attended Boston Public Latin Grammar School, but at that time his father died and he became the sole support of his mother. He found employment in Wharton and Bowes, a bookshop in Boston, and thoroughly learned the bookseller's trade. On his twenty-first birthday he opened his own shop, the London Book-Store, which garnered him a comfortable income. For British army officers he carried a stock of military treatises, many of which he read in his spare time. In 1768 he enlisted in a local artillery company and four years later joined the Boston grenadier corps as second in command. In 1773 he lost the third and fourth fingers of his left hand when a musket exploded on a hunting expedition. Despite the opposition of her parents, he married Lucy Flucker (d. 1824), daughter of Thomas Flucker, the royal secretary of Massachusetts, on 16 June 1774. They had twelve children, nine of whom died during childhood.

Following the outbreak of the American War of Independence in April 1775, Knox determined that he would fight against the British. Two months later he and his wife abandoned Boston, and he joined the American forces besieging that town. Accepted as a volunteer by General Artemas Ward, he acted in that capacity for the next five months. He met General George Washington, newly appointed commander of the continental army, on 5 July and quickly became one of the commander's most trusted friends and military advisers. On 17 November the portly, genial, and enterprising Knox was commissioned colonel of the continental line and given command of the army's sole artillery regiment, which unfortunately had little artillery. With Washington's approval he immediately journeyed to Fort Ticonderoga in upstate New York to retrieve British ordnance that had fallen into American

Henry Knox (1750–1806), by Gilbert Stuart, c.1805

hands. In late January 1776 he returned with 59 cannon, mortars, and howitzers, 2000 muskets, and a large quantity of cannon and musket balls. Using these guns to fortify Dorchester Heights, Washington compelled the British to evacuate Boston in March. Thereupon, Knox was dispatched to Connecticut and Rhode Island to work on fortifications along the coast.

Knox rejoined the American army at New York and commanded the army's artillery during all the battles consequent to Washington's retreat across New Jersey in the summer and autumn of 1776. He was promoted brigadier-general on 17 December and assisted Washington in the battles of Trenton (26 December) and Princeton (3 January 1777). In the spring of 1777 he established an arsenal at Springfield, Massachusetts, then rejoined Washington for the battles of Brandywine (11 September) and Germantown (4 October). He spent the winter at home but returned in time to fight in the battle of Monmouth on 28 June 1778. During the next two years he advised Washington on military matters and also was the commander's close friend and confidant. In 1780 he was a member of the court that tried and convicted Major John André, and at Yorktown, Virginia, in October 1781, he emplaced the cannon that helped force the surrender of Charles, Lord Cornwallis, on 19 October. On 15 November 1781 he was appointed a brigadier-general and in 1782 commanded American forces at West Point, New York. He organized the Society of the Cincinnati in May 1783, served as its first national secretary, and was elected vice-president in 1805. In January 1784 he resigned his army commission and returned home to Boston.

Immediately drawn back into public service, Knox in

June 1784 was appointed by the legislature a commissioner to deal with Penobscot Indians in Maine. On 8 March 1785 he accepted an offer by congress to become secretary of war, with an annual salary of $2450. As the army at that time numbered a mere 700 men, his duties were largely clerical. He spent part of his time on Indian affairs, negotiating treaties with the Iroquois and various Northwest Territory tribes. Meantime, he urged congress to accept a more robust military system for America. In response to Shays's rebellion in Massachusetts he successfully prodded congress in 1787 to increase the authorized size of the army to 2040 men, but only a few hundred soldiers actually enlisted, and they soon were dismissed. He also advocated the establishment of service academies to train army and naval officers, and in 1790 he proposed to congress a comprehensive national militia system. None of his ideas was accepted.

When the new constitution went into effect in 1789, Knox was appointed on 12 September secretary of war in President Washington's first cabinet. In the next few years he allied himself with Alexander Hamilton in cabinet battles against Thomas Jefferson, but he was angered when Hamilton managed to transfer procurement of military supplies to the treasury department. During the whiskey insurrection in 1794 Knox and Hamilton had serious differences as to how the government should respond, and Knox successfully petitioned Washington for a leave of absence to look into his business affairs in Maine. He was more successful in advocating an increase in the strength of the navy; at his urging congress voted to construct six new frigates for use in the Mediterranean against the Barbary pirates. His main concern was the Northwest Territory, where the Indians, at the urging of the British, were repudiating treaties and warring on American settlers. In October 1790 General Josiah Harmar was defeated by an Indian army, and on 4 November 1791 General Arthur St Clair suffered an even greater drubbing. In 1792 Knox implemented a policy of negotiating with the Indians in hopes of a peaceful solution, while assisting General Anthony Wayne in creating a new and better-trained army to fight again if necessary. His attempts at negotiation failed, but when Wayne thoroughly defeated the Indians in the battle of Fallen Timbers on 20 August 1794, his policy was vindicated. Despite his ultimate success, Knox sensed that Washington for some reason had lost faith in his abilities, and so on 31 December 1794 he resigned.

Knox and his wife settled in Thomaston, Maine, on an estate that Mrs Knox had inherited from her maternal grandfather, Samuel Waldo. At their imposing mansion, Montpelier, they entertained sumptuously, adding extra inches to their already imposing girths and making themselves a bit ridiculous in the eyes of their neighbours. Mrs Knox, fancying herself a social arbiter, was an object of derision for those who disliked her tactlessness and social blundering. Knox occupied his time on his vast estate of 2 million acres by pursuing a number of projects, such as shipbuilding, lumbering, cattle raising, brick making, fishing, and lime quarrying. In the quasi-war with France of 1798–1800 he was mentioned by President John Adams as a likely person to serve as a major-general, but he was quickly eliminated from consideration when he declared that he would not serve under Alexander Hamilton as commander-in-chief. He died at Montpelier on 25 October 1806, from the effects of a chicken bone that had lodged in his intestines, and was buried three days later at Thomaston churchyard. Knox's was a record of valuable military and governmental service that was equalled by few of his contemporaries. He was survived by his wife, who died on 20 June 1824.

PAUL DAVID NELSON

Sources N. Callahan, *Henry Knox: General Washington's general* (1958) · N. Brooks, *Henry Knox: a soldier of the revolution* (1900); repr. (New York, 1974) · F. S. Drake, *Life and correspondence of Henry Knox* (1873) · H. M. Ward, 'Knox, Henry', *ANB*, vol. 12 · N. Callahan, 'Henry Knox: American artillerist', *General Washington's generals*, ed. G. A. Billias (1964) · H. M. Ward, *The department of war, 1781–1795* (1962) · R. C. Knopf, ed., *Anthony Wayne, a name in arms* (1960)
Archives L. Cong., Washington MSS · Mass. Hist. Soc., MSS | National Archives and Records Administration, Washington DC, MSS of the continental congress
Likenesses G. Stuart, oils, c.1805, Museum of Fine Arts, Boston, Massachusetts [see illus.]
Wealth at death 2 million acres of forest in Maine (fishing, farming, shipbuilding, etc.): Ward, 'Knox, Henry'

Knox [née Craig], **Isa** [pseud. Isa] (**1831–1903**), poet and campaigner for women's rights, the only child of John Craig, hosier and glover, was born in Edinburgh on 17 October 1831. Both her parents died when she was a child, and she was raised by her grandmother. At the age of nine she left school for what she called 'a life of toil' (Knox, vii). But independent study developed her literary tastes; and after contributing verses to *The Scotsman* under the name of Isa, she was regularly employed on the paper in 1853. Her first volume, *Poems by Isa*, was published in 1856.

Isa moved to London in 1857 and became part of the newly formed Langham Place circle and other feminist groups in order to work for 'the elevation and refinement' of women of her class. A protégée of Bessie Parks, she was one of the first staff members of the *English Woman's Journal* and the first female assistant secretary of the National Association for the Promotion of Social Science, a position she held for ten years despite public scorn. Her greatest accolade, however, came in 1859, when she won first prize for her ode on Robert Burns, recited on the Burns centenary on 25 January to a 6000-strong crowd at the Crystal Palace in London. She did not attend—she thought she had lost—so the master of ceremonies read her poem. There had been 621 candidates, including Frederic William Henry Myers, Gerald Massey, and Arthur Joseph Munby. Yet her ode, with its ringing lyrics and arresting imagery, was the best she had written. Four years later, in 1863, she published *Poems: an Offering to Lancashire*, and in 1864 published *Duchess Agnes, a Drama, and Other Poems*, which included several anti-slavery pieces. Isa married her cousin John Knox, an iron merchant of London, in May 1866. This easy marriage left her much time, and she became a regular contributor to *Fraser's*, *Good Words*, and *The Quiver*. She also edited *The Argosy* and published several more volumes of poems, novels, and juvenile histories which were designed specifically for the education of women. Her *Songs of Consolation* (1874) was very popular, as was *Little Folk's History of England* (1872), which by 1899 had reached its 30,000th printing. A sparkling, happy-go-lucky person, Isa was loved by all who knew her. She died at Brockley, Suffolk, on 23 December 1903, nearly thirty years after she had retired from public life.

T. W. BAYNE, *rev.* KATHARINE CHUBBUCK

Sources A. Japp, 'Isa (Craig) Knox, 1831', *The poets and poetry of the century*, ed. A. H. Miles, 7 (1898), 459–62 · Blain, Clements & Grundy, *Feminist comp.* · I. Knox, *Poems by Isa* (1856), foreword · C. Rogers, *The modern Scottish minstrel, or, The songs of Scotland of the past half-century*, 6 vols. (1855–7) · D. H. Edwards, *Modern Scottish poets, with biographical and critical notices*, 2 (1881) · J. G. Wilson, 'Isa Craig Knox', *The poets and poetry of Scotland*, 2 (1877), 477 · A. H. Miles, ed., *The poets and the poetry of the nineteenth century*, 9 (1907)

Knox, John (*c.*1514–1572), religious reformer, was born at Giffordgate in Haddington. His mother was a Sinclair, a name he occasionally adopted as an alias when in hiding, and his father was William Knox, whose family had a long and proud tradition of service to the earls of Bothwell. William, probably an elder brother, was the only other known member of his immediate family. John seems to have been educated in the local burgh school and, though not taking a degree, continued his studies at St Andrews University where he was taught by John Mair, the great scholastic thinker who had returned there in 1528. Pursuing a conventional career pattern, Knox entered the church, being ordained deacon and priest in the late 1530s by William Chisholm, bishop of Dunblane. Using his training in canon law, by 1540 he was practising as a notary in and around Haddington.

First encounters with reform In 1543 the fledgeling underground protestant movement within Scotland was given added impetus by Regent Arran's brief flirtation with evangelical reform. The authorized preaching tour of Lothian by Thomas Guilliame, a former Dominican prior of Inverness, provided Knox with his first introduction to protestant ideas. Nothing else is known about his conversion, though on his deathbed Knox asked to hear John 17, where, as he recollected, 'I cast my first ancre' (*Works*, 6.643). The major formative influence upon the future reformer was George Wishart, whose rousing sermons in 1544–5 had a revitalizing effect upon supporters of reform. By this time Knox had become a tutor in East Lothian to Francis and George, sons of Hugh Douglas of Longniddry, and Alexander, the eldest son of John Cockburn of Ormiston. Under his supervision the three boys studied Latin grammar and literature, the Bible, and a catechism. Their fathers were members of the group of lairds supporting and protecting Wishart, and from about January 1546 Knox was one of the preacher's entourage, proudly carrying a two-handed sword during meetings. On the night of his arrest Wishart took the sword from Knox and ordered him back to his bairns, saying 'One is sufficient for one sacrifice' (ibid., 1.139). After his trial for heresy in St Andrews Wishart was executed there on 1 March 1546.

Believing he was in danger as one of Wishart's known associates, Knox went into hiding, even considering flight to Germany. This proved unnecessary, and at Easter 1547 he and his pupils entered St Andrews Castle. It was held during a protracted and half-hearted siege by protestant sympathizers who had murdered Cardinal David Beaton, partly in revenge for Wishart's death. Knox quietly resumed teaching his charges, lecturing in the castle chapel on the passage in the gospel of John that they had reached in their studies. This exposition was heard by two protestants, John Rough and Henry Balnaves, who tried to persuade Knox to become a preacher. He refused outright, protesting vehemently that he had not been called by God. Rough and Balnaves consulted Sir David Lindsay of The Mount, an advocate of religious reform who had been negotiating with the castle on behalf of the Scottish government. Rough then delivered a sermon explaining how a congregation could call its minister and concluding with a specific charge to Knox to accept such a call. Overcome, Knox burst into tears and ran off to his room. For several days he wrestled miserably with his conscience, before finally accepting his vocation.

During the siege the St Andrews parish church of Holy Trinity had been treated to two series of sermons, one putting the protestant case by Rough, and the other defending Roman Catholicism by John Annand, the principal of St Leonard's College in the university. With Annand getting the better of the argument, Knox had been supplying Rough with notes to refute his opponent's points. When Annand asserted that only the church could judge heresy, Knox challenged him, adding he could prove the pope was Antichrist and that the Roman church was 'the synagog of Sathan' (*Works*, 1.189). Although his opponent refused, the congregation enthusiastically accepted the offer, insisting Knox speak so that the non-literate could follow his reasons. This left Knox with no option but to preach for the first time the following Sunday.

Knox's initial sermon, which the St Andrews wiseacres predicted would get him burnt for heresy, set the tone for the rest of his ministry. It was a hard-hitting attack striking at the roots of papal authority and brim full of fire and thunder. The chosen text, Daniel 7: 24–5, spoke of the last beast, also identified with the Antichrist of the book of Revelation, signalling that even at this early stage Knox was interpreting the contemporary situation in apocalyptic terms. Most of the sermon argued that the papacy's doctrine and rules were contrary to the laws of God. With characteristic self-confidence, Knox concluded by challenging those present to refute him. The congregation included Mair, his former teacher, and John Winram, the subprior of St Andrews, as well as many other canons and friars. As part of his own reforming programme, Winram then staged a disputation in St Leonard's College upon issues raised by Knox's sermon. During this inconclusive debate, Knox faced the inept Franciscan John Arbuckle. Winram's burgh reformation continued with further sermons at Holy Trinity, university and priory men preaching in turn on Sundays and Knox during the week. In a radical departure, communion was administered in a reformed manner. The limited reformation within the ecclesiastical capital was brought to an abrupt halt by the arrival in July of a French fleet which recaptured St Andrews Castle. For the remainder of his life Knox retained a deep respect for Winram, even though the subprior remained within the Catholic church right up to 1559.

In the galleys After the castle's fall the captured nobles were imprisoned in French castles while Knox and the other commoners were sentenced to serve on the galleys. The nobles, turning to Knox as their spiritual adviser, consulted him about the morality of escaping. The French galleys passed the winter on the Loire before returning to Scotland in the summer of 1548 to fight against the English invasion. In his later *History of the Reformation in Scotland* Knox gave few personal details of his nineteen-month captivity. He concentrated instead on incidents illustrating how the Scots upheld their protestant faith, including his own story of throwing overboard a picture of the Virgin Mary he had been ordered to kiss, though he first prudently checked he was not observed. While in Scottish waters Knox became so sick that he was not expected to survive. When asked if he recognized the Tay estuary he answered that he could make out the steeple of St Andrews parish church where he had delivered his first sermon and confidently predicted that he would preach there again before he died.

Although in the galleys and sometimes in chains, Knox had sufficient freedom to receive and read the treatise on justification written by Henry Balnaves during his imprisonment in Rouen Castle. Having himself been much comforted by its message, he summarized its contents for the protestants in St Andrews. In this first surviving piece of writing Knox employed themes and language which were to become his trademark. He assured the brethren that when Satan appeared about to triumph, he would be defeated, and, though the battle would be fierce, Christ the captain would prevail. He culled a string of images and quotations from Isaiah to emphasize the punishment awaiting those who condemn the law of God. Reflecting his enduring fascination with the Old Testament, Knox retained these references but omitted many of Balnaves's New Testament ones. Throughout his life Knox viewed contemporary politics through the prism of the Old Testament and paralleled his own experiences with those of the prophets, especially Isaiah and Jeremiah. His language and thought revolved around biblical concepts and his writings were saturated with Bible phraseology and imagery. Supremely confident that he understood the overall sense and unity of the scriptures, he did not hesitate to run together disparate texts. For Knox the Bible was essentially a message to be preached and, though careful and at times meticulous in his exposition, he was not a textual scholar.

During this early period of his life Knox developed the virulent anti-Catholicism which became one of his hallmarks. He was strongly influenced by Wishart's Zwinglianism but had also readily adopted Balnaves's Lutheran emphasis on justification by faith alone. Knox's personal experience of a saving faith rooted in the scriptures underpinned his spirituality throughout his life. It also upheld his calling to be a preacher which, at first accepted with reluctance, dominated his subsequent career.

Refuge in England: betrothal Knox was released from the galleys in February 1549, probably owing to English intercession with the French. He travelled directly to England where he was awarded £5 by the privy council and sent to Berwick as a preacher. This garrison town played a critical role in the Anglo-Scottish wars then in progress. As a result of this 'rough wooing' the English borough served as a refuge for Anglophile Scots. Knox was thus reunited with some East Lothian friends and became part of the colony of 'assured' Scots tolerated by their English allies. His ministry improved the behaviour of the town's soldiers, removing the worst feuding and violence and helping to promote peace and quietness. During his two years at Berwick, Knox collected a core of committed protestants around him, and for them he composed one of the most gentle and pastoral of his writings dealing with the different aspects of prayer, *A Confession and Declaration of Praiers*, published in 1553. Drawing on his own experiences, including his sufferings in the galleys, he assured his readers that, even when all hope appeared gone, God answered their prayers and saved his people.

With the support of the zealous within his congregation, Knox introduced more radical liturgical practices than those prescribed in the 1549 Book of Common Prayer, with communicants receiving bread instead of the customary wafer and sitting rather than kneeling. Judging by a surviving fragment, Knox felt free to draw up his own order of service. He joined in a protestant campaign, led by Archbishop Thomas Cranmer, attacking the Roman Catholic mass. Whether to offer a platform for his views or to censure them and his liturgical nonconformity, Knox was summoned before the council of the north. At Newcastle on 4 April 1550 he faced his ecclesiastical superior, the conservative Cuthbert Tunstall, bishop of Durham, supported by a group of scholars. Although hinting he would rather debate, Knox presented a scholastic paper. The first syllogism stated:

> All wirshcipping, honoring or service inventit by the braine of man in the religion of God, without his own express commandment, is Idolatrie: The Masse is inventit be the braine of man, without any commandement of God: Thairfoir it is Idolatrie. (*Works*, 3.34)

At the same time Knox penned a brief and simple summary of the Lord's supper, outlining the main points of belief. It denied the Roman Catholic doctrine of transubstantiation, stating that the communion elements were received spiritually, though not elaborating upon this eucharistic theology. The definition of how religion should be practised, contained in the syllogism, became the *leitmotiv* of Knox's thought. Resting upon an Old Testament viewpoint, especially the injunctions in Deuteronomy, it focused on the negative and exclusive. It asserted that any action not possessing a direct commandment from God was idolatry, and conversely that only those actions with a specific scriptural warrant were to be included within divine worship. By forcing everything into one or other category—idolatry or true worship—

Knox left no room for grey or uncertain areas or for 'things indifferent' to be regulated by the church. The adherence to a rigid biblical model was treated as a universal and absolute rule applying everywhere and at all times.

While at Berwick, Knox had met the family of Robert Bowes, the captain of nearby Norham Castle. Bowes's wife, Elizabeth, already a protestant, had sought the preacher's aid during recurring spiritual crises. Finding him helpful and comforting she became a close friend and encouraged his courtship of her fifth daughter, Marjory (d. 1560). Although the rest of the family did not approve, Marjory became formally betrothed to Knox in 1553. In his dealings with his mother-in-law the preacher drew on a reservoir of patience not normally evident in his public life. With compassion and tenderness he guided Mrs Bowes's tentative steps along her doubt-ridden inner journey of faith. In his pastoral letters to her Knox felt able to express his own religious uncertainties and fears for the future, providing a vivid contrast to the brash and self-confident assertions of his polemical writings. In the spring of 1551 Knox moved to Newcastle where he met John Willock, a fellow preacher and a future leader of Scotland's Reformation. Although the peace treaties of 1550–51 had ended the Anglo-Scottish wars, many Scots within England had gravitated towards Newcastle, forming a nucleus of fellow countrymen around Knox. As at Berwick, Knox concentrated his attention on the committed core of his congregation. He occupied the pulpit of St Nicholas, the town's principal church, preaching in the presence of Newcastle's élite. In October 1551, on an inspection tour of the north, Knox had in his congregation the duke of Northumberland. The man who was governing England for young Edward VI was sufficiently impressed to extend his patronage to the preacher. By the end of 1551 Knox had moved to London to become a royal chaplain, receiving a salary of £40 per annum, with a roving preaching commission including sermons before the king and court.

Royal chaplain Preaching before Edward VI during the late summer of 1552 Knox attacked the practice of kneeling at communion as part of a radical campaign pushing for additional revisions to the draft 1552 Book of Common Prayer. As a result the privy council had its printing halted while the views of the royal chaplains were considered. Furious that changes could even be contemplated after parliament had approved, Archbishop Cranmer labelled Knox and his radical allies 'unquiet spirits' bent on upsetting good order. He singled out the proposition so dear to Knox, that what is not commanded in scripture is unlawful, stigmatizing it as a heretical Anabaptist error. Cranmer was prepared, however, to draft an additional rubric for the new liturgy, explaining that kneeling to receive communion did not imply adoration of the elements, as maintained by Roman Catholic doctrine. Printed on an inserted slip in black, rather than the normal red, it became known as the 'black rubric'. This represented a concession, but it was not the resounding liturgical victory traditionally attributed to Knox.

While still complaining about kneeling, Knox and the other royal chaplains signed a statement, the forerunner of the forty-two articles, acknowledging that the Book of Common Prayer agreed with scripture. News of his acceptance reached the north and provoked criticism from his former congregations. In a letter to Berwick, Knox explained he was not prepared to break the bonds of Christian charity nor the authorized, uniform order of the church over kneeling at communion, and he recommended conformity to the new prayer book. The long epistle was full of the troubles faced by the elect, warning them to hold fast to the gospel message and anathematizing any who taught otherwise.

The kneeling controversy suggested to Northumberland that employing Knox in the south against the Anabaptists would make it easier to establish liturgical uniformity in the north. He also decided that, if the preacher were appointed bishop of Rochester, he could be used to propel his episcopal neighbour, the archbishop of Canterbury, in a more radical direction. Still angry over kneeling and possibly anxious to avoid becoming a cat's paw of Northumberland, Knox declined a bishopric in the Edwardian church. Much later he gave the reason for his refusal as foreknowledge of the problems Mary's accession would bring. In the short term Knox's behaviour infuriated his patron, who thought him ungrateful and impossible to please. The preacher had not assisted his cause by questioning the duke's religious sincerity. Despite such provocation Northumberland still tried to get 'poor Knox' settled, and in February 1553 Knox was offered one of the best livings in London—All Hallows, Bread Street. Knox publicly refused the benefice before the privy council, in April, and launched a diatribe against the lack of discipline within the Edwardian church. In his last sermon before the king he pointedly preached about the danger of godly princes being surrounded by ungodly advisers, drawing specific Old Testament parallels with certain courtiers.

While based in London, Knox had been befriended by a group of merchants and their wives, such as Anne Locke and Mrs Hickman. As well as the more prosaic gifts of hospitality and financial support, they provided the firm backing of a small godly community within which Knox thrived. Throughout his ministry Knox was able to share his own spiritual heights and depths with the close female friends he made in the towns and cities where he worked. When apart, they became his regular and trusted correspondents to whom he readily disclosed his secret hopes and fears. By calling upon his pastoral expertise to unravel their doubts and difficulties, they brought him to a deeper understanding of his own faith and gave him the confidence to help others to overcome their spiritual tribulations. Knox's considerable pastoral gifts formed a counterpoint to his abrasive polemical style and help to explain the loyalty and affection he evoked among many of his parishioners.

Despite his outspoken criticisms of the regime, Knox remained a royal chaplain and in June 1553 was sent to preach in Buckinghamshire and Kent. He was thus absent from the capital when Edward VI died, on 6 July. After the

Roman Catholic Mary had triumphantly claimed the English throne, he chose not to return to London to join his fellow royal chaplains at Edward's funeral. Although Mary's regime strongly encouraged the departure of all the foreign protestants, Knox did not immediately leave the country. He returned to the north in the final months of 1553 but was too well known to stay there long. He went into exile at the start of the new year.

Explaining defeat In England during the opening months of Mary's reign, Knox wrote private letters as well as his *Godly Letter* and *Comfortable Epistles* to his former congregations; the latter were published in Dieppe once he had reached safety. In common with other clerical exiles Knox felt the need to counter the accusation that he had deserted his flock. His main task in these writings was to comfort those who remained and to explain the dramatic reversal of protestant fortunes when political power and control over the English church had been lost. This was a straightforward matter for Knox, who during all his ministry had stressed the apocalyptic struggle against Antichrist's forces and the imminent arrival of the plagues God sent to punish sin. Though underscoring the justice of divine punishment, unlike his fellow exiles Knox did not dwell on the positive aspects of suffering for the faith. With his deep reliance on the Old Testament he placed the covenant model at the centre of his message, especially in the *Godly Letter*, which contained an extended comparison between England and Judah with himself in the role of Jeremiah. This emphasized twin points to his readers: the need to avoid idolatry—participating in Roman Catholic worship—and the call for repentance, which involved a national return to covenant obedience. It was not only religious apostasy which offended him. Particularly in the *Faithful Admonition* (July 1554), Knox bemoaned the loss of English political independence through Mary Tudor's marriage to Philip of Spain. Characteristically, his grief expressed itself through a vitriolic denunciation of England's queen. Although he did not advocate direct resistance, he did pray for a second Jehu, to overthrow this English 'Jezebel'.

Knox had become closely identified with his adoptive land and, as he confessed to his mother-in-law in his *Exposition upon the Sixth Psalm* (1554), he was more deeply affected by England's plight than Scotland's troubles. During his English stay he had held his first continuous ministerial charges, thereby developing his confidence as a pastor and familiarizing himself with preaching every week. Among the committed protestants in Berwick, Newcastle, and the south, many of them women, he had discovered the spiritual support on which he relied so heavily. This experience encouraged his perception of the church as a godly minority surrounded by the actively hostile and the half-committed. The fear that hypocrisy would corrupt the faith and compromise the gospel message was greatly increased by his association with high politics in 1552–3. In common with most of the religious radicals, by the end of Edward's reign Knox had become deeply disillusioned. He thought the pace of religious change had been too slow

and that protestantism had become tainted by its association with Northumberland's regime.

This pessimistic interpretation of events during Edward's and Mary's reigns became locked deep in Knox's mind. He believed he had witnessed in his own times a repetition of the troubled history of Old Testament Israel. Through its official acceptance of protestantism the English kingdom had entered God's covenant, but like the Israelites had refused full obedience to divine commands. Therefore, God had punished England by replacing its godly prince with an idolatrous female tyrant. Although the circumstances were different, after Scotland's Reformation Knox continued to be haunted by the fear that this pattern would repeat itself.

Germany and Switzerland Knox's four-year exile from Marian England crystallized his ideas and he developed much of the radicalism traditionally regarded as the chief characteristic of his thinking. With more leisure to write, he composed the bulk of his polemical writings during this period. In the atypical and hothouse atmosphere of the exile congregations he refined and put into practice his liturgical and ecclesiological ideas. Through his new contacts, the perspectives gained from his visits to other protestant communities in France, Germany, and Switzerland, and his discussions with their leading reformers, he experienced the diversity of international protestantism. For the remainder of his life he remained in contact with his European friends and acquaintances and valued his membership of this broad religious brotherhood.

At the start of 1554 Knox travelled via Dieppe to Switzerland to visit Heinrich Bullinger in Zürich and John Calvin in Geneva, seeking advice on the English situation. The questions he put to them provide an indication of the direction in which his ideas were already moving. They touched upon the political authority of a minor (Edward VI) and a woman (Queen Mary), as well as the thorny problem of obedience when idolatry was being enforced (the re-Catholicization of England). In view of the extreme sensitivity of these subjects, the reformers gave Knox equivocal answers. Having visited Dieppe in April, to collect news and to publish the tracts written while on the run in Marian England, he returned to Geneva the following August, hoping to settle in Calvin's reformed city.

At this point the English exile community in Frankfurt asked Knox to become one of their ministers. The magistrates there had provided a church, and it was hoped that as many exiles as possible would join the congregation. After pressure from Calvin, Knox accepted the Frankfurt invitation in November 1554. Once there he became embroiled in the debates about the liturgy to be followed by the English exile church. The congregation reached a provisional settlement in February 1555, but the following month its arrangements were disrupted by the arrival of a large contingent from Strasbourg. The next Sunday, Knox, upset by the flouting of the agreement, preached an inflammatory sermon criticizing the Book of Common Prayer. In his attack upon the failings of the Edwardian church he censured named individuals, some of whom were present. The congregation polarized. In what Knox was convinced was a conspiracy against him, the opposing faction laid information before the Frankfurt magistrates concerning his writings. The unflattering comparison of Charles V to Nero ensured that the city council, anxious to keep the emperor's good will, requested Knox to leave. After an emotional sermon and a tearful farewell to about fifty diehard supporters, Knox left on 26 March 1555 for Geneva.

Return to Scotland: marriage Knox's personal affairs next occupied his attention. He planned to return secretly to Northumberland to marry and bring his bride and mother-in-law back to Switzerland. Having sailed to the Scottish east coast in the autumn of 1555, he travelled to Berwick to meet Marjory and Mrs Bowes and the wedding was probably celebrated in the spring of 1556. Although the sweet-natured Marjory remains a shadowy figure, especially by comparison with her mother, her affection and unstinting support were crucial to Knox during their married life and he was devastated when she died in December 1560. Marjory's own learning enabled her to shoulder most of her husband's secretarial tasks, in addition to her own domestic duties. The couple had two sons, Nathaniel and Eleazer, who after their mother's death were brought up in England by her kin and eventually sent to St John's College, Cambridge, where both became fellows.

In 1555–6 Knox's original plans were altered by his reception in Scotland. During the autumn, winter, and spring he preached to the underground churches, moving around Edinburgh and the Lothians, north to Angus, and west to Ayrshire and Renfrewshire. Members of the Scottish nobility protected him from persecution by the ecclesiastical authorities. When faced with heresy proceedings, Knox was able to appear in Edinburgh on 15 May 1556 surrounded by so many supporters that the process was quietly dropped. He was caught off guard by the rapid progress the Scottish reform movement had made since 1549. He found a network of well-organized 'privy kirks' with a growing body of sympathizers who viewed his arrival as an opportunity to acquire experienced clerical leadership. Knox found himself giving advice about acceptable religious behaviour for Christians 'under the cross'. His sermon on Matthew 4, letters to his 'sisters' in Edinburgh, and his *Answers to Some Questions Concerning Baptism* reflected these pastoral concerns. Knox told his hearers not to attend mass, which he uncompromisingly labelled idolatry. By attempting to persuade the regent, Mary of Guise, to adopt a policy of reform, his 1556 *Letter* expressed the movement's political aspirations. The report of her cool and insulting reception of the *Letter* probably encouraged Knox to leave Scotland. Even when the protestant fourth earl of Argyll, head of Clan Campbell, offered him complete protection, he could not be persuaded to remain. At this stage Knox was extremely reluctant to become the leader of the Scottish reform movement, and he sailed for France early in the summer of 1556.

Years in Geneva By September 1556 Knox had returned to Geneva, which he regarded as his exile home. Having finally triumphed over his opponents in 1555, Calvin had, in Knox's admiring testimonial, transformed the city into the 'maist perfyt schoole of Chryst … In other places I confesse Chryst to be trewlie preachit; but maneris and religioun so sinceirlie reformat, I have not yit sene in any uther place' (*Works*, 4.240). The Scot treasured this visible lesson in the implementation of discipline which he tried to reproduce when he returned to his native land. While Knox had been away, the radical group from Frankfurt had obtained a church in Geneva and in November 1555 formally constituted themselves as a congregation, electing Christopher Goodman and Knox as their ministers. By the time he had returned to accept this call, the congregation had already published a full liturgy, *The Forme of Prayers*, and was becoming the largest and most important of the English exile communities. Although Knox's own contribution was slight, the exiles produced the Geneva Bible, a new translation later officially adopted in Scotland. This dynamic congregation also boasted an efficient ecclesiastical organization which maintained strict discipline. By preserving their internal harmony as well as their zealous commitment, they provided Knox with a working model of a perfect reformed congregation. Although subsequently he strove hard, Knox was unable to replicate this achievement within Scotland. In his rose-tinted memory the entire Genevan experience remained as a tantalizing ideal of complete and successful reformation.

Knox's sojourn in Geneva was probably the happiest period in his life. In the midst of the English exiles Knox felt secure and valued and his domestic contentment was increased by the arrival in 1556 of Marjory, his wife, and the births of their two sons in 1557 and 1558. The deep friendships Knox made in the city sustained him for the rest of his life. He grew particularly close to Goodman, his ministerial partner, with whom he could share all his troubles and debate and formulate his political and theological ideas. Together they served a congregation of like-minded and deeply committed protestants, who responded to Knox's prophetic preaching and pastoral encouragement. In return the exiles furnished the intimate spiritual support that Knox craved, continually strengthening his sense of vocation while permitting him the freedom to travel. Leaving his charge in Goodman's capable hands, Knox could respond to what he understood as God's will whenever and wherever it called him.

Having left Scotland in the summer of 1556 Knox was faced, as he had been two years before in the English context, with the charge of abandoning others to face persecution while himself going into a safe exile. From Dieppe in July 1556 he sent his *Letter of Wholesome Counsel to the Brethren in Scotland* and maintained a steady correspondence with his Edinburgh 'sisters'. He reiterated his advice to stand firm and renounce the mass and gave practical guidance on conducting clandestine worship. The reform-minded nobles, anxious to sustain the political momentum achieved during Knox's visit, wrote to him in Geneva in March 1557 asking him to return. Loath to leave Geneva, Knox hesitated, torn between conflicting roles; eventually he left Switzerland in September, after Calvin had sharply reminded him of his duty to Scotland. In October, on his arrival in Dieppe, there was a letter from the Scottish lords asking him to wait. This provoked an angry reply from Knox, accusing the nobles of contaminating the religious cause with political opportunism. It was an unfair charge, reflecting Knox's ambivalence about his own role rather than the situation within Scotland.

Political writings: *The First Blast* During winter 1557–8 Knox used his enforced leisure in Dieppe to write. He composed his most famous tract, *The First Blast*, while by translating into English and amplifying an *Apology* addressed to the French king he also publicized the persecution faced by the Huguenots. Between January and March 1558, when he returned to Geneva, he travelled through France visiting the protestant towns of La Rochelle and Lyons. Once back in the Swiss city *The First Blast* was printed anonymously, but Knox's name was placed on his later Scottish titles, *The Letter to the Regent Augmented*, *The Appellation to the Scottish Nobility*, and *The Letter … to the Commonalty*. Together these 1558 tracts constitute Knox's major political writings.

The First Blast of the Trumpet Against the Monstrous Regiment of Women is the best-known, and least understood, of Knox's writings. Instead of the stirring image of serried ranks of marching women, the title more prosaically refers to non-natural (monstrous) female rule (regiment). The thinking of the English exiles, especially those based in Geneva, had been radicalized in response to the burnings of protestants by the Marian regime which had begun in 1555. By 1558 a number of Knox's friends, most notably his partner Goodman, had written tracts advocating resistance to the queen, and *The First Blast* was part of this campaign. Knox's main proposition was stated in the opening sentence of the main text:

> To promote a Woman to beare rule, superioritie, dominion, or empire, above any Realme, Nation or Citie, is repugnant to Nature; contumelie to God, a thing most contrarious to His reveled will and approved ordinance; and finallie, it is the subversion of good Order, of all equitie and justice. (*Works*, 4.373)

In the sixteenth century the assertion that women should not wield political authority at any level was neither novel nor particularly controversial. Several aspects of Knox's book, however, caused a considerable stir when it was published and have maintained interest ever since. In characteristic manner Knox presented his case in stark black and white terms, permitting no middle ground, and establishing a single immutable law to provide a moral imperative for radical action. He declared it was the law of God and of nature that women must not rule. Most unusually, instead of relying exclusively on the Bible, Knox cited as wide a range of authorities as he could muster to support this claim. He could thus dismiss the normal loopholes permitting female rule based upon custom or specific law codes. For Knox this law of God was a springboard

for action, for if a woman had by mistake or ignorance been permitted to rule, she should be deposed forthwith.

The timing of *The First Blast* added to the notoriety created by its style of argument and revolutionary conclusion. Its main target was Mary Tudor, the Roman Catholic queen of England, but on her death in November 1558 she was succeeded by her half-sister, Elizabeth, the great hope of English protestants. Scotland was also experiencing female rule with the regent, Mary of Guise, governing on behalf of her daughter, Mary, queen of Scots. The universalized nature of Knox's arguments ensured they were regarded as a direct attack upon each of these women. In one sense this was not what he had meant, as he later tried (unsuccessfully) to explain to both Elizabeth and Mary, queen of Scots. The predicament arose because of Knox's general tendency to get carried away by an idea in the heat of writing, without pausing to consider all its ramifications. As Calvin later noted, Knox's 'thoughtless arrogance' in *The First Blast* had unfairly brought opprobrium upon Geneva (Robinson, 2.35). The Scot firmly believed his central ideas were revelations to be communicated: the prophet must deliver the message he had received from God. Although *The First Blast* was conceived within this general framework, its non-religious arguments and sources of authority were distinctive. Knox's dependence upon syllogisms and scholastic proofs was a reaction to the worsening English situation. He broadened his arguments in a desperate attempt to convince Englishmen of all religious persuasions to depose their queen. By targeting Mary's gender, he chose an undeniable and unalterable characteristic of her reign. The result was a generalized attack on all female rule, presented as a logical argument.

Even within the book, the preacher struggled to hold his prophetic thunder under control, and towards the end he poured forth his denunciation of Mary's idolatrous reign. In his mind the queen's 'monstrous' rule, which denied the constraints imposed by her gender, was inextricably linked to her religious policy of re-Catholicizing England and persecuting protestants. In the light of this link, Knox was puzzled by the book's adverse reception among fellow protestants, and he wrote sadly to Anne Locke that it 'hath blowne from me all my friends in England' (*Works*, 6.14). He was equally surprised when Queen Elizabeth did not accept that he had written primarily against her half-sister. He was willing to recognize her royal authority on condition Elizabeth rested her claim upon divine providence which could override the general law forbidding female rule. In 1561 he offered a similar type of recognition to Mary, queen of Scots. While Knox saw no inconsistency between *The First Blast* and these offers, others did.

The politics of religion The centrality of his religious preoccupations and their impact on his political thinking were demonstrated in Knox's four propositions for his projected *Second Blast*, published in July 1558. They envisaged the 'election' of a ruler according to divine ordinance and allowed for the deposition and punishment of a tyrant. However, these broad principles were only applicable to kingdoms already in a covenant relationship with God. At the time of writing they applied to England, which had publicly embraced protestantism in Edward's reign even though it had committed apostasy under Mary; they did not extend to either Scotland or France, which in 1558 remained under Roman Catholic rule.

Such a crucial distinction meant that Knox's advice in his 1558 tracts for his fellow Scots was different from that to Englishmen. Since his return to Geneva in 1556 his personal correspondence and Scottish publications had betrayed an underlying ambiguity. On the one hand he sought the recognition of protestantism by the authorities. On the other he was fearful that the religious cause would be contaminated by political motives. In 1556 he had hoped Mary of Guise could be persuaded to implement religious reform, but he was far less sanguine when he reissued his *Letter to the Regent* with substantial critical additions in 1558. It accompanied *The Appellation* and *A Letter … to the Commonalty*, addressed to the Scottish nobility and Commons respectively. In the first tract Knox produced his own version of a constitutionalist theory previously employed by the German Lutherans and later adopted by the Huguenots. He explained that, because the Scottish nobility were 'magistrates' in their own right, receiving their power directly from God, they owed a duty to uphold the laws of God and protect true religion. Specifically Knox urged the nobles to introduce protestant worship within Scotland, even if that entailed defying the crown. On the basis of the spiritual equality of all men and women, the preacher also appealed to the common people, who possessed no political authority of their own. He argued that, because the word of God was essential for salvation, the people were entitled to demand that the scriptures be preached to them. These were radical proposals which, if implemented, would have led to far-reaching consequences, but the Scottish tracts were not straightforward calls for revolution.

Knox's attention remained fixed primarily upon the English situation. Just before Queen Mary's death in November 1558, the open letter addressed to his old congregations at Berwick and Newcastle indicated his deep awareness of the apocalyptic struggle being waged between the forces of Christ and Antichrist. He treated his former parishioners as soldiers in this great battle and collected a list of English martyrs, published a few months later. Having been so direct in *The First Blast* about the need to depose Mary, within this pastoral context Knox was reluctant to urge outright resistance on his correspondents; he dwelt instead on the fearful consequences of God's further punishments, reminding Berwick of the fall of Calais, its sister fortress town.

The situation was transformed by Elizabeth's accession on 17 November 1558. In the tract that Knox rushed out in January 1559, just before leaving Geneva, the Scotsman stressed how the English should welcome this great act of divine mercy. Like Old Testament Israel, God had given the kingdom the opportunity to renew its covenant and rebuild Jerusalem. In response England must re-establish true religion, which meant introducing only those practices authorized in the scriptures and exercising discipline throughout church and kingdom. The compromises and half-hearted uncertainties which Knox believed had condemned the Edwardian Reformation must be left behind.

The implications of predestination Knox wrote his longest work in Geneva, during the summer, autumn, and winter of 1558. When he returned home the manuscript was left in the city and guided through the press in 1560 by his friend William Whittingham. Concerning the difficult theological doctrine of predestination, *An Answer to a Great Nomber of Blasphemous Cavillations* was a refutation section by section of a piece by an anonymous English Anabaptist, probably Robert Cooche. The latter's tract, entitled *The Confutation of the Errors of the Careless by Necessity*, had attacked Calvin's explanation of the decrees of election and reprobation, asserting that the Swiss reformer depicted a cruel God ordaining the majority of mankind to condemnation, and a human existence devoid of choice or responsibility. Knox's rebuttal of it differs from his other writings in its length and its aim of elucidating a single doctrine. He retained his normal, destructive, polemical style, sharpened by a personal edge because, having been friends with his adversary, Knox now labelled him a blasphemer and liar. Employing an atypical device, he explicitly followed Calvin's doctrinal lead, employing long quotations from the reformer's writings on predestination. Disguised by his robust language, Knox's own discussion was sometimes tentative or, when dealing with the reprobation of the wicked, not entirely consistent. Although neither theologically original nor penetrating, the work was an impassioned defence of God's election to salvation of the invisible church. For Knox this represented the foundation of his own and every Christian's faith, humility, and obedience and the bedrock upon which he grounded his sermons.

In Knox's mind predestination was associated with the cosmic battle between the two armies, the church of God and the synagogue of Satan. Although predestination was essentially a message of salvation and consolation, Knox was acutely aware that identifying the elect was not a simple matter. The reprobate might themselves display signs of faith and sanctification for a time, making it impossible in this world to distinguish them from the elect. Knox pressed home the point that the visible church was bound to contain many such hypocrites. Throughout his life this proposition provided a constant spur for him to be tireless in his admonitory preaching, and in his final years it came to dominate his thinking. In countering the charge that predestination removed the need to preach repentance and salvation, he explained the purpose of his sermons:

> for to those that have by publicke profession received Christ Jesus, be they elect, or be they reprobate, do appertein exhortations, threatening, the doctrine of repentance, consolation prophecying and revelation of things to come; but to those that yet remaine manifest enemies of the trueth, apperteine onlie the common calling to embrace the trueth, with the threatning of destruction if they continue unfaithfull. (*Works*, 5.270)

Whatever the eternal consequences for the listeners, the warnings must be given: this conviction lay at the heart of Knox's own vocation as a preacher. The vehemence of his attack on the Anabaptist flowed from the serious threat he was seen to pose to the fundamentals of the faith Knox preached. Once the Scot had identified such an enemy he was not prepared to compromise, discuss, or debate, only to denounce.

In response to the persecution in Marian England, especially the burnings, Knox developed a ruthlessness and an increasingly radical edge to his thinking. In his writings he demonstrated his mastery of polemical invective, creating rolling denunciations filled with hyperbole and biblical imagery. Having identified the failings of the Edwardian church, which had brought such divine punishment upon the country, he concluded that compromise had been disastrous and a complete and rapid reformation was the only viable policy. In his future dealings with both British kingdoms he was driven by the fear that the Edwardian mistakes would be repeated. He therefore demanded total and complete adherence to what he deemed to be the ordinances of God for his people. He also became obsessed by the threat from those secret enemies who undermined the church, the hypocrites. By the time he left the continent, Knox had become more convinced than ever of the need to apply one fundamental principle:

> In religioun thair is na middis: either it is the religioun of God, and that in everie thing that is done it must have the assurance of his awn Word, and than is his Majestie trewlie honourit, or els it is the religioun of the Divill. (*Works*, 4.232)

Scotland reformed, 1559–1561 Having been refused permission to enter or travel through England because of *The First Blast*, Knox sailed to Leith, where he docked on 2 May 1559. He plunged straight into the middle of a Scottish crisis. To secure radical ecclesiastical reform, the protestant nobles had placed increasing pressure on the queen regent and Roman Catholic hierarchy. The ending of the 1559 provincial church council removed any hope of an accommodation, leaving a deep religious divide. Tension mounted when the regent outlawed the leading protestant preachers. At this point Knox travelled to Perth, and in St John's Church preached a provocative sermon, 'vehement against idolatrie' (*Works*, 1.321), which provoked an iconoclastic riot. It signalled the beginning of the armed confrontation between the regent and the protestant lords of the congregation. Knox was immediately drawn into the centre of the rebellion, spreading the iconoclasm to the north Fife ports, and the climax came in a sermon on 11 June in St Andrews. Knox made his most decisive contribution as a preacher who could inspire fiery and militant zeal, but he also acted as the congregation's secretary, helping to compose their manifestos and handling their correspondence. In the quest for English support he maintained a low profile so as not to arouse Queen Elizabeth's displeasure.

In the autumn of 1559 Knox became minister at St Andrews, a leading protestant centre. He accompanied the troops as a chaplain, and after their dispiriting retreat from Edinburgh his rousing sermon at Stirling on 5 November helped to rally the army. During this struggle Knox composed a narrative to justify the protestant cause which became the basis for his *History of the Reformation in Scotland*, not published until 1587. In his tale he painted the queen mother as the arch-enemy supported by the Roman Catholic clergy, who were described as agents of Antichrist. The regent's death on 11 June 1560, which opened the way for the peace secured by the treaty of Edinburgh on 6 July, provoked some of the most unpleasant of Knox's asides, revealing the fear and hatred he felt for opponents, and above all for Mary of Guise.

The summer of 1560 was a time of great triumph for Knox, when his dream of Scotland openly embracing protestantism was realized. In August the Reformation Parliament accepted the Scottish confession of faith and abolished papal jurisdiction and the celebration of the sacraments according to Roman Catholic rites. The protestant leaders were intensely busy as they strove to create a new church for the whole realm. Although extremely important as a figurehead, Knox was none the less a member of a team which together produced the key documents and the organizational framework for the new kirk. The first Book of Discipline and probably the confession of faith were the work of a committee of six men, all called John: Willock, Spottiswood, Winram, Row, Erskine of Dun, as well as Knox. Scotland's kirk adopted the Geneva Bible and that exile congregation's liturgy became the Book of Common Order. These founding texts of Scottish protestantism were closely associated with Knox and vigorously championed by him. However, they reflect a variety of sources and influences and cannot be treated as exclusively his work. Even when credited with sole authorship, Knox drew upon existing church practice for *Orders of Fasting* (1566) and *Excommunication* (1569).

During that momentous summer in 1560 Knox became minister at St Giles's in Edinburgh. He enjoyed being at the heart of political affairs as the leading preacher in the nation's capital. It was a conspicuous and, for such an outspoken man, potentially perilous position and he was twice forced to withdraw from the city. Nevertheless, at the centre of an efficient national and international information network, he exploited to the full his watching brief to keep the church informed of developments between meetings of the general assembly. His general letter of 8 October 1563, telling all protestants to gather in Edinburgh to support those arrested for disrupting the mass at Holyrood, led to his being accused before the privy council of treasonably assembling the queen's subjects. He was acquitted after a spirited defence and later received the assembly's endorsement, though not all protestants agreed with his firm and independent line. Knox could rally contingents of zealous supporters, but his brand of militant protestantism alienated as many as it attracted in his own congregation and the burgh at large. This left him nostalgic for his fellow Genevan exiles, and in 1566 made him reluctant to leave the godly warmth of his Ayrshire sympathizers when he withdrew from Edinburgh. In his ecclesiology it also encouraged the emphasis on the faithful remnant constantly suffering persecution, and downplayed the all-encompassing national church.

Edinburgh town council demonstrated its appreciation by providing Knox with a well-furnished manse. He moved, shortly before his death, into the comfortable and spacious Netherbow property, now John Knox House. With his exceptionally generous stipend, worth £566 6s. 8d., and with even some of his servants' wages being supplied from royal tax revenues, he was one of the best-paid clergymen in the land. From 1562 John Craig worked as his assistant and the burgh's second minister. His appointment made it easier for Knox to act as a general assembly commissioner to undertake visitations, such as his three-month inspection in 1562 of churches in the south-west. In the running of the national kirk Knox was employed in such specific roles as drafting articles, letters, and liturgical documents, and though he carried out some visitations he never became a superintendent. He was asked to open or close the assembly with prayers or a sermon but never served as moderator, which required the diplomatic skills of chairmanship which he manifestly lacked. Knox's strength did not lie in routine administration, as his colleagues well understood. By shouldering these burdens themselves they freed him to pursue his calling 'to instruct the ignorant, comfort the sorrowfull, confirme the weake, rebuke the proud, by tong and livelye voyce' (Works, 6.229). In his role as a prophet of wrath and judgment Knox became increasingly detached from the work of consolidation and the local implementation of reform which preoccupied the kirk in its first decade of existence.

In between his other duties Knox continued to write polemical tracts, directing his fire at the Scottish Roman Catholics. While on his 1562 visitation he held a public disputation on the mass at Maybole with Quentin Kennedy, abbot of Crossraguel, and the debate was subsequently published. Knox was also persuaded in 1568, though the result was not published until 1572, to refute a tract which James Tyrie, a Scottish Jesuit, had written to his elder brother, David Tyrie of Drumkilbo, to persuade him to return to the Roman Catholic church. It sparked a controversy about the nature of the true church which continued to rage after Knox's death. A more combative opponent, and one whom Knox declined to answer in writing, was Ninian Winzet, the Roman Catholic master of the grammar school at Linlithgow. Winzet had enjoyed pointing out the inconsistencies between the reformed kirk's theology and its practice and had criticized all its leaders. As part of his attack upon Knox, Winzet had ridiculed the highly Anglicized Scots which the reformer employed in his writings and his speech. It scored a polemical point at the time but has perhaps been taken too seriously by subsequent generations. Although he had acquired a slight English accent during his travels, Knox had no intention of abandoning his native tongue. The pragmatic adoption by the kirk of an English liturgy, the

Book of Common Order, and of the Geneva Bible, a translation into English, had a far greater effect upon language within Scotland than either Knox's writings or his oratory.

Relations with Mary, queen of Scots The return to Scotland from France of Mary, queen of Scots, on 19 August 1561, transformed the reformer's political position and his outlook. On her first night in her native country Knox led a delegation to Holyrood Palace to sing psalms as a pointed reminder of Scotland's religious allegiance. The preacher feared the presence of a Roman Catholic queen in the country and was implacably opposed to the concession granted by the protestant nobles that she could hear mass in private. He supported those who unsuccessfully stormed the Royal Chapel to disrupt the queen's mass on 24 August, the first Sunday. With his fondness for startling hyperbole, Knox had asserted, 'That one Messe … was more fearful to him then gif ten thousand armed enemyes war landed' (Works, 2.276). As he let slip in a letter in October 1561 to his dear friend Anne Locke, he had even considered the extreme option of summoning the godly to arms. Such an unyielding approach brought conflict with his former allies, the protestant leaders of the congregation who were now the queen's closest advisers. With the focus firmly on the queen and the royal court, Knox found himself marginalized. This revived his deep-seated distrust of court politics as a mixture of sycophancy and the unprincipled pursuit of power, which had been formed in Edwardian England. Believing Scotland was engaged in a war against Antichrist, Knox was convinced that any compromise with Roman Catholicism would be disastrous because, as he warned in October 1561, 'by permission Satan groweth bold' (ibid., 6.131).

Despite the myth so firmly embedded in the Knoxian legend of a titanic struggle between the Roman Catholic queen and the protestant preacher, Knox's direct contacts with Mary were limited. His own History provides the main source for the four royal interviews, with their magnificent drama and memorable lines. Written in the bleak period of 1566, the narrative for 1561–4 was spiced throughout with his biting assessments of royal policy and motives. Drawing on his English experience, Knox assumed that all Roman Catholic queens were Jezebels intent upon introducing idolatry and persecuting God's prophets and people. There was the additional danger, in his eyes, of a royal marriage bringing a Roman Catholic prince to rule in Scotland, as Philip II had in Mary Tudor's England. The reformer always viewed Mary Stewart as an enemy and believed that Scotland could not be safe while a Roman Catholic ruled. When the queen failed to act in 'character', he explained away her friendly or conciliatory gestures as 'craft' or 'deceit'.

The first interview took place at the start of September 1561, a few weeks after Mary's return. While defending his First Blast, Knox conceded that he accepted the queen's authority, though with his accustomed tactlessness he employed as an illustration St Paul living under the emperor Nero. When pressed by the queen on the wider issue of obedience, Knox endorsed the right of subjects to resist their rulers. The pair then sparred over the interpretation of the scriptures and how the true church could be recognized. Knox bluntly informed Mary that the Roman Catholic church was Antichristian and that the Bible contained self-evident truth. Yet, despite their lack of agreement on any topic, at the end of the interview Knox wished Mary well, even suggesting she might become a second Deborah. Though there was again no meeting of minds, the subsequent two interviews in December 1562 and April 1563 also ended on civil terms. In summer 1563 Mary and Knox were able to work together amicably to delay marital breakdown between the earl and countess of Argyll. However, fearful that it was a trap to lure him into preaching less critical sermons, Knox refused Mary's request to become her personal spiritual adviser at court.

The final interview in June 1563 was the most stormy, provoked by a sermon in which Knox had denounced a foreign, Roman Catholic marriage. Aware of the secret negotiations underway for a Spanish alliance, he explicitly cautioned the nobility that they banished Christ from the realm once they accepted an 'infidel' to rule the kingdom. When the queen demanded what Knox had to do with her marriage and what role he had in the kingdom, he produced the famous reply 'A subject borne within the same … Madam. And albeit I neather be Erle, Lord, nor Barroun within it, yitt hes God maid me … a profitable member within the same' (*Works*, 2.388). Justifying his harshness he explained that his duty as a preacher was to forewarn of dangers in blunt terms. In response to Mary's angry tears he clumsily assured her that he did not enjoy seeing her weep, but could not avoid speaking God's truth.

His sermons in St Giles's, which had lost none of their passion and charisma, enabled Knox to maintain a running commentary on political events during 1561–5. He constantly called for repentance for the public sins which he believed were disfiguring Scotland. These were headed by the idolatry of the queen's mass, which was polluting the entire realm, and any association with the Roman Catholic powers of Europe, especially Mary's uncles of Guise, who were fighting the French protestants. To Knox's stern eye, vice and hypocrisy sprang from the frivolity and flattery of the royal court and its politics. These constant attacks alienated many protestant nobles whose participation in Mary's government and unwillingness to follow his political direction were denounced by Knox as a lack of religious zeal. Writing his *History* in 1566 with the certainty of hindsight, he accused the courtiers of betraying the gospel; they 'declyned from the puritie of Goddis word and began to follow the warld; and so againe to schaik handis with the Devill, and with idolatrie' (*Works*, 2.265). The most dramatic breach came after a bitter argument with Lord James Stewart, earl of Moray, when the two close friends refused to speak to each other for eighteen months. Knox's harsh condemnation of the politicians stands in contrast to his more generous understanding of the motives and actions of his clerical colleagues. He did not openly criticize those, such as John Winram or John Row, who had remained within the Roman Catholic church until the Reformation crisis before transferring to leading positions within the protestant kirk. Similarly, John Erskine of Dun's friendly and conciliatory attitude towards the queen did not provoke a censorious blast.

Upholding God's covenant Although policy differences divided the protestant party at all levels, in his *History* Knox presented this as a split between the kirk and the courtiers. At the general assembly of June 1564 the divide was revealed in a debate between Knox and the queen's secretary, William Maitland of Lethington, over Mary's mass. The argument broadened to the question of the legitimacy of resistance to political authority and provoked Knox's clearest and most radical statements on that subject. Within a covenanted nation, such as Scotland, he maintained that the common people possessed a right to resist based upon the universal religious obligation to punish idolatry or other breaches of divine law. Knox considered that upholding the ten commandments was a public and political duty, not solely a personal, moral goal. The kingdom's willingness to punish those who broke divine law was the litmus test of its commitment to the covenant. This 'suppressing of vice … [and] abolishing of all suche thingis as myght nureise impietie within the Realme' (*Works*, 2.264) was the national dimension of the ecclesiastical discipline enforced by the kirk. Since the queen's return Knox had increasingly focused upon this aspect of the covenant relationship. He had become convinced that Scotland was failing this test and called with increasing stridency for a change of heart. Such a rejection of its covenant obligation would bring the terrible plagues of divine displeasure. With a frightening sense of *déjà vu* Knox identified within Scotland the same lack of discipline in church and kingdom which had caused the downfall of Edwardian England.

In March 1564 Knox married his second wife, Margaret (1546/7–c.1612), the seventeen-year-old daughter of Andrew Stewart, second Lord Ochiltree, a trusted friend and long-time supporter. With Knox aged fifty, the age gap was noted, though such discrepancies were common in second marriages. What excited greater interest, particularly from the queen, was his wife's distant royal connections because she was 'of the bludde and the name' (*Works*, 6.533). The marriage was a happy one, with his 'yokefellow' acting as secretary and nurse and comforter when he was ill. They had three daughters, Martha, Margaret, and Elizabeth, all of whom survived into adulthood, and the younger two themselves married ministers of the kirk.

Domestic happiness was unable to dispel Knox's growing sense of unease and powerlessness during Mary's personal reign. Having broken with many of the protestant nobles and deliberately rejected any close advisory role at the royal court, he concentrated upon his prophetic admonitions. From his earliest writings Knox had constructed a world of moral absolutes and imperatives which he had deduced from his interpretation of the scriptures. As he had explained to his friend John Foxe, 'to me it is yneugh to say that black is not whit, and man's tyrannye and foolishnes is not Goddes perfite ordinance' (*Works*, 5.5). He now found himself trapped within these constraints. The arrival of a Roman Catholic queen in Scotland had triggered his warnings about another Jezebel. Mesmerized by the fear that Scotland was reneging on its covenant commitments, he relied on the lessons he believed he had learned from the Old Testament prophets and the downfall of Edwardian England. They dictated that any compromise with Roman Catholicism was anathema and only total commitment to the moral discipline of the nation and unwavering zeal for the protestant cause would avert disaster. Mindful of his earlier shortcomings as one of the Edwardian preachers sent by God to be the salt of the earth, he was determined that this time he would redouble his warnings and in Scotland not hold 'backe the salt where manifest corrupcion dyd appere' (ibid., 3.270).

Calling Scotland to repentance Knox's prophecies appeared to be coming to pass in the crisis over Mary's marriage to Darnley. His belief that many of the protestant nobility had abandoned their religious commitment encouraged him to rely on spiritual remedies rather than political resistance. Although convinced that the marriage posed a threat to protestantism, Knox did not join Moray and Argyll in open rebellion against the queen. Instead he used the pulpit to warn about the dangers facing kirk and nation. Darnley was present in St Giles's on Sunday 19 August to hear Knox's sermon on Isaiah 26: 13–21. Mary's new consort was offended by the pointed references to Ahab not restraining the idolatry of his wife Jezebel and to God punishing his people by allowing them to be ruled by children and women. Knox was summoned to court and forbidden to preach as long as the royal couple remained in Edinburgh. Although the burgh council protested, Knox's preaching was probably restricted. Contrary to his usual practice, he wrote down and later published the offending oration, providing his only entire sermon text to survive. It encapsulated all the major concerns of this stage of his career.

Knox began by explaining that rulers had two tasks, to know God's will as revealed in his word and to implement his laws. With Scotland exhibiting the same disobedience as Israel had in Isaiah's time, similar disasters would surely follow. The country faced many enemies: open opponents, like the 'infidel' Ottoman Turks and the 'idolatrous' Catholics, and the more dangerous hidden foes— the hypocrites and those who had turned their backs on God and his laws. Knox warned that the 'day of temptation' was approaching fast. The godly would heed his warnings and demonstrate their obedience to God by humbling themselves, whereas the hypocrites would remain proud and scoff at God's prophets. The preacher reassured the faithful remnant that God would preserve them during persecution and, as the history of the church had demonstrated throughout the ages, in the long term they would triumph. It was a deeply pessimistic sermon

reminiscent of Knox's sentiments a decade earlier during the burnings of the Marian martyrs, though the situations were not alike. Despite the militant language of fighting under the banner of Christ against the forces of Satan, this was not a call to arms. In a marked change from 1559–60 Knox now advocated the spiritual weapons of prayer and humility and a reliance upon faith and hope, rather than armed confrontation.

During the autumn and winter of 1565 Knox left Edinburgh, and was probably travelling through the borders fulfilling the general assembly's commission to visit those areas without a superintendent. Having witnessed the queen's defeat of the rebellion known as the Chaseabout raid, and her espousal of policies favourable to Roman Catholicism, Knox was profoundly gloomy, assuming that Mary was implementing the Scottish section of a Roman Catholic conspiracy against European protestantism. In late 1565 rumours circulated that the French and Spanish monarchs had agreed at Bayonne to a crusade against the protestants. Mary, queen of Scots, was thought to be part of this league, backed by the pope and authorized by the Council of Trent. Knox even passed on details of a supposed Tridentine decree calling for the extermination of all protestants.

The *Order of a General Fast*, commissioned by the general assembly in December 1565, reflected Knox's preoccupations during these difficult months. Before the liturgy of the fast, a long doctrinal introduction explained its purpose. Parallel to Old Testament Israel, Scotland was a covenanted nation bound to uphold divine law against the threats of idolatry and social injustice. The fragility and vulnerability of the Reformation were emphasized and the dangers of lukewarm protestant commitment highlighted. A general public fast provided the ideal opportunity to demonstrate true repentance, thereby averting God's punishment of his people. The fast was a call for national repentance and the means by which the godly could demonstrate their obedience. It combined the two different concepts of the church, the comprehensive organization encompassing the covenanted nation with the persecuted faithful remnant.

The general assembly also asked Knox to compose a pastoral letter exhorting all ministers to remain in their charges despite arrears in their pay. It emphasized that a minister's vocation could not be abandoned in the face of difficulty or privation. Ironically, shortly afterwards Knox departed from his Edinburgh charge. Whether or not he had prior knowledge of the conspiracy, the preacher approved of David Riccio's murder on 9 March 1566, which he categorized as the slaying of an idolater whose influence upon the queen had been malign. However, in Knox's prayer written three days after the murder the dominant emotion was despair, not joy, as he begged God to release him from the miseries of the world. When Mary returned to the capital on 17 March, intent upon punishing the assassins, Knox departed. In a deeply depressed mood he withdrew to his friends and close personal supporters in Ayrshire, where he quietly spent the following months revising and extending his *History* to include the period 1561–4.

Civil conflict, 1566–1570 Knox's spirits were lifted by the birth of a daughter and the comfort provided by his fervent adherents in the south-west. Relieved to be outside the political and religious mainstream, by the autumn of 1566 he had agreed to act as Ayr's minister, though those in Edinburgh wanted him to resume his charge. He also welcomed the suggestion by his close friend Goodman that they resume their partnership, this time in a mission within Ireland. Although nothing came of this proposal, in December 1566 Knox obtained leave from the general assembly to visit his sons, who were living with the Bowes family in co. Durham. During his English trip he may have visited London to see members of his old Genevan congregation and to deliver the general assembly's letter concerning the controversy over vestments. He encouraged Goodman to write a pamphlet against wearing vestments and was in close touch with other radical English protestants who sought his advice on whether to secede by rejecting the Book of Common Prayer. Despite his trenchant criticisms of this liturgy, he counselled them to be patient and not separate themselves from the Church of England. Owing to his English travels Knox missed the upheavals of February–July 1567—Darnley's murder, Mary's marriage to Bothwell, the couple's defeat at Carberry, and the queen's imprisonment at Lochleven. For eighteen months he had withdrawn from public life into semi-retirement, his depression and quietism possibly linked to a bout of ill health.

By the end of June 1567 Knox had returned to Edinburgh, immediately making known his views on Mary's fate. In a sermon on 19 July he went so far as to demand her execution as an adulteress and murderess, presenting this as a test case of covenant obedience to demonstrate that, within Scotland, breaking the ten commandments would be punished, irrespective of rank. To the preacher it was a final chance for the Scots to prove their loyalty to the covenant. He therefore dismissed Mary's abdication as a half-hearted compromise which would store up future trouble. Ten days later in his sermon at James VI's coronation he struck a more optimistic note, comparing the new reign to that of Joash, the young Old Testament king. Moray became regent for the baby James and set about re-establishing the kirk on a firmer financial and constitutional footing, a cause dear to Knox's heart. To bolster these efforts, in December, Knox preached a rousing sermon at the opening of a parliament which re-enacted the 1560 Reformation legislation. Having buried his old quarrels with Moray, the preacher decided not to publish his *History*, which had documented them in bitter detail. Though advising the regent, Knox was reluctant to return to the heart of political affairs and seems instead to have contemplated retirement. In February 1568 he made the remarkable suggestion that he would like to serve again his former Genevan congregation, probably based in London, though it is difficult to imagine how he would have fitted into the Elizabethan church. During the next few years there was a marked deterioration in his health and

he became increasingly melancholy, failing to write regularly to his friends and, when he did so, speaking of his imminent and longed-for death.

During summer 1568 Knox finished the first draft of his tract against James Tyrie. The debate gave him an opportunity to mount a spirited defence of the Scottish kirk. It was his most positive description of the achievements of the Reformation, resting upon an affirmation of a visible church coterminous with the kingdom. Knox asserted that, by publicly rejecting the Roman Antichrist of the papacy and by adopting the laws of God, the Scottish realm had affirmed its covenant relationship. It had thereby entered the same league made by Christ with the apostles, establishing a true apostolic succession for the church, not the historical continuity claimed by the Roman Catholics. On the awkward charge of doctrinal diversity among protestant churches, Knox blithely stated that there was European agreement on the principles of the faith, and within Scotland no controversy at all because the preachers agreed over doctrine. In contrast to this triumphalist note, the appendix which Knox added in 1572 was introspective and gloomy. It reflected his sense of being part of a persecuted minority rather than a leader of a vibrant national church. Stung by accusations of impropriety, Knox also appended a letter of 20 July 1554 to Elizabeth Bowes demonstrating that his relationship with his mother-in-law was entirely pastoral.

During a period of great upheaval in Scotland, Knox was unusually quiescent, taking no active part in the dramas which ended the queen's personal rule. Initially he seemed to have withdrawn to concentrate on writing, but after Mary's fall he returned somewhat reluctantly to Edinburgh. Although neither willing nor able to act once more as a revolutionary leader, he did resume an interest in political and ecclesiastical matters during Moray's regency. His declining health probably exacerbated a general feeling of disillusionment and a desire to finish his ministerial career.

Moray's assassination by James Hamilton of Bothwellhaugh on 23 January 1570 was an immense blow to Knox, arousing in him a vehement and abiding hatred for all Hamiltons. Conscious of echoes of the godly Edward VI's early demise, he interpreted the regent's death as a mark of divine displeasure. God's people had once more failed to appreciate his gifts, which Knox listed: Scotland had first been delivered from French tyranny, then from Roman Catholic idolatry, and finally from the rule of 'that wretched Woman, the mother of all mischief' (*Works*, 6.569). Moray, in whom Christ's image had shone, had rescued the realm from disaster only to be murdered by the devil and his wicked servants. At the funeral on 14 February, Knox preached on the text 'Blessed are they that die in the Lord', reducing the congregation of 3000 to tears with his eulogy for the 'good regent'.

In the last two years of his own life Knox grew increasingly bitter and isolated, feeling encircled by enemies and with the work of reformation seemingly in tatters around him. In October 1570 he suffered a slight stroke which weakened both his voice and his body. He saved his strength for the weekly sermon in St Giles's, which became the chief outlet for his views upon current affairs. With Scotland embroiled in civil war between Queen Mary's supporters and those of King James, in his customary way Knox reduced the struggle to polar opposites. By treating it as a religious conflict, he turned the queen's party into Satan's agents and castigated its protestant members as backsliders from their faith. In December 1570 he launched a particularly vitriolic attack on his previous ally, William Kirkcaldy of Grange, who held Edinburgh Castle for Mary. When Grange complained of Knox's slander to the city's kirk session a feud began between the two men. Relying on the generalized right of a minister to admonish sinners, Knox continued to use the pulpit to fight his case. His Ayrshire friends joined the dispute by writing a threatening letter to Grange defending Knox as 'the first planter and chief waterer of the Kirk amonges us' (*Works*, 6.585). Within the Edinburgh congregation support was less wholehearted for the minister's outspoken stance, which served instead to deepen the existing divide between the political factions.

Rumours and propaganda leaflets circulated in the capital accusing Knox of undermining all political authority, of inconsistency in attacking female rule in *The First Blast* but then approving Queen Elizabeth, and more generally of being too good a friend to England at Scotland's expense. The preacher defended himself vigorously and urged the general assembly, to which some specific accusations had been addressed, to vindicate him. But although it supported him, the assembly did not provide the ringing endorsement which Richard Bannatyne, Knox's secretary, demanded. When clerical friends privately suggested he moderate his criticisms, Knox remained unrepentant, declaring, 'The kirk may forbid me preiching, but to stop my toung being in the pulpit it may not' (*Works*, 6.590). Such an impassioned defence of his prophetic vocation was an indication of how Knox's world had contracted to the arena of his sermons.

Last sermons and death, 1571–1572 Knox's continued denunciation of the queen's party, especially the hated Hamiltons, made Edinburgh unsafe when it occupied the burgh in May 1571. Persuaded that his presence posed a threat to his supporters, Knox left for St Andrews. Writing to his Edinburgh congregation he likened himself to the prophet Jeremiah, reminding them that continued persecution was one of the signs of election. Lodged within the priory, Knox found a more conducive atmosphere in St Andrews, especially when surrounded by the admiring students of St Leonard's College, who lionized him. His health had deteriorated to such an extent that walking unaided was difficult and he could not travel to the general assembly. Though requiring to be helped into the pulpit, as his sermons progressed he came alive, vigorously beating the pulpit and causing his hearers to quake with fear at his warnings.

Knox's sermons expounded Daniel and were packed with topical allusions, especially attacks upon the occupiers of Edinburgh Castle, William Maitland of Lethington, and the Hamiltons. They offended Robert Hamilton, minister of St Andrews, who challenged Knox's condemnations. In reply the St Leonard's students staged a play depicting the castle's fall, which Knox had foretold and had yet to happen. It became a focus for the existing rivalry between St Leonard's and St Salvator's colleges, leading to bitter feuding within the university. Knox, entangled in this dispute, wrote in August 1572 to the general assembly solemnly warning the kirk against the bondage of the universities. Now deeply suspicious of anyone who opposed him, he became embroiled in further rows with John Rutherford, principal of St Salvator's College, and with John Douglas, the newly appointed archbishop of St Andrews. By now, even in St Andrews, Knox felt opponents were fighting him at every turn.

The news of the St Bartholomew's eve massacre of the Huguenots in August 1572 increased Knox's sense of being encircled by the enemies of true religion. His warm affection for, and continued contacts with, French protestants made it a particularly bitter blow which signalled worse disaster to come. With Edinburgh now safe, Knox accepted an invitation to return. Defending at all costs his calling to be a watchman, he made it a condition that his preaching should not be restricted. He continued his attacks upon those inside Edinburgh Castle, including a denunciation of William Maitland as an atheist. When he resumed preaching in St Giles's on 31 August his voice was so weak he was henceforth moved to the smaller Tolbooth section of the building. With grim determination he continued until his final sermon on 9 November 1572, delivered at the admission of James Lawson, his replacement. Afterwards he was too sick to leave his house, being afflicted with a violent cough which heralded the onset of bronchopneumonia. In his last fortnight he was visited by many of his supporters. Attended by his wife and friends, he died at 11 p.m. on 24 November. Two days later he was buried in the churchyard of St Giles's, at a funeral attended by many nobles, including the fourth earl of Morton. The newly appointed regent made his famous tribute, 'Here lyeth a man who in his life never feared the face of man; who hath beene often threatned with dagge and dagger, but yet hath ended his dayes in peace and honour' (Calderwood, 2.242).

Knox had made his will six months earlier, leaving his wife and daughters as executors, and it was proved at the commissary court on 13 January 1573. In addition to the usual testament noting his debts and making his bequests, he penned a 'legacy', a justification of his life and vocation addressed to the faithful, the papists, and the unthankful world. It rehearsed the prominent themes of his final years: the persecution and threat of martyrdom which he and the faithful remnant of the kirk had suffered; and the failure to heed his admonitions of punishment to come, especially the destruction of Edinburgh Castle. Knox defended his vocation, asserting that by preaching the death of Christ he had striven to beat down the pride of the proud and encourage the faithful, without seeking financial reward or being tainted by corruption. Sensitive to the criticisms of partiality, he declared he had never gone beyond the scriptures in his references to contemporary events. Finally, he called for the faithful to be constant, even in the midst of troubles, and they would find that God protected them as he had Knox.

Knox firmly believed that, like Ezekiel, he had been called to act as a watchman of the Lord forever crying warnings of the enemy's approach. In his declining years he had withdrawn into this watchtower mentality and identified as enemies all those who failed to share his views. Chronically ill and embittered, he clung to the idea of the church as a persecuted minority who, like the exiled Jews, would be vindicated in the end. While this biblical parallelism had fitted with his earlier experience of Marian exile and persecution, it seemed less appropriate for a period when the Scottish kirk was putting down its roots and the kingdom was ruled by protestant regents on behalf of a young protestant king. Knox's 'legacy' formed a sad and defensive conclusion to his life, assessing the present in negative terms and full of fear for the future. It displayed little appreciation of his own vital contribution to the mighty achievement of planting a protestant kirk in his native land.

Images of Knox A proper likeness of Knox has always been difficult to construct. No contemporary portrait survives, though a verbal sketch was penned by his friend Sir Peter Young in 1579 indicating that Knox was short and stocky with broad shoulders. His dark blue eyes were set deep in their sockets under prominent eyebrows, and his narrow forehead was surrounded by black hair while a thick beard flecked with grey fell to his chest. Within his oval face, his long nose contrasted with a full mouth and large lips highlighted by his swarthy complexion. His normally grave countenance gave him an air of authority, but when angry his frown was deep and could be fearsome. By contrast the lineaments of Knox's personality have been less easy to draw. They have been dominated by his public role which has obscured the brief glimpses of the private individual also present in his writings. For Knox his calling as a preacher completely defined his life. His constant striving to live up to the responsibilities of his prophetic vocation allowed him no relaxation from his duty to act as the 'watchman of the Lord'. Once in the pulpit he believed he was no longer master of himself, but became instead the mouthpiece of the Holy Spirit. He was proud of this calling and jealously defended his right to preach, sure that he was defending God's honour and not his own. In a revealing aside he defined humility not as a lack of pride but as a consciousness of sin, and in that sense he knew himself to be a humble man.

The stern preacher who thundered God's warnings with complete conviction frightened many of his hearers, causing some to tremble with fear. In tracts and sermons he confronted his audiences with a stark black and white world in which the choice between good and evil was plain with little excuse for following the wrong way. There was no distinction in Knox's mind between the doctrinal certainties found within his biblical texts and their direct 'application' to the contemporary situation. He

viewed his political commentaries as a necessary and natural consequence of his vocation. Since his Edwardian days, Knox had feared the contaminating influence of court politics. He therefore elevated direct speaking into a distinct virtue, condemning the use of tact or diplomacy as obsequious flattery or shoddy political compromise. As with all successful myths, the image of Knox as the harsh, ranting cleric has its element of truth, though it does scant justice to the charismatic preacher whose sermons could be more rousing than 500 trumpets sounding together.

Convinced he understood the 'sense' of scripture and that the meaning of the word was self-evident to all who sought it, Knox found it extremely difficult to accept alternative interpretations. On the few occasions he recognized the need to apologize he did so clumsily, which sometimes made matters worse. This general inflexibility was linked to an absolute confidence in identifying the 'enemies of the evangel'. His 'holy' hatred for such people allowed him to dismiss out of hand any good points they might possess. In the final years of his life, Knox's attitude towards opposition from any quarter verged on paranoia. With his failing health, he became bitter and pessimistic about the future of protestantism, viewing death as a release from the onerous burden of his public duty.

Although certain of the righteousness of his cause, in private Knox could be assailed by doubt, lapsing into depression which would produce bouts of anger and frustration or withdrawal and relative passivity. During such periods he leaned even more heavily upon the support provided by his wives and an intimate circle of his spiritual sisters and brothers. In the glimpses afforded by his correspondence of these personal relationships a different Knox emerges. As a pastor he could be sympathetic, even tender, and extremely patient with the spiritual dilemmas facing his flock. In such contexts he was willing to moderate and adapt to the practical circumstances the moral imperatives that his pulpit rhetoric had declared were inflexible. Secure within the company of the godly, especially during his Geneva days, the gentler side of Knox flourished. This aspect of his personality helped to inspire the deep loyalty and affection so evident among his friends and supporters within his various congregations.

Although his writings were infused by Old Testament concepts and language, on his own admission Knox's spirituality began and ended with John 17. He found in this, the chapter of the fourth gospel containing Christ's prayer for his disciples before his betrayal, both a personal assurance of salvation and a complete world view. Knox's general apocalyptical perspective and an understanding of his vocation rested on the sharp distinction between Christ and the world running through the first sections of the chapter. In the remainder of the chapter Christ's celebration of being one with his followers, through which they are brought into the unity of the Father and the Son, underpinned Knox's ecclesiology, his predestinarianism, and his own faith. These key themes of covenant and apocalypticism, predestination and ecclesiology which

Knox found entwined in John 17 provide the crucial link between the public and private aspects of his personality.

Knox in national memory Almost immediately after Knox's death his supporters and detractors began the dispute which has continued ever since concerning his legacy and character. In 1573 John Davidson, a fervent admirer, published two poems which eulogized those aspects of his life which Knox had emphasized during his final years. Described as a model of uprightness, he was portrayed as a servant of God who, hated and persecuted by the world, had not flinched from his duty to rebuke sinners and defy tyrants. Accounts of Knox's last illness by his secretary Richard Bannatyne, and by his successor James Lawson, were published to demonstrate his 'godly death', thus vindicating his memory against Roman Catholic attacks.

The first publication in 1587 of Knox's *History* took place in London, where Andrew Melville and other Scottish presbyterians were in exile, and included book 5, covering 1564–7, written by a continuator and giving greater prominence to Knox himself. The *History* has usually been read as the first of the great presbyterian histories of the Church of Scotland, which has tended to abstract it from its place among Knox's other writings and dislocate it from its contemporary contexts. Knox's fine eye for the telling, and often humorous, detail and his enjoyment in coining a pithy or alliterative phrase give his *History* great immediacy. Its lively narrative of a crucial episode in Scottish history has maintained interest in it both as a historical source and a literary work, ensuring a succession of editions down to the present. The impact of the *History* has been immense, and it continues to provide indispensable evidence for the period, especially the revolutionary crisis of 1559–60.

Knox has been accused of giving himself undue prominence in this work. Yet the *History* is not an autobiography in disguise, for it conceals as much as it reveals about Knox's life; for example, it offers only a couple of sentences to cover his entire stay in England. It is instead a record of the Scottish struggle between the 'light of Christ's Evangel' and Satan's 'kingdom of darkness'. Knox was convinced that events in Scotland formed part of the cosmic battle between Christ and Antichrist. He fashioned his *History* within this apocalyptic framework, deliberately choosing to fill it with biblical imagery and metaphors. Knox's sections of the *History* (books 1–4) were revised in the dark days of 1566, which strongly coloured both his interpretation and his memory of the events he was recording. Nevertheless, within the framework imposed by its purpose and interpretation, the *History* is a relatively reliable record, even though in many key instances, such as the famous interviews with Mary, queen of Scots, this is difficult to verify because there are no other full accounts.

The initial association of Knox's *History* with the Scottish presbyterian opposition was solidified in the 1620s and 1630s by David Calderwood, whose own *History of the Kirk of Scotland* depended heavily on Knox's papers and publications. This was so successful that Knox's authorship of the *History* was denied by Archbishop John Spottiswood in an attempt to retain Knox within the episcopal tradition as the acceptable Scottish reformer. These struggles produced the most enduring and influential of Knox's images, as the founding father of the Scottish Reformation and of presbyterianism.

Having acquired iconic status, it was inevitable that Knox should be claimed at one time or other by virtually all Scottish protestants and deemed an anti-hero and arch-heretic by the Roman Catholics. Although dismissed as a fanatic by the rational Enlightenment, Knox remained in view because of his appearance in William Robertson's influential *History of Scotland*, first published in 1759. The fight over Knox's memory became particularly bitter during the ecclesiastical divisions of the nineteenth century, especially after the Disruption of 1843 when the Free Church battled to claim the reformer for themselves. The dramatic visual impact of David Wilkie's 1830s paintings of Knox preaching in St Andrews in 1559 and celebrating communion during 1555–6 reinforced the assumption that Knox had reintroduced apostolic purity to the kirk. Reflecting the revival of interest in Scottish history, the statues erected in Edinburgh's New College in 1896, and in Parliament Square in 1904 (now inside St Giles's), commemorate Knox as a preacher devoted to a rigorous biblicism.

Knowledge of the reformer was raised to a new level by David Laing's publication of the comprehensive six volumes of Knox's *Works* between 1846 and 1864. The corpus of material was completed in 1875 by Peter Lorimer's book *John Knox and the Church of England*, presenting the reformer as the founding father of puritanism and nonconformity. Strongly associated with the image of Knox the churchman, in its many guises, was that of the great anti-Catholic crusader, providing a model for a partisan protestant national identity within modern Scotland. Knox became an ideological patron for such anti-Catholic organizations as the Scottish Reformation Society, the Protestant Alliance, and the Orange order. Between 1909 and 1923 the Knox Club flourished, promoting Scottish Reformation history, and aiming to reduce Roman Catholic influence within Scotland and to defend the protestant succession to the throne. Among its publications were works by its vice-president, David Hay Fleming, for instance *The Last Days of John Knox* (1913).

Though he was firmly associated with Scotland, Knox's English and continental associations gave him an international reputation. He was included among the other major Reformation leaders in his friend Theodore Beza's *Icones* and is commemorated by a statue in Geneva's Reformation Wall, erected in 1917. He is remembered most widely throughout the presbyterian world in countless churches and several educational institutions from the United States to Korea. From the Elizabethan period Knox was enthusiastically adopted by the puritan wing of the Church of England and later by the nonconformist and dissenting traditions. Ever since Richard Bancroft's sermon at St Paul's Cross in 1589, Knox's political views have been vilified by their episcopal opponents as revolutionary and subversive.

A less controversial role for Knox to play was as patron of Scottish education, both at school and university levels. In the late nineteenth century his memory was employed to defend Scotland's system against 'Anglicizing' tendencies and justify comprehensive educational provision. This image was connected to the earlier characterization of Knox as a champion of democracy, emphasizing his revolutionary political thought and principled defiance of royal authority. Such an interpretation owed much to the ground-breaking and highly influential biography by Thomas McCrie first published in 1813. By using Knox's own letters and tracts, McCrie depicted him as the personification of the spirit of the Scottish Reformation. His book became an immediate best-seller, provoking an upsurge of interest in Knox to complement the massive enthusiasm for Scotland's past generated by Sir Walter Scott. In 1825 this was given visual expression in the erection of a statue of the reformer mounted on a high pillar in the Glasgow necropolis. The Chartists even celebrated him as a forerunner of their movement. The emphasis upon his heroic qualities was carried a stage further by Thomas Carlyle, who immortalized Knox as the 'one Scotchman to whom, of all others, his country and the world owe a debt' (Carlyle, 133).

The most abiding popular picture of Knox places him in opposition to Mary, queen of Scots. As a deliberate foil to her romantic image, he has been employed by Mary's supporters and critics alike. The dramatic interviews between the pair became the best-known parts of his life, providing ideal material for large numbers of historical paintings, plays, and films. By treating Knox alongside Mary, greater emphasis was given to his relationships with, and attitude towards, women and upon his criticisms of court life. Over time these characteristics were transmuted within popular imagination into Knox the woman-hater and killjoy. In the late twentieth century this negative image was highlighted by Hugh MacDiarmaid's cultural circle as the main barrier to a positive Scottish national identity. More recently, the confidence brought by devolution and the growing interest in Scotland's history has permitted a more humorous acceptance of Knox the icon, though his name is still capable of stirring up controversy.   JANE E. A. DAWSON

Sources The works of John Knox, ed. D. Laing, 6 vols., Wodrow Society, 12 (1846–64) · John Knox's History of the Reformation in Scotland, ed. W. C. Dickinson, 2 vols. (1949) · R. Mason, ed., John Knox: on rebellion (1994) · P. Lorimer, John Knox and the Church of England (1875) · T. Thomson, ed., Acts and proceedings of the general assemblies of the Kirk of Scotland, 3 pts, Bannatyne Club, 81 (1839–45) · CSP Scot., 1547–74 · J. Petheram, ed., A brief discours of the troubles begun at Frankfort 1554 (1846) · R. Bannatyne, Memoriales of transactions in Scotland, 1569–1573, ed. [R. Pitcairn], Bannatyne Club, 51 (1836) · D. Calderwood, The history of the Kirk of Scotland, ed. T. Thomson and D. Laing, 8 vols., Wodrow Society, 7 (1842–9) · The autobiography and diary of Mr James Melvill, ed. R. Pitcairn, Wodrow Society (1842) · H. Robinson, ed. and trans., The Zurich letters, comprising the correspondence of several English bishops and others with some of the Helvetian reformers, during the early part of the reign of Queen Elizabeth, 2 vols., Parker Society, 7–8 (1842–5) · L. Glassey, J. Kirk, and J. Dawson, 'John Knox's letter to Christopher Goodman, 27 October 1566', SHR [forthcoming] · T. McCrie, Life of John Knox (1813) · T. Carlyle, Heroes, hero worship and the heroic in history, ed. P. C. Carr (1925) · DNB · DSCHT, 465–6 · G. Krause, G. Müller, and S. Schwertner, eds., Theologische Realenzyklopädie, 19 (Berlin, 1990), 281–7 · I. Hazlett, 'A working bibliography of writings by John Knox', Calviniana, ed. R. Schnucker, Sixteenth Century Essays and Studies, 10 (Kirksville, MO, 1988), 185–93 · R. A. Mason, ed., John Knox and the British reformations (1998) · J. Dawson, 'The two John Knoxes: England Scotland and the 1558 tracts', Journal of Ecclesiastical History, 42 (1991), 555–76 · D. H. Fleming, ed., The last days of John Knox, Knox Club, 35 (1913)

Archives PRO, SP 52 · U. Edin., Laing MSS

Likenesses line engraving, pubd 1586 (after A. Van Somer), BM, NPG · statue, 1825, Glasgow Necropolis · statue, 1896, U. Edin., New College Quadrangle · statue, 1904, St Giles's Cathedral, Edinburgh · statue, 1917, Reformation Wall, Geneva · R. Cooper, line engraving (after unknown artist), NPG · A. Voersoun, portrait, Scot. NPG · mezzotint (after unknown artist), NPG · portrait (after A. Voersoun), U. Edin., Talbot Rice Gallery · watercolour, Scot. NPG · wood-engraving (after A. Voersoun), repro. in T. Beza, Icones (1580)

Wealth at death £1526 19s. 6d. plus £375 13s. 2d. (Deadis part): testament and inventory, 13 May 1572, confirmed at commissary court, Edinburgh, 13 Jan 1573, printed in Knox, Works, 6.53–4

Knox, John (c.1555–1623), Church of Scotland minister, was the son of William Knox; it is unclear whether this William was the merchant of Prestonpans in Haddingtonshire who was the brother of the reformer John *Knox, or this William's eldest son, also William, minister of Cockpen, Edinburghshire, from 1567 to 1592. After graduating MA at the University of St Andrews in 1575, Knox was admitted to the ministry at Lauder, Berwickshire, in April 1576. When he refused to baptize the illegitimate child of one David Douglas, the latter assaulted and wounded him, prompting him to complain to the privy council, which in June 1590 declared Douglas an outlaw when he failed to appear.

Knox is first recorded as attending the general assembly of the Church of Scotland in October 1581; during his career he participated in at least twelve of these meetings. He left Lauder to become minister at Melrose, Roxburghshire, in 1584. Committed to presbyterian polity, he refused to subscribe the articles of religion issued by the king's secretary, John Maitland of Thirlstane, the following year. In October 1586 Knox was elected moderator of the synod of Merse and Teviotdale. On 6 March 1590 the privy council appointed him a commissioner for the preservation of protestantism and the examination of ministers in Roxburghshire, and two years later he was commissioned to send information about the activities of Roman Catholics and their supporters to the Edinburgh minister Walter Balcanquhall. In 1595 Knox persuaded the general assembly to permit William Knox the younger, who had succeeded his father at Cockpen three years earlier, to move to Selkirk, but William decided to stay where he was.

Knox was active in support of the Presbyterian church at a time when it was making far-reaching claims for its own authority, even at the expense of the crown. When the general assembly established a commission in 1596 to reside at Edinburgh and monitor the actions of the excommunicated Roman Catholic earls of Huntly and Erroll and their supporters, Knox was one of the representatives for southern Scotland. However, the privy council ruled the commission illegal on 24 November 1596, and ordered its members to leave Edinburgh. Knox was one of the commissioners appointed by the general assembly in March 1598 to prepare a report on ecclesiastical representation in parliament. Two years later the assembly named him to a commission to establish ministers in towns devoid of them, and also to deal with actions by ministers that offended James VI. As a member of the assembly in 1601, he voted against the king's proposed transfer of ministers. The following year the assembly made Knox a visitor for the examination of ministers in Annandale and Nithsdale. It appointed him to a commission to advise James about the church's enemies, and included his name on a list of men that the king could present to empty benefices. Although Knox was unwilling to serve as the assembly's moderator, he accepted an appointment as moderator of Melrose presbytery in January 1607. The following year he was one of twenty ministers (ten per side) selected by the assembly to seek a compromise between advocates of presbyterian and episcopal polities. He also served as a commissioner to accompany the archbishop of Glasgow on a visitation of churches in Dumfriesshire.

Knox participated in the Falkland Palace conference on 4 May 1609 that discussed differences of opinion on church government and discipline. He quarrelled with the archbishop of St Andrews over the king's five articles on worship at the general assembly in 1617. After the articles were approved by the general assembly at Perth the following year, despite the objections of Knox and others, he preached against them in a synod at Peebles, beseeching his listeners, 'with tears, to stand to the Libertie and Government of the Kirk Established before the erection of the late Bishops' (Calderwood, 717). Knox was married to Christian, née Paterson. He died, probably at Melrose, in 1623, his wife surviving him.

John Knox (d. in or after 1654), probably the son of the Melrose minister, graduated MA at St Andrews in 1613 or 1614. King James presented him to the living at Bowden, Roxburgh, on 22 November 1621. A member of the assembly in 1638, he served on the commission (the assembly's standing committee) in 1646 and 1648. He was married to Margaret, née Douglas, and was still minister at Bowden on 26 July 1654; it is not known when he died. Their sons, Henry, who attended Charles II in exile, and John, both became ministers, the latter at North Leith, until his ejection on 11 June 1662.

RICHARD L. GREAVES

Sources Fasti Scot., new edn · Reg. PCS, 1st ser., 3.290; 4.466; 5.332–33; 6.379; 7.301; 12.241; 14.353 · D. Calderwood, The true history of the Church of Scotland, from the beginning of the Reformation, unto the end of the reigne of King James VI (1678) · J. Spottiswood, The history of the Church of Scotland, ed. M. Napier and M. Russell, 3, Bannatyne Club, 93 (1850), 10 · J. Kirk, ed., The records of the synod of Lothian and Tweeddale, 1589–1596, 1640–1649, Stair Society, 30 (1977) · A. F. Mitchell and J. Christie, eds., The records of the commissioners of the general assemblies of the Church of Scotland, 1–2, Scottish History Society, 11, 25 (1892–6) · DNB · The autobiography and diary of Mr James Melvill, ed. R. Pitcairn, Wodrow Society (1842) · R. Wodrow, Analecta, or, Materials for a history of remarkable providences, mostly relating to Scotch ministers and Christians, ed. [M. Leishman], 4 vols., Maitland Club, 60 (1842–3)
Likenesses engraving, pubd 1580 (after A. Vanson), Scot. NPG

Knox, John (d. in or after 1654). See under Knox, John (c.1555–1623).

Knox, John (d. 1688), Church of Scotland minister and army chaplain, was the younger son of John *Knox (d. in or after 1654) [see under Knox, John (c.1555–1623)], minister of Bowden in Teviotdale, Roxburghshire, and his wife, Margaret Douglas. He was the grandson of John *Knox (c.1555–1623), minister of Melrose, who was thought to have been the nephew of the great reformer; the family took conspicuous pride in this link. He was educated at the University of Edinburgh and graduated MA on 15 July 1641. Little is known of his activities during the following decade. It is possible that he remained in the Scottish capital, where his father enjoyed an influential position in the assembly of commissions, but it appears that he did not immediately seek a parish and that by 1650 he had instead become private chaplain to Archibald Douglas, earl of Ormond (1609–1655).

As the army of the Commonwealth surged northwards in the summer of 1650, Knox sought refuge behind the walls of the Douglas stronghold of Tantallon Castle and became garrison chaplain. Since the English forces under Major-General Monck were insufficiently equipped to impose a stranglehold on the area, Knox was able to lead the countess of Ormond and her sister-in-law, Lady Alexander Douglas, to the safety of a waiting fishing vessel at North Berwick—despite being marooned on a sandbank at low tide, deserted by his military escort, and assailed by Commonwealth soldiers. Forced to surrender in order to buy more time in which to effect the escape, Knox then charmed his captors over glasses of wine before seizing the horse of an English lieutenant and riding it back to the safety of the castle gates. Thereafter he continued to distinguish himself in the eyes of the royalist garrison by his gallantry and cunning, and was even able to capture a merchant vessel which had been running in supplies to the besieging army across the Firth of Forth. However, the arrival of heavy artillery in February 1651 profoundly changed the nature of the conflict and effectively sealed the fate of the garrison. After a twelve-day bombardment, the castle surrendered on 23 February 1651, though Knox received 'very good conditions' upon his own capitulation (Wodrow, 2.352). He was probably freed almost immediately.

Knox then became chaplain to Sir John Brown's regiment of horse, in the royalist army raised by David Leslie. He was with the troops who blocked the passage of the Commonwealth army across the fords of the River Forth near Stirling in early July 1651. On 20 July he appears to have fought with the detachment which gave battle to Lambert's numerically superior English host at Inverkeithing, and taken part in the furious counter-charges made that day by Scottish lancers. Following the final flight of the royalists, however, he was arrested and taken to Edinburgh. From his prison cell he maintained a lively and useful correspondence with the exiled royalist court, where his elder brother Henry was a courtier and royalist agent. A letter from Charles II, dated 31 August 1653, promised that the king would use 'all the endeavours I can to free you' (Rogers, 72) and in return asked if Knox might find 'some way … to assist me with money, which would be a very seasonable obligation, and could never be forgotten by me' (Wodrow, 2.352–3). Knox was released from custody late that year, and having been only a probationer during his military service he was finally ordained and became minister for North Leith. He probably did raise money for the royalist cause at this point, and it is clear that he acted as a conduit for secret correspondence between the exiled king and his Scottish supporters. In the mid-1650s the billeting of English soldiers in his church forced him to preach from the citadel of North Leith until he was ejected by the military from his makeshift pulpit. On 23 June 1659 he married the eighteen-year-old Jean Dalgleish of Cramond.

Despite his past loyalties, the Restoration did not bring Knox any improvement in his fortunes. He was firmly committed to the self-government of the kirk and bitterly resented the reintroduction of episcopacy. In defiance of the authorities, he led public worship at Newhaven and as a result was deprived of his parish by parliament on 11 June 1662 and by the privy council on 1 October. Although he was advised to journey to London to petition the king, Knox appears to have remained in Scotland, living near his former parish. He was one of those ministers who accepted the terms of the earl of Lauderdale's second indulgence of 1672 and was licensed to preach again in September of that year. He was given the parish of West Calder but soon fell out with his fellow incumbent, William Weir, who had refused both to appear before the privy council and to quit his manse in favour of Knox and his family. The row deepened and, having been summoned to Edinburgh on 5 September 1673 in order to affirm his own loyalty to the government and the episcopate, Knox appears to have used the occasion to push home his allegations of misconduct against his rival. Having heard that Weir had spoken against the king and had also 'by severall indirect and unhandsome wayes circumvein and abuse[d] the said Mr. John [Knox] and forced him to desert the said charge' of his parish, the privy council found against Weir. He was branded a rebel and dismissed from the parish, while Knox was confirmed as the sole incumbent and rewarded with the whole 'stipend of that Kirk for the year 1673' (Reg. PCS, 4.98–9, 101).

A regular income failed to materialize, however. Knox was widowed on 26 October 1673 and, with a young family to support, he felt impelled to petition the Scottish privy council in February 1675 and June 1677 for the payment of his arrears stretching over several years. Financial hardship may have driven him into hardening his attitude towards the hierarchy in both church and state. Charges of refusing to celebrate the king's birthday and of refusing to read out in church the order proclaiming a thanksgiving day for the deliverance of Charles II from the Rye House plot were brought against him in late November 1684 and he was once again brought before the privy council. Despite listing his services to the royal cause during the Commonwealth and protectorate periods, his refusal to sign a bond promising that he would never preach illegally again effectively condemned him in the eyes of the councillors and he was committed to the Tolbooth until such a time as he learned the proper 'cautione' (Reg. PCS, 10.38). He was not, as has been sometimes suggested, sent to serve out part of his sentence on the infamous Bass Rock: from November 1684 to March 1685 he was closely confined in Edinburgh's Tolbooth gaol. By the spring of 1685 poor conditions there had undermined his health, and in March he was paroled for one month on a bond of 5,000 Scottish merks so that he might undertake 'a course of phisick' (ibid., 171). This parole was subsequently extended twice more in April and once in June, 'in regard of his continowd sickness and infirmitie' and on account of his case being so 'singular and his loyaltie notourlie known' (ibid., 38). It was obvious that Knox represented no threat to the established order and he moved hurriedly to embrace the new offers of indulgence made in February and April 1687. Once his release was confirmed as being permanent, he returned to his old parish at North Leith, where he ministered to his congregation without interference or event until his death in March 1688. He was buried in Leith churchyard.

Knox was survived by at least three of his four children. His son John later served as the garrison chaplain to Edinburgh Castle, and in 1691 one of his daughters, Jean, married John Tullidelph, the minister of Dunbarney. Though undistinguished in terms of his preaching style and theological reflections, John Knox managed to combine for most of his career a commitment to both the presbyterian Church of Scotland and the house of Stuart. His move into opposition later in his life reflected the increasing strains placed on the Restoration settlement by its chief beneficiaries in Edinburgh and Whitehall.   JOHN CALLOW

Sources R. Wodrow, The history of the sufferings of the Church of Scotland from the Restauration to the revolution, 2 (1722) · C. Rogers, Genealogical memoirs of John Knox and of the family of Knox (1879) · Fasti Scot. · Reg. PCS, 3rd ser. · Memoirs of Rev. John Blackader, ed. A. Crichton (1823) · T. M'Crie, ed., The Bass Rock: its civil and ecclesiastic history (1848) · W. Stephen, History of Inverkeithing and Rosyth (1921) · J. K. Hewison, The covenanters: a history of the church in Scotland from the Reformation to the revolution, 2nd edn, 2 vols. (1913) · A. Williamson, The Bass Rock: its historical and other features (1908) · D. Stevenson, Revolution and counter-revolution in Scotland, 1644–1651, Royal Historical Society Studies in History, 4 (1977) · F. D. Dow, Cromwellian Scotland, 1651–1660 (1979)

Knox, John (1720–1790), bookseller and economic improver, was born in Scotland; details of his parents are unknown. About Knox's early life before he moved to London to become a successful bookseller in the Strand, or his domestic circumstances, almost nothing is known. His London business was well established by the 1760s, and to his staples of selling and dealing in books he added some publishing, including in 1767 a seven-volume New Collection of Voyages and Travels, prepared (or so his preface alleged) not because he thought the work would be likely to sell, but 'because it was wanting' (*Monthly Review*, 37, 1767, 57). Another venture with which he was closely associated was William Guthrie's popular *New System of Commercial Geography*, the first edition of which appeared in 1770. Although there is no internal corroboration—the frontispiece merely states that it was 'Printed for J. Knox'—he is said to have been the real compiler of this work (Watt, *Bibl. Brit.*, 1824, 1.453). In the section on Scotland there are certainly themes with which Knox was to be closely identified, such as the value of fishing to the north, a cause which in later life he made his own. Though resident in London, Knox retained the strongest connections with his native Scotland, especially, it seems, in the Clyde area at Old Kilpatrick in Dunbartonshire; the minister there, John Davidson, was one of the two executors of his will. Among the beneficiaries was a stepson, John Morrison, also resident there. Davidson and Knox may have shared similar politics, with both being seen as pro-American because of their opposition to the war with the American colonists. Knox's contribution to the cause is thought to have included a pamphlet, published in 1777, *The American Crisis* (T. R. Adams, *The American Controversy*, 1980).

There had been for many decades an established community of expatriate Scots in London: linen factors, bankers, and the like. But it was with the Highland Society of London, established in 1778, that Knox formed particularly strong links, channelling his time, abilities, and moneys into acquiring first-hand knowledge of conditions in northern Scotland. He made a series of tours from 1764 onwards to both the west and east coasts of Scotland, sixteen times in twenty-three years, a formidable undertaking in an era when travel in remote areas was still difficult. His journey in the autumn of 1786, published in the following year as *A Tour through the Highlands of Scotland and the Hebride Isles*, showed how the sea-crossings by open boat at that season of the year were especially hazardous. Nor was travel on foot much safer in the far north. As Knox wryly remarked, Sutherland with its bogs and precipices was a country where the traveller needed to climb like a goat and jump like a grasshopper. In 1784 appeared his *View of the British Empire, More Especially Scotland*, which argued—understandably—that transport links in the highlands had to be improved, and advocated the construction of what became the Crinan and Caledonian canals.

Knox became known as an expert on the possibilities for fishing, and, to draw on his expertise, the Highland Society of London invited him in March 1786 to lecture on his schemes for some forty planned fishing settlements from Dornoch to Arran. Knox's ideas, which were quickly rushed into print under the title *Observations on the Northern Fisheries*, were much in vogue that year. There was a general context of anxiety about how to retain a productive population in the highlands, the region being seen not as a haven for rebels, as it once had been, but as an essential reservoir of seamen and soldiers. While linen had been tried, fishing appeared to offer much more potential. Parliament took an active interest, with Knox giving expert evidence to a House of Commons committee on the British fisheries. The committee's findings gave rise to legislation, including a premium per barrel of herring caught, as well as a tonnage bounty on fishing boats. A private joint-stock company, the British Fisheries Society, was formed to buy land in the north for lease to fishermen and curers. When the list opened at London in May 1786, Knox was among the first subscribers, and he was also active later that year in Scotland, helping to raise additional capital. He was commissioned by the society to make the tour mentioned above in October 1786, and recognition of its value came in the form of a gold medal for Knox, support for its publication, and the implementation of many of his recommendations, such as the choice of Ullapool and Tobermory as suitable places to locate fishing stations.

But Knox's attention was not solely focused on fisheries. His travels in the north had made him aware of the growing enthusiasm for Scotland as a tourist destination, a market into which he intended to tap: 'Travelling through the Northern parts of our island, besides being conducive to health, has now become a fashionable amusement during the summer and harvest months' (*GM*, 59.326). In November 1789 Knox announced a scheme for a complete set of Scottish scenic and architectural views. Some preliminary work had already taken place on his proposed book *The Picturesque Scenery of Scotland*, for which the artist Joseph Farrington, who was in Edinburgh during July 1788, had made the first sketch of a view of Edinburgh Castle. However, the project was abandoned following Knox's death, at Dalkeith, on 1 August 1790.

ALASTAIR J. DURIE

Sources DNB · J. Dunlop, *The British Fisheries Society, 1786–1893* (1978) · M. Andrews, *The search for the picturesque* (1989) · 'Plan of Knox's *Picturesque scenery of Scotland*', GM, 1st ser., 59 (1789), 326–8 · GM, 1st ser., 60 (1790), 857
Wealth at death small bequests, incl. £100 to John Morrison: will, PRO, PROB 11/1198

Knox, Sir (Thomas) Malcolm (1900–1980), academic administrator and philosopher, was born on 28 November 1900 at Birkenhead, Cheshire, the elder son of James Knox (1871–1956), Congregational minister of Tillicoultry, Clackmannanshire, and his wife, Isabella Russell Marshall. His parents were both of Scottish descent, and although he was educated in England, Knox was always strongly conscious of his Scottish roots. His first wife (whom he married in 1927), Margaret Normana McLeod Smith, came from Tarbert, Harris, and this underlined the Scottish attachment. Bury grammar school and the Liverpool Institute provided the principal elements of his early education. A scholarship at Pembroke College, Oxford, was followed by a first in *literae humaniores*. In 1923 he became secretary to the first Lord Leverhulme, and this connection with Lever Brothers was continued in various secretarial and executive positions in firms managing the conglomerate's west African interests, 1925–31. Not long after the tragically early death of his wife, in 1930, he returned to academic life at Oxford, first as bursar and lecturer in philosophy at Jesus College, where his experience in business was combined with his scholarly prowess, and subsequently as fellow and lecturer in Greek philosophy at Queen's College. In 1934 he married Dorothy Ellen Jolly (d. 1974) of Thornton-le-Fylde, Lancashire, who was a much cherished companion and hostess. There were no children of either marriage.

By 1936 Knox was ready for a major move, which entailed his 'spiritual return' to Scotland and his appointment to the chair of moral philosophy in the University of St Andrews. Henceforth his entire career, until his retirement in 1966, was spent at, and indeed devoted to, Scotland's most ancient seat of learning, assisted by his wife, who became chatelaine of University House, St Andrews. The older and more conservative tradition of teaching and of 'doing' philosophy was then still alive at St Andrews, and this trend was eminently suited to Knox's mindset and experience. He rapidly acquired the reputation of an excellent and exacting teacher and that of a man of affairs in the administration of the university. It was largely due to those latter attainments that he was elected to the court of the university (the governing body in Scottish universities), which gave him a position of influence in academic and administrative developments.

When the health of Sir James Irvine, the principal and vice-chancellor of St Andrews, began to fail, Knox became the obvious choice to step into the breach as deputy (subsequently acting) principal (1951–3), and this led eventually (1953) to the substantive appointment as vice-chancellor and principal of the university. Now fully in charge, he embarked at once on some overdue reforms: he arranged for the words 'to engage in research' to be written retrospectively into the contracts of all lecturers and readers, where the pursuit of research (in contrast to professorial contracts) had (deliberately?) been omitted. He took immense trouble over professorial appointments in particular: the first two chairs to fall vacant during his term of office were those of Greek (filled by Kenneth Dover, later chancellor of St Andrews University) and of moral philosophy, Knox's own former chair, now to be occupied by A. D. Woozley. He saw to it that the academic reputation of St Andrews University was re-established in all its ancient glory.

Two further problems required Knox's most urgent attention. The financial situation of the university was extremely precarious and needed immediate amelioration. His financial skills and tough governance succeeded in placing the university's fiscal position on a sound footing in record time. Furthermore, the relationship between St Andrews and its constituent college at Dundee had long been tense. Knox managed to reconcile the two sectors of the university by winning the confidence of his Dundee colleagues, who became the new principal's keenest supporters. Yet the Robbins report on higher education (1964) and the virtual doubling of the number of British universities led inexorably to the establishment in 1966 of Dundee as an independent university. Knox, with characteristic excess of rectitude, saw in this development the failure of his stewardship and decided—quite unnecessarily—to resign at the same time.

Knox's principalship had been a marked success. He himself had set an example in thrifty administration and in the continuance of his scholarship—despite heavy burdens of management. He worked hard himself in order to persuade his colleagues to engage in research rather than waste their time in committees. He favoured old-fashioned academic virtues and preferred minimalism to gratuitous expansion of the sort proposed by the report of the Robbins committee. He enjoined his closest friends to see to it that any future memoir written about him should contain the words of opprobrium (considered by him as praise), uttered by a highly placed leader of academe at a meeting of the vice-chancellors and principals committee in the early 1960s, that he was 'an academic dinosaur'. He was knighted in 1961, and a number of honorary doctorates were conferred on him.

Knox's extra-curricular *savoir-faire* imposed on him demands to serve on a number of government-appointed commissions, such as the Catering Wages Commission, the national reference tribunal for the UK coal industry, the Scottish Tourist Board, the Advisory Council on Education in Scotland, and the review body on doctors' and dentists' remuneration. He was also chairman of governors of Morrison's academy, Crieff. His academic duties and pleasures were never neglected, especially not his work on Hegel, to which he remained single-mindedly devoted. Thus he was invited to deliver the prestigious Gifford lectures at Aberdeen University (1965–8) and was elected to membership (later to the vice-presidency) of the Royal Society of Edinburgh.

Knox owed his initial interest in Hegelianism to his father, who had studied under Edward Caird at Glasgow. He first began to explore the wider implications of Hegelianism during his undergraduate years at Pembroke, when he came under the influence of Robin Collingwood. Caird had brought out its theological significance, its capacity for countering destructive scepticism, for reanimating moral and religious convictions, for resolving the apparent conflict between science and faith. Collingwood, while he was tutoring Knox, was in the process of thinking through what he had learned from immersing himself in the Italian tradition, in the writings of Vico, Croce, and Ruggiero—in clarifying his ideas on truth and error, on aesthetics, and on the relationship between history and philosophy.

It was this spectrum of general preoccupations which established the framework for the whole of Knox's subsequent approach to Hegel studies. When he returned to Oxford in 1931, he was concerned primarily with the interdisciplinary potential of Hegel's systematic work—he gave lectures on the *Encyclopedia*, and prepared but did not publish an article on the *Philosophy of Nature*. By 1932 he had begun to appreciate the importance of the work Dilthey and Lasson had done on Hegel's development, especially on account of the light it threw on the mature conception of the relationship between ethics, politics, and religion. It was this that came to dominate his thinking, and the publication of Michael Foster's book on the political philosophies of Plato and Hegel (1935) which finally persuaded him to start work on a new translation of the *Philosophy of Right*.

At the time, concerning oneself with Hegel's political philosophy was bound to create a stir and give rise to criticism, and in 1940 (*Philosophy*, 15, 1940, 51–63) Knox felt obliged to publish an article on 'Hegel and Prussianism', in which he pointed out the foolishness of simply writing this philosophy off as a glorification of the state and a precursor of Nazism. The publication of the translation by the Clarendon Press in 1942 proved to be a milestone in the development of British Hegel studies, since for the very first time one of the key texts was presented with a full-scale commentary, placing the subject matter in its historical context and analysing the cogency of the expositions.

It was this work, which he brought out in a revised edition in 1945 and which was then reissued five times over the next twenty years, which established Knox as the leading authority on Hegelianism in the English-speaking world. He followed it up by co-operating with Richard Kroner on an edition of the *Early Theological Writings*, published in America in 1948, and with his pupil Zbigniew Pelczynski, tutor and lecturer at Pembroke College, Oxford, on a corresponding edition of Hegel's minor *Political Writings*, published by the Clarendon Press in 1964. He also continued to cultivate his wider interests, planning a comprehensive account of Hegel's development, preparing a draft translation of parts of Boumann's edition of the *Philosophy of Subjective Spirit*, and after his retirement working steadily on the *Aesthetics*, the two magnificent volumes of which he finally saw through the press in 1974. During his last years he was working on the standard text of the lectures on the history of philosophy.

Knox had decided views on the general philosophical significance of attempting to create an informed and up-to-date Hegelian culture in the English-speaking world. He was anything but enthusiastic about the growing preoccupation with the phenomenological approach and, when G. R. G. Mure's study of the *Logic* appeared in 1950, greeted it with a suitably appreciative review (*Philosophy*, 26, 1951, 180–83). He stated publicly, thirty-five years after the event, that when he first read the *Tractatus logico-philosophicus* soon after its publication, the book made no impression on his mind whatever:

> It seemed to me to be ingenious, to be about problems other than those with which in my study of philosophy I was trying to grapple, and to be not altogether exempt from what I took to be philosophical errors. If I had been told at that time that in the course of forty years I would see philosophical and historical theology eclipsed and find the philosophical scene dominated by doctrines which owed far more to Wittgenstein than to my own masters in the subject, I would have been altogether incredulous. ('Two conceptions of philosophy', *Philosophy*, 36, 1961, 289–308)

During his retirement Knox did all he could to further what he saw as worthwhile developments in Hegel studies, and in 1978 made a substantial financial contribution to the founding of the Hegel Society of Great Britain.

Knox was stocky with a markedly round head and strong rimless glasses. The obituarist in *The Times* rightly pronounced him 'a wily committee-man, a coiner of sharp aphorisms, and a master of formidable silences' (*The Times*). Once convinced of someone's loyalty, he gave his friendship unstintingly. His musical knowledge and tastes were discriminating; he played the piano well; theology and a wide range of history and literature mattered to him; vintage claret was much favoured—as was the company of a select circle of close friends. He died of cancer at his home, 19 Victoria Terrace, Crieff, Perthshire, on 6 April 1980 and was buried at Perth on 10 April.

EDWARD ULLENDORFF and MICHAEL JOHN PETRY

Sources *The Times* (16 April 1980) · personal knowledge (2004) · private information (2004) [Ian Knox, Alan Meakin, staff of St Andrews University Library]
Archives U. St Andr. L., corresp. and MSS · University of Dundee Library, corresp. | U. St Andr. L., corresp. with Cedric Thorpe Davie
Likenesses H. A. Freeth, oils, U. St Andr. · H. A. Freeth, oils, University of Dundee
Wealth at death £94,994.52: probate, 12 Aug 1980, NA Scot., SC 49/31/498/3415–27

Knox, Robert (1641–1720), merchant and writer on Ceylon, was born on 8 February 1641 on Tower Hill, London, the second child of Robert Knox (*bap.* 1606, *d.* 1661) and Abigail, *née* Bonnell (*d.* 1655/6). The Knox family came from Nacton, Suffolk, and later moved to Wimbledon, Surrey, where Robert suffered 'no affliction and lived without want'. His father was a ship's captain operating profitably between England and the Levant. Robert's early education was under the deeply religious direction of his mother. He was then sent to the boarding-school at Barnes, Surrey, where he was taught by James Fleetwood, later bishop of Worcester.

In 1655 Knox's father took delivery of a new ship, the *Anne*, and on 7 December 1655 sailed with his son for India: first to Fort St George, Madras, then to Bengal, before returning to London in July 1657. The voyage was successful and the elder Knox promptly began preparations for a second passage. In the meantime Oliver Cromwell had issued a charter granting the East India Company a new monopoly of trade to the East, which required Knox to put his vessel and crew in the company's service (13 November 1657). The *Anne* sailed from England on 21 January 1658 to the Coromandel coast and Persia. During a voyage of limited commercial success she was dismasted in a storm at Masulipatam (19 November 1659). Captain Knox was instructed to take her to Kottiar Bay, Ceylon, to step a new mainmast and to engage in whatever trade was possible.

At this time Ceylon was ruled by the king of Kandy, Rajasinha II, with whom the Dutch had a long-standing but increasingly tense alliance. The Dutch helped to rid Ceylon of the Portuguese in return for total control over the cinnamon trade. Under Rijklof van Goens the Dutch policy was to keep Rajasinha in debt, to promise food and housing to all inhabitants who would settle in areas under Dutch control, and to expand the Dutch frontiers inland at every opportunity. They had expelled the Portuguese from Colombo (1656), but had not honoured their promise to return the town to the king. Rajasinha was justifiably disenchanted with the activities of Europeans in his country. On his arrival Knox's father made the grave mistake of not sending a letter explaining his presence along with the customary present to the king to ensure his protection. Robert Knox states that this lapse in courtesy was the 'main reason of our Suprize', because Rajasinha, 'Who looking upon himself as a great Monarch, as he is indeed, requires to be treated with sutable State' (Knox, *Historical Relation*, pt 4, chap. 1).

Between 4 and 10 April 1660 sixteen members of the *Anne*'s crew were taken captive by Rajasinha's troops. The Knoxes were separated from the other captives (16 September 1660) and put together in open detention in a village about 30 miles from Kandy. Both men suffered from malaria, and after a long illness the elder Knox died (9 February 1661). Robert Knox was moved around Ceylon, managing to establish himself as a farmer, moneylender, and pedlar. Eventually he and his close associate Stephen Rutland escaped to the safety of the Dutch fort at Aripu (18 October 1679), bringing to an end a captivity of over nineteen years. After generous treatment by the Dutch on Ceylon and at Batavia, Knox arrived at the English settlement at Bantam in Java (4 February 1680), from where he travelled to London (24 February 1680), arriving in September 1680.

During the voyage to England, Knox wrote the manuscript of what became *An Historical Relation of the Island Ceylon, in the East Indies*. His manuscript came to the attention of the directors of the East India Company, who recommended its publication. It was rearranged with the help of his cousin the ecclesiastical historian and biographer Revd John Strype and encouragement from Robert Hooke of the Royal Society. The book, published in 1681, was widely read, and translated into German, Dutch, and French during Knox's lifetime, and made him famous. The book influenced the work of contemporaries such as Daniel Defoe, who drew from Knox's experiences much of the context for, and the aspirations of, his hero in *Robinson Crusoe* (1719). He also carefully summarized Knox's experiences in the novel *Captain Singleton* (1720). The direct and idiomatic language used by Knox, his acute observation of details, the importance of practical self-sufficiency and strength of character, and his use of factual reality as the basis for fiction were influential in shaping the evolution of the 'English novel'. Likewise his close focus offered a detailed and objective study of Sinhalese topography, economic and social life (especially of the ordinary people), cultural characteristics, and conditions in the interior of the country, which has ensured that his book remains a fundamental source for the economic history and anthropology of mid-seventeenth-century Ceylon.

On his return to England in 1680 Knox gained the patronage of Sir Josiah Child, chairman of the East India Company, and after he had successfully studied navigation he was employed as captain of the *Tonqueen Merchant*, for four voyages to the East over the next thirteen years. He experienced mixed fortunes and an increasing disillusionment with the East India Company's regulations covering the private trade of ships' officers. By 1694 he

could no longer tolerate the company's removal of 'the Indulgence, as they call it, which is leave to bringe whome toyes and small things of little value free of mults' (Knox, 'Autobiography', fols. 46 and 62). He quarrelled with Child and the company, which dispensed with his services.

On 3 May 1698, after four years during which he 'grew wary of a Idle and droneish life' (Knox, 'Autobiography', fol. 59), Knox took advantage of the ending of the East India Company's monopoly (1694) and invested in a private venture in the *Mary*, via Cadiz, bound for Surat, where he arrived on 1 February 1699. There was much dissension on board, and the voyage, under the direction of Thomas Lucas, was not a success. Knox returned to England in 1701, completing his seventh and final voyage to the East. Now, aged sixty, he decided he had enough of a competency to retire. He settled in London, where he spent most of his time writing further observations about Ceylon, accounts of his life, and letters to various people. On 12 April 1703 he engaged in a successful lawsuit to recover a small portion of land (in Biggery Meede, manor of Wimbledon) bought by his father on 24 April 1654, and resumed by the current lord of the manor on the grounds that the Knox family was extinct (ibid., fols. 71–5).

Robert Knox died at St Peter-le-Poer, London, on 19 June 1720 and was buried in Wimbledon church, possibly beside his mother. In his will he left numerous personal belongings of value: books, manuscripts, silverware. As well there were specific bequests of money amounting to at least £1370. The remainder of the estate and the quarter-acre block in Wimbledon went to his executor, Edward Lascelles, son of Knox's sister Abigail.

I. B. WATSON

Sources DNB · R. Knox, *An historical relation of Ceylon*, ed. J. Ryan (1911) · R. Knox, 'An historical relation of Ceylon', *Ceylon Historical Journal*, 5 (1956–7) [special issue, ed. S. D. Saparamadu]; 2nd edn pubd sep. as *An historical relation of Ceylon* (1966) · R. Knox, autobiography, Bodl. Oxf. · E. F. C. Ludowyk, *Robert Knox in the Kandyan kingdom* (1948)
Archives BL, Lansdowne MS 1197, fols. 12–13 · BL, Stowe MS 988, fols. 11b–24b · BL, Add. MSS vol. 5833 · BL OIOC, original corresp., court books, letter-books · Bodl. Oxf., *An historical relation of Ceylon* bound up with his 'Autobiography' | Bodl. Oxf., MS Rawl. A. 303, Art. 48, fol. 216 · CUL, letters to John Strype
Likenesses R. White, engraving, 1695, Bodl. Oxf.; repro. in Ryan, ed., *An historical relation of Ceylon* (1911) · P. Trampon, oils, c.1708, NMM
Wealth at death comfortable; many valuable bequests, plus specified sums totalling £1370; approx. ¼ acre of land at Wimbledon: will, 30 Nov 1711, PRO, repr. *Historical relation*, ed. Ryan

Knox, Robert (1791–1862), anatomist and ethnologist, descended from a family of Kirkcudbright tenant farmers who claimed kinship with the ancient family of Ranfurly in Renfrewshire, which included the reformer John Knox, was the eighth child and fifth son of Robert Knox (d. 1812), philosophical and mathematical master at Heriot's Hospital, Edinburgh, and member of the Jacobin-inspired Friends of the People. His mother was Mary Sherer or Schrerer (d. 1838), daughter of a farmer of German ancestry. Knox was born on 4 September 1791 at Edinburgh.

Education and early career Knox was first educated at home by his father after suffering from smallpox which left him

Robert Knox (1791–1862), by David Octavius Hill and Robert Adamson

blind in one eye and severely disfigured. From 1805 he attended Edinburgh high school, where he was *dux* and gold medallist. In November 1810 he began medical school at Edinburgh University, where he was twice president of the Royal Medical Society before his graduation. Having failed once in anatomy, partly owing to the incompetent teaching of Alexander Munro (*tertius*), he became a pupil at John Barclay's extramural school and gained a masterly knowledge of the subject. He graduated MD in 1814 with his impressive thesis, 'On the effects of stimulants and narcotics on the healthy body'. This was followed in January 1815 by an important paper, 'The diurnal variations of the pulse and other functions' (*Edinburgh Medical and Surgical Journal*, 11.52–65, 164–7). He finished this phase of his education as a pupil of the surgeon John Abernethy at St Bartholomew's Hospital, London, and was able to apply Abernethy's theories after Waterloo, when he obtained a commission as assistant surgeon in the army in 1815 and was sent to Brussels.

Knox returned to England in charge of a large party of invalids and was for a time attached to the Melsea Hospital in Hampshire. In April 1817 he was sent to the Cape of Good Hope with the 72nd highlanders to serve in the Cape Frontier War of 1819. It was here that he formulated many of the radical opinions he held throughout his life (such as an unpopular stance against colonial policy) and energetically embarked on ethnological, zoological, geographical, and medical researches which formed the basis of his study for the rest of his life. In 1820 he was involved in an

altercation with a fellow officer for which he was officially censured and unofficially and publicly horsewhipped (Stephen, 1). The cause of the dispute remains obscure but it may have arisen from his anticolonialist opinions, for Knox was a steadfast if not proud and stubborn defender of his own beliefs. He returned to Britain, wishing to be with his family, on half pay, on Christmas day 1820.

Knox remained in Edinburgh, contributing papers to the Wernerian Society on subjects suggested to him by his recent research. In the autumn of 1821 he began a year's study in Paris under Cuvier, Geoffroy St-Hilaire, De Blainville, and Larrey. He returned to Edinburgh at the end of 1822, and remained on army half pay until 1832. In 1824 he married Mary Russell (*d.* 1841), whom his student and biographer Henry Lonsdale described as of inferior rank. Lonsdale suggested that he may have maintained an 'official' residence with his sister Mary taking on the social role as wife, and a private residence for his young family. To others this seems unlikely for a man known to be devoted to his family (Rae, 49).

During the next few years Knox continued to contribute zoological and anatomical papers to the Wernerian Society and the Royal Society of Edinburgh. The most important of these was 'Observations on the comparative anatomy of the eye', in which the discoveries on the structure and physiology of the eye secured for Knox a niche in the annals of medical history. He embarked on a difficult relationship with the College of Surgeons of Edinburgh after persuading it to form a reputable museum of comparative anatomy and pathology. He was eventually appointed its conservator in 1825 after becoming a fellow of the college on 18 March, and superintended the purchase and transfer of the collection of Sir Charles Bell. He worked actively and enthusiastically in the museum until 1831.

Meanwhile, on 2 March 1825, Knox signed articles of partnership with his old teacher John Barclay, taking on the bulk of the work. When Barclay died in 1826 he left the anatomical school entirely under Knox's control. Knox built up a formidable reputation as a teacher and lecturer and almost single-handedly raised the profile of the study of anatomy in Britain. His classes increased dramatically in size until his school could be said to be the largest of its kind in Britain, attracting barristers, the clergy, the aristocracy, artists, and men of letters. His students numbered 504 in 1828–9, when the demand was such that he lectured three times daily.

Knox was probably one of the most skilled teachers Edinburgh had ever known and it is conjectured that without him British surgery might not have advanced in the way that it did (Rae, 125). Knox's approach to anatomy was refreshingly different from that of his predecessor and his university counterparts, inspiring in his students 'a desire to know the unknown; a love of the perfect; an aiming at the universal' (Knox, 22). Building on the comparative anatomy of Barclay but drawing on his knowledge of Cuvier and the French school, Knox invested anatomy with a new emphasis, infusing the mere mechanics of anatomy with a caustic wit and with a philosophy which elevated his subject to 'the hope of detecting the laws of organic life, the origin of living beings and the transcendental laws regulating the living world in time and space' (ibid., 141–2). As John D. Comrie has assessed, 'his forte was not in relation to surgery and medicine, but in bringing comparative anatomy to the explanation of human anatomy' (Comrie, 2.502). Knox's lectures were rehearsed with great care down to his physical appearance, which he embellished with fine clothes and jewellery.

Burke and Hare However, Knox's success as a teacher was to have a concomitant negative effect on the reputation of anatomical teaching. Demand had placed an added burden on the supply of suitable human subjects for dissection, legally confined to the bodies of executed murderers, and the entire practice of anatomy had become surreptitiously and illegally dependent on the work of the so-called 'resurrectionists' or grave-robbers. Knox was not alone in procuring subjects in this way, but through a combination of bad luck and bad judgement his name became inextricably linked with those of William *Burke and William *Hare [see under Burke, William]. Knox started receiving subjects from Burke and Hare on 29 November 1827. Burke's confession testifies that this first body, the only one not murdered by Burke and Hare, was originally meant for Alexander Munro, professor of anatomy at the University of Edinburgh, but one of Knox's zealous students redirected the men to Knox's rooms at 10 Surgeon's Square with the promise of a larger fee (Ball, 83). By 2 November 1828, when they were charged, Burke and Hare, attracted by the high prices he was offering, had brought Knox twelve murdered bodies which were received and prepared by his assistants for dissection.

Knox was not called as a witness in the trial and subsequently withdrew from the public eye. Privately, and naïvely, he was incredulous that he could be seriously linked with Burke and Hare. In a second confession published in the *Edinburgh Courant* shortly before his execution in January 1829, Burke stated that Knox had received the bodies with no knowledge of the murders. Not convinced, the public and many of his colleagues charged Knox with guilt by association, while others accused him of being the advocate and instigator of the crimes. John Wilson in *Blackwood* (*Noctes*, March 1829) savagely attacked him for ignoring the 'thumb marks on the neck' of the bodies brought to him. Sir Walter Scott's censure remains the most memorable, referring to Knox as the 'learned carcass-butcher' (Currie, 43). Knox was vilified in popular ballads and caricatured in lithographic prints as Richard III looking for Tyrell. On 12 February 1829 the public took matters into their own hands by strangling, hanging, and destroying an effigy of Knox in front of his home in Newington.

For months the atmosphere in Edinburgh was vengeful but Knox still made no attempt to defend himself. To investigate the charges against him a committee was formed which included John Robinson, secretary to the Royal Society of Edinburgh, and William Pultanay Alison, professor of medicine. This committee reported that they had 'seen no evidence that Dr Knox or his assistants knew that murder was committed in procuring any of the subjects brought to his rooms' and 'firmly believed' in his innocence. There were circumstances calculated to excite suspicion of murder (such as the freshness of the bodies), but because all the bodies had been smothered there was no visible proof (Knox and many of his contemporaries did not possess the knowledge required to ascertain ante- and post-mortem signs of violence). The committee merely rebuked Knox for acting incautiously in reception of subjects, and especially in allowing his assistants to receive them without investigating the source of the supply.

In Burke's official confession he states that Knox was present on two occasions when murdered bodies were received, and that in one case he had been impressed by the freshness of the corpse but had made no further inquiries. In a pamphlet published by a former doorkeeper at Knox's school, David Paterson alleged that several of the bodies had been delivered with suspiciously bloodied eyes, ears, and mouths, and moreover that the head and feet were severed from the body of 'daft Jamie', a recognizable Edinburgh figure, when it became known that he was missing. On the 17 March 1829 Knox addressed a letter to the *Caledonian Mercury* with the findings of this committee, publishing his only statement of vindication. He offered no statement of apology or regret but there is evidence from his personal catalogue that Knox ceased all research on human anatomy after 1828 (Ross and Taylor). However, the report did not alleviate the pressure of public opinion, as Knox's chief assistants T. W. Jones, William Fergusson, and Alexander Miller also took a share in his unpopularity. Sir Robert Christison, who had examined the body of the final murder victim, concluded that Knox had 'rather wilfully shut his eyes to incidents which ought to have excited the grave suspicions of a man of his intelligence' (*Life*, 1.310).

Current opinion remains divided as to the scale of Knox's guilt. He has a staunch and sympathetic defender in biographer Isobel Rae while social historian Ruth Richardson points to the more insalubrious nature of Knox's 'necrophiliac voyeurism' regarding the body of murder victim Mary Paterson, whom witnesses claim Knox kept preserved for three months so that her body could be admired and painted by students (Richardson, 101). Richardson takes Knox's failure to prosecute for libel those accusing him of complicity as 'tantamount to an admission of guilt' (ibid., 97). Anticipating the ensuing furore, Knox had drafted a letter to Robert Peel dated 3 November 1828 in which he outlined the 'obstacles which impede the progress of anatomy in Great Britain' (Rae, 62). The letter was never sent, but in it Knox hoped that the Burke and Hare scandal would force the government to publish their report on the laws governing dissection. In 1832 a new Anatomy Act extended the supply of anatomical subjects to include the poor and the homeless.

Aftermath During this period Knox ignored the picketing at Surgeon's Square and continued to publish and lecture, winning the support at least of his students who presented him with a gold vase on 11 April 1829. In 1832 he moved to larger premises vacated by the College of Surgeons and in 1833 took William Fergusson and John Reid into partnership for the practical classes. But despite his students' loyalty he was gradually frozen out of official university life. The College of Surgeons' museum contrived to be rid of him and he finally resigned in 1831. In the 1830s Knox reneged on his earlier position of silence and entered into embittered wrangles with colleagues and critics such as John Stark, who accused him of plagiarism.

Knox became a satirist and cynic, using the press and subsequent failed applications for university positions (chair of pathology in 1837, chair in physiology in 1841, and lecturer in anatomy at the Scottish Academy) to publicize his opinions concerning the administration of the study of medicine within the university and to attack colleagues including John Reid. His anti-Christian wit did nothing to endear him to the university authorities, and moreover he spoke of the chairs of the university as having 'fallen much below the income of a steady-going retail grocery or bakery' (*DNB*). In this latter respect he was correct: Edinburgh's medical teaching was falling behind London's in popularity and prestige. For this reason and compounded by the blows that Knox's reputation had suffered by 1834, the number of students attending his classes had fallen off. In 1836 John Reid left him and Fergusson virtually gave up his work as his assistant. Knox now relied almost wholly on his younger brother Frederick, with whom he had anatomized a whalebone whale in 1831–4. Knox's *Edinburgh Dissector*, brought out anonymously in 1837 to compete with Harrison's *Dublin Dissector*, was not a success. The nadir was reached in the early 1840s on the death of his wife from puerperal fever after the birth of their sixth child in 1841, and the death in 1842 of his son John, aged four.

The arrival of Knox's partner and future biographer Henry Lonsdale in May 1840 seemed to signal a slight change in his professional fortunes. Knox replaced Alexander Lizars at the Argyle Square extramural medical school as lecturer in anatomy. But this good luck was short-lived. Knox recommended his own lectures on anatomy and physiology but could not attract a class. He crossed swords with John Reid over the rights to a discovery concerning the placenta, claiming Reid's original discovery as his own (Lonsdale, 219–20, 257). This was perhaps the final humiliation. Knox placed his household in charge of his nephew and daughter Mary and left Edinburgh for London. From 1842 to 1846 he was very unsettled. He joined the small Portland Street school of medicine in Glasgow in November 1844 but returned fees to his students before the end of the month. Allowed no admittance into the ranks of London surgeons, he embarked on lecture tours, translated French anatomical textbooks, and wrote prodigiously for medical journals.

According to Rae, Christison's comment that Knox was at this time a showman to a travelling party of Ojibwe Indians was probably wishful thinking on Christison's part (p. 132). This notion, however, was undoubtedly encouraged by Knox's 1846 popular lecture tour, entitled 'The races of men', which visited Newcastle upon Tyne, Manchester, and Liverpool, where his outspoken and lamentable views on Jews were the cause of much debate in local newspapers. After the Burke and Hare scandal this phase of Knox's career remains the most engrossing to historians. Building on his studies of black peoples in the Cape, and using anatomical method to study human history, Knox theorized, remarkably early in the history of European racist philosophy, that the human race was composed of a highly systematized group of distinct species based on a sliding scale of civilizational aptitude (Biddiss, 15–20). Within this scheme a vast gulf separated white from black and it led Knox into an unfortunate analogy: '[The black man] is no more a white man than an ass is a horse or a zebra' (R. Knox, *Races of Men*, 1850, 245). Knox firmly believed that races were inherently antagonistic, immutable, and properly adapted to one single habitat. It was a thoroughly pessimistic and anti-progressive view of human history, perhaps reflecting his own outlook on life at this time as well as being the logical development of years of study through biological method. According to this theory Knox even explained the 1848 revolutions as racial struggles.

Although Knox was fundamentally racist it has recently been argued that he used his theories to mount a savage critique of colonialism. Eveleen Richards states that all Knox's inquiries into race were infused with a philosopher's concern for the social and political implications of natural law (Richards, 379). But here the paradoxes of his views are most pointed: while he despised slavery and British colonial policy, he devised a scheme when in Glasgow to found a colony in South Africa which would make it the 'best wool producing company in the world' (NL Scot., MS 2618, fol. 288). Knox's ideas later found popularity with James Hunt, founder of the Anthropological Society of London; and other contemporaries thought that *Races of Men* was 'his great work, by which he will live' (*The Lancet*). Owing to this work Knox was made an honorary fellow of the Ethnological Society of London in 1860 and honorary curator of its museum in 1862. Early in 1861 he was elected foreign member of the Anthropological Society of Paris.

Despite success in this field, during the late 1840s and 1850s Knox's life was marred by ignominy and misfortune, including the deaths of his son Robert in May 1854 and his daughter Mary in 1858. Scandal pursued him again, this time in the shape of John Henry Osborne, who had falsely obtained a certificate from Knox testifying to six months' study. Knox had been testing the patience of the Royal College of Surgeons by failing to comply with their administrative regulations (Creswell) and the college took this opportunity to ban him from performing official lectures; this later debarred him from an invitation to lecture at the Royal Free Hospital medical school. In 1848 Knox was struck off the roll of fellows of the Royal Society of Edinburgh. In the 1850s applications for a government appointment in Africa, for a surgical position in the Crimea, and for office at the British Museum were rejected.

While the last few years of his life were financially stringent, Knox did at least find some professional reward in London, in an appointment as pathological anatomist to the Cancer Hospital at Brompton; he also practised medicine in Hackney, supported by his sister and latterly his only surviving son, Edward. In the summer of 1862 his strength began to fail, and on 9 December he suffered an apoplectic seizure after returning from his duties at the Cancer Hospital; he died without gaining consciousness on 20 December at his home at 9 Lambe Terrace, Hackney. Following his wishes and lifelong deist views he was buried in the nonconformist sector of Brookwood cemetery in Woking, Surrey, on 29 December.

CLARE L. TAYLOR

Sources letter, 15 Sept 1844, NL Scot., MS 2618, fol. 288 · I. Rae, *Knox, the anatomist* (1964) · K. Stephen, *Robert Knox* (1981) · H. Lonsdale, *A sketch of the life and writings of Robert Knox* (1870) · R. Richardson, *Death, dissection and the destitute*, pbk edn (1988) · M. D. Biddiss, 'The politics of anatomy: Dr Robert Knox and Victorian racism', *Proceedings of the Royal Society of Medicine*, 69 (1976), 245–50 · E. Richards, 'The "moral anatomy" of Robert Knox: the interplay between biological and social thought in Victorian scientific thought', *Journal of the History of Biology*, 22 (1989), 373–436 · J. A. Ross and H. W. Y. Taylor, 'Robert Knox's catalogue', *Journal of the History of Medicine and Allied Sciences*, 10 (1955), 269–76 · C. H. Creswell, *The Royal College of Surgeons of Edinburgh: historical notes from 1505–1905* (1926) · J. D. Comrie, *History of Scottish medicine*, 2nd edn, 2 (1932) · *The Lancet* (3 Jan 1863) · A. S. Currie, 'Robert Knox, anatomist, scientist, and martyr', *Proceedings of the Royal Society of Medicine*, 26 (1932–3), 39–46 · *The life of Sir Robert Christison*, 1 (1885) · J. M. Ball, *The sack-'em-up men: an account of the rise and fall of the modern resurrectionists* (1928) · *Medical Times and Gazette* (27 Dec 1862) · R. Knox, *Great artists and great anatomists* (1852)
Archives BL, corresp., Peel MS 40601, fols. 50, 51 · Royal College of Surgeons, Edinburgh, records · U. Edin., Anatomy section, catalogue | NL Scot., Goodsir, linked memories, Fife Coast, etc., MS 170 · Royal Anthropological Institute, London, Ethnological Society of London minutes
Likenesses D. O. Hill and R. Adamson, photograph, Scot. NPG [*see illus.*] · A. Edouart, silhouette, Scot. NPG · caricature, repro. in Rae, *Knox* · etching, BM · photographs, repro. in Rae, *Knox*

Knox, Robert (1815–1883), minister of the Presbyterian Church in Ireland, was the third son of Hugh Knox, for forty years a ruling elder of the parish of Urney, co. Tyrone. He was born at Clady, in that parish. He entered Glasgow University in 1834 and graduated MA in 1837. He subsequently studied in the collegiate department of the Royal Belfast Academical Institution, where during his student days he was an active promoter of the union between the synod of Ulster and the Secession synod, which resulted in the formation of the general assembly of the Presbyterian Church in Ireland in 1840. He was licensed to preach in 1840, being ordained by the presbytery of Strabane, co. Tyrone, in April of that year, and was sent as a missionary to the south of Ireland. Several congregations owed their origin to his labours. On 10 June 1842 he was installed as assistant and successor to the Revd John Whiteside, pastor of the Second Congregation of Coleraine. Next year he became minister of the Linenhall Street Church, Belfast.

Knox was soon one of the most energetic of the Belfast clergy, being particularly active in promoting the erection of new churches and schoolhouses, and in furthering the work of the town mission, of which he became honorary secretary. He established and edited a monthly periodical entitled the *Irish Presbyterian*, and published many sermons. A prolonged newspaper controversy with the Revd Theophilus Campbell of Trinity Church, Belfast, afterwards dean of Dromore, on the question of baptismal regeneration, brought him into much prominence. The letters were subsequently collected and published. In 1861 he received the degree of doctor of divinity from Union College, Schenectady, New York. He was one of the founders of the Sabbath School Society for Ireland in connection with the Presbyterian church, and one of the earliest and most enthusiastic promoters of the Presbyterian alliance, in which all the Presbyterian churches of the world are represented.

In 1870 Knox married the daughter of William Gilbert, of Belfast. After his death she married the Revd George Matthews DD of Quebec. Knox died at his home, Windsor Park, Belfast, on 16 August 1883 and was buried in the borough cemetery.

THOMAS HAMILTON, *rev.* DAVID HUDDLESTON

Sources *Belfast Witness* (17 Aug 1883), 4 · *McComb's Presbyterian Almanac* (1884), 91 · C. H. Irwin, *A history of presbyterianism in Dublin and the south and west of Ireland* (1892), 113–17 · J. E. Mullin, *New Row Presbyterian Church, Coleraine, 1727–1977* (1976), 69–71 · J. M. Barkley, *The Sabbath School Society for Ireland, 1862–1962* (1961), 10 · W. T. Latimer, *A history of the Irish Presbyterians*, 2nd edn (1902), 465 · *A history of congregations in the Presbyterian Church in Ireland, 1610–1982*, Presbyterian Church in Ireland (1982), 151, 324 · A. V. Raymond, *Union University: its history, influence, characteristics and equipment* (1907), 3. 176 · CGPLA Ire. (1883)
Likenesses engraving, repro. in Mullin, *New Row Presbyterian Church*
Wealth at death £1842 18s. 11d.: probate, 7 Sept 1883, CGPLA Ire.

Knox, Robert Bent (1808–1893), Church of Ireland archbishop of Armagh, was the second son of the Hon. Charles Knox (d. 1825), archdeacon of Armagh, and his wife, Hannah (d. 1852), the daughter of Robert Bent MP, and widow of James Fletcher. He was born at Dungannon Park House, the residence of his grandfather Thomas Knox, first Viscount Northland (d. 1818), on 25 September 1808. Though generally thought to have been named Robert Bent, the only name given to him at baptism was Robert. He was educated at Trinity College, Dublin, graduating BA in 1829, MA in 1834, DD per lit. reg. in 1849, and BD and DD in 1858; he was also made LLD from Cambridge in 1888. In 1832 he was ordained deacon and priest by Beresford, bishop of Kilmore. On 7 May 1834 he was collated chancellor of Ardfert, and on 16 October 1841 he was collated to the prebend of St Munchin's, Limerick, by his uncle Edmund Knox (d. 7 May 1849), bishop of Limerick, who made him his domestic chaplain. On 5 October 1842 he married Catherine Delia (d. 1897), the daughter of Thomas Gibbon Fitzgibbon of Ballyseeda, co. Limerick. They had three sons, including Charles Edmond (later lieutenant-general), and two daughters, who survived him.

In March 1849 Knox was nominated by Lord Clarendon to the see of Down, Connor, and Dromore, vacated by the death (2 November 1848) of Richard Mant. He was consecrated bishop on 1 May, and enthroned on 3 May at Lisburn and on 5 May at Dromore. Samuel Wilberforce, who was in Ireland in 1861, reported in his diary (26 August) some gossip which was circulating about the appointment: James Henthorn Todd described Knox as 'very foolish, without learning, piety, judgment, conduct, sense, appointed by a job, that his uncle should resign Limerick'; the dean of Limerick, Anthony La Touche Kirwan (d. 1868), said that Knox 'used, when made to preach by his uncle, to get me to write his sermon, and could not deliver it' (Wilberforce, 25).

Knox, as a whig, was not immediately popular in his diocese. Like his predecessor, he resided at Holywood, co. Down. He made no secret of his unpopular opinion that disestablishment was inevitable. He had at first hoped to build a cathedral in Belfast (to add to the three existing cathedrals of the diocese), but abandoned this extravagant plan in order to achieve the more modest aim of increasing the number of churches. The Belfast Church Extension Society was founded by him in 1862; its work enabled him to consecrate forty-eight new or enlarged churches in the diocese. Prior to disestablishment, he organized in 1862 diocesan conferences, and founded a diocesan board of missions. In the House of Lords in 1867, and before the church commission in 1868, he proposed a reduction of the Irish hierarchy to one archbishop and five bishops. He was not a man of great presence or of genial warmth, being quiet and restrained. But his pragmatism and frankness made him an able administrator and an effective speaker. His involvement with many public bodies and charities meant that he became a respected figure within the community.

When the archbishop of Armagh and primate of all Ireland, Marcus Gervais Beresford, died on 26 December 1885, Knox was chosen as his successor. He left Belfast and was enthroned as archbishop of Armagh on 1 June 1886. As president of the general synod of the Irish church, his qualities of fairness and moderation came to the fore. He was active to the last, presiding at the Armagh diocesan synod a fortnight before his death. He died at the archbishop's palace, Armagh, on 23 October 1893, and was buried on 27 October in the old church (a disused ruin) at Holywood. Besides a sermon (1847), charges (1850 and 1858), and a brief address, 'Fruits of the revival', in Steane's *Ulster Revival* (1859), he published an *Ecclesiastical Index (of Ireland)* (1839), a valuable reference book.

ALEXANDER GORDON, rev. DAVID HUDDLESTON

Sources *Northern Whig* (24 Oct 1893) · *Northern Whig* (30 Oct 1893) · J. R. Garstin, *Anglican archbishops of Armagh* (1900) · H. B. Swanzy, *Succession lists of the diocese of Dromore*, ed. J. B. Leslie (1933) · R. B. McDowell, *The Church of Ireland, 1869–1969* (1975) · Burke, *Peerage* (1970) · *Belfast News-Letter* (24 Oct 1893) · *Belfast News-Letter* (30 Oct 1893) · J. B. Leslie, ed., *Clergy of Connor: from Patrician times to the present day* (1993) · D. H. Akenson, *The Church of Ireland: ecclesiastical reform and revolution, 1800–1885* (1971) · H. E. Patton, *Fifty years of disestablishment* (1922) · D. Bowen, *The protestant crusade in Ireland, 1800–70* (1978) · R. G. Wilberforce, *Life of the right reverend Samuel Wilberforce … with selections from his diaries and correspondence*, 3 (1882), 25

Archives Bodl. Oxf., corresp. with Lord Kimberley
Likenesses Way, oils, The Palace, Armagh, co. Armagh, Ireland · lithograph, repro. in Patton, *Fifty years of disestablishment* · wood-engraving (after photograph by Chancellor of Dublin), NPG; repro. in *ILN* (29 May 1866) · wood-engraving, NPG; repro. in *ILN* (25 June 1892)
Wealth at death £10,571 1s. 1d.: probate, 21 Nov 1893, *CGPLA Ire.*

Knox, Ronald Arbuthnott (1888–1957), Roman Catholic priest and writer, was born on 17 February 1888 at Kibworth rectory, Leicestershire, the youngest of the four sons and two daughters of the strongly evangelical Edmund Arbuthnott *Knox (1847–1937), later bishop of Manchester, and his wife, Ellen Penelope French (1854–1892), daughter of Thomas Valpy *French (1825–1891), the heroic evangelical missionary bishop of Lahore. On his father's side Knox was of Scots–Irish Presbyterian descent, although his paternal grandfather, George Knox, had also been an Anglican clergyman. His three older brothers, Edmund George Valpy *Knox, (Alfred) Dillwyn *Knox, and Wilfred Lawrence *Knox, were all to be distinguished, as was one of the daughters, Winifred, and the household culture was one of elaborate verbal games.

Early life and education Despite the early death of his mother from influenza when he was nearly four, Knox's childhood was an idyllic one made happy first by a clerical uncle, Lindsey Knox, and then by his father's second wife, Ethel Newton. Knox was famously precocious, declaring at the age of four that 'at night I think about the past' (Fitzgerald, 46), reading Virgil at six, and contributing a Latin serial, *Publius et Amilla*, to the family magazine. In 1896 Knox was sent to the preparatory school of Summer Fields, in north Oxford. In 1900 he entered Eton College, where he was a notable scholar and personality. He was elected to the self-selecting Eton Society, 'Pop', and became captain of the school, delegating his responsibility for corporal punishment to another boy. He won the first Balliol scholarship and Davies scholarship from Eton to Oxford, and was *proxime accessit* for the Newcastle scholarship taken by his friend and rival, Patrick Shaw-Stewart. In 1906 he joined Julian Grenfell and Charles Lister to found *The Outsider*, a magazine which tweaked the nose of authority. He also dedicated to his Eton master, Cyril Alington, *Signa severa* (1906), a collection of comic verses celebrating the Etonian ethos, most of them in English, but also in Latin and Greek.

In 1906 Knox went up to Balliol. He found the university an anticlimax after Eton, though his academic honours continued to accumulate, with the Hertford (1907), Ireland (1908), and Craven (1908) scholarships and the Gaisford Greek and chancellor's Latin verse prizes (1908 and 1910). For the Gaisford he translated Robert Browning into Theocritan hexameters. He edited *Isis*, was secretary, junior librarian, and president of the Oxford Union (in Hilary term, 1909), and was reputed one of the finest speakers of his generation. He achieved only a second in classical moderations, having neglected to read the set commentaries, but took a first in Greats in 1910. He published a second volume of comic verse and prose, *Juxta salices* (1910), the oldest of them dating from his days at Eton, dedicated

Ronald Arbuthnott Knox (1888–1957), by Howard Coster, 1938

to Patrick Shaw-Stewart as the only man able to understand all his jokes.

Anglo-Catholicism and early writings Knox's interest in Anglo-Catholicism began at Eton, and was originally inspired by R. H. Benson's *The Light Invisible* (1903), on the near reality of the spiritual world, and H. O. Wakeman's *Introduction to the History of the Church of England* (1896), which canonized the Tractarians. When only seventeen, still at Eton, he made a private vow of celibacy. At Oxford he worshipped with the Cowley fathers and at Pusey House, went to confession, and cultivated a circle of Anglo-Catholic friends. Knox considered various careers, but decided to accept a fellowship at Trinity College, Oxford, with a view to ordination to the college chaplaincy. In 1910 he was private tutor to the young Harold Macmillan, but lost the post when he refused the nonconformist Mrs Macmillan's request not to discuss religion with her son. Macmillan recalled that Knox was 'the only man I have ever known who really was a saint … and if you live with a saint, it's quite an experience, especially a humorous saint' (Horne, 18).

Knox was ordained priest in the Church of England on 22 September 1912, in St Giles's, Reading, and on 24 September he said his first mass in the fashionable London church of St Mary's, Graham Street. By 1912 he had won his reputation as an Anglo-Catholic *enfant terrible* by publishing in *The Oxford Magazine* 'Absolute and Abitofhell', a satire imitating Dryden's famous poem *Absalom and Achitophel*, on the forthcoming liberal Anglican volume of essays, *Foundations* (1912). The spoof had a greater success than its target. In a similar vein were the essay 'Studies in the literature of Sherlock Holmes' (*The Blue Book*, 1912), a satire on the German methods of biblical scholarship as well as a tribute to the great detective, and a more serious attack upon *Foundations*, *Some Loose Stones* (1913).

Knox was also associated with the Society of Saints Peter and Paul, a publishing house and seller of ecclesiastical furnishings founded by the Revd Maurice Child with the aim of converting Anglican high-churchmanship from a taste in Gothic to baroque. The society published in lavish seventeenth-century type Knox's *Reunion All Round, or, Jael's*

Hammer Laid Aside (1914), a satire in Swift's manner on contemporary ecumenism, and *Bread or Stone* (1915), Knox's Holy Week addresses. His teaching methods as a don at Trinity College included ingenious mnemonics and a game of snakes and ladders illustrating the missionary journeys of St Paul. His collegiate circles included his 'Ronnie's Bar', serving port and bananas to undergraduates, 'Spike Teas' with honey sandwiches for Anglo-Catholics, and a smaller group of more intimate friends including Guy Lawrence and Harold Macmillan, who were to figure as B and C in Knox's *A Spiritual Aeneid*.

Knox did not share in the popular exultation at the outset of the war, reminding a friend that the Curé d'Ars had run away from conscription, though Knox's book of prayers, *An Hour at the Front* (1914), sold 70,000 copies on behalf of the Prince of Wales' Relief Fund. With Oxford almost empty in 1915 he joined Cyril Alington, now headmaster of Shrewsbury, as an assistant master at the school, succeeding his friend Evelyn Southwell, of whom he wrote 'one of the best memorial poems ever written' (C. A. Alington, *A Dean's Apology*, 1952, 63–4) when Southwell fell in battle. He taught Greek and Latin by verbal games and jigsaws and translated some of Belloc's *Cautionary Tales* and other verses for *The Salopian*.

Conversion to Catholicism and ordination, 1917–1919 Knox's Roman Catholic leanings caused great suffering to his sensitive but militantly anti-ritualist father, who struck him from his will, although he loved him and took pride in him. The bishop wrote of his sons, none of whom shared his evangelical protestantism, that in the number of their publications 'They cannot be far behind the illustrious family of Archbishop Benson' (Knox, *Reminiscences*, 300). Ronald's Anglo-Catholic brother Wilfred was more understanding. Knox was received into the Roman Catholic church on 22 September 1917 by the abbot at Farnborough Abbey. He was confirmed on 6 October by Cardinal Bourne. He justified his conversion theologically in *The Essentials of Spiritual Unity* (1918) and then in *A Spiritual Aeneid* (1918), an autobiographical account of his religious history which remains a literary classic; Knox felt bound to translate the quotations from Virgil which are the framework for the book when it was republished in 1950. On Bourne's wise advice he prepared for the priesthood by living at the Brompton Oratory during thirteen months when he seems to have had some experience of the higher states of prayer. The deaths of Edward Horner, Patrick Shaw-Stewart, and his dearest intimate, Guy Lawrence, completed the near total slaughter of his old Etonian and Oxonian friends. He wrote a memoir, *Patrick Shaw-Stewart* (1920). He was ordained a priest on 5 October 1919 'on his own patrimony', having received £3000 left him in his mother's will. His *Meditations on the Psalms* appeared in the same year.

'The wittiest young man in England', 1919–1926 In 1919 Bourne sent Knox as an assistant master to the college-seminary of St Edmund's, Ware, which the cardinal wanted to turn into a fashionable school and the nursery for a better educated clergy. Knox remained seven and a half years at St Edmund's. During these years he also wrote regularly for the *Daily News*, the *Evening Standard*, the *Morning Post*, and *The Universe*. In 1924 the *Daily Mail* called him 'the wittiest young man in England' (Fitzgerald, 173). However, the newspapers heavily criticized him for his spoof BBC news broadcast on 15 January 1926, entitled 'Broadcasting from the barricades', an account of a demonstration of the unemployed who were exhorted by Mr Popplebury, secretary of the National Movement for Abolishing Theatre Queues, to sack the National Gallery, and went on to roast alive the philanthropist Sir Theophilus Gooch, and to march on Broadcasting House: the broadcaster signed off as they approached his door.

Chaplain and detective story writer, 1926–1938 Knox's detective stories (*The Viaduct Murder*, 1926; *The Three Taps*, 1927; *The Footsteps at the Lock*, 1928; *The Body in the Silo*, 1933; *Still Dead*, 1934; *Double Cross Purposes*, 1937) had as hero-detective Miles Bredon, employed by an insurance company, the Indescribable, which gave him an excuse for being at the scene of the crime. The books were written according to rules which Knox set out in his introduction to *The Best Detective Stories of the Year* (1928). These were rewritten as the oath of initiation of the Detection Club, founded in 1929, whose members met for harmless hilarity and included G. K. Chesterton, Agatha Christie, and Dorothy L. Sayers. His best stories have remained in print in collections of detective stories.

This literary activity had a purpose. In 1926 Knox was appointed chaplain to the small number of Catholic male students at Oxford; the detective stories were written during the vacation, brought in about £600, and paid his living expenses for a year. He delivered to his congregations the conferences revised for publication as *In Soft Garments* (1942). The talks in *The Hidden Stream* (1952) were given by invitation back to Oxford after his departure; the title refers to the underground waterway beside the Old Palace which houses the Catholic chaplaincy. Knox travelled tirelessly to preach and he was the church's star performer on great occasions, as well as for the requiems of friends like Chesterton (1936) and Hilaire Belloc (1953). He was also a tireless memorialist of friends.

Knox's apologetics included *The Belief of Catholics* (1927). At Frank Sheed's suggestion, Knox gently dissected the confusions in the attacks on Christianity by such literary luminaries as H. G. Wells, Arnold Bennett, Rebecca West, Hugh Walpole, and Conan Doyle in his *Caliban in Grub Street* (1930). His reply to the popular scientism also hostile to religion was *Broadcast Minds* (1932). Arnold Lunn, who had attacked him in *Roman Converts* (1924), suggested an exchange of letters about Roman Catholicism which was published as *Difficulties* (1932). Knox handled his opponent with intellectual delicacy and converted him: Lunn went on to become 'the most tireless Catholic apologist of his generation' (Waugh, 236).

Knox's duties in Oxford were undemanding, though he built a chapel and suffered moral anguish over the more wayward of his charges. He was much in demand for light papers on comic subjects, such as 'The Man who Tried to Convert the Pope'. His love of Trollope inspired his twentieth-century continuation of the Barchester novels with *Barchester Pilgrimage* (1935). Cardinal Bourne was said to disapprove of his detective stories, but Knox stood higher in the favour of Bourne's successor, the amiable Cardinal Hinsley, and of his own diocesan, Archbishop Williams in Birmingham. In 1936 Knox was appointed a domestic prelate to the pope, with the title of Monsignor, and in the same year became a member of a committee to revise the *Westminster Hymnal*, though he was tone-deaf, enriching it with four of his own hymns and forty-seven of his translations from the Latin. The new edition appeared in 1940. He also rewrote much of the vernacular Roman Catholic *Manual of Prayers* published in 1942. In 1943, after Hinsley's death, a number of Catholic bishops including Williams took exception to its alleged inaccuracies, and it was withdrawn from sale. The incident magnified Knox's sense of discouragement in translating the Bible.

Knox's own personal life, however, was rejuvenated by his platonic love affair with the young Daphne, Lady Acton. On a Hellenic cruise in 1937 the other passengers complained that Knox and Lady Acton kept exclusively together. He instructed her in the faith and received her into the church in 1938. Under her benign influence at the family home of Aldenham Park in Shropshire he wrote for her his secular masterpiece, *Let Dons Delight* (1939), the record, in an account of every fifty years from 1588, of the conversations of the senior common room of the imaginary Oxford college of Simon Magus, a junior member of one generation becoming the senior member of the next. The fellows are notable for wrong predictions: thus in 1788, 'I do not think we shall have much trouble with the Irish' (p. 167), and talk in comic ignorance of the storms of history about to break around their heads, but there is also a plangent running theme of the Roman Catholic exile from Oxford, and the ultimate failure of the successor Church of England. The debates are interspersed with biographies of the characters in pastiche styles from Anthony Wood to Mark Pattison.

At Aldenham Park, 1938–1947 In 1938 Knox decided to resign from the Oxford chaplaincy, and having declined the offer of the presidency of St Edmund's, retired in 1939 to Aldenham Park to work on the replacement of the existing Douai–Challoner translation of the Vulgate Bible, beginning by learning Hebrew. The New Testament was published in 1945. The Old Testament received the Westminster archdiocesan *imprimatur* in 1948, was printed 'for private use' in 1949, and was subjected to minute criticism by outside experts before its publication in 1955, when Knox's *Commentary on the New Testament* also appeared.

This work was achieved despite the distractions of war. Knox wrote and broadcast some allied propaganda and did his ineffectual best to help Lady Acton with her farm, lending her the money to buy a tractor. Aldenham was also occupied by evacuee Assumptionist nuns and their schoolgirl charges from 1940. Knox liked the girls; he said mass for them, preached them retreats, and gave them talks after Sunday benediction. The talks became books— *The Mass in Slow Motion* (1948), *The Creed in Slow Motion* (1949), and *The Gospel in Slow Motion* (1950)—dedicated to three of his Aldenham favourites. His monthly 'lightning meditations' for the *Sunday Times* were later published as *Stimuli* (1951). He was one of a minority in feeling revulsion at the American nuclear bombing of Japan, but his *God and the Atom* (1946), on the implications of this Promethean atrocity, fell stillborn from the press.

Knox embodied his retreat addresses on Old Testament themes in *A Retreat for Priests* (1946), and published his lay addresses in *A Retreat for Lay People* (1955). A further volume on the daily round of priestly duties, *The Priestly Life: a Retreat* (1959), appeared after his death. He published a selection of his replies to correspondents on religious themes as *Off the Record* (1953), and his sermons on the Blessed Sacrament, preached at Corpus Christi, Maiden Lane, as *The Window in the Wall* (1956).

Later life and reputation, 1947–1957 Knox was uprooted in 1947 when the Actons decided to farm in Rhodesia, and was invited to board in Mells in Somerset by Mrs Katharine Asquith, the sister of his long dead friend Edward Horner. Knox had received her daughter, Lady Helen, into the church, and her son, Lord Oxford and Asquith, had lodged with Knox in the Old Palace. At Mells he completed his long meditated and favourite work, *Enthusiasm* (1950). The book was conceived polemically but was completed eirenically. It spans two thousand years of religious heroism and eccentricity: though the scholarship is dated, it still has some literary merit, as well as passages of great wisdom and wit.

Knox was honoured by his church. He was elected to membership of the Old Brotherhood of the English Secular Clergy in 1949. In 1951 he became a protonotary apostolic *ad instar*. In 1954 he was made an honorary DLitt by the National University of Ireland and, in 1956, a member of the Pontifical Academy. Balliol made him an honorary fellow in 1953. Rare new friends included the poet Siegfried Sassoon and the novelist Anthony Powell, with whom he bottled wine. He made a rare excursion abroad in 1954 to visit the Oxfords in Zanzibar and the Actons in Rhodesia, where he worked on his translation of *The Imitation of Christ* which he was to leave incomplete. In 1956 he began his translation of the original texts of the *Autobiography* of St Theresa of Lisieux (1958). In 1957 he was operated upon for cancer of the colon, which turned out to have spread into the liver. He delivered his Romanes lecture, *On English Translation*, at Oxford on 11 June, his face like a bright yellow stain against his white clerical collar. His audience knew he was dying. Speaking of his translation of St Theresa, he remarked with significant pauses that 'It is not a simple process to put yourself inside the skin of a young … French … female … Saint' (Corbishley, 88). Knox went on to stay with the prime minister, Harold Macmillan, at 10 Downing Street, where Sir Horace Evans confirmed the diagnosis of fatal cancer. Macmillan accompanied Knox to Paddington in his official car. The pope sent him a commendation of his work on scripture and a relic of Innocent XI. He died on 24 August at the Manor House, Mells, Somerset. His body was taken to Westminster Cathedral, where a requiem mass was celebrated on 29 August; Cardinal Griffin presided and Father Martin D'Arcy preached. On 30 August he was buried at Mells.

Three volumes of Knox's sermons were published posthumously (1960–63), and there were published appreciations by Robert Speaight (1959 and 1966) and Thomas Corbishley (1964). A biography by Evelyn Waugh appeared in 1959. Yet despite these tributes to his significance, Knox's reputation rapidly waned. The Second Vatican Council and new theological fashions marked the eclipse of his type of Roman Catholicism, and modern popular culture has destroyed his own high culture, while more recent translations of the Bible have displaced his version among Roman Catholics. His style has an absolute clarity and simplicity which pass into the restraint and reserve of his devotional writings. A master of prose, he remains compulsively readable to those who read him, but he has yet to be rediscovered as a master of the spiritual life, and except among a discriminating clientele, it is not clear how much of his work will survive.

SHERIDAN GILLEY

Sources E. Waugh, *The life of the Right Reverend Ronald Knox fellow of Trinity College, Oxford, and protonotary apostolic to His Holiness Pope Pius XII* (1959) • P. Fitzgerald, *The Knox brothers: Edmund ('Evoe'), 1881–1971; Dillwyn, 1883–1943; Wilfred, 1886–1950; Ronald, 1888–1957* (1977) • R. Knox, *A spiritual Aeneid* (1918) • T. Corbishley, *Ronald Knox the priest* (1964) • R. Speaight, *A modern Virgilian: a memorial lecture to Monsignor Ronald Knox* (1959) • R. Speaight, *Ronald Knox the writer* (1966) • E. A. Knox, *Reminiscences of an octogenarian* (1934) • G. Marshall, 'Two autobiographical narratives of conversion: Robert Hugh Benson and Ronald Knox', *Recusant History*, 24 (1998–9), 237–53 • M. T. Walsh, *Ronald Knox as apologist* (1985) • A. Horne, *Macmillan*, 1: *1894–1956* (1988) • *DNB* • *CGPLA Eng. & Wales* (1957)

Archives Eton, corresp. and papers • NRA, priv. coll., corresp. and papers | BL, corresp. with G. K. Chesterton and others, Add. MS 73195 • Bodl. Oxf., letters to Shane Leslie • Bodl. Oxf., letters to Elizabeth Wansbrough • Eton, letters to Shane Leslie • Georgetown University, Washington, DC, corresp. with Sir Arnold Lunn • Lancs. RO, corresp. relating to New Testament translation | SOUND BL NSA, recorded talks

Likenesses P. Evans, pen-and-ink drawing, c.1926, NPG • H. Coster, photograph, 1938, NPG [*see illus.*] • S. Elwes, oils, c.1952, Catholic chaplaincy, Old Palace, Oxford • H. Coster, photographs, NPG • A. Pollen, terracotta head, Manor House, Mells; repro. in Waugh, *Life* • bronze cast (after A. Pollen), Trinity College, Oxford

Wealth at death £22,401 0s. 5d.: probate, 20 Dec 1957, *CGPLA Eng. & Wales* • £7049: probate, 31 Jan 1958, *CGPLA Eng. & Wales*

Knox, Thomas Francis [*name in religion* Francis] (1822–1882), Roman Catholic priest and scholar, was born in Brussels, Belgium, on 24 December 1822. He was the eldest son of the Hon. John Henry Knox (1788–1872), the third son of the second Viscount Northland, first earl of Ranfurly, and of his wife, Lady Mabella Josephine, *née* Needham (1801–1899), daughter of Francis *Needham, first earl of Kilmorey. The Knoxes were Irish protestants long settled in co. Tyrone. Knox was educated at a private school in Hampshire. In 1840 he was admitted as a pensioner to Trinity College, Cambridge, where he matriculated in Michaelmas 1841, became a scholar in 1843, and took a first-class BA degree in 1845, coming third in the classical tripos, and being among the senior optimes in mathematics and second chancellor's medallist. Because he had resigned his parish in 1843, J. H. Newman refused to become Knox's spiritual director in March 1845, but offered him a home at his retreat outside Oxford at Littlemore. Later in the same year Knox was staying with F. W. Faber when Faber and his followers decided to convert to Catholicism. He was received into the Catholic church with them by Bishop Wareing at Northampton on 17 November. He told the Oxford Movement's leader, Edward Bouverie Pusey, that the Church of England was 'a delusion of Satan' (Chapman, 119). His worried father suggested that he should travel for two years, and he left at Easter 1846 for North America and the West Indies.

Wanting to see 'the Church in all its splendour' in Mexico (Kerr, 2.61), he took a mail steamer, the *Tweed*, sailing from Havana to Vera Cruz, but on 12 February 1847 the ship foundered on the Alacranes Reef 95 miles off the north coast of Yucatán. Nearly everyone who was travelling with him in the fore part of the ship perished, but he clambered over the bulwarks and clung overnight to the ship's side, saying the rosary and the *Memorare* and vowing to the Virgin Mary to enter the ecclesiastical state if saved. Though unable to swim, at daybreak he rode on a spar through boiling breakers to the reef, where the aft of the ship lay aground with the surviving passengers and crew. After two and a half days of standing on the reef, much of the time in tidal water, he and his companions were rescued on 15 February by the Spanish brig *Aemilio*.

Knox was detained from keeping his vow by revolution in Yucatán but travelled to the United States. He was at first uncertain of his father's financial support and decided to prepare for ordination in France. On 28 June 1847 he enrolled in the Séminaire de St Sulpice at Issy near Paris, preparatory to entering the Parisian Grand Séminaire. On Newman's urging, he came at the beginning of November to Rome, where Newman and his friends were staying at Santa Croce while serving their novitiate to become Oratorians. He accompanied Newman and Ambrose St John on 3 December 1847 to the Vatican to present the brief for the English Oratory, and met Pope Pius IX: 'Knox was in raptures,' Newman reported to John Dobrée Dalgairns; 'the Pope called him Padre Francesco, and Knox declares he won't part with it' (Newman to Dalgairns, 21 Dec 1847, *Letters and Diaries*, 12.135). Knox chose Francis as his name in religion when he was admitted as an Oratorian novice at Maryvale, Old Oscott, near Birmingham, on the inception of the community on 1 February 1848. He accompanied Faber to London in 1849 to establish the London Oratory, which remained his home for the remaining thirty-three years of his life. On 2 June 1849 he was ordained priest by Bishop Nicholas Wiseman at St Edmund's College, Ware, and said his first Mass the following day, Trinity Sunday. In 1865, he succeeded Father J. D. Dalgairns as the London Oratory's third superior, a post which he held for one term (until 1868).

Knox has been accounted 'the most learned of all the fathers of that time' by the principal historian of the London Oratory, Ralph Kerr (Kerr, 2.62), though this title should probably go to Dalgairns. He became the Westminster diocesan archivist when, in 1876, Manning entrusted the archives to the Oratorians, and he wrote the introductions for *The First and Second Diaries of the English College, Douay* (1878), and *The Letters and Memorials of William Cardinal Allen, 1532–1594* (1882), which he edited with Fathers Richard Stanton and Stephen Keogh and other Oratorians. These works appeared as the first and second volumes of the Records of the English Catholics under the Penal Laws, the only ones to be published. This task of publishing Catholic records was later taken up by the Catholic Record Society. He also wrote *The Last Survivor of the Ancient English Hierarchy: T. Goldwell, Bishop of St. Asaph* (republished from *The Month*, 1876), and translated the autobiography of the fourteenth-century mystic Blessed Henry Suso (1865).

Knox's learning was also put to practical effect. He became the *defensor matrimoniorum* of the archdiocese of Westminster and, in 1874, the notary in the diocesan process for the canonization of the English Catholic martyrs, preliminary to the beatification of John Fisher and Sir Thomas More. He was a member of the council of the Catholic Union, secretary to a commission of inquiry on Catholic education in England, and lecturer on canon law to ordinands at the diocesan seminary. A high ultramontane, his treatise *When does the church speak infallibly? or, The nature and scope of the church's teaching office* (1867) took a maximalist line on its subject, but its dry and moderate tone attracted Italian theologians who wanted a work on papal infallibility for international dissemination which was 'not controversial but doctrinal, learned yet popular, brief and yet pithy' (Kerr, 2.63–4). Father Cardella accordingly translated Knox's work into Italian. Pius IX sent Knox a special commendation in 1870, and conferred a doctorate upon him in 1875. He died at his home in London, the Oratory, Brompton, of heart disease on 20 March 1882, and was buried in south London at the Oratorian private cemetery in Sydenham.

THOMPSON COOPER, rev. SHERIDAN GILLEY

Sources R. Kerr, 'The Oratory in London', 2 vols., The Oratory, London · *The letters and diaries of John Henry Newman*, ed. C. S. Dessain and others, [31 vols.] (1961–), vols. 11–12 · *The Tablet* (25 March 1882) · *The Tablet* (1 April 1882) · *The Times* (25 March 1882) · *Weekly Register* (25 March 1882) · R. Chapman, *Father Faber* (1961)
Archives Birmingham Oratory · Brompton Oratory, corresp. and papers | Birmingham Oratory, Knox MSS · NRA, Oratory MSS
Likenesses portrait; possibly at the London Oratory
Wealth at death £6350 6s. od.: probate, 19 May 1882, CGPLA Eng. & Wales

Knox, Sir Thomas George (1824–1887), consul, was born in January 1824, the eldest surviving son of James Spencer Knox (1789–1862), rector of Maghera, co. Londonderry, and his wife, Clara (d. 1862), youngest daughter of the Hon. John *Beresford (son of the first earl of Tyrone); he was grandson of William *Knox, bishop of Derry. Of robust constitution and always strongly anti-French, Knox arrived in Siam in 1851, after selling out of the army in which he had served in India and China. Like other countries in the East, Siam under King Mongkut was just beginning to open its doors to Westerners after nearly two centuries of fairly strict seclusion; Knox was involved from the start in local politics, first as a military adviser, and then as the husband of a woman of the local nobility,

Prang (d. 1888), daughter of Phraya Somkok of Bangkok, with whom he had a son and two daughters.

In 1857, in the interval following the death of the first British consul, Knox was appointed to the indispensable office of interpreter to the new consulate. In 1864 he succeeded the second consul, Sir Robert Schomburgk, and was successively promoted consul-general and agent and consul-general.

These were years marked by complicated political upheavals in Siam, quite beyond the comprehension of Knox's Foreign Office chiefs in London. Rather than backing British imperial interest in the country, Knox seems to have seen himself as a champion of its sovereignty, and, after the succession of the young King Chulalongkorn (r. 1868–1910), as his virtual guardian. Inevitably this provoked suspicion and jealousy among some Siamese, including the king himself, and Knox's successor as consulate interpreter, Henry Alabaster, after quitting the service in 1871 joined Knox's enemies. In late 1874, when he was on home leave, other consular subordinates tried, with only limited success, to prevent the king's party upsetting the existing power balance; in 1879 another faction seized power in protest at the elopement of Knox's elder daughter, Fanny, with Phra Pricha Kolakan, an associate of the king. Knox asked for a gunboat to bolster his position, but, amid Afghan and Zululand crises, Lord Salisbury instead colluded in what was really a huge blow to British prestige in the area by recalling Knox and retiring him with the KCMG as a consolation. His wife remained behind in Bangkok, and his son-in-law was executed.

Knox died at Eaux Chaudes in the Pyrenees on 29 July 1887, his wife the following year in Siam. His widowed elder daughter lived a migratory life between Europe and south-east Asia, while his younger daughter, Caroline, married Louis Leonowens, the teak trade magnate, only son of Anna, the governess made famous by the film *The King and I*. In the meanwhile, the so-called Siam question over the fate of the country, the climax to the late nineteenth-century colonial scramble for south-east Asia, came properly to a head despite the best efforts of Knox's successors, W. G. Palgrave and E. M. Satow.

N. J. BRAILEY

Sources PRO, Foreign Office archives · FO List · PRO, Ernest Satow MSS · DNB · N. J. Brailey, *Two views of Siam on the eve of the Chakri reformation* (1989) · D. K. Wyatt, *The politics of reform in Thailand* (1969) · R. J. Minney, *Fanny and the regent of Siam* (1962) · Burke, *Peerage*
Likenesses photograph, repro. in Minney, *Fanny and the regent of Siam*

Knox, Vicesimus (1752–1821), headmaster and writer, was born on 8 December 1752 at Newington Green, Middlesex, the only son of the Revd Vicesimus Knox (1729–1780), a clergyman and schoolteacher, and Ann, daughter of Devereux Wall. From 1764 the younger Knox, who signed himself first Nock and then Knock until the age of twenty, was educated at the Merchant Taylors' School, London, where his father was a master. He matriculated at St John's College, Oxford, on 13 July 1771 and in the following

Vicesimus Knox (1752–1821), by William Ward (after Archer James Oliver, exh. RA 1809)

year his father was appointed headmaster at Tonbridge School, Kent, so beginning an association which lasted over seventy years and involved three generations of the Knox family. The younger Vicesimus graduated BA in 1775 and became a fellow of St John's. He looked back fondly on his time at Oxford, recalling in a later essay 'the blissful region of the common room fire-side! Delightful retreat where never female showed her head' (Knox, *Essays*, 2nd edn, 1779, 1.325). Regardless of these views, Knox, who later became an active proponent of women's education, left St John's in 1778 to replace his father as headmaster at Tonbridge where he remained for the next thirty-four years. Here he met his wife, Mary (d. 1809), daughter of a local man, Thomas Miller; they married on 26 December 1778 at St James's, Westminster. The couple had a daughter, Sarah, and three sons, one of whom, Holles Josiah, died in infancy; of their surviving sons Vicesimus (d. 1855) became a barrister and recorder of Saffron Walden while Thomas (1784–1843) succeeded his father at Tonbridge in 1812. Ordained in the late 1770s, Knox combined his teaching duties with those of rector of Runwell and Ramsden-Crays, Essex, and, at Lord Vane's bequest, minister of the parochial chapelry of Shipborne, Kent.

Teacher and educationist Tonbridge School, governed by the Skinners' Company since its foundation by Sir Andrew Judde in 1553, had not prospered under the headship of the elder Vicesimus Knox. In his six years as headmaster the number of pupils recorded in the school lists averaged just over twenty, the lowest of the century, and chronic ill health forced his resignation in 1778; he died two years later. By contrast, the arrival of the 26-year-old Vicesimus Knox the younger galvanized the school and pupil numbers soon topped eighty, the majority of whom were boarders. With his income swelled by the fees from the boarding pupils, Knox was able to live in fine style. One pupil, Henry Woodgate, writing to his father in 1781, described how the school's fortunes had changed: 'Mr Knox of Tunbridge has a new coach just come out spick and span with a pair of long-tail greys. Is not this quite the thing? My aunt says "Lor' sir, a schoolmaster's is a vastly fine trade"' (G. Woodgate and G. C. G. Woodgate, *A History of the Woodgates*, 1910, 247). Knox's initial success at Tonbridge was principally due to the high reputation as a scholar that he had acquired at Oxford and to the popularity of his first work, *Essays Moral and Literary* (1778), whose authorship quickly became known. Three years later he further publicized the school by publishing *Liberal Education, or, A Practical Treatise on the Method of Acquiring Useful and Polite Learning* (1781), which effectively was both a manifesto and a prospectus. Eagerly purchased by the public, *Liberal Education* successfully targeted two influential audiences, for it proved indispensable as a professional handbook for fellow schoolmasters and an invaluable guide for parents who were debating how and where to educate their children. Above all, it fulfilled Knox's principal aim of providing a practical, rather than theoretical, treatise on education.

In the introduction to the study Knox defined his ideal of an enlightened education in comparison with a purely functional schooling, the one

> confined, the other enlarged; one which only tends to qualify for a particular sphere of action, for a profession, or an official employment; the other which endeavours to improve the powers of understanding for their own sake; the sake of exalting the endowments of human nature, and becoming capable of sublime and refined contemplation. (*Liberal Education*, 8–9)

Conscious of the competition from private tutors and commercial schools and the criticism of educational and moral standards at contemporary grammar schools, Knox grounded his argument in favour of a public (that is, school-based) rather than private (home-based) education for boys on the assumption that grammar schools had reformed themselves into ideal educational institutions, such as Tonbridge. While maintaining that Greek and Latin were indispensable in a liberal education, he was adamant that the curriculum should include English, French, history, and geography, and ornamental accomplishments such as music, art, and fencing. 'English biography' he particularly recommended as 'more entertaining, and perhaps more useful, than civil history at large'; furthermore he called for a 'biographical work' to be compiled for the use of schools, one that should be 'elegantly written, and consist principally, but by no means entirely, of the lives of the learned' (Knox, *Works*, 1824, 4.45). He also discussed extra-curricular activities, such as private study and foreign travel, and did not neglect to outline his views on the need for reform in the universities. He set out

his opinion on female education in two chapters. Although he advised parents to educate their daughters at home, he insisted that the content of their education should not be limited by its domestic setting. In recommending an expansive literary education for girls he asserted that the female 'mind is certainly as capable of improvement, as that of the other sex' (*Liberal Education*, 235–6). Furthermore it was essential for women to be liberally and rationally educated since, as mothers, they were responsible for the pre-school instruction of their sons. Knox used his experience as a schoolmaster to underline his point:

> A sensible and well-educated mother is, in every respect, best qualified to instruct a child till he can read well enough to enter on the Latin grammar. I have indeed always found those boys the best readers, on their entrance on Latin, who have been prepared by a careful and accomplished mother. (ibid., 17)

Evidence of how far Knox put into practice at Tonbridge the educational principles outlined in *Liberal Education* is limited. The dominance of the classics is clearly seen in a surviving curriculum from 1781 which records that boys studied the Latin Testament in the first form and graduated to Homer and Livy in the sixth; the head boy of the time, J. H. Stewart, clearly outstripped his classmates, for his studies include Hebrew and Demosthenes. On Skinners' day, the annual celebration in May of the school's founder, Knox encouraged the boys to show off their debating and oratorical skills. Moreover the pupils were examined by visiting clergy from London. Clearly Tonbridge fulfilled parents' expectations, for the school roll remained steady until the early 1790s, when pupils fell away, reaching a low of twenty-six in 1794. Knox's controversial politics, which were broadcast when *The Times* reported his involvement in a fracas in the Brighton theatre in August 1793, are usually blamed for the school's failing fortunes. However, during the turbulent years of the war with France he neither resigned nor was asked to leave by the school's governors, and by the time he retired in 1812, forty-one pupils were enrolled.

Writer on conduct Running parallel with Knox's work as an educationist was his considerable career as a writer on conduct, especially that of children and young adults. Certainly the majority who knew Knox as an educator discovered him through his numerous, much reprinted, and ever-expanding collections of essays and sermons. Writing and teaching ran in tandem. In the year of his appointment at Tonbridge his *Essays Moral and Literary* were published on the recommendation of Samuel Johnson. In the preface to the first, anonymous edition, Knox established his didactic intentions which, as in his later work, he grounded in a practical relationship between writing, education, and personal and societal development: 'to publish without improving' was, he believed, equivalent 'to increasing the weight without adding to the value of the coin', the 'real utility of literary labours' being 'the extent of their influence on the national manners' (*Essays*, 1778, iv; 1779, 2.5). To this purpose Knox's first edition of thirty-eight essays combined traditional studies on classical literature, philosophy, and the arts with commentaries on contemporary standards of taste, and the work of modern authors such as Joseph Addison. Knox's insights proved popular and a second larger, and attributed, edition appeared a year later; by 1815 the collection, now in three volumes and numbering 174 essays, reached its seventeenth edition. In these later editions Knox addressed an increasingly diverse range of subjects, among them gardening, household management, the work of Bede, the usefulness of capital letters in correspondence, and the unacceptability of masculine dress for women. The spirit of improvement implicit in these pieces was expressed more directly in numerous articles on the achievement and practice of good conduct within a series of military, civilian, religious, commercial, and mercantile contexts.

From such studies there developed a Knoxian behavioural ideal—stable, moderate, integrous, and independent—which became a staple of his writing in this and other fields and the desired end point for these general exercises in national education. To an extent this archetype was a restatement of a much discussed (and many feared lost) eighteenth-century civic ideal. Yet it is equally true that his depiction of the moral personality was also more innovative, optimistic, and receptive to then fashionable late-century behavioural codes such as sensibility. Though an energetic and, to modern readers, often relentless moralist, Knox was invariably more persuasive than puritanical, being more accommodating of recent social and economic trends than many later critics, too keen to identify him as a conservative, have been prepared to acknowledge. No doubt it was this receptiveness which contributed to the popularity of his advice. Thus Knox's ostensibly stoical ideal is better characterized by an attachment to a modern sensibility manifest in intimate social relations, acts of philanthropy, and displays of emotional compassion by men and women alike. For Knox it was principally via these qualities, rather than those of classical hardiness, that the goal of personal and national improvement was to be achieved.

It was an attachment which, alongside better-known contemporaries such as Henry Mackenzie and Hannah More, also makes Knox an important contributor to the late eighteenth-century debate on the meaning and application of sensibility, not least because of his unusual readiness to direct these ideals to the cause of political reform. Highly protective of sensibility in its purest and most edifying form, he was also highly critical of what he considered its abuse through affectation, triviality, and ostentatiousness (subjects which exercised him greatly), and in particular the growing fashion for irresponsible modern novels. His concern over aspects of contemporary fiction focused on its popularity among the same middle-class readership to whom he energetically promoted his alternative characterization of the morally robust and civically responsible man and woman of feeling. Ever the educator, Knox was motivated to communicate in an accessible manner which he believed best served by the

essay format, about which he wrote and which he also employed in a second collection on conduct, *Winter Evenings, or, Lucubrations on Life and Letters* (1788), and an anthology of 'polite' eighteenth-century sermons, *Family Lectures, or, Domestic Divinity* (1791). His own series, *Sermons; Chiefly Intended to Promote Faith, Hope and Charity*, appeared in the following year. Here, as in his earlier works, Knox complemented the accessibility of the essay or sermon format with a self-consciously unpretentious style. The result, as he seldom tired of repeating, was an honest and unsensational message directed not 'to deep, erudite, and subtle sages' but to 'the liberal merchant, the inquisitive manufacturer, the country gentleman [and] the various persons who fill the most useful departments in life' who 'have no objection to kill a little time, by perusing … the pages of a modern volume' (*Winter Evenings*, 1.v). Indeed, so frequent were these claims that it is hard not to see them as his attempt to cast as affected and haughty those who questioned the value of another set of homilies. Others suspected a more underhand motive for his apparently disingenuous approach. In the introduction of his *Sermons*, for example, Knox offered the now familiar denial of intended offence or controversy, though he stated that he was resigned to condemnation from less generous unitarian commentators sceptical of his commitment to the Trinity. Yet to critics like John Disney, minister at London's Essex Street Unitarian chapel, Knox's declaration presented an unduly severe characterization of unitarianism, by which he abused his reputation as a polite moralist in order to precipitate the very contest he claimed to avoid through 'responsible' ecumenicalism.

Religion, politics, and literature The content and tone of Knox's theology, like that of his conduct advice, was predominantly reassuring and nurturing. Religion's purpose was 'to afford the poor human nature a BALSAM FOR THE WOUNDS OF THE HEART', and its achievement the socialization of man to a level where, *pace* unitarians, it became impossible to maintain factionalism in a society dedicated to shared Christian virtues. In contrast to earlier secular writers on social performance, Knox understood refinement and religion to be intimately connected. The personal qualities that ensured the truly civilized individual—benevolence, sincerity, and humility—were also those of the Christian, and their display further enhanced the religious individual's capacity for a morally valid sociability. The importance Knox attributed to sensibility as a route to true sociability led him to identify sentimental culture as central to a wider religious vision as set out in subsequent collections, including his *Christian Philosophy, or, An Attempt to Display the Evidence and Excellence of Revealed Religion*, published in 1795. Social and religious ideals came together in the sensitive and compassionate figure of the weeping Christ.

Though keen to avoid controversy, Knox was committed to an essentially benign religious vision which prompted him to speak out on contentious issues, notably British involvement in military action against revolutionary France. In August 1793 he preached at Brighton parish church against a war which he believed driven by a 'military machine' serviced by a corrupt and misguided administration. Knox's call for 'universal peace' offended members of the Sussex regiment who were present and who confronted him and secured his ejection from the town's theatre several days later. Knox responded in November with a *Narrative of Transactions Relative to a Sermon*, in which he denounced the cowardice of his assailants and reiterated his belief of 'offensive war' as 'at once detestable, deplorable and ridiculous' (p. 96). His translation of Erasmus's *Antipolemus, or, The Plea of Reason, Religion and Humanity Against War*, appeared in the following year.

For Knox, Britain's readiness to fight was evidence of its corruption and of the prevailing 'spirit of despotism', a phrase which served as the title of his most polemical and best-known study in political science. The study, which defended the early revolution and its British supporters like Charles James Fox, was published in London in 1795. However, with the French government becoming increasingly tyrannous, Knox soon after attempted to recall the work and thereafter refused publication until an anonymous edition appeared in 1821. Though clearly prompted by William Pitt's early response to the revolution, Knox conceived of and discussed his subject in the broadest terms. Man, born in a 'state of simplicity' and possessed of a natural 'benevolence, improvement [and] cheerfulness', had been gradually corrupted by dishonest politicians, courtiers, and manipulative churchmen who sought through a 'spirit of despotism' to maintain the fiction of a 'progress to civilization' (Knox, *The Spirit of Despotism*, 1821, 5).

As in his theology, Knox linked politics to questions of personal conduct and to the potential for reform at the level of the individual reader. Perpetrators of despotism, whom in Britain he identified as tories and Jacobites, were characterized as selfish, unfeeling, duplicitous, and aggressive—war being for Knox a calculated means of subduing those who demanded justifiable political reform. By contrast, (whig) defenders of the liberties enshrined by the 1688 settlement were 'men of feeling and good minds' who embodied 'manly sentiment' and displayed an integrity born of a sound educational programme like that in his earlier *Personal Nobility, or, Letters to a Young Nobleman* (1793), dedicated to Fox. Here Knox combined civic and sentimental languages by calling on the country's natural aristocratic leaders to participate in self-analysis so as to best fulfil their political responsibilities. In *The Spirit of Despotism* he looked also to a free press, to the judiciary, and to 'the middle ranks of the People'—in whom he believed the 'Spirit of Truth, Liberty and Virtue' to be strongest—to resist further erosion of national liberties. It was the duty of such groups to maintain the separation of legislature and judiciary, to resist government attempts to pack the Lords with placemen, and in the Commons to place the principles of political liberty above the demands of party affiliation. Written quickly in response to a charged political situation, it is perhaps not surprising that *The Spirit of Despotism* provides a number of contradictory statements which undermine its effectiveness as a work of political science. Thus, man is both able

(and should be encouraged) to progress and yet is corrupted, not civilized, by that progression; medieval society was both less corrupt and yet also more greatly restricted by a chivalry defended by advocates of despotism such as Edmund Burke; it is the middle class who will restore liberty while bourgeois commercialism exists as one of the means to promote despotism. This said, for a writer who is often wrongly identified for his platitudes and conservatism, *The Spirit of Despotism* provided whig reformers with a passionate and positive critique both of tory resistance to political change and of former supporters, like Burke, whose defence of the 1688 settlement was thought less progressive than nostalgic.

Knox's final area of study was English literature. In 1783 he published an anthology, *Elegant Extracts, or, Useful and Entertaining Passages in Prose*, which reached its tenth edition in 1816 (also abridged in 1791 as *The Prose Epitome*), following this with *Elegant Extracts … in Poetry* (1789; 8th edn, 1816; also abridged in 1791), and *Elegant Epistles, or, A Copious Collection of Familiar and Amusing Letters* (1790). As before, Knox's motivation was the education and improvement of a youthful and middling readership—'the man of a liberal profession … [and] the mercantile classes'—otherwise too busy to study classical literature in full (*Extracts … in Poetry*, 1805, vi). As in his own writing, the non-fiction essay and its modern exponents, among them Addison, Johnson, Richard Steele, and Hugh Blair, featured prominently in his selection of prose writers. While not ignoring classical writers, one of Knox's principal aims was to identify and introduce to the canon those elements of modern literature he believed of particular benefit for 'the commerce of ordinary life'. His focus also resulted in a noticeably generous coverage of eighteenth-century women writers, including Anna Aiken, Hester Chapone, and Catharine Macaulay (*Extracts … in Prose*); Elizabeth Rowe, Elizabeth Carter, Helen Maria Williams, and Ann Yearsley (*Extracts … in Poetry*); and Elizabeth Montagu, Anna Seward, and the ladies Wortley Montagu, Luxborough, and Bradshaigh (*Elegant Epistles*). Appreciative of established talents and alert, here and in other works, to the potential of female students, Knox combined his promotion of modern women's writing with an ongoing campaign against sources of false learning. Principal among these was the reading of modern fiction—for Knox an alarmingly introspective, and predominantly female, experience of no discernible social benefit—whose dangers he believed reached new levels with the current vogue for 'fine sentimentalists' like Laurence Sterne. Knox's own literary tastes, and their influence, are clearly reflected in the coverage of the Tonbridge School library during his mastership. Well stocked with writers featured in the three series of *Elegant Extracts*, the catalogue lists only a handful of continental authors, among them Cervantes and Fenelon, and no works of British fiction before an edition of Walter Scott's novels was purchased in 1819, seven years after Knox's retirement.

Final years and reputation After his wife's death in May 1809 and his retirement from Tonbridge School three years later, Knox moved to Adelphi Terrace, Strand, London. His final decade was spent supervising enlarged and improved editions of his *Extracts* and, latterly, with a return to the debate on education. When a proposal to diversify the role of grammar schools, by compelling them to offer tuition in reading, writing, and arithmetic to the poor, came before parliament in 1821, Knox dashed off a lengthy protest. In his *Remarks on the Tendency of Certain Clauses in a Bill now Pending in Parliament to Degrade Grammar Schools* he robustly defended the continued value of a classical education as a training for adult life and argued that a grammar school education should be claimed by 'the mass in middle life ... as their birthright' (Knox, *Works*, 1824, 4.280). He was insistent that the classical curriculum that had been taught in grammar schools for several centuries should not be debased by the addition of elementary education in the three Rs. However, he was by no means an opponent of the education of the lowest orders and in a sermon delivered in 1814 had supported the efforts of the National Society to set up more schools where the poor would be taught according to the precepts of the Church of England. Soon after his pamphlet was published the parliamentary bill to reform the grammar schools was shelved.

Knox's popularity, particularly as a conduct writer and literary commentator, is evident from the numerous editions to which his studies ran, as well as from their publication in the United States where his contribution to the morality of a new nation was recognized with a doctorate from the College of Philadelphia. In Britain Knox's reputation was sufficient for him to be cited in contemporary works, such as Jane Austen's *Emma* (1816), in which Mr Martin reads aloud to his family from *Elegant Extracts*. That Martin, a plain, middling farmer, sought edification through the anthology would no doubt have pleased its compiler greatly. Some, of course, were less favourable to Knox's campaign for moral and literary self-improvement. For John Aikin his work suffered from an overly prescriptive focus, his 'great fault' being to set out 'with too confined a view of the ends of education ... Does he not breed them all for clergymen and schoolmasters?' (L. Aikin, *Memoirs of John Aikin, MD*, 2 vols., 1823, 1.59); an interesting observation given Knox's emphasis in *Liberal Education* on learning as more than vocational. Others questioned the consequences of his attempt to reach a broad readership. The *Critical Review*, for example, was sceptical of the intellectual value or utility of essays written for those unused 'to deeper studies, to accurate investigations, or a long train of reasoning' (48, 1779, 120), a view shared by Emma Woodhouse, though not necessarily by Austen who gave a copy of the *Extracts* to her niece. Supporters, by contrast, commended Knox's ability, the breadth of his writing, and his efforts to promote learning: the *European Magazine* 'ranked the writer with the English Classics' (81, 1822, 196); James Boswell believed the *Essays Moral and Literary* superior to his own *Hypochondriack* papers for the *London Magazine*, while the *Monthly Review* attributed the 'extensive popularity of his writings', though inferior to Johnson's *Rambler* studies, to

Knox's 'not inconsiderable' merit (I. S. Lustig and F. A. Pottle, eds., *Boswell: the English Experiment, 1785–89*, 1986, 19; *Monthly Review*, 58, 1778, 141).

Given Knox's contemporary popularity it is striking that he is now so little known. Certainly some of his work has not aged well. Knox was an exhaustive and often exhausting writer who clearly liked the sight of his own pen. The account of the officers' conduct at Brighton, for example, which Knox himself dismissed as trivial, ran to 102 pages and included close analysis of reported exchanges. Modern references to Knox have tended to criticize an intellect and literary style which fell far short of Johnson's. More recently he has become a quotable source in cultural histories of manners and sentimental culture to which he was, undoubtedly, an important contributor. The predominant image to emerge from these accounts is of a social and political conservative peddling an unoriginal message. In certain areas, such as his writing on family relations, this judgement is fair. However, to treat Knox solely as a behavioural writer is to miss his advocacy of civic regeneration, pacifism, and the politics of reform. Attempts by the libertarian right to view his critique of state corruption as promoting freedom born of individualism likewise overlook a commitment to socially responsible conduct. Certainly the range of his output generates contradictions and unanswered questions. And yet common to all areas is the figure of the sociable, benevolent, civic-minded, and politically responsible citizen. In Knox, therefore, sensibility served less as an excuse for fashionable solipsism than as an exercise in individual and societal improvement in which the personal and political were as one.

Knox died at Tonbridge on 6 September 1821 and was buried in the parish church of St Peter and St Paul where a monument commemorates his dedication 'to the moral and intellectual improvement of man'. His son Thomas remained at Tonbridge School until his death in 1843.

PHILIP CARTER and S. J. SKEDD

Sources biographical introduction, *The works of Vicesimus Knox*, 7 vols. (1824), vol. 1 · R. W. Uphaus, 'Vicesimus Knox and the canon of eighteenth-century literature', *The age of Johnson*, ed. P. Korshin, 4 (1991), 345–61 · P. L. Goldsmith, 'Education for the nation and the individual: the works of Vicesimus Knox II of Tonbridge, 1752–1821', PhD diss., University of Western Australia, 1980 [copy in Tonbridge School library] · D. C. Somervell, *A history of Tonbridge School* (1947) · S. Skedd, 'The education of women in Hanoverian Britain, c.1760–1820', DPhil diss., U. Oxf., 1997 · J. Disney, *Letters to the Revd Vicesimus Knox, DD. occasioned by his reflections on Unitarian Christians* (1792) · M. Ellis, *The politics of sensibility: race, gender and commerce in the sentimental novel* (1996) · P. Carter, *Men and the emergence of polite society, Britain 1660–1800* (2001) · will, PRO, PROB 11/1649, fols. 26r–27r · IGI

Likenesses A. J. Oliver, portrait · J. Thomson, stipple (after A. J. Oliver), BM, NPG; repro. in *European Magazine* (1822) · W. Ward, mezzotint (after A. J. Oliver, exh. RA 1809), NPG [*see illus.*]

Knox, Wilfred Lawrence (1886–1950), Church of England clergyman and theologian, was born on 21 May 1886 in Kibworth, Leicestershire, the third son and fourth of the six children of Edmund Arbuthnott *Knox (1847–1937), suffragan bishop of Coventry and subsequently bishop of Manchester, and his wife, Ellen Penelope (1854–1892),

Wilfred Lawrence Knox (1886–1950), by unknown photographer

daughter of Bishop Thomas *French of Lahore (1825–1891) and his wife, Mary Anne. Knox was educated at Rugby School and Trinity College, Oxford, where he graduated with first-class honours in classical moderations (1907) and in *literae humaniores* (1909).

After working as a junior examiner at the Board of Education, Knox moved to London to be warden of Trinity College mission settlement in Stratford, east London. During this time his sympathies with the labour movement developed: Christianity, he felt, could work with and through the labour movement in order to alleviate the poverty in areas like London's East End. This conviction was closely connected to his growing Anglo-Catholic identity. In 1913 Knox proceeded to study theology at St Anselm's College, Cambridge; he was ordained deacon in 1914 and priest in 1915 to the title of St Mary's, Graham Street, London, where he was assistant curate. Despite his pacifist convictions, he attempted to join up as an army chaplain, but was rejected.

In his first pamphlet, *At a Great Price Obtained I this Freedom* (1918), Knox argued for the separation of church and state, and for the church to give up all property and patronage derived from its relationship with the state. In 1920 he joined the Oratory of the Good Shepherd (becoming its superior in 1941). In 1922 he moved to St Saviour's, Hoxton, as assistant priest. In an essay published in 1926 he combined his commitment and devotion to the Catholic tradition with an ardent quest for the truth. In his view,

> the fear of 'Modernism' seems to suggest a lack of trust in the power of the Church to eliminate false teaching from her system … but the Christian should have sufficient confidence in the inherent strength of the Catholic system to view with equanimity the exploration of every possible avenue of inquiry … If his fears are unfounded, it can only lead to a fresh apprehension of the truth and the enrichment of Christian devotion. (Knox, 'The authority of the church', 116)

Knox believed that the proof of the Christian and Catholic faith could only be found in the person of Jesus as revealed in the gospels and in the sacraments of the church; it could not depend on the belief of individual human beings or the Christian church. From this, according to Knox, sprang the error of 'modernism'. He argued that 'The ultimate argument for Christianity must always be that of the disciple who brought his friend to Jesus with the argument "Come and See"' (Knox, *Catholic Movement*, 29). Only this would convert those who refused to admit that human effort could produce any valuable result. 'To those who are honestly ready to "come and see" the divine gift of faith will not be lacking' (ibid., 29).

While his elder brother Ronald Arbuthnott *Knox (1888–1957) converted to Roman Catholicism and became an influential priest and writer, Knox himself became an outspoken representative of the Anglo-Catholic movement in the Church of England. As a writer of popular and theological apologetics, he outlined the differences between Anglo-Catholicism and Roman Catholicism in *The Catholic Movement in the Church of England* (1923) and (with Alec Vidler) in *The Development of Modern Catholicism* (1933). Together with Eric Milner-White he responded to the convert Father Vernon Johnson in *One God and Father of All* (1929). He also wrote devotional texts, the best-known of which was *Meditation and Mental Prayer* (1927), an introduction for lay people to the spiritual life in the Catholic sacramental tradition.

As a New Testament scholar whose main interest lay in the Hellenistic background of the New Testament and the apostle Paul, Knox regarded the Hellenization of the gospel as inevitable; it had to be accommodated to the theological conceptions of the Greek world in which it was to be preached. His most important publications in this area were *St Paul and the Church of Jerusalem* (1925) and *St Paul and the Church of the Gentiles* (1939). In 1941 Knox became chaplain of Pembroke College, Cambridge, where he was elected to a fellowship after the war. In 1942 Knox delivered the British Academy Schweich lectures, which were published in 1944 as *Some Hellenistic Elements in Primitive Christianity*. He was awarded a doctorate of divinity in 1945 and was the Anglo-Catholic representative on the committee for Christian doctrine. He became a fellow of the British Academy in 1948. He died of cancer on 9 February 1950 in Addenbrooke's Hospital, Cambridge. His funeral service was held in Pembroke College chapel. At the time of his death, Knox had been working on *The Sources of the Synoptic Gospels* which was edited by Henry Chadwick and published posthumously (1953–7).

NATALIE K. WATSON

Sources P. Fitzgerald, *The Knox brothers* (1977) • *The Times* (10 Feb 1950) • W. L. Knox, 'The authority of the church', *Essays Catholic and critical*, ed. E. G. Selwyn (1926), 101–19 • W. L. Knox, *The Catholic movement in the Church of England* (1929) • E. L. Mascall, *Saraband: the memoirs of E. L. Mascall* (1992) • b. cert. • d. cert. • *CGPLA Eng. & Wales* (1950)
Archives NRA, priv. coll., corresp. and papers
Likenesses photograph, British Academy, London [*see illus.*]
Wealth at death £4576 4s. 4d.: administration, 4 May 1950, *CGPLA Eng. & Wales*

Knox, William (1732–1810), government official and pamphleteer, was born at Monaghan, Ireland, the youngest child of Thomas Knox (d. 1760), a physician, and his wife, Nicola, the daughter of John King, of co. Fermanagh. He received his early education in local Church of Ireland schools, and particularly benefited from the tutelage of Philip Skelton, the curate at Monaghan, a respected scholar and author of theological treatises. Some time during the late 1740s or early 1750s he took up residence in Dublin, where he not only attended Trinity College but also received the 'first rudiments' of his political education under the patronage of Sir Richard Cox, a prominent member of the Irish House of Commons and a leader of the opposition during the Anglo-Irish political crisis of 1753–6—one of those episodic eruptions of the latent tensions between the Irish parliamentary leaders and the English-dominated executive.

In 1756 Knox, through the influence of his Irish connections, was appointed provost marshal in the colony of Georgia. During the five years he spent in America he became increasingly alarmed by the constitutional practices which prevailed in most of the continental colonies where, as he observed, the lower houses of the legislatures exercised unwarranted sway over governors and their councils. From his perspective as a royal official he viewed such relationships as unduly weighting the balance of colonial constitutions in favour of the democratic elements in America, thus posing a potential threat to the exercise of imperial authority. As a member of the Georgia council from 1757 to 1760 he played a prominent role in the development and implementation of policies and practices which established Georgia as a model royal colony. While in Georgia he also attained the status of a substantial rice planter, who within a decade would earn an income of between £1500 and £2000 per annum from his colonial properties.

Despite the remarkable success that Knox achieved in only a few years in Georgia, his ambitions and attachments drew him back irresistibly towards the centre of the empire. He arrived in London in 1762 during the last stages of the Seven Years' War, and, with his first-hand experience of America, was provided with numerous opportunities to share his expertise with politicians and imperial officials who were attempting to incorporate newly won territories into the expanded empire. Several of his specific recommendations, particularly those regarding a projected colony in East Florida, were incorporated in the proclamation of 1763 which would establish boundaries and administrative structures in the new imperial possessions in America. In London he acted officially as Georgia's colonial agent and for three years conducted the business of the province to the complete satisfaction of his constituents. In 1765, however, the Georgia assembly summarily dismissed him from his agency after he published a defence of the Stamp Act in the *Claim of the Colonies to an Exemption from Internal Taxation*. In this pamphlet, although he questioned the expediency and the equity of the stamp duties, particularly in consideration of the unique circumstances of American colonials, Knox nevertheless simultaneously repudiated the arguments raised in America against the right of parliament to tax Americans. This heresy, by Knox's own account, earned him the honour of being 'hung & burn'd in Effigy with Lord Bute and Mr. Grenville at Boston and Savannah' (Dartmouth MS, D. 1778, 2:1817a).

On 23 September 1765, in Dublin, Knox married Letitia Ford (b. c.1741), the daughter of a fellow Irishman, James Ford. Their marriage was long and contented. They had seven children, three daughters and four sons, and Letitia Knox was a gracious hostess whose hospitality substantially enhanced her husband's social and professional status. She also brought him a 'large fortune' (P. Skelton to W. Knox, 25 Oct 1765, Knox MSS) that was more than sufficient to support his pursuit of an official appointment. During the hiatus following the loss of his Georgia agency his interests were advanced by the patronage of Lord Grosvenor, who was so impressed with his knowledge and ideas about imperial affairs that he provided him with an introduction to George Grenville. The former prime minister, who had also been dismissed from office in 1765 and had subsequently assumed a leading role in the parliamentary opposition to the Rockingham administration and its American policies, found use for Knox's colonial expertise and his talents as a writer of political tracts. In collaboration with Grenville, Knox published two pamphlets that established his reputation—historically as well as contemporaneously—as a major theorist and commentator on imperial policy. The first of these treatises, *The Present State of the Nation* (1768), provided the best and most comprehensive expression of his imperial vision—one which postulated an imperial system in which political and economic advantages and responsibilities would be equally distributed to the mutual benefit of Great Britain and the colonies. More specifically he argued that Great Britain, menacingly burdened by enormous debts arising from the successful prosecution of the great war for empire, had every reason to expect that the American colonies, the great beneficiaries of that war, should bear at least part of the escalating costs of defending the expanded empire. In return, he recommended significant concessions to the colonies in keeping with their enhanced status within the empire: allowing them the opportunity to raise imperial contributions by their own means rather than by parliamentary taxation; revising the navigation system to create new trade advantages for American colonies; and providing for colonial representation in parliament. He also expanded the scope of his imperial reforms to encompass Ireland, which was to be assigned obligations and granted concessions commensurate with those extended to the American colonies. Since Knox's *The Present State of the Nation* contained explicit attacks on the Rockingham whigs, it not surprisingly drew an immediate response from Edmund Burke, who, in his *Observations on the State of the Nation* (1769), categorically rejected Knox's analysis of Britain's fiscal difficulties and, characteristically, dismissed his systematic prescriptions for imperial reform. Contemporary critics none the less praised both Knox's and Burke's works in unison for providing the best published representations of the major competing arguments in the current debate over imperial policy. Within a year Knox published a second tract, *The Controversy between Great Britain and her Colonies Reviewed* (1769), which, in its polemical tone and partisan purpose, marked a sudden and drastic departure from the broader perspectives of his earlier work. Apparently alarmed by evidence that the American position on imperial issues was hardening—an impression shared by an increasing number of Britons—and stung by Grenville's uncompromising repudiation of his previous advocacy of concessions for America, he produced a legalistic indictment of the various arguments raised against imperial taxation and uncompromisingly asserted the absolute sovereignty of parliament over the colonies.

In 1770 Knox's reputation as a political pamphleteer won him an appointment as an under-secretary in the American department. Here, in the years before the American Revolution, by his own account Knox found himself in the remarkable position of promoting both the coercion and conciliation of America. On various occasions he recommended policies of moderation to avoid undue provocation of the colonies; however, as the British government grew increasingly resistant to American rejection of parliamentary authority, the North administration found his talents as a pamphleteer useful in providing published defences of such policies as the Quebec Act and the Coercive Acts of 1774. With the outbreak of the American war he not only proved himself an effective administrator: he also contributed to the development of major policies, particularly projects for using loyalist forces in America and proposals for peace settlements. When the strains of war precipitated another serious breach between the Irish parliament and the British government during the years 1778 to 1780, Knox played a prominent role in the campaign of conciliation that kept Ireland from going the way of America. At his urging the North administration adopted many of his earlier recommendations for trade concessions as a means of reconciling the Irish to the imperial connection and also sent him to Ireland, where he assisted in the negotiations that brought an amicable resolution of the crisis.

The end of the American war brought calamity to Knox's private and public fortunes. In America his plantation properties were confiscated by the revolutionary government of Georgia, while at home he was dismissed from office after the Rockingham government, spurred on by his nemesis Burke, dismantled the American department. He experienced a brief but satisfactory reprieve from political exile when, in 1783, acting as an unofficial adviser to the Fox–North government, he drew up the order in council that effectively cut off the valuable American carrying trade with Britain's West Indian colonies. After the fall of this short-lived administration, however, he found himself relegated to the role of supplicant in a lengthy campaign to obtain compensation for his American losses. He maintained an official presence in governmental circles by acting as the provincial agent for the loyalist colony of New Brunswick, but, when the loyalist claims commission honoured his petition for compensation in 1788, he finally withdrew from active politics. During the two decades of his retirement he produced an extraordinary number and variety of publications, ranging over such subjects as slave holding, political reforms in England and Ireland, and theology. He died on 25 August 1810 at his home in Ealing, Middlesex, survived by all seven of his children.   LELAND J. BELLOT

Sources L. J. Bellot, *William Knox: the life and thought of an eighteenth-century imperialist* (1977) · L. J. Bellot, 'William Knox asks what is fit to be done with America?', *Sources of American independence*, ed. H. Peckham, 2 vols. (1978), 1.140–89 · L. J. Bellot, 'Evangelicals and the defense of slavery in Britain's old colonial empire', *Journal of Southern History*, 37 (1971), 19–40 · U. Mich., Clements L., William Knox MSS · *Report on manuscripts in various collections*, 8 vols., HMC, 55 (1901–14), vol. 6 [Captain H. V. Knox] · W. Knox, *Extra official state papers*, 2 vols. (1789) · Staffs. RO, Dartmouth MSS · R. Koebner, *Empire* (1961) · IGI · DNB

Archives PRO, corresp., PRO 30/55 · U. Mich., Clements L., corresp. and papers | BL, letters to George Grenville, Add. MSS 42086–42087 · BL, letters to Frederick Haldimand, Add. MSS 21703–21705, 21732–21734 · PRO, Colonial Office MSS, CO 5 · Staffs. RO, Dartmouth MSS · U. Mich., Clements L., Lord George Germain MSS

Likenesses photograph (after oil painting by Baroness de Tott, 1803), U. Mich., Clements L.

Wealth at death granted and bequeathed sons real properties and church living in Wales and Trinidad, plus cash settlements; house and effects at Ealing to eldest daughter; portions of £5000 each to two younger daughters

Knox, William (1762–1831), Church of Ireland bishop of Derry, was the fourth son of Thomas, first Viscount Northland, a title afterwards merged in the earldom of Ranfurly. He was born on 14 June 1762 and was schooled in England and then, from the age of fifteen, was educated at Trinity College, Dublin. He graduated BA in 1781. On 10 September 1785 he married Anne (d. 1834), daughter of James Spencer. They had fifteen children, ten daughters and five sons, the eldest, James Spencer Knox, being the father of Sir Thomas George Knox. In 1786 Knox became rector of Pomeroy in the diocese of Armagh, after which he obtained the rectory of Callan in the diocese of Ossory, and became chaplain to the Irish House of Commons. On 21 September 1794 he was consecrated bishop of Killaloe in St Peter's Church, Dublin, and in 1803 he was translated to the see of Derry, where he was enthroned on 9 September. During his episcopacy at Derry he became widely known for his philanthropy and charitable works, helped to restore the cathedral, and published several sermons. He died in George Street, Hanover Square, London, on 9 July 1831 and was buried at the chapel of North Audley Street, London.

THOMAS HAMILTON, *rev.* DAVID HUDDLESTON

Sources J. B. Leslie, *Derry clergy and parishes* (1937), 19–20 · *GM*, 1st ser., 101/2 (1831), 175–6 · Burke, *Peerage* (1970)
Archives BL, letters to Lord Hardwicke, Add. MSS 35646–35764 · PRO NIre., letters to Sir Henry Bruce

Knox, William (1789–1825), poet, was born on 17 August 1789 at Firth, parish of Lilliesleaf, Roxburghshire, the eldest son of Thomas Knox, a farmer, and his wife, Barbara (*née* Turnbull), the widow of Mr Pott of Todrig. After schooling at Lilliesleaf parish school and Musselburgh grammar school he farmed unsuccessfully at Wrae, near Langholm, Dumfriesshire, from 1812 to 1817. He 'became too soon his own master', wrote Scott, 'and plunged into dissipation and ruin' (*Journal*, 29–30). His farming career over, Knox returned to his parents at Todrig. In 1820 the family settled in Edinburgh, and Knox became a writer with the support of John Wilson and Scott, who frequently gave him money.

As well as contributing to journals such as the *Literary Gazette*, Knox published *The Lonely Hearth* (1818), *The Songs of Israel* (1824), and *The Harp of Zion* (1825). 'Mortality', in *The Songs of Israel*, was reputedly a favourite with President Lincoln. He died in Edinburgh, a few days after a stroke, on 12 November 1825. T. W. BAYNE, *rev.* SARAH COUPER

Sources C. Rogers, *The modern Scottish minstrel, or, The songs of Scotland of the past half-century*, 3 (1856), 112–13 · Chambers, *Scots.*, rev. T. Thomson (1875), 2.452–3 · *The journal of Sir Walter Scott*, ed. W. E. K. Anderson (1972), 29–30 · J. G. Lockhart, *Memoirs of the life of Sir Walter Scott*, 6 (1837), 152–3 · J. C. Goodfellow, *Border biography* (1890), 29–33 · Anderson, *Scot. nat.* · J. G. Wilson, ed., *The poets and poetry of Scotland*, 2 (1877), 106–7

Knoydart, Seven Men of (*act.* 1948), protesters on the Scottish highland land question, became famous for a land raid on the Knoydart estate of Lord Brocket in which they sought to establish their claim to have smallholdings created by the department of agriculture for Scotland. **Alexander Macphee** (*b. c.*1893), **Donald Macphee** (*fl.* 1948)—brother of Alexander Macphee—**Duncan MacPhail** (*b. c.*1914), **Henry MacAskill** (*fl.* 1948), **John** [Jack] **MacHardy** (*fl.* 1948), **Archibald MacDonald** (*fl.* 1948), and **William Quinn** (*b. c.*1911) were not crofters in the strict legal sense of the word, but they all lived on the Knoydart peninsula on the west coast of Scotland and worked, or had done so, for the proprietor. Duncan MacPhail had spent six years in the Royal Artillery during the Second World War. An eighth man, **Archibald MacDougall** (1927–1999), did not participate in the raid as he was absent due to military service, but he was associated with the claim as land was staked out on his behalf by his neighbour, MacAskill.

MacDougall, the last survivor of the protest, did most to keep the memory of the Knoydart land raid alive, publishing a book on the subject (1993), and his name was used by the Scottish National Party in November 1999, shortly after his death, in association with propaganda on land reform. The men were assisted in their correspondence with government agencies, and in publicizing the raid and its aftermath, by the local Roman Catholic priest, Father Colin *Macpherson, later bishop of Argyll and the Isles. Arthur Ronald Nall Nall-Cain, second Baron Brocket (1904–1967), a millionaire landowner and brewery director, and former Conservative MP, was demonized at the time and in subsequent memory as a Nazi sympathizer: an accusation based on visits to Germany in the 1930s and views on the regime expressed on such occasions.

The events which occasioned the seven men's notoriety began on 8 November 1948 when they took possession of land on farms at Scottas and Kilchoan on Knoydart. This form of land protest had been common in the Hebrides from the 1880s to the 1920s, a period which saw Scottish land-reform legislation. The raid was to some extent a publicity exercise; photographers as well as newspaper reporters had been informed, and were present to witness the seizure. A series of especially well-informed articles appeared in *The Scotsman* of Edinburgh in the days following the raid. The proprietor of the land immediately responded by taking out an interdict in the court of session against the raiders. These interdicts were served on the raiders, once again with attendant photographers, and they agreed to withdraw from the land. Duncan MacPhail later recorded his regret at this decision, taken on legal advice: 'we would have been far better to have done what the old boys in the olden days did, stick on the ground until they put you to gaol' (Grigor, 77).

The proceedings in the court of session revealed much hostility between Brocket on one hand, and the raiders and Father Macpherson on the other. Brocket's legal representatives remarked in the course of these proceedings: 'It is denied that the Respondents have all been bred to agriculture, denied that they have sufficient capital and denied that they have sufficient skill or knowledge to work new holdings successfully' (NA Scot., CS275/1952/4). The same source refers to a petition organized by Brocket, which, allegedly, demonstrated that the rest of the population of Knoydart disapproved of the raid. Most of the signatories were in the landowner's employment. Brocket was certainly willing to use coercive tactics and did so against one of the raiders late in 1949. Jack MacHardy had been working as a gardener on the estate prior to the raid and in October 1949 sought such employment once again. Brocket demanded, and received, an 'unqualified apology and undertaking never to repeat such acts as those on November 9 1948' before granting MacHardy's request (NA Scot., CS275/1952/4).

This public phase of the events surrounding the Knoydart estate was a culmination of longer-running events which had taken place with less fanfare. Lord Brocket's estate management had been heavily criticized during the Second World War when he had allowed the sheep stock on the estate to dwindle. The government had requisitioned the estate in 1940 in an effort to counter this neglect and to increase food production. As late as 1947 accusations of neglect were still being levelled at the proprietor. In that year Father Macpherson had submitted a scheme to the department of agriculture for Scotland proposing that forty-six new holdings be created on the estate. The subsequent investigations of that department reached the conclusion that the land could sustain only nineteen such holdings, but that areas of the estate were suitable for afforestation. The background to these ideas was the rapidly declining human population of the estate; this had been as high as 500 in the 1870s but had fallen away to 148 by 1939. The aftermath of the raid saw a revisitation of these schemes as an attempt was made to find a solution to the problems of Knoydart. The Scottish Office appointed John A. Cameron, a well-known farmer and former member of the Scottish land court, to report on the matter. His investigation included a hearing for the views of the parties involved, including the raiders, at Mallaig in December 1948. His report, published in 1949, concluded that neither the 'Father Macpherson scheme' nor the proposals of the department of agriculture for Scotland for the creation of small-holdings were viable, on the grounds that the expense of providing roads and other infrastructure would be excessive. He recommended, although with some regret, that the estate could best be run as a single unit with stock grazing, forestry, and sport as the principal enterprises. Arthur Woodburn, the secretary of state for Scotland, accepted Cameron's recommendations. The seven men responded by sending a 'Memorial' to Woodburn, attacking Cameron's conclusions and claiming that he was 'blind to the lessons of the past' and had failed to perceive the significance of the facts placed before him at the Mallaig meeting (NA Scot., SEP12/7/3).

The Knoydart land raid was an isolated event and, unlike such raids in the 1920s, did not influence the government to create new holdings for landless people. Nevertheless, it was commemorated in several ways. The noted folklorist Hamish Henderson wrote his 'Ballad of the Men of Knoydart' soon after the event; this song saw the raid as a possible starting point for a nationalist revival in Scotland. Politicians such as Dr Robert Macintyre, of the Scottish National Party, and John Macdonald Bannerman, of the Liberal Party, used the event as a stick with which to beat the Labour government over its perceived neglect of highland and Scottish questions. In 1993 a cairn was erected to the memory of the 'Seven Men of Knoydart', an event which sought, like Henderson's song, to make wider political points from the events of 1948. The inscription on the cairn reads:

> In 1948, near this cairn, the Seven Men of Knoydart staked claims to secure a place to live and work. For over a century Highlanders had been forced to use land raids to gain a foothold where their forebears lived. Their struggle should inspire each new generation of Scots to gain such rights by just laws. History will judge harshly the oppressive laws that have led to the virtual extinction of a unique culture from this beautiful place. (Withers, 335)

In 1999, after a long struggle against absentee and corporate ownership, Knoydart was purchased by the community which lives there.   EWEN A. CAMERON

Sources A. MacDougall, *Knoydart: the last Scottish land raid* (1993) · I. F. Grigor, 'The seven men of Knoydart', *The complete odyssey: voices from Scotland's recent past*, ed. B. Kay (1996), 71–7 · NA Scot., court of session papers, CS 275/1952/3-4 · Scottish economic planning department files, NA Scot., SEP12/2; 12/7/1–3 · *The Scotsman* (10–12 Nov 1948) · *The Scotsman* (26 Nov 1948) · *The Scotsman* (23 Dec 1948) · *The Scotsman* (26 March 1949) · *Scots Independent* (Dec 1948–June 1949) · J. A. Cameron, *Knoydart estate* (1949) · H. Henderson, 'Ballad of the men of Knoydart', *Collected poems and songs*, ed. R. Ross (2000), 128–30 · C. W. J. Withers, 'Place, memory, monument: memorializing the past in contemporary highland Scotland', *Ecumne*, 3 (1996), 325–44 · *Bannerman: the memoirs of Lord Bannerman of Kildonan*, ed. J. Fowler (1972)
Archives NA Scot., court of session papers, CS 275/1952/3-4 · NA Scot., Scottish economic planning department files, SEP 12/2, SEP 12/7/1–3
Likenesses portraits, repro. in MacDougall, *Knoydart*

Knutsford. For this title name *see* Holland, Henry Thurstan, first Viscount Knutsford (1825–1914); Holland, Sydney George, second Viscount Knutsford (1855–1931).

Knyvet, Sir Edmund (d. **1539**). *See under* Knyvet, Sir Edmund (*c*.1508–1551).

Knyvet, Sir Edmund (*c*.1508–1551), landowner and member of parliament, was the eldest son of Sir Thomas *Knyvet (*c*.1485–1512) of Buckenham Castle, Norfolk, and his wife, Muriel (d. 1512), daughter of Thomas Howard, second duke of Norfolk, and widow of John Grey, second Viscount Lisle. His father was a prominent courtier (he was master of the horse) who was killed in a sea battle near Brest in August 1512. The family's extensive estates in Norfolk and Suffolk were still in the hands of Edmund's great-grandfather Sir William Knyvet, who did not die until 1515. Edmund's wardship was then purchased by his father's friend Charles Brandon, duke of Suffolk, who had also been the guardian of Knyvet's half-sister Elizabeth Grey. It appears that Suffolk subsequently sold Knyvet's wardship to Sir Thomas Wyndham, who at his death instructed his executors to sell it on to Anthony Wingfield for £400 or, failing that, to the highest bidder. It was not only the fact that he was a minor that delayed Edmund Knyvet's entering upon his inheritance. Edmund's long-lived great-grandfather had married as his second wife Joan, daughter of the first duke of Buckingham, and he left Buckenham Castle and other lands in Norfolk to his eldest son from this marriage, Sir Edward Knyvet. It was not until the latter's death in 1528, followed by that of his heir Robert, that the family lands reverted to Edmund, who secured them only in 1533. At his death they were valued at about £215 a year.

It was principally as a Norfolk landlord that Edmund Knyvet made his mark. In the early 1530s he warned the third duke of Norfolk that the parishioners of Mendelsham, Suffolk, a village of which he was himself the absentee landlord, were holding large assemblies as members of an independent Christian brotherhood, and in 1536 he joined Norfolk in suppressing the Pilgrimage of Grace. Knighted in 1538 or 1539, he was involved in the election of knights of the shire for Norfolk for the parliament of 1539: the king and his chief minister, Thomas Cromwell, favoured Edmund Wyndham and Richard Southwell, but Knyvet coveted election himself and, always irascible, was angered when he was not chosen. He quarrelled so violently with Southwell that bystanders, fearing public disorder, brought the two men before the duke of Norfolk, who bound them in £2000 each to keep the peace. In a letter to Cromwell, Norfolk described Knyvet as a young man who trusted too much to his wit and was ruled by three or four 'light naughty knaves of Welshmen and others' rather than by his father-in-law (Sir John Shelton) and the duke (*LP Henry VIII*, 14/1, no. 800). In November 1539 Knyvet was named sheriff of Norfolk and Suffolk, possibly in an attempt to mollify him. He attended Norfolk at the reception of Anne of Cleves early in 1540. In April that year he was licensed to buy the chantry or college of Thompson, near Thetford, with its estates in Norfolk and Cambridgeshire, and a year later he had a formal grant of them. But almost at once he sold them to John Flowerdew and Edmund Grey.

Late in April 1541 Knyvet again showed his hotheadedness, when he was charged with striking Thomas Clere, a servant of Henry Howard, earl of Surrey, within the king's tennis court. A recent statute had stated that anyone guilty of such violence at court should have his right hand struck off, and arrangements were made to inflict the penalty—the statute specified in detail how this should be done, the king's master cook wielding the knife and the sergeant of the poultry providing a cock to test its sharpness. Possibly because Knyvet begged to have his left hand amputated instead, so that his right might still do the king good service, he received a pardon before the blow could be struck. In January 1546 he was required to serve with 200 men in the army that Henry VIII was preparing for his war with France.

Increasingly at odds with the Howards, and especially with the earl of Surrey, Knyvet testified against the latter when he was charged with treason in December 1546. On this occasion he also claimed to have urged Surrey to speak no ill of the dead when in 1540 the earl was exulting over the execution of Thomas Cromwell. Knyvet benefited from the disgrace of the Howards, receiving a lease of some of their lands, including the Norfolk manor of Wymondham, and purchasing additional estates from the king. In 1547 he was finally elected to the Commons as a knight of the shire for Norfolk. He successfully withstood the Norfolk rebels in 1549, and went on to serve under John Dudley, earl of Warwick, in the suppression of Ket's rebellion. He died in London on 1 May 1551, before the end of the parliament. His very brief will, made on 18 April 1550, left all his goods and chattels to his wife, Anne, the daughter of Sir John Shelton of Carrow, Norfolk. He was survived by his wife and two sons, and settled a manor on the younger son. Although he named his wife and John Flowerdew executors of his estate they renounced the duty and administration was granted to his elder son, Thomas. Despite his bad relations with the Howards it is possible that Knyvet was the poet 'E.K.' who contributed several verses to the famous anthology compiled by Mary Shelton (Knyvet's sister-in-law) which also included poems by Sir Thomas Wyatt and Surrey. Knyvet's younger brother Sir Henry was a gentleman of the privy chamber and in 1540 was sent as ambassador to Charles V.

Knyvet has often been confused with his uncle, another **Sir Edmund Knyvet** (*d.* 1539), the second son of Edmund Knyvet of Buckenham Castle and his wife, Eleanor, a sister of Sir James Tyrell. This Sir Edmund, the younger brother of Sir Thomas Knyvet, was sergeant-porter to Henry VIII and received several grants from the king, including an annuity of 50 marks, a manor in Northamptonshire, a lease of land in Shropshire, and the office of receiver of revenues from Denbigh. Through his marriage to Joan, the only surviving child of John Bourchier, second Baron Berners, he acquired the manor of Ashwellthorpe, Norfolk. He was a great-nephew of Christian Knyvet, the mother of John Colet, the dean of St Paul's, and was named in Colet's will as his chief heir should the dean's mother not survive him (which she did). As porter at the gate he attended Henry VIII at the Field of Cloth of Gold. He died in 1539 and was buried at Ashwellthorpe.

STANFORD LEHMBERG

Sources HoP, *Commons, 1509–58*, 2.482–3 · *LP Henry VIII*, vols. 1–21 · will, PRO, PROB 11/34, fol. 229*v* · D. MacCulloch, *Suffolk and the Tudors: politics and religion in an English county, 1500–1600* (1986) · C. Wriothesley, *A chronicle of England during the reigns of the Tudors from AD 1485 to 1559*, ed. W. D. Hamilton, 2 vols., CS, new ser., 11, 20 (1875–7)
Wealth at death £215 p.a.: HoP, *Commons, 1509–58*, 2.482–3; will, PRO, PROB 11/34, fol. 229*v*

Knyvet, Sir Henry (1537?–1598), soldier and member of parliament, was the first son of Sir Henry Knyvet (*d.* 1546?) and his wife, Anne, daughter of Sir Christopher Pickering. In 1563 he married Elizabeth, daughter of Sir James Stumpe of Charlton, near Malmesbury, Wiltshire. She died in 1585, and he subsequently (by 1595) married Mary, daughter of Sir John Sydenham. Knyvet's grandfather Sir Thomas *Knyvet was master of the horse to Henry VIII, and his father a gentleman of the privy chamber and soldier.

In 1560 Knyvet became a gentleman pensioner to Queen Elizabeth I. This connection, and the links he sustained with prominent men in Wiltshire, helped to ensure his position among the office-holding gentry, despite enmities fostered by land disputes persisting throughout the 1560s and 1570s. He was a justice of the peace, served as sheriff of the county, and became a deputy lieutenant in 1585. He was knighted in 1574. In 1587 either Knyvet or a member of his family served in the Netherlands, suggesting protestant sympathies. Knyvet was instructed to raise 2000 Wiltshire men towards the national defences when the Armada threatened in 1588, and his contribution to county military affairs was much valued.

In parliament Knyvet represented either Wootton Bassett or Malmesbury from 1571 to 1597, but he never became knight of the shire. Though considered by one observer to have been a bore, he seems to have done valuable service on a number of committees, many of them dealing with bills concerning arms and defences. In later years relations with court and council were more strained. By January 1593 an incident involving a royal servant coming to serve process on a member of his household had resulted in two spells in prison. In March he probably did his credit no good in the House of Commons when he appears to have argued that proceedings in the subsidy bill should be kept secret, even from the queen herself.

The army was a major part of Knyvet's life. He was wounded at the siege of Leith in 1560 and nine years later he stood against the northern rising, subsequently advising on the defence of the northern border. His *Defence of the Realm*, written in 1596, was prompted by the fall of Calais to the Spanish. Like many before and since he was concerned about the ability of England to resist an invader, should the navy fail as first line of defence. His concern about the organization of the militia was timely, but his intended reliance on the longbow was hardly forward-looking.

Knyvet provides an interesting illustration of the problems faced by the crown in raising revenue. At his death he owed the queen £4000 from rents on forest land in his care as sub-warden, but there was a suggestion that he settled lands on his daughters so as to deprive the queen of her due. Yet in parliament in 1593 he had apparently spoken of the need to maximize yields from royal assets in order to finance the strong army which he thought so important. Knyvet died at Charlton, Wiltshire on 14 June 1598. There is a fine monumental effigy of him with Elizabeth, his first wife, in the church at Charlton, where he was buried on 25 July 1598. He had two sons and four daughters; three of his daughters with Elizabeth, including the eldest, Katherine [see Howard, Katherine], married into families holding the earldoms of Suffolk, Lincoln, and Rutland.　　　　　　　　　　　T. E. HARTLEY, rev.

Sources HoP, *Commons, 1558–1603* • H. Knyvet, *Defence of the realm*, ed. C. Hughes (1906) • J. E. Neale, *Elizabeth I and her parliaments*, 2 vols. (1953–7) • A. Wall, 'Faction in local politics, 1580–1620', *Wiltshire Archaeological Magazine*, 72–3 (1977–8), 119–33 • D. Dean, *Law-making and society in late Elizabethan England: the parliament of England, 1584–1601* (1996)
Likenesses effigy on monument (with first wife), Charlton church, Wiltshire

Knyvet, Sir John (d. 1381), justice and administrator, was the eldest son of Richard Knyvet of Southwick, Northamptonshire (d. 1353), the keeper of Rockingham Forest in that county, and Joanna, daughter and heir of Sir John Wurth. Knyvet was practising in the courts by 1347; in 1354 he became serjeant-at-law, and from 1356 to 1361 served as a king's serjeant. On 24 June 1361 he was appointed a justice of the court of common pleas and was knighted, and on 29 October 1365 he was raised to the office of chief justice of the king's bench. In the parliament of 1362 he served as a trier of petitions for Aquitaine and other lands overseas, and afterwards in each parliament until 1380, except while he was chancellor, was a

trier of petitions for England, Scotland, Wales, and Ireland.

On 5 July 1372, after the death of Sir Robert Thorpe, Knyvet was appointed chancellor. His period of office may have seen significant developments in chancery's emerging function as a court of equity. Speeches which he made at the openings of parliament in 1372, 1373, and 1376 are recorded in the parliament rolls. However, in January 1377 Edward III's government reverted to the custom of appointing ecclesiastical chancellors, and Adam Houghton was appointed to succeed Knyvet on 11 January. But the former minister remained in high standing with the court, for on the day after his dismissal Knyvet was retained for life as a member of the king's council, with an annuity of £200 payable from the hanaper of the chancery. Before he was replaced Knyvet was also appointed *ex officio* as one of Edward III's executors. He did not again hold judicial office, but was appointed to the first continual council of Richard II's minority government (July–October 1377) and had his annuity confirmed by the new king on 27 February 1378.

Knyvet's principal residence probably remained Southwick, where the hall shows evidence of extensive rebuilding during his tenure. He held large estates in Northamptonshire and throughout East Anglia, and his local connections are reflected by his frequent appointment as justice of assize, gaol delivery, and oyer and terminer in the central and eastern counties. During the 1350s he was also regularly appointed as a justice of the peace in Northamptonshire, and more occasionally in Bedfordshire, Buckinghamshire, Norfolk, and Suffolk. He had close connections with the royal family, serving as steward of Queen Philippa's estates, counsellor of the Black Prince, and justice of the forest in Lancashire to John of Gaunt. He received fees from the abbot of Ramsey and was in the service of William de Bohun, earl of Northampton, becoming guardian to the latter's son Humphrey.

About 1358 Knyvet married Eleanor (d. 1388), daughter and coheir of Ralph, Lord Basset of Weldon. They left five children: John, Robert, Richard, Henry, and Margery, and their descendants established themselves as a leading family in Norfolk. Knyvet died on 16 February 1381; a few months later the escheators' investigations of his lands were disrupted by the outbreak of the peasants' revolt.

W. M. ORMROD

Sources Sainty, *King's counsel* • Sainty, *Judges* • Baker, *Serjeants* • G. O. Sayles, ed., *Select cases in the court of king's bench*, 7 vols., SeldS, 55, 57–8, 74, 76, 82, 88 (1936–71) • Tout, *Admin. hist.* • RotP • CIPM, 15, no. 364 • *Northamptonshire*, Pevsner (1961) • HoP, *Commons* • Chancery records • S. Walker, *The Lancastrian affinity, 1361–1399* (1990) • G. A. Holmes, *The estates of the higher nobility in fourteenth-century England* (1957) • J. R. Maddicott, *Law and lordship: royal justices as retainers in thirteenth- and fourteenth-century England* (1978)

Knyvet, Sir Thomas (c.1485–1512), courtier and sea captain, was the eldest son of Edmund Knyvet of Hilborough, Norfolk (d. 1503/4), himself the eldest son of Sir William Knyvet of Buckenham, Norfolk (c.1448–1515). Thomas's mother was Edmund's wife, Eleanor (d. after 1540), daughter of William Tyrell of Gipping. He came to notice at court towards the end of Henry VII's reign, jousting in the tournaments of May and June 1507 and serving as an esquire for the king's body. He was closely attached to the Howard family from the time of his marriage, by 9 July 1506, to Muriel (d. 1512), daughter of Thomas *Howard, earl of Surrey and later second duke of Norfolk (1443–1524), and his first wife, Elizabeth Tilney (d. 1497), and widow of John Grey, Viscount Lisle (d. 1504). From 1509 he emerged as one of the favourites of Henry VIII, taking a leading part in many tournaments and revels at court. The king made him knight of the Bath at his coronation on 23 June 1509 and appointed him bearer of the king's standard on 27 July 1509 and master of the horse on 22 February 1510. He was also rewarded with local offices on the crown lands, customs licences, and a lease of those Lisle estates not already allocated to his wife in dower. Muriel served as a lady-in-waiting to Queen Katherine, and their links with the queen were presumably reflected in the names of two of their children, Katherine and Ferdinand; another, Anne, would serve the queen in the 1520s and receive a dowry from her mistress.

On the outbreak of war with France in 1512 Knyvet was given command of the *Regent*, one of the two largest ships in the fleet led by his brother-in-law, Sir Edward *Howard. On 10 August, in an engagement outside Brest, the *Regent* grappled and boarded the *Cordelière*, the largest ship in the French fleet. The *Cordelière* caught fire and both ships burnt, killing some 600 or 700 men on the *Regent* and 900 or more on her opponent. Sir Thomas, who according to one report was killed by gunfire before the conflagration, was among the dead. Sir Edward Howard vowed to avenge Knyvet's death before he saw the king again, and was killed in the attempt in April 1513. Knyvet's widow died in childbirth between 13 and 21 December 1512, leaving their three sons and two daughters to be brought up by their grandmother, Eleanor Knyvet. The eldest son, Edmund (1508–1551), eventually succeeded to most of his great-grandfather's estates, while his brother Henry (d. 1546) became a gentleman of Henry VIII's privy chamber. Four of Sir Thomas's five brothers also served the king at court or in the navy. Sir Thomas Knyvet's portrait, which does not survive, was painted by the Venetian artist Antonio da Solario, and he was commemorated in a poem by John Leland; his fatal encounter with the French inspired a poetic exchange between Thomas More and Germain de Brie.

S. J. GUNN

Sources R. Virgoe, 'The earlier Knyvetts: the rise of a Norfolk gentry family [pt 2]', *Norfolk Archaeology*, 41 (1990–93), 249–78 · *LP Henry VIII*, vols. 1–2 · St Thomas More, *Latin poems*, ed. C. H. Miller and others (1984), vol. 3/2 of *The Yale edition of the complete works of St Thomas More*, 218–27, 284–9, 429–694 · 'Some unpublished poems by John Leland', ed. L. Bradner, *Publications of the Modern Language Association of America*, 71 (1956), 834–5 · A. Spont, ed., *Letters and papers relating to the war with France, 1512–1513*, Navy RS, 10 (1897) · will, PRO, PROB 11/17/17

Likenesses A. de Solario; formerly in possession of Sir Brian Tuke (now lost)

Wealth at death manor of Cranworth and some purchased lands within manor: will, PRO, PROB 11/17/17

Knyvet, Thomas. *See* Knyvett, Thomas, Baron Knyvett (1545/6–1622).

Knyvett, Charles (1752–1822), musician and singer, was born on 11 February 1752 in the parish of St Margaret's, Westminster, the son of Charles Knyvett (1710–1782) and his wife, Jane, *née* Jordan (1714–1785). Educated at Westminster School from 1762, he was a boy chorister at Westminster Abbey under Benjamin Cooke and was appointed joint organist (with William Smethergell) of All Hallows Barking in November 1770. On 16 June 1772, at St Marylebone, he married Rose Alleway (c.1752–1807). Her family came from Sonning in Berkshire and Knyvett later acquired property there.

Knyvett performed occasionally at the theatre: among his engagements, in May 1775 he was paid for fourteen nights' harpsichord playing at Drury Lane, and in June 1790 he accompanied Mrs Billington when she sang Purcell's 'Mad Bess' in character as Ophelia in *Hamlet*. When he joined the Royal Society of Musicians in 1778 he was described as 'a Sober Industrious Man' (Matthews, 87). He was an organist in the oratorios at Covent Garden from 1789 to 1792, sang in the Chapel Royal choir from 1786, and was appointed organist there in 1796.

Knyvett was a principal alto at the Handel commemoration concerts from 1784. The 'Two Master Knyvetts' in the 1784 choir were his sons Charles [see below] and Henry (1774–1843), who became an army officer; a third son, the singer and composer William *Knyvett, was born in 1779. Between 1785 and 1799 the elder Charles sang every year at the Concerts of Ancient Music. He played the organ at the Three Choirs meeting in 1780 and sang at the Cambridge festival during the 1780s. With the tenor Samuel Harrison he founded the Vocal Concerts, a fashionable subscription series which ran each spring from 1792 to 1795. Knyvett appeared as singer and piano accompanist in these concerts, which featured English songs and glees. He sang for the Noblemen's and Gentlemen's Catch Club, the Je ne sais quoi Club, and the Anacreontic Society. Parke described him as 'perhaps the best catch singer in England' (Parke, 2.236), while Stevens remembered his 'rich strain of humour' (*Recollections of R. J. S. Stevens*, 76) at these convivial meetings. Knyvett moved on terms of friendship with aristocratic patrons of the catch clubs and Concerts of Ancient Music. In 1800 he edited *A Collection of Favorite Glees* submitted by candidates for two prizes given by the prince of Wales (afterwards George IV), one of which was won by his son William. The younger Charles and William performed with their father, and a number of three-part glees were published as sung by the Messrs Knyvett. Charles senior died at his house in Blandford Place, Pall Mall, on 19 January 1822 after a lingering illness.

Charles Knyvett (1773–1852), musician and singer, was born on 23 March 1773 in the parish of St George's, Hanover Square, London. The *Dictionary of National Biography* says that he was a chorister of Westminster Abbey under

Charles Knyvett (1752–1822), by William Daniell, pubd 1812 (after George Dance, 1799)

Sir William Parsons, but this statement is not supported by the records. Apprenticed to his father for five years, by the age of twenty-one he was a professional pianist, singer, and music teacher. He married Jane Laney (d. in or after 1807) on 1 September 1795; they had seven children. In 1802 he was appointed organist of St George's, Hanover Square, and his *Selection of Psalm Tunes* as sung at that church appeared in four editions between 1823 and 1850. He also published some keyboard works and glees and became an eminent teacher of thoroughbass and piano. Knyvett died on 2 November 1852, having retired to the estate he inherited at Sonning, Berkshire, after his father's death.   OLIVE BALDWIN and THELMA WILSON

Sources *Recollections of R. J. S. Stevens, an organist in Georgian London*, ed. M. Argent (1992) • W. T. Parke, *Musical memoirs*, 2 (1830) • B. Matthews, ed., *The Royal Society of Musicians of Great Britain: list of members, 1738–1984* (1985) • S. McVeigh, *Concert life in London from Mozart to Haydn* (1993) • *Old Westminsters*, vols.1–2 • J. Doane, ed., *A musical directory for the year 1794* [1794] • *GM*, 1st ser., 92/1 (1822), 94 • C. Burney, *An account of the musical performances … in commemoration of Handel* (1785) • programme books of the Concerts of Ancient Music, 1785–99 • D. Lysons and others, *Origin and progress of the meeting of the three choirs of Gloucester, Worcester and Hereford* (1895) • D. J. Reid, 'Some festival programmes of the eighteenth and nineteenth centuries [pt 2]', *Royal Musical Association Research Chronicle*, 6 (1966), 3–22 • G. W. Stone, ed., *The London stage, 1660–1800*, pt 4: *1747–1776* (1962) • C. B. Hogan, ed., *The London stage, 1660–1800*, pt 5: *1776–1800* (1968) • D. Dawe, *Organists of the City of London, 1666–1850* (1983) • H. J. Gladstone, G. Boas, and H. Christopherson, *Noblemen and Gentlemen's Catch Club* (1996) • 'Knyvett, Charles', *The catalogue of printed music at the British Library to 1980*, ed. R. Balchin, 33 (1984) [all compositions except the 1800 edn of glees are by the younger Charles] • [J. S. Sainsbury], ed., *A dictionary of musicians*, 2 vols. (1825), vol. 2 • A. Ashbee and J. Harley, eds., *The cheque books of the*

Chapel Royal, 2 vols. (2000) • parish register, St Margaret's, Westminster [baptism] • parish register, Marylebone Road, St Marylebone [marriage] • will, Feb–May 1822, Family Records Centre, London, PROB 11/1653, fols. 84–5 [copy] • *IGI* • parish register, St Margaret's, Westminster [burial: Charles Knyvett, father of the elder Charles] • parish register, Southwark, St Olave [baptism: Jane Jordan, mother of the elder Charles] • parish register, Hanover Square, St George [baptism: Charles Knyvett the younger]

Likenesses G. Dance, drawing, pencil and colours, 1799 • G. Dance, drawing, pencil and colours, 1800 (Charles Knyvett the younger) • W. Daniell, soft-ground etching, pubd 1803 (Charles Knyvett the younger; after G. Dance, 1800), BM, NPG • W. Daniell, soft-ground etching, pubd 1812 (after G. Dance, 1799), BM, NPG [*see illus.*] • G. H. Harlow, group portrait, oils, *c.*1817 (*Court scene for the trial of Queen Katherine*), priv. coll.; autograph replica, Royal Shakespeare Memorial Theatre Museum, Stratford upon Avon, Warwickshire; copy (after Harlow), Garr. Club • G. Clint, mezzotint, pubd 1819 (after G. H. Harlow), BM • J. Thompson, stipple (after Charles Knyvett the younger by A. Wivell), BM, NPG

Wealth at death £33,300 in legacies (almost completely funded by two mortgages); estate at Sonning, Berkshire inherited by son: will, 1822, PRO, PROB 11/1653, fols. 84–5

Knyvett, Charles (1773–1852). *See under* Knyvett, Charles (1752–1822).

Knyvett [Knyvet], **Thomas**, Baron Knyvett (1545/6–1622), courtier, was the younger son of Sir Henry Knyvet (or Knyvett; d. 1546), soldier, gentleman of the privy chamber, and sometime ambassador to the emperor Charles V, and his wife, Anne, heir of Sir Christopher Pickering of Killington, Westmorland, and widow of Sir Francis Weston (executed in 1536). After his father's death, Knyvett's mother married John Vaughan (d. 1577). His grandfather Sir Thomas *Knyvet of Buckenham, Norfolk (c.1485–1512), had been master of the horse to Henry VIII, while his elder brother Henry *Knyvet (1537?–1598), of Charlton, Wiltshire, a soldier and distinctly belligerent country gentleman, was MP for Wootton Bassett and Malmesbury in several Elizabethan parliaments.

Thomas Knyvett was a fellow-commoner at Jesus College, Cambridge, in 1564–5 and attended Gray's Inn in 1566. He was admitted to the privy chamber by 1572, and remained a gentleman of the bedchamber to Queen Elizabeth and to James I for the rest of his life. He was returned as a knight of the shire for Westmorland in 1572, and was elected as an MP for Westminster in all but one parliament between 1584 and his elevation to the Lords. He was seneschal of Penrith Castle in 1577. On 21 July 1597 he married Elizabeth, widow of Richard Warren, an Essex gentleman, who had died the previous March. Elizabeth was the eldest daughter of Sir Rowland *Hayward, lord mayor of London in 1570–71 and 1591, and his wife, Joan (née Tyllesworth). Knyvett's marriage may explain the timing of a lease in reversion of lands in Yorkshire, granted to him that same year, without fine, in consideration of his loyal service to the crown. He and his wife had no children. Elizabeth was appointed governess to King James's two youngest daughters, Mary and Sophia, both of whom died young.

Knyvett was steward and receiver of the lordship of Pickering from 1597 to 1599. He was created an honorary MA at Oxford when accompanying Queen Elizabeth on her visit to the university in 1592. Warden of the Tower mint from 27 September 1599, he was thereafter constantly at odds with the man he replaced, Sir Richard Martin, who remained a master of the mint. Some doubt surrounds the date of his knighthood, but he was probably knighted in 1601 between April and October (most likely in May). In favour with the new king, James I, Knyvett was given the manor of Stanwell, Middlesex, on 5 August 1603.

By 1597 Knyvett had been appointed keeper of Whitehall Palace and it was in this capacity that he conducted a search of the vaults under the House of Lords on the night of 4 November 1605, an operation which resulted in the arrest of Guy Fawkes, posing as John Johnson, servant to the earl of Northumberland's kinsman Thomas Percy, and standing guard over 18 hundredweight of gunpowder. Knyvett's promotion to the peerage as Lord Knyvett of Escrick, Yorkshire, may have been intended as a reward for this great service to the crown, or, more likely, as a recognition of his long and distinguished career at court. He took his seat in the Lords on 4 July 1607, and served as a privy councillor to Queen Anne. Knyvett's will, made in 1620, bequeathed his estate to his wife and strikingly declared his religious faith; by God's goodness he had attained 'thorough many conflictes in this my pilgramage to the three skore and fifteeneth yeare of my life'; he firmly asserted his belief in:

> one Supreame eternall infinite and omnipotent power divine by the most Glorious name of god The father the sonne and the holie ghost Three personns and one God in essence and power of Creatinge Redeeminge and governinge all his creatures accordinge to his good will and pleasure I beleeve withall every Article of the Nicen Athanasian & Apostolike Creed literallie with out ambiguitie or doubt by which profession I was receyved at my Baptisme to be a member of the Church of Christ. (will)

Knyvett died at his house in King Street, Westminster, on 27 July 1622 and was buried on 1 August. His widow died that September and, despite Knyvett's testamentary request for a modest monument, they were buried together in a magnificent tomb at Stanwell church. This may be the work of their descendants, for the tomb is of a somewhat later style. The Escrick estate was inherited by Knyvett's niece, Katherine *Howard, countess of Suffolk (d. 1638), daughter of Sir Henry Knyvet of Charlton and wife of Thomas Howard, first earl of Suffolk.

MARK NICHOLLS

Sources state papers domestic, Elizabeth I and James I, PRO, SP12 and SP14 · will and sentence, PRO, PROB 11/140, sig. 78; PROB 11/141, sig. 37 · GEC, *Peerage* · HoP, *Commons, 1558–1603*, 2.420–24
Archives Norfolk RO, corresp.
Likenesses N. Stone, marble tomb effigy, 1623, St Mary's Church, Stanwell, Middlesex
Wealth at death see will and sentence, PRO, PROB 11/140, sig. 78; PROB 11/141, sig. 37

Knyvett, William (1779–1856), singer and composer, was born on 21 April 1779 in London, the third and youngest son of Charles *Knyvett (1752–1822), a musician, and his wife, Rose, *née* Alleway (c.1752–1807). He was educated by his father, by the glee composer Samuel Webbe, and by

Giambattista Cimador. In 1788 he sang in the treble chorus at the Concerts of Ancient Music, and in 1795 appeared there as the principal alto. In 1797 he became a gentleman of the Chapel Royal and shortly afterwards a lay clerk at Westminster Abbey. He was appointed composer of the Chapel Royal in 1808, succeeding his father. He helped his father run the Vocal Concerts at Willis's Rooms, and in 1811, with his brother Charles and Thomas Vaughan, established the Vocal Subscription Concerts, which continued until 1822. From 1832 to 1840 he conducted the Concerts of Ancient Music, and he also conducted at the Birmingham festivals from 1831 to 1843 and the York festival in 1835.

One of the finest alto singers of his day, Knyvett sang in London and at provincial festivals, and formed a trio with Samuel Harrison and James Bartleman. The glee 'With sighs, sweet rose' was composed for him by John Wall Callcott.

Knyvett was a popular composer for the voice, and his songs and glees included 'My love is like the red, red rose' (1803), 'The Bells of St Michael's Tower' (1810), 'The Boatie Rows' (1810), and 'As it fell upon a day' (1812). His glee 'When the fair rose' was awarded the prince of Wales prize at the Harmonic Society in 1800. He was also commissioned to write anthems for the coronation of George IV ('The king shall rejoice') and Queen Victoria ('This is the day the Lord has made').

Knyvett was married twice. His second wife, whom he married in 1826, was Deborah Travis (1790–1876), a singer, of Shaw, near Oldham, Lancashire. She was one of the Lancashire chorus singers at the Concerts of Ancient Music from 1813 to 1815, and appeared as a principal from 1815. She was much in demand, especially as an oratorio singer, until her retirement in 1843. Knyvett died in poverty on 17 November 1856 at Clarges House, Ryde, Isle of Wight.

G. C. BOASE, *rev.* ANNE PIMLOTT BAKER

Sources H. W. Shaw, *The succession of organists of the Chapel Royal and the cathedrals of England and Wales from c.1538* (1991), 14 · *New Grove* · Grove, *Dict. mus.* · D. Baptie, *Sketches of the English glee composers: historical, biographical and critical (from about 1735–1866)* [1896] · *GM*, 3rd ser., 2 (1857), 621–2
Likenesses W. Daniell, soft-ground etching, pubd 1812 (after G. Dance), BM, NPG · G. H. Harlow, group portrait, oils, c.1817 (*Court scene for the trial of Queen Katherine*), Royal Shakespeare Memorial Theatre Museum, Stratford upon Avon, Warwickshire · print, Harvard TC
Wealth at death poor: *DNB*

Koch, Ludwig Karl (1881–1974), broadcaster and sound recordist, was born on 13 November 1881 at Eschersheimer Landstrasse 20, Frankfurt am Main, Germany, the second of the three children of Karl Theodor Koch, businessman, and his wife, Auguste Hess. Ludwig Koch's parents, both of whom were Jews, were enthusiastic music-lovers who introduced him into Frankfurt's rich musical scene where, while still a boy violinist, he was admitted to Clara Schumann's music circle. Later Koch studied singing, subsequently enjoying a short though successful career as a concert singer which was ended by the outbreak of the First World War. On 30 May 1912 Koch married Nellie Sylvia Herz, *née* Ganz (1892–1973), and they had a son and a

Ludwig Karl Koch
(1881–1974), by
Fred Kormis, c.1960

sound recordings had become universally familiar. His extraordinary, yet attractive and rather musical, Germanic pronunciation of English undoubtedly accounted in some measure for his popularity on the radio. As a broadcaster, Koch became especially associated with the natural history radio programmes emanating from Bristol from 1946 onwards. In 1948 the BBC purchased his entire collection of animal recordings and he joined the staff to make more of them by undertaking fieldwork throughout the British Isles. For several years after his retirement in 1951 from the BBC he continued to undertake expeditions to record wildlife sounds, including one to Iceland when he was seventy-one. His entire collection is now housed in the National Sound Archive at the British Library.

To the radio listeners of the 1940s and 1950s, Ludwig Koch, who was appointed MBE in 1960, was the man who brought the sounds of the countryside into their homes in a way that had been impossible before. He was a happy, humorous character whose magnetic radio personality played a significant role in heightening the British public's appreciation of wildlife. On 4 May 1974, aged ninety-two, he died peacefully in Harrow, Middlesex; he was cremated at Pinner cemetery, Harrow, on 13 May.

JOHN F. BURTON

Sources L. Koch, *Memoirs of a birdman* (1955) · J. Burton, 'Master of nature's music: Ludwig Koch, 1881–1974', *Country Life*, 157 (1975), 390–91 · private information (2004) [family] · J. F. Burton, 'Our debt to Ludwig Koch: master of nature's music', *Recorded Sound*, 74–5 (1979), 36–7 · personal knowledge (2004) · *The Times* (7 May 1974)

Archives BL, corresp. with Society of Authors, Add. MS 63280 · Sci. Mus. · Society of Authors, London, corresp. | FILM BBC WAC · BFI NFTVA, 'Fit for a queen', BBC2, 12 Nov 1997 | SOUND BBC WAC · BL NSA, 'Ludwig Koch's 75th birthday programme', 74941-4WR R1/TR1 R1 · BL NSA, performance recording

Likenesses F. Kormis, bronze resin bust, c.1960, priv. coll. [see *illus.*] · photographs, priv. coll. · photographs, BBC Natural History Unit Picture Library · photographs, repro. in Koch, *Memoirs*

Wealth at death £10,741: probate, 13 Aug 1974, *CGPLA Eng. & Wales*

daughter. His fluent French led to Koch's joining military intelligence early in the war, where he gained a special expertise in matters pertaining to prisoners of war. On the signing of the armistice in 1918, he was appointed chief delegate for repatriation for the French-occupied zone of Germany. However, he gradually resumed his participation in musical activities, giving up his work for the German government in 1925. In 1928 he was invited by the German subsidiary of Electric and Musical Industries (EMI) to organize a cultural branch of the gramophone industry; this coincided with a revival of his childhood interest in animals.

In 1889, when Koch was eight, his father had presented him with an Edison phonograph and a box of wax cylinders purchased at the Leipzig fair; so Ludwig commenced recording the voices of his numerous pets. His new responsibility for the development of cultural gramophone recording enabled him to begin, from 1929, the recording of animal sounds in earnest, using up-to-date equipment. Among several innovations, he conceived the idea of the sound-book: attaching gramophone records to an otherwise normal illustrated book.

Being a Jew, Koch's life under the Nazi regime became increasingly intolerable. Following confrontations with minor officials, he decided early in 1936 to flee to Britain. He was obliged to leave some of his precious recordings behind, but, encouraged by Sir Julian Huxley, he succeeded in interesting the ornithologist and publisher Harry Witherby in his plan for a sound-book of British wild birds. By a fortunate coincidence, E. M. (Max) Nicholson had been commissioned by Witherby to write a book on British birdsongs and he readily offered to collaborate with Koch and make it a sound-book. Koch immediately set about recording birds in the English countryside with tremendous enthusiasm. Before the end of 1936 *Songs of Wild Birds* was published, followed by two other sound-books by 1938.

Early in the Second World War, Huxley suggested to Koch that he offer his services to the BBC, and by the end of the war his unmistakable voice accompanying his

Koch de Gooreynd [*formerly* Koch], **William Julien Maurice** (1853–1919), stockbroker, was born on 14 October 1853, the second son of Franciscus Josephus Koch (*b.* 1815) and Josephine Emile de Laska of Belgium. He settled in Britain, probably at Brighton, some time prior to 1877. In that year he joined the London stockbrokers Panmure Gordon & Co. which had been formed a year earlier by Harry Panmure Gordon. Koch took British citizenship on 28 July 1883 and about 1913 added de Gooreynd to his surname by special permission of Leopold II who, it is said, would have ennobled Koch on account of his services to Belgium had he not already assumed British citizenship. Under Gordon's flamboyant leadership Panmure Gordon became well known, but Willy Koch made the key contribution; 'he was the brains of the firm', wrote the company promoter H. Osborne O'Hagan in 1929, 'although for many years Panmure Gordon was the dominating person and his partners did not much figure' (O'Hagan, 1.368). Koch was admitted a partner in 1889 and became senior partner in 1902, following the death of Gordon and the resignation of others.

Koch built Panmure Gordon into London's leading broking house for foreign government loans in the two decades before the First World War, when issues boomed and fortunes were made. In 1906 the leading merchant bankers, Morgan Grenfell, were 'impressed with the way Panmure Gordon's do their business now … they are intelligent and their methods are more sound than in the days of old PG'; a year later they believed the firm to be 'probably the most important firm in London' (Kynaston, *The City of London*, 310). Panmures specialized in foreign loans for sovereign states. The firm was especially pre-eminent as brokers for Chinese and Japanese government bond issues and worked closely with leading houses such as the Hongkong and Shanghai Bank and Barings; by 1914 twelve Chinese government and railway loans, worth £40 million, and thirteen Japanese government issues, exceeding £100 million, had been sponsored. The large and important Japanese issues negotiated with Baron Takahashi and marketed on continental and American bourses for the first time during the Russo-Japanese War were of particular note.

Koch's firm acted as brokers to a wide range of issues—from those of the city of Moscow to the Ottoman government, and from the state of São Paulo to the Union Pacific Railway. Industrial issues figured less, but Panmures' clients included many breweries, and weighty names such as Liptons Tea and Shell Transport and Trading. Apparently it had a weakness for foreign industrials, and anything outside the ordinary which it was 'quite unable to underwrite', according to the leading banker, Emile D'Erlanger (Kynaston, *The City of London*, 310). Notwithstanding, at the negotiating table Koch equalled the bankers—thereby enjoying a prestige rarely given to his profession—and offered a priceless combination of unrivalled placing power, coupled, when needed, with discretion. For example, he courted Lord Revelstoke, the imperious head of Barings, before the banker left to negotiate with the Russian government for an issue of imperial bonds in 1905. 'Should it be any "comfort" to you to syndicate 5,000,000 before you go St Petersburg', he counselled the banker, 'I think that this could be done quietly, and privately so to speak, without much fear of indiscretion' (ING Baring archives, 200243). This was placing power indeed.

Koch also figured in the affairs of the stock exchange, where he sat for a considerable time on the general purposes committee. His moment came in August 1914 when, with the markets on the threshold of collapse, he 'was one of the most indefatigable minds in saving the situation by getting the House closed and a moratorium established and later in assisting the Treasury and the City Financial Committee to formulate a scheme for the reopening' (*Financial Times*, 2).

Koch's lifestyle was opulent and, unusually for a broker, rivalled those of London's merchant bankers. His London home from about 1907 was 1 Belgrave Square, where footmen wore knee-breeches and black satin and where clients were lavishly entertained. 'Grand affair', wrote the banker Charles Addis after one such occasion in 1908; '12 guests and 6 serving men. Moet 93. Well done and less boring than usual' (Kynaston, *The City of London*, 331). Koch's Belgian links were also maintained. From at least 1910 he owned an estate at Gooreynd, near Antwerp, which he visited frequently, and during the First World War he worked for charities supporting Belgian refugees. Having a white beard, blue eyes, and a short, stocky build, he bore a striking resemblance to Edward VII, with whom he was frequently confused when taking the cure at Karlsbad. He had a passion for music and artists such as Jan Paderewski and Jelly D'Arányi were regularly invited to play at his Belgrave Square home.

On 10 September 1891 Koch married Manuela Joanna Joaquima Maria (*d.* 1936), a Polish cousin and daughter and coheir of Alexandre de Laski of London and Paris and sometime governor of the Bank of Poland. They had three sons and two daughters. His eldest son, Alexander, changed his surname by deed poll to Worsthorne although in 1937 reverted to Koch de Gooreynd; a grandson was the newspaper editor and journalist Sir Peregrine Worsthorne. His second son, Gerald, succeeded him at Panmures and was a partner there from 1924 until his death in 1953. William Koch died at his London home on 6 February 1919, leaving an estate in Britain of £0.75 million. His funeral on the 10th, presided over by a bishop, took place at the Roman Catholic cathedral, Westminster.

JOHN ORBELL

Sources B. H. D. MacDermot, *Panmure Gordon & Co., 1876–1976: a century of stockbroking* (privately printed, London, [1976]) • D. Kynaston, *The City of London*, 2 (1995) • *Daily Telegraph* (7 Feb 1919) • *Financial Times* (7 Feb 1919) • *The Times* (7 Feb 1919) • *The Times* (11 Feb 1919) • D. Kynaston, 'Gordon, Harry Panmure', *DBB* • H. O. O'Hagan, *Leaves from my life*, 2 vols. (1929) • *CGPLA Eng. & Wales* (1919) • ING Barings, London, Barings archives, 200243 • Burke, *Gen. GB* (1965)
Archives ING Barings, London, corresp.
Wealth at death £750,000: probate, 22 Feb 1919, *CGPLA Eng. & Wales*

Koczwara, František (*c*.1750–1791), musician, was born in Prague about 1750. He seems to have been an itinerant musician in Germany and the Netherlands but had moved to England by 1775. He lived in various places around England; the string quartets (op. 3, 1775) indicate that he lived in Bath, whereas the trios (op. 5) of a year later give a London address. In 1783 he moved to Dublin, where he played violin in the band at the Smock Alley Theatre; he also performed at the Chester music festival in September of that year (presumably on his way to Ireland). While in Ireland he composed perhaps his most popular work, *The Battle of Prague* (op. 23, *c*.1788), and performed for the Irish Musical Fund.

According to Pohl, Koczwara was engaged to play double bass at the new Italian opera house in London by Giovanni Gallini in 1790, but as that theatre was being rebuilt that year and did not open until March 1791 it is possible that as an interim measure he played for Gallini and Giardini at the Little Haymarket Theatre. He had certainly returned to London by May 1791, as he played in the

Concerts of Ancient Music and the Handel commemoration of May 1791. Fétis claimed to have performed, at the age of eight, a Mozart sonata and Koczwara's own *Battle of Prague* (the latter at sight) for the composer when he visited his father's house in Mons, although his dating of spring 1792 is clearly erroneous. Fétis also described how Koczwara played the violin, viola, cello, piano, oboe, flute, bassoon, and cittern.

Koczwara's compositions are mainly piano works and chamber music for piano and stringed instruments. *The Battle of Prague*, a sonata for piano and optional violin and cello, was extremely popular, particularly in Boston, USA, where it was 'indispensable to climax every concert'. According to Parke, Koczwara often sought to pass off his own works as being by more popular (and commercially successful) composers such as Haydn and Pleyel, although Newman decries 'the utter banality and triteness of this [*Battle of Prague*] sonata'.

Koczwara is most famous for the manner of his death. Although more polite generations would describe his death merely as suicide, the book *Modern Propensities, or, An Essay on the Art of Strangling* (London, *c*.1792) contained the memoirs of Susannah Hill, the woman tried at the Old Bailey on 16 September 1791 for the composer's murder. At her trial, Hill described how, on 2 September 1791 at a house of ill repute in Vine Street, Covent Garden, Koczwara had drunk a great deal of brandy and asked to be hanged in order to raise his passion. When she cut him down minutes later he was dead. Although auto-erotic asphyxia was not defined for another two hundred years, the case against Hill was dismissed.

THOMAS SECCOMBE, *rev.* MARK HUMPHREYS

Sources *Modern propensities, or, An essay on the art of strangling … illustrated with several anecdotes … with memoirs of Susanna Hill, and a summary of her trial at the Old Bailey on Friday, Sept. 16, 1791, on the charge of hanging Francis Kotzwara at her lodgings in Vine Street* (*c*.1792) • *New Grove* • Highfill, Burnim & Langhans, *BDA* • P. Wagner, *Eros revived: erotica of the Enlightenment in England and America* (1988), 24–7 • R. Wolfe, 'The hang-up of Franz Kotzwara and its relationship to sexual quackery in late eighteenth-century London', in P. Wagner, *Sex and eighteenth-century English culture: studies on Voltaire and the eighteenth century* (1984), 47–67 • W. T. Parke, *Musical memoirs*, 1 (1830), 181 • C. F. Pohl, *Mozart und Haydn in London*, 2 vols. (Vienna, 1867); repr. in 1 vol. (New York, 1970), 136 • A. Loesser, *Men, women and pianos* (New York, 1954), 243, 449 • W. S. Newman, *The sonata in the classical era* [1963], 769
Likenesses engraving, repro. in *Modern propensities*

Kodicek, Egon Hynek (1908–1982), biochemist and nutritionist, was born on 3 August 1908 in Kamenny Ujezd, Bohemia, the son of Emma and Samuel Kodicek. In 1915 his father, a doctor, moved with the family to Budweis, as medical chief of the military hospital there. Egon attended the local *Gymnasium* (*c*.1918–1927), where he read widely, cultivating a lasting interest in philosophy. He was good at sports, which he continued to enjoy during his medical course at Charles University in Prague. A brilliant scholar, he graduated as MD in 1932. He then joined the university's department of internal medicine and began his lifelong research on vitamins. The greatest influence on his career came from his studies with J. Heyrovský at the Physicochemical Institute, which convinced him of the importance of measurement in biological research. Heyrovský had invented the analytical technique of polarography, for which he received the 1959 Nobel prize for chemistry. Kodicek's early polarographic determinations of vitamin A and folic acid (a vitamin required for production of blood cells) in foods and animal tissues gained him several awards, including the Masaryk Fund prize for research (1938).

The German occupation of Prague in March 1939 made it imperative for Kodicek, who was of Jewish origin, to leave Czechoslovakia. He was offered a place at the Dunn Nutritional Laboratory in Cambridge, only just managing to avoid arrest while awaiting a visa. He reached Cambridge in June 1939. On arriving in Cambridge, Kodicek registered as a research student at Trinity College and was awarded a PhD in 1942 for his research on nicotinic acid. Kodicek had in 1936 married Jindriska (Jindra) E. M. Hradecká, an ophthalmic surgeon who had been a fellow student at medical school. She and their daughter Jana finally escaped in August, and the family lived initially on a grant from the Society for the Protection of Science and Learning. Their second daughter, Ivana, was born in 1943. Cambridge became the family's permanent home, and the Dunn Laboratory for thirty-four years the base for Kodicek's wide-ranging work. Vitamins and hormones formed the core of his research, and he developed methods of analysis of their often minute concentrations in tissues. Kodicek's measurements of vitamin C, riboflavin, and nicotinic acid helped government assessments of the nutritional value of wartime diets. His shrewd applications of new physical techniques, notably isotopic labelling, fluorimetry, ultracentrifugation, and chromatography, promoted recognition of nutritional research as a respected science.

Kodicek declined offers from the USA, and in 1947 the family became naturalized British subjects. He continued investigations on nicotinic acid (later named niacin). This compound is responsible for the prevention of pellagra, a serious disease associated with diets based on maize. Kodicek found that much of the niacin in cereals was bound in a macromolecular matrix, and was nutritionally unavailable. Severe deficiency of vitamin C (ascorbic acid) was known to impair healing of wounds, and Kodicek explored this effect extensively at the Dunn Laboratory, demonstrating abnormalities in connective tissue proteins and carbohydrates; but the biochemical complexities were beyond the scope of existing techniques.

Kodicek's frustrations on the vitamin C front were compensated by manifold achievements in research on the steroidal vitamin D (calciferol), which is essential for the control of calcium absorption and metabolism; serious deficiency leads to the soft bones characteristic of rickets. The term vitamin D comprises two compounds of very similar structure, vitamin D_2, derived from yeast, and vitamin D_3, derived from cholesterol. The vitamins are produced (both in nature and commercially) by the action of ultraviolet light on precursor sterols. Studies of vitamin D_3 (cholecalciferol), in which hydrogen atoms in certain

C-H bonds had been partly replaced by radioactive tritium, indicated loss of tritium—and correspondingly of hydrogen—from two sites during metabolism. It transpired that C-H was being converted into C-OH, yielding hydroxy-vitamins responsible for bioactivity. H. F. DeLuca at Wisconsin identified 25-hydroxycholecalciferol, while 1α,25-dihydroxycholecalciferol (calcitriol), discovered in Kodicek's laboratory in 1969, proved to be the hormone, metabolically elaborated from the vitamin, that stimulated calcium uptake by the intestine. Kodicek's magnificent contribution to the elucidation of the action of vitamin D was his crowning achievement, and a vindication of his appointment in 1963 as director of his laboratory. After retirement in 1973, he continued research, until overtaken by ill health, at the Strangeways Research Laboratory, Cambridge, investigating his hypothesis (which few accepted) that vitamin D was directly active in bone formation. After his death, it was shown that the bone-forming cells were indeed targets for the action of 1α,25-dihydroxycholecalciferol.

By virtue of his experience, wisdom, and encyclopaedic knowledge—leavened by beamish geniality—Kodicek chaired innumerable national and international committees. His many awards included the British Nutrition Foundation prize, and (jointly with DeLuca) the 1974 Roussel prize. A long-standing Biochemical Society member, and Ciba medallist, he also became an honorary member of the Nutrition Society, after being president from 1971 to 1974. He was elected FRS in 1973 and appointed CBE in 1974.

Kodicek's lifelong enthusiasm was an inspiration to his students, and to attenders at meetings who experienced his warm avuncularity (gently spiked with incisive criticism). He died at his home, 11 Bulstrode Gardens, Cambridge, on 27 July 1982.　　　　　C. J. W. BROOKS

Sources D. R. Fraser and E. M. Widdowson, *Memoirs FRS*, 29 (1983), 297–331 · D. R. Fraser, *British Journal of Nutrition*, 49 (1983), 167–70 · private information (2004) · *WWW* · personal knowledge (2004) · *CGPLA Eng. & Wales* (1982)
Archives Wellcome L., corresp. and notes | Bodl. Oxf., Society for Protection of Science and Learning and home office files · CUL, corresp. with Peter Mitchell
Likenesses G. Argent, photograph, 1973, possibly RS; repro. in Fraser and Widdowson, *Memoirs FRS*, 297
Wealth at death £31,629: probate, 21 Sept 1982, *CGPLA Eng. & Wales*

Koehler, George Frederick (1758–1800), army officer, was born on 14 January 1758, the only child of George Frederick Koehler (1732–1763), a bombardier in the Royal Artillery and a native of Frankfurt am Main, Germany, who had emigrated to England in 1753, and his English wife, Elizabeth (Betty) Dean, *née* Haley (d. 1793). In 1758 Koehler senior was given a Bengal cadetship and sailed to India; he was promoted second lieutenant, Bengal artillery, in October 1761 and was killed on 12 August 1763 at the battle of Gheria. The infant Koehler was baptized at Woolwich, Kent, on 7 May 1758. He was raised on the proceeds of the £2000 (presumably from loot or trade) which his father had left to him and his mother and attended the Royal Military Academy, Woolwich, as a private student. In his fortifications examination on 15 December 1779 he submitted 'the completest series of drawings ever produced at the Academy' (*Records of the Royal Military Academy*, 26), and as a consequence was offered, on 20 January 1780, a second lieutenantcy in the Royal Artillery.

In 1781 Koehler sailed with Admiral Darby's relief fleet to the besieged fortress of Gibraltar. There he soon gained the confidence of the governor, General George Augustus Eliott, who appointed him his aide-de-camp and assistant engineer. After the famous sortie against the Spanish lines of 26–7 November 1781, Eliott presented Koehler with his own sword in recognition of his conduct. Koehler also demonstrated his technical expertise by inventing a gun carriage which allowed the gun barrel to be depressed to an angle of 70°, which enabled accurate counter-battery fire against the Franco-Spanish siege cannon, sited far below the Rock. At the first trial, on 15 February 1782, twenty-eight shots out of thirty fired took effect in one traverse of the San Carlos battery, at a distance of 1400 yards. Koehler's accomplished drawings of the siege were also well regarded: Eliott sent some to London with his dispatches; others were later published as engravings by T. Malton.

Once the defence of Gibraltar had been brought to a successful conclusion, Koehler used a twelve-month passport granted him by Eliott and travelled in Italy and Germany, returning to England in October 1784. His close connection with General Eliott (later Lord Heathfield) continued in the following years. In 1789 Koehler accompanied him on a tour of Germany and the Low Countries. When the Brabant rebellion broke out soon after, Heathfield's warm endorsement of Koehler's abilities was remembered, and in December 1789 Count Dillon, acting for the Belgian Congress, asked Koehler (although still only a first lieutenant) to be colonel commandant of its artillery. In the event, he also received the rank of major-general. It was a measure of his creditable performance as a commander of horse and foot as well as of artillery that when, in November 1790, the Austrians crossed the Meuse and approached Brussels, the congress, desperate to stave off defeat, appointed Koehler general commandant of its entire army. But by then the situation was irretrievable and, after the fall of the Belgian republic, Koehler retired to England.

In the summer of 1791, in the wake of the Ochakov crisis, the British government sent Koehler to survey the defences of European Turkey. He remained there two years. On his return he was offered the post of deputy quartermaster-general at Toulon (then occupied by the British at the invitation of the Toulon anti-Jacobins), which entailed his promotion from brevet captain to brevet major (October 1793). Koehler, however, arrived only in time to play a role in the port's evacuation, commanding the artillery at Fort La Malgère so as to cover the British withdrawal and then spiking the guns. He was sent afterwards to Corsica with Sir Gilbert Elliot and Lieutenant-Colonel John Moore to reconnoitre the French defences (14–20 January 1794). Their report favoured a British attack, and Koehler remained ashore to liaise with

General Paoli, the Corsican resistance leader, pending the fleet's arrival. In the operations which followed, Koehler played his part in the capture of San Fiorenzo but became disillusioned by the indecision of his commanders before Bastia, the chief French garrison. At the end of March 1794, claiming pressing personal affairs, he returned to England. He married, on 30 June 1794, Ann Pass (1771–1800), of St Marylebone, Westminster. They set up home at Etchilhampton, near Devizes, Wiltshire.

Koehler's unscheduled return to England was not approved by the military authorities. He was even rebuked by his patron, the master-general of the ordnance, the duke of Richmond. Koehler's dissatisfaction increased. Although now a captain-lieutenant of artillery and (since 12 April 1794) a brevet lieutenant-colonel, he felt undervalued. In early 1795 he would have accepted an offer to enter the Turkish service had not the government, worried by the possibility of an adverse Russian reaction, expressed its reservations. For the next three years he occupied staff positions at home as assistant quartermaster-general of the southern and north-eastern districts successively. He was promoted captain of artillery on 9 December 1796.

Koehler's chance of accelerated advancement came when, in 1798, Napoleon Bonaparte invaded Egypt and the British government, anxious to help the Turks expel the French, decided to send a military mission, including artillery, stores, and 100 personnel, to Constantinople. With his knowledge of Turkey, Koehler was an obvious choice to take command. Having stipulated that, to reflect his status, he must have the local and temporary rank of brigadier-general (8 November 1798), the permanent rank of colonel (gazetted 1 January 1800), and remuneration of £1000 per annum, Koehler left England with the officers of his party in December 1798 and travelled overland to Constantinople, where he arrived in March 1799. Once he was there the Turks asked him to inspect the defences of the Dardanelles. When, in September, they tried to get him to repeat the exercise, Koehler realized that the Turks were not keen to have him join their army in Syria. Indeed, rather than have Koehler to hand urging them to fight, the Turks preferred to negotiate a French withdrawal from Egypt, a policy in which Britain's acting minister at Constantinople, Spencer Smith, and his brother Commodore Sidney Smith, the hero of Acre, were actively colluding. To this end both brothers intrigued against Koehler. The arrival in November of the new ambassador, Lord Elgin, eventually secured permission for Koehler to go to the Turkish army at Jaffa; but Elgin implied that Koehler, whose exaggerated pretensions irritated his hosts, had contributed to his own difficulties: 'General Koehler … claims to himself the respect paid to a Bonaparte or a Suvorov' (*Fortescue MSS*, 6.91).

Koehler arrived at Jaffa in July 1800, after undertaking a mission to Cyprus. As he discovered, the battleworthiness of the Turkish army left much to be desired: he believed 2000 European troops to be the match of 15,000 Turks. In October, during a respite from his duties, Koehler and his wife, who had accompanied him to the East, visited Jerusalem. Shortly after their return, however, there was an outbreak of plague in the Turkish camp at Jaffa. First his wife died, and then, fifteen days later, on 29 December 1800, Koehler himself succumbed. He was buried at Jaffa the next day.

Koehler died intestate and with no known relatives. His property, valued at £7842 8s. 4d., went to the crown. In 1820 there began the protracted case of *Bauer v. Mitford*, by which Koehler's German relatives attempted to establish their kinship. The proceedings passed to the court of chancery, and in 1859 judgment was delivered in the family's favour. Following the rejection of the crown's appeal by the House of Lords on 24 July 1861, the original value of Koehler's estate, together with £14,429 12s. 6d. interest, was paid to the descendants of Koehler's paternal uncles.

ALASTAIR W. MASSIE

Sources *Bauer v. Mitford*, including Koehler's papers, 1766–1800, PRO, Treasury Solicitor (TS) 11/1083–1115 · Foreign Office MSS, Turkey, 1791, 1798–1800, PRO, FO 78/12A, 25–27 · *The diary of Sir John Moore*, ed. J. F. Maurice, 2 vols. (1904) · *The manuscripts of J. B. Fortescue*, 10 vols., HMC, 30 (1892–1927), vols. 4–6 · E. Ingram, *Commitment to empire* (1981) · W. Wittman, *Travels in Turkey, Asia-Minor, Syria, and across the desert in Egypt, during the years 1799–1801* (1803) · J. Drinkwater, *A history of the late siege of Gibraltar*, 2nd edn (1786) · P. Mackesy, *British victory in Egypt, 1801: the end of Napoleon's conquest* (1995) · H. D. Buchanan-Dunlop, *Records of the Royal Military Academy, 1741–1892*, 2nd edn (1892) · F. Duncan, ed., *History of the royal regiment of artillery*, 2nd edn, 2 vols. (1874) · E. Preston, *Unclaimed money* (1878) · V. C. P. Hodson, *List of officers of the Bengal army, 1758–1834*, 2 (1928)
Archives priv. coll., corresp. with Lord Elgin · PRO, Treasury Solicitor (TS) 11/1083–1115
Likenesses T. Malton, double portrait, engraving, 1782 (with General Eliott; after G. F. Koehler), repro. in T. H. McGuffie, *The siege of Gibraltar* (1965) · J. Trumbull, group portrait (*The siege of Gibraltar*), Cincinnati Art Museum
Wealth at death £7842 8s. 4d.: Preston, *Unclaimed money*, 21

Koenig [*married name* Tuckman], **Ghisha** (1921–1993), sculptor, was born on 8 December 1921 at 81 St Mark's Road, Kensington, London, the younger of the two children of (Mendel) Leo Koenig (1898–1970), art critic and writer, and his wife, Fanny Hildebrand (*fl.* 1900–1940), formerly a Yiddish actress. The family was Jewish and culturally conscious, though not observant. Koenig adopted her father's strong left-wing politics—'The Zionists called him a Communist and the Communists called him a Zionist' (private information)—and his immersion in the arts. Poverty notwithstanding, the family home was the centre of a circle of Jewish artists and writers, including the painters Josef Herman and David Bomberg, who became role models for Koenig. She was educated at Hendon county grammar school where, perhaps because of her lifelong ill health, caused by asthma, she failed to shine academically.

In 1939, defying advice from her school, Koenig won a scholarship to study sculpture at Hornsey College of Art. She joined the Auxiliary Territorial Service in 1942 and was posted to Leeds. She was transferred to London in 1944 to edit the army's *London Educational Bulletin*, which involved visiting factories to investigate work opportunities, a formative experience for her subsequent career.

Ghisha Koenig (1921–1993), by unknown photographer, 1956 [in her studio at St Mary Cray]

Determined to study with Henry Moore, she attended Chelsea School of Art from 1946 to 1948, before moving to the Slade School of Fine Art for a year. Moore discouraged her, as a woman, from practising sculpture—which, given her obstinacy, was probably an important stimulus. On 5 January 1951 she married Emanuel (Manny) Tuckman (b. 1921/2), medical doctor and son of Lewis Tuckman, company director. Tuckman's practice took them to Kent, where he worked on a new housing estate in St Paul's Cray. They moved to Sidcup in 1967 and, on his retirement in 1986, to north London, where Koenig worked in the studio previously owned by the sculptor Naum Gabo.

A solitary worker, Koenig never used assistants but relied on Tuckman for much essential help, from lifting to casting and burnishing. She was a perfectionist, obsessively devoted to her work, which she recorded meticulously. Tuckman's support enabled her to work singlemindedly even after their daughter, Sarah, was born in 1955. The working process that Koenig initiated in 1951 was precisely attuned both to the circumstances of her life and to her political orientation. Both Koenig and Tuckman were consistently left-wing politically; if not members of the Communist Party, they were for a time far from unsympathetic to it. Koenig sold the *Daily Worker* outside

University College, London. They were politically active, taking part in the first Aldermaston march in 1958, and later holding Labour Party ward meetings in their home. Koenig would spend weeks or months at a local factory with a manual labour force involved in a craft process such as paper making or button carding. She worked in at least ten such factories, the first being the vegetable parchment mills in St Mary Cray. She habitually sketched each stage of the production process, then made enlarged working drawings in the studio as the basis of her reliefs and free-standing figures. They were made in terracotta and sometimes cast in bronze. *The Machine Minders* (mixed media, 1956; Tate collection), one of her largest free-standing groups, portrayed two men working at the Coates ink factory in St Mary Cray. Koenig modelled her figures on individual workers and though she never talked to them in the factory, she would invite them to see the completed work. She was best-known for such series of reliefs as *The Tentmakers* (bronze, terracotta, 1980). Either these followed the Renaissance model of figures in a stage-like illusory space, or much of the background was omitted, so that the figures were almost free-floating.

Belying her small stature and fragility, Koenig had a strong personality, emphasized by her oversize spectacles. Insecure but driven by ambition, she could be aggressive and short-tempered, though she was highly sociable and loved parties. Close friends included the historian Eric Hobsbawm who, as jazz critic of the *New Statesman & Nation*, arranged for her to draw at a dance club in Oxford Street when she was commissioned in 1963 to make a dance trophy (*The Twisters*) for Arnold Wesker's Centre 42. She had a pronounced sense of humour and a taste for gossip, good food, and luxury items. She enjoyed theatre and travel; she and Tuckman made long trips to southern Europe and visited the United States several times.

Like many women artists of her generation, Koenig exhibited relatively little. Ferociously independent, she avoided professional groups and disliked the commercial art world, though Eric Estorick's Grosvenor Gallery, which she joined in 1963, did much to promote her work. The high point of her exhibiting career was an Arts Council retrospective at the Serpentine Gallery, London, in 1986, with a simultaneous exhibition of smaller works at Agi Katz's Boundary Gallery in north London. It was there that her memorial exhibition was held in April 1994. Virtually throughout her career, Koenig's work was unfashionable. Her small, narrative, profoundly socialist pieces defied the critical focus on very large abstract sculpture. Nevertheless the commissions, including portraits, that punctuated her career indicated that she was never entirely overlooked. Among the most memorable were *Crucifixion* (terracotta, 1961) for St John's, Earlsfield, arranged by Nevile Wallis, *The Observer*'s art critic, and the *Blind School* series (bronze, terracotta, 1985–6) made at Dalton House School for the Blind, Sevenoaks, Kent, in which she recorded the school's many activities. Her last work was a relief based on children at a local sports centre in north London. She died of chronic bronchitis and emphysema on 15 October 1993 at University College Hospital, Camden, London, and was cremated at Golders Green. She was survived by her husband and daughter.

MARGARET GARLAKE

Sources *Ghisha Koenig: sculpture, 1968–74* (1974) [exhibition catalogue, Bedford House Gallery, London, 1974] · *Ghisha Koenig: sculpture, 1968-86* (1986) [exhibition catalogue, Serpentine Gallery, London, 17 May – 15 June, 1986] · *The Independent* (19 Oct 1993) · *The Tate Gallery, 1986–88: illustrated catalogue of acquisitions* (1996), 395–8 · N. Wallis, 'Church as patron', *The Spectator* (19 April 1976) · A. Jones, 'Koenig, Ghisha', *Dictionary of women artists*, ed. D. Gaze (1997), 793–5 · b. cert. · m. cert. · d. cert. · private information (2004) [Emanuel Tuckman]
Archives Henry Moore Institute, Leeds, sketchbooks · priv. coll., papers · Tate collection, sketchbooks
Likenesses photograph, 1956, Graves Art Gallery [*see illus.*] · photograph, repro. in *The Independent*
Wealth at death £201,652: probate, 14 Dec 1993, *CGPLA Eng. & Wales*

Koestler, Arthur (1905–1983), novelist and journalist, was born on 5 September 1905 in Budapest, Hungary, the only child of Henrik Koestler (1869–c.1940), Jewish businessman, and Adele Zeiteles (1871–1963), who came from a prosperous Jewish family in Prague. He admired his father, but had a difficult relationship with his mother which lasted until her death. He was educated at Budapest's Real Iskola but in 1919 the Koestlers fled Hungary in the wake of a right-wing coup which deposed the ruling communists, and in 1922 Koestler began studying engineering and physics at the Vienna Technische Hochschule, where he encountered Jewish nationalism.

In 1925 Koestler left the university for a kibbutz in Palestine, but soon discovered that he was temperamentally unsuited to communal life. He moved to Tel Aviv, where he began to concentrate on journalism, publishing articles in Budapest's *Pester Lloyd* and in several Zionist papers. In 1927 he was employed by the Ullstein press as their correspondent in the Middle East. Koestler's journalistic work is considered by some to contain his best writing. As his reputation as a writer grew, so too did his disenchantment with Zionism. In 1929 he abruptly left Palestine for Ullstein's Paris office, and in 1930 he moved to Berlin to take up his new position as science editor. Koestler was keenly aware of the threat posed by the increasingly powerful Nazis, and in 1931 he joined the Communist Party, partly because of its opposition to fascism but also because it occupied the space left by his loss of faith in Zionism. He was dismissed from his post, but the Communist International paid him to write about the USSR's first five-year plan. He travelled extensively through the USSR to research for the book but it was rejected by the Soviet authorities for containing several criticisms of communism.

Koestler scraped a living in Paris writing journalism and guidebooks, and on 22 June 1935 he married Dorothea Ascher, a Communist Party worker. In the following year he was employed by the anti-Franco *News Chronicle* to go to Spain as a special correspondent. But in 1937 he was captured by Franco's troops and imprisoned in Malaga and Seville from February to June, under daily threat of execution. Dorothea's tireless efforts to save him finally persuaded the British government to intervene, but the experience marked him profoundly.

Upon his release Koestler travelled to England, where Victor Gollancz commissioned him to write a book about his experiences. *Spanish Testament* was published to considerable acclaim in 1937. Although his first language was Hungarian, he wrote in German and French, and then almost exclusively in English from 1940. In 1938 Koestler left the Communist Party, appalled at Stalin's show trials and at what he had observed in republican Spain. In 1939 he published his first novel, *The Gladiators* (translated from the German), which uses the history of Spartacus as an allegory for the corruption of Russian socialism by Stalinism. In September of that year Koestler was arrested in France, wrongly assumed to be a security risk, and was interned as a political prisoner in Le Vernet concentration camp until January 1940. His experiences here formed the basis of *Scum of the Earth* (1941), his first book written in English. On his release he joined the French Foreign Legion, but deserted in 1941 and returned to England via Lisbon. By this time his second novel had been published and he became internationally famous. Clearly influenced by his experiences in the condemned cells in Spain, *Darkness at Noon* (1940) describes the arrest and imprisonment of Rubashov, one of the early Bolsheviks, during the purges of 1936. During his numerous interrogations Rubashov reviews his career and his unthinking allegiance to communism. At the end of the novel, as he is beginning to doubt the party, he is shot in the back of the head. The novel was an immediate critical as well as commercial success. The novel became 'a weapon in the arsenal of the Cold war' (Cesarani, 176), and remains one of the best-known and most widely read political novels of the twentieth century.

Koestler joined the British army in 1941, but the discipline of the Pioneer Corps was irksome to him and in 1942 he was formally discharged. He began working for the Ministry of Information film unit and for the BBC, while beginning his third novel, *Arrival and Departure* (1943). In 1944 Koestler met Mamaine Paget (1916–1954), who became his second wife on 15 April 1950. By the end of the war Koestler's Zionism was revivified and for many years he was a highly vocal advocate of the Jewish national cause. He returned to Palestine in 1945 with the aim of writing a book about that cause, published as *Thieves in the Night* (1946). It was well received in England and was enormously successful in America; Koestler visited the United States in 1948, eventually buying a house in Pennsylvania. Throughout his life Koestler was a compulsive purchaser of properties; heedless of practicalities, he bought homes in Britain, France, and Austria.

In 1948 Koestler became a British citizen, and in 1951 he published his fourth novel, *The Age of Longing*. From 1952 to 1955 he worked on his two most celebrated volumes of autobiography: *Arrow in the Blue* (1952) and *The Invisible Writing* (1954). Lucid, analytical, yet emotional, Koestler depicts himself in his autobiographical writings as both a unique human being and a representative, universal voice of the twentieth century. From the late 1950s Koestler wrote extensively on science; just as communism replaced Zionism in his youth, now, in his later years, politics was being replaced by science. *The Sleepwalkers* (1959), for example, was an examination of Renaissance science, arguing rather for the aesthetic nature of the mental processes suggested by Copernicus's and Kepler's astronomical discoveries.

On 8 January 1965 Koestler married Cynthia Jefferies, *née* Paterson (1927/8–1983), who had been his secretary and occasional lover since 1948. Although Koestler had no children with any of his wives, he had a daughter, Christine (*b.* 1955), with Janine Graetez. Koestler was short, handsome, and energetic, and attractive to women. He was, however, sexually predatory all his life—among other affairs he was the co-respondent named in Bertrand Russell's divorce from his third wife, Patricia Spence—and he was capable of treating women brutally. There are first-hand accounts of his violence towards women in David Cesarani's controversial biography, which seriously damaged Koestler's reputation when it was published in 1998. A chain-smoker and heavy drinker, he could be arrogant, dogmatic, and violent, but he was financially generous, especially to continental intellectuals and refugees, and he was considered a welcoming host, and very lively, often too lively, company.

In 1968 Koestler received the Sonning prize from the University of Copenhagen, and an honorary doctorate from Queen's University, Ontario. In 1972 he was appointed CBE, and in 1974 a companion of the Royal Society of Literature. He became increasingly interested in para-science and parapsychology, was particularly intrigued by extra-sensory perception and psychokinesis, and wrote extensively about these subjects in *The Ghost in the Machine* (1967), *The Case of the Midwife Toad* (1971), and *The Call Girls* (1972), which were all very popular with the general reading public, particularly the young, but were savagely derided by the scientific establishment. In 1976 Koestler was diagnosed as having Parkinson's disease and his health deteriorated over the next seven years, during which he also succumbed to terminal leukaemia. On 3 March 1983 Koestler and Cynthia were found dead in their flat at 8 Montpelier Square, Kensington, London. They had killed themselves with a mixture of tuinal and alcohol. The double funeral was held at Mortlake crematorium on 11 March 1983, and a memorial service took place at the Royal Academy of Arts several weeks later. Koestler and Cynthia left bequests which totalled almost £1 million to further the study of parapsychology and a chair was established at Edinburgh University for this purpose.

KEVIN McCARRON

Sources D. Cesarani, *Arthur Koestler: the homeless mind* (1998) • I. Hamilton, *Koestler* (1982) • A. Koestler, *Spanish testament* (1937) • A. Koestler, *Arrow in the blue* (1952) • A. Koestler, *The invisible writing* (1954) • M. Koestler, *Living with Koestler* (1985) • d. cert.
Archives BL, corresp. relating to abolition of capital punishment, Add. MSS 56455A–56459B, *passim* • Central Zionist Archive, Jerusalem • U. Edin. L., corresp. and papers | BL, corresp. with Society of Authors, Add. MS 63280 • Bodl. Oxf., corresp. with Sir Alister Hardy • ICL, archives, corresp. with Dennis Gabor • JRL, letters to the *Manchester Guardian* • U. Warwick Mod. RC, corresp. with Victor Gollancz • UCL, corresp. with George Orwell | SOUND BL NSA, documentary recordings • BL NSA, performance recordings
Likenesses bronze bust, U. Edin. • photographs, Hult. Arch.
Wealth at death £325,291: probate, 9 June 1983, *CGPLA Eng. & Wales* • approx. £1,000,000: Cesarani, *Arthur Koestler*

Koguetagechton. *See* White Eyes (*d.* 1778).

Koizumi, Gunji (1885–1965), judo master and oriental art expert, was born into a Buddhist family on 8 July 1885 in Komatsuka Oaza, Takadamura (later Edosakimachi), Inashiki Gun, Ibaraki province, Japan, a village about 20 miles north of Tokyo. He was the second son of Shukichi Koizumi (1853–1903), a tenant farmer, and his wife, Katsu (1855–1920). Koizumi's elder brother was Chiyokichi (1879–1923) and the youngest of the family was his sister Iku (*b.* 1888); another sister died in infancy.

After eight or nine years' schooling Koizumi left home in July 1900 for Tokyo where he enrolled in a government-subsidized school for telegraphists. After training he spent two years at the central post office; then, realizing the nature of a governmental bureaucracy still hidebound with feudalistic traditions, he sought a fresh career in an occupation offering more freedom of spirit. He decided to venture into the new electricity industry, intending first to study the subject in America. Leaving Japan in 1903 he worked his passage from port to port, landing in north Wales in May 1906. In August 1906 he reached London, where ju-jitsu was then very popular; stage shows were put on and there were two authentic schools run by Japanese, in one of which he became an instructor while saving for the final trip to America. This was the last time he taught professionally. Thereafter he was a strict amateur.

In May 1907 Koizumi reached America, where he spent three years studying and working with electricity, returning to London in time for the Anglo-Japanese exhibition of 1910. In January 1911 he started a business as an electrical fittings supplier but he had insufficient capital to be successful. In 1912 he opened a lacquerware studio, an occupation more in keeping with his aesthetic inclination. The business thrived and he counted among his clientele Queen Mary and Lord Kitchener. On 6 April 1912 he married Ida Celine Winstanley (1876–1947). By 1913 the couple were living at 83 Ebury Street, Victoria, above the studio. There was one daughter, Hana (*b.* 1920). In 1935 they moved to 15 Eccleston Street. Koizumi published a book, *Lacquer Work* (1923), and during 1924 and 1925 he was adviser to the Victoria and Albert Museum in revising the catalogue of Japanese and Chinese lacquer.

Koizumi continued his avid interest in the ancient fighting arts of his homeland, with a strong commitment to their spiritual and moral training aspects. Late in 1917 he organized the Budokwai (Way of Knighthood Society), an institute for the study of the martial arts and their related cultural and underlying philosophy. The Budokwai, which was at Koizumi's insistence a democratic body run and owned by its members, opened at 15 Lower Grosvenor Place, Victoria, on 26 January 1918. One of the earliest judo societies to be founded outside Japan—the Seattle (*c.*1903) and Cambridge University (1906) clubs predated it—the Budokwai played a major part in the spread of judo in Britain, providing instructors for many of the clubs which subsequently came into existence, often having been founded by Budokwai members. Demonstrations by the Budokwai were televised in 1938. Among the members of the society were Christmas Humphreys, Ernest Marples, and Enid Russell-Smith. Possessed of a strong social conscience, Koizumi also organized in 1919 a mutual-aid society for Japanese nationals in England (who numbered about 1600 in the mid-1930s, mainly living in London and Newcastle).

In July 1948 Koizumi convened two meetings in London; at one the British Judo Association was formed, and the other resulted in the European Judo Union to standardize judo rules and procedures. A further meeting, in 1951 in a Soho restaurant, created the International Judo Federation. In 1962 his efforts were recognized by the Kodokan, the headquarters of judo in Tokyo, with the award of 8th dan, the grade of a past master.

Koizumi wrote extensively, publishing over 100 articles in the *Budokwai Quarterly Bulletin* and numerous pamphlets as well as articles for foreign journals. His major work was *My Study of Judo* (1960). He has been credited with transforming the practice of judo in Britain from 'a collection of surprising tricks' to a method of character training whose technique was studied on a scientific basis (Leggett). He disliked the distortion of judo into a sport, believing that championships led to medal hunting and the intrusion of money, and always insisted that the purpose of contests was training and nothing more.

Koizumi was a man of wisdom, impeccable integrity, great courage, and iron determination. His personal charm included a keen, very English sense of humour. He laughed often and others usually joined in. He could be unexpectedly hard: for instance, when he heard that an old friend had been afraid of dying he burst out, 'The coward! Nobody should be afraid of dying' (personal knowledge). Lightly built and slightly over 5 foot 6 inches tall, he had a distinctive cat-like gait, the ball of his foot going down first. He invariably wore a black suit with cream shirt and black bow-tie, except for his country walk on Sundays when he adopted the garb of a gamekeeper—a Norfolk jacket with breeches buckled just below the knees and long, heavy, knee-length stockings.

In old age Koizumi moved to 1 Carmalt Gardens, in Putney, and there on the night of 15 April 1965, increasingly infirm and feeling he had done all he could for humanity, he brought his life to an end. A Japanese tradition is that if a man has completed his service to the world and can do no more, he is permitted to cut himself off radically, after clearing up all his affairs. It is held that only a man of pure heart can do this. He was cremated at Putney Vale cemetery, following a Christian service, and his ashes were interred in his wife's grave. Thousands in Britain and abroad mourned his death. Two days before he died he was asked what he would like to happen and answered: 'To see people thinking for themselves and not being led like sheep' (personal knowledge). On Chelsea Embankment, a few yards from Sir Thomas More's statue, a Japanese cherry tree was planted, with a plaque at its foot naming the father of British judo: Gunji Koizumi.

RICHARD BOWEN

Sources T. Leggett, *The Times* (20 April 1965) • priv. coll., archive on the history of judo in Britain • R. Bowen, 'A history of British judo' [unpubd typescript in author's possession] • personal knowledge (2004) • H. Cortazzi, ed., *Britain and Japan: biographical portraits*, 4 (2002) • R. Bowen, 'Origins of the British Judo Association, the European Judo Union, and the International Judo Federation', *Journal of Asian Martial Arts*, 8/3 (1999), 43–53 • K. Itoh, *The Japanese community in pre-war Britain: from integration to disintegration* (2001) • d. cert.
Likenesses oils, Budokwai, South Kensington, London • photographs, priv. coll.
Wealth at death £288: probate, 27 May 1966, *CGPLA Eng. & Wales*

Kokoschka, Oskar (1886–1980), artist and writer, was born on 1 March 1886 at Pöchlarn, a small town on the River Danube about 60 miles west of Vienna, the second of four children of Gustav Josef Kokoschka (1840–1923), originally from a Prague family of goldsmiths but then working as a jewellery salesman, and Maria Romana Loidl (1861–1934), the daughter of a forester from near Hollenstein in the Lower Austrian Alps. In 1887 the family settled in Vienna where Kokoschka was educated at the Währinger Staatsrealschule (secondary school) in the eighteenth district. In 1904 he was awarded a state scholarship to the Kunstgewerbeschule (school of applied arts). At the start of his third year there, in October 1906, he entered the faculty of painting to study under Carl Otto Czeschka, who also taught him printmaking. In the following year, helped by Czeschka's successor, Berthold Löffler, he became an associate of the Wiener Werkstätte (WW), the geometrizing design workshops founded by the architect Josef Hoffmann and the painter Koloman Moser. In 1908 Kokoschka held evening classes at the Kunstgewerbeschule, where he taught the practice of drawing naked figures in motion, with circus children and street urchins as his models.

Early work Kokoschka's early work, which is predominantly graphic (for example, posters, postcards, *ex libris* designs), shows the influence of Gustav Klimt and the mannered art of the Vienna Secession. But in *Die träumenden Knaben* ('The Dreaming Youths'), a 'fairy tale' with text and images by Kokoschka, published by the WW in 1908, the Secessionist fondness for sinuous ornament gives way to harsh rhythms and a more expressionist figure style. Kokoschka's complete break with Secessionist decoration occurred in 1909 with his poster for the international Kunstschau (art show) in Vienna, where his proto-expressionist drama *Mörder, Hoffnung der Frauen* ('Murderer, hope of women') was first performed to a public more amused than scandalized. The poster depicts a union between a man and a woman whose anguished faces and contorted bodies reflect the theme of explicit sexual conflict in the play. At the Kunstschau itself Kokoschka was impressed by the paintings of Munch and Van Gogh; he was also familiar with the morbid portraits of the Austrian artist Anton Romako (1832–1889). Encouraged and assisted financially by the radical architect Adolf

Oskar Kokoschka (1886–1980), self-portrait, 1937 [*Portrait of a 'Degenerate Artist'*]

Loos, he broke from the WW, left the Kunstgewerbeschule, and, over the next two years (1909–11), painted an astonishing series of portraits which, in their merciless exposure of the nervous inner life of his sitters, are an important contribution to expressionism as well as to the history of modern art.

These portraits are characterized by a complete indifference to notions of taste and style, which led critics to complain of their ugliness. Isolated against anonymous backgrounds, Kokoschka's subjects (who included Loos, the satirist Karl Kraus, and the poet Peter Altenberg) appear alienated and even ill. In 1910, while living in Berlin, Kokoschka drew a number of heads for Herwarth Walden's expressionist periodical *Der Sturm*, in which an incisive network of marks and lines suggests wounds or nervous tics: however diseased-looking, his sitters seem to vibrate with life.

The first substantial exhibition of Kokoschka's work took place at Paul Cassirer's gallery in Berlin in June 1910. His first museum show was held in August of the same year at the Folkwang Museum, Hagen, which was also the first public collection to buy a painting of Kokoschka's. He had returned to Vienna by 1911, where his style gradually became more sophisticated: forms are now fully modelled, greater attention is paid to colour and light (and their relationship), and there is a hint of cubist fragmentation. Finally, an engagement with old master painting—El Greco, Austrian baroque, but especially Venetian art—helped liberate his brushwork and broaden his vision to include religious narratives and allegorical themes. The large symbolic paintings of 1913–14, in which Kokoschka celebrated his passionate love for Alma Mahler (widow of the composer Gustav Mahler) or foretold the end of their turbulent affair, combine painterly fluency with sustained emotional intensity. Kokoschka also immortalized the relationship in two magisterial lithographic cycles, *Bach-Kantate* ('Bach cantata') and *Der gefesselte Kolumbus* ('Columbus in chains'), both published in Berlin in 1916. The affair ended in early 1915 but its impact was to be felt in his art for several more years—most notoriously in the life-size articulated doll that he had constructed in Alma's likeness and which he used as the model for his painting *Woman in Blue* (1919; Staatsgalerie, Stuttgart) and related studies.

The war years A few months after the outbreak of the First World War, Kokoschka enlisted in a smart cavalry regiment, the 15th Imperial–Royal regiment of dragoons, and in the summer of 1915 was seriously wounded in action on the Russian front. Discharged from hospital in February 1916 he served briefly as a liaison officer for war artists on the Isonzo (Slovenian–Italian) front; here he produced pastel drawings of gun batteries, trenches, and a church damaged by shellfire which are remarkable for their factual accuracy. He was again hospitalized, this time suffering from shell-shock, but late in 1916 managed to travel to Germany, first to Berlin, where he signed a contract with Cassirer, and eventually to convalesce in Dresden, where he became friendly with a crowd of pacifists, mainly expressionist actors, playwrights, and poets, who feature in two important group portraits of this period, *The Exiles* and *The Friends*. At the same time (1917) the Zürich Dada artists performed his play *Hiob* ('Job'), the final version of which was given its première in Dresden on 3 June 1917, together with Kokoschka's *Murderer, Hope of Women* and *The Burning Bush*, in a triple production directed and designed by the author–artist.

Landscapes In 1919 Kokoschka was appointed professor of painting at the Dresden Academy. From his studio balcony, which overlooked the Elbe, or from a neighbouring roof, he painted a total of ten views (1919–23) across the wide river, with its elegant bridges, to the baroque buildings on the opposite bank. The Dresden landscapes are composed of strips and patches of pure, contrasting colour—green, blue, yellow, red—which have the luminosity of stained glass. It is the closest Kokoschka came to the saturated colours of German expressionists such as Emil Nolde.

In 1922 Kokoschka represented Germany at the Venice Biennale with the three giants of German 'impressionism', Max Liebermann, Max Slevogt, and Lovis Corinth. The following year he left Dresden; he spent the years 1924 to 1930 travelling in Italy, France, Spain, Switzerland, Holland, Ireland, England, Scotland, north Africa, and the Middle East. Landscape, and particularly cityscape, preoccupied him—he painted the first of many views of the

River Thames, a river which never ceased to fascinate him—while his output of portraiture declined. In these elevated panoramas, with their rejection of single vanishing-point perspective in favour of an 'all-over' illusionistic space, Kokoschka reveals most clearly his debt to the baroque. Kokoschka's first exhibition in Britain took place at the Leicester Galleries in London in June 1928. In 1930 he was elected a member of the Prussian Academy of Arts in Berlin. He settled in Paris for a year (autumn 1930 to autumn 1931), during which a one-man show of his work at the Galeries Georges Petit made a favourable impression; but after the dissolution of his contract with Cassirer, straitened financial circumstances forced him to return to Vienna to live with his family.

'Pictures with a political meaning' In Vienna the socialist council ('Red Vienna') commissioned Kokoschka to paint a picture for the city hall. He chose as his subject a children's home housed in a former Habsburg palace, Schloss Wilhelminenberg, a few minutes' walk from his mother's house on the western edge of the city. Kokoschka concentrated on the children themselves, playing in the palace grounds, in a deliberate allusion to Brueghel's *Children's Games* in the Kunsthistorisches Museum. Each of the games depicted by Kokoschka requires the use of a different sense—touch, sight, hearing, and so on. At the back of his mind he had the ideas of Jan Amos Comenius, the seventeenth-century Moravian theologian, pacifist, and pedagogue, who stressed the importance of developing reason through direct sense experience rather than received opinion or second-hand knowledge. Kokoschka's own belief in visual and constructive education independent of nationalist or militaristic concerns, which he outlined in essays and lectures throughout the 1930s and during the Second World War, was also inspired by Comenius. He later referred to *Vienna, View from the Wilhelminenberg* as his 'first picture with a political meaning' (Hoffmann, 197).

A few months after Hitler's accession to power in 1933, Kokoschka published an article in a prominent German newspaper defending Liebermann, who, as a Jew, had been forced under the 'Aryan paragraph' to resign from the Prussian Academy of Arts. Kokoschka's anti-Nazi credentials were impeccable. Throughout the thirties he spoke out against their cultural and educational policies, while more and more of his works in German public collections were confiscated by the Nazis. In 1937 eight of his paintings were included in the Nazi exhibition 'entartete "Kunst"' ('degenerate "art"') in Munich. His response was to paint the ironically titled *Portrait of a 'Degenerate Artist'* (priv. coll., on loan to Scottish National Gallery of Modern Art, Edinburgh), a powerfully moving statement of defiance. The following year (1938) he was himself dismissed from the Prussian Academy.

Throughout this period Kokoschka was living in Prague. In 1934 he had received permission to paint Thomas Masaryk, first president of the Czechoslovak Republic. Democratic government having collapsed in Austria, Kokoschka, now freed from family responsibilities by the death of his mother, moved to Prague (where his sister was living) in autumn 1934. He found its cosmopolitan atmosphere congenial, and immediately began the first of a series of sixteen views of the city, which he was to paint more times than any other, including London. In his allegorical portrait of Masaryk (1935–6; Museum of Art, Carnegie Institute, Pittsburgh), the aged humanist and reformer is explicitly identified with Kokoschka's hero Comenius. Masaryk, who died in 1937, helped Kokoschka obtain Czech citizenship. In Prague the artist also met the young law student Olda Palkovská (*b.* 1915), his future wife. It was she who persuaded Kokoschka to leave Prague after the Munich agreement of September 1938 had effectively delivered Czechoslovakia into Hitler's hands. The couple managed to fly to London on 18 October 1938.

By the following summer Kokoschka had more or less given up hope of recognition in England, where he was not well known in spite of being included in a large exhibition of modern German art in London in July 1938. In August 1939 he and Olda Palkovská moved to Polperro in Cornwall, where they remained until summer 1940. In Cornwall, Kokoschka painted the first of half a dozen anti-war pictures, which draw on various sources—Brueghel, baroque allegory, but above all the tradition of English caricature—to make their sarcastic point about the conduct of both axis and allied powers. Back in London he became actively involved in the various anti-Nazi émigré organizations. As a Czech citizen, he was in a good position to campaign against the internment as 'enemy aliens' of numerous refugees from Hitler whose misfortune was to have arrived bearing German or Austrian passports.

Kokoschka married Olda Palkovská in London in 1941. From 1941 until the end of the war they made regular trips to Scotland, where, in response to the natural world, he took up watercolour again—a medium he had hardly touched since the 1920s—and made his first drawings in coloured pencil. In 1942–3 he painted a portrait of the Soviet ambassador to Britain, Ivan Maysky (Tate collection), donating his fee to the Stalingrad Hospital Fund: he held markedly pro-Soviet views at the time.

Although helped by the Czech government in exile during the war, Kokoschka realized afterwards that, with the expulsion of German-speaking Czechs from Czechoslovakia, there would be no place for him in his own country. In 1946 he applied for British nationality, which was granted the following year. The large retrospective of his work that took place in Basel and Zürich in 1947 helped to establish his international reputation. In 1948 he showed at the Venice Biennale and was given an important travelling exhibition in the USA. His output of portraiture increased, his subjects including several of the architects of post-war European reconstruction, such as Theodor Körner, mayor of Vienna and later president of Austria, and the German chancellor Konrad Adenauer. His townscapes became ever more broken and atmospheric in style, the best of them evoking a cosmic or apocalyptic dimension (for example, *Berlin, 13 August 1966*; priv. coll., Berlin).

Post-war work Kokoschka's post-war work will be best remembered for the paintings and numerous lithographic cycles inspired by classical, mythological, and biblical subjects, most notably two large commissioned triptychs of the early 1950s—*The Prometheus Saga* (Kunsthalle, Hamburg) and *Thermopylae* (Coutauld Institute Galleries, London). Worried by the international vogue for abstract art after the war, Kokoschka saw his role as defending 'the artistic tradition of Europe' (Hodin). He put his ideas into practice every summer from 1953 to 1963 in the painting course that he taught, under the title 'Schule des Sehens' ('School of seeing [or looking]'), at the Salzburg International Festival.

In 1959 Kokoschka was made a CBE, and in 1963 he was given an honorary doctorate by the University of Oxford. Important retrospectives of his work were held at the Tate Gallery, London, in 1962, in Zürich (1966), and in Vienna (1971). His autobiography, *Mein Leben*, was published in 1971 (English edn, 1974). Four volumes of his writings appeared in German in the 1970s, while his letters, co-edited by Olda Kokoschka, came out after his death, also in four volumes (English selection, 1992). Kokoschka died on 22 February 1980 at Montreux in Switzerland, where he and Olda had settled in 1953, in a modest house of their own design overlooking Lake Geneva. He was buried on 27 February in the cemetery at Clarens, near Montreux.   RICHARD CALVOCORESSI

Sources R. Calvocoressi and others, eds., *Oskar Kokoschka, 1886–1980* (1986) [exhibition catalogue, Tate Gallery, London, 11 June – 10 Aug 1986, and Guggenheim Museum, New York, 9 Dec 1986 – 15 Feb 1987] · *Oskar Kokoschka: Briefe*, ed. O. Kokoschka and H. Spielmann, 4 vols. (Düsseldorf, 1984–8) · *Oskar Kokoschka: das schriftliche Werk*, ed. H. Spielmann, 4 vols. (Hamburg, 1973–6) · J. Winkler and K. Erling, *Oskar Kokoschka die Gemälde, 1906–1929* (Salzburg, 1995) · F. Whitford, *Oskar Kokoschka: a life* (1986) · O. Kokoschka, *My life* (1974) · E. Hoffmann, *Kokoschka, life and work* (1947) · E. H. Gombrich, *Kokoschka in his time* (1986) · S. Keegan, *The eye of God: a life of Oskar Kokoschka* (1999) · W. J. Schweiger, *Der junge Kokoschka: Leben und Werk, 1904–14* (Vienna, 1983) · J. P. Hodin, *Oskar Kokoschka: the artist and his time* (1966), 190–93
Archives Österreichische Galerie, Vienna, works and papers · Courtauld Inst., works and papers · Guggenheim Museum, New York, works and papers · Kunsthaus, Zürich, works and papers · Kunstmuseum, Basel, works and papers · Museum der Stadt Wien, Vienna, works and papers · Museum of Modern Art, New York, works and papers · National Gallery, Prague, works and papers · Phillips collection, Washington, DC, works and papers · Scottish National Gallery of Modern Art, Edinburgh, works and papers · Staatliche Museen, Berlin, neue Nationalgallerie, works and papers · Universität für angewandte Kunst, Vienna, Oskar Kokoschka-Zentrum, archives | BL, letters to Sydney Schiff and Violet Schiff, Add. MS 52918 · Tate collection, corresp. relating to his portrait of Ivan Maisky · Tate collection, papers relating to his life and pupils [photocopies] · V&A, corresp. with Bernhard Baer
Likenesses O. Kokoschka, self-portrait, oils, 1913, Museum of Modern Art, New York · O. Kokoschka, self-portrait, oils, 1917, Von der Heydt Museum der Stadt, Wuppertal, Germany · K. Vogel, painted plaster head, c.1924–1939, NPG · O. Kokoschka, self-portrait, lithograph, c.1935, Kunstsammlungen der Veste, Coburg, Germany · O. Kokoschka, self-portrait, oils, 1937 (*Portrait of a 'degenerate artist'*), priv. coll.; on loan to the Scottish National Gallery of Modern Art, Edinburgh [*see illus.*] · photographs, c.1955–1968, Hult. Arch. · O. Kokoschka, self-portrait, lithograph, 1965, NPG · D. Wynne, bronze head, 1965, Tate collection · O. Kokoschka, self-portrait, pencil drawing, St Louis City Art Museum, Missouri · O. Kokoschka, self-portrait, polychrome clay plaque, Museum of Fine Arts, Boston · O. Kokoschka, self-portraits, Tate collection · photographs, Universtität für angewandte Kunst, Vienna, Oskar Kokoschka-Zentrum · photographs, Österreichische Nationalbibliothek, Vienna, Bildarchiv

Kollmann, Augustus Frederic Christopher (1756–1829), music theorist, was born on 21 March 1756 in Engelbostel near Hanover, Germany, the elder son of Christoph Johann Heinrich Kollmann, the Engelbostel organist and schoolmaster, and his wife, Sophia Margaret Hachmeister. After studying in Engelbostel and at the Hanover Gymnasium, Kollmann became a pupil of and assistant to Johann Christoph Böttner, organist of the Marktkirche, the principal church in Hanover. In his autobiographical account of about 1824 Kollmann described Böttner as 'an able organist in J. S. Bach's style' (Sainsbury, 2.22). In 1779 Kollmann was admitted to the Königliches Schullehrer-Seminar, the academy in Hanover where schoolteachers were trained; his masters included Böttner. Kollmann said in his autobiographical account that he learned there his 'methodical and systematical manner of teaching, which has been very advantageous to him, not only for school instruction, but also in teaching music, and particularly in writing his musical treatises' (ibid.).

On 10 December 1781 Kollmann was appointed organist and schoolmaster of Kloster Lüne, a former convent near Lüneburg which had been converted to a protestant home for noble ladies. Although he remained there only until the following July, his loss was felt deeply, the superintendent recording that in Kollmann all didactic talents had been combined and were elevated by the best moral character.

Kollmann left because he had been selected by the Hanoverian government to fulfil George III's command that someone be found to serve as organist and schoolmaster of the Royal German Chapel in St James's Palace, London. According to the Chapel Royal cheque book Kollmann was sworn as porter of His Majesty's Lutheran Chapel on 17 September 1782. He remained at the chapel for the rest of his life, living in apartments in the friary court of the palace. Until Queen Charlotte's death in 1817, when the chapel school was closed, he spent part of four days every week teaching German and music to boys under the age of twelve. One of his scholars was the bookseller and publisher Henry George Bohn (1796–1884).

Kollmann married Christina Catherina Ruel (1745–1823) at St Luke's, Chelsea, on 26 October 1783. They had two children, **Johanna Sophia Kollmann** (1786–1849) and **George Augustus Kollmann** (1789–1845), who succeeded his father as organist of the Royal German Chapel.

Kollmann endeavoured to develop a theory that would account for every note in a musical composition. His 'particular study', he explained in his *New Theory of Musical Harmony* (1806), was 'to find out a simple method, by which every note, that is useful in music, might obtain as positive a rule, as it denotes a positive sound' (2nd edn, 1823, 4). In this theory the 'regularity' of a musical composition could be proved by showing how it could be derived from a simple musical entity by successive application of a small number of rules. Kollmann's theory was a pioneering attempt to provide what would now be called a generative theory of tonality, the 'musical language' that has governed most European music composed from about 1600 to 1900 and much composed subsequently. Exploiting the ancient analogy between music and language, Kollmann divided his theory into grammatical and rhetorical parts. His most mature statement of these parts is in the 1823 edition of the *New Theory* and the 1812 edition of his *Essay on Practical Musical Composition* respectively.

Kollmann also exemplified aspects of his theory in musical compositions with 'theoretical explanations'. Although some of these compositions curiously transcend the common practice of their time, Kollmann noted in his autobiographical account that he had applied himself principally to music's 'theoretical department' and his achievements are most significant there.

Kollmann was one of the earliest advocates of the music of J. S. Bach in England. Besides printing several Bach compositions in his treatises and, in 1806, a separate edition of Bach's 'Chromatic' fantasy, he proposed in 1799 an edition of Bach's forty-eight preludes and fugues, the *Well-Tempered Clavier*, which had not yet been published anywhere in its entirety. After Kollmann's proposal was noticed in a German music periodical by Professor Johann Nicholas Forkel of Göttingen University, three European publishers produced editions of the '48' and Kollmann abandoned his plan. However, he assisted Samuel Wesley in 1808–10 with information about Bach and lent a manuscript of the '48' to Wesley and Charles Frederick Horn when they were preparing their edition of this work. Kollmann translated excerpts from Forkel's biography of Bach in his 1812 magazine the *Quarterly Musical Register*.

Kollmann died, probably in his apartments at St James's Palace, on 19 April 1829. His funeral on 27 April proceeded to St Mary's German Lutheran Church at the Savoy, where he was buried in the same vault as his wife. The funeral service, which included one of Kollmann's own hymns, was read by Frederick William Blomberg, chaplain to the royal household.

George Kollmann was born in London on 30 January 1789, probably at St James's Palace. He made his début performing his father's piano concerto in London in 1804. He designed and manufactured a novel pianoforte featuring down-striking action, for which he received a patent in 1825. His keyboard skills, shown particularly in a series of 'grand concerts' demonstrating this invention in 1838–9, received critical acclaim, but he was declared bankrupt in 1840. He also received patents in 1836 and 1839 for improvements in railways and locomotive carriages. Despite various efforts these inventions were never adopted. He died on 19 March 1845 at St James's Palace, having been suffering from kidney disease following a spinal injury, and was buried at St Mary's German Lutheran Church at the Savoy.

Johanna Kollmann was born on 20 July 1786, probably at St James's Palace, and first appeared publicly as a singer in 1806. She assisted her brother in his pianoforte business and succeeded him as organist of the Royal German Chapel. She died at St James's Palace on 11 May 1849 and was buried at St Mary's German Lutheran Church at the Savoy on 21 May. MICHAEL KASSLER

Sources M. Kassler, 'Kollmann', *New Grove* · A. F. C. Kollmann, autobiographical letter to the proprietors of the *Dictionary of musicians*, Northwestern University, USA [printed in edited form in [J. S. Sainsbury], *A dictionary of musicians from the earliest ages to the present time*(1824)] · [J. S. Sainsbury], ed., *A dictionary of musicians*, 2 vols. (1824) [incl. Kollmann's autobiographical letter] · 'The funeral of the late A. F. C. Kollmann, esq.', *Morning Post* (4 May 1829), 3 · registers of Kloster Lüne, Kloster Lüne, near Lüneburg · registers of Royal German Chapel, St James's Palace, London, PRO, RG 4/4569 · new cheque book of the Chapel Royal, Archive of the Chapel Royal, St James's Palace · tombstones, Savoy cemetery, Colney Hatch, Middlesex [A. F. C. Kollmann, G. A. Kollmann, J. S. Kollmann] · parish archives, Engelbostel, Germany
Archives BL, corresp. with J. W. Callcott, Add. MSS 27674, 27688–27689, 30022
Likenesses E. Kendrick, watercolour (J. S. Kollmann) · J. Kendrick, bust
Wealth at death £600

Kollmann, George Augustus (1789–1845). *See under* Kollmann, Augustus Frederic Christopher (1756–1829).

Kollmann, Johanna Sophia (1786–1849). *See under* Kollmann, Augustus Frederic Christopher (1756–1829).

Kolnai, Aurel Thomas (1900–1973), philosopher, was born on 5 December 1900 in Budapest, Hungary, the second son of Ármin Stein (*b.* 1858), a savings bank director, and his wife, Valéria Glück (*b.* 1871), both Liberal Jews. Kolnai completed his secondary education (1910–18) with distinction at the Lutheran Obergymnasium, one of the best schools in Budapest, though his love of England, and his support of the allied cause in the First World War, created difficulties with the staff. His studies at Budapest University (1918–19) were interrupted by the bourgeois and Bolshevik revolutions, and in 1920 he emigrated to Vienna, where he tried to make a living as a writer. Despite the encouragement of Oscar Jászi, exiled leader of the Hungarian liberals, and his early success with *Psychoanalyse und Soziologie* (1920), he could not support himself. His father made him take a business course, but then in 1922 allowed him to enrol at Vienna University.

In the years from 1918 to 1926 Kolnai abandoned his youthful positivism, and then the 'psychoanalytic worldview'. He interpreted the evolution of Hungarian politics as a warning against any form of doctrinaire leftist or rightist government. His discovery of the writings of G. K. Chesterton and Max Scheler helped him to find his own distinctive and subtle 'common-sense' voice in philosophy. They also led him to embrace the Roman Catholic faith. On 10 July 1926 Kolnai was awarded his doctorate *summa cum laude* and on the same day he was baptized. His dissertation, *Der ethische Wert und die Wirklichkeit*, was published by Herder in 1927. This systematic exploration of the constraints of reality on moral value constitutes a powerful attack on 'abstract' ethical theory. In its second, anti-Utopian, chapter it also anticipates Karl Popper's theory of piecemeal social engineering.

Ethics, in a broad sense, was always the centre of Kolnai's philosophical interest. In 1930 he published *Sexualethik*, a work of exceptional range and originality. Among other themes, it pointed to the indispensability to the human psyche of notions of purity and defilement. The year before, Husserl's phenomenological yearbook had contained Kolnai's long essay *Der Ekel* ('Disgust'). But his strongly ethical view of politics made it inevitable that contemporary political developments would distract him from strictly academic philosophy. He had little hope of a university post, moreover, and needed to try and support himself by journalism.

By the beginning of the thirties Kolnai seems to have been the only prominent Catholic journalist in Austria still championing democracy and the Christian-liberal heritage of the west. This was an enduring strand of his thought. It led in due course to *The War Against the West* (1938), a monumental critique of Nazi ideology quoted in a debate in the House of Lords at the time of Munich. In Kolnai's view, Nazism was not an inexplicable efflorescence of unfathomable evil, but the result of a pathological overemphasis on some human values at the expense of others. Much of the work was written in the Vienna cafés frequented by the local Nazis.

During 1936 Kolnai realized that he had no future in Austria, so he came to England in 1937, and then spent the next two and a half years in France, with an interlude in Switzerland and two spells of internment. This long period of indecision and wretched health was relieved by his marriage on 19 February 1940 to Elisabeth Gémes (1906–1982) and their eventual escape, late in 1940, to New York. He also completed an unpublished anti-pacifist book, in which he argued that absolute non-violence precludes moral responsibility.

The Kolnais acknowledged the 'unparalleled benevolence' of America, thanks to which they were able to live in decent poverty, but they felt constantly at war with the American way of life. Salvation came in 1945, when Kolnai was appointed to the Catholic Laval University in Canada to teach the history of philosophy. His main works in political philosophy, many of them dating from this period (see A. Kolnai, *Privilege and Liberty and Other Essays in Political Philosophy*, ed. D. J. Mahoney, 1999), owed much to his American experiences, as did the anti-communist writings which followed, notably *Errores del anticomunismo* (1952). Among the untimely themes of this work was the affinity that Kolnai claimed existed between liberal democracy and communism.

Kolnai arrived in Quebec in full knowledge of the 'privileged status' accorded to Thomism in Catholic universities. But as the cold war unfolded and Thomism was increasingly emphasized at Laval, his deeply ingrained tendency to play the 'anarchical heretic' gradually turned to implacable hostility. In 1955 he obtained a grant from the Nuffield foundation in England to study the idea of Utopia, and left Quebec to settle in London. He collated a mass of material and published various preliminary studies, but could not finish the major work. The completed chapters have appeared posthumously in *The Utopian Mind and other Papers* (ed. F. Dunlop, 1995). The theme of Utopia lies at the heart of Kolnai's thinking. His chief claim is that 'the utopian perversion' does a disservice to the aboriginal human impulse to conceive ideals, because it constantly confuses imperfection with evil. In so doing, it 'will operate both ways: attack imperfection as an intolerable evil, and justify evil as a "transitory" and "inevitable" means to the realization of the ideal', even though the perfect 'reality' which is to replace the imperfect cannot even be thought or imagined through (*Utopian Mind*, 113). The most important thing, Kolnai claimed, is that human idealism should come to terms with imperfection and engage in projects to improve an existing order. Apart from their application to totalitarianism, Kolnai used his analyses to illuminate other questions, such as those of national identity and moral theory.

These early years in England, when the Kolnais had to live on research grants and the generosity of relatives, were profoundly disheartening. But in due course Professor H. B. Acton, of Bedford College, University of London, found means to employ Kolnai to give a course of lectures. He was then given a part-time visiting lectureship, which Acton's successors ensured that he retained until his death.

During this time Kolnai produced a remarkable series of analytical papers which drew simultaneously on the methods and insights of Husserl, Scheler, von Hildebrand, G. E. Moore, W. D. Ross, and J. L. Austin, as well as on older traditions. Few subsequent thinkers have so successfully deployed this fruitful combination of phenomenology and linguistic analysis. A representative collection of these original explorations of moral and aesthetic experience was published posthumously in *Ethics, Value and Reality* (ed. F. Dunlop and B. Klug, 1977). Kolnai died at New End Hospital, Hampstead, London, on 28 June 1973, and was buried in Hampstead cemetery. His wife survived him.

Kolnai could be witty, charming, and entertaining, but always on his own terms. He never had the self-confidence that comes with an established status. His writing was too personal and complex to make quick converts. His scrupulous and meticulous philosophical thinking did not reach any large audience, despite the adherence of a discerning group who recognized its power and originality and determined to secure it a wider recognition among philosophers. By the turn of the millennium Kolnai was probably better known in mainstream philosophy than he was during his lifetime.

DAVID WIGGINS and FRANCIS DUNLOP

Sources A. Kolnai, *Political memoirs*, ed. F. Murphy (1999) · F. Dunlop, *The life and thought of Aurel Kolnai* (2002) · personal knowledge (2004) · d. cert.
Archives priv. coll., MSS
Likenesses photograph, 1952, repro. in *Ateneo, Las Ideas, El Arte y Las Letras, Revista de los Ateneos de España*, 18 (27 Sept 1952), pp. 12–13
Wealth at death £1777: administration, 4 Sept 1973, *CGPLA Eng. & Wales*

Komisarjevsky, Theodore [Teodor Komisarevsky] (**1882–1954**), theatre producer and designer, born in Venice on 23 May 1882, was the son of Teodor Komisarevsky (who was first tenor of the St Petersburg Opera and taught Stanislavsky) and his wife, the Princess Kurzevich. Vera Komisarjevskaya, the actress, was his sister.

Educated at a military academy and the Imperial Institute of Architecture in St Petersburg, Komisarjevsky directed his first production in his sister's theatre in 1907. In 1910, the year of her death, he founded his own school of acting in Moscow, to which in 1914 he added a studio-theatre in her memory. From 1910 to 1913 he was producer at the Nezlobin Theatre in Moscow, and after an interlude with the Imperial Grand Opera House he became producer at Ziminne's Opera House, with which he remained when it became the Soviet Opera House. After the revolution he was also appointed director of the Moscow State Theatre of Opera and Ballet (previously the Imperial Grand Opera) and he was allowed to continue to direct his own small theatre. In 1919, believing that he was about to be arrested by the Cheka, he fled to Paris, where Diaghilev advised him to go to England. Within four weeks of his arrival he was entrusted by Sir Thomas Beecham with a production of *Prince Igor* at Covent Garden, which immediately led to further opera productions in Paris and New York. On his return to London he began, at a time when the English theatre was inclined to insularity, a series of productions of plays by Russian authors including Chekhov, Gogol, Andreyev, Tolstoy, and Dostoyevsky.

In 1925 Komisarjevsky converted a small cinema at Barnes into a theatre with its own company which included John Gielgud, Charles Laughton, Jean Forbes-Robertson, Jeanne de Casalis, and Martita Hunt. The standard of production in the English theatre (to quote from *The Times* of that day) was 'sloppy and slovenly'; there was little attempt at ensemble playing and the settings and lighting were dull and unimaginative. Komisarjevsky's productions at Barnes (1925–6) had an immediate effect on the English theatre by making the critics aware of its deficiencies. At a time when English acting had a glossy veneer which concealed its shallowness, Komisarjevsky demanded from his actors a new intensity of feeling and a deeper understanding of the characters they were playing. He introduced a method of acting based on the theories of Stanislavsky, although he never accepted them unconditionally and to some of them he was strongly opposed.

In 1932 Komisarjevsky became a British subject. It was the year of the first of his productions at Stratford upon Avon; productions which were unorthodox and provocative, sometimes brilliant, sometimes merely wayward; all of them valuable as a means of making critics and audiences realize how conventional and humdrum had been the routine Stratford productions of Shakespeare. As a Shakespearian producer Komisarjevsky's weakness was that he had little respect for the text and small appreciation of the rhythms of the verse.

Komisarjevsky saw little to attract him to the ordinary West End theatre, although Sir Charles Cochran managed to persuade him to produce three plays there. He preferred to spend his time producing an extraordinary variety of plays in London, in the provinces, and on the continent for any theatre or society (such as the Stage Society) which was leading rather than following theatrical tastes. His productions included *The Pretenders*, in Welsh, in a gigantic marquee at Holyhead; two productions for the Oxford University Dramatic Society; *The Cherry Orchard* at the Leeds Civic Playhouse; *The Wild Duck* in Riga; *Peer Gynt* in New York; *The Dover Road* (in English) in Paris; and *Cymbeline* in an open-air theatre in Montreal.

Besides being a great producer, Komisarjevsky was also a brilliant stage designer. Almost invariably he designed his own sets and costumes. He had nothing in common with the photographically realistic English designers. His settings reduced factual realism to a minimum, stressing mood rather than detail. The effectiveness of his settings was enormously enhanced by the skill and subtlety of his lighting which made dramatic use of highlights, shadows, and halftones to give emphasis to his beautifully composed groupings.

Komisarjevsky was a small man, completely bald, with a beak nose and inscrutable brown eyes set in a pale face which seemed all the paler because of the small bright red scarf which he invariably wore at rehearsals. His rather melancholy air concealed a mischievous sense of humour which had a streak of cruelty in it. At work he was the quietest of producers. He would seldom give an actor an intonation or say how a line should be spoken. He preferred to discuss what a character was thinking or feeling, and leave it to the actor to work it out. Unfortunately, if he decided that an actor had no particular talent he took no trouble over his performance but concentrated all his attention on the better actors; so under his direction good actors usually surpassed themselves while dull actors seemed duller than ever.

In 1939, when war broke out, Komisarjevsky was working in the United States. He felt that as he had become a British subject he should return to England, so offered his services to the Entertainments National Service Association. But he was unable to get back, and spent the rest of his life in America, devoting his time mainly to lecturing and teaching. He died at Darien, Connecticut, on 17 April 1954.

During his twenty years working in the English theatre Komisarjevsky had more influence than any other producer on methods of direction, acting, setting, and lighting. On his death Sir John Gielgud described him in a letter to *The Times* as 'a great *metteur en scène*, an inspiring teacher, and a master of theatrical orchestration'.

Komisarjevsky was three times married: first, to Elfriede de Jarosy; second, to the actress Peggy *Ashcroft (1907–1991), whom he married on 1 December 1934; and third, to Ernestine Stodelle. The first two marriages were dissolved. He had two sons and one daughter.

NORMAN MARSHALL, *rev.*

Sources *The Times* (19 April 1954) · T. Komisarjevsky, *Myself and the theatre* (1929) · personal knowledge (1971)

Kompfner, Rudolf (1909–1977), electronics engineer and physicist, was born in Vienna on 16 May 1909, the only son and elder child of Bernhard Kömpfner, accountant, and his wife, Paula Grotte, of Vienna. In 1931 he graduated from the Technische Hochschule zu Wien with a diploma in engineering (architecture). This was a difficult time for Jews in Austria and, in 1934, helped by Roy Franey, his cousin's English husband, Kompfner went to London. He joined Franey's building firm as managing director (1936–41) and a house that he designed is described in H. M. Wright (ed.), *Small Houses, £500–£2,500* (1937).

Kompfner spent his evenings reading about physics in the Patent Office library, keeping a series of notebooks which he maintained until his death. These notebooks (later acquired by Stanford University) soon contained original concepts, and his first patent (BP 476311), a television camera tube, was accepted in 1937. In 1939 Kompfner married Peggy, the daughter of John Mason, a musician. They had a son and a daughter. In June 1940 Kompfner was interned as an enemy alien on the Isle of Man, where he shared quarters with a mathematician, Wolfgang Fuchs, with whom he discussed physics. Before his internment he had sent a paper on magnetrons to the *Wireless Engineer*, whose editor, Hugh Pocock, showed it to the Admiralty. This brought Kompfner's abilities to the attention of Frederick Brundrett, who sent him to the physics department at Birmingham University when he was released in December 1940. There, within two years, he invented the travelling wave tube (see his *Invention of the Traveling-Wave Tube*, San Francisco Press, California, 1964), the first of a family of devices, many developed by Kompfner and his associates, which were used for many years in radar and space communications.

In 1944 Kompfner was transferred to the Clarendon Laboratory, Oxford, where he remained until 1951, obtaining a DPhil in physics that year. He became a British subject on 19 March 1947, and was appointed a principal scientific officer in the Admiralty, attached to the Services Electronics Research Laboratories under R. W. Sutton. The years at Oxford (where he was a member of Queen's College) were not particularly fruitful in inventions, although they saw the genesis of the backward wave oscillator. However, the Clarendon was a lively centre of low temperature and microwave physics and Kompfner's interests rapidly broadened while he was there, while from D. K. C. MacDonald he gained an understanding of noise and fluctuations that influenced his later thinking.

In December 1951, at J. R. Pierce's invitation, Kompfner joined the Bell Laboratories as associate director, communication science (systems) research. He became a US citizen in 1957. This period was the culmination of his career. While he concentrated on microwave tubes he was stimulated by collaboration with Pierce and H. T. Friis, and as his research group grew, his interests widened still further. His talent as a director of scientific and engineering enterprises was outstanding. He was influential in the programmes for the maser amplifier, superconducting magnets, lasers, and optical communications. When Pierce interested him in communication satellites Kompfner and his team designed the first of these, Echo, launched in 1960, and its successor, Telstar. Later, in 1963, two scientists whom he had recruited, A. A. Penzias and R. W. Wilson, discovered the three-degree cosmic radio noise for which they received the Nobel prize in 1978. Kompfner became director of the new Crawford Hill Laboratory, where much of the technology of optical communication was developed.

After retiring from Bell in July 1973, he divided his time between Stanford as research professor of applied physics and Oxford as a research professor of engineering science and fellow of All Souls College, working there on acoustical and optical microscopes. He skied and swam, read widely, and was devoted to music. A spirited conversationalist, he was above all generous and warm-hearted. These qualities caused him to be surrounded by devoted friends and, allied with his originality, made him a fine director of research. His stimulating, but gentle, guidance had an abiding influence on his younger colleagues, many of whom subsequently achieved eminence. He was a member of the National Academy of Engineering (1966) and the National Academy of Sciences (1968) of Washington and his other principal honours included the Duddell medal of the Physical Society (1955), the Stuart Ballantine medal of the Franklin Institute (1960), the David Sarnoff award (1960) and medal of honour (1973) of the Institute of Electrical and Electronics Engineers, the John Scott award from the city of Philadelphia (1974), the Silvanus Thompson medal of the Röntgen Society (1974), and the president's national medal of science (1974). He also received honorary doctorates from Oxford (1969) and Vienna (1965). Kompfner died at Stanford, California, on 3 December 1977.   F. N. H. ROBINSON, *rev.*

Sources J. R. Pierce, 'Kompfner memorial lecture', *International Journal of Electronics*, 48 (1980) · private information (1986) · personal knowledge (1986)
Archives Stanford University, California

Konig, Charles Dietrich Eberhard (1774–1851), botanist and mineralogist, was born in Brunswick and educated at the University of Göttingen, where he studied botany. In 1800 he was invited to England to arrange the natural history collections of Queen Charlotte at Kew Palace. The following year Konig went to work for Sir Joseph Banks in Soho Square, London, as assistant to Jonas Dryander, Banks's librarian. During this period he launched and edited *Annals of Botany* in conjunction with Dr John Sims, writing, translating, and illustrating many of the articles. In 1807 he became assistant keeper in the British Museum's department of natural history and modern curiosities, and turned his attention to mineralogy, cataloguing and arranging the whole collection over the next ten years.

In 1813 Konig succeeded Dr Shaw as keeper of the department. He continued to spend most of his time on the minerals, although he did rearrange and name the bird collection in the early 1820s; he was said to show an 'excessive contempt for fossils' (Torrens, 69) in 1819. In spite of this he published a paper on the human skeleton from Guadeloupe in the *Philosophical Transactions of the*

Royal Society in 1814, and the first part of *Icones fossilium sectiles* in 1825. Konig also wrote many of the geological articles for Abraham Rees's *Cyclopaedia* (1802–20), after September 1811. In 1837 he was relieved of responsibility for botany and zoology, becoming keeper of the museum's mineralogical and geological branch. Konig was a difficult man, and had bad relations with both John E. Gray, keeper of the zoological branch, and Robert Smirke, architect of the new British Museum building. Konig died suddenly at the museum on 29 August 1851, while still in office.

JOHN C. THACKRAY

Sources GM, 2nd ser., 36 (1851), 435–6 · Ward, *Men of the reign* · A. E. Gunther, *A century of zoology at the British Museum through the lives of two keepers, 1815–1914* (1975) · W. C. Smith, 'A history of the first hundred years of the mineral collections in the British Museum', *Bulletin of the British Museum (Natural History)* [Historical Series], 3 (1962–9), 237–59 · E. Miller, *That noble cabinet: a history of the British Museum* (1973) · H. S. Torrens, 'Patronage and problems: Banks and the earth sciences', *Sir Joseph Banks: a global perspective* [London 1993], ed. R. E. R. Banks and others (1994), 49–75
Archives NHM, archives, official corresp. and reports · NHM, earth sciences library, diaries, memoranda books and manuscripts | Linn. Soc., corresp. with Sir James Smith · NL NZ, Turnbull L., letters to G. A. Mantell
Likenesses H. Eddir, lithograph, 1831, NHM · Turner, lithograph (after E. U. Eddis), BM, NPG

König, Karl (1902–1966), paediatrician and educationist, was born on 25 September 1902 in Vienna, Austria, the only child of Aron Ber (Adolf) König, shoe shop owner, of Vienna, and his wife, Bertha Fischer, whose father was a dressmaker in Iglau, Austria. He was educated at secondary school in Vienna and at the University of Vienna, where he graduated in medicine in 1927. His medical special interests were embryology, paediatrics, and homoeopathy. These, combined with a particular interest in curative education for children with mental and physical handicaps, he developed over the next eleven years in the course of attachments to children's hospitals and homes in Austria, Switzerland, and Silesia (in Germany at that time), and, by 1936, in private practice in Vienna. In 1929 he married Tilla, daughter of Ludwig Maasberg, cloth merchant of Gnadenfrei, Silesia; they had two sons and two daughters.

Following the Nazi annexation of Austria in 1938, König went to London, then to north-east Scotland. When war broke out he had to endure four months' internment as an enemy alien. In late 1940 he established at the estate of Camphill, near Aberdeen, a small residential school for children in need of special care. He was joined there by a succession of members of a group of young Viennese associates, fellow exiles from Europe, who were attracted by König's vision of therapeutic residential communities where children with learning difficulties and behaviour problems arising from organic disorders and emotional disturbances could receive a broad education to the fullest extent that their individual capabilities would allow, within a caring, sharing, self-governing, Christian 'family' setting.

König had from student days interested himself deeply in the life and works of Rudolf Steiner (1861–1925), the Austrian philosopher and founder of anthroposophy. Steiner's insights into the nature of human handicap, within his concept of the true spiritual nature of all people, inspired König and his unremunerated co-workers to plan practical implementation of many novel concepts of teaching, learning, and healing for young people with handicaps—up to the age of about nineteen.

But König's interest in schools spread predictably to provision for disabled people beyond school age. By 1955 he had founded, on an estate at Botton in Yorkshire, the first of many Camphill village communities, with emphasis again on the importance of the individual, on living with total dignity in 'family' households, on the provision of workshops for the making of marketable goods, and on cultural, artistic, and spiritual activities in generous measure.

That both kinds of Camphill therapeutic communities, schools and villages, increased in number in several countries both in and after König's lifetime—by 1987 there were over seventy centres in eighteen countries—was testimony to their success in answering a need, albeit continuously in pioneering mode and therefore not without mistakes. It was testimony also to the founder's vision, dynamic personality, and restless energy. König was small in stature, could be testy, and was impatient of any blocking of his plans. He had massive difficulties to overcome, concerned with funding, the medical profession, and not least the rough reception he got in wartime in what, in a letter written two weeks before he died, he called the 'human desert in the North of Scotland'. But in all his face-to-face contacts with disabled people—and with worried parents—he radiated a great warmth of strong, friendly reassurance. The many lectures he gave throughout his life were delivered, noteless, in an attractive broken English that spellbound his audiences. In 1963 he received the gold medal of the Tutzinger star at Tutzing, Germany. König died in Überlingen, Lake Constance, Germany, on 27 March 1966.

HAROLD WATT, *rev.*

Sources *The Times* (31 March 1966) · *The Times* (4 April 1966) · A. Weihs, *Fragments from the story of Camphill* (1976) · C. Pietzner, ed., *A candle on the hill: images of Camphill life* (1990) · personal knowledge (1993) · private information (1993) [incl. members of Camphill movement]

Königsmark [Coningsmark], **Karl Johann, Count Königsmark** in the Swedish nobility (1659–1686), army officer and accused accessory to murder, was of Swedish origin and was born at Nieuburg auf Fühnen in Germany on 15 May 1659. He was the son of General Kurt Christoph Königsmark (d. 1673) and his wife, Marie Christina Wrangel. His brother was Philip Christoph Königsmark, who was the lover of Sophia Dorothea of Celle, the wife of George, elector of Hanover and later George I of Great Britain, and who met his death under mysterious circumstances in 1694.

Königsmark was privately educated at home at the

castle of Agathenburg and at Hamburg and Stade. He subsequently from the mid-1670s travelled throughout Europe, selling his sword and engaging in a number of adventures. He saw action in the forces of the Maltese knights of St John against the Barbary corsairs. After a supposedly single-handed assault against a corsair galley Königsmark was rewarded by his installation as a knight of the order. He eventually went to England to seek service in Charles II's forces and to make some money by his other main talent as a card-sharp.

Königsmark fought in action at Tangier and on his return to England he was favoured by the king and was enough of a gallant at this time to attempt a liaison with and even proffer marriage to Lady Elizabeth Percy, styled countess of Ogle (1667–1722). She was heir to the inheritance of the earls of Northumberland and had been widowed for the first time when not quite fourteen. She was seduced by the count's charms, but Königsmark was considered a very unsuitable match for the heir to one of the great estates of England and so her guardians rebuffed him. Instead she was given to the wealthy Thomas Thynne of Longleat, which angered Königsmark, although the marriage was never consummated and Elizabeth soon absconded to the Netherlands. While Königsmark hoped for an annulment of the marriage, Thynne, anxious to retain Elizabeth's property, sought legal redress and the return of his wife. Königsmark, still feeling the insult of the marriage, planned his vengeance against Thynne. He sent a number of challenges to Thynne through his retainer Captain **Christopher Vratz** (d. 1682), army officer and murderer, a professional soldier of German origin who had previously served as a mercenary in many of Europe's armies. Vratz had also at some point received a serious head injury, and latterly lived a dissolute life in Hamburg, having already spent some time as a highwayman in Poland. In Hamburg his arrogance led to his imprisonment and then expulsion. He then obtained a commission in the Dutch army and commanded a forlorn hope at Mons. His bravery was undoubted and one contemporary noted that he was as 'hard as flint' (Burnet and Horneck, 198). As a result of his bravery Vratz had obtained a lieutenancy in the Dutch guards and the king of Sweden was said to have given him command of a troop of horse. However, insubordination led to his further expulsion and he took service in the French army under Turenne. With the peace of Nijmegen, Vratz made his way to Paris and then to London before ending up in Tangier, where he made the acquaintance of Königsmark.

It was later claimed that Thomas Thynne ignored the many challenges sent by the count and had hired men to kill Königsmark and Vratz. An attack apparently took place, but failed and left Vratz wounded. Soon afterwards Vratz recruited Lieutenant **John Stern** (1640/41–1682), army officer and murderer, to his design. Stern, who was in his forty-second year at his execution in 1682, was the illegitimate son of a Swedish baron who had been educated in Germany before becoming a professional soldier in the forces of the elector of Brandenburg. He had then spent twenty-three years or so wandering Europe in pursuit of his trade. In October 1681 he also had made his way to the kingdom of Charles II hoping to gain a place in one of the guards regiments. Falling in with him Vratz told Stern that he had a quarrel with an English gentleman and needed a second in order to duel with him. Stern agreed to fill this role. However, Vratz was also in communication with Königsmark, who was lying low in London, allegedly recovering from a venereal disease.

Planning continued, and when **Charles George Borosky** [Boratzi, Borodzycz; *called* the Polonian] (d. 1682), murderer, a Polish servant of Königsmark's, arrived in England he was immediately handed over to Vratz and told to obey the captain. On Sunday 12 February 1682 Vratz told Borosky that he had a quarrel with an English gentleman, had sent him two challenges, and had been ignored; moreover, he said, the Englishman had attempted to have both himself and Königsmark murdered. Vratz told him that he was bent on revenge and gave him a musquetoon. Borosky was reassured that, as in Poland, servants were not held responsible for carrying out the orders of their masters and together the pair, with Stern, ambushed Thynne's coach in Pall Mall at 8 o'clock that evening. As Stern moved in front of the coach Vratz and Borosky came up alongside. Borosky immediately fired his weapon into the coach and the blast struck Thynne in the stomach and hip, mortally wounding him. Sir John Reresby, in his capacity as a Middlesex magistrate, was able to arrest the trio quickly. Königsmark's role was soon revealed and he fled. He was caught at Gravesend attempting to escape to Sweden. Brought back to London he arrogantly denied any complicity in the murder and claimed he had left only because he feared the possible fury of the English mob when he heard that he had been accused. He was committed to Newgate, but Reresby, for one, believed that Charles II was not keen to see the young man suffer for his crime. Indeed, at the ensuing trial Königsmark, assisted by pressure from foreign ambassadors and judicious bribery, was the only one of the men actually released. Vratz claimed that he had wished only to get Thynne out of the coach so that he could duel with him; unfortunately a bemused Borosky had fired into the coach first. Vratz, Stern, and Borosky were all found guilty.

In prison Vratz, Stern, and Borosky were visited by two leading clergymen, Gilbert Burnet and Anthony Horneck, eager to bring these notorious murderers to a proper state of their sins and to ensure that they made a public, properly repentant, and godly end. Stern and Borosky showed the greatest signs of repentance and their confessions were duly published; Stern's was a lengthy and impassioned mix of autobiography and confession with prayers and spiritual meditations. Vratz was the most recalcitrant, though on the night before the execution Burnet detected signs of repentance. To Horneck, 'honour and bravery was the idol [Vratz] adored'; the captain regarded God

as some generous, yet partial, prince, who would regard
men's blood, descent, and quality more than their errors;
and give vast grams of allowance to their breeding and

education: and possibly the stout behaviour of some of the ancient Roman bravos (for he had read history) might roll in his mind.   (Burnet and Horneck, 204)

Vratz, Stern, and Borosky were hanged at the site of the murder on Pall Mall on 10 March 1682, the day after Thynne's burial in Westminster Abbey. Narcissus Luttrell contrasted Stern's and Borosky's penitent and 'dejected' demeanour with Vratz's 'very undaunted temper' on the gallows (Luttrell, 1.170). To Sir John Reresby, to whom Vratz bowed 'with a steady look' from the cart carrying him to his place of execution, 'his whole carriage, from his first being apprehended till the last, relished more of gallantry than religion' (*Memoirs of Sir John Reresby*, 257). The bodies of Stern and Vratz were given to their friends for burial; Borosky's was left to hang in chains at Mile End, 'being the road from the seaports where most of the northern nations doe land' (Luttrell, 1.171).

Königsmark sought consolation for the loss of Lady Elizabeth Percy in fresh military adventures. The authorities prevented any duels with whig lords, who still accused him of complicity in the crime, and he went to serve Louis XIV in his army, serving in 1683 and 1684 in the War of the Reunions between France and Spain and its allies. He was wounded at the action around Courtrai, and on his recovery served in Spain under Marshal Bellefonds and saw distinguished service in the French attack on Genoa. Eventually he went with his uncle Count Otto Wilhelm Königsmark to Greece to fight against the Turk. There are various accounts of Königsmark's death. He was either killed in action at Argos, or subsequently died of wounds and disease there, on 26 August 1686. He was later interred at the family mausoleum in Stade.

Königsmark was the classic Restoration bully and bravo. There is no doubt that he possessed a popular reputation for gallantry with women, as well as a headstrong nature. A short-tempered and violent man, who frequently stood upon his honour and engaged in a number of duels, he was also an excellent card player. Despite his protests at the trial and his subsequent release there is little doubt that he had been culpable in Thynne's murder. The fact that at the trial he was less concerned about the murder and more with having been placed in Newgate gaol, which he thought was 'a stain to his blood', says a great deal about his character (Lucas, 172).   ALAN MARSHALL

Sources K. G. H. Krause, 'Konigsmark, Karl Johann', *Allgemeine deutsche Biographie*, ed. R. von Liliencron, 15 (Leipzig, 1882), 530–31 · *N&Q*, 5 (1852), 183 · *The tryal and condenation of George Borosky alias Boratzi, Christopher Vratz, and John Stern, for the barbarous murder of Thomas Thynne Esq., together with the trial of Charles John, Count Conigsmark, as accessory before the fact to the same murder, who was acquited of the said offence at the session of the old Bailey, Tuesday February 28 1681* (1682) · N. Luttrell, *A brief historical relation of state affairs from September 1678 to April 1714*, 6 vols. (1857) · *Memoirs of Sir John Reresby*, ed. A. Browning, 2nd edn, ed. M. K. Geiter and W. A. Speck (1991) · T. Lucas, 'Lives of the gamesters', *Games and gamesters of the Restoration*, ed. C. H. Hartmann (1930) · E. Godley, *The trial of Count Königsmark* (1929) · G. Burnet and A. Horneck, *The last confession, prayers and meditations of Lieutenant John Stern, delivered by him on the court immediately before his execution* (1682); repr. in W. Oldys and T. Park, eds., *The Harleian miscellany*, 8 (1811) · *The true confession of the three notorious and bloody murtherers of Thomas Thynne* (1682) · *A hue and cry after blood and murder, or, An elegy on the most barbarous murder*
of Thomas Thynne Esq. (1682) · *State trials* · H. Vizetelly, *Count Königsmark and 'Tom of Ten Thousand'* (1890) · Hodgkin papers, BL, Add. MS 38855, fol. 114 · *CSP dom., 1682* · [J. G. Muddiman], 'The murder of Thomas Thynne', *TLS* (20 Feb 1930) [review of *The trial of Count Königsmark*] · L. B. Faller, *Turned to account: the forms and functions of criminal biography in late seventeenth- and early eighteenth-century England* (1987)
Likenesses R. White, engraving, 1682, Magd. Cam.

Konwatsi tsiaienni. *See* Brant, Molly (*c.*1736–1796).

Kook, Abraham Isaac (1865–1935), rabbi and Zionist, was born on 6 September 1865 in the small town of Greiva in Latvia (then part of tsarist Russia), the son of Rabbi Shlomo Zalman Kook and his wife, Faigah Leah. Born into a strictly Orthodox Jewish family, Kook attended the famous Lithuanian Talmudic academies of Volozhin (1884–6) and Ponovezh (1887–8). Ordained while still a teenager, he was appointed rabbi of Zaumel, Lithuania, in 1888 and of Bausk, Lithuania, in 1895. He married Batsheva Rabinowicz-Teumim; and after her death in 1890 he married Raiza Rivka Rabinowicz-Teumim, with whom he had a son. In 1904 he rejected offers of even more illustrious communal positions in eastern Europe and emigrated to Palestine, then part of the Ottoman empire, becoming rabbi of Jaffa and of the Jewish colonies recently established in the surrounding region.

This move reflected the depth and uniqueness of Kook's religious commitment to Zionism, the modern Jewish national movement which had been formally inaugurated with the convention of the First Zionist Congress at Basel in 1895. The vast majority of contemporary rabbinical authorities opposed Zionism, considering it a sinful attempt by avowed secularists to bring Jewry's divinely ordained exile to a premature end. Kook, however, argued that the impulses underlying modern Jewish nationalism constituted authentic testimony to the presence of sacred properties within the Jewish soul. Moreover, he regarded Zionism, in its organized form, as an agency which would facilitate the advent of the Messiah. In Jaffa, Kook developed these themes, increasingly stressing the mystical dimensions of Jewry's attachment to the Holy Land. He also composed a series of erudite *responsa*, which supplied practical solutions within the framework of Orthodox Jewish law to the ritual dilemmas arising from the resumption of Jewish agricultural enterprise in Palestine. He thereby laid the intellectual foundations for a brand of religious Zionism which sought to harmonize the requirements of traditional practice with the realities of the Jewish national revival.

In the summer of 1914 Kook visited Europe with the purpose of generating wider support for his ideas, only to be stranded on the continent by the outbreak of the First World War. Unable to return to Jaffa, he set up home in Switzerland until accepting, in 1916, an invitation to serve in England as rabbi of the Spitalfields Great Synagogue (*Machazike ha-Dat*, 'upholders of the faith'), an immigrant Orthodox community located in Brick Lane in the East End of London. This fortuitous circumstance placed Kook at the very focus of Zionist activity during the period of diplomatic negotiations which culminated in the publication on 2 November 1917 of the Balfour declaration (which expressed the British government's support for the establishment of a Jewish national home in Palestine). Convinced that he was living out the 'end of days' foretold by the biblical prophets, Kook regarded British official approval of Zionism as a crucial step towards ultimate Jewish redemption. He invested considerable energy in advertising this view to Anglo-Jewry, appearing on numerous public platforms alongside proponents of alternative—and sometimes competing—brands of Jewish nationalism. The support of so illustrious a rabbinical figure was undoubtedly of some help to the Zionists in their struggle for local communal legitimacy. In practical terms, however, Kook was a more doubtful asset. As one Zionist leader wrote to another, his ideas were thought to be 'too full of *sancta simplicitas*' to be of much utility (Nahum Sokolow to Chaim Weizmann, 6 March 1917, Weizmann Archives, file 213).

At the end of the First World War, Kook called for renewed efforts to strengthen the spiritual aspects of the Jewish national revival in *Degel Yerushalayim* ('The flag of Jerusalem'), published in London, 1918. In the summer of 1919 he himself returned to Jaffa, and two years later was elected the Ashkenazi (occidental Jewish) head of the new rabbinic court of appeals established by the British mandatory government of Palestine. As such, he effectively functioned as the Ashkenazi chief rabbi of Palestine, a post which he held with distinction until his death in Jerusalem on 1 September 1935.

In office Kook demonstrated a rare ability to combine a deeply mystical outlook with an intense involvement in communal affairs. Thus he seriously prepared himself for future office as priest of a restored temple cult while also supporting the foundation of a secular Hebrew university. Unusually for a rabbi he composed poetry, but also established a traditional seminary of advanced Jewish learning in Jerusalem. Above all Kook, although himself always rigorous in the observance of traditional Jewish practices (and dress), sought tirelessly to promote religious–secular understanding. He regarded all of the Jewish pioneers in mandatory Palestine, self-confessed heretics included, as unwitting instruments of the imminent redemption, and insisted that they be respected as such. The manifest love of the heavily bearded rabbi for all his fellow Jews, whatever their personal beliefs, was widely reciprocated, and his funeral in Jerusalem, on 1 September 1935, occasioned a rare demonstration of Jewish communal unity.

Never a systematic thinker, and prone to compose his thoughts in a rather esoteric Hebrew style, Kook's principal intellectual influence was posthumous. His subsequent renown as a Zionist theorist owed much to the efforts of his only son, Rabbi Zevi Yehudah Kook (1891–1982), who succeeded him as head of the Central Kook Academy in Jerusalem. It was the younger Kook who saw many of his father's edited writings through the press, notably *Orot* ('Lights'), first published in Jerusalem in 1942, thereby making them accessible to wider groups of disciples. However, the full text of his manuscripts, entitled *Shemonah kevatzim* ('Eight collections'), was not published until 1999, and even then in only a limited edition. Aspects of Kook's school of thought, and especially those which stressed the immanent sanctity of the Holy Land, became influential in national religious circles in Israel after the Six Day War of 1967, when they were frequently cited by supporters of the Jewish settler movement.

STUART A. COHEN

Sources A. I. Kook, *The lights of penitence; The moral principles; Lights of holiness; Essays, letters and poems*, ed. and trans. B. Z. Bokser (New York, 1978) · L. J. Kaplan and D. Schatz, eds., *Rabbi Abraham Isaac Kook and Jewish spirituality* (1995) · C. Roth, ed., *Encyclopaedia Judaica*, 16 vols. (Jerusalem, 1971–2) · S. Raz, *Angels as humans* (1993) · B. Homa, *A fortress in Anglo-Jewry* (1953) · Weizmann Archives, Rechovot, Israel
Archives priv. coll., archive

Koops, Matthias (*fl.* 1789–1805), paper manufacturer, was born in Pomerania, the son of Matthias and Katharine Dorothea Koops, both also of Pomerania. Very little is known of his early life, though he stated that he had 'for several years served in different distinguished military characters, under the late Emperor of Germany, and King of Prussia'. By 1789 Koops was in England. On 12 September his marriage to Elizabeth Jane Austin (*d.* 1815) took place in London. His application for naturalization was accepted on 1 April 1790 and in June, as a merchant of Edmonton, Koops was made bankrupt. He eventually capitalized on his knowledge of Europe by publishing in 1796 both a set of five maps of the Rhine, Meuse, and Scheldt, and a survey entitled *A Developement of the Views and Designs of the French Nation*, which sought to warn the English of certain French activities. In the following year Koops set up the Minerva Universal Insurance Office in Pall Mall, Westminster. This enterprise lasted less than a year.

Koops then became interested in the long-standing problem of making paper from materials other than linen and cotton. His work on it led him to prove that paper made from straw, wood, and recycled waste paper could be produced commercially; this achievement earns him a place in the history of paper making. By 1800 Koops had experience of manufacturing from waste paper at Neckinger mill in Bermondsey, and in 1800–01 three patents were granted to him: one for extracting inks from printed and written paper before pulping, and the other two for making paper fit for printing from straw, hay, thistles, waste, and refuse of hemp and flax. In 1800 his *Historical Account of the Substances which have been Used to Describe Events* was printed on straw paper.

Having proved the possibility of making good paper from such materials, Koops set up a company, the Straw Paper Manufactory, raised over £70,000 by issue of shares, and in 1801 erected a paper-making mill at Millbank in Westminster. Contractors for the machinery included John Rennie, the engineer, and the firm of Boulton and Watt. This paper mill was easily the largest in the country. The enterprise, however, was over-ambitious and undercapitalized. Koops himself was the principal shareholder in the venture and on the strength of this offered to satisfy his creditors. His failure to discharge his bankruptcy by

1802 compelled Koops's creditors to issue a writ, *inter alia*, for seizure of the Straw Paper Manufactory's assets, and in the end its proprietors could not keep the enterprise solvent. The Millbank paper mill and its equipment were eventually offered for sale by auction in October 1804, thereby ending the possibility of England challenging the European paper industry by using more easily available materials for making paper. Koops himself, optimistic to the end, is last heard of in 1805 soliciting subscriptions for his river maps; his widow died in 1815.

R. J. GOULDEN, *rev.*

Sources D. Hunter, *Papermaking*, 2nd edn (1957) · A. Chick, 'Paper from straw: Matthias Koops in London', *Antiquarian Book Monthly Review*, 12 (1985), 140–45 · R. J. Goulden, 'The shadow limn'd: Matthias Koops', *Factotum: Newsletter of the XVIIIth-Century Short Title Catalogue*, 27 (Nov 1988), 16–21

Korda, Sir Alexander [*real name* Sándor László Kellner] (1893–1956), film producer and director, was born on 16 September 1893 in Pusztatúrpásztó, near Túrkeve in Hungary, the eldest of three sons of Henrik Kellner, the steward of an estate leased by the Salgó family, and his wife, Ernesztina Weisz (*d.* 1921/2). The Kellners, like the Salgós, were Jewish and Sándor began his education at the Jewish school at Túrkeve, but at the age of nine he won a secondary school scholarship and moved to a school in Kisújszállás, a small settlement 10 miles north of Túrkeve, and then to one in Mezotúr, a larger town to the south. In October 1906 Henrik Kellner died of a ruptured appendix and the family moved to Kecskemét to live with Henrik's father, Károly.

Early years Sándor resented his grandfather's discipline and persuaded his mother to send him to Budapest to live with his cousins. There he attended the Barcsay Gymnasium and the commercial high school, where one of his teachers, the left-wing Hungarian patriot Oscar Faber, introduced him to politics and philosophy and encouraged him to write for a Budapest newspaper, *Független Magyarország* ('Independent Hungary'). In 1909 Sándor arranged for his mother and brothers—Zoltán (*b.* 1895) and Vincent (*b.* 1897)—to join him in Budapest. The family rented an apartment and took in lodgers, and Sándor worked at night in the offices of *Független Magyarország*. At the end of the year he left school and became a full-time reporter for the paper. While at school he had used the pseudonym Sursum Corda ('lift up your hearts') for his journalism; around 1910 he changed this to Sándor Korda.

In June 1911 Korda moved to Paris. He quickly learned French and became fascinated by the film-making activity at the Pathé studios, then the largest in Europe. But neither at the studio nor through his writing could he earn enough to make a living and in August 1912 he returned to Budapest. Two months later he established a weekly film journal, *Pesti Mozi* ('Budapest cinema'), and while continuing to write for *Független Magyarország* began working for Ungerleiders Projectograph Company, writing Hungarian titles for the foreign films distributed by the company. When war broke out in 1914, Korda was exempted from

Sir Alexander Korda (1893–1956), by unknown photographer, 1936 [on location filming *Rembrandt*]

military service because of his poor eyesight (an eye infection he caught as a child had been misdiagnosed, leaving him with permanently impaired vision in one eye), and he was able to take advantage of the disruption of the international film market which deprived Hungary of French and American films to launch his own career as a filmmaker. After co-directing three films in 1914 he made his début as sole director with *A tiszti kardbojt* ('The officer's swordknot') in 1915. By the time the war ended in 1918 Korda vied with Mihály Kertész (Michael Curtiz) as Hungary's leading film director and Korda had the advantage of his own purpose-built studios (Corvin, named after the Renaissance Hungarian king Matthias Corvinus) and ownership of *Mozihét* ('Ciné weekly'), the leading film journal.

When Count Károlyi formed his republican government in November 1918, Korda was appointed commissioner of film production, and despite the fact that he now enjoyed a lavish bourgeois lifestyle, he assumed a similar position under the communist government of Béla Kun. He fared less well under the right-wing regime of Admiral Horthy which came to power with Western support in the autumn of 1919. Horthy's government was ruthlessly reactionary and rabidly antisemitic—a harbinger of what was later to come in Germany—and Korda was arrested. He was released after the intervention of his brother Zoltán, who had a distinguished military record, and his own wife, Maria Farkas (*b.* 1898). The latter was a beautiful, volatile actress whom Korda had helped become an international star and married earlier in 1919. Korda was assured that his arrest was a mistake but he was sufficiently unsettled by his experience to give up everything and begin the life of an expatriate. In November he left for Vienna with Maria; he never returned to Hungary. Symbolically, when he arrived in Vienna he shed something of his Hungarian identity by changing his name Sándor to Alexander.

Vienna, Berlin, Hollywood, Paris Though Korda had lost his studio, his film journal, and his position at the head of the Hungarian film industry, when he arrived in Vienna he was still only twenty-six, married to an internationally known star, and widely recognized as an enterprising and talented film-maker. He went into partnership with Count Alexander Kolowrat-Krokowsky, an Austrian nobleman who had contributed articles to *Mozihét*, to make an adaptation of Mark Twain's *The Prince and the Pauper* (released in 1920 as *Seine Majestät das Bettelkind*) with Alfred Schreiber as Henry VIII. It was a success and Korda felt sufficiently settled to bring his mother and Zoltán to Vienna. Two further films were made for Kolowrat's company Sascha-Film, but Korda resented his patron's interference and in 1922 ended their collaboration. He also underwent upheavals in his domestic life. Maria, whose insistence on spelling her name Corda gives some indication of her determination to pursue an independent career, gave birth to a son, Peter Vincent, in 1921; and soon after his mother, with whom he was very close, died. In January 1923, after making a biblical extravaganza, *Samson and Delila* (1922), as a starring vehicle for Maria, the Kordas moved to Berlin.

In Berlin, Korda found fellow Hungarians prepared to back him. Gabriel Schwarz provided finance for a new company, Korda-Film, to make *Das unbekannte Morgen* (*The Unknown Tomorrow*, 1923), an appropriate title for a film shot in the middle of Germany's currency crisis. Josef Somlo, the head of the foreign division of the UFA film corporation, provided finance for Korda's next film, *Jedermanns Frau* (*Everybody's Woman*, 1924), and the banker Imre Gross backed Korda's expensive and ambitious *Tragödie im Hause Habsburg* (1924). Again Korda spent too much on the production and the film lost money, but he recouped his reputation with two light, topical films for Somlo (who had set up his own company with Herman Fellner)—*Der Tänzer meiner Frau* (*Dancing Mad*, 1925) and *Eine Dubarry von heute* (*A Modern Dubarry*, 1926)—and with *Madame wünscht keine Kinder* (*Madame Wants No Children*, 1926) for the American Fox Film Corporation. In 1926 Maria and Alexander were offered a contract by First National to work in Hollywood.

All six of Korda's German films had starred Maria; it was she, rather than her husband, who was wanted in Hollywood. Korda was supremely adept at grasping opportunities, but he felt frustrated and baffled by Hollywood. He missed the café society of the great European cities, and complained to a friend that: 'At night there is nothing to do, nowhere to go, it's like being in the Foreign Legion at Sidi-bel-Abbés' (Korda, 83); and though he admired the technical proficiency of the Hollywood studios, he disliked the strictly regimented timetabling and the curbs on the creative control of the director. In a letter to his friend Lajos Biró he bemoaned the fact that 'the stupidest producer can give orders to a director, and everybody's nephew is a producer. I should have come here as a producer myself, I think, or better yet, as a nephew' (ibid., 82).

None the less, Korda's career with First National can hardly be counted a failure. He directed two films starring Maria Corda (*The Private Life of Helen of Troy* in 1927 and *Love and the Devil* in 1929) and four with Billie Dove (Douglas Fairbanks's co-star in *The Black Pirate*, 1926). Maria was much in demand as a silent film star, but by 1929 Hollywood had adopted sound and Maria proved incapable of changing her guttural broken English into the sort of seductive European drawl that Garbo and Dietrich were to perfect. Her career abruptly ended and Korda found a bitterly discontented wife even more difficult to cope with than an ebulliently successful one. In 1930 the couple divorced. Korda planned to return to Europe but his savings were wiped out in the Wall Street crash of 1929 and he signed a $100,000 a year contract with the Fox Film Corporation. After making two films, Korda fell foul of two of the company's production chiefs, Sol Wurtzel and Winfield Sheehan, and rather than cling on in an increasingly unwelcoming environment he surrendered his contract and returned to Europe.

With the Horthy regime still ensconced in Budapest, Berlin was the obvious place for Korda to resume his European career, but he felt threatened by the rise of the Nazi party and moved to Paris instead. Here he established a fruitful relationship with the American company Paramount, and in 1931 made French and German versions of its Hollywood film *Laughter* (as *Rive gauche* and *Die Männer um Lucie*) and of Marcel Pagnol's play *Marius*. The French version of *Marius*, released in October 1931, was a critical and commercial success and assured Korda of a future in the French film industry, but he had already arranged to work in Britain. Together with two other Hungarians, Lajos Biró and Steven Pallos, Korda intended to set up a production company of his own.

Henry VIII and the Prudential Assurance Company Korda arrived in Britain in November 1931 with responsibility for Paramount's UK operation. His first film, *Service for Ladies* (1932), starring one of Paramount's rising Hollywood contract players, Leslie Howard (who was born in Britain of Hungarian parents), was a success. Korda was anxious to establish his independence, however, and in February 1932 set up London Film Productions, with Big Ben as its trademark. After directing *Wedding Rehearsal* (1932) for Gaumont-British, Korda assumed the role of producer on a number of modestly budgeted films, but in the spring of 1933 he began directing a more ambitious production which he hoped would establish the name of London Films, *The Private Life of Henry VIII* (1933).

Korda had suffered mixed fortunes with his costume films. *Seine Majestät das Bettelkind* was a success but *Samson and Delila* and *Tragödie im Hause Habsburg* had been too expensively made to recoup their costs; and *The Private Life of Helen of Troy* had too European a sensibility to appeal to American audiences. For *The Private Life of Henry VIII* Korda was determined to get the formula right. He recruited his youngest brother, Vincent (who had worked with him in France on the *Marius* adaptations), to build the sets, using economy and ingenuity rather than large amounts of money; he worked with his old colleague Lajos Biró and the Englishman Arthur Wimperis on the script; he brought over the distinguished French cinematographer Georges Périnal as lighting cameraman; he expanded the script (which had originally been concerned solely with the relationship between Henry and Anne of Cleves) so that Merle Oberon, Binnie Barnes, and Wendy Barrie—whom he had contracted to London Films—could play Henry's other wives; and he persuaded Charles Laughton, a British actor who had already established himself in Hollywood, to play the king. Nevertheless, he found it difficult to raise money for the film. Eventually the American company United Artists agreed to provide around a quarter of the £60,000 budget and the balance was provided by Ludovico Toeplitz de Grand Ry and from Korda's own funds. Once the film was completed, Douglas Fairbanks senior, one of the United Artists partners, became convinced of its commercial potential and in October 1933 *The Private Life of Henry VIII* was premièred at the Radio City Music Hall in New York. It broke box office records, and within a year had grossed £500,000. The wave of optimism created by the film fostered the idea that Britain was capable of creating an international film industry which could challenge Hollywood, and within three years of arriving in Britain Korda became the leading figure in the UK film industry.

By September 1935 Korda had become a full partner in United Artists (alongside Douglas Fairbanks, Mary Pickford, Charlie Chaplin, and Sam Goldwyn) and he had won the financial backing of the Prudential Assurance Company. Though film-making was inherently risky, the assessment of risk was the business of insurance companies, and the success of Korda's film seemed to indicate that the industry was ripe for development. The fact that Britain and America shared a common language meant that the British market was particularly vulnerable to Hollywood imports but, in theory at least, British films had the same opportunity to penetrate the American market. In fact there were economic barriers and cultural differences which made this difficult, but in 1934 the only major obstacle appeared to be the under-funding of British films and the lack of modern studio facilities. Korda reached agreement with the men from the Prudential (Percy Crump and Sir Connop Guthrie) that he would be given financial backing for his films and for building a seven-stage studio at Denham. Korda made use of his link with United Artists to star Douglas Fairbanks senior in *The Private Life of Don Juan* (1934) and Douglas Fairbanks junior alongside Elizabeth Bergner in *The Rise of Catherine the Great* (1934). Both films cost more and earned much less than *The Private Life of Henry VIII*, but Korda consolidated his reputation as an enterprising and innovative producer with his next three films: *Sanders of the River* (1935), *The Ghost Goes West* (1935), and *The Scarlet Pimpernel* (1934). Construction began at Denham in June 1935 and the studios were completed by May the following year. Korda himself directed the first film to be made there in its entirety, *Rembrandt* (1936), an unusually personal film that reflected Korda's own deep love of painting. It was not a commercial success and it was five years before Korda directed another film.

With seven stages to fill, Korda had to rent out space to independent production companies, but he had no intention of becoming merely a studio manager and undertook an expensive and ambitious production programme of his own. A number of European films were acquired to be remade in English—*Men are not Gods* (1936), *Moscow Nights* (1935), *The Challenge* (1935), *Forget-me-Not* (1936), *The Rebel Son* (1939), and *Prison without Bars* (1938)—but none of these was particularly successful and Korda gradually turned to contemporary or near-contemporary British subjects for his medium-budget films. The best of these films—Victor Saville's *Storm in a Teacup* (1937) and *South Riding* (1938), as well as Michael Powell and Emeric Pressburger's *The Spy in Black* (1939)—can be seen as harbingers of that authentic idiom which was to distinguish British films made during the Second World War. Korda himself was more interested in big-budget films. These included those which might be expected to have an international appeal (such as *Knight without Armour*, 1936, for which Marlene Dietrich was reputedly offered a salary of $350,000, and his two H. G. Wells adaptations—*Things to Come*, 1936, and *The Man who Could Work Miracles*, 1936), but also films which celebrated Britain's past (such as *Fire over England*, 1937) and gloried in its imperial achievements (such as *The Drum*, 1938, and *The Four Feathers*, 1939).

Korda managed to survive the financial crisis which broke over the British film industry in 1937 but he faced increasingly hostile criticism of his extravagance; early in 1938 the Prudential decided to cut its losses and remove Denham from his control. Korda was certainly guilty of extravagance and waste, but his achievements were considerable, given the problems he faced. The United Artists deal was not as advantageous as it seemed. Unlike the other major Hollywood companies, United Artists did not own cinema chains into which they could book their films, and the constitution of the company disallowed the practice of selling packages of films. Thus each of Korda's films had to be sold individually to independent exhibitors and, despite their international casts, they were often viewed with suspicion in provincial America and were insufficiently promoted to dispel the doubts of the mass audience. Returns on most of the films were pathetically small, making their budgets, although not excessive by Hollywood standards, uneconomic.

Korda's problems with the American market were compounded by the rapid changes he himself had initiated in the British film industry. His own success in raising finance in the City of London was mimicked by producers with less acumen and ability, leading to an inflation in budgets and a demand for studio space. This resulted in rebuilding and expansion at Shepperton and Elstree, and in the construction of new studios at Pinewood which were as well equipped and more practically designed than those at Denham. When the production bubble burst in 1937 there was substantial over-capacity, and once Korda had relinquished control over Denham a merger was arranged with Pinewood. Only for a brief period after the war were both studios fully operational, and in 1952 Denham was closed down permanently.

Korda continued to make films at Denham; he was fortunate that *The Four Feathers*, directed by his brother Zoltán, was almost completed when the axe fell. It proved to be one of his best and most popular films. In March 1939 he embarked on *The Thief of Bagdad* (1940), which, like *The Drum* and *The Four Feathers*, was to be made in Technicolor, using the facilities of Denham film laboratories in which Korda continued to have a controlling interest. Relieved of the responsibility of running a studio, Korda was able to devote his talents to film-making, but he saw the loss of Denham as a major blow. He had created stars (Vivien Leigh, Merle Oberon, Robert Donat), had brought internationally acclaimed directors (René Clair, Jacques Feyder, Josef von Sternberg) to Britain, and had attempted to make films on a scale which would rival those of Hollywood. Though he would achieve much in the remainder of his career, he would look back on his Denham years as a golden age.

Second World War On 3 June 1939 Korda married Merle *Oberon (1911–1979), the Tasmanian-born actress he had helped to become an international film star. Between 1935 and 1937 she had worked in Hollywood (though still under contract to London Films) and she was to draw Korda back there. On the day war between Britain and Germany was declared, Korda began production on *The Lion has Wings* (1939), a propaganda film, part fiction, part documentary, contrasting British and German values and displaying the effectiveness of Britain's air defences. Despite doubts about its complacency, it was well received in Britain and America but requisitioning and mobilization cast doubt over Korda's future in Britain. Over the next few months he made three trips to Hollywood, where Merle Oberon had returned under contract to Warner Brothers. He was able to raise loans of $3.6 million for film production, but only on condition that the films were made in America. In June 1940 he moved the production of *The Thief of Bagdad* to Hollywood, where he was to remain until May 1943.

Although he faced accusations of having 'gone with the wind up', there were good reasons for Korda to leave Britain. The details remain surrounded in mystery, but it is clear that Korda had close links with the British secret services and his contacts among the rich and famous in America were considered worth cultivating. More mundanely, the future of British film production beyond documentary and informational films was uncertain, and prospects for the sort of big-budget films with which Korda was associated looked unfavourable. Korda's friends in the government thought he would be more useful making films in Hollywood. Churchill was convinced that Britain could win the war only with American support, and films which swayed American opinion towards intervention on Britain's side would be inestimably valuable.

The Thief of Bagdad was completed in October 1940 and Korda began work on *That Hamilton Woman* (1941), starring Laurence Olivier and Vivien Leigh. When it was released in April 1941 it was not only commercially successful—in Britain, America, and even the Soviet Union—but by drawing very clear parallels between Napoleon and Hitler, it effectively pleaded Britain's cause. It was also one of Churchill's favourite films. Korda was subpoenaed to appear before the senate committee on foreign relations to answer charges of 'inciting the American public to war', but the hearing was forestalled by the Japanese attack on Pearl Harbor which brought the United States into the war.

Korda continued to operate in Hollywood, working with Merle Oberon on *Lydia* and with his brothers Zoltán and Vincent on an adaptation of Kipling's *The Jungle Book* (1942), but he had no intention of settling there. He had become a British citizen in 1936 and he made frequent trips home, despite the fact that the only means of transport was in the bomb bay of planes being delivered to the RAF. In June 1942 he was knighted, an affirmation of how valuable a contribution he was considered to have made to the war effort. In May 1943 he merged London Films with MGM's British operation and moved back to Britain. In December an ambitious programme was announced, but the shortage of studio space and disagreements between Korda and his Hollywood boss, Louis B. Mayer, meant that only one film—*Perfect Strangers* (1945), starring Deborah Kerr and Robert Donat—was made, and in October 1945 Korda extracted London Films from the merger and resigned from MGM.

Korda and British Lion In April 1944 Korda had sold his shares in United Artists for $900,000 and used the money to secure a controlling interest in a distribution company, British Lion, and two studios, Worton Hall and Shepperton. But he found it difficult to re-establish the former pre-eminence of London Films. Most of the major actors and directors were contracted to J. Arthur Rank, and though there was a gradual drift from Rank to Korda, his resources were rashly committed to three films—*Bonnie Prince Charlie* (1948), *Anna Karenina* (1948), and *An Ideal Husband* (1948; the last film Korda directed)—which turned out to be expensive flops. The government recognized how its own policies, which had provoked a Hollywood boycott between August 1947 and March 1948, had disrupted the industry, and in November 1948 agreed to loan British Lion £3 million. Korda's subsequent success with Carol Reed's *The Third Man* (1949), Frank Launder and Sidney Gilliat's *The Happiest Days of your Life* (1950), and Jack Lee's *The Wooden Horse* (1950) appeared to vindicate this decision. Film-making in the 1950s, however, with a declining market encroached upon by television, presented difficulties, and Korda found it impossible to repay the loan. In June 1954 the government foreclosed and declared British Lion bankrupt. As with Denham and the Prudential in 1938, Korda was able to continue operating as a film-maker, but again he considered it a humiliating setback.

Korda looked forward to working in the new medium of television, and founded two new companies, Big Ben Television and London Films (Television Services) in 1955, but on 23 January 1956 he died of a heart attack at his home at 20 Kensington Palace Gardens. He was cremated at Golders Green. He had suffered earlier attacks in January 1946 and soon after the government take-over of British Lion in the summer of 1954. He was a man who, like his friend Winston Churchill, smoked cigars constantly, abhorred exercise, and slept badly. He and Merle Oberon had divorced in June 1945 and he married a Canadian, Alexandra Irene Boycun (1928–1966), in June 1953. Ironically, in view of his complaint to Merle Oberon that she treated him as a father figure, his third wife was more than thirty years his junior. None of his marriages ultimately brought him much happiness and his closest relationships were with his brothers Zoltán and Vincent, who, despite their own considerable talents, were always prepared to support him and fit in with his plans.

Korda's silent films were received with enthusiasm at the Pordenone Silent Film Festival in the late 1990s, but they have yet to be assessed, and the films he directed in the 1930s and 1940s reveal him as a clever, but not outstanding, director. His knowledge and experience often made it difficult for him to function merely as a producer, facilitating the vision of others, though this is what he did very successfully with Carol Reed's collaborations with Graham Greene's *The Fallen Idol* (1948) and *The Third Man*. Where he felt that a film was not being made in the way he wanted, he did not hesitate to interfere and he could be cruel and ruthless. In 1936 C. A. Lejeune reported that 'he is tiresome, unaccountable, outspoken and cold-blooded in his judgements, he suffers fools not only not gladly, but not at all' ('The private lives of London films', *Nash's Magazine*, September 1936). And in his family memoir Michael Korda balances the picture he paints of the kindness and generosity of his uncle by detailing the humiliations to which he subjected the director Ludwig Bergner in order to drive him from the set of *The Thief of Bagdad*. Korda's style, extravagance, and charm made him an almost mythical figure. The film mogul Napoleon Bott, in Jeffrey Dell's novel *Nobody Ordered Wolves* (1939), is clearly modelled on Korda, and Karol Kulik's biography is aptly titled *The Man who could Work Miracles* (1975). As Sir Ralph Richardson recalled: 'Korda was the nearest thing to a magician that I ever met. He could make the impossible seem possible' (Sasdy).   ROBERT MURPHY

Sources K. Kulik, *Alexander Korda: the man who could work miracles* (1990) • M. Korda, *Charmed lives: a family romance* (1980) • P. Tabori, *Alexander Korda* (1959) • R. Vas, *The golden years of Alexander Korda*, 1968 [BBC TV documentary] • P. Sasdy, *Alexander Korda*, 5 Oct 1993 [*Omnibus* TV documentary] • P. Sasdy, *Alexander Korda*, 12 Oct 1993 [*Omnibus* TV documentary] • W. Duncalf, *The epic that never was*, 1965 [BBC TV documentary on abandoned Korda film, *I Claudius*] • S. Street, 'Denham studios: the golden jubilee of Korda's folly', *Sight and Sound*, 55 (1985–6), 116–22 • 'Alexander Korda', *Film Dope*, 31 (Jan 1985), 20–22, 24, 26 • J. R. Taylor, 'Tales of the Hollywood raj: Alexander Korda, showman or spy?', *Films and Filming* (July 1983), 16–18 • S. Street, 'Alexander Korda, Prudential Assurance and British film finance in the 1930s', *Historical Journal of Film, Radio and Television*, 6 (1986), 161–79 • WWW

Archives FILM BFI NFTVA, 'Korda interviews', 4 March 1956 • BFI NFTVA, 'The golden years of Alexander Korda', 27 Dec 1968 • BFI NFTVA, 'Britain in the thirties', 12 May 1993 • BFI NFTVA, *Omnibus*, 5 Oct 1993 | SOUND BL NSA, performance recording

Likenesses photographs, 1933–68, Hult. Arch. [*see illus.*] • Y. Karsh, bromide print photograph, 1949, NPG • H. Coster, photograph, NPG • A. Wysard, pencil and gouache, NPG

Wealth at death £385,684 11*s*. 9*d*.: probate, 15 May 1956, CGPLA Eng. & Wales

Korn, Arthur (1891–1978), architect and planner, was born in Breslau, Lower Silesia, Germany, on 4 June 1891, the son of Moritz Korn, a machine tool dealer, and his wife, Martha Ebstein. Following studies at the Luisenstädtisches Gymnasium in Berlin, Korn attended a carpentry trades school (*c*.1908–1909), and later completed his professional studies at the Royal Art and Trade School in Berlin (1909–11). Subsequently he worked as an architectural assistant and, for a short time, in the city planning office of greater Berlin, where he came under the influence of Raymond Unwin's recently translated *Town Planning in Practice* (1909).

Following war service as a volunteer, Korn went into practice with Eric Mendelsohn in Berlin; although the association was short-lived, Korn recalled it as critically formative: 'I owe all my further development to Mendelsohn' (Korn, '55 years', 264). From 1919 to 1922 he worked solo, subsequently forming a partnership with Siegfried Weitzmann, with whom he built a number of houses, shops, offices, and industrial buildings in Berlin and elsewhere. During the 1920s Korn was actively associated with German modernist architectural groups such as the Novembergruppe and the Ring. Photographs of Korn and Weitzmann's Villa Goldstein in Berlin were published in Walter Gropius's visual anthology of the new architecture, *Internationale Architektur* (1924); Korn himself published a seminal survey, *Glas im Bau und als Gebrauchsgegenstand* (1929), which drew attention to the potential of the new architecture and new materials.

In 1929 Korn's interest in town planning was sharpened by a trip to the USSR as a consultant, during which he made contacts with Soviet modernist architects and planners. In the same year he co-founded the Collective for Socialist Building, and made proposals for the future development of Berlin, which were exhibited in 1930. After Hitler's accession to power and the incorporation of the Bund Deutscher Architekten (BDA) in the Reichskulturkammer, Korn was forbidden to practise in Germany. He emigrated to Yugoslavia, where he worked as an independent architect and planner in Zagreb between 1935 and 1937.

Korn first visited England in 1930 and again in 1934, as a delegate of the Congrès Internationaux d'Architecture Moderne, and in 1937 he settled in Britain. Here, too, he associated himself actively with modernist tendencies: he joined the Modern Architectural Research (MARS) Group; he worked as an assistant to F. R. S. Yorke and E. Maxwell Fry; and he was a consultant for Jack Pritchard's Isokon Furniture Company, for which he proposed new developments on the eve of war. As chair of the MARS Group's town planning subcommittee from 1938, Korn was instrumental—in collaboration with Fry, Eugene Kent, Godfrey Samuel, and others—in the development of the MARS plan for London (published in 1942) which drew, in part, on the proposals he had made for Berlin in 1929–30: the plan envisaged a radical reconfiguration of the city, organized around evenly distributed neighbourhood units, linked by a rationalized and integrated transport system. It was chiefly through his ideas about town planning, promulgated through his writing and particularly through his teaching, that Korn would be influential in Britain in the first two decades after the Second World War.

Interned as an enemy alien during the early part of the

war, from 1939 to 1940, Korn's career took a new turn after his release when, from 1941, he began to teach. He taught architecture and planning first at the Oxford School of Architecture (1941–5)—now part of Oxford Brookes University—and subsequently, until his retirement, at the Architectural Association in London (1945–65). In 1953 he codified some of his ideas on town planning in a book, *History Builds the Town*. Former students and colleagues respected him not only for his firsthand association with the rise of European modernist architectural design and planning but for his infectious enthusiasm as a teacher: 'What was wonderful about Arthur was that he showed us how town planning could make the impossible possible' said Leslie Ginsburg, a former Architectural Association student and friend of Korn. Korn not only had a 'most un-English' enthusiasm for architecture in general but, as the title of his book suggests, he sought to locate his planning precepts in a historical continuum, enthusing about the lessons to be drawn from historic English type forms (such as those of the Cambridge quads and formal London squares) as much as from recent examples. Nevertheless, he insisted that his students should not treat such lessons as mere formulae. As Ginsburg observed:

> Korn's ebullient but sharply perceptive methods of teaching shook us out of the complacent feeling that once we had carried out the planning 'motions' all would be well … he insisted that it was our duty to aim high, to design for the best. (Sharp and others, 11/3)

Before he settled in Britain Korn had married Elizabeth von Friedlaender, a painter and teacher. On 21 March 1942 he married Emanuela Georgina Krizan (*b*. 1899/1900), daughter of Franz Krizan, a chemist. He nursed her devotedly in her final years. Korn had two daughters. Following his retirement, Korn settled in Austria in 1969; he died at Klosterneuberg, Austria, on 14 November 1978.

CHARLOTTE BENTON

Sources B. Housden, 'Arthur Korn, 1891 to the present day', *Architectural Association Journal*, 73 (1957), 114–35 · D. Sharp and others, *Architectural Association Quarterly*, 11 (1979), 49–54 · A. Korn, '55 years in the modern movement', *Arena* (April 1966), 263–5 · H. A. Strauss and W. Röder, eds., *Biographisches Handbuch der deutschsprachigen Emigration nach 1933 / International biographical dictionary of central European émigrés, 1933–1945*, 3 vols. (1980–83) · C. Benton and others, *A different world: emigré architects in Britain, 1928–1958* (1995) [exhibition catalogue, RIBA, 23 Nov 1995 – 20 Jan 1996] · m. cert. [Arthur Korn and Emanuela Krizan]

Likenesses photograph, *c*.1928, Hult. Arch.

Korner, Alexis (1928–1984), blues singer and guitarist, was born in Paris on 19 April 1928. His father was a former Austrian cavalry officer, and his mother was Greek. He was brought up in France, Switzerland, and north Africa. The family left France in 1940 in one of the last ships to leave the country during the Second World War and settled in London. Korner studied at St Paul's School and while there developed a keen interest in jazz and blues, mainly by way of gramophone records, with a special liking for the music of such pianists as Albert Ammons and Jimmy Yancey. He had learned the piano from the age of five but, with his growing interest in the blues, took to the guitar and did his utmost to emulate the American blues singers in spite of a current conviction in those days that it was essentially the province of black musicians. On leaving school he served for a while in the army, then had various short-lived jobs with a shipping firm, the BBC, and several record companies—including Decca, where he worked in the catalogue section. Friendships formed at this time led to his contributing some valuable blues sections to *Jazz on Record* (1960) by Charles Fox, Peter Gammond, and Alun Morgan. In 1951 Korner married Roberta Melville, the daughter of the art critic Robert Melville; they had three children, Sappho, Nicholas, and Damian, and settled in a flat in Bayswater. Anyone who evinced any interest in the blues was invited to the flat for long and smoke-laden sessions at the turntable and was inevitably introduced to a lot of names on race record labels that were still unfamiliar to most people in Britain. When Big Bill Broonzy visited London in October 1955 (and recorded two albums for the Nixa label) he stayed at the Korners' home.

From 1948 to 1950 Korner led his own blues quartet, which played as an intermission group with Chris Barber in 1949. He was a member of Barber's skiffle group in 1952–4 and recorded with Ken Colyer in 1954–5 (including such works as 'Midnight Special'). During the mid-fifties, in partnership with the harmonica player Cyril Davies (who died of leukaemia in 1963), he ran the Roundhouse Blues Club in an upstairs room above the pub in Brewer Street, where he not only supplied his own blues but also lured such prestigious guests as Muddy Waters, Sonny Terry, Jimmy Rushing, and Brownie McGhee. It was there that rhythm and blues first found an outlet in London. Korner and Davies founded the band Blues Incorporated in 1961 and in 1962, on St Patrick's day, opened the Ealing Rhythm and Blues Club in a basement beneath a cinema, which became their centre of operation. Other players included the saxophonist Dick Heckstall-Smith and the drummer Charlie Watts. Mick Jagger was in attendance and soon became a regular singer with the band, as did Brian Jones. The Rolling Stones was formed as a group to deputize for Blues Incorporated when the group was engaged elsewhere. As Blues Incorporated became better known it moved to the Marquee Club under the Academy Cinema, where it played a music that, as one obituary put it, 'merged Charlie Mingus with Muddy Waters'. Musicians who played with the group during the next few years included Graham Bond, Jack Bruce, Eric Clapton, Paul Jones, John Mayall, Phil Seamen, Art Themen, and Danny Thompson, some making their first mark with the band. The LPs *R & B from the Marquee*, *Red Hot from Alex*, *At the Cavern*, and *Alexis Korner's Blues Incorporated* were recorded in 1962 and 1964 for Decca. Korner never sought popularity or played anything other than the music he believed in, which made him always a little ahead of his time and never *Top of the Pops* material. The strong jazz influence always remained as evident in his *Red Hot from Alex*, and his own liking was for guitarists like Lonnie Johnson and Big Bill Broonzy. He was hailed as the 'father of modern British rhythm and blues', though he strongly disclaimed any such distinction and amended it to 'grandfather', meanwhile steering clear of the excessive displays of the pop world, preferring a sustained family life, much of it spent in a converted Methodist chapel in Wales, and enthusiastic discourse with friends. He never became as famous or as rich as some of his protégés, but earned the solid respect that he deserved.

Korner left the band in 1968 to work as a soloist; he recorded *I Wonder Who* (1967), *A New Generation of Blues*, and *Both Sides of Alexis Korner* (1969); then there were periods with the groups New Church (1969–70), with whom he recorded, and CCS (1970–73), featuring the singer Peter Thorup and Korner himself in some typical gruff vocals; and for a time he was resident band leader for the children's television show *Five O'Clock Club*. In 1972 Korner and Thorup toured the USA with the group Humble Pie. This was followed by a fruitful musical partnership with the bass player Colin Hodgkinson from 1973 to 1980, during which he worked both in Britain and abroad, and always preferring the intimate live performance. Recordings from this period included *Mr Blues* (1974), *Alexis Korner* (1974), *Get off my Cloud* (1975), and *Just Easy* (1978). In the latter years much of his time was taken up by broadcasting, his BBC Radio 1 programme being a model of erudition, wit, and the well-turned phrase. He was an elegant writer and a man of great courtesy and charm. His gravelly voice was frequently used to good effect as the background to television commercials. He was always a smart dresser, a great connoisseur of food, drink, and art, and a keen follower of cricket and rugby, having played the latter in his early army days. His heavy smoking habits took their eventual toll, and he died of lung cancer in the Westminster Hospital, London, on 1 January 1984, aged fifty-five; he was survived by his wife. A number of compilations of his recordings appeared in the 1980s.

PETER GAMMOND

Sources P. Gammond, *The Oxford companion to popular music* (1991) · B. Kernfeld, ed., *The new Grove dictionary of jazz*, 2 vols. (1988) · d. cert. · *CGPLA Eng. & Wales* (1984) · *The Guinness encyclopedia of popular music* (1992) · *The Times* (3 Jan 1984) · H. Shapiro, *Alexis Korner* (1996)
Wealth at death £46,760: probate, 25 June 1984, *CGPLA Eng. & Wales*

Korsakov, Nikolay Ivanovich (1749–1788). *See under* Industrial spies (*act. c.*1700–*c.*1800).

Kossoff, Paul (1950–1976), rock musician, was born on 14 September 1950 in Hampstead, London, the second son of actor David Kossoff (*b.* 1919), and his wife, Jennie, *née* Jenkins. He took up the guitar at the age of eight, inspired by classical, flamenco, and blues music. Even as a child his powers of concentration and ability to memorize finger positions impressed his guitar teacher. He bought his first electric guitar—a Gibson Les Paul—after seeing Eric Clapton play with John Mayall's Bluesbreakers. Kossoff left school at fifteen and went on tour, supplying live music for one of the plays in which his father was involved. By his sixteenth birthday he was working in Selmer's music shop in Charing Cross Road, where he met Jimi Hendrix, another formative influence.

In 1968 Kossoff formed the group Free with Paul Rodgers (vocals), Simon Kirke (drums), and Andy Fraser (bass). With the encouragement of Alexis Korner they signed to Chris Blackwell's Island Records. Free's début album, *Tons of Sobs*, was released in November 1968, and was followed by *Free* (1969). The band found its own variant on the bluesy rock popularized at the time by artists such as Cream and Hendrix. Free covered some blues standards and wrote material that showed off both Kossoff's guitar-playing and the mournful blues-inflected vocals of Rodgers in arrangements with a good sense of space and dynamics.

In 1970 the band scored a massive hit with the punchy 'All Right Now', since regarded as a rock classic. Free released *Fire and Water* (1970) and played at the Isle of Wight festival that August. A mellower fourth album, *Highway*, was not so well received, despite the fact that the plaintive quality of songs such as 'Be my Friend' was beyond the range of most rock bands at that time, with the possible exception of Peter Green's Fleetwood Mac. Despite the commercial success of the single 'My Brother Jake', tensions in the group, exacerbated by touring and Kossoff's burgeoning drug habit, led the band to split in May 1971. After *Free Live* (1971), the band reunited for *Free at Last* in 1972, another hit single 'Little Bit of Love', and a brief, troubled spell of touring. Kossoff was too unwell to contribute much to Free's last album, *Heartbreaker* (1973), and its chart single 'Wishing Well', on which vocalist Rodgers had to play some fine pastiche of Kossoff's style. Further attempts to tour and hold the band together proved unsuccessful and Free split for the last time in 1973.

Kossoff attempted to revive his career with a band called Back Street Crawler, which released two albums. Its chances were undermined by his struggle against drugs and the unwelcome attention of parasitical acquaintances who often robbed him of royalties by getting him to sign cheques when he was not aware of what he was doing. In 1974 Kossoff was hospitalized and brought back from the brink of death. He turned twenty-five and seemed to have a chance of recovering a normal life. Back Street Crawler went to the USA at the start of 1976 but Kossoff could not stay away from drugs. Eventually, his system could take no more, and he died of heart failure on a flight from Los Angeles to New York on 19 March 1976. He was unmarried.

Exploiting Marshall and Orange amplification and a vintage Gibson Les Paul, Kossoff produced an expressive tone and an inimitable vibrato. His lead guitar style was founded on a 'less is more' approach. Almost never flashy, he worked short phrases and played single bent notes of great soul. His most famous break, in 'All Right Now', shows tasteful construction, patiently building the solo to a memorable climax. Along with Eric Clapton, Jimmy Page, Peter Green, and Jeff Beck, Paul Kossoff deserves to be remembered as one of the UK's best rock lead guitarists of the 1960s.

RIKKY ROOKSBY

Sources *The Guitarist* (March 1996) · C. Larkin, ed., *The Virgin encyclopedia of popular music*, concise edn (1999) · I. Herbert, ed.,

Who's who in the theatre, 16th edn (1977) · T. Guerra, 'Paul Kossoff: a retrospective', www.tomguerra.com/Paul-Kossoff.html **Wealth at death** £19,515: administration, 9 Sept 1976, *CGPLA Eng. & Wales*

Kosterlitz, Hans Walter (1903–1996), pharmacologist, was born on 27 April 1903 in Berlin, the son of Bernhard Kosterlitz, medical practitioner, and his wife, Selma, *née* Lepman. Both Kosterlitz and his brother followed their father into medicine. Kosterlitz was educated at the universities of Heidelberg, Freiburg, and Berlin. His leanings were towards laboratory-based research, and he wrote his first scientific papers while still a medical student in Berlin. He gained his MD in 1928, and remained in Berlin for five years as an assistant in the first medical department, following his early interest in biochemistry, and studying the altered sugar metabolism in diabetic patients.

Though not Jewish, Kosterlitz was evidently dismayed by developments in Germany, and in 1934 he decided to join the laboratory of John James Rickard Macleod, the regius professor of physiology in Aberdeen. Macleod had recently returned from Toronto, and was famous as one of the co-discoverers, with Frederick Grant Banting and Charles Herbert Best, of insulin. Though Aberdeen may have seemed a somewhat remote scientific outpost, Macleod's laboratory had great appeal for researchers in the field of diabetes. Macleod died only a year after Kosterlitz joined his laboratory, but the latter carried on his research into carbohydrate metabolism for another fifteen years. He was appointed a Carnegie teaching fellow in 1936 (the year in which he received his Aberdeen PhD), and lecturer in physiology in 1939. On 9 March 1937 he married Johanna Maria Katharina (Hanna; *b.* 1905/6), daughter of Heinrich Gresshöner, farmer. They had one son, Michael.

Early in the Second World War Kosterlitz was briefly interned, but he soon returned to Aberdeen to contribute to the training of medical students, and to work on what he saw as a more urgent topic than diabetes, namely the effects of nutrition on liver function. He was appointed senior lecturer in 1945, and reader in physiology in 1955. In the early 1950s he decided to change direction scientifically, and he turned his attention to the autonomic nervous system, particularly the control of peristalsis, the rhythmical propulsive action of the gastrointestinal tract. A brief period at Harvard in 1953–4, working with Otto Krayer (a distinguished expatriate German pharmacologist whom Kosterlitz had known in Berlin), kindled his interest in pharmacology, and he learned of a paper published by Paul Trendelenburg in 1917 showing that the plant alkaloid morphine powerfully inhibited peristalsis. In Aberdeen he devoted himself to studying the peristaltic reflex in isolated segments of intestine suspended in organ baths, and using this preparation to analyse the actions of morphine on the nerves involved in peristalsis. At that time several other laboratories were studying morphine's effects on the brain, and there was scepticism about the relevance of Kosterlitz's painstaking pharmacological work on the intestine. He revealed much later that

Hans Walter Kosterlitz (1903–1996), by Godfrey Argent Studios

he had harboured from the beginning the idea that morphine, a plant-derived substance, might be acting as a surrogate for an endogenous chemical mediator, and that his undisclosed ambition had been to discover its nature.

Kosterlitz remained a reader in physiology at Aberdeen for thirteen years until 1968 when, at the age of sixty-five, he became professor and head of the newly created department of pharmacology at Aberdeen. This finally gave him the opportunity, denied for many years, to build up and lead his own department, and he made the most of it. His group turned its attention to carrying out careful quantitative pharmacological studies of the effects of morphine-like drugs on different animal tissues. Through these studies, they showed unequivocally the existence of three types of opiate 'receptor' (specialized binding molecules through which drugs exert their specific physiological effects). Simultaneously, other groups in Sweden and the United States came to similar conclusions by studying the binding of opiate drugs to different tissues. The discovery of specific receptors suggested the existence of an endogenous chemical mediator which, like morphine, produces physiological effects when it becomes attached to the receptor; Kosterlitz's long cherished belief in the existence of endogenous 'opioids' thus gained considerable credibility.

At this critical point Kosterlitz, then seventy, had to retire from his university post, but he stayed on as director of a new, independently funded unit for research on addictive drugs, which he led for another twenty-two years. John Hughes, deputy director, played a major part in the unit's very successful research. They immediately set about identifying the mysterious endogenous substance, starting from copious extracts of pig brain, and using the pharmacological assays for morphine-like substances that they had perfected. After many set-backs, they succeeded in 1975 in isolating two novel peptides (leu- and met-enkephalin), which were the elusive endogenous opioid peptides. These short peptides, containing only five amino acids, were soon found within the sequence of much longer peptides (endorphins) produced by the pituitary gland, which also belong to the endogenous opioid family. This family of mediators, and the associated receptors, quickly became the focus of intense worldwide research activity, and proved to be involved in many brain functions, including pain perception, drug dependence, learning and memory, endocrine secretions, and much else. Kosterlitz's discovery thus represented an important scientific breakthrough, which was the basis for many subsequent advances in the pharmacology of the nervous system.

Kosterlitz had an infectious enthusiasm for his work, and reciprocated the affection and respect of numerous younger colleagues. His many distinctions included fellowship of the Royal Society of Edinburgh (1951), the Schmiedeberg Plakette of the German Pharmacological Society (1976), fellowship of the Royal Society (1978), the Albert Lasker award (1978), the royal medal of the Royal Society (1979), and honorary degrees from the universities of Liège, Aberdeen, St Andrews, and Dundee. Despite two serious strokes, and other illnesses in later life, he remained active as a scientist in Aberdeen (publishing his last paper in 1991) until shortly before his death, of bronchopneumonia and cerebrovascular disease, at Rowan Court, Cults, Aberdeen, on 26 October 1996; he was buried at Newhills cemetery, Aberdeen. He was survived by his wife, Hanna, and son, Michael, professor of theoretical physics at Brown University.   H. P. RANG

Sources G. M. Lees, 'Hans Walter Kosterlitz', *Aberdeen University Review*, 57 (1997–8), 139–48 · A. T. McKnight and A. O. Corbett, 'H. W. Kosterlitz', *British Pharmacological Society handbook* (1998), 194–9 · G. M. Lees, 'A tribute to the late Hans W. Kosterlitz', *Canadian Journal of Physiology and Pharmacology*, 76 (1998), 244–51 · H. W. Kosterlitz, 'The best laid plans …', *Annual Review of Pharmacology*, 19 (1979), 1–12 · J. Hughes, 'H. W. Kosterlitz', *Nature*, 384 (1996), 418 · *The Times* (13 Nov 1996) · WWW · personal knowledge (2004) · private information (2004) [G. M. Lees] · m. cert. · d. cert.

Archives RS, personal file · U. Aberdeen, Special Libraries and Archives, papers | Bodl. Oxf., corresp. relating to Society for Protection of Science and Learning |SOUND U. Aberdeen

Likenesses Godfrey Argent Studios, photograph, Godfrey Argent Studios, London [*see illus.*] · photograph, repro. in *The Times*

Wealth at death £218,980.97: confirmation, 16 Jan 1997, NA Scot., SC/CO 972/132

Kotzé, Sir John Gilbert (1849–1940), judge in South Africa, born at Leeuwenhof, Cape Town, on 5 November 1849, was a descendant of Jan Kotzé, who emigrated from Amsterdam in 1691, and the youngest son of Petrus Johannes Kotzé, who was twice mayor of Cape Town. His mother was Susanna Maria, eldest daughter of Johannes

Sir John Gilbert Kotzé (1849–1940), by unknown photographer

Gysbert Blanckenberg. He was educated at the South African College (afterwards the University of Cape Town) from 1864 to 1868, and in 1869 he became a student at London University and the Inner Temple. He qualified for the LLB degree in 1872, and on 17 April of that year he married Mary Aurelia (d. 1931), fourth daughter of Daniel Bell of Milton House, Clapham, London; they had six sons and a daughter.

In 1874 Kotzé was called to the bar and returned to South Africa where he began to practise as a barrister, first in Cape Town and then in Grahamstown. In March 1877, when he was only twenty-seven, President Burgers offered him the office of chief justice of the South African Republic (Transvaal). Kotzé accepted it, but before he assumed duty the Transvaal was annexed by Great Britain and on his arrival at Pretoria the administrator suggested that he should take his seat as sole judge of the high court about to be constituted. He agreed but reserved his right to claim the position of chief justice.

In 1879 the high commissioner for South Africa, Sir Bartle Frere, drew up a constitution for the Transvaal, based upon the principles of crown colony government. He submitted it to Kotzé, who told him that it was in conflict with the annexation proclamation and would not be accepted by the Boers. The constitution was nevertheless introduced and aroused widespread dissatisfaction. In the same year Kotzé drew up a minute objecting to the appointment of an attorney-general who had not been admitted as a barrister and signed it in his capacity as chief justice; he sent it to the governor, Sir Garnet Wolseley, to be forwarded to the secretary of state. The governor declined to do so on the ground that Kotzé was not chief justice and had no right to sign in that capacity. This led to a controversy which the governor settled, temporarily, by appointing Jacobus Petrus de Wet as chief justice and Kotzé as puisne judge. Kotzé protested and petitioned the privy council but nothing further was heard of the matter because the Boers, dissatisfied with the new constitution, established their own government on 16 December 1880, which led to the First South African War. After the war Kotzé was appointed in 1881 chief justice of the Transvaal, but he found his position difficult. In the following year he was offered a seat on the bench of the high court of Griqualand West; he accepted the offer but did not take up the appointment because he was persuaded to continue as chief justice, and thereafter, from 1882 to 1898, he presided over the supreme court of the South African Republic (the name which the country resumed in 1884).

In spite of the fact that he was on the bench, Kotzé took an active interest in political questions and in 1893, without resigning from the bench, he became a candidate for the presidency: however, he received only 81 votes, against 7854 cast for Kruger.

In 1897 a serious constitutional crisis arose out of some of Kotzé's judgments. In 1884 he had, in a considered judgment, examined the constitutional powers of the Volksraad in relation to the *grondwet* (constitution) of 1858 and had decided that supreme power in the republic was vested in the Volksraad, that it had power to make laws which were in conflict with the *grondwet*, that it could legislate by mere resolution (*besluit*), and that the supreme court had no jurisdiction to pronounce on the validity of its enactments. Subsequently he began to have doubts about the matter, and in 1895 he announced, by way of *obiter dictum*, that his views had changed and that he now regarded the *grondwet* as a rigid constitution on the lines of the American constitution and that the supreme court had jurisdiction to inquire into the validity of acts of the Volksraad. On 22 January 1897 he carried these new views into effect in a judgment (*Brown* v. *Leyds*) which caused considerable embarrassment to the government. The Volksraad immediately passed a law authorizing the president to ask the judges whether they claimed the right to inquire into the validity of the Volksraad's legislative acts and, if they did not repudiate such a right, to dismiss them. The judges protested but the president put the question. The chief justice of Cape Colony, Sir John Henry de Villiers, although his views on the constitutional issue differed from those of Kotzé, hastened to Pretoria to mediate in the dispute. A temporary compromise was effected, but after a while Kotzé considered that the president was not carrying out his side of it and communicated his views to him very pointedly. Kruger promptly acted under the provisions of the law and dismissed Kotzé (16 February 1898). Despite an appeal to the people by Kotzé, the sensation caused by his dismissal was soon overshadowed by the outbreak of the Second South African War in 1899.

In 1900 Kotzé was appointed attorney-general of Southern Rhodesia. In 1902 he took silk; in 1904 he was appointed to the bench of the Cape eastern districts court at Grahamstown, and on 8 July of that year he became its judge president. In 1913 he accepted a puisne judgeship in the Cape provincial division of the supreme court of South Africa at Cape Town and in 1920 he became judge president of that court. In July 1922 he was appointed a judge of appeal and held that post until his retirement in 1927. His first wife died in 1931, and in 1933 he married Margaretha

Jeldina, daughter of Hendrik Doornbos of Groningen in the Netherlands.

Kotzé was knighted in 1917, having in 1896 been appointed by the king of Portugal a knight grand cross of the order of the Conception. He received the honorary degree of LLD from the universities of the Cape of Good Hope (1912), Cape Town (1927), and Witwatersrand (1939). He died at Cape Town at the age of ninety, on 1 April 1940, survived by his second wife. He was buried in Maitland cemetery.

Kotzé's best-known legal work was a translation, with notes, of Simon van Leeuwen's *Commentaries on Roman-Dutch Law* (2 vols., 1881–6). He also published a monograph entitled *Causa in the Roman and Roman-Dutch Law of Contract* (1922) and contributed several learned articles to the *South African Law Journal*.

Kotzé was proud of having been on the bench, with a short interval, for fifty years. He was a stout upholder of the principles of judicial independence. He was deeply imbued with the principles of Roman-Dutch law, and was an earnest student of the medieval authorities. He was undoubtedly one of the most distinguished judges and jurists of his day in South Africa. His valuable collection of legal works, some of great rarity, became part of the library of the appeal court of South Africa.

E. F. WATERMEYER, rev. LYNN MILNE

Sources J. G. Kotzé, *Biographical memoirs and reminiscences*, 1 (1934) · J. V. G. Hiemstra, 'Kotzé, Johannes Gysbert (Sir John Gilbert)', *DSAB* · T. R. H. Davenport, *South Africa: a modern history*, 4th edn (1991) · P. Kruger, *The memoirs of Paul Kruger*, trans. A. Teixeira de Mattos, 2 vols. (1902) · E. A. Walker, *Lord de Villiers and his times: South Africa, 1842–1914* (1925) · Burke, *Peerage* (1939) · *Kelly's Post Office London directory* (1966) · personal knowledge (1949)

Likenesses G. Wheatley, bust; library of appeal court of South Africa, 1949 · photograph, repro. in Kotzé, *Biographical memoirs* [see illus.]

Krabtree [Crabtree], **Henry** (1642/3?–c.1693), astrologer and Church of England clergyman, may be the Henry Crabtree born in Norland or Sowerby, in the parish of Halifax, who was admitted sizar at Christ's College, Cambridge, early in 1664, aged twenty-one. He acted as a curate of Todmorden, a chapelry in the parish of Rochdale from 1662, was ordained deacon by the archbishop of York on 6 November 1664, and was licensed as curate on 8 August 1665. Krabtree's modest fame rests on his *Mercurius rusticus 1685, or, A Country Almanack, yet Treating of Courtly Matters*, which dealt with the Ottoman invasion and siege of Vienna in 1683. It had been composed that autumn, in response to the alarmist works of John Holwell and others, but Krabtree missed the Company of Stationers' deadline and issued the same text with a revised calendar for 1685. He identified the Turks as the Little Horn of Daniel and the Habsburg empire as part of the Fourth (Roman) Monarchy, arguing from scripture that, as the Fourth Monarchy must last until the world's end, the Turks could never prevail. At Todmorden, Krabtree kept the first registers of births, marriages, and deaths, in which he made astrological and humorous remarks, and he was noted as a fierce enemy of the local Quakers. The curacy brought only £12 a year; this he supplemented by marrying Mary, widow of John Pilling of Stanisfield Hall, Todmorden, where he took up residence, and by practising medicine. His involvement in 1688–9 with the notorious case of the 'Surey demoniack' (the epileptic Richard Dugdale) led to lingering suspicions of sorcery. Another man was serving the cure at Todmorden in 1682–3, perhaps as an assistant, and kept the registers in 1693, the probable date of Krabtree's death; he had certainly been dead for some time by 1697. His wife, who survived him, was buried at Todmorden on 15 December 1718.   BERNARD CAPP

Sources J. Holden, 'Todmorden antiquities', *Transactions of the Halifax Antiquarian Society* (1907), 203–11 • B. S. Capp, *Astrology and the popular press: English almanacs, 1500–1800* (1979) • [T. Jollie], *The Surey demoniack* (1697) • Z. Taylor, *The Surey impostor* (1697) • T. Jollie, *A vindication of the Surey demoniack* (1698) • Lancs. RO • Ches. & Chester ALSS • Venn, *Alum. Cant.*

Krahmer, Carlo [*real name* William Max Geserick Krahmer] (1914–1976), jazz drummer and record producer, was born on 11 March 1914 at 22 Cropley Street, Shoreditch, London, the son of William Henry Charles Krahmer, hairdresser's assistant, and his wife, Phoebe Murrell. He suffered from defective vision from birth and taught himself to play the drums. He subsequently received tuition from Max Abrams and at the age of thirteen commenced playing with local bands, turning professional two years later. Always known as Carlo Krahmer, during the mid-1930s he was a member of the National Institute for the Blind dance band, led by Claude Bampton (George Shearing was also in the band), before co-leading the Lewis–Krahmer Chicagoans with guitarist Vic Lewis. He led his own quartet at the Cotton Club, London, in 1940 before joining the band of trumpeter Johnny Claes for a year.

The war was a busy period for Krahmer, who played at many of London's West End clubs, often appearing at three in one night. It was during this period that he extended his musical activities to encompass the vibraphone. He led the regular house band at London's Feldman Club at 100 Oxford Street each Sunday from 1943 to 1950 and in 1948 he appeared at the Nice jazz festival on the same bill as Louis Armstrong and Earl Hines. The following year he took his own band to play at the Paris jazz fair, an event also attended by such American visitors as Sidney Bechet, Charlie Parker, and Miles Davis.

In 1947 Krahmer established the Esquire record label with his partner Peter Newbrook, a director of photography then working in the film industry. Krahmer's Bloomsbury flat, 76 Bedford Court Mansions, Bedford Avenue, where he lived with his wife, Gertrude Rosina (Greta; *d*. 1979), had become a focal point for young British jazz musicians anxious to hear the latest new recordings from America. Krahmer had always been an avid collector (he owned over 100 different versions of 'Tiger Rag') and had many contacts at a time when foreign records were difficult to obtain in Britain. He and Newbrook set up a recording studio in the basement of the flat and recorded the early work of such artists as Ronnie Scott, John Dankworth, Cleo Laine, and Victor Feldman long before the major record companies became aware of their talents.

It was then very difficult to do financial deals outside the UK, but Krahmer and Newbrook succeeded in exchanging Esquire masters with French and Swedish companies, resulting in the British release of material by Charlie Parker, Don Byas, Sidney Bechet, and Stan Getz. In 1950 Esquire negotiated a formal leasing arrangement with the American Prestige record company and for the next fourteen years important and influential recordings by Miles Davis, Sonny Rollins, the Modern Jazz Quartet, John Coltrane, and others appeared on the small British label. Krahmer also documented the work of local traditional-style jazz groups and even released recordings by the Happy Wanderers, a quartet of musical buskers frequently to be found trudging along Oxford Street.

With the termination of the Prestige deal Krahmer fell back on issuing blues and jazz material from small American labels, but the heyday of Esquire was over. After Krahmer's death, from cancer, at 76 Bedford Court Mansions, on 20 April 1976, his widow, Greta, and Newbrook continued to run the company. Following her death in 1979 Newbrook kept the label going until the mid-1980s. He concentrated on the reissue of earlier material and privately made recordings from the war years with Krahmer playing drums in small groups containing musicians from the American navy band then based in London. Krahmer's own career as a working musician had come to an end in 1950 when the task of running the Esquire label became a full-time occupation.   ALUN MORGAN

Sources J. Chilton, *Who's who of British jazz* (1997) • J. Godbolt, *A history of jazz in Britain* (1984) • B. Kernfeld, ed., *The new Grove dictionary of jazz* (1994) • *CGPLA Eng. & Wales* (1976) • b. cert. • d. cert. • private information (2004) [Peter Newbrook]
Wealth at death £28,425: probate, 11 Aug 1976, *CGPLA Eng. & Wales*

Kramer, Jacob (1892–1962), painter and graphic artist, was born on 26 December 1892 in Klintsy, in the province of Chernigov in Ukraine, the only son of Max (Meir) Kramer (*d*. 1915), a court painter who worked in a naturalistic style and who had studied under Ilya Repin at the St Petersburg Academy of Arts, and his wife, Celia, a distinguished opera singer and authority on Slavonic folk-songs, whose father had established a circuit of small rural theatres. Kramer had two sisters, Millie and Sarah. He was unusual among Anglo-Jewish immigrant artists in coming from an artistic family. His uncle, Boris (Cion) Kramer, was also a Russian court painter who exhibited at the World's Columbian Exhibition in Chicago in 1893.

Kramer's family settled in Leeds, which had a sizeable Jewish immigrant community, in 1900, when he was eight years old. He attended Darley Street council school, where his talent was soon recognized, and assisted his father in his photographic studio. In 1902, aged ten, he ran away to Liverpool and went to sea for six months. On his return he did odd jobs in a number of northern towns, including Manchester, where he attended evening classes at the school of art. In 1907 he attended evening classes at the Leeds School of Art and a year later won a scholarship to study there full-time for three years. Michael Sadler, vice-chancellor of Leeds University, was an important early mentor and patron. Between 1913 and 1914, supported by the Jewish Educational Aid Society, he was a student at the Slade School of Art in London. The financial support, however, came with the following warning: 'The Society has been given to understand that you have not always worked at Leeds with that seriousness and assiduity which is expected of their students. ... They trust that they will hear no complaints on this score during your short stay in London' (Roberts, 11).

In 1915 Kramer was invited—although he was not an official member—to contribute to the first exhibition of the vorticist group at the Doré Galleries in London, and was elected a member of the London Group. His first one-man show took place in 1916 at Matthews and Brooke in Bradford, Yorkshire. In 1918 he joined the Russian labour corps and was sent to south Wales, where he worked as the camp's librarian. He was naturalized on 16 January 1922.

Exposed at the Slade to avant-garde influences (notably post-impressionism, cubism, and futurism), Kramer gradually abandoned the naturalism of his earliest works, most of them portraits clearly influenced by Augustus John, in favour of a dramatically simplified, hieratic style indebted to the example of the vorticists (William Roberts—who would later marry his sister Sarah, C. R. W. Nevinson, and David Bomberg were fellow students) and Mark Gertler in particular. His most distinctive works were stylistically radical depictions of Jews at study or at prayer, such as *The Day of Atonement* (1919, Leeds City Art Gallery). Rhythmically powerful, and sombre in colour, with the figures isolated against a bare background, these paintings are intensely devotional, even though Kramer early on ceased to be an observant Jew. In 1918 he wrote to Herbert Read that 'the degree of expression in a work is the measure of its greatness—a spiritual discernment is more essential than the reproduction of the obvious' (10 March 1918, Victoria, British Columbia, University of Victoria).

Loyalty to his mother and sisters following his father's death in 1915 caused Kramer to return to the family home in Beecroft Grove in Leeds, where financial necessity eventually impelled him to lay artistic experimentation to one side and to concentrate on more marketable naturalistic portraits. Israel Zangwill and Jacob Epstein, both close friends of the artist, were among those who sat for him, and in 1921 Epstein produced a bronze portrait bust of Kramer, a physically striking individual (casts in Tate collection and Leeds City Art Gallery). In the 1930s his sitters included such eminent figures as Mahatma Gandhi and Frederick Delius. (The portrait of the latter is in the Leeds City Art Gallery.) His later work is generally less innovative, though works of the late 1920s such as *The Talmudists* (1929, Leeds City Art Gallery) represent an attempt to revive the harshly geometric style of works such as *The Day of Atonement*. Similarly, a commission in the late 1940s to design book jackets for the Soncino Books of the Bible enabled him to recapture something of the graphic boldness of the work which he produced between about 1915 and the early 1920s.

Kramer became a familiar figure in Leeds, which remained his home for the rest of his life, founding the Yorkshire Luncheon Club (intended to stimulate an interest in the creative arts) in 1931 and teaching at the City of Leeds Branch College of Art, which in 1968 was renamed the Jacob Kramer College of the City of Leeds in his honour. He died of cerebral arteriosclerosis (the death certificate also mentions Parkinson's disease and chronic bronchitis as secondary causes of death) on 4 February 1962 in the Jewish Home of Rest at Balham, London, and was buried on the 7th in the Jewish cemetery at Gildersome, near Leeds. He remained unmarried and had no children.

MONICA BOHM-DUCHEN

Sources J. Roberts, ed., *The Kramer documents* (1983) · H. Read, S. Thorndike, and others, *Jacob Kramer: a memorial volume* (1969) · *Jacob Kramer reassessed* (1984) [exhibition catalogue, Ben Uri Art Society, London] · *The immigrant generation: Jewish artists in Britain, 1900–1945* (1983) [The Jewish Museum, New York, exhibition catalogue] · F. Spalding, 'The day of atonement', *Art and Artists*, 211 (April 1984), 24–6 · d. cert.
Archives U. Leeds, Brotherton L., corresp. and papers
Likenesses J. Epstein, bronze bust, 1921, Leeds City Art Gallery · J. Kramer, self-portrait, lithograph, 1930, NPG · cast (after bronze bust by J. Epstein, 1921), Tate collection

Kranich, Burchard [*known as* Dr Burcot] (d. **1578**), physician and mining entrepreneur, came from southern Germany ('High Almain'); his name suggests that he was from Kronach, upper Franconia, near the mining area of the Erzgebirge. He is first heard of in 'The suit of Burghard touching the mines' (*CSP dom.*, no. 826), on 3 June 1553. The following year Kranich was licensed to prospect for, mine, and smelt any kinds of minerals in England. After being involved in lead-smelting in Derbyshire, he moved to Cornwall, being commissioned 'to dig ... such mines of gold, silver and copper as he hath already ... tried out' (*APC, 1554–6*, 211). He is credited with using the first water-wheel type hammers ('stampers') in England. However, his Cornish mines were taken over, and for the years 1557–9 he was granted protection from creditors, 'on account of certain causes ... touching the king and queen and the realm' (*CPR, 1555–7*).

On 14 June 1561 Kranich was granted denization, and during 1562 was paid 100 marks (£66 13s. 4d.), with no reason given. In August, John Somers wrote that 'My Lady Marquis [the marchioness of Northampton] is in great danger by the jaundice. The physicians half despair, but Burcot, the Dutchman, at a pinch is like to do some good' (*CSP for.*). In October, Queen Elizabeth was taken ill with smallpox: the story of the insulted Kranich being threatened with a dagger before he would attend her is a later invention. The physician William Bullein made good-natured references to 'Dr Tocrub', while Gervase Markham's *The English Hus-Wife* (5) attributed unspecified prescriptions to a manuscript (unidentified) of Kranich and Eliseus Bomelius.

Amid growing doubts, Kranich alone insisted that the ore brought home (1577–8) by Martin Frobisher contained gold, and demanded for extracting it a daily wage of £1, and £200 pension—without success. Kranich designed a new hearth, and—someone said—'doctored' the melt with gold and silver coins. In the event, the influential investors lost their money, and his reputation suffered.

In 1568 Kranich was said to adhere to the English church; the report, ten years later, that he had heard mass at a private house was probably untrue, and his will is in the protestant form. Kranich lived in St Clement's churchyard, just outside Temple Bar, in Westminster. On 20 September 1578 a Susan Burcott 'from Doctor Burcotts' was buried at St Clement Danes: 'the death of a child of his' hastened Kranich's end, William Fleetwood believed (Hatfield House, Salisbury (Cecil) MSS, no. 660).

On 7 October 1578 Kranich, suffering from gout and infirmity, made his will, leaving his dwelling-house to his wife, who was to receive the proceeds from the sale of his Holborn properties, after payment of his debts. Following legacies to his servants and the poor, the residue, likewise, would go to his widow and executrix. By a codicil (19 October), his servant William Deane would have any proceeds over £700 from the sale, and also his (unspecified) medical books and instruments; Kranich promised a silver-gilt bowl with a cover, given him by 'my Lord', to a friend.

Kranich died later that month, and was buried at St Clement Danes on 22 October 1578; probate was granted on 21 November to his widow, Agnes.   JOHN BENNELL

Sources *CPR*, 1553–4, 159, 160; 1555–7, 554; 1557–8, 308; 1560–63, 97, 392, 409, 495 · *APC*, 1554–8 · *CSP for.*, 1562 · M. B. Donald, 'Burchard Kranich (*c*.1515–78), miner and queen's physician', *Annals of Science*, 6 (1948–50), 308–22, pl. IV · will, proved, 21 Nov 1578, PRO, PROB 11/60/41 · R. E. G. Kirk and E. F. Kirk, eds., *Returns of aliens dwelling in the city and suburbs of London, from the reign of Henry VIII to that of James I*, Huguenot Society of London, 10/3 (1907), 416 · M. B. Donald, *Elizabethan monopolies: the history of the Company of Mineral and Battery Works from 1565 to 1604* (1961), 167 · *Calendar of the manuscripts of the most hon. the marquis of Salisbury*, 2, HMC, 9 (1888), nos. 660, 1217 · *CSP dom.*, 1547–53, nos. 826, 829; *addenda, 1566–79* · parish registers, St Clement Danes, City Westm. AC · F. E. Halliday, 'Queen Elizabeth and Dr Burcot', *History Today*, 5 (1955), 542–4 · G. Markham, *Countrey contentments, in two books … the second intituled, The English hus-wife* (1615); repr. in G. M. [G. Markham], *A way to get wealth* (1631), pt 5

Krapf, (Johann) Ludwig (1810–1881), linguist of Swahili and missionary in Africa, was born on 11 January 1810 at Derendingen near Tübingen, in the kingdom of Württemberg, the youngest of four children of Johann Jakob Krapf (1773–1846), peasant farmer, and his wife, Katherina Maria Braun (1776–1846). In 1823 Ludwig Krapf entered the Anatolian school in Tübingen, where Latin, and later Greek and Hebrew, were among the subjects he learned. When he was still in the first form his father bought him an atlas of the world, and the young Ludwig wondered why so much of north-eastern Africa had been left blank; a little later a bookseller in Tübingen lent him an odd volume of Bruce's *Travels to Discover the Source of the Nile*, from which he learned of the existence of hyenas. At seventeen he entered the missionary college at Basel and remained there for two years. After a break to reconsider his vocation he returned to the college and was duly ordained in the Lutheran faith.

Krapf's original plan was to go to Smyrna as a missionary, so he began learning Turkish and modern Greek but,

in 1836, the secretary of the London-based Church Missionary Society was recruiting missionaries in Basel, and offered him a post in Abyssinia. He accepted, and was to remain with the society for nineteen years. In 1837, aged twenty-seven, Krapf travelled to Egypt, and thence to Abyssinia, where a Church Missionary Society mission had been founded in 1830 by Samuel Gobat. At first he worked in the Adwa area of Tigré. Then, in June 1839, he moved to Ankober, the capital of the kingdom of Shoa, at the invitation of King Sahela Sellasie. In 1841 an English embassy under Major Cornwallis Harris arrived at Ankober and Krapf was able to render assistance as an interpreter. During this time he and another missionary assembled a collection of more than seventy Ethiopic manuscripts, which they presented to the British Museum. Krapf remained in Shoa until 1842, when he returned to Egypt. In that year he was awarded a doctoral degree by the University of Tübingen.

At the end of 1842 Krapf and his wife, Rosine Dietrich (1817–1844), from Basel, whom he had married that year in the British chapel at Alexandria, returned to Abyssinia, hoping to re-enter Shoa, but permission was refused. In 1843 Rosine gave birth to a daughter, who lived for only a few hours. Frustrated in his endeavours to work among the Oromo (Galla) people, largely on account of opposition from Christian Abyssinians and from rival Roman Catholic missionaries, Krapf and his wife sailed for Zanzibar in 1843. In March 1844, armed with a letter of introduction from Sayyid Saʿid bin Sultan al Busaʿidi (who had recently transferred his capital from Muscat to Zanzibar), the Krapfs arrived in Mombasa, the first Christian missionaries in east Africa in modern times. In July 1844 Rosine Krapf died, and was followed to the grave a few days later by her second infant daughter; both were buried at Mkomani, on the mainland north of Mombasa.

Krapf's first major task was to learn the Swahili language, which is both the language of the Swahili coast and also, in an attenuated form, the lingua franca of the east African interior. Indeed, Krapf was probably the first European to realize the potential of Swahili as a lingua franca, and the first to grasp that Swahili belonged to the 'Bantu' family of languages (as they were later to be called). In 1849 he had published the first printed text in Swahili (three chapters of Genesis in roman script), and in 1850 the first systematic Swahili grammar appeared in Tübingen. In 1854 Krapf donated two Swahili manuscripts to the library of the Deutsche Morgenländische Gesellschaft, the first to reach Europe. In 1882 *A Dictionary of the Suahili Language* was published posthumously in London. The interest of this great pioneer lexicon is now historical rather than practical, but it also contains many valuable notes on Swahili customs. Altogether there are some twenty-five publications credited to Krapf's name, many concerned with language. He is considered the father of Swahili studies.

In 1844 Krapf had paid a brief visit to the Rabai, a people settled in Mombasa's hilly hinterland. In 1846 he was joined by a compatriot, Johannes Rebmann (1820–1876), and the two men went to live among the Rabai who, from this time onwards, were to experience almost continuous exposure to Christian missionaries. In 1848 Rebmann became the first European to see the snow-capped peaks of Kilimanjaro, Africa's highest mountain, while in the following year Krapf became the first European to see Mount Kenya.

After visiting Württemberg in 1850, Krapf returned to east Africa in 1851. In 1854 he visited Church Missionary Society headquarters in London, when it was decided that he should go to Jerusalem at the end of that year to confer with Bishop Samuel Gobat. He returned briefly to Abyssinia in 1855, when he met Emperor Tewodros. In 1856 his connection with the Church Missionary Society ended, and he returned to Württemberg, devoting much of his time to translation work. In 1858 the publication of his *Reisen in Ostafrika* ('Travels in east Africa') set an early, but seldom equalled model of careful observation. In 1867 he was again in Abyssinia, as an interpreter attached to the British army which Sir Robert Napier led to Magdala. Krapf had married again in 1857 and had had one daughter. His second wife died in 1868 and in 1869 he married Nanette Schmid; they had no children. He died at his home in Kornthal, Württemberg, on 26 November 1881, and was buried there. In 1998 a museum commemorating the work of Rebmann and Krapf was opened in Rabai.

Krapf's journeys prepared the way for the exploration of the great lakes and the sources of the Nile, while his contribution to evangelization, linguistics, and geography increased the tempo of the European scramble for Africa in the 1880s. From time to time Krapf has been compared to David Livingstone, but, in truth, Krapf was overshadowed by Livingstone, and never experienced the popularity that he enjoyed. P. J. L. FRANKL

Sources J. L. Krapf, *Reisen in Ostafrika* (1858) • J. L. Krapf, *Travels, researches and missionary labours … in eastern Africa*, abridged version (1860) • U. Birm. L., special collections department, Church Missionary Society archive • Ledderhose, 'Krapf, Johann Ludwig', *Allgemeine deutsche Biographie*, ed. R. von Liliencron and others, 17 (Leipzig, 1883), 49–54 • H. J. Rieckenberg, 'Krapf, Johann Ludwig', in Otto, Graf zu Stolberg-Wernigerode, *Neue deutsche Biographie* (Berlin, 1953–) • *The Times* (21 Dec 1881) • P. J. L. Frankl, 'Johann Ludwig Krapf and the birth of Swahili studies', *Zeitschrift der Deutschen Morgenländischen Gesellschaft*, 142 (1992), 12–20 • 'The missionary career of Dr Krapf', *Church Missionary Intelligencer*, 33 (1882), 65–81, 133–46 • J. L. Krapf, *Travels, researches and missionary labours … in eastern Africa*, 2nd edn (1968), bibliography

Archives U. Birm. L., Christian Missionary Society MSS

Likenesses portrait, repro. in J. L. Krapf, *A dictionary of the Suahili language* (1882), frontispiece

Krasker, Robert (1913–1981), cinematographer, was born on 13 August 1913 in Perth, Australia, the youngest of five children. His parents were both French. One of the most celebrated cameramen in British cinema history, Robert Krasker was brought up in Australia and France. After studying art in Paris and photography in Dresden he gained his first job as a clapper boy at the Paramount Studios in Joinville, north-east France. He subsequently moved to England and joined Alexander Korda's London Films, where he quickly graduated to operator for the company's senior cameraman, Georges Périnal, on prestige productions such as *Rembrandt* (1936), *The Four Feathers*

(1939), and *The Thief of Bagdad* (1940). Krasker remained at Denham Studios after it had been purchased by J. Arthur Rank and in 1943 he gained his first solo credit as lighting cameraman on *The Lamp Still Burns*, directed by Maurice Elvey. He soon established himself as a major new talent and his artistry contributed a great deal to the considerable improvement in British cinema's critical reputation during the 1940s.

Krasker's first big production was *Henry V* (1944), Laurence Olivier's rousing cinematic version of Shakespeare's play, which is perhaps the most famous British Technicolor film of the war years. While much of the film adopted the typical high-key Technicolor style, there were some interesting low-key sequences: the death of Falstaff and the eve of the battle stand out in their use of looming shadows and careful highlights, anticipating the kind of crisp, high-contrast photographic style (although primarily in black and white) with which Krasker tends to be associated. The triumph of *Henry V* led to assignments with some of Britain's top directors including David Lean and Carol Reed. Krasker photographed Lean's *Brief Encounter* (1945), a restrained but delicately crafted tale of the unconsummated love affair between a respectable suburban housewife (Celia Johnson) and a doctor (Trevor Howard). Set in the middle of winter, much of the action takes place in dimly lit locations, and the prevailing ideas of deception and guilt are effectively evoked by the skilful manipulation of light and shade.

Krasker's meticulous deployment of expressionistic lighting and camerawork to underscore themes and reveal psychological states was perhaps most effectively demonstrated in two thrillers which he photographed for Carol Reed. *Odd Man Out* (1946), set in Belfast, starred James Mason as a mortally wounded IRA gunman on the run, while *The Third Man* (1949), shot on location in the rubble of allied-occupied, post-war Vienna, featured a strong international cast, including Joseph Cotten, Trevor Howard, Alida Valli, and Orson Welles as Harry Lime. The action in both takes place largely at night, with the visual impact created through a combination of low-key lighting, wide-angle compositions, and dramatic camera angles. In *The Third Man* there is also the celebrated use of 'Dutch' tilts, strongly angled compositions which forcefully convey a sense of uncertainty, unease, and confusion. Krasker won an Oscar for some of the most inspired atmospheric lighting achieved on location in the history of cinema.

During the 1950s Krasker moved increasingly into the international arena with films such as *Cry, the Beloved Country* (1951), *Romeo and Juliet* (1954), *Senso* (1953), *Alexander the Great* (1956), and *Trapeze* (1956). This allowed him to explore a wide range of photographic and lighting situations, and he excelled in both black and white and colour, in academy and wide-screen formats. Krasker's versatility was demonstrated by work ranging from *The Criminal* (1960), Joseph Losey's gritty black and white drama inspired visually by Victorian prison photographs, and *Billy Budd* (1962), shot in black and white Cinemascope, which successfully combined high contrast and depth of field, to such colourful wide-screen epics as *El Cid* (1961) and *The Fall of the Roman Empire* (1964), both directed by Anthony Mann. Ill health had dogged Krasker's career since he contracted malaria in Egypt on *The Four Feathers* in 1939. This resulted in chronic diabetes, which caused problems throughout his career and led to an early retirement from feature production in the mid-1960s. Krasker died on 16 August 1981 at St Stephen's Hospital, Chelsea, London.   DUNCAN PETRIE

Sources K. Desmond, 'A glimpse of Krasker, part 1', *Eyepiece* (Sept–Oct 1990), 24–32 · K. Desmond, 'A glimpse of Krasker, part 2', *Eyepiece* (Nov–Dec 1990), 27–30 · D. Petrie, *The British cinematographer* (1996) · J. Huntley, 'Henry V', *British technicolor films* (1949), 62–9 · R. Krasker, 'Photographing the stars', *Eyepiece* (Jan–Feb 1991), 20–23 · H. A. Lightman, '*Odd man out*: suspense in black and white', *American Cinematographer* (Aug 1947), 276–7 · H. A. Lightman, 'The photography of *El Cid* in Technirama-70', *American Cinematographer* (Jan 1962), 30–48 · S. Murray, 'Robert Krasker', *Cinema Papers*, 115 (1997), 18–19 · D. Elley, 'Robert Krasker', *Focus on Film*, 13 (1973), 45 · B. Baker and M. Salmi, 'Robert Krasker', *Film Dope*, 32 (1985), 1 · A. White, 'Illuminations', *Film Comment* (Sept–Oct 1989) · *CGPLA Eng. & Wales* (1982) · d. cert.
Archives BFI, corresp. and papers relating to various projects | FILM BFI NFTVA, documentary footage
Wealth at death £65,704: probate, 27 Jan 1982, *CGPLA Eng. & Wales*

Kratzer, Nicolaus (*b.* 1486/7, *d.* after 1550), astronomer and maker of scientific instruments, was born in Munich, probably the son of a saw smith, named Hans. The date of his birth can only be deduced from a portrait by Hans Holbein the younger from 1528 (Paris, Louvre), which bears the inscription 'Imago ad vivam effigiem expressa Nicolai Kratzeri monacensis qui Bavarus erat quadragesimum primum annum tempore illo complebat 1528' ('Live portrait of the monk Nicholas Kratzer who was Bavarian, done in 1528 when he was forty-one').

Kratzer was probably trained in his father's craft. He left his native town for Cologne and matriculated at the university there on 18 November 1506, and took his BA in 1509. Then he went to the University of Wittenberg. During the following years Kratzer probably practised instrument making, but until his arrival in England in 1517 or 1518 almost nothing is known except the fact that about 1515 he copied out some astronomical treatises in the Carthusian monastery of Maurbach, near Vienna. The purpose of his move to the court of Henry VIII is shrouded in mystery, but the background was obviously known to Erasmus of Rotterdam and his correspondents. In 1517 Peter Giles wrote to Erasmus that Kratzer was on his way to England with astrolabes, armillary spheres, and a Greek book. In 1520 Kratzer, now called 'deviser of the King's horologes', was given leave of absence for a diplomatic mission. In Antwerp he became acquainted with Albrecht Dürer, who made a silver-point portrait of him, now lost. How long Kratzer stayed in the Low Countries is not certain, but in the spring of 1521 he was in the service of Thomas More, then treasurer of the exchequer, in England. It has been frequently stated that in 1517 Kratzer was among the first fellows of Corpus Christi College, Oxford, but there are no contemporary references extant. That he

Nicolaus Kratzer (*b.* 1486/7, *d.* 1550), by Hans Holbein the younger, 1528

stayed in the town is certain, but his status in the university is open to considerable doubt. On his own evidence he was lecturing at the king's command on elementary astronomy, the construction of the astrolabe, and Ptolemy's geography. Probably, like his colleague, the Spanish humanist Juan Luis Vivès, he was one of Cardinal Wolsey's lecturers residing at Corpus. Between 11 February and 23 March 1523 Kratzer was incorporated, first as BA, then as MA.

When on 21 April 1521 the assembly of divines under the chairmanship of Cardinal Wolsey condemned Luther's doctrines, Kratzer was commissioned to commemorate the event by erecting a sundial outside St Mary's Church, together with a notice on the condemnation by the Oxford divines. (This dial survived until 1744, but disappeared during rebuilding of the church wall.) Soon after his arrival in Oxford in 1521 Kratzer made another dial which stood in the orchard of Corpus. It was a polyhedral dial combined with a hemispherical dial on the upper surface of a carved stone, topped with a spherical dial supported by iron arches. This dial vanished before 1710, but Robert Hegge, a fellow of Corpus enthusiastic about sundials, had made a description and executed a drawing which is preserved in the college library. A portable dial made for Cardinal Wolsey and resembling in shape and function the stone dial in Corpus is preserved in the Museum for the History of Science at Oxford, and recently a fragment of a stone dial has been attributed to Kratzer.

Concerning his activities as an astronomer, it seems that Kratzer was mainly engaged in making scientific instruments (especially sundials), although in 1529 Kratzer, Hugh Bozvell, and Hans Bour were sent to Cornwall to survey the King's woods and mines, and to try to smelt the ore. Whether he was responsible for the construction of the dial for an astronomical clock at Hampton Court palace executed by the French clockmaker Nicolas Oursian is not certain. Two manuscripts by Kratzer are extant. One is a set of instructions for an instrument which he called *horoptrum*, the other is a collection of treatises on scientific instruments copied by Kratzer when he stayed in Maurbach. They deal with portable sundials, ring dials, the cross-staff, the 'new' quadrant of Profatius, the celestial globe, the astrolabe, and equatoria for calculating planetary positions. While this is not original, Kratzer made at least one unique design for an adjustable vertical dial with a semicircular scale which may be classified as a compound solar instrument.

Hans Holbein the younger was greatly interested in time and horology, and he and Kratzer became intimate friends. In the portrait of 1528 Kratzer is depicted as a maker of astronomical instruments surrounded by rulers, compasses, and sundials. Some of these instruments also appear on the famous double portrait of the French ambassador Jean de Dinteville and his friend George de Selve, painted by Holbein in 1533 (London, National Gallery). In the representation of scientific instruments Holbein certainly relied on instructions given to him by Kratzer, and there is good reason for thinking that Kratzer collaborated with the artist in the overall esoteric design of the painting. When he was about fifty Kratzer married, his wife's name being Christiana; they had at least one daughter. In the preface to Guido Bonatti's *Tractatus de astronomia* (1550), edited by Nicolaus Prugner, then professor for astronomy in Tübingen, Kratzer is mentioned. In all probability he died shortly afterwards, since no reference to him after Prugner's preface has been found. Some of Kratzer's books passed into the possession of John Dee and Richard Forster, physician to the earl of Leicester.

GÜNTHER OESTMANN

Sources J. D. North, 'Nicolaus Kratzer: the king's astronomer', *Science and history: studies in honor of Edward Rosen* (1978), 205–34 · M. Maas, 'Nikolaus Kratzer, ein Münchner Humanist: ein biographischer Versuch', *Beilage zur Münchner Allgemeinen Zeitung* (18 March 1902), 505–8, 515–18 · *LP Henry VIII*, vol. 3 · P. Pattenden, *Sundials at an Oxford college* (1979) · T. Fowler, *The history of Corpus Christi College*, OHS, 25 (1893) · Emden, *Oxf.* · P. I. Drinkwater, *The sundials of Nicholas Kratzer* (1993) · G. S. J. White, 'A stone polyhedral sundial dated 1520, attributed to Nicholas Kratzer and found at Iron Acton Court, near Bristol', *Antiquaries Journal*, 67 (1987) · L. Evans, 'On a portable sundial of gilt brass made for Cardinal Wolsey', *Archaeologia, or, Miscellaneous Tracts relating to Antiquity*, 57 (1901), 331–4 · J. Peschall, *The ancient and present state of the city of Oxford by Anthony Wood* (1773) · A. Dürer, *Schriftlicher Nachlass*, ed. H. Rupprich, 3 vols. (1956–69) · *The correspondence of Sir Thomas More*, ed. E. F. Rogers (1947) · Wood, *Ath. Oxon.*, 1st edn · C. K. Aked, 'The ambassadors', *Antiquarian Horology and the Proceedings of the Antiquarian Horological Society*, 10 (1976–8), 70–77 · E. G. R. Taylor, *The mathematical practitioners of Tudor and Stuart England* (1954); repr. (1967) · M. Thausing, *Dürer: Geschichte seines Lebens und seiner Kunst* (1876) · *Opus epistolarum Des. Erasmi Roterodami*, ed. P. S. Allen, 2: 1514–1517 (1910) · M. F. S. Hervey, *Holbein's Ambassadors: the picture and the men* (1900) · O. Pächt, 'Holbein and Kratzer as collaborators', *Burlington Magazine*, 84 (1944), 134–9 · P. I. Drinkwater, 'A cold look on Kratzer's "polyhedral" sundial', *Bulletin of the British Sundial Society* (1993), 8–10, 20 · Maar Maas, 'Kratzer, Nicolaus R', *Allgemeine deutsche Biographie*, ed. R. von Liliencron and others, 51 (Leipzig, 1906), 369–72 · J. D. North, *The ambassadors' secret: Holbein and the world of the Renaissance* (2001)
Likenesses H. Holbein the younger, oils, 1528, Louvre, Paris [*see illus.*]

Krause, William Henry (1796–1852), Church of Ireland clergyman, was born on 6 July 1796 on the island of St Croix, West Indies. At an early age he was brought to England, and educated at a school in Fulham, Middesex, and afterwards at another in Richmond, Surrey. In 1814, having made up his mind to enter the army, he obtained a commission in the 51st light infantry, then in the south of France. In the next year he took part in the battle of Waterloo. At the end of the war he was placed on half pay, and soon afterwards returned to St Croix, where his father still lived.

In 1822, while staying with a fellow officer in Ireland, Krause underwent a religious conversion and resolved to take holy orders. He also met Miss A. E. Ridgeway and they were married on 13 January 1823. She died on 17 September 1824 after their only daughter was born. Krause returned to England and sought ordination from the established church but was unsuccessful. In 1826 he was appointed by the earl of Farnham 'moral agent' on his Irish estates, his duty being to look after the schools and to promote the religious and moral welfare of the tenantry. While carrying out these functions he entered himself at Trinity College, Dublin, on 5 April 1826. He graduated BA in 1830 and MA in 1838. On 26 March 1838 he was ordained for the curacy of Cavan by the bishop of Kilmore, and for two years ministered there. He also acted as secretary to the local Hibernian Bible Society. In 1840 he was appointed incumbent of the Bethesda Chapel, Dublin, where he became one of the best-known evangelical clergymen. He died in Dublin on 27 February 1852, probably of a heart attack, having preached twice on the Sunday before his death. Three volumes of his sermons were published posthumously in 1859.

THOMAS HAMILTON, rev. DAVID HUDDLESTON

Sources C. S. Stanford, *Memoir of the Reverend William Henry Krause* (1854) · *GM*, 2nd ser., 37 (1852), 423 · [J. H. Todd], ed., *A catalogue of graduates who have proceeded to degrees in the University of Dublin, from the earliest recorded commencements to … December 16, 1868* (1869), 328 · Burtchaell & Sadleir, *Alum. Dubl.*, 2nd edn
Likenesses W. H. Collingridge, lithograph (after daguerreotype by Gluckman), NPG · engraving, repro. in Stanford, *Memoir*

Kray brothers (*act.* 1926–2000), criminals, became icons of a very British form of criminality inextricably linked with memories of the 1960s. There were three brothers, **Charles James Kray** (1926–2000), born on 9 July 1926 at 26 Gorsuch Street, Shoreditch, London, and the twins **Reginald Kray** (1933–2000) and **Ronald Kray** (1933–1995), born on 24 October 1933 at 68 Stean Street, Hoxton, London. Their parents were Charles David Kray, a hawker and wardrobe dealer, a door-to-door dealer in second-hand clothing and jewellery, who was seldom at home, and his

Kray brothers (*act.* 1926–2000), by William Lovelace, 1966 [Ron Kray (right), with his twin brother, Reg Kray]

wife, Violet Lee (*d.* 1982). The adult males of the extended family prided themselves on their fierce independence; Charles senior spent most of the Second World War avoiding military service. The boys were brought up by their protective mother at 178 Vallance Road, Bethnal Green, London; although 60 per cent of the children in that area were malnourished, and 85 per cent of its housing stock was deemed officially unsatisfactory, Bethnal Green was better than Hoxton. Ron suffered from a series of serious illnesses as a child, and developed as a somewhat slower and more reserved individual than his identical twin, with an active fantasy life based on his charismatic leadership of a gangster firm. Despite their father's frequent absences the boys did not lack male role models: legendary local underworld characters such as Jimmy Spinks, Dodger Mullins, and their own grandfathers, Cannonball Lee and Mad Jimmy Kray, were hugely influential. The eldest brother, Charles, who looked after the twins during their wartime evacuation to Suffolk, was instrumental in training them as boxers. All three were soon accomplished in the sport.

But the twins were primarily street fighters, and their reputations for sheer viciousness and ferocity ensured that by the time they formally left Daneford Street School at fourteen they readily adapted to the opportunities offered by the vibrant street life of the East End of London.

By the time they became professional boxers at the age of seventeen the Kray twins had already appeared in the Old Bailey after a dance-hall brawl; on this occasion the serious assault charges were dropped. Many myths surround the boxing careers of all three brothers, but only Charlie was a real contender. The twins fought as lightweights, Reg showing some natural ability, but their boxing careers effectively ended outside the ring when Ron assaulted a young police constable, whose vengeful colleagues left him bloodied in a cell. Reg immediately retaliated, seeking out the original policeman and punching him in the face. After the intervention of a local priest the twins were placed on probation. The Kray twins were called up for national service in 1952, but their total disregard for military authority ensured that they spent most of their service time in military prisons, and they were both dishonourably discharged after fifteen months in 1954. They soon took over a billiard hall on the Mile End Road and began a career in extortion.

The end of rationing and the ageing of the underworld establishment created an opening for enterprising newcomers, and the Krays seized the opportunity. The twins attracted a potent collection of established criminals, crooked businessmen, and aspiring young villains, enabling Ron to live out his military and gangster fantasies to the full, acquiring the nickname the Colonel. The Kray firm used the billiard hall as a base for various scams and low-level extortion enterprises, all accompanied by their characteristic, stylized violence. The Krays were courted by the two major criminal organizations of the day, and eventually aligned themselves with Billy Hill, the self-styled 'Boss of Britain's Underworld'. Hill, who was planning to retire from crime, tutored the three brothers in the world of illegal gambling, and when the industry was legalized in 1961, the twins moved their operation into the West End.

Ron Kray had become increasingly volatile during the 1950s, and in 1956 was sentenced to three years in prison for grievous bodily harm; he was certified insane two years later, suffering from paranoid schizophrenia. He escaped from the secure hospital, having changed places with Reg, but eventually gave himself up and served out his sentence. The firm had thrived during Ron's incarceration, buying into clubs and gambling establishments in both the east and west ends of London; their base was to be the Double R, in Bow Road, and, after it lost its licence, the Kentucky on the Mile End Road. The violence increased in intensity as business disputes and personal feuds were played out against the backdrop of the capital's nightlife. Ron's mental illness became increasingly intrusive, and when Reg was sentenced to eighteen months for his part in a protection racket their enterprises fell into a decline. But on his release the Krays once more became the darlings of fashionable 1960s London: showbusiness and sporting personalities frequented their clubs, encouraged by Reg and Charlie, while Ron established some powerful and influential alliances among politicians and members of the aristocracy.

The Krays appeared invulnerable to the law—corruption was rife in the Metropolitan Police, they had powerful friends, and witnesses were frightened into silence. In 1966 Ron murdered George Cornell, shooting him in the crowded saloon bar of the Blind Beggar pub in the Mile End Road: no one was willing to identify Ron. They engineered the escape from Dartmoor prison of Frank 'Mad Axeman' Mitchell, and were later acquitted of his murder. Looking to expand abroad they plotted with the American mafia. Ron's mental condition was deteriorating, but Reg kept a firm grip on the firm's criminal and legitimate enterprises. On 19 April 1965 Reg had married Frances Elsie Shea (1943/4–1967); her suicide in the summer of 1967 devastated Reg, who consoled himself with alcohol. The firm span out of control in a series of shootings and knifings. Encouraged by the ever more violent Ron, Reg butchered Jack 'the Hat' McVitie, a troublesome member of their own gang.

It was no longer viable for the police to ignore the Kray twins. Police Superintendent Leonard 'Nipper' Read pursued them doggedly, and once they were in custody witnesses started to come forward. The twins offered no defence at their murder trials in 1969 (although Ron did call the prosecuting counsel a 'fat slob'); they were sentenced to life, with a recommendation that they serve at least thirty years. Charlie was convicted on the lesser charge of helping to dispose of McVitie's body, despite maintaining his innocence, and was sentenced to ten years. The punitive sentences were perhaps out of proportion to the offences with which the Krays had been charged: intended as a deterrent to others their sentences have been seen as the retribution of a beleaguered establishment against the dizzying changes in society wrought by the so-called swinging sixties.

The twins were originally sent to Parkhurst on the Isle of Wight, but Ron's mental condition deteriorated and he was certified as a paranoid schizophrenic in 1979, and spent the rest of his life in the secure mental hospital, Broadmoor, under heavy medication. He married twice while in prison; his first wife, whom he married on 11 February 1985, was Elaine Mildiner (née Zelma Elaine Hussein; b. 1955/6), from whom he was divorced in 1989. Then, on 6 November 1989, he married Kate Howard (née Kathleen Anne Reville; b. 1955/6), from whom he was divorced in 1994. Ron Kray died from a heart attack in Wexham Park Hospital, Slough, on 17 March 1995. His funeral and burial at Chingford Mount cemetery brought the East End to a standstill: it was thought to be the biggest funeral since that of his boyhood hero, Winston Churchill. It was widely asserted that his estate amounted to less than £10,000: the implication was that his charitable donations had used up the fortune made in crime. His aunt had told him as a child that he was 'born to hang': only the abolition of the death penalty falsified the prediction.

Reg Kray remained in prison for the rest of his life, where, on 14 July 1997, he married a media researcher, Roberta Rachel Jones (b. 1958/9), and apparently became a 'born-again' Christian. There was a vigorous campaign for his release, but he continued to maintain that his conviction for murder was justified, thereby denying himself the chance of parole. He was allowed out of prison for his mother's funeral in 1982, for Ron's funeral in 1995, and again for Charlie's funeral in April 2000. When he was diagnosed with bladder cancer in August 2000 the home secretary ordered his release on compassionate parole. He died on 1 October 2000 at Thorpe St Andrew, Norwich, Norfolk, and was buried, like his parents and brothers, in Chingford Mount cemetery. His wife survived him.

Charlie Kray, after his release from prison in 1975, had dedicated himself to the high life, to (fitful) campaigning for the release of his brothers, and to brokering the various film and book deals that exploited and enhanced the Kray legend. In 1973 he was divorced from his wife, Doris Moore (b. 1926/7), a machinist whom he had married on Christmas day 1948, and he was devastated by the death of his son from cancer in 1996. After a police sting operation in 1996 he was sentenced to twelve years' imprisonment for supplying 2 kilograms of cocaine, and promising to supply cocaine to the value of £39 million. He died at Parkhurst prison on the Isle of Wight on 4 April 2000.

As crime came to be dominated by drugs an entire nostalgic industry grew up around the Krays. Despite their mindless violence they came to be seen as icons of a more innocent age, when crooks had good manners, gangsters loved their mothers, and murderers could be pillars of their local communities. All three brothers published accounts of their lives: Charlie published *Me and my Brothers* (1988) and *Doing the Business* (1993); Ron's autobiography *My Story* appeared in 1993, and *Our Story* (written with Reg) in 1988. Reg put his years in prison to prolific use, his name appearing on, among others, *Born Fighter* (1990), *Villains we have Known* (1993), and *Reg Kray's Book of Slang* (1984). But this was not all: friends, family, business partners, and associates all cashed in on the Kray name to sell their memoirs, and numberless accounts of the Krays' lives appeared, starting with John Pearson's *The Profession of Violence* (1972), which remains authoritative. A film, *The Krays* (1990), directed by Peter Medak, brought the family to a new audience, and several internet sites were devoted to information about the family. RICHARD HOBBS

Sources J. Pearson, *The profession of violence* (1972) · A. Donoghue, *The Krays' lieutenant* (1995) · D. Hobbs, *Doing the business* (1988) · T. Lambrianou, *Inside the firm* (1991) · *The Independent* (18 March 1995) · *The Independent* (6 April 2000) · *The Independent* (2 Oct 2000) · *The Times* (21 July 1995) · *The Guardian* (6 April 2000) · *The Guardian* (2 Oct 2000) · *Daily Telegraph* (18 March 1995) · b. certs. [Charles James Kray, Reginald Kray, Ronald Kray] · m. certs. · d. cert. [Ronald Kray] · CGPLA Eng. & Wales (1995) [Ronald Kray] · CGPLA Eng. & Wales (2001) [Reginald Kray]

Likenesses D. Bailey, photograph, 1960–69, repro. in *The Guardian* (2 Oct 2000) · W. Lovelace, photograph, 1966, Hult. Arch. [see illus.] · photographs, Hult. Arch.

Wealth at death under £125,000—Ronald Kray: administration with will, 19 July 1995, CGPLA Eng. & Wales · under £210,000—gross and net; Reginald Kray: probate, 26 Sept 2001, CGPLA Eng. & Wales

Kray, Charles James (1926–2000). *See under* Kray brothers (*act.* 1926–2000).

Kray, Reginald (1933–2000). *See under* Kray brothers (*act.* 1926–2000).

Kray, Ronald (1933–1995). *See under* Kray brothers (*act.* 1926–2000).

Krebs, Sir Hans Adolf (1900–1981), biochemist, was born on 25 August 1900 at Hildesheim, Germany, the elder son and second of the three children of Dr Georg Krebs, an otolaryngologist, and his wife, Alma Davidson, the daughter of a banker. After serving in the army for two months in 1918 he undertook pre-clinical medical studies at the universities of Göttingen and Freiburg-im-Breisgau, clinical work in Munich (from which university he graduated in 1923 with first-class marks overall), and two years of hospital experience in Berlin. Whenever possible Krebs combined these traditional pursuits with direct experience of work in research laboratories; this confirmed him in his resolve not simply to practise medicine but to concentrate on basic medical research. But his proper education in research techniques began only in 1925 when he was appointed research assistant to Professor Otto Warburg, the leading biochemist of that time. Krebs remained with Warburg for five years. He adhered steadfastly to his determination to undertake research, despite positive discouragement from his mentor.

After various vicissitudes Krebs, in 1931, secured a post at Freiburg in which, despite heavy clinical responsibilities, he could at last test his own abilities to advance learning through empirical enquiry. To his (and possibly others') surprise, his work was immediately and spectacularly successful. Assisted by a medical student, Kurt Henseleit, Krebs elucidated in less than a year the chemical steps that enable the liver to form urea (the main nitrogenous material excreted by animals in their urine) from ammonia and carbon dioxide. Most remarkably, this sequence was revealed to be cyclic in form: the starting materials entered, and urea left, a set of reactions in which the initial reactant was ultimately regenerated.

The publication in 1932 of this urea cycle was widely recognized as a milestone in biochemistry. Of particular importance to Krebs's subsequent fate was that Sir Frederick Gowland Hopkins was so impressed by this work that he not only referred to it in his presidential address to the Royal Society on 30 November 1932 but also invited Krebs to visit him in Cambridge. Two months later Hitler came to power; four months after that Krebs, as a Jew, found himself ignominiously dismissed from Freiburg. Hopkins immediately repeated his invitation and arranged temporary financial assistance from the Rockefeller Foundation; in July 1933 Krebs was at work in Cambridge.

After two years there Krebs accepted a lectureship at Sheffield. This enabled him to build up his own small research team, and to apply the techniques and ideas that had proved so successful in the study of urea formation, to unravelling the chemical steps by which muscle and other cells oxidize sugars to carbon dioxide and water. Again

Sir Hans Adolf Krebs (1900–1981), by Elliott & Fry, 1958

working with a student, W. A. Johnson, Krebs, in 1937, elucidated this process and found it also to be cyclic in form; however, the validity of this tricarboxylic acid cycle was not universally accepted until it had been fully vindicated some years later. The widest recognition of its fundamental importance as the terminal route for oxidation of virtually all food materials also had to wait until the end of the Second World War, when novel procedures (particularly the use of radioactive tracers and of spectroscopes for studying chemical reactions in living matter) became available to biochemists. Krebs was naturalized as a British citizen in 1939; he married, on 22 March 1938, Margaret Cicely (b. 1913/14), daughter of Joseph Leo Fieldhouse of Wickersley, Yorkshire, who owned shoe shops in Rotherham. The couple had two sons and one daughter; the younger son, John Krebs FRS (b. 1945), followed a career in the life sciences and was later knighted.

Krebs's discoveries led to an avalanche of honours. He had not been granted the title of professor until 1945, when he was also given honorary direction of a research unit of the Medical Research Council. Thereafter he was elected FRS (1947), awarded a half share in the Nobel prize for physiology or medicine (1953), and appointed to the Whitley chair of biochemistry at Oxford (1954), where he became a fellow of Trinity College (1954–67). He was knighted in 1958. By the end of his life he had also been awarded honorary degrees from twenty-one universities; honorary or foreign membership of at least thirty-five learned societies and academies; many medals, including a royal (1954) and the Copley (1961) medal of the Royal Society; and—in view of his past, most pleasing to him—the German order of merit. He became FRCP in 1958.

Despite the near veneration that was increasingly accorded him, particularly by the young, Krebs remained all his life simple, approachable, unaffected, and totally devoid of malice and arrogance. He also continued to be active in the laboratory. Krebs published more than 100 papers between 1954 and his retirement from the Oxford chair in 1967, and a further 100 from the research laboratory in the Radcliffe Infirmary in which he, his faithful colleagues, and a constant stream of academic visitors worked for the subsequent fourteen years. Krebs died at the Radcliffe Infirmary, Oxford, on 22 November 1981. He was survived by his wife.   HANS KORNBERG, *rev.*

Sources H. Kornberg and D. H. Williamson, *Memoirs FRS*, 30 (1984), 351–85 · J. R. Quayle, *Journal of General Microbiology*, 128 (1982), 2215–20 · *The Times* (23 Nov 1981), 10g · H. Blaschko, *BMJ* (2 Jan 1982), 59; (13 Feb 1982), 517 · H. L. Kornberg, *The Lancet* (5 Dec 1981), 1299 · J. Alton and P. Harper, eds., *Catalogue of the papers and correspondence of Sir Hans Adolf Krebs … deposited in Sheffield University Library*, 3 vols. (1988) · F. L. Holmes, *Hans Krebs*, 2 vols. (1991–3) · m. cert. · d. cert.
Archives University of Sheffield Library, corresp., diaries, papers, research notes | Bodl. Oxf., Society for the Protection of Science and Learning file · CUL, corresp. with Peter Mitchell · UCL, corresp. with Ernest Baldwin · Wellcome L., corresp. with Henry McIlwain
Likenesses two photographs, 1953–6, Hult. Arch. · Elliott & Fry, photograph, 1958, NPG [*see illus.*] · G. Napoli, photograph, *c.*1981, Hult. Arch. · photograph, repro. in Kornberg and Williamson, *Memoirs FRS* · photograph, repro. in Quayle, *Journal of General Microbiology*
Wealth at death £266,721: probate, 26 Jan 1982, CGPLA Eng. & Wales

Kris, (Walter) Ernst (1900–1957), art historian and psychoanalyst, was born in Vienna on 26 April 1900, the son of Leopold Kris, a lawyer, and his wife, Rosa. Precocious and prolific, he graduated in 1922 from Vienna University under Julius von Schlosser, with a PhD thesis on the bizarre ceramics—incorporating casts from life—of the French Renaissance potter Palissy. He was appointed assistant curator of the rich Habsburg collections of the Kunsthistorisches Museum, and among the fruits of a productive decade (during which he became an expert of international standing), was what became the standard work on the subject, *Meister und Meisterwerke der Steinschneidekunst in der italienischen Renaissance* (2 vols., 1928), and monographic studies on the outstanding holdings of the collections.

Kris's marriage on 10 November 1927 to Marianne Rie (*b.* 1900), the daughter of Oskar Rie, one of Freud's intimates, opened for him a new world of ideas to which he remained committed throughout his life. Having undergone psychoanalysis with Helene Deutsch, Kris divided his time between psychoanalytic practice in the mornings and evenings, and with Leo Planiscig, the radical reorganization of the Habsburg collections displayed on the ground floor of the Vienna museum. There the traditional arrangement according to materials was replaced by a chronological panorama of dynastic patronage and taste.

A detailed monographic study of a series of grimacing heads by the eccentric eighteenth-century sculptor Franz Xaver Messerschmidt allowed him to combine both interests, and led to two separate publications: 'Die Characterköpfe des Franz Xaver Messerschmidt' in *Jahrbuch der Kunsthistorischen Sammlungen in Wien* (1932); and a piece in *Imago*, 19 (1933); the latter was reprinted in English as chapter 4 of *Psychoanalytic Explorations in Art* (1952). The conflict between museum studies and psychoanalytic research was to some extent resolved for Kris when, recognizing his exceptional gifts, Freud appointed him editor of *Imago*, a journal concerned with the applications of psychoanalysis to the humanities.

As the range of his interests expanded, Kris felt in need of assistants, the first of whom, Otto Kurz, collaborated with him on an investigation into the myth of the artist and his magic powers, using insights gained from Freudian theory. *Die Legende vom Künstler* was published in Vienna in 1934. A revised English translation was published in 1979, with a preface by E. H. Gombrich, under the title *Legend, Myth and Magic in the Image of the Artist*. Inspired by Freud's famous study of verbal wit and its relation to the unconscious, he next embarked on a major investigation of the art of caricature, this time in collaboration with E. H. Gombrich. Political events prevented publication in its entirety, but 'The principles of caricature' in the *British Journal of Medical Psychology*, 17 (1938) and *Caricature* (1940) contain what was published of the results.

After the Anschluss, Kris was dismissed on account of his race, and with his family he followed Freud to England in April 1938, where he was consulted by the BBC on aspects of psychological warfare. This interest resulted in a book, written jointly with Hans Speier, entitled *German Radio Propaganda* (1944). In the same capacity he was sent in 1940 first to Canada and later to New York, where his wife practised psychoanalysis and he established himself as a training analyst and gave courses at the new School of Social Research.

The fertility of his mind, the boldness of his ideas, and his mastery of the bibliography of analytic research gained Kris a wide following. After the war, and jointly with his wife, Kris turned his attention to psychological problems in children, with a longitudinal study of child development. He was a founding editor of the journal *The Psychoanalytic Study of the Child*. Heinz Hartmann and Rudolph Loewenstein were his collaborators in a number of papers on aspects of the development of 'ego-psychoanalysis', originally pioneered by Anna Freud, and it was with Anna Freud and Marie Bonaparte that he edited Freud's correspondence with Wilhelm Fliess (*The Origins of psychoanalysis: letters to Wilhelm Fliess, drafts and notes, 1887–1902, by Sigmund Freud*, 1954), to which he wrote the introduction. As leader of his research teams, Kris found an outlet for his creative imagination to which his publications do not fully do justice. There he was mainly concerned with countering popular misunderstandings of psychoanalysis, emphasizing the complexity and subtlety of Freud's theories of the mind.

Outside the circle of his friends and family (his children

Anna and Anton O. Kris achieved distinction in their parents' calling), Ernst Kris had little small talk, but became immensely lively and impressive when conversation touched upon his own wide-ranging interests. Having acquired a holiday retreat in Stamford near New York, he devoted much care and love to his garden which, he said, satisfied the aesthetic leanings that had first led him to the study of art. Never of robust health, Kris succumbed to a heart attack in New York on 27 February 1957.

E. H. GOMBRICH

Sources personal knowledge (2004) · E. H. Gombrich, *Tributes* (1984) · F. Alexander, S. Eisenstein, and M. Grotjahn, eds., *Psychoanalytic pioneers* (1966)

Krishna Kanta Nandy [*known as* Kantababu; Cantoo Baboo] (*c.*1720–1794), banian, came to prominence in the service of Warren Hastings, the first British governor-general of Bengal. On 18 February 1788 Edmund Burke said: 'Whoever has heard of Mr Hastings's name with any knowledge of Indian connection, has heard of his Banyan, Cantoo Baboo' (*Writings and Speeches*, 6.384). Kantababu, the eldest of five brothers, was born in Cossimbazar, in the district of Murshidabad in Bengal, in one of three huts built by his father, Radhakrisna Nandy (*d.* 1754), that were being transformed into a house. Radhakrisna's grandfather migrated from the village of Sijna in the *taluk* of Manteswar in the Bengal district of Burdwan with his eldest son, Sitaram. The family traded in silk, betel-nut, areca-nut, and cotton fibres and were able to buy a small piece of land near the factory of the British East India Company, to which Radhakrisna supplied silk and cotton piece goods until his death in 1754. Kantababu, as he is known to posterity, as the head of the family, took charge of the business and trade, finding patronage and friendship with the young Warren Hastings posted there, and becoming his banian, or steward and business agent, from 1754 to 1763. On Hastings's departure from India, Francis Sykes, newly appointed as the company's resident at the court of the nawabs of Bengal at Murshidabad and chief of the Cossimbazar factory, chose Kantababu to serve as his banian until 1769. Hastings returned as governor of Bengal in 1772 and became governor-general in 1774. Kantababu again served him as his trusted banian from 1772 to 1785. On the death of his first wife in 1760, Kantababu had married a second time, to Anangamanjari from the village of Kurumba in Burdwan. Their only son, Lokenath, was born in 1764.

Francis Sykes became directly involved in the salt business from October 1768. Kantababu took a lease of the coastal salt-producing areas and ran the salt business in the name of his son, Lokenath, who became salt merchant for some of them, while Kantababu used his own name in others. He organized his trade well. At the behest of Hastings, however, he ceased to be a manufacturer or contractor of salt under the East India Company's monopoly. Instead, he conducted a wholesale business in salt from 1774 to 1776, sending salt in boatloads to different parts of Bengal. Kantababu's family business in silk was much larger. His silk account with the East India Company was

successfully closed in 1780. From 1787 to 1789 he manufactured silk by the new filature factory methods. The family had depended on the silk trade for 100 years. Their fortunes rose with the importance of silk. When the business was no longer profitable, it was wound up.

Kantababu started buying property—land, houses, orchards, and rights to collect revenue—when the Maratha invasions overran western Bengal in 1742–51 and the value of property dropped. Between 1752 and 1756 he bought eight properties, and after the battle of Plassey (1757) established the supremacy of the British he bought more, purchasing as many as twenty-three properties between 1758 and 1763. After the British victory at the battle of Buxar (1764) he bought property without reservation all over Bengal. He was in the list of revenue 'farmers' recorded on 4 November 1766, when the company leased out large blocks of land to contractors for the taxation collected from it. He appears under the name of his nephew Baisnabcharan (or Busunchurn). The names of Kantababu and his son appear in April 1777 as the holders of revenue farms that yielded nearly Rs 600,000 (£60,000). At Hastings's request Kantababu eventually relinquished farms worth Rs 80,000.

In 1781 Kantababu travelled to northern India with Hastings and was caught up with him in the revolt of the raja of Benares against Hastings's attempt to exact a heavy fine from him. He was present at the siege and capture of Bijaigarh, the last of the raja's forts, where he escorted to safety the raja's mother and the women of her household. An English version of his narrative of these events, 'Narrative of Bijaygarh', survives in the British Library (Add. MS 29205, fols. 118–21). During Hastings's impeachment in 1791 Kantababu sent his old master a draft for £1000.

Kantababu died between the noons of 9 and 10 January 1794 at Cossimbazar and was cremated there. The Cossimbazar raj family he founded has been an important influence on the social, religious, cultural, and industrial development of Bengal into modern times.

SOMENDRA C. NANDY

Sources S. C. Nandy, *Life and times of Cantoo Baboo (Krisna Kanta Nandy), the banian of Warren Hastings*, 2 vols. (1978–81) · 'The territorial aristocracy of Bengal, no. 5: Cossimbazar raj', *Calcutta Review*, 57 (1873), 188–200 · *The writings and speeches of Edmund Burke*, ed. P. Langford, 6: *India: the launching of the Hastings impeachment, 1786–1788* (1991) · *The history of the trial of Warren Hastings* (1796) · BL, Add. MS 29172, fols. 293–310 · BL, Add. MS 29205, fols. 113–18
Archives BL, Hastings MSS · BL, Vansittart MSS · BL OIOC, East India Company MSS · West Bengal Archives, Calcutta, East India Company MSS
Likenesses F. B. Solvyns, engravings, 1790 (of Krishna Kanta Nandy?), repro. in F. B. Solvyns, *Les Hindous*, 4 vols. (1808–12)
Wealth at death Rs 600,000 p.a.: Nandy, *Life and times of Cantoo Baboo*

Krishnamurti, Jiddu (1895–1986), religious teacher, was born on 11 May 1895 at Madanapalle, between Madras and Bangalore, the eighth son of Narianiah, a Telugu-speaking Brahman employed by the British as a rent-collector, and his wife and cousin, Jiddu Sanjeevama (*d.* 1905). When compulsorily retired, Narianiah found work at the international headquarters of the Theosophical Society at

Adyar, Madras, and moved there with his four youngest and only surviving sons, of whom Krishna (as he was known) was the second. At that time the majority of theosophists believed that the World Teacher, the Lord Maitreya, was soon to come to earth in human form, and were looking for a suitable vehicle for this incarnation. An influential clairvoyant, C. W. Leadbeater, found Krishna soon after his arrival in Madras and chose him as the vehicle, despite his physical and mental limitations: Krishna had suffered from bouts of malaria all his life, which kept him away from school.

Annie Besant, president of the Theosophical Society, adopted Krishna and his younger brother Nityananda, known as Nitya (b. 1898), and with Leadbeater founded the Order of the Star in the East to prepare the theosophists for the 'coming'. Krishnamurti was made the head of this order. In 1912 Annie Besant took both boys to England where they were educated by tutors. Others befriended them, including the American Mary Dodge, who settled on Krishna an annuity of £500, the only personal income he ever had. During their nine-year absence from India Nityananda suffered from tuberculosis, from which he was thought to have been cured; Krishna, having three times failed the entrance examination for London University, had at least acquired fluent French, having spent some time with a family in France.

The brothers were recalled to India in 1921. Krishnamurti dreaded the future planned out for him, but from affection for Annie Besant accepted his role and the duties of preparing for the 'coming'. These took him to Australia, where Leadbeater now lived, and on the journey back to Europe they stayed at Ojai in California, to the north-west of Los Angeles, where a house had been lent to them in a climate thought likely to be beneficial for Nitya's health. There Krishna underwent a series of mystical experiences, both spiritual and physical; the latter were to recur intermittently throughout his life, accompanied by intense pain. Thereafter, he was eager to share his experiences. The house in Ojai, and land there, were purchased with money raised by Mrs Besant, and it became his home between speaking tours which took him back to India and Europe. From 1924 he held an annual camp at Ommen in the Netherlands, where 5000 acres and a castle had been given for the work by Baron Philip von Pallandt. Nitya died from tuberculosis in 1925, the one great sorrow of Krishna's life.

In 1927 Mrs Besant announced publicly, but without the agreement of all her supporters, that the 'coming' had taken place. But Krishna had taken control of his own life, and at the Ommen camp of 1929 he dissolved the Order of the Star in the East, and declared that he did not want followers: those who sought truth must find it for themselves. But his endeavours to help them to do so became even more intense, and he spent most of the following fifty-seven years giving public talks, and holding discussions with distinguished persons of varying interests across three continents, edited versions of which were widely published. He spent the war years at Ojai, and when the war was over transferred the annual camps to Saanen in Switzerland.

The teaching which drew in his audiences was original, and unrelated to that of the Theosophical Society, from which Krishna had resigned in 1930. When asked to define its substance, Krishna replied that he did not himself know. He always spoke without preparation, and covered a wide range of topics. He believed that the division between the teacher and the taught was basically wrong, and that truth could only be found by discarding all preconceptions, particularly those derived from religious organizations, and those which gave rise to conflict. To set people free was his single declared aim: it was not guidance that was needed, but self-awakening.

Krishnamurti thought that these principles should be applied to the education of the young who, he believed, would discover true values through unbiased investigation and self-awareness. Education should be concerned with the cultivation of the total human being, helping both student and educator to flower naturally. A school based on these principles was founded at Rishi Valley, close to Krishna's birthplace, as early as 1924. It was followed by four others, including one at Brockwood Park, Hampshire (opened 1969), which became Krishna's second home. All the schools remained active at the end of the century. Visiting the schools for discussions with staff and students became an essential part of his work. He planned a residential centre for Krishnamurti studies at Brockwood Park, independent of the school, but it was completed only after his death.

Krishnamurti was heterosexual, deeply affectionate, and a most engaging companion. He enjoyed cars, light reading, and entertainment, and recorded classical music. A lifelong vegetarian, 'the body' in his care was his constant concern. He remained clean-shaven and kept his boyish figure throughout his life, and always dressed well and in accordance with local custom. Except for Buddhism, he was uninterested in the religious or philosophical teaching of others. His own teaching, as he allowed it to be called for want of a better description, was carried out predominantly through the spoken word. He spoke without rhetoric, often with hesitation, sometimes with passion; his unique style of presentation was captured on the many video recordings made of his later talks. Before video there were audio recordings, and printed books containing edited versions, numbering more than forty in English. A single work written in his own hand, *Krishnamurti's Notebook* (1976), gives some access to the nature of his personal thought. He made no attempt to explain the source of his perception, and privately expressed the hope that others would be able to do so.

Krishnamurti continued speaking publicly until seven weeks before his death. He died from pancreatic cancer at his house at Ojai, California, on 17 February 1986. He was cremated at Ventura, California, the same day.

MARY LUTYENS

Sources Theosophical Society archive, Adyar, Madras · Krishnamurti Centre archive, Brockwood Park, Hampshire, England · Krishnamurti Foundation of America archive, Ojai, California ·

personal knowledge (2004) • M. Lutyens, *Krishnamurti*, 3 vols. (1975–88) • P. Jayakar, *J. Krishnamurti: a biography* (1986) • M. Lutyens, *The life and death of Krishnamurti* (1990)
Archives Krishnamurti Centre, Brockwood Park, Hampshire • Krishnamurti Foundation of America, Ojai, California • Krishnamurti Foundation of India, Rishi Valley, Madras, Andhra Pradesh and Adyar | SOUND BL NSA, *The Levin interviews*, NP5 132R BD1 • BL NSA, documentary recording
Likenesses photographs, *c.*1910–1938, Hult. Arch. • two group portraits, photographs, *c.*1920–1925, Hult. Arch. • A. Bourdelle, bust, 1927, Bourdelle Museum, Paris • photograph, 1933 (with A. Besant), Hult. Arch. • photographs, Krishnamurti Centre, Brockwood Park, Hampshire • photographs, Krishnamurti Foundation of America, Ojai, California • photographs, Krishnamurti Foundation of India, Madras, Andhra Pradesh and Adyar, India
Wealth at death only personal effects (incl. clothes, watches, books, records); only personal income was £500 annuity

Kronberger, Hans (1920–1970), physicist and nuclear reactor engineer, was born in Linz, Austria, on 28 July 1920, the younger child and only son of Norbert and Olga Kronberger. His parents were Jewish and his father had inherited the family leather merchant business. At the German invasion, Kronberger managed to leave Austria and he travelled to England where King's College, Newcastle, accepted him in the 1938 entry as a student in mechanical engineering. In May 1940 he was interned as a friendly enemy alien, first in the Isle of Man and then in Australia, but he was able to continue his studies to some extent and learn from more experienced fellow internees. After being released in 1942, he returned to King's College and in 1944 took a wartime honours degree in physics. He began a PhD for Birmingham University, which he completed in 1948. In 1946 he joined F. E. Simon's team in the Tube Alloys project—the cover name for the British atomic bomb programme. In 1946 he heard that his mother and sister had died in a Nazi concentration camp.

Simon was an exceptionally fine director and Kronberger learned quickly. Heinz London was also a member of the team and he and Kronberger became close friends and collaborators. London had deep scientific insight and Kronberger showed rare ability in extending a scientific idea into practical hardware. Soon they were both transferred to the new atomic energy establishment at Harwell.

Kronberger first worked with London on the separation of carbon-13 and oxygen-18 by means of columns and low-temperature distillation. Next he made some of the early important contributions to the separation of the isotopes of uranium by means of a bank of centrifuges. Here, and in some of his later work, he found scope for his considerable mathematical talents. He married, on 17 July 1951, Joan Hanson, *née* Iliffe (1924/5–1962), a scientific assistant at Harwell, and widow of Dr John Hanson, who had been killed in a climbing accident. She already had a young son; her marriage to Kronberger brought two daughters. Within a year of their marriage, however, she was diagnosed as having a brain tumour, from which, after a long illness, she died.

The government decision to build a uranium diffusion

Hans Kronberger (1920–1970), by Walter Bird

plant at Capenhurst, Cheshire, had put a great strain on the atomic energy organization. American information and knowledge were not available and qualified staff were scarce. Kronberger in 1951 was the obvious choice as research manager of the components development laboratory. Many novel components and control devices had to be invented; new instruments had to be developed and older types of instruments had to be modified. Kronberger's performance was scintillating. In the language of the scientific laboratory, he had wonderful hands. Those same hands would sometimes make deeply felt music. After two years he was promoted to be head of the Capenhurst development laboratories and in 1956 he became chief physicist, under Leonard Rotherham, of the research and development branch of the industrial group of the Atomic Energy Authority. As part of these wider duties he continued a personal association with the Capenhurst laboratories where various methods of isotope separation were being applied to hydrogen, lithium, and boron, and where the centrifuge method of separating the isotopes of uranium continued to receive attention. Kronberger succeeded Rotherham as director in 1958.

By the early sixties the authority was committed to operating an experimental fast reactor at Dounreay; to developing the prototypes of two thermal reactor systems at Windscale and Winfrith respectively; and, because of the encouragement of Sir John Cockcroft, to having a large share in the Organization for European Economic Co-operation's Dragon reactor at Winfrith. By then Kronberger was scientist-in-chief of the reactor group, one of the groups arising from the split of the industrial group. He was faced with streams of problems, some familiar and some new. Many of them arose from the need for special materials that could survive reactor conditions. Some were solved by skilful technology (such as use of impregnated graphite) and some were avoided by cancelling elements of the project—for example, abandoning beryllium as a reactor material. As work proceeded, the reactors all seemed to be successful but when they were being extended to the stage of large nuclear power stations additional engineering problems arose which could only be solved by an integrated national effort, including the most powerful nuclear engineering companies. This was the position when Kronberger died, a year after he had been appointed a member of the Atomic Energy Authority.

Much of Kronberger's work on the diffusion project at Capenhurst remained secret or is not attributable to him, but he did become well known from his lectures on hydrostatic extrusion and on the desalination of sea water. He served as a member of the United Nations scientific advisory committee and of the advisory committee of the International Atomic Energy Agency. He was appointed OBE in 1957 and CBE in 1966; he was elected FRS in 1965 and was awarded the Royal Society's Leverhulme tercentenary medal in 1969.

Life brought to Kronberger some happy times when his sunny disposition blossomed, but he had more than his normal share of grief, and his life ended by suicide. He was found hanging in the garage of his home at 3 Smiths Lawn, Holly Road, South Wilmslow, Cheshire, on 29 September 1970. PENNEY, rev.

Sources L. Rotherham, *Memoirs FRS*, 18 (1972), 413–26 · *The Times* (30 Sept 1970), 1h · *The Times* (1 Oct 1970), 14f–h · *The Times* (3 Oct 1970), 14f · *Nucleonics Week* (8 Oct 1970) · personal knowledge (1981) · PRO, Kronberger MSS, AB 38 · m. cert. · d. cert.
Archives PRO, papers, AB 38
Likenesses W. Bird, photograph, repro. in *Memoirs FRS* [*see illus.*] · photograph, repro. in *The Times* (1 Oct 1970), 14
Wealth at death £35,459: probate, 14 Dec 1970, *CGPLA Eng. & Wales*

Kropotkin, Peter [Pyotr Alekseievich] (1842–1921), anarchist and scientist, was born on 27 November 1842 OS at 26 Shtatny pereulok in Moscow, the son of Prince Aleksey Petrovich Kropotkin (1805–1871), an army officer who came from an old aristocratic family, and Yekaterina Nikolayevna Sulima (1810–1846), who was of a Cossack military family. He was educated at the Corps of Pages, the élite military school in St Petersburg, and served as an officer in the Far East, spending much time in geographical exploration. As a boy he repudiated his title, and as a man he soon became alienated from the tsarist regime, and resigned his commission in 1867. He studied mathematics at St Petersburg University (1867–8) and worked as a professional geographer, specializing in the orography and glaciology of Asia. He adopted populism and then socialism, and during a visit to western Europe in 1872 he turned to anarchism. On his return he joined the revolutionary movement in St Petersburg, working in the Tchaikovsky circle until he was arrested in 1874. He was held without trial, but escaped from prison hospital in St Petersburg in 1876 and went into exile in the West. On 8 October 1878 he married Sofiya Grigoryevna Ananyeva-Rabinovich (1856–1938), a biologist and writer from a Ukrainian Jewish family, in Geneva.

Kropotkin soon took a leading part in the international

Peter Kropotkin (1842–1921), by Nadar, after 1871

anarchist movement, helping to shift it from the mutualism of Proudhon and the collectivism of Bakunin to a more ambitious ideology which became known as anarchist communism. After speaking and writing actively in several countries, he was arrested in France and imprisoned in 1883. When he was given amnesty in 1886 he took refuge in England, where he earned a living as a scientific journalist but also continued to develop and expound his social and political philosophy. This was a combination of biological evolution, naturalistic ethics, populist historiography, integral education, economic decentralization and self-management, political anarchy, and self-government, the final stages to be inaugurated through mass insurrection and popular revolution. He explained his ideas in lucid language and attractive arguments, remaining the best-known and best-liked figure in the anarchist movement for more than forty years, and exercising considerable and even excessive influence over it.

Kropotkin contributed both to leading liberal magazines and to radical papers, and he collaborated on several anarchist periodicals in several languages, helping to found *Freedom* in Britain in 1886. Some of his huge number of articles were reprinted as pamphlets and many were collected in a series of books: *Words of a Rebel* (1885), *In Russian and French Prisons* (1887), *The Conquest of Bread* (1892), *Fields, Factories and Workshops* (1899), *Mutual Aid: a Factor of Evolution* (1902), *Modern Science and Anarchism* (1901, 1913), *Ideals and Realities in Russian Literature* (1905), *The Great*

French Revolution (1909), and *Ethics: Origin and Development* (1922). *The Conquest of Bread* was his most impressive exposition of anarchist communism, and *Mutual Aid* was his most influential book of all. During a visit to the United States in 1897 he was commissioned to write his autobiography, *Memoirs of a Revolutionist* (1899), which became his most popular book. He contributed several scientific articles to the *Encyclopaedia Britannica*, and also the authoritative 'Anarchism' to the eleventh edition (1910).

In Britain, Kropotkin had a wide circle of friends and admirers in all walks of political and social life, and he did much to make anarchism almost respectable in progressive circles. At the end of his life he moved towards liberalism, and in the First World War he favoured the allies against the central powers, which alienated him from most of his former comrades. He was amiable and charming in company, but could be dogmatic and intolerant in controversy.

Kropotkin was a leading member of the Russian revolutionary movement in exile, and he supported the abortive revolution of 1905 and the successful revolution of 1917. He returned to his native land in June 1917 and settled in Moscow. He followed a moderate line and opposed the Bolshevik regime which took power in November 1917, occasionally protesting against its excesses. He moved to the village of Dmitrov, near Moscow, where he died on 8 February 1921 NS. His funeral in Moscow on 13 February was the last open anarchist demonstration in Russia for more than sixty years; he was buried at Novodevichye cemetery. Kropotkin's wife, Sofiya, died in Moscow in 1938. Their only child, Alexandra, who was born in Harrow in 1887, lived in several European countries before settling in the United States, where she died in 1966.

NICOLAS WALTER

Sources P. Kropotkin, *Memoirs of a revolutionist* (1899) · P. A. Kropotkin, *Zapiski revolyutsionera* (1924–9) · N. Walter, introduction and notes, in P. Kropotkin, *Memoirs of a revolutionist*, ed. N. Walter (1988) · M. A. Miller, *Kropotkin* (1976) · G. Woodcock and I. Avakumović, *The anarchist prince* (1950) · J. Grave, ed., *Kropotkine*, 2 vols. in 1 ([Paris], 1921) · M. Nettlau, 'Kropotkin at work', *Freedom* (Feb 1921), 11–13 · J. Ishill, ed., *Peter Kropotkin: the rebel, thinker and humanitarian* (1923) · E. Malatesta, 'Ricordi e critice di un vecchio amico', *Studi Sociali* [Montevideo] (April 1931), 1–3 · J. A. Rogers, *Peter Kropotkin: scientist and anarchist* (1957) · N. M. Pirumova, *P. A. Kropotkina* (1972) · V. A. Markin, *P. A. Kropotkin* (1985) · *Funeral of P. A. Kropotkin* (Berlin, 1922)

Archives BLPES, letters · Internationaal Instituut voor Sociale Geschiedenis, Amsterdam, corresp. and papers · Russian State Archive of Literature and Art, Moscow · Russian State Historical Archive, St Petersburg · Russian State Library, Moscow · State Archive of the Russian Federation, Moscow | BL, letters to May Morris, Add. MSS 45345–45347 · BL, letters to Alfred Dryhurst and Hannah Dryhurst, Add. MS 46473 · Internationaal Instituut voor Sociale Geschiedenis, Amsterdam, letters to Raphael Friedeberg · Internationaal Instituut voor Sociale Geschiedenis, Amsterdam, letters to Alfred Marsh · Internationaal Instituut voor Sociale Geschiedenis, Amsterdam, corresp. with Max Nettlau · Internationaal Instituut voor Sociale Geschiedenis, Amsterdam, letters to Vasilij P. Zuk · L. Cong., George Kennan MSS · London School of Economics, Melgunov collection · London School of Economics, Tyurin collection · Newcastle Central Library, Joseph Cowen MSS ·

Stanford University, California, Hoover Institution · state archives, Paris · state archives, Brussels · state archives, Neuchâtel · state archives, Bern · U. Lpool, corresp. with J. Bruce Glasier · University of Toronto, Thomas Fisher Rare Book Library, corresp. with James Mavor and MSS

Likenesses Nadar, photograph, after 1871, NPG [*see illus.*] · photograph, Internationaal Instituut voor Sociale Geschiedenis, Amsterdam

Kruger, Stephanus Johannes Paulus [Paul] (1825–1904), president of the Transvaal, was born in the Cradock district of Cape Colony, probably on the farm Bulhoek, on 10 October 1825, the third child and second son of Casper Jan Hendrik Kruger (1801–1851), a farmer, and Elsie Francina Steyn (*b.* 1806), of whom little is known save that she bore four more children after Paul, and died in 1834 at the age of twenty-seven.

Early career Educated entirely by his parents, save for three months under the tutelage of a migrant teacher, Paul acquired simple literary skills, reflected in rather laboured handwriting throughout his life, with one notable flourish: a small arc over the letter 'u', wherever it occurred, which in the view of F. J. du T. Spies is best understood as a common device of many Cape writers of Nederlands, going back to the seventeenth century, and not as a token German umlaut. His leading biographer, D. W. Krüger, therefore omits the umlaut in spelling Kruger's surname (Krüger, *Paul Kruger*, 1.11). This is normal among South African Krugers.

But Kruger's education for life went deeper. The Calvinism believed and practised by the Krugers and other families of *trekboers* along the southern watershed of the Orange was valued as a shield against the threat of rebarbarization latent in frontier life. In its uncompromising adherence to biblical precepts it provided a moral stiffening against danger and temptation. The sovereignty of the divine will, and its identification in the combined will of the faithful community, excluded the need for sentimentality in religion and gave a sobering legitimacy to whatever needed to be done for the nation of believers to survive as migrants in rough neighbourhoods.

Casper Kruger emigrated across the Orange with his second wife and family in 1835, and spent about a year on the Caledon River. Paul recalled, in an interview with *Land en Volk* on his thirty-third birthday, that Hendrik Potgieter's party went past them to engage Mzilikazi, the Ndebele (Matabele) ruler, in the battle at Vegkop, which has led Uys to argue that Paul had no part in that battle, against the accepted view that he did, as an eleven-year-old. But his presence is mentioned both by Theal (*History*, 6.292) and by van Oordt (J. F. van Oordt, *Paul Kruger en de Opkomst der Z. A. Republiek*, 1898, 29), both predating the account in the Kruger *Memoirs* which Uys rightly suspects. Kruger recalled in old age that after his family had then joined Piet Retief's trek into Natal they experienced a Zulu attack after Retief's murder, and beat it off. He spoke of children pinioned to their mothers' breasts by spears, or with their brains dashed out on waggon wheels. But 'God heard our prayer and delivered us out of the hands of our enemy',

Stephanus Johannes Paulus Kruger (1825–1904), by Elliott & Fry, 1877

and 'we followed them and shot them down as they fled, until more of them were dead than those of us they had killed in their attack'. 'I could shoot moderately well', he explained, 'for we lived, so to speak, among the game' (Krüger, *Paul Kruger*, 1.16–17).

Kruger seems to have played down his exploits against wild animals rather more than he did those against human enemies. Such tales abound in the *Memoirs*, usually involving lion, elephant, or buffalo. In any case Kruger, like most frontiersmen, hunted for food, hides, or to eliminate predators, rather than for the sport. Survival was the objective, and life was full of hazards. The oft-repeated story of how Kruger cut off his left thumb with a clasp knife when his gun exploded during a bout with a rhinoceros is not for the squeamish. But it is also noteworthy that Kruger was officially but only marginally involved in his old age in the setting up of a game sanctuary along the eastern border of the Transvaal between the Sabie and Crocodile rivers, the nucleus of the later Kruger National Park.

After their traumatic experiences in Natal the Krugers returned with Potgieter to the highveld in 1839, first to the district of Potchefstroom, one of the two administrative centres of the new Boer republic. In 1845 they went to the new settlement at Ohrigstad in eastern Transvaal, later the Lydenburg republic, again following Potgieter. Paul thus came to know all the main districts of Voortrekker settlement.

Entry into public life Appointed an assistant *veld-kornet* in 1840 at age sixteen, Kruger became a citizen of the republic in 1841, qualifying as of right for his first farm, Waterkloof, south of Rustenburg. This farm, and Boekenhoutfontein (acquired in 1860) remained in his hands for life, though he acquired and sold many properties over the years (Krüger, *Paul Kruger*, 1.76–81). In 1842 he married his first wife, Maria du Plessis, a Voortrekker's daughter originally from the Tarka, eastern Cape; but in 1846, after four hard years, during which they had moved to the farm Swartkop on the Steelpoort River, she died—perhaps from malaria. In the following year he married Maria's cousin Gezina Susanna Frederika Wilhelmina (Sanna) du Plessis (1831–1901). She lived to support him, despite periodic illnesses and sixteen pregnancies in twenty-eight years—nine sons and seven daughters—until she died in 1901 in Pretoria; she had been too ill to travel when her husband went into exile the previous year.

The peace of the Voortrekker community was broken when Potgieter fell out with the Volksraad party in Lydenburg over the latter's decision to abolish the post of head kommandant in 1846. At this, Potgieter and his followers moved well to the north to establish a new settlement, later named Schoemansdal, in 1848. To keep the peace, the Volksraad later decided to appoint separate head kommandants over four distinct regions, and allow the burgers to choose under whom they would serve. Paul Kruger considered this a weak solution, but accepted the ruling. His problem of allegiance was resolved only when Andries Pretorius, the kommandant-general for the Magaliesburg district, appointed him *veld-kornet*. In this capacity he attended the Sand River negotiations in 1852, which confirmed the independence from Britain of trekkers north of the Vaal.

During the 1850s and 1860s, when the Voortrekkers, as self-appointed successors to the defeated Ndebele, were seeking to turn their republic into a territorial state, Kruger was fully occupied with peace preservation and the flow of labour to the farms. He did not shrink from the practice, which he saw as normal, of distributing women and children left homeless by conflict as labourers to farmers. He took part in two major campaigns in his new role. The first was against Sechele, the Kwena leader, one of the main contenders for power among the Tswana, in 1852. Sechele was well supplied with firearms (Agar-Hamilton, *Native Policy of the Voortrekkers*, 143–53). As part of a commando 500 strong, Kruger's troop controlled a 4-pounder shrapnel field-piece. They met with much resistance, and Kruger was wounded. During this campaign David Livingstone's mission at Kolobeng was ransacked, and firearms taken by both sides, though the extent of Kruger's involvement is not clear. Two years later Kruger was sent against the northern Sotho chief Makapane in the Waterberg, south of Schoemansdal. The chief, under provocation, had massacred a hunting expedition, including its leader, Potgieter's brother Piet, a close friend of Kruger, and then raided white settlements over a wide area. The commando under M. W. Pretorius took terrible retribution on Makapane's followers who retreated into a large cave, taking with them Piet's dead body. Kruger, who commanded the Rustenburgers, went into the cave and recovered the body—an act of daring in a vindictive twenty-five-day siege which sent nearly 3000 Africans of all ages to their deaths (Theal, 3.415–19; Krüger, *Paul Kruger*, 1.41–2).

Hendrik Potgieter died in December 1852 and Andries Pretorius in July 1853. Andries's son M. W. Pretorius was subsequently chosen as kommandant-general, and in 1855 elected president under a new constitution which Kruger had helped to draft (Engelbrecht, *Nederduitsch Hervormde kerk*, 125ff.). Kruger doubted his competence, but supported him, and was required to lead the invading force when he determined to amalgamate the Transvaal and the Orange Free State (OFS), whose independence had been restored in 1854. The Free Staters threatened to resist their intervention; but Kruger brokered a settlement by stepping between the two rival commandos, shouting the OFS leader down, and arranging a disengagement which sent the two presidents home again (Krüger, *Paul Kruger*, 1.50–51). Four years later he came to the help of the OFS again, when they were at war with Moshoeshoe's Sotho, by visiting Moshoeshoe at his mountain stronghold of Thaba Bosiu and procuring peace. All in all, he had shown a loyalty to authority in political disputes, devotion to duty as an officer, and a real capacity for power play (*kragdadigheid* in Afrikaans).

The constitution which Kruger had helped to draft in 1855 did not satisfy all parties, and ultimately led to civil war between community leaders divided in both their religious and political affiliations. The religious divisions referred to arose out of the rejection of the great trek by the Cape Nederduits Gereformeerde kerk (NGK). It had led to the establishment of a new Nederduits Hervormde kerk (NHK) under D. van der Hoff in 1853 as the church of the republic. The Krugers stayed in the NGK. With their fellow Rustenburgers they objected to the singing of hymns not based on the Psalms, as containing 'poison mixed up with good food'. They worked to bring in a dominee of their own persuasion, D. Postma, under whom a splinter Gereformeerde (or 'Dopper') kerk (GK) was set up in 1858. Although the constitution limited voting rights to members of the NHK, the Volksraad immediately removed this restriction, on 20 September 1858, and gave the vote to burghers 'of whatever religious persuasion they might be'—a right soon extended to include *raad* membership as well (Engelbrecht, *Nederduitsch Hervormde kerk*, 126).

At the time of his adherence to the GK, Kruger appears to have experienced a spiritual crisis about which he later spoke very little. He set off on foot into the Magaliesberg to seek guidance in prayer, and was missing for several days. A search party found him 'nearly dead from hunger and thirst'. Krüger suggests a touch of fanaticism (*dwepery*) (Krüger, *Paul Kruger*, 1.47–8). Van Oordt linked the event with Postma's arrival (J. F. van Oordt, *Paul Kruger en de Opkomst der Z. A. Republiek*, 1898, 17). At all events, Kruger's adherence to the GK encouraged him to get to grips with the neo-Calvinist tenets of its very explicit theology, to

which he remained faithful for the remainder of his life. It sharpened his predestinarian view of life, notably by strengthening a belief in providential care for the Afrikaners as a 'chosen people', to be triumphantly vindicated in 1881, and still clung to with resignation in his dying days on Lake Leman. It would also lead him to seek and value contacts with like-minded thinkers, notably S. J. Du Toit (see below).

Kruger had already begun to stiffen Pretorius's religious convictions in order to prevent breakaway moves by Schoemansdal trekkers under Stephanus Schoeman in 1856–7 (Krüger, *Paul Kruger*, 1.46–9). Schoeman had built up a support base among the Boers of Lydenburg and Utrecht near the Natal border, and with President Boshoff of the Orange Free State against Pretorius. Boshoff encouraged the rebel Transvalers to elect a rival Volksraad, and reject the Kruger committee's constitution. In April 1857 Schoeman declared war on Pretorius; but Kruger brought them together through his brother Douw, violence was averted, and a revised constitution, known as the Rustenburg *grondwet*, was formally adopted by delegates from all the Transvaal communities, meeting in the new town of Pretoria in September 1859 as the first proper Volksraad of the South African Republic.

But Pretorius, reacting now to a positive approach from the Orange Free State, decided to stand as president of the OFS for a second time, and was duly elected to that office in January 1860. In its disenchantment the Transvaal Volksraad elected a senior member, J. H. Grobler, as their acting president in his place. Schoeman would have none of it, and claimed the role for himself as kommandant-general. Pretorius at first agreed to retire; but he withdrew his offer after a larger meeting in Potchefstroom had rejected Grobler in favour of Schoeman, and the Volksraad had then decided to appoint Schoeman when Grobler resigned for want of support. Returning from a retreat in the OFS, Pretorius persuaded the Volksraad to arrange the election of a new *raad*. It obliged, the *raad* duly met in April 1862, and through a bipartisan committee appointed an acting president, J. H. Jansen van Rensburg, in place of Schoeman, who predictably rejected his authority. Paul Kruger was then proposed by the *raad* as a candidate for a regular presidential election.

Schoeman's membership of the GK meant that Kruger had to tread warily; but he had already drawn Schoeman's wrath by calling out his commando in reaction to Schoeman's behaviour. When Schoeman seized Pretoria in January 1863, and drove out a court which was sitting on his misdemeanours, Kruger's Rustenburg commando drove Schoeman out and restored the court, which ordered new elections for the presidency and the kommandant-generalship. After complex proceedings involving two elections for each office van Rensburg narrowly beat Pretorius, and Kruger was overwhelmingly elected as kommandant-general. The Schoeman party made a further bid for power under J. H. Viljoen of Marico; but Kruger had martial law declared and went after Viljoen in the Magaliesberg, forcing his surrender. Peace was concluded at the Crocodile River in January 1864. A fresh election now enabled Pretorius to resume the presidency for a further seven years, with Kruger as his kommandant-general. By trying throughout these years to determine where legitimacy lay, and again by intervening at critical moments either to reconcile opponents or to strike down those who threatened to prolong the conflict by their actions, Kruger had made personal enemies; but he had done much to set the republic back on its feet.

The South African Republic and the chiefdoms But even now the republic's troubles were far from over. The government's ability to assert its power against chiefdoms over which it claimed sovereignty was weakened by economic collapse, leading to over-printing of paper money, and failure to raise revenue on account of the political breakdown. Black respect for the white community fell as a result of the civil war. Many burghers refused to turn out for commando service, so that Kruger, as kommandant-general, was stretched to keep the peace. On the republic's eastern border, settlers in the Lydenburg region were meeting resistance from Mabhogo's Ndzundza and Maleo's Kopa, whose lands had been cut down and beaconed off in the interest of Boer settlement in 1859–60, so forcing many Africans into the labour market. Potgieter's alliance of 1846 with the Swazi, however, enabled Kruger to call on them to break their opposition. Pretorius's government was fortunate not to have to make war against the Zulu and Pedi chiefdoms at that time, for their presence would seriously undermine the ability of the republic to resist British annexation in the 1870s. Kruger tried, but unsuccessfully, to agree on a common border with the Zulu. He did become involved in conflict with Moshoeshoe's Sotho, and defeated his general Molapo in 1865; but his men quarrelled over the booty and he could not stop them returning home.

Far more serious were the failures in the Soutpansberg (Krüger, *Paul Kruger*, 1.87–93; Theal, 4.473–91), where the long arm of the republic tried to assert its authority in the 1860s by raising tribute from the Lovedu through Tsonga middlemen, and by a policy of divide and rule among the Venda. In this area, where the 'most lawless' white people in all southern Africa, according to Theal, were engaged in ivory trading on a big scale, linked to a market at Schoemansdal, well-armed black communities, often in conflict with each other, now realized that white middlemen were not essential to their prosperity. Fighting broke out in 1864 when a party of white men looking for a black fugitive attacked his protector, and took women, children, and livestock. Pretorius and Kruger went north, learned of the retaliatory raids on white settlements, and called up a commando of 1200 men, of whom barely 500 turned out. The campaign had to be deferred. In 1867 Kruger set off with 400 men; but they had not equipped themselves properly, they mutinied, and Kruger, not for the first time, was unable to keep them at their posts. The residents of Schoemansdal fled their homes and Kruger ordered the evacuation of the settlement in July 1867—for which he was much criticized, but later exonerated by the Volksraad. It did, however, censure him for distributing numerous women and children among his burghers on

his own authority. But Kruger, not deterred from his purpose, decided that if northern Transvaal was to be won back and neither men nor ammunition were available, the followers of Makapane and Mapela would have to be smoked out of their caves and their houses fired. Even so, he met resistance from his burghers, to say nothing of the rising criticism by the British authorities of the republic's handling of the black population, and it was ultimately an attack by the Swazi in 1869 which broke the chiefdoms (Krüger, *Paul Kruger*, 1.92–6).

From Burgers's presidency to the First South African War So questionable was the viability of the South African Republic during the late 1860s that a desire on the part of leading burghers to seek a change of president was understandable, above all after Pretorius's diplomacy signally failed to secure the diamond fields to which the republic laid claim in 1871 (Agar-Hamilton, *Road to the North*). When the electors' choice fell in 1872 on Thomas François Burgers, a dominee of the NGK who had been declared a heretic for his liberal theology and deprived of his pulpit, Kruger was disturbed. Branches of the Cape NGK had been set up in the Transvaal in 1866, challenging the NHK and the GK by their presence and often preaching a liberal policy towards black people. Kruger had urged William Robinson (brother of J. B. Robinson, the mining magnate of later years) to stand for president; but he accepted Burgers on his election as lawful leader. Because Gezina was seriously ill just at the time, he obtained release from his Volksraad duties in March 1873. Burgers then had the kommandant-generalship abolished in peacetime, and Kruger, perhaps taking offence, resigned from the executive council as well. Kruger was not totally opposed to Burgers's policies, however. He supported his plans in the Volksraad for railway expansion, and he was less hostile than is sometimes supposed to Burgers's educational reforms, which at first disallowed confessional instruction in school hours (Engelbrecht, *Burgers*, 101–2, 191–2). But in 1876 he declined Burgers's invitation to lead a campaign against the Pedi, with the explanation—according to the *Memoirs*, and to Burgers's later 'Vindication' (Uys), on which Engelbrecht is silent—that the president's approval of Sunday dancing would deprive the expedition of God's blessing and ensure its failure (Krüger, *Paul Kruger*, 1.112–16). Kruger also attacked Burgers's demand for a special war tax. Yet he supported Burgers for president in an election called for February 1877, with some qualifications, in a letter to Piet Joubert on 7 November 1876 (Engelbrecht, *Burgers*, 191–7), and then let his own name go forward as a rival candidate. Whether Kruger equivocated in these ways in the hope that Burgers would destroy his chances by failure must be seen as an open question.

The presidential election was postponed for a year in February on account of political uncertainty arising from Sir Theophilus Shepstone's threat to annex the state to Britain. Before it adjourned on 8 March the Volksraad instructed the government to negotiate with Shepstone 'with the object of maintaining the independence of the state'. Shepstone nevertheless took over the Transvaal on 9 April 1877, the very day on which the executive council, to which Burgers had appointed Kruger as vice-president, held its first and only meeting. Burgers's formal protest at the annexation changed nothing.

Kruger neither wanted the annexation to happen, nor knew how to prevent it; but he accepted an appointment to travel to Britain with Dr E. J. P. Jorissen, the secretary for justice, to deliver the council's protest to the Colonial Office. They set off in August 1877, interviewed the high commissioner, Sir Bartle Frere, in Cape Town, and were politely received by Lord Carnarvon in London. Kruger, with almost no English, depended on Jorissen's interpretation. Jorissen, Burgers's appointee, was not disposed to take a strong stand, as his memoirs imply (Jorissen, 35), though Shepstone and Frere had told Carnarvon that he need not take their plea for repeal of the annexation seriously. The delegates reported failure on their return, even of their request to hold a referendum. Kruger was heavily attacked and maligned for his ineffectiveness, but was prepared in April 1878 to return to London, with evidence which he had not previously had of widespread feeling against the annexation among fellow Boers. His associate this time was Piet Joubert, of whose desire for freedom there was no doubt. This time they presented a better informed case as to the state of Transvaal opinion; but Carnarvon's successor, Sir Michael Hicks Beach, cut the interview short after hearing their case, and he conceded nothing in later correspondence. The best the deputation could achieve was to renew supportive contacts made in 1877 with Leonard Courtney, the only helpful MP, and friends in the Netherlands, and extend their contacts to France and Germany.

After their return the deputation met with a demand for armed resistance when they faced over 2000 people at Wonderfontein near Potchefstroom in January 1879; but Kruger, repeating advice given in January 1878, counselled them first to explore other avenues for at least eighteen months (Krüger, *Paul Kruger*, 1.151, 173). When Frere spoke to the Boer leadership outside Pretoria in April, having previously talked of provincial self-government under a federal system, he declined to accept a demand for the restoration of independence. Kruger, as spokesman for the Boers, insisted on a return to the Sand River convention. Frere would forward another petition to the British government asking for repeal of the annexation; but he was not prepared to support it. Sir Garnet Wolseley, after taking over the high commissionership for south-east Africa from Frere, later confirmed in September that the British government was firmly committed to retaining the Transvaal within the British empire. So, in response, the Boer leadership convened an assembly in mid-December at Wonderfontein, where Kruger again set the tone of proceedings, asking the audience to count the cost before pitting the *volkswil* (with which Kruger identified the will of God) against a usurping government. The assembly resolved on 15 December that the time for petitions was past. That was seen as defiance. Wolseley arrested M. W. Pretorius and Edward Bok (the chair and secretary of the people's committee who had signed the motion) on treason charges, but released them.

The British grand strategy between 1868 and 1880 was to bind southern Africa together in a federation, the rationale for which might vary. But its association with Shepstone's seizure of the Transvaal had utterly alienated Afrikaner opinion. Kruger and Joubert visited the Cape in May 1880, and in a vigorous political campaign denounced a federal bill then before parliament so effectively that it was withdrawn. This undercut the real motivation of British policy for the Transvaal. It therefore presented Gladstone, who had just succeeded to power, and who had denounced the annexation in his Midlothian election speeches, with an opportunity to restore Transvaal independence. However, perhaps anxious to retain control over policy towards the black population and possibly acting in the belief that the Boer leaders were fearful of making a determined stand, and certainly because the cabinet neglected the Transvaal question between July and December on account of misinformation from South African officials and a greater concern over the crisis in Ireland, Gladstone neglected to give the South African question sufficient attention, and later admitted his mistake (Krüger, *Paul Kruger*, 1.195; Schreuder 83, 91–2).

The Boer leaders therefore decided to act as if there had been no legal transfer of power at all. Kruger supported the action of a burgher in Potchefstroom whose refusal to pay taxes except to the republican government led to a riot. At Paardekraal, south-west of Pretoria, on 10 December 1880 a crowd of over 8000 heard Kruger, speaking as vice-president, outline a plan devised mainly by Jorissen to carry out the decision of the previous December. In the absence of Burgers, he now summoned the Volksraad to an extraordinary session in Heidelberg. The executive authority was reconstituted in a triumvirate consisting of himself, Joubert as kommandant-general, and ex-President Pretorius. Jorissen resumed as state attorney and Bok took over as state secretary. A press in Potchefstroom was seized to promulgate their decisions. Landdrosts were appointed in all the main towns. Commandos now re-emerged, and British troops, after the mauling of one column at Bronkhorstspruit, retreated to Standerton. The surprised British administrators were besieged in Pretoria, and the territory was in Boer hands within a week. A British relieving force from Natal under Sir George Pomeroy Colley, the new high commissioner, had suffered two military setbacks before the end of January but was poised on the border.

In this difficult situation, Kruger tried to make contact with Colley on 12 February 1881, offering a cease-fire; but he was called away to Rustenburg to handle a potential Tswana rising. Only on his return on the 28th did he receive the British offer of a royal commission to restore self-government in return for an end to the rebellion, but a 48-hour time limit imposed by Colley had already expired and his forces had taken possession of Majuba, and a Boer force had already retaken the mountain and killed Colley (Krüger, *Paul Kruger*, 2.225–8). After the battle of Majuba Hill, when the triumvirate still realized that they were in no position to dictate terms of their own choosing, Kruger offered the British government peace on the basis of complete self-government under British suzerainty, with a British resident in Pretoria. Hard bargaining ensued between the triumvirate on the one hand and Sir Evelyn Wood, acting high commissioner, on the other, with President Brand and Sir Henry de Villiers, the Cape chief justice, as mediators. The gist of Kruger's terms was accepted, and a royal commission appointed to finalize the agreement completed its work with the signing of the Pretoria convention on 3 August 1881, within an agreed six-month time limit. After the restoration of self-government a new Volksraad was elected, and the triumvirate, which had gone into abeyance before the Pretoria convention, re-emerged as a *de facto* executive until a presidential election led to the installation of Kruger as state president on 9 May 1883.

Kruger as president of the South African Republic In 1881 Kruger moved to Church Street, Pretoria (to a house opposite the Dutch Reformed church later bought by the South African government and converted into a museum). Here, as president, sitting with his coffee cup and his meerschaum pipe in the early mornings, he would greet callers of all kinds, bringing his personal style to government in this homely fashion.

Kruger did not try to turn the South African Republic into a Calvinist 'Cromwellian' commonwealth, as is sometimes supposed. In his public utterances on government and politics he reflected very closely the values of the Gereformeerde kerk, with its emphasis on the will of the people as the will of God, and the necessary separation of church and state, each sovereign in its own sphere, as articulated by Dr Abraham Kuyper, founder of the Free University of Amsterdam and later prime minister of the Netherlands. Kruger associated closely with S. J. Du Toit, whom he met in 1873, shortly before Du Toit became involved in a neo-Calvinist crusade at the Cape, and in the founding of the Afrikaner Bond. He attracted Du Toit to Pretoria in 1883 as his superintendent-general of education, to launch a campaign for 'Christian National' public schooling. He also took him to Europe in 1883 (after Du Toit had artfully had Jorissen excluded from the deputation and removed from his governmental post). On that occasion he was introduced by Du Toit to Kuyper. Kruger might well have kept Du Toit in his service for longer but for Du Toit's errant performances in other fields (see below).

To assess Kruger as a head of state it is necessary to look beyond his orthodoxies to his personal role in public affairs. As the president of the executive council (his official title), he operated under a written constitution which was flexible in the sense that constitutional amendments required no special majority in the Volksraad. The power of the sovereign people was shared in practice with the Volksraad, the president, and the courts. The will of the people was reflected in a measure of direct democracy through presidential and *raad* elections, the regular use of petitions, and the reference back of legislation; yet the Volksraad 'interpreted' that will, and, as Kruger himself insisted, his own responsibility to guide the Volksraad entitled him to unlimited speaking rights, especially as he

had no vote. He accepted that the Volksraad could reject his policies. It quite often did so, notably over his own land rights in 1868–71, when the *raad* at first refused to grant him transfer of a property on which Chief Makgato had customary title but which he did not occupy; Kruger applied pressure on the executive council, which ordered transfer; but the landdrost, backed by two other whites, objected on the ground that Potgieter had granted the land to Makgato under a Volksraad resolution of 1853; Kruger eventually won his battle when it was shown that he had actually sold the land to another party in 1871 and needed transfer to validate the sale (Krüger, *Paul Kruger*, 1.77–80). He was clear that if outvoted on a key issue he would resign; but he often took opposition very personally, as in the above land case, and especially if his Hollander officials were attacked. He threatened to walk out of sessions, and occasionally did so, extracting apologies thereby (Smit, 140–52). Carl Jeppe observed that 'even when he lost his temper he never lost his head' (C. Jeppe, *Kaleidoscopic Transvaal*, 1906, 167). That opposition could be substantial, and it often had stamina. He was at loggerheads with members of the Burgers faction during the 1870s, with Volksraad 'hawks' over the Pretoria convention and subsequent frontier policies, and with opponents of his railway policy in the late 1880s and his concessions policy in the 1890s. For the greater part of his presidency, not only during the years 1890–95 and over and above the Uitlander lobby, an embryonic opposition group existed in the Volksraad, centred on the personality of P. J. Joubert, Kruger's triumviral colleague after Majuba but his unsuccessful opponent in all four presidential elections which he contested (1883, 1888, 1893, and 1898).

As president, Kruger had the prerogative of clemency, but on one occasion misused it by applying it, on behalf of A. H. Nellmapius, a Hollander, before the judicial process had been completed: the court had Nellmapius rearrested, but decided on review that Kruger was right on the evidence, and let him go. In the more serious crisis of 1897, when Kruger confronted and in the end dismissed his chief justice, Sir John Gilbert Kotzé, after the latter had ruled that a Volksraad resolution (*besluit*) did not have the force of law because it had not been taken through requisite legislative procedures (involving a three-quarters majority and referral to the constituencies), Kruger acted because he saw that if Kotzé was right this would create legal uncertainty over a wide area. As a result, the right of the courts to test legislation—a 'right of the Devil', as Kruger dubbed it—became anathema in South Africa for close on 100 years. Kruger saw the point—that the constitution needed to be changed; but his other argument, that some clauses in the constitution obviously required formal amending procedures, whereas others did not, did not hold water.

It is often not appreciated that, as a 'Dopper', Kruger was in principle concerned to widen rather than restrict political rights. Thus the 1889 revision of the constitution disestablished all churches to make them 'sovereign in their own spheres', eliminated official status for the Dutch Reformed religion, gave toleration to other forms of

Christian worship, and extended membership of the Volksraad to other protestant congregations (article 31). Kruger himself deplored discrimination against Roman Catholics and Jews, even if he was averse to their teachings, because it implied persecution (Smit, 4, 12; Krüger, *Paul Kruger*, 2.87, 187). A friend of the tycoon Sammy Marks, he opened the Orange Grove Synagogue in 1892, with the comment: 'I see most of you are Jews: I have come to convert you.'

But although, in his political thinking, Kruger's acceptance of the voice of the people as the voice of God made him a logical democrat, his logic was bounded by the difficulty of all 'ox-waggon' republicans faced with the task of converting their society into a territorial state. His tolerance of other believers marked the limit beyond which he felt unable to bridge the logical gap. He could be paternal towards black people, and admit them to legal rights but not to political equality, least of all in a state which, until 1898, was struggling to bring all people within its boundaries under governmental control. The same consideration, but not quite to the same degree, applied to Uitlanders from overseas; but as Uitlanders shared a common Euro-Christian background with his own people, they could be offered a second (but inferior) Volksraad—this was Kruger's idea—as compensation for obstacles in the way of their voting rights. Pragmatism clashed with ideology in Kruger's mind; and his 'Christian National' assumptions, which told him that a community needed cultural as well as political coherence to survive, reinforced his belief that the ultimate question was one of power. In the end this was his undoing.

Kruger and the outside world At the signing of the Pretoria convention Kruger's simple objective had been a return to the isolation of the Sand River convention: the Voortrekkers must receive back the 'promised land' given to them for their tribulations. The Pretoria convention, by emphasizing the queen's suzerainty over the Transvaal, and empowering a British resident in Pretoria to control the government's external policy, its troop movements, and its relationship with internal black communities, constituted a real restriction on its independence.

This mattered initially with regard to frontier policies, for settlers from the Transvaal and from the Cape had ignored the borders on the edge of the Kalahari fixed under the Keate award of 1871. There had been major intrusions onto land belonging to Tswana chiefdoms, which had led to instability, and also enabled the Transvaal to straddle the trade route along the edge of the Kalahari between central Africa and the Cape. Whether to advance the interests of Boer settlers, or to enforce peace in the area, Kruger sought to have the frontier revised. His attitude on a visit to London in 1883 was clearly assertive (Schreuder, 259ff.). He went further, and supported S. J. Du Toit in 1884 when he raised the flag of the South African Republic over two mushroom Boer republics which had been set up in the area in 1882. This was a mistake on Kruger's part, based on a belief that Britain would not intervene. He had to cancel the annexation, and trim the wings of P. J. Joubert as well as those of Du Toit, for the former

was promoting expansion into northern Zululand as well. The upshot was an agreement with Lord Derby to extend the Pretoria convention boundary westwards, but not so as to cut the 'road to the north', or allow a common border between the Transvaal and the new German protectorate in south-west Africa. The London convention (1884), superseding that of Pretoria, and Britain's proclamation of the Bechuanaland protectorate in 1885 sealed off the Transvaal's westward expansion.

The years 1886–91 witnessed major changes in the economic balance of southern Africa with the discovery of the Rand goldfields, the amalgamation of the diamond industry in Kimberley under control of De Beers, and the opening up of central Africa to exploitation by the British South Africa Company, all enterprises closely associated with Cecil Rhodes, who was also prime minister of the Cape from 1890. These developments, linked to the growing interest of European powers in Africa, made nonsense of the isolation of the Transvaal, which was coming to be seen as a new focal point of economic power in the region. For Rhodes and his associates it meant the incorporation of the Transvaal in a larger economic entity, for Kruger the defence of his republic against a massive invasion by alien birds of passage seeking gold and rights, and the safeguarding of independence by obtaining direct access to the outside world through its own sea port.

Kruger's attempt to get a harbour failed. Despite the launching of the new republic in Zululand in 1887, and its incorporation in the Transvaal with British agreement, Kosi Bay on the coast was declared non-viable. This meant that for Kruger a second-best option was the building of a railway line to Pretoria from Delagoa Bay—a dream which he had supported since Burgers's day, and began to promote again through an American firm on becoming president. Both schemes administratively were badly conceived, but Kruger's found new life with his decision to engage the Netherlands-South Africa Company in 1884. He was unable on account of financial difficulties to complete this line until 1894, and then only thanks to an offer of help from Rhodes conditional on the prior admission of a line from the Cape; but at least Delagoa Bay remained an independent port, for the Portuguese held off attempts by Rhodes to buy it. By again breaking the London convention, Kruger tried to neutralize Cape railway competition in 1895 by placing high countervailing tariffs on the Cape route and then closing the Vaal drifts to road traffic; but this led to a confrontation with Britain in 1895, and he had to climb down. Ironically, in his enthusiasm to reach the sea, Kruger always discouraged attempts by his fellow Transvalers to establish rights north of the Limpopo, beyond negotiating an abortive understanding with Lobengula (the Grobler treaty of 1887), as is shown in his handling of the Bowler and Adendorff treks of 1890 and 1891.

The encirclement of the Transvaal was never quite achieved, but Kruger's success in stalling Rhodes's efforts to achieve this end forced the British government to look harder at the strategic significance of an economically independent Transvaal in a subcontinent where other powers, notably Germany, appeared to be taking an interest, especially as Kruger's relationship with Germany was cordial, and investment by German and other continental businesses on the Rand was strong. In 1894–5 two schemes were drawn up, one by High Commissioner Sir Henry Loch the other by Rhodes, to topple Kruger's government by projecting a rising of the Uitlander community on the Rand to be helped by a supporting column from Bechuanaland—in Loch's case of British troops, in Rhodes's of company police. Only the latter, the Jameson raid, was attempted. Its failure, and the manner in which Kruger handled it, added enormously to his public image as he 'waited for the tortoise to stick its head out' then struck, and then, after the leaders of the Rand rising had been convicted of treason, commuted their death sentences to fairly heavy fines, while Jameson himself was handed over to Britain for punishment. In a masterly fashion too Kruger censured the German Kaiser for giving him excessive telegraphic support.

The Jameson raid poisoned the relationship between the republic and Britain. Kruger, for his part, rearmed heavily with purchases of rifles and heavy armaments from Germany and France. Rhodes was discredited for two years, but almost managed through a new political party, the Progressives, to regain power in 1898. This in itself showed how inflamed feelings among English-speakers had become. These were reflected in counter-propaganda alleging an Afrikaner plot, much of it seizing on the sentiment in a letter in the *Staats-Courant* as far back as 16 February 1881: 'Freedom shall arise in Africa as the sun out of morning clouds: … then shall it be from Zambesi to Simons Bay: Africa for the Afrikaner.' (Such utterances had since become rare in the Dutch/Afrikaans press.)

An understandable but politically negative result of the post-raid hysteria was the impact which it had on the Uitlander residents of Johannesburg as they looked up at the fort on the Berea recently built by Kruger's government for their control. The Uitlander leaders had begun to chafe at the government from about 1892; but after the raid their anger at governmental hostility, at police behaviour, at the government's concession policy (which was seen as disfavouring the mines), and at new obstacles placed in the way of the Uitlander franchise intensified. It was matched by fresh criticisms from the Colonial Office to the effect that Kruger's government was in breach of the London convention yet again, over its immigration and aliens expulsion legislation (Marais). The franchise issue took centre stage—not because most Uitlanders necessarily wanted the vote, but because Kruger's government set out to weaken mining-house opposition by driving a wedge between capital and labour, to which an obvious answer from the Uitlander perspective was to pick an issue which could unite rather than divide them. It would probably have been easier to reform Kruger's government than to remove it, because there were signs that by 1897 it was trying to meet criticism of its undoubted inefficiencies, notably in its mining and labour legislation. But the climate was wrong. The failure of the 'great deal' between the government and the chamber of mines in March 1899 was the signal for a major Uitlander petition which Alfred Milner, the high commissioner, used to take Kruger to the brink in the hope that he could be forced to yield without the use of force.

Kruger's attitude during 1899 was no longer that of the brash opportunist of the Stellaland annexation or the drifts crisis. He left that to his angry state attorney, J. C. Smuts. Kruger was once more the conciliator of 1879–81 who would put off the day of reckoning if at all possible, and certainly not fight without counting the cost. When pressed on the issue of franchise reform, he was prepared on two occasions in that year to give ground to meet Milner's demands; but when presented with an ultimatum which seemed to require him to hand over his country, as was the case when Milner confronted him at Bloemfontein in May, and Chamberlain rejected the Smuts–Green compromise in September, his 'No' was decisive (Marais).

The Second South African War and exile, 1899–1904 When war seemed inevitable in September 1899 Kruger accepted Smuts's advice that it would be better to declare war himself and take advantage of surprise than to wait for the inevitable to happen. He took care to see that President Steyn of the Orange Free State was fully behind his stand, and sent an ultimatum to Britain on 9 October. Strategic decisions once war had started belonged to the kommandant-general, Joubert, who was beyond the president's call while on campaign. Kruger stayed mainly in Pretoria, but was nearly captured on a visit to the OFS in March 1900. He took part in the decision to go over to guerrilla warfare when the fall of the capitals seemed imminent, but agreed to leave for Europe via Delagoa Bay after the fall of Pretoria in the vain hope of being able to win continental help for the Boer cause, and left on 11 September 1900, on a ship supplied by the queen of the Netherlands.

Kruger spent his declining years in Europe, separated from his dying wife. He travelled up the east coast and went via Marseilles and Paris to the Netherlands, lionized by the crowds, but greeted with respect without high protocol treatment or offers of material help from the French government, while from the German authorities he received a cool reception. The Dutch government by contrast were warm, and provided homes in Hilversum, and later at Utrecht. Finally, after a short stay on the French riviera, he went to his last home at Clarens, Switzerland, in May 1904, and died there on 14 July. His body was temporarily buried at The Hague, and finally interred, after ceremonial lying in state in Cape Town, in the old cemetery, Pretoria, on 16 December 1904.

Assessment Kruger's career has split the critics. Some have seen him as an anachronistic throwback to the seventeenth century. They stress his intellectual unsophistication, his literalist biblical outlook with a slight suggestion of 'flat-earthism' (Krüger, *Paul Kruger*, 1.134). Others prefer to see a shrewd interpreter of events and people, able even to confute judges on points of law.

He was a tragic folk hero, faithfully defending the rights of a maligned people, whose performance has engendered much debate. Alternatively, he was a stubborn trickster, the shifty defender of an immoral cause, 'dribbling out reforms like water from a squeezed sponge', and tough on the black population. His image has now steadied, and grown with time, but perhaps his least recognized quality was noted by Reginald Statham when he wrote that 'there is no man who, while holding strong opinions of his own, is more ready to respect the opinions of others' (Statham, 92).

T. R. H. DAVENPORT

Sources D. W. Krüger, *Paul Kruger*, 2 vols. (1961–3) [Afrikaans] · D. W. Krüger, *DSAB*, 1.444–55 [incl. iconographical list] · C. J. Uys, *Paul Kruger van die wieg tot die graf* (1956) · F. P. Smit, *Die staatsopvatting van Paul Kruger* (1951) · B. Spoelstra, *Die 'Doppers' in Suid-Afrika, 1760–1899* (1963) · S. P. Engelbrecht, *Geskiedenis van die Nederduitsch Hervormde kerk van Afrika* (1953) · J. A. I. Agar-Hamilton, *The native policy of the Voortrekkers, 1836–58* (1928) · J. A. I. Agar-Hamilton, *The road to the north: South Africa, 1852–1886* (1937) · C. F. Goodfellow, *Great Britain and South African confederation, 1870–1881* (1966) · D. M. Schreuder, *Gladstone and Kruger* (1969) · Gladstone, *Diaries* · F. R. Statham, *Paul Kruger and his times* (1898) · N. G. Garson, 'The Swaziland question and a road to the sea, 1887–95', *Archives Year Book* (1957), pt 2 · C. T. Gordon, *The growth of Boer opposition to Kruger, 1890–95* (1966) · J. van der Poel, *The Jameson raid* (1951) · J. S. Marais, *The fall of Kruger's republic* (1961) · I. R. Smith, *The origins of the South African war, 1899–1902* (1996) · T. Pakenham, *The Boer War* (1979) · P. J. van Winter, *Onder Krugers Hollanders*, 2 vols. (1937–8) · F. A. van Jaarsveld, 'Die veldkornet en sy aandeel in die opbou van die Suid-Afrikaanse republiek tot 1870', *Archives Year Book* (1950), pt 2 · J. J. van Heerden, 'Die kommandant-generaal in die geskiedenis van die Suid-Afrikanse republiek', *Archives Year Book* (1964), pt 2 · J. S. du Plessis, 'Die ontstaan en ontwikkeling van die amp van staatspresident in die Zuid-Afrikaansche republiek, 1858–1902', *Archives Year Book* (1955), pt 1 · T. R. H. Davenport, *The Afrikaner Bond* (1966) · S. P. Engelbrecht, *Thomas François Burgers: a biography* (1946) · J. A. Mouton, 'Generaal Piet Joubert in die Transvaalse geskiedenis', *Archives Year Book* (1957), pt 1 · W. K. Hancock, *Smuts, 1: The sanguine years, 1870–1919* (1962) · L. E. van Niekerk, *Kruger se regterhand: biografie van dr. W. J. Leyds* (Pretoria, 1985) · R. Mendelsohn, *Sammy Marks: the uncrowned king of the Transvaal* (1991) · N. J. van der Merwe, *Marthinus Theunis Steyn*, 2 vols. (1921) · F. V. Engelenburg, *General Louis Botha* (1929) · E. J. P. Jorissen, *Transvaalsche herinneringen* (1897) · J. G. Kotzé, *Biographical memoirs and reminiscences*, 2 vols. (1933–54) · H. C. Bredell, *Dagboek, 1900–04*, ed. A. G. Oberholster (1972) · J. Carruthers, *The Kruger National Park* (1995) · L. S. J. Changuion, *Fotobiografie von Paul Kruger* (1973) · G. M. Theal, *History of South Africa*, 4th edn, 11 vols. (1915–27), vols. 3–4, 6
Archives National Cultural History Museum, Pretoria | National Archives of South Africa, Pretoria, Transvaal archives depot, H. C. Bredell, F. V. Engelenburg, Mrs L. J. Jacobsz, and G. S. Preller collections · National Archives of South Africa, Pretoria, Transvaal archives depot, W. J. Leyds archive
Likenesses Elliott & Fry, photograph, 1877, NPG [*see illus.*] · J. G. Achard, statue, Rustenburg town hall, South Africa · C. Leandre, portrait, repro. in Krüger, *Paul Kruger*, vol. 2, p. 232 · L. Lipshitz, bronze bust, University of Cape Town, South Africa, Macmillan Press Cutting Collection · E. Mayer, charcoal drawing, War Museum, Bloemfontein, South Africa · E. Mayer, portrait, War Museum, Bloemfontein, South Africa · M. Postma, statue, Krugersdorp, South Africa · C. W. H. Schröder, oils, Kruger House, Pretoria, South Africa · C. Steynburg, statue, railway headquarters building, Johannesburg, South Africa · A. Van Wouw, statue, Church Square, Pretoria, South Africa · A. Van Wouw, statue, Kruger House, Pretoria, South Africa · F. Wichgraf, portrait, National Cultural History Museum, Pretoria, South Africa · F. Wolf, portrait, Africana Museum, Johannesburg, South Africa · photographs, Cape Archives Depot, Elliott Collection

Kubrick, Stanley (1928–1999), film director, was born on 26 July 1928 at the Lying-in Hospital, 307 Second Avenue, Manhattan, New York, the son of Jacques Leonard Kubrick (1901–1985), physician, and Gertrude Perveler (1903–1985), who were both of mid-European Jewish extraction. Conscious of the boy's mediocre academic accomplishments, Kubrick's father encouraged an interest in chess and photography. He bought him a Graflex camera for his thirteenth birthday, with which Kubrick snapped street scenes and classmates at William Howard Taft School. Yet the teenage Kubrick's real passion was jazz, and he hoped to progress from playing drums with the Taft Swing Band. However, in 1945 he received $25 from the magazine *Look* for a photograph of a mournful newsboy proclaiming President Roosevelt's death, and he abandoned his musical ambitions to start work as a staff photographer.

Early films During his four-year spell at *Look* Kubrick enrolled as a non-matriculating student at Columbia University and became a voracious reader, with a questing imagination that eventually led to every conversation becoming an inquisition. He also spent many hours at the cinema, leavening the lessons learned from masters like Max Ophüls at the Museum of Modern Art with the latest releases from Hollywood. As he later confessed, 'I was aware that I didn't know anything about making films, but I believed I couldn't make them any worse than the majority of films I was seeing. Bad films gave me the courage to try making a movie' (Turner, 545). On 29 May 1948 he married Toba Metz (*b.* 1930).

Kubrick decided to attempt the transition from still to motion pictures with *Day of the Fight* (1950), a sixteen-minute documentary focusing on Walter Cartier, a boxer he had already featured in a 1949 photo spread entitled 'Prizefighter'. It was an apt beginning, for as his biographer Vincent LoBrutto suggested, 'the nature of photography itself—light, depth, space, composition, and seizing the reality perceived through the eye of the photographer—throbs at the heart of every Stanley Kubrick film' (LoBrutto, 23). Moreover, it also proclaimed his hands-on approach to film-making, for in addition to directing, Kubrick shot and edited the footage and recorded the sound.

Kubrick made $1000 profit when he sold the short to RKO for $4000. Yet it was his second film, *The Flying Padre* (1951), about the Revd Fred Stadtmueller and his 400-mile parish in the deep south-west, that reached audiences first. Unable to raise the funds for a feature, Kubrick directed a number of sponsored documentaries. However, by 1952 he had managed to borrow $10,000 from his father and an uncle in order to complete the Korean War drama *Fear and Desire*. It too was largely a one-man operation, as he wrote the screenplay, as well as directing and photographing the action. Yet he subsequently disowned the picture, despite the fact that it considered such recurring themes as the plight of the individual confronting an

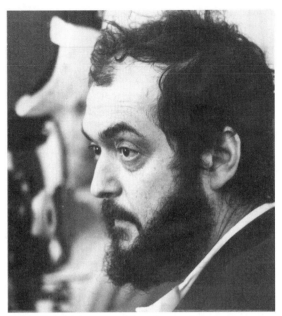

Stanley Kubrick (1928–1999), by unknown photographer, 1971

unseen enemy and humanity's inability to learn from experience.

Shot on location around New York on a budget borrowed from friends, *Killer's Kiss* (1955) demonstrated a remarkable maturity for a second feature. Its storyline, about a boxer who gets mixed up with a brutal nightclub boss, was strictly 'B' fare. But Kubrick's use of *noir*-ish shadows, symbolic doubles, and negative footage in the nightmare sequence was sufficiently impressive to persuade United Artists to offer him and his new producing partner, James B. Harris, a contract to adapt Lionel White's pulp novel *Clean Break* into the thriller *The Killing* (1956). Tackling another favourite theme, the individual bucking the system, the film marked Kubrick's first critical success and also established a career-long predilection for acquiring literary properties and then tailoring them to his own artistic purposes. Moreover, it also boasted art direction by his second wife, Ruth Sobotka (1925–1967), whom he had married on 15 January 1955, following his divorce from Toba Metz four years earlier. This second marriage ended in divorce in 1957.

Although it subsequently achieved cult status, *The Killing* lost money, and United Artists was only too happy to see Harris and Kubrick defect to MGM. Initially tempted by Stefan Zweig's novel *Burning Secret*, the duo eventually opted to adapt *Paths of Glory*, Humphrey Cobb's pacifist denunciation of military injustice in the First World War. However, a front office coup led to their contract being cancelled, and only the commitment of Kirk Douglas's Bryna Productions ensured its completion. Filmed on location in Germany, the film employed an assured blend of political comment, character motivation, and courtroom tension which enabled Kubrick to explore what would become another perennial theme, the abuse of power. Yet despite enthusiastic notices, *Paths of Glory*

(1957) not only was a commercial disappointment, but was also banned in France for its unflattering depiction of the army.

The only female member of the cast was the German-born artist Christiane Susanne Harlan (*b.* 1932), who became Kubrick's third wife in 1958. They had two children, Anya and Vivian, and Kubrick brought up Harlan's child from a previous marriage, Katharina, as his own daughter. Several projects were considered over the next couple of years, including a television series with Ernie Kovacs and *One-Eyed Jacks*, a western that Kubrick spent six months developing before falling out with Marlon Brando over casting. But nothing sufficiently intriguing materialized, and he was forced to endure his only experience as a jobbing director, when he replaced Anthony Mann on Kirk Douglas's Roman epic *Spartacus* (1960). Shot in Super-Technirama, this was the most expensive picture then attempted in Hollywood and has continued to rank among the period's most proficient widescreen blockbusters. It even aroused a little controversy, when a bathing sequence, in which Laurence Olivier and Tony Curtis discussed the relative merits of snails and oysters, incurred the censor's displeasure, owing to its homoerotic nature. The scene was eventually reinstated for the film's reissue in 1990.

Kubrick's cult movies Despite his new-found status, Kubrick was no longer willing to compromise his vision for commercial considerations. He later admitted:

> If ever I needed convincing of the limits of persuasion a director can have on a film when someone else is the producer and he is merely the highest paid member of the crew, *Spartacus* provided proof to last a lifetime. (Turner, 547)

Consequently, he moved to Britain to secure both the autonomy and the Eady plan funding he needed to realize his adaptation of Vladimir Nabokov's *Lolita*.

Kubrick persuaded James Mason to play Humbert Humbert, the middle-aged academic who falls passionately in love with the under-age Lolita Haze (Sue Lyon), and Peter Sellers to essay his nemesis, Clare Quilty. Then he began reworking the screenplay Nabokov had fashioned from his *succès de scandale* to create a mirror image of the source that reflected his own preoccupation with doubles, predetermined doom, and the manipulative misuse of responsibility.

The critics were divided on whether he had missed Humbert's humanity or the novel's poetic grace. But thenceforth no Kubrick film was ever to be accorded universal approbation. Indeed, such was the polarity of the debate that Michel Ciment could declare him 'one of the most demanding, most original and most visionary filmmakers of our time', while the equally respected David Thomson could dismiss him as 'the most significant and ornate dead end in modern cinema' (Turner, 552).

Having toyed with a further exploration of teenage sexual mores in *The Passion Flower Hotel*, Kubrick parted company with James Harris and reunited with Peter Sellers for his pitch-black cold war satire, *Dr Strangelove, or, How I Learned to Stop Worrying and Love the Bomb* (1964). Kubrick earned three Oscar nominations, for best picture, best direction, and best adapted screenplay, while Sellers landed one for best actor for his portrayal of three different characters in this irreverent take on Peter George's novel *Red Alert*, which had originally been published as *Two Hours to Doom*. The film's iconic moment saw the United States Air Force pilot Slim Pickens rodeo-riding an atomic bomb as it hurtled towards Soviet territory, although it would surely have been surpassed had Kubrick retained his original finale, in which a pie fight breaks out in the deliciously subversive war room created by the art director Ken Adam.

Now resident at Abbots Mead in Hertfordshire, Kubrick embarked on his most ambitious project, a $10.5 million, 161-minute adaptation of Arthur C. Clarke's science-fiction story *The Sentinel*. Treatments for *Journey beyond the Stars* were completed in 1964, but such was Kubrick's now legendary obsession with meticulous preparation that shooting began at Borehamwood and Shepperton studios only in 1965 and lasted well into the following year. The pioneering special effects also took many months to complete. Yet *2001: a Space Odyssey* (1968) fulfilled Kubrick's desire to create 'a non-verbal experience' that not only dispensed with traditional narrative conventions, but also pushed back visual frontiers in almost every frame. Winning an Oscar for its effects and nominations for its direction and adapted screenplay, it gave science fiction a new respectability, while also paving the way for the epoch-making space operas of the 1970s.

Frustrated in his ambition to mount a biography of Napoleon, Kubrick launched his new association with Warner Bros. with *A Clockwork Orange* (1971). Yet despite receiving the now customary Oscar nominations for best picture, best direction, and best adapted screenplay, this deeply pessimistic version of Anthony Burgess's novel encountered censorship difficulties in the United States and sparked a debate about the impact of sex and violence in cinema when the British media linked it to murders in Blackpool and Oxford. Unwilling to have his film made a scapegoat for society's ills, Kubrick withdrew it from British circulation in 1974, and it remained unavailable up to his death.

Later works Declining invitations to direct *The Exorcist* and an adaptation of Albert Speer's *Inside the Third Reich*, Kubrick alighted upon a novel of 1843 by William Makepeace Thackeray, which he determined to shoot in natural light in the style of contemporary English paintings. Another work focusing on an essentially amoral character, *Barry Lyndon* (1975) was much admired for its rich textures and unique candlelit interiors. But while it won Oscars for its design and cinematography, Kubrick again missed out as both producer and director, and the film was coolly received outside Europe.

Devotees rallied to the cause, but the *New Yorker*'s Pauline Kael was not alone in lamenting of Kubrick's work that 'everything has become serious. The way he's working, in self-willed isolation, with each film consuming years of anxiety, there's no ground between masterpiece

and failure. And the pressure shows' (Turner, 551). Moreover, following his move to Childwickbury Manor, near Harpenden, in 1977, Kubrick was increasingly portrayed as an eccentric recluse, who not only surrounded himself with gadgets and files of useless information, but also refused to fly, and insisted on being chauffeur-driven at under 30 m.p.h. This caricature was not helped by his habit of telephoning Warners or individual theatres whenever he learned of the shoddy projection of his films.

Yet each new Kubrick picture was greeted as a significant cultural event. In 1980 he further demonstrated his versatility with a reworking of Stephen King's horror novel *The Shining*. Making imaginative use of the Steadicam system, he created some memorable images and coaxed a supremely unhinged performance from Jack Nicholson. But critics bemoaned an increasing psychological detachment, and following a disappointing opening in America, Kubrick drastically reduced the running time.

Seven years elapsed before Kubrick resumed his career with *Full Metal Jacket* (1987), a bleak study of life in boot camp and the Vietnam war zone based on Gustav Hasford's book *The Short-Timers*. With derelict ground in London's docklands standing in for the site of the Tet offensive, the film was another remarkable technical accomplishment and earned Kubrick his fourth Oscar nomination for adapted screenplay. It seemed an inauspicious swansong, especially as projects like *A.I.* and *Wartime Lies* stalled in development.

Yet Kubrick returned after a twelve-year hiatus with *Eyes Wide Shut* in 1999. Based on Arthur Schnitzler's *Traumnovelle* (which he had previously contemplated in 1971) and starring the celebrity Hollywood couple Tom Cruise and Nicole Kidman, the project was shrouded in secrecy, with rumours abounding as it turned into the longest shoot in screen history. On 7 March 1999, only days after completing the release print, Kubrick died of a coronary thrombosis at Childwickbury Manor and was thus spared both the underwhelming box office and the typically ill-informed frenzy of superlatives and brickbats that greeted his final work. His third wife, Christiane, survived him.   DAVID PARKINSON

Sources V. LoBrutto, *Stanley Kubrick* (New York, 1997) • J. Baxter, *Stanley Kubrick* (1997) • A. Walker, *Stanley Kubrick directs* (1999) • F. Raphael, *Eyes wide open* (1999) • A. Turner, *World film directors*, ed. J. Wakeham, 2: 1945–85 (1988) • *The Times* (8 March 1999) • *Daily Telegraph* (8 March 1999) • *The Guardian* (8 March 1999) • *The Independent* (8 March 1999) • d. cert.
Archives priv. coll.
Likenesses photographs, *c*.1963–1975, Hult. Arch. [*see illus.*]

Küchemann, Dietrich Friedrich Gustav (1911–1976),

aerodynamicist, was born in Göttingen, Germany, on 11 September 1911, the eldest of three children and only son of Rudolf Küchemann, schoolmaster, and his wife, Martha Egener. Between 1921 and 1930 he attended the Oberrealschule, Göttingen, at which his father taught and from which, in 1933, his father was to be dismissed for his refusal to subscribe to National Socialist doctrine: this was the culmination of a long and determined opposition, shared, but more circumspectly displayed, by his son Dietrich. He entered the faculty of mathematics and physics in the University of Göttingen in 1930, and eventually studied for his doctorate in theoretical aerodynamics under Ludwig Prandtl, who later described Küchemann as the best research student of his generation.

In 1936 Küchemann married Helga Janet, daughter of Surgeon-Admiral Viktor Praefcke of the German navy; they had a son and two daughters. On the successful completion of his dissertation in 1936, Küchemann joined the Aerodynamische Versuchsanstalt, Göttingen, where, after some early work on bird flight, he began, in 1940, his monumental study of the aerodynamics of aircraft propulsion. It was a subject upon which he concentrated during the remainder of the Second World War, and he initiated a collaboration with Dr Johanna Weber that continued for the rest of their working lives. Their treatment, systematic, comprehensive, and refreshingly original, was subsequently described in their book *Aerodynamics of Propulsion* (1953). He volunteered for the army and was called up for short periods of training in the Luftnachrichtentruppe (signals) in 1938 and 1939, but he saw no real active service during the war.

Küchemann left Göttingen in September 1946 for the Royal Aircraft Establishment, Farnborough, on a temporary basis, to be joined soon afterwards by Dr Weber and then, in 1948, by his family. In that year he indicated his willingness to become a naturalized British subject, and was given a permanent appointment in 1951 (he was naturalized in 1953). Thereafter, his ascent through the hierarchy of the scientific civil service was singularly rapid: senior principal scientific officer on individual merit 1954, deputy chief scientific officer 1957, chief scientific officer and head of the aerodynamics department 1966. He held the latter post until his nominal retirement in 1971, but remained in the department as an individual research scientist until his death. Throughout, whether officially charged with administrative responsibilities or not, he maintained a continuous flow of original publications over a wide range of aerodynamic problems, embodying, as a central and developing theme, concepts of aerodynamic design, bold, elegant, revolutionary, which were to lead to the slender wing characteristic of the Concorde aeroplane. Those concepts were summed up in his last work, *The Aerodynamic Design of Aircraft* (1978).

That the success of Küchemann's civil service career was accompanied by none of the envy such achievement could generate was due, partly, to the incontrovertible evidence of his brilliance and originality, but mainly to his character. While resolute in the pursuit of his scientific ideas and the challenge they presented to aerodynamic convention, in his relations with colleagues, junior or senior, he was invariably gentle, courteous, modest, inclined to dwell upon problems that perplexed him in preference to those he had successfully solved; and at all times prepared to listen with genuine sympathy to their difficulties, eager whenever possible to offer help and encouragement.

Küchemann's warmth and sensitivity were at their most apparent in his response to music. He was a gifted cellist, and his standard of playing was high enough to have led him at one time to consider a professional career as a musician. As it was, he performed in many orchestras and, to his special delight, quartets, both in Germany and in England, once remarking that such activity provided him with the feeling, at its most intense, of belonging to a community: a feeling not narrowly experienced, since in science he was a dedicated internationalist and played an influential part in fostering research collaboration in aerodynamics among the nations of Europe.

Küchemann was elected a fellow of the Royal Society in 1963. He was appointed CBE (1964) and awarded the silver medal (1962) and the gold medal (1969) of the Royal Aeronautical Society, and, in the same year, the Enoch Thulin medal of the Swedish Society for Aeronautics and Astronautics. He received the Prandtl ring of the Deutsche Gesellschaft für Luft- und Raumfahrt (1970), and was granted honorary doctorates by the Cranfield Institute of Technology (1973), the Technical University of Berlin (1975), and the University of Bristol (1975). From 1972 he was visiting professor in the department of aeronautics, Imperial College, London. Küchemann died in Farnham, Surrey, on 23 February 1976.   PAUL OWEN, *rev.*

Sources P. R. Owen and E. C. Maskell, *Memoirs FRS*, 26 (1980), 305–26 · R. W. Slaney, *Royal Aircraft Establishment Library bibliography* (1976) · private information (1986) · personal knowledge (1986) · *WWW* · *CGPLA Eng. & Wales* (1976)
Archives Cranfield University Library, papers · Royal Air Force Museum, Hendon
Likenesses photograph, repro. in Owen and Maskell, *Memoirs FRS*
Wealth at death £15,587: probate, 27 April 1976, *CGPLA Eng. & Wales*

Kuczynski, Robert Rene (1876–1947), demographer, was born in Berlin on 12 August 1876, the son of Wilhelm Kuczynski, a banker, and his wife, Lucy Brandeis. He attended the French *Gymnasium* in Berlin and later the universities of Freiburg, Strasbourg, Berlin, and Munich. He was a student of Lujo Brentano, the historian, with whom he later collaborated, but a more important intellectual stimulus came from Richard Boeckh, a distinguished statistician and demographer who was director of the Berlin statistical office, which Kuczynski joined in 1898. Between 1900 and 1902 he worked in the census office, Washington, and then became director, first of the statistical office of Elberfeld (1904–5), and subsequently of that of Berlin-Schoeneberg (1906–21). In 1903 he married Berta Gradenwitz (d. 1947); they had a son and five daughters.

Kuczynski's interests showed a range remarkable even for his generation. In addition to his work as an administrative statistician he produced pioneer studies on the history of wages, on German economic and financial problems, on food production, and on labour problems. He edited two weekly economic news letters and published, during the inflation years, his own weekly cost-of-living index. He took an active part in politics, and was perhaps best known for his association, after the war, with the plebiscite for expropriating the Kaiser and the princes who were receiving substantial pensions from the Weimar republic. He had already made important contributions to demography when in 1926 he became a member of council of the Brookings Institution of Washington and began to concentrate on the population studies which marked the second main phase in his career: *The Balance of Births and Deaths* (1928, 1931), *Birth Registration and Birth Statistics in Canada* (1930), and *Fertility and Reproduction* (1932).

In 1933 Kuczynski left Germany and made England his home, joining the staff of the London School of Economics and Political Science, initially as research fellow and later (1938) as reader in demography, the first such university appointment to be created in Britain. He continued to contribute to the methodological side of his subject—*The Measurement of Population Growth* (1935) is ample evidence—but he also focused increasingly on British colonial territories. After the appearance of *Colonial Population* (1937) and *The Cameroons and Togoland* (1939), and his retirement from the readership in 1941, he became demographic adviser to the Colonial Office (1944). He became a British subject in 1946. Age did not affect his productivity. Until a few weeks before his death he was actively engaged with promoting new and more accurate censuses, especially in the West Indies. He also found time to undertake a massive *Demographic Survey of the British Colonial Empire*, completed with the assistance of his daughter Brigitte and published in three volumes (1948–53) after his death. He was in addition a most active member of the statistics committee of the royal commission on population.

Kuczynski's influence on demography did not derive primarily from his theoretical contributions, although the gross reproduction rate which he devised is a fertility index of considerable importance. His systematic analysis of population and vital statistics was an even more significant contribution, and one to which he brought a unique combination of insight, vast common sense, and impeccable scholarship. He was a man of great personality and charm, stimulating others by his own example and by his help and advice. No one who met him could fail to be impressed by his warmth and generosity. He died at University College Hospital, London, on 25 November 1947, a few months after the death of his wife.

D. V. GLASS, rev.

Sources private information (1959) · personal knowledge (1959) · *Population Studies*, 2/1 (June 1948) · *CGPLA Eng. & Wales* (1948)
Likenesses B. Kuczynski, charcoal drawing, priv. coll.
Wealth at death £2322 14s. 8d.: probate, 5 May 1948, *CGPLA Eng. & Wales*

Kuffeler [*formerly* Koffler], **Johannes Sibertus** (1595–1677), chemist and inventor, was born Johannes Sibertus Koffler on 6 January 1595 at the city of Cologne in Germany, in the Holy Roman empire, the eldest son of Jacob Koffler (1569–1607), the elector of Brandenburg's resident at Cologne, and Margareta von Rendinkhoven (1575–1638). Though Cologne was a Catholic city, the family's connections with Brandenburg-Prussia make it likely that they were protestant, and probably of a Calvinist orientation. Koffler matriculated at Padua University on 11 November 1617 and graduated MD on 6 March 1618. After his graduation, he and two of his brothers settled in the Netherlands (where Koffler became Kuffeler). His younger brother Abraham (1598–1657), and a fourth brother, moved to London in 1620, where they were joined two years later by Kuffeler and his brother Gilles (1596–1658).

On 1 May 1623 Kuffeler married Catharina Drebbel (*b.* 1609, *d.* after 1694), daughter of the inventor Cornelis *Drebbel; in the same year his brother Abraham, with whom his career was to be closely linked, married her sister, Anna Drebbel. The two brothers became closely involved in the business activities of their father-in-law, a prolific inventor who enjoyed the patronage of James I, from whom he received a house and a workshop in Trinity Minories, London. Collaborating closely, they helped to develop and promote Drebbel's inventions, possibly working with him on the Dutch reclamation of the fens, and they ran his Stratford-le-Bow dyeworks when he died in 1633.

In June 1642, shortly before the outbreak of civil war, Kuffeler, together with his brother, left England and settled in the Netherlands, first at The Hague and subsequently at Arnhem, where they set up a dyeworks. His brother gave up his share in the business and returned to England in 1652. Kuffeler stayed behind until 1656, when, after several false starts, he signed a tripartite agreement on 20 June 1656 with Samuel Hartlib and Ezerel Tonge, offering his services to the Commonwealth as an inventor. He and his family (several of his sixteen children born between 1628 and 1649 died young) then moved to Stratford Langton, West Ham, Essex (on the opposite bank of the River Lea to Stratford-le-Bow). He declined an appointment as professor and fellow of the new Durham College (devised in 1656 and established in 1657) and he took over the management of the Stratford-le-Bow dyeworks on the death of his brother Abraham in 1657. Their dyehouse was associated with the famous Bow scarlet, or Color Kufflerianus, also sometimes known as Kuffeler's bay. This scarlet was produced using a tin or pewter mordant to dye with cochineal; according to Kuffeler, it had been invented by his father-in-law after some Dutch merchants had stumbled upon a similar process. The method of dyeing was kept secret by Kuffeler in the hope of obtaining a patent but some aspects of the discovery were publicized by Robert Boyle in his works. Many first-hand details of the process, supplied by Thomas Fletcher (*d. c.*1640), are included in a document (1669) at the Royal Society, possibly intended for a committee report on dyeing. In 1656 Kuffeler guaranteed to Hartlib the dyefastness for twenty years of the petticoats of his 'Scarlet Women of England' (Sheffield University, Hartlib MSS, fol. 29/5/91B).

Dutch claims that Kuffeler was physician-in-ordinary to the duke of York (later James II) remain unsubstantiated, nor is he known to have practised medicine in England. Instead, he devoted himself to chemistry and alchemy in the Helmontian tradition of iatrochemistry, as attested by Boyle, Henshaw, and many other early scientists. He and his brother Abraham met and discussed alchemy with John Winthrop the younger, subsequently governor of

Connecticut, in London in 1635 and in the Netherlands in 1642, and they also corresponded with him. The Hartlib papers are a particularly rich source of information about Kuffeler's inventive skills in these spheres, as well as in metallurgy, dyeing, agriculture, and chemical medicine. Peiresc wrote that Kuffeler owned Drebbel's laboratory book, and 'Collections of approved receipts of chymical operations' (Cambridge University Library, MS 2206), mostly compiled by his son Augustus in 1666, undoubtedly reflect much of Kuffeler's own experimental work.

Kuffeler obtained no English patents for developing Drebbel's technical inventions. Chief of these was a sea-petard, or torpedo, offered by him to the Protector in 1653 during the first Anglo-Dutch War, pre-empting a bid by Louis XIV for £15,000. The device was successfully demonstrated at Deptford on 4 August 1658, making a breach 12 feet by 17 in a ship, but because Cromwell died soon afterwards the £10,000 which he had promised was never paid, despite approaches to Richard Cromwell in 1659 and the Admiralty in March 1662, and widespread interest in the weapon. He was equally unsuccessful in persuading the Dutch statesman Jan de Witt, between February and July 1659, to adopt the torpedo and two other types of grenades for the United Provinces of the Netherlands.

Kuffeler developed and marketed a water-still and a bread oven from Drebbel's originals. In May 1633 he acquired a ten-year patent for his water-still from the states general's patent office at The Hague. The compact, portable still, consisting of a special alembic, produced 14½ gallons of distilled water in twenty-four hours, used very little fuel, and was later tested in London; Kuffeler's son Jacob helped to make William Fitzgerald's still, patented in 1683. By 1635 Kuffeler was planning to ship ceramic models of his bread oven, made in the Netherlands, to England. He described the ovens, in his 1653 proposals to Cromwell, as iron- or copper-plated, 2½ feet by 3, weighing only 300 lb, economic on fuel, baking 1500 lb of tasty bread in a day, and transportable on wagons (with a larger model available). Evelyn mentions that the prince of Orange's army had used the ovens; and Kuffeler told Monconys and Oldenburg, who visited an exhibition of his inventions at Stratford in 1663, that the duke of York, as head of the Admiralty, was buying his water-stills and ovens for ships sailing to the Indies. The bread oven (which also cooked meat) and Kuffeler's improved version of Drebbel's chicken-incubator oven, which intrigued his contemporaries, both operated on semi-self-regulatory, thermostatic principles.

Kuffeler is described as loyal, persevering, and courteous. His wife, Catharina, a knowledgeable woman, assisted with his work. He died in London on 4 March 1677, but his will and burial place have not been traced.

JOHN H. APPLEBY

Sources F. C. van der Meer van Kuffeler, *Stamboek van het geschlacht van Kuffeler* (privately printed, 1952) • P. C. Molhuysen and P. J. Blok, eds., *Nieuw Nederlandsch biografisch woordenboek*, 2 (Leiden, 1912), 734–5 • C. Webster, *The great instauration: science, medicine and reform, 1626–1660* (1975) • Royal Society anonymous classified papers, Cl.P.iii.38, xxiv. 80, 81 • F. M. Jaeger, *Cornelisz Drebbel* (1922) • F. W. Gibbs, 'The furnaces and thermometers of Cornelius Drebbel', *Annals of Science*, 6 (1948–50), 32–43 • G. Tierie, *Cornelisz Drebbel* (1922) • A. Ferwerda, *Adelyk en aanzienlyk wapen-boek*, 2 (1912), 734–5 • *The works of the Honourable Robert Boyle*, ed. T. Birch, 5 vols. (1744) • J. J. Blanksma, 'Bereding van drinkwater doer destillatie van zeewater', *Chemisch Weekblad*, 42 (1946), 237–40 • *The correspondence of Henry Oldenburg*, ed. and trans. A. R. Hall and M. B. Hall, 13 vols. (1965–86) • P. S. Wilkinson, 'The alchemical library of John Winthrop, Jr.', *Ambix*, 11 (1963), 33–51 • R. C. Black III, *The younger John Winthrop* (1960) • University of Sheffield, Hartlib MSS

Archives priv. coll., Van Kuffeler Family Association archives | CUL, MS 2206, L.1.v.8 • Mass. Hist. Soc., Winthrop MSS • RS, Cl.P.iii. 38, xxiv. 80, 81 • University of Sheffield Library, Hartlib MSS

Kuhe, Wilhelm (1823–1912), pianist and impresario, was born in Prague on 10 December 1823, one of three sons of a music-loving father and an amateur singer and pianist mother. He studied in his native city with Joseph Proksch and Václav Tomášek, and also had lessons with Sigismond Thalberg. After a successful concert tour of Germany, he arrived in London with the baritone Jan Pišek on 1 May 1845. He quickly befriended other influential foreign musicians domiciled in England, especially Ignaz Moscheles and Julius Benedict, and gave successful concerts at the Musical Union; he also deputized at short notice for Henry Litolff at the Hanover Rooms before leaving in June. He soon returned, and from 1847 was permanently established in England as a popular teacher and pianist, giving regular concerts and teaching at the Royal Academy of Music from 1886 to 1904.

Kuhe's most distinctive contribution to English musical life was in Brighton, which in 1847 still boasted a social season lasting from August to October. Kuhe saw that there was a place for music, and put his energies and talents into concerts at which he played himself and to which he was able in his first season to draw artists of the stature of Marietta Alboni; later guests included Clara Schumann (with whom he played a duet) and Joseph Joachim, as well as the leading English artists of the day. He settled in Brighton about 1850, while continuing a busy career at the centre of London musical life, giving concerts both in the capital and at provincial festivals. On 22 June 1854 he married Jessie, the daughter of William Morris of Hove. What the *Musical Times* described as 'his genial and optimistic personality [which] endeared him to all with whom he had relations' meant that the Brighton festival, which he founded in 1871 after he had paved the way with some subscription concerts in 1869–70, was able to attract the best performers of the day. A vigorous promoter of new music, Kuhe performed works by Gounod, Sullivan, Benedict, Costa, Sterndale Bennett, Cowen, and Macfarren, among others. He also commissioned and gave first performances of works including J. F. Barnett's *The Good Shepherd* and George Osborne's *La pluie des perles* (1876), Frederick Clay's *Lalla Rookh* and Charlotte Sainton-Dolby's *The Legend of St Dorothea* (1877), Cowen's *The Deluge*, Macfarren's *Pastoral Overture*, Alfred Cellier's *Suite symphonique*, and William Shakespeare's piano concerto (with Kuhe's daughter Nanette as soloist) (1878), and Ebenezer Prout's organ concerto and Macfarren's B♭ symphony (1880). Instead of pandering to popular taste with excerpts, he gave complete performances of earlier symphonies and oratorios. However, local support was erratic. He sustained an average personal loss of £500 on the festivals, and was compelled to discontinue them when the 1882 festival, despite a performance of Mendelssohn's *Elijah* with Emma Albani, Sophie Robertson, Zélia Trebelli, Edward Lloyd, and Charles Santley, lost him £1000.

Kuhe's autobiography, *My Musical Recollections* (1896), provides a vivid and entertaining account of European and especially English musical life during his long career. His earliest memories included hearing first-hand stories in Prague about Mozart from musicians who had played in the première of *Don Giovanni*, and he lived to admire virtuosos whose careers lasted well into the twentieth century. He had heard Hummel and played to Metternich, whom he also befriended in Brighton; he was on cordial terms with most of the leading singers of the day (above all, Jenny Lind), and was able to retail stories and anecdotes from his friendships with Liszt, Rossini, Chopin, Berlioz, and Rubinstein, among many others. His own music includes many piano pieces, among them *Lieder ohne Worte*, *Das Glockenspiel*, *Romance sans paroles*, *Le feu follet*, and fantasias on the British and Austrian national anthems. A freemason, he was from 1874 organist of the grand lodge of England. In appearance he was of distinguished bearing, with strong features; he wore a moustache to which was added, in his last years, a full white beard. He eventually became blind. He died at 71 Longridge Road, Kensington, on 8 October 1912 after falling downstairs. His daughter Nanette had a modest career as a pianist; his son Ernst (*b.* Brighton, 1870; *d.* London, June 1936) worked as a music critic on the *Daily Telegraph*.　　JOHN WARRACK

Sources W. Kuhe, *My musical recollections* (1896) · Grove, *Dict. mus.* · *MT*, 53 (1912), 722 [regular comments and reviews from 1850 onwards] · m. cert. · d. cert.

Likenesses R. Bentley & Son, photograph, 1896, repro. in Kuhe, *My musical recollections*, frontispiece · photograph (in old age), repro. in *MT* (1 Dec 1912), 795

Wealth at death £519 5s.: probate, 23 Nov 1912, *CGPLA Eng. & Wales*

Kuhn, Heinrich Gerhard (1904–1994), physicist, was born in Breslau, Silesia, then part of the German empire, on 10 March 1904, the second son of Wilhelm Felix Kuhn (1868–1927), solicitor, magistrate, and notary public, and his wife, (Pauline Caroline) Marthe Hoppe (1868–1946), who was of part Polish descent. Wilhelm Kuhn was of Jewish descent but was baptized into the Lutheran church on his marriage. His mother was Charlotte Henschel, whose half-brother was Sir George *Henschel (1850–1934), at one time conductor of the Boston Symphony Orchestra. Wilhelm Kuhn's interests were wide, and under his guidance Heini Kuhn made many experiments in physics and chemistry at home. He was educated at a primary school in Lueben, near Breslau, and then at the *Real Gymnasium* there. He studied chemistry at the University of Greifswald (near the Baltic coast) from 1922 to 1924 and then physics at Göttingen, where his teachers included James Franck, Richard Courant, and Max Born, founders of atomic and molecular quantum physics. Kuhn received

Heinrich Gerhard Kuhn (1904–1994), by Elliott & Fry, 1954

his doctorate in 1926 for work under Franck's supervision. His research then and subsequently was on molecular spectroscopy and in 1931 he received the *venia legendi* (*Habilitationsschrift*) from Göttingen University, together with the status of *privat-docent*. He married Marie Bertha (Mariete) Nohl on 10 September the same year. Her father, Herman Nohl, was a professor of philosophy at Göttingen and her mother, Bertha, *née* Oser, was a cousin of the philosopher Ludwig Wittgenstein. The Kuhns had two sons, both scientists.

When Hitler came to power in 1933 Kuhn, like others with a parent of Jewish descent, was dismissed from the university, forbidden to enter the laboratory, and deprived of the *venia legendi*. Franck, who resigned his professorship and left for the USA, helped younger non-Aryan physicists to move abroad; he introduced Kuhn to Frederick Alexander Lindemann, who invited him to move to Oxford to join Derek Jackson in work on spectra of atoms, supported by a research grant from ICI. Lindemann brought to the Clarendon Laboratory refugees from Nazi Germany whose groups brought distinction to Oxford after 1945 by their work on atomic spectroscopy and low-temperature physics.

When Kuhn first arrived in Oxford he collaborated with Jackson on high-resolution spectroscopy of light elements, with results in good agreement with theoretical calculations by the new quantum mechanics. He took British citizenship in 1939, and in 1940 joined the team working on isotope separation of uranium for the nuclear bomb project. He spent about six weeks in the USA in winter 1943. Jackson left Oxford for Paris after the end of the war, and Kuhn became responsible for high-resolution spectroscopy when it restarted in Oxford in 1947. He always used a Fabry-Perot interferometer, which can give a very high resolution, far greater than limits imposed by the random thermal motions of the atoms (Doppler broadening). Before the war Kuhn and Franck had used beams of molecules in absorption spectroscopy to reduce the Doppler broadening; after the war Kuhn and his group cooled discharge sources for emission spectroscopy with liquid hydrogen.

In his early work Kuhn recorded photographically the fringes formed in the Fabry-Perot interferometer, but that had several disadvantages, and he developed a method of scanning in which the light transmitted by the interferometer was recorded photoelectrically while the optical length of the interferometer was slowly changed by altering the pressure, and therefore the refractive index, of the air inside it. With those techniques Kuhn and his colleagues studied three fundamental problems in atomic physics. The spectra of hydrogen-like atoms had been calculated to high precision by relativistic quantum mechanics and quantum electrodynamics, and Kuhn's study of the deuterium atom confirmed the important results. Spectra of isotopes differ one from another in three ways. Isotopes of even mass number have no nuclear spin nor hyperfine structure, but the wavelengths of lines depend on the masses of the nuclei and, for heavy elements, their volumes. Odd isotopes, with non-zero nuclear spin, have hyperfine structure. Kuhn's group made important studies of isotope shifts. The third topic to which Kuhn contributed was pressure broadening, that is, the perturbation of transitions by the forces between atoms. Kuhn worked with the Fabry-Perot interferometer for almost the whole of his career, while refining it by scanning with photoelectric recording; in his hands he confronted fundamental questions of theoretical atomic physics with powerful experiments.

Kuhn was appointed a university demonstrator in the Clarendon Laboratory in 1945, subsequently becoming a lecturer. He lectured regularly on optics to undergraduates and was responsible for devising and running the undergraduate laboratory course on optics and spectroscopy, something of an innovation at the time. He had taught as a college lecturer for University College from 1941, and in 1951 he was elected to a fellowship at Balliol. He was elected to the Royal Society in 1954 and to a university readership in 1955. He became a senior research fellow of Balliol in 1969 and an emeritus fellow (and emeritus reader in physics) following his retirement in 1971.

Kuhn resumed his connections with German scientists shortly after the end of the Second World War, but despite attractive offers he never considered leaving England for Germany. Following decisions of the German federal and state governments to compensate those who had been forced to leave Germany in the 1930s, Kuhn was declared *Professor ausser Dienst* in 1957 and received the pension of a full professor. In 1976, exactly fifty years after he had

received his original DPhil, the University of Göttingen reaffirmed his doctorate, an action equivalent to conferring an honorary degree. He received the honorary degree of doctor of science from the University of Aix-Marseille in 1958, and the Holweck prize of the British and French Physical societies in 1967. He died in Oxford on 26 August 1994 after a long and difficult illness. He was survived by his wife and two sons.　　　ALAN COOK

Sources B. Bleaney, *Memoirs FRS*, 42 (1996), 221–32 • *The Times* (3 Sept 1994) • *The Independent* (3 Sept 1994) • S. Lukes, 'Interview with Heini Kuhn', *Balliol College Annual Record* (1987), 42–53 • *WWW*, 1991–5 • personal knowledge (2004) • private information (2004) • naturalization cert., PRO, HO 334/154/A2 14294 • *CGPLA Eng. & Wales* (1994)
Archives RS, personal record | Bodl. Oxf., corresp. relating to Society for Protection of Science and Learning | FILM Balliol Oxf., video of interview by Steven Lukes, 3 July 1986
Likenesses Elliott & Fry, photograph, 1954, NPG [*see illus.*] • W. Stoneman (J. Russell & Sons), photograph, *c*.1954, RS; repro. in Bleaney, *Memoirs FRS*, 220 • photograph (as a young boy), repro. in Bleaney, *Memoirs FRS*, 222 • photograph, repro. in *The Times* • sketch, repro. in Lukes, 'Interview with Heini Kuhn', 42
Wealth at death £173,266: probate, 4 Nov 1994, *CGPLA Eng. & Wales*

Kuper, Sir Augustus Leopold (1809–1885), naval officer, son of William Kuper DD KH (*d*. 27 Nov 1861), later chaplain to Queen Adelaide, was born on 16 August 1809. He entered the navy in April 1823, and after serving on the South American and Mediterranean stations was promoted lieutenant on 28 February 1830. During the next seven years he served almost continuously on the home station, and the coast of Spain or Portugal. He married, in June 1837, Emma Margaret, (*d*. 1877), eldest daughter of Sir Gordon Bremer; they had no children. In July 1837 Kuper was appointed first lieutenant of the *Alligator* (28 guns) with his father-in-law. He assisted Bremer in forming the settlement of Port Essington in north Australia, and on 27 July 1839 was promoted by him to the command of the *Pelorus* (18 guns). In a violent hurricane at Port Essington the *Pelorus* was driven on shore, high and dry, and was got off with great difficulty and labour after eighty-six days. On 5 March 1840 Bremer, then senior officer in India, appointed Kuper acting captain of the *Alligator* (5 guns), and in June 1841 moved him to the *Calliope* (26 guns), in which he was confirmed by the Admiralty with seniority from 5 June 1841. In the *Alligator*, and afterwards in the *Calliope*, he was active during the First Opium War, and was honourably mentioned for his conduct at the capture of Chusan (Zhoushan) in July 1840, at the capture of the Bogue (Humen) forts in February 1841, and in the operations leading up to the surrender of Canton (Guangzhou). He was made a CB on 21 January 1842. From 1850 to 1853 he commanded the frigate *Thetis* in the Pacific, and for a few months in 1855 the *London* in the Mediterranean.

On 29 July 1861 Kuper was promoted rear-admiral, and in the autumn of 1862 succeeded Sir James Hope as commander-in-chief in China, in the aftermath of the Taiping uprising. Kuper's first task was to capture the Taiping stronghold Kahding (Jiading), which he did on 23

October 1862. He was quickly called away to arrange matters in Japan, where the great nobles were angry at the treaties with Western nations, and the threatened introduction of foreigners and foreign customs. On 14 September 1862 a small party of British riding in the country was savagely attacked by retainers of the daimio of Satsuma, and one was killed. Reparation and compensation were demanded both from the imperial government and from the prince of Satsuma, and as they were not given, Kuper was requested to bring the squadron into the Bay of Yokohama. He arrived there in March 1863, and under this threat, following the suspension of diplomatic relations, the Japanese government agreed to pay the £100,000 demanded. But Satsuma proved less compliant, and on 14 August Kuper brought the squadron before Kagosima. The next day three steamers belonging to the prince were seized. Thereupon his batteries opened fire, and were speedily silenced. Satsuma's palace was shelled, and by an accident the greater part of the town was burned. On 16 August 1863 the prince submitted to the British demands.

The following year the daimio of Nagato, whose batteries commanded the Strait of Simonoseki, the ordinary and most convenient channel into the inland sea, closed the navigation to foreigners. The French and Dutch squadrons, and one United States warship, made common cause with the British, and acted under the orders of the British admiral. The ships opened fire at 4 p.m. on 5 September, and by the next day all the batteries had been silenced and stormed. On 7 September negotiations began, and it was soon agreed that all ships of all countries passing through the Strait of Simonoseki should be treated in a friendly manner. The battle led not only to the opening of the inland sea, but to the downfall of the old 'country' party in Japan, and to a social and political revolution there.

In 1865 Kuper returned to England. He had no further service. He had been made a KCB on 25 February 1864, for his services at Kagosima; and on 2 June 1869 he was made GCB. On 6 April 1866 he became a vice-admiral, and on 20 October 1872 admiral. Kuper died at his home, The Rock, South Brent, near Totnes, Devon, on 29 October 1885.

J. K. LAUGHTON, rev. ANDREW LAMBERT

Sources G. S. Graham, *The China station: war and diplomacy, 1830–1860* (1978) · W. L. Clowes, *The Royal Navy: a history from the earliest times to the present*, 7 vols. (1897–1903), vol. 7 · O'Byrne, *Naval biog. dict.* · *Annual Register* (1863) · D. F. Rennie, *British arms in China, 1860, 1862* (1864) · *Hansard 3* (1864), 173.335–422 · 'Correspondence respecting affairs in Japan', *Parl. papers* (1864), 66.175, no. 3242; 66.297, no. 3303 [attack on British legation] · *The Times* (10 Nov 1864) · *The Times* (17 Nov 1864) · *The Times* (19 Nov 1864) · Boase, *Mod. Eng. biog.* · Kelly, *Handbk* (1879) · *CGPLA Eng. & Wales* (1886)
Archives Bucks. RLSS, letters to duke of Somerset
Likenesses wood-engraving, NPG; repro. in *ILN* (20 Feb 1864)
Wealth at death £21,726 7s. 10d.: probate, 3 Feb 1886, *CGPLA Eng. & Wales*

Kurti, Nicholas [*formerly* Miklós Mór Kürti] (**1908–1998**), physicist, was born on 14 May 1908, in Budapest, the only son and younger child of Károly Kürti, formerly Karfunkel (1868–1911), vice-director of the Commercial Bank of Pest, and his wife, Margit, *née* Pintér (1882–1943). Both parents were Jewish. His father (who had changed his surname to

Nicholas Kurti (1908–1998), by unknown photographer

Kürti before 1900) died when Miklós was three, and the latter's great-uncle, József Pintér, helped and advised his widowed mother over the education of Miklós and his sister Hedwig. He first attended the Lutheran elementary school, then the Trefort *utcai* or Minta Gimnázium (1920–26), a small élite secondary school under the control of the University of Budapest rather than the ministry of education. Although study at the university was open to him, despite being a Jew, the options of studying for a professional career in law, medicine, or chemical engineering did not appeal to him. Although he was an accomplished musician, he was not accepted by the Budapest Academy of Music for training as a professional pianist. Instead, he chose to study for a career in physics outside Hungary, supported by his great-uncle and with the help of a grant from his father's bank.

Kürti's undergraduate studies at the Sorbonne (1926–8) were followed by his doctoral period in Berlin (1928–31) under Franz *Simon. During these years, the University of Berlin was the centre for the development of quantum physics, and with Einstein, Hertz, von Laue, Nernst, Planck, Schrödinger, and Wigner providing inspiration, Kürti's interests turned towards the low-temperature manifestations of quantum physics. In 1931 Simon took over from Professor A. Eucken at the Technische Hochschule in Breslau. He took Kürti and his fellow student Kurt Mendelssohn with him as 'private post-doctoral assistants', leaving them there in 1932 when he himself went to the University of California at Berkeley for a semester.

By 1933 the future for Simon, Mendelssohn, and Kürti as Jews in Germany was bleak. Their luck changed dramatically when Professor F.A. (Frederick) Lindemann invited all three to Oxford to build up low-temperature physics at the Clarendon Laboratory. Kürti was enchanted by Oxford from the day he arrived, on the pillion of Kurt Mendelssohn's motor cycle, in September 1933: 'we came over Magdalen Bridge, the sun was shining; it was like fairyland; why should I ever leave? … and of course I never did' (video interview by R. Berman). Kürti, as assistant to Simon, came to develop magnetic cooling—the adiabatic demagnetization of paramagnetic electron and nuclear spin systems. After William Francis Giauque had carried out the first successful magnetic cooling in 1933 at Berkeley, Simon in 1934 allowed Kürti to repeat this experiment using the same salt, gadolinium sulphate. In 1935 they reached the much lower temperature of 0.038K, using iron ammonium alum with the largest magnetic field available. Higher fields up to 2.5T could be produced at Bellevue, near Paris, using the 100-ton iron-cored magnet there. This magnet was then used with experiments until 1939, being literally carried from Oxford to Paris, while the infrastructure for a low-temperature laboratory was being built up by Lindemann and Simon.

Kurti became a naturalized British citizen just before the outbreak of the Second World War, by which time he had amended his name from Miklós Kürti to Nicholas Kurti. He became involved with the Tube Alloys (atomic bomb) project, in particular with the development of the gaseous diffusion process for the separation of the isotopes of uranium in the hexafluoride gas, working first in Oxford and then, from 1941, in the United States. He remained in the United States in 1944–5 to set up membrane testing for the Kellex Corporation at Columbia University, New York. During the war, he met his future wife, Georgiana (Giana) Shipley (b. 1913), daughter of Brigadier-General Charles Tyrell Shipley, an army officer. They married on 24 September 1946 and had two daughters, Susannah and Camilla.

Kurti returned to his academic studies after the war. He was appointed university demonstrator in physics at Oxford University in 1945 and was elected to a senior research fellowship at Brasenose College, Oxford, in 1947. His aim to build a high-current, high-magnetic-field facility was not fully realized until 1949, when a 2MW DC generator (bought from Manchester corporation) was finally installed and commissioned. One disadvantage was the need for night-time working only, to keep down the power costs, using the off-peak tariff. In order to realize the full benefit of this generator, to produce magnetic fields using high-current, water-cooled solenoids in the absence of iron cores, Kurti had to create a multidisciplinary team of academic and technical staff and postgraduate students. From 1950 onwards this team enabled him to explore, very successfully, the applications of high fields to quantum physics, the thermodynamic properties of paramagnetic salts, nuclear orientation with all its facets of nuclear physics (including proof of the non-conservation of parity in beta decay), and nuclear thermometry. His crowning glory, in 1956, was the successful adiabatic demagnetization of nuclear spins with cooling down to one millionth of a degree kelvin. He repeated the experiment live on television for *Tomorrow's World* in 1960.

Kurti was an inspiration to his students and also great fun. On midnight picnics he would introduce his students to some of his gastronomic delights. 'Meals with the Kurti family, including the young Susannah and Camilla, were a revelation … Nicholas and Giana demonstrated their culinary talents from a kitchen which, to students in the 1950s, resembled a science laboratory' (private information). The multidisciplinary team which Kurti ran was

unique in the 1950s in marking a break from the tradition of a research scientist working on his own with one or two students. It was also extremely successful and productive in research output. Kurti was elected a fellow of the Royal Society in 1956 (serving as its vice-president in 1965–7), and promoted reader in physics at Oxford in 1960 and professor of physics in 1967 (emeritus professor from 1975).

Kurti soon found that his team had a research momentum of its own, allowing him to devote an increasing proportion of his energy and enthusiasm to membership of national and international committees and panels, including the Electricity Supply Research Council (1960–79), the Advisory Committee for Scientific and Technical Information (1966–8), and the Advisory Committee for Research on Measurements and Standards (chairman, 1969–73). In recognition of this work he was appointed CBE in 1973. In his modest way he described himself as an irritant, but he was much more effective than that. For example, he became treasurer of the committee on data for science and technology of the International Council of Scientific Unions (1973–80); a member of council of the Royal Society (1964–7), the Société Française de Physique (1957–60 and 1970–73), and the Institute of Physics (1969–73); and editor-in-chief of *Europhysics Letters* (1985–9).

Kurti chaired the cryogenics panel of the Science Research Council throughout the 1960s, playing a leading role in cryogenic developments in the UK. The cryogenics panel also enabled him to exercise his human touch, in view of his own hard experience in getting established as a research scientist in the 1930s. He was particularly supportive of young lecturers, providing priming research grants and suggestions—unsolicited support which bore fruit in many successful ventures. For example, his support from 1956 for Martin Wood, as a research student and later as an industrial entrepreneur working from within the university base, paved the way for the Oxford Instrument Company to develop into a successful industry in the 1960s, pioneering the later growth of University Science Parks. Kurti was also supportive in the establishment of postgraduate courses in cryogenics and in the creation of the Mullard Cryomagnetic Laboratory at Oxford and the Institute of Cryogenics at Southampton, unique establishments in the 1970s. Having helped his students, Kurti continued to keep a watchful eye on their careers, and to give a prod where appropriate. Many came to regard him as a distant parent in Oxford.

Throughout his life Kurti had a preoccupation with 'cooking, enjoying its results and judiciously applying physics to the noble art of cookery' (*WW*). In 1968, when he was invited to give one of the regular Friday evening discourses in the Royal Institution, he chose the subject 'The physicist in the kitchen'. His discourse was a memorable event, with dramatic cookery demonstrations, and attracted the attention of both the gastronomic world and the media. It included his famous remark, 'I think it is a sad reflection on our civilization that while we can and do measure the temperature in the atmosphere of Venus we do not know what goes on inside our soufflés' (Kurti, 'The physicist in the kitchen', *Proceedings of the Royal Institution*,

42/199, 1969, 451–67). It also led to many further gastro-nomic adventures which absorbed his energy and talent as a showman after his retirement. For example, he collab-orated with Hervé This-Benckhard of the Collège de France in organizing a series of international workshops on molecular and physical gastronomy, held in pleasant surroundings at Erice, Sicily. These workshops in 1992, 1995, and 1997 were restricted to 65 participants and were attended by chefs and scientists from around the world. Subsequent workshops in 1999 and 2001 were dedicated to his memory.

As he approached ninety, Kurti made a remarkable recovery from a hip replacement operation, when cancer was first diagnosed. Six months later his other hip joint was replaced, but this time recovery was slow: he died a few weeks later at Sobell House, Churchill Hospital, Oxford, on 24 November 1998. His body was cremated after a private service in Oxford on 30 November 1998. He was survived by his wife and two daughters. A memorial meeting, attended by friends from Britain, Hungary, France, and the USA, was held on 27 March 1999 in the Sheldonian Theatre, Oxford. On 14 May 1999, the anniver-sary of his birth, his ashes were placed in a part of the Hungarian national cemetery, Budapest, reserved for members of the Hungarian National Academy of Sci-ences, to which he had been elected in 1970.

RALPH G. SCURLOCK

Sources J. H. Sanders, *Memoirs FRS*, 46 (2000), 301–15 · R. Berman and N. Kurti, video interview, 1996, U. Oxf., Clarendon Laboratory, archive · R. Evans and N. Kurti, video interview by R. Evans, 1996?, U. Oxf., Clarendon Laboratory, archive · *The Times* (27 Nov 1998) · *The Independent* (27 Nov 1998) · *The Guardian* (28 Nov 1998) · *Daily Telegraph* (4 Dec 1998) · *WWW* · personal knowledge (2004) · pri-vate information (2004) · m. cert.
Archives University of Bath, National Cataloguing Unit for the Archives of Contemporary Scientists | Bodl. Oxf., corresp. relat-ing to Society for Protection of Science and Learning · CAC Cam., corresp. with R. V. Jones · CUL, corresp. with and relating to Gor-don Sutherland · CUL, corresp. with Peter Mitchell | FILM Claren-don laboratory archive, R. Berman, video interview · Clarendon laboratory archive, R. Evans (BNC), video interview
Likenesses photograph, 1956, repro. in *Memoirs FRS*, 300 · photo-graph, 1960, repro. in *The Independent* · photograph, News Inter-national Syndication, London [*see illus.*] · photograph, repro. in *The Guardian* · photograph, repro. in *Daily Telegraph* · photographs, RS · photographs, priv. coll.
Wealth at death under £200,000: probate, 26 Oct 1999, *CGPLA Eng. & Wales*

Kurtz, Andreas (1781–1846), chemical manufacturer, was born on 16 September 1781 at Reutlingen, in the Swabian Alps, the son of Erard Kurtz, trader in a variety of local manufactures, and his wife, Anna Barbara Shaefer. Kurtz was one of nine children. His mother was a woman of strong character who survived the tumult of the Napo-leonic wars to reach the age of ninety-seven, after seeing her family scattered east and west. The war destroyed the Kurtz home and ruined his father's trade, so at the age of about thirteen Andreas set off to seek his fortune, never to return. He reached Paris. Little is known for certain about the next twenty years of his life but it is likely that he was employed in a chemical factory at Grenelle run by the father of the later distinguished Anselme Payen (1795–1871). The elder Payen was a determined educator and his influence on his own son seems to have encouraged young Kurtz to learn a great deal of chemistry from the outstand-ing group of French chemists of the day including Gay-Lussac, Berthollet, and Thenard. When Kurtz left France he had been recognized by minor rank in the Légion d'honneur.

On 15 August 1815 Kurtz left Paris for England but went on for a short time to America where he hoped to exploit an invention he had made in the manufacture of gunpow-der. His hopes were dashed and in 1816 he returned to Eng-land where he took over a small chemical works at Thames Bank, formerly run by a Mr Sandemann (or Sand-man) who had carried out a variety of chemical manu-factures and had been involved in the early work on the fabrication of platinum. About 1818 Kurtz married Sandemann's widow, whose forename is not known. They used the factory mainly for soap boiling. In 1820 he moved to Manchester, and also made efforts to develop chemical manufacture in Dublin, St Helens, and Liverpool. How-ever, he was more interested in research than in its profit-able exploitation. He had a succession of business part-ners; one with a Richard Niven was particularly success-ful, but Kurtz was not easy to get on with and they quarrelled and parted. Thereafter Kurtz had difficulty making ends meet. Regarded always as an excellent tech-nical chemist, he specialized in the manufacture of borax and of pigments, particularly a chrome yellow based on potassium dichromate which became fashionable in aris-tocratic circles.

Kurtz was known as a liberal host, was a friend of the leading naturalist Sir Richard Owen, and had a wide circle of scientific acquaintance. He spoke and wrote in at least three languages—German, French, and English—but he had been so long from his roots that his mother tongue, German, became the one he used least. In his later years he was involved in a long succession of law cases arising from disputes over the alleged infringement of patents, which impoverished him. At the height of the most com-plex of these, in opposition to J. C. Gamble (1776–1848), he died in Manchester of a heart attack on 31 March 1846. Kurtz's scientific talents were inherited by his son, Andrew George Kurtz, who had to abandon a legal train-ing to take over his father's affairs, which he did with great success.

FRANK GREENAWAY

Sources J. Fenwick Allen, *Some founders of the chemical industry: men to be remembered*, 2nd edn (1907) · J. R. Partington, *A history of chemis-try*, 3–4 (1962–4)
Likenesses portrait, repro. in Allen, *Some founders of the chemical industry*

Kurz, (Wilhelm) Sulpiz (1834–1878), botanist, was born on 5 May 1834 at Augsberg, Bavaria, the son of Aloys Kurz, an engineer. His father died in 1842 and he and his mother moved to Munich where he attended school. He then entered Munich University where he was a pupil of C. F. P. von Martius, the professor of botany and traveller in Bra-zil. In 1854, having quarrelled with his family, Kurz went to Delft in the Netherlands, where he worked as an apothecary. In 1856 he enlisted in the subordinate medical services of the Dutch East India army under the alias of Johann Amann. He arrived at Batavia in September 1856, and subsequently served at Banka and the Celebes, taking advantage of his travels to collect plants widely. On his return to Batavia in September 1859 he was appointed to assist at the botanical garden at Buitenzorg, a post which he occupied until 1863. In that year he was induced by Thomas Anderson, superintendent of the Royal Botanic Garden, Calcutta, who was visiting the Dutch possessions, to return with him to Calcutta as curator of the herbarium. This appointment he held until his death.

Kurz became very familiar with both Indian and Malayan floras, and was frequently dispatched on botanical missions. In 1866 he spent three months on the Andaman Islands, the subject of a detailed report published in 1870. Two expeditions to Burma, in 1867–8 and 1870–71, prepared him for his most important work, his *Forest Flora of British Burma* (2 vols., 1877). In November 1877 Kurz went on leave, and proceeded on a tour to Burma and the Straits Settlements for the benefit of his health. He died at Pulo-Penang on 15 January 1878 of fever complicated by a thigh abscess. A monument in his memory was erected in the Royal Botanic Garden, Calcutta.

Kurz published over sixty reports and papers, seventeen of which appeared in the *Journal* and *Proceedings* of the Asiatic Society of Bengal, of which he was elected a member in 1869. Other papers were published principally in the *Journal of Botany, British and Foreign* (1866–76) and *Flora* (1871–5).   ANDREW GROUT

Sources *Indian Forester*, 4 (1878), 1–4 · *Flora*, 36 (1878), 113–19 · C. G. G. J. Van Steenis, ed., *Flora Malesiana*, 1st ser., 1 (1950), 305–6 · *Journal of Botany, British and Foreign*, 16 (1878), 127–8 · F. A. Stafleu and R. S. Cowan, *Taxonomic literature: a selective guide*, 2nd edn, 2, Regnum Vegetabile, 98 (1979), 708–9 · G. King, *Annual Report of the Royal Botanic Garden, Calcutta, 1877–1878* (1878), 7

Kyan, Esmonde (1750–1798), Irish nationalist, was the third son of Howard Kyan (1711–1766), landowner, of Mount Howard, and Frances Esmonde (d. 1785), daughter of Lawrence Esmonde and sister of Sir James Esmonde, seventh baronet (1701–1767), of Ballinastragh, co. Wexford. Early in his life he served as an artillery officer in the British army. After leaving the army he lost his left arm, having been fired on by a debtor; he was subsequently fitted with an artificial arm. However, this did not inhibit his activity as a United Irish artillery officer during the insurrection of 1798. He was married twice, first to Mary Ann Byrne on 16 March 1774 in the Franciscan chapel at Wexford. They had five daughters. After her death he married Margaret Furlong of Kincone, Ferrybank, Wexford, and they had two sons, who both died young, and one daughter.

5 feet 6 inches in height and regarded as handsome, Kyan was one of the outstanding figures in the social, commercial, and political life of co. Wexford. He was a senior partner in the banking and minting firm of Kyan and Carnac. His instinct for humour and wit was noted by friends and even recorded by enemies in battle. He became an early adherent to the United Irish Society and, because of his army experience, achieved military rank at colonel level in the north-east (Ballaghreen) area of co. Wexford. At the outbreak of the rebellion in co. Wexford on 26 May 1798 he was arrested and lodged with other suspects in the market house at Gorey. Following the remarkable rebel victory at nearby Tubberneering he was rescued from imminent execution, and he immediately took command of the captured artillery pieces with such effect that the crown forces under General Loftus abandoned north Wexford. He was badly injured at the battle of Arklow and never completely recovered.

Kyan was recuperating at his wife's family home at Ferrybank when, on 21 June, he heard of the killing of loyalists by a mob on the adjacent Wexford Bridge; he crossed the bridge, confronted the crowd, and saved several lives. He marched north with the insurgent division which headed for the Wicklow Mountains following defeat at the major battle of Vinegar Hill on 21 June 1798. Unable to withstand the rigours of the march, he returned to Ferrybank, where he was arrested. He was tried and then hanged on 24 June 1798 on Wexford Bridge within twenty-four hours of his arrest. Had he reached the Wicklow Mountains his life would have been saved under the surrender terms arranged with General Dundas. His brother-in-law, Patrick Furlong, recovered his body from the Slaney River and had it interred beside the Furlong family grave in Ardcavan churchyard, Castlebridge, co. Wexford. A simple monument was erected in 1938 to mark Kyan's last resting place.   NICHOLAS FURLONG

Sources C. Dickson, *The Wexford rising in 1798* (1955) · *Wexford People Newspapers* (16 April 1898) · *The Bridge*, 1/2 (1997) · *Memoirs of Miles Byrne*, ed. F. Byrne, 3 vols. (1863) · D. Gahan, *The people's rising: Wexford, 1798* (1995) · N. Furlong, *Fr. John Murphy of Boolavogue, 1753–1798* (1991) · W. Nolan and K. Whelan, eds., *Wexford: history and society: interdisciplinary essays on the history of an Irish county* (1987) · H. F. Hore and P. H. Hore, eds., *History of the town and county of Wexford*, 5 (1906), 88 · R. J. Hayes, ed., *Manuscript sources for the history of Irish civilisation*, 11 vols. (1965) · Burke, *Gen. GB* · private information (2004) [Furlong family]
Likenesses portrait, repro. in Nolan and Whelan, eds., *Wexford*, pl. XXVII

Kyan, John Howard (1774–1850), inventor of kyanizing, was born on 27 November 1774 in Dublin, the son of John Howard Kyan of Mount Howard, Ballymurtagh, in co. Wicklow. His father was the owner of valuable copper mines in co. Wicklow, and for some time at the end of the eighteenth century worked them himself. Kyan was educated to take part in the management of the mines, but soon after he entered the concern its fortunes declined, and in 1804 his father died almost penniless. In the same year, Kyan married his cousin Ellen Kyan, daughter of James Kyan of Carlow. They had three sons, the eldest of whom was the Revd William Edward Kyan of Ballymurtagh, and seven daughters. For a time Kyan was employed at a vinegar works at Newcastle upon Tyne, but subsequently moved to London, to Greaves's vinegar brewery in Old Street Road.

The decay of the timber supports in his father's copper

mines had already directed Kyan's attention to the question of preserving vegetable substances, in particular timber, and as early as 1812 he began experiments with a view to discovering a method of preventing the decay. Eventually he found that bichloride of mercury (or corrosive sublimate) gave the best results, having first applied it to timber in 1825. Without revealing the nature of the process, he submitted a block of oak impregnated with that substance to the Admiralty in 1828 and it was placed in a so-called 'fungus pit' at Woolwich, where it remained for three years exposed to all the conditions favourable to decay. When taken out in 1831, it was found to be perfectly sound, and after further trials it still remained unaffected. Kyan patented his discovery in 1832 (nos. 6253 and 6309), extending the application of the invention to the preservation of such materials as paper, canvas, cloth, and cordage. A further patent was granted in 1836 (no. 7001). The preservative action of a solution of bichloride of mercury was previously well known, and Kyan's process merely consisted in the submersion of timber or other materials in a tank containing a solution of corrosive sublimate in water (1 lb bichloride of mercury to 5 gallons of water). Kyan maintained that permanent chemical combination took place between the mercurial salt and the woody fibre, but this was contested. The process attracted great attention and Michael Faraday chose it as the subject of his inaugural lecture at the Royal Institution on 22 February 1833, on his appointment as Fullerian professor of chemistry.

In 1835 the Admiralty published the report of a committee appointed by the board to inquire into the efficacy of the process and the effect if any on health from the use of a mercury compound. Tests were largely inconclusive, but a number of ships were built with 'kyanized' timbers and a great future was predicted for the method. In 1836 Kyan sold the patent rights to the Anti-Dry Rot Company, an act of parliament being passed which authorized the raising of share capital of £250,000. Tanks were constructed at Kyan's timberyard at Grosvenor basin, Pimlico, at the Grand Surrey Canal dock, Rotherhithe, and at the City Road basin. The idea of kyanizing caught the imagination, to judge from the opening verse of a song that appeared in *Bentley's Miscellany* for January 1837:

Have you heard, have you heard, Anti-dry Rot's the word?
Wood will never wear out, thanks to Kyan, to Kyan!
He dips in a tank any rafter or plank,
And makes it immortal as Dian, as Dian!

Among the early applications of the process was the kyanizing of the palings round the Inner Circle, Regent's Park, which was carried out in 1835 as an advertisement, small brass plates being attached to the palings at intervals stating that the wood had been submitted to the new process. Kyanized timber was used in the construction of a number of large buildings in London and elsewhere. When wooden railway sleepers became general (in place of the stone blocks used on the early lines), a very profitable business for Kyan's company was anticipated, and for a time these hopes were realized. But it became evident that iron fastenings could not be used in wood treated by the method, on account of corrosive action, and it was said that the wood became brittle. The salt was somewhat expensive, and Sir William Burnett's method of preserving timber by chloride of zinc, and afterwards the application of creosote for that purpose, proved severe competitors. Doubts began to be expressed as to the real efficacy of kyanizing and the process gradually ceased to be employed.

Besides the invention with which his name is associated, Kyan took out patents in 1833 (no. 6534) for propelling ships by a jet of water ejected at the stern, and in 1837 (no. 7460) for a method of obtaining ammoniacal salts from gas liquor. He was also the author of *The Elements of Light and their Identity with those of Matter Radiant or Fixed*, 1838. He died on 5 January 1850 at New York, where he was engaged on a plan for filtering the water supplied to that city by the Croton aqueduct.

R. B. PROSSER, rev. R. C. COX

Sources 'Admiralty committee on Mr Kyan's patent for the prevention of dry rot in timber', *Parl. papers* (1835), 48.91, no. 367 · *Act 6 William IV* (19 May 1836), cap. 26 · H. P. Burt, 'On the nature and properties of timber', *PICE*, 12 (1852–3), 206–43, esp. 216–31 · B. Green, 'Description of the arched timber viaducts on the Newcastle and North Shields Railway', *PICE*, 1 (1840), 88–92, esp. 91 · Burke, *Gen. GB*

Kyd, Robert (1746–1793), botanist and army officer, was born in Forfarshire. Little is known of his family and early life. He may have studied medicine at Edinburgh. In 1764 he obtained a cadetship and was appointed ensign in the Bengal Engineers. The following year he was promoted to lieutenant. He became captain on 3 April 1768, major on 29 May 1780, and lieutenant-colonel on 7 December 1782. On the latter date he was appointed secretary to the military department of inspection in Bengal, a post he seems to have held until his death. He was a man of cultivated tastes, fond of botany, and had amassed a fine collection of plants at his home near Calcutta.

In April 1786 Kyd proposed to the government of Bengal the establishment of a garden to grow nutritious plants such as certain palms, the sago from Malaya, and the Persian date. He suggested that these should be propagated and then distributed throughout British India as alternative sources of food in times of famine. Encouraged by a favourable response, he submitted a more ambitious plan a few months later, greatly extending the range of crops to be grown, and, for the first time, calling his project a 'botanical garden'. However, he made it quite clear that he did not envisage a traditional botanical garden but rather a nursery raising 'stock for disseminating such articles as may prove beneficial to the inhabitants, as well as to the natives of Great Britain, and which ultimately may tend to the extension of the national commerce and riches' (Kyd to governor-general, 1 June 1786, Natural History Museum, London, Dawson Turner collection, 7, fols. 57–67). That summer a site for the garden was chosen on the west bank of the River Hooghly a few miles from Calcutta. With Kyd in charge of operations, the ground was cleared, plants were acquired from overseas and from other parts of the Indian subcontinent. Kyd was made honorary

Robert Kyd (1746–1793), by unknown engraver

superintendent in May 1787. By 1790 about 4000 plants were in cultivation. Kyd was disappointed by the poor response to his appeal for plants useful in horticulture. Nevertheless, during the six years he was in charge he laid the foundations of what was eventually to be the premier botanical garden in Asia. When the young Joseph Hooker visited it in 1848, he declared that it had 'contributed more useful and ornamental tropical plants to the public and private gardens of the world than any other establishment before or since' (J. D. Hooker, *Himalayan Journals* 1, 1854, 3–4).

Kyd died at Calcutta on 26 May 1793, and was buried in the South Park Street cemetery there. A memorial urn, executed by the sculptor Thomas Banks, was put up in 1795 on a site selected by William Roxburgh in the botanical garden. *Kydia*, a genus of the plant family Malvaceae in Sikkim and south-east Asia was named after him by Roxburgh.   RAY DESMOND

Sources [G. King (?)], 'A short account of Colonel Kyd, the founder of the Royal Botanic Garden, Calcutta', *Annals of the Royal Botanic Garden of Calcutta*, 4 (1893), 1–11 · R. Desmond, *The European discovery of the Indian flora* (1992) · I. H. Burkill, *Chapters on the history of botany in India* (Calcutta, 1965) · NHM, DTC 7, fols. 57–67
Archives BL OIOC, papers, MS Eur. F 95 · RBG Kew, papers | NHM, corresp. with Sir Joseph Banks
Likenesses crayon drawing, repro. in King, 'A short account of Colonel Kyd' · engraving, NHM [*see illus.*]
Wealth at death see will, [King (?)], 'Short account of Colonel Kyd'

Kyd, Stewart (*d.* 1811), radical and legal writer, a native of Arbroath, Forfarshire, was educated at Arbroath grammar school and, from the age of fourteen, at King's College, Aberdeen. Abandoning a design of entering the church, he settled in London, and was called to the bar from the Middle Temple. He became a firm friend of the radical politicians Thomas Hardy and John Horne Tooke, whose political opinions he admired. In November 1792 he joined the Society for Constitutional Information. On 29 May 1794 he was arrested and examined by the privy council, but was soon discharged. He was again summoned before the council on 4 June, and three days later was committed to the Tower on a charge of high treason, with Hardy, Tooke, and ten others. On 25 October all were brought up for trial before a special commission at the Old Bailey, but after the acquittal of Hardy, Tooke, and Thelwall, the attorney-general declined offering any evidence against Kyd, and he was discharged. In June 1797 he ably defended Thomas Williams, a bookseller, who was indicted for blasphemy in publishing Thomas Paine's *Age of Reason*. The substance of his defence was printed during the same year in a collection entitled *The Speeches at Full Length … of Thomas Erskine, and Stewart Kyd*. He was also the author of a number of legal works, including *A Treatise on the Law of Awards* (1791) and the two-volume *A Treatise on the Law of Corporations* (1793–4). Kyd died in the Temple, London, where he was living, on 26 January 1811.

GORDON GOODWIN, *rev.* STEPHEN M. LEE

Sources *GM*, 1st ser., 81/1 (1811), 190 · *State trials* · [R. W. Bridgman], *A short view of legal bibliography* (1807) · J. D. Reuss, *Alphabetical register of all the authors actually living in Great Britain, Ireland, and in the United Provinces of North-America*, 1 (1804), 589 · [D. Rivers], *Literary memoirs of living authors of Great Britain*, 2 vols. (1798) · *N&Q*, 6th ser., 2 (1880), 12 · A. Wharam, *The treason trials, 1794* (1992)
Likenesses stipple, pubd 1794, NPG · engraving (after portrait)

Kyd, Thomas (*bap.* 1558, *d.* 1594), playwright and translator, was baptized on 6 November 1558 at the church of St Mary Woolnoth in London, the son of Francis Kyd and his wife, Anna (*d.* 1605).

Early life and education Kyd's father achieved distinction as warden of the Company of Scriveners in 1580. Thomas entered Merchant Taylors' School in 1565, and may have remained a pupil there under the noted educationist Richard Mulcaster until 1575. The school curriculum included Latin, French, and Italian, a good grounding for the future translator. At Merchant Taylors', plays in both Latin and English formed part of the boys' training, and Kyd is likely to have taken part in these exercises. He may have performed before Queen Elizabeth at court, and before a paying audience in Merchant Taylors' Hall early in 1574, in the first known commercial production by a boys' company (Shapiro, 14). His failure to attend either Oxford or Cambridge university has been attributed to hints of Catholic sympathies in his writings, but the evidence is very slender.

Kyd may have taken up his father's profession of scrivener, as his neat handwriting in the few surviving holograph scraps suggests, and as Thomas Nashe's gibe about his following 'the trade of *Noverint*' possibly confirms ('Preface' to Robert Greene's *Menaphon*, 1589). According to Thomas Dekker's pamphlet *A Knight's Conjuring* (1607) Kyd was a playwright for the Queen's Men between 1583 and 1585. None of his early work is known to survive.

The Spanish Tragedy If evidence for the details of Kyd's life is scant, evidence for his authorship of the works associated with him is no less so. *The Spanish Tragedy* (1587?) was not formally attributed to him until 1773, when Thomas Hawkins, the editor of a three-volume play-collection, *The Origin of the English Drama*, cited a passing reference in Thomas Heywood's *Apology for Actors* (1612) to 'M. Kid, in the *Spanish* Tragedy'. The date of composition of the play is unknown, with speculation ranging from 1583 to 1591. It must have been written before 23 February 1592, for on that date it was performed at the Rose Theatre by Lord Strange's men for Philip Henslowe. This is unlikely to have been the play's first performance, since Henslowe did not mark it as 'ne' (new). A balance of evidence suggests a date of composition before 1588, given the absence—in a play about Spain—of any reference to the Armada, and given plausible allusions in Nashe's 'Preface' to *Menaphon* (1589) and in his *Anatomie of Absurdities* (1588-9). The year 1587 fits the known facts and plausible speculation.

The *Spanish Tragedy* proved excellent box-office. Philip Henslowe, who held the early rights, recorded twenty-nine performances between 1592 and 1597, a record almost unsurpassed among his plays. The publication record is still more impressive, with at least eleven editions between 1592 and 1633, a tally unequalled by any of the plays of Shakespeare. There are more than one hundred allusions to *The Spanish Tragedy* in contemporary literature (Dundrap, 2.607-31). Additions and revisions were commissioned, from Ben Jonson among others; Anne Barton, arguing a case from Jonson's engagement with Elizabethan literature generally, takes the view that Jonson, commissioned by Henslowe to refurbish a dated though still theatrically potent text, may have assumed a style not his own, in a bold and arguably successful act of theatrical ventriloquism. It is, however, unlikely that the 'Additions' which have survived (printed 1602) are Jonson's. Their authorship is unknown. Stage success was not confined to England. Six adaptations, three in German and three in Dutch, have survived, and performances are recorded in Frankfurt (1601), Dresden (1626), Prague (1651), and Lüneburg (1660) (R. Schönwerth, *Die niederländischen und deutschen Bearbeitungen von Thomas Kyds 'Spanish Tragedy'*, Litterarisch-Historische Forschungen, 26, 1897; Erne, 154).

By 1587-8 Kyd had acquired a patron to whom he refers, but whom he does not name, in a letter written in later years in connection with his difficulties with authority. The patron, according to the letter, was patron of a company of players, which narrows a wide field considerably. Ferdinando Stanley, Lord Strange (after 1593 earl of Derby), has been mooted, as has Henry Radcliffe, earl of Sussex, but neither suggestion is wholly convincing. Lukas Erne's advocacy of Henry Herbert, second earl of Pembroke, has the advantage of placing Kyd in relationship to an influential literary circle, and of making sense of his dedication of *Cornelia* (1594; translated from Garnier) to Mary Herbert, countess of Pembroke, wife of Henry Herbert and herself the author of a translation of Garnier's *Antoine* (1592) (Erne, 274-8).

The conflict with authority The most substantial information about Kyd's later life concerns his serious brush with authority in May 1593. On 11 May the privy council instructed its officers to seek out the source of certain 'libels', or inflammatory writings, directed against foreigners resident in London. During the investigation Kyd's rooms were searched and the officers found, not what they were looking for, but material considered equally incriminating. This was a three-page manuscript consisting, according to an endorsement by one of Kyd's accusers, of 'vile heretical Conceiptes denying the deity of Jhesus Christe o^r Savio^r' (BL, Harley MS 6848, fols. 187-9). The 'concepts' have been identified in the twentieth century as transcripts from an Elizabethan theological tract, John Proctour's *The Fall of the Late Arian* (1549), a tract which, in rebutting them, quotes 'heretical', or unitarian, views, possibly those of a parish priest, John Assheton (W. D. Briggs, 'On a document concerning Christopher Marlowe', *Studies in Philology*, 20, 1920, 153-9; G. T. Buckley, 'Who was the late Arian?', *Modern Language Notes*, 49, 1934, 500-03). The zealous officers were presumably unaware of the origin of the manuscript's contents, as Kyd must also have been, and he was arrested and imprisoned.

From his prison cell, and afterwards, Kyd wrote to the lord keeper, Sir John Puckering, pleading his innocence. In one of his letters, he explained that the incriminating documents were not his but Marlowe's 'shufled wth some of myne (unknown to me) by some occasion of wrytinge in one chamber twoe yeares since' (BL, Harley MS 6849, fols. 218-218v). In a second letter Kyd wrote more fully about Marlowe's notoriously subversive views, accusing his fellow playwright of being blasphemous, disorderly, holding treasonous opinions, being an irreligious reprobate, and 'intemperate & of a cruel hart'. Marlowe was arrested on 18 May, but was released from prison two days later. On 30 May he died in a pub brawl at Deptford, the victim, it has been suggested, of shady dealings associated with the spymaster Sir Francis Walsingham (C. Nicholl, *The Reckoning: the Murder of Christopher Marlowe*, 1992; see also J. Masten, *A New History of Early English Drama*, ed. J. D. Cox and D. S. Kasten, 1997, 357-82). Both of Kyd's letters follow the date of Marlowe's death. Whether Marlowe's arrest was prompted by verbal accusations from Kyd to privy council officers can only be a matter of speculation. The 'conceipts', it has been suggested, were possibly a deliberate plant, put in place by the officers as part of an officially inspired effort to blacken Marlowe's name (Nicholl, 288-9). Kyd's release from prison preceded his death in 1594, perhaps hastened by torture, by no more than a year. He was buried at St Mary Colechurch in London on 15 August 1594.

Lesser works and reputation Of Kyd's other writing, little has been said in print. A major problem is one of attribution. The theatrical entrepreneur Philip Henslowe refers on twenty-two occasions between February 1591 and January 1593 to performances of plays he names *Jeronymo*, *The Comedy of Jeronymo*, *Spanes comodye donne oracioe*, and *The Comodey of Doneoracio*, with further variations of spelling. Recent scholars take *Jeronimo*, in its several forms, to refer to *The Spanish Tragedy*, while the various 'comedy' titles are thought to refer to *The First Part of Ieronimo*, a play printed in quarto in 1605. This play deals with events which precede the action of *The Spanish Tragedy*, and may have been written by Kyd as a forepiece or first part for his famous tragedy. It was so edited and published by Andrew S. Cairncross (1967). Equally, the play may have been written, possibly by a hack writer, to cash in on the success of *The Spanish Tragedy*. Accurate determination is made difficult by the poor state of the printed text. Lukas Erne proposes a complex origin, arguing that the play preserves elements of Kyd's original forepiece (which he calls *Don Horatio*), in particular that play's 'political level', but suggests that this has been incorporated by a lesser writer into a new drama, with a new storyline substituted for the 'private level' of Kyd's play. The theory is attractive but unproven. The play as it survives is unsatisfactory not only textually, but as a piece of theatre, though it offers features that make attribution to Kyd not implausible.

Soliman and Perseda, entered on the Stationers' register in November 1592, may have been written in 1588 or 1589. Its relation to *The Spanish Tragedy* is once again a matter of speculation. It may have been written to capitalize on the earlier play's success, since it represents a scaling-up of the tragedy's play-within-the-play. The evidence for Kyd's authorship, including an apparent allusion noticed by Helen Gardner in one of Donne's poems (*John Donne: the 'Elegies' and the 'Songs and Sonnets'*, 1965, 112–18) is attractive if inconclusive. The play's most notable character, Basilisco, a boastful, amorous, and inventive *miles gloriosus* prefigures Shakespeare's Falstaff, especially in his *ubi sunt* meditation on the deceits of honour (*Soliman and Perseda*, v.iii, ll. 67–92).

Cornelia, Kyd's translation of Robert Garnier's tragedy-of-grief *Cornélie*, was entered on the Stationers' register on 26 January 1594, and dedicated to Lady Bridget Fitzwalter, countess of Sussex, as well as to the countess of Pembroke, perhaps in a bid to win her patronage after the débâcle of May 1593. The translation, a free one, was probably known to Shakespeare (analogies have been found with *Julius Caesar*), but the neo-Senecan genre proved a dead end in English theatre. Kyd's other acknowledged translation, *The Householder's Philosophy*, renders Tasso's *Il padre di famiglia* in vigorous prose, expanding on the original's account of home and estate management.

Kyd's authorship of a *Hamlet* earlier than Shakespeare's holds an extensive if shadowy place in the annals of English scholarship. The case rests on the interpretation of phrases in Nashe's 'Preface' to *Menaphon* (1589), and has been both supported and rejected by leading scholars. Most recently, Lukas Erne has argued that Nashe's satiric phrases do indeed imply that Kyd was the author of an early *Hamlet*. He also reinforces suggestions, made by E. K. Chambers and W. W. Greg, among others, that traces of a Kydian *Hamlet* may be found in a small section of the first quarto of Shakespeare's *Hamlet*. Shakespeare's debt to Kyd, however, remains no more than speculation.

The Spanish Tragedy has been successfully revived on the modern stage, though the record is blank before the twentieth century, except for a performance watched by Pepys at a minor theatre, the Nursery, on 24 February 1668

(Pepys, *Diary*, 9.90). Notable twentieth-century productions have included those directed by Michael Bogdanov for the National Theatre (Cottesloe and Lyttleton, opened 22 September 1982), and Michael Boyd's production for the Royal Shakespeare Company (Swan Theatre, Stratford upon Avon, opened 30 April 1997).

The play's importance to the literary historian is considerable. As the first, or one of the first, in a line of tragedies of revenge, *The Spanish Tragedy* inaugurates an influential genre. Assuming the 1587 dating is correct, the play features the first Machiavellian villain (Lorenzo), and may be the first to include a play-within-the-play. Equally significant, Kyd developed in *The Spanish Tragedy* a robust and serviceable blank verse which, though some of its rhetorical practices soon came to seem outmoded, nevertheless provided Elizabethan theatre with its earliest convincing voice. This, together with his creation of memorable character, his development of the framing action, and his exploration of the double plot, confirms Kyd as the most important innovator, with Marlowe and Shakespeare, of the great age of English drama.   J. R. MULRYNE

Sources A. Freeman, *Thomas Kyd: facts and problems* (1967) • L. Erne, 'Beyond *The Spanish tragedy*: a study of the works of Thomas Kyd', DPhil diss., U. Oxf., 1998 • P. B. Murray, *Thomas Kyd* (1969) • M. Shapiro, *Children of the revels* (1977) • C. Dundrap, 'La tragédie espagnole face à la critique élizabéthaine et jacobéene', *Dramaturgie et société … aux XVIe et XVIIe siècles* [Nancy, 1967], ed. J. Jacquot and others, 2 vols. (1968) • P. Edwards, *Thomas Kyd and early Elizabethan tragedy* (1966) • F. Carrère, *Le théâtre de Thomas Kyd* (1951) • S. A. Tannenbaum, *Thomas Kyd: a concise bibliography* (1941–67) • J. R. Díaz Fernández, 'Thomas Kyd: a bibliography, 1966–1992', *Bulletin of Bibliography*, 52/1 (1995), 1–13 • *Henslowe's diary*, ed. R. A. Foakes and R. T. Rickert (1961) • A. Barton, *Ben Jonson, dramatist* (1984)
Archives NRA, priv. coll., letters and literary MSS
Wealth at death not known, but possibly died in debt: Freeman, *Thomas Kyd*, 38

Kydd, Samuel McGowan (1815–1892), Chartist and barrister, was born on 22 February 1815 in Arbroath, Forfarshire, the second son of James Kydd. He first came to public attention in 1837 in York when he issued a pamphlet which contributed to a national debate about joint-stock banks; his arguments that such banks should issue paper money were an early indication of a deep interest in financial and economic matters. Kydd's circumstances had dramatically changed by the early 1840s when he featured in the Chartist press as a Glasgow shoemaker. He was soon in demand as a Chartist lecturer. Throughout the north of England in 1843–4 he sought to refute the arguments of the Complete Suffrage Union and the Anti-Corn Law League. Having established himself as Chartism's most persuasive protectionist lecturer, Kydd relocated to London. As secretary of the Chartist executive in 1848–9 he was at the centre of the movement's activities. Unlike other executive members he managed to escape arrest, and, without going to the official polls, was twice (in Greenwich in 1847 and the West Riding in 1848) a Chartist parliamentary candidate. During these years Kydd continued to undertake extensive lecture tours, especially in the north and in Scotland.

Though greatly liked and respected by the Chartist rank

and file, Kydd decided to realign himself. By 1850 he was a close associate of Richard Oastler and a fully fledged tory radical, arguing in his lectures and journal articles for factory reform and the reintroduction of tariffs. He became Oastler's secretary, and, using the memorabilia he now had access to, produced, under the pseudonym Alfred, a *History of the Factory Movement* (1857); it remains a valuable document for students of the subject. Kydd had long desired to enter the legal profession. In 1858 he was admitted to Gray's Inn, and in 1861 was called to the bar. Kydd lived during the second part of his life with his wife, Mary Ann Appleford (d. 1898), in Sutton, Surrey, and operated from chambers in the Middle Temple. Until the late 1880s he practised on the northern circuit and appeared at the York assizes. Shortly before his death he published *A Sketch of the Growth of Public Opinion* (1888). A man of outstanding ability, Samuel Kydd died at his home, Holly Cottage, Sutton, on 21 December 1892. He left no children.

STEPHEN ROBERTS

Sources S. Roberts, 'Samuel Kydd', in S. Roberts, *Radical politicians and poets in early Victorian Britain* (1993), 107–27 • *Arbroath Herald* (19 Jan 1893) • *Newcastle Weekly Chronicle* (14 Jan 1893) • J. Foster, *Men-at-the-bar: a biographical hand-list of the members of the various inns of court*, 2nd edn (1885) • d. cert.
Archives Newcastle upon Tyne Central Library, letters
Wealth at death £10,898 2s. 4d.: probate, 11 Jan 1893, *CGPLA Eng. & Wales*

Kyffin, Edward (1557/8–1603). *See under* Kyffin, Maurice (*c.*1555–1598).

Kyffin, Maurice (*c.*1555–1598), author and soldier, is more than likely to have been the son of Thomas Kyffin and Catrin Llwyd, who are known to have had four children. If so, he may have been born before his parents were married. Both his probable parents belonged to landed families in or near Oswestry, then a largely Welsh-speaking town. Kyffin's coat of arms is depicted as the end-piece of his best-known work, *Deffynniad Ffydd Eglwys Loegr*. He was clearly a man of learning, but all that is known about his education is that he studied poetry under the most famous Welsh bard of his age, Wiliam Llŷn, who lived in Oswestry, and that in London, from 1578 to 1580, he was one of the pupils and friends of the polymath John Dee. About 1580 to 1582 he was tutor to Lord Buckhurst's three sons, whom he prepared for entry to Oxford University. He appears to have been on close and friendly terms with a wide circle of scholars and littérateurs, who numbered among them such celebrated figures as John Dee, William Camden, Edmund Spenser, Sir John Harington, William Morgan, Dr David Powel, Gabriel Goodman, Roger Cook, and his own brother, Edward. He wrote a considerable amount of verse in English and Welsh, and many of his Welsh poems are preserved in manuscript form. His most celebrated English poem is *The Blessednes of Brytaine*, the first impression of which was printed in 1587 and the second in 1588. Inspired by the dire threat to Elizabeth and her realm from her Catholic enemies at home and abroad, it praised in lavish terms the 'inestimable benefits', especially in religion, conferred upon the kingdom by the queen's 'incomparable blessed rule'. It was dedicated to the earl of Essex and recounted the close, but unspecified, connection between its author's father and the earl's father and grandfather. In 1588 Kyffin also published an English prose translation of the comedy *Andria*, written by the Latin poet Terence. In the same year he was appointed surveyor of the muster rolls to the English army in the Netherlands and in 1591 deputy treasurer to the English forces in Normandy.

Maurice Kyffin returned to London in 1594 to complete his literary masterpiece, *Deffynniad Ffydd Eglwys Loegr*, a translation into Welsh of Bishop John Jewel's *Apologia* for the faith of the Church of England, which had originally appeared in 1562. Kyffin's Welsh text, published in 1595, became one of the classics of the language. In spite of its author's having lived much of his adult life outside Wales and his being reluctant to publish in Welsh, believing that he might achieve greater fame by writing in English, his book is remarkable for its smooth and powerful expression. He avoided the pitfalls which often beset translators, for instance of being too dependent on the style and idiom of the original author. Yet his own misgivings were not wholly unjustified; his name was virtually unknown in Wales until 1671, when a second edition of *Deffynniad Ffydd* was published. A Welsh poem written by him *c.*1595 indicated that he spent some time in the Fleet prison. He also directed an English sonnet to Sir Robert Cecil asking for his help in distress and a petition to the queen seeking service in France.

It was not in France, but in Ireland, however, that in 1596 Kyffin found an opening as comptroller of the musters to the army, although the eighteen months or so that he spent there proved to be a very stormy period. In his dispatches to Burghley and others he described the appalling conditions he encountered in Ireland: a country devastated by famine, rebellion, brutal warfare waged by both sides, and especially the exploitation of populace and soldiers as a result of the corrupt practices of commanders and officials. He was particularly downcast by the intrigues and peculation indulged in by his colleague Sir Ralph Lane. Kyffin himself was praised by Burghley and other leading figures for his honesty and conscientiousness. He died on 2 January 1598 and was buried in Christ Church, Dublin, though his grave has since been lost. In his will, drawn up in 1595, he did not mention his parents but only his brother, Edward, to whom he left £130 and most of his books, and two sisters, Elyn Kyffin, or Davies, and Thamesine (later Onslow). The will was emphatically protestant in its opening phrases and provided legacies for the poor of the French church (£3) and the Italian church (£1) in London, and £3 for the poor, especially the parents of maimed and diseased children. His brother was his executor and proved the will on 20 April 1599.

Edward Kyffin (1557/8–1603), Church of England clergyman and author, is believed to have been 'my brother Edward Kyffyn preacher', who is named in, and proved, the will of Maurice Kyffin. He was born at Oswestry and educated at Jesus College, Cambridge, but does not seem to have graduated. He was ordained deacon at London on 14 May 1585, at the age of twenty-seven, and priest at

Bangor on 28 September 1590. He was also recorded as a witness at an ordination in Bangor on 26 September 1593. He was curate of St Martin Outwich, London, and it may have been there that he died from the effects of the great plague in 1603. Since his brother, Maurice, refers in the preface to his *Deffynniad Ffydd* to the urgent need for a metrical version of the psalms in clear, intelligible Welsh verse, it may have been at his instigation that Edward undertook his translation. He was the author of *Rhann o Psalmae Dafydd Prophwyd Iw canu ar ôl y dôn arferedig yn Eglwys Loegr* ('Part of the psalms of the prophet David to be sung according to the tune customary in the Church of England'), which was printed by Simon Stafford for T[homas] S[alisbury] in 1603. In a letter to Sir John Wynn of Gwydir, Thomas Salisbury claims that Kyffin had composed about fifty metrical psalms before falling victim to the plague. However, the printed version, of which only one copy is known to be extant and which may never have been published, contains only the first twelve psalms and the first five verses of the thirteenth. They are set in simple free stanzas, known in Welsh as *awdl gywydd*, side by side with the biblical text. In the dedicatory epistle to his fellow countrymen, Kyffin explained that his reasons for undertaking the translation were that he believed Welsh to be one of the oldest languages in creation and that it had been preserved by God's providence down the centuries with some particular object in mind—presumably to bring the Reformation to the Welsh in their own tongue.

GLANMOR WILLIAMS

Sources DWB · M. Kyffin, *Deffynniad Ffydd Eglwys Loegr*, ed. W. P. Williams (1908) · M. Kyffin, *The blessednes of Brytaine* (1587); repr. (1885) · BL, Add. MS 14965 [Maurice Kyffin's Welsh verse] · *CSP Ire.*, 1596–9 · T. Parry, *A history of Welsh literature*, trans. H. I. Bell (1955) · W. J. Gruffydd, *Llenyddiaeth Cymru: rhyddiaith o 1540 hyd 1660* (1926) · A. I. Pryce, *The diocese of Bangor in the sixteenth century* (1923) · J. Ballinger, *The Bible in Wales: a study in the history of the Welsh people* (1906) · E. Kyffin, *Rhann o Psalmae Dafydd Prophwyd*, ed. J. Ballinger (1930) · G. Williams, *Wales and the Reformation* (1997) · W. Ll. Davies, 'Welsh books entered in the Stationers' Company's registers; part 1, 1554–1660', *Journal of the Welsh Bibliographical Society*, 2 (1916–23), 167–88

Archives NL Wales, account of Lord Buckhurst's embassy to Netherlands

Kyle, James Francis (1788–1869), vicar apostolic of the northern district of Scotland and historical collector, was born at Quarryholes, near Abbeyhill, in Edinburgh, on 22 September 1788, the eldest son of the four children of James Kyle (d. 1799), commissioner of roads and bridges for the war office, and his wife, Margaret Strachan, daughter of a Banff doctor. Although the elder James Kyle was a protestant, after his premature death, his son was brought up in his mother's faith as a Catholic. He was educated for three years at Edinburgh high school, before attending the Roman Catholic seminary at Aquhorties in Aberdeenshire from October 1799. His maternal uncle wanted to make him heir to his East India Company fortune and connections, but Kyle chose instead to enter holy orders, being ordained as priest in 1812. He remained at Aquhorties for twenty-seven years, becoming a master in 1808 and later prefect of studies. His scholarly instincts,

James Francis Kyle (1788–1869), by unknown engraver, pubd 1867

however, were not to be truly fulfilled: in January 1826 he was sent as a missioner to the parish of St Andrew in Glasgow, where he spent several arduous years and much family money in the Clyde Street church. On 13 February 1827 he was appointed bishop *in partibus* of Germanicia and vicar apostolic of the newly created northern district of Scotland. He was consecrated at Aberdeen by Bishop Alexander Paterson of the eastern district on 28 September 1828.

Kyle proved to be an effective vicar apostolic, though he initially faced the problems relating to the new seminary at Blairs. This house and estate had been donated to the Scottish missions by the wealthy John Menzies of Pitfodel, and Kyle had been appointed mainly to manage the new foundation. The donor's disappointment with the educational system developed at the seminary, and conflicts over the tenancy of the accompanying land, plagued Kyle's early career as vicar apostolic. He was supported, however, by the coadjutor of the western district, Bishop Andrew Scott, whose active and energetic character complemented Kyle's more cautious and intellectual one. A portrait of Kyle, probably painted about this time, shows a long-faced man with dishevelled dark hair: his expression is solemn and rather reserved.

Owing to the intractability of Menzies and Charles Gordon (1772–1855), who was overseeing the conversion of Blairs, Kyle chose to fix his episcopal headquarters at the parish of St Gregory, Preshome, from where he presided over a district of 13,000 square miles. With the foundation of the new district, new finances had become available, and Kyle was able to build many new chapels and schools. His high view of the position of the priest—he had opposed the mixing of clerical and secular students at Aquhorties, and he now deplored the tendency of highland priests to supplement their incomes by farming—

further indicated the vigorous new direction of Scottish Catholicism.

Despite a useful episcopal career, Kyle was more significant as a collector of early historical documents relating to the history of Catholic Scotland, some of which were formerly in the Scots College in Paris. He numbered his letters and papers at 30,000, but a modern estimate suggests that he collected up to 75,000. Kyle supplied Prince Aleksandr Lobanov-Rostovsky with sources for his publication of the letters of Mary, queen of Scots, and he also succeeded in deciphering the secret letter code of the queen. Kyle died at Preshome on 23 February 1869, and was buried in the church there. His collections are now deposited at Columba House in Edinburgh: to him the Scottish Roman Catholic church owes the best part of its pre-Reformation archives.   ROSEMARY MITCHELL

Sources J. Darragh, *The Catholic hierarchy of Scotland: a biographical list, 1653–1985* (1986) · J. K. Robertson, 'Young Mr Kyle and his circle', *Innes Review*, 1 (1950), 35–47 · J. K. Robertson, 'The bishop looks at his diocese', *Innes Review*, 3 (1952), 22–32 · C. Johnson, *Developments in the Roman Catholic church in Scotland, 1789–1829* (1983) · *DNB* · *DSCHT*

Archives Scottish Catholic Archives, Edinburgh, corresp. and papers · St Gregory's, Preshome, family MSS

Likenesses engraving, repro. in J. F. S. Gordon, *Ecclesiastical chronicle for Scotland* (1867) [*see illus.*] · oils, St Gregory's, Preshome

Kyle, Sir Wallace Hart (1910–1988), air force officer and governor of Western Australia, was born on 22 January 1910 in Kalgoorlie, Western Australia, the youngest of eight children of Alfred Kyle, sexton, of Perth, Western Australia, and his wife, Christina Ellen Beck Winning. He was educated at Guildford grammar school, Perth, where he excelled at swimming, football, cricket, and athletics, and was school champion in tennis and badminton. Kyle became captain of athletics, perhaps his best sport. In 1927 he won a governor's scholarship to the RAF training college at Cranwell in Lincolnshire, where his hut commander labelled him Digger to distinguish him from a fellow Australian and former student of Guildford grammar school, Edmund Huddleston. Digger was a name Kyle retained throughout his career. In 1930 he passed out of Cranwell into the RAF where his early training was on Tiger Moths and Bristol Bulldog fighters. Over the next ten years Kyle served with 17 squadron (1930–31), with the Fleet Air Arm (1931–4), and as a flying instructor (1934–9). During this period he returned to Australia, where he undertook instructional work with the fledgeling Royal Australian Air Force. It was on this tour of duty that he led a squadron of Hawker Hart biplanes on the first east–west flight across Australia.

In Britain again at the commencement of war in 1939 Kyle was on the staff of Training Command but in November 1940 took command of 139 (Jamaica) squadron of Blenheim light bombers which, despite their slowness and vulnerability, were used on daylight bombing raids over enemy territory. Kyle's bravery and leadership qualities came to the fore. A daring daylight raid on a German seaplane base at Sylt in the North Friesian Islands was followed in 1941 with another on the iron and steel works at Ijmuiden in the Netherlands. In this raid Kyle led his squadron at low level from the sea, and his planes released their bombs from a height of only 50 feet, inflicting substantial damage. With great skill and courage he then managed to elude enemy ground fire and waiting Me 109s by flying close to sea level where enemy planes could not bring their guns to bear without the risk of crashing. For extricating his squadron from almost certain destruction Kyle was subsequently awarded the DFC (1941). In 1941 he married Mary (Molly) Rimington, daughter of the late A. G. Wilkinson, of Yattendon, Berkshire. The marriage was happy, and they had three sons and one daughter.

After a short period of training Kyle was put in charge of the bomber station at Horsham St Faith, Norfolk, where he supervised the formation of the first Mosquito day bombing squadron. From there he went to RAF Marham, whose Mosquitoes flew missions for the path finder force. Kyle continued to fly operations, being awarded the DSO (1944) for perfecting the bombing techniques of Mosquitoes. In the same year he was appointed CBE. By the end of the war Kyle was on the staff of Arthur 'Bomber' Harris, commander-in-chief of Bomber Command, involved in planning raids.

After the war Kyle served at the RAF Staff College, Cranwell (1945–7), and with the Middle East air force (1948–50), before being appointed assistant commandant of Cranwell (1950–52). He was director of operational requirements at the Air Ministry (1952–3), and was then appointed air officer commanding Malaya (1955–7), where low-level bombing by his force of Lincoln bombers contributed significantly to the suppression of communist insurgents. After returning to England he filled several administrative positions including those of assistant chief of the air staff (1957–9) and commander-in-chief of technical training command (1959–62). He replaced his compatriot Sir Edmund Huddleston as vice-chief of the air staff in 1962.

In 1965 Kyle was appointed commander-in-chief of Bomber Command, and in 1968, when Bomber Command and Fighter Command were combined, he was appointed the first commander-in-chief of the newly established Strike Command. To mark the occasion he flew a Lightning jet fighter at 1000 m.p.h., thus qualifying for membership of the Ten Ton Club.

From 1949 to 1966 Kyle was closely associated with the monarchy, holding the positions of aide-de-camp to George VI in 1949 and of aide-de-camp (1952–6) and later air aide-de-camp (1966) to Elizabeth II. He was made a CB in 1953, a KCB in 1960, and GCB in 1966. Kyle retired from the RAF in 1968 and in 1975 was invited to become governor of Western Australia, a position he held with distinction, although not without controversy, until 1980. Not frightened to speak his mind, Kyle became involved in issues such as republicanism and nuclear energy. He hosted the queen's tour of Western Australia during her silver jubilee year, and the visit of the prince of Wales on the occasion of the 150th anniversary of the founding of the state. He worked closely with the government of Western Australia and was considered one of the state's most popular and successful governors. He was appointed

KCVO in 1977. Outside official duties, Kyle enjoyed golf. In 1980 he became president of the Fairbridge Society, and he held honorary doctorates from the Western Australian Institute of Technology and the University of Western Australia.

Survived by his wife and children, Digger Kyle died peacefully at his home, Inglewood, Sway Road, Lymington, Hampshire, on 31 January 1988 after a long illness which he bore with characteristic cheerfulness and courage. His whole career had been in keeping with that of many Australians who served the 'mother country' with distinction and, in so doing, brought great credit to the land of their birth. BRIAN WIMBORNE

Sources *The Times* (2 Feb 1988), 16 · *West Australian* (2 Feb 1988), 1, 32 · T. Hungerford, ed., *Tall stories: an anecdotal history of Guildford grammar school, 1896–1996*, 371–2 · *Who's who in Australia* (1959), 456 · Burke, *Peerage* (1970) · *West Australian* (20 Nov 1967), 17 · *West Australian* (15 Sept 1975), 1, 5 · *West Australian* (1 June 1978), 3 · *West Australian* (25 Nov 1975), 1, 14 · *WWW, 1981–90* · d. cert.
Likenesses photograph, repro. in *The Times*
Wealth at death £175,801: probate, 12 April 1988, *CGPLA Eng. & Wales*

Kylmington, Richard. *See* Kilvington, Richard (*c.*1305–1361).

Kylsant. For this title name *see* Philipps, Owen Cosby, Baron Kylsant (1863–1937).

Kyme family (*per. c.*1080–*c.*1380), gentry, holding lands in Lincolnshire and several other counties, were probably descended from **William** [i] (*d.* in or before 1116), the tenant of Waldin the Engineer in 1086. He was possibly the same man as William, son of Anschetil, tenant of the bishop of Durham and the de la Haie fee *c.*1100. William was succeeded by his son, **Simon** [i] (*d. c.*1162), who married, probably before 1120, Agnes, possibly the heir of Baldric 'de Lindissi' (that is, probably, of Lindsey), most of whose considerable estates, held of the earls of Chester in Lincolnshire, Simon acquired. Simon greatly augmented his lands. In 1166, in addition to a small tenancy-in-chief and about fifteen knights' fees held of the earl of Chester, his son Philip [i] [*see below*] held over fourteen knights' fees of ten lords in five counties, especially Lincolnshire, which made him more powerful than many barons. Simon married secondly Sybil, and in his later years farmed the earldom of Chester during the minority of Earl Hugh (1158–61), and Doncaster (1160–61).

Under Simon his family emerged as one of the most important in Lincolnshire. This is reflected in, and partly resulted from, the connections Simon established with other influential Lincolnshire families. His daughter, Agnes, married Herbert, son of Alard, lord of Orby and constable of the Gant fee. His second son, Simon [ii], married Isobel, daughter and heir of Thomas of Cuckney. More importantly, before 1147 his eldest son, **Philip** [i] **of Kyme** (*d.* 1192x4), married the heiress Hawise of Kyme (*d. c.*1207), who was possibly a descendant of Ralph of Kyme (*fl.* 1087–1095), a tenant, and possibly steward, of the Gant fee. The marriage brought Philip a considerable Gant tenancy in Lincolnshire, and was probably arranged by Ranulf (II), earl of Chester, partly (perhaps) as a means both of

rewarding Simon, who was a prominent member of his entourage in the 1140s and 1150s, and also of attaching the Gant family to his orbit. After the marriage Philip adopted the surname Kyme, and by 1149–50 was steward of the Gant fee.

Thereafter the Kymes were more closely involved with the Gants than with the earls of Chester, though this may have owed more to the growing independence of Lincolnshire knightly families from their lords than to any shift in Kyme allegiance. This independence is possibly also reflected in the construction of a castle in the Kyme manor of Bullington and in the religious patronage of the family. The Kymes played a significant role in promoting the monastic expansion of the mid- and late twelfth century. About 1155 Simon [i] founded a Gilbertine priory at Bullington, which became the main focus of Kyme religious patronage, and his son Philip established an Augustinian priory at North Kyme. Simon [i], Philip [i], and Philip's brother, Simon [ii], made grants to about twenty other religious houses, mainly in Lincolnshire, which seriously depleted the family resources. These benefactions reflect the wealth and extensive familial and tenurial connections of the Kymes.

Under Philip of Kyme the prestige and status of the family continued to increase through royal service and marriage alliances. Philip took over the farms of Doncaster and Tickhill *c.*1162, was sheriff of Lincolnshire from 1167 to 1170, remained loyal to Henry II during the rebellion of 1173–4, attested Henry's adjudication of the dispute between the kings of Navarre and Castile in 1177, and farmed the earldom of Chester from 1181 to 1184. He married one daughter, Hawise, before 1190, to Robert, son of Richard, a cadet of the Legbourne family, and another daughter, Sybil, to Roger of Benniworth, an important Roumare tenant. A possible third daughter, Agnes, may be the Agnes who married Thomas of Saleby, son of William, son of Hacon, the sheriff of Lincolnshire in the 1130s. More importantly Philip married his two eldest sons, Simon of *Kyme (*d.* 1220) and William [ii] of Kyme, to Rohese (or Rohaise) and Margaret, the daughters and coheirs of Robert fitz Robert, who was the steward of the Percy fee, by 1176. These marriages brought them considerable lands in the Percy lordship.

Despite his successes Philip left his son and heir, Simon, with a legacy of encumbered estates and substantial debts which increased as Simon became more closely involved than any of his predecessors in national politics and administration. He paid dearly for his prominent role in the baronial rebellion against King John, being forced to pay ransoms for his son and heir, **Philip** [ii] **of Kyme** (*d.* 1242), taken at the siege of Rochester in 1215, and for himself two years later when he was captured at Lincoln. By 1220 the period that had seen the greatest rise in Kyme power and prestige was over. Simon left his son a depleted inheritance and many unpaid debts. Although Philip [ii] enjoyed some prominence as a royal justice in 1227–8, he was unable to escape this legacy of debt. In 1227 with his mother, Rohese, he granted the manors of South Elkington and Cawthorpe, Lincolnshire, to the bishop of

Lincoln for ten years for 200 marks. In 1230/31 it was arranged for him to pay 200 marks per annum for his royal debts, and 100 marks per annum for his debts to Jewish moneylenders. At about the same time Philip accounted at the exchequer for debts in excess of £700.

Philip had two sons, **Simon** [iii] **of Kyme** (d. 1248), who succeeded him in 1242 and whose period of lordship was relatively uneventful, and **William** [iii] **of Kyme** (d. 1259), who succeeded Simon, and a daughter, Sybil, who married Walter de Ver, an important landholder in Lincolnshire and Yorkshire. By 1251 William owed 320 marks to Jewish moneylenders. In 1259 he demised to John of Swaneborn his manor of Baumber for seven years, and owed Gui de Lusignan, the king's half-brother, over £95, which he had used to repay his father's debts. Although indebted, William endowed the chapters of Nun Appleton, Louth Park, Bullington, possibly Haverholme, and Lincoln Cathedral. He married Lucy de Ros with whom he had a son and heir, **Philip** [iii] **Kyme**, first Lord Kyme (d. 1323). In 1259 the king granted the custody of William's lands and two sons and a daughter to the justiciar, Hugh (III) Bigod, for £3000.

Under Philip [iii] the fortunes of the Kyme family appear to have revived through service to the crown. Philip was summoned many times to fight in Wales and Scotland between 1282 and 1317, served in Gascony in 1294 and 1295, fought at the siege of Caerlaverock in 1300, had charge of Bolingbroke Castle in 1311, and was summoned to join the king to confront Thomas, earl of Lancaster, at Boroughbridge in 1322. Philip acted as a commissioner of array in Lincolnshire and Rutland in 1301, requisitioned provisions in Lincolnshire in 1309, and delivered the gaol of Lincoln Castle in 1311. He was summoned to parliament from 1295 to 1313. He also found time for economic development and religious devotion. In 1299–1300 he secured the right to hold a weekly market at Burwell, Lincolnshire, and he was a benefactor of the religious houses of Bullington, Haverholme, North Kyme, Newhouse, and Louth Park. In 1318–19 he was about to set out on pilgrimage to Santiago de Compostela.

Philip [iii] married Joan, daughter of Hugh (III) *Bigod, and was succeeded by his son, **William** [iv] **Kyme**, second Lord Kyme (c.1283–1338), who was also an active servant of the crown. William was summoned several times to serve against the Scots or in Gascony between 1315 and 1335, fought with the king at Boroughbridge in 1322, held a number of local administrative posts between 1320 and 1335, and was summoned to parliament from 1323 to 1335–6. He married Joan, daughter of Humphrey Littelbury, and, having no children, was succeeded by the son of his sister Lucy and her husband, Robert Umfraville, Gilbert *Umfraville, ninth earl of Angus (d. 1381) [see under Umfraville, Gilbert de].

The family's arms were in 1256 chevron between ten cross-crosslets, and in 1321/2 gules a chevron croisely d'or, with a label argent.   PAUL DALTON

Sources C. J. Wales, 'The knight in twelfth-century Lincolnshire', PhD diss., U. Cam., 1983 · B. Golding, 'Simon of Kyme: the making of a 1214 rebel', *Nottingham Medieval Studies*, 27 (1983), 23–36 · W. Farrer, *Honors and knights' fees*, 3 vols. (1923–5), vols. 1, 2 · F. M. Stenton, ed., *Documents illustrative of the social and economic history of the danelaw* (1920) · *Pipe rolls*, Henry II, Richard I · B. Golding, 'The Gilbertine priories of Alvingham and Bullington: their endowments and benefactors', DPhil diss., U. Oxf., 1979 · M. R. Abbot, 'The Gant family in England, 1066–1191', PhD diss., U. Cam., 1973 · Dugdale, *Monasticon*, new edn, vol. 6 · P. Dalton, 'Aiming at the impossible: Ranulf II earl of Chester and Lincolnshire in the reign of King Stephen', *Journal of the Chester Archaeological Society*, 71 (1991), 109–34 [G. Barraclough issue, *The earldom of Chester and its charters*, ed. A. T. Thacker] · Rymer, *Foedera*, new edn · H. Hall, ed., *The Red Book of the Exchequer*, 1, Rolls Series, 99 (1896) · W. Stubbs, ed., *Gesta regis Henrici secundi Benedicti abbatis: the chronicle of the reigns of Henry II and Richard I, AD 1169–1192*, 2 vols., Rolls Series, 49 (1867), vol. 1 · GEC, *Peerage*, new edn · *Calendar of the charter rolls*, 6 vols., PRO (1903–27), vols. 1–4 · *CPR, 1232–58; 1272–81* · C. Roberts, ed., *Excerpta è rotulis finium in Turri Londinensi asservatis, Henrico Tertio rege, AD 1216–1272*, 2 vols., RC, 32 (1835–6) · *CCIR, 1279–88* · *Calendar of chancery warrants, 1: 1244–1326* (1927) · I. J. Sanders, *English baronies: a study of their origin and descent, 1086–1327* (1960) · *CIPM*, vol. 1 · *Close rolls of the reign of Henry III*, 14 vols., PRO (1902–38) · C. W. Foster and K. Major, eds., *The registrum antiquissimum of the cathedral church of Lincoln*, 10 vols. in 12, Lincoln RS, 27–9, 32, 34, 41–2, 46, 51, 62, 67–8 (1931–73), vols. 9–10 · C. Robinson, ed., *The memoranda roll of the king's remembrancer for Michaelmas 1230–Trinity 1231*, PRSoc., 49, new ser., 11 (1933) · *Curia regis rolls preserved in the Public Record Office* (1922–) · BL, Cotton MS Vespasian E.xviii [Kirkstead Abbey cartulary], fol. 72 · A. H. Thompson, *The Premonstratensian abbey of Welbeck* (1938) · H. M. Colvin, *The white canons in England* (1951) · A. Farley, ed., *Domesday Book*, 2 vols. (1783)

Archives Belvoir Castle, Leicestershire, Add. MSS 98 and 105 · BL, Add. MS 35296 · BL, Cotton MS Vespasian E.xx · BL, Lansdowne MS 415 · BL, Harley charters, 52.G.19–52.G.32; 52.G.34–52.G.35; 52.G.37; 52.G.39–52.G.41 · BL, Cotton MS Vespasian E.xviii · BL, Harley MS 742 · BL, Add. MS 46701 · Lincoln Cathedral, Registrum antiquissimum, no. 597

Kyme, Philip of (d. 1192x4). *See under* Kyme family (*per. c.*1080–*c.*1380).

Kyme, Philip of (d. 1242). *See under* Kyme family (*per. c.*1080–*c.*1380).

Kyme, Philip, first Lord Kyme (d. 1323). *See under* Kyme family (*per. c.*1080–*c.*1380).

Kyme, Simon of (d. 1220), administrator, was a member of a substantial knightly family originating at Kyme in Lincolnshire and with its *caput* at Sotby in the same county. Sotby ranked as a barony (albeit a minor one), but the family held very little land in chief, and its importance derived rather from the twenty-eight fees which it held as undertenancies, from one of which it derived its name, and which it held in Lincolnshire and Yorkshire from some of that region's most powerful magnates, including the Gants, the Mowbrays, and the earls of Chester.

Simon's father, Philip of *Kyme (d. 1192x4) [see under Kyme family], was a royal administrator under Henry II, farming royal estates and serving as sheriff of Lincolnshire from 1167 to 1170. On Philip's death in the early 1190s he was succeeded by Simon, the eldest son of his marriage to Hawise. In 1190 Simon of Kyme became keeper of the Galtres forest in Yorkshire, and in 1191 he was appointed a royal justice in the same county. Between 1194 and 1197 he served as sheriff of Lincolnshire, and until 1207 fulfilled a number of other administrative functions in the county.

His absence from royal service thereafter may have contributed to his joining the baronial rebellion against King John in 1215. Moreover, he had inherited substantial debts from his father and was by now heavily encumbered: in 1211/12 the principal and interest on his debts to Jewish moneylenders amounted to over £1250, which he compounded to repay at £1000 over the next three years. The king may well have used these debts to enforce loyalty: if so, he failed.

As the political crisis deepened from 1212 Kyme was again found at court, and in 1213 he was one of those who urged reforms on the king at Lincoln. He may have openly joined the rebels at Stamford at Easter 1215; not long afterwards he was one of those excommunicated by name by Pope Innocent III (r. 1198–1216). In October the sheriff of Lincolnshire was ordered to put the sheriff of Yorkshire, Geoffrey de Neville, in seisin of Kyme's lands, and shortly afterwards Kyme's son and heir, Philip, was among those captured at the siege of Rochester. Kyme was unable to raise his ransom and in 1217 was himself, it seems, captured at Lincoln. Though he made his peace the following year, when he was with the royal army at Newark, the cost was a heavy one, and he was obliged to demise all the lands he held of the earldom of Chester and Lincoln.

Simon of Kyme's anti-royalist activities were probably also encouraged by ties of kinship and neighbourhood. He was married by 1176 to Rohese (or Rohaise), the daughter of Robert fitz Robert, steward to William de Percy (d. 1245), and the Percys were active rebels. Rohaise's father had married the widow of Gilbert de Gant, representative of another rebel family, and of whom the Kymes were tenants. Among the lesser Lincolnshire aristocracy, Gilbert of Benniworth and John of Orby were both cousins and near neighbours of Kyme and, like him, were rebels, as was another neighbour and associate, Thomas of Moulton (d. 1240).

On Kyme's death in 1220 he was succeeded by his eldest son Philip, who was immediately obliged to mortgage some of the family estates in order to pay off his father's outstanding debts. Of the brothers and sisters of Simon of Kyme less is known, though one, Walter, died on the third crusade in 1190, another, Roger, was probably a Gilbertine canon, while his sister, Joanna, was a nun in the Gilbertine priory of Bullington, Lincolnshire. This house, where Kyme's heart was buried, was the family foundation, but Simon of Kyme was also a patron of Nun Appleton, Yorkshire, founded by his wife's mother, and of a number of other communities in Lincolnshire and Yorkshire.

BRIAN GOLDING

Sources B. Golding, 'Simon of Kyme: the making of a 1214 rebel', *Nottingham Medieval Studies*, 27 (1983), 23–36 · C. J. Wales, 'The knight in twelfth-century Lincolnshire', PhD diss., U. Cam., 1983 · J. C. Holt, *The northerners: a study in the reign of King John* (1961) · W. Farrer, *Honors and knights' fees … from the eleventh to the fourteenth century*, 2 (1924), 118–27 · Pipe rolls · *Curia regis rolls preserved in the Public Record Office* (1922–) · Chancery records · H. C. M. Lyte and others, eds., *Liber feodorum: the book of fees*, 3 vols. (1920–31) · C. Roberts, ed., *Excerpta è rotulis finium in Turri Londinensi asservatis, Henrico Tertio rege, AD 1216–1272*, 1, RC, 32 (1835) · BL, Add. MS 6118, 717

Kyme, Simon of (d. 1248). *See under* Kyme family (*per. c.*1080–*c.*1380).

Kyme, William of (d. 1259). *See under* Kyme family (*per. c.*1080–*c.*1380).

Kyme, William, second Lord Kyme (c.1283–1338). *See under* Kyme family (*per. c.*1080–*c.*1380).

Kymer, Gilbert (d. 1463), dean of Salisbury and physician, is first noticed in university records as principal of Hart Hall, Oxford, in 1411, a post he still held in 1414. He received his MA in 1412, and was in that year senior proctor of the university. His DM was awarded about 1423 and he was bachelor of civil law by 1433. He was elected university chancellor on 10 December 1431 and had resigned by March 1434. During that time, he rented a school from University College. Elected chancellor again in February 1447, he resigned on 11 May 1453. As chancellor, he resided in Durham College in March 1449, in Lincoln College in July 1450 and January 1451, and in Coventry Hall in June and July 1452.

Some sources say Kymer married before 1420, but left his wife so as to be able to take holy orders. He came to hold numerous livings, starting with Lutterworth in Leicestershire, and was successively treasurer and dean of Salisbury, where he died on 16 May 1463, and was buried in the cathedral; his effigy survives in the window of the south transept. His will, dated 14 October 1462, was proved on 12 July 1463 and shows him a wealthy and generous man.

In 1423 Kymer appears to have migrated from Oxford to London. There, he joined forces with university-educated physicians and learned surgeons to form a *Comminalte* ('commonalty') for the regulation and education of medical practitioners, modelled perhaps on the inns of court or on one of the medical licensing bodies associated with urban universities on the continent. It was to be governed by a rector of physicians (*rector medicorum*), the first being Kymer himself. The ordinances of the *Comminalte* were presented to the mayor and aldermen of the City of London and were granted on 15 May 1423. Kymer's associates were the physician John Somerset, medical bachelor Thomas Southwell, and surgeons John Harwe and Thomas Morstede. On 10 September 1424 the *Comminalte* judged a legal case, when Harwe and others were charged with incompetence by a patient, William Forest. Kymer presided and found for the defendants, ruling that malign astrological influences had caused Forest's misfortune. By 10 November 1424 the organization had faded from the London scene.

Kymer's only surviving medical writing dates from 1424, a regimen of health for Humphrey, duke of Gloucester, which is dated 6 March of that year and was written in Hainault, Flanders. The document, which survives in a single fifteenth-century manuscript (BL, Sloane MS 4, pp. 63–102), has twenty-six short chapters, dealing in detail with the duke's mode of living. The table of contents and two chapters, largely on the ill effects of the duke's sexual appetite, were printed by T. Hearne in *Liber niger Scaccarii*

(2.550–59). In 1456 Kymer was one of several physicians and others to obtain a licence to practise alchemy from Henry VI. His associates included William Hatteclyffe, John Faceby, John Kirkeby, and Wolfard Koer. The outcome of their enterprise is not known, but Thomas Norton, in his *Ordinal of Alchemy* (c.1490), mentions that Kymer had written a work on alchemy, now lost. Duke Humphrey's famous gift of books to Oxford University seems to have been made at least in part on Kymer's advice. His first gift, in 1439 of 120 books, was delivered by Kymer himself. Kymer owned a considerable collection of medical books, including Bodleian Library, MS Bodley 362, which includes a copy of John Gaddesden's *Rosa anglica* with works by other medical authors, including Bernard de Gordon. This book was copied by Kymer's own scribe, Hermann Zurke of Greifswald, Mecklenburg.

FAYE GETZ

Sources F. M. Getz, 'The faculty of medicine before 1500', *Hist. U. Oxf.* 2: *Late med. Oxf.*, 373–405 · C. H. Talbot and E. A. Hammond, *The medical practitioners in medieval England: a biographical register* (1965) · F. Getz, 'Medical practitioners in medieval England', *Social History of Medicine*, 3 (1990), 245–83 · T. Norton, *Ordinal of alchemy*, ed. J. Reidy, EETS, 272 (1975) · T. Hearne, ed., *Liber niger Scaccarii*, rev. edn, 2 vols. (1771) · Emden, *Oxf.*, 2.1068–9
Archives BL, Sloane MS 4, pp. 63–102
Likenesses effigy, Salisbury Cathedral
Wealth at death wealthy: will, proved 12 July 1463

Kynaston, Edward (*bap.* 1643, *d.* 1712?), actor, the son of Thomas Kynaston, was baptized at Oswestry, Shropshire, on 20 April 1643. One source suggests that Edward 'was well descended. The Kynastons were anciently possessed of a genteel estate at Oteley in Shropshire' (Betterton, 116). On 5 July 1654 he was bound as an apprentice to John Rhodes in the Company of Drapers for nine years. With Thomas Betterton, Kynaston was introduced to the stage in Rhodes's troupe at the Cockpit, Drury Lane, in March 1660. In the first season Edward played several female parts, including the title role in John Suckling's *Aglaura*, Ismena in Beaumont's and Fletcher's *The Maid in the Mill*, and Arthiope in William Davenant's *The Unfortunate Lovers*:

> he being then very Young made a Compleat Stage Beauty, performing his Parts so well … that it has since been Disputeable among the Judicious, whether any Woman that succeeded him so Sensibly touch'd the Audience as he. (Downes, 19)

How far Kynaston was successful in these roles, even in a theatrical world infected by the continental preference for actresses, is hinted at by his performance as the Duke's Sister in Thomas Heywood's *The Royal King and Loyal Subject* on 18 August 1660, where Pepys thought him 'the loveliest lady that ever I saw in my life, only her voice not very good' (Pepys). Cibber recalls that 'Ladies of Quality prided themselves on taking him with them in their Coaches to Hyde-Park in his Theatrical Habit, after the play' (Cibber, 67). When the Rhodes company was absorbed into the two patent house monopoly, Kynaston became a player with Thomas Killigrew's King's Company at the Vere Street Theatre. He was sworn in on 6 October 1660, and for the first season continued to play these female roles, mixing

Edward Kynaston (*bap.* 1643, *d.* 1712?), by unknown artist

them with young male parts, such as Otto in Fletcher's and Massinger's *The Bloody Brother*, Corporal Cocke in Heywood's *The Royal King*, and the more troubling title role in Ben Jonson's *Epicoene*, a woman who turns out to be a boy in disguise.

The Burney collection notes record that Edward married Maria in 1661, which might be the marriage registered in the parish of St Giles-in-the-Fields, London, between Edward Kynaston and Mary Carter on 6 March 1662. According to the parish registers, this Edward and Mary had five surviving children, John, Elizabeth, Arabella, Sarah, and Anne. Kynaston quickly became a leading player within the King's Company and had the means to acquire a whole acting share by 1663. His roles at Vere Street and the new theatre in Bridges Street, Covent Garden, where the company moved in 1663, included Roseilli and Caraffa in John Ford's *Love's Sacrifice*, the idealistic Acacis in John Dryden's and Robert Howard's *Indian Queen*, the flawed leader Mahomet Boabdelin in both parts of Dryden's *The Conquest of Granada*, and the excessively honourable Guymor in his *The Indian Emperor*, and the title role in Orrery's *The Black Prince*. He also managed young comedic leads such as Peregrine in Jonson's *Volpone*, Valentine in William Wycherley's *Love in a Wood*, and probably Volscius in the duke of Buckingham's *The Rehearsal*.

Edward's involvement in the scandalous *Rehearsal* play was not his only foray into satirical personation. Pepys records that a performance of William Cavendish's *The Heiress* was cancelled because 'Kinaston, that did act a part therein, in abuse to Sir Charles Sedley, being last night exceedingly beaten with sticks, by two or three that assaulted him, so as he is mightily bruised and forced to keep his bed' (Pepys, 1 Feb 1669). Kynaston had recovered enough to act by 9 February and the incident did no harm to his reputation. After the disastrous burning of the Bridges Street Theatre in 1672, the King's Company occupied the old Lincoln's Inn Fields Theatre and then moved into the rebuilt Drury Lane playhouse in March 1674. Kynaston continued to take important, theatrically demanding roles such as the powerful, controlling Scipio in Lee's Sophonisba, Harcourt in Wycherley's The Country Wife, Freeman in his Plain Dealer, the villainous Morat in Dryden's Aureng-Zebe, and Leonidas in his Marriage à la mode.

As well as being a key player in the company, Kynaston had become involved in the management of the troupe: by May 1676 he held 1¼ shares, worth 6s. 3d. every acting day for life, with £100 to his executors. After a breakdown in company management in September 1676 the lord chamberlain appointed Kynaston and three other leading actors, Charles Hart, William Cartwright, and Michael Mohun, to lead the group. This management committee did not take adequate steps to right the company's difficulties, and Hart was appointed with sole responsibility shortly after this, although Kynaston continued to figure on the many documents related to the company's battle with its patent holder, Charles Killigrew. Kynaston announced his decision to retire in 1677 and no new roles are recorded for him, although the King's Company roster was in great disarray during this period. Matters came to a head when, on 14 October 1681, Kynaston and Hart signed a secret agreement with the rival Duke's Company. The King's Company was in dire financial straits by the early 1680s with poor returns for shareholders. All the same, the terms the fifth columnists were prepared to accept are startling. For 5s. a day each they agreed not to 'play among or effectually assist the King's Company of Actors' and to make over to the Duke's Company 'all the Right, Title and Claim which they or either of them may have to any Plays, Books, Cloaths, and Scenes in the King's Playhouse'. In addition they promised to:

> promote with all their Power and Interest an Agreement between both playhouses, and Mr Kynaston for himself, promises to endeavour, as much as he can, to get free, that he may act at the Duke's Playhouse, but he is not obliged to play unless he have ten Shillings per Day allowed for his Acting, and his Pension then to cease. (Gildon, 8–9)

The companies merged in 1682 and moved into the Drury Lane Theatre. Kynaston appears to have maintained a position as shareholder within the new company and in September that year Charles Hart died and bequeathed his share to Kynaston. Edward was clearly not without means and he may have been the Edward Keynaston of the fashionable Great Queen Street, listed in the baptism registers of St Giles-in-the-Fields on 1 March 1684, and the Kinnaston with property in St Martin's Lane, St Paul, Covent Garden.

In the enlarged United Company it was a sign of how highly Kynaston was regarded that he was immediately encouraged to perform, adding a range of new roles, the first of which was the King in Dryden's and Lee's The Duke of Guise, a late tory contribution to the Exclusion crisis, on 28 November 1682. Roles he originated included the domestic despot Lord Bellguard in John Crowne's Sir Courtly Nice, Don Antonio in Thomas D'Urfey's Banditti, and the faithful lover Bellmour in Aphra Behn's The Lucky Chance. In his playing of Muley Moloch in Dryden's Don Sebastian, Cibber thought 'he had a fierce Lion-like Majesty in his Port and Utterance that gave the Spectator a kind of trembling Admiration' (Cibber, 68). Cibber recalls his 'piercing eye, and in characters of heroick life, a quick imperious vivacity, in his tone of voice, that painted the tyrant truly terrible'. He found him particularly noteworthy as the King in Henry IV where 'every sentiment came from him, as if it had been his own, as if he had himself, that instant, conceiv'd it, as if he had lost the player and were the real king he personated' (Cibber, 69). Kynaston's range as a performer is illustrated by the roles he tackled, and Cibber also praised the variety Kynaston could offer within roles, finding moments of bathetic laughter as the villain in Aureng-Zebe and quiet menace in Henry IV, where lesser actors might have chosen bullying volume.

By the 1690s Kynaston was earning £3 a week but acting less frequently, according to a complaint filed by Christopher Rich and Thomas Skipwith, who were trying to stop the older players from defecting to form a new company in 1695 (Milhous, 244). However, Kynaston continued to take on new roles in the Actors' Company including Hystaspes in John Bank's Cyrus the Great, Friendly in fellow actor Doggett's The Country Wake, the avenging prince of Libardian in Delariviere Manley's The Royal Mischief, Paulinus in Charles Hopkins's Boadicea, and the earl of Warwick in Mary Pix's Queen Catherine. A manuscript cast of Southerne's Fatal Marriage lists Kynaston as the heartless father-in-law, Count Baldwin, which might indicate that Kynaston was still playing as late as 24 April 1701. Little is known of the last years of his life, although he remained a ground rent shareholder at the Drury Lane Theatre. He is probably the Edward Kynaston who was buried in St Paul's, Covent Garden, London, on 30 July 1712.

J. MILLING

Sources Highfill, Burnim & Langhans, BDA • W. Van Lennep and others, eds., The London stage, 1660–1800, pt 1: 1660–1700 (1965) • T. Betterton, [W. Oldys and others], The history of the English stage (1741) • J. Downes, Roscius Anglicanus, ed. M. Summers, [new edn] (1928) • C. Gildon, The life of Mr Thomas Betterton (1710); repr. (1970) • J. Milhous, Thomas Betterton and the management of Lincoln's Inn Fields (1979) • PRO, Lord Chamberlain 3/25, p. 157 • Pepys, Diary • C. Cibber, An apology for the life of Mr. Colley Cibber, new edn, ed. R. W. Lowe, 2 vols. (1889) • private information (2004) [D. Kathmann]
Likenesses R. Cooper, stipple, pubd 1818 (after P. Lely), NPG • R. B. Parkes, engraving (after lost portrait by P. Lely), repro. in Cibber, Apology • portrait; Christies, 7 Nov 1980, lot 68 [see illus.]

Kynaston, Sir Francis (1586/7–1642), writer and founder of an academy of learning, was born in Oteley, Shropshire, the eldest son of Sir Edward Kynaston (d. after 1638), gentleman, and his wife, Isabel, daughter of Sir Nicholas Bagenall. He matriculated at Oriel College, Oxford, on 11

December 1601, aged fourteen, and graduated BA from St Mary Hall on 14 June 1604. Admitted to Lincoln's Inn on 9 October 1604, he was called to the bar in 1611. He was awarded an MA degree from Trinity College, Cambridge, in 1609. His marriage in 1613 to Margaret, daughter of Sir Humphrey Lee, bt, produced one son. Knighted by James I on 1 January 1618, he represented Shropshire in the parliament of 1621. Named taxor of Cambridge University in 1623, he was proctor in 1634. In 1625 he became esquire of the body to Charles I.

Kynaston was almost certainly responsible for a substantial tract entitled 'True presentation of forepast parliaments', probably written in 1629. It survives in at least five manuscript copies and was the subject of extensive notes by Secretary Francis Windebanke, which identify the author as 'Sir Fr: Ken:' (PRO, SP 16/233/51–2). Kynaston was provoked into writing by an anonymous book exalting the antiquity and authority of parliament, and more generally by what he perceived as the exaggerated reverence for the House of Commons and disrespect for kingship by many MPs in the 1620s. True parliaments, he argued, did not exist under the ancient Britons or Saxons, but instead originated in an assembly convoked by Henry I for the purpose of taking oaths of fealty from his subjects after he had usurped the crown. An elected House of Commons emerged still later through an edict of Henry III, proving that medieval kings had the authority to alter parliamentary procedures and privileges. Parliament's proper function was to offer the king advice and assistance solely with respect to those issues he and his council laid before it. Although parliaments often helped to draft laws, ultimate legislative authority remained in the king alone. Kynaston strenuously objected to the idea that MPs were mainly responsible to their 'countries' rather than the king, which he thought had spread dangerously in recent years. He also criticized counties and boroughs for electing inappropriate representatives in order to please powerful local patrons.

Between 1633 and 1635 Kynaston published three works of translation. *Musae querulae: de regis in Scotiam profectione* (1633) presented Latin poems on the king's journey to his coronation in Edinburgh and English renditions by Kynaston on facing pages. *Musae aulicae autore Ionstono* (1635) did the same for Latin panegyrics to Charles and Henrietta Maria by Arthur Jonston, a Scottish physician to the king. In *Amorum Troili et Creseidae libri duo* (1635) Kynaston published a translation of Chaucer's *Troilus and Cressida* on facing pages with the original. The text was prefaced by a large number of Latin and English dedicatory poems hailing Kynaston for having rescued Chaucer from the oblivion into which his antiquated language had thrust him, by making it possible for readers to appreciate his wit 'without a dictionary' (W. Cartwright, prefatory poem).

In 1635 Kynaston also founded an academy, the Musaeum Minervae, at his house in Bedford Street, Covent Garden. For this he obtained a licence under the great seal, a grant of arms, and a common seal. Charles I contributed £100 to the project. The text of a masque written by Kynaston and presented to Prince Charles to mark the opening of the academy was printed under the title *Corona Minerva* (1635). The next year Kynaston published *The Constitutions of the Musaeum Minervae*, describing the academy's regulations and curriculum. Only sons of peers and gentlemen were to be admitted, for training by a regent and six 'professors' in subjects that men of high birth needed to understand. These included heraldry, the rudiments of the common law, antiquities, coins and medals, husbandry, anatomy, physiology and 'physic', astronomy, optics, navigation and cosmography, various branches of mathematics, music, ancient and modern languages including Hebrew, Greek, Latin, Italian, French, Spanish, and High Dutch, and skill at weapons. Additional instruction in riding, dancing and behaviour, painting, sculpture, and writing rounded out the curriculum. Strong emphasis was to be placed on ideals of honour and lineage, conveyed by 'exciting' students to emulate the accomplishments of old English 'worthies' and their own virtuous ancestors.

Late in 1636 Kynaston became involved with a Covent Garden neighbour, Edward Mae, in a project to develop a 'hanging furnace' for use by the Royal Navy. This apparently consisted of an enclosed stove suspended by iron bars, intended to replace the heavy brick piles used to contain cooking fires on board ship. The invention received a trial, though with unknown results. By the late 1630s Kynaston had run heavily into debt and was in danger of being disinherited by his father. Francis Windebanke and the king himself interceded on his behalf.

Kynaston's last published work appeared in the year of his death, 1642. This was a facetious and slightly bawdy romance set in ancient Britain, entitled *Leoline and Sydanis*, to which Kynaston appended a number of love poems. In the dedicatory epistle he described himself as 'old and stricken in years', and claimed to have a number of pieces of 'solid learning' ready for the press, none of which has since been identified. He was buried at Oteley. The Musaeum Minervae does not seem to have survived his death and the outbreak of the civil war. Letters of administration of his estate were granted to his son, Edward, on 13 November 1649.   R. MALCOLM SMUTS

Sources Foster, *Alum. Oxon.* · W. P. Baildon, ed., *The records of the Honorable Society of Lincoln's Inn: admissions*, 1 (1896), 138 · *DNB* · 'A true presentacon of forepast parliaments to the view of the present time and posterity', Harvard U., law school, bound MSS 5104 · Windebanke's notes, PRO, SP/16/233/51–2 · F. Kynaston, *The constitutions of the Musaeum Minervae* (1636) · G. Chaucer, *Amorum Troili et Creseidae libri duo priores Anglico-Latini*, trans. F. Kynaston, 2 pts in 1 (1635) · F. Kynaston, *Leoline and Sydanis: an heroick romance of the adventures of amorous princes together with sundry affectionate addresses to his Mrs under the name of Cynthia* (1642) · *CSP dom.*, 1635–8 · description of the 'hanging furnace', PRO, SP/16/338/33 · G. Burgess, *Absolute monarchy and the Stuart constitution* (1996), esp. 37–40
Archives Folger, MS V. 6.189 | BL, Lansdowne MS 213 · BL, Stowe MS 331 · Bodl. Oxf., Ashmole MSS 1149
Wealth at death probably indebted: PRO, SP/16/387/164

Kynaston, Herbert (1809–1878), headmaster, second son of Roger Kynaston (c.1777–1847), and Georgiana, third daughter of Sir Charles Oakeley, governor of Madras, was born at Warwick. From 1821 he was educated at Westminster School, where he was badly injured by an explosion of fireworks in his pocket. He was elected to a studentship at Christ Church, Oxford, in 1827, where he obtained the college prize for Latin verse in 1829, took a first class in classics in 1831, and was appointed tutor and Greek reader in 1836. He graduated BA in 1831, MA in 1833, and BD and DD in 1849. He was university select preacher in 1841. In 1834 he was ordained, and served as curate of Culham, Oxfordshire. Four years later, at the early age of twenty-eight, he was elected to the high-mastership of St Paul's School, London, on the retirement of Dr John Sleath. On 2 August 1838, shortly after his appointment, he married Elizabeth Selina, daughter of Hugh Kennedy of Cultra, co. Down.

During the thirty-eight years of his successful rule at St Paul's, Kynaston carried through many innovations. The practice of taking boarders ceased, a mathematics master was appointed, and teaching in modern languages was instituted. M. M. Demogeot and Montucci, the French commissioners who visited the school in 1866, especially mentioned the paternal manner in which the high-master dealt with the boys (*De l'enseignement secondaire en Angleterre et en Écosse*, 1868, 241). School tradition suggests that his benign regime, in which he declined to use corporal punishment, was ineffectual. In 1864 the public-school commissioners noted a decline in the academic performance of the school, though this was largely attributable to the unsuitability of the school's location. Kynaston, however, opposed its removal to a more salubrious site.

In 1850 Lord Truro, an old Pauline, presented Kynaston to the City living of St Nicholas, Cole Abbey, with St Nicholas Olave, which he held until the parishes were amalgamated with St Mary Somerset in 1866. He resigned the mastership of St Paul's in 1876, and the only preferment that he held at the time of his death was the prebendal stall of Holborn in St Paul's Cathedral, to which he was presented by Bishop Blomfield in July 1853. He died at 31 Alfred Place West, South Kensington, on 26 October 1878, and was buried at Friern Barnet on 2 November.

Kynaston's taste and scholarship led to his nomination as a candidate for the chair of poetry at Oxford in 1867, but he was defeated by his college contemporary, Sir Francis Hastings Doyle. Few scholars of his age surpassed him as a composer of Latin verse. He was the author of numerous poetical compositions in praise of Dean Colet, the founder of St Paul's School, which were produced each year at the apposition. Among these the *Number of the Fish* (1855), and the *Lays of the Seven Half-Centuries* written for the seventh jubilee (1859), were the best-known. To the wider world he was most familiar as a writer and translator of hymns, of which he published two volumes, in 1862 and 1864.   G. C. BOASE, rev. M. C. CURTHOYS

Sources Old Westminsters, vols. 1–2 · Boase, Mod. Eng. biog. · 'Two city schoolmasters: Dr Mortimer and Dr Kynaston', *Leisure Hour*, [29] (1879), 179–82 · A. H. Mead, *A miraculous draught of fishes: a history of St Paul's School* (1990) · J. Julian, ed., *A dictionary of hymnology*, rev. edn (1907)

Likenesses W. Walker, mezzotint, pubd 1856 (after Miss Walker), BM · G. Halse, marble bust, 1892, St Paul's School, London · engraving, 1892, St Paul's School, London
Wealth at death under £1500: resworn administration with will, Sept 1879, CGPLA Eng. & Wales (1878)

Kynaston [*formerly* Snow], **Herbert** (1835–1910), classical scholar and Church of England clergyman, was born in London on 29 June 1835, the second son of Robert Snow and his wife, Georgina, daughter of Roger Kynaston and sister of Herbert Kynaston, high-master of St Paul's School. His maternal grandmother was Georgiana, daughter of Sir Charles Oakeley, governor of Madras. From 1844 to 1847 Herbert Snow was at a private school at Beaconsfield, and from 1847 to 1853 was an oppidan at Eton College, where he was among the selected candidates for the Newcastle scholarship, and made his mark on the football field and the river, rowing in both the *Britannia* and *Monarch*. In 1853 he gained a scholarship at St John's College, Cambridge.

Snow's university career was brilliant and exceptionally versatile. In 1855 he won the Porson scholarship, which was then awarded for the first time, together with the Camden medal for Latin hexameters and the Browne medal for a Latin alcaic ode, and in 1857 he was bracketed senior classic with John Robert Seeley and two others. He became fellow of St John's College on 22 March 1858, graduating BA in 1857 and proceeding MA in 1860, when he vacated the fellowship on his marriage on 8 August to Mary Louisa Anne, daughter of Thomas Bros, barrister. Nor was it only in scholarship that Snow excelled as an undergraduate. He rowed seven in the university boat in the Oxford and Cambridge race of 1856, and was stroke in 1857. He was a member of the Alpine Club from 1862 to 1875. He was one of the earliest members of the Amateur Dramatic Club, and became a freemason. Throughout his life he was devoted to the craft, passing the chair in Foundation Lodge, Cheltenham, and afterwards being grand chaplain of England and one of the founders of Universities Lodge, Durham.

In 1858 Snow returned to Eton as an assistant master and was ordained deacon in 1859 and priest in 1860. His first wife died in 1864, and on 8 August 1865 he married Charlotte, daughter of Revd John Cordeaux of Hooton Roberts. He had four sons and three daughters. After sixteen years at Eton, Snow was elected principal of Cheltenham College in 1874. In 1875 he assumed his mother's family surname of Kynaston. In 1881 he proceeded BD and the next year DD at Cambridge; for the former degree he wrote a Latin thesis on the use of the expression 'the kingdom of God' in the New Testament, and for the latter an English essay entitled 'The influence of the Holy Spirit on the life of man'.

Kynaston's time at Cheltenham was neither happy nor particularly successful. The masters were divided, with considerable rivalry between the classical and modern sides, and Kynaston found little support for the reforms he felt important. Resigning from Cheltenham in 1888, he was for nearly a year vicar of St Luke's, Kentish Town. In 1889 Bishop Lightfoot appointed him canon of Durham and professor of Greek in the university, in succession to the distinguished scholar and teacher Thomas Saunders Evans. Kynaston remained at Durham until his death, at Eastbourne, Sussex, on 1 August 1910.

Always devoted to music, of which he had a practical as well as a theoretical knowledge, Kynaston had a good tenor voice. As a linguist he was at home in five or six languages, and could improvise effective poetical translations. An admirable composer in Greek and Latin, Kynaston was too fastidious a writer to make any contribution to scholarly literature commensurate with his capacities. His best-known book is a school edition of Theocritus with English notes (1869). He also produced several textbooks on composition and a volume of sermons.

HENRY ELLERSHAW, *rev.* RICHARD SMAIL

Sources E. D. Stone, *Herbert Kynaston* (1912) · Venn, *Alum. Cant.* · *The Times* (2 Aug 1910) · *The Times* (8 Aug 1910) · *The Eagle*, 33 (1911–12), 69–70 · J. U. Powell, *Classical Review*, 24 (1910) · *CGPLA Eng. & Wales* (1910)
Likenesses photograph, repro. in Stone, *Herbert Kynaston*
Wealth at death £2464 2s. 11d.: probate, 17 Oct 1910, *CGPLA Eng. & Wales*

Kynaston, John (1728–1783), author and literary scholar, was born on 5 December 1728 at Chester, son of Humphrey Kynaston, mercer of Chester. On 20 February 1745 he was admitted to Manchester grammar school; he proceeded with an exhibition to Brasenose College, Oxford, where he matriculated on 20 March 1746. He was elected a scholar on 1 August following, and graduated BA on 16 October 1749 and MA in 1752. He was elected fellow on 14 June 1751. In 1752 he left Oxford and moved to Wigan.

In 1761 Kynaston published a Bridgman oration spoken in Brasenose College chapel, *De impietate C. Cornelio Tacito falso objectata*. In 1764 he issued *A collection of papers relative to the prosecution now carrying on in the chancellor's court in Oxford, against Mr. Kynaston, by Matthew Maddock, clerk ... for the charge of adultery alleged against the said Matthew Maddock*. He was a frequent contributor to the *Gentleman's Magazine*, and in his obituary the editor, John Nichols, wrote that Kynaston's 'friendly labours have frequently embellished our Magazine', and that Nichols's own 'literary labours were facilitated by his valuable correspondence' (*GM*, 627–8). Those friendly and literary labours were some thirty or more letters to that periodical, contributions that establish Kynaston as a scholar and critic, some of whose letters, notably on the plays of Shakespeare, should be better known. He wrote to some considerable extent on *The Tempest*, *Hamlet*, and *Othello*, and also on *Macbeth*, *A Midsummer Night's Dream*, *Antony and Cleopatra*, *All's Well that Ends Well*, *The Two Gentlemen of Verona*, *Titus Andronicus*, *Julius Caesar*, and *Richard II*. In some of his observations he anticipated later scholars and editors, such as Edmond Malone, both in emendations and glosses, and he took courteous issue with a few of Dr Johnson's notes on the plays. He was the first to explain Hamlet's 'A little more than kin, and less than kind', quoting the old play *Gorboduc* in illustration. His letters show his familiarity with the Greek and Roman writers, and also with the Elizabethan dramatists, eighteenth-century poets, and French literature. His most

extended effort was six letters, dating from January 1772 to November 1773, on 'Two curious tesserae theatrales found near Herculanem'. He wrote the Latin inscription on the monument of Dr Peter Francis le Courayer in Westminster Abbey. He also took an active part on behalf of Mary Blandy, the patricide hanged on 6 April 1752. A writer in the *Gentleman's Magazine* states that Kynaston was much with her 'from the time of her conviction till her body was secured from indecent treatment' (*GM*, 803). He died at Wigan in June 1783.

GORDON GOODWIN, *rev.* ARTHUR SHERBO

Sources *GM*, 1st ser., 53 (1783), 627–8, 803 · A. Sherbo, 'John Kynaston (1728–83), a neglected Shakespearean', *Letters to Mr Urban of the Gentleman's Magazine* (1997) · Foster, *Alum. Oxon.*

Kynder, Philip. *See* Kinder, Philip (b. 1597, d. in or after 1665).

Kynewulf. *See* Cynewulf (*fl.* 9th cent.).

Kyngesbury [Kyngusbury], **Thomas** (*fl.* 1351–1396), Franciscan friar, was a member of the Franciscan convent at Oxford by 1351, and had taken the degree of DTh there by *c*.1369. He was twenty-sixth provincial minister of the English Minorites from 1379 or 1380 to 1390 or 1392. At the beginning of the great schism he induced the English Franciscans to take an oath of adherence to Urban VI (*r.* 1378–89). He was in favour at court; about 1390 Richard II urged Boniface IX (*r.* 1389–1404) to provide him to the next vacant bishopric, and he preached before Richard on 25 March 1396. In August of that year Robert Morton of Bawtry, Nottinghamshire, escheator and knight of the shire, made a bequest of £10 to him.

Kyngesbury was buried at Nottingham. Although no writings of his remain, he clearly encouraged the study of science in his order. Thus in 1380, at the instance of Joan, princess of Wales (d. 1385), he requested the friar John Somer to write a *kalendarium* for the years 1387–1462. He also authorized a treatise on music entitled the *Quatuor principalia musice*, which was written by the Oxford Minorite John Tewkesbury (though sometimes erroneously attributed to Simon Tunstede), 'with the authority and consent of Friar Thomas de Kyngusbury, Master, Minister of England, A. D. 1388' (Little, 250–51).

A. G. LITTLE, *rev.* LINNE R. MOONEY

Sources A. G. Little, *The Grey friars in Oxford*, OHS, 20 (1892), 241, 250–1 · Emden, *Oxf.* · J. S. Brewer, ed., *Monumenta Franciscana*, 1, Rolls Series, 4 (1858), 538, 561 · L. Mooney, ed., *The kalendarium of John Somer* (1998)
Archives BL, Cotton MS Faustina A.ii, fol 2 · BL, Royal MS 2 B.viii, fol. 1 · BL, Cotton MS Vespasian E.vii, fol. 7 · Bodl. Oxf., MS Selden supra 90, 1, fol. 1

Kynnesman, Arthur (1682–1770), schoolmaster, was born in London on Christmas day 1682, the son of Harold Kynnesman, a mercer. He was educated at Christ's Hospital and, with an exhibition from his school, was admitted sizar to Trinity College, Cambridge, on 30 June 1702, whence he graduated BA (1706) and MA (1709). He was ordained deacon on 23 September 1710 and priest on 22 March 1713.

For some time Kynnesman was an usher at Westminster

School but in 1715, recommended by Robert Freind, headmaster of Westminster, he was appointed master of the grammar school at Bury St Edmunds. Here he adopted the system of teaching practised at Westminster, expanded the school to some 150 pupils, and secured for it an excellent reputation. The dramatist Richard Cumberland was a pupil and left an affectionate account of his headmaster. Kynnesman was extremely proud of his school and of his pupils' achievements, and he once boasted to his college friend Richard Bentley (Cumberland's grandfather) that he would make Cumberland as good a scholar as his grandfather, to which Bentley replied joshingly, 'Pshaw! Arthur, how can that be, when I have forgot more than thou ever knewst?' (*Memoirs*, 24). Kynnesman continued the tradition of performing school plays to audiences of parents and the local gentry, and raised money to buy books for the library by taking a collection after each play. Cumberland described him as 'an excellent master, a very sufficient scholar', who had 'all the professional requisites of voice, air and aspect, that marked him out at first sight as a personage decidedly made on purpose—*habere imperium in pueros*' (ibid., 23).

Kynnesman resigned as headmaster in 1745 and took up the post of rector of Barnham, Suffolk; for a few months in 1751 he was reader of St James's, Bury, and in 1766 he obtained the living of Eriswell in Suffolk. In 1768 he published his only work, *A Short Introduction to Grammar* (2nd edn, 1775). His wife, a former Miss Maddocks of Troston, Suffolk, died in 1766. He himself died on 10 July 1770 at Bury and was buried on 17 July at Barnham, next to his wife. W. A. J. ARCHBOLD, *rev.* S. J. SKEDD

Sources R. Cumberland, *Memoirs of Richard Cumberland written by himself* (1806), 22 ff. · Davy's Suffolk collections, XC, BL, Add. MS 19166 · Venn, *Alum. Cant.* · Nichols, *Lit. anecdotes*, 8.433; 9.554 · Nichols, *Illustrations*, 3.290–91, 848; 4.319, 376 · R. W. Elliott, *The story of King Edward VI School, Bury St Edmunds* (1963)
Likenesses J. Watson, mezzotint (after Webster) · Webster, oils; at Bury St Edmunds grammar school in 1892 · group portrait, oils; at Troston Hall, Suffok, in 1892

Kynoch, George (1834–1891), ammunition manufacturer, was born on 22 August 1834 at Peterhead, Aberdeenshire, the youngest son of John Kynoch, a journeyman tailor, and his wife. They lived in humble circumstances and after education at the local national school, Kynoch obtained employment first in an insurance office in Glasgow and then as a bank clerk in Worcester. After a short while he moved to a larger bank in Birmingham as ledger clerk. By about 1856 his financial ability and ambitious nature were already apparent and very soon he exchanged his safe employment for the dangerous manufacture of copper cap igniters and ammunition, by going to work for Pursall and Phillips of Whittall Street, Birmingham. In 1859 the factory was destroyed by explosion and nineteen of the seventy employees killed, but by September 1861 Pursall had acquired the lease of 4 acres of land at Witton in the parish of Handsworth, 3 miles northwest of Birmingham. The area was thinly populated and was close to the River Tame and the Grand Junction Railway, so ideally suited for this rapidly developing industry.

In 1862 work was conducted in two wooden sheds, the staff consisting of twelve girls supervised by Kynoch; after a short while the lease was conveyed to him. On 3 February 1863 he married Helen, the daughter of Samuel Birley, a well-to-do jeweller at Edgbaston, from whom he later separated. Aided perhaps by capital from his father-in-law as well as his own ability, Kynoch's business prospered and by 1864 Kynoch & Co. had obtained contracts for the supply of ammunition to the war department and the Turkish government.

The cartridge made of coiled brass strip and developed by Colonel Boxer, superintendent in the royal laboratory, was giving trouble and the war department wished to replace it. Kynoch, in partnership with his manager, William Whitehill, filed a patent on 1 April 1868 for improvements in cartridge construction, namely, to make the case of solid drawn brass. The Lion Works, as it became known, at Witton by now comprised large workshops and well-spaced loading sheds; Kynoch's love of speculation led him into cash flow problems and in 1870 he sold his rights to the Witton land for £8000, only to buy them back two years later with 19 acres of freehold land adjoining for £9000. The firm's rapid expansion in such a hazardous trade was not accompanied by the close attention to safe procedures that it deserved and there were four serious accidents in two years, the last in November 1870. The manufacture of ammunition, including copper percussion caps for cartridges, continued and by the late 1870s orders for up to 150 million were being handled. In 1877 Kynoch leased a metal-rolling mill in Water Street and so could control the quality of his cartridge brass.

By 1883 Kynoch was living the life of a gentleman at Hamstead Hall in Handsworth and enjoying the shooting on the 300 acre estate, while Kynoch & Co. had depots and agencies in many parts of the world. All this cost money and in 1884 a new company, G. Kynoch & Co. Ltd, was set up, with six directors and Kynoch as managing director; he was to receive a salary of £500 a year and 10 per cent of the profits. His original company was sold to this organization for £110,000.

In 1886 Kynoch was elected MP for Aston as a tory and the following year became president of the Aston Villa Football Club. These activities did not go happily with his commitments to the company and, with pursuit of his personal business interests, frequently resulted in his absence from Witton. He was well known in the Russian, Turkish, and Romanian royal courts, where he travelled to make sales. Differences with the London-based directors led to non-co-operation and friction resulted.

The first year's trading profit of the new company was £30,000 but the board required a bank overdraft which one year later stood at £50,000. Ominously, government inspectors rejected a million cartridges and the directors drew Kynoch's attention to defective supervision. In 1886 the profit was marginal: this was converted into a loss in 1887 which was increased fourfold in 1888. By 1887 relations between the board and Kynoch were seriously strained and, having obtained an independent report, the directors recorded their opinion that the constant supervision required at Witton was incompatible with the duties of a member of parliament. Early in 1888 the shareholders became aware of the company's plight and formed a committee of investigation which during the year identified the problems and outlined the remedies, in particular stressing the shortcomings of the managing director. Kynoch was asked to resign which he did by letter 'owing to the state of my health'. An action in the court of queen's bench was necessary to liquidate the debt of £14,000 he owed the company. He himself, by then a very sick man, left England for South Africa in 1890. He died in comparative poverty at Johannesburg, on 28 February 1891, and was buried there the following month.

D. H. L. BACK

Sources Under five flags: the story of Kynoch Works, Witton, Birmingham, 1862–1962 (privately printed, Birmingham, 1962) · G. Boothroyd, 'The lion's share', Shooting Times and Country Magazine (23–9 July 1992), 39–42 · D. Thomas, The Eley story, 1828–1978 (1978) · G. Kynoch & Co. records, Birm. CL, IMI archives, MS 1422 · m. cert.
Archives Birm. CL, IMI archives, G. Kynoch & Co. Ltd
Likenesses group portrait, photograph, 1887, A. Wilkes & Son, West Bromwich · colour tinted photograph, Imperial Metal Industries plc headquarters, Birmingham

Kynsige. See Cynesige (d. 1060).

Kynton, John (1450s–1536), Franciscan friar and theologian, was born in the 1450s, perhaps in Lincolnshire or Yorkshire where he is known to have had personal ties. He entered the Franciscan order at the Stamford convent, probably while still in his teens. His age might explain the fact that although he took minor orders in December 1472, he was not ordained to the priesthood until March 1477. Kynton remained at Stamford until the early 1480s when he was sent to study at the Franciscan convent at Oxford. Nothing is known of him during this period, but it seems he acquired a considerable reputation as a scholar. He incepted for his doctorate early in 1495 and was permitted to remain at the university as a teacher.

Kynton's teaching took him, unusually for a regular, beyond his own convent into the wider academic community. In 1502 he was appointed praelector in theology at Magdalen College, a residential position that he held for almost two decades. During this period Kynton emerged as one of the most influential figures in the faculty of theology. He was elected senior theologus three times between 1502 and 1530 and was deputed to preach the Easter day sermon in 1515. He also became prominent in university government, serving as the chancellor's commissary for no fewer than seven terms between 1503 and 1517. Kynton's stature as a scholar also brought him to the attention of church leaders. In 1521 he was one of five scholars called upon by Cardinal Wolsey to examine the teachings of Martin Luther. It may have been as a result of this that he was appointed to the university's most prestigious chair, the Lady Margaret professorship in theology. Kynton remained in post for several years, but early in 1530 his reputation was badly damaged when the archbishop of Canterbury, William Warham, accused him of forgery. The details of the case are obscure, but it is likely to have precipitated his resignation from his chair in October 1530. In spite of these troubles Kynton remained at Oxford and was involved in scholarly discussions of the king's divorce in 1531. He died at Oxford on 20 January 1536 and was buried in Durham College chapel.

JAMES G. CLARK

Sources Emden, Oxf., 2.1053 · LP Henry VIII · W. D. Macray, A register of the members of St Mary Magdalen College, Oxford, 8 vols. (1894–1915) · Hist. U. Oxf. 3: Colleg. univ. · [J. Raine], ed., Testamenta Eboracensia, 4, SurtS, 53 (1869), 69n.

Kynyngham, John. See Kenningham, John (d. 1399).

Kynynmound, Gilbert Elliot Murray [formerly Gilbert Elliot], **first earl of Minto** (1751–1814), governor-general of Bengal, was born on 23 April 1751, at Grey Friars, Edinburgh, the eldest son of Sir Gilbert *Elliot, third baronet (1722–1777), of Minto, Roxburghshire, and Agnes (d. 1778), daughter and heir of Hugh Dalrymple-Murray-Kynynmound of Melgund, Forfarshire, and Lochgelly and Kynynmound, Fife.

Education and early career Despite his impoverished estate, Elliot's father made enough from government office as a 'king's friend' between 1756 and 1777 to have Elliot and his brother Hugh *Elliot (1752–1830) educated privately by the future diplomat Robert Liston from 1762, and then sent to Paris between 1764 and 1766, where the philosopher and historian David Hume arranged for their education at the Pension Militaire, Fontainebleau. Their classmates included the future revolutionary Honoré-Gabriel Riqueti, comte de Mirabeau. Two years at Edinburgh University (1766–8) followed, after which Elliot went to Christ Church, Oxford, matriculating on 9 November 1768, and entered Lincoln's Inn on 18 April 1769. After a further visit to Paris in 1770 and a tour of the Low Countries and the Rhineland in 1773, he was called to the bar in May 1774. He practised on the northern circuit and in arguing election petitions at Westminster, where his defence of Charles James Fox over the disputed election at Poole, in which Fox had been defeated, earned the latter's respect. In July 1776 Elliot was returned as MP for Morpeth by Frederick Howard, fifth earl of Carlisle, who later worked closely with Elliot's brother-in-law, William *Eden, later first Baron Auckland (1744–1814), in a series of offices in North's ministry. On his father's death in January 1777 Elliot succeeded him as fourth baronet and in the Minto estate, and in February 1777 he also succeeded his father as MP for Roxburghshire, a seat he retained until 1784. On 3 January 1777, at St George's, Hanover Square, Elliot had married Anna Maria (1752–1829), eldest daughter of Sir George Amyand, first baronet; he had first met her in London in 1772. They had four sons and three daughters. On his mother's death on 28 December 1778, he inherited his mother's Fife and Forfarshire estates, and assumed the additional names of Murray Kynynmound, although he seems to have continued to be known as Sir Gilbert Elliot.

Elliot assumed the role of an independent supporter of government in the Commons. At North's request he made his maiden speech on 18 November 1777 in seconding the

Gilbert Elliot Murray Kynynmound, first earl of Minto (1751–1814), by George Chinnery, c.1811–12

address to the throne, which he delivered well, though he admitted to being 'vastly terrified' (*Life and Letters*, 130). Particular political influences on him were Eden, the diplomat Sir James Harris, later first earl of Malmesbury, husband of his sister-in-law, and, increasingly, the opposition spokesman Edmund Burke, whose eloquence he admired and whose interest in Indian issues he shared. Elliot was a diffident speaker and became disillusioned with the government's conduct of the American war. He applied himself to prison reform, becoming one of the three supervisors of the new penitentiaries established by the first session of the 1780 parliament. He also paid attention to Indian issues, as an active member of the Commons select committee on the Bengal judiciary, to which he was nominated on 14 February 1781. As an East India Company proprietor, whose brother Alexander (d. 1778) was secretary to and a protégé of Warren Hastings, he trod a difficult path as attacks developed against the latter's governor-generalship.

In 1781 Elliot toured the major courts of central and eastern Europe, visiting Berlin, St Petersburg, Warsaw, and Vienna, while bringing his wife's sister back from Russia. This convinced him that all Europe favoured American independence, and defeats in America persuaded him

that the war was impracticable. He broke ranks with the North ministry to vote for Henry Seymour Conway's motion on 22 February to end the war, and declared to the Commons on 27 February 1782 'that the nation, the House of Commons and the ministers had been for a long time in the wrong; and he could no longer, with justice to his constituents, support their measures' (Cobbett, *Parl. hist.*, 22.1084). When a long-time silent supporter of North's government spoke out in this way, the effect was sensational: 'The effect … was to fix all the wavering well-wishers in the same line with Sir Gilbert' (Lord Loughborough to Eden, 1 March 1782, BL, Add. MS 34418, fol. 337). On 15 March he again voted against the tottering ministry, which resigned on 20 March. Though ignored by the new Rockingham administration, Elliot admired Fox's abilities, and followed Fox into opposition after Rockingham's death in July, rejecting offers of place from Rockingham's successor, William Petty, earl of Shelburne. Pulmonary disease took him in the autumn to recover in Nice; he returned in early 1783 to take Mirabeau (expensively) into his society for the latter's tour of Britain. At this point the coalition of Fox and North to eject Shelburne united his new and former friends in power. Burke and Fox consulted him on their controversial East India bill, and he was nominated as one of the seven parliamentary commissioners to administer Indian affairs. However, when the bill was defeated and the coalition fell, his name among the unpopular 'seven kings' (H. Twiss, *Life of Lord Eldon*, 1844, 1.163) wrecked his repeated attempts to win a seat at the ensuing 1784 general election.

Opposition to Pitt the younger Elliot's diffidence had prevented him from speaking out against what he felt to be William Pitt's reprehensible snatching of power by an unconstitutional intrigue, Pitt having allegedly collaborated with the crown against the interest of the Commons. 'If his passions were equal to his abilities, he would play a leading part', declared his brother-in-law Eden (*Life and Letters*, 283–4). He lacked ambition to play the political game at the highest level. 'My philosophy or my indolence makes me well satisfied with the prospect of some leisure for self improvement', he admitted (ibid., 284). He was also in financial difficulty with the Treasury, which demanded repayment of £10,000 of his father's balances as treasurer of the chamber. Eden, on the point of joining Pitt's government, persuaded Pitt to defer payment, but Elliot's hostility was still such that when he did return to the Commons, for Berwick upon Tweed in 1786, he rejoined the ranks of opposition.

Despite Burke's exhortation that 'You *must* be less modest … You must be all that you can be, and you can be everything' (*Life and Letters*, 1.114), delicacy about his dead brother, who was potentially implicated in the charges against Warren Hastings, kept Elliot from taking a leading part in bringing the charges against Hastings, though he eventually became one of the Commons' managers of Hastings's impeachment in 1788. Instead he took the lead in bringing charges against the Bengal chief justice, Sir Elijah Impey, but despite a brilliant opening speech on 12 December 1787 the charges were rejected in the following

May. On the death of the speaker of the House of Commons, Charles Wolfran Cornwall, during the regency crisis, the opposition nominated him on 5 January 1789 for the chair. The opposition talked of him as a possible chancellor of the exchequer, should they get into power. Both their leader, William Henry Cavendish Bentinck, third duke of Portland, and the prince of Wales (afterwards George IV), made use of his drafting skills for letters and memorials during the crisis, and in June 1789 he was again unsuccessfully opposition candidate for the speakership.

At the dissolution in 1790 Elliot again withdrew from politics, disillusioned by opposition failures and deterred by the potential cost of re-election at Berwick, but appeals from the duke of Portland and the offer of a seat at Helston in Cornwall, obtained for him by Malmesbury, brought him back to the Commons in December. His concern for civil liberties led him into moving unsuccessfully a petition to abolish the Test Act for members of the Church of Scotland in May 1791, and into supporting the attempt to abolish the slave trade in April 1792. However, he took Burke's side in the growing split within the opposition over the French Revolution and political reform within Britain, joining Malmesbury in efforts to persuade its leader, Portland, to speak out against Fox's attacks on government measures against sedition. In a speech supporting the Aliens Bill on 28 December 1792, he publicly exposed the split between Portland and Fox, claiming Portland's authorization. When Portland retracted, the Foxites blamed Elliot for deliberately exacerbating divisions and precipitating the break-up of the opposition that followed.

Viceroy of Corsica In February 1793 Elliot was among those who seceded from the Whig Club, along with William Windham, forming a 'third party' to support government measures from outside the ministry. In May his wife's concern for their young children's health led him to decline a government offer of the governorship of Madras, and in June he rejected the Irish secretaryship, before finally agreeing in August to be civil commissioner of Dunkirk, should the siege be successful and the port fall to the allies. Elliot had interested himself in the plight of the French émigrés in London, and when the siege of Dunkirk failed he was the obvious choice to take up a similar position at Toulon after it surrendered to the protection of the British fleet under Samuel Hood, Baron and later first Viscount Hood. His appointment and admission to the privy council followed on 25 September 1793, but Toulon fell within weeks of his arrival. Hood then entrusted him with negotiations with the Corsican leader Pascal Paoli for the cession of Corsica to Britain in January 1794. While returning from the island to Leghorn, he was twice rescued from shipwreck. Between March and May 1794 he was British minister to the Italian states, working to promote a confederacy for permanent defence against French attack. He moved to Corsica as provisional viceroy in June. Portland, now home secretary in the Pitt ministry, recommended his confirmation to George III for 'the moderation, the prudence, the judgement & the general ability' (*Later Correspondence of George III*, 2.252–3) he had

shown in his successful negotiations. The king gave his approval on 23 August and Elliot finally received his commission on 1 October, becoming the first and last British viceroy of Corsica.

Elliot's two years and four months as viceroy were controversial. He had difficulty asserting his authority over Paoli and his followers, and ultimately requested permission and was allowed to expel the Corsican leader from the island. He also had difficulty asserting his authority over the prickly army commander, Major-General (later Sir) Charles Stuart, and faced repeated disputes over military–civil relations. Stuart threw up his command, in February 1795, and Elliot had to require the recall of the able Lieutenant-Colonel John Moore, who he felt was taking Paoli's part against him. Elliot was accused of falling too much under the influence of the Corsican president of the council of state, Pozzo di Borgo, who had broken with Paoli, and of making too many concessions to appease Corsican unrest.

Nevertheless Elliot kept endemically unruly Corsica in British hands until October 1796, when Spanish entry into the war compelled British evacuation of the Mediterranean. Elliot withdrew to Naples, leaving in January 1797 on an adventurous voyage during which, with Captain Horatio Nelson, he escaped a pursuing Spanish squadron and was then eyewitness to Sir John Jervis's victory over the Spanish fleet at Cape St Vincent on 14 February. He landed at Plymouth on 5 March, somewhat under a cloud after his turbulent viceroyalty, and remained without employment. After some months of pressure Pitt compensated him with a peerage instead, telling the king that 'he will certainly not be useless in the house of Lords as a man of business' (*Later Correspondence of George III*, 2.262). On 20 October 1797 he was made Baron Minto of Minto, Roxburghshire. His additional surnames of Murray Kynynmound had been confirmed by royal licence on 2 October 1797.

Diplomacy and politics In the Lords, Minto experienced the same diffidence in speaking as he had in the Commons and, despairing of making his way by that means, he offered himself in January 1799 to the foreign secretary, William Wyndham Grenville, Baron Grenville, to undertake any diplomatic mission on the continent. A year earlier Grenville had rejected the king's similar suggestion for fear of Minto's 'too great eagerness & zeal' (ibid., 3.9–10), but Minto's standing improved with a powerful speech in favour of union with Ireland on 11 April (subsequently published), so that, after two others turned down the post of envoy-extraordinary and minister-plenipotentiary to Austria, Grenville offered it to Minto in June. Taking Pozzo di Borgo, who thereby began a distinguished diplomatic career that climaxed in Russian service, he reached Vienna in August. In 1799 relations between Britain and Austria were at a low ebb, yet co-operation was vital in fighting the renewed continental war. He was initially unable to persuade the Austrian minister, Johann Amadeus Franz de Paula Thugut, Baron Thugut, to co-operate in British plans, but later incurred Grenville's wrath on the grounds that his relations with Thugut were excessively close. Minto's elegantly composed but prolix dispatches aroused adverse comment and even Minto apologized for their length. His good relations with Thugut paid off in the following year when the withdrawal of Russia from the war brought Britain and Austria into a new alliance, concluded on 20 June 1800. Its effect was immediately nullified, however, by the Austrian defeat at Marengo, after which Minto again incurred Grenville's displeasure by failing to send frequent reports on the situation, and he offended the Austrian court by his efforts to maintain the pro-war Thugut in power. Austria's withdrawal from the war in February 1801, followed by news of the resignation of Pitt, Grenville, and his fellow Burkeite, Windham, over the issue of Catholic emancipation which he warmly endorsed, led him to request recall, arriving in London at the end of November.

Minto's fear of the French Revolution led him to throw in his lot with Grenville and Windham, who opposed the peace that Henry Addington's government negotiated with France. In February 1803 he was elected a fellow of the Royal Society and of the Royal Society of Edinburgh. He followed Grenville and Windham into the combined opposition with Fox, which helped bring down Addington's ministry in April 1804, rejecting Pitt's attempts to lure him away from them and into his new ministry. He told his wife that he would act with those with whom he had been connected all his life in friendship as well as politics, adding that

> I am not at all insensible to the attractions of power or the private conveniences of office; but it is fortunate for me that my ambition has always been temperate and could never interfere with what I thought my public duty or disturb my private tranquillity and comfort.   (*Life and Letters*, 3.329)

Governor-general of Bengal Office came when Grenville succeeded to the premiership on Pitt's death in January 1806. Fox thought the newness of Minto's peerage would make him unacceptable to the Scottish nobility for the great seal of Scotland; Grenville offered him instead the presidency of the Board of Control for India but without its former seat in the cabinet. Although it was the office 'which I should have preferred almost to any other, in many respects' (*Life and Letters*, 3.379), Minto was quickly moved on in July to the governor-generalship of Bengal (with authority over all British possessions in India) as compromise candidate when James Maitland, eighth earl of Lauderdale, proved unacceptable to the East India Company directors. He accepted, reluctantly, in order to acquire the fortune to back his title, telling his wife that 'the general benefit of all those who depend on me for the comforts that extend beyond my own short period, would undoubtedly be best provided for by this measure' (ibid., 3.394). The diarist Joseph Farington was later told that Minto realized £245,000 from his governor-generalship (Farington, *Diary*, 13.4617), but this is unlikely as his stipend was only £25,000 a year and most reports of his character suggest that he was too honest to be involved in corruption. The unhealthy tropical climate led his wife and daughters to stay behind with his oldest son Gilbert [*see* Kynynmound, Gilbert Elliot Murray, second earl of Minto], but he sailed in a frigate commanded by his naval son, George [*see* Elliot, Sir George], and in which his youngest son was a midshipman, and was reunited with his third son, John Edmund, who had gone to India as an East India Company writer in 1805 and whom he made his private secretary.

Minto reached Calcutta at the end of July 1807. Traditionally his tenure of office has not been well regarded by historians, being seen as part of the quiet interval between the dynamic and expansive governor-generalships of Richard Wellesley, Marquess Wellesley, and Francis Rawdon Hastings, first marquess of Hastings. Leaving Britain when the outcry against Wellesley's costly conquests was at its height, and arriving after a sepoy rebellion at Vellore in 1806 showed underlying unrest fuelled by religious tensions, he intended a policy of retrenchment so that India might enjoy repose in which prosperity could be restored. One of his earliest steps was to restrain the aggressive publications and preaching of Christian missionaries operating from Serampur, in which he received the backing of the company and the home government but the fury of the evangelicals.

Concern to avoid disruption within India, however, led Minto into a policy of forward defence when Napoleon's treaties with Persia and Russia in 1807 and a French military mission to Persia seemed to presage an overland advance on India. Encouraged by Wellesley's former protégé, John Malcolm, in 1808 Minto sent missions to Persia, Afghanistan (the first British mission there), Lahore, and Sind, to drive out French influence and seek allies. These prototype attempts at a north-west frontier policy beyond India's borders met with little success, as the states to which they were addressed were more interested in securing British help against each other than against the French. British–Persian relations were rescued from the damage of Malcolm's bullying only by the more tactful diplomacy of Sir Harford Jones, sent from London by the Foreign Office, with whom Minto allowed himself to become embroiled in a battle of jurisdictions. A treaty concluded with the ruler of Afghanistan in April 1809 was immediately nullified by his overthrow. When the wily Raja Ranjit Singh of Lahore evaded attempts to tie him down, Minto decided to curb his power and advance British influence by taking under company protection the Sikh confederacies between the Jumna and the Sutlej.

In the meantime, the Spanish revolt in 1808 removed fears of Napoleon's presumed plans against India, enabling Minto to take a wider view of the British presence in the East. He exploited British naval supremacy and military power in India by launching a series of amphibious expeditions to remove threats to British trade in the area. In 1809 expeditions were sent against the corsairs of the Persian Gulf, and to assume protection of the Portuguese trading factory at Macao on the southern coast of China. Though the latter had to be withdrawn in the face of Chinese opposition, further forces occupied the Dutch spice island of Amboyna, and the rest of the Moluccas early in

1810. Sustained by the economic recovery of the subcontinent, Minto then embarked in 1810–11 on his most ambitious and successful operations: the seizure of the Isle de Bourbon and Mauritius from France (1810), and of Java from the Dutch (1811). The attack on Java was prepared in consultation with Minto's agent to the Malay states, Stamford Raffles. He took the extraordinary step of accompanying the Java expedition himself in his son's frigate, asserting the need to 'see all the political work done to my mind' (*Minto in India*, 249–50) with regard to future relations with the Dutch and with the native rulers, but probably seeking an escape from 'this torrid zone of trouble and fatigue' (ibid., 83) in which he wearied of the immensely bureaucratic straitjacket of Indian administration. His presence speeded the success of the enterprise when he overbore the caution of the naval commander, Commodore Broughton.

Minto returned to Calcutta in late 1811, when he applied himself to reforming the East India Company bureaucracy to accommodate the new conquests. Having sanctioned the creation of a new finance department from within the public department in 1810, he then established a colonial department to administer the new overseas conquests in 1812.

Minto was allowed to continue in office when Grenville's ministry fell in 1807, but lack of strong backing in London thereafter restricted his freedom of action. When it was finally decided to recall him in 1813, he was compensated with promotion in the peerage to Viscount Melgund and earl of Minto on 24 February. He left India in October and reached Britain in May 1814, but caught a chill at the funeral of his brother-in-law, Auckland, which weakened his constitution as he sought to travel on to Scotland, and he died at Stevenage, Hertfordshire, on 21 June 1814, of 'a stranguary, a complaint to which he had long been subject' (Farington, *Diary*, 13.4617). He was buried in Westminster Abbey on 29 June 1814.

Shelburne's commendation of Minto's 'good manners and good sense' (G. Elliot, *Life and Letters*, 1.82, n. 1) was among many. His private letters show him as attentive to his family, but so much correspondence exists because for at least part of most years after 1786, when his wife barely survived the difficult birth of short-lived twins, they led separate lives as his wife disliked London. But Minto had his detractors. Elizabeth Vassall Fox, Lady Holland, thought his display of private virtues those of 'a crafty hypocritical man, with *moeurs* in his mouth and sin in the heart' (*Journal of Elizabeth, Lady Holland*, 1.161), and 'it was a well kept secret' that he had a second family, 'without benefit of clergy' (Thorne).   MICHAEL DUFFY

Sources *Life and letters of Sir Gilbert Elliot, first earl of Minto, from 1751 to 1806*, ed. countess of Minto [E. E. E. Elliot-Murray-Kynynmound], 3 vols. (1874) · *Lord Minto in India: life and letters of Gilbert Elliot, first earl of Minto, from 1807 to 1814*, ed. E. E. E. Elliot-Murray-Kynynmound (1880) · E. Haden-Guest, 'Elliot, Gilbert', HoP, *Commons, 1754–90* · R. G. Thorne, 'Elliot Murray Kynynmound, Sir Gilbert', HoP, *Commons, 1790–1820* · DNB · D. Gregory, *The ungovernable rock: a history of the Anglo-Corsican kingdom and its role in Britain's Mediterranean strategy during the Revolutionary War, 1793–1797* (1985) ·

A. Majumder, 'Lord Minto's administration in India, 1807–13', DPhil diss., U. Oxf., 1962 · M. E. Yapp, *Strategies of British India: Britain, Iran and Afghanistan, 1798–1850* (1980) · P. Kelly, 'Strategy and counter-revolution: the journal of Sir Gilbert Elliot, 1–22 September 1793', EngHR, 98 (1983), 328–48 · E. E. E. Elliot Murray Kynynmound, countess of Minto, ed., *A memoir of the Rt Hon. Hugh Elliot* (1868) · Cobbett, *Parl. hist.*, vol. 22 · *The later correspondence of George III*, ed. A. Aspinall, 5 vols. (1962–70), vols. 2–3 · *The journal of Elizabeth, Lady Holland, 1791–1811*, ed. earl of Ilchester [G. S. Holland Fox-Strangways], 2 vols. (1908), vol. 1 · Farington, *Diary*, 13 · GEC, *Peerage*, new edn, 8.713–14 · W. P. Baildon, ed., *The records of the Honorable Society of Lincoln's Inn: admissions*, 2 vols. (1896)

Archives BL OIOC, corresp. and papers relating to India, Home misc. series · BL OIOC, corresp. and papers relating to Java, MS Eur. F. 148 · Cleveland Public Library, letters · NL Scot., corresp. · NL Scot., corresp. and papers · NMM, corresp. and papers as commissioner at Toulon and viceroy of Corsica | BL, letters to Lord Auckland, Add. MSS 34415–34457, *passim* · BL, corresp. with Francis Drake, Add. MSS 46825, 46833 · BL, corresp. with Lord Grenville, Add. MS 58945 · BL, corresp. with Lord Nelson, Add. MSS 34901–34913, *passim* · BL, corresp. with Sir Arthur Paget and Count Von Colloredo, Add. MS 48395 [some copies] · BL, corresp. with William Windham, Add. MS 37852 · Hants. RO, corresp. with William Wickham · Herefs. RO, corresp. with Sir Harford Jones · NA Scot., letters to Colonel Drinkwater · NA Scot., letters to Sir Alexander Hope · NA Scot., corresp. with Lord Melville · NL Scot., corresp. with Sir Robert Liston · NL Scot., corresp. with Lord Melville · NMM, letters to Lord Nelson · NRA, priv. coll., corresp. with Lord Elgin · PRO NIre., corresp. with earl of Caledon · Sheff. Arch., corresp. with Edmund Burke · Shrops. RRC, corresp. with Lord Berwick and Joseph Brame

Likenesses Lawrence, portrait, *c*.1793 · G. Chinnery, portrait, *c*.1811–1812, Scot. NPG [*see illus.*] · J. Atkinson, oils, NPG

Wealth at death see Farington, *Diary*, vol. 13, col. 4617

Kynynmound, Gilbert Elliot Murray [*formerly* Gilbert Elliot], **second earl of Minto (1782–1859)**, diplomatist and politician, was the eldest son of Gilbert Elliot Murray *Kynynmound, first earl of Minto (1751–1814), and his wife, Anna Maria (1752–1829), daughter of Sir George Amyand, first baronet; in 1797 the elder Gilbert Elliot took, by royal licence, the additional name of Murray Kynynmound. The younger Gilbert was born at Lyons on 16 November 1782 into one of the great whig families, and was first educated privately by a Mr Somerville before attending Eton College (1796–9). He was admitted at Edinburgh University in 1801 and at St John's College, Cambridge, in 1803, and was afterwards trained for the diplomatic service, without, however, any immediate object. On 4 September 1806 he married Mary Brydone (1786–1853), eldest daughter of Patrick *Brydone of Lennel House, near Berwick. They had five sons and five daughters.

In 1806 and 1807 Kynynmound was member of parliament for Ashburton, Devon, and he sat for Roxburghshire from 1812 until March 1814 (being styled Viscount Melgund during 1813–14) as Lord Minto. On the death of his father he took his seat in the House of Lords as Lord Minto. On the formation of Lord Grey's ministry he was sworn of the privy council on 15 August 1832. In that month he went as British ambassador to Berlin, where he remained for two years. Although his tenure of office was uneventful, following his return on 16 September 1834 he was

Gilbert Elliot Murray Kynynmound, second earl of Minto
(1782–1859), by George Zobel, pubd 1851 (after Sir Francis Grant,
1842)

awarded the GCB. On the appointment of Lord Auckland
as governor-general of India, Minto succeeded to his post
as first lord of the Admiralty in September 1835, and continued to preside over naval affairs until 1841. It was said at
the time that his period of office was distinguished only
by the outcry raised at the number of Elliots who found
places in the naval service.

In Lord John Russell's cabinet of 1846 Minto, whose second daughter, Frances Anna Maria *Russell, had married
Lord John in 1841, became lord privy seal, and in September 1847 he was dispatched on a diplomatic mission to
Italy to ingratiate Sardinia and Tuscany, to assist in
carrying out the reforms suggested by Pius IX on his accession, and generally to report to the home government on
Italian affairs. Partly owing, no doubt, to the French revolution of 1848, the tour was an acknowledged failure. Its
sole practical result was that Minto induced the king of
Naples to grant the Sicilians a separate parliament. The
papacy claimed that Minto gave it to understand that the
British government would be favourable to the parcelling
out of England into Roman Catholic episcopal sees.

On his return Minto resumed his ministerial duties,
encouraging Lord John Russell in his plans for a reform
bill. After Russell's resignation in 1852 he continued to sit
and vote in the House of Lords, but otherwise took no part
in politics. He was an indifferent speaker and was undistinguished by administrative capacity, but possessed considerable political influence. He was a fellow of the Royal
Society, a trustee of the British Museum, an elder brother

of Trinity House, and deputy lieutenant for Roxburghshire. Minto died, after a long illness, at 48 Eaton Square,
London, on 31 July 1859.

ALSAGER VIAN, rev. H. C. G. MATTHEW

Sources GEC, *Peerage* · Boase, *Mod. Eng. biog.* · HoP, *Commons,
1790–1820*, 3.692–3 · Venn, *Alum. Cant.* · *The Times* (2 Aug 1859) · *GM*,
3rd ser., 7 (1859), 306 · P. Mandler, *Aristocratic government in the age of
reform: whigs and liberals, 1830–1852* (1990)
Archives NL Scot., corresp. and papers · NMM, Admiralty
corresp. and papers | BL, corresp. with Sir Charles Napier, Add.
MSS 40020–40039 · BL, corresp. with Lord Palmerston, Add. MSS
48480–48482 · NA Scot., letters to Thomas, Lord Cochrane · NA
Scot., letters to Sir John Dalrymple, eighth earl of Stair · NL Scot.,
letters to Sir John Murray · NMM, letters to Sir Charles Napier ·
NMM, letters to Sir William Parker · PRO, corresp. with Lord Granville, PRO 030/29 · RS, letters to Sir John Herschel · U. Edin. L., let-
ters to David Laing · U. Southampton L., corresp. with Lord Pal-
merston · W. Sussex RO, letters to W. S. Badcock · W. Sussex RO,
letters to duke of Richmond · Woburn Abbey, letters to Lord
George William Russell
Likenesses G. Zobel, mezzotint, pubd 1851 (after F. Grant, 1842),
BM, NPG [*see illus.*] · Butler, oils (after F. Grant), Gov. Art Coll. · plaster medallion; replica, Scot. NPG
Wealth at death £30,423 12s. 9d.: inventory, 4 Dec 1859, NA Scot.,
SC 62/44/31/317 · £18,556 7s. 11d.: additional estate in Scotland, 4
Dec 1859, NA Scot., SC 62/44/31/317 · £11,867 4s. 10d.: additional
estate in England, 4 Dec 1859, NA Scot., SC 62/44/31/317

Kynynmound, Gilbert John Elliot Murray, fourth earl
of Minto (1845–1914), governor-general of Canada and
viceroy of India, was born in London on 9 July 1845, the
eldest son of William Hugh Elliot Murray Kynynmound,
third earl of Minto (1814–1891), and his wife, Emma Eleanor Elizabeth (Nina) (d. 1882), the daughter of Lieutenant-
General Sir Thomas *Hislop.

Early life Born at his maternal grandfather's home in London, Kynynmound grew up and received his early education at Minto Castle, near Hawick, Roxburghshire, in the
Scottish lowlands. He entered Eton College in 1859, and in
1864 went to Trinity College, Cambridge, where he
enjoyed an academically undistinguished but socially
happy life devoted largely to sports, principally racing. In
1859, on the death of his grandfather, he inherited the
courtesy title Viscount Melgund. On his graduation in
1867 his family purchased him a commission in the fashionable Scots guards, where, apart from his minimal military guard and ceremonial duties, he spent the next two
years pursuing his passions for hunting, rowing, and
racing. He then joined his friend Cat Richardson at the
Machell stables in Limber Magna, Lincolnshire, where he
raced under the name Mr Rolly—his most notable success
being the French grand national in 1874 at Auteuil. Twice
during these years he served as a war correspondent: in
1870 to report for *The Scotsman* on the Paris commune, and
in 1874 for the *Morning Post* on the Carlist cause, for which
he had a great sympathy. When a racing accident terminated his racing career in 1876 Melgund embarked on a
number of military adventures. In April 1877 he served as
war correspondent for the *Morning Post*, reporting on the
Russo-Turkish War; and in November of the following
year he set off for the Second Anglo-Afghan War as a freelance adventurer whom Major-General Frederick Roberts

Gilbert John Elliot Murray Kynynmound, fourth earl of Minto (1845–1914), by Philip A. de Laszlo, 1912

subsequently made his aide-de-camp. Finally, in 1882, his family friend Sir Garnet Wolseley gave him a place in the expeditionary force sent out to subdue Arabi Pasha. He sustained a slight hand wound in battle, a token of military engagement sufficient to press his claim for promotion to major.

First contact with Canada On 28 July 1883 Melgund married Mary Caroline (1858–1940), the daughter of General Sir Charles Grey, private secretary to Queen Victoria. She was a charming, intelligent person closely connected to the court. His marriage, together with his father's declining health, obliged him to adopt a more stable, conventional life. Just before his marriage, Lord Lansdowne, a close family friend and the newly appointed governor-general of Canada, offered to make Melgund his military secretary. Since the position was scarcely demanding, Melgund accepted this and a number of other assignments which broadened his knowledge of Canada. In August 1884 he supervised the recruitment and dispatch of a contingent of 367 Canadian boatmen to assist Sir Garnet Wolseley's relief force sent to rescue General Charles Gordon at Khartoum. Shortly before, he had served on a small committee created by the Canadian minister of militia, A.-P. Caron, to

examine the condition of Canada's coastal defences against the United States. Melgund's report recommended, among other things, the creation of a naval militia. Perhaps Melgund's most significant Canadian position was as chief of staff to Major-General F. D. Middleton during the north-west rebellion. Appointed to this post in March 1885, Melgund remained almost to the end of the campaign, when he was sent to Ottawa with Middleton's instruction to sound out the Canadian government on the possibility of seeking British regular reinforcements, a request made unnecessary by the restless Canadian militia's successful decision to storm Batoche and end the métis resistance. Three months later Melgund returned to Britain, owing to family pressures and his deteriorating relations with Lansdowne. His knowledge of Canada had been deepened and his ambitions whetted by the prediction of the Canadian prime minister, John A. Macdonald, that someday Canada would welcome him back as governor-general.

Meanwhile, in June 1886 Melgund unsuccessfully contested the Hexham constituency in Northumberland for the Liberal Unionists. He then returned to the routine management of his ailing father's 16,071 acre Scottish lowland estates, a responsibility which entailed numerous local civic duties. In 1886 he became deputy lord lieutenant of Roxburghshire and in 1892 deputy lord lieutenant of Selkirk. The increasing tedium of these responsibilities and his failing efforts to improve the solvency of his family's estates encouraged his interest in alternative activities, which was only partially satisfied by his continued interest in the military, especially his promotion of the voluntary movement.

Governor-general of Canada In March 1898 Minto, as he had become after his father's death on 17 March 1891, heard of Lord Aberdeen's imminent retirement as governor-general of Canada. He began a discreet campaign to succeed him, and achieved his aim with the assistance of his wife's court influence, War Office support, and the active solicitations of his Liberal Unionist brother Arthur. Contrary to what Liberal autonomist Canadian historians have written, Minto was not Joseph Chamberlain's first choice or that of the Colonial Office. Later he frequently disagreed with the colonial secretary's actions, and the Colonial Office did not always approve of Minto's vice-regal behaviour.

Minto's first years as governor-general were turbulent. Inspired by the British court, he was determined to establish more formal social protocol at Rideau Hall, in preference to Aberdeen's more casual and democratic regime. His misjudgement and misunderstanding of the Canadian government's initial reluctance to dispatch Canadian troops to South Africa in October 1899, and his public criticism of their actions, convinced many at the time and since that he had dragooned Canada into participation in this war. In fact Minto had little sympathy for Chamberlain's pre-war policy in South Africa, doubted the need for Canada's participation, and warned Chamberlain against pushing the Canadian government too hard on this issue. Similarly his partisan support for the military reforms proposed by his friend Major-General E. T. H. Hutton, the general officer commanding the Canadian militia, and Minto's ill-advised and abortive attempts to stop the Canadian government from dismissing the general in January 1900 for insubordination, nearly led to the Canadian government's resignation. It also alarmed the Colonial Office, which promptly arranged for the general's recall and dispatch to South Africa. All these factors combined to create the impression that Minto was little more than an autocratic proconsul, out of touch with Canadian life. But he learned from his early mistakes, and in 1904, when one of Hutton's successors, Lord Dundonald, quarrelled with the Canadian government and had to be returned to Britain, Minto lost no time seeking his recall.

Nevertheless Minto retained a very broad view of his viceregal powers and responsibilities, and he was prepared to enter into some unseemly disputes with the Canadian government over the bestowal of honours, the right to recommend Canadians for commissions in the British army, and arrangements for an official commemorative service for Queen Victoria. He was particularly insistent on advising on military questions which he felt had imperial implications. In 1900 he attempted to prevent the minister of militia, Frederick Borden, from restoring paragraphs in the Canadian Militia Act's orders and regulations granting seniority in the Canadian militia by date of appointment in the Canadian militia, which would have disadvantaged imperial officers loaned to the Canadian militia who brought their seniority with them. More important were his attempts to block Borden's revisions to the Militia Act which proposed investing the post of commander-in-chief of the Canadian militia in the king rather than in the governor-general, opening command of the Canadian militia to an officer of the militia, and ending the requirement that the militia be brought under the king's regulations in time of war. He also opposed the committee of imperial defence's agreement to turn over command of the British garrisons in Halifax and Esquimalt to the Canadian government. His public endorsement of Chamberlain's campaign for imperial preference aroused a chorus of opposition from Canadian opponents of the idea.

More successful, though not necessarily less controversial, was Minto's use of his office to protect minorities from administrative abuse. This concerned especially native people, for whom he felt a particular obligation, but also the northern miners. His actions did nothing to endear him to his political advisers. During his Canadian tenure he organized the National Patriotic Fund to care for Canada's soldiers from the Second South African War and their dependants; he founded the Canadian Association for the Prevention of Tuberculosis; and he supported Joseph-Elzear Bernier's Arctic explorations, which aimed to establish Canadian Arctic sovereignty. He also attempted to rescue Canada's historical heritage from destruction and donated the Minto cup for senior amateur lacrosse.

Although his tenure was not a propitious one for the settlement of Canadian–American differences, through encouragement and social diplomacy Minto attempted to resolve difficulties during meetings of the Joint International High Commission in 1898–9 and throughout his years in Ottawa. He intervened on several occasions to encourage a settlement of the contentious Alaska boundary dispute, naively insisting that Wilfrid Laurier honour the Canadian commitment even after the Americans had violated the terms of the agreement for settlement by appointing partisan 'jurists'. Consequently he was angered by the unfavourable outcome. He was convinced that his friend Lord Alverstone, England's lord chief justice, had made a diplomatic rather than a judicial decision, and did not mince his words in private correspondence in telling him so.

Although many Canadians saw him as a stiff and wooden stickler for protocol, unfamiliar with life outside the stifling confines of Rideau Hall, Minto in fact enjoyed breaking away from the constraints of official life. He toured extensively and developed a sympathetic knowledge of, affection for, and understanding of Canada, especially the exhilarating Canadian west. Before he left the country on 18 November 1904 he toyed with the idea of building a home at the foothills of the Rockies in sight of the Bow River and making Canada his home.

Viceroy of India However, Minto's career as an imperial statesman was not over. After eight months' rest at home in Scotland he was appointed in August 1905 by the Conservative government as viceroy of India to succeed Lord Curzon, whose term in office had proved highly controversial. Mary, countess of Minto, said that the appointment came as a 'bolt from the blue'. Only a fortnight after the Mintos arrived in India in November 1905 a new Liberal government was elected with a large majority, and John Morley, the admirer and biographer of Burke, Cobden, and Gladstone, was made secretary of state for India. Morley and Minto were to serve together for five years and to give their names jointly to a set of Indian constitutional reforms passed in 1909. Although the two men broadly agreed on the principles of policy in India, there was a good deal of jockeying for supremacy between them. This was partly a matter of a clash between two strong personalities from opposite ends of the political spectrum, but partly also an attempt by Whitehall to reassert the correct constitutional standing between London and Simla after the previous viceroy had tilted the balance in favour of the latter. Morley was very aware of his radical reputation and of his future place in history, and thus reacted strongly to any measures that seemed to assert the more autocratic side of the government of India. Minto, the soldier–administrator, felt that few Westminster politicians understood the position in India correctly and that interference from them endangered the continuation of British rule in India, which rested on firm and good government. The differences between the two men were outlined in a very full correspondence, which was published in part (and selectively) by Morley in his *Recollections* (1917) and in *India, Minto and Morley* by the countess of Minto (1934).

Minto arrived in India in November 1905 when the country was in political turmoil, as Curzon's partition of the province of Bengal was being implemented. In his pursuit of good government Curzon had alienated the Western-educated Indian élite, especially the politically advanced Bengalis, by undermining their power bases in local institutions: his attitude was contemptuous of the so-called babus. Minto, on the other hand, was much more willing to accept the reality of the growing force of Indian nationalism and the need to take the more moderate element among the nationalists into account in any future reforms in India. However, Minto still shared the Anglo-Indian bureaucracy's mistrust of the educated classes, and he preferred to emphasize the incorporation of the traditional Indian élites, particularly the landowners and princes, into the political system. Minto shared with Morley the belief that Britain's democratic parliamentary system was not suitable for transfer to India. He argued that India's political system should be made more representative of key elements in Indian society so that the rulers were better informed about their subjects, but that the British needed to retain the reins of government. Minto aimed at a form of 'constitutional autocracy' that would blend the best in British and Indian political traditions.

The reforms process, which began with informal suggestions from Morley in June 1906, was very long, taking up another four years. Both viceroy and secretary of state knew that, despite the Liberal government's large majority, they had to tread carefully in view of the power of conservative interests both at home and in India. Morley, who had discussions with the moderate Indian nationalist leader G. K. Gokhale in the summer of 1906, was careful always to ensure that the initiative for the reforms was seen to come from the government of India. One reform in particular caused a good deal of opposition inside and outside government circles, and that was the plan to introduce an Indian member into the viceroy's executive council. Minto held to this measure more strongly than Morley, and in 1909 S. P. Sinha, the advocate-general of Bengal, was created law member of the viceroy's council. The opposition to this measure, which reached all the way up to the king, gives some idea of the difficulties faced by Morley and Minto. Two Indians were, however, added to the secretary of state's council in August 1907. The main change brought about by the 1909 reforms was the expansion and liberalization of the legislative councils in India. The central legislative council retained its official majority, but the provincial legislative councils gained a majority of non-officials, some of whom were to be nominated and some elected. The elections were indirect except in the case of the Muslims and landlords. The councils were given greater opportunity to debate matters such as the budget and to move resolutions. The reforms were welcomed broadly by mainstream Indian politicians, but there was widespread disappointment at the conservative way in which the rules and regulations under the act were framed. Minto retained for the viceroy the power to disqualify any candidate that he deemed unfit. In retrospect the Morley–Minto reforms seem very cautious—a continuation of the policy implemented in 1861 and 1892 of associating Indians with the administration rather than leading on to the much more significant constitutional reforms of 1919.

An important motivation for the reforms was the need to encourage moderate nationalists such as Gokhale and to separate them from their extremist colleagues, such as B. G. Tilak, B. C. Pal, and Aurobindo Ghose. Curzon's partition of Bengal had led to a much more active campaign than the normally sedate Indian National Congress had been used to. Russia's defeat by an Asiatic power—Japan—in 1904–5 had encouraged the growth of Indian nationalism, and economic and political resentments in the localities fuelled this movement. In 1907, at its annual session in Surat, the Indian National Congress broke up in disagreement between the moderates and extremists, who were not to be formally reconciled until 1916. This was a serious blow to the nationalist movement which suited the British well. In frustration some young nationalists turned to individual acts of terrorism against British officials. In 1907 an unsuccessful attempt was made on the life of the lieutenant-governor of Bengal, and in the following year a bungled assassination attempt on a judge at Muzaffarpur left two English women dead. Minto, who was himself the target of assassination attempts, was convinced that the men of violence were encouraged by politicians and journalists and that a firm hand needed to be taken to stamp out sedition at root.

A number of repressive laws were passed to control the press and to prevent sedition. The most notorious of these was the Press Act of 1910, which required newspapers to tender deposits which could be confiscated in case of their misbehaviour. Tilak was arrested in 1908 for sedition and sentenced to six years' imprisonment. Other political leaders, such as Lajpat Rai, were simply deported, a measure which to Morley smacked of tsarist Russia. Relations between Minto and Morley became much more tense in 1908 as Morley chided his opposite number while realizing his own impotence in influencing the viceroy's decisions on such matters. Minto's firm policies had the desired effect of stifling Indian agitation, at least in the short-run, but also alienated some moderate Indian political support.

Perhaps historically the most controversial of all Minto's measures was the encouragement he gave to Muslim separatism, which some historians have seen as leading ultimately to the creation of a divided subcontinent in 1947. The Muslims of British India were concerned by the announcement in July 1906 that the government was considering constitutional reforms, and particularly worried by the influence of Gokhale and the Hindu majority in Congress over those reforms. Muslim leaders were given permission to present their views to the viceroy in the so-called Simla deputation of 1 October 1906. The Muslims argued that their interests as a special community should be preserved in any reforms and that separate electorates for Muslims should be used in any electoral system to ensure that any Muslims elected truly represented Muslim interests. Minto promised in broad terms to meet these requests, and, despite Morley's preference for an electoral college system, he was able to incorporate separate electorates into the final reforms. It is now known that Minto did not orchestrate this deputation but that it did accord with his view that British rule should balance the interests of the various communities in India. Of course, a by-product of such protection was the encouragement of Muslim loyalism, and after the meeting Muslims set up their own organization, the All-India Muslim League, which was more than three decades later to prove the most serious challenger to Congress's national leadership.

Minto's great strengths were his sympathy and charm, which won over almost everybody with whom he came into contact. His qualities of 'gentlemanliness' were particularly appreciated by India's ruling princes and by neighbouring rulers. He allowed the princes a relatively loose rein, preferring that reform should come from within the states rather than be imposed from outside. Minto invited the amir of Afghanistan, Habibullah, to visit India in 1906–7, and this visit proved very successful in building up friendly relations. However, Minto's freedom to pursue his own foreign policy was very much circumscribed by Morley's Gladstonian concerns that India should have no opportunity to pursue an expensive forward policy on the frontier. In 1907 the British and Russian governments signed a convention that, among other things, recognized Afghanistan as a British sphere of influence. However, Minto was not allowed, as he had requested, to inform the amir of the convention before it was publicly announced, and thus the new relationship was unnecessarily tested.

The Mintos left India in November 1910: Minto had gained enormously from the loyal support of his wife, who had family connections with India and had gained a very firm grasp of its politics. On occasions she had acted as an intermediary between her husband and the hypersensitive John Morley. Exhausted by the very demanding duties of his office, Minto was able to retire to his Scottish home, but unfortunately he was taken ill suddenly in the autumn of 1913 with what turned out to be colonic cancer. He died at Minto Castle on 1 March 1914 and was buried at Hawick on 4 March. He was survived by his wife and their two sons and three daughters.

Lord Minto was a perfect example of the aristocratic pro-consul who was so much the backbone of the running of the British empire. He seemed to be the embodiment of the British belief in the superiority of character, sporting prowess, and integrity over bookish brilliance.

CARMAN MILLER and PHILIP WOODS

Sources C. Miller, *The Canadian career of the fourth earl of Minto* (1980) • N. Minto, *Notes from Minto manuscripts* (1862) • H. P. Gundy, 'Sir Wilfrid Laurier and Lord Minto', *Report of the Canadian Historical Association* (1952) • M. Kynynmound, *India, Minto and Morley, 1905–1910* (1934) • J. Morley, *Recollections*, 2 vols. (1917), vol. 2 • R. J. Moore, *Liberalism and Indian politics, 1872–1922* (1966) • M. Bence-Jones, *The viceroys of India* (1982) • J. Buchan, *Lord Minto: a memoir* (1924) • S. R. Mehrotra, *India and the commonwealth, 1885–1929* (1965) • M. N. Das, *India under Morley and Minto: politics behind revolution and reforms* (1964) • M. Gilbert, *Servant of India: a study of imperial rule from 1905 to 1910 as told through the correspondence and diaries of Sir James Dunlop-Smith* (1966) • P. Hardy, *The Muslims of British India* (1972) • S. E. Koss, *John Morley at the India Office, 1905–1910* (1969) • B. R. Nanda, *Gokhale: the Indian moderates and the British raj* (1977) • S. R. Wasti, *Lord Minto and the Indian nationalist movement, 1905 to 1910* (1964) • S. A. Wolpert, *Morley and India, 1906–1910* (1967) • d. cert.

Archives Kings Own Scottish Borderers Regimental Museum, Berwick upon Tweed, letter-book relating to volunteer corps • NL Scot., corresp. and papers • NL Scot., family corresp. | BL, E. T. H. Hutton MSS • BL OIOC, corresp. with Lord Ampthill, MS Eur. E 233 • BL OIOC, letters to Sir Harcourt Butler, MS Eur. F 116 • BL OIOC, letters to Arthur Godley, MS Eur. F 102 • BL OIOC, letters to Viscount Morley of Blackburn, MS Eur. D 573 • BL OIOC, corresp. with Sir Henry Richards, MS Eur. F 122 • BL OIOC, corresp. with Sir James Dunlop Smith, MS Eur. D 686 • BL OIOC, corresp. with Sir Herbert White, MS Eur. E 254 • CAC Cam., corresp. with Alfred Lyttelton • CUL, corresp. with Lord Hardinge • NA Canada, Wilfrid Laurier MSS • NA Canada, corresp. with Sir George Parkin • PRO, letters to Lord Kitchener, PRO 30/57, WO 159 • U. Birm. L., corresp. with Joseph Chamberlain

Likenesses group portrait, photograph, 1909, NAM • P. A. de Laszlo, photogravure, 1912, BL OIOC [*see illus.*] • W. G. John, bronze equestrian statue, 1913, Calcutta • P. A. de Laszlo, oils, Victoria Memorial Hall, Calcutta • Spy [L. Ward], chromolithograph cartoon, NPG; repro. in *VF* (29 June 1905) • oils, NA Canada

Kyriell, Sir Thomas (1396–1461), soldier, was born in Kent, the son of William Kyriell (1379–1413) of Eynsford. Thomas served as a man-at-arms in the retinue of Sir Gilbert Umfraville in the French expedition of 1417. By this time he was already a knight, and by 1420 was described as king's knight. He was appointed JP for Kent on several occasions from 1424 to 1430, and mustered troops embarking from the county in 1426 and 1428. In February 1431 he succeeded in gaining the reversion of the manor of Sarre on the Isle of Thanet previously held by a collateral line of the family, and also held the manor of Westenhanger. He served in France from 1429, being present, early in 1430, at the siege of Torcy under Edmund Beaufort. Soon afterwards he led a raid from Gournay into the Beauvaisis, and repulsed the French in a skirmish by placing his archers behind defensive stakes, but he may have been captured by the French later in the year. From 1432 to 1438 he was again active in the French wars. He was captain of Gournay and Gerberoy from at least December 1432 until the end of 1438, of Gisors from before March 1432 to May 1434, and he briefly held the captaincy of Le Crotoy in 1436. Early in 1436 he distinguished himself in a sortie from Rouen against La Hire and Poton de Saintrailles. In 1437 and 1438 he campaigned under John, Lord Talbot, while between November 1439 and August 1442 he was lieutenant of Calais. He was a knight banneret by 1443, in which year he crossed again to France under John Beaufort, earl of Somerset, but he seems to have spent the remainder of the 1440s in England.

There can be no doubting Kyriell's military reputation and experience, but he also faced complaints about his conduct. He had been discharged from the lieutenancy of

Calais under a cloud. At some point before 1446 Talbot, acting as marshal of France, adjudged in Normandy that Kyriell had withheld wages from his garrison at Gisors. This charge had been upheld by John, Lord Beaumont, as constable of England, but Kyriell appealed, and in November 1446 a commission was set up to determine the case. The outcome is not known, but the case may have formed part of a wider inquiry into corruption, made during the truce years of the mid-1440s. Kyriell's links with the Beauforts were by no means as strong as those of his kinsman and lieutenant at Gournay, John Kyriell, who was Edmund Beaufort's receiver at Harcourt. Thus it was his military experience and dedication to the cause of Lancastrian France, rather than his Beaufort connections, that led to his presence on the last campaign to Normandy. Thomas Kyriell was one of the few veteran captains prepared to serve in a relieving force in the late summer of 1449 after the French had invaded the duchy. But even he delayed the sealing of his indenture until December 1449, and the difficulty in finding funds to pay the troops—which also led to the murder of Adam Moleyns at Portsmouth—postponed his departure for the Cotentin until March 1450. 'Advised by dyvyson and controversie of hys pety capteyns' (Stevenson, 2.595), he did not march straight to Caen to relieve Edmund Beaufort, but instead recovered Valognes on 12 April 1450. Three days later, he was defeated and taken prisoner at the battle of Formigny.

The length of Kyriell's captivity in France and the terms of his ransom are not known, but by 1455 he was living once more in Kent, serving as MP in 1455 and 1460, and was active in local government, especially in defensive measures. On 28 August 1457 he rallied a counter-attack against the French raid on Sandwich, driving the French back to their ships. He was also lieutenant to Humphrey Stafford, duke of Buckingham, as constable of Dover and warden of the Cinque Ports from 1456 to 1460. But he gave his support to the earl of Warwick and the Yorkist party in June 1460, being elevated to the Garter on 8 February 1461, although he was never installed. At the second battle of St Albans (17 February 1461) he and Lord Bonville were entrusted with the guarding of the king. The battle lost, they were promised their safety by Henry VI, but were summarily executed two days later at the instigation of the queen, who had the young prince of Wales give the orders. In 1437 Kyriell had licence to marry Cecily (d. 1472), daughter and coheir of John Stourton of Preston Plucknett, Somerset (d. 1438), cousin of John, Lord Stourton, and widow of John Hill of Spaxton, Somerset (d. 1434). Through her dowry from John Hill, Kyriell came into possession of lands in Devon and Somerset. He was succeeded by his daughter, Alice, who married Sir John Fogge (d. 1490).   ANNE CURRY

Sources J. C. Wedgwood and A. D. Holt, *History of parliament*, 1: *Biographies of the members of the Commons house, 1439–1509* (1936) • *Chancery records* • N. H. Nicolas, ed., *Proceedings and ordinances of the privy council of England*, 7 vols., RC, 26 (1834–7), vols. 3–6 • PRO, special collections, SC • PRO, exchequer accounts various, E101 • PRO, warrants for issue, E404 • PRO, issue rolls, E403 • PRO, French rolls, C76 • Bibliothèque Nationale, Paris, collection Clairambault, MSS français, nouv. acq. françaises • BL, add. charters • *CIPM* • J. Stevenson, ed., *Letters and papers illustrative of the wars of the English in France during the reign of Henry VI, king of England*, 2 vols. in 3 pts, Rolls Series, 22 (1861–4) • R. A. Griffiths, *The reign of King Henry VI: the exercise of royal authority, 1422–1461* (1981) • *Recueil des croniques … par Jehan de Waurin*, ed. W. Hardy and E. L. C. P. Hardy, 5 vols., Rolls Series, 39 (1864–91) • *Archaeologia Cantiana*, 18 (1875), 359–60 • T. G. F. [T. G. Faussett], 'Family chronicle of Richard Fogge, of Danes Court, in Tilmanstone', *Archaeologia Cantiana*, 5 (1862–3), 112–32, esp. 126–7 • J. R. Dunlop, 'Pedigree of the family of Crioll or Kyriell of co. Kent', *Miscellanea Genealogica et Heraldica*, 5th ser., 6 (1926–8), 254–61 • J. S. Davies, ed., *An English chronicle of the reigns of Richard II, Henry IV, Henry V, and Henry VI*, CS, 64 (1856) • J. Gairdner, ed., *Three fifteenth-century chronicles*, CS, new ser., 28 (1880) • J. Gairdner, ed., *The historical collections of a citizen of London in the fifteenth century*, CS, new ser., 17 (1876) • *CPR, 1436–41*, 59 [marriage licence, 6 June 1437]

Archives PRO, SC 6/1119/17 • PRO, ministers' accounts, SC 6/977/7

Kyrle, John [*called* the Man of Ross] (**1637–1724**), philanthropist and landscape designer, was born on 22 May 1637 at the White House, in the parish of Dymock, Gloucestershire, the eldest son of three children of Walter Kyrle (d. 1660) of Ross, Herefordshire, barrister, JP, and MP for Leominster in 1640, and his wife, Alice Mallet (d. 1663), daughter and heir of John Mallet of Berkeley, Gloucestershire. The family of Kyrle or Crull had been settled in the vicinity of Ross-on-Wye since the thirteenth century. Kyrle was educated at Gloucester and at Balliol College, Oxford, where he matriculated on 20 July 1654. He was admitted a student of the Middle Temple in 1657, but retired to Ross without being called to the bar. He inherited an estate worth £500 per annum but added to this considerably during his lifetime, eventually assembling a mixture of freehold and copyhold property scattered throughout Herefordshire and west Gloucestershire. He was also the owner of New Mill, the principal corn mill in Ross, and he derived £100 per annum from the fallage of timber in Dymock Wood. Kyrle never married but lived with his kinswoman Judith Bubb, who was his 'active assistant' in good works and, in his own words, 'a very good and fine girl and a great scholar' (Davies Herefordshire Collection, AB/50, fol. 234). He spent all his life in Ross, living in a three-storied framed house adjoining the market place, which was said to have been built by his father in 1620. In politics he was a staunch loyalist and had a monogram cut into the wall of the new market hall which read 'Love Charles to the Heart'. The only local office he held was high sheriff in 1683. He declined the office of JP.

Kyrle owes his fame largely to the eulogy of him in Alexander Pope's third 'Moral Epistle', published in 1732, eight years after his death. During his lifetime he had already earned the title of the Man of Ross or, according to Thomas Hearne, the Great Man of Ross. Kyrle never officially practised as a lawyer, but he seems to have regularly acted for his neighbours in litigious matters. For instance, in 1674 he settled a dispute about the distribution of local taxes between the borough of Ross and its rural parish. In an informal way Kyrle appears to have acted for the absentee lord of the manor of Ross, Lord Weymouth. He was called upon to arbitrate in a dispute over the traditional dole for the poor of the town, paid out of the tolls of the market place. A deed of 1690 indicates that he insisted that the keeper of the market pay the poor people of Rudhall's Hospital 56s. 8d. a year. He also left £40 in his will to the recently founded Blue Coat School. The eulogist literature which proliferated around the Man of Ross during the next two centuries claims many other virtuous acts. He provided portions for poor brides, ensured the poor had decent funerals, enabled debtors to re-establish themselves in trade, paid the fees of poor apprentices, and provided simple medicines for the sick.

It was this pattern of philanthropy on Kyrle's part which came to the attention of Pope, perhaps on one of his several visits to Holme Lacy House, a few miles from Ross, but most of his information came from his publisher, Jacob Tonson, who lived near Ledbury. He was looking for an exemplary character 'to distinguish real and solid worth from showish or plausible expense, and virtue fro' vanity' (*Correspondence of Alexander Pope*, 3.290–91). Not all contemporaries were as impressed as Pope was with Kyrle's good character. Thomas Hearne was informed by Matthew Gibson, the rector of Abbey Dore, that his wife, Kyrle's niece, regarded the Man of Ross as the 'vainest man living' who 'always hated his relations' (Money-Kyrle, 227). In the late eighteenth century Thomas Dudley Fosbroke and Charles Heath, both local writers, were able to confirm Pope's claims using the reminiscences of, among others, Mrs Clarke of Hill Court and the sexton of Ross church, William Dobbs.

Pope was also attracted to Kyrle because of his delight in horticulture, architecture, and urban improvement. Beyond Ross churchyard, on the sandstone cliff above the Wye, Kyrle acquired from Lord Weymouth, on a lease of 500 years, the Clevefield, which he planted and laid out as an ornamental promenade. The Prospect, as the town end of the walk became known, was also enhanced by a fountain supplied by water pumped up from the Wye, which, via a reservoir, also fed public cocks in the town. It was surrounded by walls with three classical gateways, two of which survive today. It was made accessible to the public.

Below the Prospect the causeway towards Wilton Bridge was also planted, while round the churchyard Kyrle established his favourite tree—the elm. His hands-on approach to gardening was regarded as something of an oddity, but Pope applauded this man who consulted 'the Genius of the Place' and engaged in extensive gardening where good sense rather than fashion was the guiding principle. Indeed, a later writer commented that Kyrle had 'a taste for what is now termed the picturesque' (*Saturday Magazine*, 165), creating in a precocious manner a landscape essential for the role that Ross was to play in the late eighteenth century as a centre for the Wye tour.

Kyrle was said by Fosbroke to be 'skilled in Architecture, (and a great patron of workmen)' (Fosbroke, 10). In 1721 he supervised the replacement of the top of the spire of Ross church and designed some new pinnacles. The vicarages of Foy and Much Marcle in Herefordshire were 'rebuilt or altered under his direction' (ibid., 152), and Hill Court, close to Ross, rebuilt by Richard and Joseph Clarke about 1700, has also been attributed to him. Nearly a century later, the elderly Mrs Clarke remembered that Kyrle had frequently been a guest of the Clarkes, and in the garden there is a gateway very close in style to those on the Prospect.

Kyrle died in Ross on 7 November 1724 in his eighty-eighth year and, following an extended period of mourning, he was buried on 20 November. In his will he asked to be buried in the chancel of Ross church, at the feet of the late rector, Dr Whiting, his friend and the founder of the town's Blue Coat School. The grave was marked with a simple stone inscribed with the initials J. K. Pope noticed that he lacked a memorial, but in a letter to Tonson assumed this was a deliberate act of self-effacement. In 1749 an inscribed stone was provided which commemorated Kyrle and his heir Vandrewort Kyrle. But this was far from satisfactory for the Wye tourists, who demanded something more impressive. This was satisfied in 1776 with the erection of a pyramidical tablet in variegated marble with a bust in relief, paid for by the will of Lady Constantia Dupplin.

Kyrle's landscaping continued to be admired, although Heath referred to vandalism caused by 'idle people' in 1799. Few agreed with William Gilpin, who found the walks 'amusing' but decided, according to his strict criteria, the view was 'not picturesque' (Gilpin, 14). Several prints of the period show the elms, burgeoning woods, and summerhouse, which terminated the walk, but the tourists wanted more, and Kyrle's own garden behind his house, now the King's Arms, became a place of pilgrimage.

Public access to the Prospect continued until 1837, when the landlord of the newly built Royal Hotel annexed the walks, demolished one of the gates, and planted part of the area with cabbages. This event became a *cause célèbre* in Ross in the 1840s and a riot occurred in 1848. Eventually, about 1860, the lease was recovered and the Prospect was given in perpetuity to the inhabitants of the town. In the nineteenth century another generation of pious philanthropists rediscovered Kyrle, and the story of his life was often repeated in campaigning magazines such as *The Sketch* and the *Saturday Magazine*. In 1877 the Kyrle Society was founded by Miranda and Octavia Hill to promote gardening among the industrious classes.

DAVID WHITEHEAD

Sources C. J. Robinson, *A history of the mansions and manors of Herefordshire* (1872) · T. D. Fosbroke, *The Wye tour, or, Gilpin on the Wye* (1818) · C. Heath, *The excursion down the Wye from Ross to Monmouth* (1799) · C. L. Money-Kyrle, 'John Kyrle—the Man of Ross and the Kyrle family', *Memorials of old Herefordshire*, ed. C. Reade (1904), 223–35 · *The correspondence of Alexander Pope*, ed. G. Sherburn, 5 vols. (1956) · B. Butcher, 'Ross, John Kyrle and the Prospect', *Country Life* (Sept 1971), 8–10 · 'Original letters of the Man of Ross', *GM*, 2nd ser., 33 (1850), 493–4 · Hereford City Library, Davies Herefordshire Collection, AB/50 · Hereford City Library, Pilley Collection, 2269 · *Saturday Magazine* (Oct 1832), 164–6 [copy in Hereford City Library bound with Heath, *Excursion*] · *The Sketch* (2 June 1897) · W. Gilpin,

The Wye tour (1800) · Herefs. RO, various collections, esp. local deeds

Archives Herefs. RO, papers

Likenesses marble bust in relief?, 1776, Ross-on-Wye church, Herefordshire · J. Van Aken, oils, Hereford City Art Gallery · oils, Balliol Oxf. · portrait, repro. in Fosbroke, *The Wye tour*, frontispiece

Kyshe, James William Norton- (1855–1920), colonial official and legal writer, was probably born in Mauritius, the second son of Henry Kyshe and Esther Norton. He once described himself as 'one of the Jewish race, closely connected to the Jews of the best birth and highest standing in England' (Wesley-Smith, 285), though the latter claim seems doubtful. First employed as a clerk in Mauritius, he was appointed deputy registrar of the supreme court of Penang in 1880. His call to the bar (Lincoln's Inn) in 1888 was followed by appointments as sheriff of Singapore (1892) and registrar of the supreme court of Hong Kong (1895). He left Hong Kong in 1904 on compulsory retirement, after many disputes with colleagues and an extraordinarily cantankerous episode involving the chief justice, William Meigh Goodman (1847–1928). He had been diagnosed as suffering from nervous debility in Hong Kong and his retirement was on medical grounds: Colonial Office officials doubted his 'mental equilibrium', and in 1916 a receiver was appointed to administer his estate under the Lunacy Acts.

Intensely ambitious, arrogant, provocative, disputatious, tactless, paranoid, and utterly vain, Norton-Kyshe was described by Hong Kong civil servants and Colonial Office officials as a 'damned liar' who 'fancies he is a man with a grievance', 'an impossible' and 'bumptious man' 'with an unwarrantably good opinion of himself', and 'a liar of the first water' who 'has ability' but 'no moral foundation'. Norton-Kyshe, however, considered himself 'one of the greatest writers, if not *the* greatest, on legal matters in the Colonial Service—not by any means a mere compiler' (Wesley-Smith, 279).

Norton-Kyshe's claim to fame rests, indeed, on his writings. His four volumes of Straits Settlements law reports (with extensive historical preface) and his index to Straits Settlements laws ensure that his name will forever adorn the Singapore and Malaysian legal systems. He wrote a number of rather forgettable books on such subjects as colonial attorneys-general and the law and custom relating to gloves, but his principal work is probably the two-volume *History of the Laws and Courts of Hong Kong* (1898). This tome, reprinted in 1971, is a major contribution to the colony's legal history. It is somewhat flawed, being perilously close to 'mere compilation' of anything remotely connected to Hong Kong legal affairs, but it repays both light reading and careful study. Ironically he blamed it for causing great jealousy and animosity against him among government officials, yet both the book and its author were still referred to in late twentieth-century Hong Kong when his detractors were long forgotten.

Norton-Kyshe died of double pneumonia on 1 March 1920, at his home, 24 Victoria Road North, Southsea, Hampshire. He was married, with at least one son, though nothing further is known of his family; since his Mauritius pension was paid until 1936 it seems likely that his wife survived him until then.   PETER WESLEY-SMITH

Sources P. Wesley-Smith, 'James William Norton-Kyshe', *Hong Kong Law Journal*, 2 (1972), 278–93 · PRO, CO 129/319, 321, 322, 327 · *CGPLA Eng. & Wales* (1920)

Wealth at death £2526 6s. 5d.: probate, 17 July 1920, *CGPLA Eng. & Wales*

Kyte, Francis (*fl.* 1710–1745). *See under* Cooper, Edward (d. 1725).

Kyteler [Kettle], **Alice** (*fl.* 1302–1324), alleged witch, was a member of the Kyteler family of Flemish merchants who settled in Kilkenny in the thirteenth century. Her parentage is unknown but she is likely to be related to William le Kyteler, merchant of Ypres, who was trading in Ireland in 1277, to Joseph de Keteller who was buried in Kilkenny c.1280, and to William le Kyteler, sheriff of Kilkenny in the early fourteenth century. She married four times, each husband being a member of a wealthy and well-connected family in the Kilkenny area. Her first husband was William Outlaw, merchant and moneylender of Kilkenny, whom she probably married c.1280–85 as their son, also William Outlaw, was sovereign (mayor) of Kilkenny in 1305. She may also have had a daughter, Rose, with her first husband. By 1302 she was married to her second husband, Adam Blund of Callan, with whom she engaged in moneylending activities. Their wealth is exemplified by a legal case in that year involving the sum of £3000, which they had entrusted to William Outlaw. In June 1303 the king acknowledged a debt of £500 to Adam Blund and Alice his wife, a loan to help finance the Scottish wars. Not long before his death in 1307–8 Adam Blund quitclaimed to his stepson, William, all his goods and chattels, moveable and immoveable, jewels, gold, and silver and renounced all debts owed to him by William. By 1309 Alice was married to her third husband, Richard Valle, a landholder of Tipperary; in 1310 they assigned to William Outlaw two debts of 200 marks and £200 owed to them by others. After Valle's death c.1316 Alice took proceedings against her stepson, Richard, for the recovery of her widow's dower. Between that year and 1324 Alice married her fourth husband, John Poer.

It is for the accusations of sorcery and witchcraft brought against her by Richard Ledred, bishop of Ossory, in 1324 that Alice is chiefly known. The principal source is the *Narrative of the Proceedings Against Dame Alice Kyteler*, a detailed account probably drawn up by or on behalf of Bishop Ledred to justify and defend the part played by him in prosecuting Alice and eleven co-accused. It tells a dramatic story, portraying the bishop as a staunch defender of the faith and upholder of the jurisdiction of the church against a 'diabolical nest of heretics' combined with the might of leading members of the royal administration and ecclesiastical and lay magnates of the lordship of Ireland. The *Narrative* opens with accusations of heresy and witchcraft against Alice, following a visitation of the diocese. Seven charges are listed but the sixth charge stands out as the one which must have given rise to the whole affair. It states that the sons and daughters of Alice's four husbands had brought accusations before the bishop that she had used sorcery to kill some of her husbands and to infatuate others, and that she had so enfeebled their senses that they had given all their possessions to her and her son, to the impoverishment of their own children. Her fourth husband, John Poer, is said at this time to be totally debilitated by her sorceries but to have discovered in her possession a sackful of detestable items which he brought to the bishop. As a successful moneylender and a thrice widowed lady Alice must have amassed a considerable fortune, and it is not surprising to find a charge of sorcery being brought against her by her stepchildren, who resented the wealth inherited at their expense and the favour shown to her son William. The co-accused are not listed until later in the *Narrative* but it is soon apparent that William Outlaw is among them. Such charges were traditionally tried at common law and up to this time were regarded only as serious as the harm done to the victim; they bore no heretical implications.

The other charges brought against Alice and her co-accused concerned denial of the faith, making sacrifices to a demon, invoking the aid of demons in the practice of their sorceries, concocting potions in the skull of a decapitated robber using assorted unsavoury ingredients, and finally Alice's employment of an incubus known as Robin Artisson, a lesser demon of hell. What is so remarkable about the Kyteler case is the introduction of charges of demonic association, unknown at this time in the British Isles. This is probably attributable to the presence of Bishop Ledred as prosecutor. At the time of his appointment to the see of Ossory in 1317 he was resident at the papal court at Avignon where the recent case against the templars had given currency to the notion that the practice of magic implied demonic association. Thus, when a casual charge of malefice and sorcery was brought against Alice by her stepchildren, Ledred was bound by his training at Avignon to look for evidence of consorting with demons, and the use of the inquisitorial procedure meant that confirmation of such fears was readily forthcoming. It seems likely that the lurid details of the 'charges' listed at the beginning of the *Narrative* did not emerge until the examination under torture of some of the accused, especially Petronella of Meath. Petronella's confessions are detailed later in the course of the *Narrative* and are clearly reflected in the list of charges appearing at the beginning. Without the protection afforded to Alice by her influential relatives and friends, Petronella was burnt at the stake on the morrow of All Souls' (3 November 1324).

Bishop Ledred pursued the case against Alice with determination fortified by conviction, but he encountered strong opposition to his attempts to have her arrested. The seneschal of the liberty of Kilkenny, Arnold Poer, was contemptuous of the bishop's efforts and obstructed him at every move. When a day had been appointed for William Outlaw to appear before the bishop to answer the charges against him, Poer had the bishop imprisoned until the appointed day had passed. The bishop next wrote to Roger Outlaw, chancellor of Ireland from 1322 and a close relative of William, demanding the arrest of all the accused but he refused on the grounds that he could not issue a warrant until they had been excommunicate for forty days. When the bishop summoned Alice to appear before him she fled to Dublin before the day appointed. Bishop Ledred was himself twice summoned to Dublin to answer to the archbishop for having placed his diocese under interdict and on a countercharge of defamation brought by Alice. The tide had begun to turn in Ledred's favour when the justiciar, John Darcy, lent his support, and writs for the arrest of the accused were finally issued in July 1324. Some were arrested and interrogated by the bishop, others were released on payment of securities, but the 'mistress of all', Alice Kyteler, fled to England with Basilia, daughter of Petronella of Meath.

With the departure of Alice, William Outlaw now became the focus of the bishop's attention. He was summoned to appear before the bishop to answer thirty-four charges, including heresy, aiding and abetting heretics, usury, perjury, adultery, and clericide. But when the council met in Kilkenny in July 1324 the chancellor, Roger Outlaw, and the treasurer, Walter Islip, took up residence with William and held court there, to the consternation of the bishop. Clearly William was not to be yielded up as readily as the less fortunate Petronella. Although the *Narrative* states that the bishop had to refuse money offered by William's friends to secure his favour, a form of compromise was reached. William confessed to the charges in return for which a prison sentence was commuted to a penance, namely, to hear mass at least three times a day for one year, to feed a certain number of the poor, and to roof the chancel of the cathedral of St Canice with lead. Evidently William proved recalcitrant as in January 1325 the bishop had him committed to prison and cited to answer new charges. But the power of William's supporters was such that the new agreement reached on 17 January 1325 required only the addition of securities for his behaviour. On 25 January Roger Outlaw and ten of the principal landholders of Kilkenny acknowledged a debt of £1000 to the bishop of Ossory.

The events of 1324 were largely responsible for Bishop Ledred's enforced and prolonged exile from his diocese which commenced in 1329. Arnold Poer, convicted of heresy by the bishop, died excommunicate in a Dublin prison in 1329; the chancellor, Roger Outlaw, accused of aiding and abetting Poer in his heresy, purged himself of the charge at the parliament in Dublin in 1329. But the ultimate fate of the chief protagonist, Alice Kyteler, is unknown to history.

ANNE R. NEARY

Sources F. de Ledrede, *A contemporary narrative of the proceedings against Dame Alice Kyteler*, ed. T. Wright, CS, 24 (1843) · E. Tresham, ed., *Rotulorum patentium et clausorum cancellariae Hiberniae calendarium*, Irish Record Commission (1828) · J. T. Gilbert, ed., *Chartularies of St Mary's Abbey, Dublin: with the register of its house at Dunbrody and annals of Ireland*, 2 vols., Rolls Series, 80 (1884) · *The annals of Ireland by Friar John Clyn and Thady Dowling: together with the annals of Ross*, ed. R. Butler, Irish Archaeological Society (1849) · *Jacobi Grace, Kilkenniensis, Annales Hiberniae*, ed. and trans. R. Butler, Irish Archaeological Society (1842) · NA Ire., Rec. Comm. RC8/10–18 · J. Mills and others, eds., *Calendar of the justiciary rolls … of Ireland*,

3 vols. (1905–56) · *CPR* · A. Neary, 'The origins and character of the Kilkenny witchcraft case of 1324', *Proceedings of the Royal Irish Academy*, 83C (1983), 333–50 · L. S. Davidson and J. O. Ward, *The sorcery trial of Alice Kyteler* (1993) · N. Cohn, *Europe's inner demons* (1975)

Kytson, Sir Thomas. *See* Kitson, Sir Thomas (1485–1540).

La Tournelle, Mrs. *See* Hackett, Sarah (1737/8–1797).

La Warre. For this title name *see* Warr, Roger de la, first Lord La Warre (*d.* 1320) [*see under* Warr, de la, family (*per. c.*1250–1427)].

Laban, Rudolf Jean-Baptiste Attila (1879–1958), dancer and dance theoretician, who developed a comprehensive system of movement notation, was born on 15 December 1879 at Donaulande 12, Bratislava, in the Austro-Hungarian empire, the first among the four children of Field Marshal Rudolf von Laban and his wife, Marie Bridling.

Early life Laban's parents were both Hungarian, but his father's family came from the south of France, and his mother's family was from Yorkshire. His father was an army officer whose final command was as governor of the provinces of Bosnia and Herzegovina. As he grew up Rudolf often accompanied his parents on their travels. This early exposure to differing cultures, work patterns, and indigenous dance had a strong influence on Laban's later creative work.

Although he became a military cadet, Laban opted instead to study painting. This particularly displeased his father, who had expected his son to follow him in a respectable military career; however, he capitulated, providing his son with a small stipend. In 1900 Laban met and married an art student, Martha Fricke. The two moved to Munich where Laban began his first formal art studies. Here he became aware of the idea that the practice of art involved the spirit as well as the intellect.

In 1900 the young Labans moved to Paris to study painting and architecture at the École des Beaux Arts. Laban became fascinated with theatre, with its architecture, design, décor, and costumes. These interests led to experiments in form and colour, which engendered his later study of spatial 'forms' and movement 'colour' or quality. During these heady Parisian days he also began his investigations into the development of a dance script. In addition he created his first dance-dramas and dance choruses. While in Paris, Laban discovered Rosicrucianism. Its practices underlined his growing conviction that the body holds truths to which one can sensitize oneself. Rosicrucian subjects appeared in his later choreography and his high regard for such semi-mystical ideas as the golden mean fed into his fascination with harmony in movement.

The Labans had two children, but disaster struck soon after Martha's second pregnancy. In 1907 she died; the children were looked after by Martha's mother. Laban, devastated, succumbed to the first of many bouts of depression. He returned to his parental home in Vienna. Rejuvenation came in 1910, when Laban met and married Maja Lederer, a singer; they were to have five children. The

newly-weds moved to Munich, a city teeming with new ideas about art. Here Laban encountered the pioneering thinking of the painter Kandinsky, the educator Steiner, the composer Schoenberg, the intellectuals Wolfskehl and George, the theosophist Blavatsky, and the *Körperkultur* movement of Mensendieck and Bode.

Perennially in debt, Laban worked as a freelance illustrator. He created costumes and arranged lavish entertainments for the *Fasching* carnivals, public festivals. Soon he became known for his ability as a director of movement. At the end of the 1912 carnival season, Laban, whose health was never very vigorous, retired to the Weisser Hirsch sanatorium outside Dresden. There began his lifelong search for a basic theory of human movement. And there he met and entered into a liaison with Suzanne Perrottet, a disciple of Émile Jaques-Dalcroze, the originator of eurhythmics. Their affair continued for many years with the tacit consent of Maja, resulting in a *ménage à trois*. In 1917 both Maja and Suzanne bore his children: Roland Laban and Allar Perrottet.

Experiments with dance In 1912–13 Laban definitively turned his attention to dance. He formed a small group of student followers to further his experiments with its rhythmic and dramatic content. Summer 1913 proved a turning point in the history of dance. Laban founded a summer school at Monte Verità, Ascona, in the Swiss province of Ticino. An alternative-living colony already existed at the Mountain of Truth, embracing vegetarianism, nudism, psychoanalysis, and a relaxed attitude to sex. The choreographer and dancer Mary Wigman (Marie Wiegmann) attended that first summer school. Her relationship with Laban remained forever problematic. She was fascinated and in love with him, found his work inspiring, attributed much of her knowledge to his teaching, and nursed her resentment of his casual sexual encounters with more than a few other women. Later she blamed him for not sufficiently respecting her gifts.

At Monte Verità Laban trained his group using 'swinging scales', further developed his ideas of body–mind oneness, and created his first theatre dance works. During the following busy season Wigman caused a sensation in her solo début, dancing the *Hexentanz* ('Witch Dance'). She established a pattern *vis-à-vis* Laban that continued with others throughout his life. He would think through a problem, develop its framework, and then depend on one of his followers to embellish it and give it practical application. He served the role of prime mover; Wigman applied his ideas into the theatre.

A second summer at Monte Verità began against the gathering international storm that resulted in the First World War. By the end of July all the students had fled, leaving 'the Master' and Wigman time for the intensive work that was involved in developing Laban's framework for human movement. During 1914–19, having sought refuge in Zürich, Laban produced leaps forward in his theoretical development; however, the time was financially, domestically, and healthwise a nadir for Laban. He was constantly in debt, concerned about looming conscription, fighting for papers to allow him to stay in Switzerland, and overwhelmed by the domestic responsibilities of sustaining his wife, his lover, his six children, his mother, and his sister.

In Zürich Laban founded a new freemason lodge, deepening his experience of mysticism. Here also, as he became acquainted with the work of Carl Jung, Laban increasingly believed there existed a direct relationship between psychic function and the four motion factors of time, weight, space, and flow. He also further developed his emerging system of dance notation. He continued his search for basic ways of defining and ordering human expression through movement, developing his theories of choreutics and eukinetics. The former is the study of spatial forms, exercises based on scales. Eukinetics encompasses the study of the rhythm and dynamics of movement. Much of Laban's training method centred on swinging exercises and movement sequences built from reaching from one point in space to another. This led to his development of a spatial model, the icosahedron.

Disaster struck again in 1918–19. Maja and the children left Laban, his affair with Suzanne waned, and he became a victim of the influenza epidemic. All his work fell apart as he moved from hospital to sanatorium, desperately ill and indigent. When sufficiently recovered, Laban moved to Nuremberg with his newest assistant, Dussia Bereska. He turned his mind to one of the recurring themes in his life: dance as a celebratory and spiritual experience for the non-professional. He organized classes particularly for the youth left disaffected in the aftermath of the war.

The stay in Nuremberg was short-lived. In April 1920 Laban once again uprooted, this time to Stuttgart, where he had finally found a publisher for his first written *magnum opus*, *Die Welt des Tänzers* ('The dancer's world'). The book was received as a work of genius, gaining Laban much-needed recognition and even more needed funds. Here a young music and drama student, Khadven Joos (Kurt Jooss), became interested in Laban's work; this was the beginning of the long-term collaboration of the two men.

Laban schools founded In 1921 the Mannheim National Theatre invited Laban to become guest choreographer, and there he presented his first major choreographic effort, *Die Geblendeten* ('The deluded'), with his own group. They went on to perform in Stuttgart to rave reviews. In the succeeding five years Laban's fame spread. Laban schools were founded in Basel, Stuttgart, Hamburg, Prague, Budapest, Zagreb, Rome, Vienna, and Paris, each under the direction of one of his students. This was a high point in his career as a mesmerizing performer, a charismatic teacher, and an inventive choreographer. He interested himself in both dance as a celebratory community activity and dance as art. He founded the first of his renowned movement choirs in 1922.

Laban moved to Hamburg with his newest *amor* Dussia Bareska, with whom he conceived a child. In 1923 he redesigned and established his own performance venue and founded two professional performing groups:

Kammertanz and Tanzbühne. Kammertanz gave regular performances in his theatre; Tanzbühne undertook a highly praised tour which had an enormous impact on European dance. Plagued by financial worries, the company was stranded and forced to disband in Zagreb before completing the planned itinerary.

In summer 1926 Laban made his only journey to the New World, on a lecture-tour throughout the United States and Mexico. Laban was not enraptured with what he found. What he deemed 'American zeal' rather overwhelmed him. Meanwhile Laban had established a choreographic institute in Würzburg with the help of Bareska and his latest collaborator/lover, Gertrud Loeszer. In addition to the institute a group, Kammertanzbühne Laban-Bareska, toured successfully. In Nuremberg on 15 December, Laban's birthday, he leapt off the stage at a performance of *Don Juan*, but the mattresses that should have caught him were not in place. He sustained an injury that permanently ended his performing career.

Movement notation During this period Laban continued his passionate work of developing a system of 'written dance'. In 1928 the system, variously called Kinetography Laban and Labanotation, was published by Universal Edition in a journal, *Schrifttanz*. Of Laban's many contributions to the world of dance, this system of movement notation is one of the most important. In the years since his death, with the continuing development by his colleagues Albrecht Knust and Ann Hutchinson, it has become an important tool in the documentation and preservation of dance all over the world.

The first public exposure of the notation system had come the year before, at the Laban-organized First Dancers' Congress in Magdeburg; there it was welcomed as an important contribution by a wide-ranging group of dancers. In 1928 the choreographic institute moved to Berlin, remaining there for two years, and attaining the peak of its success. In 1930 Laban accepted the important post of ballet master of Berlin's Unter den Linden Opera House. He had also been engaged, in 1929, to direct the Viennese Festzug der Gewerbe (Festival Procession of Crafts and Industries) and organized a moving and triumphal procession of some 10,000 participants. And in May 1930 he served as guest choreographer to the Bayreuth Wagner festival.

When his one-year contract in Berlin was extended for another three years, and Bayreuth invited him back, Laban applied for German citizenship. The rise of Nazism had begun. Questions linger of whether Laban's motive was the temporary embracing of National Socialist ideas or was simply that he wished to keep his employment. In spite of his successes at the opera house, it became clear by 1934 that he could no longer hold the post, as his German citizenship had not yet come through. Consequently he took on the directorship of the Deutsche Tanzbühne. He organized a dance festival in December 1934. Over the next two years Laban continued teaching and directing the Tanzbühne, finally gaining his German naturalization. In summer 1935 his autobiographical *Ein Leben für Tanz* ('A life for dance') was published.

In anticipation of the 1936 Olympics the Meisterwerk-stätten für Tanz was created with Laban as director. He organized a gigantic performance with 1000 participants. Goebbels, head of the propaganda ministry, attended the final rehearsal. Goebbels's fateful words marked the beginning of the end of Laban's German career: 'I do not like it. That is because it is dressed up in our clothes and has nothing whatever to do with us' (Preston-Dunlop, *Rudolf Laban*, 196). The performance was forbidden and thereafter Laban was hounded by investigations, castigated for having been a freemason, unveiled as not being a member of the Nazi party, and discovered to be living with a Jewish woman. Sick and disheartened, with no possibility of earning a living, Laban left for Paris, where Jooss found him in a state of mental and physical collapse. Jooss invited Laban to come to England.

For the next years Laban lived at Dartington Hall as a guest of Jooss's hosts, the Elmhirsts. Since he was a German alien, the government permitted him to stay only if he agreed not to seek employment either paid or unpaid. In any event his ill health forbade his working. A former student, **Elisabeth Maria Martha** [Lisa] **Ullman** (1907–1985), who had been born in Berlin on 17 June 1907, befriended him and began nursing him back to health. Thus began a new phase in Laban's life.

Last decades During the difficult war years Ullman, an inspiring teacher of dance in education, acted as Laban's spokeswoman. He planned what she so beautifully taught. In 1940 the government ordered them, as aliens, to leave the nurturing environment of Dartington, which was close to the naval base at Dartmouth. In 1942 they established themselves in Manchester where Lisa, with the support of the Elmhirsts, opened a school. Laban returned to lecturing and writing. The school flourished. Much later, in 1953, it moved to more spacious quarters in Addlestone, Surrey. Laban movement training, as conceived by Laban and taught by Ullman, became a pedagogical tool used in schools throughout Britain. After Laban's death Ullman devoted herself to translating and editing his writings. She became a naturalized British citizen in 1947. Ullman died in Chertsey, Surrey, on 25 January 1985.

The eminent industrialist Frederick Lawrence heard of Laban's work and became convinced that the training might have a practical application in the factory. Thus began a whole new area of exploration. Along with Lawrence, Laban developed ways of retraining employees for unaccustomed kinds of work, most notably preparing women to take over the work of men. Laban was permitted at last to earn his own way in Britain and to contribute to the war effort. His collaboration with Lawrence resulted in the publication of *Effort* (1947), a small book describing how to graph natural effort patterns in order to match innate patterns with needed work skills.

Never happy being too far from theatre and movement as art, Laban also revived his interest in movement training for actors, which culminated in the publication in 1950 of his *Mastery of Movement on the Stage*. In his final ten years Laban began to work on his newest area of interest:

how movement could be used therapeutically. He engaged in research into personality, stress, and intervention techniques, a study which occupied him until his death on 1 July 1958 in Weybridge, where he was buried.

Rudolf Laban, charismatic teacher, brilliant dreamer, philosopher, dancer, choreographer, author, and experimenter, was a man with a rare combination of personal magnetism and genius. His work ranged from the methodical to the fantastic, from the disciplined to the wildly imaginative. His contribution has permanently changed what we see as the place of movement in our lives.

MURIEL TOPAZ

Sources V. Preston-Dunlop, *Rudolf Laban: an extraordinary life* (1998) • M. Topaz, *Elementary Labanotation: a study guide* (1996) • I. Bartenieff and A. Hutchinson, 'A tribute to Rudolf Laban', *Dance Observer* (Dec 1949) • S. J. Cohen, 'Rudolf Laban dies at 78', *New York Times* (3 July 1958) • 'Biography of Rudolf Laban, parts 1 and 2', Dance Notation Bureau, New York, archives • V. Preston-Dunlop, 'Laban and the Nazis', *Update Dance USA* (Aug/Sept 1989) • E. Hinks, 'Lisa Ullman', unpublished • *CGPLA Eng. & Wales* (1959)
Archives Dance Notation Bureau, New York • Laban Centre, London, Laban Art of Movement Trust, archives and papers • NYPL for the Performing Arts
Wealth at death £1166 4s. 9d.: probate, 23 Feb 1959, *CGPLA Eng. & Wales*

L'Abbé, Anthony (*b.* 1666/7, *d.* in or after 1753), choreographer and dancing-master, about whose birth and parentage nothing is known, joined the Académie Royale de Musique in Paris as a dancer in 1688, at the age of twenty-one. He left in 1698 when Thomas Betterton, the manager of Lincoln's Inn Fields Theatre, invited him to London as the first of a spate of dancers from the Paris Opéra to dominate performances of dance in the London theatres for the next decade. L'Abbé remained in London for the next thirty years, and became one of the most highly respected dancing-masters of his day.

After Betterton failed to renew his theatre contract in June 1703, L'Abbé performed for a while only in subscription concerts, and wrote a letter of complaint to the lord chamberlain's secretary in January 1704. From that December onwards he performed at Sir John Vanbrugh's new Queen's Theatre in the Haymarket, as well as continuing to appear in danced entertainments at court on Queen Anne's birthdays. He was invariably partnered by the English dancer Mrs Elford, and also worked with French dancers including Philippe Du Ruel and René Cherrier at Drury Lane and the Queen's Theatre. The advertisements from 1705 to about 1713 also refer to a brother, sometimes known as 'Mons. L'Abbé's scholar' or 'young L'Abbé', and it is sometimes difficult to distinguish between the two brothers in the performance rosters, as both worked at various times in all the main London theatres.

In 1719–20 L'Abbé became involved in plans to establish a Royal Academy of Music for the production of Italian opera under Handel's leadership, but the academy operas were not a lasting success. At some time in the mid-1720s a collection of thirteen of his own theatrical dances, some of them for Elford, Hester Santlow (Cherrier's protégée), and other dancers with whom he had worked between 1706 and 1722, was published by the dancing-master F. Le Roussau.

L'Abbé made his name also as a creator of sophisticated dances for presentation at court balls, and some of these dances were subsequently performed on stage. The dedication to Princess Anne of his dance *The Princess Royal* in 1715 confirms that she was his pupil; that dance was the first of a series of annual ball-dances, many of which were named after members of the royal family. By 1720, despite his foreign birth and religious status (he is described in the land tax returns of 1717 and 1718 as a papist), he had been granted official status as dancing-master to the three young princesses Anne, Amelia, and Caroline, granddaughters of George I, at an annual salary of £200. He held this post until at least 1737, at a salary which rose to £240 as opposed to the £200 paid to Handel as Princess Anne's music-master. Thirteen engraved notations of the annual ball-dances created by L'Abbé during this period still survive in the British Library, together with one theatrical solo published in 1711, all published by the dancing-master Edmund Pemberton.

Little is known of L'Abbé's work as a teacher of social dance outside his employment by the royal family. It seems likely, however, that he, like several of his colleagues, taught private pupils both in London and at their own houses in the provinces. His connection with the household of the prominent Catholic Sir William Gerard at Garswood near Warrington was noted by Nicholas Blundell in his diary entry for 20 September 1711: 'I went to Garswood and dined there with Mrs Walmesley, Mr Scarisbrick, Mr John Gelibrond &c … Sir William Gerard took physick. Mounsuer La Abbe taught Mrs Walmesley &c to Dance at Garswood, I saw them Dance' (*Great Diurnal of Nicholas Blundell*, 1.301). Although it is not known precisely who Mrs Walmesley was, other references in Blundell's journal suggest that she may have been connected with the Walmesleys of Dunkenhalgh (who in turn were connected with the Petres of Ingatestone in Essex) as well as with the Gerards of Garswood. Indeed it is feasible that L'Abbé, himself a Catholic, by 1711 was teaching members of several significant recusant families. However, the absence of his name from the list *Roman Catholics, non-jurors and others who refused to take the oaths to His Majesty King George 1715* (1745, reprinted 1862) serves as a reminder of how highly he rated the patronage of the Hanoverian royal family, although this does not reveal whether he stopped teaching Catholic families following the Hanoverian succession in 1714.

John Essex noted that L'Abbé:

> is an excellent Master, and was a great Performer when upon the Stage … Nobody gave greater Satisfaction to the Spectators than he did in his performances. His Talent chiefly lay in the grave Movement … and what more eminently makes him shine, is his excellent Instructions of those of the Royal family whom he hath the Honour to teach. (Essex, xii)

Anthony L'Abbé's name (with variant spellings) appears in London parish rate books for Newport Court in the parish St Anne's, Soho (1700), Gerrard Street in the same parish (1702–9), and Fountain Court in the parish of St Clement Danes (1709–10). In 1710 he returned to Soho and lived until 1719 at one of the fashionable addresses in King's Square Court (in the house subsequently owned by Thomas Mulso, father of the essayist Hester Chapone). From 1722 until 1737/8 he lived in Broad Street, in the parish of St James Piccadilly.

It is not known whether L'Abbé married or raised a family, although the wedding of an Anthony L'Abbé and Martha Turner, which took place on 6 November 1726 at Lincoln's Inn Chapel in Holborn, may be his wedding or that of a close relative.

Parfaict confirms that L'Abbé returned to Paris in 1738 (Parfaict, 3.252), and by 1740 was succeeded as dancing-master to the princess's London household by Leach Glover. Parfaict also notes that L'Abbé was still living in Paris in 1750–53 (the period during which the *Dictionnaire* entries were first compiled), by which time he was nearly ninety. The date of his death is not known.

JENNIFER THORP

Sources W. Van Lennep and others, eds., *The London stage, 1660–1800*, pt 1: *1660–1700* (1965) • E. L. Avery, ed., *The London stage, 1660–1800*, pt 2: *1700–1729* (1960) • J. Milhous and R. D. Hume, 'The London stage, 1660–1800, part 2: draft of the calendar for volume 1, 1700–1711', typescript, 1996, Bodl. Oxf. • A. H. Scouten, ed., *The London stage, 1660–1800*, pt 3: *1729–1747* (1961) • *The present state of the British court* (1720) • J. Chamberlayne, *Magnae Britanniae notitia, or, The present state of Great Britain*, 34th edn (1741) • J. Essex, *The dancing master* (1728) • E. Pemberton, *An essay for the further improvement of dancing* (1711); facs. edn (1970) • Highfill, Burnim & Langhans, *BDA* • C. Parfaict, *Dictionnaire des théâtres de Paris*, 3 (Paris, 1767) • *The great diurnal of Nicholas Blundell of Little Crosby, Lancashire*, ed. F. Tryer and J. J. Bagley, 1–2, Lancashire and Cheshire RS, 110, 112 (1968–70) • A. L'Abbé, *A new collection of dances* (c.1725); facs. edn (1991)
Archives Harvard U., lord chamberlain's papers, papers relating to work in the theatre • PRO, lord chamberlain's papers, papers relating to work in the theatre • U. Nott. L., Portland papers, papers relating to work in the theatre

Labelye, Charles (*bap.* 1705, *d.* 1781?), engineer and mathematician, was born in Vevey, Switzerland, and baptized on 12 August 1705, the son of François Dangeau La Bélye and his wife, Elisabeth, *née* Grammont. The baptismal entry of a subsequent child in 1709 described the father as 'Monsieur François Dangeau, Sieur de la Bélye, refugié en cette ville par sa Religion' (*DNB*). Labelye's Huguenot father is thought to have been related to the marquis de Dangeau, a prominent member of the court of Louis XIV and author of a volume of memoirs. Another child was baptized in 1714: one of the godparents was Madame de Warens, the associate of J. J. Rousseau (Chavannes, 262).

Labelye moved to England in the early 1720s: 'I was neither born nor bred in England, but in Swisserland; and never heard a word of English spoken, till I was near twenty years of age' he wrote in 1739 (Labelye, vi), but he claimed in 1736 that he had been resident in London for some sixteen years. He soon made contact with Huguenot circles, in particular with J. T. Desaguliers (1683–1744), and joined a French masonic lodge in 1725. He travelled to Madrid in 1727–8, and is known to have visited the Low

Countries at some point. By November 1728 he was back in London, and embarked on his career as a mathematician and engineer. In 1734 he supplied maps and plans of the Thames to promoters of a scheme to erect a bridge at Westminster, and in April 1735 wrote a letter to Desaguliers concerning the prevalent laws of motions and their mathematical implications which was subsequently published in Desaguliers's *Course of Experimental Philosophy* (1745, 2.77). Labelye's calculations concerning water flow were used by Nicholas Hawksmoor (1661–1736) in his *Propositions for Erecting a New Stone Bridge at Westminster* in 1736. They were the first contribution to bridge building in Britain made by scientific theory. In that year he produced the 'Mapp of the downes … together with the soundings at low water, places of anchorage and all the necessary leading marks', in which he described himself as an 'Engineer, late Teacher of Mathematics in the Royal Navy' (PRO, MPH 218).

It was the building of Westminster Bridge that brought Labelye to prominence. An act of parliament (9 Geo. II, cap. 29) was passed in 1736, entitled 'An act for building a bridge across the River Thames, from the New Palace Yard in the City of Westminster to the opposite shore in the county of Surrey'. In June 1737 Labelye was one of five persons instructed to provide the commissioners of the bridge with surveys of the river, and in May 1738 he was appointed engineer at a yearly salary of £100, with daily expenses of 10s. The selection of a foreigner for a work of such national prestige caused considerable resentment among Labelye's disappointed rivals: he had already been attacked as 'the Swiss imposter' by the disappointed Batty Langley (1696–1751). The various schemes were reviewed in a work published by John James (*d.* 1746) in 1736. The first pile for the bridge's foundations was driven in September 1738, and the first stone laid in January 1739 by Henry Herbert, ninth earl of Pembroke, the most active of the many Westminster Bridge commissioners.

Labelye's commission initially extended only to the erection of stone piers; the design of the superstructure was not decided upon until 1740, when a modified version of Labelye's 1738 design was agreed upon. The final result consisted of a stone bridge of fifteen arches and fourteen piers. Labelye was assisted considerably in the architectural treatment of the bridge by the earl of Pembroke. Of particular significance was Labelye's employment of caissons—huge open wooden boxes, built on the shore and sunk into the river bed—within which the stone piers were constructed. The method was not new, but had never been tried on such a scale. Labelye published *A short account of the methods made use of in laying the foundation of the piers of Westminster Bridge* in 1739, and the anonymous *Present State of Westminster Bridge* is believed also to be by Labelye. A prospectus for a large work on the bridge was issued in 1744, but not proceeded with. Labelye's *The Description of Westminster Bridge*, a slightly expanded version of his 1739 work, appeared in 1751, and the caisson design was published in Belidor's *Architecture hydraulique* (vol. 4, 1752). The bridge was substantially complete by late 1746 but some piers had begun to show signs of excessive settlement.

Labelye was obliged to oversee an expensive programme of repair, while Batty Langley saw fit to publish *A Survey of Westminster Bridge, as 'tis now Sinking into Ruin*, in which Labelye was termed 'an insolvent ignorant, arrogating Swiss', and attacked in a cartoon. The bridge was not opened to traffic until November 1750.

In a petition to the bridge commissioners of February 1751 Labelye observed how much money he had saved the project, and how much he had suffered on behalf of the commission, 'in whose service I have spent above 12 years and the prime of my life, and greatly impaired my health having contracted asthma (daily growing upon me) by my constant attendance on the works, especially on the water in winterly and rainy weather' (Ruddock, 17). He also claimed to have turned down several lucrative offers from abroad. He was accordingly granted a gratuity of £2000 from the bridge commissioners, and was retained as engineer at a salary of £150. The largest stone bridge built up to that time in Britain, Westminster Bridge attracted considerable attention at home and abroad and was depicted in numerous paintings and engravings. In 1752 the bridge was described as 'the most magnificent monument of our times' (Belidor, 4.191).

Other projects occupied Labelye, although his only other bridge was that over the Thames at Brentford, commenced in 1740 and completed in 1742. He was consulted in 1746 by the corporation of London concerning London Bridge, but his proposals were not acted upon. Labelye's design for a harbour at Sandwich was engraved by Harris about 1740, and in 1747 he prepared a report on Yarmouth harbour. He also produced a report in 1748 on the improvement of the River Wear and the port of Sunderland.

Labelye enjoyed the patronage of John Russell, fourth duke of Bedford, as well as that of the earl of Pembroke. In 1744 the duke asked him to prepare a report on the drainage of the fens: this was published in 1745 as *The Result of a View of the Great Level of the Fens*, and revealed Labelye's familiarity with continental drainage systems. Late in 1745 Labelye was asked to prepare a report on the viability of repairing the Howland Great Wet Dock in Rotherhithe. The resulting report, written in April 1746, recommended selling the dock to the Royal Navy: that the duke of Bedford was first lord of the Admiralty cannot have escaped Labelye's attention.

Labelye was naturalized by act of parliament in 1746 (19 Geo. II, cap. 26), but the criticisms of Westminster Bridge and the effect upon his health resulted in a decision to leave England. Little is known of his later life. In April 1752 he departed for southern France, and in 1753 he was encountered in Naples. He subsequently lived in Paris, where he became acquainted with Jean-Rodolph Perronnet, head of the École des Ponts et Chaussées, to whom he bequeathed papers and a model of Westminster Bridge. The *Gentleman's Magazine* reported his death as having occurred in Paris in 1762, but other evidence indicates that it was probably on 17 December 1781. He is not known to have married, or fathered any children. Westminster Bridge was rebuilt in 1854–62.

ROGER BOWDLER

Sources Colvin, *Archs.* · *DNB* · R. J. B. Walker, *Old Westminster Bridge: the bridge of fools* (c.1979) · T. Ruddock, *Arch bridges and their builders, 1735–1835* (1979) · N. Kent, 'Innovator in stone: Charles Labelye, 1705–82', *Country Life*, 174 (1983), 1374–6 · J. Chavannes, *Les refugiés français dans le pays de Vaud Lausanne* (1874) · C. Labelye, *A short account … of Westminster bridge* (1739), VI · J. James, *A short review of the several pamphlets and schemes … in relation to building a bridge at Westminster* (1736) · B. F. de Belidor, *Architecture hydraulique*, 4 (1752)
Archives Inst. CE · LMA · Norfolk RO, report on Yarmouth harbour
Likenesses R. Ryle, portrait (of Labelye?), repro. in Sotheby's sale catalogue (31 Oct 1990), lot 275

Lablache, Fanny Wyndham (1821?–1877). *See under* Lablache, Frederick (1815–1887).

Lablache, Frederick (1815–1887), singer, eldest son of Luigi *Lablache (1795–1858) and his wife, Teresa Pinotti, was born in Naples on 29 August 1815, and trained by his father. He made his début in 1835 at the Théâtre Italien, Paris, as the Count in Bellini's *La sonnambula*, and his London stage début at the Lyceum in Donizetti's *L'elisir d'amore* (16 November 1837). Until 1852 he sang bass-baritone parts in some of his father's London and Paris seasons; at Naples in 1836 he created the part of Edoardo III in Donizetti's *L'assedio di Calais*. Most of his career was in the British Isles. In the late 1840s he appeared in Jenny Lind's highly successful provincial tours, managed by Michal Balfe; the critic J. W. Davison then called him 'a clever intelligent artist'. He also toured with his wife, the contralto **Fanny Wyndham Lablache** [*née* Frances Wilton] (1821?–1877), a Scot who had studied at the Royal Academy of Music in London (1836–7) and then made her début at Covent Garden (*Quasimodo*, February 1836), afterwards appearing at Her Majesty's. They both retired from the stage about 1865 and taught at the Royal Academy of Music. Fanny died in Paris on 23 September 1877, Frederick at their home, 51 Albany Street, Regent's Park, London, on 30 January 1887. Their son Luigi (or Louis), an actor, died in 1914.   G. C. BOASE, rev. JOHN ROSSELLI

Sources A. Soubies, *Le Théâtre-Italien de 1801 à 1913* (1913) · *From Mendelssohn to Wagner: being the memoirs of J. W. Davison, forty years the music critic of The Times*, ed. H. Davison (1912) · private information (2004) · *The Times* (4 Feb 1887) · R. Ajello and others, *Il Teatro di San Carlo*, 2 vols. (Naples, 1987) · d. cert.
Likenesses print, Harvard TC
Wealth at death £10,831 17s. 11d.: probate, 26 Feb 1887, *CGPLA Eng. & Wales*

Lablache, Luigi (1795–1858), singer, son of Nicolas Lablache (d. 1799), an émigré Marseilles merchant, and his wife, Marie Francesca Bietagh (of Irish descent), was born at Naples on 6 December 1795. In 1806 he entered the Conservatorio della Pietà dei Turchini, the only survivor of the famous Naples music schools. His education, lasting until 1812, made him a thorough musician. In that year he won an engagement at the Teatro San Carlino, home of popular comic opera. In 1813 he married the singer Teresa Pinotti; they had thirteen children, several of them, notably Frederick *Lablache, likewise singers.

After several years singing at Palermo (1816–20),

Lablache was by 1821, when he appeared at La Scala, a finished singer—a bass-baritone with an even two-octave range from E to E and the ability to sing both traditional comic parts and the new virtuoso serious roles of Romantic opera. Through Domenico Barbaja, who from 1823 ran the leading opera houses of Milan, Naples, and Vienna, Lablache quickly became known in all three cities; in 1827 he took part in Beethoven's funeral. He showed his versatility by singing at various times all three lower parts in Rossini's *Il barbiere di Siviglia* as well as the florid, sinister part of Assur in his *Semiramide*.

From 1829 to 1851 in Paris, and from 1834 to 1855 in London, Lablache divided his career largely between the Italian opera houses of the two richest countries in the world. He still created roles in new operas: in Bellini's *I puritani* (Paris, 1835) as one of the '*Puritani* quartet' (with Grisi, Rubini, and Tamburini), long remembered as the finest of singers; in ten of Donizetti's operas, including *Don Pasquale*, his most famous comic performance (Paris, 1843); and in one by Verdi (*I masnadieri*, Her Majesty's, 1847). In London he taught singing to Princess (later Queen) Victoria. A late sensation was his Caliban in Halévy's *La tempesta* (Her Majesty's, 1850), and from 1852 to 1857 he sang each year at St Petersburg. In 1857 his health declined rapidly; he died in Naples on 23 January 1858, and was buried with his wife at Maisons-Laffitte, near Paris.

Lablache was a very big man, yet graceful in his movements; his voice was likewise huge but under firm control. In a long career he was universally admired as a matchless singing actor, to the critic Henry Chorley 'one of the greatest musicians and artists ever seen or heard'.

JOHN ROSSELLI

Sources H. Weinstock, 'Luigi Lablache', *Opera*, 17 (1966), 689–95 · private information (2004) · H. F. Chorley, *Thirty years' musical recollections*, 2 vols. (1862) · F. Regli, ed., *Dizionario biografico dei più celebri poeti ed artisti … che fiorirono in Italia dal 1800 al 1860* (Turin, 1860) · A. Soubies, *Le Théâtre-Italien de 1801 à 1913* (1913) · H. Rosenthal, *Two centuries of opera at Covent Garden* (1958) · R. Edgcumbe, *Musical reminiscences, containing an account of the Italian opera in England from 1773*, 4th edn (1834), 205–6 · Castil-Blaze [F. H.-J. Blaze], *L'opéra-italien de 1548 à 1856* (Paris, 1856)
Likenesses J. P. Dantan, bronze and plaster statue, 1831, Musée Carnavelet, Paris, France · F. Salabert, lithograph, 1835, BM · H. Robinson, stipple, pubd 1846 (after T. Carrick), BM · W. Corden, oils, 1852 (after F. Winterhalter), Osborne House, Isle of Wight · Gros, oils (as young man), Museo Teatrale alla Scala, Milan, Italy · L. Lablache, self-portrait, sketch, Archives Nationales, Paris, France, AJ[13] 1168 · D. Maclise, sketch, V&A · C. F. Tomkins, caricature drawings, BM · F. Winterhalter, oils, Royal Collection · caricature (as Giorgio in *I puritani*), Bibliothèque de l'Opéra, Paris, France · drawings and lithographs, repro. in Weinstock, 'Luigi Lablache' · lithograph, repro. in Soubies, *Le Théâtre-Italien*, 127 · prints, BM, NPG

Labouchere, Sir George Peter (1905–1999), diplomatist and art collector, was born in London on 2 December 1905, the only son of Lieutenant-Colonel Francis Anthony (Frank) Labouchere, a senior civil servant in the Post Office, and his wife, Evelyn Mary Caroline Lihla (b. 1877), only daughter and only surviving child of Sir Walter George Stirling, third baronet, of Faskine, Lanarkshire. His father was highly regarded as an authority on British butterflies. The Laboucheres were descended from a French Huguenot family who, as a result of the revocation of the edict of Nantes in 1685, took refuge in the Netherlands. Among his forebears was Henry Du Pré (Labby) Labouchere (1831–1912), the Victorian radical and founder of the journal *Truth*.

After studying at Charterhouse and the Sorbonne, in November 1929 Labouchere joined the diplomatic service as a third secretary. He was transferred to Madrid in October 1930, then Cairo in November 1932. Promoted second secretary in November 1934, he returned to London in April 1935, but was again posted abroad in January 1937, to Rio de Janeiro. Transferred to Rome in January 1940, he returned after Italy's entry into the Second World War in June 1940. He was promoted first secretary in December 1940, and transferred to Stockholm in February 1943. While there he married, on 10 May 1943, Rachel Katharine (1908–1996), the former wife of Malcolm Findanus MacGregor, and only daughter of Eustace Scott Hamilton-Russell, sixth son of Gustavus Russell Hamilton-Russell, eighth Viscount Boyne. They had met in London after Labouchere's return from Italy; she endured a hazardous journey over the North Sea in order to marry and join him in Sweden and thereafter was a firm, lifelong source of support. There were no children of the marriage.

Labouchere's postings over the next twenty years were rarely without excitement. As counsellor in Nanking (Nanjing) from July 1946 to July 1948, he witnessed the decline of Chiang Kai-shek's nationalist regime, though not its ultimate demise. He then spent two and a half years in Buenos Aires at a time when Eva Perón's power was at its height. Appointed deputy commissioner in Vienna in December 1950, he took part in the delicate negotiations for the Austrian peace treaty. He then served as envoy-extraordinary and minister-plenipotentiary in Budapest from July 1953 to October 1955, the period immediately preceding the Hungarian uprising of 1956. From then until June 1960 he was British ambassador to Belgium, then regarded as a relatively peaceful appointment, but even there he was thrust into public prominence, following publicity about the end of Princess Margaret's romance with Group Captain Peter Townsend, Britain's air attaché in Belgium at that time. Labouchere's greatest challenge, however, occurred during his final appointment, as ambassador to Spain, from June 1960 to March 1966. Following the election of the Labour government in 1964, the prime minister, Harold Wilson, cancelled an order for £14 million to build frigates for the Spanish navy, thus provoking an angry response from the Spanish authorities, which resulted in the closing of the frontier with Gibraltar. Despite all Labouchere's efforts to restore a more cordial atmosphere, diplomatic relations remained strained. For his services as a diplomat, he was appointed CMG in 1951, KCMG in 1955, and GBE in 1964.

In 1966, on retiring from the diplomatic service, Labouchere took up residence in Dudmaston Hall, near Bridgnorth, Shropshire, a late seventeenth-century mansion surrounded by a 2300 acre estate, which had belonged to his wife's family since 1126 and been left to her by her maternal uncle Geoffrey Wolryche-Whitmore. At Dudmaston Hall the Laboucheres were able to pursue their artistic interests. The house was completely redecorated with seventeenth-century Dutch flower paintings, French furniture, and Chinese porcelain that had been collected by Lady Labouchere's family. For many years Labouchere himself had been keenly interested in contemporary art, initially favouring British artists such as Henry Moore, Barbara Hepworth, Lynne Chadwick, and Ben Nicholson but later extending his interests to the Parisian and American schools, including such figures as Soulages, Poliakoff, Dubuffet, Ernst, and Vasarely. During his period in Spain he expressed great enthusiasm for the work of the young Spanish painters Suarez and Tàpies, and after his retirement from the diplomatic service he continued to build up his collection of sculptures and ironwork. His wife, a skilled botanical artist, was a founder of the Ironbridge Gorge Museum. Dudmaston was given to the National Trust in 1978, though the Laboucheres continued to live there. In addition to membership of four London clubs, Labouchere belonged to the Society of Dilettanti and was president of the Friends of the Tate Gallery. Although most of his life had been spent in an urban environment, he enjoyed the freedom and tranquillity of country life. He was president of the Shropshire branch of the Council for the Protection of Rural England.

Labouchere was the perfect diplomat, witty, courteous, and impeccably groomed. An excellent raconteur, he was an amiable host who enjoyed good living and the company of friends and only rarely expressed his personal opinions in the press; an exception came in 1976, when he made a passionate plea against government cuts in diplomatic expenditure. He died on 14 June 1999 at Dudmaston Hall from Alzheimer's disease, his wife having predeceased him in 1996.   G. R. SEAMAN

Sources *Daily Telegraph* (17 June 1999) · *The Independent* (13 July 1999) · *The Times* (15 July 1999) · Burke, *Peerage* · *WWW* · *FO List* **Likenesses** photograph, 1964, repro. in *Daily Telegraph* · photograph, repro. in *The Independent* · photograph, repro. in *The Times* **Wealth at death** £1,813,731—gross; £1,796,227—net: probate, 14 Jan 2000, *CGPLA Eng. & Wales*

Labouchere, Henry, Baron Taunton (1798–1869), politician, was the elder son of Pierre César *Labouchère (1772–1839) [*see under* Hope family] of Hylands, Essex, and Over Stowey, Somerset, and his wife, Dorothy Elizabeth (*b.* 1771), third daughter of Sir Francis *Baring, first baronet; he was born on 15 August 1798 at St Marylebone, Middlesex. The Huguenot family of Labouchère had left France at the time of the edict of Nantes, and established themselves in Holland. Pierre César Labouchère, a partner in the great mercantile firm of Hope, was the first of his family who settled in England. His son Henry was educated at Winchester College, and on 24 October 1816 matriculated at Christ Church, Oxford, where he took a first class in Greats in 1820, and graduated BA 1821, and MA 1828. He was admitted a member of Lincoln's Inn on 30 April 1817, but was never called to the bar. In 1824 Labouchere travelled with Edward Stanley, J. E. Denison, and John Stuart

Henry Labouchere, Baron Taunton (1798–1869), by William Menzies Tweedie, exh. RA 1863

Wortley (afterwards lords Derby, Ossington, and Wharn-cliffe) through Canada and the United States.

At a by-election in April 1826 Labouchere was returned as a whig for St Michael's and held the seat at the 1827 general election. He soon obtained a reputation as a competent Commons speaker. His first reported speech in the house was made during the debate on the civil government of the Canadas in May 1828 (*Hansard 2*, 316–18), when he drew attention to the abuses of the system of government, and declared that if 'we cannot keep the Canadas with the good will of the inhabitants, we cannot keep them at all'. At the general election in August 1830 he was returned at the head of the poll for the borough of Taunton, and represented that constituency until his retirement from the House of Commons. In June 1832 he was appointed a lord of the Admiralty in Grey's administration, a post which he resigned on Peel's accession to office. He then became master of the Royal Mint in Melbourne's government in 1835 and on offering himself for re-election was opposed at the last minute by Disraeli, whom he defeated by 452 to 282 votes. He was sworn of the privy council on 6 May and was further appointed vice-president of the Board of Trade. He was under-secretary for war and the colonies from February to August 1839, when, resigning the vice-presidentship but retaining the mastership of the mint, he became president of the Board of Trade (29 August) in succession to Poulett Thomson, and was admitted to the cabinet. As president, he introduced measures lowering general rates of duty in the

West Indies and North America. On Melbourne's resignation in September 1841, Labouchere retired from office with the rest of his colleagues, and on the formation of Russell's first administration in July 1846 became chief secretary to the lord lieutenant of Ireland (John William Ponsonby, earl of Bessborough). The authorization of 'reproductive' employment (that is, public works) by the famous 'Labouchere letter' of 5 October 1846 failed as a remedy for the widespread distress in Ireland; its terms were 'so guarded as to be not clearly intelligible' (Woodham-Smith, 130). He was reluctant to concede that fever accompanied famine. Soon after Bessborough's death Labouchere was succeeded as chief secretary by Sir W. M. Somerville, and was reappointed president of the Board of Trade (22 July 1847) in the place of Lord Clarendon, the new lord lieutenant. While holding this office Labouchere successfully—though with several false starts—carried through the House of Commons the bill by which the navigation laws were repealed (12 & 13 Vict. c. 29), in spite of the strong opposition of the shipping interest (which, with Gladstone's help, persuaded Labouchere to leave coastal trade unchanged). He was also instrumental in passing the Mercantile Marine Acts (13 & 14 Vict. c. 93; 14 & 15 Vict. c. 96) and the Seaman's Fund Act (14 & 15 Vict. c. 102). He retired with the rest of his colleagues on Russell's overthrow in February 1852, and was one of the whigs left out by Aberdeen when he formed his government at the end of 1852.

Though not an original member of Palmerston's first ministry, Labouchere was appointed secretary of state for the colonies (21 November 1855), in the place of Sir William Molesworth, after the refusal of the post by Lord Derby and Sidney Herbert, and continued to hold this office until Palmerston's resignation in February 1858. As colonial secretary he was efficient, high-principled, and even-tempered, and was willing to make allowances for the difficulties of his governors. He supported Sir George Grey's plans for the establishment of Natal as a separate colony and supported Gore Brown's attempts to arrange a compromise between settler interests and the Maori in New Zealand. On Palmerston's return to power Labouchere was created Baron Taunton, of Taunton in the county of Somerset, by letters patent dated 18 August 1859. He took his seat in the House of Lords for the first time on 24 January 1860, but though he took part in the debates from time to time, he held no further ministerial offices. He continued, however, to play an important part in public life as a commissioner. He had been one of the commissioners of the 1851 exhibition and had presided over the royal commission on the City of London in 1853–4. He was chairman of the schools inquiry commission of 1864–7, which generated twenty-one volumes of evidence on endowed, private, and proprietary schools which had not been investigated by the Newcastle and Clarendon commissions. The Taunton commission was one of the most thorough of all Victorian inquiries. He was a trustee of the British Museum from 1860.

Labouchere married, first, on 10 April 1840, his cousin Frances, the youngest daughter of Sir Thomas Baring, bt, with whom he had three daughters. She died on 25 May 1850, and on 13 July 1852 he married Lady Mary Matilda Georgiana (1823–1892), the youngest daughter of George *Howard, sixth earl of Carlisle; they had no children, and his nephew Henry *Labouchere (1831–1912) was his financial heir. In default of male issue the barony of Taunton became extinct upon his death, which occurred at his home, 27 Belgrave Square, London, on 13 July 1869. He was buried at Over Stowey church on 20 July. Though usually described as a whig, Labouchere was really a moderate Liberal, one of those who linked the whig party to what became the Liberal Party of the 1860s.

G. F. R. BARKER, rev. H. C. G. MATTHEW

Sources GEC, *Peerage* · A. Thorold, *Henry Labouchere* (1913) · S. Palmer, *Politics, shipping and the repeal of navigation laws* (1990) · W. P. Morrell, *British colonial policy in the mid-Victorian age* (1969) · J. B. Conacher, *The Aberdeen coalition, 1852–1855* (1968) · *The Greville memoirs, 1814–1860*, ed. L. Strachey and R. Fulford, 8 vols. (1938) · K. B. Nowlan, *The politics of repeal* (1965) · C. B. F. Woodham-Smith, *The great hunger: Ireland, 1845–1849* (1962) · C. Kinealy, *This great calamity: the Irish famine, 1845–52* (1994)

Archives Bodl. RH, corresp. and papers · NA Canada, corresp. and papers relating to Canada · W. Sussex RO, Bessborough MSS, Labouchere MSS | Bodl. Oxf., letters to Samuel Wilberforce · Borth. Inst., letters to Sir Charles Wood · Harrowby Manuscript Trust, Sandon Hall, Staffordshire, letters to Lord Harrowby · Lambton Park, Chester-le-Street, co. Durham, corresp. with first earl of Durham · NA Scot., letters to second Lord Panmure · National Library of South Africa, Cape Town, letters to Sir George Grey · NRA, priv. coll., corresp. with Lord Bessborough and others · PRO, corresp. with Lord John Russell, PRO 30/22 · Trinity Cam., letters to Lord Houghton · U. Durham L., corresp. with third Earl Grey · U. Nott. L., letters to J. E. Denison · U. Southampton L., corresp. with Lord Palmerston

Likenesses B. Thorvaldsen, plaster bust, 1828, Thorvaldsen Museum, Copenhagen, Denmark · W. M. Tweedie, oils, exh. RA 1863, NPG [*see illus.*] · G. Hayter, group portrait, oils (*The House of Commons, 1833*), NPG · F. C. Lewis, stipple (after J. Slater; Grillion's Club series), BM, NPG · C. Silvy, carte-de-visite, NPG · C. W. Wass, stipple (as a child; after T. Lawrence), BM, NPG · photograph, NPG

Wealth at death under £140,000: probate, 9 Sept 1869, *CGPLA Eng. & Wales*

Labouchere, Henry Du Pré (1831–1912), journalist and politician, was born in London, on 9 November 1831. He came of a Huguenot family established in Holland since the revocation of the edict of Nantes. His grandfather, Pierre César Labouchère, was head of the great financial house of Hope, at Amsterdam, and left a very large fortune. The first of the family to settle in England, Peter Labouchere purchased the estates of Hylands, Essex, and Over Stowey, Somerset, and married Dorothy Elizabeth, third daughter of Sir Francis Baring. The elder of their two sons was the whig politician Henry *Labouchere, created Baron Taunton in 1859. His brother John, of Broome Hall, Dorking, was a partner in the firm of Hope, and later a partner in the bank of Williams, Deacon, Thornton, and Labouchere. He married Mary Louisa, second daughter of James Du Pré, of Wilton Park, Buckinghamshire. Henry Du Pré Labouchere was the eldest child of their family of three sons and six daughters.

All his life Labouchere was a rebel against constituted authority. He was educated at Eton College (where he was

Henry Du Pré Labouchere (1831–1912), by Walery, 1890

accused of bullying), and afterwards went to Trinity College, Cambridge, where in two years he ran up debts amounting to £6000. At the age of twenty-one he was sent to South America, where his family had important commercial interests. He found his way to Mexico and there wandered about for a year or two, fell in love with a circus lady, and joined the troupe. For six months he lived in a camp of Ojibwe Indians.

Meanwhile, without his knowledge, his family had secured him a place in the diplomatic service, and he learned, while in Mexico in 1854, that he had been appointed an attaché at Washington. He remained in the service for ten years and, after leaving Washington, was stationed in succession at Munich, Stockholm, Frankfurt, St Petersburg, Dresden, and Constantinople. According to his own accounts, he was insubordinate and indolent, and his passion for gambling shaped and coloured this period of his life wherever he went. But a man of his independence of mind would not have remained in the service for ten years unless he were really interested in it. The end came oddly. In 1864, at Baden-Baden, he was informed by the foreign secretary, Lord John Russell, of his appointment to a second secretaryship at Buenos Aires. He replied accepting the post, if he could fulfil the duties of it at Baden-Baden. This was not the first joke that he had tried on Russell, and he was dismissed from the service. It was his impish way of resigning, since his mind was already turning to a political career.

In 1865 Labouchere was elected member of parliament for Windsor as a Liberal, but was unseated on petition.

Two years later he was returned for Middlesex. He lost this seat in 1868, failed at Nottingham in 1874, and had to wait until 1880 before he was again in the House of Commons. Meanwhile, he speculated in theatre productions and won fame as a journalist. He invested in a syndicate that ran the Queen's Theatre in London and produced a number of plays. In 1868 he married one of his actresses, Henrietta *Hodson, with whom he had one daughter, Mary Dorothea (Dora). He inherited a great fortune from his uncle Henry *Labouchere, Baron Taunton (1798–1869). He wrote much for the *Daily News*, of which he had become part proprietor in 1868; his witty letters from Paris during the siege of 1870 secured the *Daily News*'s finances and were republished as *The Diary of a Besieged Resident* (1871). He wrote on finance for *The World*, founded (1874) and edited by his friend Edmund Yates; then, in 1876, he established a weekly journal, *Truth*, which for many years was by far the most successful of personal organs in the press. Labouchere was a first-class journalist. His reputation as a wit was well established; he had an easy, lucid style, and he wrote with candour about his own adventurous life and the follies and failings of his contemporaries. Labouchere used his inside information about the affairs and activities of the court and the political establishment to devastating effect. Though often exaggerated, the gossip in *Truth* almost always had a base in fact. Above all, *Truth* won admiration and gratitude by its fearless exposure of fraudulent enterprises of all sorts. This brought upon him a long series of libel actions. Most of them he won, and they were such good advertisements for his paper that he could afford to be indifferent to his irrecoverable costs amounting to scores of thousands of pounds. He died a very wealthy man.

In 1880, with Charles Bradlaugh as his colleague, Labouchere began his twenty-five years' parliamentary representation of Northampton (a two-member constituency). For a dozen years an influential section of the nonconformist electors of Northampton had successfully opposed the candidature of Bradlaugh because he preached atheism. Labouchere, too, was a lifelong agnostic, but a silent one, and these same people gave him enthusiastic support: in his scoffing way Labouchere used to call himself the 'Christian member for Northampton'. He soon became one of the most powerful radicals in the Commons. His only hatred in politics was reserved for the whigs, who still retained an influence in the Liberal Party disproportionate to their numbers and to their support in the country. He attacked their methods and their purposes alike in home and foreign policy, and although publicly he always treated Gladstone with respect, inventing the term 'the Grand Old Man', privately he mocked at his fervour and 'mystifications'. He did not object, he once said, to Gladstone's always having the ace of trumps up his sleeve, but only to his pretence that God had put it there. Throughout the parliament of 1880–85 Labouchere worked for an 'all-radical' government with Joseph Chamberlain at its head. Even before the episode of the 'Hawarden Kite' in December 1885 (when Gladstone's home-rule explanations were unexpectedly disclosed), Labouchere

exploited his intimacy with the Irish nationalists in his campaign against the moderate Liberals. A resourceful intriguer, he employed all his arts in the early months of 1886 to bring Chamberlain, Gladstone, and the Irish nationalists into agreement, using each in turn to further his plan of 'dishing the whigs'. When Chamberlain decided to vote against the first Home Rule Bill, it was the greatest disappointment of Labouchere's life, for it ruined his main enterprise. Thereafter his political zeal, though unabated, was diverted. The reorganization of the Liberal Party and doctrine, for which he had worked, and which might have altered the course of history, had become impossible. The cause of home rule owed much to him, and he assisted in exposing the forgeries of Richard Pigott, by which it was sought to represent Parnell as inciting to assassination. Pigott's confession, after his cross-examination by Sir Charles Russell, was written at Labouchere's house, 24 Grosvenor Gardens. Russell was a close friend, as were J. M. Whistler and Sir Henry Irving.

If political services were the chief qualifications, there were good reasons why Labouchere should have been given a place in the Liberal government of 1892–5. His exclusion was due to the objection of Queen Victoria, who held that the proprietor and editor of *Truth* ought not to be given office under the crown, though Gladstone may, on this occasion, have been relieved at the queen's stand. Moreover, Labouchere had led a radical campaign in 1889 against a new settlement of royal grants. Shortly afterwards he suffered another rebuff. He suggested himself for the vacant ambassadorship at Washington, but Rosebery, who was then foreign secretary, would not recommend the appointment. Even if it had been a suitable opportunity, it was scarcely reasonable to expect Rosebery to appoint his most unsparing critic as the mouthpiece of his policy in the United States.

Though in general libertarian, Labouchere was a strong opponent of homosexuality; it was his clause added to the Criminal Law Amendment Act 1885 by which Oscar Wilde was tried; Labouchere regretted that Wilde got only two years' hard labour; his original proposal would have permitted seven. Labouchere gained distinction and notoriety by being unlike any English politician of his time. His scepticism and realism were of the French rather than of the English cast, and he was the only English politician of the nineteenth century who made himself popular by cynical wit. For the forms of the British constitution he had little respect. He was hostile to the royal prerogative, to hereditary legislators, and to the formalisms and circumlocutions of diplomacy; he instinctively distrusted the appeal of idealism.

An industrious student of politics, Labouchere was an especially dangerous critic in foreign affairs. His parliamentary reputation was founded on the skill with which he attacked the Egyptian policy of Gladstone's second administration. Yet—in this respect true to the tradition of the radical school to which he belonged—Labouchere was never a 'little Englander'; and in his advocacy of an independent Egypt he recognized the need for British control of the Suez Canal. He speculated heavily and on the whole successfully in Egyptian bonds between 1870 and 1884. The Egyptian settlement for which he pleaded in the 1880s was, indeed, much like that embodied in the treaty of forty years later. He led the demand for inquiry into the behaviour of Rhodes's British South Africa Company in Rhodesia in 1893–4 and was an effective critic of imperial policies. He was among the most energetic opponents of the Chamberlain–Milner policy in South Africa. He took a prominent part in the commission of inquiry into the Jameson raid of 29 December 1895, and while he admitted that there was no proof of Colonial Office complicity, he complained that access to some important documents was denied, a position subsequently vindicated by historians. On the whole, he was unsuccessful in persuading Liberals and radicals to support him on this matter. In the Second South African War he was one of the leaders of the peace party, and this was perhaps the only period of his career in which he was personally unpopular. His constituents mobbed him at Northampton, and the worries of the time injured his health. Labouchere met his match in Henry Hess of *The Critic*, who in 1905 exposed one of his share-rigging deals in a pamphlet. Labouchere did not stand at the general election in 1906, but lived his remaining years near Florence. Although he said that he did not wish for office, he was disappointed that Campbell-Bannerman, whom he had staunchly supported, did not ask him to join his new government in December 1905. His only political reward on retirement was a privy councillorship.

In spite of his brilliant gifts and his industry for a quarter of a century, Labouchere has left no permanent mark on English politics. The worldliness of his radicalism made collaboration with nonconformist radicals difficult and, though a serious politician behind the wit, he found it difficult to convince contemporaries that he was so. But his genial personality, his wit, and his unconventional ways became established in many legends. Of no other politician in his generation were so many stories told. In appearance as in mind he was more French than English. He was an early and a heavy smoker. Universally known as 'Labby' (spelt 'Labbi' by Gladstone), his slight, well-formed frame, shapely head, and bearded face were familiar to the British public for a third of a century. Nothing seemed to ruffle his composure. The voice was gentle and the manner bland, and he delivered his witticisms in a drawl that caught the fancy of his audiences whether on the platform or in the House of Commons. In his personal relations he was kindly and sometimes generous.

Retired in Florence, the Laboucheres played an active part in the life of the English community together with their daughter, the marchesa di Rudini. Henrietta Labouchere died on 31 October 1910 and was buried in San Miniato. Friends realized that Henry Labouchere was very ill when he stopped smoking. As he lay dying, a lamp was overturned accidentally: 'Flames? Not yet, I think', he murmured. He died at Villa Cristina, Florence, on 15 January 1912 and was buried in the same grave as his wife in San Miniato, the usual rules against the burial of non-Roman Catholics being temporarily suspended by the accident that the cemetery was briefly in the hands of the municipal authority.

HERBERT SIDEBOTHAM, rev. H. C. G. MATTHEW

Sources A. L. Thorold, *Life of Henry Labouchere* (1913) · R. J. Hind, *Henry Labouchere and the empire, 1880–1905* (1972) · H. Pearson, *Labby* (1936) · Gladstone, *Diaries* · J. Butler, *The liberal party and the Jameson raid* (1968) · E. Pakenham, *Jameson's raid* (1960) · G. R. Searle, *Corruption in British politics, 1895–1930* (1987)

Archives BL, papers, Add. MSS 44342, 44515 | BL, letters to Sir Henry Campbell-Bannerman, Add. MS 41222 · BL, corresp. with Sir Charles Dilke, Add. MS 43892 · BL, corresp. with Lord Gladstone, Add. MSS 46015–46016 · BL, corresp. with W. E. Gladstone, Add. MSS 44473–44515, *passim* · Bodl. Oxf., corresp. with Sir William Harcourt and Lewis Harcourt · Bodl. Oxf., corresp. with Lord Kimberley · CAC Cam., corresp. with Lord Randolph Churchill · CKS, letters to Aretas Akers-Douglas · News Int. RO, letters to Moberly Bell · NL Scot., corresp. with Lord Rosebery · Theatre Museum, London, letters to Lord Chamberlain's licensee · U. Birm. L., corresp. with Joseph Chamberlain · W. Yorks. AS, Leeds, letters to Lord St Oswald

Likenesses Walery, photograph, 1890, NPG [*see illus.*] · B. Stone, photograph, 1897, NPG · Ape [C. Pellegrini], chromolithograph caricature, NPG; repro. in *VF* (7 Nov 1874) · G. Brogi, photograph, NPG · H. Furness, pen-and-ink caricature, NPG · F. C. Gould, two drawings, NPG · S. P. Hall, pencil sketches, NG Ire.; NPG · F. Pegram, pencil sketch, V&A; repro. in *Pictorial World* (7 March 1889) · Stuff [Wright], chromolithograph caricature, NPG; repro. in *VF* (25 Nov 1897) · E. A. Ward, oils, Reform Club, London · photograph, repro. in Thorold, *Life of Henry Labouchere*, frontispiece

Wealth at death £550,020 7s. 1d.: resworn probate, 1912, *CGPLA Eng. & Wales*

Labouchère, Pierre César (1772–1839). *See under* Hope family (*per. c.*1700–1813).

Laby, Thomas Howell (1880–1946), physicist, was born at Creswick, Victoria, Australia, on 3 May 1880, the youngest of three children of Thomas James Laby (1825–1888), a well-to-do miller, and his wife, Jane Eudora Lewis (1845–1910). The family subsequently moved to New South Wales, the father having invested in a ropeworks not far from Sydney. The business failed, however, and when the father died soon afterwards, Laby's mother took on a small country boarding-school for girls. Laby attended various country schools before finding employment in 1898 in the colony's taxation department and then in the chemical laboratory of the department of agriculture. Here his talent for precise experimental work became apparent. When a vacancy appeared at the University of Sydney in 1901 for a junior demonstrator in chemistry, the head of his department, F. B. Guthrie, recommended him for the post.

This appointment entitled Laby to attend evening classes at the university even though he had not qualified to matriculate, and during the next few years he undertook systematic study in chemistry, physics, and mathematics. He also began research that led to two papers presented to and published by the Royal Society of New South Wales. These provided the basis on which, in 1905, despite lacking any formal qualification, he was awarded an 1851 Exhibition science research scholarship that took him first to Birmingham to work with J. H. Poynting and then to the Cavendish Laboratory in Cambridge.

Laby's research blossomed in Cambridge where, under the leadership of J. J. Thomson, radioactivity and the ionization of gases dominated the physics research agenda. Ingenuity and skill in experimental technique were a *sine qua non*, and there was a continuing tradition of precision measurement which became the hallmark of Laby's work. His experimental skills were honed on measurements relating to the ionization of gases; he developed an improved version of an extremely sensitive quartz-thread string electrometer that found application in various investigations of radioactivity, and he acquired great discrimination in assessing experimental data. This last gave rise to a lifelong collaboration with his fellow Cavendish researcher, G. W. C. Kaye, leading to the publication in 1911 of the first edition of their well-known *Tables of Physical and Chemical Constants*, in which they brought together and judiciously weighed the best available determinations of an astonishing variety of physical and chemical quantities. The work filled a need. It was quickly translated into Spanish, and eight subsequent English editions followed during their lifetimes, with others posthumously.

After two years in Cambridge Laby was awarded the degree of BA by research. An extension of his scholarship and the award of others by his college (Emmanuel) and by the Royal Society enabled him to stay on for a further two years, and then in 1909 he applied successfully for the newly created chair of physics at Victoria University College in Wellington, New Zealand. There he found himself in a radically different environment, with few students and almost no facilities. Nevertheless, he quickly established the only research programme in physics in the country and in due course saw his first research students awarded 1851 Exhibition scholarships and follow in his footsteps to the Cavendish Laboratory. He also threw himself into the movement that was then pressing for reform of the New Zealand university system. In addition Laby, in 1910, became a founding member of the New Zealand chapter of the Round Table movement devoted to strengthening the bonds of empire, a move that brought him into contact with leading figures in New Zealand, Britain, and later also in Australia. On 17 February 1914, while visiting London, Laby, a tall, spare, and rather diffident man, married Beatrice Littlejohn (1891–1975), daughter of a prominent Wellington jeweller. They had two daughters who both became scientists.

In 1915 Laby took up the chair of natural philosophy at the University of Melbourne. He immediately joined the Melbourne Round Table group and soon became secretary. While chafing at his inability to participate directly in the war effort, he undertook a number of war-related scientific projects. Then in 1918 he prepared an influential report on the classification of professional and scientific officers in the commonwealth public service. With the war ended he was able to begin building up his department. He was a poor lecturer, but compensated with a well-organized system of laboratory work modelled on Cambridge. This and his strong commitment to research, unusual in Australian universities at the time, resulted in

a stream of well-qualified research students emerging from the department and a steady stream of publications. Close links developed between Laby's department and the Cavendish Laboratory's new director, Ernest Rutherford. During the inter-war period, the Melbourne physics department largely monopolized the Australian list of 1851 Exhibition science research scholarships, with twelve of Laby's students winning these prestigious awards (of which there were only two each year for the whole of Australia, in all fields of science). Several other students of his also went to Cambridge, supported by other scholarships. Laby and Rutherford were close friends. Rutherford respected Laby's judgement and would always make a place at the Cavendish for a student he recommended; Laby was careful only to recommend students who he was confident would do well.

In his own research Laby maintained his commitment to precision measurement of physical quantities. One lengthy investigation yielded a new standard value for 'J', the mechanical equivalent of heat; another, on X-ray spectra, led to an extremely sensitive method of chemical analysis by X-ray emission spectrography; a third, carried out in the late 1930s, sought to reconcile the slightly different values yielded by different methods of determining the charge on the electron. He was consulting physicist to the Imperial Geophysical Experimental Survey that worked in Australia for several years in the late 1920s and co-edited its report. He was also consultant to the Commonwealth Radium Laboratory when this was established by the Australian government in 1929 in the grounds of the University of Melbourne, and in this capacity had a significant influence on the use in Australia of radiation methods for the treatment of cancer. He was a founding member of the Australian Radio Research Board, established in 1927; until it was closed in 1941, one of the board's two research groups was based in his laboratory and worked under his direction on problems relating to signal noise and fading.

Laby was awarded a DSc by Cambridge University in 1921, and was elected FRS in 1931. Throughout the 1920s and 1930s he was indisputably Australia's leading physicist. Whenever the government needed advice in matters of physics, it was his that was sought; and when an Australian branch of the (British) Institute of Physics was formally established in 1939, he automatically became president.

Following the outbreak of the Second World War Laby was anxious once again to bring his science to bear on problems of national importance. In mid-1940 the government, faced with an acute shortage of optical components to meet the needs of the armed services, established an optical munitions panel with Laby as chairman. During the next few years, on top of his university duties, he oversaw the creation in Australia, from scratch, of a design and manufacturing capability of high-quality optical instruments. However, the heavy workload took its toll on his health. He had never been an easy man to work with on committees and on several occasions disagreements had led to his resigning in spectacular fashion. As his health declined, his inability to compromise became steadily more pronounced. In 1942 he relinquished his university chair in controversial circumstances, and in 1944 he was forced to resign from the optical munitions panel. Laby died of arteriosclerosis on 21 June 1946 and was cremated in Melbourne.   R. W. HOME

Sources D. K. Picken, *Obits. FRS*, 5 (1945–8), 733–55 · R. W. Home, 'The beginnings of an Australian physics community', *Scientific colonialism: a cross-cultural comparison*, ed. N. Reingold and M. Rothenberg (1987), 3–34 · E. Muirhead, *A man ahead of his times: T. H. Laby's contribution to Australian science* (1996) · W. F. Evans, *History of the Radio Research Board, 1926–1945* (1973) · L. Foster, *High hopes: the men and motives of the Australian Round Table* (1986) · private information (2004)

Archives CUL, letters to Lord Rutherford · University of Melbourne, Laby papers

Likenesses photograph, *c.*1935, repro. in Muirhead, *A man ahead of his times*, frontispiece · photograph, *c.*1943, University of Melbourne, School of Physics · photograph, repro. in Picken, *Obits. FRS*

Lacaita, Sir James Philip (1813–1895), scholar and politician, the only son of Diego Lacaita of Manduria, in the province of Lecce, Italy, and of Agata Conti of Agnone in the Molise, was born at Manduria on 4 October 1813. He took a law degree at the University of Naples, was admitted an advocate in 1836, and practised his profession. An acquaintance with Enos Throop, the United States' chargé d'affaires at Naples, begun in December 1838, helped him in the study of English, and this knowledge gained him the post of legal adviser to the British legation at Naples, and the friendship of the minister, Sir William Temple, at whose table he met many distinguished English travellers.

Lacaita's political opinions were liberal but moderate, and he never belonged to any of the Italian secret societies. He was an unsuccessful candidate for the representation of the city of Naples in 1848, and on 7 April was appointed secretary to the Neapolitan legation in London, but did not start for his post, which he resigned after the fall of the liberal Troya ministry in May. In November 1850 he met Gladstone, who was in Naples for family reasons and was beginning to collect information about Bourbon misrule. This meeting led to the arrest of Lacaita on 3 January 1851, and he remained in custody for nine days. In a letter from Gladstone to Panizzi, in September, he is referred to as 'a most excellent man, hunted by the government' (Fagan, *Life of Panizzi*, 2.97, 205–6). Lacaita's friendship with Gladstone, which lasted the rest of their lives, did much to establish the respectability of the Risorgimentists among the Peelites.

The publication of Gladstone's *Letters to Lord Aberdeen*, for which Lacaita supplied many of the details, aroused the hostility of the court and clerical partisans in Italy, and Lacaita found it advisable to leave Naples for London, where he arrived on 8 January 1852. He was at Edinburgh on 14 February, in May he was an unsuccessful candidate for the office of librarian of the London Library, and on 15 June 1852 he married Maria Clavering (*d.* 1853), daughter of Sir Thomas Gibson Carmichael, seventh baronet. His means were small, but he made many powerful friends in

Sir James Philip Lacaita (1813–1895), by Georgio Matarrese, 1894

the best political and literary circles in London and Edinburgh. From November 1853 until April 1856 he was professor of Italian at Queen's College, London, was naturalized in July 1855, and published *Selections from the Best Italian Writers* (1855; 2nd edn, 1863). In the winter of 1856–7 he accompanied Lord Minto to Florence and Turin. From 1857 to 1863 he acted as private secretary to Lord Lansdowne, and towards the close of 1858 went with Gladstone to the Ionian Islands as secretary to the mission, being made KCMG for his services in March 1859.

Lacaita was entrusted by Cavour with a delicate diplomatic negotiation in 1860 connected with schemes to prevent Garibaldi from crossing from Sicily to Calabria, and subsequently the Neapolitan government offered him the post of minister in London with the title of marquess, both of which he declined (Fagan, *Life of Panizzi*, 2.208). In December 1860, after the expulsion of the Bourbons, he revisited Naples, caused his name to be reinstated on the municipal registry, and in July 1861, while back in England, was returned as deputy to the first Italian legislature. He generally supported the new Italian government. After the dissolution of 1865 he did not seek re-election, and was made a senator in 1876. Though speaking but seldom in the chamber, he exercised a considerable influence upon public affairs between 1861 and 1876 through his intimacy with Ricasoli, La Marmora, Minghetti, Visconti-Venosta, and other leading political figures. Florence became his headquarters in Italy after the removal of the government thence from Turin, and so it remained even after the transfer of the capital to Rome. He spent a portion of each year in England, and during the last fifteen years of his life wintered at Leucaspide, near Taranto, where he had made large purchases of monastic lands in 1868. He was a director of the Italian company for the southern railways from its formation, and took a share in the management of several Anglo-Italian public companies. Besides his English title, he was a knight of the Brazilian Order of the Rose, and knight commander of SS. Maurizio e Lazzaro and of the Corona d'Italia.

During his earlier years in England Lacaita frequently lectured on Italian subjects at the Royal Institution, the London Institution, and elsewhere. He wrote nearly all the Italian articles for the eighth edition of the *Encyclopaedia Britannica*, and revised several editions of Murray's *Handbook for South Italy*. In 1865 he edited the third, or album, volume of the great edition of the *Inferno di Dante* (3 vols., 1858–65), after the death of Lord Vernon, having helped in the production of the former volumes. He compiled the *Catalogue of the Library at Chatsworth* (4 vols., 1879) for the seventh duke of Devonshire, and edited the first complete publication of the famous Latin lectures on Dante of Benvenuto da Imola, delivered in 1375, *Comentum super Dantis Aldigherii Comoediam nunc primum integre in lucem editum, sumptibus Guil. Warren Vernon* (5 vols., 1887).

Lacaita died at Posilipo, near Naples, on 4 January 1895, in his eighty-second year, leaving an only son, Charles Carmichael Lacaita, later his biographer and Liberal MP for Dundee. During forty-five years his life and interests were divided between Britain and Italy; in the one a polished Englishman, in the other a vivacious Neapolitan and a conscientious landowner. He was a notable Dante scholar, an excellent bibliographer, a man of wide reading and intellectual sympathy, of great social tact and goodness of heart.   H. R. TEDDER, rev. H. C. G. MATTHEW

Sources C. Lacaita, *An Italian Englishman: Sir James Lacaita* (1933) · Gladstone, *Diaries* · *The Times* (8 Jan 1895) · *The Times* (10 Jan 1895) · *Lettere ad Antonio Panizzi*, ed. L. Fagan (1880) · L. Fagan, *The life of Sir Anthony Panizzi*, new edn, 2 vols. (1886) · private information (1901)
Archives U. Mich., Clements L., corresp. and autograph collection | BL, corresp. with W. E. Gladstone, Add. MSS 44233–44234 · BL, letters to Sir Austen Layard, Add. MSS 38988–39100 · BL, corresp. with Sir Anthony Panizzi, Add. MSS 36716–36725, 42177 · Herts. ALS, letters to Lord Lytton · NL Scot., letters to second earl of Minto · NL Scot., corresp. with Lord Rutherford and Lady Rosebery · NRA, priv. coll., letters to Lord Stanmore
Likenesses G. Matarrese, bronze statuette, 1894, NPG [*see illus.*]
Wealth at death £12,048 5s. 9d.: probate, 13 Feb 1895, CGPLA Eng. & Wales

Lace, Isabelle. *See* Steiger, Isabelle de (1836–1927).

Lacey, Sir Francis Eden (1859–1946), cricket administrator, was born on 19 October 1859 at Bestwall House, East Stoke, Wareham, Dorset, the youngest son of William Charles Lacey, solicitor, and his wife, Elizabeth, *née* Baker. Educated at Sherborne School, he was admitted in 1878 to Gonville and Caius College, Cambridge, where he won blues for association football (1881) and cricket (1882), and graduated BA in 1882. A little over 6 feet tall and

powerfully built, Lacey was 'a stylish bat … a capital field, and a slow round-arm bowler with deceptive flight' (Green, 529).

During his first year at Cambridge Lacey began playing for Hampshire and he captained the county from 1888 to 1893, before it was granted first-class status. Among a number of notable performances were innings of 211 and 92 not out against Kent at Southampton in 1884, and 323 not out against Norfolk in 1887, which was then the highest score on record in a county match. In 1889 he was called to the bar at Inner Temple and for a time he was lost to the game of cricket. In April 1898, though, he was appointed secretary of the MCC on the retirement of the long-serving Henry Perkins. Soon afterwards, on 9 April 1890, he married Lady Helen Alice Carnegie (1867/8–1908), only daughter of George John Carnegie, ninth earl of Northesk; they had one son and one daughter.

On taking up the reins at Lord's, Lacey found the Marylebone club 'in none-too happy a condition, and he devoted himself at once to tightening up the finances and in general to restoring a waning prestige' (*The Times*, 28 May 1946). Meticulous where his predecessor had been flamboyant, he enforced economies and introduced administrative reforms. The MCC was a growing concern and Lacey divided its rapidly multiplying affairs between a number of separate departments, each under the overall control of the main committee. His approach required an 'absolute observance of the rules and regulations' and meant a change in the easy-going ways to which some members of the club, and even the staff, had become accustomed. Inevitably the new regime had its critics. Lacey acquired a reputation for being 'stern and grim' in office and he was thought by many to be 'over-rigid, a cold personality who never dropped his official guard' (Lewis, 157). But he enjoyed a good working relationship with Lord Harris, the dominant presence on the committee; and if, as a 'new broom', he 'swept a little too clean', the Marylebone club ultimately benefited from his firmness (Green, 529).

Lacey was at bottom a cricketer and never lost the outlook of a player. In 1902 he began the Easter coaching classes for young cricketers, which became an important part of the MCC's encouragement of the modern game. He was also behind the advisory county cricket committee which was established in 1904. This brought together representatives from the first-class and minor counties, under the chairmanship of the president of the MCC or another senior member. It was an important forum, through which the MCC kept in touch with developments in the game. Lacey was involved, too, in establishing the Imperial Cricket Conference (27 July 1909), which was set up to regulate test cricket within the empire. During the First World War he served with the secret service.

Lacey was a central figure at Lord's during a time of important change in world cricket. He paid painstaking attention to detail and was undoubtedly inflexible at times. Sir Pelham Warner recalled an awkward moment when he 'refused the twelfth man of Eton admission to the pavilion on the grounds that his instructions were to admit the Eton eleven'. But Warner also remembered Lacey as 'a man of high character and integrity', who was held in genuine esteem at the MCC (*The Times*, 6 June 1946). When he retired in 1926, after nearly three decades as secretary, he was knighted, the first cricket figure thus honoured. He was also elected a trustee of the Marylebone club. After the death of his first wife he married, on 11 December 1926, Mary Marshall Walker, widow of J. Campbell Walker, of Rickmansworth, and daughter of Robert Ramsay, a merchant of Melbourne, Australia. Lacey died on 26 May 1946 at his home, Sutton Veny House, Sutton Veny, near Warminster, Wiltshire. His second wife survived him.

MARK POTTLE

Sources *The Times* (4 May 1926) · *The Times* (28 May 1946) · *The Times* (6 June 1946) · T. Lewis, *Double century: the story of MCC and cricket* (1987) · B. Green, ed., *The Wisden book of obituaries* (1986) · WWW · Venn, *Alum. Cant.* · b. cert. · m. certs. · d. cert.
Likenesses G. Spencer Watson, portrait, 1928, Lord's Cricket Ground, London · photograph, repro. in Lewis, *Double century*, 159
Wealth at death £69,332 15s. 4d.: probate, 12 Oct 1946, CGPLA Eng. & Wales

James Harry Lacey (1917–1989), by unknown photographer

Lacey, James Harry [Ginger] (1917–1989), air force officer, was born at Fairfield Villas, Wetherby, Yorkshire, on 1 February 1917, the son of Charles Lacey, a cattle dealer, and his wife, Mary Brown Smith. The later nickname Ginger came from his shock of carroty hair. He was educated from 1927 to 1933 at King James's Grammar School, Knaresborough, where he enjoyed sport and left with a school certificate. His father died in 1933 and Lacey, lacking interest in a farming career, trained as a pharmacist, passing intermediate exams in 1936. However, his heart was set on flying, so he joined the newly formed RAF volunteer reserve. He trained as a sergeant-pilot at Scone in Scotland, being the first on the course to fly solo, and passed out 'above average'; he then flew on training sessions each weekend at Brough. With increasing experience on biplanes, from Tiger Moths to Hawker Harts, he was accepted in 1938 as an instructor with Yorkshire Airways Ltd. In January 1939 he was attached briefly to 1 squadron at Tangmere, where his keen eyesight and marksmanship were noted. When the squadron re-equipped with Hurricanes he soon flew one; he had then put in 250 hours of service flying.

Lacey was called up in September 1939 and joined 501 County of Gloucester auxiliary squadron at Filton as a sergeant-pilot. Their main action began on 10 May 1940 when they joined the air component of the British expeditionary force in France as the French campaign opened. The squadron was quickly under pressure from greater Luftwaffe numbers. Lacey made his mark on 13 May by shooting down a Messerschmitt Bf 109, a Heinkel He 111, and a Messerschmitt Bf 110 before breakfast, a feat rewarded with the French Croix de Guerre. By 18 June, when the squadron returned to England, he had scored five victories and had a narrow escape from a crash-landing.

During the battle of Britain, Lacey shot down a Bf 109 over the channel on 20 July. Then, flying from Gravesend, he was in regular action, flying up to six sorties daily and suffering their attendant stress. On 8 August he destroyed

a Junkers Ju 87 Stuka and claimed two 'possibles'. Four days later he accounted for two aircraft, and then another on the 24th. He was awarded the DFM on 23 August. On 30 August, while attacking Heinkel He 111s head-on, his aeroplane was hit and oil sprayed into the cockpit, yet he managed skilfully to coax his Hurricane back to Gravesend. By 5 September he had accounted for five further aircraft and was already a respected ace during the period of greatest pressure on Fighter Command, especially on 11 group.

On 13 September 1940 Lacey shot down a Heinkel He 111 which had earlier bombed Buckingham Palace. In the action his radiator was damaged and he baled out, suffering minor burns. In his log book he wrote a reminder to leave bombers alone: 'they are shooting me down much too often' (Bickers, 95). On the 15th he destroyed three enemy aircraft, but two days later he was himself shot down again and had to parachute to safety. By the end of October he claimed four more Bf 109s, and on 26 November he received a bar to his DFM.

During the battle Lacey achieved the RAF's top score, with eighteen aircraft destroyed. It was no coincidence that thirteen were Bf 109s, considered by Luftwaffe pilots to be comprehensively superior to the Hurricane. His boyish looks belying his years and experience, Lacey had scored with superb airmanship resulting from many hours of pre-war training. Sharp eyesight, gritty determination, and skilful shooting brought him success—and a charmed life.

Although he was always content as a sergeant-pilot, in January 1941 Lacey was awarded a commission. He then flew on sorties over France, destroying four further aircraft, three of them Bf 109s. After 300 hours on active operations he was posted away to be an instructor with 57 operational training unit. In March 1942 he re-entered action with 602 squadron, then, after flying with them from Kenley, he moved on to 81 group as tactics officer. Later he experimented with rocket armament at Boscombe Down before going on to Northumberland and instructing in low-level attack.

An overseas posting arrived in March 1943 when Lacey sailed to India; later he took command of 17 squadron in

Assam. Towards the end of the Burma campaign he led offensive operations against the Japanese, and he gained his final success in February 1945 by shooting down a Nakajima 'Oscar', bringing his total to twenty-eight. After the war he took his squadron to a base near Hiroshima in Japan, and was the first pilot to fly a Spitfire over that country.

During his voyage to India, Lacey had met (Maureen) Sheila Latchford on board ship. They married on 8 July 1945 at the Sacred Heart Church, Kodaikanal, and later had three daughters—Diana, Wendy, and Susan.

Back in Britain, Lacey was awarded a permanent commission and stayed in the RAF. He served variously as a fighter controller in Hong Kong, the Isle of Man, and Burma, flew early jets, and worked as an instructor at home and abroad. In March 1967 he retired, as a squadron leader. Later he ran a small air-freight business and taught budding pilots to fly in Yorkshire; they could have had no better tutor.

Lacey died from cancer at Castle Hill Hospital, Nottingham, on 30 May 1989, and his funeral service was held in the priory church, Bridlington. A modest, yet independent and straightforward man, he was the finest exemplar of the many sergeant-pilots of the volunteer reserve who so ably served their country during the battle of Britain.

JOHN RAY

Sources RAF service record, RAF Insworth, Gloucestershire, personnel management centre, 60321 · R. T. Bickers, *Ginger Lacey: fighter pilot* (1962) [repr. 1997] · C. Shores and C. Williams, *Aces high* (1994), 383–4 · *Daily Telegraph* (1 June 1989) · private information (2004) [J. Young, Battle of Britain Fighter Association] · L. Deighton, *Fighter* (1977), 67, 144, 192 · E. Kennington, *Drawing the R.A.F.* (1942), 72–3, pl. 19 · J. Terraine, *The right of the line: the Royal Air Force in the European war, 1939–1945* (1985), 202 · R. A. Hough and D. Richards, *The battle of Britain* (1989), 202 · K. G. Wynn, *Men of the battle of Britain: a who was who of the pilots and aircrew* (1989)
Likenesses E. Kennington, drawing, repro. in Kennington, *Drawing the R.A.F.* · C. Orde, drawing · photograph, IWM [*see illus.*]
Wealth at death under £70,000: administration, 28 June 1989, *CGPLA Eng. & Wales*

Lacey, Janet (1903–1988), charity director, was born in Sunderland on 25 October 1903, the younger child and younger daughter of Joseph Lacey, property agent, who had been born within the sound of Bow Bells, and his wife, Elizabeth Smurthwaite, from the north of England. Her father died when Janet was ten, and her sister, Sadie, died of cancer in mid-life. She went to various schools in Sunderland before going to drama school in Durham. Her family were fairly narrow Methodists, mostly teetotal, though her father 'drank whisky like water'. It may have been her father's death that caused Janet's mother to send her to live with an aunt in Durham.

Although she toured in the theatre world for three years, Janet Lacey found it hard to make a living. At the age of twenty-two she applied to the Young Women's Christian Association (YWCA) for work, and in 1926 was sent to the YWCA at Kendal to train as a youth leader. She stayed there for six years. Her skills in drama were fully used, and she received her first introduction to theology. Later she became an Anglican. During the general strike of 1926 she

saw much poverty in Durham pit villages and became a Labour supporter. In 1932 she moved to Dagenham, London, to a job which used many of her gifts, in a mixed YMCA–YWCA community centre at the heart of a vast new housing estate which provided activities 'from the cradle to the grave'.

In 1945 Lacey became YMCA education secretary to the British army of the Rhine, which was slowly being demobilized. It was typical of her that she used the post to bring young British soldiers together with young Germans and with refugees. She learned much about running programmes of social aid and made her first contacts with ecumenical church leaders such as Bishop Hans Lilje and Bishop George Bell. She said she would go about whispering to herself: 'I must not get used to this devastation.' Her capacity for compassion shaped her career.

Lacey was appointed youth secretary of the British Council of Churches in 1947, a job which introduced her to the World Council of Churches. She was a significant presence at its four assemblies: at Amsterdam, Evanston, New Delhi, and Uppsala. For the second assembly she wrote and produced a dramatic presentation, *By the Waters of Babylon* (1956). She got to know intimately many of the leaders of the world church, such as Visser't Hooft. In Britain the peak of her work was the Bangor youth conference in 1951.

By 1952 Lacey needed a task which would use her full talents. In December that year she was appointed secretary (the term 'director' was only used later) of Inter-Church Aid (from 1960 Christian Aid), a post she held until 1968. She worked from both Geneva and London, helping to establish many other important bodies such as Voluntary Service Overseas and World Refugee Year, but her greatest contribution was to conceive Christian Aid Week. This was wholly her idea and she executed it with characteristic flair. The first week raised only £25,000 but by the time she retired it was raising £2 million a year. 'Need not creed' was her slogan as she stumped not only Britain but the world.

Lacey was tough and stocky; without being tall she confronted others as being a tower of strength. She was a formidable, autocratic leader, often infuriating, but her compassion in action caused even her critics to admire her. She was blunt to a fault. She was a skilled manager, but not as humane in her management as the really good manager needs to be, so that after she retired from Christian Aid, her years as director of the Family Welfare Association (1969–73) were not a total success. She more successfully reorganized the Churches' Council for Health and Healing (1973–7). Although she could run huge organizations, she could not boil an egg: nevertheless she loved entertaining her friends—at restaurants. She adored the theatre, music, and sculpture.

After her great contribution to World Refugee Year, she was appointed CBE in 1960. In 1967 she became the first woman to preach in St Paul's Cathedral. In 1970 her autobiographical volume, *A Cup of Water*, was published. Late in life she was prepared for confirmation by Father St John Groser, the socialist East End priest. She was awarded an honorary DD from Lambeth in 1975. Her retirement in her Westminster flat was happy—she would welcome her many friends from all corners of the globe—until she became a victim of Alzheimer's disease. She died, unmarried, in a nursing home at 11–13 Ladbroke Terrace, Kensington, on 11 July 1988, after having spent several years living there.　　　　ERIC JAMES, *rev.*

Sources J. Lacey, *A cup of water: the story of Christian Aid* (1970) · *The Times* (14 July 1988) · *The Independent* (20 July 1988) · personal knowledge (1996) · *CGPLA Eng. & Wales* (1988)

Wealth at death under £70,000: probate, 25 Aug 1988, *CGPLA Eng. & Wales*

Lacey, Thomas Alexander (1853–1931), religious writer and controversialist, was born at Nottingham on 20 December 1853, the younger child and only son of George Frederick Lacey, a tailor and draper, and his wife, Susan Woodward, a native of Stamford, Lincolnshire, who was ill-treated and deserted by her husband, being left to bring up two infants. Lacey was nominated to a free place in the grammar school at Nottingham, founded in 1513, which in 1868 was re-established as the high school, and the excellence of his Latin paper in the Oxford senior local examination resulted in his being offered in 1871 an exhibition at Balliol College, Oxford, where T. H. Green was his tutor. He gained a second class in *literae humaniores* in 1875. He became one of the most accomplished Latinists of his time, and it is related that when he was in Rome in connection with the inquiry into Anglican ordinations Pope Leo XIII said that he wished that he had a cardinal who could write such Latin as Mr Lacey. In 1876 he was ordained while a master at Queen Elizabeth Grammar School, Wakefield, where he taught for two years, before serving as curate at Ardwick. He was an assistant master at Denstone College (1885–9) when he married, in 1888, Dorothy, only daughter of William Stott Banks, solicitor, of Wakefield. There were three sons and three daughters of the marriage. He was vicar of St Edmund's Church, Northampton, from 1892 to 1894, and of Madingley, near Cambridge and its libraries, from 1894 to 1903.

In 1894 Lacey embarked upon the most important task of his life. He had been a member of the council of the high-church English Church Union since 1891 and assisted the attempt by the union's president, Viscount Halifax, to achieve a reconciliation between the Roman Catholic and Anglican churches. Discussion of the subject had begun in 1893 after the publication of the Abbé Portal's treatise upholding the validity of Anglican ordinations. The pope himself encouraged the process and took the initiative in appointing a commission on Anglican orders. In collaboration with Edward Denny, Lacey composed a *Dissertatio apologetica de hierarchia Anglicana* (1895). In March 1896 the commission appointed by Leo XIII to investigate the question assembled in Rome. In April, at the desire of the Abbé Duchesne and of Cardinal Gasparri, Lacey, accompanied by Frederick William Puller of the Society of St John the Evangelist, Cowley, went to Rome to give further help. He remained in Rome until June, and in *A Roman Diary* (1910) gave a graphic account of the comings and goings in the antechambers of the cardinals, the differences among the

Roman theologians, the enthusiasm of Leo XIII, the high expectations, and finally the successful neutralizing efforts of the English Roman Catholics, led by Cardinal Vaughan, to get Anglican ordinations condemned.

During the middle years of his life Lacey was a member of the editorial staff of the *Church Times*, the organ of the high-church party. From 1900 he contributed a weekly essay under the pseudonym Viator and anonymously was the author of brilliant leading articles ranging over an immense variety of topics. He increasingly took his own line, however, and was dismissed by the editor, E. Hermitage Day, in February 1920, after signing a resolution at a conference at Mansfield College, Oxford, in favour of reunion between the Church of England and the free churches. A collection of his essays from the *Church Times* and elsewhere, *Wayfarer's Essays*, was published in 1934. In politics he was a strong supporter of Irish home rule and women's suffrage, but was opposed to the admission of women to the priesthood.

As a proctor in convocation (1922–9) Lacey's speeches were provocative, paradoxical, and disconcerting; he was not always discriminate in his use of sarcasm and ridicule. He wrote learnedly on liturgical and historical subjects, including *Marriage in Church and State* (1912). In 1917 he delivered the Bishop Paddock lectures at the General Theological Seminary, New York, published the same year as *Unity and Schism*. He was one of the editors of the *English Hymnal* (1906), to which he contributed many translations of ancient Latin hymns. His original hymn 'O faith of England, taught of old' was widely used. In 1903 he became chaplain, and from 1910 to 1919 was warden, of the London Diocesan Penitentiary, Highgate. In 1918 he was appointed canon residentiary of Worcester Cathedral, and was treasurer from 1922 until his death at a nursing home at Worcester, where he was recovering after an operation, on 6 December 1931. His wife survived him. He received the honorary degree of DD from St Andrews University in 1926.　　　　C. B. MORTLOCK, *rev.* M. C. CURTHOYS

Sources *Church Times* (11 Dec 1931), 702 · C. L. Wood, *Leo XIII and Anglican orders* (1912) · private information (1949) · personal knowledge (1949) · I. Elliott, ed., *The Balliol College register, 1833–1933*, 2nd edn (privately printed, Oxford, 1934) · B. Palmer, *Gadfly for God: a history of the Church Times* (1991) · b. cert.

Archives LPL, corresp. | Borth. Inst., corresp., incl. some of his wife, with second Viscount Halifax · LPL, letters and papers to Archbishop Benson relating to reunion · LPL, corresp. with Edwin Palmer

Likenesses photograph, repro. in *Church Times* · photograph, repro. in T. A. Lacey, *Wayfarer's essays* (1934), frontispiece

Wealth at death £669 7s. 7d.: probate, 24 Feb 1932, *CGPLA Eng. & Wales*

Lacey, William. *See* Wolfe, William (1584–1673).

La Chapelle, Victor Octave Xavier Alfred de Morton de, Count de La Chapelle in the French nobility (1863–1931), lawyer and wildfowler, was born in Périgord, France, in 1863, son of the Count and Countess de La Chapelle. His mother was descended from the Scottish earls of Morton. The first eight years of his life were spent on the family's extensive estates, comprising the Château de Montcuque in the region of Périgord and the Château

Giomer on the edge of the marshes of St Valery-sur-Somme. Following the abdication of Napoleon III in 1871, his father's estates were confiscated and the family moved initially to Italy. There he developed his lifelong love of wildfowling, using a 28 bore shotgun. His inherited wealth enabled him to attend shooting forays in Italy, France, England, and North America (Dakota territory), where he worked for a time among the Sioux Indians.

La Chapelle settled in London, and was admitted a solicitor in 1888. He founded a firm of solicitors in Gresham Street in the City of London, which handled many important cases and boasted foreign links with Paris, Geneva, Brussels, Berlin, Alexandria, Florence, Bucharest, Melbourne, and New York. He was legal councillor to the royal Romanian litigation, which played a part in persuading Romania to enter the First World War on the side of the allies in August 1916. From 1907 La Chapelle spent weekends and holidays with his family—he had a wife, Rachel (1875–1970), and a daughter—at Tollesbury, Essex. He was a keen punt-gunner, famed for his adventures with his two boats, which toured the Essex Blackwater estuary. He acquired an extensive collection of guns and other shooting memorabilia which were retained at his residence, Heron Lodge. His reputation among the local inhabitants was enhanced by his unwillingness to shoot wildlife on many of the mudflats vital to their living, confining his wildfowling to the adjacent coastal stretches. His exploits were extensively documented by friend, fellow shooter, and journalist James Wentworth Day.

The count (La Chapelle was known by his French title) was a popular figure, who privately funded a London jazz band which he personally conducted. In the late 1920s his legal practice suffered from misappropriations by a trusted member of staff. La Chapelle suffered a nervous breakdown. After returning to work after a period of recuperation, he was found dead with a bullet wound to his head and a revolver by his side, in his office at 34–6 Gresham Street, London, on 9 June 1931. His funeral, held in Tollesbury, was attended by representatives of the Wildfowlers' Association (which he had co-founded) and the royal Romanian litigation. Respected as the 'king of the Blackwater punters', he was buried on 13 June at the West Street burial-ground, Tollesbury, with 'his face to the sea, his feet to the marshes, Sea Lavender in his grave, the sea wind blowing above him' (*The Field*, 20 June 1931, 898).

JOHN MARTIN

Sources J. W. Day, *Coastal adventure* (1949) · J. W. Day, *The modern shooter* (1952) · *The Field* (20 June 1931), 898 · *Daily Mail* (10 June 1931), 11 · *Essex Chronicle* (12 June 1931), 12 · *Essex Chronicle* (19 June 1931), 5 · J. W. Day, *The modern fowler* (1973) · J. W. Day, *Book of Essex* (1979) · *Essex Countryside Magazine*, 16/131 (Dec 1967), 28 · *Essex Countryside Magazine*, 17/150 (July 1969), 56 · *Essex Countryside Magazine*, 19/170 (March 1971), 42 · *Essex Countryside Magazine*, 20/190 (Nov 1972), 50 · *Essex Countryside Magazine*, 22/212 (Sept 1974), 58 · *Law List* (1890), 355 · *The Times* (12 June 1931), 8 [inquest] · gravestone, Tollesbury, Essex · d. cert.

Likenesses photograph, repro. in Day, *Coastal adventure* · photograph, repro. in *The Field*, 898

Wealth at death £2168 8s. 5d.: probate, 14 Nov 1931, CGPLA Eng. & Wales

La Chapelle, Vincent (*fl.* 1733–1736), cook and writer on cookery, was one of the most influential cooks in the early eighteenth century, but almost nothing is known about his personal life. When he published *The Modern Cook* at his own expense in 1733, he was described as having lately been the principal cook of the fourth earl of Chesterfield. A year later an advertisement for his book described him as cook to the count of Montijo; in 1736, the title page announced that he was now chief cook to his highness the prince of Orange. Before entering the service of Lord Chesterfield, La Chapelle claimed, he travelled widely and visited, among other places, India. His book reflects a curiosity about cookery throughout the world and includes recipes for such dishes as 'Calf's head Hanover style', 'Tripe the Polish way', 'Hare the Swiss way', and 'Chicken the Jamaican way'. Not only are there numerous recipes 'à l'Anglaise', but the work manifestly indicates La Chapelle's respect for English food and cooking. His culinary philosophy is revealed in his very first pages, where he wrote that: 'A cook of genius will invent new delicasies to please the palates of those for whom he is to labour, his art, like all others, being subject to change' (Hyman and Hyman, 'La Chapelle and Massialot', 45).

When his book was published in French, again at the author's expense, in 1735 under the title *Le cuisinier moderne*, La Chapelle warned his French readers that he was not writing solely for them. Nevertheless, his cookery fitted into the French mould—partly because many of his recipes were reproduced (without proper acknowledgement) from François Massialot's *Cuisinier royal et bourgeois* (1691)—one of the most popular French cookery books of the time. Despite its heavy borrowings from this older treatise, La Chapelle's book was original in many respects. It is a monumental work (from three large volumes in 1733, it grew to five in the second French edition of 1742), illustrated with sixteen engravings of imposing dimensions. Virtually every branch of cookery is treated, and it was the first eighteenth-century French cookery text to announce a rupture with the past and vaunt the merits of *cuisine moderne*, claiming it to be simpler, healthier, and more elegantly served than former styles of cooking.

La Chapelle not only introduced the French to such English dishes as 'Rosbif', 'Beef steks', and 'Potin' (pudding), but also incited French chefs to be more adventurous and to draw upon other culinary traditions for inspiration. *Le cuisinier moderne* is no doubt one of the most influential of all the cookbooks published in the eighteenth century. Antonin Carême (1833) judged it 'digne de mon attention' ('worthy of attention'; Hyman and Hyman, 'Vincent La Chapelle', 35) and a century later Auguste Escoffier included a 'Sauce Vincent' in his classic, *Le guide culinaire* (1921 edn), adding that 'this sauce was created by Vincent La Chapelle, one of the great master chefs of the 18th century' (p. 36).

PHILIP HYMAN and MARY HYMAN

Sources P. Hyman and M. Hyman, 'La Chapelle and Massialot: an eighteenth century feud', *Petits Propos Culinaires*, 2 (Aug 1979), 44–54 · P. Hyman and M. Hyman, 'Vincent La Chapelle', *Petits Propos Culinaires*, 8 (June 1981), 35–40 · V. Maclean, *A short-title catalogue of*

household and cookery books published in the English tongue, 1701–1800
(1981) · B. K. Wheaton, *Savoring the past* (1983)

Lachlen, Elizabeth. *See* Appleton, Elizabeth (*c*.1790–1849).

Lachmann, Gustav Victor (1896–1966), aeronautical
engineer, was born on 3 February 1896 at Dresden, Saxony, the younger son of Gustav Anton Lachmann, industrialist, and his wife, Leopoldine Wilvonseder; both were
Austrian and their elder son, Edward, became professor of
literature and German philology at Innsbruck University.
In 1902 the family moved to Darmstadt, where Gustav
entered the *Realgymnasium* and in 1908 joined fellow students in building a glider in emulation of Otto Lilienthal
and the Wright brothers. In 1914 he volunteered for the
24th Hessian life dragoons and was assigned to the eastern
front, being commissioned in 1917, wounded in action,
and awarded both the Eisenkreuz and the Hessische
Tapferkeits Medaillon. After transferring to the
Fliegerkorps as a fighter pilot he crashed, sustaining a
broken jaw and leg injuries; in hospital he contemplated
the cause of the stall that had interrupted his flying career, deducing that sudden loss of lift at high incidence and
low airspeed could be due to airflow stagnation. With the
aid of a ladies' hairdrier he used tobacco smoke to visual-
ize the airflow round a simple wooden model wing which
had spanwise slots discharging air from the under surface
tangentially on to the upper surface, so as to re-energize
the boundary layer; the smoke behaved exactly as
expected. In February 1918 he drafted a patent specification to protect his invention, which he believed would
prevent stalling. After rejoining his unit on the western
front, he was wounded in aerial combat and awarded a
second Eisenkreuz.

On being invalided out in 1918, Lachmann found that
the German patent examiners refused to accept the principle of his invention; he then enrolled at Darmstadt Technical University for a three years' course in mechanical
engineering and aerodynamics, graduating in June 1921 as
Diplom-Ingenieur. By chance, he saw an account in
Flugsport of the previous year's demonstration at Cricklewood of a slotted wing patented by Frederick Handley
Page and immediately challenged its priority. The German patent examiners insisted on experimental proof, so
Lachmann asked Professor Ludwig Prandtl to conduct the
requisite wind-tunnel tests, for an agreed fee of DM1000
(£50), which Lachmann borrowed from his mother; the
result (65 per cent increase in lift) convinced the patent
office, which granted the original application backdated
to February 1918, some eighteen months earlier than
Handley Page's master patent, which, however, Lachmann could not afford to contest in court. In August 1921
the two inventors met amicably in Berlin and agreed to
collaborate, retaining their separate rights in their own
countries, but pooling them elsewhere; Handley Page
retained Lachmann as his consultant during his forthcoming three years' research in Prandtl's Aerodynamic Institute at Göttingen, thus providing useful income for Lachmann at trivial cost to himself, because of the prevailing
low value of marks in relation to sterling.

In 1923 Lachmann's thesis, 'The slotted wing and its
importance for aviation', was accepted by Aachen Technical University for the degree of doctor of engineering,
the oral examination being passed with distinction,
coupled with the award of the Borchers plaque. Having
gained workshop experience in the Opel motor car factory at Russelheim, Lachmann spent one year as a
designer at the Schneider aircraft works in Berlin, then in
1925 became chief designer at the Albatros aircraft works
at Johannisthal, where he designed two biplanes, the
single-engined L72 for express delivery of a Berlin newspaper and the twin-engined L73 eight-passenger transport; both had slotted ailerons and flaps for low-speed control, but only the L72 had leading-edge slots. In 1926,
before the L73 had flown, Lachmann resigned from
Albatros to join the Ishikawajima aircraft works in Tokyo
as technical adviser on the design of a biplane, which he
also flight-tested, as no test pilot had been engaged. The
following year Lachmann married Evelyn Wyatt Haigh,
widow of the late British vice-consul at Tokyo; their only
daughter, Evelyn Leopoldine, was born in 1929, when they
moved to England, where Lachmann became engineer in
charge of aerodynamics, stressing, and slot development
at Handley Page Ltd.

In 1932 Lachmann became chief designer at Cricklewood, to exploit Herbert Wagner's 'tension-field' system
of stressed-skin metal construction for cantilever mono-
planes; he was responsible for the HP47, Harrow, and
Hampden bombers, while George Volkert dealt with production problems arising from the new technology. In
1936 Volkert resumed as chief designer, while Lachmann
initiated a research department at Edgware to develop an
advanced tailless monoplane. The Second World War
broke out before this had flown and Lachmann, still technically an 'enemy alien', was interned in Canada, from
where Lord Brabazon of Tara secured his transfer to the
Isle of Man, where he undertook non-military design studies until 1947. Lachmann became a naturalized British
subject in 1949. However, internment had affected his
marriage, which was dissolved in 1950. On 16 March the
following year he married Catherine Elizabeth Doreen (*b*.
1917/18), daughter of John Beggs, a farmer; there were no
children.

In 1953 Lachmann became head of the Handley Page
research department at Radlett, to develop laminar airflow control by suction, a difficult technique promising
enhanced performance and economy for long-range aircraft. This project ended in 1965, when Lachmann retired
to continue his researches privately at his home, Alan-
dale, Berry Lane, Chorleywood, where he died suddenly
on Whit Monday, 30 May 1966, survived by his second
wife.

Gus, as Lachmann was known to his colleagues, combined generous chivalry with an excellent command of
English (his publications were numerous) and a lively wit,
matching that of Sir Frederick Handley Page, whom he
was prepared to defy on any important point of principle.
His honours included fellowship in 1938 of the Royal
Aeronautical Society (which awarded him both the Taylor

and the Wakefield gold medals), the honorary degree of DEng of the Technical University of Aachen in 1959, and honorary fellowship of the Wissenschaftliche Gesellschaft für Luft und Raumfahrt in 1962.

C. H. BARNES, *rev.*

Sources *The Times* (1 June 1966), 14f · private information (1981) · m. cert. [Catherine Elizabeth Doreen Beggs] · d. cert.
Wealth at death £16,413: administration, 10 Jan 1967, *CGPLA Eng. & Wales*

Lachtín mac Tarbín (*d. 622/627*). *See under* Munster, saints of (*act. c.450–c.700*).

Lack, David Lambert (1910–1973), ornithologist, was born on 16 July 1910 in London, the eldest in the family of three sons and one daughter of Harry Lambert Lack, ear, nose, and throat surgeon, and his wife, Kathleen, an actress, daughter of Lieutenant-Colonel McNeil Rind, of the Indian army. Lack was educated at Gresham's School, Holt, Norfolk (1924–9), and Magdalene College, Cambridge, where he read zoology and found it very dull, for at that time there was almost no interest in field studies. He obtained a second class in both parts of the natural sciences tripos (1931 and 1933). His first paper—a study of nightjars—was completed while he was still at school.

After leaving Cambridge, Lack became a schoolmaster at Dartington Hall, Devon, from 1933 to 1940. While there, initially to interest the pupils, he started to put colour-rings on the local robins. From this emerged his *The Life of the Robin* (1943), one of the pioneer monographs on a bird population.

Encouraged by Julian Huxley—at that time one of the very few professional zoologists with an enthusiasm for field studies—Lack went in 1934 to visit R. E. Moreau in Tanganyika, and in 1935 to the USA, where he met, among other people, Ernst Mayr; both these became lifelong friends and important academic associates. In 1938–9 he spent a year in the Galápagos studying Darwin's finches; from this emerged his *Darwin's Finches* (1947, reprinted 1983).

By the time Lack returned to England the Second World War had broken out. He joined the army operational research group (1940–45), was engaged to work on radar research, and became one of the first people to realize that the masses of small, slow-moving objects on the radar screens were migrating birds. In the late 1950s he used radar to make important contributions to the study of migration.

In 1945 Lack became director of the Edward Grey Institute of Field Ornithology at Oxford, a post which he held until his death. He built the institute into a unit of international standing; among the things he initiated was an annual student conference in bird biology. He was a fellow of Trinity College from 1963. Following visits to the Netherlands, where he was impressed by H. N. Kluijver's studies of the great tit, Lack began studies of the same species. The great tit, a hole-nesting bird which is easy to monitor during the breeding season, became a major study species of the institute. As a result of both this and

David Lambert Lack (1910–1973), by Elliott & Fry, 1952

the Dutch studies, it became one of the bird 'classics'. Shortly after this, Lack also started work on swifts.

In 1949 Lack married Elizabeth Theodora Twemlow, second child of John (Jack) Silva, director of a factory manufacturing starch. They had three sons and a daughter.

In 1954 Lack produced *The Natural Regulation of Animal Numbers*, a book which covered a wide range of animal groups. This had more impact than his other books and made him a leading figure in the arguments about population regulation. Since Lack strongly believed that an understanding of natural selection played an important part in ecology, he became involved in another long-running debate—the importance of group selection in comparison with individual selection.

Lack was so devoted to his family and his research that he tended to steer clear of committees. He was also a devout Christian, and wrote *Evolutionary Theory and Christian Belief* (1957). He was interested in music and an avid reader.

Lack was awarded his ScD in 1948 and was elected a fellow of the Royal Society in 1951, largely, as he put it, on his achievements as an amateur. His main honours included the Godman–Salvin medal of the British Ornithologists' Union (1958), presidency of the International Ornithological Congress (1966), and, probably the one that pleased him most, the Darwin medal of the Royal Society (1972). Lack died in Oxford on 12 March 1973.

C. M. PERRINS, *rev.*

Sources W. H. Thorpe, *Memoirs FRS*, 20 (1974), 271–93 · D. Lack, 'My life as an amateur ornithologist', *The Ibis*, 115 (1973), 421–31 · *CGPLA Eng. & Wales* (1973)
Archives Scott Polar RI, journals · U. Oxf., Edward Grey Institute of Field Ornithology, corresp. and papers | Rice University, Houston, Texas, corresp. with Sir Julian Huxley · U. Birm. L., letters to C. T. Onions
Likenesses Elliott & Fry, photograph, 1952, NPG [*see illus.*] · photograph, repro. in *Memoirs FRS*, 270
Wealth at death £82,607: probate, 10 Aug 1973, *CGPLA Eng. & Wales*

Lackenheath [Lakingheth], **John** (*d.* 1381), Benedictine monk, derived his name from Lakenheath, a few miles north-west of Bury St Edmunds. Having been appointed keeper of the barony there, Lackenheath found that the archives of the abbey were still in a state of disorder as a result of the sack of the abbey by the townsfolk of Bury in 1327. He reorganized those archives and, c.1380, compiled an elaborate register (now BL, Harley MS 743) which provided a finding aid for the records. He is also recorded in court records as making decisions on seigneurial dues payable to the abbey. His activities on behalf of his house made him very unpopular, and during the rising of 1381 the Suffolk rebels, at the instigation of the Bury townsfolk, demanded that Lackenheath be surrendered to them. In order to prevent the destruction of the monastery, Lackenheath gave himself up to the rebels and on 15 July was beheaded in the market place, where his head was set upon the pillory.

Another Benedictine monk and near namesake, **John Lakyngheth** (d. 1396), was a member of the order at Westminster, holding a number of offices there, most notably as treasurer of the abbey at various times between 1363 and 1392. In 1386 Richard II unsuccessfully sought to secure his election as abbot of Westminster. Lakyngheth has been proposed as the author of the Westminster chronicle (in Cambridge, Corpus Christi College, MS 197A), which ends in the year of his death and includes a vivid account of the Salisbury parliament of April–May 1384 which was attended by him. However, it seems unlikely, from the description of the attempt to make him abbot, that he was responsible for this chronicle. As Barbara Harvey has observed, 'It hardly seems likely that the author who chose to record this episode—according to the evidence of the rest of his chronicle a self-effacing man—was himself the abbot *manqué*' (*Westminster Chronicle*, xl).

ANDREW PRESCOTT

Sources R. M. Thomson, *The archives of the abbey of Bury St Edmunds*, Suffolk RS, 21 (1980), 23–33, 129–31 · *Thomae Walsingham, quondam monachi S. Albani, historia Anglicana*, ed. H. T. Riley, 2 vols., pt 1 of *Chronica monasterii S. Albani*, Rolls Series, 28 (1863–4), vol. 2, p. 3 · A. Réville, *Le soulèvement des travailleurs d'Angleterre en 1381*, ed. C. Petit-Dutaillis (1898), 175–82 [appeal of John Wraw] · BL, Harley MS 743 · R. H. Hilton and T. H. Aston, eds., *The English rising of 1381* (1984) · L. C. Hector and B. F. Harvey, eds. and trans., *The Westminster chronicle, 1381–1394*, OMT (1982) · J. Taylor, *English historical literature in the fourteenth century* (1987) · E. H. Pearce, *The monks of Westminster* (1916)
Archives BL, Harley MS 743 | CCC Cam., Westminster chronicle, MS 197A

Lackington, George (1768–1844), bookseller and publisher, was the son of George Lackington, a thriving coal merchant. He was third cousin of James *Lackington (1746–1815), bookseller and publisher. In 1781 George's father purchased a share in James Lackington's business for his son, and George, who was 'well educated and gentlemanly' (Nichols, *Lit. anecdotes*, 8.51b), began work in the bookshop which was then located at Chiswell Street, London. When in 1794 the firm moved to the building in Finsbury Square known as the Temple of the Muses, it was a very successful business which dealt in cheap remaindered books sold for cash, and at the height of its prosperity was said to employ more than 100 people. When James

Lackington retired in 1798, George was made head of the firm, which became known as Lackington, Allen & Co.

By 1803 Lackington, Allen & Co. were also considerable publishers: one of their advertisements lists forty-three items including their latest 'Catalogue of Ancient and Modern Books, comprising upwards of 800,000 volumes, the largest collection for sale in Europe'. Their sales list for the same year had widened to include classical texts and contemporary writers such as Tobias Smollett. The list also includes William Turton's *Medical Glossary* (Turton was a relative of James Lackington by marriage), and William Fordyce Mavor's *Natural History* (Mavor's son became one of the partners of the firm).

On 18 March 1805 George Lackington married Miss Bullock, daughter of Captain Bullock RN. They had a daughter in 1806 and a son in 1818. Between 1815 and 1817 Lackington, Allen & Co. suffered losses amounting to £2198 under the Copyright Act which, in an amendment of 1814, contentiously required the deposit of eleven copies of new publications in certain libraries. Lackington's correspondence with Sir Egerton Brydges, MP for Maidstone, who was attempting to bring in reforms to the act, was printed in Brydges's pamphlet *Reasons for a Further Amendment of … the Copyright Act of Queen Anne* (1817). It also contains letters Lackington exchanged with James Bean, assistant keeper of printed books in the British Museum. Lackington, Allen & Co. were publishing a number of expensive works in parts by subscription, several of which had commenced before 1814 (notably Dugdale's *Monasticon*), and they were unwilling to supply the earliest parts. In 1815 Lackington was forced to comply with a demand from the British Museum.

By 1822 the business was conducted under the name Lackington, Hughes, Harding, Mavor, and Lepard. Joseph Harding was one of the early partners who had served his apprenticeship with his father, John Harding, agricultural bookseller of St James's Street. Between 1825 and 1827 George Lackington bought from William Bullock the building then known as Bullock's Museum situated at 170–71 Piccadilly. Under his ownership it was known as the Egyptian Hall and in 1831 he turned part of the building into an exhibition hall (it was demolished in 1905).

After Lackington's retirement the firm moved to Pall Mall East and was known as Harding and Lepard. Lackington, who always had a facility for financial affairs, was in later years, according to Nichols, an official assignee of bankrupts. Lackington died on 31 March 1844 at his home in Circus Road, St John's Wood, London. The last link with Lackington ended in December 1886 with the death of James Kanes Ford, who had worked for Lackington until 1821, when he left to set up his own bookselling business in London at Upper Street, Islington.

BRENDA J. SCRAGG

Sources GM, 1st ser., 75–6 (1805–6); 87–8 (1817–18) · *The Bookseller* (Dec 1886) · *The parish of St James, Westminster*, 1/2, Survey of London, 30 (1960) · S. E. Brydges, *Reasons for a further amendment of … the Copyright Act* (1817) · Nichols, *Lit. anecdotes* · Nichols, *Illustrations*
Archives Herefs. RO, letter-book · Yale U., Beinecke L., letter-book

Lackington, James (1746–1815), bookseller and publisher, was born in Wellington, Somerset, on 31 August 1746, the eldest of the eleven children of George Lackington, a journeyman shoemaker, and his wife, Joan Trott, the daughter of a poor weaver in Wellington. James's early life owed little to his father, who was a drunkard, and he claimed to be indebted to his mother for everything. He received only a few years' schooling because the family was unable to afford it, and James was required to help with the care of his brothers and sisters. At the age of ten he left home to live with a pie merchant, and entered into the business of selling pies with considerable success.

When Lackington was fourteen he went with his father to Taunton and was apprenticed for seven years to George and Mary Bowden, shoemakers; here he learned to read and first attended a Methodist meeting. With only a few months of his apprenticeship left to run his freedom was purchased by friends of the two candidates then contesting the election of 1768 in Taunton. He moved to Bristol, where he lodged with John Jones, a shoemaker, and together they plied their trade. Though he was still unable to write, Lackington composed several songs and ballads, one of which he sold for a guinea, and a number of which were printed. No evidence of these has been traced. In Bristol, Lackington first heard John Wesley preach in Broadmead, and this reawakened his enthusiasm for Methodism. He moved to lodgings in St Philip's Plain where his room overlooked the churchyard, and converted Jones and his friends to Methodism. At this time the idea of selling books first attracted Lackington and Jones, and all the spare money they accumulated was spent in purchasing books (although it was some years before Lackington became a bookseller). In 1770 he married Nancy Smith, whom he had first met in Taunton seven years before, at St Peter's Church, Bristol.

In August 1773 Lackington moved to the City of London, lodging first in Whitecross Street. He was soon joined by his wife, who died that November. In the same month his grandfather George Lackington, a gentleman farmer at Langford, near Wellington, died leaving James a legacy of £10. In June 1774 Lackington opened his first bookshop in Featherstone Street, with stock consisting of a few books and some scraps of leather together worth about £5. He acquired an interest-free loan of £5 from the Methodists to enable him to purchase more stock. Six months later his business had prospered sufficiently for him to move to 46 Chiswell Street, where he remained for fourteen years. Here Lackington would occasionally hold literary suppers attended by, among others, Henry Lemoine, the bookseller, who after Lackington had published his memoirs in 1791 wrote what he described as 'The real life of Lackington'. Another member of the circle was Thomas Hood, father of the poet. On 30 January 1776 Lackington married Dorcas Turton, a schoolmistress who had attended Nancy during her final illness. She was a great reader of novels and lover of books, and helped her husband in the shop while he was away buying stock. Lackington, who was at this time reading Thomas Amory's *Life of John Buncle*,

James Lackington (1746–1815), by Edmund Scott, pubd 1792 (after John Keenan)

experienced a change in attitude towards Methodism, and spoke publicly in criticism of it.

In 1778 Lackington took into business John Denis, son of an oilman in Cannon Street, who provided the capital to allow the stock of books to be doubled. In 1779 the firm of Lackington & Co. published its first catalogue, which contained 12,000 items. The partnership with Denis was dissolved in 1780 because of a dispute over who should buy the stock. The original agreement was that Lackington bought the stock and Denis provided the finance, but Denis questioned Lackington's purchases. Catalogues were issued annually, increasing in size (that for 1784 contained 30,000 books). All books were for sale at the lowest possible price for cash only, with no credit given. Lackington purchased large quantities of books as remainders and sold them very cheaply, causing acrimony among the trade (other booksellers bought remainders in order to destroy them and increase the price of those left). He emblazoned his carriage with the motto 'Small profits do great things', and claimed he had 'Been highly instrumental in diffusing the general desire for reading, now so prevalent among the inferior orders of society' (*Memoirs*, letter 25). Lackington was meticulous in keeping his accounts, and profits were calculated each week. His account books were kept publicly in his shop as he never saw any reason for concealing them. He sold more than 100,000 volumes annually. In 1787 he visited Edinburgh by way of York and Newcastle, returning through Glasgow, Carlisle, Leeds, Lancaster, Preston, and Manchester. He was not impressed with the bookshops he visited, saying that nothing but trash was to be found. He visited Edinburgh again in 1790 and his opinion was unchanged.

Lackington published the first edition of his *Memoirs*, which ran into many subsequent editions, in 1791. It is the principal source of information about him; in addition to the particulars of his life, the work is full of curious anecdotes and many quotations from a wide range of authors. At the time of publication his profits were £4000; in 1792 they had increased to £5000. Lackington had also extended his business into publishing a number of works, many of them theological, as is shown by a sales list of about 1791. In 1794 Lackington first issued tokens, in the form of metal coins, worth a halfpenny and a penny; the halfpenny had on the obverse a full-face portrait of Lackington, while the reverse pictured an angel blowing a trumpet and the inscription 'halfpenny of J. Lackington and Co.' It is believed that more than 700,000 Lackington tokens were issued (only valid in Lackington's business). They were all struck by Lutwyche of Birmingham.

In 1794 Lackington also moved to larger premises in Finsbury Square and called his new shop the Temple of the Muses. Built in 1789, it was one of the wonders of London (it burned down in 1841). It was of a considerable size and surmounted by an immense dome; its large circular counter was in such a spacious room that a coach and four horses drove round it after the opening day. Over the entrance was inscribed 'Cheapest Bookseller in the World' (tokens issued from these premises reproduced this as a legend). It was said that a million books were on display (*Repository of Arts*, 1, 1809). Between the First and Second world wars a street near Finsbury Square was renamed Lackington Street.

With this greater prosperity Lackington purchased a house at Merton in Surrey. It was here on 27 February 1795 that his wife died; her husband wrote the lengthy epitaph on her headstone in Merton churchyard. Later that year on 11 June Lackington married Mary Turton, the younger daughter of William Turton, an attorney of Alveston, Gloucestershire, and a relative of his second wife. He retired in 1798 and made over his business to his third cousin George *Lackington (1768–1844), who had been brought up in the business since the age of thirteen. Thereafter the business was known as Lackington, Allen & Co. Robin Allen had also worked for James Lackington from a young age. The other partners, Patrick Kirkman, Richard Hughes (a lessee of Sadler's Wells), and Thomas Hasker, had been made partners in 1794. James Lackington retired to Thornbury near Alveston, where he erected a small chapel and purchased two small estates. He engaged in a number of charitable ventures and also made a contribution to the newly erected Arminian Methodist chapel at Weymouth.

By 1804 Lackington regretted his early criticism of Methodism and published *The Confessions of J. Lackington*. These were thirty 'Letters to a Friend' expressing his opinions and attitudes to Methodists and their beliefs, to make amends for having 'publicly ridiculed a very large and respectable body of Christians' (*DNB*). Like his *Memoirs* they show considerable evidence of his wide reading of classical and religious works, and of contemporary writers, especially poets. In 1806 he moved back to Taunton

and erected the Temple Methodist Church at a cost of £3000. There is no record of its use until about five years later when it was acquired by the Wesleyan Methodists of Taunton. He moved to Budleigh Salterton in 1807 and built his house, Ash Villa, which later became the Methodist manse. In the same year he also spent £2000 to build the first Temple Church there. He endowed it with £150 a year for the minister's stipend. The present church, built in 1904, now stands on the same ground. James Lackington died on 22 November 1815 and was buried in the East Budleigh churchyard. His third wife survived him.

All subsequent biographical notices of Lackington draw on his *Memoirs*. Lackington was not always consistent in his information, and he was a self-opinionated and vain man who claimed in the preface 'that my performance possessed so much intrinsic merit, as would occasion it to be universally admired by all good judges, as a prodigious effort of human genius'.

BRENDA J. SCRAGG

Sources *Memoirs of the forty-five first years of the life of James Lackington* (1794) · 'Remarkable memoirs of the life of the celebrated James Lackington, Esq. … together with observations on his confessions lately published', *Granger's Original Wonderful Museum*, 4 (1806), 47–8 · *The confessions of J. Lackington* (1804) · D. Bank and others, eds., *British biographical archive* (1984–98) [microfiche; with index, 2nd edn, 1998] · *GM*, 1st ser., 61 (1791) · *GM*, 1st ser., 65 (1795) · *GM*, 1st ser., 71 (1801) · *GM*, 1st ser., 82/1 (1812), 673 · R. G. Doty, 'English merchant tokens', *Perspectives in numismatics*, ed. S. B. Needleman (Chicago, 1986) [available online, www.chicagocoinclub.org/projects/PiN] · *Repository of Arts*, 1 (1809) · P. Pindar, *Ode works*, 3 (1809), 274 · H. Morris, *Trade tokens of British and American booksellers and bookmakers* (Newtown, Pa., 1989) · *Wesley Historical Society Proceedings*, 1 (1898) · *N&Q*, 10th ser., 4 (1905), 54, 177–8 · *N&Q*, 11th ser., 5 (1912), 16–17 · A. N. Walton, 'James Lackington and Methodism in Budleigh Salterton', *Wesley Historical Society Proceedings*, 18 (1931–2), 85–92 · C. H. Timperley, *Encyclopaedia of literary and typographical anecdote*, 2nd edn (1842); repr. (1977), vol. 2, p. 862 · C. Knight, *Shadows of the old booksellers* (1865) · A. H. W. Houchin, *150th anniversary, 1812–1962: Temple Methodist Church, Budleigh Salterton* (1962) · F. Munby, *Romance of bookselling* (1810) · E. Marston, *Sketches of booksellers of other days* (1901) · A. L. Humphreys, 'Lackington and his memoirs', *Bookworm*, 1 (1888), 197–200, 242–5 · I. Maxted, *The London book trades, 1775–1800: a preliminary checklist of members* (1977) · *DNB*

Likenesses caricature, etching, pubd 1795, NPG · J. Goldar, print (after E. Maybry), BM, NPG; repro. in *Granger's Original Wonderful Museum* · Jackson, engraving (after Fuseli), repro. in C. Knight, *London*, 5 · E. Scott, stipple (after J. Keenan), NPG; repro. in *Memoirs* (1792) [*see illus.*]

La Cloche, Jacques de

La Cloche, Jacques de (1644/1647?–1669), pretended son of Charles II, may have come from Jersey, but nothing is known of his early life or true parentage. He claimed to be the son of *Charles II (1630–1685) and he named a woman in his will as 'Dona Maria Stuarda, della famiglia delli baroni di S. Marzo'. According to La Cloche, her 'nearness and greatness of blood was the cause … that his Majestie would never acknowledge him' (Kent, letters to Joseph Williamson, PRO, SP 85.10, fol. 111). Whom La Cloche meant by this is unclear, but Lady Mary Stuart, duchess of Richmond and Lennox and countess of March (1622–1685) [*see* Villiers, Mary], has been suggested. A previous identification of his mother as Marguerite de Carteret (1625–1713) of Jersey, who in 1656 married Jean de La Cloche, son of

Étienne de La Cloche, rector of St Ouen, seems improbable. The first contemporary notice of La Cloche occurred when he was admitted to the Jesuit novitiate in Sant' Andrea al Quirinale, Rome, the register of novices recording the admission on 11 November 1668 of Jacobus de La Cloche, from the island of Jersey, aged twenty-four.

La Cloche brought with him apparently significant documents whose authenticity, however, is disputed. Two, purporting to have been signed and sealed by Charles II, recognized La Cloche as his son. A third, supposedly supplied by Queen Kristina of Sweden, also certified La Cloche's paternity. Further letters, dated in August 1668 and seemingly by Charles II, were sent to Father Oliva, general of the Jesuits. These also acknowledged La Cloche's royal paternity and suggested that La Cloche come to London and begin negotiations for Charles II's conversion to Roman Catholicism. Father Oliva may have been convinced as, following his instructions, on 14 or 15 October 1668 La Cloche began a journey to London, going at least as far as Paris in the company of a Jesuit priest. Whether he reached London is unverified, but he returned to Rome, apparently with another letter from Charles, dated 18 November, which promised a donation and compensation for La Cloche's expenses.

Tiredness from the journey and the rigours of winter had undermined La Cloche's health. He therefore decided to delay another journey to London and await milder temperatures. Perhaps on the advice of Oliva, he transferred to Naples. Finding accommodation at the home of Francesco Corona, a poor but respectable gentleman, and his wife, Annuccia d'Amicij, Jacques fell hopelessly in love with his hosts' daughter Teresa, and married her in Naples Cathedral on 19 February 1669, styling himself Giacomo Enrico de Boveri Roano Stuardo, not before giving his father-in-law money and jewels in such quantity as to arouse suspicion that he was in reality a counterfeiter. Indeed, in early March, as he himself related in two letters to Cardinal Francesco Barberini dated 6 and 10 April 1669, he was arrested by order of the Spanish viceroy of Naples, Don Pedro of Aragon, and confined in the castle of Sant'Elmo, from where on 20 March he was transferred to the fortress of Gaeta. Among the papers confiscated from him emerged two certificates attesting his royal parentage, one apparently signed by Kristina of Sweden, the other by Father Oliva. In Naples excitement grew about the English prince and the new princess, referred to as La Reginella. The news may have reached England for it seems that Charles II wrote to the viceroy denouncing the prisoner as an impostor. La Cloche was soon released, perhaps through the intervention of the cardinal and Father Oliva. He hoped to take his family to Venice but a violent fever ended his life. He died on 26 August 1669, and was buried in the church of San Francesco di Paola, outside Porta Capuana. In La Cloche's extravagant and pretentious will he named Louis XIV executor, whom he called 'Cousin'.

On 10 December (or 11 November) 1669 a son, Giacomo, was born posthumously to Jacques de La Cloche and baptized the same day in the parish church of Santa Sofia. Giacomo lived in Naples until 1708, when he left for Rome,

where he married D. Lucia Minelli della Riccia. On 4 October 1711, for this marriage, he was arrested as a vagabond and impostor by Pope Clement XI and tried by the Roman court for an entire year, until he was recognized as a genuine descendant of Charles II. In this capacity he was welcomed by numerous Italian and European courts, and he wandered from one to another, begging respect and munificence. He died in Naples in 1752 or 1753. It seems he was survived by a son, Giuseppe (1722–1783), who resided at the court of France, and has been said to have acted as a double for Charles Edward Stuart, the Young Pretender, when he was away on secret missions. He was apparently the last of the line.   GIOVANNI TARANTINO

Sources 'Conversiones principum', Documenta a P. Jos. Boero collecta. E./Litterae Caroli II regis Angliae de filio suo naturali Iacobo de la Cloche, qui domum probationis S. Andreae anno 1668 ingressus est. Testimonia et informationes variae de eodemvalde ambiguo viro, Archivum Romanum Societatis Iesu, Rome, OPP.NN.174/175, 2/3 • Vatican Library, Vatican City, Jacques de La Cloche to Cardinal Francesco Barberini, MS Barberini Lat. 8620, fols. 184–5 • giornali d'Innocentio Fuidoro, National Library, Naples, MS X.B.15, vol. 3, 1668–71, fols. 55–6; MS XI.E.14, fols. 32–36r • Rome Gazette, Kent's letters to Joseph Williamson, PRO, SP 85/10, fols. 28v–29, 32v, 34v, 55r–v, 97–102, 104–8, 111r–v, 114–115r • Delle lettere del Signor Vincenzo Armanni nobile d'Ugubbio, scritte a nome proprio, e divise in tre volumi con la vita di lui nel primo, ed. G. Piccini, 3 (1674), 198–210 • papers of Luigi Gualtiero, BL, Add. MS 20646, fols. 56–8 • Bliss transcripts from the Milan Archives, PRO, 31/2, fols. 37–55r • Manifesto in cui si dimostra la identità e real nascita del Principe D. Giacomo Stuardo, figlio postumo del Principe Giacomo Enrico Stuardo, e nipote di Carlo II, re della Gran Bretagna (1752) • Lord Acton, 'Secret history of Charles II', Home and Foreign Review (July 1862), 146–74; repr. in Lord Acton, Historical essays and studies (1908), 85–122 • G. Boero, 'Historia della conversione alla Chiesa Cattolica di Carlo II, re d'Inghilterra, cavata da scritture autentiche ed originali', Civiltà Cattolica (1863), 28–69 • T. D. Hardy, Report to the right hon. master of the rolls upon the documents in the archives and public libraries of Venice (1886), 86–90 • L'Italia reale della Domenica [Naples], 10 (Galiani), ser. 2, no. 15 [L'Italia Reale, 2/113, pp. 450–51] (24 April 1881) • W. Mazière Brady, 'The eldest natural son of Charles II', Anglo-Roman Papers (1890), 93–119 • A. F. Stuart, 'The Neapolitan Stuarts', EngHR, 18 (1903), 470–74 • A. Lang, 'The master hoaxer, James de La Cloche', Fortnightly Review, 86 (1909), 430–39 • G. S. H. L. Washington, King Charles II's Jesuit son (1966); rev. edn (1968); new rev. edn (1979) • M. J. A. Stewart, The forgotten monarchy of Scotland (1998) • parish register, Santa Sofia in San Giovanni, Carbonara, 10 Dec 1669 [birth of son] • C. E. O'Neill, 'La Cloche, Jacques de (Stuart, James), "Hijo de Carlos II"', Diccionario histórico de la Compañia de Jesus biográfico temático, ed. C. E. O'Neill and J. M. Domínguez, 4 vols. (2001), 3.2240 • G. Tarantino, 'New disclosures on Jacques de la Cloche (c. 1647–1669), a Stuart pretender in the seventeenth century', Archivum Historicum Societatis Iesu [forthcoming]
Archives Archivum Romanum Societatis Iesu, Rome, documenta a P. Jos. Boero collecta, OPP.NN.174/175 • Biblioteca Apostolica Vaticana, Vatican City, MS Barberini Lat. 8620, fols. 151–3 • National Library, Naples, MS X.B.15, fols. 55–6 • National Library, Naples, MS XI.E.14, fols. 32–36r • PRO, SP 85/10 | BL, Add. MS 20646 • PRO, 31/2
Wealth at death according to report, 50,000 scudi; his mother's property and fortune; the marquisate of Juvignis: will, Naples, 24 Aug 1669, Naples, National Library, MS XI.E.14, fols. 32–36r; PRO, SP 85/10, fols. 97–102, 104–8, 114–115r

Lacroix, Alphonse François (1799–1859), missionary, was born at Lignières, in the canton of Neuchâtel, Switzerland, on 10 May 1799. His father died between 1799 and

1805, and Lacroix was brought up by an uncle, M. Chanel. He was educated privately and then at a mission seminary in Berkel, near Rotterdam. In 1816 he became a tutor in Amsterdam and there learned of the Tahitians' abandonment of their idols, whereupon he was stirred to offer himself for missionary labour. He arrived in the Dutch colony of Chinsura, Bengal, in March 1821, as the sole Indian representative of the Netherlands Missionary Society. On 17 May 1825 he married Hannah, daughter of Gregorius Herklots (1768–1852), a native of Bremen and fiscal or mayor of Chinsura.

On 1 March 1827, following Chinsura's transfer from Dutch to English control, Lacroix joined the London Missionary Society (LMS). Two years later he shifted to Calcutta. He was a tall, strikingly handsome man and an animated, expressive talker which, coupled with his fluency in Bengali, ensured him a reputation as an eloquent street-preacher in Calcutta and its surrounding villages and on the swampy islands of the Sundarbans. A persuasive opponent of education and proselytization solely in the English language, Lacroix devoted many hours to revising the existing Bengali translations of the Bible and ran theological classes in Bengali at his home.

In December 1841 Lacroix travelled with his family to Europe for the first and only time. He toured Britain, France, and Switzerland, and in Geneva he raised considerable funds for itinerant preaching in Bengal. He returned to India in January 1844. In September 1855, as one of the longest-serving and most popular missionaries in Calcutta, he presided over a session of the General Conference of Protestant Missionaries. In 1856 the LMS invited him to retire to England, but he declined the offer. Nevertheless, his health was failing and he died on 8 July 1859 at his home, 55 Upper Circular Road, Calcutta. His interment at the dissenters' burial-ground, also in Circular Road, was attended by almost 1000 mourners of all Christian denominations.

Lacroix was survived by his wife and several children, including a daughter, Hannah Catherine (1826–1861), who married the LMS missionary Joseph Mullens. In 1862 Mullens published an affectionate memoir of his father-in-law. KATHERINE PRIOR

Sources J. Mullens, *Brief memorials of the Rev. Alphonse François Lacroix* (1862) · S. Neill, *A history of Christianity in India, 1707–1858* (1985) · M. A. Laird, *Missionaries and education in Bengal, 1793–1837* (1972) · R. Lovett, *The history of the London Missionary Society, 1795–1895*, 2 (1899) · B. H. Badley, *Indian missionary directory and memorial volume*, 3rd edn (1886) · *Friend of India* (14 July 1859), 656 · *The Englishman* (9 July 1859) · Bengal ecclesiastical records, BL OIOC · C. R. Wilson, ed., *List of inscriptions on tombs or monuments in Bengal* (1896) · accountant-general's records, BL OIOC [Bengal wills, 1859] · A. G. Roussac, *The new Calcutta directory for 1859* (1859)

Likenesses J. Cochran, stipple (after H. Room), NPG · lithograph, repro. in Mullens, *Brief memorials*

La Croix, Michael. *See* Cross, Michael (*fl.* 1633–1660).

Lacy, Alice, *suo jure* **countess of Lincoln, and countess of Lancaster and Leicester** (1281–1348). *See under* Thomas of Lancaster, second earl of Lancaster, second earl of Leicester, and earl of Lincoln (*c.*1278–1322).

Lacy, Edmund (*c.*1370–1455), bishop of Exeter, was the son of Stephen Lacy of Gloucester and his wife, Sybil; his brother Philip later became an esquire in his household. Edmund Lacy was educated at Oxford, where he is first mentioned as a master of arts in 1391; he had graduated BTh by 1400 and DTh by 1414. He also held a fellowship of University College (*c.*1391–1396), serving as bursar (1396–7) and master (1398–9, and perhaps until *c.*1401). After ordination as priest about 1399 he soon gained entry to royal service. By November 1400 he had become a king's clerk and began to receive preferment from Henry IV and others, including canonries at Windsor (1401), Hereford (1412), and Lincoln (1414). References to his employment on diplomatic missions, however, result from confusion with John Catterick (*d.* 1419); Lacy made his mark primarily as a theologian and liturgist, and with Henry V rather than his father. On 14 April 1414 Henry V made him dean of the Chapel Royal; he went on the French campaign of 1415 and was present at Agincourt. Election as bishop of Hereford followed, evidently at the king's wish, between 21 January and 17 February 1417, and Lacy was consecrated at Windsor in Henry's presence on 18 April. In 1420 he was translated to the larger and wealthier diocese of Exeter by papal provision dated 3 July. When Henry promoted the reform of the Benedictine order in May 1421, Lacy was one of those who conferred with the order, and he preached before its monks and the king at Westminster.

After Henry's death in the following year Lacy was one of the late king's executors, but he subsequently centred his activities upon his diocese of Exeter, except for occasional visits to London—in 1428 he presided in convocation. When, by 1435, he developed a disease of the shin bones which prevented his riding, he was excused attendance at royal councils and parliaments. As long as his health permitted he was active in visiting his diocese (Cornwall as well as Devon), but in 1447 he was obliged to appoint a suffragan on account of his own advanced age and infirmity. Lacy was clearly a conscientious bishop whose diocesan registers for both Hereford and Exeter survive—that for Exeter contains 874 folios, yet still fails to include all his sealed acts. It contains large numbers of grants of indulgences and licences for chapels. At Exeter Cathedral he increased the stipends of the vicars-choral and choristers at a time of economic hardship by appropriating the tithes of Cornwood, Devon, to their use in 1430–32. He issued indulgences to encourage the completion of the cathedral cloister, and defended the dean and chapter in disputes with the city of Exeter which reached a crisis in the late 1440s. His preferred interests, however, were intellectual and spiritual. He wrote *De quadruplici sensu Sacre Scripture*, now lost, and took a particular interest in music. The John Dunstavylle whom he appointed canon of Hereford Cathedral in 1419 may have been the composer John Dunstaple (*d.* 1453), while at Exeter, Lacy maintained a chapel choir and patronized such musicians as Richard Smert, Nicholas Sturgeon, and John Trouluffe.

He had a particular devotion to the Virgin, in whose honour he instituted an antiphon and prayers in the cathedral, and to the Archangel Raphael, patron of healing—a more unusual attachment, perhaps reflecting his own infirmity. In 1444 the pope approved a liturgy composed by Lacy for a festival of Raphael on 5 October, and the bishop tried to promote the festival, which won acceptance at Exeter, Hereford, and (in 1454) York. He gave Exeter Cathedral numerous vestments, ornaments, and books.

Lacy lived to be at least eighty, acquiring a reputation for sanctity; in 1447–8 the mayor of Exeter, albeit an opponent, referred to 'his blessedness, holy living and good conscience' (*Letters and Papers of John Shillingford*, 44). He died at the bishop's manor of Chudleigh, Devon, on 18 September 1455, and was buried in a plain altar tomb on the north side of the choir in Exeter Cathedral. The tomb became the centre of an unofficial cult, attracting pilgrims and monetary donations. Wax votive offerings found near the tomb in 1942 suggest that the devotees often suffered (like the bishop) from diseases of the limbs; the cult was suppressed about 1538 by the then dean of Exeter, Simon Haynes. NICHOLAS ORME

Sources Emden, *Oxf.* · A. T. Bannister, J. H. Parry, and others, eds., *Registrum Edmundi Lacy … AD MCCCCXVII–MCCCCXX*, 1, CYS, 22 (1918) · F. C. Hingeston-Randolph, ed., *The register of Edmund Lacy, bishop of Exeter*, 1: *The register of institutions, with some account of the episcopate of John Catrik, AD 1419* (1909) · *The register of Edmund Lacy, bishop of Exeter*, ed. G. R. Dunstan, 5 vols., CYS, 60–63, 66 (1963–72) · R. Barnes, ed., *Liber pontificalis of Edmund Lacy, bishop of Exeter: a manuscript of the fourteenth century* (1847) · W. A. Pantin, ed., *Documents illustrating the activities of … the English black monks, 1215–1540*, 3 vols., CS, 3rd ser., 45, 47, 54 (1931–7), vol. 2, p. 107 · *Thomae Walsingham, quondam monachi S. Albani, historia Anglicana*, ed. H. T. Riley, 2 vols., pt 1 of *Chronica monasterii S. Albani*, Rolls Series, 28 (1863–4), vol. 2, p. 337 · *CPR, 1429–36*, 453 · G. Oliver, *Lives of the bishops of Exeter, and a history of the cathedral* (1861), 322–54 · *Letters and papers of John Shillingford, Mayor of Exeter, 1447–50*, ed. S. A. Moore, CS, new ser., 2 (1872) · G. R. Dunstan, 'Some aspects of the register of Edmund Lacy, bishop of Exeter, 1420–1455', *Journal of Ecclesiastical History*, 6 (1955), 37–47 · N. Orme, *Exeter Cathedral as it was, 1050–1550* (1986) · N. Orme, 'The early musicians of Exeter Cathedral', *Music and Letters*, 59 (1978), 395–410, esp. 399–403 · N. Orme, 'Two saint-bishops of Exeter', *Analecta Bollandiana*, 104 (1986), 403–18 · Exeter Cathedral, dean and chapter archives

Archives Devon RO, register, Chanter X · Exeter Cathedral, archives · Hereford diocesan registry, Hereford, register

Lacy, Francis Anthony, styled Count de Lacy (1731–1792), army officer and diplomatist in the Spanish service, was born in Spain, the second son of Patrick Lacy, an army officer in the Spanish service, and his wife, a daughter of the marquis d'Abbeville (Osly). Lacy's father, from Bruree, co. Limerick, had left Ireland with James II in 1691 and took military service in France and then Spain.

In 1747 Lacy joined the Spanish army as an ensign with the Irish regiment of Ultonia—the Lacys' chosen corps of service. The regiment served with the Irish brigade in the campaign in Italy of that year against the Austrians in support of Spanish claims to the crowns of Naples and Sicily and the duchy of Milan. In 1762, aged thirty-one, he was promoted colonel of the regiment, which served with the Irish brigade in the war against Portugal; it captured the frontier fortress of Miranda do Douro and occupied Braganza and Chaves, before retiring across the frontier to Extremadura with the rest of the Spanish army.

Lacy then turned to diplomacy, and served as the Spanish minister at the courts of Stockholm and St Petersburg. From Russia he wrote a series of reports to the Marquess Grimaldi between 1772 and 1775 concerning the Russian expedition to Kamchatka and drawing attention to Russian interest in the northern coast of California. This led the Spanish government to send a rival expedition to the coast of Kamchatka, to establish relations with local tribes.

Upon his return Lacy was made commandant-general of the coast of Granada, member of the supreme war council, and inspector-general of artillery and ordnance establishments (1780). He was responsible for improved discipline at the school of artillery in Segovia and for the introduction of classes for chemistry, mineralogy, and pyrotechnics. As lieutenant-general he commanded the artillery at the siege of Minorca in 1781, where the British defenders held out for six months. Thereafter he commanded the Spanish artillery at the unsuccessful siege of Gibraltar, which lasted until 1783. For his services Lacy was granted the grand cross of Charles III and the rank of commander of the cross of St Iago. He was also made titular of the rich commanderie of Las Cazas Buenas, Merida.

In March 1789 Lacy was appointed governor and captain-general of Catalonia, where he worked hard to prevent the spread of French revolutionary doctrines among the Catalans. He died, unmarried, at Barcelona on 31 December 1792, at the age of sixty-one, and was buried in January 1793 at the parish church of Santa Maria del Mar in the city. His success, according to James Grant, in his book *Cavaliers of Fortune* (1859), owed less to military talent and more to an imposing stature, a ready wit, and a steadfast loyalty to the court he served.

Lacy's elder brother, Patrick, who also joined the Ultonia regiment, where he rose to the rank of lieutenant-colonel, married a lady from Cork, with whom he had three children. Among these was Louis de Lacy (1775–1817), who enjoyed a distinguished military career in Spain under the Bourbons, the Napoleonic regime, and then again the Bourbons, only to be executed for rising in defence of the 1812 constitution. JONATHAN SPAIN

Sources Delacy-Bellingari, *The roll of the house of Lacy* (1928) · C. Oman, 'The Irish troops in the service of Spain, 1709–1818', *Journal of the Royal United Service Institution*, 63 (1918), 1–8, 193–9, 450–53 · J. O'Hart, *Irish pedigrees; or, The origin and stem of the Irish nation*, 3rd edn (1881), appx 87 · J. O'Hart, *Irish landed gentry* (1884) · W. D. Griffin, 'Irish generals and Spanish politics under Fernando VII', *Irish Sword*, 10 (1971–2), 1–9 · J. Grant, *Cavaliers of fortune* (1859), 164–77 · D. Gates, *The Spanish ulcer: a history of the Peninsular War* (1986) · F. Forde, 'The Ultonia regiment of the Spanish army', *Irish Sword*, 12 (1975–6), 36–40 · C. E. Chapman, *Catalogue of materials in the Archivo General de Indias for the history of the Pacific coast and the American southwest* (1919) · J. Drinkwater, *A history of the late siege of Gibraltar* (1785)

Lacy, Gilbert de (*fl.* 1133–1163), baron, was the son of the Roger de Lacy disinherited and banished in 1096. He had succeeded his father on the family's Norman estates of

Lassy and Campeaux by 1133. He returned to England and was with King Stephen at Easter 1136, but was disappointed of any hope of recovering those of his father's extensive lands in the Welsh borders which had been given after 1096 to Pain fitz John, Joce de Dinan, and Miles of Gloucester.

In the civil war Lacy sided with the empress: in 1138 his kinsman Geoffrey Talbot fortified Weobley (one of Lacy's chief castles) unsuccessfully against Stephen; the two then led an army which attacked Bath. He witnessed charters issued by the empress in 1141 and by her son Duke Henry in 1154–5. By 1141 Joce and Miles had deserted Stephen, but there is no evidence that Lacy ever rejoined the king. Instead he profited from the anarchy which prevailed in the southern marches and in the end recovered most of his father's lands. In the late 1140s Miles's son Roger, earl of Hereford, was making alliances against him and in 1150 attacked a party of Lacy's knights in a churchyard. Lacy also fought Joce de Dinan for possession of Ludlow, though the details remembered in the later romance *Fouke le Fitz Waryn* are unhistorical. He was well known as an able and wily commander. He gave churches at Weobley and Clodock (near his seat of Ewyas Lacy) to the family monastery of Llanthony, the manor of Guiting to the knights templar, and land to Hereford Cathedral.

In 1158 or 1159 Lacy resigned his lands to his eldest son, Robert (who was himself succeeded by his brother Hugh de *Lacy in 1162), and joined the templars. At Whitsuntide 1160 he was in France with the templars who guaranteed the peace treaty between Henry II and Louis VII. Later in 1160 or 1161 he had reached Jerusalem and he became preceptor of his order in the county of Tripoli, where in 1163 he was among the leaders of a crusader army resisting Nur-ad-Din. The year of his death is unknown, though the date of 10 November was later commemorated at Hereford.   C. P. LEWIS

Sources W. E. Wightman, *The Lacy family in England and Normandy, 1066–1194* (1966) · R. W. Eyton, *Antiquities of Shropshire*, 12 vols. (1854–60), vol. 5, pp. 238–79 · H. M. Colvin, 'Holme Lacy: an episcopal manor and its tenants in the twelfth and thirteenth centuries', *Medieval studies presented to Rose Graham*, ed. V. Ruffer and A. J. Taylor (1950), 15–40 · K. R. Potter and R. H. C. Davis, eds., *Gesta Stephani*, OMT (1976) · *Willelmi Tyrensis archiepiscopi chronicon*, ed. R. B. C. Huygens, 2 vols. (Turnhout, Belgium, 1986) · E. J. Hathaway and others, eds., *Fouke le Fitz Waryn* (1975) · R. Rawlinson, *The history and antiquities of the city and cathedral-church of Hereford* (1717), appx, p. 28 · *Reg. RAN*, vol. 3 · B. A. Lees, ed., *Records of the templars in England in the twelfth century: the inquest of 1185 with illustrative charters and documents*, British Academy, Records of Social and Economic History, 9 (1935) · *Letters and charters of Gilbert Foliot*, ed. A. Morey and others (1967) · *Pipe rolls* · L. Delisle and others, eds., *Recueil des actes de Henri II, roi d'Angleterre et duc de Normandie, concernant les provinces françaises et les affaires de France*, 4 vols. (Paris, 1909–27) · Z. N. Brooke and C. N. L. Brooke, 'Hereford Cathedral dignitaries in the twelfth century', *Cambridge Historical Journal*, 8 (1944–6), 1–21 · R. H. C. Davis, 'Treaty between William earl of Gloucester and Roger earl of Hereford', *A medieval miscellany for Doris Mary Stenton*, ed. P. M. Barnes and C. F. Slade, PRSoc., new ser., 36 (1962), 139–46 · D. Walker, 'A letter from the Holy Land', *EngHR*, 72 (1957), 662–5

Lacy [*née* Taylor], **Harriett Deborah** (1807–1874), actress, the daughter of William Taylor, a wine merchant, was born in London. With her parents' agreement she was given lessons in elocution by the actress Sarah Bartley. She made her début as Julia in *The Rivals* under the management of Bellamy at the Bath theatre on 5 November 1827. She was almost instantly popular and in the course of the next two seasons played important roles there. Her first appearance in London was at Covent Garden, where, on 30 October 1830, she played Nina in Dimond's *Carnival of Naples*, earning a very positive review from the *Theatrical Journal*. Subsequent parts included Rosalind and—much to his pleasure—Helen to Sheridan Knowles's Hunchback in his play of that name. In 1837 she was Aspatia to W. C. Macready's Melantius and Miss Huddart's Evadne in *The Bridal* under Benjamin Webster's management at the Haymarket, where she earned a reputation for playing with distinction in sentimental comedy. The following year she joined the company with which Macready began his management of Covent Garden. There, in August 1838, she played Lady Teazle to the Surface of Walter *Lacy (1809–1898), whose real name was Walter Williams. She married him on 22 June 1839. For the last part of her career she performed various roles, including some of Madame Vestris's repertory. Among her best parts were Nell Gwynne in Jerrold's play of that name, in which the song 'Buy my oranges' was heard, the original heroine in the same writer's *The Housekeeper*, and Ophelia, a part in which, according to Madame Vestris, she surpassed any actress of her time. She retired from the stage about 1845, having made her farewell appearance at the Olympic, and died on 28 July 1874 at her home in Montpelier Square, Brompton, London.   THOMAS SECCOMBE, *rev.* J. GILLILAND

Sources W. C. Russell, *Representative actors* (c.1875) · Boase, *Mod. Eng. biog.* · *The life and reminiscences of E. L. Blanchard, with notes from the diary of Wm. Blanchard*, ed. C. W. Scott and C. Howard, 2 vols. (1891) · W. Archer, *W. C. Macready* (1890) · *The Era* (2 Aug 1874) · Hall, *Dramatic ports.* · E. Kilmurray, *Dictionary of British portraiture*, 2 (1979) · m. cert. · Mrs C. Baron-Wilson, *Our actresses*, 2 vols. (1844) · *Tallis's drawing room table book of theatrical portraits, memoirs and anecdotes* (1851)

Likenesses R. J. Lane, two lithographs, pubd 1838, NPG · seven prints, Harvard TC

Lacy, Henry de, fifth earl of Lincoln (1249–1311), magnate, was born in December (perhaps on the 19th) 1249, the son of Edmund de Lacy, earl of Lincoln (1230–1258), and Alice (*d.* in or before 1311), elder daughter of Manfred (III), marquess of Saluzzo.

Early years in royal service Henry de Lacy succeeded his father at the age of eight and a half in 1258, his mother receiving custody of her late husband's lands and heirs until Henry reached legal age. The king granted £300 per annum for his maintenance during his minority. In 1269 he was involved in a quarrel with John de Warenne, earl of Surrey (*d.* 1304), as to certain pastureland, which was decided in his favour. On 5 April 1272 he was made keeper of Knaresborough Castle, and on 13 October of that year he was knighted on the occasion of the wedding of Edmund, earl of Cornwall. He appears to have taken seisin of his lands and titles at about this time, and from soon thereafter he was to be found in near constant royal service, proving himself to be one of Edward I's most reliable, faithful, and trusted servants and friends. In 1276 and 1277 he served in the Welsh war with a force of about 100 cavalry, and took Bauseley in Montgomeryshire. In January 1278 he went to Brabant to arrange the future marriage of the king's daughter Margaret to John, son and heir of the duke of Brabant, and in March of that year he was one of the escort appointed to attend Alexander III, king of Scots, on his visit to England. On 27 April 1279 he was appointed joint lieutenant of England along with the bishops of Worcester and Hereford and the earl of Cornwall, during the king's absence in France, which lasted until 19 June. In 1282 and 1283 he was again in Wales, and received substantial grants in the north from the king, forming the great lordship of Denbigh. In 1284 when Edward I celebrated the conquest of Wales with a round table, Lincoln captained one side of the tournament that ensued.

Lincoln accompanied the king on his three years' visit to Gascony, from 1286 to 1289. In 1287 he served as one of the commissioners who tried and convicted the former seneschal of Gascony, Jean de Grailly, for misconduct while in office. One of the *bastides* built by the king during this period, Nichole, bears his name. Following the king's return from Gascony, Lincoln was appointed in October 1289 to a commission charged to hear complaints against royal officials. About 1000 defendants were named, most notably Ralph Hengham, chief justice of the king's bench. Lincoln was also one of the commissioners appointed to treat with the guardians of Scotland in June 1290, and in this capacity was present at the negotiations that produced the treaty of Birgham on 18 July. He was also present at Norham in 1291 and at Berwick in 1292 during the deliberations relative to the Scottish succession, and in the latter year was one of those appointed to decide on the claims of William de Ros and John de Vaux. In 1292 Lincoln was one of the sureties for Gilbert de Clare, earl of Gloucester, in his dispute with the earl of Hereford over territories in the Welsh march, and he also served as one of the co-executors of Eleanor of Castile following her death. In May 1293 Lincoln accompanied Edmund, earl of Lancaster, on an embassy to arrange a truce with France. In the following year he set out for Gascony, but while still at Portsmouth was recalled by the outbreak of war in Wales. While proceeding to relieve his castle of Denbigh he was defeated by his own Welshmen on 11 November; Lincoln himself escaped without difficulty, and remained in Wales until the spring of 1295.

Lieutenant of Aquitaine On 3 December 1295 Lincoln was appointed king's lieutenant in Aquitaine, a position he held until the spring of 1298. On 14 January 1296 he sailed from Plymouth with Edmund of Lancaster, on his way to Gascony with a very large force of infantry. Lincoln served the king under contract, being paid 2000 marks per annum. After pillaging St Matthieu, near Cape Finisterre, his force sailed up the Gironde to Bourg and Blaye. They marched against Bordeaux without success. An attack on St Macaire failed when Robert, count of Artois, relieved the besieged French garrison. On the death of Edmund of Lancaster, on 5 June, Lincoln was chosen to succeed him by the voice of the whole army and his appointment as lieutenant was renewed. He defeated the count of Artois before Bourg-sur-Mer, and besieged Dax for seven weeks in July and August with great vigour, but was at length forced to retire to Bayonne. In January 1297 the citizens of Bellegarde, who were besieged by the French, appealed for assistance. Lincoln marched out to their aid, but was ambushed by Artois. John de St John was taken prisoner, and heavy casualties were sustained, while the English were forced to retreat once more to Bayonne. However, in the summer Lincoln made a successful raid towards Toulouse, which lasted until Michaelmas. He then went back to Bayonne where he remained until after Christmas, and about Easter 1298 he returned to England. He had been replaced as king's lieutenant in Aquitaine by Guy Ferre by 25 April 1298.

Service in Scotland On 15 May 1298 Lincoln was appointed to arrange the marriage between Edward, prince of Wales, and Isabella of France. He was one of the nobles who swore to the earls of Hereford and Norfolk on the king's behalf that Edward I, would reconfirm the charters on his return from the Scottish war, and then accompanied Edward to Scotland, where he was present at the battle of Falkirk on 22 July. He was rewarded with the position and lands of James, the steward of Scotland, which included the barony of Renfrew. In July 1299 he was summoned to attend the council at York on the affairs of Scotland. On 12 September 1299 Lincoln was present at the marriage of Edward I to Margaret of France in Canterbury, where the king turned to him to resolve a dispute over who should receive the cloths used as a canopy over the heads of the royal couple. In 1300 he was again in Scotland, and present at the siege of Caerlaverock in July, when he commanded the first division. In November 1300 he was sent with the elder Hugh Despenser on a mission to the pope in Rome to complain of the injury done by the Scots, having also been entrusted with a mission to the king of France on 14 October.

In March 1301 Lincoln was directed to attend the prince of Wales in person on his invasion of Scotland at midsummer, and during September and October he was engaged in Galloway. During the next two years he was constantly employed in the negotiations with the French king that resulted in the treaty of Montreuil on 20 May 1303. In June of that year he went to Aquitaine in the company of Otto de Grandson and Amadeus, count of Savoy, to take seisin of the duchy in Edward's name and proceed with its reorganization; he remained there for the following year. On 16 September 1305 he was one of the commissioners appointed in the parliament at Westminster to arrange the affairs of Scotland, and in the same parliament was a receiver and trier of petitions from Gascony. On 15 October he was sent along with Grandson and Walter Langton on an embassy to Pope Clement V which resulted in the suspension of Archbishop Winchelsey from office. He returned to London on 16 February 1306, and was publicly received by the mayor. Later in the year he went to Scotland with the prince of Wales, who was ordered to act by his advice. In January 1307 he was one of the commissioners appointed to hold a parliament at Carlisle. In the summer he accompanied Edward on his advance towards Scotland, and was present at the king's death on 7 July, even though on the following day he was one of three individuals, the other two being the queen and the prince of Wales, to whom letters were drafted by the household, presumably notices of the king's passing.

Elder statesman At the death of Edward I, Lincoln was without question the most senior of the English earls, and he remained extremely influential until his death in 1311. He attended Edward II into Scotland in 1307, and along with six other earls gave his assent to the creation of Piers Gaveston as earl of Cornwall in August. Indeed, the author of the *Vita Edwardi secundi* reports that it was Lincoln who confirmed that the king could lawfully alienate the earldom of Cornwall, saying it had been done twice before by other kings. The same writer goes on to say that after the king, Lincoln was Gaveston's chief supporter, but that through the favourite's ingratitude he came to be the chief of his enemies. Whatever the cause, by January 1308 Lincoln was associated with the rising baronial discontent. He not only witnessed the so-called 'Boulogne declaration' of that month that anticipated the parliament of April 1308 in drawing a distinction between the loyalty due to the crown and that due to the person of the king; he very likely played a major role in shaping this position. Nevertheless, following Gaveston's exile Lincoln quickly returned to the king's inner circle. During the second year of the reign he appears as a witness in the charter rolls no fewer than thirty times, including two occasions on which grants were made to Gaveston in June 1309. All too soon, however, he was alienated from the king and favourite, the latter having bestowed the nickname 'Burst-Belly' (*Boele-Crevée*) on him.

The insolence of the favourite, coupled with the king's perceived abuse of patronage, led Lincoln to join with his son-in-law, *Thomas of Lancaster, and other discontented magnates in calling for reform of the royal household and government. Lincoln was one of the petitioners who demanded the reforming ordinances, and was himself one of the *Lords ordainer. Although it does not appear that he played a major role in the drafting of the ordinances, he was supportive of their programme. When Edward II ordered the removal of the exchequer and both benches to York in October 1310, Lincoln threatened to resign his position as keeper of the realm. Edward relented, and the two were reconciled. Lincoln spent Christmas 1310 at Kingston in Dorset, and soon afterwards returned to London, where he died at his house in Holborn on 5 February 1311. He was buried in the lady chapel of St Paul's Cathedral on 28 February. His death had a destabilizing effect on the king's already strained relations with his magnates, and particularly with Thomas of Lancaster, whose wealth and power were greatly increased by his succession to the Lacy inheritance.

The Lacy inheritance Henry de Lacy married twice. His first wife was Margaret, daughter and coheir of William (II) *Longespée (d. 1250), a union that had been arranged as early as 1256, and which brought Lacy the earldom of Salisbury; they were married in 1257. His two sons, Edmund and John, predeceased him, and on 28 October 1294, presumably under pressure of some kind from Edward I, Lincoln and his wife made a settlement of their estates which, while reserving a life interest for themselves, entailed most of them on their son-in-law, Thomas of Lancaster, who had just married their daughter, Alice, and on Thomas's father, the king's brother *Edmund, earl of Lancaster. The settlement was such as to ruin the expectations of any collateral heirs Alice might have, to the ultimate advantage of the house of Lancaster. Margaret died in 1309, and by 16 June 1310 Lincoln had married Joan, daughter of William, Lord Martin, and his wife, Eleanor Fitzpiers. Following Lincoln's death, and before 6 June 1313, Joan married, without royal licence, Nicholas, Lord Audley; she died shortly before 27 October 1322. The properties that his marriage brought to Thomas of Lancaster stretched virtually across the whole kingdom, with particularly large concentrations in Lincolnshire, Yorkshire, Derbyshire, and what is now Denbighshire in Wales. Lincoln's revenues from his estates have been estimated at 10,000 marks per annum. It is difficult to assess the extent of his personal involvement in the network of receiverships, treasuries, and audits revealed by the surviving accounts, but given his reputation for integrity and responsibility it seems unlikely that he had no involvement in the direction of a household that has been described as 'a model of economy and practical efficiency' (Baldwin, 189). Lincoln also appears to have been a literate and cultivated man. He commissioned an abridgement of the *Brut* chronicle, the so-called *Petit Bruit* (BL, Harley MS 907), and in his early days appeared in a short poem by Walter of Bibbesworth, datable to c.1270, in which Walter tries to persuade the earl, who has taken the cross but is now trying to escape his obligations because of his love for a lady, to fulfil his crusading vow. It was with justice that Henry de Lacy, both then and later, was perceived as one of the foremost English magnates of his time.

J. S. HAMILTON

Sources M. Prestwich, *Edward I* (1988) • Rymer, *Foedera*, new edn, vols. 1–2 • J. R. Maddicott, *Thomas of Lancaster, 1307–1322: a study in the reign of Edward II* (1970) • *Chancery records* • J. R. S. Phillips, *Aymer de Valence, earl of Pembroke, 1307–1324: baronial politics in the reign of Edward II* (1972) • *Calendar of the charter rolls*, 6 vols., PRO (1903–27) • PRO, charter rolls, C53 • N. Denholm-Young, ed. and trans., *Vita Edwardi secundi* (1957) • W. Stubbs, ed., *Chronicles of the reigns of Edward I and Edward II*, 2 vols., Rolls Series, 76 (1882–3) • J. F. Baldwin, 'The household administration of Henry Lacy and Thomas of Lancaster', *EngHR*, 42 (1927), 180–200 • *CIPM*, 1, no. 418; 5, no. 279 • GEC, *Peerage* • K. B. McFarlane, *The nobility of later medieval England* (1973), 263 • M. D. Legge, *Anglo-Norman literature and its background* (1963) • R. P. Lawton, 'Henry de Lacy, earl of Lincoln (1272–1311) as *locum tenens et capitaneus* in the duchy of Aquitaine', PhD diss., U. Lond., 1974 • *CClR*, 1247–51; 1272–9

Archives Notts. Arch., manorial and household accounts

Likenesses effigy, BL, Add. MS 6728, fol. 80 • sculpture; formerly at Denbigh

Lacy, Hugh de (*d.* 1186), magnate, was the son of an unknown mother and of Gilbert de *Lacy (*fl.* 1133–1163). In 1158 or 1159 Gilbert became a knight templar and by 1159–60 had been succeeded as lord of Weobley, Herefordshire (one of the family's chief castles), by his son Robert. By 1162 Robert, in turn, had been succeeded by Hugh, presumably his younger brother. Hugh de Lacy thus became an important tenant-in-chief of the crown. He held fees hereditarily in Normandy at Lassy and Campeaux; additionally about 1172–3 he obtained by purchase of 200 livres angevins the honour of Le Pin from Robert, count of Meulan, to be held of Henry II for 2 knights' fees. In 1166 he made a return to the king stating that in England he had 54¼ fees of old feoffment, of which, however, 3½ fees were not acknowledged as his by their holders; he also had 5½ fees of new feoffment, land worth 800s., and 9 resident knights maintained in his household. In 1167/8 scutage was calculated on 51¼ knights' fees, indicating that Lacy had not recovered the contested fees. Lacy did not pay scutage in 1164/5, suggesting that he participated in person in Henry II's campaign from Shrewsbury into north Wales in 1165.

Lacy accompanied Henry II to Ireland in October 1171. Gerald of Wales certainly exaggerated, if he did not entirely invent, a meeting at the River Shannon between Lacy, William fitz Aldelin, and Ruaidrí Ua Conchobair, king of Connacht and claimant to the high-kingship, at which the latter supposedly offered submission to Henry II. Hugh de Lacy had definitely attained a prominent position in the king's entourage. Before Henry left Ireland in April 1172 he granted Lacy the kingdom of Mide for the service of 50 knights, as well as custody of the city of Dublin which the king retained as royal demesne. The terms suggest the king's determination that tenure of the Irish lordships should be more strictly controlled than that of the semi-autonomous Welsh marcher domains. Such had been the confusion over the kingship of Mide in the previous twenty years that Henry specifically granted the kingdom 'as it had been held by Murchad Ua Máel Sechlainn' (Orpen, 1.285–6), who had died in 1153. One Irish contender for the lordship of Mide, Tigernán Ua Ruairc, king of Bréifne, had made such inroads into Mide in the immediate pre-Norman period that he is actually termed 'king of Mide' by Gerald (*Expugnatio*, 95, 113). Lacy assassinated Ua Ruairc at the hill of Tlachtga (Ward, Meath) in 1172 while negotiations between the two were in progress.

Lacy was back in England by 29 December 1172, the anniversary of the death of Archbishop Thomas Becket, when he was at Canterbury, probably *en route* for Normandy. In the summer of 1173 he fought on Henry II's behalf in Normandy and in July held the castle of Verneuil against Louis VII of France, although eventually it was forced to capitulate. Lacy can be traced intermittently in Henry's entourage up to 1177. In May 1177 he was present at the Council of Oxford, when arrangements were made for the administration of the Angevin lordship in Ireland following the death in April 1176 of Richard fitz Gilbert de Clare (Strongbow), earl of Pembroke and Striguil and lord of Leinster. According to Gerald of Wales, Lacy was appointed as the

king's *procurator generalis* in Ireland (*Expugnatio*, 183), but the diplomatic of royal records indicates that it was William fitz Aldelin who exercised the role of principal royal agent in Ireland at this time. The king may have considered that his bond with William fitz Aldelin, a long-standing administrator and member of the royal *familia*, was more dependable than his personal relationship with Lacy as a tenurial vassal. Few such administrators were available to Henry in Ireland, however, and in 1177 Lacy retained custody of the royal demesne of Dublin. Extant documents testify to his administrative role. In 1176/7 the sheriff of Shropshire accounted for 200 bushels of wheat sent to Lacy in Ireland; in 1177/8 he received 200 bushels from Dorset and Somerset and 300 from Gloucestershire, while 500 bushels were shipped with his servants in 1178/9 for the use of the king's *familia* in Ireland. None the less, Henry II evidently remained wary of Lacy's intentions, and in the summer of 1177 took into his hand Lacy's demesne castle of Ludlow, which he retained for the remainder of Lacy's life: this would have had the effect of weakening Lacy power in the central Welsh march and may therefore have been intended as a mechanism of royal control in case Hugh de Lacy overstepped his position in Ireland.

The so-called *Song of Dermot and the Earl* gives an account of Hugh de Lacy's subinfeudation of Mide. The details of the process are obscure as only three charter-texts of enfeoffment survive. Settlement seems to have proceeded on the basis of pre-existing units—the charters give the Irish names of the lands and their previous holders—which were now held by knights' service, orientated towards a castle. The precise number of castles that Lacy built in Mide is unknown. His castle at Trim was to become the *caput* of the Anglo-Norman lordship of Mide. Some of his castles reused royal sites of the pre-Norman kingdom of Mide. Gerald of Wales praised Lacy in contrast to William fitz Aldelin, for fortifying Leinster and Mide with castles and pacifying Ireland. Lacy also dispensed religious patronage from his new lordship. He endowed Llanthony Prima, in Gwent, and Llanthony Secunda, in Gloucestershire, with extensive ecclesiastical benefices and lands in Mide, founding a cell of Llanthony Prima at Colp and a cell of Llanthony Secunda at Duleek. He founded a Benedictine alien priory at Fore, Westmeath, as a dependency of St Taurin, Évreux, and was a benefactor of St Thomas's Abbey, Dublin, the Augustinian priory of Kells, Meath, and the archbishopric of Dublin.

Some of Lacy's activities did nothing to lessen the king's suspicion of him. In 1178 he reached an accommodation with Ruaidrí Ua Conchobair, who had repulsed him after he had plundered the ecclesiastical site of Clonmacnoise, co. Offaly, with the Dublin garrison. Without Henry II's permission, Lacy married Ua Conchobair's daughter around this time, which apparently displeased Henry, and may have led to Lacy's recall to England in 1179 and again in 1181. In late 1181 or 1182, however, Lacy returned to Ireland, this time as the king's principal agent, though a royal clerk, Robert of Shrewsbury, was to oversee his actions. In September 1184 he was recalled again and replaced by a royal *familiaris*, Philip of Worcester, one of whose first actions was to seek the recovery of Saithne, in the north of the county of Dublin, which Hugh de Lacy was deemed to have misappropriated from the royal demesne of Dublin. When Henry II's son John went to assume the lordship of Ireland in person in 1185, he is said by the annals of Loch Cé to have reported back to Henry that Lacy had prevented the Irish kings from giving him tribute or hostages.

Hugh de Lacy was assassinated at Durrow on 26 July 1186. He was beheaded with an axe by Gillaganinathair Ó Miadaig of Bregmuine at the direction of In Sinnach Ua Ceithernaig, king of Tethba, perhaps to avenge the killing of the latter's son in battle against the Anglo-Normans eight years earlier. The annals of Loch Cé describe Lacy at the time of his death as 'king of Mide and Bréifne, and Airgialla', and further state that 'it was to him that the tribute of Connacht was paid' (*Annals of Loch Cé*, 1.173). Roger of Howden and William of Newburgh claim that news of Lacy's death was welcomed by Henry II, while Newburgh adds that the king intended to send John back to Ireland to seize Lacy's lands and castles. Lacy was buried at Durrow in 1186. His honour of Weobley was in the hands of the crown until his son and heir, Walter de *Lacy (*d.* 1241), came of age in 1189. In 1195, in moves probably linked to the assumption of the lordship of Mide by Walter, Hugh de Lacy's body was recovered at the instigation of Muirges Ua hÉnna, archbishop of Cashel and papal legate, and John Cumin, archbishop of Dublin, and removed to Bective Abbey, Meath, while his head was buried at St Thomas's Abbey, Dublin. Further controversy over his remains ended in 1205 with a papal judgment in favour of removal of the body to St Thomas's, where it was buried alongside that of his first wife, Rose, widow of Baderon of Monmouth (*d.* 1170x76), and mother of his sons, Walter, Hugh de *Lacy (*d.* 1242), Gilbert, and Robert. Rose died some time before 1180, by when Lacy had taken as his second wife the daughter of Ruaidrí Ua Conchobair, the elder, with whom he had a son, William Gorm, deemed to be illegitimate, who was to act in close concert with his half-brothers.   M. T. FLANAGAN

Sources M. T. Flanagan, *Irish society, Anglo-Norman settlers, Angevin kingship: interactions in Ireland in the late twelfth century* (1989) • *Pipe rolls*, Henry II – Richard I • H. Hall, ed., *The Red Book of the Exchequer*, 1, Rolls Series, 99 (1896), 41, 279, 281–3, 300 • Giraldus Cambrensis, *Expugnatio Hibernica / The conquest of Ireland*, ed. and trans. A. B. Scott and F. X. Martin (1978), 95, 105, 113–15, 183, 191–5, 199, 235, 251 • G. H. Orpen, ed. and trans., *The song of Dermot and the earl* (1892), lines 2606, 2656, 2716, 2727, 2940, 3129–76, 3222, p. 310 • W. Stubbs, ed., *Gesta regis Henrici secundi Benedicti abbatis: the chronicle of the reigns of Henry II and Richard I, AD 1169–1192*, 2 vols., Rolls Series, 49 (1867), 1.30, 49–50, 161, 163–5, 221, 270, 350, 361 • R. Howlett, ed., *Chronicles of the reigns of Stephen, Henry II, and Richard I*, 1, Rolls Series, 82 (1884), 239–40 • *Radulfi de Diceto ... opera historica*, ed. W. Stubbs, 2: *1180–1202*, Rolls Series, 68 (1876), 34 • R. Bartlett, 'Colonial aristocracies of the high middle ages', *Medieval frontier societies*, ed. R. Bartlett and A. Mackay (1989) • M. T. Flanagan, 'Anglo-Norman change and continuity', *Irish Historical Studies*, 28 (1992–3), 385–9 • J. Everard, 'The "justiciarship" in Brittany and Ireland under Henry II', *Anglo-Norman Studies*, 20 (1997), 87–105 • W. E. Wightman, *The Lacy family in England and Normandy, 1066–1194* (1966), 187–94, 222, and *passim* • J. T. Gilbert, ed., *Register of the abbey of St Thomas, Dublin*, Rolls Series, 94 (1889), 13, 348–51, 420 • *Gir. Camb. opera*, 7.69 • L. Delisle and others, eds., *Recueil des actes de Henri II, roi d'Angleterre et duc de Normandie, concernant les provinces françaises et les affaires de France*, 1 (Paris, 1909), 253 • W. M. Hennessy, ed. and trans., *The annals of Loch Cé: a chronicle of Irish affairs from AD 1014 to AD 1590*, 2 vols., Rolls Series, 54 (1871), 1185, 1186 • M. P. Mac Síthigh, 'Cairteacha Meán-Aoiseacha do Mhainistir Fhobhair (XII–XII céad)', *Seanchas Ardmhacha*, 4 (1960–61), 171–5; calendared in J. H. Round, *Documents preserved in France, 918–1206* (1899), 105 • E. St J. Brooks, ed., *The Irish cartularies of Llanthony prima and secunda*, IMC (1953), 18, 79, 82–3, 219 • *CPR, 1388–92*, 300 • J. T. Gilbert, ed., *Crede mihi* (1897), 37, 48 • G. H. Orpen, *Ireland under the Normans*, 4 vols. (1911–20), vol. 1, pp. 285–6 • *Chronica magistri Rogeri de Hovedene*, ed. W. Stubbs, 2, Rolls Series, 51 (1869), 34, 309

Lacy, Hugh de, earl of Ulster (*d.* 1242), magnate and soldier, was the son of Hugh de *Lacy (*d.* 1186) and his first wife, Rose of Monmouth, and younger brother of Walter de Lacy, lord of Meath (*d.* 1241). Hugh was a minor on his father's death, but had reached his majority by 1195 when he and John de Courcy led an army to Athlone and negotiated a treaty with Cathal Crobderg Ó Conchobair, king of Connacht. At about this time he was also the recipient of a speculative grant from William de Burgh of ten cantreds in Connacht, a grant confirmed by John, count of Mortain. From his brother Walter he received in Meath the barony of Ratoath and land in Morgallion, and by his marriage, some time between 1194 and 1199, to Lesceline de Verdon, daughter of Bertram de Verdon (*d.* 1192) and sister of Thomas and Nicholas de Verdon, he acquired the Cooley peninsula, Louth, and land north of Dundalk. In 1201 Lacy and Courcy supported an attempt by Cathal Crobderg to regain the kingship of Connacht from his great-nephew Cathal Carrach Ó Conchobair, but they were heavily defeated. Lacy then arrested Courcy and Cathal Crobderg but released them soon after. King John had grown suspicious of Courcy and used Lacy against him. In 1203 Lacy defeated Courcy at Down and in the following year captured and released him again. In November 1204 Hugh and Walter de Lacy were granted eight cantreds in Ulster and on 29 May 1205 Hugh was granted all Ulster as earl to hold as Courcy had held it on the day he was captured by Lacy.

In 1206 Lacy plundered Armagh, causing the archbishop of Armagh, Echdonn Mac Gilla Uidhir, to travel to England to complain to the king. In 1208 he attacked the Meath lands of the justiciar, Meiler fitz Henry, and captured his castle of Ardnurcher in Westmeath. This was done in support of William (I) Marshal whose position in Ireland was being undermined by King John. At the same time John had begun to persecute his former friend William (III) de Briouze who had quarrelled with the king over the murder of Arthur of Brittany. Briouze held land in Limerick and his daughter was married to Walter de Lacy. John hounded him for money owed to the crown and in 1209 he and his family fled to Ireland. Briouze returned to Wales the same year but his family were sheltered by Hugh de Lacy. In 1210 John arrived in Ireland to crush his opponents there. As Lacy moved north into Ulster he ravaged north Louth, thereby revenging himself on his brother-in-law, Nicholas de Verdon, who had objected to the marriage portion assigned to Lacy and attempted to claw some of it back. Lacy was chased from Ulster and fled to Scotland, where he spent a short time at St Andrews. Either before his expulsion or following his restoration in 1227 he granted the church of Carlingford in Louth to St Andrews. He and Walter de Lacy appear to have travelled to France and may have sheltered among the monks of St Taurin in Évreux. Hugh de Lacy later participated in the Albigensian crusade, being present at the siege of Toulouse in 1216 and the death of Simon de Montfort on 25 June 1218.

Negotiations for Lacy's restoration were already underway by the time of John's death. Soon after the coronation of Henry III in 1216 he was given safe conduct to meet the Marshal, and this was repeated in February 1217. Lacy, however, appears to have remained in France until 1219. The death of the Marshal in that year and the rise to power of Hubert de Burgh signalled a less sympathetic approach by the government. In 1220 Lacy responded by joining Llywelyn ab Iorwerth of Gwynedd in attacking the lands of William (II) Marshal in Wales. Attempts were again made to reach a compromise with a safe conduct being issued to Lacy to travel to England in 1221. He seems to have been confident of success at this point and in 1222 used the title earl of Ulster when witnessing a grant by Ranulf (III), earl of Chester, whose nephew and eventual successor, John the Scot, was married to Llywelyn's daughter Helen.

In December 1222 Lacy was offered his land in Meath and his wife's land in Louth, but he demanded the return of Ulster. The king offered to place it instead in the custody of the earls of Chester, Salisbury, and Gloucester and Walter de Lacy for five years, but in the summer of 1223 these lords refused to accept it. By this time Lacy was preparing to invade Ireland and the king sent letters from the pope to the archbishop of Dublin excommunicating anyone who aided him. Henry III's sister, Joan, the wife of Alexander II, king of Scotland, wrote to her brother to inform him that Alexander would not aid Lacy but that the king of Norway might do so. Lacy was involved in supporting one candidate for the kingship of Man and the Isles, Olaf, against the incumbent ruler, his brother Ragnvald. In 1224 the kingdom was divided between them with Ragnvald keeping Man and some of the isles and Olaf taking the rest. The latter subsequently supported Lacy's invasion of Ireland.

Lacy arrived in Ireland late in 1223 and went to Meath where he joined his half-brother, William Gorm de Lacy, in plundering his enemies. On 19 June 1224 the new justiciar, William (II) Marshal, arrived in Ireland and with the support of Walter de Lacy besieged Trim Castle which had been taken by adherents of Hugh. Marshal sent his cousin William le Gros with a force to relieve Carrickfergus Castle in Ulster which was being besieged by Hugh. Trim was taken and Hugh de Lacy abandoned the siege of Carrickfergus and joined his ally Áed Méith Ó Néill, king of Tír Eoghain, in destroying the castle of Coleraine which

had been built by Thomas of Galloway after Lacy's expulsion in 1210. He and Áed then turned south and harried the Verdon lands around Dundalk. A large force under William Marshal met them at the Ulster passes in October and Lacy surrendered. His captivity, however, seems not to have been onerous. About May 1225 he was granted 200 marks by the king at the instance of Marshal and in May of the following year all his lands were placed in the custody of Walter de Lacy, with Marshal acting as guarantor. Finally in April 1227 Ulster was restored to Hugh as earl, with the proviso that it would return to the crown in the absence of a male heir.

The lands of the Galloway lords Alan and Thomas were also excluded from the grant to Hugh de Lacy, but he continued to undermine their position. In 1228 he rebuilt Coleraine Castle for himself. In 1229 his daughter married *Alan of Galloway but the Scottish lord did not recover his interests in Ulster. When Alan died in 1234 he left three daughters and an illegitimate son, Thomas. Alexander II was determined that Galloway would be divided between the daughters, but in 1236 an unsuccessful invasion was launched from Ulster by Thomas, with Lacy's support. As part of his attempts to neutralize Galloway involvement in Ulster, Lacy also introduced into the earldom the family of Bisset of Moray, some of whose members murdered Patrick the son of Thomas, earl of Atholl, Alan of Galloway's brother, in 1242.

In 1230 Lacy's ally and client Áed Méith Ó Néill died and in the ensuing succession contest Lacy supported not Áed's son Domnall but his rival Domnall Mac Lochlainn. In 1234–5 Mac Lochlainn killed Ó Néill but soon turned against the earl. In 1238 the Irish of Ulaid (Antrim and Down) revolted against Lacy and appealed to Mac Lochlainn for help. Lacy was expelled but returned the following autumn with the justiciar Maurice Fitzgerald (d. 1257). Domnall was banished to Connacht and Brian Ó Néill, a nephew of Áed Méith, was set up in his place. Mac Lochlainn regained power in 1239 but in 1241 he and his family were finally destroyed by Ó Néill.

In 1228 Hugh de Lacy was summoned by the king to fight in France and in 1234 he demonstrated his loyalty to Henry III by participating in the murder of Richard Marshal on the Curragh. Considering the favour shown to Lacy by both Richard's older brother and father this was a particularly unpleasant incident in the earl's career. In the following year he was involved in the conquest of Connacht by Richard de Burgh. His reward was the revival of the grant made to him almost forty years earlier by Richard's father William. He was granted five cantreds in Sligo for the service of ten knights. Apart from founding the manor of Meelick, Lacy did not involve himself personally in Connacht and granted most of his lands there to others such as Maurice Fitzgerald, Jordan of Exeter, Gerald de Prendergast, Peter of Birmingham, and Miles de Nangle. In 1235 he also reached agreement with Roesia de Verdon, daughter of Nicholas de Verdon and niece of his wife, Lesceline, about the half of the Verdon lands he had acquired by his marriage. For a payment of £200 these were returned to Roesia on condition that the men enfeoffed there by Lacy remained undisturbed. In 1237 Lacy opposed the piratical attacks of the Mariscos in the Irish Sea and arrested Scottish merchants then in Ulster. His rehabilitation into royal favour was shown by two summonses he received to give counsel to the king in 1234 and 1237.

Hugh de Lacy died shortly before 26 December 1242 in Ulster. It is possible but not certain that he was buried at the Franciscan house in Carrickfergus, which he may have founded. He certainly founded the Franciscan house at Down in 1240. He had no surviving sons and his lands reverted to the crown. He married twice. With his first wife, Lesceline de Verdon, he had at least two sons and at least three daughters. His sons Walter and Roger were alive in 1226, but both predeceased him. One of them, or possibly another son, was killed fighting Mac Lochlainn in 1238. Of the daughters of Lacy and Lesceline one, Matilda, married David, baron of Naas, and brought as her marriage portion Lesceline's lands around Carlingford as well as Lacy's lands in Meath and Limerick. She died at a great age in 1281. Another daughter married Miles de Nangle and on her death in 1253 was buried at Boyle Abbey. A third daughter, Rose, married Alan of Galloway and was still alive in 1237. Lacy's second wife was Emeline, daughter of Walter of Ridelisford, with whom he had no children. Shortly after Lacy's death she married Stephen Longespée, a kinsman of Henry III, bringing with her as dower Lacy's Connacht manor of Meelick.   B. SMITH

Sources G. H. Orpen, *Ireland under the Normans*, 4 vols. (1911–20) · A. J. Otway-Ruthven, *A history of medieval Ireland* (1968) · T. W. Moody and others, eds., *A new history of Ireland*, 2: *Medieval Ireland, 1169–1534* (1987); repr. with corrections (1993) · H. S. Sweetman and G. F. Handcock, eds., *Calendar of documents relating to Ireland*, 5 vols., PRO (1875–86), vol. 1 · K. Simms, 'The O Hanlons, the O Neills and the Anglo-Normans in thirteenth-century Armagh', *Seanchas Ardmhacha*, 9 (1978–9), 70–94 · K. J. Stringer, 'Periphery and core in thirteenth-century Scotland: Alan, son of Roland, lord of Galloway and constable of Scotland', *Medieval Scotland: crown, lordship and community: essays presented to G. W. S. Barrow*, ed. A. Grant and K. J. Stringer (1993), 82–113 · Paris, *Chron.*, 4.232

Lacy, James (1696–1774), actor and theatre manager, was descended from an old Anglo-Irish family. Although the Lacys possessed a vast estate before the civil war, their loyalty to the house of Stuart served only to ruin them, their descendants as a consequence being 'forced to follow Fortune in almost all the different Services of Europe' (Victor, 83). Little is known of the early life of James Lacy, but by 1722 he was living in Norwich, where he earned a living as 'a reputable Dealer in the Manufactures of that City' (Victor, 64). With his business failing, however, he looked towards the stage, and made his first appearance with the Norwich company in the season 1723–4. Soon afterwards he moved to London, where he appears to have found employment with John Rich's company at Lincoln's Inn Fields. The date of his stage début in London is uncertain, but on 2 May 1727 he made an appearance as Herodorus in David Lewis's *Philip of Macedon*.

Lacy remained at Lincoln's Inn for a further year, before moving to the Haymarket Theatre for the 1728–9 season. His roles there included Acasto in Thomas Otway's *The Orphan* and Worthy in George Farquhar's *The Recruiting Officer*. The following year he appeared both at the New Haymarket and with Odell's troupe at Goodman's Fields. He then spent a further season at the Haymarket before engaging with the Covent Garden company in the autumn of 1732. He left Covent Garden in the summer of 1734, possibly to rejoin the players at Lincoln's Inn, with whom he is known to have appeared in the summer of 1735. In the autumn of 1735 Lacy returned to the Haymarket to work under the direction of Henry Fielding. As a member of 'the Great Mogul's Company of English Comedians', he appeared in two popular farces by Fielding, taking the parts of Fustian in *Pasquin* (1736) and Sour-Wit in *The Historical Register* (1737). On 4 May 1737 Lacy appeared in an afterpiece of his own, *Fame, or, Queen Elizabeth's Trumpets*, advertised as 'a new Satyrical, Allegorical, Political Farce'.

The passage of the Licensing Act in 1737 brought an end to all performances at the Haymarket. In December 1737, and in a direct challenge to the terms of the Licensing Act, Lacy began to offer public 'lectures' at the York Buildings in Villiers Street. These readings, which comprised a number of separate speaking parts shared out between Lacy and his assistants, were dramatic performances in all but name. Lacy was consequently arrested and sent to Bridewell, where he remained until the end of February 1738. After being released from prison he continued to defy the Licensing Act, offering a further series of 'orations' at the York Buildings. In 1740 he negotiated the lease of Ranelagh House and gardens, where he designed and built a theatre.

In May 1742 Lacy returned to the London stage, taking the title role in a Drury Lane performance of Thomas Southerne's *Oroonoko*. In 1744 he was approached by Amber and Green, city bankers keen to take an interest in the Drury Lane theatre. The two men, perhaps encouraged by Lacy's reputation for 'candor and integrity' (Victor, 73), entered into an agreement whereby they loaned him the money to buy the theatre patent from Charles Fleetwood. David Garrick, who had himself been offered the patent by Fleetwood, quickly fell out with Lacy. The refusal of the new manager to honour Fleetwood's debts incensed the young actor, who in the summer of 1745 quit London for Dublin. The absence of Garrick and the turmoil of the Jacobite rising caused the receipts at Drury Lane to fall alarmingly.

In the spring of 1747 Lacy made his peace with Garrick, and offered the actor the opportunity to buy a half-share of the business, including patent, theatre lease, properties, and costumes, for £12,000. The partnership was immediately successful, and by the summer of 1750 the accumulated profits already outweighed the sum of each partner's original investment. In addition to a handsome share of the profits at the season's end, Lacy paid himself a salary of £500 per year. He ran the financial side of the business, ensuring the theatre remained in good condition, and that the props, costumes, and sceneries were paid for. Garrick managed the actors, and supervised all artistic business. The association between Garrick and Lacy continued until the latter's death in 1774.

In January 1728 a 'Mrs Lacy' appeared alongside James Lacy in a performance of John Gay's *The Beggar's Opera* at Lincoln's Inn Fields. It is assumed that this actress was Lacy's wife. The same actress appeared with Lacy at the Bartholomew and Southwark fairs in the summer of 1730 and spent the following season at the Haymarket. This Mrs Lacy revisited the fairs in 1734 and 1736, and made her final appearance at Southwark in 1740 in a performance of the pantomime *Harlequin Faustus*. Some time before 1748 James Lacy began a relationship with Ann Willoughby, an actress in the Drury Lane company. Willoughby made her début at Drury Lane in September 1748, and remained there for four seasons. She retired at the end of the 1752 season, and died on 11 November 1768. Although she styled herself as a second 'Mrs Lacy', there is no firm evidence that she and Lacy were married.

According to one report, despite the financial success of Drury Lane, Lacy's attraction to increasingly outlandish forms of speculation caused him to lose much of his fortune, a significant part of which was wasted 'searching for coal-mines in Oxfordshire' (*GM*, 1st ser., 69, 1779, 172). On 21 January 1774 Lacy died at his home, Turk's House, Isleworth, Middlesex. He was buried in the churchyard of St James's Church, Paddington, on 30 January.

In 1774 Willoughby Lacy (1749–1831), the son of James Lacy and Ann Willoughby, inherited his father's share of the partnership with Garrick. The same year he appeared on stage in Birmingham, in Norwich, and then at Drury Lane. In 1778, following Garrick's decision to sell the moiety of his patent and other interest in the Drury Lane theatre, Lacy followed suit, selling his half-share in the theatre to the partnership of Sheridan, Linley, and Ford. The sale of the Lacy share raised £45,000, half of which was already owed to Garrick. Following the sale Lacy spent time as an itinerant actor, appearing in London in 1784, and Dublin in 1785. A recipient of a series of theatre benefit performances between 1798 and 1801, he seems to have fallen heavily into debt in later life. In 1813 he published a direct appeal to the public for financial assistance. He died, aged eighty-two, on 17 September 1831.

CHARLES BRAYNE

Sources B. Victor, *The history of the theatres of London and Dublin*, 1 (1761), 65–87 • *GM*, 1st ser., 49 (1779), 171–2 • *GM*, 1st ser., 44 (1774), 47 • D. Lysons, *The environs of London*, 2nd edn, 2/2 (1811), 602 • Highfill, Burnim & Langhans, *BDA* • *GM*, 1st ser., 101/2 (1831), 282–3 • W. S. Clark, *The Irish stage in the county towns, 1720–1800* (1965), 365 • S. Rosenfeld, *The theatre of the London fairs in the 18th century* • G. W. Stone and G. M. Kahrl, *David Garrick: a critical biography* (1979) **Likenesses** engraving, 1802 (for *European Magazine*, July 1802), repro. in Stone and Kahrl, *David Garrick* **Wealth at death** half-share of Drury Lane theatre, value £32,000, £20,000 of which was owed to Garrick; Turk's House, Isleworth, and another in Berners Street, London; freehold estate in Eynsham, value £500 p.a.: Highfill, Burnim & Langhans, *BDA*, 9.97

Lacy, John de, third earl of Lincoln (*c*.1192–1240), magnate, was the eldest son and heir of Roger de *Lacy, constable of Chester (*d*. 1211), and his wife, Maud or Matilda de Clere, erroneously identified as Matilda de Clare in a fifteenth-century chronicle. Since he was almost certainly a minor at the time of his father's death, and did not obtain possession of his lands until September 1213, John appears to have been born *c*.1192. His early years are obscure. The only possible reference to him before 1213 occurs in a letter of Philip Augustus, king of France, responding to an offer by a John de Lacy made in 1209 or early 1210 to foment rebellion in England and Ireland. This may, however, refer not to the seventeen-year-old John, but to the Anglo-Irish baron Walter de Lacy.

In September 1213 John de Lacy obtained possession of his father's extensive estate, comprising more than 100 knights' fees together with the northern baronies of Pontefract, Clitheroe, Penwortham, Widnes, and Halton, held by descent in the female line from the Lacy lords of Pontefract, and in the line of direct male descent as heir to the lands and office of the constables of Chester. In return for his lands he was forced to offer a massive fine of 7000 marks repayable over the coming three years, in the meantime surrendering his chief castles of Pontefract in Yorkshire and Donington in Leicestershire, to be garrisoned by the king at Lacy's expense, on pain of confiscation should Lacy rebel. In 1214 he accompanied the king to Poitou, being restored to possession of Castle Donington in July in return for the surrender of hostages including his younger brother. He was still at court on 4 March 1215, when he took the cross at the same time as King John. On the following day he was pardoned the 4200 marks still owing from his fine of 1213.

As late as 31 May 1215 Lacy was assumed to be loyal. However, with the fall of London he threw in his lot with the rebels, being named at Runnymede in June 1215 as one of the baronial council of twenty-five, and being entrusted with command of the rebel forces in Yorkshire and Nottinghamshire. Thereafter he veered opportunistically between the rebel and royalist camps. On 1 January 1216, perhaps in light of the king's capture of Castle Donington, he sought terms with John, once again surrendering his brother as hostage and repudiating all the terms of the settlement embodied in Magna Carta. In April he was restored to possession of the manor of Lytham in Oxfordshire, detached from the Lacy barony of Pontefract for much of the previous century. In May he was in Kent with the king, but he had rebelled again before John's death in October. Thereafter, with the defeat of the rebel army at Lincoln, he once again returned to the royalist camp, being readmitted to fealty in August 1217. In the following month he was commanded to oversee the restoration of Carlisle Castle by the king of Scots. However, his thoughts now turned to the crusade, and in May 1218, in company with his chief lord, Ranulf (III), earl of Chester, he embarked for Damietta.

John de Lacy's activities in the East are unrecorded, save for an award he made at Damietta for the establishment of a chapel at Pontefract in honour of the holy sepulchre and the holy cross. He did not return to England until August 1220, still following in the train of the earl of Chester. Thereafter his fortunes were linked closely to those of the earl, an alliance cemented in 1221 by his marriage to *Ranulf (III)'s niece. In February 1221, during the rebellion of the earl of Aumale, Lacy was commanded to assist in the siege of Skipton Castle, and in the following year he was appointed to forest inquiries in Nottinghamshire and Yorkshire. In the winter of 1223–4, together with the earl of Chester, he was among the leaders of the opposition to the justiciar, Hubert de Burgh, but made his peace with the king, attending the siege of Bedford in 1224, witnessing the reissue of Magna Carta in 1225, and assisting in the collection of the tax bestowed in return for the charter's reissue. In 1226 he was appointed a justice on eyre in Lincolnshire and Lancashire.

In 1227 Lacy served as one of the royal envoys to Antwerp in negotiations with the German princes, and in 1230 accompanied the king's expedition to Brittany and Poitou, receiving the manors of Collingham in Yorkshire and Bardsey in Lincolnshire in reward for his service. After August 1230 he helped to negotiate an Anglo-French truce. During the political crisis of 1232 he once again sided with the earl of Chester against Hubert de Burgh, in October being appointed to inquire into Hubert's escape from sanctuary and thereafter supplying one of the four knights appointed to serve as Hubert's gaolers at Devizes Castle. However, his adherence to the new regime headed by Peter des Roches was no more than half-hearted, and sprang principally from his desire to obtain royal favour at a crucial moment in his own affairs. Following the death of Ranulf of Chester on 26 October 1232, Lacy was permitted to benefit from an arrangement agreed before Ranulf's death, whereby Ranulf's title as earl of Lincoln was conveyed to Hawise, Ranulf's sister, and thence to John as Hawise's son-in-law. On 22 November 1232 John was granted the third penny of the county of Lincolnshire, and was thus created an earl. Although Ranulf's principal Lincolnshire barony of Bolingbroke was retained by Hawise (d. 1243), John acquired other portions of the Chester estate, including a share in the manor of Leeds, from John the Scot, Ranulf's successor as earl of Chester.

In autumn 1233 Lacy helped to defend the Welsh marches against the rebellion headed by Richard Marshal. The chronicler Roger of Wendover claims that John was bribed by des Roches to abandon the marshal: an allegation substantiated by the award to John of the wardship of the heir and lands of Nigel de Mowbray in return for a relatively modest proffer of 1000 marks. With des Roches's fall John none the less retained his position at court, emerging as a leading royal counsellor. In 1236 he discharged a ceremonial role at Queen Eleanor's coronation. In the following year, besides assisting in negotiations with Scotland and Wales and witnessing the reissue of Magna Carta, he was granted custody of the earldom of Chester on the death of Earl John the Scot. His familiarity with the king, and his purchase for 3000 marks of the marriage of Richard de Clare, heir to the earldom of Gloucester, for his eldest daughter, Maud, are said to have been resented by the king's brother, Richard of Cornwall, leading to a threat of rebellion by Richard in 1238. Thereafter Lacy's

influence at court appears to have waned, perhaps as a result of the prolonged ill health from which he is said to have suffered in his final years. He died on 22 July 1240 and was buried near his father in the choir of the Cistercian abbey of Stanlaw, his bones being moved to Whalley when the monks transferred there in the 1290s.

The fifteenth-century chronicle of Stanlaw credits Lacy with a first wife, Alice, daughter of the Anglo-Norman baron Gilbert de l'Aigle, who is said to have died childless and to have been buried at Norton Priory. Lacy's only certainly documented marriage occurred in 1221, to Margaret [see Lacy, Margaret de, countess of Lincoln], daughter of Robert de Quincy (d. 1217), eldest son of Saer (IV) de Quincy (who died at Damietta in 1219), and Hawise, sister of Ranulf, earl of Chester. Although in theory heir to her grandfather's earldom of Winchester, Margaret's claims were passed over in 1219 in favour of those of her uncle, Roger de *Quincy, a fact that may have fuelled her husband's dissatisfaction with the regime headed by Hubert de Burgh, and which must have made his eventual acquisition of the earldom of Lincoln all the more satisfying. Margaret, who eventually succeeded to part of the Quincy estate in Dorset and to her mother's portion of the Chester inheritance, long outlived her husband. In 1242 she married Walter Marshal, earl of Pembroke (d. 1245). A wealthy widow for the next twenty years, and a member of the friendship network of Queen Eleanor, Margaret died in March 1266 at Hamstead Marshall and was buried in the church of the hospitallers at Clerkenwell. Her son from her marriage to John, Edmund de Lacy, probably born in 1230, permitted to succeed to his father's estates in May 1248, at the age of only eighteen, and by 1255 at the latest was styled earl of Lincoln, receiving the third penny of the county. In May 1247 he married Alice, daughter of Manfred, marquess of Saluzzo, a kinsman of Queen Eleanor, and died on 2 June 1258, being buried at Stanlaw.

Besides making awards to the religious, principally of Pontefract and Stanlaw, John de Lacy issued the first surviving borough charter for the men of Rochdale. His arms are recorded on his seal as earl of Lincoln and by Matthew Paris as quarterly or and gules, a bend let sable and a label of four points argent, derived perhaps from the Mandeville earls of Essex via the marriage of Lacy's grandfather to a Mandeville kinswoman.

NICHOLAS VINCENT

Sources Chancery records [PRO and RC] · Pipe rolls · Paris, Chron. · R. C. Christie, ed. and trans., Annales Cestrienses, or, Chronicle of the abbey of S. Werburg at Chester, Lancashire and Cheshire RS, 14 (1887) · Ann. mon. · GEC, Peerage, 7.676–81 · G. Barraclough, ed., The charters of the Anglo-Norman earls of Chester, c.1071–1237, Lancashire and Cheshire RS, 126 (1988) · J. C. Holt, The northerners: a study in the reign of King John, new edn (1992) · L. Wilkinson, 'Pawn and political player: observations on the life of a thirteenth-century countess', Historical Research, 73 (2000), 105–23 · Byron cartulary, Bodl. Oxf., MS Rawl. B. 460, fol. 76v · Stanlaw chronicle, BL, Cotton MS, Cleopatra C.iii, fols. 315r–318r · MS, BL, additional charter 7465 · T. D. Tremlett, H. Stanford London, and A. Wagner, eds., Rolls of arms, Henry III, Harleian Society, 113–14 (1967) · R. Holmes, ed., The chartulary of St John of Pontefract, 2 vols., Yorkshire Archaeological Society Record Series, 25, 30 (1899–1902) · W. A. Hulton, ed., The coucher book, or chartulary, of Whalley Abbey, 4 vols., Chetham Society, 10–11, 16, 20 (1847–9)

Lacy, John (*c*.1615–1681), playwright and actor, born in the vicinity of Doncaster, Yorkshire, went in 1631 to London where he was apprenticed to the dancing-master John Ogilby, who ran a school in Gray's Inn Lane. Later renowned for dialect-based performances, Lacy is said (by John Aubrey in his *Letters Written by Eminent Persons*, 1813) to have furnished Ben Jonson with northern dialect terms and proverbs for his 1630s drama (critical opinion varies as to whether this was for *A Tale of a Tub*, *c*.1633, or *The Sad Shepherd*, 1637, although the north midlands setting of the latter makes that the more likely choice). Aubrey quotes Lacy on Jonson elsewhere in his manuscripts. In 1639 Lacy is recorded as acting in the company of the Cockpit Theatre. A wife, Margaret, is referred to by certain contemporaries but little more is known of her personal life. Elias Ashmole's diary refers to the baptism of Lacy's second son on 17 March 1665.

During the English civil wars Lacy served as a lieutenant and quartermaster under Colonel Charles Gerard, later the earl of Macclesfield. At the Restoration he was a founder member of Thomas Killigrew's King's Company at the Theatre Royal and rose to become one of that company's star performers. Like other early Restoration actors, he appears to have played some female parts, despite the advent of professional women performers, taking the lead in *The French Dancing Mistress* in 1662. Among other roles, he played Scruple the nonconformist in John Wilson's comedy *The Cheats* in 1662 and Teague in Sir Robert Howard's *The Committee* in 1663. Samuel Pepys witnessed the latter performance, remarking that it was 'a merry but an indifferent play' but that Lacy's performance as an Irish footman was 'beyond imagination' (Pepys, 4.181, 12 June 1663). On seeing Lacy in the part on a subsequent occasion, Pepys observed that his role was 'so well performed that it would set off anything' (ibid., 8.384, 13 Aug 1667). John Evelyn also saw Lacy perform this role, praising it in his diary. It has been argued that Lacy's performances in these two roles along with that of Monsieur Galliard (the dance reference was highly apposite) in *The Variety* by William Cavendish, duke of Newcastle, are enshrined in a triple portrait of him by John Michael Wright which hung in Windsor Castle until the early nineteenth century. Other scholars have disputed this attribution, however, and argued that the roles represented are those of Galliard, Wareston from John Tatham's *The Rump*, and Ananias from Ben Jonson's *The Alchemist*, parts Lacy can be assumed to have played in the first two years of the Restoration prior to this painting's execution about 1662 (it is datable from a reference in Evelyn, *Diary*, 3.338–9; Cooper, 759). A later copy of this painting is owned by the Garrick Club.

In addition to playing in new dramas, Lacy made a name for himself in several revivals of pre-civil war play texts, including James Shirley's *The Changes, or, Love in a Maze*—of which Pepys remarked 'The play is pretty good, but the life of the play is Lacy's part, the Clowne' (Pepys, 4.179, 10 June 1663)—and several plays by Jonson: between 1664 and 1665, as well as Ananias, he played Captain Otter in *Epicoene, or, The Silent Woman* and Sir Politic Would-Be in *Volpone*.

John Lacy (*c*.1615–1681), by John Michael Wright, *c*.1668–70 [in three roles]

About this time Lacy began to write his own plays, some of which were adaptations of existent texts. *The Old Troop, or, Monsieur Raggou* made use of his own civil war experiences and influenced Sir Walter Scott's nineteenth-century novel *Woodstock*. Lacy is believed to have played the part of Raggou, a French servant, in the original 1664–5 production. The play, which was not published until 1672, deals with the resentment felt in the English countryside (justified according to the play's representations) towards the cavalier soldiers who were billeted on villages between 1642 and 1649.

In 1666, as well as speaking the 'Epilogue' in Sir Robert Howard's *The Vestal Virgin*, Lacy played Sir Roger in a revival of Beaumont and Fletcher's *The Scornful Lady*; he also wrote an adaptation of Shakespeare's *The Taming of the Shrew*, entitled *Sauny the Scot*. This was performed at the Theatre Royal in 1667. It has been suggested that Lacy played Petruchio in an earlier revival of Shakespeare's drama and this inspired his version. There is no firm evidence of this but *Sauny the Scot* in many respects stays close to its Shakespearian forebear until the final act. The influence of John Fletcher's own version, *The Woman's Prize, or, The Tamer Tamed* (*c*.1611), can also be registered. Nevertheless, Lacy's appropriation of the play for the Restoration is significant. He turns a largely verse drama into prose, and relocates Shakespeare's story from Renaissance Italy to contemporary London. Lucentio, the Paduan student of the original, becomes Winlove, an Oxford graduate, and an opposition between town and country is established in the play, recognizable from other Restoration comedies. Margaret is the equivalent of Katherina and it is perhaps indicative of the changing sexual and social mores of the Restoration period that her part is considerably expanded to allow for a more sustained rebellion against Petruchio in the final act. The title character, Sauny, is a Scottish version of Grumio, Petruchio's servant, and is most likely to have been played by Lacy, considering his propensity for dialect parts: Sauny makes comic matter of English niceties and is constantly 'Scratten and Scrubben' himself (II.i.25).

Another dialect part figures in Lacy's *Sir Hercules Buffoon, or, The Poetical Squire*, staged presumably in 1684. In this play, a Yorkshire heiress speaks in a dialect form redolent of Lacy's native Doncaster: 'Marra, the devilst learn French for me. By my saul, ean Yorkshire word, nuncle, s'worth ten thousand French eans' (II.ii). The title character is a country squire, the nephew of Alderman Buffoon. Anxious to see the players while he is in London, he falls prey, in the tradition of country gulls, to wiser city folk who make him an apprentice of their poetical society by forcing him through an initiation ceremony. Buffoon exhibits his lack of judgement by preferring John Taylor the Water Poet over Ben Jonson (whom Lacy imitates at various points elsewhere in the play).

In 1667 Lacy appeared in Edward Howard's controversial satire on the court of Charles II, entitled *The Change of Crowns* (which was never published). The king and queen went to see the production on 15 April 1667. By the time Samuel Pepys tried to see it again the next day the play text had already been altered. Lacy, according to Pepys, 'did act the Country Gentleman come up to Court, who doth abuse the Court with all the imaginable wit and plainness, about selling of places and doing everything for money' (Pepys, 8.167–8, 15 April 1667). The king was said to have been so angered by the play that he detained Lacy in the porter's lodge. He was pardoned but the play remained under censure. The dramatist Howard (younger son of the earl of Berkshire and brother to playwright Sir Robert Howard) and his star performer are said to have quarrelled shortly after.

In 1667, despite serious illness, Lacy performed in a revival of *The Changes*. Subsequent parts included Bayes in the second duke of Buckingham's *The Rehearsal* in 1671 (a role based on Dryden), Drench in his own play *The Dumb Lady, or, The Farrier Made Physician* (1672), an adaptation (not much liked) of Molière's *Le médecin malgré lui* and *L'amour médecin* (about this time he also played the lead role in Molière's *Tartuffe*), Alderman Gripe in Wycherley's *Love in a Wood, or, St James's Park* at Lincoln's Inn (still with Killigrew's company), and Intrigo in Sir Francis Fane's *Love in the Dark, or The Man of Business*. He is also reputed to have played Falstaff.

The Dumb Lady, as its title suggests, tells the story of a woman about to be married (Olinda) who appears to have fallen mute. Certain characters reflect that this is unsurprising in view of the fop she is to be married to: the aptly named Squire Softhead. They inform her father who is anxious for the match: 'Do you think your daughter had not better be dumb and dead than marry such a ridiculous brute as this?' (I.i, p. 14). Once again, Lacy's drama exhibits considerable empathy for its women characters. A physician is sent for to attend to Olinda's ailment and Jarvis and Softhead are tricked by Isabel into believing her husband Drench (the part played by Lacy) to be a physician. A great deal of knockabout farce ensues. Indeed farce in the French style appears to have been the form Lacy most favoured in his own compositions. It has been argued that Lacy's adaptation of Molière influenced that by Henry Fielding in the eighteenth century (Colmer, 35–9).

Contemporary satires alleged that Lacy had a relationship with the king's mistress Nell Gwyn. Certainly, he gave her acting and dancing lessons. He clearly kept up his dancing skills in later life, adding dances to the entr'actes of, for example, *Horace* in 1668. Financial issues seem to have pursued him in later life. In 1673 he was sued by one Mary Bennett, presumably for debt, and in 1674 he became embroiled in a debate over the pay of French dancers at the court. Lacy died on 17 September 1681 at his address in Drury Lane after a long and successful career and was buried in the churchyard of St Martin-in-the-Fields two days later.   JULIE SANDERS

Sources Highfill, Burnim & Langhans, *BDA*, vol. 9 • W. Van Lennep and others, eds., *The London stage, 1660–1800*, pt 1: *1660–1700* (1965) • J. Maidment and W. H. Logan, memoir, in *The dramatic works of John Lacy*, ed. J. Maidment and W. H. Logan (1875) • Pepys, *Diary* • C. W. Cooper, 'The triple portrait of John Lacy', *Proceedings of the Modern Language Association of America*, 47 (1932), 759–65 • *Letters written by eminent persons … and 'Lives of eminent men' by John Aubrey*, ed. J. Walker, 2 (1813) • Evelyn, *Diary* • Ben Jonson, ed. C. H. Herford, P. Simpson, and E. M. Simpson, 11 vols. (1925–52) • *DNB* • D. Colmer, 'Fielding's debt to John Lacy in *The mock doctor*', *English Language Notes*, 9 (1971–2), 35–9 • S. Clark, *Shakespeare made fit* (1997) • M. Butler, *Representing Ben Jonson* (1999) • A. Nicoll, *A history of Restoration drama, 1660–1700* (1923) • A. Barton, *Ben Jonson, dramatist* (1984) • G. Langbaine, *An account of the English dramatick poets* (1691) • J. Downes, *Roscius Anglicanus*, ed. J. Milhous and R. D. Hume, new edn (1987)
Archives Bodl. Oxf., MS Aubrey 6, fol. 108 • Bodl. Oxf., MS Aubrey 8, fol. 54
Likenesses J. M. Wright, oils, c.1668–1670, Royal Collection [*see illus.*] • J. M. Wright, oils, copy, Garr. Club

Lacy, John (*bap.* 1664, *d.* 1730), self-styled prophet, was baptized on 30 May 1664 in Saffron Walden, Essex. He was the fifth son of Jerome Lacy (*fl.* 1630–1670) and his wife, Elizabeth (*née* Pypes; *fl.* 1630–1670), formerly of Toppesfield, Essex. He acquired a rudimentary knowledge of Latin but, unlike his brothers, did not attend Cambridge University. In the early 1680s he became a successful London merchant, living at Tottenham. Soon after 3 April 1688 he married Susanna (*fl.* 1670?–1715), daughter of Edward Rudge, and moved to St Giles, Middlesex, but no surviving children were born before 1699. As a member of the millenarian 'religious society for the reformation of manners', Lacy was associated with Anglicans, but he attended the Presbyterian chapel in Tothill Street, Westminster. In 1704 he actively supported Edmund Calamy's election as his chapel's minister, and also published a letter defending the practice of occasional conformity.

At a time when his situation was aggravated by the loss

of a lawsuit Lacy espoused the cause of the French Prophets (Camisard refugees by origin), who had arrived in England in 1706 but whose utterances and miracles were dismissed as spurious by the Huguenot authorities. His translation of François Maximilien Misson's *Théâtre sacré des Cévennes* was published in March 1707 as *A Cry from the Desart*. In April, when a mob attacked some of the Prophets, Lacy and Sir Richard Bulkeley, another sympathizer, obtained a warrant for the arrest of some of the rioters, and in June Lacy rented the Barbican (formerly used by Presbyterians) as a licensed meeting-house for the French Prophets. However, to the consternation of his wife and others, Lacy soon believed himself, also, to be inspired. In July, shortly before three of the French Prophets were due to be tried on charges of blasphemy and sedition, Lacy began to prophesy in tongues, during which time his body was curiously agitated and contorted. His prophecies were delivered as the words of God speaking in the first person, and Lacy claimed that similar messages were contained in his automatic writing. His earlier prophecies, published in three instalments during 1707 as *Prophetical Warnings*, were preoccupied with the prospect of divine judgment. The third earl of Shaftesbury's *Letter Concerning Enthusiasm* (1708) originated from his observation of Lacy prophesying in poor Latin 'under an agitation' ('Letter', 1.32). Although they were referred to as the French Prophets, Lacy was the first of several English enthusiasts involved with the movement. At times the leaders were faced with public hostility, as when Lacy's announcement that the guns of the Tower of London 'would roar in a few days' proved to be a false alarm, and they temporarily withdrew from London to gather outside the capital. Although the Prophets performed ecclesiastical functions, Lacy was a reluctant separatist and later claimed that they had continued to frequent 'those several forms of Congregations, to which their Inclinations before used to lead them' (Lacy, *Relation*, 17).

Lacy's expectation of public rejection, and his concern for the encouragement of those within the movement, may help to explain his most notorious prediction. Early in December 1707, when three of the French Prophets were being publicly pilloried, another member of the sect, Thomas Emes, fell sick. Lacy announced that if he died, God would raise him. When Emes was buried in Bunhill Fields on 25 December another Prophet, rasher even than Lacy, predicted his resurrection on 25 May 1708, designating Lacy as the one who would raise him. For some Prophets, belief in the expected miracle became the acid test of commitment, but their claims were severely dismissed by critics including Edmund Calamy and William Whiston. By 29 April Lacy was acknowledging that several of his earlier predictions had been mistaken and he indicated that he would not be at the graveside on 25 May. The scornful incredulity of the unruly onlookers was later cited by Lacy as the hindrance which had prevented the miracle.

Meanwhile Lacy's domestic life was in crisis. Late in 1708 he petitioned parliament for a revision of his marriage settlement to benefit his four younger children. His brother Roger and relatives of his wife were among the trustees of the new settlement, which may have been prompted by their anxieties about Lacy's prophetic activities. Increasingly he found himself in the company of Elizabeth (Betty) Gray (b. c.1692), whom he had claimed to cure of temporary blindness in 1707. Described by critics as 'a wild skittish girl' and a 'pretty and hansome [sic] … young wench', she had been associated with the thespian world of Drury Lane (Kingston, 45; *Correspondence of Alexander Pope*, 1.35). In a *Letter to Thomas Dutton* (a lawyer and one of the French Prophets), published in March 1711, Lacy explained that his wife's refusal to recognize his prophetic gifts was tantamount to fornication, and that he had therefore seen fit to take Betty Gray, 'a prophetess', to his bed. Thenceforth the trustees of his estate paid him an allowance with which he was able to move to Lancashire, where he lived and had two children with Betty Gray. His anonymous *General Delusion of Christians with Regard to Prophecy* (1713) was revised for a further defence of the French Prophets entitled *The Scene of Delusions* (1723). The extent of his audience may be gauged from a letter to Lacy written by Cotton Mather of Boston in 1719. Its tone is sympathetic, while troubled that the matters in Lacy's prophecies were 'too low, too mean, too trivial and jejune' (*Selected Letters*, 271). Lacy died in obscurity in the early months of 1730. TIMOTHY C. F. STUNT

Sources Saffron Walden parish records, Essex RO · R. Kingston, *Enthusiastick impostors no inspired prophets, an historical relation of the rise and progress and present practices of the French and English pretended prophets* (1707) · J. Lacy's petition to the House of Lords, MS 2519 with annexes A–C · minute book of House of Lords committee, vol. 1704/10, fols. 337–8 · J. Lacy, *A relation of the dealings of God* (1708) · Earl of Shaftesbury [A. Ashley Cooper], 'A letter concerning enthusiasm', *Characteristics of men, manners, opinions, times*, ed. J. M. Robertson, 2 vols. (1964) [1708] · *The correspondence of Alexander Pope*, ed. G. Sherburn, 1 (1956), 35 · Jean Allut to François Moult, 5 May 1730, with endorsements by Nicolas Fatio, Bibliothèque publique et universitaire, Geneva, MS fr. 605, fol. 3r · E. Calamy, *An historical account of my own life, with some reflections on the times I have lived in, 1671–1731*, ed. J. T. Rutt, 2 (1829), 76–8, 94–9, 113–14 · J. R. Sutherland, 'John Lacy and the modern prophets', *Background for Queen Anne* (1939), 36–74 · H. Schwartz, *Knaves, fools, madmen and that subtile effluvium: a study of the opposition to the French Prophets* (1978) · H. Schwartz, *The French prophets: the history of a millenarian group in eighteenth-century England* (1980) · J. R. Michaels, 'Marginalia to the *General delusion of Christians*: a preliminary report', *Harvard Theological Review*, 83 (1990), 213–18 · *Selected letters of Cotton Mather*, ed. K. Silverman (1971) · W. C. Pepys, *Genealogy of the Pepys family, 1273–1887* (1887), table 7

Archives BL, letter to Edmund Calamy, 3 Sept 1701?, Stowe MS 748, fol. 63

Wealth at death estate valued at £2500 p.a. in 1708: HLRO, MS 2519, annexe B

Lacy [*née* Quincy], **Margaret de**, **countess of Lincoln** (*d.* 1266), noblewoman, was the daughter of Robert de Quincy (*d.* 1217), eldest son of Saer de *Quincy, earl of Winchester, and of Hawise, fourth daughter of *Hugh, earl of Chester (1147–1181). Before 21 June 1221 she had married John de *Lacy (*c.*1192–1240), constable of Chester. She and John had one son, Edmund, born probably in 1230, and three daughters of whom Matilda married Richard de *Clare, earl of Gloucester and Hertford (*d.* 1262), in 1238.

Between 1230 and 1232 Ranulf (III), earl of Chester, resigned his earldom of Lincoln to his sister Hawise, Margaret's mother, and soon after Ranulf's death in 1232 Henry III recognized Hawise as countess of Lincoln. Shortly afterwards, at Hawise's request, the earldom was granted by the king to her son-in-law John de Lacy; the grant specified that the earldom was to be held by John and by his and Margaret's heirs for ever, thus implying that John became earl by right of his wife. Hawise's share of the lands of the earldom of Chester passed to Margaret after her mother's death which took place before 3 March 1243. John de Lacy died after a long illness on 22 July 1240, and early in 1242 Margaret married Walter Marshal, earl of Pembroke, who died childless three years later. At some point before 7 June 1252 Margaret made a third marriage, to Richard of Wiltshire. She died in March 1266 at Hamstead Marshall in Berkshire, and was buried near her father in the church of the knights hospitaller at Clerkenwell.

In the interval between the death of John de Lacy and her second marriage, Margaret was presented with *Les reules Seynt Roberd*, rules for the good management of the countess's household and estates, which were probably adapted by Robert Grosseteste, bishop of Lincoln, from rules which he had written for the management of his own episcopal estates.   JENNIFER C. WARD

Sources *CPR, 1232–66* · *Close rolls of the reign of Henry III*, 3–13, PRO (1908–37) · *Calendar of the charter rolls*, 6 vols., PRO (1903–27), vol. 1 · Paris, *Chron.*, vols. 3–4 · *Ann. mon.* · *Walter of Henley, and other treatises on estate management and accounting*, ed. D. Oschinsky (1971) · C. Roberts, ed., *Excerpta è rotulis finium in Turri Londinensi asservatis, Henrico Tertio rege, AD 1216–1272*, 1, RC, 32 (1835) · Dugdale, *Monasticon*, new edn
Archives PRO, chancery records
Wealth at death approx. £200 in dower lands from first husband; dower lands from second husband; inheritance from mother

Lacy, Mary [alias William Chandler] (b. **1740**), shipwright and author, was born on 12 January 1740 at Wickham, Kent, the eldest of the three children of William Lacy (d. c.1770) and his wife, whose maiden name was Chandler. Shortly after Lacy's birth the family moved to neighbouring Ash. Lacy's parents were very poor and sent her to a charity school so that they both could work. There she learned to read and write, before entering domestic service at the age of twelve.

In May 1759, on a sudden impulse, Lacy stole a set of men's clothes and ran away. Walking and hitching rides, she reached Chatham where, under the name of William Chandler, she joined the newly launched *Sandwich* as servant to the ship's carpenter. She enjoyed life as a ship's boy, even during tedious months of blockading the French coast, and in spite of the beatings her master gave her whenever he was drunk. In 1760 a crippling attack of rheumatism sent her to Haslar, the naval hospital, and by the time she was released the *Sandwich* had sailed. She was then assigned to the *Royal Sovereign* at Portsmouth where the boatswain helped her get a seven-year carpenter's apprenticeship.

On 4 March 1763 Lacy was bound apprentice to work at the royal dockyard at Portsmouth. She was passed from one dissolute master to another and was often impoverished. Her only pleasure was flirting with a number of young women, and she became engaged to a housemaid, Sarah Chase.

No portrait of Lacy exists; dock workers described her as a little man whose girlfriend was too large for him. When a rumour spread that Chandler was a woman, the men agreed that 'there is not the least appearance of it in the make or shape of him' (Stark, 160).

In 1770 Lacy became a shipwright, but within a year she was so debilitated by rheumatism that she could no longer work. She bade farewell to Sarah Chase and moved to London to apply for a pension. On 28 January 1772, aged thirty-two, she was awarded £20 per annum. In the following year there appeared Lacy's autobiographical *The History of the Female Shipwright*. In the last two paragraphs of her history Lacy claims she married a Mr Slade, but this marriage was probably fabricated by her publisher, M. Lewis, to reassure readers that she was, after all, heterosexual. Nothing is known of Lacy after 1773.

SUZANNE J. STARK

Sources S. J. Stark, *Female tars: women aboard ship in the age of sail* (1996) · M. Slade, *The history of the female shipwright; to whom the government has granted a superannuated pension of twenty pounds per annum during her life: written by herself* (1773) · PRO, ADM 36/6767 · PRO, ADM 36/6768 · PRO, ADM 36/6769 [muster bks, *Sandwich*] · 30 March 1761, PRO, ADM 36/6770 [William Chandler's request for discharge] · PRO, ADM 36/6799 · 1762, PRO, ADM 36/6800 [muster bks, *Royal Sovereign*] · 28 Jan 1772, PRO, ADM 3/79, 78–79 [pension of Mary 'Lacey']

Lacy [de Lacy], **Maurice** (1740–1820), army officer in Russia, was born during the great frost of 1739–40 in co. Limerick, one of two sons and four daughters of Patrick de Lacy (d. 1790) of Rathcahill and Templeglentan and his wife, Lady Mary Herbert (d. 1795). The de Lacys, an extensive and prominent Catholic family of Anglo-Norman ancestry, had suffered heavily in the Irish defeats of the seventeenth century. Nothing is known of Lacy's early life. His kinsmen included some of the leading immigrant Irish Catholic soldiers in Russia and the Habsburg empire and, as a young man, he took advantage of these connections to leave Ireland and enter the Russian service. He fought against the Turks and achieved general's rank. In 1792–3 he revisited Ireland. In 1799 he participated with Prince Suvorov in the defeat of the French in the north of Italy.

In 1805 Lacy was sent to Naples to command an Anglo-Russian force against the French. Ostensibly intended to bolster the Bourbon kingdom's resistance to Napoleon, the real objective was to divert French resources from the north. After Lacy's preliminary reconnaissance in May a treaty of alliance between Russia and Naples was signed in September, and towards the end of November 11,000 Russian troops from Corfu and 6000 British from Malta, under Sir James Craig, disembarked in the Bay of Naples. Lacy had landed infirm after a rough voyage and was brought from the coast in a litter to comfortable quarters at the Angri palace, where his expenses were defrayed by King Ferdinand. Sir Henry Bunbury, the British quartermaster-general, alleged that Lacy lacked talent or knowledge but considered him a simple, kind-hearted old gentleman who, in his own words, was 'always for fighting' (Bunbury, 191). Although it was stated that he best expressed himself in Russian, he also had a knowledge of French and, of course, English, which he spoke with an Irish accent. He was known to don his nightcap during councils of war and sleep, leaving discussion to others. King Ferdinand, who had less faith in his Russian allies than Queen Caroline, thought him a comical figure when he appeared in full uniform at an audience at Portici and boasted that his sword would not return to its sheath until the king's enemies had been vanquished.

Having made Teano his headquarters Lacy deployed his forces in a defensive position on the north-west border, posting the British along the River Garigliano, the Russians to cover the narrow Mignano Pass, and the Neapolitans on the Abruzzi frontier. Napoleon's victory at Austerlitz in December and his subsequent armistice with the tsar removed the *raison d'être* of the Russian military presence in Naples. When news came that a French army under Masséna, accompanied by Napoleon's brother Joseph, was preparing to invade the kingdom Lacy first spoke of retiring to Calabria but instead, as ordered by the tsar, in mid-January 1806 he evacuated his force from Baia and returned to Corfu. This was a bitter disappointment to the Neapolitans, who were left defenceless against the advancing French, the British having departed. In 1807 Napoleon, with the tsar's permission, wrote to Lacy from Tilsit, suggesting that he organize an Irish force against England but nothing came of this. Lacy played no prominent part in subsequent campaigns and took up the post of governor of Grodno, in Belorussia, where he possessed estates. He died there, unmarried, in January 1820, 'the last male descendent, direct, of the great Hugh de Lacy' (*Sketch Pedigree*), leaving an estate valued at £100,000.

HARMAN MURTAGH

Sources *Sketch pedigree of the family de Lacy, and of General Maurice de Lacy of Grodno, in Russia, and of the county of Limerick, who died 1820* (1847) [only known copies in BL] · M. Lenihan, *Limerick: its history and antiquities* (1866), 332–4 · H. M. M. Acton, *The Bourbons of Naples, 1734–1825* (1956); repr. (1974), 508–28 · H. Bunbury, *Narratives of some passages in the great war with France, from 1799 to 1810* (1854), 191–2 · J. B. B., 'A late eighteenth-century military manuscript', *Irish Sword*, 4 (1959–60), 199 · M. Lacy, letter to J. Craig, 4 Oct 1805, BL, Add. MS 37050 · T. Bartlett and K. Jeffery, *A military history of Ireland* (1996)
Archives NAM, corresp. with Sir James Craig · NL Scot., corresp. with Hugh Elliot
Wealth at death £100,000: J. B. B., 'A late eighteenth-century military manuscript'

Lacy, Michael Rophino (1795–1867), violinist, was born on 19 July 1795 at Bilbao in Spain. His father was an Irish merchant, his mother Spanish. He began learning the violin at the age of five, and when he was six made his public début at a concert given in Bilbao by Andreossi, an Italian violinist, playing a concerto by Giovanni Giornovichi. It is said that he was so small that he had to stand up on a table before the audience could see him, but the performance was very well received. As an infant prodigy he was patronized by the court of Madrid until 1802, in which year he commenced his schooling at Bordeaux. After eighteen months there he proceeded (in 1803) to a *lycée* in Paris to finish his education. While in Paris he was a pupil of Rodolphe Kreutzer, under whom he made rapid progress, and towards the end of 1804, as 'le petit Espagnol', he played a violin solo before Napoleon at the Tuileries.

Meanwhile, his father had been ruined by some American speculations, and Lacy was brought to England at the end of October 1805 to study under Giovanni Battista Viotti. On the journey he played in various Dutch towns, and became a great favourite in The Hague. It is reported that, at the time of arriving in England, when he was ten years and three months, he was able to speak fluent English, French, Italian, and Spanish, and had a fair knowledge of Latin. He was at first known merely as 'the young Spaniard', for his real name was not publicly revealed in England until May 1807, when an engraved portrait of him by Cardon (from a drawing by Smart) was published. Among his patrons were the prince of Wales, the duke of Sussex, the duchess of York, and Count Stahremberg, the Austrian ambassador. His first concert in London was given at the Hanover Square Rooms, and soon afterwards he played at Angelica Catalani's first concert in Dublin, during a visit to Ireland of Michael Kelly's opera company. On this occasion his patrons were the lord lieutenant, the duke of Richmond, and his wife. Performances at Natale Corri's concerts in Edinburgh followed, for which he received the large fee of 20 guineas per night.

In obedience to his father's will, Lacy subsequently abandoned the musical for the theatrical profession, and for about ten years (1808–18) filled 'genteel comedy parts' in Edinburgh, Dublin, and Glasgow, playing the violin in public only at his benefits. In 1818, at the invitation of the directors, he succeeded Felix Yaniewicz as leader and director of the Liverpool concerts, the musicians for which were recruited from the best talent in London. At the end of 1820 Lacy returned to London and became leader of the ballet orchestra at the King's Theatre, where he is said to have directed the ballets and composed most of the ballet music for the Italian opera. However, in 1823, following disagreements with the musical director, he returned to the management of the Liverpool concerts, though he resumed his position at the King's Theatre in 1824.

For the rest of his professional life Lacy employed his musical and linguistic skills principally in the adaptation of foreign librettos for the English stage, as well as translating several French plays and arranging the music of well-known French and Italian operas. It was Lacy who made the first English adaptations of several of Rossini's operas, including *Semiramide* (first performed at Covent Garden, 7 March 1829) and *La Cenerentola* (Cinderella; Covent Garden, 13 April 1830). Contemporary conventions allowed a great deal of artistic licence to be exercised, and Lacy often used music from different operas in a single adaptation. For example, *Cinderella* includes music from Rossini's *Maometto II*, *Armida*, and *Guillaume Tell*, while the 'dramatic oratorio' *The Israelites in Egypt* (Covent Garden, 22 February 1833) is a pasticcio combining Handel's *Israel in Egypt* and Rossini's *Mosè in Egitto*. Other adaptations include music from operas by Mozart, Auber, Meyerbeer, and Weber. Lacy also arranged favourite airs for beginners to play in public (1826). Among his compositions are a set of three rondos for the piano, a quintet for two violins, viola, flute, and cello with piano accompaniment, numerous fantasies on operatic themes (mainly for piano), and songs. He assisted with the research for Victor Schoelcher's biography of Handel during the 1850s. Lacy died at Pentonville, London, on 20 September 1867.

DAVID J. GOLBY

Sources [J. S. Sainsbury], ed., *A dictionary of musicians*, 2 vols. (1824) • F.-J. Fétis, *Biographie universelle des musiciens, et bibliographie générale de la musique*, 2nd edn, 5 (Paris, 1863), 158 • A. Pougin, ed., *Biographie universelle des musiciens, et bibliographie générale de la musique: supplément et complément*, 2 (Paris, 1880), 59; repr. (1881) • W. H. Husk and B. Carr, 'Lacy, Michael Rophino', *New Grove*
Archives BL, papers on Handel, Add. MSS 31555–31575 | BL, letters to George Colman, Add. MSS 42932–42940
Likenesses A. Cardon, stipple, pubd 1807 (after drawing by J. Smart), BM, NPG

Lacy, Peter (*c*.1310–1375), administrator, is first recorded in 1337, as a clerk in the household of Prince Edward, the eldest son of Edward III, who had recently been made duke of Cornwall. By 1339 he was parson of Whitstone, Cornwall, but was described as being 'of Rendlesham' in Suffolk. An association with Suffolk occurs again in a joint recognizance (1343) to him and Nicholas Lacy, parson of Chelmondiston, presumably a kinsman, but thereafter the surviving records relate only to his official career.

While William Hoo was Prince Edward's keeper of the wardrobe (before 1341), Lacy was Hoo's cofferer, and in 1344–5 he visited Cornwall for the duke's council. The major change in Lacy's career came on 12 November 1346, when he was appointed to send to the prince in France the revenues collected from his English estates. At first John Pirye remained receiver to collect the rents while Lacy sent them on, but Pirye was gradually displaced after 20 December, when Lacy was appointed receiver of the prince's moneys from Wales, Cornwall, Chester, and elsewhere in England, all paid to the prince's exchequer in Westminster. By 6 March 1347 Lacy's title was receiver-general, and this remained his office until 1371. Lacy was also, from this date or earlier, keeper of the prince's great wardrobe. Although Lacy's office was called 'receiver', the surviving registers (1346–8 and 1351–65) show far more disbursement orders than income reports; payments required more considered decisions, but also typified the prince's extravagant attitude to finance. Barber calls Lacy the prince's 'long-suffering receiver' (Barber, 174), but in fact he was one of the advisers who endorsed many of the prince's irresponsible generosities.

Lacy's own rewards were extremely modest. He was attorney for the parson of Northfleet, Kent, in 1356, and by 1363 he was the priest there himself. (In 1343 this living was valued at 100 marks p.a.) By then he was said to have two prebends, Wolverhampton and Bisley, which he was

Peter Lacy (*c*.1310–1375), memorial brass

instructed to resign in 1366/7 for an expected prebend in Lichfield, and he was given the Dublin prebend of Swords on 12 March 1368. On 21 February 1369 he was given a wardship in Sussex. These last changes are associated with Lacy's final promotion to keeper of the king's privy seal on 27 October 1367, in succession to, and probably through the influence of, William Wykeham, who had become chancellor in September, and who had worked with Lacy in the prince's household years before. On 4 June 1369 (not 4 July 1368 as in Tout, 3.253) Lacy witnessed Wykeham's reply to a papal letter and was himself described as a royal notary.

Lacy witnessed other official acts, and received a new seal when Edward III resumed his title of king of France on 3 June 1369 (not 11 July as in Tout, 5.141). More actively, on 28 November 1370 he was appointed to discuss a Genoese complaint about ships seized by the English. He was still Prince Edward's receiver-general, drawing large sums from the exchequer for the prince's use while taking his own unusually low privy seal salary. The latter was last collected on 1 March 1371, showing that Lacy was removed as keeper when, under parliamentary pressure, Wykeham resigned as chancellor on 24 March. Lacy continued as Prince Edward's receiver-general, however, until at least

16 December 1371, when he accepted plate given by London to the prince, but he had been replaced by January 1372.

Peter Lacy spent his last years as priest of Northfleet, donating a lodging to Prince Edward's foundation at Canterbury in July 1372. He died on 18 October 1375, according to his brass, which is still in St Botolph's Church, Northfleet (although remnants of its stone canopy went to the British Museum). His true memorial may be the legend of the Black Prince, for whose exploits he provided the necessary finance.   JOHN L. LELAND

Sources M. C. B. Dawes, ed., *Register of Edward, the Black Prince*, 4 vols., PRO (1930–33) · *Chancery records* · Rymer, *Foedera* · PRO, exchequer of receipt, issue rolls, E 403 · Tout, *Admin. hist.* · R. Barber, *Edward, prince of Wales and Aquitaine: a biography of the Black Prince* (1978) · W. H. Bliss, ed., *Calendar of entries in the papal registers relating to Great Britain and Ireland: petitions to the pope* (1896), 59 · *Fasti Angl., 1300–1541* · R. P. Dunn-Pattison, *The Black Prince* (1910) · B. Emerson, *The Black Prince* (1976) · R. H. Ellis, ed., *Catalogue of seals in the Public Record Office: personal seals*, 2 (1981) · R. R. Sharpe, ed., *Calendar of letter-books preserved in the archives of the corporation of the City of London*, [12 vols.] (1899–1912), vol. G

Likenesses copper etching (after memorial brass), Etchmasters Ltd, Prospect Road, Alresford, Hampshire · engraving (after memorial brass), repro. in C. Boutell, *The monumental brasses of England* (1849), pl. 7 · memorial brass, St Botolph's Church, Northfleet, Kent [*see illus.*]

Lacy, Peter, Count Lacy in the nobility of the Holy Roman empire (1678–1751), army officer in the Russian service, was born in Killeedy, co. Limerick, Ireland, on 29 September 1678, the son of Peter Lacy (Pierce de Lacy) of Coylross and his wife, Maria de Courtenay. His military career dates from 1691, when at the age of just thirteen he saw action as an ensign at the second siege of Limerick. Following five years in French service he entered that of Peter the Great, being among the first group of 100 western European officers recruited in 1700 at the start of Russia's Great Northern War against Charles XII of Sweden. The talent Lacy showed in the earliest Russian campaign in the Baltic territories of Livonia and Ingria ensured him rapid promotion: from captain in 1701 to colonel in 1708. In 1706 he was given command of the Polotsky regiment as well as three newly raised regiments to train. In December 1708 he attacked and captured the headquarters of Charles XII at Rumna, and the delighted tsar rewarded Lacy with the prestigious command of a grenadier regiment. He went on to become 'one of the most famous soldiers of the 18th century. Indeed no Irish family has attained greater fame in the military history of Europe' (MacLysaght, 205).

In July 1709, at the battle of Poltava, the Swedes lost to a Russian army twice their size, thereby precipitating their eventual defeat. Lacy's advice to the tsar on musketry methods is said to have played a decisive role in Russia's celebrated victory. Crucially, he insisted that the musketeers should hold their fire until coming within a few yards of the enemy. Consequently Charles was defeated and in one action lost the advantage of nine previous campaigns. In 1711 Lacy married Martha Philippine von Funcken, of the Livonian family of Löser. They had five daughters and three sons: Peter Anthony, who became a general in the

Polish service; Francis Maurice, an Austrian field marshal and chancellor of the Holy Roman empire; and Patrick Boris, a general of infantry.

In 1719, newly promoted to the rank of major-general, Lacy led a devastating raid on several Swedish coastal towns and villages. In a similar action two years later, by which time he was lieutenant-general in command of 5000 troops, he razed Sundsvall. This set-back was enough to prompt the Swedish negotiators at Nystadt to yield Livonia to Russia, thus affording her direct access to the Baltic Sea and so paving the way for the treaty of Nystadt, which was at last concluded in September 1721.

After Russia's victory over Sweden, Lacy's rise continued apace. In 1723 he became a member of the war college. In 1725 Catherine I made him a knight of the order of St Alexander Nevsky on the very day of its institution, 21 May. He was appointed general-in-chief of infantry and commander of all forces garrisoned in St Petersburg, Ingria, and Novgorod. In the general staff list for 1728 his name ranked third among the six full generals in the Russian army. As a foreigner, his annual salary was 3600 roubles whereas Russians received only 3120. A further indication of Lacy's standing at this time is the fact that his signature always occupied first place on war college reports to Catherine I.

In 1727 Lacy was ordered to expel Maurice de Saxe from the duchy of Courland. Maurice, much to Russia's irritation, had managed to have himself elected duke of Courland. The duchess of Courland was Anna, the daughter of Peter the Great's half-brother Ivan. She later became empress of Russia, on the death of Peter II in 1730. Her request to marry Maurice de Saxe had been rejected by Catherine I and led to the decision to expel him and his retinue from the duchy. Lacy's successful execution of this task confirmed him as the most influential foreigner at the Russian court. This position, however, was not without its dangers. Lacy was always careful to avoid court intrigue. Indeed, it is precisely to this quality that his remarkable survival throughout the 'era of palace revolutions' is generally attributed. But his high standing caused resentment among the many ambitious Germans at the court of Empress Anna (1730–40). The most powerful threat came from Burkhardt Munnich (Minikh), one of Anna's Courland favourites, who was determined to achieve sole authority over Russia's military affairs.

The rivalry between Lacy and Munnich grew when they saw action together in 1733 in the Russians' march on Warsaw in support of Augustus of Saxony's candidacy as king of Poland against that of Stanislas Leszczynski, who was supported by France. The ensuing War of the Polish Succession, which was concluded in 1735, gave both men the opportunity to display their military prowess. Of the two, in the view of the military historian Maslovsky, it was Lacy, overall commander of Russian forces in Poland, who had the better war. After successfully raising the siege of Danzig in 1733, Lacy further distinguished himself the following year at the battle of Wisiczin. Then, at the decisive battle of Busawitza, although outnumbered ten to one, he completely routed Leszczynski's forces. Following victory in the War of the Polish Succession, Lacy was created a knight of the order of the White Eagle of Poland by Augustus III. He spent the next two years assisting Augustus to consolidate his position as king of Poland, defeating counter-attacks in a series of remarkable actions. Lacy then visited Vienna, where he was warmly received by the emperor and empress and presented with gifts. It was on his return from the Austrian capital to St Petersburg that he was made a Russian field marshal. This was the first time in Russia's history that there had been two foreigners serving as field marshals in imperial service—the other being Munnich.

Lacy's first mission as field marshal was to prepare for the siege of Azov in anticipation of the long-expected war with Turkey, which was waged from 1735 to 1739. During the ensuing siege he was wounded and fortunate not to fall into Turkish hands. Azov capitulated to Lacy's forces in July 1736.

In 1737 Lacy was appointed to the order of St Andrew and made commander of a new campaign to annex the Crimea. Two previous attempts to do so, Leontyev's in 1735 and Munnich's in 1736, had ended in failure. Lacy eagerly accepted this new challenge and rose to it with characteristic brilliance. To the astonishment of the Crimean khan, Lacy bridged the Azov Sea at a narrow point near Perekop. Within four days his entire army crossed it and began marching on Arabat. As one commentator wryly observed, 'the parallel to a well-known incident in the book of Exodus was sufficiently striking to make an immense impression upon the superstitious Russian soldiers' (Jane, 73). Then, on learning that the khan had reached Arabat before him, Lacy decided to spring a further surprise by fording the sea separating him from the rest of the Crimea. By the use of typically imaginative strategy Lacy successfully completed his mission. Nevertheless, the Crimea was not finally annexed to the Russian empire until 1783.

Meanwhile, Lacy's relationship with Munnich deteriorated. The Irishman's achievements in the field, together with his popularity among his troops and at court, so antagonized the Courlander that on one occasion he drew his sabre and attacked Lacy. Fortunately, a third party, General Levashov, managed to separate the two field marshals before any serious damage could be done.

In 1740 Lacy was made a count, and in the spring of 1741 he was made commander of Russian forces in Finland mobilizing for renewed war with Sweden. Following Sweden's declaration of war that July, he advanced at the head of 30,000 troops on Villmanstrand and defeated its 11,000 Swedish defenders under General Wrangel. However, lack of reinforcements and supplies compelled him to return to St Petersburg. There, in December, Elizabeth, the daughter of Peter the Great, became empress literally overnight as a result of a palace revolt. Lacy, suddenly challenged to declare his support for Anna of Brunswick, regent for the boy emperor Ivan VI, or Elizabeth, judiciously indicated his support for 'the party of the reigning empress', an answer which apparently satisfied Elizabeth. Her accession brought down the so-called German party

at court. Senior Courlanders, among them Ostermann, Biron, and Munnich, were disgraced and exiled. Lacy, however, became the principal field marshal in the Russian service. An immediate consequence of Elizabeth's policy of Russifying the court and the armed forces was an outbreak of xenophobic riots in the capital. Lacy promptly implemented a system of strict policing of army personnel in St Petersburg, thus averting potentially much more dangerous disturbances between Russian and foreign serving officers in the capital. After the three-month truce with Sweden following Elizabeth's accession, Lacy returned in June to Swedish Finland at the head of a large force. He took Fredrikshamn, which had been torched and abandoned by the Swedes. There was jubilation at the capture of what was the only fortified town in Swedish Finland without the loss of a single man. Lacy pursued the retreating Swedish army and eventually surrounded it near Helsingfors (Helsinki). He cut off its further retreat to Abo by leading his forces along an unmapped road which had been built during the campaigns of Peter the Great and was revealed to the field marshal by a Finnish peasant. The surprised Swedish army capitulated, leaving all Finland subject to the Russian empire. Lacy thus returned with renewed triumph to the Russian court.

In 1743 Lacy was made a senator. At the start of Russia's operations against Sweden in that year Elizabeth boarded the field marshal's ship in St Petersburg to present him with gifts and to bless his newest enterprise, which, in the event, was pre-empted by the treaty of Abo (August 1743). Once more he returned in triumph to St Petersburg, this time aboard a yacht sent by the empress herself. After the peace celebrations, which marked the culmination of his fifty years' active service, Lacy retired to his estates in Livonia as governor of the province, a post to which Peter II had originally appointed him back in 1729. Over the years Lacy had acquired a number of properties at Riga in Livonia, among them Grosser Rop, Alt-Kalzenau, Segewold, Lindenhof, and Dahlen. There he resided until his death, in Riga on 30 April 1751 at the age of seventy-two, survived by his wife. John Cook, the doctor who attended Lacy in his last months, recalled that the citizens of Riga so mourned the field marshal's death that 'they tolled their bells eight days' (Cook, 622). He left a large fortune (£60,000 sterling) and sizeable estates, acquired, as his will states, by way of an epitaph, 'through long and hard service and with much danger and uneasiness' (ibid., 498).

Lacy was a popular commander who combined qualities of unusual ability and sound judgement. He had a notoriously quick temper, but, in the words of one English historian, 'he was generous to a fault, as brave as a lion and incapable of committing a mean action' (Bain, 219). In the course of his remarkable career he served five eighteenth-century sovereigns, and he partnered a sixth, the future Catherine II, at her wedding dance in 1745, when she was sixteen years old. Unquestionably his most affectionate imperial patron was Elizabeth. This is evident not only from the various attentions she showed him, but also from the fact that other foreign officers regarded him as the best channel for reaching the empress themselves. Moreover, when she was told that Lacy's health was improving (during what was to be his final illness), 'she expressed as great satisfaction as if he had been her father' (Cook, 617). What impressed Russians about Lacy was his loyalty to their country: 'He differed markedly from the other Russian commanders of foreign birth in that he always pursued Russia's interests, never his own' (*Russkii biograficheskii slovar*, 86). The admiration he aroused was typically expressed in a common soldier's view, as recorded by Sergey Solovyov: 'Even though he was a foreigner, he was a good man' (*Voennaya entsiklopediya*, 1914, 517). In 1891 a division of the Russian army—the 13th Belozersky infantry regiment—was named in his honour.

P. J. O'MEARA

Sources P. O'Meara, 'Irishmen in eighteenth-century Russian service', *Irish Slavonic Studies*, 5 (1984), 13–25 • Genealogical Office, Dublin, MS 162, MS 176, MS 177 • NL Ire., MS 8800, MS 8379, MS 10534 • Russian State Historical Archive, St Petersburg, fond 1343, opis' 26, delo 2964; opis' 46, delo 1311 • A. A. Polovtsov, ed., *Russkii biograficheskii slovar*' [Russian biographical dictionary], 10 (1904) • *Deutschbaltisches biographisches Lexikon, 1710–1960* (1970) • J. C. O'Callaghan, *History of the Irish brigades in the service of France*, [new edn] (1870) • D. Maslovskii, 'Russkoe voyennoe delo pri Fel'dmarshale Graf Minikh', *Voennyi Sbornik* [St Petersburg], 7 (1891) • J. E. McGee, *Sketches of Irish soldiers in every land* (1881), 104 • R. N. Bain, *The pupils of Peter the Great: a history of the Russian court and empire from 1697 to 1740* (1897) • J. Cook, *Voyages and travels through the Russian empire, Tartary and part of the kingdom of Persia* (1770) • D. N. Bantysh-Kamenskii, *Biografii russkikh generalissimusov* (1840) • E. Amburger, *Geschichte der Behördensorganisation Russlands von Peter dem Grossen bis 1917* (1966) • E. Schuyler, *Peter the Great* (1884), vol. 2 • F. T. Jane, *The imperial Russian navy: its past, present and future* (1904) • E. MacLysaght, *Irish families* (1957)
Archives NL Ire., MSS
Wealth at death £60,000: Cook, *Voyages and travels*

Lacy, Roger de (d. 1211), soldier and administrator, was son of *John, soldier and landowner, and Alice de Vere, who was a cousin of William de Mandeville, earl of Essex, and niece of Aubrey (III) de Vere, earl of Oxford. Roger's father, who was lord of Halton in Cheshire, was son of Richard fitz Eustace, and Aubreye, daughter of Robert de Lisours and cousin of Robert de Lacy (d. 1193), the last direct male descendant of Ilbert de Lacy, lord of Pontefract in the late eleventh century. John the constable was briefly placed in charge of Dublin in 1181, and, later going on crusade, died at Tyre on 11 October 1190. He founded Stanlaw Abbey, Cheshire, about 1172 (it was afterwards transferred to Whalley in 1296, by his descendant Henry de Lacy, earl of Lincoln), and also the hospital of Castle Donington.

On his father's death Roger de Lacy became constable of Chester. In 1191, having been entrusted by the chancellor with the custody of the castles of Tickhill and Nottingham, he hanged two knights who had conspired to surrender these castles to Count John, who in revenge plundered Lacy's lands. On 21 April 1194, several months after Robert de Lacy's death, Roger acquired from his grandmother, Aubreye (Robert's cousin and heir), Robert's lands, and adopted the Lacy name (derived from Lassy in Calvados).

Now lord of Pontefract, on 6 June 1194 he granted its burgesses a charter of liberties. In April 1199 he was among the barons who agreed to swear fealty to John only after they were promised restoration of what they alleged to be their rights. One of his claims was to twenty fees which Guy de Laval held of the honour of Pontefract, a claim which was realized by 1203. Between 25 August and 6 December 1199 Lacy attended John in Normandy, Maine, Touraine, and Poitou, and on 23 September 1199 was installed as castellan of Chinon. In the same year he recovered his castle of Pontefract, which the king had retained. He was obliged to surrender his eldest son as a hostage, but from this time he remained in high favour with the new king. He was sent in October or November 1200 to escort William the Lion to Lincoln, and was present when the Scottish king did homage there to John on 22 November. In 1201 he was sent, with William (I) Marshal, earl of Pembroke, in command of one hundred knights each, to check the assaults of the king's enemies on the borders of Normandy. In 1202 he was controlling shipping along the Seine, and in April 1203 he acted as surety for the loyalty of Earl Ranulf (III) of Chester. In 1203 he successfully proffered £1000 for the custody of the land and heir of Richard de Montfichet.

In 1203 Philip Augustus of France besieged Lacy in the famous Château Gaillard, which he defended with incomparable fidelity for several months, and only surrendered through stress of famine on 6 March 1204. Matthew Paris relates that the French king, in recognition of his gallant defence, put him in free custody. Lacy was ransomed by John's assistance for £1000. He was further rewarded by being made sheriff of Yorkshire and Cumberland, offices that he held until 1209. In the winter of 1204–5, when northern England was on the verge of rebellion, he remained loyal to John, fortifying Carlisle, and in the spring of 1205 he helped to organize the host against a threatened French invasion. In the years that followed, Lacy was often in attendance upon the king, and was one of John's gambling partners. In 1205 he acquired the Lancashire barony of Penwortham after paying off the debts of its previous lord, Hugh Buissel. In 1210 he was dispatched with troops to restore order in the Welsh marches, and is said to have rescued Earl Ranulf of Chester who was besieged by the Welsh at Rhuddlan, Flintshire. His fierce raids against the Welsh are said to have earned him the name of 'Roger of Hell'.

Lacy married Maud de Clere, sister of the treasurer of York Cathedral; they had at least two sons, John de *Lacy, earl of Lincoln, and Roger, and possibly a third son, Robert, who is said to have been appointed constable of Flamborough. Lacy's principal residences were at Pontefract (Yorkshire), Clitheroe (Lancashire), and Halton. He died on 1 October 1211 at Stanlaw Abbey, and was buried there. He was a benefactor of that abbey, and also of Byland, Fountains, Kirkstall, Kirkstead, Pontefract, Sallay, and Watton. He was described by Roger of Wendover as a 'great and warlike man' and as a 'noble man and outstanding knight' (*Flores historiarum*, 2.8, 58).

C. L. KINGSFORD, *rev.* PAUL DALTON

Sources *VCH Lancashire*, 1.299–304 · J. C. Holt, *The northerners: a study in the reign of King John*, new edn (1992) · S. Painter, *The reign of King John* (1949) · K. Norgate, *John Lackland* (1902) · W. Farrer and others, eds., *Early Yorkshire charters*, 12 vols. (1914–65), vol. 3 · *Chronica magistri Rogeri de Hovedene*, ed. W. Stubbs, 4 vols., Rolls Series, 51 (1868–71) · *Rogeri de Wendover liber qui dicitur flores historiarum*, ed. H. G. Hewlett, 3 vols., Rolls Series, [84] (1886–9) · *Pipe rolls* · Paris, *Chron.* · *Chancery records* (RC) · Kirkstead cartulary, BL, Cotton MS Vespasian E.xviii · Whalley cartulary, BL, Egerton MS 3126 · Kirkstall coucher, PRO, duchy of Lancaster MS Misc. BKs 7 · Pontefract Priory cartulary, W. Yorks. AS, Leeds, Yorkshire Archaeological Society, M. E. Wentworth papers

Archives BL, Whalley cartulary, Egerton MS 3126 · BL, Kirkstead cartulary, Cotton MS Vespasian E. xviii · PRO, Kirkstall coucher, duchy of Lancaster MS Misc. BKs 7 · Yorkshire Archaeological Society, Leeds, M. E. Wentworth papers, Pontefract Priory cartulary

Lacy, Thomas Hailes (1809–1873), actor, playwright, and theatrical publisher, was born Thomas Lacy Hailes in Bethnal Green, London, the son of Thomas Hailes, gentleman. He made his London début on 7 April 1828 as Lenoir in William Dimond's *The Foundling of the Forest* (Olympic). He then acted in the provinces before undertaking management of the Windsor Theatre for Montague Penley, whom he then succeeded as lessee. For a short period from 1841 he was manager of the Theatre Royal, Sheffield. After provincial engagements in Nottingham and Doncaster, he returned to London in 1844 to act at the Pavilion and Victoria theatres. In May he joined Samuel Phelps's new company at Sadler's Wells, where Frances Dalton, under her stage name Fanny Cooper [*see below*], whom he probably married on 25 January 1842 at St Paul's, Covent Garden, was also engaged. On 29 May 1844, the opening night of the season, Lacy was Banquo to Phelps's Macbeth. Other parts that season included Tobias in Benjamin Thompson's *The Stranger*, Antonio in *The Merchant of Venice*, and Appius Claudius in Sheridan Knowles's tragedy *Virginius*. In the 1844–5 season he appeared in Manchester. He was a serviceable actor, capable of a variety of roles, but he never received serious critical attention.

Lacy's activities as a playwright consisted mostly of collaborative adaptations of novels. He adapted Moncrieff's versions of Dickens as *The Pickwickians* (1837) and (with T. H. Higgie) *Martin Chuzzlewit* (Queens, 29 July 1844); (also with Higgie) W. H. Ainsworth's *The Tower of London* (City of London theatre, 26 December 1840); and, via a French version by Jules Janin (with John Courtney), Samuel Richardson's *Clarissa Harlowe* (Princess's, 28 September 1846), in which Charles Mathews played Lovelace. At Sadler's Wells on 5 August 1846 his one-act farce *A Silent Woman* was the afterpiece, with Fanny Cooper as Miss Sandford. His pieces are unremarkable; several, however, were published in his acting edition, and *A Silent Woman* was also printed in New York in De Witt's series. Lacy edited anthologies of recitations (1864, 1866) and collections of costume plates (1865, 1868, 1872). He also projected publication of an updated edition of Baker's *Biographia dramatica* (1812), for which he collected new material, six manuscript volumes of which are now in the British Library, along with four annotated copies of Baker's original.

Thomas Hailes Lacy (1809–1873), by unknown photographer

Lacy's main contribution to the theatre was in publishing. In 1849 he opened a theatrical booksellers at 17 Wellington Street, Strand, and in 1857 he moved to larger premises at 89 Strand. He proved an astute, if not especially scrupulous, businessman and from about 1852 onwards bought out the lists of venerable competitors such as John Cumberland, G. H. Davidson, and John Duncombe, and (about 1856) more recent rivals such as Samuel G. Fairbrother, with the evident intention of cornering the market in printing cheap editions of plays. Lacy's Acting Edition, begun in 1850, with full stage directions and business, rapidly became the largest enterprise of its kind, catering for amateurs and professionals alike. All plays in the series, available individually at 6*d*. or in volume sets, were kept continuously in print; an up-to-date listing of pieces in Lacy's proprietorship was published separately in 1864. By his retirement in 1873 the series comprised ninety-nine volumes and 1458 plays. His performance fees were deliberately pitched lower than those of the Dramatic Authors' Society, which simply acted as a fee-collecting agent for its members. Lacy specialized in buying up copyrights at knock-down prices from impecunious dramatists; but on occasions he assumed copyright without authority. F. C. Burnand, who as an inexperienced playwright in the early 1860s had reason to mistrust him on both accounts, portrayed him as a rather roguish figure in 'dirty shirt sleeves', 'muddling about with books and papers in a very ill-lighted and grimy shop' (Burnand, 1.368). For his cavalier attitude to copyright Lacy was successfully brought to court for unauthorized dramatizations of copyright novels in *Reade v. Lacy* (1862) and *Tinsley v. Lacy* (1863). At his decease the Dramatic Authors' Society claimed from his estate in unpaid or misappropriated copyright fees the sum of £700, which after negotiation with the executor was reduced to £250.

Having sold his business early in 1873 to the New York publisher Samuel French, Lacy retired to Surrey, but died at his home in Benhill Street, Sutton, on 1 August. He was buried at Sutton church on 6 August. His library was sold by auction between 24 and 29 November 1873 for £2650 and his theatrical portraits on 8 December for £1970. In his will the 'interest, profits, and rentals' derived from a capital sum of £8000, copyright and acting rights on Cumberland's *British Theatre* and *Minor Theatre*, and property (including 9, 11, and 13 Garrick Street) he left to a charity for needy actors and actresses, the Royal General Theatrical Fund, of which he was a long-serving board member. Known as the 'Lacy Bequest', it provided the fund with much of its income for the rest of the century and beyond.

His wife, **Fanny Cooper** [*real name* Frances Charlotte Dalton] (1814–1872), actress, was born in Greenwich, Kent, in 1814, the daughter of William Dalton. She was the leading actress in Mrs Thomas Robertson's company on the Lincoln circuit in 1837 and made her London début as Lydia in Knowles's *The Love Chase* at the Haymarket (16 April 1838), when *The Times* (17 April) was much impressed by her 'chaste quiet piece of performance', 'genuine feeling', and 'desire to give distinctness to the text'. At Drury Lane in the 1839–40 season she acted a repertory of minor parts such as Margaret in Philip Massinger's *A New Way to Pay Old Debts* and Catherine in Colman's *The Heir-at-Law*. On 7 September 1840 she joined Madame Vestris's company at Covent Garden, where in November she played Helena in *A Midsummer Night's Dream*. Although, according to *The Times* (17 November 1840), 'her manner was constrained and artificial … there was still evident desire to give the words their meaning [and] that evident knowledge of feeling that the part required'. She revived the role in January and February 1842. Fanny Cooper's marriage to Lacy, which is said to have taken place on 25 January 1842 (in Sheffield or London), has not been traced in the official records. In her first season at Sadler's Wells in 1844, she sometimes performed alongside Lacy, as Countess Wintersen in *The Stranger*, Nerissa in *The Merchant of Venice*, and Virginia in *Virginius*. Other parts in her repertory included Aspatia in Knowles's *The Bridal* and Mary in Massinger's *The City Madam* (1844 season), Margaret Aylmer in G. W. Lovell's *Love's Sacrifice* (August 1846), and Mildred in a revival of Browning's *A Blot in the 'Scutcheon* (November 1848). But she maintained her affection for Shakespearian comedy and was occasionally rewarded by important parts such as Rosalind (November 1847) and Olivia (January 1848). In late summer 1850 she left Sadler's Wells, where for four seasons she had been increasingly overshadowed by Laura Addison, for the Surrey Theatre under William Creswick. The move, though short-lived and not entirely successful, enabled her to extend her Shakespearian repertory: Lady Macbeth (September) and Volumnia in *Coriolanus* (December). Fanny Cooper never quite made the first rank as actress but she was very popular with audiences and was perfectly suited to the ensemble acting for which Sadler's Wells under Phelps became renowned. Phelps re-engaged her for two further seasons from autumn 1853, when she resumed her old role of Helena in *A Midsummer Night's Dream* (a performance which left Henry Morley in *The Examiner* rather unimpressed because she was 'too loud and real') and took on a variety of new ones, including Desdemona (November 1853), Portia, and Thaisa (March and October 1854). She died at her home, 89 Strand, on 21 April 1872. There was an only son, Thomas junior, said to be mentally unstable, who died unmarried in 1895.   JOHN RUSSELL STEPHENS

Sources *The Era* (10 Aug 1873) • *The Era* (30 Nov 1873) • Boase, *Mod. Eng. biog.* • *DNB* • *Era Almanack and Annual* (1868) • *Era Almanack and Annual* (1873) • *Era Almanack and Annual* (1874) • W. Trewin, *The Royal Theatrical Fund: a history, 1838–1988* (1989) • J. R. Stephens, *The profession of the playwright: British theatre, 1800–1900* (1992) • F. C. Burnand, *Records and reminiscences, personal and general*, 2 vols. (1904) • *ILN* (20 Sept 1873) • A. Nicoll, *A history of English drama, 1660–1900*, 6 vols. (1952–9), vols. 4–5 [bibliography] • *Catalogue of additions to the manuscripts: plays submitted to the Lord Chamberlain, 1824–1851*, British Museum, Department of Manuscripts (1964) • *British Museum general catalogue of printed books … to 1955*, BM, 128 (1962), bibliography • d. cert. • S. S. Allen, *Samuel Phelps and Sadler's Wells theatre* (1971) [Fanny Cooper] • *The Times* (17 April 1838) [Fanny Cooper] • *The Times* (17 Nov 1840) [Fanny Cooper] • H. Morley, *The journal of a London playgoer, 1851–1866*, 2nd edn (1891); repr. (1974) [Fanny Cooper] • T. Marshall, *Lives of the most celebrated actors and actresses* [1846–7] [Fanny Cooper] • Hall, *Dramatic ports.* [lists engravings of Fanny Cooper] • d. cert. [Fanny Cooper] • census return for 89 Strand, London, 1861; 1871 [Mrs Thomas Hailes Lacy] • m. cert.

Archives BL, press mark 11795 df. and k. • BL, letters to Royal Literary Fund, Loan 96

Likenesses Greatbach, engraving (Fanny Cooper; as Helena in *A midsummer night's dream*), repro. in *Tallis's drawing-room table book* • Paine, daguerreotype (Fanny Cooper), repro. in *Tallis's Dramatic Magazine* • photograph, Theatre Museum, London [*see illus.*]

Wealth at death under £10,000: resworn probate, Jan 1874, *CGPLA Eng. & Wales* (1873) • £8000 capital; property at 9, 11, 13 Garrick Street; Benhill Street, Sutton, Surrey; £2650 realized from auction of library; £1970 realized from auction of theatrical portraits

Lacy, Walter de (d. 1085), magnate, was a Norman who made a great fortune for himself in the conquest of England. He and his brother Ilbert, from whom the Lacys of Pontefract were descended, shared a Norman estate centred on Lassy, from which they were named and which they held as men of the bishop of Bayeux. In England, however, they were independent operators, and Walter, who clearly already had a military reputation, was set up by King William in the southern Welsh marches alongside Earl William fitz Osbern in 1067. Together they fought the Welsh of Brycheiniog and Gwent. Walter's lands in Herefordshire and Gloucestershire—where the bulk of his possessions lay—had belonged to the rich Englishman Eadwig Cild and other lesser thegns; Walter made his main headquarters at Weobley, Herefordshire, which had been Eadwig's principal manor. Until 1075 Walter was second in the region only to Earl William and his son Roger de Breteuil, but the idea that he was their man can be discounted: they certainly gave him some manors as a tenant in Herefordshire and Oxfordshire, but he also forged links with Roger de Montgomery, earl of Shrewsbury, and the bishops of Hereford and Worcester, among others, which extended his lands into Shropshire and Worcestershire and made him a significant figure throughout the western midlands.

On the rebellion of Roger de Breteuil in 1075, Walter de Lacy remained loyal to the king and helped ensure that the revolt failed, no doubt being additionally rewarded in the aftermath. From 1075 he was the leading baron in the region, and made new links with his fellow marcher lords, including those who had been fitz Osbern's men: a niece, for example, married fitz Osbern's former follower Ansfrid de Cormeilles. Walter had some two dozen tenants on his English estates, mostly his own men rather than other tenants-in-chief, and some of them English; the leading men of his honour of Weobley witnessed the charter by which his son Roger renewed his agreements with the bishop of Hereford in 1085. A benefactor of Gloucester Abbey, he also founded and endowed the collegiate church of St Peter in Hereford. Walter died on 27 March 1085, perhaps (as later family legend had it) falling off the scaffolding while inspecting the building works at another favoured church in Hereford, St Guthlac's. He was buried in the chapter house at Gloucester Abbey.

Walter was survived by his wife, Ermeline, and succeeded by his son Roger de Lacy, who rebelled against William II in 1088 and again in 1094–5, after which he was dispossessed and sent into exile, though the king allowed his brother Hugh to succeed. On Hugh's death, perhaps before 1115, his daughter Sibyl and her husband *Pain fitz John received only part of the family's lands, but under King Stephen, Roger's son Gilbert de *Lacy recovered most of it. A third son of Walter de Lacy entered Gloucester Abbey as a child and was its abbot from 1130 to his death in 1139, while a daughter became a nun at Winchester.   C. P. LEWIS

Sources A. Farley, ed., *Domesday Book*, 2 vols. (1783) · W. H. Hart, ed., *Historia et cartularium monasterii Sancti Petri Gloucestriae*, 3 vols., Rolls Series, 33 (1863–7) · V. H. Galbraith, 'An episcopal land-grant of 1085', *EngHR*, 44 (1929), 353–72 · C. P. Lewis, 'The Norman settlement of Herefordshire under William I', *Anglo-Norman Studies*, 7 (1984), 195–213 · W. E. Wightman, *The Lacy family in England and Normandy, 1066–1194* (1966) · D. Bates, ed., *Regesta regum Anglo-Normannorum: the Acta of William I, 1066–1087* (1998), nos. 153, 156, 341

Lacy, Walter de (*d.* 1241), magnate, was the eldest son of Hugh de *Lacy (*d.* 1186) and Rose (*d.* before 1180), widow of Baderon of Monmouth (*d.* 1170×76), and the elder brother of Hugh de *Lacy (*d.* 1242).

Recovery of his inheritance A minor at the time of his father's death in 1186, Walter de Lacy succeeded to Hugh's estates in England, Wales, and Normandy during the final quarter of the year 1188/9. He had difficulty gaining possession of his father's Irish lordship of Mide, because John, son of Henry II, sought to retain it in his own hands

to maximize his wealth as lord of Ireland. It was not until John had rebelled against King Richard and the king had assumed lordship of Ireland in person in 1194 that Lacy gained full possession of Mide. King Richard appointed Lacy and the lord of Ulster, John de Courcy, as his justiciars in Ireland in place of John's agents, Peter Pipard and William Petit. When the latter resisted their removal, Lacy and Courcy waged war against them. Following John's reconciliation with King Richard, Lacy and Courcy were replaced by John's nominee, Hamo de Valognes. About the same time, John issued a charter restoring Mide to Lacy to hold on the same terms as had his father on the day of his death. On 5 July 1194 Lacy established a borough at Drogheda, conferring on it the customs of Breteuil, an early indication of his interest in the economic exploitation of his Irish lordship.

In 1198 Lacy negotiated a proffer of 3100 marks to recover King Richard's goodwill and his Norman and English lands (except Ludlow Castle), an earlier offer of 1000 marks in 1197 having been rejected. An order issued by King John shortly after his accession hints at why this was necessary. The king instructed his justiciar in Ireland on 4 September 1199, in the context of restoring to royal favour Henry Tirel, to inquire whether Henry 'had sided with John de Courcy and Walter de Lacy and aided them in destroying the king's land of Ireland' (*Rotuli de oblatis et finibus*, 74). It may be that John, as lord of Ireland, had persuaded King Richard to sequestrate Lacy's lands in England and Normandy for actions taken in Ireland; alternatively, Richard may have taken exception to Lacy's subsequently reaching an accommodation with John in respect of his Irish lands, and sought to maintain his overriding lordship there.

Service to King John Between September 1199 and March 1201 Walter de Lacy witnessed charters issued by King John, suggesting that he was retained in the royal retinue, while about October 1200 Meiler fitz Henry, justiciar in Ireland, was directed to take hostages from Lacy's principal tenants in Mide. About November 1200 Lacy's marriage was arranged to Margaret or Margery, daughter of William (III) de *Briouze, a baron with extensive holdings in the Welsh marches, who had been newly created lord of the honour of Limerick. The alliance was of mutual benefit: Briouze supervised Lacy's estates in the marches, while Lacy in turn guarded his father-in-law's Irish interests.

On 10 February 1204 the king, in a letter requesting an aid from the clergy of Ireland for his campaign in Normandy, stated that he was sending Lacy as a messenger to them. In that year, however, Walter de Lacy lost his Norman lands at Lassy, Campeaux, and Le Pin to King Philip Augustus of France, who had granted the greater part of them to his own nominees by 1205. In the meantime Lacy acted on King John's behalf in negotiations with Cathal Ó Conchobhair, king of Connacht, and between Meiler fitz Henry and William de Burgh. On 31 August 1204 the king addressed a letter jointly to the justiciar and Walter de Lacy ordering the summons to the king of Lacy's former ally John de Courcy. If Courcy failed to respond, eight cantreds of his land nearest Mide were to be granted to Lacy and to his brother Hugh. Walter assisted Hugh in the expulsion of Courcy from Ulster, and when in 1205 Courcy attempted to retake Ulster by force with the help of his brother-in-law Ragnvald, king of Man, it was Walter de Lacy who repulsed them. On 30 June 1205 the king ordered Meiler fitz Henry as justiciar to take heed of the advice of Hugh de Lacy, newly created earl of Ulster, who was to be his coadjutor, and of Walter.

Conflict with King John Walter de Lacy's ties with his father-in-law, William de Briouze, probably served only to extend to Lacy the mistrust that John already felt towards Briouze; in any case the king was suspicious of the power of magnates like Lacy, Briouze, and William (I) Marshal, who held substantial lands both in the Welsh marches and in Ireland. On 2 November 1204 the king had instructed Lacy to hand over to Meiler fitz Henry Limerick, custody of which Lacy was exercising on behalf of Briouze. By 23 August 1205 the king had changed tack and restored the custody of Limerick to Briouze, on whose behalf Lacy was still acting, provided that Briouze gave sureties for arrears that he owed for the farm and tallage of the city. A drastic deterioration in Lacy's relations with the king was signalled on 21 February 1207, when John addressed a letter to the barons of Mide and Leinster thanking them for their loyalty in the dispute between Meiler fitz Henry and Walter de Lacy over the city of Limerick. On 14 April 1207 Lacy was summoned to England to answer charges, pending the hearing of which his lands in Ireland were not to be confiscated. On 26 May 1207 the king had to rebuke his barons in Leinster and Mide for demands that they had made of his justiciar, seeking restoration of Uí Failge in north Leinster to the lord of Leinster, William Marshal, without the consent of the king. Meiler had earlier taken Uí Failge into the king's hand by royal order. There was then a concerted move by William Marshal and Walter de Lacy against Meiler, who was a tenant of both magnates. A substantial force from Leinster harried the lands that Meiler held of Lacy in Mide and besieged the castle of Ardnurcher for five weeks; shortly thereafter Meiler was taken prisoner and obliged to give hostages for his good conduct to William Marshal's wife, Isabel, at Kilkenny Castle. Thus forced to compromise, by 5 December the king had reached an accommodation with Lacy, granting him custody of the cantred of Ardmayle, Tipperary. On 19 March 1208 Meiler was instructed that Lacy enjoyed the king's peace and that Meiler was not to wage war on him, his men, or his lands in Ireland. On 24 April 1208 Lacy received a revised charter confirming Mide for fifty knights' fees, but under more restricted terms.

The period of harmony between John and the Anglo-Norman magnates did not last. By 1210, when John mounted an expedition in person to Ireland, Walter de Lacy's relations with the king had again worsened. He became embroiled in the conflict between John and his father-in-law, William de Briouze, after Briouze had fallen from grace, rebelled, and fled across the Irish Sea. After the king's landing in Ireland, Lacy's seneschal, William

Petit, proffered submission on his behalf to John on 28 June 1210, seeking to dissociate Lacy from the plunder committed by his brother Hugh in Ulster and Mide, and pleading that both Walter and his tenants had suffered much at the hands of Hugh. Nevertheless, Walter de Lacy's English and Irish estates were confiscated by the king. The profits accruing to the crown from the lordship of Mide are indicated in detail on the surviving Irish pipe roll from John's reign for 1211/12 and amounted to a substantial annual income in excess of £770, not including renders in kind.

Reconciliation and recovery of lands The baronial revolt in England afforded an opportunity for Walter de Lacy's reconciliation with King John. The alliance formed between the baronial opposition and the Welsh ruler Llywelyn ab Iorwerth threatened the security of the Welsh marches and made Lacy a natural ally of the king. On 1 July 1213 John granted Walter permission to travel to England, probably from Normandy. On 29 July 1213 his English lands were restored, except Ludlow Castle, which was not recovered until 1215. Lacy took part in John's expedition to Poitou in 1214. On 5 July 1215 he recovered his Irish lands, apart from the castle of Drogheda, having proffered 40,000 marks. His son was to remain as a hostage until full payment was completed. On 18 August 1216 Lacy was appointed castellan and sheriff of Hereford (an office that he exercised until Henry III's partial coming of age in November 1223). On 30 August 1216 he was appointed *custos* of the vacant see of Hereford. He was a witness to King John's will at Newark in October 1216.

Lacy played an important part in ensuring the loyalty of the Welsh marches during the civil war, and he subsequently served on the early council of regency at the beginning of Henry III's minority. These activities allowed him little time to visit his estates in Mide, and he appears to have looked to his half-brother, William Gorm (d. 1233), whose mother was a daughter of Ruaidrí *Ua Conchobair, king of Connacht, to represent his interests there. William had been taken captive by King John during his Irish expedition, but Lacy negotiated his release by 10 February 1215. The annals of Clonmacnoise recount that William's arrival in Ireland in 1215 aroused 'great contention and wars between the English of the south of Ireland' (*Annals of Clonmacnoise*, 228), obliging Lacy to give the king security for the past excesses and future behaviour of his half-brother.

Return to Ireland In 1220 Walter de Lacy was back in Ireland after a ten-year absence. He led a great hosting against Ó Raghallaig of east Bréifne and captured his crannog (island fortification) on Lough Oughter. In 1221 Lacy granted Bréifne from Lough Oughter to Lough Erne to his vassal, Philip de Angulo; however, a letter written in 1224 by Cathal Ó Conchobhair, king of Connacht, to Henry III complained that Bréifne had been seized by William Gorm. About 1223 Lacy's brother Hugh, having failed to negotiate the recovery of the earldom of Ulster that King John had taken from him, arrived in Ireland and proceeded to wage war against the Anglo-Norman colonists in alliance with Aodh Ó Néill, king of Tír Eoghain. By 10 June 1224, when Walter de Lacy and the justiciar William (II) Marshal were sent to restore order, war had engulfed Mide and Ulster. In consideration of the excesses committed by the men of Mide in harbouring Hugh de Lacy and pillaging the king's land, Walter had been obliged about March 1224 to agree to the delivery of his castles of Ludlow and Trim into the king's hand for two years. On 13 May 1225 Walter de Lacy was charged 3000 marks for recovery of his Irish lands which had been taken by the king 'because of the war waged against the king by Hugh de Lacy in Ireland' (*Rotuli litterarum clausarum*, 2.39b).

Religious patronage, bankruptcy, and death   Walter de Lacy's fines to the king in 1198, 1213, and 1225, together with his castle building activities in Mide and on the Welsh marches, as well as his ecclesiastical benefactions, involved him in considerable financial liabilities. None the less he was able to make donations in Ireland to Llanthony Prima, Gwent, which had a cell at Duleek in Meath, and Llanthony Secunda, Gloucestershire, which had a cell at Colp, also in Meath, to Fore Priory, Westmeath, and to St Thomas's Abbey, Dublin; he founded a house of Benedictine nuns at Ballymore Loughswedy in Westmeath and a small Cistercian house at Beybeg, Meath, as a daughter house of Beaubec in Normandy, and a Grandmontine house at Craswell, Herefordshire. For more than two decades before his death in 1241 he was heavily reliant on money loans from Jewish financiers to service his debts. A plea roll of the exchequer of the Jews of 1244, which records details of debts owing in that year to the family of Hamo of Hereford, reveals that at the time of his death Walter de Lacy was in debt to Hamo to the sum of £1266 13s. 4d. During the minority of Henry III Lacy had been able to postpone payment of the annual sums due from his fines; the fact that he was sheriff of Hereford from 1216 to 1223 had also facilitated mutually advantageous relations with Hamo. However, after Hamo's death in 1232, when his family had to meet a relief of 6000 marks imposed by the crown, it became necessary for them to pursue creditors more urgently. Following representations by a number of Jews for recovery of debts owed by Lacy, the crown on 19 November 1240 issued orders for the distraint of his estates.

At the time of his death in early 1241, apparently before 28 February, Walter de Lacy was blind and feeble, bankrupt, and without male heirs. His only son, Gilbert, who married Isabella, daughter of Ralph Bigod, died in 1234, leaving a son, Walter, and two daughters, Matilda and Margaret. This Walter was alive in 1238, and married a daughter of Theobald *Butler (d. 1205), but predeceased his grandfather without heirs. Henry III took this opportunity to dispense patronage by arranging the marriages of the Lacy sisters, now coheirs of the Lacy estates, to noted royal servants. Margaret married John de Verdon, and Matilda married Pierre de Genevre and afterwards Geoffrey de *Geneville.   M. T. FLANAGAN

Sources administrative records of the English royal chancery and exchequer, 1186–1242 · O. Davies and D. B. Quinn, eds., 'Irish pipe roll of 14 John, 1211–1212', *Ulster Journal of Archaeology*, 3rd ser.,

4 (1941), 16–19, 34–5 [suppl.] · index and corrigenda, *Ulster Journal of Archaeology*, 3rd. ser., 53, index 1–6 · J. Mills and M. J. McEnery, eds., *Calendar of the Gormanston register* (1916), 177–8, 180–81, 190 · P. Meyer, ed., *L'histoire de Guillaume le Maréchal*, 3 vols. (Paris, 1891–1901), lines 10289–340, 13679–786, 14181–232 · Paris, *Chron.*, 4.93, 174 · W. M. Hennessy and B. MacCarthy, eds., *Annals of Ulster, otherwise, annals of Senat*, 4 vols. (1887–1901), vol. 2, s.a. 1195, 1201, 1203, 1204, 1205, 1207, 1222 · W. M. Hennessy, ed. and trans., *The annals of Loch Cé: a chronicle of Irish affairs from AD 1014 to AD 1590*, 2 vols., Rolls Series, 54 (1871), s.a. 1207, 1221, 1223, 1233, 1234, 1241 · J. Hillaby, 'Colonisation, crisis management and debt: Walter de Lacy and the lordship of Meath, 1189–1241', *Ríocht na Midhe*, 8/4 (1992–3), 1–50 · D. Murphy, ed., *The annals of Clonmacnoise*, trans. C. Mageoghagan (1896); facs. edn (1993), 228 · E. St J. Brooks, ed., *The Irish cartularies of Llanthony prima and secunda*, IMC (1953), 82–4, 213–16, 220–21, 245–6 · Dugdale, *Monasticon*, new edn, 6/2.1035 · M. P. Mac Síthigh, 'Cairteacha Meán-Aoiseacha do Mhainistir Fhobhair (XII–XII céad)', *Seanchas Ardmhacha*, 4 (1960–61), 171–5; calendared in J. H. Round, *Documents preserved in France, 918–1206* (1899), 105 · J. H. Round, ed., *Calendar of documents preserved in France, illustrative of the history of Great Britain and Ireland* (1899), 105–6 · G. Mac Niocaill, 'Cairt le Walter de Lacy', *Galvia*, 11 (1977), 54–6 · G. Mac Niocaill, *Na Buirgéisí, XII–XV aois*, 1 (Dublin, 1964), 172–3 · J. T. Gilbert, ed., *Register of the abbey of St Thomas, Dublin*, Rolls Series, 94 (1889), 11–13, 419–20 · J. Brownbill, ed., *The coucher book of Furness Abbey*, 2/3, Chetham Society, new ser., 78 (1919), 716–18 · Rymer, *Foedera*, new edn, 1/1.144–5 · T. D. Hardy, ed., *Rotuli de oblatis et finibus*, RC (1835), 74 · T. D. Hardy, ed., *Rotuli litterarum clausarum*, RC, 2 (1834)

Lacy, Walter [*real name* Walter Williams] (**1809–1898**), actor, the son of a coach-builder named Williams in Bristol, was educated for the medical profession and went as a young man to Australia. He was first seen on the stage in Edinburgh, in 1829, as Montalban in *The Honeymoon*, played there again in 1832, and acted also in Glasgow, Liverpool, and Manchester.

Lacy's London début was at the Haymarket, on 21 August 1838, as Charles Surface. On 22 June 1839 he married Harriett Deborah Taylor (1807–1874), an actress [see Lacy, Harriett Deborah]. At Covent Garden he appeared, about 1841, as Captain Absolute opposite Madame Vestris and at Drury Lane as Wildrake in Sheridan Knowles's *The Love Chase*. He then joined Charles Kean at the Princess's for seven years. On 18 September 1852 he created the part of Rouble in Boucicault's *The Prima Donna*, and he made a great success as Château Renaud in *The Corsican Brothers*. Opposite Kean, he played John of Gaunt in *Richard II*, Edmund in *King Lear*, Gratiano, and Lord Trinket in Colman's *The Jealous Wife*. On 30 June 1860, at the Lyceum, he performed the Marquis of Saint Evrémont in *A Tale of Two Cities*, and at Drury Lane, on 17 October 1864, was Cloten to Helen Faucit's Imogen. He appeared as Flutter in *The Belle's Stratagem* on 8 October 1866 at the St James's, where he was, on 5 November, the first John Leigh in Boucicault's *Hunted Down, or, Two Lives of John Leigh*. He played Mercutio in two Lyceum revivals of *Romeo and Juliet*. On 12 August 1868 he was, at the Princess's, the original Bellingham in Boucicault's *After Dark*.

Other parts in which Lacy was seen were Benedick, Comus, Faulconbridge, Malvolio, Touchstone, Prospero, Roderigo, Henry VIII, Young Marlow, Sir Brilliant Fashion, Goldfinch, Tony Lumpkin, Bob Acres, Dazzle, Flutter, Dudley Smooth, Megrim in *Blue Devils*, the Ghost in *Hamlet*, My Lord Duke in James Townley's farce *High Life below Stairs*, Jeremy Diddler, and Puff. After a long absence from the stage, occupied as professor of elocution at the Royal Academy of Music, Lacy reappeared at the Lyceum in April 1879 as Colonel Damas in Sir Henry Irving's revival of *The Lady of Lyons*. He died on 13 December 1898 at his home, 13 Marine Square, Brighton, and was buried at Brompton cemetery on the 17th.

Lacy was a respectable light comedian, but failed as an exponent of old men and was a wretched Sir Anthony Absolute. He was a familiar figure at the Garrick Club, and was almost to the last a man of much vivacity, and of quaint, clever, unbridled, and characteristic speech.

JOSEPH KNIGHT, *rev.* KATHARINE COCKIN

Sources C. E. Pascoe, ed., *The dramatic list*, 2nd edn (1880) · Hall, *Dramatic ports.* · private information (1901) · personal knowledge (1901) · *The Era* (17 Dec 1898)

Likenesses A. S. Cope, oils, 1886, Garr. Club · J. W. Gear, lithograph (as Narciss Boss in *Single life*), BM, Harvard TC

Lacy, William (*c.*1610–1671), Church of England clergyman, was the son of Thomas Lacy of Beverley in the East Riding of Yorkshire and his wife, Elizabeth, daughter of Richard Franceys of Beckingham, Nottinghamshire. His date of birth is derived from the information that he was aged fifty-six (or in his fifty-sixth year) in 1666. The Lacy family had long been known for recusancy and in September 1631 Thomas was examined by the president of the council in the north for alleged involvement in furthering the Catholic cause. William Lacy was admitted, probably before 1629, to St John's College, Cambridge, graduated BA in 1632, and proceeded MA in 1636. Admitted as a fellow of his college on 5 April 1636, he acted as tutor during 1640–42. He proceeded BD in 1642 and was made preacher at St John's at Michaelmas 1643.

Lacy was a co-author with John Barwick and others of *Certain Disquisitions and Considerations Representing to the Conscience the Unlawfulness of the Oath Entituled, a Solemn League and Covenant* (1644); the sheets were seized by the parliamentarians, but the book was reprinted at Oxford. Ejected from his fellowship in 1644 Lacy attached himself to the royalist army, and evidently became chaplain to Prince Rupert, for he was present at the storming of Bridgwater by Sir Thomas Fairfax on 23 July 1645 and was listed shortly afterwards as 'Lacy, priest to Prince Rupert' (*Fairfax's Letter*, 6). In prison, he soon became impoverished, but survived thanks to the generosity of John Barwick. It seems that Lacy inherited his father's property at Beverley, though he may have been forced to sell. On 19 April 1648 he was listed as one of the Hampshire persons already sequestrated. Before 1 September 1651 he compounded for a fine of £26, one-sixth of the value of his estate, but on 21 November of the same year he claimed in a deposition to the committee of 'debts he owed to several persons before 20 May 1642, total £44. Also that £30 debts, for which he compounded, have since become desperate, and are not likely to be paid' (Green, 3.1382).

On the return of Charles II, Lacy was restored to his fellowship by a warrant from the earl of Manchester dated 27 August 1660 and executed on 2 November. He was also presented by the king on 1 October 1660 to the prebend of South Cave in the diocese of York, but the appointment did not take effect and the prebend lapsed. At Cambridge, Lacy was admitted on 4 November 1661 to a senior fellowship; he was recommended by the king for the degree of DD on 3 October 1662, an honour awarded the following year. In 1669 he contributed £5 towards the building of the third court at St John's College. On 13 October 1662, now aged over fifty, at St Mary's Church, Leicester, Lacy married one Ann Dan (*d.* 1686), a widow; this was probably Ann, daughter of William Sherman, a gentleman of Newark, Lincolnshire, baptized in the same parish on 11 January 1618; the couple appear to have had one child, a son, William, who was born on 25 July 1663 but who was buried a few days later on 12 August. Ten days after his marriage, on 23 October 1662, Lacy was presented by Sir George Savile to the rectory of Thornhill, near Dewsbury, in the West Riding of Yorkshire, in the place of the ejected minister. The parish register records that on 8 November 1662 'Dr Will. Lacy inducted into the Rectory of Thornhill and Joshua Witton overturned' (Charlesworth, 1.172). There he rebuilt the rectory house, destroyed during the civil wars. It was evidently a very substantial building, for Lacy was assessed in 1666 for nine hearths.

Lacy died at Thornhill on 12 May 1671 and was buried next day in the church, where a stone was laid to his memory. In his will, dated 7 September 1670, he provided £350 in reversion, for two exhibitions of £8 each, to be taken up at St John's by boys from Beverley grammar school.

STEPHEN WRIGHT

Sources W. Dugdale, *The visitation of the county of Yorke*, ed. R. Davies and G. J. Armytage, SurtS, 36 (1859) · J. Charlesworth, ed., *The register of the parish of Thornhill*, pts 1–3, Yorkshire Parish Register Society, 30 (1907); 43 (1911); 53 (1915) · Venn, *Alum. Cant.* · *Walker rev.* · *VCH Yorkshire East Riding*, vol. 6 · *Fasti Angl., 1541–1857*, [York] · P. Barwick, *The life of … Dr John Barwick*, ed. and trans. H. Bedford (1724) · *Sir Thomas Fairfax's letter to the honourable William Lenthall … concerning the taking of Bridgwater* (1645) [Thomason tract E 294(6)] · T. D. Whitaker, *Loidis and Elmete* (1816) · B. H. Nuttall, *A history of Thornhill* (1963) · M. A. E. Green, ed., *Calendar of the proceedings of the committee for advance of money, 1642–1656*, 3 vols., PRO (1888) · *Dugdale's visitation of Yorkshire, with additions*, ed. J. W. Clay, 2 (1907), 427 · *CSP dom., 1661–2*, 24 · IGI · parish register, Thornhill, 13 May 1671 [burial]

Lacy, William (1788–1871), singer, was a pupil of Venanzio Rauzzini (1747–1810) at Bath about 1795. He appeared at various concerts in London a few years later before going to Italy for further study. Lacy had an excellent bass voice, with especially fine lower notes, and while in Italy he was offered lucrative engagements at the Milan and Florence operas. On his return to England soon after 1800, he frequently sang at the Lenten oratorios and at other important concerts, but poor health prevented him from pursuing a successful career in England.

In 1812 Lacy married **Jane Bianchi** (1776–1858), the widow of Francesco Bianchi (1752–1810), an Italian opera composer and the teacher of Henry Bishop. She was the daughter of John Jackson, an apothecary in Sloane Street, Chelsea, London, and had married Bianchi in 1800. Like Lacy, she was a well-known singer; she had made her début in London on 25 April 1798, and performed at the Concerts of Ancient Music in 1800. As Mrs Bianchi she often sang at Windsor in the presence of George III and Queen Charlotte, and was considered one of the finest exponents of Handel's music, though in 1809 the *Morning Chronicle* considered that 'her unaffectedness, her propriety of action, and her good taste' compensated for 'the defects of a very bad voice' (*BDA*). With Lacy she took part in the concerts given by Elizabeth Billington, Giuseppe Naldi, and John Braham at Willis's Rooms on 1 March 1809, and at the Vocal Concerts in the Hanover Square Rooms on 2 March 1810.

In 1818 the Lacys accepted an engagement in Calcutta, where they remained for seven years, giving frequent performances at the court of Oudh. After returning to England about 1826 they retired into private life. For some years they lived in Florence, but eventually settled in England; Jane Lacy died at Ealing on 19 March 1858, William Lacy in July 1871 while on a visit to Devon.

R. H. LEGGE, rev. ANNE PIMLOTT BAKER

Sources Grove, *Dict. mus.* • *Quarterly Musical Magazine and Review*, 1 (1818), 333–40 • Highfill, Burnim & Langhans, *BDA*

Ladbrooke, Henry (1800–1870). *See under* Ladbrooke, Robert (1768–1842).

Ladbrooke, John Berney (1803–1879). *See under* Ladbrooke, Robert (1768–1842).

Ladbrooke, Robert (1768–1842), landscape painter, was born at Norwich. Little is known of his early life, though his parents are said to have been humble. He was apprenticed early to an artist and printer named White, and for several years worked as a journeyman printer. As an apprentice he met and befriended John Crome, his contemporary, who was working for a house and sign painter. They became firm friends, sharing a small studio and devoting their spare time to sketching and copying. On 3 October 1793 Ladbrooke married Mary Berney (*d.* 1807) and purchased a house at Scoles Green, Norwich. He set himself up as a drawing-master and worked in partnership with Crome, who was now his brother-in-law, having married Mary Berney's sister. Initially Ladbrooke painted portraits but he subsequently turned to landscape painting, in which he established his reputation. Along with Crome, Ladbrooke took a leading part in the establishment of the Norwich Society of Artists in 1803 and, after a tour of Wales in 1804, he sent fourteen works to its first exhibition in 1805. He also sent works to the Royal Academy between 1805 and 1815. Mary Berney died in 1807, and Ladbrooke later remarried, his second wife dying in 1828.

In 1809 Ladbrooke was nominated president of the Norwich Society of Artists; he continued to exhibit his work regularly. In 1816, with Joseph Stannard, John Thirtle, and several other members, he seceded from the society, having attempted unsuccessfully to modify some of its rules. The precise nature of the dispute is unclear but may have involved the proposed exclusion of amateurs from the society and questions about financial management. Ladbrooke's faction formed a rival society and held their own exhibitions in a hall adjoining the Shakespeare tavern on Theatre Plain, Norwich. This venture, however, proved a failure, and was abandoned after only three

years. Ladbrooke therefore sent works to the British Institution for exhibition in 1819, 1820, and 1822. Between 1821 and 1822 he devoted himself to a collection of 700 lithographs of Norfolk churches with the assistance of his son John Berney Ladbrooke [*see below*]. This project was published only posthumously in five volumes in 1843. By 1822 Ladbrooke's interests in art dealing and picture framing allowed him to hand over his work as a drawing-master to his son. In 1824 he was reconciled with the Norwich Society of Artists under the presidency of his nephew, John Berney Crome; he sent two paintings to the exhibition that year and continued to send works intermittently until 1833. Success in business ventures led him to retire many years before his death, and in these later years Ladbrooke began to invest in property, leaving a significant estate including land in Beer Street and the Shakespeare tavern at his death on 11 October 1842 at his house on Scoles Green. He was buried at St Stephen's, Norwich.

Few of Ladbrooke's paintings appear to have survived. He published aquatints of two of his pictures, *A View of the Fellmongers on the River Near Bishop's Bridge* and *A View of Norwich Castle*, besides the posthumous *Views of the Churches of Norfolk*. Two of Ladbrooke's sons were well-known artists.

Henry Ladbrooke (1800–1870), the second son, was born at Norwich on 20 April 1800. His early desire to enter the church was discouraged by his father, and Henry Ladbrooke became the pupil of his uncle John Crome. He acquired a reputation as a landscape painter, especially for his moonlight scenes, and exhibited intermittently at the Norwich Society of Artists between 1818 and 1833. He then exhibited at the British Institution in 1834 and 1836 as well as at the Suffolk Street Gallery between 1836 and 1865. He worked as a drawing-master, first in North Walsham, and later in Valenger's Road, King's Lynn, and was assisted in his teaching by his daughter, Fanny. He died on 18 November 1870 and was buried at Norwich cemetery.

John Berney Ladbrooke (1803–1879), Robert Ladbrooke's third son, was born on 31 October 1803 in Norfolk. He studied under his uncle John Crome, whose style he acquired, and excelled in the representation of woodland scenery. He exhibited at the Royal Academy in 1821, 1822, and 1843 as well as at the British Institution between 1823 and 1859 and at the Suffolk Street Gallery up to 1873. He worked as a drawing-master in Norwich, and at some stage before 1850 he made a tour of the Netherlands and France. In 1859 he built a house and studio on Mousehold Heath, Norfolk, which was named Kett's Castle Villa. He died at the house on 11 July 1879 and was buried at the Rosary cemetery.

F. M. O'DONOGHUE, rev. MATTHEW HARGRAVES

Sources *Norwich Mercury* (15 Oct 1842) • J. Wodderspoon, *John Crome and his works* (privately printed, Norwich, 1858) • Graves, *RA exhibitors* • Redgrave, *Artists* • *The Times* (29 July 1879) • W. F. Dickes, *The Norwich school of painting: being a full account of the Norwich exhibitions, the lives of the painters, the lists of their respective exhibits, and descriptions of the pictures* [1906] • J. Walpole, *Art and artists of the Norwich school* (1997) • H. A. E. Day, *East Anglian painters*, 2: *The Norwich school of painters* (1968), 120–58 • A. W. Moore, *The Norwich school of artists* (1985)

Likenesses J. B. Ladbrooke, lithograph, 1839, NPG · Wageman, oils?, repro. in Day, *Norwich school*, 120

Lade, Michael (*d.* **1799**), racehorse owner and miser, emerged from obscurity after taking the lease of Cannon Park, Kingsclere, Hampshire, in May 1787. He was soon racing horses, but only at nearby meetings to save money. His first appearance in the sporting press in 1794 set the tone for most future comment. His racing groom and jockey, John Scott, had sued for unpaid wages, an action which Lade, as a lawyer, stopped by an injunction in the exchequer. Scott had to have this put aside at Hampshire assizes, where an agreed arbiter ordered the payment to Scott of the considerable sum of £165 as damages and all legal costs.

Lade made two excursions to Newmarket, where he enjoyed his one and only major success as a racing man by winning the important Oatland Stakes in 1797 with his bay colt by Dungannon out of Letitia. There then followed an impressive list of failures—at Ascot Heath, Stockbridge, Burford, Egham, and Reading. Newmarket in the following year proved equally disastrous and Lade died some months later with his stable completely neglected and his horses looking so wretched at auction that many went for only 2 or 3 guineas.

Personally, Lade was as unattractive as his horses. He appeared to have few if any friends, and was reported as seldom seen in company on the racecourse or anywhere else; he was also said to be 'cynically rigid and innately parsimonious'. His obituary in the *Sporting Magazine* pulled no punches and referred both to his titled wife who brought him some £5000 a year but who was mentally incapacitated, and to the ladies he kept in Pall Mall and at Turnham Green, though 'he was a total stranger to the powers of attraction and we may safely presume that *his amours* were regulated much more (on the part of the ladies) by interest than affection'. In short, 'he *lived* without regard, so he *died* without *regret*' (*Sporting Magazine*, vol. 15). His death occurred in December 1799, probably at his London address, Stamford Brook, Hammersmith.

DENNIS BRAILSFORD

Sources *Sporting Magazine*, 8 (1796) · *Sporting Magazine*, 9 (1796–7) · *Sporting Magazine*, 10 (1797) · *Sporting Magazine*, 13 (1798–9) · *Sporting Magazine*, 14 (1799) · *Sporting Magazine*, 15 (1799–1800) · J. Weatherby and others, eds., *The racing calendar*, 25 (1797) · Scott settlement detail, Hants. RO, Cannon Park property transactions
Archives Hants. RO

Ladyman, Samuel (**1625/6–1684**), Church of Ireland clergyman, was probably born at Dinton, Buckinghamshire, the son of John Ladyman. Aged seventeen, Ladyman, a servitor, matriculated at Corpus Christi College, Oxford, on 3 March 1643, graduating BA on 13 July 1647. Appointed a fellow by the parliamentary visitors in 1648, he proceeded MA on 21 June 1649. According to Anthony Wood he began preaching in the Oxford area about this time, becoming well known in presbyterian circles. On 20 August 1652 the government allocated £50 and £20 respectively to Edward Wale and Ladyman, who were commissioned to go to Ireland with Charles Fleetwood as chaplains. They departed the next month, sailing from Bristol to Waterford. In Ireland, Ladyman became the minister at Clonmel, perhaps at the suggestion of Joseph Eyres, his friend and contemporary at Corpus Christi. Initially Ladyman received £100 per annum at Clonmel, but in 1655 he was earning £170. When Edward Worth founded the Cork Association in 1657, initially to ordain ministers but with the ultimate goal of imposing uniformity through a national church, Ladyman and Eyres participated. Henry Cromwell invited Ladyman and approximately thirty other clergymen to Dublin in the spring of 1658 to discuss church finances and other issues. With eighteen others Ladyman drafted an address to Cromwell in May, praising his support of protestantism and interest in settling clerical maintenance. Although Cromwell invited Ladyman to move to Dublin, he opted to remain at Clonmel.

Ladyman's only published work is *The Dangerous Rule* (1658), from a sermon preached at Clonmel before the Munster judges on 3 August 1657. In it he articulated the defining characteristic of his career, namely, the subordination of conscience to 'the guidance and superintendency of known Laws' (p. 8). Conscience, he argued, is defective, uncertain, and arbitrary unless guided by law, and it must therefore be subordinate to understanding. If the consciences of the few become a law for all, the result is tyranny. He pointed to Jan of Leyden and the Quakers as examples of what could happen if claims of conscience were pre-eminent, and he urged his readers to 'behold the Monstrosity & rugged deformity of Conscience, when seated upon the Throne, as Queen Regent; whilst standing Laws are constrain'd to lie gasping under her Imperious Feet' (ibid., sig. a1v). Freedom of opinion, he warned, would lead to liberty in practice and the destruction of people's souls.

On the eve of the Restoration, Ladyman was one of the twenty highest-paid clergymen in Ireland, earning £200 in 1659. He was now assisted at Clonmel by Galatius Hickey, formerly a minister in the diocese of Killaloe. True to his belief in the supremacy of law Ladyman conformed at the Restoration, remaining at Clonmel as vicar, though he did not undergo episcopal ordination until February 1665. Three years later as archdeacon of Limerick he was receiving £120 per annum. By 1677 Dr Ladyman was prebendary of Cashel. His wife, Grace, daughter of Dr William Hutchinson of Oxford, whom Ladyman had married before 1655, had died in March 1663 or 1664. Three of their children, Samuel, Francis, and Grace, died in infancy, and the others died young—John on 9 December 1675, aged twenty, and Jane on 27 September 1681, aged twenty-one. Following his own death in February 1684 Ladyman was interred in the chancel of St Mary's, Clonmel. By his will, he left £5 per annum for the education of ten poor children, and £5 per annum to be distributed in alms.

RICHARD L. GREAVES

Sources Foster, *Alum. Oxon.*, 1500–1714 [Samuel Ladiman] · *CSP dom.*, 1651–2, 374 · *CSP Ire.*, 1666–9, 677 · Wood, *Ath. Oxon.: Fasti* (1820), 121 · *DNB* · St J. D. Seymour, *The puritans in Ireland, 1647–1661* (1912) · T. C. Barnard, *Cromwellian Ireland: English government and* *reform in Ireland, 1649–1660* (1975) · J. S. Reid and W. D. Killen, *History of the Presbyterian church in Ireland*, new edn, 2 (1867), 558, 560–62 **Archives** BL, Lansdowne MSS, 822, fol. 170; 823, fols. 51, 177 · Bodl. Oxf., Carte MSS, 160, fol. 6; 221, fol. 130

Laeghaire. *See* Lóegaire mac Néill (*fl.* 5th cent.).

Laet, Johannes De [Johannes Latius] (**1581–1649**), merchant and scholar, was born in Antwerp in the autumn of 1581, the son of Johannes De Laet (*d. c.*1605), merchant; his mother's name is unknown. After the fall of Antwerp in 1585, the family, like thousands of Flemish protestants, fled to the northern Netherlands, where Johannes attended the Latin school in Amsterdam. He moved to Leiden to study philosophy, matriculated on 4 September 1597, aged fifteen, and resided with the theologian Franciscus Gomarus; Joseph Scaliger was among his teachers. After graduating on 30 January 1602, the following year he settled in London, where on 3 July 1604 he married, at Austin Friars, Jacquemine Vanlore (1587–1606), eldest daughter of Peter *Vanlore (baronet, 1628), merchant and prominent member of the large Dutch Calvinist community in London. Through this marriage he became brother-in-law to government officials such as Sir Edward Powell, Sir Charles Caesar, and Sir Thomas Glemham, and on 16 August he obtained denization.

Two years later, however, Jacquemine died, and in 1607 de Laet took up residence again in Leiden, where in April 1608 he married Maria Boudewijns van Berlicum (*d.* 1643). There he made a fortune through overseas trade and land investments, at home and at Laetburg, near Albany, in New Netherland. In 1619 he was appointed a director of the Dutch West Indies Company, a position he held until his death.

In the ongoing religious quarrels which troubled Holland, de Laet sided with the counter-remonstrants (Gomarists) against the remonstrants (Arminians), an allegiance evident in his *Commentarii de Pelagianis et Semi-Pelagianis* (1617). In 1618 he was delegated for Leiden to the Synod of Dort, where he befriended the theologian Samuel Ward, master of Sidney Sussex College, Cambridge, one of the several English delegates. In his leisure time he proved a prolific, many-sided scholar with a keen interest in theology, geography, botany, classical philology, and comparative historical linguistics. Still of importance are his lavishly illustrated books on the Americas—*Nieuwe wereldt* (1625), which he also translated into Latin (1633) and French (1640), a detailed account of the early years of the Dutch West Indies Company (1644), and *Historia naturalis Brasiliae* (1648). He contributed eleven volumes to the Elzevier *Republicae* series, including ones on Scotland and Ireland (1627), England (1630), and India (1631). In a magisterial polemic with Hugo Grotius, he disproved Grotius's claims that the Native Americans originated from China, Ethiopia, and Norway (1644). His de luxe edition of Vitruvius's *De architectura* (1649) includes his Latin translation of Sir Henry Wotton's *The Elements of Architecture* (1624). De Laet was an astute Anglo-Saxonist, corresponding and co-operating with (but also envied by) such antiquaries as William Camden, Sir Henry Spelman, Sir

John Spelman, Abraham Wheelock, Sir Simonds D'Ewes, John Selden, and Patrick Young. Archbishop James Ussher lent him the famous 'Caedmon' manuscript (Bodl. Oxf., MS Junius 11) for an Old English–Latin dictionary he was compiling. His correspondence with John Morris reflects contemporary Anglo-Dutch intellectual exchange, while his unpublished epistolary exchange with Sir William Boswell (*d.* 1649), English ambassador in The Hague, is a particularly rich quarry for evidence of political and economic interchange between England and Holland.

In 1638 de Laet visited England for several months both in connection with his dictionary and to obtain denizenship for his son Samuel, who had married Rebecca, daughter of Timothy Cruso of London. During another visit in 1641 parliament asked his advice on the prospects for an English West Indies Company and Charles I requested him to provide the genealogy of his future son-in-law, William II of Orange. De Laet died of a stroke in Leiden on 9 December 1649 and was buried there in the Pieterskerk on 15 December, survived by five children, of whom his son Johannes settled in England in 1656.

ROLF H. BREMMER JUN.

Sources *Correspondence of John Morris with Johannes De Laet (1634–1649)*, ed. J. A. F. Bekkers (1970) · R. H. Bremmer, 'The correspondence of Johannes de Laet (1581–1649) as a mirror of his life', *Lias*, 25 (1998), 139–64 · W. J. Cameron, *A bibliography in short-title catalogue form of seventeenth-century books written or edited by Johannes de Laet* (1986) · B. Schmidt, 'Space, time, travel: Hugo de Groot, Johannes de Laet and the advancement of geographic learning', *Lias*, 25 (1998), 177–200 · H. Florijn, 'Johannes de Laet (1581–1649) and the Synod of Dort, 1618–1619', *Lias*, 25 (1998), 165–76 · P. J. Hoftijzer, 'The library of Johannes de Laet (1581–1649)', *Lias*, 25 (1998), 201–16 · K. Dekker, *The origins of Old Germanic studies in the Low Countries* (1999)
Archives Bibliothèque Nationale, Paris, corresp. · BL, corresp. and MSS · Bodl. Oxf., corresp. · University of Leiden, book collection · Utrecht University, corresp.
Likenesses J. Husnik, portrait, 1642 · J. van Bronckhorst, etching (after J. Husnik)
Wealth at death considerable: Bremmer, 'Correspondence'

Lafayette, James. *See* Lauder, James Stack (1853–1923).

Laffan, Sir Joseph de Courcy, baronet (**1786–1848**), physician, third son of Walter Laffan of Cashel, Ireland, and Eleonora, daughter and coheir of Richard de Courcy, a distant relative of the family of Kinsale, was born at Cashel on 8 May 1786. His eldest brother was Robert Laffan (*d.* 1833), Roman Catholic archbishop of Cashel, and Laffan himself was originally destined for the Roman Catholic priesthood, and studied at Maynooth College. He then proceeded to Edinburgh University and turned his attention to medicine. He graduated MD on 24 June 1808, and became a licentiate of the Royal College of Physicians in London on 22 December 1808. From then until 1812, he practised in London, in Orchard Street, Portman Square.

In October 1809 Laffan offered his services to the government on behalf of the fever-stricken troops lately returned from the Walcheren expedition. These were accepted, and the aptitude which Laffan showed for military practice led to his appointment in 1811 as physician to the forces, and later as assistant inspector of hospitals. He served in Spain and Portugal during the latter part of the Peninsular War, and he was eventually made physician-in-ordinary to the duke of Kent. At the end of the war Laffan stayed in Paris, and practised there with brilliant success until the desire for a more peaceful life led him to Rochester in Kent. In 1815 he married Jemima (d. 1839), daughter of Paul Pilcher of Rochester, and widow of Michael Symes, formerly English envoy at Ava, in Burma.

Laffan's successful treatment of an illness of the duke of York, brother to George IV, led to his being created a baronet by patent dated 15 March 1828. He was gentleman of the bedchamber to the lord lieutenant of Ireland in 1829, and in 1836 he was also created a knight of the Royal Guelphic Order.

After the death of his wife Laffan settled in Otham, Kent, having retired because of ill health. He died at Vichy in France on 7 July 1848; as he left no children the baronetcy became extinct. His body was returned to Rochester and interred there in a family vault in St Margaret's Church, also in 1848. Laffan devoted the greater part of his wealth to found a cancer ward for women in the Middlesex Hospital.

THOMAS SECCOMBE, *rev.* CLAIRE E. J. HERRICK

Sources *GM*, 2nd ser., 30 (1848), 318 · A. Peterkin and W. Johnston, *Commissioned officers in the medical services of the British army, 1660–1960*, 1 (1968), 221 · Munk, *Roll* · *BMJ* (9 Aug 1848), 448 · *The Lancet* (12 Aug 1848), 196 · *The pantheon of the age, or, Memoirs of 3000 contemporary public characters, British and foreign*, 2nd edn, 2 (1825), 521 · private information (1892)
Likenesses portrait, Middlesex Hospital, London

Laffan, Sir Robert Michael (1819–1882), army officer, third son of John Laffan of Skehana, cos. Clare and Limerick, was born on 14 August 1819. Educated at the college of Pontlevoy, near Blois, France, he went to the Royal Military Academy, Woolwich, in September 1835, and on 5 May 1837 was commissioned second lieutenant in the Royal Engineers.

After two years at Chatham and Woolwich, and becoming first lieutenant on 1 April 1839, Laffan was sent to south Africa and employed in frontier service. He was one of the officers summoned by the governor, Sir George Napier, to plan the relief of Colonel Smith and the garrison of Natal, then beleaguered by Boers under Pretorius. Laffan organized the engineering arrangements of the expedition under Sir Josiah Cloete, which relieved the British garrison.

From the Cape, Laffan was sent to Mauritius, where he was promoted captain on 1 May 1846. On his return home in 1847 he was appointed commanding royal engineer at Belfast, and at the close of the year was nominated an inspector of railways under the Board of Trade, an office he held until 1852. On 29 April 1852 he married Emma, daughter of W. Norsworthy. They had one daughter and four sons, and she survived him.

In July 1852 Laffan was elected Conservative MP for St Ives. He retained the seat until March 1857. In the autumn of 1852 he was sent to Paris and Antwerp to report on their defences for Sir John Burgoyne, inspector-general of fortifications. In 1854 he was appointed commanding royal

engineer in the London district, and in 1855 he was sent by the duke of Newcastle, secretary of state for war, with two others to report on the organization of the French ministry of war. On his return to England in May 1855 Laffan was appointed deputy inspector-general of fortifications. He was promoted major on 26 October 1858 and lieutenant-colonel on 28 November 1859.

From 1858 to 1860 Laffan was on sick leave in the south of France and Switzerland. On his return he was stationed at Portsmouth for a short time, but in late 1860 he was sent to Malta as commanding royal engineer. He remained there for five years, during which the armament of the defences was modernized. He was promoted brevet colonel on 28 November 1864.

In 1865 Laffan was sent to Ceylon as a member of a commission on its defence and also reported to the secretary of state for war on the Suez Canal. In 1866 he was appointed commanding royal engineer at Aldershot, where he devised manoeuvres and transformed the appearance of the camp by planting trees and grass: the former Queen's Birthday Parade was later renamed Laffan's Plain in his memory. In January 1872 he was sent to Gibraltar as commanding royal engineer, and remained there five years.

On 27 April 1877 Laffan was appointed governor of the Bermudas, arriving on 7 August. On 30 May the same year he was made a KCMG, and on 2 October 1877 was promoted major-general (antedated to 8 February 1870). He was promoted lieutenant-general on 1 July 1881.

Laffan's ability made him a popular and successful governor of the Bermudas at a critical time in the political history of the colony. He restored relations with the assembly, reformed local government, and reorganized the colony's defences amid rumours of impending Fenian attack. Laffan died in Bermuda, at Mount Langton, on 22 March 1882. He was buried at St John's Church, Pembroke, Bermuda, two days later.   R. H. VETCH, *rev.* ALEX MAY

Sources *Army List* · *Hart's Army List* · J. Foster, *The peerage, baronetage, and knightage of the British empire for 1882*, 2 vols. [1882] · *Parliamentary Pocket Companion* (1853–7) · *Bermuda Royal Gazette* (28 March 1882) · C. M. Watson, *History of the corps of royal engineers*, 3 (1915); repr. (1951) · H. C. Wilkinson, *Bermuda from sail to steam*, 2 (1973) · *CGPLA Eng. & Wales* (1882)
Likenesses Grillet & Co., carte-de-visite, 1869, NPG · portrait, repro. in *The Graphic*, 25 (1882), 528
Wealth at death £12,598 15s. 9d.: probate, 1 Aug 1882, *CGPLA Eng. & Wales*

La Fléchère, Jean Guillaume de. *See* Fletcher, John William (bap. 1729, d. 1785).

Lafont, Eugene (1837–1908), teacher of science in Bengal, was born on 26 March 1837 at Mons, Belgium, the son of Pierre Lafont, an army officer, and his wife, Mari Soudar. Educated at St Barbara's College, Ghent, he joined the Society of Jesus in December 1854. After preliminary training offered by the order he studied philosophy and natural science at Namur College. Henry Depelchin, the minister of Namur College, later founded St Xavier's College in Calcutta, from where, in 1865, he requisitioned the service of the young and talented Lafont. In 1867 Lafont was promoted from the school department to take charge of the natural philosophy department. Gradually he equipped the college with a fine meteorological observatory and a physical laboratory. As a teacher he was peerless.

Lafont did not confine himself to the classroom teaching in which he excelled. His meteorological prediction and observation of a terrible cyclone which struck Calcutta in November 1867 made his name well known among its citizens. For the next forty years he popularized science through illustrated lectures and demonstrations at numerous academic and literary venues there. Among the many contemporary topics covered by him were: spectrum analysis (1872), the barometrograph (1885), balloons (1886), laws of vibration of strings (1886), Edison's phonograph (with a live demonstration, 1886), measurement of velocity of light (1886), Röntgen rays (1896), telegraphy without wires (1897), colour photography (1898), and radioactivity (1907). When Mahendralal Sircar founded the Indian Association of Cultivation of Science in 1876 without any government assistance, Lafont supported him against heavy odds. Lafont gave weekly honorary lectures at the association for several years and also served as its senior vice-president. Lafont was ordained priest by Archbishop Steins in the church of Sacred Heart, Calcutta, in 1870. He was rector of St Xavier's College from 1871 to 1878 and again from 1901 to 1904. Apart from teaching physics he regularly delivered religious instruction in the college, defending Catholic tenets. He saw no contradiction between science and faith.

In recognition of his educational work the British government in India made Lafont a CIE in January 1880; in 1898 the king of Belgium made him a knight of the order of Leopold. From 1877 he served the University of Calcutta in various capacities—as a fellow, a senator, a member of syndicate, and dean—and he was made an honorary DSc in 1908. He was for many years an associate member of the Asiatic Society and he was a foreign member of the Institution of Electrical Engineers.

In early 1908 ill health and medical advice forced Lafont to retire to North Point College (later St Joseph's College), Darjeeling. On Good Friday (24 April) Lafont preached from the college pulpit. The next day he treated the students to a gramophone entertainment in the college hall but it had to be curtailed as he fell sick. On 26 April he was moved to the nearby Eden Sanatorium where he died on 10 May. He was buried in the North Point cemetery, Darjeeling, on the same day.   DEEPAK KUMAR

Sources Catholic Herald of India (13 May 1908), 305 · Nature, 78 (1908), 35 · A. K. Biswar, Karigar O Bijnani Coritmala Father Lafont [forthcoming] · S. Ghosh, Kaler Shahar Kolkata (1991)

LaFontaine, Sir Louis-Hippolyte, first baronet (1807–1864), politician in Canada, born at Boucherville, in the county of Chambly, Lower Canada, on 4 October 1807, was the third son of Antoine Ménard, called LaFontaine (1772–1814), a carpenter, and his wife, Marie-Josephte Fontaine, called Bienvenue, and the grandson of Antoine Ménard Lafontaine, a member of the legislative assembly of Lower Canada. He was educated at Montreal, and in 1825 proceeded to study law by entering the office of François Roy.

His political reputation was considerable while he was yet a clerk, and after his call to the bar in 1828 he quickly acquired a large practice among French Canadians. On 9 July 1831 he married Adèle (d. 1859), the daughter of Amable Berthelot. He was returned to the legislative assembly of Lower Canada at the general election of 1830 for the county of Terrebonne, for which he continued to sit until 1837. He was at first a follower of Louis-Joseph Papineau, whom he vigorously urged on in his resistance to the British government. But as the parti patriote became more intransigent he began to seek compromise. At the outbreak of rebellion in 1837, he travelled to Westminster to plead unsuccessfully for constitutional reform. On the outbreak of a second rebellion in November 1838 he was imprisoned, but released without trial. He then became the leader of the French-Canadian moderate reformers.

Although LaFontaine considered it fundamentally unjust, he did not oppose the union of Upper and Lower Canada in 1840. On 21 September 1841, after contesting Terrebonne unsuccessfully, he was returned to the parliament of the united provinces for the fourth riding of York, a county in Upper Canada, chiefly through the influence of Robert Baldwin. He was at once recognized as the leader of the French Canadians in the new assembly. In September 1842, on the urging of the governor-general, Sir Charles Bagot, he formed the LaFontaine–Baldwin administration, in which he held the portfolio of attorney-general for the lower province. During his term of office he obtained a cessation of proceedings against the rebels of 1837, including Papineau. The ministry resigned on 28 November 1843 in consequence of a difference with Bagot's successor, Sir Charles Theophilus Metcalfe (afterwards Baron Metcalfe), with regard to the control of the nomination of government officials. In November 1844 LaFontaine was again returned for Terrebonne, which he represented during the whole period of his opposition. In March 1848, after a stormy election in which several people were killed, he was returned for the city of Montreal, which he represented during the remainder of his public life.

In March 1848 the Reform Party triumphed at the general election, and LaFontaine was commissioned by the governor-general, Lord Elgin, to form a ministry based on the principle of responsible government. He thus became the first prime minister of Canada in the modern sense of the term. During this, his second, administration, he demonstrated the achievement of responsible government by the passage of the Rebellion Losses Bill, despite fierce opposition and violent demonstrations. His ministry also passed an Amnesty Act to forgive the 1837–8 rebels, secularized King's College into the University of Toronto, incorporated many French-Canadian colleges, established Laval University, adopted important railway legislation, and reformed municipal and judicial institutions. LaFontaine retired from political life towards the close of 1851, and was created a baronet on 28 August 1854.

His first wife having died in 1859, on 30 January 1861 LaFontaine married Julie-Elizabeth-Geneviève (Jane;

1822–1905), the widow of Thomas Kinton, a merchant of Montreal. They had one surviving son, Louis-Hippolyte, on whose death, in 1867, the baronetcy became extinct. On 13 August 1853 LaFontaine was nominated chief justice of Lower Canada, and continued to hold the office until his death, at his home in Montreal, on 26 February 1864, following an apoplectic fit the previous day. He was buried on 29 February in the Côte-des-Neiges cemetery, Montreal.   JACQUES MONET

Sources J. Monet, 'La Fontaine, Sir Louis-Hippolyte', *DCB*, vol. 9 · J. Monet, *The last cannon shot* (1969) · J. Monet, 'Les idées politiques de Baldwin et de LaFontaine', *Les idées politiques des premiers ministres du Canada*, ed. M. Hamelin (Ottawa, 1968), 11–30 · J. M. S. Careless, *The union of the Canadas: the growth of Canadian institutions, 1841–1857* (1967) · L. P. Cormier, *Lettres à Pierre Margry* (1968) · W. G. Ormsby, *The emergence of the federal concept in Canada* [1969]
Archives Archives Nationales du Québec | NA Canada, Bagot MSS, Colonial Office dispatches · NA Canada, Hincks MSS, Colonial Office dispatches · NA Canada, Metcalfe MSS, Colonial Office dispatches · NA Canada, Neilson MSS, Colonial Office dispatches · Robarts Library, Toronto, Baldwin MSS · U. Mich., Henry Vignaud MSS
Likenesses oils, Legislature of Ontario, Toronto, Canada · photographs, NA Canada · portraits, NA Canada · statue, Parliament Hill, Ottawa, Canada · statue, National Assembly, Quebec, Canada · statue, LaFontaine Park, Montreal, Canada

La Fontaine, Robert. *See* Le Maçon, Robert (1534/5–1611).

Laforey, Sir Francis, second baronet (1767–1835). *See under* Laforey, Sir John, first baronet (1729?–1796).

Laforey, Sir John, first baronet (1729?–1796), naval officer, was the second son of Lieutenant-Colonel John Laforey (d. 1753), governor of Pendennis Castle, and Mary Clayton, daughter of Lieutenant-General Jasper Clayton. He was descended from the French Huguenot family of La Forêt which settled in England during the 1690s. On 12 April 1748 he was promoted lieutenant, and on 24 May 1755 Commodore Augustus Keppel made him commander of the *Ontario*. In the *Hunter* he was with Admiral Edward Boscawen's fleet at Louisbourg in 1758. On 25 July he commanded a force of boats which burnt the *Prudent* and captured the *Bienfaisant* in Louisbourg harbour, and he was posted captain of the *Echo* by Boscawen on the following day. He took part in the conquest of Quebec in 1759 and then served in the West Indies, taking part in Admiral George Rodney's capture of Martinique in 1762. At Antigua in 1763 he married Eleanor, daughter of Colonel Francis Farley, member of the council and one of the judges of that island. Laforey commanded the *Pallas* for a short time in 1770. He commissioned the *Ocean* in September 1776 and in her took part in the battle of Ushant on 27 July 1778; at the subsequent court martial he gave evidence supporting Admiral Keppel.

In November 1779 Laforey was appointed naval commissioner on the Leeward Islands station, his principal duty being to speed up repairs and cleaning of warships at English Harbour dockyard, Antigua, where he was based. Because naval captains sometimes refused to obey Laforey, claiming he did not have a military commission and was merely a civilian in charge of the dockyard, Rodney reinforced his authority by making him a commodore in

August 1780. Unfortunately Laforey later fell out with Rodney over the purchase of naval stores captured at St Eustatius in 1781. Admiral Hugh Pigot replaced Rodney in 1782, but although he was also a supporter of Keppel, Laforey had disagreements with him about the purchase and commissioning of prizes. After the peace in 1783 Laforey returned to England and became naval commissioner at Plymouth Dockyard. He was still there when he was passed over in a promotion of flag officers on 24 September 1787. As in the disputes over his authority during the American War of Independence, it was alleged that his post was only a civil appointment. He challenged the decision and was eventually promoted rear-admiral on 10 November 1789, but with seniority to date from 24 September 1787. He was also created a baronet on 2 December 1789 and was appointed commander-in-chief on the Leeward Islands station.

Laforey was promoted vice-admiral on 1 February 1793; he was still in the West Indies when war broke out with France, and in April 1793 he captured Tobago. He returned to England in July, but was re-appointed to the Leeward Islands command in 1795, going out in the *Amiable*, commanded by his son, Francis Laforey [*see below*]. He became an admiral on 1 June 1795. During 1795–6 he helped suppress slave revolts on St Vincent, Grenada, and Dominica, while capturing the Dutch colonies of Demerara, Essequibo, and Berbice. In 1796 he handed over naval command to Sir Hugh Christian before the planned attack on St Lucia and sailed for England in the *Majestic*. He died at sea of yellow fever on 14 June 1796 and was buried in the governor's chapel at Portsmouth on 21 June. At the time of his death he owned a number of plantations in Antigua.

His only son, **Sir Francis Laforey** (1767–1835), was born in Virginia on 31 December 1767 and also joined the navy. He was promoted lieutenant on 26 August 1789, commander on 22 November 1790, and captain on 5 June 1793. He succeeded to the baronetcy in 1796, and commanded the *Spartiate* at the battle of Trafalgar in 1805. Laforey was promoted rear-admiral on 31 July 1810 and was commander-in-chief on the Leeward Islands station between 1811 and 1814. He was made KCB on 2 January 1815, and promoted vice-admiral on 12 August 1819 and admiral on 22 July 1830. He died, unmarried, on 17 June 1835 at Brighton and the baronetcy became extinct.

J. K. LAUGHTON, *rev.* ALAN G. JAMIESON

Sources *Letters and papers of Charles, Lord Barham*, ed. J. K. Laughton, 3 vols., Navy RS, 32, 38–9 (1907–11) · A. G. Jamieson, 'War in the Leeward Islands, 1775–1783', DPhil diss., U. Oxf., 1981 · GEC, *Baronetage* · M. Duffy, *Soldiers, sugar, and sea power: the British expeditions to the West Indies and the war against revolutionary France* (1987) · PRO, PROB 11/1277
Archives Berks. RO, corresp. and papers | NMM, letters to Sir Charles Middleton · PRO, ADM MSS

Laguerre, John (d. 1748). *See under* Laguerre, Louis (1663–1721).

Laguerre, Louis (1663–1721), painter, was born in France at Versailles, the son of the keeper of the royal menagerie there, a Catalan. Louis XIV is said to have been his god-father. Intending to join the priesthood, Laguerre was educated at the Jesuits' college in Paris, but his first career aim was thwarted by a speech impediment and, having a talent for drawing, he then studied at the Académie Royale de Peinture et de Sculpture. In 1682 he won third prize in the prix de Rome for a painting entitled *Cain batit la ville d'Hénoch*, and another third prize the following year, for his sculpture *Invention des forges ... par Tubal-Cain*. According to George Vertue he also spent a short time in the studio of Charles le Brun, and then, about 1684, moved to England, where he first worked as an assistant to the Italian decorative painter Antonio Verrio.

From about 1688 when he was employed at Thoresby, Nottinghamshire, Laguerre seems to have been working as a master decorator in his own right. His first major independent commission was for William Cavendish, first duke of Devonshire, at Chatsworth, Derbyshire, where between 1689 and 1697 he painted at least six interiors, including the hall and chapel, with mythological and religious subjects. Thereafter he was much in demand for decorative schemes in the baroque manner. He was employed by William III at Hampton Court Palace, where his work included a series of roundels illustrating the labours of Hercules on the exterior of Fountain Court. In 1698 he painted the ballroom at Burghley House, Cambridgeshire, with scenes from the story of Anthony and Cleopatra. Other documented commissions include several interiors at Canons, Middlesex, for James Brydges, first duke of Chandos, staircases at Buckingham House and Marlborough House, London, and at Petworth House, Sussex, and the saloon at Blenheim Palace, Oxfordshire. An early eighteenth-century painted scheme illustrating episodes from the *Aeneid*, uncovered in the staircase hall at Frogmore House, Berkshire, in 1984, has also been attributed to Laguerre.

Laguerre was a director of Sir Godfrey Kneller's Academy of Painting, founded in 1711. His chief rival after the death of Verrio in 1707 was a fellow director of the academy, James Thornhill. In 1715 Laguerre was awarded the commission to paint the interior of the dome of St Paul's Cathedral, but 'by some political contrivance' (Vertue, *Note books*, 2.125) he was replaced by Thornhill shortly after starting work. The following year Thornhill became governor of the academy, an appointment that Laguerre might have been expected to win. Although best-known as a decorative painter of interiors on a large scale, Laguerre also painted easel pictures, including portraits, and made designs for engravings and tapestry. His restoration of *The Triumph of Caesar* by Andrea Mantegna, at Hampton Court Palace, was praised by his contemporaries.

In interiors Laguerre normally painted in oil on plaster, a technique commonly used by decorative painters in England from the mid-seventeenth century, in an attempt to prevent damage caused by damp. Typically the overall format for Laguerre's interior decorative schemes takes the form of mythological scenes set in fictive 'pavilions' on side walls, with columns framing the figures, and ceilings, crowded with more figures, illusionistically treated so as to appear to be open to the sky. In this Laguerre's work is similar to that of Verrio, but his manner is more sedate, and his use of colour generally more sober. Alexander Pope's reference to

> painted Ceilings …
> Where sprawl the Saints of *Verrio* or *Laguerre*
> (*Epistle to the Right Honourable Richard, Earl of Burlington*, 1731)

memorably both links the two painters, and was written when their critical fortunes were beginning to decline. The reputations of both artists, perhaps unreasonably high in their lifetimes, have since sunk very low, probably equally unjustly, since much of their work in domestic interiors has been restored and overpainted, often many times, inhibiting assessment of its original quality.

Laguerre was first married to Eleanor, daughter of Jean Tijou, the ironworker. His second wife, Sarah, survived him. His two sons **John Laguerre** (d. 1748) and Louis (*bap.* 5 Jan 1717) were also painters, though John, the elder, became better known as an actor. He also painted scenery for the theatre and made a series of drawings, *Hob in the Well*, engraved by Charles Dubose, which were popular. His portrait of the impostor Mary Tofts was engraved by John Faber. He died in impoverished circumstances in March 1748. Louis Laguerre also had two daughters, Sarah (*bap.* 26 April 1719) and Anne (*bap.* 28 Aug 1720), who, like their brother Louis, were baptized at St Martin-in-the-Fields, Westminster, where their mother's name was recorded as Sarah. He died suddenly of apoplexy on 20 April 1721, at Lincoln's Inn Theatre, London, where his son John was performing in *The Island Princess*. He was buried in the churchyard of St Martin-in-the-Fields.

NICOLA SMITH

Sources E. Croft-Murray, *Decorative painting in England, 1537–1837*, 1 (1962) • Vertue, *Note books*, vol. 2, pp. 124–6 • *DNB* • N. Smith, 'Laguerre, Louis', *The dictionary of art*, ed. J. Turner (1996) • N. Smith, 'Frogmore House before James Wyatt', *Antiquaries Journal*, 65 (1985), 411–17 • will, PRO, PROB 11/693, sig. 266
Archives W. Yorks. AS, Leeds, Yorkshire Archaeological Society, agreement with duke of Leeds for decorations at Kiveton
Likenesses A. Bannerman, line engraving, NPG; repro. in H. Walpole, *Anecdotes of painting in England* (1762)

Laidlaw [*married name* Thomson], **Anna Robena Keddy** (1819–1901), pianist, was born on 30 April 1819 at Bretton, Yorkshire, the daughter of Alexander Laidlaw, a merchant, and his Irish wife, Ann Keddy. Her father came from an old landowning family in southern Scotland who were close friends of Sir Walter Scott. In 1827 she went to Edinburgh, where she learned the piano with Robert Müller. She moved with her family to Königsberg in 1830, and studied with Georg Tag and Louis Berger, but by 1834 was in London, taking lessons from Henri Herz.

In 1834 Laidlaw played at William IV's court and at Paganini's farewell concert. After returning to the continent in 1836, she gave successful piano recitals in Berlin and performed in Warsaw, St Petersburg, Dresden, and Vienna. While in Leipzig in 1837 she met and became a close friend of Schumann. Following her performance at one of the Gewandhaus concerts in July of that year he wrote of her playing as 'thoroughly good and individual. This artiste, in whose culture are united English solidity and natural amiability, will remain a treasured memory to all who have made her closer acquaintance' (*Neue Zeitschrift für Musik*, 11 July 1837). Schumann also dedicated his *Fantasiestücke*, op. 12, written in September 1837, to her, and at his suggestion she changed the original order of her names from Robena Anna to Anna Robena.

Anna Laidlaw was appointed court pianist to the queen of Hanover, and remained in Germany until 1840, when she settled in London. From 1842 until 1845 she toured northern Europe, and on her return to London she invited her parents to join her. She supported them until her marriage to George Thomson, a Scot, manager of an insurance office, on 27 October 1852. She then retired from public life, and devoted herself to the upbringing of their four daughters. She died at 12 Colville Square, London, on 29 May 1901, and, after cremation, her remains were buried at Woking.   J. C. HADDEN, *rev.* ANNE PIMLOTT BAKER

Sources A. W. Patterson, *Schumann* (1903), 105–17 · Grove, *Dict. mus.* · private information (1912) · m. cert. · d. cert.

Laidlaw, John (1832–1906), United Free Church of Scotland minister and theologian, born at Edinburgh on 7 April 1832, was the only child of Walter Laidlaw and his wife, Margaret Brydon. He was brought up in a strict and traditional family: his ancestors for generations had been sheep farmers, and his parents were members of the strongly Calvinistic Reformed Presbyterian church. Laidlaw was educated at elementary schools in Leith and Edinburgh, before studying at the normal school of Edinburgh. He intended to teach, but ultimately decided to prepare for the ministry. At Edinburgh University, where he matriculated in October 1851, he distinguished himself in classics, mathematics, and philosophy, winning four gold medals and several university prizes. In 1854 he was made MA *honoris causa*.

After spending three sessions in the Divinity Hall of the Reformed Presbyterian church, Laidlaw joined the Free Church of Scotland in 1856 and studied for two sessions (1856–8) at New College, Edinburgh. During the summer of 1858 he attended classes at Heidelberg and other German universities. After assisting at a church in Edinburgh, he began his ministry at Bannockburn in 1859. Here he passed three years of 'peaceful happiness' (Mackintosh, 7). On 6 August 1863 he was inducted to the Free West Church, Perth. Here the membership greatly increased during his ministry and a new church was opened in 1871, in Tay Street. In December 1869, he married Elizabeth, daughter of Samuel Hamilton and sister of his college friend, James Hamilton.

At Perth, Laidlaw built up a reputation as a popular preacher. His sermons, which always focused on the great texts of the Bible and the key doctrines of the Christian faith, were extremely well arranged and free of digressions: attuning his addresses to the average intelligence, Laidlaw spoke with a 'fine simplicity', and dwelt firmly 'not [on] the soul in its ups and downs, but Christ in His unchanging glory' (Mackintosh, 24, 40). His devotion to straightforward preaching of great themes was ironically revealed in his later critique of a rambling and pompous sermon submitted to him by a student: he commented that it 'reminds me of nothing so much as a long and stately avenue, with an extremely small cottage at the end of it' (Mackintosh, 40). Laidlaw's stature in the pulpit soon won him recognition: in 1868 he received, but declined, an invitation to become the colleague of Robert Smith Candlish at Free St George's, Edinburgh, one of the leading churches in his denomination. In 1872 he accepted an invitation to become minister of the Free West Church, Aberdeen.

In 1878 Laidlaw delivered the Cunningham lectures, taking as his theme 'The biblical doctrine of man'; the lectures were published in 1879, and recast in a new edition in 1895. This significant work, which was well regarded in both the Free Church and the (remanent) Reformed Presbyterian church, exhibited the conservatism of Laidlaw's theology, which rested on the works of Reformation theologians, and adhered to the Westminster confession of faith. Laidlaw, although unsympathetic to modern biblical scholarship, was not harsh to its disciples: he was willing to discuss higher criticism in private, and in 1880, in the general assembly, he supported an unsuccessful resolution to confine the assembly's censure of William Robertson Smith to a general admonition of caution in his public statements on the theological questions in dispute.

Promotion followed Laidlaw's Cunningham lectures: in 1880 he was made an honorary DD of the University of Edinburgh, and on 25 May 1881 he was appointed to the chair of systematic theology at New College, Edinburgh, which he held until 1904. He was a conscientious teacher, although his pedagogic methods were generally uninspired. He published several other works of theology during these years, including his most popular book, *The Miracles of Our Lord* (1890), which also originated in a course of lectures, and *Foundation Truths of Scripture as to Sin and Salvation* (1897). His *Studies in the Parables, and other Sermons* appeared posthumously in 1907.

Laidlaw was an ardent advocate of the reunion of Scottish Presbyterianism, it was largely owing to his influence that the union of the Reformed Presbyterian church with the Free Church of Scotland was brought about in 1876. Nine years later, in 1885, he was active in persuading representatives of the three large Presbyterian churches to debate the possibility of union. This unsuccessful conference bore some fruit in the 1900 union of the United Presbyterian and Free churches to form the United Free Church of Scotland. Laidlaw on several occasions attended and addressed the Keswick Convention, thus manifesting further his commitment to conservative evangelicalism. A cultured man, Laidlaw particularly enjoyed the poetry of Browning and tours of Germany, during one of which he traced the footsteps of Luther. After some years of ill health, he died at Edinburgh on 21 September 1906, and was buried in the Grange cemetery there. His wife survived him with one daughter.

W. F. GRAY, *rev.* ROSEMARY MITCHELL

Sources H. R. Mackintosh, 'Introductory memoir', in J. Laidlaw, *Studies in the parables, and other sermons* (1907) · *The Scotsman* (22 Sept 1906) · *DSCHT* · private information (1912) · *CCI* (1906)
Likenesses Horsburgh & Co., photograph, *c.*1890–1899, repro. in Laidlaw, *Studies*, frontispiece
Wealth at death £1173 18*s.* 4*d.*: confirmation, 26 Nov 1906, *CCI*

Laidlaw, Sir Patrick Playfair (1881–1940), medical scientist, was born at Glasgow on 26 September 1881, the third of the six sons of Robert Laidlaw MD and his wife, Elizabeth Playfair. At the time of Laidlaw's birth, his father was superintendent of the Glasgow Medical Mission; later he was a magistrate and medical officer in the Seychelles. Laidlaw's mother was a member of a family which produced several eminent men of science and medicine; among these were Lyon Playfair, first Baron Playfair, and his brother W. S. Playfair, well known as a specialist in obstetrics and gynaecology. Laidlaw himself never married.

Sir Patrick Playfair Laidlaw (1881–1940), by Walter Stoneman, 1936

Having suffered an attack of infantile paralysis which permanently weakened his health, Laidlaw first attended a private Quaker school in north London; from there he went to the Leys School, Cambridge, where he met Henry Dale, and in 1900 he began his medical studies as a scholar at St John's College, Cambridge. In October 1904 he won a scholarship to Guy's Hospital, London, where he completed his medical course and then became a demonstrator in physiology in the medical school. In 1909 he joined Dale, then the director of the Wellcome Physiological Research Laboratories at Herne Hill. George Barger's work there on the biologically active constituents of ergot had raised several interesting questions, and Laidlaw joined in various physiological and pharmacological researches. With Arthur James Ewins he investigated the metabolism of tyramine in the body and showed that the liver was the main site of its destruction, it being both deaminized and oxidized to phenol acetic acid. Also in association with Ewins he found a method of producing indolethylamine by synthesis and studied its metabolic breakdown. In collaboration with Dale he elaborated the powerful physiological actions of histamine, recently discovered in ergot, and suggested that it might have a role in pathological syndromes, as was confirmed later.

In 1913 Laidlaw was appointed to the Sir William Dunn lecturership in pathology at Guy's Hospital. Since most of his interest up to this point had been in pharmacology and physiology, he decided to spend some months in Vienna and Freiburg, studying new developments in research and teaching on pathology before taking up this appointment. However, the outbreak of war in 1914 found Laidlaw with a large hospital department to run but little opportunity for research. He was fully occupied in teaching and organizing the examination of post-mortem material at Guy's Hospital. Even these arduous duties could not suppress Laidlaw's ingenuity, and in 1915 he first described a technique that used hydrogen and spongy platinum to remove the last traces of oxygen from a bacteriological culture tube and its medium, thus greatly improving conditions for growing anaerobic bacteria. The method was further developed by Paul Fildes and James McIntosh and passed into routine use. Also during the war Laidlaw collaborated again with Henry Dale and with A. N. Richards, of Philadelphia, on the subject of histamine shock and its physiological relations. This work was widely acclaimed at the time, not only because of its intrinsic merit but also because it was thought to explain traumatic shock, a condition of the utmost importance during the war. While the investigation undoubtedly led to a great improvement in the treatment of wounded persons by transfusion of blood and other fluids, it later became clear that the release of histamine from the injured tissue is not the cause of wound shock.

Laidlaw's work at Guy's Hospital ended in 1922 when he joined the staff of the Medical Research Council at the National Institute for Medical Research, where he again came into contact with Dale. From then onwards Laidlaw concentrated almost entirely on bacteriological and virus research. One of the diseases first investigated was dog distemper, of great practical importance to all those who kept dogs; a considerable proportion of the necessary funding was raised by *The Field* magazine. With the collaboration of George William Dunkin MRCVS, Laidlaw found a means of transmitting the disease to ferrets, thus greatly widening the scope of the study, and before long conclusive evidence was obtained in support of earlier claims by Henri Carré that the primary infective agent responsible for true dog distemper is a filterable virus. Two methods of inducing immunity to this disease in dogs were then developed. By the first method partial immunity was obtained by injection of the virus inactivated by treatment with formaldehyde, followed by a small injection of the active virus; this caused an abortive attack and left the animal with a strong and lasting immunity. By the second method the animal received simultaneous injections of the active virus and a serum rich in the protective antibodies. Again, permanent immunity was established.

Experience gained in this work laid the foundation for Laidlaw's research on epidemic influenza. In collaboration with Christopher Howard Andrewes and Wilson Smith, he showed that the ferret was also susceptible to influenza virus, as obtained from the human patient. By accident one of the research team became infected with influenza from one of the ferrets, thus completing the evidence that the infective agent was transmissible in both directions. At a later stage the technique was modified and extended to mice. On the basis of this work Laidlaw and his colleagues proved that the infective agent of human epidemic influenza is a virus, a discovery which has been confirmed all over the world. The influenza work was not brought to the same satisfactory conclusion as the canine distemper research, partly because it was discovered that epidemics in different parts of the world are caused by different viruses and partly because such epidemics are so unpredictable that large numbers of people have to be inoculated in preparation for an outbreak which may or may not occur. However, experience did go on to indicate that some immunity can be built up by influenza virus vaccine.

Laidlaw was interested in many other branches of medical science: with Harold Dudley he examined the biochemistry of the tubercle bacillus; and with Clifford Dobell he investigated the cultivation of dysentery and other parasitic amoebae. The first part of this latter investigation was the development of a new method for growing amoebae in the laboratory, using grains of rice starch as the supply of carbohydrate in the nutrient medium used for growing the organisms. Having obtained rapidly growing cultures by this method, Dobell and Laidlaw then studied the action of the alkaloids of ipecacuanha on such cultures, thus making an important contribution to knowledge of the treatment of amoebic dysentery with this drug.

Laidlaw was elected FRS in 1927 and received a royal medal from the society in 1933 for his work on distemper in dogs; he was knighted in 1935 for his contributions to medicine. He gave the Linacre lecture, 'Epidemic influenza: a virus disease', in 1935, and the Rede lecture, 'Virus disease and viruses', at Cambridge, in 1938.

Laidlaw had a modest and retiring nature and disliked publicity. One of his chief characteristics was his ability and willingness to advise and assist in research work those who consulted him on almost any problem. In 1936 he succeeded Stewart Ranken Douglas as head of the department of pathology and bacteriology and as deputy director of the National Institute for Medical Research, of which Dale was director. Shortly afterwards his health, never robust, began to fail, and he was found dead at his home, 31 Wentworth Road, Golders Green, Middlesex, on 20 March 1940, after heart failure during the previous night. It happened a day or two after his election to an honorary fellowship at St John's College, Cambridge.

E. MELLANBY, rev. E. M. TANSEY

Sources H. H. Dale, Obits. FRS, 3 (1939–41), 427–47 · BMJ (30 March 1940), 551 · The Lancet (30 March 1940) · The Times (23 March 1940) · E. M. Tansey, 'Protection against dog distemper and dogs protection bills: the Medical Research Council and anti-vivisectionist protest, 1911–1933', Medical History, 38 (1994), 1–26 · C. Andrewes, The common cold (1965) · H. C. Cameron, Mr Guy's Hospital, 1726–1948 (1954) · personal knowledge (1949) · CGPLA Eng. & Wales (1940)
Archives Medical Research Council, London · National Institute for Medical Research, London | RS, Dale MSS
Likenesses photograph, 1927, RS · W. Stoneman, photograph, 1936, NPG [see illus.] · photograph, Wellcome L. · photographs, National Institute for Medical Research, London · portrait, repro. in Dale, Obits. FRS · portrait, repro. in BMJ · portrait, repro. in The Lancet
Wealth at death £44,278 18s. 6d.: probate, 12 July 1940, CGPLA Eng. & Wales

Laidlaw, William (bap. 1779, d. 1845), friend of Sir Walter Scott and James Hogg, was born at Blackhouse farm in Yarrow, Selkirkshire, and baptized on 28 November 1779, the eldest of three sons of James Laidlaw, tenant of Blackhouse farm, and his wife, Catherine Ballantyne. After receiving a basic education at Peebles grammar school, he assisted his father in sheep-farming. James Hogg, the Ettrick Shepherd, served his father as a shepherd for ten years, and formed a close and lifelong friendship with Laidlaw. According to Hogg's Memoir, 'he was the only person who, for many years, ever pretended to discover the least merit in my essays, either in verse or prose' (Hogg, Memoir, 12). An even more significant literary friendship was made in 1802, when he helped to procure materials for The Minstrelsy of the Scottish Border for Sir Walter Scott. About 1803 Laidlaw began farming for himself at Liberton near Edinburgh, and on 8 April 1810 married his cousin Janet Ballantyne (1786–1861), of Whitehope farm in Yarrow. Of the children of the marriage four daughters survived. Laidlaw contributed three songs anonymously to Hogg's The Forest Minstrel (1810), of which the best-known is 'Lucy's Flittin''. Subsequently he farmed at Traquair, near Peebles.

In 1817, his farming unsuccessful, Laidlaw found a congenial home and employment at Kaeside on the Abbotsford estate, acting as Scott's steward, valued companion, and literary assistant. When Scott was too ill to write, he dictated to Laidlaw the end of The Bride of Lammermoor (1819), most of A Legend of Montrose (1819), and part of Ivanhoe (1820). Lockhart claims in his life of Scott that the idea for Saint Ronan's Well (1824) arose from Laidlaw's suggestion that Scott should devote a novel to 'Melrose in July 1823' (Lockhart, 5.285). Scott's influence procured paid literary work for Laidlaw with periodicals like the Edinburgh Annual Register and Blackwood's Edinburgh Magazine. 'Sagacity of a Shepherd's Dog' (Blackwood, 2.417–21) is an interesting demonstration of the literary interaction between Laidlaw, Scott, and Hogg. During a visit to Abbotsford, Hogg wrote to William Blackwood on 5 January 1818, 'Along with Scott's and Laidlaw's contributions to your miscellany I also inclose my mite … Now that Laidlaw has

William Laidlaw (*bap.* 1779, *d.* 1845), by Sir William Allan

furnished one anecdote of the Shepherd's dog mine will follow better next month.' Scott and Laidlaw wrote 'Sagacity of a Shepherd's Dog' and Hogg, having read it, clearly tailored his own piece on the subject ('Further Anecdotes of the Shepherd's Dog') to suit with and refer to the earlier article. Scott's ruin in 1826 ended Laidlaw's life at Kaeside temporarily, but he was able to return in 1830.

After Scott's death in 1832, Laidlaw became a factor in Ross-shire, first to Mrs Stewart Mackenzie of Seaforth, then to Sir Charles Lockhart Ross of Balnagowan. Retiring in feeble health, he died in the house of his brother James at Contin, near Dingwall, Ross-shire, on 18 May 1845, and was buried in Contin churchyard.

T. W. BAYNE, *rev.* GILLIAN HUGHES

Sources bap. reg. Scot. [Yarrow] · family papers, NL Scot., Laidlaw MS Acc. 9084, nos. 8, 9; letters to Hogg, Laidlaw MS 2245, esp. fols. 232–3, 256 · J. G. Lockhart, *Memoirs of the life of Sir Walter Scott*, 7 vols. (1837–8) · *The letters of Sir Walter Scott*, ed. H. J. C. Grierson and others, centenary edn, 12 vols. (1932–79) · J. C. Corson, *Notes and index to Sir Herbert Grierson's edition of the letters of Sir Walter Scott* (1979) · J. Hogg, *Memoir of the author's life and Familiar anecdotes of Sir Walter Scott*, ed. D. S. Mack (1972) · 'Essay on the text', W. Scott, *The bride of Lammermoor*, ed. J. H. Alexander, Edinburgh edition of the Waverley Novels (1995); *A legend of the wars of Montrose*, ed. J. H. Alexander (1995); *Ivanhoe*, ed. G. Tulloch (1998); *Saint Ronan's well*, ed. M. Weinstein (1995) · *Blackwood*, 2 (1817–18), esp. 82–6, 417–21, 621–6 · R. Borland, *Yarrow: its poets and poetry* (1890) · C. Rogers, *The modern Scottish minstrel*, 2 (1856) · *GM*, 2nd ser., 24 (1845), 428–9 · J. Hogg, *The forest minstrel* (1810) · J. Hogg, letter to W. Laidlaw, LUL, [S. L.] V. 14

Archives NL Scot., corresp. and papers · NL Scot., family papers | U. Edin., Laing collection, Laidlaw's recollections of Scott
Likenesses W. Allan, chalk drawing, Scot. NPG [*see illus.*] · drawing, Scot. NPG

Laidler, (Gavin) Graham [*pseud.* Pont] (**1908–1940**), cartoonist, was born in Newcastle upon Tyne on 4 July 1908, the only son and younger child of George Gavin Laidler, owner of a painting and decorating business, and his wife, Kathleen, *née* Crosby. He was educated at Newcastle upon Tyne preparatory school and later at Trinity College, Glenalmond, Perthshire. His father died when he was thirteen and his family moved south, eventually settling in the village of Jordans, Buckinghamshire. He started drawing cartoons when still a schoolboy and was determined to earn his living in that way. But in 1926, as a result of family pressure, he enrolled at the London School of Architecture.

Laidler became seriously ill shortly after taking his first job in a surveyor's office. A tubercular kidney was diagnosed and he was advised to give up office work and to spend his winters abroad. He concentrated on drawing cartoons and in 1932 had his first acceptance from *Punch*, the beginning of a partnership which established him as a major comic artist and one of the most original talents in the long history of the magazine. His exceptional talent was eventually recognized by the editor, E. V. Knox, who placed him under an exclusive contract, an almost unprecedented arrangement. His cartoons, done under the name Pont, were in the *Punch* tradition of George Du Maurier and Frank Reynolds, poking fun at the middle classes. But his drawings were remarkable for their acuteness of observation and their complete lack of sentimentality, qualities which placed them in a different league. He excelled at grumpy antisocial males, harassed mothers, and their stony-faced domestic servants. His most successful series, called The British Character (later published as *The British Character Studied and Revealed*, 1938, with an introduction by E. M. Delafield), included a number of his most memorable drawings, with such titles as 'Weakness for Old Beams', 'Strong Tendency to Become Doggy', and 'Love of Travelling Alone' (a bowler-hatted man who has covered the seats of his railway compartment with his umbrella and briefcase).

Laidler, who became an associate of the Royal Institute of British Architects, came into his own at the outbreak of war in 1939. Another book, *The British Carry on* (1940), portrayed the atmosphere of the phoney war and the national response to the threat of invasion. Examples of this are his fierce-looking lady (to a heavily armed German soldier advancing over the lawn): 'How *dare* you come in here!'; or a placid scene in a country pub where the radio on the bar is tuned to the German propaganda station: 'Meanwhile, in Britain, the entire population, faced by the threat of an invasion has been flung into a state of complete panic.' These cartoons have frequently been used to illustrate the social history of that period.

Laidler was a tall, good-looking man, quiet and observant, who remained cheerful in spite of his illness. He was remembered with great affection by all who knew him in the course of his short life. He travelled widely, usually for reasons of health, which gave him an opportunity to observe the habits of British tourists. He died, unmarried, of polio on 23 November 1940 at the County Hospital, Hillingdon, near Uxbridge, Middlesex, at the age of thirty-two. During his brief career he had drawn over 400 cartoons, enough to furnish the material for five books, two of which were published posthumously.

RICHARD INGRAMS, *rev.*

Sources Pont [G. G. Laidler], *Pont* (1942) • Pont [G. G. Laidler], *The British character: studied and revealed* (1938); repr. (1982) • Pont [G. G. Laidler], *The world of Pont*, ed. R. Ingrams (1983) • A. B. Hollowood, *Pont* (1969) • *CGPLA Eng. & Wales* (1941) • *100 years of cartoons* (1999) [exhibition catalogue, Rae-Smith Gallery, London, 1999]
Wealth at death £3153 4s.: administration, 30 April 1941, *CGPLA Eng. & Wales*

Laing, Alexander (1778–1838), antiquary, the illegitimate son of an Aberdeen advocate named Michie, was born at Coull, Aberdeenshire. He was reasonably well educated and highly talented, but his career was hampered by an erratic temperament. For some years before his death he was employed as an itinerant bookseller and stationer, which earned him the nickname Stashie Laing. The first of Laing's antiquarian writings, *The Caledonian itinerary, or, A tour on the banks of the Dee, with historical notes from the best authorities*, was published at Aberdeen in 1819. During the next three years Laing edited an annual, the first two issues of which were entitled *The Eccentric Magazine*, and the third *The Lounger's Commonplace Book*; this was a collection of anecdotes and curiosities. In 1822 he published *Scarce Ancient Ballads Never before Published, with Notes*, and in the following year a similar collection, entitled *The Thistle of Scotland*. In 1828 he published his chief work, *The Donean Tourist, Interspersed with Anecdotes and Ancient National Ballads*, a useful collection of folklore.

Laing's last work was *An Cluaran Albannach: a repository of ballads, many never before published, to which are appended copious notes, historical, biographical, illustrative, and critical* (1834). Laing died at Boltingstone, a roadside inn between Tarland and Strathdon, and was buried in the churchyard of Coldstone, Aberdeenshire.

THOMAS SECCOMBE, rev. H. C. G. MATTHEW

Sources John Bullock, 'Notes', c.1892 • Irving, *Scots.* • S. Maunder, *The biographical treasury*, new edn, rev. W. L. R. Cates (1870) • *The poetry of Scottish rural life, or, A sketch of the life and writings of Alexander Laing* (1874)

Laing, Alexander [nicknamed the Brechin poet] (1787–1857), poet, was born on 14 May 1787 at Brechin, Forfarshire, the son of James Laing, an agricultural labourer. He spent only two years at school, and became a cowherd at the age of eight; he devoted much of his leisure time to reading and writing. At the age of sixteen he was apprenticed to a flax-dresser, and followed this occupation until he was permanently disabled by an accident fourteen years later. From this point on he earned a modest living as a pedlar.

Laing contributed verse to local newspapers and to several miscellanies, including R. A. Smith's *Scottish Minstrel* (1820) and *Whistle-Binkie* (1832–47). He also supplied anecdotes for *The Laird of Logan* (1835), and edited popular editions of the works of Burns and Robert Tannahill. A collection of his own verse, *Wayside Flowers*, appeared in 1846, and was followed by a second edition in 1850. Laing combined elements of pathos and humour in a vigorous lowland Scots. Known as the Brechin poet, he died at Brechin on 14 October 1857.

T. W. BAYNE, rev. DOUGLAS BROWN

Sources Boase, *Mod. Eng. biog.* • A. Jervise, *Epitaphs and inscriptions from burial grounds and old buildings in the north-east of Scotland*, 2 vols. (1875–9) • C. Rogers, *The modern Scottish minstrel, or, The songs of Scotland of the past half-century*, 6 vols. (1855–7) • J. G. Wilson, ed., *The poets and poetry of Scotland*, 2 (1877)
Archives NL Scot., letters and poems, MSS 3115, 7181, 20441 • Wordsworth Trust, Dove Cottage, Grasmere, account of his pilgrimage to the Lakes

Laing, Alexander Gordon (1794–1826), army officer and explorer in Africa, was born in Edinburgh on 27 December 1794, the eldest son of William Laing, a schoolmaster and the founder of a classical academy in Edinburgh, and his wife, Margaret, the daughter of William Gordon of Glasgow Academy. With teaching on both sides of his family, Laing seemed destined for a career of scholarship. He entered Edinburgh University at the age of thirteen, and, on graduating at seventeen, became a schoolmaster. But, having joined one of the local volunteer corps then being formed, he opted for a military life, was commissioned in 1810 ensign in the Prince of Wales's Edinburgh volunteers, and in 1811 went to Barbados, where his uncle was deputy quartermaster-general. In 1813 he was appointed ensign in the York light infantry, a corps which served in the West Indies, and in 1815 was promoted lieutenant. After the corps was disbanded at the peace, Laing exchanged into the 2nd West India regiment in Jamaica. He fell ill with a liver complaint, was sent to Honduras, and then returned home, where he was put on half pay in 1818. In 1820 he was brought back into the 2nd West India regiment and posted to Sierra Leone, where in 1822 he transferred, as captain, to the Royal African Colonial Corps.

Laing's posting to Africa awakened a long-desired dream of exploring the interior and finding the still uncharted Niger. Soon after his arrival he was sent by the governor, Sir Charles MacCarthy, on two successive missions to Forecariah in the coastal country (later Guinea) north of Sierra Leone, to mediate in a war between two rulers which was disrupting trade. While there, he found that one of them was receiving help from an army sent by the ruler of Solima Yalunka, an inland kingdom over a hundred miles from the coast, with its capital at Falaba, still unvisited from the colony. On his return, suspecting that it might open his way to the Niger, he offered to MacCarthy to visit Falaba to open up trade.

In 1822 Laing set out with a small escort up the Rokel River, through the mountainous Koranko country to Falaba, where he was well received by the ruler. He went on and found the source of the Rokel, but though he viewed the upland where the Niger rises he was not allowed to go on and had to return disappointed. He was, however, able to establish, by taking its height, that the Niger could not, as some still supposed, possibly flow into the Nile. His *Travels*, published in 1825, give a lively account of his adventures, including not only observations on the customs of the peoples he encountered, illustrated with his own rather amateurish drawings and a good map, but also an oral history of Solima Yalunka back

Alexander Gordon Laing (1794–1826), by Samuel Freeman

to the seventeenth century, useful to later historians. Laing was transferred to the Gold Coast in 1823 and edited the first newspaper to be published there. Then, stationed on the frontier, he participated in some skirmishes with the Asante army before the disastrous battle of Nsamanko, in which MacCarthy and almost all his men were killed. Now in poor health, he was sent home to report the news of the defeat to the colonial secretary, Lord Bathurst, with whom, to the annoyance of his senior officers, he ingratiated himself. In 1824 he was sent, with the local rank of major, on an official mission to seek the elusive Niger.

The Niger quest had now become a race. Hugh Clapperton, having returned from the expedition that he, Dixon Denham, and Walter Oudney had made southwards across the Sahara from Tripoli, was now convinced that the Niger flowed into the Atlantic and set out in 1825 for the Atlantic coast. Laing, instructed to go via Tripoli, proposed to travel south-eastwards across the Sahara to Ghadames, then to Timbuktu, still a name of glamour and mystery to Europeans, and thence to follow the Niger to its mouth. He arrived in Tripoli in May 1825, and was warmly welcomed by the British consul-general Hanmer Warrington, whose friendly relations with the ruling Turkish pasha, Yusuf Karamanlı, had made it possible for Denham's mission to travel safely across the desert. Laing, ignorant of the difficulties of Saharan travel, had budgeted for a sum far below that which Yusuf Karamanlı required, so he was delayed in Tripoli while Warrington wrote to London asking for more. Meanwhile Laing fell in

love with Warrington's daughter Emma (*d.* 1829), and, despite her father's dismay at this 'Wild, Enthusiastic and Romantic Attachment' (PRO, FO 76/19, 1725), they were married on 14 July 1825, four days before his departure for Timbuktu (her father prudently insisting that the marriage remain unconsummated).

Bathurst refused the requested subvention—and may thus be held indirectly responsible for Laing's eventual death. Denham's mission had been subsidized by a grant that guaranteed the protection of the two powerful rulers whose territories they crossed, Yusuf Karamanlı and Sultan Bello of Sokoto. Laing set out, on 18 July, without official protection, across a vast desert notoriously infested by Tuareg marauders. Sheikh Babani, a merchant long resident in Timbuktu, accompanied him as a guide. His party included two west African boat builders, to build a boat when they reached the Niger, Jacob Nahun, a Jewish interpreter, and his servant, Jack le Bore. Born in the Caribbean (San Domingo), le Bore had served all over Europe as a trumpeter in Napoleon's armies, then, at the peace, volunteered for the British army, and while stationed in Sierra Leone had accompanied Laing to Falaba.

Following a circuitous route across the desert, the party reached Ghadames, where they stayed six weeks (Laing sketched the Roman ruins), then moved westwards, making the detour to suit Babani's interests, to Ensala, where they were joined by a large trading caravan. Delayed by rumours of warfare between Tuareg and Arab clans, they eventually left on 9 January 1826. Sixteen days later they were attacked by Tuareg. Laing was fearfully wounded, with sabre cuts on his head, body, arms, and legs. Astonishingly he survived, tended by a kindly sheikh, Sidi Muhammad, who lived nearby. He set out again on 1 July, with one black servant, Bungola, his other companions, including Babani and the invaluable le Bore, being now dead.

On 13 August Laing reached Timbuktu, where he stayed for several weeks, researching into old manuscripts. But the city was now under the control of Ahmadu, the Fula ruler of Masina, who refused to let him go further. Nevertheless he again set out and (the full details are uncertain) was attacked and killed by a party who came out after him from Timbuktu on 24 September 1826. Bungola survived, and returned two years later to Tripoli with the news.

Overwrought at the death of his son-in-law, Warrington wildly accused the pasha of having conspired with the French consul, Baron Rousseau, to have Laing killed and his journals, which had not surfaced, spirited away to France. His accusations were taken seriously in London, gunboats were sent to Tripoli, and the British and French governments were involved in several years of acrimonious diplomatic correspondence. The story was even believed by some historians, including the author of Laing's entry in the *Dictionary of National Biography*. Laing himself was quietly forgotten. Not until 1931 did the Royal African Society have a memorial plaque put on the house where he stayed in Timbuktu. His surviving letters and papers, edited by E. W. Bovill, were finally published by the Hakluyt Society in 1964.   CHRISTOPHER FYFE

Sources E. W. Bovill, ed., *Missions to the Niger*, 1, Hakluyt Society, 2nd ser., 123 (1964) · A. G. Laing, *Travels* (1825) · T. Nelson, *A biographical memoir* (1830) · b. cert.
Archives RS, letters and papers | PRO, FO 76/26, 33 · PRO, CO 2/15, 16, 20 · PRO, CO 267/53, 58
Likenesses S. Freeman, stipple, NPG, Scot. NPG [*see illus.*] · portrait, priv. coll.; repro. in Chambers, *Scots.*, vol. 2

Laing, Andrew (1856–1931), marine engineer, was born in Edinburgh on 31 January 1856, the son of George Laing, a builder and contractor, and his wife, Janet Thomson. It was thought that he would enter his father's business, and he was educated with this in mind. After attending the Edinburgh normal school he went to James Baillie's private school in Morningside, where there was an emphasis on commercial education. Instead of entering the family firm he was apprenticed to Hogg and Walker, engineers and millwrights, in Edinburgh. In 1877 Laing entered the drawing office of the shipbuilders John Elder & Co. in Glasgow as an engineering draughtsman. During the early years he worked under Dr A. C. Kirk, the renowned developer of triple-expansion engines. His arrival coincided with the development of fast Atlantic liners, such as the Guion liner *Arizona*. Laing was promoted rapidly, becoming chief draughtsman in 1881, assistant manager in 1885, and engine-works manager in 1887. Finally, in 1890, he was appointed a director of what had now become the Fairfield Shipbuilding and Engineering Company. He was responsible for the engining of a number of Cunard liners, as well as warships, Castle liners, and Norddeutscher Lloyd vessels. Under him the engine and boiler works were redeveloped, and the company he served remained at the forefront of technical innovation.

It was therefore something of a surprise when Laing moved to Tyneside as the manager of the engine works of the Wallsend Slipway and Engineering Company in 1896. The move was apparently prompted by a dispute with his fellow directors over remuneration, a situation probably not helped by Laing's forceful manner, but for which he would probably have remained in Glasgow. Fairfield's loss was undoubtedly Wallsend's gain, as Laing's influence transformed a business hitherto devoted to the construction and repair of machinery for ordinary cargo vessels. Laing's first important design at Wallsend was the machinery for the Russian icebreaker *Ermak*, and in 1900 the company secured its first Admiralty contract. As the company history puts it:

> Andrew Laing was a man of outstanding energy and imagination, and his talents were exactly what the company needed at this period of rich possibilities in ship-propulsion technology. To his already considerable reputation, he was soon to add the title of the man who 'sold' the turbine engine to the sponsors of the *Mauretania*. (*Launching Ways*, 34)

The contract for the *Mauretania* was of such a scale that it precipitated a reorganization of the industry on Tyneside. The merged company of Swan, Hunter, and Wigham Richardson Ltd took a controlling interest in the Wallsend Slipway and Engineering Company, who built the quadruple-screw turbine propelling machinery for the giant liner. During the First World War the company engined sixty-eight vessels of all types, including the battleships *Queen Elizabeth* and *Malaya*. The need to improve engine performance led Laing to develop the Wallsend-Howden system of oil firing, which began manufacture in 1909. Sir Reginald Skelton recalled Laing's 'vigour and independence of thought and his accurate judgment ever inclining towards prudence and caution, but well tempered by an appreciation of the necessity for continuous progress' (Skelton, 48).

Laing, who had become a director at Wallsend in 1903, eventually became a director of Swan, Hunter as well as of the Newcastle and Gateshead Gas Company. He was appointed CBE in 1917 for his war work, and in 1930 the North-East Coast Institution of Engineers and Shipbuilders bestowed its highest distinction on him, an honorary fellowship. He was a member of the Institution of Civil Engineers, a vice-president of the Institution of Naval Architects, and a member of the Institution of Engineers and Shipbuilders in Scotland, the American Society of Naval Architects and Marine Engineers, and the American Society of Naval Engineers. He also served on a number of technical committees and research bodies. Although he was deeply interested in research, Laing's only publication was 'Fifty years of steamship machinery installations', which appeared in the *Marine Engineer* in June 1929.

A life of high achievement was lived with a narrow focus, for Laing was unmarried and had no interests outside marine engineering. At his death he and his close contemporary Sir Charles Parsons were considered to be on a par, 'as being the two greatest marine engineers in the world' (*Transactions of the North-East Coast Institution*, 432), since when he has been comparatively overlooked. In his lifetime he was reckoned to have supervised the construction of engines amounting to 5 million horsepower. During a business trip to London, Laing caught a chill that developed into pneumonia. He died at his home, 15 Osborne Road, Newcastle upon Tyne, on 24 January 1931 and was buried in Morningside cemetery, Edinburgh, on 29 January.   LIONEL ALEXANDER RITCHIE

Sources *The Times* (26 Jan 1931) · *Newcastle Journal* (26 Jan 1931) · *The Engineer* (30 Jan 1931) · *Engineering* (30 Jan 1931) · *Shipbuilding and Shipping Record*, 37 (29 Jan 1931) · *Transactions of the Institution of Naval Architects*, 73 (1931) · *Transactions of the North-East Coast Institution of Engineers and Shipbuilders*, 47 (1930–31) · R. W. Skelton, 'The work of Andrew Laing', *Transactions of the North-East Coast Institution of Engineers and Shipbuilders*, 49 (1932–3), 29–51 · W. Richardson, *History of the parish of Wallsend* (1923) · *Launching ways: published on the occasion of their jubilee*, Swan, Hunter, and Wigham Richardson Ltd (1953) · *WWW*, 1929–40 · private information (2004)
Archives Mitchell L., Glas., Glasgow City Archives, Upper Clyde Shipbuilders collection · Tyne and Wear Archives Service, Newcastle upon Tyne, Wallsend Slipway and Engineering Co. Ltd records
Likenesses photograph, repro. in *Transactions of the North-East Coast Institution of Engineers and Shipbuilders* · photograph, repro. in *Transactions of the Institution of Naval Architects* · photograph, repro. in *Shipbuilding and Shipping Record*
Wealth at death £298,799 15s. 3d.: confirmation, 17 April 1931, CCI · £1200: probate calendars, High Holborn

Laing, David (*bap.* **1775**, *d.* **1856**), architect, was born in London and baptized there on 9 March 1775 at St Dunstan-in-the-East, the son of David Laing, a cork-cutter of Tower Street, London, and his wife, Ann. He was articled to John Soane in 1790, and was still in Soane's office when he exhibited a design for a saloon at the Royal Academy in 1795. The following year he established himself in private practice. Laing's career began slowly but with promise; in 1800 he erected a villa for one Griffith Jones at Abbots Langley, Hertfordshire, and in 1803 he designed cottages at Easthampstead, Berkshire, for the marquess of Downshire. In 1800 he followed one of the time-honoured routes for aspirant architects by publishing a book of his designs: *Hints for Dwellings, Consisting of Original Designs for Cottages, Farm Houses, Villas, etc.* It was a popular work, reprinted in 1804, 1823, and 1841. He followed this in 1818 with *Plans etc. of Buildings, Public and Private, Executed in Various Parts of England, Including the Custom House*. Several of the designs were for specific patrons, such as the 'villa to be erected for a gentleman' at Ballmahon in co. Longford, illustrated in *Hints*, or the house 'erected' for General Sir J. Taylor at Castle Taylor, Ardrahan, Galway, in *Plans* (although Laing's role is unclear, and the house has been demolished).

In 1810 Laing was appointed surveyor to the customs. The expansion of Britain's trade, and consequently of the customs' business, promised to make this a valuable post. In the same year he began the new custom house in Plymouth, finished in 1811. It is a sober building of granite, five bays wide, the ground floor with rock-faced rustication, the upper floor with smooth ashlar masonry and five arched windows recessed in arched surrounds. Laing's design is distinguished and powerful, and betokened a brilliant career. In 1818–19 he also rebuilt the church of St Dunstan-in-the-East, drawings of which were exhibited at the Royal Academy, although his obituary suggested that most of the design work was done by William Tite, his then assistant; it was destroyed by bombing in 1941. Laing also built the corn exchange, High Street, Colchester (1825), a nine-bay building with an elegant colonnade of Greek Doric columns spanning the pavement in front.

In May 1812 came Laing's great opportunity, to rebuild the custom house on Thames Street in London, replacing Thomas Ripley's building of 1718. His original scheme, for a building on the north of Thames Street, approached by new docks on either side, was not accepted. Laing produced a simpler scheme for a massive rectangular block. The centre was of two storeys, with vaults for the 'king's warehouse' below and the great 'long room' above. To either side were great four-storey wings housing the offices. Laing's design for the façades was strong and innovative, and his long room, spanned with three shallow domes and clearly showing Soane's influence, would have been one of the finest neo-classical interiors in Britain. Laing's estimate was £209,000, plus £12,000 for piling and £7000 for contingencies; the contractors, Miles and Peto, won the job with a tender of £165,000.

The building of the custom house proved, however, to be one of the major architectural scandals of the nineteenth century, and the ruin of Laing's career. The problems centred on the failure of Laing's piled foundations, and his failure to supervise the contractors properly. Construction was dogged by delays and disputes between Laing and Miles and Peto. By late 1817 work was nearing completion, and the cost had soared above the estimates. A detailed series of reports by the office of works uncovered glaring discrepancies between what Laing had specified and the work executed, and he was suspected of fraudulent collusion with the contractors. This was never proved, but in 1821 Laing's conduct was widely believed to be in the highest degree improper and reprehensible. More seriously, cracks had appeared in the vault of the king's warehouse in 1820, and in 1824 part of the long room's river façade collapsed, followed by the king's warehouse vault and the long room floor. Sir Robert Smirke, called on to investigate, uncovered huge discrepancies between what was specified and paid for, and the work executed. Smirke carried out the reconstruction, underpinning the custom house with concrete foundations and rebuilding the central section as it stands today; by 1829 the total cost had risen to £435,000. J. Mordaunt Crook observed that what the custom house gained in solidity it lost in architectural interest, as Smirke rebuilt Laing's long room and river façade to his own, more pedestrian, designs.

Following Smirke's damning report Laing was dismissed, his career destroyed by the fiasco. The only significant works by him after 1824 are Lexden Park, Colchester, Essex, for J. F. Mills (1825), altered beyond recognition in the 1850s, and the Royal Universal Infirmary for Children, Waterloo Road, London, of 1833–4 (dem.). In 1837 he found some work providing illustrations of public buildings for Peter Nicholson's *Practical Masonry, Bricklaying and Plastering*. In the 1840s he was living in Brighton, though no buildings by him are known there. Laing was reduced almost to destitution and lived on the charity of the Artists' General Benevolent Institution, the Fund for Distressed Architects, and the Surveyor's Club. He died at Brompton, where he had been living since *c*.1850, on 27 March 1856, aged eighty-two. A long and strikingly generous obituary in *The Builder* (5 April 1856) sought to exculpate Laing from blame for the custom house disaster; it noted that such eminent architects as Charles Fowler and Sir William Tite had been his pupils, 'and have been happily more fortunate than their kind-hearted master' (*The Builder*, 198).   STEVEN BRINDLE

Sources Colvin, *Archs.* · J. M. Crook, 'The custom house scandal', *Architectural History*, 6 (1963), 91–102 · *The Builder*, 14 (1856), 189 · J. M. Crook and M. H. Port, eds., *The history of the king's works*, 6 (1973), 422–30 · Graves, *RA exhibitors* · IGI

Laing, David (**1793–1878**), antiquary and librarian, was born in North St David Street, Edinburgh, on or shortly after 20 April 1793, the second son of William *Laing (1764–1832) and Helen Kirk (1767–1837). His father, by profession a publisher and bookseller specializing in second-hand, antiquarian, and foreign literature, was ultimately to have twelve children, nine of whom, four sons and five daughters, survived until adulthood. Laing was educated at the Canongate grammar school between about 1800 and 1805, and thereafter attended Greek classes at Edinburgh University, but these formal studies ended when in 1806, at the age of thirteen, he began work in his father's thriving business, recently moved to 49 South Bridge. Laing made the most of this change in circumstance, reading as much of the stock as he could, with Scottish history and literature proving a particular passion. The learning he thus acquired, and his youthful enthusiasm, soon came to the notice of the many literary people who found Laing's shop an irresistible attraction. He attended several important London auction sales, such as the Porson (1809) and Roxburghe (1812); and, following his father's example, made purchasing trips on the continent in 1816 and 1819. The latter visit was to Scandinavia, and it was on this occasion that he purchased around 1500 items from the library of the Icelandic scholar Grímur Thorkelin, a collection later to be sold to the Advocates' Library in Edinburgh. The 1816 journey, to the Low Countries and northern France, was undertaken in the company of Adam Black and James Wilson (brother of 'Christopher North'), and when in Holland he made the acquaintance of John Gibson Lockhart. Lockhart referred to Laing in a poem published in *Blackwood's Edinburgh Magazine* in July 1818 as:

> the most sagacious and the best,
> As all Old Reekie's erudites opine,
> Of Scottish Bibliopoles …
> A famous Bibliomaniac, and a shrewd,
> Who turns his madness to no little good.
> (*Blackwood's Edinburgh Magazine*, 407)

The following year Lockhart, in *Peter's Letters to his Kinsfolk* (letter 43, 2.182) again praised Laing, describing him as 'by far the most genuine specimen of the true old-fashioned bibliopole that I ever saw exhibited in the person of a young man'.

In 1819 Laing was a candidate for the vacant keepership of the Advocates' Library, but, despite support for Laing from Walter Scott, Dr David Irving was elected in 1820.

Laing's youth no doubt counted against him, but another likely factor was his close links with William Blackwood and his circle, whose satirical writings infuriated many. Laing made a second attempt to become keeper of the Advocates' Library after Irving's retirement in 1848, but withdrew his application, and the post went to Samuel Halkett.

In 1821 Laing became a partner in his father's business. In that same year he issued the first results of his deep love of early Scottish poetry: an edition of the poems of Alexander Scott; an edition (with David Irving) of the poems of Alexander Montgomerie; and the first part of *Select Remains of the Ancient Popular Poetry of Scotland*. From then on, publications, mainly editions of Scottish historical and literary material, poured from him unabated until his death.

On 27 February 1823 Sir Walter Scott founded the Bannatyne Club, for the purpose of printing hitherto unpublished or long out-of-print material relating to the history and literature of Scotland. Membership was restricted to thirty-one members. Scott was president until his death, and Laing became the first and only secretary, seeing through to publication well over a hundred volumes, at least thirty-nine of which were edited or part-edited by himself, before the society was dissolved in 1861. It was Laing who held the club together and saw that the publication schedule did not flag, either for want of editorial industry or dearth of patrons, as well as ensuring that the clubbable aspects of membership were kept green.

On 9 February 1824 Laing was elected to a fellowship of the Society of Antiquaries of Scotland, having been blackballed at an earlier attempt in 1820. In 1827 his application to become a fellow of the Royal Society of Edinburgh was likewise blackballed, but here he never allowed his name to go forward for re-election, although encouraged to do so. As with the Bannatyne Club, Laing was of inestimable importance to the Society of Antiquaries: for over fifty years there was scarcely a volume of the society's publications to which he did not provide a contribution, and it has been estimated he read over one hundred papers to

David Laing (1793–1878), by Sir William Fettes Douglas, 1862

the society. He helped to edit the society's irregular *Transactions* and was joint editor of the annual *Proceedings* from their first appearance in 1851/2 until his death. As treasurer between 1836 and 1852 he steered the society through a particularly difficult period, when it seemed possible that its museum might have to be sold to meet debts. The situation was resolved when the government undertook in 1851 to maintain the collections, an important step towards the formation of a national museum of antiquities. Laing was also a vice-president (1859–62 and 1865–8), acting secretary (1839–41), and a secretary for foreign correspondence (1852–78).

Throughout the 1820s and most of the 1830s Laing continued as a bookseller. Between 1825 and 1827 he also found time to supervise the rebinding of older books and to help with the rearrangement of stock in the university library, at that time moving premises. On 21 June 1837 he was elected librarian to the Society of Writers to H. M. Signet, the professional body for Scottish solicitors, in succession to Macvey Napier. His candidature was supported by many luminaries, such as Robert Southey, T. F. Dibdin, John Lee, Sir William Hamilton, J. G. Lockhart, Sir Henry Ellis, and Sir Frederic Madden. Thereafter, Laing gave up his bookselling business, as he undertook to do in his letter of application, selling at auction the stock he did not want for his personal library. The Signet Library when Laing took over had 40,000 volumes; when he died forty-one years later, still in office, it had 70,000. Laing masterminded the production of a printed catalogue of the holdings: the volume covering A–L appeared in 1871, and letter P was reached by 1878.

Laing's own library became very large and impressive. The printed books possibly numbered 20,000 by his death, despite the sale of over 1200 items at auction in London in June 1856. His massive manuscript collections contained much highly important literary and historical material, mainly of Scottish interest, and including 3326 charters, mainly of Scottish provenance, as well as over 120 medieval manuscript volumes. He also collected old master prints and drawings, portraits of Scots, and other items of Scottish historical importance. He undoubtedly used continental visits, especially frequent in the 1850s, as well as travels within Britain, to build up his collections, but also used every opportunity nearer to home, including arrangements with at least one Edinburgh waste paper merchant.

Laing lived an equable bachelor existence, blessed with robust good health, with a wide circle of friends, acquaintances, and correspondents, although to strangers on first acquaintance he could appear brusque, testy, and impatient. He gave freely of his time to help other scholars, and Cosmo Innes declared in 1864 that 'no wise man will undertake a literary work in Scotland without taking counsel with Mr David Laing' (*The Scotsman*, 21 April 1864). David Masson declared Laing to be 'the prince of the Scottish literary antiquarians of this century' (*The Scotsman*, 30 Oct 1878). Laing's principal biographer, Gilbert Goudie, listed Laing's publications in 1913: they number 214, although some multi-volume works received entries

for each volume. On the other hand, some anonymous notices, articles, and reviews no doubt slipped through Goudie's net. Laing not only edited material for, and involved himself in the affairs of, the Bannatyne Club and the Society of Antiquaries, but he also performed editorial and organizational work for the plethora of Scottish historical clubs which sprouted in emulation of the Bannatyne, such as its Glasgow equivalent the Maitland Club, and the Abbotsford, Spalding, Hunterian, and Wodrow clubs. For the last-named Laing undertook his most important work, an edition of the writings of John Knox which appeared in six volumes between 1846 and 1864, although the club itself collapsed in 1848. No collected edition has appeared since. Many of Laing's other editions are likewise still the most accessible and accurate available, for example his edition of the letters of Robert Baillie (Maitland and Bannatyne clubs, 1841) or his edition of the diary of Alexander Brodie (Spalding Club, 1853). Laing's editorial methods were of the highest calibre according to the standards of his day, and Scottish literary and historical scholars owe him an immense debt of gratitude.

Laing's knowledge of Scottish art was on a par with his acquaintance of Scottish history and literature, a fact recognized in 1854, when he was elected honorary professor of antiquities to the Royal Scottish Academy; in 1861 he became honorary professor of ancient history there. In 1862 he declined an LLD from St Andrews University, but he accepted the same degree from Edinburgh University two years later. In 1865 Thomas Carlyle, an old friend, was elected rector of Edinburgh University, and Laing was nominated by him his assessor to the university court for the three-year period concerned.

Following his mother's death in January 1837, Laing's youngest sister, Euphemia, acted as housekeeper. Until 1843 he stayed at the family home of Ramsay Lodge, Lauriston Place, but from 1845 he lived at East Villa, 12 James Street, Portobello, to the east of Edinburgh. It was there he died, on Friday 18 October 1878, of kidney failure. He was buried in the family plot in the new Calton cemetery on 23 October.

Laing's collections had varying fates: the manuscripts, including his own correspondence comprising some 9000 items, were bequeathed to Edinburgh University Library. By his express testamentary direction, his printed books were sold by auction in London: Messrs Sotheby, Wilkinson and Hodge conducted the sale between 1 December 1879 and 24 February 1881. The same firm also sold Laing's finest prints on 21 February 1880. Altogether, there were 11,743 lots of books and 213 of prints, and the total amount realized was almost £17,000. A Scottish bibliophile of the next generation, David Murray, called the dispersal of Laing's library 'a national misfortune' (Murray, 362). Laing's impressive collection of old master drawings were bequeathed to the Royal Scottish Academy, whence they were later transferred to the National Gallery of Scotland. A large residue of prints and drawings, the latter mainly Scottish and dating from after 1800, were sold at

auction in Edinburgh: the drawings in 347 lots on 22 and
23 December 1879; and the prints in two sales, 16–19
December 1879 and 13 January 1880.

Murray C. T. Simpson

Sources G. Goudie, *David Laing, LLD: a memoir of his life and literary work* (1913) [incl. Laing's 1866 autobiographical fragment] · T. G. Stevenson, *Notices of David Laing LLD* (1878) · D. Murray, 'David Laing, antiquary and bibliographer', *SHR*, 11 (1913–14), 345–69; pubd separately (1915) · M. Ash, *The strange death of Scottish history* (1980) · J. Small, 'Introduction', *Select remains of ancient popular romance poetry of Scotland*, ed. D. Laing (1885) · W. Black, 'Biographical notices of some eminent Edinburgh librarians', *Third annual meeting of the Library Association* [Edinburgh 1880], ed. E. C. Thomas and C. Welch (1881), 30–48 · parish register (births and baptisms), Edinburgh, St Andrews, 1793 · d. cert.
Archives NL Scot., corresp. · Queen's College, London, corresp. · U. Edin. L., corresp. and papers | BL, corresp. with W. C. Hazlitt, Add. MSS 38898–38913 · BL, corresp. with Sir Frederic Madden, Egerton MSS 2838–2847 · BL, letters to J. Martin, Add. MSS 37965–37967 · Bodl. Oxf., corresp. with Sir Thomas Phillipps · NL Scot., corresp. with Carlyle, John Lee, and Sir Walter Scott · U. Aberdeen L., letters to Peter Buchan relating to his literary work · U. Edin. L., corresp. with James Halliwell-Phillipps
Likenesses J. Faed, mezzotint, pubd 1819 (after R. Herdman), BM, NPG · photograph, *c.*1860, repro. in Stevenson, *Notices of David Laing* · W. F. Douglas, oils, 1862, Scot. NPG [*see illus.*] · R. Herdman, oils, 1874, Scot. NPG · D. W. Stevenson, plaster bust, 1880, Scot. NPG · F. Harrison, etching, BM
Wealth at death £11,967 7s. 11d.: confirmation, 27 Feb 1879, CCI · £13,548 0s. 3d.: additional inventory, 28 Aug 1880, CCI

Laing, James (*c.*1530–1594), theologian, was born in the diocese of St Andrews. According to Thomas Dempster he died at the age of ninety-three and was therefore born in 1500 or 1501, but the course of his career makes a date of birth about 1530 more credible. Having probably studied at King's College, Aberdeen, he continued his studies at the University of Paris, where he applied himself to theology and took holy orders. In the university records he is described as a Scot, of the diocese of St Andrews, and of the German nation. On 20 October 1556 he was elected procurator of his nation, entitling him to represent it in the rector's court, the governing body of the university. This honour was conferred on him on many later occasions—on 27 August 1558, 27 October 1560, 10 February 1561, at some date in 1564, on 14 January 1571, and in 1590. He was also quaestor (bursar) on 21 October 1568. In September 1571 he was described as bachelor of theology, but was doctor by the date of his first book in 1581. He preached during several years in Paris. Jean de Rouen, privy councillor, royal almoner, rector, and censor of the university, in a treatise on the Sorbonne, mentions Laing in very laudatory terms.

A lifelong Catholic, Laing was a violent enemy of the Reformation, and very insulting in his personal attacks on the reformers. In 1581 he wrote *De vita et moribus atque rebus gestis haereticorum nostri temporis*. The notices of Calvin and three others are translated from the French of J.-H. Bolsec's *Histoire des vies des quatre principaux hérétiques de nostre temps* (1580). There were two editions in 1581, dedicated to Queen Mary and James VI, translated into

German in 1582 at Ingolstadt. Laing's first sentence regarding Knox concludes, 'ab initio suae pueritiae omni genere turpissimi facinoris infectus fuit' ('from his earliest childhood he was infected with every kind of the basest ill doing'; p. 113 and verso). In 1585 he wrote a second treatise, based on Bolsec's *Histoire de la vie de Théodore de Bèze* (1582), *De vita et moribus Theodori Bezae, omnium haereticorum nostri temporis facile principis, et aliorum haereticorum brevis recitatio, cui adjectus est libellus de morte patris Edmundi Campionis et aliorum quorundam Catholicorum qui in Anglia pro fide catholica interfecti fuerunt, primo die Decembris, anno domini 1581, authore Jacobo Laingeo, doctore Sorbonico*. The Campion work translated here appeared in Lyons in 1582 and Laing's book is, like his first, dedicated jointly to Queen Mary and to James VI. He is said to have written other unpublished works of a less polemical nature, including a commentary on Aristotle's philosophy, which Dempster claims he saw in manuscript with the author shortly before his death. Laing's name is appended to a document in the form of an oath of fealty signed and addressed by the principal members of the Paris faculties to Henri IV on his accession (22 April 1594). He died during this year, and was buried, according to his wish, in the chapel of the Sorbonne.

J. G. Fotheringham, *rev.* John Durkan

Sources J. Laing, ed. and trans., *De vita et moribus atque rebus gestis haereticorum nostri temporis* (Paris, 1581) · J. Laing, *De vita et moribus Theodori Bezae* (Paris, 1585) · *Thomae Dempsteri Historia ecclesiastica gentis Scotorum, sive, De scriptoribus Scotis*, ed. D. Irving, rev. edn, 2, Bannatyne Club, 21 (1829), 438–9 · C. E. Du Boulay, *Historia universitatis Parisiensis*, 6 (Paris, 1673), 943 · Acta rectoria, Bibliothèque Nationale, Paris, MS lat 9955, fol. 20 · Archives Nationales, Paris, H3 2589, fol. 41 · Archives Nationales, Paris, H3 2590, fol. 12r (1564); fol. 20 (1566); fol. 46 · A. F. Allison and D. M. Rogers, eds., *The contemporary printed literature of the English Counter-Reformation between 1558 and 1640*, 1 (1989), 30, 98 · G. Conn, *De duplici statu religionis apud Scotos*, 2 pts in 1 (Rome, 1628)

Laing, Sir James (1823–1901), shipbuilder, was born at Deptford House, Sunderland, on 11 January 1823, the only son of Philip Laing (*d.* 1852) and his second wife, Anne Jobling (*d.* 1854). His father, originally from Pittenweem in Fife, had established a shipbuilding business in partnership with his brother John at Monkwearmouth, Sunderland, in 1793. Their partnership was dissolved in 1818, the year of the move to the Deptford yard. James was groomed to succeed his father, which he did in 1843.

One of Laing's first innovations was to use teak for the exterior planking of vessels he constructed, including his first, the *Agincourt*. Laing was later convinced, by personal observation of the durability of the stranded iron steamship *Great Britain*, that iron was the building material of the future. The *Amity* (1853) was his first iron ship, and the first built on the Wear, though Laing continued to build in wood until 1866 and launched composite vessels up to 1875, the last of which was the celebrated *Torrens*. Laing married Mary Tanner (1816–1850) in 1847, and they had a daughter and a son. After his wife's death Laing married Theresa Talbot Peacock, in 1855, and they had eight daughters and five sons, two of whom predeceased him.

Laing's shipyard first concentrated on passenger-carrying clippers and later built cargo-passenger steamers. The mail steamer *Mexican*, launched in 1882, was the largest passenger-vessel ever built on the north-east coast, and when the potential of the oil-tanker market was appreciated the *Tuscarora*, launched in 1898, became the largest tanker then afloat. The firm also undertook a great deal of repair and ship-conversion work in its two graving docks, and it also maintained an extensive copper and brass works. The Laings proved unusual in their longevity as a shipbuilding family, second only to the Scotts of Greenock, and much of this was due to James Laing's vision and flexibility in embracing the changes which affected the industry in the nineteenth century.

Laing was, however, involved in more than just his own thriving shipyard. He served on the River Wear commission from 1859 and was chairman from 1868 to 1900. In 1883 he became president of the chamber of shipping of the United Kingdom and concluded an agreement with the Suez Canal Company, which met the grievances of British shipowners. He later became a director of the company. He was also a director of the North Eastern Railway, the Sunderland and South Shields Water Company, and the Sunderland Gas Company, as well as being the principal proprietor of the Ayres Quay Bottle Works. In addition the Laing family had always maintained extensive financial interests in shipping. For many years James Laing was a member of the board of Lloyd's register of shipping, as well as being on the council of the Institution of Naval Architects and of other technical societies. He served as vice-president of the Board of Trade's load-line committee. Surprisingly for a man with so many professional affiliations, he never became a member of the North East Coast Institution of Engineers and Shipbuilders.

In public life Laing was not attracted to elected office, though he did stand as a Liberal parliamentary candidate for North Durham in 1881, when he was defeated by Sir George Elliot. He was a JP for the counties of Northumberland and Durham and was high sheriff of Durham in 1879. He received recognition for his many services in 1897, when he was knighted, though it was suggested that a peerage had been offered and declined. Though raised as a Presbyterian, he was latterly associated with the Church of England and he and Lady Laing were described as 'peerless in local acts of Christian charity' (*Sunderland Herald*, 16 Dec 1901). Certainly Laing was associated with many of the borough's philanthropic institutions, and he took a special interest in the affairs of the infirmary. His business became a limited liability company in 1898 under the name Sir James Laing & Sons Ltd.

In failing health Laing spent his last years at Etal Manor, Cornhill, Northumberland, where he died on 15 December 1901 after a short illness, survived by his wife. His body was returned to Sunderland for burial in Bishopwearmouth cemetery on 18 December. At the time of his death Laing was considered to be Sunderland's most prominent citizen. His portrait suggests a patriarchal figure, whose baldness was more than offset by a flowing white beard.

Obituaries emphasized his honesty, frankness, and kindly nature, while acknowledging his occasional brusqueness of manner.   LIONEL ALEXANDER RITCHIE

Sources *Sunderland Herald and Daily Post* (16 Dec 1901), 3 · *Sunderland Daily Echo* (16 Dec 1901), 2–3 · *The Engineer* (20 Dec 1901), 633 · *Engineering* (20 Dec 1901), 846 · *The Times* (16 Dec 1901), 9 · *Transactions of the Institution of Naval Architects*, 44 (1902), 310 · J. F. Clarke, 'Laing, Sir James', *DBB* · D. H. Pollock, *Modern shipbuilding and the men engaged in it* (1884), 177–80 · J. W. Smith and T. S. Holden, *Where ships are born: Sunderland, 1346–1946*, rev. edn (1953), 20–30 · *WWW* · *Shipping World* (7 Oct 1936), 363–5 · Burke, *Gen. GB* (1906) · Kelly, *Handbk* (1900) · *CGPLA Eng. & Wales* (1902)

Archives Tyne and Wear Archives Service, Newcastle upon Tyne, Sir James Laing & Sons Ltd records

Likenesses portrait, repro. in Pollock, *Modern shipbuilding*, following p. 178 · portrait, repro. in Clarke, 'Laing, Sir James'

Wealth at death £121,402 16s. 2d.: probate, 11 Feb 1902, *CGPLA Eng. & Wales* · £129,558: Clarke, 'Laing, Sir James'

Laing, John (*d.* 1483), administrator and bishop of Glasgow, came of the family of Laing of Redhouse, Edinburghshire. He was appointed rector of Tannadice in Angus and vicar of Linlithgow, and by the beginning of 1474 he was rector of Newlands in the diocese of Glasgow. He was also involved in secular government. Described in a charter of 1463 as secretary to Mary of Gueldres, the widowed queen of James II, he had become royal treasurer by 17 September 1470 and held that office at least until his provision to Glasgow, and probably afterwards—he cannot be shown to have been replaced until 29 May 1476. In addition he was clerk register in 1473. Following the death of Andrew Durisdeer, bishop of Glasgow, on 20 November 1473 Laing was provided to the see on 28 January 1474, when Sixtus IV referred to him as councillor to the king of Scots. Laing may earlier have shared in the disquiet created in the Scottish church by the elevation of Patrick Graham to metropolitan status at St Andrews in 1472, particularly since one of his own benefices was granted for the maintenance of the archbishop's household.

In 1476 Laing founded a Franciscan friary in Glasgow. Two years later James III confirmed Laing's grants of land and tenements in Edinburgh to St Kentigern, Glasgow Cathedral, and the altar of St Duthac in the church of St Giles, Edinburgh. A further grant, made on 9 February 1482, gave the rent from two booths in Edinburgh to pay for 6 stones of wax yearly for candles for the choir of Glasgow Cathedral. The crisis precipitated by the seizure of James III by members of the Scottish nobility in July 1482 led to abrupt changes in government, and Laing had replaced Andrew Stewart, Lord Avondale, as chancellor by 25 August. Laing's long record of service to the crown as a councillor, witnessing royal charters from 1470 onwards, meant that he was not too closely identified with the unpopular James III, and consequently his appointment as chancellor would seem to have been acceptable to both the king and his opponents. During the crisis of 1482–3 he was the nominal head of an administration which rejected William Scheves, archbishop of St Andrews; as a particular favourite of James III, Scheves was resented by the wider political community, frustrated by what it saw as its exclusion from royal policy making. Laing held the position of chancellor of Scotland until his death on 11 January 1483, when he was succeeded in office by Bishop James Livingston of Dunkeld.   C. A. McGladdery

Sources C. Innes, ed., *Registrum episcopatus Glasguensis*, 2 vols., Bannatyne Club, 75 (1843); also pubd as 2 vols., Maitland Club, 61 (1843) · J. Dowden, *The bishops of Scotland … prior to the Reformation*, ed. J. M. Thomson (1912) · J. M. Thomson and others, eds., *Registrum magni sigilli regum Scotorum / The register of the great seal of Scotland*, 11 vols. (1882–1914), vol. 2

Laing, John (1809–1880), bibliographer, was born on 16 February 1809 at Edinburgh, but grew up at nearby Dalmeny, where his father, also John, was for many years factor to the earl of Rosebery; his mother was Mary Fyfe, of a Banffshire family. He lost the sight of one eye in his youth. After attending the high school in Edinburgh, he took arts classes at Edinburgh University between 1823 and 1826, and divinity classes between 1827 and 1831. Having been licensed as a clergyman by the presbytery of Edinburgh on 5 October 1841, he was ordained assistant and successor to John Robertson, minister of Livingston, Linlithgowshire, on 13 January 1842. At the Disruption in the following year he joined the newly formed Free Church, and continued his ministry in the same parish. On 29 August 1843 he married, at Dalmeny, Catherine Fyfe (d. 16 Feb 1869), daughter of a West India proprietor. There were three daughters: Mary (who died young), Catherine, and Fanny.

In 1845 Laing had a physical, spiritual, and mental collapse and went abroad for a time, becoming a chaplain to the British forces on Gibraltar and Malta. He resigned his parish in March 1847. Late in 1850 he was appointed an assistant librarian at the recently completed New College of the Free Church; in 1854 he became acting librarian following the death of the incumbent, William Rowand, the previous year. This post he held until his own death. Throughout his librarianship the collections grew rapidly and Laing organized the publication of a substantial catalogue of the printed books and manuscripts in 1868. After the death of his friend Samuel Halkett in 1871, the materials collected by the latter for a dictionary of anonymous British literature were entrusted to him, and Laing more than doubled the store. The work, *A Dictionary of Anonymous and Pseudonymous Literature of Great Britain*, was published posthumously in four volumes between 1882 and 1888, prepared for the press, apart from the unsatisfactory indexes, by Laing's daughter Catherine. 'Halkett and Laing' soon established itself as an invaluable reference work, relied upon for its accuracy and admired for the concise way in which it cited the sources for its attributions. An expanded edition in nine volumes appeared between 1926 and 1962. Laing died in Edinburgh, where he had lived, on 3 April 1880 and was buried in the Grange cemetery there.

James Kennedy, *rev.* Murray C. T. Simpson

Sources P. Muirhead, 'The Rev. John Laing…', *Free Church of Scotland Monthly Record* (1 Feb 1881), 43 · *Fasti Scot.*, new edn, 1.221 · W. Ewing, ed., *Annals of the Free Church of Scotland, 1843–1900*, 1 (1914), 203 · matriculation records, U. Edin. L., special collections division, university archives · U. Edin., New Coll., archives · E. C. T.

[E. C. Thomas], 'Halkett and Laing's *Dictionary of anonymous and pseudonymous literature*', *Library Chronicle*, 5 (1888), 148–50

Laing, Sir John William (1879–1978), builder and civil engineering contractor, was born on 24 September 1879 at 21 Newcastle Street, Carlisle, the third but only surviving son of John Laing (1842–1924) and his wife, Sarah, *née* Wood (1845–1924). His father was the son of James Laing (1818–1882), who had founded the family construction business in 1848. Laing received his primary education in Carlisle and Sedbergh and then attended Carlisle grammar school. He was brought up in a strict religious environment, his parents having joined the congregation of the Carlisle Brethren following their marriage in 1874. He joined the family firm in January 1895 at the age of fifteen and served a three-year apprenticeship as a bricklayer and mason. In 1902 he went to work on the company's first major civil engineering contract—the construction of a reservoir at Uldale in Cumberland—and spent some two years with a navvy gang of 200 men which gave him a good understanding of the construction labourer. On 28 September 1910 Laing married Beatrice Harland (1885–1972), the daughter of a chartered accountant from Stockton-on-Tees; they had two sons. The Harland family also belonged to the Brethren movement and became strongly linked to the Laing family with the preparation of the Laing company's annual reports and the marriage of Laing's sister to Beatrice's brother.

By 1908 Laing had taken over the firm's management and two years later became the sole proprietor on the retirement of his father. He was a pioneer in perceiving the importance of accurate costing and control of performance during construction and he introduced work-study methods. The First World War saw great expansion of the Laing company, largely due to government contracts. During this period Laing undertook a contract for Barrow in Furness corporation which brought him up against unforeseen and costly natural hazards and led to a law suit, which he won. His Christian commitment was strengthened at this time and he drew up a financial plan for giving away on a graduated system anything from one-eighth to one-third of his income.

Laing was deeply interested in experimental building work and developed in 1919 his own system of *in situ* concrete housing construction. This helped overcome the post-war shortage of skilled labour and it was patented as Easiform in 1924 when it featured at the Palace of Housing at the 1924–25 Wembley British Empire Exhibition. Another development of the same period was a suspended patent fireproof flooring method known as Ferrobrick. A tendering and costing system which he developed was one of the finest of its time in the industry, and he believed that the key to sound contract financing was accuracy of estimating and labour productivity.

Laing exercised a benevolent paternalism over his workers and in 1922 he introduced a scheme for employee shares. These were frequently purchased in instalments but were sometimes given as part of the distribution of company profits and they had to be returned on leaving the company's employment. A 'pupils' scheme', started in

Sir John William Laing (1879–1978), by Arthur Ralph Middleton Todd, exh. RA 1949

1924, was a form of indenture training for grammar or public school leavers, and this was later to incorporate training for professional qualifications. Laing was respected by his employees for his absolute integrity. Productivity bonuses and payments for time lost by wet weather were introduced well ahead of the industry generally. Long-service employees were always found employment during slack periods and he built up a stable and loyal workforce. A charitable trust for employees was started in 1932 and this was followed by the first holidays-with-pay scheme within the industry in 1934.

In the late 1920s, at a time of decline in the construction market, Laing launched into speculative private house building, particularly in the Greater London area. His company had built up sufficient resources to be able to finance the development of both shopping and factory precincts where they did not already exist near to his new estates. His advocacy of owner-occupation was very significant at the time; his house specification and building standards were high so his houses were more expensive than some others on the market, but they still sold readily.

Laing supported the foundation of the National House Builders' Registration Council, formed in 1937, which registered builders and guaranteed their houses. His estates were always carefully planned with preserved trees and shrubs lining road verges. He, along with others, promoted a builders' pool system, an arrangement with the building societies which reduced the cash deposits required for mortgages. A visit to Russia in 1935 had a profound influence on his practical thinking. The great blocks of Russian flats with their communal kitchens and facilities were contrasted unfavourably with his own housing estates where each house possessed its own gardens and kitchen.

At this time the company began to grow as a result of the award of government military contracts, and because of the urgency of these, the normal lengthy procedures of competitive tendering were impractical and they had to be negotiated. Laing had always disliked the cost-plus type of contract which had been extensively used during the First World War. He considered it to be inefficient, destructive of enterprise, and open to questionable practice. The company already had a long association with the Air Ministry which had led to a relationship of mutual respect and Laing was able to negotiate a 'target' form of contract. A target cost would be set and if the actual cost of labour and material proved to be less than this figure the contractor was paid cost and profit, plus a sliding-scale bonus based on the savings; if he exceeded the target, he was penalized.

The Second World War brought a tremendous expansion of the firm, which constructed fifty-four airfields, the underground headquarters of RAF Bomber Command at High Wycombe, munitions factories, and sections of the D-day Mulberry harbour. Laing reached sixty-five in 1944 but as his two sons were serving in the forces he carried on running the business alone. He also served as a consultant to the wartime government and sat on several committees. After the war, and confronted with a chronic housing shortage, Laing launched his company into Easiform construction again, supporting it with a research and development programme. The company's rapid growth continued and, despite his characteristic reluctance to delegate, he slowly transferred the firm's management to his sons, William Kirby and John Maurice. Financial and management decentralization was to follow and the business was converted into a public limited company in 1952. The Laing family and their charitable trust held sufficient ordinary shares in the company to retain control.

Laing finally retired as chairman in 1957 and became the company's life president. In that year his company was awarded the so-called 'power and the glory' contracts—Berkeley nuclear power station (decommissioned in 1989) and the rebuilding of Coventry Cathedral (consecrated in 1962). The following year the company won the contract for the first 55 miles of the M1, a new activity in which it became a national leader and which derived from its wartime airfield construction experience. For his services to the industry, Laing was appointed CBE in 1951 and knighted in 1959. His two sons attained distinction in the business world, Kirby becoming president of the Institution of Civil Engineers and Maurice a director of the Bank of England and also of Rolls-Royce, both being knighted in the 1960s.

To the end of his life Laing, supported by his wife, remained a generous benefactor of evangelical Christian enterprise. In 1922 he gave nearly 40 per cent of his personal ordinary shares in the company to a Brethren charitable holding foundation, the Steward's Company Ltd. This applied its income to missionary, evangelistic, and poor relief work. A wide range of Christian international organizations benefited from Laing's support, including the London Bible College, the British and Foreign Bible Society, the Missionary Aviation Fellowship, Fact and Faith films, and the Billy Graham crusades. Paternalistic and dominating, Laing gained a reputation for straightness in his personal and business dealings. Pursuit of efficiency and quality and close personal control marked his business style, as did his policy of extensively ploughing back profits; his frugality was expressed in his preference for the works canteen or sandwiches instead of an expensive restaurant. He also worked immensely hard, enjoyed physical fitness and held a simple, bold Christian faith until his death, aged ninety-eight, at 8A Wellington Place, Westminster, London on 11 January 1978. He was buried on 16 January 1978 in Paddington new cemetery.

ALAN THORPE

Sources R. Coad, *Laing: the biography of Sir John Laing CBE (1879–1978)* (1979) · D. J. Jeremy, 'Laing, Sir John William', *DBB* · G. Harrison, *Life and belief in the experience of John W. Laing* (1954) · *Teamwork: the story of John Laing and Son Ltd* (1950) · *Serving a nation at war, 1939–1945: a review of the building and civil engineering work of John Laing and Son Ltd* (Laing & Co., 1946) · *Building and engineering works: John Laing and Son Ltd* (Laing & Co., 1937) · *CGPLA Eng. & Wales* (1978) · b. cert. · m. cert. · d. cert. · b. cert. [Beatrice Harland] · d. cert. [Beatrice Harland] · private information (2004)
Likenesses A. R. M. Todd, oils, exh. RA 1949, repro. in Coad, *Laing*, jacket [*see illus.*]
Wealth at death £74,592: probate, 17 March 1978, *CGPLA Eng. & Wales*

Laing, Malcolm (1762–1818), historian and advocate, was the eldest son of Robert Laing (d. 1805), a merchant and provost of Kirkwall in 1788–92, who came of an old Orkney family; his brother was Samuel *Laing (1780–1868). Laing was born at the paternal estate of Strynzie (or Strenzie), on the island of Stronsay. He was educated at Kirkwall grammar school and Edinburgh University, and was called to the Scottish bar on 9 July 1785, but his practice remained small. His speeches in the court were neither eloquent nor pleasing, though in parliament he was considered an able speaker. Lord Cockburn highly praised his speech in 1794 defending Joseph Gerrald (1763–1796), a delegate from the London Corresponding Society, charged with sedition.

Turning from legal work, Laing devoted much of his time to historical studies. On the death of the historian Robert Henry, at the request of Henry's executors, he completed *The History of Great Britain*, adding chapters 5 and 7 and the appendix to volume 6 (1793). In 1800 Laing published *The history of Scotland, from the union of the crowns on the accession of King James VI to the throne of England, to the union of the kingdoms in the reign of Queen Anne, with two dissertations, historical and critical, on the Gowrie conspiracy, and on the supposed authenticity of Ossian's poems*. Though written in a somewhat awkward and overelaborate style, his *History* 'was full of useful research and displayed a breadth of

knowledge that Robertson's *History of Scotland* might not have commanded' (Price). The dissertation on the *Poems of Ossian* is a severely negative and insensitive criticism of James Macpherson's supposed Gaelic translations. Laing could not set aside the charges of forgery against Macpherson and remained contemptuous of the poet's genius. In 1804 Laing published a second and corrected edition of his *History of Scotland* in four volumes, with a preliminary 'Dissertation on the participation of Mary, Queen of Scots, in the murder of Darnley'. Here he attempted to establish the authenticity of the casket letters, and his dissertation was an able statement of the case against the queen. In the same year he edited *The Historie and Life of King James VI*, and in May and June 1805 published a heavily annotated edition of *The poems of Ossian, containing the poetical works of James Macpherson in prose and verse, with notes and illustrations*.

Laing was a strong-minded liberal in politics, a Scottish Foxite, who along with seven other Edinburgh whig lawyers, known as the Independent Friends, opposed the machine-politician Henry Dundas and his tory coalition. He joined the Whig Club in 1796 and helped C. J. Fox to write his own historical work. After a number of broken pledges to bring Laing into parliament, his Scots and English colleagues finally arranged his appointment. In the general election of 1807 Laing was named to the uncontested seat of Orkney and Shetland and held the office until 1812.

Laing married Margaret Carnegie, daughter of Thomas Carnegie of Craigo, Forfarshire, on 10 September 1805; the couple had no children. Soon after, in 1808, he left London and Edinburgh and returned to Orkney. Growing physical ailments in his last years forced his retirement from an active career. Sir Walter Scott described a visit paid to him at Kirkwall in August 1814. 'Our old acquaintance,' he wrote, 'though an invalid, received us kindly; he looks very poorly, and cannot walk without assistance, but seems to retain all the quick, earnest, and vivacious intelligence of his character and manner' (J. G. Lockhart, *Memoirs of Sir Walter Scott*, 5 vols., 1914, 2.380). Laing died on 6 November 1818 at Kirkwall. There is a tablet to his memory on the wall of the north nave of Kirkwall Cathedral. 'Depth, truth, and independence as a historian were', Lord Cockburn commented, 'the least of his merits, for he was a firm, warm-hearted, honest man, whose instructive and agreeable companionship was only made the more interesting by a hard, peremptory Celtic manner and accent' (*Memorials*, 202–3).

T. F. HENDERSON, rev. PAUL J. deGATEGNO

Sources Chambers, *Scots.* (1835) · R. P. Fereday, *The Orkney Balfours, 1747–1799* (1990) · *Memorials of his time, by Lord Cockburn*, rev. edn, ed. W. Forbes Gray (1946) · *The letters of Sir Walter Scott*, ed. H. J. C. Grierson and others, centenary edn, 12 vols. (1932–79) · P. J. deGategno, *James Macpherson* (1989) · HoP, *Commons* · J. V. Price, 'Ossian and the canon in the Scottish enlightenment', *Ossian revisited*, ed. H. Gaskill (1991) · F. J. Stafford, *The sublime savage: a study of James Macpherson and the poems of Ossian* (1988) · A. Bell, 'Cockburn's *Account of the Friday Club*', *Lord Cockburn: a bicentenary commemoration, 1779–1979*, ed. A. Bell (1979) · *Journal of Henry Cockburn: being a continuation of the*

'*Memorials of his time*', *1831–1854*, 2 vols. (1874) • *The letters of John Ramsay of Ochtertyre, 1779–1812*, ed. B. Horn (1966)
Archives BL, Blair Adam MSS • BL, corresp. with C. J. Fox, Add. MS 47578 • BL, Fortescue MSS • NA Scot., letters to Archibald Constable • NA Scot., MacLeod MS • NRA, priv. coll., papers relating to reception of his history by the Macleods
Likenesses S. Laing, wash drawing, 1804, Scot. NPG • wash drawings, Scot. NPG

Laing, Robert. *See* Shields, Cuthbert (1840–1908).

Laing, Ronald David (1927–1989), psychiatrist and psychoanalyst, was born on 7 October 1927 at 21 Ardbeg Road, Glasgow, the only child of David Park McNair Laing, electrical engineer, and his wife, Amelia Elizabeth Kirkwood. He was educated in Glasgow at Cuthbertson Street primary school, Hutcheson's Boys' Grammar School, and the University of Glasgow medical school, from which he graduated MB, ChB in 1951. After a year at the Glasgow and western Scotland neurosurgical unit in Killearn (1951), he worked as a psychiatrist in the army (1952–3) and, after demobilization, in the department of psychological medicine, Glasgow (1953–6).

In 1956 Laing moved to London, having been accepted for training as a psychoanalyst under an experimental scheme, by which promising young psychiatrists from the provinces could be trained within the National Health Service by the Institute of Psychoanalysis while working as registrars at the Tavistock Clinic. Despite opposition from some of his teachers, who found him arrogant and were offended by his failure to attend lectures regularly, he qualified as an analyst in 1960.

From 1956 until 1967 Laing worked at the Tavistock Clinic and Institute, first as a registrar and then as a research fellow of the Foundations fund for research in psychiatry, and principal investigator for the schizophrenia and family research unit. During his time at the Tavistock he was the leading co-author of two works, *Sanity, Madness and the Family* (1964) with A. Esterson, and *Interpersonal Perception: a Theory and a Method of Research* (1966) with H. Phillipson and A. R. Lee. In the former he produced clinical data in support of what became in the 1960s and 1970s the fashionable 'anti-psychiatric' idea that schizophrenia is not an illness but a mode of being into which the patient has been forced by his family. As Laing put it in *The Politics of Experience* (1967):

> when one person comes to be regarded as schizophrenic, it seems to us that *without exception* the experience and behaviour that gets labelled schizophrenic is *a special strategy that a person invents in order to live in an unlivable situation.*

This idea that schizophrenics and, by extension, neurotics are victims, the damaged but heroic survivors of impossible inhuman family and social pressures, was, coupled with Laing's charm and literary skill, largely responsible for the fact that he became a leading cult figure of the counter-culture of the 1960s.

In 1960 and 1961 Laing published the two books by which he became best known, *The Divided Self* and *The Self and Others*, the declared aims of which were to 'make madness, and the process of going mad, comprehensible' and to describe how one person can drive another one insane.

Ronald David Laing (1927–1989), by HAG (Ian Hargreaves), 1978

They describe the subjective experiences of future or potential schizophrenics in language conspicuously free of the (pseudo-) objectifying jargon of psychoanalysis and psychiatry.

About 1960 Laing came under the influence of Dr E. Graham Howe, a psychotherapist much interested in both Christianity and Eastern religions, who in the 1930s had worked with Krishnamurti. This influence presumably explains the mystical, religious element which enters— some would say obtrudes—into Laing's writings from the mid-1960s onwards, and the fact that in 1971–2 he spent a year in Ceylon learning meditation with masters of the Hinayana Buddhist tradition. In 1962 Howe appointed Laing chairman of the Langham Clinic, a body which provided low-fee psychotherapy and trained psychotherapists. But in 1965 Howe asked him to resign on account of his interest in psychedelic drugs.

In the same year Laing was one of the founders of the Philadelphia Association, an organization devoted to establishing and running residential communities in which schizophrenics could find sanctuary and make their own 'journey through madness' unimpeded by conventional psychiatric treatment. One of these communities, Kingsley Hall (1965–70), acquired fame and notoriety as a place where people could regress into infantile and uninhibited behaviour and then resurface with a new, true, and authentic sanity.

In 1972, after his return from Ceylon, Laing began a retreat from the extreme position he had taken in the 1960s. He had, he now maintained, never been an apostle of the drug culture, or an anti-psychiatrist, or an enemy of the family. In *The Politics of the Family* (1971) he had merely tried to show how families can go wrong. His writings of the 1970s and 1980s, notably *The Facts of Life* (1976), *The Voice of Experience* (1982), and the autobiographical *Wisdom, Madness and Folly* (1985), are characterized by a sense of perplexity and uncertainty and marred by unbridled speculation. It is difficult to take seriously the idea that we are all traumatized by separation from 'our intra-uterine twin, lover, rival, double', the placenta.

Despite Laing's intelligence, charm, energy, and many talents—he wrote poetry and was a gifted pianist (LRAM, 1944; ARCM, 1945)—and his remarkable gift for rapport with the mentally disturbed, he was a flawed character. His ideas on schizophrenia were more derivative than his way of expressing them revealed; he maintained that his rise to fame had been more of a solitary struggle than in fact it was; and his account of his childhood in *Wisdom, Madness and Folly* is not strictly truthful. In his relation to his 1960s followers, he must be convicted of playing to the gallery. His appearance was striking. He was dark and slender, with intense black eyes, and had an air of abstraction about him.

Laing was married and divorced twice. He married Anne, daughter of Thomas George Charles Hearne, customs and excise officer, in October 1952. The couple had two sons and three daughters; they divorced in 1970. In March 1974 he married Jutta, daughter of Max Werner, clerk; they had two sons and one daughter, and in 1986 they were divorced. He also had two illegitimate children. Laing died of a heart attack in St Tropez, France, on 23 August 1989.   CHARLES RYCROFT, *rev.*

Sources *The Times* (25 Aug 1989) · *The Independent* (25 Aug 1989) · *The Times* (16 Aug 1994) · A. Laing, *R. D. Laing: a biography* (1994) · personal knowledge (1996) · private information (1996) · *CGPLA Eng. & Wales* (1991)
Archives U. Glas. L., papers
Likenesses S. Meagher, two photographs, 1967, Hult. Arch. · R. Moreton, photograph, *c.*1975, Hult. Arch. · HAG [I. Hargreaves], platinum print photograph, 1978, NPG [*see illus.*] · V. Crowe, oil on hardboard, 1984, Scot. NPG
Wealth at death £31,221: probate, 11 June 1991, *CGPLA Eng. & Wales*

Laing, Samuel (1780–1868), author and traveller, son of Robert Laing (*d.* 1805), a merchant and provost of Kirkwall in 1788–92, of an old Orkney family and younger brother of Malcolm *Laing, was born at Kirkwall, Orkney, on 4 October 1780. He was educated at Kirkwall grammar school and the University of Edinburgh. Leaving Edinburgh without a degree about 1797, he spent eighteen months at Kiel in Schleswig-Holstein studying German. In 1805 he entered the army as an ensign in the staff corps stationed at Hythe and with which he served in the Peninsular War. He returned to Britain in 1809, sold out from the army, and, through his brother's influence, was appointed manager of mines at Wanlockhead, in southern Scotland. In March that year he married Agnes, daughter of Captain Francis Kelly of Kelly. Shortly before her death they had a daughter, Elizabeth, and a son, Samuel *Laing. In 1818 he returned to Orkney where he successfully organized the coastal herring fishery for a London firm.

When his brother died childless in 1818, he inherited the heavily encumbered estates at Strynzia or Strenzie, Orkney. He lived at Kirkwall, of which he was for some years provost, and was engaged in the reduction of kelp to alkali for glass manufacture.

At the general election of 1832–3 Laing unsuccessfully contested Orkney and Shetland as a radical, and in his *Address to the Electors* (1833) accused the lord advocate of interfering on his opponent's behalf. Reduced to comparative poverty by the development in 1832 of synthetic alkali which ended demand for kelp and ruined many in the west highlands and islands, he left Orkney in 1834. He lived in Norway from 1834 to 1836 and visited Sweden in 1838, the previous death of his wife, the marriage of his daughter, the successful start in his career of his son, and the departure after a quarrel of his wife's sister Mary who had kept house for him, leaving him unencumbered by domestic responsibilities. His widely read accounts of his journeys were less travel books than works of political economy and attracted notices comparing him to Arthur Young and von Humboldt. In *Journal of a Residence in Norway* (1836) he gave unqualified praise to the free, upright Norwegian peasantry. His praise accorded with his own belief that a relatively egalitarian distribution of property led to a virtuous society and with the tendency in nineteenth-century Norway to idealize the peasantry, through whose veins was thought to course the moral and economic life-blood of the nation. His *Tour in Sweden* (1839) was as critical of Sweden as the earlier book was enthusiastic about Norway, despite the similarities between the two countries. His criticism stemmed in part from his sympathy with the Norwegians, who in 1814 had been compelled to exchange Danish rule for personal union with Sweden, and in part from his use of the comprehensive Swedish statistics on crime, illegitimacy, and poverty which led him to conclude that the Swedes lived 'in a more demoralised state than any nation in Europe' (S. Laing, *Tour in Sweden*, 1839, 108), even while admitting that these findings did not accord with his own observations. He reserved his fiercest criticism for the ubiquitous state and state church whose hold over the people was judged insidious and evil. His grossly partisan account was widely accepted, for example by James Kay-Shuttleworth who agreed with Laing's opinion that in the degenerate Swedish social system 'some of the worst institutions of feudalism corrupt a people aroused from the incurious apathy of the middle ages' (Kay-Shuttleworth, 215). Count Magnus Björnstjerna, Swedish ambassador to St James, responded with a pamphlet *On the Moral State and Political Union of Sweden and Norway* (1840) to which Laing published a trenchant rejoinder in the *Monthly Chronicle* (November, 1840), reprinted in *Notes of a Traveller* (1842). Much of the latter book was devoted to Prussia whose people Laing likened to slaves. A German translation of this section by Adolf Heller appeared in Mannheim in 1844. Laing made a similar judgement on the Austrians and Neapolitans. Laing's purpose in these sweeping judgements on various peoples was always to analyse the political and economic régimes in operation in each country, not to point to any inherent or 'natural' characteristics of the people.

His translation of Snorri Sturluson's *Heimskringla* or chronicle of the kings of Norway (3 vols., 1840) was thought in Laing's lifetime to be his most important work. Although his introduction and the translation itself show his characteristic preference for enthusiasm rather than measured judgement, he deserves praise for setting the chronicle before the English public. Mistrust of the Roman Catholic church, evident from his *Notes of a Traveller*, led Laing to oppose the Maynooth grant and to write critically in 1845 of the pilgrimage of one and a half million people to see the alleged holy coat at Trier. He returned to travel and in *Observations on ... the European People* (1850) admitted some of the disadvantages of peasant proprietorship. For this he was reproached with inconsistency by J. S. Mill who, influenced by *Residence in Norway*, had argued in favour of that mode of land tenure in his own *Political Economy*. Laing's *Observations on ... Denmark and the Duchies* (1852) showed a similar retreat from his earlier radical views.

Laing spent the rest of his life in Edinburgh, where he died at the house of his daughter, Elizabeth Baxter, who had been widowed in 1837, on 23 April 1868. He was buried in the Dean cemetery. His translation has long been superseded, but his other work commands interest for its views of Scandinavian society in general, and in particular of peasant proprietorship and its relation to population growth and to the distribution and increase of wealth. Most recently he has been cited in debates as to whether economic and cultural developments are necessarily antithetical.   ELIZABETH BAIGENT

Sources private information (1892) · Boase, *Mod. Eng. biog.* · *Army List* (1806) · R. J. P. Kain and E. Baigent, *The cadastral map in the service of the state: a history of property mapping* (1992) · J. Kay-Shuttleworth, *Four periods of public education* (1862); repr. with introduction by N. Morris (1973) · B. Porter, '"Monstrous vandalism": capitalism and philistinism in the works of Samuel Laing', *Albion*, 23 (1991), 253–68 · B. Porter, 'Virtue and vice in the north: the Scandinavian writings of Samuel Laing', *Scandinavian Journal of History*, 23 (1998), 153–72 · Allibone, *Dict.*
Archives Orkney Library, Kirkwall, MS autobiography

Laing, Samuel (1812–1897), politician, author, and railway executive, was born in Edinburgh on 12 December 1812. He was the son of Samuel *Laing (1780–1868), author of *Tours* in Norway, Sweden, and Denmark, who was younger brother of Malcolm *Laing, the historian of Scotland. His mother was Agnes Kelly. Laing was educated at Houghton-le-Spring grammar school, and privately by Richard Wilson, a fellow of St John's, Cambridge. He entered that college as a pensioner on 5 July 1827, graduated BA as second wrangler in 1831, and was also second Smith's prizeman. He was elected a fellow of St John's on 17 March 1834, and remained for a time in Cambridge as a mathematical coach. He was admitted a student of Lincoln's Inn on 10 November 1832, and was called to the bar on 9 June 1837. He married in 1841 Mary, daughter of Captain Cowan RN; they had two sons and three daughters.

Soon after being called to the bar Laing was appointed private secretary to Henry Labouchere, afterwards Lord

Samuel Laing (1812–1897), by W. & D. Downey

Taunton, then president of the Board of Trade. Upon the formation of the railway department of that office in 1842 he was appointed secretary, and thenceforth distinguished himself as an authority upon railways under successive presidents of the Board of Trade. He declared that 'the public have never permanently benefited from competition from different lines of railway'. He advocated stricter vetting of railway bills to avoid wasteful competition, but was opposed to government interference in matters of railway operation. He opposed railway trade unionism, but supported self-help benefit societies of railway employees.

At Laing's suggestion there was included in Gladstone's Railway Act of 1844 the requirement that each newly authorized railway should provide, in each direction of its lines, third class, covered carriages, in which the charge per passenger mile should not exceed 1*d*. The trains so provided became known as parliamentary trains. This legislation was largely responsible for the proportion of third class passengers to total railway passengers rising from under 28 per cent in 1844 to over 78 per cent in 1875. In 1845 Laing was appointed a member of the railway commission, presided over by Lord Dalhousie, and drew up the chief reports on the railway schemes of that period.

In 1846 Laing resigned his position as secretary at the Board of Trade and two years later was appointed chairman and managing director of the London, Brighton, and South Coast Railway. Under his management passenger traffic nearly doubled in five years and shareholders were paid a steady 6 per cent dividend.

However, in 1852 Laing resigned his chairmanship of the Brighton line to pursue his interests in the City of London. In 1860 he was, for a few months, financial secretary to the Treasury before Lord Palmerston persuaded him to become financial minister to the crown in India. At this post he was successful in reducing military expenditure during a brief period of peace.

During Laing's absence from the chair of the Brighton company (1852–67) and his period of service in India, the directors of the company were less circumspect than they had been under his authority. In the boom years of 1865–6, they built many branch lines to protect the company's territory from incursions from the South Eastern Railway. Following the failure of the firm of Overend and Gurney in October 1866, when the Brighton company was on the verge of bankruptcy, as a result of its speculative railway ventures, its directors, in some desperation, persuaded Laing to resume the chair.

With the able and dedicated assistance of Sir Allen Sarle, who was company secretary from 1867, and secretary and general manager from 1886, Laing led an innovative and financially successful company until his retirement in 1894. In 1881 the company pioneered electric lighting in passenger carriages while the comfort of its customers was enhanced by the widespread introduction of Pullman cars.

Laing resigned from the chairmanship of the Brighton line in 1852. In July of that year he was returned to parliament as a Liberal for the Wick district, which he represented until 1857 (when he lost his seat for opposing British intervention in China). He was re-elected in April 1859. He was financial secretary to the Treasury from June to October 1860, then appointed as financial minister in India on the governor general's council; a post he held until 1865 when he was again elected MP for Wick in July 1865. He was rejected for that constituency in 1868, but was returned for Orkney and Shetland in 1873, and sat without interruption until he retired from parliament in 1885. Though a staunch Liberal, he was opposed to what he considered the anti-imperialist leanings of Gladstone; he published in 1884 a careful and moderate indictment of what would now be called Little Englandism in *England's Foreign Policy*.

It was not until Laing had turned seventy and retired from parliament that he came before the public prominently as an author. His *Modern Science and Modern Thought* appeared in 1885 and was very widely read, being, in fact, an admirable popular exposition of the speculations of Darwin, Huxley, and Spencer, and the incompatibility of the data of modern science and 'revealed religion'. A supplementary chapter to the third edition (1886) contained a fairly crushing reply to Gladstone's defence of the book of Genesis. It was followed by *A Modern Zoroastrian*, 1887, *Problems of the Future, and other Essays*, 1889, *The Antiquity of Man*, 1891, and *Human Origins*, 1892, all written in a similar easy and interesting style. Without possessing in themselves any great scientific value, these works showed Laing's

reading, especially in anthropology, to have been extremely wide, and furnished people with general ideas on subjects of importance which, if discussed in a less attractive form, would probably have passed unheeded.

Laing died, aged eighty-six, at his home, Rockhills, Sydenham Hill, London, on 6 August 1897, and was buried on 10 August in the extramural cemetery, Brighton.

Laing's writings are remarkable as the relaxations of a man who had spent over half a century almost exclusively immersed in business affairs. He never attained to quite the same thoroughness and grip of his subject as his father, but he had much the same gift of lucid exposition, and the same freedom from self-consciousness or affectation.

THOMAS SECCOMBE, *rev.* PHILIP S. BAGWELL

Sources H. Parris, *Government and the railways in nineteenth-century Britain* (1965) · S. Laing, *Observations on Mr Strutt's amended Railway Regulation Bill now before parliament* (1847) · 'Evidence of Samuel Laing to the select committee on railway and canal amalgamation (1852–3)', *English historical documents*, 12/1, ed. G. M. Young and W. D. Hancock (1956), no. 101 · S. Laing, *Letter to the working men in the employment of the London, Brighton and South Coast Railway Company, on the present contest between the Amalgamated Society of Engineers and the employers* (1852) · J. Simmons, *The Victorian railway* (1991) · S. Laing, *England's foreign policy* (1884) · S. Laing, *Modern science and modern thought* (1885) · S. Laing, *The antiquity of man* (1891) · S. Laing, *Human origins* (1892) · *Railway Review* (13 Aug 1897) · d. cert. · CGPLA Eng. & Wales (1897) · DNB

Archives BL, corresp. with W. E. Gladstone, Add. MSS 44373–44527 · NA Scot., Dalhousie MSS · PRO, 'Rail' papers

Likenesses W. & D. Downey, photograph, NPG [*see illus.*] · Spy [L. Ward], chromolithograph caricature, NPG; repro. in *VF* (16 Aug 1873)

Wealth at death £96,861 18s. 2d.: resworn probate, Dec 1897, CGPLA Eng. & Wales

Laing, William (1764–1832), bookseller and publisher, was born in Edinburgh on 20 July 1764, the son of William Laing (1729–1795), merchant tailor, and Mary, *née* Strachan (b. 1721). After education at the Canongate Grammar School, he was an apprentice compositor between 1778 and 1784. Thereafter, owing to weak eyesight, he set himself up as a bookseller and stationer, and prospered. Specializing in secondhand material, particularly foreign books, he filled a lacuna in the Edinburgh trade. His business was first situated at the head of the Canongate, but subsequently moved eastwards to Chessel's Court. He became a burgess and freeman of the burgh of the Canongate on 13 March 1786, and in September of that year he married Helen Kirk (1767–1837). They had twelve children, of whom four sons and five daughters reached adulthood. In 1804 he moved his business to 44 South Bridge, but finally settled at 49 South Bridge in 1805. His second son, the antiquary David *Laing (1793–1878), joined the thriving business in 1806. From 1786 Laing issued annual catalogues. William Laing travelled abroad several times for stock, notably to Paris in 1793, Copenhagen in 1799 (to buy duplicates from the Royal Library), and France and the Netherlands in May 1802.

By the late 1780s Laing had also expanded into publishing. The publications dearest to his heart were editions of Greek classics, with Latin translations: Thucydides (six volumes) in 1804; Herodotus (seven volumes) in 1806; and Xenophon (ten volumes) in 1811. Laing would have liked to continue with Plato and Demosthenes, but editorial difficulties proved insurmountable.

Another business venture, financially very rewarding, was involvement in the establishment of the Commercial Bank in 1810, of which Laing became a director in 1825. Having moved home several times, Laing purchased Ramsay Lodge, a large house on Lauriston Place, in 1803. He died there on 10 April 1832, and was buried in the new Calton cemetery on 12 April 1832.

MURRAY C. T. SIMPSON

Sources G. Goudie, *David Laing, LLD* (1913) · *Caledonian Mercury* (28 May 1832) · *DNB* · Laing family documents, U. Edin. L., MS La.IV.7 · Chambers, *Scots.*, rev. T. Thomson (1875), 2.459–60 · *GM*, 1st ser., 102/2 (1832), 278–9 · [J. G. Lockhart], *Peter's letters to his kinsfolk*, 2nd edn, 3 vols. (1819)
Archives U. Edin. L., corresp., LA.iv.17–18 · U. Edin. L., family documents, MS La.IV.7
Likenesses J. G. Lockhart, caricature, c.1810–c.1817, NL Scot. · A. Edouart, silhouette, 1830, Scot. NPG · miniature, c.1830, U. Edin. L., MS La.IV.7
Wealth at death £14,879 4s. 9d.: 15 Dec 1832, will and inventory, NA Scot., SC 70/1/48, pp. 13–34

Laird, John (1805–1874), shipbuilder, was born in Greenock on 14 June 1805, the eldest son of William Laird and Agnes Macgregor, and brother of Macgregor *Laird. His father moved south in 1810, eventually establishing a boiler works on Merseyside, the Birkenhead ironworks. After his education at the Royal Institution, Liverpool, and after training as a solicitor, Laird entered the business in 1828. He married, in 1829, Elizabeth, daughter of Nicholas Hurry of Liverpool, with whom he had a family, including at least one daughter. At about the same time the works built an iron lighter of 60 tons, the *Wye*, for use on inland waterways in Ireland. It was the first of a number of iron vessels to be constructed by Laird. In 1833 a paddle-steamer, the *Lady Lansdowne*, followed. Like the *Wye* it was built in sections for reassembly and use in Ireland. In 1834 he built another prefabricated vessel, the *John Randolph*, for G. B. Lamar of Savannah, the first iron ship to be built for an American owner. Another paddle-steamer, the *Garryowen*, was built at this time, again for use in Ireland. Prefabricated riverboats became a speciality and Laird provided the *Tigris* and *Euphrates* in 1835, with which F. R. Chesney explored the Euphrates. Other achievements included the construction of the *Rainbow*, then the largest iron ship of its day; the *Robert F. Stockton*, a screw-steamer; and the *Nemesis*, a gunboat which established a formidable reputation in the opium wars with China. The Admiralty eventually joined the East India Company as customers, ordering the *Dover* in 1839.

The momentum of innovation slackened somewhat after this, although the yard was later to provide mortar vessels and gunboats for service in the Crimean War, as well as the river boat *Ma Robert* for David Livingstone in 1858. In 1861 Laird retired from the business, which was carried on by his three sons, William, John, and Henry, under the style of Laird Brothers, eventually becoming Cammell Laird & Co. Ltd in 1903. Laird was elected as a

Conservative to be Birkenhead's first MP in December 1861, a position he retained until his death. He had occupied a prominent position locally for some years prior to this, serving as a member of the Mersey Docks and Harbour Board and as chairman of Birkenhead Improvement Commission. He died on 29 October 1874 at his home, 63 Hamilton Square, Birkenhead, following a riding accident.

J. K. LAUGHTON, rev. LIONEL ALEXANDER RITCHIE

Sources Cammell Laird & Co. Ltd, *Builders of great ships* (1959) · Boase, *Mod. Eng. biog.* · *WWBMP* · L. A. Ritchie, ed., *The shipbuilding industry: a guide to historical records* (1992) · *The Times* (30 Oct 1874) · personal information (1892) · *Practical Magazine*, 3 (1874), 401–8 · *CGPLA Eng. & Wales* (1874)
Archives Birkenhead Central Library, Cammell Laird archives
Likenesses J. Macbride, bust, 1863, Birkenhead Hospital, Cheshire · C. S. Keene, three pencil sketches, c.1872, NPG · W. Barnes Boadle, oils, c.1877 · A. B. Joy, bronze statue, c.1877, Hamilton Square, Birkenhead · T. Brock, bust, Williamson Art Gallery and Museum, Birkenhead · T. M. Maguire, lithograph · J. V. R. Parsons, oils · Spy [L. Ward], chromolithograph caricature, NPG; repro. in *VF* (17 May 1873) · J. & C. Watkins, carte-de-visite, NPG · photograph, Williamson Art Gallery and Museum, Birkenhead · portrait, repro. in *Practical Magazine*
Wealth at death under £200,000: probate, 11 Dec 1874, *CGPLA Eng. & Wales*

Laird, John (1887–1946), philosopher, was born at Durris, Kincardineshire, on 17 May 1887, the eldest son of the Revd D. M. W. Laird and his wife, Margaret, daughter of John Stewart, schoolmaster. His father was the third in succession to enter the ministry of the Church of Scotland, and this hereditary connection was not without its influence on young Laird. The place of his birth was symbolic of his character. His home was set just where the Dee valley becomes smoother as it approaches the sea, but in the distance there are glimpses of lofty mountains; and in Laird's nature there was an unusual mingling of rugged strength with tenderness and kindliness. The locality was also suggestive of his philosophical work, for in the adjacent parish was born Thomas Reid, the Scottish philosopher whose metaphysical realism Laird afterwards discovered that he shared.

Laird's education at the village school of Durris was simple but effective and the headmaster had an awakening influence. Two years at the grammar school of Aberdeen followed, and then the family moved to Edinburgh, where he entered the university. Although in the eyes of his fellow students he soon established himself as one of the most brilliant of their number, he himself was not enthusiastic about his Edinburgh days. He admired A. S. Pringle-Pattison, the best-known member of the philosophical faculty, but thought his lectures 'smelled of lavender'. He graduated MA with a first class in philosophy in 1908 and in that year was awarded the Shaw fellowship, the blue riband of Scottish philosophical scholarship.

Laird's philosophical awakening came at Cambridge, where he himself said that he 'began all over again'. Beginning again was an abiding characteristic; his life-long attitude is suggested in the opening paragraph of his first book: 'a complete or final answer ... is of course unattainable until the day when all speculative problems have found their solution'. He was a senior scholar of Trinity College and was placed in the first class in both parts of the moral sciences tripos (1910, 1911). After a year as assistant in St Andrews University and another short period as professor of philosophy at Dalhousie University, Nova Scotia, he went in 1913 to Queen's University, Belfast, as professor of logic and metaphysics. In 1919 he married Helen Ritchie, daughter of John Forbes, linen manufacturer, of Belfast; they had one son, who died in childhood.

Laird's wish to be a Scottish professor was fulfilled in 1924 by his appointment as regius professor of moral philosophy in Aberdeen, where he remained for the rest of his days, resisting temptations to move to any wider sphere to which his growing reputation would have given him entrance. He accepted, however, several invitations to give special lectures in other universities—the Gifford lectures in Glasgow (1939), the Herbert Spencer lecture in Oxford (1944), the Forwood lectures in Liverpool (1945), and others. In Aberdeen he made his influence forcibly felt, not only in the work of his chair but in the wider administration of the university, and he left behind him a reputation for penetrative insight and fair dealing.

From his special subject of moral philosophy Laird frequently escaped in the direction of metaphysics, which he alleged were 'always breaking in'. His first book, *Problems of the Self* (1917), an expansion of his Shaw lectures, was a manifesto of his philosophical intention, and his *Study in Realism* (1920) defines further his prevailing epistemological and metaphysical position. In it he claimed that 'knowledge is a kind of discovery in which things are revealed or given to the mind' and that 'the fact of being known does not imply any effect upon the character or existence of the thing which is known'. These views were in direct opposition to idealist contemporaries such as F. H. Bradley and H. H. Joachim at Oxford. The particular type of realism which he adopted is stated with great clearness in his brilliant contribution to *Contemporary British Philosophy* (1924). One or two more purely ethical books followed, and then he turned his attention for a while to the history of philosophy, and produced three valuable short studies—on Hume and on Hobbes, and *Recent Philosophy*. He returned to more strictly ethical writing in his *An Enquiry into Moral Notions* (1935), but its somewhat critical reception slightly disappointed him, as he thought the importance of the subject (the relation between the 'right' and the 'good') called for more sympathetic attention. He therefore very willingly accepted the opportunity, which the Gifford lectures gave him, of turning his attention once more to metaphysics, and these lectures provided the substance of his two greatest books, *Theism and Cosmology* (1940) and *Mind and Deity* (1941).

Laird was a slightly repressive guardian in respect of all theological speculation, but seemed to think that theologians might be justified if they did not overreach themselves and were careful about the solidity of their foundations. Perhaps he himself was excessively nervous about his foundations, but in the latter book he raises a more conspicuous superstructure, and reaches securely the

firm conviction that theism, which in his earlier days he had described as 'a decrepit metaphysical vehicle harnessed to poetry', could carry arguments of considerable weight. *The Device of Government* (1944), wartime lectures to the troops, attracted considerable attention. Several smaller books appeared shortly after his death. One of these, *Philosophical Incursions into English Literature* (1946), is in lighter vein than the rest of his works, and shows his abiding literary interests. He received the honorary degrees of LLD from the University of Edinburgh (1935), and of DLitt (1945) from Belfast, and was elected FBA in 1933. He died at his home, Powis Lodge, Old Aberdeen, on 5 August 1946, his wife surviving him.

W. S. URQUHART, rev. MARK J. SCHOFIELD

Sources *Aberdeen University Review*, 32 (1947–8) · W. S. Urquhart, *PBA*, 32 (1946), 415–32 · private information (1959) · personal knowledge (1959) · S. Brown, 'John Laird', *Biographical dictionary of twentieth-century philosophers*, ed. S. Brown, D. Collinson, and R. Wilkinson (1996) · *CGPLA Eng. & Wales* (1946)
Archives U. Aberdeen L., corresp. and papers
Wealth at death see confirmation, sealed in London, 27 Nov 1946, *CGPLA Eng. & Wales*

Laird, Macgregor (1808–1861), shipbuilder and explorer, was born in Greenock, the younger son of William Laird, founder of the Birkenhead firm of shipbuilders, and Agnes Macgregor; he was the brother of John *Laird. On leaving school in Edinburgh he was given a partnership in the business by his father.

The existence of the Niger River, rumoured since antiquity, was confirmed by explorers who had struck its course inland, but failed to discover its mouth. In 1830 the problem of the mouth of the Niger was suddenly solved by Richard and John Lander, who had sailed down the river from Busa, emerging into the Atlantic Ocean from the River Nun, one of the 'oil rivers', where African coastal middlemen were shifting attention from the slave trade (made illegal for British subjects in 1807) to supplying palm oil to Liverpool traders for the growing soap industry in Cheshire.

Laird was so fired by enthusiasm at this discovery that he left his father's firm to form the African Inland Company. Richard Lander joined the enterprise, advising that a profit could be made from ivory and indigo trading. Laird built two paddle-wheeled steamers designed to make the ocean voyage to west Africa and ascend the shallow waters to be found on much of the Niger. One of them, the *Alburkah*, 55 tons, would make maritime history as the first vessel constructed entirely of iron to complete an ocean voyage. Laird unsuccessfully approached the British government for financial subsidy. He saw his ambitions for trade, shipping innovation, and exploration as serving the higher purpose of striking 'a mortal blow to that debasing and demoralizing traffic which had for centuries cursed that unhappy land' and 'to be the means of rescuing millions of … fellow men from the miseries of a religion characterized by violence and blood, by imparting to them the truths of Christianity' (Howard and Plumb, 388).

As a technical and exploration venture, the expedition

of 1832–4 was successful; the *Alburkah* proved the feasibility of the iron steamship and Laird and his crews penetrated the 550 miles from the sea to the confluence of the Niger and Benue, and a further 80 miles up the latter. Overall, however, the expedition was a disaster. Trading was not profitable, and the ships were attacked returning down the Niger at Aboh by African middlemen traders, despite the fact that Laird had wisely, on Lander's advice, kept out of the palm-oil trade. Lander and three others were killed in this affray. The toll of disease was dreadful. Of the forty-eight white men who began the venture in 1832, only nine survived when it ended in 1834. The major killer was malaria, for which there was no treatment. Laird himself was seriously ill, and his health never fully recovered. He vowed to make no more inland expeditions until a cure could be found.

For almost twenty years thereafter Laird remained mainly an observer of the west African scene, publicly resisting efforts at inland penetration such as the disastrous Niger expedition of 1841, sponsored by the antislavery movement with government support, whose death rate amply justified Laird's warnings. Until the end of the 1840s Laird concentrated on the development of transatlantic steamships. In 1837 he was one of the founders of the British and North American Steam Navigation Company, whose vessel the *Sirius* made the first completely steam-powered Atlantic crossing in 1838. He remained immersed in the problems of iron steamship technology, taking out a number of patents in the field, until 1850, by which time he had moved from Birkenhead to London.

In 1851 Laird made the decision to concentrate his activities once again on west Africa, this time by providing a regular ocean steamship service to the main ports. He pressed the British government for help, and in January 1852 was awarded a mail contract for ten years with annual subsidies starting at £23,250 and decreasing to £18,750 in the final year. Laird was then able to found the African Steamship Company, with a paid-up capital of £132,842. Though experiencing financial difficulties in the first few years, the company was well established and profitable by 1860, operating seven steamships carrying mail, cargo, and passengers on a regular basis from Liverpool (to which it moved from London in 1856), calling at the main ports where British traders were present between Freetown and Fernando Po. Small traders, including Africans, began to ship goods and compete with the larger firms.

In 1854 Laird returned once again to his earlier ideas of Niger penetration. The catalyst appears to have been William Balfour Baikie, surgeon and naval officer in west Africa, who proposed to give daily doses of quinine, an ancient South American Indian malaria treatment hitherto ignored by European medical authorities. Laird secured a British government contract to build and equip a vessel to ascend the Niger and Benue. The expedition of 1854, under Baikie's command, was as successful as that of 1832–4 had been disastrous. Thanks to quinine, not a single member of the expedition died. Laird now moved to

place the Niger enterprise on a permanent footing. In 1857 he contracted with the Admiralty to send a steamer up the Niger annually for five years in return for a subsidy. These new expeditions, however, were less successful. The African coastal middlemen, armed by Liverpool traders, were determined to keep others out of the palm-oil trade of the lower Niger. In 1859 Laird's steamer laden with produce was attacked. Soon afterwards his station at Aboh was sacked. For the next two years he was involved in bitter exchanges with the Foreign Office over the failure of the navy to protect his vessels, and what subsidies he should be paid.

None of these questions were resolved when Laird died at 1 Surbiton Crescent, Surrey, on 27 January 1861, aged fifty-two. He had been married and he left children, but no further details are known. His career epitomized beliefs and qualities that came to symbolize the Victorian age. An ardent evangelical protestant and opponent of the slave trade, he shared the view that Africa could be 'civilized' through the beneficent alliance of Christian missionary activity and 'legitimate commerce' replacing trade in human beings.   JOHN FLINT

Sources M. Laird and R. A. K. Oldfield, *Narrative of an expedition into the interior of Africa by the River Niger in the steam vessels Quorra and Alburka in 1832, 1833 and 1834*, 2 vols. (1837) · M. Laird, 'Steam communication with west Africa', letter to Earl Grey, 25 March 1851 [repr. in C. W. Newbury, *British policy towards west Africa: select documents, 1786–1874* (1965), p.114] · 'Select committee on the west coast of Africa', *Parl. papers* (1842), 11.573, no. 551 [memorandum on trade and slavery] · W. B. Baikie, *Narrative of an exploring voyage up the rivers Kwora and Bi'nue (commonly known as the Niger and Tsa' dda) in 1854* (1856) · P. N. Davies, 'The African Steamship Company', *Liverpool and Merseyside: essays in the economic and social history of the port and its hinterland*, ed. J. R. Harris (1969) · J. E. Flint, *Sir George Goldie and the making of Nigeria* (1960), 13–21 · P. N. Davies, *Sir Alfred Jones: shipping entrepreneur par excellence* (1978) · K. O. Dike, *Trade and politics in the Niger delta, 1830–1885* (1956) · A. C. G. Hastings, *The voyage of the Dayspring* (1926) · H. S. Goldsmith, 'MacGregor [sic] Laird and the Niger', *Journal of the African Society*, 31 (Oct 1932) · C. Howard and J. H. Plumb, *West African explorers* (1951), 388 · d. cert.

Archives Merseyside Maritime Museum, Liverpool, letters to his wife · PRO, Foreign Office, 2nd ser.

Wealth at death £25,000: probate, 22 Feb 1861, *CGPLA Eng. & Wales*

Laisrén mac Decláin (*fl.* 6th cent.). *See under* Connacht, saints of (*act. c.*400–*c.*800).

Laisrén mac Feradaig (*d.* 605). *See under* Iona, abbots of (*act.* 563–927).

Laithwaite, Sir (John) Gilbert (1894–1986), civil servant and diplomatist, was born on 5 July 1894 in Dublin, the eldest in the family of two sons and two daughters of John Gilbert Laithwaite, of the Post Office survey, of Dublin, and his wife, Mary, daughter of Bernard Kearney, of Clooncoose House, Castlerea, co. Roscommon. He was educated at Clongowes, whence he won a scholarship to Trinity College, Oxford, of which he became an honorary fellow in 1955. He obtained a second class in both classical honour moderations (1914) and *literae humaniores* (1916).

During the First World War, Laithwaite served in the front line in France in 1917–18, as a second lieutenant with the 10th Lancashire Fusiliers, and was wounded. In 1971 he published (privately printed in Lahore) a record of part of this service in *The 21st March 1918: Memories of an Infantry Officer*, which includes a lively, detailed account of the German attack at Havrincourt, near Cambrai, on 21 March 1918.

In 1919 Laithwaite was appointed to the India Office, and thus started a long career involved with the subcontinent. He became a principal in 1924 and in 1931 he was specially attached to the prime minister, J. Ramsay MacDonald, for the second Indian round-table conference in London. Two important secretaryships followed, of the Indian franchise (Lothian) committee under R. A. Butler, which toured the subcontinent in 1932, and of the Indian delimitation committee from August 1935 to February 1936. From 1936 to 1943 he was principal private secretary to the viceroy of India, the second marquess of Linlithgow. It was a time of growing political tension following the India Act of 1935 and with provincial autonomy in 1937 imminent. The strains and stresses were greatly increased by the approach of war. Laithwaite gave staunch support to the viceroy and his policies and deserves to share with Linlithgow the credit for ensuring that India's vital role as supply centre for the war effort, as well as a source of military manpower, was quickly and efficiently organized and maintained.

In 1943 Laithwaite returned to England with Linlithgow and was appointed assistant under-secretary of state for India. He was then appointed an under-secretary (civil) of the war cabinet (1944–5) and secretary to the Commonwealth ministerial meeting in London in 1945. As deputy under-secretary of state for Burma in 1945–7, he twice visited Rangoon and had a formative share in the negotiations leading to Burmese independence early in 1948. He was deputy under-secretary of state for India in 1947 and for Commonwealth relations in 1948–9, and he acted as one of the official secretaries of the conference of Commonwealth prime ministers in 1948.

In 1949 Laithwaite became the United Kingdom representative to the Republic of Ireland, a post upgraded to ambassador in 1950. In 1951 he was sent as high commissioner to Pakistan, where he already had friendly relations with members of the government, officials, and other leaders. He steadfastly promoted the British policy of friendship with both India and Pakistan in their disputes over the future of Kashmir and the distribution of the canal waters of the Punjab, and supported the efforts of the United Nations to reconcile the two countries. He left Pakistan in 1954 to be permanent under-secretary of state for Commonwealth relations from 1955 to 1959, first visiting Australia and New Zealand. From 1963 to 1966 he was vice-chairman of the Commonwealth Institute.

Laithwaite was also a governor of Queen Mary College, London, from 1959; president of the Hakluyt Society, 1964–9; vice-president of the Royal Central Asian Society in 1967; president of the Royal Geographical Society, 1966–9; and a member of the Standing Commission on Museums and Galleries from 1959 to 1971. After retirement in 1959 he played an active part in the life of the City as a director of Inchcape and of insurance companies. He

was admitted a freeman of the City of London in 1960 and was master of the Tallow Chandlers' Company in 1972–3.

Laithwaite was an industrious and efficient worker, with an impressive grasp of problems and a reputation for fairness. He was rather tall and solidly built, dignified and precise in manner, but exceptionally friendly in a social context, even on first acquaintance, though still with a trace of formality. His outstanding qualities and affability, together with his sense of humour, made him many friends both at home and abroad. His diverse interests included a strong appreciation of fine artefacts and while in India and Pakistan he collected carpets and rugs with discrimination.

Laithwaite came from a Lancastrian Roman Catholic family and adhered devoutly to that faith, which contributed to his success in the embassy in Dublin. In 1960 he was appointed a knight of Malta. He was appointed CIE (1935), CSI (1938), KCIE (1941), KCMG (1948), GCMG (1953), and KCB (1956). Laithwaite was a homosexual and unmarried. He died in London on 21 December 1986.

MICHAEL MACLAGAN, *rev.*

Sources *The Times* (24 Dec 1986) · G. Laithwaite, *The 21st March 1918: memories of an infantry officer* (privately printed, Lahore, India, 1971) · G. Laithwaite, *The Laithwaites: some records of a Lancashire family* (privately printed, New Delhi, 1941; rev. edn (privately printed, Karachi, 1961) · personal knowledge (1996) · *CGPLA Eng. & Wales* (1987)
Archives BL OIOC, papers, MS Eur. F 138 · Lancs. RO, corresp. and papers · NRA, corresp. | BL OIOC, corresp. with Sir H. E. Rance, MS Eur. F 169 · JRL, corresp. with Auchinleck
Wealth at death £294,414: probate, 20 March 1987, *CGPLA Eng. & Wales*

Lakatos, Imre [*formerly* Imré Lipsitz] (1922–1974), philosopher of mathematics and of science, was born Imré Lipsitz on 9 November 1922 in Debrecen, Hungary, the only child of Jacob Márton Lipsitz, a wine merchant, and Márgit Herczfeld, both Hungarian Jews. His father left the family home shortly after Imre was born and he was raised by his mother and maternal grandmother. Imre studied at the Jewish Real Gymnasium and later at Debrecen University. An outstanding student, he graduated in 1944 in mathematics, physics, and philosophy.

Lakatos had become an active and influential Marxist while at university. When Germany invaded Hungary in 1944, he fled with Éva Révész (to whom he was married briefly in 1947) to Nagyvarad (now the Romanian town of Oradea). There they were kept in hiding by non-Jewish families. (Meanwhile his mother and grandmother were forced into the Debrecen ghetto and later killed in Auschwitz.) Lakatos lived in Nagyvarad on false papers under the name of Molnár. He organized a communist cell among the group of Jews in hiding and their host families; and he is alleged to have led the group in deciding on the 'forced suicide' of one of its members, Éva Iszák. There are various explanations of his role in this affair—his own seems to have been that Iszák, an anti-fascist activist who had fallen out with her host family and who therefore needed new accommodation and papers, was in some danger of arrest by the Gestapo and hence a threat to the security of the whole group. One of the most striking features of the episode is that she herself seems to have put up no resistance to the decision.

At the end of the war Lakatos returned briefly to his ransacked house in Debrecen where, among little else, he found some of his old shirts monogrammed 'I. L.' (or rather, in the Hungarian convention, 'L. I.'). He took the opportunity to change his name for a second time: to the working-class Imre Lakatos. An influential member of a circle of élite communist intellectuals in Budapest, he obtained a post in the ministry of education and became active in (controversial) educational reform. He received a PhD with highest honours from the Eötvös Collegium in 1947 for a thesis that he later insisted was 'worthless' on the sociology of science. In 1948 he won party agreement to study theoretical physics at Moscow University. He had made influential enemies, however, and in 1950, after a mysterious end to his stay in Moscow, he was—for reasons that remain unclear—called by the central committee to a hearing on the Éva Iszák affair, and expelled from the Communist Party. He was interrogated and held in solitary confinement for six weeks by the state security police (AVO). He was then taken to the labour camp at Recsk, where he was interned in appalling conditions for three years. On his release he worked at the Mathematical Research Institute at the Hungarian Academy of Science.

Although Lakatos's communist faith seems to have survived the Recsk experience, he began to question it shortly afterwards. At the time of the Hungarian revolution in 1956 he followed his second wife, Éva Pap (whom he married in 1955), and her family out of the country and soon obtained a Rockefeller Foundation scholarship to study at Cambridge for a second PhD. From 1959 onwards he regularly attended Karl Popper's seminar at the London School of Economics (LSE). The LSE appointed him to a lectureship in logic in 1960, and he was promoted to a personal chair (in logic, with special reference to the philosophy of mathematics) in 1970.

Lakatos's second PhD thesis became the basis for his *Proofs and Refutations*. This work, published initially as journal articles in 1963–4 and in book form only posthumously in 1976, constitutes his major contribution to the philosophy of mathematics. A dialogue between a group of frighteningly bright students and their teacher, it reconstructs the process by which Euler's famous conjecture about polyhedra (that they all satisfy the formula: number of vertices *plus* number of faces *minus* the number of edges equals two) was proved and, in the process, heavily modified and transformed. Lakatos's claim was that, although the eventual proof of the theorem in mathematics may be cast as a straightforward deduction, the way in which the proof is found is a more exciting process, involving counterexamples, reformulations, counterexamples to the reformulations, and careful analysis of 'failed' proofs leading to further modifications of 'the' theorem.

Lakatos thought of himself for some years as a 'Popperian', simply extending Popper's fallibilism to the seemingly unlikely field of mathematics. However, he

eventually began to discern faults in Popper's philosophy of natural science, and began in 1968 to develop his 'methodology of scientific research programmes' (all the relevant papers are reprinted in his *Philosophical Papers*, vol. 1, 1978). Lakatos claimed that science was best viewed as consisting, not of single isolated theories, but rather of broader 'research programmes'. Each programme issues in a series of theories, governed not only by empirical refutations of earlier theories, but also by certain specifiable heuristic principles operating on the programme's central assumptions or 'hard core'. Lakatos saw this methodology as giving a more accurate view of the rationality of science than Popper's—in fact, as a synthesis of the best elements of the accounts of Popper and of Thomas Kuhn. It remains influential.

Lakatos was a short, wiry, energetic man—a 'twenty-four hours a day' intellectual. A great advocate of the power of reason, he was a convinced atheist—indeed he held all his views with conviction. In the West he retained strong political interests. Like many who had suffered under a left-wing dictatorship, he swung far to the right in political, if not always in social, terms—being a vigorous opponent of the student movement of the 1960s and an equally vigorous supporter of the domino theory and hence of American involvement in Vietnam. He made several visits to give lectures in the USA in the 1960s and 1970s. He had a sharp tongue and an exceptional wit. He engendered intense friendships and intense enmities in roughly equal measure. After his divorce from Éva Pap in 1960 he had a series of affairs, some of them with women much younger than himself. He then settled into a close relationship with Gillian Page, with whom he was living at the time of his death. He had no children.

Lakatos survived a heart attack in early 1974 but, after discharging himself against medical advice, suffered a further and fatal heart attack at his home, 5 Turner's Wood, Hampstead, London, on 2 February 1974 and was declared dead on arrival at New End Hospital, Hampstead.   JOHN WORRALL

Sources I. Lakatos, *Proofs and refutations: the logic of mathematical discovery*, ed. J. Worrall and E. Zahar (1976) • I. Lakatos, *The methodology of scientific research programmes*, ed. J. Worrall and G. Currie (1978) • I. Lakatos, *Mathematics, science and epistemology*, ed. J. Worrall and G. Currie (1978) • J. Long, 'Lakatos in Hungary', *Philosophy of the Social Sciences*, 28 (1998), 245–311 • BLPES, Lakatos MSS • d. cert. • private information (2004) • personal knowledge (2004)
Archives BLPES, corresp. and papers
Wealth at death £55,581: probate, 20 Jan 1975, *CGPLA Eng. & Wales*

Lake, Arthur (*bap.* 1567, *d.* 1626), bishop of Bath and Wells, was the son of Almeric Lake (1519–1594), a burgess of Southampton; he was a younger brother of Sir Thomas *Lake, secretary of state to James I. He was baptized in St Michael's Church, Southampton, on 30 September 1567 and educated at King Edward's Grammar School, Southampton, during the headmastership of the eminent Walloon divine, Adrian (or Hadrian) Savaria. From there, in each case as a scholar, he went first to Winchester College, in 1581, and then to New College, Oxford, in 1587. He graduated BA in 1591 and proceeded MA in 1595, and BD

Arthur Lake (*bap.* 1567, *d.* 1626), by Richard Greenbury, 1626 [replica]

and DD in 1605, when he was allowed to defer some of the academic exercises owing to his work in London on the translation of the New Testament, for what became the King James Bible. Lake was fellow of New College from 1589 to 1600, and fellow of Winchester from 1600. Several letters survive from his time as an Oxford tutor, including reports to parents on their sons' progress accompanied by accounts to be settled such as bills for lessons in French and singing, and for broken windows.

Lake received a series of benefices in his native Hampshire, first at Havant (1599–1601) from the crown, then at Hambledon (1601–3) and Chilcomb (1603–6) from Bishop Thomas Bilson of Winchester, and at Stoke Charity (1605–8) on the presentation of Sir Thomas Clark. By 1603 Bilson had made Lake his chaplain, and in 1605 he promoted him to the archdeaconry of Surrey. Although most of the archidiaconal records for his time are lost, Lake did sit as a judge in the diocesan high commission at Bishop's Waltham from 1606 to 1608 and was one of Archbishop Richard Bancroft's commissaries for his visitation of Winchester diocese in 1607.

Lake's major patron was his brother, Sir Thomas, who secured him the mastership of St Cross Hospital in Winchester in 1603, the deanery of Worcester in 1608, the wardenship of New College in 1613, and, in 1616, the bishopric of Bath and Wells. As dean of Worcester Lake helped to recover a lease let contrary to law, and together with the organist, Thomas Tomkins, oversaw the construction of a new organ and in 1612 composed an anthem, 'Know ye not that a prince, a great prince, is fallen this day in Israel', for the funeral day of Prince Henry. Lake's wide intellectual interests led him in 1616 to endow lectureships in mathematics and Hebrew at New College, and volumes on history, geography, and Arabic grammar as well as theology are well represented in the substantial benefaction of books he made to the college in 1617. On his return to New College in 1613 he acquired the rectory of Stanton St John, a college living, and served as vice-chancellor of Oxford in 1616/17, remaining at Oxford until the end of the academic year despite his consecration as bishop of Bath and Wells on 8 December 1616.

Thereafter Lake lived in his diocese, where he was an energetic governor in spiritual and secular affairs. He personally conducted his three visitations of 1617, 1620, and 1623, and regularly heard disciplinary cases, usually in his episcopal palace at Wells. His diocesan government was facilitated by his friendship with many key officials, including Archdeacon Timothy Rivett of Bath, Archdeacon Samuel Ward of Taunton, his chancellor, Arthur Duck, and, from 1621, the new dean of Wells, Ralph Barlow. Lake's central concern as bishop was to spread the gospel. At Oxford he had been a distinguished preacher, with no less a figure than John Rainolds procuring copies of his sermons, and at Bath and Wells he delivered courses of sermons in the cathedral, and also preached on visitation, at the ordination of ministers, and at the public penance of those found guilty of incest, schism, and other crimes, the latter being a practice unparalleled among his fellow bishops. Lake probably also preached at local combination lectures, and certainly maintained close links with the clerical preaching élite of Somerset, which included puritans such as Richard Bernard of Batcombe and William Sclater of Pitminster; Sclater, indeed, became Lake's chaplain.

Lake brought into the diocese a number of preachers educated at New College, and was the last Jacobean bishop to require non-preaching ministers to undertake theological exercises to deepen their knowledge and improve their chances of qualifying for preaching licences. He also founded a public library at Bath Abbey for the benefit of local clergy. His evangelical fervour even embraced the New World, for in a fast sermon before the House of Lords in July 1625 he urged that the gospel be taken to the American Indians, and told John White of Dorchester, his fellow collegian and founder of the Massachusetts Bay Company, that but for his age he would accompany him to the New World.

Although Lake was merely one of a number of preaching pastors on the Jacobean bench of bishops, his career and diocesan work is unusually well documented. Often indulgent towards moderate puritans, Lake did not share their entrenched hostility to the Church of Rome, and counted among his friends at least one former recusant, Lady Elizabeth Booth of Bath. Lake espoused a moderate Calvinism, holding to the doctrine of hypothetical universalism, and was acutely conscious of the divisive consequences for parish religion of controversial divinity, a point which he emphasized in his sermons, and in private advice to Samuel Ward in 1618, while Ward was attending the Synod of Dort. Lake is the only Jacobean bishop whose diocesan sermons survive in bulk, and many contain clear expositions of scripture and hark on perennial themes such as repentance, faith, and self-knowledge.

Lake never married. He fell ill in London while attending parliament, and died on 4 May 1626, having made his last confession to his friend, Bishop Nicholas Felton of Ely. He was buried in Wells Cathedral, though without the pleasing epitaph, a play on Ezekiel 47, which he had specified in his will. On the other hand, Lake's expressed wish that his sermons be published 'for the good of younger students' (PRO, PROB 11/152/99) was observed: a folio volume appeared in 1629, containing ninety-nine sermons preached at Oxford, London, and the court, as well as in Somerset, together with eleven religious meditations, all prefaced by 'A short view of the author' by John Harris, who had been a fellow under Lake at New College. Harris's panegyric places Lake in the tradition of primitive episcopacy, and though some of his claims are unverifiable or dubious, others are vindicated by the record. *Ten Sermons upon Severall Occasions*, originally preached at Paul's Cross and Winchester, appeared in 1640, and Lake's 'Theses de Sabbato' was published in 1641, appended to *Of the Morality of the Fourth Commandment* by William Twisse, another fellow of New College in Lake's time as warden. Six sermons by Lake at Worcester in 1613 were prepared for publication in 1661 but remained in manuscript (Folger Shakespeare Library, V.a.394).   KENNETH FINCHAM

Sources J. Harris, 'A short view of the author', in A. Lake, *Sermons with some religious and divine meditations* (1629) · will, PRO, PROB 11/152, sig. 99 · K. Fincham, *Prelate as pastor: the episcopate of James I* (1990) · P. Collinson, *The religion of protestants* (1982) · parish register, Southampton, St Michael's, Hants. RO · T. Bilson, bishop's register, 1597–1616, Hants. RO, Winchester diocesan records, 21M65.A1/29 · admissions register, New College, Oxford, MS 9750 · *Hist. U. Oxf.* 4: 17th-cent. Oxf. · I. Walton, *The life of Dr Sanderson, late bishop of Lincoln* (1678) · J. Ley, *Sunday a Sabbath* (1641), 108 · New College, Oxford, MS 14.753 · Hunt. L., STT 1208 · Bancroft's register, LPL, fol. 217v · high commission act book, 1606–8, Hants. RO, Winchester diocesan records · Christ Church Oxf., Mus. MS 706 · T. B. James and A. L. Merson, eds., *The third book of remembrance of Southampton*, 4, Southampton RS, 22 (1979), 88
Archives New College, Oxford | Bodl. Oxf., Tanner MSS · Hants. RO, diocesan and parochial records · Som. ARS, diocesan and capitular records
Likenesses R. Greenbury, oils (replica), 1626, Winchester College, Hampshire [*see illus.*] · J. Payne, line engraving, pubd 1629, BM, NPG · portrait, New College, Oxford

Lake, Sir Edward, baronet (1596x1600–1674), royalist army officer, was the eldest son of Richard Lake of Irby-le-Marsh, Lincolnshire, and Anne, youngest daughter and coheir of Edward Wardell of Keelby in the same county. He graduated BA from St Catharine's College, Cambridge in 1626, was incorporated in the same degree at Oxford on 15 December 1627, and was admitted bachelor of civil law on 24 January 1628 as a member of St Alban Hall, Oxford. He ultimately took his doctor's degree, practised as a civilian, and in May 1639 became advocate-general for Ireland, where he served as MP for the borough of Cavan from 1639 until his expulsion on 9 November 1640.

On the outbreak of the civil war Lake both fought, and reputedly wrote, on the king's side; *A Just Apology for his Sacred Majestie* (1642) has been attributed to him. At the battle of Edgehill he earned fame, and royal gratitude, for a signal act of heroism when, having lost the use of his left hand by a shot, he placed his horse's bridle between his teeth and fought with his sword in his right hand. He received sixteen wounds, was taken prisoner, and detained seven weeks at Great Crosby, Lancashire. He managed to escape and by Christmas 1642 was safe at Bangor, Caernarvonshire. On 20 October 1643 he arrived at Oxford, and on the 23rd, the anniversary of Edgehill, was kindly received by the king. He was promised a baronetcy, granted by a warrant for a patent which never passed the great seal, as well as the honour of an augmentation to his arms incorporating a royal lion, besides some compensation for the loss of his estate in England and Ireland. Two months afterwards the king sent him to Worcester. At the Restoration, Lake petitioned importunately for preferment claiming he had been promised mastership of the rolls in Ireland and a grant of forfeited lands worth £600 a year, but had to content himself with the chancellorship of the diocese of Lincoln. He was granted the title of baronet by a patent dated 10 July 1661.

At Lincoln, Lake occupied the front line in the war between orthodoxy and dissent, having played his own small part in the unfolding Restoration church settlement with the publication in 1662 of his *Memoranda: Touching the Oath ex officio*. In 1666 a nonconformist barrister named Edward King of Ashby, Lincolnshire, charged him before the committee of parliament for grievances with extortion and illegal conduct. King printed his petition and circulated it throughout the county. Lake published an elaborate *Answer* which apparently satisfied the committee, but his struggles with the highly litigious, and highly effective, King ran the chancellor ragged. Although Lake fought back, he was repeatedly worsted, then left high and dry by his royal master's declaration of indulgence against which he protested in 1672. He died on 18 July 1674, and was buried in Lincoln Cathedral on 20 July, where his monument describes him as of Bishop's Norton, Lincolnshire. His wife, Anne, eldest daughter and coheir of Simon Bibye of Buckden, Huntingdonshire, died in or before 1670. The couple had at least one child, Edward, who died an infant before 1666. Lake was succeeded in his title by his grand-nephew, Bibye Lake (1684–1744), who petitioned Queen Anne on the nature of Charles I's award to his great-uncle; Lake was granted the title of first baronet in 1711.

GORDON GOODWIN, *rev.* SEAN KELSEY

Sources GEC, *Baronetage*, 3.313 · E. Green, ed., *The visitation of the county of Lincoln made by Sir Edward Bysshe*, Lincoln RS, 8 (1917) · Venn, *Alum. Cant.*, 1/3.34 · Foster, *Alum. Oxon.*, 1500–1714, 3.869 · Wood, *Ath. Oxon.: Fasti* (1815), 435 · R. Lascelles, ed., *Liber munerum publicorum Hiberniae … or, The establishments of Ireland*, 2 vols. [1824–30], vol. 1, pt 2, p. 5; vol. 2, p. 100 · *CSP dom.*, 1637–8, 401; 1660–61, 41–2, 53; 1672, 539 · *CSP Ire.*, 1660–62, 360 · *Sir Edward Lake's account of his interviews with Charles I*, ed. T. P. Taswell-Langmead (1859) · C. Holmes, *Seventeenth-century Lincolnshire*, History of Lincolnshire, 7 (1980), 225–6, 228–9 · will, PRO, PROB 11/348, fols. 197v–198r
Archives Hunt. L., corresp.

Likenesses engraving (after oil painting), repro. in J. Thane, *British autography*, 3; priv. coll.
Wealth at death see will, PRO, PROB 11/348, fols. 197v–198r

Lake, Edward (1641–1704), Church of England clergyman, was born in Exeter on 10 November 1641, the son of James Lake (1612/13–1678), rector of St Pancras in that city, later vicar of Veryan, Cornwall (1642–61), and canon of Exeter Cathedral (1660–78). Edward Lake matriculated (as Andrew Lake) from Wadham College, Oxford, on 31 July 1658 as a commoner and was elected a scholar of his college on 23 September 1659, but moved to Cambridge before graduating; however, there is no record of his college or graduation at Cambridge. In his early career he seems to have been connected to the family of John Grenville, first earl of Bath. He was made rector of Norton, Kent, in 1669, a living that he held until 1683.

About 1670 Lake became chaplain and tutor to the princesses Mary and Anne, daughters of James, duke of York. Lake's published diary for 1677–8 gives details of Mary's marriage to William of Orange and of the appointment of William Sancroft as archbishop of Canterbury (an appointment that surprised Lake, given Sancroft's then relatively lowly position as dean of St Paul's). When Princess Anne was taken ill with smallpox, the duke of York forbade Lake from attending her. Lake suspected that this was not to prevent the spread of the disease, but so that Anne's Catholic nurse could exert a greater influence over her. When Lake took his concerns to Henry Compton, bishop of London, the bishop contradicted James's orders and insisted that Lake minister to the princess.

Lake was disappointed in his hope of accompanying Princess Mary to Holland but nevertheless, despite this friction, went on to serve as chaplain to the duke of York in what seems to have been an effective and cordial working relationship, accompanying him to Scotland in 1679 and, while there, interviewing the Cameronian rebels in prison. Lake was appointed a prebendary of Exeter on 13 December 1675 and archdeacon of Exeter on 24 October 1676. That same year he was created DD at Cambridge by royal mandate. On 5 January 1681 he was elected a brother of St Katharine's Hospital (a charitable foundation attached to St Katharine by the Tower), of which he was also a commissary. (He resigned his patent for this last office on 10 November 1698.) On 30 November 1682 he was instituted to the rectory of St Mary-at-Hill, London, to which was annexed in 1700 that of St Andrew Hubbard.

Lake is best known as the author of *Officium eucharisticum* (1673), a devotional manual which was designed for his royal pupils but which became very popular and went through more than thirty editions. Later versions of the work featured additions that some felt smacked of Catholicism, but these alterations do not appear to have been the work of the author. He was also a popular preacher, delivering a sermon in 1684 to the lord mayor of London on the political dangers of all types of puritanism. As evidence he related his experience of the covenanter rebels while in Scotland in the service of the duke. Despite his closeness to James II, Lake appears to have had no problems in giving his allegiance to William III in 1689. Indeed,

he seems to have been overtly hostile to some nonjurors, Sancroft accusing him of spreading malicious rumours about him in 1690.

With his wife, Margaret (1638–1712), Lake had three daughters who survived him, Mary, Ann, and Frances, who married William Taswell DD on 21 May 1695 at St Mary-at-Hill. Taswell later published a collection of sixteen of Lake's sermons. Lake died on 1 February 1704, probably in the parish of St Mary-at-Hill, and was buried at St Katharine by the Tower, London. The inscription on his monument in the church shows that his friends thought he had been inadequately rewarded for his efforts. An engraved portrait of Lake was made by M. Van der Gucht and is reproduced in some copies of Lake's *Officium eucharisticum*.   EDWARD VALLANCE

Sources DNB · *Walker rev.* · Venn, *Alum. Cant.*, 1/3 · R. B. Gardiner, ed., *The registers of Wadham College, Oxford*, 1 (1889), 226 · 'Diary of Dr Edward Lake … in the years 1677–8', ed. G. P. Elliott, *Camden miscellany, I*, CS, 39 (1847) · W. Taswell, 'Autobiography and anecdotes', ed. G. P. Elliott, *Camden miscellany, II*, CS, 55 (1853) · will, PRO, PROB 11/474, sig. 44
Archives Bodl. Oxf., MSS Rawl.; Tanner MSS
Likenesses C. Van der Gucht, engraving (after earlier engraving by M. Van der Gucht), repro. in E. Lake, *Officium Eucharisticum* (1673) · M. Van der Gucht, line engraving, BM, NPG; repro. in E. Lake, *Sixteen sermons preached upon several occasions* (1705)

Lake, Edward John (1823–1877), army officer, born at Madras on 19 June 1823, was the son of Edward Lake (d. 1829), major in the Madras engineers, who served with distinction in the Anglo-Maratha War of 1817, and was author of *Sieges of the Madras Army*. Sent to England with a sister at an early age, Edward was left an orphan when six years old by the sinking at sea of the ship *Guildford*, in which his parents with their four younger children were returning home. He was brought up by his grandfather Admiral Sir Willoughby Lake, who sent him to Mr Stoton's private school at Wimbledon. He afterwards entered Addiscombe College (1839–40), passing in three terms instead of the usual four and winning the first mathematical prize. Commissioned second lieutenant, Bengal Engineers, on 11 June 1840, he spent a year at the Royal Engineer Establishment, Chatham, and then went to India. He arrived on 30 July 1842, and was posted to the Bengal Sappers and Miners at Delhi.

Shortly after his arrival at Delhi, Lake was sent with a company of sappers to suppress an outbreak at Kaithal, near Karnal, where he made the acquaintance of Henry and John Lawrence. He was for a time employed in road making under Henry Lawrence. He was promoted lieutenant on 19 February 1844. During the autumn of 1845 he served as a settlement officer in the Ambala district under Major George Broadfoot. On the outbreak of the First Anglo-Sikh War that year he was ordered to the Sutlej, and joined Lord Hardinge in time to be present at the battle of Mudki on 18 December, when he had a horse shot under him and was himself severely wounded in the hand. After the battle he was sent to the frontier station of Ludhiana, where he strengthened the defences and forwarded troops and supplies to the army in the field. When Sir Harry Smith's camp equipage fell into the hands of the enemy just before the battle of Aliwal—at which Lake was present—Lake was able to replace it, and received the commendation of the governor-general.

On the restoration of peace in March 1846, the trans-Sutlej territory of the Jullundur Doab was made over to the British as a material guarantee. John Lawrence was appointed commissioner for the newly acquired territory, and Lake was nominated one of his assistants and placed in charge of the Kangra district, with headquarters at Nurpur, but was soon moved to Jullundur. In May 1848, when Sir Henry Lawrence, the commissioner of the Punjab, had left India on furlough to England, open hostility was shown by Mulraj, governor of Multan, and his turbulent Sikhs; Patrick Alexander Vans Agnew and Lieutenant Anderson were murdered, and the Punjab was ablaze. Herbert Edwardes, who was in political charge of the Dera Ismail Khan district and nearest to Multan, hastily collected a body of Pathans and managed to hold his own against Mulraj. Lake was specially selected as political officer to the friendly Muslim nawab of Bahawalpure, whose territories adjoined the Punjab, and in virtual command of the nawab's troops he co-operated with his old friend Edwardes. He took part on 1 July in the second battle of Suddoosam, close to Multan, and for seven months was engaged in the operations for the capture of Multan before it fell. Lake, then only a lieutenant like Edwardes, was in fact commander-in-chief of the Davodpootra army, and although directed to co-operate with Edwardes, and in no way under his orders, he nevertheless magnanimously subordinated himself, and was content to do his utmost to further his friend's plans. On the fall of Multan, Lake was again in the field, and took part in the final victory of Gujrat on 21 February 1849. He accompanied General Gilbert to the Indus in his pursuit of the Afghans, and was present at Rawalpindi when the Sikh army laid down its arms.

Lake next went to Batala, and for two years had charge, under John (afterwards Lord) Lawrence, of the northern portion of the country between the rivers Beas and Ravi. In 1852 he went home on furlough, travelling through Russia, Prussia, Norway, and Sweden. He returned to India in 1854, having been promoted captain on 21 August and brevet major on 22 August for his services in the Punjab campaign. He took up his old charge in the trans-Sutlej province at Kangra as deputy commissioner. In 1855 he was appointed commissioner of the Jullundur Doab. When the Indian mutiny broke out in 1857, Lake occupied and secured the fort of Kangra against the mutineers, and held it until the rising was suppressed. His calmness and resource were an asset to the government throughout the crisis.

In 1860 Lake's health failed, and he was obliged to go to England. He was promoted lieutenant-colonel on 18 February 1861. In July 1861 he married Elizabeth Penrose, youngest daughter of T. Bewes of Beaumont, Plymouth; their only child died at Lahore in 1864. Lake returned to his post at Jullundur in the same year. In 1865 he was appointed financial commissioner of the Punjab, and the following year was made a CSI. In 1867 ill health again

compelled him to go to England, and subsequently to decline Lord Lawrence's offer of the much coveted appointment of resident of Hyderabad. He had been promoted colonel on 31 December 1868. On 1 January 1870 he retired on a pension with the honorary rank of major-general. After he left India the Lake scholarship was founded by public subscription in January 1870 in his honour at the Lahore high school.

About 1855 Lake had undergone a religious conversion. In India he held Bible study for officers, and Bible readings for soldiers, and helped missions. He became in 1868 honorary secretary of the East London Mission Relief Fund, of which his friend Lord Lawrence was chairman, and worked hard between 1869 and 1876 as honorary lay secretary of the Church Missionary Society. From April 1871 to June 1874 he was sole editor of the *Church Missionary Record*, and contributed articles to the *Church Missionary Intelligencer*, the *Sunday at Home*, and other publications. In 1873 he edited the fifth edition of the *Church Missionary Atlas*, and was engaged on another edition at the time of his death. He disliked 'departures from the simple forms of a reverent and reasonable service' (Barton and Maclagan, 79).

Lake was a man of slight and delicate frame, with a cheery and lovable disposition. He had great aptitude for business, and much tact in relations with Indians, who called him Lake Sahib, and by whom he was reportedly much loved. Lord Lawrence, Sir Robert Montgomery, and other eminent administrators had a very high opinion of him. In the summer of 1876 lung disease made it necessary for Lake to move from London to Bournemouth, and in the following spring he went to Clifton. He died at 10 Prince's Buildings, Clifton, near Bristol, on 7 June 1877, and was survived by his wife. He was buried on 13 June in Long Ashton churchyard, near Clifton.

R. H. VETCH, rev. ROGER T. STEARN

Sources J. Barton and R. Maclagan, *In memoriam Edward Lake: two memoirs* (1878) • H. B. Edwardes, *A year on the Punjab frontier in 1848–49*, 2 vols. (1851) • *Royal Engineers Journal*, 7 • H. M. Vibart, *Addiscombe: its heroes and men of note* (1894) • B. Bond, ed., *Victorian military campaigns* (1967) • C. Hibbert, *The great mutiny, India, 1857* (1978) • T. A. Heathcote, *The military in British India: the development of British land forces in south Asia, 1600–1947* (1995) • E. W. C. Sandes, *The military engineer in India*, 2 vols. (1933–5) • *CGPLA Eng. & Wales* (1877)

Archives NAM, letters to David Wilkie

Wealth at death under £18,000: probate, 29 June 1877, *CGPLA Eng. & Wales*

Lake, Gerard, first Viscount Lake of Delhi

Lake, Gerard, first Viscount Lake of Delhi (1744–1808), army officer, the elder son of Lancelot Charles Lake (*d.* 1751) of Flambards, Harrow on the Hill, Middlesex, and his wife, Letitia (*d.* 1760), daughter of John Gumley, glass manufacturer and army contractor, of Isleworth, Middlesex, was born on 27 July 1744.

Early career and parliament Educated at Eton College (1755–6), he was appointed ensign in the 1st foot guards on 9 May 1758, and served with the 2nd battalion in the campaigns in Germany in 1760–62. After displaying enterprise at the battle of Wilhelmstadt, near Kassel, he was appointed aide-de-camp to General Sir Richard Pearson, and lieutenant and captain on 3 January 1762. He married on 26

Gerard Lake, first Viscount Lake of Delhi (1744–1808), by R. Cooper [left, with his son Lieutenant Colonel George A. F. Lake]

June 1770 Elizabeth (1751–1798), only daughter of Edward Barker, sometime consul at Tripoli, of St Julian's, Hertfordshire: they had three sons and five daughters.

In 1776 Lake was promoted captain and lieutenant-colonel and appointed to the household of the prince of Wales, probably because the king hoped he would have a beneficial influence on the prince. His relationship with the prince was close, at least in the early years. In 1781 he went with drafts to America and served in the campaign in North Carolina under Lord Cornwallis. With the force trapped in Yorktown at the end of September 1781, on 16 October he led one element of a desperate attempt under Lieutenant-Colonel Robert Abercromby to force redoubts and destroy guns threatening the encampment. After the surrender of Yorktown, Lake was a prisoner on parole until the end of the war. He was appointed a regimental major on 20 October 1784.

First equerry to the prince of Wales, 1780–86 and 1787–96, and gentleman attendant on him from 1796 until his death, Lake devoted several years chiefly to managing the prince's stables. He also indulged his own passion for gambling. At a by-election in 1789 he unsuccessfully contested the venal householder borough of Aylesbury, Buckinghamshire. Supported by his fellow members of the Buckinghamshire Independent Club, led by the duke of Portland, Lake spent lavishly at Aylesbury. He was elected unopposed at the 1790 general election, and again in 1796. He voted with the whig opposition on the Ochakov question (April 1791 and March 1792), and in December 1792

was listed as 'supposed attached' to the duke of Portland. He retired from parliament at the 1802 dissolution.

Lake became a major-general in 1790 and a regimental lieutenant-colonel in 1792. In February 1793 he embarked in command of a brigade composed of the 1st battalions of the three regiments of foot guards. This force was present at the siege of Valenciennes and achieved a significant if costly local victory against the French at Lincelles, near Lille. Lake was invalided home in September 1793 and, although able to rejoin the duke of York briefly the following year, was again sent home in April 1794. That month he was appointed colonel of the 53rd foot and in November 1796 transferred to the 73rd foot.

Ireland 1796–1798 In December 1796 Lake was appointed to the command in Ulster, under Henry Luttrell (later Lord Carhampton) as commander-in-chief. He became a lieutenant-general in January 1797. In early spring 1797 Lake, in command of a mixed force of militia, yeomanry, and fencibles, was ordered by John Jeffreys, Earl Camden (lord lieutenant 1795–8), to use all methods to disarm Ulster. The Irish government 'meant to strike terror' (Camden to Portland, 3 Nov 1797, Bartlett, 270) and the harsh measures of house burning, flogging, and mass arrests greatly weakened the United Irishmen and secured large quantities of arms. When General Sir Ralph Abercromby, commander-in-chief from late 1797, who had indicated his disapproval of the policy of Dublin Castle, in February 1798 issued a general order condemning the absence of control of the Irish armed forces, especially the militia, Camden welcomed his resignation, and Lake succeeded to the command on 25 April 1798.

Lake again used harsh methods, including an order to take no prisoners, following the outbreak of rebellion in the south of Ireland on 24 May 1798. Although the rebels gained Wexford, they failed in an assault on Arklow and withdrew. After reinforcements arrived from England, Lake was able to assemble the army which, after an artillery attack and two hours of desperate fighting at Vinegar Hill, near Enniscorthy, finally crushed the rebellion in Wexford; Lake entered Wexford on 22 June 1798. Following the arrival of Cornwallis as lord lieutenant and commander-in-chief on 20 June 1798, Lake reverted to the command in Leitrim. After a French force of some 1100 men commanded by General Joseph Humbert landed in Killala Bay in late August, Lake was sent to Galway. Lake confronted the French at Castlebar with a mixed force of Irish militia, English and Scottish fencibles, and some regulars. His force broke in panic before a French bayonet charge. However, other detachments converged on Humbert, who had not been reinforced from France, and on 8 September the French surrendered at Ballinamuck. Lake was elected to the Irish parliament as member for Armagh to help secure passage of the Act of Union, but left Ireland in 1799.

India, 1801–1807 In 1800 Lake was appointed commander-in-chief and second member of the supreme council in India. After landing at Calcutta on 31 January 1801, and making an initial tour of inspection, he set up his head-quarters at Cawnpore. He devoted much attention to improving military method in the Bengal army and introduced galloper guns into the cavalry and light troops into the infantry. After the conclusion of a treaty with the nawab of Oudh in November 1801, Lake was involved in the spring of 1802 in the pacification of parts of the Jumna-Ganges Doab, including the territory of Balwant Singh of Sasni.

The Second Anglo-Maratha War (1803–5) was the climax of Lake's military career. In March 1803, following the conclusion of the treaty of Bassein with the Peshwa Baji Rao, the Madras government assembled a considerable force in the northern part of Mysore, to aid him in the restoration of his authority within the Maratha confederacy. The governor-general, Richard, Marquess Wellesley, left it to Lake to decide whether he should command this force himself or remain in Oudh. As the force assembled at Harihar under the command of Major-General Arthur Wellesley moved forward into Maratha territory, Lake prepared the force in Oudh designed to bring pressure on Daulat Rao Sindhia of Ujjain to accept the changed relationship of the Peshwa to the East India Company. Lake knew that the French adventurer General Perron, whose control of part of northern India under the nominal sovereignty of Sindhia amounted to independent statehood, was both creating a further brigade of infantry and seeking permission from Wellesley to withdraw into British territory. In early May 1803 Lake was directed to prepare a force to be based near the Jumna for use after the monsoon. The movement of Raghoji Bhonsla of Nagpur with his army to unite with Sindhia in early June was seen as indicating a hostile intention, and at the end of June Lake took precautionary measures. Word of these crossed with instructions from the governor-general that gave to both Lake and Arthur Wellesley wide delegated political and military powers. The alliance of the Maratha rulers was expected to 'vanish upon the approach of the British force' (R. Wellesley to Lake, 28 June 1803, *Despatches*, 3.164). This optimism was shared by Lake: 'I think Perron once beat ... little is to be apprehended' (Lake to R. Wellesley, 9 July 1803, BL, Add. MS 13742, fol. 46). The governor-general sent Graeme Mercer as a political adviser. Lake, who had visited Agra, felt able to assure Fort William that he would consider its seizure 'by a *coup de main*' (Lake to M. Shawe, 17 July 1803, BL, Add. MS 13741, fol. 144). Lake had information on the deployment and the strength of Perron's force, hoped to negotiate the withdrawal of Perron from the command of Sindhia's army in Hindustan, and believed that some of his European officers could be suborned.

Lake moved forward, planning to proceed to the frontier, 'where I shall assemble my force and where I shall hope shortly to accomplish your wishes, by negotiation or otherwise' (Lake to Marquess Wellesley, 2 Aug 1803, BL, Add. MS 13742, fol. 101). He considered that letters from the Deccan 'fully authorise me ... to commence hostilities if M. Perron does not incline to negotiation, which from his opening a correspondence with me I rather believe he does' (Lake to Marquess Wellesley, 10 Aug 1803, BL, Add. MS 13741, fol. 151). By 18 August Lake knew that Perron was removing treasure from Coel, possibly to Agra. Four days later he had confirmation of the intended desertion of officers in the service of Sindhia. On 27 August the force of three brigades of cavalry, four of infantry, and 65 guns crossed the Maratha frontier.

On 29 August Lake was able to displace a Maratha infantry and cavalry force and establish a position before Aligarh. He hoped to secure this fortress by bribery, but on 4 September resolved to attempt it by assault. It was captured by an hour's heavy fighting, aided by guidance of an officer who had recently left Sindhia's service. Perron negotiated with Lake, and secured a personal safe conduct. Lake moved forwards towards Delhi. On 11 September at Patpanganj the pickets found the Maratha army encamped in a strong position at close quarters. Lake reconnoitred, and attempted an assault with cavalry, who were exposed to casualties from Maratha artillery. He then feigned a withdrawal with the cavalry, which led the Maratha brigades incautiously to move forward, and moved his own infantry through the cavalry and then ordered a general charge with the bayonet. The Marathas retreated headlong, suffering some 3000 casualties, against British casualties of about 350. Lake could now move towards Delhi, and on 15 September was able to report that a group of French officers formerly in the service of Sindhia had surrendered. One of the symbolic scenes in the history of British India followed on 16 September, when Lake was received in the Red Fort by the Mughal emperor Shah Alam.

Lake engaged irregular forces lately in the service of Perron for service with the British forces, and was able to report that 'no French officer of any consequence now remains in Sindhia's service' (Lake to R. Wellesley, 1 Oct 1803, *Despatches*, 3.390). Lake moved on to Agra, where the sepoys had arrested their European officers, but had no single alternative leader. Lake attempted, as he had done at Aligarh, to secure the fort by offering liberal terms of surrender, but this venture failed. On 10 October in an expensive operation, involving heavy casualties on both sides, Lake, using only Indian troops, took possession of the town and cleared the ravines to the south of the fort of Maratha forces. In the ravines was placed a powerful siege battery, the effectiveness of which led the divided garrison within the fort to release a French officer and through him agree terms of surrender. The extensive treasure in the fortress was distributed to the troops as prize money.

Lake had known in early July that an extensive reinforcement of disciplined infantry had been sent northwards by Sindhia from the Deccan. They had been commanded in the first instance by the Frenchman Dudrenec, who deserted, and were now led by Ambaji Inglia, who, having been appointed by Sindhia to succeed Perron, himself had ambitions to rule again in Hindustan, and secretly negotiated with Lake. These forces moved away from Agra towards Jaipur. Lake left his heavy artillery, and by forced marches, eventually with cavalry only, arrived in the environs of the entire Maratha force, near Laswari. Lake ordered a cavalry assault which, although it pressed home, failed to dislodge the Maratha artillery and supporting infantry. There was a lull in the fighting during the middle of 1 November. On the British side the infantry had now arrived. On the Maratha, battalions not involved in the morning fighting had rejoined, and a double line of defences was created near the walled village of Mohalpur. Ambaji Inglia offered a conditional withdrawal secured by surrender of his guns, but failed to complete the negotiation in the limited time allowed. In a second attack with both infantry and cavalry, Lake attempted to outflank the Maratha position, which was strongly protected by artillery. The 76th suffered severely and Lake saved its position with a cavalry charge. He personally led two sepoy regiments in an attack on Mohalpur, while on the Maratha left flank the Deccani cavalry were put to flight, and the circle of cavalry units about the doomed Maratha infantry was completed by the movement of the two other brigades. A costly victory (822 men killed and wounded of a total force of 8000) at Laswari was also complete. It had, as Lake explained to Lord Wellesley, annihilated the regular force in northern India in Sindhia's service commanded by French officers.

In negotiation Lake and Mercer now secured the transfer of the fortress of Gwalior and the conclusion with Ambaji Inglia of a treaty, destined not to be honoured, which gave him a position as a British ally. When troops were moved forward to secure Gwalior, the commander refused to yield it, although within twenty-four hours it was secured by negotiation: Ambaji Inglia was later informed that the action of the commandant had rendered the treaty with him invalid. Meantime, in the Deccan campaign of 1803, Arthur Wellesley had successively defeated the formed brigades of Sindhia at Assaye on 23 September and a force of both Sindhia and Raghoji Bhonsla at Argaon on 30 November, and captured Gawilgarh on 15 December. After negotiations conducted in his camp, Arthur Wellesley concluded the treaty of Deogaon on 17 December with Raghoji Bhonsla and, on 30 December, the treaty of Sarji Arjangaon with Daulat Rao Sindhia, securing as a result of the two campaigns, his own and that of Lake, extensive territorial cessions.

The other major Maratha, Jaswant Rao Holkar, had stood aloof from the events of 1803, and while Sindhia and Bhonsla were preoccupied, had plundered extensively in central India. Lake sent to the governor-general letters from Holkar, friendly in tone, but noted that Holkar's 'actions do not appear to accord with his words' (Lake to Lord Wellesley, 28 Dec 1803, *Despatches*, 3.556). While hoping to avert hostilities, Lord Wellesley again gave Lake delegated political authority. Holkar agreed to send agents to negotiate, but continued to attempt to create hostile alliances. The agents presented hubristic demands in Lake's camp on 18 and 19 March 1804, and these Lake and Mercer rejected. In April Lake reported that he saw little prospect of peace with Holkar, and that forbearance had been ineffective. He feared that if he advanced, Holkar would enter and pillage recently acquired territory. On 16 May Lord Wellesley determined to initiate hostilities against Holkar, relying on a prospect of support from Sindhia, with whom a subsidiary alliance treaty had been concluded.

Holkar withdrew precipitately from before Jaipur, after Lake had moved forward a detachment under Colonel the Hon. W. Monson, which was ordered to secure passes near Bundi and Lakheri. A limited force from Sindhia moved north from Ujjain. But Holkar had withdrawn onto his strength, artillery and infantry. Although Monson was able to move beyond Bundi through the Mukhandra Pass and capture Hinglaishghar, the news of a retreat near Badnawar on 1 July of a force under Colonel Murray that had advanced from Gujarat led Monson in turn to withdraw, and at this point Holkar was able to turn his full force upon him. An initial limited retreat, at first to Rampura, became by the persistent pressure of Holkar a disordered rout, ultimately to Agra at the end of August, with extensive desertions of both regular and irregular forces.

To attempt to reverse the consequences of this defeat, Lake marched from Cawnpore on 2 September 1804, and reached Agra by the end of the month. Holkar besieged Delhi, and its capture was averted by a skilled defence commanded by Colonels David Ocherlony and James Burn. When Holkar attempted a cavalry irruption into British territory east of the Jumna, Lake after some noteworthy forced marches defeated him with a cavalry force at Farrukhabad on 16 November. General J. H. Fraser had meantime defeated an infantry and artillery concentration near Dig. The reunited army achieved the capture of the fortress of Dig on 25 December. Lake turned to the siege of Bharatpur, whose raja had repudiated an earlier subsidiary alliance, although having 'at his disposal fewer than 8,000 men and less than eighty pieces of ordnance' (Pemble, 388). The first two rushed attacks failed because the batteries had been laid too far from the walls and there had been insufficient reconnaissance. In a third assault the trench designed to give the storming parties cover was inadequate and the troops were exposed to withering fire. The fourth assault failed because the ladders were too few and too short. Ironically, after such a costly and prolonged blunder (450 men had been killed and 2500 wounded) word of Lake's appointment to the peerage arrived at this point—he was created Baron Lake of Delhi and Laswary and Aston Clinton, Buckinghamshire, on 13 September 1804—and the raja agreed to terms. The army had been before Bharatpur for three months and twenty days.

Holkar had not been within Bharatpur, although his cavalry had contributed to the harrying of attackers and of convoys. In the last stages of the siege Mir Khan, one of the most successful of Holkar's commanders, had attempted a prolonged incursion into Rohilkhand, from which he had been expelled. At the same time Sindhia, who had permitted an attack on the camp of the British resident, moved north, ostensibly to mediate between the company and Holkar, but in reality with the intention of joining him. The combined forces of Sindhia and Holkar were assessed as 5000 regular infantry, 12,000 silledar horse, 12,000 pindaries, and 146 guns. Lake deployed his force during the monsoon in advanced positions and the two Maratha chiefs quarrelled, separated, and withdrew. At the end of his governor-generalship, when about to be succeeded by Lord Cornwallis, Lord Wellelsey again authorized Lake, now stationed at Mathura, to make preparations for active operations.

Instructions from Cornwallis led to a rift between himself and Lake. Cornwallis considered the British in India over-extended; there were constant 'calls for reinforcements of men and for remittances of money' but 'little other profit except brilliant Gazettes' (Cornwallis to Lake, 30 Aug 1805, *Correspondence of … Cornwallis*, 3.544). Lake reacted badly to a statement by Cornwallis of their respective authority, Cornwallis having been again appointed, as in 1786, governor-general and commander-in-chief. Instructions from Cornwallis gave authority for an approach to Sindhia to secure a peace settlement, negotiated by Colonel John Malcolm and concluded in the treaty of Mustaphapur on 22 November. This settlement was significantly varied by Sir George Barlow, who had succeeded as governor-general on the death of Cornwallis (5 October 1805), under protest from Lake, in a way that ended British connections with states to the south and west of the Jumna. Lake at the same time received instructions drastically to reduce irregular forces to stem the drain on the finances. Lake formed a defensive line against Holkar, and in early November, as Holkar escaped into Sikh territory, attempted to secure their co-operation against 'a plunderer whose existence in any degree of power is I fear incompatible with the full restoration of peace in India' (Lake to Barlow, 11 Nov 1805, BL, Add. MS 13605, fol. 191). On receiving from Barlow instructions on a peace settlement with Holkar, which would transfer to Holkar extensive territories, including areas south of the Tapti, Lake followed him into the Punjab, crossing the Sutlej, and on the banks of the Beas, Malcolm presented agents from Holkar with a draft treaty, to be ratified in a limited time. An attempt to vary its terms was rejected, and on 7 January 1806 Lake was able to send Barlow the text of an agreed treaty. Barlow varied this treaty also, again under protest from Lake, giving further territorial cessions to Holkar. Lake then slowly withdrew his army, pausing at Delhi to complete arrangements with the Mughal emperor, proceeded to Cawnpore, and thence to Calcutta. He sailed for Britain on 9 February 1807.

Last period, 1807–1808 Lake was advanced to a viscountcy under the same designation as his barony on 4 November 1807 and took his seat in the House of Lords on 21 January 1808. He held various sinecures, including the receiver-generalship of the duchy of Cornwall from March 1807. Following a violent cold, caught while attending the court martial at Chelsea on 18 February, of Lieutenant-General Whitelocke, Lake died at his residence in Lower Brook Street, London, on 20 February 1808, aged sixty-three; he was buried on 5 March 1808 at Aston Clinton.

A soldier's general, Lake achieved much on the battlefield by ferocious energy and tactical skill. Lake could command, and he retained the adherence of his soldiers. But he lacked political skill and the capacity to interpret intelligence, and by his misjudgment of Holkar in 1804 and his impetuosity before Bharatpur in 1805 he contributed to the failure of the last year of the governor-generalship of Richard Wellesley. He professed indifference to money and, despite gaining considerable prize money in 1803, his massive accumulated gambling debts ensured he did not die wealthy. On 29 February in the House of Commons, Lord Castlereagh proposed a pension of £2000 to Lake's next two heirs in succession. After a long debate—in which opposition MPs opposed the pension and the reformer William Smith had 'brought £140,000 from India, although the property of which he died possessed did not exceed £40,000 with an estate of £800 a year' (*GM*, 248)—the pension of £2000 was settled on the next two successors to the title, which became extinct after the death of Lake's second son, Warwick, the third viscount, on 24 June 1848.

ANTHONY S. BENNELL

Sources *The despatches, minutes and correspondence of the Marquess Wellesley … during his administration in India*, ed. M. Martin, 5 vols. (1836–40) • H. Pearse, *Memoir of the life and military services of Viscount Lake, Baron Lake of Delhi and Laswarree, 1744–1808* (1908) • *Correspondence of Charles, first Marquis Cornwallis*, ed. C. Ross, 3 vols. (1859) • W. Thorn, *Memoir of the war in India conducted by … Lord Lake … and Sir Arthur Wellesley … from 1803 to 1806* (1818) • *Bengal, Fort St George and Bombay papers presented to the House of Commons, pursuant to their orders of the 7th of May last, from the East India Company, relative to the Mahratta war in 1803* (House of Commons, 1804) • F. Lewis Smith, *Sketch of the rise, progress and termination of the regular corps formed and commanded by Europeans in the service of the native princes of India* (Calcutta, [1804]) • J. Grant Duff, *History of the Mahrattas*, 3 vols. (1826) • Govind Sarkharam Sardesai, *New history of the Marathas*, 3 vols. (1948) • Sir J. Sarkar, *The fall of the Mughal empire*, 4 vols. (1950) • J. Pemble, 'Resources and techniques in the Second Maratha War', *HJ*, 19 (1976), 375–404 • T. Bartlett, 'Defence, counter-insurgency and rebellion: Ireland, 1793–1803', *A military history of Ireland*, ed. T. Bartlett and K. Jeffrey (1996), 247–93 • HoP, *Commons, 1790–1820* • GEC, *Peerage* • R. F. Foster, *Modern Ireland, 1600–1972* (1988) • *GM*, 1st ser., 78 (1808), 182, 248

Archives BL OIOC, corresp. relating to India, home miscellaneous series • BL OIOC, letters, MS Eur. F 176 • NAM, Guards Brigade order book, 8512-15-4 | BL, corresp. with earl of Chichester, etc., Add. MSS 33102–33105, *passim* • BL, corresp. with Lord Wellesley, Add. MSS 37282–37284, 37309, *passim* • BL, corresp. with Marquess R. Wellesley, Add. MSS 13578, 13710–13712, 13737–13742 • BL OIOC, corresp. with Sir Richard Jones, MS Eur. C 234 • BL OIOC, letters to Henry Wellesley, MS Eur. E 175 • CKS, corresp. with Lord Camden, U840/0165 • Morgan L., letters to Sir James Murray-Pulteney, MA 1267 (vol. 10) • PRO NIre., letters to Lord Castlereagh, 3030 • U. Southampton L., corresp. with Lord Wellesley, MS 61

Likenesses J. Nollekens, marble bust, 1814, Royal Collection • R. Cooper, stipple, BM [*see illus.*] • Ridley and Blood, stipple (after S. Drummond), BM, NPG; repro. in *European Magazine* (1808) • bust (after J. Lake), Oriental Club, London • oils, Oriental Club, London

Lake, Sir Henry Atwell (1808–1881), army officer, third son of Sir James Samuel William Lake, fourth baronet (*d.* 1832), and his wife, Maria (*d.* 1866), daughter of Samuel Turner, was born at Kenilworth, Warwickshire, on 15 December 1808. He was educated at Harrow School and at

Sir Henry Atwell Lake (1808–1881), by unknown engraver, pubd 1856 (after John Watkins)

Addiscombe College. On 15 December 1826 he was commissioned second lieutenant in the Madras engineers, then went to India. Until 1854 he was employed in the public works department, principally on irrigation works. He became lieutenant on 4 March 1831, brevet captain on 22 July 1840, regimental captain in 1852, and brevet major on 20 June 1854. He married, on 14 April 1841, Anne (d. 8 Jan 1847), daughter of the Revd Peregrine Curtois of The Longhills, Lincolnshire; they had two sons and two daughters. One son, Atwell Peregrine Macleod Lake (1842–1915), became an admiral. On 22 February 1848 he married Ann Augusta (d. 20 Dec 1877), daughter of Sir William Curtis, second baronet; they had four sons and three daughters.

While on leave in England in 1854 Lake volunteered for the Crimean War, and was sent to Kars as chief engineer and second in command to Colonel William Fenwick Williams. He became lieutenant-colonel on 9 February 1855. He strengthened the fortifications of Kars, and took a gallant and prominent part in the defence, including the repulse of the Russian forces under General Muravyov on 29 September 1855. On the surrender of Kars he was sent, with the other British officers, as a prisoner of war to Russia, where he remained until the peace in 1856.

For his services at Kars, Lake received the thanks of parliament, was transferred to the British army as an unattached lieutenant-colonel, and was made a CB, aide-de-camp to the queen, and colonel in the army from 24 June 1856. He received the second class of the Mejidiye and the Légion d'honneur, and was given the rank of major-general in the Turkish army. On his arrival in England he was presented with a finely ornamented sword of honour and a silver salver by the inhabitants of Ramsgate, where his mother then resided, and where his family was well known. He published *Kars and our Captivity in Russia* (1856) and *Narrative of the Defence of Kars, Historical and Military, from Authentic Documents* (1857).

Lake was placed on half pay on 12 September 1856, but next year accompanied the earl of Eglinton, lord lieutenant of Ireland, to Dublin as principal aide-de-camp, and in the following year retired from the army on his appointment as a commissioner of the Dublin Metropolitan Police, subsequently becoming chief commissioner of police in Dublin. In 1875 he was made a KCB of the civil division, and in 1877 he retired. He died at 63 Regency Square, Brighton, on 17 August 1881.

R. H. VETCH, *rev.* JAMES FALKNER

Sources *Indian Army List* · *Army List* · W. Porter, *History of the corps of royal engineers*, 2 vols. (1889) · *ILN* (2 Aug 1856) · Hart's *Army List* · H. Lake, *Kars and our captivity in Russia* (1856) · Boase, *Mod. Eng. biog.* · Burke, *Peerage*

Likenesses C. Baugniet, lithograph, pubd 1857, BM · engraving (after J. Watkins), NPG; repro. in *ILN* [see illus.] · engraving, repro. in *The Graphic*, 24 (1881), 389 · stipple, NPG

Wealth at death £7720 14s. 1d.: probate, 14 Sept 1881, *CGPLA Eng. & Wales*

Lake, John (*bap.* 1624, *d.* 1689), bishop of Chichester, was born in Petticoat Lane, Halifax, Yorkshire, and was baptized on 5 December 1624, the first of the three children of Thomas Lake (d. 1649), yeoman, 'grocer' to the local woollen trade, and Mary Moakson. He was educated in the Halifax grammar school and on 4 December 1637, at the age of thirteen, was admitted to St John's College, Cambridge. He became a Constable scholar on 9 November 1641 and graduated BA on 20 April 1642. After the war began, his college became a prison and he was confined for expressions of his loyalty to the king. He escaped to Oxford where he joined the king's army and continued to serve in it for about two years, receiving many dangerous wounds. He was at Basing House when it was taken and at Wallingford, one of the last garrisons that held out for Charles I. In 1647 he returned to Halifax, where he preached his first sermon on 26 July and on 19 October received clandestine ordination from Thomas Fuller, bishop of Ardfert. He married Judith Deane (1629–1700), daughter of Gilbert Deane of Exley Hall, one of the six clerks in chancery; they had eight children, but no grandchildren. As he was known to be a disaffected 'malignant', he moved to Prestwich-cum-Oldham in Lancashire where he became the curate in 1649 and acquired a house at Chadderton Fold near his royalist patron. Holding the living by subterfuges, he was able to defy the Manchester classis and was even approved briefly by the committee for plundered ministers. Eventually he lost the rectory of Prestwich and later, by the close of 1654, the chapel of Oldham.

After the Restoration, Dean Marsh of York promoted Lake on 10 April 1661 from the curacy of Halifax to the vicarage of Leeds, but the presbyterians, who preferred the popular Edward Bowles as vicar, raised such opposition that at his induction soldiers had to be called in to keep the peace. The opposition then entered a petition in chancery which failed. In 1661 Lake sought and received a royal mandate for the degree of DD from Cambridge University. Having been chosen to preach the first convocation sermon at York after the Restoration, he had attracted the attention of Gilbert Sheldon, bishop of London, who later sent for him to hold the living of St Botolph without Bishopsgate (22 May 1663). While in London, he formed a friendship with William Sancroft, then dean of St Paul's,

John Lake (*bap.* 1624, *d.* 1689), by Mary Beale, 1685

and after diligent service during the great plague and the fire he received the prebend of Holborn (1667–82). Two sermons were printed in 1671: a funeral sermon entitled *Stephanos pistou, or, The True Christian Character and Crown Described*, and one preached at Whitehall before the king on 29 May 1670.

Dean Hitch of York made Lake his procurator in 1670 and resident prebendary of Fridaythorpe from 1670 to 1684. Lake also acquired the benefices of Prestwich-cum-Oldham (1669–85) and Carlton in Lindrick (1670–82), the prebend of Halloughton, Southwell (1670–82), and Bawtry Hospital (1671–82). As magistrate of the cathedral precinct, he attacked the bad custom of boys noisily walking about the nave of York Minster during divine service, often pulling off the hats of boys whom he found wearing them. In 1673, disregarding the advice of other canons, he determined to put a stop to a revel held by the apprentices in the bell tower on Shrove Tuesday and so antagonized the revellers that two files of musketeers had to be brought in to restore order. Although advised to compromise, he persisted until he succeeded in putting a stop to the desecration of the minster. A new dean, installed in 1677, curtailed his responsibilities, so Lake and his college friend Samuel Drake edited the cavalier poetry of their Cambridge supervisor, John Cleveland, in *Clievelandi vindiciae* (1677).

Lake was archdeacon of Cleveland in 1680–82, and in 1682 the earl of Derby offered him the bishopric of Sodor and Man. After one summer on the isle he was willing to exchange it for turbulent Bristol, surrendering his residency at York in 1684. The new bishop of Bristol in 1684–5

was prepared to see his chancellor prosecute dissent rigorously, while he himself struggled with a vociferous dean who opposed him in his projects for improving the cathedral, especially his attempt to establish weekly communion. He complained piteously about his plight to his friend Archbishop Sancroft, who soon translated him to the more desirable see of Chichester in 1685. Before the move was complete, however, the accession of James II and subsequent rebellion of Monmouth required his return to Bristol where, at Keynsham Bridge, he narrowly escaped the rebels. In the interim between sees he carried out an arduous visitation of the diocese of Lichfield and Coventry for Sancroft, and in 1686 he conducted another commission for him at Salisbury.

As bishop of Chichester from 1685 to 1689, Lake carried out a primary visitation which produced an account of the lamentable state of the church in Sussex. Although suffering from gout, he was energetic in his efforts to raise standards and at the cathedral he established weekly communion. In 1687, in an attempt to placate dissenters and to preserve a common protestant front against royal policies, he moved the sermon from the choir to the nave where it could be better heard. Always obedient to Sancroft, he hurried to Lambeth in May 1688 to sign the petition to be excused from reading the king's declaration of indulgence, thus becoming one of the seven bishops committed to the Tower. After being acquitted and hailed as a national hero, he made another 'charitive' visit throughout his rugged diocese and was received by the clergy and gentlemen of Sussex with great respect and good humour. Even the duke of Somerset gave him a warm reception at Petworth. But the euphoria was short-lived, because Lake was one of those bishops who were so committed to the doctrine of the divine right of kings and to the sacred nature of the oath to James II that they could not take the new oaths of allegiance to William and Mary in 1689. He believed that the day of judgement was as certain as the day of his deprivation, and in a correspondence with Thomas Comber, precentor of York, he worked out many 'Gordian knots' in his own arguments. This correspondence, however, was cut short and Lake did not live to suffer actual deprivation. Suddenly falling ill from a summer fever and knowing his end was near, he dictated a profession of faith to his chaplain, Robert Jenkin. In this he solemnly asserted his fidelity to the Church of England and his adherence to its distinctive doctrine of non-resistance and passive obedience. The bishop signed this in the presence of five friends, who received communion with him, and three days later, on 30 August, he died, in the parish of St Olave Jewry, London. He was buried on 3 September in the church of St Botolph without Bishopsgate. The paper was published as *The declaration of the Right Reverend Father in God John late bishop of Chichester upon his death-bed*. It was, in part, a final answer to Comber, but it was widely misunderstood to be a polemic against the revolution settlement and this caused many disputatious pamphlets to be published on the subject. One defence of the profession was published anonymously by Jenkin, who gives the earliest account of the bishop's life. 'He was not easily moved but sedate and undaunted', Jenkin said, 'and he thanked God he never much knew what fear was, when he was satisfied in the Goodness of his cause' (Jenkin, 60).

H. H. POOLE

Sources The declaration of the Right Reverend Father in God John late bishop of Chichester upon his death-bed (1689) · R. Jenkin, A defense of the profession which John Lake, bishop of Chichester, made upon his deathbed, &., together with an account of some passages of his life (1690) · H. H. Poole, 'John Lake, D. D., bishop of Chichester, 1624–1689', PhD diss., University of Delaware, 1981 · R. Bretton, 'Bishop John Lake', Transactions of the Halifax Antiquarian Society (1968), 89–96 · S. Deem, 'Fidei defensor', an account of the life of John Lake, the non-juring bishop of Chichester, 1928, Oldham Public Library, MS 82, LA3 · S. Deem, 'Fidei defensor', an account of the life of John Lake, the non-juring bishop of Chichester, 1928, Man. CL, MF 542 [microfilm of Oldham text] · DNB · A. Strickland, 'Dr. John Lake', in A. Strickland and [E. Strickland], The lives of the seven bishops committed to the Tower in 1688 (1866), 104–31 · J. Watson, The history and antiquities of the parish of Halifax, in Yorkshire (1775), 483–7 · R. Thoresby, 'John Lake D. D. vicar of Leeds', Vicaria Leodiensis (1724), 98–105 · will, 1689, PRO · wills, 1649 and 1661, Borth. Inst. [Thomas Lake; Gilbert Deane]

Archives BL, Add. MSS 4274–4276 Birch · BL, Add. MSS 5799–5801 Cole · Bodl. Oxf., Tanner MSS · Bodl. Oxf., MSS. Eng. Hist. e 47 · Bodl. Oxf., MSS J. Walker · Bodl. Oxf., MSS Rawlinson · Bodl. Oxf., Add. MS C. 180 · Chetham's Library, Manchester, Raines MSS, vol. xxxii · Cumbers Hall, Shropshire, Kenyon MSS, DDKe 9 · PRO, State papers, domestic, series 29 and 44 | All Souls Oxf., MS All Souls 241, fol. 121; 252, fol. 494 · LPL, MSS Comm. · Man. CL, MS. F 942.72 R121, and MSS Kidson, xii and xiii · Parish Church Library, Leeds, MS A/22, 24 · PRO, Dawson v. Lake, Chancery series C/33/215, 1661 · York Minster Library, MSS U 2(2) 1/1

Likenesses M. Beale, portrait, 1685, St John Cam. [see illus.] · G. Bower, silver medal, 1688, NPG · D. Loggan, line engraving, 1688, BM · D. Loggan, engraving, AM Oxf. · J. Overton, engraving, AM Oxf. · W. Vincent, engraving, AM Oxf. · group portrait, oils (The seven bishops) · group portrait, oils (The seven bishops committed to the Tower, 1688), NPG · group portrait, print (The seven bishops), NPG · oils, St John's College, Oxford · oils, bishop's palace, Chichester · stained-glass window, Chichester Cathedral

Wealth at death £200 and two properties in Pontefract to James Lake; £200 to William Lake and his father's books listed in Catalogus librorum (1691); £2 bequeathed to a widow, and £8 to the poor; remainder of the estate went to wife (might have included the house at Chadderton Fold, Lancashire, and messuages, houses, cottages, and lands in Halifax and elsewhere which the bishop inherited from his father): will, PRO

Lake, Kirsopp (1872–1946), biblical scholar, was born in Southampton on 7 April 1872, the son of a physician and surgeon, George Anthony Kirsopp Lake, and his wife, Isabel Oke Clark. He was educated at St Paul's School, and at Lincoln College, Oxford, where he won a second class in theology in 1895, and was Arnold essay prizeman in 1902. He was curate of Lumley, Durham, from 1895 until 1896 when he was ordained priest. From 1897 to 1904 he was curate of St Mary the Virgin, Oxford. Here one of his most important works was written, The Text of the New Testament (1900; 6th edn, ed. S. New, 1928). He also edited Codex 1 of the Gospels and its Allies (1902) the group of manuscripts now known as 'Fam. 1' or the 'Lake group', and also various texts from Mount Athos. In 1904 he married Helen Courthope, daughter of Sidney Mills Forman, a businessman of Newcastle upon Tyne. They had one son and one daughter.

From 1904 to 1914 Lake was professor ordinarius of early Christian literature and New Testament exegesis at the University of Leiden, where in addition to further research and writings in the field of textual criticism he produced two major works, The Historical Evidence for the Resurrection of Jesus Christ (1907) and The Earlier Epistles of St Paul (1911). The latter, characterized alike by wide learning and careful judgement, was a kind of prolegomenon to his work, undertaken with F. J. Foakes Jackson, The Beginnings of Christianity (5 vols., 1920–33), as an immense introduction to the book of Acts. Lake gave to many readers of the Earlier Epistles a sense of their relation to the contemporary world of the first century, a realization of the importance of Koine Greek and of the ubiquitous and all-pervasive influence of the Jewish and Hellenistic religions in the world of St Paul and his earliest converts. All later New Testament study has been influenced by this book. In 1911 he published, with his wife, his photographic facsimile Codex Sinaiticus Petropolitanus: the New Testament, the epistle of Barnabas, and the shepherd of Hermas.

In 1914 Lake moved to the United States and became professor of early Christian literature at Harvard; in 1919 he became Winn professor of ecclesiastical history and in 1932 professor of history. Between 1934 and 1939 he published in ten fascicles a series of examples, Dated Greek Minuscule Manuscripts to the Year 1200. In 1938 he retired as emeritus. His marriage was dissolved in 1932 and in that year Lake married Silva Tipple New, daughter of Bertrand Tipple, who survived him. There was one son of the second marriage.

As an archaeologist and palaeographer Lake made many summer visits to Mount Athos and other libraries; during his Harvard days he headed the archaeological expeditions (1930, 1935) to Serabit in the Sinai peninsula, to Samaria (1932, 1934), and to Lake Van in Turkey (1938, 1939). He was elected an honorary fellow of Lincoln College, Oxford, in 1941, was a fellow of the American Academy of Arts and Sciences, a corresponding member of the Preussische Akademie der Wissenschaften, and in 1936 was awarded the British Academy medal for biblical studies. He received the honorary degrees of DD from St Andrews (1911), ThD from Leiden (1922), LittD from Michigan (1926), and PhD from Heidelberg (1936).

Lake's chief contributions to scholarship were in the historical field, especially the study of St Paul and the Acts of the Apostles, and in textual criticism, where he not only popularized the study and introduced it to many students, but made marked, permanent progress in such new areas as the identification of the Lake group of manuscripts and of the so-called Caesarean text, the type of text associated with the ancient library of Pamphilus at Caesarea. Kirsopp Lake died at South Pasadena, California, on 10 November 1946.

F. C. GRANT, rev.

Sources The Times (23 Nov 1946) · personal knowledge (1959) · private information (1959) · F. L. Cross, ed., Oxford dictionary of the Christian church, 3rd edn, ed. E. A. Livingstone (1997)
Archives BL, corresp. with Macmillans, Add. MS 55107
Likenesses J. S. Sargent, drawing, Lincoln College, Oxford

Lake, Sir Percy Henry Noel (1855–1940), army officer, was born at Tenby, Wales, on 29 June 1855. He was the eldest son of Captain Percy Godfrey Botfield Lake of Grenfell, Canada, who had served in the 54th and 100th regiments, and his wife, Margaret, second daughter of William Philips of Quebec. He was educated at Uppingham School and commissioned to the 59th foot as lieutenant on 9 August 1873. He served in the first stage of the Second Anglo-Afghan War (1878–9), when he became assistant field engineer, southern field force. He was promoted captain on 31 October 1883 and graduated with honours from the Staff College in 1884.

In 1885 Lake served in the Sudan as deputy assistant adjutant and later quartermaster-general with the forces under Sir Gerald Graham, operating from Suakin. He took part in the actions at Hashin and Tofrek and in the advance on Tamai. From 1887 to 1890 Lake served as staff captain and deputy assistant adjutant-general for intelligence at the War Office. In 1891 he acted as secretary to R. J. Lindsay, Lord Wantage, chairman of the committee on terms of service in the army, and was promoted major on 1 July 1891. He married, on 18 August 1891, Hester Fanny, only daughter of Henry Woodyer, architect, of Grafton, Surrey. They had no children, and she survived him.

In 1892 Lake was made deputy assistant adjutant-general at the headquarters of the Irish command, Dublin district. In 1893 he sailed for Canada to become quartermaster-general, Canadian militia. During the next five years he did excellent work, and was promoted lieutenant-colonel on 11 January 1899. The same year he went to India as assistant quartermaster-general for intelligence duties, but at the outbreak of the Second South African War he was brought back to the War Office to become assistant adjutant-general (afterwards assistant quartermaster-general) for mobilization and chief staff officer, 2nd army corps. He was promoted colonel on 11 January 1902 and appointed CB later in the year. He remained at the War Office until 1904, when he once more left for Canada to become chief of general staff, Canadian militia.

During the next three years Lake did much to increase the efficiency of the militia and urged the formation of a general staff on the British army model. He also extended the period of training and formed new cadet corps. He was promoted major-general on 23 March 1905, and appointed CMG in 1905 and KCMG in 1908. In the latter year he was nominated inspector-general, Canadian militia, and chief military adviser to the Canadian government, appointments which he held until the end of 1910, when he returned to England.

Lake was promoted lieutenant-general on 9 March 1911, and was again sent to India as division commander (7th Meerut division). On 21 February 1912 he became chief of general staff at Simla. During the next few years as a member of the army in India committee he argued strongly for higher military expenditure and army reform.

Lake was still chief of general staff in 1915 when a force was sent from India to Mesopotamia to ensure the safety of the oilfields. After the first failure to relieve Charles Townshend, besieged in Kut al-Amara, Lake became commander-in-chief in Mesopotamia, and with the Tigris

force made a second attempt, which again failed. With large reinforcements he prepared for a fresh campaign, but in August 1916 F. S. Maude took over and Lake came home to give evidence before the Mesopotamia commission. Maude testified to his excellent foundation work and he was appointed KCB in 1916 and given a post in the Ministry of Munitions in May 1917. Lake retired from the army on 20 November 1919 and returned to Canada to make his home in Victoria, British Columbia, where he died on 17 November 1940. C. V. OWEN, rev. ALEX MAY

Sources Army List · Hart's Army List · Indian Army List · Debrett's Peerage · The Times (20 Nov 1940) · Who's who in Canada (1927) · G. F. G. Stanley, Canada's soldiers, 1604–1954 (1954) · F. J. Moberly, ed., The campaign in Mesopotamia, 1914–1918, 4 vols. (1923–7) · CGPLA Eng. & Wales (1941)
Likenesses photograph, c.1890, NAM · Elliott & Fry, photograph, c.1916–1918, NAM · W. Stoneman, photograph, 1917, NPG
Wealth at death £3210 4s. 0d. — effects in England: probate, 23 June 1941, CGPLA Eng. & Wales

Lake, Sir Thomas (bap. **1561**, d. **1630**), administrator and politician, was the son of Emery (or Almeric) Lake (1519–1594), a minor customs official in Southampton. His date of birth is not known, but he was baptized on 11 October 1561 at St Michael's Church, Southampton, and according to one report was educated at the town's grammar school. It was presumably there that he acquired the good command of Latin which helped advance his career.

The rising administrator By 1584 Lake was in the service of Sir Francis Walsingham, principal secretary of state, and earned the nickname of Swiftsure for his speedy dispatch of business. A sign of Lake's increasing importance was his appointment as one of the clerks of the signet in 1589. It may have been to provide against the possibility of Walsingham's death that Lake acquired the reversion of the town clerkship of Southampton in 1584, but when the secretary did die, in 1590, Lake salvaged his career by adhering to the powerful Cecil family, through whose influence he was elected to the parliaments of 1593 and 1601. On 29 June 1591 he married Mary (1575–1642), the daughter of William *Rider, alderman and later mayor of London. His first child, Thomas, was probably born in 1595. His second son, Arthur, was baptized in 1598, at which time Lake was living near Charing Cross.

Following Queen Elizabeth's death in March 1603 the council sent Lake to Scotland to inform King James of the state of affairs in his new kingdom. Lake made a good impression, not only on the king but also upon his Scottish followers, and in May 1603 was knighted. There are indications that Robert Cecil, James's principal English minister, resented Lake's growing influence, but he could not counter the influence of the Scots at court, who continued to support their protégé. Lake also had the advantage of accompanying James on his frequent hunting expeditions, during which, if Sir Anthony Weldon is to be believed, he 'would tell tales, and let the king know the passages of court, and great men … and discovered their bawdry, which did infinitely please the king's humour' (Weldon, 1.368). In June 1604 the Spanish count of Villa Mediana, on a special embassy to England, reported that

James held Lake in high esteem 'as he trusts him the most and gives him many duties to perform. He is mentioned for the office of First Secretary which Cecil now holds' (Loomie, 54).

Lake sat for Launceston in the first parliament of James I's reign, and took advantage of his membership to pilot through a bill securing his title to the Canons estate at Stanmore in Middlesex, which he had purchased two years earlier.

Continuing tensions between the ambitious Lake and Robert Cecil, now earl of Salisbury, came to the surface in 1609 when the minister lessened his workload by dividing his secretarial duties between Lake and Sir Thomas Edmondes. Lake was to be responsible for home affairs, which implied continuous attendance upon the king, but when James left town for Royston in November, Salisbury ordered Edmondes to accompany him. Lake, regarding this as a calculated slight, protested so forcefully that Salisbury reversed his decision. James's attitude was indicated by his appointment of Lake as his Latin secretary in December 1609.

From the death of Salisbury to the parliament of 1614 In April 1612 Salisbury, by now a dying man, set out for Bath to take the waters. He left the signet in Lake's hands 'and gave him many good words to the King at the delivery of it' (*Letters of John Chamberlain*, 1.346). Following Salisbury's death in May, James ordered that all official communications should be sent to Lake, but he declined to give him the title of secretary, retaining it for future bestowal. Lake's financial position had been improved by the death of Sir William Rider, his father-in-law, in 1611, and he now offered £15,000 for the secretaryship. However, James still temporized. One well-informed observer suggested that there were two major impediments to Lake's appointment. The first arose from doubts about 'his soundness in religion'; the second from the arrogance and ill temper of his wife, who was frequently compared to Xantippe, the termagant spouse of Socrates (*Letters of John Chamberlain*, 1.367). There is little doubt that Lake was a covert Catholic, in contrast to his younger brother, Arthur *Lake, who became bishop of Bath and Wells in 1616. Lake's London house was next door to that of the Venetian ambassador, who allowed him to make a gateway through the party wall so that he and his family could attend Catholic services in the embassy chapel. The ambassador also reported that at various times Lake and his wife sent him 'devotional things, to take care of them, when they were afraid that the house might be searched' (*CSP Venice*, 1615–17, 597–9).

Lake's Catholic leanings won him the patronage of the lord treasurer, the earl of Suffolk, who by March 1614 had persuaded James to appoint him as secretary. However, the committed protestants on the council warned the king that this would be unacceptable to members of the forthcoming parliament and would frustrate James's hopes of a harmonious session. James therefore appointed Sir Ralph Winwood, whose protestantism was unequivocal. Lake had to be content with being made a privy councillor. He sat in the 1614 parliament as a knight of the shire for Middlesex and made an early attempt to resolve the dispute over the prerogative taxes known as impositions by proposing that a conference should be held in James's presence. Some weeks later he warned the Commons against drawing up a petition against the new order of baronets on the grounds that this 'would not only call the prerogative but the judgment and discretion of the King in question' (Jansson, 157, 326). As the session drew to its unhappy close he urged members to choose the constructive course of voting supply, rather than being 'dissolved without doing any other good' (ibid., 423), but the house was in no mood for compromise, and the Addled Parliament ended in failure.

Secretary of state and family scandals Many Catholic sympathizers distrusted parliament as an institution that gave voice to extreme anti-popish sentiments, but Lake seems to have been an exception. When the privy council discussed how to improve the royal finances in September 1615 he argued that a satisfactory relationship between the king and parliament was essential for the monarchy's reputation. He therefore advocated summoning another parliament, but only after the king had agreed to curb his extravagance.

Lake's implied criticism of James's open-handedness might well have harmed his chances of promotion, but the situation was changing in his favour as the king, disillusioned with parliament, turned towards Spain. Lake's pro-Spanish leanings—no doubt strengthened by the Spanish ambassador's award to him of an annual pension of £500 in 1614—now made him acceptable to James, and in January 1616 he was at last appointed secretary of state. Foreign relations remained the province of Winwood, as senior secretary, but Lake strengthened his position by arranging a marriage between his daughter, Anne [*see* Cecil, Anne], and Lord Ros, grandson of the earl of Exeter, who was himself the son of Elizabeth I's chief minister, William Cecil, Lord Burghley. Ros was a Catholic, and Lake persuaded James to appoint him ambassador-extraordinary to Spain in order to promote good relations between the two courts.

Further evidence of Lake's standing with the king came in 1617 when he was chosen to accompany James on his state visit to Scotland. However, when Winwood died, in October 1617, the king rejected Lake's request to be given the post of principal secretary. He offered him a barony instead, but when it was pointed out that this would create resentment among the other barons, since Lake, by virtue of his office, would take precedence over them, James changed his mind. Lake was given a choice between the peerage and the secretaryship and chose the latter.

Despite the fact that he was still only junior secretary, Lake seemed well placed for future advancement. But at this very moment he was overtaken by a crisis brought on by his own family. Lake's daughter, Anne, and her husband, Lord Ros, were an ill-assorted couple, and they were soon living apart. Lady Ros insisted that her husband should provide for her upkeep by transferring to her a property in Essex. Failing that, she would make public details of his sexual inadequacy. Lake added to the pressure by threatening that unless Ros complied no exchequer funding would be available for his mission to Spain. Ros was prepared to give way, but his grandfather, the earl of Exeter, had some rights in the property, which he refused to relinquish. This enraged Lady Ros, who had a domineering temperament. She and her mother joined forces to attack the countess of Exeter, the earl's young wife, whom they blamed for his intransigence. They accused her of attempting to poison Lady Ros, and produced a paper, said to be in the countess's hand, in which she acknowledged her guilt. The countess denounced this as a forgery, and the case was brought before the court of Star Chamber.

The entire Lake family, as Chamberlain observed, had now 'fallen into a labyrinth, whence they know not how to get out' (*Letters of John Chamberlain*, 2.145). Lake was not directly implicated, but mounting evidence that his wife and daughter were guilty of forgery as well as slander did little for his reputation. His position was further weakened by accusations of bribery made against his patron, the lord treasurer. Lady Suffolk, who was said to have received the bribes paid to her husband, had taken temporary refuge in the country, but could not for long resist the delights of London. When James heard she was back in town he threatened to have her forcibly removed. Lake reported this to Suffolk, but James accused him of betrayal and virtually suspended him from office. Lake sought assistance from James's new favourite, George Villiers, marquess of Buckingham, offering £15,000 by way of inducement. Buckingham spurned the offer, but Lake was more successful in his appeal to the favourite's mother, who persuaded him to intercede with James on Lake's behalf.

Downfall and last years By August 1618 Lake appeared to be once more securely established in office, but in February of the following year the Star Chamber gave its judgment in the Exeter case. The countess's charges against Lake's wife and daughter were upheld, and the two women were fined £15,000 and committed to the Tower of London. Lake himself was condemned on the grounds that he had used his official position to secure the imprisonment of two servants of the Ros and Exeter families who had declined to give false evidence against their masters and mistresses. Lake was stripped of the secretaryship, fined £5000, and sent to join his family in the Tower.

Lake remained incarcerated until July 1619, when he was released on health grounds. He continued to protest his innocence of the charges made against him, but he had no wish to return to prison and in January 1620 he reluctantly agreed 'to make his personal submission and acknowledgement in the Star Chamber … and to confess the judgment there given upon him to be most just for his gross credulity, indulgence and ignorance' (*Letters of John Chamberlain*, 2.284).

Lake did not give up hope of recovering his position, particularly after the disgrace of Secretary Naunton in January 1621. Yet his exclusion from power turned out to

be permanent, and he blamed this upon Buckingham. Following his election to parliament in 1626 Lake took an active part in the impeachment proceedings against the favourite, but the failure to topple Buckingham merely confirmed that Lake's political career was over. He lived a retired life at Canons until his death on 17 September 1630; he was buried on 19 October in the parish church of Little Stanmore.

King James is said to have described Lake as 'a minister of state fit to serve the greatest prince in Europe' (Fuller, 14), and there is no doubt that he was a speedy, efficient, and trustworthy administrator. However, Lake's Catholic tendencies and pro-Spanish leanings ceased to be advantages after the collapse of the Spanish marriage negotiations in 1623, and even if James had restored him to the secretaryship it is unlikely that he would have continued in office under Charles I. Lake did not welcome his enforced retirement, but, as Fuller observed, he had the consolation of 'having achieved a fair fortune, which he transmitted to posterity' (Fuller, 14).

ROGER LOCKYER

Sources CSP dom., 1595–1629 · *The letters of John Chamberlain*, ed. N. E. McClure, 2 vols. (1939) · A. Weldon, 'The court of King James', *Secret history of the court of James the First*, ed. W. Scott, 1 (1811), 313–482 · A. Weldon, 'The character of King James', *Secret history of the court of James the First*, ed. W. Scott, 2 (1811), 1–12 · G. Goodman, *The court of King James the First*, 2 vols. (1839) · [T. Birch and R. F. Williams], eds., *The court and times of Charles the First*, 2 vols. (1848) · *Letters of John Holles, 1587–1637*, ed. P. R. Seddon, 3 vols., Thoroton Society Record Series, 31, 35–6 (1975–86) · Fuller, *Worthies* (1840), vol. 2 · *Report on the manuscripts of the marquis of Downshire*, 6 vols. in 7, HMC, 75 (1924–95), vols. 2–6 · *Calendar of the manuscripts of the most hon. the marquis of Salisbury*, 24 vols., HMC, 9 (1883–1976), vols. 7–21 · *CSP Venice, 1610–23* · A. D. Thrush and J. P. Ferris, 'Lake, Sir Thomas', HoP, *Commons, 1604–29* [draft] · A. J. Loomie, *Toleration and diplomacy: the religious issues in Anglo-Spanish relations, 1603–05* (1963) · *The letters and life of Francis Bacon*, ed. J. Spedding, 7 vols. (1861–74), vols. 3–7 · E. R. Foster, ed., *Proceedings in parliament, 1610*, 2 vols. (1966) · M. Jansson, ed., *Proceedings in parliament, 1614 (House of Commons)* (1988) · W. B. Bidwell and M. Jansson, eds., *Proceedings in parliament, 1626, 2–3: House of Commons* (1992) · W. A. Shaw, *The knights of England*, 2 (1906), 109 · E. Freshfield, ed., *The register book of the parish of St Christopher le Stocks*, 3 vols. in 1 (1882), vol. 1, p. 24 · G. E. Cokayne, *Some account of the lord mayors and sheriffs of London, 1601–25* (1897) · G. J. Armytage, ed., *Middlesex pedigrees*, Harleian Society, 65 (1914), 152 · *Report on the manuscripts of Lord De L'Isle and Dudley*, 1, HMC, 77 (1925), 227 · *VCH Middlesex* · D. Lysons, *The environs of London*, 4 vols. (1792–6), vol. 3, p. 413 · BL, Add. MS 29974, fol. 138 · parish register, Little Stanmore, St Lawrence, 19 Oct 1630 [burial] · A. L. Merson, ed., *The third book of remembrance of Southampton, 3: 1573–1589*, Southampton RS, 8 (1965)

Archives BL, corresp. · Hatfield House, Hertfordshire, letters and papers | Arundel Castle, West Sussex, corresp. with earl of Shrewsbury · CKS, letters to earl of Leicester

Lake, William Charles (1817–1897), dean of Durham, was born in London on 9 January 1817, the eldest son of Captain Charles Lake, an officer in the Scots Fusilier Guards who was wounded at Waterloo and thereafter lived in retirement, and his wife, Anna Louisa, youngest daughter of Henry Halsey of Henley Park, Surrey. Some of his childhood was spent in France and the Channel Islands before the family settled in Rugby, where he attended Rugby School as a day boy under Dr Wooll and Dr Arnold. He became head of the school and formed close friendships with A. P. Stanley and C. J. Vaughan. In 1834 he won a scholarship at Balliol College, Oxford, and in 1838 gained first-class honours in the classical school. He was a friend of A. C. Tait, with whom he travelled to the continent in vacations, a member of the celebrated debating society, the Decade, and president of the Oxford Union Society in 1838. As an undergraduate he came under the influence of Newman, and his election to a Balliol fellowship in 1838 with membership of the common room brought him into frequent contact with W. G. Ward. Ordained in 1842, and in the same year appointed a tutor of Balliol (where his nicknames Serpent, Puddle, and Piddle suggested a degree of unpopularity with the undergraduates), he was one of the liberals who opposed the measures taken against the Tractarian leaders by the university's hebdomadal board. Illness caused his absence from Oxford between 1845 and 1847.

On his return to Oxford, Lake played a prominent part in university reform. He gave evidence to the royal commission (1850), was senior proctor in 1852, and took a leading part in the Oxford Tutors' Association, which promoted the moderate settlement, protecting collegiate and clerical interests, carried through by W. E. Gladstone in 1854. His most significant achievement was in organizing the introduction of modern history into the undergraduate curriculum, serving as examiner in the first examinations in law and modern history in 1853 and 1854. His association with modern studies and knowledge of European languages led to his appointment in 1855 as an examiner of candidates for army commissions and, in 1856, as a member of the War Office commission set up following the reverses in the Crimean War to investigate the training of army officers. After visiting military academies on the continent, Lake and his colleagues recommended the establishment of a staff college in Britain. He was also an academic representative, with H. M. Butler, on the royal commission on military education (1868–70). In June 1858 he was appointed a member of the royal commission chaired by the duke of Newcastle to investigate elementary education in England. Its report (1861) foreshadowed the Education Act of 1870.

In October 1858, to the surprise of his friends, Lake turned his back on academic life and accepted the Balliol College living of Huntspill in Somerset, becoming a canon of Wells in 1860. He had been an unsuccessful candidate for the vacant chair of ecclesiastical history at Oxford in 1856, and he felt a growing estrangement from the direction of Oxford liberalism, believing that the theology of Jowett and Stanley was encouraging doubt and unbelief. For this reason he disliked *Essays and Reviews*, though he publicly defended Frederick Temple, one of the contributors, in 1869. He remained a Liberal in politics and one of the high-church adherents of Gladstone, who on 9 August 1869 nominated him to the deanery of Durham, which carried with it the wardenship of Durham University. Gladstone urged him to infuse life into the moribund university, whose student numbers had fallen below fifty. Lake rejected the idea of making Durham a miniature

Oxford, but instead concentrated on its development as a leading school of theology, while the needs of higher scientific and technical education in the north-east were served by the foundation, in 1871, of the Durham College of Science at Newcastle. During his wardenship the Durham College of Medicine was also incorporated into the university.

As dean of the cathedral Lake had to overcome the conservatism of the canons, and relations were not always harmonious. He lacked a winning manner—an archdeacon described him as 'imperious', 'impetuous', and 'impertinent' (Barrett, 48)—and he was obliged to rely on a legal opinion to affirm his authority over cathedral services, which shocked him on his arrival by their lack of decorum. He succeeded in imposing order and reverence, restored the eucharist to a high place, and, in the face of determined opposition from C. T. Baring, the bishop of Durham, oversaw the restoration of the cathedral interior, carried out by Gilbert Scott (1876).

On 2 June 1881 Lake married Katherine, daughter of John Neilson Gladstone, brother of the prime minister. In collaboration with R. W. Church and H. P. Liddon he used his influence with his old college friend Archbishop Tait to dissuade him from taking extreme measures against ritualist clergymen under the Public Worship Regulation Act, and he supported those clergy who were imprisoned under the act. He was a member of the ecclesiastical courts commission (1881–3). A vice-president of the English Church Union and a governor of Pusey House, Oxford, he opposed attempts to encourage secessions from the Roman Catholic churches on the continent, protesting in 1888 against the Anglican mission to convert Italy. Latterly he broke with Gladstonian Liberalism as he opposed Irish home rule. He resigned the deanery on 2 November 1894, owing to failing health. Lake went to live at Kanescombe in Torquay, where he died on 8 December 1897. He was survived by his wife.   M. C. CURTHOYS

Sources K. Lake, ed., *Memorials of William Charles Lake, dean of Durham, 1869–1894* (1901) • Boase, *Mod. Eng. biog.* • W. R. Ward, *Victorian Oxford* (1965) • P. Barrett, *Barchester: English cathedral life in the nineteenth century* (1993) • Gladstone, *Diaries* • J. Jones, *Balliol College: a history, 1263–1939* (1988)

Archives BL, corresp. with W. E. Gladstone, Add. MS 44230 • Durham Cath. CL, letters to J. B. Lightfoot • LPL, letters to A. C. Tait • U. Newcastle, Robinson L., letters to Sir Walter Trevelyan

Likenesses photograph, 1901, repro. in Lake, ed., *Memorials of William Charles Lake*, frontispiece

Wealth at death £84,535 4s. 4d.: resworn double probate, Jan 1899, CGPLA Eng. & Wales (1897)

Lakeman, Enid (1903–1995), political reformer, was born on 28 November 1903 at Broadview, Hadlow, near Tonbridge, Kent, the only child of Horace Bradlaugh Lakeman (1874–1962), an excise officer, and Evereld Simpson (1867–1950), youngest daughter of John Harwood Simpson and his wife, Jane Ann. Enid's grandmother had supported a number of Liberal causes, including the Proportional Representation Society, and was a candidate at the London School Board election of 1879. When she died the family had moved to Kent, and settled at Tunbridge Wells. There Enid attended the County Grammar School for Girls, where she gained distinction in the school certificate and higher school certificate. In 1923 she was awarded the Arnott scholarship to study chemistry at Bedford College, London, and graduated with first-class honours in 1926. She maintained close contact with both school and college, serving as a Bedford College governor from 1957 until it amalgamated with Royal Holloway College. After graduation she worked in the chemical industry, translating from German to English, and while living in Germany saw at first hand the dangers of national socialism. She also worked as a teacher, and then became information officer for the British Flour Millers' Association. In 1941 she volunteered for the WAAF and trained as a radar operator.

Lakeman became a Liberal Party activist at an early age, serving that party, its women's section, and later the Liberal Democrats in numerous capacities—locally, nationally, and internationally—all her life. In 1938 she was encouraged to stand for parliament, but because of the war she was not adopted until 1944. She stood at St Albans in 1945, being one of only three servicewoman candidates, then at Brixton in 1950, and at Aldershot in 1955 and 1959. The post-war period was not a fruitful era for Liberal candidates, and she retained her deposit only once, in 1959. Electoral success did not entirely evade her; she was elected to Tunbridge Wells borough council in 1962, and served a three-year term. In 1946 she wrote her only party-orientated book, *When Labour Fails*.

Following demobilization in 1946 Lakeman joined the staff of the Proportional Representation Society (later the Electoral Reform Society), as research secretary, and became its director in 1960. She undertook the society's routine work, cultivating sympathetic politicians, addressing meetings, dealing with enquiries, and—at that time—counting votes and administering elections for other organizations. She drafted a number of submissions for the society—including those for the speaker's conference of 1965, the Hansard Commission on Electoral Reform, and the electoral arrangements of countries being decolonized—as well as pamphlets and contributions to other publications. Her writing style is notable for its clarity and economy of words; this ensured a high publication rate when responding to press opportunities, but brevity could lead to sharpness of tone.

When the society decided to produce a new book on electoral systems Lakeman and James Lambert were asked to undertake it jointly. The first two editions, under the title *Voting in Democracies*, appeared in 1955 and 1959. Lakeman was the sole author of the third and fourth editions, published in 1970 and 1974 as *How Democracies Vote*. The work came to be recognized as a valuable source book, and the American Political Science Association considered it worthy of their George Hallett award, for having encouraged interest in electoral systems. An unofficial Russian translation was published in the Soviet Union. Lakeman wrote a simpler book, *Power to Elect*, published as a paperback in 1982, and a brief history of the Electoral Reform Society, *The Best System* (1984), for the society's centenary. To provide a simple description of the electoral systems of the EU she wrote *Nine Democracies* (1973) and, when the EU was enlarged, *Twelve Democracies* (1991).

Lakeman's most significant campaigns were in the Irish republic, when two attempts were made to abandon the single transferable vote (STV) form of proportional representation used to elect the Dáil. In 1958 the Irish prime minister, Eamon De Valera, proposed adopting the British single-member relative majority electoral system. Since the change required a constitutional amendment, its adoption was subject to a national referendum. This took Lakeman to Ireland to help the STV supporters to campaign for its retention. Among those with whom she worked were the Nobel peace price winner Sean McBride and, later, Dr Garret FitzGerald. A presidential election was held simultaneously with the first referendum in 1959, when the voters elected De Valera president but rejected the proposed change to the electoral system. At the second referendum, in 1968, the same proposal was defeated by a larger margin. During the late 1960s the society started building contacts in Northern Ireland, which had abandoned proportional representation forty years earlier. This was a society team effort, and saw success in 1972, when William Whitelaw announced the return of the single transferable vote. Lakeman formally retired in 1980, and was appointed OBE, but continued to help the society and promote its cause until she died.

By 1970 arthritic hips made walking difficult for Lakeman, although she did not let this restrict her activities; she later had two hip replacement operations. She followed a simple diet—mainly of salads, fresh fruit, nuts, cheese, and herbal tea—but ate meat if vegetarian food was not available. Her Electoral Reform Society work promoting the single transferable vote overshadows her other interests. She supported organizations promoting universal free trade, land value taxation, and international co-operation, including the United Nations Association and the European Movement. Lakeman also supported many women's organizations, encouraging women and young people to interest themselves in public affairs. She promoted an essay competition at her old school, while the society's members promoted a Lakeman lecture at her old college; the Politics Association has recognized her support with a lecture at their conference.

Enid Lakeman died on 7 January 1995 at her home—37 Culverden Avenue, Tunbridge Wells—and was cremated on 24 January at Tunbridge Wells, after a humanist meeting celebrating her life. E. M. SYDDIQUE

Sources personal knowledge (2004) · private information (2004) · b. cert. · d. cert. · b. certs. [H. B. Lakeman; E. Simpson] · m. cert. [H. B. Lakeman and E. Simpson] · d. certs. [H. B. Lakeman; E. Lakeman] · *WW* · *The Times* (23 Jan 1995) · Enid Lakeman, private MSS, priv. coll. [to be lodged at Royal Holloway College, Egham, Surrey]
Archives Electoral Reform Society, London · priv. coll., personal papers and private corresp.
Likenesses photograph, 1980–89, McDougall Library, London
Wealth at death £145,000: probate, 17 Oct 1996, *CGPLA Eng. & Wales*

Lakensnyder, Katherine (d. 1394). *See under* Women in trade and industry in York (*act. c.*1300–*c.*1500).

Laker, James Charles [Jim] (1922–1986), cricketer, was born at Frizinghall, Bradford, Yorkshire, on 9 February 1922, the youngest child and only son—he had one sister and three older half-sisters—of Charles Henry Laker (1887–1931), stonemason, originally of Sussex, and Ellen Taylor Oxby (1878–1945), teacher, of Blackerhill, Worsborough, Barnsley. He was educated at Salts high school, Saltaire, Yorkshire, where, as a schoolboy, he was something of a batsman and quick bowler.

It was the old Yorkshire professional B. B. Wilson who, coaching Laker in the early war years, advised him to concentrate on off-spin. During his army service in the Middle East he had the chance to try his new skill against competent players. Before demobilization he was billeted at Catford, Surrey, and played for the local club. Its president, Andrew Kempton, recommended him to Surrey County Cricket Club. As Yorkshire had shown no interest, he was signed up by Surrey, made his first-class début in 1946, and soon made his place secure. He made an early start to test cricket, visiting the West Indies in the winter of 1947–8, but for some years he failed to become an England regular and he had an especially difficult summer when the Australians visited in 1948. This was despite his tremendous attainments for Surrey, for whom, in lethal spinning partnership with the left-handed Tony Lock, he produced so many great feats which were instrumental in Surrey being the outstanding county team of the post-war period. Surrey were county champions in seven successive seasons from 1952 to 1959.

It was in 1956 that Laker made his name legendary, taking forty-six wickets, at an average cost of just 9.6 runs, in the Australian series. These included the fabled nineteen wickets for 90 runs in the Old Trafford test match in July 1956, all taken while he was bowling from the Stretford end, with his co-partner Tony Lock desperately trying to make inroads from the other end. Although the conditions were favourable to Laker, it was certainly the most comprehensively effective display of bowling in cricketing history, and one of the most remarkable days in the history of cricket. No one has ever taken so many wickets in a match—players have taken 17 wickets in a game on eighteen occasions, and these are his closest rivals. To capture all but one wicket in a match would be triumph enough, but to achieve this in a test match for England against Australia added immeasurably to the glory. He also took 10 for 53 against the Australians for Surrey in 1956, becoming the only man to take ten wickets in an innings twice in the same season. Equally a part of cricketing folk-lore is his car journey home southwards after his Old Trafford success. He recalled how he sat in a Lichfield pub, drinking his beer and eating his cheese sandwich, while other customers enthused over his 19 wickets without recognizing that the brilliant perpetrator of the deed was one of their company.

All in all, Laker had a career tally of 1944 first-class victims, at an average of 18.41, and he took 100 wickets in a season on eleven occasions. His best total was in 1950, when he took 166 wickets at an average of 15.32. It was in

James Charles [Jim] **Laker** (1922–1986), by unknown photographer, 1950

that year that he produced his other memorable analysis—14 overs, 12 maidens, 8 wickets for 2 runs—at Bradford for England versus the rest in a test trial.

Laker took 193 wickets (average 21.24) in his forty-six tests. His international career lasted from 1946–7 to 1958–9, and this included tours to South Africa and to Australia and New Zealand as well as the West Indies. As a lower-order batsman he made a few useful runs on occasion, ending with a tally of 7304 first-class runs (average 16.60), and this included a couple of centuries. He also took 270 catches.

A squarely built man, 6 feet in height, dark-haired, and taciturn, Laker was sometimes compared as a bowler, for instance by John Arlott in broadcasting commentary, with the policeman on his beat. There was a distinct flavour of the old-fashioned bobby about him, large, placid, knowing, and unbending. The measured rhythm of his few paces to the wicket betokened the impeccable balance that was the base of his achievement. This was matched by the shrewd use of angles, both in his position at the crease and in his length and 'loop' of delivery, and by the firm twang of his off-spin, for few right-handers have spun the ball with such venomous thrust. He believed that potency of spin was the key, although such fierce twisting damaged his spinning finger with savage rips—he treated his fingers constantly with Friar's Balsam—and eventual arthritis. His accuracy meant that it was safe for fielders to perch close to the bat and snaffle up the inevitable catches. He was assuredly the leading off-spinner of his generation, and some critics would argue that Jim Laker was the finest exponent of off-spin in cricket's long saga.

At the end of his career Laker played some thirty games in the summers of 1962–4 for Essex as an amateur, while his memoirs, *Over to me*, published in 1960, were plain-spoken enough to cause a degree of ill feeling among the cricketing authorities. Good relations were restored and, at the time of his death, Jim Laker was chairman of the Surrey cricket committee. After a modest flirtation with industry, he found a pleasing career as a television cricket commentator, to which role he brought the traits of knowledgeable, laconic calm which had characterized his playing career. He was married on 27 March 1951 at Kensington, London, to Lilly Gingold (it was her second marriage), secretary, who was born in Vienna, Austria, in 1920. They had two daughters, Fiona and Angela. Septicaemia set in following a gall bladder operation, and Laker died at Putney, London, where he lived, on 23 April 1986, survived by his wife.   ERIC MIDWINTER

Sources A. Hill, *Jim Laker: a biography* (1998) · *Wisden* (1987) · J. C. Laker, *Over to me* (1960) · J. C. Laker, *Spinning round the world* (1957) · J. C. Laker, *The Australian tour of 1961* (1961) · D. Lemmon, *The official history of Surrey county cricket club* (1989)
Archives FILM BFI NFTVA, '4th test: Laker's great feat!' All 10 wickets', 1956 · BFI NFTVA, documentary footage · BFI NFTVA, sports footage
Likenesses photographs, 1949–77, Hult. Arch. [*see illus.*] · photographs, repro. in Lemmon, *Official history of Surrey county cricket club* · photographs, repro. in Laker, *Over to me*
Wealth at death £163,035: probate, 10 June 1986, *CGPLA Eng. & Wales*

Laking, Sir Guy Francis, second baronet (1875–1919), antiquary and museum curator, was born on 21 October 1875 at 5 Cleveland Road, Westminster, London, the only son of Sir Francis Henry Laking, baronet (1847–1914), physician-in-ordinary and surgeon apothecary to Queen Victoria and to her two successors on the throne, and physician to the royal household, and his first wife, Emma Ann Mansell (d. 1905).

Educated at Westminster School and Westminster School of Art, Laking very early developed an overwhelming interest in antiques and works of art, and, above all, in early arms and armour, and devoted most of his spare time to studying them. He often visited Christie's salerooms, only a short distance from his parents' home in Pall Mall, where he attracted the attention of one of the firm's partners, T. H. Woods, to whom he became a kind of unofficial apprentice. The association eventually led to his joining Christie's as art adviser, a position he continued to occupy for the rest of his life, despite being involved in many other activities. On 21 July 1898 he married Beatrice Ida, daughter of Charles Mylne Barker, a solicitor, with whom he had a son and a daughter.

Laking's father's royal appointments, and the location of the family residence, meant that, in Francis Sheppard's phrase, he was 'brought up almost literally within the shadow of royalty' (Sheppard, 46). There can be little doubt that the post at Christie's, with its all-embracing title, was created for him with an eye to the business that the firm hoped his royal and aristocratic connections might produce as much as in recognition of his expert knowledge. That he possessed the latter is, however, demonstrated by the quality of his first catalogue for Christie's (of the Zschille collection), produced at the beginning of 1897 when he was only just twenty-one, and by the speed with which he established thereafter a reputation as a leading expert on the decorative arts in general, and especially on medieval and later arms and armour.

In 1900 Laking was appointed honorary inspector of the armouries at the Wallace Collection—recently bequeathed to the nation—where he was already busy compiling a catalogue of the European pieces that went through four editions and two reprints between that year and 1910. Shortly afterwards he wrote a catalogue of the armoury of the knights of St John at Valletta (published in 1903), and in 1902 Edward VII created the post of keeper of the king's armoury at Windsor specially for him. This led to his producing a massive catalogue of its European pieces in 1904, followed in 1905 and 1907 respectively by catalogues of the furniture at Windsor Castle and of the Sèvres porcelain both there and at Buckingham Palace. He had achieved all this by the time he was thirty-two, while also carrying on his work for Christie's together with related activities, leading an extremely active social life, and raising a family.

In 1911 Laking was made the first keeper and secretary of the London Museum (now part of the Museum of London), which was then little more than an idea. He has been described as the greatest holder of this office, and so far as its collections were concerned he was certainly the museum's founder, since he was responsible for forming them from scratch and arranging them in Lancaster House, its first home. His long-standing connections with the royal family, some of whom took a personal interest in the museum, as also with the art and antiques trade, were specially advantageous, and the opening to the public on 23 March 1914, towards which he worked with tireless energy, was immensely successful. On the death of his father in that year he became the second baronet.

While organizing the new museum, Laking was also involved in, among other things, gathering material for what was to be the other achievement for which he will be most remembered: his *magnum opus*, *A Record of European Armour and Arms through Seven Centuries* (5 vols., 1920–22). It was unfinished at his death—he lived only to see an advance copy of the first volume—and was completed by his literary executor, F. H. Cripps-Day. It remains the largest and most fully illustrated survey of its subject ever published.

Laking's capacity for hard concentrated work was to some extent masked by a playboy image. A man of extraordinary charm—he seems to have been loved by everyone who knew him, not least by women—he was also known for his great kindness, immense generosity, and wild extravagance. He had expensive tastes in all the good things of life, including the collection of works of art, above all of fine early arms and armour. His friend Oswald Barron wrote of him that he spent his money 'like one who has a store of gold angels and gold nobles in an iron chest rather than as one who draws cheques on a banking account' (Barron, 43), and many stories used to be told about his extravagances. The most celebrated is probably that of his entertaining the members of the Meyrick Society (of arms and armour collectors) to a medieval feast at his home, which included a roast peacock in its feathers and his children's governess in armour handing round a loving-cup. In order to maintain his lifestyle he appears to have supplemented his income by giving expert advice to both collectors and dealers about works of art. There is considerable evidence to suggest that his need for money was so great that he did not always behave ethically when doing so.

Laking died on 22 November 1919 at his home, Meyrick Lodge, 16 Avenue Road, Regent's Park, and was buried in Highgate cemetery. He was survived by his wife. His son, Guy Francis William Laking (1904–1930), succeeded as third and last baronet.   CLAUDE BLAIR

Sources WW · WWW, 1916–28 · The Times (24 Nov 1919) · Daily Telegraph (24 Nov 1919) · The Londoner [O. A. Barron], 'Sir Guy', Day in and day out (1924), 41–4 · C. J. ffoulkes, Arms and the tower (1939) · J. F. Hayward, 'Sir Guy Francis Laking', Armi antiche (Bolletino dell'Accademia di San Marciano, Turin, 1964), 266–70 · F. Sheppard, The treasury of London's past: an historical account of the Museum of London and its predecessors, the Guildhall Museum, and the London Museum (1991) · C. Blair, The Meyrick Society, 1890–1990 (1991) [privately printed for circulation to members] · C. Blair, 'Crediton: the story of two helmets', Studies in European arms and armor: the C. Otto von Kienbusch collection in the Philadelphia Museum of Art (Philadelphia, 1992), 152–83 · C. Blair, 'Introduction', in G. F. Laking, A record of European armour and arms through seven centuries, 5 vols. (2000) [facs. reprint] · b. cert. · m. cert. · d. cert. · CGPLA Eng. & Wales (1920) · private information (2004)
Archives Bodl. Oxf., corresp. with Lewis Harcourt
Likenesses photograph, repro. in Blair, 'Introduction' · photograph, repro. in Blair, 'Crediton: the story of two helmets' · photograph, repro. in Daily Telegraph · photograph, repro. in Hayward, 'Sir Guy Francis Laking' · photograph, repro. in Sheppard, Treasury of London's past · photographs, Museum of London
Wealth at death £32,728 16s. 4d.: probate, 2 Jan 1920, CGPLA Eng. & Wales

Lakingheth, John de. See Lackenheath, John (d. 1381).

Lakyngheth, John (d. 1396). See under Lackenheath, John (d. 1381).

Lallóc (fl. 5th cent.). See under Connacht, saints of (act. c.400–c.800).

Lalor, James Fintan (1807–1849), Irish nationalist, was born on 10 March 1807 at Tenakill, Queen's county, the eldest of eleven children of Patrick Lalor (1781–1856) of Tenakill and his wife, Anne Dillon (d. 1835). Patrick was a gentleman farmer and middleman who took a prominent part in the anti-tithe movement of the 1830s and was MP for his county, 1832–5. Peter *Lalor was a younger son. James Fintan was set apart by physical deformity and ill health. He was educated at home until at the age of seventeen he spent a year (1825–6) in Carlow College. His lack of formal education was compensated for by the fierce energy and independence of his mind. In due course he rejected the mainstream O'Connellite movement in which his father and brothers were prominent. His search for an alternative led him into friendly correspondence with Sir Robert Peel in 1843. But long before this he had identified radical change in the landholding system as the great answer to Irish problems.

In January 1847 Lalor secured a place among the contributors to The Nation, and wrote a series of letters that were remarkable for their passionate rhetoric. He advocated a scheme for a strike against rent, which, in spite of the strong disapproval of Charles Gavan Duffy, he induced John Mitchel to adopt. On 18 September 1847 he summoned a meeting of tenant farmers at Holycross, co. Tipperary, to found a tenant association on the footing of a 'live and thrive' rent, but his want of practical ability and his fierce self-opinionatedness caused the failure of the meeting. His resolutions were carried, but the association was abortive.

The events of 1848 drew Lalor, as so many others, towards political revolution. On 26 May of that year John Mitchel was transported and the United Irishman suppressed. Thereupon John Martin arranged for the publication of the Irish Felon, successor to the United Irishman. The first number was dated 24 June 1848, and Lalor was the chief contributor. After Martin's arrest in July, Lalor practically edited the newspaper. It came to an end on 22 July with its fifth number. Lalor was arrested on 28 July. He was imprisoned under the Habeas Corpus Suspension Act, but his health having become impaired, he was released in November 1848.

Lalor was one of the leaders in a revolutionary conspiracy, largely involving artisans in the towns of Leinster and Munster, which flourished for much of 1849 before petering out after a failed attempt at rebellion in September. He was at work on plans for a new newspaper when he fell ill and died, unmarried, at his lodgings in Great Britain Street, Dublin, on 27 December 1849. A large procession followed his funeral to Glasnevin cemetery three days later. Half a century on his ideas, seldom fully comprehended, became grist to the mill of another generation of Irish nationalists. For James Connolly he provided the rare and welcome precedent of a nationalist with an appreciation of socio-economic structure. To Patrick Pearse he was, along with Tone, Davis, and Mitchel, one of the evangelists of Irish nationalism.   R. V. COMERFORD

Sources T. Ó Neill [T. P. O'Neill], Fiontán Ó Leathlobhair (1962) · T. P. O'Neill, 'Fintan Lalor and the 1849 movement', An Cosantóir (April 1950) · T. P. O'Neill, 'The economic and political ideas of James Fintan Lalor', Irish Ecclesiastical Record, 74 (1950), 398–409 · C. G. Duffy, Young Ireland, 2: Four years of Irish history, 1845–1849 (1887) · D. N. Buckley, James Fintan Lalor: radical (1990) · L. Fogarty, James Fintan Lalor: patriot and political essayist, 1807–1849 (1918)
Archives NL Ire., corresp. and papers | BL, Peel MSS · NL Ire., Luby MSS

Lalor, John (1814–1856), journalist and author, was born on 23 April 1814 in Dublin, son of John Lalor, a merchant. He was educated at a Roman Catholic school at Carlow and at Clongowes College. On 6 June 1831 he entered Trinity College, Dublin, where he graduated BA in 1837. After collecting evidence as an assistant poor-law commissioner, he left Ireland in 1836 and began working with the daily press in London, first as a parliamentary reporter and afterwards, for five or six years, as one of the principal editors of the Morning Chronicle, dealing with social and domestic questions. In 1834 he was admitted to Gray's Inn, and went on to the King's Inns in 1838. In 1839 he obtained the prize of 100 guineas awarded by the Central Society of Education for his essay 'The expediency and means of elevating the profession of the educator in society'. Lalor was brought up as a Roman Catholic, but about 1844 he joined the Unitarian church and became editor of the Unitarian weekly paper *The Inquirer*. He himself contributed influential articles on the Factory Bill, Ireland, and on education. Lalor died, after years of ill health, at Holly Hill, Hampstead, London, on 27 January 1856. He was much revered as an educator through his journalism, and his work on Ireland and on the reform of factory legislation was important.   G. C. BOASE, rev. MARIE-LOUISE LEGG

Sources *GM*, 3rd ser., 1 (1856), 319–20 · E. Keane, P. Beryl Phair, and T. U. Sadlier, eds., *King's Inns admission papers, 1607–1867*, IMC (1982) · Burtchaell & Sadleir, *Alum. Dubl.* · *The Inquirer* (9 Feb 1856) · private information (1892) · d. cert.

Lalor, Peter Fintan (1827–1889), politician in Australia, was born on 5 February 1827 at Tenakill, Queen's county, Ireland, the last of the eleven children of Patrick Lalor (1781–1856), a tenant farmer and MP, and his wife, Anne Dillon (d. 1835). One of his brothers was James Fintan *Lalor. He was baptized on 11 February 1827, and was educated at Raheen primary school. From 1845 onwards the family fortunes worsened with the onset of the great famine. After the discovery of gold in Australia, Lalor sailed for Melbourne in 1852 with his brother Richard (1823–1892), Richard's wife, Margaret, and their sister Margaret and cousin Maria Lalor. From October 1852 to December 1853, together with another Irishman, they operated as Phelan, Lalor & Co., 'wine, spirit, and provision merchants', at the corner of Elizabeth and La Trobe streets in Melbourne. In late December 1853, Lalor travelled to the goldfields at Ballarat, taking with him liquor supplies at wholesale rates costing £804, as well as general store items costing £202. Under cover of a miner's licence, he operated a 'sly grog' store. The rest of the family, however, returned to Tenakill. In December 1854 a rebellion by goldminers broke out at Ballarat. By law, diggers had to pay a monthly licence to the government, but at a meeting on 29 November 1854 it was decided not to pay the licence, and many licences were burnt. Known to the insurgents, most of them Irish, through his sly grog dealings, Lalor was elected commander-in-chief of the insurgents at the Eureka stockade, where a stand was taken for 'liberty', and, in particular, equality before the law. The stockaders objected to the acquittal of a former convict, James Bentley, the owner of the biggest hotel on the Ballarat diggings, for the murder of a miner, James Scobie, and sought to substitute a gold tax for the licence system. For Lalor, it was a stand based chiefly on conscience.

Parties of the 12th and 40th regiments, accompanied by police, attacked the miners on 3 December at the Eureka stockade, when twenty-four of the rebels were killed and twelve wounded. 125 were taken prisoner. Lalor was wounded by gunfire, resulting in the amputation of his left arm. Assisted by Father Patrick Smyth, Lalor escaped to Geelong, to his future wife, the schoolteacher Alicia Dunne (d. 1887). He recovered, and they married on 10 July 1855. He was described as being 5 feet 11 inches tall, with blue-grey eyes, and 'rather good looking'. A reward of £200 offered for his capture did not result in his arrest.

Representation was later given to the goldfields. On 10 November 1855 Lalor was elected without opposition as member for Ballarat, but he was uneasy on either side of the house. He was, however, appointed inspector of railways. Because he refused to vote for manhood suffrage, at the next election, in 1856, he was returned for the more conservative seat of South Grant, which he represented until 1871 and again from 1875 to 1888. In August 1875 he was appointed commissioner for customs in Graham Berry's first radical administration. As chairman of the Clunes water commission, through his efforts a bill was carried in 1871 for the Clunes waterworks, which cost £70,000. In 1877 Lalor was appointed commissioner for trade and customs, and in 1878 he became postmaster-general as well. In 1880 he was elected speaker of the house, a post which he filled with distinction until September 1887, when he retired in consequence of ill health. He was thereupon awarded a grant of £4000. He died at his home, Goodwood Street, Richmond, Melbourne, on 9 February 1889, having outlived his daughter Anne Lempriere and his wife. He was buried in Melbourne general cemetery. He was survived by his son Joseph P. Lalor, a medical doctor.   COLM KIERNAN

Sources NL Ire., Lalor MSS · P. Lalor, 'To the colonists of Victoria', *The Argus* [Melbourne] (10 April 1855) · R. Carboni, *The Eureka stockade* (1855) · C. Kiernan, 'Peter Lalor: Ireland and Victoria', *Victorian Historical Journal*, 59 (1988), 16–29 · C. Kiernan, 'Peter Lalor: the enigma of Eureka', *Labour and the goldfields*, ed. B. Mitchell (1968), 11–23 · T. J. Kiernan, 'The Irish background of Peter Lalor', *The Irish exiles in Australia* (1954), 135–51 · J. Lynch, *Story of the Eureka stockade* (1940) · C. Turnbull, *Eureka: the story of Peter Lalor* (1946) · C. H. Currey, *The Irish at Eureka* (1954) · J. O'Hanlon, E. O'Leary, and M. Lalor, *History of the Queen's county*, 2 vols. (1914) · I. Turner, *Peter Lalor* (1974) · W. Bate, *Lucky city: the first generation at Ballarat, 1851–1901* (1978)

Archives NL Ire.

Likenesses L. Becker, portrait, c.1852, repro. in A. Cairns, *The dangers and duties of the young men of Victoria* (1856)

Lam, Katherine (d. 1494). *See under* Women in trade and industry in York (act. c.1300–c.1500).

Lamb. *See also* Lambe.

Lamb, Sir Albert [Larry] (1929–2000), newspaper editor, was born on 15 July 1929 at 3 Holgate Avenue in the Yorkshire pit village of Fitzwilliam, the son of Henry Lamb, colliery surface blacksmith, and his wife, Coronetta Small. They never called him anything but Albert, but he adopted the name Larry from the lovable lamb in *Toytown*, the BBC *Children's Hour* radio series. He left Rastrick grammar school in 1945 at the age of sixteen to earn his keep as a clerk at Brighouse town hall, where his militant membership of the National and Local Government Officers' Association won him the nickname 'Red Larry'. He was twenty-four before he got his first newspaper job, on the *Brighouse Echo*, and moved on rapidly to the *Shields Gazette*, *Newcastle Journal*, *London Evening Standard*, and *Daily Mail*. On 7 November 1953 he married Joan Mary Denise Grogan, a gown shop manager from Huddersfield. They had three children, a daughter and two sons. Lamb joined the *Daily Mirror* under Hugh Cudlipp as a sub-editor in 1958 and rose to deputy night editor, before moving to Manchester as northern editor of the *Daily Mail* in 1968.

Lamb's big chance came a year later when Rupert Murdoch bought *The Sun* from the Mirror group, which had launched it in 1964 as 'The paper born of the age we live in'. It was altogether too precious for popular success, and sales had collapsed to 650,000. Murdoch and Lamb met for dinner in Rules restaurant; three bottles of Pouilly Fumé later, Murdoch invited him to create a tabloid challenger to the *Daily Mirror*, then selling some 4.9 million copies and grown high-minded in the absence of competition. Lamb's remit as editor was to 'be what the *Mirror* used to be—strident, campaigning, working-class … a thorn in the side of the Establishment' (Lamb, 5). But it needed to be a lot more fun too, and Lamb beckoned to the readers with a formula tailored to television advertising, on a scale hitherto unknown in Fleet Street. The package of sex, sport, showbusiness, competitions, and offers was increasingly balanced by hard news content, but *The Sun*'s silly season would always run from January to December. The paper was launched on 17 November 1969, under the *Mirror*'s cast-off slogan, 'Forward with the people'. It led with 'HORSE DOPE SENSATION', serialized Jacqueline Susann's *The Love Machine*, offered a soccer wallchart for collectable stick-on club crests, and ran an interview with the prime minister, Harold Wilson.

A year on, *The Sun* was selling 1.51 million copies daily, and on its first birthday, Lamb introduced the prototype 'page three girl' (a topless model). In 1971 the *Financial Times* noted 'a soaraway, crest of the wave' feel about the paper, and the circulation was 2.08 million. It rose to 2.63 million in 1972 and Lamb, by now group editorial director, left the editorial chair for three years to oversee Murdoch's expansion in New York and Texas, before returning to *The Sun* in 1975. Sales of *The Sun* (2.93 million in 1973, 3.30 million in 1974, 3.44 million in 1975) hit 4 million and it overtook the *Mirror* in 1978. Then Express Newspapers launched the *Daily Star*. Lamb did not share Murdoch's concern that the *Star* might do unto *The Sun* what *The Sun* had done unto the *Mirror*. As sales slipped to 3.7 million, Lamb was becoming a disciple of the Conservative leader, Margaret Thatcher—though 'it was not until 1979 that I was able to bring myself to vote Tory' (Lamb, 167). He backed her enthusiastically in his paper; his polling day editorial in May 1979 filled the first three pages, urging readers to vote for her. Victorious, she wrote to him that she would 'strive to be worthy of *The Sun*'s confidence'. Lamb observed 'Humility is not one of the qualities for which she is normally given credit' (ibid.). His own reward came in the next honours list, when he was knighted 'for services to journalism', the first tabloid editor so honoured. Murdoch was not happy about the editor of the 'people's paper' going over to the establishment, and their relationship deteriorated. Lamb now wanted to be editor of *The Times*, which occupied the other end of the Murdoch spectrum of eminence, gravitas, and profitability. He later said he understood why Murdoch did not offer him *The Times*: 'I had a reputation of being the architect of all the tit and bum in the world … a reputation I had

acquired at his behest and in his interest … I'm not naturally a pop journalist' (*The Independent*, 7 Nov 1989).

Lamb suffered what he (like Winston Churchill) called 'black dog' depressions, during which he would be more a Heathcliff than a Northcliffe. He wrote 'Rupert used to call me, with some justice, a prickly Pommy bastard'. Even a compliment could enrage him. Murdoch rang from New York one day. '"You were the best of the tabloids this morning", he said. "*Harry told me*."' Harry was Harold Evans, who had been appointed to the job at *The Times* which Lamb had coveted. Lamb was 'distinctly unamused that Harry and the Chairman were discussing the merits of that day's *Sun* before the Chairman had seen fit to discuss them with me' (Lamb, 99). In 1981 Lamb and *The Sun* parted company, Lamb making way as editor for Kelvin MacKenzie, who introduced bingo, said 'bollocks' a lot, and got sales back to 4 million.

Lamb went to Australia, headhunted by another Australian media tycoon to build up an empire based on the Perth *Western Mail*, but Robert Holmes à Court was no Rupert Murdoch, and Lamb rejoined his old boss in 1982 as editor-in-chief of *The Australian*. After nine months he returned to Britain to take over the *Daily Express*. Two years spent striving to heave the paper up the down escalator ended in a heart bypass operation in 1986. His convalescence coincided with yet another change of ownership, and he retired. Lamb set up as a consultant and published his autobiography, *Sunrise* (1989). He likened editing *The Sun* to captaining an aircraft-carrier, though his triumph had surely been all the greater for being achieved by a 'dirty British coaster', butting past posh liners as champagne-swilling ABC1 readers leant over the rails to scoff at its impertinence. Students of popular journalism dipping into his index would make their own evaluations of entries which included 'Crudeness, merit in'; 'Knickers, *Sun* full of'; 'Nudges, winks and leers'; and 'tits and bums'.

Sir Larry Lamb died in London on 18 May 2000; he was cremated at Mortlake crematorium. He was a big, handsome man, more a lion than a lamb. The rage and ambition within him fuelled the demonic drive that took *The Sun* to the moon. His fluency belied his truncated education. He would lovingly roll words around his tongue, marshalling prepositions away from the end of sentences. He could quote Mark Antony at an executive commending a valiant reporter: 'So is my horse; and for that I do appoint him a store of provender.' He was most at ease playing host, dispensing champagne on his Cotswolds croquet lawn, or analysing a tasselled wine list. Once, at the Boulestin, when Murdoch called for the house white, the sommelier sniffed, 'I don't think Mr Lamb would much care for that, sir.' Media and political critics blamed Lamb (and the need to compete with him) for the all-round lowering of standards in tabloid journalism and public morality, symbolized by his introduction of the page three girls. But it was historically more significant that *The Sun*'s success became the launchpad for the global and multimedia expansion of Murdoch's business empire.

BERNARD SHRIMSLEY

Sources L. Lamb, *Sunrise* (1989) · P. Chippindale, *Stick it up your punter!* (1990) · S. Regan, *Rupert Murdoch* (1976) · R. Grose, *Sun-sation* (1989) · *The Sun* (20 May 2000) · *The Times* (20 May 2000) · *The Guardian* (20 May 2000) · *The Independent* (20 May 2000) · b. cert. · WW · CGPLA Eng. & Wales (2001) · m. cert.
Likenesses photograph, repro. in *The Times* · photograph, repro. in *The Guardian* · photograph, repro. in *The Independent*
Wealth at death £210,791: probate, 2001, CGPLA Eng. & Wales

Lamb, Andrew (1565?–1634), bishop of Galloway, was probably related to Andrew Lamb of Leith, a lay member of the general assembly of 1560. He became minister of Burntisland, Fife, in 1593, and was translated to Arbroath in 1596 and to South Leith, near Edinburgh, in 1600. In that year he was appointed one of the members of the standing commission of the church to advise the king between general assemblies, and in 1601 he became a royal chaplain, in which capacity he accompanied the earl of Mar on an embassy to England to ensure James VI's succession to the English throne. Lamb was one of the ministers chosen by James to accompany him on his journey south in 1603, and he received a pension from the abbey of Arbroath for services to the king and to the church.

Lamb was made titular bishop of Brechin in 1607, and he presented a brass chandelier of Flemish workmanship to Brechin Cathedral in 1615. He was a member of the general assembly of 1610 which restored the full powers of the episcopate, and was one of the three Scottish bishops consecrated at London on 21 October 1610. He was one of four bishops who signed a letter of remonstrance to the king regarding the images ordered for the decoration of the Chapel Royal at Holyrood on the occasion of James VI's visit in 1617. Several biographers of Samuel Rutherford have suggested that Lamb gave tacit consent to his ordination by the laying on of presbyterial hands. While there is no clear evidence of this, Lamb was believed to be more tolerant than some of his contemporaries of those who did not conform to the ecclesiastical practices prescribed in the five articles of Perth. At the general assembly of the kirk in August 1618 he conceded that he knew of nothing in 'Scripture, Reasone, nor Antiquitie that inforceth kneeling', but, since he considered the practice as a thing indifferent, advocated its acceptance for the sake of conformity to the king's wishes (MacDonald, 163).

In 1619 Lamb was translated to Galloway, but in his later years became blind and resided chiefly in Leith, where he owned property. He died in 1634, leaving a son, James, and two daughters, both of whom married landowners in the stewartry of Kirkcudbright. His wife's name is unknown.

SHARON ADAMS

Sources *Fasti Scot.*, new edn · D. Calderwood, *The history of the Kirk of Scotland*, ed. T. Thomson and D. Laing, 8 vols., Wodrow Society, 7 (1842–9) · J. Row, *The history of the Kirk of Scotland, from the year 1558 to August 1637*, ed. D. Laing, Wodrow Society, 4 (1842) · J. Spottiswood, *The history of the Church of Scotland*, ed. M. Napier and M. Russell, 3 vols., Bannatyne Club, 93 (1850) · T. Thomson, ed., *Acts and proceedings of the general assemblies of the Kirk of Scotland*, 3 pts, Bannatyne Club, 81 (1839–45) · W. Scot, *An apologetical narration of the state and government of the Kirk of Scotland since the Reformation*, ed. D. Laing, Wodrow Society, 19 (1846) · A. R. Macdonald, *The Jacobean kirk, 1567–1625: sovereignty, polity and liturgy* (1998)

Lamb, Benjamin (*fl.* 1715), composer, was organist of Eton College and verger of St George's Chapel, Windsor, about 1715. He wrote a few songs, and some church music. Four of his anthems and an evening service in E minor are among the Tudway collection in the Harleian MSS in the British Library.   R. H. LEGGE, rev. K. D. REYNOLDS

Sources W. H. Husk, 'Lamb, Benjamin', Grove, *Dict. mus.* (1927)

Lamb [née Ponsonby], **Lady Caroline** (1785–1828), novelist, was born in London on 13 November 1785, fourth child and only daughter of Frederick *Ponsonby, third earl of Bessborough (1758–1844), and his wife, Henrietta Frances *Ponsonby (1761–1821), daughter of the first earl of Spencer and younger sister of the duchess of Devonshire. Her chaotic upbringing was cosmopolitan and cultured. As a young child, she accompanied her parents on a protracted tour of Italy. From the age of nine, owing to the ill health of her mother, she alternately ran wild with her cousins at Devonshire House or was restrained by sojourns with her austere grandmother Lady Spencer. She later regretted her lack of formal education (she seems briefly to have attended Miss Rowden's school, Hans Place, Kensington), for the family had been advised by Dr Warren, a specialist in nervous diseases, that study would exacerbate the violent mood swings which occasionally threatened her sanity. She grew up into a combination of bluestocking autodidact and tomboy: 'For myself, I preferred washing a dog, or polishing a piece of Derbyshire spar, or breaking in a horse, to any accomplishment in the world' (*Lady Morgan's Memoirs*, 2.212). With her slight androgynous figure and cropped fair curly hair, she enjoyed dressing as a page-boy, as depicted in Phillips' famous 1814 portrait. A high-spirited eccentric who feared 'nobody except the devil', she read Mary Wollstonecraft's *Vindication of the Rights of Woman* in 1809 and 'became a convert' (ibid., 2.211). Lady Caroline was a brilliant conversationalist: 'A creature of caprice and impulse, and whim, her manner, her talk, and her character shifted their colours as rapidly as those of a chameleon' (Lytton, 1.119).

Caroline married the Hon. William *Lamb (1779–1848) on 3 June 1805, and afterwards resided either in Melbourne House, Whitehall, or Brocket Hall, Hertfordshire. Their tempestuous marriage scandalized the nineteenth century, temporarily paralysing Lamb's political career. It was to be depicted in Thomas Lister's *Granby*, Benjamin Disraeli's *Vivian Grey* and *Venetia*, Mrs Humphry Ward's *The Marriage of William Ash*, Bulwer Lytton's *De Lindsey*, and Lady Lytton's *Cheveley, or, The Man of Honour*. Lady Caroline suffered the deaths of premature babies in 1806 and 1809; her only surviving child was a mentally handicapped son, Augustus, born on 29 August 1807. The marriage survived these tragedies and Caroline's subsequent open infidelities, the most notorious being a brief theatrical affair with Byron in 1812. She famously recorded her first impressions of the poet as, 'Mad, bad and dangerous to know' and 'That beautiful pale face is my fate'. So well did

Lady Caroline Lamb (1785–1828), by Thomas Phillips, 1814

she forge Byron's handwriting that she fraudulently obtained from John Murray a miniature of the poet destined for her rival, Lady Oxford. In revenge for her dismissal by Byron she portrayed him as the satanic villain of an anonymous Gothic romance, *Glenarvon* (1816), written by night in male attire, and kept secret from her husband until the day of publication (*Lady Morgan's Memoirs*, 2.202). As Byron sardonically commented, 'the time was well chosen' (*Byron's Letters and Journals*, 5.85) to capitalize on the scandal surrounding his failed marriage. The *roman à clef* also lampooned the Holland House set, and thus effected Lady Caroline's own ostracization from whig high society. William Lamb inaugurated but abandoned a legal separation; nor was he capable of halting publication of the book which publicized both his cuckoldry and the humiliating fact that his mother had also fallen under Byron's spell, becoming his 'greatest *friend*, of the feminine gender' (ibid., 6.23). Four British editions came out by 1817, the second of which was revised and included a justificatory preface. The novel was published in America and translated into French. It is still of interest as the first critique of Byronism and the Byronic hero by a woman writer. Byron commented: 'If the authoress had written the *truth*, … the romance would not only have been more *romantic*, but more entertaining. As for the likeness, the picture can't be good—I did not sit long enough' (ibid., 5.131). In *Don Juan* he too satirized the Regency aristocracy, including Caroline. Lady Caroline responded to Byron's *Don Juan* with two anonymous *ottava rima* parodies: *A New Canto* (1819) and *Gordon: a Tale* (1821), and

caused a sensation when she attended a masquerade dressed as Don Juan, escorted by a throng of devils.

Two more anonymous novels followed: *Graham Hamilton* (1822) and *Ada Reis* (1823). The latter, about an Englishwoman's love for a corsair, was printed by John Murray, formerly Byron's publisher. William Lamb had read the manuscript and advised on revisions. Lady Caroline also wrote verse for the annuals, some of which was set to music and posthumously published by Isaac Nathan in *Fugitive pieces and reminiscences of Lord Byron with some original poetry, letters and recollections of Lady Caroline Lamb* (1829). Increasingly ostracized by the aristocracy, Lady Caroline enjoyed the company of literary friends such as Lady Morgan. The Lambs also helped William Godwin and William Blake financially, and adopted a child, Susan Churchill. In 1824 they were riding near Brocket Hall and saw Byron's funeral cortège passing by on its way to Nottinghamshire. In 1825 William's family persuaded him to instigate a legal separation. Lady Caroline spent lonely drunken last years at Brocket Hall, likened to Bedlam by Emily Lamb, who unkindly referred to her afflicted nephew as 'Frankenstein'. Her husband returned from his official duties in Ireland to be with her when she was dying, aged forty-two, of oedema. She died on 26 January 1828 in Melbourne House, and was buried in Hatfield church on 7 February.

Although Lady Caroline strove to be taken seriously as a writer, popular biographies and films continue to dwell on apocryphal stories of her scandalous escapades, such as the dinner party at which she had herself served up naked in a soup tureen. However, even her famous passion for Byron was literary in origin: she had first fallen in love with his hero, Childe Harold. In Robert Bolt's film, *Lady Caroline Lamb* (1972), she was played with some style by Sarah Miles.   CAROLINE FRANKLIN

Sources L. G. Mitchell, *Lord Melbourne, 1779–1848* (1997) · D. Cecil, *The young Melbourne and the story of his marriage with Caroline Lamb* (1939) · E. Jenkins, *Lady Caroline Lamb* (1972) · H. Blyth, *Caro, the fatal passion: the life of Lady Caroline Lamb* (1972) · *Lady Morgan's memoirs: autobiography, diaries, and correspondence*, ed. W. H. Dixon, 2 vols. (1862) · Earl of Bessborough and A. Aspinall, eds., *Lady Bessborough and her family circle* (1940) · *Byron's letters and journals*, ed. L. A. Marchand, 12 vols. (1973–82) · V. Lytton, *The life of Edward Bulwer, first Lord Lytton, by his grandson, the earl of Lytton*, 2 vols. (1913) · *Lord Melbourne's papers*, ed. L. C. Sanders (1889) · GEC, *Peerage*, new edn · *The letters of Lady Palmerston*, ed. T. Lever (1957) · S. Smiles, *A publisher and his friends: memoir and correspondence of the late John Murray*, 2 vols. (1891)

Archives BL, letters, Add. MS 50142 · BL, papers · Bodl. Oxf., letters · Herts. ALS, corresp. and sketches | BL, corresp. with Lady Cowper, Add. MS 45548 · BL, corresp. with Lady Melbourne and others, Add. MSS 45546, 45548, 45911 · Bodl. Oxf., letters to Michael Bruce · Bodl. Oxf., corresp. with Lord Byron and Lady Byron · Bodl. Oxf., corresp. with William Godwin · Castle Howard, letters to countess of Carlisle · Chatsworth House, Derbyshire, letters to sixth duke of Devonshire · CKS, letters to Lady Stanhope · Herts. ALS, corresp. with William Lamb · Herts. ALS, corresp. with Sir Edward Bulwer-Lytton · Northumbd RO, Newcastle upon Tyne, letters to Thomas Creevey · V&A, letters, mainly to Henry Colburn

Likenesses F. Bartolozzi, engraving, pubd 1788 (as a child; after miniature by R. Cosway), BM · J. Hoppner, oils, c.1805, Althorp, Northamptonshire · Smythe, engraving, 1809 (after J. Hoppner) ·

E. H. Trotter, oils, c.1809, NPG · T. Lawrence, oils, c.1810 (unfinished), Bristol City Art Gallery · T. Phillips, oils, 1814, Chatsworth House, Derbyshire [see illus.] · E. E. Kendrick, miniature, V&A · H. Meyer, stipple (after miniature), BM, NPG; repro. in *New Monthly Magazine* (1819)

Wealth at death £3000 p.a. from husband, although complained of poverty

Lamb, Charles

Lamb, Charles (1775–1834), essayist, was born at 2 Crown Office Row in the Temple, London, on 10 February 1775, the son of John Lamb (c.1725–1799), a servant, and Elizabeth, *née* Field (d. 1796).

Family and early years John Lamb was the son of a cobbler, and grew up near Stamford in Lincolnshire before entering domestic service, first in Lincoln and Bath, and then in London, where he had arrived by 1746. He spent the final decades of his working life acting as indispensable and versatile factotum to Samuel Salt, a bencher of the Inner Temple, a role in which Lamb commemorates him (as Lovel) in his essay 'The old benchers of the Inner Temple'. Salt, a widower, had been the whig MP for Liskeard since 1768, and served on the governing board for several hospitals, including Christ's Hospital. He lived in chambers above the Lambs, and owned a fine library, to which the young Charles was given access. John Lamb was the author of *Poetical Pieces on Several Occasions* (published about 1777), so he may have passed on a literary disposition to his son; less happily, his family was said by some to have a history of the lunacy whose effects so strongly shadowed his son's life.

Lamb's mother's mother, Mary Field, had been in domestic service with William Plumer of Blakesware; after his death she continued in service with Plumer's widow, and then stayed on as caretaker of Blakesware. The young Charles was a visitor there, as he records in his evocative essays 'Blakesmoor in H—shire' and 'Dream-children'.

Of John and Elizabeth Lamb's seven children only three survived infancy. The eldest, John, was born in 1763, and left home to continue his education at Christ's Hospital when he was five. Mary Anne *Lamb, to be known as Mary, was born on 3 December 1764. She seems not to have been a favourite with her mother, and freely bestowed her affection on her brother Charles, born ten years later.

The Lamb household, full of strong female influences, also included Sarah Lamb, known as Hetty, the sister of Charles's father. She and Elizabeth hated each other 'with a bitter hatred', according to Mary in 1803, though they were somewhat reconciled in their last years. Hetty, who doted on the young Charles, was one of the first eccentrics whom he cherished. Her theological reading, in particular, was ecumenical and unorthodox to the point of impropriety: she appears in the essay 'My relations' and in the story of Maria Howe in *Mrs Leicester's School*.

There are few details of the first years of Charles Lamb's life. From his earliest years he was a chronic stammerer. Some reports suggest he contracted smallpox when five years old. It seems that he took lessons with a Mrs Reynolds, *née* Chambers, on whom, with characteristic loyalty, he later conferred a pension. About 1781 he passed on

Charles Lamb (1775–1834), by William Hazlitt, 1804

to the academy of Mr William Bird off Fetter Lane, London. One early story nicely anticipates his habits of humorous and independent thought: the young Charles, puzzled by the uniformly eulogistic character of graveyard inscriptions, turned to his sister and asked: 'Mary, where are the naughty people buried?' (Courtney, 8).

Christ's Hospital Lamb was formally entered for Christ's Hospital on 7 July 1782, and he was able to begin his education there when a vacancy occurred on 9 October of that year. It was through the patronage of Salt, a governor of the school, that Lamb in spite of the relatively straitened family finances was able to follow his brother John in profiting from the liberal education offered at one of the best schools of the day. The school was at this time located in Newgate Street, opposite the prison, and was presided over in disciplinarian style by the Revd James Boyer, headmaster from 1778 to 1799, though the severity of his influence was balanced by the delinquent laxity of another teacher, the Revd Matthew Field. However, the main influence on the young Charles came not from his teachers, but from his schoolmate Samuel Taylor Coleridge (three years Lamb's senior), with whom he maintained a close friendship. The school in these years was distinguished by remarkable students, including Leigh Hunt and Valentine LeGrice. There was an expectation that the abler boys would proceed from the school to university and then the church; but Lamb's stammer (like Hunt's) was thought to make him unfit for this, and so he left at only fifteen. Lamb has left us a wonderfully vivid record of the school in his two essays 'Recollections of Christ's Hospital' (1813) and 'Christ's Hospital five-and-thirty years ago' (1820). In the first of these he suggests that the school endowed pupils with a sense of right and wrong, and a strong religious consciousness; but he also emphasizes the possibilities of freedom within its régime, and a turn for romance which it fostered in him. The second essay is written as if in reply to Coleridge's grumbling at the idealism of the first, and it adds some darker notes, including much detailing of punishments, and mention of the constant shortage of food for those pupils who didn't, like Lamb, have a devoted aunt bringing them daily food packages.

From Christ's Hospital to the death of Mrs Lamb Lamb left Christ's Hospital in 1791, and his first employment thereafter was as a sort of secretary to the kindly businessman Joseph Paice, whose character is commemorated in the essay 'Modern gallantry'. As Samuel Salt had done, Paice offered Charles access to his fine library, and his taste for Elizabethan literature may have influenced the young Lamb. At some point after this Lamb had a temporary position at the South Sea House, but by February 1792 he was staying at Blakesware with old Mrs Field, who was dying of cancer. It was at this time that he met Ann Simmons, the Anna of his early love sonnets. It is hard to know how far this love was an affair of the imagination only, but at any rate it inspired some of Lamb's early poetry of 1792–5, and is probably also reflected in the love of Allan Clare and Rosamund Gray in the novel *Rosamund Gray*. Not much is heard of Ann Simmons until 1799, when she married John Thomas Bartram and moved to London. According to Southey, she dined twice with Lamb in May 1799 and was then pronounced by him to be 'a stupid girl' (Courtney, 77).

On 15 April 1792 Lamb joined the East India Company, where he served for thirty-three years as clerk in the accountant's department, never seeking promotion, probably to safeguard the time he could devote to looking after his sister in her ill health. De Quincey's *Literary Reminiscences* includes a vivid account of his first meeting with Lamb ('positively the most hospitable man I have known in this world') at work. His job seems at times to have kept him consumingly busy, but at other times left him free to write long letters at work.

Lamb resumed an intense friendship with Coleridge during the latter's time in London in December 1794. His enthusiasm for Unitarianism, especially that of Joseph Priestley, was no doubt influenced by his former schoolfriend, and he looked above all to Coleridge for support, as his correspondence records, during the tribulations of the following years. The earliest of these was the collapse of Lamb's own mental health: he spent six weeks in an asylum in Hoxton in 1795, when he wrote to Coleridge: 'I am got somewhat rational now, & *don't bite any one*. But *mad* I was—& many a vagary my imagination played with *me*, enough to make a *volume* if all *told*' (*Letters of Charles Lamb*, 1.4). The association of lunacy, imagination, and literary output should serve as a reminder of how much Lamb's literary origins borrow from the extremities of English Romanticism, even though he was to temper

his later and best-known writings to a quieter style. Lamb never again lost his own sanity, but the fear that he might do must have added a terrible anxiety to his life.

The decisively dreadful incident of madness, however, was not to be Charles's, but that of his sister Mary. In September 1796 Mary Lamb in a fit of mania killed their mother Elizabeth. The jury bringing in a verdict of lunacy, Mary was removed to Hoxton asylum; her sanity recovered, she was to be allowed to return home only on condition that a family member undertook her care. In doing so, Charles made the momentous decision to devote his life to his sister, a resolve he kept to steadily. Whatever his later religious convictions, his letters of this time suggest that he drew on a deep vein of religious feeling in finding strength to deal with the family tragedy. Procter's *Memoir* suggests that he lived in a state of constant anxiety about his sister's health, which most years required her to spend time in an asylum. The history of Mary's madness was not disclosed to the public until Thomas Noon Talfourd's *Final Memorials of Charles Lamb* (1848). Charles and Mary lived together until his death, but moved lodging eight times between 1799 and 1823, probably on occasions because Mary's history was known to neighbours. However, in her calmer periods, Mary acted as a stabilizing influence on her brother, and her good sense, kindness, and social competence were attested by many contemporaries.

Early writings, literary associations, 1796–1802 The late 1790s saw Lamb commencing a quietly promising literary career. At Coleridge's instigation, he contributed fifteen poems to *Poems, second edition, by S. T. Coleridge, to which are now added poems by Charles Lamb, and Charles Lloyd*, published in June 1797. Lamb and Lloyd appeared again together in May 1798 as co-authors of *Blank Verse*: Lamb's friendship with the Quaker Lloyd family fed into his essay 'A Quaker's meeting'. The brilliant but perverse Charles Lloyd also dedicated his novel *Edmund Oliver* (1798) to Lamb, which prompted a brief falling-out with Coleridge, the thinly disguised prototype of the title figure. *Blank Verse* included the poem which was to become Lamb's most enduringly popular, 'The Old Familiar Faces'—a strikingly elegiac work from its young author. Edmund Blunden comments on Lamb's early poems that:

> These sonnets of lost or fancied love, these soliloquies on altered fortune, on family history, on friendship and on loneliness, on the mystery of things and the eternal foundations of man in the divine, form altogether quite an individual 'progress' of poetry.   (Blunden, 19)

Lamb continued to compose poetry throughout his life, but he turned increasingly to prose, like his contemporaries Scott and Coleridge. His early versatility is suggested by the appearance in the summer of 1798 of his novel *Rosamund Gray*, one of whose admirers was Percy Shelley.

In July 1797 Lamb had been able to accept Coleridge's invitation to visit him and his young family in Nether Stowey in Somerset—a visit which required leave of absence from East India House, and arrangements to be made for the care of Lamb's increasingly senile father (Aunt Hetty had died in February 1797). There he met (among others) Thomas Poole, John Cruikshank, Gilbert Burnett, and above all William and Dorothy Wordsworth, who remained lifelong friends. The visit has also become famous for Coleridge's poem 'This Lime-Tree Bower my Prison', with its warm tribute to Lamb as 'my gentle-hearted Charles'—whose gratitude was tempered by exasperation at 'gentle': it 'almost always means poor-spirited' (*Letters of Charles Lamb*, 1.218), he wrote in one letter to Coleridge, and in another 'substitute drunken dog, ragged-head, seld-shaven, odd-ey'd, stuttering, or any other epithet which truly and properly belongs to the Gentleman in question' (ibid., 1.224).

In 1799 Lamb's father died, and Mary moved in with Charles at 36 Chapel Street in Pentonville. In 1799–1800 he was on close and friendly terms with William Godwin, through whom he met Richard Porson, Horne Tooke, and James Perry, among others who remained friends. (Lamb's biographers tend to find themselves dealing with this period of his life in terms of his friendships; in both his life and writings friendship is of central importance.) Both Lamb and Godwin were working on plays at this time, Lamb on *John Woodvil* and Godwin on *Antonio*, staged at Drury Lane Theatre. Lamb provided the prologue and epilogue for the disastrous *Antonio*, and had some stage-struck but doomed hopes for its success. Lamb kept belief in *John Woodvil*, which has some fine passages, and shows how deeply he had been influenced by Elizabethan and Jacobean drama, notably the plays of Beaumont and Fletcher and of Massinger.

Theatre and children's literature, 1802–1815 During the 1800s Lamb tried his hand at journalistic writing, theatre, and children's literature. Daniel Stuart employed him for the *Morning Post* to write joky poems and prose, first for five or six weeks in early 1802, then for a longer period from September 1803 until probably April or May 1804. He later feelingly reminisced on the drudgery of producing drollery on demand, partly a relief from the routines of office work at the East India Company, but partly a supplementary routine of its own. When this work ended, he—and soon Mary as well—began writing for children, at the instigation of the Godwins, who published books for children (albeit not under Godwin's own controversial name). Their first effort was the children's verses of *The King and Queen of Hearts* (1805), and the more enduring *Tales from Shakespear*, re-casting the plays as prose narratives suitable for children. The tales were published under Charles's name in January 1807, Charles having written half of the preface and adapted some of the tragedies, while Mary had completed the substantial rest of the collection. Lamb's *Adventures of Ulysses* came out in 1808, as did the collaboration with Mary on *Mrs Leicester's School* (though it is dated 1809), of which Charles wrote three of the ten stories. Brother and sister collaborated again on *Poetry for Children*, published in two volumes in 1809 by Mrs Godwin. The two unmarried siblings write engagingly for children, emphasizing the virtues of 'charity, tolerance, thoughtfulness' (Lucas, 1.296), as Lamb's biographer E. V. Lucas says.

Charles was also actively engaged in drama during the decade, both theatrical criticism and writing for the theatre. In June 1806 his farce *Mr. H* was accepted for playing at Drury Lane Theatre. It opened on 10 December, disastrously, with Lamb, according to Crabb Robinson, joining in the audience's hissing. In America, by an odd quirk of cultural history, it did rather well. Charles was not so far deterred that he failed to undertake a further farce, *The Pawnbroker's Daughter*, drawing on the lessons learned, but still weak: Lamb had a genius for comedy, but not for the theatre. He spent his summer holidays in 1807 working in the British Museum on the *Specimens of English Dramatic Poets who Lived about the Time of Shakespeare*, a project to which he had given desultory attention over many years, and which was published by Longmans in 1808. The work was at once recognized for its critical insight and originality, and Lamb himself remained proud of the book, which Edmund Blunden has called 'the most striking anthology perhaps ever made from English literature' (Blunden, 22).

These were years in which Lamb became well known to many of the most interesting and influential figures in the London literary world. Among them was the other great essayist of the generation, William Hazlitt, who painted his portrait of Lamb as a Venetian senator in 1804, and with whom Lamb shared a critical enthusiasm for painting. Lamb was a collector of both prints (especially of the Renaissance masters) and books. Crabb Robinson brings out the spirit of Lamb's bibliophilia charmingly, describing 'the finest collection of shabby books I ever saw; such a number of first-rate works of genius, but filthy copies, which a delicate man would really hesitate touching' (Lucas, 2.121). Charles and Mary started giving weekly soirées in 1806, at first on Wednesday evenings and later Thursdays; accounts of these convivial and eclectic occasions are among the main biographical sources we have. Lamb's drinking was often a social help and sometimes a social problem; Mary was already writing to Dorothy Wordsworth in 1803: 'Charles is very well and very *good* I mean very sober but he is very good in every sense of the word' (*Letters of Charles Lamb*, 2.118). Drink seems to have been important to Lamb, partly because it helped him overcome his stammer and partly in more general terms as a way of releasing inhibitions; but at times he got disgracefully drunk, as can be read between the lines of the loyal reminiscences of his friends. These were after all Regency times, though Lamb tends not to be thought of as a Regency author; and Lamb's drinking did not at any rate prevent him from holding down his job and meeting his other onerous responsibilities. Probably it helped him. Lamb's own 'Confessions of a drunkard' was published in 1813; there has been some dispute about how far the piece is autobiographical—Crabb Robinson for one thought it pretty accurate. He sometimes tried to give up alcohol, but not so frequently as tobacco, his other ruling vice as he tended to see it.

In 1809 Charles and Mary moved from Mitre Court Buildings, where they had lived since 1801, to 4 Inner Temple Lane. Lamb's literary output slowed down after the publication of the *Dramatic Specimens*, but he contributed four essays to Leigh Hunt's *The Reflector* (1810–11), an important foretaste of his major literary efforts to follow. That he was friends with Hunt during this period, visiting him in gaol and contributing to *The Examiner* risky verses hostile to the prince regent, indicates how far his political allegiances were and remained on what would now be regarded as the liberal left.

London life and the essays of Elia, 1815–1825   During the next decade Lamb became well known among the main figures on London's cultural scene. Not only was he as a writer rich in reminiscences, but he was the frequent occasion of reminiscences in the essays and correspondence of his contemporaries—notably Hazlitt, De Quincey, Procter, Haydon, and Crabb Robinson. One of the most memorable of these accounts is Haydon's description of the 'immortal dinner' Lamb hosted in December 1817, with a gathering including Keats, Wordsworth, and a Mr Kingston, Wordsworth's superior in his office as distributor of stamps. The occasion was described by Haydon as a genial battle of Bohemia versus bureacracy, with Lamb featuring as by some way the unruliest of the poets.

Life at the East India Company seems to have become easier for Lamb in the middle of the decade. In 1816 his salary went up, and his duties diminished (though these always fluctuated with the contingencies of trade). The Olliers published his *Works* in two volumes in 1818, partly through the friendly influence of Leigh Hunt. Lamb's literary output had fallen away in the preceding years, so he may in 1818 have thought this edition likely to be his main literary monument. He complained in a letter of this year (to Mary Wordsworth) that he was plagued by visitors (as often, disguising a real unhappiness with a jocular tone), and the joint demands of his job and his companionableness made it difficult for him to find time for writing.

In 1818 Lamb proposed marriage, evidently with Mary's blessing, to the actress Fanny Kelly. He had praised her in print, but was very little acquainted with her. She declined the offer, but they became firm friends. She died unmarried at ninety-two.

In 1820 Lamb began writing essays under the pseudonym Elia for John Scott's *London Magazine*. Elia was, to those who knew him, recognizably Lamb himself, and he drew freely on his memories and his own correspondence for the essays, but Elia was somewhat more unworldly, whimsical, and elegiac than his author; and the contrivance of the dramatic persona released an easy eloquence and emotional fluency seldom seen in Lamb's previous writings. Over the next few years Lamb wrote most of the essays for which he is best remembered, collected as *Elia* (1823) and *The Last Essays of Elia* (1833).

Among Lamb's publications of 1823 is the remarkable 'Letter to Southey', written in response to an incidental remark of Southey's in the *Quarterly Review* calling *Elia* 'a book which wants only a sounder religious feeling, to be as delightful as it is original'. Lamb responded with unusual anger, in his self-defence impugning both Southey's judgement and his character. The nature of Lamb's religious beliefs puzzled some of his friends. Crabb Robinson reported that his 'impressions against religion are unaccountably strong, and yet he is by nature pious', concluding: 'It is the dogmatism of theology which has disgusted him, and which alone he opposes' (Lucas, 2.122). His conversation was at times daringly and provocatively anti-religious, at times more playfully unsolemn. 'I am determined', he said, 'that my children shall be brought up in their father's religion if they can find out what it is' (*Letters of Charles Lamb*, 3.247). The 'Letter to Southey' espouses an ecumenically tolerant sense of the varieties of religious experience: 'the shapings of our heavens are the modifications of our constitution' (Lucas, 2.109), he wrote, in a fine phrase unlikely to please either party of contemporary zealots, the atheistical or the orthodox Anglican. A magnanimous exchange of letters soon reconciled Lamb and Southey; Lamb's part in the brief controversy also impressed Hazlitt enough to prompt him to seek a reconciliation of the falling-out he had had with Lamb. In 1824 Hazlitt included as many as eighteen of Lamb's poems and two excerpts from *John Woodvil* in his *Select British Poets*, and in the following year wrote a fine appreciation of him in *The Spirit of the Age*.

The year 1821 was darkened by the death of Lamb's elder brother John, recalled as Cousin James Elia in 'My relations', and remembered also in the essay 'Dream-children' published in the following year. In 1823 Charles and Mary moved to Colebrooke Row in Islington, at this time a semi-rural setting. Their house stood next to the New River. In this year they adopted Emma Isola, the daughter of Charles Isola, who had served in the position of esquire bedell at Cambridge University. The Lambs first met Emma in Cambridge in the summer of 1820 when she was nine; after that she frequently visited them for holidays, and they adopted her when Charles Isola, her only surviving parent, died.

Years of retirement, 1825–1834   In 1825, after thirty-three years' work, Lamb was able to retire from the East India Company on the grounds of his declining health. His salary at this time was £730 per annum, leaving him with a comfortable pension of £450. At first delighted by the new freedoms, Lamb came to miss the companionship at work, and the anchoring regularity it brought to his life, as he wrote in the essay 'The superannuated man'.

Despite his new leisure, Lamb wrote less in the last decade of his life. There were some contributions to William Hone's *Table Book*, and Hone became one of many friends for whom Lamb effectively petitioned in times of financial hardship; and he also wrote for other periodicals including the *New Monthly Magazine*, *Blackwood's*, the *Englishman's Magazine*, and *The Athenaeum*. Lamb also published two books: *Album Verses and other Poems* (1830), a volume whose modest title did not prevent it being roughly reviewed; and, more important, *The Last Essays of Elia* (1833), issued at the expensive price of 9s. Lamb continued in these years to meet many authors, and to be sought out by younger writers. Carlyle visited in 1831, and found Lamb deplorably wanting in earnestness, amid other sins which he denounced with even more than his usual violence in his journal. On the other hand, Landor, also noted for his stringency, expressed great affection and esteem for both Charles and Mary.

In 1827 the Lambs moved to Enfield, Middlesex. Lamb became a great walker in these latter years, often fuelled by beer—though it was when he went to London that his drinking became less controlled. Mary's illnesses increased in severity and length as the 1820s continued, and this in turn took a toll on Charles's health, though the loving co-dependence of the two never wavered. However, as Lamb's biographer E. V. Lucas wrote in 1905 (in what is—remarkably—the most recent full-length biography), 'the history of his life between 1825–1834 makes sad reading' (Lucas, 2.146). Accounts often suggest he was in a bad way, through depression, or nervous exhaustion, or just drinking too much. It seems clear that Lamb in his later years had become what would now be called an alcoholic. Crabb Robinson in 1834 referred to 'the destruction he is rapidly bringing on himself' (ibid., 2.262). The great joy of these later years, to Charles and Mary, was Emma Isola, whom they had raised amid their own vicissitudes with devoted care. She became engaged to Edward Moxon (the young publisher of Lamb's last two works) in 1833, and married him that summer. The death of Coleridge in July 1834 was a grief which hastened Lamb's own end: 'His great and dear spirit haunts me … He was the proof and touchstone of all my cognitions.' (ibid., 2.266) Lamb died on 27 December 1834 following a fall at his home, Walden's Cottage, Church Street, Edmonton, Middlesex, where he and Mary had moved in 1833, and was buried in the churchyard at Edmonton. Mary, his elder by ten years, survived him by thirteen years, only intermittently in her right mind, and was buried alongside him in 1847.

Assessment There is a pivotal moment in the responses to Lamb's writings in Dorothy Richardson's novel *Pilgrimage* (c.1915), when Richardson's heroine Miriam reads 'The superannuated man' and says it 'looks charming on the surface and is beautifully written and is really perfectly horrible and disgusting' (Aaron, 85). It would be too simple to suggest that the nineteenth century found the charm and beauty in Lamb, leaving the twentieth to discover the horror and disgust; but there is an element of truth in the simple scheme. Victorian critics in particular made of Lamb a figure exemplary for fine feeling in his writing and self-sacrifice in his life. At one extreme, Thackeray is reported to have exclaimed, on reading one of Lamb's letters, 'Saint Charles!' (Lucas, 2.133) A generation later Swinburne waxed rhapsodic about Lamb's lovable merits as man and writer. Lamb's contemporaries preserved a sharper sense of the darker undercurrents in his work, the thwartings of impulse and experience of defeat which his comedy could at once contain and express. Lamb's friend P. G. Patmore, for instance, called him 'a gentle, amiable and tender-hearted misanthrope. He hated and despised men with his mind and judgment' (Courtney, 77–8); while William Hazlitt, who remains probably Lamb's best critic, noted that 'His jokes would be the sharpest things in the world, but that they are blunted by his good-nature'. Hazlitt continued: 'he wants malice,

which is a pity' (Lucas, 2.139), which brings out the difference in temperament between the two great essayists. Lamb's combination of levity and seriousness has been, and remains, a challenge to the flexibility and sense of nuance in his readers, as it was to his hearers; John Stoddart, for instance, noted of Lamb in conversation that his 'bantering way with strangers was often employed by him as a mode of trying their powers of mind' (Courtney, 289), and he could also at times use his stutter as a weapon in comic timing.

Lamb's writings were held in highest esteem, probably, in the fifty years from about 1870 to 1920. The qualities in him that could be seen as whimsy and sentimentality meant that his reputation fared less well during the professionalization of English literary studies, especially in its Leavisite phase. Later writers wishing to act as Lamb's advocates have looked to the more unsettling and darker notes of his writing, detecting in him another artist of Romantic anxiety (if not agony), and like Thomas McFarland finding in his charm 'a politics of survival' (McFarland, 26). On the other hand, Lamb has never been short of readers who respond to the forgiving friendliness of his manner, the novelistic vitality of his portraits, and the odd combination of the colloquial and the erudite in his prose style.

Early biographers and critics of Lamb tended to isolate his domestic circumstances from other contexts, but recent work of a historicist turn has given a fuller account of his involvement in historically turbulent times. After Lamb's death the editor Daniel Stuart said: 'Of politics he knew nothing; they were out of his line of reading and thought' (Courtney, 323). This view has been convincingly challenged, especially in relation to the years 1795–1802, when Lamb's literary associations (especially with Coleridge and Lloyd) were enough to have him categorized as a radical. Politically minded critics have also linked Lamb's partiality to drink, to theatre, and to conversational rudeness with late eighteenth-century expressions of sociopolitical discontent from Londoners oppositional to the governments of the day. In the mingling in his works of acquiescence with hints of protest, recent criticism has concentrated more on the latter strain. He continued to maintain boldly public associations with such provocatively dissident liberals as Leigh Hunt, Hazlitt, and (in his later years) William Hone. However, partly because of the lack of a recent biography, a convincing account of Lamb's political allegiances in the 1820s and 1830s is still lacking.

PETER SWAAB

Sources E. V. Lucas, *The life of Charles Lamb*, 2 vols. (1905); rev. edn (1907) · *The works of Charles Lamb*, ed. E. V. Lucas, 7 vols. (1903–5) · W. F. Courtney, *Young Charles Lamb, 1775–1802* (1982) · *The letters of Charles Lamb: to which are added those of his sister, Mary Lamb*, ed. E. V. Lucas, 3 vols. (1935) · *The letters of Charles and Mary Lamb*, ed. E. W. Marrs, 3 vols. (Ithaca, NY, 1975–8) [3 vols. of 6 so far pubd] · J. Aaron, *A double singleness: gender and the writings of Charles and Mary Lamb* (1991) · D. Cecil, *A portrait of Charles Lamb* (1983) · E. Blunden, *Charles Lamb* (1954) · *Charles Lamb: selected prose*, ed. A. Phillips (1985) · C. A. Prance, *A companion to Charles Lamb* (1980) · *Charles Lamb Bulletin* (1973–) · T. McFarland, *Romantic cruxes: the English essayists and the spirit of the age* (1987)

Archives Brown University, Providence, John Carter Brown Library, papers · Harvard U., Houghton L., papers · Hunt. L., letters and literary MSS · Morgan L., papers · NYPL, papers · Princeton University Library, letters and MSS from and about Lamb · Ransom HRC, papers · Rosenbach Museum and Library, papers · University of Kentucky Library, papers · V&A NAL, corresp. and literary MSS · Victoria University, Toronto, papers · Yale U., Beinecke L., papers | BL, letters to Bernard Barton, Add. MS 35256 · CAC Cam., letters and notes to Charles Wentworth Dilke · DWL, letters to Henry Crabb Robinson · U. Leeds, Brotherton L., letters, mainly to Charles Cowden Clarke
Likenesses R. Hancock, pencil and chalk drawing, 1798, NPG · W. Hazlitt, oils, 1804, NPG [*see illus.*] · G. F. Joseph, watercolour stipple, 1819, BM · T. Wageman, portrait, 1824/5, repro. in T. N. Talfourd, *Letters of Charles Lamb* (1837) · H. Meyer, oils, 1826, BL OIOC; copy, NPG · F. S. Carey, double portrait, oils, 1834 (with his sister), NPG; *see illus. in* Lamb, Mary Anne (1764–1847) · W. Finden, stipple, pubd 1836 (after T. Wageman), NPG · H. Furniss, pen-and-ink, NPG · D. Maclise, etching, NPG · D. Maclise, sketch, V&A; repro. in *Fraser's Magazine* · B. Pulman, caricature, etching, BM · print (after B. Pulman), BM
Wealth at death £2000; plus £120 p.a. pension for Mary Lamb: Lucas, *Life*, 2.282, rev. edn, 682

Edward Buckton Lamb (*bap.* 1805, *d.* 1869), by unknown photographer

Lamb, Edward Buckton (*bap.* 1805, *d.* 1869), architect, was born in London and baptized on 26 June 1805 at St Mary Magdalen, Old Fish Street, London, the son of James Lamb, a senior civil servant, amateur artist, and occasional exhibitor at the Royal Academy, and his wife, Frances. One of the most daringly original Gothic revivalists, he was apprenticed to Lewis Nockalls Cottingham and exhibited regularly at the Royal Academy from the age of eighteen. He entered the Royal Academy Schools on 22 October 1827. By 1828 he was practising independently at 9 Hamilton Place, London, and in 1830 he published *Etchings of Gothic Ornament* (4 vols.). Around 1831 he met the landscape gardener and horticultural writer John Claudius Loudon and, for the next twelve years, busied himself with various designs and essays for Loudon's publications, principally the *Encyclopaedia of Cottage, Farm and Villa Architecture* (1833; rev. 2nd edn with supplement, 1842) and the *Architectural Magazine* (1834–8).

Lamb's vigorous interpretation of Loudon's principles became the mainstay of his creative endeavour. In *Studies of Ancient Domestic Architecture* (1846), and in several lectures and writings during his later life, he championed architecture as a progressive art, fusing the picturesque (aesthetic) past with the functional (ethical) future. Elected a fellow of the Institute of British Architects in 1837, Lamb resigned in 1844, only to be re-elected in 1860. He entered designs to some of the most prodigious architectural competitions of his day, and earned much critical praise. Between 1845 and 1869 his small practice generated over 100 buildings, mainly churches and country houses, but also town halls and corn markets, parsonages, cottages, schools, mechanics' institutes, a London hotel, and a consumption hospital. His entire career was founded upon the patronage of the landed aristocracy. Between 1862 and 1863 he remodelled Hughenden Manor, Buckinghamshire, for Benjamin Disraeli, having beforehand designed a monument to Disraeli's father.

Lamb was the 'arch-rogue' of High Victorian inventiveness—the *bête noire* of the Ecclesiologists. His quasi-

centralized church plans in the tradition of Wren, and his highly mannered interpretation of late English Perpendicular Gothic, earned him but the bitter enmity of the pious Camdenians. His most innovative churches include Christ Church, Hartlepool (1850), St Stephen, Aldwark, Yorkshire (1851–3), St Martin, Gospel Oak, London (1864), and St Mary Magdalene, Addiscombe, Croydon (1868–9).

Having overspent dwindling proceeds on a large country house for himself in Kent, Lamb died, bankrupt, at his London home, 3 Hinde Street, Manchester Square, on 29 August 1869. He was survived by his wife, Caroline Frances (*b.* 1820/21), possibly *née* Nixon, a music teacher, a son, Edward Beckitt Lamb, architect, and two daughters.

DAVID FARRINGTON

Sources *The Builder*, 27 (1869), 720 · *IGI* · Graves, *RA exhibitors* · nomination papers, RIBA BAL, MS SP/4/13 · E. Kaufman, 'A case study in Victorian patronage', *Art Bulletin*, 70 (1988), 314–45 · H. S. Goodhart-Rendel, 'Rogue architects of the Victorian era', *RIBA Journal*, 56 (1948–9), 251–9 · J. N. Summerson, *Victorian architecture: four studies in evaluation* (1970) · H. R. Hitchcock, *Early Victorian architecture in Britain*, 2 vols. (1954) · P. Howell and I. Sutton, *Faber guide to Victorian churches* (1989) · M. A. Winduss, 'E. B. Lamb: the development of a nineteenth century architect's career', MA diss., University of Manchester, 1978 · J. Gloag, *Mr Loudon's England* (1970) · J. Myles, *L. N. Cottingham, 1787–1847, architect of the Gothic revival* (1996) · *CGPLA Eng. & Wales* (1869) · census returns, 1861
Archives RIBA BAL, original drawings, works, and papers · V&A, original drawings, works, and papers
Likenesses photograph, RIBA BAL [*see illus.*]
Wealth at death under £450: administration, 12 Nov 1869, *CGPLA Eng. & Wales*

Lamb [*née* Milbanke], **Elizabeth, Viscountess Melbourne** (*bap.* 1751, *d.* 1818), political hostess and agricultural improver, was baptized on 15 October 1751 at Croft-on-Tees, Yorkshire, the only daughter of Sir Ralph Milbanke, fifth baronet (1721?–1798), of Halnaby Hall, Yorkshire, landowner and politician, and his wife, Elizabeth Hedworth (*d.* 1767), the daughter of John Hedworth, whig MP for co. Durham from 1713 until his death in 1747. Nothing is known of her education. In 1769 she was introduced to Sir Peniston Lamb, second baronet (1745–1828), at that

Elizabeth Lamb, Viscountess Melbourne (*bap.* 1751, *d.* 1818), by Sir Thomas Lawrence, *c.*1800

time MP for Ludgershall, Wiltshire, by his sister Charlotte, Lady Belasyse, subsequently Countess Fauconberg, and on 13 April they were married at the London house of the groom's uncle Robert Lamb, bishop of Peterborough, in Great George Street, Hanover Square. Her husband owned the estates of Brocket Hall, Hertfordshire, and Melbourne, Derbyshire, both acquired by his father, Sir Matthew *Lamb.

Political hostess Residing at first with her husband in Sackville Street, Lady Lamb quickly became known for her 'vivacity' and 'beauty' (Bank and Esposito, 56). Nathaniel Wraxall, the diplomat, paid tribute to her 'commanding figure, exceeding the middle height, full of grace and dignity' (*Historical and Posthumous Memoirs*, 5.371). Her husband, by contrast, was, as the 1812 satire *The Court of Love* would describe him, a 'Paragon of Debauchery'—generous, foolish, and indolent. After only ten months of marriage he began an affair with Sophia Baddeley, the celebrated actress. Lady Lamb was undaunted, adhering to her principle that 'Life is a tragedy to those who feel and a comedy to those who think' (Cecil, *Young Melbourne*, 20). In 1770 the Lambs moved to a larger house in Piccadilly, designed for them by William Chambers. Lady Lamb's social activities probably helped raise her husband's political profile; he was created an Irish peer as Lord Melbourne, baron of Kilmore, on 8 June 1770, and promoted to Viscount Melbourne, also in the Irish peerage, on 11 January 1781. Lady Melbourne was an enthusiastic manager of her husband's political interest: on 25 October 1774 Agneta Yorke wrote to Jemima, Marchioness Grey, that 'Lady Melbourne and Mrs Brand entered the Town in Triumph at the Head of the Melbourne Party with an open

Landau filled with Musicians playing before them' (Beds. RO, L/30/9/97/36).

During her marriage Lady Melbourne had six surviving children: Peniston Lamb (1770–1805); William *Lamb (1779–1848), later second Viscount Melbourne and prime minister; Frederick James *Lamb (1782–1853), later third Viscount Melbourne; George *Lamb (1784–1834); Emily (1787–1869) [*see* Temple, Emily, Viscountess Palmerston]; and Harriet (1789–1803); twins died in infancy in 1778. Only the paternity of Peniston was certain, and it seems that after coming to terms with her husband's infidelity and limited intellect she chose talented fathers for her subsequent children. Possibly as early as 1773 she began a lifelong attachment to the art patron George O'Brien *Wyndham, third earl of Egremont (1751–1837). Egremont was probably the father of William and Emily and perhaps also of Frederick; their relationship became 'so well known that it was an established channel for patronage proposals' (Mitchell, 6). Lady Melbourne took their relationship sufficiently seriously to prevent Egremont from marrying Lady Mary Somerset in 1774, and Lady Charlotte Maria Waldegrave in 1780.

The duchess of Devonshire and the prince of Wales In 1774 Lady Melbourne's position as a political hostess was challenged by the marriage of Lady Georgiana Spencer to William Cavendish, fifth duke of Devonshire. Lady Melbourne realized that the new duchess of Devonshire would eclipse her and chose to become the duchess's close friend and adviser. She was nicknamed Themire (goddess of justice) by the duchess of Devonshire, and the Thorn by the duchess's sister Harriet Ponsonby, countess of Bessborough. Her leading place in the Devonshire House circle was recognized in Daniel Gardner's painting *Witches Round the Cauldron* (July 1775), where she appears as one of the three witches in *Macbeth*, alongside the duchess of Devonshire and Anne Damer. The painting also captures her mischievous personality. She demonstrated the duchess's trust by sheltering the duke of Devonshire's illegitimate daughter, Charlotte Williams, at Brocket Hall during the Gordon riots in 1780. Lady Melbourne encouraged the duchess's cynical attitude towards marriage. Her opinions were recorded by the duchess of Devonshire in her novel, *The Sylph* (1779). 'Marriage now is a necessary kind of barter, and an alliance of families' (Devonshire, 1.136), says Lady Besford, who represents Lady Melbourne; 'the heart is not consulted:—or, if that should sometimes bring a pair together—judgment being left far behind, love seldom lasts long' (ibid., 1.138). Always circumspect, she later advised the duchess to restrain her conduct with Charles Grey, and they corresponded when the duke of Devonshire banished the duchess abroad. From November 1791 until September 1793 she became the duchess's only confidential correspondent.

Another relationship with lasting effects on Lady Melbourne's life was that with George, prince of Wales [*see* George IV (1762–1830)], which began when her first son was at Eton; there, on 8 August 1782, she danced 'something in the cow stile' with the prince, 'but he is *en extase* with admiration at it' (Ilchester and Stavordale, 2.34–6).

From February 1782 to May 1786 satirists linked Lady Melbourne and the prince in drawings such as *Monuments Lately Discover'd on Salisbury Plain* (15 June 1782); *The Ladies Church Yard* (22 September 1783); and *The Cock of the Walk* (31 May 1786). It was the prince of Wales, not her husband, who was believed to be the father of her son George, born in 1784. Lady Melbourne's friendship with the prince, and her adherence to whig society, shaped the remainder of her husband's political career. Having until that point been a follower of Lord North, Melbourne abstained in the vote of no confidence on 15 March 1782, and became a supporter of the prince and Charles James Fox. Melbourne became gentleman of the bedchamber to the prince in 1783, 'which no doubt is procured him by his Lady', Lady Mary Coke observed (Birkenhead, 24; Mitchell, 16), and retained the post until the prince was forced to reduce the size of his household in 1795. He was a lord of the bedchamber from 1812 until his death in 1828, and was created a United Kingdom peer as Baron Melbourne of Melbourne in 1815.

During the long period of opposition to William Pitt's government Lady Melbourne formed relationships with younger Devonshire House whigs. Her affair with Francis *Russell, fifth duke of Bedford (1765–1802), was well established by 8 December 1791, when he lent the prince of Wales's brother Frederick, duke of York, £30,000 to facilitate his purchase of the Melbournes' London house in Piccadilly; as part of the arrangement Lady Melbourne (and her husband) acquired Frederick's house on Whitehall. She celebrated the transaction at an elegant dinner party with the prince of Wales as a guest. Her influence helped keep Bedford's considerable financial resources at the disposal of the whigs. Lady Melbourne was as defensive of her relationship with Bedford as she was of that with Egremont, and in 1802 sought to delay Bedford's proposed marriage to the youngest daughter of the duchess of Gordon, the leading Pittite hostess, but any dispute was prevented by Bedford's death.

Throughout this period Lady Melbourne paid close attention to the development of her husband's estate. Early in their marriage the Melbournes supervised the reconstruction of Brocket Hall by the architect James Paine the elder; Brocket became their favourite country residence. Lady Melbourne was a skilled businesswoman who encouraged her husband to invest in the Cromford Canal, giving him a financial relationship with industrial pioneers Richard Arkwright and Benjamin Outram. She also supervised the deforestation of the Melbourne estate in Derbyshire. She learned much about agriculture from Egremont and Bedford. Arthur Young noted that she owned one of Robert Salmon's Woburn chaff-cutters, a device that could bruise oats and beans at the same time, and she introduced drill husbandry to the Hertfordshire countryside. In his account of agricultural innovations in the Hertfordshire countryside, Young singled out Lady Melbourne's garden for special praise.

The younger generation: Byron Lady Melbourne's male friends continued to help her children as they grew older. Egremont encouraged Lady Melbourne to send William Lamb to Glasgow University, which he attended from 1799. Both Emily and William made use of Egremont's box at the opera, and visited his homes at Brighton and Petworth, where their portraits hung. On 30 November 1803 the prince of Wales promised he 'never' would 'neglect an opportunity in which I can be of use to any of you' (BL, Add. MS 45548, fol. 109) and on 26 February 1812, having become regent, offered William a position on the Treasury board, which was declined (BL, Add. MS 45546, fol. 2; Gross, 53). Frederick, however, accepted the prince of Wales's invitation to join the 10th hussars. Lady Melbourne came to regret her own success in furthering Frederick's career when the prince regent appointed him to a series of diplomatic positions in Europe. She wrote to the prince on 4 February 1811 to try to have Frederick placed in the Home Office, and even tried to use Earl Grey as an intermediary when this did not succeed. In 1816 Lady Melbourne reconciled her youngest son George with his wife, Caroline St Jules, after the latter's affair with Henry Brougham in Europe.

Lady Melbourne has been described as a 'man's woman' (Cecil, *Young Melbourne*, 29). Certainly, she was the favourite of a number of young men with political and literary ambitions, including Henry Luttrell; Peter Leopold Cowper, fifth Earl Cowper (who in 1805 married her daughter, Emily); and the diplomat Robert Adair, who relied on her for political advice from as far away as Constantinople. For a brief time she helped procure naval appointments for young men through her friendship with Thomas Grenville. In 1812 she befriended the poet Lord Byron, assisting him in ending his affair with her daughter-in-law, Lady Caroline Lamb, and advising him on other liaisons with Lady Frances Webster, the countess of Oxford, and Augusta Leigh. Lady Melbourne's letters to Byron, written between 1812 and 1816, record regency society manners in great detail. He referred to her conversation as 'champagne' to his spirits (14 May 1813, Byron, 3.48). Her letters contain numerous references to Napoleon, Madame de Staël, and the prince regent. In autumn 1812 Byron asked Lady Melbourne to forward his proposal of marriage to her niece, Anne Isabella (Annabella) Milbanke, which was rejected. Writing on his own behalf two years later, he was accepted and took his honeymoon at Lady Melbourne's ancestral estate, Halnaby Hall, in January 1815. Lady Melbourne selected the house in London which they rented from Elizabeth Cavendish (*née* Foster), duchess of Devonshire. During the separation that ensued after Annabella's departure on 15 January 1816, Lady Melbourne took Byron's part and became estranged from her sister-in-law, Judith, Lady Noel (her brother Sir Ralph Milbanke having taken his wife's maiden name in 1815), who faulted her for her secretive correspondence with Byron. Later in life Lady Melbourne tried to repair her relationship with Annabella, whom she now pitied. She advised Annabella on the importance of sea air for her daughter, Ada, and continued to write to her and Lady Noel, though her letters were not always answered.

Assessment Lady Melbourne wrote a witty epigram entitled 'The Bed' which was published on 5 October 1792 in *The Times*, but her correspondence with the duchess of Devonshire and especially Lord Byron form the best record of her wide-ranging friendships and influence. Lady Melbourne disliked, and hence avoided, public scandal, despite her cynical view of marriage. '[W]hen any one braves the opinion of the World, sooner or later they will feel the consequences of it' (13 April 1810, Gross, 107), she wrote to Lady Caroline Lamb after the latter's affair with Sir Godfrey Webster.

Lady Melbourne did not 'brave' the opinion of the world. Instead, she became a keen barometer of it. She managed to maintain respectability in eighteenth-century English society by receiving more confidences than she imparted. At the same time she served as a conduit of information for those socially more established than herself, continually making herself useful. In a letter to the duchess of Devonshire, for example, she reported on political gossip, and denied the duke of Richmond's divisive suggestion that she and the duchess were 'rival queens' (correspondence with duchess of Devonshire, Chatsworth, 401.1). She is well captured as Lady Pinchbeck in Byron's *Don Juan*, a woman who knew the world 'by experience rather than by lecture' (*Byron's Letters and Journals, Don Juan*, 12.46) and who gained friends in high society by being more forgiving and intelligent than 'prudes without a heart' (ibid.). Other literary depictions of her include those by Richard Sheridan (Lady Sneerwell in *The School for Scandal*) and by Lady Caroline Lamb (Lady Margaret Buchanan in *Glenarvon*).

Surrounded by privileged women ruled by their heart more than their head, Lady Melbourne served as their adviser and remained remarkably self-possessed. She had few vices of the age, such as gambling or drinking, and only a slight inclination to corpulence; as long as she served as the confidante of the beloved duchess of Devonshire and the friend of the prince of Wales, she was, to a large degree, immune from social criticism. Her self-control, intelligence, and ambition, as well as her good sense and helpful advice, go far towards explaining her social ascendancy. Byron, who profited by her advice but could not follow her example, remembered her as 'the best friend I ever had in my life, and the cleverest of women' (*Byron's Letters and Journals*, 3.219).

Lady Melbourne died of rheumatism at Melbourne House, Whitehall, London, on 6 April 1818 after a 'very painful' (Caroline St Jules, 8 April 1818, Lovelace MSS, 92, fol. 110) illness of four months' duration. The long baths prescribed by Dr Pelham Warren did little to relieve her pain. She was buried at Hatfield on 14 April 1818. Her husband survived her, and died at Melbourne House on 22 July 1828. JONATHAN DAVID GROSS

Sources J. Gross, ed., *Byron's 'corbeau blanc': the life and letters of Lady Melbourne* (1997) • Mabell, countess of Airlie, *In whig society, 1775–1818* (1921) • M. Elwin, *Lord Byron's wife* (1962) • S. Birkenhead, *Peace in Piccadilly: the story of Albany* (1958) • R. G. Thorne, 'Lamb, Sir Peniston', HoP, *Commons, 1790–1820* • J. M. Collinge and R. G. Thorne, 'Lamb, Hon. William', HoP, *Commons, 1790–1820* • H. A. Tipping, 'Brocket Hall, Hertfordshire: the seat of Sir Charles Nall-Cain', *Country Life*, 53 (1925), 16–22, 60–67, 96–103 • W. M. Torrens, *Life of Lord Melbourne*, 2 vols. (1878) • *The letters of Horace Walpole, fourth earl of Orford*, ed. P. Toynbee, 16 vols. (1903–5); suppl., 3 vols. (1918–25) • Lovelace MSS, Bodl. Oxf. • BL, Lamb MSS, Add. MSS 45546–45548 • Lady Melbourne's letters, John Murray, London, archives • letters to prince regent, Herts. ALS, F7 D/Elb, F9/2 D/Elb • D. Cecil, *The young Melbourne, and the story of his marriage with Caroline Lamb* (1939) • D. Cecil, *Lord M., or the later life of Lord Melbourne* (1939) • *Byron's letters and journals*, ed. L. A. Marchand, 12 vols. (1973–82); suppl. (1994) • L. G. Mitchell, *Lord Melbourne* (1997) • Mabell, countess of Airlie, *Lady Palmerston and her times*, 2 vols. (1922) • *The memoirs of Sophia Baddeley*, ed. E. Steele, 6 vols. (1787) • *The life and letters of Lady Sarah Lennox*, ed. M. E. A. Dawson, countess of Ilchester and Lord Stavordale, 2 vols. (1901) • D. Bank and A. Esposito, eds., *British biographical index*, 4 vols. (1990) • A. Crawford, T. Hayter, and others, eds., *The Europa biographical dictionary of British women* (1983) • D. Gage, 'Firle Place, East Sussex', *Antiques* (June 1984), 1326–30 • GEC, *Peerage* • A. Young, *A general view of the agriculture of Hertfordshire* (1813) • J. Brooke, 'Milbanke, Sir Ralph', HoP, *Commons, 1754–90* • M. M. Drummond, 'Lamb, Peniston', HoP, *Commons, 1754–90* • R. R. Sedgwick, 'Hedworth, John', HoP, *Commons, 1715–54* • Burke, *Peerage* (1939) • A. Foreman, *Georgiana, duchess of Devonshire* (1998) • *The historical and the posthumous memoirs of Sir Nathaniel William Wraxall, 1772–1784*, ed. H. B. Wheatley, 5 vols. (1884) • correspondence with Georgiana, duchess of Devonshire, Chatsworth House, Derbyshire • Georgiana, duchess of Devonshire, *The sylph*, 2nd edn, 2 vols. (1779)

Archives BL, family corresp., Add. MSS 45546–45549, 45911 • Herts. ALS, letters • Melbourne Hall, Derbyshire • priv. coll., letters | Bodl. Oxf., Lovelace MSS, corresp. with Noel and Byron families

Likenesses F. Cotes, pastel, *c*.1770, Herts. ALS • T. Lawrence, portrait, *c*.1800, Melbourne Hall, Derbyshire [*see illus.*] • R. Cosway, miniature, Newberry Library, Chicago, Illinois • R. Cosway, oils, Royal Collection • J. Finlayson, engraving (after portrait by J. Reynolds), BM; repro. in Gross, ed., *Byron's 'corbeau blanc'* • D. Gardner, oils • T. Lawrence, oils, BM • T. Phillips, oils, repro. in Foreman, *Georgiana, duchess of Devonshire*; priv. coll. • G. Romney, oils, priv. coll.

Lamb, Frederick James, Baron Beauvale and third Viscount Melbourne (1782–1853), diplomatist, was born on 17 April 1782, the third son and third of six surviving children of Elizabeth *Lamb, *née* Milbanke, Viscountess Melbourne (d. 1818). It seems probable that his father was not her husband, Peniston Lamb, first Viscount Melbourne (1745–1828), but George O'Brien *Wyndham, third earl of Egremont (1751–1837). His elder brother, William *Lamb, second Viscount Melbourne, was to be prime minister, and his sister Emily [*see* Temple, Emily Mary, Viscountess Palmerston] was to be the wife of another. They were to be separated for much of their lives, but Fred remained close to William and Emily, and they carried on a voluminous correspondence.

Fred Lamb was educated with William at Eton College, at Glasgow University under Professor John Millar, and at Trinity College, Cambridge, where he took his MA in 1803. He initially joined the army, as a cornet in the Horse Guards (1803), but in 1811 joined the diplomatic service as secretary of legation to Naples, moving in the same capacity in 1813 to Vienna. The prince regent (who was probably the father of at least one of the other Lamb children) took an interest in launching his career. In 1815 he went as minister-plenipotentiary to Munich, remaining there for five years. He was sworn of the privy council in 1822, in which year he went to Frankfurt as minister. From 1825 to

1827 he was minister in Madrid, and in the latter year was appointed GCB.

In December 1827 Sir Frederick was sent to Lisbon as ambassador to Portugal, where Dom Miguel, the uncle of the queen, was attempting to usurp the throne. A British force previously sent to support the constitutionalist queen was due to leave Portugal, but Lamb detained them on his own responsibility, in an unsuccessful attempt to frustrate Dom Miguel's plan. Although the Wellington ministry endorsed his actions, the troops were nevertheless recalled; in England the following August, Lamb made no secret of the fact that he thought the government had acted 'very ill and foolishly in first encouraging and then abandoning the wretched constitutionalists to their fate' (*Greville Memoirs*, 1.141). On 13 May 1831 Lamb was appointed ambassador at the court of Vienna, and remained there until the whigs fell from office in 1841. A 'hard-headed reactionary' (Bourne, 461), Lamb bombarded his brother (as home secretary and then prime minister) with warnings against the radicals in the whig government, and his conservatism in foreign policy brought him into conflict with the foreign secretary, Palmerston. Lamb was, however, more at home in Metternich's Vienna than he would have been in Paris (to which his seniority and skill probably entitled him); there his differences with Palmerston could scarcely have been contained. Lamb was created Baron Beauvale in 1839, and succeeded his brother as third Viscount Melbourne in 1848.

Fred Lamb was a thorough whig (despite his political conservatism), by upbringing and position. A product of the eccentric social, political, and moral *milieu* of the Melbourne and Devonshire House set, he tended to see 'life in the most degrading light, and he simplifies the thing by thinking all men rogues and all women [whores]' (Lady Granville, cited in Mitchell, 10). He had a constant succession of mistresses, both amateur and professional (including Harriette Wilson, who gave him a friendly write-up in her notorious *Memoirs*), until his very late marriage on 25 February 1841. His wife, the Countess Alexandrina Julia Theresa Wilhelmina Sophia (Adine) von Maltzahn (1818–1894), daughter of the Prussian minister at Vienna, was some thirty-five years his junior, but the marriage was successful (if childless), and Lady Beauvale was devoted to her ageing, increasingly valetudinarian husband. Frederick's relationship with his brother Melbourne resumed the closeness of their youth in the 1840s, and the Beauvales took the burden of responsibility for Melbourne in his final years. Frederick retained his liking for political gossip, and his letters continued unabated: his sister remained his most important correspondent, but he also remained in touch with the Russian Princess Lieven. He died, the third and last Viscount Melbourne, at his home, Brocket Hall, Hertfordshire, on 29 January 1853, having suffered terribly with gout for some time. His young widow was genuinely prostrated with grief, but eventually recovered and in 1856 married John George, second Baron Forester. The Lamb estates passed to his sister, Emily Palmerston.   K. D. REYNOLDS

Sources *The Greville memoirs, 1814–1860*, ed. L. Strachey and R. Fulford, 8 vols. (1938) · K. Bourne, *Palmerston: the early years, 1784–1841* (1982) · L. G. Mitchell, *Lord Melbourne, 1779–1848* (1997) · *The letters of Lady Palmerston*, ed. T. Lever (1957) · Mabell, countess of Airlie, *Lady Palmerston and her times*, 2 vols. (1922) · *Memoirs of Harriette Wilson*, 4 vols. (1825) · *DNB*
Archives BL, corresp. and papers, Add. MSS 60399–60483 · BL, family corresp., Add. MSS 45546–45552, 45911 · Herts. ALS, diplomatic corresp., papers, personal letters, and dispatches | BL, corresp. with Lord Aberdeen, Add. MSS 43088, 43108–43109 · BL, corresp. with Lord Holland, Add. MS 51613 · Bodl. Oxf., letters to earl of Clarendon · Durham RO, corresp. with Lord Stewart · PRO, corresp. with Lord Granville, PRO 30/29 · PRO NIre., corresp. with Lord Castlereagh · U. Durham L., letters to Viscount Ponsonby · U. Southampton L., corresp. with Lord Palmerston · Woburn Abbey, Bedfordshire, letters to George William Russell
Likenesses F. Bartolozzi, group portrait, stipple, pubd 1791 (*The Lamb Family*; after J. Reynolds, 1785), BM · J. Partridge, oils, 1846, NPG; repro. in Lever, *Letters*

Lamb, George (1784–1834), politician and writer, had a disputed parentage. His mother was certainly Elizabeth *Lamb (*bap.* 1751, *d.* 1818), daughter of Sir Ralph Milbanke, and wife of Peniston Lamb, first Viscount Melbourne (1745–1828). His father was generally believed to have been *George IV (1762–1830). That monarch took a benign and lifelong interest in his career and stood as his godfather. Lamb was therefore the half-brother of William *Lamb, the future prime minister; of Frederick *Lamb, the future Lord Beauvale; and of Emily Lamb, successively the wife of lords Cowper and Palmerston [*see* Temple, Emily Mary, Viscountess Palmerston]. Born on 11 July 1784, Lamb followed his brothers first to Eton College, from 1796 to 1802, and then to Trinity College, Cambridge, from 1802 to 1805. Unlike them, he spent no time in Scottish universities, but proceeded straight to Lincoln's Inn. He was called to the bar in 1809 and practised on the northern circuit.

Red-haired and red-faced, Lamb's immoderate intake of alcohol enhanced the Lamb family's reputation for high spirits. Melbourne described him as 'very intemperate … He drank a great deal, much more than we did' (Queen Victoria's journal, 6 June 1838). According to Lady Harriet Cavendish, 'he really has not half an hour's good behaviour in him … he is like a schoolboy, when he has been good and quiet for a long time for him, he begins making a noise, teizing [*sic*] the dogs, spoiling the furniture and then we say, "Don't, George, pray be quiet, dear George. Oh, leave that alone," just as I do to your children when they question' (*Hary-O*, 268–9). Animal spirits were moderated by a genial good nature that made him for some 'a most agreeable man'. Within his family he was known as 'Curly Pate'.

On 17 May 1809 Lamb married Caroline Rosalie Adelaide St Jules, the illegitimate daughter of Lady Elizabeth Foster and the fifth duke of Devonshire. She was henceforth known as 'Caro George' or, unflatteringly, as 'Cleopatra'. Generously, the duke settled £20,000 on the young couple, together with an annuity of £500 per annum. After the death of the first Viscount Melbourne in 1828 their income rose to £3,000 per annum. In spite of this the marriage was somewhat uneven. In 1816 Lamb's wife

George Lamb (1784–1834), by Richard Dighton, 1819

rooms were sacked and he himself had to go into hiding. Losing the seat the following year, he was returned (on the Devonshire interest) for the Irish borough of Dungarvan in 1822, and represented that constituency until his death. He spoke in the house 'in a sensible and intrepid style', supporting such radical measures as triennial parliaments, the abolition of corrupt boroughs, and the setting up of an inquiry into the Peterloo massacre. He was a friend of both Daniel O'Connell and Francis Place. When his brother became home secretary, in November 1830, Lamb was appointed under-secretary in the same department, a post he held until his death. By all accounts Lamb showed himself to be an efficient and effective administrator. He was used as an intermediary between the government and the radicals in the difficult years before and after the passing of the first Reform Bill. William Lamb later called George 'his great favourite' (Queen Victoria's journal, 14 June 1838); and after her husband's death, Caro George felt the prime minister must suffer 'a pang' whenever he went into 'that room, where they were so happy together' (Panshanger MSS, D.ELb F 81). George Lamb died suddenly on 2 January 1834 at his house in Whitehall Yard, Westminster, London, and was buried at Hatfield on the 9th.   L. G. MITCHELL

Sources *GM*, 1st ser., 79 (1809), 477 · *GM*, 2nd ser., 1 (1834), 437–8 · Queen Victoria, journal, Royal Arch. · Castle Howard, Castle Howard MSS · BL, Lamb MSS · D. M. Stuart, *Dearest Bess: the life and times of Lady Elizabeth Foster* (1955) · HoP, *Commons* · Herts. ALS, Panshanger MSS · *Hary-O: the letters of Lady Harriet Cavendish, 1796–1809*, ed. G. Leveson-Gower and I. Palmer (1940)
Archives Herts. ALS, letters · Melbourne Hall, Derbyshire, papers | BL, corresp. with Lady Melbourne, Add. MS 45547 · Castle Howard, Yorkshire, Castle Howard MSS · Lpool RO, letters to E. G. Stanley
Likenesses M. Cosway, portrait, 1786 · R. Dighton, caricature etching, 1819, BM, NPG, Wellcome L. [*see illus.*]

decamped to Italy with Henry Brougham to conduct a much-publicized *affaire*, describing herself as the victim of neglect and drunkenness. Byron unkindly called Lamb 'Gay Thalia's luckless victory' and all his relations that 'cuckoldy family' (Stuart, 159–60). The couple were reconciled in 1817 and remained together until Lamb's death. There were no children from the marriage.

From a very early age Lamb evinced a passion for the theatre, first as an actor and writer in private theatricals, and then as a dramatist. In 1807 his play *Whistle for It* was produced at Covent Garden. This was a Gothic piece, brimming over with brigands and talk of daggers. In the denouement, however, a pair of young lovers are rescued by an anti-hero called Andrew, who cheerfully admits that he has never killed anyone in his life. In 1815 Lamb joined the management committee of Drury Lane, and, six years later, gave up the law completely as an unwelcome distraction from his dramatic pursuits. His sister observed that 'his heart is in Drury Lane, and he thinks of nothing but plays and epilogues and prologues'. He was also a classical scholar of some quality. A translation of the poems of Catullus was published in 1821. He thought, perhaps significantly, that the Roman poet 'inclined to constancy in love, had his constancy met with return'.

In politics Lamb was the most radical member of his family. In 1819 he agreed to 'rough it' by contesting Westminster for the whigs. He won, though his committee

Lamb, Henry Taylor (1883–1960), painter, was born in Adelaide, South Australia, on 21 June 1883, the third son and fifth of the seven children of Sir Horace *Lamb (1849–1934), mathematician and physicist, and his wife, Elizabeth Mary, *née* Foot (d. 1930), a former ladies' companion and the daughter of Simon Foot, a Dublin solicitor and JP. Lamb's eldest sister, Helen, became a don at Newnham College, Cambridge; his eldest brother, Ernest, was a professor of engineering at Queen Mary College, London; and his next eldest brother, Sir Walter Lamb, was secretary of the Royal Academy. Brought up in Manchester, where his father was professor of mathematics at the university, Lamb spent 'eight years of misery' (20 April 1932, artist's questionnaire replies) at Manchester grammar school, from September 1894 (first on the classical side, then in the mathematical sixth form), and, destined for medicine, four years at Manchester University medical school, where he obtained a graduate scholarship in 1904. Despite this success, he abandoned medicine for painting (his desire to become an artist had been strengthened by a visit to Italy with his father at Easter 1904) and settled in London in the summer of 1905. He had already received training and encouragement from Joseph Knight, art master at Manchester grammar school, and from Francis Dodd and

Muirhead Bone. From January 1906 Lamb studied at the art school run by Augustus John and William Orpen in Flood Street, Chelsea, supplementing a small allowance from a patron, Bernard Calman Alexander of Manchester, with occasional commissions from the *Manchester Guardian* for drawings of famous London buildings such as Westminster Hall. In 1907–8 he continued his studies in Paris at La Palette under Jacques-Émile Blanche.

After returning to London Lamb took a studio at 8 Fitzroy Street (1909–10), while the summers of 1910 and 1911 were spent in Brittany, followed by some months in Ireland (1912–13). He had first exhibited at the New English Art Club in 1909, and his allegiance to the progressives in English art soon showed itself when he became a founder member of the *Camden Town Group in 1911 and of the London Group in 1913. On the outbreak of war he returned to medicine, entering Guy's Hospital, London, as a full student in November 1915 and qualifying there in July 1916. Gazetted captain, he served as battalion medical officer with the 5th (Inniskilling) fusiliers in Macedonia, Palestine, and France, was gassed, and was invalided home. He was awarded the MC in 1918 and demobilized in January 1919.

Lamb's early style was strongly influenced by the work of Augustus John, and his fine drawings of Dorelia John and of his first wife, Nina (Euphemia) Lamb (1886x9–1957), daughter of Arthur Forrest (whom he married on 10 May 1906 and from whom he separated a few years later and was divorced in July 1928), executed between 1907 and 1910, equal John's in their firm brilliance. His distinctive artistic personality first flowered in a series of paintings of Breton subjects, such as *Death of a Peasant* (1911) and *Lamentation* (1911, both Tate collection). In these paintings austere realism, a restrained palette, and striking, deceptively simple composition are qualities characteristic also of much of his later work. With the exception of *Phantasy* (1912, Tate collection), a group of male nude equestrians perhaps inspired by the circus scenes of Picasso's rose period, Lamb seems to have been almost impervious to the revolutionary movements in contemporary French art. This may account for the antipathy of the art critic Roger Fry towards his painting; nor did Lamb share the pacifist beliefs of some of the Bloomsbury group. Yet it was the large portrait of Lytton Strachey, completed in 1914 (Tate collection), which brought him public notice and featured in his first one-man exhibition at the Alpine Club Gallery in May and June of 1922. Strachey, whom he first painted in 1912, is shown seated against a large window in Lamb's studio in the Vale of Health, Hampstead, and, although avoiding caricature, Lamb has relished emphasizing Strachey's gaunt, ungainly figure and the air of resigned intellectual superiority with which he surveys the world from his incredible slab-like head. The trees in the vista seen through the window are painted in a rhythmic, decorative manner which suggests that Lamb had taken from the innovations of the Nabis and Matisse what seemed consistent with his own essentially academic approach. Browns, violets, and greens predominate—

colours which were subtly woven into many later compositions, making his work easily distinguishable from that of others in group exhibitions. Other writers who sat to him were Evelyn Waugh (1930) and Lord David Cecil (1935).

Lamb's wartime experiences inspired two large paintings, *Irish Troops in the Judaean Hills Surprised by a Turkish Bombardment* (1919, Imperial War Museum, London) and *Advanced Dressing Station on the Struma, 1916* (1920, Manchester City Galleries), the earlier of which is a remarkably vivid bird's-eye view of wounded soldiers being moved from an outpost under fire. During the early twenties he painted several portrait groups of distinction, such as that of the architect George Kennedy and his family (1921, formerly J. L. Behrend), some details of which relate to the work of Stanley Spencer, whom from 1913 he had encouraged and to whom he had given a room in his house at Poole, Dorset, after the war, in 1922 from summer to that December, and again in the summer of 1923. The rooftops, warehouses, and narrow streets of the town delighted Lamb and inspired many carefully observed compositions during this period. While good at official portraits, he particularly enjoyed capturing children's likenesses, and the son and two daughters of his second marriage—in August 1928 to Lady (Margaret) Pansy Felicia Pakenham (b. 1904), an interior designer and novelist and the eldest daughter of the fifth earl of Longford—appear in many family portraits of the thirties and forties. During the Second World War he was an official war artist, attached to the army, and painted portraits of servicemen and foreign military attachés.

Failing health, especially acute arthritis, towards the end of his life forced Lamb to abandon painting landscapes, to concentrate on still life, and latterly to rework earlier themes of Breton and Irish life. He had lived at Brookside, Coombe Bissett, near Salisbury, Wiltshire, since the summer of 1928 and died in the Spiro Nursing Home in Campbell Road, Salisbury, on 8 October 1960. He was buried in the churchyard at Coombe Bissett.

Of medium height, slightly built, and agile, Lamb was fond of riding and sailing, though his constitution was permanently weakened after the First World War. He had wide intellectual interests, was an accomplished performer on the piano and clavichord of the music of Mozart, Beethoven, and Bach, and was impatient of convention. Elected ARA in 1940, he became an RA in 1949. He was a trustee of the Tate Gallery (1944–51), and of the National Portrait Gallery (1942–60), which owns two self-portrait drawings of 1950 and 1951, a fine earlier self-portrait in oils of 1914, and a drawing of him by Powys Evans; a self-portrait drawing of 1905 is in the Ashmolean Museum, Oxford. Manchester City Galleries have a portrait of him (1905) by Francis Dodd. A memorial exhibition was held at the Leicester Galleries, London, in December 1961. Portraits by him are in many British universities, a notable example being that of the principal of St Hugh's College, Oxford, Miss Barbara Gwyer, and four fellows studying the plans for the Mary Gray Allen building in

1936 (St Hugh's College, Oxford University). Lamb is widely represented in the Tate collection and in provincial museums.   DENNIS FARR

Sources private information (1971) [Lady Pansy Lamb] · artist's questionnaire replies, 20 April 1932, Tate collection · *The Times* (10 Oct 1960) · K. Clements, *Henry Lamb: the artist and his friends* (1985) · artist's catalogue file on Henry Lamb, Tate collection · [G. L. Kennedy], *Henry Lamb* (1924) · *CGPLA Eng. & Wales* (1960) · *WWW*
Archives IWM · Man. City Gall. · NPG | Tate collection, letters to Richard Carline · Tate collection, letters to Christopher Fleming · Tate collection, corresp. with Stanley Spencer
Likenesses F. Dodd, oils, 1905, Man. City Gall. · H. T. Lamb, self-portrait, pencil, 1905, AM Oxf. · H. T. Lamb, self-portrait, oil on panel, 1914, NPG · P. Evans, pen-and-ink drawing, c.1928, NPG · D. Carrington, photograph, 1929, Hult. Arch. · H. T. Lamb, group portrait, oil on plywood, 1940–43 (*The artist's family*), Tate collection · H. T. Lamb, self-portrait, oils, c.1950, repro. in Clements, *Henry Lamb*, following p. 178; priv. coll. · H. T. Lamb, two self-portraits, pencil and red chalk drawings, 1950–51, NPG
Wealth at death £11,673 2s. 3d.: administration, 19 Dec 1960, *CGPLA Eng. & Wales*

Lamb, Sir Horace (1849–1934), mathematician, was born on 27 November 1849 at Stockport, Cheshire, the son of John Lamb and Elizabeth Rangley. His father, a cotton-mill foreman (said to have invented an improvement of the spinning machine), died while he was a child, and his mother married again. He was brought up by her sister, Mrs Holland, a kind but severely puritan lady. He was educated at Stockport grammar school, and then, for a year, at Owens College, Manchester, before entering Trinity College, Cambridge, where he was a scholar 1870–72, having matriculated in 1868.

Lamb was fortunate in his teachers. While at grammar school he came under the influence of the Revd Charles Hamilton, an admired headmaster who imparted to him an abiding interest in Greek and Latin poetry. At Owens College, where his main studies were in mathematics, he was taught by the iconoclastic Thomas Barker, and in Cambridge he attended the lectures of Maxwell and Stokes. He graduated in 1872 as second wrangler and second Smith's prizeman, and was made a fellow and lecturer of Trinity in the same year.

Lamb taught at Trinity College until 1875 when he married Elizabeth Mary (d. 1930), daughter of Simon Foot, a merchant from Blackrock, co. Dublin. She was a sister-in-law of his former headmaster, Charles Hamilton. They had four daughters and three sons, one of whom was Henry Taylor *Lamb, a distinguished artist and portrait painter. The rule of celibacy was still in force in Cambridge colleges, and after their marriage they moved to Adelaide, Australia, where Lamb became professor of mathematics at the newly founded university. He held this post from 1876 to 1885, when he returned to Manchester to take up the chair of pure mathematics at Owens College, by then part of the newly incorporated Victoria University, which had been vacated by his former teacher Thomas Barker. He held this post until 1920.

Lamb was a talented and inspiring teacher, whose lectures to generations of mathematics, engineering, and physics students at Manchester were remembered for their lucidity and judgement. His most distinguished pupil was probably Arthur Eddington. Of his many books his most noted was *Hydrodynamics* (1895; 6th edn, 1932). This work, an extended version of an earlier *Treatise on the Motion of Fluids* (1879), was a seminal contribution to the field and is still in use; a model of clarity and acute scientific judgement, it has been held up as one of the finest texts in applied mathematics in the twentieth century.

In addition to hydrodynamics Lamb worked on acoustics, elasticity, and mechanics, and wrote a number of books and papers in these areas. He also wrote an introductory textbook, *Infinitesimal Calculus* (1897), especially noted for its combination of Lamb's usual clarity of expression with a high standard of mathematical rigour. His forte was the application of analysis to those physical phenomena in which wave transmission is a central feature, and he made significant and lasting contributions to the solution of many problems in this field. A triumphant example of the confidence of his approach to the many different areas of natural science that touched upon his interests is his 1904 paper 'On the propagation of tremors over the surface of an elastic solid' (*PTRS*, 203A, 1904, 1–42) which forms the basis of much modern work in theoretical seismology. His contemporaries admired his ability to keep up to date with new developments in a variety of sciences at the same time as he remained primarily a mathematician. Lord Rutherford is said to have identified Lamb as the closest approximation to an ideal university professor that he knew.

In 1884 Lamb was elected a fellow of the Royal Society, which awarded him a royal medal in 1902 and its highest accolade, the Copley medal, in 1923. Among his many other honours were a knighthood (1931) and the presidency of the British Association (1925), of the London Mathematical Society (1902–4)—he was awarded its De Morgan medal in 1911—and of the Manchester Literary and Philosophical Society. He received honorary doctorates from the universities of Glasgow, Oxford, Cambridge, Dublin, St Andrews, Manchester, and Sheffield.

On his retirement from Manchester, Lamb returned to Cambridge where Trinity College gave him an honorary fellowship and the university made him an honorary (Rayleigh) lecturer; he lectured there for fourteen years. He retained his high mathematical powers, which in most mathematicians wane with age, and continued to produce elegant and important papers. During the First World War he had given valuable help to the Admiralty and to aeronautical research, and he continued to serve the latter for a time (1921–7) as a member of the Aeronautical Research Committee. On many other councils and committees (as previously at Manchester during his long membership of the university senate) his wide knowledge and the wisdom of his outlook were highly esteemed.

Lamb travelled widely, especially in Italy and Switzerland, and was an early climber of the Matterhorn. He read much in French, German, and Italian, and had many artistic interests. His cultural hinterland is sometimes seen as the key to the 'artistry' of organization and exposition in his much emulated *Hydrodynamics*. A man of great personal dignity, conservative in temper, he was a good representative of the ideal of the secular scientist of broad culture that held sway in his day. He died at his home, 6 Selwyn Gardens, Cambridge, on 4 December 1934.

SYDNEY CHAPMAN, *rev.* JULIA TOMPSON

Sources *The Times* (5 Dec 1934), 19 · A. E. H. Love and R. T. Glazebrook, *Obits. FRS*, 1 (1932–5), 375–92 · Venn, *Alum. Cant.* · *DSB* · R. Porter, ed., *The Hutchinson dictionary of scientific biography*, 2nd edn (1994) · A. Ben Menahem, 'A concise history of mainstream seismology', *Bulletin of the Seismological Society of America*, 85 (1995), 1202–25 · *CGPLA Eng. & Wales* (1935)

Archives JRL, lecture notes | Air Force Cambridge Research Laboratories, Cambridge, Massachusetts, letters to Lord Rayleigh · CUL, corresp. with Lord Kelvin · CUL, letters to Sir George Stokes

Likenesses H. Lamb, oils, before 1913, Manchester University · W. Stoneman, photograph, 1922, NPG · Lafayette, photograph, repro. in Love and Glazebrook, *Obits. FRS* · H. Lamb, pencil drawing, Trinity Cam. · Maull & Fox, photograph, RS · photograph, RS

Wealth at death £27,617 12s. 6d.: probate, 4 Feb 1935, *CGPLA Eng. & Wales*

Lamb, Hubert Horace (1913–1997), climatologist, was born on 22 September 1913 at 4 Beverley Crescent, St Paul, Bedford, the son of Ernest Horace Lamb (1878–1946) and his wife, Lilian, daughter of the Revd G. H. Brierley. His grandfather was the mathematician Horace *Lamb, who published textbooks used by meteorologists, and his father was a professor of engineering. Given that as a young boy Lamb often took tea with his family at the house of Lewis Richardson (who attempted the first-ever numerical prediction of the weather), it might be thought that there was a certain inevitability to his eventual career. Although he ceded to family pressure at Oundle School by abandoning history and languages in favour of the natural sciences, he rebelled at Cambridge University by switching from natural sciences to geography, ending up with a mongrel degree which his father told him he would regret all his life. In fact, it provided the springboard for him to steer climatology out of the sleepy academic backwaters, and encouraged him to question conventional scientific thought. Other early influences which profoundly affected the eventual course of his career were Richardson's Quaker philosophy, which he adopted soon after graduation, and regular conversation with the libertarian Trevor Huddleston (the future bishop), a family friend.

Lamb started employment with the UK Meteorological Office in 1936, claiming modestly that he got the job only because the director had been a student of his grandfather. He soon produced a well-regarded paper on the formation of North Sea fogs but, with war looming, its publication was suppressed because of its potential use to the enemy. The war affected Lamb's career more directly. The outcome of his refusal to work on the meteorology of gas spraying led to a transfer to the Irish meteorological service. There he was charged with producing weather forecasts for the new transatlantic passenger flights, having to rely mainly on information from flight crews in the absence of access to observations. His perfect safety record reflected his deep intuition of weather systems.

Hubert Horace Lamb (1913–1997), by unknown photographer

This insight served him well when he returned to the Meteorological Office in 1946, and he was posted as expedition meteorologist on an Antarctic whaler. His sharp powers of observation allowed him to challenge successfully the received wisdom that the discontinuities between warm and cold waters in the Southern Ocean were invariant. On 7 February 1948 he married (Beatrice) Moira Milligan, with whom he had a son and two daughters.

One of Lamb's outstanding contributions to climatology was published in 1950. It was a study of weather types and natural seasons in Britain, and introduced the Lamb Weather Type classification which gave an enormous impetus to climatological research. About the same time, by good fortune, Lamb was posted to the Meteorological Office's climatology department, which contained probably the most complete and unstudied meteorological archive in the world. He reconstructed monthly atmospheric circulations over Europe and the north Atlantic back to the 1750s, confirming his growing conviction that climate changed on time-scales of significance to modern humankind. His catholic training and his growing questioning stance meant that he was very receptive to the notion of collaborating with scientists from other disciplines. He started to work with botanists, geographers, and historians in his quest to reconstruct past climates. As his interest in climate variations started to extend further back in time, he also started to think about their cause. In 1970 he published the results of a prodigious effort to produce a measure of the volcanic dust in the atmosphere following every single eruption since 1500. His name again entered the scientific literature as others used the Lamb Dust Veil Index as the starting point for their own analyses.

At the beginning of the 1970s Lamb started to feel increasingly uncomfortable over what he saw as an over-reliance on numerical methods and computers at the Meteorological Office, and left to found the climate research unit at the University of East Anglia. This was a very brave decision so late in his working career, and with all the uncertainties of university funding. Many were dubious about such a venture, and the early years were indeed difficult and stressful. However, before his retirement in 1978, he and his new colleagues in the climate research unit had convinced the remaining doubters about the reality of climate variations on time-scales of decades and centuries. He had also built such a firm base for the unit, and recruited such talented individuals, that over the next twenty-plus years it secured an international reputation for climate research. His period at East Anglia saw the completion of his greatest work: a triumph of scientific synthesis and interpretation, *Climate: Present, Past and Future* appeared in two volumes, published in 1972 and 1977. An irony is that, although the world is now very aware of climate change over decades and centuries, and Lamb did more than any other scientist to establish its acceptance, right to the end of his life he maintained a guarded attitude towards what was known as 'greenhouse gas' warming. He felt that others were too reluctant to consider the full range of other potential causes, and he included members of the climate research unit in that category.

In 1963 Lamb had been awarded a special merit promotion in the Meteorological Office, mainly for his work in the Antarctic. His research was recognized formally through awards such as the Murchison award of the Royal Geographical Society, the Symons gold medal of the Royal Meteorological Society, and the gold medal of the Swedish Geographical Society. He was appointed emeritus professor at the University of East Anglia in 1978. Lamb's modest appearance belied his achievements. He was deeply concerned about the state, and fate, of humankind, and his contribution to climate science has been immense: he is universally recognized as the greatest climatologist of his age. He died on 28 June 1997 at Kelling Hospital, High Kelling, Norfolk, survived by his wife.   TREVOR DAVIES

Sources T. D. Davies, 'Hubert Lamb', *Weather*, 53/7 (July 1998), 198–201 · *The Guardian* (30 June 1997) · *The Independent* (9 July 1997) · personal knowledge (2004) · private information (2004) · b. cert. · d. cert.
Likenesses photograph, repro. in *The Guardian* · photograph, University of East Anglia, school of environmental sciences [see illus.]
Wealth at death £227,351: probate, 10 Oct 1997, CGPLA Eng. & Wales

Lamb, James. See Lambe, James (*bap.* 1599, *d.* 1664).

Lamb, John (1789–1850), college head and dean of Bristol, born at Ixworth, Suffolk, on 28 February 1789, was the eldest surviving son of John Lamb (*d.* 1842), perpetual curate of Ixworth, vicar of Haxey, Lincolnshire, and rector of Stretton, Rutland, and his wife, Maria, daughter of William Hovell of Backwell Ash, Suffolk. He studied at Corpus Christi College, Cambridge, where he graduated BA in 1811 as fifteenth and last wrangler, and proceeded MA in 1814, BD in 1822, and DD in 1827. In January 1822, at an unusually young age, he was chosen master of his college, in succession to Philip Douglas. On 19 March 1822 he married Ann (*bap.* 1801), third daughter of Benjamin Hutchinson, rector of Cranford, Northamptonshire. He was vice-chancellor of Cambridge University in 1823–4. In 1824 he was presented by the college to the perpetual curacy of St Benedict in Cambridge; on 20 October 1837 he was nominated by the crown to the deanery of Bristol; and in 1845 he was instituted, on the presentation of the dean and chapter of Bristol, to the vicarage of Olveston, Gloucestershire, which he held until his death, with his mastership and deanery. In politics he firmly maintained whig principles, which led to a conspiracy to prevent his holding the office of vice-chancellor a second time. He died on 19 April 1850, at the lodge of Corpus Christi College, Cambridge, and was buried on the 26th in a vault under the college chapel. He had ten sons and four daughters; one of the daughters, Emily, married Norman Macleod Ferrers, sometime master of Gonville and Caius College, Cambridge.

Lamb's principal works were *An Historical Account of the XXXIX Articles* (1829; 2nd edn, 1835); *Masters's history of the college of Corpus Christi in the University of Cambridge; with additional matter and a continuation to the present time* (1831); *Hebrew Characters Derived from Hieroglyphics* (1835; 2nd edn, 1835); *A collection of letters, statutes, and other documents from the MS library of Corpus Christi College, illustrative of the history of the University of Cambridge during the time of the Reformation* (1838). Some minor writings are noted in P. Bury, *The College of Corpus Christi* (49).

THOMPSON COOPER, rev. JOHN D. PICKLES

Sources *GM*, 2nd ser., 9 (1838), 333 · *GM*, 2nd ser., 33 (1850), 667 · P. Bury, *The college of Corpus Christi and of the Blessed Virgin Mary: a history from 1822 to 1952* (1952) · *Romilly's Cambridge diary, 1832–42: selected passages from the diary of the Rev. Joseph Romilly*, ed. J. P. T. Bury (1967) · *Romilly's Cambridge diary, 1842–47: selected passages from the diary of the Rev. Joseph Romilly*, ed. M. E. Bury and J. D. Pickles, Cambridgeshire RS, 10 (1994) · P. Bury, 'John Lamb's diary', *Letter of the Corpus Association*, 58 (1978), 27–32 · Burke, *Gen. GB* · Venn, *Alum. Cant.*
Likenesses W. Beechey, oils, *c.*1825, CCC Cam.

Lamb, Lynton Harold (1907–1977), artist and book designer, was born in Hyderabad, India, on 15 April 1907, the second son of a Methodist minister, the Revd Frederick Lamb, and his wife, (Charlotte) Annie Brown. He was educated at Kingswood School, Bath, and at the Central School of Arts and Crafts, London (1928–30), where he studied painting under William Roberts and Bernard Meninsky, and engraving under Noel Rooke and R. J. Beedham. A. S. Hartrick introduced him to lithography and gave him a lasting affection for the work of the French intimistes, Edouard Vuillard and Pierre Bonnard. He knew the painter Victor Pasmore well, sharing a studio with him in the 1930s, and featuring in Pasmore's painting *The Parisian Café* (1936–7; Manchester City Galleries).

On 25 March 1933 Lamb married Barbara Grace (known as Biddy; *b.* 1907/8), daughter of the Revd John Henry Morgan, with whom he had two sons.

In 1930 Lamb joined Oxford University Press to design bindings for prayer books and bibles at their London office, Amen House. He returned to the Central School to study bookbinding under Douglas Cockerell, succeeding Cockerell as instructor in the school of book production, 1935–9, and developed a fine book design technique that brought him the tasks of designing the commemorative binding for the lectern Bible for St Giles's Cathedral, Edinburgh, in 1948, and the Bible used at the coronation of Elizabeth II in 1953. At the press he developed an interest in typography and produced many book covers and wrappers.

The Second World War interrupted Lamb's career as a painter and designer. He was commissioned into the Royal Engineers as a staff officer (camouflage), serving between 1940 and 1945. He was in congenial company, for among others, the painter William Coldstream, the stage designer Oliver Messel, the book engraver Blair Hughes-Stanton, Brian Robb, and John Lewis, the original contributor of this article, were fellow officers.

In 1946 Lamb returned to Amen House and, with the appointment of Geoffrey Cumberlege as publisher to the university, he found a sympathetic employer. One of their happiest collaborations was in producing the Oxford Illustrated Trollope, for which Lamb designed a simple and attractive format, and he himself illustrated *Can you Forgive her?* His tentative drawings illuminated Trollope's political scene, yet he was not a particularly strong draughtsman. His resolve never to do any preliminary pencil work and his belief that 'groping for the form' was an essential part of drawing found little sympathy from his friend the artist and author Edward Ardizzone. In contrast to his pen drawings, the wood-engravings he made in the 1930s, particularly for an unpublished edition of Thomas Browne's *Religio medici* and *Urne Buriall*, were most assured and accomplished pieces of work. Lamb illustrated over sixty books, but, working with the most economical means to achieve his effects, his book jackets were among his most successful graphic designs.

As a painter Lamb's aims were modest. He was a member of the London Group from 1939, and in 1951 was one of the fifty artists invited by the Arts Council to contribute a large painting for the Festival of Britain travelling exhibition 'Fifty Paintings for 1951'. During his career he showed regularly, his first exhibition being at the Storran Gallery in 1937, the last at the Radlett Gallery in the year before he died. The critic Clive Bell made a wounding remark about Lamb, which might have been intended as a compliment: 'How useful minor artists are', Bell wrote, 'in instances when the minor artist has something to say about contemporary life' (*New Statesman*, 13, 1937, 1003). Lamb was a good teacher, becoming head of lithography at the Slade School (1950–71), and lecturing on methods and materials of painting at the painting school, Royal College of Art (1956–70).

Lamb was president of the Society of Industrial Artists and Designers (1951–3); he served on the art panel of the Arts Council (1951–4), on the Council of Industrial Design (1952–5), and on the graphic panel for the National Council for Diplomas in Art and Design (1962), visiting numerous art schools as an external examiner. He designed the postage stamps for the new reign (1955) and the airmail stamp (1957). Lamb became fellow of the Society of Industrial Artists in 1968, fellow of the Royal Society of Arts in 1953, and royal designer for industry in 1974.

Lamb was charming, elegant in his dress, a most witty speaker, and as happy in the Reform Club as he was on the village cricket field. He wrote clearly and urbanely. In 1974 he suffered a series of strokes which left him partially paralysed, but he continued to see his friends and to write, with considerable difficulty, the most amusing letters. He died at Sandon, Essex, on 4 September 1977.

Lamb's publications included *The Purpose of Painting* (1936), *County Town* (1950), *Preparation for Painting* (1954), *Cat's Tales* (1959), *Drawing for Illustration* (1962), *Death of a Dissenter* (1969), *Materials and Methods of Painting* (1970), *Worse than Death* (1971), *Picture Frame* (1972), and *Man in a Mist* (1974). He also wrote articles for *Graphis* (1950), *Studio* (1951), *Signature* (1947 and 1951), and *Penrose Annual* (1956), and, with Quentin Bell, was co-editor of the Oxford paperback Handbooks for Artists.

JOHN LEWIS, rev. JAMES HAMILTON

Sources G. Mackie, *Lynton Lamb: illustrator* (1979) · B. Laughton, *The Euston Road School* (1986) · J. Selborne, *British wood-engraved book illustration, 1900–1940* (1998) · J. Lewis, 'The drawings and book decorations of Lynton Lamb', *Alphabet and Image*, 5 (1947), 57–74 · J. Lewis and J. Brinkley, *Graphic design* (1954), 159–60 · personal knowledge (1986) · private information (1986) · m. cert. · CGPLA Eng. & Wales (1977)
Archives V&A, corresp. and papers
Wealth at death £83,824: probate, 4 Nov 1977, CGPLA Eng. & Wales

Lamb, Mary Anne (1764–1847), children's writer, was born on 3 December 1764 in the Inner Temple, London, the second of the three surviving of the seven children of John Lamb (*c.*1725–1799), waiter at the Inner Temple, and his wife, Elizabeth (*d.* 1796), daughter of Mary Field, housekeeper at Blakesware House in Hertfordshire. Charles *Lamb (1775–1834) was the third surviving child. In contrast to her two brothers, John and Charles, both educated at Christ's Hospital, Mary received little formal schooling, apart from a few years at a local day school. Apprenticed to a needlewoman, she was soon contributing to the family income as a mantua maker.

A voracious reader throughout life—a habit developed in childhood when she was granted free range of the library of her father's employer, Samuel Salt, a bencher of the Inner Temple—Mary Lamb also taught herself Latin, French, and Italian in her later years. After Salt's death in 1792 her parents were obliged to quit the Temple, and moved with their two younger children, Mary and Charles, to cramped and impoverished lodgings in 7 Little

Mary Anne Lamb (1764–1847), by Francis Stephen Cary, 1834 [with Charles Lamb]

Queen Street, Lincoln's Inn Fields. It was there, on 22 September 1796, that Mary Lamb, in a sudden and violent fit of insanity, killed her mother with a knife stab to the heart; the accumulated strain of nursing a senile father and a bedridden mother, while also maintaining the family through her needlework, had exacerbated a psychological disorder subsequently categorized by her brother's twentieth-century biographers as a manic-depressive illness. In 1796 the law allowed violent lunatics to be released into the care of their relatives, if sufficient surety was given that they would be cared for as potentially dangerous for the rest of their lives. This surety her brother Charles gave, thus saving his sister from incarceration in Bethlem Hospital; he acted against the wishes of the remaining members of the family. Subsequently Mary and Charles lived together until Charles's death in 1834; neither ever married, and their 'double singleness', as Charles described it, was interrupted only by Mary's periodic illnesses, which often necessitated her removal to private madhouses. But both made great efforts to maintain a cheerful and convivial domestic life, and in 1823 they adopted and successfully reared Emma Isola, an orphan of Italian extraction, who later married Charles Lamb's publisher, Edward Moxon.

In the winter of 1805–6, Mary Lamb was commissioned by Mary Jane *Godwin (the second wife of William Godwin), who had established a publishing venture concentrating on material for children, to write a prose version of Shakespeare's plays. When *Tales from Shakespear, Designed for the Use of Young Persons* was published in 1807, however, it appeared under Charles Lamb's name; not merely the gender prejudices of the period but more significantly, perhaps, her history, and the manner of her mother's death, probably left his sister disinclined to draw any public attention to herself. Charles had also contributed to the volume, writing its versions of the tragedies. They subsequently prepared together two further volumes for Mrs Godwin's Juvenile Library, *Mrs Leicester's School, or, The History of Several Young Ladies, Related by themselves* and *Poetry for Children, Entirely Original*, both of which were published anonymously in 1809. In each case, as with *Tales from Shakespear*, about two-thirds of the texts were Mary's work. Her books for children are marked by an unpretentious lucidity of style, and a capacity to enter into the point of view of her readers, also evident in her letters and in the one piece of writing for adults she published, the essay 'On needlework' contributed to the *British Lady's Magazine and Monthly Miscellany* (1 April 1815). In this essay, and in *Mrs Leicester's School*, she shows a particular concern for the well-being of disadvantaged women and girls. Her remonstrations on such issues as the lack of remunerative female employment, and the vulnerability of young women to social and parental pressures, show her attempting to spare others through her writing stresses she had herself experienced; some of her stories in *Mrs Leicester's School* clearly have an autobiographical content. Mary Lamb outlived her brother by a number of years, her last decades darkened by increasingly lengthy periods of insanity; she died at her home, 40 Alpha Road, in St John's Wood, London, on 20 May 1847, and was buried on 28 May in Charles Lamb's grave in Edmonton churchyard, Middlesex.

JANE AARON

Sources E. V. Lucas, *The life of Charles Lamb*, 2 vols. (1905) · C. A. Prance, *Companion to Charles Lamb: a guide to people and places, 1760–1847* (1983) · J. Aaron, *A double singleness: gender and the writings of Charles and Mary Lamb* (1991) · L. J. Friedman, 'Mary Lamb: sister, seamstress, murderer, writer', PhD diss., Stanford University, 1976 · W. F. Courtney, *Young Charles Lamb, 1775–1802* (1982) · *The letters of Charles Lamb: to which are added those of his sister, Mary Lamb*, ed. E. V. Lucas, 3 vols. (1935) · *The letters of Charles and Mary Lamb*, ed. E. W. Marrs, 3 vols. (1975–8) · d. cert.
Archives Harvard U. · Hunt. L., letters · Morgan L. · State University of New York, Buffalo, Lockwood Memorial Library · U. Texas | NYPL, Berg collection
Likenesses F. S. Cary, double portrait, oils, 1834 (with Charles Lamb), NPG [see illus.]
Wealth at death residue of annual income of £210

Lamb, Sir Matthew, first baronet (1705?–1768), politician and lawyer, was probably born in 1705, the second son of Matthew Lamb (d. 1735), an attorney of Southwell in Nottinghamshire and land agent to the Coke family of Melbourne, Derbyshire. His elder brother Robert (1702–1769) became dean of Peterborough in 1744 and bishop of Peterborough in 1764. It is likely that Matthew Lamb also had a sister for, in August 1738, a Miss Lamb, 'Sister of — Lamb of Lincoln's-Inn, Esq.' was married to Richard Middlemore (*GM*, 435).

Lamb was admitted to Lincoln's Inn on 26 January 1726 and called to the bar on 26 April 1733, having received his legal training from his uncle Peniston Lamb who was a successful pleader 'under the bar', that is, a conveyancing lawyer holding a position between that of an attorney and counsel. It was said of Peniston Lamb, who had himself been admitted to Lincoln's Inn in 1708, that he was skilled in 'pleading and demurring, weaving settlements and ravelling threads of adverse wills' (Torrens, 11). When Lamb's uncle died on 29 January 1735 he left him a fortune estimated at £100,000 as well as his chambers in Lincoln's Inn.

Through his uncle, the executor of the will and guardian of the children of John, second Earl Fitzwilliam, Lamb became land agent, legal adviser, and moneylender to many members of the aristocracy. The sums he lent were considerable. This is demonstrated by Sarah, first duchess of Marlborough's complaining that she and Lord Godolphin were not receiving their jointures because the third duke was paying interest to Lamb at the rate of no less than £9000 a year out of the trust estate (Rowse, 53). Lamb managed the financial affairs of Lord Holdernesse from 1739 to 1768 and in the latter year made him a loan of £6000 secured by a bond (BL, Egerton MS 3497, fols. 1–76, 121). He was also legal adviser to Lord Salisbury and Lord Egmont, and enriched himself at their expense. By way of explaining to a visitor to Brocket Hall how a right of fishing through part of the property, almost up to the park, belonged to Lord Salisbury, his grandson the second Viscount Melbourne said: 'Well, I believe that my grandfather did the Salisburys out of some land in that direction, and was generous enough to leave them the fishing' (Hayward, 332).

The intimate knowledge which Lamb possessed of the affairs of the aristocracy gave him an influence which he well knew how to wield, and upon whom. Therefore, when Robert Lamb was nominated to the see of Peterborough in 1764 he almost certainly owed that preferment to his younger brother's pressing his claims to the bishopric upon the duke of Newcastle. Lamb was appointed solicitor to the revenue of the Post Office in 1738. He also held the office of counsel to the Board of Trade and Plantations. However, a proposal in 1746 to appoint him king's counsel met with opposition from the legal profession because 'he never was an hour in Westminster Hall as a counsel in his life' (Polwarth MSS, 5.186). In August 1756 Lamb was appointed *custos rotulorum* for the liberty of Peterborough in the county of Northampton, gaining power thereby over appointments to the magistracy. Despite the earlier opposition to his appointment as king's counsel, he finally attained that dignity in 1754.

Lamb was returned to parliament for the constituency of Stockbridge in 1741, and in 1747 was elected to Peterborough, a seat which he managed in the Fitzwilliam interest until his death. He was created a baronet on 17 January 1755, perhaps through the intercession of the duke of Newcastle. About 1740 Lamb married Charlotte, daughter of the Right Honourable Thomas Coke, a privy councillor and vice-chamberlain to Queen Anne, and sister and heiress of George Lewis Coke. Through his marriage he acquired Melbourne Hall as a residence on George Coke's

unexpected death in 1751. He had already acquired Brocket Hall, Hertfordshire, by purchase from the representatives of Sir Thomas Winnington in 1746. Lamb and his wife had three children: Peniston (1745–1828), who succeeded to the baronetcy, and was created Lord (1770) and Viscount (1781) Melbourne in the Irish peerage and Lord Melbourne in the English peerage (1815); Charlotte, who married Henry, second Earl Fauconberg in 1766, and died in 1790; and Anne, who died unmarried in 1768. Lamb's grandson was William Lamb, second Viscount Melbourne (1779–1848).

In 1756 Lamb moved from Red Lion Square, London, an area inhabited by judges and senior counsel, to the more fashionable Sackville Street in Piccadilly. Before moving to Sackville Street he entered into abortive negotiations in 1754 with Lord Strafford for the purchase of a house in Albemarle Street which had been occupied by the late Lady Strafford. He died after a short illness on 5 November 1768 and was buried at Bishop's Hatfield, Hertfordshire. His will was proved in November 1768 when his property, half of which was in personalty, was valued at nearly £1 million.

ROGER TURNER

Sources BL, Add. MSS 35604, fol. 332; 32852, fol. 75; 32870, fol. 303; 32933, fol. 258 · BL, Add. MS 22254, fols. 58–60 · BL, Egerton MS 3497, fols. 1–76, 121 · HoP, *Commons, 1715–54*, 1.195–6 · GEC, *Baronetage*, 5.100 · W. M. Torrens, *Memoirs of the Right Honourable William, second Viscount Melbourne*, 2 vols. (1878), vol. 1, pp. 10–13 · A. Hayward, *Sketches of eminent statesmen and writers, with other essays*, 1 (1880), 331–2 · *Lord Melbourne's papers*, ed. L. C. Sanders (1889), 2 · A. L. Rowse, *The later Churchills* (1958), 53 · J. W. F. Hill, ed., *The letters and papers of the Banks family of Revesby Abbey, 1704–1760*, Lincoln RS, 45 (1952), 90 · *Report on the manuscripts of Lord Polwarth*, 5, HMC, 67 (1961), 186 · W. P. Baildon, ed., *The records of the Honorable Society of Lincoln's Inn: the black books*, 3 (1899), 302, 355–6 · *GM*, 1st ser., 8 (1738), 435 · *GM*, 1st ser., 8 (1738), 547 · *London Magazine*, 4 (1735), 99 · *Manuscripts of the earl of Egmont: diary of Viscount Percival, afterwards first earl of Egmont*, 3 vols., HMC, 63 (1920–23), vol. 1

Archives Herts. ALS, accounts · Melbourne Hall, Derbyshire, papers · NL Wales, papers | BL, Add. MSS 35604, fol. 332; 32721, fol. 21; 32852, fol. 78; 32870, fol. 303; 32933, fol. 258; 22254, fols. 58–60; 33573, fols. 355, 362, 366; 47014A, fol. 163 · BL, Egerton MSS 3497, fols. 1–76, 121; 3437, fol. 7; 3439, fols. 86, 90 · Sheff. Arch., corresp. with Countess Fitzwilliam

Likenesses R. Carriera, pastels, Melbourne Hall, Derbyshire · oils (after T. Hudson), Melbourne Hall, Derbyshire

Wealth at death approx. £1,000,000 of which one half was personalty: GEC, *Baronetage*

Lamb, Patrick (*c*.1650–1708/9), royal cook, was the second of seven children of Patrick Lambe (1613–*c*.1683) and Martha, *née* Russell (*d*. 1687), of the parish of St Martin-in-the-Fields, London. Lamb's father was involved in victualling and in 1660 held a crown warrant as the sole retailer of tobacco in the precincts of Whitehall. Lamb's own career in the royal household began in or before 1661, as an untitled servant in the pastry, one of the chief departments of the household below stairs. In March 1662 he was granted the lowest named rank in this office, youngest child of the pastry, a position he held until September 1671. In April 1672 he appears in the kitchen ledgers as a child of the queen consort's kitchen. The humble title belies an increasingly profitable position; he not only received boardwages, but was also eligible to collect those fees and perquisites due to his position.

In August 1677 Lamb was appointed as master cook to the queen consort, held in tandem with the office of sergeant of his majesty's pastry in ordinary, to which he was elevated in November 1677. Finally, in February 1683, Lamb attained the status of master cook to the monarch. He was reappointed to this post under the successive household regulations of James II, William and Mary, and Anne, and was removed from it only by death. His services as a royal cook encompassed the provision of prepared dishes for daily and extraordinary consumption by the monarch and his guests at table. He also undertook provisioning contracts for the pastry and kitchen departments of the household, supplying commodities such as flour, eggs, and condiments. Lamb appears to have continued to hold his father's privileges in purveying wine, spirits, and tobacco at the court, revealed in a royal warrant of January 1683.

Lamb's culinary skills were most effectively demonstrated in extraordinary events, and his claims for large expenditures on such occasions as the Westminster visit of the Venetian ambassadors in December 1685 testify to the splendour of these. Most spectacular of all were his arrangements for the coronation feasts of James II in 1685, William and Mary in 1689, and Anne in 1702, recorded in extensive detail in the lord steward's accounts for those years. The 1689 coronation cost £4931 to stage, and Lamb was presented with £100 for his pains in its planning.

These and other junkets are evoked in the text of *Royal Cookery*, published posthumously in London under Lamb's name by John Morphew and Abel Roper in 1710, and subsequently reprinted in 1716, 1726, and 1731. The text incorporated recipes for elaborate dishes alongside engravings of lavish table layouts for occasions such as royal suppers. Such details suggest that the text was drawn from Lamb's papers, rather than being speculatively published under his name as some contemporaries contended.

Lamb married Mary Froswell on 28 October 1672 at St Marylebone Church, Middlesex. The couple had at least four children: Patrick, William, Mulys, and Mary. It is not known precisely when or where Lamb died, but it was some time between 25 September 1708 and 28 February 1709, probably in London. His wife predeceased him. There is no surviving memorial to Lamb, who was unusual in being an English cook at a time when French cooks were pre-eminent within English aristocratic households. *Royal Cookery* is nevertheless a testament to his culinary talents.   S. M. PENNELL

Sources P. Lamb, *Royal cookery, or, The complete court cook, containing the choicest receipts in all the paricular branches of cookery … etc.* (1710) · Lord Steward's records, Charles II to Anne, PRO, LS 8–9, 13 · W. Bruce Bannerman, ed., *The registers of marriages of St Mary le bone, Middlesex*, 1, Harleian Society, 47 (1917) · H. F. Westlake and L. E. Tanner, eds., *The register of St Margaret's, Westminster, London, 1660–1675*, Harleian Society, register section, 64 (1935) · will, 21 July 1708, PRO, PROB 11/508, sig. 90 · will, 13 Feb 1686, LMA, AMP/PW 1687/32 [Martha Lamb, widow] · Establishment list, Queen Anne's household, 1702, BL, Add. MS 30232 · *Calendar of the manuscripts of the marquess of Ormonde*, new ser., 8 vols., HMC, 36 (1902–20), vol. 7, p. 339 ·

R. Smith, *Court cookery, or, The compleat English cook, containing the choicest and newest receipts, etc.* (1723) · inventory of Martha Lamb, widow, of Whitehall, 9 Dec 1687, LMA, AMP/P1(i), 1687/111 · G. E. Aylmer, *The king's servants: the civil service of Charles I, 1625–1642*, rev. edn (1974) · IGI

Archives PRO, Lord Steward's accounts, LS 8–9, 13

Wealth at death over £1500 in monetary bequests: will, PRO, PROB 11/508, sig. 90

Lamb, Thomas (*d.* 1686), linen draper and philanthropist, was for many years confused with a namesake, a soapboiler by trade: remarkably, both men were prominent General Baptists. The overwhelming evidence that they were not the same individual includes a petition subscribed in 1656 by two London Baptist congregations, each in fellowship with a different Thomas Lamb. The soapboiler was to stay with the Baptists for the rest of his life, but the linen draper soon abandoned them. This was neither his first nor his last change of judgement about the nature of the church.

We first hear of Lamb in 1641, when he was listed in the poll tax returns for London as a freeman of the Leathersellers' Company, trading at the premises of the liveryman leatherseller Henry Heald of Gracechurch Street. The following year he invested £50 in the Irish Adventurers; later, he was involved in exporting cloths to France and acquired interests in the excise farm. He was a member of the church gathered in the London parish of St Stephen's, Coleman Street, by John Goodwin. For some time, during the civil war, Lamb kept the company of William Walwyn. They sampled the wide range of sermons then available in London and debated the issues which now divided the parliamentarian camp. In matters both of church government and of civil politics the gathered, or 'independent', churches, and not least that of John Goodwin, were exerting great influence in London and aroused the hostility of the presbyterian ministers. But by 1646–7 there had crystallized a Leveller current, whose spokesmen, including and especially Walwyn, attacked the Independents from the left. Thomas Lamb was saddened by his criticism of Goodwin's writings, and the two men became estranged.

Lamb remained in the Coleman Street church and became one of its elders; in 1651 he composed one of the hymns of thanksgiving sung by the congregation after the battle of Worcester. This work is not of the highest poetic quality, but it is still of interest. At once pious, patriotic, and radical, Lamb rejoiced that God had frustrated the designs of the defeated royalist 'princes and great men':

> He crusht their rage and cruelty
> The proud which did advance;
> The wicked he hath now brought low,
> And trodden down their place …
> Oh ye sons, ye saints of God,
> What say you to this sight,
> Shall not the goodness of your God
> Be greatly your delight?
> (Goodwin, *Hymns*, 8–10)

Lamb formed a lasting friendship with another prominent member of Goodwin's church, the merchant William Allen (who must also be distinguished from a namesake, the adjutant-general). In 1653 Allen, influenced by the former clergyman and future Quaker Samuel Fisher, was converted to the cause of anti-paedobaptism. Thomas Lamb soon followed suit, and after briefly espousing mixed communion the two men led twenty of Goodwin's members out of his congregation. Despite protestations of mutual respect, an unbrotherly exchange of pamphlet-fire followed. Lamb's contribution was *Truth Prevailing Against the Fiercest Opposition* (1655), an attack upon Goodwin's *Water Dipping No Firm Footing for Church-Communion* (1653); other salvoes were released by Allen, a more dedicated and effective controversialist than his friend, and, for Goodwin, by John Price.

Lamb and Allen had shared in John Goodwin's Arminianism, and this helps explain why it was to the General Baptists that they now attached themselves. More was involved than a shift from one set of church ordinances to another. Goodwin's congregation was wealthy and sophisticated, and its former members seem initially to have sought fellowship with another which might match 'such means of Edification as they had left' (Sylvester, appx 3.51). This, however, could not be found, and a new congregation was gathered in Lothbury. Lamb and Allen were able to attend an intercongregational meeting of General Baptist churches in London, signing as elders its resolution, *The Humble Representation and Vindication* (1654). This document noted the religious freedom which the protectorate seemed to promise, and urged local churches not to be drawn into agitation against it. But Lamb's congregation was one of several which protested at the imprisonment in 1655 of John Biddle, whose unorthodox Christological views were attracting some General Baptists.

In 1656 a second intercongregational meeting passed a resolution condemning mixed marriages. Lamb did not sign this, perhaps partly because within the churches of his new faith there were few potential partners whose social position matched that of his unmarried daughters. But principles were also involved. Hostility to mixed marriages was part of a larger trend within General Baptism towards the erection of barriers between the saints and the profane world. Lamb was provoked to a wider questioning of the road he had chosen. He reread works by such men as Richard Baxter and his old pastor John Goodwin, and began to waver once more on the issue of baptism.

By 1658, Thomas Lamb had become deeply concerned about the whole basis of his religious communion. At this point his wife, Barbara, played a vital role—perhaps not for the first time, for John Goodwin charged that 'a female head' had engineered the schism of 1653 (J. Goodwin, *Triumveri*, 1658, preface, section 4). She certainly initiated the correspondence which led to the prodigal's return. On 12 August 1658 Barbara wrote secretly to Richard Baxter, revealing her husband's inner turmoil. Conversations with the presbyterian Thomas Manton and with the presbyterian and future bishop Edward Reynolds, she reported, had strengthened his growing sense that he had

been mistaken in opting for a narrow communion. Lamb could no longer keep silent about his doubts. As a result, the congregation which looked to him for leadership, now 120 strong, 'grow offended and disturbed' (Keeble and Nuttall, 1.325). Barbara Lamb grasped well the main lines of her husband's difficulties. In choosing Baxter as confidant, she also showed her understanding of the means to resolve them. Concern was growing at this time for a more settled accommodation between the godly of several persuasions. Richard Baxter was a veteran campaigner in this cause. When Lamb wrote to him in September, Baxter simply encouraged him to explore further the logic of his own development. Once more, William Allen seems to have travelled the same road as his friend, and the two may well have exerted reciprocal influence. Both men now found that they had erred in rejecting the operational significance for Christians of the concept of the universal church. Gently encouraged by Baxter, Lamb and Allen now began to canvas among their Baptist friends the merits of open communion with the unbaptized.

In the pursuit of this goal, Lamb's early candour undermined his credit with his church. For a while, his colleague William Allen was listened to with more sympathy, and they succeeded in involving other leading Baptists in discussions. But most members were unalterably opposed to opening their communion, and the larger drive towards accommodation with religious moderates foundered when the end of the protectorate brought to the radicals sweeping, if ephemeral, gains in influence. By January 1659 Lamb had already resumed his attendance at Goodwin's lectures. Acutely aware of the poverty of his congregation, he hesitated to abandon it, and vowed to stay until midsummer. But his authority in Lothbury was already fatally undermined. He was forced to listen to the 'Reproaches of my dear friends that pour contempt upon me daily, as a most dreadful Apostate, a Judas' (T. Lamb to R. Baxter, 15 Jan 1659, Sylvester, appx 3.64). The hostile reception accorded to his ideas probably deepened Lamb's estrangement from his church and its democratic habits, for he became 'clog'd with scruples about popular government' (ibid., 65). Half the congregation now boycotted his services, and steps were taken to subject him to disciplinary proceedings. In April Lamb resigned, and soon repudiated as schismatic not only his second baptism but also religious Independency itself: this, he now thought, was incorrigibly opposed to the universal church. By early July, reported William Allen, Lamb had begun to see as schismatic the Reformation itself; shortly after, he stayed with Baxter at Kidderminster, and it may be that the veteran controversialist was able to help his unstable visitor renew his confidence in the foundations of protestantism. (Baxter, however, explicitly stated that he was not responsible for the abandonment by Lamb and Allen of their belief in believers' baptism.)

After the Restoration, Lamb penned two books against the Independent religion, including *A Fresh Suit Against Independency* (1677), which was honest enough to recall his own youthful errors, and which paid tribute to his friend

William Allen, now dead. He was probably resident, during these years, at a house, mentioned in his will, at St Bartholomew's Close; it was from St Bartholomew-the-Great that Barbara Lamb had appealed to Baxter. The 'Mr Lamb of Bell Alley, Coleman Street' listed in 1677 as a London merchant may very well be our man, since our main source for his later life is Richard Lucas, vicar of Coleman Street. The reference is probably to Lamb's business address. He must certainly have prospered in his trade, for he was elected master of the Leathersellers' Company in 1673–4. Many years before, the impoverishment of his Baptist brethren had troubled Lamb's conscience. Troubling memories and present prosperity may each have sharpened his awareness of poverty. At any rate, philanthropy became his consuming interest: 'continually thronged by flocks' of impoverished clients, 'several hundred prisoners, were by him, with great travail and expense set free' (Lucas, 20, 19). So recalled Lucas, who preached the sermon at Lamb's funeral on 23 July 1686, dedicating the published account to his eldest son, John Lamb (1649/50–1708), the vicar of Wheathampstead, Hertfordshire. Barbara Lamb, 'an extraordinary intelligent woman' as Richard Baxter remembered her (Keeble and Nuttall, 1.323), had died, probably shortly before her husband.   STEPHEN WRIGHT

William Lamb, second Viscount Melbourne (1779–1848), by John Partridge, 1844

Sources DWL, Baxter correspondence, 6 vols. · *Calendar of the correspondence of Richard Baxter*, ed. N. H. Keeble and G. F. Nuttall, 1 (1991) · *Calendar of the correspondence of Richard Baxter*, ed. N. H. Keeble and G. F. Nuttall, 2 (1991) · *Reliquiae Baxterianae, or, Mr Richard Baxter's narrative of the most memorable passages of his life and times*, ed. M. Sylvester, 1 vol. in 3 pts (1696), pt 3, appx 3–4, pp. 51–67 · M. Tolmie, 'Thomas Lambe, soapboiler, and Thomas Lambe, merchant, General Baptists', *Baptist Quarterly*, 27 (1977–8), 4–13 · W. Walwyn, *Walwyn's Just defence* (1649); repr. in W. Haller and G. Davies, eds., *The Leveller tracts, 1647–1653* (1944), 350–98, esp. 355–6, 374, 391–2, 396 · E. S. More, 'Congregationalism and the social order: John Goodwin's gathered church, 1640–60', *Journal of Ecclesiastical History*, 38 (1987), 210–35 · R. Baxter, *Mr Baxter's review of the state of Christian infants* (1676) · K. S. Bottigheimer, *English money and Irish land* (1971) · R. Lucas, *A sermon preacht at the funeral of Mr. Thomas Lamb 23 July 1686* (1686) · G. F. Nuttall, 'Thomas Lambe, William Allen and Richard Baxter: an additional note', *Baptist Quarterly*, 27 (1977–8), 139–40 · J. Goodwin, *Philadelphia, or, XL. queries* (1653) · J. Goodwin, *Water-dipping no firm footing* (1653) · J. Goodwin, *Two hymns, or spiritual songs sung in Mr Goodwins congregation* (1651) · W. A. [W. Allen], *An answer to Mr J. G. his XL queries* (1653) · T. Lamb, *Absolute freedom from sin* (1656) [soapboiler] · T. Lamb, *Truth prevailing against the fiercest opposition* (1655) [merchant] · [T. Lamb], *A fresh suit against Independency* (1677) · T. C. Dale, 'The members of the City companies in 1641 as set forth in the return of the poll tax', 1935, U. Lond., Institute of Historical Research [based on poll tax returns in PRO] · *A collection of the names of the merchants of London* (1677) [unpaginated] · W. H. Black, *History and antiquities of the Worshipful Company of Leathersellers, of the City of London* (privately printed, London, 1871), 67 · will, GL, MS 9171/40, fol. 150v [Thomas Lamb]
Archives DWL, Baxter correspondence

Lamb, William, second Viscount Melbourne (1779–1848), prime minister, was born in London on 15 March 1779 at Melbourne House, Piccadilly (later divided into the apartments known as the Albany), in law the second child of Peniston Lamb (1745–1828), a substantial landowner in Derbyshire and Hertfordshire, for many years an MP of no

distinction, and from 1770 an Irish peer as first Baron Melbourne (Viscount Melbourne from 1781). His mother was Elizabeth (1752?–1818), only daughter of Sir Ralph Milbanke, bt, of Halnaby, Yorkshire, but owing to the desuetude of her marriage his true father was widely held to be anyone but Lord Melbourne; contemporary suspicion rested on the fabulous aesthete Lord Egremont [see Wyndham, George O'Brien, third earl of Egremont]. Only the eldest son, Peniston, had a sound claim to legitimacy; there followed after William two brothers, Frederick (Fred) James *Lamb (later first Baron Beauvale) and George *Lamb (MP for Westminster), and two sisters, Emily, successively Lady Cowper and Lady Palmerston [see Temple, Emily], and the short-lived Harriet.

Lamb was born into a family of no great fame or antiquity, but into a social circle of high-pitched wit, wealth, and rather febrile emotion. His father was coarse and neglectful and hugged the background, often in retreat at Melbourne Hall in Derbyshire. Lady Melbourne, in contrast, was a jewel of high whig society, admired for her hospitality at Melbourne House, her great charm, and forcefulness of character. Beneath the surface of verve and cheerful self-confidence, however, lay a current of hardness and sadness, derived perhaps from the personal sacrifices that had been necessary to make her way in society without the aid of her husband. She worked hard to cultivate and promote her sons. Already in 1785 the little Lambs were well publicized by Reynolds's portrait of Peniston, William, and Fred, engraved as *The Affectionate Brothers*. Peniston was an early disappointment to Lady

Melbourne, taking after his father and inclining to sensual pleasures and the turf, so her hopes rested increasingly on William. He was entered at Eton College in November 1788, a spoilt and bookish child, in love with his mama and with Shakespeare. Yet a certain poise was already evident and he escaped the worse bullying to become a social success. At Trinity College, Cambridge, where he arrived in October 1796, he ran with the fastest crowd, but to his mother's delight showed more real enthusiasm for Rousseau and poetry than for fools and horses. His prize declamation, 'The progressive improvements of mankind', attracted Charles James Fox's attention and was commended by him in the House of Commons.

After taking his degree in July 1799, Lamb was sent with his brother Fred to Scotland to study for a few terms with the Glasgow *lumière* John Millar. This course of treatment did not have the desired effect, in that Lamb's intellectual development never leaned towards the kind of social, political, and metaphysical speculation for which the Scottish Enlightenment was famed; he preferred the classics, history, literature, and religious speculation only at a distance (Tudor and Stuart controversies were a favourite). He found Millar's Francophilia to be slightly ridiculous and, in the political circumstances of the time, even dangerous. He began to question some of his inherited whig opinions.

The whig, 1800–1815 Yet on entering 'the World' after his return from Scotland, Lamb quickly became a darling of whig society. Physically he presented a commanding figure, tall and conventionally good-looking, with masses of curling hair and dark, beetling brows. His wide reading and keen perception made him a brilliant conversationalist, especially popular with the ladies of the Devonshire House set. Unusually in the fast crowd with which he still ran, he abstained from the crudest sexual importuning and preferred the pleasures of flirtation and gourmandizing. His mother's only anxiety was for his growing tendency to inactivity and introspection.

This tendency she was not able to halt by finding Lamb profitable occupation. He had been entered at Lincoln's Inn in July 1797, so as to keep his terms concurrently with Cambridge, but was called to the bar only at Michaelmas 1804. After a single brief on the northern circuit the death of his elder brother, Peniston, on 24 January 1805 required him to consider an occupation better suited to a future peer. With glee Lady Melbourne prepared for him a glorious career in politics. He joined Brooks's Club in April with Fox as his sponsor, and in January 1806 was brought into parliament for Leominster in the place of his friend Arthur Kinnaird. Too much the débutant to win a place in the 'ministry of all the talents', he was nevertheless asked by Lord Howick to move the address in December 1806; it was his maiden speech. His whig patrons moved him to the Haddington burghs in the election of 1806 and to Portarlington in 1807. Thereafter he remained a promising young man for several years, making occasionally effective interventions in debate but displaying little zeal or talent for oratory. Both his indecisiveness and his political

scepticism were showing. He had little taste for the rhetorical excesses of opposition and, though he generally voted with the whigs because he found loyalty the easiest option, at heart he shared ministers' anxieties about outdoor agitation and their desire to prosecute war with Napoleon to the utmost.

Lamb's political difficulties were compounded in these years by romantic difficulties of a spectacular kind. His marriage on 3 June 1805 to Lady Caroline Ponsonby (1785–1828) [*see* Lamb, Lady Caroline], daughter of his Devonshire House friend Lady Bessborough, had only exacerbated his latent psychological conflicts. The two were never able to establish a normal family life. After a miscarriage in January 1806, in August 1807 Caroline bore a son, Augustus, who was prone to convulsions and developmentally retarded, and then a daughter in January 1809 who died after a few days. No further pregnancies ensued, but subsequently a number of shadowy 'adopted' children appeared for brief periods in the Lambs' household. Even had these efforts to rear a family not proved abortive, William and Caroline might not have made a happy couple. His firmness and confidence were too superficial to provide the constant attention and discipline that her flights of fancy, even lunacy, seemed to require. Within a few years of marriage she had launched into a series of public liaisons, most disastrously with the poet Lord Byron in 1812–13. Byron's repudiation of her led to a theatrical suicide attempt at Lady Heathcote's ball in July 1813, after which her grip on sanity, never firm, loosened progressively. Posterity remains divided in assigning the blame for this disaster: William's indecisiveness, Caroline's erratic behaviour, the Lamb family's hostility, and Byron's callousness all played a role. But certainly William's inability to grapple with Caroline's problems led to the long, drawn-out dénouement; no formal separation was arranged until 1825, after which date Caroline lived alone at the Lamb country houses, Brocket and Melbourne.

It seems reasonable to see Lamb's private disappointments as contributing to his deepening political disappointments, that is, both his failure to shine as a House of Commons man and his disillusionment with whig idealism. Always prone to scepticism and detachment, he was now more than ever reluctant to commit himself to great causes or to reveal what deep feelings he did hold. During Perceval's ministry he showed signs of supporting Canning's line in foreign policy and the conduct of the Peninsular campaign, but he declined disdainfully the minor office offered to him by Perceval in early 1812. He seemed hardly bothered by the loss of his seat at the general election of that year, a sentiment shared by Brougham, who regarded him as little short of a tory.

The Canningite, 1815–1830 Lamb did not think much of Canning personally but he was drawn inexorably to his centrist politics, without either whig rhetoric or tory bigotry. Social considerations made it easier for him to distance himself from the whigs. Lamb had become friendly with J. W. Ward, and he admired greatly William Huskisson; by 1816 his beloved sister, Emily, though married to

Lord Cowper, had become the acknowledged lover of the Canningite Lord Palmerston. The death of Lady Melbourne in 1818 removed another obstacle. Consequently when he returned to parliament in April 1816, brought in for Peterborough by Lord Fitzwilliam, he insisted on taking an independent line, reaffirming to Lord Holland his commitment to the whig principles of 1688 but not to 'a heap of modern additions, interpolations, facts and fictions' (Ziegler, 70). He spoke against parliamentary reform and for a firm response to domestic sedition, serving on the secret committee to consider civil disorder in February 1817 and voting subsequently to suspend habeas corpus. He took equivocal positions on Peterloo and the Queen Caroline affair.

And yet the role of hanger-on to a centrist leader-in-waiting was hardly one to set the political juices flowing. In 1819 Lamb accepted a more dignified constituency, the county of Hertfordshire, but did little with it, and when faced with whig opposition at the 1826 election he simply withdrew. Thus when Canning's moment finally arrived, upon Lord Liverpool's death in April 1827, Lamb had to be found a ministerial borough—briefly Newport, then Bletchingley—in order to qualify for office. That office was the pivotal chief secretaryship of Ireland, which he won not by dint of administrative merit or knowledge of Ireland but because his whig connections and known sympathies for the Catholic claims secured for Canning crucial whig votes.

Lamb was surprisingly successful as chief secretary, an office he continued to hold after Canning's death in the Goderich and Wellington ministries. He found some resolution to his political contradictions in a style that was superficially liberal and tolerant, and particularly alive to the importance of symbolic nuance in influencing public opinion, but was scornful of legislative reforms and favoured a strong, deflating, disciplinary response to extra-parliamentary agitation. He supported Catholic emancipation without believing it would improve the condition of the Irish people one whit, and he won popularity among Catholic eminences by appearing sympathetic and open-minded without pursuing any particular line of reform.

Fortuitously, Lamb found a similar resolution in his private life. Liberated by his separation from Caroline, he embarked on a liaison with the Dublin hostess Elizabeth La Touche, Lady Branden, in the autumn of 1827, probably a sexual attachment, certainly a deeply affectionate one that persisted at a distance after his departure from Dublin in 1828. Less demanding than Caroline, Lady Branden could appeal in moderation to both sides of Lamb's character—his pose of cool detachment and his well of feeling. As Philip Ziegler's biography reveals, a game of male chastisement of female misbehaviour featured in their correspondence. This relationship was not much affected by Lamb's citation as co-respondent in Lord Branden's divorce suit of May 1828, which was dismissed for lack of evidence after Lamb paid Branden off.

Despite his personal opposition to parliamentary reform, Lamb resigned from office with his fellow Huskissonites in May 1828 over the disposition of East Retford's disfranchised seats. Huskisson's inheritance of the moderate leadership from Canning had helped to cement Lamb's loyalties there, as had Emily's unfolding role as a Huskissonite hostess at Panshanger, near Lamb's country house at Brocket in Hertfordshire. Particularly after Caroline's death in January 1828 made Brocket once more safe to approach, Lamb spent more and more of his time there and at Panshanger. His father's death in July 1828 also cleared the occupancy of Melbourne Hall, and further freed him from House of Commons responsibilities, as Lamb inherited the English peerage his father had added to his Irish titles in 1815. Henceforward he was known as Viscount Melbourne and sat in the Lords. As such, the vicissitudes of politics would catapult him into an unlikely role as a leader not only of the whig party but of whig government.

Home secretary, 1830–1834 The Canningites were again in a powerful position when, after the 1830 general election and Wellington's resignation in November, they provided the key votes in the construction of a whig majority. Melbourne was one of the 'three viscounts' of the Canning party—the others were Palmerston and Goderich—who monopolized the secretaryships of state in Lord Grey's new government. Huskisson's sudden death in a railway accident thrust Palmerston into a position of leadership, and he secured for himself the Foreign Office and for his lover's brother the Home Office. This latter appointment surprised many people and shocked many whigs, who did not rate either Melbourne's administrative abilities or his party fidelity. Yet again Melbourne confounded the doubters. As with his Irish appointment, Melbourne's combination of superficial sympathy and firm disciplinary handling proved useful to a precarious reforming government seeking both to flatter public opinion and to reassure the forces of order by a firm administration of the law.

Melbourne took little interest in the great parliamentary business of the Grey government. Never a principled believer in parliamentary reform, he accepted the argument that it was necessary to restore popular confidence in government and even acted as some slight restraint on Palmerston's efforts to dilute the government's bill. He spoke only briefly in the Lords' debates on the measures. In social reforms that might be thought to come within the Home Office's ambit, he took little more part. He sat on the cabinet committee that framed the new poor law but hardly contributed to its deliberations. That business, as well as legislation to limit the hours of factory labour, he left to Althorp, Brougham, and teams of commissioners nominally working under his supervision. He did not care even to hear about the living and working conditions of the poor, believing them to be part of the natural order of things and certainly irremediable by legislation. 'The whole duty of government', he pronounced, 'is to prevent and punish crime, and to preserve contracts' (Cecil, 305). But he accepted with equanimity his colleagues' assurances that positive legislation was necessary to secure the acquiescence of the governed.

Against breaches of the law, however, Melbourne acted

both vigorously and sensitively, and it was for this function that his reforming brethren thanked him heartily. In dealing with the Swing riots of 1830–31 he checked tory magistrates' alarmism and was reluctant to resort to the army or even the yeomanry, but urged magistrates to use fully their ordinary powers, augmented by special constables and large bounties on the arrest of rioters and incendiaries. He appointed a special commission to try about a thousand of those arrested, but ensured that strict justice was adhered to—a third of those tried were acquitted, and although a fifth were sentenced to death most of the sentences were commuted to transportation. The same balancing act was carried off in dealing with the reform disturbances of 1831–2. Melbourne rebuffed calls for extraordinary measures, such as the extensive employment of spies, but used existing powers of prosecution and regulated assemblies rigorously.

Melbourne's antipathy to new legislation did not wholly apply to questions of public order. He considered various ways of systematically improving police and punishment. One of his first acts in office was to appoint the political economist Nassau Senior to inquire into the legality of industrial combinations, but in the end he rejected Senior's recommendation for a more severe repression of such combinations. Trade unions, he felt, were unreasonable and absurd, contrary to the law of nature but not susceptible to the law of humans. He told manufacturers that 'the Government would repress violence and punish crime', but that as for combinations, 'nothing will open the eyes of the working people, but the blowing out of forges, the stopping of mills, and the leaving the men … to indigence and beggary' (UCL, Brougham MSS 43498). However, in one famous case—that of the 'Dorchester labourers', or *Tolpuddle Martyrs—he did not entirely follow his own advice. He allowed tory magistrates to prosecute six agricultural trade unionists to such an extent as to arouse a massive protest movement, and left it to his successor, Lord John Russell, to calm the waters by commuting sentences. More positively, Melbourne devised in 1832 a bill that would have extended London's system of a stipendiary magistracy and police force to the provinces. Although this bill was never introduced—it was overshadowed first by the Reform Bill and later by poor-law reform—it shows that Melbourne was willing and able to grasp the nettle of administrative reform where matters close to his heart were touched.

Melbourne did not always win the credit he deserved for his firm hand on the helm. In September 1831 Grey sought to replace him on grounds of indolence. Holland successfully parried the accusation, maintaining that 'a dislike to meddling legislation and his careless nonchalant Manner might give him the character of an indolent man with the inobservant, but those who had business with the office did not find him so' (H. R. V. Holland, *The Holland House Diaries, 1831–1840*, ed A. D. Kriegel, 1977, 48). Melbourne had only himself to blame for such scrapes. The lazy manner he had devised to indulge his sense of fun and at the same time disguise his vulnerabilities was ill suited to a senior statesman. He received deputations with every appearance of cool carelessness. He surrounded himself with like-minded cronies, notably his brother George (who served as under-secretary at the Home Office until his death in early 1834) and his private secretary, Tom Young, sometime purser on the duke of Devonshire's yacht. In cabinet and in society he pretended to know and care far less than he did. These traits grew more pronounced as he aged. What had in his youth been viewed as stylish insouciance now came to appear more eccentric. Strangers could be alarmed by his habits: barking out imprecations, rubbing his hands gleefully at some private joke, audibly muttering to himself while by-standing in the Lords, occasionally weeping silently when mysteriously touched by some happenstance.

Nevertheless, Melbourne had by this stage achieved a happiness that had escaped him earlier. He had won the prominence that he had always felt to be his desert. He no longer allowed himself to be hurt or spurned or disappointed. And in 1831 he found a substitute for Lady Branden in Caroline Norton (1808–1877), granddaughter of his hero Sheridan and wife of an abusive husband. This relationship followed roughly the pattern of its predecessor; it is less likely to have been sexual, but it provided Melbourne with the same emotional reassurance, while allowing him to play mild games of hot-and-cold flirtation and discipline. It, too, led to a brush with the law. George Norton cited Melbourne as co-respondent in 1836 and, unlike the Branden affair, this one had its day in court. Acquittal was never in doubt, but Melbourne was bruised by the public exposure and his ardour for Mrs Norton cooled with what she felt to be indecent suddenness. He was soon engaged in the lists with Lady Stanhope, apparently a former mistress of his brother Fred.

Prime minister, 1834–1841 It was precisely Melbourne's lack of commitment on the major issues of the day that led to his premiership, when Lord Grey resigned in a huff over Irish affairs in July 1834. His doubts about reform reassured the king and the conservative sections of the whig majority, and yet his acquiescence to the lead then being taken on Irish tithe reform by Lord John Russell secured the support of the forward party. Furthermore, like Grey, he had the authority to play the honest broker among his fractious colleagues; he was, thought Durham, 'the only one of whom none of us would be jealous' (Ziegler, 169). Greville claimed that Melbourne's languor nearly overcame his ambition on this occasion, but that he was persuaded to take the premiership by Tom Young: 'Why, damn it, such a position never was occupied by any Greek or Roman, and, if it only lasts two months, it is well worth while to have been Prime Minister of England'. 'By God that's true', Melbourne is said to have replied, 'I'll go' (*Greville Memoirs*, 3.76).

Yet Melbourne did not show much enthusiasm for the job, declining to move into Downing Street and lingering at Lady Holland's dinner table as late as ever. When, in October, Althorp resigned on the inheritance of his peerage and the king took advantage of the moment to dismiss the government, Melbourne was accused by Brougham and the radicals of giving up office too easily. He then left to Duncannon the business of organizing whig candidates for the ensuing general election, and to Duncannon and Russell the strategy for the new session of parliament. He agreed to employ his personal authority to persuade James Abercromby to contest the speakership and allowed Russell to make Irish tithe appropriation the point of principle on which the tory government was to be challenged, but kept aloof from the Lichfield House compact of 18 February 1835 by which Irish and radical votes were secured for these causes. He was not, therefore, the architect of his own return to the premiership in April 1835.

Melbourne was not much more the architect of the new government. On one point, the exclusion of Durham and Brougham—who had offended him on personal as well as political grounds—he was insistent. But otherwise much of the running in the appointment of ministers and the determination of policy was to be made by Russell, and in foreign affairs by Palmerston. Melbourne's principal task, as before, was to mediate between different sections of the party. He continued to feel that the maintenance of the whigs in power was necessary to cement the people's affections to government, but he had no personal enthusiasm for specific legislative objectives. His task was paradoxically made somewhat easier by the small size of the majority (smaller still after the 1837 election), which to some extent cowed the radicals. In the Lords, where he and the equally lukewarm Lansdowne presided, it was a matter simply of accepting gracefully repeated tory vetoes, particularly on Irish tithes and corporations. As in 1834 this exposed him to accusations of insufficient zeal, on occasions almost treachery, but his critics knew that Russell held the real power in the Commons and that a more pushful premier would hardly have had better luck with the Lords. On a few issues, such as English municipal reform, Melbourne's influence may have been crucial in persuading the tories not to obstruct.

Though he took no lead in policy, in other respects Melbourne was a worthy premier. As Greville observed, he was 'a gentleman, liberal and straightforward, with no meanness, and incapable of selfish trickery and intrigue' (*Greville Memoirs*, 3.118). He kept order in cabinet and handled some fragile egos with frank good humour. He took his patronage responsibilities seriously and was fairly meritocratic, though he deluded himself in thinking Lord Lichfield one of the ablest as well as one of the pleasantest men in England. His bold appointment in 1836 of the heterodox R. D. Hampden to the regius professorship of divinity at Oxford aroused a storm of controversy, against which Melbourne persisted, but his ecclesiastical appointments were thereafter less adventurous. In foreign affairs he mediated capably between cabinet Francophiles such as Lord Holland and the irrepressibly aggressive Lord Palmerston.

After the 1837 election, which again reduced the whig majority, Melbourne's level of political activity dwindled further. Russell handled most of the complicated negotiations necessary to retain the support of the radicals. The central issues of domestic policy—Irish and English poor laws, the penny post, education—held no appeal for Melbourne and were also delegated to Russell. He had a little more appetite for some contentious issues that arose in colonial policy. The rehabilitation of Lord Durham, appointed governor-in-chief of British North America in January 1838, was an imaginative move—a radical sent to suppress rebellion and at the same time lay the foundation for self-government—although it foundered finally on the bad personal relations subsisting between governor and premier. On Canada and also on Jamaica, Melbourne had cause to criticize his colonial secretary, Lord Glenelg, but personal loyalty to this old Canningite caused him to stave off calls for his resignation until early 1839, when he finally accepted Glenelg's replacement, first by Lord Normanby and then by Lord John Russell.

The courtier, 1837–1841 Aside from habitual inclination, the principal reason for Melbourne's progressive disengagement from politics after 1837 was his involvement in a new romance, one peculiarly justifiable as in the line of duty. The object of his affections was the young Queen Victoria. She came to the throne in June 1837, aged eighteen and unmarried, and immediately latched onto Melbourne as a mentor preferable to her domineering mother, the duchess of Kent. Melbourne, for his part, was lonely. He had been hurt by the Norton fiasco of 1836 and also, in a different way, by the death of his invalid son, Augustus, in November of the same year. He now recognized the potential for the most satisfying relationship of his life. As her subject (and a sixty-year-old one, at that) flirtation with Victoria was not in question. But he could expose all of his foibles—his loose talk, his cynicism, his odd mannerisms, indeed his occasional outbursts of naked emotion—without fear of reproof or ridicule from a devoted young woman, while simultaneously doing his duty as man and statesman by tutoring her in society and politics. For her part, she could depend on him totally without impropriety, and yet by virtue of her status and her own strong will never quite appear dependent or lose the power to command. Melbourne liked both her dependence and her authority: she was Caroline within safe bounds.

Most of the attention lavished on their relationship has necessarily focused on its impact upon the monarch—her education and character formation. Its impact upon Melbourne was greatly to increase his happiness and also to limit further his political effectiveness. Riddance of William IV, who had carped at and quarrelled with Melbourne incessantly, would have benefited any premier. But only this one would have wasted the time gained—and more—in *causerie* with the queen. He acted as her private secretary and had his own bedroom at Windsor.

In 1839 this excessive intimacy got Melbourne into two bad scrapes. Early in the year, Victoria developed the idea that two of her *bêtes noires* at court—her mother's agent, Sir John Conroy, and a tory lady-in-waiting, Lady Flora Hastings—were romantically involved. When Lady Flora began to display signs of illness and a distended stomach, this idea budded into the notion of an illicit pregnancy. Melbourne's idle chatter encouraged this notion and at first he did nothing to ascertain its truthfulness. Rumour was allowed to fester and ultimately Lady Flora was submitted to a humiliating examination by the queen's doctor, Sir James Clark. Her relatives and their political allies generated much righteous indignation. Melbourne was made to seem cruelly partisan and manipulative. The affair flared up again when Lady Flora died in July—a post-mortem revealed the 'pregnancy' to be an enormous liver tumour—and both premier and queen were heckled in public.

By then, however, their relationship had already plunged Melbourne into a second, more severe crisis. On 6 May enough radicals had voted against the government in a division on the government of Jamaica to bring their majority down to five. Melbourne and Russell agreed that resignation was the only recourse. Victoria was appalled. 'All, ALL my happiness gone', she keened to her journal. 'That happy peaceful life destroyed, that dearest kind Lord Melbourne no more my minister' (Ziegler, 273). Again Melbourne indulged the queen in her partisanship. He encouraged her to think she could keep her whig ladies-in-waiting and, perhaps inadvertently, gave her courage to rebuff Peel's and Wellington's requests on the composition of her court. His partiality was to the queen rather than to office; he had to be pressed by the cabinet to make a political point of the queen's wishes. The upshot of this 'bedchamber' crisis was that the whigs were kept in office. 'I will not abandon my Sovereign in a situation of difficulty and distress', Melbourne told the Lords on 14 May. Again it appeared that the elderly subject was unchivalrously manipulating the young monarch for personal gain. The radicals were brought back into line by the minor concession of a free vote on the ballot—it lost comfortably—and the government carried on, as it might have done anyway, had Melbourne not resigned in the first place. Further damage from this anomalous situation was prevented by arrangements for the queen's marriage to her cousin, Albert of Saxe-Coburg and Gotha.

The loss of intimacy this marriage entailed deprived Melbourne of his last compelling reason to remain in office. Yet the circumstances of his departure were no more under his control than had been his arrival. After dealing with the royal marriage his main preoccupation in 1840 was the old one of mediating between Palmerston and Holland over relations with France. Palmerston had become the premier's brother-in-law in December 1839, when he had finally been able to wed his lover, Emily, upon Lord Cowper's demise. He was now insisting on a check to French pretensions in the Middle East, where France's client Mehmet Ali was undermining the integrity of the Ottoman empire. The threat of war with France hung over the cabinet all summer and into the autumn. Ultimately war was averted and still Mehmet Ali was contained—a victory for Palmerston's sabre-rattling policy, though some said also for Melbourne's quiet diplomacy within the cabinet and with the French.

At the start of 1841 Russell and the more committed whigs proposed a partial embrace of the anti-cornlaw issue as a device, if not to avert loss of office, at least to leave office on a point of liberal principle. Cabinet discussions over the 1841 budget were heated and divided over whether and how much to reduce the corn duties. The story goes that after the climactic meeting in March, Melbourne stopped his departing colleagues to ask:

> By the bye, there is one thing we haven't agreed upon, which is, what we are to say. Is it to make our corn dearer or cheaper, or to make the price steady? I don't care which: but we had better all be in the same story. (Walpole, 1.369)

True or not, the anecdote reproduces accurately Melbourne's attitude at the time; in principle opposed to reducing protection, he was in practice willing to accept his cabinet's judgement on matters of political necessity. Russell hoped to be beaten on the corn duties and to go to the country on the issue, but before it was broached Peel won a vote of no confidence on the reduction of duties on sugar. At this stage (4 June) Melbourne wanted to resign, but his colleagues were keen to have their election and forced him to dissolve parliament instead. To Melbourne's great relief, the government lost its majority in the ensuing election and he resigned at the end of August. Maintaining his reputation for probity to the end, he declined the queen's pressing offer of the Garter.

Retreat and retrospect, 1841–1848 Melbourne confessed to the queen that he had aged greatly during his last year in office. Freedom from responsibility lightened his step somewhat, though he missed his frequent meetings with the queen and regretted her new absorption in her husband. He made few moves actively to oppose Peel's government, but neither did Russell. He spent more time with the Palmerstons and resumed more frequent contact with Mrs Norton. But his temper was shorter and his manners in public more abrupt; he began finally to lose his good looks (hitherto retained despite a certain middle-aged portliness) and his sensual appearance of indulgence and self-indulgence. Then in October 1842 he was brought down by a stroke which paralysed the left side of his body. Recovery was only partial, and thereafter he was increasingly confined to Brocket, where he was cared for by his brother Fred (now Lord Beauvale) and his sister-in-law, Adine.

Whig opposition revived gradually but Melbourne was not a participant. Yet when it looked for a moment in December 1845 as if Russell might be able to form a government, some people imagined that Melbourne might return, if only in a decorative role. Melbourne ruled himself out on the grounds that he was unsympathetic to repeal of the corn laws, but this was merely a graceful excuse. He was by now making only rare forays from home and, after a series of seizures, he died at Brocket on 24 November 1848, some months short of his seventieth birthday. He was buried in the family vault at Hatfield, near Brocket.

Melbourne has always been more interesting to posterity as a psychological than as a political study. Able to view him safely as the product of a bygone age, even earnest Victorians retailed with relish anecdotes of his incredible carelessness and cynicism, and of his relations with Caroline, Mrs Norton, and Victoria. Many of these stories derive from Greville, who was perhaps inclined to exaggerate Melbourne's illiberalism, owing to Greville's own politics and his friendship with Melbourne's half-tory brother Fred. The general impression of political frivolousness and sexual peccadillo was then greatly reinforced by Lord David Cecil's brilliant two-volume biography (1939, 1954). In particular the first volume, *The Young Melbourne*, with its panoptic prologue on Regency high society, 'The World', gave a seductive portrait of aristocratic wit and sensuality before the dark Victorian night set in that appealed greatly to both dandies and moderns.

Cecil's view was that Melbourne was psychologically complex but politically simple, an aristocratic amateur, and thus in the 'industrial age' a political anachronism. Little evidence was presented to complicate this portrait until Philip Ziegler's more detailed, more accurate, and better-documented political biography of 1976. Ziegler accepted much of Cecil's psychologizing—and added new evidence relating to Lady Branden—but hotly disputed the political conclusion, arguing that Melbourne's diplomatic and tactical skills were crucial to keeping together the whig cabinets of the 1830s and holding the middle ground between toryism and radicalism. Ziegler's revision has been supported to some extent; certainly Melbourne's aristocratic background is no longer viewed as a handicap. But Melbourne had no part in the new moral, economic, and religious thinking that allowed other aristocrats—including his fellow Canningites, even Palmerston—to refurbish their image as governors for a wider audience and to deal with modern problems of legislation. His peculiar noncommittal style was unique. It did allow him to play political umpire and serve as a reassuring anchor of integrity in the troubled seas of reform. But the limits to this role are underscored by L. G. Mitchell in his biography *Lord Melbourne* (1997), which returns to the social and psychological ground broken by David Cecil. Future biographies may well follow in Cecil's and Mitchell's path, for whatever depths William Lamb may still be hiding from us are probably more of private than of public import.   PETER MANDLER

Sources P. Ziegler, *Melbourne* (1976) · D. Cecil, *Melbourne* (1965) · L. G. Mitchell, *Lord Melbourne, 1779–1848* (1997) · W. M. Torrens, *Memoirs of the Right Honourable William, second Viscount Melbourne*, 2 vols. (1878) · *Lord Melbourne's papers*, ed. L. C. Sanders (1889) · K. Bourne, *Palmerston: the early years, 1784–1841* (1982) · J. M. Prest, *Lord John Russell* (1972) · HoP, *Commons* · E. Jenkins, *Lady Caroline Lamb* (1932) · I. Newbould, *Whiggery and reform, 1830–41* (1990) · P. Mandler, *Aristocratic government in the age of reform: whigs and liberals, 1830–1852* (1990) · *The Greville memoirs, 1814–1860*, ed. L. Strachey and R. Fulford, 8 vols. (1938) · *Hansard* · U. Southampton L., Broadlands MSS · UCL, Brougham MSS · A. H. Graham, 'The Lichfield House Compact, 1835', *Irish Historical Studies*, 12 (1960–61), 209–25 · E. Hobsbawm and G. Rudé, *Captain Swing* (1969) · J. Marlow, *The Tolpuddle Martyrs* (1971) · D. Philips and R. D. Storch, 'Whigs and coppers: the Grey ministry's national police scheme, 1832', *Historical Research*, 67 (1994), 75–90 · S. Walpole, *The life of Lord John Russell*, 2 vols. (1889)

Archives Herts. ALS, corresp., journals, papers · Melbourne Hall, Derbyshire, estate papers · Royal Arch., Melbourne MSS · Royal Arch., corresp. and notebooks · U. Southampton L., political corresp. | BL, letters to members of his family, Add. MSS 44546, 45548 · BL, corresp. with James Frampton, Add. MS 41567 · BL, corresp. with Lord Holland, Add. MSS 51558–51559 · BL, corresp. with Lady Holland, Add. MS 51560 · BL, corresp. with Sir Robert Peel, Add. MSS 40394-40572 · BL, letters to Lord Spencer, p13 · BL, corresp. with Lord Wellesley, Add. MSS 37297–37312, *passim* · BL OIOC, corresp. with J. C. Hobhouse, MS Eur. F 213 · Bodl. Oxf., letters to Lady Byron · Bodl. Oxf., letters to John Wodehouse · Exeter Cathedral, letters to Henry Phillpotts · Herts. ALS, corresp. with Lord Dimsdale · Herts. ALS, corresp. with Lord Lytton · Lambton estate office, Lambton Park, Chester-le-Street, co. Durham, corresp. with Lord Durham · Lpool RO, letters to Lord Stanley · NA Canada, corresp. with Lord Durham · NA Scot., letters to James Loch · NA Scot., letters to Lord Panmure · NL Scot., letters to Edward Ellice · Norfolk RO, letters to John Wodehouse · Notts. Arch., letters to Thomas Barber · NRA, priv. coll., letters to Henry Duncan · Oriel College, Oxford, letters to R. D. Hampden · PRO, corresp. with Lord John Russell, PRO 30/22 · PRO NIre., corresp. with first marquess of Anglesey · Sheff. Arch., letters to Lord Fitzwilliam · Staffs. RO, letters to Lord Hatherton · Staffs. RO, corresp. with duke of Sutherland · TCD, letters to R. S. Carew · U. Durham L., corresp. with third Earl Grey · U. Nott. L., corresp. with duke of Newcastle · U. Southampton L., corresp. with Lord Palmerston · U. Southampton L., letters to duke of Wellington · UCL, Brougham MSS · W. Sussex RO, letters to duke of Richmond · Woburn Abbey, Bedfordshire, letters to duke of Bedford

Likenesses F. Bartolozzi, group portrait, stipple, pubd 1791 (after *The Lamb family* by J. Reynolds, 1785), BM · J. Hoppner, oils, 1796, Royal Collection · T. Lawrence, oils, 1800, NPG · F. Chantrey, bust, 1828, priv. coll. · T. A. Prior?, line engraving, c.1830 (after an oil painting by T. Lawrence, 1805), NG Ire. · E. Landseer, oils, 1836, NPG · F. Grant, group portrait, 1837 (*Party at Ranton Abbey*), Shugborough, Staffordshire · G. Hayter, pencil drawing, 1837, NPG · D. Wilke, group portrait, oils, 1837 (*Queen Victoria's first council*), Royal Collection · F. Chantrey, pencil drawing, 1838, NPG · J. Francis, bust, 1838, Royal Collection · G. Hayter, oils, 1838, priv. coll. · C. R. Leslie, group portrait, oils, 1838 (*The Queen receiving the sacrament after her coronation*), Royal Collection · R. Moody, bust, 1838, Royal Collection · F. Grant, group portrait, 1839 (*Queen Victoria riding at Windsor Castle*), Royal Collection · F. Chantrey, marble bust, 1841, Royal Collection · S. Diez, pencil and wash drawing, 1841, NPG · J. Partridge, oils, 1844, NPG [*see illus.*] · J. Doyle, caricature drawings, BM · J. Doyle, group portraits, lithographs, NG Ire. · G. H. Harlow, oils on panel, NG Ire. · G. Hayter, group portrait, oils (*The trial of Queen Caroline, 1820*), NPG · G. Hayter, group portrait, oils (*The House of Commons, 1833*), NPG · G. Hayter, group portrait, oils (*Queen Victoria's coronation*), Royal Collection · J. Partridge, group portrait (*The Fine Arts Commissioners, 1846*), NPG · engraving (after G. Hayter), NPG

Wealth at death under £35,000; plus under £200 additional estate; settled estate (principally land at Melbourne Hall, Derbyshire, and Brocket Hall, Hertfordshire) yielding £19,000 p.a. at death: Ziegler, *Melbourne*, 361; will, PRO, death duty registers, IR 26/1841

Lamb, Winifred (1894–1963), archaeologist and museum curator, was born on 3 November 1894 at Holly Lodge, Campden Hill, London, the only child of Edmund George Lamb (1863–1925), landowner, colliery proprietor, and former Liberal MP for North Herefordshire (1906–10), and his wife, Mabel (1862–1941), daughter of Stephen Winkworth, a Manchester cotton mill owner, and his wife, Emma. Her father educated her at home, at Borden Wood in Sussex (near Liphook), and at Holly Lodge, the home of her maternal grandparents and previously that also of Lord Macaulay, who had purchased it in 1856. In 1913 she was admitted to Newnham College, Cambridge, which her mother had also attended, to read classics; Winifred's maternal grandparents had been early benefactors of the college. Winifred became interested in classical archaeology, partly through the endeavours of Jane E. Harrison.

Lamb completed the classical tripos with a double first in 1917, and joined the naval intelligence department (Room 40) at the Admiralty, where the classical archaeologist John D. Beazley worked. Beazley's help is detected in Lamb's first published article in the *Journal of Hellenic Studies* (1918) which discussed seven Greek pots that she had acquired at the sale of the Hope antiquities at Christies in July 1917. Lamb was clearly influenced by the new 'science of vases', the attribution of works to largely anonymous Athenian pot-painters; Beazley was later to name one of these painters, 'the Lamb painter' ('der Lamb Maler'), in her honour.

After the war, Lamb decided to pursue her interests in classical archaeology. In 1919 Sydney Cockerell invited her to become honorary keeper of Greek and Roman antiquities at the Fitzwilliam Museum in Cambridge in succession to F. H. Marshall of Emmanuel College; she accepted, and held the position until 1958. Lamb was able to bring order to this significant collection, which contained antiquities presented to Cambridge University by Professor E. D. Clarke and Dr John Disney. One of the significant developments was the creation of a prehistoric gallery, which was to display material obtained through the fieldwork of members of the British School at Athens. Sadly, one of Lamb's key acquisitions of a marble figure of a Cretan goddess, made with the support of Sir Arthur Evans, turned out to be a forgery.

In October 1920 Lamb was admitted as a student of the British School at Athens; one of her fellow students was Bernard Ashmole. In May 1921 Lamb joined the British excavations at Mycenae, and in the 1922 season acted as second in command to the director, A. J. B. Wace; her parents were financial supporters of the excavation. She was to publish a series of studies on the palace at Mycenae in the *Annual of the British School at Athens* (1921–3).

Lamb's interests lay in the field of prehistoric Greece, and by early 1924 she was excavating with W. A. Heurtley, the assistant director of the British School, at Vardaroftsa in Macedonia. However, in March 1924 she joined the British School's major excavations at the classical site of Sparta under A. M. Woodward. Lamb was responsible for the publication of the bronze finds, in the *Annual of the British School at Athens* (1926–7). Despite the frustrations of the excavation, Lamb wrote home to her mother, 'Archaeology is a wonderful life', and expressed the view that she was now ready to start excavating on her own.

Lamb's father died in January 1925, and it was not until the autumn of 1928 that she opened a trial excavation at Methymna on the island of Lesbos, although the lack of stratigraphy meant that she abandoned future plans to work there. Frustrated, she resumed field walking the island with R. W. Hutchinson on the look-out for a suitable place to excavate. At Thermi they recognized a prehistoric site which had been partly eroded by the sea, and in April

of the following year a series of excavations was started, largely at Lamb's own expense; they continued until 1933. The site was to be published in the monograph *Excavations at Thermi in Lesbos* (1936). In 1940 Lamb was awarded a ScD by the University of Cambridge on the basis of the volume; it was examined by Professor Gordon Childe of Edinburgh and Carl Blegen of the American School at Athens, who had respectively reviewed the book for the *Journal of Hellenic Studies* (1937) and the *American Journal of Archaeology* (1938).

During the excavations of Thermi, Lamb conducted minor excavations at Antissa on Lesbos, in part to look for evidence of the Late Bronze Age and archaic period. With the Thermi excavations complete, she initiated the excavation of the archaic temple of Apollo at Kato Phana on the island of Chios. Lamb had visited Troy in 1929, and her excavations at Thermi had raised certain key questions about the contact between the Aegean and mainland Anatolia. In the spring of 1935 she selected the site of Kusura near Afyon as a possible site for excavation. Three seasons of work were carried out and published in *Archaeologia* (1936, 1937).

In spite of this busy excavating programme, Lamb continued to develop the Greek collections of the Fitzwilliam, in part through the donation of objects that she had obtained on her travels. She was later to be recognized as one of the most significant benefactors to the classical collections. This museum work allowed Lamb to concentrate on ancient bronzes, and which was to culminate in *Greek and Roman Bronzes* (1929). Her earlier interest in Greek pottery also led her to prepare the two Cambridge fascicles of the *Corpus vasorum antiquorum* (1930, 1936), which replaced Ernest Gardner's *Catalogue of Vases* (1897).

With the outbreak of the Second World War, Lamb settled at the family home of Borden Wood to look after her now frail mother, who died in August 1941. This freed her to accept the post of Greek language supervisor at the BBC, and in 1942 she transferred to the Turkish section of the Near Eastern department of the BBC, where she worked until 1946. During the final stages of the war, Lamb was badly injured when a German V2 rocket hit her lodgings in north London; her housemates were killed.

Lamb's pre-war fieldwork in Turkey led her to join in the creation of the British Institute of Archaeology at Ankara under the initiative of John Garstang. Lamb was to serve as the institute's honorary secretary from 1948 to 1957, and subsequently as a vice-president. Although her excavating days were over, she made a number of trips to eastern Anatolia which resulted in papers for *Anatolian Studies* (1954, 1956).

Lamb became an associate of Newnham College in 1926, was awarded a life studentship of the British School at Athens in 1931, and was elected a fellow of the Society of Antiquaries in 1932. In 1958 Lamb's health started to fail her. She resigned from her honorary keepership at the Fitzwilliam Museum and retired to Borden Wood; she never married and died at the Cottage Hospital, Easebourne, Sussex, of a stroke on 16 September 1963. Her funeral took place in the Roman Catholic church at Midhurst in Sussex, and she was buried in the Midhurst cemetery.

DAVID GILL

Sources G. Caton-Thompson, 'Winifred Lamb, 1894–1963 (Newnham, 1913–17)', *Newnham College Roll Letter* (1964), 50–52 · *The Times* (18 Sept 1963) · A. M. Woodward, *The Times* (21 Sept 1963) · R. D. Barnett, 'Winifred Lamb', *British School at Athens Annual Report* (1962–3), 16–18 · *Annual Report of the British Institute of Archaeology at Ankara*, 15 (1963), 2–3 · R. Hood, *Faces of archaeology in Greece: caricatures by Piet de Jong* (1998) · D. W. J. Gill, 'Winifred Lamb and the Fitzwilliam Museum', *Classics in 19th and 20th century Cambridge*, ed. C. A. Stray, Proceedings of the Cambridge Philological Society, suppl. 24 (1999), 135–56 · K. Butcher and D. W. J. Gill, 'The director, the dealer, the goddess and her champions: the acquisition of the Fitzwilliam Goddess', *American Journal of Archaeology*, 97 (1993), 383–401 · R. W. Hutchinson, 'Winifred Lamb', priv. coll. [unpublished MS] · W. Lamb, 'Byways in Attica', *Newnham College Roll Letter* (1922), 70–73 · H. Waterhouse, *The British School at Athens: the first hundred years* (1986) · G. Caton-Thompson, 'Mrs Edmund Lamb (Mabel Winkworth), 1880–1881', *Newnham College Roll Letter* (1942), 35–7 · D. W. J. Gill, '"A rich and promising site": Winifred Lamb (1894–1963), Kusura, and Anatolian archaeology', *Anatolian Studies*, 50 (2000), 1–10 · A. Hamlin, *Pioneers of the past* (2001), 39–42 · b. cert. · d. cert.

Archives British School at Athens, corresp., photograph albums · FM Cam., letters, artefacts, incl. bequest · priv. coll., photograph album | priv. coll., diaries and papers

Likenesses P. de Jong, cartoon, 1924, repro. in Hood, *Faces of archaeology in Greece*; priv. coll · photograph, British School at Athens, Greece; repro. in Hood, *Faces of archaeology in Greece*

Wealth at death £492,366 15s. od.: probate, 15 Oct 1963, *CGPLA Eng. & Wales*

William Lambarde (1536–1601), by unknown artist

Lambarde, William (1536–1601), antiquary and lawyer, was born on 18 October 1536 in the parish of St Nicholas Acons, London, the elder son of John Lambarde or Lambert (1500–1554) and his first wife, Juliana (d. 1540), daughter of William Horne (d. 1544), grocer of London. His father, a younger son of William Lambert of Ledbury, Herefordshire, and Alice Baker, was a warden and master of the Drapers' Company, merchant adventurer, alderman of London from 1547, and sheriff of the city in 1551–2. He purchased numerous properties in London and Southwark, the manor of Hedington, Wiltshire, and the manor of Westcombe in East Greenwich, Kent, and he secured a coat of arms on 15 July 1551. At his death on 4 August 1554 and the subsequent death of his second wife, Alice, the following 12 August, his two sons and heirs, William and Giles (1538–1581) were under age. William, the ward of Edmund Hensley, esquire, was found to be of legal age on 23 November 1557. Retaining Westcombe and some London property, he sold most of the remainder of his inheritance between 1559 and 1574 for a total of £1868. Giles, apprenticed in 1554 to his father's friend and fellow draper, John Calthorp, inherited property valued at £52 3s. 4d. per annum and became a controversial, litigious freeman of the Drapers' Company.

Lambarde's early education is obscure. He may have been the William Lambert enrolled in 1549 at Jesus College, Cambridge, but he later stated in his *Alphabetical Description of the Chief Places in England and Wales* (1730) that he owed more to Oxford University than to Cambridge, and he was an early donor to the library of Christ Church. On 15 August 1556 he entered Lincoln's Inn, and was named a master of the inn's revels in 1558 and a Christmas steward in 1559. A powerful case has been made that he was the William Lambert who sat for Aldborough, Yorkshire, in the two sessions of the parliament which began in 1563. This individual played a vital role in the debate on the royal succession, and in 1584 wrote an innovative treatise, 'Notes on the procedures and privileges of the House of Commons', first published anonymously in 1641. On 5 November 1566 Queen Elizabeth forestalled a petition from parliament on her marriage and the settlement of the succession by informing a delegation from the Lords and Commons that discussion of these topics should cease. On 8 November Lambarde reopened the issue in the Commons with a learned oration advocating a return to the proceedings. This action led directly to the queen's express commandment forbidding debate, Paul Wentworth's questioning of this possible breach of the liberty of free speech in the Commons, and Elizabeth's eventual, reluctant withdrawal of her prohibition. Lambarde's treatise of 1584 later identified these events as constituting an important precedent for the house, but his involvement was the direct result of his staunch protestantism and concern at the prospect of a Catholic succession, rather than abstract constitutional principle.

Following his call to the bar on 15 June 1567, for two decades Lambarde devoted himself to county administration, his estates, and his scholarship. His first historical researches, undertaken at Lincoln's Inn with the encouragement of Lawrence Nowell and originating within the antiquarian circle of Archbishop Matthew Parker, who promoted Anglo-Saxon research as a firm foundation for the Church of England, led to the publication of

Archaionomia (1568), dedicated to Sir William Cordell. Only the second book to print Old English, this was a pioneering collection and paraphrase in Latin of Anglo-Saxon laws and treaties, together with laws of Edward the Confessor and William I. It was heavily dependent on Nowell's 'improved' translation of the originals and at this date some significant manuscripts like the Textus Roffensis were known to neither Nowell nor Lambarde; the latter recognized this later and amended accordingly his own copies of the book, which survive in the Bodleian and Huntington libraries. However, the work was immediately highly influential, and was crucial to subsequent scholarship. Lambarde's achievement was commended by Parker and acknowledged by John Foxe, and had particular importance in an age when the definition and direction of historical studies were intimately connected to the religious and political conditions and when antiquarianism was an essential part of the search for precedent and authority in all aspects of life and thought.

Lambarde's involvement in county administration began with his appointment in 1568 as a commissioner of sewers for Kent, where he had been acquiring small additional plots of lands for the previous five years. On 11 September 1570 he married Jane (1553–1573), eldest daughter of George Multon (1504–1588), esquire and justice of the peace of St Clere, Ightham, Kent, and Agnes Polhill (1515?–1591). Jane's dowry included the lease of St Clere manor; although she died childless on 21 September 1573, Lambarde resided there until 1583 and held the manor until 1588. It was on his marriage and move to the county, as he later explained to Sir Henry Sidney, that, having already collected some notes for a topographical dictionary, he conceived the novel idea of a systematic survey of Kent. What was in time intended as the first instalment of a historical topography of England was completed in draft in 1570, read in manuscript by Parker and Lord Burghley, and published as *Perambulation of Kent: Containing the Description, Hystorie and Customs of that Shyre* (1576). The earliest county history, based on wide and critical reading (partly informed by Lambarde's protestant suspicion of monks and their works), it draws also on Domesday Book and on royal charters, and includes in its climatic, economic, social, religious, and historical survey a short investigation of the see of Canterbury; a discussion of the local inheritance custom of gavelkind is appended. While Lambarde was uninterested in pre-Anglo-Saxon history (unlike William Camden) and exhibited no appreciation of landscape, his book 'is packed with learned information' and 'eminently readable' (McKisack, 137). The project to publish on other counties was eventually abandoned in 1585, when Lambarde learned of Camden's similar undertaking, but his interim researches were finally published as *Dictionarium Angliae topographicum et historicum* (1730) and his marginal notations survive in the books he consulted now in the British Library, including John Price's *Historiae Brytannicae defensio* (1573) and Alexander Neville's *De furoribus Norfolciensium Ketto duce* (1575).

Lambarde was put on the county commission of the peace on 6 August 1579 (sworn on 3 June 1580) and became of the quorum in 1584. For the first eight years of his service in the western division of Kent he kept a memorandum book, his 'Ephemeris', containing notes on some aspects of his work, including the issuing of recognizances for keeping the peace, the licensing of ale houses, and provision for bastards. Twenty-nine of his erudite, contemplative charges to the quarter sessions juries and local commissions between 1582 and 1601 survive in the Folger Shakespeare Library; they probably represent only a quarter of those he actually delivered. He praised English justice, but was sharply critical of the shortcomings of the juries, which had led government to circumvent them through such agencies as Star Chamber, and thus curtail liberty. Extolling the blessings of peace and deploring the disorders attendant on war, he showed a dislike of foreigners and inveighed, among other things, against ale houses, vagabonds, and engrossers, but he made little reference to national problems and none to felony or murder. His own activities in local government, alongside his friends and associates William Brooke, Lord Cobham, Sir Thomas Fane, Thomas Leveson, and Thomas Wotton, included the recusancy commission (not mentioned in 'Ephemeris'), the organization of musters, beacons, and markets, prerogative taxation, the stewardship of the manor of Gravesend, and the wardenship of Rochester Bridge corporation. His desire to study the historical development of every office he held led to the highly praised *Eirenarcha, or, The Office of the Justices of Peace* (1582). Reprinted twelve times before 1620, this treatise long remained the standard authority.

On 28 October 1583 Lambarde married his second wife, Sylvestra or Silvester (1554–1587), widow of William Dallison (d. 1581) of Gray's Inn, daughter-in-law of Sir William Dallison, justice of queen's bench, and daughter and heir of Robert Deane or Dene (d. 1577) of Halling, Kent, and Margaret White (d. 1594). After Sylvestra's death on 1 September 1587 from complications following the birth of their twin sons, Lambarde secured the wardship of her son Maximilian Dallison (d. 1631) and a lease of their Halling residence. He made a third marriage locally, on 13 April 1592, to Margaret (b. 1544), widow successively of John Meryam and Richard Reder (d. 1582), yeoman, both of Boughton Monchelsea, and daughter of John Payne of Frittenden, yeoman. In 1598 the Lambardes moved to Westcombe.

In his 'Ephemeris' Lambarde emphasized the rule of law as the foundation of society, 'the outward guides and masters of our lives and manners' (Lambarde, *Ephemeris*, 76). By 1591 he had completed his greatest achievement in legal history, 'Archeion, or, A discourse upon the high courts of justice in England', which although it circulated extensively in manuscript, was published by his grandson only in 1635. Here he propounded a vision of political society grounded in historically validated laws and customs. He sought to trace the two essential components of this system of government, the common law and the prerogative, to an equally distant Anglo-Saxon past. As for parliament, Lambarde wrote, 'I see not how I can derive it from any other time, than from that, in which the *German* or

English did set their first foot on this *Land*, to invade it' (W. Lambarde, *Archeion*, ed. C. H. McIlwain and P. L. Ward, 1957, 126–7). For him, the establishment of a firm basis for contemporary society could only mean an appeal to the past, and his conclusions were considered valid by those who began, as he did, with a belief in the continuity of institutions which could change their name and structure but not their essential functions. The precise extent of the prerogative and of the common law was a contentious issue, and Lambarde's writings and actions revealed a consistently high opinion of the latter, although not at the expense of the essential function of the former.

Lambarde was a consistent and vocal proponent of ethical propriety and reform in the practice of the law. His direct employment by the crown was long delayed, his career perhaps impeded by his controversial action in 1566, and employment at Westminster came only with the rise to prominence of his close friends, especially Sir Thomas Egerton. In 1589 Lambarde was made deputy to Lord Burghley as master of the alienations office of chancery, in June 1592 a master in chancery extraordinary, and in 1597 a master in ordinary and deputy keeper of the rolls (to Egerton). It was in chancery that his direct influence was most effective, especially when he acted in association with Egerton. Here he attempted to restrict the growing equity jurisdiction to justifiable causes. It was he who prepared the earliest collection of chancery precedents, the so-called Cary's reports, printed in 1650, which quickly became authoritative and had a pronounced effect on moulding court procedure. As in his treatises on the House of Commons and the office of alienations, it was the identification and codification of precedents that comprised his contribution to the establishment of theory out of past and contemporary practice.

On 14 June 1597 Lambarde, who had been active in the Society of Antiquaries, and who on this occasion was described as 'a man of great reading, learning and experience' (*Black Books*, 2.51), became a bencher of Lincoln's Inn, having been an associate bencher since 1579. In January 1601 he became keeper of the records in the Tower of London and quickly produced a historical description of the royal manuscripts, 'Pandecta rotulorum'. When he presented this to the queen, in an audience at Greenwich Palace he recounted in notes preserved among his family papers, he found Elizabeth an intelligent and appreciative recipient, who questioned him in detail over the content and its meaning. Having dispensed her equally elderly guest from the necessity of kneeling before her, she reportedly avowed that 'she had not received since her first coming to the crown any one thing that brought so great delectation unto her' and finally left him with a 'Farewell, good and honest Lambarde' (McKisack, 82).

While in royal service Lambarde made his most sustained land purchases. Between 1593 and 1597 he paid £1760 for the Kentish properties that comprised his most significant acquisitions. Together with Westcombe they formed the basis for his family's landed estate. The earlier sales of portions of his inheritance had all been directed towards the costs of £2739 for the foundation of his model

almshouse, the College of Queen Elizabeth, at East Greenwich in 1576. Later, as an executor for the estate of William Brooke, Lord Cobham (*d.* 1597), he adopted the college's rules for use in Cobham's newly established almshouse, of which he and Thomas Leveson were the first presidents.

Having already obtained an unparalleled reputation for learning, piety, civic virtue, and trustworthiness, Lambarde died at Westcombe at 3 a.m. on 19 August 1601, and was buried in the parish church of St Alphege, East Greenwich; his funeral monument was moved in 1710 to the Lambarde chapel in St Nicholas's Church, Sevenoaks. He had complained of diminished eyesight since 1587, and in August 1586 had told Egerton that he had been gravely sick three times in the previous three years, 'in these Dogdays and (as it were) hearde 3 peales rong for me' (Hunt. L., MS EL 39). By the terms of his will, dated 16 May 1597, the estates in Kent descended to his eldest son, Multon (1584–1634), of Lincoln's Inn; Multon was knighted in 1608 and married Jane (1594–1674), daughter of Sir Thomas Lowe, alderman and sometime lord mayor of London. Lambarde's younger sons, Fane and Gore, the twins born in 1587, were given equal life interests in the London property on attaining the age of twenty-two; both appear to have died young and childless. Their only sister, Margaret (1586–1611), received a marriage portion of £800. On 5 May 1609 she married Thomas Godfrey (1585–1664) of Kent, then gentleman servant to Henry Howard, earl of Northampton, and later sewer of the chamber to James I and father of Edmund Berry Godfrey. Lambarde's library remained at Sevenoaks until 1924, when it was dispersed by sale and bequest.   J. D. ALSOP

Sources *William Lambarde and local government: his 'Ephemeris' and 'Twenty-nine charges to juries and commissions'*, ed. C. Read (Ithaca, NY, 1962) · *William Lambarde's note on the procedures and privileges of the House of Commons (1584)*, ed. P. L. Ward (1977) · [J. Randolph], 'Memoirs of William Lambarde, esq; an eminent lawyer and antiquary', *Bibliotheca topographia Britannica*, ed. J. Nichols, 8 vols. (1780–90), vol. 1, pp. 493–530 · 'The Lambarde diary', *Miscellanea Genealogica et Heraldica*, 2 (1876), 99–114 · W. Camden, *Camden's Britannia*, 1695, ed. S. Piggott (1971) · J. Nichols, ed., *The progresses and public processions of Queen Elizabeth* (1788), vol. 1, pp. 325–7 · W. Dunkel, *William Lambarde, Elizabethan jurist, 1536–1601* (New Brunswick, 1965) · R. M. Warnicke, *William Lambarde, Elizabethan antiquary, 1536–1601* (1973) · J. D. Alsop and W. M. Stevens, 'William Lambarde and the Elizabethan polity', *Studies in Medieval and Renaissance History*, 8 (1987), 233–65 · J. D. Alsop, 'Reinterpreting the Elizabethan Commons: the parliamentary session of 1566', *Journal of British Studies*, 29 (1990), 216–40 · W. Prest, 'William Lambarde, Elizabethan law reform, and early Stuart politics', *Journal of British Studies*, 34 (1995), 464–80 · P. L. Ward, 'William Lambarde's collections on chancery', *Harvard Library Bulletin*, 7 (1953), 271–98 · N. M. Fuidge, 'Lambarde, William', HoP, *Commons, 1558–1603* · M. McKisack, *Medieval history in the Tudor age* (1971), 79–82, 133–7 · G. S. Fry and S. J. Madge, eds., *Abstract of inquisitiones post mortem relating to the City of London*, 3 vols., British RS, 15, 26, 36 (1896–1908), vol. 1, pp. 133–5, 153; vol. 3, pp. 62–4, 302–4 · W. P. Baildon, ed., *The records of the Honorable Society of Lincoln's Inn: the black books*, 1 (1897) · J. S. Cockburn, ed., *Calendar of assize records, Kent indictments, Elizabeth I* (1979) · PRO, PROB 10/28, 29 · Staffs. RO, Leveson papers, D 593, 868, 4092, 4193, 4401 D(W)o/5–6 · GL, archdeaconry court of London, will register 9051/4, fols. 232v–233 · BL, Add. MSS 4521, 5123, 15644; Stowe MSS 415, 543; Lansdowne MSS 17, 43, 54, 61, 71, 145, 155, 235 · Hunt. L.,

MSS EL 39, 688, 2649, 2649B, 2914, R.B. 17273, 62135 · CUL, MS Ii.6.29 · J. Philipott, 'The visitation of the county of Kent taken in the year 1619 [pt 1]', *Archaeologia Cantiana*, 4 (1861), 241–72 · J. Conway Davies, ed., *Catalogue of manuscripts in the library of the Honourable Society of the Inner Temple* (1972), 741–2, 846, 851, 910 · *CPR, 1553–82* · W. J. Jones, *The Elizabethan court of chancery* (1967) · *Correspondence of Matthew Parker*, ed. J. Bruce and T. T. Perowne, Parker Society, 42 (1853), 424–6 · J. Strype, *Annals of the Reformation and establishment of religion … during Queen Elizabeth's happy reign*, new edn, 4 vols. (1824), vol. 3/1, pp. 723–4, vol. 3/2, pp. 501–2 · P. Boyd, ed., *Rolls of the Drapers' Company of London* (1934), 111 · N. R. Ker, 'Books at Christ Church, 1562–1602', *Hist. U. Oxf. 3: Colleg. univ.*, 499–500 · R. Flower, 'Laurence Nowell and the discovery of England in Tudor times', *PBA*, 21 (1935), 46–73 · E. G. Box, 'Lambarde's "Carde of this shyre"', *Archaeologia Cantiana*, 38 (1926), 89–95 · P. Wormald, 'The Lambarde problem: eighty years on', *Legal culture in the early medieval west: law as text, image and experience* (1999), 139–78 · *Calendar of the manuscripts of the most hon. the marquis of Salisbury*, 11, HMC, 9 (1906), 350–51 · R. M. Warnicke, 'The merchant society of Tudor London: John Lambarde—a case study', *Indiana Social Studies Quarterly* (1984), 57–69 · *The diary of Henry Machyn, citizen and merchant-taylor of London, from AD 1550 to AD 1563*, ed. J. G. Nichols, CS, 42 (1848), 67 · S. Robertson, ed., 'Dalison documents', *Archaeologia Cantiana*, 15 (1882–3), 391–402 · W. P. Baildon, ed., *The records of the Honorable Society of Lincoln's Inn: the black books*, 2 (1898)

Archives BL, draft of *Eirenarcha*, Add. MS 41137 · BL, historical collections, Cotton MS Vesp. A.v I · BL, annotations to the papers and transcripts by Lawrence Nowell, Add. MSS 43703–43710 · BL, *Perambulation of Kent*, commonplace book, and papers, Add. MSS 4521, 5123, 11750, 20063, 20709 · BL, second draft of his history of Kent, Sloane MS 3168 · BL, revision of part of *Eirenarcha*, Egerton MS 3676 · Bodl. Oxf., papers · Bodl. Oxf., printed copy of *Perambulation of Kent* with his corrections and additions · CKS, MS of his *Perambulation of Kent* · Drapers' Company, London, Lambarde manuscripts, H/W.L. 1–2, A.L.1–4, Add. 1–54 · Drapers' Company, London, papers incl. accounts and pedigree · Folger, diary and papers of Kent justice of the peace · Harvard U., law school, legal papers and copy of his *Archeion* · University of Virginia, Charlottesville, papers | BL, Cotton, Stowe, Lansdowne, and Add. MSS · CKS, corresp. with Sir John Leveson [copies] · CUL · GL · Hunt. L. · Inner Temple · Lincoln's Inn · Staffs. RO, corresp. with Sir John Leveson

Likenesses G. Vertue, line engraving, 1729, BM, NPG · G. Vertue, line engraving, 1730 (after unknown artist), BM, NPG · oils (after type of, *c.*1570–1575), NPG · portrait, priv. coll. [*see illus.*] · print, NPG

Lambart. For this title name *see* Lambert, Oliver, first Baron Lambart of Cavan (*c.*1560–1618).

Lambart, Charles, first earl of Cavan (*c.*1600–1660), army officer and landowner, was the eldest son of Oliver Lambart, first Baron Lambart in the Irish peerage (*d.* 1618), servitor in co. Cavan, and Hester, daughter of Sir William Fleetwood of Carrington Manor in Bedfordshire. He became second Baron Lambart on his father's death between 1 and 10 June 1618 and was given in wardship to his mother on 26 April 1619. The Lambarts were lineally descended from Ralph de Lambart, a soldier of fortune, who fought at Hastings in 1066. Prior to his death Oliver Lambart had sold and mortgaged the lands he had been granted in co. Cavan and elsewhere. However, in the plantation schemes for the province of Leinster in 1622 his son Charles had a grant of 1296 acres in co. Westmeath and King's county. In 1626 and 1628–9 Charles sat in the English House of Commons representing the borough of Bossiney in Cornwall. On 4 November 1634 he spoke for the first time in the Irish House of Lords, where he was to become a leading speaker. He married Jane, daughter of Richard Robartes, Lord Robartes, of Truro, and sister of the first earl of Radnor. They had a large family of whom Richard, the second earl, died a lunatic in the same year as his father. Oliver, their third son, having survived the second son, succeeded to the family estates under the terms of his father's will. The family maintained possession of their estates in Beauparc, Slane, co. Meath, until late in the nineteenth century, thereby living up to the family motto *Ut quocunque paratus* ('Prepared on every side').

On 6 March 1627 Lambart was made seneschal for the government of co. Cavan and the town of Kells in co. Meath. The seneschals were established in the mid-sixteenth century in Ireland and the powers of the office included the exercise of martial law. Although intended to be a temporary expedient, the system continued late into the Tudor century to stabilize Gaelic lordships until conventional sheriffs could be appointed. Lambart's military expertise was recognized when he took over Lord Moore's infantry company on 17 May 1628. He was not, however, a provident estate manager, for in 1633 he conveyed various manors around Carrick in co. Westmeath, and Crover and Mountnugent in co. Cavan—a few of his father's inheritances—to a Richard Nugent. The Lambart estates suffered much on the outbreak of the 1641 Ulster rising.

In the Irish House of Lords Lambart played a prominent part in pressing home the attack for the impeachment of Wentworth. This was a courageous action because the Irish lords were predominantly Old English. Lambart was particularly vocal on the side of the New English to back up the English House of Commons in the attack on Wentworth. His speeches in the House of Lords and his letters indicate a forthright temperament and a just and fair man devoted to the public good. His support was important constitutionally because under Poynings' law (1494) the Irish parliament could claim the right of impeachment only by claiming that English precedents were legally binding in Ireland. Wentworth had used that ancient law as a weapon against the legislature in his tyrannical government of Ireland.

When the Ulster rising of 1641 threatened to engulf the entire country Ormond ordered Lambart to raise a regiment of foot, one of three such regiments, in November 1641. Many of his recruits were refugees from Ulster, and Richard Lambart, his brother, was appointed to a captaincy. Lambart's diplomatic skills were also now recognized when the government chose him as one of the commissioners to negotiate peace with the Ulster rebels. Their efforts failed. In the ensuing warfare that preceded Oliver Cromwell's descent on Ireland, Lambart distinguished himself as a military commander. When Sir Charles Coote left Dublin in 1642 Lambart became military governor of the city, and on receipt of the news of Coote's death he was confirmed in that post by order of council of 12 May 1642. At the same time he was appointed a privy councillor. In February 1643 he aided Ormond in the rout of the rebels at Kilsallaghan, 8 miles north of Dublin near Swords. By May 1643 his cavalry incursions into the south Dublin suburbs at Dean's Grange, Carrick-mines, and north Wicklow cleared the Dublin environs of rebel activity. In the disposition of his troops for the defence of the city, Lambart's men were stationed in the streets surrounding the castle—especially in Francis, Thomas, and Patrick streets. As a commander, Lambart inevitably clashed with the civil authorities because he often rode roughshod over the dictates of the common law in precipitate military procedures.

Charles I sent Edward Somerset, earl of Glamorgan, as his personal envoy to Dublin to assist Ormond, but more immediately to get troops sent into England to aid the king as quickly as possible. The northern confederates distrusted Glamorgan; so too did Ormond, who had him arrested in December 1645 six months after his arrival in Ireland. Lambart then became involved in the examination of Glamorgan and may have helped to procure his release in January 1646. Throughout Ormond's peace efforts in 1646 Lambart supported him. He pointed out to him that those opposed to peace were planning an attack on Kilkenny, where the supreme council held its sessions, 'to keep moderate and well affected men from attending the assembly' (J. Lowe, ed., *Clanricarde Letter Book*, 1983, 342). He was made earl of Cavan and Viscount Kilcoursie in April 1647, but under the parliamentary army control of Ireland the royalist earl of Cavan was reduced to straitened circumstances.

For the last decade of his life Cavan seems to have lived in comparative obscurity. He got a lease of the manors of Clontarf and Arlaine with a pension of 30s. a week for himself and £1 for his wife, who died in 1655. Cavan died on 25 June 1660, in Dublin, and was buried in St Patrick's Cathedral, Dublin.   J. J. N. McGURK

Sources Burke, *Peerage* (1999) • J. Lodge, *The peerage of Ireland*, rev. M. Archdall, rev. edn, 1 (1789), 343–50 • G. Hill, *The plantation in Ulster*, facs. edn (1970) • Burke, *Peerage* (1841) • K. Nichols, ed., *Calendar of fiants of the reign of Elizabeth in Ireland* (1998) [leases of O. Lambart] • F. E. Ball, *A history of the county Dublin*, 6 vols. (1902–20), vol. 1, p. 51, vol. 3, p. 133 • *The manuscripts of the marquis of Ormonde*, [old ser.], 3 vols., HMC, 36 (1895–1909), vol. 1, pp. 129–39, 149, 159, 193 • B. C. Donovan and D. Edwards, *British sources for Irish history*, IMC (1997) • A. Clarke, 'The history of Poynings' Law, 1615–1641', *Irish Historical Studies*, 18 (1972–3), 207–22 • *Journal of the Irish House of Lords*, 1 (1779–1800), 166 • J. T. Gilbert, ed., *A contemporary history of affairs in Ireland from 1641 to 1652*, 3 vols. (1879–80) • R. Bagwell, *Ireland under the Stuarts*, 3 vols. (1909–16); repr. (1963) • A. Clarke, *The Old English in Ireland, 1625–42* (Dublin, 1966); repr. (2000) • T. Dooley, ed., *Sources for the history of landed estates in Ireland* (Maynooth, 2000) • M. Ó Siochrú, *Confederate Ireland, 1642–1649* (Dublin, 1999) • *DNB* • E. T. Bewley, *The Irish branch of the Fleetwood family* (1908) • P. Woulfe, *Irish names and surnames*, rev. edn (1992) • 'Lambert', *Returns of landowners in Ireland* (1988)

Archives Sheff. Arch., corresp., Wentworth muniments, WWM Str. f. 16 and 1n (1637) batch 342 — letter of 1634/5 | Glos. RO, letters, Hicks Beach uncat. D12440 MSS Box no. 44

Wealth at death lease of manors of Clontarf and Arlaine; pension of 30s. a week

Lambart, Sir Oliver. *See* Lambert, Oliver, first Baron Lambart of Cavan (c.1560–1618).

Lambart, Richard Ford William, seventh earl of Cavan (1763–1837), army officer, born on 10 September 1763, was the only son of Richard, sixth earl (d. 1788), and his second wife, Elizabeth (d. 1811), eldest daughter of William Davies, a commissioner of the navy. He succeeded his father in 1778. He was appointed ensign in the Coldstream Guards on 2 April 1779, lieutenant in 1781, captain-lieutenant in 1790, captain and lieutenant-colonel on 23 August 1793, second major on 9 May 1800, and first major on 19 November 1800, having in the meantime attained major-general's rank in 1798. He was wounded at Valenciennes on 3 January 1793, and commanded a brigade in Ireland (Londonderry) in 1798–9, and in the Ferrol expedition and before Cadiz in 1800. He commanded a line brigade in Egypt in 1801, and, when General George James Ludlow was removed to a brigade of the line on 9 August, Cavan succeeded to the command of the brigade of guards. As part of Eyre Coote's division the brigade was sent to attack Alexandria from the westward. The city surrendered on 2 September 1801. When Lord Hutchinson left in October, Cavan succeeded to the command of the whole army remaining in Egypt, including the troops under David Baird. Cavan held a brigade command in the eastern counties in England during the invasion alarms of 1803–4, and in 1805 was lieutenant-general commanding in the Isle of Wight. He was a knight of the Crescent, and was one of the six officers, besides Lord Nelson, who received the diamond aigrette. He became a full general in 1814, and was in succession colonel-commandant of a 2nd battalion 68th foot, and colonel of the 2nd West Indian and 45th regiments. He was governor of Calshot Castle, Hampshire, from 1813 until his death.

Cavan married first, on 8 July 1782, Honora Margaretta (d. 1813), youngest daughter and coheir of Sir Henry *Gould (1710–1794), and second on 11 August 1814, Lydia, second daughter of William Arnold of Slatswood, Isle of Wight. With his first wife he had three sons and three daughters; the only surviving son, George Frederick Augustus Lambart, Viscount Kilcoursie, predeceased his father, leaving a large family. With his second wife, who died on 7 February 1862, Cavan had three sons and a daughter. He died at Stanhope Place, Hyde Park, on 21 November 1837, and was succeeded by his grandson.

H. M. CHICHESTER, rev. K. D. REYNOLDS

Sources GEC, *Peerage* • *GM*, 2nd ser., 9 (1838), 92

Archives Som. ARS, corresp. and papers | National War Museum of Scotland, Edinburgh, corresp. with Sir David Baird

Likenesses attrib. P. de Loutherbourg, drawing, NPG • bust, Military Academy, Sandhurst, Camberley, Surrey

Lambart, (Frederic) Rudolph, tenth earl of Cavan (1865–1946), army officer, was born on 16 October 1865 at the rectory, Ayot St Lawrence, Hertfordshire, where his maternal grandfather, John Olive, was rector. Descended from Oliver Lambart, who was knighted at the storming of Cadiz in 1596, he was the eldest son of Frederick Edward Gould Lambart (1839–1900), at that time Viscount Kilcoursie, and his wife, Mary Sneade Olive (1846–1905). Initially (1870–75) he was educated at home but at the age of ten he was sent to the Revd Stephen Cornish's school at Clevedon, Somerset. There he began 'to show great powers of application and concentration if he was interested in his subject'

(Lambart, 3). His love of sports and games reflected the influence of his father, who encouraged him to learn to ride. The young Lambart fell more than forty times off his pony before his father declared him proficient to follow the Hertfordshire hunt, of which he was himself a member. His religious convictions and love of books and music came from his disciplined home background.

Eton and the guards Lambart entered Eton College at thirteen, joining the house of Henry Luxmoore, who provided a stimulating environment in which his confidence grew. 'All through my life I felt I had behind me the man who guided my early steps' (Cavan MSS). His housemaster never made it easy for his pupil to succeed, but challenged him constantly. On the death of his former housemaster in 1926 he wrote:

> As his captain I sought his advice always, and in his inimitable way he used to make me answer all my difficulties myself, whether it was a tough passage of a Greek play or a nice point of cricket, football, or fives. He would draw me out and make me wrestle with the question, while his piercing eye wrinkled with pleasure at the struggle. I loved him, and am proud to have kept our friendship to the end, so mercifully quick. (*Daily Telegraph*, 1926)

In 1880 Rudolph applied to join the Eton College rifle volunteers but was rejected on account of his height. The following year he was accepted when he reached the regulation 5 feet 4 inches. In 1882 he passed the preliminary examination for entry to the Royal Military College, Sandhurst. Two years later in the direct examination he was seventh among the 96 candidates who passed (Lambart, 11). He entered the college in January 1885. As a reward his father gave him four weeks' hunting with the Devon and Somerset hunt.

Six months later Lambart was commissioned and became a second lieutenant in the Grenadier Guards. At his first parade he was told that his 'trousers were a foot too short and a yard too broad in the seat!' (Cavan MSS). As a result his contemporaries nicknamed him Fatty, a name that stuck with him throughout his army career. He served at first in London before going to Dublin for a year where off-duty he rode in many point-to-point races. In 1887 his grandfather died and his father became ninth earl of Cavan. Rudolph now used the courtesy title Viscount Kilcoursie. He was foolhardy, began betting, and ended up with debts of £2000. His father was unforgiving; though he later paid the debt, he reduced his son's allowance and tried to persuade him to leave the guards. Rudolph now sought a foreign appointment and in 1891 he went to Canada as aide-de-camp to the governor-general, Lord Stanley of Preston, later earl of Derby. There he spent two happy years, and his duties gave him plenty of time for cricket, tennis, salmon fishing, and shooting ducks in the Rocky Mountains. He returned to England in 1893 and was married to the elder sister of one of his school friends, (Caroline) Inez (1870–1920), daughter of George Baden Crawley. After a honeymoon in Scotland, Kilcoursie returned to his regiment which served spells of duty in Dublin, London, Aldershot, and Windsor. In the Second South African War

(1900–02), which he found a leisurely affair, his no.7 company marched 3000 miles. He wore out five pairs of boots. He remarked 'we very rarely saw a Boer and we did not have an unfortunate incident. I suppose we heard as many bullets in the whole war as we heard in one day of the 1915–16 battles' (South African diary, Cavan MSS). His father died in July 1900 and he became tenth earl of Cavan. The war finished in time for him to return home and attend the postponed coronation of Edward VII in August 1902. He became regimental adjutant in 1904, second in command of the 1st battalion in 1906, and colonel of the 1st battalion Grenadier Guards in 1908. Two years later he was among those who were created MVO (4th class). In 1912 Cavan retired from the army and became master of the Hertfordshire hunt.

First World War At the outbreak of the First World War Cavan was appointed brigade commander of the 2nd London Territorial Force. While on a march near Bisley in early September he was ordered to go to France to replace Brigadier-General Scott Kerr who had been wounded. Having been promoted temporary brigadier-general, he was told by the general officer commanding (GOC) of the 2nd division, General Munro, on arrival: 'your brigade is on that hill, see they stick to it.' ('Recollections', Cavan MSS). At the first battle of Ypres in November Cavan made his reputation. In his report of the 1st corps to Sir John French Sir Douglas Haig wrote: 'I sent Cavan to take command of the units on our right flank near the Zillebeke road, south-east of Ypres, where for nearly a fortnight, by his decision, sound military judgement and personality he has maintained our position with troops greatly reduced in numbers. Lord Cavan inspires those under him with confidence as well as those above him' ('Lights and shadows', Cavan MSS). During the darkest days of the battle the 4th guards brigade's forces were enlarged by the arrival of the 1st battalion of the Hertfordshire regiment, one of the first territorial units sent to the western front.

The following June, Cavan was appointed to command the 50th (Northumbrian) division, but when he was home on leave in July 1915, he was summoned to Windsor to be invested with the CB and was told that he was to command a new guards division. The new division went to France to train and later to take part in the battle of Loos. Of that battle Cavan wrote 'the defence of my line has been a really glorious chapter in the annals of the Guards' (letter, 11 Oct 1915, Cavan MSS). The prince of Wales was attached to the guards division and remained on Cavan's staff for much of the war until the autumn of 1918.

Further promotion followed in December 1915 when Cavan became commander of the 14th corps which fought in the Ypres salient until August 1916. After the opening of Talbot House, at Poperinghe, Cavan became a regular visitor. The chaplain, Philip (Tubby) Clayton was his cousin. On one occasion in spring 1916, when the war was going badly for the allies, Cavan used the Talbot House chapel for prayer and left spiritually refreshed. He kept this experience to himself, revealing it eight years later at a public meeting in Woolwich town hall. In mid-August 1916 the 14th corps moved from the Ypres salient to the Somme. Setting up his headquarters near Bray-sur-Somme, he made preparations for an attack in September 1916 east of Ginchy to secure the villages of Lesboeufs and Morval. Heavy losses were incurred, though two of the three objectives were achieved, and the corps remained on the Somme throughout the winter of 1916. During 1917 his corps returned to the Ypres salient and fought in the third battle of Ypres. That autumn the chief of the Imperial General Staff (CIGS), Sir William Robertson, sent for him and told him 'Look here Cavan, my lad, you've got to go to Italy and put new heart into our allies' ('Recollections', Cavan MSS). Cavan found a dispirited army in retreat and with little discipline. Almost immediately the war cabinet changed its priorities and he handed over command to General Sir Herbert Plumer, remaining in Italy in command of the 14th corps. Plumer was recalled to the western front in spring 1918 and Cavan resumed command of the British forces in Italy. He had to work hard to keep the new CIGS, Sir Henry Wilson, informed of changing attitudes by the Italians on a possible offensive against the Austrians, whose troops were defeated when they attacked at Asiago in June 1918 (Cassar, 165). In July, when the CIGS visited Italy, Cavan was promoted full general in recognition of his leadership qualities. In the autumn Cavan was given command of the Tenth Army made up of British and Italian forces. In October, by forcing a way across the River Piave which was in full flood, they secured the complete rout of the enemy in the battle of Vittorio Veneto. An armistice was signed between the Austrians and Italians, and hostilities ceased on 4 November 1918 in Italy. George V wrote to him 'with all my heart I congratulate you … for your great services I thank you'. Earlier in 1918 he had been made a KCB. He now received the grand cross of the Italian order of St Maurice and St Lazarus from the king of Italy, and after his return to England in December 1918, the American DSO. The commander-in-chief of the Italian army, General Diaz, paid tribute to Cavan's skill 'in overcoming difficulties and the brilliant manner in which his army deputed the enemy and attained its objectives' ('Italy, 1917–18', Cavan MSS). In 1916 he had been made a knight of St Patrick and took his seat as a representative Irish peer in the House of Lords. On returning to Hertfordshire he received the freedom of the city of St Albans and was fêted by Hertfordshire county council and the members and followers of the Hertfordshire hunt.

The inter-war years At home Cavan waited for news of future appointments. He considered resigning from the army, but his wife, Inez, who was in poor health advised him to wait, and he again became master of the Hertfordshire hunt. Lady Cavan died in 1920 and was buried at Ayot St Lawrence. Having been appointed lieutenant of the Tower of London in April 1920, Cavan was offered and accepted the post of commander-in-chief of the Aldershot command, where he remained for nine months before being sent to the USA as military adviser to Arthur Balfour at the Washington conference in November 1921. During the conference, he was invited to become CIGS in succession to Sir Henry Wilson, whose four-year term of office

was to expire in February 1922 ('Recollections', Cavan MSS). He was diffident in accepting the offer, as he realized that he lacked War Office experience and that more senior officers with Staff College experience and education had been set aside. Also he was looking forward to returning to Aldershot to train his troops there. However, he replied 'I feel that you would not have asked for me if you had not wanted me, and I am proud to accept the compliment' ('CIGS', Cavan MSS). He was asked to report to the War Office as soon as possible after his return from Washington so that he could take part 'in consideration of the Geddes report and consequential questions affecting army organisation' (ibid.). There is no question that he presided over an army that was drastically reduced in size and demoralized. In a speech of November 1923 he declared that 'the Army of to-day is determined to make itself a harder hitting, quicker moving instrument for all its diminution in size, and the keenness with which all ranks of the Regular and Territorial Army have applied themselves to this task is the outstanding feature of this year's training'. In 1922 he met and married Lady (Hester) Joan Mulholland (*née* Byng; 1888–1976), youngest daughter of the fifth earl of Strafford, who was lady in waiting to Princess Mary, and widow of Captain Andrew Mulholland, who had been killed in action in 1914. They met at a ball in Buckingham Palace and were married at North Audley Street in October 1922. The new CIGS's appointment was popular within the army, though public perception of the army was not very high. The family house and estate at Wheathampstead was auctioned in 1924 and they moved to central London. A daughter, Elizabeth, was born to Lady Cavan on 15 October 1924.

Cavan was CIGS at a time when there were frequent changes in appointments of secretary of state for war. He always made it plain that he was there to serve the needs of his political master, and though he is criticized for making little real progress, he presided over an army which had reduced financial resources and limited military objectives. Cavalry officers were told that no longer would expenses be met by the army when they entered international horse shows. In 1925 he reported on the first post-war manoeuvres held by the British army and argued that orders given should be in simple and clear English. He received the GCVO in 1922 and GCB in 1926. Honorary degrees were presented to him by Cambridge (LLD 1919) and Oxford (DCL 1926).

In February 1926 Cavan's four-year term as CIGS ended and he finally retired. He became colonel of the Irish Guards. Cavan and his wife were invited to accompany the duke and duchess of York on their world tour in 1927, he as chief of staff and Lady Cavan as the duchess's lady in waiting. On their return to England in 1927 he was made a KBE. A second daughter, Joanna, was born to Lady Cavan in 1929. Cavan became involved with the National Playing Fields Association, and was later its chairman. From 1929 to 1931 he was captain of the gentlemen of arms. In 1932 he was appointed field marshal and received his baton in December. Two years later, in 1934, he visited India, stayed with the viceroy, and inspected the Hertfordshire and

Bedfordshire regiment stationed there, of which he had become colonel in 1929. At the coronation of George VI in May 1937 he commanded the troops in the procession, and took his seat in Westminster Abbey as an earl. As a member of the War Graves Commission in Italy, he regularly visited Italy and was a popular figure with Italians and the Italian army. In October 1938 he was invited to meet the king of Italy and Mussolini, to whom he spoke 'soldier to soldier' ('Recollections', Cavan MSS).

Second World War At the outbreak of war he made arrangements to move out of central London, but kept in touch with the Irish Guards and the National Playing Fields Association on a fortnightly basis. Before orders were received he removed the ribbons of his Italian decorations awarded by a grateful Italy in 1918. He enrolled in the Hertfordshire Local Defence Volunteers and was made commanding officer. In December 1940 he became one of twelve chairmen of selection boards for granting commissions in the Home Guard. He made his personal preparations for any possible invasion by digging a slit trench on one of the approaches to Ayot St Lawrence and equipped it with firearms. Initially he moved to Wrotham Park, near Barnet, and then to North Berwick, near Edinburgh, where he and his family remained until 1944. When the army benevolent fund was created in 1944, Cavan was made its president. Throughout the war he continued to work on drafts of his memoirs, which he had begun in 1926, and carried out engagements at home while corresponding with members of the general staff. During August 1946 he became ill and went into a nursing home. Following a prostate operation he suffered a heart attack and died on 28 August at the London Clinic, Devonshire Place, London. He was buried on 31 August in the family grave at Ayot St Lawrence in the old churchyard opposite the house in which he was born. A memorial service was held in St Paul's Cathedral, London, a week later. His brother, the Venerable Horace Edward Samuel Sneade Lambart, archdeacon of Shropshire, succeeded to the titles as eleventh earl of Cavan. In his will, Field Marshal Lord Cavan left the bulk of his estate to his nephew, who became the twelfth earl of Cavan in 1950.

Cavan never attended Staff College and learned his 'trade' from observing the actions of his contemporaries and serving as a battalion and regimental officer. He believed that successful officers need to read widely, travel abroad, and learn appropriate foreign languages. He himself followed that advice. First and foremost he was a gentleman, and was brought up to respect order and discipline. In battle he believed in communicating orders in a way that was readily understood by his subordinates. He believed in order and discipline. On the battlefield he applied what he had learned, giving clear instruction. Henry Page Croft called him a 'commonsense general'. He became the best corps commander on the western front. There are few adverse comments about the career of Lord Cavan, who remained immensely popular within the army for the remainder of his life. 'He retained a great simplicity, single-mindedness of purpose, devotion to duty and deep and abiding religious faith which stood him in good stead throughout his whole life; his modesty and sincerity gained him hosts of good friends' (Godley, *Household Brigade Magazine*, 1946). When he became CIGS Sir Henry Wilson considered him an 'innocent' but there was no malice in the comment. 'Those who knew him were apt to comment on his dependability, imperturbability and friendliness' (Lindsay, 1995). JOHN G. E. COX

Sources earl of Cavan, 'Recollections: hazy but happy', priv. coll., Cavan MSS [memoirs, 1926–46] · E. Lambart, Fatty Cavan's life, by his sister, priv. coll., Cavan MSS · earl of Cavan, South African diary, 1900–02, priv. coll., Cavan MSS · earl of Cavan, 'Lights and shadows', priv. coll., Cavan MSS, vols. 7, 8 · earl of Cavan, scrapbook containing letters to his sister (Lady Ellen Lambart), 1914–18, priv. coll., Cavan MSS · earl of Cavan, scrapbooks headed 'Italy, 1917–18', 'Field Marshal, 1932', 'CIGS', priv. coll., Cavan MSS · countess of Cavan, newspaper cuttings books, 1922–4; 1924–33; 1933–74, priv. coll., Cavan MSS · J. E. Edmonds, ed., *Military operations, Italy, 1915–1919*, History of the Great War (1949) · J. E. Edmonds, ed., *Military operations, France and Belgium, 1916*, 2, History of the Great War (1938) · J. E. Edmonds, ed., *Military operations, France and Belgium, 1917*, 2, History of the Great War (1948) · T. Lever, *Clayton of Toc H* (1971) · B. Bond, *British military policy between the two world wars* (1980) · G. H. Cassar, *The forgotten front: the British campaign in Italy, 1917–18* (1998) · H. P. Croft, *Twenty-two months under fire* (1917) · A. Godley, *Household Brigade Magazine* (autumn 1946) · O. Lindsay, *Once a grenadier: the grenadier guards, 1945–1995* (1995) · *CGPLA Eng. & Wales* (1947) · *Debrett's Peerage* · GEC, *Peerage*
Archives CAC Cam., memoirs · CAC Cam., papers · PRO, papers, WO79/66–72 | IWM, corresp. with Sir Henry Wilson · NA Scot., corresp. with Arthur Balfour · NL Ire., letters to John Redmond · NL Scot., Earl Haig MSS · St George's Chapel, Windsor, Berkshire, letters to Stafford Crawley and Austice Crawley; letters to his wife [copies] | FILM BFI NFTVA, news footage · IWM
Likenesses P. A. de Laszlo, oils, 1912, priv. coll. · S. A. Chandler, photographs, c.1917, NPG · F. Dodd, charcoal and watercolour drawing, 1917, IWM · J. S. Sargent, group portrait, oils, 1922 (*General officers of World War I*), NPG · photograph, c.1937, priv. coll. · W. Orpen, oils, Cavalry and Guards Club, London · W. Stoneman, photographs, NPG · photograph, IWM · photograph, priv. coll. · portrait, priv. coll.
Wealth at death £98,693 14s. 1d.: probate, 1 Jan 1947, *CGPLA Eng. & Wales*

Lambe, Sir Charles Edward (1900–1960), naval officer, was born at Stalbridge, Dorset, on 20 December 1900, the only son of Henry Edward Lambe, solicitor, of Grove House, Stalbridge, and his wife, Lilian Hope, daughter of John Bramwell, of Edinburgh. He was descended from Rear-Admiral Sir Thomas Louis who fought at the battle of the Nile and served with distinction in the Napoleonic wars. Joining the Royal Naval College, Osborne, as a naval cadet in 1914, he was a midshipman in the battleship *Emperor of India* from 1917 until the end of the First World War. After serving at home and overseas he joined the *Vernon* at Portsmouth in 1925 to qualify as a torpedo specialist. A good horseman, a keen shot, and skilful amateur pilot, he showed also much professional promise.

After service in the Mediterranean and qualifying at the Naval Staff College, Lambe joined the East Indies flagship, the cruiser *Hawkins*, in 1932, being promoted to commander in 1933. He next served on the staff of the rear-admiral, A. B. Cunningham, commanding all Mediterranean destroyer flotillas. Cunningham soon recognized

Lambe's exceptional talents at handling men and affairs. Returning to England in 1935 Lambe became the commander of the *Vernon*, and was later appointed equerry to Edward VIII and later to George VI. He married in 1940 Lesbia Rachel (b. 1905), daughter of Sir Walter Orlando Corbet, fourth baronet, formerly wife of V. I. H. Mylius; they had one son and one daughter.

Promoted to captain in December 1937, shortly after his thirty-seventh birthday, Lambe commanded the cruiser *Dunedin* for the first year of the Second World War until in October 1940 he joined the joint planning staff in Whitehall as naval assistant director of plans. He soon became deputy director and then director of plans, serving as such until April 1944. This covered the period when virtually all the major strategic decisions of the war were taken. The agonizing military alternatives which faced the government in the early part of this period together with the tremendous problems arising from the Russian, Japanese, and American entries into the war were the principal concern of the joint planning staff, who advised the chiefs of staff, and who in their turn were presided over by Winston Churchill.

Lambe's influence was far-reaching with his service colleagues, and with the chiefs of staff. His judgement, his serenity of outlook, his ability to explain, persuade, and listen to all sides, and above all his imagination and ability to see the heart of a problem proved of exceptional value to his country.

On leaving Whitehall Lambe commanded the aircraft-carrier *Illustrious* in the Indian and Pacific oceans. Hit once by a Japanese suicide aircraft, *Illustrious* took part in many operations. Soon after the end of the Japanese war he returned to the Admiralty as assistant chief of staff (air) as an acting rear-admiral and went on to appointments where his knowledge of air problems both human and technical were of special value: flag officer, flying training (1947–9), admiral commanding 3rd aircraft-carrier squadron (1949–51), and flag officer (air) home (1951–3). He became commander-in-chief, Far East station, in 1953 and served there with particular success in the difficult time following the Korean War. Later, in 1955 as second sea lord his sympathy for the less fortunate was of much value when heavy reductions were being made in naval personnel. Promoted to vice-admiral in 1950, admiral in 1954, and admiral of the fleet in 1960, Lambe was appointed CVO in 1938, CB in 1944, KCB in 1953, and GCB in 1957. Finally, after being commander-in-chief, Mediterranean (1957–9), he became first sea lord in 1959 to the delight of the navy, which was much saddened by the illness which led to his retirement in May, and his death on 29 August 1960, at his home, Knockhill House, Newport, Fife.

Lambe did many things well and often much better than other men, but there was something elusive about him. Endowed with much personal charm and greatly liked, he had a first-rate intellect which never tolerated insincerity—yet there was perhaps an inner sanctum in him which few penetrated but many sensed. His clear well-ordered mind saw through most problems, and also the most practical ways of solving them. His tastes were catholic and his enthusiasm infectious. Added to a love of outdoor pursuits he had a deep appreciation and understanding of many artistic things. He was a pianist quite out of the ordinary in performance, an accomplished watercolour painter, a lifelong member of the Bach Choir, and had an abiding appreciation of Shakespeare and Andrew Marvell's sonnets which he enjoyed quoting. Yet for all this, his love of the navy and sense of service took priority over all else.   WILLIAM DAVIS, rev.

Sources *The Times* (31 Aug 1960) · *WWW* · S. W. Roskill, *The war at sea, 1939–1945*, 3 vols. in 4 (1954–61) · personal knowledge (1971) · *CGPLA Eng. & Wales* (1961) · Burke, *Peerage* (1980) · b. cert.
Archives NRA, priv. coll., corresp. and papers | FILM IWM FVA, actuality footage
Likenesses W. Stoneman, photograph, 1951, NPG · *Times of Malta*, photograph, 31 Dec 1958, Hult. Arch. · E. I. Halliday, oils, *HMS Vernon*, Portsmouth
Wealth at death £26,638 9s. 8d.: probate save and except settled land, 8 March 1961, *CGPLA Eng. & Wales* · £23,240 1s. 7d.: probate limited to settled land, 11 April 1961, *CGPLA Eng. & Wales*

Lambe, James (bap. 1599, d. 1664), oriental scholar, was baptized on 2 February 1599 at All Saints, Oxford, the son of Richard Lambe and his second wife. He attended Magdalen College School, matriculated from Brasenose College on 2 July 1613, graduated BA on 13 December 1615, and proceeded MA (from St Mary Hall) on 11 December 1619. He spent much of his life as chaplain to Thomas Wriothesley, fourth earl of Southampton, in whose gift were the ecclesiastical livings which Lambe held. He became rector of Botley, Hampshire, in 1639, and subsequently vicar of Titchfield in the same county (the location of Southampton's seat) but, no doubt because of his patron's royalist sympathies in the civil war, this living was sequestered in 1647. Lambe married Elizabeth Beeston (née Bromfield), widow of William Beeston, after 1636. They had no children, but by his marriage Lambe became stepfather to William *Beeston (1636–1702), later lieutenant-governor of Jamaica, and Henry Beeston (later master of Winchester College and warden of New College).

Lambe acquired expertise in oriental languages, especially Arabic, presumably by independent study since he left Oxford before an Arabic lectureship was established. He published nothing but his reputation was such that Edmund Castell invited him in 1658 to join in compiling the 'Heptaglot lexicon' (he refused). Among the papers which he bequeathed to Henry Beeston were nine notebooks, which Beeston donated to the Bodleian Library in 1669 (MSS Lambe). These illustrate his assiduity in studying Arabic grammar and vocabulary, to which (apart from excerpts from the Syriac Bible) they are all devoted. They also reveal that Lambe's learning was derived from a very narrow range of materials, principally the publications of the Dutch oriental scholar Erpenius, especially his Arabic grammar and his edition of al-Makin's history, the *Historia Saracenica* (1625).

After the Restoration, Lambe was rewarded by the king with a canon's prebend at Westminster (23 July 1660) and the title of DD Oxon. (9 August 1660), and by Southampton with the rectory of St Andrews, Holborn (4 January 1663). He died in the canon's lodgings at Westminster, survived by his wife, on 18 October 1664, and was buried in Westminster Abbey two days later. G. J. TOOMER

Sources Wood, *Ath. Oxon.*, new edn, 3.668 • will, 4 Oct 1664, PRO, PROB 11/315, fol. 117 • J. L. Chester, ed., *The marriage, baptismal, and burial registers of the collegiate church or abbey of St Peter, Westminster*, Harleian Society, 10 (1876), 161 • Foster, *Alum. Oxon.* • *Reg. Oxf.*, 2/2.331 • *Reg. Oxf.*, 2/3.341 • *Walker rev.*, 186 • G. Hennessy, *Novum repertorium ecclesiasticum parochiale Londinense, or, London diocesan clergy succession from the earliest time to the year 1898* (1898), 90, 447 • E. Castell, letter to Samuel Clarke, BL, Add. MS 22905, fol. 15 • *Brasenose College quatercentenary monographs*, 1, OHS, 52 (1909), monographs iv–vii; 2/1, OHS, 53 (1909), 50 • W. D. Macray, *Annals of the Bodleian Library, Oxford*, 2nd edn (1890), 135 • *Calamy rev.*, 370 • committee for plundered ministers, BL, Add. MS 15671, fol. 25r • J. Walker, *An attempt towards recovering an account of the numbers and sufferings of the clergy of the Church of England*, pt 2 (1714), 298 • parish register, Oxford, All Saints, 2 Feb 1599, Oxon. RO [baptism]
Archives Bodl. Oxf., MSS
Wealth at death approx. £2000: will, 4 Oct 1664, PRO, PROB 11/315, fol. 117

Lambe, John (1545/6–1628), astrologer, of unknown parentage, probably originated in Worcestershire. According to his own later evidence he was first a teacher of reading and writing in English to the families of gentry. Without any training he began to practise medicine, assuming the title of 'doctor', then took up fortune telling. He was arrested in 1608, the charges being that during the previous December, at Tardebigge, Worcestershire, he attempted to disable or sap the strength of Thomas, sixth Lord Windsor, and in May 1608, at nearby Hindlip, he invoked evil spirits. Lambe was held in Worcester Castle, where he contrived to demonstrate his skill and powers to his many visitors. At his trial judgment was suspended on the first charge and stayed on the second.

Within two weeks of Lambe's trial some forty people, including sheriffs, justices, and others who had been present in court, died. The true cause was probably gaol fever, carried by an infected prisoner into the court, but a petition was raised for Lambe's transfer, and he was moved to London's king's bench prison. There he lived in some comfort in two rooms, with servants. He employed laundresses, who worked partly in his rooms and found their custom in the surrounding district. He continued to receive visitors and to practise as before, and during this period he met and became a protégé of George Villiers, duke of Buckingham and favourite of James I.

This comfortable if confined life was brought to an end on 16 June 1623 when Lambe, then aged seventy-seven, was indicted for the rape of Joan Seger, a girl of eleven who had been sent to his rooms at the prison with a basket of herbs. He was found guilty and sentenced to hang, but was first questioned by James Ley, lord chief justice. Details of Lambe's early life emerged from Ley's report to the secretary of state summarizing Lambe's evidence and defence. Ley found that the girl's father owed Lambe money, and that the charge of rape had only been laid

some weeks later when Lambe tried to recover this debt. Ley decided that on the evidence the rape charge was not proved and on 4 June 1624 Lambe was pardoned and released. He then rented a house near parliament, where he lived for over a year.

Lambe's relationship with the hated Buckingham and his supposed magical powers on Buckingham's behalf were common knowledge, which was why the mob continuously watched him. On 12 June 1626 a freak storm caused a mist to rise from the Thames near to York House, Buckingham's residence. 'This occasioned the more discourse among the vulgar, in that Dr Lamb appeared there upon the Thames, to whose Art of Conjuring they attributed that which had happened' (Rushworth, 391). Buckingham's mother consulted Lambe about her son's fate; he showed her in a glass the figure of a big fat man with a long dagger, who would kill her son. Lambe was cited as a lover and supplier of charms to Lady Purbeck, Buckingham's sister-in-law. Charges of sorcery and adultery in that matter, made in November 1627, were later dropped, but in December he was again imprisoned, for inducing a Westminster scholar 'to give himself to the Devil' (Birch, 252).

For some time Lambe had claimed that he had been licensed to practise as a physician by the bishop of Durham. However, on 18 December 1627 he was examined by the College of Physicians of London and found to be ignorant of the language and practice of medicine. His plea was that he just pretended to examine and treat people, in order to acquire a little money.

On Friday 13 June 1628 Lambe went to the Fortune Theatre, a popular haunt of the lower classes. He was recognized by some lads, who waited outside for him and then followed him, attracting thereby a larger gathering; Lambe's reaction was to hire some sailors to act as a bodyguard. They kept the crowd at bay while he supped at the Horseshoe tavern off Moor Lane. He then entered the City at Moorgate, followed by a now hostile crowd who pelted him with stones. He took shelter in the Windmill tavern, at which the crowd took vengeance on his bodyguard. The tavern keeper, fearful for his own safety, forced Lambe to leave; he managed to sneak out unseen and find refuge in a nearby house, but was discovered by the mob and again ejected. Emerging on the street, he was surrounded, and stoned and clubbed into unconsciousness. He was carried into a compter (a small lockup) in the Poultry, where he died early on 14 June. In his pockets were found a crystal ball, knives, pictures, a gold nightcap, and 40 shillings. He was buried the next day in the churchyard of St Mildred Poultry. Buckingham was stabbed to death two months later.

No one was ever brought to trial for Lambe's killing. The City authorities were severally admonished for failing to prevent his death and find his killers, and in 1632 the king's bench imposed a fine of £1000 on them, which was raised by a levy on the City companies. In September or October 1628 there appeared *A briefe description of the notorious life of Iohn Lambe, otherwise called Doctor Lambe. Together with his ignominious death.* Supposedly published in Amsterdam, it bore no author's or printer's name; it was, however, printed in London, and was followed by many broadsheets and ballads commemorating a strange life and a horrific death. ANITA McCONNELL

Sources L. M. Goldstein, 'The life and death of John Lambe', *Guildhall Studies in London History*, 4 (1979–81) · J. Rushworth, *Historical collections*, 5 pts in 8 vols. (1659–1701), vol. 1, p. 391 · [T. Birch and R. F. Williams], eds., *The court and times of Charles the First*, 1 (1848), 252 · *Analytical index, to the series of records known as Remembrancia, preserved among the archives of the City of London*, Corporation of London, ed. [W. H. Overall and H. C. Overall] (1878), 455 · G. Clark and A. M. Cooke, *A history of the Royal College of Physicians of London*, 1 (1964), 259
Likenesses line engraving (after woodcut, 1628), BM, NPG · print (modern copy; after woodcut, 1628), BM, NPG
Wealth at death 40s. with him when he died

Lambe, Sir John (*c*.1566–1646), civil lawyer, was the first of four children of John Lambe of Northampton and Elizabeth Aylett. He matriculated in 1583 from St John's College, Cambridge, where a novel conformist divinity was developing, and graduated BA in 1587. He then made a pilgrimage to Rome, returning to proceed MA in 1590. His ruthlessly ambitious career began in the Peterborough diocesan courts in 1590, and from 1603 until 1628 he held the office of registrar. By 1607 he was married either to Anne Crompton (*d.* 1624) or to an unknown first wife; he and Anne had two daughters (born in 1619 and 1621), one of whom, Barbara, married Basil Feilding, later earl of Denbigh.

In Northampton Lambe joined an embattled faction of avant-garde conformists led by John Buckeridge, Richard Butler (a close university friend), and David Owen, whose outlook was characterized by political absolutism, rabid anti-puritanism, anti-sabbatarianism, and an insistence on full ceremonial conformity. Thus in 1604 Lambe wrote to another university friend, Richard Neile, describing the anti-papist panic in Northampton following the recent clerical deprivations for nonconformity as a puritan threat to social order. He lodged with Butler at Spratton from 1605. During 1606 there commenced legal disputes with Lewis Tresham over land at Rothwell and with Jerome Lowe, who had violently interfered with Lambe's collection of tithes from the leased rectory of Yardley Hastings. As a result of the latter, Lambe and his wife were lampooned as papist sympathizers in satirical poems circulating among his puritan enemies around Northampton. In retaliation Lambe in 1607 brought proceedings against his opponents in the Star Chamber by raising, in a letter to James I, the spectre of a popular puritan threat to monarchy in the wake of the midland revolt. After 1608 he moved back to Northampton and at some time before 1615 lived at Tower Close. From 1611 until 1617 Lambe was the surrogate of Christopher Wyvell, the chancellor of Lincoln diocese, and there became associated with John Williams, to whose patronage, according to Williams's biographer, John Hacket, Lambe, who allegedly possessed the mien of a prize-fighter, owed his rise to power.

Between 1615 and 1629 Lambe was chancellor of Peterborough diocese, and supported a clique of like-minded clergymen whom he appointed his surrogates in the church courts—the most zealous being Robert Sibthorpe (his brother-in-law), David Owen, and Samuel Clarke. Lambe now tried to turn the Calvinist evangelical Jacobean church in a conformist direction. The county town bore the brunt of their campaign: ceremonial conformity, particularly lay reception of the communion kneeling, was enforced with a severity and a contempt for puritan equivocation almost unknown in the Jacobean church; the godly practices of holding prayer meetings and gadding to sermons were proscribed, and an abortive attempt was made to enforce the anti-sabbatarian Book of Sports (1618) and the observance of various holy days. In 1616, when his puritan enemies in Northampton and Sir Edward Montague retaliated by bringing articles to Judge Sir Edward Coke's attention charging him with persecuting them in the church courts, Williams persuaded Cambridge University to award Lambe an LLD. This made him eligible for the commissaryship of the archdeaconry of Leicester to which Neile, now bishop of Lincoln, appointed him in 1617. From 1619 until 1640 Lambe served as a JP for Northamptonshire: in 1620 he moved to Rothwell. When his Northampton opponents sought redress for a second time from the 1621 parliament, Williams, now lord keeper, again saved him—Lambe's letter to James I describing a puritan conspiracy to undermine royal authority—by securing a knighthood which was conferred on 26 July 1621 at Castle Ashby, Northamptonshire. The king appointed him the same year to the court of delegates. When Archbishop Abbot accidentally killed a gamekeeper Williams recommended that the duke of Buckingham seek legal advice from Lambe on how to proceed. After 1624 Lambe married Elizabeth Kimbould; there were no children of this union, and she predeceased him. A quarrel arose in 1626 over the registrarship of the archdeaconry of Leicester, Lambe backing his subordinate, Henry Allein, against John Pregion. In an emergent split from Williams, Lambe's party accused the now bishop of Lincoln of stymieing a high commission investigation into Leicester puritanism. Allein (backed by Lambe and Sibthorpe) in 1627 charged Pregion with leniency towards, and sympathy with, puritans. Williams rejected the case, and when Allein appealed to the privy council in 1628 Lambe and Sibthorpe gave evidence against Williams. But unlike his erstwhile patron, Lambe was secure in royal favour: appointed a high commissioner in 1629 he obtained through Neile a royal pardon for Sibthorpe's defence of the royal prerogative (*Apostolike Obedience*), which the parliament of that year condemned. Examined by parliament, Lambe was saved by the dissolution. Williams's attempts to oust Lambe from his own Leicester office and replace him with his secretary, Walter Walker, led to a verdict for Walker in the court of king's bench, whose judge, Sir James Whitelocke, claimed Lambe had given 'the greatest affront to the Court that ever was' (Slater, 55), but Lambe in 1632 persuaded Charles I to issue a royal command halting proceedings at common law. The matter had become part of the continuing Laud / Williams rivalry which climaxed in the latter's suspension from office.

Promoted to dean of the court of arches by his ally Archbishop William Laud in 1633, Lambe enforced as zealously as anyone the conformist policies he had so long preferred. In 1634 he advocated Laud's right to visit the diocese of Lincoln when Williams proved obstructive, and provided legal advice to Sir Thomas Wentworth on the Irish church. Lambe blocked the appeals of provincial parishes against Laudian policies, as in the cases of the churchwardens of All Saints (Northampton) and Upton, who were punished by Sibthorpe and Clarke for opposition to the altar policy: puritan scruples were condemned as seditious. As a high commissioner Lambe participated in the highest profile prosecutions of the personal rule, including those of Henry Burton, John Bastwick, William Prynne, Peter Smart, John Lilburne, and Sir Robert Howard. According to Laud at his trial, Lambe disobeyed the archbishop's order in 1638 to suppress John Cowell's absolutist work *The Interpreter*. He reinforced the actions of his Peterborough subordinates by prosecuting Miles Burkit for opposing the altar policy and Sir Richard Samwell for aiding him. The puritan prayer meetings of several Northamptonshire JPs were also targeted. By 1635, as commissary for the archdeaconry of Buckingham, he punished leaders of opposition to the Book of Sports, while in Leicester archdeaconry he enforced the strictest Laudian altar policy. Lambe was a leading promoter of Laud's metropolitical visitation in Lincoln and Peterborough dioceses, accompanied the archbishop on his visitation of St Paul's Cathedral, successfully upheld the archbishop's right to visit Oxford University, and personally acted as visitor of Merton College. As one of the visitors of Waddesdon in Buckinghamshire archdeaconry, Lambe ordered the raising of an annual levy to support a church organ and organist. He intervened repeatedly in Sibthorpe's many local disputes and shared the view that opposition to the prerogative tax of ship money was the result of puritan sedition. Lambe also brought Sibthorpe's defence of George Plowright against impressment for the bishops' war to the attention of the privy council, where the verdict went against Sibthorpe.

At the zenith of his fortunes Lambe was chancellor to Queen Henrietta Maria from 26 January 1640 until 1642, and played a leading role in convocation's framing of new ecclesiastical canons. In August 1640 he detected a group of London clergy meeting to oppose the 'etcetera oath' and proceeded in arches against clergy meeting at Kettering, who refused to swear the oath as illegal and sympathized with Scottish propaganda in the bishops' war. Lambe shared Sibthorpe's view that the conflict was the culmination of a puritan plot to subvert church and state. A flurry of petitions of grievance led in 1641 to his being sent for as a delinquent by the Long Parliament, which declared illegal many of the verdicts in which he had participated, fined him heavily, and sequestrated his property. Parliament even considered impeaching him; scurrilous pamphlet literature and cartoons linked him

closely with the archbishop. By 1642 church court activity had ceased. Lambe was named in the commission of array for Northamptonshire, and after the outbreak of civil war he fled to royalist headquarters at Oxford in 1643, was incorporated as a member of the university on 9 December, and remained until the surrender in 1646. On his return to London to compound for his estates he died intestate (leaving a fortune reputedly valued at £5000), probably at The Bell inn, Carter Lane, and was buried at the church of St Andrew by the Wardrobe, London, on 21 November 1646. J. FIELDING

Sources A. J. Fielding, 'Conformists, puritans and the church courts: the diocese of Peterborough, 1603–1642', PhD diss., U. Birm., 1989, 34–5, 37–8, 42–3, 60–61, 65–6, 70–86, 97, 101, 105, 107–8, 115–16, 127, 129, 135, 139, 247, 261 • M. D. Slatter, 'A biographical study of Sir John Lambe, c.1566–1646', BLitt diss., U. Oxf., 1952 • J. Davies, *The Caroline captivity of the church: Charles I and the remoulding of Anglicanism, 1625–1641* (1992), 166, 193, 237–8, 257, 267–9 • J. S. Hart, *Justice upon petition: the House of Lords and the reformation of justice, 1621–1675* (1991), 72, 76–7, 97–8, 115–16 • wills, PRO, PROB 6/22, fol. 68r [Susan Hill, *alias* Lambe, Sir John's niece]; PROB 6/48, fol. 41v [Edward Hill, son of Susan Hill] • *DNB* • B. P. Levack, *The civil lawyers in England, 1603–1641* (1973), 246–7 • A. Foster, *The Church of England, 1570–1640* (1994), 106
Archives E. Sussex RO, letters to Sir Thomas Holland
Likenesses satirical cartoon, 1641, repro. in T. Stirry, *A rot amongst the bishops, or, A terrible tempest in the sea of Canterbury* (1641)
Wealth at death approx. £5000: Levack, *Civil lawyers*, 246

Lambe, Robert (*bap.* 1711, *d.* 1795), Church of England clergyman and antiquary, was baptized at St Nicholas's Church, Durham, on 15 August 1711, the son of John Lambe, mercer, of Durham. He was educated at Durham grammar school and at St John's College, Cambridge, whence he matriculated in 1728 and graduated BA in 1734. He was ordained deacon at Lincoln on 23 September 1733 and priest at Norwich in October 1735, whereupon he was appointed a minor canon of Durham Cathedral. In 1747 he obtained the curacy of South Shields and a few weeks later received the living of Norham, Northumberland, which had become vacant. He remained at Norham for the rest of his life and married there, on 11 April 1755, Philadelphia Nelson (*d.* 1772), the daughter of a Durham carrier. According to James Raine's account of his courtship Lambe had seen her only once, many years before he suddenly decided to propose. In his proposal letter he invited her to meet him on Berwick pier and asked her to carry a tea caddy so that he could identify her; he then absentmindedly failed to meet her on the appointed day but none the less his suit was successful. The couple had a daughter, Philadelphia (*b.* 1756), who married Alexander Robertson of Berwick, and two sons, Robert (1759–1771), and Ralph, who died in infancy in 1764.

Lambe's publications reflect his wide-ranging historical interests; the first was *The History of Chess* (1764; 2nd edn, 1765). His principal work, *An Exact and Circumstantial History of the Battle of Flodden* (1774), appears to have been based on Thomas Gent's edition of a manuscript belonging to John Askew of Pallinsburn, Northumberland, and was embellished with Lambe's notes, which, he claimed, recorded authentic historical events. However, stories such as his description of St Cuthbert's body floating down the Tweed in a stone coffin were the product of his mischievous imagination. Likewise he maintained that his poem 'The Laidley Worm of Spindleston Heugh' was translated from a song composed by a mystical bard living in the Cheviots in the thirteenth century. This hoax fooled William Hutchinson, who included the poem in his history of Northumberland, and some of Lambe's purported archaeological discoveries were also practical jokes intended to catch out his fellow antiquaries.

Lambe died at Edinburgh on 7 May 1795 and was buried in Eyemouth churchyard, Berwickshire. His wife, who had predeceased him, had been buried at Gilligate, Durham, on 13 January 1772.

W. A. J. ARCHBOLD, *rev.* M. J. MERCER

Sources R. Welford, *Men of mark 'twixt Tyne and Tweed*, 3 vols. (1895) · Venn, *Alum. Cant.*, 1/3.37 · *N&Q*, 5th ser., 4 (1875), 308, 392, 492, 520 · *N&Q*, 5th ser., 10 (1878), 337 · J. Raine, *The history and antiquities of north Durham* (1852), 264 · Nichols, *Illustrations*, 7.391–3

Lambe, Thomas (*fl.* 1629–1661), Baptist preacher and soap-boiler, must be distinguished from another Thomas Lamb, a merchant and also for a time a prominent Baptist. Lambe the soapboiler is probably first encountered at Colchester, Essex, where on 23 March 1619 he married Dorcas Prentice at the parish church of St Nicholas. For the next twelve years he lived in the parish of St Giles in the town. In October 1629 he was accused before the archdeaconry court of non-attendance at church and failing to receive communion at Easter. This was perhaps the first of his many conflicts with the established church. On 1 July 1636 Lambe and his wife were excommunicated, having refused to attend services or have their child baptized; he is said to have also vowed 'that he would be burned before he would receive the holy sacrament after this manner' (Essex RO, D/AC/A51, fol. 122). In 1637 Lambe was reported for 'working on his trade by boyling of sope on Sunday [21 May]' (Essex RO, D/AC/A52, fol. 93r) and on 26 April 1638 the churchwardens testified that when they had demanded 4d. towards a rate for the repair of the church he refused with the remark that 'he did wish that all churches were layd in the dust' (ibid., fol. 233r).

At the end of November 1639 Lambe was in trouble with the high commission, for keeping a conventicle, and was arrested. On 6 February 1640 he appeared with Francis Lee, also of Colchester. Both had refused to take the oath *ex officio*, and were committed to prison, where their keepers were instructed to 'restrain them from company, and keeping of conventicles and private exercises of religion' (PRO, SP 16/434, fol. 88). On 25 June Lambe petitioned for release, on the grounds that 'he had for 20 weeks last past been a prisoner lying in the Fleet by means whereof his wife and six small children were utterly deprived of their maintenance, he being by trade a weaver'; the petition was allowed, on security to be determined by the bishop, provided Lambe would confer about the legality of the oath, keep from conventicles, and 'not offer to preach or baptize anie children' (ibid., fol. 221). The court may not have been rightly informed and the change in trade is puzzling, but this last phrase marks him as a separatist, and

not an anti-paedobaptist. Shortly after release Lambe evidently moved from Colchester; the last reference to him in the archdeaconry act book, dated 30 July, cryptically notes that he, his wife, and four others had 'forsaken their church' (Essex RO, D/AC/A54, fol. 159v). It may be that it was about this time that he became a Baptist; in mid 1642, after his departure from Colchester, there were two independent reports of other Baptists in the town. When on 15 October 1640 Lambe next appeared before the high commission, it was with Henoch Howet, a long-standing Baptist from Lincolnshire. On 17 January 1641 Lambe appeared as a resident of Whitechapel in London with about sixty others, charged with conventicling in that parish. Some of those named were soon associated with various Baptist congregations in London who, between late 1640 and early 1642, inaugurated the rebaptism of believers by immersion.

By the winter of 1641–2, Lambe was rebaptizing new recruits in the River Severn not far from Gloucester. While there he revealed plans for a second evangelistic visit, to Norwich, though nothing further is known of this. The outbreak of civil war may have disrupted such activities. Lambe set about building a Baptist church in London. In 1642 he was listed as a subsidy payer, rated at 2s. in goods, living in Holywell Street, Whitechapel, and it is possible his congregation met there for a time. Certainly by 1645 it was to be found at Bell Alley, Coleman Street, in the northern suburbs of the City. Most of Lambe's known early contacts had been with those who were or became General Baptists, but his congregation was at first very far from unified around the theological positions later associated with that denomination. Among its early members were (probably) Thomas Patience, and (certainly) Benjamin Cox, shortly to be leaders of the Particular Baptists, and perhaps the Leveller Richard Overton; it was to prove a breeding ground for other future Levellers. The vicar of Terling in Essex, Timothy Batte, a physician, was the senior spokesman for the church, and in 1644 he spoke alongside Lambe at a disputation with John Stalham; but the theological views which Batte set down only a little later were of a high-Calvinistic Antinomian stamp. Lambe himself was anxious to stress that Christ died for all men—the central proposition which came to distinguish the General Baptist denomination. But while rejecting both federal covenant theory and preoccupation with external discipline, he also defended the orthodox view that God had predestined an elect to salvation, and contended vigorously with advocates of free will the concept of falling away and the rejection of formal ordinances. It is unclear how, by 1642, Lambe had arrived at these elements of a renovated Calvinistic orthodoxy. His theological outlook helped to underpin an energetic programme of evangelism, which left far behind those more conservative groups who stressed the corporate bonds between members and individual obedience to the precepts of the law.

For several years Lambe was the most influential leader of the most dynamic and notorious church in England. Its emissaries preached in areas controlled by parliament, at first usually near London, though even in 1643 Cox travelled as far as Coventry. In 1644 Lambe toured in Kent and Essex, and the following year he was sighted at Guildford, Surrey, and at Portsmouth, Hampshire. In 1643 and 1644 sharp factional disputes disturbed Lambe's congregation, in which some had reached the view that all would be saved, while others, notably Batte and Cox, contested against general redemptionism, decamping with their followers in 1644–5. Something of the story of these arguments can be constructed from Lambe's book *Christ Crucified* (1646) and the two editions of his *Fountain of Free Grace Opened* (1644, 1648). Soon the activities of another colleague, Samuel Oates, were causing official alarm in several eastern counties. Back in London, Lambe was perfectly prepared to use parish churches to put across his message. On 5 November 1644 he preached at St Benet Gracechurch, drawing 'a mighty great audience' (*Gangraena*, 1.92). These proselytizing activities enraged Thomas Edwards, but the church's activities in London provided him with equally scandalous material. This by no means dispassionate observer exposed what he saw as its practice of helping members enter informal marriages, unenforceable at law, and commented on the anarchic results of its admitting all comers: 'there is such a confusion and noise, as if it were at a Play; and some will be speaking here, some there; yong youths and boyes come hither, and make a noise while they are at their Exercises' (ibid.). Above all there was the apparent willingness of Lambe to allow almost any theological proposition to be discussed, no matter how unorthodox; on 5 February 1646 he is said to have debated publicly for five hours against Overton and Batte over the mortality of the soul. The dispute was held, in defiance of the mayor's marshal, in Spitalfields, at the north end of Bishopsgate, and it is likely that the church had just moved there from Coleman Street.

Lambe may have already begun to involve himself in political struggle. On 9 December 1644, as Thomason noted on its face, a single printed sheet attacking the earls of Essex and Manchester was 'scattered about the streets in the night'. An apprentice, George Jeffery, examined by the Lords, named 'Thomas Lamb, an oilman' as one of its distributors, and this may be the soapboiler (*JHL*, 7.91). The army was already becoming politicized, partly because of the growing influence of radical separatists and Baptists opposed to plans for a presbyterian settlement; in September 1646 Lambe was with his colleague Jeremy Ives in Devizes, Wiltshire, at a meeting with many soldiers. On 15 March 1647 the Commons were informed that the Independent-Leveller *Humble Petition of many Thousands* presented that day had earlier been discussed at the Spital meeting place. After his sermon and prayers Lambe had listened while the petition was read, correcting the reader several times. He was summoned to the Commons committee of examinations chaired by Colonel Leigh, to answer questions about his involvement in the organization of the petitioning campaign in London. It is clear that this campaign continued for several weeks, and Lambe and his friends were very probably involved in it. William

Walwyn later recalled that they were extremely active in street politics in this period, while the leading Independents were nowhere to be seen. A little later it appears that Lambe also travelled to Northamptonshire, where Oates was reportedly distributing copies of the *Agreement of the People*. A contemporary sneered that the celebrated paper worn in the soldiers' hats at Ware, Hertfordshire, should rightly be entitled, 'The agreement of the people of the Spital' (*Mercurius Pragmaticus*, 73).

By the end of 1647 there had been sharp exchanges on theological issues between Lambe and leaders of the London Particular Baptists, notably Cox, who had just adopted a confession of faith phrased more conservatively than its 1644 predecessor. The denominational divergence reflected different political alignments and these controversies also affected the development of Lambe's church. In 1646 John Griffith (*d.* 1700), with help from the Kentish pastor Francis Cornwell, established the right for newly baptized members to be admitted to the congregation by the laying on of hands if they so wished, but, having failed to make the procedure compulsory, seceded with his followers. The new group quickly developed quietist tendencies and may fairly be seen as embodying a conservative response to the very radical direction in which Lambe had led the church. In April 1649, after the assumption of power by the army generals, William Kiffin and other Particular Baptist and Independent leaders issued a pamphlet repudiating the Levellers. Lambe angrily challenged them to debate the matter in public, but his opponents were now cutting with the grain. Radicalism no longer defined the immediate political agenda in the capital. Soon, Ives and Oates both enlisted as army chaplains, but Lambe is probably not to be identified with the chaplain of the regiment of Thomas Hunckes in Ulster granted £40 a year for maintenance in 1652. According to the title-page of his *Absolute Freedom from Sin* (1656), which he signed on 12 May, Lambe was then 'dwelling at the sign of the tun in Norton Fall-gate in London' (T. Lambe, *Absolute Freedom from Sin*, 1656, title-page). The work sought to defend his theological outlook (against John Goodwin) in much greater detail than had seemed necessary in the action-packed and optimistic years of the 1640s. It explicitly defended both the proposition that Christ had died for all men and that God had elected some to salvation. Lambe addressed the preface to Oliver Cromwell, whom he recalled as 'formerly appearing to me in my behalf upon several occasions' (ibid., preface). In January 1661 Lambe, together with prominent General and Particular Baptists, signed a joint declaration, *The Humble Apology of some Commonly called Anabaptists*, repudiating the insurrectionism of Venner. He may have been the Thomas Lamm committed on 26 October 1663 to the New Prison, but after this nothing more is known of him.

STEPHEN WRIGHT

Sources T. Edwards, *Gangraena* (1646) • archdeaconry act books, Essex RO, D/AC/A47–54 • M. Tolmie, 'Thomas Lambe, soapboiler, and Thomas Lambe, merchant, General Baptists', *Baptist Quarterly*, 27 (1977–8), 4–13 • *JHC*, 5 (1646–8) • [J. Stalham], *The summe of a conference at Terling* (1644) • W. Haller and G. Davies, eds., *The Leveller* tracts, 1647–1653 (1944) • J. C. Jeaffreson, ed., *Middlesex county records*, 4 vols. (1886–92), vol. 3 • *Mercurius Pragmaticus* (16–22 Nov 1647) • PRO, SP 16/434 • M. Tolmie, *The triumph of the saints: the separate churches of London, 1616–1649* (1977) • K. Lindley, *Popular politics and religion in civil war London* (1997) • J. Walter, *Understanding popular violence in the English revolution: the Colchester plunderers* (1999)

Lambe, Thomas. *See* Lamb, Thomas (d. 1686).

Lambe, Walter (*fl.* **1476–1504**), composer, is of unknown origins. Nor is anything known for certain about his education; there is no compelling reason to concur with speculation that the composer may be identifiable with the boy of this name who, having been born in Salisbury in 1450 or 1451, was elected a king's scholar of Eton College on 8 July 1467. The composer first occurs during 1476–7, as a lay clerk of the choir of Holy Trinity collegiate church, Arundel. On 5 January 1479 he was entered on the payroll, and on 13 February formally admitted, as a lay clerk of the choir of St George's Chapel, Windsor. During the autumn of 1479 he was appointed in addition to the office of master of the choristers, and he continued to occupy both posts until his departure between 1 October 1484 and 30 September 1485. In fact, he returned to Arundel, where he was once again a lay clerk during 1490–91; eventually, however, he returned to his former lay clerkship at Windsor on 1 July 1492. The rationale behind this curious career pattern is not at all evident. He was not reappointed as master of the choristers, but continued in employment as a lay clerk at least until 30 September 1504; because of loss of documentation at Windsor, his career beyond that date cannot be traced, and his date of death is unknown.

Lambe's surviving compositions comprise one setting of the Magnificat and seven Marian votive antiphons. All this music is preserved in the Eton choirbook, compiled *c.*1502–1505 for use by the choir of Eton College chapel. A further four pieces, listed in the index, have been lost from the manuscript; indeed, only John Browne was represented by a greater number of compositions, and certainly Lambe's work was well known and widely circulated. The text of *Stella celi* is an invocation for deliverance from plague, and may have been written in the summer of 1479, when an outbreak assailed the staff of St George's; beyond this, no chronology for his work can be suggested. Lambe emerges as among the two or three most accomplished representatives of that generation of composers who brought to maturity the uniquely English manner of late fifteenth-century composition. He wrote with equal assurance both for ensembles of men's voices and for full choir in up to six parts; his work is extended in scale, virtuosic in the demands which it makes on its performers, and no less imaginative in melodic invention than in the sonorities drawn from his ensemble.

ROGER BOWERS, *rev.*

Sources F. L. Harrison, ed., *The Eton choirbook*, 2nd edn, 3 vols., Musica Britannica, 10–12 (1967–73) • F. Harrison, 'The Eton choirbook', *Annales Musicologiques*, 1 (1953), 151–75 • Arundel Castle archives, West Sussex • N. Sandon, 'Lambe, Walter', *New Grove*, 2nd edn

Lambe, William (d. **1580**), philanthropist, was the son of a lesser gentleman of Sutton Valence in Kent. A man about whom, had it not been for his acts of philanthropy, little at all would have been known, his charity was celebrated in a posthumous life by Abraham Fleming, the compiler of Holinshed's chronicles, who in fashioning him as an exemplar of protestant piety made sure that his reputation endured. According to his biographer, Lambe

> hath bene seene and marked at Powles crosse to have continued from eight of the clock until eleven, attentively listening to the Preachers voice, and to have endured the ende, being weake and aged, when others both strong and lustie went away.   (Fleming)

It was also reported that during his last illness he was visited by Alexander Nowell, dean of St Paul's, and by John Foxe the martyrologist. Lambe was apparently the author of his own book of prayers, *The Conduit of Comfort* (1579), but it was probably ghost written by Fleming. The preamble to his will seems to breathe the spirit of the godly, as he looked forward to being accepted as 'one of the children of Abraham' (PRO, PROB 11/62, fol. 157). But Fleming felt it necessary to defend Lambe against 'privie whisperings' that he was a papist sympathizer, and there is no doubt that he had moved in a much more conservative milieu in his early life.

Stow describes Lambe as a gentleman of the royal chapel under Henry VIII (Stow, 1.316), but it would be more accurate to say that he had held a post in the chapel vestry, for which there is evidence from the chapel lists of 1520 and 1524. The men of the vestry were responsible for looking after the chapel accoutrements and plate. Lambe's friendships towards the end of his life, both with establishment figures such as Alderman Rowland Heyward and with the much more conservative master of the rolls, Sir William Cordell (the latter two being his executors), suggest that like many of his generation he stood precariously between two worlds. Although prosperous, he was never a tycoon—his subsidy assessments of £100 in 1541 and £50 in 1577 placing him among the top 700 to 800 citizens, but at the bottom of that group. He had dabbled in monastic lands, and in 1543 bought a package of metropolitan properties formerly belonging to the foundations of Rowley, St John Jerusalem, and St Bartholomew, Smithfield. He resided from 1541 in a property in Mugwell (or Monkwell) Street, adjacent to the former hermitage chapel of St James at London Wall.

The acquisition of property brought its inevitable tensions with the principles of charity, so that even this paragon, who during his lifetime is supposed to have distributed moneys anonymously among the poor of St Giles Cripplegate, was cast as one of the social villains of the metropolis when required by the court of aldermen in February 1574 to enter a recognizance not to take more poor tenants into his 'pestered' alley in Cripplegate. Lambe's close friendship with Heyward explains his entry to the Clothworkers' Company by redemption in 1568 at an unusually advanced age, and his evident willingness to vest the company with responsibility for the management of his charities perhaps explains the extraordinary step that they took in electing him to the mastership in 1569 after a very brief association with their guild. Lambe's willingness to participate in civic administration is confirmed by his service on the court of governors of Christ's Hospital from 1571 to 1579.

In spite of having married three times (the identity of his wives is unknown apart from their forenames, Joan, Alice, and Joan), Lambe was childless, and it was this circumstance which encouraged his philanthropy. Among the major projects he undertook during his lifetime was the foundation of almshouses at Sutton Valence in Kent in 1574, followed by a grammar school there in 1576, and the building of Holborn conduit (the latter at a cost of £1500) in 1577. The Clothworkers, who administered the Sutton Valence charities, were also the recipients of properties in the parishes of St Stephen, Coleman Street, and St Olave, Silver Street, together with the chapel of St James on London Wall, the former hermitage of the abbey of Gerendon in Leicestershire. In return the company were instructed to see that sermons were preached in the chapel four times a year and that a chaplain say divine service three times a week, as well as providing clothing each year for twelve poor men and twelve poor women, and an annuity to the poor of the parish of St Faith. Lambe's charity had its sharp edge: while requiring that his servants be kept for up to six months after his death, he nevertheless insisted that they should be treated in this way only if 'they repair to church and sermons and spend their time in other godly exercises' (PRO, PROB 11/62, fol. 157). He died on 21 April 1580 and was buried in a vault under a tomb he had already constructed in the parish church of St Faith under St Paul's.   IAN W. ARCHER

Sources A. Fleming, *A memoriall of the famous monuments and charitable almesdeedes of the right worshipful Meister William Lambe* (1580) · *An epitaph for William Lambe* (1580) · will, PRO, PROB 11/62, sig. 19 · F. L. Kisby, 'The royal household chapel in early Tudor London, 1485–1547', PhD diss., U. Lond., 1996 · London Clothworkers' Company, court minutes · M. Benbow, 'Index of London citizens involved in city government, 1558–1603', U. Lond., Institute of Historical Research, Centre for Metropolitan History · *LP Henry VIII* · F. T. W. Blatchley-Hennah, *A short history of Sutton Valence school* (1952) · repertories of the court of aldermen, CLRO · W. Dugdale, *The history of St Paul's Cathedral in London*, new edn, ed. H. Ellis (1818) · J. Stow, *A survey of London*, rev. edn (1603); repr. with introduction by C. L. Kingsford as *A survey of London*, 2 vols. (1908); repr. with addns (1971)
Likenesses portrait, 16th cent., Clothworkers' Hall, Mincing Lane, London · line engraving (after monument), BM

Lambe, William (1765–1847), physician and vegetarian, one of the four children of Lacon Lambe, an attorney, and his second wife, Elizabeth, daughter of John Berington and sister of the Catholic divine Joseph Berington (1746–1827), was born in St Peter's parish, Hereford, on 26 February 1765. He was educated at Hereford grammar school and St John's College, Cambridge, where he graduated BA in 1786, MB in 1789, and MD in 1802. He became a fellow of his college on 11 March 1788.

In 1794 Lambe married Harriet Mary (d. 1804), daughter of Captain John Walsh. They had six children: Harriet (b. 1794); Mary (b. 1796), who married the lawyer Saxe Bannister (1790–1877); Lacon William (1797–1871), who became a physician; Anne (b. 1800); Augusta (b. 1801); and Elizabeth (d. 1804). After his wife's death from scarlet fever Lambe married in 1809 Sophia Ann (c.1772–1815), daughter of Arthur Saunders, a physician; they had a daughter, Catherine (1810–1860).

Following his marriage in 1794, Lambe gave up his fellowship at Cambridge and moved to Warwick, where he succeeded to the practice of a friend, Walter Landor (father of the poet Walter Savage Landor). Here he also became friendly with Samuel Parr and William Roughead, and he soon published his analyses of the Leamington spring water. The results of further chemical examination of these waters were published by him in the *Transactions* of the Philosophical Society of Manchester and formed the basis of several later books.

Lambe moved to London shortly after 1803, and became a fellow of the Royal College of Physicians on 22 December 1804. He held both the censorship and Croonian lectureship on several occasions between 1806 and 1828, and he was Harveian orator in 1818. His London practice was neither very large nor remunerative. Lambe lived in Kentish Town, but kept a consulting room in 2 King's Road (later 14 Theobald's Road), Bedford Row, where he attended his patients three times a week. Many of them were poor people, from whom he would accept no fees. He also taught botany at the Aldersgate Street school of medicine, and was appointed physician to its dispensary in 1810.

Lambe's ill health led him to become a vegetarian at the age of forty-one. He also preferred to drink only distilled water. In 1813 he wrote that his only regret about such a regimen was that it had not been adopted much earlier in his life (Wyndham, 9). He published *A medical and experimental enquiry into the origin, symptoms, and cure of constitutional diseases* (1805) and *Reports of the effects of a peculiar regimen on schirrhous tumours and cancerous ulcers* (1809). Lambe's ideas were supported by Shelley, with whom, along with Keats, he was acquainted. Later in life Lambe became somewhat rigid in his vegetarianism. It is said that 'he carried his convictions about vegetable diet to such an extent that it well-nigh became a religious belief and he its despotic high priest' (ibid., 23). One of Lambe's grandsons later recalled:

> the old man's sudden appearance at the garden gate while the family were breakfasting off (among other things), a ham, great commotion was caused, the ham being thrust into a cupboard and all stray pieces heaped on the plate of a carnivorous governess, who, being ignorant of the reason, looked on in bewildered amazement.   (Wyndham, 24)

Shelley's biographer, Jefferson Hogg, wrote that the last time he met Lambe 'he told me he had breakfasted on one cauliflower and was just about to dine on another' (Wyndham, 27).

Lambe retired from practice about 1840, and died at Henwood, Dilwyn, Herefordshire, on 11 June 1847. He was buried in the family vault in the churchyard of that parish.   PATRICK WALLIS

Sources Munk, *Roll* · Venn, *Alum. Cant.* · [P. B. Shelley], *A vindication of natural diet* [1813] · [W. MacMichael and others], *Lives of British*

physicians (1830) · H. Wyndham, *William Lambe MD … a pioneer of reformed diet* (1940)

Lambert. *See also* Lambart.

Lambert, Aylmer Bourke (1761–1842), botanist, was born on 2 February 1761 at Bath, the only son of Edmund Lambert (d. 1802), landowner, of Boyton House, Wiltshire, and his first wife, the Hon. Bridget Bourke (d. 1773), daughter and heir of John Bourke, eighth Viscount Mayo. As a child he began to collect objects to form a little museum, and amassing botanical collections, together with horticulture, became a lifelong obsession. He was educated at Newsome's School in Hackney but spent his holidays at Hanford, Dorset, with Henry Seymer (1714–1785), brother of his father's second wife, a keen naturalist and gardener. Through Seymer, young Lambert came to know Richard Pulteney (1730–1801), the botanical historian, and Margaret, dowager duchess of Portland (1715–1785), likewise a botanist and gardener.

In January 1779 Lambert entered St Mary Hall, Oxford, as a gentleman commoner. However, although he became well acquainted with the Oxford botanists Daniel Lyons (1762–1834) and John Sibthorp (1758–1796) and continued to develop his interests in the subject, he left Oxford in 1782 without taking a degree. In December that year he married a young widow, Catherine Webster, *née* Bowater (d. 1828), whose gracious hospitality and charm endeared her to Lambert's many botanical friends. Among these were Sir Joseph Banks (1743–1820) and James Edward Smith (1759–1828).

When Smith, together with Samuel Goodenough (1743–1827) and Thomas Marsham (d. 1819), founded the Linnean Society of London in 1788, Lambert became a member and was appointed a vice-president in 1796. (At his death in 1842 he was the last remaining original member.) He contributed to the society's *Transactions* a few small papers.

A keen field botanist, Lambert formed a herbarium of British and Irish plants. He was elected a fellow of the Royal Society in 1791. Interested in many branches of natural history, in 1829 he joined the Wiltshire historian Sir Richard Colt Hoare (1738–1838) in the excavation of tumuli, subsequently becoming a member of the Society of Antiquaries. Near Boyton he found, for the first time in Britain, *Cirsium tuberosum* (*Cnicus tuberosus*), a rare species of thistle.

In 1789 Lambert went to Connaught in Ireland and in 1790 he did much botanizing in Mayo. There he met the ailing veteran Irish botanist Patrick Browne (1730–1790), who gave him his list of plants of Mayo and Galway. Lambert ultimately gave the list to Smith, but it remained unpublished until 1995. In 1797 Lambert published *A Description of the Genus Cinchona* but he was already planning a grand folio book on conifers, *A Description of the Genus Pinus*, with engraved plates drawn by Ferdinand Bauer (1760–1826), among the finest (and most expensive) conifer illustrations ever produced. The latter was published in seven parts between 1803 and 1807 in a manner so irregular that copies vary in contents; a plain copy cost 10 guineas, a coloured one 40 guineas. A second volume,

largely the work of Lambert's herbarium curator and librarian, David Don (1799–1841), was published in 1824. A second edition, published between 1828 and 1837, included conifers other than *Pinus*, together with an account of Lambert's herbarium by Don. The variation between copies, indicative of Lambert's lack of control over their issue, has made the work, Lambert's major claim to botanical fame, a bibliographer's nightmare.

On his father's death in 1802 Lambert became a wealthy man of leisure, owning Boyton House (the family property since 1527) and houses in Salisbury and London. He also received income from sugar plantations in Jamaica and estates in England and Ireland. Year by year he acquired, both by gift and by lavish purchases, many collections of dried plants (herbaria). However, he did not organize these into one scientific sequence for research purposes—as Banks, Hooker, Lindley, and Bentham did—but merely kept them as separate lots, which made their consultation difficult and led ultimately to their sale and disastrous dispersal in 1842. Yet Lambert did make his collections freely available for study by others, particularly foreign visitors such as Augustin Pyramus de Candolle (1778–1841). He was overjoyed when such visitors found species new to science within the herberia. David Don, especially, based accounts of genera on the specimens under his care, as also did his brother George Don (1798–1856) in his *A General System of Gardening and Botany* (1831–8).

Lambert, a genial and generous (if eccentric) man, needed and enjoyed the intellectual support and friendship of strong-willed botanists such as Banks, Smith, David Don, and William Jackson Hooker (1785–1865). Of these, only Hooker survived during Lambert's last years. Towards the end, Lambert's income greatly diminished but his expenditure did not. His financial and domestic affairs became chaotic, his debts staggering. Ill health and family disputes marred the end of his life. He died on 10 January 1842 at Kew and was buried in the church at Boyton House.

Lambert's will directed that his herbarium should be offered to the British Museum provided the trustees paid his debts, apparently amounting to £2500 even after sale of his London house, botanical library (comprising 689 items), and paintings. This the trustees declined to do. As a result, his botanical acquisitions, described at the time as being in a state of great confusion, were dispersed in three days (27–29 June 1842) by auction. A detailed study of the history and subsequent whereabouts of Lambert's collection (*Taxon*, 19, 1970, 489–656) showed that it had been widely dispersed. Portions of the collection were preserved at Cambridge, Geneva, Florence, Kew, Oxford, and Philadelphia; the part which had gone to Berlin was destroyed in the Second World War. It was a sad end to Lambert's ambition and efforts, and a disaster to botany through the scattering of type-specimens. The generic name *Lambertia* Smith commemorates him.

WILLIAM T. STEARN

Sources *Proceedings of the Linnean Society of London*, 1 (1838–48), 137–9 · H. S. Miller, 'The herbarium of Aylmer Bourke Lambert: notes on its acquisition, dispersal, and present whereabouts',

Taxon, 19 (1970), 489–656 • H. W. Renkema and J. Ardagh, 'Aylmer Bourke Lambert and his *Description of the genus Pinus*', *Journal of the Linnean Society of London—Botany*, 48 (1928–31), 439–66 • A. T. Gage and W. T. Stearn, *A bicentenary history of the Linnean Society of London* (1988) • A. L. Lambert, correspondence to J. E. Smith, 1789–1827, Linn. Soc. • W. J. Hooker, correspondence with D. Turner, 1839–42, Royal Collection • *Catalogue of the valuable botanical library of the late A. B. Lambert* (1842) [sale catalogue, S. Leigh Sotheby, Lower Grosvenor Street, 18 April 1842] • *Catalogue of the botanical museum of the late A. B. Lambert* (1842) [sale catalogue, R. L. Sotheby, London, 27–29 June 1842] • *The letters of Asa Gray*, ed. J. L. Gray (1843)

Archives BL, corresp. and papers, Add. MSS 28545, 28610–28612 • RBG Kew, corresp. and catalogue of books | Bodl. Oxf., Radcliffe Science Library, genus *Pinus* • Bodl. Oxf., corresp. with Harriett Pigott • Devizes Museum, Wiltshire, Wiltshire Archaeological and Natural History Society, letters to William Cunningham • Linn. Soc., corresp. with Richard Pulteney • Linn. Soc., corresp. with Sir James Smith • NHM, letters to members of Sowerby family • RBG Kew, letters to Sir William Hooker

Likenesses Holl, stipple, 1805 (after J. Russell), NPG • Landseer, engraving, c.1807 (after pastel drawing by Russell), repro. in R. Thornton, *The Temple of Flora* (1981) • J. Russell, drawing, c.1808, Linn. Soc. • W. Evans, stipple, pubd 1810 (after H. Edridge), BM, NPG; repro. in Miller, 'The herbarium of Aylmer Bourke Lambert', 490 • A. C. Lucas, miniature plaster bust, 1834, Linn. Soc. • S. C. Smith, chalk drawing, BM

Wealth at death bankrupt; London house sold for £2000; library and paintings £1140; herbarium £1171; creditors received 15 shillings to the pound: Miller, 'The herbarium of Aylmer Bourke Lambert'

Lambert, Brooke (1834–1901), social reformer and Church of England clergyman, was born in Chertsey, Surrey, on 17 September 1834. He was the fourth son and fifth of the eight children of Francis John Lambert (1798–1876), younger son of Sir Henry Lambert, fourth baronet (1760–1803). Sir John Lambert, the first baronet (d. 1723), belonged to a Huguenot family of the Île de Ré, and settled as a merchant in London soon after 1685. Brooke's mother, Catherine (d. 1851), only daughter of Major-General Wheatley, an army officer, was of Welsh descent. The family moved during Brooke's childhood to Kensington.

After education at home and at a small school kept by James Chase, a clergyman of strong evangelical views, Lambert went in 1849 to Brighton College. After deciding to seek holy orders, he became a student at King's College, London. The excitement caused by the ejection of F. D. Maurice in 1853 from his professorship there stirred in Lambert a regard for Maurice which influenced his churchmanship for life. In 1854 he matriculated at Brasenose College, Oxford, as a commoner, and in 1858 he graduated BA; he proceeded MA in 1861 and BCL in 1863. He chose a pass degree in order that he might pursue his own course of reading, as well as sporting and social activities, without interference. He attended A. P. Stanley's lectures on ecclesiastical history and formed a friendship with him.

At Whitsuntide 1858 Lambert was ordained deacon, and was successively curate of Christ Church, Preston, Lancashire (1858–60), and of St John's, Worcester (1860–63). After some months at Hillingdon, near Uxbridge, he became curate to the Revd R. E. Bartlett, vicar of St Mark's,

Whitechapel, London. On the promotion of Bartlett, Lambert succeeded to the vicarage in 1865.

As vicar of St Mark's, Lambert performed many duties which lay outside the ecclesiastical range. He joined the Whitechapel board of trustees and the vestry and became a member of the board of works and a guardian. He began a thorough study of poor-law administration and local government, and gave expression to his developing views in *Pauperism: seven sermons preached at St. Mark's, Whitechapel, and one preached before the university, Oxford, with a preface on the work and position of clergy in poor districts* (1871). Lambert here put on record the results of a census that he made of a portion of his parish and of careful inquiries into the earnings of the district, with calculations of the cost of living. He thus anticipated the scientific statistical methods of Charles Booth, as well as the doctrines of the Charity Organization Society, of which Lambert was an early member, on the uselessness of indiscriminate charity. The book was regarded as a valuable contribution to economic science and to history. It is perhaps the most important of his published works which, as well as sermons and lectures, include contributions to the *Contemporary Review* and other periodicals.

In the year of Lambert's appointment there was an outbreak of cholera in the parish. He circulated papers of directions, organized the distribution of medicine, and visited the sick assiduously; he noted that on one day he buried forty-four corpses. He founded a penny bank, a soup kitchen, a working men's club, and a mutual improvement society; he also renovated the church. At the general election of 1868 he arranged a course of sermons in his church on the duties of electors. Among the preachers were H. R. Haweis, Stopford Brooke, F. D. Maurice, and J. R. Green.

Under the constant strain of work Lambert's health broke down, and he resigned the living in 1871. He spent the winter abroad with J. R. Green, then vicar of St Philip's, Stepney, and a visit to the West Indies, where his family had property, subsequently restored his health. In June 1872 Lambert was instituted to the living of Tamworth, Staffordshire, where he remained for six years. There he made a careful and thorough restoration of the fine old parish church, nearly completed two district churches, and was instrumental in establishing a school board. But he found a provincial town more impervious to new ideas and methods than east London. In this parish, as elsewhere, he was attacked for his willingness to work with Roman Catholics and nonconformists. Although an evangelical by background, he was a broad-churchman in practice and regarded himself always as the vicar of the whole parish, not just of the congregation. A serious falling off in his private income owing to the decline of the West Indian sugar trade led to his resignation at the end of 1878.

On leaving Tamworth, Lambert engaged in London in voluntary work for the London school board, and took a particular interest in educational problems. He helped to establish the London University Extension Society, and in June 1879 became organizing secretary. He was chairman of the Local Centres Association from 1894 to 1900 and vice-chairman of the society in 1898 and 1899. In the autumn of 1879 he became curate-in-charge of St Jude's, Whitechapel, while the vicar, Canon Barnett, was abroad. In August 1880 he was appointed by W. E. Gladstone vicar of Greenwich, where he remained until his death twenty years later. The position afforded an almost unlimited field for public work. The income of the charities of the ancient royal borough amounted to nearly £20,000 per annum, and into the work of administration Lambert threw himself with energy. Boreman's Educational Foundation, and the Roan Trust, which maintained two large secondary schools, absorbed much of his attention, and he was also chairman of all the Greenwich groups of elementary schools. He was a member of the Greenwich board of works and a guardian, being the chairman of the infirmary committee and interesting himself minutely in the management of the poor-law schools.

In his parish work Lambert was equally successful. The parish church was renovated with sound aesthetic judgement. He entrusted his parish council with control of finance and consulted it with regard to changes in worship and ritual. When this council became aware in 1888 of the smallness of the vicar's stipend it established a vicar's fund which contributed £400 per annum to Lambert's income until his death.

A university extension centre and a committee of the Charity Organization Society were successfully established in Greenwich, and in 1885 the Greenwich Provident Dispensary was founded, which quickly reached a membership of 3000. Lambert was a member of the Mansion House committee appointed in 1885 to inquire into the economic distress in London during the previous year, the departmental committee appointed in 1894 by the Local Government Board to inquire into the management of poor-law schools, and the departmental committee appointed in 1895 to consider reformatory and industrial schools. From 1880 until his death he was first chairman of the Metropolitan Association for Befriending Young Servants. In the kindred Association for Befriending Boys, founded in 1898, he was also active. As early as 1883 he helped to found the Art for Schools Association, and remained its chairman until 1899.

Lambert, who was a prominent freemason and past grand chaplain of England, combined in his endeavours high ideals with business aptitudes. He travelled widely in his vacations. His health failed in 1899, and a long journey to South Africa and then up the Nile to Khartoum failed to restore it. He died unmarried at his home, Greenwich vicarage, on 25 January 1901, and after cremation was buried at Old Shoeburyness parish church.

RONALD BAYNE, rev. C. A. CREFFIELD

Sources R. Bayne, ed., *Sermons and lectures of the late Rev. Brooke Lambert, with a memoir by J. E. G. de Montmorency* (1902) · *The Times* (26 Jan 1901) · *The Spectator* (2 March 1901) · *The Guardian* (30 Jan 1901) · *The Guardian* (6 Feb 1901) · C. W. Stubbs, *A thanksgiving for Brooke Lambert* (1903) · G. K. Clarke, *Churchmen and the condition of England, 1832–1885* (1973) · *CGPLA Eng. & Wales* (1901)
Archives University of Iowa Libraries, Iowa City, corresp.

Likenesses A. B. Joy, marble bust; Roan Schools, Greenwich, 1812
Wealth at death £6262 14s. 9d.: administration with will, 5 March 1901, *CGPLA Eng. & Wales*

Lambert, Christopher Sebastian [Kit] (1935–1981), popular music manager and producer, was born on 11 May 1935 at 7 Mills Buildings, Knightsbridge, London, the son of Constant Leonard *Lambert (1905–1951), composer and critic, and his wife, Florence Chuter, who gave her name as F. Kaye on her marriage certificate. His parents divorced when he was a child and his father played little part in his upbringing. Lambert attended Forres preparatory school, Northwood, Middlesex, whence he proceeded to Lancing School, Sussex (1949–54). He spent his national service as a junior field officer in Hong Kong before going to Trinity College, Oxford, in 1956, where one contemporary recalled him as 'pretty louche and almost perpetually tight'; another compared his appearance to that of 'a young Charles Laughton' (Motion, 283). Nominally he read history, emerging in 1959 with a fourth. Afterwards he attended film school in Paris, and on returning to London took a number of jobs in the film industry. A trip, undertaken with his Oxford friend Richard Mason, into the Brazilian jungle in 1961 to shoot a documentary film ended in tragedy when Mason was killed by a local tribe.

Lambert returned to London, where he and a fellow assistant film producer, Chris Stamp—brother of the actor Terence Stamp—determined to make a film about a rock band. After seeing the London-based rhythm and blues group the High Numbers in summer 1964, they decided instead to manage them, and bought out the contract of the previous manager, Pete Meaden. The band—Roger Daltrey (vocals), Pete Townshend (lead guitar), John Entwistle (bass guitar), and Keith Moon (drums)—were attracted by what they saw as Lambert's business acumen, though he had no experience of the music industry and little knowledge of (or prior interest in) popular music. He had, however, an undeniable flair for publicity, with—according to Tony Stratton-Smith, the owner and manager of Charisma Records—'the charm and the intellect which gave another dimension to the razzmatazz and brilliant promotional ideas' (Rogan, 171). By November 1964 the band had been renamed The Who, and Lambert and Stamp had begun an energetic series of promotions, including a sixteen-week residency at the Marquee Club in Soho—publicized by the now legendary black-on-white poster promising 'Maximum R & B'. Lambert in particular was adept at identifying The Who with 'Mod' subculture (a narcissistic and predominantly male youth subculture marked out by smart, sharp clothes, black music, and amphetamine consumption). His personal allegiance to 'Mod' was minimal; it was simply a way of getting a ready-made audience for his protégés.

Lambert encouraged The Who to 'auto destruct' at the end of gigs by destroying their equipment—a gesture, begun accidentally by Townshend, for which the band became notorious. Replacing smashed equipment became costly, but the recompense came in media coverage, increasing recognition, and commercial success. Lambert's and Stamp's film background also ensured that many Who singles were backed with a promotional film—forerunners of the promotional videos that became commonplace a generation later.

Lambert also produced many of the group's recordings, though this came about as much from financial necessity as for artistic reasons. Unhappy with the group's recording contract with American Decca and its British subsidiary Brunswick (he claimed that both were inexperienced in rock music and paid low royalties, from which the previous producer Shel Talmy took a hefty percentage), Lambert brokered a new deal with Atlantic Records, receiving a large advance to pay bills for damaged equipment. But on the release of the single 'Substitute' in March 1966, Talmy took out an injunction. After a settlement was reached, Lambert took over as producer for 'I'm a Boy', recorded in August. He subsequently produced such important recordings as 'Happy Jack' (1966), 'Pictures of Lily', 'I Can See for Miles' (both 1967), 'Magic Bus' (1968), and 'Pinball Wizard', and all The Who's albums up to and including the rock opera *Tommy* (1969). As lead guitarist and main songwriter, Pete Townshend was undoubtedly The Who's creative force, and best understood the mechanics of producing a recording. Lambert's crucial role—apart from personal management—was in encouraging Townshend to introduce new and unusual subjects and themes to the group's material ('Pictures of Lily', for example, concerned male masturbation). Musically, Townshend credited Lambert with introducing him to 'baroque'—or suspended chords, first evident in the song 'If the Kids are Alright'—'it did a lot to create that churchy feel and has a lot to do with the way I play' (Clark, 1279).

Lambert and Stamp launched Track Records in 1967—a 'hip' independent record label (although Lambert, lacking the necessary finance, secured the involvement of Polydor, a recording 'major'). Track enjoyed three good years; apart from signing The Who, it acquired the services of the Jimi Hendrix Experience—Lambert, along with Stamp and Townshend, was among the first to 'notice' Hendrix in the UK—Arthur Brown, and Thunderclap Newman. The label was innovatory in its (relative) independence and in its approach, notably in making stereo singles. Its success turned Lambert and Stamp into record-company executives, which reduced the time they devoted to The Who. But it was the foundering of a project to turn the rock opera *Tommy* into a film, with Universal Studios, that led to Lambert being first sidelined and then replaced as their manager. Pete Townshend, hitherto his closest ally, became alienated from him; The Who single 'The Seeker' (1969) was produced by the band themselves, and they recorded the *Who's Next* album with Glyn Johns. By mid-1973 Lambert had *de facto* ceased to manage them, and the Track label had become effectively a Polydor imprint. The associated Fly label had also hit difficulties, notably in losing Marc Bolan's T-Rex (Bolan was another artist whom Lambert had helped earlier in his career,

drafting him into the Track band John's Children in 1968).

Lambert continued to draw royalties from The Who in line with his 1964 agreement; this was challenged by the group, and an out-of-court settlement reached in mid-1975. The Who left Track Records, which closed in 1978—by which time the punk/new wave scene had spawned a plethora of similar independent labels. Stamp left the music business, and Lambert, bitter at never receiving the credit he felt due for *Tommy*, embarked on a life of excess in London and Venice, where he had bought a palace. He had frequently tottered on the brink of financial and personal crises; a notorious drinker, his consumption of drugs escalated to an increasing use of heroin in the last twelve years of his life. In 1976, facing bankruptcy and incapable of handling his affairs, he became a ward of the court of protection. He died on 6/7 April 1981 at Central Middlesex Hospital, Park Royal, from injuries sustained after falling down the stairs at his mother's house. He was cremated at Golders Green and a memorial service was held on 11 May at St Paul's, Covent Garden.

Lambert received massive publicity during the 1960s, and his significance has occasionally been overstated. At times he lacked business acumen; he was prone to treat many people in the music industry with upper-class disdain and frequently exaggerated both his anarchic spirit and his homosexuality (except—in the latter case—in dealings with his family). Certainly his encouragement of The Who's destructive tendencies and extravagant projects was entirely in keeping with aspects of his own personality. His long-sighted entrepreneurship, however, was undoubted; he helped to raise group management into areas—such as label ownership—that had previously been the preserve of large music corporations. He also took a genuine interest in artists developing and exhibiting an awareness of their own artistic potential, most notably in the case of Pete Townshend. Lambert was one of a new breed of group-orientated popular music managers who came to the fore in the 1960s; others included Andrew Loog Oldham, who handled the Rolling Stones, and Simon Napier-Bell, manager of, among others, The Yardbirds. The progress of British rock music as a worldwide phenomenon was due in no small part to their efforts.

MICHAEL BROCKEN

Sources A. Motion, *The Lamberts: George, Constant and Kit* (1986) · D. Clarke, ed., *The Penguin encyclopedia of popular music* (1992) · J. Rogan, *Starmakers and svengalis* (1988) · P. Clark, 'The seeker', *History of rock* (1985) · E. Hanel, 'Mods and rock operas', *History of rock* (1985) · private information (2004) [A. Powers] · d. cert. · b. cert.
Likenesses Sasha, double portrait, photograph, 1937 (with his mother), Hult. Arch.
Wealth at death £90,742: administration, 28 May 1981, *CGPLA Eng. & Wales*

Lambert, (Leonard) Constant (1905–1951), composer and conductor, was born on 23 August 1905 at St Clement's Nursing Home, 302 Fulham Palace Road, Fulham, London, the younger son of George Washington Thomas Lambert (1873–1930), a painter with an American, British, and Australian background, and his wife, Amelia Beatrice Absell

(Leonard) **Constant Lambert** (1905–1951), by Christopher Wood, 1926

(1872–1964). His elder brother was the sculptor Maurice Prosper *Lambert (1901–1964). As a child Constant Lambert was delicate, and throughout his life he was plagued by ill health, the only outward hint of this being a slight limp. Educated at Christ's Hospital from 1915 until 1922, he won a scholarship to the Royal College of Music (1922–5), where he studied under Ralph Vaughan Williams and R. O. Morris.

While still a student Lambert was introduced by Edmund Dulac to Serge Diaghilev and thus began a life-long interest in French and Russian music as well as ballet. As a result Diaghilev commissioned him to write a ballet for his company, and he became the first British composer to be thus honoured. The work, entitled *Romeo and Juliet* comprised thirteen short movements, was choreographed by Bronislava Nijinska, and was first produced in Monte Carlo in May 1926. Its production was not without incident: Lambert had serious disagreements with Diaghilev, particularly over his interfering with the choreography, and at one stage even threatened to withdraw his music. Grateful for his support, Nijinska commissioned a work, and his second ballet *Pomona* was given in Buenos

Aires in September 1927. He was seen as being extraordinarily gifted. Dame Ninette de Valois would later speak of him as 'our only hope of an English Diaghilev' (Kavanagh, 110).

By this time Lambert had already begun to move in artistic and bohemian circles, mixing with the Sitwells and the composers Philip Heseltine (Peter Warlock), Cecil Gray, and Bernard van Dieren. He had been a reciter in one of the early performances of William Walton's settings of Edith Sitwell's poems, *Façade*, in 1926. Lambert then began extending his work as a composer, writing eight songs on poems by Li-Po (1926) originally with piano accompaniment (later expanded to use a chamber orchestra). This was followed by what is arguably his most important purely orchestral work, *Music for Orchestra* (1927), scored for large forces and influenced by the current jazz craze. *Elegiac Blues* (1927, for small orchestra and piano), written in memory of the black singer Florence Mills, further shows Lambert's increasing interest in the jazz idiom. This influence found its full fruition in his fine setting of Sacheverell Sitwell's poem *The Rio Grande*, for piano, chorus, and an orchestra that includes colourful percussion effects. Broadcast in 1928, it was given its first performance by the Hallé orchestra in Manchester in December 1929, with Lambert conducting and Hamilton Harty (the orchestra's conductor) at the piano. This has remained his most popular work.

On 5 August 1931 Lambert married Florence Chuter, the daughter of Frederick Chuter, deceased. On the marriage certificate 'Flo', as she was also known, signed her name as 'F. Kaye' and gave her age as eighteen, but she was probably younger. She was said to be extraordinarily beautiful: according to Lambert's biographer her mother had lived near the London docks; her real father was probably a visiting sailor from Java or Malaya. The couple had a son, Christopher, known as Kit *Lambert (1935–1981), who became the manager of a famous rock group, The Who. His parents' marriage had to cope with financial problems from the beginning. Constant Lambert's heavy drinking made a stable family life unlikely.

The composition of two large-scale works for piano occupied Lambert during the late 1920s and early 1930s: a sonata (1928–9) and a concerto (1930–31) which, though cast in the classical mould, show once again the jazz influences that permeate his earlier works. The concerto for soloist and nine players was dedicated to the memory of his friend Philip Heseltine (Peter Warlock), who had died tragically young in 1930, an event that affected Lambert profoundly. In that same year Lambert returned to the world of ballet with an appointment as conductor of the Camargo Society, recently founded with the intention of continuing the work of Diaghilev, who had recently died. He thus resumed what was to be a long and distinguished career in the world of ballet. The Vic-Wells (later the Sadler's Wells) grew from the Camargo Society, and Lambert became its first musical director, a post which he held until 1947, although he continued as an artistic adviser and an occasional guest conductor. In 1949 he participated in the company's first tour of America. His knowledge and experience as a sympathetic conductor of ballet made him one of the leading figures in this field.

An award of the Collard fellowship of the Musicians' Company in 1934 made it possible for Lambert to compose his largest and most ambitious work, the choral masque *Summer's Last Will and Testament*, a setting of poems by Thomas Nashe. It was first performed in January 1936 at the Queen's Hall, London, with Lambert conducting. Cast, like earlier works, in classical forms, it shows a consummate skill in the handling of both voices and orchestra. His next work, the ballet *Horoscope* (1937), was first performed at Sadler's Wells in 1938 with choreography by Frederick Ashton. It is especially notable for a unique palindrome at the opening, which Lambert believed to have been dictated to him by his recently deceased friend Bernard van Dieren. In the late 1930s Lambert's marriage collapsed. Frederick Ashton described him as being 'incapable of being faithful to anybody for very long' (Motion, 211), and in 1937 Lambert began a passionate affair with a young ballet dancer called Margot *Fonteyn (1919–1991). Lambert and his wife separated and were subsequently divorced; Kit stayed with his mother. The relationship with Fonteyn was over by 1947.

Lambert's later works included a setting for male voices and strings, *The Dirge from Cymbeline* (1940). The same year Lambert was touring with the Sadler's Wells Ballet in the Netherlands and narrowly escaped capture during the German invasion. His short orchestral work *Aubade héroïque* (which contains contrasting pastoral and warlike features) expresses Lambert's emotions as a result of this experience. It was dedicated to Vaughan Williams on the occasion of his seventieth birthday. Lambert's last work, the ballet *Tiresias*, was performed at Covent Garden in July 1951 shortly before his death and was choreographed by Ashton with décor by Lambert's second wife. This was Isabel Agnes Delmer, née Nicholas (b. 1912), the former wife of the war correspondent Sefton Delmer. They married on 7 October 1947.

Constant Lambert died in the London Clinic, 20 Devonshire Place, London, on 21 August 1951, the causes of his death being a combination of broncho-pneumonia and undiagnosed diabetes; after cremation his ashes were laid in Brompton cemetery on 26 August. His punishing schedule and lifestyle, especially his heavy drinking habits, undoubtedly hastened his early death. His early 'lean and alert' appearance had given way to a figure 'distinctly boozy and sybaritic' (Motion, 214). Tom Driberg described him as 'Bulky, untidy, in exuberance and girth a young Chesterton' (ibid.). At the time of his death he had become 'a heavy, stooped, prematurely aged figure' (ibid., 235).

During his time as director of the Sadler's Wells Ballet Lambert made arrangements for the company of music by composers as diverse as Purcell, Boyce, Liszt, Meyerbeer, Auber, and Chabrier. He also edited works by Boyce, Handel, and Thomas Roseingrave. As a conductor he appeared with the Hallé and Scottish orchestras and at the Promenade Concerts, where he was associate conductor (1945–6);

he broadcast unusual, lesser-known works on the BBC Third Programme, and conducted Purcell's *The Fairy Queen* and Puccini's *Manon Lescaut* and *Turandot* at Covent Garden. He wrote a book on the music of the twenties, *Music Ho!* (1934), subtitled 'A study of music in decline'. Written with a brilliant fluency, it shows his wide-ranging interest in the arts and literature, though some of his dogmatic statements were not to everyone's taste. He also wrote musical criticism for the *New Statesman*, *Figaro*, and the *Sunday Referee*. His friend Humphrey Searle described him as a brilliant composer, conductor, and conversationalist with a 'warm and generous personality … a man of enormous knowledge who made a unique contribution to English music during the last twenty-five years of his short life' (*DNB*). He was immortalized in fiction as the composer Hugh Morland in Anthony Powell's twelve-volume novel *A Dance to the Music of Time*.   BARRY SMITH

Sources A. Motion, *The Lamberts: George, Constant and Kit* (1986) · R. Shead, *Constant Lambert* (1973) · H. Foss, 'Constant Lambert', *MT*, 92 (1951), 449 · J. Kavanagh, *Secret muses: the life of Frederick Ashton* (1996) · *DNB* · H. Spurling, *Handbook to Anthony Powell's Music of Time* (1977) · b. cert. · m. certs. · d. cert.
Archives King's AC Cam., letters to John Maynard Keynes | FILM BFI NFTVA, documentary footage | SOUND BL NSA, documentary recordings · BL NSA, 'Lambert Ho!', H3676/1 · BL NSA, *Music weekly*, NP7054 BW C1 · BL NSA, oral history interviews · BL NSA, performance recordings · BL NSA, *Talking about music*, 165, 1LP0200592 S1 BD1 BBC TRANSC
Likenesses C. Wood, oils, 1926, NPG [*see illus.*] · M. Ayrton, oils, Tate collection · G. Lambert, oils, Christ's Hospital, London · M. Lambert, sculptured head, priv. coll. · C. Wood, oils, Covent Garden, London

Lambert, Daniel (1770–1809), the most corpulent man of his time in England, was the elder of two sons of a Daniel Lambert who had been huntsman to the earl of Stamford. He was born in Blue Boar Lane, Leicester, on 13 March 1770 and was apprenticed to Benjamin Patrick of Messrs Taylor & Co., an engraving and die-sinking firm in Birmingham; but in 1788 he returned to live with his father, who was keeper of the bridewell in Leicester. The elder Lambert resigned in 1791, and the son succeeded to his post. It was at this time that Lambert began to amass the bulk for which he was later to achieve fame. By 1793 he weighed 32 stone, despite his athletic enthusiasm for activities such as walking, swimming, and hunting. Moreover, he drank only water, and slept less than eight hours a day. The prison closed in 1805 and Lambert was granted an annuity of £50.

The next year Lambert decided to profit from his previously merely annoying corpulence. He had a special carriage constructed and went to London, where in April 1806 he began 'receiving company' from midday until 5 in the afternoon at 53 Piccadilly. Lambert's exhibition of himself aroused curiosity, leading to the publication of descriptions of him. 'When sitting' (according to one account) 'he appears to be a stupendous mass of flesh, for his thighs are so covered by his belly that nothing but his knees are to be seen, while the flesh of his legs, which resemble pillows, projects in such a manner as to nearly

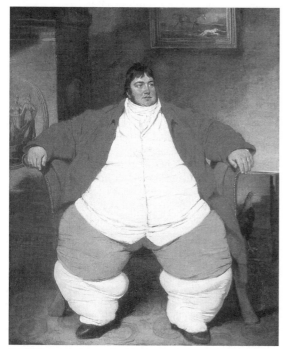

Daniel Lambert (1770–1809), by Benjamin Marshall, exh. RA 1807

bury his feet'. Lambert's limbs, however, were well proportioned; his face was 'manly and intelligent', and he possessed a quick wit. He was a well-known breeder of fighting cocks and was famous for his greyhounds. He revisited London in 1807, when he exhibited himself at 4 Leicester Square, before making a series of visits in the provinces. He was at Cambridge in June 1809, and proceeded to Huntingdon and Stamford, where, according to a newspaper, he 'attained the acme of mortal hugeness'. He died at the Waggon and Horses inn, 47 High Street, Stamford, on 21 June 1809. His coffin was built on two axles and four wheels and required 112 square feet of elm wood for its construction. His body was rolled down a gradual incline from the inn to the burial-ground of St Martin's, Stamford Baron (for Lambert's epitaph see *Notes and Queries*, 4th ser., 11.355).

Lambert's sudden death was probably caused by the stress placed on his heart by his immense proportions. At his death he was 5 feet 11 inches in height, and weighed 52¾ stone (336 kg). His waistcoat had a girth of 102 inches (with his other clothes, it is preserved in Stamford Museum). This weight greatly exceeded that of the two men hitherto especially famed for their corpulence, John Love (*d.* 1793) of Weymouth (26 stone) and Edward Bright (*d.* 1750) of Malden (42 stone). An American contemporary, Miles Darden, outweighed Lambert at 71 stone. For a time after Lambert's death his name became a synonym for hugeness; George Meredith, in *One of our Conquerors*, describes London as the 'Daniel Lambert of cities' and Herbert Spencer, in his *Study of Sociology* (1873), refers to a 'Daniel Lambert of learning'. There are several portraits of

Lambert; the best is an oil by Benjamin Marshall in Leicester Museum and Art Gallery. Lambert's portrait also appeared on a large number of public house signs in London and the eastern midlands.

THOMAS SECCOMBE, *rev.* E. L. O'BRIEN

Sources *Stamford Mercury* (23 June 1809) · *Stamford Mercury* (30 June 1809) · D. T. D. Clark, *Daniel Lambert* (1981) · H. Lemoine and J. Caulfield, *The eccentric magazine, or, Lives and portraits of remarkable persons*, 2 (1813), 241–8 · *Morning Post* (5 Sept 1812) · *N&Q*, 6th ser., 8 (1883), 346 · G. Smeeton, *Biographia curiosa, or, Memoirs of remarkable characters in the reign of George the Third* (1822) · H. Wilson, *Wonderful characters*, 1 (1821)
Archives Stamford Museum | CUL, Add. MS 7721
Likenesses B. Marshall, oils, exh. RA 1807, Leicester Museum and Art Gallery [*see illus.*] · engravings (after B. Marshall), BM, NPG · etching, BM · line engraving, BM

Lambert, Dame Florence Barraclough (1871–1957), physician and public health administrator, was born on 13 August 1871 at Northwick, Harrow, Middlesex, the daughter of Thomas Henry Lambert, a solicitor and a partner in the firm of Lambert Brothers, coal exporters, and his wife, Sarah Ann Harrison.

Florence Barrie Lambert, as she was known most of her life, was educated in France and then trained between 1895 and 1898 as a nurse at the London Hospital. In 1899 she went to South Africa as a nursing sister with the imperial yeomanry, and served until 1901. After returning to England she studied medicine at the London School of Medicine for Women, where she qualified MB BS (Durham), on 9 October 1906. Her main interest from then onwards was in public health, and in 1907 she obtained a diploma in public health from Cambridge University.

Lambert was fortunate in being able to devote time to voluntary work, in particular to child welfare. She became honorary director of the Central Council for Infant and Child Welfare, honorary secretary of the Central Council for the Care of Cripples, and an active member of the Invalid Children's Aid Society. This work channelled her interest into physical medicine, and she undertook postgraduate study at the University of Stockholm. As a result of this she was appointed physician in charge of the mechano-therapeutic department of the Charing Cross Hospital, London, and assistant physician in similar departments in London at St Mary's Hospital and the Royal Free Hospital. In 1913 she was elected a member of the State Medical Service Association, the precursor of the Socialist Medical Association.

Lambert's specialized knowledge of what became known as physiotherapy led to her appointment, in 1915, as inspector of military massage and electrical services, with the honorary rank of major in the Royal Army Medical Corps; she was also a member of the electro-medical committee of the War Office. She held these posts until 1919, when she was appointed a medical officer of the newly formed Ministry of Health. This office involved the inspection of child welfare and orthopaedic work carried out by local authorities throughout the country, which gave her a valuable insight into local government.

In 1921 Lambert resigned from the Ministry of Health in order to devote her talents to public service in the political field, and in March 1922 she was elected an alderman of the London county council (LCC). Throwing herself wholeheartedly into the work of the council she served on the public health committee from the year of her election, and chaired the committee from 1928. She was still chair in 1930 when, with greatly increased functions, it became the central health committee and subsequently the hospital and medical services committee. These bodies were charged with the enormous task of taking over the seventy-six hospitals (42,000 beds) previously administered by the Metropolitan Asylums Board. Lambert personally visited all these hospitals, and in spite of the economic crises of 1931 and 1933, when the Municipal Reform Party lost its majority at County Hall, she brought about or set in train many necessary changes.

After 1934 Lambert was 'leader of the opposition' on the hospitals and medical services committee, but both she and her successor, Somerville Hastings (1878–1967), had similar objectives and a keen desire to improve the public health and municipal health services in London, and they worked together in close co-operation. Appointed a CBE in 1920 for her war work, Lambert was made a dame commander in the Most Excellent Order of the British Empire in 1938. When hospitals were nationalized in 1948, she was appointed a member of the South-East Metropolitan Regional Hospital Board, and she chaired the nursing committee. She retained her membership of the LCC health committee and strove to effect a close liaison between the work of the local health authorities and that of the regional hospital boards.

Lambert, who was also vice-president of the Medical Defence Union, resigned from her office as county alderman in 1952. She died at her home, 1 Langton Ridge, Langton, Speldhurst, Kent, on 11 December 1957. Not having married she left most of her estate to two nieces, Patricia Ainsworth Barnard and Joan Barrie Lambert. According to 'A.D.', writing in *The Lancet*:

> Dame Barrie was indefatigable in her visits to hospitals. She had a tenacious memory and was an excellent debater. She was a firm supporter in time of trouble and tough when she felt she was right. She was no political partisan and was prepared to fight within her own party to get more money for hospitals. She was generally successful. She had vision and insight; these combined with her toughness enabled her to overcome obstacles. Few Londoners realise how much they owe to her for the whole-hearted energy with which she attacked the enormous problem of transforming the poor-law hospitals into a co-ordinated hospital system providing a first-rate service for the public. (*The Lancet*, 21 Dec 1957)

COLIN J. PARRY

Sources *The Lancet* (21 Dec 1957) · *The Times* (12 Dec 1957) · *WWW*, 1951–60 · London county council, minutes of proceedings, 1922–57, LMA · b. cert. · d. cert. · private information (2004)
Likenesses photograph, repro. in *The Lancet* · photograph, repro. in *The Times*
Wealth at death £32,646 17s. 3d.: probate, 21 May 1958, CGPLA Eng. & Wales

Lambert, George (1699/1700–1765), landscape and scene painter, is of unknown parentage. His birth date is computed from Vertue's note on him in September 1722 as 'a young hopefull Painter in Landskape aged 22 much in imitation of Wotton. Manner of Gasper Pousin', adding that he 'learnt of … Hassel' (Vertue, *Note books*, 3.6). The suggestion that he was therefore a pupil of the portrait painter Warner Hassels (*fl.* 1680–1710) remains conjectural. A book-plate for 'George Lambart' (an occasional early spelling of his name), flanked by figures of Music and Painting and displaying arms shared by the Lamberts of Banstead, Surrey, and the earls of Cavan, is accepted as having been designed by William Hogarth for him. According to Samuel Ireland it was vouched for by Lambert's pupil John Inigo Richards, who recalled that it 'was stuck in all his books; and that his library consisted of seven or eight hundred volumes' (Ireland, 1.155). Lambert is not known to have travelled abroad, married, or fathered children. He seems to have lived most of his life in some comfort in London in a rented house in the Great Piazza, Covent Garden, and travelled about the country sketching houses and views. By all accounts a jovial, clubbable man, his reputation, according to Edwards, was that of a 'person of great respectability in character and profession' (Edwards, 19). His friend the actor William Havard extolled his virtues, adding that 'He was modest to a Fault—for it hurt him in his Profession' (Highfill, Burnim & Langhans, *BDA*). Lambert was named executor in the wills of the distinguished and wealthy carver John Boson (*d.* 1743) and the painter John Thornhill and had a lifelong involvement in the affairs of artists as a professional body. He was a signatory to Hogarth's copyright bill of 1735, and in 1746 he was one of several leading artists elected governors of the Foundling Hospital, to which he presented a large overmantel landscape in 1757 (still with the Thomas Coram Foundation, London). Like many artists he was also a freemason and is recorded as a member of the Fountain Lodge in the Strand in 1723.

Lambert appears to have divided his artistic career equally between the theatre and landscape painting. From December 1726 he is traceable on the payroll of Lincoln's Inn Fields Theatre run by John Rich, with whom he moved to the newly built Covent Garden Theatre in 1732, remaining there for the rest of his life. From 1740 he received £100 a year, paid quarterly. In its painting room Lambert is said to have 'wrought day and night in his vocation' (Rosenfeld and Croft-Murray, 104), and it is there that the impromptu gatherings of artists, eminent craftsmen, men of letters, and fashionable society became consolidated in 1735 into the famously convivial Beef Steak Club, which still exists. Lambert's highly regarded scenery remained in use until destroyed by fire in 1808.

In 1725 Vertue mentions Lambert's portrait by John Vanderbank, now known only from Faber's engraving of 1727. It is lettered 'Georgius Lambert, Chorographiae Pictor', echoing the fact that he was indeed the first English artist to devote himself exclusively to landscape painting. Richards's sale in 1811 included a 'Portrait of Mr. Lambert by Wilson'; a portrait of him by Thomas Hudson is said to

George Lambert (1699/1700–1765), by John Faber junior, 1727 (after John Vanderbank)

have graced the Beef Steak Club, and in 1782 Samuel Ireland claimed to own a portrait of him by Hogarth. Lambert's output can be followed through signed and dated paintings for almost every year of his life, from 1722 until 1764. It includes paintings in the classical mode inspired by Gaspard Dughet, straight copies or adaptations of Nicolas Poussin, Claude, Salvator Rosa, and the Dutch masters, topographical English landscapes and country-house views, pastoral and rustic scenes, and decorative overmantels and overdoors. A number were engraved from 1734 onwards by E. Kirkall, G. Vandergucht, F. Vivares, E. Burtenshaw, J. Mason, and P. Canot. Lambert himself produced, at some unspecified date, two etchings after Salvator Rosa, and one architectural ruin scene dedicated to James Robinson of Wandsworth. According to Vertue, Lambert took up pastel painting about 1742, and about half a dozen examples, dated between 1742 and 1746, survive; most are versions of his oil paintings. The figures in his landscapes, which vary greatly in quality, were as a rule added by other hands, among them Francis Hayman's and Hogarth's; a number of other artists such as J. I. Richards, Samuel Wale, Thomas Dall, and Jacopo Amigoni, with whom he worked in the theatre, are likely candidates. Contemporaries also often ascribed his figures to Ferg, presumably Francis Paul. In views which required shipping he collaborated with Samuel Scott, as in 1731–2 with his first major commission, a set of six views of the settlements of the East India Company (office of Foreign and Commonwealth Affairs, London) for its house in Leadenhall Street, and later in the lost set of five views of

Mount Edgcumbe and Plymouth of 1754–5 (known from engravings).

Lambert's early style in the 1720s is close to that of John Wootton in its broad handling and strong colours. Lambert, however, understood better the principles of harmonious composition which underlay the style of Gaspard Dughet, then overwhelmingly in vogue with collectors. As a result some of his most successful pictures are confident interpretations of Gaspard's ideal landscapes (for example, *Classical Landscape*, 1745, Tate collection), a skill which earned him the accolade of 'the English Poussin'. His greatest merit is to have been the first to apply these rules to the English landscape itself. His four views of Westcombe House, Blackheath (1733, Wilton House, Wiltshire), set a new bench-mark for the genre. Having broken away from the hitherto standard head-on house portrait, Lambert integrated the house into the landscape in a way which is both naturalistic and picturesque. His two panoramic views of Box Hill, Surrey, also of 1733 (Yale U. CBA; Tate collection), are the first known views of the English landscape pure and simple, painted for its own sake, without the excuse of a hunt or a country house. With his views of *The Great Falls of the Tees* (pastel, 1746, priv. coll.) and *The Entrance to Cheddar Cliffs* (1755, Englefield House, Berkshire) he is also the first to give English landscape a dramatic status equal with the famous views of Italy. Successful compositions were frequently recycled in various sizes: at least six versions of *View of Dover Castle* were painted between 1735 and 1751. He often painted compositionally balanced sets and pairs, contrasting evening with morning, or tranquil scenes with stormy ones, and he was also the first to introduce a sense of local weather into his views. The best examples of this are his views of Copped Hall, Essex (1746, priv. coll.), where two aspects of the distant house are contrasted by giving one a tranquil sunny setting and the other a dramatically wind-tossed one. But perhaps his greatest innovation was to combine, from the 1730s onwards, the two genres of ideal and topographical landscape into 'capriccios' of his own devising. Good examples are *Arcadian Landscape with Sarcophagus, and (?) Beeston Castle* (1736) and *Capriccio with Pope's Villa at Twickenham* (1762, both priv. coll.), in which the Thames valley is nearly overwhelmed by wild mountain scenery. From about 1760 his works show a greater feeling for light and hazy distance, suggesting an affinity with his younger colleague Richard Wilson, and not surprisingly some of his later works (such as *Hilly Landscape with Coastal Inlet at Sunset*, 1763, Cardiff) were long ascribed to Wilson.

From 1755 Lambert sat on a committee, under the chairmanship of Francis Hayman, which advocated the establishment of a national academy of arts. In December 1761 he was elected chairman of the newly established Society of Artists of Great Britain. Between 1761 and 1764 he exhibited sixteen oils at the society's annual exhibitions. In November 1764 the society petitioned for incorporation by royal charter, with Lambert as its first president. It received the royal seal on 26 January 1765, and one hopes that Lambert was aware of this before he died at his lodgings in the Great Piazza, Covent Garden, a few days later, on 31 January. He was buried on 5 February in the church close at the end of the church warden's pew door at St Paul's, Covent Garden. In his short will, dated 29 December 1764, he left everything to his faithful servant Ann Terry and named his 'dear good friend' John Moody of Twickenham sole executor. The handsome contents of his lodgings and a large collection of his own paintings were sold at Langfords, Covent Garden, on 18 December 1765.

Lambert is known to have taught John Inigo Richards, Theodosius Forrest, John Collet, and the Norie brothers, and possibly William Taverner, Jonathan Skelton, and C. W. Bampfylde. His best-documented pupil, however, is **Richard Beauvoir** (1730–1780), painter, whose work has only recently surfaced. Born in London on 27 May 1730, he was a younger son of the wealthy East India merchant Osmond Richard Beauvoir (1680–1757) of Downham Hall, Essex, and his wife, Elizabeth, *née* Beard (1700–1772). After a brief career in the East India trade, he dedicated himself to artistic pursuits, largely, it seems, under the tutelage of Lambert. From 1757 onwards his cash book records regular payments to Lambert, along with purchases of Lambert's paintings (£27 for *View of Cheddar Cliffs* in 1758), prints, artist's materials, and subscriptions to the Society of Arts and Sciences from 1759 to 1764 (Berkshire MRO, Reading, Benyon MSS). A group of twenty-four landscape watercolours of some quality, dated between 1759 and 1778, by Beauvoir and three oil paintings, dated between 1770 and 1776, have descended in the Benyon collection at Englefield House, Berkshire, together with five oils by Lambert. Beauvoir's technique, especially in watercolours, is very close to Lambert and many of his drawings are clearly copies of pictures by his teacher, thus recording some which are now lost. A watercolour of unidentified ruins was acquired in 1992 by the British Museum, London. Beauvoir's last entry in his cash book regarding Lambert is a consignment to him of two dozen bottles of claret on 19 January 1765, presumably to celebrate his becoming the first president of the incorporated Society of Artists of Great Britain. In 1763 Beauvoir, as 'An Honorary Exhibitor', showed 'Four landskip drawings; stained from nature' at the society (Graves, *Soc. Artists*, 28). He died, unmarried, on 20 August 1780 at his home in Hill Street, Berkeley Square, London, and was buried on 26 August at St Margaret's, Downham, Essex.

ELIZABETH EINBERG

Sources Vertue, *Note books*, vol. 3 · S. Ireland, *Graphic illustrations of Hogarth*, 1 (1794) · S. Rosenfeld and E. Croft-Murray, 'A checklist of scene painters working in Great Britain and Ireland in the 18th century [4 pts]', *Theatre Notebook*, 19 (1964–5), 6–20, 49–64, 102–13, 133–45 · Highfill, Burnim & Langhans, *BDA*, vol. 9 · E. Einberg, *George Lambert* (1970) [exhibition catalogue, Iveagh Bequest, Kenwood, London] · M.-L. Schnackenburg, *Der englische Landschaftsmaler George Lambert* (1995) · E. Edwards, *Anecdotes of painters* (1808); facs. edn (1970) · Graves, *Soc. Artists* · *GM*, 1st ser., 50 (1780), 395 · *GM*, 1st ser., 50 (1780), 495 [Richard Beauvoir; correction] · burial register, 5 Feb 1765, London, St Paul's, Covent Garden · *London Evening-Post* (8–10 April 1736) · *London Evening-Post* (2–4 June 1757) · W. Musgrave, *Obituary prior to 1800*, ed. G. J. Armytage, 4, Harleian Society, 47 (1900), 6 · East India Company, letter-books, 1748–9, BL [R. Beauvoir] · cash book of R. Beauvoir, 1757–80, Berks. RO, Benyon MSS · private information (2004) [C. Posner, R. Beauvoir] · parish register (burial), 26 Aug 1780, Downham, St Margaret's [R. Beauvoir] · E. Einberg, 'The perfect pupil: Richard Beauvoir (1730–80), painter in oils and watercolours', *British Art Journal*, 1 (1999), 35–7 · E. Einberg, 'Catalogue raisonné of the works of George Lambert', *Walpole Society*, 63 (2001), 111–200
Archives Berks. RO, Benyon MSS, Richard Beauvoir's cash book, 1757–1780 · BL OIOC, East India Collections, correspondence of Richard Beauvoir, East India Co. letter-books, 27/E · Essex County Council RO, Downham Hall MSS, D/DBe F3 · RSA, Richard Beauvoir's subscription book · St Margaret's, Downham, Essex, parish burial records
Likenesses J. Faber junior, mezzotint, 1727 (after J. Vanderbank), NPG [*see illus.*] · A. Bannerman, line engraving, *c*.1762 (after mezzotint by J. Faber), repro. in H. Walpole, *Anecdotes of painters* (1766) · H. Robinson, line engraving, *c*.1827 (after mezzotint by J. Faber)
Wealth at death will, 29 Dec 1764, PRO, PROB 11/906, sig. 62 · at least £69 13s. realized at Langford's sale, 18 Dec 1765: annotated catalogue, Rijksbureau voor Kunsthistorische Documentatie, The Hague

Lambert, George (1842–1915), real tennis player, was born on 31 May 1842, the third son of Joseph (John) Lambert (1814–1903), who was employed at Hatfield House, Hertfordshire, as a professional tennis player by the second marquess of Salisbury. George Lambert's first engagement was under Thomas Sabin at the Merton Street real tennis court in Oxford, where he learned the game. His progress was very rapid, and in a few years he was in the forefront of tennis. In 1866 he became manager of the court at Hampton Court Palace, and three years later he was appointed head professional at the Marylebone Cricket Club's court at Lord's, at that time regarded as the best in London, where he remained for twenty years. He married in 1869 Jane Mellows.

It was during the earlier part of his time at Lord's that Lambert reached the zenith of his career. In 1869 he was narrowly defeated by John Moyer Heathcote but soon afterwards he began to surpass that fine player. In 1871 Lambert became world champion when the holder, Edmund Tompkins, yielded to his challenge without playing a match. Lambert himself then held the title unchallenged for fourteen years but in 1885, when he was nearly forty-three years of age, he was challenged and narrowly defeated in a great match at Hampton Court Palace by the aggressive 25-year-old American Tom Pettitt, of the Boston Athletic Association. Lambert was also beaten in 1886 by Charles Saunders, who thereby became champion of England, and his match-playing career ended soon afterwards. In 1889 he left Lord's and for two years he leased the East Road court in Cambridge, though this was not a financial success. In later years he suffered from gout. He died at his house in north London on 1 December 1915.

George's son Alfred Lambert, the eldest of his four children (three sons and one daughter), became tennis professional to the fourth marquess of Salisbury at Hatfield; Henry, the youngest, held the same post to the third Baron Leconfield at Petworth. Clearly the Lamberts were a tennis dynasty. George's eldest brother, Thomas, worked with Sabin at Oxford; his younger brother William held positions at Hampton Court, Lord's, and Hewell Grange; his next brother, Alfred, was the professional at the Prince's

Club in Knightsbridge, London; and the youngest brother, Charles, had a similar position at the Hatfield court. Both William's son Stanley and Charles's son Edgar also became professional players, though not to the standard of George.

Lambert, perhaps more than any other player, marked the transition from the old to the new tennis. He was the first leading professional to adopt modern stringing for his racquets, and he added an unprecedented pace and severity to the game, utilizing a superb forehand stroke with a heavy cut.   E. B. NOEL, *rev.* WRAY VAMPLEW

Sources Lord Aberdare [M. G. L. Bruce], *The Willis Faber book of tennis and rackets* (1980) • J. Marshall, *The annals of tennis* (1878) • J. M. Heathcote and others, *Tennis, lawn tennis, rackets, fives* (1890) • E. B. Noel and J. O. M. Clark, *A history of tennis*, 2 vols. (1924)
Likenesses photographs, repro. in Aberdare, *Willis Faber book of tennis and rackets*

Lambert, George, first Viscount Lambert (1866–1958), politician, was born at South Tawton, Devon, on 25 June 1866, the eldest son of George Lambert (d. 1885) of Spreyton, near Crediton, Devon, and his wife, Grace, daughter of Thomas Howard of South Tawton. His father's family had for many generations been small landowners and yeoman farmers. He was educated at the local grammar school, and at the age of nineteen he was farming 800 acres of his own land. He developed an early interest in politics, and in 1889, at the age of twenty-three, he became a Devon county councillor; he was made an alderman in 1912 and did not retire until 1952.

In 1891, aged twenty-five, Lambert won a notable victory as a Gladstonian Liberal at a by-election in South Molton, Devon, which he represented from 1891 to 1924 and from 1929 to 1945. In all he fought fourteen elections, was four times unopposed, and only once beaten (1924—because of the overconfidence of his supporters).

Lambert married on 30 July 1904 Barbara (d. 1963), daughter of George Stavers, shipowner, of Morpeth, Northumberland; they had two sons and two daughters. In 1905 he was made civil lord of the Admiralty, an appointment which caused surprise as most expected him to go to the Board of Agriculture and Fisheries. 'A farmer sent to sea' was the contemporary jibe (*The Times*). He was sworn of the privy council in 1912. At the outbreak of war, in August 1914, Asquith was under pressure from Churchill to replace Lambert with Ivor Guest but the prime minister kept him on: '[Lambert] is not very competent but to boot him out at the moment would be cruel' (*Letters to Venetia Stanley*, 161). He remained at the Admiralty until the formation of a coalition government in May 1915. He subsequently refused invitations by Asquith and later Lloyd George to join the government, citing in 1917 his disapproval of the government's naval policy, the sacking of Lord Jellicoe, and the under-use of Admiral Fisher. Lambert was particularly close to Fisher, for whom his feelings were akin to hero worship. On Fisher's death Lambert became his literary executor.

Lambert was one of the senior Liberal MPs outside the government, and during 1919–21 he was chairman of the group of backbench MPs who supported the Lloyd George

coalition. He was on the right of the party and strongly opposed to any form of state intervention. After 1929 he became increasingly opposed to the support given by the Liberal Party to the Labour government, and was among the first to make overtures in favour of a national government, formed by Ramsay MacDonald with the Conservatives and the newly constituted Liberal National Party in August 1931. He remained an outspoken backbencher, known for straightforwardness and honesty rather than subtlety, until his retirement from the House of Commons, when he was elevated to the peerage as first Viscount Lambert (23 July 1945).

In parliament Lambert gained a reputation as an expert on farming and rural life. Early in his career he promoted a private bill to give tenant farmers fair compensation for disturbance and to enable them to grow what they chose, provided that the fertility of the soil was maintained. The bill lapsed with the general election of 1895. Lambert was, however, successful in putting on the statute book an act by which parish council elections were to be held every three years instead of annually. He served on the royal commission on agriculture appointed in 1893. He was popular among the farmers and labourers of his native county, where he was known as Devonshire Jarge. Through his friendship with C. H. Seale-Hayne, whose executor he became, he was able to devote substantial sums to the building of the Seale-Hayne Agricultural College at Newton Abbot, of which he became the foundation chairman. He was a good sportsman, a good shot, and a steady golfer.

Lambert died at his home, Cofyns, Spreyton, near Crediton, Devon, on 17 February 1958. His elder son, George (1909–1989), MP for South Molton (1945–50) and for Torrington (1950–58), succeeded to the title. His younger daughter, Margaret (1906–1995), was from 1951 editor-in-chief for the Foreign Office of the captured archives of the German foreign ministry.

GEOFFREY SHAKESPEARE, *rev.* MARC BRODIE

Sources *The Times* (18 Feb 1958) • Burke, *Peerage* (1999) • H. H. *Asquith: letters to Venetia Stanley*, ed. M. Brock and E. Brock (1982) • T. Wilson, *The downfall of the liberal party, 1914–1935* (1966) • WWBMP • CGPLA Eng. & Wales (1958)
Archives CAC Cam., corresp. with Lord Fisher
Likenesses A. Hacker, oils, 1913, priv. coll. • R. G. Eves, oils, 1934, Seale-Hayne Agricultural College, Newton Abbot, Devon • photograph, repro. in *The Times*, 11
Wealth at death £50,600 15s. 5d.: probate, 13 Oct 1958, CGPLA Eng. & Wales

Lambert, George Jackson (1794–1880), organist and composer, the son of George Lambert, organist of Beverley Minster, was born at Highgate, Beverley, Yorkshire, on 16 November 1794. He had his first lessons from his father, and from the age of sixteen he studied in London under Samuel T. Lyon and William Crotch. In his early career he performed at the Royal Chapel, Chelsea College, and Royal College, Windsor. He also played in the band of the Royal Italian Opera. He was a skilled violin, viola, and cello player, and is said to have became a great favourite of the prince regent. In 1818 Lambert succeeded his father as organist at Beverley, and held the post until 1874, when ill health and deafness compelled him to retire. His father, who died on 15 July 1818, was organist at the minister for forty-one years, according to the epitaph on his tombstone in the graveyard, so that the office of organist at Beverley was held by father and son for the almost unprecedented period of ninety-seven years.

The younger Lambert was an excellent organist and published several compositions, including overtures, instrumental chamber music, organ fugues, and piano pieces. Some quartets and a septet were played at the meetings of the Society of British Musicians but never published. His *Grand quattuor* for piano, violin, viola, and cello was played at the fourth concert of the Beverley Musical Society in May 1876; another piece was performed by the Hull Philharmonic Society. Lambert was also a talented artist and painter. He executed cork models of Melrose Abbey, Beverley Minster (which took him seven years), and St Mary's Church, where his sister Elizabeth (d. 1830) was organist for some years. He married a sister of J. M. Robinson of Beverley and had two sons, George (d. 1872), who took holy orders, and Henry William (d. 1872), who adopted music as a profession. Lambert's wife predeceased him in 1877. Lambert himself died at Highgate, Beverley, on 24 January 1880, in the same house in which he had been born. His funeral took place at Beverley Minster on 28 January, and he was interred in the private burial-ground in North Bar Street Within.

J. C. HADDEN, rev. NILANJANA BANERJI

Sources *Beverley Guardian* (31 Jan 1880) · Grove, *Dict. mus.* · Brown & Stratton, *Brit. mus.* · J. D. Brown, *Biographical dictionary of musicians: with a bibliography of English writings on music* (1886) · [J. S. Sainsbury], ed., *A dictionary of musicians*, 2 vols. (1824) · D. Baptie, *A handbook of musical biography* (1883) · MT, 21 (1880), 133
Wealth at death under £2000: resworn probate, May 1880, CGPLA Eng. & Wales

Lambert, Harold Ernest (1893–1967), Swahili scholar and ethnographer, was born on 4 September 1893 at Pield Heath, Hillingdon, Middlesex, the second of three sons of George Lambert (1863–1915), gardener, and Amy Hearn (1868/9–1937), both of Hillingdon. Lambert attended Bournemouth School from 1905 to 1912 when he was admitted to Queens' College, Cambridge, as a minor scholar. On the outbreak of the First World War he was commissioned temporary lieutenant in the Gloucestershire regiment in 1916; in 1917 he was seconded to the King's African rifles. His name remained on the college books for the duration, but it seems that he never took his degree.

In April 1919 Lambert was appointed temporary assistant district commissioner in the East Africa Protectorate (renamed the colony and protectorate of Kenya in the following year), the appointment being confirmed in 1923. For the next two years he was stationed at Shimoni, which was close to the island of Wasini, a stronghold of Swahili culture, where Lambert acquired his mastery of kiVumba (the local dialect of Swahili), composed poetry in that dialect, and learned to write Swahili in Swahili-Arabic script. He was referred to by the local literati as Shaykh Lambert, and people later recalled with approval that during the

fasting month of Ramadan he did not eat, drink, or smoke in public during the hours of daylight. He also had a reputation for being neatly dressed. On 9 June 1925, while on leave in England, he married Grace Beatrice (1885–1972), daughter of Tom Firr, formerly huntsman with the Quorn hounds. In 1929, for some six months, he was district commissioner of Lamu, on the coast north of Mombasa and, like Wasini, a stronghold of Swahili culture. There he sat at the feet of Muhammad Kijumwa al-Bakri, an exceptional poet and scholar. In 1939 Lambert was made OBE; in his recommendation, the governor, Sir Robert Brooke-Popham, wrote: 'Wherever he serves he succeeds in winning the full confidence of Settlers and Natives alike.' From 1944 until his retirement in 1950 he was seconded to the African settlement and land utilization board in Nairobi, during which time he prepared ethnographic material on the peoples of the Meru and Embu districts, and on the Kikuyu. A good example of this phase is his *Social and Political Institutions of the Kikuyu* (1955). During Lambert's career he trained a number of colonial administrators, such as Richard Turnbull and Walter Coutts, who later held important posts.

Able though Lambert was in matters anthropological, it was his mastery of Swahili as spoken by the Swahili people on which his claim to fame rests (a mastery which was all the more amazing since he had served only twice at the coast, and then for comparatively short periods). He began to make his erudite contributions to the *Journal of the East African Swahili Committee* only in the early 1950s, after his retirement. His three *Studies in Swahili Dialects* (1956–8) remain, like the *Grammaire des dialectes swahilis* (1909) by Charles Sacleux, outstanding; and *Wimbo wa kiEbrania* ('Hebraic Songs'), based on the erotic Song of Solomon, is a clever *jeu d'esprit*. A collection of Lambert's Swahili poems appeared posthumously in 1971. He and W. E. Taylor were the only Europeans ever to have published Swahili poetry acceptable to the Swahili.

H. E. died in Nairobi on 28 May 1967. Grace died in Nairobi on 15 April 1972. There were no children. It is relevant to add that few foreign scholars have any reputation among the Swahili people themselves, although the names of Krapf and Taylor are invariably recognized. It is with these that H. E. will be remembered.

P. J. L. FRANKL

Sources P. J. L. Frankl, 'H. E. Lambert (1893–1967): Swahili scholar of eminence (being a short biography together with a bibliography of his published work)', *Journal of African Cultural Studies*, 12/1 (1999), 48–53 · CGPLA Eng. & Wales (1968) · b. cert. · d. cert.
Archives Nairobi University | Bodl. RH, east African Swahili committee MSS, Afr. s. 1705 (7)
Wealth at death £327 effects in England: probate, 9 March 1968, CGPLA Eng. & Wales

Lambert, Henry (d. 1813), naval officer, younger son of Captain Robert Lambert (d. 1810), entered the navy in 1795 on the *Cumberland* in the Mediterranean, and in her was present in the action off Toulon on 13 July 1795, when the *Alcide* struck to the *Cumberland*. He afterwards served in the *Virginie* and *Suffolk* on the East India station, and having passed his examination on 15 April 1801 was promoted lieutenant of the *Suffolk*, from which he was moved in October to the *Victorious*, and in October 1802 to the *Centurion*. Continuing on the East India station, he was promoted commander of the *Wilhelmina* on 24 March 1803, and captain of the *San Fiorenzo* on 9 December 1804. In February 1805 he distinguished himself by the capture of the French frigate *Psyche*, commanded by Captain Bergeret; he was confirmed in his rank on 10 April 1805.

In June of the following year Lambert returned to England. In May 1808 he was appointed to the *Iphigenia*, which he took first to Quebec and afterwards to India. In 1810 the *Iphigenia* was employed in the blockade of Mauritius; she was also one of the squadron under Captain Samuel Pym in the disastrous attack on the French squadron in Grand Port beginning on 22 August, which resulted in the loss or destruction of three of the four frigates. On the afternoon of 27 August the fourth frigate, the *Iphigenia*, with the men of two of the others on board, and with little or no ammunition remaining, was attempting to warp out of the bay, against a contrary wind, when three other French frigates appeared off the entrance. Disabled, unarmed, and crowded with men, the *Iphigenia* could not resist. Lambert surrendered, on an agreement that he, the officers, and crew should be sent on parole to the Cape of Good Hope or to England within a month. In the event the prisoners were detained in Mauritius, and were released only when the island was captured by the British on 3 December, and the *Iphigenia*, then in French service, was recovered. Lambert was then tried by court martial for the loss of his ship, and was honourably acquitted.

In August 1812 Lambert commissioned the frigate *Java* (38 guns), formerly the French *Renommée*, captured off Tamatave on 21 May 1811. On the voyage to the East Indies she fell in with the United States frigate *Constitution*, off the coast of Brazil, on 29 December 1812. Lambert could have avoided action, but he chose the bolder course, hoping to damage the *Constitution* enough to cause her commander, Commodore Bainbridge, to abandon his cruise. Poorly manned and heavily laden with stores, the *Java* was at a considerable disadvantage during the engagement. After about an hour Lambert was fatally wounded by a musket-shot in the breast; the defence continued until the *Java*, close to sinking, was forced to haul down her colours. On the second day she was cleared out and set on fire. On 3 January 1813 the *Constitution* anchored at San Salvador, where the prisoners were landed, and where, on 4 January, Lambert died; he was buried on the following day.

J. K. LAUGHTON, rev. NICHOLAS TRACY

Sources *Naval Chronicle*, 25 (1811), 72–4, 157–64, 234–8 · *Naval Chronicle*, 29 (1813), 346–9, 402–8, 414–17, 452–3 · W. James, *The naval history of Great Britain, from the declaration of war by France, in February 1793, to the accession of George IV in January 1820*, 5 vols. (1822–4) · T. Roosevelt, *The naval war of 1812* (1882) · C. S. Forester, *The naval war of 1812* (1957)

Lambert, Jack Walter (1917–1986), journalist and writer, was born on 21 April 1917 at 28 Gaynesford Road, Lewisham, London, the only son of Walter Henry Lambert, surveyor, and his wife, Ethel Mary, *née* Mutton. Lambert was educated at Tonbridge School, and from there went straight into journalism (his university, he used to remark, was the same as Gorky's). He spent three years before the Second World War gaining experience on trade journals, and at the age of twenty-two was appointed editor of *The Fruit-Grower, Florist and Market Gardener*. He also published *The Penguin Guide to Cornwall* in 1939. On 17 August 1940 Lambert married Catherine Margaret Read (*b.* 1918/19), the elder daughter of Alfred Read. She was a young actress, later to become a distinguished speech teacher. They had a son and two daughters.

Also in 1940 Lambert joined the Royal Navy as an ordinary seaman; he left it as lieutenant-commander. He served on convoy escort duties in the Atlantic and Arctic, and during the latter part of the war was with the light coastal forces in the channel. Among other adventures, his ship fished out of the Atlantic, in which she was drifting, the celebrated Greek actress Katina Paxinou. Lambert commanded first a motor gunboat and later motor torpedo boats (MTBs) charged with interdicting the channel to German enemy boats during the passage of the D-day invasion force. On D-day itself none of these potential foes ventured from harbour. Lambert recalled spending that longest day with his crew in MTB 691, 'lying off the Pointe de Barfleur, rolling our guts out'. But, in the period after the invasion, the tactics he and his fellow MTB commanders had evolved against German light forces ruled the narrow seas. For his part in these operations Lambert was mentioned in dispatches and awarded the DSC.

By the end of the war the dashing naval officer was a tall, elegant fellow with humorous eyes, an aquiline nose, fair, wavy hair, and an attractive actorish voice. Lambert was recruited for the *Sunday Times* as assistant literary and arts editor in 1948. In 1960 he became literary and arts editor, and he acted in this capacity for sixteen years, during a time when that newspaper rose to dominate the newsstands. Throughout his career he straddled the two worlds of newspaper administration and cultural criticism. In the Gray's Inn Road, Jack Lambert was a dedicated backroom boy; outside it J. W. Lambert was the distinguished critic. A broadcaster of grip and fluency, Lambert was a key member of the BBC's *The Critics* and its successor, Radio 3's *Critics' Forum*, and of ABC Television's *The Bookman*. This was withdrawn in 1961 after a season, because it was 'too serious' for a mass medium. This was a ludicrous charge to bring, against Lambert at least. He banned the word 'middlebrow' from all reviews on the grounds that everything that the *Sunday Times* tried to interest its readers in ought to be middlebrow. In addition to his parallel careers as newspaper executive and critic, Lambert edited *The Bodley Head Saki* in 1963, and in 1974 published the useful survey *Drama in Britain, 1964–73*.

Lambert was famous for his sympathy towards all kinds of writers. His credo of the function of a books page remains a model (seldom achieved):

> Our choice, not only of books but of reviewers, reflects our own beliefs and tastes. But that point of view must be, as a matter of prudence as well as courtesy, not too arrogantly remote from that of our potential readers—yet a little ahead of them as well. Our reviewers can and do, for all the arts,

influence public taste. They do so not necessarily by campaigning or preaching but by offering one side of a conversation between intelligent people. They have to be able to inform those who don't know and do so without condescension, remind those who have forgotten, yet manage not to irritate the many other experts who will be reading them. (Hobson, Knightley, and Russell)

Lambert sat on a very large number of cultural committees. He was a member of the Arts Council from 1968 to 1976, and served on the committee of the Royal Literary Fund. He was also a member and chairman (1968–76) of the Drama Panel. In addition he was on the council of the Royal Academy of Dramatic Art, and a member of the board of management of the British Drama League. Another of Lambert's interests was Opera 80, which evolved out of Opera for All in order to create greater sophistication of production in a small touring company. (As its first chairman, he saw the company through difficult early days, protecting his artistic staff from political pressures.)

Lambert's devoted service to the arts led to his being made a CBE in 1970. He was a pillar of the Garrick Club, and an urbane, humorous, cultivated man, who sang his favourite *lieder* with a voice that he liked to call a lyric baritone. He died at the Royal Free Hospital, Camden, London, on 3 August 1986, after suffering a stroke. His life demonstrated a consistent ability to mix the olive oil of the arts with the vinegar of professional journalism.

PHILIP HOWARD

Sources WW (1984–6) · H. Hobson, P. Knightley, and L. Russell, *The pearl of days: an intimate memoir of the Sunday Times, 1822–1972* (1972) · News Int. RO, The Times and Sunday Times MSS · *The Times* (6 Aug 1986) · *Sunday Times* (10 Aug 1986) · *The Guardian* (8 Aug 1986) · b. cert. · m. cert. · d. cert.
Archives Bodl. Oxf., corresp. and papers · University of Bristol Library, corresp. and statements relating to trial of *Lady Chatterley's lover* | Bodl. Oxf., corresp. with R. B. Montgomery · CUL, corresp. with W. A. Gerhardie
Wealth at death £239,658: probate, 3 Nov 1986, *CGPLA Eng. & Wales*

Lambert, James (*bap.* 1725, *d.* 1788), watercolour painter and topographical artist, was baptized on 29 December 1725 at Willingdon, near Eastbourne, Sussex, the youngest of the eight children of John Lambert (1690–1764), a flax dresser, and his wife, Susan Bray (1687–1771), daughter of Thomas Bray of Chiddingly, Sussex. About 1730 the family moved to the Cliffe, a suburb of Lewes, Sussex, where Lambert lived for the rest of his life. He attended a common writing-school and later received instruction from a music-master. From 1745 until his death he served as the parish organist, publishing volumes of psalms (1756) and hymns (2nd edn, 1774) and teaching music at least from 1756 until 1758. By 1754 he was in business as a sign painter and gilder and by 1758 as a stationer.

Lambert's ambition was to be a landscape painter. He probably received instruction from a distant relative, George Smith (*c.*1714–1776), of Chichester, perhaps after his marriage on 29 April 1760 at Stopham, Sussex, to Mary Winton (1736–1810), daughter of Francis Winton of Sompting, Sussex, a farmer. (Their one child died in infancy.) He exhibited at the Free Society of Artists

James Lambert (*bap.* 1725, *d.* 1788), by unknown artist

between 1768 and 1773 and at the Royal Academy between 1774 and 1778. His pictures combined elements both of Claudean pastoral and of Dutch picturesque rustic imagery; some featured sheep and cattle prominently. For one such the Society of Arts awarded him a premium of 15 guineas in 1770. About 1776, William Groombridge was his pupil in landscape painting.

More remunerative, from about 1772, was Lambert's quick response to the rising demand for topographical watercolours, with the assistance of his less talented nephew James Lambert (1741–1799). While local gentry commissioned views of their houses, John Elliot (1724–1782) requested images of Lewes's antiquities and Jasper Sprange views for engravings in his *Tunbridge Wells Guide* (1786); visitors ordered copies from Lambert's shop stock. His largest client was Dr William Burrell (1732–1796), for whom he worked between 1776 and 1784 and who bequeathed to the British Museum in London 269 watercolours, mainly of medieval buildings, by the two Lamberts. The Sussex Archaeological Society also has many of the Lamberts' works. Those pictures entirely by the elder Lambert are competent but uninspired compositions.

The elder James Lambert died, probably in the parish of St Thomas-at-Cliffe, on 7 December 1788 in straitened circumstances, administration of his estate being granted to creditors. He was buried on 19 December at St John-sub-Castro Church, Lewes. He was survived by his wife. His natural diffidence and taciturnity had held him back from the London art world beyond the exhibitions, but in eastern Sussex he was the first painter to be an artist rather than solely an artisan.

JOHN H. FARRANT

Sources J. H. Farrant, 'James Lambert, senior and junior, landscape painters of Lewes', *Sussex Archaeological Collections*, 135 (1997), 249–63 · W. H. Challen, 'Baldy's garden, the painters Lambert, and other Sussex families', *Sussex Archaeological Collections*, 90 (1952), 102–52 · [P. Dunvan], *Ancient and modern history of Lewes and Brighthelmston* (1795), 323–5 · W. H. Godfrey and L. F. Salzman, eds., *Sussex views, selected from the Burrell Collections*, Sussex RS (1951) [jubilee vol.] · J. H. Farrant, *Sussex depicted: views and descriptions, 1600–1800,*

Sussex RS, 85 (2001), 39–45 · monument, St John-sub-Castro Church, Lewes, Sussex
Archives BL, Burrell collection, Add. MSS 5676–5677 · BL, Add. MS 71714
Likenesses J. Lambert?, self-portrait?, Sussex Archaeological Society, picture collection, 4170; repro. in Challen, 'Baldy's garden', 138 · silhouette, BL, Burrell collection, Add. MS 5676, fol. 1 [see illus.]
Wealth at death administration to creditors: will, PRO, PROB 11/1176, sig. 99, abstracted in Challen, 'Baldy's garden', 140

Lambert, James (1742–1823), Church of England clergyman and classical scholar, was born and baptized on 7 March 1742 at Melton, Suffolk, the son of Thomas Lambert (bap. 1703), vicar of Thorp, near Harwich, and afterwards rector of Melton, and his wife, Anne. His father had been educated at Trinity College, Cambridge (BA, 1723), and he himself followed suit. After being educated at the grammar school of Woodbridge he was admitted a sizar of Trinity College, Cambridge, on 23 April 1760, aged eighteen. He graduated BA as tenth wrangler and senior medallist in 1764, and proceeded MA in 1767, having obtained a fellowship in 1765. Ordained deacon at Norwich on 12 August 1764, he served the curacies of Iken, and of Alderton and Bawdsey, in Suffolk. He was assistant tutor of Trinity College for some years, and on 7 March 1771 was elected regius professor of Greek, after delivering a prelection, 'De Euripide aliisque qui philosophiam Socraticam scriptis suis illustravisse videntur'. There was no other candidate. Lambert is principally known for having promoted the education of the eminent classical scholar Richard Porson after Porson, aged eleven, had impressed him in an examination at Trinity.

Lambert gave up his assistant tutorship in 1775 and for some years superintended the education of Sir John Fleming Leicester (1762–1827) and his brothers in London and at Tabley, Cheshire. He returned to Trinity with his pupil in 1782, having resigned the Greek professorship on 24 June 1780. Lambert was unorthodox in his theology and increasingly adopted Arian views, which caused him to refuse any preferment in the church. He supported the Feathers tavern petition of 1772 that called for an end to subscription to the Thirty-Nine Articles. The controversial Socinian content of his lectures on the Greek New Testament caused the master of Trinity to bar undergraduates from attending them. He was also a strong supporter of John Jebb, of Peterhouse, in his proposal for annual examinations at Cambridge, and was a member of the syndicate appointed in 1774 to consider schemes for this and other improvements in the university course of education; their proposals, however, were all thrown out by narrow majorities in the senate. In 1789 he was appointed bursar of his college, and he held the office for ten years. His radical religious and political opinions continued to cause friction in the college and the university. With Thomas Jones, tutor of Trinity, he was an ally of the Unitarian William Frend when Frend was tried by the university in 1794 for promoting Jacobinism.

Lambert died on 28 April 1823, aged eighty-one, at Fersfield parsonage, Norfolk, where he was staying with his friend Mr Carter, the incumbent. He was buried in the parish church. A road near Cambridge, connecting the Trumpington and Hills roads, is known as Via Lambertina.   H. R. LUARD, rev. S. J. SKEDD

Sources GM, 1st ser., 93/1 (1823), 572; 93/2 (1823), 84–5 · Venn, Alum. Cant. · J. Gascoigne, Cambridge in the age of the Enlightenment (1989) · IGI
Likenesses D. Gardner, oils, 1767, Trinity Cam.

Lambert [formerly Nicholson], **John** (d. 1538), religious radical, was a native of Norfolk. His family name was Nicholson, but at an unrecorded date he changed his surname to Lambert. He was educated at Cambridge, where he graduated BA in the year 1519/20. Shortly afterwards he was the subject of an exchange of letters between Queens' College and its patron Katherine of Aragon. It would appear that Lambert (as he was already known) aspired to become a fellow and had gained the support of the queen. The master and fellows were reluctant to admit him, and asked for the right of free election, but must ultimately have submitted, since Lambert is subsequently recorded as a fellow, though only between Michaelmas 1521 and Easter 1522. It is possible that during the early 1520s he attended the gatherings for religious discussion held in Cambridge's White Horse tavern; according to John Bale it was at this time that he was exposed to the evangelical teaching of Thomas Bilney, a leading figure at these meetings.

Lambert left Cambridge some time after 1522, and his subsequent movements are obscure. He himself later told Archbishop William Warham that he had been ordained within the diocese of Norwich. John Foxe states that Lambert was forced to leave England and take up residence in Antwerp, where he became preacher and chaplain to the English House. Foxe also suggests that during the late 1520s Lambert met John Frith and William Tyndale in the Low Countries. There is uncertainty, too, over the events in Lambert's life in the early 1530s. Foxe claims that he was 'disturbed' by Sir Thomas More and carried back from Antwerp to England to answer charges relating to the translation of heretical texts. He was probably examined on a charge of heresy before convocation on 27 March 1531, and was certainly imprisoned during the period 1531–2 and questioned by Warham, firstly at Lambeth and later at the archbishop's manor house at Otford. Foxe prints forty-five articles which were 'ministered' against Lambert, together with the latter's replies to them. Lambert is careful not to answer directly questions relating to the sacrament of the altar. He does, however, express a number of proto-protestant views including rejecting 'ear-confession', denying knowledge of purgatory, and questioning the efficacy of going on pilgrimages. In these replies Lambert also refers to the doctrine of justification by faith stating that, 'it is the usage of Scripture to say, faith only doth justify, and work salvation, before a man do any other good works' (Foxe, 1583, 1117). There is no record of the result of these examinations and Lambert appears to have been discharged following the death of Warham on 25 August 1532. After this Lambert may have resigned from the priesthood—Foxe records that he taught Latin and Greek, and claims that he contemplated getting married and joining the Grocers' Company. It is not clear, however, that he actually took either of these steps.

Some time before 13 March 1536 Lambert was accused of heresy by the duke of Norfolk, who complained of attacks made by Lambert upon the worship of saints. Questioned by Archbishop Cranmer and bishops Shaxton and Latimer, Lambert refused to change his beliefs concerning saints despite being offered a compromise by his examiners, who were afraid that his extremism would discredit their own reforming cause. How Lambert's examination ended is uncertain, but for the next two years he was active in evangelical circles in London, one of a group of gospellers whose impassioned sermons proclaimed 'only belief, only, only, nothing else' (Brigden, 266). Finally, in 1538 he was accused of holding heretical views on the sacrament of the altar. Imprisoned by Cranmer, he appealed to Henry VIII.

Lambert's trial before Henry on 16 November 1538 was a grand political and public occasion that gave rise to much contemporary comment. John Husee writing to Lord Lisle gives a detailed description of how the King's Hall of York Place was set out with 'scaffolds, bars and seats' on both sides of the hall. At noon, according to Husee, Lambert was brought before Henry, the latter sitting with 'the most parts of lords temporal and spiritual' and was confronted with a number of articles, the most important of which concerned the sacrament of the altar. Husee writes that, 'It was not a little rejoicing unto all his Grace's commons, and also to all others that saw and heard, how his Grace handled and used this matter; for it shall be a precedent while the world standeth' (Lisle Letters, 5.1273). Sir Thomas Elyot voiced a similar view of this event in the preface to his Dictionary, writing of:

> a divine influence or spark of divinity which late appeared to all them that beheld your Grace sitting in the throne of your royal estate as Supreme Head of the Church of England next under Christ, about the division and condemnation of the pernicious errors of the most detestable heretic, John Nicolson, called also Lambert.

In his Actes and Monuments John Foxe gives a very different version of this event. He describes the king in extremely negative terms, telling how during the examination Henry's brows were 'bent unto severity' showing 'a mind full of wrath and indignation'. He recounts a number of exchanges between Henry and Lambert, perhaps the most famous being one concerning the sacrament of the altar.

> Lambert: I answer, with St. Augustine, that it is the body of Christ after a certain matter.
> The King: Answer me neither out of St Augustine, nor by the authority of any other; but tell me plainly whether thou sayest it is the body of Christ or no.
> Lambert: Then I deny it to be the body of Christ.
> The King: Mark well! for now thou shalt be condemned even by Christ's own words, Hoc est corpus meum.
> (Foxe, 1583, 530)

A number of bishops also took part in the examination of Lambert, notably John Stokesley and Cranmer, although it seems unlikely that Stephen Gardiner took the leading role given to him by Foxe. By the end of the day Lambert had been condemned with the sentence of death being read out by Thomas Cromwell. Lambert was executed by burning at Smithfield on 22 November 1538.

John Bale credited Lambert with translating some of the writings of Erasmus into English, but the only work that can be safely ascribed to him is A treatyse made by Johan Lambert unto Kynge Henry the viii concernynge hys opynyon in the sacrament of the altar (1548?; STC 15180). In this text Lambert bases his arguments concerning the nature of the sacrament of the altar on the writings of the 'ancient doctors' of the church and not on the work of continental protestant writers. His views as expressed both in this treatise and during his examinations place him within the same tradition of native English religious teaching as Thomas Bilney and John Frith. It should be noted, however, that Lambert's Treatyse was edited by Bale, and that although it is not particularly radical in terms of mid-Tudor protestantism it is possible that Lambert's views as originally uttered were more extreme then those presented in this tract. The chronicler Charles Wriothesley records that in 1538 Lambert was charged and convicted of holding some relatively radical views, for instance that infants were not to be baptized and that Christ did not partake of the flesh of Mary, as well as of such mainstream protestant beliefs as the rejection of the real presence in the mass and the view that the scriptures could not be interpreted without faith.   TOM BETTERIDGE

Sources A treatyse made by Johan Lambert, ed. J. Bale (1548?) [incl. introductory notes by J. Bale] • J. Foxe, Actes and monuments (1563) • J. Foxe, Actes and monuments, 4th edn, 2 vols. (1583) • LP Henry VIII, vol. 13/2 • C. Wriothesley, A chronicle of England during the reigns of the Tudors from AD 1485 to 1559, ed. W. D. Hamilton, 1, CS, new ser., 11 (1875) • S. Brigden, London and the Reformation (1989) • D. MacCulloch, Thomas Cranmer: a life (1996) • M. St C. Byrne, ed., The Lisle letters, 6 vols. (1981) • T. Elyot, The dictionary (1539) • W. G. Searle, The history of the Queens' College of St Margaret and St Bernard in the University of Cambridge, 2 vols., Cambridge Antiquarian RS, 9, 13 (1867–71), 164–6 • Venn, Alum. Cant., 1/3.37

Lambert [Lambart], **John** (bap. **1619**, d. **1684**), parliamentary soldier and politician, was baptized on 7 September 1619 at Kirkby Malhamdale, near his home at Calton, Yorkshire. Lambert (who sometimes spelled his name Lambart) was possibly the younger son from Josias Lambert's second marriage, to Anne Heber. The family had been established at Calton by his great-grandfather, also John Lambert (fl. 1516–1566). It is probable that Lambert was educated at Trinity College, Cambridge, and at the inns of court before returning to Yorkshire to marry Frances Lister (d. 1676), daughter of Sir William Lister of Thornton in Craven, on 10 September 1639. This marriage cemented his links with the Lister family that had been established before the death of his greatly indebted father, Josias, in 1632. The Lister connection brought him further into the orbit of some of the leading Yorkshire gentry families such as the Fairfaxes and Belasyses. With the outbreak of civil war Lambert aligned himself, with his Lister kin, with the forces of Lord Fairfax.

Military and early political career Lambert was immediately a very active participant in the numerous skirmishes

John Lambert (*bap.* 1619, *d.* 1684), after Robert Walker, *c.*1650–55

and battles of the northern army. He was noted for his part in the sally from Hull (11 October 1643) and at the battle of Nantwich (25 January 1644), and he played a prominent role in the successes at Bradford (March 1644) and Selby (April 1644). At Marston Moor Lambert was part of the right wing of cavalry that was routed by Goring but which with Sir Thomas Fairfax and five or six troops forced itself through the royalists and joined Cromwell's victorious left wing. Following Sir Thomas Fairfax's appointment as commander of the New Model Army Lambert, then commissary-general of Lord Fairfax's army, was temporarily in charge of the northern forces. In March 1645 he was wounded when Sir Marmaduke Langdale raised the siege of Pontefract. In January 1646, with the end of the war in the north, Lambert was given the command of Montagu's foot regiment in the New Model and participated in the south-west campaign.

Lambert's conduct during his successful military career marked him out for increasing political employments. Recovering from injury in London during December 1644 Lambert kept Sir Thomas Fairfax informed of political developments, including the self-denying ordinance. (In this and his few other remaining letters of this period he signed himself Lambart.) At York in 1644 Lambert had been one of the treaty negotiators. He later acted in this role, alongside Henry Ireton, at the capitulations of Truro, Exeter, and Oxford, in the last of which he remained as governor. Such employments established links between leading army officers, particularly Ireton and Lambert, and those royalists such as Sir John Berkeley who came to favour negotiation with them.

With the dispute between parliament and army in 1647

Lambert was prominent among the officers who opposed enlisting for Ireland before their demands had been met. On 17 April 1647 a meeting of over 100 officers chose a powerful committee, including Lambert, to represent their views. Lambert and the committee of officers represented the sense of the army in *The Petition and Vindication of the Officers of the Armie*, which was laid before parliament on 27 April. The regiments proceeded to make their grievances known through regimental returns. Lambert was very active in organizing and directing this action. On 15 May in Saffron Walden church the officers met to listen to these regimental grievances. Colonel Sheffield and other 'presbyterian' officers questioned the right of Lambert and others to collect these regimental grievances without informing the troops fully of parliament's latest offers. Lambert in turn told them they had cut themselves off from their comrades by volunteering for Ireland and by their failure to endorse the army's March petition. A committee was formed, including Lambert, to present a summary of the regimental returns. In *A Vindication of 167 Officers* (26 June 1647) Lambert was accused of manipulating the presentation of the regimental returns. The unity of the army was restored however by the resignation of Sheffield and other like-minded officers in the face of the determination of Lambert and the majority to resist parliament. On 2 July Lambert was one of the five army commissioners in the first meeting to treat with parliament's commissioners. At a council of war at Reading on 5 July Lambert was also one of the officers appointed to draw up charges against the eleven members whom the army branded 'incendiaries'.

It is in line with these employments, and his collaboration with Ireton, that Lambert's contribution to the projected settlement of 1647 needs to be considered. In June 1647 Lambert and other officers met the king at Childerley Hall, near Cambridge. When Charles arrived at Newmarket, Lambert, with Colonel Robert Hammond, took him a message from Fairfax. The result of the army's control of the king was *The Heads of Proposals*, which according to Berkeley 'Ireton had drawn', though probably with some input from the army's allies in parliament ('Memoirs of Sir John Berkeley', 363). Bulstrode Whitelocke believed Lambert had assisted Ireton in drawing up the heads, and when Ireton presented them to the army council on 17 July 1647 it was Lambert who clarified some issues for Cromwell (Firth, 1.212).

When, in the summer of 1647, the northern forces revolted against their commander Poynts and sought firmly to align themselves with the New Model, Lambert was sent north to command them. His close links with the northern troops, established since 1642, and in particular with those, such as Captain John Hodgson, who had led the revolt against Poynts, coupled with his leadership skills, quickly calmed the situation in the north. Indeed at the time some believed his appointment was due to his connections with the 'adjutators' in the northern forces. Lambert succeeded in disbanding the supernumerary forces, restoring discipline, and mending the relationship with the civilian population, leading to him receiving much praise for his 'fairness, civility and moderation' (*Perfect Diurnall*, 13–20 Sept 1647, 1734).

With the revolt of northern royalists and the invasion of Hamilton's Scottish army in July 1648, Lambert once more showed himself to be a skilled military leader. He forced Langdale into Carlisle before capturing Appleby and neighbouring castles. Lambert's military strategy around Carlisle forced the Scots to advance to Langdale's aid before their army was properly prepared. In the face of the royalist control of Pontefract, the defection of Scarborough, and the weight of Hamilton's forces Lambert led an organized retreat of his forces to Bowes and Barnard Castle, aiming to hold Stainmore Pass against Hamilton. From there he had to retire further to Richmond and then Knaresborough. There, on 13 August, Cromwell arrived, and their combined forces defeated the Scots at Preston (17–19 August 1648). Lambert pursued Hamilton, who surrendered at Uttoxeter (25 August 1648). In October 1648 Lambert was sent to Edinburgh with an advance party of six regiments of horse and one of dragoons to support Argyll's party.

Lambert supported the *Remonstrance of the Army* (16 November 1648), and *The Declaration of Lambert's Brigade* (12 December 1648) justified the army's actions and expressed the bitterness felt by army officers towards parliament. Although named to the court to judge Charles I, Lambert was preoccupied by the northern royalist revolt and particularly the siege of Pontefract, whose resistance he finally ended in March 1649. He did not however oppose the court's proceedings or the subsequent execution of the king.

During the invasion of Scotland in 1650–52 Lambert, now a major-general, was second in command to Cromwell but emerged as the leading fighting commander, even to the extent of being judged to have saved the ailing Cromwell and the English forces from disaster. Still only thirty-one, Lambert's military genius became more evident as the campaign proceeded and as the 51-year-old Cromwell's health collapsed. Taking over command of his kinsman John *Bright's foot regiment Lambert again led his forces from the front, being twice wounded and briefly taken prisoner at Musselburgh (30 July 1650). At Dunbar (3 September 1650), according to Captain John Hodgson, Lambert, backed by Cromwell, persuaded the council of war to adopt the tactics which ultimately led to victory. Having spent most of the previous day observing the Scottish forces Lambert saw how their left wing, being piled up against the steep slope of Spott Burn glen, would be unable to assist their right wing if subjected to a concentrated attack. Lambert was nominated to head the English attack and implement this plan. Lambert led a brigade of three regiments to secure the pass over the Berwick Road which would protect the passage of the main force across Spott Burn ford so that it could fall on the Scots' right. Following an hour-long struggle Lambert's brigade achieved its objective but was then charged by the Scots' cavalry. When Lambert was reinforced by Major Packer, leading Cromwell's horse regiment, the Scots were pushed back. A second combined horse and foot charge ensured the collapse of the Scots' right. The rest of the Scottish forces were then engaged and crushed.

Lambert followed the victory at Dunbar with further blows against Scottish forces. On 1 December he routed an attack on his quarters at Hamilton, destroying the western army and capturing its leader, Colonel Ker. With further success at Aire, Lambert secured the surrender of Colonel Strachan. Briefly in charge of all forces during Cromwell's illness, Lambert forced the surrender of Blackness.

July 1651 witnessed Lambert's most notable personal victory. Managing to cross over into Fife, something which Cromwell and Monck had previously failed to achieve, Lambert, though outnumbered, destroyed a force of 4000 led by Sir John Browne at Inverkeithing. Deciding not to occupy the town Lambert prepared to defend the excellent ground provided by the Ferry hills. Lambert, with a few of his cavalry, led the Scots towards his main body and a party of infantry set to ambush them. Receiving news that Cromwell had withdrawn to Linlithgow and would not be reinforcing him, Lambert, rather than facing being trapped on a peninsula, decided to attack. Concentrating three-quarters of his total force on his right wing and leaving his left wing to prevent him being outflanked Lambert charged up the face of the ridge on the heights of which the Scots had drawn up. Two thousand Scots were killed and Lambert took between forty and fifty colours and 1400 prisoners. 'Such was the gallantry of Major-General Lambert, that had it not been for his armor he had been lost, a brace of bullets being found between his coat and his arms' (*Mercurius Politicus*, 24–31 July 1651, 965). Inverkeithing was a decisive victory. At the time it was seen as ending all of Charles II's hopes of using the Scots to secure his three kingdoms; and more recently the victory has been seen as more decisive than Dunbar.

With Charles II now forced to advance into England Lambert, with Cromwell's cavalry, harried his rear and succeeded in joining with Thomas Harrison at Warrington (15 August 1651) briefly to check the Scots. At Worcester Lambert captured Upton Bridge (28 August 1651), thus securing passage of the Severn for the English forces. Ludlow claimed that Lambert was prominent in the tactical decisions for the attack on Worcester. During the actual assault on Worcester (3 September 1651) Lambert's horse was shot from underneath him.

Lambert's military record bears comparison with that of any of his contemporaries. By the time of Worcester, although still only thirty-two, Lambert had been in arms for nine years. The enthusiasm of his troops to serve under him was testimony not only to his care of them but also to an awareness of his tactical appreciation and the preparation that preceded his most notable successes at Dunbar and Inverkeithing, crucial elements in a general campaign that otherwise would have seen an ageing Cromwell out-generalled.

Entry into civilian politics, 1651–1653 Lambert did not hold a civil office of real political importance until he became one of the eight commissioners for Scotland on 22 October 1651. He was widely seen as the unofficial head of the commissioners for Scotland and his main task was to prepare for the union of the two former kingdoms. At the same time he still led the army in suppressing those Scots who held out. It was while settling Scotland that, on 23 January 1652, Lambert, following the death of Ireton, was appointed lord deputy of Ireland.

Lambert arrived in London on 24 February to prepare to leave for Ireland. When he bought the rectory of Wimbledon on 13 May Lambert was referred to in the deed of enrolment as the lord deputy (PRO, C54/3676/23). On 17 May it was reported that Lambert would begin his journey on 24 May. On 19 May, however, parliament, which had appointed him for only six months, 'considered of the businesse of Ireland, and passed a Vote, that no Commission be granted to any Lieutenant of Ireland after the expiring of the present Commission to the Lord Deputy Lambert' (*Perfect Diurnall*, 17–25 May 1652, 1887). Lambert was offered the posts of commander-in-chief and commissioner for the civil government. These appointments would simply have made him *primus inter pares* in the Irish council. Lambert refused the commission and Cromwell secured the place for Charles Fleetwood, but requested that £2000 out of his arrears as lord lieutenant should go to Lambert. Following Lambert's refusal of the lesser post he also declined a similar position in Scotland. Despite the fact that he held no official position in either country, Lambert was later to be heavily involved in the affairs of Scotland and Ireland through his role on the council of state under the protectorate. It was he who reported on the ordinances for the Union with Scotland, chaired the committee on Irish lands, and headed the Irish committee.

Some contemporaries believed the loss of the lord deputy post was due to Cromwell and that when Lambert later realized this it began the rift between the two men. Lucy Hutchinson, who attacked Lambert for laying out £5000 on his preparations, believed that this had all been a scheme of Cromwell's to get the position for Fleetwood, who had recently married Cromwell's daughter, and Ireton's widow, Bridget. In connection with Fleetwood's appointment, Hutchinson remarked on the bitterness between Frances Lambert and Bridget Fleetwood. Edward Ludlow regarded this episode as a design by Cromwell to turn Lambert against the Rump, and he claimed that Lambert now began to press Cromwell for the dissolution of parliament.

Whatever Cromwell's part in the revocation of the Irish post, the political manoeuvres of the republicans in the Rump and especially those of Sir Arthur Hesilrige also played a part. Between Hesilrige and Lambert there was real animosity. On 31 January 1652 Hesilrige was appointed president of the council of state for a month. In early February the house debated a report recommending Lambert as commander of military forces in Ireland. The tellers in parliament for the motion to abolish the post were Hesilrige and Henry Marten. However, Lambert, like many in the army, had other reasons for antagonism towards the Rump. Legislation that the army had pushed for had been long delayed. Even that which was passed, for example the Act of General Pardon and Oblivion (24 February 1652), did not fully meet the demands of the army. Since Worcester the army had wanted fresh elections and a new parliament. The revocation of the Irish post just added to Lambert's frustration with parliament.

On 20 April 1653, when Cromwell first dissolved the parliament and then moved on to dismiss the council of state, Lambert and Harrison were with him. Harrison's wish for a council of seventy was opposed by Lambert, who believed power should be entrusted to a much smaller body of about ten or twelve. The subsequent parliament of 139 'puritan notables' appeared to signify a defeat for Lambert. Although elected to the interim council of state for the first time in April 1653, where he was its first president, co-opted to sit as an MP in July, and chosen for the first council of state, appointed on 9 July, Lambert took no part in Barebone's Parliament once it was convened. It was said that 'Lambert forbeares the Parlt and Councel much of late, he solaces at Wimbleton, and hath the visits of the most eminent of the Northerne Gentry' (Bodl. Oxf., MS Clarendon 46, fol. 113). Lambert was not chosen as a member of the second council of state (1 November).

The 'Instrument of government' and the establishment of the protectorate From mid-October at the latest Lambert was preparing an alternative settlement. He appears to have been biding his time while the radicals in parliament discredited themselves. On 19 November he returned from Yorkshire. On 24 November it was reported that 'There hath been some late discontents between the General and Harrison in so much as Harrison is retired, and its said Lambert is sent for up hither' (Bodl. Oxf., MS Clarendon 47, fol. 113). The council had sent for Lambert and on 23 November appointed a committee under Cromwell to confer with him and other officers concerning the Scottish situation.

The moderates in the parliament, led by Sir Charles Wolseley, William Sydenham, Sir Gilbert Pickering, Edward Montagu, Philip Jones, Sir Anthony Ashley Cooper, Henry Lawrence, and John Desborough, all of whom were on the council of state and would be on the new council established under the protectorate, organized a resignation and abdicated their power to Cromwell. Colonel Goffe and Lieutenant-Colonel White entered the parliament with musketeers and dispersed the members who had remained there. It is most likely they were acting under orders from Lambert. It is perhaps significant that in council on 26 December it was ordered that 'the warrant issued by Major-General Lambert on 12 December for restraining all boats and vessels from the port of Dover, be taken off' (*CSP dom.*, 1653, 311). One contemporary simply commented, 'what Lambert hath aimed at he has affected' (Thurloe, *State papers*, 1.632).

Lambert's settlement, the 'Instrument of government', introduced on 16 December, was the written constitution that was the foundation of the protectorate. At the installation of Cromwell as protector it was Lambert who had a prominent place in the proceedings. He rode with Cromwell in his carriage and it was Lambert who handed Cromwell the sword of state. At the time there was comment that Lambert was to be made a duke and general of the three nations and would be the next protector. However, the army was not one united body behind the instrument. In the hectic days before 16 December accounts state that Lambert was presenting the majority of officers with a *fait accompli*. The most visible army opposition came in the three colonels' petition (18 October 1654). Most disagreement was based on the power given to the single person, especially the power to oppose parliament. It was also noted that Cromwell's successor, probably Lambert, might use the army totally to destroy parliaments.

The height of his power, 1653–1657 Lambert's central role in the new regime is demonstrated by his activity in council, membership of key committees, and by his role in promoting important ordinances made by the council before 3 September 1654. For example, Lambert was on committees for chancery regulation, the duchy court, and the regulation of JPs. He was also involved in the army committee and in managing the affairs of Ireland and Scotland. He was also on all the committees considering how best to raise the necessary moneys to fund the army, navy, and civil administration. Indeed, the reorganization of the exchequer has been seen as a significant achievement of the protectorate, and his part in this was central. Alongside this Lambert played a key role in the establishment of Durham University.

The instrument, through its separation of the legislative and executive powers and its concentration of authority in the council as a body and not in the protector, placed tight restrictions on Cromwell's position. In the months leading up to the first protectorate parliament Lambert had his wish of a small council controlling affairs and ruling by ordinance. Contemporaries clearly saw Lambert as the dominating influence in the protectorate, appearing to be semi-independent of Cromwell through his various offices and increasing wealth. Lambert was a major-general, colonel of two regiments, a leading member of the council, warden of the Cinque Ports, and was estimated to have an income of about £6500 per annum.

Despite Lambert's influence the protector was far from being controlled by him and the protectorate councillors were not a unified group following a single line. Indeed, most had stronger links with Cromwell than with Lambert. There was policy disagreement, Lambert's opposition to Cromwell and other councillors' determination to follow the 'western design' being a notable example. Gradually, however, a much more serious rift opened between Lambert and Cromwell with regard to their respective views on the nature of a political settlement.

The pragmatic imposition of central government on the localities through the major-generals has widely been attributed to Lambert, though it was probably a wider council measure. Lambert was, however, prominent in the introduction of the original and the additional instructions of 22 August and 4 October 1655 and 19 June 1656. He was major-general of five northern counties—Yorkshire, Durham, Cumberland, Westmorland, and Northumberland—but, because of his other duties, this work was undertaken by two deputies, colonels Charles Howard and Robert Lilburne. When the major-generals came under attack in parliament Cromwell abandoned them and thus piqued Lambert. Lambert vigorously defended them and pushed for the decimation tax to be continued: 'The quarrel is now between light and darkness, not who shall rule, but whether we shall live or be preserved or no' (*Diary of Thomas Burton*, 1.319). Lambert and the major-generals believed that they could control parliament, through the elections and expulsion, and that the issue over the direction of settlement had finally to be decided. When the parliament reassembled it was clear that the major-generals had not got the house they wanted. Cromwell's opposition to decimation and the militia severely undermined Lambert's position. The outwardly religious dispute that followed merely deepened the split.

When Lambert's former quartermaster, the Quaker James Nayler, was brought before parliament accused of 'horrid blasphemy' Lambert, who was on close terms with many of radical religious views, was the leading officer to support him. His own religious preferences, behind his outward latitudinarianism, remain as obscure as they were to his contemporaries, who regarded him at various times as anything from a Catholic to an atheist. Lambert's position with regard to the Nayler case needs to be seen in light of the disputes over the major-generals and decimation. For Lambert the constitutional issues crucially underpinned the religious issues. The political framework of Lambert's instrument was the safeguard for a tolerant religious approach. A close associate of Lambert, Adam Baynes, made the point that 'for the Instrument of Government says, all shall be protected that profess faith in Jesus Christ' (*Diary of Thomas Burton*, 1.59). The essence of Lambert's defence of Nayler was that he did not want parliament to have unlimited judicial power. He was worried that future parliaments might attempt to prosecute those who had acted in the name of past parliaments. The instrument had, in part, sought to counter the power of parliament with a more influential council.

Kingship and resignation, 1657 Cromwell's apparent indecision over whether to take the title of king seems to have driven the final wedge between the two men. Although Cromwell asserted that the title of king had been in an early draft of the instrument, in 1657 Lambert led the army's opposition to kingship, a crucial factor in Cromwell's decision not to accept the title. Some contemporaries believed Lambert's opposition was not motivated by principle. Similarly they attributed his removal from office to Cromwell's fear of what he might achieve. That he was solely motivated by ambition would be a misreading of the issues at stake. Lambert saw that kingship represented a wholesale shift towards civilian government. The main issue for Lambert was that those who had won the war, the military, had to maintain a powerful voice in government. The men behind 'The humble petition and advice' could not be expected to act as trustees of the army's interest.

On 24 June 1657 parliament decided to impose an oath on all councillors. Lambert opposed this move, refused to take the oath of loyalty required by the new constitution, absented himself from the meetings of the council, and removed himself to Wimbledon. On 23 July 1657 Cromwell sent for him to resign his commands.

Wealth and financial activities Lambert's estate at the outbreak of civil war was worth less than its nominal £300 value. Lambert claimed that the military impact of the civil war lessened its value further as well as disrupting the wool trade in which he had an interest. However, the success he made of his military career and his subsequent political role saw a significant rise in Lambert's fortunes. Lambert was attacked as one of the officers whose 'parks and new houses and gallant wives had choked them up' (Griffith, 18–19). As well as his army pay Lambert received various gifts and grants of land for his military success, the most notable being £300 p.a. of land in Pontefract and £1000 p.a. in Scotland (9 November 1651). His new wealth was spent on various purchases such as Kirkby Malhamdale fee-farm rent, Ampleforth, Braunton Dean, and Nonsuch as well as works of art, through Baptist Gaspars, fine clothing, and books.

However, there was a less obvious element to Lambert's participation in land speculation. Lambert acted on behalf of his kin in relation to property in Ripon, Burton, Wennington, and Ecclesall. A notable example was his securing of Sheriff Hutton for the royalist Sir Thomas Ingram. Similarly, he acted with various royalists, including his Catholic kinsman John, Lord Belasyse, to secure property for the Vavasors. Such actions belie his increasingly hardline public attitude to royalists. They are, however, in line with the workings of his kinship network prior to 1642 which had kept his own estates secure following the death of his father. They are also mirrored by the actions of his royalist kin, Belasyse and Ingram, after the Restoration to protect Lambert's estates during his long imprisonment. Kinship was thus a determining factor in many of Lambert's investments.

The most notable of Lambert's purchases was the manor of Wimbledon. Following his purchase of the rectory of Wimbledon Lambert, on 17 May 1652, purchased Wimbledon House, formerly belonging to Henrietta Maria, for £16,822 17s. 8d. It was there that Lambert tended his notable gardens and followed his artistic pursuits. Lambert is most associated with the Guernsey lily, *Nerine sarniense*, and his gardening led him to be satirized in 1660 as the Knight of the Golden Tulip, but, following his dismissal, it also was an opening for royalist advances to him. As lord of the manor Lambert held regular manor courts under his own steward, a fellow soldier, William Claxton.

Re-emergence and defeat, 1658–1660 Despite Lambert's dismissal in July 1657 Cromwell allowed him a pension of £2000 per annum. Some saw this as a means to prevent any further opposition from Lambert. The royalists tried to exploit Lambert's dismissal but despite numerous royalist approaches, including a scheme by which his eldest daughter would be married to either Charles II or the duke of York, Lambert kept to his gardens. In the last six

months of his life Cromwell received Lambert at Whitehall and appears to have attempted a reconciliation. It was recorded that 'Cromwell fell on his neck, kissed him, inquired of dear Johnny for his Jewell (so hee calls Mrs Lambert) and for all his children by name' (Bodl. Oxf., MS Clarendon 57, fols. 175–6).

With Richard Cromwell as protector Lambert slowly returned to national politics. Sitting in the 1659 parliament as MP for Pontefract Lambert spoke in favour of Richard but also sought to limit his powers over the military and his negative voice in legislation, commenting that 'The best man is but a man at the best. I have had great cause to know it' (*Diary of Thomas Burton*, 3.189). Lambert also objected to the admission of the Irish and Scottish members and generally he appears to have been trying to ingratiate himself with the republican grouping.

Despite having no official position within the army Lambert maintained some contacts with those junior officers intriguing at Wallingford House. His exact role in their pressure which led to the dissolution of parliament (22 April 1659) is, however, not clear. When the junior officers forced the recall of the Rump, Lambert was restored to his commands and became colonel of two regiments. Naturally for someone of his ability and past record as soon as he had been invited onto the general council Lambert took a leading role. He was prominent in the negotiations which preceded the restoration of the Rump, and in the presentation of the army's declaration to Lenthall which invited the Rump to return (7 May) and a larger declaration which stated their political demands (13 May). The restored parliament made Lambert a member of a committee of safety (9 May) and council of state (13 May) as well as a member of the seven-man commission for the nomination of officers (4 June). Lambert's response to the long-delayed Indemnity Act, however, reflected his continued ambivalent attitude to parliaments. 'I know not why they should not be at our mercy as well as we at theirs' (*Memoirs of Edmund Ludlow*, 2.100).

Despite this, parliament had little choice but to send Lambert, its most capable commander, to face the rising of Sir George Booth. Lambert efficiently destroyed Booth's forces at Winwick Bridge, Cheshire (19 August), before recapturing Chester (21 August) and Chirk Castle (24 August). Lambert used the £1000 jewel parliament had voted him to pay his troops. These troops took up Fleetwood's submission to the parliament that Lambert be made, once more, a major-general.

This demand, with calls for godly reform, a senate, a proper command structure, and for no officer to be dismissed without court martial, was voiced in Lambert's officers' Derby petition. Although Lambert's role in this was unclear it aroused further suspicion of his motives among many MPs who had long feared his talents and questioned his ambition. Such doubts could only have been heightened by Lambert's strengthening of his links with Sir Henry Vane when he returned to London, for both favoured rule by a small élite. The general council of the army, however, vindicated the petition and repeated its request for arrears. When parliament learned that Lambert, Desborough, and other leading officers were seeking subscriptions to their petition they cashiered Lambert and those whom they regarded as his accomplices (12 October 1659). In response, Lambert appealed to the troops around London, most of whom responded and marched on Westminster with him. On 13 May Lambert's force surrounded the regiments of Morley and Moss and the Horse Guards that were drawn up to protect parliament. Finding the gate of Scotland Yard barred by the Horse Guards Lambert walked forward to them alone and persuaded the soldiers to join his own. When Lenthall arrived to attempt to enter parliament Lambert ordered him home. Hesilrige and the MPs soon capitulated and ordered their last defenders, Morley's troops, back to quarters. As they marched out of Westminster Hall these troops gave Lambert an ovation. Lambert now recovered his position as a major-general and became a member of the committee of safety which took over from parliament's council of state.

This body sent Lambert to deal with the advancing forces of Monck, who had declared for parliament (3 November). For Monck, Lambert in many ways represented the factors that had driven him to declare for parliament, the spectre of military rule and particularly the increasing Quaker threat, many being in his forces and his attitude to the sect seemingly tolerant. Although Lambert had a larger force he sought to avoid conflict. His delay saw the disintegration of his army, which, unlike Monck's, had not received any money. Fleetwood and Desborough in London had an increasingly fragile grip on power and as Portsmouth (3 December) and the fleet (13 December) declared for parliament the troops in London itself also acknowledged its authority (24 December). When Lambert's old commander Thomas Fairfax led the Yorkshire gentry in support of parliament (1 January 1660) the Irish brigade in his forces deserted him and his force dissolved. Offered a general indemnity, along with all his soldiers, Lambert submitted. Ordered to retire to his Yorkshire house (26 January), Lambert was further ordered to repair to Holmby, Northamptonshire. This was followed by a proclamation for his arrest (13 February) claiming that he had been in London provoking a mutiny. When he appeared before the council of state on 5 March Lambert hoped to be permitted to enter the Swedish army but he was unable to meet the £20,000 security demanded of him and was placed in the Tower.

On 10 April Lambert escaped from the Tower and attempted to rally forces against the approaching Restoration, staging a rendezvous at Edgehill. Lambert's actual aim was unclear, his personal motivation was still questioned, and his increasing identification in many minds with the Quaker threat meant he was an isolated figure. Despite this he still managed to assemble a number of officers and about six troops of horse. However, these soldiers had no will to fight when approached by troops under colonels Ingoldsby and Streeter near Daventry (22 April). Lambert was taken prisoner and escorted to London. At forty-one his career was over.

Trial, imprisonment, and death, 1660–1684 Although not a regicide, Lambert was initially excepted by the Commons from the Act of Indemnity for punishment not extending to life, but when the Lords voted that he be wholly excepted both houses then stated that if he was attainted they would petition that the death penalty be remitted. Lambert was sent from the Tower to close confinement in Castle Cornet, Guernsey, in October 1661. His wife, Frances, petitioned that she and their ten children be allowed to reside in a house that the king had allowed him to have. On 17 February 1662 a licence for Frances and three of her children 'to go and remain with her husband' was directed to Sir Hugh Pollard, then governor of Guernsey (*CSP dom.*, *1661–2*, 276). In July 1661 the Cavalier Parliament demanded that Lambert should be proceeded against. After repeated requests Charles II finally agreed to bring Lambert back from Guernsey.

At the start of April 1662 the duke of York sent ships for Lambert and Vane, who was imprisoned on the Isles of Scilly, to be returned to the Tower for trial. On 25 April the then governor of the Tower, Sir John Robinson, received a warrant to allow Lambert's wife and her children 'to have access to her husband, and to converse with him in the presence of his keeper' (*CSP dom.*, *1661–2*, 350). Lambert was arraigned in the king's bench for high treason. On 19 June Lambert stood before the bar,

> trying to excuse and justify the crimes of which he was accused. He was for all the world not upset about them and did not speak to deny his deeds, but tried all the time to make them appear less serious, and appealed to the King's Mercy, by which he won the judges' hearts. (Exwood and Lehmann, 92–3)

Although Lambert was sentenced alongside Vane to be executed, the king commuted his sentence to life imprisonment. He was returned to Castle Cornet.

At times Lambert was allowed out of close confinement. In 1663–4 Frances petitioned that she be allowed to live with her husband, whom she felt should have more liberty because he was ill. A warrant allowing Lambert more liberty was issued in November 1664. At times of danger, however, Lambert was put under increased scrutiny. When a plot to free him was discovered in late 1664 it was ordered that he 'be kept a close prisoner and if at any time an enemy should appear before the island that he be shot for having had correspondence with the king's enemies' (PRO, SP 47, MS calendar). Again at the time of a threatened invasion in July 1666 orders were given that Lambert should be shot if troops arrived on the island. One of the reasons given by Charles II for dismissing Lord Hatton as governor was his failure to keep a strict vigilance over Lambert. Given Hatton's pre-1660 links with Lambert and the marriage of Mary Lambert to one of his sons, Charles Hatton, the authorities were also probably worried about his loyalty.

During his long imprisonment it is clear that Lambert's financial problems and general affairs were managed by those who had been part of his kinship circle before the civil war and others with whom he had become connected as a result of his military and political career. In December

1667, after an appeal by Lord Belasyse, Viscount Fauconberg, and Sir Thomas Ingram, Lambert was allowed to take a house with his wife and family on the island. Of Lambert's kinship circle, also notable in helping him were his sons-in-law: John Blackwell, Daniel Parrott, John Hooke, and Dr Daniel Cox. In 1670 Lambert was transferred to St Nicholas Island. While he was imprisoned off Plymouth, Samuel Pepys, Miles Halhead, James Yonge, Charles II, and the duke of York are all recorded as having visited Lambert. In 1676 his wife, Frances, died. Lambert remained imprisoned on St Nicholas Island until his own death in March 1684. He was buried in St Andrew's parish church, Plymouth.

Lambert played a significant role in the events of 1642–60. Militarily he ranks with any of his contemporaries and during the Scottish campaign he arguably surpassed his older commander Cromwell as the leading general of the English forces. His evident military genius and care for his troops saw him worshipped by them and described by one contemporary as the 'Armyes Darling' (Bodl. Oxf., MS Carte 131, fol. 189). It was this military genius and popularity alongside his youthful dynamism, rather than a close relationship with Cromwell, that saw him rise to the height of his power in the 1650s. However, it was the very same factors that also earned him the distrust of many. This in turn, when added to his general religious tolerance and personal links with those of Catholic to Quaker beliefs, while appearing to hold no firm views himself, was to prove fatal to his cause in 1659–60. Although an aesthete his experience since 1642 ensured he would always seek to preserve military influence in government. Politically Lambert is most remembered as the author of the instrument and as prominent in the establishment of the protectorate, but this is to overlook the scale of his general role, especially in the years 1653–7, when, still in his thirties, he was one of the most influential men in the state and would almost certainly have been chosen by the council as protector if Cromwell had died at this point. The survival of a Lambertian protectorate, however, would, as the events of 1659–60 suggest, have been limited by his narrow power base.   D. N. FARR

Sources D. Farr, *Major General John Lambert, 1619–1684* (2003) · D. Farr, 'The military and political career of John Lambert, 1619–57', PhD diss., U. Cam., 1996 · D. Farr, 'New information with regard to the imprisonment of Major General John Lambert, 1662–1684', *Cromwelliana* (1998), 44–57 · Calton deeds, W. Yorks. AS, Leeds, Yorkshire Archaeological Society · PRO, C7/216/48 · BL, Add. MSS 21417–21427 · Bodl. Oxf., Clarendon MSS · *CSP dom.*, 1644–83 · *Diary of Thomas Burton*, ed. J. T. Rutt, 4 vols. (1828) · *The Clarke papers*, ed. C. H. Firth, [new edn], 2 vols. in 1 (1992) · I. Gentles, *The New Model Army in England, Ireland, and Scotland, 1645–1653* (1992) · A. Woolrych, *Commonwealth to protectorate* (1982) · A. Woolrych, *Soldiers and statesmen: the general council of the army and its debates, 1647–1648* (1987) · *The memoirs of Edmund Ludlow*, ed. C. H. Firth, 2 vols. (1894) · 'Memoirs of Sir John Berkeley', *Select tracts relating to the civil wars in England*, ed. F. Maseres, 1 (1815), 353–94 · *The writings and speeches of Oliver Cromwell*, ed. W. C. Abbott and C. D. Crane, 4 vols. (1937–47); facs. edn (1988) · A. Griffith, *Stena Vavasorensis* (1654) · Wimbledon manor records, Northants. RO · Thurloe, *State papers* · W. H. Dawson, *Cromwell's understudy: the life and times of General John Lambert* (1938) · R. Hutton, *The Restoration: a political and religious history of England and Wales, 1658–1667* (1985) · M. Exwood and H. L. Lehmann, *The journal of William Schellinks' travels in England, 1661–63*, CS, 5th ser. (1993), vol. 1 · A. Woolrych, introduction, in *Complete prose works of John Milton*, ed. D. M. Wolfe, 7, ed. R. W. Ayers (1980), 1–228 · B. Reay, *The Quakers and the English revolution* (1985) · parish register, Kirkby Malhamdale, Yorkshire, 7 Sept 1619 [baptism] · parish register, Kirkby Malhamdale, Yorkshire, 10 Sept 1639 [marriage] · J. Yonge, *Plymouth memoirs* (1951) · D. Farr, 'The education of Major-General John Lambert', *Cromwelliana* (2000) · D. Farr, 'The shaping of John Lambert's allegiance and the outbreak of the civil war', *Northern History*, 36 (2000), 247–66 · D. Farr, 'Kin, cash, Catholics, and cavaliers: the role of kinship in the financial management of Major-General John Lambert', *Historical Research*, 74 (2001), 44–62

Archives BL, letters to Captain Baynes, Add. MSS 21417–21427 · BL, letters to Colonel C. Fairfax, Add. MS 36996, *passim* [copies] · BL, letters to Sir Thomas Fairfax, Sloane MS 1519, fols. 37, 39 · Leics. RO, letters to Sir Arthur Hesilrige, 1648, DG 21 · Sheff. Arch., letters to John Bright · W. Yorks. AS, Leeds, Yorkshire Archaeological Society, Calton deeds

Likenesses F. Place, mezzotint, *c.*1670–1679 (after R. Walker), BM, NPG · M. Vandergucht, engraving, 1713 (after oil painting; after R. Walker), BM; repro. in E. Ward, *The history of the grand rebellion*, 3 vols. (1713) · J. Houbraken, mezzotint (after R. Walker), BM, NPG; repro. in T. Birch, *The heads and characters of illustrious persons of Great Britain*, 2 vols. (1743–51) · portrait, Ribbesdale collection · T. Simon, medal, repro. in H. Walpole, *Anecdotes of painting in England*, 4 vols. (1762–71), vol. 2, p. 362 · oils (after R. Walker, *c.*1650–1655), NPG · pen-and-ink drawing, NPG · portrait (after R. Walker), NPG · portrait, Eshton Hall; repro. in E. Hailstone, *Portraits of Yorkshire worthies*, 1 (1869), no. 83 · portrait (after R. Walker, *c.*1650–1655), priv. coll. [*see illus.*] · two silver medals, BM

Wealth at death imprisoned; dependent on kin

Lambert, Sir John (1772–1847), army officer, was born on 28 April 1772, the son of Captain Robert Alexander Lambert RN (*c.*1732–1801), second son of Sir John Lambert, second baronet, and his wife, Catherine, daughter of Thomas Byndloss of Jamaica. He was commissioned ensign in the 1st foot guards on 27 January 1791, and promoted lieutenant and captain on 9 October 1793. He served at the sieges of Valenciennes and Dunkirk, and was in the action of Lincelles in 1793. He was adjutant of the 3rd battalion in the campaign of 1794, served with it in Ireland during the uprising of 1798, and in the expedition to the Netherlands in 1799. He was promoted captain and lieutenant-colonel on 14 May 1801. He served in Portugal and Spain in 1808, was present at Corunna, and commanded the light companies of the guards in the Walcheren expedition of 1809. He became colonel in the army on 25 July 1810, and embarked for Cadiz in command of the 3rd battalion on 30 May 1811. In January 1812 he was sent to Carthagena with two battalions. He remained there three months, and in October joined Wellington's army at Salamanca.

On 4 June 1813 Lambert was promoted major-general, and was appointed to a brigade of the 6th division. He commanded it at the battles of the Nivelle, the Nive, Orthez, and Toulouse, and was mentioned in dispatches. He received the thanks of parliament and the gold cross, and was made KCB on 2 January 1815. Having been sent to America, he joined the army under Sir Edward Pakenham below New Orleans on 6 January 1815, with the 7th and 43rd foot regiments. In the unsuccessful attack on the

American trenches, made two days afterwards, he commanded the reserve. When Pakenham was killed, and General Gibbs mortally wounded, the chief command devolved on Lambert. He decided not to renew the attack, withdrew the troops which had been sent across the Mississippi, and, after retreating on 18 January, re-embarked his force on the 27th. It went to the Bay of Mobile, where Fort Bowyer was taken on 12 February, and next day news arrived that peace had been signed.

Lambert returned to Europe in time to command the 10th brigade of British infantry at Waterloo. The brigade joined the army from Ghent only on the morning of 18 June, and was at first posted in reserve at Mont-St Jean. After 3 p.m. it was moved up to the front line to support the 5th (Picton's) division, and one of its regiments, the 27th, which had to be kept in square near La Haye-Sainte, lost two-thirds of its men, a heavier loss than that of any other regiment. Lambert received the thanks of parliament, the order of St Vladimir of Russia (3rd class), and that of Maximilian Joseph of Bavaria (commander). He commanded the 8th infantry brigade in the army of occupation in France. On 19 October 1816 he married Jane (d. 22 May 1864), daughter of John Morant of Brocklehurst Park, New Forest.

Lambert was promoted lieutenant-general on 27 May 1825, and general on 23 November 1841. He was given the colonelcy of the 10th regiment on 18 January 1824, and was made GCB on 19 July 1838. He died at Weston House, Thames Ditton, Surrey, on 14 September 1847, aged seventy-five. E. M. LLOYD, rev. ROGER T. STEARN

Sources GM, 2nd ser., 28 (1847), 539 · Burke, *Peerage* (1959) · F. W. Hamilton, *The origin and history of the first or grenadier guards*, 3 vols. (1874) · J. Philippart, ed., *The royal military calendar*, 3 (1816) · *The dispatches of … the duke of Wellington … from 1799 to 1818*, ed. J. Gurwood, 13 vols. in 12 (1834–9) · H. T. Siborne, ed., *Waterloo letters* (1891) · W. Porter, *History of the corps of royal engineers*, 2 vols. (1889) · W. James, *Military occurrences of the late war between Great Britain and the United States of America*, 2 vols. (1818) · R. Muir, *Britain and the defeat of Napoleon, 1807–1815* (1996)
Likenesses W. Salter, group portrait, oils (*Waterloo banquet at Apsley House*), Wellington Museum, Apsley House, London · W. Salter, oils (study for *Waterloo banquet at Apsley House*), NPG

Lambert, John (b. c.1775, d. in or after 1811), traveller and painter in Canada, was born in England. In 1806 he went to Lower Canada with his uncle James Campbell, who had been sent by the privy council committee for trade to promote the cultivation of hemp in the colony after established supplies from northern Europe had been cut off by Napoleon. Although Lambert was reported to have been involved in the hemp project (see *DNB*), this seems unlikely, as in 1806, well before the failure of the scheme in 1810, he had set off on his travels around the continent. His journey was recorded in *Travels through Lower Canada, and the United States of North America* (3 vols., 1811), which ran to four editions in the absence of much competition. The text is a dense compilation of statistics and detailed description relieved by lithographs after his own watercolours. The work has proved valuable to later historians for his description of local life, which reflects his desire to be just and the fact that he mixed with people from all walks of life. He also edited Washington Irving's *Essays* (1811) and helped secure for Irving a wider English audience. Nothing is known of his later life.

ELIZABETH BAIGENT

Sources DCB, vol. 5 · J. R. Harper, *Early painters and engravers in Canada* (1970) · Allibone, *Dict.* · [J. Watkins and F. Shoberl], *A biographical dictionary of the living authors of Great Britain and Ireland* (1816) · DNB

Lambert, Sir John (1815–1892), civil servant and musicologist, was born on 4 February 1815 at Bridzor, near Wardour Castle, Wiltshire, the youngest surviving son of Daniel Lambert, a surgeon, of Hindon, and afterwards of Milford Hall, Salisbury, and his wife, Mary Muriel, the daughter of Charles Jinks of Oundle, Northamptonshire. He was a Roman Catholic, and in 1823 he entered St Gregory's College, Downside, near Bath. In 1831 he was articled to a Salisbury solicitor and he practised in Salisbury from 1836 to 1857. In 1838 he married Ellen Reade (d. 1891), the daughter of Henry Shorto of Salisbury. They had three sons and four daughters, of whom two sons and three daughters survived. Lambert took a leading part in local politics, and was a strong advocate of free trade; he was involved in anti-cornlaw agitation, and reformed the sanitary condition of the city. In 1854 he was elected mayor of Salisbury, the first Roman Catholic to be mayor of a cathedral city since the Reformation. In 1857 he was appointed a poor-law inspector.

In 1863 Lambert went to London at the request of C. P. Villiers, president of the poor-law board, to advise on the measures necessary to deal with the poverty caused by the American civil war, and the Union Relief Acts and Public Works (Manufacturing Districts) Act of that year were prepared as a result of his recommendations. After the passing of the Public Works Act Lambert superintended its administration. In 1865 he prepared statistics for the Representation of the People Acts, which were introduced in 1866 by Russell and Gladstone, and gave similar assistance to Disraeli in connection with the Representation of the People Bill of 1867. Before the resignation of Russell's administration he was offered the post of financial minister for the island of Jamaica, which he declined. In 1867 he drew up the scheme for the Metropolitan Poor Act, and under it was appointed receiver of the metropolitan common poor fund.

Lambert was a member of the parliamentary boundaries commission of 1867, and of the sanitary commission which sat for two or three years. In 1869 and 1870 he went to Ireland at Gladstone's request to gather information in connection with the Irish church and land bills, and prepared special reports for the cabinet. From 1871 to 1882 he was permanent secretary of the new Local Government Board, and was entrusted with the organization of the department. As a member of the sanitary commission he compiled in 1872 a summary of the sanitary laws, and in the same year he was chairman of the commission which drew up the census of landed proprietors in Great Britain. This was issued as a blue book, known as 'The Modern Domesday Book', and provided the raw material upon which John Bateman based his statistical compilation *The

Great Landowners of Great Britain and Ireland (1876). In 1879 Lambert prepared a report for the select committee of the House of Lords on the conservancy of rivers, and also reorganized the audit staff of the Local Government Board. He was chairman of the boundaries commission of 1884–5. In 1885 he was sworn of the privy council.

Lambert was a gifted musician, and was especially interested in medieval church music. He helped to revive the singing of plainchant, and at the end of his life was converted to the new theory of plainchant from the Solesmes congregation in France. He was a member of the Academy of St Cecilia at Rome, and received a gold medal from Pius IX for his services in promoting church music. His musical publications included *The Vesper Psalter* (1849), an edition of Janssen's *A Grammar of Ritual Music* (1849), *First Series of Hymns and Songs for the Use of Catholic Schools and Families* (1853), and *Dulcis Jesu memoria* (1856), a Gregorian hymn from the Sarum Graduale in modern notation. His works were widely used in Europe, especially in Belgium. Lambert was also the author of *Catholic Sacred Songs* (1853), *Modern Legislation as a Chapter in our History* (1865), and *Vagrancy Laws and Vagrants* (1868). He was very fond of flowers, and published papers on the cultivation of orchids.

Lambert was made a KCB in 1879. He died on 27 January 1892 after a long illness, at his home, Milford House, Elms Road, Clapham Common, London, and was buried at St Osmund's Church, Salisbury, which he had founded.

W. A. J. ARCHBOLD, rev. ANNE PIMLOTT BAKER

Sources Gillow, *Lit. biog. hist.* · 'The Right Honourable Sir John Lambert', *Downside Review*, 8 (1889) · *The Times* (29 Jan 1892) · *Downside Review*, 11 (1892) · Boase, *Mod. Eng. biog.* · *Debrett's Peerage* · Gladstone, *Diaries*

Archives BL, corresp. with W. E. Gladstone, Add. MS 44235

Likenesses Maull & Fox, photograph, repro. in *ILN* (6 Feb 1892), 166 · etching, repro. in *Downside Review* · photograph, Salisbury Corporation · print, Salisbury Corporation · wood-engraving, repro. in *ILN* (6 Feb 1892)

Wealth at death £25,898 19s. 3d.: probate, 9 March 1892, *CGPLA Eng. & Wales*

Lambert, Leslie Harrison [pseud. A. J. Alan] (1883–1941), radio broadcaster and intelligence officer, was born on 11 November 1883 at 14 Mapperley Park Drive, Basford, Nottingham, the son of Thomas Harrison Lambert, hosiery manufacturer, and his wife, Kate Everington. Educated at Rugby School, Lambert served articles as a surveyor for seven years before becoming a magician. A member of the Magic Circle and much admired for his dexterity, he regularly performed for leading members of society, including the royal family. It appears that he continued what was a highly successful magical career until about 1909 and that from one job involving secrets he was to become involved in another. Although he wrote some of his later correspondence on Foreign Office headed notepaper and his death certificate gives his occupation as Foreign Office official, Lambert was part of the Government Code and Cypher School at Bletchley Park on the outbreak of the Second World War, and became an important figure in military intelligence, concerned with naval strategy and overseas naval affairs.

However it was in broadcasting that Lambert made his name. After listening to a story broadcast by Sir William Bull MP, he called on Rex Palmer, the London station director of the then British Broadcasting Company, and told Palmer one of his own stories over a cup of tea. Palmer was so struck by his personality that Lambert—or A. J. Alan as he chose to be known—was engaged, and broadcast his first story, 'My Adventure in Jermyn Street', on 31 January 1924. His story and intimate presentation made an immediate impact and he quickly became one of the most popular broadcasting personalities of the time. In order to maintain the high standard he set himself and to keep his audience wanting more, he limited the number of broadcasts he gave to around five a year, and often spent two or three months perfecting each story he wrote. Alan's stories were written in an almost conversational style, as if he were relating a coincidence or unusual event in which he was personally involved. They invariably started in a low-key manner but quickly built up in suspense before culminating in an often satisfying twist.

A. J. Alan was a masterful performer and went to great lengths to ensure his broadcasts were as he wanted. He used to sit on a high stool close to the microphone, and began with a friendly, 'Good evening, everyone'. He never smoke or drank for at least a week before each broadcast and, to prevent the sound of rustling paper, pasted his scripts on card. Also, having read that the lights had once gone out during a news broadcast, he insisted on having a candle in the studio for back-up lighting—just in case!

Throughout his broadcasting career, and with the help of the BBC, he kept his true identity and official position a secret. This too helped build up the mystery surrounding him and only once, in 1933, did anyone successfully guess his true identity. This was a listener in Jamaica who remembered Alan's voice from his school days in Rugby. In view of the popularity of his stories, many found their way into print, appearing in magazines, newspapers, and the collections *Good Evening, everyone!* (1928) and *A. J. Alan's Second Book* (1933).

In appearance Alan was tall and slim; he was known by his neighbours as the Man with the Monocle. He was married to May (d. 1951); they had no children. He lived at Holland Park, London, and had a bungalow at Potter Heigham, Norfolk, from where he could sail his boat, *Muggins*. He was also an experienced amateur radio transmitter and authority on good eating and rare wines.

Lambert underwent an operation in 1937 and thereafter remained in indifferent health. He continued his work in the intelligence services although, with the growing 'international what not', as he described it, and his department being 'in a very over worked condition', he cut down on his broadcasts (BBC WAC, 910 L. H. Lambert, 10 June 1939). His last broadcast was on 21 March 1940 and he died at Grove House Nursing Home, 77A Newmarket Road, Norwich, on 13 December 1941. He was buried on 17 December.

NEIL SOMERVILLE

Sources contributor files and A. J. Alan special collection, BBC WAC, 910 L. H. Lambert · M. Smith, *Station X: the codebreakers of Bletchley Park* (1998) · *Magic Circular*, 67 (1973), 75–8 · *Magic Circular*,

69 (1975), 171–3 • E. A. Dawes, *A rich cabinet of magical curiosities* • b. cert. • d. cert.
Archives BBC WAC, A. J. Alan special collection, Leslie Harrison Lambert, S 200/1–12 | SOUND BL NSA, performance footage
Wealth at death £1134 18s. 4d.: probate, 24 March 1942, *CGPLA Eng. & Wales*

Lambert, Mark (1781–1855). *See under* Bewick, Thomas, apprentices (*act.* 1777–1828).

Lambert, Maurice Prosper (1901–1964), sculptor, was born in Paris on 25 June 1901, the elder son of George Washington Thomas Lambert ARA (1873–1930), the painter who towards the end of his life also turned his attention towards sculpture, and his wife, Amelia Beatrice Absell (1872–1964), an Australian. He was the brother of the musician Constant *Lambert. His father was born in St Petersburg of an American father and an English mother. When Maurice Lambert later applied for a passport he found he had no official nationality, and had to apply for nationalization as a British subject. He was educated at Manor House School, Clapham, London. From the age of seventeen he was apprenticed to F. Derwent Wood and worked as his assistant for five years, helping him to complete the machine-gun corps memorial at Hyde Park Corner. From 1920 to 1925 he attended life classes at Chelsea School of Art.

Lambert's work first appeared in public in spring 1925, at a mixed exhibition in the Goupil Gallery, Regent Street, London. He exhibited fourteen pieces, mainly bronze portraits, in various styles derived from Jacob Epstein, Frank Dobson, Constantin Brancusi, and others. But it was at the November exhibition at the same gallery that he demonstrated his true talent with a head, *Ceres*, carved from hard red African sandstone. Its simplicity yet realism indicated the direction in which Lambert might be moving and this impression was confirmed at his first one-man exhibition with the Claridge Gallery in 1927. African sandstone *Stone Heads* were exhibited side by side with a *Kneeling Torso* in alabaster, and a series of portraits in bronze, lead, and aluminium. This interest in materials was evident in his exhibition at Messrs Tooths' Gallery in 1929 where his talent as a carver became particularly apparent. He used a variety of materials—for example, marble, alabaster, African hardwood, Portland stone, metal—and, in some cases, combined more than one of these. One work, for example, entitled *Hooked Fish*, was made of aluminium, plate glass, three-ply wood, selenite, and concrete. On 27 July 1926 Lambert married Olga Marie Stuart (1895–1977), daughter of Stuart Gordon Morrison; they had no children.

In 1932 the Tate Gallery accepted a gift of an alabaster carving, *The Swan*, which had been exhibited in Lambert's next one-man show at the Lefevre Galleries. This was a just reward, since an offer of his *Man with Bird* had been rejected by their trustees three years earlier, though it was later accepted by the Victoria and Albert Museum. The verde di prato marble *Father and Son* of this period (Leeds City Art Gallery) shows the father twisting away from the

child and reveals a concern with movement which differentiates the work from that of contemporary figure groups by Henry Moore.

Lambert first exhibited at the Royal Academy in 1938. His exhibit, *Head of Woman*, in bronze, was purchased under the terms of the Chantrey bequest, the second of his works to be housed in the Tate. In the late 1930s he carried out some commissions for ocean liners: he designed a 50 foot frieze for the *Queen Mary* and his bronze *Oceanides* was placed in the first-class foyer of the *Queen Elizabeth*. In 1939 he also undertook some large scale commissions such as the 40 foot high figure which was to represent the 'Spirit of Britain' at the New York World Fair and the 20 foot high *Modern Mercury* for the centennial exhibition in Wellington, New Zealand.

Although elected as an associate of the Royal Academy in 1941, Lambert did not exhibit there again until 1945 because of his war service, at first in the ranks of the London Welsh regiment and subsequently as a captain in the Royal Welch Fusiliers. After the war he exhibited regularly in the summer exhibition. He was a fellow of the Royal Society of British Sculptors from 1938 to 1948, when he resigned; he was re-elected in 1951. In 1949 he was awarded that society's silver medal for *Pegasus and Bellerophon*, which had been exhibited at the Royal Academy during the previous year. From 1950 to 1958 Lambert was master of the Royal Academy sculpture school, and was elected Royal Academician in 1952.

Lambert's best-known work, a life-size bronze statue of the ballerina Dame Margot Fonteyn, was another Chantrey bequest purchase in 1956 which is now owned by the Royal Ballet School, White Lodge, Richmond Park. Another well-known work, *The Lark Ascending*, made from a 250-year-old church oak gatepost, was acquired for the Rutherston collection, Manchester City Art Gallery.

Lambert's other works include an equestrian statue of George V for Adelaide, South Australia; a statue of Viscount Nuffield for Guy's Hospital; the *Symbol of Communication* for the Time-Life building, London; the duke of Edinburgh's trophy for shooting and running (a drinking cup in silver and gold); a fountain for Basildon, Essex, and another for the presidential palace, Baghdad, on which he was at work during his last illness. He also did many portrait busts including those of William Walton, Dame Edith Sitwell, J. B. Priestley, Adrian Stokes, the maharani of Cooch Behar, Frank Herbert, Sir Gerald Kelly, Sir Henry Rushbury, Lord Devlin, and his brother Constant. (Some of these are in the National Portrait Gallery, London.) Among them there are bronzes of rare distinction, in which a sense of repose and unity does not detract from the character portrayal.

Lambert's undoubted early promise as a sculptor was never really fulfilled. However, the breadth of his imagination, especially using such varied media, is evident throughout his work, and this contribution to advancing sculptural interpretation was the signpost to the future. He took a particular delight in feats of virtuosity, such as a flight of fish going through the arms of a sea god. It was this skill and experience as well as his perfectionism which made him such a fine teacher in the Academy Schools. He was physically strong and had been a boxer in his early days. As a young man he spent much of his time at London Zoo studying the animals and birds and also took daily early morning runs round Regent's Park. He died of cancer of the colon in Guy's Hospital, London, on 17 August 1964.

HANS FLETCHER, rev. VANESSA NICOLSON

Sources T. Friedman, 'A modernist masterpiece by Maurice Lambert', *Leeds Arts Calendar*, 102 (1988), 20–26 · *Maurice Lambert, 1901–1964* (1988) [exhibition catalogue, Belgrave Gallery, London] · *The Times* (20 Aug 1964) · *Daily Telegraph* (20 Aug 1964) · A. Motion, *The Lamberts: George, Constant and Kit* (1986) · P. G. Konody, 'The art of Maurice Lambert', *Artwork*, 3 (1927–8), 190–93 · *CGPLA Eng. & Wales* (1964) · private information (2004) [Elizabeth Morrison, niece] · V. Nicolson, *The sculpture of Maurice Lambert* (2002)
Archives Mitchell L., NSW, letters [copies, V&A] · RA, press cuttings, letters, drawings · Tate collection, letters
Likenesses photographs, Courtauld Inst. · photographs, RA
Wealth at death £44,443: administration, 2 Nov 1964, *CGPLA Eng. & Wales*

Lambert [Lambart], **Oliver**, first Baron Lambart of Cavan (*c*.1560–1618), soldier and administrator, was son and heir of Walter Lambert (*d*. 1596?), alderman of Southampton, and his first wife, Rose, daughter of Sir Oliver Wallop of Farleigh Wallop, Hampshire. He was educated at Furnival's Inn and Lincoln's Inn from 1578, but became a professional soldier. He went to Ireland in the early 1580s, probably through his Wallop connection. There he served under Sir John Norris in an expedition by the lord deputy, Sir John Perrot, against the Scots in co. Antrim and co. Down in 1584, in which he was wounded; captured by two sons of Shane O'Neill on his way to Dublin in October, he was used by them as an intermediary.

Lambert returned to England in March 1585, with recommendations to Burghley and Walsingham from both Perrot and Norris and his uncle Sir Henry Wallop. In June 1585 he received a pension of £50 per annum and in August (under the treaty of Nonsuch) he accompanied Norris to the Netherlands. There he took part in the capture of Doesburg in September 1586 and was appointed its governor by the earl of Leicester. Later, in an important offensive in the Dutch revolt, he distinguished himself in the recapture of Deventer in June 1591. In June 1592 he took part in the siege of Steenwijk, but being wounded there was sent to Ostend rather than to campaign in France, and later returned to England for a time. Early in 1596 he was sent from the Low Countries by Sir Francis Vere to the earl of Essex with a warning of a plot against the queen and a strong recommendation for employment. Accordingly, he took part in the English expedition against Cadiz in 1596, as colonel and quartermaster, and was knighted by Essex for his valour.

In the aftermath of this expedition, and amid English fears of a Spanish response, Lambert was selected to organize defences in Hampshire, with recommendation to noblemen there, including Lord Mountjoy. His military appointments in England in 1597 and early 1598 included the superintendence of the musters in Wiltshire and the responsibility, in recognition of his knowledge and

experience in martial affairs, to transfer soldiers levied in Kent to Ostend. Now, also, he was returned to parliament for Southampton and served on parliamentary committees in December 1597 and January 1598. In 1598, back in the Low Countries, he was a captain in the English garrison at Flushing and, in 1598 also, joint promoter of a minor privateering voyage conducted from Southampton. In 1598 he married Hester (1579?–1639), daughter of William Fleetwood, then receiver-general of the court of wards and later an advocate for him with Sir Robert Cecil.

In April 1599 Lambert returned to Ireland with soldiers withdrawn from the Netherlands to support Essex's appointment and campaign there against Hugh O'Neill and his confederates. To Essex, Lambert was one of only few officers there with any substantial experience of warfare, and when Essex left Ireland prematurely in September, he left Lambert as chief commander in Leinster answerable to the earl of Ormond, and, provisionally, marshal of the camp. Acutely conscious that his association with Essex could jeopardize his new position, Lambert sought to assure it by overtures to the now-ascending Sir Robert Cecil. The ongoing war in Ireland contributed to his success in this. The privy council and the queen commended him to the new lord deputy, Mountjoy, as, unlike many, a commander of activist temperament; and, now involved in various engagements especially in Leinster, from 15 April 1600 he was sergeant-major of the army there. In the summer of 1601 Mountjoy appointed him governor of Connaught (from September, and constable of Athlone Castle from 1 October), for which office he had offered Cecil £500 in February. This was essentially a military command in that province, but he was also to act in restraint of O'Donnell should a rumoured Spanish landing in Ireland occur. His advancement, however, provoked jealousies, with another officer informing Cecil that not only was Lambert still ill-disposed towards Cecil himself but that he acted sternly and oppressively in Connaught also. After the defeat of the Spaniards and their Irish allies at Kinsale, in which he took part, Lambert suppressed the uprising in the province and was by March 1602 arguing that the instruments of civil government through the assizes and the collection of composition rents should be brought into force there again. At both Galway and Sligo in 1602 he carried out some work of fortification as precaution against a further Spanish landing.

With the end of war in 1603 a new phase in Lambert's Irish career began. On instructions from London on 9 September, he was made a privy councillor in the Dublin government, ordered to benefit from a grant of confiscated lands of £100 annual valuation, and replaced (with a pension) in Connaught by the earl of Clanricarde. By 1606 he had built up an estate, some of it at Kilbeggan, Westmeath, where he now lived, and a house in Dublin; as an indication that he intended to build his fortune in Ireland, he sold property in Southampton in 1607. In the summer of 1606 he took part in a journey into counties Monaghan,

Cavan, and Fermanagh by Lord Deputy Sir Arthur Chichester to investigate landownership, with a fee of £1 per day. After the flight of the earls in 1607, one of whom, O'Donnell, pronounced him to have been opprobrious, Lambert was sent to London to report, and returned in November with confirmation of a lease of termon lands in co. Cavan. On the outbreak of O'Doherty's rising in April 1608 he was one of those dispatched north to repress it, and in 1609 was one of the commissioners appointed to survey the escheated lands in the six Ulster counties in preparation for plantation there. In 1610 he was a commissioner to implement that plantation, and was paid for that and for a later visit to London on government business which lasted until 1611.

Lambert benefited personally from the plantation in Ulster, receiving an estate by patent in June 1611 as a servitor in Clonmahon barony, co. Cavan. Later he got custody of O'Reilly's old castle at Cavan provided he carry out defensive building there at his own expense. When parliament was summoned in 1613, he was returned for co. Cavan amid controversial circumstances and with the native Irish freeholders protesting that he did not live in that county. The final military episode of his life was a naval one involving Scotland. Late in 1614 he was dispatched from Ireland with an expedition to retake Dunyvaig Castle on Islay which had been held as a royal fortress (under the command since 1610 of Andrew Knox, formerly bishop of the Isles and now of Raphoe) as a curb on the MacDonalds of the Isles, and which they had again recently seized. This was achieved early in February 1615, after which Lambert returned to Ireland. In April the king instructed Chichester to thank him for his success, and on 17 February 1618 Sir Oliver was created Baron Lambart of Cavan.

Lambart died on a visit to London later that year, probably on 9 June, and was buried on 10 June in Westminster Abbey. He had two sons, Charles, who succeeded him as second baron, and Carew, the latter inheriting lands in co. Roscommon. One daughter died young and the other two married in England. By the time of his death, he had, by acquiring another grantee's estate, extended his holdings of plantation land in Cavan, rented mostly to its Irish occupiers, and had built two flankered bawns at strategic places there. His wealth lay essentially in the lands accumulated in Ireland, which were confirmed by patent to his widow and sons in 1622. By his will he provided that his two daughters should receive an inheritance of £1500 each, and made smaller bequests to others including John Wallop and Thomas Fleetwood. If he were one of the more successful English figures in the Ireland of his times, and if his career manifests the many and interlinked theatres in which England operated in that era, it demonstrates also the magnitude of the change brought about in Ireland during his lifetime.   R. J. HUNTER

Sources CSP Ire., 1574–85; 1599–1625 • J. S. Brewer and W. Bullen, eds., Calendar of the Carew manuscripts, 3–5, PRO (1869–71) • APC, 1587–1604 • Calendar of the Irish patent rolls of James I (before 1830) • F. Moryson, An itinerary containing his ten yeeres travell through the twelve dominions, 2–3 (1907–8) • The miscellaneous papers of Captain Thomas Stockwell, 1590–1611, ed. J. Rutherford, 2 vols., Southampton RS, 32–3 (1932–3) • HoP, Commons, 1558–1603, 2.432–4 • PRO, AO1/287/1081–290/1089 • PRO, PROB 11/131, fols. 421–421v • PRO, SP 84/57, fols. 58–59v • K. R. Andrews, Elizabethan privateering: English privateering during the Spanish war, 1585–1603 (1964), 139, 269 • G. Hill, An historical account of the plantation in Ulster at the commencement of the seventeenth century, 1608–1620 (1877), 468 • W. H. Rylands, ed., Pedigrees from the visitation of Hampshire … 1530 … 1575 … 1622 … 1634, Harleian Society, 64 (1913), 145 • CSP dom., 1611–18 • GEC, Peerage, new edn, 3.116

Archives Southampton Archives Service, Stockwell MSS, SC 4/6/1–198

Wealth at death large estate in Ireland, perhaps 10,000 acres; retained some of Southampton land; house in Dublin; military salary; fees; farm land income recommenced c. time of death: will, 1618, PRO, PROB 11/131, fols. 421–421v.

Lamberton, William (d. 1328), administrator and bishop of St Andrews, came of a family which first settled in Berwickshire, but which held lands in north-east Scotland by the late twelfth century and later in Stirlingshire also. Details of his birth, education, and early career are not certain; he had certainly received a university education by early 1293 and become a canon of Glasgow. By the time of his appearance at King John's first parliament in February 1293 he was chancellor of Glasgow Cathedral. He seems to have been sent abroad for further study by Bishop Robert Wishart of Glasgow, probably in the year or two before July 1295.

In common with most of the Scots nobles and prelates, Lamberton swore fealty to Edward I in 1296 following the English invasion and the deposition of King John. He was also, however, a supporter of the rebellion against the English occupation which culminated in Wallace's victory at Stirling Bridge on 11 September 1297. Shortly before the battle Bishop William Fraser of St Andrews had died in exile, and on 3 November 1297 Lamberton was elected to the vacant see, no doubt with the backing of both William Wallace and his co-leader, Andrew Murray. (Fordun states that it was Lamberton who brought Fraser's heart back to St Andrews for burial, which, if true, may indicate that he was in France at the time of Fraser's death.) Lamberton was consecrated at the curia in June 1298 and used his time there and his journey home through France to further the diplomatic aims of the Scots in their conflict with the English king.

Lamberton returned to Scotland in the summer of 1299 and was immediately embroiled in the difficult political situation. There were extreme tensions within the Scots guardianship which had been elected to rule in the name of the ousted King John—in August that year a dispute between supporters of the two guardians (John Comyn and Robert Bruce, earl of Carrick) ended in a brawl in the council chamber in the presence of an English spy. The dispute was settled by imposing Lamberton as a third, and senior, guardian, an arrangement which lasted for some months. Even after Bruce's resignation from the guardianship Lamberton remained in office, until in October 1300 he and his fellow guardians were replaced by Sir John Soulis, perhaps as sole guardian.

It is possible that Lamberton's demission of office as

guardian was designed to allow his participation in further diplomatic efforts abroad. Certainly, for much of 1301 he was out of the country, and may have gone with the important embassy to Rome which was led by the canon lawyer Baldred Bisset. Two of Bisset's companions on the embassy were clerks of Lamberton from the St Andrews diocese, and it seems that preparation of the famous instructions issued to the embassy, and of the *Processus* presented by Bisset, may have been influenced by those active in Lamberton's circle, if not by the bishop himself. Whether or not he visited the curia at this time, he was undoubtedly involved in negotiations at the French court in late 1301, attempting to avert the possible signing of an Anglo-French treaty without the inclusion of the Scots. Although he visited France again with a similar mission in 1302–3, his errand was unsuccessful, and the Anglo-French treaty went ahead in May 1303, leaving the Scots diplomatically isolated. Negotiations continued, but in February 1304 most of the Scots nobles submitted to Edward I, one of the conditions of their surrender being that Lamberton and Matthew Crambeth, bishop of Dunkeld, were to be included among those offered the English king's peace. Following his return to Scotland Lamberton swore fealty to Edward in May 1304. The sincerity of his commitment to Edward I must be open to question, since only a few weeks after his submission he entered into a covert bond of friendship with Robert Bruce, earl of Carrick, who was to seize the throne less than two years later. The bond's terms are vague, but must be taken to indicate that Lamberton now accepted that the political future lay with Bruce rather than with King John or his supporters, such as Wallace.

During the period which followed Lamberton seems to have gained the trust of the English king. Late in 1305 he was appointed to be part of Edward's council in Scotland, and indeed led that council by the turn of the year. In September 1305 (less than a month after the execution of Wallace), however, Edward I had issued an ordinance for the government of Scotland, which was, in effect, an act for the incorporation of Scotland in the English dominions. The implications of such an act for the ecclesiastical government of Scotland cannot have endeared it to Lamberton or the other Scottish bishops and, notwithstanding his position of trust, may have incited him to further support and encourage the intended coup by Bruce. When Bruce eventually made his bid for the kingship in March 1306, Lamberton celebrated mass for the new king after the enthronement ceremony, thus placing himself firmly on the side of those backing the new regime and in opposition to the English king. Lamberton was among the 'traitors' sought by Edward as early as May 1306, and his men fought for King Robert in the defeat at Methven on 19 June. Lamberton himself was captured by the English soon after the battle, and only his priesthood saved him from execution. He was imprisoned until May 1308, after which, in accordance with a papal demand, he received a conditional release. He was not allowed to return to Scotland until the following year, when he may have been a member of a team negotiating a truce. Later in the same

year he represented Bishop Antony (I) Bek of Durham in Scotland, making inquiry into the affairs of the templars, and, remaining there, he was then able to set about restoring the administration of his diocese, which had been severely disrupted by the wars for many years. He seems to have done this with the agreement of the English authorities, even although the work involved much contact with what the latter regarded as the rebel administration of Scotland.

By the early months of 1312, however, Lamberton had once again made it clear that his loyalty lay with the Scottish king and government. He was active as a diplomatic agent for King Robert in the later phases of the war, and was also able effectively to continue the reconstruction of his diocese. In July 1318 a major landmark was reached for both diocese and kingdom: the dedication of the new cathedral of St Andrews, a symbol not only of the restoration of the see, but also of the victory of the national church and kingdom over attempts at subjection from the south.

The position of both national church and government grew stronger, yet in the later years of the reign relations between the Scottish government and the papacy again became strained, resulting in 1319 in the excommunication of the king and his supporters, including Lamberton and other bishops. All the excommunicates ignored their summonses to the curia, and Lamberton continued to act as bishop, politician, and diplomat for some years to come. He was regularly involved in negotiations for truces and for peace, although he was not among those who eventually negotiated the 'final' peace with the English. This was agreed upon shortly before Lamberton's death, which took place in St Andrews on 20 May 1328. He was buried in his cathedral on 7 June.

Lamberton's career as Scotland's senior bishop had spanned the entire course of the wars of independence. His allegiance to the 'national' cause was not as unwavering as that of some others—in that respect he has sometimes been unfavourably compared with Bishop Wishart of Glasgow—but the political realism which led him to submit to the English power when it was in the ascendant gave him a position from which he was able to influence the path of the kingdom despite the fluctuations of the political, military, and diplomatic struggle. His contribution to the ecclesiastical and political fortunes of the country in that difficult period was therefore immense.

A. H. MILLAR, *rev.* NORMAN H. REID

Sources M. Ash, 'William Lamberton, bishop of St Andrews, 1297–1328', *The Scottish tradition*, ed. G. W. S. Barrow (1974), 44–55 · D. E. R. Watt, *A biographical dictionary of Scottish graduates to AD 1410* (1977), 318–25 · *Johannis de Fordun Chronica gentis Scotorum / John of Fordun's Chronicle of the Scottish nation*, ed. W. F. Skene, trans. F. J. H. Skene, 2 (1872) · G. Burnett and others, eds., *The exchequer rolls of Scotland*, 23 vols. (1878–1908) · W. Bower, *Scotichronicon*, ed. D. E. R. Watt and others, new edn, 9 vols. (1987–98), vol. 3

Lambespringe, Bartholomew (*fl.* 1449–1454). *See under* Austen, William (*fl.* 1449–1454).

Lamborn, Peter Spendlowe (1722–1774), engraver and miniature painter, was born at Cambridge, the son of John

Lamborn (d. 1763) and his second wife, Elizabeth Susanna Spendlowe. He went to London to study engraving under Isaac Basire and while there probably also engraved for the publisher John Boydell. The opportunities for teaching may have drawn him back to Cambridge, where from 1756 he engraved the majority of the forty-eight plates for James Bentham's *History of the Cathedral Church of Ely* (1771). He married on 6 January 1762 Mary, daughter of Hitch Wale of Little Shelford, Cambridgeshire, with whom he had three sons and a daughter; she and Lamborn exhibited at the Society of Artists in London from 1764; he was elected fellow in 1771. Besides his views of Cambridge colleges, Lamborn provided various other topographical illustrations and plates, mostly relating to East Anglia, but including illustrations for Martyn's and Lettice's translation (1773) of Bayardi's *Antiquities of Herculaneum*. His portraits included *Samuel Johnson*, drawn from life, *Oliver Cromwell*, after the Cooper portrait at Sidney Sussex College, and other university notables. The historian Thomas Dodds considered that Lamborn's views of colleges were 'more harmonised with the graving tool' than his earlier dry-point work (BL, Add. MS 33402, fol. 246). At his death in Cambridge on 5 November 1774 Lamborn was living in Free School Lane, in St Edward's parish, though his wife and children were settled on the farm that he had purchased at Little Shelford. He was buried on 8 November at Great St Mary's, Cambridge.

L. H. CUST, rev. ANITA MCCONNELL

Sources J. M. Morris, 'A checklist of prints made at Cambridge by Peter Spendlowe Lamborn (1722–74)', *Transactions of the Cambridge Bibliographical Society*, 3 (1959–63), 295–312 • L. R. Schidlof, *The miniature in Europe in the 16th, 17th, 18th, and 19th centuries*, 1 (1964), 462 • Thomas Dodd's 'History of English engravers', BL, Add. MS 33402, fol. 246 • C. H. Cooper, *Annals of Cambridge*, 4 (1852), 374 • R. Willis, *The architectural history of the University of Cambridge, and of the colleges of Cambridge and Eton*, ed. J. W. Clark, 4 vols. (1886) • parish register, St Benedict, Cambridge, Cambs. AS, 6 Jan 1762 [marriage] • will, PRO, PROB 11/1009, sig. 237

Lambourne. For this title name *see* Lockwood, Amelius Mark Richard, first Baron Lambourne (1847–1928).

Lambourne [Lamborn], **Reginald** (*fl.* 1351–1377), astrologer, was a fellow of Merton College, Oxford, in 1353, where he served as second bursar in 1353–4 and where he associated with William Rede (d. 1385), a colleague devoted to the study of astronomy and astrology. Lambourne composed an astrological weather prediction for the years 1368–74, evidently addressed to Rede upon his elevation as bishop of Chichester in 1368. Still a fellow of Merton in 1357, Lambourne had entered the Benedictine order by 1363, when he is recorded as a monk at Eynsham Abbey, Oxfordshire. In that year he wrote a letter discussing the astrological interpretation of lunar eclipses of March and September. The recipient is not specifically indicated, but the name 'Jo. London' appears at the end of the letter, suggesting identification with John of London, a monk of St Augustine's Abbey, Canterbury, who had an abiding interest in astronomical calculations. Lambourne was still at Eynsham in 1367; some time afterwards he migrated to St Mary's Abbey, York. But apparently he could not settle down at St Mary's and in January 1377 he made a direct appeal to the Holy See 'fearing attacks from his enemies upon his status and good name' (Emden, *Oxf.*, 2.1086). The nature of the dispute is unclear, but it was severe enough for Lambourne to leave the Benedictine order. Later in the same year he returned to Oxford and joined the Franciscan order; he was styled MA and DTh at this time. Lambourne died at Northampton, but the year of his death is not recorded.

KEITH SNEDEGAR

Sources Emden, *Oxf.* • H. M. Carey, *Courting disaster: astrology at the English court and university in the later middle ages* (1992) • R. Lambourne, astrological letters, Bodl. Oxf., MS Digby 176
Archives Bodl. Oxf., MS Digby 176 • Merton Oxf., Merton College records

Lambton, George (1860–1945), racehorse trainer and writer, was born on 23 November 1860 at Fenton, Northumberland, the fifth son of George Frederick D'Arcy Lambton, second earl of Durham (1828–1879), and his wife, Lady Beatrix Francis Hamilton (d. 1871). Educated privately before proceeding to Eton in 1873, Lambton was a keen huntsman from the start, 'blooded' at the age of seven. After only three years at Eton he moved to a tutor in Dorset before going up to Trinity College, Cambridge, in 1879. The university was not, however, to his taste and, following the death of his father after his first term there, he left for a crammer at Storrington where he prepared to enter the army. It was later said of Lambton's education that he 'found Eton rather too near Ascot and Cambridge rather too near Newmarket' (*The Times*), and he left the crammer after a short time also, having decided to make racing his career.

Lambton began as an amateur rider, although as a younger son he was not rich and, unlike most of his colleagues, depended on betting to live. His family was steeped in racing and at the time that he rode his first winner, Pompeia, at Nottingham in October 1880, six of his brothers had thoroughbreds in training. He enjoyed a successful racing career, winning the Grand Steeplechase de Paris on Parsang, before a heavy fall at Sandown Park in 1892 forced his retirement. During his convalescence he wrote sporting articles for *St Stephen's Review*.

Lambton now turned to training and with the help of William Brett, Baron Esher, set up at St Mary's Yard at Newmarket, Suffolk. It was an unusual step for the son of an earl to take, for training was still seen as very much a plebeian concern. But where other 'training grooms', as they were once called, were referred to by their surnames in press reports, the Honourable George, as he was known to the racing fraternity, was always *Mister* Lambton. He cared little about what society thought, and his indifference and example helped change the status of his chosen profession. But his connections served him well and after some success for Esher, principally with the influential mare Hetty Sorel, he became in 1893 private trainer to Frederick Stanley, sixteenth earl of Derby.

By 1894 Derby had built Bedford Lodge stables for Lambton and had purchased a number of yearlings, including the 1896 Royal Oaks winner, Canterbury Pilgrim, at the sale of the stock of Caroline Agnes, duchess of Montrose. Moving to Derby's newly built Stanley House stables at Newmarket in 1903, he enjoyed considerable success, becoming champion trainer in 1906, when he won his second Oaks with Keystone II. On the death of Derby in 1908 Lambton continued to work for his successor, the seventeenth earl, and between 1908 and 1926 Stanley House sent out eight classic winners and won the trainers' championship twice.

On 7 December 1908 Lambton, known for his dapper dress and handsome appearance, married Cecily Margaret (d. 1972), the daughter of Sir John Horner of Mells. They had four children: John; Edward, who succeeded his father as a trainer; Ann, whose middle name, Swynford, commemorated one of her father's St Leger winners; and Sybil, who similarly recalled the 1917 One Thousand Guineas winner, Diadem. Cecily Lambton was herself extremely knowledgeable about horses and a constant support to her husband throughout their long and happy marriage.

In 1926 old age encouraged Lambton to surrender his training responsibilities in favour of managing Derby's horses, but in 1930 financial pressures forced the earl to dismiss his trainer, Frank Butters, and Lambton combined the roles of trainer and manager until 1933. In that year he enjoyed probably his greatest success, winning the Derby and the St Leger with the magnificent Hyperion. It therefore came as a particular shock when in November Derby wrote informing him that he would not be required as trainer for the following year. Lambton's ill health was undoubtedly a factor in Derby's thinking and he offered a generous pension to his trainer, whom he expected would now retire. In fact Lambton was determined to continue, and hoped to provide a platform for his son Edward, and he felt that his prospects had been harmed by Derby's actions. It was particularly sad that one of the great partnerships in English racing should thus end acrimoniously.

Lambton next purchased the Kremlin House stables and trained the horses of his nephew the fifth earl of Durham, and after an indifferent start began winning again, securing his last classic, the Irish One Thousand Guineas, with Major Dermot McCalmont's Lapel in 1938. During the war he made an influential appeal for the continuation of racing, on the same grounds that he had defended it during the First World War, arguing that a prolonged break would destroy the industry and that the public in any case wanted racing to continue. He won the Lincolnshire handicap in 1941 and sent out his last winner, Golden Cloud, at Windsor early in June 1945. He was too ill, though, to see it win, and died at his home, Mesnil Warren, in Newmarket on 23 July 1945. He was deeply mourned by the racing community and not least by Derby, with whom there had been a rapprochement in later years.

As well as enjoying success as a trainer Lambton was also the first to demonstrate to a sceptical Jockey Club the potential influence of doping in racing. The practice of using cocaine as a dope had been brought to Britain by American trainers and jockeys in the late 1890s, and by 1900 it had become 'a serious menace' (Lambton, 254), threatening to undermine the whole bloodstock business. In 1903 its influence was so harmful that Lambton decided to act, informing one of the Jockey Club stewards of his intent. He doped five of his more mediocre charges, what he called the 'biggest rogues in training' (ibid., 255), and watched four of them win and one come second; he was careful not to bet on any of these races. The stewards, having seen reluctant and incompetent animals transformed into unstoppable athletes, banned doping, which in 1904 became a criminal offence. He was not solely acting to protect the business interests of the racing community but was concerned equally for the welfare of the animals involved and his love of horses and respect for them is conveyed strongly in his 1924 memoir *Men and Horses I have Known*, from which he emerges as a genial and opinionated professional. Discursive and entertaining, it is a record of every celebrity of the turf during the heyday of English racing and it remains, like its author, one of the most popular of its kind in the sport. EMMA EADIE

Sources Burke, *Peerage* · G. Lambton, *Men and horses I have known* (1924) · R. Mortimer, *History of the Derby stakes* (1973) · R. Mortimer, R. Onslow, and P. Willett, *Biographical encyclopedia of British flat racing* (1978) · M. Seth-Smith, *A classic connection: the friendship of the earl of Derby and the Hon. George Lambton, 1893–1945* (1983) · *The Times* (24 July 1945) · Venn, *Alum. Cant.*
Likenesses oils, Jockey Club rooms, Newmarket, Suffolk · photograph, repro. in *The Times*
Wealth at death £87,552 18s. 8d.: probate, 28 Feb 1946, CGPLA Eng. & Wales

Lambton, John (1710–1794), army officer, born on 26 July 1710, was the fourth and youngest son of Ralph Lambton (d. 1717), landowner, and his wife, whom he married in 1696, Dorothy, daughter of John Hedworth of Harraton, Durham. His elder brothers were Henry Lambton (1697–1761) and Major-General Hedworth Lambton (d. 1758), who was an officer in the Coldstream Guards from 1723 to 1753 and in 1755 raised the 52nd (originally 54th) foot at Coventry. Educated at Westminster School, John was appointed ensign in the Coldstream Guards on 12 October 1732, became lieutenant in 1739, was regimental quartermaster from February 1742 to January 1745, and became captain and lieutenant-colonel on 24 January 1746. On 28 April 1758 he was appointed colonel of the 68th foot (later 1st Durham light infantry), then made a separate regiment. It had been raised two years previously as a second battalion of the 23rd Royal Welch Fusiliers, but had been chiefly recruited in Durham, a local connection subsequently maintained. During the Seven Years' War Lambton commanded the regiment in the unsuccessful attack on St Malo, Brittany, in September 1758. When county titles were bestowed on line regiments in 1782, it was styled the 'Durham' regiment. Lambton, who became a full general, retained the colonelcy until his death. He succeeded to the Lambton estates after the deaths of his elder brothers. In the second half of the eighteenth century the freeman franchise Durham city was represented in parliament by members of the Lambton and Tempest families. Following the death on 26 June 1761 of his brother Henry, MP for

Durham city since 1734, Lambton stood. He was opposed by Ralph Gowland, the candidate of Henry Vane, first earl of Darlington, and his party, who by creating new honorary freemen, mostly unconnected with the city, gained a majority. However, on petition Lambton, who asserted the rights of the historic resident freemen, was seated in May 1762. An independent, he voted sometimes for and sometimes against the government, and there is no record of his speaking in the house. He represented the city in five succeeding parliaments until his acceptance of the Chiltern Hundreds in February 1787, and was said to be popular with the citizens for the stand he made for their rights and privileges. Reportedly in 1793 he refused a peerage. Lambton married on 5 September 1763 Lady Susan Lyon (d. 1769), daughter of Thomas, eighth earl of Strathmore, and they had two sons and two daughters. He died on 22 March 1794. His elder son, William Henry Lambton (1764–1797), MP for Durham city (1787–97), was father of 'Radical Jack', John George *Lambton, first earl of Durham (1792–1840).

H. M. CHICHESTER, rev. ROGER T. STEARN

Sources Debrett's Peerage (1831) · R. S. Lea, 'Lambton, John', HoP, Commons, 1715–54 · L. B. Namier, 'Lambton, John', HoP, Commons, 1754–90 · Burke, Peerage (1967) · GM, 1st ser., 64 (1794), 385 · D. Mackinnon, Origin and services of the Coldstream guards, 2 vols. (1833) · E. Porritt and A. G. Porritt, The unreformed House of Commons, 1 (1909) · Old Westminsters, vol. 2 · J. Black, Britain as a military power, 1688–1815 (1999)
Archives Lambton Park, Chester-le-Street, co. Durham, papers, and estate material

Lambton, John George [nicknamed Radical Jack], first earl of Durham

(1792–1840), politician, was the eldest son of William Henry Lambton, MP for the city of Durham, and his wife, Lady Anne Barbara Frances Villiers, second daughter of George, fourth earl of Jersey; he was born in Berkeley Square, London, on 12 April 1792. His father, a supporter of Charles James Fox, died in 1797. 'I have never felt the blessing of a father's care or advice', Lambton wrote in 1817, 'and, I fear, I have suffered much from it' (New, 17).

Family, wealth, and health The Lambtons were a Durham landed family. By 1826 coalmines were earning the estate £50,000 annually, although Lambton was reported to be £900,000 in debt: he economized by limiting expenditure during a visit to Paris to £1000 a month. He told Thomas Creevey that 'a man *might jog on*' with an annual income of £40,000 (Creevey Papers, 374). Creevey called him King Jog.

Lambton (as he was known to his family) suffered recurrent poor health—he complained in 1822 that it was 'damned hard that a man with £80,000 a year can't sleep!' (Creevey Papers, 391)—which probably explains his outbursts of temper, lovingly chronicled and sometimes exaggerated in contemporary diaries. A sympathetic observer noted in 1832 that 'his haughty and disdainful demeanour as well as petulant and ungovernable temper' made him 'generally unpopular' (Holland House Diaries, 166). J. C. Hobhouse saw insecurity behind the arrogance: 'he did not attach so much value to his character, or opinions, as to give himself a sufficient amount of self-

John George Lambton, first earl of Durham (1792–1840), by Thomas Phillips, 1820 [replica; original, 1819]

confidence in matters of importance' (Hobhouse, 5.75–6). Lambton acknowledged that 'there is no one who more keenly feels a slight than myself'—in cabinet in 1831 he treated opposition 'as a personal reflection upon himself' (Holland House Diaries, 8)—but such attitudes mainly characterized his dealing with social equals. He accepted sharp criticism from Joseph Parkes and Charles Buller. 'Everybody has always been afraid of him' (Lord Melbourne's Papers, 434–5), a puzzled Melbourne noted in 1838. Although acknowledged as a fine orator, he was intimidatingly taciturn, 'lacking the slightest power or turn for conversation' (Creevey Papers, 391). Florid colouring created an impression of smouldering intolerance: he looked 'like a picture by Murillo of a young Spanish Jesuit' (Sheil, 2.45). In 1832 Palmerston, an unfriendly observer, described him in cabinet as 'sullen, silent, & sulky … not condescending to take part in the discussions of mortal men' (Bourne, 524).

Education, marriage, and sport At the age of six Lambton was entrusted to the Bristol physician Thomas *Beddoes, a radical supporter of the French Revolution, who laid the foundation of a broad education which enabled him to survive three undistinguished years at Eton College. Beddoes gave him a grounding in chemistry (Lambton later encouraged the experiments of Humphrey Davy with the miners' safety lamp, and his Durham home, Lambton Castle, was one of the first houses in Britain to be lit by gas).

When Lambton left Eton in 1808 his guardians wished to

send him to Edinburgh University, but he insisted on joining the army, and was commissioned as cornet in the 10th hussars on 9 June 1809. By 1811 he had tired of military life. He fell in love with Henrietta (Harriet) Cholmondeley, illegitimate daughter of Lord Cholmondeley, and evaded his guardians' disapproval by marrying her in Scotland on 1 January 1812. An Anglican ceremony followed at Malpas in Cheshire on 28 January 1812. Harriet Lambton died on 11 July 1815, leaving three daughters.

Keen on cricket—he took 61 wickets and scored 600 runs in 1812—and horse-racing, Lambton also had a feeling for his family inheritance and marked his coming of age in 1813 by resuming massive reconstruction of Lambton Castle to the design of Joseph Bonomi, commissioned by Lambton's father in 1796. Creevey thought the 'highly collegiate' dining-hall like a 'family vault'.

Early radical politics Barely twenty-one, on 20 September 1813 Lambton was returned at a by-election as MP for co. Durham, declaring himself a reformer but 'no friend … to wild and improbable theories' (Reid, 1.68). His election brought him into contact with the whig aristocrat Earl Grey [see Grey, Charles, second Earl Grey], whose daughter Louisa Elizabeth Grey he married on 9 December 1816. Loyalty to the Grey clan led him to oppose J. C. Hobhouse at the Westminster by-election in 1819, and to fight a duel in 1826 with his Eton contemporary T. W. Beaumont, who was defending his Northumberland seat against Lambton's brother-in-law Lord Howick.

Lambton's radical reputation was founded on a few set-piece orations, beginning with his maiden speech on 12 May 1814, in which he attacked the transfer of Norway to Sweden. He made a similar protest over Genoa on 21 February 1815. In May 1817 he criticized the expense of Canning's embassy to Portugal. At a Durham county meeting on 21 October 1819 Lambton denounced the use of troops against a Manchester reform meeting (the Peterloo massacre). Brougham later claimed that Lambton, 'in no profession, independent in fortune', might have done more to oppose repression (Thomas, 360). He had done enough to be regarded as a danger to the established order, as Sir Thomas Liddell bluntly told him when refusing his electoral support in 1820.

On 6 December 1819 Lambton proposed a sweeping measure of parliamentary reform, including shorter parliaments, a wide franchise, and a redistribution of seats. His initiative was overtaken by Lord John Russell's specific proposal for the disfranchisement of the corrupt borough of Grampound. On 17 April 1821 Lambton renewed his proposal, but was humiliated by being accidentally prevented from voting for his own motion. He ceased to be a frequent Commons speaker, and spent the winter of 1826–7 in Italy for his health. On his return Lambton leaned towards support of the new prime minister, the liberal tory George Canning, placing some strain on his relations with Grey. From Canning's successor, Lord Goderich, Lambton received the peerage which he claimed 'as a matter of right' (New, 94), since his whig grandfather had refused a title from the tainted Pitt in 1793. In 1833 he claimed that he had accepted a title so that 'one who was

born, bred, and educated among the people' (Reid, 1.341) might argue their cause in the upper house. Lambton was created Baron Durham on 29 January 1828.

Office and parliamentary reform It was claimed in 1829 as 'a well-known fact' that Durham wanted a Wellington–Grey coalition (*Creevey Papers*, 543), but on 22 November 1830 he became lord privy seal in his father-in-law's cabinet, though refusing to accept the £2000 salary. Grey quickly commissioned Durham to draft a reform bill. Durham convened a committee of himself, Russell, Duncannon, and Sir James Graham, which worked intensively at his London house, 13 Cleveland Row, and produced a bold scheme on 14 January 1831. Durham overcame Russell's reluctance to include the secret ballot, perhaps because he did not wish to be upstaged as he had been in 1819, but the cabinet struck out the proposal.

Throughout the reform crisis Durham opposed compromise. He successfully pressed the cabinet on 21 April 1831 to call an election on the issue. To circumvent procedural devices designed to delay a dissolution, ministers persuaded William IV to prorogue parliament in person. Durham's role in the plot was to chivvy the master of the horse, Lord Albemarle, from his breakfast to summon the king's carriage. When the protesting Albemarle asked 'Is there revolution?', Durham replied 'There will be if you stay to finish your breakfast' (Brock, 191). Durham also favoured a large creation of peers to force the bill through the Lords, and stalked out of a cabinet dinner on 7 March 1832 when Grey prevented him from arguing his case. He was in a minority of one when he pressed the issue to a vote on 11 March. Only the likelihood that his departure would trigger the collapse of the ministry deterred him from resignation. He spoke in support of the bill in the second reading debate in the Lords on 13 April, and on 22 May, probably from a brief by Francis Place, defended the creation of new constituencies in the London suburbs. On 7 June 1832 he was one of four commissioners who signified the royal assent on behalf of the king.

Family disasters Durham felt himself excluded from a political battle fought largely in the Commons, although Grey replied, deploring his ill-tempered refusal to discuss amendments on their merits. Durham was under great stress in 1831–2 caused by a tragic series of bereavements. On 24 September 1831 Charles, his 'beautiful and remarkable son', died aged thirteen after a long illness. Durham's mother died unexpectedly on 21 April 1832. After 'terrible sufferings' the youngest daughter from his first marriage, Harriet, followed on 30 May. 'In eight months I have lost son, mother, and daughter', Durham wrote. 'I shudder to think who could be the next victim' (Reid, 1.299). It was not long before he knew. His second daughter, Georgiana, died on 3 January 1833. In December 1836 the surviving child of his first marriage, Fanny, 'the blessing of my life from her earliest childhood', died in Ireland just two months after her marriage (New, 284).

Durham was devastated by these blows: he needed laudanum to sleep. On 30 November 1831, his first cabinet appearance after his son's death, he 'lost all command of himself' in a violent clash with Grey. Durham felt that the ministry was losing its resolve over reform, and that the high personal price he had paid for his political involvement entitled his views to more consideration. The diary of Lord Holland, who witnessed the 'distressing' scene (*Holland House Diaries*, 88–9), does not support Greville's version, recorded third-hand, that the diatribe included an accusation that Grey contributed to the boy's death by forcing Durham to remain in London throughout his illness (*Greville Memoirs*, 2.226–7). 'No two men are more unlike than Durham when in good humour, and Durham in his angry, tetchy and, I am afraid one must add, usual mood', Holland noted in December 1831 (*Holland House Diaries*, 93).

Resignation and earldom Durham resigned from the cabinet on 14 March 1833, and on 23 March he received the earldom for which 'he had long panted with childish vanity' (*Holland House Diaries*, 207). Out of office Durham followed a threefold strategy. First he disputed the leadership of the radicals with Brougham, especially in speeches at Edinburgh on 15 September and Glasgow on 29 October 1834. Secondly he energetically cultivated the press, and was thought to have *The Times* and *Morning Chronicle* 'under his immediate control' (Aspinall, 380). In the publicity battle Durham broke cabinet confidentiality to claim responsibility for the Reform Bill. Thirdly he exploited a longstanding friendship with Leopold, king of the Belgians, to cultivate his sister, the duchess of Kent, as 'the avenue to Court favor' (H. R. V. Holland, 391) when her daughter, Princess Victoria, came to the throne. At Cowes in September 1833 Durham entertained Victoria with a firework display including the Lambton motto, *Le jour viendra*.

Ambassador to Russia, 1835–1837 The re-formed whig ministry under Melbourne appointed Durham ambassador to St Petersburg in July 1835, perhaps to get him out of the country. Durham had undertaken a special mission there in 1833, and relations with Russia were cordial during his term—not surprisingly, since Durham was 'completely bit by the Emperor Nicholas' (*Greville Memoirs*, 2.2), whose critics he termed 'Russophobites'. Durham's return to Britain in June 1837 coincided with the death of William IV, and there was speculation that he would join Melbourne's weak ministry.

Canada and 'the Durham report', 1837–1838 On 22 July 1837 Melbourne asked Durham to consider tackling the problem of Canada. In the mainly French-speaking province of Lower Canada (later Quebec) the elected assembly had reached stalemate in quarrels with successive governors-in-chief over the control of the colonial government. Durham decided to 'have nothing to do with the settlement of that unfortunate question' (Martin, *Durham Report*, 13). In December 1837 news arrived of rebellion in Lower Canada. Ministers were forced to suspend the constitution and required a governor-in-chief who could be trusted to wield dictatorial power. Durham's motives for accepting the task in January 1838 remain conjectural. His later claim that he had been 'told that their Existence as a Govt' depended on his acceptance suggests that he assumed

that he had acquired the whip hand over his former associates. The critical Greville marvelled at 'the general applause' (*Greville Memoirs*, 4.54) for his appointment. Realization that Melbourne controlled access to the young queen may also have persuaded him that the day predicted in the Lambton motto had not yet arrived.

Durham's mission quickly ran into problems. Although appointed to tackle a crisis, he delayed his departure until 24 April 1838. The interval was spent in assembling a lavish outfit, even including musical instruments, prompting Sydney Smith's explanation 'that Durham is going to make overtures to the Canadian people' (Reid, 2.165). On 2 April a motion to limit Durham's expenditure was defeated by just two votes in the Commons. Durham made two controversial appointments to his staff: both his legal adviser, Thomas Turton, and the colonization theorist Edward Gibbon Wakefield had been involved in sex scandals. Even the easy-going Melbourne felt that if 'their abilities … were superhuman they would not counterbalance the discredit of their characters' (*Lord Melbourne's Papers*, 428–9).

Durham arrived in Canada on 29 May 1838 with wide powers as governor-in-chief of British North America and high commissioner. Ruling Lower Canada through a special council, composed mainly of his own associates, he began to overhaul all aspects of the administration. To pave the way for a general amnesty, on 28 June 1838 Durham issued an ordinance exiling eight imprisoned rebel leaders to Bermuda, on pain of death should they return. Brougham attacked this as an abuse of power. It soon transpired that Durham had no authority over Bermuda. Ministers briefly attempted a defence, but were forced to disallow the ordinance. Unluckily, Durham learned of this from an American newspaper on 19 September. Melbourne suspected that Durham would 'concoct a general arrangement … boast of the effect he produced while there' and blame any failures 'on the manner in which he has been treated' (*Lord Melbourne's Papers*, 432). On 9 October 1838 Durham issued a forthright proclamation announcing his resignation. He departed on 1 November, after barely five months in Canada.

On his return Durham intended to 'be the plaintiff & not the defendant' (Martin, 'Durham myth', 54), but found the political world unsympathetic. The Bermuda ordinance proved that Turton's 'law is not a jot better than his morals' (*Greville Memoirs*, 4.123), and the proclamation was generally condemned. As Melbourne had predicted, when Durham arrived at Plymouth on 30 November he boasted of his success in Canada, but news quickly followed of a second revolt in the province, and his critics now alleged that he had fled from problems of his own creation.

The unauthorized publication of Durham's 'Report on the affairs of British North America' in *The Times*, beginning on 8 February 1839, caused another sensation. Wakefield was probably responsible, possibly because ministers were pressing for deletion of his ideas on land policy. Durham's enemies denied that that he was the author of the report, alleging that he merely signed the dubious production of his shady entourage. Durham's work on the

Reform Bill and a major report he produced on Russian affairs in 1836 are testimonies to his intellect. The production of a text of 120,000 words in two months suggests collaboration, and a persistent tradition points to Charles *Buller, his secretary, as co-author.

Durham's report recommended the union of Lower Canada with English-speaking Upper Canada (now Ontario) to Anglicize the French Canadians and as a step to a union of all the British North American provinces. He avoided the contentious term 'responsible government', but argued for limited colonial self-government, reserving tariffs and the disposal of public lands to Britain, and brushing aside the problem of enforcing imperial authority. Because of the brevity of his stay in Canada and his magnificent isolation from ordinary settlers—his three-week visit to Montreal and Upper Canada in July 1838 was like a royal progress—Durham hardly acquired any profound understanding of its problems.

Durham's report was later hailed by historians as the blueprint for the Commonwealth, a hagiography which in the 1970s provoked exuberant rebuttal. Although Melbourne expected that legislation would 'probably be based, at least to some degree' on Durham's proposals (Maxwell, 1.159), the verdict of 'Magna Carta of the Second British Empire' (R. Coupland, ed., The Durham Report, 1945, xlvi) cannot be sustained. Durham's fame as a proconsul has died with the British empire, but in modern Quebec he remains a symbolic cultural threat.

Durham's 'Report on the affairs of British North America' was published as a parliamentary paper (Parl. papers, 1839, 17). Editions were published by Ridgway (1839) and Methuen (1902), without named editors. C. P. Lucas published an extensive edition (3 vols., 1912) and R. Coupland a short version (1945). G. M. Craig edited An Abridgement (1963) with the Carleton Library, published by McClelland and Stewart (Toronto). A French translation, edited by M.-P. Hamel, was published in Quebec in 1948.

Death and reputation Durham's health suffered in Canada, and he took little part in politics after his return, speaking in the Lords 'like a man of great decision, mixed with some impatience' (Leeds Mercury, 23 Feb 1839). By May 1840 he was gravely ill, probably with tuberculosis. He died on 28 July 1840 at Cowes, and was buried at Chester-le-Street. Tradition related that on his deathbed Durham had said, 'The Canadians will one day do justice to my memory.' In contemporary usage, 'the Canadians' usually referred to French-Canadians: Reid, in 1906, emended this to 'Canada' (Reid, 2, title-page). Durham was survived by his son George and three daughters, one of whom, Mary, married in 1846 Lord Elgin, the governor-in-chief of British North America who presided over the province's transition to self-government. Their vow, as newly-weds, 'to build a monument' to Durham's memory added a sentimental note to his mythic role in Canadian nationhood. More tangibly, a Greek temple was erected by public subscription on Penshaw Hill in 1844, and still looms over the Durham countryside.

Durham left £250,000, all to his widow. The estate had liabilities of £635,000, but much of this was probably planned refinancing of the Lambton collieries. In religion he was a liberal Anglican, and a strong foe of reactionary clergy such as Henry Phillpotts. Durham favoured freemasonry as a means of uniting classes. He became deputy grand master for England in May 1834.

Essentially, Durham was an eighteenth-century figure. So were many of his contemporaries. The most notable among them were granted lifespans sufficient to adjust to the Victorian world. Durham died at the age of forty-eight with his personal and political contradictions unresolved.   GED MARTIN

Sources C. W. New, Lord Durham: a biography of John George Lambton, first earl of Durham (1929) • S. J. Reid, Life and letters of the first earl of Durham, 1792–1840, 2 vols. (1906) • W. Thomas, The philosophic radicals: nine studies in theory and practice, 1817–1841 (1979) • D. Spring, 'The earls of Durham and the great northern coalfield, 1830–1880', Canadian Historical Review, 33 (1952), 237–53 • F. Ouellet, 'Lambton, John George', DCB, vol. 7 • Lord Holland [H. R. V. Fox] and J. Allen, The Holland House diaries, 1831–1840, ed. A. D. Kriegel (1977) • L. Cooper, Radical Jack: the life of John George Lambton, first earl of Durham, 1792–1840 (1959) • G. Martin, The Durham report and British colonial policy (1972) • G. Martin, 'Attacking the Durham myth: seventeen years on', Journal of Canadian Studies, 25 (1990), 39–59 • The Greville memoirs, 1814–1860, ed. L. Strachey and R. Fulford, 8 vols. (1938) • The Creevey papers, ed. H. Maxwell, 3rd edn (1905); repr. (1912) • Baron Broughton [J. C. Hobhouse], Recollections of a long life, ed. Lady Dorchester [C. Carleton], 6 vols. (1909–11) • Lord Melbourne's papers, ed. L. C. Sanders (1889) • A. Aspinall, ed., Three early nineteenth-century diaries (1952) [extracts from Le Marchant, E. J. Littleton, Baron Hatherton, and E. Law, earl of Ellenborough] • M. Brock, The Great Reform Act (1973) • R. L. Sheil, Sketches, legal and political, ed. M. W. Savage, 2 vols. (1855) • County Durham, Pevsner (1983) • The journal of the Hon. Henry Edward Fox, ed. earl of Ilchester [G. S. Holland Fox-Strangways] (1923) • K. Bourne, Palmerston: the early years, 1784–1841 (1982) • H. E. Maxwell, Life and letters of George William Frederick, fourth earl of Clarendon, 2 vols. (1913) • J. Ajzenstat, The political thought of Lord Durham (1988) • P. A. Buckner, The transition to responsible government: British policy in British North America, 1815–1850 (1985)

Archives Lambton estate office, Lambton Park, Chester-le-Street, co. Durham, corresp. and papers • NA Canada, corresp. and papers relating to Canada | A. K. Bell Library, Perth, Perth & Kinross council archives, letters to Lord Kinnaird • BL, letters to J. C. Hobhouse, Add. MSS 36459–36466 passim • BL, letters to Sir Robert Wilson, Add. MSS 30108–30112 passim • Durham RO, letters to Lord Londonderry • Herts. ALS, corresp. with Lord Lytton • NL Scot., corresp. with Edward Ellice • Royal Arch., Melbourne MSS • U. Durham L., corresp. with second Earl Grey • U. Durham L., letters to Viscount Ponsonby • U. Durham L., corresp. with Sir Cuthbert Sharp • U. Southampton L., corresp. with Lord Palmerston • W. Sussex RO, letters to duke of Richmond • Woburn Abbey, Bedfordshire, letters to George William Russell

Likenesses T. Phillips, oils, 1819, Howick Hall, Northumberland • G. Hayter, group portrait, oils, 1820 (The trial of Queen Caroline, 1820), NPG • T. Phillips, oils, copy, 1820, NPG [see illus.] • T. Lawrence, portrait, 1829, Lambton; repro. in Reid, Life and letters, vol. 1 • C. Turner, mezzotint, pubd 1831 (after T. Lawrence), BM, NPG • J. Knight, group portrait, lithograph, c.1832 (William IV holding a council), BM • C. E. Wagstaff, mezzotint, pubd 1838 (after T. Lawrence), BM, NPG • C. E. Wagstaff and G. Dalziel, mixed-method engraving, pubd 1841, BM • J. Doyle, caricature drawings, BM • R. J. Lane, lithograph (after Count D'Orsay), NPG • S. W. Reynolds, group portrait, oils (The Reform Bill receiving the king's assent, 1832), Palace of Westminster, London • S. W. Reynolds, mezzotint (after T. Phillips), BM, NPG •

oils (after T. Lawrence), Reform Club, London · woodcut silhouette, NPG
Wealth at death £250,000: GEC, *Peerage*

Lambton, William (1753x69–1823), army officer and geodesist in India, was born at Crosby Grange, near Northallerton, in the North Riding of Yorkshire. The date of his birth is a matter of some conjecture, and he seems to have been at some pains to keep both his birth and his parentage a mystery. Davison Ingledew gives his date of birth as 1756, Phillimore has 1753/1756, and Keay suggests some time in the 1760s. No parish registers have been found to answer the question conclusively, and Lambton's childhood remains obscure. It is assumed that his parents were of humble means. He is known to have had a sister, Dorothy (*d.* 1827). He was educated at Borrowby, after which some neighbouring gentlemen and a clergyman entered him at the grammar school at Northallerton, where there was a foundation for four free scholars. He finished his education under the mathematician Dr Charles Hutton, though at which institute, if any, remains a mystery.

On 28 March 1781 Lambton was appointed ensign in Lord Fauconberg's foot, a 'provincial' or home-service regiment. In 1782 he transferred with the rank of ensign to the 33rd (West Riding) regiment, later the 1st battalion duke of Wellington's regiment, and joined the regiment in New York. While serving with the 33rd he was, according to some reports, briefly taken prisoner at Yorktown. In 1783 he went with the 33rd to Nova Scotia and subsequently New Brunswick. On 9 May 1784 he was promoted lieutenant. The following year he was appointed barrack-master at Saint John, New Brunswick, by both the war office and the Board of Ordnance. Since it was a double appointment, his post of barrack-master carried a double salary, namely £400 per annum. In New Brunswick Lambton helped divide and allot land to British loyalist refugees from the United States and was involved in surveying and delineating the boundary between the United States and Canada. While observing a solar eclipse in Canada he failed to attach a smoked glass lens to his telescope and suffered permanent damage to his left eye, which thereafter gave him a rather distracted and glazed expression. During the period he was surveying in New Brunswick a mountain was named Lambton's Mountain after or by him. This name appears on some early maps, but the peak later became known as Big Bald Mountain. In 1795 Lambton's regiment was ordered home, but he remained in Canada, apparently because family responsibilities would not allow him to relinquish his large salary.

The 33rd regiment was ordered to the East Indies in 1796, and Lambton was then obliged to choose between his civil and military positions. He chose to go to India with his regiment, which was then commanded by Arthur Wesley, later Wellesley. Lambton sailed for England and from there went with the regiment to the Cape in 1796, to Bengal in 1797, and subsequently to Madras in September 1798. He had not served with his regiment for twelve years and, though middle-aged, was still a lieutenant. Through a letter of introduction from his Canadian patron, Brooke Watson, to Sir Alured Clark, commander-in-chief in India,

he soon secured the staff position of brigade major to the king's troops under Fort St George (1799). Two papers, on the 'Theory of walls' and on the 'Maximum of mechanical power and the effects of machines in motion', were communicated by Lambton to the Asiatic Society about this time (*Asiatic Researches*, vol. 6). Both exhibit an impressive command of mathematics and astronomy, and this was noticed by Wesley, who became a useful patron, inviting Lambton to share his quarters in Madras. Lambton appears to have acquired his scientific knowledge through his own studies while in Canada.

Lambton served as brigade major to General David Baird in the expedition against Seringapatam, Tipu Sultan's stronghold, in the Fourth Anglo-Mysore War. Lambton's ability to find directions by the stars saved his brigade during a night march in the course of the campaign, when Baird was mistakenly leading his troops south towards enemy lines rather than north to safety. Lambton corrected the mistake. After the storm and capture of Seringapatam on 4 May 1799, in which he played an active and very creditable part, Lambton accompanied his brigade in its march to secure the surrender of the hill forts in Mysore. His journal from August to December 1799 is among the Mornington papers (BL, Add. MS 13658). When the brigade was broken up Lambton was appointed brigade major of the troops on the Coromandel coast, antedated from 22 August 1799.

In 1799 Lambton presented a memorial to the governor of Madras in council, suggesting a trigonometrical survey connecting the Malabar and Coromandel coasts. Lambton stressed to the government the practical benefits which would flow from his geodetic survey: it would provide an extendable lattice into which more detailed but less geodetically accurate local or regional surveys could be fitted. No less pressing was his desire to 'accomplish a desideratum still more sublime, viz., to determine by actual measurement the magnitude and figure of the earth' (Phillimore, 2.250). It was this scientific end which finally secured approval for Lambton's scheme. The Madras governor, Edward Clive, engaged the support for the scheme of his uncle Nevil Maskelyne, the astronomer royal. Their backing won over an initially hostile James Rennell and secured moneys to fund and continue the survey, which, like all others, dramatically overran its budget. Colonel Colin Mackenzie had already secured permission to undertake a survey in Mysore. Mackenzie's survey had broad topographical aims, recording the historical, natural, and economic character of the area; Lambton's was strictly trigonometrical. The two surveys were authorized to proceed in co-operation with one another. Phillimore's account shows the two to have been on cordial terms and that they co-operated professionally. Edney, however, suggests that relations were far from cordial and that Mackenzie resented what he regarded as the undue favour shown to Lambton.

Lambton's survey proposals were approved on 6 February 1800, and he began work immediately. Between 1800 and 1802 he conducted a preliminary survey in Mysore, measuring a base-line at St Thomas's Mount, Madras, in

1802. His next task, between 1802 and 1803, was the measurement of a degree along the Coromandel coast. Between 1803 and 1806 he measured triangles across the peninsula from east to west and started the measurement of the central arc, then between 1806 and 1807 he took the triangulation down the south coast to Tanjore. From 1807 to 1810 he extended the central arc to Cape Comorin and undertook a general survey and the construction of a map of the southern part of the peninsula. Between 1811 and 1815 he extended the central arc through the ceded districts into Hyderabad, with a connection to the eastern coast at Guntur. In 1815 he measured his sixth base-line, at Bidar, extending his arc to this point. Lambton was exacting in the demands he made for instruments and punctilious in their use, modelling his instrumentation and practice on those of William Roy. His theodolite was by William Carey, once apprenticed to Jesse Ramsden, and modelled on that used by Roy. His chain was also modelled on Roy's. In 1817 he submitted his third report, which described his progress up to 1815. The composition of such reports, the making of astronomical observations, and particularly the computation to reduce errors made in field observations occupied more and more of his time, and he increasingly left fieldwork to his assistants.

Lambton became captain in the 33rd foot, without purchase, on 25 June 1806, and purchased his majority in the regiment on 1 March 1808. When the 33rd returned home from Madras in 1811, Lambton remained behind as superintendent of the Indian survey at the company's expense. He became lieutenant-colonel by brevet on 4 June 1814 and was placed on half pay in consequence of the reduction of the army on 25 December 1818. In June 1818 his survey was transferred from Madras to be under the control of the supreme government at Fort William and was named the great or grand trigonometrical survey (GTS) of India. Against the wishes of Colin Mackenzie, who since 1815 had been the first surveyor-general of India with authority over all the surveys in the three presidencies, and who had argued that the trigonometrical survey should also come under his authority, Lambton's GTS was thus answerable only to government and not to Mackenzie. Lambton was elected a corresponding member of the French Academy (1817) through the influence of his French former assistant John Warren, and a fellow of the Royal Society (1818) and of the Asiatic Society.

In 1818, his third report complete, Lambton proposed extending the arc northwards, and the government agreed Agra as an appropriate end point. With this in mind, in 1822 he began to move his headquarters from Hyderabad to Nagpur. But Lambton never reached Nagpur. He died of heart disease according to some reports, of pulmonary tuberculosis according to others, and of his doctor's treatment according to yet others, at Hinganghat, 50 miles south of Nagpur, on 20 or 26 January 1823 and was buried there at what later became the Christian cemetery. His fine instruments, library, and papers were disposed of hastily and against the express wishes of his assistants, notably George Everest, at a camp auction, and some autobiographical notes, numerous other private papers, and some of his instruments were lost. Everest, who had been appointed Lambton's chief assistant in 1817, describes him at that period as 6 feet tall, erect, well-formed, bony, and muscular. He was a fair-complexioned man, with blue eyes, and he seemed 'a tranquil and exceedingly good-humoured person, very fond of his joke, a great admirer of the fair sex, partial to singing glees and duets, and everything, in short, that promoted harmony and tended to make life pass easily' (Phillimore, 3.468).

Lambton died unmarried, but in his will he named two natural children, William Lambton (*b.* Pondicherry, 12 July 1809) and Eliza Lambton (*b.* Hyderabad, 6 August 1819), and their respective mothers, Kummerboo, an Indian Muslim woman, and Frances, a half-European, half-Indian woman. He had a second natural son, John William (*b.* 26 December 1820), whose mother may have been Frances, and who is thought to have died young. William and Eliza were bequeathed substantial legacies, their mothers nominal allowances. William also received his father's small theodolite and his silver case of mathematical instruments. The residue of his estate was bequeathed to the two sons of his sister Dorothy, then in Yorkshire. Lambton's will was disputed acrimoniously in chancery, with the two natural children claiming that their bequests had not been honoured, yet the one surviving residuary legatee was receiving moneys.

Lambton's great arc was, by the time of his death, nearly 10 degrees or over 700 miles long. It was longer than the European arc which Lambton so much admired, and a model of its time. It was Everest who completed the arc after Lambton's death, but the project was Lambton's, as was the dedication and skill which ensured the establishment of the GTS as the then foremost geodetic establishment in the world. Lambton's results reflected the prevailing limits on instrumentation, method, and scientific understanding of effects such as local attraction, and within fifty years were superseded by a retriangulation; but his achievement remained formidable and the foundation for the subsequent achievements of others.

ELIZABETH BAIGENT

Sources R. H. Phillimore, ed., *Historical records of the survey of India*, 1–3 (1945–54) · J. Philippart, ed., *The royal military calendar*, 3rd edn, 5 vols. (1820) · J. Warren, 'Biographical sketch of the late Col. Lambton, superintendent of the Trigonometrical Survey of India', *Gleanings in Science*, 15 (March 1830), 73–82 · J. Keay, *The great arc: the dramatic tale of how India was mapped and Everest was named* (2000) · M. H. Edney, *Mapping and empire: the geographical construction of British India, 1765–1843* (1997) · C. J. Davison Ingledew, *History and antiquities of North Allerton in the county of York* (1858) · will, PRO, PROB 11/1679, sig. 697, fols. 60r–60v · J. R. Smith, *Everest* (1999)
Likenesses T. Hickey, oils, 1800, Stratfield Saye, Hampshire · W. Howell, oils, 1822, Royal Asiatic Society, London; repro. in Edney, *Mapping and empire*, 156
Wealth at death assets in India and Egland: will, PRO, PROB 11/1679, sig. 697, fols. 60r–60v

Lamburn, Richmal Crompton [*known as* Richmal Crompton] **(1890–1969)**, children's writer and novelist, was born on 15 November 1890 in Manchester Road, Bury, Lancashire. She was the daughter of the Revd Edward John

Richmal Crompton Lamburn (1890–1969), by Bassano, 1934

Sewell Lamburn (1854–1915), schoolmaster and curate, and his wife, Clara, *née* Crompton (1861–1939). She had an elder sister and younger brother, and was named Richmal after her mother's sister: this unusual forename, a derivation of Richard and Mary, had been in her mother's family since the early 1700s. Her father taught at Bury grammar school and the family lived in Bury for many years.

Richmal Crompton attended St Elphin's Clergy Daughters' School in Warrington, Lancashire, and later in Darley Dale, Derbyshire. She gained a founder's scholarship to Royal Holloway College, London, in 1911. She was awarded a university scholarship in 1912, and the college's Driver scholarship in classics in 1914. While a student she supported the campaign for women's suffrage (although she was never militant), was a member of the hockey, tennis, and boating clubs, and took a leading part in college theatricals.

After gaining second class honours in classics (1914) at London University, Crompton taught from 1915 to 1917 at her old school, St Elphin's. She then became classics mistress at Bromley High School for Girls in Kent from 1917 to 1924. During this period she began to write short stories, including one featuring the robust, anarchic schoolboy William Brown. This was published in the *Home Magazine* in February 1919. Further stories about William appeared in this monthly publication. The series was then transferred to the *Happy Mag.*, and in 1922 George Newnes published a selection in two books entitled *Just William* and *More William*. Other William books followed, becoming so

popular that between 1922 and Crompton's death in 1969 the series ran to thirty-eight titles. In 1990 a new William book, *What's Wrong with Civilizashun*, was published, consisting of some of her previously uncollected magazine articles. Her William stories contained sharp social observation of suburban mores, and have been a good deal quarried by social historians. By 1996 some 10 million William books had been sold, and translations have been made in fourteen languages. By 1996 there had also been four William films, several radio series, four television series, and several best-selling audio cassette readings. Crompton by her own account at first considered William a 'pot-boiler', and her ambition was to write adult novels. She produced thirty-nine of these, but these family sagas, although enjoyable, never achieved a fraction of the success of her William books.

After an attack of poliomyelitis in 1923 Crompton lost the use of her right leg. Although able to walk with a stick, she was advised in 1924 by her doctor to give up teaching because of the difficulty in travelling. This was the turning point in her life as she was then able to give her energies wholeheartedly to writing. Some years later, when her niece made a sympathetic reference to her disability, Crompton declared that she had led 'a more interesting life because of it'. In the 1930s Crompton developed breast cancer and had a mastectomy, but characteristically she never allowed this or her other disability to cloud the humour of her writings.

During the Second World War, Crompton was a voluntary worker in Bromley's fire service. (Her irritation with some of the officialdom she encountered is reflected in one or two comical William episodes, especially in *William Does his Bit*, 1941.) Most of her adult life was spent in Kent— some thirty-six years at Bromley Common, and over fifteen years at Chislehurst. She did not marry. As her stories suggest, Richmal Crompton was quick-witted and amusing. Despite sometimes appearing vague, she was extremely well-ordered and methodical. Towards the end of her life she became interested in mystical interpretations of Christianity while remaining a staunch member of the Church of England. Politically she was a Conservative, although her early William books are an interesting critique of Conservative values.

Crompton supported several charitable organizations, including the Muscular Dystrophy Group and the British Polio Fellowship. Always drawn to young people, she kept a drawerful of toys at her home for child visitors, and happily accepted arduous roles in children's games. She loved teaching, and many of her former pupils were grateful for the help and extra coaching which she gave them. The character of William Brown was partly inspired by episodes in the lives of members of her family: when first writing about William she drew upon events in the childhood of her brother, John, and, later, that of her nephew, Tom Disher, and great-nephew, Edward Ashbee.

Crompton created other attractive fictional characters, including Jimmy, a younger boy, in 1949, and she made two or three attempts at young girl heroines, but William Brown eclipsed them all. Tough and resilient, he became typical of the outdoor, non-bookish child. His author's insight, acute observation, and engaging irony have ensured his appeal. William's name acquired meaning even for people who had never read the stories in which he featured. Crompton continued to write about him until shortly before she died of a heart attack, on 11 January 1969, at Farnborough Hospital, Kent. She was buried at Eltham on 16 January.　　MARY CADOGAN

Sources M. Cadogan, *Richmal Crompton: the woman behind William* (1986) · K. Williams, *Just Richmal: the life and work of Richmal Crompton Lamburn* (1986) · M. Disher, *Growing up with Just William* (privately published, London, 1990) · P. Craig and M. Cadogan, 'That boy again', *Sunday Times Magazine* (6 Feb 1977) · B. Doyle, *The who's who of children's literature* (1968) · M. Cadogan, *The William companion* (1990) · M. Cadogan, *Just William through the ages* (1994) · private information (1981) · *CGPLA Eng. & Wales* (1969)
Archives priv. coll.
Likenesses Bassano, photograph, 1934, NPG [*see illus.*] · photograph, 7 June 1948, Hult. Arch. · photographs, priv. coll.
Wealth at death £59,418: probate, 25 April 1969, *CGPLA Eng. & Wales*

Lamerie, Paul Jacques de (1688–1751), goldsmith, was born on 9 April 1688 in 's-Hertogenbosch, Netherlands, the only child of Paul Souchay de la Merie and his wife, Constance le Roux. His father, an officer in William III's army, moved to London in 1689 and Paul was apprenticed to his fellow Huguenot, the goldsmith Pierre Platel, in August 1703. In February 1713 de Lamerie set up his own workshop in Windmill Street, where he rapidly established his prominence as both manufacturer and retailer. Early customers included Sir William Trumbull, Baron Foley, and the jewel house of George I.

Between 1723 and 1728 de Lamerie was in partnership with Ellis Gamble, the latter apparently running the retail side of the business. Gamble had been the master of William Hogarth, who trained as an engraver on silver before turning to copperplate-engraving and painting. The Gamble–de Lamerie partnership (discovered in the late twentieth century) supports the long-standing attribution to Hogarth of the engraving on the famous exchequer seal salver made for Sir Robert Walpole.

In 1738 de Lamerie moved to Gerrard Street and served as captain and later major in the Westminster volunteer association. In 1737–8 he served on a committee of the Goldsmiths' Company, promoting the Plate Offences Act, and moved up through the hierarchy of the court, only failing to serve as prime warden. He supplied a magnificent ewer and rose water basin to the company's order in 1741, richly chased with rococo ornament. Characteristically, he charged considerably more than had been agreed for the work; the ewer and basin weighed 570 ounces, substantially more than the requested maximum.

De Lamerie was always ready to flout the company's regulations, failing to register two alternative versions of his new sterling (Britannia) mark, and was criticized by the company for failing to submit plate for assay and hallmarking in 1717. He evaded the duty payable from 1719 on newly wrought plate by inserting already hallmarked discs into newly made wares. His wares made up the largest individual parcel in a massive consignment of plate exported to the Tsarina Anna in 1726, much of which again had paid no duty.

Since no ledgers survive, the size of de Lamerie's business and the names of his suppliers can only be suggested. His was for thirty-five years the pre-eminent retail business at the upper end of the market, supplying tableware and massive buffet plate to the jewel house and the Russian court (tsarinas Anna and Catherine, and Count Bobrinsky). His long-standing clients included Sir Robert Walpole, the earl of Ilchester, the earl of Thanet, Viscount Tyrconnel, the duke of Bedford, Baron Anson, and a cross-section of the English nobility and gentry.

The diversity and volume of silver bearing de Lamerie's mark is far greater than can have emerged from a single workshop and it came to be generally acknowledged, after a century dominated by the concept of the maker's mark, that de Lamerie, in common with many other goldsmiths registering marks at Goldsmiths' Hall, not only fulfilled orders with other goldsmiths' wares but also subcontracted orders to a range of London workshops, although striking the finished wares with his own punch. His choice of modellers, chasers, and other specialists was the key to his commercial success. His marks appear overstruck by that of Paul Crespin on ambassadorial plate issued to the earl of Chesterfield in 1727; although George Wickes supplied the Bath presentation cup to Frederick Louis, prince of Wales, in 1739, it has much in common with a contemporary series of cups with de Lamerie's mark.

For twenty years de Lamerie's silver shows a strong dependence on French *régence* designs, and techniques such as heavy formal cast and applied ornament, but from the late 1720s his work demonstrates asymmetry, with rich figurative chasing and a revival of the auricular and *massive* motifs of a century earlier. The distinctive style of the modeller James Shruder, who was in his employment in 1751 and sorted out his estate, can be recognized in de Lamerie's output from the 1730s, as can that of Charles Frederick Kandler I.

By the late twentieth century de Lamerie's silver was to be found dispersed across the world: a pair of chandeliers in the Kremlin Armoury, Moscow; a massive fountain and cistern in St Petersburg; a large collection in the Los Angeles County Museum; and in Great Britain important silver bearing his mark at the Victoria and Albert Museum, the Ashmolean Museum, and the Mansion House.

On 11 February 1717 de Lamerie married Louisa Juliott. They had two sons and four daughters. De Lamerie died in London on 1 August 1751 and was buried at St Anne's, Soho. Obituaries stressed his standing as master silversmith, 'very instrumental in bringing that Branch of Trade to the Perfection it is now in'.

PHILIPPA GLANVILLE, *rev.*

Sources P. A. S. Phillips, *Paul de Lamerie, citizen and goldsmith of London: a study of his life and work, AD 1688–1751* (1935) · S. Hare, ed., *Paul de Lamerie, 1688–1751* (1990) [exhibition catalogue, Goldsmiths' Hall, London, 16 May – 22 June, 1990]

Lamington. For this title name *see* Baillie, Alexander Dundas Ross Cochrane-Wishart-, first Baron Lamington (1816–1890); Baillie, Charles Wallace Alexander Napier Ross Cochrane-, second Baron Lamington (1860–1940).

Lamond, Mary (1862–1948), Church of Scotland deaconess, was born on 22 February 1862 at 1 Albyn Place, Edinburgh, the daughter of William Lamond, advocate, and his wife, Elizabeth Thomas Deans. Mary Lamond had strong features and an upright bearing. She was noted for her eloquent public speaking, her calm but gracious assertiveness, and her strong sense of humour. She built an impressive career in the service of the Church of Scotland Woman's Guild, and she devoted her time, means, and talents to the development of women's work within the national Church of Scotland. The Woman's Guild was established in 1887 to organize and direct the expanding contribution of women at parish and national levels to the life and work of the church. Central to the structure and purpose of the guild, as devised by Archibald Charteris, was a revival of the ancient order of deaconesses—women trained and set apart for dedicated lifetime service. Such women were to be skilled in nursing and pastoral care, but were also to provide guidance and leadership to the envisaged mass movement of women in congregational branches of the guild. After training at the Deaconess Training Institute in Edinburgh, Lamond was among the first women to be set apart as a deaconess of the Church of Scotland (DCS), at a service in Morningside church, Edinburgh, on 1 April 1894.

In 1901 Mary Lamond took over from Catherine Charteris as editor of the Woman's Guild supplement to *Life and Work* (the monthly magazine published by the Church of Scotland), and from 1905 to 1911 she was the full-time honorary secretary of the guild. In this capacity she was responsible for the organization and administration of a rapidly expanding movement, with well over 40,000 members in hundreds of local branches. The national leadership of the guild held annual conferences and initiated special schemes and projects. During her years as the supplement editor and national secretary Lamond played a key role in establishing the guild as a significant organization with a strong identity and sense of common purpose. While in some respects, with its strongly middle-class character and leadership, the guild simply confirmed and extended the traditional perception of women's place in church life, it also developed the talents and self-confidence of many able women during the years before the First World War.

In 1911 Mary Lamond was appointed superintendent of Deaconess House, which offered preparation, not just for deaconesses, but also for other women who wished to serve the church in home and foreign missionary work. The students in her charge received their practical training in the guild's own Deaconess Hospital and in an inner-city mission parish. Under the authority of the church's life and work committee, the superintendent had to direct and organize all aspects of the curriculum. However, the diaconate was always characterized as a separate, subordinate, and exclusively female ministry. Mary Lamond's own experience and vision went well beyond those limitations. During the final twelve years of her work with the Woman's Guild she developed a strategy of reorganization to meet the demands of changing times and aspirations. From 1920 to 1932 she was the most prominent woman in the church during her time as the guild's national president. She brought all her zeal, organizational ability, and clarity of thought to bear in a major process of change, strengthening the representative character of guild structures, and linking all the women's organizations for missions and temperance under the aegis of the guild. From 1926 Lamond was a dynamic and persuasive leader of the negotiations between women of the Church of Scotland and the United Free Church, prior to church union in 1929. She worked with others to ensure that the reunited national church had at its heart a co-ordinated network of women's organizations to parallel the courts of the church and promote the fuller involvement of female members. By 1930 the guild had nearly 70,000 members, and Mary Lamond was optimistic about the future: 'The inspiration and impetus given by the act of uniting will lead to new enterprises and fresh effort for the remedying of social evils at home, and the extension of Christ's Kingdom throughout the world' (*Life and Work*, 1930, 28). It was said of her that 'Among all the succession of talented women who have contributed so largely to the success and growth of the Guild, there has been no one who has played a more notable part than Miss Lamond' (*Life and Work*, 1948, 84). But she was not content simply to build up the guild as a separate woman's organization; she was committed to real equality. As the only female speaker at the union assembly in 1929 she 'brilliantly vindicated women's place in the church by a speech of very singular power and charm' (ibid.), declaring, 'The women workers of the Church of Scotland … are quite worthy of any encouragement. Perhaps they are also worthy of a greater share in Church counsels than you have yet given them' (*Proceedings and Debates of the General Assembly of the Church of Scotland*, October 1929). In her retirement she continued to advocate the worth and rights of women, and was an honorary vice-president of the Fellowship of Equal Service in the Church, whose objects included the ordination of women.

Mary Lamond, who lived latterly at 10 Forbes Road, Edinburgh, was a unique and inspiring leader during a period of great change. She died unmarried in the Deaconess Hospital, Edinburgh, on 15 March 1948.

LESLEY ORR MACDONALD

Sources M. Magnusson, *Out of silence: the Woman's Guild, 1887–1987* (1987) · L. O. Macdonald, *A unique and glorious mission* (2000) · D. P. Thomson, *Women of the Scottish church* (1975), 308 · *Life and Work* (1891–1924) [Woman's Guild suppl.] · *Life and Work* (1928–30) [Woman's Guild suppl.] · *Life and Work* (1948), 48 · *Proceedings and Debates of the General Assembly of the Church of Scotland* (Oct 1929) · DSCHT · CCI (1949) · b. cert. · d. cert.
Likenesses photograph, 1920–29, repro. in Magnusson, *Out of silence* · G. F. Watt, oils, 1933

Wealth at death £11,234 11s. 3d.: confirmation, 19 April 1949, *CCI* · £116 1s. 10d.: additional estate, 27 Aug 1949, *CCI*

Lamont, David (1753–1837), Church of Scotland minister, was born on 20 April 1753, the son of John Lamont (1700–1776), minister of Kelton, Kirkcudbrightshire, and Margaret (*d.* 1795), daughter of John Affleck of Whitepark. His grandfather John Lamont of Newton in Fife was descended from Allan Lamont, second minister of Scoonie, Fife, after the Reformation. He was licensed by the presbytery of Kirkcudbright in May 1772 and ordained as minister for the parish of Kirkpatrick-Durham in that county in August 1774. He was made DD by the University of Edinburgh in 1780 and was appointed chaplain to the prince of Wales in 1785. On 24 July 1799 he married Anne (*d.* 1857), daughter of David Anderson, an excise officer; they had one son, John (1805–1873), an advocate, afterwards a brewer in London. In 1822 Lamont became moderator of the general assembly of the Church of Scotland and chaplain in ordinary for Scotland two years later. As moderator of the general assembly he read an address to George IV and preached before him in St Giles's, Edinburgh, during his visit to Scotland.

A liberal in politics and theology Lamont held a prominent place among the moderate clergy who dominated the Church of Scotland at the time. Contemporaries described him as a popular preacher, an able debater in church courts, and an eloquent platform speaker. A considerable landowner, he divided his property into small holdings, promoted local manufactures, formed benevolent societies among his tenants and parishioners, and was said to have 'gained the affection and esteem of all who witnessed his generous and enlightened exertions'. Between 1780 and 1797 he published six works, including *Sermons on Important Subjects* (1780–97) and *Subscription of the Confession of Faith of the Church of Scotland* (1790). He also contributed an 'Account of the parish of Kirkpatrick-Durham' to Sir John Sinclair's *Statistical Account of Scotland* (1791–9). He died on 7 January 1837.

G. W. SPROTT, *rev.* MARY CATHERINE MORAN

Sources *Fasti Scot.* · R. Heron, *Observations made in a journey through the western counties of Scotland*, 2 vols. (1793) · *Caledonian Mercury* (Jan 1837)

Lamont, Sir James, first baronet (1828–1913), Arctic yachtsman, was born at Knockdow on 28 April 1828, the only son of Lieutenant-Colonel Alexander Lamont of Knockdow, Toward, Argyll, and Jane, daughter of T. Chrystie of Balchrystie, Fife. He was proud that his family was the senior cadet branch of the clan Lamont and was later president of the Clan Lamont Society. He was educated at Rugby School and the Edinburgh military academy. In 1846 he became ensign and second lieutenant in the 91st Argyllshire regiment of foot serving at the Cape of Good Hope, but resigned in 1849 when his uncle left him a fortune. He then gave his time to managing his Scottish and West Indian estates and to travelling, mainly in the Arctic; between his travels he lived in London.

Lamont took his Board of Trade certificate as master to enable him to command his own ship. In 1858 he took the yacht *Ginevra*, 142 tons, to Svalbard, Edge Island (where he had to winter), Kelihau Bay, and Kalvpunter—all poorly charted. There he caught seals, walrus, and grouse. In 1859 he chartered the walrus hunter *Anna Louisa* for a sporting voyage to Edge Island, Bell Sound, Ice Fjord, Green Harbour, Thousand Islands, and Hope Island. In 1862 he went to Nova Scotia and Labrador. He also went on pleasure and sporting trips to the Mediterranean (in 1863–4) and to South Africa. In 1869 Lamont took the *Diana*, 179/230 tons, to Novaya Zemlya, Matochkin Shar, the Kara Sea, the west of Svalbard, the east coast of Spitsbergen, Fairhaven, and Bell Sound, charting a reef. The next season he took the *Diana* to Kolguyev, Novaya Zemlya, Vaigach Island, Matochkin Shar, and Jan Mayen. In 1871 he went to Edge Island, Barents Island, Cape Mitra Smeerenburg and Prince Charles Foreland, and to lat. 80°50′ N, long. 17° E. He sailed thousands of miles in Arctic waters, recording his voyages in *Seasons with the Sea-Horse* (1861) and *Yachting in the Arctic Seas* (1876), both of which contain information about land and marine natural history and about navigation, tides, currents, and meteorology. They also contain maps and views by an artist taken by Lamont to record the landscapes. Two of the views have long remained in the *Arctic Pilot*, published by the hydrographic office to help pilots recognize the coast.

Lamont was a fellow of the Royal Geographical Society, from 1861 until 1887 when he resigned because he was out of sympathy with it, and of the Geological Society. After unsuccessfully contesting Paisley as a Liberal in 1857, he was Liberal MP for Buteshire in 1865–8. He favoured reducing property qualifications for voters and the relief of dissenters from all tests and disabilities. In 1868 he married Adelaide Eliza, second daughter of Sir George William Denys, second baronet, and they had two sons (one of whom died young) and a daughter. He was created baronet on 16 July 1910. As well as his travel books he published *A Lecture on the Civil War in America* (1864) and wrote for the *Scottish Field* on natural history and country life. After a year bedridden he died at Knockdow on 29 July 1913. He was survived by his widow and was succeeded by his son Norman (*b.* 1869). His attractively written books brought knowledge of the Arctic to a wide audience.

A. G. E. JONES

Sources *WWW* · Burke, *Gen. GB* · A. G. E. Jones, *Sportssaileren i Arktis* (1979), 50–57 · *CCI* (1913) · *Dod's Parliamentary Companion*
Wealth at death £19,785 12s. 10d.: probate, 1913, Scotland. *CCI*; £6,150 7s. 2d.—additional estate: 1914

Lamont, Johann von [*formerly* John Lamont] (1805–1879), astronomer and geophysicist, was born John Lamont on 13 December 1805 in Corriemulzie, near Braemar, Aberdeenshire, the only child of Robert Lamont, forester, and his second wife, Elspeth Ewan. In 1817, after his father's death Father Gall Robertson recruited him for the Scottish Benedictine monastery of St James in Regensburg, Bavaria, while his mother and stepbrother emigrated to the United States. The prior of the monastery, Benedikt Deasson, devoted himself to the boy's education in mathematics and mechanics. During the summer of 1827 Lamont spent his vacation at the observatory in Bogenhausen, near

Munich. The director, Johann Georg von Soldner, appreciated Lamont's work and appointed him as his assistant in March 1828. Two years later Lamont obtained a doctorate from the University of Munich. After Soldner's death in 1833 Lamont provisionally headed the observatory, and he was appointed director in July 1835. He enjoyed the support of Friedrich von Schelling, president of the Bavarian Academy of Sciences, of which he became an extraordinary member in 1835 and an ordinary member in 1836. In 1837 he began lecturing on practical astronomy at the University of Munich and succeeded Franz von Paula Gruithuisen as professor of astronomy on 20 December 1852. For a short period Lamont was a member of the senate of the University of Munich (1857-9).

Lamont's scientific work focused on astronomy, meteorology, and terrestrial magnetism. In order to do precise measurements in these fields he devised numerous new instruments in a private workshop that ultimately became part of the observatory in 1853. An outstanding 10.5 Paris inch refractor (approximately 11.25 standard inches) with a focal length of 15 feet, built by the famous workshop of Utzschneider-Fraunhofer, served him in the late 1830s for observing objects of relatively low luminosity, such as the satellites of Saturn and Uranus, the relative motion of star clusters, and Halley's comet in 1836. After 1840 Lamont's astronomical work focused mainly on positional astronomy and resulted in a catalogue of 80,000 stars, of which 12,000 had been previously undiscovered ('Observationes astronomicae in specula regia Monachiensi institutae', published as *Annalen der Königlichen Sternwarte bei München*, 20 vols. in ten bound books, 1848-74). Lamont was also the first in Europe to devise a chronometer for recording the transit time of stars across the meridian (1850).

In the 1840s Lamont's attention was drawn to meteorology and terrestrial magnetism. As atmospheric conditions determined the quality of astronomical observations, he became interested in the study of weather and proposed a network of meteorological stations. In an effort to co-ordinate measurements he founded a meteorological association in 1842, and published the *Annalen für Meteorologie und Erdmagnetismus* from 1842 to 1844. His work, though remaining fragmentary due to lack of funding, laid the foundation for meteorological science in Bavaria and introduced new meteorological measuring and recording devices.

Lamont's interest in geophysics and terrestrial magnetism, to which he contributed his most important works, was closely linked to the initiative by C. F. Gauss and W. Weber that aimed at obtaining data on the earth's magnetic field by means of regular and simultaneous measurements at different observatories all over the world. Having built a magnetic observatory in 1840 with funds from the Bavarian government Lamont participated in the international campaign between 1841 and 1845, and he devised a whole range of new instruments, such as automatic recording apparatuses and portable theodolites, which were suited for expeditions (see J. von Lamont, *Handbuch des Erdmagnetismus*, 1849). In the late 1850s he

extended his measurements to many places in Bavaria and travelled to France, Spain, Portugal, Belgium, Holland, and Denmark. Beside these main lines of work Lamont also participated in triangulation measurements between Austria and Bavaria, established statistics on Bavarian population, wrote on issues of law, health, and royal genealogy, and held popular lectures.

Lamont, of modest character and liberal to charities, did not marry and led a solitary life, though he did take part in the reunions of the 'Catholic Casino' in Munich. Lamont was a member of numerous European academies, including the Royal Society of London, and received among other honours the order of Gregory the Great (conferred by Pius IX) and the order of the crown of Bavaria, the latter bringing with it the title of nobility. Lamont died on 6 August 1879 from the effects of a youthful spinal injury and was buried in the churchyard in Bogenhausen. On his gravestone was engraved: 'et coelum et terram exploravit' ('he explored the sky as well as the earth'). Upon his death he bequeathed his savings to a foundation which he had established in 1853 to support students of astronomy, mathematical physics, and mathematics, and whose capital amounted to 160,000 marks. **M. DÖRRIES**

Sources C. von Orff, 'Johann von Lamont', *Vierteljahresschrift der astronomischen Gesellschaft*, 15 (1880), 60-82 · von Schafhäutl, 'Johann von Lamont', *Historisch-politische Blätter für das katholische Deutschland*, 85 (1880), 54-82 · N. N., 'Johann von Lamont', *Sirius* (Sept 1880), 191-6 · N. N., 'Johann von Lamont', *Sirius* (Oct 1880), 214-18 · J. MacPherson, *John von Lamont, astronomer royal of Bavaria* (1930?) · R. Häfner, 'Die Zeit Johann von Lamonts an der Königlichen Sternwarte zu Bogenhausen', *Sterne und Weltraum* (Jan 1990), 13-18 · D. B. Heerrmann, 'Lamont, Johann von', *DSB* · F. Litten, 'Johann von Lamont', *Biographisches Handbuch des Lehrkörpers der Universitäten Ingolstadt, Landshut, München* [forthcoming] · F. Schmeidler, 'Johann von Lamont', *Neue deutsche Biographie*, ed. Otto, Graf zu Stolberg-Wernigerode (Berlin, 1953-), 451-2 · K. Stöckl, 'Johannes von Lamont', *Natur und Kultur* (Sept 1929), 321-5 · *DNB*

Wealth at death 160,000 marks: von Orff, 'Johann von Lamont', 15

Lamont, John (*fl.* 1636-1671), diarist, was probably the son of Thomas Lamont (*c*.1586-1636), minister of Scoonie, Fife, from 1614 onwards, and his wife, Margaret Cockburn, and grandson of Allan Lamont, also minister of Scoonie, and of Kennoway, whose ancestors came from Argyll. He is known chiefly because of his diary, which runs from March 1649 to April 1671 but is plainly incomplete both at the beginning and at the end. It covers a particularly significant period of Scottish history, which includes the proclamation of Charles II as king of Scotland, the Cromwellian invasion, the enforced union with England in the 1650s, and the Restoration, but such nationally important events are only briefly recorded. In addition the diary records births, marriages, and deaths in various Fife families, including Lamont's own, as well as in various Scottish noble families, making it of considerable genealogical interest. It is particularly informative about the affairs of the family of Lundin of Lundin, to which his brother Allan was factor and chaplain at Lundie. It is possible that Lamont may himself have been factor to this family at some time, but details of this are unknown.

Judging by the diary Lamont never married, and died some time after 1671. His most likely heir would have been his brother Allan's son John, born in 1661, who probably inherited the manuscript diary among Lamont's other papers. This John Lamont was, like his father, factor at Lundie, and was at some time a skipper in Over Largo. In 1695 he acquired the estate of Newton in the parish of Kennoway. This caused confusion when the diary was first published by Archibald Constable as *The Chronicle of Fife* in 1810. It was described as the diary of John Lamont 'of Newton', and attributed to the nephew rather than the uncle, who never owned the Newton estate. This mistaken identification was repeated when the diary was published a second time in 1830 by the Maitland Club. The confusion was resolved by Walter Wood in an appendix to his *East Neuk of Fife* (1887), which differentiated between uncle and nephew and identified the former as the diarist; the latter was the grandfather of David *Lamont (1753–1837), the prominent Church of Scotland minister.

ALEXANDER DU TOIT

Sources H. McKechnie, *The Lamont clan, 1235–1935* (1938), 471–7 · W. Wood, *The East Neuk of Fife: its history and antiquities*, ed. J. W. Brown, 2nd edn (1887), 469–75 · *The diary of Mr John Lamont of Newton, 1649–1671*, ed. G. R. Kinloch, Maitland Club, 7 (1830) · A. Constable, ed., *The chronicle of Fife, being the diary of John Lamont of Newton from 1649 to 1671* (1810) · *Fasti Scot.*, new edn, 5.116

Archives U. St Andr. L., diary

La Mothe, Claude Groteste de (1647–1713), Reformed minister and religious controversialist, was born in Orléans, France, the second of four sons of Jacques Groteste, sieur de la Buffière (*d.* in or after 1685), advocate of the Paris *parlement* and elder of the Reformed church at Charenton, and of his wife, Anne Groteste du Chesnay. Like his brothers he took the title of a family property, in his case that of La Mothe. Having gained a doctorate in law from the University of Orléans in 1664, the following year he was received as an advocate by the Paris *parlement*. After theological study, in 1675 he became minister of the protestant church at Lisy-sur-Orcq, near Meaux, in the Île-de-France. By contract dated from Paris on 23 June 1679 he married Marie (*d.* 1726/7), daughter of Jean Berthe, a Parisian banker, and his wife, Suzanne Marchand; the bride brought a dowry of 36,000 livres. Called in 1682 to the wealthier and more prestigious church at Rouen, Groteste de La Mothe entered into the charge there, but when the vacancy at Lisy proved impossible to fill he returned to his original post. When the last protestant provincial synod was held at Lisy in August 1683, he acted as clerk and gained general approval for his wisdom.

That year, in what was celebrated by the Jesuits as a significant coup, Groteste de La Mothe's brother Marin Groteste, sieur des Mahis (1649–1694), abjured his protestantism; in time he became a Catholic priest and apologist. Subsequently his parents and youngest brother, Abraham, also converted. However, with the revocation of the edict of Nantes in 1685, Groteste de La Mothe and his wife were granted permission to leave France, taking some of their substantial property (perhaps as much as 60,000

livres), while the rest was confiscated or entrusted to relatives. By 23 November they were in London. Here in 1686 Groteste became minister of the conformist French church at St Martin Orgar; he was naturalized on 16 December 1687. He transferred to the linked churches of Swallow Street in 1689 and Hungerford Market and le Quarré in 1690; by September that year he seems to have been acting as secretary of a nascent association of refugee ministers in London. By this time he habitually signed himself C. G. de La Mothe.

In 1691 La Mothe also became a chaplain to the duke of Schomberg. In this capacity, and as spokesman of the ministers' conference, he wrote in French a work translated as *Two Discourses Concerning the Divinity of our Saviour* (1693), an assertion of their collective orthodoxy on this point and a firm rejection of the Socinian position of which they had been suspected. Stephen Nye in *Reflections upon Two Discourses* (1693) mocked him as 'an eminent Demagogue of the French Nation', and the 'Refugees for Conscience' in general as uncomprehending 'Informers and Persecutors', vainly trying to influence the English bishops and law courts, but La Mothe was undaunted (pp. 3, 21). His *The Inspiration of the New Testament Asserted* (1694) was located in a well-tilled area of apologetics, but he considered there was still scope to counter 'Libertinism' with a more thoroughgoing exposition of the divine inspiration of scripture. That February his colleagues at the four conjoined churches noted that, without their consent, La Mothe had accepted a call to the chief conformist French church at the Savoy; he apparently suffered no lasting resentment, and was to remain there for the rest of his life.

La Mothe, whose well-connected relatives included his nephew Jean or John *Robethon, secretary to William of Orange since before 1688 and later a servant of George I as elector and king, was in contact through correspondence with men of influence in France, the Netherlands, and Germany. Combining pre-eminence among the French pastors and friendship with Englishmen of varying shades of political opinion, including the whiggish Archbishop Thomas Tenison, the tory Francis Atterbury, and the suspected Jacobite George Smalridge, he became a bridge between the Anglican establishment and other European protestants. Having collected quotations from sermons preached by English clergy in support of Queen Anne's appeal of 1703 on behalf of protestant refugees from the new French province of Orange, he published them at The Hague as a demonstration of Anglican charity. *Correspondance fraternelle de l'église anglicane avec les autres églises réformées et étrangères* (1705) claimed a close relationship between the Church of England and the continental Reformed churches. La Mothe's criticism of high-churchmen who through their 'rigidity' refused to acknowledge this provoked a backlash, which in turn prompted him to publish the much more ambitious *Entretiens sur la correspondance fraternelle* (1707). This traced a flourishing partnership since the Reformation, which had cooled only in the days of Archbishop Laud; taking up the mantle of the founder minister and apologist of the

Savoy, Jean Durel, he appended letters from Geneva and elsewhere approving both the church and episcopacy.

In April 1706 and December 1707 respectively, La Mothe became the first naturalized Englishman to be elected to the newly founded Society for Promoting Christian Knowledge (SPCK) and to the Society for the Propagation of the Gospel (SPG). Actively involved in both, he channelled donations from his own community, organized relief for persecuted Vaudois protestants and French versions of the Book of Common Prayer for Huguenots in North America, and helped examine potential missionaries. He proclaimed to foreigners the worth of the SPG in *Relation de la Société établie pour la Propagation de l'Évangile* (1708), a translation of White Kennett's 1706 work accompanied by sermons of his own. Applauding recent British initiatives such as charity schools and parish libraries, it called on all protestants to join in the formidable task of converting the nations. In April 1708 the SPCK in its turn formally thanked La Mothe for his *Caractères des nouvelles prophécies* (1708), four sermons exposing the so-called Cévenol or French Prophets. When these three exiled leaders of an unsuccessful protestant rising had arrived in London in 1707 and solicited political support through the medium of 'divinely inspired' warnings, the Savoy and Threadneedle Street churches had united to dissociate themselves from co-religionists who were undermining their credibility. In his *Nouveaux mémoires pour servir à l'histoire des trois Camisars* (1708) La Mothe offered the evidence they had collected for the 'fraud', which he perceived as favoured by Socinians and infiltrated by papists. The latter were the target of his *Politique du papisme en Angleterre*, published at Rotterdam the following year. Convinced that England was the primary target of Rome's onslaught on the Reformed, he decried what he saw as a fifth column sowing division between the Anglicans and their brethren, and between the French refugees and their hosts; in response he proposed a society dedicated to combating Catholicism. La Mothe consistently regarded Lutherans as partners of the Reformed. When the conversion and subsequent marriage of Elizabeth Christine of Wolfenbüttel to Charles III of Spain tarred them with popery, La Mothe gained the gratitude of Tenison and other supporters of the Hanoverian succession with his well-researched defence of Lutheran conduct, *Mémoires de la prétendue déclaration de l'Université de Helmstad* (1710). In the final years of his life he collected material for another apology for his adopted church and country, *Charitas Anglicana*, but it is unclear where and when it was published.

In 1712 La Mothe was elected a member of the Royal Society of Berlin. In July 1713, in collaboration with Henri de Massue de Ruvigny, earl of Galway, he was busy collecting funds for Huguenots released from the galleys. However, in his last years he was overtaken by a long and serious illness. Being 'within two fingers of death' concentrated his mind on the duties of the suffering and recovering believer, laid out during a brief respite in *Les devoirs du chrétien convalescent* (1713). His will, made on 3 September 1713 from Chelsea, made no reference to his physical condition but gave evidence of his varied interests and connections. Beneficiaries included the French church at the Savoy, the charity house in Soho, the SPG, 'the society which meets at Mr Shute's, minister, in Bartlet Buildings', and a cousin in the Netherlands. Apart from Madame La Mothe's, the largest bequests were to his eldest brother, Jacques Groteste, sieur de la Buffière (whose financial sufferings and insecurity as a protestant remaining in France feature in surviving correspondence), his youngest brother, Abraham (whose Catholicism had not impaired good relations), and his nephew Robethon, then in Brunswick. La Mothe died on 30 September 1713 and was probably buried at the Savoy Chapel, Westminster. Condolences from many quarters reached his widow and executor. Until her death, between late October 1726 and early January 1727, she continued to correspond with family and friends abroad; many of the couple's letters (those from 1703 written to and from a house in St Martin's Lane, Westminster, 'by the French pewterer's') survive among the papers of La Mothe's colleague at the Savoy, Israel Antoine Aufrère, deposited at the Huguenot Library, London.   VIVIENNE LARMINIE

Sources P. Bultmann and W. A. Bultmann, 'Claude Groteste de la Mothe and the Church of England, 1685 to 1713', *Proceedings of the Huguenot Society of London*, 20 (1956–64), 89–101 · W. Turner, ed., *The Aufrère papers*, Huguenot Society quarto series, 40 (1940), esp. 75–112 · W. H. Manchée, 'Huguenot clergy list, 1548–1916', *Proceedings of the Huguenot Society of London*, 11 (1915–18), 263–92 · D. C. A. Agnew, *Protestant exiles from France, chiefly in the reign of Louis XIV, or, The Huguenot refugees and their descendants in Great Britain and Ireland*, 3rd edn, 2 vols. (1886), 239–41 · E. Haag and E. Haag, *La France protestante*, 10 vols. (Paris, 1846–59), vol. 5 · W. A. Shaw, ed., *Letters of denization and acts of naturalization for aliens in England and Ireland, 1603–1700*, Huguenot Society of London, 18 (1911), 198, 212 · W. Minet and S. Minet, eds., *Register of the church of Hungerford Market, later Castle Street*, Huguenot Society quarto series, 31 (1928), ix–xiii · W. Minet and S. Minet, eds., *Registers of the churches of the Chapel Royal, St James and Swallow Street*, Huguenot Society quarto series, 28 (1924), 14–15 · R. D. Gwynn, ed., *Minutes of the consistory of the French Church of London, Threadneedle Street, 1679–1692*, Huguenot Society quarto series, 58 (1994), 326

Archives BL, corresp., Stowe MS 223 | UCL, Huguenot Society Library, Aufrère papers, corresp.

Wealth at death property in England and France

La Motte, John (1577–1655), merchant, was born in Colchester on 1 May 1577, the son of Francis La Motte, a weaver and cloth merchant who had fled to the town in 1564 from Ypres in Flanders. Presumably he was apprenticed in his father's craft. By the second decade of the seventeenth century, during which he moved to London, he had become a highly successful merchant. In 1615 he was residing in the parish of St Bartholomew by the Exchange; by 1618 he lived in Broad Street and had become a freeman of the Weavers' Company. About this time he married Anne Tivelyn from the Dutch/Walloon community in Canterbury; the couple had two daughters, Hester and Elizabeth.

Initially La Motte joined his local parish church, and throughout his life he continued to attend godly lectures there. After having served as constable in 1619, he became church warden in 1621. Five years later he was elected an

John La Motte (1577–1655), by William Faithorne the elder, pubd 1656

died in Broad Street, London, on 13 July 1655 and was buried at St Bartholomew by the Exchange. By this time he owned the manors of Ramsey and Brudwell, in Essex, and lands at Fowlmer, in Cambridgeshire. His will, proved on 8 August 1655, divided his considerable estate, half going to his grandson Maurice Abbot, son of Elizabeth La Motte and Sir Maurice Abbot, and the other half to his surviving daughter, Hester, who had married Sir Thomas Honeywood, and her family and other relatives and friends. La Motte's deep concern for Christian charity, evident in his funeral sermon and in many donations during his lifetime to the Dutch community in London, was also reflected in his will. He left bequests for the inmates of Bridewell, of which he was a governor, and for the poor in Christ's Hospital; to the Dutch churches of London, Colchester, Sandwich, and Canterbury; and to the parishes of Fowlmer and St James, Colchester; as well as to the Weavers' Company. La Motte's piety and godliness impressed his contemporaries: while John Goodwin, minister of Coleman Street, had dedicated one of his early works to him, Samuel Clarke included him in his hagiography of great puritan men and women.

OLE PETER GRELL

Sources J. H. Hessels, ed., *Ecclesiae Londino-Batavae archivum*, 3 vols. (1887–97) · GL, MSS 7397/7 and 8 · F. Bellers, *Abrahams interment* (1656) · S. Clark [S. Clarke], *The lives of sundry eminent persons in this later age* (1683) · O. P. Grell, *Calvinist exiles in Tudor and Stuart England* (1996) · O. P. Grell, *Dutch Calvinists in early Stuart London: the Dutch church in Austin Friars, 1603–1642* (1989) · E. Freshfield, ed., *The vestry minute books of the parish of St. Bartholomew Exchange in the City of London, 1567–1676* (privately printed, London, 1890) · R. E. G. Kirk and E. F. Kirk, eds., *Returns of aliens dwelling in the city and suburbs of London, from the reign of Henry VIII to that of James I*, 4 vols., Huguenot Society of London, 10 (1900–08) · A. B. Beaven, ed., *The aldermen of the City of London, temp. Henry III–[1912]*, 1 (1908) · A. Plummer, *The London Weavers' Company, 1600–1970* (1972)
Likenesses W. Faithorne the elder, line engraving, BM, NPG; repro. in Bellers, *Abrahams interment* [see illus.]

Lampe, Geoffrey William Hugo

Lampe, Geoffrey William Hugo (1912–1980), theologian, was born at Southbourne on 13 August 1912, the only child of Bruno Hugo Lampe, musician, originally from Alsace, and his wife, Laura Mary Burton. From Blundell's School he won a scholarship to Exeter College, Oxford, where he achieved first-class honours in *literae humaniores* in 1935 and in theology in 1936. After training at Queen's College, Birmingham, he was ordained deacon in 1937 to serve as curate of Okehampton. Following ordination to the priesthood in 1938 he became assistant master and assistant chaplain of King's School, Canterbury (1938–41). In 1938 he married Elizabeth Enid, daughter of Arthur Griffith Roberts, a civil engineer. They had a son and a daughter. For the last four years of the Second World War he gave distinguished service as a chaplain to the forces, which led in 1945 to the award of the MC for bravery under fire.

The remainder of Lampe's career was spent in the work of theological teaching and research in three English universities: chaplain and fellow of St John's College, Oxford, until 1953; Edward Cadbury professor of theology in the University of Birmingham, 1953–9; Ely professor of divinity at Cambridge, 1959–70, and regius professor there

elder of the Dutch church in London, unusually without having first served the community as a deacon. By that time La Motte had become a widower, and in 1626 he married the extremely wealthy Elizabeth van Poele, widow of the former clerk of the signet, Sir Levinius Munk (*d.* 1623), who had been a prominent member of the London Dutch church. La Motte's business acumen and financially astute marriages guaranteed him a place among the London merchant élite, and in 1629 he was elected upper bailiff of the Weavers' Company. He was also able to play a leading part in one of the major charitable causes of his age, the collections for the Reformed refugees from the Rhine Palatinate, which commenced in England in 1628. Among his many business ventures was an interest in the East India Association, organized by another member of the Dutch church, Sir William Courten, to compete with the East India Company, and licensed in 1635. In this capacity he collaborated closely not only with a group of wealthy Dutch and Walloon merchants resident in London, but also with a group of 'new' English merchants in the City, of whom the most prominent was Maurice Thomson.

In March 1648 La Motte was elected an alderman of the City of London, but, pleading old age and infirmity, he was discharged the following month on payment of a fine of £600. Despite his frailty, he lived another seven years and continued to serve as an elder of the Dutch church. He

Geoffrey William Hugo Lampe (1912–1980), by unknown photographer

from 1970 until his retirement in 1979. He was a fellow of Gonville and Caius College from 1960. Academic honours were soon forthcoming: BD and DD of Oxford (1953), honorary DD of Edinburgh (1959), and FBA (1963). His three major publications reflect the range of his scholarly interests. *A Patristic Greek Lexicon*, an indispensable tool for all patristic scholars, on which work had started before he was born, was finally completed under his editorship and with substantial contributions from his own pen, appearing in five volumes between 1961 and 1968. But his interest was not primarily philological. *The Seal of the Spirit* (1951) is a detailed historical and doctrinal study of Christian initiation in the early church, a subject prompted not only by purely historical but also by contemporary pastoral concerns, arising out of his experience as an army chaplain. And in his Bampton lectures (1975–6), published as *God as Spirit* (1977), he once again drew on his extensive patristic learning to illuminate an even more central issue of contemporary debate, the Christian doctrine of God.

Lampe's scholarship, though detailed and precise, was never narrowly conceived. He was both a historian of doctrine and a theologian in the liberal tradition. He was not afraid to ask challenging and radical questions about traditional beliefs. At times, as with his broadcast Easter sermon in 1965, these gave rise to public controversy. But such questioning was always undertaken with the positive goal of making faith more real and more accessible in the world of today. The breadth of his interests was reflected in the wide range of ways in which he contributed to the life of the universities in which he worked, and of the wider church. For his last three years in Birmingham, for example, he was vice-principal of the university and at Cambridge he held office as chairman of the board of extramural studies. For many years he served as a proctor in convocation and as a member of the general synod of the Church of England. There his scholarship, his personal friendliness, and his evident concern for the furtherance of Christian faith in the ordinary life of the church ensured that he was always listened to with great attention and respect, even when he was advocating causes which were unacceptable to the majority of members. He was a passionate advocate of the ordination of women to the historic ministry of the church, and of increasing ecumenical co-operation between the churches. He was also the leading figure for many years in a series of Anglo-Scandinavian conferences, an activity recognized not only by an honorary doctorate of theology of the University of Lund in 1965 but also by his appointment as a commander of the Northern Star by the king of Sweden in 1978.

Lampe was a product of the old 'liberal evangelical' tradition in the Church of England, but was always a man of wide and catholic sympathies. He was a large man physically and the largeness of his physique matched the largeness of vision with which he approached the issues alike of scholarship and of life. He had a great gift for friendship, was a splendid raconteur, and could be the life and soul of a party. He never gave evidence of being anxious or in a hurry, however many the engagements or great the load of work that he had undertaken. His calmness and courage were never more unostentatiously but conspicuously displayed than in the way he faced critical illness in 1976 and 1978. In spite of that illness and the treatment it necessitated, the last years of his life were lived with undiminished zest and generosity until his death at Cambridge on 5 August 1980.   MAURICE WILES, *rev.*

Sources C. F. D. Moule, 'Geoffrey William Hugo Lampe, 1912–1980', *PBA*, 67 (1981), 399–409 · C. F. D. Moule, ed., *G. W. H. Lampe, Christian, scholar, churchman: a memoir by friends* (1982) · *The Times* (7 Aug 1980) · personal knowledge (1982) · *CGPLA Eng. & Wales* (1980)
Likenesses photograph, British Academy, London [*see illus.*]
Wealth at death £19,013: probate, 21 Nov 1980, *CGPLA Eng. & Wales*

Lampe, John Frederick (1702/3–1751), composer and bassoonist, of unknown parentage, was said to be a native of Saxony (Burney, *Hist. mus.*, 2.1001), and, according to his tombstone epitaph, was born in late 1702 or early 1703. Lampe's treatise *A Plain and Compendious Method of Teaching Thorough Bass* (1737) states he was 'Sometime Student at HELMSTAD in SAXONY'; he was therefore assumed to have been born in Helmstädt, but his birth is not recorded in Helmstädt archives. Record of Lampe's 1718 matriculation as a law student at the university there, however, links him to nearby Brunswick, and he has also been connected with St Catherine's School in that city. Nothing is known of his career before he arrived in London about 1725, when he became a bassoon player in the opera band. According to Burney, Handel had the first British contrabassoon made for Lampe to play for George II's 1727 coronation (Burney, *Account*, 'Introduction', 7).

The pantomime *Diana and Acteon* (1730), written for the Drury Lane dancing-master Roger, is the earliest theatre work attributed to Lampe. *Wit Musically Embellish'd* (1731), a collection of original ballads, was his first musical publication; in it he says that most of the songs were written for his students or patrons. The poet Henry Carey may have

John Frederick Lampe (1702/3–1751), by James Macardell (after S. Andrea)

numbered among those students (Hawkins, 2.895). In 1732, as part of a concerted English opera 'revival', Lampe set Carey's *Amelia* for the Little Theatre in the Haymarket. The following season Lampe wrote music for Thomas Lediard's masque-like *Britannia* and arranged John Gay's *Dione* and also Henry Fielding's *Tragedy of Tragedies* as *The Opera of Operas*. For the 1733–4 season he was employed at Drury Lane, where he achieved his first major success with the pantomime *Cupid and Psyche, or, Columbine Courtezan*. Theatre politics meant Lampe wrote little theatrical music from 1734 to 1737, and he instead completed his thorough-bass treatise.

In 1737 Lampe returned to the Haymarket Theatre with his enormously successful *Dragon of Wantley*, a burlesque opera by Carey. Reputedly a favourite with Handel and with George II, it was performed every season until Lampe's death and its popularity continued throughout the century, though its 1738 sequel, *Margery, or, A Worse Plague than the Dragon*, was less successful. The composer married his leading lady, Isabella *Young (*bap.* 1716?, *d.* 1795) [*see under* Young family], on 31 January 1737. Lampe continued to work in satirical and comic vein, writing music for pantomimes and mock operas such as *Pyramus and Thisbe* (1745). He wrote another treatise, *The Art of Musick* (1740), and composed many songs, published in the collections of others—such as *British Melody* (1739) and *The Musical Entertainer* (1737–40)—and in collections of his own, for instance *Lyra Britannica* (1741). Lampe's two hymn collections set to words by Charles Wesley demonstrate the Wesleys' influence on him from 1745 onwards. John Wesley's diary for 29 October 1745 reveals that Lampe 'had

been a deist for many years, till it pleased God, by the *Earnest Appeal*, to bring him to a better mind' (*Journal*, 3.226).

In September 1748 Lampe, Isabella, and a small company went to Dublin at Thomas Sheridan's invitation, where he conducted theatrical performances and concerts. Benjamin Victor called the musicians Sheridan's 'woeful Bargains', as 'the Tot of their Salaries … was near fourteen hundred Pounds a Year' (Victor, 1.143). In November 1750 Lampe moved to Edinburgh for a similar engagement at the Canongate Theatre. He died in Edinburgh on 25 July 1751, and was buried on 28 July in Canongate churchyard, where his monument predicted, somewhat over-optimistically, that his 'harmonious compositions shall outlive monumental registers, and, with melodious notes, through future ages, perpetuate his fame'.

SUZANNE ASPDEN

Sources D. R. Martin, *The operas and operatic style of J. F. Lampe* (1985) · G. W. Stone, ed., *The London stage, 1660–1800*, pt 4: *1747–1776* (1962) · C. B. Hogan, ed., *The London stage, 1660–1800*, pt 5: *1776–1800* (1968) · J. Hawkins, *A general history of the science and practice of music*, 5 vols. (1776); new edn, 3 vols. (1875) [repr. 1875–83] · Burney, *Hist. mus.*, new edn · B. Victor, *The history of the theatres of London and Dublin*, 2 vols. (1761) · O. E. Deutsch, *Handel: a documentary biography* (1955) · J. F. Lampe, *A plain and compendious method of teaching thorough bass* (1737) · Highfill, Burnim & Langhans, *BDA* · R. Fiske, 'Lampe, John Frederick', *New Grove* · *The journal of the Rev. John Wesley*, ed. N. Curnock and others, 8 vols. (1909–16) · C. Burney, *An account of the musical performances … in commemoration of Handel* (1785) · *Daily Post* [London] (8 Nov 1732)
Likenesses S. Andrea?, portrait; formerly priv. coll. [now lost] · J. Macardell, mezzotint (after S. Andrea), BM [*see illus.*]

Lamphire, John (1614–1688), college head and physician, was the son of George Lamphire, apothecary, of the parish of St Lawrence, Winchester. He entered Winchester College as a scholar in 1627, and on 19 August 1634 matriculated from New College, Oxford, where he was elected fellow in 1636, graduated BA in 1638, and proceeded MA in 1642. In 1640 he wrote Latin verses for an Oxford collection celebrating the birth of Prince Henry—the first of seven such contributions over the next thirty years. By the time the parliamentary visitors expelled him from his fellowship in 1648, he was college bursar. Through the 1650s, Lamphire practised as a physician in and around Oxford. Among the royalist wits who met at a city coffee house in 1655, he was, according to Anthony Wood (later his patient) 'sometimes the naturall droll of the company' (*Life and Times of Anthony Wood*, 1.201). In 1654 he was associated with the publication in Oxford of Hugh Lloyd's *Phrases elegantiores*.

In late April 1660 Lamphire was one of thirty-nine Oxfordshire royalists whose *Declaration* disavowed revenge. The restoration of his fellowship was ordered on 19 May by the House of Lords, and on 16 August he was elected Camden professor of history in succession to Lewis du Moulin. Six weeks later, on 30 October, he was created MD, and he continued to practise medicine, treating Anthony Wood's deafness. Lamphire's edition of his friend Thomas Masters's 1642 oration, *Monarchia Britannica sub Elizabetha, Jacobo*, appeared for the first time in 1661. On 2 September 1662 Clarendon appointed him principal of New Inn Hall, from where on 30 May 1663 he was translated to the headship of Hart Hall. When parliament went to Oxford in 1665 to escape plague it was at Lamphire's suggestion that the Commons moved that the university be thanked formally for its defiance of the parliamentary visitors in 1647.

Wood called Lamphire 'a public spirited man, but not fit to govern', being 'much given to his pleasures'; he 'layd out much on the Principal's lodgings' (*Life and Times of Anthony Wood*, 1.475, 2.56). As a justice of the peace, Lamphire improved Oxford's roads and drainage; he also corresponded with secretaries of state Joseph Williamson and Leoline Jenkins, exchanging gifts which included his bottled 'fountain water that has crossed the equinoctial line four times' without corruption and had a secret antiscorbutical ingredient (*CSP dom.*, 1676–7, 151–2). On 27 February 1679 his election as university MP was frustrated when 'the vice-chancellor shew'd himself false' (*Life and Times of Anthony Wood*, 2.443).

Lamphire was associated with further Oxford publications: Lancelot Andrewes's *Preces privatae* (1675), Robert Pinck's *Quaestiones* (1680), and Thomas Lydiat's *Canones chronologi* (1675), printed from Lamphire's twenty-two volumes of Lydiat manuscripts, part of his substantial manuscript collection. He died, unmarried, at Hart Hall on 30 March 1688 and was buried in New College chapel on 2 April. His will, dated 9 December 1681, provides for relatives, numerous friends, and various Oxford institutions; it includes books and manuscripts for the university library and £50 'towards the mending of the Heighway betwixt St. Clements Church and the bottom of Hiddington Hill'.   HUGH DE QUEHEN

Sources Wood, *Ath. Oxon.*, 2nd edn · *The life and times of Anthony Wood*, ed. A. Clark, 5 vols., OHS, 19, 21, 26, 30, 40 (1891–1900) · *Hist. U. Oxf. 4: 17th-cent. Oxf.* · F. Madan, *Oxford books: a bibliography of printed works*, 2–3 (1912–31) · S. G. Hamilton, *Hertford College* (1903) · Foster, *Alum. Oxon.* · T. F. Kirby, *Winchester scholars: a list of the wardens, fellows, and scholars of … Winchester College* (1888) · M. Burrows, ed., *The register of the visitors of the University of Oxford, from AD 1647 to AD 1658*, CS, new ser., 29 (1881) · A. Wood, *The history and antiquities of the colleges and halls in the University of Oxford*, ed. J. Gutch (1786) · will, proved 7 April 1688, Oxford

Lampitt, Leslie Herbert (1887–1957), food chemist, was born on 30 September 1887, at 27 Hutton Street, Aston, Warwickshire, the son of Daniel Lampitt, a vegetable salesman, and his wife, Eliza, *née* Haywood. He was educated at Birmingham Technical School and entered Birmingham University as a Priestley scholar in 1906, gaining a first-class honours degree in chemistry and biochemistry. This combination of subjects reflected the dual interests of his professor, P. F. Frankland. Scholarships enabled him to proceed to the degrees of MSc and DSc. On 6 October 1915 he married Edith Potter (*b.* 1888/9), daughter of George Potts; they had one son.

Lampitt's first appointment was as chief chemist to a flour mill in Brussels, La Meunerie Bruxelloise. When war was declared he immediately rejoined the Officers' Training Corps, to which he had belonged at university; he served in France throughout the war and reached the rank of major. Through a chance meeting with Montague Gluckstein, chairman of the catering firm J. Lyons & Co., he was invited to become its first chief chemist and to set up a laboratory for food testing and research. He accepted, and eventually became a director of the firm.

Lampitt's scientific work was particularly concerned with the hygienic protection and sterilization of foodstuffs. He examined the adulteration of honey, measured incipient rancidity, and devised new methods for estimation of trace metals (such as aluminium and copper) and of such organic contaminants as furfural in sugar. His early research into foodstuff composition ranged from fresh fruits to milk products. Studies on vitamin retention included analysis of vitamin C in potatoes, vegetables, and oranges (where much was shown to be concentrated in the peel). Lampitt's most important work related to the physico-chemical nature of the main components of starch, adding substantially to fundamental knowledge of that material.

In the inter-war years food scientists tended to be fairly isolated individuals and Lampitt saw the importance of scientific association, encouraging his staff to share his view. It is for his work with a variety of chemical organizations that he will probably be most remembered. He first made his mark in the Institute of Chemistry, becoming a fellow in 1920 and giving four terms of service on the council, starting in 1928. He was vice-president from 1942 to 1945. It was, however, the Society of Chemical Industry that engaged him most. In 1932 he founded a food group of the society and, from 1936, held continuous office until the day of his death, serving as treasurer (1936–46), president (1946–8), and foreign secretary (1948–57). In the last capacity he formed the first overseas section in 1952. He received the society's medal in 1943 and was the first recipient of its international medal in 1949. He was treasurer for the International Union of Pure and Applied Chemistry and, from 1938 to 1945, chairman of the Chemical Council, set up in 1935 to bring societies closer together.

Lampitt held tenaciously to the Christian faith, being a keen churchman and for many years vicar's warden of St Mary's Church, Harrow on the Hill, near his home, Thornlea, Mount Park, Harrow. He died of heart disease in the Hospital of St John and St Elizabeth in London on 3 June 1957; his wife survived him. The funeral sermon by Canon Edward Carpenter of Westminster paid tribute to his commitment to both science and Christianity.

COLIN A. RUSSELL

Sources E. B. Hughes, *Chemistry and Industry* (6 July 1957), 942–3 [incl. funeral address by Canon Edward Carpenter] · F. P. Dunn, *Proceedings of the Chemical Society* (1957), 366–7 · b. cert. · m. cert. · d. cert.
Likenesses photograph, repro. in Hughes, *Chemistry and Industry*
Wealth at death £37,099 18s. 2d.: probate, 15 Aug 1957, *CGPLA Eng. & Wales*

Lamplugh, Thomas (*bap.* 1615, *d.* 1691), archbishop of York, was the son of Christopher Lamplugh (*d.* in or before 1625) of Little Riston, Yorkshire, and his wife, Anne (1594/5–1661), daughter and coheir of Thomas Roper of

Octon in the East Riding of Yorkshire. There is an interpolation in the register of Lamplugh, Cumberland, dating Lamplugh's baptism as taking place on 13 June 1615, but he was probably born and baptized at Thwing in Octon. It appears that Lamplugh went to live with his uncle Thomas Lamplugh of Ribton Hall, Bridekirk, near Cockermouth in Cumberland, and he was sent to St Bees grammar school. He matriculated at Queen's College, Oxford, on 10 October 1634, aged sixteen, as the son of Thomas Lamplugh of Dovenby, Cumberland, but this entry has been altered with the original stating that he was the son of Christopher Lamplugh and aged nineteen. This alteration may be explained by the fact that Cumbrian students received privileges at Queen's which were not available to those from Yorkshire.

Lamplugh graduated BA on 4 July 1639 and proceeded MA on 1 November 1642, the same year in which he became a fellow of his college. Lamplugh survived the parliamentarian visitation in 1648, taking the covenant, but it seems that he used his weekly lectures each Sunday at St Martin's, Carfax, to uphold the doctrines of the Church of England where, according to Thomas Hearne, 'all the honest loyal men in Oxford came to hear him' (*Remarks*, 2.48). He also travelled to Bishop Robert Skinner's house at Launton to assist in the private ordination of Church of England clergymen. He proceeded BD on 23 July 1657, and became minister of Holy Rood, Southampton, according to his will 'the place where I first began to exercise my ministry publicly' (Jabez-Smith, 'Joseph Williamson and Thomas Lamplugh', 156–7). In 1659 he became rector of Binfield, Berkshire, and Charlton-on-Otmoor, Oxfordshire.

Following the Restoration, Lamplugh was able to show his true colours. He was named to the royal commission charged with reinstating ejected members of the university. He was created DD by royal mandate on 9 November 1660. Anthony Wood, for one, was unimpressed by Lamplugh's skill in retaining his fellowship, 'a great cringer formerly to Presbyterians and Independents, now to the prelates and those in authority' (*Life and Times*, 1.365). In 1661 Lamplugh was elected to convocation as a proctor by the Oxfordshire clergy. He was presented by the king on 3 July 1663 to the archdeaconry of Oxford, but the appointment was challenged by Thomas Barlow, who received a favourable verdict at the Oxford assizes in March 1664. On 9 November 1663 Lamplugh was licensed to marry Katherine (1633–1671), daughter of Dr Edward Davenant of Gillingham, Dorset. They had five children, three of whom predeceased their mother; one son, also Thomas, survived his father. The king then presented him to the archdeaconry of London, Lamplugh being collated on 27 May 1664. He also became rector of St Anthony's, London. He was admitted principal of St Alban Hall in August 1664, prompting Wood to comment that he had a wife and 'looked after preferment; neglected the Hall' (ibid., 2.19) during his nine-year tenure. He was incorporated at Cambridge University in 1668. He was presented to a prebend of Worcester by the king on 23 May 1669. On 1

July 1670 he was collated vicar of St Martin-in-the-Fields, London, remaining there until his elevation to the episcopate. In November 1672 a warrant was issued by the king for Lamplugh to be made dean of Rochester, and he was installed on 6 March 1673, a successor being presented in 1676.

On 3 October 1676 Lamplugh was elected bishop of Exeter, being consecrated on 12 November at Lambeth Palace. Lamplugh was a diligent diocesan, attending services in his cathedral and seeking to win over moderate dissenters to the church. Moreover he promoted the repair of parochial churches. He received a writ of summons for a seat in the House of Lords on 10 February 1677, where he supported the court, holding two proxies at the beginning of the October 1678 session. He delivered the 5 November sermon to the House of Lords in 1678, which was subsequently printed—his only publication. On 15 November he voted to add the test on transubstantiation to the oaths of allegiance and supremacy in the new Test Bill, thereby evincing his anti-Catholicism. He was also one of eleven peers on 29 November who supported an address from the Commons asking the king to remove the queen from Whitehall. Generally he supported the earl of Danby during this session of parliament. Lamplugh went on visitation in autumn 1679 and was very active in the tory reaction in his diocese, ordering the laws against dissenters, whether protestant or papist, to be put into execution. In April 1680 he reported to Archbishop Sancroft on the suppression of meeting-houses in his diocese. He voted in the Lords on 23 November 1680 against a joint committee with the Commons to consider the safety of the kingdoms.

Lamplugh was one of the few bishops to order James II's second declaration of indulgence to be read in his diocese in May 1688. However, on 28 May he added his signature to the seven bishops' petition for its withdrawal. Lamplugh left Exeter shortly before the prince of Orange arrived in November 1688, after exhorting his flock to remain loyal to King James. His return to London to wait on James resulted in his appointment to the archbishopric of York which had been vacant for over two years. He joined with Archbishop Sancroft and several other bishops on 17 November in petitioning James II for a free parliament. He was duly elected to the see of York on 28 November and was confirmed on 8 December 1688. Thus, following the king's initial flight from London, Lamplugh was a senior figure when the peers assembled on 11 December to oversee the government of the city. Indeed he was often the most senior peer present. On James II's return to London, Lamplugh was one of the bishops attending the king to negotiate concessions to the church. On the eve of the king's second departure Lamplugh said that 'if he saw His Majesty's face no more, he hoped that they should meet together in heaven' (Beddard, 60). However, he supported the request that Prince William take on the administration of the government until the Convention met.

Lamplugh voted for a regency on 29 January 1689 and opposed a motion on 31 January to declare William and

Mary monarchs. He voted on both 4 and 6 February against King James having abdicated the throne but he took the oaths to William and Mary on 4 March. On 11 April 1689 he assisted Bishop Compton in crowning the new monarchs. In the Lords, Lamplugh voted against the rehabilitation of Titus Oates in May and July 1689.

Lamplugh died at the archiepiscopal residence, Bishopthorpe, on 5 May 1691, and was buried in York Minster. His will of 2 May prayed for the end to breaches in the unity of the church 'that they may no longer rend and tear out the bowels of their tender indulgent but now sadly afflicted mother' (Jabez-Smith, 'Joseph Williamson and Thomas Lamplugh', 156-7). He remembered Dr Christopher Potter and Dr Gerard Langbaine, both provosts of Queen's College, with bequests to their sons. His son Thomas was his executor.   STUART HANDLEY

Sources Foster, *Alum. Oxon.* · A. R. Jabez-Smith, 'Joseph Williamson and Thomas Lamplugh', *Transactions of the Cumberland and Westmorland Antiquarian and Archaeological Society*, new ser., 86 (1986), 145-61 · S. Taylor, 'The family of Lamplugh of Lamplugh in Cumberland', *Transactions of the Cumberland and Westmorland Antiquarian and Archaeological Society*, new ser., 38 (1938), 102-18 · A. R. Jabez-Smith, 'An interpolation in a Lamplugh parish register', *Transactions of the Cumberland and Westmorland Antiquarian and Archaeological Society*, new ser., 61 (1961), 120-30 · Wood, *Ath. Oxon.*, new edn, 4.878-80 · *The life and times of Anthony Wood*, ed. A. Clark, 1-3, OHS, 19, 21, 26 (1891-4) · J. L. Chester and G. J. Armytage, eds., *Allegations for marriage licences issued from the faculty office of the archbishop of Canterbury at London, 1543 to 1869*, Harleian Society, 24 (1886), 74 · *Remarks and collections of Thomas Hearne*, ed. C. E. Doble and others, 11 vols., OHS, 2, 7, 13, 34, 42-3, 48, 50, 65, 67, 72 (1885-1921) · *Fasti Angl.* (Hardy), vol. 1 · *Fasti Angl., 1541-1857*, [St Paul's, London; Ely; Canterbury; York; Bristol] · R. Beddard, ed., *A kingdom without a king: the journal of the provisional government in the revolution of 1688* (1988) · R. Davis, 'The "presbyterian" opposition and the emergence of party in the House of Lords in the reign of Charles II', *Party management in parliament, 1660-1784*, ed. C. Jones (1984), 1-21 · E. Cruickshanks, D. Hayton, and C. Jones, 'Divisions in the House of Lords on the transfer of the crown and other issues, 1689-94', *BIHR*, 53 (1980), 56-87, esp. 87 · J. Spurr, *The Restoration Church of England, 1646-1689* (1991) · E. H. Plumptre, *The life of Thomas Ken*, 2 vols. (1888)
Archives Cumbria AS, Whitehaven, corresp. and papers · Queen's College, Oxford, corresp. and papers | Bodl. Oxf., corresp. with Sancroft, etc.
Likenesses G. Kneller, oils, 1689, Bishopthorpe Palace, York; versions, Queen's College, Oxford, York Art Gallery · G. Gibbons, standing effigy, 1691, York Minster · statue, *c*.1694, Queen's College, Oxford · portrait, Queen's College, Oxford; repro. in Jabez-Smith, 'Joseph Williamson', 147

Lamport, William [Guillén Lombardo] (**1611/1615-1659**), soldier and spy, was born in Wexford, Ireland, probably on 25 February 1615, although his brother affirmed that his birth was in 1611. He was the youngest of four children of Richard Lamport (*d.* 1636?), merchant and scion of a noble Catholic Anglo-Irish family, and his wife, Alfonsa Sutton (*d.* 1625?). He was educated first by the Augustinians and Franciscans in Wexford and by the Jesuits in Dublin. In 1628 he went to London to study, but was compelled to leave because of his political opinions and then became acquainted with a gang of pirates. He left his comrades in 1630 and fled to Santiago de Compostela, Spain, to study at

St Patrick's College, where he Hispanicized his name to Guillén Lombardo. Subsequently the duke of Olivares, chief minister of Philip IV, called him to the court of Spain. In 1632-3 he studied both at San Lorenzo in the Escorial and at San Isidro College, Madrid. In 1634-5 both Peter Paul Rubens and Anthony Van Dyck painted portraits in which he appeared as small and handsome with red hair and flashing eyes.

As a captain in the Spanish army Lamport fought at Nördlingen (1634) and Fuenterrabia (1638) against Swedish and French troops. After returning to Madrid, in 1639 he supported Richard Nugent's secret mission to get money and soldiers for rebellion in Ireland. The following year Olivares sent him to Mexico to spy on the new viceroy, Villena, whom he suspected of treason. He moved in the highest social circles, all the time collecting evidence against Villena. He became engaged to a rich heiress, Antonia Turcios, having left behind in Spain his mistress, Ana Cano y Leiva, and a daughter, Teresa. On 9 June 1642 Villena was arrested by Palafox, who became viceroy for a few months. During this period of disorder Lamport tried to overthrow Spanish rule with the help of former viceroy Cadereyta, whose wife, it is said, was probably his mistress. On 26 October Lamport was arrested by the Inquisition, which accused him of conspiring against Spain to liberate the American Indians and black slaves, and of attempting to set himself up as king of an independent Mexico.

Lamport spent seven years in prison, becoming a leader of the prisoners, who were mostly Jews or converted Jews. Helped by the new viceroy, Alba Aliste, and Palafox supporters he managed to escape from prison on 26 December 1650, but he remained in Mexico City. He denounced the crimes of the inquisitors and plastered the city walls at night with posters made by pasting cigarette papers together. Captured again after a few days he was gaoled for a further nine years. While in gaol he wrote many pamphlets in Spanish, attacking the Inquisition, and also almost one thousand beautiful psalms in Latin. Having apparently compromised his Catholicism he was condemned to burn at the stake in an *auto-da-fé* on 19 November 1659 at the plaza de l'Alameda, Mexico City, but before the fire was lit he managed to strangle himself to death with the rope used to tie him to the stake.

Lamport's fame survived his death: his deeds made him a hero in the eyes of the American Indians and the underprivileged and among the Franciscans. In 1872 Vicente Riva Palacio, a retired Mexican general, wrote a historical romance about him, *Memorias de un impostor*. In 1919 Johnston McCulley, a New York journalist, rewrote the tale, giving to the hero a new name, Diego Vega, alias Zorro. The following year saw the appearance of the first film featuring Zorro, *The Mark of Zorro*, starring Douglas Fairbanks; his characterization spawned many offshoots. Fairbanks played both father and son in *Don Q, the Son of Zorro* (1925). Tyrone Power remade the original story in *Mark of Zorro* (1940); Linda Sterling played a female Zorro in the 1944 serial, *Zorro's Black Whip*; Guy Williams starred in the popular

Walt Disney television series (1958–9); George Hamilton played in *Zorro the Gay Blade* (1981); Anthony Hopkins played the ageing Zorro, who teaches Antonio Banderas to become the new Zorro, in *Mask of Zorro* (1998).

FABIO TRONCARELLI

Sources Archivo General de la Nación, Mexico City, Inquisición, 1496–1497 · Archivo Histórico Nacional, Madrid, Inquisición, 1731, 53, 4 · L. González Obregón, *Rebeliones indígenas y precursores de la independencia Méxicana en los siglos XV, XVI, XVII* (Paris and Mexico, 1908) · [documents of Lombardo], Instituto Tecnologico, Monterrey, Nuevo León, Mexico, Biblioteca Cervantina · G. Méndez Plancarte, 'Don Guillén Lombardo y su "Regio Salterio"', *Abside*, 12 (1948), 125–92, 287–372 · F. Troncarelli, *La spada e la croce: Guillén Lombardo e l'Inquisizione in Messico* (Rome, 1999)
Archives Archivo General de la Nación, Mexico, Inquisición · Archivo Histórico Nacional, Madrid, Inquisición, 1731, 53, 4 | Archivio Vaticano, Vatican City, Congregazione Riti, *Processi* 2129 B1S · Biblioteca Cervantina, Monterrey, Nuevo León, MS · National University of Ireland, Maynooth, Salamanca archives, S/33/1/15
Likenesses P. P. Rubens, oils, 1634–5, Timken Museum, San Diego, California · A. Van Dyck, oil sketch, 1634–5, Szépművézseti Museum, Budapest

Lampson, Sir Curtis Miranda, first baronet (1806–1885), fur merchant and telegraph cable promoter, the fourth son of William Lampson of Newhaven, Vermont, USA, and his wife, Rachel, daughter of George Powell of Louisborough, Massachusetts, was born in Newhaven, Vermont, on 21 September 1806. He worked first as a clerk in a store in Newhaven, before moving to New York in 1825. He married on 30 November 1827, in New York, Jane Walter, youngest daughter of Gibbs Sibley of Sutton, Massachusetts; they raised three sons and one daughter, Hannah Jane, who married Frederick Locker-Lampson. The eldest son, George Curtis (1833–1899), became second baronet. He moved to England in 1830, and set up in business as a fur merchant, in Friday Street, in the City of London. He was afterwards senior partner in the firm of C. M. Lampson & Co. at 9 Queen Street Place, Upper Thames Street, London. On 14 May 1849 he was naturalized a British subject. On the formation of the company for laying the Atlantic telegraph cable in 1856, he was appointed one of the directors, and soon after vice-chairman. For ten years he devoted much time to its organization. The great aid he rendered was acknowledged in a letter from Lord Derby to Sir Stafford Northcote, who presided at a banquet given at Liverpool, on 1 October 1866, in honour of those who had been active in laying the cable, and on 16 November Lampson was created a baronet of the United Kingdom. He was deputy governor of the Hudson's Bay Company, and one of the trustees of the fund that was given by his friend George Peabody for the benefit of the poor of London. Shortly before his death he was elected to the Athenaeum in recognition of his distinguished service.

He died at his London house, 80 Eaton Square, Westminster, on 12 March 1885; the value of his personalty in England was sworn at around £400,000.

G. C. BOASE, *rev.* ANITA McCONNELL

Sources *The Times* (13 March 1885), 10a · *ILN* (21 March 1885), 300 · *ILN* (8 Dec 1866), 545, 558 · J. G. Wilson and J. Fiske, eds., *Appleton's cyclopaedia of American biography*, 3 (1887), 602 · trade directories, London · *DAB*
Archives Yale U., Beinecke L., corresp. with Frederick Locker and Hannah Locker
Likenesses wood-engraving (after photograph by Mayall), NPG; repro. in *ILN* (8 Dec 1866), 545
Wealth at death £397,022 2s. 10d.: resworn probate, Feb 1886, CGPLA Eng. & Wales (1885)

Lampson, Frederick Locker- [*known as* Frederick Locker] (1821–1895), poet, was born on 29 May 1821 at the Royal Naval Hospital, Greenwich, Kent, where his father, Edward Hawke *Locker (1777–1849), held the office of civil commissioner, an appointment gained in part through Frederick's grandfather William Locker, a naval captain and friend of William IV. His mother, Eleanor Mary Elizabeth Boucher (1793?–1861), was the daughter of the Revd Jonathan *Boucher, vicar of Epsom, Surrey, a book collector and a former friend of George Washington. Frederick was the third child, and a younger brother was the novelist Arthur *Locker (1828–1893). All were raised to revere their illustrious seafaring heritage, and were regaled with tales of Nelson over dinner, and surrounded by books and maps.

Frederick was sociable, if not quick—at the age of nine he could not yet read—so rather than attend Eton College, his father's school, he pursued a nondescript education at various schools—at Clapham in London, at Yateley in Hampshire, at Greenwich, and elsewhere—before becoming, on 18 September 1837, a junior clerk in a colonial broker's office in Mincing Lane in London. He followed this uncongenial calling for some years. Then, on 30 March 1841, he obtained from Lord Minto, first lord of the Admiralty and son of the governor-general of Bengal, a temporary clerkship in Somerset House. On 12 November 1842 he was transferred to the Admiralty, as a junior in Lord Haddington's private office, and he subsequently became deputy reader and précis writer, which he enlivened by his ready wit and poetry. A rhyming version of a petition from an importunate lieutenant seems to have sent Lord Haddington into ecstasies, and Locker continued his career under Sir James Graham and Sir Charles Wood until ill health gained him a leave of absence on 23 May 1849, after which he toured the continent.

On 4 July 1850 Locker made a brilliant match in Paris with Lady Charlotte Christian Bruce (d. 1872), a daughter of Thomas *Bruce, seventh earl of Elgin, who brought the Elgin marbles to England. Along with giving him an entrée to royal circles—he and his wife used to summer at Frogmore, as Lady Charlotte was friendly with Queen Victoria—his marriage enabled him to quit government service, and in 1857 he published, with Chapman and Hall, his first collection of verse, *London Lyrics*, a small volume of ninety pages, which, under its various editions and revisions, constitutes his poetical legacy. Ironically, he had trouble having editors respond to his poetry, but he had an ally in Thackeray, who once told him 'I have a sixpenny talent (or gift), and so have you; ours is small-beer, but, you see, it is the right tap' (Locker-Lampson, *My Confidences*,

Frederick Locker-Lampson (1821–1895), by Julia Margaret Cameron, c.1867

300). A second issue appeared in 1862, and in 1865 Moxon included a selection from its pages in *Miniature Poets*, illustrated by Richard Doyle. In 1868 another issue was privately printed for John Wilson of Great Russell Street, with a frontispiece by George Cruikshank. Eight further editions appeared between 1870 and 1893. In the United States *London Lyrics* was printed in 1883 for the Book Fellows' Club of New York, with some fresh illustrations by Randolph Caldecott; and in 1895 the Rowfant Club of Cleveland, Ohio, named from Locker's home in Sussex, put forth a rare little volume of his verse, chosen by Locker himself, entitled *Rowfant Rhymes*. The latter includes a preface by Austin Dobson and a poem by Robert Louis Stevenson. More reprints were put forward throughout the twentieth century, assuring Locker a place in England's literary history.

London Lyrics was not Locker's only work, and in 1867 he published the anthology *Lyra elegantiarum*, composed of specimens of *vers de société* and *vers d'occasion* gleaned from his ample experiences of high society. Although chronic ill health and dyspepsia made it impossible for him to follow any active calling, they did not prevent him from being a member of several clubs or enjoying the friendship of many distinguished people. Along with Thackeray, he was on intimate terms with Anthony Trollope, Tennyson, Lord Houghton, Lord Lytton, George Eliot, Dickens, Robert and Elizabeth Barrett Browning, Alexander William Kinglake, George Cruikshank, Alphonse de Lamartine, Franz Liszt, George Du Maurier, the royal family, and the shah of Persia, and he took great pains to see them

introduced to his daughter Eleanor, who married Tennyson's son Lionel in 1878. In the meantime Lady Charlotte had died on 26 April 1872, and she was buried at Kensal Green. On 6 July 1874 Locker married his second wife, the children's writer Hannah Jane Lampson, the only daughter of Sir Curtis Miranda *Lampson, first baronet (1806–1885), of Rowfant, Sussex, and he took the Lampson name in order to succeed to the family estate in 1885. At this time his wife was a more prolific writer than Locker, who was caught up in *London Lyrics*, but he did publish *Patchwork* in 1879.

Locker's general characteristics are well summed up by his son-in-law, Augustine Birrell KC, who became his principal biographer. Birrell said that Locker was 'essentially a man of the world; he devoted his leisure hours to studying the various sides of human nature, and drawing the good that he could out of all sorts and conditions of men' (Birrell, appendix to *The Rowfant Library, a Catalogue*). As a poet he belonged to the school of Matthew Prior, Winthrop Mackworth Praed, and Thomas Hood. His chief endeavour, he said, was to avoid flatness and tedium, to cultivate directness and simplicity both in language and idea, and to preserve individuality without oddity or affectation. Thus, his work is always neat and clear, restrained in its art, and refined in its tone. Many of these characteristics may be glimpsed in the writings of his son, Godfrey Locker-Lampson, the eldest child of his second marriage. Oliver Locker-Lampson (1880–1954), his second son, became a commander in the Royal Navy, a war hero, and a member of parliament.

Locker lived out his last years at his home, Rowfant, with his wife and children—for along with Godfrey and Oliver he had two more children, his daughters Dorothy and Maud—and it was for them that he wrote *My Confidences*, a mix of genealogy and reminiscences of famous people which was published by Birrell after Locker died. Birrell also put together a catalogue of his books, once known as the 'Rowfant library'. The catalogue comprises, in addition to its record of rare Elizabethan and other volumes, many interesting personal and bibliographical memoranda which he had collected, along with his Louis XVI furniture, old masters, Chinese porcelain, and east Asian antiques. After Locker's death at Rowfant on 30 May 1895, an appendix to the *Rowfant Library* was issued, but the library itself was sold to an American bookseller in 1905 and dispersed.

AUSTIN DOBSON, *rev.* KATHARINE CHUBBUCK

Sources F. Locker-Lampson, *My confidences: an autobiographical sketch addressed to my descendants*, ed. A. Birrell, 2nd edn (1896) · A. Birrell, *Frederick Locker-Lampson: a character sketch* (1920) · J. B. Matthews, 'Frederick Locker', *Century Magazine*, 25 (1883), 594–8 · A. H. Miles, 'Frederick Locker-Lampson', *The poets and the poetry of the century*, ed. A. H. Miles, 9 (1894), 423–4 · A. Birrell, 'Frederick Locker', *Scribner's Magazine*, 19 (Jan 1896), 39–44 · B. Perrett and A. Lord, *The czar's British squadron: the story of Oliver Locker-Lampson* (1981) · *CGPLA Eng. & Wales* (1895) · F. Locker-Lampson, *The Rowfant Library, a catalogue* (1886) [with an appx by A. Birrell]

Archives BL, letters, Ashley B 3594–3595 · Harvard U., Houghton L., corresp. · Hunt. L., diaries, letters · Ransom HRC, corresp. · Yale U., Beinecke L., corresp. and papers | BL, letters to Royal Literary Fund, loan 96 · Bodl. Oxf., letters to Bertram Dobell · CUL, letters to marquess of Crewe • Harvard U., Houghton L., letters to Austin Dobson • JRL, corresp. with John Leicester Warren • Lincoln Central Library, letters to Emily, Lady Tennyson • LUL, letters to Austin Dobson • Mitchell L., Glas., Glasgow City Archives, letters to Sir William Stirling-Maxwell • NA Scot., letters to earl of Rosslyn and countess of Rosslyn • NL Scot., letters to Blackwoods • St John Cam., letters to James Sylvester • Trinity Cam., letters to Lord Haughton

Likenesses J. M. Cameron, photograph, c.1867, NPG [see illus.] • G. Du Maurier, pen-and-ink drawing, repro. in F. Locker–Lampson, *London lyrics* (1857) • J. Millais, etching, repro. in *Moxon's Miniature poets*, ed. J. B. Payne, 10 vols. (1865–9) • C. W. Sherborn, etching (after G. Du Maurier), BM • etching (after J. Millais?), NPG • photograph, repro. in Locker-Lampson, *My confidences*

Wealth at death £30,419 14s. 2d.: probate, 1 July 1895, *CGPLA Eng. & Wales*

Lampson, Miles Wedderburn, first Baron Killearn (1880–1964), diplomatist, was born at Killearn, Stirlingshire, on 24 August 1880, the second among the four sons and the fourth among the six children of Norman George Lampson (1850–1894), justice of the peace for Surrey and London, and his wife, Helen Agnes (d. 1929), the fourth daughter of Peter Blackburn (1811–1870), Peelite MP for Stirlingshire from 1855 to 1865. Sir Curtis Miranda *Lampson, first baronet, promoter of the Atlantic cable, was his grandfather, and Colin *Blackburn, Baron Blackburn of Killearn, lord of appeal in ordinary, was his great-uncle. Educated at Eton College from 1894 to 1898, Lampson entered the Foreign Office as a clerk in March 1903. He was secretary to Prince Arthur of Connaught's garter mission to Japan in 1906, and served as second secretary at Tokyo from September 1908 to December 1910. He then had a spell as second secretary at Sofia, from October 1911 to January 1912. On 6 July 1912 he married Rachel Mary Hele Phipps (d. 1930), the younger daughter of William Wilton Phipps, of Chelsea. They had two daughters and a son.

Lampson returned to Tokyo with Prince Arthur of Connaught's special mission for the funeral of Emperor Meiji from August to September 1912. After a period in London he was posted as first secretary to Peking (Beijing), where he served from September 1916 to April 1920. During this appointment he was from November 1919 to February 1920 acting high commissioner in Siberia. His time in Siberia was brief but interesting, coinciding with the collapse of the White regime of Admiral Kolchak. Lampson acquitted himself well in difficult circumstances, and his performance earned the commendation of Lord Curzon, the foreign secretary. He then spent the early 1920s at the Foreign Office. He was a member of the British delegation to the Washington conference from October 1921 to February 1922, after which he became head of the central European department. In October 1925 he was a member of the British delegation at Locarno, where his work impressed the foreign secretary, Sir Austen Chamberlain. Promoted counsellor in January 1922, he was appointed CMG in 1922 and CB in 1926.

In October 1926 Lampson was sent as minister to Peking, a post he held until December 1933. It was a fascinating time to be in China. The state of Chinese domestic politics was, to put it mildly, turbulent, with an aggressively anti-foreign nationalist mood prevailing in the country. To

Miles Wedderburn Lampson, first Baron Killearn (1880–1964), by Vandyk, 1953 [with his daughters Jacquetta and Roxana]

complicate the situation, there was a brief war with the Soviet Union in 1929, and the Japanese seized Manchuria in 1931–2. There was a further crisis following the Japanese attack at Shanghai in 1932. Lampson (who was knighted KCMG in 1927) was in the thick of all this, for until 1931 Great Britain, the premier imperialist power, was the main target of the anti-foreign nationalism. He was involved in almost five years of continuous negotiations with the Chinese government, on the return of territorial concessions, on tariff reform, and on extraterritoriality. Some issues remained unresolved, but considerable progress was made by the time the Manchurian crisis erupted in September 1931. Lampson must take considerable credit for this. His approach to the Chinese was pragmatic. At the beginning of his time in China he wrote to Chamberlain saying how he proposed to proceed in his negotiations with the Chinese government: '1. To be fair. 2. To be firm when you are in the right. 3. To show them that you are in a position to be firm if they drive you too far' (Lampson to Austen Chamberlain, 26 Dec 1926, priv. coll.). These principles characterized his performance in China, and were later to guide him when he moved to Egypt. The high point of Lampson's time in China was his handling of the Shanghai crisis in 1932. He was at the centre of three months of complicated negotiations, and it was the combination of patience, tact, and firmness he displayed that was vital to the achievement of a settlement in May 1932. Arguably it was his finest hour as a diplomatist.

Lampson's years in China were marred by the death of his first wife, Rachel, in January 1930. Nevertheless he found happiness in his second marriage, on 18 December 1934, to Jacqueline Aldine Leslie Castellani, the only daughter of Professor Marchese Count Aldo Castellani, a bacteriologist and parasitologist. They had a son and two daughters.

In December 1933 Lampson was appointed high commissioner for Egypt and the Sudan, where he remained for twelve and a half years. It was a case of out of the Chinese frying pan and into the Middle-Eastern fire. The British representative in Cairo had to cope with rising nationalism and anti-British agitation in Egypt, irreconcilable differences over the future of the Sudan, and the vagaries of the young and temperamental King Farouk. The situation became even more troubled and the outlook bleaker with the outbreak of the Second World War in September 1939 and the Italian declaration of war in June 1940, and the serious threat to Britain's position in Egypt and the Middle East posed first by the Italians and then by Rommel. It changed for the better with the victory at El Alamein in November 1942. Lampson's part in all this was crucial to maintaining British interests. He had a key role in the conclusion of the Anglo-Egyptian treaty of alliance in August 1936. Following the conclusion of the treaty, Egypt became independent and Lampson became the first British ambassador; he was promoted GCMG in 1937. The treaty set relations on a new course and withstood the stresses of the critical war years from 1939 onwards. During the war it was Lampson's steadfastness and determination that ensured a stable base in Egypt. His most controversial action came in February 1942 when, supported by an armed escort, he drove to the Abdin Palace and delivered an ultimatum to Farouk to recall the Wafd leader Nahas Pasha to office or to abdicate. Farouk chose the former course. Historians have argued about the correctness of Lampson's action and about its longer-term effects on Anglo-Egyptian relations, but it resolved the immediate crisis and ensured stability in the crucial months before El Alamein. Lampson was sworn of the privy council in 1941 and raised to the peerage as Baron Killearn of Killearn in 1943.

In March 1946 Killearn was appointed special commissioner in south-east Asia, based at Singapore. This was an emergency post, created to cope with the problems arising after the Japanese surrender. In his two years there Killearn played a key role in overcoming a critical food crisis throughout the region, and played a part in the negotiations between the Dutch and the Indonesians that led to the Linggajati agreement of November 1946 and its eventual ratification in March 1947. He retired in May 1948.

Lampson seemed to have a talent for holding particularly interesting and difficult posts, and for being present when big or at least unusual things were happening: Siberia in an armoured train in 1919; the Washington conference; Locarno; China in the turmoil of the nationalist revolution and the onset of Japanese aggression; Egypt with all the drama and danger of the desert campaigns from 1940 to 1943; and finally Singapore with south-east Asia in

post-1945 chaos. It is clear from his diaries and correspondence that he enjoyed a crisis. As he put it to Walford Selby in February 1932, while *en route* for Shanghai to sort out the crisis there: 'I would not have missed this business for anything in the world' (Lampson to Selby, 10 Feb 1932, priv. coll.). He was considered for other high offices, notably ambassador to Berlin and to Washington in the late 1930s, and viceroy of India in 1943. It is intriguing to speculate what might have happened had he gone to Berlin instead of Nevile Henderson, or to India instead of Wavell.

Physically Lampson was a very big man—over 6 feet 5 inches tall and weighing 18 stone—and he had an undoubted presence. To the Chinese he was the man-mountain unmoved by a hundred cups of rice wine. An outstanding negotiator, he was undaunted in handling critics, adversaries, and menacing situations. He was a man of enormous energy, a great worker, and a great player. Whatever the crisis, however long and wearisome the hours of negotiation, he would find time for golf, racing, shooting, collecting Chinese porcelain, and an evening game of bridge. After his retirement, he attended the House of Lords regularly. He died at the Royal East Sussex Hospital, Hastings, on 18 September 1964, survived by his second wife, Jacqueline, and his six children. He was succeeded as second baron by the son of his first marriage, Graham Curtis Lampson (1919–1996), who in turn was succeeded by his half-brother (Lampson's son from his second marriage), Victor Miles George Aldous Lampson (*b.* 1941). DAVID STEEDS

Sources DNB · M.W. Lampson, first Baron Killearn, diaries, 1926–48, St Ant. Oxf., Middle East Centre, GB165-0176 · *The Killearn diaries, 1934–1946*, ed. T. E. Evans (1972) · T. E. Evans, *Mission to Egypt, 1934–46* (1971) · D. Steeds, 'The British approach to China during the Lampson period, 1926–1933', *Some foreign attitudes to republican China*, ed. I. Nish (1980), 26–51 · N. Tarling, '"Some rather nebulous capacity": Lord Killearn's appointment in southeast Asia', *Modern Asian Studies*, 20 (1986), 559–600 · D. Steeds, '"The ending of a highly discreditable enterprise": Miles Lampson in Siberia, 1919–20', *The Russian problem in East Asia*, ed. I. Nish (1981), 1–26 · *The Times* (19 Sept 1964) · *The Times* (22 Sept 1964) · *The Times* (23 Sept 1964) · *The Times* (24 Sept 1964) · Burke, *Peerage* · WWW · FO List (–1949) · CGPLA Eng. & Wales (1965)
Archives Bodl. RH, papers · priv. coll., papers relating to service in Peking · St Ant. Oxf., Middle East Centre, diaries | U. Durham L., letters to Sir Harold MacMichael | FILM BFI NFTVA, documentary footage · BFI NFTVA, news footage
Likenesses W. Stoneman, photograph, 1918, NPG · Vandyk, photograph, 1953, NPG [*see illus.*] · C. Beaton, photograph, NPG · photograph, repro. in *The Times* (19 Sept 1964) · photographs, Hult. Arch.
Wealth at death £57,603: probate, 15 Sept 1965, *CGPLA Eng. & Wales*

Lancashire witches. *See* Pendle witches (*act.* 1612).

Lancaster. For this title name *see* Edmund, first earl of Lancaster and first earl of Leicester (1245–1296); Thomas of Lancaster, second earl of Lancaster, second earl of Leicester, and earl of Lincoln (*c.*1278–1322); Henry of Lancaster, third earl of Lancaster and third earl of Leicester (*c.*1280–1345); Lacy, Alice, *suo jure* countess of Lincoln, and countess of Lancaster and Leicester (1281–1348) [*see under*

Thomas of Lancaster, second earl of Lancaster, second earl of Leicester, and earl of Lincoln (c.1278–1322)]; Henry of Lancaster, first duke of Lancaster (c.1310–1361]; John, duke of Aquitaine and duke of Lancaster, styled king of Castile and León (1340–1399); Blanche of Lancaster (1346?–1368) [see under John, duke of Aquitaine and duke of Lancaster, styled king of Castile and León (1340–1399)]; Katherine, duchess of Lancaster (1350?–1403).

Lancaster, Charles William (1820–1878), gun maker, the eldest son of Charles Lancaster, a gun maker, of 151 New Bond Street, London, and his wife, Mary, née Warrington, was born at 5 York Street, Portman Square, London, on 24 June 1820. He was educated at a private school and left at an early age to enter his father's factory, where he learned the business of a gun maker, and soon became a clever designer of models and a competent mechanic. The study of rifled projectiles and the construction of rifles was his chief pleasure, and he soon attained the highest skill as a rifle shot.

In 1846 Lancaster constructed a model rifle, with which he conducted successful experiments at Woolwich over distances of 1000 and 1200 yards; the duke of Wellington then ordered some similar guns for the rifle brigade at the Cape of Good Hope. During 1844 and 1845 Lancaster devoted himself to solving the problem of rifled cannon. In July 1846 he submitted to the Board of Ordnance a plan for firing smooth-sided conical projectiles from rifled cannon, and imparting the necessary rotatory motion by modifying the form of the base of the projectile. Further experiments, however, did not encourage him to go on with this scheme. In 1850 he conceived the idea of the oval bore as the proper form for all rifled arms and cannon, and his name will always be associated with this system. In order to make his invention known, he constructed full-size working models of the 68-pounder, the largest gun then in the service, for the Great Exhibition of 1851. At the request of the government these models were not exhibited, but a 68-pounder oval-bore gun, made and rifled at Birmingham, with accurately turned shells, was sent to Shoeburyness for trial. The shooting of this gun directed attention to the oval-bore system, and Lancaster assisted the war department with subsequent experiments made at Woolwich, and for some time superintended production of the guns in the Royal Arsenal. He was elected an associate of the Institution of Civil Engineers on 6 April 1852, and wrote a paper, in their *Minutes of Proceedings* (40.115), 'On the erosion of the bore in heavy guns'.

In 1852 Lancaster experimented upon the .577 pattern Enfield rifled musket, and some carbines bored to his own specification were sent to the School of Musketry at Hythe, and found to be effective. In January 1855 the Lancaster carbine was adopted as the arm for the Royal Engineers, and was used by that corps until it was superseded by the Martini-Henry rifle in 1869. During the Crimean campaign oval-bored rifle cannon were used and did good service; they were, it is said, the first rifled guns used in active service by the army and navy. Shortly after the war heavier guns were required for armour piercing, and experiments

carried out at Shoeburyness, in which Lancaster assisted, led to a complete revolution in rifled artillery. For the oval-bore system of rifling he received £4000 from the government in 1867. His transactions with the War Office, however, led to disputes, and he set out his grievances in a pamphlet. Between 1852 and 1860 he had received awards totalling £16,600 but considered these sums an inadequate reward for his services. Lancaster took out upwards of twenty patents, chiefly in connection with firearms, between 1850 and 1872. His last invention was a gas-check, applicable to large rifled projectiles. He travelled much in Russia, where the tsar had a special gold medal of large size struck in his honour.

In 1868 Lancaster married Ellen, daughter of George Edward Thorne and Ann Thorne of Old Stratford, Northamptonshire; they had two daughters. While making arrangements for retiring from business Lancaster was seized with paralysis, and died at his house, 11 Redcliffe Road, Brompton, west London, on 24 April 1878. His wife survived him.   G. C. BOASE, rev. ANITA MCCONNELL

Sources PICE, 53 (1877–8), 289–92 · Sporting Mirror, 3 (1882), 21–2 · Globe Encyclopedia, 5 (1879), 379 · 'Report of Major-General Harding … on the building erected for the Lancaster shot manufactory', Parl. papers (1854–5), 32.683, no. 396 · 'Return of amount of public money advanced … for experiments', Parl. papers (1860), 41.657, no. 386 [weapons of war] · 'Ordnance select committee on the trials in firing shot from … competition guns', Parl. papers (1865), 32.707, no. 459 · private information (1892)
Wealth at death under £10,000: resworn administration with will, March 1879, CGPLA Eng. & Wales (1878)

Lancaster, Elizabeth of. See Elizabeth of Lancaster (1364?–1425).

Lancaster, Henry of. See Henry of Lancaster (c.1280–1345); Henry of Lancaster (c.1310–1361).

Lancaster, Henry Hill (1829–1875), essayist and advocate, born on 10 January 1829 at Glasgow, was the son of Thomas Lancaster, a Glasgow merchant, and his wife, Jane, née Kelly. He was educated first at the high school, Glasgow, and afterwards at Glasgow University. A distinguished student, he proceeded in 1849 as a Snell exhibitioner to Balliol College, Oxford. In 1853 he obtained a first class in *literae humaniores* as well as third class honours in the new school of law and modern history, and in the following year he was awarded the Arnold prize for an essay on 'The benefits arising from the union of England and Scotland in the reign of Queen Anne'. He graduated BA in 1853 and MA in 1872. He settled in Edinburgh on leaving Oxford, passed as an advocate there in 1858, and proved himself an able and industrious lawyer. He defended the university in *Jex Blake v. the University of Edinburgh*, and *The Athenaeum* in the action brought against that journal by Keith Johnston. In 1862 he married Margaret (b. 1836/7), daughter of John Graham of Skelmorlie Castle, Ayrshire, and his wife, Elizabeth; they had at least one son and two daughters.

During Gladstone's first government (1868 to 1874) Lancaster was advocate-depute. He took an active interest in the cause of education. In 1858 he served as secretary to a commission of inquiry into the state of King's and Marischal colleges, Aberdeen; and in 1872 was a member of a royal commission on Scottish educational establishments.

In his leisure Lancaster contributed to the daily Edinburgh press, and in November 1860 he began a connection with the *North British Review* with an article on 'Lord Macaulay's place in English literature'. He took a strong interest in Scottish political history, and was a contributor on that subject for the *Edinburgh Review*. He died suddenly from apoplexy, on 24 December 1875, at 5 Ainslie Place, Edinburgh. In 1876 his more important essays were reprinted privately in two volumes, with a prefatory notice by Benjamin Jowett, and many were published as *Essays and Reviews* (1876). His son, Thomas Harvey Lancaster, was rector of Edinburgh Academy.

T. B. SAUNDERS, *rev.* H. C. G. MATTHEW

Sources The Scotsman (25 Dec 1875) · The Athenaeum (1 Jan 1876), 24–5 · Journal of Jurisprudence, 20 (1876), 107 · Boase, Mod. Eng. biog. · m. cert. · d. cert. · CGPLA Eng. & Wales (1876)
Wealth at death £5984 19s. 7d.: confirmation, 4 July 1876, CCI

Lancaster, Hume (d. 1850), marine painter, was born to unknown parents. Many of his paintings, which were often executed on a large scale, show the coasts of France, the Netherlands, and south England, and views of the Scheldt River in Belgium. From 1836 to 1849 he exhibited paintings at the Royal Academy, the British Institution, and the Society of British Artists, of which he was elected a member in 1841. On 30 December 1834 Lancaster married Dinah Flood, painter, at the church of St John the Evangelist, Lambeth, London. Their son, Henry Hume Lancaster, was baptized on 20 May 1843 at St Pancras Old Church, London. Dinah Lancaster exhibited a landscape at the British Institution in 1840. Some of Hume Lancaster's pictures were engraved in the prize annual of the Art Union of London for 1848. Although his talent was undisputed, Lancaster made little money from his work. He was living in poverty and without appropriate recognition when he died at Erith in Kent on 3 July 1850.

L. H. CUST, *rev.* L. R. HOULISTON

Sources Art Journal, 12 (1850), 240 · M. H. Grant, A dictionary of British landscape painters, from the 16th century to the early 20th century (1952) · D. Brook-Hart, British 19th-century marine painting (1974) · Wood, Vic. painters, 3rd edn · J. Johnson, ed., Works exhibited at the Royal Society of British Artists, 1824–1893, and the New English Art Club, 1888–1917, 2 vols. (1975), 276–7 · Graves, RA exhibitors · Graves, Brit. Inst. · Redgrave, Artists · Bryan, Painters · Graves, Artists · S. W. Fisher, A dictionary of watercolour painters, 1750–1900 (1972) · D. T. Mallett, Mallett's index of artists (1935) · IGI

Lancaster, Isabel of. *See* Isabel of Lancaster (d. 1349).

Lancaster, Sir James (1554/5–1618), merchant, was one of at least three sons of James Lancaster of Basingstoke. He was born at Basingstoke and brought up among the Portuguese, as a gentleman, soldier, and merchant. He returned to England before February 1587 and in 1588 commanded the *Edward Bonaventure*, a merchant ship of 250 tons, serving in the fleet against the Armada. He commanded the same ship in the first English voyage to the East Indies

with George Raymond as general in the *Penelope* and Samuel Foxcroft in the *Merchant Royal*. They left Plymouth on 10 April 1591, were becalmed for nearly a month in the doldrums, and reached Table Bay on 1 August, the first English ships to use the roadstead. Losses from scurvy had been such that the *Merchant Royal* was sent home to allow adequate manning of the other ships. A few days after rounding the Cape the *Penelope* was lost with all hands in a storm. In another storm four men were killed and many injured by lightning. In an affray at the Comoros they lost the master, some thirty men, and their boat. After refitting at Zanzibar they made a difficult voyage to Penang, losing many men from sickness. They put to sea again on 1 September, plundered three ships, and called at Junkceylon and the Nicobars. Forced by a mutinous crew to head for home, they were becalmed for some six weeks in the doldrums, ran short of victuals, and made for the West Indies. Lancaster and others landed on Mona Island but one of those left on board cut the cable; the ship drove to Hispaniola and was surrendered to the Spaniards. Lancaster and his companions were taken off by a French ship and landed at Dieppe, whence they reached Rye on 24 May 1594. The voyage had been financially disastrous but had revealed the vulnerability of the Portuguese monopoly in the East.

The object of Lancaster's second voyage was to plunder Pernambuco. He left with three ships in October 1594, took prizes, and was joined at the Cape Verde Islands by John Venner in return for a quarter of the booty. The town was easily taken, and they captured the contents of an East India carrack that had been unloaded for transshipment. Three Dutch and four French ships were chartered to transport the plunder. A party landed to attack a redoubt built to command the harbour entrance. They succeeded but, against the orders of Lancaster, who was ill, they pursued the Portuguese, were repulsed, and lost thirty-five men. They left for England the same evening with fifteen ships, all laden. They reached home safely, though not together; the booty made Lancaster a rich man. In 1598 he was made a commissioner for managing the earl of Cumberland's voyage, but seems not to have taken part in it. In 1601 he was receiving a pension of £50 per annum but it is not known why and he surrendered it in 1610.

In 1600 Lancaster became a director of the newly founded East India Company. He was in command of the four ships of its first expedition, the *Hector*, *Susan*, *Ascension*, and the *Red Dragon*, of at least 400 tons, in which he himself sailed. They left Woolwich on 13 February 1601 but were delayed by contrary winds and did not leave Torbay until 20 April. Becalmed in the doldrums they did not reach Table Bay until 9 September; by then they had lost 105 men from scurvy, the flagship having lost fewer than the others because Lancaster had provided his crew with lemon juice. They called at St Mary's Island and spent from Christmas until 6 March at Antongil Bay. After spending nearly three weeks in the Nicobars they sailed to Achin, where the sultan readily permitted them to trade without paying custom dues. Lancaster sent the *Susan* to

Priaman to buy a full lading of pepper, and joined the Dutch in plundering a richly laden Portuguese vessel. The *Ascension* and *Susan* were sent home while the *Hector* and *Red Dragon* went to Bantam. Terms for trade there were agreed and a factory established, while a pinnace bought from the Dutch was sent to the Moluccas to obtain cloves and nutmegs. Lancaster was given a letter and present for Queen Elizabeth and left Bantam on 20 February 1602. When near the Cape the *Red Dragon* was so badly damaged in a storm that the crew wanted to abandon her, which Lancaster refused to do. He ordered the *Hector* to leave him and make for home, but his order was disobeyed. Both ships anchored in the Downs on 11 September. Lancaster was received by the king and knighted for his achievements in the following year.

Lancaster lived in London in Bevis Marks, served as a director of the East India Company more than once, and was consulted by members. His interest in the north-west passage is attested by the name Baffin gave to Lancaster Sound when he discovered it in 1616. Lancaster died in London on 6 June 1618 and was buried on the 9th in All Hallows parish church, London Wall. His will does not mention a wife or children, but does mention a surviving brother Peter and another, deceased, John, and a brother-in-law Hopgood. The bulk of his property he bequeathed to various charities, especially in connection with the Skinners' Company, of which he became a freeman in 1579, and to Mistress Thomasyne Owfeild for distribution to the poor. C. F. BECKINGHAM

Sources R. Hakluyt, *The principal navigations, voyages, traffiques and discoveries of the English nation*, 2nd edn, 2 (1599), 102–10; 3 (1600), 708–15 • S. Purchas, *Purchas his pilgrimes*, 4 vols. (1625), vol. 1, bk 2, 147–64 • H. Roberts, 'Lancaster his allarums', in *The voyages of Sir James Lancaster to Brazil and the East Indies, 1591–1603*, new edn, ed. W. Foster, Hakluyt Society, 2nd ser., 85 (1940) • J. Lancaster, 'A true and large discourse', *The voyages of Sir James Lancaster to Brazil and the East Indies, 1591–1603*, new edn, ed. W. Foster, Hakluyt Society, 2nd ser., 85 (1940) • *The voyages of Sir James Lancaster to Brazil and the East Indies, 1591–1603*, new edn, ed. W. Foster, Hakluyt Society, 2nd ser., 85 (1940) • W. Foster, *England's quest of Eastern trade* (1933) • J. F. Wadmore, *Some account of the Worshipful Company of Skinners of London* (1902) • Records of the Skinners' Company, Skinners' Hall, London • will, PRO, PROB 11/131, sig. 65 • sentence, PRO, PROB 11/132, sig. 121

Likenesses oils, 1596 (after type, 1596), Skinners' Hall, London; repro. in Foster, *Voyages of Sir James Lancaster*

Lancaster, John (1569/70–1619), Church of Ireland bishop of Waterford and Lismore, was a native of Prescot, Lancashire, and probably the third son of Thomas Lancaster of Rainhill, Lancashire. Educated at Eton College, he was admitted to King's College, Cambridge, on 28 August 1587, aged seventeen, graduated BA in 1592, proceeded MA in 1597, and held a college fellowship during 1590–97. A chaplain to James I, he arrived in Ireland in 1607 bearing a letter from the king directing that he be granted the first available bishopric. On 5 January 1608 he was nominated to Waterford and Lismore, a see long held *in commendam* by the pluralist Miler Magrath, archbishop of Cashel.

Lancaster was Waterford's first resident bishop for nearly thirty years. Churches and communities had been devastated in the uprisings of Elizabeth's reign, and much of the see land had been alienated by the four previous bishops, especially in the west, where the episcopal manors of Lismore and Ardmore were now held by Richard Boyle, earl of Cork. Lancaster's episcopate was marked by a determined effort to increase the revenues of his diocese, which he calculated at no more than £40 for Waterford and £60 for Lismore. In 1610 he was awarded a grant *in commendam* of various benefices in his own and adjacent dioceses, to which in 1614 was added the vicarage of Mothel, co. Waterford. He introduced a bill into the Irish House of Commons to have his predecessors' sales of diocesan property declared null and void, but, owing to the intervention of the earl of Cork, 'by a general clamour and consent [it] was cast out of the house' (Grosart, 2.101). In 1618 he succeeded in obtaining for his diocese a grant of 546 acres of escheated land in co. Wexford.

In Waterford the great majority of the citizens were Roman Catholic, and the city was imbued with the spirit of the Counter-Reformation. Lancaster built a new episcopal residence, provoking the hostility of the mayor by using timbers and other materials from St Peter's Church. His determination to assert his authority by refusing to allow the mayor to hold up his sword of office in the cathedral precincts resulted in an angry complaint to the government. In March 1618, successive mayors and sheriffs having refused to take the oath of supremacy, the corporation was abolished, the city being placed under direct rule from Dublin.

Lancaster appears to have been twice married. By his first marriage he had two sons. The elder, John, was precentor of both Lismore and Waterford. In 1616 Boyle granted him the vicarage of Mothel, 'and he promised me to assure his mother-in-law [i.e. stepmother] £30 a year during her life', to commence after the bishop's death (Grosart, 1.125). The younger John Lancaster married Elizabeth, second daughter of Sir Edward Harris, justice of the common pleas, and had a son, John, admitted to Trinity College, Dublin, in 1638 aged fifteen. He died on 18 April 1630. There is a monument to his wife in Kinsalebeg churchyard near Youghal. The bishop's younger son, Joshua, of Grange, co. Tipperary, married Mary, daughter of Gilbert Waters of Cullen, co. Tipperary, and had a daughter, Elizabeth. He died in October 1634.

In 1619 Lancaster was at Ardfinnan attempting to wrest the episcopal manor from Miler Magrath's daughter when fire destroyed the hut containing his personal effects and records, including the 1487 rental of the diocese known as the black book. Magrath commented acidly that its destruction was a greater loss to the church than if all the protestant bishops of Munster had been drowned. Shortly after this (at some time between April and July 1619) Lancaster died; he was buried in Waterford Cathedral.

JULIAN C. WALTON

Sources *The whole works of Sir James Ware concerning Ireland*, ed. and trans. W. Harris, 1 (1739), 539 [annotated copy with notes by John Lodge (master of the rolls), Royal Irish Academy] • H. Cotton, *Fasti ecclesiae Hibernicae*, 2nd edn, 1 (1851), 125; 5 (1860), 19 • 'Joshua Boyle's accompt of the temporalities of the bishopricks of Waterford', ed. W. H. Rennison, *Journal of the Cork Historical and Archaeological Society*, 2nd ser., 32 (1927), 42–9, 78–85; 33 (1928), 42–7, 83–92;

35 (1930), 26–33; 36 (1931), 20–25 • P. Power, 'The protestant diocese of Waterford in 1615', *Journal of the Waterford and South-East of Ireland Archaeological Society*, 8 (1902–5), 103–15 • P. Power, 'Waterford city churches temp. James I', *Journal of the Waterford and South-East of Ireland Archaeological Society*, 14 (1911), 49–55 • P. Power, 'Material condition of the churches of Waterford', *Journal of the Waterford and South-East of Ireland Archaeological Society*, 16 (1913), 114–21 • *CSP Ire.*, 1606–8, 197, 249, 388–9, 421–2; 1608–10, 214, 439–40; 1611–4, 81; 1615–25, 187, 303 • *The Lismore papers, first series: autobiographical notes, remembrances and diaries of Sir Richard Boyle, first and 'great' earl of Cork*, ed. A. B. Grosart, 5 vols. (privately printed, London, 1886), vol. 1, pp. 125, 215, 227, 287; vol. 2, pp. 101, 147, 362, 376; vol. 3, pp. 29, 243–4 • Venn, *Alum. Cant.* • *Calendar of the Irish patent rolls of James I* (before 1830); facs. edn as *Irish patent rolls of James I* (1966), 106, 115, 182, 260, 423, 431, 460 • *The journals of the House of Commons of the kingdom of Ireland*, 1 (1796), 16–18 • C. Holywood, 'Annual letter for 1619. Residence of West Munster. Clonmel', Jesuit Archives, Dublin, MacErlean Transcripts • 'Interesting letter contributed by Father Hogan', *Journal of the Waterford and South-East of Ireland Archaeological Society*, 6 (1900), 101–22 [letter of Fr Muzio Vitillischi, SJ, recounting events in Waterford, 1617] • W. H. Rennison, 'From Declan to disestablishment', Library of the Representative Church Body, Dublin [unpublished history of the Church of Ireland diocese of Waterford and Lismore] • 'Some funeral entries of Ireland', *Journal of the Association for the Preservation of the Memorials of the Dead, Ireland*, 7 (1907–9), 80–81, 205 [appx] • W. H. Rennison, *Succession list of the bishops, cathedral and parochial clergy of the dioceses of Waterford and Lismore* (1920), esp. 194 • D. Cowman, 'The Reformation bishops of the diocese of Waterford and Lismore', *Decies: Journal of the Old Waterford Society*, 27 (1984), 31–8 • J. C. Walton, ed., 'Calendar of the MSS of the dean and chapter of Waterford, 1210–1833', Waterford Municipal Library [to be published by the Irish Manuscripts Commission; copy of the typescript] • J. C. Erck, ed., *A repertory of the inrolments of the patent rolls of chancery in Ireland, commencing with the reign of James I*, 1 (1846–52), 353, 404–5 • P. Power, 'The ancient ruined churches of co. Waterford: … Kinsalebeg', *Journal of the Waterford and South-East of Ireland Archaeological Society*, 4 (1898), 200–01 • Burtchaell & Sadleir, *Alum. Dubl.*, 2nd edn, 480

Lancaster, Joseph (1778–1838), educationist, was born in Kent Street, Southwark, London, on 25 November 1778, the youngest son of Richard Lancaster (1742–1821) a former soldier working as a cane sieve maker. Joseph's mother, Sarah Lancaster, *née* Faulkes (d. 1811), who had borne ten children, kept a small shop near St George's Fields. Lancaster received little formal education, attending local schools in Southwark and working for his father. The accounts of his early life are vague and contradictory. At the age of fourteen he attempted unsuccessfully to get to Jamaica as a naval volunteer 'to teach the poor blacks the word of God' (Corston, 2). Later he decided to become a dissenting minister and joined the Society of Friends, changing to teaching as the Quakers had no ministry. According to his first biographer, William Corston, Lancaster set up his first day school with the help of his father about 1798, after working as an assistant in other schools. This school moved into larger premises when numbers began to increase. He was well suited to be a schoolmaster as he had enormous enthusiasm, great self-confidence, a fluent tongue, and an instinctive understanding of young children, assets helped by a somewhat impressive appearance. He also possessed a capacity for self-advertisement which attracted help from local supporters. At a time when child labour was uncontrolled and parents expected their offspring to add to the meagre family income as soon

Joseph Lancaster (1778–1838), by John Hazlitt, *c.*1818

as possible, such children as attended any school rarely stayed long or learned much. Lancaster had little difficulty on this score, as he provided free meals in addition to charging low fees.

Borough Road School and the monitorial system About 1801 Lancaster established a 'free-school' in a barn-like building near Borough Road, Southwark, advertising free instruction to those who could not afford to pay even a moderate fee. Before long the numbers of children at Lancaster's school were overwhelming and to avoid paying assistants he adopted the method whereby the older boys, the monitors (led by a monitor-general), taught the younger children under the general supervision of the master. What was forced on him by necessity was turned into an advantage and Lancaster set about proclaiming the effectiveness and cheapness of his monitorial plan. Many of his claims were exaggerated, not least his assertion that by his method a great proportion of children could finish their education in the 'three Rs' in twelve months. Lancaster possessed considerable organizing powers. Some of his maxims, such as 'a place for everything and everything in its place' and 'let every child at every moment have something to do and a motive for doing it' became proverbial. A soldier's son, he sometimes compared his pupils to well disciplined troops and, like soldiers, his best monitors and pupils were rewarded with silver-plated badges worn on their caps or suspended by a chain. A keen rivalry was fostered among his pupils by an elaborate system of rewards, including toys or money for the diligent, while the mischievous, or unsuccessful, were dealt with by a system of humiliating penalties which were designed to expose the victim to the ridicule of his fellows. Lancaster's expenses were reduced by the device of using sand tables and slates instead of writing books, as well as sheets pasted on the walls instead of reading books. Groups of children, under the control of a monitor, learned the alphabet by repeating simple words, and practised figures. Passages extracted from the Bible or suitably pious books furnished scripture lessons. Lancaster himself was a keen reader and stressed the need for a good library.

By 1803 Lancaster's success in coping with several hundred boys simultaneously was attracting interest outside Southwark. The first of several editions of the book explaining his aims and describing his monitorial methods, *Improvements in Education as it Respects the Industrious Classes of the Community* (1803), was well subscribed. Eminent visitors from all over London came to see the remarkable school at Borough Road, many of them donating funds for the furtherance of the work. According to William Corston, 'foreign princes, ambassadors, peers, commons, ladies of distinction, bishops and archbishops, Jews and Turks, all visited the school with wonder-waiting eyes' (Corston, 11). Soon the attention of the prodigiously rich duke of Bedford and other nobility was directed to Lancaster's methods. The climax of interest in the school came in 1805 when Lancaster was given an audience by George III, who congratulated him on his achievement and donated a subscription of £100 from himself and suitably graduated subscriptions from the rest of the royal family. No doubt some of the enthusiasm for Lancaster's school arose out of public curiosity to view an unusual and well-advertised spectacle. But there was also a genuine interest, for Lancaster appeared to have solved one of the social problems of the day—how to provide a basic education for the rapidly increasing numbers of illiterate children in city streets without employing large numbers of teachers and great quantities of equipment. Most of the upper class believed that the children of the poor should at least be taught to read the Bible and learn habits of subordination and obedience. Witness George III's words to Lancaster, which were displayed in large letters in the schoolroom at Borough Road: 'It is my wish that every poor child in my dominions is taught to read the Holy Scriptures.'

Establishing Lancasterian schools   Lancaster was never known for his personal modesty (the Quaker reformer, Elizabeth Fry, noticed a want of humility in his manner) and the extent of his fame began to go to his head. He envisaged the foundation of monitorial schools all over the country erected in the image of what he now called the Royal Free School. He spent such funds as supporters donated to him in setting up at Borough Road a slate factory, a printing office, and a girls' school run by two sisters. He maintained his best monitors, his 'house lads', as apprentice schoolmasters, preparing them to go out like educational missionaries and start monitorial schools elsewhere. In *Improvements in Education*, he emphasized the importance of well trained and well remunerated teachers. On 5 June 1804 Lancaster married, in Sarah Trimmer's words, 'a pretty Quaker', Elizabeth Bonner (*c*.1780–

1820), daughter of Henry Bonner of Southwark, and she gave him his only child, also named Elizabeth (Betsy). Soon after his marriage he set out on the first of a series of extravagant coach tours around the country, publicizing the merits of his system and whipping up a good deal of local enthusiasm. At Maiden Bradley in Wiltshire he established a rural monitorial school which for a time absorbed his interest and his money, though it eventually fell into neglect. After the first of several visits to Ireland in 1806, establishing schools, he returned to Southwark heavily in debt to local tradesmen and was confined in the king's bench debtors' prison. Even after his release the constant risk of being arrested again persuaded Lancaster to spend much of his time on lecturing tours in the provinces and Ireland, accompanied by some of his young apprentices, many of whom were devoted to him. Meanwhile the Borough Road monitorial school was left mainly in the hands of his assistants.

Financial difficulties, however, were not Lancaster's only problem. He had opened his school for children of all religious denominations and though the Bible was read diligently, no sectarian instruction was given. At first the Anglican clergy had donated subscriptions to the school, especially when it received royal approval. But this support changed into opposition when in 1805 Sarah Trimmer, after visits to Lancaster's school at Southwark, began to attack him in her correspondence and pamphlets as the 'Goliath of Schismatics' and his school at Borough Road as inimical to the interests of the established church. Mrs Trimmer particularly attacked Lancaster's methods of 'emulation and reward', complaining that his medals and orders of merit for his 'nobility' gave the children ideas above their station in life. She asserted that Lancaster had taken many of his ideas for his monitorial system from Dr Andrew Bell, whose Madras System, pioneered by Bell in India, was regarded favourably by the Anglican church. Lancaster had admitted his debt to Bell for some of his ideas and Bell had also professed his admiration for Lancaster's school. But after Mrs Trimmer's attack had divided their supporters, they drifted into hostility, widened by Bell's jealousy of the royal patronage given to Lancaster.

The Anglican attack helped to rally nonconformist and secular support to Lancaster, including a powerful defence of his system in the whig *Edinburgh Review*. In 1808 a small committee was formed to raise money to pay off his debts and put the finances and administration of the institutions at Borough Road on a sounder basis. The earliest of these supporters included Corston and Joseph Fox, a leading member of the Baptist sect. But the most influential member of the group was William Allen, a wealthy manufacturing chemist and well-known Quaker philanthropist, who was greatly impressed on his first visit to Borough Road in 1808. Allen, who became treasurer to the new committee, had friends in high places, including the royal dukes of Kent and Sussex. It was due to Allen more than to anyone else, that the Borough Road institutions were established on a permanent footing. But in spite of the financial support and economies of the committee, the need for funds remained pressing, especially as Lancaster's tours brought a demand for teachers of his monitorial system, the reputation of which was beginning to spread overseas, as well as throughout the British Isles. In 1810, therefore, an enlarged committee was formed under the presidency of the duke of Kent including, in addition to Allen and his friends, such educational enthusiasts as James Mill, Henry Brougham, and Samuel Whitbread, who had introduced a bill into parliament aiming to set up a national system of elementary schools based on Lancaster's system. This enlarged committee called itself the Royal Lancasterian Institution for the Education of the Poor of Every Religious Persuasion. Meanwhile the rival followers of Bell set up the National Society for Promoting the Education of the Poor in the Principles of the Established Church, with the support of the tory *Quarterly Review* and the Anglican clergy.

Resignation Between 1808 and 1811 Lancaster produced a number of pamphlets at The Royal Free School Press, including *The British System of Education* and *Report of J. Lancaster's Progress from the Year 1798*, recording fifty new schools for 14,000 pupils and acknowledging the financial assistance of his supporters. But he was, in fact, increasingly resentful of the control exercised by Allen and the committee. In 1812, without any reference to his trustees, he opened a boarding-school at Tooting for wealthy pupils, using money subscribed for Borough Road. He persuaded some of the apprentice schoolmasters to join him at Tooting and sent the committee a bill for their maintenance. Eventually after long and often acrimonious negotiations between Lancaster and the committee, a general meeting held at the Freemasons' Tavern in 1813 and attended by Lancaster and the leading members of the committee accepted a constitution and rules for the Institution for Promoting the British System for the Education of the Labouring and Manufacturing Classes of Society of Every Religious Persuasion. Lancaster was offered the position of salaried superintendent, the collapse of the Tooting project leaving him again heavily in debt. He agreed to these arrangements with reluctance accusing the leading members of the new society of usurping his authority and seizing his property. These arrangements soon came to an end, for in 1814 an unsavoury scandal made Lancaster's removal inevitable. According to Francis Place, who had joined the committee in 1812 and played a prominent part in its affairs for a time, a youth named William Brown, who was still apprenticed to Lancaster, informed Corston that Lancaster 'used to flog his apprentices for his own amusement' (BL, Add. MS 27823). On the evidence of an inquiry into Lancaster's conduct towards his apprentices, which ran contrary to his moral pronouncements in *Improvements in Education*, he was called before the committee but forestalled further action by resigning as superintendent. Meanwhile he advertised a new monitorial school in Westminster to be financed by money sent to him by a supporter in Spain. After Lancaster's final withdrawal, the institution was renamed the British and Foreign School Society, much to the resentment of Lancaster

who in *Oppression and Persecution* (1816) accused his 'pretended friends', Allen and Fox, of driving him away from the institutions he had created at Borough Road and excluding his name from the title of the society 'as if Britons and foreigners had combined in its invention'. The Westminster project having collapsed, he resumed his travels around England, Ireland, and Scotland, lecturing on his monitorial system and establishing local committees. But his extravagance became increasingly wild. He had already been declared a bankrupt and disowned by the Society of Friends which disapproved of his spendthrift conduct and ostentatious appearance. His wife's mental illness had disrupted his family life. Eventually a few friends, including David Holt, a Quaker mill owner from Manchester, organized a subscription to pay for Lancaster's passage to America and in 1818 he crossed the Atlantic with his wife and daughter.

United States and Venezuela Monitorial schools on the Lancasterian plan had already been set up in New York and Philadelphia and for a time Lancaster regained something of his old popularity. He was warmly welcomed by supporters in the United States and received by the president in Washington. But plans to establish model schools at Philadelphia and elsewhere collapsed because of Lancaster's ill health, his preference for lecture tours, and disputes over payment for himself and his assistants. Early in 1820 Lancaster moved to Baltimore where he opened another school and produced a treatise entitled *The Lancasterian System of Education with Improvements by its Founder* (1821). On 6 December 1820, however, his mentally afflicted wife, Elizabeth, died at Baltimore. Six years later, on 23 February 1827, he married Mary Robinson, the widow of an English miniature painter, John Robinson, who had emigrated to America. By that date Lancaster had left the United States and established himself at Caracas in the new state of Venezuela. Simón Bolívar, the president of Columbia (which then included Venezuela) had met Lancaster during a visit to Borough Road in 1810 and a proposal for a monitorial school at Caracas had already been made. Again, however, the results were disastrous, as problems of language, of religious instruction (for Catholicism was dominant in Caracas), and of finance inevitably arose. Relations between Lancaster and the British consul, who regarded him as an impostor and resented Lancaster's attitude to himself, rapidly deteriorated. After a brief period of cordial relations with Bolívar, who attended Lancaster's marriage to Mary Robinson in Caracas, Lancaster was abandoned by the 'liberator', being left heavily in debt. Both he and his second wife, who had three children by her first marriage, were obliged to leave Caracas at some personal risk to themselves. Meanwhile Lancaster's daughter, Elizabeth, had married Richard Jones, one of several former apprentices who had joined Lancaster in America and they had settled in Mexico with their family.

Back in the United States, Lancaster returned to New York and after visiting various cities on the north-eastern seaboard of America, established himself at Montreal in September 1829 where, as at other Canadian cities, he was at first welcomed, though his schools failed to flourish. During these years of increasing penury, he became virtually estranged from his wife, Mary, though she eventually rejoined him in the United States. On his return again to New York, some of his old friends, such as Roberts Vaux, tried to assist Lancaster and a subscription list was opened in America and Britain, to which Allen and other former supporters contributed, to purchase him an annuity. In 1833 he produced his last attempt at self-justification, *An epitome of some of the chief events and transactions in the life of Joseph Lancaster, containing an account of the rise and progress of the Lancasterian system of education and the author's future prospects of usefulness to mankind.* He also reopened correspondence with Corston in England, giving him the impression that he was still received everywhere with enthusiasm. 'With properly trained teachers and monitors', he wrote in 1838, 'I should not scruple to undertake to teach ten thousand pupils in different schools all to read fluently in three weeks to three months, idiots, absentees and truants excepted' (Salmon, 64). But shortly after writing this letter, he was seriously injured in a street accident in New York and died a day later, on 23 October 1838. He was buried at the Friends' burial-ground in Houston Street, New York.

'Be assured I shall stand in my place here and hereafter,' Lancaster wrote to an acquaintance in 1834 (McCadden, 73), when enthusiasm for monitorial methods was already declining, in spite of the original impact of the system of mutual instruction at home and abroad following the success of the Borough Road model school. Lancaster himself had become an increasing embarrassment over the years. Place's unkind dictum that Lancaster was 'adapted to the teaching in the school but to nothing else' and became 'mischievous, ridiculous and childish' as he was 'caressed by the great' (BL, Add. MS 27823) was sadly true of a life which was mainly one of failed prospects, broken engagements, sordid quarrels, and endless debts. Even his relations with his own family deteriorated into mutual recriminations and neglect. 'That old serpent, Mr Lancaster,' wrote the British minister in Caracas, 'is the most black and dangerous being in the place' (Dickson, 246) and this was an opinion shared by many acquaintances, though some few friends never lost faith in him. His biographer, David Salmon, was probably correct in suggesting that Lancaster's creative energy, which had achieved much for the children of the poorer classes, had been pretty well exhausted at thirty and it would have been better for his reputation if he had died many years earlier. Even so, his name was to survive in English educational history as one of the foremost pioneers of mass schooling and effective teacher training in the early industrial era.

G. F. BARTLE

Sources D. Salmon, *Joseph Lancaster* (1904) · M. Dickson, *Teacher extraordinary: Joseph Lancaster* (1986) · W. Corston, *Life of Joseph Lancaster* (1840) · H. Dunn, *Joseph Lancaster and his contemporaries* (1848) · G. F. Bartle, 'Joseph Lancaster and his biographers', *Biography and education: some eighteenth and nineteenth century studies*, ed. R. Lowe (1980) · E. Vaughan, *Joseph Lancaster in Caracas, 1824–1827*, 2 vols. (1987–9) · J. M. McCadden, 'Joseph Lancaster in America', *The Social Studies*, 28 (1937), 73–7 · C. F. Koestle, *Joseph Lancaster and the monitorial school movement* (1973) · *DCB*, vol. 7 · BL, Add. MS 27823

Archives American Antiquarian Society, Worcester, Massachusetts, corresp. and papers · Boston PL, corresp. · Church of Ireland College of Education, corresp. relating to educational matters · Col. U. · Hist. Soc. Penn. · Pembrokeshire RO, letters and biographical papers | BL, papers relating to Lancastrian schools and Association, Add. MS 27823 · Brunel University, Middlesex, British and Foreign School Society archives, letters to William Allen and others · PRO NIre., corresp. with John Foster

Likenesses watercolour miniature, *c*.1810 · J. Hazlitt, oils, *c*.1818, NPG [*see illus.*] · Dequevauvillier, stipple and line engraving, NPG · T. Rowlandson, cartoon, BM · Vigneron, engraving (after silhouette by T. Pole, 1809), repro. in J. Hamel, *Mutual instruction* (1818) · engraving, Haverford College, Pennsylvania

Lancaster [*née* Rawlinson], **Lydia** (1683–1761), Quaker minister, was born on 8 March 1683 at Graithwaite, Lancashire, the seventh of the eight children of Thomas Rawlinson (*d.* 1689) and Dorothy (1644–1737), only daughter of Thomas Hutton of Rampside. Brought up in a Quaker family Lydia described herself as one drawn to thoughts of God from infancy. When she was about seven years old she was moved to floods of tears by the ministry of a visiting Friend, and from the age of fourteen she struggled with the conviction that she was being called to be a minister herself. She resisted this calling for ten years—a period which her contemporaries saw approvingly as a time when she grew in wisdom and experience but which she herself remembered as a 'long howling wilderness' of unfaithfulness (*Extracts from the Letters*).

Soon after the beginning of her ministry, in 1708, Lydia began to travel, at first to local meetings and then, in 1710, as far as London. In 1712 she went to Ireland, in 1717 to Scotland, and in 1718 she visited America in the company of her brother Abraham's wife, Elizabeth Beck Rawlinson (1670–1750), and Thomas Chalkley, among several others. Lydia's travels, however, although undertaken under a sense of religious duty, were, as she says herself, 'sometimes pretty trying, not having such care taken at home in my absence as might have been desired' (*Extracts from the Letters*). She had married, on 21 January 1707, Bryan Lancaster (1686–1747), a tanner of Kendal. There were no children of the marriage and there are hints in contemporary records of sorrows and affliction, some of it possibly financial, brought upon Lydia by her 'nearest temporal connexion', her husband (testimony to Lydia Lancaster from Lancaster monthly meeting, 1762, Lancs. RO, Preston). Bryan Lancaster's name is conspicuous in its absence from Quaker records. In 1729 Lydia moved with her aged mother to Colthouse, near Hawkshead, a small rural settlement next to a Quaker meeting-house, but there is no mention of her husband on the removal certificate. Her mother died in 1737, and by 1743 Lydia was evidently living at Colthouse with her husband, who died in 1747.

Lydia Lancaster's ministry was generally acknowledged to be expressive and powerful but her experience gave her another dimension for 'being instructed in sorrow she was favoured with a sympathizing heart and knew how to partake in the affliction of others' (testimony to Lydia Lancaster from Lancaster monthly meeting, 1762, Lancs. RO, Preston). Throughout her ministry Lydia was a staunch supporter of Quaker women's meetings for business at local level. In 1746 she put her name to a petition aimed at extending them to national level, although this was not accepted and no such body was set up until 1784. Lydia was not concerned with the equality of women as such but that they might be encouraged to take up their religious duties as much as the men were. In her local meetings Lydia, drawing on her own experience, was both stern and encouraging, 'particularly to the timorous and backward' (ibid.). She is remembered as always bidding farewell with a sort of blessing to those women who made the effort to come to women's meetings, and she continued to attend meetings herself right up to her last days.

At the end of her life Lydia lived in Lancaster, free from financial worries and, she says, 'mostly alone, for that is what I most delight in and have done most of my time' (*Extracts from the Letters*). She still travelled in the ministry, taking long journeys in 1749 and in 1754. In 1760 she and Grace Chamber travelled together to Welsh yearly meeting, to Bath, Bristol, and to London. Lydia died on 30 May 1761 at Lancaster and was buried there in the Quaker burial-ground. Though she published nothing in her lifetime her influence continued. Many years after her death, in 1840, her family descendant and namesake, Lydia Ann Barclay, edited and published a selection of extracts from her letters, feeling that they might be of use to future generations.   GIL SKIDMORE

Sources 'Dictionary of Quaker biography', RS Friends, Lond. [card index] · *Extracts from the letters of Lydia Lancaster*, ed. L. A. Barclay (1840) · RS Friends, Lond. · B. Carré, 'Early Quaker women in Lancaster and Lancashire', *Early Lancaster friends*, ed. M. Mullet (1978), 43–53 · Lancaster quarterly meeting minute-books, Lancs. RO · E. E. Moore, *Travelling with Thomas Story: the life and travels of an eighteenth-century Quaker* (1947) · M. H. Bacon, ed., *Wilt thou go on my errand? Three eighteenth-century journals of Quaker women ministers* (1994) · R. Labouchere, *Abiah Darby* (1988)
Archives Lancs. RO · RS Friends, Lond.

Lancaster, Matilda of. *See* Matilda of Lancaster (*d.* 1377).

Lancaster [*née* Perkins; *other married names* Field, Tree], **Nancy Keene** (1897–1994), interior decorator, was born on 10 September 1897 at The Cottage, Mirador, Albemarle county, Virginia, USA, the second daughter of (Thomas) Moncure Perkins (1865–1914), the owner of a provisioning and meat-packing business, and his wife, Elizabeth (1867–1914), the daughter of Colonel Chiswell Dabney Langhorne. She was brought up in Richmond, Virginia, and attended a convent in Territet, Switzerland, and a *lycée* in Tours. She first visited England in 1910, when she saw the funeral procession of Edward VII and stayed with her aunt Nancy, Viscountess Astor, in London and Cliveden. Her parents separated in 1910 and both died within a fortnight in 1914, after which she was brought up by her aunt Irene, the wife of the artist Charles Dana Gibson, herself famous as a Gibson girl. Her education was completed at Foxcroft, Middleburg, Baltimore. In 1915 she paid another visit to Nancy Astor in England, and that winter was launched as a débutante in New York City and Richmond, Virginia.

In February 1917 Nancy married Henry Field, a grandson of the store magnate Marshall Field; Cole Porter was an

Nancy Keene Lancaster (1897–1994), by unknown photographer

usher. Field died five months later, having spent three months in hospital after a tonsil operation. He left her a rich widow. On another voyage to Britain she met Field's cousin (Arthur) Ronald Lambert Field Tree (1897–1976), and they were married in London on 5 May 1920. Tree was an Anglo-American who loved Britain and led a full political and public life there.

In the early years of their married life the Trees lived in about six houses, including the family home in Virginia, Mirador, which they bought in 1922. This Nancy improved, helped by the architect William Delano, who taught her to consider the garden as an extension of the house. In New York they lived in a house on East 96th Street, formerly owned by Ogden Codman, the celebrated Boston architect and decorator. Interior decorating soon became Nancy's passion, combining elegance and comfort.

The Trees moved to England in 1926, and Ronald Tree served as Conservative member of parliament for the Harborough division of Leicestershire from 1933 to 1945. For hunting they rented Cottesbrooke, and later Kelmarsh Hall, both in Northamptonshire. In 1933, when Tree came into his inheritance, they bought Ditchley Park, Oxfordshire. They restored both house and garden over two years and redesigned the terrace from plans found in Sir John Soane's Museum. Nancy furnished it with eighteenth-century furniture, pointing out that the eighteenth century provided plenty of variety. She also decorated Eydon Hall for Lord Brand (the husband of another of her Langhorne aunts) and Champion Lodge for Crawley Champion de Crespigny.

Ditchley was the scene of much entertaining: the couple's guests included politicians—although politics bored Nancy—and aristocrats, notably Anthony Eden and Lord Cranborne (later fifth marquess of Salisbury), and celebrities and film stars, such as Noël Coward and David Niven. During the war Winston Churchill was a frequent visitor: Ditchley was thought safer than Chequers when the moon was full. Churchill's presence dominated the house, as he worked with his private secretary through the morning, invited his own guests, and received visits from military leaders. Nancy herself commanded a corps of mobile canteens which took food to bombed areas. Her canteen was the first into Coventry after the bombing, and eventually she had a fleet of more than a hundred.

The Trees had two sons and one daughter (who died soon after birth). Their marriage broke down, and they were divorced in 1947. On 24 August 1948 Nancy married Claude Granville (Juby) Lancaster and returned to be mistress of Kelmarsh Hall. That marriage lasted only three years, and the verdict of her sons was that it was Kelmarsh that she loved, not Lancaster, although she kept his name for the rest of her life.

Meanwhile Ronald Tree bought her Sibyl Colefax's share of the decorating business Colefax and Fowler, in Avery Row, off Brook Street, London, for £15,000, and she entered into a formidable partnership with John Fowler. Always known for her perfect taste, she liked to create the atmosphere of rooms that had developed gradually over many decades with an accumulation of possessions. Fowler was the perfect foil for her. He was the observant outsider, an expert on the eighteenth century, and an artist, reviving stippling and dragging, while she preferred the overall look, applying her yardstick of elegance and comfort. They adorned many an English country house and garden, among them the duke of Norfolk's new house in the park at Arundel, as well as Boughton and Badminton, and the duke of Windsor's mill at Gif-sur-Yvette, near Paris. Between 1945 and 1957 Colefax and Fowler gave Nancy the opportunity to scour the countryside for unusual furniture and antiques for the shop and for her clients. It is impossible to overvalue the contribution the pair made to English country-house decoration on the grand scale: in the 1930s Nancy had led the way with the introduction of American-style plumbing and bathrooms in country houses, which had previously relied on picturesque but labour-intensive and inefficient methods of sanitation.

In 1954 Nancy Lancaster settled at Haseley Court, in Oxfordshire, redesigning the house with John Fowler's help and the garden with advice from Sir Geoffrey Jellicoe. This was her last great creation, but after a serious fire she sold it in 1975 and moved into the coach house by the drive, where she lived until her death, at home, on 19 August 1994.   HUGO VICKERS

Sources R. Becker, *Nancy Lancaster* (1996) · J. M. Robinson, *The latest country houses* (1984) · *The Times* (20 Aug 1994) · *The Independent* (25 Aug 1994) · personal knowledge (2004) · private information (2004) · m. cert. [3rd marriage] · d. cert.

Likenesses C. Beaton, photograph, 1958, repro. in *The Independent* · photograph, News International Syndication, London [*see illus.*] · photographs, repro. in Becker, *Nancy Lancaster*

Wealth at death £131,351: probate, 1 June 1995, *CGPLA Eng. & Wales*

Lancaster, Nathaniel (1601–1661), Church of England clergyman, was born in Rainhill, Lancashire, son of Gabriel Lancaster of Rainhill and of Margery (*b.* 1571), daughter of the celebrated puritan John *Bruen of Bruen Stapleford, Cheshire. He followed in the family religious tradition: educated at Oxford University, he graduated BA in 1622 from All Souls and proceeded BD in 1634 from Brasenose, the Oxford college most closely linked with the north-west. He was ordained on 20 December 1624 and took up his first appointment as curate at Thornton in the Moors, Cheshire. By 1631 he was well established at St Michael's, Chester, and received bequests in that year from Peter Drinkwater, alderman, and from Alice Lloyd. Appointed in 1638 to the rectory of Tarporley, Cheshire, he remained there for the rest of his life.

The strict religious regime which Lancaster established in his parish had its opponents as well as followers, and loud complaints against the rector and his curate John Jones were directed to the quarter sessions in 1642 and 1643. Traditionalists deeply resented his many departures from prayer book practice in the way in which communion services, baptisms, and burials were conducted. The use of the surplice had been abandoned and stained glass and crosses in the church had been broken. Sick visiting had been set aside, and catechizing was being ruthlessly used, Lancaster's opponents declared, to regulate access to the communion table. Sabbatarianism was vigorously upheld in this parish in a way to be expected from one of the Cheshire clergymen who had exhorted John Ley to publish *Sunday a Sabbath* in 1641. Faced with all these tribulations, withholding tithe payments was the counter-revolution under parochial review at the time the second complaint was lodged in 1643.

When civil war came in 1642 Lancaster, it was claimed, preached that all who were against parliament would be trodden under foot. Events in the short term proved otherwise. Lancaster's own farm stores were plundered by Colonel Hastings and Lord Cholmondley. The rector, in the latter's judgement, was 'a stinking rascal' who 'lost too little if he lost all' (Urwick, xviii), and Lancaster was still, unsuccessfully, seeking redress seven years later in 1649. For two years after 1644 Lancaster, by this stage identified among presbyterians, served as chaplain and clerk to the army of Sir William Brereton. During this time he published a narrative of the protracted siege of Chester, and sent a timely (and handsomely rewarded) account to the speaker of the House of Commons of military proceedings at Denbigh. No slavish admirer of Brereton, Lancaster in his account of the military operations at Chester played down the commander and gave disproportionate credit to his lieutenants. His departure from the army chaplaincy in 1646 was perhaps not unconnected with these earlier events, although he was more conservative than Brereton in religion, and was replaced by Samuel Eaton, an Independent. Lancaster was a signatory to the Cheshire attestation in 1648.

Lancaster was related to the Dones, Crewes, and Bruens, all significant Cheshire gentry families, and another index of this rector's gentry links is that he married Elizabeth (c.1598–1658), daughter of Peter Legh. It is no surprise to find this well-connected clergyman dining regularly in the 1650s with local gentry families such as Thomas Mainwaring. Glimpses of his correspondence with the gentry survive (Bennett and Dewhurst, 136–7). Lancaster's wife was buried on 28 September 1658. Of his children, Peter (bap. 16 July 1630) moved through Trinity College, Cambridge, to a career in the law. Nathaniel Lancaster saw in the Restoration but died on 9 January 1661 before the real testing time for presbyterians began.

R. C. RICHARDSON

Sources Cheshire Sheaf, 3rd ser., 38 (1943) · R. C. Richardson, Puritanism in north-west England: a regional study of the diocese of Chester to 1642 (1972) · G. Ormerod, The history of the county palatine and city of Chester, 2nd edn, ed. T. Helsby, 3 vols. (1882) · W. Urwick, ed., Historical sketches of nonconformity in the county palatine of Cheshire, by various ministers and laymen (1864) · J. S. Morrill, Cheshire, 1630–1660: county government and society during the English revolution (1974) · J. H. E. Bennett and J. C. Dewhurst, eds., Quarter sessions records with other records of the justices of the peace for the county palatine of Chester, 1559–1760, Lancashire and Cheshire RS, 94 (1940) · The letter books of Sir William Brereton, ed. R. N. Dore, 1, Lancashire and Cheshire RS, 123 (1984) · The letter books of Sir William Brereton, ed. R. N. Dore, 2, Lancashire and Cheshire RS, 128 (1990) · Ches. & Chester ALSS, QSF 4/24 [quarter sessions, 1642] · Foster, Alum. Oxon. · parish register, Tarporley, Cheshire [burial, Elizabeth Legh]

Lancaster, Nathaniel (b. in or after 1700, d. 1775), Church of England clergyman and satirist, was born in Cheshire, though further details of his parentage and childhood are unknown. The earl of Cholmondeley was an early patron, and through him Lancaster was introduced to 'the exalted scenes of polished life' (Nichols, 2.379). He was appointed rector of St Martin's, Chester, on 12 June 1725, and in January 1733 was made chaplain to Frederick, prince of Wales. On 17 February 1733 he married the widow of Captain Brown, who brought with her an inheritance of £20,000; they had two daughters. In February of the following year he was created doctor of divinity by the archbishop of Canterbury, and in September 1737 became rector of Stanford Rivers, near Ongar, Essex, where he remained for the rest of his life.

As a young man Lancaster had been a talented and witty conversationalist in polite society. In later years he turned to writing as a way of satirizing what he came to see as the excessive delicacy of modern manners. His treatise The Pretty Gentleman, or, Softness of Manners Vindicated (1747) offered a spoof defence of refined gentlemen such as the fictional fop William Fribble, recently satirized in David Garrick's play Miss in her Teens. Ostensibly a critique of Garrick's bluff tone, Lancaster's study was equally critical of what he saw as the enervated demeanour of overly delicate British manhood. Two further publications—a sermon, 'Public virtue, or, Love of our country' (1746), and The Plan of an Essay upon Delicacy (1748)—addressed the same

problem from different perspectives: the first offered a civic-minded call for public duty in the face of encroaching temptation, and the second a detailed guide to the correct ways for men and women to adopt a refined or delicate character. A similar dichotomy can be seen in Lancaster's work as a JP for Essex: a letter to the London bookseller Jacob Robinson tells how he frequently felt both compassion for defendants and a sense of duty to uphold the law (GM, 1784, 345).

A man 'of strong natural parts, great erudition, refined taste, and master of a nervous, and at the same time elegant style' (Nichols, 2.379), Lancaster published only one further work, a long rhapsodical poem, Methodism Triumphant, or, The Decisive Battle between Old Serpent and Modern Saint (1767). Whatever else he wrote was regularly burnt, in a life which became increasingly reclusive and penurious. Indeed, so great was this indebtedness that after Lancaster's death, on 20 June 1775, the rectory was pulled down on account of the state of disrepair into which it had fallen during his tenancy.

PHILIP CARTER

Sources DNB · Nichols, Lit. anecdotes, 2.379–80 · GM, 1st ser., 54 (1784), 345–6 · GM, 3rd ser., 17 (1864), 637 · R. Norton, Mother Clap's molly house: the gay subculture in England, 1700–1830 (1992)

Wealth at death penurious

Lancaster, Sir Osbert (1908–1986), cartoonist and designer, was born in London on 4 August 1908, the only child of Robert Lancaster (d. 1916) and his wife, Clare Bracebridge Manger. His grandfather, Sir William Lancaster, became secretary of the Prudential Assurance Company and his father had a job in the City but enlisted in the army in 1914. He was killed in the battle of the Somme. Lancaster was sent to St Ronan's preparatory school in Worthing, and then to Charterhouse School, an appropriate school for a caricaturist, as John Leech, W. M. Thackeray, and Max Beerbohm had all been there. (In the 1950s Lancaster received Beerbohm's warm compliments when he painted murals in the Randolph Hotel, Oxford, illustrating scenes from Zuleika Dobson.)

Lancaster did not shine at school (the headmaster's final report pronounced him 'irretrievably gauche') but was admitted to Lincoln College, Oxford, in 1926. Like his friend John Betjeman, Lancaster became a 'figure' at Oxford. He wore loud checks, sported a monocle, and grew a large moustache. He contributed cartoons to Cherwell, the university magazine. He and Betjeman were fascinated by the Victorians and their architecture, an interest which began half in a spirit of mockery, but ended in expert championship. Lancaster obtained a fourth-class degree in English (1930) after an extra year of study. Intended for the bar, he failed his bar examinations.

He then went to the Slade School of Art, where he met his first wife, Karen Elizabeth (d. 1964), the second daughter of Sir Austin Harris, vice-chairman of Lloyds Bank. They were married in 1933 and had one son and one daughter. Lancaster found work alongside Betjeman as an assistant editor at the Architectural Review. In 1936 his Progress at Pelvis Bay began the long sequence of his books satirizing architecture and social life. He was appointed cartoonist to the Daily Express in 1939 and on 1 January the first

Sir Osbert Lancaster (1908–1986), by Georges Maiteny

of his pocket cartoons appeared in its William Hickey column. He drew roughly 10,000 cartoons, with only brief interruptions, over the next forty years, many of them appearing on the front page. Lancaster's fusion of topicality and urbane wit was consistent. He depicted the world he knew—that of Canon Fontwater, Father O'Bubblegum, Mrs Frogmarch (the Tory lady), and, his most enduring creation, Maudie, countess of Littlehampton, and her dim, monocled husband Willy. Lancaster's satire was not splenetic, and, except in the cause of good architecture, he was never a crusader.

In the Second World War, Lancaster joined the press censorship bureau (1939) and was sent to Greece, with which he fell in love, as a Foreign Office press attaché (1944–6). The British ambassador was being too high-handed with the press, and Lancaster effectively smoothed things over. His first book published after the war was *Classical Landscape with Figures* (1947), a descriptive work based on his Greek experience. *The Saracen's Head* (1948) and *Draynflete Revealed* (1949) were in the manner of his pre-war satires, though the former was pitched as a children's book.

In 1951 Lancaster worked with John Piper on designs for the Festival of Britain. In the same year, on Piper's recommendation, he designed his first stage set, for *Pineapple Poll* at Sadler's Wells. This and the many stage designs that followed (several for Glyndebourne) released him from the austerity of line and allowed him to indulge in the Mediterranean colour he loved. In 1953 the Lancasters moved to Leicester House, a stucco Regency mansion at Henley-on-Thames. Karen died in 1964 and in 1967 Lancaster married Anne Eleanor Scott-James, journalist and author, the daughter of Rolfe Arnold Scott-*James, also journalist and author.

The 1960s with their fashionable fads and fantasies were perfect fodder for Lancaster's type of social satire. He would come into the *Express* office after lunching at one of his four clubs and hold court for a while, telling jokes, before settling down with the day's newspapers. George Malcolm Thomson, right-hand man to Lord Beaverbrook, said of Lancaster: 'The annoying thing at the *Express* was, not only was he the only one who could draw; he could also *write* better than anyone in the building'. The prose, admittedly, was an acquired taste, and it had to be taken on its own terms. When Betjeman wrote to congratulate Lancaster on 'that deliciously convoluted prose you write', the implied censure was not lost on Lancaster. The prose had to be taken as part of the rich plum-cake fruitiness of the character Lancaster had created for himself. It was often said that he looked like one of his own cartoon characters and, as he aged, he resembled more and more an effigy of the English gentleman on a French carnival float: bulging eyes, bulbous nose, buffalo-horn moustache, bald head, striped shirt, pinstripe suit from Thresher and Glenny, old-fashioned shoes with rounded toes.

'Osbert, it quickly becomes clear', wrote the architect Sir Hugh Casson, 'was a performance, meticulously practised and hilariously inflated and at times disturbing.' What, he wondered, was behind that 'elaborately woven yashmak of subsidiary clauses, this defensive portcullis of anecdotes, cranked into place at one's approach?' Lancaster was a work of art as memorable as any he created. It was as if he had chosen to be a 'living museum' exhibit, representing not the period of his own life but that of his lost father.

Lancaster was appointed CBE in 1953 and knighted in 1975, in which year he also received an honorary DLitt at Oxford. He also received honorary degrees from Birmingham (1964), Newcastle upon Tyne (1970), and St Andrews (1974). He was a fellow of University College, London (1967), an honorary fellow of RIBA and of Lincoln College, Oxford (1979), and was made RDI (1979). He died in Chelsea on 27 July 1986 and was buried at West Winch, Norfolk.

BEVIS HILLIER, *rev.*

Sources *The Times* (29 July 1986) · O. Lancaster, *All done from memory* (1953) · O. Lancaster, *With an eye to the future* (1967) · *Strand Magazine* (Feb 1947) · *Sunday Times* (25 July 1954) · M. Piper, 'Osbert Lancaster', *The Spectator* (1 Aug 1986) · E. Lucie-Smith, ed., *The essential Osbert Lancaster* (1988) · R. Boston, *Osbert: a portrait of Osbert Lancaster* (1989) · *CGPLA Eng. & Wales* (1987)

Likenesses B. Brandt, bromide print, 1942, NPG · J. Bown, photograph, repro. in *The Observer* (9 Sept 1979) · G. Maiteny, photograph, NPG [*see illus.*] · photographs, Hult. Arch.

Wealth at death £676,363: probate, 1987, *CGPLA Eng. & Wales*

Lancaster, Thomas of. *See* Thomas of Lancaster, second earl of Lancaster, second earl of Leicester, and earl of Lincoln (*c.*1278–1322).

Lancaster, Thomas (*d.* **1583**), Church of Ireland archbishop of Armagh, was possibly a native of Cumberland.

He had graduated BTh by 1536, probably from Oxford University. He was the rector of Offekerque in the pale of Calais from 1536 to 1540.

About 1550 Lancaster published a tract, 'The ryght and trew understandynge of the supper of the lord and the use thereof faythfully gathered out of ye holy scriptures', a copy of which is in the British Library. The book was dedicated to Edward VI but was published under a *nom de plume* (Johan Turke) as its eucharistic theology was more advanced than that authorized in the first Book of Common Prayer. Lancaster's protestantism commended him to Sir James Croft, Edward VI's viceroy in Ireland, and he was nominated to the vacant see of Kildare in April 1550. He was consecrated on 11 July 1550. He was allowed to hold the deanery of Kilkenny *in commendam* on account of the poverty of Kildare.

Bishop Lancaster was married, although his wife's name is unknown, and on that ground he was deprived of his ecclesiastical offices by a Marian royal commission in 1554. With the accession of Elizabeth to the throne, however, Lancaster was made a royal chaplain. He was granted the rectory of South Hill, Cornwall, and was presented to the treasurership of Salisbury Cathedral by the queen in 1559. He was highly favoured by John Jewel, bishop of Salisbury, becoming vicar-general and official principal of Salisbury as well as Jewel's suffragan bishop of Marlborough in 1560–61. He was a member of the lower house of convocation and on 5 February 1563 was in the minority of fifty-eight who approved of the proposed six formulas committing the established church to ultra-protestant doctrine and practices, as against the fifty-nine who opposed the change. In the same year he signed the petition of the lower house of convocation for reform of church discipline. He was admitted as principal of St Edmund Hall, Oxford, on 26 February 1565, an office which he held until 1568.

When Sir Henry Sidney became Elizabeth's viceroy in Ireland Thomas Lancaster secured a royal licence in October 1565 to attend upon him and to absent himself from his spiritual duties. He accompanied Deputy Sidney throughout much of his time in Ireland. It was probably on Sidney's recommendation that Elizabeth decided to promote Lancaster as the Church of Ireland archbishop of Armagh and primate in the summer of 1567. Cecil was pleased that the 'lusty good priest, Lancaster' was to be promoted (*CSP Ire.*, Elizabeth, xxi, no. 70). On 28 March 1568 Elizabeth informed the Irish lords justices that she had chosen

> Thomas Lancaster, one of our ordinary chaplains, heretofore bishop of Kildare in our said realm, and therein for his time served very laudably, and since that time has been very well acquainted in the said part of Ulster, having been lately in company with our said deputy in all his journeys within our said realm, and has preached right faithfully. (ibid., xxiii, no. 86)

Because the see of Armagh was left virtually bankrupt by his predecessor, Adam Loftus, Lancaster was allowed to retain the treasurership of Salisbury and the rectories of

South Hill and Sherfield, Hampshire, *in commendam*. He was also granted the archdeaconry of Kells and the rectory of Nobber, Meath diocese, and the prebend of Stagonil, Dublin. Furthermore, Lancaster was loaned £200 by the queen to allow him to become established in Armagh and she secretly made provision to lend him further sums not exceeding £50 if he so required. Archbishop Lancaster was reconsecrated with episcopal orders on 13 June 1568 by Archbishop Loftus of Dublin, Bishop Brady of Meath, and Bishop Daly of Kildare in Christ Church, Dublin. He preached his own consecration sermon on the subject of regeneration.

Elizabeth ordered that Armagh Cathedral and other ruined churches in Ulster be renovated after the devastation wrought by the wars waged by Shane O'Neill, lord of Tyrone. She ordered too that the residence of the archbishop at Armagh be restored, but she secretly intended it to house a provincial council which was to govern the north of Ireland on her behalf. The restoration proceeded slowly, but Elizabeth's provincial council for Ulster was never established. Archbishop Lancaster himself was unable to visit Armagh city in person for fear of his life and was obliged to confine his ministry to those parishes of his archdiocese which were situated in the English pale. It cannot be said that Lancaster's ministry was blessed with much success. The advent of his successor, John Long, was greeted with the hope of a fresh start for the Reformation in Ireland. Archbishop Long himself was of the opinion that there were not forty Irish born Christians in the whole of Ireland, a sorry reflection on Lancaster's fifteen years as primate of the Church of Ireland.

Archbishop Lancaster died at Drogheda in December 1583. He was buried in the vault of Primate Octavian del Palatio in St Peter's Church, Drogheda. Lancaster had intended to found a grammar school by the name of Queen Elizabeth College in Drogheda, and to endow eight exhibitions tenable for scholars at St Edmund Hall, Oxford, but the project failed to materialize as his deathbed will was successfully challenged on the grounds that he was 'crazed and sickly' and surfeited with red herring and alcohol when he composed it (TCD, MS 553). He was survived by a son and two daughters.

HENRY A. JEFFERIES

Sources *The whole works of Sir James Ware concerning Ireland*, ed. and trans. W. Harris, rev. edn, 1 (1764) · *CSP Ire.* · Emden, *Oxf.*, 4.338–9 · J. Jewel, bishop's register, Wilts. & Swindon RO · litigation about will, TCD, MS E.4.4 (553) · J. Morrin, ed., *Calendar of the patent and close rolls of chancery in Ireland, of the reigns of Henry VIII, Edward VI, Mary, and Elizabeth*, 1 (1861) · J. Turke [T. Lancaster], *The ryght and trew understa [n]dynge of the supper of the Lord* [1550]

Lancaster, Thomas William (1787–1859), Church of England clergyman and writer, born at Fulham, Middlesex, on 24 August 1787, was the son of the Revd Thomas Lancaster of Wimbledon, Surrey. He matriculated from Oriel College, Oxford, on 26 January 1804, and graduated BA (with a second class in *literae humaniores*) in 1807, and MA in 1810. In 1808 he was elected to a Michel scholarship at Queen's

College, and in the following year to a fellowship on the same foundation. After being ordained deacon in 1810 and priest in 1812, he became in the latter year curate of Banbury, Oxfordshire, and vicar of Banbury in 1815. He resigned his fellowship at Queen's on his marriage in 1816 to Anne, *née* Walford (1775/6–1860), of Banbury. They had no children.

Lancaster's relations with his parishioners were not happy, and although he retained the living of Banbury for over thirty-three years, he lived in Oxford for about half that time. In 1849 the bishop of Oxford, Samuel Wilberforce, persuaded him to exchange Banbury for the rectory of Over Worton, a small village near Woodstock. He did not find the new living more congenial than the old, and continued to live in Oxford, where he frequented the Bodleian Library. In 1831 he preached the Bampton lectures, taking for his subject the popular evidence of Christianity. He was appointed a select preacher to the university in 1832, and a public examiner in 1832–3. From 1840 to 1849 he acted, with little success, as undermaster (*ostiarius*, or usher) of Magdalen College School, and was for a time chaplain to the dowager countess of Guilford.

Lancaster was one of the old-fashioned 'high and dry' school, opposing the broad church and the Tractarians with equal fervour from the university pulpit. Besides his Bampton lectures, Lancaster published quite widely, engaging in the theological pamphlet wars of the 1830s but also writing works such as *The Harmony of the Law and the Gospel* (1825), *A Treatise on Confirmation* (1830), an edition (1834) of Aristotle's *Nicomachean Ethics* widely used in its day, and *Vindiciae symbolicae* (1848), a treatise on creeds and articles. Lancaster had partly prepared for press a collection of his sermons when he died, on 12 December 1859, at his lodgings in High Street, Oxford. He was buried in Holywell cemetery, and his sermons were published by subscription (1860). His wife died on 8 February 1860, aged eighty-four. W. A. GREENHILL, *rev.* H. C. G. MATTHEW

Sources *GM*, 3rd ser., 8 (1860), 188 · personal knowledge (1892) · *Oxford Journal* (17 Dec 1859) · J. R. Bloxam, *A register of the presidents, fellows … of Saint Mary Magdalen College*, 8 vols. (1853–85) · Boase, *Mod. Eng. biog.*

Archives Bodl. Oxf., papers

Wealth at death under £300: probate, 30 Jan 1860, *CGPLA Eng. & Wales*

Lancaster, William (1649/50–1717), college head, was the son of William Lancaster of Sockbridge in Barton parish, Westmorland. He was born in Barton and for some time taught at the parish school there. The school was near Lowther Castle, and when Sir John Lowther's son, afterwards Lord Lonsdale, went to Queen's College, Oxford, Lancaster went with him as his servitor. Lancaster was entered as a batteler at the college on 23 June 1670, and matriculated on 1 July that same year, aged twenty. He graduated BA on 6 February 1675, proceeded MA on 1 July 1678 (although the degree was initially stopped for some words Lancaster had said against the proctor, John Clerke of All Souls), BD on 12 April 1690, and DD on 8 July 1692.

William Lancaster (1649/50–1717), by George Vertue, 1718 (after Thomas Murray)

His career at Oxford was interrupted for a while by a stay in Paris on a state grant to which he had been recommended by Sir Joseph Williamson. On his return to England Lancaster continued to spend most of his time in college, though he was appointed domestic chaplain to the earl of Denbigh and was collated to the vicarage of Oakley, Buckinghamshire, on 1 September 1682. On 15 March 1679 he was made a fellow of Queen's, a post that he retained until his marriage in 1696; from 1686 to 1690 he was first junior and then senior bursar of his college.

From 1690 onwards Lancaster appears to have spent more time in London than in Oxford. He became domestic chaplain to Henry Compton, bishop of London, who nominated him on 22 July 1692 to the vicarage of St Martin-in-the-Fields (vacated by Thomas Tenison when he became bishop of Lincoln), but the rights of presentation were claimed by the queen, who installed Nicholas Gouge instead. Lancaster was finally instituted into the living on 31 October 1694, following Gouge's death. He continued to work closely with Compton, supervising a fund for dispossessed Scottish episcopalian clergy on the bishop's behalf. His wife, the daughter of Mr Wilmer of Sywell in Northamptonshire, was a relative of Compton. Through Compton's favour he was later collated (29 March 1705) to the archdeaconry of Middlesex, a post that he held until his death. Lancaster was also a part of the circle of his fellow

Cumbrian and student contemporary, William Nicolson, in London, along with John Waugh, White Kennett, Edward Gee, and Dean Grahme. Nicolson's son, Joseph, studied at Queen's College, and was shown much favour by Lancaster. In return Nicolson appears occasionally to have performed Lancaster's duties at St Martin-in-the-Fields when he was away in Oxford. Lancaster was a popular preacher and on 30 January 1697 he delivered a sermon before the Commons commemorating the death of Charles I. He used the occasion to decry the evil of rebellion, claiming that the greatest danger to William III, who had recently survived an assassination plot, came from the continued belief in a lawful right of resistance. A whig reply to this sermon was belatedly published in 1710, probably to coincide with the trial of Henry Sacheverell.

On 15 October 1704 Lancaster was elected as provost of Queen's College, but the election was disputed as contravening the college statutes. Lancaster's opponents claimed that only present, and not past, fellows of the college could hold the office. In response, Lancaster appealed successfully to the visitor, the archbishop of York, who confirmed the election on 18 November 1704. It was under Lancaster that the rebuilding of the college in the Palladian style was begun, with the provost sinking an estimated £4000 of his own money into the work. His efforts for the corporation of Oxford were repaid with a 1000-year lease to the college of a plot of land on the High Street.

From 1705 to 1709 Lancaster acted as vice-chancellor of Oxford. In administrative terms he rescued the university from the financial chicanery of his predecessor, William Delaune, who had embezzled the profits from the publishing of Clarendon's *History*. Academically, he tried to curb the influence of Lockean ideas in Oxford, blocking the appointment of John Wynne, a popularizer of Locke's *Essay Concerning Human Understanding*, as Lady Margaret professor of divinity in 1705. However, his intellectual influence was not solely negative. He was a keen promoter of literary talents and promoted the writings of Joseph Addison and Thomas Tickell. Lancaster was a tory, but the expectation that he would be another zealot like Delaune was disappointed. He generally appears to have acted to quell political controversy, taking the decision not to invite Sacheverell or his high-church supporters to preach again after May 1707. Lancaster attempted to co-operate with the government, helping to propose an address on the union of Scotland and England, despite opposition from many university members. His willingness to work with the Godolphin administration brought accusations of 'trimming', but also the possibility that he might be rewarded with a bishopric (St David's and Chichester were both rumoured). Such political pragmatism earned Lancaster the contempt of the arch-tory Thomas Hearne. Lancaster was 'smoothboots', the 'Northern bear' (a sneer at the lowly social origins of a man who had risen from village schoolmaster to vice-chancellor of the University of Oxford), and an 'old hypocritical, ambitious, drunken sot' (*DNB*).

However, once Sacheverell's trial effectively became a

verdict on the revolution of 1688, Lancaster was reluctantly forced to come to his defence. On 14 December 1709 Lancaster took Sacheverell to the House of Lords in his own coach and stood with him at the bar. On 13 January 1710 he put up £3000 bail for him. Clearly, though, there were limits to Lancaster's loyalty to the tory cause and he refused to give a personal testimony to Sacheverell's good character. Lancaster remained an important figure in Oxford after 1709, acting as pro-vice-chancellor, and with Bernard Gardiner of All Souls worked effectively to block the attempts of Francis Atterbury, dean of Christ Church, to reassert tory dominance within the university. In league with Gardiner and Arthur Charlett, Lancaster kept the university politically passive while the country waited to see what changes the death of the queen would bring.

Lancaster died in Oxford on 4 February 1717 of a 'gout of the stomach' (*DNB*) and was buried in the old church of St Martin-in-the-Fields on 8 February. He left £1000 in his will for the further rebuilding of Queen's. His portrait by T. Murray hangs in the college hall.

EDWARD VALLANCE

Sources DNB · *Hist. U. Oxf.*, 4.425; 5.78–96 · G. V. Bennett, *The tory crisis in church and state* (1975), 148–9 · *The London diaries of William Nicolson, bishop of Carlisle, 1702–1718*, ed. C. Jones and G. Holmes (1985) · E. Carpenter, *The protestant bishop, being the life of Henry Compton, 1632–1713, bishop of London* (1956), 310 · S. P., *A letter written in the year 1697 to Dr Lancaster* (1710) · W. Lancaster, *A sermon preached before the hon. House of Commons* (1697) · J. R. Magrath, *Queen's College*, 2 vols. (1921), vol. 2, pp. 76–84 · *Remarks and collections of Thomas Hearne*, ed. C. E. Doble and others, 5, OHS, 42 (1901) · Foster, *Alum. Oxon.* · will, PRO, PROB 11/556, sig. 38
Archives Bodl. Oxf., Ballard MSS, letters to A. Charlett
Likenesses G. Vertue, line engraving, 1718 (after T. Murray), BM, NPG [see illus.] · T. Murray, oils, Queen's College, Oxford
Wealth at death left £1000 to college: Magrath's *Queen's College* (1921), vol. 2, pp. 76–84

Lancaster, William Joseph Cosens [*pseud.* Harry Collingwood] **(1843–1922)**, children's writer, was born on 23 May 1843 at Concord Place, Weymouth, Dorset (most references except his birth certificate give his date of birth as 1851). He was the oldest son of Captain William Lancaster, a master mariner, and Anne, *née* Cosens. He was educated at the Royal Naval College, Greenwich, where he won a number of prizes and joined the Royal Navy as a midshipman, aged fifteen. Defective eyesight meant that Lancaster had to abandon a career in the navy; instead, he qualified as a civil engineer. He specialized in sea and harbour work and hydrology. In this capacity he travelled widely and in the course of his work visited the Baltic and the Mediterranean, the East and West Indies, and the coasts of Africa. At one stage in his career he lived for eight years in Natal. In York, on 10 July 1878, he married Kezia Hannah Rice Oxley (*b.* 1850/51), the daughter of George Oxley, a provisions dealer. They reportedly had one son although little else is known of Lancaster's private life, and his death was registered by a nephew, Harold G. Smellie.

Lancaster began to write his sea stories for boys in 1878 and continued to do so for the next forty years, publishing over fifty books for boys altogether. He always wrote under the pseudonym Harry Collingwood (the name chosen out of admiration for Vice-Admiral Cuthbert Collingwood, Nelson's second-in-command at Trafalgar). Lancaster's books were 'widely appreciated by many thousands of young readers' (*The Times*, 17 June 1922). His travels as a civil engineer in sea and harbour work provided him with authentic background material for his stories. Although most of his boys' stories were about the sea, he also wrote several about flying. His first book was *The Secret of the Sands* (1879), which was followed over the years by such titles as *Voyage of the 'Aurora'* (1885), *The Rover's Secret* (1888), *The Pirate Slaver* (1895), *An Ocean Chase* (1898), *With Airship and Submarine* (1907), and *A Middy of the Slave Squadron* (1910).

Lancaster was a keen sportsman and enjoyed swimming, shooting, riding, and cycling. Like his more famous contemporary, G. A. Henty, he was also a keen yachtsman and racer as well as a yacht designer. His other hobbies included watercolour painting, photography, and music. He died at 40 Liverpool Road, Chester, on 10 June 1922 and was buried in the city on the 15th; he was survived by his wife.   GUY ARNOLD

Sources WWW, 1916–28 · Allibone, *Dict.* · *The Times* (17 June 1922) · B. Doyle, *The who's who of children's literature* (1968) · b. cert. · m. cert. · d. cert. · *CGPLA Eng. & Wales* (1922)
Wealth at death £866 11s. 8d.: probate, 12 July 1922, *CGPLA Eng. & Wales*

Lancastre, de. For this title name *see* Lancastre Saldanha, Adeline Louisa Maria de, Countess de Lancastre (1824–1915).

Lancastre Saldanha, Adeline Louisa Maria de [*formerly* Adeline Louisa Maria De Horsey], **Countess de Lancastre** [*other married name* Adeline Louisa Maria Brudenell, countess of Cardigan] (**1824–1915**), aristocrat, was born on 24 December 1824, in Charles Street, Berkeley Square, London, the eldest of the three children and only daughter of Spencer Horsey Kilderbee (from 1832, De Horsey; *d.* 1860) and Lady Louisa Maria Judith (*d.* 1843), daughter of John Rous, first earl of Stradbroke. Educated at home by French governesses, she became fluent in five languages and an accomplished musician. Adeline De Horsey made her society début in the 1842 season, and rapidly acquired a reputation as an unconventional, ambitious flirt, substantiated by her engagement in 1848 to the Carlist pretender to the Spanish throne, the count of Montemolin. His failure to take the throne led directly to the ending of the engagement.

Rumours about De Horsey's morals burgeoned when society observed her blossoming relationship with a friend of her father's, James Thomas *Brudenell, seventh earl of Cardigan (1797–1868), army officer, who was married (albeit formally separated from his wife). In defiance of social convention, Adeline De Horsey was regularly seen riding in Hyde Park with the earl, without benefit of chaperon. In 1857, the remonstrances of her father caused her to leave his house, initially for a hotel in Hyde Park Square, and subsequently for a furnished house in Norfolk Street, Park Lane, where she was established by

Adeline Louisa Maria de Lancastre Saldanha, Countess de Lancastre (1824–1915), by Alice Hughes

Cardigan as his mistress. She remained there until Cardigan arrived with the news of the death of his wife in July 1858. They sailed to the Mediterranean in August and were married in Gibraltar on 28 September. Lady Cardigan joined her husband in his favourite pursuits, hunting, yachting, and racing, and became a notable member of the 'sporting set'; the courtesan Skittles referred to her as 'the head of our profession' (Thomas, 306). She was never welcomed in polite circles or at court. After Cardigan's death, childless, on 27 March 1868, Lady Cardigan took over the management of the family estates, which had been left to her for her lifetime; the improvements which she carried out and the repayment of heavy mortgages on the estates were a source of pride to her.

On 28 August 1873, Adeline Cardigan was married again, to Don Antonio Manuelo de Lancastre Saldanha, conde de Lancastre (*d.* 1898), having unsuccessfully sought to marry Disraeli. Following the marriage, she spent some time in his native Portugal, and in Paris, where the count preferred to live. By 1879, the countess of Cardigan and Lancastre (as she styled herself) had returned to Deene Park, ostensibly to oversee the management of the estates, while her husband remained in Paris, where he died in 1898.

In 1909 she published a volume of memoirs, *My Recollections*, which caused tremors to run through high society. Written by a publisher's assistant from notes of conversations, the book is full of scandal and malicious gossip, some half-remembered, some evidently fabricated, from the mid-Victorian period, without the customary discretion as to persons. The timing of the publication—coinciding with anxieties over Lloyd George's budget—was a particular source of concern. Lady Dorothy Nevill remarked: 'What people are afraid of is that when the election comes these Radical demons will cut pieces out just to show what the upper classes are' (Nevill, 194). Lady Cardigan remained unrepentant; eccentric and autocratic to the last, she died at Deene Park on 25 May 1915, and was interred in the parish church at Deene, with her first husband.   K. D. REYNOLDS

Sources countess of Cardigan and Lancastre [A. L. M. Saldanha], *My recollections* (1909) • R. Nevill, *Life and letters of Lady Dorothy Nevill* (1919) • GEC, *Peerage* • D. Thomas, *Cardigan: the hero of Balaclava* (1974) • J. Wake, *The Brudenells of Deene* (1953) • *The Times* (27 May 1915) • Burke, *Peerage* • *WWW* • private information (2004)
Archives Deene Park, Northamptonshire
Likenesses E. Boehm, bust, Deene Park, Northamptonshire • A. Hughes, photograph, unknown collection; copyprint, Women's Library, London [*see illus.*] • portraits, repro. in countess of Cardigan and Lancastre, *My recollections* • portraits, Deene Park, Northamptonshire
Wealth at death £21,678 2s. 0d.: resworn probate, 7 Aug 1915, CGPLA Eng. & Wales

Lance, George (1802–1864), still-life painter, was born in the manor house of Little Easton, near Dunmow, Essex, on 24 March 1802. His father was the adjutant of the Essex yeomanry, while his mother was the daughter of Colonel Constable of Beverley, Yorkshire. His parents had eloped while his mother was still at boarding-school. The family moved to London during Lance's childhood, when his father became inspector of the Bow Street horse patrol. One contemporary biographer noted that Lance was 'born an artist' like 'most of those who have achieved distinguished eminence in art' (Bryan, *Painters*, 103). He favoured picture books over other toys. His family sent him as an adolescent to Leeds to work as a clerk in a factory, a position that is said to have damaged his health. The thirteen-year-old Lance soon returned to London, unhappy with his foray into commerce and determined to become an artist. While studying in the British Museum, he approached Charles Landseer, who was sketching there. During conversation Lance learned that Landseer was a pupil in the studio of Benjamin Robert Haydon and soon after Lance went to Haydon's studio and offered himself as a pupil. He remained there for seven years, studying at the Royal Academy Schools at the same time.

It was in Haydon's studio that Lance fixed upon his artistic speciality: fruit painting. As part of his artistic training Lance produced cartoons of the Parthenon frieze in the British Museum, completed courses in dissection, and also executed studies of fruit and vegetables. A fruit study prepared for a scene from Homer's *Iliad* attracted the attention of the collector Sir George Beaumont, who purchased the study. Soon after, both the duke of Bedford and the earl of Shaftesbury commissioned fruit pieces. Haydon himself noted the improbability that an artist trained in his studio would excel at fruit painting rather than history painting; he reportedly told Lance, 'it seems a

pity to cast off the nobler walk of Art, but I am so convinced you will have no competitor in that you are now following' (*Art Journal*, 1857, 306).

On 15 May 1823 Lance married Sarah Rawles, with whom he had at least two daughters, Mary Elizabeth and Eliza, and a son, George Edmund, a cotton broker of Liverpool. The following year Lance began to exhibit works publicly, sending still-life paintings to the British Institution and to the Society of British Artists. In 1828 he contributed his first work to the Royal Academy exhibition, another still life. Lance continued to exhibit his work publicly throughout his career, with thirty-eight works shown at the Royal Academy, forty-eight at the Suffolk Street Gallery, and 135 at the British Institution. Lance completed more than 400 fruit and other still-life paintings during his career, judged by a contemporary as 'wonderful alike for the variety of interest displayed in them, and for the splendour and truthfulness of their execution' (Bryan, *Painters*, 103). During his lifetime his paintings were compared to those of the Dutch old masters and lavishly praised: 'his "fruit-pieces", which are his speciality, have never been surpassed in luxuriance and richness of colour, in truth, and in effective and most harmonious grouping' (*Art Journal*, 1857, 305). Works by Lance are currently held in the National Gallery, the Tate collection, and the Victoria and Albert Museum, London.

Although known for his still-life works, Lance frequently produced paintings in other genres. In 1836 he won the prize for best historical picture of the season at the Liverpool Academy with *Melancthon's First Misgiving of the Church of Rome* (Manchester City Galleries). In addition, he executed portraits, such as *Dr. William Forbes* (NPG) and *Rev. William Harness* (Tate collection). Self-portraits of Lance are in the collections of both the Victoria and Albert Museum and the National Portrait Gallery, London. However, after 1845 he painted exclusively still-life works, exhibiting publicly for the last time in 1862. Throughout his career Lance accepted pupils, including Sir John Gilbert and William Duffield—reputedly his favourite pupil—whose death at the age of thirty-one greatly affected Lance.

Little is known of Lance's personal life. He lived for most of his life in London, retiring for health reasons to Cheshire in 1862. He died at Sunnyside, New Brighton, Wallasey, Cheshire, on 18 June 1864. Interestingly, a contemporary biographer notes: 'a daughter of Mr. Lance follows in her father's career, evincing considerable ability' (Bryan, *Painters*, 103).   MORNA O'NEILL

Sources 'British artists, their style and character: no. XXIX, George Lance', *Art Journal*, 19 (1857), 305–7 • Bryan, *Painters* (1876); (1903–5) • Graves, *Brit. Inst.*, 328–30 • J. Johnson, ed., *Works exhibited at the Royal Society of British Artists, 1824–1893, and the New English Art Club, 1888–1917*, 2 vols. (1975), 277 • *Art Journal*, 26 (1864), 244 • K. Powling, 'Lance, George', *The dictionary of art*, ed. J. Turner (1996) • Redgrave, *Artists* • *IGI* • *CGPLA Eng. & Wales* (1864)
Archives Edinburgh Central Reference Library, signed note describing a picture entitled *The ballad* • FM Cam., signed note regarding the collection of his picture, *The grandmother's blessing*, MS 3–1966 n.45 • V&A, letters | Mitchell L., Glas., Glasgow City

Archives, corresp. with or relating to Sir William Stirling-Maxwell, concerning *The boar hunt* by Velasquez, MS T–SK 29/58/1–18 **Likenesses** G. Lance, self-portrait, oils, *c.*1830, V&A · G. Lance, self-portrait, pencil drawing, NPG · G. Lance, self-portrait, water-colour drawing, BM · Maull & Co., carte-de-visite, NPG · Maull & Polyblank, two cartes-de-visite, NPG · J. Smyth, line engraving (after G. Clint), BM, NPG; repro. in *The Art-union*, 9 (1847) · aquatint, BM · wood-engraving, NPG; repro. in *ILN* (21 Dec 1861) · woodcut (after drawing by J. Gilbert), BM **Wealth at death** under £14,000: probate, 26 July 1864, *CGPLA Eng. & Wales*

Lancecrona, Agnes (*fl.* 1382–1388). *See under* Vere, Robert de, ninth earl of Oxford, marquess of Dublin, and duke of Ireland (1362–1392).

Lancelene, Edith de (*fl.* 1133–1138/9), monastic patron and abbess of Godstow, was the widow of William de Lancelene and the originator of the community of nuns at Godstow, Oxfordshire. According to the preface of the fifteenth-century cartulary of Godstow, she came from Winchester, the only child of noble parents, and was fair and comely. On the death of her husband some time before 1133, she obeyed a vision and led a solitary life at Binsey, Oxfordshire, before founding a community of nuns at Godstow. She was helped in this by Henry I and her nunnery benefited from royal and episcopal support. A confirmation charter of the bishop of Lincoln, issued in 1138–9, probably at the time of the dedication of the church at Godstow, underlined the importance of her role in the foundation. It stated that the nunnery was founded through her generosity and under her direction, and that she built the church and helped to gather the endowments. She entered the community and ruled it as the head for a long time—according to a note in the Latin cartulary for fifty-one years. If she married young, and lived to an old age, this is a possibility, but it may reflect confusion with her successor as abbess, apparently a second Edith.

According to the cartulary Edith had two daughters, Emma and Hawise, who both entered the community and became prioress, as well as a son, John, who became abbot of Abingdon.   S. P. THOMPSON

Sources A. Clark, ed., *The English register of Godstow nunnery*, 2 vols., EETS (1911), 1.26–7; 2.674–5 · PRO, MS E 164/20, esp. fols. 5, 13, 68, 183*v* · D. M. Smith, ed., *Lincoln, 1067–1185*, English Episcopal Acta, 1 (1980), 20, n. 33 · W. Holtzmann, ed., *Papsturkunden in England*, 1 (Berlin), Abhandlung der Gesellschaft der Wissenschaften zu Göttingen, new ser., 25 (1930–31), 41, 259–60 · D. Knowles, C. N. L. Brooke, and V. C. M. London, eds., *The heads of religious houses, England and Wales*, 1: *940–1216* (1972), 211–12 · H. E. Salter, ed., *Eynsham cartulary*, 2, OHS, 51 (1908), 361 · *VCH Oxfordshire*, vol. 2

Lancey, Oliver De (*c.*1749–1822), army officer and politician in America, was born in New York, the son of General Oliver De Lancey (1718–1785), an army officer who fought against the revolutionaries during the American War of Independence, and Phila Franks, daughter of Jacob Franks of Philadelphia. His father's brother was James *DeLancey, the celebrated New York lawyer, who was chief justice of that colony between 1733 and 1760 and lieutenant-governor from 1753 to 1760. De Lancey's father and uncle were sons of Etienne De Lancey, a wealthy

Huguenot of Caen in Normandy, who had emigrated to America following the revocation of the edict of Nantes (1685), and bought large estates in New York, where the brothers ranked among the colony's wealthiest and most powerful citizens.

Oliver De Lancey was educated in England and entered the British army as a cornet in the 14th dragoons on 1 October 1766. He was promoted to lieutenant on 12 December 1770 and to captain into the 17th dragoons on 16 May 1773. When the American War of Independence broke out in 1775 he was at once dispatched to New York to make arrangements for the accommodation and remounting of his own regiment. In the following year his father raised, equipped at his own expense, and commanded three battalions of American loyalists. De Lancey meanwhile accompanied his regiment to Nova Scotia and to Staten Island in June 1775. He participated in the expedition to Long Island, where he commanded the cavalry outposts in the action of 28 August, in which the American General Woodhull surrendered to him, but was unfortunately murdered by De Lancey's soldiers. At the battle of Brooklyn he commanded the advance of the right column of the British army under Sir Henry Clinton and Sir William Erskine, served at the capture of New York and the battle of White Plains, and was promoted major in his regiment on 3 July 1778. With this rank he covered the retreat of Knyphausen's column in Clinton's retreat from Philadelphia, was present at the battle of Monmouth court house, and was in temporary command of the 17th dragoons. He also commanded the outposts in front of the New York lines from mid-1778 to the end of 1779. De Lancey was then appointed as deputy quartermaster-general to the force sent to South Carolina, and after serving at the capture of Charles Town he became aide-de-camp to Lord Cornwallis, and eventually succeeded Major André as adjutant-general to the army at New York.

On 3 October 1781 De Lancey was promoted lieutenant-colonel of the 17th dragoons, and he retired to England with his father at the end of the war. The king appointed De Lancey, on Lord Sydney's recommendation, to settle the military claims of the American loyalists, and as head of a commission to settle all the army accounts connected with the war. On 18 November 1790 he was promoted colonel and made deputy adjutant-general at the Horse Guards. In 1792 he became superintendent-general of barracks and in 1794 received the post of barrack-master-general, with an income of £1500 a year. On 20 May of the following year George III appointed him colonel of the 17th dragoons. In September 1796 he entered parliament as MP for Maidstone, a seat which he held until June 1802.

De Lancey was promoted lieutenant-general on 1 January 1801, but in November 1804 the commissioners of military inquiry found serious mistakes in his barrack accounts. He was removed from his post as barrack-master-general, but in spite of the violent attacks of the political opposition, headed by John Calcraft, he was not prosecuted, and was treated rather as having been culpably careless than actually fraudulent. He did not contest his seat in 1802, and in 1806 his property of Effingham Hill in Surrey was seized to meet his liabilities. He remained a member of the consolidated board of general officers, however, and was promoted general on 1 January 1812. He eventually retired to Edinburgh, where he died on 3 September 1822. He was survived by his only son, Oliver De *Lancey (1803–1837), army officer.

H. M. STEPHENS, rev. TROY O. BICKHAM

Sources B. Murphy, 'De Lancey, Oliver', HoP, Commons, 1790–1820 · E. R. Fingerhut, 'De Lancey, Oliver', ANB · L. S. Lanitz-Schürer, 'Whig-loyalists: the De Lanceys of New York', New York Historical Society Quarterly, 56 (1972), 179–98
Archives BL, corresp. · PRO, corresp.
Likenesses H. Benbridge, oils, Pennsylvania Museum, Philadelphia

Lancey, Oliver De (1803–1837), army officer, was born in Guernsey, the only son of General Oliver De *Lancey (c.1749–1822), barrack-master-general from 1794 to 1804. He entered the army as a second lieutenant in the 60th rifles on 30 March 1818, and joined the 3rd battalion in India in the same year. He was promoted first lieutenant on 17 June 1821, and after serving as aide-de-camp to Lieutenant-General Sir Charles Colville, commander-in-chief at Bombay, was promoted captain on 7 August 1829, and joined the 3rd battalion at Gibraltar, where he learned Spanish and took a keen interest in Spanish politics. His battalion returned to England in 1832, but De Lancey still kept up his interest in Spain, and was one of the first English officers who volunteered to join the Spanish legion which was being raised to serve under the command of Major-General Sir De Lacy Evans against the Carlists.

De Lancey sailed for Spain in 1835 with one of the first drafts from England, and on the way out showed his courage when his ship struck in a fog on the rocks off Ushant. On landing he was placed at the head of a regiment of the legion, and, after serving as acting adjutant-general at the action of Hernani, accompanied Lieutenant-Colonel Greville in command of the expedition to relieve Santander, which was then hard pressed by the Carlists. The expedition was successful, and De Lancey received the cross of San Fernando and was appointed deputy adjutant-general to the legion. He distinguished himself in the defence of San Sebastian, especially in the action of 1 October, and was sent on a delicate mission to Madrid, which he carried out to the satisfaction of his general.

Not long after his return to San Sebastian the Carlists attacked the town, on 15 March 1837, and De Lancey was killed at the head of his regiment, just as his more famous cousin, Sir William Howe De *Lancey, Wellington's quartermaster-general, was killed at Waterloo. His tomb is in the fort at San Sebastian.

H. M. STEPHENS, rev. JAMES LUNT

Sources GM, 2nd ser., 8 (1837)

Lancey, Sir William Howe De (c.1778–1815), army officer, probably born in New York, was the son of Stephen De Lancey (1747/8–1798), clerk of the city of Albany and later governor of Tobago, and his wife, Cornelia, daughter of the Revd H. Barclay of Trinity Church, New York. The scion of a wealthy and influential loyalist family, he is thought to have attended Harrow School (1789–91) before being

commissioned a cornet in the 16th light dragoons in 1792. Despite his youth he did duty with his regiment and by October 1794 was a captain in the new raised 80th regiment, which he joined in Holland in December that year; he first saw action at Tuil on the 28th. On the way to India with the regiment in 1796, his youthful good looks and infectious high spirits caught the attention of General John St Leger who, in March 1797, took him to Calcutta as his aide-de-camp in readiness for an expedition to Manila, an enterprise in which the 33rd foot, under its young colonel, the future duke of Wellington, was also to take part. William Hickey records in his diary two lively occasions when the two men were among his guests.

On returning to England in late 1798 as captain in the 17th light dragoons (a regiment of which his uncle, General Oliver De Lancey, was colonel), De Lancey spent some months in Canterbury before his uncle procured his promotion as major in the 45th, then serving in the West Indies. Granted leave to await its return, he put the interval to good use by entering the Royal Military College at High Wycombe that had been recently established for the education of staff officers. Although he possessed a facility for drawing, he probably took this step at the suggestion of his uncle by marriage, General Sir David Dundas, then quartermaster-general of the forces. He stayed for eighteen months until September 1802 and reached, as few did, the class of the chief instructor, General François Jarry, an achievement which, in the opinion of Dundas, qualified him to become in 1804 one of the half-dozen officers on the permanent staff of the quartermaster-general, the branch of the staff responsible for troop movements. As such he served in the Yorkshire district (1806) and Ireland (1807) before sailing in 1808 as the senior assistant quartermaster-general first to Sweden and then, in August, to the Iberian peninsula. In Sir John Moore's campaign he had to conduct Sir John Hope's division by a long detour to Salamanca, and he stayed with it during the retreat to Corunna. As lieutenant-colonel on the permanent staff, he returned to Portugal early in April 1809 and became deputy quartermaster-general under Colonel George Murray, a position he held for the remainder of the war. Murray reported to Major-General Alexander Hope on 6 October 1809 that he was: 'Intelligent, zealous and anxious to be employed in any way in which he can promote the service' (Luffness MSS), and a junior officer in the department found him 'everything I could wish as a commanding officer' (Captain Tryon Still to General Le Marchant, 30 June 1810, Le Marchant MSS). In 1812, during Murray's absence, he headed the department until the arrival in August of Colonel James Willoughby Gordon; he headed it again from December 1812 to March 1813. While unable to react to Wellington's wishes quite as Murray had done, De Lancey's operation orders nevertheless satisfactorily interpreted Wellington's memoranda for those bold initiatives that culminated in the battle of Salamanca. Later, after experiencing Gordon's meddlesome methods, Wellington was able to say that De Lancey did the job much better. Murray, upon his return, gave De

Lancey in May 1813 the exacting but flattering task of conducting the powerful left wing of the army under Sir Thomas Graham for the advance into Spain, and he continued to act with this wing until the end of the war. He was promoted colonel in June 1813 and on 1 January 1815 he was rewarded with a knighthood in the Order of the Bath.

At the peace De Lancey was appointed head of the department in Scotland. He married in Edinburgh on 4 April 1815 Magdalen, daughter of Sir James *Hall of Dunglass, fourth baronet (1761–1832), and Lady Helen Douglas (1762–1837). A few days later he responded loyally to an appeal to rejoin Wellington who, on assuming command in the Southern Netherlands, had inherited in Sir Hudson Lowe a quartermaster-general whom he could not abide, and whom he succeeded in getting posted elsewhere. Though expressing disappointment at being no more than deputy pending Murray's return, De Lancey hastened to Brussels on 9 May and from 15 June onwards was occupied day and night. He conducted the retreat from Quatre Bras on 17 June and marked out the position the troops were to occupy at Waterloo on the 18th—to the rear, apparently, of the ground originally chosen by the duke. Late in the battle of Waterloo, while talking to Wellington, he was struck in the back by a spent cannon-ball that broke eight ribs. Left for dead on the field for thirty-six hours, he was taken up and carried to a farmhouse in Mont-St Jean where, though devotedly nursed by his young wife, he died on 26 June 1815. His remains were buried on the 28th in the protestant cemetery of St Joost-ten-Node, from where they were removed in 1889 to nearby Evere. His widow, who married Henry Harvey in 1819, died in 1822.

All who spoke of De Lancey testify to his engaging manner and cheerful temper, a character borne out in his letters. If he had a fault as a staff officer, it was in his failure sometimes to distance himself from those to whom he had to give orders, but this was a largely unavoidable consequence of his naturally easy-going disposition.

S. G. P. WARD

Sources PRO, WO 25/745, no. 72 (1809) · PRO, WO 31/52 · PRO, WO 31/89 · NL Scot., Murray MSS, Adv. MSS 47.1.22–47.3.6Y · NRA Scotland, Luffness MSS, GD 364 [Murray to Hope] · Royal Military College, Sandhurst, Le Marchant MSS, WO 99/13 · MS Entry Book, Staff College Library, Camberley · *A week at Waterloo: Lady De Lancey's narrative*, ed. B. R. Ward (1906) · C. M. Duncan-Jones, *Trusty and well-beloved: letters of William Harness (80th)* (1957) · *Memoirs of William Hickey*, ed. A. Spencer, 4 vols. (1913–25) · *The dispatches of … the duke of Wellington … from 1799 to 1818*, ed. J. Gurwood, 13 vols. in 12 (1834–9) · *Supplementary despatches (correspondence) and memoranda of Field Marshal Arthur, duke of Wellington*, ed. A. R. Wellesley, second duke of Wellington, 15 vols. (1858–72) · E. Longford [E. H. Pakenham, countess of Longford], *Wellington*, 2 vols. (1969–72) · S. G. P. Ward, *Wellington's headquarters: a study of the administrative problems in the Peninsula, 1809–14* (1957) · *The Harrow School Register* (1999) · J. Philippart, ed., *The royal military calendar*, 2 (1815), 232

Likenesses miniature, c.1800, repro. in Ward, ed., *Week at Waterloo* · portrait, c.1813–1814, repro. in Ward, ed., *A week at Waterloo* · T. Heaphy, steel engraving, c.1814

Lanchester, Edith (1871–1966), socialist and feminist, was born at 1 St John's Terrace, Hove, Sussex, on 28 July 1871,

the fifth child in the family of eight children of Henry Jones Lanchester (1834–1914), an architect, and his wife, Octavia Ward (1834–1916). Her brother Frederick William *Lanchester (1868–1946) formed the Lanchester Engine Company in 1899 and introduced the Lanchester motor car in 1901; another brother, George Herbert *Lanchester (1874–1970), was also prominent in the firm. After attending the Birkbeck Institution and the Maria Grey training college, Edith (known to her intimates as Biddy) was first a teacher and then a clerk-secretary. When she came to prominence in October 1895 she was working for a firm in the City of London.

Edith Lanchester was a convinced socialist and a member of the Social Democratic Federation (SDF), Britain's leading Marxist body, lodging in Battersea with working-class SDF comrades. Her celebrity or notoriety resulted from events which followed her announced intention to live with her lover, James Sullivan (d. 1945), without marrying him. Her view was that marriage reduced a wife to the position of a chattel. Sullivan, who was also an SDF member, worked in a black lead factory but he had intellectual ambitions and worked hard at self-education. He later became a short-hand typist and bookkeeper.

One can speculate on Edith's family's reaction had her lover been of a higher social class and not borne an Irish name. As it was, they were determined to stop the union. At the behest of her parents and brothers she was interviewed at her lodgings on 25 October 1895 by George Fielding Blandford, a leading mental specialist and the author of *Insanity and its Treatment* (1871; 4th edn, 1892). Although Blandford had warned in the book against mistaking immorality for irrationality he signed a medical certificate to confine her to a mental institution. Under section 11 of the Lunacy Act of 1890 a single certificate was adequate for seven days' compulsory incarceration in cases of urgency, but a second certificate was obtained shortly afterwards. Dr Blandford explained that as he would have certified her if she had threatened suicide, he was justified in preventing her from trying to commit 'social suicide'. Edith forcibly resisted her father and brothers, but in the end she was dragged off to a carriage and driven to The Priory institution, Roehampton.

The affair led to enormous publicity and the intervention of John Burns, MP for Battersea and formerly a member of the SDF. The *New York Times* commented (3 November 1895) that the affair had 'rivet[ed] the attention of three kingdoms' and that '[n]o penny paper had printed less than ten columns on this engrossing subject during the week'. But according to the report of the commissioners of lunacy, when the papers on the case were put before them on Monday 28 October it was the first they had heard of Edith Lanchester. They took care, however, to visit her at Roehampton the same afternoon, conducted an 'interview of some duration' and 'satisfied themselves that she was not then insane'. She was freed the following day under section 75 of the Lunacy Act, as a patient 'detained without sufficient cause' (*Report*, 53). She had been in the institution for four days.

Lanchester and Sullivan continued to live together without ever marrying, though socialist and feminist opinion in 1895 suggested that in the conditions of existing society it would have been more sensible to do so. For a period Edith was employed in a clerical capacity by Karl Marx's daughter Eleanor.

The couple paid a considerable price for their refusal to observe the conventions. According to their daughter Elsa *Lanchester (1902–1986), the actress whose autobiography is the source for her mother's later life, Edith never saw her father again. (Perhaps she would not have done so even if she had married Sullivan.) She did, however, re-establish friendly relations with her mother, who left her £400. Her socialist, vegetarian, and atheist beliefs may have contributed to alienating her daughter, who wrote that she was never able to like her mother (Lanchester, 5, 11, 32, 49, 314).

Edith Lanchester was a militant though apparently not very active supporter of women's suffrage. She was a pacifist during the First World War and afterwards joined the Communist Party. She assisted her son Waldo, who after release from prison as a conscientious objector became a puppet maker and weaver. After James Sullivan's death in 1945 Edith moved to Brighton where she spent the remainder of her long life. Elsa wrote that she remained a communist, displaying posters outside her Brighton flat, and attending political meetings so long as she was physically active enough to walk to the bus (ibid., 316–17). Edith Lanchester died at her home, 18 Highcroft Villas, Brighton, Sussex, on 26 March 1966.

The Lanchester affair had no immediate impact on the lunacy laws, for there was no major legislation until 1959. After the public obloquy to which Dr Blandford had been subjected in 1895 the laws may have been interpreted with more care, at least where middle-class women were concerned. Edith Lanchester's action in defying social convention and her own family at whatever cost was one of many gestures by women in the 1890s to increase their freedom and civil rights. As such she deserves to be remembered as a pioneer of the freedom of her sex.

DAVID RUBINSTEIN

Sources New York Times (3 Nov 1895) · 'Commissioners in lunacy: fiftieth report', Parl. papers (1896), vol. 39/1, no. 304 · Y. Kapp, Eleanor Marx, 2 (1976) · H. D. Sears, The sex radicals: free love in high Victorian America (1977) · E. Lanchester, Elsa Lanchester herself (1983) · E. Showalter, The female malady: women, madness, and English culture, 1830–1980 (1985) · D. Rubinstein, Before the suffragettes: women's emancipation in the 1890s (1986) · b. cert. · d. cert.
Likenesses photograph, repro. in Lanchester, Elsa Lanchester herself, following p. 26

Lanchester [married name Laughton], **Elsa Sullivan** (1902–1986), actress and entertainer, was born on 28 October 1902 at 48 Farley Road, Lewisham, London, the second child of James Sullivan (d. 1945), factory worker and later commercial clerk, and Edith *Lanchester (1871–1966), daughter of Henry J. Lanchester of Brighton. Her parents were militant socialists, pacifists, and vegetarians who caused a scandal when, true to their free love beliefs, they decided to live together in 1895 without marrying. Edith's

Elsa Sullivan Lanchester (1902–1986), by Doris Clare Zinkeisen, exh. RA 1925

family was so outraged that they kidnapped her in collusion with a psychiatrist who committed her to a lunatic asylum. Her cause was taken up by fellow members of the Social Democratic Federation (she had been secretary to Eleanor Marx) and her release was secured when she was found not to be insane.

Unsurprisingly, Elsa Lanchester was brought up in a family environment that stressed rebellion and nonconformity. Moving around a variety of houses in south London, she received relatively little formal schooling despite attending a council school and Mr Kettle's progressive school in Clapham Common. Her precocious talent for dancing led to a scholarship at the age of eleven to Isadora Duncan's Bellevue School in Paris, an episode cut short by the First World War. She then formed her own dance club and began to teach dancing at the Margaret Morris School in Chelsea. After the war she rented a small hall in Charlotte Street, London, that became the Children's Theatre (1918–21), recruiting local children for musical entertainments. It was shut down by the London county council for exploiting child labour. In 1921 she co-founded the Cave of Harmony in Gower Street, a nightclub devoted to presenting late-night cabaret and avantgarde plays that became a fashionable haunt for the bohemian London of which she was a part. A red-haired gamine with a snub nose, she excelled in musical turns. She paid her way by working as an artist's model, posing for Jacob Epstein, and (on occasion) acting as a co-respondent in divorce cases.

Lanchester's first theatrical appearance was in *Thirty Minutes in a Street* at the Kingsway Theatre in 1922, followed by the Larva in the Capek brothers' *The Insect Play* for Nigel Playfair, who cast her in several further productions. Evelyn Waugh, a friend, wrote an amateur film in which she appeared in 1924. Another friend, H. G. Wells, wrote three short films for her which were made about 1927. Appearing on stage in Arnold Bennet's *Mr Prohack* in 1927, she met the young actor Charles *Laughton (1899–1962). They lived together in Soho before marrying on 10 February 1929. Shortly after the wedding, Lanchester discovered that Laughton was a homosexual following an incident with a rent boy who wanted more money. Theirs was a complex marriage that lasted up to Laughton's death. Lanchester remained loyal and supportive to Laughton as his career took off and he became one of the leading actors of his time. She was inevitably overshadowed by him and in any case possessed a different kind of talent. Not being a conventional beauty, she found herself playing supporting roles in films, often opposite Laughton.

Lanchester was Anne of Cleves to Laughton's eponymous character in Alexander Korda's *The Private Life of Henry VIII* (1933) which she then followed by acting with her husband in the 1933 Old Vic Theatre season. She was particularly successful as Ariel to Laughton's Prospero in *The Tempest*. In 1935 she went to Hollywood to play *The Bride of Frankenstein* opposite Boris Karloff. Although she was on screen only for a short time (she also played Mary Shelley in the opening scene) this remains her most iconic role and the one with which she will always be associated. The following year she played opposite Laughton on film in *Rembrandt* and on the London stage in the title role of *Peter Pan* (Laughton played Captain Hook). Hers was the last Peter Pan to be approved by J. M. Barrie.

Lanchester and Laughton moved permanently to the United States in 1939 and became American citizens in 1950. Lanchester had a regular film career playing spinsters, eccentrics, and other character parts and was nominated for the best supporting actress Oscar for *Come to the Stable* (1949) and for her role as Laughton's nurse in *Witness for the Prosecution* (1958). However, she really came into her own at the Turnabout Theatre, Los Angeles, where from 1941 to 1951 she appeared in cabaret, reviving some of her old turns from the Cave of Harmony and adding new songs by Forman Brown to her repertoire, with Ray Henderson as piano accompanist. She later toured the country appearing to packed houses. In 1960 Laughton directed her in a successful one-woman show, *Elsa Lanchester Herself*. After Laughton's death in 1962 she continued to act on television and in films. She also performed cabaret, appeared on chat shows, and released several albums. Her autobiography, *Elsa Lanchester Herself*, was published in 1983. She died of bronchopneumonia in Los Angeles on 26 December 1986, and was buried there.

Lanchester claimed she lacked ambition for the great stage roles which is why she threw herself into cabaret. She told an interviewer: 'I only wanted to do vaudeville ... I like to get a laugh. I'm a vaudevillian, not an actor' (*Guardian*). Nevertheless she will be remembered as one of the finest character actresses of the twentieth century.

ROHAN MCWILLIAM

Sources E. Lanchester, *Elsa Lanchester herself* (1983) · E. Lanchester, *Charles Laughton and I* (1938) · S. Callow, *Charles Laughton: a difficult actor* (1987) · C. Higham, *Charles Laughton: an intimate biography* (1976) · *The Times* (29 Dec 1986) · press cuttings microfiche, BFI, Elsa Lanchester · F. Roberts, 'Elsa Lanchester', *Films in Review* (Aug–Sept 1976), 385–404 · *The Guardian* (10 Sept 1983) [interview with Elsa Lanchester] · E. Waugh, *A little learning: the first volume of an autobiography* (1964) · *The diaries of Evelyn Waugh*, ed. M. Davie (1976) · E. Lanchester, *A gamut of girls* (1988) · K. Hunt, *Equivocal feminists: the Social Democratic Federation and the woman question, 1884–1911* (1996) · b. cert. · m. cert.
Archives BFI, Joseph Losey Collection, corresp. with Joseph Losey, items 355 and 390 | FILM BFI NFTVA, documentary footage · BFI NFTVA, performance footage | SOUND BL NSA, 'Elsa Lanchester reminisces', 1967, 1 LP0135968
Likenesses D. C. Zinkeisen, oils, exh. RA 1925, NPG [*see illus.*] · photographs, 1927–57, Hult. Arch. · photographs, repro. in Lanchester, *Elsa Lanchester herself* · photographs, repro. in Lanchester, *Gamut of girls*

Lanchester, Frederick William [*pseud.* Paul Netherton-Herries] (1868–1946), car and aircraft designer and engineer, was born on 23 October 1868 at 4 Sandfield Terrace, Lewisham Road, Lewisham, London, the fourth of the eight children of Henry Jones Lanchester (1834–1914), architect, surveyor, and part-time inventor, and his wife, Octavia, *née* Ward (1834–1916), a tutor of mathematics and Latin. He enjoyed an informative youth, living at 1 St John's Terrace, Hove, and attending, in nearby Brighton, a preparatory and boarding-school, where he excelled in maths and science. In 1882 he was accepted at the Hartley Institution (later incorporated in the University of Southampton) and after three years of study won a national scholarship to the combined Normal School of Science (now the Royal College of Science) and the Royal College of Mines. He set up a laboratory in the family's London home at 7 Balham Grove, Balham, and, in 1887, he attended Finsbury Technical College to accelerate his rate of learning.

Lanchester's first invention was a 'pendulum accelerometer', a device which measured the acceleration and retardation of an object, later used with road and rail vehicles. After his 'radial cursor' invention, which was later produced by an instrument maker, he became impatient with his routine studies and left the school without bothering to finish the course. Shortly afterwards came the first of his 426 varied patent applications, his 'isometrograph' to assist draughtsmen, which was bought soon after by a manufacturing company.

At the age of twenty and with no formal qualifications, Lanchester so impressed the owner of the Forward Gas Engine Company of Birmingham that he was offered the position of assistant works manager. Within six months Lanchester had invented his 'pendulum governor' to control engine speeds, and the following year, after his promotion to works manager and designer, his 'gas engine starter'; both devices were highly successful. His ideas multiplied and in 1892 he designed and built the world's first direct-coupled engine–dynamo installation. After more successes he resigned as works manager in 1893, after first securing the position for his younger brother, George *Lanchester.

Since 1891 Lanchester had been developing his theories on heavier-than-air flying machines and considered raising money to fund the development of an aero-engine. He was warned, however, that his reputation would be ruined if his far-reaching proposals were publicized and he was therefore forced temporarily to abandon them. He turned instead to motorized-carriage design and began by designing and building a 2 hp single-cylinder, high-revving, vertical engine. In 1893 and 1894, in the garden of his home at Fairview, St Bernard's Road, Olton, near Birmingham, Lanchester built a flat-bottomed river launch as a test bed for this engine, which he installed to drive a stern-mounted paddle-wheel. Launched in 1894, this was the first all-British motor boat. The engine's success led to the design and construction of a single-cylinder motor car. Occasionally assisted by his brothers George and Frank he built it to his own original design and incorporated a 'live' rear axle instead of one continuous shaft, epicyclic gears from which the modern automatic gearbox has evolved, and a direct-drive top-gear ratio; it was also the first car ever designed to run on pneumatic tyres. It was completed late in 1895 in his workshop in Saltley, Birmingham—the first all-British four-wheel petrol car. It was later redeveloped, and this, together with the success of two experimental cars, one of which received a gold medal in 1899 for its 'excellence of design and performance', led the three brothers to form the Lanchester Engine Company in November 1899. The directors appointed Frederick general manager, works manager, and chief designer.

Lanchester moved to 53 Hagley Road in Birmingham, his home for the next twenty years, which was within easy reach of a newly acquired factory for the company's production cars. Like their predecessors, these employed vibrationless and quiet engines, silent gears, powerful brakes, and other qualities far in advance of contemporary vehicles. His inventions for general use included splined shafts, roller bearings, turbocharging, four-wheel brakes, four-wheel drive, and interchangeability of parts to assist mass production methods.

The directors declined, however, to provide sufficient capital to service the products and the level of sales that were being achieved and the company went into receivership in 1904. Following reconstruction it emerged as the Lanchester Motor Company with a greatly enlarged capital of £250,000. Lanchester became, however, increasingly disillusioned with his directors' antics, and in 1910 resigned most of his responsibilities to become their part-time consultant and technical adviser. In 1914 he resigned from this position also, although his design concepts continued with the cars and armoured cars of the First World War.

In 1909 Lanchester had taken employment with the Daimler Motor Company as its consultant and technical adviser. His work for it, and soon after for its parent company, Birmingham Small Arms, over the next twenty years, included the design of his world-famous 'crankshaft vibration damper' and his 'harmonic balancer', both of which are still in use in various forms. His aeronautical interests, although never far from his thoughts, had necessarily taken second place to motor car design. His 1894 paper to the Birmingham Natural History and Philosophical Society was entitled 'The soaring of birds and the possibilities of mechanical flight' and it far-sightedly dealt with his theory of 'vortex of lift' acting on an aircraft's wing. It was revised and presented three years later to the Physical Society. It was rejected. This profound work, not then understood by the society's eminent scientists, lay untapped until Lanchester published two books, *Aerodynamics* in 1907 and *Aerodonetics* in 1908, jointly entitled *Aerial Flight*. The work was universally acclaimed and became the standard reference for aircraft designers; it was later translated into French and German. At this time he met other pioneers of flight in various countries in order to exchange views. However, the trial and error experiments of the Wright brothers were anathema to Lanchester whose own work was solidly based on calculation and theory.

In the two years from 1909, as consultant to the White and Thompson aeroplane concern, Lanchester gave their biplane many innovative features such as aluminium-clad wings instead of fabric, braced in triangular form by tubular steel struts. He resigned from the company when he felt the work had become incompatible with his increasing responsibilities as a member, from 1909, of the government's advisory committee for aeronautics. He foresaw the major contribution that aircraft could play in wartime, much to the chagrin of the military command, who still espoused traditional means of warfare, and he publicized his views in his book *Aircraft in Warfare: the Dawn of the Fourth Arm* (1916). This included his research into operational strategy, termed 'the N-square law', copies of which were dispatched to both the British and the USA military commands. His tireless work was later acknowledged in his brother's statement that 'The rapid evolution of British aircraft during the First World War was largely due to his energy and foresight' (Clark, *Lanchester Legacy*, 1.162). He received no national honour, however, perhaps having upset too many important people by his blunt and forthright manner. He had often been frustrated by the apparent slowness of thought of other experts and had shown little tact or diplomacy, especially in his patriotic quest for rapid progress. In one instance, Lanchester wrote of a high-ranking member of the exalted Air Board 'A terrible lot of time has been wasted by a long discourse from the Chief Engineer, and if every designer in the country were heard at that length, they would not get down to work until next Christmas' (Clark, *Lanchester Legacy*, 1.161). In 1919 Lanchester married Dorothea, daughter of Thomas Cooper, vicar of St Peter's Church at Field Broughton near Windermere; they had no children.

Lanchester gradually withdrew from the advisory committee after the war and moved back to Birmingham in

1924. After rejecting a house design from his architect brother, Henry, in typical independent fashion he designed one himself. It was duly built and named Dyott End, in Oxford Road, Moseley. From here, consultancy work was undertaken for a number of companies, including Lanchester, Wolseley, and Beardmore, and later for Sir Malcolm Campbell on his Bluebird record-breaking car. Lanchester founded a new company in 1925, named Lanchester's Laboratories Limited, to promote, among other inventions, his experimental work on petrol–electric transmission systems and a superior range of wireless and sound-reproducing equipment.

However, Lanchester's business acumen was not as astute as his inventive mind and this, coupled with his strong loyalty and trust in others, helped to render him a poor man in his later years. He could afford no car, new books, or clothes and his house mortgage was taken over by a charity, an event this proud man must have hated. Despite failing eyesight and Parkinson's disease his brain was unimpaired, and he produced a diversity of inventions and papers in the 1930s and 1940s on such things as the musical scale, self-steering wheelbarrows, vision, vehicle suspension, relativity, politics, and, under the pseudonym of Paul Netherton-Herries, poems and limericks.

Lanchester was a stockily built man of some 15 stone and nearly 6 foot in height. He always worked to his own ideas from first principles and was dismissive of designing to accommodate fashion, as 'it does not bring logical progress' (interview, *Autocar*, 25 March 1938). He was respected by most as a far-sighted genius. His wide range of interests led him to write more than sixty technical papers for various institutions and organizations. Although he was distressed never to receive national recognition in the honours list, he was nevertheless honoured by various institutions during his lifetime. In 1919 he was awarded an honorary degree of Doctor of Laws by Birmingham University. Among other honours and awards were fellowship of the Royal Society in 1922; honorary membership in 1937 and the James Watt international medal in 1945 of the Institution of Mechanical Engineers; membership in 1910 and the Ewing gold medal in 1941 of the Institution of Civil Engineers; presidency of the Institution of Automobile Engineers in 1910; fellowship in 1917 and the gold medal in 1926 of the Royal Aeronautical Society; and the American Guggenheim gold medal in 1931 and associate membership of the Institution of Naval Architects. After suffering two strokes Lanchester died at home on 8 March 1946; his ashes were buried in his parents' grave at Lindfield, near Haywards Heath, in Sussex.   C. S. CLARK

Sources C. S. Clark, *The Lanchester legacy, 1: 1895–1931* (1995) • P. W. Kingsford, *F. W. Lanchester: the life of an engineer* (1960) • A. Bird and F. Hutton Stott, *Lanchester motor cars* (1965) • C. S. Clark, *The Lanchester legacy, 2: 1931–1956* [forthcoming] • F. W. Lanchester, patents, 1888–1939 • J. Fletcher, ed., *The Lanchester legacy, 3: A celebration of genius* (1996) • private information (2004) • b. cert.

Archives Coventry University, corresp. and papers • CUL • Institution of Mechanical Engineers, London, diagrams • Sci. Mus. • U. Southampton L., papers • University of Warwick, Royal Aeronautical Society collection, corresp. | Birmingham Museum of Science and Industry, corresp. and papers • CAC Cam., corresp. with A. V. Hill • Institution of Mechanical Engineers, London, corresp. with Sir Henry Grey relating to donations to Institution of Mechanical Engineers • Solihull Public Library | FILM BFI NFTVA, one-minute film, 1902 Lanchester

Likenesses R. Main, oils, Institution of Mechanical Engineers, London • photographs, Coventry University, Lanchester Library Collection • photographs, Institution of Mechanical Engineers, London

Wealth at death £5633 7s. 2d.: probate, 22 June 1946, *CGPLA Eng. & Wales*

Lanchester, George Herbert (1874–1970), engineer and car designer, was born on 11 December 1874 at 1 St John's Terrace, Hove, Sussex, the youngest of eight children of Henry Jones Lanchester (1834–1914), architect, surveyor, and part-time inventor, and his wife, Octavia, *née* Ward (1834–1916), a tutor of mathematics and Latin. He attended a nursery and then a boarding-school in Brighton, and after the family moved to 7 Balham Grove, Balham, London, in 1886, Clapham high school. He was greatly influenced by his talented family and especially by his brother Frederick William *Lanchester, who later gained world renown as an inventor and engineer. George watched and helped him conduct experiments in the basement workshop at home, and their close association was to endure all their lives.

In October 1889 Lanchester left home to become an apprentice at the Forward Gas Engine Company in Birmingham, where Frederick was assistant works manager. From lowly beginnings, George became respected by both the workforce and management for his technical skills. His high level of craftsmanship encouraged his growing self-confidence and he voluntarily attended evening classes in engineering at the Midland Institute, although he missed so many classes through enforced overtime that he never took his final examinations. At the end of his apprenticeship he spent a year in the drawing office. In 1893, aged only nineteen, he was appointed works manager when his brother resigned the position. Besides his normal duties, George often deputized for his brother, who had remained as consultant and designer, and his occasional trips abroad helped mould his character.

At this time, Frederick, George, and another brother, Frank, designed and constructed a river boat, complete with an advanced, high-revving engine. It was launched late in 1894 and was the first all-British motor boat. Lanchester also helped Frederick with the design and construction of his 5 hp car, destined to become, in 1895, the first all-British, four-wheel petrol car. George's passion for motor vehicles was set after he accompanied his brother on the car's first run. He later proclaimed: 'It was a great thrill, and sufficiently successful to instil in me an enthusiasm beyond expectation for the new mode of transportation'. In 1897 Lanchester resigned his company position in order to join Frederick as his chief assistant, for the purpose of development and construction of Lanchester cars. He oversaw the development work on the experimental models, one of which was awarded a gold medal in 1899 for its 'excellence of design and performance'.

When the Lanchester Engine Company was formed in

George Herbert Lanchester (1874–1970), by unknown photographer

1899, with Frank as company secretary, Lanchester continued as Frederick's personal assistant. Although their production cars were praised for their unique design and precision construction, the company, which was seriously undercapitalized, went into receivership and had to be reformed in 1904, with an increased capital. Lanchester was employed by the Lanchester Motor Company in the same position as previously, implementing Frederick's design concepts during his absences, and contributing greatly to its growing reputation.

In 1910, after Frederick's partial withdrawal from the company, Lanchester was appointed chief designer. He immediately modernized the coachwork design to attract new customers, a policy which gained much acclaim, and he subsequently modified the mechanical features of the four- and six-cylinder cars. During the First World War, his 38 hp armoured cars operated successfully in Europe, mostly on the Russian front.

His brother's resignation from the company in 1914 allowed Lanchester to emerge from Frederick's shadow. His first post-war car design was the famous 40 hp of 1919, an advanced vehicle with a 6 litre, overhead camshaft engine. His methods of coachbuilding incorporated the world's first use of oxy-acetylene welding for aluminium body panels. The car, which remained available until 1931, was deemed by many to be the finest in the world and was bought by the rich and famous—Princess Elizabeth was

first seen by the public, as a baby, in her father's Lanchester 40 hp limousine. Lanchester's next design, the 21 hp model, was thought by many to be better than its Rolls-Royce competitor and his eight-cylinder 30 hp model of 1928 was acclaimed as the best Lanchester of all. Also, from 1927, he developed a 40 hp armoured car which was Britain's first armoured vehicle designed as such, rather than one converted from a commercial chassis. Supplied to the 11th hussars and the 12th lancers, it allowed them to become the first mechanized regiments of the British army.

By the end of the decade Lanchesters' success was fading. After its bank called in its relatively small overdraft, Lanchester was one of the board who reluctantly agreed to the sale of the company to the BSA group in 1931, in order to avoid bankruptcy. He continued as chief engineer, but the different business environment prompted his resignation in 1936.

Lanchester then joined the Alvis Motor Company as assistant chief engineer, in charge of design and management for its motor car division. During the first eighteen months of a three-year contract, he successfully produced the Silver Crest and 12/70 models, which laid the basis for Alvis's subsequent pre- and post-war cars. His remaining period with the company saw him in charge of the Alvis-Straussler mechanical warfare department, which made armoured cars and light tanks. In 1939 he joined the Sterling Armament Company as technical adviser and consultant, demonstrating his versatility by supervising the production and progress of six squadrons of sound-ranging vehicles for the Dutch government. Once this contract was completed, he turned his attention to the design and construction of his Lanchester sub-machine gun, which was used by both the British and Australian navies.

In 1943, the year in which he was appointed president of the Institution of Automobile Engineers, Lanchester became technical adviser to the Sterling Engineering Company, organizing the manufacture of war-related equipment. After two years he became technical adviser to the Russell Newberry Company, working on various projects, especially diesel engines. When this company's ownership changed, he commented: 'I was then given the sack in June 1961, as being too old' (he was eighty-seven). His twelve post-war patented inventions, supplementing the fifteen pre-war motoring patents dating from 1906, included such varied innovations as earth-drilling apparatus, optical projectors, electric torches, and the design and manufacture of firearms.

Lanchester had a strict Victorian attitude to life, and his great interest, other than engineering, was listening to classical music. He had a commanding build, and was 6 foot tall and 14 stone in weight. He was a modest and kind man, with an incredible memory for detail, always willing to give advice and encouragement to owners of Lanchester cars which dated from the turn of the century. His in-depth knowledge and experience of motor vehicles led to his popular appointments as president of the Veteran Car Club in 1958 and 1959, patron of both the Lanchester

Register and the Daimler and Lanchester Owners' Club, and consultant editor of the international *Automobile Engineers' Reference Book.*

In April 1907 Lanchester married Rose (*d.* 1953), elder daughter of a contractor, William Thomas, whose other daughter had married Lanchester's brother Frank; they had two children. In 1961, Lanchester married Lilian Mary, an old family friend and daughter of William Stevenson, a silversmith. While recovering from a two-year illness, Lanchester died of a heart attack at his home, The Hill, Chulmleigh, Devon, on 13 February 1970. He was cremated shortly afterwards in Exeter.　　　C. S. CLARK

Sources C. S. Clark, *The Lanchester legacy*, 1: *1895–1931* (1995) • A. Bird and F. Hutton Stott, *Lanchester motor cars* (1965) • C. S. Clark, *The Lanchester legacy*, 2: *1931–1956* [forthcoming] • private information (1995) • J. Fletcher, ed., *The Lanchester legacy*, 3: *A celebration of genius* (1996) • d. cert.

Archives Coventry University • Solihull Public Library • University of Warwick | FILM BFI NFTVA, a one minute film of 1902 Lanchester

Likenesses photograph, repro. in Bird and Hutton-Stott, *Lanchester motor cars*, facing p. 16 [*see illus.*] • photographs, Coventry University, Lanchester Library collection

Lanchester, Henry Vaughan (1863–1953), architect and town planner, was born on 9 August 1863 at 18 Alma Square, St John's Wood, London, the first of the eight children of Henry Jones Lanchester (1834–1914), an architect and surveyor with offices in London and Brighton, and his wife, Octavia Ward (1834–1916). Frederick William *Lanchester, inventor of the Lanchester motor car, was a brother, and Elsa *Lanchester, the actress, a niece. Lanchester designed many major public buildings in the first half of the twentieth century, and was one of the earliest proponents of the town planning movement in Britain and India. Brought up in Hove and educated at a preparatory school there, he was articled to his father in 1879, and subsequently employed by a number of London architects. He attended the National Art Training School at South Kensington, and then the part-time schools of the Architectural Association and Royal Academy, and won travelling studentships from the Architectural Association in 1888 and the Royal Institute of British Architects (RIBA) in 1889–90.

In the 1890s Lanchester was an assistant in the lively London office of George Sherrin, and there met his future partners James S. Stewart (1865/6–1904) and Edwin Alfred Rickards (1872–1920). About 1897 they set up together as Lanchester, Stewart, and Rickards. The firm became one of the most successful teams in winning the copious architectural competitions of the Edwardian era. According to Lanchester, their designs were the result of the efficient co-ordination of skills: he relished the intellectual challenge posed by planning and construction, while Rickards concentrated on the design of the façade, fittings, and interior. Rickards, a sociable and exuberant character, was one of the finest architectural draughtsmen of the period, and had a capacity rare among Englishmen for designing in a swaggering European baroque—a taste fully shared by Lanchester. Rickards's friend the writer Arnold Bennett described his art as 'that rarest gift,

common sense in imagination' (A. Bennett, ed., *The Art of E. A. Rickards*, 1920, 6) and used him as the model for the hero in *The Roll Call* (1918). Rickards's most successful independent design was the Edward VII Memorial Fountain, Bristol (1910–13), with sculpture by Henry Poole. He died of tuberculosis in Bournemouth at the age of forty-eight.

Lanchester's first major commission was an office building for Bovril Ltd in Finsbury, London (1896–9; dem.), notable for its early steel frame and reinforced concrete floors. This was overshadowed in 1897 by his firm's triumph in the competition to design the town hall and law courts for Cardiff's new civic centre at Cathays Park. Erected in 1901–5, these vigorously baroque buildings seemed to C. H. Reilly 'full of the glorious life we all wanted but could not afford' (C. H. Reilly, *Scaffolding in the Sky*, 1938, 53). The buildings that followed, Deptford town hall (1903–5), Hull School of Art (1903–5), and Colnaghi and Obach's Gallery (1911–13), continued in reduced scale the sculptural theme of the more opulent ensemble in Wales. The up-to-date construction of the conspicuous Methodist Central Hall, Westminster (1905–11), and the heating and ventilation systems of the Third Church of Christ Scientist, Mayfair (1910–12, with later tower), confirm Lanchester's lifelong interest in technique, and may reflect experience gathered in his tour of American and Canadian cities in 1907.

On 17 February 1909 Lanchester married Annie Gilchrist (Nancy) Martin (*b.* 1882), a comedy musical actress and daughter of Robert Martin, a colliery manager. His niece Elsa Lanchester, who used to visit their home in Weybridge (designed by Lanchester), recalled how she was 'swept off [her] feet' by 'aunt Nancy's singing' (E. Lanchester, *Elsa Lanchester Herself*, 1983, 39). The couple had two sons and a daughter: Henry Robert (1912–1941), who was briefly a partner in his father's firm before he was killed in 1941, Frederick Gilchrist, and Pauline, who was disabled.

After Rickards's death in 1920 Lanchester teamed up with Geoffry Lucas and, from 1923 to 1952, T. A. Lodge; Lanchester, Lucas, and Lodge (later Lanchester and Lodge) developed a cooler classical style better suited to the interwar years. While continuing to build for municipal clients, for example Beckenham town hall (completed 1932) and Hackney town hall (1934–7), they won many competitions for university buildings, notably Leeds University, where the Brotherton Library is outstanding. Their winning submission for the Queen Elizabeth Hospital, Edgbaston (1933–8), created a demand for them as specialists in hospital architecture. Such successes owed much to Lanchester's ability to plan a complex building during a weekend or a few days.

From 1912 until 1937 Lanchester pursued an additional career in India, where he spent from two to six months almost every year. This originated in his short-term appointment as consultant to the town planning committee for the layout of New Delhi, to the chagrin of Edwin Lutyens, who was principally interested in securing the design of Viceroy's House and saw Lanchester as a rival. The revised urban plan Lanchester proposed in July 1912 was essentially carried through, though with many modifications by other hands. He undertook a tour of Indian cities with Patrick Geddes in 1915, and in 1920–30 had an office in Lucknow to look after his numerous projects in the city, among them the council chamber, the Christian college, and the post and telegraph office. The most spectacular of his Indian commissions, at a scale almost rivalling Viceroy's House, was the Umaid Bhawan Palace (1929–44; now a hotel) for the maharaja of Jodhpur.

Through his writings and lectures on town planning and his activity as an adviser and planner to colonial and Indian governments (for example at New Delhi, Madras, Lucknow, Rangoon, and Zanzibar) Lanchester became an authority in what was just becoming recognized as a specialist field. He was president of the Town Planning Institute (1922–3), lectured in civic design at University College, London, was consultant planner to the University of London, and in 1944 drew up an outline of studies in town planning for the RIBA. His book of 1925 *The Art of Town Planning* emphasized outward form and advocated a synthesis between picturesque and Beaux-Arts ideas. Despite this adherence to traditional and visual ideas, Lanchester steadfastly opposed the clearance of ancient Indian cities by means of axial boulevards and sympathized with the biological analysis of cities advocated by his friend Geddes.

Lanchester was also much involved in professional and educational affairs. He served on the council of the RIBA for over thirty years and was twice its vice-president; he received the institute's gold medal in 1934. Life and work were entwined, and he wrote books and articles on many subjects, including a biography of the Austrian baroque architect Fischer von Erlach (1924). In 1940 a short newsreel film he made for Gaumont, called *Toys from Waste*, was released in cinemas. He died at Stoneleigh Nursing Home, Cornfield Road, Seaford, Sussex, on 16 January 1953, and was buried in Brighton. His wife survived him.

ALEXANDRA GERSTEIN

Sources C. H. Reilly, 'H. V. Lanchester', *Representative British architects of the present day* (1931), 113–25 · J. Burchell, *The history of Lanchester & Lodge* (1986) · *The Builder*, 184 (1953) · *RIBA Journal*, 60 (1952–3) · *Journal of the Town Planning Institute*, 39 (1953) · *Birmingham Post* (17 Jan 1953), 72 · *The Times* (17 Jan 1953) · 'Architects of the day: Messrs. Lanchester and Rickards', *Builders' Journal and Architectural Engineer*, 30 (1909), 337–51 · 'The royal gold medal: presentation to Mr Henry Vaughn Lanchester, FRIBA', *RIBA Journal*, 41 (1933–4), 549–56 · *Architecture Illustrated*, 33 (1952), 52–68 · 'Henry Vaughn Lanchester', *Architect and Building News*, 138 (6 April 1934), 3–4 · *Modern examples of architecture: Lanchester, Lucas & Lodge*, Technical Art Series · Pevsner · 'The maharaja's palace, Jodhpur', *The Builder*, 178 (1950), 49–55 · P. Davies, *Splendours of the raj: British architecture in India, 1660–1947* (1985) · N. Evenson, 'Modern planning and the colonial city', *The Indian metropolis: a view towards the West* (New Haven, 1989) · H. Richardson, ed., *English hospitals 1660–1948: a survey of their architecture and design* (1998) · b. cert. · m. cert. · d. cert. · *The Builder*, 87 (1904), 184

Archives priv. coll. · RIBA | Keele University Library, LePlay Collection, corresp. and minute book entries as member of Sociological Society committees

Wealth at death £17,694 17s. 2d.: probate, 15 Sept 1953, CGPLA Eng. & Wales

Lanczos, Cornelius [*formerly* Kornél Löwy] (1893–1974), mathematician and mathematical physicist, was born on 2 February 1893 in Székesfehérvár, Hungary, the first of four children born to lawyer Károly Löwy (1854–1939) and his wife, Adél Hahn. Lanczos attended a Jewish elementary school and graduated from the local Catholic school in 1910. From 1911 he studied at the University of Budapest under Fejér and Eötvös. After graduating in 1915 until 1920 he worked at the Technical University of Budapest as physics assistant to Tangl. In 1921 Lanczos received his doctorate at the University of Szeged under Ortvay (a student of Sommerfeld).

Owing to antisemitism in Hungary, Lanczos spent the next ten years in Germany, first as a lecturer at the University of Freiburg in Breisgau, then, from 1924 to 1931, at Frankfurt am Main.

In papers of 1922 and 1923 Lanczos was the first to show that the de Sitter solution could be written in a form which avoided singularity at the mass horizon. He wrote a significant paper in 1924 on the surface distributions of matter in Einstein's theory and, in a series of papers published in 1925, developed a new approach to the problem of radiation, using the general theory of integral equations. In the same year ground-breaking papers in quantum mechanics were published by Heisenberg, Born, and Jordan. Lánczos recognized that by reformulating the matrix theoretical method of Heisenberg–Born–Jordan into integral equations, he would have the method to construct physical problems within a fluid field theory. In December 1925 he showed how the techniques of matrix mechanics could be represented in terms of integral equations, but the form of the universal kernal function in the integral equations remained unsolved. Schrödinger solved this and published four weeks later (in January 1926), so preceding Lanczos's idea of the field-like representation of quantum theory.

In 1928–9 Lanczos, who in 1922 had published a paper on the Einsteinian equations of gravity, was granted leave to work with Einstein at the University of Berlin. It was during this time that Lanczos met such people as Schrödinger and von Neumann and he continued a lively correspondence with Einstein throughout the following years. He married in 1927, Maria Rupp (d. 1939); they had a son.

In 1931 Lanczos was invited to the United States as professor of mathematical physics at the University of Purdue, Indiana. He had published his first paper on the quadratic action principle in relativity that year, but his main research area at Purdue was numerical analysis. In 1938 Lanczos developed his well-known theory of economization of polynomials (the Lanczos–Tau method). He also published two papers in 1942 on practical techniques of Fourier analysis which anticipated the Fast–Fourier Transform. In 1943–4 he was seconded to the National Bureau of Standards to work on the mathematical tables project in New York.

In 1946 Lanczos left Purdue to become senior research engineer at the Boeing Company in Seattle. A year later he was appointed Walker–Ames lecturer at the University of Washington, Seattle. From 1949 to 1952 he worked at the

Institute for Numerical Analysis at the University of California. In 1949 his first book, *Variational Principles of Mechanics*, was published and in 1951 he published the first exact method for obtaining all the eigenvectors and eigenvalues of an arbitrary matrix.

It was in 1952 that Lanczos was invited to join Dublin Institute for Advanced Studies in Ireland as a visiting lecturer. He returned to the United States in 1953–4 as a computer specialist with North American Aviation, then took up a permanent position at the Dublin Institute as senior professor in 1954. He married Ilse Hildebrand in 1955. During his time in Dublin Lanczos held visiting professorships at a number of institutions in the United States. He was professor emeritus at Dublin from 1968 until his death. This period spent in Ireland was remarkably fruitful and productive. Lanczos wrote seven books on the topics of applied analysis, linear differential operators, Fourier analysis, number, geometry, and on Albert Einstein, in addition to over 120 papers during his lifetime. Significantly, Lanczos wished to be remembered for introducing a new type of mathematical textbook; he wrote with great clarity, possessing a very personal style.

Lanczos's mathematical research centred on Fourier series, Fourier analysis and synthesis, Fourier transforms, matrix eigenvalues and eigenfunctions, Chebyshev polynomials, the gamma function and numerical analysis; in physics he worked on relativity theory, quantum mechanics, classical mechanics, and electromagnetism, and published about a hundred scientific papers. In 1960 he was awarded the Chauvenet prize by the Mathematical Association of America for his fundamental paper on the decomposition of an arbitrary matrix, first published in 1958.

Despite his extreme humility Lanczos received much recognition throughout his distinguished career, including membership of the Royal Irish Academy and honorary doctorates from Trinity College, Dublin (1962), National University of Ireland (1970), University of Frankfurt am Main (1972), and University of Lancaster (1972).

Lanczos was a member of many professional bodies, including the American Mathematical Society, the American Physical Society, the Society for Industrial and Applied Mathematics, and the Mathematical Association of America. He was a fellow of the American Association for the Advancement of Science, a member of Sigma Xi, and an honorary member of Sigma Pi Sigma.

A devoutly religious man Lanczos was proud of his Jewish heritage and ministered as a Levite at the synagogue. He was fluent in three languages and was an accomplished pianist, holding regular ensembles at his home in Dublin, in addition to taking a keen interest in the arts. Towards the end of his life Lanczos was still active in research and had been working in the field of Fourier analysis in the days before he died. It was at the Roland Eötvös University in Budapest while on a lecturing visit that Lanczos suffered a heart attack, on 25 June 1974. His funeral was held on 5 July in Budapest, where he was buried. He was survived by his second wife.

JENNIFER L. ATKINSON

Sources J. D. Brown and others, eds., *Cornelius Lánczos International Centenary Conference* [Raleigh, NC 1993] (1994) · R. Butler and H. G. Hopkins, 'Cornelius Lánczos, mathematician and mathematical physicist', *Advance*, 15 (Oct 1974), 53–6 · *The Times* (9 July 1974) · B. K. P. Saife, ed., *Studies in numerical analysis: papers presented to Cornelius Lánczos* (1974) · W. Yourgrau, 'Cornelius Lánczos, 1893–1974', *Foundations of Physics*, 5 (1975), 19–20 · private information (2004)
Likenesses J. Chirnside, charcoal, University of North Carolina · photograph, University of Manchester Institute of Science and Technology · photograph, University of Manchester Institute of Science and Technology, mathematics department

Land, Edward (1815–1876), pianist and composer, was born in London. He began his career as one of the children of the Chapel Royal, and made his name as the accompanist to John Wilson, the celebrated Scottish singer. After Wilson's death he acted in a similar capacity to David Kennedy. On the formation of the Glee and Madrigal Union he was appointed as accompanist, and appeared on occasion as a second tenor. He was also secretary of the Noblemen and Gentlemen's Catch Club for several years. As a composer, his output included a number of songs which were popular in their day, such as 'Bird of Beauty' (1852), 'The Angel's Watch' (1853), and 'Birds of the Sea' (1858). In addition, he harmonized or arranged a good deal of miscellaneous vocal music, wrote many original pieces for the piano, and made piano arrangements of various Scottish melodies and other compositions. He died at his home, 4 Cambridge Place, Regent's Park, London, on 29 November 1876. He was unmarried.

J. C. HADDEN, *rev.* DAVID J. GOLBY

Sources *MT*, 18 (1877), 17 · Brown & Stratton, *Brit. mus.* · *CGPLA Eng. & Wales* (1876)
Wealth at death under £14,000: probate, 15 Dec 1876, *CGPLA Eng. & Wales*

Landau, Henry (1892–1968), intelligence officer, was born in Transvaal, on 7 March 1892, of a Dutch mother and an English father. Educated at Durban high school, in 1910 Landau went to Gonville and Caius College, Cambridge, to study natural sciences. Fluent in French, German, and Dutch, he travelled widely in Europe and after graduation joined the London School of Mines. On the outbreak of the First World War in August 1914 he joined the Australian Volunteer Hospital, and was soon in France. In December 1914 Landau enlisted in the Royal Field Artillery and, after brief training, returned to France in April 1915 as second lieutenant. However, in May 1916 he successfully applied for a transfer to the intelligence corps and was seconded to Commander Mansfield Cumming, head of the British secret service. The Germans had recently broken up Cumming's spy network monitoring troop movements in occupied Belgium and northern France, and he informed Landau that 'it is up to you to reorganise the service' (Landau, *All's Fair*, 43). Landau was dispatched to Rotterdam to work with Richard Bolton Tinsley, one of Cumming's senior agents.

In Rotterdam Landau headed Tinsley's military section, running train-watching networks in the eastern half of Belgium under an agreement with British general headquarters, which ran its own networks in the western half. His agents monitored the distribution of German forces, passing messages across the electrified barrier which the Germans had constructed along the Dutch–Belgian border. The most significant of his networks was La Dame Blanche, which by the end of the war included over 900 agents and ninety observation posts. By October 1916 Landau's networks were producing results, while the general headquarters' systems were in decline. By July 1917 the general headquarters' networks were in such poor shape that Sigismund Payne Best was sent to Rotterdam to reorganize them. Best heard rumours that Landau had been poaching general headquarters' agents, but more significantly he found Tinsley to be 'a most thorough-paced scoundrel' (Payne Best correspondence, Walter L. Leschander Collection), heavily involved in blackmailing Dutch businessmen through the allied blacklist of firms known to trade with Germany. By September 1917 Tinsley was under official investigation and Best claimed that on two occasions Tinsley sent agents to beat him up, although Landau tipped him off. In November 1917 general headquarters was obliged to transfer Best to London, after official complaints from Colonel Oppenheim, military attaché at The Hague.

In June 1918 Cumming recalled Landau to London, noting in his diary that he 'won't speak but gives me the impression that there is "something rotten"' (Judd, 416). According to Best:

[Landau] was put through a proper interrogation. … He was quite ready to quit and he told us all about the conspiracy being run by Tinsley and Laurence Oppenheim over the 'black book'. He said that they got millions out of the Dutch business people by threatening to have them put on the black book unless they paid for their names to be omitted. (Payne Best MSS)

Despite these revelations Landau was permitted to return to Rotterdam and Cumming declined to take action against Tinsley, who survived a second investigation some months later and was said to have ended the war £200,000 richer.

After the war Landau joined Best on the inter-allied intelligence commission in Brussels, with responsibility for awarding medals and compensating the families of agents captured and executed. In August 1919 the London Gazette carried the names of almost 1400 of Landau's former agents, and the same month saw the creation of a new passport control department, providing diplomatic cover for Cumming's agents abroad. Landau was assigned to Berlin as senior passport control officer for Germany, but he was dissatisfied with this posting and resigned in 1920.

Landau claimed to have tried a number of business ventures, including freelance work for Cumming, before returning to South Africa in 1924. According to Best he left hurriedly after staging his own suicide, taking with him a large amount of what may have been secret service money. In 1927 he travelled to the United States, and seven years later further embarrassed the British secret service by publishing his detailed memoir All's Fair: the Story of the British Secret Service behind the German Lines, followed in 1935 by Secrets of the White Lady, dealing with La Dame Blanche.

The British secret service was particularly concerned that one of the agents described in All's Fair was still working in Germany, and when he was arrested and executed in October 1939 they blamed Landau. When the United States entered the war in December 1941 some attempt was apparently made to have Landau arrested, but there was never any firm evidence that his revelations had compromised operations. Landau died in retirement in Cocoa Beach, Florida, in May 1968.   NICHOLAS HILEY

Sources H. Landau, All's fair: the story of the British secret service behind the German lines (1934) • H. Landau, Secrets of the White Lady (1935) • H. Landau, Spreading the spy net: the story of a British spy director (1938) • I. Kirkpatrick, The inner circle: memoirs of Ivone Kirkpatrick (1959) • Bodl. Oxf., MSS Francis Oppenheimer • IWM, Irene Kirkpatrick papers • IWM, Sigismund Payne Best papers • correspondence of Sigismund Payne Best, Stanford University, Hoover Institution, Walter L. Leschander Collection • A. Judd, The quest for 'C': Mansfield Cumming and the founding of the secret service (1999)

Landauer, Fritz Josef (1883–1968), architect, was born in Augsburg, Bavaria, in Germany on 13 June 1883, the middle child of Joseph Landauer (1853–1929), a Jewish textile manufacturer, and Anna Rahel Feisenberger (1861–1913). He had an older brother Otto (b. 1882) and a younger sister Ida (b. 1886). After completing his schooling at the Königliches Realgymnasium in Augsburg in 1902 he studied architecture at the Munich Technische Hochschule under Friedrich von Thiersch and Carl Hocheder. He also studied at the Karlsruhe Technische Hochschule in 1904–5. He qualified in 1907 and set up in independent practice in Munich in 1909. He was a member of the Vereinigung Münchner Privatarchitekten and the Bund Deutscher Architekten.

Landauer designed important synagogues at Augsburg (with Heinrich Lömpel, 1912–17, restored) and Plauen, the Reform Synagogue (1928–30, destroyed). The former building, late historicist in style, shows the influence of his teachers von Thiersch and Hocheder, whereas the latter building has been described as 'one of the purest International Style synagogues ever built' (Krinsky, 304). In addition, he unsuccessfully entered design competitions for Würzburg (1922), Vienna (Hietzing) (1924), and in Hamburg the Oberstrasse Liberal Synagogue (1929).

Landauer laid out a number of cemeteries and war memorials and worked on commercial, public, and residential projects, including apartment blocks, mainly in Munich and his native Augsburg, but also in Fürth and Nürnberg. From about 1926 he worked in a consistently modernist style, one of the few modernist architects active in south Germany at the time. The Villa Strauss (Nibelungenstrasse 17), built in 1930 for a wealthy Jewish family in Augsburg, was one of his most celebrated 'Neues Bauen' projects, as was his Villa Hirschmann in Fürth (1930–31). In these projects he demonstrated his holistic approach to architecture, greatly influenced by the Deutscher Werkbund (Munich, 1907) and Bauhaus schools. He published a number of papers both on synagogue architecture and on the theory of modernism. A quiet, intense, and stubborn man, he paid obsessive attention to detail. The design of door knobs and light fittings was as important to him as was the form of the building. Landauer also designed furniture, although Dr Rudolph Strauss, the son of the family who lived at the Villa Strauss, found his old Biedermeier chairs more to his taste than Landauer's contemporary pieces.

As a Jew (he was a member of the Liberal Jewish communities of Augsburg and Munich), Landauer decided to leave Germany when the Nazis came to power and arrived for the first time in England in September 1933. He had married Else Hirschmann (b. 1888) in Germany on 24 October 1909 and two children were born in Munich, Gertrud (b. 1912) and Walter, afterwards Landor (1913–1995). Walter went ahead to England in 1931, where he briefly studied at Goldsmiths' College, London University, before leaving for America on the outbreak of war. Landor was to make a name for himself as a pioneer of corporate design.

While endeavouring to organize his emigration, Fritz Landauer carried on working in Germany, designing Jewish cemeteries in Munich in 1933 and in Stuttgart in 1935. However, in 1934 he was forced to close down his office in Munich. In 1936 he was given permission to stay indefinitely in the UK and in 1937 settled with his wife in London. He found employment with the Jewish Reform movement, which was at this period heavily augmented by central European refugees. In association with Wills and Kaula, the latter a Hungarian refugee, Landauer designed the North Western Reform Synagogue, Alyth Gardens, Golders Green (1935–6), and Willesden United Synagogue (1936–7), the latter being a rare example of direct modernist influence on Jewish architecture in London; the striking Heathfield Park façade was particularly successful. The corner site was used to good effect, with the architects treating the forecourt as a segment of a circle and setting within it the façade angled in the shape of a chevron. Further interest was created by the expressionist Hebrew lettering in the grille-work of the window over the main entrance and the positioning of a side wing with a large semicircular window to the south-west. The *Architects' Journal* described the building as 'designed by' Landauer and it certainly seems that he was responsible for the originality of the concept, which, with its exposed brick walls, was reminiscent of Plauen. However, his early design for the Finchley United Synagogue, Kinloss Gardens (1934–5), was rejected in favour of one by Dowton and Hurst (1965–7) that appeared in a cartoon in the *Jewish Chronicle* as a Rolls Royce grille, because of its resemblance to the car.

Until the outbreak of the Second World War, Landauer continued his commercial work, designing shopfronts and interiors for Boots the Chemist (1933), Lyons & Co. 'cornerhouses' (1933), and Montague Burton (1939), flats in Highgate (1935), planned as an extension of High Point One by Berthold Lubetkin, and in Sheffield (1938). None of these projects was executed and between 1939 and 1955 Landauer was forced to turn to tombstone design and supply in order to make a living.

Landauer died in London at the age of eighty-five, almost forgotten, at home at 2 Maresfield Gardens, Hampstead, on 17 November 1968. He left only £527 in his will.

His son Walter Landor achieved far greater material success than his father. In 1935 he founded the Industrial Design Partnership, the first design consultancy in Britain. In America, Landor Associates designed brand logos for big-name companies including Coca-Cola, Levis Jeans, and British Airways. Landor died a millionaire in California on 9 June 1995.   SHARMAN KADISH

Sources J. Bettley and R. Raper, eds., *Catalogue of the drawings collection of the Royal Institute of British Architects: a cumulative index* (1989) · C. Benton, *A different world: émigré architects in Britain, 1928–1958* (1995) · S. Klotz, *Fritz Landauer: Leben und Werk eines jüdischen Architekten* (2001) · C. H. Krinsky, *Synagogues of Europe* (1985) · P. Lasko, 'The impact of German-speaking refugees in Britain on the fine arts', *Second chance: two centuries of German-speaking Jews in the United Kingdom*, ed. W. E. Mosse (1991), 255–74 · H. P. Schwarz, ed., *Die Architektur der Synagoge* (1988) · *Architect's Journal* (14 April 1938), 617–19, 636 · d. cert. · *New York Times* (13 June 1995) [obituary of Walter Landor] · *The Guardian* (16 June 1995) [obituary of Walter Landor] · *The Times* (19 June 1995) [obit. of Walter Landor] · *CGPLA Eng. & Wales* (1969)

Wealth at death £527: probate, 12 Sept 1969, *CGPLA Eng. & Wales*

Landel, William (d. 1385), bishop of St Andrews and diplomat, was probably a younger son of a baronial family originally established in Berwickshire. On the death of his brother John, William acquired the baronies of Hownam and Crailing in Roxburghshire, but surrendered these in 1367 to John Crichton. By then Landel's ecclesiastical and political career was well established, but his early years remain shrouded in obscurity. He may have studied in France in the 1330s, but he was only occasionally styled master thereafter, and it remains uncertain whether he graduated. A lengthy sojourn in France, whether as a student or perhaps in the entourage of the exiled King David II, would, however, explain why nothing is known of Landel's pre-episcopal career—other than that he was rector of Kinkell, Aberdeenshire, immediately before his elevation. Residence in France would similarly account for the support which both King Philippe VI of France and David II extended to Landel's episcopal appointment in a supplication to Pope Benedict XII (r. 1334–42).

Benedict appointed Landel as bishop of St Andrews on 18 February 1342; he was consecrated at Avignon on 17 March. Instructed by the pope the following day to return to his diocese, Landel was back in Scotland by the end of that year. He remained a close associate of David II, who had returned from exile in France the previous year. From 1357, after the king's release from English captivity, Landel frequently witnessed royal charters and presumably spent much of his time with the royal court, not just during its visits to the principal centres of government at Edinburgh, Perth, and Scone, but also on its occasional journeys to the west and the north-east of the kingdom. Thus he was with the king when David visited the north-east during the winter of 1362–3 in order to escape an outbreak of plague further south. Although holding no official governmental position, Landel was often entrusted with diplomatic business. Between 1348 and 1370 he was nominated to serve on almost every Scottish embassy to

England, including that which conducted the negotiations leading to the treaty of Berwick and David II's subsequent release in 1357. Spiritual activities further prolonged Landel's probably lengthy absences from his diocesan seat. He received safe conducts to undertake pilgrimages to Santiago de Compostela in 1361 and Canterbury in 1362, and to visit the papal court in 1363, and an unspecified destination overseas in 1365.

Although he crowned Robert II during the inauguration ceremony at Scone on 16 March 1371, Landel's political prominence declined after the accession of the new king, doubtless mainly due to the effects of advancing years. Although he continued to witness royal charters regularly in the early years of the new reign, his diplomatic role diminished and he probably began to spend more time in St Andrews, where he supervised the beginning of reconstruction work on his cathedral after its destruction by fire in 1378. Although by 1381 Landel was reported to be feeble and broken with age, from at least 1383 until his death he was entrusted with the custody of the king's illegitimate son, James. Landel bequeathed jewels, vestments, books, and 'other more pleasing playthings' (Wyntoun, 3.27) to his cathedral church. He was one of the first Scottish bishops able to dispose of his personal property by testament, having been instrumental in persuading the crown to grant this concession to the episcopate. Landel died on 23 September 1385 and was buried in his cathedral church. DAVID DITCHBURN

Sources G. W. S. Barrow and others, eds., *Regesta regum Scottorum*, 6, ed. B. Webster (1982) · *RotS*, vols. 1–2 · J. M. Thomson and others, eds., *Registrum magni sigilli regum Scotorum / The register of the great seal of Scotland*, 2nd edn, 1, ed. T. Thomson (1912) · G. Burnett and others, eds., *The exchequer rolls of Scotland*, 1–2 (1878) · *CDS*, vols. 3, 5 · A. Theiner, *Vetera monumenta Hibernorum et Scotorum historiam illustrantia* (Rome, 1864) · W. H. Bliss, ed., *Calendar of entries in the papal registers relating to Great Britain and Ireland: petitions to the pope* (1896) · *CEPR letters*, vols. 3–4 · Andrew of Wyntoun, *The orygynale cronykil of Scotland*, [rev. edn], ed. D. Laing, 3 vols. (1872–9) · W. Bower, *Scotichronicon*, ed. D. E. R. Watt and others, new edn, 9 vols. (1987–98), vols. 3, 6–7, 9 · D. McRoberts, ed., *The medieval church of St Andrews* (1976) · G. W. S. Barrow, *The kingdom of the Scots: government, church and society from the eleventh to the fourteenth century* (1973) · C. Burns, ed., *Papal letters to Scotland of Clement VII of Avignon, 1378–1394*, Scottish History Society, 4th ser., 12 (1976)

Landells, Ebenezer (1808–1860), wood-engraver, illustrator, and magazine proprietor, was born at Newcastle upon Tyne on 13 April 1808 and was baptized there on 15 May, the third son of Ebenezer Landells, a merchant, and his wife, Jane Graham. His paternal grandfather ran a wholesale drapery business and his maternal grandfather was the Revd William *Graham (1737–1801), minister of the Close Presbyterian Meeting-House. Landells attended Mr Bruce's academy in Newcastle and at fourteen was apprenticed to Thomas Bewick, the celebrated wood-engraver. After payment to Bewick of 5s. for indentures at the end of 1822 there is no further mention of Landells in Bewick's records. Landells served out his remaining apprenticeship with Isaac Nicholson, wood-engraver and himself a former pupil of Thomas Bewick. Nicholson's workshop was in St Nicholas's Churchyard, Newcastle. While an apprentice in 1826 and 1827 Landells exhibited

paintings at the Northumberland Institution for the Promotion of the Fine Arts, Newcastle, and at the Northern Academy, Newcastle, in 1828.

On arriving in London in 1829, through the influence of fellow Northumbrian engravers John Jackson and William Harvey, Landells secured a position overseeing the fine art engraving department of Branston and Vizetelly. Landells engraved Harvey's drawings and initial letters for the second series of Northcote's *Fables* (1833) and also drawings by H. K. Browne and Cattermole for Dickens's *Master Humphrey's Clock*, which were engraved in partnership with Charles Gray. He was married on 9 January 1832 at St Pancras New Church, London, to Anne, eldest daughter of Robert McLagan of London.

Landells earned a place at the heart of the burgeoning wood-engraving business in London as a result of his Newcastle connections, all talented pupils of Bewick. This skill was vital for providing illustrations for books and magazines for the mass market. Landells possessed great energy and enthusiasm and he had the vision to realize the potential of wood-engraving in this field. Unfortunately his lack of business acumen meant that his schemes were not always profitable.

Landells soon established his own engraving workshop and employed some of the most outstanding engravers and illustrators of the next generation, including Edward and George Dalziel, Birket Foster, and Edmund Evans. His first engraving business was run from his home in Thornhill Road, Barnsbury, in north London, where he was assisted by his brother Alexander. This was followed by a bigger workshop at 22 Bidborough Street, New Road, St Pancras, where he undertook the engravings for his own venture: a journal of fashion entitled *Cosmorama*. This was short-lived, as Landells soon became involved with journalists including Henry Mayhew, Douglas Jerrold, and Thackeray, all of whom had failed satirical magazines behind them. Landells devised a new model based upon the French magazine *Le Charivari* and provided the technical expertise and capital to produce a magazine with many small illustrations and two full-page wood-engravings. The cover was designed by Landells and executed by Archibald Henning and the political 'cut' would change every week. The first issue of *Punch, or, the London Charivari* appeared on 17 July 1841. This involved a prodigious amount of work and organization by Landells, in particular liaison between illustrators, engravers, and printers. He was so successful in this respect that Herbert Ingram consulted him about launching his new paper, the *Illustrated London News*, in 1842. Landells had a one-third share in *Punch*, but the magazine's initial fortunes were rocky, despite spectacular sales from almanack and holiday numbers. The printers and publishers Bradbury and Evans bought out the existing shareholders on 24 December 1842 and in spite of their promising to honour Landells's position as engraving chief he was soon replaced by Joseph Swain. Landells was able to vent some spleen against Bradbury and Evans in a pamphlet, *A Word with Punch* (1847), produced by Alfred Bunn, a theatrical impresario who had been lampooned mercilessly by the magazine; Landells provided the engravings for the diatribe in the *Punch* style.

Landells did not remain disaffected for long. His association with Herbert Ingram bore fruit and propelled Landells forward as an illustrator as well as an engraver. He was commissioned to make sketches of Queen Victoria's first visit to Scotland in 1842 for the *Illustrated London News*. These were so successful that the queen bought the sketches and commissioned some additional watercolours while on her tour. Landells was the paper's first artist correspondent and later accompanied the queen on her visit to the Rhine. His workshop was also responsible for a large number of stock engravings for the *Illustrated London News*.

Landells was involved with many other magazines as proprietor or engraver: the *Illuminated Magazine* (1843), the *Lady's Newspaper* (1847) ('the earliest paper devoted to female interests', according to the *Dictionary of National Biography*), the *Great Gun* (1844), *Diogenes* (1853), and the *Illustrated Inventor*. He had a knack of identifying trends in publishing: seeing the growth in the children's book market, he illustrated his own—*Boy's Own Toy-Maker* (1858), *Girl's Own Toy-Maker* (1859), and the *Illustrated Paper Model Maker* (1860). Landells undertook an enormous number of engraving projects with variable financial returns. Some of his early engraving work is quite fine, in the Bewick style, but his later work is undistinguished and merely competent. He was an exceptional teacher and encouraged his apprentices to develop their own particular strengths in drawing or engraving: Foster, Evans, and the Dalziel brothers were among those who loyally testified to this. His apprentices bestowed on him the affectionate nickname Tooch-it-oop, in imitation of his north-eastern accent, which he never lost (*DNB*).

Landells made a unique contribution to the development of the illustrated magazine in the nineteenth century. He provided the link between Bewick's inspirational use of wood-engraving for artistic purposes and the use of the same technology for the mass market. He exhibited engravings at the Society (later Royal Society) of British Artists in 1833 and 1837. Over 1000 of his wood-engraving proofs are held in the prints and drawings department of the British Museum. He died on 1 October 1860 at his lodgings in Victoria Grove, West Brompton, and was survived by his wife, two sons, and four daughters.

Landells's eldest son, **Robert Thomas Landells** (1833–1877), illustrator and journalist, was born in London on 1 August 1833. He was educated in France but studied drawing and painting in London. He began his career as special artist at the *Illustrated London News* in 1855, following his father, and in 1856 was sent to the theatre of war in the Crimea. Some of his sketches appeared in the *Illustrated London News* towards the end of the war. After the peace with Russia he went to Moscow to record the coronation of Tsar Alexander II for the *Illustrated London News*. In winter 1863 he made drawings of the war between Prussia and Denmark and was decorated by both sides. He showed great skill in depicting battle scenes and troop configurations. In the war between Austria and Prussia in 1866 he

accompanied the 1st Prussian army corps as part of the staff of the Prussian crown prince on the march to Vienna. He received the Prussian Iron Cross for bravery during the Franco-Prussian War in recognition of his exertions in aid of the sick and wounded soldiers in the winter campaign on the Loire. After this he did not undertake further foreign assignments, but concentrated on painting studies of the Thames and the Dutch coast. He was commissioned by Queen Victoria to sketch and paint state ceremonies and visits between 1857 and 1874; specimens of his work are preserved in the Royal Collection.

Robert Landells was married, on 19 March 1857, at St Pancras New Church, London, to Elizabeth Ann, youngest daughter of George Herbert Rodwell, musician and composer, and granddaughter of Liston, the comic actor. They had two sons and two daughters. Landells died on 6 January 1877 at his home, 49 Winchester Terrace, Chelsea, London.   AMANDA-JANE DORAN

Sources R. K. Engen, *Dictionary of Victorian wood engravers* (1985) · *DNB* · M. H. Spielmann, *The history of 'Punch'* (1895) · R. D. Altick, *'Punch': the lively youth of a British institution* (1997) · [G. Dalziel and E. Dalziel], *The brothers Dalziel: a record of fifty years' work … 1840–1890* (1901) · Redgrave, *Artists* · *The reminiscences of Edmund Evans*, ed. R. McLean (1967) · IGI
Archives *Punch* library, London

Landells, Robert Thomas (1833–1877). *See under* Landells, Ebenezer (1808–1860).

Landen, John (1719–1790), mathematician, was born on 23 January 1719, at Peakirk, near Peterborough, Northamptonshire, the son of Matthew Landen and Elizabeth Cole (*d.* 1750). He was brought up to the business of a surveyor, and practised at Peterborough from 1740 to 1762. From 1762 to 1788 he acted as land agent to William Fitzwilliam, Earl Fitzwilliam (1748–1833). Cultivating mathematics during his leisure hours, he was a contributor to the *Ladies' Diary* from 1744 to 1772. He published eight papers in the *Philosophical Transactions of the Royal Society* between 1754 and 1785, which particularly concerned series, areas of curvilinear figures, rectification, and rotatory motion. In 1755 he published *Mathematical Lucubrations*, and in 1764 *The Residual Analysis*, book 1 (book 2 never appeared), which followed *A Short Discourse Concerning the Residual Analysis* (1758). In these last two works he attempted to replace the fluxional calculus with an analytic method 'founded entirely on the *anciently received* principles of algebra' (*Short Discourse*, 5). According to Lacroix this was the first attempt to reduce the infinitesimal calculus to 'purely algebraic notions' (S. F. Lacroix, *Traité Du calcul différentiel*, 2nd edn, 1810–19, 1.237). Lagrange evoked Landen's theory at the very beginning of his *Théorie des fonctions analytiques* (1797) but judged it jejune and embarrassing.

The remarkable theorem, known by Landen's name, for expressing a hyperbolic arc in terms of two elliptic arcs was inserted in the *Philosophical Transactions* for 1775, and formed a worthy conclusion to researches opened in the *Transactions* of 1771. This theorem forms one of the foundation stones of the theory of elliptic functions and was generally cited in eighteenth-century literature on the subject. Specimens of its use were given in the first volume of

Landen's *Mathematical Memoirs* (1780). In a paper on rotatory motion laid before the Royal Society on 17 March 1785 Landen obtained results differing from those of Euler and D'Alembert, and he defended them in the second volume of *Mathematical Memoirs*, prepared for the press during the intervals of a painful disease, and placed in his hands, printed, the day before his death. In the same work he solved the problem of the spinning of a top, and explained Newton's error in calculating the effects of precession.

Landen was elected a member of the Spalding Society in 1761 and a fellow of the Royal Society on 16 January 1766. Although continental mathematicians gave him a high rank among English analysts, he failed to develop and combine his discoveries. Humane and honourable as an individual, he was dogmatic in society. He led a retired life, chiefly at Walton in Northamptonshire. With his wife, Elizabeth (d. 1789), he had two daughters. He died at Milton (the seat of the Fitzwilliam family), near Peterborough, on 15 January 1790, and was buried at Castor church, Northamptonshire.   A. M. CLERKE, *rev.* MARCO PANZA

Sources *GM*, 1st ser., 60 (1790), 90, 191–5 • C. Hutton, *Philosophical and mathematical dictionary* (1815) • H. G. Green and H. J. J. Winter, 'John Landen, FRS (1719–1790)—mathematician', *Isis*, 35 (1944), 6–10 • G. N. Watson, 'The marquis and the land-agent', *Mathematical Gazette*, 17 (1933), 5–17 • H. J. J. Winter, 'John Landen FRS (1719–1790)', *Annual Report of the Peterborough Natural History, Scientific, and Archaeological Society* (1943), 3–14 • N. Guicciardini, *The development of Newtonian calculus in Britain* (1989) • F. Cajori, *A history of the conceptions of limits and fluxions in Great Britain from Newton to Woodhouse* (1919) • L. J. Montucla, *Histoire des mathématiques*, 2nd edn, 3 (1793–1802), 240 • J. C. Poggendorf, *Biografisch-literarisches Handwörterbuch zur Geschichte der exakten Wissenschaften*, 1 (1863), col. 1364–1365 • *GEC, Peerage*

Lander, John (1806–1839), traveller in Africa, was born in Truro, Cornwall, the fourth son of John Lander, innkeeper, and his wife, Mary Penrose. He was the younger brother of Richard Lemon *Lander. He was apprenticed to a printer and later became compositor to the *Cornwall Gazette*, a job which he evidently enjoyed. He was also a keen student of languages and poetry, and had published several essays and poems. He helped his brother Richard prepare the journal of his first voyage for publication. He volunteered to accompany Richard without any recompense in his expedition which left England in January 1830 to explore the course and outlet of the River Niger. The journey (described in Richard Lander's memoir) established that the river flowed into the Gulf of Guinea on the Atlantic coast, disproving theories, held notably by John Barrow, that it flowed into Lake Chad. John's journal was incorporated with that of Richard in the narrative of the expedition published in 1832.

John Lander returned to Truro and married Mary Livett, sister of his brother James's wife. His share of the money paid by John Murray to publish his journal dwindled and he secured through the patronage of Lord Goderich, president of the Royal Geographical Society, a place in the customs house, first in Liverpool and, after 1835, in London, where the three of his four children who survived infancy were born. Allibone's report, that Lander 'sank under the unwholesome effects of the climate and … found a grave

in a land of strangers' was one of several which suggest a more exotic place of death than his home, 23 Wyndham Street, Bryanston Square, London, where he died on 16 November 1839, allegedly of an illness first contracted in Africa but in fact of inflammation of the lungs. His widow was given a civil pension of £75 a year.

The discovery made by Lander and his brother was a significant step in geographical discovery in Africa and also opened up the Niger, seen as the highway into central Africa, to trade, settlement, and ultimately to Nigeria's becoming a British protectorate.

ELIZABETH BAIGENT

Sources M. Mackay, *The indomitable servant* (1978) • K. O. Dike, *Trade and politics in the Niger delta, 1830–1885* (1956) • *The Niger journal of Richard and John Lander*, ed. R. Hallet (1965) • *GM*, 2nd ser., 12 (1839), 662 • Allibone, *Dict.* • S. Maunder, *The biographical treasury*, new edn, rev. W. L. R. Cates (1870) • d. cert.
Archives Cornwall RO, letters to his brother, journals, logbook, and notebook
Likenesses W. Brockedon, chalk drawing, 1834, NPG • portrait, repro. in Mackay, *Indomitable servant*, pl. 12

Lander, Richard Lemon (1804–1834), traveller in Africa, was born on 8 February 1804 at Truro, Cornwall, the third son of John Lander, innkeeper, and his wife, Mary Penrose. The fourth of six children, he was educated under a Mr Pascoe in Coombe Lane, Truro, until at thirteen he went out with a merchant to the West Indies. Here he had an attack of malaria in San Domingo which was said to have helped him resist the disease later in Africa. He returned home in 1818 and was servant to several wealthy families in London with whom he travelled in Europe. In 1823 he went to Cape Colony as servant to Major W. M. G. Colebrooke. After travelling through the colony with Colebrooke, Lander returned home in 1824.

Public interest in the African discoveries of Clapperton and Denham led Lander to offer his services to Clapperton, refusing better paid employment in South America. With Clapperton he went to west Africa and was his devoted servant during this, his last expedition. They sailed in the *Brazen* in August 1825, reaching Badagri and thence heading inland, experiencing much sickness and privation *en route*. They crossed the Niger and went on as far as Sokoto where Clapperton died in 1827. Despite his own severe illness, Lander made his way back to the coast, reporting Clapperton's death to Denham who sent the news to England. Lander followed with Clapperton's papers, arriving at Portsmouth in April 1828. He made his way to Truro in poor health and was initially unable to edit Clapperton's *Journal* which appeared in 1829 with Lander's own *Journal* appended. In 1830 with the help of his brother John *Lander, Richard produced an edited version in two volumes. While in England, on 24 August 1828 he married Anne Hughes, daughter of a London merchant, at St Margaret's, Westminster. They had a daughter and a son who died in infancy.

Dissatisfied with the menial job he had obtained at the customs' house, and at the instance of Lord Bathurst, Lander undertook another expedition to trace the source

Richard Lemon Lander (1804–1834), by William Brockedon, *c.*1835

and course of the Niger. He arranged that his wife receive £100 a year from the government during his absence and that he get £100 on his return. With his brother John he left Portsmouth on 9 January 1830 and reached Cape Coast (now in Ghana) on 22 February. Travelling via Accra and Badagri, they reached Bussa on 17 June, and thence went upstream for about 100 miles to Yelwa, the furthest point reached by the expedition. They returned to Bussa on 2 August 1830 and headed downstream in canoes with no idea where they would end up. At Kerre they were robbed and nearly killed by the locals and at Igbo Ora were imprisoned by the king who demanded a heavy ransom which was obtained only after long delay. Eventually they got through the forested delta to find that the Nun distributary flowed into the Gulf of Guinea on the Atlantic coast. This settled the vexed question of the course and outlet of the Niger which many had thought flowed inland to Lake Chad. On 1 December 1830 the brothers reached Fernando Po (Bioko) and thence arrived home in 1831.

The Landers, particularly Richard, were greeted with much enthusiasm: Richard became the first gold medallist of the Royal Geographical Society and John Murray, the publisher, gave them £1000 for their journals. Lacking formal education, the brothers were not thought capable of editing the journals themselves, and they were instead (badly) edited by A. B. Becher and published as *Journal of an Expedition to … the Niger* (3 vols., 1832); a good later edition is that by Hallet (1965). The work was immediately popular and editions appeared in Dutch, French, German, Italian, and Swedish.

Lander took a position at the customs' office in Liverpool until, early in 1832, some merchants in the city led by Macgregor Laird formed a company to send an expedition under Lander to open up trade with the countries of central Africa by establishing the Niger as a trade route. The expedition was furnished with two finely built and fitted vessels, the *Quorra* and the *Alburkah*, which were among the first ocean-going steamers. They were supported by the brig *Columbine* which carried coals and goods. Lander started from Milford Haven on 25 July and reached Cape Coast after many delays on 7 October 1832. Illness and numerous other difficulties delayed progress, but the steamers managed to get some way up the Niger before returning to Fernando Po for fresh supplies. Leaving the steamers in charge of Surgeon Oldfield, Lander returned to the Nun mouth and began going upstream. At Angiama his party was fired on and pursued by local middlemen who wanted to see European traders remain on the coast, rather than establish bases inland and thus cut out the middlemen. Lander, who normally got on well with Africans, received a shot which entered his body near the anus and lodged deep in his thigh. He was taken as quickly as possible to Fernando Po, where, the shot being lodged too deeply to be removed, the wound went gangrenous and he died on 6 February 1834 at the house of the commandant. He was buried in the Clarence cemetery, Fernando Po. The story of the expedition was told in *Narrative of an Expedition into the Interior of Africa* by Macgregor Laird and R. A. K. Oldfield (1835). Lander's fate was shared by most of the Europeans on the expedition who succumbed mainly to malaria, although contemporaries attributed their deaths to the unhealthy climate. Macgregor Laird lost his entire fortune although not his life. The failure of the expedition considerably dampened the enthusiasm for trade with west Africa which Lander's first expedition had helped to raise.

The various monuments raised to Lander had unhappy fates. That erected by his wife and daughter in the Savoy chapel was destroyed by fire on 7 July 1864. The stained-glass window erected to replace it by the Royal Geographical Society was destroyed by bombing in the Second World War. A memorial erected in Lemon Street, Truro, in 1835 fell down in 1836—its replacement was still standing in the 1990s. His grave in Fernando Po fell into disrepair until an outcry in 1910 ensured a new monument was erected in the Roman Catholic cemetery there.

A government pension of £70 a year was given to Lander's wife and a gratuity of £80 to his daughter. In person he was very short and fair. His journals show him to have been intelligent and perceptive, despite his lack of formal education, and devoutly religious. Strong and healthy, his bravery and resoluteness fitted him ideally for African travel, although he lacked the middle-class background and officer training of the stereotypical African explorer. His discovery that the Niger flowed into the Atlantic was hailed by contemporaries as an event of cardinal importance since it opened up the whole of central Africa to commerce and ultimately to settlement.

ELIZABETH BAIGENT

Sources M. Mackay, *The indomitable servant* (1978) · K. O. Dike, *Trade and politics in the Niger delta, 1830–1885* (1956) · *The Niger journal of Richard and John Lander*, ed. R. Hallet (1965) · W. H. Tregellas, *Cornish worthies*, 2 vols. (1884), vol. 2 · 'Richard Lander's grave: a national reproach', *The Times* (10 May 1910) · S. Maunder, *The biographical treasury*, new edn, rev. W. L. R. Cates (1870) · C. Knight, ed., *The English cyclopaedia: biography*, 1 (1856) · J. F. Waller, ed., *The imperial dictionary of universal biography*, 3 vols. (1857–63) · H. Williams, *Quest beyond the Sahara* (1965)

Archives Wellcome L., diary of Niger expedition | Bodl. Oxf., copy of the journal of Captain Hill of the Alburkah

Likenesses W. Brockedon, chalk drawing, 1831, NPG · W. Brockedon, oils, *c.*1835, NPG [*see illus.*] · N. N. Burnard, statue, *c.*1852 (after bust by W. Brockedon), Lemon Street, Truro, Cornwall; repro. in Mackay, *Indomitable servant*, pl. 25 · W. Brockedon, oils (after his drawing, 1831), RGS · W. Brockedon, plaster bust, RGS; related marble bust, Gov. Art Coll. · line engraving, NPG; repro. in R. Lander and J. Lander, *Journal of an expedition to explore the course and termination of the Niger*, 3 vols. (1832) · portrait, repro. in R. Lander, *Records of Clapperton's last expedition to Africa*, 2 vols. (1830) · portraits, repro. in Mackay, *Indomitable servant*, pls. 13, 18, 26 · stipple, NPG

Landmann, George Thomas (1780–1854), army officer and military engineer, was born on 11 April 1780 at Woolwich, Kent, the son of Isaac *Landmann (1741–1826), professor of artillery and fortification at the Royal Military Academy at Woolwich, and his wife, Helene. Nothing is known of his school education. He became a cadet at the Royal Military Academy on 16 April 1793 and was commissioned second lieutenant in the Royal Engineers on 1 May 1795. Stationed at Plymouth, he was employed in the fortification of St Nicholas's Island, and, while at Falmouth, similarly Pendennis Castle and St Mawes. Promoted first lieutenant on 3 June 1797, later that year he went to Canada. He was involved in the construction of fortifications at St Joseph on Lake Huron, Upper Canada, and at Quebec in 1799 distinguished himself by dousing with snow a dangerous fire on the roof of a magazine. During 1801 and 1802 he was employed in cutting a new canal at the Cascades on the St Lawrence River. He advanced to captain-lieutenant on 13 July 1802 and at the end of the year returned to England. In 1803–4 he was at Winchester and then moved to Portsmouth, where he helped to strengthen its defences and those of neighbouring Gosport.

On 13 July 1804 Landmann became second captain, and on 23 February 1806 he joined the garrison at Gibraltar. His amusing and lively journal, written there, included numerous anecdotes about social and military events, as well as acute observations on the character and demeanour of a wide range of individuals. He had several personal mishaps and adventures, which included falling off a ladder, so that 'the tip bone of my left elbow was split' (Landmann, 1.36), in July 1807 having pieces of flannel soaked in boiling water pressed liberally on his stomach to combat cholera, and, the following year, chasing a whale in a ship's boat. He showed a deep interest in, and knowledge of, botany, cultivating his own exotic garden. However, he failed to rise above 'the humblest mediocrity' when seeking to play the Spanish guitar, though he 'made some progress' in learning to paint miniatures (ibid., 1.229). His house displayed a library of more than 1000 volumes and

sixteen pictures. Promoted captain on 1 July 1806, he sailed on 14 May 1808 as commanding royal engineer with Major-General Brent Spencer's force, which took part in the blockade of six French warships anchored in Cadiz under the guns of hostile Spanish batteries. Fluent in Spanish, he went ashore to liaise with the garrison, and he witnessed at first hand the bombardment, which preceded the enemy's surrender. On 8 August Spencer's force landed at Mondego Bay to join Lieutenant-General Sir Arthur Wellesley (later duke of Wellington). Landmann was then attached to the light brigade under Brigadier-General the Hon. Henry Fane, and was present at the battle of Roliça on 17 August, when he succeeded Captain Howard Elphinstone, who was wounded, as commanding royal engineer. On 18 August he sketched a panoramic view of the battlefield, which Wellesley sent home with dispatches. During a lone reconnaissance two days before the battle of Vimeiro, Landmann was almost captured by French dragoons. In the fighting, on 21 August, for a short period he acted as aide-de-camp to Brigadier-General Robert Anstruther, then joined Fane's brigade to take part in the capture of a French field gun. After the battle, for which he received a gold medal, he delivered a sketch of the engagement to Lieutenant-General Sir Harry Burrard, who had succeeded Wellesley in command of the army. After commanding the Royal Engineers for ten days, during which he displayed his 'great repugnance to the flogging system' (ibid., 2.277) by reducing a sentence of 300 lashes to 25, he was superseded by Major Richard Fletcher on 26 August. The following month, he was sent to report on the fortress of Peniche, and when Fletcher went to Spain with Lieutenant-General Sir John Moore, he became commanding engineer in Portugal. In December he was ordered to construct a bridge of boats at Abrantes, on the River Tagus, another at Punhete, on the Zêzere, and a flying bridge at Vila Velha, all of which were completed in five days.

On his return to Lisbon, Landmann was, in February 1809, sent overland with dispatches to Bartholomew Frere, the British minister at Seville, and from there, as commanding engineer, to join Major-General Alexander Mackenzie's force at Cadiz. Soon after his arrival, rioters threatened to kill the governor, the marqués de Villel, suspecting his loyalty. Mackenzie sent Landmann to restore order, and, as he spoke Spanish so well, he was eventually able to calm the situation. For his services on this occasion he received the thanks of Ferdinand VII, the king of Spain. He was granted a commission as lieutenant-colonel in the Spanish engineers on 22 February 1809, and when Mackenzie and his troops left for Lisbon, he remained at Cadiz on Frere's request. He went back to Gibraltar in July and sent home plans of the fortifications of Cadiz, with a report which led to vigorous efforts being made to defend the port.

Following the French capture of Seville, an attack on Gibraltar was expected from the landward side. So, in January 1810, plans were drawn up to demolish forts San Felipe and Santa Barbara in the Spanish lines, for which, after difficult negotiations, Landmann secured the Spanish governor's agreement. When the French marched on Cadiz in February, he volunteered to accompany reinforcements embarked at Gibraltar, but with that force detained by a contrary wind, he hired a rowing boat, reached Cadiz on the second day, and found himself for a time commanding engineer of the British forces.

On 25 March 1810 Landmann was appointed colonel of infantry in the Spanish army, and in April he served at the siege of Matagorda. During August he returned to England through ill health, but four months later had recovered sufficiently to sail for Lisbon as one of the military agents in the Peninsula. After delivering dispatches to Wellington at Cartaxo he proceeded towards Cadiz, and on the way joined the Spanish division of Major-General Francisco Ballasteros, being present at the action at Castillejos, near the River Guadiana, on 7 January 1811, where his horse fell under him and he sustained an injury to his left eye. From Cadiz, he returned in June to Ayamonte and rode round the seacoast to Corunna. After a short stay in Galicia, he went back to Cadiz by another route.

In March 1812 Landmann sailed for England with the Spanish ambassador. His health was now so impaired that he was unable to resume active duty until July 1813, when he was sent to Ireland to command the engineers in the Lough Swilly district in co. Donegal. On 4 June 1813 he had been promoted brevet major, and he became lieutenant-colonel on 16 May 1814. In March 1815 he was appointed commanding royal engineer of the Thames district, and in May 1817 was transferred to Hull in a similar capacity for the Yorkshire district. Landmann was granted leave of absence in 1819 and appears to have continued on leave until he retired from the corps on 29 December 1824. In the 1830s he was a promoter and the chief engineer of the London and Greenwich Railway. He also revised his father's *Principles of Fortifications* in 1831. He died at Shacklewell, near Hackney, London, on 27 August 1854.

R. H. VETCH, *rev.* JOHN SWEETMAN

Sources *Army List* · G. T. Landmann, *Recollections of my military life*, 2 vols. (1854) · T. W. J. Connolly, *History of the royal sappers and miners*, 2nd edn, 2 vols. (1857) · W. Porter, *History of the corps of royal engineers*, 1 (1889) · *DNB* · *GM*, 2nd ser., 41 (1854), 422 · parish register (baptism), 31 May 1780, St Mary Magdalen, Woolwich
Likenesses oils, *c.*1800, Royal Engineers, Chatham, Kent

Landmann, Isaac (1741–1826), military educationist, was born on 17 March 1741 in Alsace. He taught projectiles and fortification at the École Royale Militaire in Paris, and, following the school's reorganization, tutored young noblemen of the same city in the art of war.

On 25 November 1777 Landmann was appointed professor of fortification and artillery at the Royal Military Academy, Woolwich. A letter from the Board of Ordnance to the lieutenant-governor of the academy introduced him as a gentleman who 'has seen a great deal of service, and acted as ADC to Marshal Broglie in the last war' (*Records of the Royal Military Academy*, 24). He was given a house at the Warren (after 1805, the Royal Arsenal) and received a salary of £100 p.a., rising by steps to £494, together with 12

chaldrons of coal and 12 pounds of candles. He also taught gentlemen attendants, students who did not intend joining the army. In 1780 he and his wife, Helene, had a son, George Thomas *Landmann, who was baptized at St Mary Magdalen, Woolwich, on 31 May.

Landmann published a number of works on fortification, artillery, mathematics, and architecture, including textbooks for the cadets of the academy. Other unpublished writings by him are preserved in the Royal Artillery Institution. He was highly thought of and was a technical scholar who had great influence over the many young men he taught for a period of nearly thirty-eight years. He retired on 1 July 1815, aged seventy-four, on an annual pension of £500 granted him by the prince regent, and died on 28 June 1826. His wife survived him.

R. H. VETCH, *rev.* P. G. W. ANNIS

Sources H. D. Buchanan-Dunlop, *Records of the Royal Military Academy, 1741–1892*, 2nd edn (1892) · C. de Beer, ed., *The art of gunfounding* (1991) · parish register, St Mary Magdalen, Woolwich, 31 May 1780 [baptism] · PRO, WO 44/691 (268) [retirement and pension papers] · PRO, WO 42/70 (205L)
Archives Royal Artillery Institution, Woolwich, London, papers

Landon [*married name* Maclean], **Letitia Elizabeth** [*pseud.* L.E.L.] (1802–1838), poet and writer, was born on 14 August 1802 at 25 Hans Place, Chelsea, the eldest child of John Landon (1756–1824) and Catherine Jane, *née* Bishop (*d.* 1854). John Landon, the son of a country rector, had begun his career as a midshipman in the navy before joining—and later becoming a partner in—the army agency of Adair & Co. in Pall Mall. Little is known about Catherine Bishop, Landon's mother, save that she was of Welsh extraction, the daughter of Mrs Bishop (*d.* 1826), a woman of independent means and a friend of Sarah Siddons, to whom Landon was to dedicate her first published collection of poetry. The Landons had two other children: Whittington Henry (1804–1883), who went into the church, and Elizabeth (1812–1825), who died aged thirteen.

Childhood and first writings At the age of five Landon began attending Miss Rowden's school at 22 Hans Place, where Mary Mitford and Lady Caroline Lamb were also educated. In 1809 the family moved to a large, if somewhat run down, country house called Trevor Park in East Barnet and John Landon carried out experiments in model farming at the nearby Coventry Farm. From this point on Landon was educated by her cousin Elizabeth and she soon showed a great interest in books and an exceptional talent for writing. With the end of the Napoleonic wars came a drop in the demand for military supplies and an agricultural depression. John Landon was seriously affected by both, and, in straitened circumstances, the family returned to London in 1815, moving first to Fulham and then, in 1816, to Old Brompton. One of their neighbours here was William Jerdan, editor of the *Literary Gazette*. Jerdan responded with enthusiasm when he saw Landon's poems, and her first published work, 'Rome', appeared in the *Literary Gazette* on 11 March 1820, signed simply with the initial 'L'. Other poems followed, and in August 1821, with the financial aid of her grandmother, Landon published *The Fate of Adelaide: a Swiss Tale of*

Letitia Elizabeth Landon (1802–1838), by Daniel Maclise, *c*.1830–35

Romance; and other Poems under the full name of Letitia Elizabeth Landon. Although noted by a number of the major reviews, this collection did not generate a great deal of public interest, partly, perhaps, because the publisher went out of business one month later. That same month, however, two more of Landon's poems appeared in the *Literary Gazette*, this time signed 'L.E.L.' Her 'Poetic Sketches' accompanied by these initials then began to appear regularly, and the identity of the unknown romantic poetess aroused much speculation; the tantalizing initials, as Laman Blanchard notes in his *Life and Literary Remains of L.E.L.*, 'speedily became a signature of magical interest and curiosity' (1.30). In addition to producing poetry for the *Gazette* Landon also became Jerdan's chief reviewer. As the *Gazette* was one of the most influential journals of the time and had a notable influence on the sales of the books reviewed in its pages, Landon wielded a significant amount of power in this role, contributing to the decline of a number of literary reputations. Unfortunately these reviews were published anonymously and most have not been identified. Landon's next collection, *The Improvisatrice, and other Poems*, was published by Hurst and Robinson in 1824. The main reviews were split in their assessments of this collection, but the mysterious L.E.L. had captured the imagination of the general public and the book went through six editions in the first year.

Mature poetry In 1824 Landon's father died, leaving his family relatively impoverished. An unexplained rift with her mother led Landon to move in with her maternal

grandmother in Sloane Street, but she continued to support her mother financially and contributed to putting her brother Whittington through Oxford. Although Landon earned a substantial amount through her writing (according to William Jerdan more than £2585 over the course of her career), most of this went towards the support of her family. Landon's next collection of poems, *The Troubadour: Poetical Sketches of Modern Pictures, and Historical Sketches*, appeared in 1825; Landon reached the height of her popularity and soon discovered the price of such fame for an independent woman of her time. Exaggerated stories about her began to be circulated. Since she wrote primarily about love, it was perhaps inevitable that many of these stories concerned her supposed conquests. As she reported with amusement:

> One young lady heard at Scarborough last summer, that I had had two hundred offers; and a gentleman at Leeds brought an account of three hundred and fifty straight from London. It is really very unfortunate that my conquests should so much resemble the passage to the North Pole and Wordsworth's Cuckoo, 'talked of but never seen'. (Blanchard, 1.50–51)

Not all the gossip was quite as harmless as this. In 1826 Landon began to be slandered in the gutter press, primarily by *The Wasp*, a short-lived satirical magazine devoted to scandalous exposés of popular personalities. One extended absence from London while visiting an uncle led to malicious reports that she had become pregnant by Jerdan and that, as the anonymous writer in *The Wasp* sniggered, 'she was ordered into the country to gather *fruit*, and to *deliver* an account thereof on her return' (*The Wasp*, 1826, 36). Landon was understandably distressed by such attacks, and accurately assessed her position in a letter to her friend Katherine Thomson:

> I think of the treatment I have received until my very soul writhes under the powerlessness of its anger. It is only because I am poor, unprotected, and dependent on popularity, that I am a mark for all the gratuitous insolence and malice of idleness and ill-nature. (Blanchard, 1.54)

Following the death of her grandmother in 1826, Landon moved into an attic room in her old school at Hans Place, now run by the Misses Lance. More independent than ever, Landon also became even more productive. Over the next few years she produced two more collections of poetry, *The Golden Violet* (1827) and *The Venetian Bracelet* (1829); she contributed to many of the periodicals of the time, and to the annuals, the expensive illustrated gift books that were published at the end of each year. Landon edited many of these annuals and frequently, in the case of such works as *Fisher's Drawing Book Scrap Book*, also composed the entire contents, writing poems to illustrate the engravings with which she was provided. As Landon grew ever more successful, so she also was increasingly imitated, and much of the popular verse of the time reveals the marks of her style. Testimony to the extent of her influence is given, if somewhat grudgingly, by *The Athenaeum*'s comment that 'as she has undoubtedly founded a poetic school, we have unfeignedly wished that she would whip some dozen of her scholars' (*The Athenaeum*, 10 Dec 1831, 793).

Landon's poetry is marked by a sense of spontaneity, no doubt the combined result of her desire to suggest she was an *improvisatrice*, and the need, given both her financial requirements and her great popularity, to produce a prolific amount of verse in a short period of time. Considering the demands placed on her by her work, it is hardly surprising that, for much of her life, Landon was plagued by illness; her letters repeatedly refer to being confined to the house by a cold, and her friends and acquaintances often comment on her tendency to suffer from headaches and nervous disorders.

Romance and Reality Landon's first novel, *Romance and Reality* (1831), revealed a completely different writing style from that which she affected in her role as the sentimental poetess L.E.L. The reviewers praised the witty commentary on modern life and remarked with approval on the new Landon that was revealed: where, asked the reviewer of *The Athenaeum*, 'till now, dwelt the brave good sense—the sarcasm bitter with medicine, not poison?' But for *Romance and Reality*, he added, 'half our island might never have awoke from the dream that L.E.L. was an avatar of blue eyes, flaxen ringlets, and a susceptible heart' (*The Athenaeum*, 10 Dec 1831, 793). In fact, Landon had dark eyes and dark hair. The reviewer's assessment that this witty satire revealed the 'true' Landon was echoed by Henry Chorley when he later observed that all three of her novels reflected:

> the conversation of their authoress—which sparkled always brightly with quick fancy, and a *badinage* astonishing to those matter of fact persons who expected to find, in the manners and discourse of the poetess, traces of the weary heart, the broken lute, and the disconsolate willow tree. (H. Chorley, 'Mrs Maclean', *The Athenaeum*, 5 Jan 1839, 14)

Now an integral part of the London literary scene, Landon became a key figure at many literary gatherings. She managed to charm most, but not all. Disraeli, describing one such gathering at the Bulwer-Lyttons' in 1832, reveals a certain class-laden disdain when he writes, 'I avoided L.E.L., who looked the very personification of Brompton—pink satin dress and white satin shoes, red cheeks, snub nose, and her hair *à la Sappho*' (R. Disraeli, ed., *Lord Beaconsfield's Letters*, 1887, 71). The suggestion that Landon had a taste for vulgar finery is not borne out by the numerous portraits made of her, although she did appear to be interested in fashion, and was particularly fond of the more exotic styles of the time—she was often depicted wearing voluminous leg-of-mutton sleeves and enormous hats. While Landon's family background was certainly respectable, as a woman living alone and making a living as a professional writer she herself was often seen as less than respectable. In response, she tended to swing between a desire to maintain an appearance of respectability and a healthy contempt for all the artificial distinctions that class would impose. Blanchard notes the difficulty of inducing her 'to condescend to be on her guard, to put the slightest restraint upon her speech, correspondence, or actions, simply because self-interest demanded it to save her conduct from misrepresentation' (Blanchard, 1.52).

In June 1834 Landon visited France; although she had the opportunity to meet such figures as Heine and Chateaubriand, she was less than pleased by her travels, complaining bitterly about sightseeing, 'the most tiresome thing in the world' (Jerdan, 202), and about the deficiencies of Parisian society—it was not the season and there were few social events of any importance to attend: 'God never sent me into the world to use my hands, or my feet, or my eyes,' she declared; 'he put all my activity into my tongue and ears' (ibid.). If Paris bored her, French literature both shocked and enchanted her; here she found 'extraordinary talent—every page full of new ideas and thoughts—they want nothing but a little religion and a little decency', and these, she added, were 'two trifling wants, to be sure' (Blanchard, 1.110).

Slander and death Before this trip to France, Landon had begun seeing John Forster (1812–1876), then editor of *The Examiner*, and they eventually became engaged. The old scandals unfortunately soon erupted: Landon was again accused of improper behaviour, now not only with Jerdan, but also with William Maginn, Daniel Maclise, and Edward Bulwer-Lytton. This time, Landon does not seem to have been aware of the rumours. Forster, however, was; he went to Landon suggesting the stories should be refuted; she sent him to speak with her friends; he did and pronounced himself satisfied of her innocence, asking her to accept his protection by marrying him immediately. Landon responded by breaking the engagement. The ostensible reason she gave was that she could not allow Forster to marry someone who had been accused of improper behaviour, and Blanchard, in his *Life*, consequently speaks of 'the self-sacrifice she deemed herself called upon by duty to make' (Blanchard, 1.129). To her good friend Bulwer-Lytton, however, she told a different story, suggesting she was unable to marry someone who had behaved with such a lack of sensitivity:

> If his future protection is to harass and humiliate me as much as his present—God keep me from it … I cannot get over the entire want of delicacy to me which could repeat such slander to myself. The whole of his late conduct to me personally has left behind almost dislike—certainly fear of his imperious and overbearing temper. (M. Sadleir, *Bulwer: a Panorama*, 1931, 426)

In October 1836, Landon was invited to a dinner party at the home of Matthew Forster, who was involved in the administration of the Gold Coast; here she met George *Maclean (1801–1847), governor of the British post at Cape Coast, west Africa. Maclean and Landon soon appear to have reached an understanding, although they do not seem to have been, officially, engaged. At the beginning of 1837, however, Maclean had second thoughts about the relationship; he went to Scotland, remaining there for more than six months. Landon was distraught, and her friends rallied round, putting pressure on Maclean to marry her. Reluctantly, he returned to London, and on 7 June 1838 they were married in a private ceremony at St Mary's, Bryanston Square, London. The marriage was not made public and Landon stayed with friends until 5 July, when the Macleans sailed from Portsmouth for Cape

Coast, arriving on 16 August. Just two months later, on 15 October 1838, Landon, at the age of thirty-six, was found dead in her room, apparently slumped against the door with an empty bottle of prussic acid in her hand. Such a mysterious and melodramatic death ensured that Landon was not soon forgotten, and even if the taste for her particular kind of poetry did not last long into the Victorian age, she had a notable influence on the Victorian women poets who followed her. Elizabeth Barrett Browning, for example, comments on the sadness of Landon's life and her isolation in 'L.E.L.'s Last Question' (1839), a reference to the words Landon supposedly spoke when she left England: 'Do you think of me as I think of you?' Christina Rossetti then takes up a line from 'L.E.L.'s Last Question'— 'Whose heart was breaking for a little love'—as the epigraph to her 'L.E.L.'. Perhaps more importantly, the women poets who followed Landon reacted against the limitations that had been imposed on her, against the emphasis on women writing only from the heart. This is particularly notable in *Aurora Leigh*, where Barrett Browning not only draws on the details of Landon's life, but also shows Aurora rejecting the notion of woman as *improvisatrice*, and gradually moving from poetess to woman poet.

Numerous memoirs written by friends and acquaintances emerged soon after the announcement of her death, all attempting to interpret the woman known as L.E.L. and offer their particular explanations of her death; the interest in Landon continued well into the twentieth century, with such fictional reconstructions as D. E. Enfield's *L.E.L.: a Mystery of the Thirties* (1928) and Clyde Chantler's *Eight Weeks: a Novel* (1965). In spite of all the attempts to solve the mystery, the circumstances of Landon's death have never been satisfactorily explained and it is unlikely any new information will come to light. An inquest was held on the afternoon of her death, and the doctor in attendance was so convinced that death was caused by the prussic acid he did not think an autopsy necessary. The depositions given by the witnesses at the inquest, including Maclean and Mrs Bailey, the woman who found Landon, are full of contradictions, discrepancies, and omissions. The conclusion of the inquest was death by accidental overdose of prussic acid, and Landon was buried early that same evening in the rectangular drill ground of the castle. GLENNIS BYRON

Sources L. Blanchard, *The life and literary remains of L.E.L.*, 2 vols. (1876) • W. Jerdan, *The autobiography of William Jerdan: with his literary, political, and social reminiscences and correspondence during the last fifty years*, 4 vols. (1852–3), vol. 3 • G. Stephenson, *Letitia Landon: the woman behind L.E.L.* (1995) • *Poetical works of Letitia Elizabeth Landon, 'L.E.L.'*, ed. F. J. Sypher (1990) • *The fate of Adelaide, a Swiss romantic tale, and other poems by Letitia Elizabeth Landon*, ed. F. J. Sypher, facs. edn (1990) • *Critical writings by Letitia Elizabeth Landon*, ed. F. J. Sypher (1996) • S. C. Hall, *A book of memories of great men and women of the age* (1871)
Archives Hunt. L., letters • Morgan L. • Rutgers University, New Jersey, Archibald S. Alexander Library, letters • University of Iowa Libraries, Iowa City, letters and literary papers | Bodl. Oxf., letters to Marie Anne Disraeli • Herts. ALS, letters to Lord Lytton • NYPL, Berg collection

Likenesses D. Maclise, pencil and black chalk drawing, c.1830–1835, NPG [*see illus.*] • D. Maclise, watercolour drawing, 1833 (study of drawing for *Fraser's Magazine*), BM • E. Finden, stipple, 1835 (after drawing by D. Maclise), BM, NPG; repro. in Sypher, ed., *Poetical works* • S. Freeman, stipple, 1837 (after J. Wright), BM; repro. in *New Monthly Magazine* (1837) • lithograph, pubd 1839, BM • C. Cook, stipple (after H. W. Pickersgill), BM, NPG • E. Finden, stipple (after drawing by D. Maclise), BM • D. Maclise, drawing, V&A • D. Maclise, lithograph, BM • D. Maclise, pencil drawing, BM; repro. in *Fraser's Magazine*, 8 (1833) • H. Robinson, stipple (after H. W. Pickersgill), BM, NPG; repro. in Jerdan, *Autobiography*

Landor, (Arnold) Henry Savage (1867–1924), explorer and artist, was born on 2 June 1867 in Florence, Italy, the second of the three sons (there was also a daughter) of Charles Savage Landor (1825–1917) and his wife, Esmeralda Armida Piselli. His grandfather was the author Walter Savage *Landor (1775–1864). He was educated at the Liceo Dante and the Istituto Tecnico, Florence, and studied portrait painting in Paris, which he abandoned in 1888 to travel round the world. He supported himself by painting the portraits of the distinguished people he met on the way, and in Japan he went off alone to live among the aboriginal Ainu. His books *Alone with the Hairy Ainu* (1893) and *Corea, or, Cho-sen, the Land of the Morning Calm* (1895) were well received and in 1896 he undertook a scientific expedition to Tibet, where he was captured and tortured. The book about his experiences, *In the Forbidden Land* (1898), was translated into all the major European languages, though his scientific data were seen to be of less importance.

In 1899 Landor climbed Mount Lumpa in Nepal and in 1900 he joined the allied march on Peking (Beijing) during the Boxer uprising. He undertook further expeditions between 1903 and 1911 over little-explored territory. He traversed the deserts of Persia and Baluchistan by camel, crossed central Africa at its widest point (which he later described in *Across Wildest Africa*, 1907), and explored the Mato Grosso of Brazil, where his men mutinied and made two attempts on his life. The party found its way back to civilization in a starving condition on an improvised raft. These experiences he recorded in *Across Unknown South America* (1913). In the Philippines he visited headhunters in Luzon and discovered the white-skinned Mansaka people in Mindanao (described in *The Gems of the East*, 1904). During the First World War he toured the western front and submitted designs for improved armoured cars, motor cycles, and airships, and a device for destroying barbed-wire entanglements. He had experimented with flying machines as early as 1893.

Landor's want of training and his impatience to press on with all speed made him an unreliable surveyor, and there were those who impugned the veracity of his hair-raising escapes; but in energy and resourcefulness, and in courage and power of endurance, he was the equal of any of the previous generation of great explorers. He scorned special equipment and was said to have appeared on a mountain or in a jungle as he would in Bond Street. His contempt for ropes and nailed boots nearly cost him his life on several occasions while mountaineering. As a painter he had the facility to produce a likeness in a single one-hour sitting, and the numerous illustrations he made for his books are competent. A bronze bust he did of his father shows real ability.

Landor was elected a fellow of the Royal Geographical Society in 1892, and a member of the Royal Institution in 1897. He died, unmarried, at his home at via Farina 10 in Florence on 26 December 1924 after being knocked down by a motor vehicle in London.

T. C. Farmbrough, rev.

Sources *The Times* (29 Dec 1924) · A. H. S. Landor, *Everywhere: the memoirs of an explorer* (1922) · RGS · *CGPLA Eng. & Wales* (1925) **Archives** Richmond Local Studies Library, London, letters to Douglas Sladen **Wealth at death** £25,271 18s. 5d.—in England: administration with will, 23 April 1925, *CGPLA Eng. & Wales*

Landor, Robert Eyres (1781–1869), writer, the youngest brother of Walter Savage *Landor, was born on 10 May 1781 in Warwick, near the east gate, the sixth of seven children of Walter Landor (1733–1805), a physician and country gentleman, and his second wife, Elizabeth (1743–1829), daughter of Charles Savage, a Warwickshire landowner. He attended Bromsgrove School, Worcestershire, until 1797 and, from that year, Worcester College, Oxford, where he graduated BA in 1801 and MA in 1802, and also held a fellowship.

Ordained in 1804, Landor was a curate at Wyke Regis in Dorset for the first part of 1805, but for the next decade his occupation and residence are unknown, except that he spent some time as a curate at Stockton in Warwickshire in 1813. In 1815 and 1816 he travelled with his brother Walter in France and Italy. From 1817 until 1824 or 1825, he was vicar of St Michael's at Hughenden in Buckinghamshire, and he was also briefly chaplain to the prince regent. He may have lived in Tenby in Wales for a few years after leaving Hughenden. He then moved to Birlingham in south Worcestershire, where he was rector of St James's Church in Nafford parish from 1829 until his death forty years later.

Originally close to his brother Walter—he helped him edit the second edition of his poem *Gebir* in 1803—he quarrelled with him in 1820 over money matters, and the two did not speak for twenty years.

Landor wrote in several genres, producing four closet dramas, two novels, one long poem, and a series of political letters on the trial of Queen Caroline. In 1824 his verse play *The Count Arezzi* won praise for its poetical language and its originality, and it sold well until Landor announced that, contrary to rumour, Lord Byron was not the author. In 1828 Landor published the narrative poem *The Impious Feast*, which was criticized for mixing romance with a biblical subject. The poem is also notable for combining rhyme with blank verse. His novel *The Fountain of Arethusa* (1848), in which two modern-day explorers engage in a series of dialogues with the ghosts of ancient Greeks and Romans, in some way resembles his brother's *Imaginary Conversations*, and in general, critics have noted a 'remarkable family likeness' in the writing styles of the two Landors (Saintsbury, 229).

Robert Landor was not well known even in his own day, and afterwards was almost totally forgotten—unjustly so, according to one of his biographers, who praises his originality, his 'moral nobility', and his elegant prose style (Partridge, 104, 103, 81–4).

Landor's personality has been variously described as ebullient and crusty (Super, 133; Elwin, 363). Although reclusive, he was, according to John Forster, 'a really brilliant talker' (Forster, 2.502). He had the same quick grey eyes as his brother Walter and resembled him in voice, but at 6 feet 2 inches was much taller. Landor died at Birlingham, Worcestershire, on 26 January 1869, leaving behind a collection of art works and a large library. He never married.

Sheldon Goldfarb

Sources E. Partridge, *Robert Eyres Landor: a biographical and critical sketch* (1927) · R. H. Super, *Walter Savage Landor: a biography* (1954) · J. Forster, *Walter Savage Landor: a biography*, 2 vols. (1869) · M. Elwin, *Savage Landor* (1941) · S. Wheeler, 'The other Landor', *The Bookman*, 58 (1920), 200–02 · F. L. Colvile, *The worthies of Warwickshire who lived between 1500 and 1800* [1870], 495–8 · G. Saintsbury, 'Robert Eyres Landor', *The Cambridge history of English literature*, 12 (1921), 228–30 · O. Elton, *Survey of English literature, 1780–1830*, 2 vols. (1912), vol. 2 · A. Symons, 'Robert Eyres Landor (1781–1869)', *The Romantic movement in English poetry* (1909), 207–9 **Archives** BL, letters to his brother and mother, MS Facs. 558 · Shakespeare Birthplace Trust RO, Stratford upon Avon, legal documents relating to Landor and family estates at Ipsley · William Salt Library, Stafford, corresp. and papers · Worcester College, Oxford, letter and MSS containing alterations for *The impious feast* | NYPL, Berg collection · Princeton University, New Jersey, Walter Savage Landor corresp. · Yale U., Osborn collection **Likenesses** photograph (late in life), repro. in Wheeler, 'The other Landor' **Wealth at death** under £20,000: probate, 17 March 1869, *CGPLA Eng. & Wales* · art collection of about fifty works incl. Rubens, Holbein, Raphael, and Caravaggio; library containing about 1600 volumes; well-stocked wine cellar: Partridge, *Robert Eyres Landor*

Landor, Walter Savage (1775–1864), poet and author, was born on 30 January 1775 at Eastgate House in Smith Street, just outside the east gate of Warwick, the eldest son of Walter Landor (1733–1805), medical practitioner, and his second wife, Elizabeth Savage (1743–1829). Both parents inherited considerable wealth, the father in 1781 coming into possession of family estates in Staffordshire, while in 1786 the mother's second cousin John Norris bequeathed to her estates at Bishops Tachbrooke, near Leamington, and at Ipsley Court, near Redditch. These properties were entailed upon the eldest son, who was thus early impressed with the idea that his future prospects were assured. That his assurance needed no reinforcement is evident from a story told by Mrs Sherwood, née Mary Martha Butt, a prolific writer for children. In 1782, when both she and Landor were seven, she accompanied her mother to the Landor household, and was startled by the boy's insolence to his mother. 'From that day this youth became the prototype, in my mind, of all that was vulgar and disobedient' (Darton, 40). She evidently had no idea that the insolent boy had, by the time of her death in 1851, become one of the most admired literary patriarchs in Britain. He never became a model of good behaviour, though in later

Walter Savage Landor (1775–1864), by Herbert Watkins, 1850s

years his courtesy, when he chose to exercise it, was elaborate and engaging.

Education and early literary career Landor's precocity was probably fostered by his early departure from home. He was only four and a half when his parents dispatched him to Thomas Treherne's school, some 10 miles from Warwick, and barely eight when, in 1783, he went on to Rugby School. There he gained a formidable reputation as a boxer, as well as proficiency in the other school sports. He was particularly renowned for his skill in fishing by casting a net, on one occasion using his net to trap and intimidate a farmer who had found him poaching. He also showed a considerable talent for the Latin verse composition so highly prized in an educational system devoted almost exclusively to the study of the classics. It was a talent that led him into serious trouble with school authority. When required to copy some of his verses into the school's 'play-book', he claimed that some of his worst composition had been chosen, and in revenge added some emphatically coarse lines by way of disavowal. Defiance of this kind, coupled with his adoption of the egalitarian principles current in the early days of the French Revolution, made his presence in the school intolerable to the headmaster, Dr Thomas James, who did not exactly expel him, but requested his departure.

Landor left Rugby at the end of 1791, spent a short time with a tutor in London, and then was settled with the Revd William Langley, rector of a parish in the neighbourhood of Ashbourne in Derbyshire. Here he spent a year apparently reading as he wished, acquiring a greater knowledge of Greek and a still greater facility in the writing of Latin. He had already become acquainted with the celebrated whig scholar Dr Samuel Parr, perpetual curate of Hatton, a village just outside Warwick. Parr greatly admired Landor's classical attainments, an admiration which was to encourage the young poet to publish rather more of his work in Latin than was commercially prudent. In January 1793 Landor entered Trinity College, Oxford. With the execution of Louis XVI and the outbreak of war between Britain and France, radical convictions were hardly acceptable in a university so dominated by the established church, but Landor was quite undaunted by this challenge and soon gained the reputation of being a mad jacobin. Although he was on good terms with his tutor, William Benwell, his contempt for most of the college fellows was notorious, and it is little wonder that his undergraduate career came to a premature end. His contemporary Robert Southey thought he had been rusticated after shooting at a fellow, but his offence was not in fact quite so gross. At a party in his rooms, in June 1794, his guests became involved in an altercation through the windows with the guests at another party. The latter eventually closed their shutters, and Landor took a shotgun with which he had been shooting rabbits and fired a volley at the closed window. Complaints followed, and Landor had to leave, although he would have been at liberty to return after two terms.

Landor spent the remainder of the summer of 1794 in Tenby in south Wales. There he made love to a young woman called Nancy Jones, celebrated in his verse as 'Ione'. In due course he took a step that looked like a determination never to return to Oxford: he removed his name from the college books. On his return to Warwick in December there was an angry exchange with his father, who had no patience with his son's rejection of a settled occupation, and Landor left home to make his literary fortune in London. Sadly, his first volume of poems found only thirty-six purchasers, and for a time he had to subsist mainly on his prospects as the heir to his father's property. He had friends who offered their assistance, including Dr Parr, who would have been happy to have Landor stay with him. Dorothy Lyttelton, heir to a considerable fortune, knew Landor's sister Elizabeth well, and encouraged him to make his peace with his father. She would have been a suitable match for Landor, but the likelihood is that Nancy Jones had a child by Landor in 1795, and he very properly rallied to her support. Eventually his father made him an allowance of £150 a year.

An elegy included in Landor's *Simonidea* (1806) indicates that Nancy Jones died while still young, and it is a natural inference that the child did not survive either (Landor, *Poetical Works*, 3.2–3). Whatever the circumstances, the relationship ended, and Landor found consolation in the family of Howell Price, who lived near Swansea and whose wife was the widow of Lord Aylmer. Her daughter by this marriage, Rose Aylmer, came to know Landor well, and it was she who lent him Clara Reeve's *Progress of Romance*, in which he found the story that formed the basis of his first major poem, *Gebir*, published in 1798. Shortly after this she went to Calcutta with her aunt, whose husband, Sir Henry Russell, was a judge in the supreme court there. She died of cholera in 1800. Her death prompted Landor to write the brief and poignant poem by which he is best remembered, 'Ah what avails the sceptred race!' (ibid., 3.77).

Gebir, mainly written in 1797, is a remarkable poem, an idiosyncratic example of modern epic, a genre which enjoyed a considerable vogue at the turn of the century. The story is one of invasion: the Spanish prince Gebir reasserts his ancestors' rights to rule in Egypt and is received with love by its queen Charoba, but is killed by a poisonous cloak presented by the queen's counsellor Dalica. The narrative is elaborate and obscure, but there are many individual passages of a haunting beauty that led Robert Southey to write a warmly appreciative notice in the *Critical Review*. Years later Shelley found the poem totally absorbing, and it had an indirect influence as well. Landor's schoolfellow Henry Francis Cary seems to have profited from *Gebir* when he came to undertake his translation of Dante's *Divina commedia*, and Cary's blank verse was an element in the revision of Keats's *Hyperion*. At the time most of the reviews were hostile, mainly because of the occasional indications in the poem of Landor's radical politics.

Landor's political interests were not confined to his poetry. In 1797 he published the first of his many political statements, *To the Burgesses of Warwick*, an attack on one of Pitt's tax-raising measures. Its language has all the violence natural to Landor's temperament, though its substance is the stuff of mainstream controversy. Dr Parr hoped that this eloquent young writer might be drawn into the constitutional opposition campaigning associated with Charles James Fox, though this would have meant keeping back some of his 'favourite and perhaps erroneous opinions' (Forster, 1.155). Landor recalled many years later that Parr took him to hear his celebrated Spital sermon, preached in April 1800 (Landor, *Letters and other Unpublished Writings*, 57). The sermon, when printed, was expanded into what amounted to a manifesto of moderate whiggism, reproving the giddy rashness of youth and commending ingenuous docility. This was counsel to which Landor paid no attention, but Parr none the less remained a warm admirer of his protégé.

For some years Landor led the life of an idle young man, enjoying the fashionable society of Bath and London and always in debt. He published a few slender volumes: *Poems from the Arabic and Persian* and *Poetry by the Author of 'Gebir'* (both in 1800) and, in Latin, *Iambi* (1800) and a translation of *Gebir* (1803). In the summer of 1802, during the brief peace of Amiens, he visited France, and was struck, as Wordsworth was, by the lack of popular fervour for the revolution or for Bonaparte himself. Landor, for his part, was intensely gratified by an opportunity that came his way to see the first consul at close quarters, and if his political sentiments were altered by his visit, it was mainly because of the dislike he conceived for the French people—a dislike that remained with him for the rest of his life.

It was on one of his visits to Bath, early in 1803, that Landor first met Sophia Jane Swift, the most enduring love of his life. She appears in his poetry as Ianthe, and was evidently a vivacious and light-hearted young woman who found Landor's choleric outbursts entertaining rather than intimidating. When she wanted to be particularly persuasive she took hold of his ears to reinforce her point, a liberty which seems to have gratified him. Unfortunately for Landor she was engaged to be married to a distant cousin in Ireland, Godwin Swifte, and marry him she did in the autumn of 1803. After her marriage she paid a number of extended visits to fashionable resorts in England, and Landor followed and flirted with her in a rather scandalous way.

Spain and friendship with Southey On 3 November 1805 Dr Landor died, and his son entered into his inheritance. He had no desire to maintain the family's estate in Staffordshire, and was ready to sell it in order to buy property in a more romantic location. A search in the Lake District proved unsuccessful, but he found what he wanted in the Black Mountains in south Wales. The picturesque countryside around the ruins of Llanthony Abbey seemed an appropriate setting for Landor's ambition to be an enlightened landlord. He had plans to improve the roads, restore the abbey, and plant thousands of trees. Unfortunately it soon became clear that managing an estate required more tact and experience than he possessed. He placed his affairs in the hands of a local solicitor, Charles Gabell, who showed little disposition to take care of his client's interests, allowing rents to be left unpaid and trees to be felled. But at first Landor had concerns more pressing than the care of his estate. When in 1808 popular enthusiasm for the long war with France was rekindled by the Spanish insurrection against their French invaders, Landor responded vigorously, and decided to join the insurgents in person. He persuaded two Irishmen to join him, and in August set off for Corunna, where he raised a company of volunteers and contributed a substantial sum to the relief of the war-stricken town of Venturada. His troop advanced eastwards along the north coast of Spain as far as Bilbao, but took no part in actual fighting. When, under the terms of the convention of Cintra, British generals allowed French forces to withdraw unscathed, he returned home in disgust. Although his expedition had lasted only three months, the Spanish authorities were grateful, and gave him the honorary rank of colonel in the king's army.

Earlier in 1808 in Bristol, Landor had met Robert Southey for the first time. He had always been grateful for Southey's favourable review of *Gebir*, and now, different in temperament though they were, the two men found in each other a source of appreciation and reassurance. Landor learned something of Southey's plans for a series of mythological poems, and of the economic obstacles in the way of his carrying them out. His impulsive response was to offer to pay any publishing costs, and Southey, although he refused to take advantage of Landor's generosity, felt encouraged to go on with *The Curse of Kehama*, sending drafts of the poem to Landor for comment and dedicating it to him when it was eventually published in 1810. This warm relationship continued until Southey's death in 1843. They met only a few times, but corresponded steadily. Although Southey suffered from dementia in his last years, he could remember Landor's name when everything else was forgotten. The durability of their mutual regard is the more surprising because of the growing contrast in their political convictions. At their first meeting they could have united in congenial denunciations of the baseness of almost all public men, but Southey soon came to fear the effects of such subversive sentiments, and by 1812 was a confirmed supporter of the tory administration. When in 1811 Landor wrote a radical commentary on a biography of Charles James Fox and dedicated it to the president of the United States, John Murray the publisher asked Southey to persuade Landor to soften the more objectionable parts. Southey's persuasions were tactful and friendly, but in the end the pamphlet had to be suppressed. He performed a similar service in 1823, when the publisher of the first series of *Imaginary Conversations* took fright at some of Landor's audacities, and Southey acted as a kind of mediator.

One result of Landor's Spanish adventure was a kindling of his interest in the earlier invasion of the peninsula by the Moors, and in 1810 he began work on his tragedy depicting the predicament of the nobleman who collaborated with the invaders: *Count Julian*. As with *Gebir*, the narrative develops obscurely, but the sublime passions of the hero are eloquently, sometimes turgidly, articulated:

> the agony
> Of an opprest and of a bursting heart.
> (*Count Julian*, v.iv, ll. 231–2)

Landor told Southey that he had laboured on it during the day, 'and at night unburdened my mind, shedding many tears' (Forster, 1.293). Southey himself was more attracted by the intimations of invulnerable endurance which were an important element in Landor's self-image, like the eagle who stands solitary:

> Upon some highest cliff, and rolls his eye,
> Clear, constant, unobservant, unabased,
> In the cold light, above the dews of morn.
> (*Count Julian*, v.ii, ll. 21–4)

Landor had some hopes of persuading John Philip Kemble to play the part of Julian, but he settled for having the play published as a closet drama. To his annoyance it was rejected by Southey's publisher, Longman, but eventually John Murray agreed to produce a small edition, provided that Landor paid for it. This appeared in 1812.

Failure as a landowner and exile The agonies of Count Julian were in part an oblique expression of the frustration Landor was experiencing in the development of his Llanthony estate. He hoped to improve matters by settling there. This needed the presence of a wife, and in 1811, after what seems to have been a rather perfunctory courtship, he married Julia Thuillier (1794–1879), the seventeen-year-old daughter of an unsuccessful banker: 'a girl without a

sixpence, and with very few accomplishments', but 'pretty, graceful, and good-tempered' (Forster, 1.323). The marriage took place on 24 May, and shortly afterwards they moved to Llanthony. The house he was having built there was unfinished, and they lived 'among ruins and rubbish' (ibid., 1.326). There were other sources of discontent: in particular he found the local people sullen and dishonest. Hoping to find a congenial English tenant, he let one of his largest farms to Charles Betham, a brother of a friend of Southey's, Matilda Betham. But Betham proved to be no more satisfactory than the scoundrelly Welshmen, and he and Landor were soon at odds over payment of rent and use of the land, with meadows that Landor wished to preserve ploughed up, and hedges neglected, allowing sheep to graze destructively in his much prized plantations. When a younger brother of Betham dug up trees that Landor had planted, he denounced him in a handbill that he personally posted up in Monmouth at the time of the assizes. A libel suit followed, and Landor had to pay £100 damages.

After Charles Gabell had shown his unwillingness to act against a refractory tenant actually recommended by himself, Landor lost all patience and found another lawyer, Baker Gabb. But he was no more successful in handling his affairs, and by 1813 the loss of income and the accumulation of debts had made it impossible for Landor to remain in Llanthony. The estate was placed in the hands of a trust managed by his brothers, and a modest income secured to him and his wife out of his mother's rents from her Ipsley estate. The long war with France had ended in April 1814, and at the end of May Landor sailed from Weymouth with a view to settling in that country. He went at first to Jersey, where his wife joined him. She had no liking for the idea of living abroad, and a bitter marital quarrel ensued: 'every kind and tender sentiment was rooted up from my heart for ever' (Forster, 1.413). He left her, sailed to Granville in an oyster boat, and then travelled on to Tours, where he spent the best part of a year. His wife sought a reconciliation, and Landor relented, meeting her at Dieppe towards the end of February 1815 and bringing her to Tours. This coincided with the return of Napoleon from his exile in Elba, and the consequent brief renewal of the war. Landor did not allow this to change his plans, scorning any anxiety about his being declared an enemy alien. He later had the satisfaction of seeing (as he claimed) the defeated Napoleon passing through Tours on his way to La Rochelle after the battle of Waterloo.

In order to secure Landor's formal consent to the financial arrangements devised by his brothers, the youngest brother, Robert Eyres Landor, came to Tours with the necessary documents in October 1815. Robert found Julia patient and submissive, and Walter as tempestuous as ever, though surprisingly popular with the local market-women. In the aftermath of defeat the country was in a disturbed state, and Walter and Julia were anxious to leave Tours. As Robert wanted to visit Italy they travelled together as far as Milan, where they separated, Robert going on to Rome and his brother and sister-in-law to

Como. There Landor engaged a house, which was his home until the autumn of 1818.

Residence in Italy; *Imaginary Conversations* Here, in the summer of 1817, Landor once again met Southey, who was touring the continent after the death of his son. Here, too, Landor's eldest son was born, in March 1818. He named him Arnold after Sir Arnold Savage, an early fifteenth-century speaker of the House of Commons who had insisted that grievances should be redressed before supplies were granted. Landor speculated that this congenially audacious figure might have been an ancestor, and devoted one of his first imaginary conversations to him. Landor's own audacity ensured a dramatic departure from Como. He had composed a series of Latin epigrams, one of which was a reply to a local poet's sonnet attacking England. The censor declared this a libel, and Landor was summoned to appear before the governor of Lombardy, who, after an angry altercation, ordered him to leave Como in a few days. Landor defiantly stayed beyond the date decreed in September 1818, but then left anyway. He spent much of the next three years in Pisa, where his daughter Julia was born. He devoted his energies mainly to the writing of Latin poetry, published in 1820 as *Idyllia heroica decem*. This volume contained his wide-ranging essay 'De cultu atque usu Latini sermonis', which included assessments of modern English poets, invoked by Southey in his denunciation of the 'Satanic School' in the preface to his *Vision of Judgement*.

In 1821 Landor moved to Florence, and it was here that he began to produce his *Imaginary Conversations*. Dialogue was a form peculiarly congenial to him, allowing him to express his opinions and prejudices in an unsystematic and wide-ranging way, sometimes with that epigrammatic sharpness which is so striking in his best-remembered verse, rather often with a grandiloquence that for his contemporaries suggested the dignity of classical literature. Julius Hare thought of it as a model of what prose composition should be: 'at its best, where the air of classic antiquity breathed about the speakers, the style seemed to him what Apollo's talk might have been, as radiant, piercing, and pure' (Forster, 2.87). Julius was a younger brother of Francis Hare, one of Landor's most sympathetic friends in Italy, and it was he who had succeeded in having the book published at all. Five publishers turned it down, and eventually Hare used his personal acquaintance with John Taylor, who owned the *London Magazine*, to persuade him to accept it. Taylor himself felt considerable anxiety about some things that Landor wrote, in particular his doubts about the efficacy of prayer. But Hare suggested that the proofs should be sent to Southey for consideration, and both Landor and Taylor agreed to accept his judgement of what was allowable. The book appeared in March 1824, and was widely reviewed, though opinions were not always favourable. Landor had already achieved some notoriety as one of Byron's targets in the feud with Southey. 'Savage Landor (for such is his grim cognomen)' features in the preface to *The Vision of Judgement* (1822) as a reviler of George III (in *Gebir*). Such publicity enhanced the initial interest in *Imaginary Conversations*, and its ambitious scope and accomplished technique established Landor's position as an important writer. The work's reputation was steadily enhanced as time went on by its association with two Victorian phenomena. The first was the cult of the hero, of the great man who shapes history. In *The Pentameron* something said by his Petrarch clearly applies to Landor himself:

> Among the chief pleasures of my life, and among the commonest of my occupations, was the bringing before me such heroes and heroines of antiquity, such poets and sages, such of the prosperous and unfortunate, as most interested me by their courage, their wisdom, their eloquence, or their adventures.

Landor created conversation suited to their characters: 'I knew perfectly their manners, their steps, their voices'; he knew them so well that he felt able to make them speak 'on subjects far remote from the beaten track of their career' (Landor, *Complete Works*, 9.273–4). Landor's impersonation of noble characters reinforced that other Victorian predilection, the ideal of Hellenism, associating the classical ethos with a tranquillity that he so evidently lacked in his personal life, but that he sought to create in his writings. The most admired of the subsequent additions to the original set of dialogues (and he published some 150 in all) were those in which classical Greek and Roman characters figured. The same ethos pervades the imagined correspondence of *Pericles and Aspasia* (1836), and, with little modification, the conversations between Boccaccio and Petrarch in the *Pentameron* (1837).

One of the more favourable assessments of *Imaginary Conversations* had been William Hazlitt's in the *Edinburgh Review*. He visited Florence with his second wife in February 1825, and boldly introduced himself to Landor. Their vehement temperaments and fiercely held iconoclastic opinions proved mutually congenial, and according to Hazlitt it was he who introduced Landor to Leigh Hunt and thus to a number of younger writers and artists in Florence whose friendship he came to value. These included the painter Seymour Kirkup, and Charles Armitage Brown, the friend of John Keats. He was also friendly with an Irish peer, the thirteenth Viscount Dillon, a man as boisterous and unconventional as Landor himself. Later, in 1827, Landor made the acquaintance of Marguerite, countess of Blessington, who was in Italy gathering materials for her *Conversations of Lord Byron*. She was deeply impressed by his 'high breeding and urbanity' (Blessington, 494), and Landor for his part thought that he had never talked with a woman more elegant or better informed (Forster, 2.139). In this sympathetic circle he found encouragement to continue with the composition of his conversations; Henry Colburn published a further volume in 1828, and James Duncan two more in 1829. Landor had quarrelled with John Taylor over delays in payment for the first volumes and the arrangements for the third, evidence that he was at last seeing himself as a professional writer who might gain an income from his pen.

As his reputation grew, Landor received many visits from visitors to Florence, notably Wordsworth's friend

Henry Crabb Robinson and the young Ralph Waldo Emerson. But there was constant friction in his relationships with local people. Slighting remarks about the Florentines in the first edition of *Imaginary Conversations* were translated into Italian and hardly encouraged friendly feeling. He became known, too, as a troublesome and violent resident. The state archives contain records of a number of cases in which Landor is alleged to have committed a variety of assaults, kicking tradesmen, knocking them down, and thrashing them. He was said to have thrown scalding water at a maidservant. By his own account his relations with the authorities were stormy. He reacted to the failure of the courts to recover stolen goods by threatening to drag the president of the Buon Governo (the minister of police) before the grand duke 'by the throat':

> The next morning I had an order from the commissary to attend him. I went; and he read to me an order from the president to be out of Tuscany in three days. 'Tell the president I shall neither be out of Tuscany nor out of Florence in three days; and let him use force if he dares; I will repel it.' (letter to Southey, July 1829; Forster, 2.218–19)

Landor soon afterwards did indeed leave the city of Florence, but only for Fiesole, 3 miles to the west, where a wealthy admirer, Joseph Ablett, enabled him to buy the Villa Gherardesca. It was a beautiful situation in itself, but the association of the neighbourhood with Boccaccio and Milton enhanced Landor's satisfaction. There were extensive grounds attached to the villa, and he embarked on an ambitious programme of planting. This led him into yet another long-running dispute with a neighbour, who complained that Landor was depriving him of water: an affair of which he gives a lively account in *High and Low Life in Italy* (1837).

Separation from his wife and return to England A second son, Walter, had been born in 1822, and a third, Charles, in 1825. Landor's children gave him boundless pleasure while they were young, but his family life was increasingly soured by tensions with his wife. A visit to Florence in 1829 by his 'Ianthe', now the comtesse de Molandé, seems to have created an insurmountable jealousy. Mrs Landor took to insulting her husband before company, and after an embarrassing scene witnessed by Charles Armitage Brown in March 1835 Landor left the house, and in September he returned to England. He had already been there on a summer visit in 1832, when he had enjoyed the prestige due to the author of *Imaginary Conversations*, meeting again with Southey, and finding his way to Wordsworth, Coleridge, and Lamb. Now, settled first in Clifton, near Bristol, and then, from October 1837, in Bath, he found himself for the next twenty-three years established as a man of letters of acknowledged distinction. He widened his circle of friends through his visits to the countess of Blessington's house in London, coming to know Charles Dickens and Robert Browning, as well as John Forster, who was to be the biographer of both himself and Dickens. He found much pleasure in the attentions of younger women, as is shown particularly in his letters to Rose Paynter, a niece of Rose Aylmer whom she greatly resembled. His own children were a continuing

disappointment to him. Arnold visited England in 1842, but gave his father little affection. Young Walter came over in both 1841 and 1843, on the second occasion accompanied by his sister Julia. Julia proved to be more responsive to her father's goodwill, but even she turned against him in later years when, in 1855, he was unable to raise money to enable her to marry a French count.

In spite of these vexations, Landor was a steadily prolific writer, in the earlier part of this period producing work in the classical mode such as *The Pentameron*, and experimenting with verse drama in *Andrea of Hungary* and *Giovanna of Naples* (1839). Forster encouraged him to prepare a comprehensive edition of his writings. He spent nearly three years overseeing this project, and the *Collected Works* appeared in two large volumes in 1846. They proved relatively successful, being reprinted three times. A collection of his writings in Latin, *Poemata*, followed in 1847. Landor also came to be something of a political figure: his *Letters of a Conservative* (1836) was a call for radical reform of the Church of England. His conservative principles were, indeed, distinctly idiosyncratic, combining fierce support for anti-monarchical movements abroad with a detestation of the moneyed interest at home. His ideas are clearly expounded in his 'Reflections on Athens at the Decease of Pericles', an essay appended to the first edition of *Pericles and Aspasia*. He contributed many letters to the newspaper *The Examiner*, where John Forster was a regular contributor and, between 1847 and 1855, the editor. Landor was exhilarated by the revolutionary upsurge in 1848, in particular championing the Hungarians and their leader Louis Kossuth. He shared the popular hostility in England to Russia, and eagerly supported the Crimean War. He was particularly notorious for his advocacy of tyrannicide (though in general he was opposed to capital punishment), and incurred much censure when in January 1858 Felice Orsini made an attempt on the life of Napoleon III. Napoleon escaped, but many bystanders were killed. Landor had indeed met Orsini, and was accused of inciting him, though there was no basis for such a charge. He was deeply shocked by the loss of innocent lives.

Second exile and death The opprobrium attaching to the Orsini affair damaged Landor's standing in a libel case that drove him a second time into exile. In 1856 he had become acquainted with a clergyman and his wife, Morris and Mary Jane Yescombe. They had taken under their care a young woman called Geraldine Hooper, whom Landor found attractive. He addressed poems to her (as 'Erminine') and gave her many gifts: these found their way into Mrs Yescombe's keeping. Eventually, early in 1857, Landor began to suspect that Mrs Yescombe was exploiting Geraldine to enrich herself, and rashly published an attack on her in a pamphlet, *Walter Savage Landor and the Honorable Mrs Yescombe*. A libel action was threatened, but John Forster persuaded Landor to sign a retractation. The offence was repeated in three poems included in Landor's next publication, *Dry Sticks, Fagoted by Walter Savage Landor* (1858). Mrs Yescombe initiated an action for libel, and when it came to court in August 1858 she was awarded £1000 in damages. The newspapers reacted with eloquent denunciations of this libeller and advocate of tyrannicide. By then, though, Landor was no longer in England. He was in poor health in the winter of 1856–7, made something of a recovery in the course of 1857, and then suffered an apoplectic stroke in March 1858. He was not disabled by this, but was in no condition to enter upon an effective defence. Two nieces, Sophy and Kitty Landor, assisted him in his escape, and he returned to Fiesole and to the reluctant care of his estranged family.

Landor came to find his position in his old home intolerable, and in June 1859 left it, walking into Florence with little money and no possessions. Robert and Elizabeth Barrett Browning were living in Florence at the time, and Robert met Landor in the street. He immediately gave him shelter, and wrote to Forster to see if Landor's family in England could support him in lodgings, which in due course they did. After a few months in Marcioni, near Siena, where he was cared for by the family of the American sculptor William Wetmore Story, he was established in rooms at 2671 via Nunziatina (subsequently called 93 via della Chiesa), Florence, not far from the Brownings' home. He was increasingly infirm, but contrived to publish one last political pamphlet, on the American civil war (*Letters of a Canadian*, 1862), and one last volume of poetry, *Heroic Idyls* (1863). He died in his rooms on 17 September 1864, and was buried in the protestant cemetery in Florence two days later. His estranged wife lived on until 17 April 1879.

Reputation A few months before his death Landor had been visited by a greatly admiring young poet, A. C. Swinburne, whose homage is a fine symbol of Landor's role as one of the forerunners of late Victorian aestheticism. He was in advance of his own contemporaries, too, in his appreciation of early Italian painting. His friends were almost unanimous in deriding what seemed to them his indiscriminate purchases of old paintings—'not esteemed at that time', as his friend Seymour Kirkup put it (Forster, 2.205). The esteem was to come with the Pre-Raphaelites, with whom, indeed, Landor had some affinity. But Landor's place in the literary landscape has never been easy to determine. For many years after his death his reputation was high, Swinburne, for example, claiming that 'he had won for himself such a double crown of glory in verse and in prose as has been won by no other Englishman but Milton' (Swinburne, 14.278). But admirers always had to concede that he was little-read; Landor made a virtue of the fact, and was consciously exclusive: 'I shall dine late; but the dining-room will be well lighted, the guests few and select' (Landor, *Complete Works*, 6.37). He took pride in his Latin publications, and made no concessions to the ignorance of the readers of his English writings. Much of his prose and poetry is a deliberate attempt to recreate the tranquil atmosphere associated by his contemporaries with the literature of ancient Greece. He constantly sought perfection of expression:

How many verses have I thrown
Into the fire because the one

Peculiar word, the wanted most,
Was irrecoverably lost.
(Landor, *Poetical Works*, 3.472)

He is remembered mainly for a few brief poems, some hauntingly tender, some fiercely scornful. The often quoted dismissal of the four Georges ('George the First was always reckoned / Vile, but viler George the Second …') has the same clear definition as a poem to Ianthe, 'Past ruin'd Ilion Helen lives …':

Soon shall Oblivion's deepening veil
Hide all the peopled hills you see,
The gay, the proud, while lovers hail
In distant ages you and me.
(ibid., 2.331, 3.114)

It is in such brief moments that Landor's genius is most apparent. His more ambitious works tend to be diffuse and long-winded, a trait particularly apparent in his *Citation and examination of William Shakspeare before the worshipful Sir Thomas Lucy Knight touching deer stealing* (1834), the one publication which he (mistakenly) expected to be popular.

Although never widely read, Landor became well known as an eccentric character, in part because of the vivid portrayal of him as Lawrence Boythorn in Dickens's *Bleak House* (1852–3). Dickens dexterously captures Landor's boisterous laugh, stentorian voice, extravagant language, and startling gentleness, and although he relishes the absurdity of his outbursts, they are a manifestation of a splendidly resilient vitality. It is strange that so little of this uninhibited vigour should find its way into the work by which Landor expected to be remembered.

GEOFFREY CARNALL

Sources *The complete works of Walter Savage Landor*, ed. T. E. Welby and S. Wheeler, 16 vols. (1927–36) · R. H. Super, *Walter Savage Landor: a biography* (1954) · J. Forster, *Walter Savage Landor: a biography*, 2 vols. (1869) · M. Elwin, *Landor: a replevin* (1958) · *The poetical works of Walter Savage Landor*, ed. S. Wheeler, 3 vols. (1937) · *Letters and other unpublished writings of Walter Savage Landor*, ed. S. Wheeler (1897) · *Letters of Walter Savage Landor, private and public*, ed. S. Wheeler (1899) · W. S. Landor, *Pericles and Aspasia*, vol. 2 (1836) · J. Field, *Landor* (2000) · J. Forster, ed., *The works and life of Walter Savage Landor*, 8 vols. (1876) · S. Colvin, *Landor* (1881) · *The life and correspondence of Robert Southey*, ed. C. C. Southey, 6 vols. (1849–50) · *Selections from the letters of Robert Southey*, ed. J. W. Warter, 4 vols. (1856) · *New letters of Robert Southey*, ed. K. Curry, 2 vols. (1965) · W. Hazlitt, 'The modern gradus ad Parnassum', in *The complete works of William Hazlitt*, ed. P. P. Howe, 20 (1934) · R. R. Madden, *The literary life and correspondence of the countess of Blessington*, 3 vols. (1855) · M. Blessington, *The idler in Italy*, vol. 2 (1839) · C. Dickens, *Bleak house* (1852–3) · R. H. Horne and E. Barrett, 'Landor', *The new spirit of the age* (1844) · *Henry Crabb Robinson on books and their writers*, ed. E. J. Morley, 3 vols. (1938) · H. C. Minchin, *Walter Savage Landor: last days, letters and conversations* (1934) · L. Whiting, *The Florence of Landor* (1905) · G. A. Treves, *The golden ring: the Anglo-Florentines, 1847–1862* (1956) · W. R. Swifte, *Wilhelm's wanderings, an autobiography* (1878) · A. C. Swinburne, 'Landor', *Encyclopaedia Britannica*, 9th edn, 14 (1882) · H. James, *William Wetmore Story and his friends*, vol. 2 (1903) · R. W. Emerson, *English traits* (1856) · F. J. H. Darton, *Life and times of Mrs Sherwood* (1910)

Archives Bath Central Library, letters and verses · BL, autobiographical notes, Ashley B 3551 · BL, family corresp., M/673 [microfilm] · BL, letters, Add. MS 47891 · BL, letters to his family, M/575 [microfilm] · Bodl. Oxf., letters · Hunt. L., letters, literary MSS, and his sister's letters · JRL, letters, mostly to his family · Princeton

University Library, New Jersey, corresp. · Ransom HRC, papers · University of Virginia, Charlottesville, Virginia, papers · V&A NAL, corresp., literary MSS, and papers · Warks. CRO, family papers · William Salt Library, Stafford, corresp. · Yale U., Beinecke L., family corresp. · Yale U., Beinecke L., letters to his brother and papers | All Souls Oxf., corresp. with Charles Stuart · Baylor University, Waco, Texas, letters to Robert Browning · BL, letters, Ashley 4889 · BL, letters to Lady Blessington, Ashley 4889, 5742–5744, B 1066 · BL, letters to Henry Landor and Robert Landor, M/672(a) [microfilm] · BL, letters to Rosenhagen, MS Facs Suppl IX · BL, letters to Mrs C. A. Southey and others, Add. MS 47891 · Bodl. Oxf., letters to Sir William Napier and Lady Caroline Napier · Bodl. Oxf., corresp. with Sir Henry Taylor · DWL, letters to Henry Crabb Robinson · Harvard U., Houghton L., letters to Lady Blessington, etc. · Harvard U., Houghton L., corresp. with Edward Twisleton · Hunt. L., letters to James Nicholas · LMA, *The cabinet* and related papers · NL Wales, letters to Baker Gabb and Baker Gabb junior · NYPL, Berg collection · University of Chicago Library, letters to John Forster · Yale U., Sterling Memorial Library, revision of *Imaginary conversations* and other papers

Likenesses W. Bewick, pencil drawing, 1826, BM · J. Gibson, marble bust, 1828, NPG · A. D'Orsay, lithograph, pubd 1839, BM, NG Ire., NPG; repro. in *Letters*, ed. Wheeler · W. Fisher, oils, 1839, NPG · N. Branwhite junior, Indian ink drawing, c.1840, BM · W. Fisher, drawing, 1840, repro. in *Letters*, ed. Wheeler · C. Branwhite, drawing, 1847, Trinity College, Oxford · J. Stewart, oils, 1848, repro. in Super, *Walter Savage Landor* · H. Watkins, photograph, 1850–59, NPG [*see illus.*] · W. Boxall, oils, c.1852, V&A · R. Faulkner, pastel drawing, c.1854–1855, NPG · photograph, 1855, Warks. CRO · W. Wetmore Story, drawings, 1859, Yale U. · W. Wetmore Story, drawings, 1859, Morgan L. · C. C. Coleman, oils, 1861, repro. in Whiting, *Florence of Landor* · G. Alinari, photograph, 1863–4, NPG · J. Brown, stipple (after N. Dance, 1804), repro. in Field, *Landor* · marble bust (after J. Gibson), NPG · portraits, repro. in Field, *Landor* · portraits, repro. in Elwin, *Landor* · portraits, repro. in Forster, *Walter Savage Landor*

Wealth at death uncertain: R. H. Super, *Walter Savage Landor*, p. 475, pp. 495–6, pp. 499–500

Landsborough [*formerly* McLandsborough], **David** (1779–1854), Free Church of Scotland minister and naturalist, was born on 11 August 1779 in Dalry, Glenkens, Kirkcudbrightshire, the only son and eldest of four children of John McLandsborough and Isabel Hugan. He was educated at the parish school and Dumfries Academy, before entering Edinburgh University in 1798. Although reading divinity, he also attended lectures in botany, anatomy, chemistry, and surgery. At university, he dropped 'Mc' from his surname, proclaiming it 'long enough' without (Rutherford, 1980, 4). Through his musical skills he became known to metaphysician Thomas Brown and to the landscape-painter John Thompson (1778–1840), the latter of whom instilled in Landsborough a taste for painting. From Edinburgh Landsborough became tutor to Sir John Hay of King's Meadows, Tweedside, and then to the family of Lord Glenlee, of Barskimming, Ayrshire. He was licensed to the ministry of the Church of Scotland in 1808, and in September 1811 was ordained minister to the parish of Stevenston, Ayrshire. In addition to his clerical duties and his daily readings in Latin, Greek, Hebrew, French, or Italian, he soon began studies of the natural history of his parish and nearby Arran. It is possible that his field studies on the Ayrshire coast were encouraged by an Edinburgh meeting with John Fleming (author of *A History of British Animals*), who had requested some 'new' crabs. In this

period, Landsborough also began cultivating the Stevenston manse garden, which he walled higher for greater shelter.

In 1817 Landsborough married Margaret (1797/8–1834), daughter of James McLeish of Port Glasgow; the couple later had four sons and three daughters, including the explorer William *Landsborough (1825–1886). Over the years his wife's health deteriorated, and she died in November 1834, aged thirty-six. It was a blow 'he never fully overcame, he laid his flute aside till his seventies and remembered the day every year' (Rutherford, 1980).

Landsborough's studies in Arran led to a first publication, *Arran, a Poem in Six Cantos* (1828); it was republished in 1847 with field-work accounts. He made collections of flowering plants but these were soon extended to embrace algae, lichens, fungi, and mosses. He contributed much material and many botanical records to works such as W. H. Harvey's *Phycologia Britannica*. His discovery of new or previously unreported marine animals (many since reassessed taxonomically) associated him with both John Fleming and George Johnston (1797–1855), although he may never have met the latter in person. For many years, Landsborough recorded the daily weather, migration movements, and flowering periods; he studied also land Mollusca and fossil plants of the Ayrshire coalfield. He published at least seven papers before 1843 in different journals, covering topics such as zoophyte phosphorescence, birds, dredging, the Mollusca of Whiting Bay, and geological deposits at Stevenston and Largs. His garden flourished with exotic plants rare for Scotland. In 1837 he produced the Stevenston parish account (48 pages), which was judged one of the best contributions to the *New [Second] Statistical Account [of Scotland]* and led to his assisting other ministers with the natural history sections and acquiring the sobriquet 'the Ayrshire Naturalist' (Rutherford, 1980).

In the Scottish church Disruption of spring 1843 Landsborough joined the Free Kirk, becoming minister at Saltcoats and losing his previous church, manse, and beloved garden. These changes reduced his income from £350 to £150 per year, and limited his natural history studies. Between about 1847 and 1853, under his direction, his daughters made and sold about 400 varying sets of algae, with varying content, labels, title-pages, and geographical origin. Entitled *Treasures of the Deep, or, Specimens of Scottish Sea-Weeds*, they are often referred to as the 'Ayrshire Albums'. Sold at bazaars and privately for discharge of the manse debts and unkeep and to support churches and schools, they retailed when bound at 15s. per album; most were probably formed of between thirty-eight and sixty-three specimens. These funds were augmented by income from lectures which Landsborough gave throughout Britain, and by annual collections in church. Creation of albums and time spent lecturing represented considerable effort by the Landsborough family; both the Saltcoats Free Kirk and other churches benefited considerably.

By the early 1840s, the Landsborough family was actively exploring Arran and its rich shores; Landsborough also dredged in the Firth of Clyde with James

Smith of Jordanhill. His experiences led to a series of papers in the *Christian Treasury* during 1845; these were included in his enlarged and revised *Arran; a Poem; and Excursions to Arran* in 1847. This book sold well, resulting in a further (1851 [1852]) edition which suffered chaotic reorganization through removal of the 1828 poem and Landsborough's overprovision of replacement text. In his preface to the 1847 edition Landsborough described the late 1840s as 'the very busiest period of my professional life'. He was invited by Lovell Reeve to write a *Popular History of British Seaweeds*: the work was well received, achieving three editions (1849; 1851; 1857), and as a result Landsborough was commissioned to prepare a *Popular History of British Zoophytes or Corallines* (1852). He was elected associate of the Linnean Society in 1849, and in the following year was instrumental in establishing the Ayrshire Naturalists' Club, of which he was the first president.

Comparatively well-travelled, Landsborough visited most parts of Scotland and Ireland on religious duties, as well as spending four months on supply ministry in Gibraltar in 1842. In 1852, in his seventies, he visited Gibraltar and Tangier, returning via the Balearic Islands, Italy, and France. During a cholera epidemic in Ayrshire in 1854 Landsborough was involved in comforting the sick and dying and himself contracted the disease; he died after a very brief illness at Saltcoats, on 12 September 1854, and was buried in a plague pit in the churchyard of Stevenston High Kirk, Ardrossan. The Ayrshire Naturalists' Club effectively died with him. JAMES H. PRICE

Sources private information (2004) · D. Landsborough, 'A memoir of the Rev. D. Landsborough, D.D., A.L.S., M.W.S., M.R.P.S.', in D. Landsborough and D. Landsborough, *Arran: its topography, natural history and antiquities*, rev. edn (1875) · letters to Margaret Gatty, Sheff. Arch. · J. J. P. Clokie and A. D. Boney, 'David Landsborough, 1779–1854: an assessment of his contribution to algal studies in the Firth of Clyde', *Glasgow Naturalist*, 19 (1979), 443–62 · A. Rutherford, 'Landsborough—the "Scottish Gilbert White"', *Arran Naturalist*, 4 (1980), 4–7 · F. [R.] Woodward, 'David Landsborough, father and son', *Porcupine Newsletter*, 3 (1985), 118–20 · J. H. Price, 'Goody two-shoes or a monument to industry? Aspects of the *Phycologia Britannica* of William Henry Harvey (1811 to 1866)', *Bulletin of the British Museum (Natural History)* [Historical Series], 16 (1988), 87–216 · D. E. Allen, *The naturalist in Britain: a social history* (1976), 131, 162 · D. H. Kent and D. E. Allen, *British and Irish herbaria*, 2nd edn (1984), 184 · A. Rutherford, 'David Landsborough', *Conchologists' Newsletter*, 11 (1964), 63 · D. Landsborough, *Arran; a poem; and excursions to Arran*, rev. edn (1847)
Archives priv. coll. | RBG Kew, Lovell Reeve & Co. letter-book, corresp. with Lovell Reeve [drafts] · Sheff. Arch., letters to Margaret Gatty
Likenesses photograph, 1830–1839? (after portrait), repro. in *Arran Naturalist*, cover · Hill & Adamson, group portrait, calotype photograph, 1843, Scot. NPG · group portrait (after calotype), Church of Scotland Head Office, Edinburgh · photograph (after portrait), high kirk of Stevenston, Ardrossan, Ayr; repro. in B. Reid, *The high kirk of Stevenston, 1833–1983* (privately printed, Stevenston, 1983), 9

Landsborough, William (1825–1886), explorer in Australia, the third son of the Revd David *Landsborough (1779–1854) and his wife, Margaret (1797/8–1834), the daughter of James McLeish of Port Glasgow, was born on 21 February 1825 at Stevenston, near Saltcoats, Ayrshire. He was one of four sons and three daughters. He was educated at Irvine Academy, Irvine. In 1841 he joined his older brothers, John and James, in Australia on their New England pastoral run. After a stint on the Bathurst goldfields from 1849, he went to Queensland in 1852 and took up Westholm in the Wide Bay district. From 1854 he explored a vast area of the Rockhampton hinterland with several fellow entrepreneurs; they surveyed and sold new pastoral runs, meanwhile retaining the choicest country, so that Landsborough held extensive leases by 1861.

That year Landsborough led an official party in an unsuccessful search for the lost explorers Robert O'Hara Burke and William Wills. After an initial foray to the south-west, Landsborough started in February 1862 from his depot on the lower Gulf of Carpentaria and crossed the continent from north to south. Some charged him with concentrating on pastoral discovery and neglecting his official duty, but Landsborough was honoured with viceregal receptions in Melbourne, Sydney, and Brisbane. His journal (*Landsborough's Expedition from Carpentaria, in Search of Burke and Wills*) was published in 1862, and in London in 1863 he received the Royal Geographical Society's presentation gold watch.

Landsborough was appointed to the Queensland legislative council in 1862 and took his seat in 1864, but resigned the following year. He was now a senior partner in Bowen Downs, a large central Queensland property, which expanded northwards in 1864 to the newly occupied Burke district on the Gulf of Carpentaria; the next year Landsborough successfully applied for the position of police magistrate in the Burke district. Here he conducted further exploration and avidly championed the Burke region, but the initial settlement was beset by adversity; Landsborough's administrative task was inordinately difficult, while his critics decried his failure to provide strong leadership, the impropriety of his interests in local business, and his suppression of a charge against a Bowen Downs associate for the alleged lynching of a Chinese labourer. By the time he was removed from office in 1870 Landsborough was financially ruined through the failure of his Burke pastoral interests.

The following year Landsborough was summarily dismissed when supervising road works near St George; thereafter he served as inspector of brands in the Moreton district. For services to exploration the government awarded him £2000 in 1881, with which he purchased Loch Lamerough near Caloundra. A devoted family man, he married Caroline Hollingsworth Raine on 30 December 1862; they had three daughters, Fanny, Janet, and Sweersena. Caroline died in 1869, and on 8 March 1873 Landsborough married a widow, Maria Theresa Carr (*née* Carter), with whom he had three sons, Sydney, Leslie, and Lionel. Landsborough died on 17 March 1886, probably of cancer, and was buried with Anglican rites at Loch Lamerough; in 1913 his remains were reinterred in Toowong cemetery, Brisbane. ANNE ALLINGHAM

Sources State Library of Queensland, Brisbane, John Oxley Library, Landsborough MSS · Queensland State Archives, Brisbane · *Queensland Parliamentary Debates*, esp. 1862, 1866, 1869–70, 1880–

81 • *Queenslander* (1864–79), esp. 19/5, 7/7, 10/11/1866 • *Port Denison Times* (1865–70) • *Sydney Morning Herald* (1862–3) • *Sydney Morning Herald* (1869) • *Examiner* [Melbourne] (23 Aug 1862) • *Examiner* [Melbourne] (6 Sept 1862) • *Examiner* [Melbourne] (4 Oct 1862) • *Examiner* [Melbourne] (15 Nov 1862) • *The Times* (3 June 1886) • *Brisbane Courier* (17 March 1886) • *Queensland Figaro* (3 June 1886) • *Journal of Landsborough's expedition from Carpentaria, in search of Burke and Wills* (1862) • *Bourne's journal of Landsborough's expedition from Carpentaria, in search of Burke and Wills* (1862) • J. Kirby, *Narrative of a voyage from Melbourne to the gulf of Carpentaria* (1862) • D. S. Macmillan, *Bowen Downs, 1863–1963* (1963) • D. S. Macmillan, 'The Scottish Australian Company and pastoral development in Queensland, 1860–1890', *Journal Royal Historical Society Queensland*, 4/2 (1959–60), 454–74 • 'Extracts of a despatch from His Excellency Sir George Bowen to the duke of Newcastle, in reference to the voyage of Captain Norman, and the routes of Mr Landsborough and Mr Walker', *Proceedings* [Royal Geographical Society], 7 (1862–3), 3–10 • E. Palmer, *Early days in north Queensland* (1903)

Archives Mitchell L., NSW • State Library of Queensland, Brisbane, John Oxley Library | Mitchell L., NSW, Ernest Henry MSS • Newcastle Central Library, Scottish Australian Investment Company records • Royal Historical Society of Queensland, Brisbane, George Phillips MSS • State Library of Queensland, Brisbane, John Oxley Library, Ernest Henry MSS

Likenesses group portrait, photograph, 1862, John Oxley Library, Brisbane, Australia; repro. in W. Landsborough, *Landsborough's expedition from Carpentaria* (1862), frontispiece • four photographs, John Oxley Library, Brisbane, Australia

Wealth at death £2500: probate, 1886, Brisbane, Australia

Landseer, Charles (1799/1800–1879), painter of historical and genre subjects, was born on 12 August 1799 or 1800 at 71 Queen Anne Street East, London, the second son to achieve adulthood among the fourteen children of John George *Landseer (1763/9–1852), engraver and antiquary, and his wife, Jane, *née* Potts (1773/4–1840). Having received early instruction in art from his father, in 1816 Charles Landseer entered the Royal Academy Schools, where he remained for approximately three years. Together with his brothers Thomas *Landseer and Edwin *Landseer, he also became a pupil of Benjamin Robert Haydon. In the 1820s Landseer accompanied Lord Stuart de Rothesay to Portugal and Rio de Janeiro on his mission to negotiate a commercial treaty with Don Pedro I. He executed numerous sketches for the latter and on his return exhibited six paintings based on his travels at the British Institution (1827, 1828) and the Society of British Artists (1827).

Charles Landseer was represented by 126 works at the British Institution (1822–46), the Society of British Artists (1824–35), the Royal Academy (1828–79), the Liverpool Academy (1830–65), and the Royal Manchester Institution (1840, 1843). Until the mid-1830s he exhibited landscapes, portraits (among unexhibited subjects were the radical journalist Thomas Jonathan Wooler, Sir Thomas Lawrence, president of the Royal Academy, and Harriet Grote), genre and literary scenes from Jonathan Richardson, Cervantes, and Laurence Sterne: his *Clarissa Harlowe in the Prison Room of the Sheriff's Office* (exh. Society of British Artists, 1833–4; Tate collection) was bought by Robert Vernon, and *Sterne's Maria* (exh. British Institution, 1836; V&A) by John Sheepshanks. The success of two ambitious paintings, *The Plundering of Basing House, Hants; Taken and Destroyed by Cromwell, Oct. 14 1645* (exh. RA, and Liverpool Academy, 1836; Tate collection) and *The Death of Douglas at the Battle of Langside* (exh. RA, 1837; ex Town and Country Estates Ltd, Ireland, 19 September 1956) led to his election as an associate of the Royal Academy in 1837 and determined the historical nature of the majority of his future exhibits. Other major paintings of this type include *The Pillaging of a Jew's House in the Reign of Richard I* (exh. RA, and Liverpool Academy, 1839 and British Institution, 1840; Tate collection) measuring 6 feet 3 inches by 7 feet 9 inches; *The Temptation of Andrew Marvell* (exh. RA, 1841; V&A); and *Charles I on the Eve of the Battle of Edgehill* (exh. RA, 1845; Walker Art Gallery, Liverpool). In the 1840s and early 1850s Charles Landseer achieved considerable success: his works were engraved for the *Art Union* and the *Art Journal*; three paintings were chosen by Art Union prize-winners for £300, £400, and £300 respectively (*The Departure of Charles II from Bentley in Staffordshire* (exh. RA, 1842), *The Monks of Melrose* (exh. RA, 1843, and lent for the Royal Jubilee Exhibition in Manchester, 1887), and *The Return of the Dove to the Ark* (exh. RA, 1844; Forbes Magazine collection).

In 1845 Landseer was elected Royal Academician and in 1851 keeper of the Royal Academy, a post which involved instructing pupils in the antique school. From the 1860s, however, Landseer's work met with increasing criticism and towards the end of his life he was renowned mainly for his puns and witticisms (he was responsible for the description of photography as a 'foe-to-graphic' art) and for his likeable nature. In May 1873 he retired from his post as keeper, with a pension equivalent to his former salary. Charles Landseer never married and always lived with members of his family. He died on 22 July 1879 at his home, 35 Grove End Road, St John's Wood, London, and was buried in Highgate cemetery, Middlesex, having bequeathed £10,000 of his considerable property (part of which he inherited from his brother Edwin) to the Royal Academy for the foundation of scholarships. A sale of the contents of his studio was held at Christies on 14 April 1880. An obituarist described his work as characterized by 'careful execution, appropriate accessories and costumes rather than by striking effects and grandeur of character' (*Art Journal*, 18, 1879, 217). Examples of his work are in the Victoria and Albert Museum, the Tate collection, the British Museum, the National Portrait Gallery, the Walker Art Gallery, Liverpool, and the Ferens Art Gallery, Kingston upon Hull.

CHARLOTTE YELDHAM

Sources *Men of the time* (1856) • *Men of the time* (1875) • R. Ormond, *Sir Edwin Landseer* (1981) • C. Lennie, *Landseer: the Victorian paragon* (1976) • Graves, *RA exhibitors* • J. Johnson, ed., *Works exhibited at the Royal Society of British Artists, 1824–1893, and the New English Art Club, 1888–1917*, 2 vols. (1975) • Graves, *Brit. Inst.* • *Engraved Brit. ports.* • R. Ormond, *Early Victorian portraits*, 2 vols. (1973) • J. Elmes, *Annals of the fine arts*, 12 (1920), 129 • J. Elmes, *Annals of the fine arts*, 17 (1920), 370–71 • E. Morris and E. Roberts, *The Liverpool Academy and other exhibitions of contemporary art in Liverpool, 1774–1867* (1998) • exhibition catalogues (1840–43) [Royal Manchester Institution] • *Art Journal*, 41 (1879), 217 • *ILN* (2 Aug 1879), 109–10 • *The Graphic* (9 Aug 1879), 128 • artist's file, archive material, Courtauld Inst., Witt Library • CGPLA Eng. & Wales (1879)

Likenesses S. Alexander, pen-and-ink drawing, 1840–49, BM • woodcut, 1879, NPG • D. Maclise, pencil drawing, V&A • W. M. Thackeray, sketch, V&A • C. Watkins, photograph, repro. in *ILN*, 109 • J. and C. Watkins, carte-de-visite, NPG

Wealth at death under £30,000: probate, 16 Aug 1879, *CGPLA Eng. & Wales*

Landseer, Sir Edwin Henry (1802–1873), animal painter, was born in London on 7 March 1802 at 88 Queen Anne Street East, Marylebone, the youngest of the three sons, and the fourth of the seven surviving children of John George *Landseer (1763/9–1852), engraver and author, and his wife, Jane, *née* Potts (1773/4–1840). His elder brothers Thomas *Landseer (1793/4–1880), a printmaker, and Charles *Landseer (1799/1800–1879), a genre and history painter, are noticed separately. The following year the family moved to 71 Queen Anne Street East (this became 33 Foley Street in 1810).

The young prodigy Edwin Landseer appears to have been educated at home, where from a very early age his artistic gifts were recognized. Under the guidance of his father (who was extremely ambitious for his children), by the age of four or five he was drawing with extraordinary precocity and was making etchings at the age of seven. His subjects were animals, not only domestic and farmyard creatures, notably cows in the fields near Child's Hill, Hampstead, London, but also lions and tigers, which he studied at Mr Cross's menagerie at Exeter 'Change in the Strand (often in the company of his boyhood friend and neighbour, the painter John Frederick Lewis) or at the Tower of London. In 1813 Landseer was awarded the silver palette from the Society of Arts for his drawing of a spaniel (RSA). Two years later he made his Royal Academy début, as an honorary exhibitor (on account of his age), with *Portrait of a Mule* and *Head of a Pointer Bitch and Puppy*. These were the property of W. W. Simpson of Maldon, Essex, his first patron. In that year the three Landseer brothers became pupils of Benjamin Robert Haydon, who encouraged Edwin's study of anatomy and of the Elgin marbles, and introduced him to some of the great literary figures of the age. Haydon took the credit for Sir George Beaumont's buying Landseer's *Fighting Dogs Getting Wind* (Louvre, Paris), exhibited in 1818 at the Society of Painters in Oil and Water Colours. This was his first fully realized sporting picture, and its 'wonder producing vitality' was acclaimed by the critic of *The Examiner*, who dubbed the artist 'our English SCHNEIDERS' (26 April 1818, 269). The composition was influenced by the animal painter James Ward as well as the seventeenth-century Flemish artist Frans Snyders; Haydon was indeed schooling his pupil to be 'the Snyders of England' (*Paintings and Drawings by Sir Edwin Landseer*, v). *Fighting Dogs Getting Wind* is typical of Landseer's early attraction to themes of violence in the animal kingdom. This may, perhaps, represent a displacement of aggression in an adolescent whose formative years were subject to the strict discipline of artistic observation rather than to the free range of boyhood fancy.

On 9 August 1816, at fourteen, Landseer entered the Royal Academy Schools. Earlier in that year he had sat to his friend Charles Robert Leslie as the model for Rutland in Leslie's *The Murder of Rutland by Lord Clifford* (exh. RA, 1816; Pennsylvania Academy of the Fine Arts, Philadelphia). Leslie remembers him at this period as 'a pretty

Sir Edwin Henry Landseer (1802–1873), by Sir Francis Grant, *c*.1852

little curly-headed boy' (Leslie, 1.39). He was known affectionately by the keeper of the schools, Henry Fuseli, as 'my little *dog boy*' (ibid.), suggesting that his reputation as an animal painter was already established. Indeed, Landseer's earliest drawing of a dog (V&A) was executed at the age of five. From a very early age he was using animals as metaphors for human situations and emotions in a way that differentiated much of his work from the tradition of British sporting art. For example, the 1814 oil paintings *French Hog* (exh. RA, 1874) and *British Boar* (exh. RA, 1874; priv. coll.), etched in 1818 by Landseer's eldest brother Thomas (BM), comment on the Napoleonic Wars in contrasting the gaunt, half-starved French beast with the well-fed, contented British one. This type of humorous juxtaposition became one of Landseer's trademarks, immortalized, for example, in *Dignity and Impudence* (exh. British Institution, 1839; Tate collection). In stark contrast is *The Cat's Paw* (exh. British Institution, 1824; priv. coll.), one of Landseer's best-known but most shocking images, which shows a monkey forcing a cat to pick up chestnuts from the top of a burning stove. Its sadism is disturbing, but this aspect did not worry Landseer's contemporaries, who on its first exhibition hailed him as 'a pictorial Shakespeare of animal expression' (*The Examiner*, 29 Jan 1824, 130). The artist, who had recently come of age, was assured of financial and critical success.

The highlands, 1824–1835 In autumn 1824 Landseer travelled north to Scotland for the first time, and the impact of the country on his life and art was profound. The highlands became both a second home to him, visited in the summer and autumn months year after year, and the inspiration for many of his greatest works. On his first trip he stayed for ten days with Sir Walter Scott at Abbotsford. Scott wrote to a friend on 6 October: 'Mr. Landseer who has drawn every dog in the House but myself is now at work upon me under all the disadvantages which my employment puts him to' (*Letters*, 8.392). Landseer made several spirited oil sketches of Scott, one of which is in the National Portrait Gallery, London.

From Scott's home in the borders Landseer travelled on to the highlands to stay with the elderly John Murray, fourth duke of Atholl, at his ancestral castle, Blair Atholl. The duke commissioned Landseer to paint *Death of the Stag in Glen Tilt* (priv. coll.), a hunting group of himself, his grandson and heir, and his keepers. This monumental work, finally completed and exhibited at the Royal Academy in 1830 under the title *Portraits of his Grace the Duke of Atholl and George Murray attended by his Head Forester John Crerar and Keepers*, is an eloquent tribute to a great highland chieftain and a famous sportsman. Another dynastic sporting group, exhibited at the Royal Academy two years earlier (priv. coll.), shows Alexander, fourth duke of Gordon, with his daughter Georgiana, duchess of Bedford, and his young grandson Lord Alexander Russell; the duke has been shooting, she and her son fishing.

On his expeditions to Scotland Landseer stayed with a variety of aristocratic hosts, including the marquess of Breadalbane and the duke of Atholl, but he was most often a guest of the sixth duke of Bedford and his wife at The Doune, a hunting-lodge near Aviemore in the Cairngorms. The duchess had constructed a series of bothies in the remote valley of Glenfeshie where she lived a simple highland life with a small circle of intimate friends. Landseer recorded the valley in a sequence of wonderfully fresh and vibrant small *plein air* studies that reveal his gifts as a landscapist. The sketches he painted in Scotland between 1825 and 1835 deserve to be better known, for they are of exceptional quality in their swift recording of highland topography and weather. (Most are in private collections, but there are examples in Manchester City Galleries, the Walker Art Gallery, Liverpool, the Tate collection, and the Yale Center for British Art, New Haven, Connecticut.) The duchess and her guests were the butt of Landseer's numerous witty pen-and-ink caricatures, which capture the spirit of camaraderie and fun typical of these parties; a large number of them are still owned by descendants of the duchess's daughter, Louisa, marchioness of Abercorn (priv. coll.).

Scenes of deer-hunting became a regular feature in Landseer's repertory. In *Highlanders Returning from Deerstalking* (1827; priv. coll.) we see a stag being brought down on an old shooting pony by two keepers, its antlers poignantly silhouetted against a stormy sky. In *Deer and Deer Hounds in a Mountain Torrent* (exh. RA, 1833; Tate collection), a terrified stag is swept away downstream along with the attacking hounds. The line dividing Landseer's bloodlust from his compassion is narrow, and out of the tension between them was born his best sporting work. Stags are wild and noble beasts but also trophies of the hunting field, as Landseer made clear in a letter of 9 September 1837 to Lord Ellesmere:

> There is something in the toil and trouble, the wild weather and savage scenery that makes butchers of us all. Who does not glory in the death of a fine stag? on the spot—when in truth he ought to be ashamed of the assassination.

Significantly perhaps, Landseer was a notoriously bad shot. 'Still', the artist continued:

> with all my respect for the animal's inoffensive character— my love of him *as a subject for the pencil* gets the better of such tenderness—a creature always picturesque and *never* ungraceful is too great a property to sacrifice to common feelings of humanity. (*Paintings and Drawings by Sir Edwin Landseer*, 29–30)

Landseer's enthusiasm for the highlands extended to the highlanders themselves, whose simple lives and rugged characters he admired. Apart from Sir David Wilkie and J. F. Lewis, there were few other artists painting such pictures in the 1820s. Landseer's superbly detailed scenes capture the very essence and texture of highland life. Among many outstanding and deservedly popular paintings are *An Illicit Whisky Still in the Highlands* (exh. RA, 1829; Apsley House, London), *The Stone Breaker* (exh. British Institution, 1830; V&A), *The Poacher's Bothy* (exh. RA, 1831; Hamburg Kunsthalle), *Interior of a Highlander's House* (exh. RA, 1831; priv. coll.), and *A Highland Breakfast* (exh. RA, 1834; V&A), a tender scene juxtaposing a mother feeding her baby with a bitch suckling two puppies. These works culminated in the large and crowded canvas *A Scene in the Grampians: the Drover's Departure* (exh. RA, 1835; V&A), an elegy for a traditional way of life that was fast disappearing.

Social and artistic success, 1826–1840 In 1826, aged twenty-four, Landseer was elected an associate of the Royal Academy (at the time no one under that age was eligible). A year earlier he had taken the lease of a 2 acre property to the west of Regent's Park, at 1 (later 18) St John's Wood Road. Improved and enlarged over the years, this remained his home for the rest of his life. His maternal aunt Barbara Potts kept house for him, to be succeeded by his sister Jessica. By the time that Landseer was elected a full Royal Academician in 1831 he had established an enviable reputation as the foremost animal painter of the day, and he had also broken into high society. He numbered several dukes among his patrons, including those of Atholl, Beaufort, Bedford, Devonshire, Gordon, Northumberland, and Wellington. They not only bought his sporting pictures and highland subjects, but welcomed him into their houses as a friend. Lively and attractive, small and puckish, funny and witty, Landseer was a good addition to any drawing-room. He helped to design the theatricals at Woburn Abbey (seat of the duke of Bedford), kept parties amused by his trick of drawing different subjects with his left and right hands simultaneously, and produced endless and highly accomplished caricatures of his friends.

Landseer was pre-eminent in his own day as a painter of dogs, even though the range of his art was much wider than that designation implies. He was the heir of George Stubbs in his profound understanding of canine anatomy and character; his early *écorché* (flayed) studies reveal the depth of his study and knowledge. What he added to his naturalistic depiction of dogs was a narrative content and an anthropomorphic interpretation that transformed them into works of the imagination. He told one patron that he simply could not paint an animal without a story; straightforward dog portraiture held no interest for him. So he invented situations for his dog subjects, giving them feelings and attitudes akin to those of human beings. In a pair of early works, *High Life* and *Low Life* (1829; Tate collection), he contrasts the common mastiff of a butcher with the elegant deer-hound of an antiquarian aristocrat. The difference in style, period, social class, and values is conveyed through the character of the two animals, who perfectly represent their absent masters, as well as in the settings of a butcher's shop and a medieval-style castle. The two works are painted with a feeling for texture and light and detail learned from a study of the seventeenth-century Flemish master David Teniers.

A Jack in Office (exh. RA, 1833; V&A) takes this allegorizing vein a stage further. A sleek and confident terrier sits atop the barrow of a cat-and-dog-meat salesman, guarding his master's property from a group of mangy and beggarly dogs. The picture may have been inspired by La Fontaine's fable of the dog who carried his master's dinner, but it also symbolizes the hard-heartedness of those who have much towards those who have nothing.

Among Landseer's dog subjects none struck such a chord with the public as those which demonstrated love and fidelity. The earliest of these, painted in 1820, is *Alpine Mastiffs Reanimating a Distressed Traveller* (priv. coll.), set in the St Bernard Pass. *Attachment* (1829; priv. coll.) records a real-life story of a terrier who stayed by the body of his dead master on Helvellyn for three months—the subject also of a poem of 1805 by Sir Walter Scott. In *Suspense* (exh. British Institution, 1834; V&A), a desperately anxious bloodhound waits at the door of a room into which his wounded master has been carried. Most moving of all is *The Old Shepherd's Chief Mourner* (exh. RA, 1837; V&A), a collie crouching against the coffin of his master in an agony of grief. This picture, revealing the character of the old shepherd through the simple accessories and lonely atmosphere of his bothy, inspired a famous passage in the first volume of John Ruskin's *Modern Painters* (1843). The great critic (not usually an admirer of Landseer's work) called it:

> one of the most perfect poems or pictures … which modern times have seen … a work of high art, [which] stamps its author, not as the near imitator of the texture of a skin, or the fold of a drapery, but as the Man of Mind.   (Ruskin, 3.88–9)

What Ruskin approved of was the pathos and imaginative force with which Landseer invested the scene, raising it above mere realism to a higher plane of feeling.

Landseer's industry during the 1830s was prodigious and it was matched by a fertile imagination and painterly finesse. As well as dog subjects and highland scenes, he painted a handful of history pictures, of which the most important is *Scene in the Olden Time at Bolton Abbey* (exh. RA,

1834; priv. coll.). This was commissioned by William Cavendish, sixth duke of Devonshire, who owned the romantic ruined abbey on the banks of the Wharfe in the West Riding of Yorkshire. Ignoring his brief to portray the abbey itself, Landseer chose instead to evoke the spirit of monastic life in the Middle Ages. A forester, his son, and his daughter lay the trophies of the hunt, painted with the artist's usual virtuosity, at the feet of a rotund abbot standing in the doorway of the abbey. What lies at the root of Landseer's picture is nostalgia for an earlier age when society was at peace with itself, when people accepted and enjoyed their lot, when the paternalism of the monastery meant something, and when the rivers and forests teemed with game.

Though he never found human likenesses easy, Landseer was frequently employed as a portraitist during the 1830s. As with his dog subjects, he liked to introduce narrative motifs into his pictures. The heir to the earl of Tankerville is seen beside a white bull of the Chillingham breed he has just shot, together with the deer-hound who saved his life, in *Scene in Chillingham Park: Portrait of Lord Ossulton (The Death of the Wild Bull)* (exh. RA, 1836; priv. coll.). The enormously wealthy earl of Ellesmere and his family are dressed in seventeenth-century style for the outdoor group entitled *Return from Hawking* (exh. RA, 1837; priv. coll.). In *Portraits of the Marquess of Stafford and the Lady Evelyn Gower: Dunrobin Castle in the Distance* (exh. RA, 1838; priv. coll.) Landseer depicts the two eldest children of George Levenson-Gower, second duke of Sutherland: Lady Evelyn is seen decorating her pet fawn with a chaplet of columbine, watched by her brother and their favourite dogs.

Three of Landseer's greatest patrons in the 1830s were, however, representative of a new breed of capitalist collector. The artist enjoyed close relations with the cloth manufacturer John Sheepshanks, the army contractor Robert Vernon, and the shipbuilder William Wells of Redleaf, near Tunbridge Wells, Kent. It is fortunate for Landseer's reputation that the Sheepshanks collection in the Victoria and Albert Museum and the Tate's Vernon collection contain so many of his finest works from this early period. Landseer's patrons carefully monitored progress on their commissions, and kept the artist up to the mark—none more so than Wells, whose superb collection is sadly dispersed. From accounts by those who stayed at Redleaf, Landseer—represented by more than twenty works—was its presiding genius. There are many anecdotes about him at Redleaf: the one most often repeated concerned a spaniel, Trim, which Landseer had promised to paint. In August 1831, when finally pressed on this much postponed commission, he waited until everyone had gone to church and painted the dog in a session of two and a half hours, to the astonishment of his host; an engraving by J. Webb, 1832, is in the British Museum, London. A later collector of a similar stamp was the chemist Jacob Bell, who became an intimate friend of the artist, and acted as his trusted adviser. He bequeathed his collection to the National Gallery in 1859, including an important group of Landseer paintings (now Tate collection).

Landseer was especially attractive to women. He had

many intimate female friends, including the duchess of Bedford and the famous beauty Mrs Caroline Norton, and he was forever falling in and out of love, but he never married. His name was scandalously linked at the time to the duchess of Bedford. He was said to have been her lover, and father of one of her children, but this is uncorroborated. There was a raffish side to Landseer's character. He enjoyed the bohemian atmosphere of Lady Blessington's circle, and was a close friend of her lover Count D'Orsay, with whom he exchanged racy gossip. He was certainly familiar with the *demi-monde* and may have enjoyed its hedonistic pleasures as a relief from the constraints of formal society.

1840 and its aftermath In May 1840, at the height of his powers and reputation, Landseer suffered a severe nervous breakdown that cast a long shadow over his subsequent career. This was attributed to various causes at the time, including the death that January of his mother. His friend Lady Holland blamed the fatigue and anxiety of being a member of the hanging committee at the Royal Academy,

> where there are so many jealousies and bickerings, & then the shock of the murder [on 6 May] of poor Ld William [Russell, grandson of the fourth duke of Bedford], with whom he was very intimate & had seen frequently just at the time … He is full of terror and horror, expecting an assassin to destroy him. It is really very shocking. (*Elizabeth, Lady Holland*, 184–5)

It was also said that his illness had been precipitated by the refusal of the duchess of Bedford (who had been widowed the previous autumn) to marry him (*Diary*, ed. Pope, 5.452). Underneath the brilliant façade that Landseer presented to the world there were evident signs of stress. He was unreliable about finishing pictures, he broke engagements on the flimsiest of pretexts, and even before his breakdown he provoked numerous quarrels with old friends. For example, about 1838 he misconstrued a request from Caroline Norton, who wrote to him: 'It would take more to offend me than a huffy note, from you, as I have seen too much gentlemanlike and generous feeling in you, not to forgive you for being touchy, even when I did think it unjust' (Ormond, *Sir Edwin Landseer*, 9).

Landseer's state of mind following the breakdown is vividly conveyed in a letter he wrote to Count D'Orsay on 13 July 1840:

> The only thing against me is *self-torture*. My unfinished works haunt me—visions of noble Dukes in *armour* give me nightly scowls and pokings … My imagination is full of children in the shape of good pictorial subjects. Until I am safely *delivered*, fits of agitation will continue their attacks. (Ormond, *Sir Edwin Landseer*, 10)

After a recuperative tour of the continent, in the care of his friend Jacob Bell, Landseer returned to London to pick up the threads of his life. His friends rallied round. Bell took charge of his business affairs and acted as general factotum (Landseer's lengthy correspondence with Bell in the Royal Institution, London, is a primary biographical source). Landseer continued to be offered lucrative commissions, from Queen Victoria downwards; he went

north to Scotland each summer as before to stay in aristocratic hunting-lodges; his popularity was undiminished. But something had changed. He would never recapture that self-confidence and blitheness of spirit which had characterized him as a young man. His later letters chart bouts of depression, nervous prostration, dyspepsia, and a host of psychosomatic ailments. By 1850, the year of his knighthood, Landseer was drinking heavily, a problem compounded by drug abuse; in the following decade there were times when he lost his mind. Though he continued to lead a busy social life, and to paint through all but the worst crises, he never recovered from the effects of his first breakdown or from the burden of mental suffering.

Later paintings The year 1840 marks not only a turning point in Landseer's personal life but also a distinct change of direction in his art. The transparency and tight detail of his early style—inspired by Rubens, Teniers, and the Flemish school—gave way to a broader style of painting. His themes became more weighty, his compositions more complex, his imagination in many ways stranger and less predictable. He was responding not only to impulses in himself but to wider trends in the field of art generally. The series of competitions for fresco decorations in the new Palace of Westminster, instituted in 1843, were symptomatic of a return to the principles of high art and moral seriousness that typified the high Victorian period. With his acute sensitivity to changes in taste, Landseer raised his game to meet this new challenge, and in doing so ensured that animal painting remained a mainstream art form. But something was also lost in the process. The surface brilliance and detail of his early works was never recaptured.

In his later dog subjects Landseer pushed anthropomorphic art to new limits, drawing on the conventions of history painting, while at the same time poking fun at them. *Laying Down the Law* (*Trial by Jury*) (exh. RA, 1840; priv. coll.) shows a large white poodle as judge and a mixed group of other canine breeds as jury in a type of composition associated with figure painting. Landseer's target is the maladministration and pomposity of the law, and he uses the dumb but expressive faces of the dogs to drive it home. The picture of *King Charles Spaniels* (exh. British Institution, 1845; Tate collection) is a skit on the vogue for popular scenes of cavaliers and roundheads; two mischievous-looking spaniels lie curled up beside a plumed hat and gilt spur. The classical subject of Alexander meeting the philosopher Diogenes is transformed by Landseer into a confrontation between a large white bull terrier, with a train of attendants, and a smaller, wily terrier in the role of the philosopher sitting in a barrel (exh. RA, 1848; Tate collection). Landseer was turning the ideals of academic art on their head, but this did not concern a contemporary audience, who read the picture as a parody of human manners and behaviour and a *tour de force* of animal characterization.

Landseer's ability to catch the mood of the moment is exemplified in his picture *Shoeing* (exh. RA, 1884; Tate collection), an image of rural peace and harmony skilfully expressed in the gleaming hide of the bay mare, her close companionship with a donkey and a hound, and the homely figure and accessories of the blacksmith. This was one of the most popular of all Landseer's paintings, with a European reputation; it was one of the works that helped to secure him a gold medal at the Universal Exhibition in Paris in 1855. While Landseer's art was thought to be quintessentially English by foreign critics, there is no doubt that it had an influence abroad, especially through the print market. The deer paintings of Gustave Courbet and Rosa Bonheur, for example, show evidence of their debt.

When the threat of war with France loomed in the later 1840s, and tensions rose on both sides of the channel, Landseer painted the companion pictures *Time of Peace* (a scene of rural tranquillity on the cliffs at Dover) and *Time of War* (a dead lancer with mangled cavalry horses; both exh. RA, 1846) to remind his fellow countrymen of the consequences of belligerent action. Both pictures were destroyed in the Tate flood of 1928. Landseer had visited the field of Waterloo when touring the continent in 1840, and this inspired one of his most extraordinary pictures, *The Shepherd's Prayer* (exh. RA, 1845; priv. coll.). With out-stretched arms, a shepherd kneels at a wayside crucifix on the field of battle as if interceding for the blood that has been spilt, while his vast flock, like a miniature army, stretches away into the far distance. Landseer later painted the aged duke of Wellington revisiting the site of Waterloo with his daughter-in-law, Lady Douro, in a work entitled *A Dialogue at Waterloo: 'But 'twas a famous victory'* (exh. RA, 1850; Tate collection). The duke was a friend and admirer of the artist, commissioning a bizarre painting of the popular lion tamer Isaac van Ambrugh (exh. RA, 1847; Yale U. CBA) looking like a latter-day Daniel in the lions' den; an earlier picture of van Ambrugh by Landseer (exh. RA, 1839) is in the Royal Collection.

Landseer's powers as an image maker and mythologist were put to good account in his service to the crown. In his pictures of Victoria and Albert he captured that spirit of idealism and role-playing which characterized the new monarchy. His full-length equestrian portrait (never finished) of the queen riding out alone in a romantic land-scape (1838–72; priv. coll.) was inspired by Van Dyck's famous picture *Charles I on Horseback with Monsieur de St Antoine* in the Royal Collection. In *Windsor Castle in Modern Times* (1840–43; Royal Collection), the returning huntsman Albert is greeted by his loving wife and daughter. The royal couple present an image of domestic bliss that reflects the well-being of the state. In a painting of 1842–6 in the Royal Collection, the queen and prince consort, dressed as Edward III and Queen Philippa for a famous cos-tume ball held at Buckingham Palace, embody the virtues of chivalry and nobility drawn from an earlier age. And it was Landseer who lent substance to their vision of them-selves as romantic highlanders. *Royal Sports on Hill and Loch*, a large work begun in 1850 and still incomplete at the art-ist's death (it was later destroyed), is best described by Queen Victoria herself:

The picture is intended to represent me as meeting Albert, who has been stalking, whilst I have been fishing, & the

whole is quite consonant with the truth. The solitude, the sport, the Highlanders in the water, & c will be, as Landseer says, a beautiful historical exemplification of peaceful times, & of the independent life we lead in the dear Highlands. It is quite a new conception, & I think the manner in which he has composed it, will be singularly dignified, poetical & totally novel.   (journal, 19 Sept 1850, Royal Archives, Windsor Castle; Ormond, *Sir Edwin Landseer*, 162)

By the mid-century Landseer was the best-known artist in Britain, as judged by the public's familiarity with his work. Over 350 of his pictures had been engraved, some of them two or three times, and the sale of prints ran into many thousands, earning Landseer large sums of money. From his surviving bank accounts it is possible to chart his rising income, from roughly £3000 per annum in the 1830s to double that figure in the following decade, and in his most lucrative year (1865) to a dizzy £17,352. The artist himself was acutely aware of the role which engraving played in popularizing his work, and went to great lengths to ensure the accuracy of the large steel plates employed in the process. Marked proofs in the British Museum reveal extensive reworkings in Landseer's own hand. He reduced engravers and publishers to despair by rejecting proofs and requesting expensive alterations; there were constant quarrels and disputes, several of them docu-mented in the correspondence with Bell. Though his behaviour was often unreasonable, Landseer was passion-ate about preserving the integrity of his work from com-mercial pressures.

The Monarch of the Glen   Landseer continued to paint scenes of ordinary Scottish life, for example *The Highland Shepherd's Home* (exh. RA, 1842; priv. coll.), *The Free Church* (exh. RA, 1849; Royal Collection), and *The Forester's Family* (exh. RA, 1849; priv. coll.), but it was in his later deer paint-ings that he forged his most enduring imagery of the high-lands. His work became almost transcendental as he pic-tured stags in life-and-death struggles on a heroic stage. In *The Sanctuary* (exh. RA, 1842; Royal Collection) an exhausted stag reaches a secluded lake at sunset. The tran-quil beauty of the scene underlines the violent end from which the stag has recently escaped. By contrast *Stag at Bay* (exh. RA, 1846; priv. coll.) is all blood and thunder; we experience the event through the rolling eyes of a defiant and terrified stag, the snapping jaws of the hounds, the broken crests of the lake in which they are immersed, and the stormy sky. *Coming Events Cast their Shadow before them* (*The Challenge*) (exh. RA, 1844; priv. coll.) represents the cruelty inherent in the natural world, rather than man's inhumanity to animals. On the shore of a lake a stag awaits his rival, who is swimming towards him in an eerie moonlit landscape that prefigures the epic battle to the death that will follow. In Landseer's largest highland painting of all, *The Drive—Shooting Deer on the Pass; Scene in the Black Mount, Glen Urchy Forest* (exh. RA, 1857; Royal Col-lection), two ghillies huddle under a plaid in the fore-ground, hoping to remain undetected as the herd of deer heads towards unseen guns.

These pictures proved extremely popular, not only with the sporting community but with the public at large. Like his friend Charles Dickens, Landseer could combine extreme violence with highly charged emotion that made his pictures live in the imagination of his audience. There was bloodshed and horror and drama, but also compassion and a terrible beauty to his work. Landseer caught the spirit of what it was that attracted people to Scotland: the wildness and splendour of the landscape, the solitariness and remoteness from civilization, the wealth of wildlife, and the spectacle of nature red in tooth and claw. His pictures contributed a Romantic vision of highland life and landscape that is still with us today. His painting of *The Monarch of the Glen* (exh. RA, 1851; priv. coll.) remains a defining image of the highlands: a majestic stag, seen in close-up, surveys the mountain tops and sniffs the morning air. The image has become a cliché through over-reproduction, but the original picture is a *tour de force*, so powerful is the rendering of the animal, so tactile its fur, so sublime its surroundings, so tragic its potential fate.

As well as his oil paintings of deer, Landseer also executed several large and impressive pastels, and a wide range of chalk drawings recording in detail the sport he loved so much.

Last years, death, and posthumous reputation Landseer's later years were clouded by episodes of dementia, inebriation, and even threats of physical violence. He was often in the hands of doctors, among them Sir Richard Quain and the eminent neurologist Dr Thomas Tuke, but drugs and rest-cures produced only temporary alleviation. To his unfailing friend and guardian Thomas Hyde Hills, Landseer confided in the later 1860s: 'My health (or rather condition) is a mystery quite beyond human intelligence. I sleep well seven hours, and awake tired and jaded, and do not rally till after luncheon' (*Cornhill Magazine*, 29, 1874, 99).

Landseer was a sick and lonely man, but he continued to inspire loyalty and affection among his friends, and in the right company he was his amusing self. The Abercorns, the William Russells, the Tankervilles, and others continued to invite him to stay. The two houses where he went most often were South Park near Penshurst, Kent, the seat of Lord Hardinge, and Stoke Park near Slough, the home of his patron E. J. Coleman. When things got too much for him Landseer instinctively turned to Stoke Park, often inviting himself for days at a time. Some of his most touching friendships were with artists younger than himself. Both William Powell Frith and John Everett Millais, whom he had championed in their early days, remained devoted to him, Millais completing four of his pictures after his death, including *Nell Gwynne* (Tate collection). Landseer's protégé, the German painter Frederick Keyl, has left detailed accounts of his evening conversations with the artist from 1866 to 1869 (Royal Archives, Windsor Castle). One can almost hear Landseer speaking, so full and graphic are Keyl's notes; the talk ranged over natural history, breeds of dog, sporting reminiscence, literature, politics, friendship, and scandal.

Landseer could also make a great impact on young social acquaintances, one of whom recalled him as:

> a short, undistinguished-looking little man, with shy manners and a rough voice, and his grey beard and moustache gave him an unkempt appearance; but it was all redeemed by the fine forehead and high brow, under which his bright sparkling eyes looked out with an expression of wistful interest and keen appreciation of whatever appealed to him or whatever he might be painting. In some ways his face often reminded me of a shaggy Scotch terrier. (Lady St Helier, *Memories of Fifty Years*, 1909, 26)

Given Landseer's unstable mental state, it is astonishing that he was able to continue painting until the end of his life, producing some of his most ambitious compositions in his last years. His application and his imagination rarely faltered, and he found solace in the discipline of the studio. In 1860 he completed *Flood in the Highlands* (Aberdeen Art Gallery), a work begun many years earlier, which conveys the psychology of fear in an acute form as animals and humans cling to the roof of a highland bothy beset by raging waters. Four years later came *Man Proposes, God Disposes* (Royal Holloway College, Egham, Surrey), a chilling scene of Arctic disaster: two polar bears dismember the human remains of a failed polar expedition in a pitiless landscape of ice and snow. While the title comes from a fifteenth-century source, *The Imitation of Christ* by Thomas à Kempis, the subject was inspired by the tragic loss of Sir John Franklin's entire expeditionary force in 1845, and shows how much the artist was in tune with contemporary events. *Rent Day in the Wilderness* (exh. RA, 1868; NG Scot.) is a large, panoramic history picture recording highland resistance to the redcoats following the 1715 Jacobite rising. *The Swannery Invaded by Sea Eagles* (exh. RA, 1869; priv. coll.) is one of those shocking scenes of extreme animal violence that had a lifelong attraction for the artist. One of the very last paintings Landseer completed is *The Baptismal Font* (exh. RA, 1872; Royal Collection), a strange religious work showing sheep (symbolizing the Christian flock) huddled below the font while above three doves flutter in the incandescent light of a fire representing the holy spirit.

What is remarkable in Landseer's late works is his willingness to experiment and push out the boundaries of his art. When asked to design the lions around the base of Nelson's Column in Trafalgar Square, London, in 1857, he cheerfully accepted the commission, although his knowledge of sculpture was extremely limited. Working in the studio of his friend Baron Carlo Marochetti, Landseer laboured on the four colossal clay models for a period of ten years, at times elated by the project, at others almost overwhelmed by its size and complexity. One of Landseer's letters to Marochetti tellingly reveals the fragile state of his nerves at this period: 'a Lion has been turned loose on me by the government. I must conquer or fall' (30 Nov 1862, priv. coll.). When in January 1867 the bronze lions were finally unveiled, Landseer was gratified by the praise of his friends and scornful of his critics.

New forces in the world of art, in particular Pre-Raphaelitism and aestheticism, had by now begun to undermine Landseer's reputation and render his style of painting old-fashioned. He had wisely refused to allow his name to be put forward for the presidency of the Royal Academy on the death of Sir Charles Eastlake in 1866, and he increasingly withdrew into himself. By 1872 his conduct had become so erratic that his family had him certified with the concurrence of Gladstone and other prominent men. His death on 1 October 1873, at his home, 18 St John's Wood Road, London, was, in the words of his loyal patron Queen Victoria, a merciful release, 'as for the past three years he had been in a most distressing state, half out of his mind, yet not entirely so' (journal, 1 Oct 1873, Royal Archives, Windsor Castle; Ormond, *Sir Edwin Landseer*, 22). Landseer's funeral on 11 October in St Paul's Cathedral, where he was buried in the crypt, was a national event, and he was the subject of many tributes and eulogies, for he had been a major force in British art for more than fifty years.

In May 1874 a major sale of Landseer's works was held by his executors at Christies, when 1410 lots raised £69,709 9s. and swelled the value of the artist's estate, which had been assessed for probate the previous November at the then colossal sum of just under £160,000. Financial success was crowned by popular acclaim—the Landseer memorial exhibition of 532 works, held at the Royal Academy in winter 1874, attracted 105,000 visitors and sold 30,000 catalogues.

In 1961 the then president of the Royal Academy, Sir Charles Wheeler, remarked that 'In this century [Landseer's] fame has been entirely eclipsed and probably in the whole of British art there is no other figure who has suffered such extremes of approbation and neglect' (*Paintings and Drawings by Sir Edwin Landseer*, iii). For the curators of the 1961 exhibition at the Royal Academy, Landseer's anthropomorphic dog subjects were deemed mawkishly sentimental; it was safer by far to concentrate on 'his portrait studies and landscapes among the oils and the brilliant figure drawings and caricatures in pen and ink' (ibid., iv). And as long as celebrations of hunting continue to offend liberal sensibilities, it is hard to envisage Landseer ever regaining widespread popularity.

The extensive circulation of his works in the form of engravings has meant that Landseer's exceptional skill as a painter has been undervalued. This was one of the revelations of his major retrospective exhibition held at the Tate Gallery, London, in 1981. As Derek Hill (a fellow painter) observed twenty years earlier: 'even in his most banal and uninteresting works (and many such exist), Landseer seldom loses the remarkable ability of translating the texture of the natural surface he represents into the equivalent texture of paint' (*Paintings and Drawings by Sir Edwin Landseer*, x).

In 2001 'Inventing New Britain: the Victorian Vision', the Victoria and Albert Museum's exhibition celebrating the centenary of the death of Queen Victoria, justifiably included some of Landseer's most famous paintings. To his contemporaries their appeal transcended class boundaries. Well over a century after his death images such as *The Old Shepherd's Chief Mourner* or *The Monarch of the Glen* remain embedded in the national consciousness, while Landseer's lions in Trafalgar Square are one of the most famous features of the London scene.

JUDITH BRONKHURST and RICHARD ORMOND

Sources R. Ormond, *Sir Edwin Landseer* (1981) [with contributions by J. Rishel and R. Hamlyn; exhibition catalogue, Philadelphia Museum of Art and Tate Gallery, London] · R. Ormond, *Early Victorian portraits*, 2 vols. (1973), vol. 1, pp. 253–7; vol. 2, pls. 364, 497–501 · *Paintings and drawings by Sir Edwin Landseer R. A., 1802–1873* (1961) [exhibition catalogue, RA] · C. Lennie, *Landseer: the Victorian paragon* (1976) · A. Graves, ed., *Catalogue of the works of the late Sir Edwin Landseer, R. A.* [1875] · *The remaining works of Sir E. Landseer, R. A. deceased* [sale catalogue, Christie, Manson and Woods, 8–15 May 1874] · C. R. Leslie, *Autobiographical recollections*, ed. T. Taylor, 2 vols. (1860), vol. 1, pp. 39 and 83 · *The autobiography and memoirs of Benjamin Robert Haydon (1786–1846)*, ed. T. Taylor, new edn, 2 vols. (1926), vol. 1, p. 248 · *The diary of Benjamin Robert Haydon*, ed. W. B. Pope, 5 vols. (1960–63), vol. 2, p. 466; vol. 3, pp. 398 and 404; vol. 5, p. 452 · *The letters of Sir Walter Scott*, ed. H. J. C. Grierson and others, centenary edn, 12 vols. (1932–79), vol. 8, p. 392 · J. Ruskin, *Modern painters*, 5 vols. (1843–60); repr. in *The works of John Ruskin*, ed. E. T. Cook and A. Wedderburn, library edn, 39 vols. (1903–12) · *The Examiner* (26 April 1818), 269 · *The Examiner* (29 Jan 1824), 130 · Landseer's bank accounts, 1821–73, ledgers, Barclays Bank, Fleet Street, London branch (formerly Gosling's Bank) · E. H. Landseer, letters to J. Bell, Royal Institution of Great Britain, London · 'Sir Edwin Landseer', *Cornhill Magazine*, 29 (1874), 99 · F. Keyl, notes on conversations with Landseer, 1866–9, Royal Arch., Keyl Papers · M. A. Stevens, 'The Royal Academy in the age of Queen Victoria', *Art in the age of Queen Victoria: treasures from the Royal Academy of Arts permanent collection*, ed. H. Valentine (1999), 32 · W. S. Sparrow, *A book of sporting painters* (1931), 198–200 · *Sir Edwin Landseer, R. A.* (1874) [exhibition catalogue, RA] · *Elizabeth, Lady Holland to her son, 1821–1845*, ed. earl of Ilchester [G. S. Holland Fox-Strangways] (1946), 184–5 · O. Millar, *The Victorian pictures in the collection of her majesty the queen*, 2 vols. (1992), vol. 1, pp. 135–57 · private information (2004) · d. cert.

Archives Bodl. Oxf., letters · FM Cam., letters · Harvard U., Houghton L., letters and drawings, MS Eng. 157 f176 · Hunt. L., letters · V&A NAL, corresp. and MSS | BL, letters to C. G. Lewis and F. C. Lewis, Add. MS 38608 · Chatsworth House, Derbyshire, letters to sixth duke of Devonshire · estate of the duke of Sutherland, Mertoun, Melrose, Roxburghshire, letters to earl of Ellesmere · FM Cam., letters to Robert Peel · Harvard U., Houghton L., letters to Count D'Orsay · National Gallery, London, corresp. with William Boxall · NL Scot., letters to Lady Ashburton · Northumbd RO, Newcastle upon Tyne, letters to M. Culley · NRA, priv. coll., letters to marquis of Breadalbane · NRA, priv. coll., letters to Lord Wemyss · Royal Institution of Great Britain, London, letters to J. Bell · Russell-Cotes Art Gallery, Bournemouth, corresp. with L. V. Flatow, 1864 · Sheff. Arch., letters to first earl of Wharncliffe · V&A NAL, letters to John Forster · V&A NAL, letters to Sir F. Grant · V&A NAL, letters to W. Wells

Likenesses J. Hayter, graphite and brown wash, 1814, priv. coll.; repro. in Ormond, *Sir Edwin Landseer*, 4 · E. H. Landseer, self-portrait, graphite drawing, 1818, NPG · E. H. Landseer, self-portrait, oils, c.1820, priv. coll. · J. Hayter, oil caricature, 1823, Shipley Art Gallery, Gateshead · G. Hayter, pen-and-ink drawing, 1825, BM · J. F. Lewis, watercolour, c.1830, priv. coll.; repro. in Ormond, *Sir Edwin Landseer*, 6 · C. C. Vogel, chalk drawing, 1834, Staatliche Kunstsammlungen, Dresden, Kupferstichkabinett · lithograph, pubd 1843 (after Count D'Orsay, 1843), NPG; related lithograph, NPG · E. H. Landseer, self-portrait, pen-and-ink caricature, 1845, Christies, 11 July 1972 · F. Grant, oil sketch, c.1852, NPG [*see illus.*] · F. Grant, oils, 1852, NPG · F. Grant, pen-and-ink drawing, 1852, NPG · J. Watkins, carte-de-visite, 1860–69, NPG, Royal Collection · carte-de-visite, 1860–69, NPG · J. Ballantyne, oils, c.1865, NPG · E. H. Landseer, self-portrait, oils, exh. RA 1865 (*The connoisseurs*), Royal Collection · C. Marochetti, marble bust, exh. RA 1867, RA · C. B. Birch, double portrait, pencil drawing, c.1870, NPG · T. Woolner, marble medallion, 1882, St Paul's Cathedral, London · Count D'Orsay, pencil drawing, Gov. Art Coll. · F. Grant, oils, RA · F. Grant, pen sketch, Athenaeum, London · H. H., caricature, woodcut, NPG; repro. in *The Mask's Album* • G. Hayter, pencil drawing, BM • E. H. Landseer, self-portrait, chalk drawing, BM • E. H. Landseer, self-portrait, pen, ink, and wash drawing, Hatfield House, Hertfordshire • J. F. Lewis, pencil drawing, RA • D. Maclise, drawing, V&A • G. S. Newton, drawing, NG Scot. • Sem [G. Goursat], watercolour and pencil caricature, V&A • W. M. Thackeray, drawing, V&A • prints (after photographs), BM, NPG • stipple (after drawing by J. Hayter, 1813), BM; repro. in *Works* • wood-engraving, NPG; repro. in *ILN* (19 Sept 1874)

Wealth at death under £200,000: resworn probate, Aug 1876, *CGPLA Eng. & Wales* (1873)

Landseer, Jessica (1807–1880), painter and etcher, was born at 71 Queen Anne Street East (later 33 Foley Street), London, one of the fourteen children (of whom seven survived infancy) of John *Landseer (1763/9–1852), painter, engraver, and author, and his wife, Jane Potts (1773/4–1840). Sir Edwin Henry *Landseer (1802–1873), the famous animal painter, was her brother. She received an art education at home from her father and first exhibited at the Royal Academy in 1816, at the precocious age of nine. She was represented by a total of forty-seven works at the Royal Academy (1816–66), the British Institution (1817–23), the Old Watercolour Society (1817–20), the Society of British Artists (1832–7), and the Liverpool Academy (1838). The majority of her early contributions were landscapes, often of scenes in Essex and Suffolk. In the 1820s she also etched plates of her brother Edwin's work, including one of a Scottish terrier, *Vixen*, and another, *Lady Louisa Russell Feeding a Donkey*, in 1826. In the 1830s her subject matter broadened: she exhibited portraits at the Royal Academy, including *Portrait of a Student of the Royal Academy* in 1835, while to the Society of British Artists she sent figure subjects and three watercolour copies of her brother's paintings of people and animals.

A couple of years after the death of their mother in 1840, Jessica Landseer went to live with her brother Edwin, who had remained a bachelor, at 1 St John's Wood Road, London, where their aunt, Barbara Potts, kept house for him. Jessica gradually took over household responsibilities and by the 1850s her brother was paying her more than £200 a year. She cared for him through the years of his greatest acclaim and success, during which he was frequently subject to illness and depression, until his death in 1873. Algernon Graves described Jessica Landseer as 'a meek, amiable little body who looked after her brother's house in a very quiet and unostentatious way' (Lennie, 165).

Jessica Landseer did not exhibit between 1839 and 1862, and it has been suggested that she was prevented from doing so by Edwin's disapproval of professional women artists, as well as by her considerable domestic duties. Evidence that she continued to work, however, is provided by three extant works: a miniature of 1844 (Victoria and Albert Museum, London) from a sketch of Mrs Bradshaw by Edwin Landseer; a watercolour copy in miniature, dated 1845 (Scottish National Portrait Gallery, Edinburgh), of her brother's portrait of Sir Walter Scott; and her own engraving of 1858 (British Museum, London) from her portrait of her brother Thomas *Landseer (1793/4–1880). In 1863 she resumed exhibiting at the Royal Academy, showing that year a painting of Edwin Landseer's dog, Lassie,

Jessica Landseer (1807–1880), by unknown photographer

and a final contribution, *A Recollection*, in 1866. Otherwise, from 1865 until her death in 1880 she was represented exclusively at the Society of Female Artists, of which she was for the same period an honorary member; her exhibits included landscapes, animals, portraits, and two copies, in miniature, of paintings by Edwin Landseer, one of which, *Beauty's Bath* (a portrait of Miss Eliza Peel with her dog, Fido), became the property of Queen Alexandra, consort of Edward VII. Edwin Landseer left his sister a substantial legacy and by 1877 she had moved to 6 Kensington Park Gardens, London, where she kept a carriage. She died, unmarried, at Folkestone, Kent, on 29 August 1880.

CHARLOTTE YELDHAM

Sources Graves, *RA exhibitors* • Graves, *Brit. Inst.* • J. Johnson, ed., *Works exhibited at the Royal Society of British Artists, 1824–1893, and the New English Art Club, 1888–1917*, 2 vols. (1975) • J. Soden and C. Baile de Laperrière, eds., *The Society of Women Artists exhibitors, 1855–1996*, 4 vols. (1996) • C. Lennie, *Landseer: the Victorian paragon* (1976) • R. Ormond, *Sir Edwin Landseer* (1981) • Wood, *Vic. painters*, 2nd edn • P. Dunford, *A biographical dictionary of women artists in Europe and America since 1850* (1990) • *DNB* • *The Royal Watercolour Society: the first fifty years, 1805–1855* (1992) • *DNB* • 'Landseer, John', *DNB* • E. Morris and E. Roberts, *The Liverpool Academy and other exhibitions of contemporary art in Liverpool, 1774–1867* (1998)

Likenesses photograph, MacKenzie Collection; repro. in Ormond, *Sir Edwin Landseer*, p. 4 [*see illus.*]

Wealth at death under £70,000: resworn probate, March 1882, *CGPLA Eng. & Wales* (1880)

Landseer, John George (1763/1769–1852), engraver and antiquary, was born in Lincoln in either 1763 or 1769. Little is known of his childhood or family except that his father was a jeweller and that, at some point during his youth, the family moved to London, where Landseer was apprenticed to William Byrne (1740–1805), a landscape engraver.

John George Landseer (1763/9–1852), by Sir Edwin Landseer, c.1848

His earliest single plates, published in Joseph Farington's *Views in the Lake Country* (1784–8), were landscape views. Similarly, his first complete series of prints was after James Moore's topographical designs for his antiquarian account *Twenty-Five Views in the Southern Part of Scotland* (1794). At the same time, along with numerous fellow engravers, he also worked on entrepreneurial publishing schemes such as Robert Bowyer's lavish illustrated edition of David Hume's *History of England* (8 vols., 1792–3), and in 1794 he engraved vignettes after Philippe Jacques de Loutherbourg for an edition of the Bible published by Thomas Macklin (8 vols., 1800). Indeed, Macklin can be said to have had a great influence on Landseer's life, as it was through this publisher that he met Jane Potts (1773/4–1840). The couple married in 1794 and moved to 71 Queen Anne Street (and later 33 Foley Street), where they had fourteen children, of whom seven survived to adulthood. These were Thomas *Landseer (1793/4–1880), a printmaker; Jane (*b.* 1795); Charles *Landseer (1799/1800–1879), a painter; Edwin *Landseer (1802–1873), the acclaimed and knighted painter; Anna Maria (1805–1871); Jessica *Landseer (1807–1880), a miniaturist; and Emma (1809–1895), who also painted miniatures. Although John Landseer remained a prolific printmaker and an occasional painter in oils who consistently exhibited work at the Royal Academy until his death, it is sometimes said that his most major contribution to the arts was the nurture and artistic training of his children, especially that of his most celebrated son, Sir Edwin Landseer.

Often described as opinionated, domineering, and embittered, Landseer, 'being somewhat deaf' (Farington, *Diary*, 11.3847), carried an ear trumpet and was renowned for having a short temper and for muttering to himself under his breath. His pugnacious character did not help to ingratiate him with his peers; only his friend Joseph Farington recognized that, although 'Landseer is warm in His temper ... He does not appear so out of doors to the world, and is not liked by those of His Profession' (Farington, *Diary*, 14.4884). Landseer's reputation for being difficult and cantankerous appears to have had little real effect upon the structure of his career. He frequently collaborated with artists: for example, he worked with the draughtsman and traveller William Alexander and the engraver J. Shirt in producing *An Authentic Account of an Embassy to China* (1807). He also engraved designs for some of the major nineteenth-century artists, including both Turner and Constable; the latter of these, on seeing his plate of *Stoke Mill* in 1814, described Landseer as 'a very superior landscape engraver' (Parris and Shields, 227). Moreover, Landseer's sense of community is nowhere better represented than in his self-appointed role as the most vociferous and constant spokesman for the liberal status of English engravers.

On 27 December 1802 Landseer delivered an address to the Royal Academy in which he proposed that four engravers should be made full academicians and that a system of medals should be instituted to encourage engraving. In so doing, he championed the grievances of engravers, whom the academy did not consider worthy of the privileged status of full academicians. Landseer's proposals were not heeded. Nevertheless, in 1806 he accepted the post of associate engraver of the Royal Academy in the hope of improving conditions from within the institution. Additionally, in the same year he delivered a series of lectures at the Royal Institution which presented the history and benefits of engraving under the belief that 'No Art can flourish in any country unless honoured as an Art' (Fox, 8). The sixth of these caused controversy as it was deemed to be a direct attack on the publisher John Boydell, who, Landseer claimed, had exploited modern engravers for his own personal gain. Although this was not technically libellous, as Boydell had died in 1804, the latter's nephew Josiah Boydell complained to the committee of the Royal Institution, and Landseer was immediately dismissed from his professorship without even the privilege of a hearing. In order to vindicate his name and to continue his campaign on behalf of engravers, Landseer published his discourses with the addition of a preface which explained his motives.

The success and perhaps the scandal of the *Lectures on the Art of Engraving* (1807) 'whetted Landseer's appetite for authorship' (Herrmann, 1.26), though he turned his attentions to more general artistic and antiquarian topics. His next venture, in 1808, was the launch of the critical *Review of Publications of Art*. Despite the fact that this journal survived for only four issues and lost him £400 in the process, Landseer attempted another similar project in 1837, with a periodical entitled *The Probe*; this also quickly collapsed. Having been elected a fellow of the Society of Antiquaries in 1807, he published an erudite and polemical essay on ancient Babylonian relics in the society's journal, *Archaeologia*, in 1817; he then returned to this topic in an independent volume called *Sabaean researches, in a series of essays on the engraved hieroglyphics of Chaldea, Egypt, and Canaan* (1823). During the later part of his career he combined his two interests and published several of his prints with pamphlets which provided additional contextual information on the subjects he engraved. This was the case with his engraving of Edwin Landseer's *Alpine Mastiffs Reanimating a Distressed Traveller* (1831) which was accompanied by his father's essay *Some Account of the Dogs and the Pass of the Great St Bernard* (1831).

Although there were few tangible results, Landseer continued to campaign for the improved rights of engravers for the rest of his life. In 1810 he proposed a plan for a society and academy of engravers and in 1836 he joined in a petition to the House of Commons which once again attempted to influence the structure of the Royal Academy. This petition was received favourably by a select committee, but a subsequent appeal to the king was unsuccessful, and it was not until 1854 that an engraver was accepted as a full academician. Nevertheless, Landseer was personally honoured when, in 1837, he was appointed engraver to William IV. He died on 29 February 1852 and was buried at Highgate cemetery, Middlesex.

LUCY PELTZ

Sources J. Landseer, *Lectures on the art of engraving, delivered at the Royal Institution of Great Britain* (1807) · Farington, *Diary* · L. Herrmann, 'John Landseer on Turner: reviews of exhibits in 1808, 1839 and 1840', *Turner Studies*, 7/1 (1987), 26–33; 7/2 (1987), 21–8 · R. Ormond, *Sir Edwin Landseer* (1981), 1–24 · C. Fox, 'The engraver's battle for professional recognition in early nineteenth-century London', *London Journal*, 2 (1976), 3–31 · Graves, *RA exhibitors* · J. Hague, 'Sir Edwin Landseer, 1802–1873', *Landseer and his world* [1972], 4–27 [exhibition catalogue, Mappin Art Gallery, Sheffield, 5 Feb – 12 March 1972] · J. Turner, ed., *The dictionary of art*, 34 vols. (1996) · Bryan, *Painters* (1866); (1903–5) · *Engraved Brit. ports.* · A. Davies and E. Kilmurray, *Dictionary of British portraiture*, 4 vols. (1979–81) · Graves, *Soc. Artists* · Bénézit, *Dict.*, 3rd edn · Thieme & Becker, *Allgemeines Lexikon*, vols. 4–36 · F. G. Stephens, *Memoirs of Sir Edwin Landseer* (1874) · *John Constable: further documents and correspondence*, ed. L. Parris, C. Shields, and I. Fleming-Williams, Suffolk RS, 18 (1975), 226–8

Archives BL, lectures and notes on art of engraving, C.60.n.2 | BL, letters to second Earl Spencer, Section G (pre-deposit list) · CUL, letters to Royal Society of Literature

Likenesses E. Landseer, oils, c.1848, NPG [*see illus.*] · E. Landseer, pencil drawing, BM · J. Scott, mezzotint (after E. Landseer), repro. in *The works of Sir Edwin Landseer, RA*, 4 vols. (1879–80)

Landseer, Thomas (1793/4–1880), printmaker, was born at 71 Queen Anne Street, London, the eldest son of the engraver John George *Landseer (1763/9–1852) and his wife, Jane Potts (1773/4–1840), and was baptized, along with the other Landseer children, in the parish of St Marylebone on 23 May 1821. He was the eldest brother of seven surviving children who all displayed artistic talents and received their earliest general training from their father. Edwin *Landseer (1802–1873) was his youngest brother. With another brother, Charles *Landseer (1799/1800–1879), he went on to study under the painter Benjamin Robert Haydon, when he was a fellow pupil of the young printmaker William Bewick (whose biography, *Life and Letters of William Bewick (Artist)*, he edited in 1871).

Having been taught various engraving techniques by his father, Thomas Landseer produced his first published print, *Study of the Head of a Sibyl* (1816), in a mixture of aquatint and etching after one of Haydon's drawings. He followed this in 1817 with a series of academic figure studies entitled *Haydon's Drawing-Book*, which he executed in softground etching to emulate chalk drawing. Before this point he had etched a number of animal sketches, such as *A Bull Marked T. W.* (1811), after sketches by his youngest brother Edwin. Throughout his career he reproduced more than 125 of Edwin's heroic animal paintings in a blend of etching and engraving, which can be seen in plates such as the *Hunted Stag* (1848) or *Monarch of the Glen* (1852). This characteristic style of engraving effectively captured the textures and tones of his brother's originals, and Sir Edwin's financial success and popular acclaim owed much to Tom's reproductions, which were usually sold for between 3 and 10 guineas, depending on whether they were artist's proofs or finished prints. Although he engraved a number of sporting subjects and satirical vignettes to illustrate respectively texts such as *The Annals of Sporting and Fancy Gazette* (1822–8) or Coleridge's *The Devil's Walk* (1831), Landseer always returned to animal subjects. Sometimes, as in the case of *Twenty Engravings of Lions, Tigers, Panthers & Leopards* (1823), these were reproductions of ennobled prototypes by Rembrandt and Rubens; at other times he appealed to more scientific concerns with his *Characteristic Sketches of Animals* (1832), which was dedicated to the Zoological Society. He also exploited graphic traditions in *Monkeyana, or, Men in Miniature* (1827), where he depicted monkeys in fashionable dress, engaged in human activities, as a way of satirizing contemporary life. Landseer was also a painter, and between 1853 and 1877 he exhibited several landscape and genre paintings at both the British Institution and the Royal Academy. However, in 1867, when he was elected an associate of the Royal Academy, it was for his talents as an engraver.

Surprisingly little is known of Thomas Landseer's private life or personality except that he was deaf, like his father, and was, according to his brother Edwin, rather dissolute and disorganized. He was the only one of his close family to marry, but the identity of his wife remains entirely unknown, probably as a result of her indiscretion. The nature of this was made clear in Haydon's diary when, in 1829, he mentioned that 'Tom Landseer … took back his wife after she had a child by another' (*Diary*, ed. Pope, 3.398). Though this reference casts doubt on the paternity of George Landseer (1829–1878), Thomas brought him up as his own, and the boy followed in the family footsteps by becoming a portrait and a landscape painter. Towards the end of his life Landseer left his wife and moved in with his brother Charles and sister Jessie, at 11 Grove End Road, St John's Wood, where he died on 20 January 1880. He was buried at Highgate cemetery on 24 January, and his will, dated 28 April 1878, was read on 13 February. In it he left a fortune of around £45,000 to his executors Thomas Hyde Hills and Arnold William White, as well as a bequest of £5000 to the Artists' Orphan Fund and substantial legacies and annuities to various friends and family, including his sisters Jessie and Emma and the widow of his late son George.   LUCY PELTZ

Sources R. Ormond, *Sir Edwin Landseer* (1981), 1–24 · *The diary of Benjamin Robert Haydon*, ed. W. B. Pope, 5 vols. (1960–63) · *The Times* (5 March 1880), 7 · T. Landseer, ed., *Life & letters of William Bewick (artist)*, 2 vols. (1871) · A. Potts, 'Natural order and the call of the wild: the politics of animal picturing', *Oxford Art Journal*, 13/1 (1990), 12–33 · J. Turner, ed., *The dictionary of art*, 34 vols. (1996) · *The Times* (30 Oct 1881), 3 · Graves, *Brit. Inst.* · Graves, *RA exhibitors* · Bénézit, *Dict.*, 3rd edn · Thieme & Becker, *Allgemeines Lexikon*, vols. 4–36 · F. G. Stephens, *Memoirs of Sir Edwin Landseer* (1874) · Redgrave, *Artists* · *Engraved Brit. ports.* · A. Davies and E. Kilmurray, *Dictionary of British portraiture*, 4 vols. (1979–81) · G. W. Friend, ed., *An alphabetical list of engravings declared at the office of the Printsellers' Association, London*, 2 vols. (1892) · *CGPLA Eng. & Wales* (1880) · d. cert.

Archives BM, MSS book

Likenesses C. Landseer, chalk drawing, 1858, NPG · J. Landseer, lithograph, 1858, BM · W. J. Edwards, stipple (after Landseer), NPG · J. & C. Watkins, carte-de-visite, NPG; repro. in Ormond, *Sir Edwin Landseer*, 3 · wood-engraving (after Watkins), NPG; repro. in *ILN* (1868)

Wealth at death under £45,000: probate, 13 Feb 1880, *CGPLA Eng. & Wales*

Lane, A. (*fl.* 1695–1700), grammarian, is known only through the evidence provided by the two grammars he has left us. He styles himself MA on the title-page of *A Rational and Speedy Method of Attaining to the Latin Tongue* (1695), but no record survives of his attendance at university. From Lane's prefatory epistle dedicated to Sir Richard Reynell, lord chief justice of Ireland, we learn that Lane had been encouraged to use his linguistic ideas to teach Latin to Reynell's eight-year-old son. As a result of the son's progress, 'several Persons of Quality thought fit (on your Lordship's Recommendation) to put their Children under the same conduct' (*A Rational and Speedy Method*, sig. A2r). By 1700, according to the title of his *A Key to the Art of Letters* (1700), he was 'A. Lane, M.A, late Master of the Free School of *Leominster* in *Herefordshire*, now Teacher of a private School at *Mile-end-green* near *Stepney*'.

Lane's two books show that he was familiar with logic and grammatical theories ranging from Priscian to Port-Royal, but his contribution to knowledge lies in the original adaptation of his material; *Method* has, in addition to a Latin grammar, the first 'universal' grammar in English, 'containing such Precepts as are common to all Languages' (title-page). His philosophy was continued into the *Key* since the rules 'are the same in all Languages how different soever they be' (preface, x).   R. D. SMITH

Sources A. Lane, *A rational and speedy method of attaining to the Latin tongue: in two parts* (1695) · A. Lane, *A key to the art of letters, or, English a learned language, full of art, elegancy and variety* (1700)

Lane, Sir Allen [*formerly* Allen Lane Williams] (**1902–1970**), publisher, was born in Bristol on 21 September 1902. He was the first of four children of Samuel Allen Gardiner Williams, an architect, and his wife, Camilla Matilda Lane. After a brief period at Telesford House School, he attended Bristol grammar school, where he was a competent but not outstanding pupil.

John Lane, founder of the Bodley Head publishing

Sir Allen Lane (1902–1970), by unknown photographer

house, was related to the boy's mother; childless himself, he suggested that young Allen come and learn the business under him, thus ensuring that both the firm and his name would continue. The Bodley Head had risen to eminence during the 1890s, and was the firm most closely associated with the literary style of that era; Bodley Head authors had included such names as Oscar Wilde and Aubrey Beardsley. In response to his uncle's wishes, Allen Williams in 1919 changed his name to Allen Lane; at the same time his parents, brothers, and sister all took on the name of Lane as well.

Allen Lane took quickly to the book trade, enthusiastically learning every aspect of it: he served as delivery boy, packer, and salesman, and he soon showed himself to be an even greater asset to the company in his dealings with both authors and customers. Living in London with John Lane and his wife, he was soon moving with ease among the circles of the most influential London publishers, and he was seen as capable, trustworthy, and amiable. Upon John Lane's death in 1925 he became a member of the board of directors, rising to chairman in 1930. The Bodley Head had become rather staid by this time, and the new ideas Lane brought with him often clashed with those of the more conservative members of the board. One of these clashes came over Lane's wish to publish James Joyce's *Ulysses*, still unavailable to the British reader except in frequently pirated continental editions. The board members were fearful of prosecution, even though an American court in 1933 had decreed the book not to be obscene. Lane won, and the Bodley Head's *Ulysses* finally appeared in 1936; there was no prosecution, and the book was financially very successful.

But the lengthy company battle over *Ulysses* had shown Lane that if he wanted to be innovative the Bodley Head was not the place for him. He had been developing an even bolder idea during this time, one involving a series of inexpensive but high-quality paperbacks. The idea had come to him, he later said, in 1934 when, returning from a weekend visit to Agatha Christie's home, he could find nothing worth reading in the railway station—only magazines and cheap fiction. He presented the idea to his brothers Richard and John (who were also working for the Bodley Head), proposing that the company acquire the rights to reprint good-quality fiction and non-fiction, produce them in tasteful paperback format, stick firmly to a price of 6*d.*, and employ an aggressive mass-marketing plan to sell them.

The other Bodley Head directors were against the plan, and indeed most publishers at the time were convinced it could not succeed. The paperback format was closely associated with the second-rate or worse, and the 6*d.* price seemed to guarantee that no profit could possibly be forthcoming. Lane insisted, though, that the combination of high quality with low prices could work if sales were high enough; the Bodley Head board gave him reluctant approval to follow up on the scheme, which they saw as at best a minor sideline for the business. Other publishers, such as Jonathan Cape, were fully convinced that the venture would fail; some willingly sold Lane the rights to some of the titles he wanted at a much lower rate than they might have.

Lane decided on an initial list of ten titles that provided a good indication of the sort of market he was seeking: respectable but not avant-garde books that had already demonstrated some popularity. The first list reprinted novels by Dorothy L. Sayers, Agatha Christie, Ernest Hemingway, and Compton Mackenzie, among others. A critical aspect of marketing the list was the packaging, and Lane came up with the idea of calling them Penguin Books, and employing cleanly designed covers in eye-catching orange and green. Edward Young, an amateur artist who worked for the Bodley Head, drew the original Penguin colophon. The image was jaunty, and the pages well-printed and readable. The traditional paperback had a lurid cover illustration, but everything about the look of the Penguins promised respectability and quality (Lane would long resist using any sort of cover illustrations at all, referring to them as mere 'bosoms and bottoms').

The success of the project depended on very large orders. Lane and his brothers set about interesting retailers in the books, with mixed success until Lane approached the Woolworth's chain. The Woolworth's buyer happened to ask his wife, as a representative of the general public, what she thought of the books; her enthusiasm prompted him to place an order with Lane for some 63,000 copies. This single sale guaranteed that the project would pay for itself, and of course it provided very wide exposure for the set of books. In 1936 Lane set up Penguin Books as a separate firm, and he soon resigned from the Bodley Head to run the new enterprise.

Sales were higher than even Lane had hoped for (by March 1936 over 1 million Penguins were in print), and soon many more titles were added to the original ten. Lane's vision for the company was broadened in 1937, when he met William Emrys Williams, who suggested to him that Penguins might serve more than just a financial aim: they could do real public good as well. With Williams's help, Lane started the series known as Pelicans, non-fiction books with an educational intent (the first title was George Bernard Shaw's *The Intelligent Woman's Guide to Socialism*, in two volumes). Pelicans were also priced at 6*d.*, and also sported lively but respectable uniform covers. The Pelicans sold very well, and Lane's wish for his books to serve the public good resulted in yet another series, Penguin Specials, which strove to educate the public about the growing threat from Germany. When war broke out in 1939 paper rationing was introduced with the portion allotted to each publisher being based on the previous two years' sales. The enormous success of Penguins meant that Lane secured a far more generous ration than other publishers. The sense of social purpose shown by the Penguin Specials was equally evident in the Armed Forces Book Club that Lane launched in 1942. With parcels going out to the troops and to prisoners of war, Penguin came to be closely identified with the war effort, and could even be seen as symbolic of the very way of life the soldiers were defending. It ensured that Penguin never suffered, as most other publishers did, from paper shortage. The 1940s also saw the launch of Puffin Books, a series for children, which likewise enjoyed superb sales figures.

E. V. Rieu, a scholar who had long worked in publishing, approached Lane in 1945 with the idea of a series to be called Penguin Classics. The first title in the series was Rieu's prose translation of the *Odyssey*, which ultimately sold over a million copies. Penguin Classics were a natural expansion of Lane's vision for his publishing house to combine social and educative responsibility with commercial success. The series soon became a mainstay of the firm, helping it gain a foothold in the lucrative American market, where Penguin had hitherto had only mixed success. The firm expanded also into Canada and Australia, where sales grew dramatically. Presiding over what had become a publishing empire, Lane at times became autocratic and eccentric, as in the famous anecdote of his departure after a visit to the Australian branch: at the airport, he suddenly turned to the three company executives who had accompanied him, and jabbed a finger at each of them, announcing, '*You're* in—*you're* out—and *you're* in.'

Aside from the pressure put on him by his increasingly complex and far-flung business, Lane's personal life was contented. He had married Lettice Lucy Orr, a psychiatric social worker, on 28 June 1941, and with her had three daughters; and he was knighted in 1952, the first of a long list of honours to be granted him. But he never ceased to innovate, and to take large (if well-calculated) risks. The most famous of these was his decision to print a complete set of D. H. Lawrence's works in 1960, thirty years after Lawrence's death. The set was to include *Lady Chatterley's Lover*, which had not been printed in England and which had become almost a byword for high-toned pornography. Lane risked prosecution, but prosecution under the new and more liberal Obscene Publications Act of 1959. The new act required that a book had to be judged as a whole, not simply on the basis of some indecent passages, and on these grounds Lane was sure he could win. The book was seized, and prosecution began on 20 October 1960. The trial, as Lane expected, made headlines, and positioned Penguin as a champion of free and open literary expression. The prosecution's case was handled rather half-heartedly and quite badly, while Lane had arranged for a long parade of high-profile defence witnesses, including Rebecca West, C. Day Lewis, E. M. Forster, and Richard Hoggart; on 2 November Lane won an acquittal along with an enormous public relations boost for Penguin. Lane had originally projected sales of 200,000, but sales soon surpassed 3 million; the projected profit of £5000 on the book came ultimately to £112,000.

Penguin and Lane continued to thrive and expand in the 1960s. In 1965 he became embroiled in a struggle for control of the firm with his chief editor, Tony Godwin, who had enjoyed wide support from the board. Things came to a head when Godwin and the board overruled Lane on the publication of a particular book. At night Lane and a loyal employee smuggled out all the copies of the book Godwin had championed, hauled them off to his farm, and burned them all. The crisis forced Godwin out, and Lane reasserted control. But three years later he was diagnosed with bowel cancer, and he died on 7 July 1970 in Mt Vernon Hospital, Northwood, Middlesex; his wife survived him. His ashes were placed in Hartland church, north Devon, and a memorial service was held at St Martin-in-the-Fields, London, on 18 August, packed with celebrities, officials, authors, and colleagues, all testifying to Lane's prominence and influence.

After Lane's death Penguin suffered a brief period of disarray, but soon righted itself and went on, in the 1970s and 1980s, to a series of expansions and acquisitions of other publishers both in Britain and abroad. In 1970 Penguin became part of Pearson Longman, and in 1975 the American branch of Penguin merged with Viking Press to become Viking Penguin. In 1986 Penguin bought out the New American Library (which had split off from Penguin in 1948); after this acquisition, Penguin had roughly equal interests in Britain and the USA. The company has continued to enjoy a success and influence far beyond what Lane could have dreamed possible back in 1935.

RAYMOND N. MacKenzie

Sources J. E. Morpurgo, *Allen Lane, King Penguin: a biography* (1979) · S. Hare, ed., *Penguin portrait: Allen Lane and the Penguin editors, 1935–1970* (1995) · W. E. Williams, *Allen Lane: a personal portrait* (1973) · C. H. Rolph, ed., *The trial of Lady Chatterley: Regina v. Penguin Books Limited* (1961) · *DNB*

Archives LUL, corresp. with Duckworth and Co. · University of Bristol Library, corresp. and statements relating to *Lady Chatterley's lover* trial; corresp.; files

Likenesses B. Kneale, portrait, repro. in Williams, *Allen Lane*; priv. coll. · R. Moynihan, group portrait (*After the conference*), repro. in Morpurgo, *Allen Lane* · photograph, Hult. Arch. · photograph, NPG [*see illus.*] · photographs, repro. in Morpurgo, *Allen Lane*

Wealth at death £1,216,474: probate, 1 Dec 1970, *CGPLA Eng. & Wales*

Lane, Charles Richard William (1786–1872), army officer, son of John and Melissa Lane, was born on 29 October 1786, and baptized at St Martin-in-the-Fields, London, on 23 November 1786. He was nominated to a cadetship in 1806, and passed an examination in Persian and Hindustani, for which he was awarded a gratuity of 1200 rupees and a sword. His commissions in the Bengal infantry were: ensign (13 August 1807), lieutenant (14 July 1812), captain (30 January 1824; army 5 February 1822), major (30 April 1835), lieutenant-colonel (26 December 1841), and colonel (25 May 1852). He shared the Deccan prize as lieutenant 1st Bengal native infantry for 'general captures'. He sought permission in 1824 to change his name to Mattenby, but the request was refused as beyond the competence of the Indian government. He served with the 2nd native grenadier battalion in Arakan during the First Anglo-Burmese War in 1825, was timber agent at Naulpore in 1828, and was in charge of the commissariat at Dinapore in 1832. He married at Calcutta, on 18 March 1829, Miss Ursula Palma: she died in Kensington on 9 September 1847, aged thirty-nine.

Lane commanded his regiment in Afghanistan under Sir William Nott in 1842, and commanded the garrison of Kandahar when the town was assaulted on 10 March 1842 by an Afghan force, which was repulsed with heavy loss. He was made CB on 27 December 1842. He married at Camberwell, on 23 March 1848, Maria, elder daughter of John Gibbs of Ballynora, co. Cork, captain in the Royal Cork city militia. He became major-general in 1854, lieutenant-general in 1866, and general in 1870. Lane died at his residence, Kandahar Villa, Jersey, on 18 February 1872, aged eighty-five.

H. M. Chichester, *rev.* James Falkner

Sources *Indian Army List* · BL OIOC · *LondG* (Sept 1842) · V. C. P. Hodson, *List of officers of the Bengal army, 1758–1834*, 3 (1946)

Lane, Edward (1605–1685), Church of England clergyman, was elected a scholar at St Paul's School, London, where he was a pupil of Alexander Gill the elder. He was admitted on 4 July 1622 to St John's College, Cambridge, graduating BA in 1626 and proceeding MA in 1629. Ordained priest on 22 September 1628 he was presented in 1631 (admitted 24 March) to the vicarage of North Shoebury, Essex, by the crown, through the lord keeper, Thomas Coventry. He resigned on 28 January 1636, being presented by the same patron to the vicarage of Sparsholt, Hampshire. He was also rector of Lainston, Hampshire, a parish adjoining, probably from 1637. On 9 July 1639 he was incorporated MA at Oxford. In 1644, being a 'time of warre', Lane was absent from Sparsholt: he was recommended by the Westminster assembly on 27 February 1645 to fill the sequestrated benefice of Sholden, Kent.

Lane's writings resulted from controversy. *Look unto Jesus* (1663) expanded a sermon first preached before the Restoration, when it had stirred up controversy because it accepted the celebration of Christmas; it was published as a defence of the restored Church of England (bound with the British Library copy is an autograph manuscript entitled 'A taste of the everlasting ffeast … in Heaven'). *Mercy Triumphant* (1680) and *Du Moulin's Reflections Reverberated* (1681) attacked the assertion of Lewis Du Moulin's *Moral Reflections on the Number of the Elect* (1680) that the elect might be fewer than one in a million as contrary to the gospel, harmful to godliness and troubled souls, and opposed to the riches of God's mercy. Postscripts to *Du Moulin's Reflections* attacked transubstantiation (and in passing, Lutheran consubstantiation) and, against the Erastian Edmund Hickeringill, defended church courts. 'A discourse of the waters of Noah', left in manuscript at his death, was a reply to Thomas Burnet's *The Sacred Theory of the Earth* (1684).

Although Lane remained an incumbent throughout the interregnum, after the Restoration he wrote of Charles I as a saint and martyr. He also then defended divine right episcopacy, bowing at the name of Jesus, and the use of set forms of prayer, which he claimed to be the general practice of the Reformed churches. He argued that those who had taken the solemn league and covenant could conscientiously disavow it. Next to scripture he sought the guidance of 'my good Mother the Holy Church of England' (*Mercy Triumphant*, 40). Roman Catholicism he considered a Babylon of error and novelty, and dissenting conventicles he scorned for blasphemy, narrowness, and sedition. Lane was convinced that the Jews would eventually be converted to Christianity.

Lane's incumbency at Sparsholt lasted fifty years. He had collected and transcribed the parish registers from 1607, and was reputed to be an exemplary parish clergyman. He died on 2 September 1685 and was buried on 4 September in the chancel of Sparsholt church. His wife, Mary, had been buried on 27 October 1669. None of his children survived him: Edward, who had been in Ireland, was buried on 17 May 1660; Henry, baptized on 11 April 1639, who had been a scholar at New College, Oxford, was buried on 6 October 1659. DEWEY D. WALLACE, JUN.

Sources Wood, *Ath. Oxon.: Fasti* (1815), 310; (1820), 127 • Venn, *Alum. Cant.* • J. F. Bailey, 'Edward Lane's "Waters of Noah"', *N&Q*, 5th ser., 10 (1878), 181–2 • B. W. Greenfield, 'Edward Lane's "Waters of Noah"', *N&Q*, 5th ser., 10 (1878), 273 • BL, Add. MS 15669, 39b • *DNB* • D. D. Wallace, *Puritans and predestination: grace in English protestant theology, 1525–1695* (1982)
Archives BL, Add. MS 15669 • BL, copy of Lane's *Look unto Jesus* (1663), containing the author's corrections; a MS presentation to Anne and Catherine Chettle; an autograph MS entitled 'A taste of the everlasting ffeast … in Heaven' • MS entitled 'A discourse of the waters of Noah'

Lane, Edward William (1801–1876), orientalist, born on 17 September 1801 at Hereford, was a younger son of Theophilus Lane (1764–1814), prebendary of Hereford, and his wife, Sophia Gardiner, of Bath, a niece of the painter Thomas *Gainsborough RA. His sister was Sophia Lane *Poole, travel writer. Two of his nephews, (Reginald) Stuart *Poole and (Edward) Stanley *Poole [see under Poole, Sophia Lane], as well as a great-nephew, Stanley Edward Lane-*Poole, shared his interest in Egyptian matters.

Edward William Lane (1801–1876), by Richard James Lane, 1829

Another great-nephew, Reginald Lane *Poole, was a historian. Lane attended grammar schools at Bath and Hereford, but much of his education was conducted by his mother, his father having died in 1814. Originally intending to study at Cambridge and enter the church, Lane instead followed his brother, Richard James *Lane, into apprenticeship as an engraver under Charles Heath in London, but during the early 1820s his imagination was captured by Egypt, then a subject of popular fascination. He decided to make the Egyptian people and their language his life's work.

Lane arrived in Egypt on 19 September 1825, likening his feelings to those of 'an Eastern bridegroom, about to lift up the veil of his bride' (manuscript draft of 'Description of Egypt', Bodl. Oxf., MS Eng. misc. d. 234, fol. 5). He lived exclusively in Muslim areas of Cairo, adopted local dress, and soon spoke Arabic fluently, moving freely in Egyptian society and recording the close observations that made his work so valuable. Although he primarily associated with the indigenous people, who knew him as Mansur Efendi, Lane also became acquainted with the small group of British Egyptologists and orientalists then assembling in Egypt: Henry Salt, John Gardner Wilkinson, Robert Hay, James Burton, Frederick Catherwood, Algernon Percy (Lord Prudhoe), Joseph Bonomi, and Major Orlando Felix. He worked extensively in Cairo and explored nearby archaeological sites such as Giza, Saqqara, and Dahshur, for he was intensely interested in ancient as well as modern Egypt during this stage of his career. Twice he ascended the Nile into Nubia as far as the second cataract. Before leaving Egypt he purchased Nefeeseh (Anastasoula Georgiou; 1820–1895), a Greek child who had been captured during the Greek War of Independence and sold as a slave in Cairo.

After returning to London in June 1828 Lane composed 'Description of Egypt', a remarkable manuscript of some 300,000 words and almost 200 illustrations. Besides recording his travels through Egypt, it included geographical studies, essays on modern and ancient Egyptian history, and a description of the Nubians. The eminent London firm of John Murray agreed to publish the work, but postponed sending it to press, initially because of the crisis over the Reform Bill of 1832. Frustrated by continuing publication delays and eager to return to Egypt, Lane took some chapters about modern Egyptian society that Murray had insisted on removing from 'Description' and proposed to develop them into a separate book. With the support of Lord Brougham, the Society for the Diffusion of Useful Knowledge contracted to publish the book and provided an advance payment which financed Lane's second trip to Egypt. When he returned to Cairo in December 1833, Lane quickly gathered his data and a year after his arrival began the fair copy of the book manuscript. A fierce outbreak of plague forced him in early 1835 to flee into Upper Egypt where he spent several months living in a tomb at Thebes before returning to England later that year. *An Account of the Manners and Customs of the Modern Egyptians* (2 vols.) became an instant success after its publication in 1836 and is still used as a basic text by both Eastern and Western students of the Arab world.

Soon after the appearance of *Modern Egyptians*, Murray cancelled plans to publish 'Description of Egypt', which was not published until almost 125 years after Lane's death. Greatly disappointed, Lane turned to other projects. One was his translation of the Arabic classic, the *Thousand and one Nights* (3 vols., 1839–41); another was *Selections from the Kur-án* (1843). Though *Selections from the Kur-án* is the least substantial of Lane's major published works, it nevertheless contains valuable material and demonstrates his conviction that essential Middle Eastern literary works should be communicated to the English reading public. This was even more the case with the *Thousand and one Nights*, which Lane believed presented 'most admirable pictures of the manners and customs of the Arabs, and particularly of those of the Egyptians' (Lane, *Modern Egyptians*, 1.vi n.). It reigned as the leading English translation of the *Nights* for decades, and its copious notes are stimulating micro-essays of enduring value.

The course of Lane's later life was set in 1841 when he accepted an offer from his friend Algernon Percy (known as Lord Prudhoe, later the duke of Northumberland) to support the compilation of a definitive Arabic–English lexicon. The first step was to travel to Egypt and gather the Arabic lexicographical texts on which such a work had to be based. Lane sailed from England in July 1842, accompanied by Nefeeseh, whom he had married on 8 July 1840, and by his sister Sophia Poole and her two sons, Stanley and Stuart. For the next seven years they lived in Cairo, always in those parts of the city inhabited by local people, as Lane collated the material for the lexicon, assisted by an Egyptian language master, Sheykh Ibrahim al-Desuqi. Lane threw himself into the daunting task so thoroughly as to become a near recluse, often not leaving his house for months at a time. With his permission Sophia took selected passages from his 'Description of Egypt' manuscript and added her own experiences to form a series of letters to an imaginary correspondent in England. Prepared under Lane's general supervision, Sophia's *The Englishwoman in Egypt* (3 vols., 1844–6) became a classic, especially prized for its observations of Egyptian women.

The Lanes and Pooles returned to England in October 1849. After briefly living in Hastings, they moved to Worthing where they eventually settled at 1 Union Place. Sophia remained there until the household was dissolved after Lane's death; Stanley and Stuart soon departed for London to begin careers at the British Museum. At Worthing, Lane intensified his dedication to the lexicon project, working on it every day from early morning until late at night, except on Sundays, which were reserved for Bible study in Hebrew, and on Friday afternoons when he received friends. Otherwise visitors were generally denied. Algernon Percy (by now duke of Northumberland) and later his widow continued their support, which the government supplemented by a civil-list pension. The first volume of the *Arabic–English Lexicon* appeared in 1863, followed by succeeding volumes at fairly regular intervals. Lane was working on the sixth volume at the time of his death. His great-nephew Stanley Lane-Poole supervised publication of the remaining volumes, the eighth and final one appearing in 1893. The *Lexicon*, a monumental work of nineteenth-century scholarship, remained an indispensable resource for scholars throughout the twentieth century. A second series of volumes that Lane had originally projected for rarer Arabic words was never composed.

Besides the works listed above, Lane published two essays in German—one on Arabic lexicography and the other on Arabic pronunciation—and he is considered to have been the anonymous author of a book about science and scripture. He also published a notable lithograph of the great pyramid in 1830, one of the few illustrations from his 'Description of Egypt' manuscript to appear during his lifetime. After Lane's death Stanley Lane-Poole selected notes from the *Thousand and one Nights* and published them under Lane's name as *Arabian Society in the Middle Ages* (1883). Another posthumous publication was *Cairo Fifty Years Ago* (1896) which consisted of revised chapters about Cairo from 'Description of Egypt'. Not until 2000 was a complete edition of *Description of Egypt* published. Lane was generally reluctant to accept honours—family tradition strongly hints that he refused a knighthood—but he received an honorary doctorate of literature from the University of Leiden and was a member of the German Oriental Society, the Royal Asiatic Society, the Royal Society of Literature, the Institut de France, and other learned institutions. He died on 10 August 1876 at his home in Worthing, survived by his wife, and was buried on 15 August in Norwood cemetery, London.

JASON THOMPSON

Sources L. Ahmed, *Edward W. Lane* (1978) • S. Lane-Poole, *Life of Edward William Lane* (1877) • A. J. Arberry, 'The lexicographer: Edward William Lane', *Oriental essays: portraits of seven scholars* (1960), 87–121 • A. Amin, 'Al-Sheykh al-Dessuki wa Mister Lane', *Fayd al-khatir* (Cairo, 1965), 39–50 • P. Stocks, 'Edward William Lane and his Arabic-English "thesaurus"', *British Library Journal*, 15

(1989), 23–34 • J. Thompson, 'Edward William Lane as Egyptologist', *Minerva*, 6 (1995), 12–17 • J. Thompson, 'Edward William Lane as an artist', *Gainsborough's House Review* (1993–4), 33–42 • J. Thompson, *Sir Gardner Wilkinson and his circle* (1992) • W. R. Dawson and E. P. Uphill, *Who was who in Egyptology*, 3rd edn, rev. M. L. Bierbrier (1995), 235 • J. Thompson, '"Of the Osmanlees or Turks": an unpublished chapter from Edward William Lane's *Manners and customs of the modern Egyptians*', *Turkish Studies Association Bulletin*, 19/2 (1995), 19–39 • J. Thompson, 'Edward William Lane in Egypt', *Journal of the American Research Center in Egypt*, 34 (1997), 243–61 • J. Thompson, 'Edward William Lane's "Description of Egypt"', *International Journal of Middle East Studies*, 28 (1996), 565–83 • d. cert. • private information (2004) • record, London borough of Lambeth, 15 Aug 1876 [burial] • E. W. Lane, draft of 'Description of Egypt', Bodl. Oxf., MS Eng. misc. d. 234, fol. 5

Archives BL, Add. MSS 34080–34088 • Bodl. Oxf. • CUL • NL Scot. • U. Oxf., Griffith Institute | Bodl. Oxf., letters to Robert Hay • Gainsborough's House, Sudbury, Gainsborough MSS • UCL, Society for the Diffusion of Useful Knowledge MSS

Likenesses E. W. Lane, self-portrait, sepia wash, 1826?, BL, Add. MS 34088, fol. 45 • portrait, 1826–34, repro. in Dawson, Uphill, and Bierbrier, *Who was who in Egyptology* • R. J. Lane, tinted pen-and-ink, 1828, priv. coll. • R. J. Lane, plaster statue, 1829, NPG [*see illus.*] • R. J. Lane, plaster bust, 1833, Bodl. Oxf. • R. J. Lane, pen-and-ink, 1835, St John's College, Oxford • C. S. Lane, watercolour, 1850, NPG • photograph, 1870–79, priv. coll. • metal engraving, 1876 (after photograph), repro. in *The Graphic* (26 Aug 1876) • R. J. Lane, lithograph, BM • wood-engraving (after R. J. Lane, *c*.1835), NPG; repro. in *ILN* (2 Sept 1876)

Wealth at death under £2000: administration, 22 Sept 1876, *CGPLA Eng. & Wales*

Lane [*née* Coulborn], **Dame Elizabeth Kathleen** (1905–1988), judge, was born on 9 August 1905 in Bowdon, Cheshire, the second of three children and only daughter of Edward Alexander Coulborn, mill owner at Bury in Lancashire, and his wife, Kate May Wilkinson. Her early years were spent in Bowdon and she was educated at home until the age of twelve. Her family moved to Switzerland in 1913, but returned in 1914 just before the outbreak of war. At Twizzletwig School in Hindhead and at Malvern Girls' College, she did not display any enthusiasm for academic studies, preferring to play games, especially hockey. Given the opportunity to study for Oxford or Cambridge, she decided not to embark on higher education and never regretted not going to university. She believed that, on leaving school, she would be 'done with academics and have a good time'.

In 1924 Elizabeth spent a year in Montreal with her elder brother, and there she met (Henry Jerrold) Randall Lane, whom she married in Didsbury parish church on 14 January 1926 when she was twenty. He was the son of a merchant of the same name. The couple went first to live in Manchester. Their only child, a son, was born in 1928. He was mentally disabled and died at the age of fourteen.

Her husband's decision to read for the bar changed Elizabeth Lane's entire life, and led to her distinguished career at the bar and on the bench. They read law together, and in 1940 she was called to the bar by the Inner Temple. She was elected a bencher in 1965. She quickly made a name for herself in a profession where few women were, at that time, in practice, and prejudice was hard to overcome. She joined the midland circuit and became a QC in 1950, only the third woman to do this. In turn she was an

assistant recorder of Birmingham (1953–61), the first woman recorder of Derby (1961–2), and a commissioner of the crown court at Manchester (1961–2). She also became a member of the Home Office committee on depositions in criminal cases in 1948 and chair of the Birmingham region mental health review tribunal (1960–62). In 1962 she was the first woman to be appointed a county court judge and she sat until 1965. She also sat as acting deputy chairman of London sessions.

In 1965 Elizabeth Lane was the first woman to be appointed to the High Court bench and was assigned to the Probate, Divorce, and Admiralty, later the Family Division. On her appointment she was made DBE, an honour corresponding to the knighthood customarily conferred upon male High Court judges. In court she concealed, under a stern and even intimidating exterior, a warm, kindly, and understanding approach to the problems of families in the throes of separation and divorce. She was particularly understanding of the needs of children. When she went on circuit she enjoyed the opportunity to try both civil and criminal cases, in which she was always courteous. She was short in stature and wore glasses; correct in manner, she was conservative in outlook. Essentially a shy and modest person, she seldom relaxed except in private, when she was with close friends. She was very much aware that she was setting standards for the women judges of the future. Her portrait, which hangs in the Inner Temple, shows a stern unbending mien, which was only part of her character. She was a kind and generous friend, with an excellent though rarely displayed sense of humour.

Between 1971 and 1973 Elizabeth Lane chaired the committee on the working of the Abortion Act, managing controversial and emotive problems with skill and understanding. Her report displayed a tolerant and unexpectedly liberal attitude.

Elizabeth Lane's husband, Randall, became legal adviser to the British Council. They were a devoted couple brought closer by the tragedy of their son. Randall was a great support to her in her career, and his death in 1975 was a very sad loss.

On her retirement in 1979 Elizabeth Lane left the Temple, where she had lived for many years, and moved to Winchester. There, at Hillcrest, 60 Chilbolton Avenue, she had a garden, which she had missed in London. From time to time she sat in the Court of Appeal and much enjoyed it. She was very proud when the western circuit made her an honorary member. She always encouraged young women contemplating a career at the bar. In 1986 she became an honorary fellow of Newnham College, Cambridge. She died in Winchester on 17 June 1988.

ELIZABETH BUTLER-SLOSS, rev.

Sources E. Lane, *Hear the other side* (1985) [autobiography] • *The Times* (18 June 1988) • *The Independent* (22 June 1988) • *WW* • private information (1996) • personal knowledge (1996) • *CGPLA Eng. & Wales* (1988)

Likenesses J. Whithall, oils, 1982, Inner Temple, London • photographs, Hult. Arch.

Wealth at death £413,293: probate, 17 Nov 1988, *CGPLA Eng. & Wales*

Lane, George, first Viscount Lanesborough (1620–1683), political administrator and politician, was born on 25 December 1620, the son of Sir Richard Lane, first baronet (*d.* 1668), of Tulske, co. Roscommon, and his second wife, Mabel, daughter and sole heir of Gerald Fitzgerald of Donore, co. Kildare. His grandfather George Lane had first gone to Ireland during the wars in Queen Elizabeth I's reign. In return for his services he was granted lands in counties Longford and Roscommon which provided the nucleus of the holdings subsequently enlarged by his successors. George Lane was admitted to Trinity College, Dublin, in 1638. Four years later he waited on Charles I at Oxford. By what means he came to the notice of the duke of Ormond, the king's lord lieutenant in Ireland, is unknown. However, probably by the spring of 1643 and certainly by 1644 he was acting as Ormond's secretary. In that capacity he was privy to the tortuous negotiations with the confederate Catholics in Kilkenny, the royal court in Oxford, and the Westminster parliament. With his fortunes so firmly linked to those of Ormond, Lane followed him into continental exile in 1650. Because of his intimacy with the duke, Lane was himself regarded as influential, not least because he could introduce suitors or their petitions to his master.

Richard Lane was connected through his mother, an O'Farrell, with a leading Catholic sept of the Irish midlands. His son, George, through his Fitzgerald mother, was part of an extensive kindred, much of which had remained Catholic. In addition, the Lanes, thanks to kinship and neighbourhood, traditionally looked to the Burkes, earls of Clanricarde, as their principal patrons in the region. In 1650 Ormond, when he quit Ireland, named the Catholic Clanricarde as his deputy. In turn, Richard Lane, mindful of his commission as sheriff of Roscommon in 1651, obeyed Clanricarde's orders and demolished his castle at Tulske. Earlier, in the 1640s, having handed Tulske to Lord Ranelagh, he had soldiered in Galway with Clanricarde. These continuing royalist affiliations meant that he was liable to forfeit much of his property. On 4 July 1656 the commissioners sitting at Loughreagh allowed him a third of what he had formerly enjoyed, but it was to be set out in a different barony of Roscommon. Somehow he eked out a penurious existence with others in similar straits. Some of the Lanes' relations, especially the O'Farrells, moved to the continent. There they entreated Secretary George Lane to intercede for them. Much of this period George spent in Paris and northern France, moving eventually with the court and Ormond to Brussels. Other than to act as a conduit through which those uprooted from the midlands could direct their requests, it is difficult to detect any distinctive stance adopted by Lane. As befitted the trusted secretary, he modestly performed the duties of amanuensis and mouthpiece. His abilities led to his employment as secretary to the king's council. In the intimate world of the exiles he built up understandings with Edward Hyde, future earl of Clarendon, and Edward Nicholas which would later prove useful. Richard Talbot, whom he first encountered in exile, would subsequently use Lane as an intermediary to overcome misunderstandings with Ormond.

Charles II's restoration brightened Lane's prospects. First in England and then, from July 1662, in Ireland, where Ormond had reoccupied the lord lieutenancy, Lane was inundated with business. Much of it related to the general settlement of Ireland and the Ormonds' tangled affairs. However, he did not neglect the opportunities to advance himself and his own. His father's sacrifices in the Stuart cause were recognized when, on 11 February 1661, he was created a baronet. Sir Richard Lane was chosen by the gentry of Roscommon to represent what they had suffered through transplantation. He sought for himself the collectorship of crown rents in counties Galway, Mayo, and Roscommon. In August 1662 a royal letter promised to restore the elder Lane to what he had lost. The younger Lane had already been knighted by the king in 1657 and granted the prestigious posts of clerk to the English privy council (in 1656), clerk of the Irish parliament, and protonotary and clerk of the crown in Ireland towards the end of the interregnum. After 1660 he enjoyed the salary, perquisites, and status which went with these posts. In 1662 he was returned, at a by-election, to the Irish House of Commons as knight of the shire for Roscommon. In the same year the Irish parliament granted him £2000 in recognition of his recent services and past sufferings. Under his long-time master, Ormond, he thrived.

In September 1664 Lane was permitted to surrender his clerkship in England (he sold it to another Irish protestant, Robert Southwell) so that he could concentrate on Irish business. In 1663 he was made secretary to the council of war in Ireland and keeper of the public records stored in the Bermingham Tower of Dublin Castle. The latter was a sensitive post, so much so that in 1669 Lane was accused of removing documents without proper authority. In November 1664 he was sworn of the Irish privy council. More solid still was the special provision made for him in the land settlement—generosity which later was criticized. In addition to his estates in the midlands he acquired at least another 8615 acres scattered across five counties. At Rathcline in co. Longford he erected and furnished a mansion of considerable grandeur. Of necessity, with his official duties, much of his time was passed in Dublin. He was much concerned with framing and executing the land settlement. It gave him ample opportunity for personal profit and earned him a reputation for venality. In Dublin, too, he had added considerably to his holdings, and dwelt in a substantial house. So closely was he identified with Ormond that the latter's dismissal in 1669 reduced Lane's power. Ormond's successor sought to suppress the secretaryship of war. By 1674 the post, which some had contended was an unprecedented one, was being treated simply as secretaryship of state for Ireland. As late as 1676 Lane was bargaining over the terms on which he would lay it down. A pension for his son and a viscountcy—of Lanesborough—for himself were the prices. Ormond later claimed that he had bestirred himself to obtain this honour for Lane in 1676. Unfortunately the viscountcy did not satisfy his former secretary, who wanted to be advanced to an earldom. Such grandiloquent hopes were not to be fulfilled. The Lanes' revenues, notwithstanding the recent supplements, yielded no more than £2000–3000 p.a., which by conventional reckoning could not support an earldom. Ormond, in advising thus, incurred Lane's enmity. Lane was left out of the civil establishment in 1683, an affront alleged to have hastened his death later that year. In vain Ormond had sought to reassure him 'that I have all the value and affection for him that a man can have for such a friend as he would trust his life and honour with' (Ormond to Arran, 9 June 1683, *Ormonde MSS*, 7.41).

Lane married three times. The brides indicated his progress from provincial Ireland into the noble society of Restoration England. His first wife was Dorcas, second daughter of Sir Anthony Brabazon, brother of the first earl of Meath. Possibly this match was contracted about April 1638 when Richard Lane entailed property on his heir. The Brabazons had origins in Ireland similar to those of the Lanes. Next, in March 1655, he married Susanna (*b.* 1627), a daughter of his colleague in exile the English secretary, Sir Edward Nicholas. After her death on 18 July 1671, he married Lady Frances Sackville, daughter of the earl of Dorset, with whose family the Orrerys had also recently allied.

On his estates around Rathcline and in the nearby borough of Lanesborough, Lane endeavoured to create English and protestant communities. In 1677 he was enlarging the protestant church there. The little that he had accomplished would be largely destroyed during the Williamite wars. Through lineage and connection he remained close to the formerly dominant Irish Catholic families of the area, notably the Nangles and O'Farrells. In addition, despite his devotion to the house of Ormond, he prided himself on his relationship to the Burkes and Fitzgeralds. But such links with Catholic Ireland did not prevent Lane from being reviled for obstructing the dispossessed when they sought reinstatement in the 1660s. To other critics his own personal rewards and his intimacies in Gaelic and Catholic Ireland exemplified what was thought to be wrong with Ormond's lax Irish administration. He died at Lanesborough on 11 December 1683.   TOBY BARNARD

Sources NL Ire., Lane MSS 8641–8646 · NL Ire., MS 16974 · Lane case papers, PRO, C 106/104–6 · Lane case papers, PRO, C 106/153, boxes 1 and 2 · Bodl. Oxf., MSS Carte, MSS Clarendon · *Calendar of the manuscripts of the marquess of Ormonde*, new ser., 8 vols., HMC, 36 (1902–20), esp. vol. 7 · GEC, *Peerage*, 7.422 · *CSP Ire.*, 1676–7, 29, 31, 236 · F. E. Ball, 'Some notes on the households of the duke of Ormond', *Proceedings of the Royal Irish Academy*, 38C (1928–9), 1–20 · *The Nicholas papers*, ed. G. F. Warner, 4 vols., CS, new ser., 40, 50, 57, 3rd ser., 31 (1886–1920) · T. C. Barnard, 'The protestant interest', *Ireland from independence to occupation*, ed. J. Ohlmeyer (1995) · T. Barnard and J. Fenlon, eds., *The dukes of Ormonde, 1610–1745* (2000) · R. C. Simington, *The transplantation to Connacht, 1654–58*, IMC (1970), 277 · Burtchaell & Sadleir, *Alum. Dubl.*, 480

Archives NL Ire., MSS 8641–8646 · PRO, C 106/104–6 · PRO, C 106/153 | BL, letters to Sir Edward Nicholas and Sir John Nicholas, Egerton MSS 2535–2539, *passim* · BL, corresp. with Robert Southwell, Add. MS 78015, *passim* · Bodl. Oxf., Carte MSS · Bodl. Oxf., Clarendon MSS

Lane, Sir Hugh Percy (1875–1915), art dealer and collector, was born on 9 November 1875 in Ballybrack House, Douglas, a suburb of Cork. His father, the Revd James William Lane (1847–1910), came from a middle-class family of lawyers and businessmen and, after ordination into the Church of England, later held parishes in Yorkshire, in Bath, and in Redruth, Cornwall. His mother, Frances Adelaide (1840–1909), was the daughter of Dudley Persse of Roxborough House, near Loughrea, one of the leading gentry of south Galway. Hugh was one of eight children born between 1870 and 1884, two of whom died young. Money worries and personality clashes drove his parents apart in the mid-1880s and this marital rupture affected Hugh, the only child born in Ireland, who shuttled back and forth between his father in Cornwall and his mother as she moved from Cork to Paris, Plymouth, and Dublin. Lack of stable parenting and money as well as poor health ruled out any formal schooling and private tutors at home brought him no closer to a university education. However, he did meet some of the luminaries of the Irish literary revival during a summer holiday at the home of his aunt, (Isabella) Augusta *Gregory, Lady Gregory, Coole Park, near Gort, co. Galway.

Move to London In 1893, at the age of seventeen, Lane found a job in London through his aunt, working for the art dealer Martin Henry Colnaghi (1821–1908), who owned the Marlborough Gallery. There the lowly apprentice cleaned paintings and ran errands for £1 a week while learning the rules of the art dealer's game. Albeit ignorant of European history, he had a flair for discerning value in old masters. If his charm impressed many customers, it grated on Colnaghi, who considered him a social climber and sacked him in May 1894. Undaunted by this rebuff, Lane went to work for Morley Turner, who ran the Carlton Gallery in Pall Mall. However, Lane soon fell out with Turner over money matters and their quarrel ended up in the courts, where Lane argued his case without benefit of a lawyer and won.

In February 1898 Lane opened his own gallery at 2 Pall Mall Place, where he sold modest paintings for immodest prices. Bereft of capital and living a spartan life, he gradually increased his inventory and profits, while earning a reputation as a shrewd gentleman-dealer. Although some rivals wrote him off as 'a damned amateur' (Lady Gregory, *Sir Hugh Lane*, 31), they had to concede his ability to spot a bargain and then sell it for four or five times what he had paid. Once he recognized a Franz Hals underneath layers of 'foreign matter'. Later he discovered a George Romney portrait beneath a Victorian one. At a Christies sale he bought Titian's *Portrait of a Man in a Red Cap* (now in the Frick Collection) for £2000 and then sold it to Arthur Grenfell for £25,000. Growing prosperity enabled him to move from Duke Street to Jermyn Street, where he lived above the ground-floor showroom. In the summer of 1900 he spent several weeks at Coole consorting with the writers and visionaries of Lady Gregory's circle, who in Yeats's fine trope 'came like swallows and like swallows went' (W. B. Yeats, 'Coole Park', 1929).

Having outgrown the Jermyn Street premises, Lane

Sir Hugh Percy Lane (1875–1915), by Antonio Mancini, exh. Royal Society of Painters 1907

decided in 1907 to share a rented house in South Bolton Gardens with William Orpen, the gifted Irish artist and a distant cousin. Despite their marked differences in temperament and taste, they remained lifelong friends. Orpen enjoyed a boisterous bohemian night-life, whereas Lane relished small and elegant dinner parties with élite guests. Orpen bestowed on him the nickname Petticoat—an allusion to Petticoat Lane, the famous East End street where secondhand goods were bought and sold. Generous to a fault with his friends, Lane preferred to buy *objets d'art* or jewellery for good friends rather than waste money on a decent lunch or a taxi for himself. In 1909 the need for more privacy and space induced him to buy the west wing of Lindsey House, an imposing town house overlooking the Thames Embankment at 100 Cheyne Walk, Chelsea. He commissioned Sir Edwin Lutyens to redesign the garden and Augustus John agreed to paint some 'decorative pictures' in the hall, but the two men quarrelled and 'the brilliant … designs' were never finished (Bodkin, 25). Serving as a private art gallery, museum, and residence as well as a saleroom, Lindsey House became a centre of cultural and social activity where the rich and famous could dine in lavish surroundings and admire the paintings and sculptures. If they took a fancy to one, they might tender a price and close the deal with a glass of good wine or champagne. In 1911 Lane proposed marriage to the daughter of an Irish aristocrat, Lady Clare Annesley of Castlewellan, who was only eighteen at the time. But the age gap proved too much and she broke off the engagement. By then a talented Irish artist, Sarah Cecilia Harrison, had fallen in love with Lane and dreamed of marrying him even though she was thirteen years older. But Lane's early death dashed all her chances, if not her dreams.

The Dublin gallery project Lane's chief claim to fame arose out of his ambition to educate the Irish people about modern continental and British art. No matter how cosmopolitan London made him, he could not forget his native country and like W. B. Yeats he wanted to enrich the aesthetic life of his countrymen. He also aspired to stir 'sleepy Irish artists … to do great things' (Lady Gregory, *Hugh Lane's Life and Achievement*, 44). In short, he set his sights on endowing Dublin with a gallery and a collection of modern and contemporary art worthy of the city. An exhibition of paintings by Nathaniel Hone and John Butler Yeats in Dublin in October 1901 opened his eyes to the talent of some living Irish artists and he commissioned Yeats to paint some of Ireland's leading citizens—a task completed by his young rival William Orpen. Had Lane continued to sell pictures to the new rich, he could easily have become another Agnew, Colnaghi, or Duveen. But his need for a greater challenge than making money spurred him to invest ever more energy, time, and wealth in the Dublin gallery project.

In the winter of 1902–3 Lane mounted an exhibition of old masters in the Royal Hibernian Academy, Dublin, after promising to underwrite all the expenses not covered by the admission fee. Backed by aristocratic patrons, this exhibition attracted many visitors. In 1904 he assembled some recent Irish paintings for display at the St Louis World Fair. But when the cost of insurance proved prohibitive, he exhibited them in London's Guildhall during May and June. The success of this show reinforced his desire to create a gallery of modern art in Dublin that would include the work of prominent Irish artists on the grounds that 'if we are to have a distinct school of painting in Ireland … it is one's contemporaries that teach one the most' (Arnold, 137). Lane learned that the superb collection of modern French and Dutch art owned by the late railway magnate James Staats Forbes was to be sold to a museum of art. Much impressed by the works of the Barbizon school in this collection—especially the Corots, Courbets, and Millets—he went to Paris with Orpen in September 1904 to study and buy some pictures from the notable art dealer and patron of the impressionists Paul Durand-Ruel. There he acquired Manet's *Portrait d'Eva Gonzalès* and Renoir's *Les parapluies* (National Gallery, London). On his return to London he arranged with the executors of the Staats Forbes estate to borrow 164 pictures for his exhibition of modern art that opened in November 1904 at the Royal Hibernian Academy of Painting, Sculpture, and Architecture in Lower Abbey Street, Dublin. Emboldened by this success, he formed a committee of art patrons who selected eighty-five paintings and drawings for display at the National Museum in Kildare Street in May 1905. Seventy-nine of these came from the Staats Forbes collection. To achieve his mission of endowing Dublin with a gallery of modern art, Lane urged his wealthy friends to buy these works for the permanent collection and encouraged Irish artists to contribute a few of their own works. He also promised to give his own modern paintings to the proposed gallery so long as the corporation paid for at least half the project and found a suitable site. At his prompting the prince of Wales, afterwards George V, commemorated his recent visit to Dublin by subscribing £1000 for the purchase of two Constables and two Corots from the Staats Forbes collection. Later the princess of Wales donated a third Constable to the cause. Lane told the corporation that he would find buyers for as many of the Staats Forbes pictures as possible, which would form the core of the gallery's holdings.

Following on the heels of this triumph, Lane exhibited some 143 modern pictures at the Free Library in Belfast during the spring of 1906. He had already organized a committee of art patrons in Dublin to raise funds for the new gallery. Besides his conversion to French modernism, he also wanted to promote what he called 'the common race instinct' in Irish art (Arnold, 139).

Despite these achievements Lane was passed over for the directorship of the National Museum of Science and Art in Kildare Street in favour of 'a safe man' (George Noble, Count Plunkett). Notwithstanding this setback, he continued to lobby for a municipal gallery of modern and contemporary art near St Stephen's Green. In 1907 the Dublin corporation finally obliged by offering him the former town house of the earls of Clonmell at 17 Harcourt Street, along with an annual grant of £500 for operating costs. Despite the poor lighting and leaky roof, Lane made the best of this compromise while insisting on free admission and evening hours for working people. Of the 280 works of art on display, some seventy of the British and French paintings belonged to the sponsor, as did John Singer Sargent's masterly portrait of Lane (1906; Hugh Lane Municipal Gallery of Modern Art, Dublin) for which his friends and admirers had paid in recognition of all that he had done for Irish art. As Orpen put it, Lane was not just a genius but a '"freak", a wonder person … a force one could not withstand. He used us all like little puppets, and we loved him and worked for him gladly' (Orpen, 49).

After receiving the freedom of the city of Dublin in 1908, Lane was honoured with a knighthood in the king's birthday honours in 1909 for his services to Irish art. And yet Lane had many detractors. Besides the Irish Ireland disciples of D. P. Moran, who resented his patrician bearing, Anglo-Irish origins, and aesthetic taste, there was Maud Gonne, who told her friend John Quinn, the New York lawyer and art collector, that Lane was a mercenary 'cur' or a swindler who preyed on poor artists and rich collectors and who had gained his knighthood by pretending to donate his French pictures to Ireland while looking for a better deal in London (Too Long a Sacrifice, 109). Quite apart from his Irish mission, Lane aided and abetted the cause of fine art in South Africa by procuring a number of modern pictures for the new art museum in Johannesburg. While delivering this consignment in person in 1910, he met General Jan Smuts, who convinced him that the National Gallery in Cape Town deserved a collection of Dutch and Flemish old masters. Lane promptly went to work and by 1913 he had bought and shipped out some sixty-eight paintings that were paid for by the South African millionaire Max Michaelis.

The inadequacies of the Harcourt Street location forced Lane to redouble his efforts on behalf of a new gallery. On 5 November 1912 he informed the lord mayor that he would withdraw his French pictures at the end of January 1913 unless the corporation found a suitable site. In response, a Dublin citizens' committee held several packed meetings at the Mansion House, where prominent supporters appealed for funds to match the £22,000 pledged by the corporation. A vigorous letter-writing campaign and a fund-raising trip to America by Lady Gregory brought in only about £11,000 of the estimated £45,000 needed for the building.

After Lord Ardilaun vetoed Lane's plan to place the gallery in the middle of St Stephen's Green, several other locations were considered before Lane embraced the bold idea of an Uffizi-like museum that would span the Liffey in place of the metal bridge. Lutyens agreed to design an imposing structure with a pillared portico arching over the river. While Lane expected this building to revitalize central Dublin, his critics dismissed the scheme as much too daring and costly. They also worried about the moisture and the noxious fumes rising from the river that would permeate the gallery. The rich and ruthless businessman William Martin Murphy announced in the papers that he 'would rather see in the City of Dublin one block of sanitary houses at low rents replacing a reeking slum than all the pictures Corot and Degas ever painted' (O'Brien, 54). At last, in September 1913 the corporation vetoed the Lane–Lutyens project to the great dismay and anger of Lady Gregory's circle. When this news reached a distraught Lane in London he ordered all his French paintings to be packed up and sent to the National Gallery in London.

On 11 October 1913 Lane drew up a will bequeathing his Sargent portrait and the paintings then on exhibition in Belfast to the Dublin Municipal Gallery and leaving his thirty-nine French pictures to the National Gallery in London. Four months later he was appointed director of the National Gallery of Ireland. Generous to the end, he donated his salary of £500 to a fund for purchasing new pictures and presented half a dozen old masters to the museum. Then on 3 February 1915 he amended his will in what Lady Gregory called 'his codicil of forgiveness' (Lady Gregory, Case for the Return of Sir Hugh Lane's Pictures to Dublin, 7), wherein he gave his French pictures to the city of Dublin 'providing that a suitable building is provided for them within 5 years of my death'. If no gallery had been built by that date, then the pictures were to be sold and the proceeds used to 'fulfil the purpose of my will'. He also appointed Lady Gregory his sole trustee. Unfortunately the lack of a witness deprived this document of any legal authority.

Death and reputation The rest is history, or tragedy—or both. In mid-April 1915 Lane boarded the *Lusitania* at Liverpool bound for New York where he was scheduled to testify in a court case involving paintings damaged in a shipboard fire. On the eve of sailing he told his closest friend

Alexander (Alec) Martin (later managing director of Christies) that he wished to leave his French pictures to the country he loved so fervently. On the return voyage a German submarine sank the *Lusitania* on 7 May off the Old Head of Kinsale not far from Lane's birthplace. Lane was among the 1200 people who drowned. He was last seen helping women and children into a lifeboat. Although a kinsman circulated a flyer with a photograph and description of his features, clothing, and jewellery, his body was never found. Many of his close friends and clients attended his memorial service at Chelsea Old Church on 20 May. He left an estate valued at £50,000 excluding his pictures in Lindsey House (worth at least £100,000). Besides modest legacies to his two brothers and sister, he bequeathed his personal effects to family and friends.

Because the British courts refused to recognize the codicil to his will, Lane's French pictures remained in storage in the National Gallery, London, before they were transferred to the Tate. A grief-stricken Lady Gregory devoted the rest of her life to lobbying for the return of these works to Dublin. But neither her entreaties nor those of prominent writers and artists in Dublin and London moved the British government to surrender the collection. In 1933 the Municipal Gallery found a new home in Charlemont House in Rutland Square, Dublin, which the taoiseach, Eamon de Valera, opened on 19 June. Not until November 1959 did the British and Irish governments agree to divide the collection into two groups that would alternate between London and Dublin for five-year periods. After a new round of negotiations in 1979 some thirty pictures remained in Dublin for the next fourteen years. Then in 1993 the Hugh Lane Gallery (so named in 1977) won possession of thirty-one pictures, while the other eight (including two by Manet, a Monet, a Degas, and a Renoir) alternated between the two cities at intervals.

Slight of build, dapper in dress, sharp of tongue, and always on the lookout for good deals, Lane made his share of enemies. His obsession with beautiful paintings, along with an inborn self-confidence, struck many as arrogance. Loving a good fight over issues that mattered, he paid a high price at times in terms of severe emotional distress. His warmth and the presents lavished on close friends inspired lasting devotion. At times he echoed Oscar Wilde by exclaiming: 'I have nothing but my taste' (Lady Gregory, *Sir Hugh Lane*, 8). But of course he also had an abundance of ambition, energy, money, connection, and courage. Frugal to the point of walking around London to save a cab fare, he drained his fortune on behalf of the municipal gallery. Afflicted with insomnia, he relaxed only when riding in Hyde Park or the countryside, playing the piano, adorning the hair of his lady friends with jewels, or stroking his beloved Pekinese dog Tinko. Owners of country houses sought him out to appraise their works of art. As Daisy, countess of Fingall observed, 'he loved beautiful things—old things especially—and would fall down and worship a picture or a piece of china' (Elizabeth, countess of Fingall, 264).

Despite his passion for French impressionism, there were strict limits to Lane's modernism. He had no time for fauvism or cubism, and dismissed Picasso's paintings as so much 'rubbish'. In his eyes the post-Monet generation lacked 'sanity, normality and health' as well as 'honesty' (Reid, 223–4). Years later W. B. Yeats celebrated Lane as an 'impetuous' man, who 'found pride established in humility' (W. B. Yeats, *Coole Park, 1929*). But Augustus John delivered the ultimate tribute by hailing him as 'one of those rare ones who, single-handed, are able to enrich and dignify an entire nation' (*Lady Gregory's Journals*, 47).

L. PERRY CURTIS JUN.

Sources Lady Gregory, *Sir Hugh Lane: his life and legacy*, Coole Edition (1973) · Lady Gregory, *Hugh Lane's life and achievement, with some account of the Dublin galleries* (1921) · T. Bodkin, *Hugh Lane and his pictures*, 1st edn (Dublin, 1932); 2nd edn (Dublin, 1956) · R. O'Byrne, *Hugh Lane, 1875–1915* (Dublin, 2000) · B. Dawson, 'Hugh Lane and the origins of the collection', *Images and insights*, ed. E. Mayes and P. Murphy (Dublin, 1993), 12–32 · B. Arnold, *Orpen: mirror to an age* (1981) · S. B. Kennedy, *Irish art and modernism, 1880–1950* (1991) [exhibition catalogue, Hugh Lane Municipal Gallery of Modern Art, Dublin, 20 Sept – 10 Nov 1991 and Ulster Museum, Belfast, 22 Nov 1991 – 26 Jan 1992] · *Tribute to Sir Hugh Lane* (Cork, 1961) · R. F. Foster, *The apprentice mage, 1865–1914* (1997), vol. 1 of *W. B. Yeats: a life* · D. T. Torchiana, *W. B. Yeats and Georgian Ireland* (Evanston, 1966) · A. Norman Jeffares, *W. B. Yeats: a new biography* (1989) · B. L. Reid, *The man from New York: John Quinn and his friends* (New York, 1968) · J. Brown, *Lutyens and the Edwardians: an English architect and his clients* (1996) · W. Orpen, *Stories of old Ireland and myself* (1925) · M. Holroyd, *Augustus John: the new biography* (1996) · J. V. O'Brien, '*Dear, dirty Dublin': a city in distress, 1899–1916* (1982) · M. L. Kohfeldt, *Lady Gregory: the woman behind the Irish renaissance* (New York, 1985) · J. Rothenstein, *The Tate Gallery* (1958) · Elizabeth, countess of Fingall, *Seventy years young* (1937) · *Too long a sacrifice: the letters of Maud Gonne and John Quinn*, ed. J. Londraville and R. Londraville (1999) · *The Gonne–Yeats letters, 1893–1938*, ed. A. MacBride White and A. N. Jeffares (1992) · *Lady Gregory's journals, 1916–1930*, ed. L. Robinson (1946), 5, pp. 283–317 · G. Moore, *Hail and farewell: ave, salve, vale*, ed. R. A. Cave, 2nd edn, 2 vols. (1925); repr. in 1 vol. (1976), pt 3 · *The collected poems of W. B. Yeats*, [new edn] (1965) · *The collected letters of W. B. Yeats*, 3, ed. J. Kelly and R. Schuchard (1994) · D. R. Pearce, ed., *The senate speeches of W. B. Yeats* (Bloomington, 1960) · I. J. Rice (law agent for the Dublin corporation), 'Statement of the Rt. Hon. lord mayor, aldermen, and burgesses of Dublin … to the committee appointed to consider the disposition of the late Sir Hugh Lane's French pictures', 25 Aug 1924, NL Ire., MS 10908 · *The Times* (8 May 1915) · *The Times* (10 May 1915)

Archives NL Ire., Hugh Lane Gallery archive, corresp. · NL Ire., papers, MS 10929; 13071–13072 · NL Ire., papers, MS 15, 750; MS 5073 | NYPL, Berg collection, Lady Gregory papers · TCD, corresp. with Thomas Bodkin · U. Glas. L., letters to D. S. MacColl

Likenesses J. B. Yeats, pencil drawing, 1905, NL Ire.; repro. in Bodkin, *Hugh Lane*, pl. 2 · S. Harrison, oils, c.1906, NG Ire. · J. Sargent, oils, 1906, Hugh Lane Gallery, Dublin · A. Mancini, oils, exh. Royal Society of Painters 1907, Hugh Lane Gallery, Dublin [*see illus.*] · W. Orpen, pen-and-ink caricature, 1907, NPG · W. Orpen, sketch, 1907 (*Lane's dinner party*), repro. in Arnold, *Orpen*, 247 · caricature, 1907, repro. in Foster, *W. B. Yeats* · G. C. Beresford, photograph, 1909, NPG, Hugh Lane Gallery, Dublin · W. Orpen, group portrait, oils, 1909 (*Homage to Manet*), Man. City Gall. · G. Kelly, oils, 1914, Crawford Art Gallery, Cork · photograph, c.1914, repro. in Gregory, *Sir Hugh Lane* · photograph, c.1914, repro. in [C. Lane], 'Lost on the Lusitania—Sir Hugh Lane', *The Times* (c.81915–10 May 1915) · M. Beerbohm, caricature, Hugh Lane Gallery, Dublin · S. Keating, oils, Hugh Lane Gallery, Dublin · W. Orpen, crayon sketch, repro. in Arnold, *Orpen*, 48 · W. Orpen, ink caricature, NG Ire. · A. Power, marble bust?, Hugh Lane Gallery, Dublin • photograph, repro. in Arnold, *Orpen* • photograph, repro. in C. Fahy, *W. B. Yeats and his circle* (1989)

Wealth at death £50,000 plus approximately £100,000 for pictures in Lindsey House, Chelsea

Lane, James Hunter (1806/7–1853), physician and medical journalist, was admitted a licentiate of the Royal College of Surgeons of Edinburgh in 1829, and graduated MD at Edinburgh University in 1830.

Lane was honorary physician to the Cholera Hospital, Liverpool, during the epidemic of 1831–2, for which he received the thanks of the board of health, and he was physician to the Lock Hospital of the infirmary there in 1833. In 1834 he collaborated with James Manby Gully in a translation, *A Systematic Treatise on Comparative Physiology*, from the German of Frederick Tiedemann of Heidelberg. Lane contributed many articles to the medical papers, and for some time edited the *Liverpool Gazette*, which later became the *Monthly Archives of the Medical Sciences*. In so doing he became well known for his 'outspoken and fearless criticism' on health questions. In 1840 he was appointed senior physician of the Lancaster Infirmary, and in the same year he brought out his *Compendium of materia medica and pharmacy, adapted to the London pharmacopoeia, embodying all the new French, American, and Indian medicines, and also comprising a summary of practical toxicology*. This was a work of considerable worth in its day. Lane was shortly afterwards elected president of the Royal Medical Society of Edinburgh. He was also a fellow of the Linnean Society.

For the last few years of his life Lane lived in London at 58 Brook Street, Grosvenor Square, and had an excellent practice. His death at Chain Pier Lodge, Brighton, on 23 June 1853, was caused by ascites.

THOMAS SECCOMBE, *rev.* PATRICK WALLIS

Sources *GM*, 2nd ser., 40 (1853), 420 • *London and Provincial Medical Directory* (1854) • *Nomina eorum, qui gradum medicinae doctoris in academia Jacobi sexti Scotorum regis, quae Edinburgi est, adepti sunt, ab anno 1705 ad annum 1845*, University of Edinburgh (1846) • T. H. Bickerton and R. M. B. MacKenna, *A medical history of Liverpool from the earliest days to the year 1920*, ed. H. R. Bickerton (1936) • d. cert.

Lane, Jane, Lady Fisher (d. 1689), royalist heroine, was the third daughter of Thomas Lane (1585–1660) and Anne Bagot (b. 1589, d. in or after 1651), who married at Blithfield, Staffordshire, on 10 February 1610. Her father, 'a person of excellent reputation', resided at Bentley Hall, near Wolverhampton, and had 'a fair estate' (Clarendon, *Hist. rebellion*, 5.199) worth £700 a year, while her mother was the sister of Sir Hervey *Bagot (1591–1660) [see under Bagot family (per. c.1490–1705)], a wealthy baronet and MP for Staffordshire in the Long Parliament. Both families were royalists during the civil war. Thomas Lane served as a commissioner of array in 1642–3, while Jane's eldest brother, John, fought in the king's army as the colonel of a cavalry regiment and in 1643–4 was successively governor of Charles I's garrisons in Stafford and Rushall Hall. In May 1644 Bentley Hall was extensively looted by parliamentary forces.

Jane Lane, Lady Fisher (d. 1689), by unknown artist, c.1660

Following his defeat at the battle of Worcester on 3 September 1651, Charles II went into hiding, and by 8 September was at Moseley Hall, a few miles from Bentley. Having availed himself of a pass which Jane had recently obtained from the parliamentary governor of Stafford to visit a pregnant kinswoman, Ellen Norton, at Abbots Leigh near Bristol, he accompanied her as a manservant, under the assumed name of William Jackson. After spending the night at Bentley, Charles set off on the morning of 10 September, mounted on horseback before 'Mistress Lane'. According to an account published at the Restoration, over the next week the king's protectress 'comported herself with extraordinary prudence and fidelity' (Eglesfield, 212), particularly in the streets of Stratford upon Avon, where she and her royal companion collided with a troop of parliamentarian cavalry, a moment of extreme danger which she surmounted by a cool composure. As one contemporary ballad had it:

In vain ye search, Bloodthirsty Men, to find
Vailed Majesty; her Virtue makes you blind;
Her faith out-acts your Malice; and your swords
(Broadley, 219)

As they were accommodated at various inns on their southward progress, 'the loyal lady' (Eglesfield, 212) was always extremely solicitous about Charles's welfare, making sure that 'a good bed' was 'provided for him' and that he received the best food, 'which she often carried herself' to his chamber (Clarendon, *Hist. rebellion*, 5.202). Her solicitude was equally on display during his four-day sojourn at Abbots Leigh, and her quick thinking provided an excuse for Charles to move on to Trent, Somerset, despite the distraction of Mistress Norton's serious illness following a miscarriage. She counterfeited a letter to the effect that her father's serious illness required her immediate departure for Bentley, a ploy which worked admirably. After accompanying Charles to Trent, on 18 September she returned to Staffordshire, only to be forced to take flight herself when on 14 October information about her involvement in his escape was presented to the council of state. While troops fruitlessly searched Bentley Hall, she trudged on foot, disguised as 'a country wench' (Dauncey, 146), to Yarmouth, from where she took ship to France.

When Jane arrived in Paris in mid-December 1651, she was welcomed by the English court in exile. Charles, who had landed in France two months before, greeted her with the salutation 'Welcome my life' (Eglesfield, 233) and conveyed her in his own coach to the Louvre to meet Henrietta Maria, with whom she developed a particularly close relationship. She was reputed a woman of 'an acute wit' and 'an excellent disputant', though no beauty, and all the émigré royalists were said to 'extremely adore her' (*French Intelligencer*, 5, 16–23 Dec 1651, 36), including John Evelyn and his wife, whom she visited on 21 December. Although *Mercurius Politicus* reported on 16 December that as 'a firm Presbyterian' (p. 1283) she refused to attend prayer book services with the king, he still held her 'in great esteem', and such was the 'merry discourse' (*French Intelligencer*, 5, 16–23 Dec 1651, 36) between them that in March 1652 Sir John Finch reported a rumour that she had become Charles's mistress. This was probably false, though in several letters of May and June 1655 Charles's sister Mary, princess of Orange, referred to her in jest as his 'wife', while in March 1656 his aunt Elizabeth of Bohemia informed him of 'a wittie' but 'foolish' and 'malicious' libel circulating in The Hague that his former preserver 'lay with your Majestie' (Thurloe, *State papers*, 1.674). Jane herself was alleged to have brushed aside 'this ogley bisness', convinced of her own 'good carettor' and hoping that her detractors would not diminish her standing with the king 'which shall be the study of my wholl [life] to preserve' (Broadley, 34).

By autumn 1652 Jane had entered the service of the princess of Orange, probably at the instigation of Charles, who wrote to her from Paris of his great debt to her. The princess proved a 'most obliging' employer, for which she was thanked by Charles (*Clarendon State Papers*, 1786, 3.153); Jane was one of her attendants when she visited Frankfurt with Charles in October 1655. By this time, however, Jane claimed he was neglecting her, an accusation he denied. Having returned to The Hague, in July 1656 she was courted by Lord Newburgh, but this came to nothing.

At the Restoration the king granted Jane an annual pension of £1000 and gave her many gifts, including portraits and a lock of his hair. On 19 December 1660 parliament, in gratitude for her service to the monarchy, gave her £1000 to purchase a jewel. Two years later, on 8 December 1662, Gilbert Sheldon, bishop of London, conducted her marriage to Sir Clement Fisher (*bap.* 1613, *d.* 1683), baronet, of Packington, Warwickshire, MP for Coventry. Fisher had served as a captain in her brother John's regiment during the first civil war and had played host to him and Lord Wilmot as they shadowed Charles during his journey to

Abbots Leigh in 1651. The Fishers had no children. After Sir Clement's death on 15 April 1683 Lady Fisher remained at Packington. By Lady day that year her state pension had fallen £6500 in arrears; this and her own extravagance placed her considerably in debt. She died on 9 September 1689, allegedly leaving 'but £10 behind' and observing that 'her hands should be her executors' (Burrows); she was buried at Packington three days later. The most famous of several surviving portraits of Jane depicts her allegorically with the crown of England in her right hand, over which she has partially drawn her lace veil to conceal it from the danger posed by a hydra (the Rump Parliament?) looming up on her left side.   JOHN SUTTON

Sources T. Blount, *Boscobel*, pt 1 (1660), pt 2 (1681) · F. Eglesfield, *Monarchy revived* (1660), dedication and pp. 212, 233 · J. Dauncey, *The history of his sacred majesty Charles II* (1660), 145–7 · [T. Birch and R. F. Williams], eds., *The court and times of Charles the First*, 2 (1848), 389–93 · Clarendon, *Hist. rebellion*, 5.199–205 · R. Plot, *The natural history of Staffordshire* (1686), 307 · D. Lloyd, *Eikon Basilike, or, The true pourtraiture of his sacred majestie Charls II*, 3 vols. in 1 (1660), vol. 2, p. 70 · M. A. E. Green, *Lives of the princesses of England*, 6 (1855), 229 · A. M. Broadley, *The royal miracle* (1912) · A. Fea, *The flight of the king after the battle of Worcester* (1897) · W. Matthews, ed., *Charles II's escape from Worcester* (1967) · C. Penruddock, *Mistress Jane Lane* (1995) · H. M. Lane, *The Lanes of Bentley* (1898) · G. Wrottesley, 'History of the Lane family', *Staffordshire Historical Collections* (1910), 186–8 · A. M. Mimardière, 'Fisher, Sir Clement', HoP, *Commons, 1660–90* · A. Bryant, ed., *The letters, speeches and declarations of King Charles II*, 2nd edn (1968), 25–6, 38 · M. Burrows, ed., *Collectanea: second series*, OHS, 16 (1890), 394

Archives LPL, MSS, vol. 646, fol. 59 | BL, letters to queen of Bohemia, Add. MS 63744, fols. 6, 15, 18, 24, 34, 57 · William Salt Library, Stafford, Salt MS 542

Likenesses oils, 1652?, repro. in Fea, *Flight of the king*, facing p. 252; formerly at King Bromley Hall, Staffordshire · P. Lely?, oils, *c.*1660, repro. in Fea, *Flight of the king*, facing p. 256; formerly at Packington Hall, Warwickshire · oils, *c.*1660, NPG [*see illus.*] · I. Fuller, double portrait, oils, *c.*1670 (with Charles II), NPG · engraving (with the king), repro. in Dauncey, *The history of his sacred majesty most wonderful preservation after the battle of Worcester*

Wealth at death £10

Lane, John (*fl.* 1600–1630), poet, is of unknown parentage, though he may have been born in Somerset as this is the residence of at least three of his friends: Matthew Jefferies, master of choristers at Wells Cathedral, George Hancocke, and Sir Thomas Wyndham of Kentsford. Further, in *Tritons Trumpet* (1621) Lane contrasts his 'western *Poetrie*' to 'eastern *Tussers* husbandry … as drewe fro *Somerset*, us to his queere'. In the dedication to his 1616 continuation of Chaucer's *Squire's Tale* he relates that he has had no university education.

The earliest date for Lane is given in an aside by Anthony Wood in his note on a John Lane who died in 1578, where Wood adds that 'there was one John Lane, a poet, about this time' (Wood, *Ath. Oxon.*, 2.189). This would seem to place Lane as early as the 1570s, if Wood's secondhand recollection can be trusted. William Riley Parker discusses a number of John Lanes living during the first half of the seventeenth century (Parker, 2.716), but there is no way to determine which is the subject of this article. In an entry in the Stationers' register, dated 23 June 1591, the title 'Tom Tell Trothe' is included among a list of some ninety works granted to Thomas Orwyn which formerly belonged to Thomas Marshe, deceased. This could be Lane's book although the plain-speaking figure of Tom Tell-Truth appears throughout the Renaissance and the 1600 edition does not mention Orwyn. The first definite record of Lane is the book in question: *Tom Tell-Troths message and his pens complaint: a worke not unpleasant to be read, nor unprofitable to be followed* (1600). This work, which Lane calls 'the first fruites of my barren braine', is dedicated to George Dowse and consists of 120 six-line stanzas which enumerate the vices of England and lament the sorry state of the two universities.

The only other poem Lane published during his lifetime was *An Elegie upon the Death of the High and Renowned Princesse, our Late Soveraigne Elizabeth*, published in 1603. This work is listed in an April 1603 entry in the Stationers' register, with the provision that the bookseller John Deane 'gett Aucthoritie for yt' before printing (Arber, *Regs. Stationers*, 3.36). No further record of Lane appears until 2 March 1615, which is the date of an imprimatur by John Taverner in Lane's continuation of Chaucer's *Squire's Tale* (Bodl. Oxf., MS Douce 170), one of three works Lane left in manuscript. The manuscript is dated 1616 in the title and includes a short poem by John Milton sen., a close friend of Lane, among its dedicatory poems; interestingly, it is mistitled 'Spencers Squiers Tale', an error Lane corrects in his 1630 revised continuation (Bodl. Oxf., MS Ashmole 53).

Lane's next work, 'Tritons Trumpet to the Twelve Monethes Husbanded and Moralized by John Lane … 1621', is a long pastoral modelled after the calendar structure of Spenser's *Shepheardes Calender*. It exists in two manuscripts, both in Lane's hand (BL, Royal MS 17 B.xv and Trinity College, Cambridge, MS O.2.68). Lane begins each month with a husbandry section, modelled on Thomas Tusser, and then follows with a moral tale. In the November section Lane celebrates the elder Milton's musical ability. His 'Corrected historie of Sir Gwy, earle of Warwick … begun by Dan Lidgate … but now diligentlie exquired from all antiquitie' (BL, Harley MS 5243) is prefaced with a commendatory sonnet by the elder Milton. Although it bears an imprimatur by John Taverner, dated 13 July 1617, the *Guy of Warwick* manuscript is dated 1621 in its title. The prose introduction to this work is printed in *Bishop Percy's Folio Manuscript* (Hales and Furnivall, 2.521–5).

On 25 May 1621 Lane and John Milton sen. bought some property at the north end of Gray's Inn Lane from a Dr Leonard Poe, which they sold on 22 April 1622 to James Kent. On 9 February 1622 Milton lent £50 to Edwarde Raymonde, who listed James Ayloffe as the surety for his debt, which was to be paid with interest in six months' time. A bond for £100 was made out to John Lane—the extra being to cover potential costs if Lane were forced to go to court to collect the debt—and throughout future legal writs on the loan Milton and Lane were usually named together. The whole matter ended in a series of lawsuits, during which time Raymonde died and Milton and Lane were forced to take Ayloffe to court to collect what remained of the debt. Ayloffe, of course, accused Milton and Lane of

acting in collusion with Raymonde, and sued the two himself in a 1 May 1624 chancery bill, which Milton answered on 10 May of that year. What finally came of all of this is unknown, but it appears that throughout the course of legal wrangling Lane was a subsidiary figure.

The next record of Lane is the 1630 revision of his earlier continuation of Chaucer's *Squire's Tale*: 'Chaucers piller, beinge his master-peece, called the squiers tale; wch hath binn given lost, for allmost thease three hundred yeares: but now fownd out, and brought to light by John Lane'. This revised manuscript, dedicated to 'the virtuous Queene Marie', omits most of the commendatory poems from the 1616 manuscript but adds a short poem, titled 'The Muse to the Fowre Windes', wherein Lane lists his works. He mentions 'more *Poetick Visions*', alluding to a two-part work which Edward Phillips lists in his 1675 *Theatrum poetarum* but of which nothing is known, and his *Alarum to Poets*, which was finally printed in quarto in 1648. The *Alarum to Poets* is Lane's final publication and is dedicated 'to the most ingenious classis laureat wheresoever'. Although the *Alarum* was probably printed posthumously Lane must have lived for some time beyond 1630, the year in which Edward Phillips was born, since Phillips claims that Lane 'was living within my remembrance' (Phillips, 111).

In his *Theatrum poetarum* Phillips writes a glowing tribute to Lane, describing him as 'a fine old Queen *Elizabeth* Gentleman' and asserting that, had his longer works been published, they 'might possibly have gain'd him a name not much inferiour, if not equal to *Drayton*, and others of the next rank to *Spencer*' (Phillips, 111–12). Lane in fact self-consciously modelled his career on Spenser's; when listing his works at the end of the *Alarum* (and elsewhere) he arranges them to suggest a move from pastoral to epic. His career, however, never blossomed, and he has had little if any influence on subsequent generations.

VERNE M. UNDERWOOD

Sources E. Phillips, *Theatrum poetarum, or, A compleat collection of the poets, especially the most eminent of all ages* (1675) · *John Lane's continuation of Chaucer's 'squire's tale'*, ed. F. J. Furnivall, Chaucer Society, 2nd ser., 23, 26 (1888–90) · J. Lane, 'Tom Tell-Troths message', *Tell-Trothes new-yeare's gift*, ed. F. J. Furnivall (1876), 107–35 · Arber, *Regs. Stationers* · J. M. French, *The life records of John Milton*, 5 vols. (1949–58) · J. M. French, *Milton in chancery* (1939) · Wood, *Ath. Oxon.*, new edn · W. R. Parker, *Milton: a biography*, 2 vols. (1968) · J. W. Hales and F. J. Furnivall, eds., *Bishop Percy's folio manuscript: ballads and romances*, 3 vols. (1867–8) · W. C. Hazlitt, ed., *Fugitive poetical tracts, 1600–1700*, 2nd ser., 2 vols. (1875)

Archives BL, Royal MS 17 B.xv · BL, Harley MS 5243 · Bodl. Oxf., MS Douce 170 · Bodl. Oxf., MS Ashmole 53 · Trinity Cam., MS O.2.68

Lane, John (1854–1925), publisher, was born on 14 March 1854 at West Putford, north Devon, the eldest child and only son of Lewis Lane (*bap.* 1829), a prosperous farmer, and his wife, Mary Grace (*bap.* 1834), daughter of John Jenn, miller and corn merchant, of Cory Mill, in the same parish. In 1857 the family moved to Fosfelle farm at nearby Hartland, and it was there that John Lane began his education at the local national school. In 1869, through the efforts of his mother and a local parson, he left Devon, having completed his schooling at Brook Hill Academy, Chulmleigh, to take up a position as a junior clerk in the railway clearing house in London. Though never particularly happy in this position, he stuck at it for over two decades, alleviating the drudgery through the pursuit of his antiquarian enthusiasms. Indeed, by the time he began his second career as a publisher, the awkward, modestly educated Devon farm boy had become an urbane, clubbable, well-connected man of the world, with an impressive personal library and a passion for various collectables, including rare books, bookplates, prints, paintings, antique glass, and furniture.

Never simply an energetic, amateur antiquary, Lane was also an ambitious young entrepreneur with an eye for business. And so it was not surprising when, in 1887, he decided to take a more professional interest in the rare book trade by starting a small second-hand bookshop, at 6B Vigo Street, London, in partnership with Charles Elkin Mathews (1851–1921), a bookseller and small-scale publisher from Exeter who was the brother of a fellow clerk. The shop, which they called the Bodley Head, after Sir Thomas Bodley, opened for business in October that year. Though the partnership lasted seven years, it was never an easy one. The younger, more enterprising Lane, who none the less cautiously kept his position at the clearing house until 1892, was the driving force, but Mathews, the more retiring antiquarian, was the principal investor who always had more to lose. Initially supported by Mathews, who continued to dabble in publishing himself, Lane soon set about transforming the bookshop into a small but distinctive publishing firm, specializing in stylish, limited editions of poetry and *belles-lettres*. Its first publication was Richard Le Gallienne's bookish collection of poems *Volumes in Folio* (1889).

Over the next decade, first with Mathews, then on his own, after the partnership ended in September 1894, Lane continued to expand the Bodley Head, making it one of the most celebrated literary publishing houses of the 1890s. Always a club man—he belonged to the Sette of Odd Volumes, the Reform, Whitefriars, Cocoa Tree, and Pilgrims' clubs in London; the Union Club, Brighton; the National Arts Club, New York; and he was vice-president of the London Devonian Association—his principal assets in this initiative were his own energy and sociability. He was a tireless networker; for instance, in 1895 he took up golf specially to widen his range of contacts, for he recognized early on that his survival, not to mention his success, as an undercapitalized new publisher depended on his ability to collaborate effectively with others. This meant the careful cultivation of relationships with well-to-do private investors, innovative fine printers in Britain and America, and, not least of all, the diverse poets, novelists, dramatists, essayists, and artists who made up his list and often worked on his staff. Young poets like Le Gallienne, John Davidson, Ernest Dowson, Arthur Symons, and Lionel Johnson, all of whom belonged to the self-consciously avant-garde Rhymers' Club; 'new woman' authors like Mary Chavelita Dunne (George Egerton), Ella D'Arcy, Evelyn Sharp, Netta Syrett, Gertrude Dix, and

Grant Allen; leading artists like Aubrey Beardsley, Charles Ricketts, Walter Crane, and William Strang; and renowned publishing ventures like the Keynotes series and, most famously, the *Yellow Book* (1894–7)—all these rapidly earned the Bodley Head its reputation as the most distinctive and innovative publishing house of its generation.

Yet Lane the publisher, like Lane the business-minded antiquary, was not simply an inspired champion of 'art'. He was an astute entrepreneur with a flair for public relations and a commitment to prudent publishing practices. Associating frequently with young, sometimes controversial but inexpensive writers, adopting a vigorous approach to marketing, and producing elegant, distinctively modern but always affordable books, he managed to cut costs and make his name by bringing the prestige of a small, avant-garde press to an increasingly mass market in Britain and America (he opened a branch of the firm in New York in 1896). In all this he was typically as cautious as he was bold. Unlike Mathews he was, for instance, happy to publish some of Oscar Wilde's more *risqué* works, but when the controversy surrounding Wilde's arrest in 1895 threatened the firm, he quickly took his books off the list, fired Beardsley who was then art editor for the *Yellow Book*, and began rethinking his business strategies. Though he continued to nurture his ties with the avant-garde—he published, among other things, Wyndham Lewis's *Blast* (1914–15), the next generation's aesthetic manifesto—and while he never lost his taste for the controversial, at the turn of the century he began to change the business once again, from a literary into a general publishing house. By the time he sold the New York firm and converted the London business into a private limited company in 1921, the Bodley Head depended as much on its always impressive list of new literary authors as on its assorted series, its reprints of the classics, and its best-sellers (William John Locke was especially popular), its translations, memoirs, biographies, travel writings, art, cookery, and gardening books.

On 13 August 1898 Lane had married Annie Philippine King (1856/7–1927), a wealthy Swiss-born Bostonian, only child of Julius Eichberg, director of the Boston Conservatory of Music, USA, and widow of Tyler Batchellor King LLD. A productive Bodley Head author in her own right, she played an important part in the development of the firm as an investor and an unofficial adviser. They had no children, but Allen *Lane (1902–1970), a distant cousin who served his apprenticeship with the firm in the 1920s, gave many of their ideals new life when he founded Penguin in 1935. John Lane died of pneumonia on 2 February 1925 at his London home, 8 Lancaster Gate Terrace, Bayswater, London. He was cremated at Golders Green, and his ashes were interred at St Nectan's Church, Hartland, Devon.

PETER D. MCDONALD

Sources J. W. Lambert and M. Ratcliffe, *The Bodley Head, 1887–1987* (1987) · J. G. Nelson, *The early nineties: a view from the Bodley Head* (1971) · J. L. May, *John Lane and the nineties* (1936) · J. L. May, *The path through the wood* (1930) · *The Times* (4 Feb 1925) · R. P. Chope, *The book* of Hartland (1940) • R. P. Chope, 'John Lane: a personal note', *Devonian Year Book* (1926) • C. H. Stacey, *Men of the west* (1926) • M. D. Stetz, 'Sex, lies, and printed cloth', *Victorian Studies*, 35 (1991–2), 71–86 • M. D. Stetz and M. S. Lasner, *England in the 1890s: literary publishing at the Bodley Head* (1990) • *WWW* • register, Anglican church, West Putford, Barnstaple RO • m. cert.

Archives BL, photographic copies of archive, RP 3208 • Ransom HRC, personal and business corresp. and papers | BL, corresp. and notes relating to Prince Hoare, Add. MS 50857 • Bodl. Oxf., notes from Kenneth Grahame • King's AC Cam., letters to Oscar Browning • Royal Albert Memorial Museum and Art Gallery, Exeter, artworks • U. Edin. L., corresp. with Charles Sarolea • U. Reading L., Bodley Head publishers' archive • U. Reading L., corresp. with Charles Elkin Mathews **Likenesses** E. L. Ipsen, oils, *c*.1921, Royal Albert Memorial Museum and Art Gallery, Exeter **Wealth at death** £15,211 15s. 5d.: probate, 7 March 1925, CGPLA Eng. & Wales

Lane, John Bryant (1788–1868), painter, was born at Helston in Cornwall, the son of Samuel Lane, chemist and exciseman, and Margaret Baldwin, his wife. Lane was educated at Truro until he was fourteen, when his interest in art was noticed by Francis Basset, baron de Dunstanville of Tehidy, whose patronage enabled him to enter the Royal Academy Schools in 1805. Lane was awarded a gold medal from the Society of Arts for a historical cartoon, *The Angels Unbound*, and soon started exhibiting works at the Royal Academy and the British Institution, including an altarpiece for a church built by Lord de Dunstanville in Cornwall (exh. RA, 1808); *Christ Mocked by the Soldiers of Pilate after Flagellation*, for the guildhall at Helston (exh. RA, 1811, British Institution, 1812); and *Eutychus Restored to Life by St Paul* (exh. RA, 1813, British Institution, 1814), for a church in London. At Lord de Dunstanville's, Lane met the landscape painter and diarist Joseph Farington, who gave him encouragement and advised him 'to turn his thoughts to Portrait Painting as a means of getting money which he might do without prejudice to his main pursuit, History Painting' (Farington, *Diary*, 12.4340, 4 May 1813). In 1817 his patron sent him to Rome, where he remained for ten years, engaged on a gigantic picture, *The Vision of Joseph*, which he refused to show during progress. In 1827 he finally exhibited it at Rome, but details in it were found offensive by the papal authorities, who expelled both the artist and his picture from the papal dominions. Redgrave states that Lane then went to Dresden to study Correggio, sending the picture to London, where in 1828 he exhibited it in a room at the royal mews, Charing Cross. Its huge size and the surrounding controversy attracted attention, but from an artistic point of view it was a complete failure, and was left to decay in the Pantechnicon in Belgrave Square. The *Gentleman's Magazine* declared that nevertheless 'with all his faults, Mr. Lane is a great painter' (*GM*, 61).

Lane settled once again in London and subsequently concentrated primarily on portrait painting. He had previously drawn and engraved a few portraits for *The British Gallery of Contemporary Portraits* (1815 and 1822, Cadell and Davies, London), and from 1831 to 1834 he sent mostly portraits to the Royal Academy, as well as a few to the Society of British Artists. Among his sitters were Sir Hussey Vivian, Davies Gilbert MP (exh. RA, 1831), and Lord de Dunstanville (exh. RA, 1831; a second portrait, *c*.1831, exh. RA, 1832, painted for the Royal Institution, Truro; Royal Cornwall Museum, Truro). Lane died, unmarried, at his home, 45 Clarendon Square, Somers Town, London, on 4 April 1868.

L. H. CUST, rev. ERIKA INGHAM

Sources Graves, *RA exhibitors* • Graves, *Brit. Inst.* • J. Johnson, ed., *Works exhibited at the Royal Society of British Artists, 1824–1893, and the New English Art Club, 1888–1917*, 2 vols. (1975) • 'Mr J. B. Lane's vision of Joseph', *GM*, 1st ser., 98/2 (1828), 61–2 • Redgrave, *Artists* • Boase, *Mod. Eng. biog.* • Thieme & Becker, *Allgemeines Lexikon* • S. C. Hutchison, 'The Royal Academy Schools, 1768–1830', *Walpole Society*, 38 (1960–62), 123–91 • R. Walker, *National Portrait Gallery: Regency portraits*, 2 vols. (1985) • Graves, *Artists* • Farington, *Diary*, vols. 10–13, 16

Lane, Joseph (1851–1920), socialist campaigner, was born on 2 April 1851 in the Oxfordshire village of Benson (or Bensington), the son of Thomas Lane, a cordwainer, and Mercy Lane, *née* Warner, who was illiterate. Lane had virtually no education, and never managed to write grammatical English. He worked on the land from an early age, and soon took an interest in politics, supporting the campaign for land reform and taking part in the general election campaign of 1865. He moved to London, where he earned his living as a carter and spent his energy on politics. He married Isabella Adams on 5 September 1874, and had children, including several sons, but his family took no interest in his public life. He took part in the radical demonstrations of the mid-1860s, and joined the agrarian and republican movements. By the end of the 1870s he was taking a leading part in several radical organizations in central London—the Manhood Suffrage League, the English section of the Social Democratic Club, the Marylebone Radical Association, and the Local Rights Association. He took part in the general election campaign of 1880, and then turned to more clearly revolutionary and socialist activity.

In 1881 Lane moved to east London, where he was involved in producing the English *Freiheit* in 1881 and *The Radical* from 1881 to 1882. In 1881 he formed the Homerton Social Democratic Club, whose meetings were suppressed by the police in 1882; he represented it as a delegate at the International Revolutionary Congress in London in 1881 and as a signatory of a manifesto calling for the revival of the International Working Men's Association in 1883. In 1882 he helped to found the socialist Labour Emancipation League and became its secretary. He organized public meetings and working men's clubs all over east London, and produced a series of propaganda leaflets. In 1884 he led its merger with the radical Democratic Federation to form the socialist Social Democratic Federation, and joined the executive, where he made friends with William Morris and enemies with H. M. Hyndman. At the end of 1884 he joined the revolutionary majority in seceding and forming the Socialist League, signing the latter's founding documents and joining its council. He became the manager and joint publisher of its paper *The Commonweal* in 1885, and was also an occasional contributor.

Lane was a leading member of the anti-parliamentarian fraction in the disputes which immediately divided and eventually destroyed the Socialist League. In 1886 he was appointed to a subcommittee attempting to draft an acceptable policy statement; in 1887, when the majority report recommended parliamentary socialism, he produced a minority report reaffirming revolutionary socialism. When both reports were rejected by the annual conference in May 1887, he published his in June 1887 as a pamphlet entitled *An Anti-Statist, Communist Manifesto*, which became a standard text of extreme revolutionary and libertarian socialism short of anarchism.

The internal disputes continued in the Socialist League, and in 1889 Lane quietly resigned, partly for private reasons (he was offended by personal slights) and partly for political reasons (he preferred William Morris's circle to the extreme anarchists). He took no further direct part in socialist activity, though he kept in touch with his old comrades and continued to collect and distribute radical literature. He published occasional leaflets from 1906 to 1912, returning to the campaign for land reform, opposing tariff reform, supporting the syndicalist movement, and attacking reformist socialists. He moved to Forest Gate, and worked for a furrier in the City until his sudden death at East Ham, Essex, on 3 September 1920.

Lane was an earnest rather than eloquent speaker or writer, but he was an inspiring agitator and organizer. He was one of the central figures in the rise of revolutionary socialism in Britain during the 1880s, and author of its most convincing exposition produced by a native working-class writer. Unfortunately he left only manuscript notes for an autobiography. William Morris wrote to him when he left the Socialist League: 'I always looked upon you as one of the *serious* members of the League' (Morris to Lane, 21 May 1889, *The Collected Letters of William Morris*, ed. N. Kelvin, 3, 1996, 68). And the anarchist historian Max Nettlau, who knew him in the Socialist League, wrote a decade after his death: 'I consider him to be the best head English socialism possessed in the years 1879 to 1889' (Nettlau, 3.349).   NICOLAS WALTER

Sources autobiographical notes, Internationaal Instituut voor Sociale Geschiedenis, Amsterdam, Nettlau collection · Socialist League MSS, Internationaal Instituut voor Sociale Geschiedenis, Amsterdam · letters, BL, John Burns MSS · letters, BL, William Morris MSS · *National Reformer* (1870–89) · *The Radical* (1880–82) · *Justice* (1884–5) · *The Commonweal* (1885–9) · M. Nettlau, *Anarchisten und Sozialrevolutionäre* (Berlin, 1931); repr. as vol. 3 of *Geschichte der Anarchie* (Glashütten im Taunus, 1972), 93 · M. Nettlau, *Die erste Blütezeit der Anarchie, 1886–1894* (Vaduz, 1981), vol. 4 of *Geschichte der Anarchie* · F. Kitz, *Freedom* (Jan–July 1912) [biographical references] · M. Kavanagh, 'Recollections and reflections', *Freedom* (Oct 1934) [biographical references] · [M. Nettlau], 'Anarchism from the root. Renewed effort in the 80's. IV. Joseph Lane and William Morris', *Spain and the World*, 1/12 (19 May 1937), 3–4 · G. Cores, 'A life's struggle in working-class movement', *Direct Action*, 7/5 (entire 60) (Nov 1952), 4 · G. Cores, '"Soldiers, don't shoot!"', *Direct Action*, 8/3 (entire 64) (July 1953), 2 · E. P. Thompson, *William Morris: romantic to revolutionary* (1955) · S. Shipley, *Club life and socialism in mid-Victorian London* [1972] · J. Quail, *The slow burning fuse* (1978) · N. Walter, 'Introduction', *An anti-statist, communist manifesto*, new edn (1978) · A. Barker, memoirs, Vestry House Museum, Walthamstow, London · b. cert. · m. cert. · d. cert.

Archives Internationaal Instituut voor Sociale Geschiedenis, Amsterdam, Nettlau collection, autobiographical notes · Vestry House Museum, Walthamstow, London, Ambrose Baker memoirs | BL, John Burns MSS · BL, William Morris MSS · Internationaal Instituut voor Sociale Geschiedenis, Amsterdam, Socialist League MSS

Wealth at death £957 2s. 2d.: administration, 30 March 1921, CGPLA Eng. & Wales

Lane, Lupino [*real name* Henry William George Lupino] (1892–1959), actor and theatre manager, was born on 16 June 1892 in London, the elder son of Harry Charles Lupino (1865–1925), a dancer and actor, and his wife, Charlotte Sarah Robinson (1863–1937), niece of the celebrated Sara Lane, actress and lessee of the Britannia Theatre, Hoxton, in whose honour the 'Lane' half of his stage name was assumed.

As designers, dancers, acrobats, pantomimists, and clowns the Lupinos had featured in London's theatrical life since the eighteenth century, and the future Lupino Lane was bred to the stage as a matter of course. He made his first public appearance at the age of four, in a benefit performance for Vesta Tilley at the Prince of Wales's Theatre, Birmingham, and his London début in 1903, under the name of Nipper Lane, at the London Pavilion. Gruelling hours of practice taught him the full repertory of family skills while he picked up many of the tricks of the trade from the great figures of the music hall such as Dan Leno and Little Tich. 'Nipper' derived from a coster song of Albert Chevalier, a hugely popular comedian in the 1890s, and originally suggested a creature physically small, quick, and neat; as his stage personality developed Nipper or Nip Lane became the embodiment of the cockney, dapper and jaunty, but with the true clown's gift of pathos—the endearing 'little man' whose cheerful resilience wins through. On 10 February 1917 he married an actress, Violet (b. 1893/4), daughter of John Propert Blyth, a sea captain; they had one son, Lauri Lupino Lane, who carried on the theatrical tradition.

Lane's progress towards a leading position in the world of revue and pantomime was not at first spectacular, but it was steady. In 1915 he appeared at the Empire in a successful *Watch your Step*, and he remained there for the next two productions; from then onwards he was seldom out of an engagement, playing 'funny man' parts of increasing importance in London, in New York (where he made a hit as Ko-Ko in *The Mikado* in 1925), or in the other principal cities on the touring network. His perfect timing disguised the all but manic physical energy demanded by low comedy (in the pantomime *Aladdin* in 1930 he dived through seventy-two stage traps in about three minutes). During the twenties he rubbed shoulders with the British colony of actors in Hollywood, where he made about forty silent films; he experimented in British films as director and author, and featured in early radio revues. By the time he was forty he was a leading comedian on both sides of the Atlantic.

It was not, however, until the part of Bill Snibson was written for him that Lupino Lane became a household name. Snibson made his first appearance, as a bookie's tout, in *Twenty to One*, a musical farce by L. Arthur Rose and

Lupino Lane (1892–1959), by Bassano, 1919

Frank Eyton, with music by Billy Mayerl, which opened at the London Coliseum on 12 November 1935, presented jointly by Lupino Lane and Sir Oswald Stoll. It ran for nearly a year and subsequently went on a long tour, turning Lane into a star performer as well as into a manager of substance, but was swiftly put in the shade by the second Snibson play, *Me and my Girl*, in which L. Arthur Rose had Douglas Furber as collaborator and the music was composed by Noel Gay.

Me and my Girl, in which Snibson is the unlikely heir of a country estate and brings his mates from the old London borough of Lambeth to revitalize an effete aristocracy, took London by storm. Directed as well as presented by Lane, it opened at the Victoria Palace on 16 December 1937 and had the phenomenal run of 1646 performances, for the first 1550 of which Snibson was played by Lane. The play was several times revived; it was the first musical comedy to be televised from a British stage, and was made into a film in 1939. At the heart of its triumph lay, undoubtedly, the song and dance which Lane created to a catchy tune by Gay, 'The Lambeth Walk'. In the late 1930s the dance became a craze right across Europe, its lyrics translated into several languages; for the British, especially during the war, its nostalgic evocation of the easygoing, indestructible cockney spirit chimed with the 'all-in-it-together' mood of the nation under bombardment. (The play was very successfully revived in 1985 with Robert Lindsay in the lead, and voted musical of the year by London's theatre critics.)

Me and my Girl left Lane a very rich man though he was never again to enjoy such success on the stage. In 1945 he published an advice book, *How to Become a Comedian*, which reads as a testament to the enormous dedication and versatility of his stage career. He came once more into the public eye in 1946 when he bought for £200,000 the Gaiety Theatre, with which his family had been connected for a hundred years. He failed, however, to find the financial backing necessary to reopen the theatre and resold the property in 1950. Lane died of a heart attack in London on 10 November 1959, at his home, 11 Grosvenor Cottages, Eaton Terrace; his wife survived him.

W. A. Darlington, *rev.* Alison Light

Sources J. D. White, *Born to star: the Lupino Lane story* (1957) · J. Parker, ed., *Who's who in the theatre*, 12th edn (1957) · Theatre Museum, London, Lupino Lane biographical file · Theatre Museum, London, *Me and my girl* file · *The Times* (11 Nov 1959) · *Daily Mail* (11 Nov 1959) · Highfill, Burnim & Langhans, *BDA*, vol. 9 · A. Light and R. Samuel, 'Doing the Lambeth walk', *Patriotism: the making and unmaking of British national identity*, ed. R. Samuel (1989), 262–71 · G. S. Jones, 'The "cockney" and the nation, 1780–1988', *Metropolis London: histories and representations since 1800*, ed. D. Feldman and G. S. Jones (1989), 272–324 · S. Lupino, *From the stocks to the stars: an unconventional autobiography* (1934) · m. cert. · CGPLA Eng. & Wales (1960) · personal knowledge (1971)

Archives FILM BFI NFTVA, documentary footage · BFI NFTVA, performance footage | SOUND BL NSA, performance recordings
Likenesses Bassano, photograph, 1919, NPG [*see illus.*] · photograph (as Bill Snibson in *Me and my girl*), repro. in White, *Born to star* · photographs, Theatre Museum, London, Lupino Lane files · photographs, Theatre Museum, London, *Me and my girl* file
Wealth at death £4688 4s. 7d.: probate, 15 Jan 1960, CGPLA Eng. & Wales

Lane, Margaret Winifred [*married names* Margaret Winifred Wallace; Margaret Winifred Hastings, countess of Huntingdon] **(1907–1994)**, novelist and biographer, was born on 23 June 1907 at 5 Abington Road, Sale, Cheshire, the only child of Harry George Lane (1881–1957), newspaper editor, and Edith Webb (1884–c.1950), daughter of a Birmingham glass dealer.

Margaret Lane's childhood was spent in London, as her father, to whom she was devoted, was editor of the *Daily Sketch* and later editor-in-chief of Northcliffe Newspapers. Margaret Lane was educated at St Stephen's, Folkestone, and St Hugh's College, Oxford. After graduating BA she followed her father into journalism, working from 1928 to 1931 on the *Daily Express* in Fleet Street, then from 1931 to 1932 in New York as a special correspondent for the *Express* and for the International News Service—where her greatest scoop was an exclusive interview with the gangster Al Capone. On her return to England she worked for the *Daily Mail* from 1932 to 1938, becoming the highest-paid woman journalist in the country. In 1935 she published her first novel, *Faith, Hope, No Charity*, which was awarded the prix Femina-Vie Heureuse, and a second, *At Last the Island*, two years later.

On 23 June 1934 Lane married Bryan Edgar Wallace (*b.* 1903/4), a film scriptwriter, elder son of the thriller writer Edgar Wallace, and her father-in-law became the subject of her first biography, which appeared in 1938. In that year Lane met the left-wing painter Francis John Clarence Westenra Plantagenet (Jack) *Hastings (1901–1990), who with his first wife had lived for some years in the South Seas, studied under Diego Rivera in Mexico, and driven an ambulance for the republican side in the Spanish Civil War. They decided to marry. Lane obtained a divorce in 1939 but Jack Hastings, who succeeded his father as sixteenth earl of Huntingdon in that year, was unable to do the same until 1943. Until then the couple remained quietly together, first in the west of Ireland, then in the village of Vernham Dean in Hampshire. They married on 1 February 1944.

In her novels Lane wrote of love and marriage in a manner which combined sharp social observation with a tender romantic strain. Her wit and a talent for delicate caricature stand in finely balanced apposition to a sometimes surprisingly bleak view of the possibility of human happiness. The ending of *Where Helen Lies* (1944), for instance, was so heart-rending that her husband insisted that she change it. She had a fondness, too, for the macabre, most disturbingly displayed in a brilliant short story, 'The Thing about Mrs Slezinger'.

After the war the Huntingdons lived in Albany, Piccadilly, from which after the birth of two daughters they moved to Roehampton, with a country house first in north Wales, then in the New Forest. It was a happy marriage and their life together was exceptionally agreeable. Although Jack Huntingdon served in Attlee's post-war Labour government, he was not ambitious, preferring to spend his time painting, attending the House of Lords, and enjoying a mildly hedonistic style of life. He and Lane had a large circle of friends in both politics and the arts, they entertained generously, travelled widely, bought houses on Elba and in Morocco, and kept a yacht on the Beaulieu River in which they sailed in summer. Impractical about financial affairs, they were fortunate that Jack Huntingdon's patrimony just lasted out their lifetimes.

Although for many years she had no room of her own in which to work, Lane was disciplined about her writing, capable of intense concentration on her novels, biographies, and on regular book reviews for the *Sunday Times* and the *Daily Telegraph*. Her highly regarded biographical works include a reassessment of Mrs Gaskell's life of Charlotte Brontë (1953) and a study of *Samuel Johnson and his World* (1975). Best known is her biography of Beatrix Potter (1985). Lane established a good working relationship with Potter's widower, William Heelis, only after it was discovered by chance that Heelis responded most happily to the hectoring tone he became used to from his wife. In *Purely for Pleasure* (1966) Lane explored some of her favourite subjects, among them Charles Dickens, Flora Thompson, the entomologist Jean Henri Fabre, and the eighteenth-century countess of Huntingdon, the 'Queen of the Methodists'.

Lane was a frequent broadcaster on radio and a member of *The Brains Trust* team on television, as well as making numerous public appearances as president of the Women's Press Club, the Dickens Fellowship, the Johnson Society, the Brontë Society, and the Jane Austen Society. Her interests were varied. A gifted amateur naturalist, she loved animals, including snakes and spiders, and once spent three months staying in memorable discomfort with the distinguished herpetologist C. J. P. Ionides in Tanganyika. Inquisitive and adventurous, she persuaded her husband to undertake an expedition in 1959 to Mozambique to look for buried treasure, a dangerous and arguably irresponsible quest vividly described in *A Calabash of Diamonds* (1962). She played the harp, the flute, and recorder, was an expert cook and needlewoman, enjoyed elaborate découpage, and in the 1980s bought and restored an old Gypsy caravan.

Margaret Lane was a very pretty woman with a good figure and a flair for clothes. A mesmerizing talker, she could be extremely funny, although a highly developed sense of irony and an occasionally daunting manner made her formidable to some. She liked to hold centre stage and was well aware that she attracted the opposite sex. At the same time she was a loyal and loving friend to an unusually broad range of acquaintants. In her maternal role she maintained a slightly lower profile, her attendances at school concerts and sports days remarkable chiefly for their extreme rarity.

Notable for their subtle wit and unfailing elegance of style Lane's novels are unlikely to be long remembered, but her essays and biographies earn her place as a highly honourable member of her profession. Margaret Lane died at Southampton General Hospital on 14 February 1994; following cremation on 26 February, her ashes were placed with her husband's at Ashby-de-la-Zouch in the Hastings chapel of St Helen's Church.

SELINA HASTINGS

Sources WW · Burke, *Peerage* (1970) · personal knowledge (2004) · b. cert. · m. cert. [Bryan Edgar Wallace] · m. cert. [Francis John Clarence Westenra Plantagenet Hastings] · b. cert. [Harry George Lane] · b. cert. [Edith Webb] · d. cert. [Henry George Lane] **Archives** Boston University, Mugar Memorial Library · NRA, corresp. · St Hugh's College, Oxford
Wealth at death £769,545: probate, 1994, *CGPLA Eng. & Wales*

Lane [*née* Parr], **Maud** [Matilda], **Lady Lane** (*c*.1507–1558/9), courtier, was the eldest of four daughters of William *Parr, later Baron Parr of Horton (*c*.1480–1547), and his wife, Mary Salisbury (1484–1555). Matilda, Lady Parr, mother of *Katherine Parr, was Maud's godmother.

On 10 December 1517 Sir William Parr took the unusual step of naming Maud heir to his entire estate, principally the manor of Horton, Northamptonshire, and betrothed her to Ralph Lane, the eight-year-old son of William Lane of Orlingbury. Her father was named guardian of the couple until Ralph's twentieth birthday. The marriage was celebrated in 1523 and, under the terms of the betrothal contract, consummated in 1527 when the groom turned eighteen. The couple had ten children: three sons, Robert (*b*. 1529), Ralph (later governor of Virginia, *d*. 1603), and William; and seven daughters, including Frances (married Sir George Turpin), Lettice (married Peter Wentworth), Mary (married Thomas Pigot), Jane (married first Lewis Montgomery and second Thomas Bawde), Dorothy (married Sir William Fielding), and Katherine (married John Osborne). Sir Ralph Lane supported the reformed religion and was a commissioner for the dissolution of the monasteries in Buckinghamshire. He died in 1540 and in June 1542 Maud paid £40 for wardship of her son.

On 20 July 1543, in the same month that Maud's cousin Katherine, or Kateryn, Parr married Henry VIII, Maud paid £980 for the reversion of the manors of Hogshaw, Buckinghamshire, and Wheatley, Warwickshire. Appointed gentlewoman to the queen, Maud was, according to John Foxe, 'great with [the queen] and of her blood; [and] … privy to all her doings' (Acts and Monuments, 5.557). Besides maintaining an absolute loyalty to her cousin, she was an avid supporter of the reformed religion and one of the queen's inner circle which promoted cheaply priced religious publications in the vernacular. In 1546 she became a key target in a plot by conservatives, led by Stephen Gardiner, bishop of Winchester, to destroy the queen. Evidence was secretly sought against her of heresy in hopes that such an investigation would implicate the queen. Plans to arrest her and two other of the queen's ladies by night and incarcerate them in the Tower were in hand when the plot failed, helping to weaken Gardiner's position in the last months of the reign. Maud retired from court soon after and lived quietly in the country until she died in 1558 or 1559.   SUSAN E. JAMES

Sources S. E. James, *Kateryn Parr: the making of a queen* (1999) · *LP Henry VIII*, vols. 17–18, 21 · *CPR, 1547–8*, 361; *1549–51*, 193, 386; *1558–60*, 99 · exchequer, king's remembrancer, accounts various, PRO, E101/423/12, fol. 3b · *The acts and monuments of John Foxe*, ed. S. R. Cattley, 8 vols. (1837–41), vol. 5 · Parr–Lane marriage settlement, 1517, Northants. RO · S. E. James, 'Lady Jane Grey or Queen Kateryn Parr?', *Burlington Magazine*, 138 (1996), 20–24 · T. Blore, *The history and antiquities of Rutland* (1811) · W. C. Metcalfe, ed., *The visitations of Northamptonshire made in 1564 and 1618–19* (1887)

Wealth at death sufficient income July 1543 to pay nearly £1000 for reversion of two manors: *LP Henry VIII*, vol. 18, i, 981

Lane, Sir Ralph (d. 1603), soldier and colonist, was of unknown parentage and education. He ranked in that restless corps of Tudor wanderers who schemed the advance of English interests in Ireland and America even as they chased fortunes for themselves. Nineteenth-century scholars presumed that he came from Horton, Northamptonshire, but those presumptions lack the sanction of unimpeachable evidence. However, it is certain that he acquired a taste for adventure through his experiences of the sea and soldiering. From the 1570s his name appears with some regularity in the correspondence of William Cecil and other crown officers, whom he relentlessly importuned for royal preferment. His persistence paid off, for by the mid-1580s he had received several Irish appointments, including the shrievalty of Kerry; he was also equerry of the queen's great stables. He then caught the attention of Sir Walter Ralegh, who recruited him in 1585 to lead a colonizing enterprise in North America.

A year earlier Ralegh had sent an expedition to seek a site more suitable for settlement than Labrador or Newfoundland, inhospitable places that his predecessors had failed to settle. He planned a second foray to America even before his scouts returned to report their discoveries to him. To that purpose he amassed seven vessels, supplies, and upwards of 300 men, whose company included the mathematician Thomas Harriot and the artist and cartographer John White. Command of the fleet went to Sir Richard Grenville, but once the convoy reached its destination it was Lane who would govern the colony.

The voyagers cast off from Plymouth on 9 April 1585. Their navigator, Simão Fernandes, a Portuguese seafarer and long-time employee of English explorers, steered towards their destination—the coast of modern North Carolina, the place Ralegh styled Virginia in honour of Elizabeth I. Stops in the West Indies gave respite from a storm-tossed crossing and allowed Lane to adapt his skill at fortification to American conditions before the flotilla sailed northwards. In June it reached Wococon, one of the barrier islands that formed the outer ring of Pimlico Sound, and Fernandes carelessly ran his flagship aground. Damage proved minor, though the accident cost dearly because the vessel sprang leaks that spoiled a major part of the colony's provisions. Undaunted by their misfortune, Lane and Grenville explored Pimlico Sound, seeking a suitable place to settle. After many disagreements they chose Roanoke Island, where Lane laid out a fort and supervised the construction of housing even as he wrangled fiercely with Grenville. By the time Grenville sailed homewards in August for more supplies the breach between the two men was unbridgeable, and each attacked the other in letters to their superiors in England. Their quarrels foreshadowed troubles that were to dog the colony to the end of its days.

Part of the difficulty lay with Lane. Vain, boastful, and fiery-tempered, he brooked little opposition. Then, too, being of a military background, he relied more upon arms than diplomacy, and that approach soured his dealings with the natives from the start. Moreover, Lane's men were suited more to fighting than to settling. They were mainly soldiers who had been recruited for wages and plunder instead of being picked for their talents as colonizers. In essence, they were a garrison in occupied territory. Everyone's survival therefore depended upon whatever forage the land and its indigenous people might yield. It was not the native way to stockpile surpluses of foodstuffs as trade goods, and so local tribes had little to spare, even though they eagerly bartered with the English until the supply of beads, bells, and other trinkets played out—as it did by December 1585. Ralegh's provisioners had also neglected to include nets and other fishing equipment, which limited the settlers' chances of partaking of abundant fish stocks. Soldierly skill at shooting did not readily translate into marksmanship that successfully brought down game.

Despite these hardships, Lane kept his men safely through the winter of 1585–6. The experience convinced him that time and diligent work might sustain a colony, but a more permanent settlement needed two things not readily found at Roanoke Island, a snug harbour and vendible commodities of high demand on English markets. In spring 1586 Lane set off to locate both. He discovered the one—extant accounts indicate how he trekked northwards to the mouth of Chesapeake Bay—but he never found the other. Instead, he had to battle the natives for survival.

With Lane gone from Roanoke, the natives plotted the destruction of the governor and the colony. The local chieftain, whose name was Pemisapan, put it about that Lane intended to attack the natives above Roanoke, which stirred them to harass the governor and his foragers. In turn, the chief tried to undermine the guardians of the fort with tales of Lane's death and attempts to coax his own tribe to forsake Roanoke Island and so cause the soldiers to die of starvation. However, Lane fought his way back to the fort and eventually defeated his enemy.

Shortly thereafter a fleet of English ships under Sir Francis Drake appeared. Drake volunteered some much needed supplies and one of his vessels to tide the settlers over until the expected arrival of Ralegh's relief convoy. A great storm blew up amid the transfer of the stores, which drove Drake's fleet out to sea and evidently broke the colonists' resolve to tarry longer. News that England and Spain neared war intensified doubts that Grenville might return any time soon, and Lane was hardly eager to confront him again. All things considered, Lane and his men opted to return to England with Drake.

Barely two days after they all left, a relief ship, which sailed ahead of Grenville's main column, appeared off Roanoke. Finding none of their countrymen, the ship's company turned round and sailed for home. Grenville arrived a few weeks later only to discover a deserted fort and huts that bore signs of hasty abandonment. He scouted the area for a time before leaving a small holding party and enough provisions to keep them for upwards of two years and making for England.

As for Lane, he landed at Portsmouth in July 1586. Thereafter he participated in preparing English coastal defences against a possible Spanish invasion. By the 1590s he was back in Ireland, where he became muster master-general of the English garrisons and fought rebel Irishmen. Knighted for his services by the lord deputy of Ireland, Sir William Fitzwilliam, Lane lived out his remaining days in Dublin. He died there and was buried in St Patrick's Church on 28 October 1603.

The most notable achievements of the Roanoke expedition were not Lane's. They belonged instead to Thomas Harriot and John White. Harriot's *A Briefe and True Report of the New Found Land of Virginia* described Virginia as a real land of plants and animals and people to be exploited by the English. White supplied beautifully accurate drawings of the Carolina flora and fauna, and in the hands of the Dutch engraver Theodor de Bry these became illustrations for multilingual editions of Harriot's volume that de Bry marketed all across Europe. Harriot and White's work also informed the writings of the greatest of all sixteenth-century promoters of English colonization, Richard Hakluyt the younger, whose tireless efforts led to the founding of Jamestown in 1607.   WARREN M. BILLINGS

Sources D. B. Quinn, *Set fair for Roanoke: voyages and colonies, 1584–1606* (1985) · D. B. Quinn, ed., *The Roanoke voyages, 1584–1590: documents to illustrate the English voyages to North America under the patent granted to Walter Raleigh in 1584*, 1, Hakluyt Society, 2nd ser., 104 (1955) · D. B. Quinn and R. A. Skelton, eds., *The pricipall voyages of the English nation by Richard Hakluyt imprinted at London, 1589*, Hakluyt Society, extra ser., 39 (1965) · D. B. Quinn, 'Preparations for the 1585 Virginia voyage', *William and Mary Quarterly*, 6 (1949), 208–36 · D. B. Quinn, 'Simão Fernandes: a Portuguese pilot in the English service, *circa* 1573–1588', *Congresso Internacional de História dos Descobrimentos: Actas*, 3 (1961), 449–65 · P. Hulton and D. B. Quinn, *The American drawings of John White, 1577–1590*, 2 vols. (1964) · J. H. Parry, *The age of reconnaissance: discovery, exploration, and settlement, 1450–1650* (1963) · J. H. Parry, *The discovery of the sea*, 2nd edn (1981) · *DNB* · M. Rukeyser, *The traces of Thomas Hariot* (1971) · *A briefe and true report of the new found land of Virginia by Thomas Hariot*, ed. R. G. Adams (1951)

Archives BL, memoir, Lansdowne MS 69 · PRO, letters | PRO, corresp. with William Cecil

Lane, Sir Richard (*bap.* **1584**, *d.* **1650**), barrister, was the first son of Richard Lane, yeoman of Courteenhall, Northamptonshire, and his wife, Elizabeth, daughter of Clement Vincent of Harpole, Northamptonshire, and was baptized at Harpole on 12 November 1584. He attended Westminster School and matriculated at Trinity College, Cambridge, as a scholar in 1602. From Cambridge he proceeded to the Middle Temple where he was admitted on 8 February 1605 and was called to the bar on 22 November 1611. Lane appears to have practised primarily in the court of exchequer—a court on whose bench he would later serve. He also served as deputy recorder of Northampton in 1615 and as recorder in 1628. He was possibly a patron or relation of the poet Thomas Randolph who dedicated to Lane his *The Jealous Lovers* of 1632. On 30 October 1629 the Middle Temple chose him as Lent reader for 1630 and in 1634 he became attorney-general to the prince of Wales. In 1635 he served as counsel to the University of Cambridge and on 12 June that year he became a bencher of his inn. He became treasurer of the Middle Temple in 1637 and in May 1638 Henry, earl of Holland, nominated him as his deputy in forest courts.

Early in 1641 Lane served as legal counsel to Thomas Wentworth, first earl of Strafford, during his impeachment and attainder on a charge of high treason in the Long Parliament. On 17 April 1641 during the debate on the bill of attainder Lane argued that the statute 1 Hen. IV c. 10 had effectively repealed the declaratory power invested in parliament by the great Statute of Treasons (25 Ed. III). As a result the Long Parliament had neither the law nor the authority to proceed against Wentworth by bill of attainder. Parliament, however, rejected this argument and Charles I reluctantly gave his assent to the bill of attainder on 10 May 1641. The unfortunate Wentworth was duly beheaded on Tower Hill on 12 May 1641.

Lane also served as counsel to the impeached ship money judge Sir Robert Berkeley from October 1641 and the imprisoned twelve bishops in January 1642. Like most of the judiciary and crown law officers he remained loyal to the king at the outbreak of general hostilities with the Long Parliament in the summer of 1642. Upon joining Charles I at Oxford the king quickly rewarded Lane and he received the degree of MA from the University of Oxford on 1 November 1642. In 1643 the Long Parliament ordered that his 'chambers, goods, chattels and books' at the Middle Temple be seized and his estate sequestered for his adherence to the king (Hopwood, 1005). From the king, however, there were only further rewards. On 4 January 1644 Charles knighted Lane at Oxford and on 23 January raised him to the degree of serjeant-at-law in a ceremony held at the philosophy school. Two days later he was made chief baron of the exchequer and on 31 January he received the degree of DCL from the University of Oxford. In January 1645 he was one of the king's commissioners at the failed Uxbridge negotiations where he resisted parliamentarian demands that parliament have sole control of the militia.

Upon the death of Sir Edward Littleton the king appointed Lane on 30 August 1645 as lord keeper of the great seal. When Oxford surrendered to Sir Thomas Fairfax on 24 June 1646 Lane acted on the king's behalf. In negotiating the articles of capitulation he struggled unsuccessfully to retain control of the great seal, the seals of the other courts, and the sword of state. Fairfax sent the items to parliament and on 3 July 1646 the Long Parliament resolved to have the king's seal destroyed. This was accomplished on 11 August 1646, the seal being ceremonially broken up by a smith and its remnants distributed between the speakers of both houses. Charles II renewed his patent and Lane remained the Stuarts' nominal lord keeper until his death. He followed the newly disinherited king into exile, landing at St Malo in March 1650 in poor health. About this time he wrote to the king asking him to make his eldest son, Richard (b. 1616), a groom of the bedchamber—a request that the king fulfilled. Lane subsequently moved to Jersey where he died on 12 May 1650 and was buried at St Helier. James, duke of York, attended the funeral. Lane's wife, Margaret, died on 22 April 1669. Although Lane had entrusted his chambers, library, and goods to his friend Bulstrode Whitelocke, the latter would later deny all knowledge when Lane's son applied for them.

Lane's lasting significance lay in his legal reporting activities, notably as the posthumous author of *Reports in the court of exchequer beginning in the third, and ending in the ninth year of the raign of the late King James* (1657), which contained an important report of Chief Baron Sir Thomas Fleming's opinion in *Bate's case* (1606). Charles Francis Morrell reprinted this set of reports in a new edition of 1884 and they were incorporated into *The English Reports* in 1914.

D. A. ORR

Sources DNB · Foss, *Judges*, 6.341–3 · Venn, *Alum. Cant.*, 1/3.41 · Foster, *Alum. Oxon.* · Baker, *Serjeants*, 396–7, 522 · W. R. Prest, *The rise of the barristers: a social history of the English bar, 1590–1640* (1986), 276–7, 375 · C. H. Hopwood, ed., *Middle Temple records*, 3: 1650–1703 (1905), 452, 542, 757, 761, 835, 1005 · R. Lane, *Reports in the court of exchequer beginning in the third, and ending in the ninth year of the raign of the late King James* (1657), 22–31 [145 ER 267] · *Lane's exchequer reports … with notes and a life of the reporter*, ed. C. F. Morrell (1884) · S. Kelsey, *Inventing a republic: the political culture of the English Commonwealth* (1997), 93 · D. A. Orr, 'Sovereignty, state, and the law of treason in England, 1641–1649', PhD diss., U. Cam., 1997, 101

Lane, Richard (1795–1880), architect, was born in London on 3 April 1795, the son of Richard Lane and his wife, Margaret (*née* Cowen). Little is known of his parents or early

life, apart from what is mentioned in an anonymous article published in the *Manchester Evening News* of 26 March 1898, where it is stated that he was taught by the mezzotint engraver Samuel William Reynolds (1775–1835), who was married to his mother's sister, before studying the rudiments of his profession in London. He is listed in 1817 as a pupil at l'École des Beaux-Arts of Achille Leclère (1785–1853), who drew upon the architecture of ancient Greece as one of his principal sources. According to the *Manchester Evening News* article Lane returned to London in 1818 and moved to Manchester in the same year. He is first listed in a Manchester directory in 1821. The demand for buildings which would reflect the wealth and social aspirations of Manchester's new mercantile élite offered openings to a man of talent and ambition, and there was not much local competition: of the nine architects listed in a directory of 1825, most were probably no more than builders. The opportunities, however, attracted strong competition from outsiders, among them Charles Barry (1795–1860) and Francis Goodwin (1784–1835). Lane found himself competing, sometimes successfully, with both during the 1820s.

During the 1820s and 1830s Lane became Manchester's principal exponent of the Greek revival style, which had been popularized in the city by Thomas Harrison (1744–1839) and by Francis Goodwin's town hall of 1819–21 (dem.). Early successes with a Methodist chapel in Stockport, Cheshire (1824–6; dem.), and club premises in Bolton, Lancashire (1824–6), were followed by Salford market hall, Lancashire (1825–7). For this Lane used an imposing pedimented portico with attached Greek Doric columns, a design he was to adapt and develop for buildings such as the Friends' meeting-house (1828–31) and the nearby Gentlemen's Concert Hall (1830–31; dem.), with its splendid portico of Corinthian columns overlooking Manchester's St Peter's Square. Like most men of his generation he also designed in the Gothic revival style, and St Mary's Church, Oldham, Lancashire (1827–30), with its fanciful neo-Perpendicular detailing, plaster rib-vaulted ceiling, and attenuated cast-iron columns, is the best of three early churches which all conform with the standard auditory type of the period.

Lane must have felt that his career was securely established when, on 20 August 1827, he married Emma Fagg (b. 1806) of Bedfont, Middlesex, with whom he had a daughter, Emma, and a son, Samuel. In his professional life he continued to prosper, and the decade following his marriage saw him experimenting with a picturesque neo-Tudor style for educational institutions, most notably the West Riding proprietary school in Wakefield (1833–4), as well as continuing to develop the Greek idiom for buildings such as the Chorlton-on-Medlock town hall, Lancashire (1830–32), and Stockport Infirmary (1832–4). That archaeological accuracy was an objective of his interpretation of the Greek style is demonstrated by his reliance on the measured drawings in J. Stuart and N. Revett, *The Antiquities of Athens* (3 vols., 1762–94) and by the Manchester corn exchange (1836; dem.), which was top-lit and had no windows to break the severity of its temple front.

Lane was at the peak of his career when the first Manchester Architectural Society was formed in 1837, and his pre-eminence among his colleagues made him the obvious choice for president. At this time he was involved in the most ambitious project of his career. On the outskirts of Manchester, Victoria Park, with its sinuous thoroughfares and crescents and villas set in their own grounds, is an early example of a planned residential suburban development. Lane designed the layout and the handful of villas which were erected in the first few years following the opening of the park in 1837; the latter are among the few known examples of his domestic architecture. After a promising start the company failed in 1842 and Lane quickly left the house he had designed for himself there and moved to Sale in Cheshire. It must have been a bitter blow and it came at a time when his career was at a watershed. Greek revival architecture had become unfashionable, and the Regency Gothic of his churches and schools represented a style which was being reviled by Gothicists influenced by the writings of A. W. N. Pugin and the proselytizing activities of the Cambridge Camden Society (later the Ecclesiological Society).

Fewer major commissions came during the 1840s, but those that did demonstrate that Lane was able to adapt. St Thomas's Church, Henbury, Cheshire (1844–5), is the model of ecclesiological rectitude, so different from the early churches that it could have been designed by another man. The Manchester Royal Lunatic Asylum (1848–50) in Cheadle, Cheshire, was commended for its enlightened design by J. Conolley in his pioneering book on mental illness, *Treatment of the Insane without Mechanical Restraint* (1856). St John's Church, Isle of Man (1849–51), seat of the traditional Manx court, the Tynwald, was his last major work.

Lane retired in 1859, and eventually settled near Ascot, where he died at his home, Fir Bank, Sunninghill, on 25 May 1880; he was survived by his wife. His career spanned a period when enormous changes were taking place in English architecture, and criticism of Regency architectural styles in general, and of his buildings in particular, appeared in the architectural press during the 1840s. In the latter half of the nineteenth century his work was overshadowed as huge commercial and civic buildings all but obliterated pre-Victorian Manchester. However, of twenty-six known major commissions fifteen survive as a testament to an architect who made an important contribution to the spread of the Greek revival style in the provinces, a scholarly and versatile man who helped to shape early nineteenth-century Manchester and was the city's first truly professional architect.   CLARE HARTWELL

Sources C. Hartwell, 'The work of Richard Lane: a preliminary review', MA diss., University of Manchester, 1990 • *Manchester Evening News* (26 March 1898) • C. Stewart, *The stones of Manchester* (1956), 28–30 • M. Spiers, *Victoria Park Manchester* (1976) • T. Allen, *Lancashire illustrated from original drawings by S. Austin, J. Harwood, G. and C. Pyne, etc.* (1831), 98, 100–01 • M. Girouard, *Cities and people* (1985), 265–6 • A. Darbyshire, *An architect's experiences: professional, artistic, and theatrical* (1897), 21–2 • A. Whitman, *Samuel William Reynolds* (1903), 2 • E. Delaire, *Les architectes élèves de l'École des Beaux-Arts 1789–1907*, 2nd edn (Paris, 1907), 311 • parish register (baptism), 28 April 1795, Piccadilly, St James, London • parish register (marriage), 20 Aug 1827, East Bedfont, Middlesex
Archives Man. CL, Manchester Archives and Local Studies, material relating to individual buildings
Wealth at death under £4000: probate, 1880, *CGPLA Eng. & Wales*

Lane, Richard James (1800–1872), lithographer and sculptor, was born on 16 February 1800 at Berkeley Castle, Gloucestershire, the second son of the Revd Theophilus Lane (1764–1814), prebendary of Hereford Cathedral, and his wife, Sophia, née Gardiner, the niece of the painter Thomas Gainsborough. He was the elder brother of the Arabic scholar Edward William *Lane. He married, on 10 November 1825, Sophia Hodges, with whom he had two sons and three daughters.

From childhood Lane showed an interest in practical and artistic things, and at the age of sixteen he was apprenticed to the line engraver Charles Heath. After completing his apprenticeship he worked as an engraver for some years, and in 1827 produced a fine print after Sir Thomas Lawrence's *Red Riding Hood*. By this time he had become dissatisfied with the commercialization of engraving and had abandoned it for lithography, a process Heath had been one of the first to practise in Britain. Lane's earliest lithographs date from 1824, and in this year his skills were recognized by the leading lithographic printer Charles Hullmandel, who employed him to produce a title vignette for his *Art of Drawing on Stone* (1824) and referred to him briefly in his text as though he was already one of the most accomplished lithographers in Britain. Lane maintained a close association with Hullmandel, who printed nearly all his early lithographs and also called on him for his *On Some Important Improvements in Lithographic Printing* (1827) to illustrate a method of making changes to a drawing on stone once printing had begun. Lane soon established a reputation for the quality of his craftsmanship in lithography and thereby helped to raise the status of this fledgeling process by achieving something of the 'finish' of engraving that was so sought after at the time. He was particularly praised for his delicate crayon work, which, especially in small-scale prints, was unsurpassed in Britain. He first exhibited at the Royal Academy in 1824 and continued exhibiting there regularly until his death, and also occasionally at the Suffolk Street Gallery. He was elected an ARA in 1827. Not long before this he had dedicated his *Studies of Figures by Gainsborough* (1825) to the president of the Royal Academy, Sir Thomas Lawrence. Lane produced most of the plates of this work in tinted lithography in imitation of Gainsborough's crayon originals, many of which were drawn on tinted paper and touched up with white. The outcome was one of the most remarkable applications of tinted lithography in the 1820s.

Lane worked mainly as a reproductive lithographer and produced several sets of lithographs which were much praised at the time, including *Illustrations of the Late John Philip Kemble* (1826) and *Lithographic Imitations of Sketches by Modern Artists* (1827). However, his specialism was portraiture, and he produced hundreds of lithographs of this kind, including portraits of Queen Victoria and members of the royal family, leading artists and actors, and other notable figures, among them Lord Byron. The quality of his portrait lithography was reflected in the fees he charged, which in 1849 were sometimes as high as £100. He also took on other kinds of reproductive work, notably some of the tinted lithographs for J. F. Lewis's *Lewis's Sketches and Drawings of the Alhambra* (1835). His total number of prints is recorded as 1046. Victoria sat for him in 1829 when she was a ten-year-old princess, and he made other portraits of her when she was queen, some of which he lithographed. In 1837 he was appointed lithographer to the queen, and three years later to the prince consort. He also made statuettes, and in 1835 he executed a life-size seated statue of his brother Edward in Egyptian dress. His bust of this brother (*c*.1833) is in the Bodleian Library, Oxford. Lane had acted as assistant to the sculptor J. E. Carew and gave evidence for his master in a lawsuit of 1840.

Towards the end of his life Lane taught at the government School of Design (later the Royal College of Art). In 1864 he took over the etching class, which had been established by J. M. Delâtre not long before; he also taught lithography there. In 1865 he was largely instrumental in securing the right of engravers to be admitted as full academicians. Perversely, he has attracted most attention since his death in connection with a set of four portraits of the North family, drawn by Ingres in Rome in 1815 and printed by Hullmandel in London in the early 1820s, which—it has been suggested—he may have put on stone. He was noted for his fine tenor voice and remarkable memory, which included the ability to recite. In addition to his circle of artist friends, he was at home with leading figures from the opera and theatre; among his closest friends were Charles Kemble (whose *Readings from Shakespeare* he edited in 1870), W. C. Macready, C. A. Fechter, and Maria Feliciá Malibran. He wrote three works, including *Life at the Water Cure, or, A Month at Malvern* (1846). He died at his home, 19 Gloucester Terrace, Campden Hill, Kensington, on 21 November 1872. He was survived by his wife.

MICHAEL TWYMAN

Sources DNB · *Library of the Fine Arts*, 1 (1831), 207–8 · Redgrave, *Artists*, 2nd edn · Graves, *Artists*, 3rd edn · W. S. Williams, 'On lithography', *Transactions of the Society for the Encouragement of Arts, Manufactures, and Commerce* (1847–8), 233–4 · J. Pennell and E. Robins Pennell, *Lithography and lithographers* (1898) · C. Hullmandel, *On some important improvements in lithographic printing* (1827) · *The Lady's Magazine*, new ser., 6 (1825), 56 · *The Lady's Magazine*, new ser., 7 (1826), 682–3 · M. Twyman, *Lithography, 1800–1850* (1970) · F. H. Man, *150 years of artists' lithographs, 1803–1953* (1953) · C. Hullmandel, *The art of drawing on stone* (1824) · *Engraved Brit. ports.* · Thieme & Becker, *Allgemeines Lexikon*, vol. 22 · R. Gunnis, *Dictionary of British sculptors, 1660–1851* (1953) · G. Ashton, *Pictures in the Garrick Club*, ed. K. A. Burnim and A. Wilton (1997) · *CGPLA Eng. & Wales* (1873)
Archives Gainsborough's House, corresp.
Likenesses E. Hodges, pencil and chalk drawing, 1839, NPG · H. Watkins, albumen print photograph, *c*.1855–1859, NPG · Elliott & Fry, two cartes-de-visite, NPG · R. J. Lane, wood-engraving (after photograph by C. Watkins), NPG; repro. in *ILN* (7 Dec 1872), 548 · Mayall, carte-de-visite, NPG · four portraits · group portrait, wood-engraving (*Members of the Royal Academy in 1857*), BM, NPG; repro. in *ILN* (2 May 1857)

Wealth at death under £2000: probate, 19 Feb 1873, *CGPLA Eng. & Wales*

Lane, Samuel (1780–1859), portrait painter, was born on 26 July 1780 at King's Lynn, Norfolk, the oldest of the five children of Samuel Lane (1749–1835), collector of taxes, and his wife, Elizabeth (1753–1832), daughter of the Revd Anthony Mayhew. At the age of seven he became deaf following an accident, said to be a fall into the river mud near his home in Purfleet Street. As a result he was never able to speak distinctly. He later went to London, where he studied under Joseph Farington for three years, and on 21 June 1800 at the age of twenty he was admitted to the Royal Academy Schools and became a pupil of Thomas Lawrence. From about 1802 he was employed by Lawrence as a studio assistant, although the arrangement was not without problems: 'I go on badly with Mr Lawrence. He does not employ me in a regular way, & I lose much time in consequence of his being undetermined how to employ me' (Farington, *Diary*, 7.2751, 7 May 1806). Despite this, he remained with Lawrence for several years and at his death in 1830 Lane completed portraits left unfinished in his studio. For most of his career Lane remained in London, living at 60 Greek Street, Soho. He contributed over 200 portraits to the Royal Academy, exhibiting almost every year between 1804 and 1857. In 1805 he received the freedom of King's Lynn after presenting to the corporation a portrait of George III, copied from the original portrait by Sir Joshua Reynolds. He exhibited with the Norwich Society of Artists between 1819 and 1829 and in London with the British Institution in 1819 and the Society (later Royal Society) of British Artists in 1832. Lane's honest, if somewhat prosaic, likenesses attracted numerous commissions. He had a wide range of sitters. They ranged from the distinguished, such as Robert Southey (1824; Balliol College, Oxford), and the exotic, Ráden Rána Dipura, a Javanese chief who accompanied Sir R. S. Raffles to England (exh. RA, 1818), to the infant son of Mr and Mrs Bartley of the Theatre Royal, Drury Lane (exh. RA, 1826). Several of the portraits were for presentation, for example a portrait of Luke Hansard (Palace of Westminster, London) painted in 1828 for the Stationers' Company and another of Thomas William Coke MP (priv. coll.) painted in 1832 for the Norwich Corn Exchange. Many were engraved by other artists. Lane retained his links with his native Norfolk, and carried out commissions for several wealthy families in the area. One of his sitters, the Revd Thomas Hankinson of King's Lynn, wrote in 1838 that he communicated with Lane in 'finger-talk'. He continued: 'I like Lane very much, and were it not for his unfortunate infirmity should hold a good deal of interesting talk with him' (*Samuel Lane Centenary*). Lane married twice. His first wife was Catherine Jane Powys of Fawley, Buckinghamshire, whom he married in 1835. A portrait by Lane of Horatio Powys Lane, Madras artillery (exh. RA, 1856), may have been of a son. His second marriage took place in 1840 to Elizabeth Murray of Petworth. In 1853 he moved to Ipswich, where he died on 29 July 1859 at his home at 2 Paragon's Buildings, Lower Brook Street. He was buried in Ipswich cemetery, and was survived by his second wife.

NORMA WATT

Sources *Samuel Lane centenary* (1959) [exhibition catalogue, King's Lynn, London] · [J. Chambers], *A general history of the county of Norfolk*, 2 vols. (1829), vol. 1 · Farington, *Diary* · Rajnai Norwich Artists archive, priv. coll. · *Norfolk Chronicle* (7 March 1835) · *Norfolk Chronicle* (15 Feb 1840) · *CGPLA Eng. & Wales* (1859) · transcript of annual register of deaths, 1859, King's Lynn, Norfolk · transcript of burials at Ipswich cemetery, Ipswich RO
Wealth at death under £200: probate, 16 Aug 1859, *CGPLA Eng. & Wales*

Lane [*née* Borrow], **Sarah** (1822/3–1899), actress, playwright, and theatre manager, was born in the neighbourhood of Clerkenwell, London, the daughter of William Borrow, cab proprietor, and of Sarah Fowles. She made her début at sixteen, as a singer at the Ironmonger-Row Saloon in Clerkenwell. She is also reported to have performed at the Bedford Saloon in Camden Town. For most of her life she was identified with the Britannia Theatre in Hoxton, where she progressed from a player in a saloon to the actress, manager, and playwright known as the Queen of the Brit.

In 1841 Samuel Haycraft Lane had opened the Britannia Saloon, where Sarah, under the name Sara Wilton, was engaged as a singer and actress in or about 1843. Following the death of Samuel Lane's first wife, he and Sarah married, probably in 1846; they had no children. During the following thirty years the Lanes built the Britannia into a large and increasingly 'respectable' venue. The saloon early on had something of an unsavoury reputation: a police report from 1844 insists that 'there can be no doubt that this place is calculated to corrupt the morals of the growing youth in that low and thickly populated neighbourhood' (PRO, LC 7/6). The saloon become a theatre in 1858, when it reopened in much-expanded and lavishly redecorated form, with a seating capacity of over 3000 and a reputation for good catering. During this time Sarah Lane became an enormously popular performer, known for saucy comic and melodramatic heroines. The *Touchstone* reported that Lane was 'chiefly remarkable for the wonderful versatility of her powers' (*Touchstone, or, The New Era*, 22 June 1878); *The Era* observed that 'a collection of the pungent and sparkling figurative sayings which this lady is accustomed to utter in her different characters could make a considerably large and amusing book of proverbs, emblems, and repartees' (*The Era*). Lane's particular speciality was the feisty female who battled the villain, stepped out of her place, and wrought the happy ending. Typical is the role of Florence Langton in C. H. Hazlewood's *Mother's Dying Child*, 1864, who, repeatedly insisting 'my natural curiosity must be satisfied', adopts no fewer than four identities as she pursues the villain who threatens her family.

The Lanes were quite prosperous by the 1860s, and spent a good deal of time and money yachting, travelling (during the summer months), and shopping. Sam Lane died in 1871; upon his death Sarah became the lessee of the Britannia Theatre, a position she held until her death in 1899. In running the theatre, Lane occasionally came into conflict with her nephew, A. L. Crauford, who replaced her as manager of the Britannia in 1882. In addition to acting and to managing the theatre, Lane also became a playwright—

she wrote eight plays for the Britannia between 1873 and 1881, usually adaptations from the French. By the mid-1880s she had ceased to be a regular performer at the Britannia, but she did continue to appear in the annual pantomime and in the Britannia Festival that closed the season in December. At the festival—unique to the Britannia—the members of the company would each appear in his or her most popular role of the season, and Sarah Lane would distribute gifts and be strewn with flowers. She made her last appearance at the Britannia during the annual festival performance in 1898. The pantomime remained to the end a great draw, attracting attention from West End critics such as George Bernard Shaw, who favourably compared the wit and wholesomeness of the Brit's pantomime to what he saw as the cynicism and lewdness of the 'expensively dreary' productions of the West End (*Saturday Review*, 9 April 1898).

In her later years Lane was much venerated in the Hoxton community, which had grown progressively poorer in the last decades of the century; she, by contrast, left a substantial personal estate. She died of dropsy, aged seventy-six, at 81 Finchley Road, London, on 16 August 1899, and was buried in Kensal Green cemetery.

HEIDI J. HOLDER

Sources *The Britannia diaries, 1863–1875: selections from the diaries of Frederick C. Wilton*, ed. J. Davis (1992) · J. Davis, 'The gospel of rags: melodrama at the Britannia, 1863–74', *New Theatre Quarterly*, 7/28 (Nov 1991), 369–89 · J. Davis, 'Sarah Lane: questions of authorship', *Playwriting and women in nineteenth-century Britain*, ed. T. Davis and E. Donkin (1999) · J. Davis and T. Davis, 'The people of the "People's Theatre": the social demography of the Britannia Theatre, Hoxton', *Theatre Survey*, 32 (Nov 1991), 137–65 · A. L. Crauford, *Sam and Sallie* (1933) · C. Barker, 'The audiences of the Britannia Theatre, Hoxton', *Theatre Quarterly*, 9/34 (1979), 27–41 · A. E. Wilson, *East End entertainment* (1954) · Carados [H. C. Newton], 'The "Old Brit"', *The Referee* (3 Feb 1924) · H. B. Baker, *History of the London stage and its famous players, 1576–1903*, 2nd edn (1904) · *The Times* (18 Aug 1899) · *The Era* (19 Aug 1899) · *Hackney Gazette* (17 Aug 1899) · d. cert.
Wealth at death £122,456 2s. 7d.: probate, 11 Oct 1899, *CGPLA Eng. & Wales*

Lane, Theodore (*c*.1800–1828), painter and etcher, is said to have been born at Isleworth, Middlesex, in 1800, but the statement is not confirmed by the parish register. His father, who came from Worcester, was a struggling drawing-master, and as a result Lane received little formal education. At the age of fourteen he was apprenticed to the miniature painter John Barrow of Weston Place, St Pancras.

Lane first came to notice as a painter of watercolour portraits and miniatures, and he exhibited four works of that class at the Royal Academy in 1819, 1820, and 1826. However, his talent was for humorous subjects, and a series of thirty-six subjects designed and etched by him, entitled *The Life of an Actor*, with a letterpress by Pierce Egan, was published in 1825. Lane also etched a number of sets of satirical and comic prints of sporting and social life, such as *The Masquerade at the Argyle Rooms*, *Scientific Pursuits, or, Hobby Horse Races to the Temple of Fame*, and *A Trip to Ascot Races*, a series of scenes on the road from Hyde Park Corner to Ascot Heath, which he dedicated to George IV in 1827.

He also illustrated with etchings and woodcuts *A Complete Panorama of the Sporting World* and Egan's *Anecdotes of the Turf, the Chase, the Ring, and the Stage* (1827).

About 1825 Lane took up oil painting, and, with the help of Alexander Fraser, rapidly attained proficiency in the medium. In 1827 he exhibited *The Christmas Present, or, Disappointment*, at the Royal Academy, and *An Hour before the Duel* at the British Institution. The following year he showed *Disturbed by the Nightmare* at the Royal Academy, *Reading the Fifth Act of the Manuscript* at the British Institution, and *The Enthusiast* at the Society of British Artists. The humorous treatment of the subjects and their delicate finish attracted much attention.

Lane's promise was not to be fulfilled, however; his life was terminated by a freak accident. While waiting for a friend at the horse repository in Gray's Inn Road, he struck his head on a skylight and suffered a fatal fall. He died at his home, 79 Judd Street, Brunswick Square, London, on 21 May 1828 and was buried at St Pancras Old Church on 28 May. He left a widow and two children, for whose benefit his best-known work, *The Enthusiast* (Tate collection), representing a gouty angler fishing in a tub of water, was engraved by Robert Graves. The work was later purchased by Robert Vernon and engraved by Henry Beckwith for the *Art Journal* (1850). A work in oils, entitled *The Mathematician's Abstraction*, which was unfinished at his death, was completed by Fraser and purchased by Lord Northwick; it was engraved by H. Graves. In 1831 Egan published *The Show Folks*, illustrated with nine woodcuts designed by Lane. The text was accompanied by a detailed and humorous memoir of the artist, emphasizing a 'mild and peaceable' character unaffected by the foibles of the theatrical and sporting worlds he depicted (Egan, 50). Examples of his work are in the British Museum and the Victoria and Albert Museum, London.

F. M. O'DONOGHUE, rev. GREG SMITH

Sources M. H. Grant, *A dictionary of British etchers* (1952), 125 · *GM*, 1st ser., 98/1 (1828), 572 · P. Egan, *The show folks* (1831)

Lane, Thomas (*c*.1640–1710), merchant, was baptized on 7 January 1641, the son of Thomas Lane, of Dodford, Northamptonshire, and his wife, Sarah, daughter of the Revd Walter Evans. The family were minor gentry with a strong clerical and colonial element: Lane had two grandfathers and an uncle in holy orders, as well as two uncles in Barbados; of his seven brothers, one later entered the church and two went to Jamaica. As the second son in a family of eight sons and four daughters, it was almost inevitable that he would follow a career that took him far from Northamptonshire. Though evidence is lacking, it is likely that during his early years he spent some time as a factor or trader overseas in the Chesapeake or elsewhere in America. He was active as a merchant in London by 1672, when he was importing tobacco from Virginia. About that time he became the partner of Micaiah Perry the elder in the firm of Perry and Lane, Virginia merchants of London. The firm prospered, rising from twelfth among London tobacco importers in 1676 to second in 1686, during years when London accounted for more than half of England's total tobacco imports. After the death in 1688 of its most important competitor, John Jeffreys, the firm moved into first place and held that position until at least 1720. This made it then the largest firm in London trading to North America.

In December 1679 Lane obtained a licence to marry Mary Puckle (1661–1727), daughter of Major William Puckle, a Cromwellian officer, functionary, and later merchant. Her mother was a daughter of Richard Hutchinson, treasurer of the navy under Cromwell. With the patronage of Robert Thomson, another former Cromwellian functionary and later deputy governor of the East India Company, Major Puckle was given a commission to inspect that company's trading stations between Madras and Bengal, where he died in 1676, leaving his daughter an orphan.

The business of Perry and Lane was particularly prosperous during the 1690s, when it added to its direct trade a considerable commission business from larger tobacco planters attracted by the higher European prices in wartime. Lane is not known to have invested in any of the great company flotations of that decade but in 1697 used £6550 of his personal fortune to purchase lands in Charwelton parish, Northamptonshire. He also owned (with the Perrys) Chester's Quay on the Thames, near the Customs House. At his death in 1710, Lane, then of Bethnal Green, left his widow an annuity of £250 derived from the income of his Charwelton lands. They had no children.

Lane took no known part in the guild or public life of London. However, in 1711, after his death, his wife's cousin, the London notary James Puckle, published *The Club*, a collection of humorous sketches, dedicated to Lane and the Perrys, 'Whose Consummate wisdom, Matchless industry, and Perfect honesty, so justly made them Live Beloved, and Die Lamented'. JACOB M. PRICE

Sources J. M. Price, *Perry of London: a family and a firm on the seaborne frontier, 1615–1753* (1992) · G. Baker, *The history and antiquities of the county of Northampton*, 2 vols. (1822–41) · H. I. Longden, *The visitation of the county of Northampton in the year 1681*, Harleian Society, 87 (1935) · will, PRO, PROB 11/518, sig. 250 · will of Mary, widow of Thomas Lane, 1727, PRO, PROB 11/617, sig. 237

Lane, Thomas (*b. c*.1660, *d.* in or after 1704), civil lawyer, was born at Glendon, Northamptonshire, the son of Francis Lane, landowner, of Glendon Hall, and his wife, Mary Bernard. Educated at a school in Higham Ferrers, Northamptonshire, he matriculated from St John's College, Cambridge, in 1673 and graduated BA in 1678. He then moved to Oxford, where he was admitted a commoner of Christ Church, and on 10 October 1678 was incorporated BA. In 1679 he was elected a probationer fellow of Merton College. His election was only one of the continuous subjects of dispute between the warden, Sir Thomas Clayton, and the fellows of Merton, but it was notable for its acrimony and for the warden's decisive defeat. Lane's champion was William Bernard (later DD), vicar of Overton, Wiltshire, and of the Merton living of Malden, Surrey. Bernard was a longstanding opponent of Clayton, and Lane was probably his kinsman.

Lane graduated MA in December 1683, read civil law, and proceeded to the DCL in July 1686. He was admitted to practice in Doctors' Commons later that year and established a strong reputation as an advocate. He was then reputed to have turned papist, and he accompanied Francis Taafe, later earl of Carlingford, on a mission to Vienna, but he was also active in the affairs of his college, where Wood believed that he had sought to build a Northamptonshire faction. Early in 1688, when Lane was serving as bursar, he left Oxford with an account undischarged and a sum of college money in his possession which the subwarden followed him to retrieve, apparently without rancour or other consequences.

In 1689 Lane took a more dramatic course. In 1685 Merton had celebrated James II's succession with bonfires and toasts in claret, and contributed volunteers to the troop raised in the university to resist Monmouth's rebellion. Now Lane went to Ireland and accepted a command in James II's army there. He was wounded and taken prisoner at the battle of the Boyne, and spent a year in captivity in Dublin. Before the end of 1691, however, he returned to Merton, and soon afterwards was in practice again in the court of arches. Wood observed, with something less than his customary sharpness, that Lane's taste for adventure had been satisfied and that he had come to value the college as a haven. In 1704 Lane was a candidate for the wardenship, which would have been a piquant climax to his career in Merton. There is no later notice of him, and he probably died soon afterwards.

Lane was evidently persuasive, and he had other qualities. His learning was not confined to the civil law. Wood says that he contributed to Moses Pitt's *English Atlas* (Oxford, 1680–84), probably collaborating directly with its literary director, William Nicolson, later bishop of Carlisle and of Derry, with whom he shared philological interests. He translated Cornelius Nepos's life of Epaminondas (1684) and took part in a scheme to reorganize the Ashmolean Museum. His enthusiasms seem never to have outrun his energies, nor yet his resourcefulness.

G. H. MARTIN

Sources DNB · Wood, *Ath. Oxon.*, new edn · Foster, *Alum. Oxon.* · G. H. Martin and J. R. L. Highfield, *History of Merton College, Oxford* (1997) · Venn, *Alum. Cant.*

Lane, Timothy (1734–1807), apothecary and natural philosopher, was born in June 1734 in London, the elder son of the two sons and three daughters of Timothy Lane (1705–1741), apothecary and member of the Society of Apothecaries in London, and his wife, Mary. On 5 April 1757 Lane became a member (by patrimony) of the society, and a few years later took over William Watson's practice at Aldersgate Street, London. On 9 June 1763 he married Ann Halford; their only child, Mary Aubrey Lane, was born the following year.

Lane shared Watson's interest in electricity and its applications, and was acquainted with some of the leading electricians of the time, including Joseph Priestley and Richard Lovett to whose works he subscribed. During the 1760s his researches concentrated on the effects of the electric fluid on minerals and living bodies. His concern with the accuracy of electrical measurements led him to the invention of a discharging electrometer that could determine the intensity of the electric shock administered by a Leiden jar. The instrument, which became known as Lane's electrometer, combined with portable electrical machines, came to be widely used as an essential component of medico-electrical apparatus. It was also used by Benjamin Franklin to demonstrate the action of electricity in atmospherical phenomena. The description of the electrometer, in the form of a letter to Franklin, was read at the Royal Society in March 1767 and published in the *Philosophical Transactions*. On 11 January 1770 Lane was elected a fellow of the society.

Lane was as well known for his work in chemistry as for that in natural philosophy. In 1769 his letter to Henry Cavendish 'On the solubility of iron in simple water by the intervention of fixed air' was published in the *Philosophical Transactions*. With Cavendish he also worked at the construction of an artificial torpedo, which mimicked the torpedo fish and could administer electric shocks. On 15 May 1777 he was appointed by the Board of Ordnance to serve on the committee investigating the most appropriate shape of lightning rods to protect buildings during thunderstorms. The committee included William Henley, Edward Nairne, and Joseph Planta, secretary of the Royal Society, and subsequently also Cavendish, Priestley, and Pringle, the society's president, among others.

Within the Society of Apothecaries Lane advanced to the rank of upper warden in 1800 and in the following year to the mastership, and it was as master that he lectured on botany to the apprentices in 1803. On 5 June 1801 he obtained a patent (no. 2511) for his invention of 'Measuring glasses for compounding medicines'. In the specification Lane stated that to distinguish the measures made under the patent the name 'Lane' was to be affixed to them. The apparatus was regarded as an effective means in preventing vendors and purchasers from being deceived by fallacious measures of the kind that were detected by the censors of the Royal College of Physicians in the years 1800 and 1801. Lane died on 5 July 1807 at his daughter's house in Hampstead.

PAOLA BERTUCCI

Sources GM, 1st ser., 77 (1807), 689 · T. Lane, 'Description of an electrometer', PTRS, 57 (1767), 451–60 · freedom admissions to the Society of Apothecaries, London, GL, MS 8206/2 · parish registers, St Edmund the King and Martyr, London · parish registers, St Botolph Aldersgate, London · *The writings of Benjamin Franklin*, ed. A. H. Smyth, 10 vols. (1907); repr. (1970) · election certificate, RS · W. Bulloch, 'Roll of the fellows of the Royal Society', index, RS · J. C. Poggendorff and others, eds., *Biographisch-literarisches Handwörterbuch zur Geschichte der exacten Wissenschaften*, 2 vols. (Leipzig, 1863)
Likenesses P. Audinet, engraving (after W. Patten), Wellcome L.

Lane, William (1745/6–1814), publisher, was probably born in Whitechapel, London, the son of John Lane, poulterer, and his wife, Mary. He became a liveryman of the Poulterers' Company in 1767, and in the same year was admitted into the Honourable Artillery Company, in which he was to achieve some eminence. He began his bookselling activities about 1770 from his father's shop, but had moved to 13 Aldgate High Street by the end of 1773; it was at this time that his first publications came out, among them the *Ladies' Museum* (1773–1814), and that he began to explore the possibilities of circulating libraries.

While retaining an interest in the artillery company (he had been elected to the office of adjutant in 1772 and in 1774 was the first captain of the Red regiment of trained bands), he resigned as adjutant in 1775 in order to concentrate on his business. He transferred to the Stationers' Company in 1777, becoming a liveryman in 1776 at the time of his move to 33 Leadenhall Street. About 1784 he set up a press there, and founded an ambitious system of circulating libraries; to anyone wishing to found such a library he offered a stock of books, a catalogue, and instructions. He was a pioneer in establishing circulating libraries in country districts; earlier they had been confined to major towns and watering-places. Also, as a means of diffusing his own publications, this time through advertisement, he was among the backers in 1788 of the first evening daily, the *Star and Evening Advertiser*; it created a precedent in offering a copy service to others. Lane's partnership with the printer of the *Star*, Peter Stuart, was curtailed in 1789 at the time of the Regency Bill, when Stuart allegedly printed anti-Pitt propaganda; in revenge, Stuart began a short-lived rival to the *Star* in which Lane was pilloried as a 'scribbling poulterer' and his paper as the 'Dog Star'. Lane's *Star* continued until 1831, when it was absorbed by *The Albion*.

In 1790 Lane adopted for his business the title Minerva Press. It was under this imprint that the light romantic novels were issued which constituted the staple fare of Lane's circulating libraries. Often written by women (including Agnes Maria Bennett and Mary Meeke), and intended for a female readership, the novels are characterized by a blend of sentiment and sensationalism with elements of the fashionable Gothic, such as the popular *The Children of the Abbey* (1796) by Regina Maria Roche; a number of them were translations from the French. The Minerva Press became synonymous with cheap fiction and into the nineteenth century the name 'meant little more than a convenient epithet of contempt' (Blakey, 1). (In recent analyses 'notorious presses' such as Minerva are held responsible for the 'constant criticism and mockery aimed at fiction by educated people in the period who saw in it an undermining of traditional classical culture' (Todd, 219–20).)

Nevertheless by the end of the eighteenth century Lane had become wealthy by profits from them and from military activities. By 1791 he had risen to the rank of lieutenant-colonel in the White regiment and first captain of the West London regiment in 1794. In his business Lane formed separate departments in printing, and in publishing and bookselling. In 1801 he took Anthony King Newman as his partner in publishing. In 1803 the company was trading as Lane, Newman & Co. When war with France was renewed in the same year his publication of *The Soldier's Companion* secured him a considerable fortune. Minerva books were circulating internationally. Lane retired from business at some time between 1803 and 1808 and settled in Brighton. He was replaced by John Darling in 1809.

Lane married twice; his second wife, Phoebe (*bap.* 1770), was the daughter of Lewis Shepheard of Richmond, Surrey. Lane died on 29 January 1814 at 3 Gloucester Place, Brighton, aged sixty-eight. He had no children. He was buried in his wife's family vault at Richmond parish church on 9 February 1814. Acquaintances credited Lane with 'strong mental powers … energy and spirit' (Blakey, 25). The development of the library system remains his most significant achievement.

ALISON SHELL, *rev.* CLARE L. TAYLOR

Sources D. Blakey, *The Minerva Press, 1790–1820* (1939) · J. Todd, *The sign of Angellica: women, writing and fiction, 1660–1800* (1989) · burial register, Richmond parish church, Surrey · *IGI* · J. Nichols and J. B. Nichols, eds., *Illustrations of the literary history of the eighteenth century*, 8 vols. (1815–58), vol. 8

Wealth at death under £17,500: Blakey, *Minerva Press*

Lane, William (1746–1819), portrait draughtsman and engraver, of whose parents nothing is known, began his career as an engraver of gems, exhibiting such works at the Royal Academy from 1778 to 1789. In 1785 Lane exhibited a crayon portrait of Mrs Siddons among others. He later became an established and successful artist in this medium, his drawings being delicate and accurately drawn. Between 1798 and 1815 he exhibited a further forty-four portraits at the Royal Academy. Lane also engraved a few small copperplates after works by Richard Cosway and Sir Joshua Reynolds. His portraits were admired for their accuracy as likenesses. He was patronized by the prince regent and many of the nobility. A portrait of Francis Russell, fifth duke of Bedford, and a composite group, *Whig Statesmen and their Friends*, also in chalk, are in the National Portrait Gallery, London. A copy by Lane of Reynolds's portrait of Charles James Fox is in the Royal Collection. A few of Lane's works were engraved, by F. C. Lewis among others. He died at his home in the Hammersmith Road, London, on 4 January 1819.

Miss Anna Louisa Lane, who was related to Lane, exhibited at the Society of Artists and the Royal Academy from Lane's address, 130 Pall Mall, London.

F. M. O'DONOGHUE, *rev.* JILL SPRINGALL

Sources Graves, *RA exhibitors* · *GM*, 1st ser., 89/1 (1819), 181 · D. Foskett, *A dictionary of British miniature painters*, 2 vols. (1972) · B. Stewart and M. Cutten, *The dictionary of portrait painters in Britain up to 1920* (1997) · Redgrave, *Artists* · *Engraved Brit. ports.* · O. Millar, *The later Georgian pictures in the collection of her majesty the queen*, 2 vols. (1969) · D. Foskett, *Miniatures: dictionary and guide* (1987)

Lane, Sir William Arbuthnot, first baronet (1856–1943), surgeon and health campaigner, was born at Fort George, near Inverness in Scotland, on 4 July 1856, the eldest child of Benjamin Lane (*b.* 1827), surgeon to the 80th regiment of foot, and his wife, Caroline Arbuthnot (*d.* 1903), daughter of Joseph Ewing, a retired inspector-general of hospitals and an Ulsterman. Benjamin Lane's family had been doctors and lawyers in Limavady, co. Londonderry, for many generations, having come to Ireland during the plantation of Ulster. At only two weeks of age Lane was taken to South Africa, where his father's regiment served in a frontier war. Until the age of twelve he travelled around the world with the regiment, which was posted to

Bengal, Corfu, Malta, Halifax (Nova Scotia), and Dublin. Between the ages of twelve and sixteen he studied under John and Thomas Braidwood, and latterly with five other pupils at Stanley House School, Bridge of Allan, near Stirling.

In 1872 Lane's family moved to Woolwich, London, and in the same year he entered Guy's Hospital as a medical student. Between 1874 and 1877 he passed through the various student posts of dresser, ward clerk, and anatomy demonstrator; he passed the MRCS examination in 1877. Following this he spent a few months as a ship's doctor in the Caribbean. His next post, as house physician at Guy's to W. Moxon and C. H. Fagge, was important in that Moxon persuaded Lane that his chances of promotion at Guy's were greater in surgery than in medicine.

Lane's surgical career started at Victoria Hospital for Children, Chelsea, as house surgeon. After gaining his MB degree (London, 1881) and becoming FRCS (1882) Lane returned to Guy's initially as an anatomy demonstrator, and later as assistant surgeon in October 1882. He became MS (London) the following year. On 25 October 1884 Lane married Charlotte Jane, the daughter of John Briscoe, a merchant of Tinvane, co. Tipperary, and the sister-in-law of his old teacher C. H. Fagge. During this period he lived at 8 St Thomas's Street. These years allowed him easy access to cadavers and patients and the time to develop the ideas which informed his controversial work. A paper he wrote on empyema led to him being wrongly credited as the first person to resect a rib for empyema, an incident typical of his work. Lane was considered to be original in outlook rather than conception, and though criticized by his seniors he was accepted, at least for a time, by his juniors and most of his contemporaries. In 1895 he moved to 21 Cavendish Square, just south of Harley Street, thus enhancing his private practice. He remained there until about 1930. Lane's move to the West End prior to his appointment as full surgeon to Guy's in 1903 was unusual and had been authorized after his wife had petitioned the treasurer of the hospital.

Lane was also a consultant at Great Ormond Street Hospital for Sick Children from 1883 to 1916. During the First World War he not only continued at Guy's but was consulting surgeon to the Aldershot command and the French Hospital. He was asked to organize and open Queen Mary's Hospital, Sidcup, which became the nursery of all modern plastic work. He was created baronet in 1913 after operating on 'a princess of the royal house' and was made CB in 1917. He was also a member of the Athenaeum and chevalier of the Légion d'honneur.

Several characteristics shaped Lane's life and work. He was an extremely skilful and competent surgeon who possessed marvellous manual dexterity, and he was among the pioneers of aseptic surgical technique. He developed long instruments which allowed the surgeon to work without touching the tissues, and he worked with nursing staff to ensure the sterility of the operating area. These skills and methods enabled him to perform surgery which would previously have been extremely dangerous to the patient. Lane's profound distrust of received wisdom was expressed in his dictum 'if everyone believes a thing it is probably untrue'. He preferred his own theories, which he formulated in the mid-1880s and used until well into his retirement. His work and activities attracted criticism and sometimes abuse all through his life, a state of affairs which he certainly did little to avoid. He was, however, softly spoken, charismatic, humorous, and often charming, and was said to treat his patients with 'unorthodox kindness'. He formed strong friendships with both senior and junior colleagues, including many of his critics. His home was evidently a happy, informal place, full of pets and frequent visitors. He was a connoisseur of porcelain and enjoyed dancing.

Lane's private practice was very successful, probably stemming from his reputation as the only man in London who could open the abdomen safely. By 1925 he had an income stated by one friend to be £20,000 per annum, and had bought an estate, Glendalough, co. Wicklow, Ireland.

The theoretical framework on which Lane based his work was the product of skeletal studies carried out while anatomy demonstrator at Guy's. A keen evolutionist, Lane began by studying the bones of working men and described changes which took place in their skeletons. Lane saw these changes as evidence of evolution occurring in a single lifetime. In the fourth edition of his book *The Operative Treatment of Chronic Intestinal Stasis* (1918) he set out the principles which he held throughout his life: 'The skeleton represents the crystallization of lines of force which when exerted in a single direction are laid down as cancellous tissue' (p. 1); and 'every change in the anatomy of the individual which develops during lifetime enables him to accommodate himself more efficiently to his surroundings [but] tends to shorten his life' (p. vi, preface).

The first and most lasting application of Lane's ideas was to the treatment of simple fractures (breaks in bone where the skin is intact). Lane was unimpressed by the results of splinting. Dockers with fractures which were supposed to have been set well complained they could not do their work. After watching them at the docks Lane realized that every broken bone had to be put back exactly into the position which the pieces had held before. Lane started to operate on these fractures, fixing them with wire or screws to realign the bones, which directly contravened the surgical conventions of the time. These operations, from which much modern orthopaedic practice was later developed, were initially opposed in Britain, despite being enthusiastically taken up in the United States and Germany. A report by the British Medical Association (BMA) was to endorse Lane's approach officially in 1912. Lane also developed neonatal operations for cleft palate and promoted breathing exercises to develop the structure of the face.

It was as an abdominal surgeon that Lane was at his most controversial. He developed the idea that once the colon became overloaded it became kinked by the crystallization of the abnormal forces acting on it, exacerbating the initial constipation. The colonic contents thus became a source of internal chronic poisoning, and Lane termed this process chronic intestinal stasis. The idea of chronic poisoning from the colon was not new, having been held by many in the medical establishment in Lane's youth, such as Sir James Paget. His thinking on this was reinforced by the ideas of Elie Metchnikoff (1845–1916), whom he met in 1904, and particularly his book *La vie humaine* (1903). Stasis could in Lane's view cause problems ranging from general debility to the development of rheumatoid arthritis, tuberculosis, or cancer. From the 1890s he prescribed paraffin as a lubricant (he took it himself thrice daily) and he removed entire colons from patients in increasing numbers from 1900 onwards. Again these treatments and the specific ideas of anatomical change were widely opposed. A special series of meetings on alimentary toxaemia was held at the Royal Society of Medicine in 1913. The operative treatment of chronic intestinal stasis was rejected at the last meeting. Lane was said to be crushed by this outcome, though other general theories of chronic poisoning from the colon or teeth remained popular with some doctors for many years.

In the early 1920s Lane became interested in the idea that cancer was the product of faulty diet and the civilized habits of life. Public and professional interest in diet was heightened at this time by the recent discovery of vitamins. Lane gave several press interviews on the subject in 1924, which attracted the censure of the BMA ethics committee, whose members interpreted such interviews as indirect advertising. Lane became publicly critical of the BMA for opposing public statements on health by doctors, and resigned his membership. This was commonly mistaken for his having either been removed from, or having removed himself from, the medical register in order to carry on his health propaganda. Lane himself repeated this latter account in his private autobiography, though he actually continued in practice and was registered until 1933.

In 1925 Lane inaugurated the New Health Society, despite the disapproval of the BMA and the rulings by the General Medical Council on indirect advertising. The society used newspaper articles and public lectures as well as books to disseminate information on healthy diet and lifestyle. It achieved a high public profile through its friendly collaboration with the press, especially the *Daily Mail*, and the impressive membership of the council, which included Lloyd George, Lord Asquith, Alfred Mond, George Lansbury, William Willcox, and Henry Wellcome. Public health education of this sort rapidly became accepted by the BMA with the encouragement of Sir George Newman, then chief medical officer. The ideas promoted by the society included the use of wholemeal bread, increasing consumption of fruit and vegetables, returning the people to the land, both as smallholders and as holidaymakers, maximizing exposure to sunlight, the importance of regular bowel habits, and physical exercise. As well as reflecting the popular interest in physical culture it also supported some of the widespread eugenic thinking of the time. The society was wound up in 1937, but the journal *New Health* remained in publication until 1963.

In 1935 Lane's first wife, Charlotte, died, and on 25 September of the same year he married Jane Mutch (*b.* 1884/5), the daughter of Nathan Mutch, a Rochdale building contractor. Jane's brother, Dr Nathan Mutch, was involved in the New Health Society, and was married to Lane's third daughter, Eileen. Lane died at his home, 46 Westbourne Terrace, London, on 16 January 1943, survived by his second wife. By his first marriage he had three daughters and one son, Sir William Arbuthnot Lane (1897–1972). His eldest daughter, Rhona, was headmistress of Wycombe Abbey School (1925–7).

Balanced accounts of Lane's life and work are rare. Many tend to focus on his work on chronic intestinal stasis, producing an entertaining but erroneous caricature. Lane was a colourful character with a dislike of convention, who was among those pioneering many lasting developments in surgery, especially orthopaedics; and he was an enthusiastic proponent of health education through the mass media.   ANDREW A. G. MORRICE

Sources T. B. Layton, *Sir William Arbuthnot Lane, bt.* (1956) · W. A. Lane, 'Autobiography', 1936, Wellcome L., GC/127/A2 · W. E. Tanner, *Sir William Arbuthnot Lane, bart.* (1946) [incl. bibliography of all Lane's pubns] · A. A. G. Morrice, '"The medical pundits": doctors and indirect advertising in the lay press, 1922–1927', *Medical History*, 38 (1994), 255–80 · *DNB* · *Medical Directory* (1902) · m. certs. · d. cert. · *CGPLA Eng. & Wales* (1943) · Burke, *Peerage*

Archives Wellcome L., autobiographical notes and papers | BL, corresp. with Marie Stopes, Add. MS 58566

Likenesses A. Wolmark, pen-and-ink drawing, 1926, NPG · E. Cock, mechanically reproduced caricature, NPG; repro. in *VF* (21 May 1913) · D. Low, caricature, pencil sketch, NPG · E. Newling, oils, Guy's Hospital, London

Wealth at death £75,968 19*s.* 0*d.*: probate, 27 March 1943, *CGPLA Eng. & Wales*

Lane-Fox. For this title name *see* Fox, Felicity Lane-, Baroness Lane-Fox (1918–1988).

Laneham, Robert. *See* Langham, Robert (*c.*1535–1579/80).

Lanesborough. For this title name *see* Lane, George, first Viscount Lanesborough (1620–1683).

Laney, Benjamin. *See* Lany, Benjamin (1591–1675).

Lanfranc (*c.*1010–1089), archbishop of Canterbury, was a Lombard by birth, who became a monk in Normandy before he was made archbishop four years after the Norman conquest of England in 1066.

Early life Lanfranc was born in Pavia, the capital of Lombard Italy, at an unknown date, probably *c.*1010 or soon after. A late and unconfirmed Canterbury tradition gave his parents' names as Haribaldus and Roza (*Works of Gervase of Canterbury*, 2.364). His father was known as a prominent and respected citizen who belonged to 'the order of those who oversaw the rights and laws of the city' (Gibson, 'Vita Lanfranci', 668). About Lanfranc's early years, his twelfth-century life contains divergent accounts. According to one, he was educated from childhood both in the liberal arts and in Lombard law; he exhibited precocious skill in pleading causes and in passing judgments; he thereby won lasting fame at Pavia; only after leaving Italy did his thoughts turn to the true wisdom of the religious life. According to the other, he lost his father at a tender age; rather than succeeding to his father's honour and dignity, he left Pavia to study the liberal arts elsewhere; he returned only when he was well grounded in them, before leaving for France. This account makes no mention of legal study or practice. Since Lanfranc's later writings and activities give scant evidence of special knowledge of or skill in Lombard law, it is best to leave open the question of how familiar with it he became.

Not before 1031 (and perhaps several years later), Lanfranc, like many Italian scholars of his time, left Italy for France, where he travelled the country with a considerable following of pupils. Probably after visiting Tours and Chartres, he eventually reached Normandy, where he taught for some time at Avranches, a city still suffering after the viking ravagings. He is likely to have taught widely in the seven liberal arts, but with some specialization in dialectic. At Avranches his vocation to the religious life developed and deepened; he decided to search for a place where there would be no *litterati* to honour and reverence him.

Lanfranc the monk Lanfranc set out alone towards Rouen. According to a perhaps apocryphal story, as he passed through a wood near the River Risle, he fell among thieves, who robbed, blindfolded, and abducted him. Upon asking passers-by to direct him to the most lowly and poor monastery of the neighbourhood, he was sent to Bec, where he found the abbot working with his own hands to build an oven. After reflecting upon the rule of St Benedict, Lanfranc asked to be, and was permitted to become, a monk there.

Lanfranc probably came to Bec in 1042. The monastery had been founded in 1034 by Herluin, a knight from the nearby castle of Brionne, who became its first abbot. The keynote of its early years as described in Gilbert Crispin's life of Herluin (itself a major source for the life of Lanfranc) was austerity and simplicity. According to these lives, Herluin and Lanfranc from the start of their association complemented each other as models of the active and the contemplative life: Herluin attended to the external business of Bec, including its legal affairs, while Lanfranc devoted himself to silence, meditation, and the observance of the monastic office. Before long, however, Lanfranc became troubled by laxity among his monastic brethren; his secret preparations to leave Bec and become a hermit were frustrated by being revealed to Herluin in a dream. Lanfranc humbled himself before his abbot and professed full obedience. About 1045 Herluin appointed him prior (or second-in-command) of the monastery, with responsibility for both internal and external affairs. During Lanfranc's eighteen years or so as prior, Bec grew in numbers and acquired churches and endowments; it became a thriving Benedictine house alongside the older monasteries of Normandy. In 1063 Duke William chose Lanfranc, despite his reluctance to leave Bec, to be the first abbot of St Étienne at Caen. Lanfranc embarked upon the construction of the abbey church and buildings. In 1068 he secured from Pope Alexander II the exemption of his abbey from the authority of the diocesan, the bishop of Bayeux.

During his years in Norman monasteries, Lanfranc's concerns were far from being limited to monastic affairs in the strict sense. He continued and greatly developed his work as a teacher. As prior of Bec, he was responsible for the claustral school in which boys were educated for life in the community; the fame of his teaching quickly and increasingly attracted young men from near and far, not least from Germany, to be equipped for employment outside the cloister. His teaching was at first mainly in the liberal arts and in 1059 Pope Nicholas II sent imperial and papal chaplains to be taught the dialectic and rhetoric that were useful in curial service, though he also referred to reports that Lanfranc had become concerned with biblical studies. Probably while Lanfranc was at Caen, Pope Alexander II wished to send him a kinsman for further education, possibly theological. Lanfranc opened his teaching to outsiders in part from a wish to raise money for the buildings and other monastic necessities at Bec which he urged upon Abbot Herluin, and especially for

Lanfranc (c.1010–1089), manuscript drawing

the removal of the monastery, c.1060, to a more suitable site. Lanfranc's pupils at Bec included the canon lawyer Ivo, bishop of Chartres (r. 1090–1115), and the anti-Berengarian writer Guitmund, later bishop of Aversa (r. 1088–c.1090x95). Anselm of Aosta, who entered Bec in 1060 (and who succeeded Lanfranc as prior there and later as archbishop of Canterbury), acknowledged a major debt to Lanfranc's instruction in learning as well as in the monastic life. Evidence that Pope Alexander II had been Lanfranc's pupil is late and inconclusive.

In Normandy, Lanfranc became Duke William's ecclesiastical adviser. There seem at first to have been stresses between them, perhaps arising from Lanfranc's criticism of the duke's marriage to Matilda of Flanders on grounds of relationship within the prohibited degrees. A story has it that William banished Lanfranc from Normandy. He set off on a lame horse, but asked the duke to give him a sound one so that he could obey his sentence of exile. The jest served permanently to restore Lanfranc to the duke's favour. In 1059, Pope Nicholas II observed with satisfaction that 'his friend' Duke William habitually followed Lanfranc's advice (Southern, 20–21); Norman sources referred to his special and beneficial place as William's spiritual director and political counsellor. As they stand, twelfth-century accounts of Lanfranc's success at Rome in 1059 as an intermediary between William and the papacy over the problem of his marriage and of his securing a papal dispensation for William in return for the foundation of the abbeys of St Étienne and La Trinité at Caen are of questionable historicity; however, they testify to his reputation for diplomatic skill and success. In 1067, after he had himself refused the archiepiscopal see of Rouen, Lanfranc secured, at Rome, Pope Alexander II's permission for the translation to it of Bishop Jean of Avranches.

Lanfranc had a series of contacts with the reforming popes of his monastic years, especially Leo IX (1049–54), Nicholas II (1059–61), and Alexander II (1061–73). In view of his duties as prior of Bec, his possibly year-long association with Leo IX (which later Bec tradition obscured) was remarkably protracted. It began at, or more probably soon after, Leo's great reforming council at Rheims in October 1049. Lanfranc was certainly with him at Remiremont on 14 November, as one of his letters shows, and he accompanied him back to Rome before a council at the Lateran beginning on 29 April 1050. Leo asked Lanfranc to stay in the papal entourage until the Council of Vercelli in September. Lanfranc thus witnessed at first hand an energetic year's work by the first significant reforming pope of the eleventh century. His return to Rome for Pope Nicholas II's council of April 1059 cannot be proved but, on balance, is probable (Southern, 22–4; Gibson, Lanfranc, 109–11 gives a different view); Lanfranc preserved on pages of his canon-law collection a dossier of documents relating to the council. An outcome of his contacts with the papacy was his high regard for the energetic reformer Cardinal Humbert of Silva Candida, in respect not only of his eucharistic theology but also of his general impact on church affairs. In 1067 ducal business again brought Lanfranc to Rome; his standing with Pope Alexander II was such that he later called him 'our most cherished member and one of the leading sons of the Roman church' (Letters of Lanfranc, 60–61).

Lanfranc the scholar While he was a monk at Bec, Lanfranc's work as a teacher was reinforced by academic and theological study. So far as the arts are concerned, he wrote a lost treatise, De dialectica. He devoted much attention to correcting the texts of the Old and New testaments in their Latin version and of the Christian fathers of the early church. His main purpose was simply to establish the best readings. His emendations passed into manuscripts which, at Bec and elsewhere, remained in use well into the twelfth century. His annotations on patristic texts included brief comments upon St Augustine of Hippo's De civitate Dei and Pope Gregory the Great's Moralia in Job. He was concerned to use such texts as a vehicle for grammatical instruction, thus seeking in a novel way to use Christian texts for this purpose. From c.1055 Lanfranc increasingly devoted himself to biblical study. His principal commentaries were one on the Psalms, which survives only in two fragments, and another on the Pauline epistles, fourteen in number since he accepted Hebrews as Pauline (Patrologia Latina, 150.105–406). He again provided much analysis of language and of rhetorical structure, but he increasingly also added excerpts from the ancient fathers, which he took from Carolingian florilegia of selected passages. He expressed his mistrust of secular learning as a means to the exploration of Christian truth. In his biblical commentaries, Lanfranc was less of an innovator than in his annotations of Augustine and Gregory. However, his commentary on the Pauline epistles circulated and was widely copied. His work was used and built upon in the schools of Laon and Paris. As a scholar, Lanfranc cannot be deemed original or creative, but his skills developed in ways that prepared for major twelfth-century advances.

Lanfranc and Berengar of Tours Lanfranc's controversy with Berengar of Tours affected every stage of his life after leaving Italy. Their principal difference concerned the presence of Christ in the eucharistic elements. According to Lanfranc, this presence was substantial in a sense akin to Aristotle's understanding of substance, so that, at the eucharistic consecration, bread and wine were in themselves changed into the body and blood of Christ; for Berengar, it was a matter of signification not of change: the material bread and wine persisted while becoming also the spiritual body and blood of Christ. Lanfranc and Berengar represented different methods of thought and looked back to different patristic and Carolingian traditions: Lanfranc to St Ambrose and Paschasius Radbertus, but Berengar to St Augustine of Hippo and Ratramnus. Berengar fuelled opposition to his position by the obscurity of his Latin and by the contentiousness of his demeanour.

Lanfranc heard Berengar lecture on logic during his early wanderings in France and formed a poor opinion. In 1049, at about the time of the Council of Rheims, Lanfranc nevertheless came under suspicion of complicity in Berengar's supposed aberrations; but at Leo IX's Easter synod of 1050, he successfully defended himself. In the following autumn, Lanfranc was present, though not in a prominent capacity, at Brionne when Berengar debated his opinions with other scholars. If Lanfranc was at Rome for Nicholas II's Easter synod of 1059, he was not present at the session when Berengar appeared before it. However, he approved of the extremely realist profession of faith, drafted by Cardinal Humbert, to which Berengar was made to swear an oath of acceptance; it is among the documents of the time that are copied into Lanfranc's canonical collection.

On returning to France, Berengar recanted his oath and returned to his former teaching. After Nicholas II and Humbert died in 1061, Lanfranc came to the fore as Berengar's leading opponent. Probably early in his years as abbot at Caen, he wrote his *De corpore et sanguine domini*, in which he began with the Easter synod of 1059 and deployed philosophical arguments and patristic citations against Berengar and in advocacy of his own position. At Pope Alexander II's request, Lanfranc in 1072 dispatched a copy to Rome; the treatise also circulated widely in northern Europe. Berengar's own principal surviving work, his *Rescriptum contra Lanfrannum*, was written in indignant reply. As archbishop of Canterbury, Lanfranc was still at pains to refute 'that schismatic Berengar', especially when he challenged the orthodoxy of St Hilary of Poitiers's *De trinitate*; Lanfranc later gave a hint that he was less than satisfied by Pope Gregory VII's eventual condemnation in 1079 of Berengar's eucharistic teaching (*Letters of Lanfranc*, 142–9, 158–9).

Canterbury: the early years At Eastertide 1070 papal legates deposed Stigand, archbishop of Canterbury since 1052. King William I summoned a reluctant Lanfranc, who was already some sixty years old, to succeed him. Lanfranc accepted only when Pope Alexander II added his own command through legates, Bishop Ermenfrid of Sion and the Roman subdeacon Hubert, who convened for the purpose a general assembly of Norman clergy and laity. Lanfranc was appointed on 15 August and consecrated at Canterbury on 29 August by Bishop Maurice of London and seven or eight other suffragans of Canterbury.

Until Alexander's sudden death on 21 April 1073, Lanfranc enjoyed and reciprocated his favour and trust to a striking degree. When Lanfranc visited Rome in autumn 1071 and received his pallium (the stole of white wool which signified a metropolitan's participation in the apostolic pastoral office), Alexander added the rare, personal grant of a second pallium which he had himself worn liturgically. After Lanfranc returned to England, Alexander told the king of major matters that he had delegated for Lanfranc to settle in England; he had so far committed his authority to Lanfranc that whatever he rightly decided should be as binding as a decision taken in the pope's presence. Lanfranc, for his part, looked to Alexander for favour and for advice in a number of particular cases including those of bishops. He commended himself to Alexander as 'a loyal follower and servant of St Peter and of yourself, and of the holy Roman church' (*Letters of Lanfranc*, 54–5; see also 32–9, 42–3, 60–63).

Lanfranc quickly claimed a primatial status for Canterbury which he deemed to be both historically justified and practically necessary for the well-being of the church in England and throughout the British Isles. At Pentecost 1070, the Norman, Thomas of Bayeux, had been nominated for the vacant see of York. Lanfranc quickly entered into a dispute about the relation of the two metropolises; a memorandum of it was included in Lanfranc's letter-collection (*Letters of Lanfranc*, 38–57). Thomas's consecration was delayed until after Lanfranc's, and when Thomas came to Canterbury, Lanfranc claimed the custom of his predecessors for requiring from him a written profession of obedience, fortified by an oath. Thomas expressed dissatisfaction with the evidence that Lanfranc adduced and departed without consecration. The king was angry because he thought Lanfranc to be claiming more than his due. But during a subsequent encounter, at which Lanfranc said that the English testified in his favour, he persuaded the king and the Normans of the justice of his claim. By royal edict Thomas had to return 'to the mother church of the whole kingdom' and to make a profession of absolute and unconditional obedience to Lanfranc in all matters of the Christian religion; as regards obedience to Lanfranc's successors, the issue was left open. Thomas made a profession of obedience, the text of which has not survived, and Lanfranc consecrated him late in 1070 or early in 1071.

According to the Canterbury account, it was Thomas (who accompanied Lanfranc to Rome in autumn 1071) by whom the question of the primacy of Canterbury over York was raised before the pope. Thomas cited the authority of Pope Gregory the Great for pleading the equal status of the two metropolises; he also claimed the obedience to himself of the bishops of Dorchester (later Lincoln), Worcester, and Lichfield. After long debate, Pope Alexander ruled that both matters should be decided in England. At Eastertide 1072 they were considered during the royal court at Winchester. Lanfranc afterwards rehearsed in a letter to the pope the arguments by which he had claimed Canterbury's primacy not only over York but of the whole British Isles including Ireland. A number were historical and derived from Bede and other sources; to the modern critic they appear somewhat weak. As 'the final core and foundation of our whole case', he named eight popes from Gregory the Great to Leo IX whose privileges and letters he asserted to bear out his claim. Most of the popes named appear among the alleged authors of forged privileges which were produced at Rome in 1123 when Canterbury's case was presented there. Scholars have long debated whether, in 1072, Lanfranc used forgeries which had already been prepared (with or without his knowledge), or whether they were subsequently drawn up on the basis of Lanfranc's list of popes. While the question remains open, there are substantial reasons for doubting that Lanfranc knowingly used forged material. Lanfranc's arguments prevailed over those of Thomas of York, who therefore made an absolute profession of canonical obedience to Lanfranc and his successors. The king's court drew up a constitution, finally reissued at the Council of Windsor at

Pentecost, which established that the church of York should be subject to that of Canterbury and should obey its archbishop as primate of the whole of Britain in all matters relating to the Christian religion; Thomas of York's claim to the obedience of the three bishops south of the Humber was disallowed.

The large measure of success which Lanfranc thus achieved in establishing the primacy of Canterbury should not obscure his difficulties and insecurity during his early years as archbishop. He was unable to secure the primacy beyond Archbishop Thomas's lifetime and could not know that Thomas would long outlive him. At Rome the powerful Archdeacon Hildebrand curtly disallowed the granting of a papal privilege to strengthen Canterbury's position unless Lanfranc again came to Rome. Moreover, 'for love of the king' (that is, probably, because the king would not allow it), Lanfranc had to abandon his claim that Thomas's profession of obedience should be reinforced by an oath of loyalty to himself (*Letters of Lanfranc*, 40–41, 46–7). There was a further difference with the king over the status of the former Archbishop Stigand: Lanfranc followed Pope Alexander in regarding his archiepiscopate as utterly vitiated and null, whereas the king had found it expedient to give him greater recognition than he had enjoyed before 1066, to the extent of allowing him to consecrate Bishop Remigius of Dorchester. Such points of difference cannot have made Lanfranc's relations with the king easy. They help to explain why, in the winter of 1072–3, Lanfranc complained to Pope Alexander of his *calamitates*, and of his sense of unprofitableness in the past and hopelessness for the future; he made a transparently sincere plea to be released from his archbishopric and to return to the cloister.

Lanfranc's work as archbishop Lanfranc would not have expected his plea to be accepted. Moreover, circumstances changed in April 1073 with Archdeacon Hildebrand's succession to the papacy as Gregory VII (1073–85). The difficulties that he had made about a papal privilege for Canterbury and Lanfranc's probable disquiet about his long suspension of judgement upon the opinions of Berengar of Tours go far to account for Lanfranc's studied coolness towards Gregory. Gregory quickly bid to resume the familiarity that Alexander had enjoyed with Lanfranc by sending a letter which tacitly accepted his primacy over the Irish. But Lanfranc consistently disregarded Gregory's summonses to pay duty, *ad limina* visits to Rome, and in 1082 Gregory threatened him with suspension from his office. From 1073 Lanfranc settled down to loyal and fruitful collaboration with King William in the spirit of the constitution of the royal court in 1072. He seldom left the province of Canterbury, although in 1077 he made a brief visit to Normandy and his old monasteries of St Étienne at Caen and Bec, where, after an emotional reunion with the aged Abbot Herluin, he consecrated the high altar of the new abbey church. However, he kept in touch by letter with leading persons in Normandy and elsewhere, notably Anselm as prior and abbot of Bec, and Archbishop Jean of Rouen.

For Lanfranc, the roles of bishop and abbot were compatible: 'If bishops bestow fatherly care upon their subjects in Christ's stead, they may not inappropriately be called abbots, that is, fathers; for the name suits what they do' (Knowles, 4). Accordingly, as archbishop, Lanfranc continued, so far as he could, to live the monastic life. At Canterbury, this was facilitated because, since the time of Archbishop Dunstan (959–88), the Christ Church Cathedral chapter comprised Benedictine monks of whom the archbishop was *ex officio* abbot. In 1067 the cathedral and monastic buildings had been devastated by fire; the monks were demoralized and few in number. Lanfranc quickly determined to perpetuate the monastic regime. He made temporary repairs to the monks' quarters and proceeded to the reconstruction of the cathedral, which by c.1077 was restored to use. By 1089 it was completed and sumptuously equipped with vestments and sacred vessels. Lanfranc also rebuilt the monastic offices, especially the cloister, cellar, refectory, and dormitory. Near the cathedral he erected a palace for the official use of the archbishop, and he surrounded the ensemble of buildings by a wall. He envisaged a monastic community of some 150 monks; at his death it probably comprised almost 100. After 1079 he compiled from various sources a body of monastic constitutions for the liturgical ordering and for the administration and discipline of the Canterbury community. They were practical in character; but liturgically, interest attaches to the Palm Sunday procession, when the consecrated host was carried in procession to the city gate, in commemoration of Christ's coming to Jerusalem. Although the day-to-day running of the community devolved upon the prior (Lanfranc summoned from Bec a monk named Henry to fill this office), Lanfranc performed so far as he could the abbot's role, both in the daily monastic round and in the pastoral oversight of the monks and their families, for which the Canterbury monk Eadmer praised him.

Lanfranc was much concerned with the administration and defence of the property of the see of Canterbury. His years as archbishop witnessed an increasingly clear division between the property of the archbishop and that of the monks. He was remembered for the many fine buildings, including churches, which he had built upon his manors, most of which were in Kent and Sussex. He was much concerned to recover the lands and other resources of his see, which had suffered severe losses both before and after 1066. He came into dispute with the king's half-brother Odo, bishop of Bayeux and earl of Kent. Their most fully recorded litigation occurred, perhaps in 1072, at a meeting of the shire on Penenden Heath. On the king's behalf, Bishop Geoffroi of Coutances judged in Lanfranc's favour about his judicial rights in Kent and about six Christ Church estates. The process of recovery which was thus started continued until the Domesday Survey.

On account of his necessarily frequent absences from Canterbury and sheer pressure of work, Lanfranc came to use the bishop of Rochester as a kind of vicar-general. He thereby abandoned the pre-conquest usage whereby a *chorepiscopus* (assistant bishop) was based at St Martin's Church at Canterbury. He made an excellent choice in Gundulf, a monk of Bec who was his prior at Caen and then his right-hand man at Canterbury from 1070. In 1077 Lanfranc himself invested Gundulf as bishop of Rochester and Gundulf thereafter relieved Lanfranc in the tasks of diocesan ordinary, such as ordaining clerks, consecrating chrism, and dedicating churches. Lanfranc devoted generous resources to building and equipping a new cathedral at Rochester, where a monastic chapter on the Christ Church model was introduced.

Lanfranc was frequently absent on royal and ecclesiastical business. He attended crown-wearings held at the three main Christian festivals when the king was in England. He was known then to admonish as well as to honour the king: when both sat at a coronation banquet and a jester, pointing to the bejewelled king, flatteringly said, 'Behold! I see God', Lanfranc insisted on the king's having the jester severely beaten; for Lanfranc recalled the fate of King Herod Agrippa, who listened to flatterers hailing him as a god and was smitten by God and eaten by worms (Gibson, 'Vita Lanfranci', 708–9; see Acts 12: 21–3).

Holding councils Lanfranc, as primate, held councils, often at the seasons of crown-wearings, for the English church in which, after 1072, Thomas of York collaborated. In many respects, they were similar to the reforming councils held in 1070, before Lanfranc's arrival, by Alexander II's legates; but they also followed the tradition of church councils as held in Normandy, though not in England, since the 1040s. Like Norman councils, Lanfranc's were subject to William's authority and direction. After the councils of Winchester and Windsor in 1072 when the issue of the primacy was settled, Lanfranc held councils at London (1074 or 1075), Winchester (1076), London (1077 or 1078), and Gloucester (1080, 1085). Until 1076 these councils issued canons which, though fragmentary and unsystematic, illustrate several of Lanfranc's main concerns. The earliest legislation sought to buttress the Norman regime by prescribing public loyalty to the king and prayer and alms on his behalf. Lanfranc required a structured and orderly church life which would complement his stringent requirement that bishops make professions of obedience to himself; in many ways he sought to ensure the bishop's authority in his diocese, and three bishoprics were moved from villages to major centres at Sarum (Old Salisbury), Chichester, and Chester. Attention was given to clerical morality: Lanfranc proscribed simoniacal practices and promoted celibacy, demanding it at once of canons but (less strictly than the papal legates in 1070) allowing the generality of priests with wives to keep them, while those who were unmarried must remain so; bishops were to require promises of celibacy from those in future ordained priest or deacon. There was some regulation of the lives of the laity, especially as regards marriage and spiritual jurisdiction over them.

The canons of the Council of London, in particular, were widely circulated; and their preamble spoke of renovation of things laid down in ancient law. Lanfranc was concerned to complement the revival in England of church

councils by facilitating the study of canon law. He summoned from Bec and presented to Christ Church, Canterbury, a collection of canons and decrees called by modern scholars the *Collectio Lanfranci*, based upon the Pseudo-Isidorian decrees (the 'false decretals') as compiled in mid-ninth-century France. It is in two parts: an abridged version of the papal decretals from Clement I to Gregory II (715–31) with certain additions, and a full, if in some ways distinctive, version of the councils from Nicaea (325) to Seville II (618). It is by no means certain that the collection was made by Lanfranc or under his supervision; more likely it came to Bec from elsewhere. In England, copies of the collection were made and circulated to cathedral libraries; until the mid-twelfth century it was a main source in England of canon law. Marginal markings seem to testify to Lanfranc's own study of the Christ Church manuscript and to correspond to references to canon law in his letters. He enjoined its study upon bishops, urging Herfast of Thetford to:

> give up the dice, to mention nothing worse, and the worldly amusements in which you are said to spend the whole day. Read sacred authors, and devote particular study to the decrees of the Roman pontiffs and to the sacred canons. Then you will find out what you do not know; having read them, you will deem worthless the devices in which you trust to evade church discipline.   (*Letters of Lanfranc*, 152–3)

If, after 1073, Lanfranc paid little heed to the presently reigning pope, he ascribed high authority to the decrees of popes long dead. Steadfast himself in spiritual reading, he was also concerned to provide and circulate in England emended texts of the Vulgate and other sacred writings upon which he himself continued to work.

Lanfranc gave comparable attention to the veneration of English saints, about some of whom he had doubts, particularly Ælfheah (Alphege), the archbishop of Canterbury whom the Danes killed in 1012; but Anselm of Bec persuaded him that Ælfheah deserved commemoration as a martyr. Lanfranc employed Osbern, a monk of Canterbury, to write lives of Ælfheah and of St Dunstan, to whom Lanfranc seems to have had a particular devotion. He made no purge of English saints; his attitude towards them seems to have been shaped by judiciousness and a strict concern for authenticity. He showed no insensitivity to English feelings; when assured of the sanctity of English saints, he duly provided for their veneration.

Lanfranc's letter collection yields glimpses of his routine business. In his terse way, he answered enquiries from several bishops—Thomas of York and Walcher of Durham as well as suffragans of Canterbury. Penance and marriage discipline were recurrent topics; Lanfranc displayed a range of attitudes from rigorous insistence upon canonical rules to pastoral leniency towards the proven penitent.

Lanfranc and monastic affairs The canons of Lanfranc's councils, especially the London Council, testify to his vigilance over the monastic order; as in non-monastic matters, he showed deference to the king. Lanfranc had a basic concern that monks should establish their way of life according to the best ancient models and that stability, obedience, oversight, and poverty should be rigorously ensured. Having found and quickly learnt to value a monastic chapter at Canterbury, he defended such a chapter at Winchester against the initial attempt of the first Norman bishop, Walchelin, to abolish it. Partly owing to his advocacy, within fifty years of the conquest nine of the sixteen English sees had cathedral monasteries—a situation unique in Latin Christendom. Although his monastic constitutions were compiled only for Canterbury, their workmanlike qualities led to their being adopted in other cathedral monasteries and elsewhere; early copies existed in some twelve houses. Lanfranc's predilection for cathedral monasteries may have indirectly retarded the constitutional development of the secular (that is, non-monastic) chapters, and have set back the spread in England, already attested before the conquest, of canons regular.

Lanfranc's letters again suggest the depth and range of his abiding concern with monastic affairs, over and above his involvement at Canterbury and Rochester. He protected individual houses: Bury St Edmunds, the abbey of his friend and physician Abbot Baldwin, against the jurisdictional claims of Bishop Herfast of Thetford; and Coventry, where Bishop Peter was to desist from harassing the monks and to make restitution. When the abbess and prioress of Barking were at loggerheads, Lanfranc insisted that Bishop Maurice of London should intervene. Many letters concerned individual monks: Lanfranc was exercised about the noviciate of his nephew, another Lanfranc, at Bec; he sent spiritual advice and a medical remedy (*marrubium*: horehound) to one seriously ill; he interceded, in terms reminiscent of St Paul's epistle to Philemon, with Abbot Adelelm of Abingdon to receive back fugitive but penitent monks; he censured both a fugitive monk of Chertsey and his lax abbot, Odo, who had permitted him to wander; but he encouraged a monk who wished to transfer to a more observant regime under Abbot Serlo of Gloucester. When Lanfranc wrongly assessed a postulant at the New Minster, Winchester, he admitted his error and asked for the case to be decided by the Winchester authorities. He humanely sanctioned the departure from the cloister of nuns who had entered religion only from fear of the Norman invaders.

Lanfranc's dealings with two non-cathedral monasteries are particularly recorded. He brought another nephew, Paul, a monk of Caen, to be abbot of St Albans (r. 1077–93), where he ruled with distinction. Lanfranc assisted him with 1000 marks towards a thoroughgoing rebuilding and equipped the church with precious ornaments; he also provided books to be copied in the scriptorium. Lanfranc's monastic constitutions were followed at St Albans which, although in the diocese of Lincoln, remained under Lanfranc's close supervision. With St Augustine's, Canterbury, Lanfranc came into severe difficulty near the end of his life. In 1087 or 1088 he consecrated as abbot, and (apparently supported by Odo of Bayeux) attempted to install, a monk of St Augustine's with the Norman name of Guy. Most of the monks (who were largely English and

who resented Lanfranc's nearby foundation of St Gregory's) refused to admit Guy and fled into the city. Lanfranc coerced or persuaded many to return, but there was soon a plot against Abbot Guy. Lanfranc interrogated the ringleader, Columbanus, who declared that he would have killed his abbot if he could; Lanfranc had him stripped naked and flogged at the abbey gate before being driven from the city. He thereby terrorized the monks into submission until his death, when trouble again erupted. Against dissident monks Lanfranc could act harshly; but, on balance, the Anglo-Saxon Chronicle declared justly upon his death that he was 'the reverend father and consoler of monks' (ASC, s.a. 1089, text E).

Extent of Lanfranc's authority Lanfranc's conception of his primacy led him to claim authority over the whole British Isles. Beyond the two English provinces, his attention was most directed to Ireland. In 1074, at the request of King Gofraid (Guthric) of Dublin, he consecrated at London an Irish monk, Patrick, who was trained and professed at Worcester, to the see of Dublin. Patrick made a profession of obedience to Lanfranc as 'bishop-elect of Dublin, the metropolis of Ireland', a phrase which may express Lanfranc's hope at this time of establishing a dependent Irish metropolis. But when, a year after Patrick's death in 1084, Lanfranc consecrated his successor Donatus (Donggus) at Canterbury where he had been a monk, his profession of obedience contained no such phrase (Richter, 29, 31; Letters of Lanfranc, 66–9). In truth, the centres of ecclesiastical and political power in Ireland lay elsewhere. In 1074 Lanfranc commended Patrick not only to the king of Dublin but also to the increasingly dominant high-king, Toirdelbhach Ó Briain of Munster, whom he urged to convene a council of bishops and religious men to remedy the country's many ills. In 1080 or 1081 he answered in fatherly terms an enquiry from Domnall, chief bishop of Munster, and others about baptism and the eucharist. As for Scotland, the concord of 1072 provided that Thomas of York should have jurisdiction 'to its farthest limits'. Lanfranc respected this provision by enabling Thomas in 1073 to consecrate, at York, Ralph, bishop of the Orkneys. His only recorded direct dealings with Scotland were with Queen Margaret, daughter of Edward Ætheling and wife of King Malcolm III Canmore. He acceded to her request that he should become her spiritual adviser and he referred to the part that Christ Church monks were taking in setting up the monastery of Holy Trinity, Dunfermline, which became the first regular Benedictine house in Scotland. Lanfranc took no authenticated action with regard to Wales—surprisingly, in view of the inflated claims to jurisdiction that Welsh bishops were advancing; it was left for Anselm to assert Canterbury's authority.

Lanfranc and secular government In English government, Lanfranc enjoyed the king's confidence and on occasion took a leading part. Later Bec tradition stated that, during William I's absences in Normandy, Lanfranc was the chief and keeper (*princeps et custos*) of England in defence, government, and peace (Gibson, 'Vita Lanfranci', 711). This takes no account of others, like bishops Odo of Bayeux and Geoffroi of Coutances, who acted as royal deputies. But it fairly epitomizes Lanfranc's part in the troubles of 1075 when, with the king in Normandy, he directed resistance to the revolt (from motives that remain obscure) of Ralph, earl of East Anglia, and Roger, earl of Hereford, who found support from the Englishman Waltheof, earl of Huntingdon. French and English forces under Bishop Wulfstan of Worcester and Abbot Æthelwig of Evesham opposed Roger, while bishops Odo of Bayeux and Geoffroi of Coutances, with William (I) de Warenne, dealt with Ralph's supporters in Cambridgeshire and Norfolk. Lanfranc's part is primarily apparent from his letters. At the outset he took a lead in implementing the king's orders that all his loyal magnates should see to the security of royal castles. After the defeat of Earl Ralph near Cambridge, he reported to the king, urging him not to return to England since such perjurers and brigands could be sufficiently dealt with by his subjects there; Lanfranc clearly felt that peace could better be restored without the wrath that William would surely apply. After the rebels' surrender of Norwich Castle, he again wrote to say that the realm had been purged of the pollution of the Bretons and that the noise of warfare was silent in the land. But he also wrote to Bishop Walcher of Durham and with good reason warned him that the Danes whom Ralph had summoned were on their way; he should fortify and victual his castle.

Lanfranc's dealings with Earl Roger are particularly interesting. His guiding purpose was to restore the earl to his proper loyalty to the king. He at first appealed to Roger on grounds of their own bond of affection, of the example of service to the king set by his father, William fitz Osbern, and of the duty that a vassal owed to his king, especially since William had been restrained and had shown willingness to hear Roger's grievances against his sheriffs. Lanfranc repeatedly offered to travel anywhere to meet Roger and to promote concord with the king. When such measures failed, Lanfranc sought to coerce Roger into loyalty by invoking his primatial authority to excommunicate him and his followers, with effect throughout England. This was in addition to Lanfranc's military dispositions. When Roger showed signs of repentance and offered to meet Lanfranc, however, Lanfranc now dared not meet him from fear of the king; but he undertook to inform the king of Roger's plea for mercy. Meanwhile, Roger should lie low and do nothing further to provoke the king. In the event, Lanfranc was unable to save Roger: when William returned to England, he condemned him to the Norman penalty for treason—life imprisonment and forfeiture of all lands. Chronicle sources show that Lanfranc was even less successful in obtaining mercy and reconciliation for Waltheof, who had at an early stage withdrawn from the revolt. On the advice of Lanfranc, he did penance and crossed to Normandy where he placed himself in the king's mercy. After his return to England, William, however, exacted the death penalty that English law prescribed. The fates of Roger, and still more of Waltheof, show the limits of Lanfranc's influence with the king and their contrasting methods of dealing with rebellion.

Lanfranc sometimes acted as a royal justice, particularly in East Anglia. Thus, in 1081, the king instructed him to settle the dispute between Bishop Herfast of Thetford and the abbey of Bury St Edmunds about episcopal rights over the abbey. After hearing witnesses from nine shires, Lanfranc gave a judgment in the abbey's favour which was confirmed by a royal writ. Thereafter, he became involved, with Bishop Geoffroi of Coutances and Count Robert of Mortain, in the latter stages of the abbey of Ely's attempts to clarify its rights and holdings of land, especially as against Bishop Remigius of Lincoln. In these, as other, cases, Lanfranc behaved as a leading tenant-in-chief of the crown rather than in any distinctive way. He took no known part in planning or executing the Domesday Survey, although in a letter he duly answered an enquiry about Canterbury lands in East Anglia. For all his personal standing with the king, he was never a courtier, nor did he make an abiding contribution to Norman administration or political institutions.

When William I died at Rouen in 1087, he is said to have sent Lanfranc instructions to crown his second son, William Rufus, king of England, which, according to Eadmer, he did with some reluctance; but Lanfranc's acceptance of William was the critical step in the new king's succession. If William of Malmesbury was right in his statement that Lanfranc had a part in William's education and dubbing as a knight, there may have already been a personal bond between them. Lanfranc is said later to have reproved the king gently for disregarding his coronation promises to his people and to the church, and to have received the answer, 'What man alive can fulfil everything that he promises?' However, Lanfranc was loyal to William during the widespread revolt of 1088, led by Bishop Odo of Bayeux (Ordericus Vitalis, *Eccl. hist.*, 4.97–8, 110–111; *Historia novorum*, 25; Malmesbury, *De gestis pontificum*, 73, and *Gest. reg.*, 2.359–60).

Lanfranc's loyalty and forensic skill were apparent in the trial before the king's court of William of St Calais, bishop of Durham, which took place at Salisbury in November 1088, and of which an almost certainly authentic eye-witness account survives (van Caenegem, 90–106). The bishop was on trial for his part in the revolt. He claimed that, as a bishop, he should be tried by an ecclesiastical court; Lanfranc argued that he was on trial in his capacity as a tenant-in-chief, not an ecclesiastic, and he claimed similarly to have judged Bishop Odo of Bayeux in 1082. Bishop William took his stand upon canon law, producing a book which appears to have been the Durham copy of the *Collectio Lanfranci*. But Lanfranc countered by turning against the bishop the canonical principle that he had extracted from it, that of the *exceptio spolii*—that a defendant who has been despoiled of his possessions must be reinstated in them before proceedings can begin. He frustrated William's appeal to it on the grounds that, before his trial, the king had by no means completely despoiled him of his possessions; when the king's court did this, Lanfranc knew that William could not effectually appeal to the pope because the pope had no means of enforcing repossession and could not, therefore, hear him. Lanfranc won lay as well as clerical plaudits in the king's court as the *vetulus ligaminarius* (probably: 'the old master of the hunting pack'), who spoke well when he challenged the bishop. Under William II, as under his father, Lanfranc was, when needed, the staunch and effective upholder of the Norman order and of the king's cause within it.

Lanfranc and papal politics If Lanfranc's loyalty to the English crown remained unshakeable, his loyalty in his last years to the papacy of Gregory VII and his followers may be questioned. In 1080 Henry IV of Germany chose Archbishop Guibert of Ravenna to be an anti-pope; at Eastertide 1084, having entered Rome, he established him as Pope Clement III. A letter of Lanfranc shows that, in 1084 or 1085, he initiated an exchange with a partisan of Clement whose name was abbreviated as 'Hu.'. He was probably Hugh Candidus, Gregory VII's long-standing and virulent opponent among the Roman cardinals. Lanfranc sent a masterly and noncommittal reply, deprecating both Hu.'s maligning of Gregory and his eulogy of Clement. He conceded that the success of Henry IV, now emperor, indicated divine favour. Yet Hu. might not himself come to England without its king's leave, and the English kingdom would take no decision until the situation was further clarified. Clement in due course sent Lanfranc three letters, highly commending him, inviting him to visit Rome, and requesting Peter's Pence. They were copied into Lanfranc's canon-law collection, but he is not known to have replied. Lanfranc thus undoubtedly made prudent contacts with the Guibertine party and kept his options open. But letters to him from Pope Urban II and Anselm of Bec, as well as contacts with others of Gregorian sympathies, make it clear that he was not known to have in any way identified himself with the opposing party.

As benefactor Lanfranc's contemporaries looked to a monk–archbishop for generous almsgiving; he amply fulfilled their expectations. Almsgiving was a keynote of his activity: at his episcopal consecration, the customary *sortes bibliae* (fortune-telling through the random selection of biblical verses) produced the text, 'Give alms, and behold! all things are clean to you' (Luke 11: 41). He was believed to have disbursed in alms £500 a year. He provided for the poor on all his manors, but his three principal charitable foundations were at Canterbury itself. In his latter years, when his main expenditure upon Christ Church was completed, he founded outside the north gate of the city the church of St Gregory, the dedication of which reflected his devotion to the pope who had sent St Augustine of Canterbury to Britain. He established there a community of clerks whom he intended to make good the pastoral ministrations in Canterbury, especially burials, which had been curtailed by reason of the expansion of the cathedral monastery, and which were to be provided for the poor without payment. Lanfranc brought to St Gregory's a rich endowment of relics of early archbishops and other saints of the Anglo-Saxon, and especially Kentish, past. Near to it, he built the hospital of St John the Baptist to relieve the sick and aged, and at Harbledown, a short distance to the west of the city, he built a leper hospital of St Nicholas. From his estates he endowed these twin hospitals with £140 yearly. Lanfranc's foundations were far from complete by his death, but they form a prominent part of the munificence which was remembered in his obit. His humane side was also evident in his concern to abolish the slave trade from England to Ireland.

Death and reputation Lanfranc died of fever on 28 May 1089, suddenly but after receiving the last rites; he had wished so to die, with memory unclouded and speech unimpaired. He was buried in the nave of his new cathedral to the west of the choir screen; but when Anselm built a new choir his body was moved. Nothing of his tomb remains. No cultus developed but at Canterbury he was held in high honour. A man of tireless and well-directed energy, to the end of his life he adapted himself surely to the needs of each change in his circumstances. The rapport which, after 1072, he achieved with William I, a master of commanding ability whom he understood and respected, enabled him to leave English church and society far stronger than he found them after the traumas of the conquest. The effect of his archiepiscopate was to equip the church in England for its place in the mainstream of Christian life during the rest of the middle ages.

H. E. J. COWDREY

Sources M. Gibson, *Lanfranc of Bec* (1978) · G. d'Onofrio, ed., *Lanfranco di Pavia e l'Europa del secolo XI, nel IX centenario della morte (1089–1989): atti del convegno internazionale di studi* [Pavia 21–4 Sept 1989] (Rome, 1993) · M. Gibson, ed., 'Vita Lanfranci', *Lanfranco di Pavia e l'Europa del secolo XI, nel IX centenario della morte (1089–1989): atti del convegno internazionale di studi* [Pavia 21–4 Sept 1989], ed. G. D'Onofrio (Rome, 1993), 659–715 · G. Crispin, 'Vita Herluini', in *The works of Gilbert Crispin, abbot of Westminster*, ed. A. S. Abulafia and G. R. Evans (1986), 183–212 · R. W. Southern, *Saint Anselm: a portrait in a landscape* (1990) · *The letters of Lanfranc, archbishop of Canterbury*, ed. and trans. H. Clover and M. Gibson, OMT (1979) · D. Whitelock, M. Brett, and C. N. L. Brooke, eds., *Councils and synods with other documents relating to the English church, 871–1204*, 2 (1981) · R. C. van Caenegem, ed., *English lawsuits from William I to Richard I*, SeldS, 1, 106 (1990) · H. S. Offler, ed., 'De iniusta vexacione Willelmi episcopi primi per Willelmum regem filium Wellelmi magni regis', rev. A. J. Piper and A. I. Doyle, *Camden miscellany, XXXIV*, CS, 5th ser., 10 (1997), 49–104 · Guillaume de Poitiers [Gulielmus Pictaviensis], *Histoire de Guillaume le Conquérant / Gesta Gulielmus ducis Normannorum et regis Anglorum*, ed. R. Foreville (Paris, 1952) · 'Acta Lanfranci', *Two of the Saxon chronicles parallel: with supplementary extracts from the others*, ed. J. Earle, rev. C. Plummer, 1 (1892), 287–92 · M. Richter, ed., *Canterbury professions*, CYS, 67 (1973) · *Willelmi Malmesbiriensis monachi de gestis pontificum Anglorum libri quinque*, ed. N. E. S. A. Hamilton, Rolls Series, 52 (1870) · William of Malmesbury, *Gesta regum Anglorum / The history of the English kings*, ed. and trans. R. A. B. Mynors, R. M. Thomson, and M. Winterbottom, 2 vols., OMT (1998–9) · *Eadmeri Historia novorum in Anglia*, ed. M. Rule, Rolls Series, 81 (1884) · Ordericus Vitalis, *Eccl. hist.* · *Patrologia Latina*, 150 (1854), 105–406 · *The historical works of Gervase of Canterbury*, ed. W. Stubbs, 2: *The minor works comprising the Gesta regum with its continuation, the Actus pontificum and the Mappa mundi*, Rolls Series, 73 (1880), 325–41, at 363–70 · Pope Alexander II, 'Epistolae et diplomata', *Patrologia Latina*, 146 (1853), 1279–430 · *Decreta Lanfranci monachi Cantuariensibus transmissa*, ed. D. Knowles, Corpus Consuetudinum Monasticarum, 3 (1967) · F. Liebermann, 'Lanfranc and the antipope', *EngHR*, 16 (1901), 328–32 · *ASC*, s.a. 1070 [text A]; s.a. 1086, 1089 [text E] · F. Barlow, *The Norman conquest and beyond* (1983),

223–44 • M. Gibson, 'Artes' and Bible in the medieval West (1993), chaps. 12–13 • Z. N. Brooke, The English church and the papacy from the conquest to the reign of John (1931), 57–83, 117–46 • J. de Montclos, Lanfranc et Bérenger: la controverse eucharistique du XIe siècle (Louvain, 1971) • H. E. J. Cowdrey, 'The enigma of Archbishop Lanfranc', Haskins Society Journal, 6 (1994), 129–52 • R. B. C. Huygens, 'Bérenger de Tours, Lanfranc et Bernold de Constance', Sacris Erudiri, 16 (1965), 358–77 • The Gesta Guillelmi of William of Poitiers, ed. and trans. R. H. C. Davis and M. Chibnall, OMT (1998)

Likenesses manuscript drawing, Bodl. Oxf., MS Bodley 569, fol. 1 [see illus.]

Lang, Andrew (1844–1912), anthropologist, classicist, and historian, was born on 31 March 1844 at Viewfield, in Selkirk, the eldest of the eight children of John Lang, town clerk of Selkirk, and his wife, Jane Plenderleath Sellar, daughter of Patrick Sellar, factor to the first duke of Sutherland.

Education and marriage Lang was educated at Selkirk grammar school, and at Edinburgh Academy. He attended the University of St Andrews for three sessions beginning in 1861, followed by a year at the University of Glasgow to qualify for the Snell exhibition, and thence in 1865 to Balliol College, Oxford, where he studied under Benjamin Jowett and T. H. Green. He took firsts in classical moderations in 1866 and literae humaniores in 1868, and was elected to an open fellowship at Merton College. On 17 April 1875 he married Leonora Blanche Alleyne, youngest daughter of C. T. Alleyne of Clifton and Barbados. They had no children. On his marriage he resigned his fellowship and settled in London, earning his living henceforth as a professional writer.

Lang's hugely prolific and successful intellectual career, which saw him achieve eminence in several fields, should be viewed against a background of unremitting writerly effort to keep the wolf from the door of 1 Marloes Road, Kensington, where he and his wife—who was also a writer and translator and very much the practical intelligence behind the Lang household—lived until his death in 1912. He was a leader writer for the Daily News, until pressure of work in the 1890s forced him to give it up. He regularly wrote reviews and other contributions for a wide range of periodicals including the Saturday Review, the Morning Post, the Illustrated London News, Blackwood's, The Academy, and Punch. His monthly column, 'At the sign of the Ship', which appeared in Longman's Magazine from January 1886 to October 1905, became a national institution. Lang's facility made even hardened pressmen gasp: he could write anything, anywhere, and with astonishing rapidity, often attending meetings and composing articles simultaneously. Even more surprising was the unwaveringly high quality of what he wrote: indeed Sir Arthur Quiller-Couch was to proclaim him the most accomplished prose stylist of his generation.

Lang made his mark first as a poet. An admirer of William Morris, Dante Gabriel Rossetti, and Algernon Charles Swinburne, he pioneered the revival of the old medieval French forms in English, the ballade, rondeau, triolet, and villanelle. In 1872 he published Ballads and Lyrics of Old France, including translations of Villon, Ronsard, Du

Andrew Lang (1844–1912), by Sir William Blake Richmond, 1884

Bellay, and others, with original lyrics of his own. A number of further slim volumes of verse were to follow, including XXXII Ballades in Blue China (1881) and Grass of Parnassus (1888), which established his characteristic manner—languorous, dream-like, elegant, and archaic, rather like Alma-Tadema in metre. But the lukewarm reception accorded to his most ambitious poem, the richly sonorous and elaborate Helen of Troy (1882), induced him to turn to other fields.

Writings on pre-history and folklore Lang's major contribution lay in the related disciplines of anthropology and folklore. His youth coincided with a dramatic increase of interest in prehistory, as a result of Darwin's theory of evolution, Jacques Boucher de Perthes's discovery of the relics of palaeolithic man, and exciting new developments in the study of mythology. Lang was a child of the borders, immersed in the old ghost and fairy lore, and his interest in its formal study dated from his undergraduate days. His advocacy of the comparative method of study actually predated the work of his mentors, J. F. M'Lennan and E. B. Tylor, the founders of the science of anthropology and comparative religion, on whose work he reared his own distinctive contribution. In an article, 'Mythology and fairy tales', in the Fortnightly Review for May 1873, he challenged the dominant philological approach to mythology whose chief spokesman was the Sanskrit scholar Professor Max Müller. Müller argued that the cradle of mythology lay in northern India, whence it had been diffused by the migrations of the Aryan peoples throughout the West. The source of myth lay in a 'disease of language', an intensely figurative habit of expression peculiar to early man which invested everything it touched with metaphoric force, resulting in personification of the forces of nature. Personal names held the key to interpretation because, thanks to a complicated series of linguistic mutations, it was from these that the familiar personal gods and goddesses of Western mythology had sprung.

In a series of papers, later collected as *Custom and Myth* (1884), Lang argued that this approach was fundamentally unsound. Scholars using it could not produce agreed results. Many tales appeared in similar versions in different cultures; but the names of the protagonists, upon which the philological school laid such stress, were subject to no sort of stability. The focus upon 'Aryan' civilization was far too narrow, since comparative anthropology showed the same practices, customs, and beliefs occurring in widely scattered societies. The secret of mythological systems lay in the doctrine of 'survivals'. European society had, Lang claimed, a thin 'progressive' upper stratum in which alone real cultural change took place, and a great sluggishly conservative underclass which had never seriously changed its ancient beliefs. Since there was a fixed course of cultural evolution through which every society passed, similar intellectual structures might be expected to appear with great regularity and stability. This made possible a comparative approach which, brushing aside superficial features such as language and geographical difference, could identify recurring underlying structures. This made it possible to compare societies at similar levels of development, wherever and whenever they might occur. It also put paid to the idea of diffusion as the dominant method of cultural transmission. Lang cited numerous examples of similar cultural practices located in communities so remote in time and space as to exclude the possibility of contact between them. The only possible explanation lay in spontaneous local creation which lent powerful support, in turn, to another key proposition of the new anthropology, namely the underlying psychic unity of mankind.

Lang's most important work in this field, *Myth, Ritual and Religion* (2 vols.), appeared in 1887. From many parts of the world he accumulated evidence for his contention that all primitive peoples have essentially the same ideas, tales, customs, and beliefs, and that these live on in the form of 'survivals' in the classical myths and in the popular traditions of the developed world. Unlike a number of his contemporaries Lang treated the savage intellect with respect, considering its operations—in its own terms—to be so powerfully speculative and resourceful as to make it reasonable to speak of a 'savage metaphysics', and he explained the 'irrational' quality frequently encountered in mythology in terms of its descent from an older world in which it had once made perfect sense. Comparative anthropology could demonstrate that the gods evolved from earlier totemic animal forms to the lofty creatures of later refined and philosophic belief without ever quite shedding the earlier accretions. This idea had many ramifications. For example, it was obvious from such a perspective that the conventional view of Scott and the brothers Grimm that folk-tales were the detritus of earlier

mythic systems, of a once high culture which had fallen into the clutches of the common people and fragmented during a long degenerative process of transmission, could not be correct. In a complex and subtle argument Lang made the case for the tales containing the genuinely archaic material out of which the epics and romances had later been reared; and was not at all uncomfortable with the consequence that the common people must, therefore, be a fundamentally important stratum in the creation and transmission of culture. *Myth, Ritual and Religion* was an influential work, being issued in a second revised edition in 1899 and translated into Dutch and French.

During the 1890s Lang revised his views and parted company with Tylor regarding the primacy of animism—the theory that all religion sprang from early man's habit of regarding the material world as suffused by spiritual life, intelligence, and purpose. In *The Making of Religion* (1898), and again in *Magic and Religion* in 1901, he claimed to have found clear traces of a pre-animistic strain of belief centring on the concept of a single high god, a benign and ethical maker of the world, later displaced by the cruder practices of animism. The point at issue was a fundamental one. If he was right, then the prevailing view of evolutionary anthropology, which pictured a smooth and inevitable ascent of human civilization from 'lower' to 'higher' cultural forms, was wrong. If cultural evolution was not inherently progressive, then the view of J. G. Frazer and the vegetable god people (scornfully dismissed by Lang as 'the Covent Garden School of Mythology') that mankind went through three intellectual stages of development, namely from magic to religion and from religion to science, was unsustainable.

The final phase of Lang's work in this field centred on the phenomenon of totemism, which, because it seemed to provide the ruling principle in the organization of savage societies, had become the central question in anthropology in the early years of the twentieth century. On it he wrote three books, *Social Origins* (1903), *The Secret of the Totem* (1905), and a final work eventually published in 1994 as *Andrew Lang on Totemism*, edited by Andrew Duff-Cooper from the manuscript which Lang completed just before his death. Lang's sense of the sophistication and complexity of savage society led him to insist that current, observable social practice could not be used as evidence of man in his primal state, and that totemic practices were much more varied and problematic than some commentators, particularly J. G. Frazer in his recently published *Totemism and Exogamy* (1910), had supposed. Duff-Cooper believed that here Lang had anticipated much of Claude Lévi-Strauss's position in *Totémisme aujourd'hui* (1962).

The Folk-Lore Society In 1878 Lang became a founding member of the Folk-Lore Society, chairing its folk-tale section, and serving as president during the year of the International Folk-Lore Congress held in London in 1891. The new discipline focused attention on traditional legends, customs, and beliefs preserved in contemporary societies in the developed world, but Lang viewed it very much as part of the larger anthropological enterprise. It seemed plain to him that the cultural forms identified as 'folkloristic' were not independent later creations but survivals from earlier stages of social evolution, and that they could be elucidated, therefore, by the familiar comparative method. Lang refused to have any truck with the tendency to narrow the range of folklore by restricting its field of enquiry to remote, unlettered, and peasant peoples. He observed that similar customs and ideas survived in the most conservative elements of the life of educated people, in ritual, ceremonial, religious traditions, and myths. He used the findings of the Society for Psychical Research (he had joined it shortly after its formation in 1882, and was its chairman in 1911–12) to demonstrate in books like *Cock Lane and Common Sense* (1894) that there were irrational 'primitive' phenomena—such as hauntings, wraiths, ghosts, clairvoyance, telepathy, and telekinesis—demonstrably present in the modern world in every social class. These phenomena, whether they were 'true' or not (and Lang was bullishly sceptical upon the latter point), existed as widely as, and over a similar time scale to, other survivals of savage institutions. He argued that the evidence clamoured for anthropological and folkloristic investigation, although these disciplines perversely refused to take it up.

Lang's friends often felt that he had wasted his outstanding powers by pursuing an intellectual career too varied and eclectic. Although formidable in several disciplines, he never quite managed to write the really big definitive book which would have allowed him, unequivocally, to dominate a single field. There seems little doubt, if things had been otherwise, what that field would have been. One night after an Oxford dinner he was walking with a friend, and sighed: 'Ah … If I had stayed on here when I was a young Fellow, and stuck to one thing, I should have been a big swell by now … I should have been a really big swell at anthropology' (*DNB*). But his virtuosity clamoured for expression, and works of apparently effortless expertise flowed from his pen in a wide variety of academic disciplines. If he had done nothing else, for example, he would be remembered as a distinguished classicist. His important translations of the *Odyssey* (1879, with S. H. Butcher) and the *Iliad* (1883, with Walter Leaf and Ernest Myers) were followed by three monographs on the Homeric question: *Homer and the Epic* (1893), *Homer and his Age* (1906), and *The World of Homer* (1910). Lang argued with passionate eloquence against the 'separatist' tradition which claimed that the *Iliad* and *Odyssey* had begun life as relatively short lays composed by oral poets and then been fashioned into a coherent whole in sixth-century Athens by an anonymous editor or editors. Lang appealed to other poems of epic length such as the Finnish *Kalevala* and the old French *chansons de geste*, produced in heroic societies at a similar stage of development, pointing to their characteristically loose and episodic arrangement to insist that the *Iliad*'s superb structure must be the work of a single, magnificently endowed mind. The problem of transmission which then arose was met by deploying the latest archaeological findings to argue that the introduction of writing in ancient Greece must be considerably earlier than had been supposed, and that the coherence of the Homeric texts must be based upon direct textual transmission.

Historian of Scotland and essayist In the 1890s Lang turned to a new field—Scottish history. His cavalier temperament and distaste for the whiggish and presbyterian bias of so much existing Scottish historiography moved him to produce a series of books devoted to a single ambitious question: was it possible to defend the Stuarts? Works such as *The Mystery of Mary Stuart* (1901), *John Knox and the Reformation* (1905), and the *History of Scotland from the Roman Occupation to the Suppression of the Last Jacobite Rising* (4 vols., 1900–07) caused some stir at the time. But in *Pickle the Spy, or, The Incognito of Prince Charles* (1897) he achieved one of the most striking contributions ever made to Jacobite historiography, and the crowning moment of a decade which witnessed a major revival of interest in the movement. Lang had been helping his old friend Robert Louis Stevenson, then at work on a Jacobite novel in Samoa, by sending out transcripts of papers from the British Museum. When these were returned on Stevenson's death, Lang resisted the impulse to complete the text as a novel, and instead used the documents as the basis of a spectacular historical coup. The notion of incorruptible highland heroism and loyalty had become a cherished establishment belief. Lang proceeded to puncture it with calculated brutality, building a powerful case against Alastair Macdonell, thirteenth chief of Glengarry, and close associate of Prince Charles Edward Stuart, as a liar, traitor, and paid government spy. That one of the great highland chiefs could behave so basely, and that Lang should be so tactless as to proclaim the fact, gave serious thought to many a Victorian reader. But the real value of the book lies in its painstaking account of Charles Edward Stuart's career after the Jacobite rising of 1745—the years of wandering around Europe, often in disguise, and seldom, thanks to people like young Alastair of Glengarry, more than one jump ahead of the British secret service, the later decline into alcoholism and enfeeblement—about all of which little was then known. The book also shows how Lang set about such tasks and how he was able to maintain his phenomenal productivity. He used research assistants, patient transcribers and checkers of references, and a web of correspondence which enabled him to tap specialist knowledge in the field, while his social standing permitted privileged access to family papers still in private hands.

Lang is remembered, also, as a scintillating essayist, with collections including *Books and Bookmen* (1886) and *Adventures among Books* (1905), and as the biographer of J. G. Lockhart (*The Life and Letters of John Gibson Lockhart*, 2 vols., 1896) and Jeanne d'Arc (*The Maid of France*, 1908). In children's literature he is well known for his 'coloured' fairy books, compilations of folk-tales from many parts of the world, beginning with *The Blue Fairy Book* (1889) and continuing through to *The Lilac Fairy Book* in 1910. Lang was also a novelist, collaborating with his friend Henry Rider Haggard in *The World's Desire* (1890), and issuing in his own right *The Monk of Fife* (1896) and *The Disentanglers* (1902), the latter a sparkling social comedy containing moments of inspired tomfoolery, such as the kidnap of a Canadian heiress from a castle on the west coast of Scotland, and an ensuing mad chase around the Minch in submarines.

Lang was a handsome man, slim and gracefully built. In manner he was languid, drawling, and reserved. Those who were able to penetrate the façade were devoted to him, inspired by his generosity and warmth. Although not particularly gifted as a sportsman, he was a keen cricketer, golfer, and angler, and wrote lovingly and wittily on these subjects. Stevenson hit him off best, in a genially malicious little squib written shortly after they met in the south of France in January 1874:

> My name is Andrew Lang,
> Andrew Lang
> That's my name,
> And criticism and cricket is my game.
> With my eye-glass in my eye,
> Am not I,
> Am I not,
> A la—dy da—dy, Oxford kind of Scot
> Am I not?
> (Green, 177–8)

Behind the calculatedly effete exterior lurked one of the most powerful and subtle intellects of his generation.

Lang was much honoured, holding doctorates from St Andrews (1885) and Oxford (1904). He was made a freeman of Selkirk in 1889 and elected an honorary fellow of Merton College in 1890. Andrew Lang died of angina pectoris at the Tor-na-Coille Hotel, Banchory, Kincardineshire, on 20 July 1912, having just completed a review for the *Manchester Guardian* of part 5 of *The Golden Bough*. His wife survived him. He was buried in the cathedral precincts at St Andrews.   WILLIAM DONALDSON

Sources R. L. Green, *Andrew Lang: a critical biography with a short-title bibliography of the works of Andrew Lang* (1946) · A. B. Webster, ed., *Concerning Andrew Lang: being the Andrew Lang lectures delivered before the University of St Andrews, 1927–1937* (1949) · A. P. L. de Cocq, *Andrew Lang: a nineteenth century anthropologist* (1968) · R. M. Dorson, *The British folklorists: a history* (1968) · A. Lang, *Adventures among books*, 3rd imp. (1912), 3–38 · A. Duff-Cooper, ed., *Andrew Lang on totemism: 1912 text of totemism by Andrew Lang* (1994) · E. L. Montenyohl, 'Andrew Lang's contributions to English folk narrative scholarship', *Western Folklore*, 47 (Oct 1988), 269–84 · E. D. S. Langstaff, *Andrew Lang* (1978) · R. Haynes, *The Society for Psychical Research, 1882–1982: a history* (1982) · J. F. M'Lennan, *Primitive marriage: an inquiry into the origin of the form of capture in marriage ceremonies* (1865) · E. B. Tylor, *Researches into the early history of mankind and the development of civilization*, 2nd edn (1870) · E. B. Tylor, *Primitive culture: researches into the development of mythology, philosophy, religion, language, art, and custom*, rev. 3rd edn, 2 vols. (1891) · *DNB*

Archives Claremont College, California · Harvard U. · State University of New York at Buffalo, New York, MSS and letters · U. St Andr., MSS and letters | BL, correspondence with William Archer, Add. MS 45293 · Bodl. Oxf., letters to Sidney Lee, Gilbert Murray · Ches. & Chester ALSS, letters to Rhoda Broughton · CUL, letters and enclosure to W. Robertson Smith · Hunt. L., letters, mainly to H. Clifford Smith · LUL, letters to Austin Dobson · NL Scot., letters to Blackwoods, Ella Christie and Alice Stewart, A. H. Millar, Mrs Maxwell Scott · NLA, letters to Daisy Bates · Norfolk RO, letters to Sir Henry Rider Haggard · U. Leeds, Brotherton L., letters to Edward Clodd, Sir Edmund Gosse · U. St Andr., letters to William Craigie, Clement K. Shorter

Likenesses W. B. Richmond, oils, 1884, Scot. NPG [*see illus.*] · P. Naumann & R. Taylor & Co., wood-engraving, 1892, BM, NPG; repro. in *ILN* (14 May 1892) · M. Beerbohm, caricature drawing, 1896, Newberry Library, Chicago, Illinois · A. L. Coburn, photogravure, 1904, NPG; repro. in *Men of mark* (1913) · M. Beerbohm, caricature drawing, 1926, U. Cal., Los Angeles, William Andrews Clark Memorial Library · H. Furniss, caricature pen-and-ink sketches, NPG · F. Hollyer, photograph, V&A · P. Portsmouth, relief portrait on memorial, Selkirk Free Library · bas-relief cameo, U. St Andr., Fife · photograph, repro. in A. Lang, *Helen of Troy*, new edn (1913) · photographs, NPG

Wealth at death £1585 3s. 9d.: resworn probate, 2 Sept 1912, *CGPLA Eng. & Wales*

Lang, (William) Cosmo Gordon, Baron Lang of Lambeth (1864–1945), archbishop of Canterbury, was born on 31 October 1864 at Fyvie manse, Aberdeenshire, the third son of the Revd John Marshall *Lang (1834–1909), then Church of Scotland minister of the parish, and his wife, Hannah Agnes (1840–1921), daughter of the Revd Peter Hay Keith, minister of Hamilton.

Early life Cosmo Lang attended the Park School, Glasgow, until at fourteen he entered Glasgow University. There he became convinced that 'The Universe is one and its Unity and Ultimate Reality is God' (Lockhart, 13). At the university debating club he emerged as a tory democrat. After less than four years he graduated as an MA and won two university prizes. He decided to go on to Oxford. Though he had now crossed the border he remained always (as he confessed) 'the enthusiastic, romantic, perhaps sentimental Highlander' (ibid., 15). He entered Balliol College in October 1882 to read *literae humaniores*. During his first term he won the Brackenbury history scholarship. In February 1883 he leapt to fame in the Oxford Union and was elected president unopposed that summer. But because of his intense social life he got a second not the expected first. The next year he worked harder and in 1886 won a first in history.

Through contacts with the East End settlements of Toynbee Hall and Oxford House, the needs of the poor began to stir Lang's conscience. But he was still determined on the bar and politics. Leaving Oxford he widened his experience by giving Oxford extension lectures to workers in the north of England. In 1887 W. S. Robson took him into his chambers. The following year Lang was elected a fellow of All Souls. In 1929 (when he became visitor) he described it as 'the centre of an abiding interest and love' (Lockhart, 61).

Early ministry But in 1889, on the eve of being called to the bar, Lang kept hearing an inner question: 'Why shouldn't *you* be ordained?' (Lockhart, 62). One Sunday at evensong in Cuddesdon parish church he heard an inner voice: 'You are wanted. You are called. You must obey' (ibid., 64). He severed his connection with the bar; he sought entrance to Cuddesdon College; he was confirmed by Edward King, the saintly bishop of Lincoln. Thereafter, Cuddesdon parish church became for Lang 'the most sacred spot on earth to me' (ibid., 86). He had known for a long time that if he became an Anglican he would identify himself with the liberal Catholicism of *Lux mundi* (1889) and the social teaching of F. D. Maurice and Charles Kingsley. These various decisions increasingly distanced himself from his family, though he kept close to his mother.

(William) Cosmo Gordon Lang, Baron Lang of Lambeth (1864–1945), by Bassano, 1937

In 1890 Lang turned down the offer of the chaplaincy of All Souls and instead chose to be ordained deacon for a curacy at Leeds parish church, where E. S. Talbot (a contributor to *Lux mundi*) was vicar. In 1891 Lang was ordained priest. For nearly all his three years as a curate, Lang chose to live in a disused public house, then in a condemned hovel in the most squalid part of Leeds. He converted a shop into a home for orphan street boys. Each Sunday he was responsible for the instruction of 80 to 100 young men. In 1893 he was appointed dean of divinity at Magdalen College, Oxford, and a year later also vicar of the university church, St Mary's. In 1896 he became vicar of Portsea. He had initially refused, depressed by its drabness, but his conscience smote him. It was a parish of 40,000 people, ministered to by a large group of curates. Long before church councils became compulsory in 1919, he pioneered their creation in Portsea. He preached twice on Sunday to large congregations and in the afternoon lectured to 300 men. In 1898 he was commanded to preach before Queen Victoria at Osborne. This inaugurated what became a particularly close relationship with the royal household.

When A. F. Winnington Ingram was translated from Stepney to London in 1901, he asked that Lang should succeed him as bishop of Stepney and canon of St Paul's. Lang was consecrated by Archbishop Frederick Temple on 1 May. During the next eight years he combined his duties in the cathedral and in the East End with travelling extensively for the East London Church Fund and addressing meetings of the Church of England Men's Society of which he became chairman. One Sunday the Labour leader George Lansbury came to Bow church where Lang was preaching. Lang drew Lansbury back to become a regular communicant again. As bishop of Stepney he was at the height of his powers and attracted many by his vivacity. 'I think he is very great' commented the young William Temple (Iremonger, 52).

Archbishop of York In 1908 Lang was nominated by Asquith, the prime minister, to be archbishop of York. It was almost unknown for a suffragan to become an archbishop without having been a diocesan, but Asquith believed that the next twenty years would be critical for the Church of England, and that a young primate was needed to be able to guide it for a generation. Lang was only forty-four, but he was already well known throughout the church. Lang was enthroned on 25 January 1909 and he and Randall Davidson, archbishop of Canterbury since 1903, quickly developed a close relationship. The bishops of the province were all much older and with one exception low-churchmen. But his tact and skill won them over. He achieved the division of his over-large diocese with the creation in 1914 of the diocese of Sheffield and in 1927 by the transfer of the rural deanery of Pontefract to Wakefield. He decided to visit each church in the diocese at least once—some had never been visited by an archbishop before.

Lang's maiden speech in the Lords (30 November 1909), supporting Lloyd George's controversial budget, caused a stir, whereas the majority of bishops, led by Archbishop Davidson, abstained. He angered many tories by voting for the 1911 Parliament Bill. Yet, just when leading figures in the church were seeking to make it more sympathetic to working people, Lang began to act as a prince of the church. His self-dramatization started to obscure the prayerful, pastoral, and self-abnegating priest behind the facade.

The First World War At the outbreak of the First World War, Lang felt 'harried with anxiety' as to whether the church should support it, but concluded it was 'righteous' (Lockhart, 246). In November 1914, during an address about the war in York, he referred to his 'sacred memory' of the Kaiser kneeling beside Edward VII at the bier of Queen Victoria (ibid., 248). The hundreds of letters which arrived denouncing his remarks depressed him by their hatred and malice. For the first time in his life he experienced hatred and scorn. The alopecia which followed turned a young-looking, dark-haired man into an elderly-looking bald man with white hair. Even friends did not recognize him.

Lang played a leading role in the national mission of repentance and hope mounted by the church in 1916 to dispel misconceptions and to call for social and personal penitence. He visited the Grand Fleet in 1915 and the western front in 1917. He met some chaplains who, realizing how irrelevant and ossified the church seemed to many servicemen, were determined on radical reform. The pressure group Life and Liberty which pressed for such reform was headed by Lang's friends William Temple and Dick Sheppard. But Lang regarded some of the chaplains' criticisms as insubordination. At the end of the war Lang was weary. His conscience was troubled by the lack of magnanimity in the Versailles treaty. But he failed to understand many of the lessons of the war for the church and the changed nature of post-war society. Yet his chairmanship of the reunion committee of the 1920 Lambeth conference showed that he was still capable of new ventures. It was he who conceived the idea of an 'Appeal to all Christian People' to press towards 'the goal of a reunited Catholic Church' (Lockhart, 269). It offered a new way forward through reciprocal commissioning by which the free churches would be united to the historic episcopate without repudiating their own past. Though little resulted from the subsequent consultations, it inspired the ecumenical endeavours of later generations.

The unofficial conversations at Malines between some Anglicans and Roman Catholics between 1921 and 1926 coincided with deep protestant concern about the Catholic direction of prayer book revision. Lang, as a catholic Anglican felt more warmly towards the conversations and the revision than Archbishop Davidson. After the rejection by parliament of the proposals in 1927 and 1928, the bishops in 1929 in effect sanctioned the use of the revised prayer book. After 1928 the church was left without any coherent and effective authority. Lang (now at Canterbury) refused to challenge parliament. In 1913, Lang, during the Lords debate on Welsh disestablishment on 12 February, had offered an almost mystical defence of the state connection. Is there, he asked, 'some ultimate sanction to which the nation looks, some ultimate ideal which it professes' (*Hansard 5L*, 13.1205)? In the 1930s George Bell's pressure for a renegotiated relationship with the state alarmed Lang, who had been ambivalent when Bell was nominated for Chichester in 1929. Bell admired Lang as a great preacher and assiduous administrator, with a great interest in politics and world affairs. But to Bell, Lang was not the reformer the church needed. After the rejection of the revised prayer book, an archbishops' commission reported on church–state relations, but no effective steps were taken to give the church that greater degree of self-government for which Bell contended.

In 1924 Lang was painted by Sir William Orpen, who portrayed him (some thought) as 'proud, prelatical and pompous'. When presented with the portrait, Lang described it as 'a portrait of a very hard-working, very well-meaning, very lonely and very disappointed man' (Lockhart, 290–91). Yet when Michael Ramsey was archbishop of York (1956–61) he found more photographs of Lang than of William Temple in the vicarages of the older clergy.

Archbishop of Canterbury Archbishop Davidson announced his resignation in July 1928. The following day Baldwin, the prime minister, nominated Lang to succeed him. William Temple was nominated for York. Lang was nearly sixty-four. Charles Gore characteristically sent the message which pierced his armour: 'Keep loyal above all

things to Jesus of Nazareth' (Lockhart, 311). On 4 December, Lang was enthroned with magnificent music and ritual in the presence of a much wider representation of people from the nation and the arts than ever before. Lang wrote to Dick Sheppard, his dear but critical friend: 'I think I have some invincible youth hiding within me, and a late lark singing' (ibid., 312). It proved not to be so.

'The job is really impossible for one man, yet only one man can do it', Lang concluded in 1935. He described his pace of life as 'incredible, indefensible and inevitable' (Lockhart, 372). He usually worked seven days a week, 8 a.m. to midnight, yet was always up for early morning chapel. But from 1914 to 1945, each summer he would spend a month or more at Ballure, a dower house on the Kintyre peninsula. The first few mornings were devoted to uninterrupted prayer. Each year he reiterated in his journal his deep sense of unworthiness, his gratitude for God's mercy, and his rededication. 'In this sacred little place, by God's mercy, watersprings break from a dry and thirsty land' (ibid., 187). He spent Holy Weeks in retreat at Cuddesdon. However, he did not use his Scottish background or visits as vantage points from which to cast a critical eye on church and society in England. For most of his ministry he maintained his unremitting work without serious damage to his health, though suppressed resentment at his regime surfaced as irritability. But during his first three years at Canterbury he was frustrated by serious illnesses. Had his anxiety as to whether Canterbury would be offered taken its toll? For some months Mervyn Haigh, his chaplain, had to act for him. On two occasions Lang convalesced by cruising in the Mediterranean on the yacht of the American millionaire J. P. Morgan. These cruises also gave him the opportunity to strengthen Anglican–Orthodox relations. During his third cruise, in April 1939, he became the first archbishop of Canterbury to visit the ecumenical patriarch at the Phanar itself—the crown of Lang's ecumenical endeavours.

Most weekends Lang spent faithfully visiting his Canterbury diocese. By 1941 he had visited almost every parish at least once. But he disliked being stared at by strangers and travelled to Canterbury only once by train. 'Never again, never again', he muttered (Lockhart, 329). Lang considered his translation to Canterbury as a vindication of the Catholic revival in the Church of England: 'he catholicised the Church of England probably more than anyone else, and largely without giving offence' (Hastings, 197). He was the first archbishop since the Reformation to live in a cassock and to wear a mitre. Though he regarded his Catholicism as more inclusive than that of Rome, he was the first modern archbishop of Canterbury to have a sympathy for Rome and an understanding of its workings. On the other hand, his Presbyterian background also enabled him to feel at home in evangelical churches.

Hewlett Johnson became dean of Canterbury in 1931, and though his communism was anathema to Lang, they got on surprisingly well. Lang remembered that Johnson was one of the few who had written to support him during the First World War when he was attacked for asserting that Germans were also children of God. When in 1931

Johnson proposed spending four months investigating the chaos in China brought about by war, Lang agreed because he too had been haunted by the suffering.

Unlike Davidson, Lang did not regularly frequent the Athenaeum to meet national leaders and usually attended the Lords only when he was due to speak. Though presiding over convocation and the church assembly was uncongenial, he was a skilful chairman. His close relationship with the Cecil family who controlled the assembly ensured that it was run along high tory lines.

Lang approached the 1930 Lambeth conference with apprehension. He had only just recovered from serious illness; he expected divisions. But it went well. Good progress was made with relations with the Orthodox and the Old Catholics and with the unity scheme for south India. The cautious approval given by the majority of bishops for the first time to contraception was the one topic which directly affected ordinary people. But Lang was curiously uninterested in the issue which he described as 'tiresome and difficult' (Lang MS 2884/146).

Lang's contribution to church unity was highlighted by Bell: 'there is no man in the whole Anglican Communion who has left a deeper impression on the Unity movement in that Communion between 1920 and 1947' (Lockhart, 273). Lang was one of the six presidents of the notable Oxford conference on 'Church, community and state' and celebrated the eucharist for the delegates from different churches at St Mary's, Oxford, an unusually generous gesture for that time.

'The name of the Archbishop of Canterbury is to-day a household word throughout the inhabited globe', Lang was told by one of his chaplains (A. C. Don) in 1937 (Lockhart, 424). His bell-like voice at the coronation had become familiar through film and wireless. He had close relationships with public figures, including Baldwin, Chamberlain, and Halifax. But it was above all his involvement in international questions and royal affairs which made him well known to the public.

International affairs Lang and his generation had been horrified by the slaughter of the First World War and were determined to do almost anything to prevent another war. Christians promoted the ecumenical movement partly as a means to peace among nations. Lang supported the appeasement policy of Chamberlain and Halifax which then seemed hopeful and Christian, and trusted that the League of Nations would be an instrument of international order. Lang was a significant figure in Anglo-German relations. The German authorities carefully monitored what Lang and other bishops said. Joachim von Ribbentrop, the German ambassador, had regular meetings with Lang, and later described him as 'a very clever man' and the Church of England as politically as well as spiritually important (Chadwick, 13). Lang hoped that his frequent strong words to Ribbentrop about Nazi policies towards the churches and the Jews might have influence.

Lang received regular information about the German situation from the Anglican bishop in Europe and his chaplains, from ecumenical figures, leaders of other churches, persecuted individuals, and the Foreign Office. The

creation of the Church of England council on foreign relations in 1933 was a mixed blessing as its chairman, A. C. Headlam, bishop of Gloucester, took a benign view of the Nazis. He was in frequent conflict with Bishop Bell who was in close contact with victims of Nazism. In March 1933 Lang began receiving reports about the persecution of the Jews. On 30 March in the Lords he asked the government to voice the deep concern of the British people. On 31 May at Canterbury convocation he strongly deplored the persecution. On 27 June he addressed a public meeting at the Queen's Hall attended by Christians and Jews. He continued to denounce antisemitism both in Germany and Britain and tried to help the many desperate Jews who wrote to him from Europe.

In the Lords on 25 October 1935 Lang strongly condemned Italian aggression in Abyssinia and recognized that this was a crucial test for the League of Nations. Lang was also deeply concerned about the oppression of religion in Russia. He worked hard, but in vain, to bring security for Assyrian Christians in Iraq who had looked to Canterbury for protection since 1886. His plea for Britain to help India towards self-government led to his appointment in 1933 to the joint committee on the Indian constitution.

Like other British leaders, Lang believed that the Versailles treaty was unjust and that its provisions could not be permanent. So when Hitler marched into Austria in 1938, he spoke in the Lords on 29 March of the inevitability of the union of the two countries. Later he regretted omitting certain qualifying phrases from his speech. After the Munich agreement, Lang declared Sunday 2 October a day of thanksgiving. Despite anguished appeals from Czechoslovak Christians, after consultation with leaders of other churches, he issued a statement which ascribed this 'sudden lifting of the cloud' to 'the great volume of prayer which … has been rising to God' (Wilkinson, 174). In March 1939, after Hitler's annexation of Czechoslovakia, Lang and Chamberlain changed their tone. In the Lords on 20 March, Lang said that the annexation demonstrated that 'pledged words cannot be trusted … there must be the massing of might on the side of right' (Hansard 5L, 112.320–21). Britain should be prepared to co-operate with Russia and to accept papal leadership in the search for peace. (However, his efforts to enlist the papacy in a joint declaration from church leaders foundered). The speech dismayed pacifists, pacifiers, and protestants and was denounced by German leaders of church and state. In May, Lambeth pressed the government to ensure that conscientious objectors were treated more fairly if war broke out.

The monarchy Lang grew close to George V (at whose coronation in 1911 he preached admirably) and to Queen Mary. The king would sign his letters 'your sincere old friend' (Lockhart, 389). In 1929 both the king and Lang convalesced at Bognor. The king, who had not allowed Davidson to minister to him in sickness, now received Easter communion with the queen from Lang. It was Lang who drafted the king's last two Christmas broadcasts, and that for the silver jubilee; also the queen's messages to the nation after the death of the king and after the abdication.

All changed with the advent of Edward VIII, who resented the fact that his father had discussed him with Lang. So he rebuffed Lang's friendly overtures. News of the king's relationship with Mrs Simpson filtered into Lambeth. Lang agonized over whether he could bring himself to crown him. But the king refused to discuss the issues with Lang. During the crisis Lang had regular consultations with Queen Mary, Baldwin, Geoffrey Dawson (editor of *The Times*), and the king's private secretary. What influence he exerted on them is not known. On 13 December 1936 Lang in his broadcast criticized Edward for surrendering his sacred trust for a relationship which was inconsistent with Christian marriage. He also included a maladroit reference to George VI's stammer. He had composed the speech himself and not consulted anyone. His words had been influenced by his sympathy for Queen Mary and by correspondents who advised him that the people felt let down. Baldwin told him that he had spoken for Christian England. A Benedictine monk in the Rhineland described it as 'an absolutely classical document of episcopal frankness, fatherly gentleness and national feeling ... It is most significant that in England the Church can speak thus' (Lang MS 192/396). But to many it seemed like kicking a man when he was down. When he had visited Baldwin in Downing Street on 6 December the crowd had booed him. Lang's reputation never recovered from the broadcast. Yet he wrote in his diary 'My heart aches for the Duke of Windsor' (Lockhart, 406).

Lang likened the new reign to waking to sunshine after a nightmare. He was already close to the new king and queen. On 12 December 1936, two days after the abdication, the queen wrote to Lang: 'for many years now, you have been so kind and wise about our troubles and joys ... I sign myself for the first time and with great affection, Elizabeth R.' (Lang MS 2864/135–6). The mystery, symbolism, and history of the coronation appealed deeply to Lang. He called the nation to a renewed faith. 'Let him not come alone to his hallowing' (Lockhart, 410).

The Second World War During the war Lang tried to maintain spiritual values and to learn lessons from the church's mistakes during the First World War. There should be no hatred, no vindictive peace settlement, and there should be restraints on the conduct of the war. On 28 June 1939 Lang had conveyed to the bishops' meeting the government's assurance that civilians would not intentionally be bombed in wartime. In 1941, at the May convocation, Lang rejected public clamour for indiscriminate bombing of Germany. In his retirement, Lang, unlike Temple, supported Bell's condemnation of obliteration bombing, in the Lords on 9 February 1944. On 20 September 1940 Lambeth Palace suffered a direct hit. Lang moved to Canterbury but continued to sleep at Lambeth when in London. Then on 10 May 1941, when Lang was in residence, the palace was rendered uninhabitable by four bombs.

In 1911 Lang had declared that if the nineteenth century was concerned with the creation of wealth, the twentieth century would be concerned with its more equal distribution. Lang's early social radicalism faded, but he was glad when Temple was appointed bishop of Manchester in 1921 because he would understand labour. On 21 December 1940 *The Times* published a letter from the two archbishops, Cardinal Hinsley, and the Free Church moderator supporting the pope's five peace points and adding standards for social policy. Temple had given it final shape. Lang signed it though he was uneasy about the proposed abolition of 'extreme inequality' (Lang MS 84/187).

Lang announced his resignation on 21 January 1942. His yearning for sympathy and his self-dramatization led him into another unfortunate remark, when he lamented his withdrawal to obscurity and his 'very slender means' (Lockhart, 441). Yet he had been granted a peerage and a grace-and-favour house in Kew by the king; he had his pension and (though it was not publicly known) £15,000 from J. P. Morgan. Over Easter he stayed at Cuddesdon and made his confession on Easter eve.

During his retirement Lang spoke in the Lords fairly frequently, enjoyed his visits to All Souls, and spent several months each year at Ballure. He was deeply shocked by Temple's early death in 1944 and on his eightieth birthday read the lesson at the funeral. On 5 December 1945 Lang died, aged eighty-one, of heart failure, hurrying to Kew Station. He was taken to the Royal Hospital, Richmond, Surrey. On 10 December a service was held in Westminster Abbey, and simultaneously a requiem was sung at Canterbury Cathedral, where that afternoon the funeral took place. After cremation, the ashes were interred in St Stephen's Chapel, Westminster, on 11 December.

Estimate J. G. Lockhart's portrayal of Lang in his 1949 biography as a brilliant but highly complex personality who disappointed the high hopes of his early ministry has stood the test of time. But he played a more important and creative role in international affairs than Lockhart suggested. Throughout his ministry he was an eloquent public speaker with an instinct for the dramatic which sometimes led him into trouble. He played a notable part in fostering ecumenism, though after listening to a speech by an evangelical he confided: 'The one form of religion I could never conceivably embrace is Protestantism' (Lang MS 2866/82). His ecumenical and international ministry developed further the worldwide role of the see of Canterbury. He was a sensitive pastor to those in pain—as his long ministry to Dick Sheppard illustrated. His legal training enabled him to understand complex legislation and to penetrate swiftly to the heart of a problem.

Lang went to Canterbury too late in life, after twenty years at York and an over-long apprenticeship to the cautious Davidson. Lacking any grand strategy he just conscientiously responded to each task as it arose. In an increasingly democratic and informal age, his patrician style made him seem remote and snobbish to ordinary people. Haigh, one of his chaplains, affirmed Lockhart's description of Lang as 'a jangle of warring personalities' (Lockhart, 458) adding, 'anyone who ever saw him arrange himself for an interview, or pass in a flash from death to fullness of vigour with a change of company or after donning a purple silk cassock, would readily recognize that fact' (Barry, 100). His smooth exterior concealed great inner struggles. 'Ah, Haigh', he would say, 'were it not for that strange Man upon his Cross!' (Barry, 100). Celibate, lonely, and normally in tight control of his private emotions, in 1911 he opened his heart to his chaplain, Wilfrid Parker, who was moving to new work:

> You can't understand … the strange way in which you have got into my heart … my life is really rather a lonely one. It needs … someone in daily nearness to love. The fact that for reasons sufficient to me I am not and do not propose to be married, does not make this need less. (Lang MS 2881/71)

Lang held twelve doctorates including the Oxford DCL (1913). He was an honorary fellow of Magdalen (1909), Balliol (1928), and All Souls (1942), and an honorary bencher of the Inner Temple (1931). He received the Royal Victorian Chain in 1923 and was appointed GCVO in 1937 and in 1933 lord high almoner.   ALAN WILKINSON

Sources LPL, Lang MSS · LPL, Bell MSS · 'Journal of A. C. Don', LPL · *DNB* · J. G. Lockhart, *Cosmo Gordon Lang* (1949) · A. Wilkinson, *Dissent or conform? War, peace and the English churches, 1900–1945* (1986) · F. A. Iremonger, *William Temple, archbishop of Canterbury* (1948) · R. Jasper, *George Bell: bishop of Chichester* (1967) · F. R. Barry, *Mervyn Haigh* (1964) · A. Hastings, *A history of English Christianity, 1920–1985* (1986) · R. Hughes, *The Red Dean* (1987) · O. Chadwick, 'The English bishops and the Nazis', *Annual Report* [Friends of Lambeth Palace Library] (1973), 3–28 · A. Chandler, 'The Church of England and the obliteration bombing of Germany in the Second World War', *EngHR*, 108 (1993), 920–46 · A. Chandler, 'The Church of England and the Jews of Germany', *Leo Baeck Institute Yearbook*, 38 (1993), 221–61

Archives Borth. Inst., official corresp. and papers · LPL, corresp. and papers | All Souls Oxf., letters to Sir William Anson · BL, corresp. with Lord Cecil, Add. MS 51154 · BL, corresp. with Sydney Cockerell, Add. MS 52729 · BL, corresp. with Albert Mansbridge, Add MSS 65254–65255B · BLPES, corresp. with E. D. Morel · Bodl., letters to Herbert Asquith · Bodl. Oxf., corresp. with Bickersteth family · Bodl. Oxf., corresp. with L. G. Curtis · Bodl. Oxf., corresp. with Geoffrey Dawson · Bodl. Oxf., letters to Sir James Marchant · Bodl. Oxf., corresp. with Lord Sankey · Bodl. Oxf., corresp. with third earl of Selborne · Bodl. RH, corresp. with Lord Lugard · Bodl. RH, corresp. with J. H. Oldham · Borth. Inst., corresp. with Lord Halifax · CUL, corresp. with Sir Samuel Hoare · Herts. ALS, letters to Lord Desborough and Lady Desborough · Lancs. RO, letter to T. H. Floyd · LPL, corresp. with Samuel Bickersteth · LPL, letters to Canon A. S. Crawley, his wife, and daughter · LPL, corresp. with Randall Thomas Davidson · LPL, corresp. with John Douglas · LPL, letters to Sir Edward Ford · LPL, corresp. with Lord Gladstone · LPL, corresp. with Arthur Headlam · LPL, letters to Claude Jenkins · LPL, letters to Lady Londonderry · LPL, corresp. with Edwin Palmer · LPL, letters to Wilfrid Parker · LPL, letters to Richard Rawstorne · LPL, corresp. with Athelstan Riley · NL Scot., letters to Sir Charles Dalrymple · NL Scot., letters to Seton Gordon · NL Scot., corresp. with Lord Haldane · NL Scot., letters to H. P. Macmillan · Shrops. RRC, letters to first Viscount Bridgeman | FILM BFI NFTVA, 'The coronation of their majesties King George VI and Queen Elizabeth', Pathé pictures, 1957 [footage of Lang conducting ceremony] · BFI NFTVA, documentary footage · BFI NFTVA, news footage · BFI NFTVA, record footage | SOUND BBC WAC · BL NSA, sound recording · BL NSA, current affairs recordings

Likenesses Rotary Photo, two postcards, photographs, *c.*1901–1908, NPG · A. Hester, cabinet photograph, *c.*1909, NPG · E. M. Sutcliffe, photograph, *c.*1909, NPG · G. F. Watt, oils, 1913, All Souls Oxf. · J. Russell & Sons, photograph, *c.*1915, NPG · W. Stoneman, three photographs, 1923–41, NPG · W. Orpen, oils, 1924, Bishopthorpe Palace, York · R. S. Sherriffs, pen-and-ink caricature, 1930–39, NPG · I. Opffer, sanguine drawing, 1934, NPG · I. Campbell, pencil and chalk drawing, 1936, NPG · W. Llewellyn, oils, *c.*1936, LPL · Bassano, photograph, 1937, NPG [*see illus.*] · P. A. de Laszlo, oils, 1937, Church House, Westminster, London · P. A. de Laszlo, oils, 1937, LPL · W. Reynolds-Stephens, bust, 1938, NPG · F. Dodd, pencil drawing, Athenaeum, London · P. Evans, print, NPG; repro. in *Saturday Review* (23 Jan 1926) · Spy [L. Ward], caricature, lithograph, NPG; repro. in *VF* (19 April 1906) · photograph, repro. in Lockhart, *Cosmo Gordon Lang*, facing p. 448

Wealth at death £29,541 16s. 9d.: probate, 20 Feb 1946, *CGPLA Eng. & Wales*

Lang, John Dunmore (1799–1878), Presbyterian minister and politician in Australia, was born on 25 August 1799 at Greenock, Renfrewshire, the eldest of the four children of William Lang (1768?–1830), a small landowner, and Mary Dunmore (1770–1844). He was educated for the ministry at the Largs parish school (1807/8–1811) and the University of Glasgow (MA 1820, DD 1825), and was licensed to preach in 1820. In 1823 he emigrated to be the first Presbyterian minister in Sydney.

The following year Lang made the first of nine visits to Britain, seeking government support for colonial education, recruiting clergy and schoolmasters, and promoting migration to Australia. On his second visit he married a cousin, Wilhelmina Mackie (1812–1891), on 25 August 1831. The marriage was happy and in all his controversies Lang was comforted by a warmly harmonious family life, though this was marred by tragedies involving his children; of ten five died in infancy.

In 1833–4 Lang again returned to Britain. As always on voyages, he wrote—this time *An Historical and Statistical Account of New South Wales* (1834). Revised editions appeared in 1837, 1852, and 1875. In 1835 he commenced a weekly, *The Colonist*, which ran until 1840. The *Colonial Observer* (1841–4) and *The Press* (1851) were also Lang papers. Lang next visited Britain in 1836–7. In 1832 he had formed the presbytery of New South Wales with other ministers, all of whom he had recruited. Too many were over-fond of the bottle and most of the others were unwilling to prosecute their fellows. Lang determined to enrol sufficient new clergy to outvote the backsliders and their abeters. He obtained twelve Presbyterian clergymen and, in Germany, three Lutheran missionaries and ten lay assistants.

Back in Sydney, Lang imprudently and schismatically established a new church court instead of relying on the increased numbers in the presbytery of New South Wales to discipline the delinquent ministers. On his next visit to Britain the rival courts combined to form the synod of Australia, which Lang joined on his return in 1841. But he was quickly affronted when it criticized his ministry, and he abandoned it, denouncing it as 'a mere synagogue of Satan'. He also renounced his government stipend, convinced that state support of religion produced a multitude of evils. He could do so because his congregation at the Scots Church was perhaps as large and wealthy as all other Presbyterian congregations combined.

In June 1843 Lang was elected to the legislative council, beginning a parliamentary career that lasted until 1869.

He was elected to the legislature seven times, three times topping the poll, and defeated only once.

In 1846 Lang again sailed for Britain to promote emigration. His continual theme for the next three years in books, pamphlets, lectures, and newspaper articles was that the grinding poverty of Britain could be relieved by the boundless opportunities in Australia. He proposed that reputable migrants who paid their own fares receive a grant of crown land. Prolonged correspondence and interviews at the Colonial Office failed to secure this concession, which was in fact illegal. Lang nevertheless recklessly arranged for about 270 migrants to sail in the *Fortitude* in September 1848, promising them they would receive free land in proportion to their passage money. By a dishonest manoeuvre he then vainly tried to trick the colonial governor into granting the migrants land on their arrival. He thus destroyed his reputation with the Colonial Office and saved it with the Australian public at large only by blustering falsehoods. Despite this fiasco, Lang dispatched six vessels with more than 1200 migrants before he returned to Australia in 1850.

In lectures in Sydney in April 1850 Lang declared that Australia should at once become a republic. He believed strongly in local self-government and abhorred the aristocratic influences in English society and politics. He set out his arguments in pamphlets and two large, learned books, *Freedom and Independence for the Golden Lands of Australia* (1852, 1857) and *The Coming Event! or, Freedom and Independence for the Seven United Provinces of Australia* (1870).

In 1851 Lang falsely accused a political opponent of dishonesty and, though he apologized for his error, was convicted of malicious libel and sentenced to four months' gaol. In 1855, when greatly provoked, in a pamphlet entitled *The Convicts' Bank*, he charged a prominent banker with 'malice prepense of the foulest character imaginable ... and a degree of low-bred brutal malignity worthy only of an incarnate demon'. That was criminal libel and it earned Lang six months in gaol, which he spent comfortably in the residence of the gaol's governor.

In 1850 Lang had established the synod of New South Wales with ministers he had enlisted on his recent visit to Britain. He then settled them throughout the colony. In 1865 this synod joined in the general Presbyterian union, which combined the Free Churchmen with those supporting the established Church of Scotland.

From 1874 Lang suffered several small strokes, but they did little to hinder his activities, and he made a strenuous round-the-world journey in 1874–5. He died, after a massive stroke, on 8 August 1878 at the Australian College, Jamison Street, Sydney. He was accorded a state funeral on 10 August, and was buried at the Devonshire Street cemetery.

Above all, Lang was a Presbyterian minister. Yet he cooperated willingly with other protestant clergymen, especially Baptists and Congregationalists, often more cordially than with fellow Presbyterians. Always parading as an upright man, he frequently condemned the sins of those in public life, including the fornication of Governor FitzRoy. Many hundreds of the poor, the homeless, and the bereaved remained deeply grateful to him as benefactor and friend. His achievements in promoting education and immigration bear comparison with those of any of his contemporaries but would have been much greater had his intense inner drive not been compounded with an equal impulse to castigate opponents or even those merely lukewarm towards his designs. His long parliamentary career included many electoral triumphs and he witnessed the achievement of almost all his political aims: the end of transportation, the separation of Victoria and Queensland, the introduction of responsible and democratic government, radical land reform, national education, and the abolition of state aid to religion.

In addition to his larger books, Lang published more than a hundred polemical, religious, or political pamphlets, and almost every day, it seems, he wrote an article for the press or at least a letter to the editor. His writings, though repetitious and egotistical, are nevertheless always vigorous and informative and often tinged with powerful sarcasm. These, together with innumerable lectures given in Sydney or in the bush on his never-ending colonial journeyings, must have had a large influence in inculcating the liberal and secular values which were dominant in Australia by the end of the nineteenth century.

D. W. A. BAKER

Sources D. W. A. Baker, *Days of wrath: a life of John Dunmore Lang* (1985) · *John Dunmore Lang: chiefly autobiographical from 1799 to 1878*, ed. A. Gilchrist, 2 vols. (1951) · I. F. McLaren, *John Dunmore Lang: a comprehensive bibliography of a turbulent Australian Scot* (1985)
Archives Mitchell L., NSW · State Library of New South Wales, Sydney, Dixson Library, letters and papers | Matlock, Derbys. RO, letters to Sir R. J. Wilmot-Horton [copies]
Likenesses W. Nicholas, watercolour, c.1840, Mitchell L., NSW · J. Backler, oils, after 1850, Mitchell L., NSW · C. Rodius, crayon, 1850, Mitchell L., NSW · oils, before 1850, Mitchell L., NSW · J. T. Gorus, photograph, 1873 (engraved by H. S. Sadd), Mitchell L., NSW
Wealth at death under £1000—goods: New South Wales Probate Office · under £2500: probate, 3 April 1879, *CGPLA Eng. & Wales*

Lang, Sir John Gerald (1896–1984), Admiralty official, was born in Woolwich on 20 December 1896, the elder son (there were no daughters) of George Thompson Lang, an engineering toolmaker, and his second wife, Rebecca Davies. There were four sons and one daughter of George Lang's first marriage. Lang was educated at Haberdashers' Aske's School, Hatcham, London, and entered the Admiralty as a second division clerk in 1914. He saw service in the First World War as a lieutenant in the Royal Marine Artillery (1917–18). After his return to the department, it was not long before he began to make a name for himself and his abilities were eventually recognized in 1930, by promotion to the administrative class as assistant principal.

In his early days Lang was engaged mainly on personnel administration but his mastery in this field was so marked that by the outbreak of the Second World War it was clear that he would go far. He became principal in 1935 and assistant secretary in 1939. During the war he was selected to fill the important post of director of labour, concerned with the recruitment, organization, and deployment of dockyard and shipyard labour. The contacts which he made with ship builders and officials of the ship-building unions were to stand him in good stead later on. From these civilian personnel tasks he moved on in 1946 to become the under-secretary concerned with naval personnel and he made a notable contribution to the reorganization of naval manpower as it was returned to a peacetime level.

By then Lang's capacity had become so widely recognized that, when Sir Henry Markham died prematurely in December 1946, Lang was the obvious choice to succeed him as secretary of the Admiralty, although this involved a double promotion. His time as secretary (1947–61) was in general one of retrenchment, and his was the guiding hand in the process of reducing the Admiralty to its peacetime size.

Lang was endowed with a photographic memory. He could recall, over several years, not merely the contents of a paper, but also its registered number. This memory enabled him to build up an unrivalled knowledge of past discussions and events and this in turn made him a formidable advocate of any policy which he decided to support. He was by nature very deliberate, and he liked to have plenty of time to consider a question from all its angles before coming to a conclusion. As a result, he developed a very mature judgement which was rarely at fault.

Lang's staff held him in high regard and affection. He led them by his example of selfless service to the department's affairs, rather than by any strict discipline. He was always accessible and invariably calm and courteous. His retirement in 1961 was widely regarded as something of an end of an era. Lang was appointed CB in 1946, KCB in 1947, and GCB in 1954. He was twice married. In 1922 he married Emilie Jane (d. 1963), daughter of Henry Shelley Goddard, interior decorator, of Eastbourne. They had one daughter. In 1970 he married her sister, Kathleen Winifred (d. 1984), widow of C. G. E. Edmeades.

In retirement Lang pursued several interests with undiminished enthusiasm, in spite of the handicap of impaired sight, which struck him not long after he left the Admiralty. From 1964 to 1971 he was principal adviser to the government on sport and for most of that time he was deputy chairman of the Sports Council. In 1969 he produced a report on crowd control at football matches, which formed the basis of many of the early measures to combat soccer hooliganism. In 1969 he headed an investigation which secured for the taxpayer a large refund on a defence contract. He was a governor and an officer of the Bethlem Royal and Maudsley hospitals (1961–70).

Lang was a vice-president of the Royal Naval Association and chairman of its standing orders committee, responsible for the running of the association's annual conferences. He was active in the Royal Institution of Naval Architects, of which he also became a vice-president (1977). He was associated with the Navy Records Society, and a member of the Worshipful Company of Shipwrights and of the Pepys Club, of which he became president. In his eighties he offered his services to Help the Aged, and though he became their adviser on VAT, to begin with he was content, with typical modesty, to perform very humble tasks for them.

Lang died on 22 September 1984, at his daughter's house at Walton on the Hill, Tadworth, Surrey. His second wife survived him by only a few days.

CLIFFORD JARRETT, rev.

Sources *The Times* (26 Sept 1984) · personal knowledge (1990) · private information (1990) · *WWW* · *CGPLA Eng. & Wales* (1984)
Archives FILM IWM FVA, actuality footage
Likenesses T. Stubley, oils, Admiralty House, London
Wealth at death £166,529: probate, 5 Dec 1984, *CGPLA Eng. & Wales*

Lang, John Marshall (1834–1909), Church of Scotland minister and university principal, was born on 14 May 1834 at the manse of Glasford, Lanarkshire, the fourth of eleven children of Gavin L. Lang (1791–1869), minister of the parish, and his wife, Agnes Roberton Marshall (d. 1886) of Nielsland. Lang received his early education with private tutors at the manse; he then spent a year at the high school in Glasgow, followed by studies at the University of Glasgow under several noted professors. However, he was not an outstanding student academically and he did not graduate. Proceeding to the divinity hall of the university, he came under the influence of several of the senior divinity students, including John Caird, A. K. H. Boyd, and G. W. Sprott. But it was only after his licensing and a short-term assistantship at Dunoon that his native ability and preaching gifts became apparent. At the young age of twenty-two years Lang was called to the important charge of the East Parish of St Nicholas, Aberdeen, where he was ordained on 26 June 1856. Experiencing some ill health, he left Aberdeen in August 1858 for the country parish of Fyvie, Aberdeenshire, where he learned much about life and ministry in a rural Scottish setting. While minister at Fyvie, Lang married, on 10 April 1861, Hannah Agnes (1840–1921), daughter of Peter Hay Keith, minister of Hamilton. They had seven sons and one daughter—the third son being (William) Cosmo Gordon *Lang (1864–1945), archbishop of Canterbury from 1928 to 1942.

In January 1865 Lang was called to Anderston, Glasgow, a newly built church in the west end of the large parish of the Barony; on 25 June 1868 he was translated to the Edinburgh suburban parish of Morningside. Lang's last, longest, and most notable experience as a parish minister was in the historic Barony Church in Glasgow, where he followed the great Norman Macleod. Inducted into the charge on 9 January 1873, he ministered there with great distinction until his appointment as principal of Aberdeen University on 31 March 1900. He served in that office until his death in 1909. Lang was one of those many Scottish presbyterian ministers who, in the latter years of the nineteenth and early years of the twentieth centuries, exercised a wide influence and provided outstanding leadership not only in ecclesiastical affairs but in the social and cultural, civic, and educational spheres of Scottish life. Like Lang, several became principals of Scottish universities in these years.

A man of broad interests and liberal sympathies, Lang was an early leader in the liturgical renewal movement of the time, and in efforts to recover catholic elements within the reformed tradition which had been neglected in contemporary Scottish presbyterianism. In his first charge in Aberdeen, at the young age of twenty-three, he preached a sermon which resulted in a censure from the presbytery. At a time when congregations sat to sing, he suggested in his sermon that if there was a reason for choirs to stand to praise, that reason applied equally to congregations. While Lang deemed it prudent to conform to presbytery's demand that he return to 'use and wont', within a few years this change had become widespread in the established church. Lang and Robert Lee of Old Greyfriars, Edinburgh, were the first ministers to introduce pipe organs into the services of worship. While much initial opposition ensued, by the 1870s the use of an organ had ceased to be an innovation in the Church of Scotland.

Lang was one of the first members of the influential Church Service Society, formed in 1865 in the Church of Scotland, which successfully promoted the restoration of elements of form and order to the often barren presbyterian worship of the time. As a member of the high-church party in the established church (sometimes referred to as Scoto-Catholics) he was also a prominent member of the Scottish Church Society founded in 1892. To this party and society the unity of the church was of fundamental importance, and its members were therefore among the most enthusiastic supporters of inter-church dialogue and co-operation. This concern was reflected in Lang's commitments and involvements: as early as 1872 he and Professor William Milligan of Aberdeen University were deputies from the Church of Scotland to the general assembly of the Presbyterian church, USA. For many years he was convener of the general assembly committee dealing with overseas reformed churches. He was a leading figure in the Pan-Presbyterian Alliance, attending and giving addresses at all its quadrennial conferences from the first at Edinburgh in 1876 to that of which he was president at Washington in 1899. Lang's endeavours nationally were no less impressive: he was made convener in 1890 of the assembly's commission 'to inquire into the religious condition of the people of Scotland'. The task occupied six years and involved a personal visit to almost all the parishes of Scotland. His annual speech, as he gave his reports, was a highlight of successive general assemblies. In 1893 he was moderator of the general assembly.

During his long ministry in Glasgow at the Barony Church, Lang became deeply involved in the public life of the city. For nine years he served on the school board and for twenty-seven years he was chaplain to the 1st Lanark volunteers; he was a member of the presbytery's commission for the housing of the poor. In his church he introduced Sunday evening services, and was instrumental in raising £28,000 for the rebuilding of Barony Church, dedicated in 1889. Lang was particularly concerned to address the rampant social evils of his day and to support the working class in their struggle for a more just and equitable society. He praised trade unions for improving the lot of workers, advocated a minimum 'living wage' for the

lowest paid, argued for an end to sweated labour, and favoured state support for working-class housing. With other prominent Scottish churchmen such as Robert Rainy he sided with the workers in the famous Scottish railway strike of 1890–91, speaking at a large union rally in Glasgow. In his moderator's address in 1893 he stressed that economic insufficiency—not immorality—was the major cause of poverty, and that workers' efforts to use their voting power upon governments to achieve social reforms—'an effort by the people for the people to realize better distribution of wealth and more equitable adjustments in condition' (Moderators' Closing Addresses, 1836–1905, 3.13)—were essentially just and praiseworthy. In one sermon preached in Barony Church he is reported to have advocated a radical redistribution of the nation's wealth (said to be £1000 million a year) from the rich to the poorer classes.

In the last decade of his life Lang proved to be a most diligent and able principal at Aberdeen University. The major event of his principalship was the opening of the new buildings at Marischal College, which his energy largely brought to completion. He was made CVO in celebration of the occasion, adding to his earlier honours from Glasgow University (DD in 1873 and LLD in 1901). Lang wrote numerous books on a variety of subjects. His major works were his 1897 Duff lectures (The Expansion of the Christian Life, 1897) and his 1901 Baird lectures (The Church and its Social Mission, 1902). In December 1908 his health began to fail, and he died at Chanonry Lodge, Old Aberdeen, on 2 May 1909. He was buried in the south transept of St Machar's Cathedral, Aberdeen.   DONALD C. SMITH

Sources Fasti Scot., new edn · DNB · J. Kerr, The renascence of worship: the origin, aims and achievements of the Church Service Society (1909), 88–90 · H. A. Lang, Memories of John Marshall Lang (privately printed, 1910) · D. C. Smith, Passive obedience and prophetic protest: social criticism in the Scottish church, 1830–1945 (1987) · Moderators' closing addresses, 1836–1905, 3 [n.d.] [annual addresses to the general assembly of the Church of Scotland] · The Scottish Pulpit: A Magazine of Religion and Life (6 July 1892), 247 · Scottish Weekly and Scottish Pulpit (15 Nov 1893) · British Weekly (15 Jan 1891)

Likenesses E. R. Calterns, portrait, U. Aberdeen · Elliott & Fry, photograph, repro. in Kerr, The renascence of worship, facing p. 88 · bronze medallion; formerly at Barony Church, Glasgow, 1911

Wealth at death £3866 0s. 11d.: confirmation, 7 July 1909, CCI

Lang, (Alexander) Matheson (1879–1948), actor, theatre manager, and playwright, was born in Montreal, Quebec, Canada, on 15 May 1879, the youngest son of the seven children of the Revd Gavin Lang of Mayfield, Inverness, Scotland (but at that time a minister of the Scottish Presbyterian church of St Andrew's, Montreal), and his wife, Frances Mary (née Corbett). Raised in Scotland, he was educated at Inverness College and St Andrews University. He was destined for the church (his cousin Cosmo Gordon Lang became archbishop of Canterbury) but decided on the stage after seeing Frank Benson and Sir Henry Irving when their companies toured Scotland. He joined Louis Calvert's repertory company in 1895, and made his début two years later at Wolverhampton in Proof. A number of small parts followed before he joined Benson's Shakespeare company, with which he made his London début, in February 1900, as Montjoy in *Henry V*. He soon graduated to larger roles (Macduff, Laertes, Bassanio, Charles Surface) before appearing in December 1902 at the Imperial as Sir Charles Croffte in *The Cross-Ways* with Lillie Langtry; he toured with her in the United States the following year.

After returning to the Imperial, Lang played Benedick in *Much Ado about Nothing* opposite Ellen Terry in 1903, before touring with her. He took leading parts in Benson's tour of the West Indies and returned to the West End in a succession of plays (1905–6) before scoring a great success in Manchester as Othello. Further successes followed, as Trevor Lerode in *John Glayde's Honour* at the St James's and as Dick Dudgeon in *The Devil's Disciple* at the Savoy, before he embarked on a programme of popular drama with Ernest Carpenter, manager of the Lyceum. This included roles as John Storm in *The Christian* (1907), Romeo in *Romeo and Juliet* (1908), and Hamlet (1909). At this time Lang was taking great interest in the promotion of a national theatre but with Carpenter's death in December 1909 the Lyceum organization broke up.

Lang appeared in December 1909 in New York at the New Theater as Charles Surface in *The School for Scandal*. In April 1910 he left to tour Australia, fitted in *Macbeth* at Stratford upon Avon the following year, then took his company on a successful tour of South Africa with a repertory of Shakespearian and modern romantic drama, repeating that success in India and the Far East. He returned to the West End in several roles (including Surface again at His Majesty's) before playing, from November 1913, Wu Li Chang in the hit *Mr Wu*, by Harry M. Vernon and Harold Owen, at the Strand, the role with which he was to be long associated. He scored again, in November 1914, as Hotspur in *Henry IV, Part 1* at His Majesty's, toured as Mr Wu in 1915 and then as Shylock in *The Merchant of Venice* with his own company before playing the latter at the St James's under his own management. For the next few years he punctuated occasional West End appearances with further touring. His style was deemed 'frank, full-blooded drama, for which his powerful presence, resonant voice and energetic temperament fitted him', but possibly he favoured touring because 'even 30 years ago there was less demand for that sort of thing in London than in the provinces and oversea' (*The Times*, 13 April 1948, 7e). However, W. Maqueen Pope was more charitable: 'He required a costume play—or a costume part—to reach his heights and when he reached them he was superb' (*The Times*, 19 April 1948, 6d).

In July 1918 Lang took on the management of the Lyric, where he adapted *The Purple Mask* and appeared as the Comte de Trevières. In February 1920 he assumed management of the New Theatre, commencing with *Carnival*, which he co-adapted from the Italian and in which he appeared as Silvio Steno. He scored a particular success later that year as Matathias in E. Temple Thurston's *The Wandering Jew*. It ran for a year and was a role to which he returned on many occasions. He also presented well-received matinées as Othello to Arthur Bourchier's Iago. In 1925 he toured as Yuan Sing in his own play *The Chinese*

Bungalow, in which he also appeared at the King's, Hammersmith. He toured Canada in 1926–7 with a repertory company and played *The Wandering Jew* at the Cosmopolitan, New York, a role he also played at Drury Lane for King George's pension fund. In 1928 he played his favourite role, Count Pahlen, in *Such Men are Dangerous* at the Duke of York's. For the next nine years he played only a few new roles (such as General Crack, Wellington, Sir Philip Holbrooke KC in *For the Defence*), and was chiefly touring, mostly in revivals, especially of *The Wandering Jew*. His last tour was with *The Chinese Bungalow* in 1937.

Lang also had a busy screen career—indeed, he was 'one of the few great stage actors to become a film star despite his theatrical style' (Gifford, 172). Many of his films were versions of his stage successes: his début was *The Merchant of Venice* (1916), followed by *Mr Wu* (1919), *Carnival* (1921), *The Wandering Jew* (1923), and *The Chinese Bungalow* (1926). Perhaps inevitably, he made sound versions of some of these, including remakes of both *Carnival* and *The Chinese Bungalow* in 1931. He made only eight 'talkies', but several were noteworthy: *Channel Crossing* (1933), *Little Friend* (where he was fine as the father), and *The Great Defender* (very good as the famous but ailing counsel Sir Douglas Rolls; both 1934), and the historical pageant of events in the reign of George V, *Royal Cavalcade* (1935). *Drake of England*, in which he starred as Drake (1935), though, was disappointing, and in his final role, as Cardinal de' Medici in *The Cardinal* (1936), he was better than his material.

Lang married on 7 December 1903 Nellie Hutin Britton (1876–1965), daughter of Thomas Britton. An actress since 1901 and with Lang in the Benson company, she subsequently toured with him, usually as a leading lady. They had no children. In 1914 they helped to inaugurate Shakespeare productions at the Old Vic under Lilian Baylis, for which Lang personally lent costumes and scenery. His wife was a member of the Old Vic's governing board for many years. In 1940 Lang wrote a volume of autobiography, *Mr Wu Looks back*. The following year he moved to South Africa, where he enjoyed many pursuits: art, literature, sailing, golf, and tennis. He died in Bridgetown, Barbados, on 11 April 1948. His funeral took place at West Church, Inverness, on 6 August and he was buried at Omnahurich cemetery.   ROBERT SHARP

Sources *Who was who in the theatre, 1912–1976*, 4 vols. (1978) · *WWW* · *The Times* (13 April 1948), 7e · *The Times* (19 April 1948), 6d · *DNB* · P. Hartnoll, ed., *The Oxford companion to the theatre*, 4th edn (1983), 472 · D. Gifford, *The illustrated who's who in British films* (1978) · m. cert.
Archives FILM BFI NFTVA, performance footage | SOUND BL NSA, documentary recording · BL NSA, performance recording
Likenesses S. MacDonald, oils (as Hamlet), University of Bristol · R. Martin, photograph, NPG
Wealth at death £31,155 16s. 5d.: probate, 10 May 1949, CGPLA Eng. & Wales · £41,845 1s. 5d.: probate, 5 Oct 1948 [revoked 10 March 1949], CGPLA Eng. & Wales

Lang, Sir William Biggart (1868–1942), machine tool manufacturer, was born on 19 September 1868 at 59 High Street, Johnstone, Renfrewshire, the youngest of five sons in the large family of John Lang (*c*.1825–1906), machine tool maker, and Annie Biggart. His father had founded his own firm in 1874 in Johnstone, a town which had seen its early growth closely linked to the development of the cotton industry. As the cotton industry began to decline, engineering expanded from the mid-nineteenth century; and John Lang & Sons was a typical example of a firm set up to serve the needs of the shipbuilding and engineering trades, and which specialized in the production of lathes.

Lang was educated at Paisley grammar school, followed by attendance at classes at the Glasgow and West of Scotland Technical College. He became an apprentice in his father's firm, learning all aspects of engineering. This pattern of education and training was similar to that followed by his brothers, three of whom also joined the family business. A fourth joined the well-known company of G. and J. Weir Ltd of Cathcart, Glasgow.

By the time that Lang joined it, the firm had established a significant presence in the engineering industry: it served every shipyard on the River Clyde, exhibited at international exhibitions, and its customers nationwide included the British Admiralty, Armstrong Whitworth & Co., and Messrs Vickers and Maxim. Expansion and modernization of the premises in 1893 and 1899, with a workforce increased to 350, established John Lang & Sons as one of the foremost machine tool manufacturers in Scotland, if not Great Britain. It was during this decade of expansion that Lang became more involved in the running of the business. He became a partner in 1895, aged only twenty-seven. The decade of the 1890s also saw Lang's marriage, on 15 June 1897, to Agnes, the daughter of James Barr, a well-known local businessman in the firm of James McDowall & Sons, saw mill engineers. They had a family of three daughters.

His father retired in 1898, and when the firm became a private limited company in 1916, Lang served as its first managing director, and also as chairman from 1927. He had few interests in other companies, devoting his business life to the family firm and to the machine tool trade. From 1912 he was a member of the North West Engineering Employers Association, serving as its president in 1921–2. John Lang & Sons played an important role in munitions in both world wars, and from 1915 Lang became chairman of the machine tool committee of the Ministry of Munitions. The first chairman (1917–22) of the Associated British Machine Toolmakers Ltd of London, he also served on the tariff advisory committee of the Machine Tool Trades Association, and in 1934 became president of the Machine Tool Trades Association. A member of the Institution of Engineers and Shipbuilders in Scotland from 1906, he also served on the various boards and committees of the Engineering and Allied Employers Federation.

Throughout his life Lang was involved in local affairs in Johnstone. He was a councillor from 1908, and in 1914 succeeded his brother John as provost. He served three consecutive terms until his retiral in 1923. A JP for Renfrewshire, he was president of the local YMCA from 1911, and a member of the committee of management of Paisley Savings Bank from 1932. For most of his life he was a member of the Johnstone High Church. In honour of his services to the local community and national contribution to the machine tool trade, he was awarded a knighthood in 1937.

Lang died at a nursing home at 121 Hill Street, Glasgow, on 17 February 1942 after a short illness, and was buried on 19 February. His wife predeceased him the year before. His death occurred at a time when John Lang & Sons was again playing a key role in the production of munitions, and especially lathes for aircraft guns and tank parts. Aided by other members of his family who were involved with the firm, Lang successfully endeavoured to keep the concern at the forefront of the machine tool industry.

SHEILA HAMILTON

Sources *Transactions of the Institution of Engineers and Shipbuilders in Scotland*, 85 (1941–2), 392 • *Glasgow Herald* (18 Feb 1942) • *Paisley and Renfrewshire Gazette* (18 Feb 1942) • *Paisley Daily Express* (18 Feb 1942) • *Engineering* (13 March 1942) • *The Times* (7 March 1942) • WWW • A. McLean, ed., *Local industries of Glasgow and the West of Scotland* (1901) • W. S. Murphy, *Captains of industry* (1901) • *Paisley and Renfrewshire Gazette* (28 Feb 1874) • *Paisley and Renfrewshire Gazette* (22 Sept 1894) • *Paisley and Renfrewshire Gazette* (8 Jan 1898) • *Paisley and Renfrewshire Gazette* (7 Nov 1914) • DSBB • d. cert. [Agnes Lang]
Wealth at death £63,794 9s. 2d.: confirmation, 16 July 1942, CCI

Lang, William Henry (1874–1960), botanist, was born in Withyham, Groombridge, Sussex, on 12 May 1874, the son of Thomas Bisland Lang (d. 1876/7), a medical practitioner originally from Bridge of Weir, Renfrewshire, and his wife, Emily Smith. Following the death of his father, Lang and his mother returned to Bridge of Weir. He was educated at the local village school, and then, as a day boy, at Dennistoun public school, Glasgow. He obtained a BSc with honours in botany and zoology in 1894 from Glasgow University and qualified in medicine, with high commendation, in 1895. But he never became an active practitioner; innate interest and the enthusiasm inspired by his teacher Professor F. O. Bower led him into professional botany.

Lang's first botanical researches were concerned with development and structure in the ferns, on which, like his teacher, he became an authority. In 1895 Lang went to the Jodrell Laboratory at Kew with a Robert Donaldson scholarship. There he began his classical observations on the enigmatic reproductive phenomena of apogamy and apospory in ferns. He made the discovery of sporangia on the prothallus of a fern (*Philosophical Transactions of the Royal Society*, 1898) which was of particular contemporary interest for biologists who were then exploring the manifestations of alternation of generations (where one generation reproduces asexually, and the next sexually) in plants and animals. All his life Lang seemed to have the knack of lighting upon interesting things. During the next thirty years he made further contributions to the same general theme, and he was usually to the fore when 'alternation', with its many vicissitudes, was under discussion.

At Kew, Lang came under the inspiration of D. H. Scott, a leading exponent of fossil botany. Rumination on the nature of plant life in Devonian and Carboniferous eras, the cautious assessment of fossil fragments, the critical evaluation of the views of others on such materials, were

William Henry Lang (1874–1960), by unknown photographer

occupations highly congenial to Lang. He had a scholarly and philosophic mind, unusual skill and patience in making the most of scanty and imperfectly preserved materials, and an almost excessive caution in the eventual written interpretation of his findings, an attitude which he later impressed, perhaps with some over-emphasis, on his students and colleagues.

In the autumn of 1899 Lang went to Ceylon and Malaya to collect material and study tropical cryptogamic species. The work led to publications on pteridophytes (ferns) and bryophytes (mosses and liverworts). In 1902 he returned to Glasgow University as a lecturer in botany. Among his colleagues were D. T. Gwynne-Vaughan, a talented plant anatomist. Bower, Gwynne-Vaughan, and Lang worked together for some twelve years as the 'Triumvirate'—of whom many good stories were told.

During this period the Glasgow department was frequently visited by Robert Kidston of Stirling, a notable investigator of the Palaeozoic flora. Gwynne-Vaughan and Lang collaborated in the production of a notable series of memoirs: 'The fossil Osmundaceae' (1907–10). Following the death of Gwynne-Vaughan, Lang joined with Kidston in investigating the Rhynie chert from Aberdeenshire which contained extremely well preserved Devonian material. This was a landmark in the history of botany. The silicified plant remains were in an excellent state of preservation and the two investigators made the most of them. Their observations, published in the *Transactions of the Royal Society of Edinburgh* (52, 1917–21), provided remarkable demonstrations of the form and structure of a group of simple leafless and rootless vascular plants of early

Devonian times—now known as the Psilophytales. *Psilophyton* had been known since 1858, but had been rather neglected and its structural features were imperfectly known. The precision with which Kidston and Lang described and portrayed essential morphological features and phylogenetic aspects of the new genera and species of the Rhynie fossils gave great impetus and new direction to the whole of this branch of botany. These memoirs made a unique, factual contribution to evolutionary theory. At the time of their publication they had a very special interest for the many botanists then seeking to establish the original flora of the land in early geological times. Other neglected fossil materials, of the same general period and affinity and often of the most fragmentary character, were subsequently investigated by Lang. Later, in collaboration with Dr Isabel C. Cookson, Lang showed, in a study of materials from the Australian Silurian, that primitive vascular plants, not unlike a lycopod in their general configuration, had flourished in geological times much earlier than the Devonian. Other ancient materials investigated by Kidston and Lang (for example, *Sporocarpon*, *Transactions of the Royal Society of Edinburgh*, 53, 1925) provoked new interest because they were made at a time when students of phylogeny were eagerly searching for evidence of possible connecting links between the algae and the first primitive land plants.

In 1900 Lang was awarded the DSc degree of Glasgow and when the Barker chair of cryptogamic botany was established in the University of Manchester, he was first choice. He took up his duties, in what was essentially a research chair, in 1909. The following year he married Elsa Valentine (d. 1957), a cousin from Dublin. They had no children. When Lang retired in 1940 he had already been father of the senate and elder statesman for many years; his work for the university and his personal pre-eminence were recognized by an honorary LLD in 1942. He was elected FRS in 1911 and awarded a royal medal in 1931. In 1932 he received an honorary LLD from Glasgow. He was a foreign member of the Swedish Royal Academy of Science and in 1956 received the gold medal of the Linnean Society of London.

Lang was tall, a distinguished bearded figure, and a keen walker, who enjoyed good health. He was an amiable and stimulating conversationalist, with an agreeable, cynical pawkiness and jollity of delivery; the words fairly fizzed out of him, enjoyed no less by himself than his hearers. But he was essentially a quiet and modest man, with a deep feeling for philosophy, especially for the restraint which it could exercise on the often superficial theorizing of contemporary botany. His memorable presidential address to the botany section of the British Association in 1915, 'Phyletic and causal morphology', was remarkable for its practical and philosophic insight into major problems of causation in plant development and evolution, and for its critical attitude to the prevailing comparative morphology of the post-Darwinian period.

Following Lang's retirement, much further research was curtailed because of his wife's ill health. They moved to Westfield, Storth, near Milnthorpe, Westmorland, where, after some years, she died. Lang himself died on 29 August 1960 at St John of God Hospital, Silverdale, Carnforth, in Lancashire.

C. W. WARDLAW, *rev.* PETER OSBORNE

Sources J. Walton, 'Professor W. H. Lang F. R. S.', *Nature*, 188 (8 Oct 1960), 102–3 · E. J. Salisbury, *Memoirs FRS*, 7 (1961), 147–60 · *CGPLA Eng. & Wales* (1960)
Archives U. Glas., Archives and Business Records Centre, letters to F. O. Bower
Likenesses photograph, repro. in Walton, *Nature*, 102–3 · photograph, repro. in Salisbury, *Memoirs FRS* [*see illus.*]
Wealth at death £15,313 15s. 7d.: probate, 31 Oct 1960, *CGPLA Eng. & Wales*

Langbaine, Gerard (1608/9–1658), college head, the son of William Langbaine, was born at Barton Kirk, Westmorland. After education at Blencow School, Cumberland, on 17 April 1625 he entered Queen's College, Oxford, from which he matriculated on 21 November 1628, aged nineteen. On 6 October 1627 he received a non-residential Dudley exhibition of Oriel College, and on 10 June 1630 a scholarship at Queen's. Having graduated BA the following 24 July, he became a tutor and grammar reader. He proceeded MA on 27 June 1633, when he had to sell his patrimony to pay debts, and was elected fellow the following 30 October. Ordained deacon in 1634 and priest in 1635, he held no ecclesiastical preferment other than the vicarage of Crosthwaite, Westmorland, obtained in early 1643.

The diarist Thomas Crosfield suggests that Langbaine was a lively presence at Queen's. In 1638 he and another fellow stocked the garden with lapwings and with a hare which died after two days from rough handling. Crosfield also noted, in 1633, Langbaine's books. These included Xenophon in Greek, dictionaries and religious, literary, political, and historical works in Italian and French, volumes on Hebrew antiquities, Sir Thomas Ridley's *A View of the Civile and Ecclesiastical Law*, and a work on the Council of Trent.

From early on Langbaine delved in Oxford libraries and their manuscript collections, and exhibited catholic interests in print. From 1625 he regularly contributed verses to celebratory academic volumes. He compiled a detailed index for John Gregory's second edition of Ridley's *View* in 1634, and two years later published a student edition of Dionysius Longinus's Greek study of the sublime including his own detailed commentary. In 1638, inspired by the dedicatee, Christopher Potter, provost of Queen's, his *A Review of the Councell of Trent* translated the work of the Gallican Guillaume Ranchin while disclaiming Catholic doctrinal content. Probably dating from his years as a tutor was a basic guide for students, *Philosophiae moralis compendium*, printed posthumously in 1698 with additional material by Thomas Barlow. According to Thomas Hearne, Langbaine was already in touch with continental scholars, sending in 1641 a transcript of Bodleian manuscripts of Ailred of Rievaulx's *De vinculo perfectionis* and *De vita inclusarum* to Jacobus Merlon Horstius of Cologne for an edition of St Bernard.

In 1641 Langbaine entered the political arena with his *Episcopall Inheritance*, defending the right of bishops to vote

in the House of Lords (which provoked a response by Cornelius Burges), and a new edition, pointedly relevant, of Sir John Cheke's *Hurt of Sedition*, entitled *The True Subiect to the Rebell*, with a preface on Edward VI's reign and a life of the author. Registered as absent from college in the protestation returns of 1642, later that year Langbaine was prominent in a delegation dealing with Sir John Byron's royal troopers and was sent by the university to Nottingham, probably in connection with providing money for the king. In 1644 his antiquarian and legal skills made him the obvious successor to Brian Twyne as the university's keeper of the archives and defender of academic privileges. It was probably he who published in that year *A Review of the Covenant*, arguing that the solemn league and covenant was unlawful.

Langbaine was chosen Camden lecturer in ancient history in 1646 but did not take up the post. He succeeded Potter as provost of Queen's on 11 March and was created DD on 22 June. Soon afterwards he married his predecessor's widow, Elizabeth (1613–1692), daughter of Charles Sunnybanke, canon of Windsor. Two sons, William and Gerard *Langbaine (1656–1692), and at least one other child, were born to the couple.

As the university's custodian of its privileges Langbaine participated in negotiations for Oxford's surrender in 1646, and his successive drafts of articles to safeguard academic freedoms survive. Later he visited London to lobby parliament through the university's MP, John Selden, for payment of rents withheld, and strove, unsuccessfully, to have the Stationers' Company pay contracted dues. Langbaine was probably largely responsible for *The Privileges of the University of Oxford, in Point of Visitation*, issued in 1647. He contributed to *Reasons for the present judgment of the University of Oxford concerning the solemn league and covenant*, printed the same year, and then translated it into Latin for publication in 1648 with a view to reaching learned men abroad. Madan conjectures that amid such employments he also edited the autobiographical *Life of Sir Thomas Bodley* (1647).

It was almost certainly Langbaine who wrote *The answer of the chancellor, masters and scholars of the University of Oxford, to the petition, articles of grievance, and reasons of the city of Oxon.*, printed in 1649 and presented to the parliamentary committee for Oxford in response to an assault by the city on academic privileges. With unrivalled antiquarian knowledge and the assistance of the learned civil lawyer Richard Zouche, Langbaine easily saw off parliamentary projects to reform the university's Laudian statutes after 1649. He was involved in the reconstitution of the chancellor's court in July 1650. In 1651 he published *The Foundation of the Universitie of Oxford* and *The Foundation of the Universitie of Cambridge*, both, as Wood noted, drawing heavily on John Scot's work decades earlier. He produced, possibly for manuscript circulation, verses on three political questions aired at the formal vespers disputations of 1651, which were published in 1658 with Sir Henry Savile's *Oratio, coram Regina Elizabetha Oxoniae habita*. His concern at the decline of the civil law led him to collaborate on Arthur Duck's *De usu et authoritate juris civilis* (1653), and in late 1654 he organized a spirited defence of the languishing faculty in Oxford. The following year, with several intruded heads of house, he sought revision of dangerous new terms of parliamentary visitation, an effort resulting in tacit forbearance.

Langbaine also adroitly defended the interests of his college against parliamentary interference. He did not take the engagement, but still survived. Writing to his scholarly friend Selden, who smoothed his path, he accepted the earl of Pembroke as chancellor. On 9 October 1648 he wrote shrewdly enlisting the aid of another friend, Francis Mills MP, active with the parliamentary committee, on behalf of the fellows of Queen's: few were lost and few intruded. Diplomacy and outward moderation were rewarded when Queen's was allowed to elect its own officers again in April 1652. From 1651 Langbaine could count on the former Queen's man John Owen, now dean of Christ Church after a period as Cromwell's chaplain. The provost seems to have been no stickler for Church of England liturgy and formulas. His second son, Gerard, born on 15 July 1656, was 'baptized by Dr. Wallis after the new cutt, without godfathers' (PRO, SP 18/129, fol. 140v).

Langbaine maintained a prudent freedom of thought and expression within Queen's, reputed in the 1650s as royalist as circumstances permitted and so attracting loyalists and young men of rank to a degree exceptional in Oxford. In 1654 Langbaine and others there contributed to support distressed bishops in exile. Remembering his own struggles with poverty Langbaine not only endowed a grammar school at Barton, his birthplace, and funded apprenticeships for two poor boys, but also sought unsuccessfully to convince selfish fellows to improve remuneration for poor scholars. On a recommendation from Richard Busby of Westminster School, he admitted in 1650 the talented young Joseph Williamson, whom he helped from his own pocket. Despite his best efforts, however, during his last years there were factional disputes, centred on Thomas Barlow, in the fellowship.

Langbaine continued his own scholarly and antiquarian work. In 1643 he began cataloguing Greek manuscripts in the Bodleian and in college libraries, becoming the indispensable expert. In 1652 he initiated the creation of a subject catalogue of the Bodleian and college libraries. This was never finished, although part of his own assignment survives. He produced a bibliographical survey of Platonic writers in Greek and Latin and the whereabouts of their work in Oxford, eventually printed by John Fell in his *Alcinoi in Platonicam philosophiam introductio* (1667). Between 1650 and 1652, at Selden's suggestion, Langbaine produced with the aid of young scholars transcriptions of musical manuscripts for Marcus Meibom of Holstein to include in his *Antiquae auctores septem, Graece et Latine* (Amsterdam, 1652). A letter of 1656 from Franciscus Junius to William Dugdale suggests that Langbaine was then working on Anglo-Saxon texts. Thomas Fuller believed he was preparing an expanded edition of Twyne's work on the antiquity of Oxford, although this was denied by Wood. Hearne says he was also working on a new edition of Francis Godwin's *De praesulibus Angliae* (1616) and that he

contributed to William Dugdale's *A Short View of the Late Troubles in England*, printed only in 1681. When Archbishop Ussher died in 1656 he left his unfinished *Chronologia sacra* to Langbaine as the only man he could trust to prepare it for publication, and Wood says the provost 'drudged much' (Wood, 3.447) in this task.

Langbaine also laboured incessantly for the learned press in Oxford. Particularly active in this field from 1647, he formally became a delegate for the press in 1653. As keeper of the archives he looked after matrices and founts of type at his lodgings and bought Hebrew founts between 1655 and 1657 and a large fount of Anglo-Saxon in 1656.

Langbaine was a vital prop to numerous scholars: 'as his Brain was the Mother of some, so was it the Midwife to other, good Books which he procured to be published' (Fuller, 1.239). It was he who encouraged Selden to obtain the restoration of Edward Pococke's stipend as Laudian professor of Arabic, drawing up the university's protest at his treatment, and he encouraged Pococke to publish his *Specimen historiae Arabum* (1650), his 1655 edition of the *Porta Mosis* of Maimonides, and his 1654–6 edition of Eutychius' *Annales*; Pococke acknowledged Langbaine as the spur to publication of his *Historia compendiosa dynastiarum, authore Gregorio Abul-Pharajio* (1663). Langbaine also supported John Greaves and Samuel Clarke in their Arabic and Hebrew scholarship, and Sir Henry Spelman and William Dugdale in their work on *The History and Fate of Sacrilege* and *Monasticon Anglicanum* respectively. His friendship and correspondence with men like Ussher, Selden, Spelman, Dugdale, and Pococke attest to his pivotal position in English scholarship in these decades. He had also been a friend of the learned Ben Jonson.

Langbaine died on 10 February 1658 'of an extream cold taken by sitting in the University-Library whole Winter days, and thence after his return home, continuing in his study whole Winter nights, without any food or fire' (Lloyd, 518), apparently working over-hard on the project left him by Ussher. He was buried in the college chapel on 13 February alongside his two predecessors. By his will, among modest bequests to his stepchildren and others, virtually everyone at Queen's, including servants, was given a small sum; the residue of his estate went to his wife. A portion of his books, his 'greatest earthly treasure', was bequeathed to the college, and another to the Bodleian Library, the curator of which was to have choice of others at fair price. In April and May 1658 Anthony Wood, who respected Langbaine highly, acquired some of his books and manuscripts.

A. J. HEGARTY

Sources J. R. Magrath, *The Queen's College*, 2 (1921), 1–32 • D. Lloyd, *Memoires of the lives … of those … personages that suffered … for the protestant religion* (1668), 517–18 • Wood, *Ath. Oxon.*, new edn, 3.258, 446–9 • *Hist. U. Oxf. 4: 17th-cent. Oxf.* • *Remarks and collections of Thomas Hearne*, ed. C. E. Doble and others, 11 vols., OHS, 2, 7, 13, 34, 42–3, 48, 50, 65, 67, 72 (1885–1921), vol. 1, pp. 110–12, 393; vol. 2, pp. 13, 44, 66, 158, 207 • chancellor's court wills, Langbaine, Oxf. UA, fols. 5r–6v • A. Milton, *Catholic and Reformed: the Roman and protestant churches in English protestant thought, 1600–1640* (1995), 263 • G. J. Toomer, *Eastern wisedome and learning: the study of Arabic in seventeenth-century England* (1996) • Foster, *Alum. Oxon.* • Fuller, *Worthies* (1811), 239 • F. Madan, *Oxford books: a bibliography of printed works*, 3 vols. (1895–

1931); repr. (1964) • *The history of the church of Crosthwaite, Cumberland* (1853), 136–7 • *The diary of Thomas Crosfield*, ed. F. S. Boas (1935)
Archives Bodl. Oxf., advercaria, papers, collections • Queen's College, Oxford, notes relating to history of Queen's College | Bodl. Oxf., letters to John Selden
Likenesses two portraits, oils, Queen's College, Oxford
Wealth at death small bequests and forgiving of debts approx. £100–£150; £100 plus residue of goods to wife; books: will, 19 Aug 1647, confirmed 7 Feb 1658, Oxf. UA, wills L, 5r–6v

Langbaine, Gerard (1656–1692), dramatic cataloguer and writer, was born on 15 July 1656 in the parish of St Peter-in-the-East, Oxford, the second of two sons of Gerard *Langbaine (1608/9–1658), provost of Queen's College, Oxford, and his wife, Elizabeth (1613–1692), daughter of Charles Sunnybanke, canon of Windsor. From about 1666 to about 1670 he attended a school in Denton, in the parish of Cuddesdon, Oxfordshire, where he was taught by William Wildgoose. When in 1670 his mother's plan to secure his admission to Magdalen College, Oxford, failed, Langbaine was sent to London and apprenticed to Neville Simmons, a bookseller in St Paul's Churchyard. He was bound to Simmons for eight years, starting from 1 February 1672, but he never took up his freedom, for within months of his arrival in London he was recalled to Oxford on the death of his elder brother, William, on 3 June 1672. He matriculated from University College, Oxford, on 25 October 1672, but he never took his degree. His studies were interrupted when, not yet nineteen, he married Mary Greenwood (d. 1724), on 18 May 1675 at Headington, and promptly left for London. After a spell in the capital he seems to have settled in Holywell parish, Oxford. The young couple's conjugal felicity did not last long. Their daughter Elizabeth died shortly after being baptized at St Cross, Holywell, in August 1681, and was buried at St Peter's-in-the-East on 23 August. Wood tells us that Langbaine 'left his wife and hous in Holywell in the beginning of June 1683 and went away with a whoreish woman named … daughter of Warnford who lived in Halywell' (Wood, *Ath. Oxon.*, 4.364).

The young heir's hasty marriage, his frequent visits to London in the late 1670s, which involved extravagant playgoing and book-buying sprees, his adulterous escapade, and his costly passion for horses—Wood refers to him as a 'great jockey' (Wood, *Ath. Oxon.*, 4.364)—meant that he soon ran out of the estate he had inherited. Apparently reconciled to his wife, Langbaine was by 1685 back in Oxfordshire, where he lived a retired life at Wick in Headington. His sons Gerard and William were born in 1688 and 1692 respectively.

The retirement afforded Langbaine the leisure to pursue his 'inclination to [Dramatick] Poetry', which, he recalls, 'has led me not only to the view of most of our Modern Representations on the Stage, but also to the purchase of all the Plays I could meet with, in the *English* Tongue' (G. Langbaine, *Momus triumphans*, 1688, sig. A2r). Langbaine's interest in the drama goes back to his brief period of apprenticeship in London where he had the opportunity to see plays, and where he is likely to have become acquainted with Francis Kirkman, a bookseller

with a strong line in playbooks which he advertised in successive catalogues of 1661 and 1671. Having begun to build his own collection of plays while in college, by 1688 Langbaine owned no fewer than 980 titles (part of his collection survives in the library of Worcester College, Oxford). His 'natural and gay geny … to dramatic poetry' (Wood, *Ath. Oxon.*, 4.364) led him to produce a series of increasingly sophisticated catalogues of plays, the earliest of which was *An exact catalogue of all the comedies, tragedies, tragi-comedies, opera's, masks, pastorals and interludes* (1680). Published anonymously, this catalogue was merely a continuation of Kirkman's latest playlist. By contrast, Langbaine's later compilations proved a landmark in the history of dramatic authorship, bibliography, source study, and criticism. *A New Catalogue of English Plays* (1688), better known under its spurious title *Momus triumphans, or, The Plagiaries of the English Stage*, was the first ever to arrange entries alphabetically by authors' surnames, thus indicating the growing status of playwriting towards the end of the seventeenth century, the first to identify the sources of individual plays, Shakespeare's prominent among them, and the first to list the most readily available editions. Langbaine was scrupulous in distinguishing between plays which could confidently be attributed and those which could not. His catalogue moves from the category of incontrovertible ascription ('Declared Authors'), through that of conjecture ('Supposed Authors'), to that of 'Anonemous Plays'. The alphabetical index of plays makes each item easy to locate in one of the three classes. The preface to *Momus*, moreover, contains the first theoretical discussion of plagiarism in the English language. Langbaine sharply distinguishes between classical imitation and modern literary theft. Imitation, he argues, involves acknowledged adoption of ancient masterpieces as models; modern playwrights, however, recycle worthless French materials or debase native dramas. He makes a further distinction between overt borrowing from canonical authors (especially Shakespeare and Fletcher) and covert adaptation of plays by less prominent writers. The latter form of appropriation is particularly rife, he claims, because there is less likelihood of its discovery.

Langbaine expanded his views of the proprieties of appropriation in his magnum opus, *An Account of the English Dramatick Poets* (1691). Arranged alphabetically by author and—in contrast to its predecessor—written in continuous prose, the *Account* supplied basic biographical information about English playwrights, listed their works, and assessed, in however rudimentary a manner, their literary merit and authorial probity in the use of sources. In contrast to *Momus*, which did not determine conclusively what the dramatist is at liberty to take from a romance, a novel, or a play, the *Account* locates the author's property in the linguistic form of a literary work. Stories, plots, and ideas can legitimately be borrowed, but the actual words of the original are barred from appropriation.

Langbaine tapped into a rich vein of public interest. Though the book was scathingly reviewed in one of the short-lived literary periodicals, *The Moderator*, on 23 June

1692, the *Account* had a lasting impact upon later dramatic bibliographers, biographers, and critics from Charles Gildon (who within eight years wrote a sequel entitled *Lives and Characters of the English Dramatick Poets*, 1699), Giles Jacob, and Theophilus Cibber to Samuel Johnson and beyond. Not only was Langbaine's work continued, but annotated copies of his playlists, *Momus* and *Account*, circulated among critics, literary scholars, and editors well into the eighteenth century. In his condemnation of literary theft and his concern about literary property, authors' rights, and the integrity of the dramatic text Langbaine anticipates eighteenth-century legal and conceptual developments, notably the official recognition of authors as owners initiated by the Copyright Act of 1710, and the emergence of ideals of originality and individual genius which are central to the Romantic conception of literary creation.

Langbaine's other works include *The Hunter: a Discourse of Horsemanship* (1685) and *The Gallant Hermaphrodite* (1688), a translation of François de Chavigny de la Bretonnière's *La galante hermaphrodite nouvelle amoureuse* (1683). He was elected inferior bedel of arts at Oxford on 14 August 1690, and on 19 January of the following year superior bedel of law. Langbaine died in Oxford on 23 June 1692 and was buried on 27 June in St Peter's-in-the-East.

PAULINA KEWES

Sources H. S. Harvey, 'Gerard Langbaine the younger', BLitt diss., U. Oxf., 1937 · Wood, *Ath. Oxon.*, new edn, vol. 4 · P. Kewes, *Authorship and appropriation: writing for the stage in England, 1660–1710* (1998) · A. Watkin-Jones, 'Langbaine's *Account of the English dramatick poets* (1691)', *Essays and Studies by Members of the English Association*, 21 (1936), 75–85 · D. F. McKenzie, ed., *Stationers' Company apprentices*, [2]: *1641–1700* (1974) · C. H. Wilkinson, *A handlist of English plays and masques printed before 1750 in the library of Worcester College* (1929)

Langdale. For this title name *see* individual entries under Langdale; *see also* Bickersteth, Henry, Baron Langdale (1783–1851).

Langdale, Alban (*fl.* 1532–1580), Roman Catholic priest and writer, was born in Yorkshire, possibly at Houghton, but nothing is known of his parentage. He was educated at St John's College, Cambridge, graduating BA in 1532, becoming a fellow of St John's in March 1534, and commencing MA in 1535. In 1539 he was one of the proctors of the university. His clerical career began in 1541 when he was ordained deacon; in the same year he was ordained priest and became university chaplain, a position he held until 1554. In 1544 he proceeded BTh. In June 1549 he was one of the Roman Catholic speakers in the debates held before the royal commissioners for the visitation of the university about transubstantiation and whether, in the communion service, there was 'none other oblation or sacrifice' than 'remembrance of Christ's death, and of thanksgiving' (*Acts and Monuments*, 6.308). In November 1551 Roger Ascham confessed to being 'sorry Mr Langdale is gone from college, although he did dissent from us in religion' (Ascham, 393), but Langdale returned to the university early in Mary's reign, commencing DTh in 1554, and being incorporated in that degree at Oxford in the

same year. Adding to his rectorship of Buxted, Sussex, he was made prebendary of Ampleforth in York diocese on 26 May 1554, archdeacon of Chichester on 16 April 1555, prebendary of Alrewas in the church of Lichfield on 19 January 1559, and chancellor of Lichfield in the following month. Mary's reign also saw him disputing with Cranmer, Latimer, and Ridley at Oxford in 1554, taking part in the third and sixth examinations of Richard Woodman in 1557, and being dispatched by Anthony Browne, first Viscount Montague, whose chaplain he had become, to 'preach in places not well affected in religion' (*CSP dom.*, 1547–80, 162) in 1558. It was also in Mary's reign that his *Catholica confutatio impiae cuiusdam determinationis D. Nicolai Ridlei* (Paris, 1556) was published.

Early in Elizabeth I's reign Langdale was one of the eight Roman Catholics appointed to take part in the abortive Westminster disputation begun on 31 March 1559. By 7 October 1559 he had been deprived of the archdeaconry of Chichester, having refused to take the supremacy oath, and, having failed to attend the visitation at York in the same year, he had lost his prebendal stall there by 7 November. After deprivation he took up residence at Lord Montague's residence at Cowdray, Sussex. In 1561 he was described as 'learned and very earnest in papistry' on a list of recusants, and ordered to remain within Lord Montague's household, or somewhere else appointed by his lordship, and to be ready to appear before the authorities on twelve days' notice (*CSP dom.*, 1547–65, addenda, 523). Richard Smith blamed Langdale for Montague's occasional conformity, describing the priest as 'a learned and pious man indeed, but fearful' (Smith, 19). In 1580 a manuscript treatise entitled 'A discourse delivered to Mr Sheldon to persuade him to conform. Arguments to prove it lawful for a Roman Catholic to attend the Protestant service' (PRO, SP 12/144/19) began to circulate among incarcerated Roman Catholics. Robert Parsons, eager to track down its author, discovered tell-tale annotations on theological works in Langdale's library at Montague's Southwark residence. Since then the work, copied and disseminated by William Clithero, and instrumental in persuading Ralph Sheldon and Thomas, third Lord Paget, to conformity, has usually, and very convincingly, been attributed to Langdale, though his authorship cannot be proved.

Crucially, the tract was not a general dispensation for conformity, but a casuistical treatment of the specific dilemma faced by people from the upper echelons of society who had been imprisoned. It also helped the cause of partial conformity, suggesting that by combining presence at services with a refusal to participate on particular occasions the risks of undermining the loyalty of one's fellow religionists could be minimized. Its main contemporary importance was the extent to which it provoked the advocates of nonconformity, and Parsons and George Blackwell collaborated on a riposte ('Against going to churche', 1580, BL, Add. MS 39830). A chief concern was the timing of Langdale's tract: its tempting advice was dispensed only a few months ahead of the harsh 1581 antirecusancy legislation. The tract's main historical significance is the rare glimpse it offers of a theologically grounded alternative to recusancy. The 'Tetrastichon' and 'Carmina diversa' appended to J. Seton's *Dialectica* (1574), are also by Langdale. His movements after 1580 are unclear, but he may have died between 1587 and 1589. Suggestions that he moved to the continent cannot be substantiated. He should not be confused with Thomas Langdale, regarded as his nephew, who was another defender of Roman Catholic conformity. JONATHAN WRIGHT

Sources Venn, *Alum. Cant.*, 1/3 · Gillow, *Lit. biog. hist.*, vol. 4 · *The acts and monuments of John Foxe*, ed. J. Pratt, [new edn], 6 (1859); 8 (1868) · 'The memoirs of Father Robert Persons', ed. J. H. Pollen, *Miscellanea, II*, Catholic RS, 2 (1906), 12–218 · 'The memoirs of Father Persons', ed. J. H. Pollen, *Miscellanea, IV*, Catholic RS, 4 (1907), 1–161 · *CSP dom., addenda, 1547–65; 1547–80* · state papers domestic, Elizabeth, PRO, SP 12/144/19 · *Fasti Angl., 1541–1857*, [Chichester] · *Fasti Angl., 1541–1857*, [York] · R. B. Manning, 'Anthony Browne, 1st Viscount Montague: the influence in county politics of an Elizabethan Catholic nobleman', *Sussex Archaeological Collections*, 106 (1968), 103–12 · A. Walsham, *Church papists: Catholicism, conformity and confessional polemic in early modern England* (1993) · J. Strype, *Annals of the Reformation and establishment of religion … during Queen Elizabeth's happy reign*, new edn, 1/1 (1824) · R. Ascham, *The English works*, ed. J. Bennet (1761) · R. Smith, *An Elizabethan recusant house, comprising the life of the Lady Magdalen Viscountess Montague*, ed. A. C. Southern (1954) · A. C. Southern, *Elizabethan recusant prose, 1559–1582* (1950) · 'Bishop Kennett's collection, volume 46: biographical memoranda', BL, Lansdowne MS 980, fol. 279 · *DNB*
Archives PRO, SP 12/144/19

Langdale [*formerly* Stourton], **Charles** (1787–1868), politician and biographer, was born on 19 September 1787, the fourth son of the six sons and six daughters of Charles Philip, seventeenth Baron Stourton (1752–1816), and his wife, Mary (d. 1841), second surviving daughter and coheir of Marmaduke Langdale, fifth and last Baron Langdale. In January 1799 he was sent to Oscott College, which he left in August 1804. In October of the same year he entered Stonyhurst College, where he finished his studies. On 24 December 1814 he assumed his mother's maiden name by royal licence, in order to comply with the conditions of the will of Philip Langdale of Houghton, Yorkshire. On 27 January 1817 he married Charlotte Mary, fifth daughter of the sixth Baron Clifford. She died on 31 March 1819, leaving him two daughters. On 1 May 1821 he married again; his second wife was May (d. 1857), eldest daughter of Marmaduke Constable of Everingham Park. They had a large family of at least five sons and six daughters.

Langdale soon became active and prominent in politics and public life. He appeared on platforms in London with other leading Catholic laymen to campaign for the emancipation of Roman Catholics in England from the legal restraints which had been imposed upon them since the Reformation. After the Catholic Emancipation Act was passed in 1829 he became one of the first Roman Catholics in the Commons, sitting for Beverley in 1832–5 and for Knaresborough in 1837–41. On the return of the Poor Law Amendment Act to the Commons in 1834 he moved and carried a resolution that the clause securing religious freedom in the workhouses, which had been struck out by the Lords, should be reinstated. He voted for the ballot, the

repeal of the Septennial Act, and for an inquiry into the pensions list; he was also involved in negotiations for the repeal of the remaining enactments against Catholics in the 1840s.

Langdale's most significant efforts, however, were in the field of Roman Catholic education, where he became 'the most important Catholic educationalist of the century' (Norman, 167). In 1838 he chaired the first meeting of the Catholic Institute, a society intended to circulate pro-Catholic tracts and to improve Roman Catholic education by promoting lectures and libraries. In 1847 he suggested and supported the foundation of the Catholic Poor Schools Committee, of which he was chairman (and the only recusant member) until his death. The activities of this effective and influential body included supporting the growth of the teaching orders and organizing training for lay teachers. Langdale's most important contribution to its work was made in the mid-1840s, when he was the leading figure in negotiations with the government to secure a share in public grants and other educational amenities for Roman Catholic schools.

During the 1850 'papal aggression' crisis Langdale publicly testified to his belief in the patronage and protection of the Virgin and the saints at a large public meeting in York. In the mid-1850s he became involved in another controversy. Lord Holland's *Memoirs of the Whig Party*, which were published posthumously in 1852, contained an assertion that Maria Fitzherbert, the reputed wife of George IV, had never believed her marriage vows to be in any way binding. Langdale, who had been a close friend of Mrs Fitzherbert in his youth, determined to write a defence. He applied for permission to see Mrs Fitzherbert's remaining papers, including her marriage certificate, which were held in Coutts's Bank and of which his brother, Lord Stourton (d. 1846), had been a trustee. The representative of the longest surviving trustee, however, refused him access, and Langdale was obliged to base his vindication solely on Mrs Fitzherbert's personal recollections, dictated to Lord Stourton. The *Memoirs of Mrs Fitzherbert* were published in 1856; only fifty copies were produced, but Langdale's narrative served to establish the religious validity of the marriage in the eyes of the Roman Catholic church, and to show that Mrs Fitzherbert firmly believed herself to be the wife of the prince regent.

Langdale died on 1 December 1868 at 5 Queen Street, Mayfair, London, having been admitted shortly before as a lay brother of the Society of Jesus. He was buried at Houghton, the family seat, and was succeeded by his eldest son, Charles Joseph Langdale (1822–1895). Father Peter Gallwey, who preached at the funeral, dwelt on his personal spiritual life, which was one of regular devotion and relative poverty, describing him as 'a father to us all' (Gallwey, 21). Langdale was a significant figure in liberal Catholic politics until his death. Bernard Ward, describing him as 'a leader in all catholic good works' (*Eve of Catholic Emancipation*, 3.282), identified Langdale and John Talbot, sixteenth earl of Shrewsbury, as the outstanding Roman Catholic figures in post-1829 politics. Langdale has been unduly neglected in modern scholarship on Roman Catholic politics and religion in the first half of the nineteenth century.   ROSEMARY MITCHELL

Sources Gillow, *Lit. biog. hist.* · Burke, *Gen. GB* · GEC, *Peerage* · WWBMP · P. Gallwey, *Salvage from the wreck: a few memories of friends departed, preserved in funeral discourses* (1890), 19–61 · A. Leslie, *Mrs Fitzherbert* (1960) · B. N. Ward, *The eve of Catholic emancipation*, 3 vols. (1911–12), vol. 3, p. 282 · B. Ward, *The sequel to Catholic emancipation*, 2 vols. (1915), vol. 1, pp. 195, 197; vol. 2, pp. 75, 80, 146–58 · J. P. Marmion, 'The beginnings of the Catholic poor schools in England', *Recusant History*, 17 (1984–5), 67–83 · E. R. Norman, *The English Catholic church in the nineteenth century* (1984), 167–9
Likenesses A. R., watercolour, repro. in Ward, *Sequel to Catholic emancipation*, vol. 1, facing p. 197 · photograph, repro. in Gallwey, *Salvage from the wreck*, facing p. 19
Wealth at death under £35,000: probate, 30 Dec 1868, CGPLA Eng. & Wales

Langdale, Marmaduke, first Baron Langdale (*bap.* 1598, *d.* 1661), royalist army officer, was the only son of Peter Langdale, esquire (*d.* 1617), and his wife, Anne Wharton (*bap.* 1576/7, *d.* 1646), daughter of Michael Wharton, esquire, of Beverley and his wife, Joane. He matriculated at St John's College, Cambridge, in 1613 and succeeded his father in 1617, inheriting from him estates at Molescroft, Pighill, Sancton, and Bainton. He then pursued a military career in Europe in the service of the queen of Bohemia. Among his comrades was his neighbour, the future parliamentarian Sir John Hotham. In 1620, under the command of Sir Horace Vere, he participated in the defence of the Palatinate against the Spanish.

The opponent of 'thorough' On 12 September 1626, at St Michael-le-Belfry in York, Langdale married Lenox (*d.* 1639), daughter of Sir John Rodes of Barlborough, Derbyshire, and his third wife, Catherine, daughter of Marmaduke Constable of Holderness. Lenox was also the sister of Sir John Hotham's first wife, Katherine Rodes. Despite his refusal to pay the forced loan in 1627 Langdale was knighted by Charles I at Whitehall on 5 February 1628. He resided at North Dalton until his purchase of Holme-on-Spalding-Moor from Sir William Constable in 1633. He spent over £12,000 on land purchases and increased his rents, bringing his family into the ranks of the county's upper gentry. They had four sons and three daughters, but on 22 July 1639 Lenox died in childbed at Holme.

Langdale became a predictable and leading opponent of Charles I's and Wentworth's policy of 'thorough'; in 1638 Wentworth referred to him as a 'Person of ill Affections I am sure, to the Provinciall Power, if not to the Regall Power' (Cliffe, 311). His rent book contains notes detailing Yorkshire's grievances during the bishops' wars, and in 1639 he led the East Riding's opposition to ship money. Wentworth reflected on 26 March 1639:

> I hear my old friend Sir Marmaduke Langdale appears in the head of this business, that gentleman I fear carries an itch about him, that will never let him take rest, till at one time or other he happen to be thoroughly clawed indeed. (Cliffe, 313)

He was appointed high sheriff of Yorkshire on 12 November 1639, and his health may have been poor as he made his will six days later. The king had rejected Wentworth's

Sr Marmaduke Langdale, the first Lord Langdale, *From a Picture of him in the Possession of Marmaduke Lord Langdale at Holme on Spaldingmore 1774.*

Marmaduke Langdale, first Baron Langdale (*bap.* 1598, *d.* 1661), by William Humphrey, 1774

suggestions for the shrievalty, intent on punishing Langdale with the appointment, reasoning that his attitude would soon change when faced with making up tax shortfalls himself. However, Langdale still took no action for months, and the king remarked that he had 'neglected to perform that service in manifest contempt of our crown and dignity, and thereby have incurred our high displeasure and indignation' (*CSP dom.*, 1640, 223). He finally agreed to collect the tax on 16 June 1640, after having been threatened with Star Chamber proceedings. Despite his opposition he remained on the commission of the peace, and on 28 July 1640 many Yorkshire gentlemen gathered at his house, where a petition of the county's grievances was framed by Sir John Hotham and Sir Hugh Cholmley.

The royalist Despite maintaining close links with key future parliamentarians until early 1642, Langdale was named a commissioner of array for Yorkshire on 18 June 1642. In July he mustered Sir Henry Griffith's trained bands regiment of foot in the East Riding, and was commissioned a colonel. In November, with parliamentarian forces blockading York, he was sent to persuade the earl of Newcastle's royalist army, north of the River Tees, to march to York's relief and accept command in the county in place of the earl of Cumberland. Langdale had seen the devastation wrought by the Thirty Years' War, and his letter to Sir William Savile dated from Newcastle on 9 November reveals his foreboding and reluctance for war:

> We in Yorkshire should have some happiness if we could make an end of the troubles and distractions of our county and so divert the war southward, that whatsoever foreign nations come they may be employed in the South where the wellspring of our miseries began, and where there is pillage enough to satisfy many armies. (*Portland MSS*, 1.70)

Langdale waited upon Queen Henrietta Maria shortly after she landed with her convoy at Bridlington on 25 February 1643, and, making a very favourable impression, equipped his regiment with some of her arms and supplies. He was also involved in important attempts to persuade his kinsmen, the Hothams, to forsake their parliamentarian allegiance. On 11 September 1643 he was commissioned colonel of a brigade of horse returned from Ireland. A mark of his military reputation, he was even authorized to summon his own council of war.

The Northern horse When the Scots covenanter army invaded England, Langdale defeated its cavalry at Corbridge on 19 February 1644. Despite the royalists' defeat at Marston Moor on 2 July he enjoyed success against Sir Thomas Fairfax in his part of the battle. He retreated with Rupert through Lancashire, fighting in engagements at Ormskirk and Malpas, where he was wounded on 26 August 1644. During these weeks he forged a new brigade composed of the remnants of the earl of Newcastle's old cavalry regiments, 1600 veterans known as 'the Northern horse'. After joining the king's main field army he fought at Donnington Castle in November and in Rupert's raid on Abingdon.

In the following year Langdale was given permission to return northwards to endeavour to relieve Pontefract Castle. On 25 February 1645 he defeated a parliamentarian force under Colonel Rossiter that intercepted him at Melton Mowbray. On 1 March 1645 he relieved Pontefract, scattering the besiegers. His report claimed to have captured 20 colours and 500 prisoners, representing one of the royalists' last major field victories in England. Returning south, he was wounded again at Lydney in Gloucestershire on 15 April. He commanded the Northern horse on the royalist left wing at Naseby on 14 June, but was outnumbered and overpowered by Oliver Cromwell, sustaining heavy losses. He was present at Rowton Heath on 24 September as a major-general, and won the royalists initial advantage before the battle was lost.

The Northern horse contributed to the king's subsequent decision to move northwards, but Charles's elevation of Lord Digby to the position of lieutenant-general in England north of the Trent eclipsed Langdale from command. Digby's poor generalship contributed to the devastation of the remnants of the Northern horse at Sherburn in Elmet, in Yorkshire, on 15 October 1645. Digby and Langdale fled through Skipton into Cumberland but were further defeated at Burgh by the Sands. On 24 October they embarked at Ravenglass for the Isle of Man, whence they took ship for Ireland. Langdale finally reached France, and on 15 May 1646 a parliamentarian agent reported his presence in Paris.

The second civil war At the outbreak of the second civil war Langdale landed in Scotland in early 1648, where he angered his Scottish allies by refusing to wait for them to complete their preparations. On 28 April 1648 he captured Berwick by surprise with only 100 men. Raising the northern royalists, he invaded England with a commission from the prince of Wales as commander of five northern counties. He rallied considerable support and his forces of English royalists grew to 3000 foot and 600 horse. His army then joined the larger Scottish engager army under the duke of Hamilton as it marched down the western side of the Pennines. Langdale's forces suffered heavy losses when Hamilton ignored his warnings and the engager army was defeated by Cromwell at the battle of Preston on 17 August 1648. Langdale was captured six days later while resting in a small alehouse near Nottingham. He wrote an account of the failed expedition (printed in Sunderland, 133–6). He was confined in Nottingham Castle and might have been sentenced to death, for on 21 November 1648 he was among the seven royalists exempted from pardon by parliament. However, Lady Savile (Sir William's widow) aided his escape and, employing a variety of disguises including that of a milkmaid, he eventually made his way to London. Sir Thomas Fairfax offered a reward of £1000 for his capture, his estates were confiscated, and he was perpetually banished as an enemy and traitor on 13 March 1649. He had reached the continent safely by April, and in June he was sent for a short time to assist the earl of Derby in the defence of the Isle of Man. He was reportedly 'a very lean and much mortified man so that the enemy called him ghost (and deservedly, they were so haunted by him)' (Sunderland, 231).

Exile, conversion, and return Langdale engaged in the Venetian service in 1652, defending Candia (Crete) against the Turks from 5 to 12 May. After war broke out between England and the United Provinces, Langdale offered to seize Newcastle and Tynemouth with the aid of the Dutch, but he was not encouraged. Now Langdale was openly Roman Catholic; Sir Edward Nicholas wrote to Sir Edward Hyde in January 1653: 'I pray by whom was the K. moved to send for Sir M. Langdale and to make him of his Council? Sir M. [is] as eager in pursuing the Papists' interest as any new Popish proselyte ever was' (*Nicholas Papers*, 2.3). Langdale was reported in the royal council as 'driving on with much fierceness the Catholics design and extolling excessively those worst of Papists in Ireland' (Newman, *Royalist Officers*, 223). He confidently expected Catholic priests to carry royalist messages for him in Yorkshire, but by favouring a Spanish alliance he distanced himself from his fellow English Catholics around the queen. Sir Edward Hyde clashed with him also, describing him as 'a man hard to please, and of a very weak understanding, yet proud, and much in love with his own judgement' (Scrope and Monkhouse, 3.135, 181). He resided in Brussels for much of 1655 where he resented his exclusion from plans for the 1655 uprisings and complained of having to deal with Richard

Overton's and Edward Sexby's Leveller involvement in royalist conspiracy: 'I am so weary of discoursinge with them that I can noe longer endure it with patience ... they are not wourth the taking notice of' (*Nicholas Papers*, 3.128). He was involved in the royalist plot uncovered in the spring of 1658, but by the later 1650s he had become extremely poor and took refuge at the English Benedictine abbey of Lambspring, in Westphalia. On 4 February 1658 at Bruges the future Charles II created him Baron Langdale of Holme-on-Spalding-Moor.

Langdale returned to Holme in 1660 and was the only pre-war JP to return to the bench in the East Riding. He was also appointed lord lieutenant of the West Riding in 1661. His estates were comparatively easy for him to recover because his confiscated manors of Holme, Pighill, Molescroft, and Gatenby had been granted to leading republicans and regicides. Nevertheless he had reportedly lost £160,000 in the royal service. On 7 April 1661 he wrote to excuse himself from attending Charles II's coronation; he pleaded that he was too poor to attend with the requisite dignity, but he was also in poor health. He died in his house at Holme on 5 August 1661, and did so without a priest, as his son reportedly could not bring himself to warn him of Langdale's impending death. He was buried on 10 August among his ancestors in the sanctuary on the right side of the altar at All Saints' parish church, Sancton, where a monumental inscription commemorated him. He was succeeded as second baron by his son and namesake.

ANDREW J. HOPPER

Sources F. H. Sunderland, *Marmaduke, Lord Langdale of Holme-on-Spalding-Moor, Yorkshire (colonel-general), and some events of his time, 1598–1661* (1926) · P. R. Newman, *Royalist officers in England and Wales, 1642–1660: a biographical dictionary* (1981) · GEC, *Peerage*, new edn, vol. 7 · J. T. Cliffe, *The Yorkshire gentry from the Reformation to the civil war* (1969) · Venn, *Alum. Cant.*, 1/3 · P. R. Newman, *The old service: royalist regimental colonels and the civil war, 1642–1646* (1993) · *The Nicholas papers*, ed. G. F. Warner, 2, CS, new ser., 50 (1892) · R. Scrope and T. Monkhouse, eds., *State papers collected by Edward, earl of Clarendon*, 3 vols. (1767–86), vol. 3 · Borth. Inst., prob. reg. 44, fol. 72 [microfilm 962] · parish register, Sancton, All Saints, Borth. Inst., microfilm 1803 · P. G. Holiday, 'Land sales and repurchases in Yorkshire after the civil wars, 1650–70', *Northern History*, 5 (1970), 67–92 · H. Aveling, *Northern Catholics: the Catholic recusants of the North Riding of Yorkshire, 1558–1790* (1966) · Gillow, *Lit. biog. hist.* · E. Hailstone, *Portraits of Yorkshire worthies*, 2 vols. (1869), 1.64 · H. Cary, ed., *Memorials of the great civil war in England from 1646 to 1652*, 1 (1842) · J. Foster, ed., *The visitation of Yorkshire made in the years 1584/5 ... to which is added the subsequent visitation made in 1612* (privately printed, London, 1875) · G. C. F. Forster, *The East Riding justices of the peace in the seventeenth-century*, East Yorkshire Local History Society, 30 (1973) · M. A. E. Green, ed., *Calendar of the proceedings of the committee for compounding ... 1643–1660*, 1, PRO (1889) · *CSP dom., 1640; 1651–2; 1660–61* · *The manuscripts of his grace the duke of Portland*, 10 vols., HMC, 29 (1891–1931), vol. 1

Archives BL, Add. MSS 37047, 40132, 40135, 40137 · Bodl. Oxf., account of his action in civil war and copy of letters patent · East Riding of Yorkshire Archives Service, Beverley, papers · W. Yorks. AS, Leeds, Yorkshire Archaeological Society, notebook | BL, letters to Sir Edward Nicholas, Egerton MSS 1048, 2534, 2535, 2550, 2551 · BL, Sloane MS 1519

Likenesses W. Humphrey, mezzotint, 1774, BM, NPG [*see illus.*] · portrait, repro. in Sunderland, *Marmaduke, Lord Langdale*

Wealth at death see Borth. Inst., microfilm 962, probate register 44, fol. 72

Langdon, John (*d.* 1434), bishop of Rochester, was a native of Kent and had at least two brothers, Thomas and Richard, both laymen; others of the surname, derived from a local village, were either in his circle, or employees of Canterbury Cathedral and diocese, or both. He was a close friend of Bishop John Cliderow of Bangor, who was a native of Romney. Admitted as a monk of Christ Church, Canterbury, in 1398, Langdon was ordained to minor orders in April and May 1401, and as priest on 24 May 1404. He graduated BTh of Oxford by 1400, and DTh by August 1411. Although he served as sub-prior of his house some time before 1411, and as its almoner by 1 December that year, he was often at Oxford; he was a scholar of Canterbury College (which was connected with his house) in 1407–8, warden there from September 1410 to after August 1411, and again a scholar in 1414–15. By then he had become widely known. He gave the opening sermon in the convocation of Canterbury on both 17 February 1410 and 1 December 1411, evidently as a preacher of reputation and perhaps engaged in opposing Wycliffite heresy. He acted as commissary for the chancellor of Oxford in 1410 or 1411, and was one of twelve Oxford scholars appointed by Archbishop Arundel in 1411 to examine the writings of Wyclif (Wilkins, 3.339–49), and also one of Arundel's five commissaries instructed on 23 June 1411 to take oaths from Oxford scholars to renounce Wyclif's errors.

On 12 March 1414 Langdon announced the election of Henry Chichele as archbishop, having played a prominent part in its process. He attended the Council of Constance, quite possibly throughout its duration and probably on behalf of his house, which on 1 November 1417 appointed him as its proctor in the curia of the new pope, Martin V. In fact he did not go to Rome, being used instead, by his own estimation, for nearly three years in France and Normandy by Henry V and Archbishop Chichele, mainly to report back to the council in England. The king and archbishop tried to have him provided as bishop of Lisieux in 1419, but the pope preferred to favour an Italian cardinal, Branda da Castiglione. Langdon was in England in March 1419, and again in October 1419 and April 1421, when twice more he gave the opening sermon in convocation, while in February 1420, May 1421, and February 1423 he took part as an examiner in the trial of the heretic William Taylor. On 17 November 1421 he was provided to the see of Rochester and consecrated on 7 June 1422 at Canterbury. Modest though the see was, undoubtedly its location was ideal for Langdon, as was its particular connection with Canterbury; Langdon had continued to be used as a proctor by his house whenever and wherever possible.

After Henry V's death Langdon was named to the regency council, on about 5 November 1422, although he rarely attended during the first seven and a half years. He attended the Council of Pavia–Siena from early summer to late 1424, defending the religious orders against reformist critics. He presided over the convocation of Canterbury on 27 April 1426, preached the opening sermon yet again (when heresy was the principal item on the agenda) on 5 July 1428, and presided on 10, 12, and 14 July.

On 15 November 1428 he was appointed to a committee of convocation to develop more effective measures against heresy. In these years he worked almost entirely from Trottiscliffe in his diocese, and evidently in good harmony with his archbishop. From April 1430 Langdon attended regularly at the king's council, and accompanied Henry VI to France for his coronation. In February 1432 he was appointed to an embassy to Charles VII of France, and thereafter he hardly saw his diocese. On 17 July following he was appointed to the first English delegation to the Council of Basel, but, instead, was in France on a mission to Charles VII from late December 1432 to February 1433, and then in England for the rest of the year. On 18 February 1434 he was appointed to the second delegation to Basel, but was still in England on 5 June, when he was appointed to speak once more with Charles VII. He left England a week later, inevitably with an extra commission to represent Christ Church, Canterbury, at the council. This time he did reach Basel. He died there on 30 September. He had made his will on 2 March 1434, supposing (like Bishop Polton two years earlier) that he might never return from such a complacently indefinite assembly; both were right. In his will he concentrated on his family and upon the cathedrals of Rochester and Canterbury, his lifelong environment, and asked for burial in the lady chapel of Rochester. He was in fact buried in the choir of the Carthusian monastery at Basel. His will was proved only on 27 June 1437, which may explain why his wish to be brought home was not met. Thomas Rodeburne in the preface to his *Historia minor*, says that he used a collection by Langdon of historical material; there is no trace of this or of Langdon's evidently influential sermons.

R. G. DAVIES

Sources Emden, *Oxf.*, 2.1093–4 [Thomas Rodeburne] · R. G. Davies, 'The episcopate in England and Wales, 1375–1443', PhD diss., University of Manchester, 1974, 3.clxi–clxiv · W. G. Searle, ed., *Christ Church, Canterbury*, 1: *The chronicle of John Stone, monk of Christ Church*, Cambridge Antiquarian RS, 34 (1902), 10, 184 · E. F. Jacob, ed., *The register of Henry Chichele, archbishop of Canterbury, 1414–1443*, 2, CYS, 42 (1937), 556–8 [will] · register, Rochester, CKS · D. Wilkins, ed., *Concilia Magnae Britanniae et Hiberniae*, 2 (1737), 339–49 · episcopal register, CKS, DRc/R6, fols. 7–111

Archives CKS, register, DRc/R6, fols. 7–111 · Rochester diocesan record office, Maidstone, register

Langdon, John (1741–1819), merchant and politician in the United States of America, was born on 26 June 1741 near Portsmouth, New Hampshire, one of six children of John Langdon, farmer, and Mary Hall of Exeter. He was educated in the classics at Samuel Hale's Latin Grammar School in Portsmouth, and in 1760 was employed as a clerk by Daniel Rindge, a local merchant. In 1763 he was appointed master of one of Rindge's merchant vessels, and within a few years was a successful shipowner of his own. In the early 1770s he became outspoken against British colonial policies when he lost a cargo of goods to customs agents because of alleged violations of the maritime laws. He played a major part in the American assault on Fort William and Mary at New Castle, New Hampshire, in December 1774 to seize munitions from the British garrison. Having been elected to the New Hampshire

assembly in 1775, he was chosen its speaker. Upon the outbreak of the American War of Independence he attended the second continental congress in Philadelphia, serving on a number of important committees. He was appointed agent for continental naval prizes in New Hampshire on 25 June 1776 and returned to Portsmouth.

For the remainder of the war Langdon served as continental agent in New Hampshire, disposing of prizes captured by American privateers. He received a percentage from each transaction, thus accumulating huge wealth from his service to the patriotic cause. He also used his political connections to secure appointment as naval agent for congress in New Hampshire and to acquire government contracts for construction of the warships *Ranger*, *Raleigh*, and *America*. He funded a number of privateers and made money on these ventures as well. Emerging from the revolution with his fortune not only intact but vastly enhanced, he was never troubled at doing well by what he considered doing good. On 2 February 1777 he married Elizabeth Sherburne (1763–1813), the sixteen-year-old daughter of John Sherburne; they had two children. In 1777 he returned to the legislature, where he served four years as speaker, working to protect propertied interests and control inflation.

When the British invaded upstate New York in 1777, Langdon organized New Hampshire's militia forces, appointing John Stark to command them and largely financing their operations. Then he led a body of militia in Stark's little army at the battle of Bennington on 16 August and in the Saratoga campaign. In August 1778 he commanded a New Hampshire militia force at Newport, Rhode Island. He served in congress again from 1783 to 1784 and in the New Hampshire senate from 1784 to 1785. He was elected president of New Hampshire in 1785 but lost elections to John Sullivan in the next two years. From 1786 to 1787 he served in the legislature as speaker. He attended the constitutional convention in Philadelphia in the summer of 1787, and in the following year supported the constitution in New Hampshire's ratifying convention. In 1788 he defeated Sullivan for president but resigned the office in 1789 to serve in the United States senate. He was elected the first president *pro tempore* and over the next twelve years supported federalist programmes to strengthen the central government.

In 1801 Langdon was offered the post of secretary of the navy but declined it. Instead he returned to New Hampshire. From 1801 to 1805 he was once more in the legislature, and during the last two years again was speaker. After losing three gubernatorial elections, he achieved the office in 1805. He was re-elected until 1811, with the exception of 1809. Offered a chance to run for vice-president of the United States in 1812, he chose instead to retire from public life. After his wife's death in 1813, he became preoccupied with religion, founding the New Hampshire Bible Society and contributing money to various religious organizations. He died on 18 September 1819 in his mansion on Pleasant Street, Portsmouth, and was entombed in the north burying-ground.

PAUL DAVID NELSON

Sources L. S. Mayo, *John Langdon of New Hampshire* (1937) • *New Hampshire Gazette* (21 Sept 1819) • J. R. Van Atta, 'Langdon, John', *ANB* • J. L. Elwyn, 'Some accounts of John Langdon', *Early State Papers of New Hampshire*, 20 (1891) • J. Daniel, *Experiment in republicanism: New Hampshire politics and the American Revolution, 1741–1794* (1970) • R. Upton, *Revolutionary New Hampshire* (1971)
Archives Hist. Soc. Penn., papers • New Hampshire Historical Society, Concord, papers • Strawbery Banke Museum, Portsmouth, New Hampshire, papers
Likenesses S. Sartain, engraving, repro. in H. Cirker and B. Cirker, eds., *Dictionary of American portraits* (New York, 1967), 368

Langdon, Richard (1729/30–1803), organist and composer, was born in Exeter, the son of Charles Langdon of Exeter, and possibly the grandson of Tobias Langdon (*d.* 1712), priest vicar-choral of Exeter. He was appointed lay vicar-choral and organist of Exeter Cathedral on 23 June 1753, and became additionally master of the choristers in 1762. He matriculated at Exeter College, Oxford, and took the degree of BMus on 18 July 1761, aged thirty-one. He resigned from Exeter Cathedral in October 1777 and in November was elected organist of Ely, moving from there to Bristol in 1778. In 1782 he was appointed organist of Armagh Cathedral. He resigned in 1794 and retired to Exeter, where he died on 8 September 1803. Langdon published songs, anthems, harpsichord sonatas, two collections of songs and cantatas (*c.*1754 and *c.*1770), one of glees (*c.*1780), and *Divine Harmony, being a Collection in Score of Psalms and Anthems* (1774).

J. C. HADDEN, rev. K. D. REYNOLDS

Sources *New Grove* • Grove, *Dict. mus.* (1927) • Foster, *Alum. Oxon.* • *GM*, 1st ser., 73 (1803), 888

Langdon, Stephen Herbert (1876–1937), Assyriologist, was born at Ida, near Monroe, Michigan, in the United States, on 8 May 1876, the elder son of George Knowles Langdon, farmer, and his wife, Abigail Elizabeth Hassinger. He was educated at the high school at Monroe and the University of Michigan, Ann Arbor, and also took degrees at the Union Theological Seminary and Columbia University in New York. He then (1904–6) studied in Paris, where he was ordained deacon (1905) in the American Episcopal church, never proceeding beyond that order, and (1906–7) at Leipzig.

In 1908 Miss Mary Wallace Shillito offered £10,000 to the University of Oxford to found a readership in Assyriology on condition that Langdon was elected; appointed on these terms, he remained in Oxford for the rest of his life. In the First World War he served with the Oxford Volunteers, and helped to load ammunition at Didcot. In 1913 he had become a naturalized British subject, and in 1919 was appointed professor on the retirement of A. H. Sayce. He was a voluminous editor and interpreter of Sumerian and Assyrio-Babylonian texts, but his work was marred by inaccuracy caused by undue haste and a defective sense of language; he wrote fluently in French and German as well as English, but all his writing betrayed his mixed education. At the same time scholarship owes him a great debt for much pioneer work, especially in making an immense number of cuneiform tablets accessible for the first time; and many flashes of brilliance lit up, if they did not always solve, the numerous problems offered by these often exceedingly obscure texts. He also found time to raise funds for the excavation of Kish and spent two seasons (1923 and 1925) personally directing the work at some risk to his health. These excavations not only made considerable additions to early Mesopotamian history but also greatly enriched the collections of the Ashmolean Museum at Oxford and the Field Museum at Chicago, which provided part of the funds. Further, before Langdon's time all British Assyriologists were either self-taught or educated on the continent, and his chief merit was perhaps to build up an English school of Assyriologists.

Langdon married in 1925 May Adelaide, younger daughter of Thomas Gregory JP, of Cardiff, owner of the Garth engineering works; they had no children. He was elected a fellow of the British Academy in 1931 and a corresponding member of the Académie des Inscriptions et Belles-Lettres in 1933; he was also Schweich lecturer of the British Academy in 1933 and Singer-Polignac lecturer at the Collège de France in 1934. Fond of golf and tennis, he enjoyed the life of Jesus College senior common room, but was never made a fellow. He died suddenly at Oxford on 19 May 1937; his wife survived him.

G. R. DRIVER, rev.

Sources *The Times* (21 May 1937) • *Oxford Magazine* (27 May 1937) • C. J. Gudd, 'Stephen Herbert Langdon, 1876–1937', *PBA*, 23 (1937) • personal knowledge (1949) • *CGPLA Eng. & Wales* (1937)
Archives U. Oxf., Griffith Institute, Sumerian notes
Likenesses W. Stoneman, photograph, 1932, NPG
Wealth at death £670: administration, 16 July 1937, *CGPLA Eng. & Wales*

Langdon, Thomas (*d.* 1638), land surveyor, was certainly practising by 1589 and possibly a year or two earlier. He had a brother, Vallence, who briefly assisted him, a sister, who married Thomas Patchet, and a relative of the same name, who was living in Lambeth in 1638. He was educated at New College, Oxford, and proceeded to the degree of BCL in July 1599, having become MA and studied civil law for three years. He probably learned his surveying skills from the land surveyor Thomas Clerke, to whom he was assistant by 1589, and possibly in 1587, and continued as such until Clerke's death in 1602.

Langdon's career as one of the leading land surveyors and map makers of his time spanned about thirty years, and flourished as landowners were coming to appreciate the value of maps both as tools of estate management and as decorative objects of prestige. Several Oxford colleges were taking greater interest in their estates and their profitable management, and Langdon surveyed land all over England for them. He succeeded his former master as surveyor to the estates of All Souls College, Oxford, and continued in the college's employment until 1605. In 1600–01 he was paid for surveying for New College, in 1602 he mapped the Cambridgeshire estates of Merton College, and in 1607 he surveyed an estate in Leicestershire for Brasenose College. Corpus Christi College employed him too, from 1605 to 1607, in 1609, and from 1615 to 1616; in his third period of working for the college he was assisted by a pupil, Henry Wilcocke. Langdon was employed not only by Oxford colleges but also by private individuals, including Sir Thomas Cecil and Sir John Byron. His last known employment as a surveyor was by the London Charterhouse, whose estates in Cambridgeshire and Wiltshire he surveyed from 1616 to 1618. Langdon's maps, drawn of estates in about fifteen counties, are distinctive and their embellishments with Elizabethan strap-work ornamentation show his skills as an artist and draughtsman.

Langdon had become curate of Tithby, Nottinghamshire, probably in 1603, and remained there for the rest of his life. He married Joan Sharples on 3 February 1606 in Langar, Nottinghamshire. Their daughter Rosamund (d. 1633) married George Darker (d. 1658) at St Peter's Church, Nottingham, on 3 July 1630. By his will, made on 1 March 1638 and proved on 11 October 1638, Langdon left bequests to his wife and granddaughter and his surveying instruments to his son-in-law, who may therefore have been his apprentice or assistant.   SARAH BENDALL, *rev.*

Sources P. Eden, 'Three Elizabethan estate surveyors', *English map-making, 1500–1650: historical essays*, ed. S. Tyacke (1983), 68–84 · F. W. Steer and others, *Dictionary of land surveyors and local map-makers of Great Britain and Ireland, 1530–1850*, ed. P. Eden, 2nd edn, 2, ed. S. Bendall (1997), 304 · J. L. G. Mowat, *Sixteen old maps of properties in Oxfordshire (with one in Berkshire)* (1888) · C. M. Woolgar, 'Some draft estate maps of the early seventeenth century', *Cartographic Journal*, 22 (1985), 136–43 · S. Bendall, 'Merton College and the mapping of its estates, 1601–1836', *Oxoniensia*, 65 (2000), 79–110

Langevin, Sir Hector-Louis (1826–1906), politician and journalist in Canada, was born on 25 August 1826 at Quebec City, the third of the seven children of Jean Langevin (1785–1870), a merchant and office holder, and his wife, Sophie (1800–1868), the daughter of Pierre Laforce, a notary. The Langevin family had farmed in Canada since 1666, and Jean was the first to follow a career in town. Hector-Louis was educated at local schools, then at the Petit Séminaire de Québec (1836–46). He studied law in the office of Augustin-Norbert Morin and with George-Étienne Cartier. Both those men were active in the political movement led by Louis-Hippolyte LaFontaine, and Langevin was drawn into it by them. Influenced by his two older brothers, Jean and Edmond, who were both priests, he played an important part in drawing LaFontaine's Liberal Party into a close alliance with French Canada's Roman Catholic clergy. In 1847–9 he was the editor of *Mélanges Religieux*, the organ of Montreal's ultramontane bishop Ignace Bourget, which, under Langevin, gave strong support to LaFontaine's party. Admitted to the bar in 1850, he opened a practice in Quebec City the following year.

Langevin's activities ranged widely. In 1853 he became the secretary of a company formed to build a railroad along the north shore of the St Lawrence; in 1855 he published a book on Canada's institutions and economic potential for distribution at the Paris World Fair. Having been elected to the Quebec municipal council in 1856, he served as mayor from 1858 to 1861. In 1857 he briefly edited a new ultramontane newspaper, the *Courrier du Canada*.

On 10 January 1854 Langevin married Justine Têtu (1833–1882), the daughter of a well-to-do merchant, in a ceremony performed by his brother Jean. The couple remained closely united until Justine's death on 29 October 1882. Of nine children born to them, only five survived infancy, and four outlived their mother.

In 1857 Langevin was elected to the legislative assembly, following his former patron, Cartier, now the leader of LaFontaine's party, which had entered a coalition with English-Canadian Conservatives and business interests. In 1864 he entered the cabinet as solicitor-general, then as postmaster-general in the 'Great Coalition' formed to pursue a British North American federation. He played an active part in the making of confederation, trying to balance the need for a strong central government to promote economic development with French Canada's need for provincial autonomy, while watching over the interests of the Catholic church, with which he was closely connected.

Langevin served as secretary of state (1867–9) and then minister of public works (1869–73) in the first federal administration, led by Sir John A. Macdonald. Implicated in the Pacific scandal that forced Macdonald's resignation in 1873, he did not return to parliament until 1876. Even then, the courts annulled his election on the grounds that the clergy had exerted excessive influence on his behalf; but he won the resulting by-election. When Macdonald returned to power in 1878, Langevin was reinstated in the cabinet and soon took back the department of public works. He was an excellent administrator, and under his direction the department erected an impressive network of public buildings and infrastructure for the young confederation.

Politically Langevin was less effective. After the death of Cartier in 1873, he seemed the natural heir to the leadership of the *bleus* (the Quebec wing of the Conservative Party), but he never fully succeeded in uniting them behind him. His principal rival, J.-A. Chapleau, rallied Montreal interests hostile to those of Langevin's Quebec City, as well as French-Canadian nationalists who felt that Langevin's commitment to an Ottawa career had caused him to lose sight of Quebec's special needs. It was outside Quebec that Langevin received his highest honours: companion of the Bath in 1868; knight commander of St Michael and St George in 1881; and knight commander of the Vatican's order of St Gregory in 1870.

Langevin's support in Quebec was seriously shaken in 1885, when he failed to prevent the execution of the Métis rebel Louis Riel, for whom French-Canadian opinion had demanded mercy. Then, in 1890, newspapers belonging to his own former protégé, Joseph-Israël *Tarte, published charges of corruption in Langevin's ministry. The scandal forced Langevin to resign the portfolio in 1891, and, although an inquiry cleared him of personal culpability, his political career was effectively ended. He retired to Quebec City in 1896, and died there, at his home, 47 rue St Louis, on 11 June 1906. He was buried at the Hôtel-Dieu cemetery on 15 June.

Solid, hardworking, unflamboyant, Langevin never had the popular appeal of Cartier or Chapleau. Today neither his ultramontanism nor his federalism is admired by most Quebeckers. But monuments to his administration survive across Canada in the public works over which he presided.   A. I. SILVER

Sources A. Désilets, *Hector-Louis Langevin: un père de la confédération canadienne* (1969) · *DCB*, vol. 13 · J. Monet, *The last cannon shot* (1969) · H. B. Neatby and J. T. Saywell, 'Chapleau and the conservative party in Quebec', *Canadian Historical Review*, 37 (1956), 1–22 · B. Young, *Promoters and politicians: the north-shore railways in the history of Quebec, 1854–85* (1978) · A. I. Silver, *The French-Canadian idea of confederation, 1864–1900* (1982)
Archives Archives Nationales du Québec, family papers · NA Canada | CCC Cam., corresp. with sixteenth earl of Derby · NA Canada, Sir John A. Macdonald MSS
Likenesses group portrait, photograph, 1864, presumed National Archives of Canada · bust, National Archives of Canada · colour lithograph, National Archives of Canada · pencil drawing, National Archives of Canada · photographs, repro. in Désilets, *Hector-Louis Langevin*; priv. coll. · sixty-nine photographs, National Archives of Canada, Edouard-Joseph Langevin collection · three cartoons, National Archives of Canada · twenty-six photographs, National Archives of Canada

Langford, Abraham (1711–1774), auctioneer, was born in the parish of St Paul, Covent Garden, London, of unknown parentage. As a young man he began to write for the stage, his first published piece being an 'entertainment' called *The Judgment of Paris*, produced in 1730. His ballad opera entitled *The Lover his Own Rival, as Performed at the New Theatre at Goodman's Fields*, though received with little acclaim, was reprinted at London in 1753 and at Dublin in 1759.

Langford had probably been employed for some time with Christopher Cock, the eminent auctioneer, for when Cock died in 1748 he continued to occupy Cock's auction rooms in the north-eastern corner of the Piazza, Covent Garden, trading for a short time as Cock and Langford. Richard Gough, the historical topographer and antiquary, discoursing on the historical progress of selling books by catalogue, said of Cock and Langford that 'none had been better assisted' (*GM*, 1066–9), and John Nichols, in his *Literary Anecdotes of the Eighteenth Century* (1812–16), frequently mentions Langford as the cataloguer of various notable libraries put up for sale.

Langford and his wife, Mary, had numerous children including Robert (1744–1785), who entered Westminster School in 1752, and Abraham (*b.* 1751), who was in business with his father as Abraham Langford & Son from 1766 until 1773, when the name changed to Messrs Langford. At the time of his death Langford owned shares in the *Daily Advertiser*, and houses in Bath and Highgate. Langford died on 17 September 1774 in London and was buried in St Pancras old churchyard in a tomb whose sides were covered by a lengthy and grandiloquent epitaph. He was survived by his wife, three sons, and a daughter, Mary. In 1776–7 the younger Abraham Langford sold George Vertu's plates and prints; he was followed in business by Barford at some time before 1783. In 1811 he was a governor of Highgate Chapel and school. The auction rooms were later occupied by George Robins, another well-known auctioneer.

                                              ANITA MCCONNELL

Sources D. E. Baker, *Biographia dramatica, or, A companion to the playhouse*, rev. I. Reed, new edn, rev. S. Jones, 1/2 (1812), 444 · D. Lysons, *The environs of London*, 3 (1795), 357 · I. Maxted, *The London book trades, 1775–1800: a preliminary checklist of members* (1977), 133–4 · D. H. [R. Gough], letter, *GM*, 1st ser., 58 (1788), 1066–9 · Nichols, *Lit. anecdotes* · *Daily Advertiser* [London] (19 Sept 1774) · PRO, PROB 11/1001, q. 341
Likenesses J. Greenwood, pencil drawing, BM · mezzotint, repro. in H. Bromley, *A catalogue of engraved British portraits* (1793), 407 · mezzotint, BM, NPG

Langford, John Alfred (1823–1903), writer and journalist, was born in Crowley's Court, Bradford Street, Birmingham, on 12 September 1823, the fourth of six sons, and one of only two to survive infancy, of John Langford, who was of Welsh descent and came from Herefordshire, and Harriet Eaton (*d.* 1857), daughter of a baker in Birmingham. After arriving in Birmingham in 1815, John Langford worked as a chairmaker and thirteen years later set himself up as a master in Bradford Street. That year, John Alfred Langford was sent to school at Mr Reynold's academy in Birchall Street, Deritend, although his early education had been carried on by his mother, who was partly paralysed by a stroke. She had a profound effect upon the minds of both her sons. Langford also attended a Wesleyan Sunday school, but his full-time education ceased when he was ten and was put to work in the women's department of his father's workplace.

In 1836 the family was visited from Radnorshire by John Langford's brother, Richard, who took his nephews to the theatre. This event made Langford pass 'through an ever-memorable turnpike in his career' ('Toiling upwards', 58). Affected by a deep passion for plays, he spent much of his meagre earnings on books. By now he was apprenticed to his father and soon after he enrolled at the Mechanics' Institute, Birmingham. Among Langford's fellow students was George Jacob Holyoake, later well known as a Chartist, secularist, and co-operator. Although Langford laboured for fourteen hours each day, he strove to improve his education by learning mathematics, English grammar, Latin, French, and German. Under the burden of so much work and study he became sickly and was sent on a trip to the Isle of Man to recover his health.

In 1842, and while still an apprentice, Langford married Anne Swinton (*d.* 1847). After he became a journeyman, the couple and their two children moved into a small, courtyard house in Bradford Place, Bradford Street, Birmingham. A teetotaller, peace advocate, and a member of a people's library, Langford was keener on social than political agitation. He believed that 'a happy future for man was built on a general, thorough education of the people—the elevation of the masses into men' ('Toiling upwards', 221). The new co-operative movement attracted him and in 1846 he was appointed honorary secretary of the newly established Birmingham Co-operative Society. The next year he gained notice through his regular contributions to *Howitt's Journal*, an organ for co-operators, and in June 1847 William Howitt described a visit to Langford (*Howitt's Journal*, 2, 1847, 242–4) on which he found the chairmaker's wife confined after giving birth to their fourth child, and Langford himself nursing the three other children. Howitt noticed a number of books on a small, round deal table and was surprised that Langford should be attempting at once to nurse and read. Among the publications was a German edition of Goethe's *Faust*. Howitt was impressed by Langford's knowledge of the language, by his ability to buy expensive books on a wage of little more than a £1 a week, and by his poetry which described the sufferings of the labouring poor. Not long after, Anne Langford died from consumption. Her death was followed by those of two of her children.

In 1848 Langford began to attend the church of the Saviour, started by the charismatic nonconformist preacher George Dawson. In a widely circulated pamphlet, Langford defended Dawson against an attack by George Gilfillan in *Tait's Magazine* (1848, 279–85), and the next year he wrote a supportive article on Dawson in the *Truth-Seeker*. On 7 April 1849 Langford married Mary Anne Price, eldest daughter of F. Price, a self-employed printer. They settled in the working-class street of Cheapside, Birmingham, and Langford continued to combine his work with his writings, issuing *Religion, Scepticism and Infidelity* in 1850. During the winter of that year he taught evening classes in the schools attached to the church of the Saviour in Edward Street and gave up chairmaking to open a small shop in New Street, Birmingham, selling newspapers and books.

A supporter of radical causes, Langford was a great admirer of Lajos Kossuth, the Hungarian patriot, and in 1851 he became honorary secretary of the Birmingham branch of the 'Friends of Italy', formed to support Mazzini and his followers. Continuing to write political pamphlets and poetry, Langford also became involved in the debate on education, writing *Religion and Education in Relation to the People* in 1852. That year he sold his shop and started a printing business with his father-in-law as the manager at 45 Anne Street, from which he published his own works and those of his friends. In 1855 he left this enterprise and became a sub-editor at the newly founded *Birmingham Daily Press*, which was the first daily newspaper in the town and of which George Dawson was a chief shareholder. The same year he had published his poem *The Lamp of Life* (1855). In 1857 his mother died, the sixth child of his second family was born, and Langford became involved in the project to buy Aston Hall Park. Between 1858 and 1864 he was manager of the place, although he carried on writing and among other works brought out *Poems of the Field and Town* (1859).

From 1862 Langford was also a contributor to the *Birmingham Daily Gazette*, a recently established Liberal-Conservative newspaper, and in 1864 he became its local editor. He resigned from his position four years later because he could not support the newspaper's backing of Conservative parliamentary candidates against the Liberals John Bright, George Dixon, and P. H. Muntz. Still, Langford's time on the newspaper had given him access to the complete files of *Aris's Birmingham Gazette*, started in 1741, and they led him to compile *A Century of Birmingham Life from 1741–1841* (1868). It was followed by *Modern Birmingham and its Institutions from 1841 to 1871* (1873–7). Both publications are indispensable for historians of Birmingham. For ten years from 1864, Langford was teacher of English literature at the Birmingham and Midland Institute, and throughout the 1870s he conducted numerous classes for men employed at the Cornwall works of his friend Sir Richard Tangye. In 1879 the workers presented him with a testimonial in recognition of his services.

Langford was a member of the Liberal Party and was twice elected to the Birmingham school board on the non-conformist list (1874–85 and 1886–91)—even though he did not attend chapel regularly. He was also active on behalf of Birmingham's public libraries, publishing an account of them and the local art gallery in 1871. His honorary degree of LLD was conferred on him in 1877 by the Greeneville and Tusculum College of Tennessee, and he was also a fellow of the Royal Historical Society. He died on 24 January 1903 at his home, 85 Fernley Road, Sparkhill, Birmingham—a road recently built for the prosperous of the working class and the lower middle class—and was buried at Key Hill cemetery, Hockley. Although his poetry was not of the highest order, Langford was characterized by his 'indomitable perseverance' ('Dr J. A. Langford', 102), and he was regarded as 'one of those men who helped to build up the public life of Birmingham' (*Birmingham Daily Mail*, 24 Jan 1903). He is a prime example of a self-taught working man who strove to better himself and his class.

CARL CHINN

Sources [N. L.], 'Toiling upwards: John Alfred Langford', *British Controversialist*, 3rd ser., 25 (1871), 54–62, 221–30, 303–12, 383–91 • *Birmingham Daily Post* (26 Jan 1903) • *Birmingham Faces and Places*, 1 (1888–9), 102–4 • *Biograph and Review*, 2 (1879), 140–43 • *Birmingham Daily Mail* (24 Jan 1903) • *Birmingham Daily Gazette* (26 Jan 1903) • *Birmingham Evening Despatch* (24 Jan 1903) • *The Times* (26 Jan 1903) • G. J. Shirley, letter, *Birmingham Daily Post* (29 Jan 1903) • 'Presentation to Dr J. A. Langford', *Birmingham Daily Gazette* (25 May 1879) • *DNB*
Archives Birm. CA, newspaper cuttings • Birm. CA, corresp.
Likenesses J. Collier, photograph, repro. in *Birmingham Faces and Places*, 102 • W. Holl, stipple (after photograph), NPG
Wealth at death £491 6s. 9d.: resworn probate, June 1903, CGPLA Eng. & Wales

Langford, Thomas (*fl. c.*1320), Dominican friar and historian, is recorded by the Italian Dominican Leandro Alberti, in his *De viris illustribus ordinis Praedicatorum* (1517), as an English Dominican who at an unspecified date wrote a history of the world from the creation to his own times. John Bale, writing some forty years later, acknowledges Alberti as a source, but supplies considerably more detail, stating that Langford was an Essex man, born not far from Maldon, who became a Dominican friar—at Chelmsford, according to Thomas Tanner. Proceeding to Cambridge University, Langford became learned in scholastic theology, obtaining the degree of DTh (again according to Tanner). Active in the years around 1320, he wrote one volume of sermons and another of disputations, as well as his universal chronicle. John Pits, who in this follows another Italian Dominican, Antonio of Siena, also attributes to Langford a commentary on Job. None of these works is known to have survived.

HENRY SUMMERSON

Sources L. Alberti, *De viris illustribus ordinis Praedicatorum* (1517) · Bale, *Cat.*, 1.394 · Antonius of Siena, *Bibliotheca ordinis Fratrum Praedicatorum* (1585), 247 · J. Pits, *Relationum historicarum de rebus Anglicis*, ed. [W. Bishop] (Paris, 1619), 413 · Tanner, *Bibl. Brit.-Hib.*, 465

Langham [*née* Hastings], **Lady Elizabeth** (1635–1664), exemplar of godly life, was born on 19 February 1635, probably at Donington Park, Leicestershire, one of the ten children of Ferdinando Hastings, sixth earl of Huntingdon (1609–1656), and his wife, Lucy *Hastings (1613–1679), daughter of Sir John *Davies and Lady Eleanor *Davies; Theophilus *Hastings, seventh earl of Huntingdon (1650–1701), was her younger brother. Her well-educated mother supervised the education of her three surviving daughters. More receptive than her sisters to this instruction Elizabeth became an extremely religious woman. From her youth she was a diligent observer of the sabbath and took care to perform her religious duties faithfully. As an aid to her spiritual pilgrimage she studied languages; she was able not only to read works by Peter Martyr in Latin and by Peter du Moulin in French but also to understand Italian authors. In a posthumous eulogy her brother-in-law William Langham claimed:

> That skill in Scripture, and in Tongues she got,
> Made her a living Bible Polyglot.
> (Clark, 207)

On 18 November 1662 Lady Elizabeth was licensed to marry, with a dowry of £10,000, Sir James Langham, baronet (c.1621–1699). She moved into the Langham homes at Cottesbrooke, Northamptonshire, and Crosby Place, Bishopsgate, London, over which her father-in-law, Sir John Langham, still presided. Before their marriage Sir James had served in parliament, most recently for Northampton in early 1662. A devoted stepmother, Lady Elizabeth took care of her husband's eleven-year-old daughter, Mary, from a previous marriage, passing on to this child, who later married Henry Booth, first earl of Warrington, her own commitment to the reading of scriptures and to the hearing of sermons. On 18 March 1664, less than two years after her wedding, Elizabeth, who was admired for her good relations with her friends, the care of her servants and household, and charity to the poor, succumbed to smallpox, taking with her to the grave her unborn child. On her deathbed at Cottesbrooke she worried about the appropriateness of her deportment, fearing she would be thought impatient with the divine plan and warning her husband that his zealous prayers for her might be a sign of 'overloving' her (Clark, 206). She overcame brief conflicts with temptation and met death willingly and courageously.

Lady Elizabeth's exemplary piety was celebrated by Samuel Clarke in his *Lives of Sundry Eminent Persons* (1683), which presented her as the epitome of a godly gentlewoman. Affixed to the study was the eulogy written by her brother-in-law William Langham, who studied medicine abroad and may have attended her in her last illness:

> O what a glorious Creature, and how rare
> A Saint 'twould be, that had what she could spare!
> (Clark, 207)

RETHA M. WARNICKE

Sources GEC, *Peerage*, new edn, vol. 6 · E. R. Edwards, 'Langham, Sir James', HoP, *Commons, 1660–90* · *Collins peerage of England: genealogical, biographical and historical*, ed. E. Brydges, 9 vols. (1812), vol. 6 · S. Clark [S. Clarke], *The lives of sundry eminent persons in this later age* (1683) · E. S. Cope, *Handmaid of the Holy Spirit: Dame Eleanor Davies, never soe mad a ladie* (1992) · W. Dugdale, 'Historical and genealogical collections of the family of Hastings, earls of Huntington', Hunt. L., HA 16250, fol. 86v

Langham, Robert (c.1535–1579/80), mercer, was reputedly the author of a description of the entertainment given by Robert Dudley, earl of Leicester, for Elizabeth I at Kenilworth Castle in the summer of 1575. All that is known for certain about him is that he was apprenticed to William Leonard and admitted to the freedom of the Mercers' Company in 1557, so that he was probably born in the mid-1530s. He received payments of £10 each April from 1573 to 1579 as keeper of the council chamber: on 13 April 1580 the sum was paid to his widow for his pains during the last year, and on 29 November of the same year letters of administration were granted to his widow, Mary, of the parish of St Mildred in Bread Street ward.

The description of the entertainment has the title *A letter: whearin, part of the entertainment vntoo the Queenz Maiesty, at Killingwoorth Castl, in Warwik Sheer in this soomerz progress 1575. iz signified: from a freend officer attendant in the coourt, vntoo hiz freend a citizen, and merchaunt of London*. It usefully complements the description given of 'The princelie pleasures at Kenelworth Castle' by George Gascoigne, one of their devisers, in an account of 1576, which survives in his *Whole Works* of 1587. The *Letter* also supplies a list of books owned by Captain Cox, a Coventry mason and leader of the Hock-Tuesday play; it is an important source for the ballads, romances, plays, and popular literature of the time. The account has been well known since it was reprinted at Warwick in 1784; it was included in John Nichols's editions of *The Progresses and Public Processions of Queen Elizabeth* (1788 and 1823). Scott drew on it in his novel *Kenilworth* (1821), in which Langham makes an appearance as a minor character.

The *Letter* survives in two editions; neither supplies any information about who printed them, when or where, but they may have been printed about 1578 and after 1580. An earlier edition, published shortly after 'this soomerz progress' in 1575, may have been suppressed. The *Letter*, dated from Worcester on 20 August 1575, is addressed to Humfrey Martyn, the son of Sir Roger Martyn, a master of the Mercers' Company: Humfrey Martyn, younger and richer than Langham, was admitted to the company by patrimony in 1570 and to the livery on 23 July 1572. The two were evidently only recently acquainted, which allows Langham to tell Martyn a certain amount about himself. In the course of the *Letter* the writer refers to himself as 'Lanham' or 'Laneham', 'Langham', 'Ro. La.', and 'R. L. Gent. Mercer', as well as 'the blak Prins' or 'El prencipe negro' (Langham, 58, 78, 36, 80).

Making use of a distinctive orthography, the writer of the *Letter* is portrayed as an egocentric and amiable buffoon, with antiquarian tastes and a love for old stories, for music and dancing, and for food and drink. The *Letter* supplies further biographical details. Langham was educated at St Anthony's and St Paul's schools in London, was apprenticed to 'Master Bomsted', travelled in France and Flanders with Bomsted and on his own, and learned foreign languages, including Spanish, through his business. He is described as a 'Merchauntaventurer, and Clark of the Councell chamber doore': an account of his day in this last office is supplied. Leicester is referred to as his patron who got him the post with the privy council as well as a 'licenz of Beanz' which, he adds, he needs to use much (Langham, 36, 76, 80); his father is said to be a servant of the earl in his stables. In London after work he frequents the establishments of Sir George Howard and Lady Sidney. His friends are stated to include Thomas Pullison, a merchant and future lord mayor of London, Thomas Smith, customer of the port of London, a 'Master thorogood' (perhaps William Thoroughgood of St Antholin, Budge Row), and another mercer, Thomas Denman.

Some of these details have a circumstantial plausibility. An Edward Langham, gentleman, was granted livery by the earl of Leicester in 1559, received payments for supplying food for his hawks, and served him in Ireland. A John Laneham was an actor and member of Leicester's theatrical company in 1572–4; later he joined the Queen's Men, of which he became a leading member, and was involved in the Marprelate controversy. 'Master Bomsted' can be identified with Christopher Bompsted, who had been freed as an apprentice mercer in 1541. No independent record, however, can be found of Robert Langham as a pupil at either of the two schools, the post of clerk of the council chamber door is otherwise unknown, and no licence for beans has been found.

The question of the authorship of the *Letter* has been much debated. Its editor, R. J. P. Kuin, has argued that it is an authentic account by Langham, but others (David Scott and Brian O'Kill) believe that it is the work of William Patten, who published it as a joke at Langham's expense: this second view has been accepted by some authorities, including the *Short-Title Catalogue* and the revisers of Halkett and Laing's *Dictionary of Anonymous and Pseudonymous Publications* (1980). The argument for Patten's authorship is based on several elements. These include similarities of form, style, subject matter, and phraseology shared between the *Letter* and Patten's acknowledged work; Patten's practice of annotating his own publications and the resemblance between his hand and the hand which appears in the two annotated copies of the *Letter*; the fact that Patten himself played a part in the Kenilworth festivities, contributing some Latin verses, which Gascoigne records as by 'M. Paten', to welcome the queen; and the distinctive orthography and language of the *Letter*, which shares forms and a fondness for archaisms and coinages used by Patten in his works. Finally, a letter from Patten to William Cecil, Lord Burghley, dated from London on 10 September 1575, among the Hatfield House papers, relates how he has heard from his 'good freend' the master of requests, Thomas Wilson, 'hoow the book waz too be supprest for that Langham had complaynd vpon it, and ootherwize for that the honorabl enterteinment be not turned intoo a iest'. Patten reports that he has sent out six

copies of the book (to Burghley, to Wilson, and to the lord keeper, Sir Nicholas Bacon), and has 'not let three more pass me, but haue & suppress them all'. Langham has seen a copy and Patten professes himself 'sory … that he takez it so noow' (Hatfield House, MS 8/52).

These strong arguments in favour of Patten's authorship leave a number of questions unanswered about his possible motivation in wishing to mock Langham, the dangers he ran of causing offence to those powerful people and institutions satirized by association in the *Letter*, and about Burghley's part in the events. Furthermore, Patten was not the only writer of the time to make use of distinctive phonetic forms (John Cornet and Leonard Staveley favoured a similar style) and archaic vocabulary, and, if he did annotate copies of the *Letter*, it does not necessarily follow that he wrote it. The circumstances in which the account was reprinted before and after Langham's death are unexplained. If the suppressed edition to which Patten refers was identical with the surviving text of the *Letter*, then it must have been printed and called in between 20 August and 10 September 1575. It is possible, however, either that the text of the *Letter* published and suppressed in 1575 was different from the one that survives in the later prints, or that Patten wrote a work, now lost, mocking Langham's account of Kenilworth which had to be withdrawn. Finally, although the *Letter* presents Langham in a comic light, it does so mainly in the last two or three out of just under ninety pages, and some of the mockery can be read as self-mockery.

H. R. WOUDHUYSEN

Sources R. Langham, *A letter*, ed. R. J. P. Kuin (1983) · D. Scott, 'William Patten and the authorship of "Robert Laneham's *Letter*" (1575)', *English Literary Renaissance*, 7 (1977), 297–306 · B. O'Kill, 'The printed works of William Patten (c.1510–c.1590)', *Transactions of the Cambridge Bibliographical Society*, 7 (1977), 28–45 · R. J. P. Kuin, 'The purloined *Letter*: evidence and probability regarding Robert Langham's authorship', *The Library*, 6th ser., 7 (1985), 115–25 · R. J. P. Kuin, 'Robert Langham and his *Letter*', *N&Q*, 223 (1978), 426–7 · PRO, PROB 6/2, fol. 211r · Hatfield House MSS, W. Patten, letter to W. Cecil, Lord Burghley, MS 8/52

Langham, Simon (*d.* 1376), administrator, archbishop of Canterbury, and cardinal, was born at Langham in Rutland, the son of Thomas Langham—his spectacular career as an ecclesiastic and royal minister contrasts markedly with his modest beginnings. He became a monk of St Peter's, Westminster, some time before 1339, and in 1346 was his abbey's proctor at the Benedictine triennial chapter in Northampton. That same year he began his studies at Oxford, but returned to Westminster in 1348, possibly with the coming of the black death, without completing his degree. If he studied theology in his years at Oxford, he was one of only four abbots of Westminster to have done so. On 10 April 1349, at the height of the plague epidemic in England, he was appointed prior and, several weeks later, on 27 May, was elected abbot of Westminster. The ravages of the plague were challenge enough for the new abbot, but Langham also had to face a crushing debt left by his predecessor and a monastic community grown slack in discipline. As abbot from 1349 to 1362 Langham worked hard to correct both defects. He managed the abbey's estates shrewdly, reviving and expanding a previous policy of leasing lands and purchasing new properties. He succeeded not only in paying off the debts, but also in bringing the abbey into a period of renewed prosperity. He oversaw new building projects, completed the cloister in the new perpendicular style, and was himself a generous benefactor to the abbey, establishing chantries and giving from his own accumulated wealth as abbot and, later, as archbishop. He is deservedly called Westminster's second founder.

Langham improved monastic discipline in his community much as he managed its estates, with sound judgement and pragmatism. The mid-fifteenth-century Westminster chronicler John Flete called him a reformer of the first rank, a wise counsellor, and an eloquent preacher. But John Reading (d. 1368/9), who lived under Langham, held a different opinion of the man, and thought him overbearing and ambitious. However much such opinions differ, there is little doubt that Langham was an excellent administrator. Edward III knew as much when he appointed him treasurer on 23 November 1360, the first religious to occupy such a high post in the royal administration in nearly a century. Meanwhile, Langham continued his duties as abbot while struggling to reduce his master's sizeable war debt. His successes were rewarded with rapid advancement. In 1361 the cathedral chapters at both London and Ely elected him bishop, but Langham chose the latter on account of its ties with the Benedictine community. The pope provided him to Ely on 22 January 1362, and Bishop William Edington (d. 1366) consecrated him bishop on 20 March at St Paul's. On 21 February 1363, Edward made him chancellor, an office Langham held until September 1367. As chancellor he promoted royal policy to legislation, including tighter restrictions on appeals to the papal court in the revised Statute of *Praemunire* (1365). He opened parliament regularly, and in 1363 broke with tradition by delivering the chancellor's formal address in English.

Langham was not only an experienced and able administrator, he cultivated like talents in other men. He was a mentor to William Wykeham (d. 1404) and appointed him keeper of the privy seal in 1363. Adam Easton (d. 1397) was to be a member of his household in later years. Pleased with Langham's achievements, Edward nominated him as archbishop of Canterbury in 1366 and the pope provided him to the see on 24 July. He was the last monk to hold this office and might have made a lasting impression on the province had his reign been longer. Still, Langham's register shows a man busy with administration and pastoral care in challenging times. He enforced new papal restrictions on pluralism, and corrected abuses in his visitations of deaneries and religious houses. He attempted to curb religious dissent by ordering John Ball (d. 1381) to cease preaching in 1367, and, in the following year, intervened in a bitter dispute between the Oxford theologians Uthred Boldon (d. 1396) and William Jordon, issuing thirty articles of his own on matters of justification, grace, and the salvation of non-believers. His own spirituality emerges in the pages of his register with three hymns written in honour of St Catherine. But Langham was archbishop for only two years; on 22 September 1368 Urban V created him cardinal-priest of St Sixtus, and Langham indicated his willingness to accept the promotion before consulting the king. While Langham may have thought himself more useful to the king as a potentially influential member of the papal court, Edward regarded the move as one of divided loyalty and compromised service to the crown. Langham's situation changed quickly: Edward seized the Canterbury temporalities before the archbishop could resign them (which he did on 28 November), leaving Langham in relative poverty, and delaying his departure for Avignon until 28 February 1369.

Langham's desire to serve church and kingdom as a peacemaker was given real opportunity in 1370 with the election of Gregory XI. For several years thereafter the 'cardinal of Canterbury', as Langham was styled at Avignon, was engaged in several diplomatic missions. Though he was frustrated by the intransigence of the French and English kings, he managed to arrange a peace between Edward and the count of Flanders in 1372. But what diplomatic successes he enjoyed went unrecognized both in England, where many of his friends regarded him as too pro-papal, and in Avignon, where the French majority of cardinals questioned his loyalty. The latter's mistrust was confirmed on one famous occasion when Langham, in the presence of the English king, removed his hat in deference. The pope was less concerned by the incident, and promoted him to cardinal-bishop of Palestrina in 1373, but the elevation did little to improve Langham's real status either at the papal court or in England. His diplomatic services were no longer required and, in spite of his benefices which included archdeaconries in Wells and York and the prebends of Brompton in Lincoln and Wistow in York, Langham was less wealthy as a cardinal than he had been as an archbishop.

Nevertheless, Langham managed to remember his brethren at Westminster in the form of generous endowments. Between 1368 and his death in 1376 Langham had a chantry established in the abbey for his own soul and the souls of his family worth 1000 marks, earning 40 marks annually in rents; he also left his community a residuary estate worth nearly £1000, along with a valuable, indeed notable, library, vestments, and plate, and donated a further £400 to the fabric fund. In 1374, with Canterbury vacant and the chapter sympathetic toward Langham's candidacy, the cardinal entertained hopes of returning to England in his former capacity. But the chapter looked elsewhere, as neither king nor pope would have approved the election. In 1376, when it was certain that Gregory would go back to Rome, Langham sought and obtained papal permission to retire to England, but he died at Avignon on 22 July, possibly from a paralysing stroke. He was buried at the Carthusian church near Avignon. In 1379 his remains were transferred to the splendid tomb built by Henry Yevele and Stephen Lote in St Benedict's Chapel, Westminster Abbey. He is the only archbishop buried in the abbey.

W. J. DOHAR

Sources Registrum Simonis Langham, Cantuariensis archiepiscopi, ed. A. C. Wood, CYS, 53 (1956) • Emden, Oxf. • J. Flete, The history of Westminster Abbey, ed. J. A. Robinson (1909) • B. Harvey, Westminster Abbey and its estates in the middle ages (1977) • J. A. Robinson, 'Simon Langham, abbot of Westminster', Church Quarterly Review, 66 (1908), 339–66 • J. Tait, Chronicon Johannis de Reading et anonymi Cantuariensis, 1346–67 (1914), 108–9 • D. Knowles [M. C. Knowles], The religious orders in England, 2 (1955), 54–6 • B. F. Harvey, 'The leasing of the abbot of Westminster's desmesnes in the later middle ages', Economic History Review, 2nd ser., 22 (1969), 17–27 • R. G. Davies, 'The episcopal appointments in England and Wales of 1375', Mediaeval Studies, 44 (1982), 306–32 • E. Carpenter, ed., A house of kings: the history of Westminster Abbey (1966), 62–6 • J. R. L. Highfield, 'The English hierarchy in the reign of Edward III', TRHS, 5th ser., 6 (1956), 115–38 • A. P. Stanley, Historical memorials of Westminster Abbey, 5th edn (1882) • RotP, 2.275, 283 • CPR, 1346–7, 330; 1367–70, 187 • CEPR letters, 3.327; 4.37 • N. Pevsner, P. Metcalf, and others, The cathedrals of England, 2: Southern England (1985)
Likenesses H. Yevele and S. Lote, alabaster tomb effigy, Westminster Abbey, London
Wealth at death approx. £666 13s. 14d. left for the endowment of a chantry in Westminster; £975 residuary estate left to the monks: Harvey, Westminster Abbey, pp. 40, 396

Langhorn, John (bap. 1744, d. 1817), Church of England clergyman and missionary, was baptized on 22 April 1744 in Shotley, Northumberland, the eldest of the four children of the Revd William Langhorn (fl. 1741–1758), assistant curate of Shotley, and his wife, Martha (1713–1798), daughter of Humphrey Hopper (1677–1760) and his wife, Jane, née Hodgson (c.1675–1752). John Langhorn grew up at Black Hedley, Shotley, just a few miles from Hadrian's Wall. The Hoppers were a prominent landed family in the parish.

Langhorn is thought to have been educated at St Bees School in Cumberland. However, his family was unable to send him to university. In 1766 he was ordained deacon and began a lengthy curacy in Cheshire. By 1780 he was connected to All Saints', Harthill, near the Welsh border. He was not ordained priest until 1784, when he was forty years of age. His rigid and ritualistic form of high-church Anglicanism seems to have been particularly influenced by the writings of the Rt Revd Thomas Wilson (1663–1755), bishop of Sodor and Man.

Necessity prompted Langhorn to choose employment in Canada as a missionary with the Society for the Propagation of the Gospel in Foreign Parts (SPG). A position overseas was a chance to increase his income and provide for his widowed mother and unmarried sister. He also had the encouragement of two prominent churchmen and supporters of the SPG, the Ven. Thomas Townson (1715–1792), archdeacon of Richmond, and the Rt Revd Beilby Porteus (1731–1808), bishop of Chester.

Langhorn arrived in Cataraqui (later Kingston) in the autumn of 1787. His initial meeting with the Revd John Stuart (1740/41–1811), a refugee of the American War of Independence and the only resident Anglican clergyman in what would soon become Upper Canada, was strained, though relations improved towards the end of Stuart's life. That first winter Langhorn and his loyalist parishioners endured harsh weather and famine. For several years the SPG was in arrears with part of his salary. He lived modestly as a tenant of a local family and indulged only in the purchase of books.

Langhorn established two principal congregations in Ernestown and Fredericksburgh townships, and six other preaching stations. For the next twenty-six years he traversed on foot an immense terrain, sparsely inhabited by a few Church of England adherents and a wide variety of dissenters, particularly Methodists and Presbyterians. The bachelor cleric soon gained a reputation as an irascible eccentric, perhaps partly due to his poor health. It cannot be denied that Langhorn attended dutifully to his professional responsibilities, but he had an unfortunate penchant for religious controversy.

Langhorn's doctrinal rigidity did not increase his popularity among people who were absorbed by the struggle for survival and had a wide choice of religious options. His refusal to show any respect for dissenters naturally brought reciprocal antagonism. Had it not been for the shortage of missionaries he would have been recalled on several occasions. However, despite his undiplomatic ways, even his detractors had to acknowledge his scrupulous honesty and selfless generosity.

Langhorn served in Upper Canada until the outbreak of the Anglo-American War of 1812–14. Having reached his seventieth year, he returned to England in 1813 and retired to Natland Millbeck, Westmorland. He died, unmarried, aged seventy-three, on 15 May 1817 and was buried in Heversham churchyard on 18 May. His carefully garnered estate of just under £3000 was left in trust to his sister and niece. His spiritual legacy was far less modest. Like Stuart, Langhorn contributed significantly to the vitality of Anglicanism in early Canada.

JOHN D. BLACKWELL and LAURIE C. C. STANLEY-BLACKWELL

Sources E. Bellasis, Westmorland church notes (1888), 1.262 • J. D. Blackwell and L. C. C. Stanley, 'Two Anglican images: John Stuart and John Langhorn', St George's Cathedral: two hundred years of community, ed. D. Swainson (1991), 167–87, 291–4 • W. Canniff, History of the settlement of Upper Canada (1869) • GM, 1st ser., 87/1 (1817), 644 • J. C. Hodgson, A history of Northumberland, 6 (1902) • Kingston Gazette (9 March 1813) • Kingston Gazette (1 June 1813) • [J. Langhorn], Anglican register, 1787–1814: Rev. John Langhorn, rector of Ernestown, ed. L. Wanamaker and M. Wanamaker (1980) • [J. Langhorn], 'Entries in the journals of the Society for the Propagation of the Gospel in Foreign Parts relating to the Revd John Langhorn', ed. A. H. Young, Papers and Records [Ontario Historical Society], 23 (1926), 534–60 • [J. Langhorn], 'More Langhorn letters', ed. A. H. Young, Papers and Records [Ontario Historical Society], 29 (1933), 47–71 • H. E. Turner, 'Langhorn, John', DCB, 5.474–7 • L. Turner, Ernestown: rural spaces, urban places (1993) • A. H. Young, 'The Revd John Langhorn, Church of England missionary, at Fredericksburgh and Ernestown, 1787–1813', Papers and Records [Ontario Historical Society], 23 (1926), 523–33
Archives Bodl. RH, Society for the Propagation of the Gospel archives
Wealth at death £3000: will, 1814, Lancs. RO

Langhorne, Daniel (c.1635–1681), antiquary, was born in London, and matriculated from Trinity College, Cambridge, in October 1649. His parentage is unknown, but his family was probably collateral to the Langhornes of Westmorland, from whom Isabella, the mother of Benjamin Jowett, master of Balliol College, Oxford, was descended. He became a scholar of Trinity, and graduated BA in 1654 and MA in 1657. He was appointed curate of the parish church of Holy Trinity, Ely, then newly constituted from the lady chapel of the cathedral, and after the Restoration was licensed by Bishop Wren in 1662 to preach there and throughout the diocese. In 1663 he was elected a fellow of Corpus Christi College, Cambridge, and having graduated BD in the following year became one of the university preachers. He vacated his fellowship in 1671 after his institution as vicar of Layston with the chapelry of Alswick, Buntingford, Hertfordshire, which he held until his death.

In accord with the quickening interest in early English history in both universities, Langhorne devoted his studies to early British history and the settlement and eventual unification of the English kingdoms. He was well versed in the evidence of the chronicles, but he wrote at a time when the wilder extravagances of the legendary British history had generally been rejected, and before archaeology, philology, and critical documentary techniques had been able to put anything else in their place. Like his contemporaries he was aware of that gap, and he said of Geoffrey of Monmouth's history, sensibly enough, that although much of it was palpably ridiculous, there might be a substratum of truth, at least in the sense of distorted recollection, remaining in it. His first study was *Elenchus antiquitatum Albionensium, Britannorum, Scotorum, Danorum, Anglosaxonum et ceterorum: origines et gesta usque ad annum 449, quo Angli in Britanniam immigrarunt, explicans* (London, 1673). It was dedicated to Sir William Montagu, attorney-general to Queen Caroline and later chief baron of the exchequer, and was followed by *Appendix ad elenchum antiquitatum Albionensium: res Saxonum et Suevorum vetustissimas exhibens* (London, 1673). An English version of the two volumes, *An introduction to the history of England, comprising the principal affairs of this land from its first planting to the coming of the English Saxons, together with a catalogue of British and Pictish kings*, appeared in 1676. In 1679, and on rather firmer ground, he published *Chronicon regum Anglorum, insignia omnia eorum gesta ab Hengisto rege primo usque ad Heptarchiae finem*, dedicated to Sir Joseph Williamson, secretary of state. There is no obvious connection between Langhorne and his dedicatees, neither of whom was an outstandingly edifying member of the political community, though Williamson, a busy man, was known sometimes to temper his customary parsimony with charitable acts.

The quest for patronage was, however, a convention as well as a resource, and Langhorne derived other satisfactions from his work. He died on 10 August 1681, with his history incomplete, as he apparently intended to carry it at least to the Norman conquest. Forty years later Thomas Hearne asked Thomas Baker, the Cambridge antiquary, for information about Langhorne, and was told, beside the facts of his career, that Baker had seen a manuscript version of the second part of the history. This was probably the handsome text later prized by the antiquary Dawson Turner. It may be that, like Dugdale, Langhorne habitually wrote an exquisite hand, but he seems also to have enjoyed matching the best of his exemplars.

G. H. MARTIN

Sources DNB · Venn, *Alum. Cant.* · *Remarks and collections of Thomas Hearne*, ed. C. E. Doble and others, 8, OHS, 50 (1907), 195 · R. Clutterbuck, ed., *The history and antiquities of the county of Hertford*, 3 vols. (1815–27)
Archives BL, Chronicle of England, part 2, Add. MS 24108

Langhorne, John (1735–1779), poet and translator, was born in March 1735 at Winton in the parish of Kirkby Stephen, Westmorland, the younger son of the Revd Joseph Langhorne of Winton and Isabel, his wife. He was educated at a school in his native village and afterwards at Appleby. At eighteen he became a private tutor in a family near Ripon, and during his residence there began writing verses. He was afterwards an usher in the free school at Wakefield, and there took deacon's orders and eked out his scanty income by taking Edmund Cartwright, reputed inventor of the power-loom, as a pupil during vacations. About this time he wrote for Ralph Griffiths's *Grand Magazine*, which had a three-year existence from 1758 to 1760. In 1759 Langhorne went to Hackthorn, near Lincoln, as tutor to the sons of Robert Cracroft. In the following year he matriculated at Clare College, Cambridge, intending to take the degree of bachelor of divinity as a ten-year man. He left the university, however, without taking any degree. He left Hackthorn in 1761 and took up a curacy in Dagenham, Essex.

That same year (1761) Langhorne wrote his first review for Ralph Griffiths's *Monthly Review*, and by November 1768, when he wrote the last review for Griffiths, he had been responsible for some 300. In 1764 he was appointed curate and lecturer at St John's, Clerkenwell, and in December 1765 was appointed assistant preacher at Lincoln's Inn by the then preacher Dr Richard Hurd, afterwards bishop of Worcester. Also in 1766 he became rector of Blagdon, Somerset, and was said to have been granted the honorary degree of DD by the University of Edinburgh in return for his *Genius and Valour: a Scotch Pastoral* (1763) in defence of the Scots against the aspersions of Charles Churchill in his *Prophecy of Famine* (1763). There is no record of such a grant. In January 1767, after a courtship of five years and an initial rejection of his proposal of marriage, he married Ann Cracroft (1735/6–1768), the sister of his old pupils, whom he had taught Italian, a language in which he was proficient. Ann died in giving birth to a son on 4 May 1768, aged thirty-two, and was buried in the chancel of Blagdon church. At her desire he published after her death their premarital correspondence under the title of *Letters to Eleonora* (1770–71).

Langhorne left Blagdon shortly after Ann's death and went to live with his elder brother William [see below] at Folkestone where they translated *Plutarch's Lives … from the original Greek, with notes critical and historical, and a new life of Plutarch* (6 vols., 1770), dedicated to Lord Folkestone. The translation went through a number of editions.

On 12 February 1772 Langhorne married the daughter of a Mr Thompson, a magistrate near Brough, Westmorland. After a tour through France and Flanders they returned to Blagdon, where he was made a justice of the peace. His second wife died giving birth to an only daughter in February 1776. Langhorne was installed a prebendary of Wells Cathedral in October 1777, and according to a writer in the *European Magazine*, almost surely Isaac Reed, 'his death was imputed to his usual substitute for the Castalian fountain, rather too frequent draughts of Burton ale, at the Peacock Inn, Gray's-Inn-Lane' (*European Magazine*, 17, 1790, 102). He died at Blagdon House on 1 April 1779 and was buried at Blagdon.

Reed, in the same article in the *European Magazine*, listed thirty-three works by Langhorne. Although enjoying some contemporary popularity for his poetry, in a number of forms and on a variety of subjects, he is largely remembered for his translation of Plutarch's *Lives*. Mention may be made of his *Solyman and Almena: an Oriental Tale* (1762); *The Viceroy: a Poem Addressed to the Earl of Halifax* (1762); and the very popular *The Letters that Passed between Theodosius and Constantia after she had Taken the Veil* (1763, followed by a second edition in 1764 and a number of subsequent editions). Langhorne published a number of sermons in 1764 with a second edition in 1773. His *Country Justice: a Poem, by one of Her Majesty's Justices of the Peace for the County of Somerset* (1774–7) was greatly praised by Wordsworth in a letter of 15 January 1837, who wrote that it 'is not without many faults in style … but these are to me trifles in a work so original and touching' (Davie, 122). Langhorne edited *The Poetical Works of William Collins* in 1765, and translated Milton's Italian poems in 1776. Both in his own writings and in his reviews in the *Monthly Review* he exerted influence on some of his contemporaries, notably on John Scott of Amwell, in the life of whom, prefatory to his posthumously published *Critical Essays* (1785), their friendship is mentioned.

William Langhorne (1721–1772), John's elder brother, was presented by the archbishop of Canterbury on 23 March 1753 (*GM*, 23, 1753, 149) to the rectory of Hawkinge and the perpetual curacy of Folkestone, Kent, and on 19 May 1756 received the Lambeth degree of MA (*GM*, 16, 1864, 637). He died on 17 February 1772 and was buried in the chancel of Folkestone church, where a monument was erected to his memory. Besides collaborating in the translation of Plutarch's *Lives*, he wrote *Job: a Poem, in Three Books [a paraphrase]* (1760), *A Poetical Paraphrase on Part of the Book of Isaiah* (1761), and *Sermons on Practical Subjects and the most Useful Points of Divinity* (1773). These last were posthumously published and seen through the press by his brother, by whom the 'advertisement' is signed, 'J. L.', 1778.   ARTHUR SHERBO

Sources *European Magazine and London Review*, 17 (1790), 101–3 · J. T. Langhorne, 'Memoirs of the author', in J. Langhorne, *Poetical works* (1804), 5–25 · D. Davie, *The late Augustans* (1958), 122 · DNB
Likenesses C. Pye, line engraving, pubd 1804 (after R. Corbould), BM; repro. in Langhorne, *Poetical works*, frontispiece

Langhorne, Nancy Witcher. *See* Astor, Nancy Witcher, Viscountess Astor (1879–1964).

Langhorne, Richard (*c*.1624–1679), barrister and victim of the Popish Plot, was probably born in London, the son of Richard Langhorne (*d*. 1635), an apothecary in London, and Dorothy Legate (*b*. 1606), daughter of Thomas Legate of Havering atte Bower, Essex. He had two brothers, Thomas and Edmund, and a sister, Elizabeth. Little is known about him before his admission to the Inner Temple on 31 May 1647 and his being called to the bar on 27 November 1654. Despite the occasional suggestion that he attended a Jesuit college on the continent there is no evidence. At an unknown date he married Elizabeth (*fl.* *c*.1659–*c*.1679). They had four children: Charles, the youngest son (1660–1723); his two older brothers, Richard (*d*. 1719) and Francis (*c*.1659–1709); and a sister, Laetitia (*d*. 1729). Charles and Francis were priests, Richard and Laetitia Catholic nonjurors. The three sons attended the English College at St Omer. In 1676 the oldest son disappeared, apparently joining the French army, and lost contact with his family. He later returned to St Omer, contacted English Jesuits there, and through their intercession re-established contact with his father, who paid for his return home. In 1677 Charles Langhorne, then a student in Valladolid, entrusted to Titus Oates a letter to his father. Oates had been expelled from the college on 30 October for serious moral lapses and returned to London. After a brief sojourn Oates travelled to St Omer with a letter of gratitude from Langhorne to the Jesuits for all they had done for his sons.

Langhorne built a successful legal practice from his quarters in the Inner Temple. Gilbert Burnet claimed that he 'passed as Protestant' (*Burnet's History*, 155) without further explanation. At least from 1664 he lived in Shire (or Sheer) Lane, Holborn. Among his clients—or at least his acquaintances—were the recusant William Blundell of Crosby; the Hatton family; William Penn; and the Society of Jesus. To the first, on 3 November 1666, he confided his disappointment that Charles II had capitulated to parliament and agreed to execute the penal laws against Catholics. Langhorne's *Consideration touching the great question of the king's right in dispensing with the penal laws* (London, 1687), written in defence of Charles II's declaration of indulgence in 1672, was edited by his son Richard and published to support James II's proclamations in 1687. For the Jesuits, Langhorne provided legal and financial advice to the Jesuit provincial and procurator, and served as their trustee.

Titus Oates and Israel Tonge unleashed the Popish Plot on 28 September 1678 with the arrest of three Jesuits and a Benedictine. Langhorne was arrested a week later. As he explained, 'I must be a perfect Mad-man to appear publickly, and not to flie or conceal my self, if I were conscious of any the least imaginable Guilt' (Langhorne, *Memoires*, 2), since he continued to work after their arrest. Charged with high treason Langhorne remained in close confinement in Newgate: Oates claimed—and William Bedloe corroborated—that the correspondence he delivered between Langhorne and the Jesuits dealt with treason and treachery. Found guilty of high treason on 13 June and sentenced to be executed on the 20th, Langhorne received a reprieve for a month on the 19th as a result of a petition by his wife (a 'true Protestant' (McCoog, 'Richard Langhorne', 499)) so that he could tidy up the financial affairs of his clients. Moreover she promised to persuade him to reveal all he knew about the plot and about Jesuit finances. Langhorne produced a potentially damaging disclosure of some Jesuit assets. On 15 July 1679 Charles Hatton told Lord Hatton that Langhorne had received the approval of the imprisoned Jesuit provincial Thomas Whitbread (alias Harcott or Harcourt) to do so, but how two close prisoners could communicate remains unexplained especially since the provincial was executed the day after the offer was made. Langhorne's disclosure about Jesuit finances was in the hands of Charles II and the privy council by 3 July. The council was not satisfied; the king ordered that no copy of it be made and, mysteriously, returned the original to the author. A copy, however, was made and can now be found in the Royal Archives in Brussels.

Langhorne was executed at Tyburn, London, on 14 July 1679. In his speech from the gibbet he made an extraordinary declaration for a man on such familiar terms with the Jesuits: he professed Charles II his 'True and Lawful Sovereign' as understood by the oath of allegiance, and denied that the pope had any right to depose monarchs (Langhorne, *Memoires*, 18). Pope Pius XI beatified him on 15 December 1929.   THOMAS M. MCCOOG

Sources G. Anstruther, *The seminary priests*, 3 (1976), 127–30 · M. Blundell, *Blessed Richard Langhorne* (1933) · *Cavalier: letters of William Blundell to his friends, 1620–1698*, ed. M. Blundell (1933) · *Bishop Burnet's History of his own time*, new edn, 2 vols. (1838) · Gillow, *Lit. biog. hist.*, 4.127–31 · E. Henson, ed., *The registers of the English College at Valladolid, 1589–1862*, Catholic RS, 30 (1930) · G. Holt, *St Omers and Bruges colleges, 1593–1773: a biographical dictionary*, Catholic RS, 69 (1979), 157–8 · W. P. Jeffcock and L. E. Whatmore, 'Some notes on the families of the English martyrs', *Biographical Studies*, 1 (1951–2), 233 · J. Kenyon, *The Popish Plot* (1972) · R. Langhorne, *Mr. Langhorn's Memoires, with some meditations and devotions of his, during his imprisonment: as also his petition to his majesty and his speech at his execution* (1679) · R. Langhorne, *Consideration touching the great question of the king's right in dispensing with the penal laws* (1687) · V. Langhorne, 'The ancestry of Blessed Richard Langhorne, c.1624–1679', *Catholic Ancestor*, 8 (2000), 51–7 · T. M. McCoog, 'Richard Langhorne and the Popish Plot', *Recusant History*, 19 (1988–9), 499–508 · T. M. McCoog, 'Apostasy and knavery in Restoration England: the checkered career of John Travers', *Catholic Historical Review*, 78 (1992), 395–412 · W. H. Cooke, ed., *Students admitted to the Inner Temple, 1547–1660* [1878] · E. M. Thompson, ed., *Correspondence of the family of Hatton*, 2 vols., CS, new ser., 22–3 (1878) · *The tryall of Richard Langhorn* (1679) · M. E. Williams, *St Alban's College, Valladolid: four centuries of English Catholic presence in Spain* (1986) · PRO, PC 2/68, 123

Archives BL, corresp. with the Hatton family, Add. MSS 29551–29557

Likenesses mezzotint, pubd 1802 (after print by Luttrell), BM, NPG · portrait, repro. in W. Richardson, *Portraits illustrating Grainger's Biographical history of England*, 2 vols. (1792)

Langhorne, Sir William, baronet (*c*.1634–1715), administrator in India, was born in the City of London, the only son of the four children of William Langhorne, an East India merchant, of the parish of St Gabriel Fenchurch, and Hitchin, Hertfordshire, and his wife, Mary, daughter of Dr Daniel Oxenbridge, a London physician. Langhorne entered Trinity College, Cambridge, on 23 October 1649.

He was admitted to Gray's Inn on 7 July 1652, and to the Inner Temple on 6 August 1664, but does not appear to have practised at the bar. He inherited his father's holding of East India Company stock, made money, and was in 1668 created a baronet.

In 1669 Langhorne was appointed by the court of committees to investigate a charge of fiscal malpractice which had been brought against Sir Edward Winter, East India Company agent and governor of Madras, with the result that Langhorne himself was made governor in Winter's stead in the course of the year. His arrival at Fort St George, Madras, on 14 June 1670 coincided with a critical period in the history of the settlement. Colbert had in 1664 projected the French Compagnie Royale des Indes Orientales, and in 1672 the French admiral La Haye seized San Thomé, just south of Madras, on the Coromandel coast. Langhorne maintained a discreetly neutral position between the French, who were at that moment the nominal allies of England, the Dutch, with whom England was at war, and the king of Golconda, who was attempting to regain San Thomé. It has been claimed that as 'a former Cromwellian who disliked Charles II's pro-French policy' Langhorne 'connived after September 1673 at a suspension of hostilities against the Dutch' (Furber, 111). However, a contemporary observer accused him of 'actively espousing the French cause to the detriment of Anglo-Indian relations' (Watson, 295). In fact, Langhorne adopted a broadly neutral pragmatic policy designed to safeguard the interests of the East India Company and of his own private trade. When in 1674 the Dutch finally took possession of San Thomé, he contented himself with expressing sympathy with the French, at the same time strengthening the defences of Fort St George. In the same year the English settlement was visited by Dr John Fryer, the English traveller, who spoke highly of Langhorne as:

> a gentleman of indefatigable industry and worth ... His personal guard consists of 3 or 400 blacks; besides a band of 1500 men ready on summons; he never goes abroad without fifes, drums, trumpets, and a flag with two balls in a red field; accompanied with his Council and Factors on horseback, with their ladies in palenkeens.   (Fryer, 38)

In 1675 Langhorne successfully resisted an attempt at extortion by Podela Lingappa, the naik (deputy governor) of the Poonamallee district, but only at the unlooked-for expense of what might have proved a perilous misunderstanding with the king of Golconda. In 1676 he showed his tolerant spirit by firing a salute upon the consecration of a Roman Catholic church in Madras, and thereby drew upon himself a rebuke from the directors at home. The code of by-laws that he drew up as governor helps to depict the contemporary social life of the settlement. Among his regulations it was enacted that no person was to drink above half a pint of arrack or brandy or a quart of wine at a time; to such practices as blaspheming, duelling, being absent from prayers, or being outside the walls after eight o'clock, strict penalties were allotted.

An over-shrewd man of business, Langhorne fell a victim, like his predecessor, to charges of private trading, by which he was said to have realized the too obviously large sum of £7000 per annum, in addition to the £300 allowed him by the company. He left Madras for England in early 1678, having been succeeded by Streynsham Master, who, antagonistic to Langhorne's 'suave' and 'easy-going' style, dispatched a 'scathing indictment of Langhorne and all his works' (*Diaries*, 1.64, 66).

In England, in 1680, Langhorne purchased from the executors of William Ducie, Viscount Downe, the estate and manor house of Charlton, in Kent, where he settled. In 1707 he also acquired Hampstead Manor. His first wife was Grace Chaworth, dowager Viscountess Chaworth of Armagh (1632–1700), second daughter of John Manners, eighth earl of Rutland. However, she died within a year of their marriage, on 15 February 1700. He married, second, on 16 October 1714, Mary Aston (d. 1730), who, after his death, married George (or John) Jones of Twickenham. At Charlton, Langhorne became a JP, and commissioner of the court of requests for the hundred of Blackheath (1689), endowed a school and some almshouses, and died with the reputation of a rich and beneficent 'nabob' on 26 February 1715. He was buried in the north aisle adjoining the chancel of Charlton parish church. By his will, proved on 8 March 1715, he left at least £1600 to be applied, after the manner of Queen Anne's Bounty, in augmenting poor benefices. Leaving no issue by either marriage, Langhorne was succeeded in his estate by his sister's son Sir John Conyers, bt, of Horden, co. Durham, and Langhorne's baronetcy became extinct. He was the author of two works arguing the case of the old East India Company against the 'interloping' new company. The first was a broadsheet, *Considerations Humbly Tendred, Concerning the East-India Company* (1688). The second was a pamphlet, *Some Considerations Relating to the East-India Trade* (1694).

THOMAS SECCOMBE, rev. ANDREW GROUT

Sources GEC, *Baronetage*, 4.45 · D. Lysons, *The environs of London*, 2 (1795); 4 (1796) · *Diaries of Streynsham Master*, ed. R. C. Temple, 2 vols. (1911) · *The visitation of London, anno Domini 1633, 1634, and 1635, made by Sir Henry St George*, 2, ed. J. J. Howard, Harleian Society, 17 (1883), 47 · G. J. Ames, *Colbert, mercantilism, and the French quest for Asian trade* (1996) · J. T. Wheeler, *Madras in the olden time*, 3 vols. (1861–2), vol. 1, pp. 68–93 · J. Fryer, *A new account of East-India and Persia* (1698) · E. Hasted, *The history and topographical survey of the county of Kent*, 4 vols. (1778–99) · H. Furber, *Rival empires of trade in the Orient, 1600–1800* (1976) · I. B. Watson, *Foundation for empire: English private trade in India, 1659–1760* (1980) · Venn, *Alum. Cant.*, 1/3 · T. C. Dale, ed., *The inhabitants of London in 1638*, 2 vols. (1931)

Archives BL OIOC, European MSS, MS Eur. D 300 · BL OIOC, factory corresp.

Wealth at death £1600; plus property: Hasted, *History*; Lysons, *Environs*, vol. 4

Langhorne, William (1721–1772). *See under* Langhorne, John (1735–1779).

Langland, William (c.1325–c.1390), poet, is known from only three sources. These are a Latin memorandum of about 1400 on the last leaf of an unfinished copy of his poem *The Vision of Piers Plowman* made about the same time (TCD, MS D.4.1 (212)), a cluster of sixteenth-century ascriptions by the antiquary John Bale (d. 1563), and the poem itself.

Origins Even the memorandum seems primarily about Langland's parentage, as if this were the object of interest:

> It was Stacy de Rokayle who was William de Langlond's father; this Stacy was of gentle birth and lived in Shipton-under-Wychwood in Oxfordshire, holding land from Lord le Spenser; the aforesaid William wrote the book called *Piers Plowman*. (Dublin, Trinity College, MS D.4.1 (212))

The memorandum is authenticated by knowledgeable local annals dated from 1294 to 1348 in the same hand above it on the page, with clear interest in the Despensers. Extension of that interest to include the poet's family is indicated by a recent discovery (Matheson) that his grandfather Peter de Rokele had been in the service of Hugh le Despenser the younger, indeed had several times been violently and unlawfully active in his interest, and that, having in April 1327 been pardoned for 'adhering' to Despenser, he was within months implicated in a conspiracy to release the captive Edward II. This Peter held land in and about Wooton Underwood in Buckinghamshire. His son Eustace (Stacy) appears in local records as a man of standing in Oxfordshire. Bale's ascriptions call the poet Robert Langland, and have him born at Cleobury Mortimer in Shropshire. The baptismal name, Robert, was a mistaken inference from a scribal error which survives in two unrelated copies of the poem; even without the memorandum Langland's given name would be established as William by an unmistakable cryptogrammatic signature in the convention of the genre, in one version of *Piers Plowman*: 'I have lived in land, my name is Long Will.' But his identification of the birthplace, which has been questioned on mistaken grounds, seems confirmed by records of deeds of gift and grants of land made by various Langlands between 1399 and 1581 not actually in Cleobury Mortimer but a bare 5 miles away in the manor of Kinlet and in adjoining Highley. This seems to have been the poet's mother's family. That he took her name need imply no more than that he was not in line to inherit through primogeniture. As to proximity, there are clear indications of Rokayle interest in Shropshire. The surname Rokele may come from the hamlet Ruckley (earlier Rucklee, Rokeley, Rokele) about 25 miles north-west of Kinlet, part of the manor of Acton Burnel where the Despensers had connections by marriage. Continued association is implied by record of a grant, in 1577, of lands named in the earlier deeds to Thomas Longland son of William Longland, by a Richard Longland of Cuddington, Buckinghamshire, 4 miles from Wooton and half a day's ride from Shipton under Wychwood. The span of dates implies a family of substance.

Dating the poet When the poet was born and died, and the circumstances of his life, have been the subject of much inference from his poem. This survives in three forms, each preserved in a substantial number of copies. The first, evidently unfinished, but already bespeaking an accomplished poet, has for coda in three copies a skilful pastiche in Langland's style by a man who names himself John But. The second, developing and extending the first and almost three times as long, has an unmistakable closure. The third is an uncompleted revision of the second. Walter Skeat, who identified these forms, called them the A, B, and C texts. Each contains unmistakable contemporary references. The mature excellence of the writing in the A text, and allusions in it to Edward III's French campaigns, and to a great storm in 1362, between them have suggested that the poet was born about 1330. Recent discovery (Matheson) that a William Rokele, who might conceivably be the poet, received the first tonsure from Bishop Wolstan of Worcester not long before 1341, suggests a somewhat earlier date, say 1325. Langland's death has long been taken, almost as a matter of convenience, to have occurred before 1387, on the basis of an early identification of the John But who signed the A coda, where the poet's death is reported, as a king's messenger who died that year. The name But, initially thought to be unusual, has proved fairly common, and about a dozen John Buts have come to light in the records. Meanwhile the date 'by 1387' has been put in serious question by the reflection of some features of the 1388 Statute of Labourers in a passage new to the C version (5.1–103). Moreover, having Langland alive after 1388 enables understanding of veiled, but unmistakably political, allusions in C. A better date for his death, taking account of fourteenth-century life expectation, would be c.1390.

The poet's circumstances By its character Langland's poem encourages speculation about him. It belongs to a genre called the dream-vision, which takes the form of a report by a first-person narrator who claims to have experienced the vision he recounts. He figures as participant, encountering personages ranging from the allegorical or fantastic to the possible, even the historical. The dreamer, if he is named, is called after the poet and, where this can be checked, has some of his attributes. He is to an indeterminable extent fashioned in the image of that poet who, for his part, comes to live imaginatively in the personage of his creation. The poet uses him as a means of engagement, obviously powerful in a time when poetry was written as if to be read aloud.

In the unfinished A text of *Piers Plowman* the Dreamer, three times involved in the action by the name Will, gradually acquires character and a temperament. In the completed B text, where the poet encloses his own name in the cryptogram, Will takes shape as a sharply defined personality. In the uncompleted C revision he is even further implicated. Here in a new passage between visions (5.1–103) Langland has set an episode from which a way of life and its circumstances have been inferred for him. The Dreamer reports how in the prime of life, given to indolence, living with his wife in a mean house in Cornhill in the city of London, he is confronted by Conscience and Reason, two personifications who in the course of the first two versions have acquired implicated significance, the former, to simplify, the unthinking impulse to good, the latter an absolute principle of right which informs creation and should govern human conduct. Reason reproaches him for being an idle wastrel, no better than a sponging beggar. From his defence he reveals that he had a clerical education, but his father and those who maintained him and paid for that education in his youth, 'many years ago', are dead now, and he supports himself (as presumably also his wife) by pious service of prayer and psalmody in the oratories of big houses, now here, now there, welcome in periodic visits during which he prays for the souls of his hosts. The tone of his defence is bitter, tinged with disappointed expectation.

This episode has seemed too particular to be an elaborate fiction. On its basis the poet who created the Dreamer has been identified as a clerk in minor orders, necessarily because of his marriage no higher than acolyte, preserving his clerical status by tonsure and habit, a kind of itinerant 'beadsman-for-the-living'. That sketch fits the concept of a younger son in a family of standing, cherished by father and 'frendes' (that is, in Middle English, 'patrons' or 'kinsfolk'), who ended a promising career in the church by an impulsive marriage and could not fit into any of the various secretarial, administrative, or legal jobs open to a minor cleric. Each detail is plausible. But the assemblage is unverifiable and based on arbitrary selection of such detail as seemed appropriate to the biographer.

Other self-revelations by the Dreamer are interpreted figuratively. Once he tells how, in a dream set within a vision, he is carried off by Fortune and three lovely girls, Concupiscence of the Flesh, Concupiscence of the Eyes, and Pride of Life, to the Land of Longing and Love. Of course Fortune deserts him, and on awakening he reproaches himself for the 'wilde wantownesse', headlong lack of restraint, of his youth. Then from the next vision he awakens almost out of his mind, like a man whose luck is out, and lives a roving beggar's life for many years. Still later, again on awakening, he describes how he is subject to periodic dementia, spells of disturbed mental balance. Near the end of the poem he tells how Old Age first tramples on and then beats him, leaving him bald, deaf, toothless, gouty, and, to the distress of his wife, impotent.

Each of these four carefully located disclosures leads up to a literally represented episode of moral insight and reorientation, of spiritual reassurance for the Dreamer. The first three have been sensitively read as the poet confronting Will with 'a momentary vision of his own life' at its middle point, with biographical implication. But the biographers ignore the fourth: it is, of course, without dignity. Yet it must seem gratuitous unless similarly read, and indeed directly upon its goliardic self-disparagement follows the ultimate spiritual reorientation of the Dreamer.

The Dreamer's confrontation with Conscience and Reason responds to similar reading. It is exquisitely staged: two personifications and a fiction named after the poet, the plot intellectually conceived, the interrogation calling to mind the Statute of Labourers of 1388. Without doubt there is underlying autobiography here, to do with acquiring insight into oneself, and in the design of the C version the episode compresses the poet through his self-projection into the perspective of the most extended set piece of the poem, the confessions of the personified capital sins, which follows directly.

But further biographical inference from this episode can seem hazardous. That Langland was a cleric would be otherwise apparent. Whether he was married is another matter: the names he gives to the wife and daughter of the Dreamer who bears his name are terms of disparagement, and the two may be no more historical than the Dreamer's three companions in the Land of Longing and Love. Above all the poem exhibits resources of mind and attitudes that would be remarkable in the self-confessed failure drifting from one kindly household to another. To write it Langland must have read extensively in French religious and secular literature. He was fluent in legal terminology. He made easy use of the techniques of sermon-building taught in the *artes praedicandi*. His hamartiology is professionally sophisticated, reflecting penitential literature, particularly the manuals for confessors, even to their pastoral tone. He was familiar with such contemporary aids to biblical study as *distinctiones* and concordances. His theology, while not that of Oxford, is embracing and judicious.

The record of a William Rokele tonsured in the diocese of Worcester some time before 1341 redirects attention to disregarded records of an ordained cleric of that name who in 1353 was by papal letter to the bishop of Norwich preferred from a living in Easthorpe, Essex, which he was required to resign, to one in the gift of the abbot of Peterborough. The prominence of Rokeles in Easthorpe, as also in Norwich, suggests that this could be the same man. The circumstances that seven copies of the earliest form of the poem, among them the three with the But coda, are of eastern county provenance, and that Rokeles and Buts appear in long and close association in Norfolk, would support a suggestion that this William Rokele was the poet who called himself Langland. The extent and degree to which already the earliest form of *Piers Plowman* is critical of the ecclesiastical establishment from parson to pope, and particularly of the consistory courts, suggests why it might have seemed to such a man advisable to sign the poem in its second form by another name, and, in the convention of the genre, to give the critic who is his speaking voice a markedly different external personality from his own. Whether or not such identification is accepted, the breadth of his knowledge, and that he had leisure to write, imply either patronage or a relatively secure place, and, moreover, access to books.

Dating the poem The three texts, in effect versions, of *Piers Plowman* cannot be dated in the modern sense. Langland evidently worked at the poem over many years, and the dates of the three occasions in its developing history when the ancestor of each was copied are not recoverable. At best each must have been copied after the latest identifiable topical reference it contains. For the A version that would appear to be after 1370. For B the date is furnished by the actual rising of 1381: the form of the letter of the radical priest John Ball in Walsingham's *Historia Anglicana* echoes this at two points (B 11.195 and 19.355–7). The latest topicality in C appears to be reference to the king's implacable hatred of Gloucester and the Arundels after the dissolution of the Merciless Parliament (C 5.194–6).

Early reception Dissemination of the poem was evidently rapid. Seventeen of the fifty-seven known copies and three fragments could, on palaeographic indication, have been made by 1400. The A version, which may not have gone into circulation during Langland's lifetime, survives in ten copies, at its longest a prologue and eleven sections which the rubrics call *passus* ('steps'); three have all or part of John But's coda. B survives in thirteen copies and a black-letter edition of 1550 printed from a lost manuscript, C in eighteen copies. Another ten copies are composites reflecting availability of exemplars; six of these complete an A version with text from C.

Before 1381 the B version was talked about enough for the name of its eponymous hero Piers Plowman to be taken up by the insurgents as a rallying cry. The author of John Ball's letters seems to have read the poem. In the early fifteenth century it was seen as a dangerous document associated with the spreading Lollard heresy: there is one copy of C from which the name 'Piers Plowman' has been systematically erased. Nevertheless it continued to be read. Seven copies can be associated with monasteries, one with a convent of friars. Among mid-fifteenth-century owners were a bencher of Lincoln's Inn and a speaker of the House of Commons. The poem is mentioned in the wills of a cathedral canon (1396), two rectors of parishes (1400 and 1431), the vicar-choral of York Minster (1409), and a member of the Mercers' Company (1434).

Chaucer knew *Piers Plowman*: the Canterbury 'Prologue' shows unmistakable influence. Soon after 1383 someone with Lollard sympathies wrote an 850 line anti-fraternal *Pierce the Ploughman's Crede*, creditably imitating Langland's metre and style. Not long after 1400 two political poems—one retrospectively justifying Richard's deposition, the other counselling his successor—were composed, enough like *Piers Plowman* for Skeat to think them by Langland. A third, written soon after 1415 commending Henry V's French campaign, is also in Langland's manner. Later verse with 'Plowman' in the title has nothing to do with Langland's poem.

For a couple of decades after Henry VIII's breach with Rome *Piers Plowman* was of immediate topical interest. Within the single year 1550 Robert Crowley issued three impressions of a B copy since lost. Following Bale he called Langland 'Roberte'; but his perception of the poet's double concern, 'he doth most christianlye enstruct the weake and sharply rebuke the obstinate blynde', and his knowledge of the poem were accurate. Like Bale and Leland a few years later, recalling the dissolution of the monasteries he was struck by what seemed fulfilment of its prophecies. A generation later it was crudely labelled a satire by Puttenham (1589) and Meres (1598). Like Webbe, who in 1586 wrote of Piers Plowman as its poet, they may not have been able to read it. In 1622 Henry Peacham attributed it to Lydgate.

Antiquaries of the eighteenth century accepted Bale's attribution and read the poem with more insight. Elizabeth Cooper, in the first volume of the Muses' Library (1737), while deploring the difficulty of its language, and, as she perceived it, the imperfect metre, observed that 'several Passages in it deserve to be immortal'. Thomas Hearne in 1725 believed it had been 'much altered at different times'; Joseph Ritson in 1782 thought it 'highly probable that the author had revised his original work'.

Modern scholarship The first modern edition of *Piers Plowman* was Thomas Whitaker's in 1813, from a copy of the C text. He dismissed Crowley's copy as a bad, late manuscript reflecting revision by the poet. In 1824 Richard Price identified a new form of the poem in the first component of a conjoint AC copy, which he thought might be a 'first draught'. In 1832 Thomas Wright published an edition of a B copy. Reviewing Whitaker in 1834, and in his second edition, he challenged him: his own text was based on the best and oldest manuscript; the differences that characterized Whitaker's copy were made by some other person, who was perhaps induced by his own political sentiments to modify certain passages, and was gradually led on to publish a revision of the whole. In 1866 Walter Skeat, having examined twenty-nine copies of *Piers Plowman*, identified five forms of the poem of which he judged three, each preserved in a distinctive manuscript tradition, to be authorial. In 1867, 1869, and 1873 he published successive editions of these from good copies, and followed in 1886 with a hugely erudite parallel-text edition of the three. He postulated that the shortest form was the earliest, the others successive revisions. It was forty years before his conclusions were questioned.

The first issue to be raised was authorship. In 1906 and at greater length in 1908 J. M. Manly argued that what he read as faults of structure, incoherencies of sense within versions, and discrepancies of sense between versions, reflected a succession of revisers, indeed as many as five. Two years later R. W. Chambers and J. H. G. Grattan launched a defence of the single authorship of the three versions in the course of which they invoked the quality of the texts from which Manly had argued. Soon, in adversarial posture, each party had committed itself to producing texts more authorial than Skeat's. Chambers's successors in his textual project saw this as involving re-examination of Manly's case for multiple authorship, and their judgement that this was not compelling has been fairly generally accepted. But in editing the C version they found that the archetype of the C manuscript tradition must have been made from copy prepared by a 'literary executor' confronted with the poet's uncompleted revision materials.

Skeat's sequence of versions has been twice questioned in a proposition that his A text, the short form of the poem, is an abridgement of B for lay persons, by a redactor (H. Meroney), possibly by Langland (J. Mann); it remains to be seen whether the latter proposition, in its newly argued form, comes to be widely accepted. In 1983 A. G. Rigg and his student Charlotte Brewer published, as the earliest form of the poem, antecedent to A, the first component of a conjoint AC copy (Bodl. Oxf., MS Bodley 851). Another view is that, as Skeat believed, this text is a copy of A written down from imperfect memory and eked out with some 200 lines mainly of pastiche, by someone who had seen the B and C versions. Skeat's view is supported by

the evident perplexity of this writer about the breakdown of Conscience at the end of the poem in B and C.

The study of *Piers Plowman*, where nothing seems to admit of absolute proof, depending accordingly on assessments of likelihood and relative plausibility of argument, is clouded by the bearing upon it of late twentieth-century literary theory and the politicization of literature. Nevertheless interest in the poem is actually growing. A vogue of scepticism about received opinions fails to diminish its power of engagement, and disagreements reflect possessive attitudes to its text, and indeed to its poet, who has been anything but marginalized, quite simply because of the quality of his poem as a memorable archive of human experience by which it has the power to engage notwithstanding the passage of six centuries.

Langland in his time Langland's subject, a culture restive in the beginnings of radical change, is of huge moment. *Piers Plowman* records a *prise de la conscience* affecting an entire society of which at least theoretically the social and economic fabric was subject to elaborately formulated religious directive. The poem is charged with deep spiritual unease, loss of confidence in the order of things, a condition for which no durable and intelligent explanation was possible because the available forms of thinking were inadequate to this. It particularized itself in a sense of discrepancy, a consciousness of oppositions that should not exist, between material and spiritual values, between moral excellence as a philosophically conceived value and the visibly prevalent imperfection of actuality, between knowledge of right conduct and failure in the possessors of that knowledge to realize it, between divine and worldly wisdom, between the *imago dei* in Adam newly created and its distortion by the fall, and, in the deepest theological sense, between the God of justice and the God of love. At the centre of this anxiety was the evident failure of the church's ministers in pastoral care.

Langland's reformist thinking about the shortcomings of the clergy was not innovative. The grand living and avarice of the prelacy, the ignorance, sloth, and vicious living of parish clergy, the diversion of educated clerics to lay office, the decay of monasticism into self-indulgent worldliness, the cynicism of the friars, particularly their venal exploitation of the sacrament of penance, the moral poisoning of the institutional church by ownership of property, the political papacy, were notorious. In many details Langland's anti-clericalism chimes with Wycliffite criticisms, but in fact *Piers Plowman* anticipates these, and many Lollard texts echo its language. Moreover, where the Wycliffites lapsed into heterodoxy, as in respect of the dogmas of penance, purgatory, and prayers to saints for intercession, *Piers Plowman* is orthodox: Langland saw himself within a different church from Wyclif's, not a convocation of the *presciti*, the elect, but one of all Christendom restored by grace to the excellence of the pristine apostolic foundation, 'a state of charity, life in love and righteousness in a single faith and doctrine, a love-knot of righteous conduct and of faith expressed in works, Christians of every kind in firm accord' (C 17.125-9).

The nature and intensity of his concern and his dream

of a regenerate church afford a perception of Langland the man, a reformer but no rebel, who identified the source of moral—or, nowadays, social—evil in the extreme fallibility of individuals rather than in defective institutions. Langland appears the poet in the typification of his ideal of regeneration, his eponymous hero the ploughman Piers, who in the course of the poem grows from a peasant of upright life to an embodiment of divine grace. Similarly the discrepant actuality which made regeneration seem remote, even unlikely, Langland represents in the bearer of the burden of original sin, his hopeless everyman Hawkyn, who regrets not having died immediately after his baptism while still in the state of grace.

Langland from his poem His poem discloses a great deal about Langland the poet. Already the first version, which he was working on in the 1360s, shows him an independent and radical innovator while Chaucer, some time after 1368, was still occupied with imitating French court poetry in *The Book of the Duchess*.

Langland's critical insight was remarkable; in the first place he perceived or sensed that a minor, often trivialized genre could bear a subject of the greatest moment. He had no literary tradition in English to draw upon, and the critical theory of his time, in Latin of course, had not developed concepts and terms for the kind of undertaking evidently in his mind. He had a sense of scale, which showed him that the moral crises of his world had the proportions of what nowadays would be called cosmic drama, and he discerned in them a shape in which to arrange his poem. Above all, whether he knew about the statutory assertion of the primacy of English over French in 1362, he was actively conscious of its serviceability as a poetic medium. And his educated choice of metre, preferring a provincial, unrhymed alliterative measure with an archaic flavour over the only practical alternative, the four-beat rhyming couplet adapted from the French octosyllabic, was inspired.

The defining features of the dream-vision are few and simple: a poet falls asleep, commonly in an idyllic setting; he experiences a dream in which he himself figures; he awakens and puts, or resolves to put, this into verse. Langland perceived that the speaking voice constantly implying identity of poet and dreamer could be used for intensely personal statement. He developed the intrinsic irony of implied identity and its practical denial into a powerful means of engagement: an authorial presence, elusive but inescapable, inhabits *Piers Plowman*. In a very real sense his poem is Langland; he is a factor in its meaning.

Langland also perceived that the genre, in not prescribing internal form, afforded almost entire liberty of organization. He could arrange discourse as appropriate to the immediate topic, on patterned criticisms of estates satire, or manuals for confessors, or biblical exegesis, or structures of theological argument, or explications of dogma, or rhetorical shapes recommended in the manuals for composing sermons. His manner of proceeding was radically unconventional. He moved his Dreamer through not one vision but a career of eight, within two of which he experiences an 'inner' dream. The time-scale and pace vary arbitrarily; progression is only formally serial, governed by contingency of topics of discourse but given the appearance of successions of events. The topics determine the settings. Langland shifts these with smooth plausibility: the road to Westminster and the king's court in judicial session there, a city of London alehouse, the way past Piers's smallholding, vast wildernesses, Piers's walled garden enclosing the Tree of Charity, Jerusalem under Pilate, Calvary, Limbo before the gates of Hell, the battlefield of Christendom ravaged by the renegade Christians of Antichrist's armies, the beleaguered citadel of Unity Holychurch.

Langland based the near surrealist narrative on a system of dominant themes marking the stages of progress, and the actual concept of such progress, in the development of perfected Christian spirituality: the subjection of material to spiritual values; return by confession and contrition to a state of grace; the ascending degrees of moral excellence; submission to God's will as the first means of attaining this; Pauline charity as its highest degree; the redemption as the supreme act of love; the church through its divine foundation the instrument of redeeming grace; its catastrophic state in the actual world.

Langland moves the Dreamer from one theme to the next by way of intricate networks of related doctrinal and moral concern. He uses their complexity to develop in each stage of the journey a sense of intensifying crisis, so that identification of the theme appears as discovery and spiritual reassurance. The reassurance mounts to a climax of comfort in the representation of the redemption as a judicial combat between Christ the knight bachelor in the cognizance of Piers Plowman and the death Satan brought into the world. At its peak, having broken the gates of Hell, Christ proclaims that in the fullness of time he will come as king and 'have the souls of all mankind out of hell' (B 18.371–2). But that is said in a dream; thereafter reassurance seems to fail when Antichrist's forces penetrate Unity Holychurch. Then the best comfort is cold: grace must be forthcoming because that God should withhold it is inconceivable.

Langland developed these crises out of oppositions inherent in the complexities of late medieval moral and eschatological thinking. His paradoxical achievement, one source of his poem's continuing power to engage when the issues it raises have lost their moment, is that his mind, devoutly orthodox, nevertheless identified the drama of such oppositions, between powerful instincts and controls dogmatically imposed by those equally subject to them; between a sense of achievement (the sin of pride) and the theologically conceived virtue of humility; between the free operation of intelligence and the anti-intellectualism of dogmatically based authority.

The style in which Langland realized these insights shows exceptional understanding and command of language. Its first appearance of artless colloquialism belies it. Close scrutiny shows him commanding interest by exploiting the rhetorical potential of syntax, the 'poetry of grammar', in figures of speech, and enforcing meaning with the principal figures of thought, personification of course, and every kind of paronomasia or pun, and a very distinctive ironic incongruous metonymy. His ear for the registers of English in a vocabulary of more than 5000 words appears flawless: he commands effects ranging from the homeliest to the sublime, moving easily from one to another. His personifications come to life from the tones of their representation. He made the alliterative long line, used with little distinction by most of his contemporaries, into a component of style, counterpointing the several stresses, of word and phrase and larger statement, with the recurrent phonemes of the formal alliteration, all to a chime of vowels, in music that conferred engagement on prosaic homilizing and, even, today, on issues long dead.

His poem shows Langland driven by two compulsions. One, externally generated, was to communicate his heightened sense of anxiety by bringing together salient instances of the moral deterioration of his age and his sense of imminent change. This seems to have amounted to a mission: *Anima*, 'Reason', a wholly authoritative personification, says to the Dreamer of the delinquency of pastoral clergy, 'I have a duty to publish this because of the moral issues involved' (B 15.28, 91). The other compulsion was that of the artist whose medium is language, for whom the act of composition is necessary to self-fulfilment. Langland undoubtedly sensed this: another of his personifications, Wit, 'Intelligence', describes 'speche', that is, words in meaningful patterns, as 'the grace of the pentecostal tongues of fire', of Acts 2: 3, 'and God's music-maker, and a celestial diversion' (B 9.103–4).

The two compulsions were both conflicting and inseparable. In Langland's rewriting of the B version it is seldom confidently discernible whether the first impulse to any change had to do with substance or with form and style. Even when this seems possible the effects cannot be separated. Thus a main difference in the last version, greatly augmented criticism of clerical corruption, affords occasion for much stylistic bravura; and the one large structural change, apparently designed to eliminate repetitious treatment of the same topic, is accompanied by substantial additions of differentiating matter.

At least once the poem seems to register Langland's awareness that his writing was a self-gratifying activity because it displaced penitential exercises and prayers for benefactors (B 12.10–27). Nevertheless he continued to write. And however deeply he may have been concerned about salvation, his own or that of fellow Christians, there is no sign in his work of modesty about his poetic gift.

There was, indeed, no ground for any. Langland was by at least a decade the first of the poets who in the second half of the fourteenth century established the standing of English as a poetic medium, and, by their works, initiated the English poetic tradition. In particular his instinctive craftsman's understanding of the quality of English, its communicative and evocative capacity, singles him out. Langland had, it seems, no models; but his example may

have fired Chaucer, who first appears restive against the ascendancy of French culture about 1380 in *The House of Fame*. The ploughman hero whom Langland created and celebrated played a role in great events, as an emotional focus for the English rising of 1381 which failed, and for the Hussite movement of religion in fifteenth-century Bohemia which changed the course of history. But even without such considerations Langland stands, for the quality of his art, with Dante and Chaucer among the supreme poets of the European middle ages.

Langland's use of Middle English is difficult even for scholars of the subject. For others his poem is accessible in two translations which do not disgrace it. One, J. F. Goodridge's *Piers Plowman: William Langland Translated into Modern English* (repr. 1975), reproduces the literal sense of Skeat's B text with respect and, by and large, accurately; the other, E. T. Donaldson's *Will's Vision of Piers Plowman: an Alliterative Verse Translation* (1990), based on the Athlone edition of B, communicates something of the effect of Langland's metre, albeit occasionally at the cost of intelligibility. To best effect the two should be read side by side.

GEORGE KANE

Sources memorandum, *c*.1400, TCD, MS D.4.1 (212), fol. 89*v*; repr. in G. Kane, *Piers Plowman: the evidence for authorship* (1965), 32–3 • Bale, *Index*, 383, 509–10 • Birm. CL, Childe family muniments, bundle 16 [relevant matter cited in G. Kane, *Piers Plowman: the evidence for authorship* (1965), 28–9, n. 6] • W. Langland, *Piers Plowman: the A version*, ed. G. Kane (1960) • W. Langland, *Piers Plowman: the B version*, ed. G. Kane and E. T. Donaldson (1975) • W. Langland, *Piers Plowman: the C version*, ed. G. Russell and G. Kane (1996) • R. W. Chambers, 'Robert or William Langland', *London Medieval Studies*, 1, pt 3 (1948), 430–62 [for 1939] • C. H. Pearson, 'Contemporary literature', *North British Review*, 52 (1870), 211–322, esp. 241–5 • R. McKinley, *A history of British surnames* (1990), 30–31 • E. Rickert, 'John But, messenger and maker', *Modern Philology*, 11 (1913–14), 107–16 • C. Barron, 'William Langland, a London poet', *Chaucer's England: literature in historical context*, ed. B. Hanawalt (1992), 102–4 • O. Cargill, 'The Langland myth', *Publications of the Modern Language Association of America*, 50 (1935), 49ff • E. T. Donaldson, *Piers Plowman: the C-text and its poet*, repr. (1966), 199–226 • L. Clopper, 'Need men labour? Langland's wanderer and the labour ordinances', *Chaucer's England: literature in historical context*, ed. B. Hanawalt (1992), 117–18, 128 • J. Burrow, *Langland's fictions* (1993) • P. Gradon, 'Piers Plowman and the ideology of dissent', *Publications of the British Academy*, 66 (1980), 179–205 • H. Meroney, 'The life and death of Long Wille', *ELH: a Journal of English Literary History*, 17 (1950), 1–35 • J. Mann, 'The power of the alphabet: a reassessment of the relation between the A and B versions of *Piers Plowman*', *Yearbook of Langland Studies*, 8 (1994), 21–50 • A. G. Rigg and C. Brewer, *William Langland Piers Plowman the Z text* (1983) • G. Kane, 'The "Z version" of *Piers Plowman*', *Speculum*, 60 (1985), 910–30 • V. DiMarco, *Piers Plowman: a reference guide* (1982) [bibliography to 1979] • *Yearbook of Langland Studies* (1987–) • L. M. Matheson, text of a lecture delivered 3 May 1997 during the Medieval Congress at Kalamazoo • G. Kane, 'The autobiographical fallacy in Chaucer and Langland studies', *Chaucer and Langland* (1989), 1–14 • G. Kane, 'An open letter to Jill Mann about the sequence of the versions of *Piers Plowman*', *Yearbook of Langland Studies*, 13 (1999), 7–33
Archives Bodl. Oxf., MS Bodley 851 • TCD, MS D. 4.1 (212), fol. 89*v*

Langley, Batty (*bap.* 1696, *d.* 1751), writer on architecture, was baptized at the parish church of Twickenham, Middlesex, on 14 September 1696, the son of Daniel and

Elizabeth Langley. Having been trained in his father's profession as a gardener, he moved into surveying and landscape gardening and was one of the earliest popularizers of the new irregular style advocated by Stephen Switzer in his *Ichnographia rustica* (1718). Langley published a few designs for irregular gardens in his *Practical Geometry* (1726), but his most important work on the subject was *New Principles of Gardening* (1728). This contained a variety of garden plans in what he called the 'arti-natural' style, replete with twisted serpentine paths or meanders that prefigure Hogarth's 'line of beauty' and signalled the emergence of the rococo style in England. Instead of pursuing the subject he knew best, however, he turned to architecture, which was more in demand but in which he had no practical experience and very limited ability.

In 1729 Langley left Twickenham for London; there he had temporary premises at Palladio's Head near Exeter Change in the Strand, from which he published *A Sure Guide to Builders* (1729). He and his second wife were residing in the parish of St John's, Smith Square, in 1732; by 1734 they had moved to Parliament Stairs, Westminster, and in 1738 they joined his younger brother Thomas [*see below*] and other members of the family at Meard's Court, Dean Street, Soho. While at Parliament Stairs, Batty started a school offering lessons in drawing, geometry, architecture, mensuration, mechanics, and garden design, advertised in *Ancient Masonry* (1736); the school continued on firmer footing at Meard's Court, where Batty Langley was assisted by Thomas. He also manufactured and sold a great variety of artificial stone ornaments for buildings, interiors, and gardens at his warehouse, the Hercules' Head, opposite St Paul's Wharf, adjoining the Falcon Stairs on the Bankside in Southwark (advertised in the *Daily Journal*, 10 March 1731). One of these, a medallion of Sir Isaac Newton, was presented by Langley to Sir Hans Sloane and is now in the British Museum.

Although Langley published advertisements (the first, dated 10 September 1736, in his *Ancient Masonry*) offering to make 'Designs for Buildings, Gardens, Parks, etc. in the most grand Taste' and to design and build 'Grottos, Cascades, Caves, Temples, Pavilions, and other Rural Buildings of Pleasure' (B. Langley, *Ancient Masonry*, 1736), he had very little success as a practising architect. His only recorded buildings were 'a curious grotesque temple *in a taste entirely new*, finely decorated within with busts of King William II, George I, and five gentlemen of the Club of Liberty' (J. P. Malcolm, *Londinium redivicum*, 4, 1807, 172), built in 1734 or 1735 for Nathaniel Blackerby, deputy grand master of the grand lodge of freemasons, whose house adjoined his in Parliament Stairs, and a brewhouse for the duke of Kent at Wrest, Bedfordshire, in 1735. He competed unsuccessfully for the Mansion House in 1735 and the new bridge across the Thames at Westminster in 1736–7. Both schemes were engraved and the latter was published with a descriptive text: it aroused a heated public controversy to which Langley contributed three more pamphlets, *A Reply to Mr John James's Review of the Several Pamphlets and Schemes* (1737), *A Survey of Westminster Bridge,*

as 'tis now Sinking into Ruin (1748), and *Observations on a Pamphlet Lately Published … by Charles Marquand* (1749).

Langley's ineffectual entry into the arena of new public building in London was a direct outcome of his examination of James Ralph's *Critical Review of the Publick Buildings … in and about London and Westminster* (1734), which he published in the *Grub Street Journal* from July 1734 to March 1735. Shielded by the pseudonym Hiram, Langley viciously attacked the foreign, Palladian taste imposed by Lord Burlington, praising Gothic architecture (or native Saxon, as he preferred to call it) and the works of Hawksmoor, who was married to the daughter of his patron, Nathaniel Blackerby.

These xenophobic views are clearly related to Langley's freemasonic determination (and obligation) to improve the status of British craftsmen, and ultimately the country's architecture, by providing them with the information they needed on geometry and the classical orders—the fundamentals of architecture—in an easily understandable and affordable form. His output was prodigious, ranging from the largest architectural book of the period, *Ancient Masonry*, an unwieldy folio compendium containing over 450 plates, and issued in parts from 1733 to 1736, to the condensed vicesimo-quarto *The Workman's Golden Rule* (1750).

Langley's best-known work, *Ancient Architecture, Restored, and Improved*, was first published in 1741–2 and reprinted in 1747 under the more explicit title *Gothic architecture, improved by rules and proportions, in many grand designs of columns, doors, windows, chimney-pieces … umbrellos, temples, pavilions &c*. It was a significant departure from the mass of instructive builders' manuals which Langley churned out. An exceptional and original work, it was a pioneering attempt to give Gothic architecture the classical respectability of orders, motivated, as usual, by his interest in English freemasonry and handsomely engraved by his brother Thomas. Its novelty and light-hearted inventiveness, although scoffed at by amateur gothicists such as Horace Walpole and Thomas Gray, were just what many country squires wanted, prompting other architectural writers—William Halfpenny, T. C. Overton, and William Pain in particular—to follow Langley's lead. Among the several works executed from his published designs are doorways at Great Fulford, Devon, and the Ludlow police station; fireplaces at Shobdon church, Herefordshire, and Tissington Hall, Derbyshire; the Gothic temple at Bramham Park, Yorkshire; and the 'show' front of the gate at Castletown, co. Kildare.

Langley was married twice: first, on 5 February 1719, to a Twickenham girl, Anne Smith, at St Anne's Church, Soho. They had four children before her death in June 1726. With his second wife, Catherine, he had ten more children: the first, John, was born in October 1732 and was followed by four sons, to whom he gave the masonic names Euclid, Vitruvius, Archimedes, and Hiram. He died at his house in Meard's Court, Soho on 3 March 1751.

His brother **Thomas Langley** (1702–1751?), engraver, was born at Twickenham in March 1702. He was employed as a sub-turnkey at Newgate prison in 1724, when Batty published his *Accurate Description of Newgate*, but was evidently trained as a gardener and contributed a few pedestrian plans for kitchen gardens to his brother's *New Principles of Gardening* (1728). He was also responsible for drawing the plates for this book, which include, apart from Batty's designs, copies of ruinscapes by Joachim von Sandrart from the brothers' remarkably large and wide-ranging collection of prints and books. By 1738 he was teaching drawing and engraving at Batty's academy in Meard's Court. His best and earliest known engravings were for *Ancient Architecture* (1741–2). This was followed in 1746 by *The Plan and Elevations of Windsor Castle*, drawn by Batty. Most of his engraved work was for his brother's books; only two independent subjects are recorded, both of St Thomas's Church, Salisbury, after drawings by John Lyons. Michael Bryan's *Dictionary of Painters and Engravers* (1895 edn) gives the date of his death as 1751, but this is uncorroborated. EILEEN HARRIS

Sources Colvin, *Archs.*, 597–8 · E. Harris and N. Savage, *British architectural books and writers, 1556–1785* (1990), 262–80 · A. Rowan, 'Batty Langley's Gothic', *Studies in memory of David Talbot Rice*, ed. G. Robertson and G. Henderson (1975), 197–215 · *DNB*
Likenesses J. Carwitham, mezzotint, 1741, BL, BM; repro. in Harris and Savage, *British architectural books and writers*, 262

Langley, Batty. *See* Etchells, Frederick (1886–1973).

Langley, Edmund de. *See* Edmund, first duke of York (1341–1402).

Langley, Francis (1548–1602), businessman and moneylender, was born near Althorpe, Lincolnshire, one of the seven children of Thomas Langley, a tenant farmer, and his wife, Agnes. Orphaned at the age of eight, Francis and his younger brother Thomas were brought up by their uncle John Langley, a prosperous London goldsmith who later became prime warden of his company, sheriff, alderman, and lord mayor (1576–7). A country youth suddenly in a prosperous household in a new urban environment, Francis soon developed a taste for the perquisites of power and affluence. Having been apprenticed to a draper, he was before long censured for taking inappropriate liberties and was finally turned out by his master. By unknown means Langley did secure his freedom in the Company of Drapers many years later, along with a reversion to the office of alnager, or searcher and sealer of woollen cloths, for the City. He took up this office in 1585 and was promptly embroiled in lawsuits charging him with extortion and fraud.

During these same years Langley also learned how the City money market worked and began a long career as a moneylender. He soon became quite adept at using loans to ensnare gullible borrowers, to their loss and his gain. When Thomas Cure defaulted on one such series of loans in the late 1580s, Langley acquired from him the lordship and manor of Paris Garden, a 100 acre tract on the south side of the Thames across from London. Langley built rental tenements on the western edge of this property, and in 1594–5 erected the Swan playhouse on its eastern edge, near the manorial millpond and the Falcon landing stairs on the riverside.

The Swan was the fifth playhouse in the environs of London and the second on the Bankside; it joined its neighbour the Rose, built almost a decade earlier by Philip Henslowe, and the two Shoreditch playhouses, the Theatre and the Curtain, built in 1576–7. (The fifth playhouse, at Newington Butts, was being dismantled even as the Swan was being built.) A year or so after its erection the Swan was described by the Dutch traveller Johannes de Witt as the largest and most magnificent of London's playhouses. But its success as a business venture never matched its opulence, and the reason for this failing lay most probably in the personality of its owner. Langley was an ambitious entrepreneur and speculator, not at all a patron of drama. His chief ambition was to be wealthy and respected; he pursued wealth on many fronts, moneylending chief among them. The ownership of a playhouse was but one move—and by no means the best move—towards his goal.

The Swan playhouse was itself built on speculation. In London at the time there were three or four companies of stage players for every available playhouse, and the imminent prohibition of inn yards as places of performance was soon to make the shortage of playing space even more acute. Langley was certain that if he built a playhouse he would attract companies of players wishing to become tenants, and he appears, initially at least, to have been right. The Swan was occupied almost immediately, though the identity of its occupants during its first year or two is unknown. Speculation has suggested that Shakespeare's company, the Lord Chamberlain's players, may have used the Swan for a time in 1596 as a way of testing out a Bankside location for their own anticipated move from Shoreditch. Indeed, Langley's name is curiously joined with Shakespeare's in a writ of attachment sworn out in 1596 by one William Wayte against 'Willelmum Shakspere Franciscum Langley' and two otherwise unknown women; Wayte claimed that these four people constituted a threat to his life and safety. Nothing further is known about this teasing claim.

The first occupants of the Swan of whom we have any record, the earl of Pembroke's players, became a topic of controversy in July and August 1597 for having performed a play called *The Isle of Dogs* that was reported to the privy council as being seditious. The charge resulted in the arrests of Gabriel Spencer, Robert Shaa, and Ben Jonson—all players in the Pembroke company, and one a playwright as well—and in the hasty flight from London of Thomas Nashe, one of the play's authors. After a few weeks the arrested players were released and the matter was quietly dropped, suggesting that the charge of sedition had been found baseless. As the play itself has not survived, there is only circumstantial evidence and the testimony of self-interested witnesses to go on. But there is strong evidence that during 1596 and 1597 Langley himself had fallen into disfavour and had incurred the enmity of Robert Cecil. Given those circumstances, the Swan was perceived from that point onwards as an undesirable playhouse, and its tenants tended more towards the transient than the stable. It was used by the Masters of Defence for exhibitions of sword-fighting from time to time and was the site of Richard Vennar's fraudulent non-performance of *England's Joy* in 1602. Before long the Swan fell into decay.

Robert Cecil's animosity towards Langley had begun when Langley became implicated in the theft of an enormous diamond from a Spanish carrack, the *Madre de Dios*, captured by English seamen in 1592. Most of the ship's cargo was plundered by its captors, and the diamond, a special prize, soon came into Langley's hands. Cecil pursued Langley for many years in an effort to recover the stone in the queen's name (the harassment at the Swan over *The Isle of Dogs* in 1597 may have been part of this pursuit). But Langley managed somehow to stay just beyond Cecil's grasp, though his evasiveness contributed to his eventual impoverishment and also destroyed the career of his brother-in-law Anthony Ashley, one of the clerks of the privy council.

Langley overreached himself in other arenas as well. After fourteen years of disgraceful performance in his post as City alnager, marked by numerous lawsuits, he was ejected from the office in 1599 by the court of aldermen. By the following year his financial adventurism had brought him into serious debt, and he was forced to sell the manor of Paris Garden, with its playhouse, to Hugh Browker, a perennially hostile neighbour.

Langley was by now in his early fifties and on the verge of bankruptcy. His final failed adventure was in Cardiganshire, where he nourished hopes of extracting silver from an abandoned lead mine which he believed he had acquired. But he was ill, and his old shrewdness was gone. Sir Lewis Lewkenor got the better of him in this scheme, and at the age of fifty-four Langley died penniless, leaving his widow, Jane, *née* Ashley (d. after 1608), with six children and a swarm of lawsuits to contend with. He was buried on 9 July 1602 in St Saviour's Church (now Southwark Cathedral).   WILLIAM INGRAM

Sources W. Ingram, *A London life in the brazen age: Francis Langley, 1548–1602* (1978) · wills, 1531–56, Lincs. Arch., Stow wills, 4 [Thomas Langley] · PRO, STAC 5/A.8/4 · parish register, St Saviour's, Southwark, 9 July 1602 [burial]
Archives CLRO · Drapers' Company, London · GL · Goldsmiths' Company, London · LMA · PRO
Wealth at death bankrupt: Ingram, *A London life*

Langley, Sir Geoffrey (c.1200–1274), administrator and landowner, was the son of Walter de Langley, minor knight with property at Siddington in Gloucestershire and at Pinley near Coventry, and his wife, Emma de Lacy (d. in or before 1222). He was probably of age by 1222, which suggests a date of birth about 1200, and first appears in royal service in 1233–4 as constable of St Briavels, Gloucestershire. He joined the royal curia, and was appointed knight-deputy to the earl marshal and marshal of the household.

The Gascon campaign of 1242–3 proved a turning point in Langley's career. On his return he was given custody of the honour of Arundel. From late 1244 to early 1250 he was associated with the general forest eyre conducted under the headship of Robert Passelewe (d. 1252). On 4 March 1250 he was made chief justice of the forest on both sides of the Trent, an office which he exercised for two and a half years until 25 October 1252. As a forest justice he earned some notoriety. According to Matthew Paris, Langley had gained a reputation for parsimony while marshal of the household. Now he was to be particularly zealous in the interests of the king. Langley's northern eyre was a very lucrative one, and undoubtedly caused murmurings.

By 1252 Langley was at the height of his power and high in royal esteem, being a particular favourite of the queen. A member of the council, he functioned as a guardian of the king's young daughter, Margaret, queen of Scots, during 1252–3, but made himself unpopular in Scotland and was removed. Then in March 1254 he took responsibility for the English and Welsh lands of the young Prince Edward. This proved to be a disaster, however, for he provoked the Welsh rising of November 1256. Paris says that he conducted himself here in a typically high-handed manner, while the Dunstable annalist writes of him as trying to bring Wales under English law, and ordering the introduction into that country of shires and hundreds, while boasting before the king and queen that he had the Welsh in the palm of his hand. Out of favour with the king, he was eventually pardoned on 14 February 1258. In 1262 he was one of the auditors investigating the accounts of Prince Edward's bailiffs. He was unpopular, however, with the opposition baronage, and was among those royalists whose lands were pillaged in the spring of 1263.

Although Langley inherited some property, and acquired other estates through marriage, it was his service to the crown that raised his family's fortunes. He added to the estates received directly from the crown by acquiring the estates of landowners indebted to Jewish moneylenders. He paid considerable attention to the improvement and consolidation of his estates. At its height his income from land must have been at least £200 per annum. In addition he was able to acquire an heiress and her estates for his eldest son, Walter. Langley was married twice, first to Christine, of unknown parentage, and second to Matilda, daughter of Robert of Brightwell. He died in 1274, by 22 September; he was buried, as were Matilda and his son Walter, in the church of the Franciscans in Coventry. The division of his estates between the two branches of his family, based in Warwickshire and Gloucestershire respectively, helps to explain why the Langleys failed to rise further, as Geoffrey's own career might well have suggested.   PETER COSS, *rev.*

Sources P. R. Coss, ed., *The Langley cartulary*, Dugdale Society, 32 (1980) · Paris, *Chron.*, vols. 4–5 · *Ann. mon.*, vol. 3 · P. R. Coss, *The Langley family and its cartulary: a study in late medieval 'gentry'*, Dugdale Society, 22 (1974) · M. Howell, *Eleanor of Provence: queenship in thirteenth-century England* (1998)
Archives BL, cartulary, Harley MS 7
Wealth at death £200 p.a. (minimum): Coss, ed., *Langley cartulary*

Langley, Sir Geoffrey (d. 1297), diplomat, was born into a Warwickshire knightly family, the son of Sir Geoffrey *Langley (c.1200–1274), who was Prince Edward's steward in north Wales in the 1250s, and his unidentified first wife, whose name was Christine. The younger Geoffrey is first recorded some time between 1252 and 1254, in the entourage of William de Ferrers, fifth earl of Derby. When William's successor, Robert de Ferrers, forfeited the earldom in 1266, Langley probably transferred his loyalties to Edward's brother Edmund, later earl of Lancaster, to whom Henry III granted the Ferrers lands and titles. In 1271 he was a member of the contingent which accompanied Edmund on a crusade to the Holy Land. It may have been this experience in the east that recommended Langley to Edward I as a suitable choice when, two decades later, he needed an envoy to send to the court of Arghun, the Mongol ruler of Persia, which the Mongols had conquered in the 1250s.

Arghun, a great-great-grandson of Genghis Khan, and the ilkhan (a title perhaps best translated as 'subject khan') of Persia (r. 1284–91), was an enthusiastic advocate of alliance with western Christendom against the mameluke rulers of Egypt and Syria. This policy—that Islam might be crushed by a pincer movement from east and west simultaneously—also had substantial support in western Europe and the Latin east, even though nothing much ever came of it in practice. In the twelfth century expectations had centred on Prester John, the mythical Christian priest–king of remotest Asia. Now it was the turn of the Mongols, who even if not exactly Christian were, it was thought, at any rate the enemies of Islam.

Arghun had sent the Nestorian Christian monk Rabban Sauma as his ambassador to Europe in 1287, and the envoy had been received by King Edward in Gascony. Another embassy from Persia, led by Buscarello Ghisolfi, a Genoese in Mongol service, reached London in January 1290, as Edward I's wardrobe accounts testify. Edward's response was to send an embassy to Persia, headed by Langley. This embassy, of which a detailed account of the expenses has survived in the Public Record Office, left England in 1291. Langley's entourage included two esquires (one of whom, Nicholas of Chartres, kept the accounts of the embassy), a chaplain, four men-at-arms, a trumpeter, a barber, three falconers (to look after some English gerfalcons, for which Arghun had specially asked), and others. Langley was fortunate in being able to travel in the company of the experienced Buscarello, who was returning to Persia.

Langley travelled to Genoa, and from there by sea to Trebizond on the Black Sea, where he arrived in April 1292. From Trebizond he proceeded overland via Erzurum to the Mongol capital, Tabriz, in the north-western Persian province of Azerbaijan. By this time Arghun had died and had been succeeded by his much less energetic brother, Geikhatu (r. 1291–5). There is no precise evidence as to where, or even whether, Geikhatu personally received Langley, but his reception appears to have been cordial, in that King Edward's gift of English gerfalcons was reciprocated by the ilkhan: a Persian leopard came back to the West with Langley, to end its days in England. But Langley brought with him no treaty of alliance: the death of Arghun had, for the time being, ended any prospect of joint operations against the mamelukes.

Langley left Tabriz in September 1292, returning to Trebizond by the same route as on the outward journey. Leaving Trebizond by sea again, he and his companions travelled via Constantinople and Otranto, reaching Genoa in January 1293. There is no record of his return to England, but he was among the knights summoned to accompany the king to Gascony in 1294. After his brief moment of prominence on the international stage Langley retired to comparative obscurity among the Warwickshire gentry. He had married a woman named Emma, and when he died in 1297 his heir was his son Edmund.   D. O. MORGAN

Sources L. Lockhart, 'The relations between Edward I and Edward II of England and the Mongol īl-khāns of Persia', *Iran*, 6 (1968), 23–31 • M. Prestwich, *Edward I* (1988) • T. H. Turner, 'Unpublished notices of the times of Edward I, especially of his relations with the Moghul sovereigns of Persia', *Archaeological Journal*, 8 (1851), 45–51 • A. A. M. Bryer, 'Edward I and the Mongols', *History Today*, 14 (1964), 696–704 • J. A. Boyle, 'The il-khans of Persia and the princes of Europe', *Central Asiatic Journal*, 20 (1976), 25–40 • C. Desimoni, 'I conti dell'ambasciate al chan di Persia nel MCCXII', *Atti della Società Ligure di Storia Patria*, 12 (1879), 540–698 • P. R. Coss, 'Sir Geoffrey de Langley and the crisis of the knightly class in thirteenth-century England', *Past and Present*, 68 (1975), 3–37 • P. R. Coss, *The Langley family and its cartulary: a study in late medieval 'gentry'*, Dugdale Society, 22 (1974) • P. R. Coss, ed., *The Langley cartulary*, Dugdale Society, 32 (1980) • W. Dugdale, *The antiquities of Warwickshire illustrated*, rev. W. Thomas, 2nd edn, 2 vols. (1730)
Archives PRO, 'Expenses of the embassy of G. de Langele to Tartary'

Langley, Henry (1610/11–1679), nonconformist minister, was the son of Thomas Langley, a shoemaker of Abingdon, Berkshire, and attended John Roysse's Free Grammar School in the town. On 6 November 1629, aged eighteen, he matriculated as one of several scholars of Abingdon from Pembroke College, Oxford. He graduated BA on 11 June 1632, proceeded MA on 30 April 1635, and was elected to a fellowship. On 16 August 1640 he was named as a lecturer at St Martin's Church, Carfax, Oxford, but appears to have stayed only about a year. On 16 April 1642 the Commons ordered that he be recommended to the parishioners of Watlington, Oxfordshire, 'to be their lecturer to preach there every Saturday in the afternoon, and likewise every Lord's day', and that Price the vicar allow him to do this 'without any lett or interruption' (*JHC*, 2, 530). On 20 June 1643 the rectory of St Mary Newington was sequestered to Langley from John Meggs. By a parliamentary order of 10 September 1646 he was named one of seven ministers authorized to preach in any Oxford church, with a view to winning support for the planned reformation of the university.

Following the death on 10 July 1647 of Thomas Clayton, master of Pembroke, the fellows hurried to elect (three days later) Henry Wightwick, but parliament vetoed the choice. Abingdon inhabitants, noting the connections between their school and the college, petitioned that Langley be chosen, and on 26 August 1647 order was given for his appointment. His standing with the new authorities was registered in the university by his nomination on 30 September as one of Pembroke's two delegates to consult with the parliamentary visitors. They confirmed his appointment as master on 8 October, and next day 'thrust out Mr Whitewicke from his Headship by virtue of an Instrument stuck up in the Common Hall', which proclaimed Langley as the rightly constituted incumbent. In accordance with a parliamentary order of 2 March 1648, Langley was appointed on 12 April by the visitors to a canonry of Christ Church in the place of the extruded George Morley. On the same day he proceeded BD, and in May was one of the twenty delegates appointed by the proctors to be answerable for the conduct of the affairs of the university. On 5 July 1648 he was made an examiner of candidates for fellowships and scholarships and on 18 December 1649 was awarded a doctorate of divinity.

During the 1650s Langley was an energetic supporter of godly reform in his college, strongly backing vice-chancellor John Owen's campaign against anti-trinitarianism. He was friendly with Samuel Hartlib and Tobias Garbrand, principal of Gloucester Hall. Langley held both his position as master of Pembroke and his canonry at Christ Church until the Restoration, when he unsuccessfully petitioned Charles II to confirm him in the latter. His leaving the college did not proceed smoothly. Wightwick complained to the commissioners on 11 October 1660 that Langley retained possession of the master's lodgings and he was ordered to vacate them within four days; the final payment to him from the college accounts was dated 19 December. On 13 May 1662 the college petitioned in chancery that he had stolen from it documents and plate, and had failed to account for donations: he denied the charges, claiming that his proposals for internal arbitration had been rejected.

Now living at Tubney near Abingdon, Langley 'instructed the sons of dissenting brethren in academical learning' including logic and philosophy (Wood, *Ath. Oxon.: Fasti*, 2.158). In 1669 he was reported to be preaching at Cogges and Tubney—'a dangerous person keeps conventicles there' (*Calamy rev.*, 314). He was granted a licence at his house in Tubney on 16 April 1672. Wood records that also at this time Langley and other former members of the university held meetings in Thames Street in Oxford. In a letter of 18 June 1672 John Penny of Christ Church wrote that, in a sermon in the city the previous Sunday, Langley had:

> held forth two houres upon the Spirit of which subject they say he preacht in the late times neare two yeares, and they say he was all the while so unintelligible that from that time to this, no body could tell whence the sound thereof came; or whither tis goeing. (*Calamy rev.*, 314)

When Langley made his will on 16 June 1679 he was already ill. He left 10s. to each of his children, Henry Langley, Elizabeth Boyland, and Elliot Langley, and the lease of his house, held from Magdalen Hall, Oxford, to his wife, Elizabeth, named executor. He died on 10 September 1679 and was buried in St Helen's Church, Abingdon.

STEPHEN WRIGHT

Sources *Calamy rev.*, 314 • D. Macleane, *A history of Pembroke College, Oxford*, OHS, 33 (1897) • *Hist. U. Oxf.* 4: *17th-cent. Oxf.*, 721, 752n., 754, 764, 859 • Wood, *Ath. Oxon.*, new edn, 4.10, 592 • Wood, *Ath. Oxon.: Fasti* (1820), 113, 157–8 • M. Burrows, ed., *The register of the visitors of the University of Oxford, from AD 1647 to AD 1658*, CS, new ser., 29 (1881) • A. E. Preston, *The church and parish of St Nicholas, Abingdon: the early grammar school to end of sixteenth century* (1929); repr. (1971) • *Fasti Angl., 1541–1857*, [Bristol] • *JHL*, 8 (1645–6) • *JHL*, 9 (1646–7) • *JHL*, 10 (1647–8) • *JHC*, 2 (1640–42) • *JHC*, 5 (1646–8) • Foster, *Alum. Oxon.* • will, Berks. RO, D/A1/94/87
Archives University of Sheffield Library, letters • Yale U., Beinecke L., commonplace book
Wealth at death see will, Berks. RO, D/A1/94/87

Langley, John (d. 1657), headmaster, was born in or near Banbury, Oxfordshire, and probably attended the grammar school there; his parents' names are unknown. In 1612 he was admitted to Magdalen Hall, Oxford, as a commoner, subscribing on 23 April 1613; he graduated BA on 5 July 1616 and proceeded MA on 24 April 1619. In 1616 Langley had been appointed usher of the King's School, Gloucester, and on 9 March 1618 was promoted to the headmastership. Although, as later became apparent, he was opposed to the prevailing regime of William Laud as dean of Gloucester, he was well regarded by the subsequent dean, Thomas Winniffe, and his chapter. In December 1627 Langley resigned to move to a better-paid post at Dorchester, but the Gloucester city fathers offered him an additional £10 p.a. to stay, and with the further encouragement of the cathedral authorities he was reinstated on 11 August 1628. It is possible that he had objected to teaching the choristers in the King's School, since on his return other arrangements were made for them. When Sir Nathaniel Brent visited the cathedral on behalf of Archbishop Laud in June 1635 Langley was threatened with suspension for refusing the oath; sentence was deferred because although he was (rightly) suspected of puritanism he was recognized as 'a very good schoolmaster' (*CSP dom.*, 1635, 40). Langley was nevertheless replaced by November. On 19 September 1639 the city council, who had found the master of the Crypt School, which they controlled, to be generally negligent and to have sent few scholars to the universities, appointed Langley usher and teacher of Greek, as he had 'given good testimony in teaching and instructing many of the burgesses sonnes of this citye and others and inabling them for the universities' (Glos. RO, GBR 3/2, 132). On 27 September they withdrew the appointment as usher, but confirmed Langley as teacher of Greek and 'other learninge' (ibid., 134). But when in 1640 there was a prospect of his becoming headmaster of this school, the king directly intervened to forbid it. A privy seal letter of 22 April, undoubtedly framed by Laud, condemned the city's 'attempt to bring in ... a man factiously sett agaynst the government of the Church of England', who had 'deserted' the dean and chapter's school after refusing to conform (ibid., 148).

But Langley's connections soon helped him to a better prize; Winniffe was now dean of St Paul's, and on 30 December 1640 he and the earl of Middlesex nominated Langley for the high mastership of St Paul's School. Among three short-listed candidates Langley was judged 'extraordinary', and he was duly elected on 7 January 1641 (McDonnell, 171). He went on to achieve great renown both within his school and without. On 20 June 1643 the Commons committed to him (and his old adversary Brent) the licensing of books in philosophy, history, morality, and the arts; the stationers would claim in 1648 that his school work impeded performance of these duties. He himself published during this period *Totius rhetoricae adumbratio* (1644), for his scholars at St Paul's, and *Gemitus columbae* (also 1644). The same year he provided evidence at the trial of Laud, instancing ritualistic practices introduced into Gloucester Cathedral during his decanate. He also alleged that, as primate, Laud had persecuted the Gloucester lecturer John Workman (whose brother Giles had been Langley's under-master at the King's School).

On 25 December 1644 Langley preached before the Commons in St Margaret's, Westminster. He retained a connection with Gloucester, being in 1656 appointed one of the collectors for repair of the cathedral. He died at his house in London on 13 September 1657 and was buried on the 21st at the Mercers' chapel, Cheapside, when Edward Reynolds preached in praise of his great and diverse learning. Langley left £30 to the Mercers' Company, £20 to the city of Gloucester to provide short-term loans to young tradesmen, £10 to Pembroke College, Oxford, to rebuild its derelict premises, and more than thirty individual bequests to London ministers and merchants. He was unmarried, and of close family his will mentions only his nieces Mary and Ann. He is said to have had 'a very awfull presence and speech' (Wood, *Ath. Oxon.*, 3.435) which, however, softened on acquaintance.   C. S. KNIGHTON

Sources VCH Gloucestershire, 2.325–6 · D. Robertson, *The King's School, Gloucester* (1974), 44–8 · M. McDonnell, ed., *The registers of St Paul's School, 1509–1748* (privately printed, London, 1977), 170–72 · CSP dom., 1635, 40; 1644, 4 · JHC, 3 (1642–4), 138; 4 (1644–6), 1 · JHL, 6 (1643–4), 377 · Wood, *Ath. Oxon.*, new edn, 3.434–6 · W. Prynne, *Canterburies doome, or, The first part of a compleat history of the commitment, charge, tryall, condemnation, execution of William Laud, late arch-bishop of Canterbury* (1646), 75 · Foster, *Alum. Oxon.* · *Seventh report*, HMC, 6 (1879), 67 · *The obituary of Richard Smyth … being a catalogue of all such persons as he knew in their life*, ed. H. Ellis, CS, 44 (1849), 45 · J. R. S. Whiting, *The King's School, Gloucester, 1541–1991* (1990), 15–17 · PRO, PROB 11/267, fol. 256 · Glos. RO, GBR 3/2, 132, 134, 148
Archives Bodl. Oxf., notes and transcripts from his collections
Wealth at death £198—specified cash bequests: will, PRO, PROB 11/267, fol. 256

Langley, John Newport (1852–1925), physiologist, was born at Newbury, Berkshire, on 2 November 1852, the second son of John Langley, schoolteacher, and his wife, Mary, eldest daughter of Richard Groom. He was educated first at home, and later at Exeter grammar school. In October 1871 he proceeded with a sizarship to St John's College, Cambridge, where he was subsequently awarded a scholarship. He was reading mathematics and history with a view to entering the Indian Civil Service, but he changed course and began to read for the natural sciences tripos, in which he gained a first-class degree in 1874. In the following year he was appointed a demonstrator. In 1877 he was elected to an open fellowship at Trinity College, and in the same year spent several months in Heidelberg, studying the salivary secretion of the cat. In 1878 he received his MA from Cambridge and a ScD in 1896.

At Michael Foster's suggestion, Langley began experimental research even before taking his degree. The action of the new drug pilocarpine as tested on the frog's heart

John Newport Langley (1852–1925), by unknown photographer

formed Langley's earliest subject of research; the work was published in the newly started *Papers from the Cambridge Physiological Laboratory*. The course of this work led Langley to the study of secretion, and he found that the new drug exerted a specific influence on the secretory process in mammalian salivary glands. This led to his study of secretion in general, which he followed with an unparalleled precision. He soon showed that, contrary to the accepted view, based on statements made by Rudolf Heidenhain of Breslau, the secretory granules accumulate when the gland is not secreting, and when secretion ensues the granules are discharged from the cell. He also conducted microscopical examination of the gland cells which were under experiment, checking his microscopical observations of the 'fixed' and 'stained' gland cells by observations on the living cells, sampled from the glands at various stages of experiment.

Langley also investigated the nervous influence exerted on the gland cells; he distinguished between the 'loaded' and the 'exhausted' states of the gland. He showed that the belief in the existence of specific 'trophic' nerve fibres for the salivary glands rested on evidence which could be explained by vascular effects concurrently produced in the local blood circulation. Besides the fundamental information contained in his papers, the form and style of these papers were generally recognized as setting an exceptionally high standard of effectiveness, clearness, and accuracy, free from speculative argument.

Langley's systematic exploration of the secretory process occupied the first fifteen years of his career in research. In 1883 he was appointed a lecturer in natural science at Trinity College, and university lecturer in physiology, confirming, both in college and university, his position as assistant to Foster, who in 1883 had been appointed professor of physiology. In 1900 Langley became deputy to Foster, and in 1903 succeeded him in the professorship.

The climax of Langley's achievement as an investigator was perhaps his research (1890–1906) into the sympathetic nervous system. Proceeding from the discovery, made by himself and his pupil, W. Lee Dickinson, in 1889, that nicotine paralyses the nerve cells in sympathetic ganglia, Langley used that procedure as a method, and subjected the whole of the sympathetic ganglionic system to exhaustive analysis, determining for each ganglion from where its paths come and to where they lead. The belief had been that sympathetic nerve paths vary greatly, and differ greatly from each other, some having one and some having many nerve cells intercalated along their course. Langley made it clear that in the sympathetic system, from its spinal to its distal goal, whether in muscle, gland, or other peripheral tissue, only one nerve cell is interposed in each and every path. Each ganglion forms the one and only relay station for the fibres interrupted there. Langley showed further that the sympathetic ganglia belong entirely to efferent paths. It became clear, therefore, that the pain accompanying visceral disease is not due to the ganglia, though they are predominantly visceral. It had been thought that the true reflex actions could be obtained from sympathetic ganglia, but Langley showed that spread of conduction along merely branched nerve fibres (axon reflexes) would explain the seemingly reflex phenomena. He furnished an excellent summary of this work in 1901 for the second volume of E. A. Sharpey-Schafer's *Advanced Text-Book of Physiology*.

In 1907 Langley, having noticed that adrenaline stimulates the cells of the sympathetic system after degeneration of the spinal fibre which conveys to them their normal stimulation, found that nicotine produces the same effect. Nicotine causes also a local contraction of muscle, which has its seat at the point of nerve entry into the muscle fibre; this local contraction is prevented by curare. Langley inferred from observations of this kind that the mechanism of excitation of one cell by another consists in a locally developed receptive substance, which sensitizes the cell for the stimulus which it receives from the cell to which it reacts. The cells of different tissues he supposed to have different and specific receptive substances.

This work was interrupted in 1914 by the outbreak of the First World War, which depleted the new physiological laboratory, completed earlier that year, of staff and students. Langley therefore directed the energies of its remaining workers into channels of direct value for wartime medicine. He collaborated with foreign visitors, mainly Japanese, to his laboratory, in investigations especially connected with the trophic changes in muscle and nerve following traumatic injury and during recovery.

When the war was over, Langley quickly returned to his former routine of research and teaching, working chiefly on various aspects of vasomotor action. The results of his later research were collected in his *Autonomic Nervous System* (1921).

From 1894 until his death, Langley both owned and edited the *Journal of Physiology*. Founded in 1876 by Foster, who retained the official title of editor until his death in 1907, the journal had an established reputation but had also incurred a sizable debt. Langley, having paid the debt and bought the unsold stock, ensured that every paper issued in the journal not only made a solid contribution to knowledge, but maintained the desired standard of form and style with succinctness, lucidity, and a minimum of speculative discussion. He would, where he judged fit, almost entirely recast a paper, his strictness often annoying, sometimes alienating, his collaborators. Many, however, came ultimately to recognize his assistance with gratitude. He declined any published acknowledgement of this labour. In the course of time the international scientific world came to recognize that by his actions he was setting a pattern in the presentation of scientific work.

Langley was elected a fellow of the Royal Society in 1883, was vice-president in 1904–5, delivered the Croonian lecture in 1906, and received the royal medal of the society in 1892. He was president of the Neurological Society of Great Britain in 1893, and of the physiological section of the British Association in 1899. He was awarded the Baly medal of the Royal College of Physicians in 1903, and the Andreas Retzius medal of the Swedish Society of Physicians in 1912. Among the other honours which he received were honorary degrees from several British and foreign universities.

Langley married in 1902 Vera Kathleen (d. 1932), daughter of Frederick G. Forsythe-Grant, of Ecclesgreig, Kincardineshire; they had one daughter. From his marriage onward he lived at Hedgerley Lodge, Madingley Road, just outside Cambridge. All his life he had a keen interest in outdoor games, especially rowing and lawn tennis, and in later life he was a keen gardener. He had also been a first-rate skater. He was of middle stature, with steel-blue eyes. He showed considerable power as a hypnotist, when, for a time, the subject of mesmerism had engaged his attention. Langley died suddenly, from an attack of pneumonia, at his home, on 5 November 1925.

C. S. SHERRINGTON, *rev.* CAROLINE OVERY

Sources G. L. Geison, 'Langley, John Newport', *DSB* · W. M. Fletcher, 'John Newport Langley. In memoriam', *Journal of Physiology*, 61 (1926), 1–27 · *The Times* (6 Nov 1925) · W. M. F., *PRS*, 101B (1927), xxxiii–xli · personal knowledge (1937) · *CGPLA Eng. & Wales* (1925)
Archives CAC Cam., corresp. with A. V. Hill · Wellcome L., corresp. with Sir Edward Sharpey-Schafer
Likenesses photograph, U. Cam., department of physiology [*see illus.*] · photogravure, Wellcome L. · portrait, repro. in *PRS* · portrait, repro. in Fletcher, 'John Newport Langley'
Wealth at death £11,235 17s. 2d.: probate, 24 Dec 1925, *CGPLA Eng. & Wales*

Langley, Thomas (c.1360–1437), administrator and bishop of Durham, was born about 1360—in 1433 he described himself as being in his seventies. He was the son of William and Alice Langley of Middleton, Lancashire. His patron was James Radcliffe of Radcliffe, member of a leading Lancashire family, from whose service he transferred to that of John of Gaunt, duke of Lancaster. He trained in the palatinate administration of Lancashire, and was rewarded with a prebend at St Martin's-le-Grand in 1395 and a canonry at St Asaph in 1397; in 1398 he was nominated an executor of Gaunt's will. He was subsequently associated with the establishment of Manchester collegiate church in 1421, and founded a chantry school at

Middleton. With the accession of Gaunt's son as Henry IV, Langley served him as secretary (1399–1401), went on the Scottish expedition of 1400, and in 1401 was appointed keeper of the privy seal. Meantime he had obtained the archdeaconry of Norfolk in October 1399, prebends at York Minster and at Bridgnorth in 1401, and, after a dispute over papal provisions, the deanery of York in July 1403. In October 1404 he was recommended by the king as bishop of London and elected, but this was overridden by Pope Innocent VII (r. 1404–6) in favour of Roger Walden (d. 1406). On 2 March 1405 the king appointed him chancellor of England, and secured his election to succeed the executed Archbishop Richard Scrope at York, a suggestion rejected by the pope. On 14 May 1406 Langley received a papal provision to the see of Durham, although his formal election was contested by Thomas Weston, archdeacon of Durham. He was enthroned on 4 September. He resigned the chancellorship on 30 January 1407, but was appointed a member of the king's council at an annual salary of 200 marks (£133 6s. 8d.).

Continuing in royal service Langley was initially active in diplomacy with France. Later in December 1408, at the northern convocation at York, he was appointed to lead the northern delegation to the general council at Pisa to end the great schism in the papacy. He reached Pisa on 7 May 1409 and returned to England in October. On 2 May 1410 Langley was appointed to the newly reconstituted king's council, but rarely attended, probably because he regarded it as unduly influenced by Prince Henry, though he was also heavily engaged in northern affairs at the time. In the summer of 1411 Langley and Bishop Robert Hallum of Salisbury were chosen by Pope John XXIII (r. 1410–15) as cardinals, but their nominations were overruled by Henry IV. That autumn the king resumed control of government and appointed a new council, including Langley, and the latter remained in attendance until the death of the king, who nominated him as an executor. Under Henry V, Langley continued on the council, and was a chief adviser on foreign policy. In January 1414 he headed the commission which concluded a general truce with France to last one year, and then was joint leader of the embassies to Paris of August–September 1414 and March 1415 which failed to avert Anglo-French hostilities. When it was decided to renew war with France, Langley was appointed to the lieutenancy council of John, duke of Bedford. In July 1415, before leaving for France, Henry V made his will, appointing Langley as one of his trustees and an executor. And when Henry V again embarked for France, Langley was appointed chancellor, on 23 July 1417, and, under Bedford, led the council which administered England when the king was abroad. One consequence of Henry's absence was a substantial increase in the amount of judicial work referred to Langley as chancellor, in his capacity as keeper of the king's (public) conscience. Following the death of Henry V on 31 August 1422, Langley resigned the great seal, but was reappointed as chancellor by parliament on 16 November. He finally surrendered the great seal on 16 July 1424, although he continued, with decreasing frequency, to came to meetings of council

until excused further attendance on the grounds of age in December 1433.

With such experience in royal administration, it is unsurprising that Langley undertook reorganization of the palatinate powers of the bishops of Durham, using former colleagues from the duchy of Lancaster as receivers-general and treasurers, stewards, and members of his council. He introduced the practice of separate enrolment in his chancery of letters patent and letters close, although chance survivals from other sources indicate that many warrants were not registered. He upheld the claim of his palatinate to immunity from parliamentary taxation by agreeing to pay a sum above that likely to be assessed. There was also an increase in the amount of litigation conducted in his chancery. The actions brought there invariably involved the bishop, a practice parallel to, and no doubt derived from, that of the common-law side of the royal chancery. The revenues of the bishop have been estimated at over £4000 a year, making Langley one of the five wealthiest men in England, in terms of income. Rents slowly declined during his episcopate, in common with elsewhere in England at that date. In 1418 Langley attempted a review of his resources and commissioned a survey of his estates and a register of all inquisitions undertaken since the second quarter of the previous century. Rents of mines and forests yielded about £250 a year; lead sold between 1428 and 1431 yielded £858. It is impossible to be more precise as to revenue, because no account of a receiver-general, Langley's chief financial officer, has survived.

Langley was responsible for substantial building operations at his castles of Norham and Durham, a new gaol at Durham, and gates to both bridges there, alterations to Durham Cathedral, and rebuilding of his manor house at Stockton and the west gate of his palace at Howden in the East Riding of Yorkshire. He loaned substantial sums of money to Henry V, and once to the abbey of St Werburgh, Chester. In 1433, probably at the instigation of Sir William Eure of Witton-le-Wear, co. Durham, a wealthy but aggressive and discontented landowner in the north-east, a comprehensive attack on Langley's palatine administration was made by a royal commission into franchisal abuses in northern England. With his defence strengthened by evidence from the cathedral muniments, Langley went to London and in June 1433 obtained confirmation from the king's chancery of charters recognizing his palatinate powers. The matter was heard in parliament, and the king's council found in Langley's favour.

In view of the proximity of his diocese to the Anglo-Scottish border, it is unsurprising that Langley was employed on various occasions as ambassador to negotiate truces with the Scots, and in 1416 and 1423–4 the release from captivity of James I of Scotland. Between 1424 and 1432, moreover, Langley was at least titular leader of commissions to negotiate settlements of border disputes with the Scots. A conscientious diocesan, he resided twice a year except in 1419. Nevertheless, routine business functioned without him. He had a vicar-general and a suffragan to act for him. Although some of his official business was recorded in his diocesan register, this provides a very imperfect guide to his ecclesiastical administration. He reformed the statutes of the three collegiate churches of Auckland, Lanchester, and Chester-le-Street, to enforce if not residence at least the provision of vicars in the prebends. He also gave new statutes to Sherburn Hospital outside Durham. Langley was reasonably regular in attendance at the northern convocation of clergy at York. He died at Bishop Auckland on 20 November 1437. A keen huntsman, Langley none the less accumulated a small library, whose contents included works of theology, canon and civil law, and history. He donated a St Cuthbert window at York Minster in 1429, and he also founded a chantry in the Galilee chapel of Durham Cathedral, his designated burial place, whose two chaplains were to teach grammar and song to poor children freely—the forerunner of Durham School. C. M. Fraser

Sources R. L. Storey, *Thomas Langley and the bishopric of Durham, 1406–1435* (1961) • 'Willielmi de Chambre continuatio historiae Dunelmensis', in *Historiae Dunelmensis scriptores tres: Gaufridus de Coldingham, Robertus de Graystanes, et Willielmus de Chambre*, ed. J. Raine, SurtS, 9 (1839), 127–56, esp. 146–7
Wealth at death est. £4000 p.a.: Storey, *Thomas Langley*, 68–74, 88–97

Langley, Thomas (*fl.* 1430), Benedictine monk and prosodist, was probably born in the last years of the fourteenth century. Nothing is known of his education or career, and even his association with the abbey of St Benet of Hulme, Norfolk, is uncertain. According to John Bale and later bibliographers Langley was a poet and metrist, the author of a series of epigrams and a treatise *De varietate carminum*, which survives anonymously in a single early fifteenth-century manuscript (Bodl. Oxf., MS Digby 100, fols. 178r–189v). A note added in a later hand indicates that the text was dedicated to a bishop of Norwich, which would seem to support the attribution. Tanner added that the bishop's name was John, although his evidence for this is obscure. Given the date of the manuscript, a likely dedicatee in this case would have been John Wakering, bishop of Norwich from 1415 to 1425.

Langley's treatise considers the whole nature of poetry. He examines scansion, rhythm, and metrical forms, and he defends his study of what was considered a pagan practice by demonstrating that it could also be found in the work of many Christian writers. His text is very similar in form and content to another fifteenth-century treatise on metre, the *Metristencheridion*, written by John Seward, a London grammar-master. Like Langley, Seward discusses variations in metrical form using examples from Horace, and in particular Boethius's *De consolatione philosophiae*. Seward wrote a generation earlier than Langley—the earliest version of the *Metristencheridion* was completed in 1415; it is very likely that Langley acquired a copy and used it as the basis for his own work.

The Seward connection may explain the putative dedication of the *De varietate* to a bishop of Norwich. The *Metristencheridion* in its earliest form was itself dedicated to Richard Courtenay, bishop of Norwich, who died in

1415; it is possible the annotator of the Digby manuscript confused the two texts when adding his note, especially given their obvious similarity. In the same way the bibliographers may also have confused Langley with Seward when they suggested that he was the author of epigrams. Seward was the author of several sets of epigrams, including one sequence dedicated to JW, who may be identified with John Wakering. This in turn perhaps explains Tanner's suggestion that Langley's patron had been a Bishop John. Alternatively the alleged epigrams may be traced to a misreading of the opening lines of Langley's prologue to the *De varietate*, or of the later rubric which identifies the prologue as 'Epigramma in primum librum de varietate carminum'. James G. Clark

Sources Bale, *Index*, 441 • Tanner, *Bibl. Brit.-Hib.*, 465 • T. Langley, 'De varietate carminum', Bodl. Oxf., MS Digby 100, fols. 178r–189v • V. H. Galbraith, 'John Seward and his circle', *Medieval and Renaissance Studies*, 1 (1941), 85–104
Archives Bodl. Oxf., MS Digby 100, fols. 178r–189v

Langley, Thomas (d. 1581), Church of England clergyman and translator, may have been the son of Thomas Langley, an Augustinian canon of Leeds, Kent, who died before 11 August 1534, in which case the younger Thomas was illegitimate. A student of Jesus College, Cambridge, in 1536/7, Langley graduated BA in 1538. In April 1546 he published an English abridgement of the eight books of Polydore Vergil's encyclopaedic reference book *De inventoribus rerum*. Dedicated to Sir Anthony Denny, a courtier sympathetic to the cause of religious reform, the abridgement is no masterpiece, not least because it is some 90 per cent shorter than its original. Langley added a number of comments of his own, which are principally of interest in showing his antipathy towards both Catholics and Anabaptists. In spite of its shortcomings the work proved popular and was reprinted several times in the sixteenth and seventeenth centuries, the last edition appearing in 1686.

No later than 1548 Langley was a chaplain to Archbishop Thomas Cranmer, in that year instituting articles of heresy against John Assheton, parson of Shiltelington. In 1552 he issued a translation, entitled *Of the Christian Sabboth*, of a work by Julius of Milayne (the Italian protestant Giulio da Milano). That year, too, he was instituted to the vicarage of Headcorn, Kent. He had resigned the living before 27 November 1554, having on 28 September been presented to the rectory of Boughton Malherbe, also in Kent, by Thomas Wotton. He held this living until 1564. Wotton, a protestant supporter of Lady Jane Grey who later corresponded with Thomas Cartwright, was imprisoned at the start of Mary's reign, and it is possible that Langley fled abroad—the Thomas Langley admitted to residence at Geneva on 14 October 1557 may have been the translator, though he is registered as 'laboureur'. In 1561 it was claimed that he was married to 'a woman who was with child in Queen Mary's days and whose husband is thought to be alive', and that no banns had been called before their marriage (Willis, 13). All this may well have had to do with the oscillations of religious policy. Langley and his wife, Anne, had at least two sons and two daughters living at the time of their father's death.

If there was uncertainty about the status of Langley's marriage it did not prevent his gaining further preferment. He was presented by Queen Elizabeth to the canonry of the ninth prebend at Winchester on 6 October 1559 and installed nine days later; in that year, too, on presentment of the crown, he was instituted to the rectory of Welford, Berkshire. He took his BTh at Oxford on 15 July 1560. In 1563 he was presented by the dean and chapter of Winchester to the vicarage of Wanborough, Wiltshire, and seems to have acquired fairly extensive properties both in that county and in Kent. By the time he made his will, on 21 December 1581, Langley could only put his seal to the document 'becawse I am blynde and cannott subscribe my name' (PRO, PROB 11/64, fol. 3v). Naming his old patron Thomas Wotton among the overseers, Langley asked to be buried in the chancel of Wanborough church. A successor was collated to his canonry on the last day of 1581. STEPHEN WRIGHT

Sources Venn, *Alum. Cant.* · Cooper, *Ath. Cantab.*, 1.447–8 · J. Strype, *Memorials of the most reverend father in God Thomas Cranmer*, 2 vols. (1848), vol. 1, pp. 255–6 · will, PRO, PROB 11/64, sig. 1 · *Fasti Angl., 1541–1857*, [Canterbury] · C. H. Garrett, *The Marian exiles: a study in the origins of Elizabethan puritanism* (1938) · *Canterbury institutions sede vacante*, Kent Archaeological Society Records Branch, 8 (1924) · L. Duncan, 'The renunciation of papal authority by the clergy of west Kent', *Archaeologia Cantiana*, 22 (1897), 293–309 · L. C. Evans, 'The Wotton monuments', *Archaeologia Cantiana*, 89 (1972), 15–29 · A. J. Willis, *Church life in Kent ... Church court records ... 1559–65* (1975) · D. Hay, *Polydore Vergil: Renaissance historian and man of letters* (1952)
Wealth at death property in Kent and Wiltshire: will, PRO, PROB 11/64, fols. 3r–3v

Langley, Thomas (1702–1751?). *See under* Langley, Batty (*bap.* 1696, *d.* 1751).

Langley, Thomas (1769–1801), topographer, only son of Thomas Langley (*d.* 1801), farmer and minor landowner, and Mary, daughter of John Higginson, was born at Marlow, Buckinghamshire, on 10 May 1769. His family had owned land in Marlow since before 1550. He entered Eton College in 1780, and matriculated from Hertford College, Oxford, on 17 May 1787; he graduated BA in 1791 and proceeded MA in 1794. Most of the cost of his education was borne by his uncle Alexander Higginson (*d.* 1793), of London. After ordination he was in 1793 licensed to the curacies of Bradenham and Taplow, Buckinghamshire. On 2 October 1800 he was instituted to the rectory of Whiston, Northamptonshire, on the presentation of a neighbouring landowner, Frederick, second Lord Boston, with an arrangement to hold it pending the ordination of the latter's son W. A. Irby (*b.* 1780).

Langley's *The history and antiquities of the hundred of Desborough and deanery of Wycombe in Buckinghamshire* was published in 1797. It contains many picturesque descriptions, but lacks scholarly method. Its principal source was the manuscripts of Browne Willis. Information was also supplied by lords of manors, members of the clergy, and others with whom Langley corresponded. In 1799 Langley was collecting material for a projected history of Burnham hundred, to be illustrated with plates.

In February 1800 Langley had completed an unpublished religious poem of some length. He died unmarried on 30 July 1801, and was buried on 5 August in the family vault at Marlow. He is commemorated by a tablet in the church there. DANIEL HIPWELL, *rev.* HUGH HANLEY

Sources Foster, *Alum. Oxon.* · parish registers, Great Marlow, Bucks. RLSS · *Catalogue of the Stowe manuscripts in the British Museum*, 1 (1895), 579 · [T. Langley], unsigned memoranda on family affairs, *c.*1800, Bucks. RLSS, Mackenzie MSS [uncatalogued] · Lincs. Arch., Lincoln diocesan records · *GM*, 1st ser., 66 (1796), 736 · *GM*, 1st ser., 67 (1797), 491 · *GM*, 1st ser., 71 (1801), 768 · A. H. Cocks, 'The intramural monuments ... of Great Marlow church', *Records of Buckinghamshire*, 8 (1898–1903), 162–203, esp. 179 · Nichols, *Lit. anecdotes*, 9.227 · *Eighth report*, 3, HMC, 7 (1881), 31 · *VCH Buckinghamshire*, 3.67, 75 · T. Langley, 'A short account of the family of Langley ... in "Book of evidences" of the estate of Thomas Langley, gentleman', 1798, Bucks. RLSS, Mackenzie MSS, 3–12
Archives BL, corresp. and papers relating to history of Desborough, incl. a copy of the printed edition with his annotations, Stowe MSS 803–804 | Bucks. RLSS, Mackenzie MSS
Wealth at death under £1000: will, PRO [PROB 11/1364, sig. 681]

Langley, Walter (1852–1922). *See under* Newlyn school (*act.* 1882–*c.*1900).

Langmead, Thomas Pitt Taswell- (1840–1882), legal writer, was the only son of Thomas Langmead, gentleman, of St Giles-in-the-Fields, London, and his wife, Elizabeth, daughter of Stephen Cock Taswell, a descendant of an old family formerly settled at Limington, Somerset. He assumed Taswell as an additional surname in 1864. He was educated at King's College, London, and on 9 May 1860 entered the Inner Temple, moving on 9 July 1862 to Lincoln's Inn, where he took the Tancred studentship and in Easter term 1863 was called to the bar. Meanwhile he matriculated in October 1862 at St Mary Hall, Oxford, where he graduated BA in 1866 with first-class honours in law and modern history. He was awarded the Stanhope prize the same year for an essay on the reign of Richard II and the Vinerian scholarship in 1867. He graduated BCL in 1869.

Taswell-Langmead practised as a conveyancer, and in 1873 was appointed tutor in constitutional law and legal history at the inns of court. He also held the post of revising barrister under the River Lea Conservancy Acts, and for the last seven years of his life was joint editor of the *Law Magazine and Review*. In 1882 he was appointed professor of English constitutional law and legal history at University College, London. He wrote articles on the need for better preservation of parochial records and drafted W. C. Borlase's abortive Parish Registers Bill of 1882. His only other important contribution to the *Law Magazine and Review* was an article entitled 'The representative peerage of Scotland and Ireland', in May 1876. In 1875 he published a textbook, *English Constitutional History*, which ran to several editions. He died unmarried at 18 Hova Villas, Hove, Brighton, on 8 December 1882 and was buried at Nunhead cemetery. J. M. RIGG, *rev.* CATHERINE PEASE-WATKIN

Sources *Solicitors' Journal*, 27 (1882–3), 134 · *Law Journal* (23 Dec 1882), 700 · *Law Times* (20 Jan 1883), 218 · C. H. E. Carmichael, *Law Magazine*, 4th ser., 8 (1882–3), 141–6 · *Oxford University Calendar* (1892), 38, 59, 175 · *N&Q*, 2nd ser., 6 (1858), 380 · *N&Q*, 6th ser., 6

(1882), 500 · *Misc. Gen. et Herald.*, new ser., 1, 255 · *Inns of Court Calendar* (1878) · Foster, *Alum. Oxon.* · *CGPLA Eng. & Wales* (1882)
Wealth at death £954 6s. 2d.: probate, 22 Dec 1882, *CGPLA Eng. & Wales*

Langridge, Edith [*known as* Mother Edith] (1864–1959), settlement worker and missionary in India, was born at 36 Marlborough Hill, Marylebone, London, on 21 March 1864, the first daughter and second of seven children (four girls and three boys) of Henry Langridge, a merchant, and his wife, Flora Jane, *née* Pope. She was educated at Queen's College, Harley Street, and at Lady Margaret Hall (LMH), Oxford, where she was awarded a scholarship and read classics (1885–8), obtaining second-class honours in honour moderations. Although mathematics had been her best subject at school Miss Wordsworth, the principal of LMH, decided 'Not mathematics, you simply can't come to Oxford and do mathematics' (Mother Edith, 'LMH, 1885–8', 48), and arranged for her to learn Latin from scratch to take the university's responsions examination just six weeks later. She was tall, moved swiftly, and had striking grey-green eyes. Fellow students regarded her as an accomplished all-rounder—academic, athletic, and practical. She enjoyed the informality of LMH life, and was thoroughly at home in its high Anglican ethos, while displaying a taste for silence that friends often attributed to the influence of her maternal grandmother, a Quaker.

In 1895 Edith returned briefly to LMH as acting vice-principal (student warden) for one term. In 1897 she was appointed first warden of the Lady Margaret Hall Settlement at 129 Kennington Road, Lambeth, a post she held until 1902. She had first discussed this project with a fellow LMH student, Maggie Benson, in 1886, two years after the opening of Toynbee Hall. They and others continued to work towards its realization even after the opening of the non-denominational Women's University Settlement in Southwark in 1887, and the former students of LMH formally adopted the specifically Anglican initiative in 1896. The bishop of Rochester, Edward Talbot, founder of Lady Margaret Hall, decided to found the proposed LMH Settlement in his diocese, which then included parts of south London now in the diocese of Southwark. Edith gained experience of church and secular social work agencies in the area in preparation for the new project. More than anyone else she established its early character, organization, and range of work among the poor of Lambeth.

Edith decided that she had a missionary vocation, and studied Swahili with a view to serving with the Universities' Mission to Central Africa. Through Bishop Talbot and Canon Charles Gore she was directed instead towards the Oxford Mission Brotherhood of the Epiphany, founded by Edmund Linwood Strong, to work with them in India and to found a sisterhood. She began to learn Bengali, she and three other volunteers were blessed by Bishop Talbot on 15 October 1902, and they sailed for India soon afterwards. Despite initial health problems she spent the rest of her life with the Oxford Mission Sisterhood of the Epiphany in India, apart from occasional periods of leave in England, including one in the summer of 1928 when she attended the golden jubilee celebrations of LMH in Oxford, and was presented to the duchess of York. She was elected an honorary fellow of LMH in 1933.

For thirty-two years Edith Langridge lived in Barisal, east of Calcutta. The bishop of Calcutta appointed her sister superior in 1903. She designed the sisters' habit, and helped devise the rule, based on Benedictine principles, which was adopted in 1907, and which placed the sisterhood under the direct religious and financial control of a warden from the brotherhood. She took final vows on 12 January 1913 and was immediately elected mother of the sisterhood, a position she retained until 1943. The community's task at Barisal was to help the brotherhood build up the Christian church in the district, through a girls' boarding-school, a home for needy girls and women, medical work, and outreach in the locality, often by boat. Mother Edith's responsibility, however, was the spiritual, personal, and practical development of the community. Her style was quiet, reserved, and non-authoritarian, but for some of the sisters, too austerely remote and impersonal. In 1928 and 1931 the regular election of the mother superior was deadlocked, with Edith being reinstated only by the action of the warden, followed up by a change in the constitution.

Mother Edith visited the foundations made elsewhere by the community, including one guiding the early development of a sisterhood in the Orthodox Syrian church, in Malabar. Other projects faced insuperable cultural problems. An equivalent of the Oxford Mission Sisterhood, for Indian women, failed. When instead the original community was opened to Indian women, only two persevered in Mother Edith's long lifetime. In a refuge for girls in Calcutta, the Christian influence of the sisters was mistrusted by the local community. But the sisterhood gradually grew modestly, attracting, among others, two former students of LMH. In 1934 Edith moved to a new venture, a student hostel in Calcutta, then in 1938 to a home for women and small boys in Behala on the city's outskirts. The Calcutta hostel closed in 1940. Political and religious circumstances in the final years of British India prevented the sisters' proposed women's college there from ever finding favour with the authorities, ending Mother Edith's hopes of involvement in higher education in India. In 1943, a new mother superior was elected, and had to face the effects of independence and partition in 1947.

Mother Edith spent her last years, 1952–9, in Shillong, high in the Assam hills, the final eighteen months in a hospital there run by a Welsh Presbyterian mission. She died at the hospital on 6 May 1959. She compiled some devotional works and wrote some articles on missionary themes.

FRANCES LANNON

Sources Sister Gertrude, *Mother Edith O.M.S.E.* (1964) · Mother Edith, 'LMH, 1885–8', *Brown Book* (1948), 46–54 · *LMH register, 1879–1952* (1955) · C. Anson, *Brown Book* (1959), 29–32 · Mother Edith, *An ancient church and a new venture of faith in it* (1928) · Mother Edith, *After this manner* (1955) · K. B. Beauman, *Women and the settlement movement* (1996) · K. B. Beauman, *Lady Margaret Hall Settlement: a short history, 1897–1980* (1980) · b. cert.
Likenesses photographs, Lady Margaret Hall, Oxford

Langrish, Browne (d. 1759), physician, was born in Hampshire, and first educated as a surgeon. In 1733 he was in practice at Petersfield, Hampshire, and published *A New Essay on Muscular Motion*, which discussed the structure of muscles and the phenomena of muscular contraction. In 1734 he became an extra licentiate of the College of Physicians, and began practice as a physician. He was elected a fellow of the Royal Society in 1734, and in 1735 published *The Modern Theory and Practice of Physic*, which described experiments in the analysis of excreta and the examination of the blood. He practised in Winchester or Basingstoke, Hampshire, and in 1746 published *Physical experiments on brutes, in order to discover a safe and easy method of dissolving stone in the bladder*. Experiments on cherry laurel water (prussic acid) were made, and Langrish concluded that it could be used in medicine with advantage. An unpublished letter (1747) to the Royal Society on oleaginous warm baths was published in an article in 1938, with critical comments from the authors F. T. Gardner and C. D. Leake (*Annals of Medical History*, 131–5).

Langrish delivered the Croonian lectures on muscular motion to the Royal Society in 1747, and they were published in 1748. In the same year he graduated MD, and published a work of thirty-five pages on smallpox which showed extensive reading and acute clinical observation. He died at Basingstoke, Hampshire, on 12 November 1759.   NORMAN MOORE, rev. JEAN LOUDON

Sources Munk, *Roll* · *GM*, 1st ser., 29 (1759), 551 · F. T. Gardner and C. D. Leake, 'Browne Langrish's letter on the usefulness of oleaginous warm baths: an example of eighteenth-century medical confusion', *Annals of Medical History*, new ser., 10 (1938), 131–5 · T. Thomson, *History of the Royal Society from its institution to the end of the eighteenth century* (1812)

Archives BL, letters to Sir Hans Sloane

Langrishe, Sir Hercules, first baronet (*c*.1729–1811), politician, was born in Knocktopher, co. Kilkenny, the second but only surviving son of Robert Langrishe (*c*.1696–1770), landowner, of Knocktopher, and Anne, second daughter of Jonathan Whitby of Kilcregan in the same county. He was educated at Trinity College, Dublin, where he graduated BA in the spring of 1753. A freeman of Kilkenny from 3 November 1750, he sat as MP for Knocktopher for six consecutive terms totalling almost forty years from 1761 until the abolition of the seat with the Act of Union in 1800. The length of his tenure as MP has received much comment as has his advocacy for repealing the penal laws against Catholics, especially his introduction of the Catholic Relief Bill of 1792. On 31 May 1755 he married Hannah (d. 1803), second daughter and coheir of Robert Myhill of Killarney, co. Kilkenny, and Mary Billingsley, and sister of Jane, wife of Charles, first marquess of Ely; they had three sons and three daughters. Their eldest son, Robert, second baronet (1756–1835), also sat as MP for Knocktopher from 1783 to 1796.

Between 1762 and 1793 Langrishe supported a number of bills in the Irish parliament to repeal a range of anti-Catholic penal laws enacted in the 1690s and early 1700s. Up to 1782 these bills (none of them successful before 1778) concentrated on extending a number of property rights to Roman Catholics, including taking out mortgages on land, obtaining leases for terms in excess of thirty-one years, and purchasing and bequeathing freehold land. The British government supported Roman Catholic relief to curb the power of Irish protestants who were beginning to demand legislative independence in the wake of the American War of Independence (1775–83).

Modern research suggests that Langrishe may have supported Roman Catholic relief bills for primarily fiscal reasons. First, he was rewarded for his support of the government with appointments to a succession of offices—commissioner of barracks (1766–74), supervisor of accounts (1767–75), commissioner of revenue (1774–1802), and commissioner of excise (1780–1802)—and by being made a baronet on 19 February 1777. He was also appointed an Irish privy councillor in 1786. Second, the Roman Catholic relief acts facilitated his manipulation of the vote in the borough of Knocktopher, which was almost entirely his property. His piecemeal acquisition of the remaining leasehold property in the borough enabled him to let holdings almost exclusively to Roman Catholic householders who were excluded from the franchise because of their religion. By 1783 there was only one protestant tenant in Knocktopher, a Dublin resident given the task of passing his vote in Langrishe's favour. The increased security of tenure experienced after 1782 by Roman Catholics limited the opportunity for any electorally unreliable protestant to move into Knocktopher.

Langrishe's politics were otherwise primarily pro-protestant. He opposed extending the parliamentary franchise to Catholics in 1784 and 1785 because, he felt, the resultant democracy would subvert the minority protestant administration in Ireland. He also opposed proposals to reform the tithe system in 1786–7, whereby concessions would be made to non-Anglicans, because this would have impoverished the Church of Ireland clergy and would have broken with 'the principles of the glorious revolution to which we owe our religion and liberty' (Kelly, 122). However, prompted by Edmund Burke's *Letter to Sir Hercules Langrishe* (1792), he introduced a moderate relief bill in 1792 that allowed Catholics, among other things, to practise law, except as judges or as king's counsel. He seconded the Catholic Relief Bill of 1793, whereby Roman Catholics with freehold property worth 40s. gained the vote, partly from a fear of French revolutionary principles which he shared with the government. His view was that the 'old dangers of Popery were extinct; [and that] new dangers had arisen against which Catholics would be the truest allies' (Fewer, 'Land tenure', 58–9). As the French revolutionary regime grew more repressive he opposed proposals to extend the franchise or further relax the penal laws in 1794, 1796, and 1797. He also acted as an official informer to the government regarding the state of co. Kilkenny during the 1798 rising.

Langrishe supported the government in other parliamentary matters by, for example, opposing the reduction of pensions and favouring the Police Bill in 1786–8. At other times he opposed the government, especially during the unpopular administration of George, fourth Viscount Townshend (viceroy, 1767–72), who had prorogued the Irish parliament between 1769 and 1771. Langrishe satirized the viceroy's administration in an anonymous essay entitled 'The history of Barataria continued' that was published in the *Freeman's Journal* (April–May 1771) and later reprinted with contributions by Henry Flood and Henry Grattan in *Baratariana*. He subsequently advocated a conciliatory policy towards the American colonists in 1775 and passively supported the legislative independence of the Irish parliament in 1782. After 1791, however, he came to support the government's desire for a legislative union between Britain and Ireland. With the passing of the Act of Union in 1800 he was subsequently compensated (as were other MPs regardless of whether they supported the act or not) for the loss of his parliamentary seat with the sum of £13,862 10s., a sum far in excess of his estate's rental, which that year amounted to just over £525. Langrishe died at his residence in St Stephen's Green, Dublin, on 1 February 1811 and was buried on 8 February at St Ann's in the same city. THOMAS G. FEWER

Sources T. G. Fewer, 'Hercules Langrishe: Catholic emancipationist or self-serving politician?', www.geocities.com/gregory_fewer/hercule.htm, 29 Jan 2003 · T. G. Fewer, 'Land tenure in south Kilkenny, c.1800–1850', MA diss., National University of Ireland, Cork, 1993, 55–62, 138–40 · *GM*, 1st ser., 81/1 (1811), 194, 289 · A. Vicars, ed., *Index to the prerogative wills of Ireland, 1536–1810* (1897) · corporation minutes, 5 Dec 1730–25 Sept 1760, Kilkenny Corporation, archives, CR/D6, 409 · Burtchaell & Sadleir, *Alum. Dubl.*, 2nd edn · Registry of Deeds, Henrietta Street, Dublin, deeds 141.496.97306 and 173.594.117563 · J. Kelly, 'The genesis of "protestant ascendancy": the Rightboy disturbances of the 1780s and their impact upon protestant opinion', *Parliament, politics and people: essays in eighteenth-century Irish history*, ed. G. O'Brien (1989), 93–128 · R. ffolliott, 'Index to biographical notices in newspapers of Limerick, Ennis, Clonmel and Waterford, 1758–1821', 1985, NL Ire. [card index] · grand roll of freemen of the city of Kilkenny from the 1st January 1760, 1760–1987, Kilkenny Corporation archives, CR/H3 · W. Wilson, *The post-chaise companion through Ireland* (1784), 215 · L. Hoyne, 'Myhills of Killarney, co. Kilkenny: their landowning predecessors and successors', *Old Kilkenny Review*, 47 (1995), 94–108 · H. Boylan, *A dictionary of Irish biography*, 2nd edn (1988) · Burke, *Peerage* (1970) · G. D. Burtchaell, *Genealogical memoirs of the members of parliament for the county and city of Kilkenny* (1888), 158–60 · *DNB* · R. Langrishe, 'A refutation', *Journal of the Royal Society of Antiquaries of Ireland*, 5th ser., 7 (1897), 434–6 · Kilkenny Archaeological Society, Rothe House, Kilkenny, Langrishe MSS · M. M. Phelan, 'Entrance structures at Killarney House', *Old Kilkenny Review*, new ser., 2/3 (1981), 271–3 · pedigree, Genealogical Office, Dublin, MS 112 Brooke, 23

Archives Kilkenny Archaeological Society, Rothe House, Kilkenny, MSS · NA Ire., MSS, BR/KK 38 · TCD, letter-book

Likenesses F. Wheatley, group portrait, oils, 1780 (*The Irish House of Commons*), Leeds City Art Gallery · G. Dance, pencil drawing, 1795, priv. coll. · watercolour, priv. coll.

Wealth at death estate rental in 1800 amounted to £525 18s. 3d.; was paid £13,862 10s. compensation for loss of parliamentary seat in 1800: Langrishe MSS, Rothe House, Kilkenny; Burtchaell, *Genealogical memoirs*; Boylan, *A dictionary*; *DNB*; Langrishe, 'A refutation'

Langshaw, John (1724/5–1798), organist and organ builder, was of unknown parentage and birthplace. In the 1760s he worked with John Christopher Smith, Handel's amanuensis, on a large mechanical organ for the earl of Bute at Luton Park. Barrel organs were widely used in English churches in the late eighteenth and early nineteenth centuries, and Langshaw's skilful work on the barrels of Bute's organ demonstrated the potential for those instruments:

> Langshaw, a very ingenious artist, was employed; and, under Smith's directions, set the barrels with so much delicacy and taste, as to convey a warm idea of the impression which the hand gives on the instrument. The organ was esteemed a masterpiece in musical mechanism. (Coxe, 53)

Langshaw was organist of Wigan parish church from 1770 to 1772 and of Lancaster Priory and parish church from 1772 until his death. He and his wife, Mary (1732/3–1800), had seven children and, in discussing his son John's musical education, he observed that 'a hundred a year (the utmost I get) will not both mentain my large family, & pay the high fees some Masters demand' (J. Langshaw to C. Wesley sen., 28 Sept 1778). Langshaw died on 3 March and was buried at Lancaster Priory on 7 March 1798.

Langshaw's son **John Langshaw** (1763–1832), organist and composer, was born in February 1763 in London. In 1778 he studied with Benjamin Cooke, organist of Westminster Abbey, but according to his father was 'no little mortified' at Cooke's method of teaching (J. Langshaw to C. Wesley sen., 28 Sept 1778). From 1778 to 1784 he continued his musical training in London with the younger Charles Wesley, with whom he formed a lasting friendship and whose brother Samuel also befriended him. Langshaw became a music teacher and in 1798 succeeded his father as organist at Lancaster Priory, a position which he held for the rest of his life. His published compositions included songs, a theme with variations for pianoforte or harp, and arrangements of works by Handel and Haydn. According to Sainsbury his use of 'the ancient style of music' was an obstacle to the publication of other works, 'perhaps more worthy of notice', including voluntaries, concertos, songs, hymns, chants, duets, and arrangements of concertos by Geminiani. Langshaw, who married Sarah Grundy (1774–1865) on or about 7 February 1800, died on 5 December 1832 and was buried at Lancaster Priory on 10 December. ARTHUR W. WAINWRIGHT

Sources parish register, St Mary, Lancaster, Lancs. RO, PR 3262/1/4, 7 March 1798 [burial] · parish register, St Mary, Lancaster, Lancs. RO, PR 3262/1/4, 15 Sept 1800 [burial] · parish register, St Mary, Lancaster, Lancs. RO, PR 3262/1/7, 19 April 1813 [baptism] · parish register, St Mary, Lancaster, Lancs. RO, PR 3262/1/40, 10 Dec 1832 [burial]; J. Langshaw (1763–1832)] · J. Langshaw, corresp. with Wesley family, 1778–1827, Emory University, Atlanta, Georgia, Robert W. Woodruff Library, John Wesley MSS · *Wesley–Langshaw correspondence*, ed. {}, A. W. Wainwright, and D. Saliers (1993) · W. Coxe, *Anecdotes of George Frederick Handel and John Christopher Smith* (1799); repr. (1979) · [J. S. Sainsbury], ed., *A dictionary of musicians*, 2 vols. (1825); repr. (New York, 1966) · W. O. Roper, ed., *Materials for the history of the church of Lancaster*, 4 vols., Chetham Society, 26, 31, 58, 59 (1892–1906) · G. T. O. Bridgeman, *The history of the church and manor of Wigan, in the county of Lancaster*, 4 vols., Chetham Society, new ser., 15–18 (1888–90) · C. Fleury, *Time-honoured Lancaster* (1891) · F.-J. Fétis, *Biographie universelle des musiciens, et bibliographie générale de la musique*, 2nd edn, 8 vols. (Paris, 1860–65); repr. (1867–83) · *DNB* · A. W. G. Ord-Hume, *Barrel organ* (1978) · Grove, *Dict. mus.* (1927)

Archives Emory University, Atlanta, Georgia, Robert W. Woodruff Library, John Wesley MSS

Langshaw, John (1763–1832). *See under* Langshaw, John (1724/5–1798).

Langston, John (1640/41–1704), clergyman and ejected minister, is of unknown parentage and background. He was educated at Worcester grammar school before matriculating from Pembroke College, Oxford, as a servitor in 1655. Having left university without taking a degree he was appointed to the sequestered curacy of Ashchurch, Gloucestershire, but was ejected in 1660. After ejection he moved to London and 'taught a private Grammar School near Spitalfields', but after the Act of Uniformity in 1662 he 'went with Captain Blackwell into Ireland partly as his chaplain and partly as tutor to his eldest son; and returned to London in 1663 and kept school again' (Calamy, *Abridgement*, 2.661). Here he acted as an assistant to William Hook (1601?–1678), and on 20 April 1672 the two men were licensed as congregationalist teachers 'in the house of Richard Loton in Spittle Yard' (Gordon, 299). After 1679 Langston preached in Bedfordshire, before settling at Ipswich. Here a rumour was maliciously spread, and widely believed, that Langston was a Jesuit, and he was forced out of the town. In 1686 he returned, having married a wife, Susanna. As he records, on 12 October 1686, following extensive preparations, including sermons, 'several days of prayer and humiliation, and several conferences together', seventeen persons 'having on this same day related to each other what God had done for their souls, embodied together as a Church of Christ, giving themselves up to the Lord and one to another'. At a meeting on 22 October these and thirty others 'elected and gave Mr Langston a call to the pastoral office' (Browne, 370). Having accepted on 29 October, he was inaugurated on 2 November. On 24 June 1687 the church held its inaugural meeting in the new chapel in Green Yard. In the mid-1690s Langston was paid by the Congregational Fund Board for work as a tutor. From November 1702 he was assisted in his ministry by Benjamin Glandfield (d. 1720). He died at Ipswich on 12 January 1704, aged sixty-three, leaving property to his wife, who survived him, and £20 to the poor of his Ipswich congregation.

ALEXANDER GORDON, *rev.* STEPHEN WRIGHT

Sources Calamy rev. • J. Browne, *A history of Congregationalism and memorials of the churches in Norfolk and Suffolk* (1877) • A. Gordon, ed., *Freedom after ejection: a review (1690–1692) of presbyterian and congregational nonconformity in England and Wales* (1917) • will, PRO, PROB 11/475, fol. 172 • E. Calamy, ed., *An abridgement of Mr. Baxter's history of his life and times, with an account of the ministers, &c., who were ejected after the Restoration of King Charles II*, 2nd edn, 2 vols. (1713) • Foster, *Alum. Oxon.*
Archives Suffolk RO, Ipswich, sermons
Likenesses Taylor, stipple, BM, NPG; repro. in *Evangelical Magazine* (1819)

Langstrother [Longstrother], **Sir John** (d. 1471), administrator and prior of the hospital of St John of Jerusalem in England, seemingly came of a well-to-do northern family, several members of which were buried in St John's Hospital, Clerkenwell. Preceptor of the order's estate at Dalby, Lincolnshire, by 1448, in 1449 Langstrother became preceptor of Balsall, Warwickshire, and receiver for the treasury of the hospital in England. For twenty years his administrative, financial, and negotiating skills commended him to the order's grand master in Rhodes, as well as to Richard Neville, earl of Warwick (d. 1471), and English kings. By 1463 he was one of Edward IV's councillors; he was the preceptory's bailiff of Eagle, Lincolnshire, and steward of the grand master by 1469. Langstrother's prominence in the order and in the realm made him the unanimous choice of his brethren as prior of the hospital in England on 9 March 1469. The office of English prior was nationally important. Its holder was normally a royal councillor, and was also premier baron of England, so it is not surprising that he needed a royal licence before he could take up office or administer his order's estates. Edward IV distrusted Langstrother for his Neville associations, and tried to impose his young brother-in-law, Sir Richard Woodville, as prior in 1469.

Following the defeat of Edward's supporters at Edgcote (26 July), Langstrother was appointed treasurer of England by Warwick, but once Edward regained his independence he was removed from the treasurership (25 October 1469). Edward refused to recognize him as prior until he swore fealty (18 November), which was regarded as a dangerous precedent by the hospital. In any case, Langstrother remained Warwick's confidant: after the Lincolnshire rising of March 1470, he kept secretly in contact with Clarence, and was put in the Tower of London when the duke and Warwick fled to France. The invasion of Clarence and Warwick in September 1470 brought him back to high office; he was with the force that released Henry VI from the Tower, and on 20 October was reappointed treasurer. Henry VI rewarded his loyalty by acknowledging the rights of his order and confirming his appointment as duly elected prior on 20 December. Langstrother helped to negotiate Warwick's treaty with France (16 February 1471), and on 24 February he and John Delves were granted the wardenship of the mint. Having been sent to France for the purpose, in April 1471 he escorted Queen Margaret and her son, Prince Edward, to England and accompanied them to Tewkesbury. At the battle (4 May) he shared command of the Lancastrian centre, and following their defeat sought sanctuary in Tewkesbury Abbey. Edward was induced to pardon him and other fugitives to the abbey, but they were subsequently taken out, and on 6 May Langstrother was tried and executed in Tewkesbury's market place. His body was allowed honourable burial, in the hospital of St John at Clerkenwell.

R. A. GRIFFITHS

Sources Chancery records • *CEPR letters*, 10.26, 161–2, 261–2, 264–5; 12.234–5 • Rymer, *Foedera*, 1st edn, vol. 20 • PRO • C. L. Kingsford, *English historical literature in the fifteenth century* (1913) • J. Warkworth, *A chronicle of the first thirteen years of the reign of King Edward the Fourth*, ed. J. O. Halliwell, CS, old ser., 10 (1839) • P. Vergil, *English history*, ed. H. Ellis (1844) • J. Stevenson, ed., *Letters and papers illustrative of the wars of the English in France during the reign of Henry VI, king of England*, 2/1, Rolls Series, 22 (1864) • J. Stow, *A survay of London*, rev. edn (1603); repr. with introduction by C. L. Kingsford as *A survay of London*, 2 vols. (1908); repr. with addns (1971) • C. L. Scofield, *The life*

and reign of Edward the Fourth, 2 vols. (1923) • C. Ross, *Edward IV* (1974) • P. W. Hammond, *The battles of Barnet and Tewkesbury* (1990) • C. Tyerman, *England and the crusades, 1095–1588* (1988) • A. Cross, *The dissolution of the Lancastrian kingship* (1996)
Likenesses manuscript illumination, University of Ghent, Belgium, 'Historie of the arrival of Edward IV', 1460–99, MS 236

Langtoft, Peter (*d.* in or after **1305**), Augustinian canon and chronicler, was a canon of Bridlington Priory by 1271 at the latest. His surname, very common in Lincolnshire and Yorkshire in the fourteenth and fifteenth centuries, is a place name of Scandinavian origin (*long toft*) attested in Domesday Book. Very little is known of his life. Until 1286 he represented Prior Geoffrey of Nafferton and the house in a series of negotiations, some of them at Westminster, but in 1293 he left Bridlington without permission from the archbishop of York, John Romanus. Probably he then settled near London and the court. But there is no further trace of him.

With twenty-one medieval manuscripts still surviving, his work seems to have been the most widely diffused Anglo-Norman chronicle after the *Brut d'Engleterre* and Wace's *Brut*. His chronicle consists in fact of three books, all of them in verse: an abridgement and adaptation of Wace's *Brut*, 3010 lines long; a history of Saxon and Norman kings until the death of Henry III, 4200 lines long; and a history of Edward I, with whom he was contemporary. This third book, which is the most informative, consists of 2022 lines in its first redaction and 2591 lines in its second.

Langtoft wrote his account of Edward I's reign long after the first two books, putting pen to parchment again only in 1294, at the request of a friend he calls Schafeld, and summing up the years 1272–94 in 370 lines. This friend was very probably John Sheffield, a royal clerk, sheriff of Durham from 1302 and of Northumberland from 1305, and a faithful supporter of Antony (I) Bek, bishop of Durham.

It is thus not surprising that, in its earliest form, the text emphasizes the military and political fight Bek put up against the Scots. After 1296 and the victory of the English foot soldiers at Dunbar, the text divides into two different redactions, neither of which, it seems, was completed by Langtoft himself. In the first, which is the closest to him in time, the text was continued until 1305 and the execution of William Wallace, or even until 1306 and the execution of the earl of Atholl. Then an adapter, probably a courtier, who was indifferent to Bek and Durham, rather Francophile, and heavily influenced by contemporary French idioms, altered this first redaction, to show Robert Bruce, future king of Scots, as a mere murderer premeditating the killing of John Comyn, his competitor for the throne, in February 1306. This report, purporting to be testimony contemporary with the event, is a masterpiece of royal propaganda.

The other redaction extends to and includes Edward's death. Most of the manuscripts containing it can be localized in north-east England; it thus seems to express the feelings of gentry dwelling there. In particular it shows distrust of Edward, who was regarded as too lenient towards the Scots and unwilling to make a proper distribution of the lands he had conquered or to limit the boundaries of the royal forests.

The three books of the chronicle were composed in Anglo-Norman alexandrines gathered into long stanzas which use a single rhyme or assonance and produce an epic flavour. The main literary feature of the third book (*The Reign of Edward I*) is the addition of a few stanzas of short satirical lines, bilingual or composed in Middle English, extremely nationalistic and anti-Scottish, with alliterative and tripartite schemes. These lines appear again as independent and purely English poems in some manuscripts of the *Brut of England* and in Robert Fabyan's *New Chronicles*.

In 1338 Robert Mannyng, a Gilbertine canon in Sixhills Priory, Lincolnshire, completed 'for the love of simple men' (Mannyng, 1.77) a Middle English adaptation of Langtoft's chronicle as a whole. But for the first book he substituted a direct translation of Wace's *Brut* and for the third he translated the second redaction only. The first redaction of this *Reign of Edward I* did in fact enter the Anglo-Norman *Brut d'Engleterre* and eventually the *Chronicles of England* printed by Caxton in 1480. Only three medieval manuscripts of Mannyng's text are still surviving, so that it seems to have been much less widespread than Langtoft's.

A Princeton University manuscript (Princeton University Library, Taylor MS 12), datable to the middle of the fourteenth century, attributes to Langtoft the translation into Anglo-Norman alexandrines of three political letters, the Latin text of which was very common in the medieval libraries of England. These letters are: a bull of Pope Boniface VIII, presented to Edward I on 26 August 1299 by Archbishop Winchelsey, declaring that Scotland had never been vassal to the king of England, but on the contrary had always depended on the Holy See; a letter sent to Boniface VIII on 12 February 1301 by the English barons proclaiming their determination to prevent the king from giving up any of his rights; and, longer than the previous letters, Edward's personal reply dated 17 May 1301, in which his suzerainty over Scotland appears to be largely grounded on the Arthurian history of Britain. Whether in the translation or in the authentic text, the spirit of this reply recalls Langtoft's chronicle itself, and the argument displayed is the one Edward I and Antony Bek expected from the monasteries when they consulted them about the succession of Scotland in 1291. These translated letters are in long single-rhymed stanzas, like those of the chronicle, and contain a total of 673 lines.

The scribe of BL, Cotton MS Julius A.v, wrongly attributes to Langtoft an allegorical poem on the passion of Christ, but with more probability a lament of the Virgin recalling St Bernard's *De planctu Virginis Marie*.

J. C. THIOLIER

Sources Peter of Langtoft, *Le règne d'Édouard Ier*, ed. J. C. Thiolier (Créteil, 1989) [incl. account of MSS] • *The chronicle of Pierre de Langtoft*, ed. T. Wright, 2 vols., Rolls Series, 47 (1866–8) • J. C. Russell,

'Dictionary of writers of thirteenth century England', *BIHR*, special suppl., 3 (1936) [whole issue], 101 · A. Gransden, *Historical writing in England*, 1 (1974), 475–86, 501 · J. C. Thiolier, 'Pierre de Langtoft: historiographe d'Édouard Ier Plantagenet', *Anglo-Norman anniversary essays*, ed. I. Short, Anglo-Norman Texts, occasional publications ser., 2 (1993), 379–94 · W. T. Lancaster, *Abstracts of the charters and other documents contained in the chartulary of the priory of Bridlington* (1912), 13, 55, 169, 351, 354, 360, 419–20 · J. C. Thiolier, 'L'itinéraire de Pierre de Langtoft', *Miscellanea mediaevalia: Mélanges offerts à Ph. Ménard*, ed. J.-C. Faucon, A. Labbé, and D. Quéruel, 2 (1998), 1329–53 · J. Raine, ed., *Historical papers and letters from the northern registers*, Rolls Series, 61 (1873), 101–2 · J. Parker, ed., *Yorkshire fines, 1246–1272*, Yorkshire Archaeological Society, record ser., 82 (1932), 178 · E. L. G. Stones, ed. and trans., *Anglo-Scottish relations, 1174–1328: some selected documents*, OMT (1965), 162–75, 192–219 · F. J. Tanquerey, *Plaintes de la Vierge en anglo-français* (Paris, 1921), 56–60, 125–35 · M. Prestwich, *Edward I* (1988) · E. L. G. Stones and G. G. Simpson, eds., *Edward I and the throne of Scotland, 1290–1296*, 1 (1978), 80–82, 92; 2 (1978), 198–9, 263, 297 · Robert Mannyng of Brunne, *Robert Mannyng of Brunne: the chronicle*, ed. I. Sullens (1996)

Archives BL, Cotton MS Julius A.v · Princeton University, New Jersey, Taylor MS 12

Langton, Lady Anna Eliza Mary Gore- (1820–1879), campaigner for women's rights, was born in February 1820, the only daughter of Richard Plantagenet Temple-Nugent-Brydges-Chandos-*Grenville, second duke of Buckingham and Chandos (1797–1861), and his wife, Lady Mary Campbell (1795–1862), daughter of John, first marquess of Breadalbane. Her father dissipated his inheritance after succeeding to the dukedom in 1839. He left England a ruined man in 1847, and the contents of Stowe, the family seat, were sold in 1848. Her parents were divorced in 1850. Nothing is known of Lady Anna's formal education, though her home life presumably gave her instruction in the realities of politics; her father had been the proposer of the Chandos clause to the 1832 Reform Bill, by which the vote in counties was conferred on £50 tenants.

On 9 June 1846, at St George's, Hanover Square, London, Lady Anna married William Henry Powell Gore-Langton (1824–1873). They had three sons and two daughters. The family's country home was Newton Park, Newton St Loe, near Bath. Her husband was a Conservative member of parliament for Somerset, but was sufficiently radical to support John Stuart Mill's attempt to include women in the Representation of the People Bill in 1867. Lady Anna had signed the petition in favour of women's suffrage that Mill presented to parliament in 1866. From 1872 she was president of the Bath committee of the National Society for Women's Suffrage, and in 1874 she became president of the Bristol and west of England branch. In April 1873 she was a speaker at a public meeting organized by the central committee of the National Society for Women's Suffrage at the Hanover Square Rooms, London. Helen Blackburn wrote of Lady Anna that 'Her speaking was thoroughly practical, and carried with it great earnestness and conviction—perhaps it was all the more convincing because it was quiet and unassuming. Her fine presence and noble face lent great dignity to all she said' (Blackburn, 113–14). In June 1877 Lady Anna was a member of a deputation to the chancellor of the exchequer, seeking his support for a bill in favour of women's suffrage that Jacob Bright was to present the next day. After this bill's disastrous defeat Lady Anna took the lead in organizing a meeting of suffrage workers at her London house in order to review the position. She was presumably riled by the suggestion, in the course of the parliamentary debate, that supporters of women's education (particularly supporters of Girton College) were not friends to women's suffrage. Lady Anna was decidedly a supporter of both; she was to leave £1000 to Girton in her will.

Lady Anna Gore-Langton was involved with several other feminist enterprises, being a director of the Women's Printing Society; a member, from 1871, of the general committee for securing a medical education to women in Edinburgh; and, by 1878, a vice-president of the London School of Medicine for Women. At a public meeting held in London on 25 June 1877 she had described how, from her own knowledge, women in English villages failed to seek medical attention because it could be had only from men; for the same reason, she thought women medical practitioners much needed in India. She was a vice-president of the National Indian Association, particularly interested in the welfare and education of women in India. She accompanied her brother, Richard Plantagenet Campbell Temple-Nugent-Brydges-Chandos-*Grenville, third duke of Buckingham and Chandos, when he was appointed governor of Madras in 1875 and spent much of the remainder of her life in India. During one of her return visits to England she gave lectures on 'The Social Conditions of Indian Women'; initiated, with Mary Carpenter, a scheme to train and send out women teachers to India; and assisted in raising scholarships for women in Indian universities.

Lady Anna Gore-Langton died of cerebral apoplexy at her London home, Langton House, George Street, Hanover Square, on 3 February 1879, shortly after returning from India. ELIZABETH CRAWFORD

Sources E. Crawford, *The women's suffrage movement: a reference guide, 1866–1928* (1999) · H. Blackburn, *Women's suffrage: a record of the women's suffrage movement in the British Isles* (1902) · *The Times* (6 Feb 1879) · d. cert. · m. cert. · Burke, *Peerage*

Likenesses photograph, repro. in Blackburn, *Women's suffrage* (1902)

Wealth at death under £120,000: probate, 14 March 1879, CGPLA Eng. & Wales

Langton, Anne (1804–1893), artist and author, was born on 24 June 1804 at Farfield Hall, near Addingham, in the West Riding of Yorkshire, and baptized there at St Peter's Church on 3 September, the second child and only daughter of Thomas Langton (1770–1838), merchant, and his wife, Ellen (1766–1846), *née* Currer, daughter of a Yorkshire clergyman. Members of the family claimed that he was connected to the Brontë family. From 1804 until 1815 the family lived at Blythe Hall, Ormskirk, Lancashire, where Anne studied French and Latin and took music lessons. In 1815 the Langtons left England and made their way through Belgium and Germany to Yverdon, Switzerland, where they stayed for almost a year. In the following four years they lived in France, Germany, and Italy. During this time Anne had lessons in art. In Rome, for example, she studied drawing, and in Paris miniature painting. For the rest of her life she worked in pencil, pen and ink, and watercolour.

In 1821 the Langtons returned to England and settled in Liverpool, but because of financial difficulties they moved again in 1826 to Bootle. Anne assisted the family financially by painting miniatures, almost all of family and friends, one of which was exhibited in 1831 and one in 1832 at the Liverpool Academy. Taking with him a series of miniatures of his family painted by Anne, her brother John Langton (1808–1894) emigrated in 1833 to Upper Canada (Ontario), where he purchased uncleared land by Sturgeon Lake, near Fenelon Falls. In May 1837 Anne, her parents, and her aunt Alice Currer (1769?–1846) sailed from Liverpool to join John on his farm, named Blythe after the family's former home. During their journey from New York city, where they arrived in July, Anne made sketches of West Point, New York, and Niagara Falls; the family arrived at Sturgeon Lake in August.

Anne Langton's life at Blythe was hard, especially after her father's death in 1838. She chopped wood, glazed windows, and made candles. She delivered clothing and medicines to poorer settlers, and from 1839 to 1841 ran a small school; in 1842 she established a lending library. She kept a journal and sketched Blythe, its inhabitants, and the surrounding area. She expected to be permanently settled at Blythe, but her brother's marriage in 1845, and the death the following year of her mother and aunt, led her to visit England in 1847. She remained for the next three years with her brother William *Langton (1803–1881) in Manchester. She continued to draw and paint, and in 1850 returned to Sturgeon Lake. There she stayed until 1852, when she moved with her brother and his family to Peterborough, Canada West. In 1855 John Langton became the auditor-general for Canada, and the Langtons moved to the cities of Toronto (1855–9), Quebec (1859–65), and Ottawa (1865–78), until they settled in Toronto in 1878. During this period Anne made three trips to England (1860–62, 1868–70, 1873–5). Throughout this time she sketched many scenes in England and Canada, some of which, including a panoramic view of the city of Quebec, she developed into finished watercolours. During her last trip to England in 1880 Anne completed *The story of our family* (1881). She died at 123 Beverley Street, Toronto, on 10 May 1893 and was buried in St James's cemetery, Parliament Street, Toronto.

Examples of Anne Langton's paintings and drawings are held in the Archives of Ontario, whose picture collections include a self-portrait and watercolour portraits of members of her family; the National Archives of Canada, Ottawa; the Metropolitan Toronto Reference Library; the University of Toronto archives; Peterborough Centennial Museum and Archives; Trent University Archives, Peterborough, Ontario; and the Committee for the Preservation for Anne Langton Articles (Fenelon Falls, Ontario). They include finished watercolours of Canadian and British landscapes, topographical drawings of backwoods views—log cabins, snake fences, and dense forests—and drawings of everyday scenes. Some of these are illustrated in *Early days in Upper Canada: letters of John Langton from the* *backwoods of Upper Canada and the audit office of the province of Canada*, ed. W. A. Langton (1926). A selection of Anne Langton's journals was edited by her nephew, Hugh Hornby Langton, and published as *A Gentlewoman in Upper Canada* (1950). They are valuable as an account of early pioneer life, especially from the point of view of a woman settler.

MARY JANE EDWARDS

Sources A. Langton, *The story of our family* (1881) • E. J. L. Philips, ed., *Langton records: journals and letters from Canada, 1837–1846* (1904) • *A gentlewoman in Upper Canada: the journals of Anne Langton*, ed. H. Hornby Langton (1964) • *Early days in Upper Canada: letters of John Langton from the backwoods of Upper Canada and the audit office of the province of Canada*, ed. W. A. Langton (1926) • *Letters of Thomas Langton to Mrs. Thomas Hornby, 1814 to 1818*, ed. E. J. L. Philips (1900) • *The letters of Thomas Langton, flax merchant of Kirkham, 1771–1788*, ed. J. Wilkinson, Chetham Society, 3rd ser., 38 (1994) • L. D. Baker, *Anne Langton and pioneering in Upper Canada* (1985) • H. E. H. Smith and L. M. Sullivan, '"Now that I know how to manage": work and identity in the journals of Anne Langton', *Ontario History*, 87 (1995), 254–69 • B. Williams, 'Langton, Anne', *DCB*, vol. 12 • *IGI*

Archives Fenelon Falls Municipal Office, Ontario, family papers, F1077 • Lancs. RO, papers, DXX/190

Likenesses Roman artist, portrait, c.1818, Archives of Ontario, Toronto, Langton family collection, F1077-9-4-3 (D-75) • A. Langton, self-portrait, miniature on ivory, 1833, Archives of Ontario, Toronto, Langton family collection, F1077-7-1-0-2 (D-65) • Fraser & Sons, photograph, c.1890, Archives of Ontario, Toronto, Langton family collection, F1077-11-0-5-1

Wealth at death C$1319: probated will, 1 Sept 1893

Langton, Bennet (*bap.* 1736, *d.* 1801), friend of Samuel Johnson, son of the Revd Bennet Langton (1696–1769) and his wife, Diana, daughter of Edmund Turner of Stoke Rochford, Lincolnshire, and descendant of the old family of the Langtons of Langton, near Spilsby in Lincolnshire, was baptized at St Cuthbert's, York, on 11 January 1736. As a young man he was so interested by *The Rambler* (1750–52) that he obtained an introduction to Johnson, who at once took a liking to him. On 7 July 1757 Langton matriculated from Trinity College, Oxford, where he became friendly with Topham Beauclerk. The two youths took Johnson for his famous 'frisk' to Billingsgate. Johnson later visited the Langtons, and declined the offer of a good living from Langton's father. Langton took the degrees of MA in 1765 and DCL 1790. He was an original member of the Literary Club (about 1764). Johnson, however, was provoked to the laughter which echoed from Fleet Ditch to Temple Bar by Langton's will in 1773, and soon afterwards caused a quarrel, which apparently lasted for some months, by censuring Langton for introducing religious questions in a mixed company.

On 24 May 1770 (*Annual Register*, p. 180) Langton married Mary, *née* Lloyd (*d.* 1785), widow of John Leslie, earl of Rothes (1698–1767), with whom he had four sons and five daughters. According to Johnson, he rather spoilt them (Fanny D'Arblay, *Diary*). His eldest son, George (1772–1819), succeeded him in his estate; Peregrine, the second, married Miss Massingberd of Gunby, and took her name. His second daughter, Jane (*b.* 1776), was Johnson's goddaughter. She died on 12 August 1854, having always worn a 'beautiful miniature' of Johnson (*GM*, 1854).

Langton became a captain, and ultimately major, in the

Lincolnshire militia. Johnson visited him in camp at Warley Common in 1778, and in 1783 at Rochester, where Langton was quartered for some time. Johnson once requested Langton to tell him in what his life was faulty, and was greatly irritated when Langton brought him some texts enjoining mildness of speech. Johnson's permanent feeling, however, was expressed in the words, 'Sit anima mea cum Langtono' ('May my soul be with Langton'; Boswell, 1282).

During Johnson's last illness Langton came to attend his friend; Johnson left him a book, and Langton undertook to pay an annuity to Francis Barber, Johnson's black servant, in consideration of a sum of £750 left in his hands. Langton was famous for his Greek scholarship, but wrote nothing except some anecdotes about Johnson, published by Boswell in his *Life* under the year 1780. Johnson and Boswell frequently discussed Langton's incapacity for properly managing his estates. He was too indolent, it appears, to keep accounts, in spite of exhortations from his mentor. Langton was very tall and thin; his gentle and amiable nature made him universally popular. According to Sir William Jones, Langton's conservative political opinions made him 'vehement against the lovers of freedom in all countries', while Hester Thrale confirmed that Langton was 'a Tory and a high Churchman up to the Eyes' (Rogers, 222). He was appointed in April 1788 to succeed Johnson as professor of ancient literature at the Royal Academy. Langton died at Southampton on 18 December 1801.

LESLIE STEPHEN, *rev.* MICHAEL BEVAN

Sources J. Boswell, *Life of Johnson*, ed. R. W. Chapman, rev. J. D. Fleeman, new edn (1970); repr. with introduction by P. Rogers (1980) · G. B. Hill, *Dr Johnson, his friends and critics* (1878), 248–79 · L.-M. Hawkins, *Anecdotes, biographical sketches, and memoirs* (1822), 144, 276 · *Autobiography, letters, and literary remains of Mrs Piozzi*, ed. A. Hayward, 2 (1861), 203 · *GM*, 1st ser., 71 (1801), 1158, 1207–8 · Burke, *Peerage* (1959) · *IGI* · *GM*, 2nd ser., 42 (1854), 403 · P. Rogers, *The Samuel Johnson encyclopedia* (1996)
Archives Yale U., Beinecke L., corresp. with James Boswell
Likenesses J. Reynolds, oils, 1761–2, Gunby Hall, Lincolnshire · C. von Breda, oils, exh. RA 1790?, Gunby Hall, Lincolnshire · G. Dance, pencil drawing, 1798, BM · attrib. J. Zoffany, oils, Samuel Johnson Birthplace Museum, Lichfield, Staffordshire · plaster bust, Trinity College, Oxford

Langton, Christopher (1521–1578), physician, was born at Riccall in Yorkshire. He was educated at Eton College between 1534 and 1538, and on 23 August 1538 went as a scholar to King's College, Cambridge. He was admitted a fellow of King's College a week later than all the other scholars of his year, on 2 September 1541, and graduated BA in 1542. He received his last quarterage as a fellow at Cambridge at Christmas 1544. Langton married Margaret Chambers of London, the marriage licence being issued on 11 January 1546.

On 10 April 1547, in London, Langton published *A very brefe treatise, orderly declaring the principal partes of phisick, that is to say, thynges natural, thynges not naturall, thynges agaynst nature*, with a dedication to Edward, duke of Somerset, in which he describes himself as 'a lernar and as yet a yong student of physicke'. The work discusses anatomy, pathology, and therapeutics according to ancient and modern methods, commending Pliny and quoting Hippocrates, Aetius, Paulus Aegineta, Celsus, Galen, and Avicenna.

In 1550 Langton published *An Introduction into Phisycke, wyth an Universal Dyet*. It is dedicated to Sir Arthur Darcye, and is largely based on the earlier work. One other book appeared: *A Treatise of Urines, of All the Colours Thereof, with the Medicines* (1552).

Langton took his MD at Cambridge in 1552, and was admitted a fellow of the College of Physicians, London, on 30 September 1552. However, he was expelled from the college for breach of the statutes and profligate conduct on 17 July 1558. On 16 June 1563, having been caught in a compromising situation with two young women, he was punished by being carted to the Guildhall and through the City. His professional ability must have been considerable, for in spite of this public disgrace he continued to have a successful medical practice. Lord Monteagle gave him a pension; both Sir Thomas Smith and Sir Richard Gresham were his patients; the latter left him a small legacy.

Langton died in 1578, and was buried in London at St Botolph's Church without Bishopsgate, on 26 October.

NORMAN MOORE, *rev.* SARAH BAKEWELL

Sources Venn, *Alum. Cant.* · Munk, *Roll* · W. Sterry, ed., *The Eton College register, 1441–1698* (1943), 206

Langton, Sir George Philip (1881–1942), judge, was born in London on 22 April 1881, the youngest of the six sons of Francis Albert Romuald Langton, of Danganmore, co. Kilkenny, civil servant, and his wife, Margaret Cecilia, daughter of John Tobin, shipowner, of Montreal. Educated at Beaumont College, in 1899 he went as a commoner to New College, Oxford, where he gained a second in modern history in 1902.

In preparation for the bar, after admission to the Inner Temple, Langton went into a stockbroker's firm in London and then into a solicitor's office. In 1905 he was called to the bar by the Inner Temple and became a pupil of Alfred Henry Chaytor; afterwards he went into the chambers of Maurice Hill and of Daniel Stephens. These chambers dealt mainly with maritime cases, the Admiralty work being heard in the Admiralty court, and the commercial work in the commercial court. Langton also joined the south-eastern circuit, and was for a time its junior, but the difficulty of combining a practice in the courts of common law and crime with one in the Admiralty and commercial courts proved insuperable, and he gradually became a specialist in maritime law, giving up other work. This may be a matter for some regret, for Langton's eloquence, humour, personal charm, and dramatic sense (he had been a highly successful president of Oxford University Dramatic Society), combined with great mental and physical vigour, would have made him a very successful advocate before a jury.

Just as Langton had begun to do well in his profession, war broke out and before the end of 1914 he had been commissioned in the Royal Garrison Artillery and was posted at Queenstown, of which he soon became garrison adjutant with the rank of captain. His extreme shortsightedness preventing him from going overseas on active service, he was transferred in 1915 to the intelligence branch of the War Office, then to the Ministry of Munitions in 1916. There, as director of the labour department and commissioner of labour disputes, he worked with Alan Barlow and used his remarkable powers of persuasion and his witty friendliness with real effect. In 1918 he was made controller of the demobilization department of the Ministry of Labour, until his own demobilization in 1919. He was appointed OBE in 1917. In 1919 he married Alice Mary Katherine, daughter of Daniel Francis Arthur Leahy, justice of the peace and deputy lieutenant, of Shanakiel, county Cork.

Langton returned to the bar at a time when several leading juniors in the Admiralty and commercial courts were taking silk, and at the same time the work in those courts was greatly increased on account of the war. He soon acquired a large junior practice, especially in the Admiralty court under Sir Maurice Hill. From 1922 until his elevation to the bench in 1930 he acted as secretary and adviser to the British Maritime Law Committee. His interest in the Comité Maritime International led to his being appointed its joint general secretary and to his presence at all their conferences; his fluent French and light-hearted humour made him a general favourite at these somewhat solemn meetings.

In order to relieve the heavy pressure of work in the Admiralty court, Sir A. D. Bateson was appointed an additional judge in 1925. Langton was obviously the man to take his place in the front row, and very shortly afterwards he took silk. At once he became one of the leaders of the Admiralty court, and during the next five years he was employed in a very large proportion of the cases tried there, as well as in many other maritime cases. He also gradually acquired work in other courts, but the question whether he would have become a prominent leader of the common law bar was to remain unanswered, for in October 1930 Hill retired from the bench and Langton was appointed in his place, receiving the customary knighthood. Shortly afterwards he was elected a bencher of the Inner Temple.

During the twelve years in which Langton sat as a judge in the Probate, Divorce, and Admiralty Division, he performed his judicial duties with ability and unflagging attention to the task. He thoroughly understood the Admiralty work, and his decisions, from which there was very seldom an appeal (and still less a successful one), were always well thought out and clearly expressed. In divorce cases he took great pains to master the law applicable to matrimonial disputes, and from time to time he found an outlet there for his humour and immense energy, which made it difficult for him to keep silent.

This exuberant energy also showed itself in physical exercise, especially lawn tennis and golf, in both of which Langton became a skilful player with a complete mastery of style. One of his qualities was an immense capacity for taking pains, and this showed itself both in his work and

in his recreations. In 1939 he was elected chairman of the executive committee of the All England Lawn Tennis Club and he held that position until his death. He died from drowning, his body being found in the River Parrett at Dunball, near Bridgwater, Somerset, on 14 August 1942; he had last been seen alive at Burnham in Somerset on 9 August 1942. There was no evidence to show how he came to be in the water. He was survived by his wife and daughter.   A. T. BUCKNILL, *rev.* ALEC SAMUELS

Sources *The Times* (15 Aug 1942) · personal knowledge (1959) · private information (1959) · d. cert.

Likenesses W. Stoneman, photograph, 1931, NPG · J. M. Crealock, oils, priv. coll.

Wealth at death £28,634 15s. 6d.: probate, 5 Nov 1942, *CGPLA Eng. & Wales*

Langton, John (d. 1337), administrator and bishop of Chichester, probably came from a family that had the lordship of the manor of West Langton in Leicestershire, and may have been related to the treasurer Walter Langton (d. 1321), whom John succeeded in the York prebend of Fridaythorpe in 1296. There is no record of university study, but in a letter from the chancellor of Oxford of c.1307–1310 he is described as 'esteemed colleague' (*confrater probatus*), and at the end of his life, in 1337, he founded a loan chest for deserving clerks at Oxford. He is first recorded in June 1278, when he became rector of Castle Sowerby, Cumberland, though only an acolyte. He may well have been the clerk of that name to whom Edward I gave two oak trees in March 1280. By May 1286 he was keeper of the rolls of chancery, the first person so to be titled. At the king's request he obtained a papal dispensation for pluralism in February 1291. He succeeded Robert Burnell (d. 1292) as chancellor in December 1292. The appointment may have caused some surprise—the Dunstable annalist comments that until then Langton had been only a chancery clerk—and the increased use of the privy seal from this date may indicate that he did not succeed to Burnell's influence; but his dissent from the policy pursued before the outbreak of war with France in 1294 was remarked upon, especially by the Worcester annalist.

The usual trawl of benefices accorded to Edward I's civil servants came Langton's way, and by 1294 he was treasurer of Wells. When the rich bishopric of Ely fell vacant in 1298, Edward I pushed hard to get him elected. But only a minority of the monks supported Langton, Archbishop Winchelsey was opposed, and, despite a visit to the curia between February and June 1299, Langton finally had his election quashed by the pope in June 1299. He was compensated with a dispensation to retain benefices—sixteen in all—to the value of £1000, and also with the archdeaconry of Canterbury. Further conflict with Winchelsey broke out over the valuable rectory of Reculver, to which Langton had been presented by the king in 1293, but which he was eventually forced to surrender in 1302. However, Langton supported the archbishop in his dispute with St Augustine's, Canterbury.

For reasons that remain obscure Langton was dismissed from the chancellorship in August 1302. Yet on 5 April

1305 he was elected to the bishopric of Chichester. Consecrated at Canterbury on 19 September 1305, in the following month he participated in a high-level mission to the new pope, Clement V (r. 1305–13), at Lyons. Following Edward II's accession, in August 1307, Langton regained his former post as chancellor, and was one of the bishops Winchelsey commissioned to crown the new king in his absence. In 1309 he was active on the king's council, and his presence at the Stamford parliament in July 1309, where the exile of Piers Gaveston was annulled, suggests support for the king. However, in March 1310 he was one of five bishops elected as *lords ordainer, and this may account for his removal from the chancellorship on 11 May. The office remained unfilled until Walter Reynolds (d. 1327) was appointed on 6 July. In the summer of 1311 Langton participated at the London trial of the templars.

At the Lincoln parliament in 1316 Langton was an auditor of petitions for England, and was sworn of the king's council. The earl of Lancaster at this time urged him to prosecute John de Warenne, earl of Surrey (d. 1347), for adultery, a course of action that in March 1315 Langton had been anxious to pass on to the archbishop of Canterbury. W. H. Blaauw, writing in 1853, contended that at some point Langton did excommunicate Warenne for adultery, and that in consequence the earl assaulted the bishop's officers, and was even himself imprisoned, but this cannot be substantiated. Langton took a large part in the negotiations between the king and Lancaster preceding the treaty of Leake of 1318 and was one of the standing council appointed as a result of the treaty. At the Westminster parliament of October 1320 he was again an auditor of petitions for England and Wales, while in July 1321 he was one of the bishops who mediated between the king and the barons.

Langton's role in public affairs decreased with age, although he was one of the commission appointed in July 1327 to give effect to the statute reversing the financial depredations of the Despenser regime. As a diocesan he vigorously contested royal attempts to convert the collegiate churches of Hastings and Bosham into royal free chapels, and in 1314 he annulled a statute of the dean and chapter on the grounds that it had been made without his permission; among its provisions was a prohibition of pluralism on the part of the cathedral vicars. He spent £341 on the window in the south transept of Chichester Cathedral beneath which he is buried, and bequeathed £100 to the cathedral fabric. A chantry was erected to him in the chapel of Sts Thomas of Canterbury and Edmund of Abingdon. He died shortly before 19 July 1337.

M. C. BUCK

Sources Chancery records • Emden, Oxf. • J. H. Denton, Robert Winchelsey and the crown, 1294–1313: a study in the defence of ecclesiastical liberty, Cambridge Studies in Medieval Life and Thought, 3rd ser., 14 (1980) • CEPR letters, vols. 1–2 • VCH Sussex, vols. 2–3 • Fasti Angl., 1300–1541, [Chichester] • J. Hughes, 'Walter Langton and his family', Nottingham Medieval Studies, 35 (1991), 70–76, esp. 75–6 • Ann. mon., vols. 3–4 • M. Hobbs, ed., Chichester Cathedral: an historical survey (1994) • W. D. Peckham, ed., The chartulary of the high church of Chichester, Sussex RS, 46 (1946) • W. R. W. Stephens, Memorials of the south Saxon see and cathedral church of Chichester (1876) • W. Stubbs, ed., 'Annales Londonienses', Chronicles of the reigns of Edward I and Edward II, 1, Rolls Series, 76 (1882), 1–251 • W. H. Blaauw, 'Warennia', Sussex Archaeological Collections, 6 (1853), 107–28, esp. 123 • register of Walter Reynolds, LPL, fols. 72v, 125v
Likenesses effigy on personal seal, repro. in VCH Sussex, vol. 2, facing p. 16
Wealth at death considerable: will, Peckham, ed., Chartulary, 903, no. 38

Langton, John (fl. 1389–1392), Carmelite friar and theologian, was perhaps born about 1340 and came, according to Bale, from the west of England: he may accordingly be the John Langton who was ordained as subdeacon at Worcester on 11 June 1362, and about 1389 was an unsuccessful candidate for the Bath and Wells prebend of Combe Sexta. Traditional accounts, however, have him originating from London and entering the order at the London Whitefriars before being sent to Oxford. He had gained the degree of BTh by 1392, but had already been described as a scholar of canon law in 1389, which probably accounts for his inclusion among the judges in the episcopal proceedings against the Cistercian Henry Crump at the Carmelite house in Stamford in 1392. It was Langton who recorded the proceedings: the main charge against Crump was that of denying the rights of the mendicants in such matters as hearing confessions, but it is more likely that the real issue was that Crump had been guilty of adopting a Wycliffite view of the eucharist as a reflection of the body of Christ rather than the true body itself. Langton is said to have compiled a collection of sayings (Collectanea dictorum) and another of questions (Quaestiones ordinariae), but neither is known to have survived. He has been, but should not be, confused with another noted anti-Lollard preacher, the Benedictine doctor of theology John Langdon (d. 1434), author of a chronicle, De rebus Anglicis, and afterwards bishop of Rochester. MICHAEL WILKS

Sources Emden, Oxf., 2.1100 • [T. Netter], Fasciculi zizaniorum magistri Johannis Wyclif cum tritico, ed. W. W. Shirley, Rolls Series, 5 (1858), 343–59 • Bale, Cat., 2.57–8 • Commentarii de scriptoribus Britannicis, auctore Joanne Lelando, ed. A. Hall, 2 (1709), 407 • Fasti Angl., 1300–1541, [Bath and Wells], 28 • J. Crompton, 'Fasciculi zizaniorum [pts 1–2]', Journal of Ecclesiastical History, 12 (1961), 35–45, 155–66, esp. 156
Archives BL, Harley MS 3838, fols. 84v–85

Langton, Robert (1470–1524), ecclesiastic and pilgrim, was born at Appleby, Westmorland, on 25 June 1470. The names of his parents are unrecorded, but he had two brothers and five sisters. He also had powerful kinsmen in the church, for Thomas *Langton, who died in 1501 as archbishop-elect of Canterbury, was his uncle, and Christopher Bainbridge, who became a cardinal and archbishop of York, was his cousin. Robert owed his education and early preferments to the former. From 1487 he studied at the Queen's College, Oxford, where his uncle was provost, doubtless financing his tuition from a series of benefices which began in 1483 with a prebend in Lincoln Cathedral. Though not recorded as having taken orders, in 1485 he was also collated to a prebend in Salisbury Cathedral, and on 25 June 1486 he became archdeacon of Dorset in Salisbury diocese, where Thomas Langton was then bishop. Then on 6 April 1493 Robert Langton was recorded at Bologna, and he probably remained in Italy until he took his DCL degree at Bologna on 14 May 1498. The degree was incorporated at Oxford in 1501, the year in which Thomas Langton died.

His uncle's death did not prevent Langton's adding livings in Devon and Wiltshire to his collection of benefices, but his principal patron was now his cousin Bainbridge, thanks to whom he was admitted treasurer of York Minster on 24 April 1509. On 23 September following, immediately before leaving England for Rome, Bainbridge appointed Langton to a commission to administer York diocese in his absence. But Langton did not stay long in England, for on 11 October 1511 Bainbridge licensed him to go on pilgrimage to Santiago de Compostela, Rome, and other places. His travels were wide-ranging, in Spain, southern France, and Italy, and eventually brought him to Rome, where he was recorded in March and April 1514. He probably returned to England soon afterwards, for by May 1514 he had resigned both his archdeaconry and his treasurership, though he retained his prebends in Lincoln (until 1518) and Salisbury, and added to them prebends in York and Southwell minsters. He took up residence in the London Charterhouse.

A wealthy man, Langton was a benefactor to the God's House hospital in Southampton (where he maintained another residence), and above all to his alma mater at Queen's. Probably beginning in 1516, he financed the building of an ante-chapel which more than doubled the size of the college chapel, at a reported cost of £300. The work was probably largely completed by 1518, a date recorded in several stained-glass panels. He also paid for work on the provost's lodgings. Langton died in 1524 in the Charterhouse, where he requested burial, between 20 June, when he drew up his will, and the 30th, when a successor was collated to his Salisbury prebend. His memorial brass at Queen's, the stylized representation of a cleric, is far removed from the portrait of him recorded as 'lately' seen in 1858, depicting 'an elderly man, with white flowing beard, moustache, and hair; the features of a pronounced character, the nose being long and aquiline, and the eye piercing' (Thompson, 347). The picture, said to have come from Annesley Hall, Nottinghamshire, is not otherwise recorded.

Langton is also commemorated by his educational benefactions and by a book. In his will he made cash bequests totalling at least £623, including £10 for poor scholars at Oxford and £200 to Queen's 'to purchase lande and to make a scole howse in Appylby where I was born' (will, fol. 166). In 1681 it was recorded that he and his younger kinsman Miles Spenser had financed the 'Litle Schole' in front of Appleby grammar school's main building, and the two men's names were still engraved on the school seal in the 1920s. Langton's book shows him in a drier light. In 1522 he published *The pylgrymage of M. Robert Langton clerke to Seynt James in Compostell and in other holy places of Crystendome* (STC 15206). Only one copy is known to survive, in Lincoln Cathedral Library, though a modern edition appeared in 1924. It is presented in the form of a travelogue, starting at Orléans and listing the places, with the distances between

them, visited on his journey to Santiago and beyond. The itinerary is followed by a series of glosses on many of the places named in it, providing details of their relics and images, and sometimes also of points of secular interest, such as the tomb of Dante at Ravenna and the famous statue of Laocoon (disinterred only in 1506) in Rome.

In 1509 Langton walked alongside John Colet in Henry VII's funeral procession, and he named Cuthbert Tunstall and Richard Pace, both members of Colet's circle of moderate humanist reformers, as supervisors of his will. Like Colet, Langton wanted to advance the provision of learning. Unlike him, he clearly believed wholeheartedly in the spiritual value of pilgrimages: in the preamble to his *Pylgrymage* Langton declares that he has lately visited Jerusalem, and the emblems on his coat of arms may indicate that he travelled to Egypt and Sinai as well. In his old-fashioned stress on the penitential benefits of pilgrimages for those who 'take peyne on them for Crystes sake and encrease of theyr merytes' (*Pilgrimage*, 39), and his omitting to record the indulgences associated with relics and shrines, Langton may nevertheless reflect the aspirations of Colet and his associates to recover a pre-scholastic piety. In the early 1520s, however, such a position was out of step with popular devotion, perhaps explaining the apparent failure of his book.

HENRY SUMMERSON

Sources *The pilgrimage of Robert Langton*, ed. E. M. Blackie (1924) • Emden, *Oxf.*, 2.1100–01 • will, PRO, PROB 11/21, fols. 165v–166r • J. R. Magrath, *The Queen's College*, 2 vols. (1921) • A. Wood, *The history and antiquities of the colleges and halls in the University of Oxford*, ed. J. Gutch, 3 vols. in 4 (1786–96), vol. 3 • J. Thompson, 'Portrait of Dr Robert Langton', *N&Q*, 2nd ser., 6 (1858), 347–8 • R. B. Tate, 'Robert Langton, pilgrim (1470–1524)', *Nottingham Medieval Studies*, 39 (1995), 182–91 • R. J. Mitchell, 'Robert Langton's *Pylgrymage*', *The Library*, 5th ser., 8 (1953), 42–5 • D. S. Chambers, *Cardinal Bainbridge in the court of Rome, 1509 to 1514* (1965) • R. P. Brown, 'Thomas Langton and his tradition of learning', *Transactions of the Cumberland and Westmorland Antiquarian and Archaeological Society*, 2nd ser., 26 (1926), 150–246 • *Fasti Angl., 1300–1541*, [Salisbury]
Likenesses memorial brass, Queen's College, Oxford; repro. in Magrath, *Queen's College*, vol. 1, facing p. 13 • portrait, repro. in Thompson, 'Portrait of Dr Robert Langton'
Wealth at death cash bequests in will totalling at least £623, excluding household goods in London and Southampton, and some silver plate: will, PRO, PROB 11/21, fols. 165v–166r

Langton, Simon (d. 1248), ecclesiastic and diplomat, was the youngest son of Henry Langton of Langton by Wragby, Lincolnshire, and brother of Archbishop Stephen *Langton, who made him archdeacon of Canterbury. A third brother, Walter, inherited the family estate, but he was childless and on his death in 1234 his lands and debts fell to Simon. Simon was probably educated at Paris, where Stephen was the leading professor of the day, and he was almost invariably titled 'master'. A number of written works have been attributed to him in the past but they have either disappeared or had their attribution questioned.

Langton first appears in public records in 1208, when his brother Stephen was seeking acceptance as archbishop of Canterbury by King John. As Stephen's agent Simon made two trips to England in 1208, and probably another in

1209, during which he proved himself a hard bargainer. When John's resistance finally ended in 1213, he welcomed Simon to England very warmly. But during the next two years Simon Langton appears as the leading member of the archiepiscopal *familia*, perhaps acting as its chancellor, in its continued opposition to the king, and he went to Rome in 1214 to rebut charges made against his brother. After he had been given rich prebends in both London and York, his fellow canons of York elected Simon Langton their archbishop in 1215, despite a papal prohibition against his seeking the office. But when he went to Rome to seek confirmation his election was quashed and he was forbidden any episcopal office without specific papal approval. Unchastened, Langton proceeded to join Louis of France in his invasion of England and to become Louis's chancellor. He flouted the orders of the papal legate who had been sent to oppose Louis, and for this disobedience he was excommunicated by name. Consequently, when Louis withdrew in 1218, Langton was forced to surrender all his benefices and go to Rome for absolution. In time he was reconciled, made a papal subdeacon, and allowed to hold a benefice in France, but he was exiled from England by both king and pope. He seems to have resided in Paris where he was a canon of Notre Dame and where he received a pension from the French crown.

A rumour late in 1220 that the pope might allow Simon Langton to return to England occasioned a passionate protest from a large group of magnates. The king remitted his ire and indignation towards the end of 1223, but it was not until 1227 that both king and pope, at the urging of the archbishop, now old and ill, permitted Langton's re-entry. Langton arrived at Dover on 25 July, having already been named archdeacon on 14 May. In December, only seven months before his own death, Archbishop Stephen issued acts granting his brother and his successors authority over all churches of the archdiocese including those of the archbishop and his chapter, giving them the power to choose and remove rural deans, and increasing the wealth of the archdeacons by appropriating to the office the rich churches of Teynham and Hackington. These acts were ratified by the monks of Christ Church, Canterbury, who were assured that no church of secular canons would be built at Hackington to compete with their church (as proposed by the last two archbishops), and furthermore, the archdeacon gave them the archidiaconal house in Canterbury. In its stead Langton built a new official mansion at Hackington which he called New Place.

For the most part the duties of Langton's office were performed by his officials, two of whom are known: Master Robert of Gloucester and Master Roger of Elham. But Langton's term of office would be marked by three great controversies with the Benedictines of the archdiocese. First in 1235 Archbishop Edmund appealed to Rome against the election by the monks of Rochester of Richard Wendene (*d.* 1250) as their bishop. Langton was the archbishop's advocate, but the action was lost and Langton was ordered by the pope to assist in the consecration and to install the monks' choice. Then in 1237 the abbey of St

Augustine renewed its ancient claims against the archdeacon's jurisdiction over their appropriated churches, particularly in vacancies, but the matter was compromised yet again. Finally, in 1238, the monks of Christ Church, Canterbury, challenged the archbishop over their liberties, rights, and customs. The case was appealed to Rome, where the archbishop was again represented by the archdeacon, who accused the monks of forging their charters. This charge was proved, the prior was deposed, and two monks were exiled to other monasteries. But then the monks elected a new prior without proper involvement of the archbishop, who proceeded to excommunicate them. Langton supported Edmund wholeheartedly, and, after the archbishop died in 1240, brought a new claim that he, not the prior, should have spiritual jurisdiction in the archdiocese. The case was closed only when the king entered the lists in favour of his own candidate for the see and threatened royal wrath.

Langton was often more involved in the service of the pope and the king than of Canterbury. From the autumn of 1229 until that of 1237 there is no evidence that he spent any time in England. A rumour of his death reached the royal court in January 1232 and led to the appointment of a replacement until the story was found to be erroneous. His destination in 1229 was given as Rome, and the monastic chroniclers blame him for having sabotaged in 1231 and 1232 the elections to the archbishopric of Ralph Neville (*d.* 1244) and John Blund (*d.* 1248) respectively. Clearly he was held in high regard by Pope Gregory IX (*r.* 1227–41), who gave him a task to perform in Paris. It was in France, too, that King Henry made use of Langton's diplomatic talents by charging him to negotiate truces with the king of France and the count of La Marche. This proved a long and complicated process that went on from November 1234 until August 1235, for which services the king was effusively grateful. Langton was back in England for the legatine council of London on 20 November 1237, where he proceeded to make an enemy of the legate by demanding that the latter's commission be read. He accompanied Archbishop Edmund to and from Rome in 1238, but he is not known to have gone abroad thereafter and in 1241 he decided that he was too old and infirm to cross the Alps again, even to pursue his feud with the monks of Christ Church. In 1242 Henry wrote specially to Langton to ask his prayers for the success of the expedition the king was leading to Gascony, but two years later had to seek to restore the reputations of royal clerks who had been given an unfavourable report to the pope by a commission that included the archdeacon of Canterbury. Langton can be shown to have remained active into 1247, and he did not die until 1248.

The Benedictines cursed his memory as persecutor and troublemaker; Matthew Paris denounced him as one who had stirred up trouble throughout England and France. But Simon Langton was remembered affectionately by the Franciscans, whom he had welcomed into England, and by the college of poor priests in Canterbury, of which he was second founder. At the University of Paris he left a library for the use of poor scholars, and at the cathedral of

Notre Dame he endowed the celebration of his own and his brother's obituaries on the feast of the translation of St Thomas Becket, a feast that Stephen Langton had added to the church calendar.   FRED A. CAZEL, JR.

Sources J. C. Russell, 'Dictionary of writers of thirteenth century England', *BIHR*, special suppl., 3 (1936) [whole issue], esp. 152–4 · F. M. Powicke, *Stephen Langton* (1965) · K. Major, ed., *Acta Stephani Langton*, CYS, 50 (1950) · E. John, 'The litigation of an exempt house, St. Augustine's, Canterbury, 1182–1237', *Bulletin of the John Rylands University Library*, 39 (1956–7), 390–415 · Paris, *Chron.* · *Chancery records* · S. Painter, *The reign of King John* (1949) · *The historical works of Gervase of Canterbury*, ed. W. Stubbs, 2 vols., Rolls Series, 73 (1879–80) · *Matthaei Parisiensis, monachi Sancti Albani, Historia Anglorum, sive … Historia minor*, ed. F. Madden, 3 vols., Rolls Series, 44 (1886–9) · W. W. Shirley, ed., *Royal and other historical letters illustrative of the reign of Henry III*, 2 vols., Rolls Series, 27 (1862–6)

Langton, Stephen (c.1150–1228), archbishop of Canterbury, was one of three sons, perhaps the eldest, of Henry Langton, a minor landowner in Langton by Wragby, Lincolnshire. A moated farmhouse to the west of the church could mark his birthplace.

Early years and career in Paris The first certain date in Langton's life is his appointment as cardinal in 1206, though he is known to have taught theology in Paris in the 1180s. By then he would have completed courses in both the arts and theology, which would have taken fifteen years, from perhaps c.1165 to 1180, and it is likely that he would have been fifteen when his studies there began. One brother, Simon *Langton, followed him to Paris. Where the brothers were first educated is unknown, though Lincoln, about 12 miles from Langton, had schools. At first the family must have supported Stephen, but later he received benefices at York and Notre Dame, Paris. Some time between 1191 and 1205 Stephen was in York, where he witnessed two charters of Archbishop Geoffrey as Master Stephen Langton. If it were Geoffrey who gave him his prebend (and it is known that another Paris master, Pierre de Corbeil, was made archdeacon by him), this would have added to his later unpopularity with King John, who never enjoyed good relations with his brother. Much later in 1226 Stephen referred warmly to his former membership of the church of York. His position at Notre Dame, on the other hand, which would have provided him with a house as well as an income, must have depended upon the approval of King Philip Augustus, another negative point for John.

About 1165 there may have been approximately 3000 students in Paris, forming one-tenth of the city's total population. The schools were concentrated on the Île de la Cité, and around, even on, the Petit Pont which joined the Île to the Left Bank. Langton's teachers in arts are not known, but when he moved, c.1170–75, to theology, he came into contact with a number of masters, of whom the most significant was Peter the Chanter. Whether he was formally Peter's pupil is a matter of dispute, but it is agreed that Peter influenced him deeply in his choice of questions to tackle, and in interpretation of scripture. Like the Chanter, Langton attracted able pupils, of whom two, probably six, had distinguished careers. Richard Poor became dean of Salisbury in 1197 and was elected to

Stephen Langton (c.1150–1228), manuscript drawing [crowning Henry III]

Chichester, the first of his three bishoprics, in 1215, while Thomas of Marlborough became abbot of Evesham (1229–36), having previously taught law in Exeter and Oxford. Henry of Sandford, archdeacon of Canterbury and bishop of Rochester (1227–35), was certainly a great admirer of Langton and, like Alexander of Stainsby, bishop of Coventry and Lichfield (1224–38), may well have been another pupil. Andrew Sunenson, archbishop of Lund (1201–24), may have been a fifth, since some of his writings follow Langton's very closely, and Bernard (II), archbishop of Santiago de Compostela (1224–37), a sixth, because he had an extensive collection of Langton's works.

Writings Langton wrote most as a teacher of theology, exemplifying the three sides of a master's work distinguished by the Chanter: disputation of theological questions, biblical commentary, and sermons. In each area the sheer scale of manuscript evidence has prevented the close study, and certainly the editing, of more than a little. The difficulties are increased because many works survive in a number of forms: as yet no consensus has emerged about whether these reflect notes (*reportationes*) made by different students of the same, or separate, verbal presentations: the contribution of Langton's own editing is also unclear. It is possible that some revision may have occurred when he was unable to exercise his archiepiscopal office for much of 1207–13 and 1216–18.

The centre of Langton's work is a series of commentaries on the whole of the New and Old testaments, with the probable exception of the Psalms. They form a far larger contribution than that made by any other contemporary scholar. Some commentaries began as lectures, indeed some only exist as notes made by others which refer to Langton as 'the master'. Normally he draws on the work of earlier teachers contained in the *Glossa ordinaria*, and on writers nearer his day, like Andrew of St Victor, and Peter Lombard. One manuscript of a commentary on Paul's epistles portrays the relationship: in the centre of the page is the biblical text, around it Lombard's comments, and circling the whole, Langton's. For some books he comments on all the traditional senses of scripture, for some the literal sense only, or merely the moral. It is quite clear that, although establishing the meaning of the text is inescapable, he lays more stress on drawing out the spiritual meaning. At the start of his commentary upon the lesser prophets, taking a verse from Ecclesiasticus, 'May the bones of the Twelve Prophets spring up out of their place' (Ecclesiasticus 49: 12), he explains the dry bones as the letter of scripture, but their marrow and fatness as the spiritual interpretation, which is harder to extract.

This extensive biblical work made Langton aware of difficulties caused by the lack of any accepted method of arranging the Bible's books, and of dividing them into chapters. He produced schemes for both of these which rapidly won approval, and were still basically those used at the end of the twentieth century. There is less agreement about his share in a handbook which soon circulated as an appendix to the Bible, explaining the meaning of Hebrew names in the Bible, usually known from its opening entries as *Aaz-apprehendens*. Some manuscripts attribute it to him, but in view of the fact that some others date back to the eighth century, Langton's share may be that of editor and popularizer. He also produced a commentary on what was then the main textbook for biblical history, the *Historia scholastica* of Peter Comestor.

Within some of Langton's commentaries there are sections where he explores a *quaestio*, and references to *quaestiones* which exist separately. The *quaestiones* themselves contain some material also in his commentaries, and some which is quite independent, and which may survive in a number of different versions. Some *quaestiones* on related topics are grouped into collections, or *summae*—the *Summa de virtutibus et vitiis*, for example, deals with the seven deadly sins. Many of the *quaestiones* generally seem to have arisen out of disputation, which by that time took place at a different time from lectures. Only recently has the first thorough catalogue of these *quaestiones* been made.

The number of Langton's surviving sermons is very considerable: Schneyer's repertory lists over 600, but Roberts based her study on 122 that survive in several named copies. It is likely that the final figure of genuine sermons will fall somewhere between these two figures. Only a handful of them have yet been edited and their discussion has to be tentative. It is generally accepted that most were preached during his Paris years, although a few can be definitely placed later. Most were aimed at clerical audiences, some at monks, rather fewer at a mixed or mainly lay audience. It is supposed, by analogy with other known preachers, like Bernard of Clairvaux, that to the laity Langton would have spoken in the vernacular, although all surviving sermons are in Latin.

The quality of Langton's thought Some characteristics are common to all Langton's work: here two will be mentioned, self-confidence and liveliness. The first arose from his thorough training and grasp of earlier literature. He was fluent and clear in speech, and familiar with both Parisian masters and the fathers. He had absorbed the work carried out by Hugh and Andrew of St Victor to establish the meaning of the biblical text, which Peter Lombard, Peter Comestor (Peter Manducator), and Peter the Chanter had all accepted was essential. Among the fathers he had read particularly Jerome, Augustine, and Gregory. This preparation gave Langton courage sometimes to agree with a modern master like Andrew rather than Augustine. Quite frequently he referred to Jewish interpretations, but at present there is no consensus about whether he had any knowledge of Hebrew. Many of his references were derived from Hebraists among his immediate predecessors, like Peter Comestor, Peter the Chanter, and Andrew, rather than Jerome, and although he seems to have talked with Jews, he did not approve of entering into disputation with them, which some of his contemporaries did. The Jews were, for him, like slaves who carried the satchels of Christians—'Iudei enim capsarii nostri sunt' (Dahan, 130).

Langton's liveliness, although it can be overlooked, is shown in his frequent use of examples to illustrate the argument. The use of *exempla*, or short stories, in sermons had a long history by his time, going back to Jesus's use of parables. Langton drew upon the Bible most regularly for such stories, but he also turned to many sides of contemporary life. His comments upon life in the schools, for example, are vivid. He knew that many students, whatever they professed to be doing, spent their time gazing at the walls of the lecture room, but justified the charging of fees to them by appeal to the tradition that Abraham had become rich by teaching astronomy in Egypt. He illustrated the effectiveness of *exempla* in a comment upon the story in Judges 3 of Samgar's killing 600 Philistines with a ploughshare when Aod only dispatched one with a sharp sword:

> See! This makes clear that a preacher should not always use polished, subtle preaching, like Aod's sword, but sometimes a ploughshare, that is rustic exhortation. Very often a popular story [*exemplum*] is more effective than a polished, subtle phrase. Aod killed one man only with a two-edged sword, Samgar six hundred with a ploughshare; so, whereas the laity are easily converted by rude, unpolished preaching, a sermon to clerks will draw scarcely one of them from his error.   (Lacombe and Smalley, 173)

Langton's serious approach to sermons may have developed when he experienced some kind of conversion through listening to the charismatic preaching of Foulques de Neuilly, in the 1190s. Jacques de Vitry says that Langton was one of seven remarkable preachers who were deeply affected by him. It must have been his forceful preaching that led to his being nicknamed Thunder-Tongued (de Lingua-Tonante) in some manuscripts. In Paris, Langton belonged to a circle of masters who were committed to the reform of the church, and one of his stories casts a curious light forward to what was to befall him when he went to England. It occurs in the same commentary on the lesser prophets when he reaches the story of Amasius, the high priest of Bethel, hiding behind King Jeroboam as he received Amos. Langton describes Amasius as representing 'a bad priest or any bad, greedy prelate … [who] for a whore or a little worldly profit' was 'ready to go two leagues or more on a winter's night, but to hear a poor man's confession … will not leave his table, even for a few minutes' (Smalley, 'Four senses', 72–3).

Amos is the reformer, fresh from Paris. To him Amasius says:

> 'Thou seer', O popular and learned doctor, who threatens us so terribly with thy piety! 'Go, flee away into the land of Judah', leave my bishopric or my parish, return to your studies in Paris, 'eat bread there and prophesy there', confine your teaching and preaching in Paris. 'In Bethel', that is my bishopric, 'prophesy no more', that is preach no more. (ibid.)

Certainly there can be no doubt that Langton, once he moved from the schools to the world, found himself faced with pressures and tensions of such complexity that they nearly tore him apart.

The Canterbury election Early in 1206 Langton's life as a successful teacher came to an abrupt end: Innocent III called him to Rome, to become cardinal-priest of St Chrysogonus; by the end of that year he had persuaded the monks of Canterbury to elect him archbishop of Canterbury. Just what considerations had moved the pope to either course are not entirely clear, but they may be connected. Both men were of similar age, and had known each other for about twenty years, since Innocent had studied in Paris before 1187. Like Langton, the pope admired Thomas Becket, whose shrine at Canterbury he visited. That experience may have made him aware how the community felt about the dead saint, with whom they had often disagreed while he was alive, and their defence of their rights in the choice of his successors. Certainly the long struggle between Christ Church and two later archbishops, Baldwin and Hubert Walter, over their plan to create a collegiate church, would have been very well known at Rome. It may be more than coincidence, then, that the pope sent for Langton not long after news of Hubert Walter's death on 13 July 1205, and the subsequent dispute, arrived in Rome.

Langton would have been able to observe closely the procession of embassies over the next months as the monks, the suffragan bishops of Canterbury, and the king all tried to make their cases. Ultimately, in December 1206, after the pope had rejected the royal and monastic nominees, and the claim of the suffragans to take part in the election, the monastic delegation elected Stephen Langton. Their choice was influenced by Innocent after the community had shown itself to be divided. To John, Langton was quite unacceptable: he was not someone he knew, had spent too much time in France, and had been chosen after a process that allowed no consideration of royal preferences. It is likely, too, that he wanted a more compliant person than Hubert Walter, with whom his relations had become very strained.

To John's objections Innocent replied by praising Langton's qualities as a 'Doctor not only in the liberal arts but also in theological learning' (Cheney and Semple, 86–90). When he added that 'as a result he was judged worthy to hold a prebend of Paris' and another at York, he struck notes, as has been observed, that would have jarred. Innocent's stance was based on the provision in canon law that, when an election took place in his presence, there was no formal need for royal approval, and he seems to

have thought that John would concede, as he had done in earlier disputed elections. His warning in the same letter, that John would find it dangerous to 'fight against God and the Church in this cause for which St Thomas, that glorious martyr and archbishop recently shed his blood', was scarcely emollient. The two parties, king and pope, saw the problem from diametrically opposed points of view, and it was to be nearly six and a half years before they could come to terms.

The unacceptable archbishop Matters stood still from the election until 17 June 1207 when Innocent consecrated Stephen Langton at Viterbo. Not long afterwards Langton wrote a long open letter to the English people which provides some hints as to why he accepted the position. The first is his feeling of deep pastoral concern for England, not surprising for one whose career had become increasingly devoted to preparing others to be priests. The second is a sense that he had only accepted because ordered to by the pope, *de mandato superioris*—again something that would spring out of his own teaching. Lastly, when he, like Innocent, claimed that the struggle involved Becket and the liberties he had established, he betrays a feeling of deep personal identification with his predecessor. Later his choice of seal was to reflect this: the reverse shows the martyrdom within an inscription which may be translated 'May the picture of a death in the external world, be for you a life of love within'. The letter, in short, suggests that Langton accepted what he must have known to be an almost impossible task because he felt deeply committed to trying to put into practice what he had taught.

The letter went on to emphasize Frederick Barbarossa's fate: he had struggled against the church, and then drowned in a stream which even a child could have waded through, because God's justice had caught up with him. Langton also, perhaps more ominously, stated that if a rebel remained in schism the church could justly absolve his men of their fealty, since he had withdrawn his fealty from God. Such words can hardly have weakened John's resolve. When he heard of the consecration, he expelled the monks from Christ Church (11 July) and began the course that led to an interdict being laid on his kingdom on 24 March 1208 and his own excommunication in November 1209.

Meanwhile the king took his revenge on Langton's family, causing his father to flee to St Andrews, where he died. His other brother, Walter, may well have gone overseas about then, since in 1211 he was fighting in the Albigensian crusade. Stephen moved into northern France and spent most time at the Cistercian monastery at Pontigny, where Becket had also passed part of his exile. In 1222 he remembered Pontigny generously, granting it an annual pension of 50 marks from the church at Romney. Sometimes he is recorded elsewhere. In October 1209 he went to Melun where he consecrated Hugh of Wells as bishop of Lincoln, and next year settled a dispute between the bishop and city of Cambrai. A year later, in 1211, he presided at the funeral of William de Briouze at the abbey of St Victor in Paris. The winter of 1212–13 was spent in

Rome, and at some time between 1210 and 1213 he undertook a preaching tour against usury in Flanders with his fellow Englishman and master of the Paris schools, Robert de Courson.

Fruitless negotiations for Langton's acceptance in England took place each year from 1208 to 1211. Stephen used his brother Simon as his representative on the first two occasions, and in October 1209 had sufficient hope to cross himself to Dover. But such parleys all foundered on two issues: the king wished to have his own position in elections formally recognized by the pope, while the archbishop and his fellow exiles wanted to bind him to compensate them for their own losses. The trust necessary for settlement was lacking. Twice, in 1208 and 1211, Langton cavilled about the terms of safe conducts provided for him and refused to negotiate in England.

Ultimately, in the autumn of 1212, the political situation forced John to give way. Some of his nobles were plotting against him, the Welsh were causing problems, and so he sent a powerful group to Rome which early in 1213 accepted terms offered in 1211. Langton and other English bishops were probably in Rome to witness this collapse. The king was to promise to obey the pope, to provide safe conducts for the archbishop, the other exiled prelates, and the monks of Christ Church, to hand over the Canterbury estates to Langton, after he had taken an oath of fealty from him, and to compensate the exiles for their losses. Innocent gave John until the beginning of June to agree. This he did on 13 May before Pandulf, the papal nuncio, and Langton entered England on 9 July. On 20 July he absolved the king from his excommunication at Winchester and celebrated mass in his presence. The struggle for Canterbury seemed to be over, but a wider struggle had already begun.

Archbishop in action The next two years were full of activity, as Langton tried to deal with the problems left by the interdict, and then to mediate between John and his restless barons. On his return Langton was about sixty years old, lacking close knowledge of either king or nobles because he had been out of England for forty years, apart from a short period in York, and a mere visit to Dover. It must have taken time for him to establish himself and to try to win the king's confidence. The task must have been almost impossible if John knew that Simon Langton had been in the pay of Prince Louis. Stephen's role was further complicated by the king's surrender of his kingdoms into the hands of Pandulf, just three weeks before his own return. Holding England and Ireland as fiefs from the pope, in return for an annual tribute of 1000 marks, like his later taking the cross (March 1215), may have protected the king against the discontented, but growing papal intervention in England was now inevitable. That was critically affected by the distance between England and Italy. A fast messenger took at least thirty days to traverse it, so by the time the pope's reaction to news of English events arrived back, at least two months had passed: again and again Innocent's orders did not fit the new situation. He got news, too, from king and papal representatives who might well paint Langton's interventions in a poor light.

Innocent's primary desire was for peace, and for the crusade: he had little understanding or sympathy with anyone who wanted to disturb the balance of things. The pope was also concerned with the great council to which he had sent out summonses on 13 April 1213, although it was not to gather until November 1215. Langton, on the other hand, clearly acquired sympathy with some of the barons' aims, as he tried to mediate between them and the king, because he suspected John's good faith. Thus, in the end, he was trusted by neither king nor pope, and suspended from office.

Innocent's instructions to Langton of 15 July 1213 told him to 'do all that you believe helpful to the salvation and peace of the king and kingdom, not forgetting the honour and advantage of the Apostolic See and the English church …' (Cheney and Semple, 155). Langton's priorities were rather different, as he became involved in two issues: the settlement of compensation for the exiles and the filling of vacant positions in the church, both being issues which brought him into conflict with king and pope. John obviously wanted to be committed to pay as little as possible; Stephen and the other exiles wanted to bind the king firmly, and had only the threat of refusing to lift the interdict to persuade him to come to terms. The situation clearly puzzled ordinary people, since Langton was forced to devote a large part of his sermon delivered at St Paul's on 25 August 1213 to it. The newly arrived papal legate, Nicolò of Tusculum, was annoyed that the bishops would not compromise, while Peter des Roches, bishop of Winchester, worked skilfully to reduce John's contribution. When finally John accepted a solution, on 17 June 1214, it satisfied no one, and entirely ignored the losses of churchmen who had stayed in England.

The task of filling vacant sees and abbeys was equally contentious. At first John attempted to proceed as though things could continue exactly as before, summoning groups of canons or monks to conduct elections in the royal chapel—a process to which Langton and the bishops objected. They hoped for a freer form of election, although they must have realized that John was unlikely to agree. The pope had put elections firmly under Cardinal Nicolò on 31 October 1213, urging him to ensure that those elected 'on your recommendation' should be 'suitable clerks who should be men not only distinguished by their life and learning, but also loyal to the king, useful to the state, and capable of giving counsel and help—the king's assent having been requested' (Cheney and Semple, 166). When John left for Poitou in February 1214 he arranged that elections were to be supervised by a committee of five: two great lay curialists, William Brewer and William (I) de Cantilupe, with the abbots of Beaulieu, Selby, and St Mary's, York. Langton was outmanoeuvred; the result was that most new bishops were king's men, and Langton had no chance to see whether reformers might be treated as he had thought they would be when he was a teacher.

Langton and Magna Carta Much the most difficult part of Langton's job was to try to work for 'the peace of the king and the kingdom', as Innocent put it, since John was planning to take a great expedition to Poitou in 1214 against the king of France, a repeat of the project of 1212–13 which had been prevented by baronial opposition. Very soon after the reconciliation with the king Langton intervened to persuade him not to punish those barons who had refused service, and from then on he was almost continually involved in negotiations. Nowadays the picturesque stories told by Roger of Wendover, of Langton's making John promise at the time of his absolution to restore the good laws of Edward the Confessor and producing a charter of Henry I at St Paul's on 25 August to the assembled barons, are discounted. There is, however, general agreement that without Langton the course of events would have been very different.

Langton's was probably the mind responsible for the attempt to set down in writing what the barons wanted, and to frame it in a way which would bind the king. His concern that a king should act according to law and after proper judgment had been themes of his teaching. At first he seems to have hoped that persuading the king to swear to repeat his coronation oath, or something like it, at the time of his absolution would be enough, but by November 1213 he seems to have realized that more was necessary. When the political balance tipped against the king following the battle of Bouvines (27 July 1214) the problems became ever more difficult. Langton lost the pope's trust. Innocent came to connect the growth of discontent in England with the archbishop's arrival, and was ready to aid the king by instructing the archbishop to denounce conspirators against him. The role given to Langton, and to other bishops, in the articles of the barons to clear up various still unsettled matters reflects the barons' confidence. The first clause in Magna Carta granting freedom to the English church, including freedom of elections, may be one achievement of the archbishop, though he and the bishops may well have been troubled by the security clause that denied royal rights which they supported.

Both the articles and Magna Carta were forced out of John by the short civil war of May 1215, but the peace they symbolized quickly broke down, despite Langton's continuous efforts to prevent this. He and the bishops, for example, tried to bring the parties together at Oxford on 16 August and at Staines on the 28th. Soon afterwards, when Innocent's letter of 7 July, which had been written in ignorance both of the charter and of renewed hostilities, arrived, it excommunicated all 'disturbers of the king and kingdom' (Cheney and Semple, 208), and laid their lands under interdict, ordering the archbishop and his suffragans to publish these sentences, or be suspended. By that time Langton had completely lost royal favour when he refused to surrender Rochester Castle (a cause of tension ever since the reconciliation of July 1213), almost certainly because by then he did not trust the king. In some senses his refusal to excommunicate the rebels, presumably on the ground that the pope lacked full knowledge of the facts, brought to an end an intolerable situation. The bishop of Winchester, the first addressee of the letter, suspended him, about the middle of September as he was leaving for Rome to attend the council. If Langton's career had ended here, his archiepiscopate might have seemed a disaster.

Last years Langton made his way south to Rome, where on 4 November 1215 Innocent confirmed his suspension. A few days later the great council opened at the Lateran, at which, perhaps unsurprisingly, Langton seems to have taken little part. Indeed, almost nothing is known about his movements until he returned to England in May 1218, having been permitted to do so by Honorius III. By then he found a very different political situation from that of 1215. The throne was occupied by a boy, but power was exercised on the young Henry III's behalf by a triumvirate: William (I) Marshal, the regent, Peter des Roches, bishop of Winchester, and Pandulf, since 1218 papal legate. In 1219 Langton took charge of the investigation into the miracles of Hugh of Lincoln, and next year presided at two great celebrations: Henry's second coronation at Westminster (17 May 1220), and two months later the translation of Becket's relics to a new shrine at Canterbury. There he emphasized Becket's essential Englishness, a nice note for a prelate who was so unused to England, and whose brother Simon was still not allowed back into the country because of his support for Prince Louis's attempt to seize the throne. That autumn he travelled to Rome to ask for the recall of Pandulf, taking with him a Becket relic as a gift for the pope. He was back by July 1221 with the order for Pandulf's return, and from then until his death he played a significant role in public affairs.

Power was still not in Henry's control, but exercised by the justiciar, Hubert de Burgh, and des Roches, along with the archbishop, who took over something of the moderating role that the Marshal had filled. Langton was involved in many critical episodes, as the justiciar and des Roches jockeyed for influence, and the body of loyal royal administrators tried to maintain peace and order. One means, the reissuing of the great charter of 1215, certainly owed something to Langton's belief in it as powerful reassurance of royal good intentions. In January 1223 he persuaded the king to confirm it verbally, and two years later was behind its reissue in what was to be its definitive form. The gesture did not placate all those being forced to disgorge castles and offices that they had long controlled, and next year occurred the one serious breakdown of internal peace since the end of the French invasion. William de Bréauté then held Bedford, on his brother's behalf, against the justiciar for eight weeks from June to August 1224. Langton was at the siege and its bloody end when the garrison was hanged. There he was acting out his earlier view that removing custody of a castle from a noble was proper if a judgment of the royal court preceded action. To Honorius the archbishop's conduct seemed extraordinary, because he believed that troops should have been fighting against the king's enemies in Poitou, but he, like Innocent earlier, suffered from having no real knowledge of what was happening in England.

Closer to his concern for reform, Langton made time to hold a provincial council for his province at Oxford in 1222. The significance of its sixty canons is reflected in their survival in sixty manuscripts. Nine of its provisions cite those of the Fourth Lateran Council, while another sixteen reflect it. Others repeat statutes issued by a synod for the diocese of Canterbury which Langton had managed to hold in 1213–14. Very quickly other bishops included the Oxford canons in their own diocesan legislation, and so Langton's work endured as the basis of the church's law. As examples of provisions affected by the Fourth Lateran Council may be cited prohibitions against clergy taking part in judgments involving the loss of blood, or celebrating mass more than twice a day save at Christmas or Easter, and attempts to insist that every vicar should receive an income of at least 5 marks a year, and that no person should occupy more than one benefice involving cure of souls (clauses 13, 11, 21, 44). Altogether a wide range of issues involving both regular and secular clergy were covered, so that the life of the later medieval church was deeply influenced by Langton's work.

In 1227, when he was in his seventies, perhaps nearly eighty, Langton retired from court, but it is striking how king and justiciar continued to maintain contact with him. On 7 July 1228 Langton took part in the celebration of the feast of the Translation of Becket in Canterbury, having seen Henry and Hubert the day before when they came to ratify the terms of a truce with France. By then he was very weak and was taken by litter to his manor at Slindon, Sussex, where he died, probably on 9 July (the sources disagree), to be buried, a few days later, at Canterbury, where his monument, as a result of a rebuilding in the 1430s, now lies protruding through the east wall of St Michael's Chapel, at the south-west end of the nave.

Changing estimates of Langton Understanding of Langton's life has changed considerably since the late nineteenth century, when interest centred primarily on the political side of his archiepiscopate, as told in chronicle sources, and particularly on his part in the negotiations that led to Magna Carta. Now a better appreciation of the complex politics of John's reign lends a different aspect to Langton's contribution, and his achievement as one of the most important theologians of the turn of the twelfth century has emerged. The change can be seen beginning in F. M. Powicke's Ford lectures of 1928 (which still set the main chronology). They were much influenced by the work of one of his pupils, Beryl Smalley, then beginning to hew out from the manuscripts an entirely new Langton. She has been followed in this task by many, but very few of his works are yet edited, or their chronology established.

Undoubtedly Stephen Langton was one of the great churchmen of the middle ages, moving at the heart of public affairs for much of his archiepiscopate. As ecclesiastical statesman he helped to make the tensions of John's reign less bloody than they might have been, to create the climate in which Magna Carta could be produced, and to see that later it was brought within the regular means of maintaining trust between king and people. As primate and diocesan he left behind relatively few *acta* compared with Baldwin or Hubert Walter, but he provided the church with a standard for reform in his legislation. At Canterbury itself he finished the great archiepiscopal hall begun by Hubert Walter. On the world of learning his

mark was as great as any of his predecessors, Anselm excepted, and he enriched the resources of prayer with one great sequence, *Veni, sancte spiritus* ('Come, Holy Ghost'). A great scholar, an indefatigable negotiator, a wise elder statesman, he deserves to be remembered, even though he might have judged his own achievements severely against the standards he had taught in the schools.   CHRISTOPHER HOLDSWORTH

Sources F. M. Powicke, *Stephen Langton* (1928) · B. Smalley, *The study of the Bible in the middle ages* (1952) · J. W. Baldwin, *Masters, princes and merchants: the social views of Peter the Chanter and his circle*, 2 vols. (1970) · P. B. Roberts, *Stephanus de Lingua-Tonante: studies in the sermons of Stephen Langton*, Pontifical Institute of Medieval Studies: Texts and Studies, 16 (1968) · J. C. Holt, *Magna Carta* (1965) · C. R. Cheney, *Innocent III and England*, Päpste und Papsttum, 9 (1976) · N. Vincent, *Peter des Roches: an alien in English politics, 1205–38*, Cambridge Studies in Medieval Life and Thought, 4th ser., 31 (1996) · D. A. Carpenter, *The minority of Henry III* (1990) · K. Major, ed., *Acta Stephani Langton*, CYS, 50 (1950) · G. Lacombe and B. Smalley, 'Studies on the commentaries of Cardinal Stephen Langton', *Archives d'Histoire Doctrinale et Littéraire du Moyen Âge*, 5 (1930), 5–266 · L. Antl, 'An introduction to the *Questiones theologicae* of Stephen Langton', *Franciscan Studies*, new ser., 13 (1952), 151–75 · N. Vincent, 'Master Simon Langton, King John and the court of France', *Speculum* [forthcoming] · *Selected letters of Pope Innocent III concerning England, 1198–1216*, ed. C. R. Cheney and W. H. Semple (1953) · F. A. Cazel, 'The last years of Stephen Langton', *EngHR*, 79 (1964), 673–97 · B. Smalley, 'Stephen Langton and the four senses of scripture', *Speculum*, 6 (1931), 60–76 · C. R. Cheney, *Medieval texts and studies* (1973), 111–37, 138–57, 185–202 · G. Dahan, 'Exégèse et polémique dans les commentaires de la "Génèse" d'Étienne Langton', *Les juifs au regard d'histoire: mélanges en l'honneur de Bernard Blumenkrantz*, ed. G. Dahan (Paris, 1985), 129–48 · A. d'Esneval, 'Le perfectionnement d'un instrument de travail au début du XIIe siècle: les trois glossaires bibliques d'Étienne Langton', *Culture et travail dans l'Occident médiéval*, ed. G. Hasenohr and J. Longère (1981), 163–75 · A. Saltman, ed., *Stephen Langton: commentary on the Book of Chronicles* (1978) · P. B. Roberts, 'Archbishop Stephen Langton and his preaching on Thomas Becket', *De ore Domini: preacher and word in the middle ages*, ed. T. L. Amos, E. Green, and B. M. Kienzle (1989), 75–92 · I. W. Rowlands, 'King John, Stephen Langton and Rochester Castle, 1213–15', *Studies in medieval history presented to R. Allen Brown*, ed. C. Harper-Bill, C. J. Holdsworth, and J. L. Nelson (1989), 267–80 · F. Stegmüller, ed., *Repertorium biblicum medii aevi*, 11 vols. (Madrid, 1950?–1980) · J. B. Schneyer, *Repertorium der lateinischen Sermones des Mittelalters: für die Zeit von 1150–1350*, 5 (Münster, 1974), 466–507 · R. Quinto, *'Doctor nominatissimus': Stefano Langton (†1228) e la tradizione delle sue opere* (Münster, 1994) · S. Ebbesen, 'The semantics of the Trinity according to Stephen Langton and Andrew Sunesen', *Gilbert de Poitiers et ses contemporains*, ed. J. Jolivet (1987), 401–35 · P. Collinson and others, eds., *A history of Canterbury Cathedral, 598–1982* (1995), 455

Archives Bodl. Oxf., commentary on Isaiah · LPL, commentaries on Pentateuch and Joshua

Likenesses manuscript drawing, CCC Cam., MS 16, fol. 56r [see illus.] · obverse seal, repro. in F. Barlow, *Thomas Becket* (1986) · seal, repro. in Powicke, *Stephen Langton*, frontispiece

Langton, Thomas (c.1430–1501), bishop of Winchester and archbishop-elect of Canterbury, was born at Appleby in Westmorland. The terms of his will imply that the year of his birth was about 1430. He had graduated MA at Cambridge by 1456 and was a fellow of Pembroke College by 1462–3, when he served as senior proctor of the university. He vacated his fellowship in 1464 to study at Padua, but soon returned to Cambridge because of a shortage of funds, and was admitted BTh in 1465. During his second stay in Italy (1468–73) Langton was created DCnL at Bologna in 1473 and DTh by 1476.

Langton's first benefice may have been the rectory of Seaham, Durham, which he held by May 1473. Described as a royal chaplain, he became a canon of Crediton briefly in November 1477, and on 18 February 1478 was collated to the treasurership of Exeter, at the king's nomination. In January 1478 he was appointed to a canonry and prebend in Wells, and in 1479 the king presented him to the rectory of Pembridge in Herefordshire, which he continued to hold until 1485. He was given the rectory of All Hallows, Bread Street, by the archbishop of Canterbury on 1 July 1480, and the rectory of All Hallows Gracechurch by the prior of Canterbury in May 1482. He was also a canon of Lincoln. On 4 July 1483 Langton was papally provided to the bishopric of St David's at the request of the protector, Richard, duke of Gloucester, who had already given him custody of the temporalities. Langton was consecrated on 7 September. As king, Richard secured Langton's translation to the more valuable see of Salisbury early in 1485. The temporalities had been in Langton's custody since March 1484, Bishop Lionel Woodville being then an attainted traitor in sanctuary.

Langton's experience of travel on the continent doubtless proved invaluable at the outset of his secular career as a diplomat. In November 1476, and again in March 1477, Edward IV appointed him to go to Castile to explore a possible marriage between the prince of Wales and the Infanta Isabella. In November 1477 and March 1478 he went to France, to try to dissuade Louis XI from his proposed attack on Burgundy. On 26 August 1478 Langton was empowered to conclude with the king of France the betrothal of Edward IV's eldest daughter, Elizabeth, with the dauphin, and was reappointed to this fruitless project in May 1479 and August 1480. Edward IV also employed Langton on missions to Maximilian, duke of Austria and later emperor, in 1480–81. On 29 February 1484 Richard III appointed Langton his proctor to the curia to swear obedience to the pope, and on 21 March empowered him to negotiate a truce with Charles VIII of France. When he was not on embassy Langton was busy at court, and he accompanied Richard III on his progress in August 1483, during which he wrote a celebrated letter to the prior of Christ Church, Canterbury, in praise of the new king, declaring that 'God hath sent him to us for the weal of us all' (Ross, 151).

According to a privy seal warrant sealed on 6 October 1485 Langton forfeited his temporalities as bishop of Salisbury by his adherence to Richard III at Bosworth; however, on 6 November he was granted full pardon and restitution of his lands and revenues, and by the end of the month he was exercising his episcopal patronage unimpeded. He immersed himself in the administration of his diocese, being particularly assiduous in his efforts to eradicate Lollard heresy, both at Salisbury and later at Winchester, visiting the royal court only when summoned to parliament or convocation. Having been excluded from Henry VII's first parliament in 1485, he was summoned to the next, in November 1487, and to all subsequent parliaments until his death. Also in November 1487 he was appointed to the commission of the peace for Wiltshire; he served in this capacity for Wiltshire, Hampshire, and Surrey until his death. In December 1487 he was elected provost of Queen's College, Oxford. The most convincing proof that Langton had gained the confidence of Henry VII is provided by his translation, early in 1493, to the see of Winchester, the richest in England. But he continued to shun the court, and occupied himself with diocesan administration and the rebuilding of the palace at Bishop's Waltham, Hampshire. When Cardinal Morton died on 15 September 1500, Henry VII secured Langton's election as archbishop of Canterbury on 22 January 1501, but only two or three days later Langton fell ill with plague, and on 27 January he died.

The text of Langton's will, dated 25 January, runs to more than one hundred items. His money legacies amount to upwards of £2000, including the provision of six exhibitions in Queen's College, Oxford, and more than a dozen other benefactions to the universities. Richard Pace (d. 1536), the future diplomat and dean of St Paul's, who had been sent as a young man to study at Padua at Langton's expense, remembered that the bishop 'befriended all learned men exceedingly, and in his time was another Maecenas, rightly remembering (as he often said), that it was for learning that he had been promoted to the rank of bishop' (Wegg, 4–5). He also advanced the fortunes of his nephews Robert *Langton (d. 1524) and Christopher *Bainbridge (d. 1514)—the latter was subsequently appointed cardinal-archbishop of York. Thomas Langton is buried in the richly decorated chantry chapel he had built at the east end of the south aisle of the retro-choir of Winchester Cathedral.   D. P. WRIGHT

Sources D. P. Wright, ed., *The register of Thomas Langton, bishop of Salisbury, 1485–93*, CYS, 74 (1985) · C. E. Woodruff, ed., *Sede vacante wills*, Kent Archaeological Society Records Branch, 3 (1914) · J. B. Sheppard, ed., *Literae Cantuarienses: the letter books of the monastery of Christ Church, Canterbury*, 3 vols., Rolls Series, 85 (1887–9) · J. B. Sheppard, *Christ Church letters*, CS, new ser., 19 (1877) · T. Langton, bishop's register, 1493–1501, Hants. RO, Winchester diocesan records, 21M65.A1/16 · J. Wegg, *Richard Pace: a Tudor diplomatist* (1932) · C. Ross, *Richard III* (1981)

Archives Hants. RO, register, MS 21M65.A1/16 · Wilts. & Swindon RO

Wealth at death over £2000: Woodruff, ed., *Sede vacante wills*

Langton, Thomas (1724–1794), flax merchant, was born at Kirkham, Lancashire, on 18 August 1724, the fourth of nine children of John Langton (1691–1762), woollen draper and merchant of Kirkham, and Elizabeth (d. 1766), natural daughter, and only child, of Thomas Brown of Kirkham, gentleman, who gave her the same advantages of education he would have accorded his legal heir.

Thomas Langton received an exclusively classical education at Clitheroe Free School under the Revd Park. He became a partner with his father and William Shepherd, a flax dresser and merchant venturer, and it is likely he received his grounding in the linen trade from Shepherd. In 1753 he married Shepherd's niece, Jane (d. 1774), elder daughter of William Leyland, merchant, of Blackburn; they had nine children, six of whom survived infancy.

The firm benefited from the improved fortunes of the English linen trade following the legislation of the 1750s, and secured several contracts for sailcloth with the Navy Board from 1756. Shepherd's brother-in-law, John Birley, became a partner in the firm on John Langton's death in 1762, and the firm eventually became Langton, Birley & Co. They imported most of their flax and hemp from the Baltic, along with subsidiary merchandise such as iron, wheat, and timber. To the American colonies they exported canvas and twine, and imported from there timber, rum, sugar, and tobacco, sometimes as part-owners, sometimes taking freight in others' ships. Occasionally they were participants in the three-cornered slave trade.

Four generations of Langtons served the public life of Kirkham. Thomas Langton was seven times bailiff. He followed his father onto the select vestry of the Thirtymen and was trustee of the girls' charity school, of which his father was co-founder. He was a visitor of the free school and trustee of charities in neighbouring villages. As a freeholder he had the franchise, with which he supported the whigs at the Lancaster elections.

Forty-eight letters written by Thomas Langton and now in the Lancashire Record Office reveal much about the public and private persona of the writer. As a man of business he was in firm command, issuing instructions how to conduct transactions, advocating the desirability of deals 'for money' and the need to avoid 'the risque of bad debts'. Prospective clients were vetted for their 'sufficiency'. No opportunity of furthering trade was to be lost. His son Will, on holiday in France, was encouraged to 'form some connections which might be of use in the mercantile line'; he was reminded that the firm was 'near enough to Liverpool to attend to the sale of any article'. Langton held that 'justice and not humanity' must be the rule in commercial affairs, but he was fair and honest in his dealings, a worthy operator in a business world where personal integrity counted for much. Although the firm experienced a cash crisis in both 1780 and 1788, his able management steered them through.

For his sons' education, Langton chose private academies offering a 'liberal education' to follow their earlier years at the Kirkham Free School, which followed the classical curriculum. Twenty-six of the letters are written to his two eldest sons at the academy of the Revd Bartholomew Booth, first at Woolton Hall, near Liverpool, and later at High Beach, Essex. He was anxious to get value for the 'great expense' the boys' schooling cost him; he continually urged them to pay special attention to writing and accounts, the basic skills of business, and they were to account for every penny they spent. He was, however, generous in what he allowed them, and they had considerable freedom in personal choice of dress and recreation. Nor was his daughter expected to spend all her time at home, even after her mother died in January 1774.

Thomas Langton's will does not survive, but his granddaughter, Anne, wrote that he 'left his property to his sons according to seniority, in diminishing ratio', his daughter receiving the same as his youngest son. He had, however, taken care to provide for his sons by placing them appropriately. His two eldest were his partners, the fourth was set up as a 'Manchester warehouseman' in London, and the youngest became a partner in a Riga mercantile house. The third, blind from childhood, was settled in Kirkham. His daughter married into the rival Hornby flax firm.

The Birleys remembered Thomas Langton as 'a proud man of very passionate temperament' but *Billings Liverpool Advertiser*, announcing his death, added 'deeply lamented by his friends and the poor'. His strong personality certainly dominated his family, but he had a real affection for his children, and his son Will may readily be believed, when he recorded that they 'deeply lamented' their father's passing. He died at his home, Ash Hall, Kirkham, on 30 October 1794 and was buried in the churchyard of Kirkham parish church, where he had worshipped with his family.   JOAN WILKINSON

Sources Lancs. RO, Langton papers, DDX/190/1–190 · *The letters of Thomas Langton, flax merchant of Kirkham, 1771–1788*, ed. J. Wilkinson, Chetham Society, 3rd ser., 38 (1994) · F. J. Singleton, 'The flax merchants of Kirkham', *Historic Society of Lancashire and Cheshire*, 126 (1977), 73–108 · Lancs. RO, Birley papers, DDD/unclassified · R. C. Shaw, *Kirkham in Amounderness* (1947) · A. Langton, *The story of our family* (privately printed, Manchester, 1881) · Clitheroe grammar school accounts, Lancs. RO, DDX/22/5 · *Billings Liverpool Advertiser* (31 Oct 1794)

Archives Lancs. RO, letters, 1771–88, DDX/190/21–68

Langton, Walter (d. 1321), administrator and bishop of Coventry and Lichfield, was probably born in Langton West within Church Langton parish, Leicestershire, where in 1306 he received a grant of free warren. At his death he still held 3 acres there. Sir Robert Peverel, son and heir of Walter's brother, Simon Peverel, had a house at Northampton in the early 1300s. When Walter died, his heir was Robert's son Edmund. The idea that he was a nephew of William Langton of Rotherfield, dean of York, arose from confusion with another Walter. It is tempting to suggest a relationship between Walter and Edward I's chancellor John Langton, but the latter name seems to have been a common one, and it is impossible to make any secure identification among the John Langtons with whom Walter Langton was associated.

Early career in church and state Guisborough describes Langton as a poor clerk; elsewhere he is said to have been in Edward I's service from his youth. Appearing first as a wardrobe clerk in 1281–2, he presented the account roll for the Welsh war of 1282–4 in lieu of the controller, Thomas Gunneys. He was in Gascony with the king in 1286 and 1289. By 1287 he was acting as cofferer of the wardrobe, by 1290 as its controller—the year in which, after some months as temporary lieutenant, he succeeded William Louth, created bishop of Ely, as keeper of the wardrobe. In that position he was responsible for improving the wardrobe's methods of accounting for its expenditure and receipts. After Chancellor Robert Burnell's death in 1292, he had temporary custody of the great seal before John Langton's appointment, while in 1295 he followed William of March (d. 1302) as treasurer of the exchequer, an office he was to retain until 22 August 1307—just over a month into Edward II's reign.

Thanks to Edward I, Langton became a notable pluralist, and when on 7 January 1296 the Lichfield chapter sought licence to elect a bishop he was chosen (19 February). Archbishop Robert Winchelsey (d. 1313) gave his assent on 11 June; the spiritualities were restored the same day. Immediately afterwards he took the oath of fealty to the vicegerent of the king and received livery of the temporalities on the 16th. His consecration by Béraud de Got, cardinal-bishop of Albano, took place on 23 December at Cambrai, where he was engaged in peace negotiations with the papal nuncios. This was irritating to a metropolitan concerned to uphold his chapter's claim to license the ceremony's performance *alibi*. On his return he had to make his profession of obedience to Winchelsey before the high altar at Canterbury, and again at the archiepiscopal manor of Teynham, an elaboration which—the continuator of Gervase of Canterbury implied—was a conscious attempt to underline the priory's rights. As might be expected he had little time for his diocese. His episcopal register contains sections for his vicars-general: Master Robert Redeswell, archdeacon of Chester, for the period 1298–1308, Master Ralph Leicester for 1312–13—there were others. Only slight indications of visitational activity can be traced, and many episcopal mandates emanate from outside the diocese.

Politics and diplomacy He attended the marriage of Edward I to Margaret of France in September 1299, and on the following Saturday in the chapel of the archbishop's palace at Canterbury he celebrated mass for the queen, who received the customary gift of wax at his hands, afterwards deposited at the shrine of St Thomas. By the end of the reign he was regarded by Walter of Guisborough as the man specially favoured by the king, dealing with the burdensome business of the entire realm, and overshadowing Chancellor Langton. Queen Margaret described Langton as 'the king's right eye' (*Liber epistolaris*, 317), and it was he, so the story goes, who was chosen by Prince Edward to present the case to his father for giving Gaveston the county of Ponthieu. This so enraged the king that, losing his temper, he pulled out tufts of his son's hair.

It has been assumed that as a curialist—a secularly minded clerk, devoted to royal service regardless of ecclesiastical susceptibilities—Langton was in bitter conflict with Winchelsey at least from 1301, when the archbishop is said by Langtoft to have demanded Langton's dismissal as treasurer at the Lincoln parliament. It has even been alleged that an accusation by John de Lovetot in that year, to the effect that Langton was living in adultery with his stepmother and had murdered her husband, the accuser's father, was brought at Winchelsey's instigation. Other charges, such as pluralism and simony may have been close to the mark, but that of communicating with the devil was a common fabrication. Winchelsey himself claimed that he knew nothing of such matters before receiving a papal mandate. In May 1301 Langton was cited to respond and suspended from episcopal office. At this as

at other times the king stood by his treasurer, making him a member of an embassy at the curia, where he had gone to plead his case. Following an inquiry by Winchelsey and the Dominican Thomas Jorz (d. 1310) he was cleared of all charges, although Boniface VIII's formal absolution was delayed until 8 June 1303. Lovetot was imprisoned for homicide and died in detention. J. H. Denton, Winchelsey's biographer, repudiates the notion that the archbishop bore any animus against Langton at this time, arguing that he promoted the accused's absolution and return to England. To what extent the treasurer in his turn disliked the archbishop, or contributed personally to his suspension in 1306 by a co-operative Clement V (r. 1305–13), is difficult to assess, but it is credible that Langton would have felt that the primate's removal smoothed the path of royal policy.

In the early 1290s Langton was closely concerned with political and diplomatic affairs, being one of the judges in the Great Cause, the succession to the Scottish throne, which in November 1292 was decided in favour of John Balliol. Two years later, with the earl of Lincoln, he counselled Edward to make a temporary surrender of Gascony to Philippe IV, who found occasion to retain it until 1303. In 1305 he was a member of an embassy sent to Lyons to secure papal absolution from Edward's oath to maintain the charters, and attended Clement V's consecration on 14 November. On 2 July 1306, jointly with Archbishop William Greenfield of York (d. 1315), Langton was appointed keeper of the realm during Edward I's absence in Scotland. Before long, however, he deputed William Carleton (d. 1309) to act for him in the treasury. He was instructed to open the parliament of January 1307 at Carlisle, where John Ferrers, claimant to the earldom of Derby, accused him of champarty—supporting a plaintiff in the courts for reward. Langton produced a royal pardon, which Ferrers alleged to be a forgery. He was not at Edward I's deathbed on 7 July, but heard the news at Wentworth in Yorkshire. By 23 July he had reached Burgh by Sands to commence his duties as the late king's executor.

Trials and tribulations On his way to Westminster to arrange the funeral he was arrested and imprisoned, variously in the Tower of London, at Windsor, and at Wallingford. The Pauline annalist gives the date of his arrest as three days after the funeral cortège's arrival at Waltham on 4 August. On 22 August Walter Reynolds replaced him as treasurer. Nevertheless, a chancery warrant dated 1 October ordered the delivery of 20,000 marks to Langton and his fellow executors for royal funeral expenses. Gaveston may be assumed to have had a hand in Langton's disgrace and he benefited financially from the confiscation of the treasurer's assets, although the exaggerated claims made concerning these by some chroniclers are contradicted by the evidence of the wardrobe books and enrolled accounts of Langton's lands. Edward, according to the bulk of chronicle opinion, was bent on revenge.

Although Langton had alienated many and shared in the unpopularity of Edward I's final years, there were those, including Thomas of Lancaster (d. 1322), who had reason to be grateful for his help and shared his dislike of Gaveston. But in Winchelsey's absence the young king's violations of ecclesiastical privilege—the impeding of an executor's functions, the seizure of clerical goods, and the imprisonment of a bishop—passed without repercussion. Langton was ordered to appear before a panel of justices to answer for trespass, misprision, and losses inflicted on the king and others. Treasurer Reynolds and the barons of the exchequer were to search the memoranda for evidence of extortions, false enrolments, the securing of wrongful judgments, and the diversion of treasure from the exchequer to his own household. Other charges concern the sale of woods and land, appointment of inadequate sheriffs, and grants by chancery writ in Edward's absence. Proceedings at the exchequer between 1307 and 1311, for the collection of debts owed to him, and also before the justices at Windsor between 1307 and 1310, are extant. Many charges he admitted. His unscrupulous manipulation of statute merchant is revealed by the existence of some eighty-five extant recognizances in his favour, while income from his property contributed over £2400 to the exchequer in 1308.

The king postponed the trial until after his coronation, for which he had hoped to enjoy Winchelsey's ministrations. By April 1308 Clement V was urging Langton's release, and Edward, in his efforts to secure the recall of Gaveston (now in exile for the second time), the rescinding of the latter's contingent sentence of excommunication, and other favours, on 3 October relinquished the bishop's temporalities. Finally, on 9 November, a date carefully noted in his episcopal register, Langton was set at liberty, being summoned to the parliament of March 1309. In August he received absolution for an unspecified offence against the papacy. June 1311 saw him imprisoned in York Castle for alleged involvement in a homicide, but in deference to clerical privilege he was transferred to the archbishop's custody, and by October he was free again. In January 1312 all charges were dropped, his lands were finally released, and he was permitted to pursue those that had been alienated as well as debts still unpaid, a task that was to occupy him and his executors for some fifty years.

Rehabilitation and last years Too able an administrator to be ignored, on 23 January 1312 he resumed the treasurership. One anonymous correspondent described him as the closest man to Edward after Gaveston, though Trokelowe thought he attained only a partial grace. He may have been behind the policy of calling in judicial estreats, cancelling atterminations, and pressurizing sheriffs to collect arrears. However, the ordainers, claiming that he had been appointed contrary to the ordinances, forcibly disrupted his work at the exchequer, and on 17 May 1312 secured his removal. According to Murimuth, Winchelsey excommunicated Langton during that year for ignoring a summons to a provincial council, arising from his reluctance to observe the ordinances. Langton defended himself at Avignon, where Winchelsey's case was promoted by Murimuth. The archbishop's death in May 1313 ensured Langton's rehabilitation, and he became a member of

Edward's council, only to be removed as 'undesirable' in 1315 during the Westminster parliament. He played a conciliatory part with other bishops in the negotiations preceding the treaty of Leake and was a member of the standing council. In 1318 he was unsuccessfully claiming compensation of £20,000. He died at his residence in the Strand, London, on 9 November 1321.

Langton gave vestments, a gold chalice and two phials (worth £80), and a bejewelled gold cross (worth £200) to Lichfield Cathedral, enfeoffed the vicars choral with houses, and provided 20s. a year for their commons. He commenced the building of the 'decorated' lady chapel, to the east of the chancel, and bequeathed money to complete it, though Edward II temporarily requisitioned this for his Scottish campaign of 1322. Within the chapel he erected a shrine for the relics of St Ceadda (Chad) at a cost of £2000, and was buried nearby on 5 December 1321. What is said to be his defaced effigy in Derbyshire marble rests in the south aisle of the choir. Following Bishop Burnell's example at Wells, Langton built and crenellated a wall round the close with fortified gates, and he constructed a new palace on the edge of the enclosure. Within the town he built 'the great bridge' and secured a grant of pavage. He repaired his London house, and completely rebuilt his residences at Eccleshall Castle and Haywood.

ROY MARTIN HAINES

Sources Walter Langton's episcopal register, Lichfield Joint RO, B/A/1/1 · Canterbury-based chronicle, Trinity Cam., R.5.41 · *Chancery records* · T. Madox, *The history and antiquities of the exchequer of the kings of England*, 2nd edn, 2 vols. (1769); repr. (1969) · Rymer, *Foedera*, vols. 1–2 · *The historical works of Gervase of Canterbury*, ed. W. Stubbs, 2: *The minor works comprising the Gesta regum with its continuation, the Actus pontificum and the Mappa mundi*, Rolls Series, 73 (1880) · *Johannis de Trokelowe et Henrici de Blaneforde … chronica et annales*, ed. H. T. Riley, pt 3 of *Chronica monasterii S. Albani*, Rolls Series, 28 (1866) · *Adae Murimuth continuatio chronicarum. Robertus de Avesbury de gestis mirabilibus regis Edwardi tertii*, ed. E. M. Thompson, Rolls Series, 93 (1889) · [H. Wharton], ed., *Anglia sacra*, 1 (1691) · K. Edwards, 'The social origins and provenance of the English bishops during the reign of Edward II', *TRHS*, 5th ser., 9 (1959), 51–79 · A. Beardwood, ed., *Records of the trial of Walter Langton, bishop of Coventry and Lichfield, 1307–1312*, CS, 4th ser., 6 (1969) · A. Beardwood, *The trial of Walter Langton, bishop of Litchfield, 1307–12* (1964) · J. H. Hill, *History of Langton* (1867) · J. C. Davies, *The baronial opposition to Edward II* (1918) · Tout, *Admin. hist.*, vols. 2–3, 5–6 · M. Prestwich, *Edward I* (1988) · J. R. Maddicott, *Thomas of Lancaster, 1307–1322: a study in the reign of Edward II* (1970) · J. H. Denton, *Robert Winchelsey and the crown, 1294–1313: a study in the defence of ecclesiastical liberty*, Cambridge Studies in Medieval Life and Thought, 14 (1980) · J. R. S. Phillips, *Aymer de Valence, earl of Pembroke, 1307–1324: baronial politics in the reign of Edward II* (1972) · R. M. Haines, *The church and politics in fourteenth-century England: the career of Adam Orleton, c. 1275–1345*, Cambridge Studies in Medieval Life and Thought, 3rd ser., 10 (1978) · J. R. Wright, *The church and the English crown, 1305–1334: a study based on the register of Archbishop Walter Reynolds* (1980) · M. Prestwich, *War, politics, and finance under Edward I* (1972) · *The liber epistolaris of Richard de Bury*, ed. N. Denholm-Young, Roxburghe Club (1950)

Archives Lichfield Joint RO, register, B/A/1/1 | PRO, wardrobe books · Trinity Cam., R.5.41

Likenesses tomb effigy, 13th cent., Lichfield Cathedral

Wealth at death wealthy: Wharton, ed., *Anglia sacra*

Langton, William (1803–1881), banker, son of Thomas Langton (1770–1838), a merchant who spent some years in

Russia and Canada, and his wife, Ellen (1766–1846), the daughter of the Revd William Currer, vicar of Clapham. He was born at Farfield, near Addingham, in the West Riding of Yorkshire, on 17 April 1803. He was educated mainly in Switzerland, and became fluent in several foreign languages, especially Italian. From 1821 to 1829 he was employed by the mercantile house of T. and W. Earle of Liverpool, latterly as agent for several Russian firms. In August 1829, after the Russo-Turkish War of 1827–9, which had disrupted the Russian trade, he joined Heywoods Bank in Manchester. He remained with Heywoods until 1854, when he was appointed managing director of the Manchester and Salford Bank, which flourished under his aegis for the next twenty-two years. He resigned in October 1876, after losing his eyesight.

Langton was one of the leading members of the influential élite which guided and dominated the cultural, intellectual, and philanthropic life of mid-nineteenth-century Manchester. He was associated with the establishment of some of its prominent institutions, and was among the founders of the Manchester Athenaeum in 1836 and the mechanics' institution two years earlier. His services were publicly recognized in 1881 by the presentation to the Athenaeum of his marble medallion bust, along with those of his co-founders, Richard Cobden and James Heywood. When the Chetham Society was founded in 1843, he was elected treasurer, and he subsequently served as the honorary secretary. He edited several volumes for the society. In 1846 he acted as secretary to a committee which was formed to promote a university for Manchester. Though unsuccessful, this scheme was instrumental in suggesting to John Owens the foundation of the college which bears his name and which formed the basis of the later university.

Langton was also, in association with Dr Kay (afterwards Sir J. P. Kay-Shuttleworth), a chief promoter of the Manchester Provident Society and of the Manchester Statistical Society, both established in 1833. In all his many cultural and philanthropic activities he was the close associate and collaborator of his friends and employers the Heywood family.

Langton married at Kirkham, Lancashire, on 15 November 1831, Margaret, daughter of Joseph Hornby of Ribby, Lancashire; the Hornbys and Langtons had had close business ties for over a century. The couple had three sons and six daughters; two of the daughters married sons of Sir Benjamin Heywood. Langton was an accurate genealogist, herald, and antiquary, a philologist, a skilful draughtsman, and a graceful writer of verse, both in his own language and in Italian. He spent his retirement at his house, Docklands, in Ingatestone, Essex, where he died on 29 September 1881. He was buried in Fryerning churchyard, Essex. C. W. SUTTON, rev. ALAN G. CROSBY

Sources *Chetham Society*, 110 (1882), iii–x · *Manchester Guardian* (30 Sept 1881) · *Manchester City News* (1 Sept 1877) · *Manchester City News* (1 Oct 1881) · L. H. Grindon, *Manchester banks and bankers: historical, biographical, and anecdotal*, 2nd edn (1878) · *The letters of Thomas Langton, flax merchant of Kirkham, 1771–1788*, ed. J. Wilkinson, Chetham Society, 3rd ser., 38 (1994) · *CGPLA Eng. & Wales* (1881)
Archives Bodl. Oxf., corresp. with Sir Thomas Phillipps

Likenesses marble medallion, c.1881; The Athenaeum, Manchester, 1892 · portrait (after marble medallion, c.1881), repro. in *Chetham Society*
Wealth at death £32,644: probate, 18 Nov 1881, *CGPLA Eng. & Wales*

Langton, Zachary (*bap.* 1698, *d.* 1786), Church of Ireland clergyman, was baptized on 24 September 1698, the third, but second surviving, son of Cornelius Langton (1668–1712), of Kirkham, Lancashire, and his wife, Elizabeth (*bap.* 1661, *d.* 1736), daughter of the Revd Zachary Taylor, of Kirkham. He was educated at Kirkham grammar school, where Zachary Taylor was headmaster. His father's will was that he be 'made a scholar and have university education if he may be thought fit and capable' (Fishwick, 152). He duly matriculated at Magdalen Hall, Oxford, on 5 April 1718 and was elected an exhibitor, under Barker's trust, on 7 September; he graduated BA on 18 December 1721 and proceeded MA on 10 June 1724.

According to his mother Langton left 'a very comfortable subsistence near London' (Fishwick, 152) in order to follow to Ireland his kinsman Robert Clayton, nominated bishop of Killala in December 1729. He may well have been the young clergyman very often seen by Mary Pendarves at Killala in 1732. Langton was collated to a prebendary of Achonry on 5 July 1735 and to a prebendary of Killala on 6 December 1735. Late in 1735 Clayton was translated to Cork. Langton was chaplain to William Stanhope, earl of Harrington, lord lieutenant of Ireland from 1746 to 1751. In Garstang, Lancashire, on 14 August 1749 he married Bridget (*bap.* 1703, *d.* 1761), daughter of Alexander Butler of Kirkland; they had no children. In 1753 he published anonymously *An Essay Concerning the Human Rational Soul*; the Dublin edition of 1759 was dedicated to John Russell, fourth duke of Bedford, lord lieutenant of Ireland from 1757 to 1761.

Bridget Langton died in Garstang on 14 November 1761, which may account for Langton's return to England in that month. He was present at Kirkham for the public recantation of a Roman Catholic priest, William Gant, on 28 May 1769. He retained his Achonry prebend until 1782 and his Killala prebend until 1785. He died in Oxford on 1 February 1786. STUART HANDLEY

Sources J. Foster, ed., *Pedigrees of the county families of England*, 1: *Lancashire* (1873) · Foster, *Alum. Oxon.* · H. Fishwick, *The history of the parish of Kirkham in the county of Lancaster*, Chetham Society, 92 (1874), 152–3 · H. Cotton, *Fasti ecclesiae Hibernicae*, 4 (1850), 89, 110 · J. P. Earwaker, ed., *Local gleanings relating to Lancashire and Cheshire*, 2 (1877–8), 127 · T. D. Whitaker, *An history of Richmondshire*, 2 vols. (1823), 2.451 · IGI · *The autobiography and correspondence of Mary Granville, Mrs Delany*, ed. Lady Llanover, 1st ser., 3 vols. (1861), vol. 1, p. 383 · *Palatine Note-Book*, 4 (1884), 148

Langtry, Lillie [*née* Emilie Charlotte Le Breton] (1853–1929), actress, was born on 13 October 1853 at St Saviour's rectory, Jersey, the only daughter and sixth of the seven children of William Corbet *Le Breton (*d.* 1888), dean of Jersey, and his wife, Emilie Davis Martin. Educated at home, she developed into a socially ambitious and remarkably beautiful young woman. In 1874 she married Edward Langtry, son of a Belfast shipowner. Within three years the couple were established in London, where Lillie

Lillie Langtry (1853–1929), by Sir John Everett Millais, 1877–8 [*A Jersey Lily*]

became celebrated, not only as a 'professional beauty'—a society woman whose photographic likenesses were on sale to the public—but as the mistress of *Edward, prince of Wales. Between 1877 and 1880 she enjoyed a period of heady social success. Her portrait was painted by most leading artists of the day; the best-known is *A Jersey Lily* by John Everett Millais, in the possession of the Société Jersiaise in Jersey.

Towards the end of her three-year liaison with the prince of Wales, Lillie met Prince Louis of Battenberg (1854–1921) [*see* Mountbatten, Louis Alexander]. In Paris, in March 1881, she gave birth to their daughter, who was christened Jeanne-Marie, with the surname of Langtry. The birth of this child coincided with the bankruptcy of Edward Langtry and the breakup of Lillie's marriage. Despite the continued support of the prince of Wales, she was ostracized by society, though she maintained a well-publicized friendship with W. E. Gladstone.

Exceptionally resilient, Lillie embarked on a new career—as an actress. Her appearance in a charity performance led to an offer to join the Bancrofts' company at the Haymarket Theatre. She made her professional début as Kate Hardcastle in *She Stoops to Conquer* on 15 December 1881. Appreciating that it was her notoriety, as the former mistress of the prince of Wales, that was attracting audiences, Lillie soon founded her own company. Between 1882 and 1889 she divided her time between tours of the United States, where she owned a ranch in California, and appearances on various London stages. Although never

more than a competent actress, she was an extremely decorative and popular one, at her best in plays about upper-class society. In 1889 she returned permanently to England. To her career as an actress, the always practical Lillie now added another: that of a highly successful racehorse owner; she won the Cesarewitch twice, with Merman and Yutoi.

In 1899, two years after Edward Langtry had died in destitution, Lillie married Hugo Gerald (1871–1940), the eldest son of Sir Henry de Bathe, fourth baronet. On the death of her father-in-law in 1907, Lillie became Lady De Bathe.

After the failure of her attempt to establish a company at the Imperial Theatre, Westminster, Lillie resumed touring. After the First World War she bought a villa, Le Lys, in Monaco. In 1925 she published a highly selective book of memoirs. She died—by no means destitute—in Monte Carlo on 12 February 1929 and was buried in St Saviour's churchyard, Jersey.   THEO ARONSON, *rev.*

Sources E. C. Langtry, *The days I knew* (1925) · P. Magnus, *King Edward the Seventh* (1964) · private information (1993) · C. Hibbert, *Edward VII* (1976) · Gladstone, *Diaries* · Burke, *Peerage* · Burke, *Gen. GB*

Archives NRA, priv. coll., corresp. with Edward VII and George V · NYPL, letters to Clement Scott, NUC MS71-1248 · Sheff. Arch., Wharncliffe muniments, to earl of Wharncliffe

Likenesses J. E. Millais, oils, 1877–8 (*A Jersey Lily*), Jersey Museum [*see illus.*] · E. Poynter, oils, *c.*1878, Jersey Museum · G. F. Watts, oils, 1880, Watts Gallery, Compton, Surrey · E. Poynter, bronze medal, 1882, BM · Lafayette, photograph, *c.*1888, U. Texas · C. Beaton, photograph, NPG · W. & D. Downey, photograph, postcard, NPG · W. & D. Downey, woodburytype, NPG; repro. in W. Downey and D. Downey, *Cabinet portrait gallery*, 1 (1890) · G. Pilotell, drypoints, BM · G. Pilotell, popular and theatrical prints, NPG · G. Pilotell, prints, Harvard TC · V. Weyde, cabinet photograph, NPG · Window & Grove, woodburytype, NPG

Wealth at death £47,445 18s. 2d.: probate, 1 May 1929, CGPLA Eng. & Wales

Langwith, Benjamin (1683/4–1743), antiquary and Church of England clergyman, was born in Yorkshire and baptized on 14 December 1684 at Holy Trinity, Goodramgate, York, the son of Oswald Langwith, clerk of the vestry of York Minster. He was educated at Queens' College, Cambridge, whence he matriculated in 1701, and was elected fellow and tutor. He graduated BA in 1705, MA in 1708, BD in 1716, and DD in 1717. The antiquary Ralph Thoresby placed his son under his care, but, owing to Langwith's negligence, was forced to remove him. Langwith was ordained priest in July 1712 and was instituted to the rectory of Petworth, Sussex, in 1718. He was made prebendary of Chichester on 15 June 1725. On 2 November 1734 he married Sarah Gregory at Headley, Hampshire.

Langwith gave Francis Drake some assistance in the preparation of his *Eboracum*. Four of Langwith's scientific papers appeared in the *Philosophical Transactions*. He also wrote *Observations on Dr. Arbuthnot's Dissertations on Coins, Weights, and Measures*, which was published posthumously in 1747, edited by his widow. It was reissued in the second edition of Arbuthnot's *Tables of Ancient Coins* (1754). Langwith died in 1743 and was buried at Petworth church on 2

October 1743, aged fifty-nine. His widow, Sarah, died on 8 February 1784, aged ninety-one, and was buried in Westminster Abbey.

GORDON GOODWIN, rev. J. A. MARCHAND

Sources Nichols, *Illustrations*, 1.298 · Watt, *Bibl. Brit.* · *IGI* · Venn, *Alum. Cant.* · *Fasti Angl.* (Hardy), 1.273 · J. L. Chester, ed., *The marriage, baptismal, and burial registers of the collegiate church or abbey of St Peter, Westminster*, Harleian Society, 10 (1876), 437 · [J. Hunter], ed., *Letters of eminent men, addressed to Ralph Thoresby*, 2 (1832), 322–3, 361–2
Archives RS, letters to James Jurin
Likenesses oils, Queens' College, Cambridge

Lanier [*née* Bassano], **Emilia** (*bap.* 1569, *d.* 1645), poet, was baptized in St Botolph without Bishopsgate, London, on 27 January 1569, daughter of Baptista *Bassano (*d.* 1576) [*see under* Bassano, Alvise], court musician, and his 'reputed wife', Margaret Johnson (*d.* 1587). The Bassanos were a family of Italian Jews, émigrés from Venice who came to be musicians and instrument makers at court in 1531. Giovanni Baptista Bassano lived near the Charterhouse but Emilia was brought up by Susan, dowager countess of Kent, whom she addresses as the 'noble guide of my ungoverned dayes'. Although we know nothing specific of her education, Emilia writes that the countess was 'directed' by a mother famed for her furtherance of protestant and humanist learning, Catharine Bertie, dowager duchess of Suffolk, and we may suppose that more than usual attention was paid to her reading.

We learn from a visit Emilia made to Simon Forman, astrologer, in 1597 that she had been a favourite at the court of Elizabeth, had become mistress of Henry *Carey, first Baron Hunsdon (1526–1596), and had been 'maintained in great pomp' until 1592, when, having become pregnant, she was married to Captain Alphonso Lanier (*d.* 1613) of the other leading family of court musicians, the Laniers, who moved to London from Rouen in 1561.

Though Emilia Lanier's outstanding achievement is undoubtedly the composition of the first original poetry by a woman to be published in the seventeenth century—a volume of religious verse entitled *Salve Deus rex Judaeorum* (1611)—she has become notorious as a result of attempts to identify her as the 'dark lady' of Shakespeare's *Sonnets* (1609), on the conjectural grounds of her racial colouring, musical ability, and promiscuity. Although there is insufficient evidence to establish the identification it illustrates a tendency that, interestingly, her own poetry strives to overcome—that is, the tendency to read a woman's emergence into the sphere of public discourse as a form of indecency, signalling promiscuity. The central poem of her volume, which celebrates the 'worthy mind' of her patron Margaret, dowager countess of Cumberland, is remarkable for managing to avoid identifying female virtue with chastity, articulating in its place a feminine mastery of those dialectical skills that constituted the humanist ideal of masculine virtue. The volume concludes with the first country-house poem published in English, an encomium of an estate at Cookham occupied by the countess, in which the passing of the seasons suggests the ephemerality of patronage relations; the walks bear 'summer Liveries', and the prospect of hills and vales appears to 'preferre some strange unlook'd for sute' only as long as their mistress is in residence.

The ambiguity of an elegy that laments the loss of constancy in relations between household and patron, yet offers itself in the public market place as a suit for favour, aptly characterizes the circumstances of Emilia Lanier's life, for court musicians were at once household servants and courtiers, suitors for office. As well as inheriting stipends and liveries Bassanos and Laniers competed among themselves for patents and privileges. From the first Emilia occupied the position of a precariously privileged dependant, and complained of 'hard fortune', her father having died when she was a child, leaving a 'miserable' estate. Though she brought a substantial dowry in money and jewels to Alphonso Lanier this was soon exhausted by his service in hope of preferment under Robert Devereux, second earl of Essex. He did, however, receive in 1612 (delayed from 1603) a lucrative patent for the weighing of hay and straw but on his death in 1613 Emilia surrendered the patent to an enterprising brother-in-law, Innocent Lanier.

Consequently Emilia Lanier was again in financial difficulties, in 1617, when she unsuccessfully attempted to set up a school in St Giles-in-the-Fields for the education of children of the nobility. When her son Henry, another court musician, died in 1633 his widow petitioned to get their four-year-old son, Henry, trained in music 'as soon as he shall be capable thereof'. In the meantime Emilia Lanier tried to provide means for this grandson and his sister, Mary, by claiming in chancery heritable rights in the patent for the weighing of hay and straw. The privy council finally ruled in her favour in 1637. Emilia Lanier was buried in St James's, Clerkenwell, Middlesex, on 3 April 1645.

LORNA HUTSON, rev.

Sources A. L. Rowse, *Poems of Shakespeare's dark lady* (1978) · *CSP dom.*, 1603–38 · Bodl. Oxf., MSS Ashmole 226, 354 · R. Prior, 'Jewish musicians at the Tudor court', *Musical Quarterly*, 69 (1983), 253–65 · D. Lasocki and R. Prior, *The Bassanos: Venetian musicians and instrument makers in England, 1531–1665* (1995) · S. Woods, *Lanyer* (1999)

Lanier, Sir John (*d.* 1692), army officer, volunteered as a young man to serve with the English troops in French pay in Flanders, during which time he lost an eye. He was promoted to lieutenant-colonel, commanding the duke of Monmouth's regiment of horse in 1674 following the battle of Enzheim, and kept that post until his return to England in May 1678, when he was knighted and commissioned as a brigadier of horse. In 1679 he succeeded Sir Thomas Morgan as governor of Jersey. He quarrelled with the states, fell out with the Carteret family over precedence, challenged Sir Edouard Carteret to a duel, and spent so much time away from the island that he was forbidden by the privy council to leave without the king's permission. He improved the defences of Elizabeth Castle by building a magazine, on the north side of which may still be seen his coat of arms set in stone. He was replaced in July 1684, although the king claimed to be 'well satisfied' with his services.

After the accession of James II he was given the colonelcy of the Queen's regiment of horse and made a brigadier-general. Lanier was one of the professional soldiers, often with experience of foreign service, who had been promoted by James but who, by the summer of 1688, were conspiring to deliver their allegiance to William, prince of Orange. James promoted Lanier major-general and, in the autumn of 1688, posted him to Ipswich with three regiments to prevent a Dutch invasion. Recalled and dispatched to the south-west upon news of William's landing, a stream of desertions from troops under Lanier's command promoted the retreat of James's army towards London. Lanier declared for William III and was sent to Scotland, where he took over the siege of Edinburgh Castle from Hugh Mackay. Lanier accepted the duke of Gordon's surrender and took possession of the castle on 12 June 1689. He was subsequently posted to Ireland, where in February 1690 he led a force from Newry to attack Dundalk, which he found strongly garrisoned by the Irish. He burnt the western suburbs, took the lightly garrisoned Bedloe Castle, and drove off 1500 cattle. Lanier led King William's advance guard of horse to the Boyne and was present in the battle on 1 July 1690. He was also present at the siege of Limerick in August, where some held him responsible for the failure to intercept Sarsfield's raid on the artillery train. He directed the abortive attempt to seize Lanesborough Bridge on the Shannon in December 1690, and took part in an ineffective raid on Ballymore in the following spring, shortly after which he was relieved of his command in Ireland and sent back to England.

In December 1691 Lanier declined an offer of a generous pension if he resigned, but was nevertheless promoted to lieutenant-general on 23 January 1692. However, so resentful was he of William's supposed favour for his Dutch and German officers that in May 1692 his name was included in a lengthy list of officers against whom Jacobite sympathies were alleged. Lanier marched with his regiment to Flanders in July, was fatally wounded at the battle of Steenkerke on 3 August 1692, and died there a few days afterwards. His corpse was returned on an Admiralty yacht to England for burial there. Although he had a wife while he was in Jersey, he died a widower and left no heirs.   PIERS WAUCHOPE

Sources J. W., *An exact account of the late action at the town of Dundalk* (1690) · *Bishop Burnet's History of his own time*, ed. G. Burnet and T. Burnet, 2 vols. (1724–34) · R. Kane, *Campaigns of King William and Queen Anne*, 1 (1745) · *The life of James the Second, king of England*, ed. J. S. Clarke, 2 vols. (1816) · R. Bell, ed., *The siege of the castle of Edinburgh*, Ballantyne Club (1828) · N. Luttrell, *A brief historical relation of state affairs from September 1678 to April 1714*, 6 vols. (1857) · C. Dalton, ed., *English army lists and commission registers, 1661–1714*, 6 vols. (1892–1904) · *CSP dom.*, 1679–85 · C. T. Atkinson, 'Feversham's account of the battle of Enzheim, 1674', *Journal of the Society for Army Historical Research*, 1 (1922) · G. R. Balleine, *A history of the island of Jersey* (1950) · P. Wauchope, *Patrick Sarsfield and the Williamite war* (1992) · J. Childs, *The army, James II, and the Glorious Revolution* (1980) · J. C. R. Childs, *The British army of William III, 1689–1702* (1987) · will, PRO, PROB 11/411, fols. 329–30
Archives NL Scot., letters to William Blathwayt, MS 3740

Lanier, Nicholas (1568–1646?). *See under* Lanier, Nicholas (*bap.* 1588, *d.* 1666).

Lanier, Nicholas (*bap.* **1588**, *d.* **1666**), musician and art dealer, was baptized on 10 September 1588 in the church of Holy Trinity Minories, London. His father, John Lanier (*d.* 1616), was a sackbut player in the royal court band or musick, and his mother, Frances (*bap.* 1566, *d.* after 1616), was the daughter of Mark Anthony Galliardello, an Italian member of the musick. The strong musical tradition in the family stemmed from Nicholas's paternal grandfather, also called Nicholas (*d.* 1612), a Huguenot musician (originally from Rouen) in the service of Elizabeth I. John Lanier's five brothers—Alphonso, Innocent, Jerome, Clement, and Andrea—were also all members of the musick.

The younger Nicholas Lanier entered the household of Robert Cecil, earl of Salisbury, as an apprentice musician, probably about 1601. Later he seems to have acted for a time as music tutor to Salisbury's heir, William, Lord Cranborne. He himself came under the influence of John Coprario, who was also attached to Salisbury's household, and of the younger Alfonso Ferrabosco. In 1610 Lanier joined Cranborne in Paris and possibly accompanied him to Italy; he certainly visited Venice in the autumn of that year as a diplomatic courier.

On 26 December 1613, in the former banqueting house of Whitehall Palace, Lanier sang his own song 'Bring away this sacred tree' in *The Squires' Masque*, an entertainment with text by Thomas Campion and music mostly by Coprario. This song marked Lanier's first tentative use of the Italianate declamatory or *recitativo* style, which was to be the main feature of his vocal compositions. Perhaps partly as a result of this début Lanier succeeded to a vacant place as a lutenist and singer in the king's musick (12 January 1616), of which John Dowland was then also a member. Lanier was in addition a skilled viol player. During the next decade he was associated with a number of court masques, mostly with texts by Ben Jonson, including *The Vision of Delight* (1616) and *The Masque of Augurs* (1621). Little of his music for these events survives, with the notable exception of the song 'Do not expect' from *The Masque of Augurs*. The masque *Lovers Made Men*, performed on 22 February 1617 at the home of Lord James Hay, was especially significant, as it seems that Lanier not only composed all the music but also designed the stage sets and costumes. Through a combination of his own talents and the influence of powerful patrons such as the duke of Buckingham and the earl of Arundel he became a member of the privileged circle surrounding Prince Charles. Here he developed as a connoisseur of art and also as a practising painter. The precise date of his appointment as master of the king's musick is unknown, but he is first named as such in documents dated 13 and 22 June 1626 (Ashbee, 3.18).

Immediately after the funeral of James I on 7 May 1625 Lanier was dispatched by the new king, Charles I, to Italy, to search out and purchase paintings for the enlargement of the Royal Collection. Through Daniel Nys, a French-

Nicholas Lanier (*bap.* 1588, *d.* 1666), by Sir Anthony Van Dyck, 1628?

born art dealer, agent, and entrepreneur, Lanier made contact with the duke of Mantua, Ferdinando Gonzaga, with a view to buying the extensive and celebrated Mantuan collection. The negotiations were long and tortuous and were not finally completed until 1628; the total price paid for this splendid collection was 68,000 scudi (then about £15,000). (Lanier was not involved in a second sequence of negotiations, which culminated in the purchase of Mantegna's *The Triumph of Caesar*.)

During this period Lanier made two separate visits to Italy, being based for the most part in Venice. At the end of his first trip he returned to England with his own portrait by Van Dyck (now in the Kunsthistorisches Museum, Vienna). As a result Van Dyck was invited to enter the service of King Charles. Lanier had already begun to collect drawings, both for himself and for his patron Lord Arundel, at a time when such pieces were considered valueless, and was the first to imprint on them a distinctive collector's mark. Among his friends were members of the Oliver family of miniaturists, and a miniature of Lanier, perhaps by Peter Oliver, was said by Vertue (Vertue, *Note books*, 1.62) to have been in the Royal Collection. Lanier may also have received instruction in painting technique from Oliver.

Lanier now returned to his musical duties at court. The murder of the duke of Buckingham on 23 August 1628 inspired him to compose his most celebrated work in *stilo recitativo*, a setting for solo voice with instrumental accompaniment of the legend of Hero and Leander, the words also being by Lanier. It shows the influence of Monteverdi, whom Lanier probably had met in Venice. Both the piece itself and Lanier's singing of it were greatly admired by

King Charles. Most of his surviving vocal compositions (about thirty songs) date from the 1630s. A handful of instrumental works in dance form also survives. On 15 July 1635 Lanier was appointed first marshal of the Corporation of Musick, a body set up to supervise standards among professional musicians.

With the outbreak of the English civil war in 1642 Lanier followed the court to Oxford, where he painted the half-length self-portrait now hanging in the faculty of music there. This shows the influence of Rubens, who had visited England in 1629. Lanier depicts himself in sober costume, in face and appearance not unlike his king, holding a brush and artist's palette, together with a *memento mori* skull and a fragment of his own music. By spring 1645 he had already left England, and he spent the next fifteen years variously in France and the Netherlands. However, his self-imposed exile was not complete; official passes (still extant) gave him permission to enter England with paintings, presumably purchases for patrons, and in 1649–50 he was present on several occasions at the gigantic sale of King Charles's art collection which he had himself largely helped to create. At the sale he managed to buy for £10 his own portrait by Van Dyck. He was joined in exile by his wife, Elizabeth, whom he had probably married about 1626; there were apparently no children.

Lanier also experimented as a printmaker. About 1636 he had produced a handful of etchings after drawings by Giulio Romano, and in 1656, possibly in Paris, he made a few more, after Parmigianino. Recent research has dispelled former doubts as to his authorship of the second set.

Following the Restoration in 1660 Lanier was reinstated in his former posts as master of the musick, marshal of the Corporation of Musick, and groom of the queen's bedchamber. However, in his will (drawn up on 5 March 1661) he was already complaining of 'divers infirmities, incident to old age', and he was by that time probably no longer fully equal to the demands of his offices. Samuel Pepys records several musical meetings in Greenwich (where he was temporarily staying because of the plague) between 30 October 1665 and 3 January 1666, at which Lanier was present and sang, 'in a melancholy method, very well, and a sober man he seems to be' (Pepys, 30 Oct 1665). Lanier died a few weeks later, apparently suddenly, and was buried on 24 February 1666, probably at St Alfege, Greenwich. His widow survived him for a further seven years and died in February 1673.

This Nicholas Lanier should not be confused with the **Nicholas Lanier** (1568–1646?), possibly a cousin, who in 1636 published some etchings from drawings by Parmigianino, and in 1638 another set of etchings after Giulio Romano. It was probably this Nicholas Lanier who was buried at St Martin-in-the-Fields, London, on 4 November 1646. MICHAEL I. WILSON

Sources CSP dom., 1571–1661 · Calendar of the manuscripts of the most hon. the marquis of Salisbury, 6–7, HMC, 9 (1895–9); 16 (1933); 21 (1970); 24 (1976) · Vertue, Note books · Pepys, Diary, vols. 6–7 · A. Ashbee, ed., Records of English court music, 9 vols. (1986–96) · M. I. Wilson, Nicholas Lanier, master of the king's musick (1994) · A. MacGregor, ed.,

The late king's goods: collections, possessions and patronage of Charles I in the light of Commonwealth sale inventories (1989) • B. L. Harrison, The Laniers and their world, 1559–1719 (1995) • New Grove • F. Lanier Graham, 'The earlier life and work of Nicholas Lanier, collector of paintings and drawings', MA diss., Columbia University, 1966 • A. Ashbee and D. Lasocki, eds., A biographical dictionary of English court musicians, 1485–1714, 2 vols. (1998) • DNB • parish register, London, Holy Trinity Minories, GL, MS 9238 • parish register, St Giles, Clerkenwell • parish register, St Alfege, Greenwich, London • PRO, SP 99/28/291 • PRO, PROB 10/1048

Archives BL, Add. MSS 10337, 11608, 14399, 33236; Egerton MS 2013 • Bodl. Oxf., MS Don. C. 57 • Bodl. Oxf., MUS. d. 238 • Christ Church Oxf., music MSS 379–381, nos. 29–30 • FM Cam., music MS 734, nos. 12–15 • LPL, MS 1041 • NYPL, Drexel MSS 4041, 4257

Likenesses G. Reni, drawing, c.1625 (Portrait of a man's head), Los Angeles County Museum of Art • A. Van Dyck, drawing, 1625?, NG Scot. • A. Van Dyck, oils, 1628?, Kunsthistorisches Museum, Vienna [see illus.] • L. Vorsterman, line engraving, c.1632 (after J. Lievens), BM, NPG • school of J. Jordaens, oils, c.1635 (David playing the harp), Musées de St Omer • W. Dobson, group portrait, oils, c.1643 (Portrait of the artist with Sir Charles Cotterell and Nicholas Lanier), priv. coll. • N. Lanier, self-portrait, oils, c.1644, U. Oxf., faculty of music

Wealth at death everything to wife except for a few bequests to nephews and nieces: will, PRO, PROB 11/320, fol. 47

Lanigan, John (1758–1828), biblical scholar and historian, was born at Cashel, co. Tipperary, the eldest child of Thomas Lanigan, a schoolmaster, and his wife, Mary Ann Dorkan. He was educated at his father's school and at a classical school kept by a protestant clergyman at Cashel. In 1776 he entered the Irish College at Rome to study for the Roman Catholic priesthood. Here his intellectual gifts attracted the attention and patronage of influential figures such as Cardinal Marefoschi and Pietro Tamburini, though he also showed evidence of a certain acerbity of temperament that led to a complaint from the cardinal to Archbishop James Butler of Cashel in 1783, shortly before his ordination. He was nevertheless ordained priest, and was then introduced to the University of Pavia by Tamburini, who had become a professor there.

Here Lanigan was deeply influenced by the 'Catholic Enlightenment', which in Italy was especially concerned with historical theology. In 1786 Grand Duke Leopold of Tuscany, brother of Emperor Joseph II, encouraged the convocation of an ecclesiastical synod at Pistoia. The acts of this synod were denounced as Jansenistic, and in fact it received little support from the clergy or laity of Tuscany. Tamburini was the leading theologian at the synod, but Lanigan declined his invitation to take part in it. Despite this, his intellectual powers made such an impression at Pavia that in the spring of 1788 he was offered the professorship of scripture, Hebrew, and ecclesiastical history. At the same time, however, Archbishop Butler wrote from Ireland to say that Francis Moylan, recently appointed bishop of Cork, was planning to open a classical school, as permitted by legislation of 1782, and would like Lanigan to be headmaster. Lanigan accepted, but laid down a list of conditions, which although individually not unreasonable sounded peremptory when taken together. In the event he accepted the professorship in Pavia. His inaugural address, 'De origine et progressu hermeneuticae sacrae', was published in 1789. Shortly afterwards he published Saggio sulla maniera d'insegnare a' giovani ecclesiastici la

scienza de' libri sacri. This was followed in 1793 by a substantial and valuable study of the history of the books of the Bible, Institutionum Biblicarum pars prima, and in 1794 he received the doctorate of divinity of the university.

Yet there are indications that Lanigan was not settled at Pavia, especially in his enquiries in 1795 to archbishops John Thomas Troy of Dublin and Thomas Bray of Cashel about the possibility of being appointed to a teaching post in the newly opened seminary at Maynooth in Ireland. Then in March 1796 Italy was invaded by the French Revolutionary army. The University of Pavia was closed, and Lanigan fled to Ireland. The news that he might apply for a post at Maynooth had already aroused misgivings, and when Lanigan landed in Cork he was coldly received by Bishop Francis Moylan, and likewise by Archbishop Bray in Cashel. He made his way to Dublin, where he was offered a post as assistant by Martin Hugh Hamill, once a fellow student in Rome and now parish priest of Francis Street Chapel. Meanwhile an appointment had been made to the chair of scripture in Maynooth, but the person appointed resigned early in 1797 and Lanigan applied for the post. This led to acrimonious exchanges, and it is not easy to be sure exactly what happened. Some of his friends claimed that he had been approached by the two most important episcopal members of the Maynooth board of trustees, the archbishops of Armagh and Dublin, but it is not easy to credit this. Another version is that he was proposed by the archbishop of Armagh, seconded by the archbishop of Dublin, and appointed, when Bishop Moylan, who had come late to the meeting, demanded that he first sign an anti-Jansenist formula. The truth is obscured by the heated exchanges that clearly took place, but Lanigan, so his friends said, turned down the appointment. The fact that there is no minute of an appointment in the journal of the Maynooth trustees does not, of course, necessarily imply that none was made, and it is clear that the taint of Jansenism that clung to Lanigan was undeserved.

This gifted scholar was now without a post. He was rescued by the Dublin Society, which appointed him in 1799 as 'translator, editor and corrector of the press', and in 1808 as librarian. In 1800 he published for the society An Essay on the Practical History of the Sheep in Spain, and of the Spanish Sheep in Saxony (1785), translated from a work by George Stumpf, a project surely dictated by financial needs rather than personal interests. He took part in the current controversies over Catholic emancipation and the veto, but his real interest became concentrated on Irish church history. He was a leading member of the group who founded the Gaelic Society in 1808, and he assiduously collected the material for his planned work. In 1813, however, the first signs of mental illness began to appear, and he was condemned to lengthening stays in an asylum in Finglas, to the north of Dublin, where he died, aged seventy, on 7 July 1828.

Lanigan's most important work, An Ecclesiastical History of Ireland from the First Introduction of Christianity among the Irish to the Thirteenth Century, was published in 1822. It ran to four volumes, including almost 2000 pages in all, and, given the state of Irish historical studies at the time, was a remarkable achievement. It was unashamedly confessional, in that it assailed the protestant historians who had written earlier, especially the most recent of them, Edward Ledwich. Lanigan's castigation of Ledwich in particular was deserved, but his tetchiness made it devastating. However, coupled with this was a remarkable knowledge of the sources then available, and a robust critical mind honed in the atmosphere of the Catholic Enlightenment in Pavia. J. F. Kenney, whose *Sources for the Early History of Ireland*, volume 1 (1929) is still in some respects the starting point for all exploration of the period, wrote, 'He became the Lingard of Irish church history, and his monumental work on that subject remains of value' (Kenney, 61).

Lanigan's personal library was sold a few months before his death. He was buried in the cemetery of Finglas parish church. In 1861 a cross with an inscription in Latin and Irish was erected over his grave.   PATRICK J. CORISH

Sources W. J. Fitzpatrick, 'Dr Lanigan: his life and times', *Irish wits and worthies* (1873) · M. J. Brenan, *An ecclesiastical history of Ireland from the introduction of Christianity to the year MDCCCXXIX* [n.d.] · A. A. MacErlean, 'Lanigan, John', *Catholic encyclopedia*, 16 (1914) · J. F. Kenney, *The sources for the early history of Ireland* (1929) · *DNB*
Archives Irish College, Rome, P. F. Moran, 'Spicilegium Ossoriense', III, 351 (1884)

Lankester, Edwin (1814–1874), public health reformer and natural historian, was born on 23 April 1814 at Melton, near Woodbridge, Suffolk. His father, William Lankester (1791–1818), was a builder who died of tuberculosis at the age of twenty-seven leaving his widow, Susan, *née* Taylor, his four-year old son Edwin, and possibly a younger daughter. Injudicious use of William's small estate left the family poor, and Edwin's schooling at local establishments ceased when he was barely twelve years old; in 1826 his mother became landlady of the Royal Oak inn, Woodbridge. Edwin was then articled to Samuel Gissing, surgeon, of Woodbridge, until 1832. After enduring two brief and unsatisfactory assistantships in Hampshire and London he became, in 1833, assistant to Thomas Spurgeon of Saffron Walden, Essex, who took pleasure in furthering the education of his employees. He gave Lankester the use of his library and helped him in his study of the classics. Lankester also became secretary of the local natural history society and curator of the town museum.

Friends then lent Lankester £300 to support him through a medical course at the newly opened University of London, where he studied from 1834 until he qualified as MRCS and licentiate of the Society of Apothecaries in 1837. During that time he became president of the college medical society, published his first medical paper, and won the Lindley silver medal for botany. (In 1846 John Lindley would name a newly discovered tropical plant, *Lankesteria parviflora*, after his former pupil.) Through Lindley, Lankester obtained the post of resident medical attendant and science tutor to the family of Charles Wood of Campsall Hall, near Doncaster, where, with his colleague Dr Leonard Schmitz and his two pupils, he was able to broaden his own scientific knowledge while playing an

Edwin Lankester (1814–1874), by Antoine Claudet, *c*.1862

active part in the Doncaster Lyceum. Here, too, he wrote his first book (published 1842), a scientific account of the neighbouring Askern mineral springs. In 1839 he travelled to Heidelberg, learned German, and graduated MB, accomplishing this feat in only six months.

Lankester then settled in London, supporting himself by means of part-time medical appointments at two dispensaries, literary work, and popular lectures. From 1842 until at least 1856 he held a lectureship at the prestigious Grosvenor Place medical school. He made many friends at this time, including Charles and Catherine Dickens, Douglas Jerrold, and Arthur Henfrey. He lodged with Edward Forbes at Golden Square and was an original member of the Red Lion Club founded by Forbes in 1839. He wrote regularly for the *Daily News*, chiefly on medical reform in support of Thomas Wakley, and for *The Athenaeum*. He was a regular attendant at the meetings of the British Association for the Advancement of Science, and from 1839 to 1864 was the secretary of section D (botany and zoology). In 1844 he became secretary of the newly formed Ray Society for which he edited *The Memorials of John Ray* (1845). He was elected a fellow of the Linnean Society in 1840 and of the Royal Society in 1845.

Also in 1845, on 3 July, Lankester married Phebe Pope

[*see* Lankester, Phebe (1825–1900)], eldest daughter of Samuel Pope of Highbury, a former Lancashire mill owner. The couple set up home at 22 Old Burlington Street, but later moved to Savile Row, and in 1872 were living at 68 Belsize Park. Phebe was a botanist in her own right, producing popular botanical books and, after her husband's death, books on health matters. Seven of their eleven children survived to adulthood. Their eldest son, Sir (Edwin) Ray *Lankester (1847–1929), was a brilliant zoologist, founder of the Plymouth marine laboratories, and director of the British Museum (Natural History).

In 1841 Lankester obtained the extra licence of the Royal College of Physicians, allowing him to practise in the provinces; he sat for the London licence five years later but failed an examination designed for students fresh from crammers. As a result, he abandoned clinical medicine as a career, turning to science and social medicine. In 1850 he obtained the chair of natural science at New College, London, holding it until the college terminated the appointment in 1872. He was a popular public lecturer, contributed to numerous encyclopaedias and reference works, wrote *The Natural History of Plants Yielding Food* (1845) and other books of popular science, translated Schleiden's *Grundzüge der Wissenschaftlichen Botanik* (1849), and edited William McGillivray's *Natural History of Deeside* (1854) for the prince consort. He also translated Kuchenmeister's *Die in und an dem Körper des lebenden Menschen vorkommenden Parasiten* (1855) which became a seminal work in British dermatology. Lankester was a skilled microscopist, was joint editor of the *Quarterly Journal of Microscopical Science* from 1852 to 1871, and was president of the Microscopical Society of London in 1859 and 1860 and of the Quekett Microscopical Club in 1865; in 1859 he published his immensely popular *Half Hours with the Microscope*. In the same year he was appointed examiner in botany for the teachers' qualification newly instituted by the Department of Science and Art. He was a juror for the international exhibitions of 1851 and 1862. In 1858 he followed Lyon Playfair as superintendent of the food collection at the South Kensington Museum, where he reorganized and relabelled the exhibits to the benefit of the lay public, and published his associated lectures (1860, 1861). His employers considered that he had exceeded his brief and terminated his appointment in 1862. From 1856 to his death both Lankester and his wife published with Robert Hardwicke. Lankester advocated the teaching of physiology in schools and held advanced views on the place of women in society.

In 1849 Lankester was elected to the vestry of his parish, St James's, Westminster, and was active on a number of its committees when, in 1854, the infamous outbreak of cholera occurred in Broad Street. John Snow, who had published his brilliant theory on the epidemiology of the disease in 1849, quickly traced the outbreak to the local pump, but it was Lankester who enabled him to prove his theory by persuading his reluctant vestry to set up a cholera committee, finance an epidemiological study, and publish the results. Lankester also made a microscopical study of water samples and was able to disprove the then prevalent fungoid theory of the cause of cholera.

In 1856, as a result of his work on cholera, the vestry appointed Lankester to be the first medical officer of health for Westminster, a part-time post which he held until his death. He aimed to reduce by half the appalling death rate in the slums, while fighting a parsimonious vestry for adequate funds. He appointed a sanitary inspector to carry out regular inspections of the slum housing, drastically reduced the number of cow-houses and slaughterhouses in the basements, and tackled the water supply and the open sewers. His vaccination policy almost halved the incidence of smallpox in the parish, and his leaflets on precautions against cholera were delivered to every household. He made fortnightly reports to his vestry and published his deliberately uncompromising annual reports.

Lankester was an active participant in a number of medical societies, and it was as a member of the Provincial Medical and Surgical Association that he played an important part in its transformation to the British Medical Association (1856). He was also deeply involved in the struggle of both associations for a Medical Reform Bill (1858), fighting the royal colleges for real reforms and taking part in or leading a number of delegations to ministers.

On the death of Thomas Wakley, coroner for central Middlesex, Lankester was chosen as the medical candidate for the post, beating the legal candidate after a hugely expensive fight from which his own finances never recovered. His unorthodox use of the coronership to investigate the social evils causing death was violently opposed by his employers, the Middlesex magistrates, who retaliated by starving him of funds. With the help of the Social Science Association he publicized workhouse deaths, infanticides, and the huge infant death rate, which was often hidden by the incomplete registration of births. He pointed out the need for local mortuaries and for pathologists trained in post-mortem work, and was active in the Coroners' Society. His published annual reports were eagerly awaited by his colleagues and the public. As always, he insisted on the need to educate the public in health matters, himself publishing further popular books.

Lankester was an attractive man, tall, rather portly, with a high complexion and dark eyes and hair; his voice was deep, his manner warm and kind, and he had many friends attracted by his genial and sociable nature. His love of the countryside and of wild plants and animals was intense. He was a sincere Christian, probably moving between nonconformism and the Church of England, and he believed that God shaped the earth over millions of years for the express benefit of man. He was a born publicist, teacher, and reformer, always fighting for the poor and defenceless, but was eventually worn out by ceaseless conflict with a class-conscious, mean, and callous establishment. A prodigious worker, he took on far too many responsibilities and this, combined with his lack of method, resulted in constant admonishments for delay.

Lankester succumbed to overwork and anxiety at the age of sixty and died of diabetes on 30 October 1874, at 7 The Paragon, Margate; he was buried at Hampstead. His estate of £2000 was seized by the receiver to cover debts accrued in his fight for the coronership. His memory has been unjustly eclipsed by that of his brilliant son Ray.

MARY P. ENGLISH

Sources M. P. English, *Victorian values: the life and times of Dr Edwin Lankester, MD, FRS* (1990) · *Quekett Journal of Microscopical Science*, 15 (1875), 59 · *The Lancet* (7 Nov 1874), 676 · parish register, Suffolk, 1912 [birth] · m. cert.

Archives DWL, corresp. · Linn. Soc. · UCL, paper on evolution theory | Coroners' Society of England and Wales, annual reports · Elgin Library, Morayshire, letters to George Gordon · Museum of Scotland, Edinburgh, letters to William Jardine · UCL, letters to Society for the Diffusion of Useful Knowledge · Victoria Library, London, vestry of St James

Likenesses A. Claudet, carte-de-visite, *c*.1862, NPG [*see illus.*] · photograph, *c*.1865, NHM, Quekett Microscopical Club · E. Edwards, photograph, NPG; repro. in *Portraits of men of eminence*, 3 (1865) · T. H. Maguire, lithograph, repro. in T. H. Maguire, *Portraits of honorary members of the Ipswich Museum* (1852) · three photographs, RS · wood-engraving, NPG; repro. in *ILN* (26 July 1862)

Wealth at death under £2000: probate, 3 Dec 1874, *CGPLA Eng. & Wales*

Lankester [*née* Pope], **Phebe** [*pseud.* Penelope] (1825–1900), writer on botany and health, was born on 10 April 1825 in Manchester, the eldest daughter of Samuel Pope, a former mill owner, and his wife, Phebe, *née* Rushton. She grew up in middle-class Highbury, a residential suburb of London, attended a dissenting ladies' academy in Mill Hill, and later received private instruction in Manchester. On 3 July 1845 she married Dr Edwin *Lankester (1814–1874), medical reformer, popular science lecturer, and writer, who was coroner for central Middlesex from 1862 until his death. They lived for many years at 8 Savile Row, London, and had eleven children, seven of whom survived; one was Sir (Edwin) Ray *Lankester (1847–1929), biologist, teacher, and later director of the British Museum (Natural History).

Phebe Lankester worked with her husband in 1846–7 on articles for the *Penny Cyclopaedia* (1833–58), and on articles for the natural history section of the *National Cyclopaedia* (1854–5). In 1859, after her last child was born, she embarked on her own writing. *A Plain and Easy Account of British Ferns* (1860) describes more than forty indigenous ferns with information on varieties, localities, and medicinal and other uses. The book, a revision of Edwin Bosanquet's manual from the 1850s, reflects the Victorian fern craze. Lankester enthusiastically promotes collecting and cultivating ferns, particularly by the use of Wardian cases, as the way 'to bring something of the verdure of a country lane into the close atmosphere of a city' (*A Plain and Easy Account of British Ferns*, ix). While acknowledging the harmful effects of the rapacity of collectors, she recommends digging up ferns found in the countryside. Her book was advertised in conjunction with a descriptive folio album into which fern collectors could paste specimens. It continued in print into the 1890s under the title *British Ferns*. Her next book, *Wild Flowers Worth Notice* (1861), published as a companion volume, had illustrations by the botanical

Phebe Lankester (1825–1900), by Sir Hubert von Herkomer, 1895

artist J. E. Sowerby. Lankester features about a hundred native plants, such as the buttercup, and discusses botanical aspects and uses of wild flowers, and legends associated with them. She celebrates the benefits of botany for people of all ages and social classes, and her preface contains a ringing call for science education in schools.

As a writer, Lankester benefited from Victorian interest in making science accessible and inviting. She contributed articles between 1861 and 1864 to the periodical *Popular Science Review*. She was conversant with botany in its technical and applied aspects, and contributed substantially to J. T. Boswell Syme's *English Botany* (1863–86), the third edition of a foundational work of botanical classification and description. This important new edition sharply distinguished between technical material and 'popular' or 'literary' information. Phebe Lankester wrote nearly 400 entries for the 'popular portion'; her entries offered historical and poetic remarks about English plants as well as general information on their uses and properties.

Phebe Lankester was widowed in 1874, aged forty-nine. She continued her writing career and cultivated a juvenile audience with *Botany for Elementary Schools* (1875), in Allman's Penny School Series, and *Talks about Plants* (1879). Her writing repertory also included books on health. *Talks about Health* (1874) features a mother and son discussing such topics as fresh air, digestion, and proper exercise. *Domestic Economy for Young Girls* (1875), another title in Allman's Penny School Series, emphasizes the importance of women's role in home management and teaches about food preparation, clothing, and household cleanliness. This book addresses daughters who will enter into domestic service, later to become wives and mothers, and encourages them to keep a penny account book and deposit money into the Post Office Savings Bank. *The National Thrift Reader, with Directions for Possessing and Preserving Health* (1880), a reading book for schools (with vocabulary lists), consists of short chapters on topics such as 'What to do with money', 'Life insurance', and 'Health is wealth'. Recurrent themes throughout Lankester's books on health topics are the tyranny of female fashion (such as high-heeled shoes) and concerns about sanitary conditions in houses, especially drainage and sanitary arrangements.

Issues of women's health, education, and social circumstances also featured in Phebe Lankester's magazine writing for *The Queen*, *Chambers's Journal*, and *Magazine of the Arts*. For twenty years after her husband's death she wrote a popular syndicated weekly column in East Anglian and other provincial newspapers under the pseudonym Penelope. Addressing women of all social classes, she discussed such topics as increasing female employment, women's welfare, female emigration, and the importance of placing women on local poor-law boards.

As a widow she lived for many years at 5 Wimpole Street, London, with her youngest son and two of her unmarried daughters. She died there on 9 April 1900, and was buried two days later beside her husband in the churchyard of the Hampstead parish church. The *Times* obituary commented on her 'wonderful energy'. A portrait of her by Sir Hubert von Herkomer shows a kind face, strength of character, and a calm, steady gaze.

ANN B. SHTEIR

Sources F. Hays, *Women of the day: a biographical dictionary of notable contemporaries* (1885) · M. P. English, *Victorian values: the life and times of Dr Edwin Lankester, MD, FRS* (1990) · J. Lester, *E. Ray Lankester and the making of modern British biology*, ed. P. J. Bowler (1995) · *The Times* (14 April 1900), 4
Archives priv. coll., family papers
Likenesses H. von Herkomer, portrait, 1895, Ipswich Museum [*see illus.*]

Lankester, Sir (Edwin) Ray (1847–1929), zoologist, was born on 15 May 1847 at 22 Old Burlington Street, London, the eldest son of Edwin *Lankester (1814–1874) and his wife, Phebe *Lankester, *née* Pope (1825–1900), eldest daughter of Samuel Pope of Highbury, formerly a mill owner in Manchester, and sister of Samuel Pope, barrister. His father was a surgeon, coroner, and natural historian who instituted many social reforms, and did important work in microscopy. His mother wrote popular works on wild flowers.

Education and public career, 1858–1907 Lankester was at first educated at home, where he was introduced to eminent scientists including Charles Darwin, T. H. Huxley, Edward Forbes, and W. B. Carpenter. He was sent to a boarding-school at Leatherhead, and then to St Paul's School, London, in 1858. In 1864 he obtained a scholarship to Downing College, Cambridge, but somewhat reluctantly moved in 1866 to Christ Church, Oxford, where he worked under Professor George Rolleston, who was introducing the teaching of biology through practical work. He

Sir (Edwin) Ray Lankester (1847–1929), by George Charles Beresford, 1902

gained first-class honours in natural sciences in 1868 and was awarded the Burdett Coutts scholarship in geology (1869) and the Radcliffe travelling fellowship (1870).

With funds from the Radcliffe fellowship Lankester studied physiology at Leipzig and Vienna, and morphology (comparative anatomy and embryology) under Ernst Haeckel at Jena. In 1871–2 he studied marine zoology with Anton Dohrn, who was then founding his Stazione Zoologica at Naples. In the summer of 1871 he worked as a demonstrator in the practical classes in biology established for schoolteachers by Huxley at South Kensington. In 1872 he became fellow and tutor at Exeter College, Oxford, where he began to agitate for the reform of science teaching at the university, annoying Rolleston and the university authorities by his persistence.

In 1875 Lankester was appointed to the chair of zoology at University College, London (which was endowed as the Jodrell chair in 1881). Here he created a highly effective department for teaching, in which many eminent biologists of the next generation were trained. He was an effective lecturer, illustrating his descriptions of animal structures with meticulously drawn diagrams, and built up a museum and laboratory for practical work. Despite his success he worried about financial security, and in 1882 accepted the regius professorship of natural history at Edinburgh. He found the conditions for teaching and research there not to his liking and resigned almost immediately, much to the annoyance of Huxley and others who had campaigned on his behalf. He was reappointed at University College, where he remained until offered the Linacre chair of comparative anatomy at Oxford in 1891. Here he was successful in reorganizing the University Museum, but encountered many frustrations when he renewed his campaign to reform science teaching in the university. He made many enemies through his intemperate attacks on those whom he considered to be defending outdated privileges. He also found Oxford social life disappointing after his years in London.

In 1898 Lankester was appointed director of the natural history departments and keeper of zoology at the British Museum, South Kensington. He made effective changes to the museum's displays, and also tried to reform its role as a research institution. He came into conflict, however, with the principal librarian, Sir Edward Maunde Thompson, who was determined to keep the natural history collections subordinate to the central museum administration in Bloomsbury. Lankester enlisted the support of many scientists in his efforts to retain autonomy, but was constantly harassed by Thompson and his supporters among the staff and governors. After several years of conflict he was forced to retire at the age of sixty in 1907, although a public outcry forced the government to increase his pension.

Lankester was created KCB shortly after his enforced retirement in 1907. He had been elected to the Royal Society in 1875 and was awarded its royal medal in 1885 and the Copley medal in 1913. He was vice-president of the society in 1883 and 1896 and president of the British Association for the Advancement of Science in 1906. He received many honours from other societies at home and abroad, and was awarded the honorary DSc by the universities of Oxford and Leeds and an honorary LLD by St Andrews.

Zoology: practical and theoretical studies Lankester had begun writing on natural history as a schoolboy, with his first publication (a letter on the fossil fish *Pteraspis*) appearing in 1862. He had a great love of nature and collected specimens on informal field trips both at home and on the continent. He undertook a dredging expedition to collect the hemichordate *Rhabdopleura* in the Norwegian fjords in 1882. He was a skilled observer with the microscope, studying protozoan parasites, the cells of the blood and other bodily fluids, and especially the internal structure and development of both invertebrates and vertebrates. He wrote almost two hundred technical articles, many illustrated by his own hand. His most important work was on the structure, development, and phylogenetic relationships of invertebrates.

Some of Lankester's earliest papers were on the physiology of the earthworm. A pioneering study of the embryology of the Mollusca was aimed at elucidating the primitive type from which the members of the class have diverged. He accepted Haeckel's view that the early stages of individual development threw light on evolutionary relationships, but noted the extent to which the presence of a large yolk in the egg could distort ancestral structures. He argued that the molluscs have evolved from an ancestry within the annelid worms, losing the original segmentation.

Lankester worked on the structure of the heart and the segmented nature of the head in the Arthropoda. His classic paper 'Limulus an arachnid' (*Quarterly Journal of Microscopical Science*, 21, 1881, 504–649) confirmed that *Limulus*, the horseshoe crab, is not a crustacean but a member of the same class as the spiders. These researches resulted in a number of general conclusions concerning the origin and relationship of the major animal types. The necessity of distinguishing between different types of body-cavity was demonstrated: the coelom of worms and vertebrates is not homologous with the enlarged blood-space or haemocoel of arthropods and molluscs. An 1870 paper, 'The use of the term homology in modern zoology' (*Annals and Magazine of Natural History*, 6, 1870, 34–43), helped to clarify the relationship between homologies (resemblances produced by common descent) and homoplasies (resemblances between distinct groups produced by convergent evolution).

Lankester also wrote on the cell-layers from which the early embryo develops: his papers 'The primitive cell-layers of the embryo' (*Annals and Magazine of Natural History*, 11, 1873, 321–38) and 'Notes on the embryology and classification of the animal kingdom' (*Quarterly Journal of Microscopical Science*, 17, 1877, 399–454) challenged Haeckel's views on the phylogenetic significance of these early stages. He introduced many terms that have become widely adopted by morphologists, including 'invagination', 'nephridium', and 'blastopore'.

Lankester was among the first to describe protozoan parasites in the blood of vertebrates (1871). He actively promoted the study of parasitology and became a member of the Royal Society's tropical diseases committee. He worked with Ronald Ross on the malaria parasite and, as director of the British Museum (Natural History), commissioned F. V. Theobald's pioneering monograph on the mosquitoes (1901). He worked on bacteria and proposed a theory of 'pleomorphism' which maintained that various cocci, bacilli, and vibrios may be phases of the same species living under different conditions. He studied the corpuscles of the blood and other body fluids, especially in invertebrates. Lankester also worked on the chordates, especially the structure of the heart in *Amphioxus* and in various fishes. He later produced the first scientific study of the newly discovered okapi, and was depicted riding on the animal's back in a *Punch* cartoon (1902).

From the start Lankester had an interest in fossils, producing a monograph on the ancient fish the Cephalaspidae in 1868. At the museum he gave popular lectures on fossils which were published as a book in 1905. At a more general level, he published an essay, *On Comparative Longevity in Man and the Lower Animals* (1870), and wrote on the significance of the larger brain of vertebrates in allowing educability to play an ever-increasing role in animals' behaviour. He was an active supporter of the theory of evolution and did much to clarify its implications.

Besides the phylogenetic studies mentioned above, Lankester published *Degeneration: a Chapter in Darwinism*

(1880), pointing out the extent to which adaptation to less stimulating conditions would lead to evolutionary degeneration. The evolutionist could easily be misled into assuming that degenerate forms were the primitive ancestors from which the highest members of a class had progressed. In his later years he became an active opponent of the Lamarckian theory of the inheritance of acquired characters and a supporter of neo-Darwinism. He had little interest, however, in the emergence of Mendelian genetics.

Activities in the scientific community In 1883 Lankester headed a public campaign to raise funds for the creation of a national laboratory for the study of marine zoology. The Marine Biological Association was founded the following year, with Lankester again playing the most active role in raising funds and ensuring government support. He contributed to the design of the laboratory that was built at Plymouth and was elected president of the association in 1890.

Another area to which Lankester contributed, with less enduring success, was archaeology. From 1910 he supported the views of J. Reid Moir, who insisted that flints found in the Red Crag deposits of Suffolk, of Pliocene age, had been worked by humans. Lankester suggested the term 'rostrocarinate' to denote the most common shape, and wrote strongly worded papers in support of their authenticity. For a while, his efforts helped to convince at least some archaeologists that Reid Moir's discoveries were significant.

In addition to contributing his technical papers Lankester played a much wider role in the area of scientific publication. His father had founded the *Quarterly Journal of Microscopical Science*, and from 1869 he became co-editor. From 1878 to 1920 he was the editor, and under his leadership it became one of the country's leading scientific journals. Lankester wrote many articles on zoological topics for the *Encyclopaedia Britannica*, some of which were collected into a separate volume in 1891. He conceived and edited the massive *Treatise on Zoology*, nine volumes of which appeared between 1900 and 1909 (Lankester himself wrote the introductions to the first two).

In addition to these fairly detailed surveys Lankester wrote for a more popular readership in a wide range of periodicals. His most important contribution at this level was the series of articles 'Science from an easy chair' which began in the *Daily Telegraph* in 1907. For several years he wrote an article every week, and many of these were collected into books which sold by the tens of thousands. He thus played a major role in establishing the field of popular science writing. His work also reached a wide public through his relationship with H. G. Wells. Lankester's views on evolutionary degeneration are reflected in Wells's story 'The Time Machine', and the two writers collaborated on the early chapters of Wells's *Outline of History* (1920) which discussed the evolutionary origin of mankind.

Character and social views Lankester held strong views on a variety of social questions, views which he expressed in a manner so forthright that it earned him many enemies among those of a conservative disposition. As a young man he had met Karl Marx, and he was one of the few people who attended Marx's funeral. His own views were meritocratic rather than socialist, however. Throughout his career he opposed the dominance of the classical mode of education in the ancient universities. He was a professional scientist, and saw science as a social and intellectual force that deserved a major role in society and government. His 1883 British Association address 'Biology and the state' noted that much more support was given to science in Germany than in Britain. In 1916 he chaired a committee on the neglect of science created to promote the role of science in the war effort and in national life generally.

Lankester was a freethinker, opposed not so much to religion as to dogmatic theology. He resisted all efforts to promote what he considered superstition, and gained wide attention through his unmasking of the medium Henry Slade in 1876. He exposed Slade as a fraud and brought him to court; although freed on a technicality, Slade soon left the country. Lankester was aware of the potential value of science for industry, but thought it short-sighted to concentrate on this side of its social impact. Far more important, he claimed, was the value of science as a force for encouraging critical thinking and a more humane vision of how people could interact together. These views were summarized in his Romanes lecture given in Oxford in 1905 and published two years later as *The Kingdom of Man* (1907). Like many of his earlier efforts on behalf of reform, the lecture generated a good deal of opposition. Lankester did not agree with those biologists who held that individual attainment is limited by heredity: he stressed the extent to which the emergence of the human mind had permitted a new level of social, rather than biological, evolution.

Lankester had a deep love of art and literature. He painted watercolours throughout his life, depicting the scenery he enjoyed in Britain and on his many continental holidays. He knew many of the Pre-Raphaelite painters and discussed art with them; he also knew the sculptor Rodin, was a great admirer of the dancer Anna Pavlova, and was on close terms with a number of literary figures, especially Wells.

Lankester was a tall man who grew corpulent in middle age. He was engaged twice but never married; both engagements were broken off through last-minute disagreements. His letters to H. G. Wells proclaim his love of feminine charms, but he could not find a partner who could combine these charms with the respectability suited to his position in life. There were persistent rumours (fanned by his many enemies) about his private life. Some hint of this surfaced in 1895 when he was arrested late at night in Piccadilly Circus for obstructing the police when they were arresting a prostitute. Lankester insisted in a letter to *The Times* that the woman was being treated with undue harshness and that he became involved only to protect her. To his many friends, Lankester was a larger-than-life figure who was always the centre of attention in any social gathering. His later life was lonely and increasingly burdened with illness. He died at his home, 44 Oakley Street, Chelsea, London, on 15 August 1929; he was cremated at Golders Green crematorium after a funeral service at St Martin-in-the-Fields.

PETER J. BOWLER

Sources J. Lester, *E. Ray Lankester and the making of modern British biology*, ed. P. J. Bowler (1995) • E. S. G. [E. S. Goodrich], *PRS*, 106B (1930), x–xv • S. J. Hickson, S. F. Harmer, E. J. Allen, and others, *Nature*, 124 (1929), 309–14 • C. Mitchell, *The Times* (10 Aug 1929), 15 • *The Times* (21 Aug 1925) • T. Fisher, *Prostitution and the Victorians* (1997), 145–8

Archives Ernst-Haeckel-Haus, Jena • Marine Biological Association, Plymouth, corresp. and papers • NHM, papers • priv. coll. • RCS Eng., lecture notes • RS • Stazione Zoologica, Naples • U. Oxf., department of zoology, corresp. • UCL, lecture notes | BL, corresp. with Macmillans and letters to J. R. Moir, Add. MSS 55219, 44968–44971 • ICL, T. H. Hayley MSS • ICL, letters to Thomas Huxley • NA Scot., letters to F. M. Maitland • NHM, letters to C. E. Fagan • NHM, corresp. with Albert Gunther and/or R. W. T. Gunther • Oxf. U. Mus. NH, letters to Sir E. B. Poulton • RBG Kew, W. Thistleton-Dyer MSS • U. Leeds, Brotherton L., letters to Sir Edmund Gosse • UCL, letters to Karl Pearson • University of Illinois, Urbana-Champaign, H. G. Wells MSS • Wellcome L., corresp. with Lister Institute

Likenesses G. C. Beresford, photograph, 1902, NPG [*see illus.*] • J. Collier, oils, 1904, Exeter College, Oxford • photograph, *c.*1907, NHM; repro. in Lester, *E. Ray Lankester* • W. Stoneman, photograph, 1921, NPG • W. Rothenstein, chalk drawing, 1922, NPG • W. Rothenstein, sanguine drawing, 1925, NPG • W. Orpen, oils, 1929, Birmingham Museums and Art Gallery • Elliott & Fry, carte-de-visite, NPG • Maull & Fox, photograph, RS • Spy [L. Ward], caricature, watercolour study, NPG; repro. in *VF* (12 Jan 1905) • W. A. P., cartoon, repro. in *Punch* (12 Nov 1902) • mezzotint, NHM; repro. in Lester, *E. Ray Lankester* • photograph, RS; repro. in *PRS*, 106B, facing p. x

Wealth at death £4612 14*s.* 6*d.*: probate, 11 Oct 1929, *CGPLA Eng. & Wales*

Lankrink, Prosper Henricus (1628–1692), painter and collector, was born in Germany, the only son of an army officer who had moved to Antwerp to take up a commission in the Flemish army. After his father's death, his mother ensured Lankrink was well educated (Vertue refers to a 'liberal' education) with the intention he would enter holy orders. However, after revealing a real talent for painting and drawing, it was agreed that he should instead serve an apprenticeship with a local painter and study at the Antwerp Academy, where he soon developed into a promising landscape artist. Formative influences at this stage were the work of Titian and Salvator Rosa which he was able to study in the collection of a local collector, Myn Heer Lyam. Following his mother's death, Lankrink is said to have visited Italy before arriving in London in the mid-1660s. He lived first in Piccadilly and then from 1686 until his death in 1692 at 2 Great Piazza, Covent Garden, in the north-west corner of this fashionable development.

During the 1670s and 1680s Lankrink enjoyed a successful independent practice as a landscape and decorative painter. An early patron was the naval commander Sir Edward Spragge who introduced him to fellow collectors and patrons, most notably Sir William Williams, who became a major collector of Lankrink's work. According

to Vertue, Williams's house was almost 'intirely furnished' with Lankrink's paintings, all of which were destroyed soon after by fire. Very few other examples of his work survive or can indeed now be identified. But from examples that do periodically appear in the sale rooms and descriptions in earlier sale catalogues, his paintings seem to have been heavily indebted to seventeenth-century Italian classical landscape artists, and characterized by a broad sweep of sky, framing blocks of foliage and classical ruins and peopled by small pastoral or biblical figures. According to one contemporary, Bainbrigg Buckeridge, writing in 1706, Lankrink's paintings were 'wonderful, both as to the invention, harmony, colouring and warmth, but above all surprisingly beautiful and free in their skies, which by general consent excell'd all the works of the most eminent Painters in that kind' (Buckeridge, 399–400). His skill in portraying small figures, Buckeridge maintained, resulted from his 'practising drawing by the life' (ibid.). On the evidence of the sale catalogue of his own collection (see below) he also produced a number of portraits including a self-portrait and a portrait of the artist and copyist Symon Stone, both 'done 3 ways' (showing the sitters in three positions). Only one print after his work, a mezzotint by John Smith after *Nymphs Bathing*, is now known.

In addition to his own independent practice, Lankrink was closely involved with the studio of Peter Lely, Charles II's principal painter, where he was employed to paint flowers, ornaments, landscape backgrounds, and occasionally draperies. Not surprisingly therefore, as someone familiar with the Covent Garden studio, he played an important part in the dispersal of its contents following Lely's death in 1680, completing a number of unfinished canvases, helping to organize the sale of artist's materials, and purchasing for himself items as varied as pigments, drawing paper, frames, '42 postures without head', '11 palettes', and '16 gross of pencils' (BL, Add. MS 16174, fol. 21v).

As well as listing his qualities as a painter, many contemporaries acknowledged Lankrink's importance as a collector. He began forming his collection in Antwerp and seems to have taken advantage of the dispersal of both Rubens's and Rembrandt's collections in the 1650s. He continued to collect after he arrived in London, regularly attending the growing number of art auctions held in Covent Garden and Lincoln's Inn Fields and buying extensively at Lely's paintings and drawings sales in 1682 and 1688. Frequent references in Constantijn Huygens's journal to Lankrink accompanying other collectors to auctions, attending sale previews, going through the stock of artist–dealer friends, and offering conservation advice about fellow collectors' drawings suggest that he was a well-known and respected figure in the art circles of Restoration London. At his death in 1692 his collection was described as 'certainly the most Curious and the most Numerous, that ever was seen in this Country, in a private man's possession'. Totalling some 464 items it comprised mainly sixteenth- and seventeenth-century Dutch and Flemish landscape, still-life and flower pieces, portraits, and subject pictures, including works by Lely, Rembrandt, and Rubens plus a handful of works 'in the manner of Tintoretto and Titian' (Cust, 30–32, 35). It was sold by auction on 23 January 1693 from his house in the Great Piazza. His collection of old master drawings, with a similar Dutch and Flemish bias, but also containing works by sixteenth-century Italian artists such as Parmigianino and Veronese, was sold the following year, having first been stamped with his characteristic PHL collector's mark.

Lankrink was described by Vertue as of a 'debonnair-temper … a good Bottle Companion, & Excellent Company but also a grate Favourite of the ladies' and was clearly popular among his many friends and acquaintances (Vertue, *Note books*, 2.145). He lived well and was often in debt; at his death at his home in 1692 his collection had to be sold to clear his outstanding debts and he had borrowed heavily from a friend and fellow collector Mr Austen to finance his purchases at Lely's sales. He appears never to have married and left no will. At his particular request he was buried facing the garden under the great porch of St Paul's, Covent Garden. The preface to his painting sale catalogue serves as a fitting epitaph to this relatively little known but intriguing and talented character:

> Mr *Lankrink* has been look'd upon as one of the most excellent Painters in *Europe*, as well in respect to the Perfection of his own Painting, as for his great Knowledge, and vast Understanding, in what is left, of the finest and most finish'd Pieces, of the greatest Masters. Other Nations have envied the Happiness we have had, of enjoying such a famous Man, for several years.   (Cust, 30)

DIANA DETHLOFF

Sources [B. Buckeridge], 'An essay towards an English school of painters', in R. de Piles, *The art of painting, and the lives of the painters* (1706), 398–480 · Vertue, *Note books*, 1.24–49; 2.5, 69, 95, 144–5 · [L. Cust], 'P. H. Lankrink's collection', *Burlington Magazine*, 86 (Feb 1945), 29–35 · D. Dethloff, 'The executors' account book and the dispersal of Sir Peter Lely's collection', *Journal of the History of Collections*, 8 (1996), 15–51, esp. 17, 19, 21, 36–7, 48 · M. K. Talley, *Portrait painting in England: studies in the technical literature before 1700* (1981), 360, 364–73 · 'Journal von Constantijn Huygens den Zoon', *Historisch Gezelschap Werken Nieuwe serie* (1862), no. 25 · executors' account book of Sir Peter Lely, 1679–91, BL, Add. MS 16174

Lanner [*married name* Geraldini], **Katharina Josefa** [Katti] (**1829–1908**), dancer and choreographer, was born in the parish of Laimgrube, Vienna, Austria, on 14 September 1829, one of the two daughters of Josef Lanner (1801–1843), a violinist and waltz composer, and his wife, Franciska, *née* Jahns. Her brother August (1834–1855) was a violinist and orchestra leader. She trained at the ballet school of the Vienna Court Opera, and made her début in *Angelica* at the city's Kärntnertortheater on 4 August 1845. For ten years she danced with the Vienna Court Opera Ballet, where her parts included Fenella in *Die Stumme von Portici* (1847), and the title roles in *Elina* (1847) and *Giselle* (1856). She also danced in Berlin, Munich, and Dresden.

In 1862 Katti Lanner took the position of ballerina and ballet mistress at the State Theatre, Hamburg, where she choreographed ten successful ballets, including *Uriella, der Dämon der Nacht* (1862) and *Sitala, das Gaukler-Mädchen*

(1863). On 11 February 1864, in Hamburg, she married the composer Johann Alfred Geraldini; they had three daughters—Sofia, Katharina, and Albertina. In the late 1860s she toured Scandinavia and Russia, and by 1869 she was leading her own company, the Viennese Ballet Company, which performed in Bordeaux (1869), New York (1870), and Lisbon (1870–71). She appeared in London at Drury Lane in 1871, and made her Paris début at the Théâtre Italien in May 1872. In 1873 she travelled again to America, with the Kathi Lanner Coreographic Combination [*sic*], and toured for the next two years. She made several appearances at Niblo's Garden, New York, in *Azrael* (1873) and *Tom and Jerry* (1875).

Lanner returned to London in 1875, and made her family's home at 40 North Side, Clapham Common. The following year she was invited to take charge of the National Training School of Dancing, which had been set up by the opera impresario James Mapleson, at 73 Tottenham Court Road. She later became sole owner of the school, with the object of 'the resuscitation of the faded glories of ballet, and to bring a thorough knowledge of the choreography art within the range of those classes among whom talent most abounds'. She was an affectionate but stern disciplinarian. From 1877 to 1881 she was ballet mistress at Her Majesty's Theatre, London, where she staged ballets for the Italian Opera Company, including *Les papillons* (1878). Lanner continued to dance herself, one of her last appearances being as Elena in *Robert le diable* at Her Majesty's on 16 July 1878. She also choreographed the ballets in Augustus Harris's pantomimes at Drury Lane and for pantomimes at the Crystal Palace. In 1887 she became ballet mistress (choreographer) at the Empire Theatre, which was then a variety theatre, and over the next twenty years she put on more than thirty ballets, some modern, some preserving classical traditions, with Adeline Genée as her principal ballerina. The music for most of these ballets was written by Hervé and Leopold Wenzl, successive musical directors at the Empire, among them being *The Sports of England* (1887), *Cleopatra* (1889), *Orféo* (1891), *The Girls I Left Behind Me* (1893), *Faust* (1895, to music by Meyer Lutz), a new version of *Les papillons* (1901), and *The Milliner Duchess* (1903). Lanner was succeeded by Fred Farren, but was called out of retirement in 1906 to put on *The Debutante*, and the following year she choreographed *Sir Roger de Coverley* to music by F. O. Carr.

Lanner was an honorary member of the Imperial Society of Teachers of Dancing and of the Society of German Dance Teachers, and was one of the first women to choreograph regularly. Her training of young dancers was perhaps her most important contribution to the profession in Britain, though she was later rather eclipsed by the arrival of Diaghilev's Ballets Russes. She died at her home at Clapham Common on 15 November 1908, and was buried at Norwood cemetery.

J. GILLILAND

Sources I. Guest, *The Empire ballet* (1962) · C. W. Beaumont, *The complete book of ballets* (1917) · S. D'Amico, ed., *Enciclopedia dello spettacolo*, 11 vols. (Rome, 1954–68) · M. Bremser, ed., *International dictionary of ballet* (1993) · I. Guest, 'An early "national school": the achievements of Katti Lanner', *Dancing Times* (Nov 1958) • S. L. Bensusan, 'The evolution of a dancer', *The Sketch* (13 March 1901) • B. Hunt, ed., *The green room book, or, Who's who on the stage* (1906) • P. Bedell, *My dancing years* (1906) • R. Mander and J. Mitchenson, *The lost theatres of London* (1968) • M. E. Perugini, *The art of ballet* (1915) • *Morning Post* (16 Nov 1906) • T. C. Davis, *Actresses as working women: their social identity in Victorian culture* (1991) • d. cert.

Likenesses photograph, 1877, repro. in Guest, *Empire ballet* • Martin and Salinow, photograph, *c.*1901, repro. in Bensusan, 'The evolution of a dancer' • print, Harvard TC

Wealth at death £6227 19*s.* 7*d.*: probate, 23 Jan 1909, *CGPLA Eng. & Wales*

Lanquet, Thomas (1520/21–1545), historian, is of unknown origins. Wood asserts that he studied at Oxford, but neither he nor the university records offer evidence to support the claim. Lanquet is known for having undertaken a history of the known world in which the fortunes of nations and peoples are summarized together year by year. His purpose was didactic and moralizing, as he explains in his introduction (Lanquet and Cooper, fols. 1–2*v*). 'In reading of historyes examples of politicall vertues and civill affayres ought to bee observed', he declares, and he eulogizes Henry VIII as a perhaps surprising illustration of the truth 'that good princis bee preserved and defended by god'. He displays humanistic leanings in a chapter devoted to 'the originall begynnyng of man, after the false opinion of the Ethnike [heathen] philosophers', but his framework is firmly Christian. Lanquet proposed to divide his history into three sections, from the creation (dated to 3962 BC) to Abraham, from Abraham to the birth of Christ, and finally down to his own time. But he died in London in 1545, aged twenty-four, having reached only the accession of Tiberius (AD 17).

Lanquet's work was completed by Thomas Cooper, later successively bishop of Lincoln and of Winchester, and it was published in 1549 as *An Epitome of Chronicles*, with a dedication to the duke of Somerset. In the epistle to the reader announcing his taking up the reins, Cooper describes Lanquet as a 'studious younge man' and acknowledges his 'greate laboure and diligence' (Lanquet and Cooper, fol. 84). The tribute was well deserved. On the evidence of references to such writers as Homer, Herodotus, Thucydides, Xenophon, Plutarch, Sallust, Julius Caesar, Eusebius, and Bede, Lanquet was widely read in Greek and Latin sources. His having consulted 'the conspiracy of Catiline, translated into english by Thomas Paynell' (ibid., fol. 82*v*), a work intended to encourage obedience to the crown, may be a further pointer to Lanquet's political position. In other respects Lanquet's views are hard to discover, possibly a sign of an eirenic temperament. He states explicitly that he finds the British and Scottish origin myths incredible, but nevertheless resolves to use them—'I wil not discent from the common opinion therof, but wil also folow it as nere as I may' (ibid., fol. 32). He knew the scriptures well but says nothing, even in his account of the life of Christ, to indicate his own religious position. In a comment on the early Jewish sects he compares the Essenes to Anabaptists, who 'condemned bothe the Lutheranes and papistes, and studyed to bee seene holyer than thei bothe' (ibid., fol. 75*r–v*), but that is the limit of his partisanship. In

1559 Robert Crowley reissued the *Epitome* with a continuation to the accession of Elizabeth, virulently anti-Catholic in its account of recent events. But in 1560 Cooper in turn brought out another edition, repudiating Crowley's and in its continuation much less violent against Rome. This edition was reissued in 1565. Lanquet is also said by Bale to have written an account of Henry VIII's capture of Boulogne in September 1544, which has not survived.

HENRY SUMMERSON

Sources T. Lanquet and T. Cooper, *An epitome of cronicles* (1549) [later edns 1559, 1560] • Bale, *Cat.*, 1.712 • Wood, *Ath. Oxon.*, new edn, 1.149–50 • Emden, *Oxf.*, 4.342 • J. McConica, *English humanists and Reformation politics* (1965)

Lansbury, George (1859–1940), leader of the Labour Party, was born on 22 February 1859 in the Thoroughfare, Halesworth, in Suffolk, the second of nine children of George Lansbury (*d.* 1875), railway timekeeper for Thomas Brassey & Co., and his Welsh wife, Mary Anne Ferries, daughter of James Ferries of Clyro, Radnorshire. He was the third eldest child, with six brothers and two sisters.

In his autobiography, *My Life* (1928), Lansbury said little about his father, but remembered the influence of his nonconformist grandmother, his mother, and the Revd J. Fenwick Kitto, an Anglican minister. By 1868 the Lansbury family had settled in the East End of London, where G. L., as Lansbury became popularly known, had an intermittent education until the age of fourteen at dame-schools and St James-the-Less, Birkbeck, and St Mary's elementary schools. Afterwards, various manual jobs included unloading coal wagons. In 1880 Lansbury married Elisabeth (Bessie) Jane Brine (*d.* 1933), his schoolfriend and the daughter of Sarah and Isaac Brine, owner of a local timber yard which Lansbury took over on his father-in-law's death. Happily married for over fifty years, George and Bessie had twelve children: their second son, William, was manager of the family business with their third son, Edgar, the father of the actress Angela Lansbury; their third daughter, Dorothy, married Ernest Thurtle MP; and their fourth daughter, Daisy, was Lansbury's secretary and married Raymond Postgate, her father's biographer. Their main home, 39 Bow Road, in the heart of the East End, became Lansbury's well-known political base throughout his life.

In 1884 the Lansburys emigrated to Australia, only to experience unemployment. On their return to London in 1886, Lansbury's campaign for accurate emigration information brought him into Liberal–radical politics. He became honorary secretary of the Bow and Bromley Liberal and Radical Association, and masterminded parliamentary election victories for Samuel Montagu and J. A. Murray Macdonald in 1886 and 1892, as well as being agent in 1889 for Jane Cobden, one of the first two women returned to the London county council.

During the late 1880s Lansbury converted to socialism, influenced by Marx and by socialists such as William Morris and H. M. Hyndman. He witnessed at first hand the poverty of outcast London and became disillusioned with

George Lansbury (1859–1940), by Felix H. Man, 1934

the Gladstonian Liberal Party's hostile attitude towards social reform, party democracy, and women's rights, particularly when the National Liberal Federation conference in 1889 declined to support a motion in favour of the eight-hour day. From 1892 to 1904 Lansbury was the leading figure in the Social Democratic Federation (SDF) in London and he was its national organizer in 1895–6. In May and July 1895 he unsuccessfully contested Walworth and, in 1900, Bow and Bromley as an SDF parliamentary candidate. By 1904 he had joined the Independent Labour Party, for which he stood unsuccessfully at Middlesbrough in 1906, where his election agent, Marion Coates Hansen, influenced his support of women's enfranchisement.

In local government Lansbury held every office: guardian (from 1893), councillor (from 1903), member of the London county council (1910–13), and justice of the peace. In Poplar the Labour group's influence under Lansbury far outweighed its minority position before 1914 and became synonymous with workhouse reform and the generous treatment of paupers. A fear that this was undermining the principles of the 1834 poor law led Sir James Davy of the Local Government Board to set up an official inquiry into the conduct of the Poplar board of guardians. Lansbury also worked closely with the American millionaire soap manufacturer Joseph Fels, who funded Lansbury's election campaigns and the establishment of Hollesley Bay and similar farm colonies for the unemployed. A member of the Central (Unemployed) Body for London, Lansbury was appointed to the royal commission on the

poor laws (1905–9) and signed Beatrice Webb's minority report.

Defeated in January 1910, Lansbury was returned to parliament as the Labour member for Bow and Bromley in December 1910. He soon became a backbench rebel, opposed to Ramsay MacDonald's alliance with the Liberal government. In 1912 he was temporarily suspended from the Commons after his clash with Asquith over the forcible feeding of suffragette prisoners. An ardent champion of the Women's Social and Political Union, Lansbury resigned his seat over women's suffrage, but lost the by-election in November 1912 and remained out of parliament for a decade. His family was active in Sylvia Pankhurst's East London Federation. In 1913 Lansbury was imprisoned after his Albert Hall speech appeared to sanction the suffragettes' arson campaign.

From 1912 to 1922, as a founder, Lansbury was editor-proprietor of the *Daily Herald* and kept the paper alive despite recurrent financial crises—a story recounted in *The Miracle of Fleet Street* (1925). With a team of outstanding journalists and a country-wide network of Herald leagues, the paper became the focus of socialist, feminist, and syndicalist dissent in the turbulent world of Edwardian politics. Between 1914 and 1918 the paper was published as a pacifist weekly and then, in the early 1920s, it became the tribune of the left. In 1921 'Poplarism' entered the political vocabulary, as the symbol of local defiance of central government. Lansbury, who had been the first Labour mayor in 1919, his son Edgar, and daughter-in-law Minnie were among the thirty councillors of Poplar, in east London, who were imprisoned for six weeks during the Poplar rates rebellion.

After an unsuccessful contest in 1918, Lansbury was returned to parliament for Poplar, Bow, and Bromley in 1922, and he retained the seat until his death. Ramsay MacDonald left him out of his Labour cabinet in 1924, mainly because the king, George V, recalled Lansbury's sympathy for the Bolshevik regime. He visited Russia in 1920, and published *What I Saw in Russia* (1920). From 1925 to 1927, with Raymond Postgate, Lansbury published *Lansbury's Labour Weekly*. He was staunchly anti-imperialist and gave unflagging support to nationalist movements, especially in Ireland and India.

In 1929 Ramsay MacDonald appointed Lansbury as first commissioner of works, the only left-winger in the cabinet. In charge of historic buildings and monuments, the veteran Lansbury amazed civil servants with a radical programme of recreational improvements for the public in the royal parks, including 'Lansbury's Lido' on the Hyde Park Serpentine. In the 1931 financial crisis Lansbury was a leading member of the minority in the cabinet which opposed the 10 per cent cut in unemployment insurance; this opposition brought the end of the second Labour government.

As the only former cabinet minister who survived the 1931 election, Lansbury became leader of the Labour Party. Between 1931 and 1935, in opposition to the National Government with over 500 MPs, he rallied the parliamentary party of forty-six MPs and the labour movement, and started important party reforms. With the rise of European fascism, his pacifist views brought him into conflict with trade union bosses within the party. Lansbury resigned the leadership after the 1935 Brighton conference, where, during the Abyssinian crisis, Ernest Bevin cruelly attacked him for 'hawking your conscience from body to body asking to be told what to do with it' (Shepherd, *George Lansbury*, 320–28). In his final years Lansbury, by then president of the Peace Pledge Union, campaigned internationally for peace and undertook visits to Hitler and Mussolini, which he described in *My Quest for Peace* (1938). He also published *My England* (1934) and *Looking Backwards and Forwards* (1935).

A member of the Church Socialist League and a teetotaller, Lansbury consistently applied his Christian socialist principles throughout his life and career, seeking neither wealth nor social status. As a cabinet minister he wore an old double-breasted blue serge suit and travelled by bus or train. He was easily recognized: a tall, upstanding figure, kind ruddy face, white hair, side whiskers, and an unmistakable friendly, ringing voice. Lansbury was a charismatic speaker and revered populist leader with a reputation as 'the most lovable figure in modern politics' (A. J. P. Taylor, *English History, 1914–1945*, 1965, 142 n. 3). He died of cancer at Manor House Hospital at Golders Green, Middlesex, on 7 May 1940. His funeral service at St Mary's, Bow, was followed by cremation, with a memorial service in Westminster Abbey. JOHN SHEPHERD

Sources J. Shepherd, *George Lansbury: at the heart of old Labour* (2002) • R. Postgate, *The life of George Lansbury* (1951) • J. Schneer, *George Lansbury* (1990) • J. Shepherd, 'Labour and the trade unions: George Lansbury, Ernest Bevin and the labour leadership crisis of 1935', *On the move: essays in transport and labour history presented to Philip Bagwell*, ed. C. Wrigley and J. Shepherd (1991) • G. Lansbury, *My life* (1928) • M. Cole, 'Lansbury, George', *DLB*, vol. 2 • D. Lukowitz, 'George Lansbury's peace missions to Hitler and Mussolini in 1937', *Canadian Journal of History*, 15/1 (April 1980), 67–82 • A. W. Purdue, 'George Lansbury and the Middlesbrough election of 1906', *International Review of Social History*, 18 (1973), 333–52 • P. Ryan, '"Poplarism", 1894–1930', *The origins of British social policy*, ed. P. Thane (1978), 56–83 • N. Branson, *Poplarism, 1919–1925: George Lansbury and the councillors' revolt* (1979) • H. Richards, *The bloody circus: the Daily Herald and the left* (1997) • B. Holton, *British syndicalism, 1900–1914* (1976) • B. Holman, *Good old George: the life of George Lansbury* (1990) • E. Lansbury, *George Lansbury: my father* (1934) • b. cert. • *CGPLA Eng. & Wales* (1940) • *The Times* (8 May 1940)
Archives Bancroft Road Library, Tower Hamlets, London, corresp. and MS of *Principles of the English poor law* • BLPES, corresp. and papers • University of Manchester, Labour History Archive and Study Centre, papers | BLPES, Independent Labour Party Archive, Francis Johnson MSS [microfilm] • BLPES, corresp. with the JLP • BLPES, Passfield MSS • Bodl. Oxf., Ensor MSS • Bodl. Oxf., letters to Lord Ponsonby • Borth. Inst., corresp. with Major D. E. Pole • Hist. Soc. Penn., Fels MSS • HLRO, Lloyd George MSS • HLRO, letters to Herbert Samuel • LPL, letters to H. R. L. Sheppard • PRO, MacDonald MSS • Ruskin College, Oxford, corresp. with James Middleton • U. Lpool L., Glasier MSS • University of Bristol Library, corresp. with Jane Cobden | FILM BFI NFTVA, documentary footage • BFI NFTVA, news footage | SOUND BL NSA, 'Lansbury's *Labour Weekly*', c.1926/1927, LA 836, tape 5143 • BL NSA, 'The Disarmament Situation', 19 Oct 1933, AA 235 • BL NSA, 'Earl Attlee recalls Lansbury becoming leader in talk on the Labour Party in 1931', May 1960, AA LP26422 • BL NSA, 'W. W. Benn, secretary of

state for India, recalling appointment by J. R. Macdonald', May 1960, AA LP26422 • BL NSA, *In Our Time*, May 1960, FE LP26422-3 [radio biography] • BL NSA, 'Reminiscences by Nellie Cressall of Lansbury and Labour Party and of Lansbury's imprisonment during Poplar rates rebellion of 1921', May 1960, AC LP26422 • BL NSA, *I remember*, 27 July 1960, LP27052 • BL NSA, 'H. Short recalling how Lansbury brought ballet to Bow in 1910', 4 Oct 1966, AA LP30476 • BL NSA, 'Memories of early days of the *Daily Herald*' by W. N. Ewer and Sir Francis Meynell (May 1960), BBC archive record LP 26423 • BL NSA, recorded talks
Likenesses photograph, c.1901, NPG • B. Stone, photographs, 1911, NPG • group portrait, photograph, 1921 (with his family), NPG • oils, c.1921, priv. coll. • E. Kapp, drawing, 1929, Barber Institute of Fine Arts, Birmingham • W. Stoneman, photographs, 1929–40, NPG • F. H. Man, photograph, 1934, NPG [*see illus.*] • H. Coster, photographs, c.1935, NPG • S. Gosse, oils, 1939, NPG • Bassano, photograph, NPG • T. Cottrell, print on cigarette card, NPG • P. Evans, pencil drawing, NPG • Lafayette, photograph (with his wife), NPG • plaque, 39 Bow Road, Tower Hamlets • portrait on plaque, Lansbury's Lido, Serpentine, Hyde Park
Wealth at death £1695 18s. 4d.: probate, 28 Aug 1940, *CGPLA Eng. & Wales*

Lansdell, Henry (1841–1919), Church of England clergyman and traveller, was born in Tenterden, Kent, on 10 January 1841, the eldest son of Henry and Julia Lansdell. Educated by his father and, between 1865 and 1867, at St John's College of Divinity, Highgate, he was ordained deacon in 1867 and priest in 1868. He was curate of Greenwich from 1867 to 1869, and between 1869 and 1879 was secretary to the Irish Church Missions on whose behalf he travelled energetically, lecturing and attending meetings, combining travel and missionary work in a pattern which was to characterize the rest of his life. He founded, and from 1874 to 1876 was secretary of, the Church Homiletical Society which aimed to improve the preaching and pastoral work of the younger clergy and which had great influence. In this connection he published two works on preaching and founded the *Clergyman's Magazine* which he also edited between 1875 and 1887. From 1885 to 1886 he was curate in charge of St Peter's, Eltham, Kent.

From the 1870s Lansdell began to travel, at first spending short holidays in the more accessible parts of Europe, but ultimately making long and often arduous journeys in little known parts of Asia until he had visited almost every part of Europe and much of central Asia, Russia, and Siberia. His object was to distribute tracts and bibles provided by London missionary societies in many languages wherever he went, most notably in prisons and hospitals in Siberia and central Asia. He published accounts of his travels in *Through Siberia* (2 vols., 1882) and *Russian Central Asia* (2 vols., 1885). The first proved extremely popular, running to five editions in England and also being published in German, Danish, and Swedish. It aroused criticism, however, because of its very favourable attitude towards Russia. In particular his largely commendatory accounts of conditions inside Russian prisons aroused angry opposition from Prince Kropotkin. Lansdell's second work continued in pro-Russian vein, being dedicated to Alexander III, repudiating the charges of Kropotkin and others that his accounts of Russian prisons had been either credulous of Russian propaganda or had deliberately obscured the true state of affairs, and declaring that the annexation of Merv by Russia in 1884 was not, as had been alleged, due to Russian subterfuge and coercion, but to the genuine wish of the people of Merv for closer ties with Russia which would conduce to their well-being. This book too, however, found an audience because of its detailed descriptions of remote places rarely before visited (descriptions often vetted by knowledgeable specialists before publication) and because of its exotic illustrations—not least the photographic portrait of the author in Khokand armour presented by the emir of Bukhara, and the line drawing of him in academic dress for his reception by the emir. An abridged popular version appeared as *Through Central Asia* (1887) which has an appendix on the 1885–6 border dispute. *Chinese Central Asia* (2 vols., 1893) recorded his last major journey to Tibet. He set off in 1888 armed with his normal tracts in the improbable hope that a letter from the archbishop of Canterbury to the Dalai Lama which he carried in a silk mount would secure his access to the closed city of Lhasa. Thwarted in his attempts to reach Lhasa from India, he sailed for China, hoping to approach from the other side; but the English ambassador in China, fearing damage to already sensitive Anglo-Tibetan relations, persuaded him to give up and sail home.

In 1892 Lansdell was appointed chaplain of Morden College, almshouses for decayed merchants at Blackheath, London, and in the same year married Mary Anne, eldest child of Charles and Mary Anne Colyer of Farningham and Greenhithe, Kent. After Tibet his travels were less extensive, but he continued to write, publishing works on scriptural and historical aspects of the tithe (1906, 1908, and 1909) and *Princess Ælfrida's Charity* (7 parts, 1911–16), an account of Morden College which had previously appeared in local newspapers. These works, however, fell quickly into obscurity. His travel experience led to his election of the Royal Asiatic Society, the Royal Geographical Society, and the British Association for the Advancement of Science on whose committee he served. He was made honorary DD by the archbishop of Canterbury in 1882. He retired from Morden College in 1912 and died in London on 4 October 1919.   ELIZABETH BAIGENT

Sources P. Schaff and S. M. Jackson, *Encyclopedia of living divines and Christian workers of all denominations in Europe and America: being a supplement to Schaff-Herzog encyclopedia of religious knowledge* (1887) • *GJ*, 54 (1919), 327 • *WWW* • *Men and women of the time* (1899) • Allibone, *Dict.* • P. Hopkirk, *The great game: on secret service in high Asia* (1990) • P. Hopkirk, *Trespassers on the roof of the world* (1982) • *The Times* (6 Oct 1919)
Archives U. Birm. L., letters to V. A. Pashkov
Likenesses line drawing, repro. in H. Lansdell, *Russian Central Asia*, 2 vols. (1885) • photograph, repro. in H. Lansdell, *Russian Central Asia*, 2 vols. (1885)
Wealth at death £1738 1s. 4d.: probate, 19 Aug 1920, *CGPLA Eng. & Wales*

Lansdowne. For this title name *see* Granville, George, Baron Lansdowne and Jacobite duke of Albemarle (1666–1735); Petty, William, second earl of Shelburne and first marquess of Lansdowne (1737–1805); Fitzmaurice, Henry Petty-, third marquess of Lansdowne (1780–1863); Fitzmaurice, Henry Thomas Petty-, fourth marquess of Lansdowne (1816–1866); Fitzmaurice, Henry Charles Keith Petty-, fifth marquess of Lansdowne (1845–1927).

Lant, Thomas (1554/5–1600/01), herald and draughtsman, was born in Gloucester, one of the seven children and four sons of Thomas Lant of Gloucester and his wife, Mayens or Mary Mounsloe of Shropshire. At the age of twelve he became a page to Richard Cheyney, bishop of Gloucester, and after Cheyney's death in 1579 page to Henry, Baron Cheyne of Toddington, with whom he remained 'some two or three years' (College of Arms, Arundel MS 40, fol. 1). He may have been the Thomas Lant who in 1580 gathered a collection of tunes on a roll of parchment (King's College, Cambridge, Rowe MS 1). Lord Cheyne recommended Lant to Sir Philip Sidney, whom he accompanied to the Low Countries in November 1585; he remained there until Sidney's death on 17 October 1586. Lant was the draughtsman of a remarkable roll measuring over 35 feet by about 7¾ inches, engraved on thirty copperplates by Theodore De Bry, recording Sir Philip's funeral procession at St Paul's Cathedral on 16 February 1587. Lant's portrait appears on the first plate; dated 1587, it gives his age as thirty-two.

Lant was next employed by Sidney's father-in-law, Sir Francis Walsingham, the secretary of state, on whose recommendation and that of Sidney's uncle the earl of Leicester he obtained appointment as Portcullis pursuivant at the College of Arms, his patent being signed by the queen on 20 May 1588 and dated under the great seal 9 January 1589. In 1589 he compiled an augmented version of the account of the English baronage by Robert Cooke, Clarenceux (BL, Sloane MS 4959). As Portcullis Lant wrote *Observations and Collections Concerning the Office and Officers of Arms* (College of Arms, Arundel MS 40), a good source of information on the College of Arms in the 1590s, which he described as 'a company full of discord and envy' (College of Arms, Arundel MS 40, fol. 6r). At the back of this manuscript his arms appear impaled with those of Houghton of Beckbury, Shropshire, reflecting his marriage at an unknown date to Elizabeth (c.1573–1629), daughter of Richard Houghton. He may be the Thomas Lant, author of *Daily Exercise of a Christian* (1590). In 1595 he presented to the queen a catalogue of officers of arms known as Lant's roll, unfortunately containing inaccuracies but purporting to show that promotion in the College of Arms was always by seniority. A number of copies survive. A manuscript in Lant's hand includes notes on the creation of peers and knights (College of Arms, MS B.P.11).

In 1596 Lant challenged the universally disliked Ralph Brooke (c.1553–1625), York herald, and never had an answer. Subsequently meeting Brooke near Temple Bar he boxed him under the right ear and 'bumbasted his shoulders & his sydes very handsomely' (College of Arms, Arundel MS 40, fol. 38v). He was created Windsor herald on 23 October 1597, though the patent was issued only on 29

Thomas Lant (1554/5–1600/01), by Theodor de Bry, 1587 (after self-portrait)

November 1600, shortly before his death. He was alive on 26 December 1600 but is thought to have died early in the new year. Letters of administration for his estate were granted to his widow on 9 May 1601. They had two children, a daughter, Theodosia, who married James Norton, and a son, Thomas, who was born after his father's death and died on 18 May 1688, aged eighty-six, as rector of Hornsey, Middlesex. Elizabeth Lant, on 28 September 1609 at the Savoy Chapel, Westminster, married the physician and alchemist Francis Anthony (d. 1623). The marriage licence describes her as aged about thirty-six, relict of Thomas Lant, gent., deceased eight years since.

THOMAS WOODCOCK

Sources W. H. Godfrey, A. Wagner, and H. Stanford London, *The College of Arms, Queen Victoria Street* (1963), 171–2 · A. Wagner, *Heralds of England: a history of the office and College of Arms* (1967), 87–8, 217–19 · 'The observations and collections of Thomas Lant, Portcullis', Coll. Arms, Arundel MS 40 · E. Goldring, 'Sir Philip Sidney and the politics of Elizabethan festival', *Court festivals of the European Renaissance: art, politics and performance*, ed. J. R. Mulryne and E. Goldring (2002), 199–224 · M. Noble, *A history of the College of Arms* (1804), 171–2 · T. Moule, *Bibliotheca Heraldica Magnae Britanniae* (1822), 34–5

Archives BL, additions to armoury of nobility gathered by Robert Cooke and Robert Glover, Royal MS 18 cxvii · Coll. Arms, in Lant's autograph, on the creation of knights and peers, MS B.P.11 | BL, augmented version of Cooke's baronage, Sloane MS 4959 · BL, catalogue of heralds, Lansdowne MS 80 (21) · BL, copy of Lant's roll, Lansdowne MS 80 · BL, copy of Lant's roll in the hand of Nicholas Charles, Harley MS 5880 · Coll. Arms, Young collection, copy of Lant's roll · Coll. Arms, 'The observations and collections of Thomas Lant', Portcullis, incl. original copy of his roll, Arundel MS 40

Likenesses T. de Bry, line engraving, 1587 (after self-portrait), BM, NPG [*see illus.*] · line engraving, pubd 1803 (after T. Lant), NPG

Lantéri, Edward [Édouard] (1848–1917), sculptor and teacher of sculpture, was born at Auxerre, France, on 1 November 1848, the son of a tradesman. Although he showed precocious talent as a violinist, in his mid-teens he accepted an offer from the academic sculptor Aimé Millet to receive training in his Paris studio; at the same time he attended the Petite École de Dessin (c.1863–c.1865). He subsequently worked for François-Joseph Duret and received a more formal sculptural education at the École des Beaux-Arts, Paris, under Pierre-Jules Cavelier and Eugène Guillaume (c.1865–c.1868). The Franco-Prussian War brought a temporary setback to Lantéri's career: for eighteen months he worked as a cabinet-maker's assistant, repairing furniture damaged during the bombardment of Paris. In July 1870 Lantéri married, probably Honorine (the name of his widow).

Through the expatriate French sculptor Jules Dalou, who was based in London, Lantéri received an offer of employment from Joseph Edgar Boehm in 1872. The critic M. H. Spielmann later claimed that Lantéri's 'extraordinary skill and intelligent perception are to be found in much of the best productions' of Boehm (Spielmann, 128). While Lantéri certainly contributed to Boehm's success, their relationship was founded on mutual respect and friendship and lasted until Boehm's death in 1890. Boehm probably helped secure Lantéri's appointment as Dalou's successor as instructor in modelling at the National Art Training School, South Kensington, in 1880. As Lantéri was little known at the time, this caused controversy and press comment, with Edmund Gosse calling the affair 'the Dalou–Boehm job' (Stocker, *Royalist and Realist*, 332).

It soon emerged, however, that Lantéri's appointment was little short of inspirational. He remained at the school (from 1896 the Royal College of Art) for thirty-seven years and was made its first professor of sculpture and modelling in 1901. Although the institution was severely criticized in two government reports in 1887 and 1911, on both occasions Lantéri's areas of activity were handsomely endorsed. Student numbers reflected his success, the total increasing from twelve in 1874 to 105 in 1899. A high point came in 1903, when Lantéri's friend Auguste Rodin visited the Royal College of Art and pronounced himself 'delighted with all the students' work' (Frayling, 84). Spielmann claimed that 'A very large proportion of the most successful British sculptors of to-day who are not more than middle-aged owe to Professor Lantéri much of the success they have achieved' (Spielmann, 1). They included Alfred Gilbert, Alfred Drury, and Albert Toft, all major figures in the New Sculpture. Lantéri's students of a later generation, such as Charles Sargeant Jagger, Gilbert Ledward, and Charles Wheeler, took sculpture into the era of art deco and early modernism. Also significant was a talented array of women sculptors, including Margaret Giles, Ruby Levick, and Gwendolyn Williams.

In response to requests to publish his notes used for demonstration classes, Lantéri compiled the three-volume text *Modelling: a Guide for Teachers and Students*

(1902–11), described as 'the classic treatise on the techniques of figurative sculpture' (N. C. Hale in Lantéri, *Modelling and Sculpture*, 1.vi); a reflection of its enduring significance was its republication in 1965 and 1985. Lantéri avoided being drily academic, stressing that 'art is essentially individual' (ibid., 2). The aim of art teaching should be 'to put within the pupil's grasp all that is necessary to help him to express his thoughts by the simplest, surest and quickest means' (ibid., 3). Lantéri regarded drawing as 'the principal foundation of sculpture' (p. 4), and knowledge of anatomy was equally essential (ibid., 4). Elaborate modelling tools were unnecessary: 'the human finger is more firm, and at the same time more sensitive, than any mechanical instrument. It is nature's spatula and should be used in preference to anything else' (Staley, 84). In handling composition he advised restraint on the teacher's part: 'For a master to impose on his pupil his own conception of a subject is entirely contrary to the rules of artistic teaching' (Lantéri, *Modelling and Sculpture*, 2.98). Lantéri practised what he preached. One of his pupils, Francis Shurrock, who later laid the foundations of sculptural education in New Zealand, recalled: 'None of Lantéri's students worked as he did, each developing in his own way, & that is just what Lantéri wanted' (Stocker, 'Francis Shurrock', 50).

Although Lantéri could only devote limited time to his own sculpture, he exhibited seventy works at the Royal Academy between 1885 and 1917. Their poor survival rate has contributed to his relatively low art historical profile. To some extent Lantéri was himself culpable: a perfectionist, he was recorded by Spielmann as having destroyed many works. His stylistic versatility is reflected in the lively rococo modelling of *Sketch for a Garden Design* and the more serene, classical carving *The Duet* (1891), a sculptural counterpart to the paintings of Albert Moore and Frederic Leighton. Surviving works—such as the busts of *The Peasant* (c.1901) and *Alfred Stevens* (1911; both Tate collection)—convey confidence in handling material and psychological insight. Lantéri's most prominently sited works are his architectural carvings for the Victoria and Albert Museum (1905–7). They were executed with assistance from four advanced Royal College of Art students and comprise *Fame* at the summit of the main tower and figures of *Sculpture* and *Architecture* below. As a medallist Lantéri was second only to Alphonse Legros in significance. Like Legros, he encouraged the revival of the cast medal and responded to Italian Renaissance precedents, seen for example in *Julio Monticelli* (1888; British Museum, London).

Lantéri died at his home at 50 Perryn Road, East Acton, Middlesex, on 18 December 1917 and was succeeded at the Royal College of Art by his former pupil Francis Derwent Wood. Apart from Sir Edmund Gosse—who unaccountably omitted Lantéri from his influential essay 'The New Sculpture'—reactions to him were invariably enthusiastic. Shurrock claimed, 'Lantéri was more than a teacher, he was an inspiration' (Stocker, 'Francis Shurrock', 50), and Gilbert called him a 'man of infinite sensibility, subtle imagination and inflexible will, endowed, too, with natural poetical instincts' (McAllister, 25). Examples of his work are in the Tate collection; the British Museum and Victoria and Albert Museum, London; and the Musée d'Orsay, Paris. His statue of Sir Samuel Sadler may be seen in Victoria Square, Middlesbrough, and that of Ludwig Mond at Winnington Lane, Northwich, Cheshire.

MARK STOCKER

Sources E. Lantéri, *Modelling: a guide for teachers and students*, 3 vols. (1902–11) [republished as *Modelling and sculpture*, 3 vols. (1965) with introduction by N. C. Hale, *Modelling and sculpting the human figure* (1985), and *Modelling and sculpting animals* (1985)] • I. McAllister, 'Edward Lanteri: sculptor and professor', *The Studio*, 57 (1912–13), 25–31 • E. Staley, 'Edward Lantéri: artist and teacher', *Art Journal*, new ser., 23 (1903), 241–5 • C. Frayling, *The Royal College of Art: one hundred and fifty years of art and design* (1987) • A. L. Baldry, 'Sculptor and professor: Edouard Lantéri', *Magazine of Art*, 25 (1900–01), 80–84 • P. Attwood, 'Lanteri, Edouard', *The dictionary of art*, ed. J. Turner (1996) • P. Attwood, *Artistic circles: the medal in Britain, 1880–1918* (1992) [exhibition catalogue] • M. H. Spielmann, *British sculpture and sculptors of to-day* (1901) • M. Stocker, *Royalist and realist: the life and work of Joseph Edgar Boehm* (1988), 332 n. 112 • M. Stocker, 'Francis Shurrock revisited', *Bulletin of New Zealand Art History*, 18 (1997), 50 • J. Darke, *The monument guide to England and Wales: a national portrait in bronze and stone* (1991) • CGPLA Eng. & Wales (1918) • d. cert.
Archives Musée Rodin, Paris, letters
Likenesses A. Legros, drawing, c.1900, repro. in Lantéri, *Modelling and sculpture* • S. E. Scott, drawing, c.1900, repro. in Baldry, 'Sculptor and professor', 80 • photograph, c.1900, repro. in Staley, 'Edward Lantéri', 242
Wealth at death £2335 7s. 1d.: probate, 11 June 1918, CGPLA Eng. & Wales

Lantfred (*fl.* 974–984), monk and author, belonged to the Benedictine community at the Old Minster, Winchester, and wrote the earliest account of the miracles that took place following the translation of the relics of Bishop Swithun there on 15 July 971. Very little is known of Lantfred's career. A contemporary Winchester author, Ælfric, describes him as 'the foreigner' (*se ofersæwisca*); and the spelling of his name as he gives it in his account of St Swithun, the *Translatio et miracula Sancti Swithuni* ('Translation and miracles of St Swithun'), implies an origin in Francia, probably West Francia (a German spelling of the same name would be Lantfrid). A Frankish origin for Lantfred is confirmed by the occurrence of various Latinized Old French words in his *Translatio*, as well as by a letter (datable to 974–84) addressed to Archbishop Dunstan by an author who signs himself as '.L.'; on stylistic grounds, the letter is unambiguously the work of the author of the *Translatio*. In this letter Lantfred reports to Dunstan that he has returned to Fleury, but, as a result of a fire there, has need of various books which he left in England in the possession of Osgar, a former Winchester monk who later became abbot of Abingdon. That Lantfred came to Winchester from Fleury at the invitation of Bishop Æthelwold (d. 984) is implied by the fact that Æthelwold, in the preface to his *Regularis concordia*, records his gratitude for advice on monastic customs given to him by monks from continental houses including Fleury—a reference, perhaps, to advice given by Lantfred.

Lantfred's *Translatio et miracula Sancti Swithuni* is one of the most polished pieces of Latin prose composed in England between the time of Aldhelm (*d.* 709/10) and the Norman conquest. From references in the text it is evident that it was composed within a few years of the translation of St Swithun in 971; Lantfred describes himself as an eyewitness for many of the miracles. The persuasive nature of Lantfred's work helped to establish the cult of St Swithun, a fact reflected in the number of manuscripts and later redactions of the work. The *Translatio* is not only a valuable account of the origin and early development of an Anglo-Saxon saint's cult, but a precious (and firsthand) witness to various aspects of Anglo-Saxon life, including pilgrimage, travel, slavery, medicine, law enforcement, capital punishment, and trial by ordeal. It is composed in extremely flamboyant Latin prose, being the earliest attested Anglo-Latin example of rhyming prose, and bristles with learned words of various kinds, including archaisms and Graecisms, mostly derived from the Greek New Testament (though, to judge from errors in declension, it is most unlikely that Lantfred himself knew any Greek). Lantfred's Latin prose is also characterized by the use of poeticisms, and of Virgilian diction in particular. Although (with the exception of the Bible) the number of works quoted in the *Translatio* is limited, Lantfred was clearly a scholar of considerable learning.

A manuscript now in Cambridge (CUL, Kk.5.34), which was written at Winchester in the late tenth century, contains three Latin poems under the rubric 'Versus .L. de quodam superbo', and there is reason to think that the '.L.' in question is Lantfred. The first two poems are conceived as high-spirited (and frequently vitriolic) master–student debate poems; the third is a sophisticated meditation of the problems of predestination and free will, which has as its nuclear image Boethius's metaphor of God observing the human race from a watch-tower. The poems share many features of diction with Lantfred's *Translatio*, and reveal that he was an accomplished poet as well as a master of Latin prose. MICHAEL LAPIDGE

Sources M. Lapidge, *The cult of St Swithun*, Winchester Studies, 4/2 (2002) • M. Lapidge, 'Three Latin poems from Æthelwold's school at Winchester', *Anglo-Saxon England*, 1 (1972), 85–137
Archives CUL, Kk.5.34

Lany, Benjamin (1591–1675), bishop of Ely, was born in Ipswich, Suffolk, the fourth of at least five sons, and one of twelve children of John Lany (*bap.* 1547, *d.* 1633), barrister and recorder of the town, and his wife, Mary (1551?–1633), daughter of John Poolie, esquire, of Badley in the same county. He matriculated as a pensioner from Christ's College, Cambridge, in July 1608, graduating BA in 1612 and proceeding MA in 1615. Elected a fellow of Pembroke College in 1616, he was ordained deacon and priest in February 1619, and became first curate of Harston, Cambridgeshire, and then, from 1619 to 1624, vicar of Madingley, also in Cambridgeshire. Meanwhile in 1622 he proceeded BD.

In 1625, at the king's request, Lany was given two years' leave of absence from Pembroke to be chaplain to Sir Edward Barrett, then appointed ambassador to France. Not only did he retain his fellowship and emoluments, but

Benjamin Lany (1591–1675), by Sir Peter Lely, 1668

he was also elected college praelector in philosophy for a year. Bishop Richard Neile of Durham recognized Lany as an impressive scholar and preacher, and perhaps assisted his preferment in 1626 to Hambledon, Hampshire. From 1627 to 1629 he was absent from Pembroke and gained other Hampshire preferments. Following Neile's translation to Winchester in 1628 the bishop presented him to Waltham Bishops and made him his chaplain in 1629, and presented him to Buriton with Petersfield; he made him a prebendary of Winchester in 1631. In the metropolitan visitation of 1635 he was active as a commissary investigating migration of English families to the Huguenot congregation in Southampton.

Meanwhile, in 1630 Lany proceeded DD. On Christmas day that year, through the considerable influence of Neile and of Bishop William Laud of London, he was elected master of Pembroke College. He did not prove a good administrator, so records from his mastership are deficient or non-existent. However, he was probably responsible for building the north side of the second court and extending the master's lodge, and was certainly responsible for the college hall. He also ensured that the chapel was repaired. Richard Crashaw, a devoted pupil, suggests that it lost its austerity in worship, and perhaps that vestments were introduced. Lany beautified the altar with tapers and many-coloured draperies and hangings, and possibly raised it at the east end. Perhaps he was responsible for the cherubim and eighty 'superstitious' pictures destroyed by the parliamentary commissioners in 1642. Much of the Sunday service was sung by a small choir, with anthems, accompanied by an organ, replacing psalms. Bowing towards the altar and facing east were stressed. The number of Arminian fellows was notable; some, like Mr Randall, insisted that students should subscribe to Whitgift's three articles before graduating. Seven were complained of in 1641. These included Eleazor Duncon, who had argued that good works were necessary to salvation and had been favoured by Lany as moderator in 1633. Another fellow, John Turnay, preached in 1634 against Roman Catholic charges of antinomianism, arguing that faith worked with love in good works, increasing justification. He was brought before the vice-chancellor's court, and was later denied his BD for repeating this. Lany successfully resisted his condemnation, and perhaps secured Charles I's intervention in Turnay's favour.

In 1632–3 Lany was vice-chancellor of the university. In this capacity he took a lead in prosecuting puritans and Calvinists, as in the cases of Richard Spinke of St John's College, who made a commonplace against clerical absenteeism, ceremonies, and chapel ornamentation, and Lionel Gatford, fellow of Jesus College, who preached against Arminianism. Later Lany was one of the group who defended it in the vice-chancellor's court. In 1634 he supported Peter Hausted of Queens' College in abusively advocating ceremonies, and attacking lectures and chaplaincies. In 1636, when John Normanton of Gonville and Caius College attacked justification by faith alone, and praised fasting and penance, Lany supported him in refusing to give a copy of his sermon to the vice-chancellor unless articles were brought against him. When in 1637 Sylvester Adams preached in Great St Mary's that confession to a priest was necessary to salvation, the non-Laudian heads of house regarded this as popish, and urged recantation. Lany was one of those dissenting because he did not wish to discourage auricular confession. In 1640 he was among the doctors who acquitted William Norwich of Peterhouse when accused of preaching that people were justified by works as well as faith. With other Arminian heads of house he repeatedly helped secure similar acquittals.

Lany's stance led to his being appointed a royal chaplain in 1634, and he served annually thereafter. In June 1639 he was made prebendary of Westminster Abbey. However, his actions and attitudes made him an object of opprobrium and suspicion to puritans, especially when protégés like John Normanton became Roman Catholics; in *Canterburies Doome* William Prynne described Lany as one of Laud's creatures. On the outbreak of the civil war Pembroke College sent all its plate, except the foundress's and anathema cups, to the king. When, with other heads of houses, Lany refused a contribution to parliament and the imposition of an oath which would have forced him to betray his colleagues, he became a prime target for sequestration. In March 1644 the earl of Manchester had him ejected from the mastership 'for opposing the proceedings of Parliament and other scandalous acts' (*DNB*).

Lany then joined Charles I at Oxford as his chaplain, and became nominally dean of Rochester, though instituted only in 1660. In 1644, with Gilbert Sheldon and others, he

was selected to debate on church government with ministers seeking further reformation before the Scots commissioners, but was refused a hearing. He also attended the unsuccessful negotiations with the Presbyterians at Uxbridge in February 1645. By May he had been sequestrated from Buriton.

After the parliamentary victory in the first civil war Lany, in danger of imprisonment, fled to France, and became one of the close-knit group of Arminian clergy there. They regarded themselves as a faithful remnant of the Church of England whose function was to preserve it against presbyterianism, and worked in hardship to nurture the faith and preserve the worship of the scattered royalist refugees. They also battled to prevent conversions to Roman Catholicism. As chaplain to the prince of Wales from his arrival in 1646 Lany played a vital role, especially when faced with pressure from Queen Henrietta Maria, and arguments from both Roman Catholics and Presbyterians for the prince's conversion from Anglicanism. Probably the resulting theological debate, including that between Bishop John Bramhall and Thomas Hobbes on free will which prompted the latter's *A Letter on Liberty and Necessity*, also led to Lany's *Observations*, eventually published with it in 1676. In it he argues against Hobbes's psychological and theological determinism, and in favour of free will as essential to the nature of virtue and vice, religion, and society itself.

By 1659 Lany's stature was sufficient for secretary Edward Hyde to consider him as a candidate for a bishopric, though doubting his willingness. He was wrong. On 2 December 1660 Lany was consecrated as bishop of Peterborough, and he was one of the twelve episcopal commissioners nominated by Charles II to review the prayer book at the Savoy conference in 1661, though he took little part. His six published court sermons, delivered between 1661 and 1666 and in 1675, elucidate his views. He emphasizes godly living and liturgical worship in the tradition of the early church, especially the eucharist, an offering of praise to honour Christ's redemptive sacrifice. Sacraments are divinely instituted; sermons are less important, and liable to be affected by man's fallibility. They should be measured against scripture, easily comprehended, and applied to the hearers' lives. He upholds episcopal ordination and emphasizes the importance of retaining creeds and confessions of faith as yardsticks of orthodoxy. The church's guidance, and skills of 'shepherds', although not infallible, are more reliable than individual interpretations. He argues that the king has a certain jurisdictional, administrative, and even authorizing power over ministry, because, presumably, he nominates bishops. Politically, he is supreme, and the only legitimate source of authority. 'The Sword is the Kings, and *He that takes it* from any hand but His, where God hath placed it, shall perish with the Sword' ('A sermon preached … at White hall, March 18th 1665', B. Lany, *Five Sermons*, 1669, 133–4). He deeply deplores schism as a sin, referring to some nonconformists as wolves in sheep's clothing who misuse phrases such as 'God's glory' and 'Christian liberty' to justify religious and political anarchy in place of constructive order and discipline. Lany deplores the Levellers' and others' preaching against minority land ownership, and the Quakers' refusal to honour their social betters, and argues that those organizing congregations, giving laws on worship and doctrine, and setting up teachers and leaders are acting outside their sphere. He regards claims to be led by the Holy Spirit as almost certainly deceptive, and is deeply distrustful of action on grounds of conscience. Such views mean that he deplores the idea of a comprehensive church. 'I think it might better have been called a Dragnet, that will fetch in all kinds of Fish, good or bad, great or small' (*The Last Sermon Preached at Court by B. L.*, 1675, 26).

Thus, as bishop of Peterborough, Lany's attitude to nonconformists was unlikely to be tolerant. At his 1662 visitation before the Act of Uniformity came into force, he told his clergy, 'Not I but the law', giving the impression that he washed his hands of dissenters (B. Lany, *Articles of Visitation and Enquiry*, 1662). Forty-one ministers in the diocese either resigned just before the St Bartholomew's day deadline and became nonconformists or were subsequently deprived and did the same, like Daniel Cawdrey of Great Billing. As the judicial affairs of the diocese were handled by the civilian lawyer Dr George Wake, vicar-general in spirituals and principal official, a very legal approach was likely. One glimmer of latitude appears in the case of Richard Gascoyne, minister of Warmington, who continued to reside, though not episcopally ordained until June 1663, presumably because he was persuaded to conform. Careful enquiries were made in Lany's primary visitation as to whether the churches had returned to all practices enjoined by law or canon, with a special admonition to forward names of confirmation candidates. Investigation of the names of heretics or schismatics took prime place in questions on parishioners' conduct.

Inheriting a ruined palace, and with his first year's revenues due to the king as first fruits, Lany continued as a prebendary of Westminster and master of Pembroke College, to both of which he had been restored in 1660. He lived mostly at his Westminster house, making excursions to the diocese for spiritual duties. He was generous in repairing civil war damage to the cathedral, and, with John Cosin's aid as dean, the nave and choir were reordered.

In 1662 Lany resigned his mastership and the following year his prebend, and in April 1663 he was translated to Lincoln diocese. His visitation articles, published in 1664, show that he followed the same policies as at Peterborough, although he admitted tolerating a few nonconformists like Samuel Ainsworth, who preached at Brampton, adjoining Lany's palace at Buckden. In 1667 he was translated to the wealthy see of Ely, and statutorily became a governor of Charterhouse, London. His generosity was notable. He rescued his nephew from ruin by a gift of £3600, helped many other poor relatives, left £500 each for the rebuilding of St Paul's Cathedral and the establishment of a grammar school in Cambridge, or the increase of Pembroke fellowships, as well as establishing a trust for apprenticing poor children at Soham, Cambridgeshire.

His monument describes him as being of terrifying acuteness. Perhaps there is truth in the anecdote that he told the new provost of Eton, who was seeking favours, that his head was too little to have anything in it. Lany was an active member of the House of Lords until 1672, taking increased responsibility on committees with greater seniority. He died unmarried at Ely House, London, on 24 January 1675, and was buried in Ely Cathedral.

ELIZABETH ALLEN

Sources DNB · Venn, *Alum. Cant.* · W. Kennett, *A register and chronicle ecclesiastical and civil* (1728), 502, 508, 579, 632, 729, 804, 813 · W. Hervey, *The visitation of Suffolk, 1561*, ed. J. Corder, 2, Harleian Society, new ser., 3 (1984), 314 · PRO, LC 5/132, p. 354; LC 5/134; LC 5/135 · *Walker rev.*, 186 · *Calamy rev.* · R. S. Bosher, *The making of the Restoration settlement: the influence of the Laudians, 1649–1662*, rev. edn (1957), 49–50, 52, 58, 60–61, 67 · BL, Harl. MS 7019, fols. 53–4, 56, 63, 65–6, 81, 86, 92 · A. Milton, *Catholic and Reformed: the Roman and protestant churches in English protestant thought, 1600–1640* (1995), 72–3, 76 · A. W. Foster, 'A biography of Archbishop Richard Neile (1562–1640)', DPhil diss., U. Oxf., 1978, 4, 217–18 · J. Twigg, *The University of Cambridge and the English Revolution, 1625–1688* (1990), 32–3 · *The complete works of Richard Crashaw*, ed. A. B. Grosart, 2 (1873), 14–15 · H. I. Longden, *Northamptonshire and Rutland clergy from 1500*, ed. P. I. King and others, 16 vols. in 6, Northamptonshire RS (1938–52), vol. 1, p. 177; vol. 2, p. 265; vol. 5, pp. 31, 147; vol. 6, p. 93; vol. 10, p. 251; vol. 15, p. 195 · *JHL*, 11 (1660–66) · *JHL*, 12 (1666–75) · will, 1675, PRO, PROB 11/347 · D. Hoyle, 'A Commons investigation of Arminianism and popery in Cambridge on the eve of the civil war', *HJ*, 29 (1986), 419–25, esp. 421 · *Fasti Angl.* (Hardy), 1.344, 578; 3.35, 358 · *CSP dom.*, 1635, 149; 1636 · P. Barwick, *The life of ... Dr John Barwick*, ed. and trans. H. Bedford (1724), 462–3 · R. Baxter, *An accompt of all the proceedings of the commissioners ... for the review of the Book of Common Prayer* (1661), A2 · J. Bentham, *The history and antiquities of the conventual and cathedral church of Ely* (1771), 202 · S. Roberts, *Pembroke College, Cambridge* (c.1947) · A. Gibbons, ed., *Ely episcopal records: a calendar and concise view of the episcopal records preserved in the muniment room of the palace of Ely* (privately printed, Lincoln, 1891), 312 · Peterborough consistory court books, Northants. RO, 70–71 · Charterhouse muniments, Sutton's Hospital, London, assembly orders C · Pembroke Cam., MS Bβ 2, fols. 56, 58, 60, 62, 63, 111 · A. L. Attwater, *Pembroke College, Cambridge: a short history*, ed. S. C. Roberts (1973), 70–73 · R. Willis, *The architectural history of the University of Cambridge, and of the colleges of Cambridge and Eton*, ed. J. W. Clark, 4 vols. (1886), 142–3, 145, 149

Likenesses attrib. W. Dobson, oils, c.1644, Pembroke Cam. · P. Lely, portrait, 1668, bishop's palace, Lincoln [*see illus.*] · school of P. Lely, oils, c.1677, Sutton's Hospital, London · portrait, Pembroke Cam. · portrait, Usher Art Gallery, Lincoln

Wealth at death wealthy: will, PRO, PROB 11/347

Lanyon, Sir Charles (1813–1889), architect and engineer, son of John Jenkinson Lanyon (1770/71–1835) of Eastbourne, Sussex, and his wife, Catherine Anne Mortimer (1772/3–1840), was born at Eastbourne, Sussex, on 6 January 1813. Having received his early education at a private school in Eastbourne, he was articled to Jacob Owen of the Royal Engineers' department in Portsmouth, later of the Irish board of works, Dublin, in preparation for the profession of civil engineer. On 2 February 1837 he married Owen's daughter Elizabeth Helen (d. 1858); they had ten children, including Sir (William) Owen *Lanyon. In 1835, at the first examination for Irish county surveyorships, Lanyon took second place; he was appointed county surveyor of Kildare, and in the following year transferred at his own request to co. Antrim. Here he executed several works of great importance, among others the constructing of the great Antrim coast road from Larne to Portrush, and he designed and erected many bridges in the county, including the viaduct of 1837 at Glendun and the Ormeau Bridge of 1860–63 over the Lagan at Belfast. He laid out several of the chief local railways, such as the Belfast and Ballymena line and its extensions to Cookstown and Portrush, later amalgamated with other lines to form part of the Belfast and Northern Counties Railway. He was also engineer of the Belfast, Holywood, and Bangor Railway, and the Carrickfergus and Larne line. He was architect of some of the principal buildings in Belfast, such as the Queen's College, now Queen's University (1846–9), the court house (1848–50), the county gaol (1843–5), the custom house (1854–7), and the Institute for the Deaf and Dumb and Blind (1843–5; dem. 1965). His palm house in the botanic gardens, Belfast, built in two phases between 1840 and 1852, although small, is notable as one of the earliest examples of curvilinear iron and glass anywhere. Much of Lanyon's work was carried out in private practice, in which he was assisted by two partners, first W. H. *Lynn (1829–1915), from 1854, and then his own eldest son, John (1839–1900), from 1860. The joint firm was one of the most prolific in Ireland, responsible for many churches, banks, and country houses throughout Ireland.

Lanyon resigned the county surveyorship in 1860, and then retired from practice completely following the breakup of his firm in 1872, to devote his energies to public life, in which he was already involved. In 1862 he became mayor of Belfast, and in 1866 Conservative member of parliament for the town. In 1868 he was defeated at the polls. In 1876 he served as high sheriff of co. Antrim. He was one of the Belfast harbour commissioners and a deputy lieutenant and magistrate of the county. In 1862 he was elected president of the Royal Institute of Architects of Ireland, and held office until 1868, when he was knighted by the duke of Abercorn, then lord lieutenant. He was also a fellow of the Institute of British Architects and a member of the Institution of Civil Engineers of both England and Ireland. For a long time he was a prominent member of the masonic body, in which he rose to be grand master of the province of Antrim. He died, after a protracted illness, at his residence, The Abbey, White Abbey, co. Antrim, on 31 May 1889, and was buried on 4 June in the churchyard of Knockbreda, near Belfast.

THOMAS HAMILTON, rev. PAUL LARMOUR

Sources Belfast News-Letter (3 June 1889) · ICE minutes of proceedings, 98 (1889), 391–3 · personal knowledge (1892) · P. Larmour, 'Sir Charles Lanyon', GPA Irish Arts Review Yearbook (1989–90), 200–06 · P. Larmour, Belfast: an illustrated architectural guide (1987) · H. Dixon and B. Walker, In Belfast town, 1864–1880 (1984) · P. Larmour, 'Lanyon, Sir Charles', The dictionary of art, ed. J. Turner (1996) · C. E. B. Brett, Buildings of Belfast, 1700–1914, rev. edn (1985) · Belfast Telegraph (13 June 1940) · J. Foster, The peerage, baronetage, and knightage of the British empire for 1882, 2 vols. [1882] · W. Budgen, Old Eastbourne: its church, its clergy, its people (1913) · CGPLA Eng. & Wales (1889)
Likenesses C. Laurie, etching, repro. in R. F. Gould, History of freemasonry (1885) · oils, Queen's University, Belfast; repro. in Larmour, 'Sir Charles Lanyon' · photograph, Royal Institute of Architects of Ireland, Dublin · photograph, repro. in Belfast Telegraph · wood-engraving (after photograph by J. Magill of Belfast), NPG; repro. in ILN (22 June 1889)
Wealth at death £10,774: probate, 19 Aug 1889, CGPLA Ire

Lanyon, Sir (William) Owen (1842–1887), army officer and colonial official, born in co. Antrim, Ireland, on 21 July 1842, was the son of the civil engineer and architect Sir Charles *Lanyon (1813–1889) of The Abbey, White Abbey, near Belfast, co. Antrim, and his wife, Elizabeth Helen (d. 1858), daughter of Jacob *Owen of the board of works, Dublin. Like his brothers, Lanyon was educated at Bromsgrove School, Worcestershire (1855–9), which then took many boys from Ireland. On 21 December 1860 he was commissioned ensign by purchase in the 6th Royal Warwickshire regiment, with which he served in Jamaica during the 1865 insurrection. The same year he was appointed aide-de-camp to the general commanding in the West Indies. He purchased his lieutenancy, 6th foot, in 1866, exchanged to the 2nd West India regiment, and in 1868 purchased a company. He was aide-de-camp and private secretary to Sir John Peter Grant, governor of Jamaica from 1868 to 1873. In 1873, and until invalided in January 1874, Lanyon served as aide-de-camp to Sir Garnet Wolseley in the Second Anglo-Asante War, suffering fever and gaining Wolseley's praise (brevet of major). In 1874 he was sent by the Colonial Office to the Gold Coast on a special mission connected with the abolition of slavery, for which he was in August 1875 made CMG. From September 1875 to April 1880 he was administrator of the diamond fields territory, Griqualand West. He improved the finances and raised and commanded the volunteer force there during the Griqua rebellion and the 1878 invasion of the Batlapin chief, Botlasitsie, whom he defeated and subdued. He was thanked by the home government and the Cape legislature (CB, November 1878, brevet of lieutenant-colonel).

Appointed by Sir Michael Hicks Beach (colonial secretary, 1878–80), from March 1879 Lanyon was administrator of the Transvaal under the successive high commissioners Wolseley and Sir George Colley. Lanyon assisted Sir Bartle Frere in his negotiations with the Transvaal Boers. Wolseley was glad to leave the Transvaal administration in 'Billy's competent hands' (Lehmann, First Boer War, 63). Lanyon concentrated on tax gathering in which he was, if sometimes acting arbitrarily and illegally, notably successful. He claimed to have produced a surplus in the former bankrupt republic. This was disputed: according to Lord Kimberley there was an 'enormous and hopeless deficit' (de Kiewiet, 279). On Wolseley's recommendation Lanyon was made KCMG in April 1880: disliking the name William, he called himself Sir Owen.

Lanyon, like Wolseley, despised the Boers, whom he considered a 'semi-civilized people'. Distant and overbearing, he ignored their wishes. They disliked him. He was tall, dark, tanned, and swarthy, and they knew of his West Indian service. They believed he had African blood, was a 'West Indian bastard', and that they were being oppressed by a 'kaffir'—a further British insult. Kruger wrote in his memoirs that Lanyon was 'absolutely unfitted for this difficult task' (Kruger, 1.154). The new Gladstone government (April 1880) retained Lanyon in post. He responded to local press criticism by imposing restrictions on newspapers. As Boer unrest increased he assured the Colonial Office that they were contented, and requested a substantial salary increase. Following his reports the imperial government reduced British troops in the Transvaal; Lanyon also sent volunteers away to the Basuto 'gun war'. In December rebel Boers declared their republic and attacked British troops (the First South African War, 1880–81). A few days before, Lanyon had written to Colley that the Boers were 'mortal cowards, so anything they do will be but a spark in the pan' (Lehmann, *First Boer War*, 101), and in January 1881 he wrote to the Colonial Office that 'the collapse will be as sudden as the outbreak' (ibid., 102). The British in Pretoria were blockaded rather than besieged. The troops there were commanded by Colonel William Bellairs, an experienced and cautious officer. In February, Lanyon urged an offensive against the Boers; Bellairs believed it imprudent but acquiesced. The attack (Red House laager, 12 February) was a disaster, with heavy British casualties. After the war, in April 1881, Lanyon was recalled and replaced by Bellairs. Lanyon's failure in the Transvaal ruined his reputation and effectively ended his career. He was criticized in the British press and later by historians: according to C. W. de Kiewiet, Lanyon was guilty of 'stupid ignorance' of the Boers, and 'his conduct as a soldier was conceited, fatuous and shortsighted' (de Kiewiet, 273). He never again held a Colonial Office post.

Lanyon served in the 1882 Egyptian campaign as colonel on the staff and base commander at Isma'iliyyah (third class Osmanieh), and also served with the Gordon relief expedition (1884–5). In 1882 he married Florence, daughter of J. M. Levy of Grosvenor Street, London; she died in 1883. Lanyon died of cancer at New York, after a long and painful illness, on 6 April 1887, aged forty-four.

ROGER T. STEARN

Sources Army List · J. H. Lehmann, *The First Boer War* (1972) · J. H. Lehmann, *All Sir Garnet: a biography of Field-Marshal Lord Wolseley* (1964) · *Parl. papers* (1874–82) [see under Gold Coast, Griqua, Transvaal] · M. Wilson and L. Thompson, eds., *The Oxford history of South Africa*, 2 vols. (1971), vol. 2 · B. Bond, ed., *Victorian military campaigns* (1967) · B. Bellairs, *The Transvaal War, 1880–1881* (1885) · *ILN* (2 July 1887) · Boase, *Mod. Eng. biog.* · WWBMP · C. W. de Kiewiet, *The imperial factor in South Africa* (1937) · P. Kruger, *The memoirs of Paul Kruger*, trans. A. Teixeira de Mattos, 2 vols. (1902), vol. 1 · W. B. Worsfold, *Sir Bartle Frere: a footnote to the history of the British empire* (1923) · *The old Bromsgrovian register* (1908) · H. E. M. Icely, *Bromsgrove School through four centuries* (1953) · *CGPLA Eng. & Wales* (1887) · DNB
Archives National Archives of South Africa, Pretoria, Transvaal archives depot, corresp., diary, and papers | Bodl. Oxf., letters and telegram to Lord Kimberley · Bodl. RH, corresp. with Sir Godfrey Langden · Glos. RO, corresp. with Sir Michael Hicks Beach · Hove Central Library, Sussex, corresp. with Lord Wolseley
Likenesses engraving, repro. in *The Graphic*, 23 (1881), 217 · photograph, repro. in Lehmann, *The First Boer War*, 192–3 · photograph, repro. in L. S. Amery, ed., *The Times history of the war in South Africa*, 2nd edn, 1 (1900), facing p. 78
Wealth at death £12,272 12s. 10d.: resworn probate, June 1888, *CGPLA Eng. & Wales* (1887)

Lanyon, (George) Peter (1918–1964), painter, was born on 8 February 1918 at the Red House, St Ives, Cornwall, the only son and second child of (William) Herbert Lanyon (1862–1936), an amateur photographer, musician, and composer whose father was a director of mines in Redruth, and his wife, Lilian Priscilla Vivian (1880–1975), widow of Gordon Smith, from Camborne. As a child, regular visits to artists' studios with his father stimulated Lanyon's early decision to become a painter. He also absorbed Herbert Lanyon's strong socialism; it underpinned his passionate concern for the lost livelihoods of Cornish miners and fishermen. Lanyon spent nearly all his life in St Ives. He took great pride in his Cornish ancestry and his contribution to defining a modern cultural identity for Cornwall was acknowledged when he was elected a bard of the Cornish gorsedd in 1961 for services to Cornish art.

Lanyon was educated at Miss Baker's primary school, St Ives; St Erbin's preparatory school, Penzance; and Clifton College, Bristol (1930–35). His formal art training consisted of eighteen months at the Penzance School of Art (1936–7), with the intention of becoming a commercial artist, some private tuition during this time from the landscape painter Borlase Smart, and two months at the Euston Road School, London, in the summer of 1939. Shortly before this, he had his first one-man exhibition in Johannesburg, during a visit with his mother and sister to the Rhodesias and South Africa, where two uncles were involved in the mining industry.

Lanyon described himself as a provincial landscape painter whose historical models were Constable and Turner. Even in the 1930s his overriding interest was landscape, explored on sketching trips with his sister Mary and reproduced on small, densely painted panels. The first significant change in his work occurred late in 1939, when Ben Nicholson encouraged him to make abstract drawings and constructions. However, it was the constructivist artist Naum Gabo, who became Lanyon's mentor and father figure, who had the most lasting impact on his work.

From March 1940 to February 1946 Lanyon served with the Royal Air Force as a flight mechanic. To his acute disappointment, migraine disqualified him from pilot training, but he took the opportunities offered by the mechanics' workshops to make abstract metal constructions. During service in north Africa, Palestine, and southern Italy he painted obsessively, alternating landscapes with complex curvilinear paintings.

In April 1946 Lanyon married Sheila St John Browne (b. 1918), who had studied at the Guildford School of Art. They lived in St Ives in the converted Attic Studio, designed and built by Lanyon's father, until they bought Little Park Owles in nearby Carbis Bay in December 1955. The couple had six children, all born between 1947 and 1957 and all baptized in the Methodist church—to emphasize their Cornish roots rather than from religious conviction. Lanyon painted his response to his homecoming and marriage in the Generation series of oil paintings (1946–7), his first body of mature work. He told Gabo that it consisted of eight paintings, though only four can be securely identified.

Ambitious and intent on developing a distinctively modern practice, Lanyon rapidly emerged as an activist among his contemporaries. He was good-looking, well-read, articulate, convivial, disputatious, and incapable of ignoring any issue about which he felt strongly, though he was intermittently disabled by severe depression caused by the stress of painting. As a founder of the Crypt Group, he took part in all three of its exhibitions between 1946 and 1948 and was also a founder member of the Penwith Society in 1949, though he resigned the following year, with several others, in one of the more acrimonious episodes in the art politics of St Ives. Thereafter he refused to show in St Ives and became a regular exhibitor with the Newlyn Society of Artists.

Lanyon's first one-man exhibition in London, at Gimpel Fils in 1949, resulted in an invitation to take part in the Arts Council's '60 Paintings for '51'. His contribution, *Porthleven* (oil on masonite, 1951), was characteristic of his idiosyncratic landscape painting. Its complexity, the ambiguity of its multiple viewpoints and sweeping brushstrokes, meant that like many of his later works it was wrongly considered to be abstract, though the realism of his colour was always recognized. Painting was an act of visual, emotional, and intellectual synthesis incorporating Lanyon's own sense of a locality with its history, topography, and, often, an erotic charge. His frequent use of Cornish place names as titles indicates the centrality of place, particularly the villages, mines, farms, and coast of West Penwith, as subject matter. Place extended into a perception of reciprocity between the body and landscape, revealed by the presence in many paintings of half-concealed, rudimentary human figures. Classical mythology, particularly the Europa myth which Lanyon absorbed and extended following a four-month stay in Italy early in 1953, was to add an elusive narrative strand to his work.

Despite regular one-man exhibitions at Gimpel Fils and vigorous participation in group shows, often with the Arts Council and the British Council, and a practice which encompassed constructions, prints, pottery, drawings, and gouaches, Lanyon sold very little in the 1950s and was constantly short of money. To compensate, he taught at the Bath Academy of Art, Corsham, Wiltshire (1951–6), and from 1954 to 1960 founded and ran a private art school, St Peter's Loft, in St Ives with the painter William Redgrave. Lanyon was a visiting lecturer at the Falmouth School of Art (1960–61) and the West of England College of Art in Bristol (1960–64). He was a regular broadcaster and published occasional, illuminating articles on his painting and on education.

In 1957 Lanyon visited New York for the first of five one-man exhibitions at the Catherine Viviano Gallery. He made lasting friendships with Mark Rothko and Robert Motherwell, both of whom visited him in St Ives. With good sales in the United States he was able to fulfil his desire to fly and received his glider pilot's licence late in 1959. Although his 'gliding' paintings are considered the most abstract of his works they alluded specifically to the experience and techniques of gliding. The spatial freedom and vast views of the pilot contributed to his three murals,

commissioned by Liverpool University (1960), Birmingham University (1963), and Stanley Seeger, his principal American patron (1962).

Lanyon was the most innovative artist of his generation; the significance of his inclusive, multidisciplinary formulation of landscape has been widely recognized since the 1980s. Yet, despite winning the Critics' prize in 1954, second prize in the John Moores exhibition in 1959, and the Marzotto acquisition award in 1962, his work baffled most critics during his lifetime and the difficulty of selling it in Britain was a goad to work abroad, preferably in the United States. Three months spent as visiting painter at the San Antonio Institute in Texas early in 1963 confirmed his enthusiasm for American culture and its vast landscape which he celebrated in vivid, exuberant paintings.

Early in 1964 Lanyon visited Czechoslovakia to lecture for the British Council and finalized arrangements to teach in Australia the following year. On a training course with the Devon and Somerset gliding club, he crashed while landing in a side wind and died at the Taunton and Somerset Hospital on 31 August 1964 as a result of injuries to his back. He was buried at St Uny's Church, Lelant, Cornwall, on 5 September 1964; his wife survived him. Examples of his work may be found in the Tate collection; the Scottish National Gallery of Modern Art, Edinburgh; City of Birmingham Museum and Art Gallery; the Whitworth Art Gallery, Manchester; and several American and Australian museums. MARGARET GARLAKE

Sources A. Lanyon, *Peter Lanyon, 1918–1964* (1990) · *Peter Lanyon* (1968) [exhibition catalogue] · A. Causey, *Peter Lanyon: his painting* (1971) · *Peter Lanyon: paintings, drawings and constructions, 1937–64* (1978) [exhibition catalogue, Whitworth Art Gallery, Manchester, 25 Jan – 15 Sept 1978] · M. Garlake, 'Peter Lanyon's letters to Naum Gabo', *Burlington Magazine*, 137 (1995), 233–41 · *Peter Lanyon: the mural studies* (1996) [exhibition catalogue, Gimpel Fils, London, 1996] · *Peter Lanyon: air, land and sea* (1992) [exhibition catalogue, London, Coventry, Sheffield, and Penzance, Dec 1992 – June 1993] · P. Garlake and M. Garlake, 'The open places: a Cornishman in Africa', *Gallery* [Harare], 5 (1995), 7–8 · *CGPLA Eng. & Wales* (1965) · private information (2004)

Archives priv. coll. · Tate collection, letters and transcripts of interviews | Yale U., Beinecke L., letters to Naum Gabo | SOUND British Council, A. Bowness, ed., 'Recorded talk', 1963 [transcript in Tate collection] · 'Landscape painting', discussion between P. Lanyon, A. Fry, and A. Forge, BBC Third Programme, 29 April 1957 [transcript in Tate collection]

Likenesses P. Lanyon, self-portrait, oils, 1938, priv. coll. · P. Lanyon, self-portrait, oils, 1939, priv. coll. · photographs, c.1942–1964, Tate collection · P. Lanyon, self-portrait, pencil and wash drawing, 1947, priv. coll. · G. Adams, print, 1952, NPG · photographs, priv. coll.

Wealth at death £33,985: probate, 6 April 1965, *CGPLA Eng. & Wales*

Lanza, Gesualdo (1779–1859), singing teacher, was born in Naples, the son of Francesco Giuseppe Lanza (c.1750–c.1812), composer and the author of *6 arie notturne con accomp. di chitarra franc. e v. a piac.* (1792) and of six trios, op. 13, and six canzonets with recitative, op. 14, who moved to London in the early 1790s and for some time was a private musician to the marquess of Abercorn. Lanza was taught music by his father, and soon became known in London as a singing teacher. Among his pupils were Catherine Stephens, later countess of Essex, and Anna Maria Tree, the sister-in-law of Charles Kean. He also had a music-selling business at Chesterfield Street, St Pancras New Road. In 1842 Lanza started singing classes at 75 Newman Street. Later in the same year he announced a series of lectures, 'The national school for singing in classes, free to the public', and on 5 December 1842 he delivered a lecture at the Westminster Literary and Scientific Institution illustrative of his new system of teaching singing in classes.

In 1813 Lanza published *The Elements of Singing*, which was highly praised. His other publications include *The Elements of Singing in the Italian and English Styles* (1809), *Sunday Evening Recreations* (1840), and *Signor Lanza's New Method of Teaching Class Singing* (1843). Lanza composed the music for *The Deserts of Arabia* (1806), an operatical entertainment written by F. Reynolds, a masque, *Spirits of Dew*, a *Stabat mater*, and a *Grand missa di gloria* (1835), as well as songs and ballads. He died in London on 12 March 1859 and was buried in Highgate cemetery. His daughter, Rosalie Lanza, was a well-known opera singer.

R. H. LEGGE, *rev.* ANNE PIMLOTT BAKER

Sources New Grove · Boase, *Mod. Eng. biog.* · [Clarke], *The Georgian era: memoirs of the most eminent persons*, 4 (1834), 528 · *Quarterly Musical Magazine and Review*, 1 (1818), 351
Likenesses H. Minasi, stipple, 1809 (after T. Cheesman), V&A; repro. in G. Lanza, *The elements of singing* (1813)

Laon, Martin of. See Martin of Laon (819–875).

Lapidge, Edward (1779–1860), architect and surveyor, was the eldest son of Samuel Lapidge (*d.* 1806), the chief gardener at Hampton Court and before that an assistant to Lancelot Brown; he was the brother of Rear-Admiral William Lapidge (1793–1860). He is known to have had three sons: Charles, William Frederick, and Samuel. Samuel trained to be an architect but, after financial difficulties, emigrated to New Zealand.

In 1808 Lapidge sent to the Royal Academy a view of the garden front at Esher Place, in 1814 a drawing for a villa at Hildersham in Cambridgeshire, and in later years various other drawings. In 1824 he was appointed surveyor to the county of Surrey. Between 1825 and 1828 he was engaged in building his most important work, the new bridge over the Thames at Kingston. His prime interest was in civil engineering, and in 1850 he exhibited at the Royal Academy a design for a suspension bridge. Between 1827 and 1840 he designed and built a number of churches, including St Peter's, Hammersmith, Middlesex (1827–9), and Doddington church, Cheshire (1836–7). However, these buildings, while competent, were not inspired. In 1836 he was an unsuccessful competitor for the new houses of parliament, and in 1837 for the Fitzwilliam Museum at Cambridge.

Lapidge was elected a fellow of the Institute of British Architects in 1838. He had two pupils: George Wightwick and H. H. Russell. He died on 19 February 1860 at Hampton Wick, Middlesex, and was buried there.

L. H. CUST, *rev.* JANE HARDING

Sources Colvin, *Archs.* · *CGPLA Eng. & Wales* (1876)

Archives Surrey HC, papers relating to rebuilding of Esher Place
Wealth at death under £7000: probate, 13 April 1860, *CGPLA Eng. & Wales* · £7000: further action, 5 Dec 1876, *CGPLA Eng. & Wales*

Laporte, George Henry (1802–1873). *See under* Laporte, John Peter (1761–1839).

Laporte, John Peter (1761–1839), watercolour painter, may have been born in Dublin. He may be identified with the John Peter, son of Gabriel and Anne Laporte, who was baptized at St Anne's, Soho, on 29 March 1761. When first definitely heard of in London he was a pupil of the Dublin-born Huguenot landscape painter John Melchior Barralet, in whose house, 3 Orange Street, he was living in 1779. A fellow pupil of one of the Barralet brothers, perhaps John James, was William Frederick Wells, later the moving spirit behind the foundation of the Society of Painters in Water Colours; another lifelong friend of Laporte was the sporting painter H. B. Chalon.

Laporte first exhibited at both the Royal Academy and the British Institution in 1785, habitually showing landscapes. During the 1780s he changed address frequently, living for the most part in the artists' quarter around Tottenham Court Road and Soho. For some years from about 1789 he lodged at 4 Gresse Street, sharing with the topographical artist John Hassell in 1792–3. By 1802 he had moved to 21 Winchester Street, Edgware Road, which remained his home until about 1830. In his *Tour of the Isle of Wight* (1790), Hassell records meeting him at Alum Bay in 1789, and they probably visited Wales together in 1792. Laporte was a regular visitor to the Lake District from 1790 and to Ireland from 1795. It is possible that he travelled to Madeira in 1807 or 1808, and later to Italy and Switzerland, but equally his exhibited views may have been worked up from other travellers' drawings.

Laporte built up a considerable practice as a drawing master, but the repeated claim that he was professor of drawing at the Addiscombe military academy is a confusion with Wells. Probably his most distinguished pupil was Dr Thomas Monro, the patron of Girtin and Turner, to whom he sold drawings to the value of £500 or £600, according to Joseph Farington. He may well have met Turner, either at Monro's house in the Adelphi, where he dined frequently, or through their mutual friend Wells. In any event, Laporte's work does occasionally show hints of Turner's early style, although for the most part it remains true to the Sandby tradition. His favourite compositional form leads the eye 'along the line of some high object (in one case the side of a wood, in the other an almost precipitous hill) diagonally across the picture to the skyline' (Williams, 62).

Occasionally Laporte produced oil paintings, one of which is in the Derby Art Gallery. However, his best-known works are in gouache, and he also worked in pure watercolour. His 1812 lesson book *The Progress of a Water-Coloured Drawing* illustrates both his teaching and his painting technique. Step-by-step instructions were fashionable, but Laporte's guide was more than a painting-by-numbers exercise, since the pupil was supposed to create the basic composition. The sample composition was typically Claudian, and the insistence on a 'dead coloured' grey ground for distance was also becoming old-fashioned. Laporte did not join the Society of Painters in Water Colours, but was a member of the rival Associated Artists in Water-Colours which held exhibitions between 1808 and 1812. This does not imply a break with Wells, since in 1819 they collaborated on a series of seventy-two soft-ground etchings after landscape drawings by Gainsborough. His other publications were *Characters of Trees* (1798–1801), *A Drawing Book* (1800), and *Progressive Lessons Sketched from Nature* (1804). He died from 'decay of nature' at 2 Upper Coleshill Street, Pimlico, on 8 July 1839. Examples of his work are in the British Museum and the Victoria and Albert Museum, London, and the art galleries at Aberdeen, Accrington, Leeds, Leicester, and Newport.

Laporte's daughter Mary Anne (*b.* c.1795) painted portraits and fancy subjects. She exhibited at the Royal Academy and the British Institution from 1813 to 1821, and was a member of the New Society of Painters in Water Colours from 1835 until 1846, when she retired because of ill health. Laporte's son **George Henry Laporte** (1802–1873), animal and military painter, worked in both oil and watercolour, shared his father's address until 1827 or before, and may well have been taught by H. B. Chalon. He exhibited at the Royal Academy and elsewhere from 1818, and was a member of the New Society of Painters in Water Colours from 1834. He was animal painter to the duke of Cumberland and king of Hanover from 1836, and he contributed forty-three plates to the *Sporting Magazine*. His work declined after the 1830s, when both horses and landscapes had shown considerable strength. He died at 13 Norfolk Square, Paddington, on 23 October 1873. His wife, Eliza, *née* Elgie, whom he married in the autumn of 1850, predeceased him, and their only child, Georgina Dora Laporte (1852–1884), died unmarried.

HUON MALLALIEU

Sources B. Long, 'John Laporte', *Walker's Quarterly*, 8 (July 1992), 1–59 · I. O. Williams, *Early English watercolours and some cognate drawings by artists born not later than 1785* (1952) · H. L. Mallalieu, *Understanding watercolours* (1985), 2nd edn, 1.15–28 · S. Mitchell, *The dictionary of British equestrian artists* (1985) · d. cert. [John Peter Laporte] · d. cert. [George Henry Laporte] · *IGI* · Farington, *Diary*, 6.2074 · *DNB* · *The exhibition of the Royal Academy* [exhibition catalogues]

Likenesses J. Hay, miniature, exh. RA 1804

Lapraik, John (1727–1807), poet, was born at Laigh Dalquhram, near Muirkirk, Ayrshire. After education in the parochial school he succeeded his father on the estate, which was of considerable extent, and had been in the family for generations. He also rented the lands and mill of Muirsmill, in the neighbourhood. In 1754 he married Margaret Rankine, sister of Burns's friend, 'rough, rude, ready-witted Rankine'. She died after the birth of her fifth child, and in 1766 Lapraik married Janet Anderson (1740/41–1826), a farmer's daughter, who bore nine children, and survived her husband by nineteen years.

Ruined by the collapse of the Ayr Bank on 12 August 1773, Lapraik had first to let and then to sell his estate, and after an interval to relinquish his mill and farms, on which for several years he struggled to exist. Confined for a time during 1785 as a debtor, he figured as a prison bard.

Early in 1785 Burns heard the song 'When I upon thy bosom lean' at a 'rocking', or social gathering, in his house at Mossgiel Farm, Muirkirk. Learning that Lapraik was the author, he made his acquaintance, and within the year addressed to him his three famous 'Epistles'. Lapraik's other significant connection with Burns, according to local legend at least, is that he helped inspire the sentiments of 'Is there for honest poverty' ('A Man's a Man for a' that'). Burns sent an improved version of Lapraik's song to Johnson's *Scots Musical Museum*. An early version of the song may be one of the lyrics published in the *Weekly Magazine*, 14 October 1773.

Burns's generous patronage encouraged Lapraik to publish his verses, which appeared at Kilmarnock in 1788 as *Poems on Several Occasions*. The volume contains nothing equal to 'When I upon thy bosom lean'. James Maxwell of Paisley notices Lapraik unfavourably in his *Animadversions on some Poets and Poetasters of the Present Age* (1788).

After 1796 Lapraik opened a public house in Kirk Street, Muirkirk, conducting also the village post office on the same premises. Here he died on 7 May 1807 and was buried in the churchyard of Muirkirk parish church. A cairn was erected in 1914 by the 'Lapraik Burns Club' of Muirkirk to mark the spot where Lapraik's house once stood at Laigh Dalquhram. T. W. BAYNE, *rev.* GERARD CARRUTHERS

Sources C. P. Bell, 'The Lapraik family in Muirkirk', *Burns Chronicle*, 24 (1915), 99–124 · G. Sprott, *Robert Burns: pride and passion* (1996), 122 · *The letters of Robert Burns*, ed. J. de Lancey Ferguson, 2nd edn, ed. G. Ross Roy, 2 vols. (1985) · *The poems and songs of Robert Burns*, ed. J. Kinsley, 3 (1968) · J. D. Ross, *Who's who in Burns* (1927) · T. Crawford, 'Lowland song and popular tradition in the eighteenth century', *The history of Scottish literature*, ed. C. Craig, 2: 1660–1880, ed. A. Hook (1988), 123–39

Wealth at death house and furnishings plus £17 cash to widow: Bell, 'Lapraik family in Muirkirk'

Lapthorne, Anthony (1572–1658/9), Church of England clergyman, was probably the son of James and Robiga Lapthorne of Modbury, Devon. He graduated BA at Balliol College, Oxford, in 1593, and the same year migrated to Exeter College, where he became a fellow and in 1596 proceeded MA. He relinquished his fellowship on his marriage in 1600 and that same year acquired the rectory of Landrake, Cornwall, on the presentation of Sir Henry Killigrew. His biographer, John Quick, states that Lapthorne was also a royal chaplain, first to Elizabeth I, from 1597, and then to James I.

Lapthorne had a stormy career as a result of his nonconformist practices, forthright preaching, and trenchant views, which even extended to reproving James I for swearing. As his biographer put it, 'he was no self-seeker, nor time-server, nor man-pleaser' (DWL, 34, MS RNC 38.1.386). He also had godly admirers, among them the third earl of Pembroke, the first Viscount Conway, and Sir Francis Rous. Lapthorne lost his living at Landrake in 1605 for refusing to conform, and presumably also his royal chaplaincy, and moved to Somerset, where in 1606 he was prosecuted for unlicensed preaching. In 1613 he became incumbent of Minchinhampton, Gloucestershire, on the presentation of the crown, but in June 1618 was deprived by the high commission and degraded from the ministry, doubtless for nonconformity. He then found employment as a lecturer at Lewes, Sussex, until his suspension in May 1623 for contravening the royal directions on preaching issued in 1622.

In 1625 Lapthorne published *Spirituall Almes*, in which he argued that the Christian duty of exhortation or admonition was essential, if unpopular. It was dedicated to Pembroke, whom Lapthorne thanked for many favours, and about 1624 or 1625 it was Pembroke who recommended Lapthorne to Bishop Thomas Morton of Coventry and Lichfield. Lapthorne was placed at Cannock, Staffordshire, where Morton recalled that he turned an unruly parish into 'as religious and orderly as any others' (*CSP dom.*, 1638–9, 434), though Morton was obliged at some stage to suspend him from a lectureship at Tamworth. About 1631 Lapthorne became rector of Tretire, Herefordshire, only to be deprived by the high commission in October 1634 for flagrant nonconformity, and for denouncing from the pulpit non-preaching clergy and threatening some parishioners. In December 1635 he was discovered serving the living of Great Burstead, Essex, without licence. Again he resorted to Morton, by this time bishop of Durham, who gave him the cure of Ovingham, Northumberland, which had lacked a preacher for forty years, and paid for his stipend. Although Lapthorne worked hard and with some success at Ovingham he was censured by the Durham high commission in 1639 for preaching elsewhere against ceremonies and non-preaching ministers who denied their congregations the means of salvation. During 1638 and 1639 Lapthorne was also accused of associating with Scottish covenanters, and Charles I forbade him to preach without his permission.

The 1640s brought some relief for Lapthorne. Though he was rejected for the Kidderminster lectureship because of his 'roughness and great immethodicalness and digressions' (*Autobiography of Richard Baxter*, 24), in May 1642 the House of Commons ordered that he be admitted lecturer at his old cure of Minchinhampton. If Lapthorne served there it was not for long, since the following year the Commons placed him temporarily at Great Holland, Essex; finally, in 1646 he was nominated by the committee for plundered ministers to be rector of Sedgefield, co. Durham. However, a rival candidate was put up by some parishioners and, although Lapthorne eventually took possession, in the 1650s it was alleged that he had received more income than he was due, so that as late as 1657 he was facing a suit in the court of exchequer over profits of the living. In 1656 Lapthorne was described as 'rich, childless and through age unable to preach' (*CSP dom.*, 1656–7, 147). Lapthorne's first wife had died in 1629, and his second wife, Elizabeth, was eventually his executor. Lapthorne drew up his will on 5 August 1658 and it was proved on 15 February 1659; he died near Bristol, probably in the winter of 1658–9. A detailed biography was written in 1695 by John Quick, the eminent nonconformist, who had met Lapthorne in Oxford in 1656.

Kenneth Fincham

Sources will, PRO, PROB 11/286, fols. 352–3 • L. A. [A. Lapthorne], *Spirituall almes* (1625), RSTC 15103 • J. Quick, 'Icones sacrae Anglicae', DWL, RNC 38.34, 1.380–98 • C. W. Boase, ed., *Registrum Collegii Exoniensis*, new edn, OHS, 27 (1894), 84 • K. Fincham, *Prelate as pastor: the episcopate of James I* (1990), 224–5, 259, 317, 324 • *CSP dom.*, 1634–5; 1638–40; 1656–8; 1625–49 • W. H. D. Longstaffe, ed., *The acts of the high commission court within the diocese of Durham*, SurtS, 34 (1858), 190–92 • *Sixth report*, HMC, 5 (1877–8), 147 • *Walker rev.*, 143, 148, 173 • Bodl. Oxf., MS Rawl. A. 328, 36 • *The autobiography of Richard Baxter: being the Reliquae Baxterianae abridged from the folio* (1696), ed. J. M. Lloyd Thomas (1925) • W. N. Landor, 'Staffordshire incumbents and parochial records, 1530–1680', *Collections for a history of Staffordshire*, William Salt Archaeological Society, 3rd ser. (1915 [i.e. 1916]), 270, 275 • commissary act book, 1634–6, Essex RO, fol. 120r
Archives DWL, RNC 38.34, 380–98
Wealth at death reasonable list of bequests: will, PRO, PROB 11/286, fols. 352–3

Lapworth, Arthur (1872–1941), chemist, was born on 10 October 1872 in Galashiels, Selkirkshire, the elder son in the family of two sons and one daughter of Charles *Lapworth (1842–1920), professor of geology at the University of Birmingham, and his wife, Janet, daughter of Walter Sanderson of Galashiels. He went to school in St Andrews and to King Edward VI's School, Birmingham, and graduated in 1893 from Mason College, Birmingham. He then studied chemistry at the City and Guilds Central Technical College under F. S. Kipping, who became his friend. His studies laid the foundations for his later researches on camphor and the mechanism of aromatic substitution. He took a DSc at London University in 1895.

Lapworth's academic career began as lecturer in chemistry at the School of Pharmacy in Bloomsbury; in 1900 he moved to the Goldsmiths' Company's institute at New Cross as head of the chemistry department. In the same year he married, in Bridgwater, Somerset, Kathleen Florence, youngest daughter of William Thomas Holland JP. There were no children. Kathleen's two elder sisters married the chemists F. S. Kipping and W. H. Perkin respectively. In 1909 he was appointed senior lecturer in inorganic and physical chemistry at the University of Manchester, where he succeeded W. H. Perkin as professor of organic chemistry in 1913 and became Sir Samuel Hall professor of inorganic and physical chemistry and director of the laboratories in 1922, appointments which show his remarkable versatility.

At Manchester, Lapworth studied the molecular constitution of camphor and its derivatives; his researches suggested new interpretations of organic reaction mechanisms employing the migration of double bonds within organic molecules, and the formation of organic ions and chemical equilibria. His ideas were eagerly taken up by his assistant, Robert Robinson, who made use of them in developing his own electronic theories. The two men remained friends until Lapworth's death. Lapworth discovered new reactions and introduced improved preparative techniques. His classification of organic reagents as 'anionic' and 'cationic' paved the way for the electronic theory of organic reactions, but as the electronic formulations of C. K. Ingold were simpler these were generally adopted and Lapworth's pioneering work was largely forgotten until the late 1940s. Elected a fellow of the Royal Society in 1910, Lapworth served on its council (1927–9) and was awarded the Davy medal (1931). He received honorary LLD degrees from Birmingham and St Andrews; on retirement in 1935 he was made emeritus professor at Manchester.

Lapworth was retiring, generous, especially to his students, and sincere, though he had a sharp wit. He ran his department with firmness and wisdom; in controversy he was always courteous. He loved radio, the cinema, and the theatre and had a wide knowledge of classical music, playing the violin, cello, and viola at Perkin's musical parties in Manchester. He was a member of the council of the Manchester College of Music for many years. Carpentry, microscopy, astronomy, geology, mountaineering, golf, and fishing were among his hobbies; he was an authority on British mosses and was interested in ornithology.

Lapworth died at Sandown Nursing Home, 55 Palatine Road, Withington, Manchester, on 5 April 1941. He was survived by his wife.   N. G. COLEY, rev.

Sources R. Robinson, *Obits. FRS*, 5 (1945–8), 555–72 · G. N. Burkhardt, *Memoirs of the Literary and Philosophical Society of Manchester*, 84 (1939–41), vi–x · G. N. Burkhardt, *Nature*, 147 (1941), 769–70 · W. V. Farrar, 'Lapworth, Arthur', *DSB* · *The Times* (7 April 1941) · *CGPLA Eng. & Wales* (1941)
Archives RS, corresp. with Sir Robert Robinson, mostly relating to theoretical chemistry
Likenesses photograph, RS; repro. in Robinson, *Obits. FRS* · photograph, repro. in A. Findlay and W. H. Mills, eds., *British chemists* (1947), 353
Wealth at death £5209 13s. 4d.: probate, 27 May 1941, *CGPLA Eng. & Wales*

Lapworth, Charles (1842–1920), geologist, was born on 20 September 1842, in Faringdon, Berkshire, the second son of a shopkeeper, James Lapworth (1813–1889), and his wife, Martha Butler (1815x19–1890). The family soon moved to a farm near Buckland in the Vale of the White Horse, and Lapworth was educated at Buckland national school, famous for its environmental approach to education. Following a period as a pupil-teacher he went, in 1862, to Culham Teacher Training College, gaining a first-class certificate in 1864.

Lapworth's first teaching post was as master of St Peter's Episcopalian School in Galashiels. In 1869 he married Janet, daughter of Walter Sanderson, a civic leader and industrialist of Galashiels. They had four children, three sons, one of whom died in infancy, and a daughter. One son, Arthur *Lapworth, became a professor of chemistry at Manchester University and fellow of the Royal Society, the second a well-known water engineer. Both his second son and daughter studied geology. It was in Galashiels that, as a hobby, he began the geological work which eventually led to the clarification and understanding of the structure of the southern uplands of Scotland. After collecting fossils in local rocks formerly thought unfossiliferous, Lapworth by 1870 had established the value of graptolites in identifying outcrops throughout the whole region. By 1872 he had begun correlating these outcrops, and as a result rejected the succession and comparatively simple structure favoured by the geological survey. Using graptolites as zonal fossils for the first time, he mapped the shale sequences in minute detail. He established the correct sequence of beds, and through this, the complex structure of the southern uplands as a series of isoclinal folds. He was also able to correlate rocks from the southern uplands with similar black shales in Scandinavia and elsewhere in Europe. His work resulted in the rejection of the theory of 'Colonies', put forward by Joachim Barrande, and enabled the older Palaeozoic rocks to be classified and correlated in as great a detail as younger rocks. During this work he established a new methodology for the geologic mapping of any area, which involved minute and exact observation and recording on maps of large scale. Often he had to enlarge and draw these base maps himself. From his work in Scotland, and also that in Wales, Lapworth was able to redefine the divisions of the Lower Palaeozoic sub-era on the basis of distinctive faunas. He proposed the Ordovician period to separate the Cambrian from the Silurian, thus resolving the controversy between Adam Sedgwick and Sir Roderick Murchison over their classification.

During the later part of his researches in southern Scotland, Lapworth had moved, in 1875, to Madras College, St Andrews, as an English teacher. However, following publication of his early major works, especially the Moffat series, in 1881 he was appointed as the first professor of geology at Mason College (later the University of Birmingham). He held this post until his retirement in 1913. On arrival in Birmingham, Lapworth began work on the mapping of the north-west highlands of Scotland, where, with the application of his detailed mapping techniques and his knowledge of tectonics, he was able to determine the structural relationship of the Lower Palaeozoic rocks to the Precambrian, and establish the presence of the Moine thrust plane. He was one of the earliest workers in Britain to apply the theories on alpine tectonics of Esher von der Linth and Albert Heim to British geology. Such was his workload that in 1883, during the final stages of the work on the north-west highlands, he suffered a major breakdown. His findings, of major tectonic movements, were confirmed by the officers of the geological survey in the memoir published on the area. His later work on fold theory, which stemmed from this and earlier fieldwork, was ahead of its time, but stimulated many other workers in this field.

Between 1901 and 1918 Lapworth edited the classic monograph, *British Graptolites*, for which he also wrote the introduction. In total, he published sixty-nine papers: his early publications were based on the geology of specific localities in southern Scotland; later ones were wider in their geographical scope, and were increasingly concerned with the fossil content of the rocks, and the use made of this in determining the structure, and biostratigraphy. Eventually, papers were published that were specifically palaeontological, dealing with various aspects of the graptolites worldwide. Work on tectonics resulted in his papers on the north-west highlands, and thereafter on fold theory on a global scale.

Lapworth was always concerned with the economic implications of any geological studies and many of his publications reflect this. When in Birmingham he undertook a great deal of consultancy work, notably on water supply and building materials. Always conscious of the importance of geological education, he wrote and lectured throughout his professional life. He built up a large and successful department, and was an inspiring teacher, both in the lecture room and in the field. He was elected a fellow of the Geological Society in 1872, served on its council in 1894, and was its president in 1902. He was awarded the society's Lyell fund in 1882 and in 1884, the Bigsby medal in 1887, and the Wollaston medal, its highest award, in 1899. Lapworth was elected a fellow of the Royal Society in 1888 and a member of its council in 1895, and in 1891 was awarded its royal medal. He was president of Section C of the British Association in 1892. In 1905 he received the Wilde medal of the Manchester Literary and Philosophical Society, and he was awarded honorary LLDs by the universities of Aberdeen (1883) and Glasgow (1912). After an illness lasting several months, Lapworth died at his home, 38 Calthorpe Road, Edgbaston, on 13 March 1920. He was buried at the Lodge Hill cemetery, Birmingham. He was survived by his wife.

BERYL AMBROSE-HAMILTON

Sources W. W. Watts, 'The geological work of Charles Lapworth', *Proceedings of the Birmingham Natural History and Philosophical Society*, 14 (1921) · J. J. H. T. and W. W. W., *PRS*, 92B (1921), xxxi–xl · U. Birm., Lapworth Museum of Geology · private information (2004) · *CGPLA Eng. & Wales* (1920) · *DNB*
Archives Birm. CA, maps and sections · U. Birm., Lapworth Museum of Geology, corresp. and papers · U. Birm. L., notebook · Ulster Museum, Belfast, drawings and papers · Warks. CRO, notes on Museum of Natural History, Warwick | BGS, letters to Finlay Kitchin
Likenesses portrait, U. Birm., department of geology, Lapworth Museum
Wealth at death £6491 3s. 4d.: probate, 12 May 1920, *CGPLA Eng. & Wales*

Lapworth, Edward (1574–1636), physician and poet, was born in Warwickshire. His father, possibly the Michael Lapworth who was elected fellow of All Souls, Oxford, in 1562 and graduated BM in 1573, was physician to Henry Berkeley.

Lapworth is probably the Edward Lapworth who matriculated from Exeter College, Oxford, on 31 January 1589. He was admitted BA from St Alban's Hall on 25 October 1592, and MA on 30 June 1595. From 1598 to 1610 he was master of Magdalen College School, and as a member of Magdalen College he supplicated for the degree of MB and for licence to practise medicine on 1 March 1603. He was licensed on 3 June 1605, and was admitted BM and DM on 20 June 1611. He was 'moderator in vesperiis' in medicine in 1605 and 1611 and 'respondent' in natural philosophy on James I's visit to Oxford in 1605. In July 1611 he had permission to be absent from congregation so that he might attend to his practice. In 1617 and 1619 Lapworth seems to have been in practice at Faversham, Kent. In 1618 at Oxford he was designated first Sedleian reader in natural philosophy under the will of the founder (though the bequest did not take effect until 1621), and on 9 August 1619 he was appointed Linacre physic lecturer. From this time he resided part of the year in Oxford, but in the summer he usually practised in Bath.

Lapworth married, first, Mary Coxhead, who was buried on 2 January 1621; and, second, Margery, daughter of Sir George Snigg of Bristol, baron of the exchequer, and widow of George Chaldecot of Quarlstone. With his first wife he had a son, Michael, who matriculated at Magdalen College in 1621, aged seventeen; he also had a daughter, Anne, who was her father's heir, and became the mother of the poet and dramatist William *Joyner.

According to Guidott, in person Lapworth was 'not tall, but fat and corpulent', a scholarly man, with a taste for poetry. At the marriage of Theophila Berkeley to Sir Robert Coke in 1613 there were, it is said, 'songs of joy from that learned physician, Doctor E. Lapworth' (Smyth, 3.401). The verses he contributed to a variety of books included lines on Elizabeth's death and on James I's accession. There were some verses of his in Joshua Sylvester's *Du Bartas, his Devine Weekes and Workes* (1605), and in the treatise of Edward Jorden on *Naturall Bathes and Minerall Waters* (1631). The lines given in MS Ashmole 781, fol. 137, as by 'Dr. Latworth on his deathbed', seem to be his; they begin 'My God, I speak it from a full assurance'. There are some notes of his as to a child with two heads being born at Oxford in 1633 (Queen's College, Oxford, MS 121, fol. 29; *CSP dom., 1633–4*, 284). He was the owner of Harleian MS 978 (Bodl. Oxf., MS James 22).

Lapworth died in Bath on 24 May 1636, a year after resigning his Oxford lectureship. He was buried in the church of St Peter and St Paul, Bath.

C. L. KINGSFORD, rev. SARAH BAKEWELL

Sources Wood, *Ath. Oxon.* · Foster, *Alum. Oxon.* · J. Smyth, *The Berkeley manuscripts*, ed. J. Maclean, 3 vols. (1883–5) · J. Nichols, *The progresses, processions, and magnificent festivities of King James I, his royal consort, family and court*, 4 vols. (1828) · R. C. Hoare, *The history of modern Wiltshire*, 5 (1837), 31–2 · AM Oxf., MS 781, fol. 137 · Queen's College, Oxford, MS 121, fol. 29 · *CSP dom., 1633–4*, 284 · Bodl. Oxf., MS James 22 · T. Guidott, *Lives of the physicians of Bath* (1677)

Lara, Isidore de (1858–1935), composer, was born on 9 August 1858 in Islington, London, the second of six children of Abraham Cohen (*b.* 1828/9) and his wife, who was probably named Sarah (*b.* 1840/41). His parents were British-born Sephardic Jews with a modest private income, who spent the 1860s at Boulogne (where the cost of living was low). French schooling made Isidore bilingual. On his return to London in 1871, he gave his first piano recital at the age of thirteen before studying at the Milan conservatory (1874–7). He called himself Isidore de Lara to sound artistic (and a Spanish Count Laurent de Lara was his ancestor).

Student prizes from Italy did not sway British music publishers. The young composer resorted to giving singing lessons at the new Guildhall School of Music (1880–92). Meanwhile, he began to work the exclusive drawing-rooms of the West End as a discreetly paid singer–song-writer, emulating Paolo Tosti. De Lara specialized in ardent love songs. To women, his big brown eyes conveyed as much as his light baritone voice when he sang 'You', 'Soirs d'amour', and 'Drifting in Dreamland'. Luxuriant dark hair, moustache, and eyebrows were definitely assets, while the piano hid the shortness of his legs.

De Lara composed a few operettas, playing Charles II in *The Royal Word* (1883), but it was the best-selling ballad 'The Garden of Sleep' (1886) that made his name. He set verses by Lord Lytton, then ambassador to France, who introduced him to Parisian salons. Duchesses doted on de Lara, who adored cultured high society. He studied composition with Édouard Lalo in Paris and attended a philosophy course in London. Quoting Schopenhauer became a habit, while his interest in Buddhism inspired *The Light of Asia*, a cantata based on Edwin Arnold's poem. Augustus Harris was persuaded to present it—as *La luce dell' Asia*—at the Royal Italian Opera, Covent Garden, in 1892. It fared well enough to justify one performance (in French) of de Lara's first proper opera *Amy Robsart* in 1893. Britain was the only major European country without a permanent operatic repertory company. Having achieved everything he could in London, de Lara decided to make Paris his base and join the raffish cosmopolitan set bridging *beau monde* and *demi-monde*.

De Lara had first met Princess Alice of Monaco (1858–1925) at a soirée about 1887, when she was the duchesse de Richelieu. Born (Marie) Alice Heine in the USA of Franco-German Jewish parentage, she married Prince Albert of Monaco in 1889. A lover of the arts, her serene highness used casino profits to transform the Théâtre de Monte Carlo into a grand opera house. Her decision to present *Amy Robsart* there in 1894 reflected her liking for de Lara, whom she engaged as her musical adviser with a commission for two new operas. He collaborated with French librettists, who had written for Camille Saint-Saëns and Jules Massenet, and his music became sophisticated. *Moïna* (1897) was set in Ireland in 1798. The adulterous affairs of a Roman empress were the subject of *Messaline* (1899).

By now de Lara's works were accounting for 40 per cent of opera performances in Monaco. Such patronage prompted comparisons with Ludwig II and Wagner, and professional jealousy and antisemitism (intensified by the Dreyfus affair) excited talk of a talentless poodle faker, who won applause because the princess spent so much on first-rate singers, magnificent scenery, and 'publicity fees' to journalists. The intimacy between musician and patroness did turn into a scandal, although it may be doubted whether any punning Monégasque ever really chalked 'Ici dort de Lara' on the wall of the Palais Princier. Prince Albert formally separated from Alice in 1902, and Monte Carlo Opera purged its repertory. But in the meantime *Messaline* had become an international hit. Of operas (as distinct from operettas) by British composers, only M. W. Balfe's *The Bohemian Girl* had previously enjoyed such success on the continent—and that never reached La Scala.

Revived in the French provinces until the 1940s, *Messaline* clocked up 3000 performances.

When not travelling to supervise new productions, de Lara divided his time between a Paris flat and Alice's Château du Haut-Buisson in La Sarthe, where he worked in a pavilion in the grounds. *Sanga* (1906), *Solea* (1907), and *Les trois masques* (1912) were all tales of passion and death in colourful locations, fairly well received by continental audiences. The belly-dancing courtesan of *Naïl* (1912) elicited a rhapsodic score, pervaded with melismatic Arab motifs. Its creator was made first a chevalier (1914) and then an officier (1925) of the Légion d'honneur. While his gifts as a melodist and orchestrator were generally admitted, critics said that music so eclectic and devoid of form could not stand repeated hearing. De Lara retorted that this was opera: his task was to summon up the immutable spirits named Love, Hate, Ambition, Envy, Heroism, and Sacrifice. He prided himself on his sense of theatre; and people thought 'theatrical' was just the word for him, as he constantly acted the roles of maestro, social butterfly, ladies' man, and bohemian. Behind the mannerisms was an amiable soul. His hobbies included boxing and cycling.

From 1914 to 1919 de Lara and the princess lived at Claridge's Hotel in London. Rejected as an army interpreter, de Lara set up War Emergency Entertainments in November 1914, a charity taking music into hospitals and barracks, engaging hard-up artistes, and promoting works by British composers. It staged 1310 concerts. Five of his operas were given in Britain (in English) between 1919 and 1930, chief among them *Naïl*. Beecham liked his music; Parry had reckoned it nauseating. In 1924 de Lara launched the abortive National Opera Trust to campaign for state subsidies (as in France).

Mainland Europe remained more receptive. *Les trois mousquetaires* (1921) appeared at Cannes, *Le prince de Marcocana* (1927) at Aix-la-Chapelle, and *Le voilier blanc* (1933) at Budapest. A cultural relic of the *fin de siècle*, de Lara died in Paris at his flat at 49 rue Copernic on 2 September 1935. He was buried in the Père Lachaise cemetery three days later.

In his day Isidore de Lara was known—in France and Belgium at least—as a successful operatic composer of the second rank. He classed himself with Frederick Delius and Ethel Smyth as a British musician whose stage works appeared abroad. However, as neither his career nor his aesthetic conformed to the ideals of the 'English musical Renaissance', its chroniclers excluded him as a virtual Frenchman (just as French authors discounted him as English). Before long, his name meant nothing even to opera lovers.

JASON TOMES

Sources I. de Lara, *Many tales of many cities* (1928) · E. W. White, *A history of English opera* (1983) · S. Sadie, ed., *The new Grove dictionary of opera*, 4 vols. (1992) · T. J. Walsh, *Monte Carlo opera, 1879–1909* (1975) · T. Beecham, *A mingled chime* (1944) · A. Edwards, *The Grimaldis of Monaco* (1992) · *The Times* (3 Sept 1935) · *MT*, 61 (1920), 135 · 'A made musician', *Punch*, 90 (1886), 253 · L. Carley, ed., *Delius: a life in letters* (1983) · J. Dibble, *C. Hubert Parry: his life and music* (1992) · C. Hirshfield, 'Musical performance in wartime, 1914–1918', *Music Review*, 53 (1992), 291–304 · *CGPLA Eng. & Wales* (1936)

Likenesses Hy. F., caricature, 1886, repro. in 'A made musician', 253 • Ape [C. Pellegrini], caricature, repro. in *VF* • E. Dulac, caricature, repro. in de Lara, *Many tales* • photographs, repro. in de Lara, *Many tales* • photographs, repro. in Carley, ed., *Delius*
Wealth at death £10,000 15s. 5d.: probate, 3 March 1936, by decree dated 27 Jan 1936, *CGPLA Eng. & Wales*

Larcher, Dorothy Mary (1882–1952), flower painter, designer, and textile printer, was born on 28 September 1882 at 47 Shirlock Road, St Pancras, London, the daughter and (presumed) only child of William Gustavus Francis Larcher, schoolmaster, and his wife, Eliza Pearce, *née* Arkell. Active during the 1920s and 1930s, she produced with her partner, the designer and printer (Mabel) Phyllis *Barron (1890–1964), innovative hand block-printed materials that had 'a perfect harmony between the fibre, the dye and the block' (Bosence, 42).

> Despite the peculiarly English feel of these textiles, they were in complete contrast to what was generally being produced in Britain in the interwar years for dress and upholstery. They stand apart even when compared to the few other well-established contemporary hand block-printed textiles that were available, such as those of Alec Walker for Crysede or Joyce Clissold at Footprints, where designs were often on a smaller scale and the results frequently busier and more fragmented, often employing more colours. (Roscoe, ed. Coatts, 61)

Larcher studied fine art at Hornsey School of Art, London, where she also later taught. In 1914 she accompanied Lady Christiana Herringham to India to help record the Buddhist frescoes in the Ajanta caves; subsequently she taught and lived with an Indian family in Calcutta, as the outbreak of war prevented her return to England until 1921. No doubt it was in India that she first saw textiles being printed by hand. Back in London 'she visited the Brook Street Gallery and was charmed with Barron's simple hand block-printed textiles. They met, and later … decided to work together' (Bosence, 45). Initially Dorothy Larcher 'joined Barron's workshop in Hampstead High Street. Soon afterwards they moved to 2 Parkhill Studios in Parkhill Road and shared a flat together which was practically next door' (Roscoe, ed. Coatts, 64–5).

In 1930 Larcher and Barron moved to Hambutts House, Edge Road, Painswick, Gloucestershire. The etcher and educationist Robin Tanner recorded his first visit in 1938. Describing Larcher as 'small' but with a 'strong personality', he wrote:

> She had a rather sad, quiet voice and a serious manner, though her sense of humour was every bit as keen as Barron's. She too was most beautifully dressed. She wore cotton printed in iron rust in her own design called *Old Flower* the very first she ever cut … [She] was a most distinguished embroideress. (Roscoe, 1993, 123)

Whereas Barron tended towards strong geometrical patterns Larcher more often based designs on plant and flower motifs such as *Little flower* and *Basket*. Responsibilities in the workshop tended to be divided: 'Dorothy Larcher was mainly responsible for the block cutting … and Barron was very good at dye mixing … Girls from the village helped with the printing, taught by Dorothy Larcher' (Bosence, 48).

The Second World War brought an end to production.

Hambutts House was sold and Barron and Larcher converted the self-contained workshop into a compact but equally comfortable home called Hambutts. Inspired by special plants from their well-stocked garden 'Larcher returned to her flower studies, each one lovingly painted—its character, colour and markings captured in a rare, discreet quality of paint [but] she completed only about forty of her favourite plants before she died' (Bosence, 48). Her death certificate records that she died of cerebral thrombosis at New Nursing Home, Cainscross Road, Stroud, on 14 August 1952 and that Barron arranged for her burial.

The Crafts Study Centre at the Surrey Institute of Art and Design, University College, Farnham, holds the major collection and archive of Barron's and Larcher's work, presented by Robin and Heather Tanner. Their textiles can also be seen at the Whitworth Art Gallery, Manchester; Cheltenham Museums and Art Gallery; and the Victoria and Albert Museum, London. BARLEY ROSCOE

Sources B. Roscoe, 'Phyllis Barron and Dorothy Larcher', *The arts and crafts movement in the Cotswolds*, ed. M. Greensted (1993) • B. Roscoe, 'Phyllis Barron and Dorothy Larcher', *Pioneers of modern craft*, ed. M. Coatts (1997) • S. Bosence, *Hand block printing and resist dyeing* (1985) • b. cert. • d. cert. • P. Barron, 'My life as a block printer', transcript of a talk given at Dartington Hall, Devon, 22 Feb 1964, Crafts Study Centre collection and archive, Farnham • R. Tanner, 'Phyllis Barron, 1890–1964', transcript of a talk given at the Holburne Museum and Crafts Study Centre, Bath, 1 June 1978, Crafts Study Centre collection and archive, Farnham
Archives Surrey Institute of Art and Design, Farnham, Crafts Study Centre collection and archive, Barron and Larcher archive | Cheltenham Museums and Art Gallery • V&A, London • Whitworth Art Gallery, Manchester | SOUND Surrey Institute of Art and Design, Farnham, Crafts Study Centre collection and archive, Barron and Larcher archive
Likenesses double portraits, photographs, *c.*1925–1945 (with Phyllis Barron), Surrey Institute of Art and Design, Farnham, Crafts Study Centre • photograph, *c.*1930, Surrey Institute of Art and Design, Farnham, Crafts Study Centre
Wealth at death £9380 16s. 2d.: probate, 30 Oct 1952, *CGPLA Eng. & Wales*

Larcom, Sir Thomas Aiskew, first baronet (1801–1879), surveyor, the son of Captain Joseph Larcom, RN (d. 1818), and Ann, daughter of William Hollis of Liverstoke, was born at Gosport, Hampshire, on 22 April 1801. He had an elder brother and three sisters. After studying at the Royal Military Academy at Woolwich he was in 1820 commissioned second lieutenant in the Royal Engineers. In 1824 he was chosen by Thomas Colby to work on the Ordnance Survey, originally in England and Wales and, after 1826, in Ireland. From 1826 to 1828 he worked with Joseph Portlock on the great triangulation by which the Irish survey was connected with that of England. In 1828 Colby appointed Larcom as his assistant in the headquarters of the Irish survey in Mountjoy, Phoenix Park, near Dublin, where he took charge of the practical side of the work and proved an exacting but popular and inspiring taskmaster. He organized the many civilians and soldiers needed to compile, engrave, and publish the remarkable 6 inch maps of Ireland. He organized the adoption after considerable controversy of the electrotype process, which allowed maps

Sir Thomas Aiskew Larcom, first baronet (1801–1879), by
Camille Silvy, 1866

to be updated more readily, and the introduction of con-
tour lines to replace hachuring. Mountjoy under Larcom
became a centre of scientific education and was visited by
numerous individuals, institutions, and businesses who
were supplied with information gathered by surveyors,
even before the maps for which it was compiled were published. Larcom believed that the work of the survey
should be expanded to include a detailed descriptive
memoir of each locality. The Irish administration
approved the scheme, but, after the publication in 1837 of
the memoir of Templemore in Londonderry, refused on
grounds of economy to authorize further memoirs. This
was perhaps not surprising given that the memoir contained such information as the diameter of every mill
wheel in the townland and the amount spent on manure
down to the nearest penny. Larcom himself, however, continued to study the Irish language and, with the help of
agents, accumulated an unrivalled store of information
about the history, languages, and antiquities of Ireland,
much of which might otherwise have been lost. He also
established the meteorological observatory in Phoenix
Park, intending it as part of a nationwide network of weather stations.

With his systematic approach and realization of the
value of maps, Larcom prompted many improvements in
the gathering and presentation of official information. He

prepared the maps needed to effect the changes caused by
the Irish Reform Bill and in 1836 compiled a remarkable
map of the country to show proposed railway building
and prepared the topographical part of the *Report on Irish
Municipal Reform*, completing elaborate maps of sixty-
seven towns in one month. In 1840 Larcom married Georgina (*d.* 1898), daughter of General Sir George D'Aguilar,
with whom he had four sons and a daughter. In 1841 he
became a census commissioner and at his instigation the
Irish census of that year included a classification of the
occupations and general condition of the population, as
well as its numbers; a permanent branch of the registrar-
general's department was formed for the collection of
agricultural statistics, and thematic maps accompanied
the census reports. The pattern set by the Irish census was
later adopted in England. In 1842 he was appointed commissioner for inquiring into the state of the Royal Irish
Society and again in 1845 in connection with the Queen's
colleges.

Although always theoretically subordinate to Colby, it
was Larcom who moulded the Irish survey to a model of a
national survey board, initiating projects and supplying
information of the highest standard to enquirers. His personal dedication to the survey's work was reflected in the
use of the term 'Larcom's survey' for the 6 inch maps of
the 1830s. Information gathered by the survey was used by
Larcom during the 1846 famine when he helped to organize road building and drainage as public relief works for
the destitute. By this time the 6 inch survey was nearing
completion and, as part of a plan to bring the Irish survey
under the control of the Southampton Ordnance Survey
headquarters, Larcom was removed from his post on 4
May 1848 leaving him with only a temporary appointment
with the famine relief commission to mark more than
twenty years of service.

Larcom's plight attracted attention, but was overshadowed by the general problems in the country. He
occupied himself preparing an edition of the
seventeenth-century 'down survey' of William Petty
(1851) and held temporary positions with poor relief and
boundary reform commissions before, in 1853, he was
appointed under-secretary for Ireland, an office which for
the first time was non-political and permanent. Under
him the administration became conspicuously more efficient and stable, although not daringly innovative. Its
most important legacy was the valuations from Richard
Griffith's cadastral survey of the country in the 1850s and
1860s, using which local taxation was reformed and other
changes made. Notable reforms were made to the poor
law, medical dispensaries, sewerage, and local government. Larcom, adopting the policy of his friend Thomas
Drummond who had also become under-secretary after
service on the survey, aimed to govern all parties disinter-
estedly, to remove abuses, and to prevent disorder by systematic vigilance through fostering a belief in the ubi-
quity of the government's power. He was promoted
major-general in 1858 and created KCB in 1860. His unique
knowledge of the country enabled him to use his position
to encourage economic growth, in particular capital

investment and schemes to help the poor. He also encouraged education, particularly the Queen's colleges for the upper classes, despite Roman Catholic opposition, and hoped to lessen religious discord by encouraging the teaching of aspects of religion which all denominations had in common. He saw a steady increase in prosperity during his term of office. Each year he drew up memoranda to be read by the lord lieutenant, showing by official returns the progress of agriculture, improvements in standards of living, and reductions in crime. They also showed his belief that copious and accurate information was the basis for good science and good government.

The final years of Larcom's administration were marked by the Fenian uprising, which he helped quell, leaving Ireland peaceful on his retirement in 1868. He was created a baronet on 24 December 1868 and was also sworn of the privy council in Ireland that year. He spent his retirement collecting information about Ireland during his term of office, which he arranged in volumes and presented to the learned societies, chiefly Irish, with which he had been associated. He died at Heathfield, near Fareham, on 15 June 1879. In appearance Larcom was of middle height and thickly set, with an imposing head. He is justly remembered for his significant contribution to the Irish survey and for establishing the need for good-quality information on which to base government administration. ELIZABETH BAIGENT

Sources J. H. Andrews, *A paper landscape: the ordnance survey in nineteenth-century Ireland* (1975) · W. A. Seymour, ed., *A history of the Ordnance Survey* (1986) · *PRS*, 29 (1879), x–xv · T. W. Moody and others, eds., *A new history of Ireland*, 5: *Ireland under the Union, 1801–1870* (1989) · Burke, *Peerage* · *DNB* · J. H. Andrews, 'Thomas Aiskew Larcom 1801–1879', *Geographers: biobibliographical studies*, 7, ed. T. W. Freeman (1983), 71–4

Archives NL Ire., corresp. and papers · Ordnance Survey Office, Southampton · TCD, corresp. and papers | Bodl. Oxf., corresp. with Lord Kimberley · NL Ire., letters to the sixth earl of Mayo · NL Ire., corresp. with John O'Donovan · TCD, corresp. with W. R. Hamilton · University of Limerick Library, letters to George Petrie

Likenesses C. Silvy, photograph, 1866, NPG [*see illus.*] · bust; formerly in Mountjoy, Phoenix Park, 1892 · photograph, NL Ire., letterbook of Peter Fitzgerald, MS 3096

Wealth at death under £6000: probate, 15 July 1879, *CGPLA Eng. & Wales*

Lardner, Dionysius (1793–1859), writer on science and public lecturer, was born on 3 April 1793 in Dublin, the son of William Lardner (d. 1808), a solicitor.

Education, marriage, and career, 1812–1831 Lardner matriculated at Trinity College, Dublin, in 1812 and graduated BA in 1817, MA in 1819, and LLB and LLD in 1827. He married Cecilia Flood on 19 December 1815; they separated in 1820. About 1820 he began a prolonged relationship with Anne Maria Darley Boursiquot (1795–1879), wife of a Dublin wine merchant; he almost certainly fathered her son Dion *Boucicault (1820–1890), the actor and dramatist, and provided him with support until 1840.

Although in holy orders Lardner never held a clerical living. Until 1827 he lived in Dublin, in the early stages of a career as a scientific writer and lecturer, contributing articles to the *Transactions of the Irish Academy*. He published a

Dionysius Lardner (1793–1859), by Alexander Craig, c.1840

variety of treatises, mostly on mathematical subjects, intended for beginners in arithmetic, geometry, and calculus. Lardner was appointed the first professor of natural philosophy and astronomy at the new London University in 1827, at which time he moved to London. After a stormy tenure he resigned his professorship in 1831; he had attempted to introduce a measure of Anglicanism into a determinedly non-clerical foundation (one of the rare times in his career when his clerical status seemed to matter), and he found the compensation inadequate for his social ambitions.

Scientific celebrity, 1827–1840 Lardner's activities and writings may be grouped in three phases, Dublin, London, and Paris. The middle, London, period (1827–40) was the most significant. In this period Lardner was a significant participant in the autodidactic and scientific cultures centred in the capital. At the height of his career, he lectured extensively on scientific and technical subjects, wrote prolifically, and became a scientific celebrity. He wrote treatises on mechanics, pneumatics, and Newton's optics for the Society for the Diffusion of Useful Knowledge, and contributed the chapters on algebra and geometrical analysis to the *Encyclopedia Metropolitana*. He oversaw seven editions of *The Steam Engine Familiarly Explained and Illustrated*, which eventually had eleven editions in Britain, as well as American editions and translations into French, German, Italian, and Danish; *The Athenaeum* called it 'the most popular mechanical treatise ever published' (962). He promoted the new *Monthly Chronicle* and edited it in 1838 and 1839. He contributed important articles to the *Edinburgh Review*, notably a clear account of Charles Babbage's calculating engine (which Babbage himself recommended), and discussions of issues relating to steam transportation.

He enjoyed great popularity as a lecturer, appearing at the Royal, London, and London mechanics' institutions; his lectures to provincial literary and philosophical societies and mechanics' institutes were eagerly awaited and widely praised as appearances of a great figure from the metropolis. Some of his lectures took the form of short courses on such general topics in the physical sciences as pneumatics or mechanics, but his forte was the single lecture on a topic of contemporary moment, delivered in a popular style to a general audience. One such lecture at the Royal Institution attracted the largest audience of the decade to the same hall where Faraday established his fame; on two occasions (1834 and 1835) he delivered popular evening lectures at British Association meetings, discussing Babbage's calculating machines and steam locomotion.

Lardner's editorship of the *Cabinet Cyclopedia*, which he had proposed to the Longman publishing group in 1827 or 1828, continued through the 1830s, bringing him into contact with leading literary figures, and it was especially important to his contemporary renown. It eventually comprised 133 volumes, published between 1830 and 1844; all but the final four volumes appeared before 1840. For the *Cyclopedia* he solicited contributions from eminent literary figures: Sir Walter Scott (two volumes on the history of Scotland), Thomas Moore (four volumes on the history of Ireland), Robert Southey (four volumes on naval history), Connop Thirlwall (eight volumes on the history of Greece), as well as translations of de Sismondi's histories of the Italian republics and of the fall of the Roman empire. Mary Shelley contributed (anonymously) to volumes of biography. He enrolled prominent scientists as well: Sir David Brewster contributed a volume on optics, while John F. W. Herschel wrote his *Preliminary Discourse on the Study of Natural Philosophy* for Lardner's project. The indefatigable Lardner himself wrote six titles (in seven volumes) for the *Cyclopedia*, expounding the topics of mechanics, hydrostatics and pneumatics, heat, arithmetic, geometry, and electricity. He promoted other literary ventures as well, including a *Cabinet Library*, of which nine volumes appeared between 1830 and 1833, and the *Monthly Chronicle*, proposed jointly by Lardner and Edward Lytton Bulwer, and edited solely by Lardner in 1838 and 1839.

Cambridge University awarded him an LLD in 1833; he had been elected a fellow of the Royal Society as well. He was twice a member of the council of the British Association for the Advancement of Science (in 1838–40), and twice a vice-president of its mechanical science section (in 1837 and 1839).

Scandal and later career, 1840–1859 In 1840 Lardner's career unravelled dramatically when he eloped with Mary Spicer Heaviside (d. 1891), wife of Captain Richard Heaviside of the 1st dragoon guards. Lardner had been divorced from Cecilia Flood in 1832 and the marriage had been dissolved by statute on 14 June 1839. When he and Mary Heaviside fled to Paris in March 1840 Captain Heaviside pursued them, subjected Lardner to a flogging, but could not

induce Mary to return with him to England. In a sensational trial in August 1840, Heaviside successfully sued Lardner (now *in absentia*, first in Paris and then in the United States) for criminal conversation, winning an £8000 judgment from a Lewes jury. The Heavisides were divorced in 1841, and after their marriage was dissolved by statute in 1845 Lardner and Mary Heaviside married in Paris, on 2 August 1846; they lived in Paris until Lardner's death.

After the 1840 scandal interrupted his London career Lardner lectured widely in the United States from 1841 to 1844. Although he reputedly prospered from both lecture fees and the subsequent publication of his American lectures, the American sojourn brought no scientific notice. In the final decade of his life, in Paris, he completed his systematic treatise *Railway Economy* (1850), and returned to elementary didactic treatises on a wide range of scientific topics, many published under the general heading of *The Museum of Science and Art*.

Steam power and scientific progress Although Lardner's activities of the 1830s seemed bewilderingly diverse, much of his energy focused on the steam engine and its applications to rail and sea transport. He was an enthusiastic promoter of the steam engine, and believed that national social and economic progress could follow from its application to railways. He eagerly anticipated the reductions in costs and the greater productivity of land that railways would allow, as well as the growth of cities, and the suburbanization which would make them pleasanter places to live in. The railway, he believed, would economically develop (and socially transform) Ireland, for rail links would carry the commerce of Britain and Europe to Ireland's west coast, the logical point for transshipment to the Americas. His pre-eminent position in the world of popular science made him for a few years in the 1830s the unofficial voice of British science on steam engines and transportation. His articles in the *Edinburgh Review*, and testimony before parliamentary committees, strengthened that position. The British Association commissioned (and subsidized) his investigations into 'railway constants'.

Lardner nevertheless became involved in a series of controversies with railway and steamship engineers and companies, and from those controversies emerged as a foolish theoretician, out of touch with the reality of engineering genius. He forecast that the speed of a train passing through the Great Western Railway's Box Tunnel would create a suffocating vacuum for the passengers; he believed that air resistance would place a broad gauge locomotive at a decisive disadvantage, and then later (in his railway constants investigation) discounted the effects of such resistance; in his most famous dispute he doubted that steamships could carry adequate coals to make a crossing from Britain to America practicable. That argument, made most dramatically at Bristol in the 1836 British Association meeting, drew strong opposition from Isambard Kingdom Brunel and stirred the passions of those who had invested money or energy in the possibility of such travel. In the next year's British Association meeting (at Liverpool) Lardner moderated his position but the successful voyages of the *Sirius* and the *Great Western* in 1838 allowed his opponents to burlesque his views. His 'impracticable' became (in the public mind) 'impossible', and his own flight to the United States in 1840—by steamship—recalled his erroneous prophecy.

At the centre of much of Lardner's writing—and career—lay the convictions that science could be easily and familiarly explained, and that technology depended on science. He wrote (and lectured) with greatest success for those who wished to improve their practical skills, and for those who hoped that some scientific veneer would enhance their gentility. He recognized little distinction between science and technology, for in his view the latter was simply a department of the former; the British Association's creation of a mechanical science section illustrated such a conviction. Learning was necessary for technique; mere practical men could not advance technology without the guiding hand of science. His controversies arose from those beliefs, for he was unwilling to cede expertise to such mere practical men as Brunel and the Stephensons. He criticized railway and steamship companies as well as engineers, arguing that their competitiveness made them secretive and hence inimical to scientific investigation. Without such research, technological progress would be stifled. He argued that national progress—economic, social, even moral—depended on the progress of technology, and that that progress could not be trusted to the greed of the marketplace. He was therefore committed to the notion that railways should be guided by rational, not market, impulses, and he supported the railway clearing house scheme of the 1840s. He favoured state regulation of railway enterprise for a number of reasons, adding, in his *Railway Economy*, financial peculation to competitive, irrational, unscientific folly as grounds for the state regulation.

Contemporary and historical assessments Lardner died at Naples on 29 April 1859. Opinions on his character and significance have been varied. His personal behaviour betrayed both social insecurity and an irregular private life. In the years of his fame he acted the parvenu, deliberately courting fashion, inviting aristocratic women to his lectures, mixing in a glittering theatrical demi-monde. However, his position in the inner circles of science remained marginal. Although his editorship of the *Cabinet Cyclopedia* made his name famous, some of the literary figures with whom it brought him in contact held him in contempt. To Dickens he was the 'prince of humbugs' (*The Letters of Charles Dickens*, ed. W. Dexter, 1938, 1.154); to Southey he was a 'knave' (*New Letters of Robert Southey*, ed. K. Curry, 1965, 2.328); Thackeray satirized him at length in his 'Yellowplush papers', in which Lardner emerged as 'the little Irishman in the whig, who et, drank, and talked as much as ½ a duzn' (*Fraser's Magazine*, 18, 1838, 196). In 1833–4 his friend William Charles Macready, the actor, repeatedly found him 'very interesting' (*Diaries*, 1.6), and a source of 'much interesting conversation, or rather information' (ibid., 1.144). Macready read his *Mechanics* (part of the *Cabinet Cyclopedia*) with 'great delight' (ibid., 1.156), but by 1836 Macready had decided that Lardner 'really *bores* me' (ibid., 1.326) and that seems to have been typical of the responses he eventually inspired. When his elopement put an end to his London career he had perhaps already outlived his success. His treatises did not progress beyond the level demanded by the autodidactic hopes that inspired mechanics' institutes, the Society for the Diffusion of Useful Knowledge, and the *Cabinet Cyclopedia*. His conversation like his writing remained at the level of elementary pedagogy, and his frantic social ambitions had worn thin his welcome.

Subsequent historical writing has generally held Lardner in low esteem. Most such critical views have come from railway historians, who have contrasted the vain and foolish cabinet philosopher with the triumphant empirical genius of engineers. Lardner made egregious mistakes: his miscalculations of steamship possibilities, his odd arguments about air resistance to locomotives; it has been easy to make him a buffoon. But such writers have also uncritically accepted the early Victorian horror at his elopement (although Lardner and Mary Heaviside seemed to have remained devoted to each other until Lardner's death), and have prolonged the satire which his pretentious classical name invited from his contemporaries ('Goodness be with us', Scott exclaimed in 1829, 'what a name'; *The Journal of Sir Walter Scott, from the Original Manuscript at Abbotsford*, 1890, 2.318). Some more modern notices, while slight, have granted his importance as a contributor to debates about government regulation of railways, and have reasserted the central position he occupied in celebrating science and technology to the readers of the 1830s. As an important mediator of the culture of the new technologies of his time, his influence should not be underestimated, and his writings are a key source for understanding nineteenth-century popular ideas about progress and its relation to technological development.

J. N. HAYS

Sources J. N. Hays, 'The rise and fall of Dionysius Lardner', *Annals of Science*, 38 (1981), 527–42 • review of Lardner's *The steam engine*, *The Athenaeum* (5 Dec 1840), 962 • *The diaries of William Charles Macready, 1833–1851*, ed. W. Toynbee, 2 vols. (1912) • R. Fawkes, *Dion Boucicault: a biography* (1979) • P. H. Theerman, 'Dionysius Lardner's American tour: a case study in antebellum American interest in science, technology, and nature', *Experiencing nature: proceedings of a conference in honor of Allen G. Debus*, ed. P. H. Theerman and K. H. Parshall (1997), 211–36 • M. Peckham, 'Dr Lardner's *Cabinet Cyclopedia*', *Papers of the Bibliographical Society of America*, 45 (1951), 37–58 • H. H. Bellot, *University College, London, 1826–1926* (1929) • *Wellesley index* • J. Morrell and A. Thackray, *Gentlemen of science: early years of the British Association for the Advancement of Science* (1981) • 'Gallery of literary characters, no. xxvi: Reverend Doctor Lardner', *Fraser's Magazine*, 5 (1832), 696–7 • W. Bates, *The Maclise portrait-gallery of 'illustrious literary characters'* (1883) • G. R. Hawke, *Railways and economic growth in England and Wales, 1840–1870* (1970) • T. R. Gourvish, *Mark Huish and the London–North Western Railway* (1972) • A. Vasquez, 'The awareness of Cournot's *Recherches* among early British economists', *Research in the History of Economic Thought and Methodology*, 15 (1997), 115–37 • E. T. MacDermot, *History of the Great Western Railway,*

rev. C. R. Clinker, rev. edn, 1 (1964) · H. Ellis, *British railway history: an outline from the accession of William IV to the nationalisation of railways*, 1 (1954) · L. T. C. Rolt, *Isambard Kingdom Brunel* (1957) · Boase, *Mod. Eng. biog.* · *The Times* (10 May 1859)
Archives Wellcome L., corresp. and papers | BL, letters to Charles Babbage and Macvey Napier, Add. MSS 37183–37200, 34614–34626 · Linn. Soc., letters to William Swainson · NL Scot., letters to Sir Walter Scott · RS, corresp. with Sir John Herschel · UCL, letters to Society for the Diffusion of Useful Knowledge
Likenesses A. Craig, portrait, *c*.1840, priv. coll. [*see illus.*] · F. de Lisle, miniature, oils, NPG · D. Maclise, lithograph, BM, NPG; repro. in *Fraser's Magazine* · lithograph (after T. Bridgwood), NPG · pencil sketch, repro. in 'Gallery of literary characters, no. xxvi', *Fraser's Magazine*, 696 · watercolour study (after D. Maclise), V&A

Lardner, Nathaniel (1684–1768), Presbyterian minister and patristic scholar, was born at the Hall House, Hawkhurst, Kent, on 6 June 1684, the elder son of Richard Lardner (1653–1740). He also had a sister, Elizabeth. His father, who was grandson of Thomas Lardner, a cordwainer at Portsmouth, was educated at the academy of Charles Morton (1626–1698) and became an Independent minister. He served between 1673 and 1732 at Deal, at Plaisterer's Hall, London, and then at Chelmsford. Nathaniel's mother was a daughter of Nathaniel Collyer (or Collier), a Southwark tradesman who in the plague year, 1665, had retired to Hawkhurst. Lardner appears to have attended a grammar school, probably at Deal, and from there went to study at the Presbyterian academy in Hoxton Square, London, under Joshua Oldfield, assisted by John Spademan and William Lorimer. Towards the end of 1699 he accompanied Martin Tomkins to study at Utrecht. Daniel Neal, later his brother-in-law and a historian of puritanism, was among his fellow students. In the winter of 1702 he studied at Leiden.

In 1703 Lardner returned to London and joined the Independent church in Miles Lane, under Matthew Clarke the younger. He continued his studies for a further six years, and it was not until 2 August 1709, in Tomkins's pulpit at Stoke Newington, that he preached his first sermon. In 1713 Lardner became domestic chaplain to Lady Treby (formerly Mary Brinley), fourth wife and widow of Sir George Treby (*d*. 1700), chief justice of the common pleas. He was tutor to their youngest son, Brinley, and in 1716 travelled with him for four months in France and the Netherlands, keeping a journal of the tour. He was a contributor to *Occasional Papers* (1716–19), its authors, six Presbyterians and two Independents, including—at that time—Lardner (in 1730 he became a Presbyterian), largely siding with Benjamin Hoadly in the Bangorian controversy, which erupted following Hoadly's sermon of 31 March 1717, in which he denied that there was biblical warrant for any visible churchly authorities.

Following Lady Treby's death at the beginning of 1721, Lardner went to live with his father in Hoxton Square, acting as his assistant (until 1729) at Hoxton Square meeting-house, though he was never formally ordained. He joined a literary club and a clerical club which met at Chew's Coffee House, Bow Lane. The death of his pupil Brinley Treby in 1723 greatly affected his spirits and health. He became

Nathaniel Lardner (1684–1768), by Thomas Kitchin, pubd 1769 (after unknown artist, *c*.1713–23)

very deaf; early in 1724 he wrote that when at public worship he could hear neither the preacher's voice nor the congregation singing. He was at this time taking part in a course of Tuesday evening lectures at the Old Jewry, instituted in 1723. Late in that year he also began another series of lectures, out of which grew a notable book, *The Credibility of the Gospel History* (12 vols., 1727–55).

The appearance in February 1727 of the first two volumes of part one of Lardner's *Credibility* brought him into the front rank of Christian apologists. Further volumes appeared until the twelfth in 1755, which was followed by a supplement in 1756. Parts of the work were translated into Dutch, Latin, and German. However, he sold the copyright in 1768 for £150, which was less than his original investment. On 24 August 1729 Lardner preached for William Harris at the Presbyterian meeting-house in Poor Jewry Lane, Crutched Friars. He had held Harris in high esteem since his youth, and the latter unexpectedly offered him a position as his assistant preacher, though he did not assume responsibility for pastoral care. At this period Lardner was engaged in an important correspondence on theological topics with John Shute Barrington, first Viscount Barrington. This eventually led to Lardner's publishing *A Letter … Concerning … the Logos* (1759).

Lardner almost died from a fever in 1728, and he experienced further ill health in 1736–7. The death of his father, with whom he had continued to live, and of his ministerial colleague William Harris occurred in the same year, 1740. He was now urged to replace Harris as minister, but worries about ordination, deafness, and literary work held him back. He eventually decided to remain as assistant, and George Benson was elected pastor in November 1740. Lardner disliked engaging in religious disputes, and it is clear that he shrank from the ordeal of a theological examination and a detailed confession of faith.

It was primarily through his many and varied publications that Lardner became renowned. The collected edition of his *Works* first appeared in 1788 and ran to eleven volumes. Lardner regarded the average reader as capable of assessing the internal evidence for the historical character of the New Testament, and thus he discussed the documentary writings of Josephus and other contemporaries of Jesus, as well as invoking later patristic authors. Lardner also brought together a pioneering collection of critically appraised materials for determining the date and authorship of New Testament books. His *A large collection of ancient Jewish and heathen testimonies to the truth of the Christian religion* appeared in 1764. He contributed extensively to patristic scholarship, and a number of works, including a history of the heretics of the first two centuries AD, were published posthumously. Lardner's scholarship was undoubtedly pioneering, and was not superseded until well into the nineteenth century.

A friend of Archbishop Secker and the bishop of Chichester, Edward Waddington, Lardner also corresponded with such dissenters as John Brekell, Samuel Chandler, Philip Doddridge, and Henry Miles. He sent Doddridge some volumes of his *The Credibility of the Gospel History* in return for several gifts of Doddridge's works, and made observations on Celsus, Julian, and the Manichaeans. Thomas Morgan, the moral philosopher, who had written against revelation, addressed himself to Lardner, thinking he 'could not talk to any man of greater impartiality and integrity' (*Memoirs of the Life and Writings*, 59).

Lardner was, however, conservative in his acceptance of the miraculous element in the biblical narrations. Yet his treatment of demoniacal possession, which he attributed to 'bodily diseases and indispositions' rather than to evil spirits as such (*The Works of Nathaniel Lardner*, ed. B. Cole, 11 vols., 1788, 1.429–96), was uncharacteristically rationalistic. All the more remarkable, therefore, was his independence of mind in relation to dogmatic theology. He regarded Christianity as 'a republication of the law of nature, with the two positive appointments of baptism and the Lord's Supper' (*Memoirs of the Life and Writings*, 81). The gospel was advantageous because people 'needed to be awakened and excited to the practice of what they did know' (ibid., 83). At Salter's Hall in 1719, where the ostensible subject of discussion, the Trinity, was overshadowed by the issue of subscription, he was a nonsubscriber. He disowned the Arian doctrine which denied the co-equality of the Son with the Father; but for a time Lardner was attracted to the modified Arianism adhered to by the Anglican philosopher and theologian Samuel Clarke (1675–1729) and the dissenter James Peirce. By 1730 Lardner adhered to what he called the Nazarene doctrine of the Saviour's miraculous conception, as distinct from the Ebionite, according to which Jesus was the son of Joseph and Mary only. This opinion he taught from the pulpit as early as 1747, but did not publish it until 1759, and then anonymously.

Lardner was of slender build and middle height. He had a frank, intelligent face, and all accounts speak of his good humour and civility. Early in 1745 he received the diploma of DD from Marischal College, Aberdeen, and in June 1746 he was appointed a London correspondent of the Scottish Society for Propagating Christian Knowledge. He retained his place as assistant until 1751; the smallness of the morning congregation was among his reasons for resigning, and he preached his last sermon on 23 June. His lack of popularity as a preacher was partly due to indistinct enunciation; he slurred his words and dropped his voice, defects to which his deafness rendered him insensible. From about 1753 communication with him was by writing only, and he amused himself when alone with looking over the sheets covered with the miscellaneous jottings of his visitors.

Lardner's old age was lonely. His brother, Richard, a barrister, died in April 1733, his brother-in-law, Daniel Neal, in 1743. In 1748, following the death of his sister Elizabeth, Neal's widow, he wrote that 'now all worldly friendships fade, and are worth little' (*Memoirs of the Life and Writings*, 97). However, his literary activity and also his benevolence continued to the end of his life, and shortly before his death he exerted himself to procure aid for foreign protestants. Joseph Priestley often visited him, but when he did so in 1767 found his memory to be failing.

In July 1768, although quite feeble, Lardner took his annual journey to Hawkhurst, accompanied by one of his nieces and her husband. Although he reached Hawkhurst, Lardner died there on 24 July 1768. He was buried in his family vault in Bunhill Fields, London. His funeral, attended by a number of nonconformist ministers, including Caleb Fleming, Thomas Amory, and Richard Price, was very simple. Lardner had not wanted a funeral sermon, and so Ebenezer Radcliffe, his successor at Poor Jewry Lane, wrote an elogium, which he delivered at the graveside. In 1789 an inscribed marble slab was erected to his memory in Hawkhurst church by his great-nephew David Jennings. His library was sold in December 1768, many books from it eventually finding a home in Dr Williams's Library in London.

ALEXANDER GORDON, rev. ALAN P. F. SELL

Sources *Memoirs of the life and writings of the late Reverend Nathaniel Lardner*, ed. J. Jennings (1769) • [S. Lee], *A collection of the names of the merchants living in and about the City of London* (1677); repr. as *The London directory of 1677* (1878) • *Protestant Dissenter's Magazine*, 4 (1797), 434–5 • *Monthly Repository*, 3 (1808), 364–5, 485–8 [enlarged repr. of *Protestant Dissenter's Magazine* (1797)] • W. Wilson, *The history and antiquities of the dissenting churches and meeting houses in London, Westminster and Southwark*, 4 vols. (1808–14), vol. 1, pp. 88–112; vol. 2, pp.

267–8 • W. Turner, *Lives of eminent Unitarians*, 1 (1840), 126–163 • A. Gordon, ed., *Freedom after ejection: a review (1690–1692) of presbyterian and congregational nonconformity in England and Wales* (1917), 55, 301 • *Calendar of the correspondence of Philip Doddridge*, ed. G. F. Nuttall, HMC, JP 26 (1979), nos. 695, 864, 959, 1042, 1433, 1733 • W. D. Jeremy, *The Presbyterian Fund and Dr Daniel Williams's Trust* (1885), 113, 131, 140, 156 • T. S. James, *The history of the litigation and legislation respecting Presbyterian chapels and charities in England and Ireland between 1816 and 1849* (1867), 688, 713, 716, 717, 721 • C. G. Bolam and others, *The English presbyterians: from Elizabethan puritanism to modern Unitarianism* (1968) • *Life and correspondence of Joseph Priestley*, ed. J. T. Rutt, 1 (1831), 37 • *The theological and miscellaneous works of Joseph Priestley*, ed. J. T. Rutt, 21 [1822], 243 • H. McLachlan, *English education under the Test Acts: being the history of the nonconformist academies, 1662–1820* (1931), 44, 127, 230, 266 • minute books of the body of protestant dissenting ministers of the three denominations in and about the cities of London and Westminster, 1727–1827, DWL [3 vols.] • T. W. Davids, *Annals of evangelical nonconformity in Essex* (1863), 467 • J. Hunt, *Religious thought in England from the Reformation to the end of the last century*, 3 (1873), 238 • J. B. Lightfoot, *Essays on the work entitled 'Supernatural religion', reprinted from the 'Contempory Review'* (1889) • J. H. Colligan, *The Arian movement in England* (1913), 152 • DWL, Jennings family MSS
Archives CKS, correspondence and papers, Kent misc. • DWL, Jennings family papers
Likenesses marble slab, 1789, Hawkhurst church, Kent • J. Hopwood, stipple, pubd 1817, BM, NPG • T. Kitchin, engraving (after portrait, c.1713–1723), NPG; repro. in *Memoirs of the life and writings of … N. Lardner [see illus.]* • T. Kitchin, line engraving, NPG

Larke, Sir William James (1875–1959), engineer and industrial administrator, was born at Ladywell, Kent, on 26 April 1875, the eldest son of William James Larke, builder, and his wife, Rosa Barton. He was educated at Colfe's School, Lewisham, and trained as an engineer with H. F. Joel & Co., Finsbury, and Siemens Brothers, Woolwich. In 1898 he joined the British Thomson-Houston Company, becoming engineer and manager of its power and mining department in 1899 and executive engineer in 1912.

Larke joined the newly established Ministry of Munitions in 1915, where he was mainly concerned with organizational and administrative matters, becoming director-general of raw materials in 1919. The administrative skill which he showed at the ministry, added to his industrial experience as an engineer, provided an invaluable combination of qualities when he was involved in the national organization of the steel industry after the war. He was able to draw on his war experience during his service as secretary of the sub-committee of post-war iron and steel requirements of the Ministry of Munitions council committee on demobilization and reconstruction. The chairman of this group was Walter Layton, the first director of the National Federation of Iron and Steel Manufacturers, whom Larke succeeded in that office in 1922.

Taking over at a time of acute industrial depression, Larke steadily advanced the arguments for control of imports and a measure of protection for the British iron and steel industry. This policy was finally accepted by the government and embodied in the Import Duties Act of 1932. As a result of the act, and of recommendations from the import duties advisory committee, which it set up, for a stronger central organization for the iron and steel industry, the British Iron and Steel Federation came into existence in 1934 and the National Federation was dissolved. Larke, who had played an important part in the transition, continued as director of the new and more powerful organization, under its chairman, Sir Andrew Rae Duncan, until his retirement in 1946.

In 1939 Larke was made chairman of the advisory committee of non-ferrous minerals at the Ministry of Supply and in 1942 he became controller of non-ferrous mineral development, a post he held until the end of the war.

Larke was continually active in promoting research and co-operation directed to technological efficiency within the iron and steel industry. Combining scientific knowledge, thorough experience of industrial affairs, and a genial personality, he fitted naturally into leading positions in a large number of industrial and professional bodies. In 1924, early in his association with the National Federation of Iron and Steel Manufacturers, the federation undertook the organization of co-operative research. This work was transferred in 1929 to the Iron and Steel Industrial Research Council, which he chaired from 1938 to 1945. He was elected vice-president of the Iron and Steel Institute in 1934, became honorary vice-president in 1946, and was awarded the institute's Bessemer medal in 1947. He was also in his time president of the Junior Institution of Engineers, of the Institute of Fuel, of the Institute of Welding, and of the British Standards Institution.

He was appointed OBE in 1917, CBE in 1920, and KBE in 1921. He received the honorary degree of DSc from the University of Durham in 1945. He married in 1900 Louisa Jane (d. 1959), daughter of James Taylor Milton, chief engineer surveyor of Lloyd's Register of Shipping, of Blackheath; they had one daughter, Joyce, and a son, William Milton Larke, who became general manager of Stewart and Lloyds, Ltd, Bilston, Staffordshire. Larke died on 29 April 1959 at his home, Cray Hill, Rectory Lane, Sidcup, Kent. WALTER TAPLIN, rev.

Sources *The Times* (1 May 1959) • *The Engineer* (8 May 1959) • J. C. Carr and W. Taplin, *History of the British steel industry* (1962) • private information (1971) • d. cert.
Likenesses W. Stoneman, photograph, 1947, NPG
Wealth at death £24,921 17s. 9d.: probate, 16 July 1959, CGPLA Eng. & Wales

Larkham, Thomas (1602–1669), Independent minister, was born on 17 August 1602 at Lyme Regis in Dorset, the eldest son of Thomas Larkham, linen draper (d. 1639), and his wife, Jane. He matriculated from Trinity College, Cambridge, in 1619 and graduated BA from Trinity Hall in 1622. On 22 June that year at Shobrooke, Devon, he married Patience (d. 1677), daughter of George Wilton, schoolmaster, of Crediton. Through his wife Larkham came into property and income which helped to support his unconventional career. Ordained priest in London on 23 May 1624, he became curate at Sandford, Devon, where his son John was baptized on 10 October that year. He proceeded MA in 1626 and on 26 December became vicar of Northam, Devon. He later claimed, in the dedication to his *The Wedding Supper* (1652), that he endured 'suffering (in the time of the prelacy) in almost all the courts in England', including high commission and Star Chamber. No evidence survives to substantiate this. He left for New England in late 1639 or early 1640, and was deprived in August 1640 for neglect by absence.

Larkham settled with his family at Dover (Paschataqua), New Hampshire, where Hanserd Knollys (1598–1691) had gathered a church. The inhabitants turned to Larkham because he was laxer about church membership, a reputation at odds with his later notoriety as a congregationalist. In 1641 Larkham opposed Knollys's antinomian preaching: Knollys excommunicated him, and his faction marched towards Larkham's house with a bible on a pole. Knollys soon left Dover. Larkham promised to stay, but in November 1642 suddenly left for England. John Winthrop noted sourly in his journal that Larkham deserted his church, and that a widow later confessed she was carrying his child (rumours of this followed him home) (*Journal of John Winthrop*, 421). In his diary, begun about 1648, Larkham noted with pleasure for many years the anniversary of setting sail from New England.

On his return Larkham went to Kent, then became a parliamentary chaplain. In 1645 the committee for plundered ministers supported his right to preach in the parish of East Greenwich. Thomas Edwards in his *Gangraena* (1646) branded him a fierce Independent. In February 1647 Larkham went to Ireland as chaplain to Sir Hardress Waller's regiment.

Larkham went to the west country with Waller at the start of the second civil war, and to Tavistock in April 1648. He preached publicly in the town, which had lost its vicar in 1643 when George Hughes (d. 1677) left for Plymouth. The patron, the earl of Bedford, had agreed to let the inhabitants select the incumbent. Larkham claimed he was the parishioners' choice. He left the army after a court martial for inciting disorder, his opponents alleged, though Larkham referred only to disagreements over soldiers' irreligious behaviour. It is not clear whether he gathered a church in the parish immediately, but he quickly caused offence by excluding from communion those he judged ungodly. He alienated trustees of the Lamerton tithe, who withheld a £50 augmentation due to the vicar of Tavistock: Larkham's diary records his dismay. In protest, he went north in August 1651. He joined his son George (1629/30–1700), who had graduated BA from Exeter College, Oxford, the previous year and gone to Cumberland earlier that year. Both were attracted by calls for preachers from the commissioners for the four northern counties.

Larkham preached in itinerant fashion near Cockermouth, Cumberland, at Cross Canonby, Dearham, and Flimby, and may have been attached to troops in the area. During the autumn he instigated a gathered church at Cockermouth, its members drawn from parishes in the neighbourhood. He held no formal office, but the church book shows he played a critical role. George Larkham, who had been ordained by his father and others on 28 January 1652, became curate of Cockermouth and pastor to the church. In both Tavistock and Cockermouth, father and son combined parish livings with ministry to gathered churches—an unusual style of ministry, though possible in the interregnum.

Larkham stayed in Cumberland until April 1652, but set off for Tavistock in response to pleas from supporters. Anticipating more controversy, he went to London to secure support from the committee for advance of money in the Lamerton dispute, and to print his *The Wedding Supper* (issued in a new edition in 1656) to defend his ministry. When he reached Tavistock his enemies locked the parish church to keep him out. If Larkham had not formally gathered a church before, he soon did so. He distinguished between duties to parish and church: as he revealed in his *A Discourse of Paying Tithes* (1656), 'I teach all in the publike meeting-house, but do only baptize the children of such as are received and allowed members of the Church, and admitted to the Lords Table' (Larkham, *Discourse*, 25). His *The Attributes of God Unfolded, and Applied* (1656) reveals an active preaching ministry, but parish records suggest half those born between 1653 and 1660 went unbaptized. What perhaps began as an attempt to refuse sacraments to the ignorant or immoral became a church defined ever more tightly, by written covenant and pastoral inquiry. By 1658 the gathered church paid Larkham to use a meeting-chamber in his house, and allied itself with Lewis Stucley's congregationalist church in Exeter. Larkham's opponents tried to persuade the authorities to remove him: those with a stake in the Lamerton dispute, such as Walter Godbeare, John Pointer, and Francis Glanville, were to the fore, with disenchanted church members like Nicholas Watts and William Hore, and ministers excluded by Larkham from Tavistock's pulpit, such as Digory Polewhele of Whitchurch and Andrew Gove of Peter Tavy. When appeals to the Devon commissioners for sequestrations, the commission for plundered ministers, and the commission for the ejection of scandalous ministers came to nothing, Glanville, Polewhele, Godbeare, Watts, and Hore produced *The Tavistock Naboth Proved Nabal* (1658), the only tract now extant from a fierce exchange of pamphlets between Larkham and his critics. Their campaign, constructed to fit the expectations of interregnum religious policy, focused on Larkham's unfit conduct as a public preacher, not on his right to gather a church. They glossed his experiments in church discipline as a way to exclude those who had preferred George Hughes's ministry, 'for … he hath often said there were two parties in the Church, the Hugonites and the Larkamites' (F. G. and others, 67). The existence of this rift is confirmed by Watts's connections with Hughes's ministerial circle (which helped Watts to establish a rival lecture-day in Tavistock in 1659), and by Larkham's isolation from the Devon association formed by Hughes. However, the vehemence of *The Tavistock Naboth*'s polemic should not obscure the poor success of the crusade to evict Larkham. Nor should evidence of local support be overlooked: his diary lists those to whom he gave or sold his printed sermons, and notes a stream of gifts from almost eighty donors, many among the town's poorer citizens. Family names that recur in the diary before and after 1660 give a sense of the loyalty to Larkham that carried Tavistock's gathered church into nonconformity.

On 21 October 1660 Larkham resigned as vicar at the patron's request, but stayed in or near Tavistock, preaching when he could. He fled to Cumberland for six months in 1663–4 to escape charges of nonconformity, but he was excommunicated in 1665. He drew up his will, as of Tavistock, on 1 June 1668, mentioning his wife, son George, daughters Patience and Jane, and grandson Thomas. He died in 1669 and was buried on 23 December in Tavistock.

SUSAN HARDMAN MOORE

Sources 'The diary of the Revd. Thomas Larkham, MA.', c.1648–1669, BL, Loan 9, Bound 717A [pubd in different edns by W. Lewis, 1871, 1888] · T. Larkham, *The wedding supper* (1652), preface · T. Larkham, *A discourse of paying tithes* (1656), preface, 25 · F. G. [F. Glanville] and others, *The Tavistock Naboth proved Nabal: in an answer unto a scandalous narrative published by Mr. Tho: Larkham* (1658) · *Calamy rev.*, 315 · S. Hardman Moore, '"Poor folkes" and the parish: Thomas Larkham in Cockermouth and Tavistock', *Life and thought in the northern church, c.1100–c.1700: essays in honour of Claire Cross*, ed. D. Wood (1999) · *The journal of John Winthrop, 1630–1649*, ed. R. S. Dunn, J. Savage, and L. Yeandle (1996), 348–50, 392, 421 · 'A register or the records of the church gathered in & about Cockermouth in Cumb[erlan]d', Cumbria AS, Carlisle, DFC/C1/6/1 · papers of the committee for advance of money, PRO, SP 19/11, fols. 364–5; SP 19/12, fols. 29, 76, 241, 341, 387; SP 19/25, fol. 11; SP 19/95, nos. 68, 89, 108–13, 115–33, 387 · *The Winthrop papers*, ed. W. C. Ford and others, 4 (1944) · parish records, Tavistock, Devon RO, Tavistock, add 2/PR1, 482A/PF135, 482A/PV1 · H. J. Hopkins, 'Thomas Larkham's Tavistock: change and continuity in an English town, 1600–1670', PhD diss., U. Texas, 1981 · G. H. Radford, 'Thomas Larkham', *Report and Transactions of the Devonshire Association*, 24 (1892), 96–146
Archives BL, diary, MS Loan 9, Bound 717A
Likenesses line engraving, 1649, NPG · T. Cross, engraving, 1652, repro. in Larkham, *The wedding supper* · engraving, 1656, repro. in T. Larkham, *The attributes of God* (1656)
Wealth at death £78 3s. 4d.—incl. books £20: *Calamy rev.* · property in Tavistock and Crediton: will

Larkin, James (1874–1947), labour leader in Ireland, was born on 4 February 1874 at 41 Combermere Street, Toxteth Park, Liverpool, the second of the six children of James Larkin (1845–1887), a forge labourer, and his wife, Mary Ann McNulty (1842–1911). His parents were part of that vast exodus from Ireland who took their place at the bottom of the English social pyramid. James Larkin, therefore, was brought up in poverty, received only a few years' formal schooling, watched his father die of tuberculosis in 1887, and was thrown on to a brutal labour market. He joined the Toxteth branch of the Independent Labour Party in 1892, and was converted to socialism. In summer 1893 he stowed away to escape unemployment and to find adventure, but returned to Liverpool the following year to take his place again among that vast army of casuals who prowled the docks in search of a day's work. He eventually found regular work as a docker, and was soon promoted to dock foreman. By 1903 he was earning £3 10s. a week and decided to marry. He had been keeping company for some time with Elizabeth Brown, whose father managed a working-class restaurant in Liverpool and was a Baptist lay preacher. Larkin courted Elizabeth by taking her to socialist meetings and speaking engagements, though she never expressed any real interest in socialism. They

James Larkin (1874–1947), by unknown photographer, 1914

were married on 8 September 1903 in a civil ceremony in Liverpool, and eventually had four sons.

When his men went out on strike in summer 1905 Larkin joined them and became their leader. Though the strike was lost he was asked to become a full-time organizer for the National Union of Dock Labourers. He quickly organized in the Scottish ports, and was then assigned to the more difficult task of doing the same in Ireland. Soon after his arrival in 1907 Larkin was involved in a series of strikes in Belfast, Cork, and Dublin, which the executive of the National Union was reluctant to support. Larkin then broke with the National Union and founded the Irish Transport and General Workers' Union late in 1908; he was the union's secretary and edited its paper, the *Irish Worker and People's Advocate*. Larkin's imprisonment on a charge of embezzlement of strike funds did not prevent the union from rapidly gaining in numbers and strength: by 1913 it was the largest and most militant union in Ireland. The building of the Transport Union, which laid the foundations of the Irish labour movement, was undoubtedly much assisted by Larkin's oratorical skills and charisma, and was the most creative achievement of his long life. Larkin believed that it was a union's responsibility to do more than merely wring better wages, hours, and conditions from reluctant employers. For him, the union was a revolutionary instrument through which he could effect not only economic change, but also a profound social transformation in Irish society.

During summer 1913 Larkin decided to consolidate his

formidable power base in Dublin by challenging the financier William Martin Murphy, whom he had demonized for several years as Dublin's arch-capitalist. Larkin began by organizing among the workers of Murphy's Dublin United Transway Company, and declared a strike in August 1913 in response to victimization. Murphy retaliated by organizing a Dublin Employers' Federation of some 400 strong, who locked out union members and those who refused to pledge never to join. The upshot was an epic struggle that lasted six months and involved 20,000 workers, during which Larkin was once more briefly imprisoned. The Dublin workers were able to sustain themselves only because of massive support from the British labour movement, which contributed £150,000 in money and food. In the midst of the lockout Larkin launched a crusade in Britain to induce the British labour leadership to declare a general strike in support of the Dublin workers. The British Trades Union Congress met in London early in December 1913 to consider the matter, but after an acrimonious debate rejected the Larkinite proposal by more than ten to one. In February 1914 the workers were finally obliged to surrender, and returned to work on the employers' terms. The Transport Union was decimated in numbers and financially ruined, but this did not prevent Larkin from assuming the presidency of the Irish Trades Union Congress. The struggle also had the effect of making him an international figure: by 1914 'Larkin' and 'Larkinism' had become household words in Britain, and in America too, the left wing had taken him up as a prime example of a socialist of the meat-eating and syndicalist variety. Even Lenin had been impressed by Larkin's revolutionary posture in 1913. With the outbreak of the First World War in August 1914 Larkin cemented his international reputation as a revolutionary socialist by immediately and unequivocally denouncing it as a capitalist plot.

In order to raise the funds necessary to rebuild the Irish Transport and General Workers' Union, Larkin decided to visit America, leaving the union in the hands of his deputy, James *Connolly. He sailed for the United States in late October 1914 and expected to be away for only a short time, but in the event it was nearly nine years before he finally returned to Ireland. While in America, Larkin was by turns a lecturer, a union organizer, a German secret agent, an Irish propagandist, a socialist agitator, a founder of the American Communist Party, and finally a 'martyred' political prisoner who served nearly three years in prison. Two overriding themes, however, gave some coherence and consistency to what otherwise seem disparate activities. The first was his implacable opposition to the First World War, and the second was his enthusiastic acceptance of the Russian revolution in November 1917. Both these stands, especially after the United States entered the war in April 1917, were very unpopular, and when the celebrated 'red scare' followed hard on the heels of the end of the war Larkin was arrested on the charge of criminal anarchy in late 1919. He was then tried, convicted, and sentenced to five to ten years in prison.

Shortly after he was pardoned by Governor Alfred

E. Smith early in 1923 in the interests of free speech Larkin was deported to Ireland. On his return home in May 1923 he found that the successful war against the British had degenerated into a fratricidal civil war, and he immediately called for peace. Within a month of his return, however, a fierce struggle for power broke out in the Transport Union, which soon extended to the Irish labour movement as a whole. The eventual result was that Larkin was suspended as general secretary of the union and finally expelled. He then founded the Workers' Union of Ireland, but was able to carry with him only a remnant of the Transport Union, mainly those members based in Dublin. Larkin's power and influence in the Irish labour movement were also greatly impaired by his open and continued support for Soviet communism. In summer 1924 he visited Moscow to attend the Fifth Congress of the Third International, or Comintern, and was elected to represent Ireland on the twenty-five-member executive council which governed that body between congresses. He was elected a member of the Dáil in 1926, but was unable to take his seat because he was an undischarged bankrupt. He was again elected to the Dáil and served in 1937–8, and 1943–4. After 1928 he began to drift out of the communist orbit, though he never repudiated his earlier affiliations. With the advent of the great depression in 1929 Larkin's power and influence were further impaired on both the trade union and political sides of the labour movement. Though his political fortunes revived slightly in the 1940s, when he managed to secure the dilution of anti-trade union legislation sponsored by De Valera, he remained a marginal figure in Irish politics until he died in Meath Street Hospital, Dublin, on 30 January 1947. He was buried in Glasnevin cemetery on 2 February.

EMMET LARKIN

Sources E. Larkin, *James Larkin, Irish labour leader, 1876–1947* (1989) • A. Mitchell, *Labour in Irish politics, 1890–1930: the Irish labour movement in an age of revolution* (Dublin, 1974) • C. MacCarthy, *Trade unions in Ireland, 1894–1960* (Dublin, 1977) • W. O'Brien, *Forth the banners go* (Dublin, 1977) • J. Gray, *City in revolt: James Larkin and the Belfast dock strike of 1907* (1985) • C. D. Greaves, *The Irish Transport and General Workers' Union: the formative years, 1909–1923* (Dublin, 1982) • M. Milotte, *Communism in modern Ireland: the pursuit of the workers' republic since 1916* (Dublin, 1984) • J. D. Clarkson, *Labour and nationalism in Ireland* (New York, 1925) • *DNB* • H. A. Clegg, A. Fox, and A. F. Thompson, *A history of British trade unions since 1889*, 1 (1964) • b. cert. • *CGPLA Éire* (1947) • private information (2004)
Archives JRL, Labour History Archive and Study Centre, letters and papers • NL Ire., corresp. and papers | NL Ire., William O'Brien papers
Likenesses photograph, 1914, Hult. Arch. [*see illus.*] • J. Cashman, photograph, 1923, repro. in Larkin, *James Larkin*, 270 • O. Kelly, statue, 1979, O'Connell Street, Dublin • M. Carney, sculpture, Hugh Lane Municipal Gallery of Modern Art, Dublin
Wealth at death £16 2s. 6d.: administration, 21 Nov 1947, *CGPLA Éire*

Larkin, Philip Arthur (1922–1985), poet, writer, and librarian, was born at 2 Poultney Road, Radford, Coventry, on 9 August 1922, the only son and younger child of Sydney Larkin (1884–1948), city treasurer of Coventry, who came from Lichfield, and his wife, Eva Emily Day (1886–1977), of Epping. He was educated at King Henry VIII

Philip Arthur Larkin (1922–1985), by Humphrey Ocean, 1984

School, Coventry (1930–40), and went up to St John's College, Oxford, in October 1940 to read English language and literature, taking a first-class degree in 1943. Unlike many of his contemporaries during the Second World War, he took the full-length, unbroken degree course, having been rejected for military service because of his bad eyesight.

Childhood influences and youthful friendships In poems (such as 'Coming' and 'I remember, I remember'), in interviews, and in casual references in his prose, Larkin implies that his childhood was unremarkable, 'a forgotten boredom' (Larkin, *Collected Poems*, 33), and that his upbringing was of no significance: 'Nothing, like something, happens anywhere' (ibid., 82). But there is a good deal of evidence that this was not so. A brief prose memoir, 'Not the Place's Fault', first published in a small Coventry arts magazine in 1959 and uncollected in his lifetime, is a vivid and acutely remembered account of his early days; and a number of his letters, early and late, to King Henry VIII School friends such as J. B. Sutton and Colin Gunner show a sharp recall of such things as the verbal peculiarities of his schoolmasters.

Larkin was powerfully influenced by his father, a man of strong views on many things: literature, politics, religion, women, and efficiency. Sydney Larkin admired much about the recovery of Germany under the Nazi regime, and took his son on two visits to Germany in 1936 and 1937. Philip loathed these experiences, chiefly (as he recalled them) because of the impenetrable language barriers. But he was always loyal to his father's shaping spirit in literature: the family library introduced him to the English classics, and also to more recent authors: Hardy, Butler, Shaw, and—more radically, in the 1930s—to D. H. Lawrence, Aldous Huxley, and Katherine Mansfield.

From childhood Larkin was hampered by a disability which lasted until his early thirties: he was a stammerer. But to some extent he compensated for this by becoming a fluent writer. His first contribution to his school magazine, *The Coventrian*, was published in 1933, when he was eleven. It is an extraordinarily assured, facetious performance for someone so young. Throughout his school years, he made his mark through his wit, and his ability to unite the acceptable and the anarchic.

Oxford gave Larkin greater scope, and brought him new friends. At first he stuck with his King Henry VIII contemporaries, such as James Sutton, who was unexpectedly in Oxford as a student at the Slade School of Fine Art, the Slade having been evacuated from London to the Ashmolean Museum. More importantly, and lastingly, there was his friendship with Kingsley Amis, who arrived at St John's to read English at the beginning of Larkin's third term, in April 1941.

Early publications From the beginning, Larkin and Amis shared tastes, in jazz, films, poetry, fiction, and jokes. They laughed at the pretensions of the leading undergraduate poets of the day (Sidney Keyes, John Heath-Stubbs), at the requirements of the English syllabus, at the dons. They constructed together wild parodies and travesties. Larkin was already beginning to write a series of pastiches of schoolgirl stories, including the Willow Gables fantasy, which became part of his first novel, *Jill*. For four terms, in 1941–2, Larkin and Amis were an almost inseparable team, until Amis was called up into the army. Their friendship continued in letters, of a highly mannered, often scurrilous kind, throughout Amis's military service and afterwards.

Later at Oxford, Larkin became a close friend of another St John's undergraduate, Bruce Montgomery, already beginning to make a reputation (under the pseudonym Edmund Crispin) as a detective-story writer, and also as a musician. It was Montgomery who introduced Larkin to a new kind of intellectual, bohemian, bon-viveur life. Larkin contributed some passages to Montgomery's early Crispin fiction, and one of Montgomery's first novels is dedicated to him.

Larkin had already made a precocious start as a poet, publishing a poem in the BBC's literary weekly, *The Listener*, within a few weeks of his arrival at St John's. At Oxford he contributed to such undergraduate journals as *Cherwell*, and some of his poems were included in the anthologies *Oxford Poetry, 1942–43* and, later, *Poetry from Oxford in Wartime*. But for all his ebullient presence, he was not counted among the most noted university writers.

The poems Larkin had written from the age of sixteen until his final year at Oxford had been marked by a devotion to W. H. Auden. Many of these early Larkin poems are exceptionally precocious; they may be Audenesque pastiches, but they are full of skill and confidence. Then, in the spring of 1943, a visit to the Oxford University English Club by Vernon Watkins supplanted Auden as an influence. Watkins read and talked about W. B. Yeats, and later

Larkin several times recalled the impact of this: 'I spent the next three years trying to write like Yeats' (Larkin, *Required Writing*, 29). It was not a helpful influence, but it was hard to shake off.

Becoming a librarian Having been awarded his first, and at home in his parents' house in Warwick (the Coventry house was badly damaged in the blitz), Larkin unsuccessfully attempted entry to the civil service. Failing in that, he worked away at his novel *Jill*. But in November 1943 a letter arrived from the Ministry of Labour, pointing out that his rejection by the civil service should not preclude his search for other war work. Almost precipitately, he applied for the first job that seemed to present itself: urban district librarian in Wellington, Shropshire. He was given the job ('single-handed and untrained'), and began work in December 1943.

Larkin had had no particular bent for librarianship, and always maintained that his entry to the profession was an accident of wartime circumstances. But, for all the bewildering drudgery of the job (he found he had to stoke the boiler as well as stamp the books, make reports to the district council, clear the reading room of derelicts, for long hours on low pay), he became a popular and influential figure. Most importantly, he formed a close relationship with a sixth-former from a local school, Ruth Bowman.

This friendship grew to become Larkin's first engrossing—and characteristically difficult—love affair. There was the discrepancy of ages: Larkin was twenty-one, Ruth only sixteen. Her family was naturally suspicious. But Ruth was deeply influenced by the literary knowledge which Larkin passed on to her, pressing books in her direction. She was flattered by his attentions. For his part, he was both infatuated and frightened: infatuated because of her devotion, frightened of what it might lead to. It was not until May 1945 that they actually became lovers; for a time they seemed destined to marry.

There was a brief engagement, but Larkin allowed it to evaporate, looking for a way of escape. In September 1946 he left Wellington and became an assistant librarian at what was then the University College of Leicester. His first novel, *Jill*, completed and accepted by the small and suspect Fortune Press, was published in that year. It received no attention; nor had his book of poems, *The North Ship*, published by the same press a year earlier.

Meanwhile, Larkin had completed a second novel, *A Girl in Winter*, which was published by Faber and Faber in 1947. This had several positive notices, and it sold 5000 copies within its year of publication. Larkin, in his university library work at Leicester, was recognized by a few as 'a writer'. Among these was (Margaret) Monica Jones (1922–2001), a young lecturer in the English department, who, without knowing him then at all, had been an Oxford contemporary.

Apart from his parents, and with the exception of the powerful but more marginal Kingsley Amis, Monica Jones was the most consistently important figure in Larkin's life. She was his confidante, frequent and finally sole companion, from the late 1940s until his death. What began rather casually in 1946 continued as an association so close and intimate that it became, in the end, almost a marriage.

Becoming a poet In spite of the small success of *A Girl in Winter*, which could have given him some credibility as a writer, Larkin had at this time by no means established himself as a poet. Indeed, he still felt himself to be a novelist. It was only later, after repeated struggles with two further novels, never completed, that he gradually discovered his true gift. In late 1947 he submitted a typescript collection of poems, *In the Grip of Light*, to the literary agent A. P. Watt, who had placed *A Girl in Winter* with Faber and Faber. This was turned down by several publishers. In March 1948 Sydney Larkin died of cancer. Larkin had the task of trying to settle his widowed mother. Troubled by this, and by his lack of literary success, it seemed to him that his effective life was over.

Already, however, Larkin had begun—at first sporadically—to write the poems which established his reputation: 'Wedding Wind', in 1946, was one of the earliest, and this is one of a handful written during his period in Leicester which, in retrospect, show the growth of his genius. They were, according to Larkin, prompted by his reading of some of Thomas Hardy's poems that year, though 'Wedding Wind' seems to carry something of an earlier admiration of D. H. Lawrence.

Then, after making sure that his mother was settled in Loughborough, in the autumn of 1950 Larkin made a decisive break with his former life, taking up the job of sub-librarian of the Queen's University in Belfast. It was Belfast that saw, as Larkin later acknowledged, his breakthrough as a poet. Within a few months he wrote some of his best and best-known poems. He had little immediate success with them, and fell back on publishing at his own expense 100 copies of a pamphlet, *XX Poems*, set up by a local printer in 1951. But soon he began to publish some of these poems in such periodicals as *The Spectator*, in a Fantasy Press pamphlet (1954), and to have them broadcast on the BBC Third Programme. Word began to spread that a new poet was on the scene. The literary editor of *The Spectator*, J. D. Scott, together with Anthony Hartley, who in the 1950s was poetry editor of the journal, had much to do with this. Scott's anonymous leading article, 'In the Movement', in October 1954, drew attention to what quickly became known as the 'Movement', and Larkin's name began to be associated with such new writers as Kingsley Amis, John Wain, and Iris Murdoch.

By early 1955 Larkin had put together a collection, initially called *Various Poems*. At that moment he was approached by George Hartley, who together with his wife, Jean, had for a year been editing a quarterly magazine of poetry, *Listen*, from a suburb of Hull. Hartley had published some of Larkin's poems in *Listen*, and was keen to launch himself as a book publisher under a new imprint, the Marvell Press, with a really good volume. His choice was Larkin, to whom Hartley wrote in Belfast.

Librarian of Hull Coincidentally, Larkin had already accepted the post of librarian at the university library in Hull. Hartley and Larkin between them drew up a list of possible subscribers to the book, which Larkin eventually entitled *The Less Deceived*. It was published at the end of 1955, by which time Larkin had arrived in Hull, where he was to spend the last thirty years of his life.

Larkin transformed the library, which was small and old-fashioned when he took it over, into one of the best university libraries in Britain: as he put it, he inherited 'a nice little Shetland pony' and made it into 'a frightful Grand National winner' (*TES*, 19 May 1972). *The Less Deceived* made his name as a poet, being picked by *The Times* as one of the books of the year, and rapidly going into several impressions. The *Times Literary Supplement* referred to Larkin as 'a poet of quite exceptional importance'. Some of the poems included quickly became in their various ways exemplars of excellence: 'Church Going', 'Toads', 'Lines on a Young Lady's Photograph Album', 'Deceptions' (a phrase from which became the title of the book), 'At Grass'. They ranged from the easily colloquial and casually humorous to the weightily rhetorical, often within the compass of a single poem.

An established poet The discovery of Larkin as an important poet almost inevitably meant that he was soon sought out as a reader of his own poems, as well as a critic and lecturer. In most cases, however, he resisted all such approaches. Nevertheless, for a time in the late 1950s he reviewed new books of verse for the *Manchester Guardian*, and in 1961 he began a longish period of reviewing jazz records for the *Daily Telegraph*. Jazz had been an important enthusiasm since his teens, and at first he welcomed the opportunity to write about it. But before long he realized, with some pain and some asperity, that his tastes were too narrow to satisfy either himself or a wider (and younger) jazz-loving audience. He did, however, eventually take the initiative in gathering together many of his *Daily Telegraph* pieces, published by Faber and Faber as *All What Jazz* in 1970.

Although Larkin was, between the early 1950s and the early 1970s, less costive a poet than he liked to pretend, he was a severe judge of his own work. After *The Less Deceived*, it was nine years before he published another book of poems: *The Whitsun Weddings* (1964). This too was published by Faber and Faber, the initiative having been taken by Charles Monteith, an editor in the firm. As long ago as 1955, Monteith, noticing 'Church Going' in *The Spectator*, had written to Larkin asking whether he would like to offer a collection to what was the most prestigious publisher of poetry in Britain. But Larkin was by then already committed to the Marvell Press. However, his growing fame, and the friendship which he developed with Monteith during the late 1950s and early 1960s, meant that the offer was taken up, though later rather than sooner.

The Whitsun Weddings set the seal on Larkin's reputation. Following its publication in 1964, a first printing of 4000 was soon exhausted and a reprint was ordered shortly after publication. It was a Poetry Book Society choice, and was given an Arts Council award. Larkin received the queen's gold medal for poetry. The book's title-poem had already become one of the talismanic poems of the period, and the book also contained others which were recognized as brilliant, moving, sharply exact moments of truth: 'A Study of Reading Habits', 'Dockery and Son', 'An Arundel Tomb'. The complexities and simplicities of his language registered a precise sensitivity to life and death, loneliness and communion, desire for the impossible and despair at the unattainable, which was recognized as both memorious and memorable.

Although Larkin was never a ready supplier of material to the many literary editors who now clamoured for his attention as reviewer and critic, he allowed himself throughout the 1960s, 1970s, and almost until his death, to write about other writers to whom he felt allegiance: Thomas Hardy, William Barnes, Christina Rossetti, Wilfred Owen, W. H. Auden, Stevie Smith. His juvenile fascination with D. H. Lawrence and with the Powys brothers, as well as with less obvious writers (Henry de Montherlant, Julian Hall, Barbara Pym), was followed in several reviews and articles. Most conspicuously, he was loyal to the work and example of John Betjeman, with whom he formed a mutual admiration society. They probably enjoyed a sense of detachment, in that they escaped both the new 'swinging' fashions of Carnaby Street and the 1960s, and the new academic taste for continental literary theory.

Ten years after *The Whitsun Weddings* appeared the last book of poems to be published in Larkin's lifetime: *High Windows*. A year earlier, in 1973, Oxford University Press brought out his controversial anthology, *The Oxford Book of Twentieth-Century English Verse*. Larkin had accepted this commission in 1966. Most of his reading for it was done during a period of two terms, 1970–71, when he was given a visiting fellowship at All Souls College, Oxford. Taking leave of absence from the University of Hull, he doggedly read his way through the century's verse in the Bodleian Library, taking photocopies of his material and brooding over it in his rooms in college lodgings in Iffley. When this anthology was eventually published, its critical reception was mixed. Some (such as W. H. Auden, John Betjeman, C. P. Snow) welcomed it as an illuminating collection. Robert Lowell, the leading American poet, saw it as 'a Larkin poem, not the best, but the longest to write' (*Encounter*, May 1973). Others, such as Donald Davie, pronounced it 'a calamity', which excluded some of the best poets of the period. With all this controversy, the anthology sold extremely well, over 175,000 copies during the next quarter-century.

High Windows (1974) followed in its wake. If 'Church Going' was the acclaimed major poem of *The Less Deceived*, and 'The Whitsun Weddings' held the same position in the book of that title, 'The Building' was the centre of attention in *High Windows*. As an authoritative testimony of the ubiquitous power of death, following the same kind of circumstantial, anecdotal, ratiocinative route as the earlier poems in their coming to terms with religion and marriage, 'The Building' made a definitive statement. Other poems in *High Windows*—the title-poem, 'Annus mirabilis', 'This be the Verse'—showed Larkin's crisp, cutting command of the resonantly colloquial, most immediately in its confrontation with sex. The opening line of 'This be the Verse' ('They fuck you up, your mum and dad') has become part of the common currency of contemporary Britain. A few years after its publication Larkin remarked in a letter that 'I fully expect to hear it recited by a thousand Girl Guides before I die' (Larkin, *Selected Letters*, 674).

Later years In the remaining eleven years of his life, Larkin wrote little poetry and published less. His final major published poem was 'Aubade', written, as was so often the case, over a long period, and finally appearing in the *Times Literary Supplement* in 1977. Feeling that his gift as a poet had come to an end, he refused Margaret Thatcher's offer of the poet laureateship after the death of John Betjeman.

But Larkin's literary career had not come to an end. In 1983 he published a gathering of prose pieces (memoirs, interviews, reviews), *Required Writing*, which was received with great enthusiasm, and won the W. H. Smith award in 1984. Indeed, his last years were marked with many honours, including a multitude of honorary doctorates (from Belfast, 1969; Leicester, 1970; Warwick, 1973; St Andrews, 1974; Sussex, 1974; the New University of Ulster, 1983; and Oxford, 1984). He was made a CBE in 1975, received the A. C. Benson silver medal from the Royal Society of Literature that same year, and the Shakespeare-Preis from the FVS Foundation in Hamburg in 1976: his brief visit to Germany to receive this was one of Larkin's very few forays into dreaded 'abroad'.

Beginning in the 1960s, Larkin made available his unusual powers as a committee man: he served at various times on the literature panel of the Arts Council of Great Britain, was active in first setting up and then guiding the Arts Council's National Manuscript Collection of Contemporary Writers in conjunction with the British Museum, was chairman for several years of the Poetry Book Society, and as a widely respected librarian was a prominent member of the Standing Conference of National and University Librarians. Having at an early stage taken his library examinations and become an associate of the Library Association in 1949, he was elected an honorary fellow of that association in 1980. In 1977 he rather surprisingly accepted the offer of being the chairman of judges for the Booker prize for fiction, and delivered a notably graceful and witty speech when the prize went to Paul Scott. His old college at Oxford, St John's, made him an honorary fellow in 1973, and he served on the board of the British Library.

In June 1985 Larkin was made a Companion of Honour. That month he was suddenly taken ill after an operation on his oesophagus, and was in intensive care for some time. He was discharged from hospital a month later, and returned to the house in Hull he had bought in 1974, the first house he had ever owned. Four months later he collapsed and was taken into the Nuffield Hospital, Hull, where he died of cancer in the early hours of 2 December 1985. His funeral was at St Mary the Virgin, Cottingham, just outside Hull, and he was buried close by on 9 December.

The obituaries, articles, radio and television programmes that followed were unprecedented for a late twentieth-century poet. Larkin's memorial service was held in Westminster Abbey on an exceptionally cold St Valentine's day, 14 February 1986. It was attended by many hundreds of admirers who had never known the man but who loved his work. Larkin's literary executors and trustees were faced with a difficult will, drawn up by Larkin in July 1985: some of its clauses were judged 'repugnant' (that is, contradictory) by a queen's counsel acting on behalf of the literary executors. Larkin's voluminous diaries had been destroyed in early December 1985: he had made his wishes clear to Monica Jones as he lay dying. But his other papers remained, including the seven manuscript notebooks of poems drafted between March 1950 and November 1980. (Larkin had presented his first notebook, covering the period October 1944 to March 1950, to the British Library in 1965.) Monica Jones, living with Larkin in Hull at the time of his death, and having been appointed by him as both trustee and literary executor, appointed his two further literary executors to edit and write three books. In 1988 Larkin's *Collected Poems* (edited by Anthony Thwaite) was published. There followed *Selected Letters, 1940–1985*, also edited by Thwaite, in 1992. In 1993 Andrew Motion published his *Philip Larkin: a Writer's Life*. All were widely and sometimes controversially reviewed. Some attacked the books and the editing and writing, some Larkin himself as someone perceived to have an overblown reputation: some attacked both.

Larkin was a very private but also sometimes surprisingly a convivial, witty, entertaining, and genial man. Against his public remarks and phrases in private letters which might suggest a loathing of women, children, foreigners, and several other categories of human being, there has to be set a number of very close friendships with women (including not only those already mentioned but also Winifred Arnott, Patsy Strang, Judy Egerton, Maeve Brennan, and Jean Hartley) and with a significant minority of children, foreigners, and left-wing intellectuals.

Physically, Larkin was tall, strongly built, imposing in his presence, heavily bespectacled, but also gradually burdened with a sense of being prematurely bald, overweight, increasingly deaf, and reminded day by day of what he memorably called 'age, and then the only end of age' (Larkin, *Collected Poems*, 153). But he never lost his love of his favoured type of jazz; or of the game of cricket, his election to the Marylebone Cricket Club being one of his most coveted honours. He was a keen photographer, and many of the images of himself were recorded, singly or with others, with his own delayed-action camera.

ANTHONY THWAITE

Sources A. Motion, *Philip Larkin: a writer's life* (1993) · P. Larkin, *Selected letters, 1940–1985*, ed. A. Thwaite (1992) · P. Larkin, *Collected poems*, ed. A. Thwaite (1988) · A. Thwaite, ed., *Larkin at sixty* (1982) · P. Larkin, 'Not the place's fault', *Umbrella* (1959) · P. Larkin, *Required writing* (1983) · P. Larkin, *All what jazz* (1970) · personal knowledge (2004) · *CGPLA Eng. & Wales* (1986)

Archives BL, notebook number 1 · BL, notebook of draft poems, Add. MS 52619 · Bodl. Oxf., corresp. · Bodl. Oxf., notes and MSS · U. Hull, papers · U. Hull, poems and family MSS · U. Hull, Brynmor Jones L., corresp. and papers, incl. MSS and workbooks; additional papers · U. Hull, Brynmor Jones L., MSS and administrative files |

Bodl. Oxf., letters to Robert Conquest · Bodl. Oxf., letters to Winifred Dawson · Bodl. Oxf., letters to Bruce Montgomery · Bodl. Oxf., letters to Barbara Pym · Hunt. L., letters to Kingsley Amis · NL Wales, letters to Dannie Abse · U. Hull, Brynmor Jones L., letters to Harry Chambers · U. Hull, Brynmor Jones L., corresp. with Colin Gunner · U. Hull, Brynmor Jones L., corresp. with Brenda E. Moon · U. Hull, Brynmor Jones L., letters to Philip Norton-Smith · U. Hull, Brynmor Jones L., letters to James Ballard Sutton · U. Hull, Brynmor Jones L., letters to Ted Tarling · U. Hull, Brynmor Jones L., letters to Anthony Thwaite · U. Leeds, corresp. with *London Magazine* · University of Tulsa, Oklahoma, McFarlin Library, letters to Patricia Avis | FILM U. Hull, Brynmor Jones L. | SOUND U. Hull, Brynmor Jones L., several recordings: Larkin reading, and in interviews **Likenesses** H. Morgan, charcoal drawing, 1979, U. Hull · H. Ocean, oils, 1984, NPG [*see illus.*] · photographs, repro. in Motion, *Philip Larkin* · photographs, repro. in Thwaite, ed., *Larkin at sixty* · photographs, repro. in Thwaite, ed., *Selected letters, 1940–1985* **Wealth at death** £297,787: probate, 14 July 1986, *CGPLA Eng. & Wales*

Larkin, William (*c*.1580–1619), portrait painter, is first recorded on 17 July 1606 when he was awarded the freedom of the City of London by redemption in the Company of Painter–Stainers. Further documentary evidence of his life and work is scanty, but because his will is listed with those in the parish of St Sepulchre, just outside the walls of the City, it has been suggested that his father may have been William Larkin, the host of The Rose inn in that parish. A brother, Richard, and his son, Benjamin, are mentioned in the will.

The fact that Larkin did not obtain his freedom to trade in London in the usual way—by patrimony or after serving an apprenticeship—is unexplained. Freedom by redemption was usually awarded to craftsmen coming from elsewhere, but the evidence of Larkin's painting style points to training in one of the London studios. In any event by 1606 he had certainly attracted patronage at the highest level: his sponsors for freedom of the City were Lady Arabella Stuart, third in line to the throne, and her future father-in-law, Edward Seymour, earl of Hertford.

In 1609 or 1610 Larkin painted the only picture which can as yet be linked to documentary evidence: a portrait of Edward Herbert, first Baron Herbert of Cherbury, which survives with its pair, of Sir Thomas Lucy (1585–1640; Charlecote Park, Warwickshire). According to an anecdote told in Herbert's autobiography, copies of the portrait were made for the queen, for Richard Sackville, the third earl of Dorset, and in miniature by Isaac Oliver, for Lady Aeres (a copy at University College, Oxford, may be one of these). In 1613 Larkin painted the third earl of Dorset and his brother, Sir Edward Sackville, later fourth earl, and shortly afterwards he or his studio was responsible for seven portraits of ladies connected with the Suffolk family. (This series is now in the collection of English Heritage.) The Rutland papers record two payments to Larkin, both of the considerable sum of £30: in 1617 for an unspecified picture, and in 1619 for a portrait of Lady Katherine Manners, who was to marry George Villiers, marquess of Buckingham, in the following year (a portrait of Buckingham in the National Portrait Gallery, London, is attributed to Larkin on stylistic and technical grounds). In the summer of 1618 Lady Anne Clifford sat to Larkin (a

bust-length portrait still at Knole, Kent, may be a copy of the original). Three portraits by Larkin are listed in a seventeenth-century inventory of pictures at Claydon House, Buckinghamshire: Lady Sussex; Frances Howard, countess of Somerset; and Anne Turner, her accomplice in the murder of Sir Thomas Overbury.

Larkin represents the end of the tradition in which a painter was regarded as an anonymous craftsman, like a possible relation, Thomas Larkin, the king's locksmith. His paintings echo the elaborate concoctions of late sixteenth-century European court portraiture, a style soon to be swept away by the tide of the baroque brought to England from Flanders by Rubens and Anthony Van Dyck.

All that is known of Larkin's domestic life derives from the parish registers of St Ann Blackfriars, where between 1612 and 1615 the baptisms and burials of three of his children are recorded, and from his will, in which he mentioned his wife and young daughter, both named Mary. There is no suggestion of worldly success, although the sums paid for his work compared well with those paid to his contemporaries, and his estate is referred to simply as 'goods and chattels and debts'. Larkin died in 1619, between 10 April when he signed his will and 14 May when it was proved.   SHEILA O'CONNELL

Sources will, 1619, GL, commissary court of London, MS 9172/30 · M. Edmond, 'Limners and picturemakers', *Walpole Society*, 47 (1978–80), 60–242 · R. Strong, *The English icon: Elizabethan and Jacobean portraiture* (1969) · S. O'Connell, *William Larkin and the 3rd earl of Dorset: a portrait in focus* (1989) [exhibition catalogue, Ranger's House, London] · R. Strong, *William Larkin: icons of splendour* (Milan, 1995) · S. Cove, 'The materials and techniques of paintings attributed to William Larkin', unpublished report for diploma in conservation, 1985, Courtauld Inst.

Larking, Lambert Blackwell (1797–1868), antiquary, was born at his father's house, Clare House, East Malling, Kent, on 2 February 1797, the eldest son of John Larking, sheriff of Kent in 1808, and Dorothy, daughter of Sir Charles Style, bt, of Wateringbury Place. He was educated at Eton College and at Brasenose College, Oxford, where he graduated BA in 1820, proceeding MA in 1823. While at Oxford he founded the university lodge of freemasons, Lodge Apollo, in 1819. In 1820, after making a grand tour of Europe with a Mr Lowther, Larking was ordained deacon and licensed to the curacy of East Peckham, near Tonbridge, Kent; he became vicar of Ryarsh, near Maidstone, in 1830, and of Burham, near Rochester, in 1837. He was also chaplain to Viscountess Falmouth, of Mereworth Castle. He married, on 20 July 1831, Frances (*d.* 1873), eldest daughter of Sir William Jervis Twysden (*d.* 1834), bt, of Roydon Hall, East Peckham, and his wife, Frances Lynch; the couple had no children. He remained vicar of Ryarsh and Burham until his death.

For many years Larking collaborated with the Revd Thomas Streatfield (1777–1848) of Chart's Edge, Westerham, in the collection and compilation of materials for a new history of the county of Kent. When Streatfield died in 1848 the materials were left in Larking's hands; he felt that it would be possible to do no more than revise and update the *History and Topographical Survey* of the county which had been published by Edward Hasted at the end of the eighteenth century. But although he continued to collect material for the project up until the time of his death, ill health compelled Larking to do little more than devote himself to his clerical duties, and it was not until nearly twenty years after his death that his brother John Wingfield Larking was able to arrange for the publication of part of the work under the editorship of Dr Henry H. Drake. *Hasted's History of Kent: Corrected, Enlarged, and Continued to the Present Time*, part 1, *The Hundred of Blackheath*, appeared in a folio edition in 1886. It was the only part ever published.

A further project very dear to Larking, an edition of *The Domesday Book of Kent*, in facsimile, with transcription, translation, notes, and appendix by him, was completed shortly before his death, when it was in process of being printed. The handsome folio edition which he had planned appeared in 1869.

Larking was a founder member of the Kent Archaeological Society in 1857, and was its honorary secretary until 1860, when he was elected a vice-president, and he contributed many articles to *Archaeologia Cantiana*, the society's transactions. For the Camden Society, of which he was a member of the council for many years, Larking edited three volumes of records, in 1849, 1857, and 1861; the second of these, *The Knights Hospitallers in England … 1338*, was taken from a document shown to him in the public library of Valletta when ill health caused him to pass the winter of 1838–9 in Malta. Larking died on 2 August 1868 at Ryarsh vicarage.   SHIRLEY BURGOYNE BLACK

Sources H. H. Drake, introduction, in *Hasted's history of Kent: corrected, enlarged, and continued to the present time*, ed. H. H. Drake (1886) · C. R. Smith, *Retrospections, social and archaeological*, 3 vols. (1883–91) · T. D. H., *Archaeologia Cantiana*, 7 (1868), 323–9 · Foster, *Alum. Oxon.* · *Clergy List* (1859) · d. cert.
Archives BL, Add. MSS 34147–34178 | U. Edin. L., letters to James Halliwell-Phillipps
Likenesses H. Smith, lithograph, 1857, NPG · engraving, repro. in Drake, ed., *Hasted's history of Kent*, frontispiece
Wealth at death under £6000: probate, 18 Sept 1868, *CGPLA Eng. & Wales*

Larkworthy, Falconer (1833–1928), banker and political economist, was born at Weymouth on 22 March 1833, the elder son of Dr Ambrose Larkworthy (d. 1850), a surgeon resident in Bombay, and Amelia (d. c.1842), daughter of John Cooke, merchant and shipowner, of Calcutta. Educated variously in London and Scotland, he completed his schooling at the Liverpool high school. He married first in 1857 Mary Agnes (1835–1861), daughter of Captain Balston of Cape Town, a sea captain with the East India Company; after she died in 1861 following the birth of their second child, he married in 1863 Elizabeth Anne, daughter of J. W. Clover of Aylsham, Norfolk. Altogether, Larkworthy had three sons and three daughters.

When Larkworthy was sixteen, in preparation for a mercantile career in Bombay his father arranged for him to join the merchant firm of Frith, Wallace & Co., which operated in Burma and India. However, before he could get to India, his father died of cholera. Instead, in 1852

Larkworthy joined the overseas service of the Oriental Bank Corporation and was appointed sub-accountant of a new branch in Mauritius.

Larkworthy was then sent to the bank's Melbourne office, arriving in Australia in early 1855. When the Oriental Bank expanded into Victoria's agricultural and goldmining districts, he became accountant of the first agricultural branch, at Kilmore. Towards the end of 1857 he opened and managed a new branch, to co-ordinate the gold-buying agencies of the Ovens goldfield, Victoria.

In 1860, Larkworthy took up an appointment in Auckland, New Zealand. When the Oriental Bank decided to withdraw in 1861, he threw in his lot with the fledgling Bank of New Zealand (BNZ). He negotiated a good arrangement with BNZ: in return for establishing branches and goldfield agencies in New Zealand's South Island, he would open its London branch, becoming its managing director. Larkworthy left for Dunedin in October 1861. His work for BNZ in South Island was successful, and after six months he duly sailed for England. For nearly thirty years Larkworthy steered BNZ's London branch effectively through some troubled times, including the Overend Gurney crisis. He joined the main board in 1865. Also in 1865, BNZ agreed to his setting up the New Zealand Loan and Mercantile Agency to provide the bank with extra capital.

In the 1880s BNZ encountered difficulties with some of its New Zealand accounts, and in 1888 Larkworthy went out to undertake an inspection. The loan company was in worse trouble than the bank, and Larkworthy recommended an independent inspection. His advice was not taken, and in 1890 he resigned. The loan company went bankrupt in 1893, its directors being held responsible by the judge in the subsequent court case. Larkworthy, however, was publicly vindicated by the judge, and by the financial press.

Thereafter, Larkworthy devoted himself to the affairs of the Commercial Union Assurance Company, on whose board he had sat since its inception in 1863. In 1898, however, he joined the court of the Ionian Bank, and from 1900 until 1920 he was its chairman. Larkworthy conceived a great affection for this small bank, which was British-owned, and an important source of British commercial influence in the eastern Mediterranean. He also exercised a beneficial influence on its fortunes: its balance sheet increased from just over £1 million in 1898 to nearly £12 million in 1919.

While Larkworthy was chairman of Ionian, his annual speeches to the shareholders were highly regarded in financial circles. They focused increasingly on currency reform. He became a strong advocate of a new international currency and exchange system, not necessarily dependent on gold. He was impressed both with the American federal reserve board procedure and the exchange fund system set up by Greece in 1910, which stabilized its exchanges. In 1924, aged ninety-one, he gave evidence before the committee on currency and foreign exchanges.

Larkworthy firmly believed that money was made for

man, not man for money. He was an evangelical Christian, who saw no conflict in reconciling a life in banking with his Christian beliefs. The greatest sin, in his view, was the hoarding of wealth; it had instead to be circulated and made to work. A founder member of the Institute of Bankers, in 1903 Larkworthy was made commander of the Royal Greek Order of the Saviour. He was the author of numerous papers on currency and exchange, as well as a volume of reminiscences. Larkworthy died, aged ninety-five, on 14 May 1928 at his home, 35 Belsize Avenue, Hampstead, London.   FRANCES BOSTOCK

Sources *91 years: being the reminiscences of Falconer Larkworthy*, ed. H. Begbie (1924) · F. Larkworthy, *Occupy till I come: a sequel to 'Ninety-one years'* (privately printed, Southampton, 1925) · *Ionian Bank Limited: a history*, Ionian Bank, Ltd. (1953) · BLPES, Ionian Bank MSS · *WWW* · d. cert.

Archives BLPES, Ionian Bank archive

Likenesses photograph, repro. in Begbie, ed., *91 years*, frontispiece

Wealth at death £6116 12s. 1d.: probate, 29 June 1928

Larminie, William (1849–1900), poet and folklorist, was born on 1 August 1849 at Castlebar, co. Mayo, the fourth child and second surviving son of William Larminie (1796–1856) and his wife, Bridget (Beda; 1812–1903), third daughter of Colonel John Jackson of Ballina, co. Mayo. The Larminies were a family of Huguenot descent, settled in co. Mayo since 1721. On his father's death Larminie's maternal uncle, the Revd William Jackson, later archdeacon of Killala, helped the family to move to Wicklow and provided his nephews with a tutor. Larminie later attended Kingstown School and Trinity College, Dublin, from which he graduated in 1871 with a moderatorship in classics.

Larminie joined the India Office in 1873 as a junior clerk in the store department, and his mother moved to England, keeping house for him in Anerley, Upper Norwood. However, Larminie, who had been writing poetry since adolescence, decided to retire from the civil service in 1887, and devote himself to folklore collecting and to literature. His mother, described by William Kirkpatrick Magee (John Eglinton) as 'brilliant and picturesque' and by Douglas Hyde as 'a terrible old woman' (Eglinton, 14), was angered by this decision, for which she never forgave him; however, she returned with her son to Bray, co. Wicklow, where they lived in some comfort at 2 Prince of Wales Terrace, despite Larminie's not having qualified for a pension. Larminie, who had learned Irish, had begun to collect oral folk tales in the west of Ireland in 1884 with the help of a friend, James Lecky. Larminie translated and edited a selection, *West Irish Folk-Tales and Romances*, in 1893; he had already allowed Douglas Hyde to use two of his orally collected tales in *Leabhar sgeulaighteachta* (1889). W. B. Yeats reviewed Larminie's collection very favourably, describing it as having 'the extravagance and tumultuous movement as of waves in a storm' (Yeats, *Uncollected Prose*, 1.328), and one of Larminie's folk tales also provided the source for part of Yeats's poem 'The Secret Rose' (1896). Hyde, who greatly admired Larminie's pioneering work and his respect for the specificity of the oral folk

tale, described him as 'the most under-rated man in Ireland' (Eglinton, 13).

In 1889 Larminie published his first collection of poetry, *Glanlua and other Poems*, a volume which, like Yeats's *The Wanderings of Oisin and Other Poems* (1889), sought to continue the tradition of Sir Samuel Ferguson's *Congal* (1872) and to realize Irish mythological subjects in English verse. In 1892 a second volume, *Fand and other Poems*, also containing much verse based on Irish mythological and legendary material, followed. Larminie also attempted to introduce prosodic forms (such as assonance) from Irish poetry into English poetry, without conspicuous success, despite the concern with prosody demonstrated in his essay 'The development of English metre' (1894).

From the mid-1890s onwards, Larminie's principal concern was with his projected translation of John Scottus Eriugena's *De divisione naturae*. In 1897 he published an article on Eriugena, 'our Irish Plato', claiming him as the forerunner of German idealist philosophy—and therefore modern philosophy (W. Larminie, 'Joannes Scotus Erigena', *Contemporary Review*, April 1897, 558). In December 1897 he began to publish his translation of Eriugena in *The Internationalist*, the journal of the Dublin Theosophical Society, of which he was a member. By 1898 he was well enough known to be recommended by Yeats to T. P. Gill as a potential contributor to the Dublin *Daily Express* in its brief nationalist phase. Yeats, who thought Larminie a 'bad but wildly eccentric poet', had been very impressed by Larminie's two articles on Norse and Irish mythology, published in the *Contemporary Review* in October and November 1895, which Yeats thought showed Larminie to be 'a profound Celtic folk lorist' and 'more philosophical than Hyde' (*Collected Letters of W. B. Yeats*, 2.307, 268). Larminie did write for the *Express* during the orchestrated cultural nationalist controversy of autumn 1898 and his contribution was reprinted by George Russell in *Literary Ideals in Ireland* (1899) as 'Legends as materials for literature'.

William Kirkpatrick Magee (John Eglinton), a fellow theosophist, who was probably Larminie's closest friend, described him as 'a tall handsome man, something of the Parnell type', and reported Beda Larminie's pride in her son's good looks (Eglinton, 12). John Eglinton, who spent most Sundays walking with Larminie in the Wicklow hills, feared that his return to Ireland (or rather to Bray) had been unwise and that the initial excitement and sense of released creativity, on his return to 'the enchanted strand' ('The Finding of Hy Brasil', *Glanlua*, 72), had diminished; however, John Eglinton, who confessed to having never read his friend's verse, was vehemently opposed to the use of Irish mythological materials in modern writing. He recalled Larminie as:

> a somewhat forlorn figure in Bray, where I have heard him characterized briefly as a 'queer fish': he was in fact a fairly normal, thoughtful, utterly unpretentious human being … the 'return of the native' was in his case as complete a failure as in Hardy's novel, and shortly before his last illness he confessed to me that time hung very heavily with him. (Eglinton, 15)

Larminie was coming into closer contact with the leading figures of the Irish literary revival at the close of his life and was a vice-president of the National Literary Society of Ireland from 1896 to 1899. He died of pneumonia following influenza at his home, 2 Prince of Wales Terrace, in Bray, co. Wicklow, on 19 January 1900, and was buried in Enniskerry churchyard, there being no protestant cemetery at Bray. He had retained the respect of contemporaries such as George Russell and Yeats. Russell wrote a eulogistic account of his verse for Brooke and Rolleston's *A Treasury of Irish Poetry in the English Tongue* (1900) expressing his bewilderment that Larminie's 'many and great gifts as an imaginative poet, should have been so coldly received' (p. 476). Yeats, in 1919, arranged for his wife to inspect the manuscript of Larminie's translation of Eriugena deposited in the National Library of Ireland, a manuscript which John O'Meara called 'a pathetic testimony to his great interest and our indifference' (O'Meara, 90). DEIRDRE TOOMEY

Sources A. Larminie, family history (typescript), before 1978 · J. J. O'Meara, 'William Larminie, 1849–1900', *Studies* (March 1947), 90–96 · J. Eglinton [W. K. Magee], 'William Larminie', *Dublin Magazine* (April–June 1944), 12–16 · *The collected letters of W. B. Yeats*, 2, ed. W. Gould, J. Kelly, and D. Toomey (1997) · W. B. Yeats, *Uncollected prose*, ed. J. P. Frayne, 2 vols. (1970–75), vol. 1 · W. Larminie, three letters to Douglas Hyde, 1888, NL Ire., MS 17, 293
Archives NL Ire., letters to Douglas Hyde
Likenesses photograph, University College, Dublin, department of Irish folklore

Larmor [Larmour], **Sir** (**John**) **Graham** (1897–1968), linen industrialist, was born on 19 March 1897 at Fairacre, Derriaghy, near Lisburn, co. Antrim, the second of five children of John Sloan Larmor (1845–1917), linen merchant, of Magheragall near Lisburn, and his wife, Harriett A. E. Glover, formerly of co. Donegal. Larmor was educated at Campbell College, Belfast, then entered the Ulster Weaving Company, the family firm founded in 1898 by his father, in partnership with John Hogg, at 47 Linfield Road, Belfast. Following his father's death from peritonitis, Graham Larmor became company chairman at the early age of twenty.

On 14 February 1924 Larmor married (Annie) Gladys Lee (d. 1960), daughter of the late George Maughan of Newcastle upon Tyne. The couple lived at Dalboyne House, Belsize Road, Lisburn, where they raised two sons and a daughter, before moving in the 1930s to Ardnabannon House, Annsborough, near Castlewellan, co. Down, their home for some thirty years, until Gladys died.

In 1924 Larmor began to diversify the company and expanded from weaving production to establish mercantile premises at Cheapside in London. Six years later the company's trading interests in America were reinforced by the opening of mercantile offices in New York which were managed by his youngest brother, Will Larmor. During the 1930s he continued to expand the company, buying the firm of James Murland Ltd, flax spinners and linen manufacturers, of Annsborough. The success of these business ventures contrasted with the depressed trading position and subsequent closure of many firms in the linen industry during the 1930s. At the outbreak of the

Second World War the Ulster Weaving Company was in a highly profitable state. At this time Larmor also took over control of Killyleagh Flax Spinning Company Ltd, and Hurst Flax Spinning Mills in Drumaness, both in co. Down, and acquired a one-third share in John Hogg & Co. Ltd, flax merchants, and a one-third share in Richardson Brothers and Larmor, yarn merchants. These business achievements indicate Larmor's advocacy of, and commitment to, the modern concept of vertical integration at a time when most of the industry consisted of small specialized firms. By 1945 he had transformed the Ulster Weaving Company from a solely weaving company into an integrated group of linen-based firms. This position was reinforced with the acquisition in the 1950s of the Old Bleach Linen Company Ltd, Randalstown, co. Antrim.

Between 1939 and 1946 Larmor was appointed agent for the Ministry of Supply and government purchase departments for Northern Ireland in providing textile equipment to the services. During the Second World War he worked tirelessly, living in a specially built apartment at his Linfield Mill premises in Belfast during the week, and returning to Ardnabannon only at weekends. Larmor was knighted in 1948 for his contribution to the war effort. After the war Sir Graham sat on numerous government and civil committees including the Northern Ireland Housing Trust (1945–57); the Northern Ireland advisory committee for civil aviation (1949–58); the Robson departmental committee on coal distribution costs (1956); the Northern Ireland advisory committee on textile education (1957–63); the Export Council for Europe (1961); and the Industrial Coal Consumers' Council (1962). He was president of the Northern Ireland board of the Institute of Directors in 1961. He was noted for his drive and determination in the promotion of good relations between Northern Ireland and the Republic of Ireland at a time when neither Stormont nor the Irish government had begun to consider co-operation appropriate. He was president of the Irish Association for Cultural, Economic, and Social Relations (1954–63).

Sir Graham was one of the leading spokesmen for the Northern Ireland linen industry during the post-war period, as a member of the Central Council of the Irish Linen Industry (1946–68), and held the positions of vice-chairman in 1956 and chairman in 1966. He was also president of the Belfast chamber of commerce in 1957. Because of his commercial acumen and forthright manner, Sir Graham was invited on occasion to act as economic adviser to the Northern Ireland government. However, he caused a sensation on the eve of the 1962 general election by publicly supporting an independent unionist, and attacking the economic policies of Lord Brookeborough's government for their lack of vision. Sir Graham Larmor was a man of strong conviction and self-discipline, who expected similar high standards of his employees and associates. He was proud of the Huguenot origins of his family, who settled in Ireland during the late seventeenth century.

Sir Graham remarried in 1964, his first wife having died

at home in Annsborough on 11 September 1960. His second wife was Barbara, daughter of Major H. Dixon of Keighley, West Riding of Yorkshire. The couple moved to 723a Antrim Road, Belfast. On 13 October 1968 Larmor died at the Royal Victoria Hospital, Belfast, following a fall. His funeral took place on 15 October 1968 at Roselawn cemetery, Belfast.
BRENDA COLLINS

Sources *Belfast News-Letter* (14 Oct 1968) · *Belfast News-Letter* (18 Feb 1924) · *Belfast News-Letter* (15 Oct 1968) · *Belfast News-Letter* (13 Sept 1960) · *Mourne Observer* (18 Oct 1968) · *WWW* · *Belfast Chamber of Commerce Yearbook* (1957–8)
Archives PRO NIre., Advisory Committee on Civil Aviation for Northern Ireland
Wealth at death £27,821 15s. 0d.: probate, 31 March 1969, *CGPLA Éire*

Larmor, Sir Joseph (1857–1942), theoretical physicist, was born at Magheragall, co. Antrim, on 11 July 1857. He was the eldest of the seven children of Hugh Larmor and his wife, Anna, elder daughter of Joseph Wright of Stoneyford, co. Antrim.

Education and early career In 1863 or 1864 Hugh Larmor gave up farming to become a grocer in Belfast. Larmor attended first a national school in Eglinton Street, and then the Royal Belfast Academical Institution, being described at the time as a 'thin and delicate black-haired boy of most precocious ability both in mathematics and classics' (Eddington, 197). He proceeded in 1871 or 1872 with a scholarship to Queen's College, Belfast, graduating BA and then MA. In 1876, a year later than planned due to a severe illness, he entered St John's College, Cambridge, reading for the mathematics tripos.

At Cambridge, Larmor was coached by Edward Routh in the methods of analytical dynamics which were central to the tripos teaching of the time. Analytical dynamics was a mathematical method of solving physical problems by applying Lagrange's equations and Hamilton's principle of least action. It could co-ordinate phenomena and allow predictions to be made about the existence of other effects without any knowledge of the underlying mechanism. Maxwell's electrodynamics exemplified the method, and, by the early 1880s, were becoming a focal point for the research of the most able mathematics graduates. Larmor remained deeply committed to analytical dynamics throughout his life, the principle of least action being, for him, 'the ultimate natural principle—the mainspring of the universe. ... Before he would admit to understanding [a theory] ... Larmor required it to be put in the form of an action principle' (Eddington, 204).

In 1880 Larmor graduated as senior wrangler (J. J. Thomson was second), first Smith's prizeman, and was elected a fellow of St John's. In the same year he was appointed professor of natural philosophy in Queen's College, Galway. Despite being cut off from the Cambridge research community Larmor continued to study Maxwell's *Treatise on Electricity and Magnetism*, which prompted his first major piece of research, a theoretical study, 'Electromagnetic induction in conducting sheets and solid bodies' (*Philosophical Magazine*, January 1884). This work exemplified the type of mixed mathematics which Larmor was to use

Sir Joseph Larmor (1857–1942), by Frank McKelvey, 1940

all his life; in an appendix to the same article he stressed that he had reduced 'the mathematical analysis to as narrow limits as possible, replacing it by a discussion of the physical phenomena' (*Philosophical Magazine*, April 1884), and he was always looking for general principles underlying phenomena, being impatient of attending to the mathematical details. This paper was rapidly followed by 'Least action as the fundamental formulation in dynamics and physics' (*Proceedings of the London Mathematical Society*, 15, 1884, 158–84).

Seeking to return to Cambridge, Larmor applied unsuccessfully for the Cavendish professorship of experimental physics in 1884. J. J. Thomson was elected, but in 1885 Larmor was appointed to succeed him in one of five recently created university lectureships in mathematics. He lived at St John's College for the rest of his working life, succeeding G. G. Stokes as Lucasian professor of mathematics in 1903.

The ether and matter In Cambridge, Larmor's research was at first devoted mainly to traditional problems in dynamics and analytical geometry. About 1890, though, his interest in Maxwellian electrodynamics was stimulated by preparing a review article on magneto-optic rotation and recent theories of light propagation. The extremely comprehensive article eventually appeared in 1893 as a British Association report, 'The action of magnetism on light: with a critical correlation of the various theories of light propagation', and it led directly to the work for which Larmor was best known, the development of the idea of electrons as the electromagnetic basis of matter. His ideas marked a fundamental break with the nineteenth-century attempts to devise a mechanical, continuous, and essentially material ether which underlay all physical phenomena, including electromagnetism. Larmor argued instead for an electromagnetic ether, discrete strain centres (called electrons) in which formed matter.

While preparing his British Association report Larmor became aware of George FitzGerald's re-analysis of James MacCullagh's rotationally elastic ether. Larmor identified himself strongly both with the school of mathematical physics at Trinity College, Dublin, to which FitzGerald and MacCullagh belonged, and with the method of least action by which FitzGerald showed that MacCullagh's mechanical ether was formally equivalent to Maxwell's electromagnetic field. Larmor became convinced that if he could ascribe the correct properties to MacCullagh's ether, then it could provide a dynamical foundation for both electromagnetism and the propagation of light.

Larmor's work, 'A dynamical theory of the electric and luminiferous medium', appeared in three parts between 1894 and 1897 in the *Proceedings of the Royal Society*. Between the three parts, and even within some parts, his theory changed considerably. FitzGerald, who refereed the first part, criticized it heavily and was largely responsible for urging Larmor to solve some of the problems by introducing 'discrete electric nuclei' into his theory. For these Larmor adopted the name 'electrons', a term already proposed by FitzGerald's uncle George Johnstone Stoney for the discrete quantities of electric charge found on the ions in electrolysis.

'Electrons' were introduced in an appendix to part 1 of *A Dynamical Theory* and profoundly affected Larmor's understanding of the relationship between the electromagnetic ether and matter. Previously these had been distinct substances and no one had succeeded in explaining how they interacted. Now if, as he supposed, matter was composed purely of positive and negative electrons, and electromagnetic effects were due to the motion of electrons, then the whole of physics would be unified into a problem of the electrodynamics of moving bodies (Larmor, *Dynamical Theory*, pt 3, 1897).

Like Lorentz, whose *Versuch* he had read in early 1895, Larmor initially thought of his electrons as about as massive as the hydrogen ion. But the discovery by Zeeman, Lorentz's student, in 1896, of the broadening of spectral lines in a magnetic field, and work by J. J. Thomson, Emil Wiechert, and Walter Kaufmann on cathode rays in 1897, both provided important experimental support for the electron idea and indicated that electrons were only about a thousandth of the size of a hydrogen ion. In analysing and explaining the Zeeman effect Larmor arrived at the three results which now bear his name: the Larmor precession, which describes the precession of electron orbits in a magnetic field (at a frequency known as the Larmor frequency, which has become important in understanding nuclear magnetic resonance); the Larmor theorem, which allows the effect of the magnetic field to be neglected to a first order approximation by transforming into a suitably rotating frame of reference; and Larmor's formula for the power radiated by an accelerating electron ('On the theory of the magnetic influence on spectra: and on the radiation from moving ions', *Philosophical Magazine*, December 1897).

The electronic theory of matter also enabled Larmor to predict the apparent absence of motion of the earth through the ether as shown by Michelson and Morley's experiment of 1887. To British Maxwellians, Larmor and FitzGerald included, who liked to think of the ether as stationary, the Michelson–Morley negative result was puzzling. In 1889 FitzGerald had suggested speculatively that it could be explained if moving matter contracted slightly in the direction of its motion through the ether. Larmor now, in 1897, showed that electron theory predicted this effect; rather than being an anomaly to be explained away, the Michelson–Morley experiment became central evidence for the validity of his theory.

In analysing the Michelson–Morley effect Larmor confronted the problem of correlating the electromagnetic fields measured by an earthbound observer, with the fields that would be measured by an observer who was stationary in the ether. By 1900 he had arrived at the space–time transformations which were later given by Lorentz and Einstein, and are now known as the Lorentz transformations. Larmor was the first physicist to state these, in his influential book *Aether and Matter* (1900), the published version of the essay with which he won the Adams prize in 1899.

Larmor's work paralleled in many ways that of Lorentz on the continent, and his electronic theory of matter bore many similarities to the electromagnetic theory of nature developed from Lorentz's work. But there were fundamental differences between the two views, the most important of which was that Larmor (unlike Lorentz and, later, Einstein) believed that the equations of electromagnetism were not fundamental but were a manifestation of the dynamical properties of an underlying ether. In practice, though, he did not investigate these ethereal properties, but worked simply with the electromagnetic equations. And his sophisticated techniques, presented in *Aether and Matter*, allowed Larmor's students to work with Lorentz's model, as developed by Einstein, without abandoning ether physics. Indeed, Ebenezer Cunningham, who is widely credited with introducing relativity theory to Britain, initially adopted Einstein's 1905 relativity theory merely as an adjunct to Larmor's work. It was not until about 1912 that the fundamental incompatibility between relativistic physics and the electronic theory of matter was widely recognized.

Other scientific work Only about half the works collected in Larmor's *Mathematical and Physical Papers* (2 vols., 1929) are about electromagnetism. The rest are 'mainly General Dynamics and Thermodynamics including the dynamical history of the Earth, Formal Optics, and Geometry' (J. Larmor, *Mathematical and Physical Papers*, 1929, 1.v). His interest in the dynamics of the earth's motion dated from 1896 when he published 'On the period of the earth's free Eulerian precession' (*Proceedings of the Cambridge Philosophical Society*, 9, 1896, 183–93), which was followed by four papers over the next twenty years. In 1906 and 1915, with E. H. Hills, he introduced a new kind of analysis of the irregular motion of the earth's rotation (*Monthly Notices of the Royal Astronomical Society*, 67, 1906, 22–34; 75, 1915, 518–21). Other papers investigated isostasy and, elsewhere, the sun's magnetism.

Larmor had first considered the effects upon the earth of a conducting layer in the upper atmosphere in his paper 'Electromagnetic induction in conducting sheets and solid bodies' (1884), where he showed how such a layer could screen the earth from external magnetic fields. He returned to the topic of the ionosphere in 1924, his interest stimulated by the experiments of Edward Appleton, another fellow of St John's. Since 1901, when Marconi had demonstrated that radio signals could be transmitted around the earth from Cornwall to Newfoundland, the mechanism guiding the radio waves had been a subject of debate. In 1902 Heaviside and Kennelly both suggested that a conducting layer in the upper atmosphere reflected the waves. After the First World War, Appleton began investigating the existence, nature, and height of this Heaviside layer, as it became called, by examining the fading of radio signals between London and Cambridge. Larmor became interested in the mechanism by which the radio waves were reflected or refracted by this layer: should one consider the ionized air as a conductor or as a dielectric? The central problem was that the layer had to bend the waves considerably without absorbing them at the same time. Assuming that the waves were refracted Larmor concluded that the lack of absorption was possible only if the air pressure was very low and the conductivity of the ionosphere was very small, so that it behaved like a feebly conducting dielectric. He published his results in 'Why wireless electric rays can bend round the earth' (*Philosophical Magazine*, 48, 1924, 1025–36). Larmor's results suggested to Appleton that the effective electrical particles in the Heaviside layer were free electrons rather than molecular ions, a conclusion that he was later able to verify.

Deeply interested in the history of thermodynamics Larmor was concerned to 'disentangle the romantic history of the evolution of foundations in that domain, with the mainly statistical outlook which its generality imposes' (Larmor, *Collected Papers*, 1929, 2.v). His obituary notice of Lord Kelvin for the *Proceedings of the Royal Society* (1908) contains an extensive survey of the developments of thermodynamics. He also contributed an obituary of Josiah Willard Gibbs to the same journal (1905), revised Maxwell's edition of the papers of Henry Cavendish (1921), and edited the collected works of James Thomson (1912), the fourth and fifth volumes (1904–5) of the works of G. G. Stokes, and the fourth, fifth, and sixth volumes (1910–11) of those of Lord Kelvin.

Public life A quiet and reserved man, Larmor nevertheless took on more than his full share of public duties. Some insight into his character and conception of public service can be gained from his comments on Henry Cavendish, who, Larmor judged, had been unfairly judged misanthropic:

> The tracking out of great discoveries which will be a possession to the human race for all time has indeed to be its

own supreme intellectual satisfaction; and once an investigator has realized, in however modest a way, his capacity for such achievement, he can feel that he is serving humanity in the most perfect manner open to him by concentrating upon that work. Yet the temptation to continual postponement of ordinary social intercourse inevitably involves increasing isolation, and growing habits of solitude … in the cooperative tasks which united the scientific men of the time … he was always ready to take unsparing pains, and to devote himself without limit to the assistance of his colleagues. (Larmor, preface to *The Scientific Papers of the Honourable Henry Cavendish*, 2 vols., 1921, 1.ix–x)

These comments might apply, in lesser measure, to Larmor himself. Larmor had few friends, but being kindly by nature 'while he lived, and they lived, he lost none' (Thompson, 13).

Elected a member of the London Mathematical Society in 1884 Larmor served on its council from 1887 to 1912, being at various times vice-president (1890–91), treasurer (1892–1912), and president (1914). In 1914 he received the De Morgan medal of the society.

Larmor was elected a fellow of the Royal Society in 1892, became a member of the associated Philosophers' Club, a dining club which existed to discuss new ways of promoting the society's scientific aims and improving its methods and organization, and in 1901 became physical secretary, a responsible and influential position which he held until 1912. In this position he was knighted, in 1909, and later received the society's royal medal (1915) and Copley medal (1921).

Possibly prompted by concern for the Irish question, Larmor entered parliament as a Unionist, being MP for Cambridge University from 1911 to 1922.

> One of his characteristic reminiscences was the defeat of the alternative vote, which he claimed to have secured by a long speech, leading the bewildered House deeper and deeper into mathematics until the whip gave him the signal that the wanted absentees had arrived. (Eddington, 206)

Larmor was for many years a member of the council of St John's College. Here he was often critical and conservative, ensuring that important points were not overlooked, and questioning modern trends. But at a more informal level Appleton recalls that he was 'friendly, considerate and generous in the attention he gave to [his younger colleagues]' (Appleton, 66). D'Arcy Thompson alleges that he was disappointed not to have been elected master of his college. His continuing commitment to Cambridge and St John's was shown by bequests which he made for medical help for junior members of the university, to the University and College Servants' Association and for prizes to be awarded annually to men of St John's College who were adjudged the most outstanding on general, rather than purely academic, grounds.

In 1932, about the time that he began suffering from pernicious anaemia, of which he eventually died, Larmor retired from Cambridge. He returned to Ireland, living at Drumadillar, Demesne Road, Holywood, co. Down, near Belfast, with four of his brothers and sisters, including his brother Alexander, who had followed Larmor to Cambridge and had subsequently become professor of natural philosophy at Magee University College, Londonderry. From there Larmor followed with interest general advances in geophysics and astrophysics, often contributed letters to *Nature* and *The Observatory* on the physical problems that they raised, and pursued metaphysics. His brothers' and sisters' deaths left him isolated, for nearly a year before he himself died at Holywood on 19 May 1942.

ISOBEL FALCONER

Sources A. S. Eddington, *Obits. FRS*, 4 (1942–4), 197–207 · *DNB* · W. B. Morton, 'Joseph Larmor', *Proceedings of the Belfast Natural History and Philosophical Society*, 2 (1942–3), 82–90 · D. W. Thompson, 'Joseph Larmor', *Year Book of the Royal Society of Edinburgh* (1941–2), 11–13 · J. Z. Buchwald, *From Maxwell to microphysics: aspects of electromagnetic theory in the last quarter of the nineteenth century* (1985) · B. J. Hunt, *The Maxwellians* (1991) · A. Warwick, 'Frequency, theorem, and formula: remembering Joseph Larmor in electromagnetic theory', *Notes and Records of the Royal Society*, 47 (1993), 49–60 · A. Warwick, 'On the role of the FitzGerald–Lorentz contraction hypothesis in the development of Joseph Larmor's electronic theory of matter', *Archive for History of Exact Sciences*, 43 (1991–2), 29–91 · A. Warwick, 'Cambridge mathematics and Cavendish physics: Cunningham, Campbell and Einstein's relativity, 1905–1911, part 1', *Studies in History and Philosophy of Science*, 23 (1992), 625–56 · E. Appleton, 'Sir Joseph Larmor and the ionosphere', *Proceedings of the Royal Irish Academy*, 61A (1960–61), 55–66 · Venn, *Alum. Cant.* · *The Times* (14 Oct 1936) · *CGPLA NIre.* (1942) · *WWW*, 1929–40

Archives RS, Larmor correspondence · St John Cam., MSS | CUL, Stokes collection, papers and correspondence · CUL, Kelvin collection, correspondence · CUL, Rutherford collection, correspondence · UCL, Lodge MSS, correspondence

Likenesses photograph, 1912, repro. in Hunt, *Maxwellians*, 211 · F. McKelvey, portrait, 1940, Queen's University, Belfast [*see illus.*] · W. Stoneman, photograph, NPG · photograph, repro. in Eddington, *Obits. FRS*, facing p. 197 · photograph, repro. in Morton, 'Joseph Larmor', facing p. 82

Wealth at death £9901 8s. 5d.: probate, 9 Nov 1942, *CGPLA NIre.*

Larmour, John (c.1764–1807), naval officer, almost certainly had a relatively humble upbringing and background before entering the navy as an ordinary seaman; no details are known of his parentage or upbringing. Larmour (nicknamed Jack) had a life and career that would have remained obscure had it not been for his influence on another younger officer, Thomas Cochrane (later tenth earl of Dundonald), whom he encountered in 1793. For Cochrane, Larmour was

> one of a not very numerous class, whom, for their superior seamanship, the Admiralty was glad to promote from the forecastle to the quarter-deck, in order that they might mould into shape the questionable materials supplied by a parliamentary influence. (Dundonald, 11)

Promoted to the rank of lieutenant in June 1784, Larmour possessed abilities that were sufficiently recognized for the Admiralty to employ him during the peace which followed the American War of Independence. In 1787 he was serving as fifth lieutenant of the new ship *Colossus* (74 guns) and by 1791 he was first lieutenant of the frigate *Hind* commanded by the Hon. Sir Alexander Cochrane. In June 1793, while the *Hind* was refitting at Sheerness, Alexander Cochrane sent his nephew Thomas on the vessel as a midshipman, where he came under Larmour's care and instruction. Cochrane was highly impressed to find Larmour dressed in the garb of an ordinary seaman complete

with marlinspike round his neck and lump of grease in his hand for treating the rigging. Contrary to the usual behaviour of the commissioned officer Larmour's 'only ideas of relaxation were to throw off the lieutenant and resume the functions of the able seaman' (Dundonald, 13). Thus Larmour provided a role model which Cochrane was himself to emulate successfully in later years.

At the end of 1793 Larmour followed Alexander Cochrane to the frigate *Thetis* serving on the Nova Scotia station; here he remained until July 1795, when he was promoted to the rank of commander. Although he probably remained unemployed on half pay for a short while, by 1797 he was commanding the *Lord Hood* (14 guns), a vessel hired by the Admiralty. Stationed in the North Sea he recaptured the *Phoenix* brig and successfully claimed salvage on a further brig, the *John & Amy*. Having been promoted post captain on 16 April 1800, Larmour commanded successively the *Wassanaer* (64 guns) and the frigate *Diadem*, both with reduced armament. His contact with the Hon. Sir Alexander Cochrane was renewed in March 1801, when Larmour was selected to assist Cochrane with the landing of Sir Ralph Abercromby's troops in Abu Qir Bay during the campaign to drive Napoleon's army out of Egypt. Following the success of this operation he was appointed to the frigate *Endymion* and then, in mid-1802, the frigate *Clyde* stationed in the North Sea. By May 1803 Larmour was commanding a small squadron responsible for the blockade of the Elbe. Towards the end of 1805 he briefly commanded the *Temeraire* and the *Audacious* before being appointed to another frigate, the *Emerald*. On 16 January 1807 he died suddenly of 'the Dropsy' while in London; he may have been buried at Lambeth, London. His obituary notice described him as 'An excellent officer, who rose, by fortunate merit alone, from the humblest situation in a ship' (*Naval Chronicle*, 17, 176).

TOM WAREHAM

Sources *Naval Chronicle*, 17 (1807), 176 · D. Syrett and R. L. DiNardo, *The commissioned sea officers of the Royal Navy, 1660–1815*, rev. edn, Occasional Publications of the Navy RS, 1 (1994) · Thomas, tenth earl of Dundonald [T. Cochrane], *The autobiography of a seaman*, ed. Douglas, twelfth earl of Dundonald [D. M. B. H. Cochrane], new edn (1890) · W. James, *The naval history of Great Britain, from the declaration of war by France in 1793 to the accession of George IV*, [8th edn], 6 vols. (1902) · D. Steel, *Steel's prize pay lists* (1802) · admiralty list books, PRO, ADM/8 series · *The Keith papers*, ed. C. Lloyd and W. G. Perrin, 3 vols., Navy RS, 62, 90, 96 (1927–55) · M. Lewis, *A social history of the navy, 1793–1815* (1960)

Larnach, Donald (1817–1896), banker and financier, was born on 17 July 1817 at Caithness, Scotland, one of at least two sons of William Larnach (d. 1829), reputedly a naval purser, and his wife, Margaret, née Smith. Little is known about his early life, but he clearly received a good education. In 1834 he joined his squatter brother, John, in New South Wales. During the 1840s' colonial depression he bought a steam flour mill in Sydney and also traded and acquired urban and pastoral property. On 3 September 1845 he married Jane Elizabeth, the eldest daughter of a leading merchant and fellow countryman, William

Walker, the influence of whose advice and guidance he later generously acknowledged.

In 1845 Larnach began his legendary association with the Bank of New South Wales, first as auditor and, from the following year, as an innovative and respected director. Compact and well-proportioned in figure and features, Larnach had a composed appearance which belied energy and confidence. Following his involvement in the reconstitution of the bank in 1850, he was elected president (1852–3). He steered his charge to notable prosperity, greatly enhanced by direct dealing in gold. Generous-minded, Larnach identified easily with a rising colonial society, and was early bent on making its first bank successful: by 1866 the 'Wales' had assets greater than any other bank in Australia.

By the age of thirty-six Larnach had laid the foundation of a personal fortune and was also a director of a gold company. After moving to London in 1852 he organized a branch for the bank that freed it from overseas agencies. He was appointed foundation managing director at Cannon Street in 1854, where for more than forty years he promoted expansion of the bank outside Australia. Ambitious to make an impression and even 'take the lead of all others', he could soon write, 'we stand as high as any Bank in London and you may say to our friends that although many of them thought it very fine to belong to English Banks, I would not exchange with any of them' (Larnach to Alexander Stuart, 2 Jan 1854, London letter-book, B/LON/2, Westpac archives).

While a steady flow of gold from Australia had no doubt helped, Larnach's fine judgement, finesse, and acute professional principles met recognition in the capital. He became director (1858–91) and president of the London Joint Stock Bank, and a director of the Chartered Mercantile Bank of India, London, and China and of the Indemnity Mutual Marine Insurance Co. During the financial crisis following the collapse of Overend, Gurney & Co. in 1866 he chaired a committee formed to contain the failure of the Agra and Masterman's Bank. In the panic he assured headquarters at Sydney that 'I always hold myself in readiness to pledge all I have in the world for the Bank here' (Larnach to Shepherd Smith, 26 Sept 1866, London letter-book, B/LON/2, Westpac archives). It was no small pledge. Larnach fully appreciated the subtleties, social and otherwise, of metropolitan financial activities. Living at Kensington Palace Gardens ('Millionaires' Row'), and riding in nearby Hyde Park, he entertained appropriately but not ostentatiously; his estate, Brambletye, in Sussex (where he was high sheriff in 1883), was close to members of the Walker family.

Larnach raised loans and development finance on the London market for the Australian colonies, adroitly reducing the consequences of unco-ordinated borrowing. His shrewdness was a byword in the Antipodes, and his advice widely depended on. He kept in close touch with the bank's Sydney management and with visitors, correspondents, and colonial politicians. In the early 1870s Larnach virtually ran the New South Wales agent-general's office in London. In 1879 he was appointed chairman of the London board and retired as managing director. Increasingly sceptical of the financial management of short-lived colonial administrations, he agreed in 1884—when the bank relinquished the New South Wales government account, held since 1868—that '… we would be as well without their business' (Larnach to Shepherd Smith, 8 Aug 1884, London letter-book, B/LON/2, Westpac archives). Larnach visited Australia, where he retained investments and property, in 1880 and 1886. A founding vice-president of the Institute of Bankers, he was acknowledged as the doyen of Australian bankers.

Survived by his wife, two sons, and a daughter, Larnach died at home, at 21 Kensington Palace Gardens, Kensington, London, on 12 May 1896.   MARGARET STEVEN

Sources R. F. Holder, *Bank of New South Wales: a history*, 2 vols. (1970) · R. S. Gilbert, 'Donald Larnach', *Australian financiers: biographical essays*, ed. R. T. Appleyard and C. B. Shedvin (1988) · *Australian Insurance and Banking Record* (15 Sept 1888) · *Australian Insurance and Banking Record* (19 May 1896) · *Australian Insurance and Banking Record* (20 March 1897) · *The Australasian* (1 April 1893) · *The Australasian* (11 July 1896) · *Town and Country Journal* [Sydney] (23 May 1896) · *Town and Country Journal* [Sydney] (11 July 1896) · New South Wales archives, Sydney, Australia, Colonial Secretary MSS · G. P. Walsh, 'Larnach, Donald', *AusDB*, vol. 5 · London letter-book, Westpac Banking Corporation archives, Sydney, Australia, B/LON/2 · New South Wales pioneers register of births, deaths, and marriages, Sydney, Australia · *CGPLA Eng. & Wales* (1896) · parish register (baptism), 27 July 1817, Watten, Caithness

Archives Westpac Banking Corporation, Sydney, Australia, archives

Likenesses photograph, Westpac Banking Corporation, Sydney, Australia; repro. in Gilbert, 'Donald Larnach', 82

Wealth at death £619,935 18s. 10d.: probate, 2 July 1896, *CGPLA Eng. & Wales* · estate sworn for probate in New South Wales at £258,383 and in Victoria £7450: Walsh, 'Larnach, Donald'

Larner, Samuel James [Sam] (1878–1965), fisherman and folk-singer, was born at Winterton, Norfolk, on 18 October 1878, one of the nine children of George Ezra Larner (*fl.* 1855?–1920?), fisherman, and his wife, Jane Amelia Powles. From the age of eight he went on occasional trips to sea, and at thirteen he signed as 'peggy' (cabin boy) on the *Young John*, a 40-ton sailing lugger. In 1894 he joined the *Snowflake* as a deckhand, and in 1899, after eight years in sail, he moved to the *Lottie*, the first of a series of steam drifters. In December 1923 Larner married Dorcas Eastick, who worked at Hill House, Winterton, in the church of her own parish, Watton, some 20 miles west of Norwich. The marriage lasted over forty years. Among the wedding celebrations was a long session of singing in the Winterton public house then kept by Larner's father. In 1933, in poor health and worn out by unremitting hard work, Larner left the sea, and he thereafter eked out a living until his retirement eight years later with periods on unemployment benefit and jobs such as tree planting and breaking stones on the road—in his own words, 'just like a convict' (MacColl and Seeger, 1).

In his own locality Larner was well known as an entertainer. By the age of eight he was picking up the songs he heard his grandfather sing at the Fisherman's Return public house at Winterton, and in the following year he was singing them himself to earn pennies from the coach parties which stopped in the village. When he joined the fishing fleet:

> We used to sing when we pulled in the nets, and I soon picked up the old songs. The ruder they were, the quicker I picked 'em up. Then we used to sing these songs to each other in the pub. There was no amusement in those days, and we had to make our own entertainment. There was one landlady who always gave me a cigar when I sang a rude un. (Anderson)

Over the years, as the fleet followed the herring, Larner sang in fishermen's concerts 'all the way from Lerwick in Scotland down to Newlyn in Cornwall' (MacColl and Seeger, 2). His repertory ran to well over sixty items—classic ballads, sea songs, broadside lyrics, music-hall pieces.

Larner was an extrovert performer, something of a showman who 'vividly savoured every line he sang' (Lloyd), lapsing from time to time into *parlando*, pausing, uttering gruff asides; 'songs excited him, and made him laugh outright, or snort with indignation, or murmur with sympathy' (ibid.). As well as zest for singing, he had a high degree of musical skill and sensitivity which ensured that when he came to the attention of the wider world, at the age of seventy-eight, he made a lasting mark. 'A man from the BBC who was doing a tour went into the local pub and asked if there was anybody in the village who could sing folk songs. Someone told him about me, and he asked me to go over' (Anderson). After the fortuitous meeting, the 'BBC man', Philip Donnellan, a distinguished producer, not only recorded Larner but brought him to the notice of Ewan MacColl and Peggy Seeger. They in turn made extensive recordings of both his speech and his singing, and also took him to London to meet the new audience of the folk revival then taking place. At the Princess Louise public house in Holborn, Larner 'sat and sang and talked to the several hundred young people, who hung on his every word as though he had been Ulysses newly returned from Troy to Ithaca' (MacColl, 318). Larner hugely relished the occasion, not least because of 'All them pretty young girls sitting down there on the front row with their short skirts' (ibid.).

Larner soon reached a still wider audience through his part in the Italia prize-winning BBC radio ballad *Singing the Fishing* (1960), by MacColl and Seeger (produced by Charles Parker). One of the songs written for the programme by MacColl, 'The Shoals of Herring', which subsequently enjoyed a great vogue in its own right, was closely based on Larner's accounts of his experiences at sea, in sail and steam, over half a century. *Now is the Time for Fishing*, an epoch-making LP of Larner's talk and singing, edited by MacColl and Seeger, came out in 1961, and in 1964 Larner featured with Harry Cox in a television film directed by Charles Parker, *The Singer and the Song*.

Sam Larner died at the St Nicholas Hospital, Great Yarmouth, on 11 September 1965 and was buried, possibly at Winterton, five days later. Interest in him continued: transcriptions of his songs appeared in anthologies, selections from Donnellan's recordings came out on LP and cassette (1974–5), and *Singing the Fishing* was issued on LP (1966),

then on CD (1999). *Now is the Time for Fishing* also reappeared on CD (1999), and in the previous year Larner's singing was represented on two of the twenty-CD series *The Voice of the People*. Several decades after his death Larner was still not only admired but held in great affection. A. L. Lloyd called him an 'exemplary singer' (Lloyd). For A. E. Green he was 'a poet of the everyday, crystallising in a few laconic and concrete phrases a lifetime of hard experience and its attendant emotions' (Green, 19). Ewan MacColl remembered the octogenarian, 'short, compact, grizzled, wall-eyed and slightly deaf, but still full of the wonder of life', whose 'one good eye still sparkled at the sight of a pretty girl' (MacColl, 318). Asked in November 2000 whether Winterton people remembered Sam Larner, a resident said: 'Remembered in the parish—will they ever forget him?' (private information).

ROY PALMER

Sources E. MacColl, P. Seeger, and S. Larner, *Now is the time for fishing* (1961) [booklet with LP record, Folkways Records, New York, FG 3507] · J. Anderson, 'Sam Larner, still a singing star at 85', *Eastern Evening News* (10 Jan 1964) · A. L. Lloyd, *A garland for Sam*, Topic records 12T244 (1974) [sleeve notes to LP record] · E. MacColl, *Journeyman: an autobiography* (1990) · A. Green, 'Sam Larner on record: a review with some comments on the singer's art', *Traditional Music*, 1 (1975), 19–21 · P. Seeger and E. MacColl, eds., *The singing island: a collection of English and Scottish folksongs* (1960) · R. Palmer, ed., *The Oxford book of sea songs* (1986) · *CGPLA Eng. & Wales* (1965) · b. cert. · m. cert.

Archives Norwich Central Library, newspaper cuttings [copies] | SOUND Birm. CL, local studies department, Charles Parker archive, performance footage · BL NSA, performance recordings · BL NSA, documentary recordings · Ruskin College, Oxford, performance footage

Likenesses photograph, repro. in *Eastern Daily Press* (14 Oct 1959) · photograph, repro. in Lloyd, *Garland for Sam* · photograph, repro. in *Now is the time for fishing*

Wealth at death £857: probate, 19 Oct 1965, *CGPLA Eng. & Wales*

Larner, William (*d.* 1672?), printer and Leveller, was the son of William Larner (*d.* in or after 1646), yeoman, of Little Rissington, Gloucestershire. He was apprenticed in London's Merchant Taylors' Company in February 1630, but about 1633 he was transferred to a new master, a London stationer. He was made free of the Merchant Taylors' Company in October 1637. Given Larner's career in the book trade, it may be significant that he completed his service with a stationer.

By the early 1640s Larner was trading as a London bookbinder and bookseller. He published unlicensed titles at the sign of the Golden Anchor near St Paul's Churchyard and at the Bible in Little Eastcheap, specializing in tracts by religious nonconformists. This and his involvement with the Levellers would suggest that he was a nonconformist, but there is no further evidence of his religious beliefs. As books by John Lilburne and Katherine Chidley and a petition attributed to Richard Overton were among the first works Larner published, he may have established early ties with future Leveller colleagues.

Larner interrupted his trade to volunteer for the parliamentarian army, serving as a sutler in Lord Robartes's foot regiment. His military career was cut short by illness, however, and by 1645 he was living in Bishopsgate Street,

London, at the sign of the Blackamoor. Here Larner kept a secret press that possibly published one of Lilburne's titles in addition to Overton's initial attacks against presbyterianism under the pseudonym Martin Marpriest. Fear of discovery led to the removal of the press outside the City to Goodman's Fields, where he continued to issue pamphlets, including Lilburne's *Englands Birthright Justified*, until the press was seized in late 1645. However, Larner soon procured the letter for a new surreptitious press that included the final Marpriest tracts in its output.

Larner was identified as a distributor of Lilburne's pamphlets by William Prynne in October 1645, arousing the suspicions of the Stationers' Company which frequently searched his premises. He was finally arrested in March 1646 when copies of a tract he may well have published, Overton's *The Last Warning to All the Inhabitants of London*, were discovered in his shop. For refusing to answer questions before the lord mayor, the committee of examinations, and the House of Lords, Larner and his two servants were imprisoned. Their case was publicized in a number of pamphlets and Larner authored two defences of himself. His tracts expressed a strong belief in the sovereignty of the people and the rule of law, and emphasized that his incarceration brought great suffering to his family.

With Larner's release in October 1646 the volume of Leveller publications gradually increased. This suggests his importance to the Levellers as their most productive and committed printer and publisher. In November 1647 Larner was among five men imprisoned by the Commons after presenting a Leveller petition in support of the *Agreement of the People*. A scurrilous royalist tract also accused the prisoners of conspiring to divide the army and murder the king. Although Larner was soon released, the Levellers' support for John Morris alias Poyntz in his protracted dispute with the clerk of the Lords saw him briefly imprisoned again in August 1648.

A warrant for Larner's arrest in April 1649 indicates that his activities as a bookseller remained under suspicion. Yet presumably he escaped prosecution as he continued to publish openly less controversial Leveller titles by William Walwyn and Humphrey Brooke. However, in October 1653 Larner and his wife were ordered to answer charges before the council of state.

Larner continued to publish unlicensed books after the Levellers' demise. In 1650 he issued *The Light and Dark Sides of God* by the Ranter Jacob Bothumley, and is almost certainly the 'W. L.' who published Gerrard Winstanley's *England's Spirit Unfolded*. In 1652 Larner moved to a shop near Fleet Bridge, from where he issued numerous attacks against tithes and a number of astrological and astronomical tracts. The final books he published were Muggletonian works by Lawrence Clarkson, the last of which appeared in 1660. He is possibly the William Larner, citizen and merchant tailor of London, who died in 1672 and whose will mentions a wife, Katherine.

P. R. S. BAKER

Sources P. R. S. Baker, 'The origins and early history of the Levellers, *c*.1636–*c*.1647', PhD diss., U. Cam. [in preparation] • H. R. Plomer, 'Secret printing during the civil war', *The Library*, new ser., 5 (1904), 374–403 • [W. Larner], *A true relation of all the remarkable passages, and illegal proceedings of some sathannicall or doeg-like accusers of their brethren* (1646) • W. Larner, *A vindication of every free-mans libertie* (1646) • K. Lindley, *Popular politics and religion in civil war London* (1997) • CSP dom., 1649–50, 529; 1653–4, 198, 438 • JHL, 8 (1645–6), 240, 242, 245, 250, 257, 274, 287–8 • Merchant Taylors' Company, apprentice binding books, vol. 10, 1629–35, GL, microfilm 316, fol. 80 • Merchant Taylors' Company, court minute books, vol. 8A, 1630–42, GL, microfilm 329, Oct 1637 • H. R. Plomer and others, *A dictionary of the booksellers and printers who were at work in England, Scotland, and Ireland from 1641 to 1667* (1907) • will, commissary court of London, GL, MS 9171/34, fol. 236r–v • Wing, STC • R. L. Greaves, 'Larner, William', Greaves & Zaller, BDBR

Laroche [Laroch], **James** [Jemmy] (*c*.1688–1710?), singer, although active in London was possibly of French origin or birth. He first came to notice as a little boy of about seven in late December 1695 in George Granville's *The She-Gallants* at the Lincoln's Inn Fields Theatre singing 'So well Corinna likes the joy' to music by John Eccles. He may well have been 'the Boy' who was 'sometimes cited in printed songs in 1696' (Highfill, Burnim & Langhans, BDA, 155). He sang in *The City Bride* in March of that year, and from 14 November 'Jemmy Laroche' appeared as Cupid in Peter Anthony Motteux's *The Loves of Mars and Venus*, a musical entr'acte to Edward Ravenscroft's *The Anatomist* with

James Laroche (*c*.1688–1710?), by unknown engraver (after Egbert van Heemskerk) [singing 'The Raree-Show']

music by John Eccles and Gottfried Finger. Appearances as the Child of Hercules in *Hercules* (June 1697) and as a Savoyard in *Europe's Revels* (4 November 1697) followed, in the latter of which (according to Highfill, Burnim & Langhans, *BDA*) he sang 'The Raree-Show'. This was the source of his subsequent fame and popularity. Laroche's raree-show was given in London and the provinces about 1710. The claim that the 'Raree show', as depicted in a print in the Harvard Theatre Collection, was played at the theatre in Little Lincoln's Inn Fields in April 1713 is doubtful, as the new theatre was not opened until December 1714.

There appears to be no record of Laroche's activities after 1710. He may have been the James 'La Roach' buried at St Paul's, Covent Garden, on 4 July 1710 (Highfill, Burnim & Langhans, *BDA*). DAVID J. GOLBY

Sources Highfill, Burnim & Langhans, *BDA* · *TLS* (17 May 1928) · *TLS* (31 May 1928) · J. Marshall, 'Laroche, James', Grove, *Dict. mus.* **Likenesses** engraving (after E. Heemskerk), BM [*see illus.*] · portrait, Harvard TC; repro. in Highfill, Burnim & Langhans, *BDA*, 155

Laroon, Marcellus, the elder (1648/9–1702). *See under* Laroon, Marcellus, the younger (1679–1772).

Laroon, Marcellus, the younger (1679–1772), painter, was born on 2 April 1679 in London, the second son of the painter Marcellus Laroon the elder [*see below*] and Elizabeth Keene. Though baptized Marcellus Lauron, he always used the name Laroon. He was trained with his brothers by his father as a painter, but also learned fencing, dancing, French, and music.

At eighteen Laroon attended the peace conference at Rijswijk, Holland, in 1697 (the congress of Ryswick) as a page, before visiting Venice with Charles Montagu, fourth earl of Manchester. After returning to London in 1698, Laroon worked briefly with his father before embarking on a career as an independent painter. He was soon obliged to find other work, as a singer for Colley Cibber at the Drury Lane Theatre, where he remained until 1706.

In 1707 Laroon joined the 1st regiment of foot guards, beginning an army career described in his autobiography (which tells little of his artistic life). His earliest attributed drawings, for example, *A Market Tent in Camp: Soldiers Making Merry* (1707; Courtauld Inst.), record army life in Flanders. On campaign in Spain in 1709–11, Laroon was imprisoned. Ransomed after two years, he resumed civilian life (on half pay) in Covent Garden; he worked at Kneller's academy of painting from 1712 to 1715, and socialized with the painter Samuel Scott at the Rose and Crown Club. In 1715 Laroon returned to soldiering, and he served in Scotland before retiring from the army, aged fifty-three, on a captain's full pay, free from reliance on art commissions.

Laroon interpreted eighteenth-century English life with sympathetic humour and refinement in paintings and drawings. Most of his conversation pieces, like *The Dinner Party*, given by Laroon to George I (1725; Royal Collection), resemble scenes from plays, often incorporating a few apparent portraits and details such as Venetian furniture and music-making which reflect Laroon's personal interests and experience. The actions of minor figures often serve as commentaries on the central action. For example, in *A Nobleman's Levée* (c.1740; priv. coll.), the boy grooming a dog in the foreground parodies the relationship between the nobleman and the valet tending his wig. Laroon's individualized treatment of servants and his gentle mockery of aristocratic pride may derive from his period as a page.

Laroon's works reveal his Franco-Netherlandish artistic heritage and his interest in contemporary French art, filtered through English cultural attitudes, as in *The Village Wedding* (1735; priv. coll.) and *Tavern Interior with Peasants* (1742; priv. coll.), which includes details reminiscent of works by Teniers and Watteau. The jolly server leaning forward at the left in *The Dinner Party* is a miniature version of a Dutch 'merry toper'. The cello propped against a stool in *A Musical Assembly* (1720) is a quotation from Watteau. (Laroon, himself a cellist, was certainly familiar with musical instruments.)

Laroon's finished drawings include a group of 'music party' scenes intended as gifts for friends. Into old age Laroon continued to compose lively crowd scenes. In his *A Fight* (1770; AM Oxf.); Laroon depicts a battle between rival serenading parties with the expertise of an army veteran.

Preliminary sketches survive for some of Laroon's finished drawings, but few for his paintings. He worked out details of individual figures on the final canvas, outlining them in brown on a greyish ground and filling them in with oil colour, which he increasingly used like watercolour wash. From the 1760s he relied on white highlights rather than chiaroscuro to create depth.

Laroon also collected art. His sale (17 March 1775) included works by Cuyp, Hobbema, Ostade, Kneller, Bril, Teniers, Van de Velde, and (allegedly) Watteau. According to Vertue, Laroon possessed portraits by Frans Hals of the portrait painter Thomas Wyck and his wife.

Laroon was high-spirited and good-humoured, judging from his writings, for example his farewell letter written on the eve of the battle of Schellenberg (Raines, 1996, 44; Weyerman, appx 4, p. 102), and from his challenge in 1729 to friends at London's Tavern Club who criticized his advice to Sir Robert Walpole on buying art. In old age, Laroon moved to Oxford. He died there on 1 June 1772 in the parish of St Mary Magdalen.

Laroon's father, **Marcellus Laroon the elder** (1648/9–1702), painter, was born at The Hague in the Netherlands, the son of Marcel Lauron, a French painter of portraits and landscapes. Lauron apprenticed his son to a history painter before taking him (after 1660) to London, where Laroon trained until about 1670 with 'La Zoon' (perhaps Hendrick Sonnius, Lely's assistant), and with Balthazar Flesshier, a painter of seascapes and portraits. He then became a portrait painter in Yorkshire (where, he told George Vertue, he met Rembrandt at Hull). After returning to London, Laroon joined the Company of Painter-Stainers in 1674. In 1675 he married Elizabeth Keene, daughter of Jeremiah Keen, a rich builder of Little Sutton, near Chiswick. Elizabeth's wealth probably enabled the Laroons to live from 1680 at 4 Bow Street, in fashionable Covent Garden. They had six children. Their three surviving sons (including Marcellus Laroon the younger) were trained by their father as painters, and received a liberal education.

Laroon's most famous works were his drawings of London street traders and entertainers. Examples are at Blenheim Palace, Oxfordshire. Engraved by different hands, these were published in 1687 as *The Cryes of the City of London Drawne after the Life* (also known as *Tempest's Cryes of London*, after its publisher Pierce Tempest). They inspired copies, children's books, and a set of Meissen porcelain figurines by Johann Kaendler (1706–1775). The final edition from the original copperplates was printed in 1821. Laroon also provided twenty-four illustrations for *The Art of Defence* (1699), a book about fencing, and erotic engravings (with titles like *The Brothel* and *A Fryer's Civil Chastisement*), for sale in 1691 at Will's Coffee House, Bow Street. Vertue recorded a *Coronation Procession of William III and Mary II* by Laroon the elder.

Laroon's masterpiece was his *Charles II* (1684) for Christ's Hospital (it measured 15 feet by 10 feet). He also produced portraits of John, Lord Lovelace (1689; Wadham College, Oxford), William Savery (1690; City Art Gallery, Plymouth), and Caius Gabriel Cibber, the sculptor. His *Deliverance of Andromeda* was engraved by John Smith. A versatile painter, Laroon also worked as a copyist, notably of the Dutch architectural artist Bartholomeus van Bassen, and painted animals (including the lost *Spaniel* and *Sparrowhawk*), small conversation pieces, 'drolls' (comic paintings), and 'fancy' paintings. He excelled in drapery painting, and became a studio assistant to Kneller.

Laroon commemorated his combative personality in a lost self-portrait showing sword-fighting scars. (He appears unmarked in portrait prints by William Humphrey and G. P. Harding.) He died of consumption aged fifty-three on 11 March 1702 at Richmond, Surrey, and was buried there, bequeathing his art collection to his three sons.   ANNE THACKRAY

Sources R. Raines, *Marcellus Laroon* (New Haven, CT, 1996) · R. Raines, *Marcellus Laroon* (1967) [exhibition catalogue, Paul Mellon Foundation for British Art, Aldeburgh, Suffolk, and Tate] · S. West, 'Laroon', *The dictionary of art*, ed. J. Turner (1996), vol. 18, pp. 796–7 · J. T. Smith, *Nollekens and his times*, 2nd edn, 2 vols. (1829), vol. 2, pp. 255–74 [incl. Laroon's autobiography] · Vertue, *Note books*, vol. 3 · R. Raines, 'Marcellus Laroon the younger', *Connoisseur*, 140 (1957), 241–5 [repr. in *Connoisseur Yearbook* (1959), 114–15] · R. Edwards, 'The conversation pieces of Marcellus Laroon', *Apollo*, 22 (1935), 193–8 · O. Millar, *The Tudor, Stuart and early Georgian pictures in the collection of her majesty the queen*, 2 vols. (1963), vol. 1, p. 174, pl. 182 · E. Waterhouse, *Painting in Britain, 1530–1790* (1983), 142–43, pl. 112 B. · S. Shesgreen, *Criers and hawkers of London: engravings and drawings by Marcellus Laroon* (1990) · [B. Buckeridge], 'An essay towards an English school of painters', in R. de Piles, *The art of painting, with the lives and characters of above 300 of the most eminent painters*, 2nd edn (1744), 354–430 · M. Spufford, review, *Costume*, 25 (1911), 113–15 [publishing related drawings] · J. C. Weyerman, *De levens-beschryvingen der Nederlandsche konst-schilders en konst-schilderessen*, 4 vols. (The Hague, 1729–69)

Likenesses G. P. Harding, print (M. Laroon the elder) · W. Humphrey, print (M. Laroon the elder) · attrib. M. Laroon, group portrait, oils (formerly attrib. W. Hogarth, *An assembly of arts*), AM Oxf. · M. Laroon, self-portrait, oils, Yale U. CBA

Wealth at death art collection, incl. works by Netherlandish and French artists: Raines, *Marcellus Laroon* (1996)

Larpent [*née* Porter], **Anna Margaretta** (1758–1832), diarist, was born at Pera, Turkey, on 4 April 1758, the second of five and eldest of three surviving children of Sir James *Porter (1710–1776), British ambassador at Constantinople (1746–62), and his wife, Clarissa Catherine (*d.* 1766), eldest daughter of Elbert, second baron de Hochepied, the Dutch ambassador at Constantinople. Her importance resides less in her activities during her lifetime than in the survival of her daily diary; some seventeen volumes, covering the years 1773 to 1830, are now at the Huntington Library, in San Marino, California (HM 31201).

Anna's brother George Porter (1760–1828) was also born at Pera, and a sister, Clarissa Catherine (Clara; 1764–1833), was born at Brussels. In 1765 the Porters returned to England, where Anna's mother died in the following year. James Porter and his children divided their time between Ham and London, socializing with politicians and intellectuals, attending the theatre, and visiting historic landmarks—all described in Anna's diary. Following her father's death, in 1776, Anna acted as mother to her sister Clara. On 25 April 1782 she married John *Larpent (1741–1824), inspector of plays in the office of the lord chamberlain from 1778 to 1824. He was a widower with a young son, Francis Seymour *Larpent (1776–1845), and she married him in part because 'I hoped the Man who felt so much for his Motherless son, wd. feel for my Orphan child' (Larpent, diaries, HM 31201, vol. 17, April 1782). Clara lived with the Larpents from 1786 to 1798, when she married the Rt Hon. James Trail, who was later secretary of state for Ireland.

The Larpents first resided in Upper Grosvenor Street, London, and at Heston, near Hounslow, but by 1790 they had moved to Newman Street, London, and Ashtead, in Surrey. In 1799 they moved to Charlotte Street, London, and in 1804 to Putney, having given up their second home in Ashtead in 1798 to Clara and James Trail. They had two children, John James (1783–1860) and George Gerard *Larpent (1786–1855), whom Anna tutored alongside her stepson, Seymour, in French, Latin, history, and natural sciences, all areas in which she was exceptionally well-read. As John Larpent's health declined in the early 1800s Anna increasingly managed his affairs, and she nursed him until his death, on 18 January 1824. From then onwards she renewed a busy social life, even travelling in 1826 to Antwerp, where her son John was British consul from 1825 to 1837.

John Larpent shared his work of reviewing English plays with Anna, who catalogued and helped to read all productions submitted for licensing. She actually served as a sort of co-censor, independently reviewing and licensing several works, including all those in Italian, a language in which she was fluent, unlike her husband. She wrote sharp, often caustic assessments of nearly all the plays submitted to him, and these portions of the diary have been selectively used by historians of the English stage. But the diary offers a richer, even overwhelming chronicle of a prosperous, learned woman's reading habits, spiritual reflections, and intimate relationships. Though other scholars have characterized it as primarily presenting a 'cerebral self' (Brewer, 228) over the years Anna occasionally revealed strong feelings about her beloved children, many dear family friends (including the Bowdlers and the Plantas), and especially her siblings, with whom she had strained relations. Through the 1790s the diary richly describes London life, English travels, and news about the French Revolution. While Anna reported landmarks and painting exhibitions in bland detail she offered pungent descriptions of trends and people, especially foreigners, the French, and Catholics. On 25 August 1803 she recounted her first Catholic (and French) mass, reporting that the duc de Berri was 'a little brown mean man, not *quite* like an Ape, nor yet like a Mulatto, a something in feature *tirant sur l'un & l'autre*' (Larpent, diaries, HM 31201, vol. 5). By 1799, as John Larpent's health declined, Anna, a devout member of the Church of England, devoted more time to spiritual reflection. She had become increasingly pious by the 1810s, and as a result less acerbic in her personal descriptions. Though she recorded all aspects of each day she invariably wrote mostly about her eclectic reading of novels, travel accounts, history, and political economy. She delighted in Jane Austen and Hannah More, but she generally questioned whether women should publish. She complained that Mary Wollstonecraft 'tires one with her feelings. I am glad she is dead & can write no more' (ibid., vol. 2, 23 July 1798). She published nothing herself but seems to have written some original essays and 'tales', which her diary implies that she circulated among intimates.

Anna Larpent frequently wrote of the moral temperament of her age. In her youth she felt self-consciously estranged from Georgian society, viewing others as frivolous and debauched, but as an older adult she often praised the restraint and piety of the new century. Periodically she reflected on the purpose of her journal, noting that at first it trained her to observe, while providing an amusing 'chat with myself' (Larpent, diaries, HM 31201, vol. 2, 1 Jan 1796); later she described it as 'a Second sort of conscience' (ibid., vol. 7, 19 Aug 1809) but she also occasionally explicitly directed her remarks to her sons, whom she imagined would someday read the journals. The last surviving volume ends with Anna selling books and possessions, including the 2398 manuscript plays that her husband had kept as censor, which she sold for £175 to John Payne Collier and Thomas Amyot. She went to live with her son George and his family at their home, Putney Park, on 24 July 1830, and died there on 4 March 1832. In her will, drawn up on 7 February 1828, she asked to be buried with her husband at Mortlake.

LISA FORMAN CODY

Sources Anna Larpent, diaries, 1773–1830, Hunt. L., HM 31201, 17 vols. · J. Brewer, 'Reconstructing the reader: prescriptions, texts and strategies in Anna Larpent's reading', in J. Raven and others, *The practice and representation of reading in England* (1996), 226–45 · *DNB* · L. W. Conolly, *The censorship of English drama* (1976) · *Guide to British historical manuscripts in the Huntington Library* (1982) · *The private journal of Francis Seymour Larpent, Esq.*, ed. G. Larpent, 3 vols. (1853) · Larpent A. M. to J., 27 Sept 1827, Hunt. L., Beaufort (Sir Francis) papers, box 36, FB 1855 · D. MacMillan, *Catalogue of the Larpent plays in the Huntington Library* (1939) · Boase, *Mod. Eng. biog.* · C. M. Colombo, '"This pen of mine will say too much": public performance in the journals of Anna Larpent', *Texas Studies in Literature and Language*, 38 (1996), 285–301 · 'A woman's view of drama, 1790–1830: the diaries of Anna Margaretta Larpent in the Huntington Library' (Adam Matthew Publications, 1995), 9 reels [microfilm copy] · *GM*, 1st ser., 102/1 (1832), 286 · will, PRO, PROB 11/1797, fols. 189v–190v

Archives Hunt. L., diaries, HM 31201 · Hunt. L., Sir Francis Beaufort collection

Larpent, Francis Seymour (1776–1845), civil servant, was born on 15 September 1776, the eldest son of John *Larpent (1741–1824), inspector of plays, and his first wife, Frances Western (d. 1777). Sir George Gerard *Larpent was his half-brother. He was educated at Cheam School under the Revd W. Gilpin. He graduated BA from St John's College, Cambridge, as sixth wrangler in 1799, was elected fellow, and proceeded MA in 1802. In 1799 he was admitted at Lincoln's Inn, and studied for some time under Bayley, the eminent special pleader, before being called to the bar (1803). He went the western circuit but did little business, though he made some useful friendships. Manners Sutton, judge-advocate-general, selected him in 1812 to go as deputy judge-advocate-general to the forces engaged in the Peninsular War, managing the courts martial. He remained until 1814 at headquarters with Wellington, who thought highly of his services (*The Dispatches of Field Marshal the Duke of Wellington*, ed. J. Gurwood, 6, 1836, 360). In August 1813 he was taken prisoner, but was exchanged almost immediately (ibid., 737, 761).

In 1814 Larpent was made a commissioner of customs. About the same time he was appointed civil and Admiralty judge for Gibraltar, where a new code was being prepared. He took part in arranging the court martial on General Sir John Murray at Winchester and was a member of the commission which investigated the escape of American prisoners from Dartmoor. He married on 15 March 1815 Catherine Elizabeth (d. 1822), second daughter of Frederick Reeves of East Sheen, Surrey.

In the spring of 1815 Larpent was invited by the prince regent to inquire into the improprieties that the Princess Caroline was alleged to have committed abroad, but he wisely insisted that his appointment should proceed from the government directly, and that he should be employed to sift rather than gather partisan evidence. Although he nominally set out to take up his work at Gibraltar, he went to Vienna, where he was accredited to Count Münster, and began his investigations into the princess's conduct, with the result that he dissuaded the prince regent's advisers from bringing her to public trial. He travelled from there to Gibraltar, where he remained until 1820, when he was again employed in secret service inquiries into Princess Caroline.

In 1821 Lord Liverpool made Larpent one of the commissioners of the board of audit of the public accounts. In 1826 he became its chairman, and in 1843 he retired. Following the death of his first wife, he married secondly, on 10 December 1829, Charlotte Rosamund (d. 1879), daughter of George Arnold Arnold of Halstead Place, Kent. Both marriages were childless. Larpent died at Holmwood, near Dorking, Surrey, on 21 May 1845, and was buried in the family vault there. When in the Peninsula, Larpent wrote descriptive letters to his stepmother, Anna Margaretta *Larpent. These were edited, with a biographical preface by Sir George Larpent, in 1853 and passed through three editions the same year.

W. A. J. ARCHBOLD, rev. M. C. CURTHOYS

Sources *The private journal of F. Seymour Larpent, judge-advocate general*, ed. G. Larpent, 2nd edn, 2 vols. (1853) · Venn, *Alum. Cant.* · *GM*, 2nd ser., 24 (1845), 99 · Burke, *Peerage*
Archives BL, private journal as judge-advocate-general at Wellington's headquarters, Add. MS 33419 · Bodl. Oxf., letter-book as chairman of the board of audit · Surrey HC, inventory
Likenesses double portrait, oils (with his wife), NPG

Larpent, Sir George Gerard, first baronet, and Baron de Hochepied in the Hungarian nobility (1786–1855), politician, was born in London on 16 February 1786, the younger son of John *Larpent (1741–1824), inspector of plays, and his second wife, Anna Margaretta *Larpent (1758–1832), daughter of Sir James *Porter, diplomatist. In 1819 he was granted permission to assume the Hungarian title of Baron de Hochepied, which came through his mother's line.

Larpent entered the East India house of Cockerell and Larpent at an early age, became chairman of the Oriental and China Association, and deputy chairman of the St Katharine's Dock Company. In May 1840 he unsuccessfully contested Ludlow as a whig, and in April 1841, Nottingham; but in June 1841 he was returned at the head of the poll for Nottingham with Sir John Cam Hobhouse. On 23 August 1841 he was created a baronet. He retired from parliament in August 1842, pending the result of a petition presented against his return. In 1847 he unsuccessfully contested the City of London. He wrote two pamphlets on trade and edited the descriptive journals written home by his half-brother, the lawyer Francis Seymour *Larpent (1776–1845); he also edited the history of Turkey written by his grandfather, Sir James Porter, continuing it and adding a memoir (1854).

Larpent's first marriage was on 13 October 1813, to Charlotte (1792–1851), third daughter of William Cracroft of the exchequer office. She died on 18 February 1851 at Bath, leaving two sons and a daughter; his second was on 17 July 1852, to Louisa Martha, daughter of George Bailey of Lincolnshire; she died at Marseilles on 23 March 1856. They had a son, Seymour George Larpent. Sir George Larpent died at Conduit Street, Mayfair, London, on 8 March 1855.

ANITA MCCONNELL

Sources *GM*, 1st ser., 89/2 (1819), 367 · *GM*, 2nd ser., 16 (1841), 311 · *GM*, 2nd ser., 43 (1855), 524–5 · Boase, *Mod. Eng. biog.*
Archives LUL, corresp. relating to Bank of India | UCL, letters to Edwin Chadwick
Likenesses wood-engraving, NPG; repro. in *ILN* (1847–8)

Larpent, John (1741–1824), examiner of plays, was born on 14 November 1741, the second son of John Larpent (1710–1797), later chief clerk to the Foreign Office, and his wife, Mary Ann, the daughter of James Pazant, of a refugee Norman family. Larpent was educated at Westminster School and entered the Foreign Office. He was secretary to John Russell, fourth duke of Bedford, at the peace of Paris in

1763 and to Francis Seymour Conway, first marquess of Hertford, when the latter was lord lieutenant of Ireland. He remained Hertford's secretary, and followed him to the lord chamberlain's department. By 1777 he had become a groom of the privy chamber. In November 1778 he was appointed examiner of plays by Hertford, to succeed William Chetwynd, who had held the post since its inception in 1738.

Larpent had married Frances, the daughter of Maximilian Western of Cokethorpe Park, Oxfordshire, on 12 or 14 August 1773. They had two sons before Frances died on 9 November 1777. The influence of Larpent's second wife, Anna Margaretta Porter (1758–1832) [*see* Larpent, Anna Margaretta], helped shape his role as examiner. She was a sharply observant diarist and enthusiastic follower of the theatre, whom Larpent married on 25 April 1782, and who was soon acting as his deputy.

Larpent's policy as examiner reflected the times. Before 1789 he was tolerant of generalized political satire, but in the heightened climate of the revolutionary and Napoleonic wars he became more sensitive, ordering revisions even to pro-government plays should they inadvertently encourage sedition. However, he was conscientious and a polite and sensitive negotiator, on several occasions successfully working with playwrights and managers to render rejected plays suitable for performance. Episodes such as Theodore Hook's attack on Larpent, which followed the suppression of his play *Killing No Murder* in 1819 on the grounds that it was excessively insulting to Methodists, were the exception rather than the rule. Larpent considered Hook's subsequent claim that he was a Methodist libellous.

Larpent died at his home in East Sheen, Surrey, on 18 January 1824. He was survived by Anna Larpent, by the elder son of his first marriage, Francis Seymour *Larpent, and by the sons of his second (there seem to have been no daughters), John James Larpent (1783–1860) and George Gerard *Larpent. He also left behind him the collection of plays built by successive examiners since the licensing act of 1737, which he and his wife had carefully maintained. The collection was not passed on to his successor, George Colman the younger, and ownership was assumed by Anna Larpent, who sold the plays to John Payne Collier and Thomas Amyot. It was acquired in 1853 by Francis Egerton, first earl of Ellesmere, and in 1917 by Henry E. Huntington, and thence passed to the Huntington Library, California.

W. A. J. ARCHBOLD, rev. MATTHEW KILBURN

Sources L. W. Conolly, *The censorship of English drama, 1737–1824* (1976) · *A woman's view of drama, 1790–1830: the diaries of Anna Margaretta Larpent in the Huntington Library* (1995) · *The private journal of F. Seymour Larpent, judge-advocate general*, ed. G. Larpent, 2nd edn, 1 (1853), x · *Old Westminsters* · Burke, *Peerage* (1889) · R. Findlater, *Banned! A review of theatrical censorship in Britain* (1967), 53–4 · IGI
Archives Hunt. L. | Hunt. L., diaries of Anna Margaretta Larpent
Likenesses portrait, repro. in Conolly, *Censorship of English drama*
Wealth at death see will, PRO, PROB 11/1681, sig. 92

Larwood, Harold (1904–1995), cricketer, was born on 14 November 1904 at 17 Chapel Street, Nuncargate, Kirkby in

Harold Larwood (1904–1995), by Howard Coster, 1933

Ashfield, Nottinghamshire, the fourth of five sons of Robert Larwood, coalminer, and his wife, Mary, *née* Sharman. He was educated at Kirkby Woodhouse board school, but left at thirteen and a year later began work at Annesley colliery. Larwood's early cricket was for the Nuncargate club. While playing for that club he was recommended to Nottinghamshire County Cricket Club. Impressed by his fast bowling, the county club engaged him for the 1923 season at £2 per week. At the end of the following summer he made his county championship début and almost from the start of 1925 won a permanent place in the county side. On 17 September 1927 he married Lois Cynthia Bird (*b.* 1906/7), daughter of William Bird, coalminer. They had five daughters.

The cricket press was quick to recognize Larwood's fast-bowling potential and he was capped by England in June 1926. The first four tests against Australia were all drawn; in the fifth and deciding game Larwood played a key role, taking six wickets. England won and regained the Ashes. In both 1927 and 1928 Larwood headed the season's first-class bowling averages. He was therefore an automatic choice for the MCC side to tour Australia in the winter of 1928–9. The tour began splendidly, England winning the first test by 675 runs; Larwood took six wickets for 22 in Australia's second innings. He also scored 70, showing himself to be no mean batsman. However, the hard pitches took their toll on Larwood's stamina and he was not so successful in the later games. England, however, won the series four matches to one.

Back in England in 1929 Larwood was an important member of the Nottinghamshire side which won the county championship. 1930 saw the Australians touring England. It was the first visit of Donald Bradman, in statistical terms the greatest batsman the cricket world has seen. With pitches conducive to run-getting Bradman dominated the 1930 tests. Larwood and his colleagues were overwhelmed. In domestic cricket Larwood's success as a fast bowler continued unchallenged. In 1931 and 1932 he was again the leading bowler in English first-class cricket. In fact, he topped the English bowling tables five times in all, a feat unequalled by any fast bowler during the twentieth century.

Larwood was chosen for the 1932–3 MCC tour to Australia under Douglas Jardine. The latter realized the necessity of reducing Donald Bradman's run-getting powers. Following pre-tour discussions Jardine decided that his fast bowlers should employ leg theory—attacking the leg stump using a semicircle of close in leg side fielders. The tactic would only work if the bowling was accurate. Larwood's renowned accuracy was thus paramount to the scheme's success. England's new stratagem got off to a brilliant start: the first test was won by ten wickets, Larwood capturing five wickets in each innings. For the second test Australia produced a pitch designed to assist spin. Having, in W. J. O'Reilly, the world's best spinner, they duly levelled the series. The Australian press had by now labelled England's bowling tactics with the evocative term 'bodyline'. This very term raised the temperature for both public and players. The teams met in Adelaide for the third test. Fast deliveries from Larwood hit the Australian batsman W. M. Woodfull several times, causing the crowd to barrack; later in the same innings a ball from Larwood hit W. A. S. Oldfield on the head, knocking him unconscious. The Australian Cricket Board cabled to London saying that unless England stopped using bodyline the series should be abandoned. So serious was the issue that talks were held at government level. Matters calmed a little and the series was played to its conclusion, England winning four matches to one. Larwood returned the outstanding figures of thirty-three wickets, at an average of 19.51.

Larwood's left foot was badly injured in the final test and he missed most of the 1933 English season. He was fit again when Australia visited in 1934. The early season was dominated by press speculation as to whether Larwood would be picked for England. The authorities asked him to apologize for his bowling in 1932–3; he said he had nothing to apologize for. He had only bowled as instructed by his captain. Neither side would climb down. Larwood's test career came to a premature end, though all acknowledged him as the greatest fast bowler of his generation.

Larwood retired from county cricket in 1938. In 1950, together with his wife and daughters, he emigrated to Australia. A quiet spoken, modest man, he lived in a suburb of Sydney for the remainder of his life. English cricket fans would make a point, when in Australia, of going to visit him and they invariably were received with courtesy. After a long campaign by his friends, both English and Australian, Larwood's outstanding service to English cricket was finally recognized in June 1993, when he was appointed MBE. He died on 22 July 1995 in Randwick, New South Wales, aged ninety, and was cremated. He was survived by his wife and five daughters.

PETER WYNNE-THOMAS

Sources H. Larwood, *Bodyline?* (1933) · K. Perkins, *The Larwood story* (1965) · P. Wynne-Thomas, *Harold Larwood* (1990) · A. W. Carr, *Cricket with the lid off* (1935) · D. R. Jardine, *In quest of the Ashes* (1933) · A. A. Mailey, *And then came Larwood* (1933) · J. H. W. Fingleton, *Cricket crisis* (1946) · file on Harold Larwood, Nottinghamshire County Cricket Club library, Trent Bridge, Nottingham · *The Times* (24 July 1995) · *The Independent* (24 July 1995) · b. cert. · m. cert.
Archives FILM BFI NFTVA, documentary footage · BFI NFTVA, news footage · BFI NFTVA, performance footage
Likenesses H. Coster, photograph, 1933, NPG [*see illus.*] · photograph, Nottinghamshire County Cricket Club, Trent Bridge, Nottingham · photograph, repro. in *The Times* · photograph, repro. in *The Independent*

Lascelles, Sir Alan Frederick (1887–1981), courtier, was born on 11 April 1887 at Sutton Waldron House, Dorset, the sixth and youngest child, and only surviving son, of Commander Frederick Canning Lascelles (1848–1928), second son of the fourth earl of Harewood. His mother, Frederica Maria (*d.* 1891), was the daughter of Sir Adolphus Frederic Octavius Liddell, son of the first Baron Ravensworth. After his mother's death Tommy (as he was known from childhood) was brought up by governesses and by his elder sisters until he was sent to Hazelhurst preparatory school in Sussex. He won a scholarship to Marlborough College but found its regime spartan and its ethos unaristocratic. In 1905 he matriculated at Trinity College, Oxford, where he joined a glittering circle of undergraduates and developed a love of books and music. During the holidays he pursued his favourite sports of hunting and fishing.

After Oxford, where he spent some of his happiest years, Lascelles had difficulty in settling into a job. Having failed to get into the Foreign Office he turned his hand to journalism and stockbroking but found them dispiriting. He joined the Bedfordshire yeomanry in 1913 and was mobilized on the outbreak of war. Most of his friends from Oxford were killed in the war; he probably owed his own survival to being a cavalry officer, for in an age of trench warfare he spent much of his time in reserve. Nevertheless he was mentioned in dispatches and was awarded the MC.

In 1919 Lascelles sailed for India as aide-de-camp to his brother-in-law Sir George Ambrose (later Lord) Lloyd, the designated governor of Bombay. In Delhi the following year, on 16 March, he married Joan Thesiger (1895–1971), eldest daughter of the viceroy, Frederic *Thesiger, Viscount Chelmsford. They had three children: a son, who died in 1951, and two daughters, one of whom married the second Viscount Chandos. Having returned to England in 1920 Lascelles was appointed assistant private secretary to the prince of Wales (later Edward VIII). Tall, wiry, and handsome, he looked every inch the courtier. Deeply cultivated, with a remarkable memory, he drafted elegant letters and speeches.

A man of moral scruple, Lascelles became increasingly

Sir Alan Frederick Lascelles (1887–1981), by Walter Stoneman, 1953

disillusioned with the prince, whom he believed to be in a state of arrested adolescence. In 1929, shortly after a tour of Africa, he turned in his resignation and used the opportunity to give the prince some candid criticism of his shortcomings. The prince took it in his stride, replying that he was 'quite the wrong sort of person to be Prince of Wales' (Ziegler, 194). From 1931 to 1935 Lascelles served as private secretary to the governor-general of Canada and was appointed CMG for his work at the Ottawa conference in 1933, which dealt with issues of free trade in the empire. He returned to royal service in 1935, as assistant private secretary to George V. When the king died a few months later he continued, despite his reservations, in the same capacity under Edward VIII. A close observer of the ensuing royal crisis, Lascelles became one of the king's harshest critics. After the abdication he told Harold Nicolson that 'nobody would ever know what they [the court] had had to endure during the last year' (Nicolson, MS diaries).

After the abdication Lascelles carried on as an assistant private secretary to George VI. He encouraged a return to the standards of George V and sought to fortify the untried king's resolve, not least in his relations with his exiled elder brother. When Alexander Hardinge, the king's private secretary, retired on health grounds in 1943 Lascelles succeeded him and retained the post until after the coronation of Queen Elizabeth in 1953. He was sworn of the privy council in 1943. As a royal adviser he was a man of old-world certainties, wary of innovation at the palace and of royal exposure; he played a leading role in opposing the attachment between Princess Margaret and Peter Townsend. In his capacity as keeper of the Royal Archives he was more flexible and promoted the writing of official royal biography. Harold Nicolson, whom he encouraged to write the life of George V, found him 'a great help ... so certain, so humorous and so friendly' (Nicolson, *Diaries and Letters*, 188).

Lascelles led an active life outside official circles, and upon retiring in 1953 became chairman (1953–63) of the Historic Buildings Council for England, chairman of the Pilgrim Trust (1954–60) and a director of the Midland Bank. He refused a peerage (life peerages had not been introduced when he retired) but accumulated honours rather as a successful business magnate accumulated dividends. For services to the sovereign he was created KCVO in 1939, promoted GCVO in 1947, and made a GCB in 1953. From 1953 until his death he was an extra equerry to the queen. An aficionado of music, he was an honorary fellow of the Royal Academy of Music. His old college made him an honorary fellow in 1948 and Oxford University gave him a DCL in 1963. Sociable, if rather austere, he was often seen in London's clubland but resigned from the Traveller's when it relaxed restrictions on the admission of women. Outside royal circles he will be best remembered for his posthumously published *Letters and Journals* (1986, 1989); they show him to be a more emotional man than was suggested by his refined exterior, and an observant witness to a privileged Edwardian generation that had to endure successive shocks to its standards and beliefs. Upon retirement he lived in the Old Stable Block at Kensington Palace, where he died on 10 August 1981.

FRANK PROCHASKA

Sources DNB · *The Times* (11 Aug 1981) · P. Ziegler, *King Edward VIII* (1990) · S. Bradford, *George VI* (1991) · B. Pimlott, *The queen: a biography of Elizabeth* (1996) · *End of an era: letters and journals of Sir Alan Lascelles, 1887–1920*, ed. D. Hart-Davis (1986) · H. Nicolson, *Diaries and letters*, ed. N. Nicolson, 3 (1971) · H. Nicolson, diaries, Balliol Oxf. · *Charles Lister, letters and recollections* (1917) · Burke, *Peerage* (1999) · CGPLA Eng. & Wales (1981)
Archives CAC Cam., diaries and papers · Royal Arch., corresp. and papers | Bodl. Oxf., letters to Lady Milner · Bodl. Oxf., corresp. with Lord Monckton · Borth Inst., corresp. with Lord Halifax · CUL, department of manuscripts and university archives, corresp. with Sir Samuel Hoare · PRO, corresp. with Lord Ismay, CAB 127/30–31 · Som. ARS, corresp. with Mary Herbert
Likenesses O. Birbey, drawing, 1922 · W. Stoneman, photograph, 1953, NPG [*see illus.*]
Wealth at death £66,662: probate, 27 Oct 1981, CGPLA Eng. & Wales

Lascelles, Sir Frank Cavendish (1841–1920), diplomatist, was born in London on 23 March 1841, the third son of the Hon. William Saunders Sebright Lascelles (1798–1851), a diplomatist who was the third son of Henry *Lascelles, second earl of Harewood. His mother was Lady Caroline Georgiana (*d.* 1881), eldest daughter of George *Howard, sixth earl of Carlisle. He was educated at Harrow School, and entered the diplomatic service in 1861. After serving for two years as an attaché in Madrid, he was transferred to Paris in 1864 and promoted to third secretary the following year. Lascelles saw the Second Empire at its apogee

at the time of the great Paris Universal Exhibition of 1867. On 25 June 1867 he married Mary Emma Olliffe (*d.* 1897), eldest daughter of Sir Joseph Francis *Olliffe (1808–1869), physician to the British embassy at Paris, and his wife, Laura Cubitt. They had two sons and one daughter, Florence, who married Sir Cecil Arthur Spring-*Rice.

Lascelles's next assignment was to Berlin, where he remained until the end of the Franco-Prussian War. He returned to Paris in February 1871, after the siege, and remained at the embassy during the commune, while the ambassador, Lord Lyons, accompanied the French government to Versailles. In the same year, with the rank of second secretary, he proceeded to Copenhagen. He then held a number of further brief appointments in Rome (1873), Washington (1876), and Athens (1878). He was three times sent to take charge of the agency and consulate-general in Cairo during the last two stormy years of the Khedive Isma'il's reign, which ended in Isma'il's enforced abdication in 1879.

In recognition of his services in Egypt, Lascelles was promoted at the end of 1879 to be agent and consul-general in Bulgaria, which had been virtually detached from the Ottoman empire and constituted into an autonomous principality, with Prince Alexander of Battenberg as its first ruler. Lascelles was in Sofia throughout the prince's troubled reign, supporting him until he was driven to abdicate and leave Bulgaria. Lascelles thus won Lord Salisbury's approval and also earned the special goodwill of Queen Victoria, who warmly favoured the prince's suit for the hand of her granddaughter, Princess Charlotte of Prussia, although Bismarck was vehemently opposed to it.

Lascelles made his way up the diplomatic ladder, and was promoted at the beginning of 1887 to be minister to Romania, where he became friendly with Count von Bülow, the future German chancellor and Prussian prime minister (1900–09), and Count Goluchowski, the future Austrian foreign minister (1895–1906). In 1891 he became minister to Persia, and in 1894 he was appointed British ambassador to Russia; then, at the end of 1895, he was specially selected to succeed Sir Edward Malet, one of his oldest friends, who had been ambassador in Berlin for twelve years. Lascelles held this embassy for the same length of time as his predecessor during a period when Anglo-German relations were entering a new and increasingly difficult stage. Within a few days of his arrival, in January 1896, the famous telegram dispatched by Kaiser William II to President Kruger became public and unleashed a storm of protest in Britain. Lascelles handled the crisis exceedingly well, but it was a foretaste of the Kaiser's impetuous and dangerous interventions in Anglo-German relations in the years that followed.

An ambassador in the old style, Lascelles set about cultivating close personal relations with the Kaiser, a task needing considerable patience and a reservoir of goodwill. The Kaiser delighted in unexpected visits, practical jokes, family confidences, and, above all, lengthy conversations of a semi-official kind, as disturbing to the Wilhelmstrasse as to British foreign secretaries. In spite of the Kaiser's not infrequent outbursts of angry temper when talking of British ministers and British policy, Lascelles was generally inclined to acquit him of any hostile designs against the United Kingdom, and he preferred to throw the blame on the sovereign's advisers, and especially on von Bülow, whom he greatly distrusted. Lascelles remained the Kaiser's intimate and a convinced advocate of an Anglo-German understanding until his retirement in 1908. Already during Lord Lansdowne's period as foreign secretary, some Foreign Office officials were highly critical of the ambassador's unduly sanguine view of German ambitions and his underestimation of the German threat to British supremacy on the high seas. Although his stay in Berlin was prolonged into the Liberal period, there was little sympathy between him and the senior hierarchy of Grey's Foreign Office. He was thought to have outlasted his usefulness and was succeeded in 1908 by Sir Edward Goschen, a man whose views were more in accord with the prevailing currents in the department. Lascelles continued right up to the outbreak of the 1914 war to use his influence, as spokesman for the Anglo-German Friendship Society, for the restoration of Anglo-German amity.

In the diplomatic service Lascelles was known to be one of the steadiest and one of the most courteous and kindest of men. He was happiest in the personal relationships so central to the 'old diplomacy' and took some pride in his reputation of being rather lazy, particularly when it came to putting pen to paper. He was created KCMG (1886), GCMG (1892), GCB (1897), and GCVO (1904), and was sworn of the privy council in 1892. Lascelles died at his home, 14 Chester Square, London, on 2 January 1920, and was buried three days later in Brompton cemetery.

VALENTINE CHIROL, *rev.* ZARA STEINER

Sources *The Times* (3 Jan 1920) · *FO List* (1919) · Z. S. Steiner, *The foreign office and foreign policy, 1898–1914* (1969) · private information (1927)
Archives CAC Cam., corresp. and papers · PRO, corresp., FO 800/6–20 | Bodl. Oxf., corresp. with Lord Kimberley · PRO, FO 371/Germany
Likenesses F. Dicksee, print, 1910, NPG · K, caricature, watercolour study, NPG; repro. in *VF* (23 Oct 1912) · P. Naumann, woodengraving, NPG; repro. in *ILN* (28 Sept 1895) · Spy [L. Ward], caricature, chromolithograph, NPG; repro. in *VF* (27 March 1902)
Wealth at death £63,417 4*s.* 4*d.*: probate, 18 March 1920, *CGPLA Eng. & Wales*

Lascelles, Henry, second earl of Harewood (1767–1841), politician, was born at Stapleton on 25 December 1767, the second son of Edward Lascelles, first earl of Harewood, and his wife, Anne, daughter of William Chaloner. On 2 September 1794 he married Henrietta (1770–1840), eldest daughter of Sir John Saunders Sebright; Queen Charlotte wrote, on his engagement: 'the gay Lothario is to wed the sedate and retired wife … beauty there is none nor fortune on the female side' (Harcourt, 6.44). Of their seven sons and four daughters, the eldest boy, Edward, died in 1839 and the second, Henry, succeeded to the title.

In 1796 Lascelles was elected unopposed as MP for Yorkshire, standing as a Pittite. He was re-elected in 1802, but did not stand in 1806, knowing that he would be opposed

Henry Lascelles, second earl of Harewood (1767–1841), by Sir Thomas Lawrence, 1823

for his hostility to restrictions on woollen manufacturing. In 1807 he was again a candidate for Yorkshire in the first contested election which had occurred for sixty-six years. The struggle was also memorable on account of the vast expense which Lascelles incurred: nearly £100,000. William Wilberforce, whose party almost entirely lacked organization, was head of the poll and Lascelles was beaten by Lord Milton; he sat instead for Westbury (bought by his father). On 6 October 1812 he was returned for Pontefract; but Wilberforce having retired from the representation of the county, Lascelles came in as his substitute on 16 October. Probably in consequence of the enormous sums he had expended in electioneering in the county, he chose to sit for the family borough of Northallerton in 1818. In the House of Commons he voted as a moderate tory and spoke fairly often. On 13 February 1800 he supported the Habeas Corpus Suspension Bill, and on 3 November 1801 voted for the preliminaries for peace with France. He seconded the appointment of Charles Abbot (afterwards first Baron Colchester) as speaker on 11 February 1802, and took the moderate side in the debate on the prince of Wales's debts on 4 March 1803. He moved the second reading of the Woollen Manufacturers Bill on 13 June 1804, the first of a series of efforts to liberalize the trade. The whigs tested him 'against the Opposition' and he opposed parliamentary reform and, once in the Lords, Catholic emancipation. He supported modest change to the 1815 corn laws and was a moderate supporter of retrenchment. After the death of his elder brother in 1814 he was styled Viscount Lascelles, and when, in 1819, Earl Fitzwilliam was removed on political grounds from the lord lieutenancy of the West Riding, Lascelles was appointed in his place. On 3 April 1820—while seeking a coronation peerage—he succeeded his father in the earldom. He took little part in the debates in the House of Lords. He was opposed to the bill of pains and penalties against Queen Caroline. On 7 October 1831 he declared himself a moderate reformer, and favoured the extension of representation, but opposed the Reform Bill. In the Lords he was of 'the middle or moderate party', a designation which reflected his general political posture.

Always something of a dandy, Lascelles was known as 'Beau Lascelles' and dressed in the fashion of George IV. His chief interest lay in country life. He maintained the Harewood hunt and died, on 24 November 1841, at Bramham in Yorkshire, just after returning from a run with the hounds.   W. A. J. ARCHBOLD, rev. H. C. G. MATTHEW

Sources GM, 2nd ser., 17 (1842), 96–8 · HoP, Commons · R. I. Wilberforce and S. Wilberforce, Life of William Wilberforce, 5 vols. (1838) · GEC, Peerage · E. W. Harcourt, ed., The Harcourt papers, 14 vols. (privately printed, London, [1880–1905])
Archives W. Yorks. AS, Leeds, Yorkshire election and lieutenancy corresp. and papers; accounts | BL, corresp. with Lord Liverpool and others
Likenesses S. W. Reynolds, mezzotint, pubd 1820 (after J. Jackson), BM, NPG · chalk drawing, c.1820, Harewood House, West Yorkshire · T. Lawrence, oils, 1823, Harewood House, West Yorkshire [see illus.] · E. U. Eddis, oils, Harewood House, West Yorkshire · M. Gauci, lithograph, BM · G. Hayter, drawings, NPG · G. Hayter, group portrait, oils (The trial of Queen Caroline, 1820), NPG · attrib. J. Jackson, oils, Harewood House, West Yorkshire · S. W. Reynolds, print, NPG

Lascelles, Henry George Charles, sixth earl of Harewood (1882–1947), husband of Princess Mary, was born in London at 43 Belgrave Square, the house of his maternal grandfather, on 9 September 1882. He was the elder son of Henry Ulick, Viscount Lascelles, later fifth earl of Harewood (1846–1929), and his wife, Lady Florence Katharine Bridgeman (1859–1943), daughter of the third earl of Bradford. From Eton College and the Royal Military College, Sandhurst, Viscount Lascelles (as he was known during his father's lifetime) joined the Grenadier Guards. He did not, however, intend to make the army his profession, and from 1905 to 1907 he was an honorary attaché in Rome, where he was able to cultivate his taste for art. He spent the next four years (1907–11) as aide-de-camp to Earl Grey, governor-general of Canada.

In a 1913 by-election, Lascelles stood as a Conservative for Keighley, in his native Yorkshire. His failure may have first given him the distaste for politics which his subsequent experiences confirmed. In later life he used to declare that every war in which Britain had been involved had been due to the inefficiency of politicians, and that

they began what soldiers had to end. From 1914 he was himself thus occupied, having joined his yeomanry unit, the Yorkshire hussars, on mobilization. But after the battle of Neuve Chapelle (10–13 March 1915), when the guards suffered very severely, he rejoined his old regiment. Wounded in the head a fortnight later, at Givenchy, he was back again in October for the battle of Loos. The end of the war saw him in Belgium, commanding the unit in which he had first served, the 3rd battalion of the Grenadier Guards. He had been wounded three times, and gassed once, and had received the DSO and bar, and the Croix de Guerre. Subsequently, his interest in military affairs was concentrated on the Territorial Army, in particular, and the welfare of ex-servicemen in general.

During the war his great-uncle, the second and last marquess of Clanricarde, died, and left practically his whole fortune of £2.5 million to Lascelles, with whom he shared a taste for the arts. These, and country pursuits in Yorkshire, were not, however, to be Lascelles's main occupations, for he became a public figure on his marriage on 28 February 1922 to the only daughter of *George V, Princess (Victoria Alexandra Alice) *Mary (1897–1965), known from 1932 as the princess royal. The marriage, which was warmly welcomed by the royal family, despite the fifteen-year age difference, was the first big pageant since the war, called by the newspapers 'the "Abbey Wedding" or the "Royal Wedding" or the "National Wedding" or even the "People's Wedding"', as the duke of York observed (Pope-Hennessy, 519). Besides helping his young wife in her many engagements, Lascelles soon acquired a reputation of his own as a businesslike chairman and an after-dinner speaker with a dry wit. Although he had, and sometimes showed, a typical dislike for the press, his obiter dicta found a ready currency in the newspapers.

On the eve of his wedding Lascelles was appointed KG. He succeeded his father as sixth earl in 1929, and was made a GCVO in 1934. He was lord lieutenant of the West Riding of Yorkshire from 1927, chancellor of Sheffield University from 1944, and president of the Royal Agricultural Society in 1929 when its show was held at Harrogate. His connoisseurship—he was versed in the classical European schools of painting and English furniture of the eighteenth century—was suitably recognized when he was made royal trustee of the British Museum in 1930. He was also an exponent of the art of petit point.

Much of Harewood's time and interest was given to racing and freemasonry. Already in 1926 senior grand warden of England, he became in that year provincial grand master in west Yorkshire. In 1943 he became grand master of the United Grand Lodge. In horse-racing of all kinds—flat, National Hunt, and pony—he was expertly versed, and he acted as co-editor of Flat Racing (1940) for the Lonsdale Library. He appeared before the royal commission on lotteries and betting in 1932 when, as a steward of the Jockey Club, he cogently expressed its views on the dangers to racing of large sweepstakes. He died at his residence, Harewood House, Yorkshire, on 24 May 1947, after some years of declining health. A great portion of the

Harewood estates were sold to meet death duties assessed at 70 per cent of the value of the estate. Harewood had two sons, the elder of whom, George Henry Hubert (b. 1923), succeeded him as seventh earl.

H. E. WORTHAM, rev. K. D. REYNOLDS

Sources T. Borenius, *Catalogue of the pictures and drawings at Harewood House and elsewhere in the collection of the earl of Harewood* (privately printed, Oxford, 1936) · private information (1959) · Lord Harewood, *The tongs and the bones* (1981) · GEC, *Peerage* · J. Pope-Hennessy, *Queen Mary* (1959)
Archives FILM BFI NFTVA, documentary footage · BFI NFTVA, news footage
Likenesses F. O. Salisbury, group portrait, oils, 1922, Harewood House, West Yorkshire · S. J. Solomon, oils, 1922, Harewood House, West Yorkshire · two group portraits, photographs, 1922, Hult. Arch. · J. S. Sargent, charcoal drawing, 1923, Harewood House, West Yorkshire · W. Stoneman, photograph, 1927, NPG · A. J. Munnings, double portrait, 1930 (on horseback with the princess royal), Harewood House, West Yorkshire · W. Nicholson, oils, 1936, Harewood House, West Yorkshire; version, Freemasons' Hall, London · J. St H. Lander, portrait, Harewood House, West Yorkshire · photographs, repro. in Harewood, *The tongs and the bones*
Wealth at death £549,120 2s. 1d.: probate, 20 Feb 1948, CGPLA Eng. & Wales

Lascelles, Rowley (1771–1841), antiquary and archivist, was born in Westminster, the eldest son of Rowley Lascelles, a merchant, of Little Ealing, Middlesex, and his wife, Ann Dunn. He was educated from 1785 at Harrow School, and was admitted to the Middle Temple in 1788 and to the King's Inns in 1806. He practised for about twenty years at the Irish bar.

In 1813 the record commissioners for Ireland selected Lascelles as successor to Bartholomew Thomas Duhigg to edit lists of all public officers recorded in the Irish court of chancery from 1540 to 1774. The lists formed part of the extensive manuscript collections concerning the history of Ireland made by John Lodge (1692–1774), deputy keeper of the rolls in Ireland. These collections had been purchased after Lodge's death from his widow by the Irish government, and were deposited in Dublin Castle. Lascelles quarrelled with the commissioners, but having gained the favour of Lord Redesdale, he was authorized by Henry Goulburn, then chief secretary for Ireland, to carry on the work in London. It was printed, financed by the Treasury, in two volumes in 1824 and 1830. The partisan tone of this book gave so much offence that, although copies were distributed to public libraries, it was practically suppressed, and Lascelles's employment ceased. Henry Cotton commented that the work contained 'a great mass of curious information carelessly put together, and disfigured by flippant and impertinent remarks of the compiler, most unbefitting a government employé' (*Fasti ecclesiae Hibernicae*, 2nd edn, 1851, 1, preface). Almost inevitably, a financial dispute between Lascelles and the Treasury followed: Lascelles maintained before a select committee of the House of Commons in 1836 that he was entitled to be paid £500 a year until the completion of the work, and he received £200 in 1832, and £300 in 1834. The

two petitions which he addressed to the House of Commons on the subject produced no result. He died on 19 March 1841 at 22 Newland Street, London.

THOMPSON COOPER, rev. MARIE-LOUISE LEGG

Sources GM, 2nd ser., 16 (1841), 323–5 · W. T. J. Gun, ed., *The Harrow School register, 1571–1800* (1934) · E. Keane, P. Beryl Phair, and T. U. Sadleir, eds., *King's Inns admission papers, 1607–1867*, IMC (1982) · H. A. C. Sturgess, ed., *Register of admissions to the Honourable Society of the Middle Temple, from the fifteenth century to the year 1944*, 3 vols. (1949) · d. cert.
Archives BL, corresp. with Robert Peel, Add. MSS 40248–40347, *passim* · TCD, corresp. with William Shaw Mason

Lascelles, Thomas (1669/70–1751), military engineer, was probably the Thomas Lascelles baptized at Leake, Yorkshire, on 16 May 1670, the son of Thomas Lascelles. He seems to have been a member of the Lascelles family who owned the small estate of Ganthorne in the North Riding of Yorkshire, but it is unclear whether he inherited any property. He served as a volunteer in Ireland from 1689 to 1691 and distinguished himself at the battle of the Boyne. He also served in the expedition led by Sir George Rooke in 1702 to Cadiz and the destruction of the plate fleet in Vigo, as a gentleman of the 2nd troop of guards volunteers. He obtained his first commission in the regular army in 1704, sharing the pay of an engineer (£100 p.a.) with John Armstrong. He served throughout Marlborough's campaigns in the Low Countries, being present at nearly all the battles and sieges. Lascelles was seriously wounded at the battle of Blenheim in 1704. When Queen Anne distributed £65,000 to the members of Marlborough's army, in recognition of their gallant services, Lascelles received £33 as his share.

Following the treaty of Utrecht in 1713 Thomas Lascelles and John Armstrong were appointed to superintend the demolition of fortifications and the razing of the harbour works at Dunkirk. Lascelles remained on this duty until 1716. He and Armstrong were initially paid 20s. per day, which was double the ordinary allowance. Later the Board of Ordnance had this sum increased by 10s. per day. Having been appointed deputy quartermaster-general in 1715, Lascelles was re-employed at Dunkirk between 1718 and 1725. Lascelles's mission (shared with Armstrong for the early part of 1718) was as much diplomatic as technical. The scheme agreed at the treaty of Utrecht was opposed by the inhabitants, who considered the closed-off old harbour a health risk, and by the merchant interest more specifically, who consistently sought ways of opening up the waterways around Dunkirk to restore their trade. Lascelles sympathized with the aspirations of the merchants and did not object to their being allowed an indirect connection with the English Channel by canal. However, his mission required him to ensure that the direct route to the sea, the old harbour, remained closed to commercial and military traffic while allowing sufficient water to pass through the barrier to prevent the harbour becoming stagnant. The situation demanded constant scrutiny of local politics as well as continual reassessment of the engineering practicalities. Exhausted, Lascelles returned to Britain in 1725.

Lascelles had been promoted director of engineers on 1 April 1722, following the death of Lewis Petit des Etans in 1720, and deputized for Armstrong as surveyor of the ordnance during Armstrong's absences abroad. Lascelles was ordered to return to Dunkirk in March 1730, where he found repairs to the port and fortifications well advanced. Sustained pressure from Lascelles and from the British embassy at Paris achieved the reduction of the new quays and jetties to ground level, but this time local grievances were more closely aligned with the aspiration of the French government to strengthen its offensive capability on its northern coast. Following a series of fruitless negotiations on this issue Lascelles left for Britain in May 1733, leaving the affair in the hands of his nephew and deputy, Joseph Day.

Britain's return to European conflict placed further pressure upon Lascelles. In 1740 he was appointed chief engineer of the train of artillery in the expedition to Cartagena led by Charles, eighth Lord Cathcart; however, by then his services were in such great demand at home that Jonas Moore had to be substituted for him. As a consequence in November 1741 Lascelles was directed to fill the office of surveyor-general of the ordnance during the illness of Major-General John Armstrong. In April 1742 he was directed to become master-surveyor of the ordnance at the Tower of London. Lascelles was further appointed assistant and deputy to the lieutenant-general of the ordnance in May 1742 and to perform the duties of that office for as long as the post remained vacant. On 1 July 1742, following Armstrong's death, he was appointed chief engineer. Lascelles visited Ostend in 1744 to report on the armament and ammunition which was to be sent there and to arrange for the repair and augmentation of the fortifications. He was further promoted inspector-general of artillery and represented the British government at The Hague for the purpose of carrying out the terms of a convention, dated 5 May 1745, between the states general of the United Provinces and George II. Lascelles was further able to determine the balance due from Great Britain to the states general for artillery and ammunition which was required to be supplied by Great Britain in the Low Countries.

Lascelles resigned from the service on 1 March 1750. In April he was granted £200 per annum for life for his long and faithful services. The same year he retired on a pension of £200 per annum; it is unclear whether or not this was an additional sum. Lascelles moved back to his native Yorkshire; in his will, dated 23 November 1750, he is described as 'of Pontefract' and possessed estates at Hunton and Scotton, which he left to his nephew Francis Lascelles, in addition to £10,000 p.a. Further legacies were distributed to other members of his family. He died on 1 November 1751, aged eighty-one; he had served through twenty-one campaigns and been present in thirty-six engagements. R. H. VETCH, rev. W. JOHNSON

Sources PRO, SP 76/3 · PRO, SP 105/6 · W. Johnson, 'Fireworkers and firemasters of England, 1662–1856', *International Journal of Mechanical Sciences*, 36 (1994), 1061–7 · D. Chandler, ed., *Oxford history of the British army* (1994), 493 · will, PRO, PROB 11/793, fols. 216– · R. F. Edwards, ed., *Roll of officers of the corps of royal engineers from 1660 to 1898* (1898) · GM, 1st ser., 21 (1751), 523 · IGI
Archives BL, corresp. with duke of Newcastle and others relating to Dunkirk, etc., Add. MSS 32689–32845

Lascelles, William Henry (1832–1885), builder, was born in Exeter, the second of four children of Henry Lascelles, a fuller, and his wife, Sarah Hutchings. He was apprenticed as a joiner in 1845, and in 1852 moved to London where he worked first with the building firm of William Cubitt, and then with that of Newman and Mann. In 1856 he became clerk to C. W. Waterlow of Bunhill Row, Finsbury, a builder specializing in window frames, doors, and shopfronts. When Waterlow retired in 1859 the firm became Clerihew and Lascelles, and in 1861 on the death of his partner, Alexander Clerihew, Lascelles became sole proprietor of the Bunhill Row 'steam-joinery works'. The firm's advertisements were soon boasting 'the largest stock in London', of prefabricated joinery, including greenhouse frames (Post Office directory, advertisements). Horticulture was a personal interest, and large bentwood conservatories were to become a speciality.

After 1870, perceiving a threat from cheap imported joinery from Sweden, Lascelles diversified his business. He made furniture, supplying thousands of desks and seats to the new London school board, and went up-market as a joiner and contractor for high-class houses. In particular he forged a close working relationship with the architect Richard Norman Shaw (1831–1912). By 1873 he was fulfilling general contracts in London and Shaw could say that Lascelles 'does a great deal of work for me' (Saint, 164). Among the houses they built were Lowther Lodge in Kensington Gore, studio homes for the painters Luke Fildes and Marcus Stone in Kensington, and Shaw's own home in Hampstead. The beautifully made staircase and other joinery in Sir William Armstrong's house at Cragside, Northumberland, were probably Lascelles's work. He also executed some fine oak furniture in Shaw's heftier Queen Anne manner. Pieces of this kind were shown at South Kensington in 1877 and at the Paris Exhibition in 1878, where Lascelles was a prominent British exhibitor. At this period he was employing some 200 men, all paid by piecework. His reputation for labour relations was excellent for a Victorian builder. He was interested in devising and improving appliances of all sorts, and among novelties at his much-visited works and showrooms were a brick-cutting machine and American wood-drying apparatus.

Lascelles's reputation as an innovator largely stems from his use of concrete. This was well established for floors and foundations in British building, and the 1870s saw much experiment in constructing walls of mass concrete or concrete blocks for cheapness. Lascelles took a wholly original approach, however, that of a frame hung with pre-cast cladding slabs of concrete, made of coke-breeze and lightly reinforced with iron bars. The frame was usually of timber but could be of concrete, and the slabs were screwed either to the outside only or to both inside and outside for extra insulation, making a cavity wall. Extra elements such as rafters, roof tiles, and window frames might also be of pre-cast concrete if desired, and he also produced concrete bricks. Lascelles patented his slabs and built his first 'concrete cottages' near his home in Croydon in 1875. The following year he explained his system to the Royal Institute of British Architects. Two cottages were erected at the 1878 Paris Exhibition; with them went a volume of sketch designs by Norman Shaw to show that the Lascelles system could be adapted to the fashionable architecture of the day. A second volume, *Sketches for Country Residences*, followed under Ernest Newton's name in 1882.

The Lascelles 'patent cement slab system' proved to be sound and enjoyed some practical success. Various cottages, small houses, and stables were built in it, and notable examples survive, including two pairs of houses in Sydenham Road, Croydon (of which one seems to have been set up as a show house and has ornamental features internally), and the former central buffet and dock manager's office at the Royal Albert Dock, London. The system was criticized from the start because it aped existing architectural styles instead of being developed along lines of its own, but Lascelles vigorously defended his approach.

Lascelles would doubtless have developed his system but about 1880 he fell seriously ill. He was obliged to retire in August 1882, and died of chronic brain and heart disease at his home, Middleheath Cottage, Sydenham Road, Croydon, on 25 October 1885. He was survived by his wife, Mary Hill, *née* Pollard, whom he married at Exeter on 7 June 1856, and by two daughters. The firm continued under the superintendence of his brother Thomas as W. H. Lascelles & Co., remaining for some years major builders in London and Croydon. The concrete slab system was still commercially available in the 1890s, but disappeared with the advent of reinforced concrete. Lascelles's principle of a frame with pre-cast concrete cladding was not again applied in Britain until the programme of housing built after the First World War.   ANDREW SAINT

Sources 'Mr Lascelles' steam joinery works, Bunhill-Row', *Building News* (23 March 1877), 286–7 · *Building News* (30 Oct 1885) · 'Concrete slab cottages', *The Builder*, 33 (1875), 731 · 'Lascelles' cement slab cottages', *The Builder*, 36 (1878), 908–9 · 'Mr Lascelles' specialties in concrete building and decoration', *The Builder*, 40 (1881), 648–9 · W. H. Lascelles, 'A chat about house building', *The Builder*, 42 (1882), 653 · A. Payne, 'Concrete as building material', *Sessional Papers of the Royal Institute of British Architects* (1875–6), 179–92, esp. 185–7; 225–38, esp. 226–7 · 'Ninety-year-old precasting system', *Concrete*, 6 (April 1972), 28–9 · P. Collins, *Concrete* (1959) · A. Saint, *Richard Norman Shaw* (1976) · H. Brooks, 'Lascelles, William Henry', *DBB* · A. E. J. Morris, *Precast concrete in architecture* (1978) · d. cert.
Archives Croydon Central Library, Helen Brooks MS
Likenesses Lombardi & Co., photograph, repro. in Brooks, 'Lascelles, William Henry'
Wealth at death £17,776 5s. 9d.: resworn probate, July 1886, *CGPLA Eng. & Wales* (1885)

Laski, Harold Joseph (1893–1950), political theorist and university teacher, was born on 30 June 1893 at Smedley House, Cheetham Hill, Manchester, the second of the three children of Nathan Laski (1863–1941), a successful cotton exporter, and his wife, Sarah Frankenstein (1869–

Harold Joseph Laski (1893–1950), by Elliott & Fry

1945). Nathan was the most prominent figure in the Manchester Jewish community and a leading local Liberal, and Sarah, who was also active in public life, was a Liberal councillor from 1925 until her death. Harold's elder brother Neville Laski was president of the Board of Deputies of British Jews from 1933 until 1939.

From the age of eleven Laski attended Manchester grammar school, where he soon revealed his precocious intellect, his ability to read and absorb the contents of books at immense speed and to write in an authoritative and witty way. He was also already an accomplished speaker, who could debate on equal terms with adults. At the age of sixteen acute appendicitis kept him away from school for almost a year and, while convalescing in Halesowen, he met (Winifred) Frida Kerry (1884–1978), who was working there as a masseuse. The daughter of Francis John Kerry of Acton Hall, Suffolk, she was twenty-five, from a landowning family, and had become an enthusiastic supporter of eugenics—the belief that social improvement could be brought about by genetic policies. Laski was immediately captivated by her and soon mastered the theory of evolution and the current controversies about heredity. He published his first article, 'The scope of eugenics', in *Westminster Review* (July 1910), and it was greeted enthusiastically by the founder of the subject, Sir Francis Galton, who was astonished to find that the author was still a schoolboy. Having won an exhibition in the autumn to read history at New College, Oxford, Laski transferred to science, and studied eugenics in London under its prime exponent, Sir Karl Pearson. On 1 August 1911 he and Frida eloped to Scotland. Although their marriage was to be extremely happy and a buttress for all his work, he was then just eighteen, and the elopement was a joint rebellion against Edwardian conventions. It also signified Laski's rejection of his parents' values, for they were totally opposed to intermarriage between Jews and Gentiles. This family crisis, which led to estrangement from his parents until 1920, had a lasting significance for him. His first (unpublished) book, 'The chosen people', written in 1912, explored the clashes between traditional Judaism and the world of science and rationality, and between traditional authority and individual freedom. His insistence on the superior claims of reason and the dictates of personal conscience would be incorporated into his subsequent theoretical work, and his willingness to act on his beliefs meant that his career would always be controversial.

Early work, 1914–1925 At Oxford, Laski showed no aptitude for science, and reverted to history after his first year. He also soon lost interest in eugenics and, partly through Frida's influence, became a militant campaigner for female suffrage, which also led him into the labour movement. After graduating with a first-class degree and the Beit memorial prize in 1914, George Lansbury offered him temporary employment on the *Daily Herald*, where he was soon writing vigorous left-wing editorials. When the war began, he volunteered for military service, but was rejected on medical grounds. In the autumn he accepted a junior lectureship at McGill University, Montreal, where he remained until 1916, and where their only child, Diana (1916–1969), was born in May. He then moved to Harvard University, where in 1917 he became book editor of the *Harvard Law Review*—the only person ever to hold this position without having a law degree. He also established many lasting friendships and associations in universities, journalism, and progressive politics and retained strong ties with the United States for the rest of his life. Of particular importance were his friendships with Felix Frankfurter, who was later to become an adviser of President Roosevelt and a supreme court judge, and with Oliver Wendell Holmes, the outstanding figure in American law. His relationship with Holmes was incongruous: when they met in 1916 Laski was only twenty-three and an ebullient, radical optimist, while Holmes was already seventy-five, politically conservative, sceptical, and even pessimistic. Yet their friendship, sustained through correspondence for almost twenty years, was undoubtedly important to both of them and in the early years Holmes's pragmatic attitude to law was an influence on Laski's thought. Later his attempt to maintain the old man's spirits by concentrating on the brighter side of life may have helped him to maintain some of his own optimism, and he was distressed when Holmes died in 1935.

While in North America, Laski's first major academic contributions were published in a series of articles, many of which were subsequently brought together in *Studies in the Problem of Sovereignty* (1917), *Authority in the Modern State*

(1919), and *The Foundations of Sovereignty* (1921). These works in pluralist theory included esoteric accounts of historical conflicts between church and state, discussions of political ideas, and analyses of practical organizational issues. Their purpose was to refute the existing orthodoxy, which emphasized the moral superiority of the state, and argued that it was 'sovereign' in the sense that it was the ultimate body which commands without being commanded. Laski was not the originator of pluralism, but he pushed it to a more radical conclusion, and expressed the ideas more provocatively, than any other writer. The state, he argued, needed to win support by acting reasonably, but could not demand it through invoking bogus doctrines to justify obedience. Associations such as clubs, churches, and trade unions gave vitality to social life and provided the channels through which individual personality was expressed. But if people were—and should be—members of associations, it followed that they had a 'plurality' of allegiances. The state should not demand exclusive or superior loyalty and Laski favoured decentralization, in which there should be thriving participation at local level, and in work-based organizations. He was also keen to dismantle state sovereignty in its external sense, so that the nation-state itself recognized a moral duty to the world as a whole, which should be embodied in international law and institutions.

These works on pluralism established Laski's contemporary reputation as a major political theorist, but their scholarly tone masked a burning political commitment, which soon brought him into conflict with conservative forces. In the midst of the post-war 'red scare' in the United States, he outraged the local élite by supporting the Boston police in their 1919 strike action. This led to his vilification as a 'Bolshevik' and also precipitated anti-semitic attacks. Although A. Lawrence Lowell, the president of Harvard, defended him against calls for his dismissal, Laski now welcomed the offer of a lectureship in government at the London School of Economics (LSE), where he remained until his death.

After returning to Britain in the summer of 1920 Laski became increasingly closely involved with the Labour Party, and he joined the executive committee of the Fabian Society in 1921. His ideas also underwent an evolution, which had already begun while in North America. Much of his early pluralism had been written as if there was a simple polarity between associations and the state, with the former regarded as positive and the latter as negative. However, by 1917–18, with the rise of industrial conflict and the Russian Revolution, he had placed class inequality at the centre of his analysis. This made a significant difference to his position for, from then on, he regarded himself as a socialist and viewed capitalism as a system incorporating inequality at every level. Henceforth he believed that liberty was inseparable from equality and that it was therefore impossible to conceive of a free society unless the working classes shared in its material and spiritual benefits. This led to a re-evaluation of the role of the state, which culminated in *A Grammar of Politics* (1925).

This was an extremely ambitious work in which Laski tried to elaborate a socialist theory and to apply this to constitutional practice, economic organization, and national sovereignty, outlining the necessary reforms in each sphere. Because he believed that the structure of inequality permeated all the institutions of society he now argued that only the exercise of state power would be effective in bringing about change. He also saw a need for a party, armed with a doctrine and a programme, to take control of the government and direct the process of reform. Nevertheless, he still adhered to a vision of participation and creativity at grass-roots level, urging an acceptance of federal authority and international controls over the nation-state. And his underlying liberalism remained evident in his stress on the fundamental importance of the individual and the sanctity of personal conscience.

While many of the detailed proposals of the book inevitably appear dated, Laski's attempt both to attain a synthesis between pluralism and Fabianism and to elucidate the practical implications of his doctrine remains impressive. Its immediate impact was his promotion to the Graham Wallas chair of political science at the LSE in 1926 at the age of thirty-two. In the same year he became a member of the industrial court, where he took his responsibilities in arbitration cases extremely seriously. As an internationally renowned political theorist, an influence on Labour Party thinking, an outstanding teacher, and a public servant, Laski appeared to be an unqualified success. However, his work was to become increasingly controversial.

The move to Marxism, 1927–1939 During the early 1920s Laski had been unsympathetic to both communism and Marxism, but he now began to re-examine them more seriously. One reason for this was the general strike, in which he had attempted to act as a mediator and had been deeply shocked by the intransigence of many figures in the Conservative Party, including Winston Churchill. This experience and research for a short book, *Communism* (1927), led to an increasing anxiety that peaceful change might not be possible. At this stage he did not believe that Marxism was valid, and feared that revolution would lead to dictatorship, but he now argued that the doctrine would inevitably appeal to those who suffered from economic oppression. The only way to counter this effectively would be 'by the alteration of the present social order by concessions larger in scope and profundity than any ruling class has so far been willing to make by voluntary act' (*Communism*, 240). *Liberty in the Modern State* (1930) was his final attempt to demonstrate the value of an egalitarian version of the liberal ideal before pessimism became a more dominant strain in his writing.

By the late 1920s Laski was also becoming increasingly doubtful about the determination of the Labour Party to institute the necessary changes, but he certainly hoped that the MacDonald government of 1929 would institute bold reforms. As an energetic member of the lord chancellor's committee on ministers' powers (1929–32), he also sought to play a practical role in facilitating this. The committee held that delegated legislation was necessary and an irreversible trend in modern government. Laski and Ellen Wilkinson, the left-wing Labour MP, went beyond the rest of the committee, in arguing that such legislation ought to be extended, and in seeking a limitation of judicial power over statutes so that the spirit behind government legislation would prevail over conservative-minded judges. However, the abrupt collapse of the Labour government in 1931, coupled with Ramsay MacDonald's defection to the premiership of a national government, reinforced his pessimism.

Arguing that MacDonald had done the most considerable disservice to constitutionalism in Britain in modern times, Laski still hoped that peaceful, constitutional change remained possible. This, he believed, meant that the Labour Party would need a 'religious enthusiasm for its ends' and the ability 'to convince its opponents that nothing can turn it from its goal' (*The Crisis and the Constitution: 1931 and After*, 1932, 55). But having also spent four months in the USA at the height of the depression in 1931, he now despaired of the survival of democracy anywhere. It was in these circumstances that in 1932 he wrote *Democracy in Crisis* (1933). In this he argued that the growth of liberal democracy had been a remarkable achievement, but that there was no guarantee that constitutional conventions would be accepted if there was a fundamental disagreement over the whole system. It was on this assumption that he proceeded to make highly controversial statements about the situation which could arise in Britain in the event of a Labour victory. Envisaging a climate of potential civil war in which privileged groups sought to resist necessary reforms, he argued that the government would need 'to take vast powers', 'suspend the classic formulae of opposition', and secure Conservative promises that 'its work of transformation' would not be repealed (*Democracy in Crisis*, 87). Such speculation indicated his state of mind, for the book was dominated by a prolonged inner debate between a fervent desire to save constitutional democracy and his growing belief that this was improbable. Such theoretical contradictions were matched by apparent inconsistencies in his public life for, although he was adamantly opposed to the National Government, he continued to participate in committees which served it. He thus remained a member of the departmental committee on local government officers from 1930 until 1934, and the lord chancellor's committee on legal education from 1932 until 1934.

The appointment in January 1933 of Hitler as chancellor in Germany made Laski still more pessimistic about the resilience of parliamentary democracy and he now adopted a personal form of Marxism, which continued to be infused with liberalism. Indeed he appeared to accept both perspectives simultaneously, striving to bring about a reconciliation between them. This attempt was manifested analytically in *The State in Theory and Practice* (1935), and historically in *The Rise of European Liberalism* (1936). At this stage he also believed that the Soviet Union might constitute a new civilization, but his deep-seated belief in individual freedom meant that he recoiled from whole-hearted endorsement of any dictatorship. His real message therefore remained that it was imperative for capitalism to accept socialist reform so that liberal values could be preserved. *Parliamentary Government in England* (1938) epitomized these contradictions, for the book simultaneously extolled constitutional democracy and argued that it was impossible to implement in an unequal society.

During this period Laski's political activities intensified and, with them, the controversies. In 1934 William Beveridge, the director of LSE, attempted to curtail his popular journalism, arguing that his utterances might be harmful to the school and, before this matter had been resolved, a series of lectures Laski delivered in Moscow caused a new furore. Although he had argued that the communist method was inapplicable to the current British situation, the *Daily Telegraph* and some Conservative MPs claimed that he had advocated revolution and called for disciplinary action against him or even a reduction of funding to LSE. These demands were resisted, but Laski agreed to end his regular *Daily Herald* articles and limit his extra-curricular political activities. These attacks, which were sometimes tinged with antisemitism, reinforced his fears about the preservation of fundamental freedoms in the current climate. However, he was simultaneously given new hope by President Roosevelt's policies, which he immediately recognized as positive. Through Frankfurter he was introduced to the president in April 1935 and a new friendship was established. Laski subsequently promoted and defended the New Deal in both Britain and the United States, and his book *The American Presidency* (1940) argued that a strong presidency was essential if the capitalist crisis now gripping the USA was to be resolved democratically.

Laski was also an advocate of a united front with the communists against fascism. In May 1936 he therefore joined John Strachey and Victor Gollancz to launch the Left Book Club, and at the beginning of 1937 he signed a 'unity manifesto' between the Independent Labour Party, the Communist Party, and the Socialist League—a left-wing pressure group in the Labour Party, of which he was a member. Although the Socialist League then dissolved under pressure from the Labour leadership, the campaign continued and Laski was elected to the constituency section of the Labour Party national executive committee (NEC) as a unity candidate at the annual conference later that year. However, he subsequently became increasingly disillusioned with Communist Party policies, and by 1939 he had no doubts that war against Nazi Germany was necessary.

The war and after, 1939–1950 Laski campaigned relentlessly for the defeat of Nazi Germany and its allies, and his pamphlet *Is this an Imperialist War?* (1940) was an influential refutation of communist arguments against the war in the period 1939–41. But he was equally adamant that the construction of a post-war world should be based on a 'revolution by consent' (*Reflections on the Revolution of our Time*, 1943, 160–61). His insistence, within the Labour Party NEC and in countless lectures, speeches, and pamphlets, on the need to introduce extensive changes, rather than simply to achieve military victory, caused conflict with both the government and the Labour Party leader, Clement Attlee. Such policy differences brought him temporary notoriety at the end of the war.

Although the coalition government was dissolved on 23 May 1945, with the election date set for 5 July, Churchill subsequently invited Attlee to accompany him to the Potsdam conference. Attlee accepted the invitation without consulting the Labour Party NEC, and Laski, who had just become the party chairman, wrote to him asking him to make it clear that neither he nor the party could be bound by any decisions taken at Potsdam. Attlee ignored this, but the dispute became public, with Laski portrayed in right-wing newspapers as a sinister influence. This was reinforced when a conservative councillor claimed that Laski had supported violent revolution in a speech in Newark on 16 June. He issued writs for libel, but remained in the public eye up to the election, with Churchill naming him in a radio broadcast on 21 June as the figure who would control a Labour government through the NEC. Before the general election Laski also urged Attlee to resign as leader, believing him to lack popular appeal, and immediately after the Labour victory he tried without success to persuade him not to go to the palace to accept the premiership until the parliamentary party had met to choose their leader. A few weeks later, after Laski had given interviews which appeared to pre-empt aspects of foreign policy, Attlee informed him that he had no right to speak for the government and that 'a period of silence on your part would be welcome' (Attlee to Laski, 20 Aug 1945, Laski MSS, University of Hull). Attlee's exasperation with his behaviour is understandable, but Laski was attempting to safeguard the position of the NEC against control by the leadership.

After the war Laski firmly opposed communist attempts to merge with social democratic parties and his pamphlet *The Secret Battalion* (1946) was extremely critical of communist tactics. Yet he continued to regard Marxism as a legitimate and important part of the socialist tradition and wrote a long introduction to *The Communist Manifesto* for a centenary edition (*The Communist Manifesto: Socialist Landmark*, 1948). However, by now his influence was already waning and this decline had been reinforced by the court action over his libel case at the end of 1946. This was an unmitigated disaster for him, as Sir Patrick Hastings, one of the most formidable barristers of the era, used passages from *Democracy in Crisis* and *The State in Theory and Practice* to demonstrate Laski's belief in revolution. Although Laski had never believed in violence, he was unable to make subtle distinctions effectively against Hastings in court. He was devastated when he lost the case and his always fragile health suffered considerably from a sense of humiliation and failure. Nor were his final years very happy in political terms for, although he was generally pleased with the domestic policies of the Labour government and the independence of India, he was highly critical of aspects of foreign policy. In particular, he was bitterly opposed to Bevin's policy in the Middle East, for the Nazi holocaust had made him a passionate advocate of a Jewish state in Palestine, and he criticized the British role in the cold war. However, he was still more disappointed by American politics after the death of Roosevelt.

The American Democracy (1948) was a monumental work, in which Laski sought to demonstrate, in considerable detail, that the spirit and institutions of democracy had been corrupted by the dominance of business over every facet of life. Both renewal at home and international peace depended, he argued, on the growth of a labour movement which would control capitalism. However, by now the USA was again in the midst of a 'red scare', with many of Laski's friends and associates in universities under intense pressure. During his final lecture tour there in 1949 he faced harassment wherever he went and the mayor of Cambridge, Massachusetts, refused to allow the Harvard law school to use a local auditorium for a talk by Laski, on the grounds that he was a communist, hostile to all religions, and an enemy of Catholicism. This atmosphere, coupled with repression and executions in the Soviet bloc, led him in his final, uncompleted, work to denounce the irrationalism of both sides in the cold war. But, while he was categorical that the West was preferable in terms of civil rights, political liberty, and democracy, he was equally insistent that only the United States could make the decisive move to end the ever more dangerous cycle of action and counter-action. It is also notable that in some of these final writings he discussed the alienating effects of large-scale bureaucracy in both capitalism and communism, and reverted to some of his earliest themes of decentralization and pluralism (The Dilemma of our Times, 1952).

Despite his reservations about the Labour government, which had led to his resignation from the NEC in 1949, Laski campaigned as vigorously as ever in the general election of February 1950, writing the introductory section of the party programme and speaking at some forty meetings. By now he was so ill with bronchitis that he could sometimes hardly stand and on 24 March 1950 he died at St Mary's Hospital, Paddington, London, from a burst abscess on the lung. The funeral, held at Golders Green crematorium where he was cremated four days later, was attended by the prime minister and eight other members of the cabinet and tributes were sent from all over the world.

Having established his reputation as a major political theorist at an unusually early age, Laski became the best-known socialist intellectual of his era, and published more than twenty books as well as hundreds of chapters, tracts, and articles. Small in stature and slight in build, he was an inspiring teacher, who influenced generations of students from all over the world. Convinced that academic life must not be confined to the 'ivory tower', he was also a political activist. His election to the Labour Party NEC for twelve successive years was an unparalleled achievement for someone who was never an MP. As a friend of leading members of President Roosevelt's New Deal administration, and a supporter of Indian independence, his influence was felt in the USA, India, and mainland Europe, as well as Britain.

While there is general agreement about Laski's standing as a teacher and as a socialist intellectual, particularly during the 1930s, there is much less agreement about the enduring importance of his work. It has been widely held that his early books were the most profound and that he subsequently wrote far too much, with polemics displacing serious analysis. Similarly, many have argued that his wish for influence led him to exaggerate his own importance and even to indulge in fantasies. There is some validity in these criticisms, but they have been overstated, particularly during the cold war era, when the focus on his personality diverted attention from his political message. Some of the criticism of his later work is also attributable to the fact that his Marxist phase was less acceptable to mainstream opinion than his pluralism. Indeed, the most interesting feature of his work was the attempt to incorporate the different phases of his thinking—pluralist, Fabian, Marxist—into a single perspective. The result was certainly contradictory, and Laski failed to bring his life's work together into an overall coherent doctrine. Nevertheless, few people have devoted such energy to a sincere attempt to combine liberty, equality, and internationalism in theoretical terms and to promote these ideals through teaching and participation in public life. He deserves full recognition for this.

MICHAEL NEWMAN

Sources M. Newman, *Harold Laski: a political biography* (1993) · I. Kramnick and B. Sheerman, *Harold Laski: a life on the left* (1993) · K. Martin, *Harold Laski (1893–1950): a biographical memoir* (1953) · B. Zylstra, *From pluralism to collectivism: the development of Harold Laski's political thought* (1968) · P. Hirst, *The pluralist theory of the state* (1989) · M. de Wolfe, ed., *Holmes–Laski letters: the correspondence of Mr. Justice Holmes and Harold J. Laski*, 2 vols. (1953) · H. A. Deane, *The political ideas of Harold J. Laski* (1955) · R. Miliband, 'Harold Laski's socialism', *Why not capitalism?*, ed. L. Panitch and others (1995) · M. Newman, 'Harold Laski today', *Political Quarterly*, 67 (1996), 229–338 · C. Attlee, letter to H. J. Laski, 20 Aug 1945, U. Hull, Brynmor Jones L., Laski papers

Archives BLPES, lecture notes · Internationaal Instituut voor Sociale Geschiedenis, Amsterdam, correspondence and MSS · L. Cong., correspondence with several individuals [incl. a large collection of Laski–Frankfurter letters] · St Hilda's Library, Oxford, MS of Civil history of India · Syracuse University, New York, George Arents Research Library, miscellaneous MSS · U. Hull · U. Hull, correspondence (1973) · U. Hull, correspondence between Frida and Harold Laski · U. Southampton, Anglo-Jewish Archive, Laski family MSS | BL, correspondence with S. Cockerell, Add. MS 52729 · BLPES, Fabian Society MSS, correspondence with Fabian Society · BLPES, Webb MSS, letters to S. Webb and B. Webb · Bodl. Oxf., correspondence relating to Society for Protection of Science and Learning · Franklin D. Roosevelt Library, New York, Eleanor and Franklin D. Roosevelt MSS · HLRO, Lloyd George MSS, letters to D. Lloyd George · HLRO, Soskice MSS, letters to David Soskice · Internationaal Instituut voor Sociale Geschiedenis, Amsterdam, correspondence with Max Beer · L. Cong., Huebsch MSS, correspondence with B. H. Huebsch · McMaster University Library, Russell Archives, correspondence with Bertrand Russell · NL Wales, J. Conway Davis MSS, correspondence with J. Conway Davis · People's History Museum, Manchester, The labour party archives · Ruskin College Library, Oxford, Middleton MSS, letters to James

Middleton |FILM BFI NFTVA, documentary footage |SOUND BL NSA, 'Laski broadcasts'

Likenesses I. Opffer, sanguine, 1930, NPG · J. Kramer, chalk and Indian ink drawing, c.1944, London School of Economics · J. Kramer, lithograph, c.1944, NPG · photograph, 1946, repro. in Newman, *Harold Laski*, cover · photograph, 1948, repro. in R. Dahrendorf, *A history of the London School of Economics and Political Science* (1995) · A. Dalkman, colour illustration, repro. in Kramnick and Sheerman, *Harold Laski*, cover · Elliott & Fry, photograph, NPG [*see illus.*] · D. Low, three pencil caricatures, NPG · cartoons, repro. in Martin, *Harold Laski*

Wealth at death £19,558 4s. 7d.: probate, 2 Sept 1950, *CGPLA Eng. & Wales*

Laski, John. *See* À Lasco, John (1499–1560).

Laski, Marghanita [*formerly* Esther Pearl] (1915–1988), writer and broadcaster, was born in Manchester on 24 October 1915, the eldest child (she had one sister, two brothers, and an adopted brother and sister) of Neville Jonas Laski, barrister (later a crown court judge), and his wife, Seraphina Gaster. Her father called her Marghanita (an affectionate adaptation of the Aramaic word for 'pearl') when she was small and she later adopted it herself. She was educated at Ladybarn House School in Manchester, at St Paul's Girls' School, London, and at Somerville College, Oxford, where she read English language and literature, giving as much time as the syllabus allowed to Old English and Middle English. She obtained a third-class degree in 1936. She also found time at Oxford for socializing and playing croquet and bridge. It was at Oxford that she met John Eldred Howard, whom she married in 1937; he became a publisher and was the founder of the Cresset Press. He was the son of John Howard, stockbroker and farmer. They lived in Oxford during the Second World War, and about 1948 moved to Capo di Monte, a picturesque house on the edge of Hampstead Heath, where they remained for the rest of their lives. About 1965 they acquired a holiday house in the south of France, and it was there that a great deal of her book reviewing and her reading for the *Oxford English Dictionary* was done.

A primary influence on Laski's early life in Manchester was her maternal grandfather, Moses *Gaster (1856–1939), scholar and chief rabbi of Sephardi Jews in England, 1887–1918, and she found his younger children, her near contemporaries, an intellectually stimulating group. She rarely spoke about her uncle Harold Laski, the political theorist, and it can be assumed that he played little part in shaping her beliefs. In view of the enduring influence of Moses Gaster it is a mark of Marghanita Laski's true independence of mind that, while remaining proud of her Jewishness, she renounced her faith even before she went up to Oxford and declared herself to be an atheist.

Marghanita Laski's first novel, *Love on the Supertax*, was published in 1944, and this was followed by numerous other works (novels unless otherwise stated), including *The Patchwork Book* (an anthology, 1946); *To Bed with Grand Music* (written under the pseudonym Sarah Russell, 1946); *Stories of Adventure* (which she edited, 1946); *Victorian Tales* (also as editor, 1947); *Tory Heaven* (1948); *Little Boy Lost* (1949); *The Village* (1952); *The Victorian Chaise-Longue* (1953); and *The Offshore Island* (a play, 1959). The film rights of *Little Boy Lost*

Marghanita Laski (1915–1988), by Mark Gerson, 1963

were sold to John Mills, and she was furious and hurt when he turned it into a musical starring Bing Crosby (1953).

In the 1960s Laski turned away from the writing of fiction, and a string of thoughtful and literary works followed, including *Ecstasy* (1961), an ambitious book subtitled: *A Study of some Secular and Religious Experiences*; a set of essays on the Victorian novelist Charlotte M. Yonge (with E. G. Battiscombe, 1965); and a series of studies of the work of Jane Austen (1969), George Eliot (1973), and Rudyard Kipling (1974). She also broadcast widely acclaimed radio programmes on the life and work of Kipling (1973, 1983).

To the general public Laski was best-known as a broadcaster. 'Her clear, immediately recognisable voice with a slight touch of petulance or arrogance always there, was heard in programmes such as *Any Questions*, *The Brains Trust*, and *The Critics*' (*Daily Telegraph*, 8 Feb 1988). She also enjoyed speaking from pulpits, and her sermons were a demonstration of her profound and continuing interest in religion.

Laski gave much time and energy from 1974 onwards to the committee of inquiry into the future of broadcasting (1974–7, chaired by Lord Annan); and to the Arts Council (from 1979), serving as its vice-chairman (1982–6) and also as chairman of its literature advisory panel (1980–84).

Laski's extraordinary contribution as a voluntary reader for the supplement to the *Oxford English Dictionary* was among her noblest deeds. From 1958 until the publication of the final volume in 1986 she supplied some 250,000 illustrative examples to the project, all copied out in her own hand. For this purpose she dredged numerous bulky

Edwardian sales catalogues for the names of domestic articles, she read much of the crime fiction published in the twentieth century, and she scoured the whole rich literary world of twentieth-century (and some older) books and magazines for their unregistered vocabulary.

At Oxford and throughout her life Laski was renowned for her beauty, her forceful personality, and her obsession with religious and secular beliefs. She died in the Royal Brompton Hospital from a smoking-related lung problem on 6 February 1988; her husband died in 1992. They had a son and a daughter.   R. W. BURCHFIELD, *rev.*

Sources *The Observer* (7 Feb 1988) · *The Times* (8 Feb 1988) · *Daily Telegraph* (8 Feb 1988) · *The Guardian* (8 Feb 1988) · *The Independent* (9 Feb 1988) · private information (1996) · personal knowledge (1996) · *CGPLA Eng. & Wales* (1988)
Archives University of Bristol Library, Lady Chatterley MSS
Likenesses M. Gerson, photograph, 1963, NPG [*see illus.*] · J. Epstein, watercolour, priv. coll. · photographs, priv. coll.
Wealth at death £205,682: probate, 15 Dec 1988, *CGPLA Eng. & Wales*

Lassell, William (1799–1880), astronomer, was born on 18 June 1799 in Bolton, Lancashire, where his father, Nathaniel (*d. c.*1812), was in business as a timber merchant and builder with James Gregson, a brother-in-law. Lassell's mother, Hannah, came from a Liverpool business family. The religious backgrounds of his family were Congregationalist and Independent, and William (who until the late 1840s was often known as William Lassell junior) completed his education at the Rochdale dissenting academy. He maintained religious interests throughout his life.

Although no record seems to have survived of the trade he entered, Lassell became an apprentice in Liverpool about 1815. By 1825 he was being listed in a Liverpool directory as a brewer. Two years later, on 8 May 1827, he married Maria King, *née* Gregson, in Toxteth, Liverpool. Maria and at least three daughters survived him. The success of Lassell's brewing business, in which he sometimes traded with various partners, enabled him to lavish many thousands of pounds on his astronomical endeavours. Even so, at his death his estate was valued at almost £70,000.

Lassell early developed strong scientific interests. These interests were linked to his fascination with machinery through the construction, as well as the use, of reflecting telescopes, a hobby he began no later than 1821. By 1837 he had completed an excellent reflecting telescope with a speculum metal main mirror 9 inches in diameter. This, his first major instrument, was followed by two much more powerful telescopes, the first a 24 inch reflector completed in 1845 (which followed an identical design to the 9 inch). A huge 48 inch that required two assistants for its operation went into service in 1861.

An innovative telescope builder, Lassell, along with Lord Rosse, was instrumental in pushing reflectors well beyond the state of the art as defined in the late eighteenth century by William Herschel. Lassell's tenacity and mechanical skills were evidenced by his mastery of the making and use of such awkward instruments (when the 24 inch was erected at the Royal Greenwich Observatory after his death, it was not a success in other hands). His

William Lassell (1799–1880), by Henry John Whitlock

main contributions were to apply equatorial mountings to large reflectors and to develop steam-driven machines for grinding and polishing big telescope mirrors in which the movements closely matched those used in polishing mirrors by hand.

Lassell was closely and directly involved in the construction of his telescopes, only some larger pieces of metalwork being contracted out. However, he was aided in his undertakings by his close friend James Nasmyth, one of the most skilled and versatile engineers of his generation, as well as an avid amateur astronomer. It was Nasmyth, for example, who built, from Lassell's design, Lassell's first successful polishing machine. Another intimate friend was William Rutter Dawes. For many years a dissenting minister at Ormskirk, Dawes was a renowned astronomical observer, and he eased Lassell's access to wider scientific circles.

The 24 inch telescope was built by Lassell while at Starfield, his first suburban mansion in Liverpool. In 1855 he moved 2 miles further from the centre of the city, to Bradstones. Here the 48 inch was assembled between 1858 and 1860. But in 1861, in order to escape the ever troublesome Liverpool atmosphere, as well as to observe from a more southerly latitude, Lassell, as he had done with the 24 inch in 1852, shipped the 48 inch to Valletta, Malta, where it served him for three years. As this was a far better site than that of Lord Rosse's 72 inch reflector, the more famous 'Leviathan of Parsonstown', in Ireland, Lassell's telescope was arguably the most powerful in the world.

When Lassell returned to England (taking up residence at Ray Lodge in Maidenhead, Berkshire), he did not re-erect the 48 inch, preferring to observe with his smaller but easier to manage 24 inch. In 1864 he offered the 48 inch as a gift to the Melbourne observatory in Australia. The Royal Society committee then charged with securing a large telescope for the observatory declined, preferring to start from scratch with a design for a new reflector by the Dublin maker Thomas Grubb, a choice with which the Melbourne authorities agreed. Eventually, in 1877, nearly all of the 48 inch was consigned to scrap.

As an observer, Lassell was little interested in the sort of painstaking positional astronomy pursued by professionals, nor did he possess the mathematical training and skills to engage in debates in theoretical astronomy. Although he did spend some time observing nebulae, he was most enthusiastic about examining the planets of the solar system (especially Saturn) and in searching for new satellites orbiting around them. His first major find was that of Triton, Neptune's largest satellite, which he first glimpsed within weeks of the discovery of Neptune itself in September 1846. In 1848 he found (almost simultaneously with W. C. Bond at Harvard) Hyperion, a satellite of Saturn, and in 1851 he detected Ariel and Umbriel, two faint satellites of Uranus. A catalogue of some 600 new nebulae was the work of his assistant, Albert Marth, an accomplished positional astronomer, whom he hired for the second stay at Malta. When Lassell engaged him, in 1862, Marth had published on, among other things, the planetary satellites of Saturn, Uranus, and Neptune, interests very much in line with Lassell's keen pursuit of new satellites. It also says much for Lassell's independence of mind that he ignored the strident advice of the then astronomer royal, George Biddell Airy, not to employ Marth.

Lassell was awarded the gold medal of the Royal Astronomical Society in 1849, and in 1858 he was one of the Royal Society's royal medallists. Active in a variety of scientific societies, he was president of the Royal Astronomical Society from 1870 to 1872. Lassell was an administrator, not a reformer who sought to take the society in a radical new direction. He died in his sleep at his home, Ray Lodge, Maidenhead, on 5 October 1880.

ROBERT W. SMITH

Sources Catalogue of scientific papers, Royal Society, 3 (1869), 866–8 • Catalogue of scientific papers, Royal Society, 8 (1879), 170 • Catalogue of scientific papers, Royal Society, 10 (1894), 521 • R. W. Smith and R. Baum, 'William Lassell and the ring of Neptune', Journal for the History of Astronomy, 15 (1984), 1–17 • A. Chapman, 'William Lassell (1799–1880)', Vistas in Astronomy, 32 (1988), 341–70 • J. A. Bennett, 'The giant reflector, 1770–1870', Human implications of scientific advance: the 15th International Congress of the History of Science [Edinburgh 1977], ed. E. G. Forbes (1978), 553–8 • J. A. Bennett, Church, state, and astronomy in Ireland: 200 years of Armagh observatory (1990) • Correspondence concerning the great Melbourne telescope, in three parts: 1852–70 (1871) • H. C. King, The history of the telescope (1955) • J. Herschel, 'Address delivered by the president', Monthly Notices of the Royal Astronomical Society, 9 (1848–9), 87–92 • Nonconformist registers (birth), Duke's Alley Chapel, 1785–1818

Archives National Museums and Galleries on Merseyside, Liverpool • NMM • RAS, papers • Whipple Museum for the History of Science, Cambridge | RAS, Dawes MSS • RAS, letters to Richard Sheepshanks • RAS, letters to Royal Astronomical Society • RS, corresp. with Sir John Herschel

Likenesses photograph, c.1850, RS • photograph, c.1870, RAS • photograph, c.1870–1879, Bolton Central Library • H. J. Whitlock, photograph, NPG [see illus.]

Wealth at death under £70,000: resworn probate, April 1881, CGPLA Eng. & Wales (1881) • £460: probate, 28 Jan 1881, CGPLA Ire.

Lassells [Lascelles], **John** (d. 1546), courtier and religious activist, was the second of three children of Richard, or George, Lassells of Gateford, Nottinghamshire (d. 1520), gentleman, and his wife, Dorothy, daughter of Sir Brian Sandford. After studying at Furnival's Inn, in the 1530s he entered Sir Francis Bryan's household. However, in 1538 his vigorous advocacy of evangelical religion led to his dismissal; he moved into the service of Thomas Cromwell through, it seems, the patronage of his guardian, Sir John Hercy. He acted as a messenger for Cromwell in 1538–9, and was rewarded in late 1539 with the post of sewer in the king's privy chamber.

The chamber was a nest of evangelicals, and Lassells quickly found himself among kindred spirits. In September 1540, in the wake of Cromwell's fall, he and three colleagues discussed their hopes for the future. They agreed that Bishop Gardiner and Thomas Howard, duke of Norfolk, were blocking further reform, but Lassells believed that the king himself remained committed to the evangelical cause. He therefore urged his more impetuous comrades

> not to be to rashe or quike in mayntenyng the scrypture, for yff we wolde lete [Gardiner and Norfolk] a lone and suffer a lettell tyme they wolde (I doubte not) ower throwe them selves, standyng manyfestlye a nenst god and theyr prynce. (PRO, SP 1/163, fol. 46r)

This optimism was rewarded in the following year, when he visited his younger sister Mary Hall in Sussex. Mary had once been in the duchess of Norfolk's household with the young Katherine Howard, so John suggested that she should approach the queen for a place. She demurred, saying that Katherine was 'light both in living and in condytions' (Proceedings ... of the Privy Council, 7.353), and describing the series of affairs which the queen had had before her marriage. She apparently did not realize how explosive this information was, but John immediately took the matter to Archbishop Cranmer, and so set in motion the process which ended with the queen's destruction. He maintained that he revealed the information to avert a charge of misprision of treason, which may well be true, but he can hardly have regretted the destruction of so prominent a Howard.

By 1546, however, Lassells's patience with the pace of reform under Henry VIII had run out. In the spring of that year he counselled Edward Crome not to recant his views on the mass, and by 11 May he was arrested, having 'boosted abrode that he was desirous to be called to the

Counseill and he would aunswer to the Pricke' (PRO, SP 1/218, fol. 45r). Although more circumspect under examination, he was committed to the Tower. He was denounced as a patron of Richard Laynam, a London prophet who predicted the imminent overthrow of the king. Even more dangerously, Lassells was linked with the sacramentarian Anne Askew. They were clearly friends: John Bale described Lassells as her 'instructour' (First Examinacyon, 67r), and A. G. Dickens has agreed that he was the 'leading spirit' (Dickens, 34) of the radical group at court. His workmanlike command of Greek certainly suggests considerable education. His Protestation, written from prison and printed after his death, describes a subtle and idiosyncratic eucharistic theology which caused his editors some embarrassment; this may, as Robert Persons later argued, have derived from the German radical Carlstadt. It was certainly enough to condemn Lassells. He was arraigned for heresy on 12 July but, 'mery and chereful in the Lorde', he refused to recant (Nichols, Narratives, 43). On 16 July, along with Askew and two others, he was burnt at Smithfield.   ALEC RYRIE

Sources PRO, state papers domestic, Henry VIII, SP 1/132, fol. 163r–v · PRO, state papers domestic, Henry VIII, SP 1/134, fol. 217r · PRO, state papers domestic, Henry VIII, SP 1/138, fol. 67r · PRO, state papers domestic, Henry VIII, SP 1/163, fol. 46r–v · PRO, state papers domestic, Henry VIII, SP 1/218, fols. 45r, 110v, 112r–v · S. Brigden and N. Wilson, 'New learning and broken friendship', EngHR, 112 (1997), 396–411 · J. Lascelles, et al., Uvicklieffes wicket … with the protestation of J. Lassels late burned in Smythfelde [1548?] · N. H. Nicolas, ed., Proceedings and ordinances of the privy council of England, 7 vols., RC, 26 (1834–7), vol. 7, pp. 352–5 · A. G. Dickens, Lollards and protestants in the diocese of York, 1509–1558 (1959) · G. W. Marshall, ed., The visitations of the county of Nottingham in the years 1569 and 1614, Harleian Society, 4 (1871) · D. Wilson, A Tudor tapestry: men, women and society in Reformation England (1972) · R. Persons, A treatise of three conversions of England, 3 pts (1603–4), pt 3, p. 498 · J. G. Nichols, ed., Narratives of the days of the Reformation, CS, old ser., 77 (1859) · The first examinacyon of Anne Askew, latelye martyred in Smythfelde, ed. J. Bale (1546) · APC, 1542–47, 419, 449 · J. G. Nichols, ed., The chronicle of the grey friars of London, CS, 53 (1852), 51

Lassels [Lascelles], **Richard** (c.1603–1668), Roman Catholic priest and travel writer, was the younger son of a Catholic gentleman, William Lascelles of Brackenborough in Yorkshire, and grandson of Sir Thomas Lascelles, a member of the council of the north; his mother was Elizabeth Tunstall, youngest daughter of Sir Francis Tunstall of Thurland Castle, Lancashire, and Anne Bold (from whom Richard and his brothers derived their religious alias 'Bolds'). About 1623, Lassels followed two of his brothers abroad to be educated in the Southern Netherlands at Douai College; Thomas and John Lassels had both been there since 1618 and were ordained as priests in 1624 and 1625 respectively. In May 1626 Richard was sent with a group of students to Paris, probably because of the plague. According to Anthony Wood he was 'an hospes for some time' at Oxford, 'as those of his persuasion have told me, but whether before or after he left England they could not tell' (Wood, Ath. Oxon., 3.818). Back at Douai he was teaching grammar in 1629 (the year when a third brother, Ralph Lassels, also arrived at the college) and syntax a year later. Richard was ordained priest there on 6 March 1632.

Almost certainly he was the author (under his alias of Richard Bolds) of The Conviction of Noveltie, and Defense of Antiquitie (1633), a slim duodecimo by 'R.B. Roman Catholicke, and one of the English Clergie, and Mission'. It is likely that he returned to England briefly, on the mission to reconvert his compatriots, after his ordination.

In 1633 Lassels returned to Paris, however, where he was employed first by the Catholic bishop in exile, Richard Smith, and then by Smith's patron, Cardinal Richelieu, as Latin secretary. In 1637 he saw through the press at Paris his Latin translation, Epistola historica de mutuis officiis (dedicated to Charles I), of Smith's work, then visited Rome, probably on clergy business, and stayed there with Peter Fitton, a fellow priest and scholar. Something of a connoisseur, and a friend of Bellori, Fitton may have introduced Lassels to Italian art and fellow scholars in this field. Lassels became familiar with the works of Vasari, Carlo Rifoldi, and Bellori, and may indeed have met the last as well as artists such as François du Quesnoy and Gianlorenzo Bernini. He also refers in his writings to the great collector the earl of Arundel, another acquaintance of Fitton's. During this time he translated the twelfth volume of Cardinal Caesar Baronius's Annales, which was published in Paris in 1639 as The Life or the Ecclesiasticall Historie of S. Thomas Archbishope of Canterbury. The civil war confirmed Lassels's residence abroad, and by 1644 he was apparently chaplain to the self-exiled Lady Anne Brudenell, in Paris. This was where he published The Way how to Heare Masse with Profit and Devotion (1644, with a dedication to Lady Anne) though historical knowledge of this edition depends upon a later manuscript transcript and published versions.

Having already acted as travelling tutor, in the jubilee year of 1650 Lassels was asked to accompany a daughter of the earl of Shrewsbury, the Lady Catherine Whetenhall, to Rome. At her death in childbirth in Padua her husband asked Lassels to write an account of their journey together (now BL, Add. MS 4217). This was the first in what became a series of continuously revised manuscript accounts of Italy based on his experience of several tours with young royalist and Catholic exiles: 'The Description of Italy' of 1654, written for David Murray, Lord Balvaird, whom he was unable to accompany in person (now NL Scot., Adv. MS 15.2.15); 'The Voyage of Italy' of about 1663 (now at North Yorkshire County Record Office); and 'The Voyage of Italy' of 1664 (now at Yale University, Beinecke Library).

During the late 1650s and 1660s Lassels was cited in correspondence now in the Westminster Cathedral Archives as a candidate to be Richard Smith's successor as bishop of Chalcedon. But Lassels died in September 1668 in Montpellier in his capacity as travelling tutor, during what would have been his sixth voyage to Italy, accompanying Richard, Lord Lumley, and Ralph Sheldon. He was buried in the church of the Discalced Carmelites, Montpellier, and left 100 florins to Douai College. His fellow priest Simon Wilson obtained the latest version of his Voyage manuscript, edited it (apparently omitting those passages likely to offend protestant taste), and published it in Paris in 1670. A still more censored version was published in London the same year.

Lassels's *Voyage of Italy* became the most influential English guidebook of the period, conditioning the first impressions of many a tourist to that country. It also provided the basis for subsequent guidebooks as well as manuscript accounts such as the Italian sections of John Evelyn's diary. The unprecedented attention it paid to art and architecture encouraged the phenomenon of the eighteenth-century style 'grand tour' (a term coined by Lassels) according to which art prevailed over all other subjects, religious or secular. It was translated and published in French and German and was still being reprinted in the early eighteenth century. Aside from Lassels's published works, notes and two or three completed pietistic manuscripts ('Collections … out of Baronius' and the two-volume 'Apologie for the Roman Catholicks') in his fine, distinctive hand survive at Oscott College.

EDWARD CHANEY

Sources C. Dodd [H. Tootell], *The church history of England, from the year 1500, to the year 1688*, 3 (1742), 304–5 • *DNB* • E. Chaney, *The grand tour and the great rebellion* (1985) • Wood, *Ath. Oxon.*, new edn • E. H. Burton and T. L. Williams, eds., *The Douay College diaries, third, fourth and fifth, 1598–1654*, 1, Catholic RS, 10 (1911) • E. Chaney, *The evolution of the grand tour*, 2nd edn (2000) • G. Anstruther, *The seminary priests*, 2 (1975), 184–5 • R. Lassels, 'The description of Italy', NL Scot., Adv. MS 15.2.15 • R. Lassels, 'The voyage of Italy', N. Yorks. CRO, ZRL 9/6/1 • R. Lassels, 'The voyage of Italy', Yale U., Beinecke L., Osborn Shelves G.324
Archives Georgetown University • Westminster Cathedral | BL, Lady Catherine Whetenhall journal, Add. MS 4217 • Oscott College, Birmingham, Oscott College MSS

Last, Hugh Macilwain (1894–1957), historian of Rome and college head, was born at Putney, London, on 3 December 1894, the only son of William Isaac Last (1857–1911), a civil engineer who became director of the Science Museum, South Kensington, and his wife, Anna Maria Quare, daughter of the medical writer George *Macilwain. At St Paul's School, of which he was a scholar, Last came particularly under the influence of T. Rice Holmes who turned his attention towards the world of Rome. In 1914 he passed with an open scholarship into Lincoln College, Oxford, where he remained a solitary undergraduate throughout the war, his heart having been affected by attacks of bronchitis. He obtained first classes in honour moderations (1916) and *literae humaniores* (1918), and established a very close relationship with his tutor W. Warde Fowler who revealed to him not only a comprehensive conception of republican Rome but also that world of international scholarship which later formed the background of his life. Last had begun his Oxford career late, and undisturbed by the normal preoccupations of undergraduate life he matured intellectually at an early age. He was able to read deeply and widely in those branches of ancient history, notably the history of the ancient Orient, which were not part of the normal curriculum. This wide reading bore valuable fruit in a sympathetic understanding of the needs of such subjects, particularly Egyptology, which Last took practical steps to promote within and without the university. It also led to a close friendship with many leading figures in these subjects, notably H. R. H. Hall. Throughout his life Last formed his closest friendships with men considerably older than himself.

When in 1919 Last was elected to an official fellowship in ancient history at St John's, his future as a Roman historian was already clear. He quickly made his mark in the college: as a teacher who, notwithstanding his confident mastery of his subject and Olympian manner, took endless pains with the second and third class men and won his pupils' affection, and in other walks of college life. He played an active part on the governing body and soon stood out as an able man of affairs with a particular interest in the agricultural and financial policy of the college. In the wider field of university affairs Last was also making a mark: he was a trenchant, if slightly ponderous, debater and his frequently contemptuous dismissal of his opponents made him many enemies. A colleague recalled 'how he killed a proposal for an honour school of anthropology with the remark that "an acquaintance with the habits of savages is not an education"'. He was already consciously building the image of himself which he presented to the world: the international scholar who was also a man of affairs. To this image Last imparted a suitable outward appearance: tall, dark, and heavily built, with a deliberate gait, and always dressed with the greatest care, his Homburg hat, his pipe, his walking stick, and the grey woollen scarf thrown back over his shoulder. There is an admirable likeness of him in Sir Muirhead Bone's interior of Blackwell's of which he is the central figure.

Last's reputation as a Roman historian was firmly established by his contributions to the first edition of the *Cambridge Ancient History* for which, with Henry Stuart-Jones, he was chosen to write on the earliest history of Rome in the seventh volume (1928). One of his only two sustained pieces of writing, these chapters reveal his historical position more clearly than his later account of republican history from the Gracchi to Sulla which appeared in the ninth volume (1932). His account of early Rome shows an unusual combination of solid erudition, developed powers of close reasoning, admirable judgement, and a certain solemn eloquence, which (in spite of some unexpected heterodoxies) gives that work a lasting value and sets it at the head of his writings. Throughout this reconstruction he showed his close kinship with the two great historians Gaetano De Sanctis and Theodor Mommsen. These greatly influenced Last's notions of the social and political development of Rome. His admiration for Mommsen was an important factor in the development of that truly astonishing capacity for constitutional detail which later provided him, as Camden professor, with the raw material for his weighty and almost oracular lectures on the Roman republican constitution. On the other hand, Last's reverence for the achievements of the nineteenth-century German historians led to some atrophy of his own wider interests (for instance in the ancient history of the Near East) and to his adoption of a rather negative attitude towards the discovery of new forms of investigation within the field of Roman history. To the end he was always captivated by the fascination of new evidence, but he remained unimpressed by many of the new approaches to the existing body of knowledge. While wholly familiar with inscriptions, papyri, and coins, these were for him simply historical material for his task of interpreting to the common man, and above all to the undergraduate, the spirit quickening Rome's history, and he rarely attempted direct technical work on them.

While developing into an authoritative and influential figure in the university and in the national field of Roman studies (he was president of the Roman Society in 1934–7), Last, who never married, still found time for other pursuits: his main recreations were nightly bridge in college with Stuart-Jones and others, golf, and occasional shooting at Bagley Wood, while in vacation he returned regularly to relax at his family home at Harlow in Essex. Of travel as an aid to the study of ancient history, he was frankly sceptical; apart from frequent visits to Italy (which gained him a facetious reputation as an admirer of Mussolini) he travelled little.

In 1936 Last, who had been university lecturer in Roman history since 1927, was appointed Camden professor and migrated to Brasenose. His influence in the sub-faculty was perhaps not much greater than it had been when he was a fellow of St John's, even if he now became less critical of academic policy. But his influence as a teacher increased: he was free to lecture both on the subject always nearest to his heart, the Roman constitution, traditionally a lecture of the Camden professor, and on some more peripheral subjects. He was able to confirm and extend his influence on young graduates beginning the advanced study of Roman history; and he used his weighty authority in public debate, both in and out of the university, in the defence of classical studies. It was undoubtedly as a supervisor of young graduates that Last scored his greatest success; he possessed unusual patience and skill in determining suitable subjects of research, and remained a constant, if not infrequently sardonic, adviser as the work developed. The influence which he exercised over young historians extended far beyond Oxford, and was acknowledged wherever Roman studies were prosecuted: he received honorary degrees from Edinburgh (1938) and Trinity College, Dublin (1948), and was elected an honorary fellow of Lincoln (1939).

Great though his professional achievement was, the passage of time brought no major work from Last's pen. With his main contributions to the *Cambridge Ancient History*, the last of which was published in 1936, his original work was largely over. Certainly he wrote much (although always with difficulty, and in an involved and unattractive style), but his published work took increasingly the form of learned and often elaborate reviews of the works of others. The intervention of the war (during much of which he was employed on government intelligence work) may have been partly responsible for this, but in fact the trend was already clear. Last had lost the most important qualities of a historian—a lively historical imagination and a lasting creative vein—and his hyper-developed critical sense made this defect only more

marked. Nevertheless, while in these years he did not write the book which many hoped for on the Roman constitution, his interests were developing in another field, largely through the influence of N. H. Baynes. Last, as if conscious of his own deficiency, always had the greatest respect for those who possessed the gift of imaginative writing; nobody excited his admiration and affection as much as Baynes, whose profound learning and dramatic eloquence had done much to stimulate the study of the Christian empire, and in these years Last's thoughts turned continually to the problems connected with the early history of Christianity. Another aspect of Roman civilization which increasingly occupied his attention was the Roman legal system; he sought to bring home in his later years the realities of the civil law to the historical student, and devoted several courses of advanced lectures to various aspects of this general problem.

In 1948, on the sudden death of W. T. S. Stallybrass, Last was offered the principalship of Brasenose which he accepted against medical advice. In the years between the wars the college had been an affluent and convivial society but now the main task which faced Last was the restoration of its financial stability. In the few years available to him he notably improved the financial position of the college and left his mark upon its intellectual standards by his full encouragement of all aspects of college life. In 1956 ill health compelled him to resign and he was elected an emeritus fellow. He died at Strathmore, Mulberry Green, Harlow, Essex, on 25 October 1957.

P. M. FRASER, *rev.*

Sources *The Times* (30 Oct 1957) · *Manchester Guardian* (1 Nov 1957) · [J. B. N.], 'In memoriam: Hugh Macilwain Last', *Brazen Nose*, 11 (1957–8), 14–19 · *Journal of Roman Studies*, 47 (1957) [vol. of papers presented to Last, incl. bibliography] · private information (1971) · personal knowledge (1971) · *CGPLA Eng. & Wales* (1957)
Archives AM Oxf., notebook · BL, correspondence with Sir Idris Bell, Add. MS 59514
Likenesses M. Bone, group portrait (*Interior of Blackwells*) · photograph, repro. in *Journal of Roman Studies*, frontispiece
Wealth at death £27,435 2s. 2d.: probate, 17 Dec 1957, *CGPLA Eng. & Wales*

Last, Joseph William

Last, Joseph William (1809?–1880), printer and journal proprietor, was probably born on 13 October 1809 in Stoke Green, Ipswich, Suffolk, the son of Joseph and Eliza Last. He married Elizabeth Smith on 8 January 1833 at St Bride's Church, Fleet Street, London. By 1839 he was described as a printer, dealer, and chapman, and had gained a considerable trade reputation in Edward Street, Hampstead, where he produced some highly successful weekly publications entitled *Clarke's Tales of the Wars* for the publisher Mark Clarke of Warwick Lane. Splendidly illustrated with either a naval or military battle on the first page, they attained an immense circulation. Last early had a reputation for as extensive a knowledge of the machinery and practicalities of printing as any man of his time. He claimed to be the first to print a six-sheet poster and was one of the earliest to execute superior work from a cylinder-press supposedly unfitted for the requirements of woodcut reproduction.

With his excellent taste in effective and fancy display

typography, from 1838 onwards Last established himself as a theatrical printer in various places near the Strand. Noteworthy in a forty-year career full of vicissitudes was his management of the Strand Printing Company and the Savoy Press in Savoy Street, the Strand (1861–3). He finally settled down in Wych Street, London, where he carried on a successful business until his death, his son, Alfred Last, being his manager. Best known, however, was 3 Crane Court, Fleet Street (1840–43), nearly opposite the Whitefriars Printing Works. Here also were born Parr's Life Pills, puffed as a longevity pill by Herbert Ingram, who for this purpose rented some rooms 'on the premises of his friend Mr Last' (*Mr. Punch: his Origin and Career*, 14). His landlord's close ancestral ties were with 'gutter papers' best known for their short shelf-life, small sales, scurrility, and sensationalism. In June 1837 Last launched *The Town*, a weekly featuring original indecorous essays for aspiring gentlemen about town, which collapsed after 156 numbers in May 1840. He owned another weekly with a rickety provenance, *The Crown*, which ran from July 1838 to April 1839. He seemingly could not exist without a comic journal, his next venture being *The Squib*, self-described as a 'granulation of wit, satire and amusement', which survived from 29 May to 17 December 1842.

With the engraver Ebenezer Landells, Last was starting a periodical called *The Cosmorama* when he introduced Landells to Henry Mayhew, a son of his solicitor. Although a coherent story of its birth remains cloudy, Last's family was to claim that the initiative lay with the master printer for the birth of an English version of Philipon's *Charivari* (a periodical built around a large satirical drawing), initially to be called the *Funny Dog* but destined to achieve immortality as *Punch, or, The London 'Charivari'*. The printer met with and discussed the project with a literary circle meeting at an inn kept by Mark Lemon, and at least one meeting took place in Last's office, where it appears a prospectus was first read and debated.

Despite bankruptcy proceedings in March 1839 and mindful of the bleak age of the 'hungry forties', when it took courage to launch a comic journal, Last contrived to invest £600, representing one-third of the new property. Another third came from Landells, who was to act as art editor, and the remaining third was divided equally between three co-editors, Mayhew, Lemon, and Stirling Coyne. The first number was printed on 17 July 1842 and distributed from 13 Wellington Street. Mayhew wanted emphasis on a whole-page political cartoon with the back left blank, but Last expressed anxiety over this ingredient for success. Less emotionally involved with the project and having to bear its start-up costs, Last soon saw little prospect of any returns and refused to go on. Rival printers Bradbury and Evans (familiarly known as the 'Whitefriars potentates') broke off negotiations to acquire Last's share, which was eventually acquired by Landells. Last's son, however, was to maintain that there had been a direct sale to Bradbury and Evans in September 1841.

Meanwhile, with the growth of mass literacy Ingram had enjoyed a remarkable success with cheap, illustrated weekly periodicals, and Last was engaged as managing printer for the *Illustrated London News* (1842). His proven ability influenced that great pictorial speculation, printed on the same machinery erected for *Punch*. While still actively engaged in business as J. W. Last & Co., Last died in St Peter's Hospital, Berners Street, London, on 23 March 1880 from a combination of peritonitis and 'exhaustion'.

GORDON PHILLIPS

Sources D. Griffiths, ed., *The encyclopedia of the British press, 1422–1992* (1992) • Boase, *Mod. Eng. biog.* • *London, Provincial and Colonial Press News* (Jan 1880), 25–6 • D. Linton and R. Boston, eds., *The newspaper press in Britain: an annotated bibliography* (1987) • R. G. G. Price, *A history of Punch* (1957) • *Mr. Punch: his origin and career* (1870) • A. Mayhew, *A jorum of 'Punch' with those who helped brew it …* (1895) • M. H. Spielmann, *The history of 'Punch'* (1895) • IGI • d. cert.

Last [*née* Lord], **Nellie** [Nella] (**1889–1968**), housewife and diarist, was born at 81 Salthouse Road, Barrow in Furness, on 4 October 1889, the daughter of John Charles Lord, a railway clerk and later an accountant employed by the Furness Railway, and his wife, Margaret, *née* Rawlinson, whose previous married name was Parkinson. Nella referred to her descent from 'the proud Rawlinsons' (directive reply, June 1939), yeoman farmers who could trace their origins back to Elizabethan times and whose tombstones are in Hawkshead churchyard. She was named Nellie, but was known as Nella, the name under which her diaries were published. After being injured in a childhood accident, Nella was unable to walk properly between the ages of five and thirteen, and she described her education as 'patchy' (directive reply, Jan 1939). The most important early influence was her maternal grandmother, a Quaker whose serene outlook provided her with an emotional touchstone throughout her life. On 17 May 1911, anxious to escape an unhappy parental home, she married at St George's parish church, Barrow, a joiner, William Last (*b.* 1887/8), son of Edward Last, a builder and joiner; he was a quiet, depressive man whose family disliked Nella 'for what they called my "fine lady ways"' (directive reply, June 1939). Apart from a brief period in Southampton during the First World War while her husband served in the navy, Nella spent her whole life in Barrow.

During the war Nella's mother and her only sister both succumbed to fatal illnesses. Uncomfortable with her in-laws and with the working-class neighbourhood in which they lived, she devoted herself to providing her two sons—Arthur and Cliff, born in 1913 and 1919 respectively—with a rounded education. By the 1930s the two boys had become her closest friends and confidants, and they were still exchanging weekly letters with their mother in the 1960s. In the early 1930s her elder son, Arthur, left home to train as a tax inspector, while her younger son, Cliff, distressed her by turning down a scholarship to the grammar school in order to join the family business. (Later, however, after serving in the army during the Second World War, he became a sculptor.) In the early 1930s Nella was active for a time in Conservative politics, canvassing at the general election of 1931 and chairing her ward party. Subsequently, with her sons growing up, she found domesticity increasingly unfulfilling and appears to have suffered a nervous breakdown. About 1936 she finally persuaded her husband to move to a modern semi-detached house at 9 Ilkley Road on a 'nice little estate' (*Nella Last's War*, 84) in the northern suburbs of Barrow, where she lived for many years.

Mass-Observation, which she joined at the beginning of 1939, and the Second World War both gave Nella Last a new lease of life. 'Next to being a mother', she wrote in October 1939, 'I'd have loved to write books … and the boys tell me I've given them more pleasure [with her letters] than if I'd written best-sellers!' (*Nella Last's War*, 19). Mass-Observation provided an outlet for both her creativity and her feelings. Writing up to 1500 words every day, Nella used her wartime diary to chart, often with great eloquence, every nuance of her anxieties about the violence of war, the difficulties of wartime domesticity, and her growing exasperation with her depressive husband. It was through her public work, above all, that Nella discovered that she was 'a really clever woman in my own line, and not the "odd" or "uneducated" woman that I've had dinned into me' (ibid., 255). She had joined the Women's Voluntary Service before the war, and by January 1941 she was serving on the committee of its hospital supply department. When the leadership of the Barrow branch fell apart during the blitz of May 1941, Nella took the initiative in re-establishing the hospital supply work. Subsequently she took on greater responsibilities, working on a mobile canteen and opening and running a Red Cross charity shop. Her descriptions of how she made time for her public work by cutting back on domestic standards, her growing self-confidence, and the shifting balance in her marriage—'peeling off the layers of "patience", "tact", "cheerfulness", "sweetness" that smother me like layers of unwanted clothes' (ibid., 222)—provide clear evidence of how war emancipated women. In Nella's case, however, the war may merely have provided the occasion for a liberating break from what she came to think of as her 'slavery years of mind and body' during the 1930s. Given the creativity and energy revealed by the diaries it is hard to believe that Nella would not have flowered into middle age, war or no war.

In 1945 Nella Last, like many other middle-class women, feared that opportunities for voluntary work would dry up, denying her the strength to resist her husband's pleas that she should resume full-time domesticity. She continued to write her Mass-Observation diaries more or less every week for the next twenty years, and her voluntary work also continued, at least into the early 1950s.

Extracts from the 2 million words of the wartime diaries were published in 1981, providing one of the most intimate insights available into the civilian experience of the Second World War. The post-war diaries, amounting in all to perhaps 6 million words, await transcription, editing, and publication. The story of her later life, which may well be as illuminating for historians as her account of the war years, will not be known until this is done. In February 1966, aged seventy-six and feeling ill, she sent in her final diary entry, wondering if her writing was ever read and 'if

the need for it is past now' (diary, 17 Feb 1966). She died at Bevan House, Stackwood Avenue, Barrow in Furness, on 22 June 1968. Her husband survived her.

JAMES HINTON

Sources *Nella Last's war: a mother's diary, 1939–45*, ed. R. Broad and S. Fleming (1981) • directive replies, U. Sussex, Mass-Observation Archive • N. Last, diaries, U. Sussex, Mass-Observation Archive • Women's Royal Voluntary Service, minutes, papers, Cumbria AS, Barrow, BDso/27/1, 2 • Old Station Business Park, Compton, Newbury, Women's Royal Voluntary Service archive, Region 10/2 • *Furness and District Year Book* (1939) • b. cert. • m. cert. • d. cert.
Archives U. Sussex, diaries
Wealth at death £5840: probate, 1968, *CGPLA Eng. & Wales*

Laszlo, Philip Alexius de [*formerly* Fülöp Elek László; Philip Alexius Laszlo de Lombos] (1869–1937), painter, was born in Budapest, Hungary, on 30 April 1869, the eldest son of the six children of Adolphus László, tailor, and his wife (*d.* 1915), who was a governess before her marriage. He was brought up in poor circumstances, having very little formal education, and while still a child of ten he worked for a scene-painter and learned photographic retouching. In 1884 he began studies at the School of Arts and Crafts and in 1885 at the Academy of Arts in Budapest. At the age of nineteen he won a state scholarship which took him to Venice, but he fell ill there and went on instead to the Akademie der Bildenden Künste in Munich, where he studied under Alexander von Liezen-Mayer. He then had a period of time (1890–91) at the Académie Julian in Paris under Jules Lefebvre and Benjamin-Constant before returning to Munich for another two years.

Although destined to become the most internationally successful and productive society portrait painter of his age, László's ambitions at this time fluctuated between *plein-air* genre scenes and historical subjects, both painted in the watered-down central European realism of the times. His *Im Hofbräuhaus* (1891, Hungarian National Gallery, Budapest), painted in Munich, contains over twenty-five figures and was a sensation at the winter exhibition in Budapest in 1892. In late 1893 he met Alexius de Lippich, an official in the fine arts department of the ministry of education, who began to secure portrait commissions for his young protégé, including in 1894 the portraits of Prince Ferdinand and Princess Marie-Louise of Bulgaria which would mark the beginning of his rapid rise as painter to the courts of Europe.

While in Sofia, László was commissioned by Prince Ferdinand to paint the Archimandrite Gregorius (1894, National Art Gallery, Sofia), which first attracted great attention at the Budapest winter exhibition in 1895. Official commissions began to flood in, including portraits of the Hungarian prime minister Sándor Wekerle (1896) and Emperor Franz Josef I (completed 1898). He was much in demand by the German nobility and began to undertake regular trips to Germany, including to Dresden in 1895, and to Weimar in 1898 to paint the grand duke. A one-man exhibition in Berlin at the Schulte Gallery early in 1898 consolidated his reputation there and attracted the attention of the imperial family. Regular showings of his work

Philip Alexius de Laszlo (1869-1937), self-portrait, 1918 [with his wife, Lucy, and son Henry]

at the Paris Salon at this time also resulted in his fame being spread beyond mainland Europe, and in 1899 he won the gold medal for his portrait of the German chancellor Prince Hohenlohe-Schillingsfürst and in 1900 for his portrait of Pope Leo XIII, both commissions from the Hungarian government for the Hungarian National Gallery.

Following his marriage on 7 June 1900 to Lucy Madeleine, sixth daughter of Henry Guinness of Burton Hall, Stillorgan, co. Dublin, László moved in 1903 from Budapest to Vienna, but finally decided in 1907 to settle in London. With characteristic thoroughness he organized an exhibition of his work at the Fine Art Society in May to precede his arrival and was rewarded with commissions from Edward VII for a sketch of Princess Victoria (National Portrait Gallery, London), followed immediately by half-lengths of the king and Queen Alexandra (Royal Collection). Early in 1908 he made the first of a number of visits to the United States and painted Theodore Roosevelt, one of four portraits he did of American presidents. The remaining pre-war years in London were an unqualified success as he cut swathes through both the aristocracy and the British establishment and consolidated his ambitions (and those of his clients) with regular one-man exhibitions at Agnew's. Between 1911 and 1914 he exhibited annually at the Royal Academy and taught occasionally at the London and New Art School in Kensington. In 1912 he was raised to the Hungarian nobility with the hereditary suffix de Lombos, and from then on he called himself de Laszlo and also used this form as his signature.

De Laszlo was not naturalized as a British subject until 29 August 1914. During the First World War he committed various indiscretions, such as sending money to his relatives in Hungary and using the Dutch diplomatic bag for correspondence. He was interned in September 1917 until in June 1919 a naturalization (revocation) committee sat to determine whether his certificate should be revoked. It found, however, no evidence of disaffection or disloyalty, and he was finally released from the house arrest under which he had been held following a nervous breakdown and his release from Holloway prison the previous May.

The remainder of de Laszlo's career was to all outward appearances as successful as it had been in the pre-war years. Few, if any, were the royal houses of Europe which could not boast a painting by de Laszlo and he continued to be in demand for portraits of the British aristocracy and establishment in the same huge quantities. In 1921 he went to the United States to paint President Warren Harding. By June 1923 he had organized an exhibition of mostly new work at the French Gallery in London and had painted Mussolini in Rome. Wartime xenophobia had, however, taken its toll and although he was awarded no fewer than twenty-one foreign orders during his lifetime, in Britain he never progressed beyond the MVO bestowed on him by Edward VII in 1910. He had been a fellow of the Royal Society of Portrait Painters since 1913 and was elected president of the Royal Society of British Artists in 1930 and vice-president of the Royal Society of Arts in 1937. Further attempts to exhibit at the Royal Academy, however, were met with rejection and it was not until 1925, when he painted the duchess of York (Royal Collection), that the royal family felt able to avail themselves once more of his services. In 1936 he suffered a heart attack and in October the following year, while beginning work on coronation portraits for faithful patrons such as the dukes of Portland and Northumberland, he suffered a further attack and died at his home, 3 Fitzjohn's Avenue, Hampstead, London, on 22 November 1937, on the eve of a large charity exhibition of his work at Wildenstein & Co., London. Five sons survived him; a daughter had died in infancy.

De Laszlo's biographer noted that:

> Although his work lay in a sophisticated world, he himself remained a man of very simple tastes. Besides golf and an occasional game of chess, he had no recreations, although he liked reading books of history and biography. He was moderate and abstemious. He needed no bodily stimulants. A cup of tea would excite him like alcohol. ... [A] passion for cleanliness showed itself in his clothes and personal habits. He was extraordinarily neat and tidy. He detested slovenly or Bohemian dress worn by the artist of popular conception. ... He was sometimes absent-minded. 'Please remember that I am at Balliol College, Oxford, *not* Cambridge', one of his sons had to tell him.   (Rutter, 393)

On his own reckoning, de Laszlo had painted over 2700 portraits during his career. In the post-war years he had the help of one studio assistant, Frederick Harwood, who can have had little time to do more than prepare his materials. Always painting *alla prima* and specializing in sketches completed at one sitting, such rapid workmanship and its considerable material rewards were, in addition to his central European origins, doubtless also grounds for suspicion among the British artistic establishment. Despite the continued huge demand for his portraits, there was also a sense that his work belonged very much to the Edwardian era, emphasized by his continued preference for dressing his female sitters in vaguely late eighteenth-century costume. His contemporaries constantly cited Reynolds and Raeburn as his influences, but there can be no doubt that, from the late 1890s onward, Sargent, whom he admired and with whom he was always unfavourably compared, must have been the deciding influence on his mature work. De Laszlo's extraordinary facility ultimately provided the elegance but also the near uniform blandness of all his portraits. He was, nevertheless, by his own standards, remarkably consistent, and there is perhaps no such thing as a 'bad' painting by de Laszlo. It is now possible to see that even portraits of the late 1920s and 1930s, such as that of the countess of Mansfield (1927, Scone Palace, Perthshire) and Princess Elizabeth (1933, Royal Collection), and a number of portraits of his wife and family, are not only very much of their own time but can be as fresh and lively as many more contemporary works. ROBIN GIBSON

Sources O. Rutter, *Portrait of a painter: the authorized life of Philip de László* (1939) [incl. de Laszlo's incomplete autobiography] · O. von Schleinitz, *Ph. A. von László* (1913) · R. de Montesquiou and O. Williams, *The work of P. A. de László* (1921) · D. Clifford, *The paintings of P. A. de László* (1969) · Thieme & Becker, *Allgemeines Lexikon*, 22.415–16 · *WWW* · *DNB*
Archives BL, signature books, Add. MSS 45095, 45096 · Courtauld Inst., Paul Laib photos of de Laszlo's paintings | NPG, photo albums
Likenesses P. de Laszlo, self-portrait, oils, 1911, Uffizi Gallery, Florence, Italy · P. de Laszlo, self-portrait, oils, 1918 (with wife and son), priv. coll. [*see illus.*] · E. O. Hoppe, photograph, National Museum of Photography, Film and Television, Bradford, Royal Photographic Society collection · P. Laib, photographs, Courtauld Inst. · D. Low, pencil, NPG
Wealth at death £141,096 13*s.* 3*d.*: probate, 11 Feb 1938, *CGPLA Eng. & Wales*

Lates, Charles (1770/71–*c.*1810). *See under* Lates, James (*c.*1740–1777).

Lates, James (*c.*1740–1777), composer, was the son of David Francisco Lates or Lattes (*d.* 1777), of Turin, a teacher of Hebrew, music, and modern languages at Oxford. He is sometimes mistakenly called John James Lates. He became a notable violinist at Oxford, playing there in the music-room orchestra from about 1759 until his death. He also seems to have been organist of St John's College. The duke of Marlborough was his patron, and he played for him for many years at Blenheim. Five works have been published, including sets of duets for violins and for German flutes, and *Six Solos for a Violin and Violoncello* (op. 3), which Stanley Sadie described as 'among the most interesting English violin solos of the period' (*New Grove*). He died at Oxford on 21 November 1777. His son **Charles Lates** (1770/71–*c.*1810) was born at Oxford, and was a pupil of the university professor of music, Philip Hayes. He

matriculated at Magdalen College on 4 November 1793, aged twenty-two, and graduated MusB the following year, when he described himself as 'organist of Gainsborough'. His exercise for the degree, an anthem, 'The Lord is my light', was performed on 7 November 1793. He subsequently published a set of sonatas for the piano and various songs. A Charles James Lates, son of Charles and Elizabeth Lates, was baptized in Gainsborough on 4 October 1796. R. H. LEGGE, *rev.* K. D. REYNOLDS

Sources S. Sadie, 'Lates, James', *New Grove* · Foster, *Alum. Oxon.* · *Hist. U. Oxf.* 5: *18th-cent. Oxf.* · *IGI*

Latewar, Richard (1559/60–1601), Church of England clergyman and poet, was the son of Thomas Latewar, a successful clothworker of London. He entered Merchant Taylors' School in 1571 and proceeded to St John's College, Oxford, on a scholarship in 1580. Latewar soon gained a high reputation as an orator, preacher, and poet. One auditor praised him as a 'poet lawreat' as early as January 1582 (Donno, 73). He became a fellow of St John's in 1583 and graduated BA on 28 November 1584. In 1586 he composed a Latin poem in commemoration of Sir Thomas White, founder of St John's, which the college paid to have printed in gold letters for display, and the next year he made substantial contributions to Oxford's *Exequiae* for Sir Philip Sidney, edited by his friend William Gager. Latewar also contributed verses to three books of commentary on Aristotle by John Case and wrote a play, *Philotas*, which (according to Samuel Daniel) won much praise when it was performed at St John's. On 23 May 1588 he proceeded MA. When Queen Elizabeth visited Oxford in September 1592 Latewar was apparently one of the scholars chosen for a public disputation of moral philosophy.

Having served as a university proctor in 1593/4 and proceeded BD on 2 July 1594, Latewar joined his friend John Buckeridge in preaching away from Oxford. The two men later incepted as DD on the same day, 5 February 1597, and the books which Latewar gave to his college suggest that he shared similar theological views to Buckeridge. As a theologian Latewar was sufficiently well regarded for Oxford to nominate him (unsuccessfully) for the inaugural divinity lectureship at Gresham College in February 1597. By 1595 Buckeridge was a chaplain to the earl of Essex and Latewar himself was clearly associated with those scholars at Oxford who looked to the earl's patronage. One of his few surviving poems in English is a riposte to 'The Lie', a poem written by Essex's sometime rival Sir Walter Ralegh. Latewar apparently became a chaplain to Essex's friend, Lord Mountjoy, by August 1596, when Mountjoy secured him the rectory of Hopton, Suffolk. Three years later Mountjoy helped him win the richer living of Finchley, Middlesex.

Latewar served as vice-president of his college in 1597/8 but left Oxford in December 1599 when Mountjoy was appointed lord deputy of Ireland and given the task of crushing Tyrone's rebellion. His colleagues at St John's voted him 20 marks 'with a fellow feeling much tendering the state of our said fellow drawn by his love and dewtye to his L[ord] into so daingerouse and yet necessary service'

(Costin, 14). Mountjoy and his entourage arrived in Ireland to begin their long campaign two months later. On 16 July 1601, during a minor skirmish at Benburb, Latewar ventured too close to the action and received a mortal gunshot wound to his head. He died the next day, aged forty-one, and was buried on 20 July at Armagh Cathedral. A monument for him was erected by his father in the chapel of St John's in 1604, for which the college paid the costs of installation. The inscription, punning on his name, memorializes Latewar's renown as a scholar and poet.

PAUL E. J. HAMMER

Sources K. J. Holtgen, 'Richard Latewar, Elizabethan poet and divine', *Anglia*, 89 (1971), 417–38 · *An Elizabethan in 1582: the diary of Richard Madox, fellow of All Souls*, ed. E. S. Donno, Hakluyt Society, 2nd ser., 147 (1976) · Bodl. Oxf., MS Tanner 179, fols. 7v, 41v · Wood, *Ath. Oxon.*, new edn · W. C. Costin, *The history of St John's College, Oxford, 1598–1860*, OHS, new ser., 12 (1958) · Foster, *Alum. Oxon.* · PRO, E334/12, fols. 61r, 132v · monument, St John's College, Oxford

Likenesses portrait, St John's College, Oxford

Latey, Gilbert (1626–1705), Quaker activist, was born at St Issey, Cornwall, in February 1626, and was baptized there on 20 March. He was the youngest son of John Latey, a prosperous yeoman, maltster, and innkeeper. His mother, whose maiden name was Hocking, was 'a gentlewoman born' and came 'of the best family then in the parish' (Hawkins, 2); her brother married a sister of Charles I's attorney-general Sir William Noy. Latey served his apprenticeship to a tailor and then worked in Plymouth but left his employment owing to doubts about his master's religious sincerity. In November 1648 he arrived in London and soon set up business as a tailor in the Strand. His nephew and biographer, Richard Hawkins, noted that 'he grew into great reputation in the world ... being employed and respected by persons of the first rank and quality' (ibid., 4).

In 1654 Latey was attending four sermons a day but was disturbed by religious doubts, for 'his mind and desires were still to find peace with the Lord' and so he remained in a 'seeking condition' (Hawkins, 4). He was convinced of the Quaker message at the house of Sarah Matthews, a widow in Whitecross Street, after hearing Edward Burrough speak. He at once joined the movement and shortly became one of its most influential members in London, testifying about 1659 against the schismatic John Perrot. As a result of his new beliefs he refused to make coats superfluously adorned with lace and ribbon and 'came under a conscientious concern not to meddle therein ... which made some say he was mad' (Hawkins, 19). Latey discussed his objections in the tract *To All You Taylors and Brokers who Lyes in Wickedness* (1660) in which he remarked that 'people look like apes and fools' rather than 'sober men and women' and deprecated such practices as the bedecking of servants in liveries (ibid., 45–6). As a consequence most of his wealthy customers left him, and his trade, which had been prosperous, for a time declined, so that he had to release his servants and go and 'work at day labour for his bread' (ibid., 20).

In 1659 Latey went to St Dunstan's Church, Fleet Street, and after the sermon openly charged the preacher, the presbyterian Thomas Manton, to prove his doctrine. As the congregation came to 'a fermentation' a constable was sent for and Latey was taken before a magistrate. The latter told him that Manton was a very learned man and could doubtless give scriptural proof for what he said; according to his nephew, Latey replied 'that was all he desired, but could not obtain' (Hawkins, 24–5). The magistrate then dismissed him with the remark that he had understood the Quakers to be 'mad, whimsical folks' but that Latey seemed rational enough (ibid., 26). Soon afterwards Latey and about sixteen others were thrown into a small dungeon at the Gatehouse, Westminster, for meeting together. The cell was dark and only 10 feet by 11, which meant that they had to take turns to lie down. Latey afterwards succeeded in proving charges of cruelty and extortion against Wickes, the master of the prison.

Following his release Latey signed the petition of 600 Friends, presented through Sir John Glanville, that they might lie body for body in place of those already in prison, though the request was refused. About 1660 Latey and George Fox attempted to arrange the release of two female Quakers from prison in Malta and the former took the matter up with Lord d'Aubigny, lord almoner to the queen mother. On one visit he was invited to her chapel and 'the power of the Lord worked so much on Gilbert, that he stepped up on ... a private altar, and the word of the Lord came to him to preach truth' (Hawkins, 54). He continued to visit d'Aubigny who eventually secured the women's release.

Latey constantly visited the numerous meetings in and around London, at Kingston, Hammersmith, Barking, and Greenwich. While riding to Greenwich on one occasion he was stoned by a mob. In 1661 he was taken by a party of the King's foot guards from a meeting in Palace Yard, Westminster, and confined under the Banqueting House in Whitehall. He was again arrested at the end of 1662 for being present at a meeting in the home of Elizabeth Trot in Pall Mall, where the Quakers continued to meet until 1666 when they moved to Westminster.

By the 1660s it would appear that Latey was taking an important role in the affairs of the central Quaker meetings. In 1668 he was one of the keepers of the society's national stock and remained so until 1682. He was frequently chosen to represent the society regarding sufferings and often did so with George Whitehead, who described Latey as his 'true companion in laborious solicitations' on behalf of Friends (George Whitehead's testimony concerning Gilbert Latey, in Hawkins, sig. A5). In 1663, for example, Whitehead procured, after a personal appeal to Charles II, the release of sixty-three Quakers imprisoned at Norwich and the remission of their fines. During the plague of 1665 Latey was in constant attendance on the sick, distributing money collected among the Friends, particularly to those confined to houses in the parishes outside Temple Bar. He caught the infection himself in October but, as he told Margaret Fell, 'the lord was good unto him, and, having further service for him to do, raised him up again' (Braithwaite, *Second*, 48). In September 1670 he held meetings in Somerset, Devon, and Cornwall, but on learning that Sir John Robinson, governor of the Tower of London, had given orders for the pulling down of several meeting-houses in London, Latey hurried back and managed to prevent the demolition of the one in Wheeler Street to which he held the title. In 1671 Latey was arrested and fined for preaching at Hammersmith in spite of the warning of his patron, Sir William Sawkell, that he had orders to arrest all who should be present.

On 23 March 1674 Latey married Mary Fielder (*d*. 1714), only daughter of John and Ann Fielder of Kingston upon Thames, Surrey. They had eleven children, most of whom died at an early age; certainly only their daughters Sarah and Mary appear as beneficiaries in Latey's will of 1705. Mary Latey gave a picture of her husband's character in a testimony to him, writing that 'he was a man given up to serve God, and his people, never sparing himself to do what good he could' (M. Latey, 'A testimony concerning my dear and well-beloved husband Gilbert Latey', in Hawkins, sig. A).

Latey was a key member of the meeting for sufferings, which met weekly from 1676. In 1679 he again went by Bath and Bristol to Cornwall where he visited Thomas Lamplugh, bishop of Exeter, hoping to moderate the persecution of Friends in the west country, a venture which, judging by a letter from the bishop of March 1684, appears to have been successful. On behalf of the meeting for sufferings Latey attended Charles II on many occasions, for example at Hampton Court in 1683, where he discussed the plight of prisoners in Norwich as well as Quaker customs such as the refusal of hat honour. Soon after the accession of James II, Latey and Whitehead, who had always been well received at court under his brother, induced the new king after long attendance at Whitehall to order the release from prison of 1500 Friends and to remit their fines of £20 a month for non-attendance at church. Subsequent interviews with James led to the discharging of other Friends in Bristol and elsewhere and, in 1686, to the restoration of meeting-houses at the Savoy and at Southwark which had been seized as guardhouses for the king. Latey's house at the Savoy communicated with the meeting-house by a stone passage and flight of steps. In December 1687 a third visit paid by Latey and Whitehead to the king was followed by another proclamation of pardon. With William and Mary, Latey's personal influence was exerted no less successfully. On their accession he presented an address on behalf of a hundred Quakers, most of whom were in prison for refusing the oath of allegiance, and was successful in securing their release. It was owing to Latey's and Whitehead's personal and persistent applications at court that parliament passed the act in 1696 by which the Quaker affirmation became acceptable instead of an oath, an act which was made perpetual in 1715.

A number of character testimonies exist for Latey, including that from his nephew and biographer, Richard Hawkins, who wrote that 'His parts were quick, and his apprehension lively; his memory good, and his judgement sound and strong; his example shining in self-denial; yet he was of a generous and free spirit' (R. Hawkins, 'The testimony of Richard Hawkins concerning … Gilbert Latey', in Hawkins, unpaginated). An unnamed 'very eminent Friend' said of Latey that 'of all the men, among Friends, that he ever knew or heard of, he never followed a man that had a sweeter character' (Hawkins, 154). Being mostly involved in organizational affairs, Latey apparently had little time for writing. Apart from his tract of 1660 he contributed to *A Salutation or Testimony of True and Brotherly Love* (1672) and was a signatory to Edward Burrough's *A Declaration from the People called Quakers* (1659).

Latey continued to preach at Hammersmith and elsewhere until his death there from consumption on 15 November 1705; he was buried at Kingston upon Thames on 20 November. His widow died eight years later, on 18 February 1714.

CHARLOTTE FELL-SMITH, *rev*. CAROLINE L. LEACHMAN

Sources R. Hawkins, *A brief narrative of the life and death of that ancient servant of the Lord and his people, Gilbert Latey* (1707) [incl. testimonies by G. Whitehead and Mary Latey] · J. Besse, *A collection of the sufferings of the people called Quakers*, 2 vols. (1753), vol. 1 · W. Evans and T. Evans, eds., *The Friends' Library*, 1 (1837) · W. C. Braithwaite, *The beginnings of Quakerism*, ed. H. J. Cadbury, 2nd edn (1955); repr. (1981) · W. C. Braithwaite, *The second period of Quakerism*, ed. H. J. Cadbury, 2nd edn (1961) · M. Webb, *The Fells of Swarthmoor*, 2nd edn (1884) · W. Beck and T. F. Ball, *The London Friends' meetings* (1869) · Boase & Courtney, *Bibl. Corn.*, vol. 1 · J. Smith, ed., *A descriptive catalogue of Friends' books*, 1 (1867) · Quaker digest registers, RS Friends, Lond. · C. L. Leachman, 'From an "unruly sect" to a society of "strict unity": the development of Quakerism in England, *c*.1650–1689', PhD diss., U. Lond., 1997 · will, PRO, PROB 11/485, sig. 246 **Archives** RS Friends, Lond., letters · RS Friends, Lond., Portfolio MSS, 16/4, 6, 7, 34, 45 **Wealth at death** approx. £1000: will, 25 Aug 1705, PRO, PROB 11/485, sig. 246

Latey, John (1842–1902), journalist, born in Wenlock Road, Islington, London, on 30 October 1842, was the only son of John Lash Latey (1808–1891) of Tiverton, Devon, a contributor from 1842, and editor (1858–90), of the *Illustrated London News*, and his wife, Eliza Bentley, of South Molton, Devon, daughter of a coal merchant. His father was a firm supporter of liberal reforms from the time of the Reform Bill of 1832, and an early contributor under the pseudonym of Lash to *Lloyd's Weekly News*. Latey was educated at Barnstaple and at the Working Men's College, London (1860–64). He married Constance, daughter of Louis Lachenal, on 1 August 1872.

In 1861 Latey joined the staff of the *Penny Illustrated Paper*, then newly founded by William Ingram of the *Illustrated London News*; from that year until 1901 he was the art and literary editor. Under his guidance the paper, which was staunchly Liberal, filled an important place in popular journalism. Harry Furniss and Phil May were among his artists; with May, he contributed in 1878 a series of 'Bird's-eye views', and from the same year until 1889 he wrote a weekly article by The Showman, genially criticizing society and affairs. For fifteen years, under the pseudonym of the Silent Member, Latey was parliamentary reporter to the *Illustrated London News*; he was also for a time drama critic, as well as literary editor, and editor of the Christmas Annual in 1899. With Mayne Reid, he was co-editor (1881–2) of the *Boys' Illustrated News*, the first illustrated newspaper for children, and from June 1899 to 1902 he was editor of *The Sketch*. Latey published several works, including *The Showman's Panorama* (1880), which appeared under the pseudonym of Codlin, and was illustrated by Wallis Mackay. He also wrote *Love Clouds: a Story of Love and Revenge* (1887), a short history of the Franco-Prussian War (1872), and a *Life of General Gordon* (1885).

Latey was a founder of the London Press Club and a fellow of the Institute of Journalists, and was also one of the earliest volunteers as a private in the Working Men's College company of the 19th Middlesex regiment. He died at his home, 18 South Villas, Camden Square, on 26 September 1902 after a long illness, and was buried at Highgate cemetery. He was survived by his wife, three sons, and a daughter, who married the graphic artist W. Heath Robinson. W. B. OWEN, *rev.* JOANNE POTIER

Sources WWW · D. Griffiths, ed., *The encyclopedia of the British press, 1422–1992* (1992) · *The Sketch* (1 Oct 1902), 414 · *ILN* (4 Oct 1902) · *Men and women of the time* (1899) · A. T. C. Pratt, ed., *People of the period: being a collection of the biographies of upwards of six thousand living celebrities*, 2 vols. (1897)

Likenesses J. E. Williams, portrait, 1873; formerly in the possession of his widow, 1912 · R. T. & Co., group portrait, woodengraving (*Our literary contributors—past and present*), NPG; repro. in *ILN* (14 May 1892) · photograph, repro. in *The Sketch* · portrait, repro. in *ILN* · portrait, repro. in *Penny Illustrated Paper* (4 Oct 1902)

Latey, Sir John Brinsmead (1914–1999), barrister and judge, was born on 7 March 1914 at 4 Osborne Mansions, Chapter Road, Cricklewood, London, the elder of the two sons of William Latey (1885–1976), journalist, and later barrister and special commissioner in divorce, and his wife, Anne Emily (Annie, or Midge), daughter of Horace G. Brinsmead. John *Latey (1842–1902), journalist, was his paternal grandfather. At the time of his son's birth William Latey was following his own father's profession of journalism but in 1919 he started to practise at the divorce bar with sufficient success to send his son John to Westminster School and Christ Church, Oxford. Latey graduated with a third in jurisprudence in 1935 and was called to the bar by the Middle Temple ('Father William's' inn) in 1936. On 20 April 1938 (for a time relying on his skill at the bridge tables of Crockfords to supplement his meagre professional earnings) he married Betty Margaret Beresford (*d.* 2000), daughter of Edwyn Henry Beresford, medical practitioner, of London. They had a son, Philip, and a daughter, Anna, known as Jill. Their eminently happy marriage was ended only by his death, sixty-one years later.

Latey (though an enthusiastic and skilled golf player) suffered from poor eyesight and on this ground was at first not accepted for military service. In 1942, however, he was commissioned in the Royal Army Pay Corps and (transferred to the judge advocate's department) established procedures whereby soldiers—the scheme did not apply to those holding commissioned rank—contemplating divorce were required to explore the prospects of conciliation before being allowed to stop the allotment of pay to

their allegedly errant wives and to institute divorce proceedings. Latey believed that in this way a large number of marriages were saved. In 1946 he urged the Denning committee on procedure in matrimonial causes of the need to co-ordinate 'the thousands of voluntary social workers' into a well publicized 'integrated (but not over-organized) network' which could (as the minutes of evidence record) 'get at' those contemplating divorce before the prospects of saving the marriage were irretrievably lost (PRO, LCo 2/3948). Half a century would pass before such ideas received government backing.

Latey built up a successful practice at the bar and was appointed queen's counsel in 1957 (seven years after his father). In 1965 the incoming Labour lord chancellor, Lord Gardiner (a committed law reformer), recommended Latey's elevation to the bench as a judge of the Probate, Divorce, and Admiralty Division of the High Court. He received the customary knighthood and served as a High Court judge for just short of twenty-five years.

Latey became a judge at a time of massive change in the family justice system. Divorce and other family business was allotted to the newly created Family Division in 1971, and the Divorce Reform Act (1969) replaced the old law which since 1858 had been based on the notion that a wholly innocent petitioner was obtaining legal relief for an offence committed by the respondent. The act of 1969 asserted that the sole ground upon which a divorce petition could thenceforth be based was that the marriage had broken down irretrievably; but the need to obtain parliamentary approval for so radical a change meant that the reforming legislation was in some respects ambiguous—how far did one party's responsibility for the breakdown affect what financial arrangements should be made, for example?—and Latey steered a skilful course in seeking to reconcile the essential justice of the cases which came before him with the statutory language.

Latey's time on the bench also coincided with greatly increased public interest in the fate of the children who were so often the victims of family breakdown. The principle that the child's welfare should be the determining factor was easy enough to state but sometimes much more difficult to apply. Should a child be known by the surname of the stepfather, for example? Latey's most celebrated case involved the future of 'Baby Cotton', born to an Englishwoman recruited by an American commercial surrogacy agency to bear for its clients a child conceived by artificial insemination. The child's welfare pointed unequivocally to allowing the commissioning parents to care for the child in the United States, but Latey subsequently emphasized the 'pitfalls, the obstacles, and the anxiety' in such arrangements (*Daily Telegraph*, 28 April 1999); and (despite the legislation following the report of the 1984 Warnock committee on human fertilization and embryology) the practice of surrogacy remained controversial. On this and other occasions Latey could be an outspoken and trenchant critic—notably in a decision of 1985 in which some practices of scientology were held to justify removing children from their home and family circle into the care of the other parent.

Latey was a firm believer in what some came to call the 'settlement culture' as the preferred method of resolving matrimonial disputes; and his addiction to the elegantly packaged *Passing cloud* cigarettes made him all the more ready to invite counsel and the parties to take time to discuss the possibilities of settlement. Although more than a hundred of his judgments are preserved in the law reports and he joined in editing the fourteenth edition of his father's authoritative text on divorce, he would not have claimed to be an outstanding lawyer; but his success as a first instance judge was recognized by his being sworn of the privy council (an unusual distinction for a puisne judge) in 1986 after twenty-one years' judicial service.

Latey's most significant achievement was in chairing the committee on the age of majority established by Lord Chancellor Gardiner in 1965. Latey approached this task with an open mind and urged the need for such an approach on the other members. He infected an outstandingly gifted team with his enthusiasm. The committee made determined efforts (for example, by commissioning opinion polls, encouraging media discussion, and making personal visits to schools and youth clubs) to discover the views of ordinary young people rather than simply relying on the opinions expressed by bodies officially concerned with the young. Although the committee's terms of reference might have appeared to confine inquiry to little more than a consideration of young people's legal capacity to make contracts and to marry without their parents' consent, the report's unequivocal message was that young people were maturing earlier than in the past, and that accordingly the age of full legal capacity in the field of private civil law should be reduced from twenty-one to eighteen.

Latey insisted that the drafting of the report should be collaborative. He personally took a very full part in this, though in a number of particularly significant passages he was able to draw on the presentational skills of the distinguished columnist Katharine Whitehorn. The outcome was that the committee's message was delivered in unusually readable prose, reflecting the committee's belief that the 'ordinary everyday problems of human beings' should not be obscured by 'technical language, overloaded by too great a weight of evidence too exhaustively explained, or run upon the shoals of difficult statistics embodied in the text' ('Report of the committee on the age of majority', *Parl. papers*, 1966–7, 21, Cmnd 3342, para. 9). Notwithstanding a powerful (and also attractively written) dissent on the general principle by Geoffrey Howe QC and the highly regarded and experienced solicitor John Stebbings, the Family Law Reform Act (1969) gave effect to the recommendation that the age of full legal capacity should fall to eighteen. Although the committee's report insisted that the majority had not disregarded the constitutional and social implications of this change to the private law, it soon became clear that a new benchmark for determining legal status had been created.

Latey retired in 1989 and died of lung cancer at his home, 1 Adderbury Park, Adderbury, Banbury, Oxfordshire, on 24 April 1999. Following cremation his ashes were interred in St Mary's churchyard, Adderbury, Oxfordshire. He was survived by his wife, Betty, and their two children.   S. M. CRETNEY

Sources *Daily Telegraph* (28 April 1999) · *The Independent* (15 May 1999) · *The Times* (3 June 1999) · WWW · G. Howe, *Conflict of loyalty* (1995) · S. M. Cretney, *Law, law reform and the family* (1998), chap. 6 · personal knowledge (2004) · private information (2004) [Lady Peirse, subject's daughter] · b. cert. · m. cert. · d. cert.
Archives PRO, LC O2/3948 · PRO, LCO 17/1–12
Likenesses photograph, 1986, repro. in *Daily Telegraph* · photograph, repro. in *The Independent*
Wealth at death £42,222 gross; £38,908 net: probate, 10 Oct 1999, CGPLA Eng. & Wales

Latham, Baldwin (1836–1917), civil engineer and meteorologist, was born on 6 December 1836 in Nantwich, Cheshire, the son of George Latham, architect and surveyor. After attending Nantwich grammar school he entered his father's office in 1851, and served the usual three-year pupillage as a civil engineer. He then moved to Sandiway, Cheshire, to work for three years with the contractors Douglas and Beckett before joining Joseph Glyn, a civil engineer and fellow of the Royal Society, in the fens at Ely. In 1860 Latham went into business on his own account in Ely, and on 24 November 1863 he married Ann Elizabeth, daughter of William Neal, draper, of Ely, with whom he moved to Croydon and raised a large family.

In 1865 John Rennie proposed Latham for associate membership of the Institution of Civil Engineers (ICE). The proposal form gave details of the many vestries, local boards, and town councils for which he had already worked, including Dorking, Merton, Rugby, Warwick, Reigate, and Croydon. By 1868 Latham had designed the sewerage, irrigation, and water works for fifteen English towns. He had also begun a series of nearly forty papers reporting on these and related matters. The minutes of the ICE *Proceedings* show him to have been a regular attender of and lively contributor to the institution meetings.

His professional interest in water, its supply, management, and disposal, led to Latham's involvement with many of the scientific societies of the day. He joined the British Association in 1870 and in 1876 he was elected a member of the Royal Sanitary Institute. In the same year he joined the Geological Society and the Royal Meteorological Society, becoming president of the latter in 1890 and 1891. He was particularly interested in rainfall, and encouraged many members of the Croydon Natural History and Philosophical Society to set up rain gauges. They sent the resulting reports to the British Rainfall Organisation set up by G. J. Symons. Latham was the first to devise a recording rain gauge. Latham became a well-known personality in the Croydon area, and his civic involvement extended to becoming a member of the Guild of Playing Card Manufacturers. His meteorological friends were startled to receive packs of playing cards instead of Christmas cards one year, with a portrait of their friend in the full regalia of the master of the guild set in the centre of the ace of spades. He belonged to the guild for forty-two years, being master twice. The guild assessed playing card design in an annual competition, and met regularly to dine

Baldwin Latham (1836–1917), by London Stereoscopic Co., pubd 1907–9

together. More usefully, they acted as a source of help for families of members and, during the First World War, arranged for thousands of packs of cards to be distributed to hospitals for soldiers both in Britain and overseas.

Latham is best remembered for his contributions to public water supply, particularly in the Croydon area. His book, *Sanitary Engineering, a Guide to the Construction of Sewerage and House Drainage* (1873, 2nd edn, 1878) was regarded as a classic in its day. In the latter part of his life, he analysed the parish records of Croydon from their commencement in 1538 to identify deaths caused by water-borne diseases. He constructed from this a summary of the state of Croydon's water year by year to 1900. His interest in the characteristics of the district's hydrology continued undiminished, and they formed the subject of the last paper he gave, to the Croydon Natural History and Philosophical Society. It was in press when Latham died, on 13 March 1917, at his home, Park Hill House, Stanhope Road, Croydon, aged eighty-one; he suffered from phlebitis and a pulmonary embolism. He was buried at Croydon cemetery on 19 March. He was survived by his wife.   JANE INSLEY

Sources F. Campbell-Bayard, *Proceedings of the Croydon Natural History and Scientific Society*, 8 (1916–17), xcviii–ci · *Symons Meteorological Magazine*, 52 (1917), 50 · J. Insley, 'Pen portraits of presidents: Baldwin Latham', *Weather*, 52 (1997), 128–9 · W. W., 'Baldwin Latham, 1836 to 1917', *Journal of the Royal Sanitary Institute*, 38 (1917–18), 99–100 [incl. portrait] · m. cert. · d. cert. · *CGPLA Eng. & Wales* (1917)
Likenesses London Stereoscopic Co., photograph, pubd 1907–9 [*see illus.*] · F. Vandamm, photograph, before 1917, repro. in Campbell-Bayard, *Proceedings of the Croydon Natural History and Scientific Society*, frontispiece · portrait, Royal Meteorological Society, Reading
Wealth at death £4643 14s.: administration, 28 April 1917, *CGPLA Eng. & Wales*

Latham [*formerly* Lathan], **Charles**, first Baron Latham (1888–1970), local politician, was born on 26 December 1888 at Norwich, the eighth of ten children of George Lathan (1852–1929), a tanner, and his wife, Sarah Ann Mason (*d.* 1933). He subsequently changed his name to Latham, apparently to avoid confusion with his eldest

brother, George Lathan (1875–1942). The latter was assistant general secretary of the Railway Clerks' Association (1912–37), Labour MP for Sheffield Park (1929–31 and 1935–42), and chairman of the Labour Party (1931–2). Charles Latham's public career was more focused on the politics and administration of London, but demonstrated a similar character—professionalism and efficiency rather than keen partisanship. He left elementary school in Norwich at the age of fourteen and worked as a clerk, first in Norwich and later in London. By 1914 he had qualified as an accountant. Active in the labour movement from 1905, he was involved in the foundation of the London Labour Party in 1914. He married, on 14 June 1913, Maya Helen (*d.* 1978), daughter of Louis George Allman of Hendon; they had one son and three daughters.

After commissioned service during the First World War with the Royal Sussex regiment Latham became first a manager with, and then a partner of, a firm of accountants. Active in the London Association of Accountants, he played a leading role in its development into the Association of Certified and Corporate Accountants. He served a three-year term as president of the latter.

Latham's attempts to win a parliamentary seat as a Labour candidate failed. Third places at Hendon in the general elections of 1922 and 1923 were followed in 1924 by defeat in a straight fight at Wandsworth Central. In suburban Hendon he was the sole Labour member of the urban district council from 1926 to 1931. His crucial breakthrough came in 1928, when he was elected to the London county council (LCC) as an alderman. This success reflected the strategy of the LCC Labour group leader, Herbert Morrison, who saw aldermanic vacancies as a valuable opportunity to strengthen Labour's professional expertise.

During the spring and summer of 1931 Latham became involved in the events that culminated in the collapse of the second Labour government. He was one of two Labour members of the committee on national expenditure, usually known as the May committee after its chairman, Sir George May, of the Prudential Assurance Company. Latham's Labour colleague was Arthur Pugh, the steelworkers' leader and a member of the TUC general council. A committee majority of actuaries, accountants, and bankers produced a report urging drastic economies; Latham and Pugh wrote a minority report that largely reflected the thinking of the TUC and its research department. Although they accepted the majority's contentious estimate of the budget deficit as £120 million and endorsed some economies, they considered the underlying economic difficulties not to be the result of excessive public expenditure, but of post-war deflation, the return to the gold standard, and the fall in world prices. An equitable solution should include taxation of holders of fixed-interest securities who had benefited from the fall in prices. Whereas the majority saw a potential conflict between fiscal rectitude and the outcomes of democratic politics, Latham and Pugh endorsed the redistributive policies that had emerged out of the war—'what they regard as "undesirable" we view as consistent with the right and proper course of democratic government and progress' (Command 3920 Minority Report, para. 5). The minority report presented an alternative strategy for which no parliamentary majority existed.

In the years following the collapse of the Labour government and the party's 1931 electoral disaster, Latham became a leading figure on the LCC. When the Labour Party achieved a majority on the LCC in 1934 Latham was elected for South Hackney, a position he retained until becoming an alderman again in 1946. Morrison appointed him chairman of the finance committee. His strict scrutiny of other committees' estimates earned him the title the Iron Chancellor. Credibility in this area was deemed vital given Labour's concern that electors might harbour doubts about the party's financial competence in the aftermath of the 1931 crisis. Moreover, Herbert Morrison lacked expertise in the area and relied heavily on Latham's judgements.

Beyond his formal position Latham also operated as part of the LCC Labour leadership. Apart from Morrison, the other members were Isaac Hayward, the chief whip, and Lewis Silkin, chairman of the housing committee. Morrison labelled this quartet the Presidium. They thrashed out issues in informal discussions and, having taken a decision, maintained unity before the remainder of the party group. Their lead was respected; the resulting cohesion strengthened Labour's credibility, and when the 1937 LCC election increased Labour's majority the legitimacy of this leadership was enhanced. Whatever Labour's broader electoral problems, these London victories and the socially progressive policies pursued by the LCC enhanced the party's reputation.

In May 1940, when Morrison entered Churchill's coalition government, Latham was his predictable successor to lead the LCC. Initially he found Morrison a hard act to follow; his predecessor's political stratagems had been flavoured with geniality, and Latham could seem aloof. However his industry and thoroughness established his position, and for those who penetrated his reserve, there was warmth and generosity.

The effectiveness of the civil defence services owed much to Latham's energy and to his successful co-operation with Sir Ernest Gowers, regional commissioner of the London Civil Defence Region. A consummate professional, Latham embodied the Morrisonian respect for the LCC's senior officers, insisting that they should give advice to politicians without concern for its political convenience. The LCC was influenced by the debates over post-war reconstruction. Latham's leadership saw the publication of the county of London plan in 1943 and the Greater London plan in the following year. Yet the LCC leadership, including Latham, were cautious about institutional reform; the reconstruction vision narrowed, and in several respects the LCC responses to post-war problems showed continuities with the successful political initiatives of the late 1930s. Latham epitomized this continuity; he was the skilled administrator implementing a political agenda that in content and style owed much to his more creative predecessor.

Latham's peerage, granted in January 1942, allowed him to strengthen the limited Labour presence in the House of Lords, but in 1947 he left the LCC and became an apolitical public servant. He had been a member of the London Passenger Transport Board—essentially a Morrisonian conception—since 1935. With the nationalization of the railways and of much road transport, the new London transport executive (LTE) came under the aegis of the British Transport Commission; Latham became the LTE's first chairman. The context was difficult. The new institutional structure reduced the autonomy for London Transport, and funds for capital investment were limited. Passenger usage peaked in 1948. Fare increases in the light of increasing costs were inevitably controversial. On a more nostalgic note Latham headed the reception committee that greeted the last London tram on completion of its final journey in July 1952.

Latham left the chairmanship of the LTE at the end of his first term of office in 1953 and returned to his accountancy practice. Some distance had developed between him and the Conservative government. The Conservative minister of transport, Alan Lennox-Boyd, had responded to backbench criticism of London Transport by establishing a committee of inquiry under the industrialist Sir Paul Chambers. The subsequent report acknowledged that London Transport had been conducted with efficiency and economy. However, in some quarters there was perhaps a feeling that Latham's chairmanship, whatever its administrative qualities, had lacked 'panache' (Elliot, 87).

Latham later joined the LCC housing committee (1957) as a co-opted member and became a member of the Metropolitan Water Board. His managerial interests were evident from 1945 in his work as a member of the Standing Advisory Committee on the Pay of the Higher Civil Service (1956–67), and of the Council of Europe (1960–62). As a lord lieutenant of Middlesex from 1945 to 1956 he enjoyed the ceremonial. Very much an 'insider' in London politics, he took part in 1963 in a last significant battle, with his old ally now Lord Morrison of Lambeth, to oppose the LCC's replacement by the greater London council.

Latham's marriage was dissolved in 1957. In March 1957 he married Sylvia May (d. 1985), widow of Alexander Kennard; she was the daughter of Alexander Newmark of London. Latham died in the Middlesex Hospital, London, on 31 March 1970. DAVID HOWELL

Sources DNB · The Times (2 April 1970) · The Times (17 April 1970) · WWW · The Labour who's who (1927) · 'Report of the committee appointed by HM treasury', Parl. papers (1930–31), vol. 16, Cmd 3920 [national expenditure] · P. Williamson, National crisis and national government: British politics, the economy and empire, 1926–1932 (1992) · The Times (1 Aug 1931) [for material from the Command 3920 minority report] · K. Young and P. L. Garside, Metropolitan London: politics and urban change, 1837–1981 (1982) · Railway Gazette (1947–53) [on Latham's period at London Transport (incl. 22/29 Aug 1947: appointment; 16 Jan 1948: first press conference; 20–27 Feb 1950: on financial issues; 11 July 1952 on last London tram; 27 Feb 1953 on decision to leave at end of term of office)] · J. Elliot, On and off the rails (1982) · Burke, Peerage (2000) · CGPLA Eng. & Wales (1970)

Archives LMA, corresp., diaries, and papers | FILM BFI NFTVA, documentary footage · BFI NFTVA, news footage

Latham, Ebenezer (*c*.1688–1754), nonconformist tutor, was born probably at Mickledale, Cheshire, the eldest son of the Revd Richard Latham (*c*.1653–1706), nonconformist minister at Wem, Shropshire, from 1696. Intended for the nonconformist ministry from an early age he was a student under Samuel Benion, and then attended Glasgow University which he entered in February 1704. After his father's death he supplied Wem, receiving a grant of £5 from the Presbyterian Fund between 1706 and 1710. He was ordained privately in Benion's house in 1707 or 1708. Fearing that he would be unable to preach because his voice had suffered as a result of smallpox, he studied medicine, graduating MD from Glasgow on 25 October 1710. He was to practise medicine throughout his ministry. In 1710 he moved to Caldwell, in Derbyshire, preaching there and at Hollington and Ashbourne. While at Caldwell he began his academy, but he was among those nonconformist tutors forced to suspend their work as a result of the passing of the Schism Act. Following the death of Thomas Hill in March 1720, who conducted an academy at Findern, Latham became his successor both as tutor and minister.

Latham was widely read. He claimed at one time to have allowed himself 'but four hours sleep' in twenty-four (*Sermons on Various Subjects*, i). He possessed a 'critical skill in the learned languages' and had 'a good acquaintance' with Jewish antiquities and history, which he applied to a study of the Old and New testaments (ibid., xii–xiii). His students were taught Hebrew so that they could study the scriptures for themselves, using Benedict Pictet's *Theologia Christiana* for their system of theology. In their logic classes they read Locke, who proved so influential in encouraging new standards of criticism. Natural philosophy, anatomy, mathematics, and history were also taught. Correspondence with Cromwell Mortimer reveals that Latham took a practical interest in astronomy. According to a former student Latham 'was master of great quickness in composing his thoughts', which were 'often striking, & his language frequently brilliant' (Hunter, 'Britannia puritanica', fol. 215r). Philip Doddridge admired his preaching in 1722.

Latham was an Arian after the school of Samuel Clarke, insisting on the sufficiency of scripture and rejecting all creeds and subscriptions. 'We have our bibles, the only complete system of divine knowledge, in our hands; by which we may improve on the best compositions of fallible men' (*Sermons on Various Subjects*, 1). Nevertheless, 'his determined resolution never to make his instruction subservient to a narrow spirited party, and supposed want of entire orthodoxy' cost him support particularly from orthodox ministers in London (Hunter, 'Britannia puritanica', fol. 215r). Latham was blamed for the increasing heterodoxy of many Presbyterian ministers educated in this period. His academy declined as a result of the growing reputation of Doddridge's at Northampton

(1729–51), which was supported by the Coward Trust. In 1745 Latham became assistant minister to Josiah Rogerson, minister of Friar Gate Presbyterian meeting, Derby, and moved there with his academy.

Latham's academy was notable for the liberal theological principles on which it was conducted and the length of its existence. The names of more than 60 students are known, but there are said to have been between 300 and 400. They included Joseph Fownes of Shrewsbury, who provided an account of the academy, John Wiche of Maidstone, William Turner of Wakefield, and Samuel Blythe, a colleague of Joseph Priestley at Birmingham. The lay students included Thomas Bentley, partner of Josiah Wedgwood, and Robert Newton, high sheriff of Derbyshire (1746). The Presbyterian Fund supported thirty-five students. In 1725 they decided to support only students at Findern, Taunton, and Carmarthen academies.

Latham published a number of ordination and funeral sermons, including one for Daniel Matlock, which included the first printed list of ministerial students at Frankland's academy. A collection of fifteen of his sermons was published posthumously with an inadequate memoir by his brother-in-law, William Willets. Latham was married, and he and his wife (*d*. 1751) had at least two daughters. One of them, Mary, who died in September 1771, daily read the Bible in Hebrew; 'tho' not gramatically learned, yet by a constant comparing [of] the parallel texts' she attained a critical understanding of the Old Testament (*Derby Mercury*, 6 Sept 1771). Latham died at his house on the Nuns Green near Derby on 15 January 1754, aged about sixty-six. By the time of his death he had very few students indeed.   DAVID L. WYKES

Sources H. McLachlan, 'Ebenezer Latham, M.A., M.D. (1688–1745), and the academy at Findern, Derbyshire', *Essays and addresses* (1950), 147–64 · A. Gordon, ed., *Cheshire Classis Minutes, 1691–1745* (1919), 187 · 'An account of the dissenting academies from the Restoration of Charles the Second', DWL, MS 24.59, pp. 27–8, 30, 54–7 · J. Hunter, 'Britannia puritanica, or, Outlines of the history of the various congregations of Presbyterians and Independents which arose out of the schism in the Church of England of 1662', BL, Add. MS 24484, fols. 214v–215r · biographical account of Latham, DWL, Walter Wilson MS, A 10.(15), a–b · J. Hunter, 'Collectanea Hunteriana volume VIII being memoirs to serve for a history of Protestant dissenters', BL, Add. MS 24442, fols. 70v–71v · notes on the academies of Mr Hill and Dr Latham, DWL, New College collection, L54/2/2–4, 6 · *Sermons on various subjects by the late Reverend Ebenezer Latham, M. D.*, ed. W. Willets (1774) · H. McLachlan, *English education under the Test Acts: being the history of the nonconformist academies, 1662–1820* (1931), 131–1 · *Derby Mercury* (6 Sept 1771) · J. B. W. [J. B. Williams], 'Original letter from Dr Ebenezer Latham', *London Christian Instructor or Congregational Magazine*, 7 (1824), 637–8 [March 1708] · 'A view of the dissenting interest in London of the Presbyterian and Independent denominations, from the year 1695 to the 25 of December 1731, with a postscript of the present state of the Baptists', DWL, MS 38.18, p. 90 · BL, Royal Society Papers, Add. MS 4434, fols. 211r–213v, 4435, fols. 237–46 · W. Tong, *An account of the life and death of Mr Matthew Henry, minister of the Gospel at Hackney, who dy'd June 22, 1714 in the 52d year of his age* (1716), 205

Latham, Henry (1794–1866). *See under* Latham, John (1761–1843).

Latham, Henry (1821–1902), college head, was born at Dover on 4 June 1821, second son of John Henry Latham, paymaster of the exchequer from 1823 to 1848, and his wife, Harriet Stringer Broderip, only child of Edward Broderip MD. His grandfather, Samuel Latham (d. 1834), was a banker. His mother died in 1824 or 1825 and his father, who had settled in Eltham, remarried in 1826 and had a second family, but since his health was thought to be delicate, Henry was raised by his maternal grandfather at Dover where he attended a day school. On returning home in 1836 he studied with tutors and began the first of his foreign travels. Admitted in 1841 as a pensioner of Trinity College, Cambridge, where his uncle John Taddy had been a fellow, he became a scholar and took an inauspicious BA as eighteenth wrangler in 1845. His health had recovered and he was by then tall and well built, and able to undertake the strenuous study for a competitive Trinity fellowship examination. Before that happened, however, he was admitted on the recommendation of his Trinity friends to Trinity Hall as the junior of the two fellow clerical tutors (December 1847), and took holy orders.

Trinity Hall had always been unusual, for it was largely a preserve of lawyers, its fellows were mostly non-resident, and it needed to increase numbers and broaden the basis of its teaching. Its ultimate success in both was due in large measure to Latham, whose chief duty was to select undergraduates, look after their welfare, help them to avoid and recover from pitfalls, receive their confidences, and reassure their parents; in short to be policeman and protector. He united a genuine interest in the students with the exercise of college authority, followed their careers and welcomed their return. He preferred character to academic success and took as much trouble with the average man as with the exceptional, taking lectures and pupils to keep in touch with the young. The numbers of undergraduates increased fourfold while he was senior tutor (1855–85), and he achieved popularity and influence among successive generations of them, who knew him as 'Ben', a joke about his height referring to Psalm 68. They paid for his portrait and founded a Latham prize in English language and literature. In university affairs he was a moderate liberal. The years of his tutorship coincided with the two royal commissions, and he anticipated William Whewell in complaining that the commissioners in 1857 were in danger of reducing colleges with different traditions to a single pattern. He withdrew as a candidate for the mastership of Trinity Hall in 1877 as did his rival Henry Fawcett in favour of Sir Henry Maine, but when Maine died in 1888 he was elected unanimously. He felt too old to serve as vice-chancellor, but had given good administrative service before. He is said to have declined church preferments to stay in Cambridge.

Besides an early work, *Geometrical Problems* (1848), Latham wrote several papers on educational matters and university reform; he knew of continental developments and contributed an article on the Maison Paternelle at Mettray to *Macmillan's Magazine* in 1869. Out of long experience came an important book *On the Action of Examinations*

Considered as a Means of Selection (1877). He set less store by examination results than by personal knowledge and deprecated constant changes in the Cambridge examination system. Late in life and to widespread surprise he produced three religious books for a popular audience, *Pastor pastorum* (1890) and its sequel *The Risen Master* (1901, reprinted twice) and a treatise—somewhat odd for the times—on angels.

Latham liked best the society of men and never married. Thomas Thornely, who entered Trinity Hall in 1873, records that he was seldom at ease in the company of ladies, and spoke of 'the difficulty he experienced in distinguishing between them … "They all look so much alike"' (Thornely, 57). In 1880 he built a large house, Southacre, at Trumpington, near Cambridge, and was a convivial though mildly eccentric host, who hated music but charmed guests with his stories. He was a keen oarsman for most of his life and encouraged rowing among students for its teamwork and self-discipline. He also played the stock market adroitly and did well from it; he was able to spend such large sums of his own on building and refurbishment that at the end of his life it was a pardonable hyperbole to describe him as a 'second founder' of Trinity Hall, and he was a generous benefactor to the college and to the university by his will. He died suddenly of heart disease at Trinity Hall lodge on 5 June 1902 and is buried in the churchyard of Little Shelford. The university library has a sale catalogue of his books and effects.

JOHN D. PICKLES

Sources C. Crawley, *Trinity Hall: the history of a Cambridge college, 1350–1975* (1976) · H. E. Malden, *Cambridge Review* (16 Oct 1902) · H. E. Malden, *Cambridge Review* (23 Oct 1902) · T. Thornely, *Cambridge memories* (1936) · J. W. Clark, *Endowments of the University of Cambridge* (1904)
Archives CUL
Likenesses R. Farren, group portrait, 1863 (*Senate House Hill: degree morning*), Trinity Hall, Cambridge; repro. in Crawley, *Trinity Hall*, pl. 13 · F. Holl, oils, 1884, Trinity Hall, Cambridge · F. Holl, oils, after 1888, Trinity Hall, Cambridge · L. Dickinson, oils, 1889, Trinity Hall, Cambridge · J. P. Clarke, photograph, repro. in H. E. Malden, *Trinity Hall* (1902), facing p. 228
Wealth at death £112,098 8s. 10d.: probate, 29 July 1902, CGPLA Eng. & Wales

Latham, James (1696–1746), portrait painter, born in co. Tipperary, was a member of a Tipperary family living near Cashel. The head of the family, Oliver Latham of Meldrum, was appointed commissioner of oaths by the second duke of Ormond in 1695, a fact which leads to the earliest attributable portraits by Latham—of James Butler of Ballyricken, then the head of the Ormond family in Ireland, and his brother Christopher, Roman Catholic archbishop of Cashel (both c.1718–c.1720, Kilkenny Castle, co. Kilkenny). No evidence exists of Latham's early education but these portraits, if somewhat crude, show many of the qualities which were to make him a most distinguished painter. In the Ormond collection of paintings in Kilkenny Castle he had an important source for study and in 1724 he is recorded as visiting Antwerp, studying for one term in the Guild of St Luke and becoming a master of the guild. Whether he went via Paris or London is not certainly known, but it is likely that he visited both cities. He settled in Dublin in 1725.

Despite his merits Latham's work was quickly forgotten, and the oval head and shoulders of Bishop Berkeley (Trinity College, Dublin) was until recently his only remembered work. It was engraved by John Brooks without a publication date. Several other works were engraved, including the whole-length portrait of Eaton Stannard and that of Charles Tottenham (both National Gallery of Ireland, Dublin), as well as likenesses of Sir John Ligonier (mezzotint by J. Brooks) and Patrick Quin (mezzotint by Andrew Miller). *Colonel Charles Janure de la Bouchtière* (Ulster Museum, Belfast), a portrait of a Huguenot officer, must date before the sitter's death in 1731 and is a splendid character study of this soldier. Latham's finest portraits were done for the Cosby family, who owned four three-quarter lengths: of Pole Cosby and his daughter Sarah, his wife with their son Dudley, another of Sarah as a child, and one of her with her parrot after her marriage. There were a further two pictures of Dudley Cosby: one, much damaged, as a baby; and another as a child, which has been cut at the bottom edge and shows a strong French influence (all ex Sothebys, 11 July 1984, lot 38; 20 November 1985, lots 36, 85, 39; and 14 March 1990, lot 49). These pictures must have been painted over a ten-year period and show that love of children revealed in all Latham's child portraits, including the one of Bishop Berkeley's son (ex Sothebys, 2 June 1995, lot 201). They are delightful character studies; Pole Cosby's gesture, for instance, holding his daughter's hand, shows how much she meant to him. Latham put on his paint with firm direct strokes; his flair for colour is displayed in Sarah Cosby's beautiful pink dress as she offers her parrot cherries, or in the magnificent waistcoats of such sitters in the 1740s as Sir Capel Molyneux (Tate collection), but he is equally at home with the silvery tones in the portrait of the fourth earl of Inchiquin (priv. coll.), in which the sitter is wearing the insignia and ribbon of the Order of the Bath. Besides the Cosby groups Latham painted a number of double portraits, including the Leslie sisters playing the harpsichord (priv. coll.) and Bishop Clayton and his wife (National Gallery of Ireland, Dublin). His beautiful brushwork with its contrasting delicacy and breadth, seen in his rendering of sparkling braids or the soft density of a powdered wig, lifts Latham above the level of more humdrum contemporaries.

According to his will, dated 1 January 1746, Latham was married to a woman named Joane and had four daughters, Elinor, Margaret, Anne, and Mary, and one son, James. He was living in Trinity Lane, Dublin, when he died in 1746.

ANNE CROOKSHANK

Sources P. Rombouts and T. Van Lerius, *De liggeren en andere historische archieven der Antwerpsche Sint Lucasgilde*, 2 (The Hague, 1876); repr. (Amsterdam, 1961), 737–8 · A. Pasquin [J. Williams], *An authentic history of the professors of painting, sculpture, and architecture who have practiced in Ireland … to which are added, Memoirs of the royal academicians* [1796]; facs. edn as *An authentic history of painting in Ireland* with introduction by R. W. Lightbown (1970), 29 · A. Crookshank, 'James Latham', *GPA Irish Arts Review Yearbook*, 5 (1988), 56– 72 · W. G. Strickland, *A dictionary of Irish artists*, 2 vols. (1913) · A. Crookshank and the Knight of Glin [D. Fitzgerald], *The painters of Ireland, c.1660–1920* (1978)
Archives NL Ire., Betham abstracts of prerogative wills

Latham, Jane Leeke (1867–1938), college head and missionary, was born on 3 August 1867 at Holbrooke Hall, Derbyshire, the home of the Revd William and Mrs Leeke, her mother's parents. She was the daughter of Edward Latham (*d.* 1883) and his wife, Jane Leeke. Her father was for seventeen years housemaster of Repton School, where Jane spent the first eight years of her life until 1875, when he became vicar of Matlock Bath, Derbyshire. She was the third of ten children, one of whom later wrote: 'I always consider that our parents brought up the first three, and they brought up the rest' (Lloyd). Jane was educated at home until in 1880 she and an elder sister were sent to Cheltenham Ladies' College. When, on the death of her father in 1883, her mother moved to Blackheath Jane continued her education at the high school there, one of the most prestigious of the Girls' Public Day School Company schools. In 1886 she won a higher local scholarship to Girton College, Cambridge, and in 1889 took a good second in the mathematical tripos (graduating MA at Trinity College, Dublin, in 1907). From 1889 to 1897 she was mathematics mistress at Cheltenham, and thus came under the influence of Dorothea Beale as both pupil and colleague. In 1897 she was appointed lady warden of the Woodard school, St Anne's, at Abbots Bromley, responsible for the girls' spiritual and moral training, the headmistress being in charge of curriculum and discipline. She was largely instrumental in founding another Woodard school at Scarborough. In 1903 she became principal and head of the training department at St Mary's College, Paddington. Founded as an Anglican school in 1874, under the care of the Wantage Sisters, it had also undertaken the training of secondary schoolmistresses. Inadequate finances caused the sisters to offer it to the Woodard trustees, who were unable to accept it as the college had a conscience clause. The warden of the Woodard schools, however, was able to form a committee which secured a scheme from the charity commissioners, and Miss Latham was offered the principalship.

The college now endowed, but still badly housed and precarious in finance, Miss Latham did 'much to raise the standard of work and to place the College on a sound financial basis' (*Girton Review*). It was inspected by the Board of Education and recognized as a training college for secondary teachers who could qualify for entry on the teachers' register, authorized by the Board of Education Act, 1899. In 1904 St Mary's was recognized as qualifying students to be registered as internal students of the University of London's department of pedagogy. Those who were qualified by degree or equivalent took the London University diploma, the rest the Cambridge teachers' certificate; Miss Latham superintended both college and school, lectured to the students, and conducted 'some criticism work'. She did not however approve of public criticism lessons, which were 'not profitable enough to repay the strain caused to the student' (Board of Education, *The Training of Women Teachers*). There is strong testimony to the quality of Miss Latham as a teacher, and her achievement was keeping this precarious structure functioning at a time when women were in the forefront of the movement for the professional training of secondary teachers. Her methods of administration were unorthodox, handing a sheaf of letters to her secretary, it is said, with the instruction, 'Write nice answers, will you?' (Lloyd).

Miss Latham was born into the world of Victorian educational reform and until this time had been actively involved within it throughout her life—the reform of a boys' public school, two of the most influential new girls' schools (boarding and day, one Anglican, one non-sectarian), the oldest women's university college, the Woodard experiment in an Anglican 'mission to the middle classes', and the creation of a trained teaching profession. She regarded education as a vocation which gave her great spiritual satisfaction, but she had, from her childhood, been attracted to work in the mission field, and in 1908 she resigned from St Mary's. She was asked to pay a six months' visit to India to prepare a report on women's education for the Edinburgh conference of 1910. Her gradual call to the mission field was reaching its consummation. In 1910 she was appointed head of the women's work of the Society for the Propagation of the Gospel mission at Ahmednagar in the Bombay diocese (from 1929 the diocese of Nasik). A second life of dedication had begun.

For the next twenty years Miss Latham was in charge of all women's work, with more than twelve women missionaries under her. She lived from 1910 to 1915 at Miri and from there her influence spread in the villages around. She never became fluent in the native languages, but 'she had a marvellous gift for getting in touch with people' and 'immense patience and willingness to listen' (Lloyd). In 1915 she went to live at St Monica's House at Ahmednagar, giving her main attention to education. The normal school was already recognized by government as a training college for teachers, and Miss Latham's gift for organization provided it with buildings and developed its work. For a short time in 1918, with her bishop's permission, she went to work among the English soldiers in Bangalore, and for this and for her work in the famine in Ahmednagar she received in 1919 the kaisar-i-Hind medal of the second class.

During these busy years Miss Latham's desire for greater simplicity of life grew, and in 1931 she resigned the headship of St Monica's and went to Malegaon in the Nasik district, where there was a derelict Church Missionary Society mission station which the bishop hoped to revitalize. With two Christian schoolmistresses she opened a small school for girls; she also began a medical relief association, and with the support of the Red Cross opened village dispensaries. While the bishop recognized that Miss Latham had brought Malegaon to life he considered the strain on her at the age of sixty-eight was too great, and before she went on furlough in 1935 he told her that on her return she must be content to lead a quiet life of prayer.

Before her return Miss Latham made a pilgrimage to the Holy Land, and when she reached India again obediently went to live a contemplative life in a tent near Kalwan. In 1936 she went far from any white people to Tarhabad, among the poverty-stricken Bhills. When the monsoon failed they faced starvation and Miss Latham set to work to arouse 'the conscience of the whole community, Indian and English, official and private' (Lloyd). With a small band of workers she began to open schools, founded a society for redeeming villagers from debt to moneylenders, and secured some training in horticulture and chicken farming for them. She interviewed the prime minister and got promises of food until harvest time. 'It is the importunate widow who comes to mind when I think of Jane Latham', said a clerical colleague. 'She was loved and revered throughout the whole countryside' as the horrified bishop wrote when he returned from furlough and discovered that 'she had begun to do all the things she had promised me she would not do' (ibid.).

For this work Miss Latham received the kaisar-i-Hind gold medal in 1936. In that year she became a tertiary of the Franciscan community Crista Prema Seva Sangha, whose mother house was at Poona, and to this she left all her property by will.

When in July 1938 Miss Latham was attacked by dysentery she was brought to the Canada Hospital in Nasik, and there she died on 5 August 1938; she was buried in Nasik cemetery. Hers had been an 'heroic and costly way of life'.   MARGARET BRYANT

Sources P. Lloyd, 'Memoir of Jane Leeke Latham', United Society for the Propagation of the Gospel archives · K. T. Butler and H. I. McMorran, eds., *Girton College register, 1869–1946* (1948) · *Girton Review*, Michaelmas term (1938) · *The training of women teachers for secondary schools*, Board of Education, pamphlet 23 (1912) · *CGPLA Eng. & Wales* (1938) · b. cert.

Archives United Society for the Propagation of the Gospel, London, missionary index archive

Wealth at death £672 11s. 9d.: probate, 3 Feb 1939, *CGPLA Eng. & Wales*

Latham, John (1740–1837), naturalist, was born on 27 June 1740 at Eltham, Kent, the eldest son of John Latham (*d.* 1788), a surgeon and apothecary. He was educated at Merchant Taylors' School, London, until the age of fifteen. He attended the London Hospital medical school, and studied anatomy under William Hunter (1718–1783). In 1763 he moved to Dartford, in Kent, where he began practising medicine, probably from a Spital Street address. In the same year, he married Ann Porter, with whom he had at least one son, John (1769–1843), and three daughters, including Ann (*b.* 1772). Latham practised medicine in Dartford for some thirty-five years, and served as doctor to the Dartford poorhouse on a number of occasions.

Once established in medical practice, Latham could begin to spend more time pursuing his interests in natural history. Ornithology and comparative anatomy were his favourite subjects (although he was also interested in archaeology). He assembled a fine collection of birds and established a museum which attracted many visitors and was of great use to fellow naturalists and artists. In 1770 his first published work appeared in the Royal Society's *Philosophical Transactions*. As early as 1771 Latham entered into correspondence with the ornithologist Thomas Pennant (1726–1798), which lasted until the latter's death. Latham also corresponded with most of the important naturalists of his time. As a result, he had access to the major collections in the country and, in time, he became an important member of the scientific community, and the leading English ornithologist of his day. In 1772 he met the natural history collector Sir Ashton Lever (1729–1788); the two men subsequently entered into friendly competition over their collections of specimens. In 1773 Latham discovered the Dartford warbler. In 1788 Lever was forced to sell part of his collections by lottery, and when in 1806, Lever's museum was sold, Latham was able to acquire some specimens for his own collection.

Latham's works depended heavily on personal observation of the collections of specimens accessible to him; his connections were such that he was in an excellent position to study both native and foreign birds. His works featured a large number of exotic birds from all over the world, including specimens from India, Australia, and the Pacific. On 25 May 1775 Latham was elected FRS, at which time Sir Joseph Banks (1743–1820), was president of the society. Banks provided Latham with a further supply of specimens and material, indeed some of the collection housed at the Royal Society's museum was gathered during Banks's voyage with Captain James Cook (1728–1779). Banks also allowed Latham access to the various paintings made during the Cook voyages (1768–71, 1772–5, 1776–80). Moreover, Latham was often given the first opportunity to view new specimens and information. His sources included the Indian bird material in the collections of Major-General Thomas Hardwicke, Lady Mary Impey (d. 1818), and Sir John Anstruther (1753–1811); specimens from Barbados were also sent by the earl of Seaforth, and Abyssinian birds were presented to him by the collector Henry Salt (1780–1827); and he made use of illustrations of Australian birds in the 'Lambert drawings' acquired by Aylmer Bourke Lambert (1761–1842), from Surgeon-General John White (1756–1832), and the notes made by the botanist Daniel Solander (1733–1782) and (Johann) Reinhold Forster (1729–1798) on Cook's voyages. It is not surprising, therefore, that he became known as the 'grandfather' of Australian ornithology, since he was the first to describe and classify a number of Australian birds, including the emu.

In 1778 Latham became a corresponding member of the Medical Society of London. It has been suggested that about 1788 or 1789, through his association either with the botanist James Edward Smith (1759–1828), who had purchased Linnaeus's library, or with Banks, Latham proposed the founding of the Linnean Society of London. In 1793 he was elected FSA and in 1794 was nominated a member of the Natural History Society of Berlin. In 1795 he received the degree of MD from the University of

Erlangen in Germany and in 1812 received the diploma of the Royal Academy of Sciences, Stockholm. In 1796, having amassed a considerable fortune, he retired from practice and settled in a large house in Middlebridge Street, Romsey, to be near his son, John, a common brewer (and JP). In 1798 Latham married his second wife, Ann Delamott, of Ealing.

During the period 1780–90, Latham's objective appears to have been the publication of a complete work of all known bird species, including an update of existing ornithological knowledge and a consideration of all new information as it occurred. In his work, he generally adopted a classification system dependent on 'Ray for his basic divisions and on Linnaeus for lower divisions'. His published works included *A General Synopsis of Birds* (1781–5), containing many new genera and species, which was followed by supplements in 1787 and 1801. In this and future works Latham, like many of his peers, drew, etched, and coloured his own plates. In the preface he wrote:

> The intent of the following sheets is to give, as far as may be, a concise account of all the Birds hitherto known; nothing having been done in this way, as a general work, in the English Language, of late years.

By publishing this work in English, rather than Latin, he provided Johann Friedrich Gmelin with the opportunity to take the credit for translating his work and allocating scientific names to his specimens.

Latham did not repeat this oversight in his next major work, *Index ornithologicus, sive, Systema ornithologiae*, which attempted to describe the known birds of his time and their habitats. This work was issued in parts between 1790 and 1801, no doubt owing to the countless new specimens that were appearing (especially from Australia and the Pacific islands). The projected second edition to his *Index ornithologicus* never materialized, probably because of the increasing volume of new material. However, the work was reissued, with additions, in Paris in 1809.

Besides papers in the *Philosophical Transactions* and the *Transactions of the Linnean Society*, Latham (helped by his daughter Ann) contributed the descriptions of a number of new birds in *The Voyage of Governor Philip to Botany Bay* (1789). He also helped to revise the part on insects for the second edition of Thomas Pennant's *Indian Zoology* in 1793. Two years later, Latham's contribution on the subject reappeared in *Faunula Indica, concinnata a Joanne Latham et Hugone Davies*, which was edited by Reinhold Forster in 1795. In 1811 Latham's revision of Pennant's *British Zoology* was published. From 1796 to 1819, while living at Romsey, he became interested in local antiquities, and wrote accounts of 'Ancient sculptures in the abbey church of Romsey' in *Archaeologia* (vol. 14, 1801) and of an engraved brass plate from Netley Abbey, which also appeared in *Archaeologia* (vol. 15, 1804).

In 1809 Latham had mentioned to Colonel George Montagu the possibility of a second edition of his *General Synopsis of Birds*, and in 1821 he embarked on this task. The enlargement of his earlier work appeared in ten volumes between 1821 and 1828, under the title *A General History of Birds*, and incorporated new information and both new and improved illustrations (designed, etched, and coloured by himself); it was dedicated to George IV, and considered his greatest work.

Pecuniary losses in Latham's old age forced him to sell a great part of his library and museum—in 1819 his son John became bankrupt and Latham endeavoured to help cover his son's debts by selling his own possessions. In the same year Latham moved to Winchester, to live with his daughter and her husband, William N. Wickham, a surgeon. In the autumn of 1836 Lord Palmerston visited Latham (then ninety-six), and described him as 'well, hearty, and cheerful, eating a good dinner at five' (*DNB*), but adds that he could no longer see to read. The ornithologist Alfred Newton (1829–1907) remarked of Latham that 'his defects as a compiler, which had been manifest before, rather increased with age, and the consequences were not happy' (ibid.). While there is a consensus of opinion that Latham was essentially a compiler whose work was not always of a high standard, his industry won him an international reputation and he dominated his field for fifty years. He died on 4 February 1837 at Winchester and was buried in Romsey Abbey, beside his first wife.

YOLANDA FOOTE

Sources private information (2004) · A. Newton, 'Ornithology', *Encyclopaedia Britannica*, 9th edn (1875–89), vol. 18, p. 6 · Nichols, *Illustrations*, 6.613 · *DNB* · Nichols, *Lit. anecdotes*, 9.26 · *The Naturalist*, 4, 26 [cf. 256, 283] · *GM*, 2nd ser., 8 (1837) · *Annual Register* (1837), 178 · M. T. Howard, *Dr John Latham, 1740–1837: Romsey's first local historian* (1990) · C. E. Jackson, *Bird etchings: the illustrators and their books, 1655–1855* (1985) · H. M. Whittell, *The literature of Australian birds: a history and a bibliography of Australian ornithology* (1954) · P. L. Farber, ed., *The emergence of ornithology as a scientific discipline, 1760–1850* (1982)
Archives NHM | Linn. Soc., letters to James Smith · Warks. CRO, Pennant MSS
Likenesses W. Daniell, engraving, 1812 (after G. Dance) · lithograph, repro. in *The Naturalist*, 4 (1838–9)

Latham, John (1761–1843), physician, was born on 29 December 1761 at Gawsworth, Cheshire, the eldest son of John Latham of Oriel College, Oxford, vicar of Siddington, Cheshire, and his wife, Sarah, formerly Podmore, of Sandbach, Cheshire. After education at Manchester grammar school he entered Brasenose College, Oxford, in 1778, graduated BA on 9 February 1782, MA on 15 October 1784, MB on 3 May 1786, and DM on 3 April 1788. From 1782 to 1784 he studied medicine at St Bartholomew's Hospital, London.

On 12 April 1784 Latham married Mary, daughter of Peter Mere, vicar of Prestbury. They had three sons: John (1787–1853) [see below], Peter Mere *Latham (1789–1875), and Henry (1794–1866) [see below]. Latham began to practise medicine in Manchester, and was honorary physician to Manchester Infirmary, but he soon moved to Oxford, where, on 11 July 1787, he became physician to the Radcliffe Infirmary. In 1788 he moved to London, and was elected fellow of the Royal College of Physicians on 30 September 1789. He was elected physician to the Middlesex Hospital on 15 October 1789, and resigned on his election to the same office at St Bartholomew's Hospital on 17 January 1793, which he held in 1802. He had a large practice at his house in Bedford Row, regularly attended the Royal College of Physicians, where he was censor the year after his election as fellow, and delivered the Harveian oration in 1794. He delivered the Goulstonian lectures in 1793, and the Croonian in 1795. He was president from 1813 to 1819 inclusive. In 1795 Latham became physician-extraordinary to the prince of Wales. He published *A Plan of a Charitable Institution to be Established on the Sea Coast* in 1791, and in 1796 *On Rheumatism and Gout: a Letter Addressed to Sir George Baker, Bart*, where he stated his opinion that neither acute rheumatism nor gout should be classed among inflammations, and that the seat of both was the radicles of the lymphatic vessels. He denied that gout was inherited, and that attacks were ever beneficial, and advocated a very elaborate system of treatment.

Latham had made a fortune and bought an estate at Sandbach before 1807. In that year he showed symptoms of advanced consumption. Dr David Pitcairn cured him, and he retired for rest to his estate for two years, but he grew tired of country life and returned to London, where he took a house in Harley Street. While continuing to practise he wrote prolifically during the years before his second retirement.

Latham's *Facts and Opinions Concerning Diabetes* (1811) consisted of long extracts from the Greek writers and from Francis Willis on the subject, followed by recorded cases. He favoured a dietetic treatment and supported the views of Dr John Rollo. Ten papers on a wide variety of topics were published in *Medical Transactions* between 1806 and 1819. Besides his printed works he wrote an elaborate 'Dissertation on asthma'. His writings show that he excelled in clinical observation and acquaintance with the materia medica.

Latham moved in 1829 to Bradwall Hall in Cheshire, where he died of stone in the bladder on 20 April 1843. He set aside a portion of his income for charity, and called this (by a term derived from Hebrew) his corban fund.

John Latham (1787–1853), poet, was born at Oxford on 18 March 1787. He was sent to Macclesfield grammar school when five years old, and to Brasenose College, Oxford, in 1803, where Reginald Heber was his contemporary and friend. Latham was a dedicated and methodical student, and thus had time to indulge his love of sports. In 1806 he won the university prize for Latin verse with a poem on Trafalgar, and in that year, while still an undergraduate, was elected a fellow of All Souls. In December 1806 he entered Lincoln's Inn, graduating BCL in 1810 and DCL in 1815. Soon afterwards he was attacked by ophthalmia, and lost all but residual sight. For fourteen years he spent several months of each year at All Souls, the rest of the time living with his father, until 24 May 1821, when he married Anne (d. 1839), daughter of Sir Henry Dampier; they took a house at Somerset Street, Portman Square, London. Their eldest son, John Henry Latham (1823–1843), an accomplished scholar, died while an undergraduate at Oxford; two sons and a daughter survived him. In 1829 he settled in Cheshire, near his father, whom he succeeded as squire in 1843. He died at Bradwall on 30 January 1853 and was buried on 4 February at Sandbach. Latham published anonymously a volume of poems (1836), and a volume of his *English and Latin Poems, Original and Translated*, was printed in 1853.

Henry Latham (1794–1866), poet, third son of John Latham, was born in London on 4 November 1794. From Manchester grammar school he entered Brasenose College, Oxford, in 1812, and there obtained a prize for Latin verse. He graduated in 1815 and was admitted a barrister of Lincoln's Inn in 1820. The three brothers went to Paris and the Low Countries in 1820, and Henry later visited North America. He subsequently entered the church; he was vicar successively of Selmeston with Alciston and of Fittleworth, Sussex. He retained a taste for classical studies, and published in 1863 a collection of translated and original Latin poems. He died of cholera on 6 September 1866, at Boulogne. He was twice married.

NORMAN MOORE, rev. ANITA MCCONNELL

Sources Munk, *Roll*, 2.393–5 · Foster, *Alum. Oxon.* · *Hist. U. Oxf.* 5: *18th-cent. Oxf.*, 695, 708 · J. Latham, *English and Latin poems, original and translated* (1853) [preliminary memoir] · E. M. Brockbank, *Sketches of the lives and work of the honorary medical staff of the Manchester Infirmary: from its foundation in 1752 to 1830* (1904) · d. cert. [J. Latham, 1787–1853]
Archives BL | BL, collection for history of Romsey, Add. MSS 26774–26780 · BL, letters to Dr J. E. Gray, Add. MS 29533
Likenesses G. Dance, chalk drawing, 1798, RCP Lond. · A. Pope, miniature, *c*.1806, RCP Lond. · J. Jackson, oils, exh. RA 1816, Brasenose College, Oxford · R. W. Sievier, bust, 1824, St Bartholomew's Hospital, London
Wealth at death under £1500—Henry Latham: probate, 7 Nov 1866, *CGPLA Eng. & Wales*

Latham, John (1787–1853). *See under* Latham, John (1761–1843).

Latham, Sir John Greig (1877–1964), politician and judge in Australia, was born on 26 August 1877 in Ascot Vale, then an outlying suburb of Melbourne, Victoria, Australia, the eldest of five children (four sons and a daughter) of Thomas Latham, a native-born tinsmith, and his Scottish-born wife, Janet Scott. He was brought up in the Melbourne suburb of Ivanhoe.

Thomas Latham served as a JP and local councillor, as well as secretary of the Victorian Society for the Protection of Animals, which he founded. He was a devout Methodist who instilled into his children an ethos of hard work and moral rectitude, discernible in John Latham throughout his life. From Gore Street primary school in Fitzroy, inner Melbourne, the serious, studious boy won a scholarship to Scotch College, one of the trio of prestigious private schools set up in Melbourne along denominational— in its case Presbyterian—lines. From there a scholarship took him to the University of Melbourne; he graduated BA in 1896 with high distinction in philosophy and logic. Following a period teaching at Hamilton Academy, a private school in rural Victoria, he returned to the university, where he graduated LLB in 1902. He was admitted to the

Victorian bar in 1904 and commenced practice in the following year. On 19 December 1907 Latham married, in a Methodist ceremony, Eleanor Mary (Ella; *d.* 1964), daughter of Richard Tobin of Northcote, Victoria. They had two sons and a daughter.

Briefs came slowly, and between 1904 and 1920 Latham combined his legal work with teaching at the university: first as resident tutor in logic and philosophy at one of its constituent colleges, then as lecturer in inductive and deductive logic, and finally as lecturer in the law of contract and personal property. He also supplemented his income by writing for the *Argus*, the more conservative of Melbourne's two morning dailies, and in 1908 became Australian correspondent of the staunchly imperialistic London *Standard*. He served as secretary of the Imperial Federation League's Victorian branch and joined the Victorian group of the Round Table, the think-tank set up by Viscount Milner to explore the link between motherland and dominions. Having rejected his father's Methodism, Latham assisted in 1907 in setting up an Education Act Defence League to oppose teaching scripture in Victoria's state schools. Two years later he helped to found the Rationalist Society of Victoria and subsequently served as its president; until his death he was connected with its successor body, the Rationalist Association of Australia.

When the First World War broke out Latham volunteered for service and simultaneously held commissions in both the army and navy. In 1915 he became secretary of the Victorian branch of the Universal Service League, crusading vigorously for conscription. Two years later, in the wake of allegations of sabotage in Australia's naval dockyards, he was appointed head of naval intelligence with the honorary rank of lieutenant-commander. As staff officer and adviser to the Australian minister for defence, Sir Joseph Cooke, Latham attended the Imperial Conference in London in 1918. In 1919 he went to the Paris peace conference as assistant secretary of the British empire delegation and as British secretary of the inter-allied commission on Czecho-Slovak affairs. He took part in framing the various classes of mandate, including that under which Australia became responsible for New Guinea. He was also attached to a subcommittee of a commission dealing with the League of Nations, and as such became convinced of the need for Australians to be better informed regarding international affairs. In 1920 he was appointed CMG for his services overseas.

Having returned to the bar in 1919, Latham saw his practice expand. He specialized in taxation and commercial and arbitration issues, yet important constitutional cases came his way. In 1922 he took silk. In the previous year, owing to his growing involvement in public affairs, he declined appointment as a judge of Victoria's supreme court. Before the war he had been an activist in Alfred Deakin's Liberal Party and in 1918 considered entering federal politics as a National Party member. At Versailles he had conceived an enduring personal and political detestation for prime minister William Morris Hughes, and in 1922—campaigning as an independent Liberal

Union candidate with the slogan 'Hughes must go'—he won the federal seat of Kooyong and entered the house of representatives. There the rural-based Country Party held the balance of power; Latham was invited to its deliberations to plot the downfall of Hughes, who resigned early in 1923. Latham's entry into parliament entailed substantial financial sacrifice, and he seemed ill-suited by temperament and attitude for the political maelstrom. He was scholarly, with an austere, aloof manner; he unswervingly refused to compromise his principles for the sake of pragmatism or popularity; he had no empathy with machine politics. That he did not return to the bar once his aim of removing Hughes was accomplished is attributable to his abiding sense of public duty. In debate he commanded from the outset respect for his cogency. But the legacy of voice and elocution lessons taken to overcome a childhood stammer was a stilted, high-pitched way of speaking better suited to a law court than to a parliamentary chamber: it was much ridiculed. Eventually he managed to vary his tone and peppered his speeches with dry witticisms.

In 1925 Latham joined the Nationalist Party, whose leader, prime minister Stanley Melbourne Bruce, appointed him attorney-general. As such, Latham demonstrated strict impartiality, and he accompanied Bruce in 1926 to the Imperial Conference in London, where he almost collapsed through overwork. He also led the Australian delegation to the League of Nations general assembly in Geneva. As seen in his book *Australia and the British Commonwealth* (1929), comprising lectures delivered during 1928 at the University of Queensland, he took a cautious approach to the Imperial Conference's attempt to redefine formally the relations between Britain and the dominions. In the federal election of 1929, against a background of worsening economic recession and industrial strife, the Australian Labor Party led by James Scullin was swept to power. Bruce was unseated, and the Nationalist presence in the house of representatives depleted. Latham's sense of public duty induced him reluctantly to accept leadership of the opposition. Harrying the government relentlessly, especially on its inability to fulfil its promises to the electorate, he proved remarkably effective.

Beset by the great depression and dissension in its ranks, the government suffered a setback with the defection of a prominent figure, Joseph Aloysius Lyons, and four Labor colleagues; they left the party in 1931, having supported a narrowly defeated motion of no confidence in the Scullin administration introduced by Latham. Lyons subsequently became associated with the extra-parliamentary and avowedly non-partisan All for Australia League, the most important among several organizations of concerned citizens formed to counter left-wing extremism with its perceived threats to Australia's security, institutions, and links with Britain. The Nationalists, realizing that they were in danger of being eclipsed by the league as a political force, decided that they should co-operate with Lyons, and authorized Latham to ask Lyons and Country Party leader Earle Page if they would agree to form a single opposition party, with one leader and a common programme. Page demurred, but Lyons agreed, accepting Latham's offer of its leadership on condition that the Nationalists unanimously concurred. This they did, and Lyons's praise for Latham's readiness to place the nation's welfare above his personal aggrandizement was widely echoed in non-Labor circles.

The resultant United Australia Party was formed in May 1931 and, having won the December federal election, took office in January 1932 with Lyons as prime minister. Latham—deputy prime minister, attorney-general, minister for external affairs, and minister for industry—played a major part in formulating policy. Among his contributions were the Financial Agreement Enforcement Act, the Crimes Act, and the Transport Workers Act. He ensured that certain sections of the statute of Westminster should not apply to Australia until specifically endorsed by the federal parliament (which occurred under John Curtin's Labor government in 1942). In 1932 he represented Australia at the League of Nations and attended the Geneva disarmament conference as well as the Lausanne conference on reparations. He was appointed privy councillor in 1933. A steadfast champion of the white Australia policy, he was nevertheless keen to develop his nation's links with south-east Asia and in 1934 led a goodwill mission to countries of that region, the first such tour undertaken by an Australian minister for external affairs. Latham retired from politics later that year and was appointed GCMG. He became chief justice of the high court of Australia in October 1935 and served until April 1952. From 1940 to 1941 he concurrently held the post of Australian minister to Japan, but since he arrived in Tokyo after that nation's pact with the axis powers had been concluded his effectiveness was blunted. As chief justice he took a strictly legalistic view of constitutional problems and was deeply interested in constitutional reform, especially in the industrial sphere. He was much concerned with issues relating to the defence power of the federal government in war and in peace. Sometimes, as in his final important case, the *Communist Party Case* of 1951, his judgment differed from that of his colleagues. Following his retirement he testified before the joint committee on the constitution (appointed 1956, reported 1958).

Latham died in the Melbourne inner suburb of Richmond on 25 July 1964. Despite his rationalist views, the cremation was preceded by a funeral service at Wesley Church. His wife had predeceased him by four months. Of his children, Richard Thomas Edwin (1909–1943), a fellow of All Souls College, Oxford, and author of *The Law and the Commonwealth* (1937), was killed while serving in the Royal Air Force; Winifred Mary (Freda) died in 1953; and Peter Greig, a lieutenant-colonel, survived him.

HILARY L. RUBINSTEIN

Sources J. Latham, 'Remembrance of things past: mainly political', *Meanjin Quarterly*, 21 (1962) · Z. Cowen, *Sir John Latham and other papers* (Melbourne, 1965) · J. R. Williams, *John Latham and the conservative recovery from defeat, 1929–1931* (Sydney, 1969) · S. Macintyre,

AusDB, vol. 10 • *Commonwealth parliamentary debates: House of Representatives* (1922–34) • L. Foster, *High hopes: the men and motives of the Australian Round Table* (Melbourne, 1986) • R. Garran, *Prosper the commonwealth* (Sydney, 1958) • NL Aus., Sir John Greig Latham papers • University of Melbourne, archives, Sir William Harrison Moore papers • University of Melbourne, archives, Australian British Trade Association papers

Archives NL Aus., papers | National Archives of Australia, cabinet papers • University of Melbourne, Australian British Trade Association papers • University of Melbourne, Sir William Harrison Moore papers

Likenesses W. Dargie, oils, High Court, Canberra

Wealth at death £74,365 Australian: *AusDB*, vol. 10

Latham, Peter Mere (1789–1875), physician, was born on 1 July 1789 in Fenchurch Buildings, London, the second son of John *Latham (1761–1843), physician, and Mary, daughter of Peter Mere, vicar of Prestbury, Cheshire. His early education was at the free school at Sandbach in Cheshire and, from 1797, at Macclesfield grammar school. In 1806 he went to Brasenose College, Oxford, where he won a prize for Latin verse, as did both his brothers, and graduated BA in 1810. He began his medical studies at St Bartholomew's Hospital and at the Public Dispensary in Carey Street, London, under Thomas Bateman; here a fellow student was Richard Bright, who became a lifelong friend. Latham obtained his BM degree in 1814 and his DM in 1816.

Latham began practice in a house in Gower Street and in 1815 was appointed physician to the Middlesex Hospital. Three years later he was elected fellow of the Royal College of Physicians and began a distinguished career in the college. During the next twenty years he was censor at various times, gave the Goulstonian and Lumleian lectures and, in 1839, demonstrated that he had not lost his youthful touch by delivering the Harveian oration in better Latin than most orators of his generation. In 1837 he was appointed physician-extraordinary to the queen and he retained that appointment until his death.

In 1823 Latham and Peter Mark Roget were asked by the government to investigate an epidemic of scurvy and dysentery among the prisoners at Millbank penitentiary. They concluded that it was due to an inadequate diet; however, it is more likely to have been cholera. In 1824, like his father before him, Latham resigned from the Middlesex Hospital and was appointed physician to St Bartholomew's Hospital. In the same year he married Diana Clarissa Chetwynd Stapleton, but she died in the following year. On 14 February 1833 he married Grace Mary Chambers (d. 1868); there were four children of this marriage. At St Bartholomew's Latham devoted himself to improving the quality of the clinical teaching, which had been deteriorating for several years. He quickly acquired the reputation of being the best clinical teacher in London—although it was said that his old friend Richard Bright ran him close. In 1836 Latham was appointed lecturer in the theory and practice of medicine in the medical school and in the same year published his *Lectures on Subjects Connected with Clinical Medicine*. He had developed a special interest in diseases of the heart; his *Essays on some Diseases of the Heart* (1826) was expanded into the much more substantial *Lectures on Clinical Medicine, Comprising Diseases of the Heart* (1845). As a result of these publications he acquired the nickname Heart Latham.

In these publications Latham demonstrated his extensive knowledge and sound judgement, and he was unusually aware of the limitations of the knowledge and practice of his day. His lucid descriptions of heart disease were balanced by the frankness with which he admitted his ignorance and the clarity with which he identified and expounded the problems still awaiting solution. He was an early convert to the use of the stethoscope, first described in 1819, and was teaching on auscultation as early as 1826—much earlier than most of his peers and senior colleagues.

As a teacher Latham was clearly conscientious to a fault; his lectures were much praised by contemporaries but the use of terms such as 'highly finished and exhaustive' to describe lectures delivered in a 'slow and formal style' raises the suspicion that some students may have found them a little tedious. Latham himself was well aware of this risk and, in his writings on medical education, especially a series of papers published in the *British Medical Journal* in his retirement, he emphasized the inferiority of lectures to the direct study of sick men and women for the aspiring physician.

Of Latham's physical appearance and character Charles West, one of his most distinguished pupils, wrote a detailed account. He was very short and spare with a slight deformity of the spine; his hair was light brown, thinning as he aged, his eyes were grey and his nose aquiline, 'almost like the great Duke's'. Despite these largely unremarkable features his appearance and demeanour seem to have been striking and, together with his voice, were calculated to command attention. A genial and cultured gentleman and a devout Christian, his sympathy with and compassion for his suffering patients was such that he is recorded as failing to keep appointments with those whose distress he could not relieve. West concluded his word picture of Latham: 'In troublous times he would have been a confessor; he might have lacked the courage to become a martyr' (Watson).

Latham's health was always delicate and his chronic asthma and emphysema compelled him to resign his appointment at St Bartholomew's at the age of fifty-two in 1841. His father also had retired early due to ill health and, like his father, Peter Latham found that relief from the stresses of hospital practice produced sufficient improvement to allow him to continue in private practice for two more decades. He finally retired in 1865 to Torquay with his wife; after her death in 1868 he was cared for by his two daughters, who never married. He died at Highwood, Torquay, on 20 July 1875.　　　　PETER R. FLEMING

Sources *DNB* • Munk, *Roll*, 2.393–5; 3.185–90 • T. Watson, 'In memoriam: Dr Peter Mere Latham', in *The collected works of Dr P. M. Latham*, ed. R. Martin, 1 (1876), xiii–xxx • W. B. Spaulding, 'Peter Mere Latham (1789–1875): a great medical educator', *Canadian Medical Association Journal*, 104 (1971), 1109–14 • private information (2004) • d. cert. • *CGPLA Eng. & Wales* (1875)

Archives St Bartholomew's Hospital, case notes | Bodl. Oxf., letters to John Taylor Coleridge · U. Birm., correspondence with Harriet Martineau · Wellcome L., case books
Likenesses F. Holl, stipple (after G. Richmond), Wellcome L. · J. Jackson, portrait, priv. coll. · engraving (after J. Jackson), RCP Lond.
Wealth at death under £35,000: probate, 4 Sept 1875, *CGPLA Eng. & Wales*

Latham, Peter Walker (1865–1953), racket sports player, was born in Manchester on 10 May 1865, the only child of William Latham, engine fitter, and his wife, Sarah Jane Hewitt. At the age of eleven he started his sporting career in the Manchester rackets club and in 1887, when not quite twenty-two, he successfully challenged Joseph Gray of Rugby for the world's championship. Gaining the title led, in 1888, to his engagement as head professional of rackets at the Queen's Club, west Kensington, where he remained for the next thirteen years. During this period he successfully defended his title against Walter Gray of Charterhouse and twice against George Standing, the second time involving a trip to New York, where he played what was probably the hardest and greatest match of his career, at one time coming within an ace of losing, but finally winning by 4 games to 3.

Latham also took up real tennis and in 1895 beat the previously invincible Charles Saunders for the world crown, becoming the only man to hold the world titles in real tennis and rackets simultaneously. He defended this successfully against Tom Pettitt of Boston in 1897 and C. (Punch) Fairs of Brighton in 1904 before losing to Fairs the next year, his sole defeat ever in a championship match. Two years later, at the age of forty-two, he defeated Fairs to regain the title. He then retired from championship play and for some years played exhibition and handicap matches in America and on the continent. He was rated scratch in professional handicaps until 1909.

In 1901 Latham left Queen's to become tennis professional to Charles Rose, first at Newmarket and later at Hardwick House, near Pangbourne. In 1916 he returned to the Queen's Club, where he did much to revive tennis after the war and was greatly sought after as a teacher of players of all standards. He was blessed with many exceptional qualities, which were not fully apparent to the spectator but were quickly discovered by his opponents. His service may not have looked remarkable but it was delivered to prevent his opponent from making his favourite return and to obtain the attack and put his adversary on the defensive. Always well balanced, he was very quick to move at the critical moment, so that it appeared as though the ball was always being hit towards him. In the words of Edgar Baerlein, an amateur who had played with Latham at his best in both games: 'He was an artist ever seeking perfection. For him it was not enough that a stroke should be a winner. It had to be that and more, the more being that even he could not improve it' (Aberdare, 94).

Latham married in 1888 Annie Sarah Carpenter, daughter of Stephen Whetham, flax cleaner for rope making, of Bridport. They had one daughter and four sons, one of whom, Emil, became a tennis professional at Queen's Club. Latham died in his home at Chiswick, Middlesex, on 22 November 1953. His *Times* obituary remarked that he was 'a peerless player of rackets and tennis' with 'no weak point in his armour'.   ABERDARE, *rev.* WRAY VAMPLEW

Sources Lord Aberdare [M. G. L. Bruce], *The Willis Faber book of tennis and rackets* (1980) · *The Times* (23 Nov 1953) · private information (1971) · personal knowledge (1971)
Likenesses J. Clark, painting (*In the Dedans at Queen's Club*); formerly in the possession of Mr P. M. Lottman-Johnson, 1971 · photographs, repro. in Aberdare, *The Willis Faber book of tennis and rackets*

Latham, Richard (1699–1767), small-holder and textile producer, was born in Scarisbrick, Lancashire, the fourth son of Thomas Latham (*d.* 1723), small-holder, and his wife. On 25 August 1723 Latham married Ann Barton; between 1726 and 1741 they had one son and seven daughters, one of whom died in childhood. In the same year Latham inherited the lease of the farm in Scarisbrick, on the death of his father; shortly after his birth he had been named as the third life on a lease for three lives, a system of tenure that was typical in south-west Lancashire during this period. Almost immediately after acquiring the farm he was plunged into debt by the purchase of stock and agricultural implements; the early years of his marriage were a lean time as he continued to stock the farm and pay off debts. Borrowing money to pay a fine of £40, relating to the renewal of his lease in 1728, put further pressure on a household that was growing rapidly. There are few indications of luxury items in the Latham household throughout its formative years. Latham is representative of a substantial number of people who were at the forefront of economic development in Lancashire during the mid-eighteenth century, though unrepresentative in that he kept a detailed account of his personal expenditure throughout his married life. His financial astuteness, to which his accounts are clear testimony, meant that within his constraints a reasonable standard of living was achieved. His family enjoyed a varied and nutritious diet, and even found the time and money for a modest social calendar, which consisted mainly of visits to friends, family, and fairs. Latham was probably Roman Catholic in religion and Jacobite in politics.

Despite being only a small-holder (after Latham's death his widow renewed a lease for 9 acres of land) Latham was a market-oriented, progressive farmer. From the first year of his marriage he was growing clover and potatoes; he expanded his crops into a wide range of vegetables and fruits in later years. At various times he also kept cattle, pigs, sheep, and poultry. In practice he probably altered his output and used his land in different ways as his family expanded and grew older, as well as in response to market changes. He was more than a subsistence farmer, although some of what he produced was consumed by his family.

Latham's progressiveness is perhaps most evident in the area of domestic textile production. The household was producing textiles throughout the period of the accounts, even during Ann's childbearing years. During the 1720s and early 1730s this production was limited to flax and wool, not all of which was produced on the farm. However, in 1736, when his eldest daughter was ten years old,

Latham purchased cotton for the first time. Three years later he purchased two spinning wheels, as well as cotton cards, spindles, and other equipment. However, cotton production failed to displace entirely the older textile industries, and for a time the Latham household was engaged in the production of flax, linen, wool, worsted, and cotton. Textile production continued at an increasing rate throughout the 1740s and 1750s as the Latham children reached their full productive capacity. It was largely this expanded textile production, rather than agricultural output, that financed Latham's higher standard of living during this period, as indicated by his purchase of luxury items such as quality furniture and fashionable clothes. By the 1760s, when the children were leaving home and Latham and his wife were elderly, expenditure on such items declined.

Latham died at his home at Scarisbrick on 5 July 1767.

A. J. GRITT

Sources L. Weatherill, *The account book of Richard Latham, 1724–1767* (1990) · L. Weatherill, *Consumer behaviour and material culture in Britain, 1660–1760* (1988) · S. Harrop and P. Perrins, *Transactions of the Historic Society of Lancashire and Cheshire*, 140 (1990) · private information (2004)
Archives Lancs. RO, Scarisbrick MSS
Wealth at death bequests of £53 5s. after death of wife: will

Latham, Robert Gordon (1812–1888), ethnologist and philologist, was born on 24 March 1812 at Billingborough, Lincolnshire, the eldest son of the Revd Thomas Latham (1770/71–1846). Educated at Eton College, and a contemporary of his future brother-in-law Sir Edward Creasy (1812–1878), he entered King's College, Cambridge, as a scholar in 1829 and became a fellow in 1832. He graduated in January 1833 and took his MA in 1836. In 1833 visits to Hamburg and Copenhagen, followed by a year of language studies in Norway, led to his delightful *Norway and the Norwegians* (1840). With Creasy he had previously translated, in 1838, Esaias Tégner's *Axel* and *Frithiofs saga*.

From 1839 to 1845 Latham was professor of English language and literature at University College, London, but he simultaneously developed a medical career, qualifying as a licentiate of the Royal College of Physicians in 1842, taking his Cambridge MD in 1844, and being elected an FRCP in 1846. Initially physician to the St James's and St George's Dispensary, in 1844 he became assistant physician at the Middlesex Hospital, London, where he lectured on forensic medicine and materia medica. He was elected a fellow of the Royal Society in 1848.

Latham's *The English Language* (1841) became a standard text until the 1870s. He wrote many other grammatical works and advocated spelling reform, but his consuming passion was ethnology—the study of the varieties of mankind and its languages, and the enigma of human origins. In *Man and his Migrations* (1851), seven years before the first pronouncement by Darwin and Wallace on evolution by natural selection, Latham speculated on human development from 'some species … lower in the scale of Nature' (p. 50).

Latham acquired a light-hearted semi-fictional existence in *Bentley's Miscellany* for 1846 as the Cambridge Travelling Bachelor, in his contributions to the Tipperary Papers with Creasy and John Sheehan. A description of the bachelor ethnologist's 'learnedly and fancifully decorated' lodgings, including the 'hunting dress of an Ojibbeway Indian and the Sunday clothes of a German Professor lying about promiscuously', carries conviction (*Bentley's Miscellany*, 19.520). On 19 July 1848 he married Elizabeth, daughter of George Cottam, engineer. As a result of his marriage he gave up his fellowship of King's (only bachelors could hold fellowships for life), and he also gave up his medical practice.

Latham's first, seminal work in ethnology was *The Natural History of the Varieties of Man* (1850), followed by other ethnological works, both general and specific, on the colonies, the British Isles, Europe, the Russian empire, and India. He was vice-president of the Ethnological Society, wrote particularly on Native American languages for the Philological Society, and was a member of several other learned societies. He was uniquely qualified for his appointment as director of the ethnological department at the Crystal Palace in 1852. Latham's independence of mind led him in 1862 to question the widely held belief that India was the Aryan motherland, an eccentricity which destroyed his reputation. Only in 1887 did Isaac Taylor, in a paper read to the Royal Anthropological Institute, revive Latham's theory that the Aryans came from southeast of Lithuania, giving impetus to further research into Indo-European origins.

After 1862 Latham's most significant works were a major new edition (1866–70) of Dr Johnson's *Dictionary* and, notably, *The 'Hamlet' of Saxo Grammaticus and of Shakespeare* (1872). By 1863 he was in financial difficulties and was granted a civil-list pension of £100. During the late 1860s and the 1870s he came to know Theodore Watts-Dunton well and introduced him to Thomas Gordon Hake, who in turn introduced them to George Borrow. Hake's *Memoirs of Eighty Years* (1892) are not kind to Latham in the 1860s, describing a decline in habits and appearance, despite his 'handsome person' and 'kindly nature'— 'like a clergyman of a less reputable type; his white necktie unlaundressed, his fine chin ill-shaven, his black coat unskilfully brushed, if at all' (Hake, 208–12). Watts-Dunton's comments in Latham's obituary (*The Athenaeum*, 17 March 1888) show greater understanding and admiration of his 'brilliance of intellect and encyclopaedic knowledge' (Watts, 340). This brilliance did not, unfortunately, lead to clarity or even accuracy of presentation. His erudite writings remain indigestible despite their historical interest.

Latham ultimately developed aphasia—a sad end to a lifetime devoted to language in all its varieties. He died on 9 March 1888 at his home at 156 Upper Richmond Road, Putney, London. He was survived by his wife, and at least one daughter, Clara.

ANN MARGARET RIDLER

Sources T. Watts [T. Watts-Dunton], *The Athenaeum* (17 March 1888), 340–41 · T. G. Hake, *Memoirs of eighty years* (1892) · R. G. Latham, biographical notice, BL, Add. MS 28511 [partly autograph], fol. 25 · I. Taylor, 'Paper presented by Canon Isaac Taylor to the Anthropological Institute of Great Britain & Ireland', *Journal of the Anthropological Institute of Great Britain & Ireland*, 17 (1888), 238–75 · *London Medical Directory* (1847) · *Bentley's Miscellany*, 19 (1846), 186, 297, 413, 520, 626 · *Bentley's Miscellany*, 20 (1846), 92 · T. St E. Hake and A. Compton-Rickett, *The life and letters of Theodore Watts-Dunton*, 2 vols. (1916) · C. Knight, ed., *The English cyclopaedia: biography*, 3 (1856), 610 · H. E. C. Stapylton, *The Eton school lists, from 1791 to 1850*, 2nd edn (1864) · Venn, *Alum. Cant.*, 2/4 · H. H. Bellot, *University College, London, 1826–1926* (1929) · m. cert. · d. cert. · *CGPLA Eng. & Wales* (1888) · Foster, *Alum. Oxon.* · private information (2004) [staff, CUL; archivist, Royal Society] · *The Post Office London directory* (1846) · letter to A. R. Wallace, 10 Nov 1864, BL, Add. MS 46435, fol. 16 · *The Guardian* (14 March 1888) · correspondence, Kongelige Bibliotek, Copenhagen

Archives BL, MSS · CUL, MSS · Kongelige Bibliotek, Copenhagen, correspondence

Likenesses E. Edwards, photograph, NPG; repro. in L. Reeve, ed., *Portraits of men of eminence*, 1 (1863)

Wealth at death £116 4s. 1d.: administration, 10 April 1888, *CGPLA Eng. & Wales*

Latham, Simon (d. 1649?), writer on falconry, has left virtually no record of his life. Although the precise relationship cannot be established, he may have been the nephew of, and was almost certainly connected with, Lewis Latham of Elveston, Bedfordshire, a professional falconer who rose through the ranks to become serjeant of his majesty's hawks in 1627. Simon Latham dedicated his treatise on falconry to Sir Thomas Monson, master of the king's hawks, but there is no evidence in the state records to support suggestions that he was employed as a royal falconer. He may, however, have been the Simon Latham who received a bequest of 5s. from his brother, William, in 1632. Although Latham is described as a gentleman in his book, the Lathams are not recorded as gentry in the visitations. It is more probable that he was the Simon Latham, yeoman of Bletsoe, whose will was proved in Bedfordshire in 1649. That would explain why he was not mentioned in the 1655 will of Lewis Latham.

Latham acknowledged that he was introduced to falconry by Henry Sadleir of Eversley, the third son of Sir Ralph Sadleir of Standon, master of the hawks, and that he wrote about falconry in response to the suggestion of a friend. He claimed no literary skill and indeed the verses which he included in his treatise are somewhat crude. His treatise, *Latham's Falconry, or, The Faulcons Lure and Cure in Two Books* appeared in two parts in 1614 and 1618 and was subsequently reissued in 1633, 1658, and 1665. Unlike many examples of the genre, it was original, practical, and of lasting value. Although he referred in passing to Geoffrey Turbeville, he claimed correctly that his book did not draw on traditional printed sources. The first part was a highly specialized study of how to train the haggard peregrine, that is, a falcon which has been trapped as an adult as distinct from one taken from the nest before it can fly. This was followed by a more conventional review of methods to prevent and treat disease in hawks and the discussion was extended to include goshawks, sparrowhawks, and lanner falcons.   RICHARD GRASSBY

Sources S. Latham, *Latham's falconry, or, The faulcons lure and cure in two books*, 2 pts (1614–18) · J. E. Harting, *Bibliotheca accipitraria: a catalogue of books … relating to falconry* (1891) · F. A. Blaydes, *Genealogia*

Bedfordiensis (1890) · J. Godber, *History of Bedfordshire, 1066–1888* (1969) · *CSP dom.*, 1603–47

La Thangue, Henry Herbert (1859–1929), painter, was born at 4 St John's Grove, Croydon, Surrey, on 19 January 1859, the son of Richard Henry La Thangue, a clerk in the General Register Office, and his wife, Clara, formerly Tiersden. He attended Dulwich College at the same time as fellow painters Alexander Stanhope Forbes and Frederick Goodall. After a brief period at Lambeth School of Art he entered the Royal Academy Schools in 1874. As a gold medallist and with the personal recommendation of the president of the Royal Academy, Frederic Leighton, he entered Jean-Léon Gérôme's atelier at the École des Beaux-Arts in Paris in 1880. Like many of his contemporaries, La Thangue was simultaneously influenced by the work of Jules Bastien-Lepage, the leading rustic naturalist painter at the Salon, and by James McNeill Whistler. His *Study in a Boatbuilding Yard on the French Coast* (exh. Grosvenor Gallery, London, 1882; NMM) refers to the whole *plein-air* naturalist movement initiated by Bastien-Lepage. Anxious to put Bastien's principles into action he worked during the summers of 1881, 1882, and 1883 in Brittany and the south of France. At Donzère in the Rhone valley in 1883 he painted *Poverty* (exh. Institute of Painters in Oil Colours, 1884; priv. coll.), a work which heavily depends upon Bastien-Lepage's *London Flower-Seller* (1882; priv. coll.). At the same time *A Portrait* ('Girl with a Skipping Rope') (exh. Grosvenor Gallery, 1883; Fine Art Society, London) echoes the aestheticism of Whistler's *Harmony in Grey and Green, Miss Cicely Alexander* (1874; Tate collection).

His French training complete, La Thangue returned to England to become a founder member of the New English Art Club (NEAC). Although he did not attend the planning meetings that took place in 1885, he had a powerful influence over the proceedings, forcefully stating his belief that the young painters of Britain should organize themselves on democratic lines to stage annual exhibitions on the scale of the Salon—and in competition with the Royal Academy. Although we have little evidence of La Thangue's personality, apart from occasional inferences in the Stanhope Forbes's letters that he could be truculent, it is clear that his polemical views did not sit easily with the ambitions of the more conservative members of the club. In particular, he deeply offended W. J. Laidlay who had agreed to underwrite the expenses of the club, and who, with the support of other members, forced his withdrawal. La Thangue's only NEAC exhibit, *In the Dauphiné* (1886; presumed des.), was also one of the most controversial in the show. A scene showing two haymakers setting off for the fields, it was striking for its broad handling and bright colour. This picture was re-exhibited later that year at the Arcadian Art Club in Bradford, of which La Thangue was president. His principal patrons at this time were Bradford mill owners with avant-garde tastes who did not object to the broad handling or 'square brush' aspect of his work. At the same time, conscious of public demands, he produced a number of large exhibition pieces addressing social issues. These began with *Leaving*

Home (1889; exh. New Gallery, London; priv. coll.), a picture of a weeping farmer's daughter setting off for life as a servant in the city. The characteristic landscape of Norfolk with its dykes, its spikey trees, and grey skies provided the backdrop.

In 1891, in company with Frederick Brown and George Clausen, the original 'irreconcilables' of the NEAC, La Thangue returned to regular Royal Academy exhibiting with a large canvas portraying a peripatetic preacher delivering a sermon, entitled *A Mission to Seamen* (Castle Museum, Nottingham). He had moved to Bosham in Sussex by this time and was painting delightful impressionist scenes of family and friends conversing under the trees in nearby apple orchards. For the Royal Academy, however, La Thangue reserved grander subject pictures such as *The Last Furrow* (exh. RA, 1895; Oldham Art Gallery) and *The Man with the Scythe* (exh. RA, 1896; Tate collection), the second of these being purchased by the Chantrey Bequest.

Increasingly disgruntled at the destruction of English rural life, La Thangue returned frequently to Provence around the turn of the century. He retained his commitment to peasant subject matter, although in paintings like *A Provencal Winter* (exh. RA, 1903; Glasgow Museums and Art Galleries) an element of picturesqueness enters his work. On many occasions, in the Chelsea Arts Club, he asked Alfred Munnings to recommend 'a quiet old world village where he could live and find real country models' (A. Munnings, *An Artist's Life*, 1951, 97–8). Munnings confesses that La Thangue never succeeded in his quest. Eventually he established a house at Bormes les Mimosas, worked at Les Martiques, and before the First World War had travelled throughout Brescia and Liguria on painting expeditions. His diploma picture, *Violets for Perfume* (exh. RA, 1914; RA) typifies his work of this period. By this stage he was painting pure landscapes and these made up the core of his solo exhibition at the Leicester Galleries in 1914. The work in this show was enthusiastically supported by Walter Sickert who declared that his canvases will 'speak to many generations to come' (O. Sitwell, ed., *A Free House! The Writings of Walter Richard Sickert*, 1947, 271). In the years up to his death, La Thangue concentrated exclusively on scenes of village life in southern France and northern Italy. However, by the end of the 1920s poor health brought him back to England. He fell into a depression when two of his pictures went down in a ship off the coast of New Zealand and he died at 20 Wimpole Street, Marylebone, on 21 December 1929 leaving a widow, Katherine (Kate). Sir George Clausen, his lifelong friend, wrote his epitaph in a letter to *The Times*, praising his 'inflexible honesty and straight conduct, both as artist and as man' (27 Dec 1929, 11).   KENNETH MCCONKEY

Sources J. S. Little, 'H. H. La Thangue', *Art Journal*, new ser., 13 (1893), 169–73 · G. Thomson, 'Henry Herbert La Thangue and his work', *The Studio*, 9 (1896–7), 163–77 · J. S. Little, 'Henry Herbert La Thangue ARA', *Magazine of Art*, 28 (1903–4), 1–6 · *A painter's harvest: H. H. La Thangue RA, 1859–1929* (1978) [exhibition catalogue, Oldham Art Gallery] · A. Jenkins, *The connoisseur: art patrons and collectors in Victorian Bradford* (1989) [exhibition catalogue, Cartwright Hall, Bradford] · *CGPLA Eng. & Wales* (1930)

Wealth at death £32,532 11s. 0d.: resworn probate, 30 Jan 1930, *CGPLA Eng. & Wales*

Lathbery, John. *See* Lathbury, John (d. 1362).

Lathbury, Sir Gerald William (1906–1978), army officer, was born in Murree, India, on 14 July 1906, the only child (a daughter born previously had died very young) of Colonel Henry Oscar Lathbury and his wife, Katherine Fanny Cobbett, granddaughter of William Cobbett. Lathbury was educated at Wellington College and the Royal Military College, Sandhurst (1924–5). He was commissioned on 2 February 1926 and gazetted to the Oxford and Buckinghamshire light infantry stationed in Germany. He was seconded to the Gold Coast regiment from 1928 to 1933. He rejoined his own regiment at Bordon and went to the Staff College, Camberley, in 1937–8.

After the Second World War broke out Lathbury served in France, being appointed MBE in 1940. He then became general staff officer, grade 2 (GSO 2), at the Staff College and GSO 1 at the War Office. He was given command of the 3rd parachute battalion and soon selected to command the 3rd Parachute brigade and then the 1st Parachute brigade in north Africa, Sicily, and Italy where he was appointed to the DSO (1943). He commanded the 1st Parachute brigade in the Arnhem operation in 1944. In 1942 he married Jean Gordon, daughter of Lieutenant-Colonel Edward Gordon Thin, of Aston Somerville Hall, Broadway, Worcestershire; they had two daughters.

After attending the Imperial Defence College in 1948 Lathbury commanded the 16th airborne division (TA) as major-general that year. He was appointed CB in 1950. He became commandant of the Staff College in 1951, vice-adjutant-general in 1954, and commander-in-chief east Africa in 1955. This was at the height of the operations in Kenya to defeat the Mau Mau rebellion and on reaching Nairobi Lathbury pursued his task with enthusiasm. It was made easier by his liking Africans and taking pleasure in the spectacular Kenya countryside—he was an ardent naturalist, conservationist, and bird-watcher. Moreover, he was able to establish friendly relations with the white settlers at an awkward time for them, given the policies of the British government during Britain's withdrawal from empire. He brought the operations to a successful conclusion and was appointed KCB (1956) for his work. Back home he was promoted lieutenant-general, and became director-general of military training in 1957. He was appointed general officer commander-in-chief, eastern command, in 1960 and promoted general. In 1961 he became quartermaster-general to the forces, a post he held until 1965 when he retired from the army.

Lathbury was governor of Gibraltar from August 1965 until April 1969. This covered a period when conditions there were becoming more difficult almost daily. Frontier restrictions were being intensified; Spanish propaganda was at its height; adverse resolutions were being passed in the United Nations; abortive and unpopular talks were held with the Spanish government; there was, until 1967, a virtual pay freeze. The people, firm and unyielding before these pressures, were none the less indignant, confused, and anxious. Throughout all these difficulties Gibraltar's stately, elegant soldier–governor radiated a serene imperturbability. This quality was in his nature, but it exactly met the need of the moment, as it helped to counter the people's anxiety and responded to and reinforced their resolve.

There were silver linings in those years as well: the fast-growing evidence of British political and moral support; the start of the development programmes; the gradual consolidation of popular feeling and pride in the community; the triumph of the referendum; and the new constitution, with its guarantees that the people would remain with Britain as long as this was their wish. In these matters, too, Lathbury remained apparently unmoved, but he deeply shared the Gibraltarians' satisfactions as well as their trials and disappointments and worked hard to promote and further their interests.

Lathbury was colonel-commandant of 1st Royal Green Jackets and the Parachute regiment from 1961 to 1965, and was much involved in planning the amalgamation of the former with the King's Royal Rifle Corps and the rifle brigade to form the Royal Green Jackets in 1966. He was also colonel of the West India regiment in 1959 and of the Jamaica regiment from 1962 to 1968. He was aide-de-camp-general to the queen from 1962 to 1965 and was appointed GCB in 1962.

Lathbury's first marriage was dissolved in 1972 and he married in the same year Mairi Zoë, widow of Patrick Somerset Gibbs and daughter of Patrick Mitchell, rubber planter in Malaya, and stepdaughter of Arthur Macmillan, the brother of Harold Macmillan (later the earl of Stockton). Lathbury died on 16 May 1978 at his home in Mortimer, Berkshire. The funeral was held at Mortimer parish church, the bearers appropriately being found from the Royal Green Jackets and the Parachute regiment.

JOSHUA HASSAN, rev.

Sources The Royal Green Jackets Chronicle, 13 (1978), 164–6 · personal knowledge (1986) · The Times (18 May 1978) · WWW · R. B. Edgerton, Mau-Mau: an African crucible (1991) · CGPLA Eng. & Wales (1978)
Archives Airborne Forces Museum, Aldershot, Arnhem diary | FILM IWM FVA, actuality footage | SOUND IWM SA, oral history interview
Likenesses photograph, 1963, Hult. Arch. · J. W., photograph, 1967 (with Joshua Hassan), Hult. Arch.
Wealth at death £42,260—in England and Wales: probate, 21 Dec 1978, CGPLA Eng. & Wales

Lathbury [Lathbery], **John** (d. 1362), Franciscan friar and theologian, was born at Lathbury, Buckinghamshire, probably at the beginning of the fourteenth century; when he died in 1362 he was, according to Bale, 'an old man' (Bale, Cat., 1.532–3). He joined the Franciscan order in his twenties, perhaps in the diocese of Coventry and Lichfield, where he was ordained subdeacon on 22 April 1329. He studied at Oxford during the 1330s and 1340s, and had become regent master by 1350. In Oxford he formed a close friendship with a German friar, Hermann of Cologne; they discussed matters of theology and exchanged stories and moral exempla, many of which Lathbury later included in his commentary on Jeremiah.

Although a schoolman, Lathbury evidently was also active in pastoral work in the surrounding districts. In 1342 he was licensed to hear confessions in the diocese of Salisbury, and in November 1352 he was given the same licence in the archdeaconry of Buckingham. At the same time he became involved in the government of his order. In 1343 he was present at a meeting of the provincial chapter, and he may have attended others. Lathbury probably remained in Oxford for the greater part of his career, retiring only in late middle age to the Reading Greyfriars, where he died and was probably buried. In 1348 he gave several of his own books to a relative, a younger John Lathbury. The gift may have coincided with the end of his active career in the schools.

The elder Lathbury was distinguished for his work as a theologian and exegete. His most influential, and probably his only completed work, was a commentary on the Lamentations of Jeremiah. It is a vast text, incorporating a wide range of sources, including notes made by Robert Grosseteste (d. 1253), whose books Lathbury had studied at first hand in the library of the Oxford Greyfriars. It is most notable, however, for its use of rare and obscure classical texts to elucidate the darker passages of scripture. Lathbury's interest in classical literature, and his willingness to use it as a tool of exegesis, places him in a tradition of English (and especially fraternal) biblical scholarship which had been inaugurated a generation earlier by the Dominican theologians Robert Holcot (d. 1349) and Thomas Waleys. Their work had done much to revive the art of exegesis and promote a 'literal' reading of scripture in the first half of the fourteenth century, but with the exception of Lathbury they had few followers or imitators. Indeed he can be seen as one of the last English scholars to employ these methods.

The commentary circulated widely in late medieval Europe; it was among the first books to be printed at Oxford in 1482, and one of the seven surviving manuscript copies was brought up from the bottom of the sea, in a fisherman's net, probably in the sixteenth century. Lathbury continually reworked and reorganized his commentary, and the revised version circulated in various different guises as part of an *Alphabetum morale*, a collection of exempla and sermons, and as a series of *distinctiones*. Lathbury may also have completed a commentary on the Psalms which is now lost. The fifteenth-century bishop Stephen Patrington (d. 1417), according to Bale, quoted 'Lathbury on the psalms' in one of his sermons. Bale also suggests Lathbury was the author of a commentary on the Acts of the Apostles, and quotes an incipit, but it is not known to survive, and it is possible that in both cases he confused Lathbury with his kinsman, John Lathbury the younger.

JAMES G. CLARK

Sources Emden, Oxf., 2.1104–5 · B. Smalley, English friars and antiquity in the early fourteenth century (1960), 221–39 · Bale, Cat., 1.532–3 · Bale, Index, 225 · F. Stegmüller, ed., Repertorium biblicum medii aevi, 3 (Madrid, 1951), 372–3

Archives Exeter College, Oxford, MS 27 · Gon. & Caius Cam., MS 57 · Inner Temple, London, commentary on Lamentations · Lincoln College, Oxford, Lat MS 66 · Merton Oxf., MS 189 · Peterhouse, Cambridge, MS 23 · Sion College, London, MS Arc L40.2/L32

Lathbury, Thomas (1798–1865), Church of England clergyman and ecclesiastical historian, was born at Brackley, Northamptonshire, the only son of Henry Lathbury. On 7 April 1821 he matriculated at St Edmund Hall, Oxford, graduating BA in 1824 and MA in 1827. Having taken holy orders, he held curacies at Chatteris, Cambridgeshire, Bath, and Wootton, Northamptonshire. In 1831 he was appointed curate at Mangotsfield, Gloucestershire, and in 1838 curate at the abbey church, Bath. In 1848 he was presented by the bishop of Gloucester and Bristol to the perpetual curacy of St Simon and St Jude, Bristol.

A liturgical scholar and antiquarian collector of printed service books, Lathbury was the author of numerous works of both ecclesiastical and liturgical history and of more popular polemic. Some of his writings were learned treatises or editions of older texts, and reflected his antiquarian and liturgical interests and historical sympathies. This category of his writings included such works as an edition of the nonjuror Jeremy Collier's *Ecclesiastical History of Great Britain*, with a life of the author (1852) and *A History of the Book of Common Prayer* (1858). Lathbury's more popular works consisted of anti-Catholic polemic, including the best-selling *Protestantism the Old Religion, Popery the New* (1838), *Guy Fawkes, or, A Complete History of the Gunpowder Plot* (1839; 2nd edn, 1840), and *The Spanish armada, AD 1588, or, The attempt of Philip II and Pope Sixtus V to re-establish popery in England* (1840).

As a writer, Lathbury suffered from apprehensions over defects in his literary skills. He could be meticulous in attention to detail but lacked originality, and a reviewer in the *British Critic* considered that his *History of English Episcopacy* (1836), his most significant work, exhibited 'no great power of writing', although he also commended the work as a perspicacious and dispassionate account of its subject. Lathbury's *History of the Nonjurors: their Controversies and Writings* (1845) represents his most accomplished work. Based on wide reading and knowledge of the sources, its particular value lies in its exposition of nonjuring political thought. It has been considered one of the most accurate and informative histories of the nonjurors.

Lathbury was a non-party, moderate, and not untypical protestant churchman of his generation. His *History of English Episcopacy* was praised in the Irish Anglican evangelical journal the *Christian Examiner* (February 1837, 129) because of its adherence to the 'moderate principles of Ecclesiastical polity … Preserving a due medium between the Latitudinarians on the one side, and the Altitudinarians on the other … and attached to the constitutional doctrines of the old Revolution Whigs'. Suspicious of the Oxford Movement, he in 1838 wrote warmly in defence of the proposed protestant Martyr's Memorial in Oxford against its Tractarian critics. Alarm at what he regarded as the rise of popery in the 1830s prompted his

numerous works of anti-Catholic polemic. Although orthodox and not latitudinarian in his churchmanship, Lathbury's *History of English Episcopacy* was criticized by its high-church *British Critic* reviewer for exhibiting a 'rationalising' tendency. The features of the work which earned the *Christian Examiner's* praise, such as his regarding Laud's notions of divine-right episcopacy as a 'novelty' and his apparent over-indulgence of continental protestant churches, caused offence to the high-church reviewer (*British Critic*, 1836, 342–3). Lathbury himself offered an article on various works concerning church reform and unity to the then editor of the *British Critic*, J. S. Boone, but it was not published. Despite his misgivings about the Tractarians, Lathbury offered another article, a review of Thomas Price's *History of Protestant Nonconformity* (1836–8) to J. H. Newman as editor in February 1838. Newman commended the article for its style and learning, but rejected it because of 'the general line of opinion' manifested in it. He explained the main ground of his difference—that he [Newman] viewed 'the church less in the light of an Establishment' (*Letters and Diaries*, 6.199).

Lathbury's moderate high-church credentials, however, were demonstrated in his cautious sympathy for the nonjurors (*History of the Nonjurors*), and in the attack on the protestant nonconformist attempt to make capital out of the bicentenary of the St Bartholomew's day ejections of nonconformist ministers in 1662 contained in his *Facts and Fictions of the Bicentenary: a Sketch from 1640 to 1662* (1862). He followed this up with another anti-dissenting polemic, *Oliver Cromwell, or, The old and new dissenters, with strictures on the lectures of N. Haycroft and H. Quick* (1862). Lathbury's firm churchmanship found its most practical expression in his championship of the church congress held at Bristol in September 1864.

Lathbury died at his residence, 3 Cave Street, Portland Square, Bristol, on 11 February 1865. His stipend at the time of his death amounted to little more than £150 per annum. He left a widow and four children, three of them sons. The eldest son, Daniel Connor Lathbury, became a barrister and journalist, and was the editor of *Correspondence on Church and Religion of William Ewart Gladstone* (1910).

PETER B. NOCKLES

Sources Foster, *Alum. Oxon.* · Crockford (1860) · *GM*, 3rd ser., 18 (1865), 385 · *Daily Bristol Times and Mirror* (13 Feb 1865), 2 · *Daily Bristol Times and Mirror* (14 Feb 1865), 2 · *Daily Bristol Times and Mirror* (15 Feb 1865), 2 · T. Lathbury, 'A history of the English episcopacy; from the period of the Long Parliament to the Act of Uniformity; with notices of the religious parties of the time, and a review of ecclesiastical affairs in England, from the Reformation', *British Critic, Quarterly Theological Review, and Ecclesiastical Record*, 20 (1836), 329–49 [review] · 'Lathbury's "History of the English episcopacy" and le Bas' "Life of Laud"', *Christian Examiner*, new ser., 2/15, 129 · J. Foster, *Men-at-the-bar: a biographical hand-list of the members of the various inns of court*, 2nd edn (1885), 267 · *The letters and diaries of John Henry Newman*, ed. C. S. Dessain and others, [31 vols.] (1961–), vol. 6, p. 199 · *DNB*
Archives Bodl. Oxf., MSS Norris
Wealth at death under £4000: probate, 24 March 1865, *CGPLA Eng. & Wales*

Lathom, Francis (1777–1832), novelist and playwright, born at Norwich, is said to have been the illegitimate son of an English peer. In early life he wrote for the Norwich Theatre, and probably acted there. His plays, including *All in a Bustle* (1795), *The Dash of the Day* (1800), and *The Wife of a Million* (performed in 1803), were successful light comedies and satires. While working for the theatre he was also channelling his taste for melodrama into Gothic romances such as *The Castle of Ollada* (1795), which shamelessly appealed to the readers of *The Castle of Otranto* and was a formulaic 'shocker' for the circulating libraries. *The Midnight Bell* (1798), published anonymously as a pseudo-Germanic translation, was notable for its use of anecdotal material from France's 'reign of terror' and for its mention as one of the 'horrid novels' in Jane Austen's *Northanger Abbey*, itself a parody of the Gothic form. Lathom was also ridiculed in Sarah Green's *Romantic Readers and Romance Writers: a Satirical Novel* (1810). *The Midnight Bell* has variously been read as a standard Gothic romance full of morbidity and portents, and as a subversion of the form (Jenkins). But for many critics it was the social satire of *Men and Manners* (1799) which was his 'masterpiece' (Summers, 316).

After 1801 Lathom moved to Inverurie (perhaps to pursue a homosexual relationship; Summers, 317), where he lodged with a baillie, and subsequently moved to Bogdavie, a farmhouse in Fyvie, Aberdeenshire, belonging to one Alexander Rennie. He was liberally provided with money and developed many eccentricities. He dressed, it is said, 'like a play-actor', drank whisky freely, interested himself in theatrical gossip, sang songs of his own composition, and continued to produce romances at a rapid rate which secured him his sizeable income. Most notable of these is *The Mysterious Freebooter, or, The Days of Queen Bess* (1806), a skilful combination of horror and historical drama. Frederick S. Frank has commented that in it 'it is possible to discern the outlines of the historical novel' (Frank, 195). In *The Fatal Vow, or, St Michael's Monastery: a Romance* (1807) he further blended history and horror. The name of his heroine was used by Coleridge in 'Christabel'. With *The Unknown, or, The Northern Gallery* (1808) he became 'increasingly committed to historical verisimilitude' (ibid., 197). After *The Romance of the Hebrides* (1809) he did not write for another eleven years.

Lathom lived comfortably during that period (it is said that in addition to income from his work his father had left him a rich man), and he was known in Fyvie as Mr Francis or Boggie's Lord, from the name of Rennie's farmhouse. His reputed wealth exposed him to frequent risk of being kidnapped by those who were anxious to secure so profitable a lodger.

Lathom returned to fiction with *Italian Mysteries* in 1820 which pleased his readers and came close to 'the psychological Gothic' (Frank, 198). He also seemed to have travelled in France and Italy and was in Philadelphia in spring 1828. In his last years he lived with Rennie at Milnfield Farm in the parish of Monquhitter. At the time of his death it was said he was training farmers for the theatre. He died at the farm suddenly on 19 May 1832 and was buried in the Rennies' burial plot in the churchyard of Fyvie.

Lathom was a prolific writer skilled in dialogue and drama who found a loyal readership during his life and for some time after his death. On the whole his romances are 'made-to-order' Gothic fictions (Frank, 193) and at worst have been seen as 'cynical exercises in an assumed manner' (Sadleir, 16). Lathom was vocal in his derision of the fashion for 'mysteries' which he nevertheless exploited: 'it is not an author's business to inquire why such is the public taste but to comply with it', he wrote in his preface to *The Unknown* (vii). But Summers sees Lathom's role as more innovative and his omission from literary history as lamentable given his part in the shift from the brooding romanticism of the Gothic form to the stark realism of historical fiction.   CLARE L. TAYLOR

Sources F. S. Frank, *The first Gothics: a critical guide to the English Gothic novel* (1987) · M. Sadleir, 'The Northanger novels: a footnote to Jane Austen', *English Association Pamphlet*, 68 (Nov 1927) · L. Jenkins, 'Introduction', in F. Lathom, *The midnight bell* (1989) · M. Summers, *The Gothic quest: a history of the Gothic novel* (1938) · *N&Q*, 2nd ser., 4 (26 Sept 1857) · F. Lathom, 'Preface', *The unknown, or, The northern gallery: a romance*, 1 (1826) · *DNB* · D. P. Varma, *The Gothic flame: being a history of the Gothic novel in England, its origins, efflorescence, disintegration, and residuary influences* (1957)

Lathy, Thomas Pike (*b.* **1771**, *d.* in or after **1819**), writer and plagiarist, was born in Exeter. Very little is known about his parentage and early life other than that he was 'bred to trade' (*Biographical Dictionary*, 196). Despite this upbringing Lathy 'chiefly devoted himself to letters' (ibid.).

While in America Lathy married Sally King Johns in Boston, Massachusetts, on 15 April 1799. The following year his prose play *Reparation, or, The School for Libertines* was performed at the Boston Theatre 'with great applause' and published for his benefit (*DNB*). He next appears as the author of a series of novels published in London in small format. *Usurpation, or, The Inflexible Uncle* was published by the Minerva Press in 1805. *The Paraclete* came out in the same year, followed by *The Invisible Enemy, or, The Mines of Wielitska: a Polish Romance* (1806), a Gothic novel of extreme incident in a largely underground setting, which was widely read. When *Gabriel Forrester, or, The Deserted Son* was published in 1807, a reviewer commented, 'we certainly think him superior to the great crowd of modern novel-writers; but he is too often warm; and sometimes too tedious' (*Monthly Magazine*). The *Monthly Review* criticized Lathy's 'indelicacy of description, and … inelegance of language'. *A Biographical Dictionary of the Living Authors of Great Britain and Ireland* assigns a further four novels to Lathy, but modern scholarship has not upheld these attributions.

Lathy reappeared in 1819 as the compiler of *Memoirs of the Court of Louis XIV*, which he dedicated to the prince regent. In the same year he took advantage of a vogue for fishing literature by selling the manuscript of a poem called *The Angler: a Poem, in Ten Cantos* to Thomas Gosden, a bookbinder and fishing enthusiast, for £30. Gosden had an engraving of himself in fishing attire inserted as a frontispiece, and had a copy printed on vellum at a cost of £10, as well as twenty copies on royal paper; the poem was also profusely illustrated. Lathy used the pseudonym Piscator, and equivocated as to the authorship of the poem in his preface. In November 1819 the poem was exposed as being largely plagiarized from Thomas Scott's *The Anglers: Eight Dialogues in Verse* (1758; reprinted 1773). Scott's great-nephew wrote to the *Gentleman's Magazine* to complain about the 'extraordinary incorporation' of the earlier poem and its notes. Lathy had removed Scott's interlocutors and had added a number of descriptive and didactic passages to Scott's material, in particular a series of enthusiastic addresses to women, whom he encouraged towards 'the union of sexes in the sport' (preface). Despite the exposure, the poem was reprinted, with Lathy's name on it, in 1822 and 1841, but nothing more of Lathy's own life is known. Watt in 1824 lists only the novels published before 1810.

PAUL BAINES

Sources [J. Watkins and F. Shoberl], *A biographical dictionary of the living authors of Great Britain and Ireland* (1816) · IGI · T. Westwood and T. Satchell, *Bibliotheca piscatoria* (1883), 131 · *GM*, 1st ser., 89/2 (1819), 407–8 · W. Pinkerton, 'Fisher's garlands', *N&Q*, 3rd ser., 7 (1865), 17–18 · *Monthly Magazine*, 24 (1807), 630 [suppl.] · *Monthly Review*, new ser., 62 (1810), 213 · M. B. Tymn, ed., *Horror literature: a core collection and guide* (1981), 100 · W. S. Ward, *Literary reviews in British periodicals, 1798–1820: a bibliography*, 2 vols. (1972) · Watt, *Bibl. Brit.* · J. Raven and others, eds., *The English novel, 1770–1829: a bibliographical survey of prose fiction published in the British Isles*, 2 vols. (2000) · D. Blakey, *The Minerva Press, 1790–1820* (1939) · *DNB*

Latimer. For this title name *see* individual entries under Latimer; *see also* Neville, Richard, second Baron Latimer (*c*.1467–1530); Neville, John, third Baron Latimer (1493–1543).

Latimer, Hugh (*c*.1485–1555), bishop of Worcester, preacher, and protestant martyr, was born at Thurcaston, a village north of Leicester. Most accounts of his life mention the passage in a court sermon of 1549 referring to his parents and their hard-won prosperity: 'My father was a yeoman, and had no lands of his own, only he had a farm of three or four pound by year' where he tilled enough to keep 'half a dozen men'. In addition to a 'walk for a hundred sheep' his mother kept a dairy and 'milked thirty kine'. Young Hugh (named for his father) was their only surviving son. Among his earliest memories was of buckling his father's armour in 1497 before the battle of Blackheath Field. His six sisters were 'brought up in godliness' and provided with good marriage portions. In his later years he came to rely upon a niece, Mary Glover (*Sermons*, 101).

Cambridge convert According to Foxe, Latimer's parents early recognized their son's 'ready, prompt, and sharp wit', and 'purposed to train him up in erudition', sending him first to the local grammar school, then to Cambridge at the age of fourteen (Foxe, *Acts and Monuments*, 1583, 1730). He graduated BA in 1511, subsequently proceeding MA in 1514 and BTh in 1524. Clare College, where he was elected a fellow on 2 February 1510, provided his titles when he was ordained subdeacon at Peterborough in March 1515, deacon at Lincoln Cathedral the following month, and priest at Lidington that July.

Hugh Latimer (*c*.1485–1555), by unknown artist, 1555

In his early years at the university Latimer (like Cranmer) demonstrated only the most conventional piety. During the chancellorship of Bishop John Fisher scholasticism at the university remained strong, particularly in the faculty of theology, though humanism was slowly providing an additional, even complementary, dimension of learning for scholars. Until matters were clarified by the papal excommunication of Martin Luther at the end of 1520 the old orthodoxy and the new learning associated with Erasmus flourished side by side and nurtured each other. Once the first ripples of continental reform began to reach the university Latimer's response was hostile. 'For I was as obstinate a papist as any was in England', he remembered in after years, and his examination sermon in 1524 for his bachelor's degree in theology denounced the opinions of Philip Melanchthon (*Sermons*, 334–5).

Under the influence of Thomas Bilney and George Stafford, who were Cambridge's greatest early catalysts for the renewal of the church outside its traditional framework of authority, Latimer's perspectives began to shift, but perhaps not as dramatically as he later remembered. Having attended his examination sermon Bilney 'perceived that I was zealous without knowledge'. Taking advantage of the utter secrecy that the sacrament of confession afforded (an early—and useful—device that reformers used to convert and hearten each other) Bilney came to Latimer's study and asked him to hear his confession. Bilney's private revelations challenged Latimer's complacent, dutiful piety. His previous studies seemed as naught. 'I began to smell the word of God, and forsook the school-doctors and such fooleries', he remembered years later (*Sermons*, 334–5). Stafford's lectures on scripture confirmed his transformation from a Saul to 'a very Paul' (Foxe, *Acts and Monuments*, ed. Townsend, vol. 7, appx 4). Writing well after the event, Foxe implied that Latimer was part of a great circle of evangelists (Bilney having 'catched' him 'in the blessed net of God's word' (Foxe, *Acts and Monuments*, 1583, 1730) who met regularly at the White Horse tavern in Cambridge to share views that were so highly charged with Lutheran and other opinions from the continent that it was known as 'Little Germany'. This is probably an exaggeration. At these early stages the opinions of Latimer and confrères like Edward Crome defy easy categorization. Many of his early opinions may have been shaped less by Luther than by the Swiss reformers. Unfortunately Latimer's correspondence with continental reformers has not been preserved, so their influence upon his thinking cannot be traced, though he enjoyed warm support from such men as Martin Bucer, Heinrich Bullinger, and Theodore Bibliander in the 1530s.

Initially the early reformers stressed the great Pauline aspiration of 'preaching Christ', of disseminating the gospel through sermons and in print to bring about a deep spiritual renewal throughout society. This could be accomplished by removing the distracting and even idolatrous practices that they felt had grown up in the Roman Catholic church in recent centuries, a process which could be accomplished through reference to scripture, against which all doctrines and usages had to be judged. Much of the received wisdom of the Catholic church (including the sacraments) had to be re-examined and where necessary cast aside, and the conservative elements of the Roman hierarchy dismantled. In his last years Latimer argued from Romans 10: 8–17 that salvation was attained not through any devotion to the mass, but through regeneration by faith, by means of the preaching and hearing of God's word.

Evangelical champion Latimer's re-evaluation of doctrinal matters proceeded gradually. Like Thomas Cranmer and other leaders he continued to adapt and expand his opinions as opportunity and circumstances allowed, in the face of resolute opposition from his theological opponents and political enemies, and the complicating conservatism of Henry VIII. As late as 1529 he praised the value of voluntary works of salvation, including pilgrimages and the ornamentation of churches. But from the beginning of the 1530s he and his friends attacked the papacy, non-preaching bishops, and the influential mendicant orders. The doctrine of purgatory, never mentioned by name in the Bible, became one of his favourite targets, and with it the elaborate traditional economy of salvation. He began to argue that if votive masses could not assist the departed in purgatory then the institutions which existed largely to celebrate masses for the dead, including the religious houses and chantries, were redundant, and should be dismantled so that their wealth could be redirected, especially towards relief of the poor and to the universities for the training of good preachers. But even as late as 1550 Latimer continued to remember the dead in a general

sense in prayer, and a mature reappraisal of the eucharist, a central element in the reform movement, did not emerge in his thinking until the late 1540s.

Once the fault lines between orthodoxy and the new learning had become apparent Latimer and his friends ran serious risks under the heresy laws, and they continued to do so until the cause of reform became intertwined with King Henry's efforts to obtain a divorce from Katherine of Aragon in the late 1520s. Then, and again later when they faced constraints imposed by Henry's supremacy over the English church, they fell back upon equivocation as a deliberate strategy to evade suppression and execution, which further hinders a complete understanding of their opinions until they were able to shape policy under Edward VI. In 1525 Bishop Nicholas West of Ely came unannounced to Cambridge to hear Latimer preach in the university church. When West asked him to denounce Luther, Latimer replied disingenuously that since no one was allowed to read his works he was not acquainted with his opinion. If Luther preached the doctrine of God from scripture, as he had just done, then Luther did not need to be confuted. Nothing pleased, West retorted that Latimer smelt of the frying pan like a heretic, and would repent 'this gear' (Foxe, *Acts and Monuments*, ed. Townsend, vol. 7, appx 4). Soon afterwards Latimer was called before Cardinal Thomas Wolsey, but managed to escape without incurring further difficulties: indeed, his licence to preach was confirmed. But at precisely this time Wolsey and Fisher staged an elaborate ceremony at St Paul's, with the burning of Lutheran books and the abjuration of Latimer's friend Robert Barnes (prior of the Augustinian house at Cambridge) as its ritual centrepieces.

In 1529 Latimer's series of Advent 'Sermons on the Card' (only one of which survives) caused fresh disruptions in the university. Referring to the traditional Christmas games to make his lessons on the ten commandments and the sermon on the mount memorable Latimer triggered an uproar with his demand that the Bible should be translated into English (which was then an offence under the law). A procession of Cambridge's conservative theologians followed him into the university's pulpits, including Bishop West and the fellows of Fisher's college, St John's. The Dominican prior Robert Buckenham countered card-playing with 'Christmas dice', arguing from the New Testament and the early church fathers that the mysteries of holy writ were too abstruse for the public to read without the guidance of the clergy as intermediaries. Latimer responded that scripture was approachable and necessary, that its figurative aspects were metaphors like those in common speech, and should be available to all directly. Only the intervention of convocation calmed matters briefly, but the result was a breach among theologians that proved irreparable. The classicist and theologian John Redman warned Latimer that Christ's seamless garment was being torn asunder through his influence.

Attacks against the reformers intensified in 1531 when Archbishop William Warham succeeded Wolsey as a leading defender of orthodoxy. Cambridge men, including Latimer and Crome, were particularly marked for their 'erroneous preachings' (*Sermons and Remains*, 218), but the chief victim was Bilney, who was burnt in August in the Lollard's pit at Norwich. Having already made one humiliating public abjuration Bilney had ultimately rejected further efforts to temporize, and he told his friends that 'he would go to Jerusalem' as Christ had done, 'and so would see them no more' (Foxe, *Acts and Monuments*, 1583, 1008). Latimer later gave an affectionate salute to his dead friend as 'Bilney, little Bilney, that blessed martyr of God' (*Sermons*, 222). Now the saving issue for reformers became the royal supremacy over the church in England. Fisher and Warham became increasingly identified with Katherine's cause, while the Cambridge reformers swiftly warmed to Henry's Great Matter. Latimer and Crome soon began to couple doctrinal change with endorsements of the king's supremacy. Anne Boleyn's enemies dismissed her as a Lutheran, but the importance of her dedication to the cause of evangelism cannot be overstated. Her patronage became the cornerstone of Latimer's rise to prominence, and he owed his most important promotions to her influence. As early as 1524 (in a letter which refers to 'the honoured' Sir Thomas More) Latimer had already established connections with the court, and could speculate about the 'royal confidence' in referring to Cambridge appointments (*Sermons and Remains*, 295–7). Henry invited him to preach his first sermon at court during Lent 1530, at Windsor Castle, 'where his majesty, after the sermon was done, did most familiarly talk with me in a gallery' (*Sermons*, 335).

Court sermons were dubious distinctions. Preachers might hope to interest the king and sway him to a particular policy, but there was also a serious danger that they would inadvertently give offence, with disastrous results. 'A prince must be turned; not violently, but he must be won little by little' (*Sermons*, 232). Latimer's later sermons are interlarded with accounts of narrow escapes in the 1530s, ones that left his friends trembling in fear on his behalf. On one of these occasions Latimer knelt before Henry and asked that he be permitted to preach at court as he thought best, in accordance with God's commandment, without the gainsaying of others. 'I thank Almighty God', he remembered, 'my sayings were well accepted of the king' (*Sermons*, 135), though it was not always so.

In January 1531 Anne's influence brought Latimer promotion to the rectory of West Kington in Wiltshire, a valuable living, where he was diligent in his cure, saying mass, preaching, and keeping hospitality. It started him in a lifelong association with the cause of reform in the west country, and gave him a springboard from which to respond to invitations to preach in London, Kent, and elsewhere (in 1522 the university had licensed him to preach anywhere in the British Isles without the permission of the local bishop, which he now turned to his advantage). The sermons he delivered at St Mary Abchurch in London, which raised questions about the sacrament of the altar, earned Bishop John Stokesley's abiding wrath. Known for being Bilney's 'ghostly father' (*Sermons and Remains*, 330) Latimer was a ready target. On 11 March 1532 he was called before convocation to face charges that he had impugned

purgatory, prayers for the dead, the intercession of saints, pilgrimages, fasting, and the veneration of the crucifix and other images. Crome had faced similar charges the previous year, but in contrast to Bilney's self-abnegating sacrifice he had provided an avenue for escape by throwing himself on the king's mercy as the highest authority under God. Latimer followed Crome's example. He was excommunicated and imprisoned at Lambeth, but his loyalty to the king ensured that he need make only a token submission to Warham before he was released in April. This episode later occasioned a bitter comment in Latimer's 1537 convocation sermon, that rather than preach and glorify God the prelates had spent their time trying to punish good men who defended the king's authority by raking them 'in the coals' (*Sermons*, 46).

Pulpit triumphs In 1533 Latimer exploited the supremacy to inflict a lasting defeat on Katherine's allies and the old orthodoxy. Invited by the mayor and clergy of Bristol to deliver a series of Lenten and Eastertide sermons, Latimer undermined justification by good works as well as the Virgin Mary's role as mediator, causing deep divisions among his hearers. Critics accused him of doing as much damage as Luther. In the bitter controversy that ensued Bristol's pulpits rang for the next two months with fierce rejoinders defending the tenet of purgatory, pilgrimages, the mediation of saints, and the use of images, led by Edward Powell (a defender of Katherine), Nicholas Wilson (a protégé of Fisher), William Hubberdine (of Oxford), and John Hilsey, the Dominican prior of Bristol. But Fisher was arrested that spring, and by early June, when Cranmer (newly raised to the archbishopric of Canterbury) crowned Anne Boleyn queen, the advantage had clearly gone to the reformers. Hilsey changed sides (Latimer denounced only abuses, he now maintained, not the substance of doctrine) and accused Powell of denigrating Henry's marriage to Anne and defending the pope's authority, charges which led to the arrest of Powell and Wilson. Soon Hilsey had a leading role in suppressing his former order throughout England, and replaced Fisher as bishop of Rochester.

Latimer's victory in Bristol was part of an important turning point for the Reformation in England as a whole. In April 1535 Sir Thomas More, who had now started on his own path towards execution after disappointing the king's expectation that he subscribe to the new Act of Succession, saw Latimer in a high-spirited moment in the garden of Lambeth Palace. Latimer was 'very merry' and laughing as he cast his arms around Cranmer's chaplains in triumph (*Correspondence*, 503).

The reformers consolidated their advantage to further 'the truth and the pure dispensation of God's word' by monopolizing the Lenten series of sermons at court in 1534. Cranmer warned Latimer and Nicholas Shaxton (Anne's almoner, another Cambridge stalwart) to speak circumspectly and for not longer than an hour and a half to avoid wearying the king and queen (*Miscellaneous Writings*, 308–9), a necessary admonishment, for Latimer's court sermons in the next reign lasted between three and four hours. In 1535, when the dioceses of Worcester and

Salisbury were divested of their absentee Italian bishops, Latimer and Shaxton were elevated to their places, unusual moves in keeping with Anne's innovative patronage; the queen lent both men £200 towards their first fruits.

Bishop of Worcester Consecrated bishop of Worcester by Cranmer on 23 September 1535 Latimer was enthroned on 20 August 1536. Once established in his diocese he embarked upon a programme of dismantling images and promoting new standards of preaching. He stripped the statue of the Virgin ('our great Sibyll') that stood in Worcester Cathedral. He removed the renowned relic of Christ's blood from Hailes Abbey (in 'bolting' it, the contents appeared to be merely an 'unctious gum', he told Thomas Cromwell; *Sermons and Remains*, 407–8). When Friar John Forest was burnt with a Welsh image in 1538 Latimer reluctantly delivered a ferocious sermon from a pulpit that was placed next to the stake, hoping that Forest would abjure rather than burn.

Latimer took his 'disciples' to Worcester with him, men he had been drawing to himself ever since Cambridge days, to serve in the diocesan administration, and as energetic preachers. They included his chaplains Rowland Taylor (burnt 1555) and Thomas Garrard. He invited Barnes to preach with him at Christmas 1537, and praised his abilities to expound scripture and undermine the traditional economy of salvation by 'setting forth of Christ' (*Sermons and Remains*, 389). Latimer and his friends (including Crome) supported the psychopannychistic view that in the absence of any place of expurgation souls departed entered into a painless state of sleep, 'the sleep of grace' (*Sermons*, 40). His convocation sermon of 1537 (the first of his sermons to be printed) was a masterful call to remove abuses, including 'our old ancient purgatory pick-purse' and the 'money-gathering' that the papacy had promoted for its own benefit, oblivious of the need of Christ's flock, who had been dying in superstition (ibid., 50–51).

Latimer took part in the theological disputations that were a feature of Queen Anne's supper parties, which Henry would attend and (alarmingly) join in himself. Once Latimer, paired with Shaxton, debated 'a question of scripture' against the king and Anne's brother ('William Latymer's chronicklle', 62). At the queen's request Latimer tried to persuade Henry not to confiscate the goods of the religious houses, but to re-found them or distribute their wealth in fulfilment of their ultimate potential as centres of learning and preaching, and continual relief of poverty. 'Abbeys were ordained for the comfort of the poor', Latimer argued in a sermon before the king and court at Paul's Cross during Lent 1536 (*Sermons*, 93). This became a perennial issue as more ecclesiastical lands and goods became available for channelling into new purposes, and Latimer and his friends tried (with limited success) to direct the flow towards education and charity, rather than allow wholesale plunder by 'carnal gospellers', who loved reformed religion less than the chance to snare some abbey or chantry lands for their own use (ibid., 320). Anne's ultimate disgrace and fall in 1536 had much to do with her high-minded desire to invest the church's wealth

in charitable causes, and Latimer's career was hobbled at crucial junctures by his tireless advocacy of relief of the poor.

Perhaps the greatest satisfaction of Latimer's episcopate was the appearance in 1537 of an officially sponsored English translation of the Bible, a design first promoted by Anne. Cromwell, as the king's vicegerent for spirituals, succeeded her in the leadership of the evangelicals, and brought their efforts to a successful conclusion, ordering bibles to be set up in every parish church in the realm. Next to Cranmer no other bishop had done as much as Latimer to encourage the project. He immediately enjoined all clergymen with cure of souls in his diocese to obtain a copy for daily study, and to encourage the laity to read 'good books' (*Sermons and Remains*, 244). On the title-page of the Great Bible of 1539 Latimer is represented standing shoulder to shoulder with Cranmer and Shaxton as they receive the sacred text from Henry's hand.

In keeping with Latimer's reputation for controversy, conservative clerics and gentry in his diocese of Worcester found him unbearable, and some openly reviled him as fit for burning because he was 'infecting' the entire diocese with heresy (*Sermons … by Roger Edgeworth*, 96). Soon after Anne's execution in 1536 they began to work with the conservative leaders, Bishop Stokesley of London and the duke of Norfolk, to obtain new legislation to inhibit reform. Cromwell countered by throwing the full weight of his protection behind Latimer, and the conservatives backed down for the time being. But by the end of the decade Cromwell himself was losing ground with the king, whose toleration of doctrinal innovation waned with shocking suddenness.

In May 1539 the bill of the six articles was presented by Norfolk for parliament's consideration at the king's instance. It represented an almost complete return to a traditional understanding of the nature of the eucharist, and a tacit recognition that masses benefited the departed. Although the words 'purgatory' and 'transubstantiation' were not used, the real presence of Christ's very body and blood in the bread and wine was endorsed, and with it the importance of 'private' masses. The six articles presented an unappetizing quandary to the evangelicals, and to Latimer in particular. He had already prepared a paper for the king's consideration that argued against the existence of purgatory, drawn mainly from the writings of the church fathers. And Henry's comments had been withering. Latimer had showed mere hypocritical 'carnal wit' in formulating his positions, the king said, and 'purgatory may yet stand', despite all the authorities Latimer had invoked (*Sermons and Remains*, 245–9). Latimer now faced an appalling choice between obeying the king as supreme head of the church and standing by the doctrine he had had a key role in developing and promoting for the past decade.

In one of the boldest stands the evangelicals ever made against Henry VIII's own policies Latimer and Shaxton spoke against the six articles in the House of Lords. Cromwell did not dare come to Latimer's aid again, and in July both men were forced to resign their bishoprics. Their disgrace caused a sensation. Crome (who had criticized the six articles in convocation) defended their reputations, preaching against the popular perception that they had surrendered their honour with their dignities. Melanchthon wrote to Henry praising their bravery. For some months Latimer was held in ward, expecting every day to be led to execution. In December, however, they were partially rehabilitated, though Latimer was not permitted to preach again while Henry lived. They were granted annual pensions of 100 marks, which was enough to give Latimer a measure of financial independence. Many of his chaplains went on to other patrons, especially to Cranmer and Cromwell. Indeed, Barnes and Garrard became inextricably associated with Cromwell as he began his final descent early in summer 1540. On 29 June, the day after Cromwell was beheaded, they ended their lives at the stake, as Powell suffered near by for treason (with two other conservative clerics) in a ruthless display of Henry's even-handed justice.

On the defensive For Latimer there followed more than seven years of silence, which he devoted to family matters and study. There are glimpses of him reading in Cranmer's magnificent library at Lambeth Palace. He arranged the marriage of his favourite niece Mary (whom he had brought up in his household upon the death of her parents) to Robert Glover (burnt 1555). For the rest of his life their Warwickshire residence at Baxterley was his home, when he was not travelling, and he was there so often that it was said he formed the greater part of her dowry.

Even when Latimer was in eclipse other reformers looked to him for advice and support, and it is testimony to his influence that he became one of the conservatives' main targets during the next great crisis in 1546. Desperate new struggles over the mass developed between evangelical and conservative courtiers as Henry's health failed, and shifts in policy became even more erratic. In April, perhaps encouraged by signals from the king that he was willing to consider new reforms, Crome preached 'to rouse the people from the vain opinion of purgatory' (Foxe, *Acts and Monuments*, 1583, 1234). Now it was the turn of chantries to be dissolved, and Crome made essentially the same case that Latimer had made for Anne Boleyn at the dissolution of the religious houses, and had then made again in his paper against purgatory: if masses did help the departed then it was wrong to abolish the institutions that supplied them. But as the king had been right to do away with them, then the correct conclusion to draw was that the mass was not the primary means of salvation. Of course Crome was aiming at the six articles, but the king's support for their reversal was not secure, and Crome had also underestimated the resourcefulness of his conservative opponents, now led by bishops Stephen Gardiner of Winchester and Edmund Bonner of London. They exploited Crome's misstep to try to bring about a wholesale eradication of evangelicals at court and throughout the realm. Latimer, Shaxton, and several dozen other reformers who had advised Crome were arrested under suspicion of heresy. Latimer's case could

not have been helped when Anne Askew asked to speak with him after she had been condemned to the stake for refusing to admit that the sacrament of the altar was 'flesh, blood, and bone' (ibid., 1239). Shaxton too was condemned.

The possibility cannot be dismissed that, like Anne Askew, Latimer had come to reject the doctrine of the real presence by 1546, and that his thinking now embraced a spiritual presence in the eucharist. Compelling proof either way, however, is elusive. He was examined at length on this point by members of the privy council and a panel of bishops who hid a scribe behind an arras inside a fireplace to record his answers to leading questions (Latimer could hear 'a pen walking' behind the cloth). Four years later he gave an incomplete account of his understanding of 1 Corinthians 11: 23–9, when he challenged the nature of the mass as a sacrifice, for 'in thanksgiving is none oblation'. How could anyone dare to offer Christ's body, when he had offered it himself once and for all time at the Last Supper? Christ's kingdom, Latimer argued, 'was a spiritual kingdom' and He was a 'spiritual judge' (*Sermons*, 275–6, 294). But even if he had stopped short of arguing that Christ's presence in the eucharist was likewise purely spiritual Latimer had to repel the implication that he had descended fatally into heresy. He told his examiners that he had been deceived into resigning his bishopric in 1539. He demanded more time for study and an opportunity to speak to the king. In the end the privy council admitted that strenuous measures were necessary 'to fishe out the botom of his stomak', and they were no wiser than they had been before they started questioning him (*State Papers, Henry VIII*, 1.489). All the same the evangelicals had suffered a severe blow. Latimer spent the remaining months of Henry's life in the Tower. Askew was burnt, Crome was humiliated, and Shaxton recanted (and returned to the conservative side for ever). But their sacrifices ensured the reformers' survival and paradoxical triumph in time for Henry's death, though the entire crisis foreshadowed the deep divisions that emerged among the evangelicals in the new reign.

Court preacher Henry died on 28 January 1547, and the subsequent manoeuvring to oust conservatives like Gardiner from their positions of influence brought Cranmer and his allies their long-awaited opportunity to implement the doctrinal changes they had desired. Late in 1547 the six articles were repealed. Upon his release Latimer resumed his stellar career as a preacher, so long interrupted.

For Latimer preaching represented the mystical meeting place between the earthly and the divine. The sermon was an aural revelation of the truth of God made possible by the action of the Holy Spirit working upon him as he stood in the pulpit. Only rarely (as in the case of his convocation sermon, delivered in 1537 as the Bishops' Book was being prepared) did he write his sermons before, or even after, he delivered them. Few of his sermons were recorded until Augustine Bernher became his amanuensis. Latimer placed himself in the tradition of being a fool for Christ, and was ready to deprecate his own considerable powers in order to move his listeners' hearts. 'I shall play the fool after my customable manner', he wrote to Cromwell before preaching at Forest's execution (*Sermons and Remains*, 391). Yet he also conveyed his message with the sense of *gravitas* necessary to remind his audiences that his represented God's own voice. Of all the reformers Latimer was the most persuasive in the pulpit, and Hilsey was only one of the many whom he won over to his views. Latimer also did not hesitate to reprove even the mightiest, and he could be relentless on issues small as well as great: the godly duchess of Suffolk was reminded that the farthingales she and her women wore were not in keeping with the abiding standard of humility that the Virgin Mary had established for all of womankind. Many of his sermons at Edward's court seem to have been fuelled by a desire to get his own back against those who had thwarted him under Henry. He had wit, and he knew how to turn phrases that stayed in his listeners' memories: on one occasion he shocked his audience by claiming that the busiest bishop in all England was the devil.

During the six years that followed the death of Henry VIII Latimer preached two sermons nearly every Sunday. Winter and summer he rose about 2 a.m. for his studies. Like Cranmer, Latimer marked the triumphant but sobering release brought about through the old king's death by growing a beard, though in his case (as the near contemporaneous painting in London's National Portrait Gallery shows) his was not a flowing patriarchal example, but a short trim version of the type eventually known as a Vandyke. Posed with his spectacles hanging by a cord around his neck and an open book in his hands, the universal symbols of his learning, Latimer put a shrewd and dignified face upon the evangelical movement. He assiduously developed his own reputation as the grand old man of reform, as a martyr in all but name, a martyr *manqué* who had reason to believe that he had already survived the worst, whose sacrifice of ambition and worldly honours (including his bishopric) was the prime token of God's sanction, one which he turned to political advantage.

Preaching a series of sermons entitled 'On the plough' at St Paul's from 1547 to early 1548 Latimer maintained that Christ's crucifixion was the only sacrifice that mattered, and that the traditional mass actually 'evacuated' the cross of Christ, and 'mingled' or diminished its true meaning (*Sermons*, 72–5). By the autumn of 1548 it was at last obvious that Cranmer and Latimer had embraced the Swiss reformers' understanding of the spiritual nature of the eucharist, to Bullinger's deep delight. In 1550 Latimer could state plainly that it was an 'abominable presumption' for the mass to be offered as a sacrifice (ibid., 275).

For the first three Lents of Edward VI's reign Latimer appeared before the court in the outdoor pulpit at Westminster. Now he had old scores to settle and new agendas to pursue. He was a merciless opponent. Although he advocated the removal of those bishops who refused to put aside the doctrine of the real presence, including Nicholas Heath of Worcester, heavy allusions to his surrender of 'mine office' did not result in his restitution once Heath was deprived in October 1551 (*Sermons*, 135–6). He delivered a shocking series of philippics in 1549

against Thomas Seymour, brother of Protector Somerset, which were unparalleled for their vitriol. He endorsed Seymour's execution, and after the axe fell declared that he had died unrepentant, and 'horribly'. Further, Latimer said that Seymour had been responsible for the seduction of a poor woman that had led her to a criminal life and the gibbet. Seymour was 'the author of all this woman's whoredom' (ibid., 161–4). These pronouncements caused great offence and Latimer remained a contentious court preacher to the last.

Even with Cranmer's domination of the Edwardian religious establishment (along with Nicholas Ridley, the new bishop of London), 'stirring, scratching and scraping' at court was still the order of the day (*Sermons*, 131), and in March 1550 Latimer retired from court. His farewell sermon formed part of a series, shared with Thomas Lever and James Courthope, in a concerted effort to defend the flow of resources to the universities, whose prestige and funding had been undermined amid the doctrinal upheavals. Latimer's sermon was a salvo against covetousness, linking the avarice he observed to the recent rebellions and calling again for proper investment of the church's former goods in learning and relief of the poor. His leavetaking was impeccably timed, for when Courthope called courtiers 'gredye spunges' shortly afterwards he was sent to the Fleet prison ('Letters of Richard Scudamore', 128).

Latimer now transferred his full attention to Katherine Brandon (later Bertie), the godly duchess of Suffolk, who had already emerged as the most important patron to the hotter type of protestants (she nursed Bucer at Cambridge in his final illness). Latimer preached several series of sermons before her household at Grimsthorpe in Lincolnshire, treading a regular pathway between Warwickshire and the duchess's court, preaching along the way in the company of Lever (and carefully arranging his journeys so that he would not be underfoot whenever Mary Glover was lying in childbed). Highly indulged, Latimer's exuberant style of extemporaneous preaching on the Lord's prayer and other topics now meandered according to his every mood. Katherine's limitless purse funded the printing of his sermons from 1548 onwards, and it was this, with the unflagging efforts of Bernher as amanuensis, that ensured their ultimate survival.

Protestant martyr The death of King Edward on 6 July 1553, followed by the triumphant coup of his Catholic sister, Mary, spelt ultimate disaster for the protestant cause. Latimer attended the young king's funeral as his chaplain, the very last of all his official functions, and then withdrew to his family at Baxterley. In the following months the new queen's policies began to reverse the achievements to which Latimer and his friends had devoted their lives. At the end of the summer John Careless of Coventry, a leading member of the circle of evangelicals Latimer had been encouraging in the west country and midlands, warned him that his arrest was imminent. Probably Mary and her advisers wished him to flee (prudently, the duchess of Suffolk withdrew to the continent after she was warned). Under Henry, Latimer had briefly considered going into exile, but now he rejected his chance. The doctrinal developments of Edward's reign had gone so far that Latimer no longer had room to equivocate, especially once it became obvious that he and the young king's other reforming bishops, Cranmer and Ridley, were to carry the blame for leading England into heresy. From the time of his arrest for sedition, on 13 September 1553, Latimer determined to 'stand unto his doctrine until his death' (*Sermons*, 322).

Initially Latimer was held in the Tower. In January 1554 he found himself thrust into the same cell with Cranmer, Ridley, and John Bradford, where, to their mutual comfort, they 'did read over the new testament with great deliberation and painful study', discussing again the meaning of Christ's sacrifice, and reinforcing their opinions on the spiritual presence in the Lord's supper (*Sermons and Remains*, 258–9). In March the three former bishops were moved to the Bocardo, Oxford's town prison, for open disputations the following month with Catholic theologians. Cannily Latimer refused to dispute in formal university fashion, pleading the infirmities of his age and the rustiness of his Latin, devices that permitted him to make a stout-hearted defence of his opinions. He maintained that he had 'forgotten all massing, and the very mass itself I do detest', dismissing the Catholic clergy as 'massmongers' who had robbed the realm 'with your sacrifice' (Bodl. Oxf., MS Bodley 53, fol. 3*v*).

With Bernher in constant attendance and able to bring small comforts from his niece Mary and other faithful women, Latimer spent the succeeding months waiting for the inevitable. Confused and frightened protestants sent for the bishops' advice on how they should behave once the Catholic mass was re-established. Latimer was held less closely than Cranmer, and in 1555 he was able to smuggle out of the Bocardo a few epistles of advice and comfort to friends and 'all the unfeigned lovers of God's truth' in uncharacteristically decorous redactions of scripture, modelled after St Paul, that urged patience under persecution (*Sermons and Remains*, 435–44). Bernher describes how the grey-haired Latimer 'beat into the ears of the Lord God' (*Sermons*, 322) petitions for the restoration of the gospel under Elizabeth. Denied other books, he re-read the New Testament many times over. By the time of his trial at the end of September Latimer complained that he had been kept 'so long to the school of oblivion' with only 'bare walls' for a library, that he could not defend himself adequately (*Sermons and Remains*, 284). The verdict was never in doubt. Still unrepentant he unleashed upon his audience a categorical attack against the see of Rome, which he characterized as the traditional enemy of the true, persecuted flock of Christ.

On 16 October 1555 Latimer and Ridley went to their deaths. The account of their burning has been shaped for all time by John Foxe in his *Acts and Monuments* (the famous 'book of martyrs'), who, however, revised and improved his story over the years, adding many of those moving details that justified the protestant agenda. Latimer followed Ridley to the stake in Oxford in 'a poor Bristol style frock all worn' and underneath a new shroud hanging down to his feet. Onlookers were struck by the depth of the calamity into which the former bishops had fallen, but a few minutes later, stripped to his shroud, Latimer now seemed less the crooked old man he had first appeared, and more 'as comely a person to them that were there present, as one should lightly see' (Foxe, *Acts and Monuments*, 1563, 1376–7). Bernher served his master to the end, and was one of Foxe's chief eyewitnesses.

The most famous element in Foxe's story is Latimer's defiant proclamation: 'Be of good comfort Master Ridley, and play the man: we shall this day light such a candle by God's grace in England, as (I trust) shall never be put out' (Foxe, *Acts and Monuments*, 1583, 1770). Did Latimer actually say these words as the flames were kindled? It may never be known. They did not appear in Foxe's first English edition of 1563, but they were added in a later emendation of his great work. Their ultimate point of origin was Eusebius's story of the death of the martyr Polycarp in the second century. Foxe may have wanted to make a general allusion to the vast procession of martyrs who have graced the history of the Christian church from its earliest days, a procession in which Latimer and Ridley occupied a distinguished place, rather than describe the event as it actually occurred. It may never be known how much Foxe expected his readers to accept as a literal account, and how much they would recognize as art. But perhaps Latimer too shaped his own story, for Bernher was the first to note that Latimer referred constantly to the writings of Eusebius in his sermons and his defence. Bernher believed that Latimer, like Polycarp, had shed his heart's blood for the sake of the gospel, and this understanding helped to supply Foxe's account with part of its great emotional power. At the last (unlike Ridley) Latimer appears to have smothered without pain.

Posthumous witness In the leadership of evangelical reform in England Latimer must be placed just after Cranmer in importance. He lacked Cranmer's breadth of mind and grasp of doctrine, and he could also be surprisingly old-fashioned in some of the stories of the saints that he told in the pulpit. But his was the most energetic voice, and his tireless efforts, as well as his manifold sacrifices, helped to determine the ultimate acceptance of protestantism in England.

Latimer's words at the stake, as Foxe supplied them, have been invoked time and again through the centuries as a model of courage in the extreme. His death, with those of the other Marian martyrs, had a key role in proving the protestant cause in England. But for a man who advocated the dismantling of images in order that their value should be used to relieve the poor, Latimer has been honoured with a surprising number of monuments in stone and stained glass, from the windows of the Cambridge church of St Edward (its pulpit is one of several he spoke from that survive to the present day) to the incongruous martyrs' memorial, with its statues of Latimer, Cranmer, and Ridley in a neo-Gothic setting reminiscent of the medieval Eleanor crosses, that was raised by Victorian Oxford near the place of the burnings. Perhaps it is appropriate that at Worcester Cathedral, where Latimer did much to turn his ideals into action, there is no modern plaque or marker to commemorate him. Beside his own letters and sermons the most important of all of the tangible memorials is the simple cross of cobblestones set in the middle of Broad Street, Oxford, under the walls of Balliol College, where workmen in the nineteenth century discovered the stump of a stake and pieces of charred bone.   SUSAN WABUDA

Sources Latimer's paper against purgatory, with Henry VIII's comments, BL, Cotton MS Cleopatra E. v. [printed in Latimer, *Sermons and remains*, 245–9] · PRO, SP1, SP6, SP10, SP11 · Augustine Bernher's papers, Bodl. Oxf., MS Bodley 53 · H. Latimer, register, Worcs. RO, b716.093 BA.2648/9 (ii) · Lincs. Arch., episcopal register 25, fols. 112, 113*v*–115*r* [ordination records] · Campeggio's register, Wilts. & Swindon RO, fol. 24*v* [institution to West Kington] · J. Foxe, *Actes and monuments* (1563) · J. Foxe, *Actes and monuments*, 4th edn, 2 vols. (1583) · *Sermons by Hugh Latimer*, ed. G. E. Corrie, Parker Society, 16 (1844) · *Sermons and remains of Hugh Latimer*, ed. G. E. Corrie, Parker Society, 20 (1845) · *Miscellaneous writings and letters of Thomas Cranmer*, ed. J. E. Cox, Parker Society, [18] (1846) · H. Robinson, ed. and trans., *Original letters relative to the English Reformation*, 1 vol. in 2, Parker Society, [26] (1846–7), esp. 321–3 · J. Foxe, *Acts and monuments*, ed. G. H. Townsend, 8 vols. (1843–9) · 'The letters of Richard Scudamore to Sir Philip Holby, September 1549 – March 1555', ed. M. Dowling, *Camden miscellany, XXX*, CS, 4th ser., 39 (1990) · 'William Latymer's chronicklle of Anne Bulleyne', ed. M. Dowling, *Camden miscellany, XXX*, CS, 4th ser., 39 (1990) · *Sermons very fruitfull, godly and learned by Roger Edgeworth: preaching in the Reformation, c.1535–c.1553*, ed. J. Wilson (1993) · *The correspondence of Sir Thomas More*, ed. E. F. Rogers (Princeton, 1947) · A. G. Chester, *Hugh Latimer: apostle to the English* (Philadelphia, 1954) · P. Collinson, 'Truth and legend: the veracity of John Foxe's book of martyrs', *Elizabethan essays* (1994), 151–77 · M. Dowling, 'Anne Boleyn and reform', *Journal of Ecclesiastical History*, 35 (1984), 30–46 · E. W. Ives, 'Anne Boleyn and the early Reformation in England: the contemporary evidence', *HJ*, 37 (1994), 389–400 · Venn, *Alum. Cant.*, 3.49 · D. R. Leader, *A history of the University of Cambridge*, 1: *The university to 1546*, ed. C. N. L. Brooke and others (1988) · D. MacCulloch, *Thomas Cranmer: a life* (1996), 197, 392–8, 408–9, 508–9 · R. O'Day, 'Hugh Latimer: prophet of the kingdom', *Historical Research*, 65 (1992), 258–76 · S. Wabuda, 'Equivocation and recantation during the English Reformation: the "subtle shadows" of Dr Edward Crome', *Journal of Ecclesiastical History*, 44 (1993), 224–42 · S. Wabuda, '"Fruitful preaching" in the diocese of Worcester: Bishop Hugh Latimer and his influence, 1535–1539', *Religion and the English people, 1500–1640: new voices, new perspectives*, ed. E. J. Carlson (1998), vol. 45 of Sixteenth Century Essays and Studies, 49–74 · S. Wabuda, 'Shunamites and nurses of the English Reformation: the activities of Mary Glover, niece of Hugh Latimer', *Women in the church on the eve of the dissolution*, ed. W. J. Sheil and D. Wood, SCH, 27 (1990), 335–44 · T. Freeman, 'Texts, lies, and microfilm: reading and misreading Foxe's "Book of martyrs"', *Sixteenth Century Journal*, 30 (1999), 23–46 · will, PRO, PROB 11/32, fols. 290*r*–291*v* [William Benson] · *State papers published under … Henry VIII*, 11 vols. (1830–52), vol. 1, pt 2, 484–9

Likenesses oils, 1555, NPG [*see illus.*] · H. E. Dawe, mezzotint (after unknown artist), NPG · G. Gyfford, line engraving, BM, NPG; repro. in *Sermons* (1635) · W. & M. van de Passe, line engraving, BM, NPG; repro. in H. Holland, *Heröologia* (1620) · engraving, repro. in T. Somer, ed., *The fyrste sermon of mayster Hughe Latimer* [1549] · oils, other versions, Clare College, Cambridge; deanery, Canterbury Cathedral; Balliol Oxf. · portrait, repro. in *Great Bible* (1539), title-page · portrait, repro. in Foxe, *Actes and monuments* (1563), frontispiece to the ninth book

Latimer, Sir Thomas (1341–1401), soldier and alleged heretic, was the third son of Sir Warin Latimer of Braybrooke, Northamptonshire, and Katherine, daughter of John de la Warr, born between 10 and 17 September 1341. He is chiefly notable as the most conspicuous, if not the most fervent, member of a group of courtiers and soldiers disparaged by the chroniclers Thomas Walsingham and Henry Knighton for their heretical views, and known collectively as the '*Lollard knights'.

Predeceased by his two older brothers Latimer proved his majority in November 1362, and thereupon inherited a sizeable estate in Northamptonshire, Leicestershire, and Somerset. Knighted by 1365 he probably began his career as a soldier in the service of Edward, the Black Prince, in whose Gascon and Spanish campaigns he fought from 1365 to 1370, and of whom he held his castle and manor of Braybrooke. He married Anne, the widow of Sir John Beysin, by April 1366. As a companion to Joan, princess of Wales, she had been present at the birth of the future Richard II in 1367, and she brought to her husband a life interest in a large estate in Staffordshire and Shropshire. Latimer also took part in the Spanish and Breton expeditions of 1373–4 and 1377–8, but in the retinue of the prince's younger brother, John of Gaunt, duke of Lancaster. It was probably his relationship with the latter that secured his election as a knight of the shire for Northamptonshire in the parliaments of January 1377 and October 1378, which were packed with Gaunt's supporters. He was also appointed to several oyer and terminer commissions there from 1378 to 1385, and sat on the peace commission from 1381 to 1385.

On 12 June 1385 Latimer was ordered by Richard II to attend upon Joan, princess of Wales, along with other Lollard knights then in the king's service. His interest in the controversial preaching emanating from Oxford may have been nurtured in the household of the king's mother, who is known to have been sympathetic to John Wyclif (*d.* 1384). After her death in 1385 Latimer retired from court altogether, ceasing to play a part in public affairs and turning his attention to religious matters. In May 1388 he was summoned to appear before the king's council 'with certain books and quires in his custody' (McFarlane, 193) said to contain erroneous doctrine contrary to the Catholic faith. No serious consequences appear to have resulted from this interview.

By early 1389 it is evident that Latimer was protecting John Wodard, a Lollard chaplain from Knebworth, Hertfordshire, who preached sermons every Tuesday at Latimer's market at Chipping Warden, Northamptonshire. An emissary of John Buckingham, bishop of Lincoln (*d.* 1399), made several unsuccessful attempts to serve Wodard with a summons to appear before the bishop, but this only provoked Latimer into suing the bishop's agent for loss of profits from his market. Buckingham responded by invoking the lay power, sending a certificate naming forty-one persons led into heresy by Wodard, some of whom were associates of Latimer.

Latimer's relationship with the other Lollard knights, particularly Sir Lewis Clifford (*d.* 1404), an overseer of his will, is also telling, as is his patronage of the notorious heretic Robert Hoke, whom either he or his wife presented to the rectory of Braybrooke. On 14 September 1401 Latimer died, and was buried in Braybrooke churchyard. Both he and Dame Anne, who died the following July, left wills in English similar to those of several of their fellow Lollards [see Lollard women (act. c.1390–c.1520)]. They emphasized their unworthiness, forbade funeral pomp, and expressed contempt for their bodies and a biblical concern for the poor. The overseers and executors of Dame Anne's will included Robert Hoke, Sir Lewis Clifford, and two Wycliffite Oxford academics—Robert Lechlade and the reformed Philip Repyndon. At their deaths the Latimer estate—valued, doubtless conservatively, at £120 yearly on Sir Thomas's death—passed to Thomas's younger brother Edward, but Braybrooke remained a centre of heresy for some years to come. In 1405, 1414, and 1425 Robert Hoke, still rector, appeared before church authorities on charges of heresy, abjuring twice, and it is clear that he enjoyed considerable local support. It was undoubtedly he who furnished two Czech scholars with a copy of Wyclif's *De dominio divino* at Braybrooke in 1407. Not surprisingly, Braybrooke has been suggested as the location of the Lollard scriptorium that flourished in the east midlands in the late fourteenth and early fifteenth centuries.

MAUREEN JURKOWSKI

Sources K. B. McFarlane, *Lancastrian kings and Lollard knights* (1972) · GEC, *Peerage · Chancery records · CIPM*, 11, nos. 108–9, 378; 18, nos. 435–9, 609–13 · G. H., 'Four ancient English wills', *The Ancestor*, 10 (1904), 13–21, esp. 13–21 · A. Hudson, 'Some aspects of Lollard book production', *Schism, heresy and religious protest*, ed. D. Baker, SCH, 9 (1972), 147–57; repr. in A. Hudson, *The Lollards and their books* (1985) · E. F. Jacob, ed., *The register of Henry Chichele, archbishop of Canterbury, 1414–1443*, 3, CYS, 46 (1945), 101–15 · J. Bridges, *The history and antiquities of Northamptonshire*, ed. P. Whalley, 1 (1791), 115; 2 (1791), 13 · A. Hudson, *The premature reformation: Wycliffite texts and Lollard history* (1988) · M. Aston, '"Caim's castles": poverty, politics and disendowment', *The church, politics and patronage in the fifteenth century*, ed. R. B. Dobson (1984), 45–81; repr. in M. Aston, *Faith and fire: popular and unpopular religion, 1350–1600* (1993) · M. C. B. Dawes, ed., *Register of Edward, the Black Prince*, PRO, 4 (1933), 375, 383, 387 · W. T. Waugh, 'The Lollard knights', *SHR*, 11 (1913–14), 55–92 · *CEPR letters*, 4.54

Archives BL, Add. charters 854, 8131, 22213–22216 · Northants. RO, Griffin cartulary 1, ZA6242, fols. 13–50

Wealth at death £120 p.a.: *CIPM*, Henry IV, 18, nos. 435–9

Latimer, Thomas (1803–1888), journalist, was born in Bristol on 9 August 1803, the son of a merchant's clerk who, some time after 1807, moved his household to London. Following an unrecorded but probably haphazard education, Thomas Latimer was apprenticed to a printer. With like-minded apprentices, among them the future comic writer and playwright Douglas Jerrold (1803–1857), Latimer pursued the self-education possible in a printing office, mastering French and Latin, with some Italian, and was caught up in Byronism and radical enthusiasms. Present in 1823 when Dr George Birkbeck (1776–1841) proposed a mechanics' institution in the capital, Latimer threw himself into the new activity, but soon withdrew and became involved in a nascent gymnastic movement on the German model.

After completing his apprenticeship Latimer worked briefly for the *Morning Post* (as a writer of jokes at 6*d.* for seven lines) and then for the radical *Albion* until the government closed it down. A walking tour of Devon in the summer of 1826 confirmed his dislike of London; settling on Exeter, he married Frances Ann Perry (1807/8–1892) of London, and they served briefly as superintendents of an infant school. Of twelve children born in the marriage, the younger son and four daughters survived him.

Soon after his arrival in Exeter Latimer was introduced to two leading figures in the Devon County Reform Club who proposed to pay his salary while he was placed with the *Devon County Chronicle*. Latimer claimed to have been the first shorthand reporter in the county; on one occasion at the Exeter assizes he and Charles Dickens matched skills. The arrangement with the *Chronicle* collapsed after a year and Latimer was engaged by the *Plymouth Journal*; in the first six months of 1830 he also edited *Philo-Danmonian*, a literary periodical.

On his return to Exeter in 1830 Latimer joined the *Exeter and Plymouth Gazette*, where he soon became acting editor. When his hard-hitting leaders, in the mounting excitement over parliamentary reform, provoked his dismissal, he was immediately hired by the less well-established but uncompromisingly radical *Western Times*. In 1835, realizing his value in a new age of opinion, local liberal leaders bought out the paper and installed him as managing editor. With the collapse of Exeter's ancient textile industry, the plight of the many poor residents engaged Latimer's deepest sympathies, though he had little use for trade unionism as a remedy. He sharply attacked the entrenched leadership of the city, giving point to the motto for the paper, 'Tempora quaeram'.

Though an Anglican, Latimer found his choicest target in Henry Phillpotts (1788–1869), an uncompromising high-churchman who had become bishop of Exeter in 1831. Phillpotts soon alienated many of his clergy and much of the population of Exeter, especially the dissenters, by his absence from the city for all but a few hours during the cholera epidemic of 1832, by his use of patronage to provide for his family, and by his intolerance of theological difference, the last reaching a climax in the Gorham controversy of 1850.

Latimer's genius for abuse fully justified his reputation as the Cobbett of the West. When on the scent he was not overscrupulous about fact or language. While notably strait-laced in habit and conversation, his humour and sarcasm led him to focus on personal frailties and to make outrageous play with names: thus, a high-church parson who was among the first to place flowers on the altar was ever after Flower-Pot Smith, and when Phillpotts appointed a son-in-law, the Revd Francis du Boulay, to a living, the unfortunate cleric became the Revd du Bouilli (the Revd Bully-Beef). Very much of its time this slashing style clearly embarrassed late Victorian journalists who were called upon to write otherwise admiring obituaries.

In the mid-1840s a long-simmering dispute between the duke of Somerset and Phillpotts boiled over. A dozen years earlier the duke had chosen James Shore, an evangelical clergyman, as curate of a chapel built to serve some new housing on the ducal estate. In 1843 a change of vicars gave Phillpotts occasion to refuse a licence to Shore. Somerset thereupon had the chapel licensed as a dissenting place of worship, but when Shore continued to officiate according to the Book of Common Prayer the bishop brought Shore to trial before the court of arches. In a judgment on 20 June 1846, later upheld by the judicial committee of the privy council, the court refused to remove Shore but ordered him admonished and to pay the costs, which led to his imprisonment for debt.

Shortly after the privy council judgment, Latimer printed a full report of a speech by the duke's son, Lord Seymour, attacking the bishop, and in an editorial Latimer denounced Phillpotts as, among other things, a 'consecrated, careless perverter of facts'. Phillpotts thereupon brought a charge of criminal libel against 'Thomas Latimer, labourer'; overriding the advice of his lawyers Latimer refused to apologize, and the case came to trial on 27 March 1848, when Latimer was brilliantly defended without fee by Alexander Cockburn (1802–1880), later lord chief justice. Phillpotts had not reckoned with the effect of Lord Campbell's act of 1843, which allowed truth to be pleaded against an accusation of libel, and, despite hostile instructions, an overwhelmingly Conservative jury acquitted Latimer, to general rejoicing in Exeter.

Although Latimer somewhat moderated his editorial tone after mid-century, he remained committed to radicalism as he understood it. He became an overseer of the poor and an improvement commissioner in 1849 and a magistrate in 1851. Physically active and a genial friend, he was handicapped only by increasing deafness, which led him in the late 1860s to turn over editorial duties largely to his son-in-law, while his younger son Hugh (1843–1920) took on the management of the highly successful paper, which had become a daily in 1866. Latimer died at his home, 143 Fore Street, Exeter, of liver cancer on 5 January 1888 and was buried in the old cemetery on 10 January. The commemorative window in the south aisle of the cathedral, like the windows in the lady chapel honouring his old adversary Bishop Phillpotts, was destroyed in an air raid in 1942.   R. K. WEBB

Sources R. S. Lambert, *The Cobbett of the west: a study of Thomas Latimer and the struggle between pulpit and press at Exeter* (1939) · *Western Times* (6 Jan 1888) · *Western Times* (11 Jan 1888) · *Evening Post* (6 Jan 1888) · cuttings from local press, Exeter Central Library, Westcountry Local Studies Department · R. Acton, 'Reminiscences of Mr Latimer', Exeter Central Library, Westcountry Local Studies Department [press cutting] · leading articles, *Western Times* (1830–39); (1866–9) · *Devon and Cornwall Notes and Queries*, 35 (1982–6), 257–8 · G. C. B. Davies, *Henry Phillpotts, bishop of Exeter* (1954) · b. cert. · d. cert.
Archives UCL, corresp. with E. Chadwick
Likenesses attrib. Mogford, portrait, c.1846, repro. in Lambert, *The Cobbett of the West*, frontispiece · H. B., lithograph (after photograph by O. Angel), repro. in *Echoes of the Exe* (9 Oct 1885), supplement · G. G. Palmer, lithograph ('Exeter election 1868. Shakespeare illustrated no. 5'), repro. in Lambert, *The Cobbett of the West*, facing p. 208 · photograph (aged about eighty), repro. in Lambert, *The Cobbett of the West*, facing p. 209
Wealth at death £4345 6s. 2d.: probate, 6 March 1888

Latimer, William, first Lord Latimer (d. 1304), baron and soldier, was the son of William Latimer (d. 1268), sheriff of Yorkshire in 1254–60 and 1266–7, and escheator north of Trent in 1258–65; his mother's identity is unknown. Born of a family landed in Yorkshire and Lincolnshire, Latimer acquired estates in Northamptonshire and Bedfordshire through his marriage, by 1268, to Alice (d. 1317) elder daughter and coheir of Walter Ledet, while his younger brother John married Alice's sister Christiana: the sisters were also heirs of the justice Henry of *Braybrooke (d. 1234) and his wife, Christiana Ledet, their great-grandparents.

Latimer the sheriff had been a trusted agent of Henry III, and in February 1270 the younger William was pardoned his father's accounting arrears in recognition of the latter's services and for a sum of 200 marks. Three months later Latimer had protection while crusading, and in 1275 he was arranging attorneys when going to Santiago de Compostela. He received protection in 1275, when he went overseas with Edmund, the king's brother, and in April 1286 when going abroad with the king; he accompanied Edward I's daughter Eleanor, countess of Bar, overseas in 1294. Latimer received military summons against the Welsh in 1276 and 1282, against the Scots intermittently between 1291 and 1303, and for service in Flanders in 1297 and 1298. His wife was granted residence in houses in Skipton Castle in August 1294 when her husband was described as setting out for Gascony. Latimer was present at the battle of Stirling Bridge (1297) and at the siege of Caerlaverock (1300). He was in this period keeper of Berwick, captain-general in Nottinghamshire, Derbyshire, Yorkshire, and Northumberland, lieutenant of the marches towards Scotland, a commissioner to exchange prisoners with the Scots, and was summoned to York in 1299 to consider the keeping of the marches and garrisoning of the king's castles in Scotland. Latimer's military feats earned contemporary praise: Walter of Guisborough three times uses the adjective 'strenuous' to describe him, and the *Song of Caerlaverock* praises his valour.

Alongside his military career Latimer took an active part in political affairs. He was a signatory to the letters of protest sent to the pope in 1290 and 1301, and was named among the grantors of the aid for the marriage of the king's daughter in 1290. From his attendance at parliament in 1290 and his summonses by writ to the parliaments of 1300 and 1302, he is considered to have become Lord Latimer. He held prestigious commissions, being appointed in 1289 to hear grievances and wrongs committed in the king's absence, and in 1298 to hear ministerial abuses in forests.

On 18 July 1302 Latimer and his heirs had a grant of a weekly market and a yearly fair at the manor of Ash, Kent, a fair at the manor of Wotton, Surrey, and a weekly market and fair at the manor of Terrington, Yorkshire. Latimer died on 5 December 1304 and was buried at Helpringham, Lincolnshire. His heir was his son William *Latimer; another son, Nicholas, was living in 1317; and a son Thomas is recorded in 1327; a daughter Joan married Alexander Comyn.   HELEN M. JEWELL

Sources GEC, *Peerage*, new edn, 7.460–65 · *Chancery records* · *CIPM*, 4, no. 330 · *The chronicle of Walter of Guisborough*, ed. H. Rothwell, CS, 3rd ser., 89 (1957), 219, 244–5, 363 · *CDS*, vols. 1–3 · J. Stevenson, ed., *Documents illustrative of the history of Scotland*, 2 (1870) · [Walter of Exeter?], *The siege of Carlaverock … with a translation, a history of the castle and memoirs of the personages commemorated by the poet*, ed. and trans. N. H. Nicolas (1828), 45 · *Chronica monasterii de Melsa, a fundatione usque ad annum 1396, auctore Thoma de Burton*, ed. E. A. Bond, 2, Rolls Series, 43/2 (1867), 268 · *The survey of the county of York, taken by John de Kirkby*, ed. R. H. Scaife, SurtS, 49 (1867) · M. Prestwich, *Edward I* (1988) · F. Palgrave, ed., *The parliamentary writs and writs of military summons*, 1 (1827), 699 · *VCH Yorkshire North Riding*, 2.336 · I. J. Sanders, *English baronies: a study of their origin and descent, 1086–1327* (1960), 33
Wealth at death wealth in Kent: *CIPM*

Latimer, William, second Lord Latimer (*c*.1276–1327), soldier and administrator, was the son of William *Latimer, first Lord Latimer (*d*. 1304), and his wife, Alice (*d*. 1317). He became a household knight of Edward I in 1294, in which year he was knighted while on the Welsh campaign. He also served alongside his father, in Gascony in 1295, and in Scotland from 1297. In March 1304, along with John Segrave and Robert Clifford, he is credited with defeating Simon Fraser and William Wallace during a raid in Lothian. He served in Scotland in 1307 with twenty-three men in the retinue of Aymer de Valence. He was initially summoned to parliament in February 1299 and continued to be called until 1326.

Latimer began the reign of Edward II as a loyal household knight. During the crisis of 1308 he was one of the few king's men who stood by Edward II. He was made custodian of Rockingham Castle as well as of the forest between the bridges of Oxford and Stamford in March, and, according to Stowe, he later led a force northward to capture Henry de Lacy, earl of Lincoln, who was at that time the leader of opposition to the crown. Latimer was sent abroad on the king's business in 1309, served with the king in Scotland in 1310–11, and witnessed royal grants made at Berwick on numerous occasions between November 1310 and July 1311. As a household knight he was regularly present at court in York between 24 January and 24 March 1312, the period during which Piers Gaveston returned from his final exile, which led to an open breach between the king and the baronial opposition that culminated in Gaveston's pursuit, capture, and execution. Significantly, Latimer was granted custody of Scarborough Castle in January 1312, which was to be Gaveston's final refuge, but Henry Percy refused to deliver it to him. Latimer continued to attend the court at Westminster and Windsor frequently between September 1312 and March 1313. In the spring of that year he was once again sent abroad on the king's business.

Latimer was taken prisoner at Bannockburn on 24 June 1314, and held at Bothwell until his release, which took place before February 1315. In April 1315 he was summoned to a council of war at Doncaster, and in August was ordered to remain in the north during the winter campaign. He was present at the parliament held at York in May 1319 at which preparations were made for a campaign to recover Berwick, which had fallen to the Scots in the previous year. At this time, on 15 May, Latimer entered the service of Thomas of Lancaster. His indenture for service to Lancaster is extant and is quite informative. His retinue, which has rightly been described as extraordinarily large, was to consist of forty men, one besides himself to be a knight-banneret, and ten to be knights. Latimer received the manor of Sedgebrook (Lincolnshire) for life, and annual sums from the manors of Rauns (Northamptonshire), Huntingdon, and Godmanchester (Huntingdonshire). He was to receive £1000 in wartime to maintain his household for a year's service in the field. He was also to receive the earl's livery, and to come to parliament when summoned. Similarly, he was liable to be ordered to provide council or assist in judgment. In 1319 Latimer did in fact receive £250 for his service at Berwick in the first quarter of the year. It has been calculated that of this £250, slightly less than half was necessary for the payment of his retinue, leaving a profit of some £128 18*s*. to Latimer himself. Only the earl of Lancaster could afford to pay his retainers so lavishly. He was present at the Sherburn assembly during the summer of 1321 at which the earl of Lancaster attempted to build a coalition of northerners and marchers as well as his own retainers with which to oppose the Despensers. Nevertheless, in the event, Latimer remained loyal to the king in the armed confrontation that followed. His indenture of service to Lancaster specifically exempted him from taking up arms against the king, and like other of the earl's retainers, he appears to have made use of this exemption. He was commissioned to raise the Yorkshire levies against the earl of Lancaster in February 1322, and he was a joint leader of the royalist forces that defeated Lancaster at Boroughbridge on 16 March 1322. In October 1322 he was appointed as custodian of the city of York. Latimer was frequently at court in Westminster in the spring of 1324. He last appeared at court when he witnessed a charter at Beaulieu on 11 April 1325. He died on 27 February 1327 and was buried at Guisborough, Yorkshire.

Latimer was married to Lucy, daughter and coheir of Sir Robert Thwing of Danby, Yorkshire, by April 1295. Their son William, born about 1301, succeeded as third Lord Latimer. This first marriage was tumultuous. In 1304 the sheriff of York was ordered to find and return Lucy to Latimer's manor of Brunne in Yorkshire. She in turn had applied to Archbishop Thomas of Corbridge for a divorce on grounds of consanguinity and cruelty. A divorce was subsequently obtained in 1312, before 22 July. Lucy, after bearing an illegitimate son to Sir Nicholas Meynell of Whorlton, married first Sir Robert Everingham and second Sir Bartholomew Fanacourt. By 18 August 1314 Latimer had remarried without the king's licence, taking as his second wife Sibill, the daughter of Sir Richard de Fourneaux and the widow of William of Huntingfield. Sibill died before 23 July 1317. Latimer held lands in Kent, Bedford, and Surrey in addition to his primary holdings in Yorkshire.

J. S. HAMILTON

Sources J. R. Maddicott, *Thomas of Lancaster, 1307–1322: a study in the reign of Edward II* (1970) · *CIPM*, 7, nos. 37, 50 · PRO, charter rolls, C 53 · *CPR* · *CCIR* · GEC, *Peerage*

Wealth at death see *CIPM*, 7, no. 50

Latimer, William, fourth Baron Latimer (1330–1381), soldier and courtier, was born on 24 March 1330, the son and heir of William, the third Lord Latimer, who died in 1335. His mother, Elizabeth, outlived her son, to die in 1384. Her long survival may have been a reason for his career of lively military and financial activity. He was already present at the battle of Crécy in 1346. By 1351 he was a knight, was in royal service at Calais, and had received a grant of land at Corby. By 1353 he had married Elizabeth, daughter of Richard (II) Fitzalan, earl of Arundel. On 5 July 1354 he was granted 500 marks a year until he obtained his mother's property. In January 1356 he witnessed Edward Balliol's surrender of the kingdom of Scotland. In 1359 he was in Gascony and by September 1360 he was the king's lieutenant there.

This precocious early military career was followed by a period in which Latimer's activity was centred in Brittany. In October 1360 he was involved in the defence of Bécherel in Brittany, a castle that was to play a large part in his career. In 1364 he fought on the side of John de Montfort, duke of Brittany (d. 1399), at Auray. He remained in Brittany at least until 1366 and was granted control of Bécherel in 1368, as a castle in the king's hands and as a pledge from the duke of Brittany. The castle was then administered by Sir John Pert and Huchoun Middleton on his behalf. Latimer appears to have been the most prominent beneficiary of a system of plundering which had been maintained by English troops in Brittany, officially defending the English ally, the duke of Brittany, against the French king, but also in fact extracting money from the unfortunate Bretons in areas that they controlled. Bécherel was under Latimer from 1359 to some time in the 1370s, and exchequer documents speak of large sums collected there as 'ransoms'. This system of extortion was no doubt one reason why in the 1370s Latimer was able to act in England as a wealthy man with cash in hand. He was a creditor of the earl of March in 1375, while in 1365 had received a licence to found a college of thirteen chaplains at Helpringham, Lincolnshire.

Latimer was summoned to the parliament of 1368 and was presumably principally in England for some years after this. He was steward of the household from 1368 to 1370, then chamberlain from October 1371 until removed by the Good Parliament of 1376. The administration of the royal household appears to have been dominated from 1371 to 1376 chiefly by Latimer and by John Neville of Raby (d. 1388), who had become steward, and who later married Latimer's daughter and heir, Elizabeth. In 1372 Latimer became constable of Dover Castle and warden of the Cinque Ports. He was able to offer 1000 marks for the wardship of Edward Courtenay in August 1372, and £1500 for that of Henry Beaumont in December 1373, which suggests again that he had ready money. He appears to have taken part in the duke of Lancaster's expedition to France in 1373, and in the same year was involved in negotiations with the king of Portugal; he was then one of the negotiators with France at Bruges in 1375.

In the Good Parliament of 1376 the Commons made serious accusations of misconduct against Latimer. The principal ones were that he and the London merchant Richard Lyons (d. 1381) had arranged the issue of licences for the evasion of the staple by exporters of wool; that they had arranged for a loan of 20,000 marks to be taken with an unnecessary rate of interest by the king; that Latimer and his lieutenants had carried out extortions at Bécherel; that he had negligently allowed the castles of Bécherel and St Sauveur to fall to the French. There is no doubt that licences to evade the staple had been granted extensively, and that payment for them had been made to the chamber, which Latimer controlled as chamberlain. The loan of 20,000 marks had been made as stated, and it was asserted in parliament that the money advanced had come partly from Latimer. Since he regularly handled large sums as chamberlain it is possible that the king's own money was being lent to the king. The Good Parliament undoubtedly unearthed an extremely corrupt court regime which had Latimer at its centre. The degree of truth in the charges relating to Brittany is more difficult to determine. There is no direct evidence of Breton complaint about Latimer's activities, but there is plenty of evidence that the people around Bécherel had been oppressed by his subordinates. The castle of St Sauveur had been sold to the French by its defenders in 1375. This may have been the result of the policy of the court with which Latimer was associated.

The Lords declared the charges against Latimer proven. He was condemned to a fine of 20,000 marks and imprisonment, and he lost his positions in the king's household and on the council. But although he ceased to be chamberlain he was quickly exonerated, being pardoned in October 1376. He was named as one of the executors of Edward III, who died in June 1377. At the beginning of the reign of Richard II he was one of the commanders of an unsuccessful naval expedition to Sluys, and claimed the right of acting as almoner at the coronation. In February 1379 he was appointed a commissioner to make peace with the Scots. In 1380 he returned to France, joining the elaborate and entirely unsuccessful *chevauchée* of Thomas of Woodstock, earl of Buckingham (d. 1397). This was his last military enterprise. He died on 28 May 1381, apparently after a stroke. Chroniclers accounted him a disreputable extortioner and wastrel. His career was also, on the other hand, a striking example of success in the Hundred Years' War and at Edward III's court. At his death Latimer held properties of the crown in a number of English counties and at Calais. His extensive estates included the manor of Danby and other lands in Yorkshire, the centre of the family inheritance, also lands in Bedfordshire, Buckinghamshire, Cumberland, Lincolnshire, and Northamptonshire, and several woolhouses at Calais. His widow, Elizabeth, had died by May 1384, and his estates descended to his daughter Elizabeth *Willoughby [see under Willoughby family (per. c.1300–1523)].

GEORGE HOLMES

Sources GEC, *Peerage* · Chancery records · G. Holmes, *The Good Parliament* (1975) · [T. Walsingham], *Chronicon Angliae, ab anno Domini 1328 usque ad annum 1388*, ed. E. M. Thompson, Rolls Series, 64 (1874) · V. H. Galbraith, ed., *The Anonimalle chronicle, 1333 to 1381*

(1927) · *Chroniques de J. Froissart*, ed. S. Luce and others, 15 vols. (Paris, 1869–1975) · *CIPM*, 15, nos. 375–88

Archives PRO, E 101

Latimer, William (*c*.1467–1545), clergyman and Greek scholar, was the son of John Latimer and came from the diocese of Worcester, perhaps from the parish of St Mary, Worcester, a church to which he gave a bequest in his will. He studied arts at Oxford University during the 1480s and (having graduated as a BA) was admitted to a fellowship tied to the study of the arts at All Souls College in 1489. Latimer left All Souls about 1496 to study Greek in Italy, residing at Padua about 1498 when he corresponded with the Venetian printer and Greek scholar Aldus Manutius (Aldo Manuzio), whom he may have visited. He took an MA degree at Ferrara in 1502 and returned to England in that or the following year. On his return, he was presented by Evesham Abbey, Worcestershire, to the rectory of Saintbury, Gloucestershire, and took holy orders, concluding with the priesthood in December 1504. He continued, however, to be involved in travels and study. In 1510 he visited Rome, where he borrowed a volume containing Plutarch's *Moralia* and Aristotle's *Ethics* from the Vatican Library. In 1513 he was living in Oxford as tutor to Reginald Pole, and hired a room there in Canterbury College at various times between 1516 and 1529. He still had a chamber in Oxford when he made his will. In 1538 he was appointed by the bishop, Nicholas Shaxton, to a canonry of Salisbury Cathedral, with the prebend of Woodford and Wilsford, which he vacated in 1543. He also became rector of Weston-sub-Edge, Gloucestershire, adjoining Saintbury, and held the benefice until his death.

Latimer was admired by his contemporaries as a scholar of Latin and Greek. His selection as Pole's tutor was one such endorsement, and he was friendly and corresponded with Erasmus and Thomas More. Erasmus rated him highly and called him 'a man in the forefront of both learnings [Latin and Greek], not inferior to [Thomas] Linacre, a true theologian, very sound and erudite' (*Opus epistolarum*, 2.479). He asked Latimer for help with his edition of the New Testament in 1516, and (in the same year) urged him to teach Greek to John Fisher, bishop of Rochester, a project which Latimer declined, pleading other concerns. In 1531 he was listed as a scholar living outside Oxford who might be consulted about the king's divorce. His will referred to his Greek and Latin books, some at home and some at Oxford, and directed his executors to give them to children apt for learning, or to the college libraries of All Souls or Corpus Christi College, Oxford. He also had some care for his parishes. He bequeathed at his death a load of wood, a strike (measure) of wheat, and a strike of barley to every cottage in Saintbury and Weston. His curate in Saintbury from 1540 to 1546, Robert Glasemund, was a good enough Latinist to become schoolmaster of Chipping Camden grammar school, and even his shepherd, Robert Williams, was an intelligent reader. An extant copy of Thomas Langley's *Abridgement of Polydore Vergil* was bought by Williams in 1546, while keeping Latimer's sheep on Saintbury Hill, because Bible-reading by ordinary people had been forbidden. Latimer's links with scholars brought him into the company of men with religious opinions ranging from More at one end to Shaxton at the other, but his allocation of money to Glasemund to pray for his soul for three years suggests his attachment to much of traditional Catholicism. He made his will on 13 April 1545, and died during the following summer, the will being proved on 17 October. He asked, if he died at home, to be buried in Saintbury church or churchyard, and to have a modest funeral.

NICHOLAS ORME

Sources Emden, *Oxf.*, 2.1106–7 · *Opus epistolarum Des. Erasmi Roterodami*, ed. P. S. Allen and others, 12 vols. (1906–58) · J. F. Mozley, *Coverdale and his bibles* (1953), 284 · N. Orme, *Education in the west of England, 1066–1548* (1976), 128 · will, PRO, PROB 11/30, sig. 38, fols. 294v–295r

La Touche, William George Digges (1747–1803), East India Company servant and banker, was born on 28 August 1747, the eldest son of James Digges La Touche (1707–1763), a poplin merchant, and his second wife, Matilda, daughter of William Thwaites. His paternal grandfather, David La Touche (1671–1745), a Huguenot, had founded the Irish branch of the La Touche family. Born near Blois in France, he fled to an uncle in Amsterdam on the revocation of the edict of Nantes and entered Caillemotte's Huguenot regiment. He travelled to England with William of Orange, served at the battle of the Boyne, and settled in Dublin after his regiment was disbanded. Having first worked as a poplin maker, he became a successful banker, establishing the La Touche bank in 1715. He married twice and had two sons with his first wife, Martha Judith Biard (the daughter of M. Noel Biard, of Belesme, and his wife, Judith Chevalier), namely David Digges (1704–1785), also a banker, and James Digges La Touche.

William La Touche entered St Paul's School, London, on 30 August 1757 and in 1764 accompanied Henry Moore, the British resident, to the Ottoman-controlled port of Basrah, where the East India Company had established an agency in the previous year. During the Persian siege of Basrah in 1775–6 shelter in the company factory was offered to the city's principal inhabitants, and after the city fell in 1776 La Touche appears to have been evacuated to Bombay. He resumed residence in Basrah presumably in 1779, when it was recaptured by the Turks; two of his letters from Basrah in 1782, addressed to Sir Robert Ainslie, British ambassador at Constantinople, are preserved in the Lansdowne manuscripts in the British Library.

Following his return to Ireland about 1784 La Touche married Grace, daughter of John Puget, a London banker. He now became a partner in La Touche's, the bank owned by his cousins in Dublin. This was by now Ireland's premier bank, and the La Touche family was among the country's leading landed and political dynasties—six sat in the last Irish parliament and six sat in the British parliament up to 1820. La Touche settled in Dublin, lending his London connections to the business, and built himself a substantial town house in St Stephen's Green. He also purchased the country house of Sans Souci, near Dublin. He died of an apoplectic fit at his house in Dublin on 7

November 1803, leaving four sons. The eldest, James Digges La Touche (1788–1827), entered Trinity College, Dublin, as a fellow commoner on 2 October 1803, graduated BA, taking a gold medal, in 1808, and managed the bank. A great supporter of Sunday schools, he married Isabella, daughter of Sir James Lawrence Cotton, bt, of Rockforest.   [ANON.], *rev.* P. J. JUPP

Sources W. Urwick, *Biographical sketches of … J. D. Latouche, banker, Dublin* (1868) · A. La Touche, 'Some records of the family of Digues de La Touche', *Proceedings of the Huguenot Society*, 11 (1915), 227–39 · R. B. Gardner, ed., *The admission registers of St Paul's School from 1748 to 1876 (1876 to 1905)*, 2 vols. (1884–1906) · J. Taylor, *Travels from England to India, in 1789, by way of the Tyrol, Venice, Scandaroon, Aleppo, and over the great desert to Bussora*, 2 vols. (1799) · Burke, *Gen. GB* (1858) · E. M. Johnston-Liik, *History of the Irish parliament, 1692–1800*, 6 vols. (2002), vol. 5, pp. 65–6

La Trobe, Benjamin (1728–1786), Moravian leader, was born on 10 April 1728 in Dublin, the only surviving child of James La Trobe (1700–1752), a merchant of Huguenot descent, and his first wife, Elizabeth Thornton (*d.* 1744). Raised with the intention that he should enter the Baptist ministry, La Trobe matriculated in 1743 at the University of Glasgow. Back in Ireland, he later came under the influence of the evangelist John Cennick, whose brief visit in 1746 shaped the course of his life. He broke with the Baptist church and formed, unaided, a large religious society in Dublin on Moravian lines.

In 1748 La Trobe was received in Germany into the Moravian church and ordained. He returned to England, where his responsibilities steadily increased. Married on 25 April 1756 to the Moravian deaconess Anna Margaretta Antes (1728–1794), daughter of a distinguished Pennsylvania German family, he became principal minister of the great settlement at Fulneck in Yorkshire.

This was a crucially important position. The church was bankrupt and its reputation was severely tarnished. Some time later it emerged that a British leader was required for the Moravian church in Britain. In 1768 La Trobe took up this post, and moved to London. For about the last ten years of his life he lived at 32 Fetter Lane, where the church's provincial headquarters were situated in the city. He proved to be a very acceptable representative of his church. True to its principles, he worked for unity between Christians, and a notable achievement was the foundation in 1785 at Fairfield, near Manchester, of that embodiment of the Moravian ideal, a settlement or Christian community.

La Trobe did much to restore the church's standing. He promoted the cause of Moravian foreign missions to the heathen, for which the church became famous, and he edited and saw through to the press a range of important Moravian publications. He was a persuasive preacher, whose eloquence attracted both Anglicans and dissenters. When it was noted at the end of 1783 that prejudices against the church had greatly abated, he had received more invitations to preach at the chapels of other denominations than he could accept. It was also characteristic of his catholic spirit that he was invited and joined that year the Eclectic Society in London, formed recently by his friend John Newton.

In the summer of 1786 La Trobe was taken mortally ill at Teston in Kent, while on a visit to Sir Charles Middleton. Nursed nearby at the vicarage of his old friend the abolitionist James Ramsay, he was moved early in November to his residence in London. He died there on 29 November, and was interred on 6 December at the Moravian cemetery at Chelsea. At his request the family were not in mourning.

The obituary which appeared in the London press was not placed by Moravians. Here it was said that La Trobe had 'firmly' restored the church's reputation, and that 'The goodness of his heart and the affability of his disposition, endeared him to all his connexions' (*London Chronicle*). La Trobe would most heartily have objected to any personal testimonial whatsoever, but few would have dissented from the tenor of these sentiments. He was survived by his widow, who died on 17 March 1794. Of their three talented sons, only Christian Ignatius *La Trobe (1758–1836) followed him into the church. Benjamin Henry *Latrobe (1764–1820) became the leading architect of his age in America, and John Frederick La Trobe (1769–1845), who lived in Germany, became known as a minor composer.   JOHN C. S. MASON

Sources 'Historical sketch of the connection of the LaTrobe family', *Periodical Accounts Relating to the Missions of the Church of the United Brethren Established among the Heathen*, 25 (1864), 79–81 · J. Mason, 'Benjamin La Trobe, 1728–1786', in J. Mason and L. Torrode, *Three generations of the La Trobe family in the Moravian church* (1997), 3–15, 28 · Pilgrim House diary, 1747–8, Moravian church archives, London · Gemeinhaus diary, 1748, Moravian church archives, London, week 38 · Fetter Lane congregation diaries, Moravian church archives, London · letter from John Wollin, 13 Dec 1786, Moravian church archives, Fulneck, near Leeds, Yorkshire, FU 86 TCMR · 'Some account of … Benj. La Trobe's last illness', Moravian church archives, Herrnhut, Germany, R.22.137.6 · *London Chronicle* (2 Dec 1786) · W. I. Addison, ed., *The matriculation albums of the University of Glasgow from 1728 to 1858* (1913), p. 29, no. 998 · *The Virginia journals of Benjamin Henry Latrobe, 1795–1798*, ed. E. C. Carter, 1 (1977), lxv–lxviii

Archives Moravian church archives, Moravian Church House, Muswell Hill, London · Moravian church archives, Fulneck, near Leeds, Yorkshire · Moravian church archives, Herrnhut, Germany

Likenesses W. Bromley, engraving, pubd 1793 (after J. Astley), repro. in Mason and Torrode, *Three generations* · J. Astley, oils, repro. in Mason and Torrode, *Three generations*; formerly in New Orleans, USA, 1993 [sold by auction, 1940] · silhouette, Moravian Church, Fulneck, near Leeds, Yorkshire

Wealth at death trustee for church property; inherited very small estate from uncle in Ireland

Latrobe, Benjamin Henry (1764–1820), architect, was born on 1 May 1764 in Fulneck, a village near Leeds, Yorkshire, and the earliest self-contained Moravian settlement in the country. He was the second son of Benjamin *La Trobe (1728–1786), a minister who became the elder of the Moravian congregation in Britain, and Anna Margaretta Antes (1728–1794), a Moravian from Pennsylvania. Christian Ignatius *La Trobe (1758–1836), Moravian minister and composer, was his elder brother.

Latrobe's early education was at the Fulneck School or

Benjamin Henry Latrobe (1764–1820), by Charles Willson Peale, *c.*1804

'choir', which he entered at the age of three. His parents moved to London eighteen months later, but he remained in the school until in 1776 he was sent to a select Moravian school at Niesky in Saxony for the children of missionaries and church officials. From there he went to another Moravian school, at Gnadenfry, Silesia. In 1782 he was moved again, to Barby in eastern Germany, the zenith of the Moravian school system. However, his lack of evangelical zeal and unorthodoxy caused him to be removed in June 1783. He had hoped to go to Vienna, to study the engineering of fortifications (despite the Moravians' pacifist ideals) but instead returned to London, where in 1784 he took up an appointment in the stamp office which allowed him to continue with other work and studies.

At Niesky Latrobe had had weekly drawing lessons and he seems to have had a certain amount of expertise already when he began his engineering studies under John Smeaton, builder of the Eddystone lighthouse and of the ill-fated Hexham Bridge. While in Smeaton's office he worked on improvements for Rye harbour in Sussex and on the Basingstoke Canal. From around 1789 until 1792 he was a pupil in the office of Samuel Pepys Cockerell, which involved him in a number of commissions for the Admiralty as well as country-house work including Warren Hastings's Indian-style mansion at Daylesford in Gloucestershire (1789–93).

A set of drawings showing a number of basic plans and elevations for Fairfield, the Moravian settlement at Droylsden outside Manchester which was founded in 1785, bear Latrobe's signature. They are among his earliest works, although whether as architect or as draughtsman is not clear. After his marriage in 1790 to Lydia Sellon (*c.*1761–1793) he set up an architectural and engineering

practice of his own, working on an (unexecuted) major project, the Chelmer and Blackwater navigation (1793), and at least two private houses, Hammerwood Lodge and Ashdown House, both in Sussex, as well as alterations to others. He also held an appointment as surveyor of the London police offices.

The death of Latrobe's wife in childbirth in 1793 devastated him. He was left with two small children, Lydia and Henry. His wife appears to have been unusually supportive and interested in his work and his immediate reaction was to start his life again, far away. America was an obvious choice, given his mother's nationality and his own inherited land in Pennsylvania. Latrobe was also an admirer of the new United States of America and could see opportunities there, now it was free of its colonial allegiances. He was also facing bankruptcy. In November 1795 he sailed for Norfolk, Virginia, where he arrived in March of the following year. He was the first fully trained European architect–engineer, and had little trouble finding work. He first ventured into engineering but on arrival in Richmond, Virginia, he was commissioned to design the Virginia state penitentiary (1797–8), on a bold semicircular plan. Following this, Latrobe moved to Philadelphia, where, following John Howard's principles, he built the Bank of Pennsylvania, completed in 1801, the first Greek revival building in the country. The Philadelphia waterworks (1798–1801) called upon his engineering skills as well as his abilities as a designer, for the Centre Square pump house in which he recalled the strictly rational neoclassicism of Ledoux.

In these early works in his American career Latrobe drew upon both his engineering and architectural expertise, which the great gentlemen amateur architects Thomas Jefferson and Charles Bulfinch could not. Latrobe also introduced the structure of the architectural profession, as it was evolving in Britain, to America. He took pupils on a formal basis (the most important of whom were Robert Mills and William Strickland) and charged a fixed 5 per cent on his design and supervision of buildings.

Latrobe's professional pre-eminence was marked by his appointment by Thomas Jefferson in 1803 as surveyor of the public buildings of the United States, which gave him the responsibility for overseeing the chequered construction of the Capitol (designed by another amateur, Dr William Thornton), including much work that was destroyed in the British attack in 1814 and substantial interior remodelling thereafter. He also designed the portico of the president's house (the White House) in 1807.

In 1800 Latrobe married Mary Elizabeth Hazlehurst (1771–1841), with whom he had six children, of whom three survived infancy. In 1815 he wrote, with justification, that since 1800 he had been 'the father of Architecture on this side the Atlantic, having been the first who pretended to more than a mechanical knowledge of the Art' (Cohen and Brownell, 2.12). He aimed to be an American Sir William Chambers and to surpass antiquity in his approach to neo-classical architecture.

The Roman Catholic cathedral in Baltimore (1805–1821),

which he designed in two variant styles, the Gothic and the Roman, is considered Latrobe's greatest work. The chosen style for the building was the classical version and Latrobe's beautifully calibrated vaulting and the sequence of domed spaces taking their light from hidden sources owed much to European precedents such as Soufflot's Panthéon in Paris or John Soane's early work at the Bank of England. No American architect had such technical or spatial competence at that date combined with a first-hand knowledge and practice of European neo-classicism.

Latrobe's correspondence and journals show him to have been a thoughtful, sensitive man who was equally versed in the theories of the sublime and the picturesque or in the ideas of appropriate ornament (he introduced a corn cob capital in the American senate) as he was in a practical approach to matters such as acoustics and complex structures such as multiple shell domes. He was a disastrous businessman, however, and found the tortuous patronage and political processes that surrounded his office as surveyor both frustrating and painful. He resigned his post in 1817 and, as had his engineer son Henry in 1816, died of yellow fever on 3 September 1820 in New Orleans, where he was buried in the protestant cemetery.   GILLIAN DARLEY

Sources *The correspondence and miscellaneous papers of Benjamin Henry Latrobe*, ed. J. C. Van Horne and L. W. Forwalt, 3 vols. (1984–8) · *Journals of Benjamin Henry Latrobe*, ed. E. C. Carter and others, 3 vols. (1977–80) · *Engineering drawings of Benjamin Henry Latrobe*, ed. D. H. Stapleton (1980) · *The architectural drawings of Benjamin Henry Latrobe*, ed. J. A. Cohen and C. E. Brownell, 2 vols. (1994) · T. F. Hamlin, *Benjamin Henry Latrobe* (1955) · W. H. Pierson, *American buildings and their architects: the colonial and classical styles* (1970) · Colvin, *Archs.* · M. M. Thomas, 'Latrobe, Benjamin Henry', *ANB*

Archives LMA, accounts and vouchers · Maryland Historical Society, Baltimore

Likenesses C. W. Peale, portrait, *c*.1804, priv. coll. [*see illus.*] · R. Peale, portrait, repro. in Stapleton, ed., *Engineering drawings*, 4; priv. coll.

La Trobe, Charles Joseph (1801–1875), colonial administrator and traveller, born in London on 20 March 1801, was the third son of Christian Ignatius *La Trobe (1758–1836) and his wife, Hannah Sims (or Anna Syms), of Yorkshire. He received a Moravian education, with a view to following his father in the Moravian ministry, but abandoned this for teaching. In 1824 he became tutor to the son of the Count de Pourtalès in Neuchâtel, Switzerland, and soon proved himself a worthy pioneer of the Alpine Club. While mountaineering, he expressed in his diary and later in *The Alpenstock* (1829) the religious feelings inspired by the grandeur of 'the work of the Creator', but dissatisfied with this apparently purposeless way of life, in September 1829 he matriculated at Magdalene College, Cambridge. However, he went back to travelling and in 1830 made a long walking tour in the Tirol, described in *The Pedestrian* (1832), in 1832 went to the USA with his former pupil, and, in 1834, to Mexico.

La Trobe returned to Europe in 1835, and on 16 September he married at Neuchâtel Sophie (1810–1854), the twenty-five-year-old daughter of Auguste de Montmollin,

Charles Joseph La Trobe (1801–1875), by Thomas Woolner, *c*.1853

a Swiss councillor of state; and when he had finished his books, *The Rambler in North America* (1835) and *The Rambler in Mexico* (1836), he needed regular employment. Helped by the influence of his elder brother Peter *Latrobe [*see under* Latrobe, John Antes] in 1837 he was commissioned to report on the education of black West Indians.

Lord Glenelg appreciated La Trobe's reports and in 1838 appointed him superintendent of the Port Phillip district of Australia, despite his administrative inexperience, for a major responsibility there would be the Aboriginal problem. He reached Melbourne on 1 October 1839, where his 'subjects' warmly welcomed him as foreshadowing greater independence from New South Wales, but in this, Governor Sir George Gipps, though personally friendly, controlled his subordinate closely and refused his pleas for more public works and more assisted immigrants. La Trobe was also unable to control the conflict with the Aborigines, although he showed his 'rambling' ability again, in fourteen years making ninety-four journeys all over the district and discovering land routes to Gippsland and Cape Otway, where he was responsible for building the important lighthouse at the entrance to Bass Strait.

Appointed acting-governor of Van Diemen's Land in 1846–7, La Trobe reformed the convict administration and his experience influenced his opposition to the imperial government's attempts to send convicts to Port Phillip in 1848–9; however, his opposition to popular election to the legislature and his failure to win more independence led in 1848 to a petition for his recall. However, in 1851 he was appointed lieutenant-governor of the newly separated colony of Victoria. Here the gold rush tripled the population in three years to 225,000 in 1854, but, while preserving law and order, he avoided conflict with the diggers. By refusing to lease land to the squatters and reserving large areas for small-scale settlement, he avoided a battle for the land, and, by promoting the Convicts Prevention Act, he limited the influx of ex-convicts from Tasmania. In Melbourne he reserved land for public parks, sponsored a piped water supply system and backed plans to establish the public library and the university. Conscientious and impeccably honest, La Trobe served Victorians well.

La Trobe sailed for England on 5 May 1854, after the death of his wife at Neuchâtel on 30 January; she had borne him one son and three daughters. On 3 October

1855 at Neuchâtel, he married his first wife's widowed sister, Rose Isabelle de Meuron, *née* Montmollin (1821–1883), and they had two more daughters. They lived chiefly in Worcester and at Litlington in Sussex. Blindness prevented La Trobe from writing his planned history of Port Phillip, but the pioneers' letters which he had collected for the project were sent to Melbourne and published in 1898. Made a CB in November 1858, and belatedly given a small pension (£333 6s. 8d.) in 1865, La Trobe died on 4 December 1875 at his home, Clapham House, Litlington, leaving £15,905. He was buried at Litlington, but in 1878 his family built a memorial chapel at Neuchâtel, to which the Victorian government donated a window on its centenary.   A. G. L. SHAW

Sources A. G. L. Shaw, 'Governor La Trobe', *Victorian Historical Journal*, 61 (1990), 17–32 • A. Gross, *Charles Joseph La Trobe* (1956) • *Gipps–La Trobe correspondence, 1839–1846*, ed. A. G. L. Shaw (1989) • L. J. Blake, ed., *Letters of Charles Joseph La Trobe* (1975) • K. Fitzpatrick, 'Charles Joseph La Trobe', *Victorian Historical Journal*, 47 (1976), 253–64 • G. Serle, *The golden age: a history of the colony of Victoria, 1851–1861* (1963) • D. McCaughey, N. Perkins, and A. Trumble, *Victoria's colonial governors, 1839–1900* (1993) • G. Serle, 'Noble vision and harsh realities: C. J. La Trobe and early Victoria', *Victorian Historical Journal*, 47 (1976), 265–76 • Garryowen [E. Finn], *The chronicles of early Melbourne, 1835 to 1852*, centennial edn, 2 vols. (1888) • J. Eastwood, 'La Trobe, Charles Joseph', *AusDB*, vol. 2 • M. Cannon, *Old Melbourne town* (1991) • D. Walker, *Beacons of hope: early history of Cape Otway and King Island lighthouses* (1991) • 'Report on negro education', *Parl. papers* (1837–8), 48.61, no. 113, 48.159, no. 520 [Jamaica, and Windward and Leeward Islands]; (1839), 34.455, no. 35 [British Guiana and Trinidad] • 'Correspondence on … convict discipline and transportation', *Parl. papers* (1847–8), 52.33–79, no. 941 [despatch on convicts in Van Diemen's Land] • *CGPLA Eng. & Wales* (1875)
Archives Public Record Office, Victoria, Australia, corresp. as superintendent and lieutenant-governor • State Library of Victoria, Melbourne | Public Record Office, Victoria, Australia, Colonial Office, UK, inward corresp. • State Archives of New South Wales, Sydney, colonial secretary's archives, New South Wales, letters
Likenesses W. Brockedon, chalk drawing, 1835, NPG • F. Grant, oils, c.1851–1854, town hall, Melbourne • T. Woolner, bronze medallion, 1853, State Library of Victoria, Melbourne, La Trobe picture collection • T. Woolner, bronze medallion, c.1853, NPG [see illus.] • F. Grant, oils, 1854?, La Trobe's Cottage [National Trust of Australia], Victoria • S. Bellin, portrait, NPG • F. Grant, oils (after F. Grant), State Library of Victoria, Melbourne, La Trobe picture collection • photograph (after S. Bellin), State Library of Victoria, Melbourne, La Trobe picture collection • photograph (after portrait at Neuchâtel), State Library of Victoria, Melbourne, La Trobe picture collection • portrait, Neuchâtel, Switzerland
Wealth at death £15,905: Eastwood, 'La Trobe' • £1500: probate, 21 Dec 1875, *CGPLA Eng. & Wales*

La Trobe, Christian Ignatius (1758–1836), Moravian minister and composer, was born on 12 February 1758 at Fulneck in Yorkshire. He was the eldest son of Benjamin *La Trobe (1728–1786), a Moravian minister, and Anna Margaretta (1728–1794), deaconess and daughter of Henry Antes of Pennsylvania. Benjamin Henry *Latrobe (1764–1820), architect, was his younger brother. Raised from infancy as a Moravian, La Trobe was educated from his early teens in Germany, first at the Moravian school at Niesky, Upper Lusatia, and then at the Moravian seminary at Barby near Magdeburg. In 1779 he returned to the school as a tutor and he taught the organ, his principal instrument. In 1784

La Trobe went to London, where he lived for fifty years. Ordained in 1788, he ministered at the Moravian chapel in the City, but he did not consider himself suited for the ministry. Instead he found his proper calling and life's work as secretary to the Moravian Brethren's Society for the Furtherance of the Gospel to the Heathen, a position which he held with considerable distinction from 1787 until 1834.

La Trobe's skill as a propagandist soon manifested itself. In 1788 he prepared at the request of Bishop Beilby Porteus a masterly treatise on the conduct of Moravian missions to slaves in the West Indies. This was well received by the government's inquiry that year into the slave trade and published as part of its evidence. In 1790 La Trobe initiated the publication of the *Periodical Accounts* of Moravian missions, an influential quarterly journal which stimulated interest in foreign missions in general, and support for the church's work overseas. The importance of his role at the interface of the British world was recognized in 1795 when La Trobe was relieved of ministerial responsibilities, raised to presbyter and appointed secretary of the international Moravian church in Britain, the 'Unitas Fratrum', in succession to James Hutton.

La Trobe, well known in evangelical circles, moved easily between denominations, and founders of new missionary societies sought his advice. In 1815 William Wilberforce, who had known him since 1788, described him 'truly as the head and hands [in England] of the Moravian mission and who manages much of their correspondence all over the world'. He was also 'a man of education, gentlemanly manners, good sense & piety, both in principle and practice'. La Trobe's comment on this was typically self-effacing (W. Wilberforce to Lord Caledon, 2 March 1815, Transactions with Government, copies, C. I. La Trobe, Moravian Church House, London).

One result of La Trobe's successful visitation in 1815–16 to the mission at the Cape of Good Hope was the publication of his *Journal of a Visit to South Africa* (1818) and the posthumous *Letters to my Children* (1851). Both unwittingly reveal the man—devout, but most companionable, and energetic in mind and body.

La Trobe received 'excellent musical instruction … in Germany' (La Trobe, *Letters*, v) where study in 1779 of Haydn's *Stabat mater* was particularly influential. A determination that his gifts should serve his Christian faith is apparent from La Trobe's six-volume *Selection of Sacred Music from the Works of the most Eminent Composers of Germany and Italy* (1806–26). This introduced works mainly new to the British public, arranged in a manner suited for home and amateur use. That many were composed for the Catholic church reflected his own and Moravian thinking. It is on this innovative project that his reputation for 'exerting a quiet influence on music' rests (Holmes, 249). La Trobe assisted Charles Burney, and Vincent Novello benefited from his outstanding music library. His own compositions and his editions of Moravian hymn tunes are considered essential for the study of the church's music.

On 25 November 1790 La Trobe was happily married to the Moravian Hannah Benigna Syms (1758–1824). Their six children all had 'musical souls' (La Trobe, *Letters*, 27) and he ensured that the four boys, including Charles Joseph *La Trobe, were well educated by Moravians at Fulneck. His eldest son, Peter *Latrobe (1795–1863) [*see under* Latrobe, John Antes], his assistant from 1821, succeeded him in the posts that he held. In 1834 La Trobe retired to Fairfield, the settlement at Droylsden, near Manchester. There he died on 6 May 1836 and was buried on 12 May.

JOHN C. S. MASON

Sources 'Historical sketch of the connection of the LaTrobe family', *Periodical Accounts Relating to the Missions of the Church of the United Brethren Established among the Heathen*, 25 (1864), 81–4 · J. Mason, 'Christian Ignatius La Trobe, 1758–1836', in J. Mason and L. Torrode, *Three generations of the La Trobe family in the Moravian Church* (1997), 16–28 · J. C. S. Mason, *The Moravian church and the missionary awakening in England, 1760–1800* (2001) · C. I. La Trobe, *Letters to my children* (1851) · C. E. Stevens, 'The musical works of Christian Ignatius Latrobe', PhD diss., University of North Carolina at Chapel Hill, 1971, appx A [The correspondence of Charles Burney, Vincent Novello and Christian I. Latrobe] · E. Holmes, 'The Rev. Christian Ignatius LaTrobe', *MT*, 4 (1850–52), 249–50, 255–6 · Moravian church archives, Moravian Church House, London · Moravian church archives, Fulneck, near Leeds, Yorkshire · Moravian church archives, Fairfield, Droylsden, near Manchester · N. Temperly, 'Latrobe, Christian Ignatius', *New Grove* · F. R. Bradlow, introduction, in C. I. Latrobe, *Journal of a visit to South Africa in 1815 and 1816* (1969) [facs. of 1818 edn]
Archives JRL, journal, English MS 1244 · Moravian church archives, Moravian Church House, London, corresp. and papers · priv. coll. · Yale U., Beinecke L. | Moravian church archives, Fulneck, near Leeds, Yorkshire · Moravian church archives, Fairfield, Droylsden, near Manchester · U. Edin., New Coll. L., letters to Thomas Chalmers
Likenesses T. Barber, oils, State Library of Victoria, Melbourne, La Trobe picture collection · S. Bellin, mezzotint (after T. Barber), BM, NPG
Wealth at death insignificant; left MSS to eldest son: will, 1837

Latrobe [La Trobe], **John Antes** (1799–1878), writer on music, was born in London, the son of the composer Christian Ignatius *La Trobe (1758–1836) and his wife, Hannah Benigna Sims (1758–1824). His family was originally of Huguenot descent, and he was named after the Moravian composer John Antes, of whom his father was a nephew. He received his education at St Edmund Hall, Oxford (BA 1826; MA 1829), and then took orders in the Church of England. He served as curate at Melton Mowbray, Tintern (Monmouthshire), and other places before finally becoming incumbent of St Thomas's, Kendal, a post which he held from 1840 to 1865. In 1858 he was made an honorary canon of Carlisle Cathedral.

Latrobe was the author of *The Music of the Church Considered in its Various Branches, Congregational and Choral* (1831), a book which was much valued in its day and which, despite its rather stilted language, provides a good description of Anglican church music before the Oxford Movement. His other publications included *Instructions of Chenaniah: Plain Directions for Accompanying the Chant or Psalm Tune* (1832), *Scripture Illustrations* (1838), and two volumes of original poetry, *The Solace of Song* (1837) and *Sacred Lays and Lyrics* (1850). He compiled the hymnbook used in his church at Kendal, in which several of his own hymns

were included. He died, unmarried, at Westmorland Villas, Cromwell Street, Gloucester, where he had been living in retirement, on 19 November 1878.

His brother **Peter Latrobe** (1795–1863) took orders in the Moravian church, and succeeded his father as secretary to the Moravian mission, also known as the Missions of the United Brethren in England. (His grandfather, Benjamin Latrobe, had been superintendent of the Moravian Brethren in England.) He too had musical talent, both as an organist and composer, and he wrote an 'Introduction on the progress of the church psalmody' for an edition of *The Moravian Hymn Book*, which demonstrated his extensive knowledge of the subject. He resided at 27 Ely Place, London, and died on 24 September 1863 at Berthelsdorf, Saxony.

Their brother Charles Joseph *La Trobe became lieutenant-governor of Victoria, Australia.

J. C. HADDEN, rev. DAVID J. GOLBY

Sources N. Temperley, 'Latrobe, Christian Ignatius', *New Grove* · *Brief notices of the Latrobe family* (1864) · J. Eastwood, 'La Trobe, Charles Joseph', *AusDB*, vol. 2 · *CGPLA Eng. & Wales* (1878) · *CGPLA Eng. & Wales* (1863) [Peter Latrobe]
Wealth at death under £4000: probate, 27 Dec 1878, *CGPLA Eng. & Wales* · under £3000—Peter Latrobe: probate, 2 Dec 1863, *CGPLA Eng. & Wales*

Latrobe, Peter (1795–1863). *See under* Latrobe, John Antes (1799–1878).

Latter, Mary (*bap.* 1722, *d.* 1777), author, was baptized at Frilsham, Berkshire, on 12 January 1722, the only child of George and Mary Latter. There is no evidence that, as early accounts stated, her birthplace was Henley-on-Thames. Her grandfather was probably the Revd Thomas Latter, rector of Frilsham from 1691 until his death in 1730. Mary subsequently recalled the idyllic years of her childhood, at large in the countryside and reading established English authors to educate herself. This agreeable spell ended when her father died, some time before 1740. He is said to have been a country attorney, but his widow and daughter were left badly off, and they moved to Reading. There they opened a linen draper's and milliner's shop in Butcher Row, but business was poor. Even so, Mary claimed to have enjoyed a busy social life, even being jilted by a well-connected suitor.

Mary Latter early developed a gift for poetic satire, and in the *Reading Mercury* of 17 November 1740 she had to disown, in verse, a sarcastic ditty she had written on 'the persons and characters of some ladies in Reading'. After her mother died in 1748, she was reduced to taking in lodgers. Despite support from some influential patrons, notably the antiquary John Loveday (1711–1789), of Caversham, and John Spicer, headmaster of Reading School, authorship brought in very little money.

In 1759 Mary published by subscription her *Miscellaneous Works, in Prose and Verse*. Although a commentator discerned 'some strokes of genius' in the volume (*Critical Review*, August 1759), it was an ill thought out mixture of a short epistolary novel with essays, letters, and verses. Latter wrote: 'My present Residence is not very far from the Market-Place, where I continue immersed in Business and in Debt … sometimes madly hoping to gain a Competency; sometimes facing Dungeons and Distress' (Latter, *Miscellaneous Works*, 80). The last-named fear became reality when she was imprisoned for debt.

Rescue from this cycle of poverty appeared to be at hand in 1761. A friend of Mary showed John Rich, manager of Covent Garden Theatre, the unfinished manuscript of her tragedy, *The Siege of Jerusalem*. Rich took the trouble to visit Reading and advance her 5 guineas, and later added £10 to clear her debts. He invited her to stay in his London home for ten weeks, allowing her to gain knowledge of playwriting by frequenting theatres. He also obtained a hundred subscriptions, at 5s. each, for *A Miscellaneous Poetical Essay* (1761), dedicated to George, first Baron Lyttelton; once again, she spread her talents too thinly. She helped Rich in revising some theatrical manuscripts, but that November he died. His successors at Covent Garden turned down *The Siege of Jerusalem*, as being of preposterous length and as too scholarly. Undaunted, she had it published in 1763, adding 'an essay on the mystery and mischiefs of stagecraft'; she was bitter at being dismissed as 'an indigent, illiterate, impertinent *female* Scribbler' (Latter, *Siege of Jerusalem*, ix). For good measure, she included a 'Lyric Ode on the Birth of the Prince of Wales', the future George IV.

In 1764 Mary Latter published her most accomplished work, a burlesque poem, *Liberty and Interest*, held by friends and commentators alike to demonstrate a lively imagery and both wit and satire reminiscent of the work of Jonathan Swift. Her only subsequent writing was *Pro and Con, or, The Opinionists* (1771), equally jumbled in its critical, political, and esoteric ideas, which led some commentators to doubt her sanity. Unlike the later Hampshire author, Mary Russell Mitford, in *Our Village* (1824–32) and *Belford Regis* (1835), Latter did not use her literary gifts of keen observation and gentle social satire to offer sketches of life in Reading and its environs. Instead, her work suffered from an obsession with the poverty that afflicted her throughout her adult life and with an associated persecution mania. Mary Latter died, unmarried, on 4 March 1777 after a very long, probably psychiatric, illness, at her home in Butcher Row where she had lately been a bookseller. She was buried on 10 March, near the grave of her mother in St Laurence's churchyard, Reading.

T. A. B. CORLEY

Sources DNB · C. Coates, *The history and antiquities of Reading* (1802), 447–8 · J. Doran, *The history and antiquities of Reading* (1835), 275 · J. Todd, ed., *A dictionary of British and American women writers, 1660–1800* (1984) · S. Markham, *John Loveday of Caversham, 1711–1789* (1984), 431–2 · M. Latter, *Miscellaneous works, in prose and verse* (1759) · M. Latter, *The siege of Jerusalem, and essay on the mystery and mischiefs of stagecraft* (1763) · *Reading Mercury* (17 Nov 1740) · *Reading Mercury* (10 March 1777) · *The letters of David Garrick*, ed. D. M. Little and G. M. Kahrl, 3 vols. (1963) · parish register, Frilsham, Berkshire, 12 Jan 1722 [baptism] · parish register, St Laurence's, Reading, 9 Jan 1748 [burial, mother] · parish register, St Laurence's, Reading, 10 March 1777 [burial]

Latter, Thomas (1816–1853), army officer in the East India Company and Burmese scholar, son of Major Barré Latter, an officer who distinguished himself in the Anglo-Nepal War of 1814–16, was born in India. He obtained a commission as ensign in 1836 from the East India Company in the 67th Bengal native infantry, then stationed in Arakan. He was promoted lieutenant in 1840. At Arakan he devoted his leisure to the study of the Burmese language, and in 1845 published a Burmese grammar, which (although subsequent to the primers of Adoniram Judson, the American missionary) was the first recognized scholarly treatise on the subject. At the start of the negotiations respecting breaches of the treaty of Yandabo (1826), Latter left his regiment to serve on attachment as chief interpreter to Commodore Lambert's expedition, and on the outbreak of the Second Anglo-Burmese War he served Sir Henry Thomas Godwin in the same capacity. On 14 April 1852 he led the storming-party against the eastern entrance of the Shwedagon pagoda at Rangoon, and acted so gallantly in the assault that Laurie, the historian of the war, called him the 'Chevalier Bayard of the expedition'. He took part in the capture of Pegu in June 1852, and when shortly afterwards the town of Prome, which was one of the chief rallying places of the enemy, was occupied, Latter was on 30 December 1852 appointed resident deputy commissioner. The post was rendered very difficult by the fact that, although open warfare had ceased, the Burmese were still hostile, a state of affairs which continued until the definitive treaty of 1862. The vigilance and determination which Latter exhibited in repressing disaffection in the neighbourhood of Prome during the following year made him specially hated by the Burmese court, and at two o'clock on the morning of 8 December 1853 he was murdered in his bed. He was buried at Prome with military honours on the following day.

THOMAS SECCOMBE, *rev.* JAMES FALKNER

Sources *East-India Register and Directory* (1837) · *East-India Register and Directory* (1844) · *East-India Register and Army List* (1853–4) · *East-India Register and Army List* (1854) · W. F. B. Laurie, *Our Burmese wars and relations with Burma: being an abstract of military and political operations* (1880)

Lattimore, Owen (1900–1989), Mongolist and Sinologist, second son of David Lattimore (1874–1965) and his wife, Margaret Barnes (1873–1958), was born in Sibley Hospital, Washington, DC, on 29 July 1900. His father was a language teacher who accepted a job with the Chinese government teaching English and French in 1901. Owen was raised in Shanghai, Paotingfu (Baodingfu), and Peking (Beijing); the children were educated at home. In 1912 Margaret Lattimore took their five children to Switzerland for formal schooling. Owen was enrolled at the *collège classique cantonal* in Lausanne until war broke out in 1914; he was then sent to St Bees School, Cumberland (1914–19), where he flourished although he failed to secure a place at Oxford. Years later, he was glad that he had not attended Oxford. He felt that he would have emerged 'an insufferable aesthete' like Evelyn Waugh or Aldous Huxley, or would perhaps have been influenced by one of the extremist ideologies of the day, fascism or Marxism, which would have pre-empted the strong empirical bent that dominated his scholarship.

After returning to China in 1919 Lattimore obtained a job with the British trading firm Arnhold & Co., first in Tientsin (Tianjin), then in Shanghai. He learned Chinese and frequently travelled to the interior, where he learned much about politics, economics, banditry, landlordism, and peasant unrest.

On 4 March 1926 Lattimore married Eleanor (1895–1970), daughter of Dr T. F. Holgate, a Northwestern University dean then living in China. The story of their honeymoon trip through central Asia was told in Owen's *Desert Road to Turkestan* (1929) and *High Tartary* (1930), and in Eleanor's *Turkestan Reunion* (1934). From India they went to Italy, England, and the United States.

From 1928 to 1929 Lattimore studied anthropology at Harvard, after which he obtained grants including the Royal Geographical Society's Cuthbert Peek grant, that enabled him to travel widely in the Chinese areas bordering the USSR between 1929 and 1934. He emerged from this study vigorously hostile toward Japanese aggression, and dedicated to the welfare of the Mongols whose autonomy he espoused for the rest of his life. He also developed the appreciation for the Soviet minority policies in central Asia that later was interpreted by American cold-warriors as pro-communist. The Mongols and other minorities that he studied had kin on the Soviet side of the Sino-Soviet border; 'democracy' to them meant the educational and economic opportunities afforded by the USSR, which contrasted strongly with Chinese repression. This was what Lattimore called Russia's 'power of attraction' for the central Asian peoples; this was a phrase that, in mid-century America, was held to be pro-communist.

In 1934 Lattimore became editor of *Pacific Affairs*, the major journal of the Institute of Pacific Relations, which he edited from a base in China. By 1937 Japanese depredations made it impossible to continue working there. Isaiah Bowman, president of Johns Hopkins University in Baltimore, offered Lattimore a job lecturing and shortly thereafter as head of the Page School of International Relations at Johns Hopkins.

In 1941 President Roosevelt nominated Lattimore political adviser to Chaing Kai-shek. Lattimore had never met Chiang but thought him the only person with the stature to lead China against the Japanese. In 1942 Lattimore resigned from Chiang's service to direct the Pacific operation of the American office of war information. He was then asked by Roosevelt to accompany Vice-President Henry Wallace's mission to Siberia and China in 1944.

After a short return to Johns Hopkins, Lattimore served on the Pauley reparations mission in Tokyo from December 1945 to January 1946. Back at Johns Hopkins, he organized a programme of Mongol studies and published some 350 articles between 1945 and 1950, many of them scholarly but most popular discussions of world affairs. His first mass-market book, *Solution in Asia* (1945), advocated entrepreneurial enterprise freed from European colonial control and endemic corruption as in China. Among many international academic honours he received by this time was the Royal Geographical Society's patron's medal (1942).

But events in China did not go as Lattimore hoped. Instead of promoting political and economic liberalization the nationalist government concentrated on destroying Mao's forces, with the aid of American arms and transport. This did not work; as whole nationalist armies defected with their American equipment to the communists, Lattimore became the most prominent exponent of the heresy that aid to Chiang was throwing good money after bad. And since Mao had won without significant Soviet aid, the people's republic established in 1949 was not a creature of the Kremlin hence not part of a monolithic world communist conspiracy. With the defeat of the American Eighth Army in Korea in 1950, this 'Mao was independent' heresy became intolerable in Washington.

In 1950 Senator Joseph McCarthy selected Lattimore not only as the scapegoat on whom to blame the 'loss' of China, but as the 'top Soviet spy' in the United States, the 'boss' of the ring to which Alger Hiss had allegedly belonged. Democratic senator Pat McCarran, a ferocious supporter of Chiang and of Francisco Franco, in 1951 assembled a senate internal security sub-committee of like-minded ultra-conservatives to probe the Institute of Pacific Relations and Lattimore as its former editor. For twelve days in 1951 Lattimore was questioned by McCarran and his sub-committee, the longest interrogation in senate history up to then. He emerged bloody but unbowed; McCarran, on the basis of testimony by former communist witnesses who were known by the FBI to be mendacious, declared him a 'conscious, articulate instrument of the Soviet conspiracy' (*Institute of Pacific Relations Report*, p. 224) and persuaded the attorney-general to indict him for perjury in December 1952. The FBI was not consulted as to whether this indictment should be sought and indeed their five costly and extensive evaluations concluded that there was no perjury (or any other) case against him. A federal judge threw out most counts of the indictment, but not until June 1955 did Attorney-General Brownell dismiss the case.

Johns Hopkins kept Lattimore on during the inquisition, but the post-indictment years there were a torment to him. He no longer had a public audience, and right-wing professors constantly attacked him. In 1963 the University of Leeds asked him to head a new department of Chinese studies, organizing it as he saw fit. He accepted gladly. At Leeds he was able to incorporate all that he believed necessary to sound scholarship: language, literature, history, economics, geography, anthropology, and sociology. Leeds's willingness to ignore conventional disciplinary boundaries, which had been stultifying at Johns Hopkins, was to Lattimore a *summum bonum*. He counted the years at Leeds the most satisfying of his life. He acquired a new audience, and his public appearances returned to what had been normal before McCarthy, with the BBC and *Times Literary Supplement* the most prominent outlets. The Foreign Office asked him to interpret for the queen when the new Mongolian ambassador presented his credentials on 14 November 1963. He gave the Chichele lectures at the University of Oxford in May 1965.

In 1961 the Mongolian people's republic invited Lattimore to visit and he visited Ulan Bator almost every year from then until he was too old to travel, becoming a major force in the small but active world of Mongol scholarship. In 1969 he became the only foreigner to hold full membership of the Mongolian Academy of Sciences, an honour that he prized above all others. Even the USSR decided in the 1960s that, capitalist apologist or not, his ideas were worth hearing, and he spent extensive periods in Moscow and Soviet Central Asia. He was invited to lecture and advise at every centre of Asian studies in Europe. As he put it in a letter to the *New York Times*, the 'outrageous Department of Justice indictment became an international passport' (23 March 1972).

In 1970 Lattimore retired from Leeds but his wife's death the same year deprived him of the support and domestic discipline that had made his earlier writings possible. From 1970 to 1985 he wandered ceaselessly. As professor emeritus at Leeds from 1970 he still visited the department to work with colleagues and students and sporadically to lecture, but his main residence was at Paris (1973–9) and then Cambridge (1979–85) where honorary links to the university and King's College gave some institutional stability in a period otherwise marked by great restlessness.

Many of Lattimore's books became classics, especially *Inner Asian Frontiers of China* (1962), but his major claim to fame was the clarity and prescience of his many predictive judgements. What were once heresies, at the turn of the century appear to be perceptive and well informed analyses of the countries of the Far East and central Asia and their relations with the West. To beleaguered American liberals, and perhaps some British people, his most important legacy was proof that it was possible for a single individual to prevail against a powerful committee of the American senate, without knuckling under, confessing imagined sins, or running away.

In 1985 Lattimore moved to Pawtucket, Rhode Island, to be near his only son, David, and six grandchildren. He was frail, but still keen of mind. He died there of pneumonia on 31 May 1989; his ashes were to be scattered on a mountain in Mongolia.   ROBERT P. NEWMAN

Sources R. P. Newman, *Owen Lattimore and the 'loss' of China* (1992) · L. Cong., manuscript division, Owen Lattimore MSS · interviews with O. Lattimore by R. P. Newman, 1977–87, priv. coll. · Federal Bureau of Investigation, HQ File, 100–24628, Owen Lattimore, espionage—R [for Russia] · *Owen Lattimore: China memoirs*, ed. F. Isono (1990) · O. Lattimore, *Ordeal by slander* (1950) · J. Cotton, *Asian frontier nationalism* (1989) · *Institute of Pacific Relations report* (Washington, DC, 1952), 224 [82nd congress, 2nd session] · private information (2004) [D. Lattimore]
Archives L. Cong., collection · priv. coll., papers | FILM BFI NFTVA, 'On the edge of the Gobi', 10 Dec 1975 | SOUND BL NSA, current affairs recording · BL NSA, performance recording · BL NSA, recorded lecture · priv. coll., tapes
Likenesses photograph, repro. in Newman, *Owen Lattimore*

Wealth at death £8097 in England and Wales: administration with will, 26 March 1990, *CGPLA Eng. & Wales*

Latto, William Duncan [*pseud.* Tammas Bodkin] (1823–1899), author and newspaper editor, was born on 4 April 1823 in Hurrel's Wynd, near Ceres, in the county of Fife, the natural son of Thomas Latto and Cecilia Methvan; one Catherine Duncan took responsibility for his upbringing (and was named as his mother by Latto's son on the death certificate). He achieved enormous fame in Victorian Scotland for his vernacular Scots essays, written under the pen-name Tammas Bodkin. Latto was perhaps the greatest of the pioneering generation of journalists who brought the burgeoning Scottish popular press into being following the repeal of the Stamp Act in 1855, and his influence on Scottish popular culture was incalculably great. Under his editorship (1860–98) the *People's Journal* grew from a local working-class paper circulating in Dundee and its hinterland into the leading popular weekly in Scotland.

Latto was brought up in poverty and received only the most rudimentary of formal schooling. At the age of fourteen he became a hand-loom weaver in the village of Ceres and his lifelong involvement in radical politics began. He was an active 'physical force' Chartist and free trader and became one of the first members of the new Free Church in Ceres when it was founded in 1843. Like many intellectuals of his generation in Scotland, he was largely self-taught. He studied English, with a copy of *Lennie's Grammar* attached to his loom. The Free Church minister lent him books and helped him with his Latin. He became teacher of a small subscription school at Baldinnie, near Ceres, and soon he was able to afford a bursary place at the Free Church Training College at Moray House in Edinburgh. In October 1849 he became the Free Church schoolmaster of the fishing village of Johnshaven, near Inverbervie, in Kincardineshire. He married a Johnshaven woman, Margaret Findlay, on 1 January 1853 in the parish of Benholm, Kincardineshire. They had eight children, five of whom died in infancy.

When the Dundee-based *People's Journal*, a radical working-class newspaper, started up on 2 January 1858, Latto, who already enjoyed a reputation as writer for periodicals, contributed a current affairs column in vernacular Scots as well as leading articles and reviews. When its sister paper, the *Dundee Advertiser*, went daily he gave up schoolteaching and became editor of the *People's Journal* in his own right. He continued his involvement in radical politics as secretary of the East of Scotland Reform Union, campaigning to extend the franchise, and in the columns of his paper he campaigned tirelessly for social and economic reform.

The most distinctive aspect of the *People's Journal* under Latto was that it was substantially written, as well as read, by working people. He commissioned leading articles, prominently printed under the heading 'The people's opinion', and actively sought imaginative writing from the readers, including stories, poetry, songs, and tunes, and even running an advice column for the authors of

William Duncan Latto (1823–1899), by unknown photographer

rejected manuscripts. The response rapidly became so great that a separate supplement and then a separate weekly, the *People's Friend*, had to be started with its own editorial staff. When Professor David Masson estimated in the early 1880s that about 200,000 people in Scotland regularly wrote poetry, this was in no small degree owing to the growth of the new mass popular literary market in Scotland spearheaded by Latto and his papers.

Latto was fertile in the creation and commissioning of features which reflected his own and his readers' passionate interest in Scottish popular culture: there were frequent series on folklore, popular song, and every aspect of social and economic history, particularly as affecting the common people. Later there was a women's column, a children's section, medical and legal advice, and some of the earliest cartoon strips to appear in the British or American press.

Latto's own powers as an essayist were developed in his Tammas Bodkin column, written in a memorably rich and inventive vernacular Scots. It began in the *People's Journal* in 1861 and ran for more than thirty years. The adventures of the fictional main character, Tammas Bodkin, a tailor in Dundee, were used as a vehicle for ideas on a wide range of social, economic, and political issues. Selections of the essays were several times published in book form, but compared to the sardonic, genial, intellectual figure who appears in the original source, the book Bodkin, severely starched and trimmed for the middle-class literary market, was rather tame and conventional. Latto was one of the most important writers in vernacular Scots since the Enlightenment; but most of his best work is at present available only in the original newspaper sources. When Latto relinquished the editor's chair at the age of seventy-five the *People's Journal* had thirteen different editions with a combined circulation of nearly a quarter of a million copies a week, the largest of any weekly paper published outside London.

Latto died of pneumonia barely six months after his retirement at Bridgend of Straloch, Kirkmichael, Perthshire, on Sunday 16 July 1899. He was buried in Westerton cemetery, Dundee.   WILLIAM DONALDSON

Sources W. Donaldson, *Popular literature in Victorian Scotland* (1986) · W. Donaldson, ed., *The language of the people* (1989) · *Dundee Yearbook* (1899), 68–71 · *Biographical Magazine* (April 1887), 334–49 · parish register (birth/baptism), 4 April and 3 Sept 1823, Ceres, Fife · parish register (marriage), 1 Jan 1853, Benholm, Kincardineshire · d. cert.

Likenesses photograph, *c*.1887, repro. in *Biographical Magazine*, 334–5 · photograph, *c*.1890, repro. in Donaldson, *Popular literature in Victorian Scotland*, 46 · photograph, repro. in Donaldson, *The language of the people* [see illus.]

Wealth at death £1014 7s. 10d.: confirmation, 28 Sept 1899, *CCI*

Latymer, Edward (*c*.1559–1627), legal official and educational benefactor, was born in Ipswich, Suffolk, the son of William *Latymer (1498/9–1583), dean of Peterborough, and his wife, Ellen or Helena (*d*. 1603), whose son from a former marriage, Edmund English (*d*. 1603), was a major benefactor of Emmanuel College, Cambridge. Save for the fact that he may have been the Edward Latimer who matriculated as a pensioner at St John's College, Cambridge, in 1571, nothing is known of his life until 1584, when he acted as executor of his father's will. In 1591 he acted with Sir Francis Gawdy (a relation by marriage of Edmund English) as agent in the acquisition by Sir Henry Warner of the tithes and patronage of Mildenhall in Suffolk.

On 11 June 1594 Latymer was appointed deputy and clerk to William Fleetwood, receiver-general of the court of wards and liveries, and in Trinity term 1601 he became one of the two attorneys in the same court, in which capacity he served until his death. From 1597 or earlier he lived in the parish of St Dunstan-in-the-West, London, latterly in a house in Ram Alley off Fleet Street. Early in 1615 he acquired for £100 a house and small estate, worth £8 a year, at Edmonton in Middlesex. In June 1622 he purchased the manor of Butterwick, near Hammersmith, with many other parcels of land in the parish of Fulham, for £1600, but there is no reason to believe that he ever lived there. In the same year he apparently founded and generously endowed a hospital, probably in Hull, but conceivably elsewhere; when the Hull antiquary Abraham Pryme found deeds relating to it nearly eighty years later, all memory of it had apparently already been lost.

Latymer died unmarried at his house in Ram Alley on 14 January 1627, aged 'about 67' according to the heralds' funeral certificate, and was buried in the St Dunstan's burying-ground of St Anne's Chapel on 20 January following; it is likely that the officiating priest was the vicar of St Dunstan, John Donne, whom Latymer mentioned several times in his will.

Latymer's will is dated 16 March 1625. Apart from monetary and valued bequests totalling £3361 10s. 2d., of which £450 was on trust for express charitable purposes, it specifies his intentions with regard to his property, referring to an indenture dated 20 March by which he made the bulk of it over to various groups of feoffees. A parcel of 5¾ acres in Fulham parish was to be held for the benefit of the poor of St Dunstan-in-the-West. The income of a further 28½ acres in the same parish, including the Butterwick property, was to pay for the education and clothing of eight poor boys and the clothing and sustenance of six poor men of the town of Hammersmith. The remaining lands in Fulham and his property in Edmonton were to meet the education and clothing of eight poor boys from the latter parish. In each case Latymer specified that the juvenile beneficiaries were to wear doublets with a 'Latymers crosse' on their sleeve. The transfer of property was accomplished by the executors in the course of 1627 and 1628, and the charities were in operation thereafter. Despite a challenge to the will mounted in the prerogative court and then in chancery by Bartrum Themilthorpe, one of Latymer's kinsmen (whose legitimacy was contested), its dispositions stood, and have lasted in Hammersmith in the form of Latymer Upper School, a boys' independent school, and Godolphin and Latymer School, a girls' school refounded in 1906 by means of a substantial donation and annuity from the Latymer foundation; while in Edmonton, the Latymer School, which became a state school under the terms of the Education Act of 1944, is a direct descendant of Latymer's original charity.

C. E. A. CHEESMAN

Sources W. Wheatley, *The history of Edward Latymer and his foundations*, 2nd edn (1953) · will, 1583, PRO, PROB 11/66, fol. 213v [William Latymer] · will, 1625, PRO, PROB 11/151, fol. 115 [Edward Latymer] · funeral certificate, 1627, Coll. Arms, record MS I. 23/22b · *The diary of Abraham de la Pryme, the Yorkshire antiquary*, ed. C. Jackson, SurtS, 54 (1870) · churchwardens' accounts, St Dunstan-in-the-West, GL · will, 1602, PRO, PROB 11/101, fol. 198v [Edmund English] · Venn, *Alum. Cant.*

Archives PRO, corresp., wards 14/3/20/2

Wealth at death monetary and valued bequests amounted to £3361 10s. 2d.; also left specified property with total annual value of £44 5s. 4d: will, PRO, PROB 11/151, fol. 115

Latymer [Latimer], William (1498/9–1583), dean of Peterborough and biographer of Anne Boleyn, was the second son of William Latymer, a gentleman of Freston, Suffolk, and Anne Bokinge. He was educated at Corpus Christi College, Cambridge, reading canon law and arts and graduating MA in 1536. He has occasionally been confused both with William Latimer, the Oxford scholar and rector of Saintbury in Gloucestershire, and with Hugh Latimer, the bishop of Worcester and Marian martyr. He is not known to have been related to either.

Perhaps through Matthew Parker, also of Corpus Christi, Latymer was brought to the notice of Anne Boleyn. He became one of her chaplains, charged with obtaining evangelical books for her. When, in 1535, a young Cambridge student named Tristram Revell angled for her patronage by translating a work by Francis Lambert for presentation to Anne, he tried to get it to her through Latymer. The gift was eventually declined, partly on the advice of Hugh Latimer. In January 1536 Latymer received his first recorded benefice, Stackpole in Pembrokeshire. A few months later he was in the Low Countries collecting books on behalf of the queen, probably from the Antwerp dealers who were supplying the English market with evangelical books. On his arrival back at Sandwich in Kent on 7 May, he was greeted with the news that his mistress was in the Tower for treason. He surrendered his books and papers for inspection, and the Sandwich authorities had him escorted to London.

Latymer survived this crisis and in September 1538 succeeded Thomas Starkey as master of the College of St Laurence Pountney in London. He remained master until the college's dissolution in 1547. He was also rector of Witnesham, Suffolk, in 1538–54 (a living in the presentation of his brother). His later benefices included Speldhurst, Kent (1558–53), St Mary Abchurch (1553–4, 1556–61), St George's, Southwark (1559–61), Kirkton and Shotley, Suffolk (1559–83), and Leake Magna, Nottingham (from 1568).

Latymer identified himself with the thoroughgoing protestantism of the reign of Edward VI, preaching at Paul's Cross on the sacrament of the altar. He was one of the proctors for the diocese of Norwich and voted in favour of clerical marriage at convocation in 1547. He took advantage of this provision, marrying Ellen, the widow of Michael English (who was however not the prominent wool merchant of that name). In the autumn of 1549, when his bishop, Edmund Bonner, was accused of failing adequately to preach on the royal supremacy, Latymer and John Hooper were the principal prosecution witnesses. The case ended in Bonner's deprivation.

As a married priest Latymer was deprived of his livings after Mary's accession. It is not known if he is to be identified with the William Latimer, parson of Kirkby in Cleveland, also deprived at this time. He seems to have spent most of Mary's reign back in his native Suffolk, in Ipswich. By separating from his wife he was able to serve the cure of St Stephen and St Laurence in Ipswich. The separation appears to have been somewhat notional since their first son, Edward *Latymer, was conceived in this period.

Latimer's prominent role within Anne Boleyn's household left him well placed for promotion when Elizabeth came to the throne. He was made a chaplain to the queen, as he had been to her mother, and was appointed dean of Peterborough in December 1559 and a prebendary of Westminster Abbey shortly afterwards. The administrative records show him active in both offices. Additionally he served as archdeacon of Westminster and as treasurer at the abbey. At some time in Elizabeth's reign Latymer composed for presentation to the queen the account of her mother which is his principal claim to fame. He is the only biographer of Anne Boleyn who can be said to have known her in her lifetime. His work confines itself to her time as queen and consists largely of set speeches by Anne in which she expounds her religious, educational, and charitable ideals, illustrated with anecdotes to show those ideals in action. While there was a clear intention to nudge Elizabeth in the direction of the values attributed to her mother, the account is not fiction and has historical value. Latymer was made DD by the queen at Cambridge in 1564, and it is possible that the biography of her mother was composed for this occasion.

Latymer died at an advanced age in 1583, and was buried on 28 August in Peterborough Cathedral as he had requested. He was survived by his wife, who lived on to 1603, and by their only known children, Edward and Joshua. While his books at Peterborough were bequeathed to Edward, his books at Westminster were left to the abbey library, where some twenty-two are still identifiable. Some contain annotations in his hand. The extensive educational and charitable bequests of his son Edward resulted in the foundation of the Latymer schools. ANDREW HOPE

Sources 'William Latymer's chronicklle of Anne Bulleyne', ed. M. Dowling, *Camden miscellany, XXX*, CS, 4th ser., 39 (1990) · W. Wheatley, *The history of Edward Latymer and his foundations … including the lives of William Latymer, dean of Peterborough, and Thomas Alured*, rev. edn (1953) · J. Foxe, *Acts and monuments*, 5 (1858) · deposition of Tristram Revell, PRO, SP 1/102/125–6 · letter of the mayor and jurates of Sandwich to Henry VIII, PRO, SP 1/103/262–3 · will, PRO, PROB 11/66, fols. 213*v*–215 · Cooper, *Ath. Cantab.*, vol. 1 · A. J. Slavin, 'The Tudor revolution and the devil's art: Bishop Bonner's printed forms', *Tudor rule and revolution*, ed. D. J. Guth and J. W. McKenna (1982), 3–23 · H. B. Wilson, *A history of the parish of St Laurence Pountney* (1831) · Venn, *Alum. Cant.*, 1/3

Archives PRO, state papers · Westminster Abbey, Westminster Abbey muniments

Wealth at death moderately well off, but not wealthy: will, PRO, PROB 11/66, fols. 213*v*–215

Laud, William (1573–1645), archbishop of Canterbury, was born in Reading on 7 October 1573, the only son of William Laud (*d.* 1594), a prosperous clothier, and his wife, Lucy, *née* Webb (*d.* 1600), the widow of John Robinson, another Reading clothier. Despite later gibes at his lowly birth (to which Laud was very sensitive) his father was a relatively wealthy man, leaving money and stock worth £1200 and three properties when he died. His mother also had far from mean connections: her brother Sir William Webb was a lord mayor of London (having married the daughter of an earlier one), who bequeathed his nephew £100 when he died in 1599. Laud was his mother's tenth child; as he later commented, 'I was the tenth, and was paid to the Church' (*Works*, 7.173). He was educated at the grammar school in Reading, a town which he remembered in later life by promoting a charter for it, as well as securing a bequest for a hospital there.

Oxford, 1589–1610 Laud matriculated in October 1589 at St John's College, Oxford—an institution which provided his home for the best part of the next thirty years. He later commented that it was the place 'where I was bred up' (*Works*, 3.253). St John's was a Marian foundation which had not therefore experienced the rigours of the Edwardian Reformation, and Laud joined the college only sixteen years after five fellows, including Edmund Campion, had defected to Rome. Catholic tendencies had not entirely left the college: three other students at St John's in the 1590s later became Benedictine monks—Leander Jones, John Roberts, and Augustine Baker. Laud shared rooms as an undergraduate with Jones, who returned to England in 1634 as Dom Leander of Sancto Martino. St John's played a crucial role in Laud's life, and it was in the college that he made most of the significant friendships of his life: Sir William Paddy, William Juxon, Humphrey May, Richard Baylie, and Francis Windebank were all members of the college. An even more important influence was wielded by his tutor, John Buckeridge. Laud was closely associated

William Laud (1573–1645), by Sir Anthony Van Dyck, *c.*1635–7

with Buckeridge until the latter's death in 1631, and thereafter he sent an annual gift to Buckeridge's widow. It was possibly Buckeridge who was the source of many of Laud's early 'high-church' views: his surviving published works reveal an exalted view of the sacraments and of episcopacy and a taste for Greek patristic literature, which are all evident in his pupil. Buckeridge was also a prebendary of Rochester Cathedral, and Bishop John Young of Rochester ordained Laud as priest and deacon in 1601. Young presumably shared many of Buckeridge's ideas: he was the tutor of Lancelot Andrewes and had preached a sermon before Elizabeth in 1576 in which he had condemned unnecessary doctrinal disputes, 'certayne vayne, curious and unnecessary questions … touching almightie God hym selfe' (Young, sig. Cvv). It was later reported (as is so often the case) that Young had prophesied great things for the ordinand, trusting that his firm foundation in patristic divinity rather than modern authors would enable him to restore the Church of England to broader principles.

Laud progressed in his studies. After gaining the scholarship for Reading boys in 1590, he was made a fellow of St John's in 1593, graduated BA in 1594, and proceeded MA in 1598. On 9 May 1601 he was elected a senior fellow, and he became a university proctor in 1603. In that first decade of the seventeenth century, however, Laud found himself almost constantly at the centre of controversy—a position with which he became familiar. In 1602 he argued for the perpetual visible continuity of the true church, probably in a divinity lecture at St John's, for which he earned the wrath of George Abbot, later archbishop of Canterbury and Laud's early nemesis. Laud later reaped his revenge by condemning, to King James, Abbot's contrasting view of the succession of the church through medieval heretical sects. Laud's BD thesis in 1604 further indicated his profound concern with the government and rituals of the established church: he maintained the absolute necessity of baptism and denied that there could be any true church without diocesan bishops. Thomas Holland, the divinity professor, complained that Laud had taken most of his argument out of the works of the Roman controversialist Bellarmine, and accused him of seeking to sow division between the Church of England and foreign (non-episcopal) Reformed churches.

A sermon preached by Laud in St Mary's in October 1606 was condemned by the vice-chancellor Henry Airay, provost of Queen's, 'as containing in it sundry scandalous and Popish passages' (Heylyn, *Cyprianus*, 54), and Laud was cited to appear before him. Laud's friend Sir William Paddy sought to avoid the inevitable disgrace that would follow by petitioning the chancellor, Lord Buckhurst, on Laud's behalf. As a result Laud avoided a public recantation, but doubtless became even more objectionable to his enemies. He was branded a papist, and his biographer Peter Heylyn later reported 'that it was almost made an Heresie (as I have heard from his own mouth) for any one to be seen in his company, and a misprision of Heresie to give him a civil Salutation as he walked the streets' (ibid.). As if this degree of ostracism were not enough, just two years later Laud was creating controversy yet again in his DD thesis, when he maintained that only a bishop can confer orders, and that episcopacy is a separate order from presbyters, and superior to them by divine right. As a result Laud was accused of unchurching the foreign Reformed churches. While both positions could be glossed in such a way as to leave a loophole for continental protestant churches, the hostile response implies that Laud had made no attempt to do so, and was comfortable for others to attempt such mental gymnastics if they so wished. The position that episcopacy was a separate order (rather than merely a higher degree of the priesthood) was a minority viewpoint at this time, but one which presumably lay behind Laud's argument in his earlier BD thesis, and he was still staunchly upholding it in the late 1630s when episcopacy was threatened in Scotland.

In the same year (1608) Joseph Hall published his *Epistles*, which included an epistle addressed to 'Mr. W. L.' berating the addressee for his strange lukewarmness and equivocation between the camps of the protestants and Catholics: 'Today you are in the tents of the Romanists, tomorrow in our's, the next day betweene both, against both. Our adversaries think you our's, wee their's' (Hall, 2.55–6). The same sentiments were echoed in a sermon preached some years later from the university pulpit by Robert Abbot, regius professor of divinity at Oxford (and brother of Laud's enemy George), in which he publicly demanded of Laud: 'What art thou, ROMISH or ENGLISH? PAPIST or PROTESTANT? Or what art thou? A Mungrel, or compound of both?' (Heylyn, *Cyprianus*, 67). Given that accusations of popery against Laud are so often taken by historians from the manifestly hostile William Prynne, it is important to

recognize that theologians of the stature of Abbot and Hall also found themselves baffled by Laud's failure to observe the standard lines of attack and defence in the conflict between Rome and protestantism. Fears of lurking popery at Oxford were also not mere puritan paranoia: Humfrey Leech, a chaplain of Christ Church, had fled from Oxford in 1608 and converted to Rome, but not before insisting that he had in Oxford supporters for his anti-Calvinist views, who may have included Laud himself. It is hardly surprising, given the frequency with which the charge of popery was made against him, and the defection of some of his own Oxford acquaintances to Rome, that Laud would in later life have a troubling dream that he was reconciled to Rome. Despite the fact that the charge of popery pursued him from his Oxford days right until his death, there is no evidence whatsoever that Laud ever seriously contemplated conversion to the Roman church, which he always seems to have regarded with distaste.

While Laud had stirred up much hostility by his refusal to provide loopholes for the foreign Reformed churches when defending the integrity of the Church of England's episcopal government, it would be unwise to assume that he was simply hostile towards all manifestations of foreign Reformed divinity at this point. The annotations which he made during a period leading up to but not beyond 1619 in his copy to Bellarmine's *Disputationes* (published in 1596–9) reveal him to be still upholding aspects of Calvinist doctrine. On issues relating to predestination, he specifically defends that paragon of Calvinist orthodoxy, Theodore Beza, against Bellarmine's attacks (*Works*, 6.696, 703), and repeatedly defends Calvin himself against the cardinal's unfair exposition of his views, in the process displaying a firm adherence to the doctrine of the perseverance of the elect (ibid., 6.698, 704). Commenting (privately again) on a Jesuit tract in the early 1620s, Laud also made a point of defending Calvinist authors from the attacks of the Lutheran controversialist Conrad Schlüsselberg. Laud does not at this stage look like an Arminian zealot, or someone instinctively hostile to foreign Calvinist divinity. What is most clear is his passionate defence of the importance of the church and its institutions, and their crucial role in salvation, doubtless combined with a profound hostility to the activities of those puritans who defied the orders and devalued the structures and rationale of the national church. The precise implications of such views for other doctrinal matters were not self-evident, and there is little to suggest that at this point Laud was keen to explore them: his concerns at this stage of his career were eminently practical, however far he had shown a readiness to create controversy by providing the most exalted doctrinal basis for the ecclesiastical structures and sacraments which he held so dear.

In this troubled first decade of the seventeenth century Laud also landed himself in hot water through his first lay patron. In 1603 he had become chaplain to Charles Blount, earl of Devonshire, and on 26 December 1605 he conducted the marriage of his patron to Penelope, Lady Rich, who had been divorced from her husband, Robert Rich, third Baron Rich (then still alive), for adultery with Devonshire. On some readings of canon law such a marriage was illegal, to most it was distasteful, and for Laud it meant a personal crisis. The matter was referred to the king, and Laud became tainted in the eyes of many of his potential supporters. He certainly toyed with the arguments that would legitimate the marriage, and possibly even had a hand in the defence produced by Devonshire, before he finally wrote a paper refuting it. There is little doubt that the whole experience was highly traumatic for Laud: over twenty years later his enemies were still seeking to blacken his name over the incident, and he always remembered the anniversary with fasting and a special prayer which he composed for the occasion in which he begged God's forgiveness for serving his ambition and the sins of others. It was probably ambition which had motivated his acceptance of a chaplaincy in the first place, as Devonshire's views were decidedly Calvinist, even puritan.

Laud was not, in the end, bereft of patrons. He was appointed to Stanford, Northamptonshire, in 1607 by Sir Thomas Cave, and was granted the advowson of North Kilworth, Leicestershire, in 1608. But it was his continuing high-profile conflicts in Oxford that perhaps attracted the attention of the man who became his most crucial supporter over the next fifteen years, and who provided Laud with his entry into the royal court, Richard Neile. Laud became Neile's chaplain in 1608 and the following year, thanks to Neile's position as clerk of the closet, he preached before the king at Theobalds; he was sworn in as a royal chaplain in November 1611, having received a grant in reversion of a prebendal stall at Westminster Abbey the previous year. In 1612 he appeared for the first time in the roster of Lent preachers at court, and he regularly preached in the series thereafter.

The 1610s In 1610–11 Laud secured the presidency of St John's in succession to Buckeridge, but not without further controversy. An attempt to head off his intended election was made by his arch-enemy George Abbot (soon to be the new archbishop of Canterbury) via the chancellor, Lord Ellesmere, whose chaplain John Rawlinson was the opposing candidate. Resolution of the matter took some nine months and a series of signet letters from the court, with conflicting indications of royal intentions, until James spent 'three hours together at least' (*Works*, 3.172) hearing the case personally at Tichborne on 29 August 1611 and concluded that the election should be confirmed as the procedural irregularities were innocently made. Even so, it took another month for a signet letter formally confirming Laud's election to be sent—all ample evidence that he had his enemies at court, and that Neile's support may well have been crucial. In the event Laud did not prove a controversial president: he worked hard to improve college finances and encourage donations, although he did oversee the beautification of the college chapel, which included new stained glass, a new organ loft, and the commissioning of anthems to be sung there. As president, he regularly preached at Woodstock, where his friend James Whitelocke was recorder.

It was not long before Laud's continuing clashes with Abbot brought him before James again. According to Heylyn, Laud in a sermon on Shrove Sunday 1615 at the university church 'insisted on some points which might indifferently be imputed either to Popery or Arminianism (as about that time they began to call it)' (Heylyn, *Cyprianus*, 66). The sermon plainly also contained Laud's by now characteristic attack on presbyterians as being as bad as papists. In response to this Robert Abbot gave his Easter Sunday sermon publicly condemning Laud, questioning his protestant allegiance, and complaining that his remarks on presbyterians maligned the many protestant churches abroad who approved and admitted presbyteries and yet 'contend for the Religion established amongst us' (ibid., 67). The charge of crypto-Catholicism was evidently carried to court and heard before King James (along with other charges against John Howson), but, with the support of Neile, Laud eventually returned to Oxford with the king's blessing and an apology from Abbot for his conduct.

In 1616 James appointed Laud to the deanery of Gloucester, and he soon proved to be a predictably controversial appointment. Having been, as he claimed, charged by James to sort out irregularities in the diocese, he began early in 1617 by placing the communion table in the cathedral altarwise at the east end of the church, and commanded people to bow towards the altar on their approach. This prompted an enraged response, not least from the bishop, Miles Smith (although the oft-repeated story that the bishop in protest never entered the cathedral again is untrue). Again it was Neile whom Laud begged to defend him at court. Neile seems to have been successful in protecting his protégé: the following year Laud was one of the clergy chosen to accompany James on his trip to Scotland, and while little is known of Laud's activities there, it is not entirely surprising that he was singled out in one report as one of the bishops who offended the Scots by insisting on wearing a surplice at a funeral. His hostility to presbyterian influences, and his readiness to associate them with opposition to the crown, can only have been confirmed by his observations in Scotland and the controversies that surrounded the articles of Perth. James later allegedly complained that, not satisfied by the ratification of the articles of Perth by the Scottish parliament, Laud had urged him to draw the Scots 'to a nearer conjunction with the Liturgy and Canons' of the Church of England (Hacket, 1.64), and presented him with two unsolicited papers of proposals on the subject. Laud's journey to Scotland was one of only two he made outside England and Wales (there was another brief visit to Scotland in 1633).

Throughout this decade Neile's support was clearly crucial to the survival of Laud's fortunes at court in the face of the hostility of Archbishop Abbot and Laud's own remarkable capacity to make enemies. As well as securing crown appointments for him, Neile also acted more directly as a patron in giving him the prebend of Buckden in 1614 and the archdeaconry of Huntingdon in 1615. He may also have been behind the attempt in 1621 to make Laud dean of Westminster (Neile's own first major ecclesiastical appointment). In the event, however, John Williams held on to the deanery on his elevation to the bishopric of Lincoln, and Laud was instead appointed bishop of the humble diocese of St David's, being consecrated on 18 November 1621. Williams later claimed credit for soliciting this appointment for Laud, but it was transparently a way of preserving the deanery for himself, and conceivably intended also as a means of distancing Laud from the court. It is often commented that King James himself was opposed to Laud's elevation, and that he warned Charles and the marquess of Buckingham (who had sought it):

> I keep Laud back from all Place of Rule and Authority, because I find he hath a restless Spirit, and cannot see when matters are well, but loves to toss and change, and to bring Things to a pitch of Reformation in his own Brain ... take him to you, but upon my Soul you will repent it. (Hacket, 1.64)

But this account is highly dubious: it derives from a later alleged report by Williams (by then Laud's sworn enemy) to his chaplain John Hacket, and besides, Laud's diary provides no suggestion that he was at this point a target for the patronage of either Charles or Buckingham (although the latter did indeed soon emerge as Laud's most important patron at court). It is also notable that Laud was appointed to the bishopric a mere ten days after he had preached at court a sermon (printed immediately by royal command) in favour of the king's preferred policy of peace at a time when parliament was baying for war. Moreover, the king was happy to appoint Laud to further positions in the following year, presenting him to the rectory of Rudbackston in March 1622, and in the following month permitting him to hold a commendam in the collegiate church of Brecon, as well as a prebendal stall at Westminster and Ibstock rectory. The king's readiness in April to employ Laud in the especially sensitive matter of the potential conversion to Catholicism of the marquess of Buckingham's mother implies a degree of trust in the skills and discretion of a cleric whom James would have known from personal experience was capable of stirring up opposition. For his part, Laud was devoted to James, and privately compiled a list of the king's virtues and accomplishments after his death.

At court, 1621–1625 Laud's appointment to the bishopric meant at least a temporary farewell to Oxford, as he resigned his presidency of St John's, although he was allegedly invited to hold the presidency *in commendam*. While he did visit his diocese in 1622 and 1625, and preached several times during his primary visitation in 1622, the court proved his new home. Neile initially secured his position there, and Laud kept his lodgings (and, apparently, his books) in Neile's palatial residence at Durham House in the Strand at least until 1626. His fellow lodgers included his old tutor Buckeridge and a clutch of younger divines, including John Cosin, who were to form the nucleus of the ceremonialist drive in Durham in the 1620s and Cambridge in the 1630s [see Durham House group]. But it was his close association with the king's favourite, Buckingham, which put Laud on the path to

success over the following years. The king's initial instructions to Laud on the issue of the countess's conversion were followed on 24 May 1622 by a conference in the presence of the countess and her son between Laud and John Fisher, the Jesuit attempting to work the conversion. Despite detailed discussions with the countess subsequently, Laud was unable to bolster her protestant commitment in the longer term. His alliance with her son, however, was sealed. He became chaplain, or confessor, to Buckingham three weeks later, and for the next six years his dedication to the favourite was absolute. While he enjoyed the approval of James, and later Charles, he was perceived most of all as Buckingham's man.

Laud's conference with Fisher was not only the springboard for his alliance with Buckingham; it also provided the occasion for his first entry into print with a work of controversy. Laud's comment in his diary at the time of publication that 'I am no controvertist' (*Works*, 3.147) should not lead the observer to neglect the extraordinarily controversial sermons and disputations that he had delivered in the past. He was certainly no stranger to religious controversy, nor a shirker from it, but he did generally show a reticence from entering into print on such matters. The genesis of this publication dated from October 1622, when Laud had written an answer to an account of the conference which Fisher had circulated in manuscript. The following Christmas he read over his answer to James, who determined that it should be published. In the event, it appeared in 1624 as a brief appendix to Francis White's substantial account of his own conferences with Fisher at court (a mere seventy-four pages in contrast to the nearly 600 pages of White's work). It was also curiously presented as being the work of 'R. B.'—Laud's chaplain Richard Baylie. Laud later claimed in the preface to the 1639 edition that this ploy had been directed by others and that he had 'submitted' to it, but his diary makes it plain that it was Laud himself who requested this, presumably out of a desire for anonymity born of his many troubles in the past. That being said, while the work coyly referred to 'a certain bishop' on its own title-page, the title-page to the whole volume identified the conference as having been with the bishop of St David's, and used 'R. B.' to stand for 'reverend bishop'. The subject matter of the conference was effectively determined by the Jesuit Fisher, and was concerned principally with the relationship of salvation to membership of particular visible churches, glancing at the authority of church and scriptures, and how far erroneous belief might impede salvation. Laud expounded a carefully moderate position, which displayed a notable reluctance to brand churches or individuals with heresy, or to speculate on which doctrines might deprive an individual of salvation (despite Laud's attendance in 1612 at the last official burning of a heretic in England). The book prompted little initial attention, however; the enormously expanded second edition of 1639 is better known, and will be discussed below.

Laud's attention was soon recalled to the divisions within the Church of England. With Neile and Lancelot Andrewes he secretly cross-questioned Matthew Wren on the latter's return from attending Prince Charles in Spain in 1623, asking 'how the Prince's heart stands to the Church of England, that when God brings him to the crown we may know what to hope for' (C. Wren, *Parentalia*, 1750, 46). The following year saw the first stirs against the anti-Calvinist publications of Richard Mountague. While Mountague did at one time or another gain crucial support from John Cosin, Richard Neile, and John Buckeridge, he was not an intimate member of the Durham House circle, and was not a very close acquaintance of Laud, although Laud certainly had a strong sympathy for his views. Mountague's stance towards Rome in his *New Gagge* and *Appello Caesarem* certainly had strong similarities with that of Laud, although the former was ready to attack directly as 'puritan' the more extreme anti-papal positions which Laud preferred simply to ignore. Despite his earlier manuscript notes on predestination, Laud also showed himself far less eager than Mountague to argue the points through in public. Consequently Mountague was not always sure of his support, commenting drily in 1624 'I hope to see him one day where he will both do and say for the Church. Interim, if in someways he concede, I blame him not' (*Correspondence of John Cosin*, 24). He could only hope that Laud would 'use his greate creditt' with Buckingham to influence episcopal appointments in an anti-Calvinist direction (ibid., 22). Ironically, however, it was the very fact of Laud's close alliance with the favourite which probably obliged him at times to restrict his open support for Mountague, especially when Buckingham's bellicose foreign policy required parliamentary support for which it might be necessary to sacrifice him. Nevertheless, there is abundant evidence that Laud supported Mountague's views. It was the latter who was stirring outrage with his talk of 'doctrinal puritanism', implying that strong anti-Catholic and Calvinist views were inherently puritanical, and it is noteworthy that in December 1624 Buckingham was asking Laud for 'a little tract' on the subject, which Laud happily provided (*Works*, 3.156). It was also in 1625 that Laud wrote a letter to Buckingham co-signed by his old tutor Buckeridge and John Howson, bishop of Oxford, in which he explicitly defended Mountague's views and warned that the positions which Mountague opposed were threatening to undermine 'civil government in the commonwealth' as well as 'preaching and external ministry in the Church'. In what became a typical association of ecclesiastical dissension with civil subversion, he added: 'if the Church be once brought down beneath herself, we cannot but fear what may next be struck at' (ibid., 6.245).

A linking of the public role and fortunes of church and state had already been a prominent theme in one of Laud's early court sermons. In 1621, echoing Richard Hooker, he preached that 'Commonwealth and Church are collective bodies made up of many into one, and both so near allied that the one, the Church, can never subsist but in the other, the Commonwealth'. Laud went much further, however, in associating the fortunes of the English monarchy tightly with the specific rights, fortunes, and health of the Church of England. He insisted that 'the

Commonwealth can have no blessed and happy being, but by the Church' (*Works*, 1.6). He argued in 1626 that anyone who was sacrilegious towards the church would inevitably offer violence towards princes too. Whatever his earlier private marginal notes on the subject of predestination, by the mid-1620s Laud had clearly convinced himself that the arguments being used against Arminianism were threatening both the established church, and by association the civil unity, which he held most dear. He warned parliament in 1626: 'divide the minds of men about their hope of salvation in Christ and tell me what unity there will be' (ibid., 1.71). His appeal for unity involved not merely a condemnation of controversies over predestination, but also an attack on the style of predestinarian piety that placed divisive issues of election at the heart of pastoral ministry. This was not enough to turn Laud into a zealous promoter of Arminian views: there seems no reason to doubt his later remark that he felt that 'something about these controversies is unmasterable in this life' (ibid., 6.292). Nevertheless, he certainly seems to have become acutely sensitive to the dangers posed by unbridled anti-Arminianism and hardline 'experimental' Calvinism to the integrity and unity of the church and her institutions, and by extension to the state.

The accession of Charles and the later 1620s   The accession of Charles to the throne at the end of March 1625 was to be a turning point in Laud's life, but it was not initially marked by any close relationship with the king, although Laud did play a significant role at the coronation and was appointed to preach at the opening of parliament in 1625 and 1626. Nevertheless, much of his contact with the king took place via Buckingham. Just a week after James's death Laud presented to the duke 'a schedule, in which were wrote the names of many Churchmen, marked with the letters O. and P.' (*Works*, 3.159)—presumably meaning 'orthodox' and 'puritan'—which Buckingham had requested in order to deliver it to Charles. But the clergyman whose advice Charles really sought was Lancelot Andrewes, and the same month Laud was dispatched to Andrewes in the role of a mere messenger, to find out 'what he would have done in the cause of the Church' (ibid., 3.160). Laud would not have found this demeaning: he had enormous respect for Andrewes, whom he dubbed in the privacy of his diary 'the great light of the Christian world' (ibid., 3.196), and later (with the assistance of Buckeridge) he edited his collected sermons. But it was only with Andrewes's death that Laud received the crucial post of dean of the Chapel Royal and the longer-term promise of the archbishopric of Canterbury (both pieces of news received within days of Andrewes's death, and both typically relayed to Laud by Buckingham, rather than told him directly by Charles). In his new court position, however, Laud was better placed to develop a closer relationship with the king. He rapidly sought to reform the Chapel Royal, asking the king to be present at prayers as well as the sermon from now on—a gentle rebuke which clearly appealed to Charles's sense of order and seemliness. By April 1627 Laud was noting in his diary that Charles had said something 'most graciously ... unto me [which] I have wrote in my heart with indelible character, and great thankfulness to God and the King' (*Works*, 3.204). Further encouragement swiftly followed. Having been nominated bishop of Bath and Wells in June of the previous year, Laud was chosen for the vacant bishopric of London in June 1627 (although he was not formally installed until July 1628). He also had his first taste of archiepiscopal authority in 1627, when he was appointed to a commission for executing the office of archbishop during Abbot's sequestration. He was also made a privy councillor at the end of April 1627.

As Laud's position at court grew more powerful, however, so it also came to seem more vulnerable. His enemies at court were constantly intriguing against him, and the Devonshire marriage was still being dredged up to poison the king and Buckingham against him. Archbishop Abbot was his inveterate enemy, but it was John Williams whose intrigues were giving Laud sleepless nights. It was inevitable that Williams and Laud would clash: Williams's great patron had been Lord Ellesmere (Laud's foe in 1611), and the future bishop had been able to exercise a certain amount of authority in Oxford through his patron's role as chancellor, as well as developing links with the vehement opponent of Laudianism in the 1620s and 1630s, John Prideaux. But it was Laud's close relationship with Buckingham, and the corresponding decline in Williams' influence, that precipitated as early as 1623 a crisis between the two churchmen. This created a permanent rift and thereafter Williams was constantly intriguing against Laud. The latter for his part was ever haunted by fears that Williams would secure his revenge, and terrified by rumours that Williams was seeking a reconciliation with Buckingham. When Laud did sleep, his dreams either spelt out his anxiety (with Williams appearing before him in chains but then freeing himself and riding away beyond Laud's reach) or provided wish-fulfilment (with reports that Williams was dead). His obsessive fears of Williams coloured his interpretation of political crises for the rest of his life: he was convinced that his enemy was behind the activities of Henry Burton, John Bastwick, and William Prynne, and even the Scottish rebellion over the prayer-book.

Laud's enemies were not just those at court, however, and in the increasingly fractious relations between Charles and parliament in the first years of his reign Laud inevitably became a target for discontent. His sermons before parliament in February 1626 and March 1628 appealed for unity and peace, but with a strong emphasis on the power of the monarch in alliance with the church, and with dire warnings of radicals who sought to undermine both. Fears of religious and political radicals had little obvious basis in fact at this time, but Laud shared Charles's fears of populist conspiracy, and in his sermon of 1626 he was already seeing fit to warn that there were those who pushed for parity in the Church of England, and who would also aim at parity in the state. His affirmations of the power and authority of the monarch were consequently unambiguous. In a court sermon in July

1626 he maintained that irreverence towards the king was sacrilege, as his office and person were sacred. In a court sermon the previous year he had declared unequivocally that the king's power 'is not any assuming to himself, nor any gift from the people, but God's power', and that 'one and the same action is God's by ordinance and the King's by execution' (*Works*, 1.94). Parliament received its influence and power from the king, and its sole function was to provide him with the money necessary for his independent authority: 'The King is the sun. He draws up some vapours, some supply, some support, from us. It is true he must do so: for if the sun draw up no vapours, it can pour down no rain' (ibid., 1.101). Here was no room for seeing parliament and the king as engaged in a series of equal exchanges and bargains.

As parliament increasingly attacked his patron Buckingham, Laud played a role in mounting defences of the favourite. He drafted a speech of self-defence for Buckingham to deliver on 11 May 1626, and a further speech of justification by Charles in the same parliament. He prepared the speeches that Charles delivered on the duke's behalf on 29 March and 11 May (*Works*, 4.354), and criticized and corrected Buckingham's defence delivered on 8 June. The text of these public speeches seems to have aimed at tact and reassurance—and the same thinking lay behind Laud's advice that the notorious sermon by Roger Maynwaring in defence of the forced loan should not be published for fear of inflaming the populace. Laud also drafted the king's reply to the Commons' remonstrance of June 1628, which stoutly defended royal policies and the behaviour of Buckingham, but still ended positively with an appeal that 'let us see moderation and the ancient parliamentary way, and we shall love nothing more than parliaments' (ibid., 7.637).

Laud's advice was not always directed towards moderation, however. In 1627 he and Neile unsuccessfully attempted to secure a conviction for treason for the author of an anonymous pamphlet attacking the forced loan, on the grounds that writing it had sowed division between the king and the people (a readiness to extend the scope of treason which Laud's opponents would prove all too eager to imitate at his later trial). A paper which Laud delivered to the king in 1627 discussing the pros and cons of calling a parliament dwelt rather heavily on the cons: he maintained that subsidies were due by the laws of God, warned that parliament tended 'to sell subsidyes and not to give them', made the pointed observation that 'they will looke to sacrifice somebody', and alerted Charles to the existence of 'factious spirits' who 'were seene to laugh outright in the last Parliament when they gott their ends upon the Kinge' (PRO, SP 16/94/88). A further memorandum by Laud to Charles on the history of parliamentary subsidies, apparently written in 1628, includes a declaration that Magna Carta 'had an obscure birth by usurpation, and was fostered and shewed to the world by rebellion' (citing Walter Ralegh's *Prerogative of Parliaments* as evidence). People should vote taxes (Laud also observed) 'without dispute', and the king could revoke Magna Carta when he pleased (PRO, SP 16/96/31). Laud also pointedly noted the occasions when the clergy had granted subsidies to the crown. Of course he had his own reasons to fear parliament. In June 1628 a Commons remonstrance named Laud and Neile as Arminians. When prospects were raised for a further calling of parliament, Laud heard reports that a resummoned parliament would mean that some would need to be sacrificed, and that Laud would be as good a one as any for this treatment: this sent him rushing to Charles for reassurance. Charles told him not to believe these reports until he saw the king forsake his other friends—an ironic presage of his desertion of Laud after the execution of Strafford. Buckingham's assassination soon afterwards could have been fatal for Laud's ambitions, but his closeness to the deceased favourite may have created a crucial extra bond with Charles, who was deeply offended by the rejoicing of others at Buckingham's death. Laud described Buckingham's assassination in 1628 as 'the saddest news that ever I heard in my life' (Trevor-Roper, 456)—worse, one assumes, than the death of his own parents—and it is remarkable that Charles (who was himself grief-stricken) was particularly solicitous towards Laud at this time, sending him sympathetic letters and speaking graciously to him when Laud returned to court for the first time after Buckingham's death, some two weeks later. Even Charles could see that Laud and Buckingham enjoyed a special intimacy that was possibly greater than his own with the favourite. In the following years Laud was ever solicitous to Buckingham's wife and surviving son, and when his widow married again Laud struggled manfully to defend her husband, the appalling earl of Antrim, to his friend Thomas Wentworth, imploring him to be kind to the couple 'in remembrance of my Lord Duke that is gone' (*Works*, 7.479). In his will Laud gave a chalice and gold paten to Buckingham's son 'as the memorial of him who had a faithful heart to love, and the honour to be beloved of his father' (ibid., 4.443).

The continuing need for parliamentary support for war with Spain after Buckingham's death may have led Laud towards a tactical retreat on the Arminian issue. In February 1629 it was being reported that he had preached against Arminianism at court, and the Commons were told by Humphrey May that Laud and Neile had been on their knees before the privy council denying that they were Arminians. The hasty dissolution of parliament in 1629 effectively removed the matter from further debate, although the final condemnation of religious innovations read out while the speaker was held in his chair can have left Laud in little doubt of what to expect the next time a parliament was called.

Chancellor of Oxford The dissolution of parliament left Laud free to pursue his objectives in the church more wholeheartedly, even though Abbot remained archbishop of Canterbury until his death on 4 August 1633. The first place where Laud's reforming zeal was evident was in fact in his alma mater. As bishop of Bath and Wells he had already acted as visitor of Wadham College in 1628, and had drafted proctoral regulations in the same year, but in 1630, apparently to his own surprise, Laud was elected

chancellor of the university. The crown's preferred candidate for the post, whom Laud was supporting, was Sir Richard Weston, the lord treasurer, but a group of dons acting unofficially promoted Laud's election, which he eventually won by the narrow margin of nine votes. As with all of Laud's appointments this one was challenged, with the supporters of his opponent, the fourth earl of Pembroke and Montgomery, unsuccessfully petitioning the king that the election had broken the university statutes. Laud's authority over the university soon became a matter of urgent concern when three fellows in a series of sermons in 1631 flouted university regulations by tackling predestination, and also 'by some not obscure passages … endeavoured to fasten the imputation of apostasy and backsliding upon some persons of eminent quality'. Laud's ally Brian Duppa warned that they 'strike at the very root of government' (*Works*, 5.49–50). Charles settled the conflict personally at a hearing at Woodstock, in the process entirely vindicating Laud and his policies—a triumph which Laud specially recorded in his diary.

Laud was anything but a figurehead chancellor. He was much more regularly involved with routine university affairs than any of his predecessors had been, and conducted a weekly exchange of letters with the vice-chancellor throughout his chancellorship as well as receiving detailed accounts of university affairs from his other allies at Oxford. Such zealous attention doubtless reflected his own consuming interest in the university, but also reflected a broader policy of reforming levels of order, discipline, and piety throughout society, with Oxford serving both as exemplar and disseminator. At the heart of his Oxford policy was the remedying of the oft-deplored failings of the university statutes by creating a new code of statutes, finally promulgated in June 1636. While convocation submitted draft proposals, the statutes have rightly been seen as essentially the work of Laud, who made many alterations to the initial draft and took a very close personal interest in the project. His interventions were often aimed at securing, among other things, the extension and clarification of the powers of the chancellor, as well as the revival and strengthening of the university's traditional requirements on discipline, residence, and teaching. The statutes were not concerned with increasing the chancellor's overview of religious matters, but Laud sought to secure this by a separate but concurrent campaign, commenced after his election as archbishop of Canterbury on 19 August 1633 and confirmation on 19 September, to secure his rights of metropolitical visitation of the university. He insisted on the right to examine the religious conformity of every single member of the university, but although his rights were acknowledged by the privy council he did not in the event exercise them, partly because the accession of more Laudian bishops to the bench and the suspension of Bishop Williams gave him the requisite control via the bishops' powers as college visitors to supplement the power already exercised by the vice-chancellors that he appointed. Laud also managed to secure a new charter confirming and extending the privileges of the university *vis-à-vis* the town of Oxford, which passed the great seal in March 1636. These achievements were capped by a royal visit to Oxford in August that year, at which Laud presided. He was also a generous benefactor—to his own college of St John's by building an impressive new quadrangle, to the Bodleian Library by donating over 1000 manuscripts as well as coins and books, and to the university as a whole by founding a lectureship in Arabic and augmenting the stipend of the professor of Hebrew.

For all Laud's determination to reform the university and to prosecute nonconformity, Caroline Oxford was not gripped in the vice of an unbending religious orthodoxy, even if the path to preferment was clear. At the royal hearing in 1631 Charles had taxed Laud to make sure that the royal declaration concerning predestination was implemented impartially, and subsequently Laud required his vice-chancellor to judge 'impartially' between Arminian and Calvinist offenders against Charles's moratorium, 'that neither one nor the other may have cause to say that you favour a party' (Works, 5.48). Laud's particular concern here and elsewhere seems to have been to avoid giving opponents of his policies the opportunity to tar them with an Arminian brush. That did not mean that he disapproved of all religious controversy. He was quite happy to direct the publication of controversial works when he had the king's support and when he deemed the matter worthy of defence, as is clear in his directions to the vice-chancellor to publish William Page's defence of bowing at the name of Jesus, thereby crossing Archbishop Abbot's attempt to stifle the pamphlet debate.

Laud's well-founded sense of vulnerability also led him to urge tactical restraint on his vice-chancellors, especially when it came to enforcing non-canonical ceremonies. When Edward Corbet, the proctor and subwarden of Merton College, petitioned Laud in 1638 to give him a direct order to bow towards the communion table when officiating at the communion at the beginning of terms, or to leave him the liberty not to do so, Laud refused, smelling a puritan trap, and stressed that he would never make any such command 'till I may be warranted myself by public authority'. He advised that Corbet should arrange for another person to substitute for him, but refused to make even this a direct command, 'that the blame may not be cast upon me' (Works, 6.206).

Ecclesiastical policy during the personal rule Laud had declared to the king that 'if it [the Church] had more power, the Kinge might have more both obedience and service' (PRO, SP 16/94/88). In his sermons at court and before parliament he had painted an image of church and state working in harmony, and the essence of his ecclesiastical policy was to oversee a strengthening of the powers of the church which would as a consequence reinforce ties of deference within society, as well as providing the crown with enhanced support independent of parliament. If Laud's aspirations are clear, it would nevertheless be unwise to attribute all the workings of the ecclesiastical policy of the personal rule to his sole inspiration. There was a tendency among contemporaries (and indeed among later historians) to attribute all aspects of policy to

Laud's direct intervention. But in fact he formed a close working partnership with the king. Charles was certainly happy to appear as the originator of policy, partly because he considered that by insisting that official policies were his own he would most effectively secure compliance. And Laud, given his troublesome past, was anxious to shield himself with royal directions whenever possible. The result was a partnership in which Laud guided Charles towards the practical policies which would achieve the results that they both desired.

Laud certainly had his own agenda too: an undated list within his diary of 'things which I have projected to do if God bless me in them' (probably initially compiled about 1630 and occasionally added to thereafter) provides a catalogue of tasks aimed at rebuilding the power, wealth, and dignity of the church. Many are concerned with boosting the economic power of the church: these include the augmentation of livings; the attaching of commendams to smaller bishoprics; the settling of tithe disputes in London; and the return of crown impropriations to the Irish church. In the latter case, at least, Laud was able to add 'Done' in the margin, and the other more long-term tasks regularly attracted his attention in the 1630s. His constant attempts to rebuild the power of the church inevitably meant infringing on lay authority: indeed, another of his specific tasks was the overthrow of the feoffees for impropriations. Various lay-funded lectureships also faced intrusion by Laud, although he was not always well enough informed to act, and he still managed to retain amicable relations with the Merchant Taylors' Company, which had long preserved close links with St John's College, and which in 1632 formally elected Laud as a member.

Some of the rebuilding of the church was to be quite literal: one of Laud's listed tasks was the restoration of St Paul's Cathedral, a task which he pursued with dogged determination throughout the decade, and which resulted in the new west front designed by Inigo Jones. A contemporary unwisely predicted that this 'will be his perpetuall monument' (Dering, sig. B2r): it was of course burnt down with the rest of the cathedral in 1666. In other cathedrals the shortcomings were administrative as much as structural and Laud pursued another of his stipulated tasks—the revision of cathedral statutes—with vigour and with no little success, thanks to his metropolitical visitation. The policy was not without its opponents: some deans and chapters complained of the interference in their jurisdiction (not least in Laud's own cathedral of Canterbury, whose dean and chapter were to prove a constant source of irritation to the archbishop), and town corporations were furious at the other side of this regularizing of the position of the cathedrals—a systematic revision of town corporations via a *quo warranto* campaign which benefited the cathedrals against the lay authorities.

While Laud was determined to rebuild the power and wealth of church and clergy, it should not be assumed that he was indulgent towards those clergy who failed to manifest proper behaviour. In a sermon before King James in

1621 in which he condemned lay sacrilege, Laud had admitted that 'so are too many of us priests guilty of other as great sins as sacrilege can be' (*Works*, 1.26), and those sins of simony, neglect, and scandalous living felt his lash in the court of high commission. Moreover, for all his determined defence of the dignity and authority of the episcopal order, Laud was not averse to humiliating those bishops who sought to avoid their duties or even tried to sabotage his campaign. Bishops Godfrey Goodman of Gloucester, John Bridgeman of Chester, and John Williams of Lincoln all encountered his displeasure directly. He was also severe on corrupt Irish bishops, opining that if one of them were to be made a public example and deprived of his bishopric it 'would do more good in Ireland, than anything that hath been there these forty years' (ibid., 6.333). Laud's pursuit of his ecclesiastical authority pitted him a number of times against his own clergy. His determined pursuit of the right to conduct a metropolitical visitation of the universities brought even Laudian heads of college ostensibly in conflict with him.

But puritan nonconformists were Laud's chief target, and ceremonial conformity was the essence of his ecclesiastical policy. He maintained at his trial that he had 'laboured nothing more, than that the external worship of God (too much slighted in most parts of this kingdom) might be preserved' (*Works*, 4.60). It was not that external, outward ceremonies were ends in themselves, but they were 'the hedge that fence the substance of religion from all the indignities which profaneness and sacrilege too commonly put upon it' (ibid., 2.xvi). The neglect of the outward forms of God's worship was echoed in the neglect of the buildings in which such worship was performed, and Laud sought to promote the reform of both. The essence of many ceremonies was also that they were observed by the whole congregation, and Laud did not underestimate the importance of uniformity. He was emphatic that 'unity cannot long continue in the church, where uniformity is shut out at the church door' (ibid., 4.60). This was the essence of his ecclesiastical vision; where some believed that a unity of minds was best preserved by casting an indulgent eye over occasional nonconformity, to Laud it was uniformity in outward observance which not only provided evidence of obedience, but which also ultimately helped to foster a broader unity.

It was Laud's conviction that in enforcing conformity in divine service and more decorous forms of church decoration and worship he was merely restoring the Church of England 'to the rules of its first reformation' (*Works*, 6.42), although this sometimes implied that matters had begun to deteriorate almost from the first days of the Reformation settlement. He was also quite frank in explaining that the Book of Common Prayer and the existing canons of the church could be improved. Nevertheless, in this return to the rules of the early Reformation, he was careful to ensure that he had the necessary 'rules' to hand. Although the rigid enforcement of conformity to the 1604 canons through his metropolitical visitations of twenty dioceses between 1634 and 1637 represented a drive for

ecclesiastical uniformity unparalleled since the Reformation, in those cases where ceremonies lacked such legal authority he trod more cautiously. Thus his metropolitical articles do not insist upon communion tables being railed at the east end of the church, which was to become the *cause célèbre* of personal-rule policy. Laud had demonstrated his enthusiasm for east-end altars when dean of Gloucester, but while his erstwhile patron Neile was happy to enforce east-end altars from early in the 1630s, Laud, although generally sympathetic, held back, apparently unsure of the precise legal significance of the king's ruling in the St Gregory's case. However, he was pleased to secure the stipulation of east-end altars in the Irish canons of 1635 and later the English canons of 1640. In his famous speech at the censure of Burton, Bastwick, and Prynne by Star Chamber in 1637, Laud maintained that the placing of the communion table was a matter indifferent and that nothing had yet been done 'by violence or command'. In the same speech, however, he made it plain that the arrangement of the communion table was not merely a matter of order and decency. He called the altar:

> the greatest place of God's residence upon earth … yea greater than the pulpit, for there 'tis *Hoc est corpus meum*, 'This is My body', but in the pulpit 'tis at most but *Hoc est verbum meum*, 'This is My word'. (*Works*, 6.57)

The reissuing in 1633 of the Book of Sports, which specifically permitted certain recreations on the sabbath, was another policy where Laud trod carefully: he later protested that he had not moved this initiative, and indeed he seems to have had little interest in the issue of pastimes as such, although he was strongly opposed to the practice of fasting on Sundays. Nevertheless, he was alive to the value of another test of the allegiance and loyalty of local ministers, and had clearly been initially concerned by the degree to which strict local sabbatarian orders represented an infringement of ecclesiastical jurisdiction by puritan lay justices.

Laud's policies were not as undiscriminatingly severe as his puritan contemporaries and posterity sought to represent them, and he occasionally showed himself ready to deal sensitively with those clergymen who gave indications that they could be persuaded to conformity; his malicious pursuit of Bishop Williams was far from typical. He was inflexible in his determination to enforce conformity, however, and his determination to close off every remaining loophole and escape route meant that ceremonial conformity was imposed more systematically than ever before. There was, too, a radical edge to Laudian reforms. While careful to ensure that he had legal support for his imposition of canonical ceremonies, Laud was happy to promote bishops and pamphleteers who stridently advocated and enforced non-canonical ceremonies, in the belief that their activities were helpful but (most importantly) could not be blamed on him directly.

Catholicism in the 1630s Laud had been accused of popish sympathies since his early days in Oxford, and the charges showed no sign of abating in the 1630s. Reports of his sympathy to Rome and hostility towards puritanism generated unwise hopes on the other side. He was twice offered a cardinal's hat in the weeks immediately following Abbot's death, probably by the English Benedictine David Codner—an offer which he rejected with the reflection that 'something dwelt within me which would not suffer that, till Rome were other than it is' (*Works*, 3.219). He made a point of refusing to meet the unofficial papal emissary Gregorio Panzani and was hostile towards the papal agent George Con. He was distressed by his friend Kenelm Digby's conversion, and after Lord Newport complained directly to him of his wife's conversion in 1637 Laud raised the problem of court conversions at the council board and secured the passage of a royal proclamation against them.

Laud's opposition to court Catholicism made the increasing charges against him of popery all the more ironic. He was, nevertheless, fully aware of the danger of such charges, and the desire to refute them lay behind his decision in 1639 to publish a much expanded version of his earlier *Conference with Fisher*. The agenda of Laud's work was again partly set by his opponent—in this case the Roman Catholic writer 'A. C.' who had replied to Laud's earlier treatise in *True Relations of Sundry Conferences* (1626), and whom Laud rightly assumed to be the Jesuit Fisher himself. There are no startlingly new insights in Laud's *Conference* but it is a thorough and careful exposition of the moderate and legalistic defence of the separation from Rome that was becoming more a feature of English protestant writing. It is most notable for what it omits—here is no sense that the pope was Antichrist, no suggestion that Rome was not a true church, only limited senses in which Rome is adjudged guilty of heresy or idolatry, and a carefully articulated sense that salvation was theoretically possible within her communion. On the question of the visibility of the church, Laud's position is notably different from that of Francis White, who had been happy to accept the relative invisibility of the 'true church' in times of oppression. Laud did also seize on the opportunity to insert very lengthy new sections, which reflected the interest that he had long had in the jurisdictional autonomy of the Church of England. Substantial new sections were thus inserted on general councils, on the historical authority of the papacy, and on the independent right of churches to reform themselves (referring specifically to the so-called 'Cyprian privilege' of the English church to be governed by her own patriarch).

As an exposition of more tactically moderate defence of the Church of England the work won its supporters. Indeed, it was praised even by those who had no personal sympathy for Laud. James Ussher was reportedly impressed and wished that it would be translated into Latin, and John Hacket called it a 'Master-Piece in Divinity' (Hacket, 1.172), while Sir Edward Dering prophesied that the book 'shall strike the Papists under the fifth ribbe when he is dead and gone' and would prove Laud's 'lasting Epitaph' (Dering, sig. B2r). The book was perhaps more internally consistent by its avoidance of some of the more vigorously anti-Catholic tenets of earlier protestant polemic, but it was the absence of these same tenets that provoked some of the more bitter responses. As a result, it

suffered the indignity of attacks from the protestant as well as the Roman Catholic side. Laud himself, however, was in no doubt that the book should provide a lasting testimony of his innocence from the charge of popery: he left £100 in his will to have the book translated and sent abroad 'that the Christian world may see and judge of my religion' (*Works*, 4.449).

At the Caroline court Laud was not merely concerned with matters of ecclesiastical policy. As a member of the privy council from 1627 he was involved in the formulation of many of the secular policies of the personal rule. Indeed, after the death of the earl of Portland in March 1635 he found himself serving for over a year on the treasury committee, as well as being a member of the committees of trade and foreign affairs. That being said, while his appetite for hard work seems to have been undiminished by these administrative burdens, and the king's trust in his diligence and integrity led to many more responsibilities, Laud does not seem to have played a major and distinctive role in other areas of policy. Here he was essentially aligned with the so-called 'Spanish faction' at court, less for any Hispanophile sentiment (Laud's insular instincts became if anything more xenophobic over the years), but because their policies aimed at peace and an avoidance of the foreign adventures that had required the king to consult his increasingly fractious parliaments in the 1620s. Laud knew that settled crown finances and a lack of parliaments were needed if his ecclesiastical policies were to be given time to succeed. If his attitude to foreign affairs aligned him with Portland and the chancellor of the exchequer, Sir Francis Cottington, however, he was on a personal level deeply distrustful towards them, all the more so after his old friend Sir Francis Windebank, for whom he had secured the post of secretary, defected to Cottington's side when the treasury commission quarrelled over the new soap patent. Laud enjoyed amicable relations with Lord Keeper Thomas Coventry and the secretary of state Sir John Coke, and was relieved when the treasurership was awarded to his old ally William Juxon, whom he had earlier secured as Neile's successor as clerk of the closet 'that I might have one that I might trust near his Majesty, if I grow weak or infirm' (*Works*, 3.216). Another close political ally appears to have been the lord deputy of Ireland, Sir Thomas Wentworth. Theirs was a political association based on mutual needs rather than constituting the political faction described by some historians—they had their disagreements over policy and allies, where their interests did not always coincide. Nevertheless, if for Wentworth the association with Laud was crucial to maintaining his influence at court, the archbishop seems to have regarded their alliance as a genuine friendship and, while he was sometimes worried by Wentworth's impetuosity or sceptical of his claims to impartiality, Laud's many lengthy surviving letters to the lord deputy display a loquaciousness, a readiness to confide, and even a ponderous sense of humour which is notably absent from his other correspondence.

Nevertheless, for all his apparent influence at court, Laud remained as fearful as ever of court intrigues against him, convinced that his arch-enemy Williams was intriguing with his court enemies Cottington and the earl of Holland. His fears of court opponents were partly based on simple fact—he had indeed made enemies. But he was also fully aware that he could never hope to compete with those better versed in the aesthetic graces and trivialities of court life. This did not mean that he was philistine in his cultural attitudes. He showed a ready appreciation of Inigo Jones's work, and posed for Anthony Van Dyck's portrait. He also seems to have appreciated music: at his death he had a harp, a chest of viols, and a harpsichord in his parlour. The real problem was that at heart Laud remained the awkward, soberly dressed, and self-righteous don. His overwhelming seriousness, fussy pedantry, and quick temper made him an easy butt for Cottington's jokes. More seriously, however, Laud did not enjoy good relations with the queen. This was not just a matter of religious differences, nor even of Laud's lack of facility with the French language (although that did not help). It is revealing that the wife of the gentleman usher, in whose house Laud later spent ten weeks in custody, allegedly commented that he was 'one of the goodest men … but with all one of the sill[i]est fellows to hold talk with a Lady that ever she met with in all her life' (Heylyn, *Cyprianus*, 465). This was no mean handicap at the Caroline court.

For all his prominence in the king's counsels, Laud was never a Richelieu or a Wolsey, or even a Williams—he was always essentially an ecclesiastic. Nevertheless, his religious vision had political implications; he saw Calvinist ideas and puritanism as subversive of the institutions of the state as well as of the church, while his political vision was based on the intimate interdependence of church and state. His organic view of society meant that, just as he was eager to uproot corruption, waste, and the pursuit of private interest in the church, so he was eager to attack the same evils in the court, and in society at large. In high commission and Star Chamber he was keen to enforce social morality, and to see the mighty humbled. One of his earliest political appointments in 1622 was to a commission on grievances to receive petitions complaining of oppression and bribery. In Star Chamber he was particularly severe against those charged over building enclosures, or hoarding grain to increase prices at times of shortage, or converting land to pasture. He professed in 1638 that he was 'a great hater of depopulations in any kind, as being one of the greatest mischiefs in this kingdom' (*Works*, 6.520), and publicly condemned grain hoarders for grinding the faces of the poor. Like his friend Wentworth, he was anxious to display the power and impartiality of the law by prosecuting the wealthy and the noble, and earned their enmity as a result.

Foreign churches and the Scottish crisis From his earliest days in Oxford, Laud had displayed little respect for or interest in the fortunes of other protestant churches, and when their different forms of church government or ceremonies were urged by puritans against the Church of England he became actively hostile. It was not surprising, therefore, that he gave a very cool response when the eirenicist John Dury approached him with his schemes for pan-protestant unity in the 1630s (although Laud did seek to make the most of his limited support of Dury when his protestant credentials were challenged at his trial). He did show mild interest when Dury assured him that the Swedish church was eager to imitate the forms of the Church of England in creating a new court of high commission. Given the importance that Laud attached to episcopal government, it is understandable that (as he made clear to Viscount Scudamore) he felt reunion with the Swedes more likely than with the presbyterian Swiss and Huguenots.

Rather than pursuing closer relations with foreign churches, Laud was involved in seeking to bring churches and individuals more into line with the Church of England. The French and Dutch stranger churches in England came under pressure to conform to the established church, Laud commenting that 'their example is of ill consequence … for many are confirmed in their stubborn ways of disobedience to the Church-government, seeing them so freely suffered'. As always he added a further political warning, that the divisions of their members from the Church of England served to 'alienate them from the state' (*Works*, 6.25–6). In the case of Englishmen abroad, however, Laud reversed his reasoning and urged that they should be brought into closer conformity with their native church rather than that of their country of residence. Already in July 1630 Laud had voiced his concern that merchant adventurers in the Netherlands did not follow the set forms of prayer, and urged the need to bring them under ecclesiastical government. By 1633 he was also trying to bring the regiments in Dutch service under episcopal control, urging that clergy who did not use the ceremonies according to the English prayer book should not continue to serve as chaplains of any English or Scottish regiments (the latter point an omen of later events).

Laud was also eager to ensure that all the territories under the crown were brought under the same basic government and liturgy as the Church of England. He explored the possibilities of reducing Guernsey to episcopal government, while also heading an important commission for the English colonies. It was this commission that ruled that no one should go to New England without a certificate of religious conformity, that instituted *quo warranto* proceedings against the Massachusetts charter, and that may also have contemplated sending out a bishop to New England.

In Ireland and Scotland, Laud had ambitious schemes to rebuild the economic power of the church. But in these cases, too, he was also anxious to ensure that the churches be brought into greater conformity with the Church of England, and was particularly attracted by the idea that the same prayer book might be observed in all of Charles's dominions. In each case, however, he recognized the need for compromise. In Ireland he was happy to see the introduction of a court of high commission and the formal introduction of the Thirty-Nine Articles, but while he would have preferred for the English canons to be adopted in their entirety, he acquiesced in the adapted Irish canons, noting with satisfaction that some improvements were thereby made to the English version. In Scotland, Laud (who had been made a privy councillor there) similarly emphasized his desire 'to conform Scotland to the Church of England', and recommended that the English prayer book should be adopted in its entirety, but was overridden by the advice of the Scottish bishops although he still reviewed their draft prayer book on the king's instructions. Laud was adamant that he was not to blame for the conflict that subsequently developed. He complained on 2 September 1639 to his ally John Bramhall that he had always warned the Scottish bishops 'to be very careful what they did and how they demeaned themselves … that they should be very moderate in the prosecution and temper themselves from all offence' (Hunt. L., Hastings MS 15172). He deplored the 'want of care and circumspection … in the way of managing the thing … and then in timely suppressing the first disorders about it' (*Works*, 7.489–90) which had created a crisis that he had been unable to avert despite regularly foretelling it.

Ironically, it was the Scottish crisis, in which Laud's involvement was least obvious, that was to prove his downfall. It led directly to the recall of parliament, and it was the Scots who were most determined to track him down subsequently and to secure his trial as one of the 'incendiaries' who had moved the king against them.

Parliament, imprisonment, trial, and execution, 1640–1645
While Laud reluctantly supported his friend Wentworth's call for the summoning of the Short Parliament, recognizing the need to raise funds to defeat the Scots, he cannot have been surprised that his religious policies soon came under attack: over a year earlier he had warned that a new parliament would cripple the church, and before this parliament he annotated Henry Neville's advice to James I on the doomed Addled Parliament. In the event, a series of speakers condemned what they regarded as the introduction of popish ceremonies, and Laud's phrase 'Hoc est corpus meum' ('this is my body') and his encouragement of bowing towards the altar were singled out for particular attack in debates. He was not the only councillor who advised the dissolution of the deadlocked parliament, and he was certainly not behind the fateful decision to continue the sitting of convocation after the dismissal of parliament (he only agreed to the policy after being provided with a guarantee of legality subscribed by the judges, although once the decision had been taken by Charles he soon set about drafting royal instructions to convocation). In the popular mind, however, Laud was regarded as solely responsible for both policies, and became the target of increasingly frenzied popular hostility, culminating in a siege of Lambeth Palace by a mob of apprentices hunting 'William the Fox' (although Laud had taken shelter at Whitehall on the king's orders). Laud had little say in the conduct of the so-called second bishops' war which followed, but he was again seen as a prime mover in it, and by late August libels in Covent Garden were calling on the apprentices to fall upon Laud during the king's absence.

Laud had no illusions of what the calling of the Long Parliament would mean for him. He declined to nominate an MP for Reading, fearing that this would merely generate further hostility, and commented a week before it opened that 'I am almost every day threatened with my ruin in parliament' (*Works*, 3.237). Unlike Strafford he seems to have nurtured no plans for a defensive strike: during the first month of parliament's sitting he busied himself with sorting out the arrangements for his charitable bequests in Reading and his gifts of manuscripts to Oxford, apparently reconciled to an impending demotion. He told John Selden on 29 November that he would be happy to ask the king to abrogate the canons passed by convocation in the spring if this were to be desired, claiming that he would have moved this at the very beginning of parliament, were it not for the fear that the Commons would take offence at it and would say 'that we did it on purpose to prevent them' (ibid., 6.589). This attempted surrender did not help him, however. On 18 December 1640 he was impeached for high treason by the Commons. In the debate Harbottle Grimston called him 'the roote and ground of all our miseries and calamities … the sty of all pestilential filth that hath infected the State and Government' (*Journal of Sir Simonds D'Ewes*, 169). The particular charges against Laud covered both secular and religious matters (in roughly equal proportion): he was accused of endeavouring to subvert the fundamental laws to bring in arbitrary government, of hindering justice, of altering the true religion and usurping papal powers, of labouring to reconcile England and Rome, of persecuting godly preachers, of sowing division with other Reformed churches, of stirring a war with Scotland, and of alienating the king from his subjects. It was the theme of popery that ran through both secular and religious charges and provided the rationale that lay behind Laud's treacherous actions. The fact that he was committed to the custody of the gentleman usher, rather than (like Strafford) to the Tower, hints that even at this stage he was not regarded as posing the same threat. When the case against Laud was brought forward again in February 1641, with fourteen articles of impeachment voted against him in the Commons on the 24th, it seems to have been intended simply to please the Scots, and just two weeks later it was being commented that Laud 'was ready to die, since the King did not now regard him' (C. Russell, *The Fall of the British Monarchies*, 1991, 268). On 1 March 1641 Laud was committed to the Tower, pursued by jeering apprentices. His own state of mind is reflected in the inspiration which he felt at the readings from chapter 50 of Isaiah and Psalm 94 at his final service in his chapel. Both refer to the assaults of enemies, but both promise a final earthly triumph over evil opponents.

Laud's enemies were not in any hurry, however. He was not regarded as dangerous, and he was not proceeded against. He was much moved by Strafford's execution, fainting when attempting to give the earl a final blessing on his way to the scaffold, and his bitter complaint that Strafford had fallen because he had served a king 'who knew not how to be, or be made, great' (*Works*, 3.443) may have reflected not only his dismay at the king's betrayal of his promise to Strafford, but also perhaps his recognition that he had himself been deserted. Certainly, the swift promotion of Laud's old enemy Williams implied that the king had turned his back on his archbishop. Laud's account book indicates that from November 1640 gifts to him from Charles abruptly ceased, something that he can hardly have failed to notice. Later it was only at Edward Hyde's prompting that the king had a royal pardon under the great seal sent to Laud in April 1644 (and in characteristic vein Laud sent it back for amendments when his counsel felt it needed adjustments), but despite his rather half-hearted production of it at the end of his trial, Laud can have had few illusions, having seen Strafford's fate, that the pardon would be effective. For the next two years he languished in gaol, his chiefest persecutors being the huge numbers of sheets, ballads, and broadsheets published against him, which he painfully but diligently purchased through his secretary William Dell. While keeping careful track of the parliamentary debates in the weekly diurnals, Laud devoted most of his enforced leisure to posterity, with one eye to the needs of his defence at a future trial. During this time he compiled his history of his chancellorship of Oxford University, wrote two very detailed responses to speeches by Lord Saye and Sele against episcopacy and the liturgy, and also commenced a history of his own troubles (for which he was never to want for material), beginning with his impeachment. His remarkable passivity and resignation in these years probably sprang in part from the fact that he had always been expecting such a reversal of fortune.

Laud would probably have continued to live neglected in the Tower, in the manner in which Matthew Wren did, were it not for complications that emerged from his continuing authority as archbishop of Canterbury, which necessitated his agreeing to new ecclesiastical appointments (he had resigned as chancellor of Oxford University in June 1641). Laud sought to comply with parliament's directions when he could, but when faced with instructions to appoint the same Edward Corbet with whom he had earlier clashed in Oxford to the rich living of Chartham in the face of counter-instructions from the king, he finally refused. This event unfortunately focused parliament's attention on their unfinished business with Laud, and the practical problems which meant that inertia was no longer an option. One of Laud's most implacable enemies, William Prynne, was unleashed, and ordered on 31 May 1643 to seize the archbishop's papers for evidence against him. Even now, however, there was little sense of urgency: it was another five months before the Commons sent up a further ten articles against Laud and the Lords required the archbishop's answer, and it was not until 12 March 1644 that his trial finally began. The trial itself dragged on until 11 October, partly because of endless delays: meetings were very infrequent, such was the pressure of other parliamentary business.

Laud's trial was a travesty of justice. He was manifestly innocent of the charges of treason and the advancement of popery that were levelled against him, and the conduct of the trial reflected badly on his accusers: witnesses were interfered with; the question of which precise pieces of evidence were intended to provide material for a charge of cumulative treason was never clarified; and apart from the speaker not one of the lords who sat in judgment was present for the whole of the trial (often being present only to hear the prosecution), while Laud was generally only given two hours to prepare answers to the prosecution charges which would occupy the whole morning. It was not until 11 October that Laud's counsel was finally heard on the points of law. Laud was clearly innocent as charged: it is remarkable that the vindictive Prynne, with access to twenty-one bundles of Laud's private papers, including his personal diary, was not able to find evidence that would substantiate the main charges against the archbishop. Gilbert Burnet's claim that Laud had burnt incriminating material is not supported by the evidence, and partly reflects the bewilderment that more damaging material had not been located.

But this is not say that Laud was spotlessly innocent of lesser charges. The injustice of the charges against him and the vindictiveness of his accusers should not disguise the fact that he was not entirely candid in his responses. This was hardly to be expected, of course. He was on trial for his life, and it is greatly to Laud's credit that it is very difficult to find examples of him consciously lying in his answers. Indeed, on occasion when he judged a principle to be of sufficient importance he stoutly defended it, even if he knew his judges were irreconcilably opposed to it, rather than disowning it. But he did appeal to documentary evidence which he knew gave a partial and misleading account, and exploited the fact that the prosecution did not have access to information that would have clinched some of their accusations. He urged the evidence of docket books when he knew they did not deliver accurate information of the working of ecclesiastical patronage; he disclaimed responsibility for promoting inflammatory figures when, as is clear from evidence that the prosecution did not possess, he was unquestionably their patron. He constantly hid behind collective, corporate decisions and policies which he himself had clearly initiated—a ploy which can be dated back to his days as dean of Gloucester. It was not in his interests to tell his prosecutors more than they knew, and he was therefore unquestionably economical with the truth, though he never entirely abandoned it. This economy also found its way into his account of his troubles, which provided what was often a rather selective account of the day's proceedings, inevitably depicting Laud defeating his opponents, and passing over some palpable hits by the prosecution and some slips and errors of his own. The records of Laud's trial show him to have been innocent of the principal charges levelled against him; but they do not present a candid account of his rule.

Laud's defence was ultimately astute enough to frustrate the attempt to convict him by normal means. Throughout the trial, indeed, he had displayed an extraordinary vigour and clear mind for a man of his age, and had at last found the self-control in the face of extraordinary provocation which he had struggled to muster in his more fortunate years. It was a triumph both for the shrewdness of his defence and of his more long-term pursuit of 'plausible deniability' (Fincham and Lake, 45) that the Commons ultimately despaired of achieving a judgment against Laud in the normal way and, as with Strafford, decided to proceed instead by a bill of attainder. After a good deal of mob pressure the Lords finally gave way and passed the ordinance on 4 January 1645, with only nineteen peers present. Laud was executed on Tower Hill on 10 January. In his speech at the scaffold he denied that he had done anything deserving death. He was harried by his opponents, in the shape of Sir John Clotworthy, even in his final moments, and after some brief responses to Clotworthy's interrogation he turned to the executioner 'as the gentler and discreeter person' (Heylyn, *Cyprianus*, 537). He was buried in the chancel of All Hallows, Barking. After the Restoration his body was finally and fittingly removed on 24 July 1663 to the chapel of St John's College, Oxford, where he was buried in a vault under the altar between the college's founder and his ally Juxon, who had been interred a few weeks previously.

Later reputation and assessment Laud proved as controversial a figure in death as he was in life. Even his speech at the scaffold prompted outraged attacks upon it by Henry Burton and Joshua Hoyle, whereas his death prompted encomiastic verses from John Cleveland and Peter Heylyn. Prynne's vituperative *Canterburies Doome* (1646) was countered by Heylyn's life of Laud, *Cyprianus Anglicus*, first published in 1668, which, while indebted to Prynne's work for some of its material, presented Laud in the most heroic guise. This dependence of Laud's supporters on Prynne's work was finally lifted when Henry Wharton enthusiastically published the surviving papers of Laud, 'that most Excellent Prelate and Blessed Martyr' in 1695 (Wharton, preface). But Laud never lacked opponents: he was condemned by Burnet and Hacket, and whig historians kept up the critical barrage in the following century, culminating in the famous polemic of Lord Macaulay, who commented in lofty tones that for Laud 'the ridiculous old bigot' 'we entertain a more unmitigated contempt than for any other character in our history'. He had to admit that some in the Church of England revered Laud, although he compared this to 'the perversity of affection which sometimes leads a mother to select the monster or idiot of the family as the object of her special favour' (*Edinburgh Review*, 95, Sept 1828, 134). Macaulay's 'ridiculous old bigot' had indeed enjoyed his high tory supporters in the eighteenth century, but it was in the Victorian period that he reached the height of his popularity among such circles. The Tractarians revered him, and seven volumes of his *Works* were published in the Library of Anglo-Catholic Theology. He was applauded as a defender of the catholicity of the Church of England (often in contrast with the early reformers), and as 'one of the Fathers of the English Reformation ... one of those to whom, under God, we owe all that we hold most dear' (Collins, 63). Others found different aspects of his career to admire. With what one hopes was conscious anachronism, C. H. Simpkinson saluted Laud in 1895 as 'the chief advocate of the Working classes, the defender of the poor, the Leader of the Education Movement, and the administrator who endeavoured to exterminate the corruption of the Civil Service' ('Laud's personal religion', ibid., 124).

Extraordinary scenes attended the ceremonies that were arranged to observe the 250th anniversary of Laud's execution in 1895. An exhibition of 'Laudian relics' was displayed in the schoolroom adjoining the church of All Hallows, Barking, and was visited by more than 2000 people. On the anniversary of the execution itself a large procession with a choir travelled to the site of the scaffold on Tower Hill, where a Te Deum was sung and the account of Laud's death from Heylyn's biography was solemnly read out. The commemoration drew enormous attention, but leading articles in newspapers repeated and wildly embellished the traditional stories against Laud: that he was a Jesuit in disguise, that he made use of 'the thumb-screw and the Scavenger's Daughter', even that he was responsible for the ejection of nonconforming ministers in 1662. Strange anonymous letters were received by the organizers of the commemoration which were oddly similar to the libels published against Laud in the early 1640s, warning that 'you are doing the work of the great Whore of Babylon and leading them to the Pope as your Laud did' (Collins, xiv). He has continued to stir up extraordinarily vehement responses among historians, being condemned even in the 1980s as 'the greatest calamity ever visited upon the Church of England' (Collinson, 90).

Part of the reason why Laud continues to divide historical opinion so fundamentally clearly derives from the long-term divisions of the civil war which engulfed him. Laud has often been either celebrated or berated as the champion of ideas which many of his pre-war contemporaries shared. He has been seen to a quite bizarre degree as the embodiment of absolutism, autocratic clericalist governance, and high-church bigotry, and thereby made vastly more significant and singular (and, it is tempting to say, more interesting) a figure than the historical facts seem to warrant. The events which surrounded his life, and particularly his death, have lent him a symbolic significance out of all proportion to his real distinctiveness and achievements. Given the magnitude of the events for which Laud is held responsible, his humble and unprepossessing personality has often inspired contempt. His social awkwardness, his superstitious fears, and his vulnerability have invited scorn rather than a sense of shared humanity, and even reputable historians have continued to dwell on his shortness of stature and red face to an obsessive degree, even when it has become clear that Laud was not guilty of many of the tyrannies of which he has been accused. Distaste for his objectives clearly lies behind much of this derision, but this strange combination of hatred and contempt is partly rooted in Laud's perceived personality.

Laud's problem—for his contemporaries and for posterity—has been one of presentation. Clarendon wrote that:

> he did court persons too little, nor cared to make his designs and purposes appear as candid as they were, by showing them in any other dress than their own natural beauty and roughness, and did not consider enough what men said or were like to say of him. (Clarendon, *Hist. rebellion*, 1.125)

This was partly true. Laud could certainly be tactless and irritable in public courts and private meetings, and his overwhelming self-righteousness meant that he expected opposition. But the fact that Laud was habituated to opposition should not lead to the assumption that he was indifferent to it. On the contrary, his concerns with it amounted to a morbid obsession. No one was more conscious of his lack of support and the hostility of his opponents. All libels and threats made against him, no matter how eccentric, were always carefully collected and noted. His diary and his dreams are full of anguished fears that he is losing influence and supporters at court. His private devotions harp obsessively on the theme of betrayal by his enemies, begging God's protection from malice and falsehood, paraphrasing the Psalms in his laments that 'the voice of the slanderer and blasphemer hath overtaken me' and 'They that hate me without a cause are more than the hairs of my head' (*Works*, 3.47, 54). In policy terms these fears helped to generate his remarkable conviction that presbyterians were everywhere in church and state from very early on, and like Charles his distrust led him to demands for evidence of loyalty and conformity which then forced potential opposition into the open.

Laud's constant fears have generated contempt on the part of some commentators, but they also surely reveal a startling degree of courage. He was anxious to drive through reforms in church and state in the certain knowledge that future parliaments would be bound to attack him; his instinctive fatalism never let him flinch from pushing forward unpopular policies. His worries did, however, prompt him towards caution. The fiery temper which he could display in personal exchanges was moderated in policy terms by his conviction that he would be called to account for his actions, and that it was crucial that he be able to offer a legal defence. Whenever possible he hid behind royal instructions, judges' decisions, and corporate actions, and the struggles of the prosecution at his trial was a testimony to the skills he had shown. His execution, however, displayed the limitations of this approach: political opposition could overturn legal niceties, and Laud's fundamental problem was that he sought to protect himself against opponents, rather than striving to placate them or even to win them over.

That is not to say that Laud was incapable of making friends. He managed to turn a violent opponent of his election to the presidency of St John's—Richard Baylie—into one of his most devoted and reliable supporters. He was also able to develop amicable relationships with former critics such as John Hales and John Selden. But while these might be skills that could work to build factions in a small college community, they were not appropriate to winning over a country. Sir Thomas Roe claimed that Laud was 'above all, mistaken by the erring world' (PRO, SP 16/178/32), but there was little in Laud's public conduct that would change the mind of that 'erring world'. Clarendon commented that 'few excellent men have ever had fewer friends' (Clarendon, *Hist. rebellion*, 3.466), but those friendships which Laud did have were plainly very intense and deeply felt, which is why he felt the betrayal of Windebank and the death of Buckingham so keenly. His diary provides cryptic evidence of other troubled and intensely painful relationships which continued well into the 1630s, with individuals referred to by mostly unidentified initials, and there are occasional allusions to deep-seated fears that secrets would be revealed. It is impossible to say whether these are allusions to a latent homosexuality (although this is not inherently improbable), but his greatest fears from his earliest days at Oxford were prompted not by his sexuality but by the gibe of 'papist', and it was this anxiety that pursued him to his end.

There is a danger that a recognition of Laud's vulnerability, along with his plodding pedantry and taste for administration, can lead to his being regarded simply as a diligent but dull and unimaginative bureaucrat, lacking any ideological preoccupations. There was an undogmatic side to him, it is true; his overwhelming interest in the institutions of the established Church of England, visible from his earliest days in Oxford, made him relatively less interested in doctrinal controversies, and created a certain common ground with writers such as John Hales and William Chillingworth, although he condemned Socinianism and was suspicious of any patterns of thought which removed the crucial role of the institutional church and her sacraments in fostering true belief and ensuring salvation for the individual. But if Laud's chosen means were legal and administrative rather than doctrinal, and were seasoned by a certain amount of careful compromise, it must be emphasized that his ends were inflexible, and were inspired by a radical vision of the nature and significance of the institutional church and of its role in society which had spilled over into his sermons and doctoral theses in Oxford. His reading of the nature of episcopacy was certainly more radical than the mainstream views of the time, and his elevated sense of the importance of the established church and its institutions and sacraments led him to be dismissive of many of the ideas and practices that had grown up in the years since the Reformation. He was not in search of some vague, ideologically neutral 'law and order': his long-term aim to restore the economic, social, and political power of the church would ultimately have involved undoing much of the effects of the Reformation, and would have transformed the social and political balance of the country as a whole. His opponents were not wrong to see a revolutionary programme here, even if their attempt to brand it as 'popery' was technically incorrect, and reflected both the elastic contemporary usage of the term and the lack of other words which could describe what was being attempted. Laud's constant paranoia was partly a reflection of his deep-seated recognition of the scope of his ambitions and the inevitability of the opposition that they would arouse.   ANTHONY MILTON

Sources *The works of the most reverend father in God, William Laud*, ed. J. Bliss and W. Scott, 7 vols. (1847–60) · *A replie to Jesuit Fishers answere … by Francis White … hereunto is annexed, a conference of the right R: B: of St Davids with the same Jesuit* (1624) · P. Heylyn, *Cyprianus Anglicus* (1668) · W. Prynne, *Canterburies doome, or, The first part of a compleat history of the commitment, charge, tryall, condemnation, execution of William Laud, late arch-bishop of Canterbury* (1646) · *The manuscripts of the House of Lords*, new ser., 12 vols. (1900–77), vol. 11 · J. Hacket, *Scrinia reserata: a memorial offer'd to the great deservings of John Williams*, 2 pts (1693) · PRO, SP 16/94/88, 96/31, 178/32 · Laud's household accounts, PRO, E101/54715 · LPL, Lambeth MSS 943, 1030 · Strafford papers, Sheff. Arch., Wentworth Woodhouse muniments, vols. 6–7, 15, 20–21 · Hunt. L., Hastings MS 15172 · *Hist. U. Oxf.* 4: *17th-cent. Oxf.* · K. Fincham, 'William Laud and the exercise of Caroline ecclesiastical patronage', *Journal of Ecclesiastical History*, 51 (2000), 69–93 · G. Westin, 'Brev från John Durie åren 1636–1638', *Kyrkhistorisk Årsskrift: Skrifter Utgivna av Kyrkhohistorika Foreningen*, 1/33 (1934) [Uppsala] · Clarendon, *Hist. rebellion* · N. Tyacke, *Aspects of English protestantism, c.1530–1700* (2001) · N. Tyacke, *Anti-Calvinists: the rise of English Arminianism, c.1590–1640* (1987) · P. Heylyn, *A briefe relation of the death and sufferings of … L. archbishop of Canterbury* (1645) · *The journal of Sir Simonds D'Ewes from the beginning of the Long Parliament to the opening of the trial of the earl of Strafford*, ed. W. Notestein (1923) · H. Wharton, ed., *The history of the troubles and tryal of the most reverend father in God, and blessed martyr, William Laud* (1695) · R. C. Johnson and others, eds., *Commons debates, 1628*, 6 vols. (1977–83) · W. Notestein and F. H. Relf, eds., *Commons debates for 1629* (1921) · K. Fincham and P. Lake, 'The ecclesiastical policies of James I and Charles I', *The early Stuart church, 1603–1642*, ed. K. Fincham (1993), 237–49 · E. Dering, *A collection of speeches* (1642) · H. R. Trevor-Roper, *Archbishop Laud, 1573–1645*, 3rd edn (1988) · W. H. Hutton, *William Laud*, 2nd edn (1896) · C. Carlton, *Archbishop William Laud* (1987) · A. Milton, *Catholic and Reformed: the Roman and protestant churches in English protestant thought, 1600–1640* (1995) · R. P. Cust, *The forced loan and English politics, 1626–1628* (1987) · *The correspondence of John Cosin D.D., lord bishop of Durham*, ed. [G. Ornsby], 1, SurtS, 52 (1869) · [T. Birch and R. F. Williams], eds., *The court and times of Charles the First*, 2 vols. (1848) · W. E. Collins, ed., *Archbishop Laud commemoration, 1895* (1895) · J. Hall, *Epistles* (1608) · W. J. Tighe, 'William Laud and the reunion of the churches: some evidence from 1637 and 1638', *HJ*, 30 (1987), 717–27 · A. Ford, 'Correspondence between archbishops Ussher and Laud', *Archivium Hibernicum*, 46 (1991–2), 5–21 · J. Young, *A sermon preached before the queenes majestie* (1576?) · J. Davies, *The Caroline captivity of the church: Charles I and the remoulding of Anglicanism, 1625–1641* (1992) · P. White, *Predestination, policy and polemic* (1992) · P. Seaver, 'Land and the livery companies', *State, sovereigns and society in early modern England*, ed. C. Carlton (1998) · P. Collinson, *The religion of protestants* (1982) · K. Sharpe, *The personal rule of Charles I* (1992)

Archives BL, corresp. and papers, Add. MS 32093 · Bodl. Oxf., MSS collection · HLRO, corresp. · LPL, corresp., MSS 943, 1030 · LPL, corresp. and papers · PRO, household accounts, E101/547/5 · Queen's College, Oxford, notes · St John's College, Oxford, diary, corresp., and papers | BL, Harley MSS, papers · Bodl. Oxf., letters to James Ussher [abstracts] · Bodl. Oxf., corresp. with Gerardus Vossius, MSS Rawl. lett. 79–84 · CUL, corresp. and papers relating to Cambridge University · Hunt. L., letters to John Bramhall · Sheff. Arch., corresp. with earl of Strafford · U. Durham L., letters to John Cosin · Wadham College, Oxford, letters to warden and fellows of Wadham College, Oxford

Likenesses bronze bust, 1635, St John's College, Oxford · A. Van Dyck, oils, c.1635–1637, FM Cam. [*see illus.*] · R. Dunkarton, mezzotint, pubd 1813 (after A. Van Dyck), NPG · attrib. H. Le Sueur, gilt terracotta bust, Bodl. Oxf. · J. Roettier, gold and silver medal, BM · A. Van Dyck, oils, other versions, LPL, Hermitage Museum, St Petersburg · mezzotint (after A. Van Dyck), NPG · watercolour drawing, NPG

Wealth at death will includes grants of land and leases and c. £4225 in cash bequests: *Works of Laud*, 4.441–51

Lauder, George (*fl.* 1622–1677), poet, was the younger son of Alexander Lauder (*d.* 1622x5) of Hatton, Edinburghshire, and Mary *Maitland (*d.* 1596), writer, third daughter of Sir Richard *Maitland of Lethington. He probably graduated MA at Edinburgh University in 1620. In 1623 he published *The Anatomie of the Roman Clergie*, a verse translation of a selection of Latin authors, detailing the abuses of the Catholic church.

Lauder seems to have entered the English army, where he attained the rank of colonel, and in 1627 it is likely that he accompanied the duke of Buckingham on the expedition to the Île de Ré. As a royalist he spent many years on the continent, living chiefly at Breda, in the Netherlands, where he printed various poems, and appears to have entered the army of the prince of Orange. The poems include funeral elegies for Henry, prince of Orange (1647), and William, prince of Orange (1650), and *A Horse, or, A New-Yeares-Gift* (1646), addressed to Sir Philip Balfour, a colonel of a Scottish regiment in the prince's army. Writing from The Hague, 1 April 1662, to John Maitland, duke of Lauderdale, Lauder thanks him for kindness to his son. In 1668 he was still living in Breda, and received the part dedication of Justus Turcq's *Bergizomii otia hagana*, a collection of verse dedicated to eminent men of the day. On 15 August 1677, when with his regiment at Embrick, Lauder refers in another letter to Lauderdale to some offer which had been made to him by Sir George Downing of a place in the guards, and says that he declined it because having 'more hungry stomachs than myne owne to fill' he required some provision to be made for his wife and children. He also asks to be 'freed from the rigour of the law and proclamation and receaved into the number of his majesty's free subjects' (BL, Add. MSS, 23116 fol. 9, 23127 fol. 201).

A reference in Sinclair's *Truth's Victory over Error* (1684) shows that Lauder reached an advanced age. In *Fugitive Scotish Poetry* David Laing wrongly makes 1670 the year of his death. In the same work (2nd series) Laing gives a 'Christmas carol' by 'F. G.', 'For the heroycall L. Colonel Lauder, patron of truth', and an 'Epitaph on the honourable Colonel George Lauder', by Alexander Wedderburn.

Lauder's poems were mainly patriotic and military. He wrote the heroic couplet with considerable vigour, and skilfully compassed an irregular sonnet especially in instances where commemorating fallen comrades. His most notable achievement was his successful memorial poem, 'Damon, or, A pastoral elegy on the death of his honoured friend, William Drummond of Hawthornden' (1650), which depicts Drummond dying of a broken heart as the old royalist culture of Britain recedes. This was prefixed to Drummond's *Poems* (1711) and provides useful biographical information on Drummond. Robert Mylne, an industrious collector, possessed a good set of Lauder's tracts; and a quarto manuscript in New Hailes Library contains several of his pieces, apparently transcribed from copies printed on the continent. Two of these, *The Scottish Souldier* and *Wight* (an appeal from the Isle of Wight for bulwarks), were printed about 1629, and republished in *Frondes caducae*, by Sir Alexander Boswell of Auchinleck in 1818 along with a list of his other writings compiled by George Chalmers. Four more poems, dating from 1622 to his poem on the death of Charles I in 1649, appeared in the second series of Laing's *Fugitive Scotish Poetry*.

T. W. BAYNE, rev. GERARD CARRUTHERS

Sources A. Boswell, ed., *Frondes caducae*, 7 vols. (1818) · *The poetical works of William Drummond of Hawthornden*, ed. L. E. Kastner, 2 vols., STS, 2nd ser., 3–4 (1913) · D. Masson, *Drummond of Hawthornden: the story of his life and writings* (1873) · D. Laing, ed., *Various pieces of fugitive Scotish poetry; principally of the seventeenth century* (1853) · *ESTC* · BL, Add. MSS 23116, 23127

Archives BL, corresp., Add. MSS 23116, 23127

Lauder, Henry, of St Germains (*d.* 1561). *See under* College of justice, procurators of the (*act.* 1532).

Lauder, Sir Henry [Harry] (**1870–1950**), music-hall singer, was born in Bridge Street, Portobello, near Edinburgh, on 4 August 1870, the eldest of seven children of John Lauder (*d.* 1882), potter, of Musselburgh and his wife, Isobella Urquhart Macleod, daughter of Henry MacLennan, of the Black Isle, Ross-shire. On his father's death in 1882 the family moved first to Arbroath, where Lauder worked part-time in a flax-mill, and then in the following year to Hamilton, where he was employed as a miner for the next decade. On 19 June 1891 he married Annie Vallance (1873/4–1927), daughter of a Hamilton coalminer. It was to be a happy marriage. Lauder quickly gained a reputation as a singer and comedian with local concert parties, eventually turning professional in 1895. Initially, he worked the smaller Scottish and northern English halls using a mixture of Scottish and Irish characterizations, although he had virtually dropped the latter by the turn of the century.

Noting that English comedians could surmount potential communication problems and succeed with Glasgow audiences, Lauder sought London bookings in March 1900, taking great care that his act, while distinctively Scottish, avoided the excessive use of dialect that had hitherto handicapped Scottish performers in the metropolis. His success was instant, a leading theatrical paper noting that:

> Harry Lauder, a Scotch comedian, who has been appearing this week as an extra turn at Messrs Gatti's Westminster Bridge Road establishment, has caused so great a furore with his three songs that he has been secured by the London Pavilion management. (*Era*, 24 March 1900)

Lauder moved rapidly to the head of the variety profession, touring the USA in 1907, performing in a private concert before Edward VII in 1908, and appearing in the first ever royal variety performance in 1912. The £1125 he received at the Glasgow Pavilion in 1913 was probably the highest weekly salary earned by a variety artist in the pre-

Sir Henry [Harry] **Lauder** (1870–1950), by Cavendish Morton, 1904

war period. During the First World War he worked tirelessly in recruiting campaigns and starred in innumerable troop concerts at home and on the western front, activities made poignant by the death in action of his only son, John, in 1916. Lauder was knighted for services to the war effort in 1919. He continued to star on the variety stage well into the 1930s, touring all over the English-speaking world: his final North American tour in 1932 was his twenty-fifth such undertaking. Effectively retired by the mid-1930s, he returned to undertake troop concerts throughout the Second World War and still made occasional radio broadcasts into the late 1940s.

Lauder's major vehicle was the comic song with an extended 'patter' routine, with his early songs in particular often built around an unfolding narrative showing the ultimate victory and native wit of a supposedly soft or foolish character. He was able to build a rapid rapport with audiences through his easy-to-assimilate characterizations, range of facial expressions, and 'pleasing and expressive baritone voice' (*The Times*). As his career progressed he also deployed a range of cheerful love songs such as 'I love a lassie' and 'Roamin' in the gloamin'', launched in Glasgow pantomimes in 1905 and 1910 respectively, as well as uplifting offerings such as 'The End of the Road' (1924) and even hymn tunes. This, coupled with his growing tendency to give short homilies to audiences and to make public protestations about the need for high moral standards in popular entertainment, has earned him something of a reputation for sanctimoniousness which obscures key elements of his comic talent. While clearly anxious to associate himself with the supposedly more refined tone of Edwardian variety, he was aware of music-hall tradition and worked comfortably within it. 'Stop your tickling, Jock' (1905) celebrated the 'treacle roly poly' that Harry and his young lady enjoyed while her parents were at the kirk; 'I'm the one they left behind' (1903) told of a lad who saw his patriotic duty as looking after the local womenfolk while his friends fought abroad; on being asked how he had lost his luggage, a character in 'The Saftest o' the Family' (1904) replies, 'the cork came oot o' the bottle'. Lauder probably wrote a considerable amount of his own material though he also collaborated effectively with a number of writers including Clifford Grafton and William Dutton, and there are suggestions that, in line with common variety practice, other writers' songs were published under Lauder's name after only minimal payment.

The first Scottish character comedian to become a major international star, Lauder, while not inventing the stage Scotsman, did much to construct and reinforce certain notions of Scottish identity. Although he did not use Scottish dress exclusively, he became best known for colourful representations involving kilt, tam-o'-shanter bonnet, and curly cromach (shepherd's stick). To this were added numerous jokes about Scottish miserliness which the anyway cautious Lauder further reinforced through a carefully cultivated off-stage persona, involving the studious avoidance of tipping and other devices. In his autobiography he answered his rhetorical 'have I carried the totally undeserved reputation for Scottish "carefulness" to a line bordering on the excessive?' with 'perhaps I have' (Lauder, 280). At his death, his estate was worth more than a quarter of a million pounds. The quaint and comically sentimental 'kailyard' version of Scotland that he tended to portray may well have generated rather limited images of his country among non-Scottish audiences and did not endear him to some fellow countrymen. However, there can be little denying his enormous popularity both in Scotland and in expatriate communities, especially in North America, and no one has more effectively combined Scottish pawky humour with sentimentality.

Although best known as a live performer, Lauder was a regular recording artist from the early 1900s and, unusually attentive to the needs of the new medium, he also became a consummate broadcaster. He appeared in a number of short films from 1907 and made three features: *Huntingtower* (1927), a silent version of the John Buchan novel in which he played Glaswegian grocer Dickson McCunn, and two sentimental family dramas, *Auld Lang Syne* (1929) and *The End of the Road* (1936). From the death of his wife in 1927, his niece Greta acted as housekeeper and companion and she nursed him through his final illness. Lauder enjoyed writing and produced three autobiographical volumes, *Harry Lauder at Home and on Tour* (1907), *A Minstrel in France* (1918), and *Roamin' in the Gloamin'* (1928). He suffered a thrombosis in August 1949 from which he

never recovered. He died at his Scottish home, Lauder Ha, Strathaven, on 26 February 1950 and was buried at Cadzow parish church, Hamilton, on 3 March. His death drew a leading article from *The Times*, tribute to his enormous standing within British public life, and only his most hostile critics would deny him a position among the leading half-dozen variety artists of all time.

DAVE RUSSELL

Sources H. Lauder, *Roamin' in the gloamin'* (1928) · *Performer* (2 March 1950) · *The Times* (27 Feb 1950) · G. Irving, *Great Scot: the life story of Sir Harry Lauder, legendary laird of the music hall* (1968) · *Francis & Day's album of Harry Lauder's popular songs* [n.d., 1930?] · b. cert. · m. cert.
Archives NL Scot., corresp. | FILM BFI NFTVA, documentary footage · BFI NFTVA, current affairs footage · BFI NFTVA, news footage · BFI NFTVA, performance footage | SOUND BL NSA, 'Roamin' in the gloamin'', H5484/5
Likenesses C. Morton, photograph, 1904, NPG [*see illus.*] · H. M. Bateman, pen and wash drawing, 1915, Scot. NPG · J. Lockhart, oils, 1916, Dundee City Art Gallery · J. McBey, oils, c.1922, Art Gallery and Museum, Glasgow · T. Roscoe, oils, Scot. NPG
Wealth at death £264,418 12s. 10d.: confirmation, 26 April 1950, CCI

Lauder, James Eckford (1811–1869), genre and landscape painter, was born on 15 August 1811 at Silvermills, Edinburgh, the son of John Lauder, tanner, and Helen (or Ellen) Tait, his wife. He was the younger brother of the painter Robert Scott *Lauder (1803–1869), from whom he received early artistic encouragement. From 1830 to 1833 he attended the antique class of the Trustees' Academy in Edinburgh, his teachers being William Allan and Thomas Duncan. Afterwards he joined his brother in Rome, where he studied and made copies from the old masters between 1834 and 1838.

James Eckford Lauder's early paintings were largely figure subjects drawn from Shakespeare or from his Italian surroundings. He exhibited from 1833 at the Royal Scottish Academy, where he was elected an associate in 1839, and a full academician in 1846. The most notable success in his career was his painting *The Parable of Forgiveness* (1847; Walker Art Gallery, Liverpool), for which he won £200 in the Westminster Hall competition. The drama is set, frieze-like, on a narrow stage before a backdrop of classical buildings. Its figure composition, with a reliance on theatrical gesture, shows his knowledge of paintings of the Italian high Renaissance. During the 1850s Lauder continued to produce biblical, historical, and literary subjects, for example *Bailie Duncan Macwheeble at Breakfast* (1854; NG Scot.) which may be regarded as the masterpiece of his career. In a finely balanced composition every texture and detail of the books, papers, vessels, and the character himself are depicted with a fineness to rival Dutch paintings of the seventeenth century. Unfortunately, he did not sustain this quality and his diploma work, *Hagar* (1857; Royal Scottish Academy), is a much weaker painting. After about 1857 he turned to landscape subjects, mainly of Scotland or Italy, possibly in the hope of improving his now slackened sales. This departure was not successful: although he worked hard to produce large quantities of paintings, he appears to have struggled financially. In later years he relied on a fellow artist and academician, D. O. Hill, to assist him by acting as an agent for his late works and also in providing cash handouts. James Eckford Lauder never married and he died at his lodgings, 14 Salisbury Street, Edinburgh, on 29 March 1869. He was buried in Warriston cemetery, Edinburgh, where he shared a headstone with his more illustrious brother, Robert Scott Lauder.   JOANNA SODEN

Sources P. J. M. McEwan, *Dictionary of Scottish art and architecture* (1994) · *DNB* · *Annual Report of the Council of the Royal Scottish Academy of Painting, Sculpture, and Architecture*, 42 (1869), 9 · Wood, *Vic. painters*, 2nd edn, 276 · R. Brydall, *Art in Scotland, its origin and progress* (1889), 428–9 · W. D. McKay, *The Scottish school of painting* (1906), 256–9 · J. L. Caw, *Scottish painting past and present, 1620–1908* (1908), 118 · C. B. de Laperriere, ed., *The Royal Scottish Academy exhibitors, 1826–1990*, 4 vols. (1991), vol. 3, pp. 15–17 · d. cert. · Graves, *RA exhibitors* · Royal Scot. Acad., RSA Archives · headstone, Warriston cemetery, Edinburgh

Archives Royal Scot. Acad., corresp.

Likenesses C. Lees, oils, exh. 1849, Royal Scot. Acad. · R. Innes, oils, Scot. NPG · J. E. Lauder, self-portrait, oils, Scot. NPG · photograph, Royal Scot. Acad.

Lauder, James Stack [*pseud.* James Lafayette] (1853–1923), photographer, was born on 22 January 1853 and baptized on 18 March at St George's parish church, Hardwicke Place, Dublin, the eldest son in the family of six sons and four daughters of Edmund Stanley Lauder (*c*.1824–1891), photographer, and his wife, Sarah Harding Stack (*c*.1828–1913), who had been matron of the union workhouse, Parsonstown, King's county. The Lauders came from minor gentry in King's county. In the 1850s Edmund Lauder opened a daguerreotype portrait studio in Dublin, later known as Lauder Brothers, where James served his apprenticeship in the 1860s and witnessed the transition of commercial photography from a trade to an industry.

By his own account Lauder studied painting in Paris and worked in a Berlin photographic studio. In 1880 he opened his own studio in Dublin, which became established as the firm of Lafayette. In 1884 he was awarded a medal for his first entry at the annual show of the Photographic Society of Great Britain and was also elected a member. In the spring of 1885 Alexandra, princess of Wales, visited Ireland and was photographed by his studio after receiving an honorary degree. This remarkable image of a princess in a scholarly role caught the public imagination and more than 60,000 prints were sold. Summoned to photograph Queen Victoria in her golden jubilee year (1887), Lauder became the first Irish photographer to be granted a royal warrant. Three months later, on 1 June, he married Annie Pierrette, daughter of the artist Felix Pierre Dinnette; they had three sons and four daughters.

Lauder continued winning medals at exhibitions, including one at the 1889 Paris Universal Exhibition. His large-scale study of a floating angel, at the World's Columbian Exhibition shown in Chicago in 1893, was noted by H. W. Vogel, professor of photography and art critic, as the 'grandest exhibit' in the English section (Vogel, 668). Years later Lauder explained his conjuring effect: the model was not suspended by wires but positioned horizontally on a sheet of glass, with the perspective background beneath,

James Stack Lauder (1853–1923), by Lafayette [standing centre, with members of his family]

and photographed from above. In the 1890s the firm of Lafayette rapidly expanded, opening up new branch studios in Glasgow, Manchester, Belfast, and London, and in 1898 it became a publicly quoted company. Lafayette's commercial success coincided with developments in the half-tone printing process which resulted in the proliferation of illustrated weekly magazines; Lauder was one of the first to recognize the opportunities offered by syndicating photographs. His studies and portraits of distinguished men and women from society and the stage appeared prominently in a series of newly launched titles, including *Madame*, *Cycling World*, and *Country Life*, and later *Car Illustrated*, *Candid Friend*, and *The Throne*, frequently providing the frontispiece and setting the tone for the publication.

When he moved to London in 1897, Lauder was already a celebrity within the circle of commercial photographers, who welcomed him with a formal dinner. A commission from the duchess of Devonshire, to record the guests at her diamond jubilee costume ball, confirmed his position in London. He remained very much in demand with high society and its followers until the turn of the century; however, his style of photography remained Victorian in flavour, and in the new century younger competitors started eroding his share of the fashionable market. In Ireland the Lafayette studio was still pre-eminent and its promotional photography for the motor cycle and the motor car explored new ways of looking at the landscape.

A talented entrepreneur and image-maker, Lauder contributed substantially to the translation of ideas from the language of the fine and performing arts into that of popular photography. Of the thousands of images credited to Lafayette, only 649 photographs registered for copyright (now in the Public Record Office, Kew, London) bear the signature of James Lauder as author. Lafayette is linked to memories of Dublin through references in James Joyce's *Ulysses* (1922) and more recently in John McGahern's *The Leavetaking* (1984). Exhibitions at the Queen's Gallery, London (1987), the Guinness Museum, Dublin (1989), and the National Portrait Gallery, London (1998), have included examples of his work. The National Portrait Gallery and the Victoria and Albert Museum in London, the Royal Archives at Windsor, and a private collection in Dublin all have large holdings of his photographs. Lauder died at the Hôpital St Jean, Bruges, Belgium, on 20 August 1923. He was survived by his wife. JANE MEADOWS

Sources registers (baptisms), St George's, Hardwicke Place, Dublin City, Representative Church Body Library, Dublin, MS Church of Ireland, 1853–70 · General Register Office, Dublin · records, town hall, Bruges, Belgium, General Registry (Burgerlijke Stand) · copyright entry forms, PRO, COPY 1: 1885–1912 · Lafayette negative collection, V&A, department of prints and drawings · *Industries of Dublin* (1888) · L. Carnac, 'Photography as a fine art', *Pearson's Magazine*, 3 (March 1897), 241–50 · *Stock Exchange Year Book* (1901–53) · *Stock Exchange Year Book* (1956) · *Stock Exchange Year Book* (1959) · *Journal and Transactions of the Photographic Society of Great Britain*, new ser., 9 (1884–5), 22, 28 · *British Journal of Photography* (10 Oct 1884), 651–2 · *Photographic News* (10 Oct 1884), 644 · *Photographic News* (7 June 1889), 370 · *Bulletin de la Société Française de Photographie*, 2nd ser., 5 (1889), 253–9 · H. W. Vogel, 'Letter from Germany: the Chicago World's Fair', *Anthony's Photographic Bulletin* (11 Nov 1893), 668 · J. K. Brown, *Contesting images: photography and the World's Columbian Exposition* (1994) · E. Chandler and P. Walsh, *Through the brass lidded eye: photography in Ireland* (1989) · F. Dimond and R. Taylor, *Crown and camera: the royal family and photography, 1842–1910* (1987) · T. Pepper, *High society: photographs, 1897–1914* (1998)

Archives FILM priv. coll., The Lafayette Project [c/o NPG]

Likenesses Lafayette, photograph, NPG [*see illus.*]

Wealth at death £3116 16s. 9d.: probate, 16 Jan 1924, CGPLA Éire · £164 13s. 4d.: probate, 8 Oct 1923, CGPLA Eng. & Wales

Lauder, Sir John, second baronet, Lord Fountainhall (1646–1722), judge and political commentator, was born at Edinburgh on 2 August 1646, the eldest son of Sir John Lauder (1595–1692), an Edinburgh merchant and bailie who was raised to the Nova Scotia baronetcy in 1688, and his second wife, Isabel Ellis (or Eleis), daughter of Alexander Ellis of Mortonhall, a Wigtownshire laird. After education at the high school and university of Edinburgh, from where he graduated MA on 18 July 1664, he proceeded to the continent to pursue his legal studies. Residing at Poitiers from 28 July 1665 to 24 April 1666, he also visited Paris, Brussels, Antwerp, and Leiden, an itinerary recounted in his *Journals*, which were eventually published in 1900. On his return to Scotland he was admitted to the Faculty of Advocates on 5 June 1668, and, along with Sir George Mackenzie, he was one of the fifty advocates who supported Sir George Lockhart in his determination to appeal from the king's courts to the Scottish parliament. Briefly debarred and banished from Edinburgh with his colleagues, Lauder nevertheless began to acquire a formidable reputation as a lawyer. On 21 January 1669 he

married Janet (1652–1686), daughter of Sir Andrew Ramsay of Abbotshall, with whom he had several children, including his eldest son and heir, John.

Lauder's career as a criminal advocate reached its peak in his defence of the earl of Argyll in the latter's trial for treason in 1681, by which time Lauder was an experienced and accomplished legal practitioner. He was also, as his extensive writings reveal, a keen and critical observer of public affairs, not only in Scotland but also elsewhere in Britain and in Europe. Published in 1848 as *Historical Notices of Scotish Affairs*, one such commentary covers the entire period 1661–88, though with particular concentration on events from the late 1670s. Here Lauder reveals himself as an instinctive royalist, a sincere presbyterian, and a political conservative—though also as a man of comparatively moderate preferences, worried by fanaticism and sedition in all their insidious manifestations: his dislike of the rebellious covenanters, for example, whom he distinguished as 'remonstrant Presbyterians', comes through clearly in his shocked response to the murder in 1679 of Archbishop James Sharp, which Lauder uncompromisingly judged 'ane barbarous act' (*Historical Notices*, 1.225).

For the 1680s Lauder's political attitudes are illustrated by what was printed in 1840 as *Historical observes of memorable occurrents in church and state, from October 1680 to April 1686*. This text, which captures his views on the Scottish sojourn of the duke of York and his subsequent accession as James VII, is far superior to the work known as *Chronological Notes of Scottish Affairs from 1680 to 1701*, edited by Sir Walter Scott in 1822, which, though it purports to be based on Lauder's writings, is in fact shot through with a rabid Jacobitism intruded by Robert Mylne, an Edinburgh lawyer who had early posthumous possession of the manuscript original. Unlike the *Chronological Notes*, which bristle with criticism of the Williamite revolution as an 'unnaturall usurpation' (*Chronological Notes*, 265), the *Historical Observes* provide an authentic insight into the views of a presbyterian royalist in increasingly difficult times.

Like many other Scots of this time, Lauder emerges as a man whose natural tolerance of James VII as legitimate sovereign was sorely tested by the authoritarianism and pro-Catholic policies of the crown, eventually leading to regretful but unambiguous support for the revolution. He was also an active politician throughout the period from James's accession to the final abolition of the Scottish parliament. Elected MP for Haddingtonshire on 23 April 1685, he represented the same county in the parliaments of 1690–1702 and 1702–7. Following the death of his first wife, on 26 March 1687 he married Marion Anderson, daughter of the laird of Balram, with whom he also had numerous children.

Given both his religion and his skills, Lauder was a predictable beneficiary of the Williamite government in its restructuring of the Scottish legal establishment. Having been knighted about 1681, he became a lord of session on 1 November 1689, with the title of Lord Fountainhall. On 27 January 1690 he became lord justiciary, further proof of his acceptability to the post-revolution administration. In April 1692 he also successfully obtained title to his father's baronetcy, which his stepmother had previously secured for her own son by alleging on its initial creation in 1688 that Lauder was disloyal to James's cause. He certainly possessed an independence of mind at which this unscrupulous accusation had probably gestured, occasionally exhibiting extreme obstinacy and several times refusing, on matters of principle, to support the government line. This attachment to the dictates of his own conscience continued to show itself even after the revolution. In 1692 he declined the opportunity to become Scotland's lord advocate: in fact, he had discovered that, if appointed, he would not be allowed to prosecute the perpetrators of the recent massacre in Glencoe, an event to which he did not share the indulgent attitude of William's blinder Scottish acolytes. Similarly in the last Scottish parliament he stoutly held out against the proposed Union with England which was forcefully advocated by Queen Anne's ministers.

In the aftermath of Union, Fountainhall suffered from increasing ill health before resigning the lord justiciarship. Nevertheless he continued to sit in the court of session for several years. He finally died in Edinburgh on 20 September 1722, and was interred three days later in Greyfriars kirkyard there. Many of his surviving manuscripts were subsequently preserved and several are now to be found in the National Library of Scotland.

DAVID ALLAN

Sources *Historical notices of Scotish affairs, selected from the manuscripts of Sir John Lauder of Fountainhall*, ed. D. Laing, 2 vols., Bannatyne Club, 87 (1848) • GEC, *Baronetage*, 4.357–8, 360–61 • *Journals of Sir John Lauder*, ed. D. Crawford, Scottish History Society, 36 (1900) • J. Lauder, *Historical observes of memorable occurrents in church and state, from October 1680 to April 1686*, ed. A. Urquhart and D. Laing, Bannatyne Club, 66 (1840) • *Chronological notes of Scottish affairs … being chiefly taken from the diary of Lord Fountainhall*, ed. W. Scott (1822) • Chambers, *Scots.*, rev. T. Thomson (1875), 2.460–64
Archives NL Scot., accounts, journals, legal papers • U. Aberdeen, Special Libraries and Archives, travel diary [copy] • U. Edin., papers, incl. narrative of his travels in France

Lauder, Robert Scott (1803–1869), painter and art teacher, was born on 25 June 1803 at Silvermills in Edinburgh, the son of John Lauder, a tannery owner, and his wife, Ellen (or Helen) Tait. Lauder was educated at the Royal High School, Edinburgh. Encouragement from the artist David Roberts, who was a neighbour and who was working at the time as a scene painter, helped steer Lauder towards an artistic career. In 1822, with the support of Sir Walter Scott, he was accepted by the Trustees' Academy, where he studied for two years with the landscape painter Andrew Wilson. A self-portrait of 1823 (Scot. NPG), already very accomplished, shows a slightly dandified young man with a fine, sensitive face and curly hair. Supported by his father, he then spent three years studying independently in London. In 1827 he exhibited at the Royal Academy for the first time from 83 Dean Street, London. He returned to Edinburgh, where in February 1828 he was elected a member of the Institution for the Encouragement of the Fine Arts in Scotland. William Allan had succeeded Andrew Wilson at the Trustees' Academy in 1826 and in November 1829, on Allan's recommendation, Lauder was appointed

Robert Scott Lauder (1803–1869), self-portrait, c.mid-1820s

as his temporary replacement during a year's leave of absence. In April the same year Lauder was elected a full member of the new Scottish Academy.

Lauder's initial intention seems to have been to become a portrait painter, and the remarkable portrait of his younger brother Henry Lauder (1827; NG Scot.), his eyes shaded by a wide-brimmed hat, shows that Lauder, more subtle than Watson Gordon and a better colourist than Thomas Duncan, was potentially the best Scottish portrait painter since Raeburn. He exhibited numerous portraits at the Royal Institution and the Royal Scottish Academy from 1826 to 1839, but from the latter date he exhibited very few, turning instead to historical narrative subjects, inspired perhaps by William Allan and by the success of David Wilkie's *Preaching of Knox before the Lords of the Congregation*, exhibited at the Royal Academy in 1832. Lauder favoured subjects drawn from Scott's Waverley novels. These, such as *The Bride of Lammermoor* (1839, MacManus Gallery, Dundee), or *The Fair Maid of Perth* (1848; Smith Art Gallery, Stirling), though often vivid in colour and handling, are rather stagy costume dramas. It is possible that he did not pursue his ambition to be a portrait painter in Edinburgh because John Watson Gordon had already assumed the position left vacant by Raeburn's death. However, Lauder did subsequently paint a number of remarkable portraits, notably of his friend David Roberts in oriental costume (exh. RA, 1840; Scot. NPG), of Professor John Wilson (exh. RA, 1843; University of Edinburgh), and an intense and moving double portrait of John Gibson Lockhart and, posthumously, his wife, Sophia Scott (c.1842; Scot. NPG).

On 10 September 1833 Lauder married Isabella Thomson

(*b.* 1808), herself a painter and daughter of the minister and landscape painter the Revd John Thomson of Duddingston. The couple then set out for Italy, arriving in Rome in November. Their first two children were born in that city in 1834 and 1837. Three further children followed in 1839, 1841, and 1844. Lauder endeavoured to make a living from portrait commissions but also painted very fine landscapes and genre studies, and even still life, as well as subject pictures. *The Trial of Effie Deans* (1839; Dundee Museums and Art Galleries), for example, was begun in Scotland and finished in Rome. Two self-portraits from this time, one in seventeenth-century costume, were hung at Hospitalfield House in Arbroath, home of Patrick Allan Fraser, a fellow painter and companion in Rome.

In May 1838 the Lauders left Italy, returning via Venice and Munich, before settling in London at 35 Upper Charlotte Street, formerly the home of John Constable. During the following years, endeavouring to establish himself in London, Lauder exhibited paintings drawn from the works of Scott, Byron, and Shakespeare as well as occasional portraits at the Royal Academy. However, though he evidently established his reputation among some of his fellow artists, he failed to be elected to the academy and, abandoning the attempt, in 1847 agreed to become president of its newly established rival, the Free Exhibition. He did not exhibit at the Royal Academy after 1848. In 1847 he entered the competition for the decoration of the new houses of parliament. His main entry, a 12 foot wide canvas, *Christ Teacheth Humility*, is rich in colour and dramatic in lighting. Its composition is based on Rembrandt's etching *Christ Healing the Sick* and with almost thirty figures, it is by far his largest and most ambitious painting. Nevertheless, he was disappointed when it was passed over by the Westminster judges. In 1848, however, it was bought by the Royal Association for the Promotion of the Fine Arts in Scotland, an organization set up with the aim of establishing a national collection and so it later passed to the National Gallery of Scotland, Edinburgh.

Disappointed in London and in some financial difficulty, on 16 February 1852 Lauder accepted an invitation to return to Edinburgh, to the Trustees' Academy. The academy had been going through a difficult time and in consequence Lauder was expected to share his teaching position with an existing incumbent, Alexander Christie. In spite of these obstacles, Lauder's teaching as director of the antique, life, and colour schools, had a significant influence on art in Scotland. Under his teaching, though it was for so brief a period, a brilliant group of students emerged. His pupils W. Q. Orchardson, John Pettie, G. P. Chalmers, and William McTaggart were the leaders among a dozen artists known simply as the Scott–Lauder school who went on to dominate Scottish painting and, indeed, to make their mark in London. The secret of Lauder's success as a teacher was his willingness to encourage his students to think pictorially from the start. One of them, Peter Graham, said:

One thing that lives in my memory, was the effective way in which he gave 'heartening' to his students. He was constantly encouraging, and urging them, even at an early

stage in their career, to begin and work upon a picture of some kind. (Gilbert, 3)

At the time this was a highly unusual approach. Generally art teaching everywhere was prescriptive, the results mechanical. Students were actively discouraged from painting, or even composing, until they had passed the first years of drawing from the antique and from life. In contrast, surviving drawings from the antique by Lauder's pupils are complete works of art and very beautiful (examples in NG Scot.). They show how he used these studio exercises imaginatively to develop in his students pictorial ideas about light and shade, and composition. Lauder's own use of rich colour and his subtle and lively technique were also an important example to his students, so much so that when in 1908 the critic James Caw sought to define the Scottish school, these were the characteristics that he chose, citing Lauder's teaching as their starting point (Caw, 491–5).

In 1858, however, following complex and bitter negotiations between the Trustees of the Board of Manufactures, hitherto responsible for the Trustees' Academy, the Royal Scottish Academy, which had always claimed the right to control teaching though it had never done so, and the Department of Science and Art in South Kensington, the Trustees' Academy was absorbed into a larger unit and Lauder's own position was downgraded. This insult combined with financial trouble and a stroke he suffered in 1861, after which he could neither teach nor paint, darkened his final years. He resigned his post in January 1864 and died at 3 Hardie Avenue, Edinburgh, on 21 April 1869. He was not forgotten by his students, however. In 1863 a group of them wrote from London a warm and touching letter of tribute. His gravestone in the Warriston cemetery, Edinburgh, adorned with a bust of the artist by his pupil John Hutchison, was inscribed 'Erected by his students of the School of Design in grateful remembrance of his unfailing sympathy as a friend and able guidance as a master'.
                                                                    DUNCAN MACMILLAN

Sources 'R. S. Lauder', *Art Journal*, 12 (1850), 12 · E. Gordon, *The Royal Scottish Academy of painting, sculpture and architecture, 1826–1976* (1976) · W. D. McKay and F. Rinder, *The Royal Scottish Academy, 1826–1916* (1917) · E. Pinnington, 'Robert Scott Lauder & his pupils', *Art Journal*, 37 (1898), 339–43, 367–71 · W. M. Gilbert, 'The life and work of Peter Graham RA', *Art Annual* (1899) [entire volume] · J. L. Caw, *Scottish painting past and present, 1620–1908* (1908) · R. Napier, *John Thomson of Duddingston* (1919) · D. Irwin and F. Irwin, *Scottish artists at home and abroad* (1975) · L. Errington, *Master class: Robert Scott Lauder and his pupils* (1983) [exhibition catalogue, NG Scot., 15 July – 2 Oct 1983, and Aberdeen Art Gallery, 15 Oct – 12 Nov 1983] · Graves, *RA exhibitors* · *Art Journal* (1869), 176 · d. cert.
Likenesses R. S. Lauder, self-portrait, pencil and chalk drawing, 1823, Scot. NPG · R. S. Lauder, self-portrait, oils, *c.*1823–1827, Scot. NPG [*see illus.*] · J. Hutchison, marble bust, 1861, Scot. NPG · T. Duncan, oils, Scot. NPG · Green, woodcut (after drawing), BM; repro. in *Art Journal* (1850) · circular medallion (after J. Hutchison), BM, NPG; repro. in *ILN* (13 Jan 1872)

Lauder, Thomas (1395–1481), bishop of Dunkeld, was the son of a nobleman, probably a Lauder of Bass, and an unmarried woman. He was educated at the University of Paris, taking the degree of licentiate of arts in 1414, and served at the Council of Basel, where he is described as *secretarius regis scotorum*, although this indicates that he held a clerical position rather than the office of royal secretary. By 1437 he was master of the hospital of Soutra in Lothian, while in 1444, when he founded a chaplainry in the church of St Giles, Edinburgh, he is also referred to as a canon of Aberdeen. He became tutor to the young James II, whom he continued to serve as both counsellor and royal clerk, and by 1449 he was the first chancellor of St Andrews.

Lauder was provided to the see of Dunkeld on 28 April 1452, confirmation of his appointment being given on 22 June. He witnessed the settlement in parliament, on 18 July 1454, between the king and James Crichton over the earldom of Moray, but he suffered from the wider ramifications of the conflict between the king and the Black Douglases, which caused a breakdown of law and order. On 26 November 1454 Lauder complained of problems in visiting his diocese in person, 'because of certain ill wishers and enemies of his' (Dunlop, 153 n. 2), and he was apparently compelled to hold his synods to the south of Perth, where he built an episcopal lodging. He was able to organize the running of the business of his diocese from the chapter house at Dunkeld, however, completed and dedicated by him in 1464. In 1454, in a measure similarly intended for administrative convenience, James II granted Lauder the incorporation of all the lands of the bishopric of Dunkeld into two baronies: Dunkeld for those north of the Forth and Aberlady for those south of the Forth.

In October 1474, being seventy-nine years of age, Lauder resigned as bishop of Dunkeld in favour of James Livingston, although he retained his episcopal dignity and received a pension of 600 gold florins from the revenue of the see. Confirmation was given of a charter by Thomas Lauder, described as formerly bishop of Dunkeld, but now a bishop in the universal church, on 17 March 1481. He died on 4 November that year and was buried in Dunkeld Cathedral.   C. A. McGLADDERY

Sources A. Myln, *Vitae Dunkeldensis ecclesiae episcoporum*, ed. T. Thomson, rev. edn, 1, rev. C. Innes, Bannatyne Club (1831) · J. Dowden, *The bishops of Scotland … prior to the Reformation*, ed. J. M. Thomson (1912) · J. M. Thomson and others, eds., *Registrum magni sigilli regum Scotorum / The register of the great seal of Scotland*, 11 vols. (1882–1914), vol. 2 · *CEPR letters*, vols. 7–13 · C. Innes, ed., *Registrum episcopatus Moraviensis*, Bannatyne Club, 58 (1837) · C. Eubel, ed., *Hierarchia Catholica medii aevi*, 2 (Münster, 1901) · A. I. Dunlop, *The life and times of James Kennedy, bishop of St Andrews*, St Andrews University Publications, 46 (1950)

Lauder, Sir Thomas Dick, seventh baronet (1784–1848), author, was a descendant of Sir John *Lauder of Fountainhall. He was the son of Sir Andrew Lauder of Fountainhall, sixth baronet (d. 1820, who had first married Isabel Dick, the heir of The Grange in Edinburgh), and his second wife, Elizabeth, daughter of Thomas Brown of Johnstonburn. For a short time he held a commission in the 79th regiment (Cameron Highlanders), but on his marriage in 1808 to Charlotte Anne Cumin (d. 1864), only child and heir of Susanna and George Cumin of Relugas, on the River Findhorn, near Forres, he took up his residence there. They

Sir Thomas Dick Lauder, seventh baronet (1784–1848), by Robert Scott Lauder, c.1833

had two sons and ten daughters. Dick Lauder succeeded to the baronetcy on the death of his father in 1820. The scenery and legends of the district gave a special bent to his scientific and literary studies. In 1815 he began to contribute papers on chemistry, natural history, and meteorology to the *Annals of Philosophy*, edited by Professor Thomas Thomson of Glasgow. He read to the Royal Society of Edinburgh in 1818 a remarkable paper on the 'parallel roads of Glenroy', in which he tried to show that the 'roads' were the result of glacial movements rather than constructions by ancient Celtic warriors. He was one of the early contributors to *Blackwood's Edinburgh Magazine*, writing for it in 1817 a tale, 'Simon Roy, Gardener at Dumphail'.

Dick Lauder's romantic view of the Moray area was set out in two historical novels, *Lochindhu* (1825) and *The Wolf of Badenoch* (1827), very popular (especially the latter) throughout the nineteenth century; they gave a lively sense of the region's geography, but showed also how much abler a historical novelist was Sir Walter Scott. Dick Lauder maintained his scientific interests with a statistical account of Moray for the *Edinburgh Encyclopaedia* and—his most original work—*An Account of the Great Moray Floods of 1829* (1830), an unusual exercise in meteorology which contains material of continuing value and is an exceptional record of the geography of a highland area.

From 1832 the Dick Lauders lived in The Grange, Edinburgh, though he continued to publish on the highlands in books such as *Highland Rambles* (3 vols., 1837) and *Legends and Tales of the Highlands* (3 vols., 1841). Though never contesting an election, Dick Lauder was an energetic whig-Liberal. Lord Cockburn wrote that he was 'the greatest favourite with the mob that the whigs have. The very sight of his blue carriage makes their soles itch to take out the horses.' He also credits him with 'a tall, gentleman-like Quixotic figure, and a general picturesqueness of appearance' (*Journal of Henry Cockburn*, 1.102). In 1839 Dick Lauder's whiggery was rewarded by appointment to the secretaryship of the board of Scottish manufacturers, which soon merged with the board of white herring fishery—Dick Lauder being secretary to the consolidated board. He wrote several works of instruction for the fishermen, some of which were translated into Gaelic. He was active in founding technical and art schools and became secretary to the Royal Institution for the Encouragement of the Fine Arts. *A Tour Round the Coast of Scotland* (1842), written with James Wilson, the naturalist, recorded his journeys as fishery secretary. His scientific interests were maintained in *The Miscellany of Natural History* (2 vols., 1833–4), edited with Thomas Brown and William Rhind, and Sir Uredale Price's essay on the picturesque (1842), which he edited. Suffering from a tumour on the spine from about 1847, Dick Lauder dictated to his daughter Susan a series of papers on Scottish rivers which were published in *Tait's Magazine* from 1847 to 1849, and reprinted after his death as *Scottish Rivers* (1874).

In Edinburgh Dick Lauder was one of the most active proponents of the building of the Scott monument and he organized the building of the Queen's Drive round Arthur's Seat. He was a deputy lieutenant of East Lothian and a fellow of the Royal Society of Edinburgh. He was an able artist, illustrating many of his books himself. He died at The Grange, Edinburgh, on 29 May 1848, his son John (1813–1867) succeeding to the title.

H. C. G. MATTHEW

Sources GM, 2nd ser., 30 (1848), 91–2 · *Tait's Edinburgh Magazine*, new ser., 15 (1848), 497 · *Journal of Henry Cockburn: being a continuation of the 'Memorials of his time', 1831–1854*, 2 vols. (1874) · T. Constable, *Archibald Constable and his literary correspondents*, 3 vols. (1873) · J. Brown, preface, in T. D. Lauder, *Scottish rivers* (1874) · I. F. Grant, *Along a highland road* (1980)

Archives NL Scot., family and personal corresp. · NRA, priv. coll., family corresp., journals, and papers | Bodl. Oxf., corresp. with George Edward Ancon · Borth. Inst., letters to Mary Ponsonby, Countess Grey · Glos. RO, letters to Daniel Ellis · NA Scot., letters to Lord Dalhousie · NL Scot., corresp. with Archibald Constable · NL Scot., corresp., incl. with Hugh Miller · NL Scot., corresp. with Sir Walter Scott · U. Durham L., letters to his wife, Charlotte

Likenesses R. S. Lauder, portrait, c.1833, priv. coll. [*see illus.*] · J. Steell, plaster bust, Scot. NPG · woodcut (after B. W. Crombie), NPG

Lauder, William (*d.* 1425/6), administrator and bishop of Glasgow, was the son of Robert Lauder, a landowner in Berwickshire and Edinburghshire, and the nephew of Sir Alan Lauder of Hatton; his mother's name was Annabella. William's education was completed at Angers University in France, and in the 1390s he held a number of benefices in the diocese of St Malo, as well as seeking preferment in his native Scotland. By 27 August 1405 he was archdeacon of Lothian. Following the death of Matthew Glendinning,

bishop of Glasgow, on 10 May 1408, Lauder was consecrated as his replacement on a date before 24 October 1408. He served at intervals as a royal envoy on embassies to England and France from 1405 onwards, and is reputed to have played a significant role in persuading the governor of the Scottish kingdom, Robert Stewart, duke of Albany (*d.* 1420), to withdraw Scottish allegiance from the Avignon pope Benedict XIII in favour of Martin V in 1418–19.

Lauder was appointed chancellor of the kingdom by Stewart's son and successor as governor, Murdoch, duke of Albany, on a date shortly before 4 January 1422. He seems to have been politically aligned with those who were keen to secure the release from captivity of the Scottish king, James I, who had been in English custody since his capture at sea in 1406, and took an active part in the negotiations with the English crown that eventually culminated in James's release in April 1424. Lauder continued to act as chancellor for James I's regime, while a number of his kinsmen appeared on the king's council during 1424. He supported the king in his struggle with the former guardian and his allies, which ended with the execution of Albany and his sons at Stirling in March 1425. Lauder retained a prominent role in government until his death between 14 December 1425 and 25 February 1426.

S. I. BOARDMAN

Sources W. H. Bliss, ed., *Calendar of entries in the papal registers relating to Great Britain and Ireland: petitions to the pope* (1896) · C. Innes, ed., *Registrum episcopatus Glasguensis*, 2 vols., Bannatyne Club, 75 (1843), 304–7, no. 324 · *RotS*, vol. 2 · G. Burnett and others, eds., *The exchequer rolls of Scotland*, 4 (1880) · J. M. Thomson and others, eds., *Registrum magni sigilli regum Scotorum / The register of the great seal of Scotland*, 11 vols. (1882–1914), vol. 2 · Rymer, *Foedera*, 1st edn, vol. 10 · D. Shaw, 'The ecclesiastical members of the Lauder family in the fifteenth century', *Records of the Scottish Church History Society*, 11 (1951–3), 160–64 · NA Scot., Abercromby of Forglen MSS, GD 185 · D. E. R. Watt, *A biographical dictionary of Scottish graduates to AD 1410* (1977), 331–3

Lauder, William (*c.*1520–1573), writer and Church of Scotland minister, was born in Lothian and incorporated in St Salvator's College, University of St Andrews, in 1537, probably with a view to taking orders, but apparently did not take the MA degree. He went to Edinburgh, possibly in some religious function, but in February 1549 he was paid £11 5*s* for a play celebrating the marriage of Lady Barbara Hamilton, daughter of the regent of Scotland, with Alexander, Lord Gordon. On 28 December 1554 it is recorded that 'the Provest, baillies, and counsale findis it necessar and expedient that the litill farshce and play maid be William Lauder be playit afoir the Quenis Grace' (*Extant Poetical Works*, vi), the queen in question being the queen dowager, the Catholic Mary of Guise, who had been proclaimed regent of Scotland while her daughter was a minor. In 1558, on the occasion of the marriage of the young queen to François, dauphin of France, Lauder was paid £10 by the same council for a celebratory play (probably a masque: it involved the seven planets and Cupid). Lauder did not however contribute to the celebrations on the arrival of Mary, queen of Scots (as she had become), in 1561. His earliest surviving work is *Ane compendious and* *breve tractate, concernyng the office and dewtie of kyngis, spirituall pastoris, and temporall jugis*, printed in black letter and with woodcut illustrations in 1556, probably by John Scot, the radical printer of Edinburgh and St Andrews. In over 500 lines of somewhat irregular octosyllabic couplets, Lauder sets out the duties of those who have power over their subjects, and the fate that awaits them if they abuse it. It may have been written with a view to influencing Mary of Guise and her counsellors.

Lauder threw in his lot with the reformers (the protestant faith was established in Scotland in 1560), and about 1563 became minister of the united parishes of Forgandenny, Forteviot, and Muckarsie, in the presbytery of Perth, with one Gabriell Creichton to assist as reader at a salary of £20. In 1567 he had a stipend of £80, with a further £20 after Lady mass 1569, perhaps connected with his holding Kinnoull 'in charge'. Lauder's other known works date from this period and are sterner in character, lambasting the sins of the rich and taking their lead from the famine and plague which were affecting Scotland. *Ane godlie tractate or mirrour: quhairintill may be easilie perceavit quho thay be that ar ingraftit in to Christ, and quho are nocht* (dated 1 February 1569) consists of over 700 lines of pentameter couplets excoriating the idolatry and carnality of Roman Catholics, but also the hypocrisy of 'gredie dissemblit fals Protestantes' (*Extant Poetical Works*, 16) who mistreat the poor. A short 'Lamentatioun of the Pure', in quatrains which all conclude 'How lang, Lorde, sall this warld indure?', was appended. *Ane prettie mirrour or conference, betuix the faithfull protestant and the dissemblit false hypocreit* (printed at Edinburgh about 1570) set out the differences between the godly and the wicked in baldly oppositional terms. To this was appended 'Ane trew & breve sentencius discriptioun of the nature of Scotland twiching the interteiment of virtewus men that laketh ryches', a complaint about the lack of respect accorded the virtuous poor, and 'Ane gude exempill. Be the butterflie, instructing men to hait all harlottrie'. These two publications, also in quarto format, black letter, with woodcuts, were confidently assigned by Dickson and Edmond to the press of Robert Lekpreuik, the printer normally used by the reformers, but more recent research has suggested that Scot was the printer of all Lauder's published works. Lauder's title-pages often present his text as 'Compylit be William Lauder', indicating a rather low-key claim to authorship, and the texts are heavily flagged with biblical sources. Lauder died at Candlemas (February) 1573. The kirk paid two-thirds of Lauder's salary to his widow, of whom nothing is known, in the year of his death.   PAUL BAINES

Sources *The extant poetical works of William Lauder*, ed. F. Hall and F. J. Furnivall (1870) · S. L. Sondergard, 'Rediscovering William Lauder's poetic advocacy of the poor', *Studies in Scottish Literature*, 29 (1996), 158–73 · *Fasti Scot.*, new edn, 4.209, 211 · P. B. Watry, 'Sixteenth-century printing types and ornaments of Scotland, with an introductory survey of the Scottish book trade', DPhil diss., U. Oxf., 1993 · R. Dickson and J. P. Edmond, *Annals of Scottish printing from the introduction of the art in 1507 to the beginning of the seventeenth century* (1890), 166–73, 268–70 · D. G. Mullan, *Episcopacy in Scotland: the history of an idea, 1560–1608* (1986), 6–7

Lauder, William (*c*.1710–*c*.1771), literary forger, was born in Scotland, but nothing more of his early life is known, though Lauder himself gave out that he was related to the Lauders of Fountainhall; he 'appears to have entered the world, with only his literature to support him' (Chalmers, 146). He was educated at Edinburgh University, subsequently becoming a private teacher of Latin. Shortly after he left college one of his legs was amputated after a wound on the knee, received while watching golf at Brunstfield Links near Edinburgh, became infected. In 1732 he dedicated *A Poem of Hugo Grotius on the Holy Sacrament, Translated into English Verse* to the provost and corporation of Edinburgh. In 1734 he applied unsuccessfully for the professorship of humanity at Edinburgh on the death of Adam Watt, whose classes he had taught during the professor's final illness; the heads of the university awarded him a testimonial on 22 May 1734, certifying that 'he was a fit person to teach Humanity in any school or college whatever' (Nichols, *Lit. anecdotes*, 2.136). Chalmers says that 'he taught the Latin language, in his private school, and in the university classes, with acknowledged approbation' (Chalmers, 146). He was also unsuccessful in his application for the keepership of the university library.

In 1739 Lauder narrowly failed in his application to become one of the masters of the high school in Edinburgh; 'though the palm of literature was assigned by the judges to Lauder, the patrons of the school preferred one of his opponents' (Chalmers, 147). In the same year he published a useful collection of sacred poems by Scottish authors, *Poetarum Scotorum musae sacrae* (1739), beautifully printed by Thomas and Walter Ruddiman at Edinburgh. This included much of Arthur Johnston's work, including his versions of the Psalms and the Song of Solomon; Lauder added a Latin life of Johnston. Copies were dispatched to various notable contemporaries, such as Alexander Cruden and David Mallett, with handwritten Latin inscriptions. Lauder was convinced that Johnston's version of the Psalms was better than George Buchanan's, and on 19 May 1740 he petitioned the general assembly of the Church of Scotland for the introduction of Johnston's version as a textbook for the grammar schools of Scotland; the petition was granted on 13 November. John Love, rector of the grammar school at Dalkeith, deplored the decision in *A Letter to a Gentleman in Edinburgh*, arguing that Buchanan (of whose paraphrase he had produced an edition) was the better poet and Latinist. Lauder responded with fury in the first part of *Calumny Display'd, or, Pseudo-Buchananus Couch'd of a Cataract* (1741). Love's *Second Letter to a Gentleman in Edinburgh* prompted Lauder's *Calumny Display'd*, parts 2 and 3 (1741), in which he accused Love of false quotation and forged evidence. No regular income ensued from the edition of Johnston and Lauder further published *Chamaeleon redivivus* (1741), in which he continued a bitter assault on his enemies as forgers and sharpers. The 'Bellum grammaticale' attracted much notice in the *Scots Magazine* and *The Patriot*.

Lauder later claimed that he sent a volume of the collection to Alexander Pope, via Mallett, in an attempt to recruit Pope to his cause. Pope responded only by ridiculing Johnston (of whom lavish editions had been published by Alderman Benson in 1741) as inferior to Milton in the revised *Dunciad* (4.111–12), thus weakening Lauder's case and causing him to abandon Buchanan as his main object of hatred in favour of Milton. In 1742 Lauder applied for the rectorship of Dundee grammar school, supported by the Edinburgh professors Peter Cumming and Colin McLaurin. On 3 September 1745, during the Jacobite rising, Lauder wrote from Dundee to the Jacobite printer and scholar Thomas Ruddiman, to declare that Milton had taken not only the plan of his poem, but also four or five thousand lines from a series of obscure modern Latin poems. He copied the substance of the argument to the secretary of the Young Pretender (Charles Edward Stuart) and appeared to think that this discovery would be of serious propaganda use for the Jacobite cause (Duncan, 159–65). He also asked for money. Ruddiman responded, perhaps fatally, by arguing that Lauder's case simply lacked the crucial evidence of exact verbal parallels extended over several lines. Ruddiman later commented: 'I was so sensible of the weakness and folly of that man, that I shunned his company, as far as decently I could' (Chalmers, 150n.). Lauder resigned his post at Dundee on 31 October 1745 and went to England the following spring. He was welcomed by William King, principal of St Mary Hall, Oxford, himself a Jacobite. In London Lauder began a series of articles in the *Gentleman's Magazine* (January–August 1747) devoted to proving by means of parallel quotations that Milton's great epic was largely plagiarized from Jacobus Masenius (*Sarcotis*, 1654), Hugo Grotius (*Adamus exsul*), Andrew Ramsay (*Poemata sacra*), and others. The proprietor of the magazine, Edmund Cave, probably introduced Lauder to Samuel Johnson, who to some degree countenanced Lauder's claims—partly no doubt out of political antipathy towards Milton, but also out of his habitual charity towards poor scholars and a genuine liking for modern Latin verse. Johnson wrote on Lauder's behalf a proposal for a subscription edition of Grotius's *Adamus exsul*, as well as a Latin Milton for schools. A controversy ensued, with a number of puffs for Lauder's scholarship and some querulous rejoinders, especially from Richard Richardson, who carried his critique of Lauder's argument into a pamphlet: *Zoïlomastix, or, A Vindication of Milton from All the Invidious Charges of Mr William Lauder* (1747). In addition Henry Fricker (writing as C. Bates) tried to suggest that Lauder's case was badly tainted by falsified evidence (September 1747, 423), but the damaging accusations in his letter were cut by the *Gentleman's Magazine* and had to be printed instead in the *British Magazine* (November 1747, 490–94).

Lauder's character was blasted in a pamphlet thought to be by the historian of Jacobitism, Andrew Henderson: *Furius, or, A modest attempt towards a history of the life and surprising exploits of the famous W. L. critic and thief-catcher* (1748); the catalogue of these 'exploits', which appears to be based on inside knowledge, was mainly devoted to proving Lauder's extreme commitment to the editing of literary texts to promote a Jacobite version of history. The

pamphlet described Lauder as 5 feet 7 in height, with 'a sallow complexion, large rolling fiery eyes, a stentorian voice, and a sanguine temper' (Chalmers, 150). Lauder, however, persisted with his claims and on 21 December 1749 produced *An Essay on Milton's Use and Imitation of the Moderns, in his 'Paradise Lost'* (dated 1750), dedicating the work to the universities of Oxford and Cambridge. The title alludes to an anonymous earlier essay, *An Essay on Milton's Use and Imitation of the Ancients*, published at Edinburgh in 1741 and sometimes ascribed to Lauder, though he refers to it as the work of another on page 1 of his own *Essay*. Some of Lauder's 'sources' had already been carried into Bishop Thomas Newton's variorum edition of the poem (published 30 November 1749). At the beginning of his assault Lauder adopts a scholarly poise, but as the list of Milton's 'borrowings' from eighteen poets (displayed in a chronological table) unfolds the tone becomes increasingly aggressive and pugnacious. The essay is framed by a preface (reused from the proposals for an edition of *Adamus exsul*) and postscript from Samuel Johnson (on behalf of Milton's granddaughter, Elizabeth Foster, and thus offered as a sort of recompense for the assault on Milton's own character). Lauder also included an advertisement trumpeting his abilities as a private teacher of Latin.

There was some initial support for Lauder in the *Gentleman's Magazine* but Warburton immediately denounced the *Essay* as 'the most silly and knavish book I ever saw' (Nichols, *Illustrations*, 2.177) and Richard Richardson again wrote to the *Gentleman's Magazine* to argue that Lauder's quotations had been radically falsified, though his letters were not acknowledged until December 1750, after Lauder had been exposed. The scholar John Bowle advertised an *Examen* of Lauder's *Essay* as early as 25 January 1750, but further evidence was discovered during the year by Roger Watkins, vice-principal of St Mary Hall, Oxford, Robert Thyer, a librarian, and Thomas Newton, editor of *Paradise Lost*. Masenius and Grotius proved unavailable, but from the combined researches it was evident that in many cases what Lauder quoted as sources for Milton were really parts of William Hog's Latin version of *Paradise Lost* interpolated into the supposed source-texts.

This material was brought together with a fine rhetorical flourish by John Douglas, later bishop of Salisbury, in *Milton vindicated from the charge of plagiarism, brought against him by Mr Lauder, and Lauder himself convicted of several forgeries and gross impositions on the public* (late 1750, dated 1751). The vindication was dedicated to his patron, the earl of Bath, to whose son (Lord Pulteney) Douglas was tutor. Bath was also the dedicatee of Newton's edition of *Paradise Lost*. Lauder apparently heard of the imminent publication; at first he tried to call their bluff, and then attempted to forestall publication by confessing, but Douglas was resolved to destroy Lauder completely. Douglas had noted Johnson's authorship of the preface and postscript while deferentially acquitting him of involvement in the fraud, and Johnson immediately caused Lauder to publish a dictated confession, apologizing for the offences listed by Douglas and revealing the other offences for which evidence was lacking. *A Letter to the Reverend Mr Douglas* was dated 20 December 1750 and published on 2 January 1751. Lauder, however, added in his own right a further series of testimonies in his favour, mostly old letters recommending him for teaching posts, and a more truculent account of his distaste for Milton, which somewhat lessened the dignity of the confession. Lauder's booksellers had interrogated him about the accusations and put out an advertisement denouncing him on 28 November 1750, and issued their own 'New preface' alongside the original *Essay*, which they continued to sell as a 'curiosity of fraud and interpolation' (p. iii); they complained of Lauder's breezy and impudent response to the charges in a further postscript (1 December 1750 and 2 January 1751). Thomas Newton gave an account of Lauder's penitence in the second edition of his *Paradise Lost* (1750), but Lauder was further attacked in two anonymous poems, *Pandemonium, or, A New Infernal Expedition* (1750) and *The Progress of Envy* (1751). Warburton wrote to Jortin with sarcastic aloofness about the case (Nichols, *Illustrations*, 2.177–8). Lauder published a further *Apology for Mr Lauder, in a letter most humbly addressed to his grace the archbishop of Canterbury* (then Thomas Herring) in March 1751, in which he repeated the story that Pope had blighted his chances with the couplet in *The Dunciad*, but exacerbated the circumstances. The archbishop allowed Lauder to dedicate a two-volume edition of *Delectus auctorum sacrorum Miltono facem praelucentium* (1752–3) to him. Milton was still 'Plagiariorium Princeps' (2.xxii) and the table of authors supposedly quarried ran to ninety-seven. Meanwhile, on 15 March 1751 Lauder wrote to Thomas Birch, who had refused to see him. Lauder cited Birch's own appendix to his edition of Milton's *Historical, Political, and Miscellaneous Works* (1738) as the source of his problems: Birch had given some credence to the story that *Eikon basilike*, supposedly Charles I's meditations in prison, had been tampered with by the regicides, and particularly by Milton, to include the prayer from Sidney's *Arcadia* which Milton complained of as impious in his *Eikonoklastes*. Lauder claimed that he had initiated the controversy over Milton's text as a kind of revenge for and animadversion on Milton's deceit in this matter of *Eikon basilike*. He wrote to Dr Mead in much the same terms on 9 April 1751. Birch dropped the appendix about *Eikon basilike* from his 1753 edition of Milton's prose, after Newton had discredited the story in the second edition of his *Paradise Lost*, but in 1754 Lauder published the anecdote in *King Charles I vindicated from the charge of plagiarism, brought against him by Milton, and Milton himself convicted of forgery, and a gross imposition on the public*. The title alludes to Douglas's rebuttal of the *Essay* and the pamphlet as a whole uses the story against Milton as a further self-exculpation. Reviewers were quick to remember the previous controversy in dismissing the book. Douglas himself responded in 1756 with a 'second edition', retitled *Milton No Plagiary* and carrying a short appendix on the new issue. Douglas was by now involved in heavy controversy against Archibald Bower; his detective zeal led to his appearance as 'the scourge of impostors, the terror of quacks' in Goldsmith's

Retaliation (1774). Johnson's involvement continued to cause comment, and he was openly accused by William Kenrick of sponsoring, if not writing, the whole of Lauder's *Essay*. After Johnson's essay on Milton in *Lives of the English Poets* appeared, Nichols showed Johnson Francis Blackburne's whiggish *Remarks* on it, which cited Johnson's involvement with Lauder to counter his anti-republican sentiments. Johnson wrote in the margin: 'In the business of Lauder, I was deceived; partly by thinking the man too frantick to be fraudulent' (Nichols, *Lit. anecdotes*, 2.551). Charles Churchill, Michael Lort, and Sir John Hawkins also testified to Johnson's forwardness in advancing Lauder's claims, but Johnson was defended with customary efficiency in Boswell's *Life*.

Lauder meanwhile emigrated to Barbados, where his behaviour was said to be 'mean and despicable' (Nichols, *Lit. anecdotes*, 2.137). For a while he taught in a grammar school in Bridgetown, but latterly ran a huckster's shop, in which he was helped by a slave woman he had bought. According to an unverified account by R. Reece, he and the slave woman had a daughter, Rachel, on whom he made an incestuous attempt. Colourful anecdotes of this daughter are told in the same article. Lauder is said to have died in miserable poverty about 1771 in Barbados, where he was also buried.   PAUL BAINES

Sources M. J. Marcuse, '"The scourge of imposters, the terror of quacks": John Douglas and the exposé of William Lauder', *Huntington Library Quarterly*, 42 (1978–9), 231–61 · M. J. Marcuse, 'The *Gentleman's Magazine* and the Lauder/Milton controversy', *Bulletin of Research in the Humanities*, 81 (1978), 179–209 · M. J. Marcuse, 'The Lauder controversy and the Jacobite cause', *Studies in Burke and his Time*, 18 (1977), 27–47 · M. J. Marcuse, 'The pre-publication history of William Lauder's *Essay on Milton's use and imitation of the moderns, in his "Paradise Lost"'*, *Publications of the Bibliographical Society of America*, 12 (1978), 38–50 · P. Baines, *The house of forgery in eighteenth-century Britain* (1999), 81–102 · G. Chalmers, *The life of Thomas Ruddiman* (1794), 146–50 · [A. Henderson (?)], *Furius, or, A modest attempt towards a history of the life and surprising exploits of the famous W. L. critic and thief-catcher* (1748) · D. Duncan, *Thomas Ruddiman: a study in Scottish scholarship of the early eighteenth century* (1965), 159–65 · Nichols, *Lit. anecdotes*, 2.136–7, 551 · Nichols, *Illustrations*, 2.177–8 4.428–32 · R. Reece, 'An unpublished page in the life of Lauder', *N&Q*, 4th ser., 5 (1870), 83–5 · A. H. Millar, 'William Lauder, the literary forger', *Blackwood*, 166 (1899), 381–96
Archives BL, letters · NL Scot., letters

Lauderdale. For this title name *see* Maitland, John, duke of Lauderdale (1616–1682); Maitland, Charles, third earl of Lauderdale (*c*.1620–1691); Murray, Elizabeth, duchess of Lauderdale and *suo jure* countess of Dysart (*bap*. 1626, d. 1698); Maitland, Richard, fourth earl of Lauderdale (1653–1695); Maitland, John, fifth earl of Lauderdale (*c*.1655–1710); Maitland, James, eighth earl of Lauderdale (1759–1839); Maitland, Anthony, tenth earl of Lauderdale (1785–1863) [*see under* Maitland, James, eighth earl of Lauderdale (1759–1839)]; Maitland, Thomas, eleventh earl of Lauderdale (1803–1878).

Laugharne, Rowland (*c*.1607–1675), parliamentarian army officer and politician, was born in St Bride's, south Pembrokeshire, of a gentry family prominent in that county from the sixteenth century. His parents were John Laugharne (b. c.1587, d. after 1644) and his wife, Janet Owen, the daughter of Sir Hugh Owen of Orielton, an estate in Castlemartin, on the other side of Milford Haven from St Bride's. As a youth Rowland acquired a place as a page in the household of the third earl of Essex, who owned land in Pembrokeshire. Laugharne may have accompanied his master in military activity in the Low Countries, but whether or not this was so, he was certainly among those in south-west Wales who declared support for parliament at the outbreak of the civil war, and was made commander-in-chief of Pembrokeshire.

With John Poyer, mayor of Pembroke, and Rice Powell, Laugharne turned Pembroke into an unofficial garrison for parliament, and doggedly resisted attempts (short of armed force) by the royalists to make the town submit to the king's will. Just as Laugharne's opponents were organizing a siege of Pembroke, in mid-February 1644 a parliamentarian naval force was driven into the haven by foul weather, and Laugharne persuaded its commander to bombard royalist fortifications. Under cover of this engagement he marched against the gentry houses of Stackpole and Trefloyne, took the royalist fort at Pill, and so demoralized the king's forces that they fled from Haverfordwest. Supported by the naval force, Laugharne's troops seemed unstoppable, and by 10 March 1644 they had secured the county for parliament; in the lightning campaign, the boldness and personal prestige of Laugharne had made a major contribution. The combination of Laugharne's land forces and naval support secured another spectacular victory in April, when Carmarthen was taken, but the arrival of Colonel Charles Gerard in south Wales ensured that by 23 June 1644 Carmarthenshire was once again under royalist control. Within a month nearly all Laugharne's gains, except Haverfordwest and Tenby, had been forfeited, and the former town fell on 22 August.

The withdrawal of Gerard to assist Prince Rupert allowed Laugharne to venture forth again from Pembroke to take a number of towns in Cardiganshire in the winter of 1644, and he was rewarded by parliament with sums totalling £3500. When Gerard returned to west Wales from the north, he routed Laugharne's troops at Newcastle Emlyn, and the parliamentarian commander was forced once more to fall back on his Pembrokeshire strongholds. Ever the military opportunist, however, Laugharne attacked Haverfordwest in July 1645, taking advantage of the concentration of royalist military forces elsewhere. The town surrendered to him on 2 August, after a battle on Colby Moor. The House of Commons voted him further supplies, and awarded his wife an allowance of £10 per week while she was in London. As in the spring of 1644, the taking of Haverfordwest was followed by a mopping-up of other Pembrokeshire towns, so that by mid-September, the county was for the second time wholly in parliamentarian hands. Once again Laugharne was rewarded by a grateful House of Commons, this time with £2000 out of the excise. The estate of Slebech

was also bestowed on him. In a further repetition of previous manoeuvres Laugharne advanced out of Pembrokeshire into Carmarthenshire, which came over to him readily enough, and from thence through Glamorgan into Brecknockshire. Having dispatched declarations of loyalty to parliament from Brecon in mid-December 1645, Laugharne returned to Haverfordwest.

As senior commander in south Wales, Laugharne oversaw the general submission of the region to parliament. He supplied arms to the leaders of the Clubman 'peaceable army' of Glamorgan, which had come into being as a reaction against the excesses of Gerard. His support for the Clubman movement was not enough to prevent a genuinely royalist upsurge in January 1646, and he underestimated the strength of royalist feeling when he refused to break off from besieging Aberystwyth to attend to the revolt in Glamorgan. Laugharne was compelled to relieve Cardiff Castle, besieged by the royalists, and fought two successful actions there between 18 and 20 February 1646. On 8 April 1647 Laugharne was confirmed by the House of Commons as commander of 100 horse and 100 dragoons in south Wales, but only by a margin of three votes, and with a New Model officer posted as his second-in-command: an indication that physical and political isolation were reducing his standing. In June, in reaction to the seizure of the king's person by the New Model Army, the royalist Glamorgan gentry grew restless again, and assembled against the county committee a force which fled on Laugharne's arrival from Carmarthen. Although the royalists expressed themselves 'without any the least meaning of opposition or disrespect' to Laugharne (Phillips, 2.337), his own account of the matter to the speaker and to Sir Thomas Fairfax implied that they had been dealt with too leniently by parliament.

Laugharne's hostility to the royalists in June 1647 is significant for an assessment of his role in the second civil war in Wales, which broke out in March 1648. He, Poyer, and Powell, the trio who had garrisoned Pembroke for parliament in 1642, had been isolated by developments in army and parliamentary circles. Laugharne sympathized with London's militia committee, led by political presbyterians, who approached him in the summer of 1647 as a military commander they favoured. While his remaining outside the New Model Army commended him to London's rulers, who shared his social conservatism, it also ensured that his soldiers, 'supernumeraries' in the jargon of the day, suffered from extensive arrears of pay and faced dispersal in the 'great disbandment' planned for 1648. Early that year Laugharne was detained at Maidenhead while returning to Wales from London, where he was doubtless in contact with his City supporters. He escaped, and in March some of his officers helped support Poyer's resistance to the New Model Army at Pembroke. Only four days before the battle of St Fagans on 8 May Laugharne asserted his command in south Wales against Colonel Thomas Horton, sent to quell the south Wales rising, but by then his troops were peeling off to join Poyer, and Laugharne's protestations of loyalty rang hollow. In open command of the rebel force at St Fagans, he suffered a decisive defeat, and was forced to surrender to Oliver Cromwell on 11 July at Pembroke. Parliament was more sympathetic to its former favourite than were the army leaders, who on 13 December 1648 secured a reversal of the Commons' vote that Laugharne should be banished. He was instead tried by court martial, and with Poyer and Powell sentenced to death on 11 April 1649. Laugharne and Powell escaped with their lives after lots were drawn by a child.

After the Restoration Laugharne claimed to have spent most of the 1650s in prison, but he had been treated with some leniency by the republican governments, and was in 1655 granted a remission of his delinquency fine of £712. He was monitored by the government when in 1659 the royalist rising of Sir George Booth was imminent, and was regarded as a reliable enough supporter of monarchy in February 1660 to have been nominated a commander in south Wales. He made an unsuccessful bid to sit in the Convention of 1660, but was returned for Pembroke Boroughs in the Cavalier Parliament. His parliamentary career was undistinguished and half-hearted, perhaps because his time and energy were absorbed in attempts to remedy his undoubted financial distress. He died in London, and was buried at St Margaret's, Westminster, on 16 November 1675. He was survived by his wife Ann, *née* Button, who died in 1681.   STEPHEN K. ROBERTS

Sources J. R. Phillips, *Memoirs of the civil war in Wales and the marches, 1642–1649*, 2 vols. (1874) · L. Naylor and G. Jagger, 'Laugharne, Rowland', HoP, *Commons, 1660–90*, 2.712–13 · *DWB* · R. Ashton, *Counter-revolution: the second civil war and its origins, 1646–8* (1994) · *The journal of Thomas Juxon*, ed. K. Lindley and D. Scott, CS, 5th ser., 13 (1999) · *A great fight in Wales: sixteen colours taken, armes and ammunition, with the prisoners, and men slain* (1648) [Thomason tract E 441(4)] · R. Laugharne, *A declaration by Major General Laughorn* (1648) [Thomason tract E 442(8)] · R. Laugharne and R. Powel, *The declaration and propositions of Maj. Gen. Laughorne, and Col. Rice Powel* (1648) [Thomason tract E 442(11)] · G. Williams, ed., *Glamorgan county history, 4: Early modern Glamorgan* (1974) · G. D. Squibb, ed., *Report of heraldic cases in the court of chivalry*, Harleian Society, 107 (1956) · parish register, St Margaret's, Westminster, 16 Nov 1675 [burials] · parish register, St Margaret's, Westminster, 1681 [burials]

Likenesses line engraving, BM; repro. in J. Vicars, *England's worthies* (1647)

Wealth at death debts of £8000, 1666; 'only 3s in the world', 1670: Naylor and Jagger, 'Laugharne, Rowland'

Laughland [*née* Jarman], **Victoria Nicola Christina** [Tory] (1944–1994), social worker and charity administrator, was born on 11 July 1944 at St John's Hospital, Weston Favell, Northamptonshire, the only daughter and youngest of the three children of Archibald Seymour (Archie) Jarman (1910–1982), flight lieutenant in the Royal Air Force and later administrator of the family estate, and his wife, Helene Mariana Klenk (*b.* 1911), who had gone to England from Germany to work as a children's nurse and later founded the Rudolf Steiner School in Brighton. After the war Victoria enjoyed many holidays on her aunt's farm in the village of Pfaffenhofen in Bavaria. Her elder brothers, Nicholas and Christopher, went to Harrow, but she attended day schools, the Lycée Français in Kensington and, later, St Mary's Hall, Brighton. She was the first of

their pupils ever to obtain a place at Oxford or Cambridge. She read French and German at St Hilda's College, graduating with a second-class degree in 1966. She then worked as an agent's reader in London. On 7 June 1969 she married (Graham Franklyn) Bruce Laughland (1931–2002), a barrister and later a judge at the Old Bailey, and the son of Andrew Percy Laughland, civil and electrical engineer.

From an early age Tory felt a strong empathy with people less fortunate than herself. Her husband described her as 'a great collector of lame ducks' (private information). He encouraged her to enrol for the diploma in social administration at the London School of Economics in 1973. She returned after a year's interval to obtain her professional social work qualification, and went on to work for Wandsworth and Westminster social services departments. Her only child, Francis, was born in 1980 after she had been married for ten years. It was a severe blow when at the age of four he was diagnosed as autistic. She managed the difficulties that arose with characteristic courage, helped by support from friends and relatives. But much though she loved Francis she needed time away from him, and other channels for her sense of social purpose.

As a guardian *ad litem* in Westminster from 1980, Laughland helped to set up a Who Cares? group to enable young people in care to speak for themselves. In 1983 the group produced the first *Who Cares?* magazine. With her enthusiasm, creativity, and sense of fun, she proved the ideal editor. From 1987 the National Children's Bureau provided a base, but as the circulation grew the magazine could no longer be run from one room with part-time assistance. Laughland decided that the way forward was to set up an independent charitable trust that would continue to publish the magazine as its core activity but would also become a campaigning organization for children in care, developing practical services in response to the needs they expressed. She found premises, recruited a board of trustees, and made use of all her connections to advance the project, which came to fruition in 1992. Although extremely modest and self-effacing personally, she had no inhibitions about approaching anyone, however important or well known, to become a trustee, provide a feature for *Who Cares?* magazine, or sponsor a fund-raising event in a prestigious location. Such was her charm and persistence that people invariably said yes. Thus the lord chief justice and the chief inspector of social services found themselves listening at first hand to the painful experiences of children in care.

Recognizing educational success as a crucial escape route, Laughland set up an education advisory group at Who Cares? and regarded the education development work as one of the trust's most important tasks. At an individual level she befriended and inspired many young people, including Fred Fever, who published a book about growing up in care, *Who Cares?* (1994), and went on to take a university degree. She had a wonderful ability to communicate with children from backgrounds entirely different from her own. They responded to her interest, her lack of condescension, and above all her sense of humour.

Readers of the magazine wrote to her regularly, feeling that 'she was a true and special friend who would always believe in you' (*Who Cares?*, 29). She always replied, often getting up at 5 a.m. to write letters before she went to work.

Laughland was also a magnificent friend to many people other than children in care. One of her assistants recalled struggling home through a snowstorm to find all her pipes frozen and in danger of bursting. To her amazement Laughland turned up to help at one o'clock in the morning, wearing rubber boots and carrying a chocolate bar, a fan heater, and a bunch of flowers. Diagnosed with mesothelioma in 1993, she insisted on knowing the prognosis but shared the knowledge only with close friends and continued to work with her customary commitment almost to the end. Although often suffering intense pain, her overriding concern, apart from her son and husband, was that the Who Cares? trust should continue and flourish. Fortunately Susanna Cheal, previously a consultant to the trust, was available to take over as director, and this proved an inspired choice. Laughland died on 19 July 1994 at Paddington Community Hospital, Woodfield Road, Westminster, ten days after celebrating her twenty-fifth wedding anniversary and her fiftieth birthday among friends. She was cremated in West London crematorium. She was survived by her husband, Bruce, and her son, Francis. The small organization that she started and nurtured had by 2001 an annual turnover of more than £1 million and the magazine circulation had grown to 30,000. The trust remained in the forefront of innovation in services for children in public care and was regularly consulted by government and official bodies.

SONIA JACKSON

Sources 'Tory Laughland: a tribute', *Who Cares?*, 29/14–15 (autumn 1994) · *The Times* (23 July 1994) · personal knowledge (2004) · private information (2004) [Bruce Laughland, Christopher Jarman, Susanna Cheal, John Simms, Pamela Norman, Fred Fever] · b. cert. · m. cert. · d. cert.

Archives Who Cares? Trust, Kemp House, London

Likenesses photograph, Who Cares? Trust, London; repro. in 'Tory Laughland', *Who Cares?* · photograph, repro. in *The Times*

Wealth at death £323,196: probate, 4 Jan 1995, *CGPLA Eng. & Wales*

Laughton, Charles (1899–1962), actor, was born on 1 July 1899 at the Victoria Hotel, Scarborough, the eldest of the three sons (there were no daughters) of Robert Laughton, a prosperous hotelier, and his wife, Elizabeth Conlon. He spent a childhood largely tormented by a glandular problem which made him constantly overweight and therefore unpopular at school and indeed at home, where his early determination to become an actor met severe parental opposition.

Brought up as a Catholic, Laughton was educated at Stonyhurst College, where even one of his few schoolfriends described him as 'the ungainliest of boys with a huge head'. He was sent, against his wishes, to study the hotel trade at Claridge's in London before being called up at the end of the First World War, but he was rapidly invalided out of the army after being gassed on the western front in 1918.

Charles Laughton (1899–1962), by Howard Coster, 1936

On returning to his parents in Scarborough, Laughton continued to train in hotel management until in 1925 he at last defied the family and enrolled as a drama student at the Royal Academy of Dramatic Art in London, where two years later he won the gold medal and was immediately given his start in the professional theatre by one of his teachers, the Russian director Theodore Komisarjevsky. His earliest stage roles at Barnes and the Everyman in Hampstead in 1926 were in classic Russian plays, but in 1928, at the Little Theatre in London, he first made his name in the type of role which was to become his hallmark: that of the neurotic, greedy, sinister villain in *A Man with Red Hair*, by Hugh Walpole. From there Laughton progressed to two more familiar roles, Poirot and Pickwick, before scoring another big success as the Chicago gangster loosely modelled on Al Capone in *On the Spot* (1930), by Edgar Wallace. He made his New York début in 1931 as the squalid murderer in *Payment Deferred* before accepting a Hollywood offer, which took him to California for *The Old Dark House* (1932) and his first Nero in *The Sign of the Cross* (1932).

It was back in England for Alexander Korda in 1933 that Laughton made his screen name in *The Private Life of Henry VIII* at the start of a sequence of major cinema biographies—*The Barretts of Wimpole Street* (1934), *Mutiny on the Bounty* (1935), *Rembrandt* (1936), and the unfinished *I, Claudius* (1936)—which were to see him at the very peak of his reflective, anguished talent for larger-than-life monsters of reality.

In 1933 Laughton joined the Old Vic Company for an

impressive range of stage work (*Henry VIII* again, *The Cherry Orchard*, *Macbeth*, *Measure for Measure*, *The Tempest*), and in 1936 he was the first English actor ever to be invited to appear at the Comédie Française in Paris, where he played Molière's *Le médecin malgré lui*. He then settled in California, where, despite occasional returns to the theatre (notably in the first production of Bertolt Brecht's *The Life of Galileo* in 1947, which he also adapted), he focused mainly on such films as *Jamaica Inn* (1939), *The Hunchback of Notre Dame* (1939), *Witness for the Prosecution* (1957), *Spartacus* (1960), and *Advise and Consent* (1962), returning only rarely to Britain and only notably for David Lean's *Hobson's Choice* in 1954.

In the following year Laughton made his only picture as director, *Night of the Hunter*, with Robert Mitchum, which is now regarded as one of the best *films noirs* ever made in Hollywood; but then, as if aware that his time was running out and his film career waning, he returned to Britain to make one last West End appearance in *The Party* (1958), for which he discovered the actor Albert Finney straight from drama school.

The following summer Laughton went to Stratford upon Avon in a remarkably starry season which also featured Paul Robeson, Edith Evans, Laurence Olivier, and Sam Wanamaker, working for such directors as Tony Richardson, Glen Byam Shaw, and the man who was immediately to succeed Shaw at Stratford and create the Royal Shakespeare Company, Peter Hall. Laughton played Bottom in *A Midsummer Night's Dream* (Finney and Vanessa Redgrave were among the young lovers) and Lear in *King Lear*, but it was already apparent that he was having trouble with his memory, and he never again appeared on stage or in Britain.

'With Charles', said Laughton's first great producer, Alexander Korda, 'acting was a kind of childbirth; what he needed was a midwife, not a director', and it is arguable that the performances that might have been, such as the abortive *I, Claudius*, were almost as important as those he actually gave. Of those performances he did give, it is the biographical (Rembrandt, Henry VIII, Captain Bligh of the *Bounty*) that stay in the memory, as well as those in which he was able to convey some aspect of the double life he had always been forced to lead on account of his homosexuality. Back in 1929, on 10 February, he had married the *Bride of Frankenstein* actress Elsa *Lanchester (1902–1986), herself also always more attracted to her own sex, and although they remained married until his death it was inevitably a relationship of convenience to them both, rather than of lifelong happiness for either. Elsa was the daughter of James Sullivan, an Irish worker in a black-lead factory, and his wife Edith *Lanchester, an active member of the Social Democratic Federation. They had no children, but remained united by a shared belief in social revolution and the desire to push out the barriers of pre-war Hollywood tolerance as far as they could safely be pushed without ruin to either career or immigrant status.

Throughout this long marriage, Laughton's homosexuality undoubtedly caused him great unhappiness, and if there was any one key to his always theatrical greatness

on screen it was perhaps this lifelong sense of being a misfit, uneasy in his own skin, and forever on the outside of social, sexual, and familial demands on his upbringing and conditioning. An American citizen from 1950, Laughton died at his Hollywood home on 15 December 1962; some years later, the Scarborough hotel that had been the root of his family fortune was washed away to sea in a cliff collapse. 'You don't direct Laughton in a picture,' noted Alfred Hitchcock, 'all you can do is referee it.'

SHERIDAN MORLEY, rev.

Sources *The Times* (17 Dec 1962) · S. Callow, *Charles Laughton: a difficult actor* (1988) · C. Higham, *Charles Laughton: an intimate biography* (1976) · K. D. Singer, *The Charles Laughton story* (1954) · E. Lanchester, *Charles Laughton and I* (1938) · personal knowledge (1993)
Archives FILM BFI NFTVA, 'Callow's Laughton', ITV, 30 Aug 1987 · BFI NFTVA, performance footage | SOUND BL NSA, The Friday feature, BBC Radio 4, 7 Aug 1987 · BL NSA, documentary recordings · BL NSA, performance recordings
Likenesses photographs, c.1928–1959, Hult. Arch. · J. W. Debenham, double portrait, photograph, 1934 (with Elsa Lanchester), Theatre Museum, London · H. Coster, photograph, 1936, NPG [see illus.] · A. Wysard, pencil and gouache drawing, 1936, NPG · A. Wysard, pencil and watercolour drawing, 1936, NPG · R. Avedon, bromide print, c.1950, NPG · B. Kneale, oils, c.1959, Castle Museum, Nottingham

Laughton, George (1735/6–1800), Church of England clergyman, was born in Bridgwater, Somerset, the son of John Laughton, 'pleb.' (Foster), of that town. He was educated at Wadham College, Oxford, where he matriculated on 3 April 1754, aged eighteen, and graduated BA in 1757 and MA, BD, and DD in 1771. He was curate of Richmond, Surrey, from 1763 to December 1775.

In 1773 Laughton published a sermon attacking the excesses and moral lapses of rich and poor. The following year he published *The History of Ancient Egypt*, which he dedicated to George III. In this work he argued that the Egyptians had played their part in the process of civilizing human society; from these early beginnings of 'barbarians formed into civilized states' mankind was able ultimately to 'soar to the grandeur and perfection of the *British* empire' (p. vii). In 1780 he published a scholarly response to Edward Gibbon's sceptical account of the growth of Christianity that had appeared four years earlier in chapters 15 and 16 of the first volume of his *History of the Decline and Fall of the Roman Empire* (1776). Laughton's reply included a wide-ranging discussion of comparative religions in Greece, Rome, India, and Egypt and their connection with Judaism. He accused Gibbon of presenting heathen narratives in so pleasing a way 'that Christianity and Heathenism seem to walk as congenial friends, equally honourable and amiable' (Laughton, *Progress and Establishment of Christianity*, 34). In words that presaged his later role as a clerical magistrate Laughton claimed that infidelity encouraged ideas of equality in the poor, which 'destroys humility and subordination, swells the inferior class of society to high notions of their own importance, makes them dissolute, prompt to riot, and become the tools of the artful, to subvert all order and government' (ibid., 38).

On 2 November 1785 Laughton became vicar of Welton,

Northamptonshire, and soon he was an established figure in that county. When in 1790 he published *Sermons on the Great Doctrines and Duties of Christianity* no fewer than four copies were bought by his close neighbours the Spencers of Althorp, as the list of subscribers reveals; but he was still remembered well enough in Richmond for Thomas Wakefield, its parish priest, also to buy four copies. In 1794 Laughton was made vicar of Chippenham, Cambridgeshire, and shortly afterwards he was appointed a justice of the peace for the county. In 1798, in the context of the war against French revolutionary ideas, he published two assize sermons preached at Huntingdon, in which he argued that while ideas of equality 'are subversive of the public good' (Laughton, *At the Assize*, 13) religion was 'the chain that keeps the mass of society in order and peace' (ibid., 16). George Laughton died in Chippenham in June 1800.   ROBERT HOLE

Sources Foster, *Alum. Oxon.*, 1715–1886, vol. 3 · GM, 1st ser., 64 (1794), 1211 · GM, 1st ser., 70 (1800), 593 · DNB · G. Baker, *The history and antiquities of the county of Northampton*, 2 vols. (1822–41) · G. Laughton, *At the assize, held at Huntingdon ... March 11 ... this sermon was preached by G. L.* (1798) [on Jeremiah 10:23] · G. Laughton, *Sermons on the great doctrines and duties of Christianity* (1790) · G. Laughton, *The history of ancient Egypt* (1774) · G. Laughton, *The progress and establishment of Christianity* (1780)

Laughton, Sir **John Knox** (1830–1915), naval educator and historian, was the second son and youngest child of James Laughton of Liverpool (1777–1859), a former master mariner who had become a successful wine merchant. His mother was Ann Potts, who came from a Cumberland family. Laughton was born in Liverpool on 23 April 1830. He was educated at the Royal Institution School, Liverpool, and at Gonville and Caius College, Cambridge, where in 1852 he sat for the mathematical tripos and graduated as a wrangler. He entered the Royal Navy as an instructor, joining his first ship, the *Royal George*, on 27 December 1853, and proceeded to the Baltic, where he served (1854–6) in the Crimean War. When it ended in 1856, he was transferred to the *Calcutta*, flagship of the commander-in-chief in the Far East. During the Second Opium War he was present at the capture of the Canton (Guangzhou) defences (1856), the battle of Fatshan (Foshan) Creek (1857), and the capture of the Taku (Dagu) forts (1858). In these actions he distinguished himself by his bravery; and while in pursuit of his ordinary duties he laid the foundations of his success as a teacher. For his services Laughton received the Baltic and Opium War medals with clasps. In 1859 he was appointed to the *Algiers* in the Mediterranean, and after serving in two other ships he came ashore in 1866, to the Royal Naval College, Portsmouth. In 1866 he married Isabella (d. 1884), daughter of John Carr of Dunfermline. They had one son and three daughters.

Laughton's pupils were half-pay captains and commanders, and, the educational fashions of the age of sail being still in vogue, the chief subject he had to teach was mathematics, though to this were added meteorology and marine surveying. There were no suitable textbooks, so Laughton filled the gap with his *Physical Geography in its Relation to the Prevailing Winds and Currents* (1870), and two years later his *Treatise on Nautical Surveying*. These works attracted attention outside the service, and led to a long connection with the Royal Meteorological Society, of which he was elected a fellow in 1873 and president in 1882. From 1866 Laughton wrote on tactics, publishing his historic papers *Essay on Naval Tactics* in 1873 and *The Scientific Study of Naval History* in 1874.

In 1873 the Royal Naval Hospital, Greenwich, became the new Royal Naval College and Laughton was promoted to take charge of the department of meteorology and marine surveying. In 1876 he began to lecture on naval history as an additional paid task. The subject had been largely neglected in the service, and although included in the original Greenwich curriculum, had been reduced in favour of technical subjects. But from this time Laughton transferred his allegiance almost wholly to his new study. He believed that only accurate historical scholarship could provide the basis for naval doctrine in an era of rapid technical change. In 1885 he was retired, although he continued to lecture on naval history at Greenwich. He became a regular contributor to the *Edinburgh Review* and to the *Dictionary of National Biography*, for which he wrote more than 900 lives, including almost all the naval memoirs. He was the third most prolific contributor to the *Dictionary of National Biography*.

In 1886 Laughton married Maria Josepha (d. 1950), daughter of Eugenio di Alberti of Cadiz; this second marriage produced three sons and two daughters, including Elvira Sibyl Maria *Mathews, later director of the Women's Royal Naval Service. Within six months of retiring from the navy he was appointed professor of modern history at King's College, London, which enabled him to continue his pioneering work in the Admiralty archive at the Public Record Office. Under the influence of Professor S. R. Gardiner he became a professional historian, editing *Memoirs Relating to Lord Torrington* for the Camden Society in 1889. In 1893, with the help of old shipmates, politicians, journalists, and historians, he founded the Navy Records Society, for the publication of documents relating to British naval history. The first two volumes, *Papers Relating to the Defeat of the Spanish Armada* (1894), he edited himself; and as first secretary of the society from 1893 to 1912, he not only directed its proceedings, but put his own vast knowledge at the disposal of other labourers in the same field. Laughton stressed the role of history in the education of the nation and the navy.

Laughton was elected an honorary fellow of Gonville and Caius College in 1895 and received the honorary degrees of several universities; and in 1910 he was awarded the Chesney gold medal by the Royal United Service Institution. In 1907 he was knighted, and in 1910, on his eightieth birthday, a number of admirers, including George V, then prince of Wales, and all the most celebrated admirals on the flag-list, presented a testimonial and an address to the 'pioneer in the revival of naval history'.

A man of striking personal appearance, tall, athletic, and handsome, Laughton continued to lecture at King's

College, London, until Christmas 1914. He then complained of ill health, and withdrew to his house, 9 Pepys Road, Wimbledon. He died there on 14 September 1915. In accordance with his request, his ashes were conveyed to sea by HMS *Conqueror* and buried in 40 fathoms at the mouth of the Thames 'in the track of the incoming and outgoing ships'. His second wife survived him.

In addition to works already mentioned, Laughton wrote two volumes about Nelson, the *Life* (1895) and *Nelson and his Companions in Arms* (1896); edited the papers of Lord Barham (1907–11); published a selection of Nelson's letters (1886); and collected his studies on tactics and strategy as *Studies in Naval History* (1887). But it is not from these books that the full value of Laughton's labour can be estimated. He was a dynamic scholar with an astonishing capacity for hard work. This allowed him to lead naval history out of the age of simple chronicles into the academic world, establishing it as a subject and as the basis for naval doctrine and strategic thought. As a pioneer he was more concerned with laying foundations than with contributing large books, but his disciples, who included most of the leading early twentieth-century naval historians—Alfred T. Mahan USN, Sir Julian Corbett, and Admiral Sir Herbert Richmond—carried his work on to a new plateau in the last years of his life. His legacy was the sound doctrinal framework of naval thought in place in 1914.

G. A. R. Callender, rev. Andrew Lambert

Sources A. D. Lambert, *The foundations of naval history: John Knox Laughton, the Royal Navy, and the historical profession* (1998) · D. M. Schurman, *The education of a navy: the development of British naval strategic thought, 1867–1914* (1965) · R. Seager, *Alfred T. Mahan* (1977) · *The writings of Stephen B. Luce*, ed. J. Hayes and J. Hattendore (1977) · D. M. Schurman, *Julian S. Corbett, 1854–1922: historian of British maritime policy from Drake to Jellicoe*, Royal Historical Society Studies in History, 26 (1981) · J. Corbett, *The revival of naval history* (1916) · F. Hearnshaw, *History of King's College, London* (1927) · *CGPLA Eng. & Wales* (1915)
Archives NMM | King's AC Cam., letters to Oscar Browning
Likenesses photographs, King's Lond.
Wealth at death £471 14s. 8d.: probate, 30 Oct 1915, *CGPLA Eng. & Wales*

Laughton, Richard (*bap.* 1670, *d.* 1723), Church of England clergyman and natural philosopher, was baptized at St Andrew's, Holborn, London, on 19 February 1670, the son of William Laughton and his wife, Anne. He was admitted as a sizar at Clare College, Cambridge, on 20 October 1684, from which he proceeded BA in 1685, MA in 1691, and DD in 1717; and to which he was elected as a fellow on 14 December 1686. About 1693 he served as chaplain to the bibliophile John Moore, then bishop of Norwich.

Laughton's fame rests chiefly on his abilities as a tutor at Clare (a post he held from 1694) and his willingness to expose his students to new currents of thought, notably those linked with the works of Isaac Newton and John Locke. Contemporaries acknowledged Laughton's high reputation as a teacher—in 1716 Thomas Greene of Corpus Christi urged a young fellow of his college to 'set Mr. Laughton, of Clare hall, as a pattern before you for the management of your pupils' (Nichols, *Illustrations*, 6.788) and in the following year John Colbatch of Trinity remarked on the 'conflux of nobility and gentry' he attracted to Clare (Whiston, 26).

Laughton's influence extended beyond his college, however, to reshape the tenor of the curriculum of the university more generally. Drawing on his own study of Newton's work, which was evident in the praise accorded to him by another of Newton's early Cambridge popularizers, Samuel Clarke, Laughton sought to encourage undergraduates to study the work of the great Cambridge natural philosopher. His chief opportunity for doing so came when he served as proctor in 1709–10. Drawing on 'a sheet of questions for the use of the Soph schools, on the Mathematical Newtonian Philosophy' that he had previously published, he 'most zealously promoted disputations on them there, to the great credit and reputation of the disputants', as his pupil, the physician Sir William Browne, put it (Nichols, *Anecdotes*, 3.322). In 1709, too, he delivered a speech in the schools underlining both Newton's scientific significance and his sound whig credentials, drawing particular attention to Newton's role in the university's struggle against the pro-Catholic policies of James II. Along with his advocacy of Newton, Laughton evidently was an early disciple of Locke for in 1704 it was to him that Lady Masham sent her account of the philosopher's last hours.

In the politically and religiously charged atmosphere of post-revolutionary Cambridge, Laughton's advocacy of such intellectual change was closely linked with his political and religious views. The promotion of new forms of natural philosophy for Laughton, as for many of his latitudinarian contemporaries, implied a sympathy for forms of theology which placed considerable emphasis on natural rather than revealed religion. Such a downplaying of the role of the church as the custodian of a supernatural revelation was also consistent with a strong sympathy for a more desacralized conception of the church and the monarchy. Laughton, then, was a vigorous supporter of the whig cause within Cambridge; and this led to a confrontation with Tory sympathizers when, as proctor, in 1710 he broke up a drinking party celebrating Dr Sacheverell's victory over his whig opponents. Such views probably also accounted for the fact that he was narrowly defeated when the mastership of Clare became vacant in 1713. He was, however, appointed to a prebend of Worcester Cathedral in 1717—the only ecclesiastical preferment he enjoyed apart from serving as vicar of Quy-cum-Stow from 1709 and as a chaplain to George I.

Laughton's theological views are evident in his two unpublished treatises, still in the archives of Clare College, 'An exposition of the articles of our church' and 'The principles of natural religion establish'd' (MS G.3.21). In them he argued for less emphasis on debatable points of doctrine, putting the view in the former that the Thirty-Nine Articles represented a departure 'from the primitive Simplicity of the first ages of Christianity'. Consistent with such a position he refused the customary subscription when he received his DD (by royal mandate) in 1717. He died in London on his way from Worcester to Cambridge on 28 July 1723.

John Gascoigne

Sources H. R. Fox-Bourne, *The life of John Locke*, 2 vols. (1876), 2.556 · Nichols, *Lit. anecdotes*, 3.322 · J. R. Wardale, ed., *Clare College: letters and documents* (1903), 128 · CUL, Add. MS 7896, fol. 28 · Nichols, *Illustrations*, 6.788 · W. Whiston, *Memoirs of the life and writings of Mr William Whiston: containing memoirs of several of his friends also* (1749), 430 · CUL, MS Oo.vi.111(3) · J. H. Monk, *The life of Richard Bentley, DD*, 2nd edn, 1 (1833), 286–8 · C. Middleton, *The miscellaneous works of the late reverend and learned Conyers Middleton*, 3 (1752), 341–3 · G. Dyer, *History of the university and colleges of Cambridge*, 2 vols. (1814), vol. 2, p. 249 · S. Clarke, *Jacobi Rohaulti physica … annotatbionibus, ex illustrissimi Isaaci Newtoni*, 3rd edn (1710) · Venn, *Alum. Cant.* · [M. D. Forbes], ed., *Clare College, 1326–1926*, 1 (1928), 156 · *IGI*
Archives Clare College, Cambridge

Laun, Henri van (1820–1896), author and French scholar, was born in the Netherlands. He was educated in France, and settled permanently in England in 1848. At first he sought to make his fortune as a journalist, but soon came to prefer the less precarious business of teaching. He was successively French master at King William's College, Isle of Man, at Cheltenham College, and at the Edinburgh Academy, where he became friends with Professor Blackie, Lord Neaves, Sir Alexander Grant, and many other noted intellectuals. Settling afterwards in London, he acted for twenty consecutive years as French examiner for the civil service commission and for the War Office. He was also at this time involved in literary and artistic circles in London, and his first publication, *A Grammar of the French Language*, in three volumes (1863–4), was followed by *The Adventures of Gil Blas* (1866), a translation of Alain-René Lesage's *Histoire de Gil Blas de Santillane*, and *Selections from Modern French Authors* (1869–88). In 1871 a *History of English Literature*, a translation of the work by his friend Hippolyte-Adolphe Taine, was first published in Edinburgh in two volumes. It ran through four or five editions, and was then published in four volumes in London in 1886. The *Dramatic Works of Molière*, translated by van Laun in six volumes, was published in Edinburgh in 1875–6, with illustrations by Lalauze. It included much out-of-the-way information, derived from Langbaine and other sources, concerning seventeenth- and eighteenth-century translations and plagiarisms, both acknowledged and unacknowledged, of separate plays.

In 1876–7 van Laun produced his own *History of French Literature*. The first volume covered the period 'from its origin to the Renaissance'; the second covered the period to 'the end of the Reign of Louis Phillipe [sic]'. It was reprinted in 1883. He next published his *French Revolutionary Epoch* (1878), a history of France in two volumes from the beginning of the first revolution to the end of the Second Empire. This was followed in 1885 by *The Characters of J. de La Bruyère, Newly Rendered into English*.

Van Laun was for some years confidential adviser to John C. Nimmo, a London publisher. He also occasionally wrote critical pieces for the press, and contributed to such journals as *Notes and Queries*. He was widely read in English dramatic literature, and possessed a great knowledge of French and English idioms as well as a large amount of scholarly erudition. He was described in his obituary in *The Times* as a 'bibliophile of exacting taste, [whose] acquaintance with *éditions de luxe* and book illustrations could scarcely be rivalled' (*The Times*, 22 Jan 1896, 10). He died of cirrhosis of the liver at 174 Lancaster Road, London, on 19 January 1896, and was buried in Brookwood cemetery, Woking, on the 23rd.

THOMPSON COOPER, rev. MELANIE ORD

Sources *The Times* (21 Jan 1893), 1 · *The Times* (22 Jan 1896), 10 · *N&Q*, 8th ser., 9 (1896), 80 · *BL cat.* · *Annual Register* (1896) · d. cert.
Wealth at death £717 7s. 10d.: probate, 18 Feb 1896, *CGPLA Eng. & Wales*

Launder, Frank Sydney (1906–1997), scriptwriter, film producer, and director, was born on 28 January 1906 at 13 Walsworth Road, in Hitchin, Hertfordshire, the son of James Sydney Launder, a builder, and his wife, Alice Butler. Educated in Brighton, he subsequently went on to work in the office of the official receiver of bankruptcy there. He also acted with the Brighton Repertory Company, for which he wrote two plays: *There was No Signpost* and *Hey-Day* (under the pseudonym Eric Jetadore). In 1928 he was recruited by British International Pictures, who were expanding their scenario department to prepare for the coming of sound films. He was put to work on an adaptation of Thomas Hardy's *Under the Greenwood Tree* (1929)—on which Sidney *Gilliat also worked—and subsequently on the adaptation of George Bernard Shaw's *How he Lied to her Husband* (1930) and *Arms and the Man* (1932). Shaw refused to allow cuts and alterations to his dialogue, and Launder found greater satisfaction creating film vehicles for comedians such as Monty Banks, Ernie Lotinga, Leslie Fuller, and Stanley Lupino.

In 1934 Launder left British International Pictures and after a brief sojourn as scenario editor at Sound City Studios, Shepperton, he joined the script department of Warner Bros. at their Teddington studio outside London. It was during this period that he began to collaborate with Sidney Gilliat, notably on a trainbound thriller, *Seven Sinners* (1936), based on Arnold Ridley's play *The Wrecker*. Gilliat had worked for Gaumont-British and its subsidiary, Gainsborough Pictures, since 1930, and on his instigation Launder was brought in as script editor at Gainsborough, where he was responsible for a number of Crazy Gang and Will Hay comedies (including *Oh Mr Porter*, 1937, for which Launder wrote the original story) as well as Carol Reed's *Bank Holiday* and Roy William Neill's *Doctor Syn* (1937). Ironically, Gilliat left Gainsborough to join MGM-British shortly after Launder joined, but in 1938 their partnership was resumed on an adaptation of Ethel Lina White's thriller *The Wheel Spins* for the American director Roy William Neill. However, production was delayed and the project might have been abandoned had not Alfred Hitchcock seen the script. The resulting film, *The Lady Vanishes* (1938), Hitchcock's penultimate work before leaving Britain for Hollywood, established Launder and Gilliat as a top writing team. Henceforth they worked on more prestigious projects such as the trilogy they wrote for Carol Reed: *Night Train to Munich* (1940), *Kipps* (1941), and *The Young Mr Pitt* (1942). But they became increasingly restive and sought greater control over what they had written. In 1942 they co-directed an eight-minute propaganda film for the

Frank Sydney Launder (1906–1997), by unknown photographer, c.1935

Ministry of Information, *Partners in Crime*. This was followed by *Millions Like Us* (1943), one of the most memorable and popular feature films of the war years.

Launder and Gilliat had collaborated amicably on the film, but they felt that having two directors on the set confused the cast and crew and they decided hitherto to alternate roles of director and producer. With hindsight they can be seen to have had quite different styles and interests. Gilliat's first film as solo director was *Waterloo Road* (1945), a gritty melodrama about a soldier going absent without leave to check on his wife's fidelity; Launder's début was *2,000 Women* (1944), a much lighter tale of escapades and intrigue in a women's internment camp in France. He followed it by two films with Irish backgrounds—a comedy thriller, *I See a Dark Stranger* (1946), and *Captain Boycott* (1947), an untypically serious film about the plight of the Irish peasantry under absentee English landlords—and an adaptation of H. de Vere Stacpoole's *The Blue Lagoon* (1949), before beginning a long run of successful comedies with *The Happiest Days of your Life* (1950). Launder's own favourites were the whimsical Celtic comedies *Geordie* (1955) and *The Bridal Path* (1959), but he is best remembered for the five films dealing with the rampaging schoolgirls of St Trinian's, which stretched from *The Belles of St Trinian's* in 1954 to *The Wildcats of St Trinian's* in 1980. Between 1958 and 1972 Launder and Gilliat

served on the board of British Lion, and their executive responsibilities reduced their capacity for making their own films. During this period Launder directed only *The Bridal Path*, *The Pure Hell of St Trinian's* (1960), *Joey Boy* (1965), and—jointly with Gilliat—*The Great St Trinian's Train Robbery* (1966).

After directing *The Wildcats of St Trinian's* Launder retired to live at Cap d'Ail in the south of France. He married twice and had two children from each marriage. His first wife, whom he married on 5 September 1931, was Alicia Maud (*b.* 1910/11), daughter of Robert Thomas Quayle, a tailor's manager. His second wife, whom he married on 8 July 1950, was the actress Bernadette Mary O'Farrell (*b.* 1923/4), daughter of Augustine Joseph O'Farrell, a bank manager. The couple met on the set of *Captain Boycott*.

Launder and Gilliat were instrumental in founding the Scriptwriters' Association in 1937, and in 1946 Launder became president. Though by this time he was also a director, he was an outspoken champion of the film writer and in October 1947 he told *Cinema and Theatre Construction* magazine:

> My complaint about established novelists and dramatists is that they will not bother to learn how to write for the screen. The great majority have no affection for the medium. They look down on it from a height, and if they are asked to write a screen play they invariably regard it purely as a money-making venture. They tear off a story with the minimum narrative value, a bunch of characters and yards and yards of dialogue and hope that some hack screen writer—whom they despise because they themselves have never bothered to master the technique—will turn their heterogeneous mass of writing, by some miraculous means, into a shootable screenplay. I have no time for these fellows. It is only those writers who devote themselves wholeheartedly to the film and regard it as the most wonderful medium of expression who can hope to become writers of good screen plays.
> (*Cinema and Theatre Construction*, 12)

Frank Launder made a vital contribution to the establishment of a British film industry capable of producing films as professional, popular, and entertaining as those made in Hollywood. He died in Monte Carlo, Monaco, on 23 February 1997, aged ninety-one. He was survived by his second wife.   ROBERT MURPHY

Sources G. Brown, *Launder and Gilliat* (1977) · *Film Dope*, 33 (Nov 1985), 26–8 · *Cinema and Theatre Construction* (Oct 1947), 12 · *The Independent* (24 Feb 1997) · *Variety* (23 Feb 1997) · *Classic Images* (April 1997), 262 · B. Cross, 'From ideas to screen', *Picturegoer* (25 May 1946), 8 · I. F. McAsh, 'A new term at St. Trinian's', *Films Illustrated* (Nov 1979), 106–7 · b. cert. · m. certs.
Archives FILM BFI NFTVA
Likenesses photographs, c.1935, Hult. Arch. [*see illus.*] · photographs, Hult. Arch.

Laune, Guillaume de. *See* Delaune, William (c.1530–1611).

Laurel, Stan [*real name* Arthur Stanley Jefferson] (1890–1965), comedian, was born at his grandfather's house in Argyll Street, Ulverston, Lancashire, on 16 June 1890, the second son in the family of four sons and one daughter of Arthur Jefferson, known as A. J., of Bishop Auckland, theatre manager, and his wife, Margaret (Madge) Metcalfe,

Stan Laurel (1890–1965), by Stagg, 1936

is usually regarded as their finest short film; it is certainly the most famous. Among their feature films, *Sons of the Desert* (1933), involving a Chicago convention and a mythical voyage to Honolulu, *Way out West* (1936), featuring the duet 'On the Trail of the Lonesome Pine', *Block-Heads* (1938), and *The Flying Deuces* (1939), with the pair joining the foreign legion, are among the best remembered. The Laurel and Hardy set piece was the ordinary situation from which sprang a spiral of disaster. Their usual guise was as everyday American hen-pecked husbands or companions, but over the years they did adopt other roles such as First World War soldiers or pilots. Whatever the location, they were soon engulfed in difficulties. Nervy, flustered, even tearful, Stan Laurel, 'the thin one', exacerbated these accumulating troubles, to the growing chagrin of 'the fat one', the ever earnest Oliver Hardy, culminating in his cry of 'Another fine mess you've gotten me into'. Laurel, in effect, made two contributions to the partnership: as Hardy was quick to concede, Laurel was the creator and rigorous controller of their comedy, as well as a member of what was widely recognized as the best comic double act of its time. An important reason for this was their eschewal of the conventional 'straight' man, two-dimensional and irritable. Each developed a detailed and complete persona of his own. The endearing bathos and crassness of Laurel found an admirable foil in the elephantine smugness of his rotund partner. Their last film, *Atoll K*, was made in 1952. Laurel and Hardy travelled extensively during the Second World War, entertaining troops, and made a variety tour of Britain in 1947, opening at the London Palladium. Oliver Hardy died in 1957, ending one of the most successful comic partnerships in history.

Stan Laurel won a special Academy award in 1960 for 'creative pioneering' on film. Much more serious and committed than his genial partner, he had devoted much time and energy to his peculiar art form. His devotion to his work might account for the chaos of his private relationships: his marital toils were convoluted and confusingly reported. The nearest to an exact listing would be to record that he was married to Lois Neilson in 1926 (with whom he had a son who died in infancy and a daughter); to (Virginia) Ruth Rogers in 1935 (after a possibly illegal ceremony in Mexico the previous year); to Illeana Shuvalova in 1938; to Ruth Rogers again in 1941; and to Ida Kitaeva Raphael, who survived him, in 1946. Stan Laurel died on 23 February 1965 in Santa Monica, California, USA, and was buried at Forest Lawn, Los Angeles.

ERIC MIDWINTER

actress, of Ulverston. He attended schools in Bishop Auckland, Gainford, and Glasgow, after which his family connections helped him to gain entry to the music-hall as a 'boy' comedian. His first appearance was in 1906 at the Scotia Music-Hall, Glasgow, which his father managed. In 1907 he joined the Fred Karno company, where his greatest success was as Jimmy the Fearless in a sketch of that name. It was while touring the United States with Karno in 1912 that he tried his luck in American vaudeville, often in a duo with his common-law wife, Mae Dahlberg, who suggested his stage name, Stan Laurel, although he did not adopt it legally until 1934. In 1915 he saw the opportunities for music-hall pantomimists in the silent movies, and sought a mixed fortune in films and on the stage. He lived in the USA from this period.

Laurel became acquainted with Oliver 'Babe' Hardy in the early 1920s, but it was in 1927, under the auspices of the Hal Roach studio, that they were first paired with any success, in *Slipping Wives*. From that point they were to make over a hundred films together, some thirty of them silent, and almost all of them produced by Roach. Their best work was probably between 1929 and 1935, when they were engaged in creating coherent and sparse twenty-minute cameos. *The Music Box* (1932), involving the delivery of a piano to a house at the top of a steep incline,

Sources F. L. Guiles, *Stan* (1980) • J. Walker, ed., *Halliwell's filmgoer's companion*, 12th edn (1997) • R. Busby, *British music hall: an illustrated who's who from 1850 to the present day* (1976) • private information (1993) [Laurel and Hardy Museum, Ulverston, Lancashire] • J. McCabe, *Mr Laurel and Mr Hardy* (1961) • *DNB*
Archives Laurel and Hardy Museum, Ulverston |FILM BFI NFTVA, *The South Bank Show*, ITV, 6 Jan 1991 • BFI NFTVA, news footage • BFI NFTVA, performance footage • BFI NFTVA, record footage |SOUND BL NSA, 'Life and times of Stan Laurel', BD3 RADIOLA • BL NSA, oral history interview • BL NSA, performance recording

Likenesses photographs, 1927–68, Hult. Arch. · Stagg, photograph, 1936, NPG [*see illus.*]

Laurence [St Laurence, Lawrence] (*d.* 619), archbishop of Canterbury, secured the Christian foundations laid by St Augustine when the survival of the Roman mission to the English was at risk. He was one of the Roman monks who had accompanied Augustine from Rome in 596, and after their establishment in Kent had been sent to report back to Pope Gregory I on their needs. On this journey he was accompanied by the monk Peter and their advice caused the pope to send a reinforcing missionary group and detailed guidance for the structure of the new church in June 601. Laurence is styled 'the priest' in Gregory's letters and by Bede, establishing that he had been ordained, perhaps in order to facilitate his part in the pastoral work of the mission. At some date between 604 and 610 Laurence succeeded to Augustine's see at Canterbury, as the second incumbent, having already been consecrated by Augustine in order that there should be no break in the episcopal succession of the young church. It is likely that, like Augustine, he was also the metropolitan bishop and that that status did not pass to London as Gregory had planned in 601, and where Mellitus had been bishop since 604. Bede records that it was Laurence rather than Mellitus who took precedence in letters seeking friendly relations with, and pastoral authority over, the churches of the Britons and of the Irish. Part of the letter of Laurence, Mellitus, and Justus to all the Irish bishops and abbots is recorded by Bede and concerns Irish departures from the 'practice of the universal church' (Bede, *Hist. eccl.*, 2.4) and their refusal to eat with the Roman missionaries. Bede believed that the calculation of the date of Easter was the principal issue in dispute, but both Britons and Irish are likely to have regarded any hint that they should be subject to an English church as politically unacceptable.

Laurence and 'all the clergy' are known to have received a letter from Pope Boniface IV, which was brought by Mellitus who had attended the pope's Roman synod of February 610 concerning the harmony of the monastic life. In 613, according to the medieval historians of the monastery of St Augustine's at Canterbury, Laurence consecrated their monastic church of St Peter and St Paul, whose construction had been begun by Augustine. The crisis of Laurence's episcopate, however, came with the death of King Æthelberht in 616 or 618. Reversions to paganism occurred both in Essex and in Kent, where Æthelberht's son and successor, Eadbald, still apparently a pagan, sought to secure his succession by marrying his stepmother. Though bishops Mellitus of London and Justus of Rochester both fled to Frankish Gaul, Laurence remained at Canterbury. Within a year the king had been baptized and married to a Christian Frankish princess and the bishops had been recalled to Kent. Canterbury tradition reported by Bede explained the king's conversion as a miracle, after Laurence had been brutally beaten in a vision by St Peter for planning to desert his flock. That attractive monastic myth may obscure the archbishop's successful engineering of Frankish pressure upon the

king to enforce his conversion. Laurence died on 2 February 619 and was buried beside his predecessor in the north porch of the church of St Peter and St Paul. In 1091 his bones were translated to the new Norman abbey church of St Augustine's and a few years later the monk Goscelin wrote a brief life, mainly based on Bede, but which claims that Laurence converted one Irish archbishop, named Terenan, to the Roman way of calculating Easter; it also claims that he travelled to Fordun in Perthshire and built a church there, which may be an attempt to explain the dedication of a church associated with Queen Margaret of Scotland. A number of brief late medieval lives have nothing further to add.   N. P. BROOKS

Sources Bede, *Hist. eccl.*, 1.27, 33; 2.4–7 · *S. Gregorii magni registrum epistularum*, ed. D. Norberg, 2 vols. (1982), 922–4, 938, 946–7, 950–51 [letters 34–35, 41, 48, 51] · N. Brooks, *The early history of the church of Canterbury: Christ Church from 597 to 1066* (1984), 9–13, 64–6, 88, 260 · T. D. Hardy, *Descriptive catalogue of materials relating to the history of Great Britain and Ireland*, 1, Rolls Series, 26 (1862), nos. 587–90 · R. Sharpe, 'The setting of St Augustine's translation, 1091', *Canterbury and the Norman conquest: churches, saints and scholars, 1066–1109*, ed. R. Eales and R. Sharpe (1995), 1–13

Laurence [St Laurence, Lorcán Ua Tuathail, Laurence O'Toole] (*c*.1128–1180), archbishop of Dublin, was probably born about 1128, the son of Muirchertach Ua Tuathail, king of Uí Muiredaig (in north Leinster). According to the compilation known as the *Ban-Shenchus* ('Lore of women'), his mother was the daughter of Cerball Mac Bríc; but according to his early thirteenth-century hagiographical life his mother was Derbail, daughter of Ua Brain (almost certainly of the north Leinster dynasty of Uí Fáeláin). The same source states that Laurence served as a hostage for his father at an early age with Diarmait Mac Murchada, overking of Leinster, who mistreated him (bearing in mind, however, that this king is accorded a consistently hostile depiction throughout the life).

Monk, bishop, and archbishop Laurence became a monk at the important north Leinster monastery of Glendalough and in 1153 succeeded to the office of abbot. According to the life he was then aged twenty-five, though in saying this the author may have been conditioned by requirements of canon law. His succession to the abbacy may be presumed to have had the approval of Diarmait Mac Murchada as provincial king of Leinster, and this is further suggested by the fact that around that time Mac Murchada married Laurence's half-sister, Mór. Laurence declined to accept promotion to the bishopric of Glendalough when it became vacant in 1157, according to his life because he had not reached the canonical age of thirty. Another possible reason is that most of the lands of Glendalough were still attached to the abbacy rather than to the cathedral church, and that acceptance of the episcopal office may not have been viewed as advancement. More ambitious motives for Laurence's refusal may be suggested by the fact that in 1162 he was prepared to accept elevation to the more prestigious archbishopric of Dublin. At the Synod of Kells of 1152, the papal legate, Cardinal Giovanni Paparo, had intended that after the death of its incumbent the diocese of Glendalough should be united to the diocese of Dublin. However, when Glendalough did fall vacant in 1157, its incorporation into Dublin was not effected, for reasons unknown.

Laurence's succession to Dublin in 1162 was almost certainly approved at the Synod of Clane held in that year, presided over by Gilla Críst (Christianus) Ua Connairche, bishop of Lismore and papal legate, and Gilla Meic Liac (Gelasius), archbishop of Armagh. He was consecrated as archbishop by Archbishop Gilla Meic Liac in his capacity as primate, assisted by Joseph, bishop of Ferns, and Malachias Ua Brain, bishop of Kildare. The participation of these two bishops, who were associates of Diarmait Mac Murchada, suggests the latter's consent to the promotion. It may also be significant that between 1160 and 1162, as abbot of Glendalough, Laurence had witnessed Mac Murchada's charter to St Mary's Abbey, Ferns, and between 1162 and 1165, as archbishop, attested his charters to Killenny and All Hallows. However, a disputed succession to the abbacy of Glendalough followed Laurence's promotion to Dublin, with his nephew (known only by his Latin name of Thomas) eventually succeeding him. This appointment is presented in the partisan life as a victory for canonical procedures, and as emphatically made on the grounds of personal merit (although there is other evidence to suggest that Thomas fathered at least one son), and in the face of an attempted intrusion by Diarmait Mac Murchada of another candidate. In 1167 Laurence attended the large assembly of clergy and laity convened by Ruaidrí Ua Conchobair, king of Connacht and claimant to the high-kingship, which suggests that he was prepared to acknowledge Ua Conchobair as high-king.

Anglo-Irish affairs Following the beginnings of Anglo-Norman intervention in Ireland, Laurence negotiated on behalf of the city of Dublin before it was taken by force by Diarmait Mac Murchada and his Anglo-Norman allies in 1170. It would be rash, however, to draw firm conclusions about Laurence's political allegiance from his role as mediator, since throughout the twelfth century Irish churchmen had been very actively engaged as peace negotiators. In 1171 Laurence is depicted by Gerald of Wales as acting in consort with Ruaidrí Ua Conchobair in seeking to raise mercenaries for the siege of Dublin, held by Richard fitz Gilbert, earl of Pembroke and lord of Striguil (known as Strongbow), and as acting with Ua Conchobair in sending letters to Godred, king of Man; Gerald attributes Laurence's motives to 'zeal for his own people' (Giraldus Cambrensis, 78–9). Laurence attended the Council of Cashel convened by Henry II, 1171–2, and in 1172 Pope Alexander III named him in letters exhorting the Irish bishops to aid Henry in ruling Ireland. The pipe roll of 1172/3 records payment of his passage to Ireland in the company of William fitz Aldelin, indicating that he had visited England and had made representations to Henry.

In October 1175 Laurence witnessed the treaty concluded at Windsor between Henry II and Ruaidrí Ua Conchobair, which delimited Leinster, Meath, and a portion of Munster as an Angevin sphere of influence, and conceded to Ua Conchobair overlordship of the remainder of Ireland, provided that he acknowledged Henry as his superior, maintained loyalty to him, and paid tribute. While in England, according to his life, Laurence survived an assassination attempt at Canterbury, made by a madman who sought to draw comparisons between him and the martyred Thomas Becket. He travelled back to Ireland in the company of Augustinus Ua Selbaig, bishop-elect of Waterford, to whose appointment Henry had assented at Windsor. The city of Waterford had been reserved by Henry as royal demesne and Laurence was clearly prepared to allow such a right of assent to the king. He presided at the burial of Strongbow in Holy Trinity Cathedral, Dublin, in April 1176. An original charter with seal attached, issued by him between 1176 and 1178, confirming a grant of Killester (in north Dublin) to William Brun, constitutes the earliest surviving original charter of an Irish bishop.

Papal legate Shortly after Christmas 1178, Laurence set out to attend the Third Lateran Council, due to be held in the following year, travelling via the court of Henry II to seek his permission to be present, and swearing an oath that he would do nothing to diminish the king's rights at the council. He secured a privilege of protection from Pope Alexander III, dated 20 April 1179, confirming him and his successor in their rights in the see of Dublin and its churches, and in its five suffragan bishoprics; he may also be considered responsible for procuring a privilege of protection, dated 13 May 1179, for Malchus, bishop of Glendalough. The pope also appointed Laurence *legatus natus* (his resident legate) in Ireland, to replace Gilla Críst Ua Connairche. On his return to Ireland, in his capacity as papal legate, Laurence convened a synod at Clonfert in 1179. An account of the synod survives only in a garbled seventeenth-century English translation of the annals of Clonmacnoise, which indicates, however, that he sought to proclaim the decrees of the Lateran Council. The location of the synod (at which is recorded the attendance of the clergy of Connacht, as well as that of Echthigern Mac Máelchiaráin (Eugenius), bishop of Meath, and Máelísu Ua Cerbaill, bishop of Louth, or Airgialla, both suffragan bishops of Armagh) suggests that it was intended to serve for the sphere of influence which had been allocated to Ruaidrí Ua Conchobair by the treaty of Windsor. Laurence's life has an account of his charitable activities during the severe winter of 1179, including the sending of a shipload of distressed Irish to England, where he arranged that they should receive aid from friendly benefactors. Early in 1180 he installed Tommaltach Ua Conchobair, bishop of Elphin and nephew of Ruaidrí Ua Conchobair, in the see of Armagh. The translation of a Connacht bishop to the primatial see of Armagh was unprecedented and suggests a close association with Ua Conchobair.

According to Roger of Howden, soon after the feast of the Purification (2 February), in 1180 Laurence was at Henry II's court, accompanied by a son of Ruaidrí Ua Conchobair; the latter was to be a pledge of Ua Conchobair's good faith in his undertaking to pay tribute owing to Henry, possibly on the basis of the treaty of Windsor, although there is no consensus among historians that the treaty was still in operation at that date. Notwithstanding the reference to tribute made by Howden (who was aware of the terms of the treaty of Windsor, the text of which he transcribed), it is also possible that Henry had objected to the appointment of Tommaltach to Armagh. Inconclusive negotiations between Laurence and Henry took place; Henry left for Normandy on 15 April 1180, and Laurence, who had been forbidden to return to Ireland before peace had been concluded, was obliged to remain in England. Late in October or early in November, Laurence crossed from Dover to Wissant near Boulogne. He was at Eu on 10 November, already suffering from a fever. On 11 November he sent a cleric named David, tutor of Ua Conchobair's son, to Henry's court, where the youth was handed over as a hostage. On 13 November David returned with news that peace had been concluded with Henry. Laurence died at Eu on 14 November 1180 and his burial there was presided over by the Roman subdeacon and papal legate, Alexis, who may have been involved in breaking the impasse in negotiations between Laurence and Henry.

Canonization and cult By 20 May 1191, when Pope Celestine replied to a petition for Laurence's canonization from Archbishop Walter of Rouen, by saying that the time was not opportune, a book of Laurence's miracles, compiled by Bishop Máelisú Ua Cerbaill, had already reached Eu. In 1206 Hugues, abbot of Eu, petitioning Innocent III for canonization, stated that this was the fifth such attempt made by the canons of Eu; in 1214 Abbot Guido petitioned again. Laurence was eventually canonized by Pope Honorius III on 11 December 1225, testimonies in support of his canonization having been provided by: the archbishop of Rouen; the abbot of Eu; John Cumin, Laurence's successor in the archbishopric of Dublin; Echdonn (Eugenius), archbishop of Armagh; Ailbe (Albinus), bishop of Ferns; and Marianus (Ua Briain), bishop of Cork. His relics were translated by Theobald, archbishop of Rouen, on 6 May 1226. It has been suggested that the earliest extant version of his life may have been compiled by Henry of London, archbishop of Dublin from 1213 to 1228. Soon after Laurence's canonization, a life, focusing chiefly on his miracles, was written by a canon of Eu, possibly Jean Halgrinus of Abbeville, later archbishop of Besançon.

Gerald of Wales twice attributes to common report the view that Laurence was a man of excessive partiality for his own people; he also asserts that Laurence incurred the displeasure of Henry II in securing privileges at the Lateran council of 1179, to which the king objected, although he does not specify any details. Gerald was mistaken in suggesting that Laurence was prevented from returning to Ireland after the council. However, he was also prepared to describe Laurence 'as a good and just man' (Giraldus Cambrensis, 196–7), and recounts a miracle relating to his final days when he refused to rest at Abbeville because, with prophetic insight of his impending death, he wished to reach the basilica dedicated to the Blessed Virgin at Eu; this miracle is also recounted in the life. The saint's feast is celebrated on 14 November and the feast of the translation of his relics on 10 May; he has a place in the painted calendar of saints canonized in the thirteenth century in the basilica of the Four Crowned Martyrs at Rome. As in the case of St Malachy of Armagh, the circumstance of Laurence's death and burial on the continent ensured his canonization; he and Malachy remained the only formally canonized Irish saints until the canonization of Oliver Plunket in 1976. Laurence's reputation as an ecclesiastical reformer also rests chiefly on the dossier compiled for his canonization. Nevertheless, his promotion of church reform, which receives important emphasis in his life, is demonstrated by his introduction of Augustinian canons of the Arrouaisian filiation into Holy Trinity Cathedral, Dublin, a step which had been taken no later than 1176–7.

M. T. FLANAGAN

Sources M. P. Sheehy, ed., *Pontificia Hibernica: medieval papal chancery documents concerning Ireland, 640–1261*, 1 (1962), 26–31, 73, 255–8 · M. V. Ronan, 'St Laurentius, archbishop of Dublin: original testimonies for canonisation', *Irish Ecclesiastical Record*, 5th ser., 27 (1926), 347–64; 5th ser., 28 (1926), 247–56, 467–80, 596–612 · C. Plummer, ed., 'Vie et miracles de S. Laurent, archevêque de Dublin', *Analecta Bollandiana*, 33 (1914), 121–86 · D. Murphy, ed., *The annals of Clonmacnoise*, trans. C. Mageoghagan (1896), 213–14 · W. Stubbs, ed., *Gesta regis Henrici secundi Benedicti abbatis: the chronicle of the reigns of Henry II and Richard I, AD 1169–1192*, 2 vols., Rolls Series, 49 (1867), 1.27, 103–4, 221, 270, 321 · *Chronica magistri Rogeri de Hovedene*, ed. W. Stubbs, 2, Rolls Series, 51 (1869), 31, 85, 171, 253 · Dugdale, *Monasticon*, new edn, 6/2.1141–2 · C. M. Butler and J. H. Bernard, eds., 'The charters of the Cistercian abbey of Duiske in the county of Kilkenny', *Proceedings of the Royal Irish Academy*, 35C (1918–20), 1–188, esp. 5–7 · R. Butler, ed., *Registrum prioratus omnium sanctorum* (1845), 50–51 · *Pipe rolls, 19 Henry II* · *Pipe rolls, 25 Henry II* · M. P. Sheehy, 'Diplomatica: unpublished medieval charters and letters relating to Ireland', *Archivium Hibernicum*, 25 (1962), 123–35 · W. Stokes, ed., 'The annals of Tigernach [8 pts]', *Revue Celtique*, 16 (1895), 374–419; 17 (1896), 6–33, 119–263, 337–420; 18 (1897), 9–59, 150–97, 267–303, 374–91; pubd sep. (1993), s.a. 1162 · *AFM*, 2nd edn, 1162–3, 1167 · Giraldus Cambrensis, *Expugnatio Hibernica / The conquest of Ireland*, ed. and trans. A. B. Scott and F. X. Martin (1978), 66–7, 78–9, 98–9, 166–7, 196–7 · G. H. Orpen, ed. and trans., *The song of Dermot and the earl* (1892), lines 1840–46 · J. T. Gilbert, ed., *Chartularies of St Mary's Abbey, Dublin: with the register of its house at Dunbrody and annals of Ireland*, 2 vols., Rolls Series, 80 (1884), vol. 1, pp. 32–3; vol. 2, pp. 266, 274, 287 · M. A. O'Brien, ed., *Corpus genealogiarum Hiberniae* (Dublin, 1962), 13 · M. C. Dobbs, ed. and trans., 'The Ban-shenchus [pt 2]', *Revue Celtique*, 48 (1931), 163–234, esp. 234 · R. Sharpe, *Medieval Irish saints' lives: an introduction to Vitae sanctorum Hiberniae* (1991), 395 · J. C. Crosthwaite, ed., *The book of obits and martyrology of the cathedral church … Dublin*, Irish Archaeological Society, 4 (1844), xlvii · D. H. Farmer, *The Oxford dictionary of saints* (1978), 240 · A. S. Mac Shamhráin, *Church and polity in pre-Norman Ireland: the case of Glendalough* (1996)

Likenesses seal, NL Ire., D.9979

Laurence del Brok. *See* Brok, Laurence del (*c.*1210–1274).

Laurence, Edward (*bap.* 1674, *d.* 1739), land surveyor, was baptized on 21 October 1674 at St Martin's Church, Stamford, Lincolnshire, the sixth of seven children (and third of four sons) of John Laurence (*d.* 1700), Church of England clergyman, and his wife, Elizabeth Stubbs, of Stibbington, Huntingdonshire. By 1699 Edward was in London and he had accommodation addresses there until 1731 with, among others, John Senex (1714–16) and Jonathan Sisson (1725–8).

Laurence worked as a land surveyor from about 1706. An early commission was to map an estate at Eltington,

Northamptonshire, the parish next to Yelvertoft where his brother John *Laurence was rector. On this map he called himself a teacher of mathematics at Northampton and advertised as a land surveyor and maker of sundials. In 1716, he still offered to teach when he was not surveying, but probably from then until 1719 he was employed surveying the estates of the duke of Kent in Bedfordshire, Gloucestershire, and Herefordshire; atlases of lands in the first two counties survive. In addition, he mapped land in Cambridgeshire and Wiltshire for other owners during these years. Laurence's first two publications also date from 1716: 'A new and familiar way to find a most exact meridian line by the Pole star' (printed as an appendix to his brother John's *The Gentleman's Recreation*); and *The Young Surveyor's Guide, or, A New Introduction to the Whole Art of Surveying Land*. This second work drew attention to possible errors when taking measurements; a second edition was published in 1717 and a third in 1736.

Laurence continued to survey and map land. He was employed by Lord Cholmondeley, Charles Tryan, Sir Walter Wagstaffe Bagot, and others, and added Essex, Staffordshire, and Surrey to counties where he worked. From 1722 to 1727 Laurence was extensively employed as a land surveyor by the trustees of Edmund Sheffield, second duke of Buckingham and Normanby; his final bill to the trustees was submitted in 1734. As well as surveying and mapping the family's estates in Essex, Lincolnshire, and Yorkshire, he also valued land and wood, let farms (at high rents), and advised the trustees on husbandry matters. The duchess of Buckingham was the dedicatee of *The duty of a steward to his lord … design'd … for the … stewards and tenants of his grace the duke of Buckingham* (1727), second and third editions of which were published in 1731 as *The Duty and Office of a Land Steward*. In it, Laurence advised on estate management, proposed covenants to be included in leases, provided model surveys, and discussed quantity surveying and particular cultivations and crops. He advertised his surveying business, in which he had been joined by William Gardiner since 1725. The junior partner surveyed estates, leaving Laurence to concentrate on estate valuing and improving. After a disagreement in 1728, the partnership appears to have been broken.

Laurence was an early example of a land surveyor who was a specialist employed by landowners, their agents, and stewards to measure land and judge its quality, value, and potential. Valuation is a skill discussed by him in *A dissertation on estates upon lives and years … with an exact calculation of their real worth* (1730). Although Laurence continued to survey estates, during the later years of his life he seems to have been more involved in antiquarian and natural philosophical matters. On his admission as a member of the Spalding Gentlemen's Society in 1731, he was described as a land surveyor and mathematician of London. In 1736, based in Stamford, he was a founder of the town's Brazen-nose Society and corresponded with his co-founders George Lynn and William Stukeley, showing his long-standing interest and abilities as an instrument maker, and his activities as a practical astronomer. Notes by him were included in the third edition of Edward Hoppus's *Practical Measuring* (1736). Laurence probably remained in Stamford, where he was buried in St Martin's Church on 3 June 1739.

SARAH BENDALL

Sources F. W. Steer and others, *Dictionary of land surveyors and local map-makers of Great Britain and Ireland, 1530–1850*, ed. P. Eden, 2nd edn, ed. S. Bendall, 2 vols. (1997) · R. V. Wallis and P. J. Wallis, eds., *Biobibliography of British mathematics and its applications*, 2 (1986) · *The family memoirs of the Rev. William Stukeley*, ed. W. C. Lukis, 1, SurtS, 73 (1882) · P. Eden, notes on Edward Laurence, BL, Map Library, Dictionary of Land Surveyors · private information (2004) · Venn, *Alum. Cant.* · A. S. Bendall, *Maps, land and society: a history, with a cartobibliography of Cambridgeshire estate maps, c.1600–1836* (1992) · Lincs. Arch., D&C Ciij 46/2/21 · J. Laurence, *The clergyman's recreation* (1714) · W. Gardiner, advertisement, *Daily Journal* (31 July 1728) · list of members, Spalding Gentlemen's Society · parish registers, Nassington and Stamford St Martin, Northants. RO

Archives Beds. & Luton ARS, Lucas MSS · Glos. RO, D1297 · Scunthorpe Museum, Sheffield MSS

Laurence, French

Laurence, French (1757–1809), lawyer and politician, was born on 3 April 1757 at Bath, Somerset, the eldest of the four children of Richard Laurence (1729–c.1773), watchmaker, and his wife, Elizabeth, daughter of John French, clothier. Both parents were natives of Warminster in Wiltshire, but their families were of Lancashire and co. Galway origins. His younger brother was the scholar and archbishop of Cashel Richard *Laurence. Laurence was educated at Winchester College and Corpus Christi College, Oxford, matriculating on 5 March 1774, and graduating with a BA on 17 December 1777. He took his MA on 21 June 1781. In 1781, intending to read common law, Laurence took chambers at the Inner Temple, but the political associations he formed with Charles James Fox and the whigs made him turn to the study of civil law. Laurence received his DCL at Oxford on 19 October 1787 and on 3 November 1788 he was admitted to the College of Advocates.

Laurence already had something of a literary reputation. In 1776 his libretto, *A Lyric Ode on the Fairies, Aerial Beings, and Witches of Shakespeare*, was set to music by Thomas Linley the younger and performed at Drury Lane. Following his move to the Inner Temple, Laurence was encouraged by Sheridan to write in the service of the Foxite whigs, most actively during the Westminster election of 1784. He published political pamphlets, had a significant share in the composition of the satirical poem the 'Rolliad', and also in 1784 wrote the preface and notes to the sixteenth and twenty-first *Probationary Odes*.

Laurence developed a working relationship with Edmund Burke as a contributor to the *Annual Register*. This soon became, on Laurence's part, a deep and abiding admiration which influenced his intellectual and moral development. While his specific role is unclear, evidence indicates that he succeeded Burke as editor of the *Annual Register* in the late 1780s. The correspondence between the two, begun in 1788, details Laurence's work during the regency crisis and his interest in Irish affairs as well as the rapid growth of his professional practice at the civil bar. The letters also demonstrate Laurence's sense of humour and his concern for others. When Burke's son Richard died in 1794 Laurence gently reminded Burke that his work would temper the hard edges of grief, while Jane

Burke 'will have no refuge' (Laurence to Burke, after 4 Aug 1794, MS, Osborn collection, Yale 21.271) from memories of their son.

Although he continued to write poetry, partisan pamphlets, and biblical commentary throughout his life, Laurence's most significant achievements were made as an active political figure. He first came to public notice as chamber counsel to the managers in the impeachment trial of Warren Hastings. Counsels' duties were to advise the managers on points of law and to draw up briefs. The appointment attests to Laurence's growing reputation because it was made during his 'year of silence', the year immediately succeeding admission into the College of Advocates when he could not plead. Laurence's dedication to the prosecution demonstrated his fellow feeling with Hastings's paramount critic, Burke, and with the whig party, receiving public praise from Fox. In 1791 he was appointed a judge of the court of Admiralty of the Cinque Ports.

That year, when Fox and Burke split the whig party over Burke's stance on the French Revolution, Laurence unhesitatingly cast his lot with Burke. Laurence acted as Burke's representative in negotiations with William Cavendish Cavendish-Bentinck, third duke of Portland, seeking the reunion of the whigs either in opposition or in the government of Pitt the younger. A decisive break came on 28 February 1793 when Laurence followed Burke in resigning from the Whig Club, of which he had been a member for seven years. Burke helped promote Laurence's attempt to find a parliamentary seat, unsuccessfully proposing that he become Earl Fitzwilliam's nominee at Malton following the death of Richard Burke. Portland, as chancellor of the University of Oxford, secured Laurence's appointment as regius professor of civil law there in 1796. His duties at Oxford were executed by his brother Richard. In October that year Laurence finally entered the Commons as member for Peterborough, nominated by Fitzwilliam after repeated lobbying by Burke.

Laurence disliked the polarization of the Commons between supporters of Pitt and Fox, and in February 1797 declared his resolve 'to keep a check over the two contending parties' (Thorne, 385). He made several speeches opposing the union with Ireland, following Fitzwilliam's concern for Irish legislative independence, his own support for Catholic relief, and his suspicion of measures that upset the existing constitutional balance. The passage of the union helped propel Laurence closer to opposition, where he remained following the formation of the Addington ministry.

In parliament Laurence was noted for his intellectual strength, wide-ranging knowledge, and retentive, capacious memory. According to contemporaries, the wit and keen intellect Laurence exhibited in written prose and verse were missing from his oral presentations. In a letter to Burke describing Laurence's first speech in the Commons, William Windham wrote: 'Dr. Laurence's first performance … succeeded perfectly well. He keeled a little in the launching which gave me some minutes anxiety. But he soon righted, when he touched the water, and shewed,

as he is, a grand first-rate' (Poetical Remains, 10). Unfortunately Laurence's elocutionary skills never matched his literary art, so that years later Gilbert Elliot described his conversation as a 'learned manuscript written in a bad hand' (Life and Letters, 1.139n.). This ineptness in conversation may have had something to do with his being blackballed three times for membership by the Literary Club before finally being elected to it in 1802. After 1804 he was also a member of Brook's Club. Laurence and Walker King were Burke's literary executors, and by 1803 they had published eight volumes of his collected works.

On 26 June 1805 Laurence was appointed a member of the committee to frame articles of impeachment against Henry Dundas, first Viscount Melville. Following the formation of the Grenville ministry in 1806 the war and colonial secretary, William Windham, who was, like Laurence, a protégé of Burke, tried to find him a judicial or administrative appointment. Unfortunately, a place could not be found that was acceptable to either Grenville or Laurence. Furthermore, Laurence was a leading campaigner for the impeachment of Richard, Marquess Wellesley, on the grounds of maladministration in India, regarded by Grenville as an unjust charge. In 1808 Laurence's health began to fail, and he was absent from the Commons that year. He died suddenly on 26 February 1809 'attacked after dinner with something like apoplexy' (Epistolary Correspondence, xxvi) during a short visit to one of his brothers in Eltham, Kent.

Laurence never married but counted among his friends and acquaintances some of the most notable men and women of his day. When he died Samuel Whitbread delivered a tribute in the Commons: 'this House and the country have, in Dr. Laurence, lost a vast fund of knowledge, an exemplary instance of public and private virtue, and a larger proportion of pure principles, and political integrity, than perhaps have ever been united in any one individual' (Hansard 1, 12, 1809, 1162–3).

ELIZABETH R. LAMBERT

Sources The epistolary correspondence of the Right Hon. Edmund Burke and Dr. French Laurence (1827) · Poetical remains of French Laurence … and Richard Laurence, ed. [H. Cotton] (1872) · The correspondence of Edmund Burke, ed. T. W. Copeland and others, 10 vols. (1958–78), vols. 7–9 · Life and letters of Sir Gilbert Elliot, first earl of Minto, from 1751 to 1806, ed. countess of Minto [E. E. E. Elliot-Murray-Kynynmound], 1 (1874), 139 n. · F. Laurence to E. Burke, Yale U., Beinecke L., Osborn collection, 21.271 · Hansard 1 (1809), 12.1162–3 · R. G. Thorne, 'French, Laurence', HoP, Commons, 1790–1820 · will, PRO, PROB 11/1494 · IGI

Archives BL, letters to T. Robinson, Add. MSS 23818–23819 · BL, corresp. with William Windham, Add. MS 37876–37909 · Bodl. Oxf., letters to Edmund Burke · Sheff. Arch., corresp. with Edmund Burke · Sheff. Arch., corresp. with Earl Fitzwilliam · U. Nott. L., corresp. with duke of Portland · Yale U., Osborn collection, 21.262–284

Likenesses J. Wright, miniature, 1805, repro. in Laurence, Poetical remains

Wealth at death small annuities (£300 a year to brothers; £100 a year to sister); plate; manuscripts; printed books: will, PRO, PROB 11/1494

Laurence, John (1668–1732), writer on gardening, was baptized on 27 October 1668 at Stamford Baron, near

Stamford, Northamptonshire, the elder son of John Laurence (d. 1700), vicar of St Martin's, Stamford Baron, and prebendary of Lincoln, and his wife, Elizabeth Stubbs. Edward *Laurence was his brother. He entered Clare College, Cambridge, on 20 May 1685, and took a BA in 1689 and an MA in 1692. He was a fellow of Clare College from 1691 to 1701. From 1700 to 1721 Laurence was rector of Yelvertoft, Northamptonshire, and he was chaplain to the bishop of Salisbury, and a prebendary of Salisbury from 1720 to 1732. In 1722 he became rector of Bishopwearmouth, co. Durham.

Laurence wrote three of his four gardening books at Yelvertoft, where he transformed a neglected garden, harvesting fruit within three years. He spent all his spare time in his garden and claimed that gardening brought him peace of mind. He was especially successful in growing pears. His first gardening book was *The Clergyman's Recreation, Shewing the Pleasure and Profit of the Art of Gardening* (1714; 6th edition 1726). This was followed by *The Gentleman's Recreation* (1716), *The Fruit-Garden Kalendar* (1718), and *A New System of Agriculture* (1726). He also published religious works, including *An Apology for Dr Clarke* (1714). There is no evidence that the poem *Paradice Regain'd* (1728) was by him.

Laurence married Mary, the only daughter of Stephen Goodwin, vicar of Horley, near Banbury, Oxfordshire. They had one son and three daughters. He died at home, at Bishopwearmouth, on 17 May 1732, and was buried at the church of which he was rector.

M. G. WATKINS, *rev.* ANNE PIMLOTT BAKER

Sources J. S. Gilmour, 'The Rev John Lawrence (1668–1732); the man and his books', *Huntia*, 2 (1965), 117–37 · R. P. Brotherston, 'The Rev John Laurence', *Gardeners' Chronicle*, 3rd ser., 27 (1900), 129–30, 413–14; 3rd ser., 28 (1900), 42 · H. W. Miles, 'John Laurence and his pears', *The fruit year book* (1958), 63–9 · 'Early writers on English gardening, no. 11: Rev. John Laurence', *Journal of Horticulture, Cottage Gardener and Country Gentleman*, 30 (1876), 270–72 · Desmond, *Botanists* · D. McDonald, *Agricultural writers from Sir Walter of Henley to Arthur Young, 1200–1800* (1908) · J. Donaldson, *Agricultural biography* (1854) · Venn, *Alum. Cant.*
Likenesses Vertue, engraving, repro. in Gilmour, 'The Rev John Lawrence', 120 · marble monument, Bishopwearmouth church, Durham

Laurence, Richard (1760–1838), archbishop of Cashel, born at Bath and baptized at Bath Abbey on 13 May 1760, was the younger son of Richard Laurence (1729–*c.*1773), watchmaker, and his wife, Elizabeth French. His elder brother was French *Laurence (1757–1809), who became the friend and literary executor of Edmund Burke. He was educated at Bath grammar school and at Corpus Christi College, Oxford, where he matriculated on 14 July 1778 with an exhibition. After graduating BA in 1782 and proceeding MA in 1785, he in 1787 became vicar of Coleshill, Berkshire, where he took pupils. He also contributed to the *Monthly Review* and edited the historical department of the *Annual Register*. Shortly afterwards he held the vicarage of Great Cheverell, and the rectory of Rollstone, Wiltshire. In June 1794 he took the degrees of BCL and DCL as a member of University College.

Upon his brother's appointment to the regius professorship of civil law, in 1796, Laurence was made deputy professor, and again settled in Oxford. In 1804 he delivered the Bampton lectures, which were published as *An attempt to illustrate those articles of the Church of England which the Calvinists improperly consider Calvinistical* (1805). The archbishop of Canterbury presented him in 1805 to the rectory of Mersham, Kent; and in 1811 he was collated to the valuable rectory of Stone, near Dartford, in the same county. Laurence's wife was Mary Vaughan, daughter of Vaughan Prince, merchant, of Faringdon, Berkshire. They had at least one daughter.

From youth Laurence read widely in theology and canon law, and in later life he studied oriental languages. Accordingly in 1814 he was appointed regius professor of Hebrew and a canon of Christ Church, Oxford. In 1822, after the death of his wife, he reluctantly accepted the archbishopric of Cashel, Ireland. He had at first declined the appointment—he was over sixty—but in the event yielded to Lord Liverpool's importunity. Together with Dr William Bisset (bishop of Raphoe) he was consecrated in the Chapel Royal in Dublin Castle, on 21 July 1822, by the archbishop of Armagh and the bishops of Kildare and Down. He resided at Cashel until the Church Temporalities Act of 1833–4 (3 and 4 Will. IV, c.37) annexed the diocese of Waterford and Lismore to that of Cashel and Emly, when he selected Waterford as the future place of residence for himself and his successors. He was the last archbishop of Cashel: under the act's provisions the united diocese became on his death a suffragan see within the province of Dublin.

Laurence's writings were models of exactness and judicious moderation. His erudition was well illustrated by the three volumes in which he printed, with Latin and English translations, Ethiopic versions of apocryphal books of the Bible. The first, the *Ascensio Isaiae vatis* (1819), which he dated AD 68 or 69, furnished in his opinion arguments against the unitarian falsification of passages in the New Testament. (He had published his *Critical Reflections* upon the unitarian version in 1811.) The second, *The Book of Enoch the Prophet* (1821), was printed from the Ethiopic manuscript which James Bruce had brought from Abyssinia and presented to the Bodleian Library. The third was the Ethiopic version of the first book of Esdras (1820).

During the baptismal controversy of the early nineteenth century Laurence published two apologetic works (in 1815 and 1816, with later editions) on the efficacy of baptism and on the interpretation of baptismal regeneration held by orthodox churchmen. He thus anticipated both mid-century baptismal controversies in England and the agonized synodical debates in the Irish church after disestablishment. He published also sermons and episcopal charges (delivered both as diocesan and as primate of Munster), works on the predestinarian and other historical controversies, and—indicative of the breadth of his scholarship—papers both on philosophical and scientific topics, and on the critical principles and classification of manuscripts relative to biblical translation. Late in life, and at a time of intense interest in the Irish church in the protestant minorities of continental Europe, he brought forward documents (one was published posthumously) on the visitation, in 1527 and 1528, of the Saxon reformed church.

Laurence's years in Ireland coincided with significant developments in the church there. Like Richard Mant, he helped to strengthen the revival of the old high-church tradition under mainly indigenous leadership. But he witnessed also the recovery of the historic, moderate Calvinism which he disdained. Although he published the third edition of his Bampton lectures in 1838, the future lord chancellor of Ireland, John Thomas Ball, would conclude with neat irony that they were 'designed to establish that the Articles of the Church of England were not framed to bear merely a Calvinistic sense' (Ball, 284). In relation again to primate Lord John George Beresford's policy of eradicating abuses in the establishment, Laurence's conniving at the holding of benefices in plurality by his son-in-law Henry Cotton—the bibliographer and future dean of Lismore—were a serious embarrassment to Beresford in his dealings with government, as his correspondence with Lord Stanley makes clear (Beresford MSS, 178/18).

Laurence died on 28 December 1838 in Merrion Square, Dublin, and was buried in the vaults of Christ Church there, in the choir of which a marble tablet was erected to his memory. The clergy of Cashel also erected a handsome monument to him in their cathedral; and in that of Waterford a small slab records the fact that it was owing to Laurence that Waterford remained the home of a resident bishop. A photograph of the archbishop was included in his *Poetical Remains*, edited (and in 1872 privately printed) by Dean Cotton, together with those of French Laurence.

GORDON GOODWIN, rev. ALAN R. ACHESON

Sources H. Cotton, *Fasti ecclesiae Hibernicae*, 2nd edn, 1 (1851), 24–30 · J. T. Ball, *The Reformed Church of Ireland, 1537–1889*, rev. 2nd edn (1890), 284 · A. R. Acheson, *A history of the Church of Ireland, 1691–1996* (1997) · Representative Church Body Library, Dublin, Beresford MSS, 178/18 · IGI · H. Cotton, 'Memoir', in *Poetical remains of French Laurence … and Richard Laurence*, ed. [H. Cotton] (1872), 1–21, 111–16 **Archives** Representative Church Body Library, Dublin | BL, corresp. with Sir Robert Peel and others · Lpool RO, corresp. with E. G. Stanley · Representative Church Body Library, Dublin, Beresford corresp. **Likenesses** monument, Cashel Cathedral, Ireland · photograph, repro. in H. Cotton, 'Memoir'

Laurence, Roger (1670–1736), nonjuror and bishop of the nonjuring Church of England, was born in London on 18 March 1670, the son of Roger Laurence, an armourer. Having been admitted on the royal mathematical foundation of Christ's Hospital, London, in April 1679, on the presentation of Sir John Laurence, merchant, of London, he was discharged on 22 November 1688. He served as a book-keeper on a Spanish merchant ship for seven years before being employed in Spain by Sir John Lethieullier, a London merchant. By 1705 he had returned to London. He married Jane Holman, who survived him.

Laurence studied divinity, became dissatisfied with his baptism among dissenters, and was informally baptized in Christ Church Greyfriars on 31 March 1708, by John Bates. His act attracted considerable attention, and resulted in the publication that year of his *Lay Baptism*

Invalid. This led the bishops of the province of Canterbury to offer to convocation a declaration affirming the validity of baptisms administered by non-episcopally ordained ministers. This declaration, offered to convocation on 14 May 1712, was rejected by the lower house after some debate.

Through the influence of Charles Wheatly, then fellow of St John's College, an honorary degree of MA was conferred upon Laurence by the University of Oxford on 16 July 1713. Although it is not known how he became involved with the nonjurors, the nonjuror bishop George Hickes ordained him deacon on 30 November and priest on 19 December 1714. He ministered at a 'chapell on College Hill within the city of London' (Macray, 3.243). In 1718 he became involved in the 'usages' controversy, which divided the nonjurors over proposed liturgical changes, but in 1729 he broke with Thomas Brett, when Brett attempted to reunite the divided nonjuror community by abandoning the liturgical changes. This break resulted in the formation of another nonjuror party, which sought to preserve the usages, under the leadership of the Scottish nonjuring bishop, Archibald Campbell. In an attempt to preserve the episcopal succession of the Usages party, in 1733 Campbell, acting alone, consecrated Laurence and Thomas Deacon as bishops. Most nonjurors did not recognize the consecrations as valid because they had been done by a single bishop.

Laurence was an able though not elegant controversialist. He was best known for his part in the lay baptism controversy. He published several works attacking lay baptism and defending his rebaptism. These works included the anonymously published *Lay baptism invalid, or, An essay to prove that such baptism is null and void when administer'd in opposition to the divine right of apostolical succession* (1708). The book was attacked by Gilbert Burnet in a sermon on 7 November 1710; by Bishop William Fleetwood in an anonymous pamphlet; by William Talbot, bishop of Oxford, in a charge (1712); and by Joseph Bingham in his *Scholastic History of Lay Baptism* (1712). Laurence offered responses to each of his critics. These included his *Sacerdotal Powers, or, The Necessity of Confession, Penance, and Absolution* (1711), *The Dissenters, and other Unauthorized Baptisms Null and Void* (1712), *The Bishop of Oxford's Charge, Consider'd* (1712), and *The Second Part of Lay Baptism Invalid* (1713). In his *Indispensable obligation of ministring the great necessaries of publick worship in the Christian church* (1732) he attacked Thomas Brett's rapprochement with the Non-usages party, which had been intended as an end to the divisions within the nonjuror movement. In the tract he also defended the necessity of continuing the liturgical changes for valid sacraments.

After a lengthy illness Laurence died, aged sixty-five, on 6 March 1736 at Kent House, Beckenham, the country residence of the Lethieulliers. He was buried in the parish churchyard at Beckenham on 11 March. His will, made on 29 February 1736, left all his property to his wife Jane.

ROBERT D. CORNWALL

Sources Foster, *Alum. Oxon.* · H. Broxap, *The later nonjurors* (1924) · 'Nonjurors: Roger Laurence, a neglected biography', *N&Q*, 2nd ser.,

5 (1858), 475–7 · W. D. Macray, 'Nonjuring ordinations', *N&Q*, 3rd ser., 3 (1863), 243–4 · G. V. Bennett, *The tory crisis in church and state: the career of Francis Atterbury, bishop of Rochester* (1975) · W. Kennett, *The wisdom of looking backward* (1715) · W. Scott, 'Preface', in R. Laurence, *Lay baptism invalid* (1841) [first pubd 1708] · *GM*, 1st ser., 6 (1736), 167 · Allibone, *Dict.* · A. P. Perceval, *An apology for the doctrine of apostolic succession* (1841) · *DNB*

Laurence, Samuel (1812–1884), portrait painter, was born at Guildford, Surrey, and early manifested a great love for art. His parentage and education are unknown. The first portraits he exhibited in London were at the Society of British Artists in Suffolk Street in 1834, and in 1836 he sent three portraits, including that of Mary Somerville (preliminary drawing in Girton College, Cambridge), to the Royal Academy. On 10 August 1836 Laurence married Anastasia Gliddon, cousin and adopted sister of Katharine, Mrs Thornton Leigh Hunt. A portrait of her in later life shows the delicate effect he achieved with the use of black and white chalks (Yale U. CBA). During his early married life he visited Florence and Venice, studying diligently the methods of the old masters, and endeavouring to discover the secrets of their success.

Early in life Laurence became closely associated with the Victorian literati, and he was to draw and paint most of the writers and thinkers of his day many times. He hosted his own literary circle in the 1840s, the Bohemian Phalanstery, based on Fourieresque principles, which involved Thornton Leigh Hunt. He was close friends with the writer George Henry Lewes and James Spedding, the editor of Bacon, whom he painted in 1881–2 (Trinity College, Cambridge). W. M. Thackeray was a close friend and helped Laurence secure many patrons: he wrote in 1853 to Bancroft: 'I think Lawrence [*sic*] is the best drawer of heads since Van Dyke' (*Letters and Private Papers*, 317). Laurence's oil portrait of the novelist reading a letter became one of the sitter's best-known likenesses and was frequently reproduced (exh. RA, 1864; NPG). His portrait of Tennyson (*c*.1840; NPG) was also much engraved and the most famous of the poet when young. In 1854 Laurence travelled to America to take a portrait of the poet, Henry Longfellow, for an illustrated edition of poems commissioned by George Routledge, Longfellow's London publisher; he remained in America until 1861. The chalk portrait (Longfellow National Historic Site, Cambridge, Massachusetts) was completed in June 1854 and was well received, Fanny Longfellow noting on 19 June in a letter to her sister Mary Mackintosh that 'all agree in thinking the best yet taken. It is full of life and with a very lively, agreeable expression' (Longfellow, vol. 2, 19 June 1854). While visiting the family at their holiday residence in Nahant in September 1857, he drew portraits of Longfellow's wife and various friends.

Laurence ceased to exhibit at Suffolk Street in 1853, but his works continued to appear regularly at the Royal Academy until 1882, when he sent a drawing of George Eliot (1860, exh. RA, 1882; preliminary sketch in Girton College, Cambridge). Among his many chalk drawings are portraits of Charles Dickens (*Sketch of Boz*, exh. RA, 1838; priv. coll.), F. D. Maurice (*c*.1846; NPG), Barbara Leigh Smith

Bodichon (1861; Girton College, Cambridge), Sir Henry Cole (1865, exh. RA, 1866; NPG), and Robert Browning (1866; exh. RA, 1869; Baylor University, Texas). About 1841–2 he did a series of chalk drawings of the Cambridge Apostles including Archbishop Richard Trench (1841; NPG) and the Revd William Thompson (1841; NPG); oil portraits of Thompson (1869) and Dr William Whewell (1845) are in Trinity College, Cambridge. One of his most successful, yet unfinished, portraits in oil is that of Leigh Hunt (1837; NPG), which was exhibited in the National Portrait Exhibition of 1868 and photographed for the frontispiece of *The Correspondence of Leigh Hunt; Edited by his Son* (2 vols., 1862). Also in oil are Thomas Carlyle (1838, exh. RA, 1841; priv. coll.), Anthony Trollope (*c*.1864; NPG), and Elizabeth Gaskell (*c*.1846).

There is a large collection of Laurence's work, in both oil and chalks, in the National Portrait Gallery, London, including Charles Babbage (exh. RA, 1845), Sir Thomas Bourchier (1846), Sir Charles Wheatstone (1868), and one of his most consistent friends and patrons, Sir Jonathan Pollock (exh. RA, 1842). A chalk drawing of Pollock (1862, exh. RA, 1863) was commissioned by Thackeray at the same time as one of himself (1862; priv. coll.), which were then exchanged, as Lady Anne Thackeray Ritchie wrote 'out of friendship for one another and the painter too' (Ormond, 381 and 458). A three-quarter length of Thackeray (1881) was commissioned by the Reform Club, London. Laurence died at his home, 6 Wells Street, Oxford Street, London, from the effects of an operation, on 28 February 1884. His obituary in *The Athenaeum* described him as the 'most venerable of our portrait painters who had so to say, outlived his once considerable reputation' (*The Athenaeum*, 1884).   R. E. GRAVES, rev. AILSA BOYD

Sources R. Ormond, *Early Victorian portraits*, 2 vols. (1973) · J. Johnson and A. Greutzner, eds., *The dictionary of British artists, 1880–1940* (1976), vol. 5 of *Dictionary of British art*; repr. (1980) · Wood, *Vic. painters*, 3rd edn · Bryan, *Painters* (1903–5) · *The Athenaeum* (8 March 1884), 318 · G. S. Haight, *George Eliot: a biography* (1968) · Graves, *RA exhibitors* · H. Longfellow, journals, transcript ed. S. C. Paterson, Longfellow House, Cambridge, Massachusetts [vol. 2, '"The second act of life's drama": Longfellow and his friends'] · *The letters and private papers of William Makepeace Thackeray*, ed. G. N. Ray, 3 (1946)
Archives Wordsworth Trust, Dove Cottage, Grasmere, letters to Joshua Stanger and Mary Stanger
Likenesses S. Laurence, self-portrait, oils, AM Oxf.
Wealth at death £1658 0s. 8d.: administration, 19 April 1884, *CGPLA Eng. & Wales*

Laurence, Thomas (1597/8–1657), college head, was born the son of a Dorset clergyman. Having obtained a Balliol scholarship in 1614 he matriculated on 11 May 1615, aged seventeen. Elected a fellow of All Souls College in 1617, he was formally admitted on 14 January 1618. He graduated BA on 9 June 1618 and proceeded MA on 16 May 1621. He incorporated his MA at Cambridge in 1627.

Ordained deacon in May 1624, Laurence subsequently became a priest and received from the college in July the vicarage of Lewknor, Oxfordshire, which he had resigned by March 1625. Perhaps about this time he became chaplain to William Herbert, earl of Pembroke, chancellor of the university. Granted the richest canonry of Lichfield

Cathedral on 31 January 1629, he took his BD on 13 March. He became a chaplain to Charles I, through Pembroke's influence according to William Laud. Secure in the chancellor's favour, in disputations at the Oxford Act on 13 July 1629 Laurence asserted not only that property consecrated to God was inalienable but also that doctrine might be defined only by churchmen at ecclesiastical synods, and that laymen could have no say in it. This was implicitly to criticize the Commons' 1628 attack on Arminianism, and John Prideaux, regius professor of divinity, furiously accused Laurence of favouring popery. In 1630 Laurence apparently resigned his fellowship, and some time after, married; his wife's name is unknown.

In 1633 Philip Herbert, who had succeeded his brother as earl of Pembroke, presented Laurence to the rich rectory of Bemerton with Fugglestone, Wiltshire, in succession to George Herbert. He took his DD on 16 July of that year. His *Two Sermons* (1635), which denounced schismatic tendencies, criticized reliance on predestination without works, defended reverencing of the altar, and proposed a high view of sacerdotal dignity, identified him publicly with Arminian positions. His *Sermon Preached before the King's Majesty* (1637), which exalted priestly dignity and defended the real presence in the eucharist, became a *cause célèbre*.

In November 1637 Laud, evidently pleased by Laurence's publications, probably engineered Laurence's succession as master of Balliol College. Evelyn thought the new master 'an accute and Learned Person' (Evelyn, *Diary*, 2.18), excusing his disciplinarian style as necessary after his predecessor John Parkhurst's neglect, but the headship was simply a first step. After some difficulty, in March 1638 Laud, worried by the ever-present Calvinistic authority of Prideaux as regius professor of divinity, finally secured Laurence's election to the Lady Margaret professorship as a counterweight. He was also promptly installed in an attached canonry of Worcester Cathedral. He was a serious scholar and his annotated manuscript index of theological works in the Bodleian, presented to the same library in 1658 by his eldest son, suggests wide reading. Laud, however, wished the controversial professor to be prudent and advised him through Gilbert Sheldon, warden of All Souls, to be 'mindful of the waspishness of these times, and to be sure to read upon no argument, that may make any the least trouble in Church or university' (Laud, *Works*, 5.186). Prosperity allowed him to buy mills at Woodstock, near Oxford (1639), and land at Long Hanborough, also in Oxfordshire (1641). Dispensed from lecturing early in 1640 owing to ill health, he was sufficiently recovered to preach the national fast on 8 December 1640.

By absence from college in early 1642 Laurence evaded the protestation, and he remained loyal to the king during hostilities with parliament. At Laud's trial Laurence's promotion was given as an instance of the archbishop's advancing the popishly affected, but his serious troubles began in 1646, when on 13 April his Wiltshire rectory was let and he had to compound. By late June, in financial straits, he borrowed £10 from the vestry of St Lawrence Jewry, a Balliol living. In July the Wiltshire committee heard that he had observed ceremonies, set up an altar, forbidden psalm-singing, permitted a maypole, and allowed a bowling green and skittle alley to be used on Sundays. He had not visited Bemerton since before the war, though his wife had lived there. Laurence refused the covenant. Attempts to secure payment of his professorial arrears were ultimately unsuccessful and in January 1648 he was listed with sequestrated Wiltshire delinquents.

One of few men of note to submit without formal reservation to the parliamentary visitors of Oxford in 1648, Laurence was allowed to resign his two offices and depart with hopes of ecclesiastical employment elsewhere. Soon afterwards, having sold his Woodstock property, he left Oxford. Colonel Valentine Walton, a parliamentarian whom he had assisted while a prisoner in royalist Oxford, relieved his needs and by 1652 secured him the chaplaincy of Colne, in the parish of Somersham, Huntingdonshire.

Charles II is said to have destined Laurence for an Irish bishopric, but he died shortly before his burial on 10 December 1657 in Colne chapel, where his wife had been interred. By his will dated 2 November 1657 he bequeathed sums amounting to £150 between four younger sons, a nephew, and a niece, household goods at Colne and at Long Hanborough to his daughter Mary, the executrix, and the residue, including curiously his barber's case and instruments, to his eldest son, Thomas.

A. J. HEGARTY

Sources Wood, *Ath. Oxon.*, new edn, 3.437–8 · M. Burrows, ed., *The register of the visitors of the University of Oxford, from AD 1647 to AD 1658*, CS, new ser., 29 (1881), lxxxii–lxxxiii, cxxv–cxxvi, 167, 181, 188, 479 · *Walker rev.*, 376 · *Reg. Oxf.*, 2.338, 3.364 · *The works of the most reverend father in God, William Laud*, 5, ed. J. Bliss (1853), 185–6, 194, 244–5 · Bodl. Oxf., MS Mus. e.40; MS DD All Souls College c. 112, item 11 · PRO, SP 16/146/94r; SP 16/271/148v–149r; PROB 11/283/585 · N. Tyacke, *Anti-Calvinists: the rise of English Arminianism, c.1590–1640* (1987); repr. (1990), 78, 83–4, 221 · LPL, MS 943, 133–4 · diary of Thomas Crosfield, Queen's College, Oxford, MS 390, 75r · *VCH Oxfordshire*, 12.165, 429 · *Fasti Angl., 1541–1857*, [Ely], 125
Archives Balliol Oxf., letters, essays, and verses · Bodl. Oxf., annotated catalogue, MS Mus. e. 40
Wealth at death see will, PRO, PROB 11/283/585

Laurens, Henry (1724–1792), revolutionary politician in America and merchant, was born on 6 March 1724 in Charles Town, South Carolina, the first son and third of the six children of Esther (Hester) Grasset (1700–1742) and John Samuel Laurens (1696–1747). Descended from French Huguenot refugees, the family had moved to South Carolina by the time of Henry's birth. After a preliminary education in Charles Town, Laurens's father, a wealthy saddler, sent him to London in 1744 to be apprenticed to the prominent merchant James Crokatt. In 1747 Henry Laurens returned to Charles Town a few days after his father's death. With a large inheritance he operated a lucrative mercantile business that exported deerskins, rice, and indigo, and imported manufactured goods, rum, and African slaves. He acquired a town house in the fashionable Ansonborough section of Charles Town, as well as plantations and land holdings totalling 20,000 acres in the

Henry Laurens (1724–1792), by John Singleton Copley, 1782

back country of South Carolina, on the coast of Georgia, and near Charles Town. He maintained his family's country residence at Mepkin Plantation, a 3000 acre estate on the Cooper River, 30 miles north-west of Charles Town.

On 6 July 1750 Henry Laurens married nineteen-year-old Eleanor (1731–1770), daughter of prominent planter Elias Ball. They had at least twelve children, only four of whom lived to maturity. Their daughters Martha and (Mary) Eleanor married David *Ramsay (1749–1815) and Charles *Pinckney (1757–1824), respectively, both wealthy, significant men in the revolutionary era. Laurens devoted much attention to the education of his sons, Henry and John, and did not remarry after their mother's death. A devout communicant at St Philip's Anglican Church, he ridiculed 'Deism or Infidelity' in favour of 'true Religion and Virtue' (*Papers of Henry Laurens*, 1.243–4). He read the Bible and regularly quoted the book of Proverbs. Although he tolerated the liberalism of his era, he preferred the personal piety of his Huguenot ancestors, and routinely resigned himself to divine will.

Henry Laurens was short, swarthy, self-righteous, sensitive about his honour, sometimes sarcastic in his speech and writings, and a frequent participant in bloodless duels. Although his personality was ill-suited for a political career, he was intellectually curious, a devoted father, kind to his slaves as well as his friends, a shrewd businessman, and intensely loyal to his country.

First elected to the Commons house of assembly in 1757, Laurens began a public career that lasted until 1784. Except for one term, he served in that body until the

American Declaration of Independence. In 1764 he declined an appointment to the royal council on the grounds that it was dominated by royal placemen who had no regard for the welfare of the province. He served as a lieutenant-colonel in the colonial militia that fought alongside British regulars against the Cherokee Indians in 1761. His childhood friend and neighbour Christopher Gadsden, who was the colonel of that militia, began to criticize royal authority vigorously for the manner in which the governor had conducted the campaign. Laurens took the royal side, arguing against Gadsden, and established himself as a moderate in the debates that led to the break with Britain.

Laurens believed that Britain should be pressured into respecting the rights of her citizens in North America, but he distrusted colonial mobs and did not want separation from the mother country. During the Stamp Act crisis of 1765, when the armed and drunken Sons of Liberty searched his basement for stamps, he declared his fealty to British law. Two years later, however, when customs officials seized two of his own vessels, he angrily yanked the nose of the customs collector, challenged corrupt vice-admiralty judge Sir Egerton Leigh to a duel, and published a vitriolic pamphlet justifying his actions. In 1769 he supported the boycott of British goods until parliament repealed the odious Townshend Acts. From 1771 to 1774, when he lived in London to supervise the education of his two sons, he found himself increasingly an apologist for South Carolina, and soon transferred his sons to a stricter school in Geneva.

From his return to Charles Town late in 1774 until the end of the war, Laurens took an active role in South Carolinian and American affairs. In 1774 he became a member of the first South Carolina congress; in 1775 he became its president. He became a member of the first council of safety, and president of the second one. He helped draft a constitution for South Carolina in February 1776, then served as vice-president. He participated in the defence of Charles Town against the British in June 1776, and attempted to avert civil war between the loyalists and the patriots. After the fighting between the colonials and British troops had begun, he reluctantly accepted inevitable separation from the mother country and mournfully declared that the word 'Independent' caused him to fear financial losses and 'cuts me deep' (27 Feb 1776, *Papers of Henry Laurens*, 11.126).

At the beginning of the war Laurens, like many other southern planters, saw the inconsistency in their argument that the mother country treated them like slaves while they themselves owned hundreds of African slaves. Although he had once dealt in slaves, in 1776 Laurens declared that he abhorred the institution and soon freed the hundreds whom he owned, the first large planter in the deep south to do so.

A delegate to the continental congress from 1777 to 1779, Laurens served as its president from 1 November 1777 to 9 December 1778. He staunchly supported George Washington, and proudly presided over congress's approval of the articles of confederation, and over ratification of the treaty of alliance with France in 1778.

On 13 August 1780 Laurens set sail from Philadelphia for the Netherlands, bound by congress to negotiate a $10 million loan from the Dutch and to offer them a treaty of friendship and commerce. Three weeks into the voyage the British captured him, transported him to England, charged him with treason, and incarcerated him in the Tower of London from 6 October 1780 to 31 December 1781. He suffered many indignities, declining health, and feelings of alienation from congress. Twice Laurens appealed to the British authorities for his release, claiming his health was poor and he needed to see his son John, and that he had attempted to prevent the struggle against the mother country. Although some members of congress questioned his loyalty to the United States, Benjamin Franklin procured his release on bail, and the British exchanged him for Charles Cornwallis, second Earl Cornwallis, the captured commander of their forces in America.

Laurens joined Benjamin Franklin, John Adams, and John Jay at the peace conference in Paris. Although he reached them only two days before they signed the preliminary treaty by which Great Britain recognized the independence of the United States, he influenced the articles that called for the sharing of Newfoundland fisheries and prohibited the British from confiscating slaves from their former colonies. He returned to New York city in August 1784, reported to congress in Philadelphia later that year, and returned to Charles Town (now renamed Charleston) early in 1785. He never recovered his health or from the tragic news that his son John had been killed near the end of the war. He died at Mepkin on 8 December 1792. One of the first Americans to be cremated, his former slaves, following his instructions, constructed and ignited his funeral pyre on his plantation. In addition to an estate of 20,000 acres and goods exceeding £25,000, he left behind a large collection of writings that became essential for the study of his era.

E. STANLY GODBOLD JR.

Sources *The papers of Henry Laurens*, ed. P. M. Hamer and others, 15 vols. (1968–) · D. D. Wallace, *The life of Henry Laurens, with a sketch of the life of Lieutenant-Colonel John Laurens* (1915) · E. McCrady, *The history of South Carolina under the royal government, 1719–1776* (1899) · E. McCrady, *The history of South Carolina in the revolution,* 1: *1775–1780* (1901) · E. McCrady, *The history of South Carolina in the revolution,* 2: *1780–1783* (1902) · E. S. Godbold and R. H. Woody, *Christopher Gadsden and the American Revolution* (1982) · J. Drayton, *Memoirs of the American Revolution,* 2 vols. (1821) · R. W. Gibbes, ed., *Documentary history of the American revolution,* 3 vols. (1853–7) · D. Ramsay, *The history of South Carolina: from its first settlement in 1670, to the year 1808,* 2 vols. (1809) · R. M. Weir, *Colonial South Carolina: a history* (1983)
Archives South Carolina Historical Society, Charleston, papers | National Archives and Records Administration, Washington, DC, continental congress papers · priv. coll., William Gilmore Simms collection
Likenesses J. S. Copley, oils, 1782, Smithsonian Institution, Washington, DC, NPG [*see illus.*]
Wealth at death 20,000 acres, plus cash, valued at more than £25,000: Wallace, *Life of Henry Laurens,* 426 n. 1

Laurent, André [Andrew Lawrence] (1710–1747), engraver, was born on 10 February 1710, the natural son of Andrew Laurent (*d.* 1726), an apothecary, of Pall Mall, Westminster. He received a liberal education, was well versed in mathematics and perspective, and had some musical accomplishments; he performed on the German flute and the violin and he composed several pieces that were published anonymously. Thereafter he spent thirteen months with Jacques Regnier, a Huguenot seal engraver and printseller in Newport Street. His father intended that he should become a physician, and in his will, written when the boy had just passed his fifteenth birthday, he provided £18 per annum for his son's support. Unfortunately by this time Laurent had fallen under the influence of one Riario, his father's journeyman. This man persuaded Laurent that they could discover the secret of changing base metals into gold, and on this he squandered the greater part of his inheritance. When they ran into poverty they moved to Boulogne and continued their quest until all was lost. Riario then went in search of another gullible youth and Laurent went to Paris in search of work. He was recommended to the great landscape engraver Jacques-Philippe le Bas, who was impressed by Laurent's engraving and offered him three years' work as an assistant at a modest wage. His etching of Wouverman's *Halte d'officiers* (1740) was the first of some seventeen large plates that he began for le Bas. He also engraved several vignettes for books. After leaving le Bas he produced a number of plates, including *Saul and the Witch of Endor,* etched for the picture dealer Andrew Hay and dedicated to the eminent physician Richard Mead, who had perhaps known his father.

When approached by the art publisher Arthur Pond, Laurent saw an opportunity to return to England, but on being told that he would receive the same meagre pay as Pond's other workmen he declined, and remained in Paris. He was frequently urged to apply for membership of the Royal Academy of Painting at Paris, but was unwilling to declare himself a Roman Catholic. From his long hours at a sedentary occupation Laurent became ill and was unable to complete his masterpiece, *The Ceiling at Versailles,* after le Brun; it was later finished by Cochin. His friend Thomas Major described him as being of middle stature, fairly tall, thin and long-visaged, with grey eyes, dark hair, and a brown complexion.

Laurent's physician ordered him to take exercise by riding, but, although a friend offered to meet the expense, he declined. A few days before he died Laurent sold all his effects before witnesses to Pierre Soubeyran to settle his debts, thus avoiding, as a protestant, seizure of all his goods. He died in the arms of Nicholas Blakey on 8 July 1747. Blakey, Major, Soubeyran, and John Ingram accompanied his body to a timber-yard outside the Porte St Antoine, the burying place for heretics. His copper plates, sold publicly, were bought by Major and taken to England in 1753 with the help of William Augustus, duke of Cumberland, who imported them free of duty as the work of an Englishman abroad.

TIMOTHY CLAYTON and ANITA MCCONNELL

Sources T. Major, 'Memoir of Andrew Lawrence', 1785, BM, 1870/5/14/2357 · D. Alexander, 'Laurent, André', *The dictionary of art*, ed. J. Turner (1996) · will, PRO, PROB 11/608, sig. 52

Laurent, Peter Edmund (1796–1837), classical scholar, was a native of Picardy in France. He studied at the Polytechnic School at Paris, where he gained several prizes. He went to England at an early age, and was for several years a teacher of modern languages at Oxford. He was also French master at the Royal Naval College, Portsmouth. He was a good mathematician, and is stated to have spoken fluently 'nearly all the European languages,' and to have been 'well versed in Arabic, Latin, and Greek' (*GM*). In 1818 Laurent left Oxford with two university friends and visited the towns of northern Italy. Starting from Venice on 9 July 1818 he visited Greece and the Ionian Islands, and went home in 1819 through Naples, Rome, and Florence. In 1821 he published an account of his travels as *Recollections of a Classical Tour*. He died in the autumn (before the end of October) of 1837 at the Royal Hospital, Haslar, Hampshire, aged forty-one. He was the father of four children, who survived him. His wife, Anne, died at Oxford on 5 January 1848, aged fifty. Besides the *Recollections* Laurent published manuals on French and German grammar, an introduction to ancient geography, and a translation into English of Herodotus. W. W. WROTH, *rev.* C. A. CREFFIELD

Sources *GM*, 2nd ser., 8 (1837), 436 · *GM*, 2nd ser., 29 (1848), 220–21

(Robert) Douglas Laurie (1874–1953), by Maurice de Sausmarez, *c.*1953–5

Laurie, (Robert) Douglas (1874–1953), founder and first president of the Association of University Teachers, was born at 10 Laurel Road, Tranmere, Cheshire, on 27 October 1874, the only son of Robert Laurie, a book-keeper, and his wife, Eleanor (*née* Ord). He was educated at Birkenhead School and subsequently took a job at the Bank of Liverpool, where he remained until 1899. What prompted him to resume his studies is unknown; however, in 1899 Laurie left his job and enrolled as a student at University College, Liverpool. In 1901, at the comparatively late age of twenty-six, he matriculated at Oxford University, where he was an exhibitioner of Merton College, obtaining third-class honours in zoology. After taking his degree in 1905 he was appointed assistant demonstrator in the department of comparative anatomy at Oxford. In 1906 he became demonstrator and assistant lecturer in zoology at the University of Liverpool, where he remained until 1918; from 1911 onwards he was also lecturer in embryology and genetics. On 9 July 1912 in Wythburn, Cumberland, he married Elinor Beatrice, daughter of George Ord, architect, of Durham; they had one daughter.

In 1909 Laurie and a fellow zoologist called a meeting of junior academic staff at Liverpool with the idea of forming an association. Laurie remarked that junior staff seldom had an opportunity to meet their counterparts from other departments, that, in fact, they were less well organized than the students. Originally conceived as a dining club, the association, like others forming at the other civic universities, soon turned its attention to the question of lecturers' pay. During the First World War the issue acquired great urgency as wartime inflation eroded already inadequate salaries. In 1917 Laurie, in his capacity as secretary of the junior staff association, called a meeting and, as an afterthought, invited representatives of other universities to come and help draft a memorandum to the Board of Education. These meetings, coupled with the refusal of H. A. L. Fisher, president of the board, to meet with junior staff, promoted unity among the university organizations and provided an opportunity for Laurie to demonstrate those powers of persuasion and tenacity for which he became legendary. In his role as chairman of the conference of university lecturers, Laurie compiled a detailed survey of the existing remuneration of university lecturers which he submitted to the Board of Education. Meanwhile, increasing dissatisfaction with the newly created pension scheme for university teachers added fuel to a move within the conference to include professors in its membership. In June 1919 the Association of University Teachers (AUT) was created with Laurie as its first president. Although he served for only a year, Laurie continued to run the AUT virtually single-handed as its honorary general secretary from 1920 to his death in 1953.

In 1918 Laurie moved to the University College of Wales, Aberystwyth, initially as an independent lecturer and head of department in zoology. In his first year the able and energetic Laurie impressed his superiors as deserving of a professorship, although he had to wait until 1922, when a private donation made possible the creation of his chair in zoology. The principal remarked that Laurie was: 'a man who knows what he wants and usually gets it'

(Ellis, 220). In 1919 Laurie annexed space for his inadequately housed department in buildings recently acquired by the college which had formerly housed a slate works. In the absence of funding to make the structure usable Laurie, his staff, and students set out to remodel the buildings themselves, a task to which they evidently brought more enthusiasm than skill. By 1929 the college capitulated and agreed to finish the job. 'A thing of beauty it is not', wrote the principal, 'but as a triumph of enthusiasm over mere finance it merits great respect' (Ellis, 220).

A man of formidable energy, Laurie was greatly respected both for his enthusiasm as a teacher and for his contributions to his own field. A former student remembered him as a friend who was always willing to help students and to find graduates posts most suited to their skills. She wrote that 'he was a keen field naturalist and some of us recall delightful days spent with him exploring the polluted waters of some of the north Cardiganshire rivers' (Newton, *Universities Review*, 36). His research interests included a study of the fauna of the sea floor of Cardigan Bay, collected using an apparatus known as the 'Petersen grab' which was worked from a motor boat. As a zoologist Laurie was interested in the application of science to social problems, he promoted the teaching of zoology in schools, and he taught summer courses in biology for teachers. He was an enthusiastic member of the Eugenics Society and vice-president of the Universities' Federation for Animal Welfare. From 1921 to 1923 he served as recorder of the zoology section of the British Association. He travelled widely both as a zoologist and as a representative of the AUT.

In the inter-war period Laurie continued to serve the AUT, visiting universities abroad and participating in delegations to the government protesting against the recurrent grant cuts which bedevilled the universities in those years. The historian of the AUT points out that Laurie was largely responsible for its development as a professional association rather than as an academic trades union, although pay and pensions formed such a large part of its agenda in the early years. In 1940 Laurie retired from teaching but in 1943 he became honorary secretary of the International Association of University Professors and Lecturers (IAUPL), an interest which gave him 'great joy in the later years of his life' (Newton, *Universities Review*, 36). Laurie died in Amsterdam on 7 April 1953 while attending the conference of the IAUPL.

Douglas Laurie has been described as the greatest amateur in an amateur professional body, and certainly the AUT was a personal project of Laurie's throughout his lifetime (Perkin, 51). It operated out of two rooms of his house in Aberystwyth, Tyn-y-gongl, and was staffed by Laurie and his devoted secretary; only after his death did it take on professional staff. This arrangement worked because Laurie possessed the skills necessary to run it: he coupled utter single-mindedness and tenacity with an appealing, tolerant friendliness that converted potential adversaries into allies, allowing him to rule with no serious challenge to his authority. One historian has called him a 'bonny, good-humoured fighter', an adversary whom no one could dislike (Ellis, 220). Laurie's modesty was such that he effaced himself from his own history of the AUT but he will be remembered as the association's single founder.

ELIZABETH J. MORSE

Sources H. Perkin, *Key profession: the history of the Association of University Teachers* (1969) • E. L. Ellis, *The University College of Wales, Aberystwyth, 1872–1972* (1972) • *Universities Review*, 26/1 (Oct 1953), 2–3, 36, 39–40 • *The Times* (9 April 1953), 8 • *The Times* (24 April 1953), 10 • *WWW, 1951–60* • T. Kelly, *For advancement of learning: the University of Liverpool, 1881–1981* (1981) • R. D. Laurie and E. E. Watkin, 'Investigation into the fauna of the sea floor of Cardigan Bay', *Aberystwyth Studies*, 4 (1922), 229–49 • matriculation records, Oxf. UA • b. cert. • m. cert.

Archives Association of University Teachers, London, history of Association of University Teachers

Likenesses M. De Sausmarez, oils, *c.*1953–1955, Association of University Teachers, London [*see illus.*]

Wealth at death £2891 12s. 4d.: probate, 25 July 1953, CGPLA Eng. & Wales

Laurie, Gilbert (*bap.* 1718, *d.* 1787), apothecary and local politician, was born in Edinburgh and was baptized there on 24 October 1718. He was the son of Gilbert Laurie or Laury (*d.* after 1765?) of Crossrig, Berwickshire, a surgeon apothecary, and the first of his three wives, Janet (*d.* in or before 1730), daughter of the late Thomas Balderston, farmer in Niddrie. Possessing no residential or family qualification, the senior Gilbert Laurie was admitted a burgess of Edinburgh in 1715 upon payment of £100 Scots. Given that Janet Balderston's family were also surgeon apothecaries, it is little wonder that the younger Laurie also took up the family trade, after attending Edinburgh University. Laurie assumed the status of Edinburgh burgess in 1742 by right of his father's qualification, and on 23 October 1755 he succeeded George Cunninghame as his majesty's apothecary and druggist for Scotland, an office he held for the rest of his life. Residing in Kinloch's Close (South), he had a shop conveniently located at the head of Niddrie's Wynd, where he traded under the sign of the Moving Head.

Laurie was the most powerful and influential Edinburgh local politician of the third quarter of the eighteenth century. His rise began when he became one of the sixteen nominated captains of the trained bands summoned to the town council's meeting-house on 20 October 1747 to restore administrative structure to the town in the aftermath of the Jacobite rising of 1745–6. He served five years as captain of the blue and white company of that civic defence organization before becoming captain of the orange colours, and therefore commander of all sixteen companies of the trained bands, in October 1752. His first civilian office was as kirk treasurer for Edinburgh in January 1752. Eight months later he became first merchant councillor, with responsibilities that extended to the bailieship of the butter, cheese, and lawncloth markets. An astute and reliable public officer, Laurie was treasurer of Edinburgh in 1756 and 1757, old treasurer in 1758, third bailie in 1759, dean of guild in 1760 and 1761, and first bailie in 1764. He also served as a director of the Royal Bank of

Scotland (1767–87) and as a manager of the Royal Infirmary. From 1755 he was a director of the social assembly, which regularly hosted dances and other social entertainments that raised considerable amounts of money for charitable causes from the town's élite.

Laurie's smooth ascent in local politics culminated in his election as lord provost in 1766, the same year that the town council approved James Craig's design for Edinburgh's famous new town. Laurie served the customary two-year term and did so again in 1772–4. His administrative skills and political affiliations were subjected to bitter personal attack, particularly for his involvement in the selection of Sir Laurence Dundas as Edinburgh's member of parliament in 1768. 'His ambition and avarice … are never to be satisfied', said one anonymous pamphlet of 1776, which added that the 'affairs of this ancient metropolis have been under the direction of Mr Lawrie about sixteen years' (*Examination of the Principles and Conduct of Edinburgh Town Council*, 18, 14). The fall from grace predicted by this pamphlet never occurred.

Laurie first married Sarah Balderstone (d. in or before 1762), with whom he had five daughters. On 7 November 1762 he married his second wife, Katherine Erskine (1729–1809), daughter of the advocate Thomas Erskine, with whom he had two more daughters. Laurie purchased the Polmont estate near Falkirk, Stirlingshire, where he died on 10 September 1787. He was buried in Polmont churchyard, and was survived by his wife, who died on 13 February 1809.   RICHARD IAN HUNTER

Sources M. Wood and T. B. Whitson, *The lord provosts of Edinburgh, 1296 to 1932* (1932) · Edinburgh old parish registers, 1716–62, NA Scot., reels 685¹/16, 17, 23–27 · J. Gilhooley, 'Dunedin and Caledonian Mercury' databases (1998) · *An historical sketch of the municipal constitution of Edinburgh* (1826) · J. H. Jamieson, 'Social assemblies of the eighteenth century', *Book of the Old Edinburgh Club*, 19 (1933) · *Scots Magazine*, 49 (1787), 467 · N. Munro, *The history of the Royal Bank of Scotland, 1727–1927* (1928) · privy seal new series, English registers, NA Scot., 8.585 [11 Nov 1755] · Mitchell's microfilm of excise records, NA Scot. · *An examination of the principles and conduct of Edinburgh town council* (1776) · deeds registers, NA Scot., 217/2, 223 and 232 · Edinburgh trained bands minute book, 1676–1779, Edinburgh City Archives · J. F. Mitchell and S. Mitchell, *Monumental inscriptions (pre 1855) in East Stirlingshire* (1972), Polmont, stone, no. 390

Archives Edinburgh City Archives, Edinburgh trained bands records · NA Scot., Mitchell's microfilm · NA Scot., registers of deeds

Likenesses portrait · portrait, priv. coll.; repro. in Wood and Whitson, *Lord provosts of Edinburgh*

Laurie, James Stuart

Laurie, James Stuart (1832–1904), educationist, was born in Edinburgh on 21 September 1832, younger son of James Laurie, chaplain to the Edinburgh Royal Infirmary, and his wife, Jean, daughter of Simon Somerville, United Presbyterian minister at Elgin. Simon Somerville *Laurie (1829–1909), later professor of education at Edinburgh University, was his elder brother. James attended universities in Edinburgh, Berlin, and Bonn before becoming a private tutor, employed at one time in the family of Lord John Russell.

In 1854 Laurie was appointed schools inspector for British and Wesleyan schools in the south-west of England. Eight years later he joined twenty-three of the current forty-nine inspectors in a memorial to Lord Granville, president of the committee of council on education, strongly refuting an accusation that the inspectorate tended to neglect the examination of younger pupils. A statement in his *Times* obituary (19 July 1904) that he resigned his inspectorship in protest against the introduction of Robert Lowe's revised code is contradicted by his final 1862 report, in which he predicted the new regulations would improve pupil attendance. After leaving the inspectorate, Laurie travelled to Australia. He noted England's apparent neglect of the colonies' educational progress, an omission he later criticized in *The Story of Australasia* (1896). In 1868 Laurie was sent by the Colonial Office to inspect education in Sierra Leone. Laurie's comprehensive, pertinent report led to the establishment of a director of public instruction, under a new board of education, and the creation of a model school to provide an educational standard for the colony. Following this success, Laurie became the first director of public instruction in Ceylon in 1869, where his recommendations for the establishment of model schools and a normal college to train pupil teachers were adopted. However, his proposals to substantially increase the number of local schools and introduce a system of payment by results on the lines of the English revised code were only partially implemented. While still in Ceylon he was appointed an assistant commissioner on the royal commission of inquiry into primary education in Ireland (the Powis commission, appointed 1868). His report on schools in the counties of Limerick and Clare in 1870 highlighted irregular pupil attendance and a general apathy among the upper classes concerning the education of the poor. His experience as a schools' inspector led him to compare unfavourably the meagre voluntary subsidies donated to schools in Limerick and Clare with the far more generous amounts available in Devon and Somerset. Together with other assistant commissioners, Laurie drew attention to the reluctance of protestant and Catholic clergy in Ireland to support schools in which both religious persuasions were represented, although many parents were willing to support 'mixed' schools.

Laurie entered the Inner Temple as a law student on 2 November 1867 and, after leaving Ceylon, was called to the bar on 6 June 1871. On 7 October 1875 he married Emily Serafina, eldest daughter of Frederick G. Mylrea. After 1870 he concentrated on writing, compiling from the early 1860s a wide range of elementary school texts; by the mid-1870s the name Laurie was synonymous with numerous graduated reading, science, and mathematical manuals, as well as with other more theoretical educational publications. He also contributed articles on educational subjects to the press. He always favoured a broad rather than a dogmatic approach to Christianity. In 1900 he published an acrimonious theological debate between himself and Frederick Temple, archbishop of Canterbury, in which Laurie alleged that true faith was in danger of being superseded by religious dogma among the Church of England hierarchy. Laurie complained bitterly that Temple treated his well-meant criticisms with 'ungracious contempt' (Laurie, *Gospel Christianity*, vi). James Stuart Laurie lived at Rosario, Canford Cliffs, Bournemouth, where he died, aged seventy-three, on 13 July 1904.

JANET SHEPHERD

Sources *The Times* (19 July 1904) · *WWW* · 'Report of the committee of council on education', *Parl. papers* (1863), 47.82–91, no. 3171 [protestant schools in Cornwall, Devon, Dorset, Hampshire, Somerset, Surrey, Sussex, and Wiltshire] · 'Memorial by the school inspectors … complaining of the unjust aspersions made upon them', *Parl. papers* (1862), 43.171–3, no. 322 · J. S. Laurie, ed., *The graduated series of reading-lesson books* (1862) · J. S. Laurie, *Gospel Christianity versus dogma and ritual: a letter to the archbishop of Canterbury* (1900) · J. S. Laurie, 'Special report on the state of public instruction in Ceylon, June 1869', *Sessional papers, Ceylon* (1869–70) · 'Royal commission on … primary education', *Parl. papers* (1870), 28/1.287–303, C. 6 [Limerick district; Ireland] · J. S. Laurie, *The story of Australasia: its discovery, colonisation and development* (1896) · C. Fyfe, *A history of Sierra Leone* (1962) · J. S. Laurie, ed., *Laurie's sixpenny manuals of instruction* (1877) · J. S. Laurie, ed., *Educational Review*, 1 (Jan 1871) · L. J. Lewis, *An outline chronological table of the development of education in British West Africa* (1953) · *DNB* · Schools Inspector Reports, Committee of Council on Education. Blue Books (1860–63)
Archives Bodl. Oxf., corresp. with Lord Kimberley
Wealth at death £50 2s. 6d.: probate, 2 Sept 1904, CGPLA Eng. & Wales

Laurie [*married name* Seyler], **Joan Ann Werner** (1920–1964), book and magazine editor, was born on 17 November 1920 at 12 Ashland House, Marylebone, London, the youngest daughter of Thomas Werner Laurie (1864–1944), publisher, and his second wife, (Elizabeth Mary) Beatrice (b. 1895), daughter of Henry Blackshaw, with whom he had had three children prior to their marriage in 1931. Her Edinburgh-born father founded the independent publishing house T. Werner Laurie Ltd in 1904 and rapidly built it into a thriving company with a reputation for eclectic titles, such as T. Francis Bumpus's series *The Cathedrals of …*, *The Encyclopaedia of Sex*, and *The History of Torture through the Ages*.

Joan Werner Laurie was educated at various private establishments, and sent to finishing school in Switzerland. She nurtured aspirations to be a doctor but these came to nothing. She married Paul Clifford Seyler (b. 1914), soldier and son of the playwright Clifford Seyler, on 1 May 1942, but joined the Women's Royal Naval Service soon after, as a clerk and then a driver. After the war she worked in an SPCK bookshop in London, and on 3 March 1946 she gave birth to a son, Nicholas Laurie Seyler. Paul Seyler left England soon afterwards, but his subsequent whereabouts and fate were unknown.

On its founder's death, T. Werner Laurie Ltd was bought by Clarence Hatry and continued to operate from offices over Hatchards bookshop in Piccadilly, London, where Joan worked as production editor. She met her life partner, Nancy Brooker *Spain (1917–1964), when the author and journalist became editor of the literary monthly magazine *Books of Today*. Nancy had envisaged T. Werner Laurie's daughter as 'an elderly spinster, grown etiolated and dry in the service of the firm' (N. Spain, *Why I'm Not a*

Millionaire, 1956, 132). Instead, she found 'a girl four years younger than me, very good looking with rather a long nose' (ibid., 133).

In 1954 Nancy Spain was approached by the National Magazine Company to be editor of a new women's monthly publication that was being planned. She declined, because of her numerous writing and broadcasting commitments, and suggested that Joan Werner Laurie would be perfect for the job. Marcus Morris, then managing director of the National Magazine Company, said in an obituary:

> Joan believed that intelligent, young-minded women, wanted to be stimulated, shocked, provoked, given cause to think by word and picture. She believed they wanted to know what was going on in the world outside their own backyard or comfortable sitting-room. Her conviction that even the most controversial subject could be tackled without offending more than a handful of readers was completely justifiable. (*She*)

Elsewhere he wrote, 'Her personality was stamped on every page' (*Sunday Times*).

Under Joan Werner Laurie's editorship, *She* smashed every last brick in the wall of taboos about what women's magazines should contain, and paved the way for the late twentieth century post-feminist titles such as *Cosmopolitan* and *Marie-Claire*. In 1963, defending an article about abortion, she was able to boast defiantly: '*She* has dealt in full detail with menstruation, hysterectomy, breast cancer, lung cancer, leprosy, brain tumours. We have even told our enchanted readers exactly what a bidet is for' (*The Listener*, 31 Oct 1963, 705). *She* contained the obligatory recipes but also regular articles on 'Ladies and the law', simple carpentry, 'Building your own boat', and consumer-tested motor cycles.

Joan Werner Laurie was less sociable and charismatic than her more famous partner, who hogged the limelight while publicly acknowledging the enormous influence Joan had on her life—including agreeing to pass off as her own child the son born to Nancy in 1952. Her less glittering social circle included Europe's leading woman racing driver, Sheila Van Damm, who shared a home with her and Nancy Spain for several years, and the romantic novelist Denise Robins. On 21 March 1964, on one of the rare occasions when Joan joined Nancy for a celebrity jaunt, they died together in the Piper Apache plane taking them to the Grand National, when it crashed just outside Aintree racecourse. Joan was cremated at Golders Green crematorium on 26 March. Joan's and Nancy's interchangeable wills resulted in both estates passing to Nicholas Seyler (later Werner Laurie), which unintentionally disinherited Nancy's son, Thomas Seyler (who later changed his surname to Carter, the same as his natural father, Philip Youngman Carter). ROSE COLLIS

Sources R. Collis, *A trouser-wearing character: the life and times of Nancy Spain* (1997) · *She* (May 1964), 35 · *Sunday Times* (29 March 1964), 15 · private information (2004) · b. cert.
Archives National Magazine Company, London, *She Magazine*
Likenesses photographs, repro. in N. Spain, *Why I'm not a millionaire* (1956)
Wealth at death £28,118: probate, 21 Sept 1964, CGPLA Eng. & Wales

Laurie, John Paton (1897–1980), actor, was born on 25 March 1897 at 3 Ryedale Terrace, Maxwelltown, Kirkcudbrightshire, the fifth of the six children of William Laurie (1856–1903), a Dumfries tweed mill superintendent and kirk elder, and his wife, Jessie Brown (1858–1935). Although born into a family rooted in covenanting traditions, Laurie soon became a 'lapsed Presbyterian'. A more significant childhood influence was Robert Burns's association with Dumfries. Laurie once introduced a Burns broadcast with 'His songs and poems were in the air I breathed' (Laurie MSS).

Leaving Dumfries Academy in 1914, Laurie joined an architect's firm. From 1916 he served with the Honourable Artillery Company at the Somme and Paschendale. Invalided out, he returned to architecture in 1918. However, in 1920, the urge to act took him to a summer school of speech and drama at Stratford. Convinced by the revelation of Bridges-Adam's productions, he abandoned architecture and went to London to study at the Central School of Speech and Drama, where the renowned voice teacher Elsie Fogerty transformed his life.

John Laurie first appeared on stage in Dumfries in 1921 in J. M. Barrie's *What every Woman Knows*. Later that year he joined the London Old Vic to play Pistol in *The Merry Wives of Windsor*. He performed regularly with the company until 1925, building an impressive list of credits in Shakespearian and classical roles under the director Robert Atkins. After a spell with the Stratford Festival Society Company in 1926, playing Autolycus in *The Winter's Tale* and Conrad in *Love's Labours Lost*, followed by a period in the West End, he returned to Stratford to play Hamlet in 1927. From 1927 to 1929 leading roles at the Old Vic included both Macbeth and Hamlet. The Old Vic director Harcourt Williams wrote of his incisive diction, his Scottish vigour, and his warm personality (Williams, 77).

In 1939 Laurie launched his screen career in Alfred Hitchcock's *Juno and the Paycock*. He made over a hundred films, including *The Thirty-Nine Steps* (1935), *The Four Feathers* (1939), and *Kidnapped* (1960). With his dark wavy hair and piercing eyes, he became familiar as the dour miser or the eccentric pessimist—usually Scottish. Until 1939 he alternated between the Old Vic, Stratford, and the West End, playing in Ibsen and in Shakespeare in roles ranging from Feste to Othello and from Malvolio to Richard III. Laurie's work then diversified and he appeared, for example, in Shaw's *Heartbreak House* (West End, 1943), *John Knox* (Glasgow Citizens' Theatre, 1947), and *Tiger at the Gates* (New York, 1955). He toured Australia with J. C. Williamson's Shakespeare Company in 1959, the USSR, America, and Europe with the Royal Shakespeare Company in 1964, and he joined the Chichester Festival Company in 1966.

Work increasingly focused on television, mainly in drama series such as *Armchair Theatre* and *Play of the Month*. In 1968 the BBC broadcast the first episode of the legendary comedy series *Dad's Army*. Ironically, Laurie's characterization of Private Fraser, with the catch-phrase 'We're all doomed', bestowed on him unprecedented popular recognition. Such fame tended to obscure his fine reputation as a classical actor of which he was rightly proud. Nevertheless he was made an honorary fellow of the Royal Scottish Academy of Music and Drama in early 1980. A man of no regrets, he gladly accepted all work offered.

As a founder member of the Apollo Society—dedicated to the performance of music and poetry—he was able to combine his principal relaxation, reading, with his profession. He was a celebrated exponent of Burns and McGonagall. EMI recorded a Burns concert, entitled *The Kindling Fire* in 1974. Laurie, with a keen sense of humour and a generous nature, was known for his outspokenness. He was invited to compile an anthology of Scottish literature in 1974 and his introduction to *My Favourite Scottish Stories*—'Actors as men of letters are rare birds'—surely revealed how he saw himself.

Laurie's first wife, the Old Vic actress Florence Mary Saunders (b. 1891), died in 1926. He married Oonah Veronica Todd-Naylor (1901–1990), a teacher, in 1928. Their only child, Veronica, was born in 1939. Ties with Scotland notwithstanding, he made his home in England. He died from emphysema and respiratory failure on 23 June 1980 in Chalfont Hospital, Chalfont St Peter, Buckinghamshire, and was cremated in July at Amersham cemetery.

P. S. BARLOW

Sources private information (2004) · C. Liddell, 'John Laurie: artist and friend', *Scottish Field* (Feb 1984), 20–22 · R. Webber, 'John Laurie: Private Fraser', *'Dad's army': a celebration* (1997), 74–8 · I. Herbert, ed., *Who's who in the theatre*, 16th edn (1977) · K. Roy, ed., *Scottish theatre directory* (1979) · H. Williams, *Old Vic saga* (1949) · *The Guardian* (26 June 1980) · *The Times* (26 June 1980) · *Daily Telegraph* (26 June 1980) · *The Scotsman* (26 June 1980) · J. P. Laurie, 'Introduction', *My favourite Scottish stories*, ed. J. P. Laurie (1974) · m. cert. [Florence Saunders] · m. cert. [Oonah Todd-Naylor]

Archives priv. coll. | FILM BFI NFTVA, documentary footage · BFI NFTVA, performance footage

Likenesses M. Gertler, charcoal drawing, 1927, priv. coll. · I. P. Williams, oils, c.1927, priv. coll. · E. Carrick, pastel drawing, c.1928, priv. coll. · photographs, 1928–74, Hult. Arch. · T. Evans, oils, 1950–59

Wealth at death £44,549: probate, 6 Jan 1981, CGPLA Eng. & Wales

Laurie, Sir Peter (1778–1861), saddler and politician, was born at Saundersdeal Farm, Haddington, on 3 March 1778, the son of John Laurie (d. 1799) and his second wife, Agnes, née Thomson. He was educated at Morham and later at Haddington grammar school, where he studied Latin with the intention of entering the ministry of the established Church of Scotland. His mother died in 1784 and his father remarried but Laurie rebelled against his stepmother and when he reached the age of twelve was sent to be apprenticed to his brother George at Jedburgh. A disagreement there led to his indenture being cancelled and he spent a year in Edinburgh before embarking on a further three years' apprenticeship to Maxton, an Edinburgh saddler. There he was at last happy, learning his craft during the day and attending classes in the evening at which he absorbed radical religious and political ideas. However, again an outburst of temper led to his departure; from Edinburgh he rode to Berwick and took ship to London where he lodged with his late brother's daughter and her husband and in due course found employment with David Pollock of Piccadilly, saddler to George III, where he soon rose to be foreman. He joined a debating society, taking part in the speech-making, discussions, and dramatic recitations, and treading the boards at Richmond theatre.

After his father died Laurie went to Scotland to settle family affairs, and appeared briefly on the Edinburgh stage before returning to London and his former post with Pollock. He was obliged to leave when Pollock's son came of age and replaced him, whereupon, in 1801, he established his own saddlery business at 293, later at 296, Oxford Street, securing contracts with the Indian army which ensured his future prosperity. Through his attendance at the Scottish chapel in Swallow Street he met the family of John Jack, and on 1 January 1803 he married Jack's daughter Margaret at St Martin-in-the-Fields. The couple at first resided in Oxford Street; there were no children of the marriage but they accumulated a family by adopting first Laurie's nephew John Laurie, then another nephew, Peter Northall Laurie, and other young relatives. Laurie's admission into the Saddlers' Company in 1812, and subsequently onto the livery, introduced him to the leading commercial and political persons of the day and in 1819 he campaigned for George Lamb, a whig candidate for Westminster. Laurie retained his ties with Scotland, holding office in the Society for the Propagation of Christian Knowledge in Scotland and in the Highland School Society. In 1820 he took his nephew John into partnership and retired from the saddlery business to live first in a newly built house in Cornwall Gardens, Regent's Park, later at nearby Park Square West, from where he could indulge his enjoyment of horse-riding.

Laurie's entry into City politics began with his election as sheriff in 1823. His travels through the City made him aware of the then public spectacle of hangings, which were often bungled by drunken and inefficient executioners, and he began to campaign for more efficient executions and better treatment of convicted prisoners. His efforts were rewarded by a knighthood on 7 April 1824. He sat as a magistrate for Westminster and, from 1826, when he was elected alderman for Aldersgate ward, for the City also, duties which he performed with great diligence and care for those arraigned before him. In 1832 he held office as lord mayor; in 1833 he was master of the Saddlers' Company.

Throughout these years Laurie divided his time between commerce and welfare. He campaigned for more open municipal government and for social advancement generally, several of his speeches and proposals being published in the form of pamphlets. He was a director of the Beacon Fire Insurance Company of Edinburgh and of the North British Insurance Company, and president of the royal hospitals of Bridewell and Bethlem, where he pressed for the adoption of the humane methods of the Quaker Retreat near York, which he had visited in 1820. He had been a youthful advocate of reform, but the riots and violence perpetrated by radical groups gradually made him a tory.

Laurie's high opinion of himself led his opponents to seek to puncture his inflated ego; the anonymous and vulgar satire of one hundred *Maxims of Sir Peter Laurie Knt, Lord Mayor of London*, published on lord mayor's day 1833, was one such dart and in 1835 his polemic against the periodical election of aldermen (he thought their appointment should be for life) generated more stinging responses from his opponents. His wife's death in 1848 left him a lonely man. In 1861 he went to Folkestone in failing health, tarried a while at Brighton, and then returned to die in his house at 7 Park Square West, Regent's Park, London, on 3 December 1861. He was buried at Highgate cemetery. The bulk of his large property went to his nephew Peter Northall Laurie, whom he and his wife had always regarded as a son.   ANITA McCONNELL

Sources P. G. Laurie, *Sir Peter Laurie: a family memoir* (1901) · *The journal of Sir Peter Laurie*, ed. E. Shepherd (1985) · *CGPLA Eng. & Wales* (1862) · d. cert.
Likenesses J. Sayers, caricature, etching, pubd 1794, BM, NPG · J. Nollekens, marble bust, 1803, Scot. NPG · J. Henning, paste medallion, 1806, Scot. NPG · J. Henning, pencil drawing, 1806, Scot. NPG · G. Hayter, group portrait, oils (*The trial of Queen Caroline*, 1820), NPG · J. Henning, pencil drawing, Scot. NPG · T. Phillips, oils, Bridewell Royal Hospital, Witley, Surrey · plaster bust, Scot. NPG
Wealth at death £160,000: probate, 30 Jan 1862, *CGPLA Eng. & Wales*

Laurie, Robert (1755?–1836), mezzotint engraver and printseller, was probably born in 1755, into a family originating from Dumfriesshire. He was apprenticed to Robert Sayer (1724–1794), a publisher of prints, maps, and charts, at the sign of the Golden Buck, 53 Fleet Street, from 1770 to 1777. In 1770 the Society of Arts awarded him a silver palette for his drawing from a picture, and in 1775 and 1776 premiums of 5 guineas and 10 guineas respectively for his patterns for calico printing. In 1776, when he was twenty, he also received an award of 30 guineas for disclosing his method of colour printing mezzotint engravings. His letter to the society explained that, after etching or engraving the outline on a copper plate, the plate was warmed and the appropriate oil colours applied on camel-hair stump brushes. The plate was afterwards wiped with a coarse gauze cloth, then with the hand, as in common practice, and again warmed before being passed through the press.

Laurie's earliest mezzotints are dated 1771, and from that time until 1774 his prints were signed variously Lowery, Lowry, Lowrie, Lawrey, Lawrie, or Laurie. Several were ambitious subjects after Kaufmann, Coypel Rubens, Rembrandt, and Vernet. Around this time he married. He and his wife, Esther, had at least one son, Richard Holmes Laurie (1777–1858), and a daughter, Esther Alicia. Richard Laurie was apprenticed to his father in the Stationers' Company and was then employed engraving mezzotints for the firm. Laurie's own plates are competent but lack any delicacy or finesse. He made a brief attempt to establish himself as an independent artist about 1779 but soon rejoined Sayer as an assistant and then a partner. His subjects included portraits of George III and Queen Charlotte after Zoffany, royal groups after his own designs, other nobility and lesser persons, actors in their own right and as stage characters, religious groups, landscapes, and allegorical scenes.

Laurie and his fellow assistant James Whittle took over Sayer's business on his retirement in 1794, and both partners moved into the Fleet Street house. Laurie rarely engraved after this time: portraits of Howe (1794) and Nelson (1797) were exceptions. The partnership inherited from Sayer a huge stock of prints as well as a comprehensive and profitable list of atlases and a range of charts covering much of the maritime world. Laurie and Whittle increased their list of charts, and added *The Oriental Navigator*, a volume of sailing directions to accompany their *East India Pilot*. They employed both in-house and independent engravers, printing on their own premises. Chart publishing was very demanding in that it required a network of specialist naval contacts to send in corrections and new information, as well as continual work to update existing charts before they were sold.

In 1812 Laurie retired; the firm continued as Whittle and Laurie, with the business conducted by his son, who on Whittle's death in 1818 became sole proprietor. Privately produced charts were now competing with the products of the Admiralty chart office and the quasi-official publications of the East India Company hydrographers, and in the 1820s Richard Laurie abandoned the chart and map business to concentrate on nautical publishing. Robert Laurie died in his house at Broxbourne, Hertfordshire, on 19 May 1836, aged eighty-one, and was buried at Broxbourne church on 26 May. He was survived by his widow, Esther, his daughter Esther Alicia, now the wife of Louis Rogers of Broxbourne, and his son Richard Holmes Laurie, who died at 53 Fleet Street on 19 January 1858.

TIMOTHY CLAYTON and ANITA McCONNELL

Sources *Transactions of the Society for the Encouragement of Arts, Manufactures and Commerce*, 2 (1784), 124, 127, 129, 145–8 • will, PRO, PROB 11/1863, sig. 369 • Bryan, *Painters* (1886–9), 2.26 • J. C. Smith, *British mezzotinto portraits*, 2 (1879), 796–810 • T. Dodd, 'Memorials of British engravers', BL, Add. MS 33406, fols. 259–260r • J. Ames, *Typographical antiquities, or, An historical account of the origin and progress of printing in Great Britain and Ireland*, ed. W. Herbert, 3 vols. (1785–90) • *GM*, 2nd ser., 6 (1836), 108; 3rd ser., 4 (1858), 561–3 • I. O. J. Gladstone, *The Lauries of Max Welton and other Laurie families* (1972) • P. H. Muir, 'The rolling press in Georgian times: the firm of Laurie and Whittle', *Connoisseur*, 116 (1948), 92–7 • S. Fisher, *The makers of the Blueback charts* (2001) • parish register, Broxbourne, 26 May 1836, Herts. ALS [burial] • C. Lennox-Boyd and others, *Theatre in the age of Garrick* (1994)

Laurie, Simon Somerville (1829–1909), educationist, was born on 13 November 1829 at Edinburgh, the eldest son of James Laurie, chaplain to the Edinburgh Royal Infirmary, and Jean Somerville, daughter of Simon Somerville, United Presbyterian minister at Elgin. His brothers included Thomas, a publisher in London, and James Stuart *Laurie, director of the Ceylon educational service. The family was not well off, and Laurie helped to pay for his own education by tutoring younger students. He was educated at Edinburgh high school (1839–44) and Edinburgh University (1844–9), where he became class assistant to the professor of Latin, James Pillans; as a former rector of the high school and an early champion of the professional

Simon Somerville Laurie (1829–1909), by George Fiddes Watt, 1904

training of teachers, Pillans no doubt helped turn Laurie's mind to educational work. After five years acting as a private tutor in London, in Ireland, and on the continent, Laurie returned to Scotland in 1855 to become secretary of the Church of Scotland's education committee; appointed at the age of twenty-five, he held this post until 1905. The committee controlled the church's 'general assembly' schools, which were mainly in the highlands and islands, and generally supervised and co-ordinated schools affiliated to the established church. It thus had a central role in Scottish education until the act of 1872 which transferred these responsibilities to the state and created the Scotch Education Department (SED). After that, the committee was chiefly concerned with the church's two (later three) training colleges, transferred to the state only in 1905.

In 1856 Laurie became visitor (secretary and inspector) of the Dick bequest, an important endowment which supported the teaching of higher subjects, especially the classics, in the rural parish schools of the counties of Aberdeen, Banff, and Moray; this regional tradition, linked through competitive bursaries with entry to Aberdeen University, came to symbolize the opportunities enjoyed by the Scottish 'lad o' pairts'. Laurie examined and inspected schoolmasters aided by the bequest, and used his periodic reports to the governors (1865, 1890, 1904) to expound his general educational principles. In the 1860s he began a prolific career as an author. The 1872 act, and its equivalent of 1870 in England and Wales, led to a great expansion of the elementary teaching profession, and Laurie's treatises on education (notably *Primary Instruction in Relation to Education*, 1867, and *Institutes of Education*, 1892), and his numerous essays and lectures which were published in collected editions, were staple reading for several generations of trainee teachers. He also enjoyed a wide readership in the United States, and was a corresponding member of the American National Educational Association. His publications included several works on the history of education, and although these were not based on original research his study of Comenius (1881) was a popular success.

Thus although Laurie never himself taught in a school, by the 1870s he was regarded as Scotland's leading educational expert, and when the Bell trustees created two university chairs of education in 1876, he was appointed to the chair at Edinburgh. This proved in some ways a frustrating experience. Laurie believed that teaching should become a profession on the same level as medicine or law—in 1891 he became president of the Teachers' Guild of Great Britain and Ireland, which campaigned for this cause—and that teachers should enjoy the liberalizing effects of a university education. The SED, on the other hand, was determined to keep the professional education of elementary teachers in the hands of the training colleges. Students at the latter were allowed from 1873 to attend some university courses, and this became an increasingly common practice for men, but Laurie's lectures on education were not officially recognized for qualifying purposes. He did persuade the university, however, to create a schoolmaster's diploma, which could be taken on a voluntary basis.

Laurie was also involved in wider educational movements. In the 1860s he supported the foundation of higher education courses for women in Edinburgh, and advocated reform of the residential 'hospitals' which provided education on charitable grounds for a limited number of children. The Merchant Company of Edinburgh, which administered several of these, commissioned a report from Laurie which condemned the boarding regime (1868), and this strongly influenced the conversion of hospitals into large day schools by the Merchant Company in 1869–70, and later by other educational trusts. In 1872 Laurie was appointed secretary of the royal commission on Scottish endowed schools chaired by Sir Edward Colebrooke, and its report of 1875, which sought to use endowed funds to create a coherent network of secondary schools throughout Scotland, was drafted by him and clearly reflected his ideas. He kept the impetus alive by founding the Association for Promoting Secondary Education in Scotland, the aim of which was at least partly achieved by legislation in 1878. While Laurie thus encouraged the development of secondary schools, his experience with the Dick bequest also made him a champion of the parish school tradition, and he sought to perpetuate its values within the evolving state system. His educational principles stressed the personal influence of the teacher and the training of the faculties, especially through the study of language, rather than the accumulation of facts. He was hostile to vocational and utilitarian approaches to education, represented at the time by the doctrines of Herbert Spencer, and argued that even in elementary schools the aim should be to give a humanistic and ethical training. By the end of his career these views appeared old-fashioned, and brought him into conflict with the policies of the SED, notably over its code of 1903, which encouraged vocational training for older pupils.

Laurie had a lifelong interest in philosophy, and derived his educational principles from a metaphysical scheme of his own devising. He published preliminary studies on ethics in the 1860s, and was an unsuccessful candidate for the Edinburgh chair of moral philosophy in 1868. More substantial work followed with *Metaphysica nova et venusta* in 1884 and *Ethica, or, The Ethics of Reason* in 1885, both initially published under the pseudonym Scotus Novanticus. In 1905–6 Laurie gave the Gifford lectures in natural theology at Edinburgh University, and these were published in 1906 as *Synthetica, being Meditations Epistemological and Ontological*. Laurie's philosophy of 'natural realism', in seeking a rational basis in experience for theism and for ethical idealism, may be seen as a late expression of the Scottish 'common-sense' tradition, and was perhaps influenced by the contemporary revival of interest in Kant. He was a close personal friend of the pioneering British exponent of Hegel, James Hutchison Stirling, but did not subscribe to the neo-Hegelianism which was then dominant in university philosophy chairs. He preferred to use his own terminology, and not to make explicit connections either with the philosophical schools of the past or with the main currents of contemporary thought. His ideas thus had little permanent influence. He did, however, attract a Belgian disciple, Georges Remacle, who translated his 1884 and 1885 books into French, and published *La philosophie de S. S. Laurie* in 1909.

Laurie resigned from his university chair in 1903, and from the Dick bequest in 1907. He received honorary doctorates from the universities of Edinburgh, Aberdeen, and St Andrews, and was a fellow of the Royal Society of Edinburgh (1870) and an honorary fellow of the Educational Institute of Scotland (1891). He was married twice: in 1861 to Catherine Ann (d. 1895), daughter of William Hibburd of Egham, and in 1901 to Lucy, daughter of Sir John Struthers, professor of anatomy at Aberdeen University; she survived her husband. There were two sons and two daughters of the first marriage. Laurie died on 2 March 1909 from heart failure at his residence, 22 George Square, Edinburgh, and was buried three days later in the city's Grange cemetery. His elder son, Arthur Pillans Laurie (1861–1949), was trained at Cambridge as a chemist and became principal of the Heriot-Watt College, Edinburgh, in 1900.   R. D. ANDERSON

Sources H. M. Knox, 'Simon Somerville Laurie, 1829–1909', *British Journal of Educational Studies*, 10 (1961–2), 138–52 [incl. list of Laurie's publications] • G. Remacle, *La philosophie de S. S. Laurie* (1909) [incl. biographical notice based on family information] • *DNB* • *WWW* •

The Scotsman (3 March 1909) · *The Scotsman* (5 March 1909) · J. B. Baillie, 'Professor Laurie's natural realism', *Mind*, new ser., 17 (1908), 475–92; new ser., 18 (1909), 184–207 · A. Morgan, 'Simon Somerville Laurie', *Makers of Scottish education* (1929), 193–209 · R. D. Anderson, *Education and opportunity in Victorian Scotland: schools and universities* (1983)

Archives NL Scot., corresp. with George Combe

Likenesses G. F. Watt, oils, 1904, U. Edin. [*see illus.*] · W. Hole, etching, repro. in W. B. Hole, *Quasi cursores: portraits of the high officers and professors of the University of Edinburgh at its tercentenary festival* (1884)

Wealth at death £10,836 19s. 9d.: confirmation, 6 May 1909, *CCI*

Laurie, William George Ranald Mundell [Ran] (1915–1998), oarsman, was born on 4 May 1915 at Manor Farm, Grantchester, Cambridgeshire, the son of William Walker Laurie, a farmer, and his wife, Margaret Grieve Mundell. He was named after an uncle killed in the First World War, was educated at Monkton Combe School, Somerset, and rowed in the school eight at Henley from 1931 to 1933. He went up to Selwyn College, Cambridge, in 1933. There he rowed in three winning boat race crews between 1934 and 1936, stroking the Cambridge crews in 1935 and 1936, and breaking the course record in 1934. At no. 7 among the crew members was **John Hyrne Tucker Wilson** (1914–1997), oarsman, who became Laurie's rowing partner and lifelong friend. The third child of Henry Elcock Wilson, formerly a doctor in southern India who had business interests in Birkenhead and Texas, and his wife, Katherine Lippet Tucker of South Carolina, Jack Wilson was born in Bristol, Rhode Island, on 17 September 1914, and educated at Shrewsbury School and Pembroke College, Cambridge. Wilson had Henley wins to his credit in the ladies' plate with Shrewsbury in 1932, the stewards' in 1933 and 1934, and the grand challenge cup in 1935 with Pembroke; Laurie had stroked the Leander club to a record in the grand at Henley in 1934.

After the boat race in 1936, Wilson, like many blues before him, joined the Sudan political service, while Laurie stroked the British eight to fourth place in the Olympic games in Berlin. He maintained that Wilson's absence cost them the title. 'He was not only the greatest mover of a boat I have ever seen, but rowing was such fun to him that he made it fun for anyone who rowed with him' (*Daily Telegraph*, 27 Feb 1997). In 1937 Laurie also joined the political service of Sudan. In 1938 he and Wilson took leave to compete at Henley, where they won the silver goblets, and were also members of the Leander four which won the stewards' challenge cup. This gave them the idea of trying for the 1940 Olympics, but they spent the next ten years in Sudan, having only chance contacts with their sport. In 1943 Wilson married Anne Elinor Alexander, a Wren, after she succeeded in getting a posting to Mombasa; they had two sons. On 10 February 1945, while on leave in England, Laurie married Patricia Laidlaw (1916/17–1989), with whom he had two sons and two daughters. During their time in Sudan Wilson, a district commissioner, was speared by an elderly woman acting on a witch doctor's orders. He disarmed her before she could do too much damage, and when Laurie rushed to his hospital bed he found Wilson out playing tennis.

In 1948 Laurie and Wilson (none the worse for his spearing) turned up in pairs at Marlow regatta, where they achieved the distinction of hitting both banks during the same race. Things went better at Henley, over the straight course. The 'desert rats', as the pair came to be called, won the goblets for the second time with ease, and were immediately selected to represent Britain in the London Olympic games a month later. They trained at Cambridge and were allowed to draw extra rations (known as 'heavy industrial'), while their wives supported their young families frugally. On the night before the first Olympic race (which took place at Henley) Laurie was up four or five times with an upset stomach, but they managed a tight victory over the Italians to reach the semi-finals. The final was described by Laurie as 'a thoroughly satisfactory race. It was the best row we ever had and we finished about a length ahead of the Swiss with the Italians two or more behind them, and we had a bit in hand' (Laurie, 15–16). A week later he was back at work in Sudan, his wife having produced their second daughter four days after the race.

Laurie left the Sudan service in 1950 to become a doctor. He qualified in 1954 and was a general practitioner in Oxford for thirty years. He twice returned to Africa to provide relief for mission doctors, for Save the Children in Biafra, and for a Methodist hospital in Kenya. He was a passionate gardener, fisherman, and cricketer. He chaired the duke of Edinburgh's award Oxford committee from 1959 to 1969, and the local branch of Save the Children from 1986 to 1989. He maintained his connections with rowing all his life: he became a steward of Henley royal regatta in 1951 and was on the management committee from 1975 until 1986. He became an umpire at Henley in 1966. In this capacity he was at the centre of a controversy when Thames Tradesmen locked oars with Trident near the finish line of the Wyfold final in 1970. He had warned both crews about their steering, and it was far from clear who was at fault when they were forced to stop. Laurie clearly did not know either, and ordered the crews to paddle on. When they drifted apart, Trident took a few gentle strokes and crossed the line. Laurie then awarded them the race, to the incredulity of all concerned. The young East Ender stroking Tradesmen broke the silence, as *The Guardian* (6 July 1970) reported, by 'attributing a part of the anatomy to the umpire which it is doubtful that he possessed'. But it was an uncharacteristic incident, and Laurie bore him no ill will.

Both of Laurie's sons were rowers; the younger, Hugh, rowed for Cambridge in 1980, before becoming more famous as a comic actor and writer. He recalled rowing a pair with his father:

> I was a teenager in full-time training, 6 foot 3 and 14 stone, he was a GP in his mid-fifties who did a spot of gardening, and I had to go like hell to keep the boat straight. The power, and the will, was almost frightening. (private information)

Laurie's wife, Pat, was diagnosed with motor neurone disease in 1988, and Ran (who had encountered only one such case professionally) nursed her single-handed until her death in 1989. On 14 July 1990 Laurie married (Eveline) Mary Arbuthnot, *née* Morgan (b. 1914/15), and moved with her to Norfolk. His robust good health deserted him shortly afterwards, and he developed Parkinson's disease. He died at his home, Hethersett Hall, Hethersett, Norfolk, on 19 September 1998.

Wilson rose to the position of deputy governor of Bahr al-Ghazal province before Sudan became independent in 1954. He returned to Britain to join the steel company Stewart and Lloyds (later part of British Steel), and became general manager of its west midland tubes division, until his retirement in 1976. He too continued to be involved with rowing, as a steward at Henley from 1953. He was also a magistrate. He died from cancer at his home, 9 Fore Street Hill, Budleigh Salterton, Devon, on 16 February 1997, survived by his wife.

Laurie and Wilson were the finest pair-oar of their generation. It was not until Steve Redgrave and Andy Holmes won at the Olympic games in 1988 that Britons again excelled in this most difficult of boats to race. The desert rats' boat is in the collection of the River and Rowing Museum at Henley. Hugh Laurie, describing a photograph of the pair receiving their medals on the pontoon at Henley in 1948, said:

> Jack is loose-limbed and dashing, my father ramrod straight to attention. I think it describes the two of them very well— or perhaps each is describing a part of the other—for these were two really remarkable men. Tough, modest, generous and, I like to think, without the slightest thought of personal gain throughout their lives. A vanished breed. (private information)

CHRISTOPHER DODD

Sources personal knowledge (2004) · private information (2004) · R. Laurie, 'The 1948 Olympics', *Regatta*, 12 (Sept 1988), 15–16 · *The Times* (1 March 1997) · *The Times* (26 Sept 1998) · *Daily Telegraph* (27 Feb 1997) · *Daily Telegraph* (28 Sept 1998) · *The Independent* (10 Oct 1998) · *The Guardian* (6 July 1970) · *Regatta*, 113 (Nov 1998), 23–5 · b. cert. · m. certs. · d. cert. · d. cert. [John Hyrne Tucker Wilson]
Likenesses photograph, 1948, Hult. Arch.
Wealth at death £322,759—gross; £319,388—net: probate, 19 May 1999, *CGPLA Eng. & Wales* · £192,189—John Hyrne Tucker Wilson: probate, 14 Aug 1997, *CGPLA Eng. & Wales*

Laurier, Sir (Henri Charles) Wilfrid (1841–1919), lawyer and prime minister of Canada, was born in St Lin, a village near Montreal, on 20 November 1841, the son of Carolus Laurier (1815–1886), a farmer and surveyor who was active in local politics, and his wife, Marcelle Martineau (1815–1848). His French Catholic forebears had resided in Canada for eight generations. When his mother died in 1848 his father took a second wife, Adeline Ethier; there were five children from this marriage.

Education, marriage, and early years in law and politics Laurier's early schooling was from his mother and in the parish school in St Lin. At the age of eleven he was sent to neighbouring New Glasgow to live with an English-speaking family and attend, for two years, an English-language primary school. In 1854 he began seven years of training at L'Assomption College, L'Assomption, where he mastered Latin and French literature, with a smattering of Greek,

Sir (Henri Charles) Wilfrid Laurier (1841–1919), by William James Topley, 1906

English, mathematics, philosophy, geography, and history. In 1861 he entered the faculty of law at McGill University in Montreal and attended lectures in English and French. Three years later he graduated BCL and began to practise law in Montreal.

Laurier's family background and early acquaintances encouraged his alliance with the *parti rouge*, inheritors of European liberal traditions, and with the anti-clericalism of the Institut Canadien of Montreal, of which he became a vice-president. He also opposed the formation of the dominion of Canada at confederation in 1867. Poor health and few clients forced Laurier to move in 1866 to L'Avenir and then Arthabaska, where he combined his law practice with running a liberally orientated newspaper, *Le Défricheur*. On 13 May 1868 he married, at her proposal, Zoe, the daughter of Napoléon-Godefoi Lafontaine of Montreal. Their fifty-year marriage remained childless.

A patient and ever-supportive companion, Zoe was not the only woman of Laurier's affection. Private correspondence discovered in 1963 revealed that for three decades he also had a close intellectual and emotional relationship with a woman whose education, culture, and charm eclipsed that of his spouse. Emilie Lavergne, the wife of Laurier's Arthabaska law partner, became a close friend. When the Lauriers moved to Ottawa, Emilie followed. She became an indispensable fixture at Ottawa social events, large and small, often co-hosting official functions at the Lauriers' home. Some readers of the correspondence decipher trysts in Laurier's affectionate messages to Emilie. Others believe the effusive, yearning language of Laurier's letters falls within the Victorian vocabulary of friendship of which he was a master. The most careful analyst of the relationship, Sandra Gwyn, reserves judgement on whether Laurier and Emilie were lovers. Gwyn asserts that the real significance of Emilie's relationship with Laurier was as a mentor to the rising politician. Having lived in Paris and London, she introduced the tall, handsome country lawyer to the elegant manner of dressing and the sophisticated conversation of the salon, which marked the aspirations of the higher social circles of the nation's colonial capital.

Laurier was elected to the Quebec legislative assembly as a Liberal in 1871. Uninspired by provincial politics, he resigned his seat in 1874, stood in the dominion general election of that year as candidate for Drummond–Arthabaska, and won. Three years later he was promoted from the back benches to become minister of Inland Revenue in the Liberal government of Alexander Mackenzie. In the 1878 general election his party was defeated by John A. Macdonald's Conservatives, but Laurier successfully contested the seat of Quebec East and continued to represent that constituency until his death. Under the leadership of Edward Blake the party lost the elections of 1882 and 1886, and when Blake resigned in 1887 he recommended Laurier, who had become leader of the Quebec party, as national leader.

Leader of the Liberal Party and prime minister Laurier's task was to unite, build into a national party, and restore to power the Liberals, who were divided among themselves on questions of French–English relations in dominion politics, especially over the hanging in 1885 of the métis insurgent Louis Riel (whom Laurier had defended). His first attempt, running on a policy of unrestricted reciprocity with the United States against Macdonald's protectionist tariff policy, failed in the 1891 general election. Two years later, at the first national party convention in Canadian political history, the Liberals adopted a more moderate trade policy—'freer trade' with both Britain and the United States. The party also eschewed a specific stance on the vexed question of French–English relations of the day, the Manitoba schools question. These carefully crafted ambiguities, together with the troubled history of the Conservatives after Macdonald's death in 1891, brought Laurier's party to power in 1896. In 1897, during the diamond jubilee celebrations of Queen Victoria and the Colonial Conference, Laurier was appointed to the imperial privy council and made knight grand commander in the Order of St Michael and St George. He remained prime minister for fifteen years, guiding his party through three more successful general election campaigns. But in 1911, running on a reciprocal trade agreement recently negotiated with the United States, the Liberals were defeated by Robert Borden's Conservative Party. Laurier remained party leader and leader of the opposition in the Canadian parliament through the troubled years of the First World War and a bitterly fought general election over conscription in 1917.

As party leader Laurier dominated the Liberal Party and, during his prime ministership, the nation. A commanding figure who grew ever more compelling in appearance and manner throughout his career, his friendly demeanour and gracious ways captured the admiration and loyalty of the humblest and the highest of Canadians and made him a captivating leader among colonial politicians on the imperial stage from 1896 to 1911. He loved to affect an attitude of casualness, even laziness, as a style of governance: but there was nothing casual about his ambitions or his sense of purpose. Of his former leader, Alexander Mackenzie, he once remarked that 'he had no zest to carry a party on' (Brown, 1980, 187). Laurier did. As early as his first election to public office, in 1871, he told a friend that his goal was 'making my ideas triumph' (ibid.). Laurier's minister of the interior from 1897 to 1905, Sir Clifford Sifton, observed that he was 'a masterful man set on having his own way and equally resolute that his colleagues shall not have their way unless this is quite agreeable to him' (Stevens, 73).

At the age of twenty-three, in an address to his McGill law school class, Laurier pledged his life 'to the cause … of concord among the different elements of this country' (Wade, 89). That, achieving and maintaining concord among Canadians, especially between French and English Canadians in national politics, was the goal of his political career. In 1904 he wrote that 'my object is to consolidate Confederation, and to bring our people long estranged from each other, gradually to become a nation'. Laurier had an abiding respect for the British political system and British political ideals, especially those of the nineteenth-century British Liberal Party. These he articulated in the most famous speech of his career in 1877, when he rose in defence of the Liberal Party in Quebec against the assault upon it by the Roman Catholic clergy of the province. He attributed the political liberty Canadians enjoyed to the achievements of Fox, O'Connell, Grey, and Russell and to 'the liberal institutions by which we are governed, institutions which we owe to our forefathers and the wisdom of the mothercountry' (Skelton, 1.153). This liberty, these institutions, together with the art of compromise at which he was deft, and the more than occasional persuasive use of his political power, were Laurier's guideposts to maintaining national unity in his party and his country.

Laurier's term of office coincided with the development of western Canada and a period of unprecedented prosperity in Canadian history. Between 1901 and 1921 Canada's population grew by 64 per cent, from 5.37 to 8.78 million people, as immigrants from the United States, Britain, and eastern Europe arrived in ever-growing numbers to work in Canada's new factories, in the forests and mines of her northern hinterland, and, most especially, opening new farm lands in the west. The times were favourable: the best lands in the United States were already settled, and rising world wheat prices and falling shipping rates for bulk goods such as wheat stimulated a boom in the export sector of the economy. Sifton refined immigration procedures to ease the way of aspiring settlers, pressured the Canadian Pacific Railway to open its millions of acres of land on the prairies to settlement, flooded the USA and Europe with Garden-of-Eden propaganda, and hired aggressive agents to recruit homesteaders. Nervous Canadians of French and British stock worried about the huge influx of foreigners, especially those from the Austro-Hungarian empire whom Sifton praised as stalwart peasants of 'good quality' (Brown and Cook, 63), who were much more likely to succeed as pioneers than were urban migrants from Britain.

English and French Canadians were, however, split in another school crisis in national politics when Laurier's government, in 1905, extended the boundaries of Manitoba and created the new provinces of Alberta and Saskatchewan. As in Manitoba in the 1890s, when the provincial government abolished the separate (Roman Catholic) school system, the question in 1905 was whether separate Roman Catholic schools would be allowed in the new provinces. The Roman Catholic population in the west, the Roman Catholic hierarchy across Canada, and Quebec's members in parliament fought for protection of minority school rights in the new provinces, while the English-Canadian majority demanded a single, secular, 'national' school system. Laurier stoutly defended initial legislation which appeared to provide for separate school systems in Alberta and Saskatchewan but, after Sifton's resignation from the government over the issue, eventually accepted a schools clause which established a secular schools system with modest provisions for religious instruction at the end of the day and the possibility of hiring Roman Catholic instructors in districts with a majority Catholic population. The compromise dangerously undermined the ever-more hesitant support a growing, powerful *nationaliste* group of young French Canadians gave to the prime minister.

Imperial–dominion relations Laurier was more successful in balancing the sharply opposed views of English-Canadian imperialists and French-Canadian nationalists on the issue of imperial relations during his prime ministership. For imperialists, especially those only a generation or two removed from the British Isles, the nation's destiny rested squarely on its imperial foundations. As Principal Grant of Queen's University put it, 'We are Canadians, and in order to be Canadian we must be British' (Brown and Cook, 28). For French Canadians, domiciled for generations in the St Lawrence valley, Canada was their only homeland. In the autumn of 1899, when imperialists clamoured for Canadian participation in the South African War, and the French-Canadian press and nationalists opposed any contribution, Laurier temporized, arguing that the British were fighting a just war in the Transvaal, but that Canada had no direct responsibility there. Then he compromised: Canada would recruit, equip, and transport volunteers for service, and in South Africa the imperial government would assume all subsequent responsibility for them. Eventually some 7000 Canadians fought in South Africa.

Laurier's South African war policy was rooted in the voluntary principle, the idea that liberty within the empire, the freedom to say yes and to say no, the liberty inherent in the political ideals of British Liberalism which he so admired, was the silken bond of unity that held the empire together. Laurier firmly and consistently resisted any schemes, British or Canadian inspired, to centralize the constitution and governance of the British empire. At the 1902 Imperial Conference he angered the colonial secretary, Joseph Chamberlain, and other centralists, who sought centralized political, economic, and military reform of the empire, by refusing all of their proposals, including a colonial contribution to imperial naval defence. Instead, he offered a vague commitment to create, in due course, a Canadian naval defence force. A South African representative stormed that 'that dam' dancing master bitched the whole show' (Schull, 410).

Laurier's commitment was put to the test in the last years of the decade. A 1909 resolution to create a Canadian naval force for coastal defence was supported by both parties in parliament, and, following consultation with imperial authorities, Laurier's Naval Service Act was passed in 1910. The new Canadian navy would have a complement of five cruisers and six destroyers, deployed on both coasts; it would be manned by a volunteer force, and there would be a naval college to train officers. It would be under Canadian command but, with parliament's consent, in wartime could be placed under imperial command. Imperialists grumbled about Laurier's 'tin pot' navy while French-Canadian nationalists angrily made their final break with Laurier Liberalism. More moderate opinion viewed the proposed navy for what it was: another compromise, a modest but important step, voluntarily taken, towards dominion autonomy within the empire.

Defeat and years in opposition The navy was the last great act of the Laurier administration. His government, once vigorous and talented, had been instrumental in developing the nation, creating new provinces, reviving the economy, chartering two new transcontinental railways, stimulating immigration, and cautiously fostering autonomy within the empire. Now it was old, tired, and tainted with corruption. It had unleashed political constituencies with which the prime minister had no sympathy. In 1911 *Encyclopaedia Britannica* observed that Laurier was 'an individualist rather than a collectivist' (Clippingdale, 180–81)—in other words, far from the cutting edge of twentieth-century British Liberalism. In Canada a growing chorus of trade unionists, Social Gospellers, women demanding to be enfranchised, and other reformers decried overcrowding, disease, and lack of a living wage in Canadian cities. 'Reforms', Laurier had remarked, 'are for the opposition' (Brown, 1980, 154). The Liberals' accommodations to business and industry, essentially continuing the protectionist tariff policies of Macdonald's Conservatives in an earlier era, stimulated increasing hostility among prairie farmers.

An American initiative in trade relations in 1910 resulted in a broadly based reciprocity agreement which required legislative approval by both nations. Introduced in January 1911, it seemed providential for the Liberal government. But the belated opposition of industrial, commercial, and transport interests, and then an aroused Conservative Party, denied its passage and forced dissolution. Robert Borden's Conservative Party forged a shaky alliance of 'the interests', provincial and national Conservative Party members, and French-Canadian nationalists soundly to defeat the Laurier government on 21 September 1911.

As leader of the opposition Laurier remained master of his party in and out of parliament. His relationship with the new prime minister was friendly and reflected the respect Robert Borden had for Canada's senior statesman. Laurier strongly opposed Borden's proposal of an emergency contribution of $35 million to the imperial navy in 1913 and engineered defeat of the bill in the Canadian senate. He also led the Liberal opposition to a bill to provide financial aid to the faltering Canadian Northern Railway, one of the two new transcontinental railways he had chartered, and, in 1917, to Borden's successful bill to nationalize it.

Laurier strongly supported Canada's participation in the First World War as long as military participation was on a voluntary basis. By 1917, when casualties mounted into the thousands and the strength of the Canadian corps in Europe was dangerously threatened, and when voluntary recruiting had dried up, Borden, after attending the first imperial war cabinet and conference, came home to announce conscription. He proposed a coalition with Laurier to carry the new Military Service Bill through parliament and a general election. Laurier temporized for several weeks, as many of his English-Canadian party members announced support for conscription and French-Canadian members roundly denounced it. He then refused to join Borden, who proceeded to form a Union of Conservatives and conscriptionist Liberals to fight the December 1917 election. It was the most bitter general election in Canadian history, marked by blatant gerrymandering and manipulation of the franchise by the government and vicious slandering of Laurier and French Canada by the English-Canadian press. The result was an overwhelming victory for Borden's Union. It captured 153 seats, only three of which, all English speaking, were in Quebec. Laurier held sixty-two seats in his native province, ten in the maritime provinces, eight of eighty-two in Ontario, and two of fifty-seven in the four western provinces. Laurier, now aged seventy-eight, was philosophical. 'I did not expect to win and therefore I feel no disappointment', he wrote to a long-time friend and wife of a former governor-general of Canada, Lady Aberdeen. 'I am conscious that I was in the right; that is quite sufficient for the present' (Brown and Cook, 273).

Final years Laurier's ambition was done. Many of his ideas had, as he had hoped in 1871, triumphed. His governments had guided the expansion and consolidation of confederation, the growth of a vibrant economy, rooted in agricultural exports with a strong industrial sector and prosperous cities, and the development of policies which had won support from both English and French Canadians.

The Liberal Party had become a political force that would command the allegiance of most Canadians through much of the twentieth century and of Quebec in every federal election until 1984.

In the early weeks of 1919 Laurier, tired, frail, and in failing health, began planning for the new session of parliament, scheduled to open on 20 February. On the preceding Saturday, 15 February, he attended a luncheon meeting of the Canadian Club and then went to his office to work. As daylight faded he rose from his chair, was struck by a stroke, and collapsed. He recovered enough to take the tram home. As he was dressing for mass the next morning he was struck again. Then, with his wife at his side, he suffered a third fatal stroke early in the morning of 17 February 1919. The customary lying-in followed, with a state funeral at St Patrick's Basilica on 22 February and a long, slow procession to Notre-Dame cemetery, Ottawa, where he was laid to rest.

ROBERT CRAIG BROWN and JAN NOEL

Sources O. D. Skelton, *Life and letters of Sir Wilfrid Laurier*, 2 vols. (1921) · J. Schull, *Laurier, the first Canadian* (1965) · H. B. Neatby, *Laurier and a liberal Quebec* (1973) · R. Clippingdale, *Laurier: his life and world* (1979) · J. English, *The decline of politics: the conservatives and the party system, 1901–20* (1977) · S. Gwyn, *The private capital* (1984) · P. Stevens, 'Wilfrid Laurier, politician', *The political ideas of the prime ministers of Canada*, ed. M. Hamelin (1969) · R. C. Brown, 'Fishwives, plutocrats, sirens and other curious creatures: some questions about political leadership in Canada', *Entering the eighties: Canada in crisis*, ed. R. K. Carty and W. P. Ward (1980) · R. C. Brown, '1896–1911: the Laurier years', in J. L. Granatstein, R. C. Brown, and others, *Twentieth century Canada* (1983); 3rd edn as *Nation: Canada since confederation* (1990) · L. O. David, *Laurier: sa vie, ses oeuvres* (1919) · J. Willison, *Sir Wilfrid Laurier and the liberal party*, 2 vols. (1903) · M. Wade, *The French Canadians, 1760–1945* (1968) · *Documents on Canadian external relations*, Canada, Department of External Affairs, 1 (1967) · R. C. Brown and R. Cook, *Canada, 1896–1921: a nation transformed* (1974)
Archives NA Canada | BL, corresp. with J. E. Burns, Add. MSS 46282 · Bodl. Oxf., corresp. with Herbert Asquith; letters to James Bryce; corresp. with Lewis Harcourt · NA Canada, Henri Bourassa MSS; John Wesley Dafoe MSS; Newton Wesley Rowell MSS; Sir Clifford Sifton MSS; Sir John S. Willison MSS · NL Scot., corresp. with fourth earl of Minto · U. Birm. L., corresp. with Joseph Chamberlain · Wilts. & Swindon RO, corresp. with Sir Michael Herbert
Likenesses G. Delfosse, portrait, 1897, NA Canada · W. J. Topley, photograph, 1906, NA Canada [*see illus.*] · S. P. Hall, pencil drawing, NPG · Spy [L. Ward], chromolithograph caricature, NPG; repro. in *VF* (19 Aug 1897)

Lauriston. For this title name *see* Law, Jacques Alexandre Bernard, of Lauriston, marquess of Lauriston in the French nobility (1768–1828).

Lauterpacht, Sir Hersch (1897–1960), international lawyer, was born on 16 August 1897 at Zolkiew, a village near Lemberg (Lwów) in eastern Galicia, Poland, the younger son in a family of three children of Aaron Lauterpacht, a timber merchant of fluctuating fortune, and his wife, Deborah Turkenkopf. He belonged to a family deeply Jewish in sentiment and sympathy. With the sole exception of his sister's daughter, who found refuge in a convent, all his relatives in Poland were massacred during the Second World War.

In 1910 the family moved to Lemberg (Lwów) to enable

Sir Hersch Lauterpacht (1897–1960), by Elliott & Fry, 1949?

Hersch Lauterpacht to receive a better secondary education. On the outbreak of war, as an Austrian subject, he was mobilized into the Austrian army but was required to serve in his father's timber factory, which was requisitioned and in a territory occupied and reoccupied by the Russian and Austrian armed forces. After the war, because of academic difficulties at Lwów, he went to the University of Vienna, where he obtained his doctorate in law in 1921 and, as a student of Hans Kelsen, a doctorate in political science in 1922. In 1923 he married Rachel, the third daughter of Michael Steinberg, resident in Palestine.

Both at Lwów and in Vienna Lauterpacht took a very prominent part in Jewish and Zionist affairs, organizing schoolchildren and students not least in order to make provision for their desperate human needs. It was this early experience which moulded his intellectual and emotional interest in human rights and their international protection. He was a founder and president of a World Federation of Jewish Students.

In spring 1923 Lauterpacht went to England, and although he could barely speak English he entered the London School of Economics as a research student under the direction of A. D. (later Lord) McNair, for whom he always retained the deepest respect and affection, regarding him as the great formative influence in his life. He obtained his LLD in 1925 with a dissertation entitled *Private Law Sources and Analogies of International Law* (published

in 1927), which has been described as a seminal work of contemporary international law, and in 1927 he was appointed an assistant lecturer at the London School of Economics. At that point he decided to attach himself permanently to this country, and he was naturalized a British subject in 1931.

Lauterpacht's career in his adopted country was truly remarkable. He became reader in public international law in the University of London in 1935. From 1938 to 1955 he held the Whewell chair of international law in the University of Cambridge, in succession to McNair. In 1946 he became a fellow of Trinity College and in 1948 of the British Academy. In 1936 he was called to the bar by Gray's Inn and he took silk in 1949. He did much advisory work at the bar, and was specially associated with the 'continental shelf' arbitrations, appearing for the Petroleum Development Company in the great *Abu Dhabi* case. During the Second World War, in the critical period of American neutrality, he was able when visiting the United States to render very valuable service to the United Kingdom. He was a member of the British War Crimes Executive in 1945–6 and attended the Nuremberg trials. He was of counsel for the United Kingdom in the *Corfu Channel* and the *Anglo-Iranian Oil Company* (interim measures) cases before the International Court of Justice at The Hague; he advised in other cases and was entrusted with the revision of the *Manual of Military Law*, eventually published by the War Office in 1958. He was a member of the Institute of International Law (associate in 1947 and titular in 1952); and he was elected to the United Nations International Law Commission in 1951, discharging his heavy duties there with great conscientiousness during four years, two of them as special rapporteur on the law of treaties. He accepted visiting professorships at many universities, particularly at Geneva and in the United States, and he delivered courses of lectures at The Hague Academy of International Law in 1930, 1934, 1937, and 1947. His lectures at Geneva were published in 1934 under the title *The Development of International Law by the Permanent Court of International Justice* (2nd and expanded edn, 1958).

Among Lauterpacht's numerous other books and articles, four require special mention: *The Function of Law in the International Community* (1933), *Recognition in International Law* (1947), and *International Law and Human Rights* (1950): the first being his most important contribution to the understanding and development of international law, the second his most comprehensive treatment of a topic of enduring and ever-increasing practical importance, the third the consecration of a lifelong interest and preoccupation. The fourth is his long anniversary article (*British Year Book of International Law*, 23, 1946) entitled 'The Grotian tradition in international law', which is a typical illustration of his own thinking and methods.

Concurrently Lauterpacht was fully occupied with his other academic duties. He took great pains with the standard course of lectures which he delivered as Whewell professor in Cambridge. The clarity of his presentation, the width of his learning, the skill of his exposition, and his own total commitment made an almost prophetical impression on a succession of audiences. The success of his lectures was an important factor in the development of international studies at Cambridge. His reputation at home and abroad gathered round him a large number of research students who have claimed it as a special distinction that they were trained under his rigorous supervision.

Lauterpacht's capacity for work was formidable, for in addition to the occupations already mentioned, he was concerned continuously with three major tasks—the editing, amplifying, and renovating of the standard two-volume textbook by L. F. L. Oppenheim on international law (now 'Oppenheim–Lauterpacht'); the editing of the *British Year Book of International Law*, of exceptional authority in this field, which was under his exclusive direction between 1944 and 1954; and the truly monumental *Annual Digest of Public International Cases* (later called the *International Law Reports*) with which he was connected from its outset and for which he had sole responsibility for the twenty-eight years from 1929 to 1956.

Lauterpacht's career culminated in his election in 1954 to a judgeship of the International Court of Justice, whereupon he was elected a bencher of his inn in 1955 and was knighted in 1956. It was universally expected that during his tenure of the nine-year office (and its probable renewals) he would add to his achievements an epoch-making series of judgments. His contributions as a judge were indeed not negligible; but he suffered a severe heart attack in 1959. He died on 8 May 1960 in the London Clinic, 20 Devonshire Place, London, as the result of an operation, at the judicially almost immature age of sixty-two, to the great and untimely loss of international legal science.

In his personal life, Lauterpacht was most simple and modest and quiet. He was exceptionally good-humoured and good-natured, dedicated indeed and devoted to his work and to his students but without solemnity, of high but straightforward moral principles, deeply attached to his wife and son and profoundly appreciative of the happiness of his home, kindly and friendly and cheerful. His only child, Elihu, himself attained distinction in the international legal world. A room in the Squire Law Library, Cambridge, was named after Hersch Lauterpacht.

C. J. HAMSON, *rev.*

Sources Lord McNair, *PBA*, 47 (1961), 371–85 · C. W. Jenks, 'Hersch Lauterpacht: the scholar as prophet', *British Year Book of International Law*, 36 (1960), 1–103; 37 (1961), 1–71; 38 (1962), 1–83; 39 (1963), 133–88 · N. Feinberg, ed., *Studies … in memory of Sir H. L.* (1961) · personal knowledge (1971) · private information (1971) · *The Times* (10 May 1960) · *WWW* · *CGPLA Eng. & Wales* (1961)
Archives Bodl. Oxf., corresp. with Lord Monckton
Likenesses Elliott & Fry, photograph, 1949?, NPG [*see illus.*] · M. Winiarska-Cotowika, bust, priv. coll.
Wealth at death £46,748 3s. 9d.: probate, 13 June 1961, *CGPLA Eng. & Wales*

Lauwerys, Joseph Albert (1902–1981), educationist, was born in Brussels on 7 November 1902, the eldest child in the family of two sons and two daughters of Henry Lauwerys, a tailor, and his wife, Louise Nagels. The family were mainly French speaking. In 1914 they fled to England just before the German occupation, establishing themselves there permanently. Lauwerys spent a year at Ratcliffe College, Leicestershire, and then completed his schooling at Bournemouth, where the family eventually settled. He left school early, and worked in a number of jobs, mainly as a shop assistant. Through the co-operative movement he was encouraged to pursue his education part-time and in 1927 obtained a first-class London University BSc general degree, from King's College. This was followed in successive years by honours degrees in chemistry and physics. He taught for a while in Stirling House, a private school in Bournemouth, but in 1928, upon the recommendation of T. Percy Nunn, of the London University Institute of Education, he became physics master at Christ's Hospital, Horsham. He was naturalized in 1928, and married in 1932 Waltraut Dorothy, from Germany, daughter of Hermann Bauermeister, publisher. They had three sons.

In 1932 Lauwerys was appointed lecturer in the methods of teaching science in schools at London University Institute of Education. During this period he wrote many science textbooks and works on scientific method and science teaching, as well as programmes for schools broadcasting. In 1946 Ghent University awarded him a doctorate for a thesis on film and radio as educational media. His interest in science teaching was lifelong.

However, the Second World War stimulated Lauwerys's different growing concern, education in other countries. In 1941 he had become reader in comparative education, and during the war led an inquiry initiated by the committee of allied ministers of education that met in London under R. A. Butler to plan educational reconstruction after the conflict. Promoted in 1947 to be the first professor of comparative education at London University Institute of Education, his work as adviser for UNESCO gave him further insights into how education might become an instrument for promoting peace and international understanding.

Lauwerys also saw his professional role as one of establishing comparative studies in education more firmly as a legitimate field of enquiry. In this, through his writings, his indefatigable development of international contacts, and his own teaching, he was eminently successful. Although he wrote no single major work his contribution as senior editor of the *World Year Book of Education* from 1947 to 1970 was invaluable. The thematic and global approach adopted in these twenty-four volumes which, for example, made more widely known such topics as economics and education (1956) and educational planning (1967), was highly innovative and acted as a catalyst for further research. His own numerous articles and monographs were equally influential. He was himself visiting professor at many universities ranging from the Americas to the Far East. He made the London Institute into the major graduate centre for comparative studies, particularly by his own charismatic lecturing. A polyglot, Lauwerys was a lively conversationalist and tenacious debater, communicating in his many varied activities an unbounded enthusiasm and zest for life.

Responsibilities and honours were showered upon

Lauwerys. Thus he was the British representative on the UNESCO conciliation and good offices commission dealing with discrimination in education. With Lord Boyle of Handsworth he co-chaired the education committee of the parliamentary group for world government. He was active in such organizations as the Council for Christians and Jews, the International New Education Fellowship, the International Montessori Association, and the Basic English movement. He saw the possibilities of using Basic English as a lingua franca for education in the 'third world'. *Professeur associé* at the Sorbonne from 1969 to 1971, he had been made a commander of the ordre des Palmes Académiques in 1961. His own university had conferred a DLitt upon him in 1958, and he was made a fellow of King's College, London.

Lauwerys retired from London University in 1970, but until 1976 was director of the Atlantic Institute of Education, Halifax, Nova Scotia. In his latter years both his Catholic upbringing and his scientific background, as well as a natural philosophical bent, led him to interest himself in Japanese efforts to establish a 'universal moral science', or 'moralogy', and in 1976 he published *Science, Morals and Moralogy*. He died at Guildford, Surrey, on 29 June 1981.

W. D. HALLS, rev.

Sources M. McLean, ed., 'Joseph A. Lauwerys, a Festschrift', *London Institute of Education Library Bulletin*, supplement 22 (1981) · V. Mallinson, 'Emeritus Professor J. A. Lauwerys (1902–1981)', *Comparative Education*, 17/3 (1981) · H. van Daele, 'Joseph Lauwerys (1902–1981) en de vergelijkende pedagogiek', *Persoon en Gemeenschap*, 24/6 (1981–2) · personal knowledge (2004) · private information (1990) · *CGPLA Eng. & Wales* (1981)
Archives U. Lond., Institute of Education, corresp. and papers
Wealth at death £109,722: probate, 15 Dec 1981, *CGPLA Eng. & Wales*

Lavelle, Patrick (1825–1886), Roman Catholic priest and Irish nationalist, was born at Mullagh, near Westport, co. Mayo, the eldest of five children of Francis Lavelle, a tenant farmer, and Mary MacManus. He entered St Jarlath's College, Tuam, co. Galway, in 1840, his education being paid for by an uncle, and in 1844 he moved on to St Patrick's College, Maynooth, to study for the priesthood. In 1851 he was ordained and spent the next three years at the Dunboyne Establishment in Maynooth. Between October 1854 and April 1858 he served as professor of philosophy at the Irish College, Paris, where John Miley was rector.

Lavelle's time in Paris saw a major confrontation with Miley. Throughout his life Lavelle was quick-tempered, aggressive, zealous, and confrontational—characteristics which first became apparent during his stay in Paris. In March 1858 Miley locked Lavelle and one of his colleagues out of the college, because of their disruptive influence, but they climbed over the back wall and refused to leave. After four days of turmoil Lavelle was expelled from both the college and Paris.

Lavelle spent the rest of his life as administrator and parish priest of Partry, co. Mayo (1858–69), and parish priest of Cong, co. Mayo (1869–86). He came to Partry at a time of much conflict between the local Catholic and Church of Ireland populations. It was alleged that evangelicals, led by the local landowner, who was also the protestant bishop of Tuam, Thomas, Baron Plunket, were proselytizing Catholics. Plunket was allegedly using his position as landlord to coerce his tenants into sending their children to the schools run by evangelicals. On his arrival in Partry, Lavelle attacked Plunket's activities and forbade his parishioners to send their children to these schools. He wrote to newspapers and addressed demonstrations denouncing Plunket and raised funds for the poor of Partry throughout Britain and Ireland. As a result of his activities in Partry, Lavelle rose to notoriety, enhancing his reputation through libel actions against Plunket's supporters. His position was helped when Plunket evicted sixty-eight people from their farms on 21 November 1860, ostensibly for burning land, but primarily because they supported Lavelle. Lavelle used this event to inform the world of the situation in Partry.

The funeral of the prominent nationalist Terence Bellew MacManus in November 1861 inaugurated a decade of conflict between Lavelle and Archbishop Paul Cullen of Dublin. Lavelle supported the MacManus funeral committee and delivered the graveside speech at Glasnevin, although Cullen had forbidden his clergy to participate in any way. His writings and speeches on the right of Catholics to revolt against unjust governments and his involvement with the National Brotherhood of St Patrick (of which he was vice-president between 1862 and 1864) also enraged Cullen. Lavelle never actually joined the Fenians and criticized them for administering a secret oath and for the 1867 rising. Nevertheless, Cullen felt he was an uncompromising Fenian and was infuriated by Lavelle's defence of revolutionary principles and the right to take up arms. While Rome stated that all secret societies were proscribed, Lavelle argued that the Fenians were not included as they were not mentioned by name. Lavelle's superior, Archbishop John MacHale of Tuam, defended him, using the opportunity to undermine Cullen's position within the Irish church. In April 1864 Cullen succeeded in persuading Rome to suspend Lavelle, although he was reinstated in 1865. Lavelle's enthusiasm for Fenianism was declining and he espoused constitutional nationalism under the influence of George Henry Moore, MP for Mayo. When the Vatican finally condemned the Fenians by name in January 1870 Lavelle's association with them ended.

Between 1868 and 1874 Lavelle was a major force in Mayo parliamentary politics and a leading member of the Home Government Association, actively supporting Captain Nolan's candidature in the 1872 Galway by-election. His political activity declined after 1874, partly because he lost the support of MacHale and partly because of the clergy's declining political dominance in Mayo. His transfer to Cong in October 1869 removed tensions with local landlords, as he had good relations with the landlord of Cong, Sir Arthur Guinness. While he attended a few Land League meetings in the early stages of the land agitation, his absence from most of its activities was conspicuous. His death on 17 November 1886 was met with indifference by a country engrossed with home rule. He was buried in Cong on 19 November. He published *The Irish Landlord since the Revolution* (1870), an examination of Irish landlord–tenant relations, and *Patriotism Vindicated: a Reply to Archbishop Manning* (1867), a defence of the Fenians' right to rebel.

GERARD MORAN

Sources G. Moran, *A radical priest in Mayo. Fr Patrick Lavelle: the rise and fall of an Irish nationalist, 1825–1886* (1994) · G. Moran, *The Mayo evictions of 1860: Fr Patrick Lavelle and the war in Partry* (1986) · G. Moran, 'The radical priest of Partry: Patrick Lavelle (1825–1886)', *Radical Irish priests, 1660–1970*, ed. G. Moran (Dublin, 1998), 113–30 · T. Ó Fiaich, 'The patriot priest of Partry, Patrick Lavelle, 1825–1886', *Journal of the Galway Archaeological and Historical Society*, 35 (1976), 129–48 · G. Moran, 'John Miley and the crisis at the Irish College, Paris, in the 1850s', *Archivum Hibernicum*, 50 (1996), 113–26 · E. Larkin, *The consolidation of the Roman Catholic church in Ireland, 1860–1870* (1987) · E. Larkin, *The making of the Roman Catholic church in Ireland, 1850–1860* (1980) · S. Gilley, 'The Catholic church and revolution in Ireland', *Terrorism in Ireland*, ed. Y. Alexander and A. O'Day (1984), 121–48 · G. Moran, 'The changing course of Mayo politics, 1867–1874', *'A various country': essays in Mayo history, 1500–1900*, ed. R. Gillespie and G. Moran (1987), 135–53 · register, St Jarlath's College, Tuam, co. Galway · register, St Patrick's College, Maynooth, co. Kildare · d. cert. · *Freeman's Journal* [Dublin] (20 Nov 1886) · *Connaught Telegraph* (27 Nov 1886)
Archives Dublin Diocesan Archives · Irish College, Paris, MSS | NA Ire., chief secretary's office · NL Ire., Isaac Butt MSS · NL Ire., Thomas Larcom MSS · NL Ire., George Henry Moore MSS · TCD, Larcom MSS
Likenesses T. Wynne, photograph, Wynne collection, Castlebar, co. Mayo

Lavenham [Lavyngham], **Richard** (*fl.* **1399–*c*.1403**), prior of the Carmelite convent, London, philosopher, and theologian, presumably came from the town of Lavenham, in Suffolk—John Leland and other early biographers report that he came from that region. He entered his order at Ipswich and completed his education at Oxford, where he advanced to the study of theology and may have earned the doctorate. Some sources from the sixteenth century and thereafter say that Lavenham became prior of the Carmelite convent at Bristol, but all such reports appear to be derived from John Bale, whose account of Lavenham is untrustworthy in other details. Bishop Robert Braybrooke's London register records that Lavenham was prior of the Carmelites at London in 1399, when he presented candidates for ordination. He was probably still active *c*.1400–03, since it was most likely at this time that he compiled a well-known list of heresies drawn from the works of the Wycliffite John Purvey.

It is sometimes said by early bibliographers and modern authors alike that Lavenham was Richard II's confessor. This view seems to be derived solely from a story in Polydore Vergil's *English History*, which mentions 'a certain Richard', a Carmelite, confessor to Richard II, who was killed on the outskirts of London together with Simon Sudbury and Sir John Hales during the peasants' revolt of 1381. Without endorsing it, Bale repeats this story and seems to have been the first to identify Polydore's Richard with Lavenham. He may be right about Polydore's intentions, but Braybrooke's register refutes the date 1381 for Lavenham's death. There appears to be no other reason for supposing that Lavenham was confessor to Richard II.

Uncertainty about the particulars of Lavenham's death dates back at least to the Reformation. There were three accounts in circulation. First, there is the story from Polydore, via Bale, that Lavenham died in 1381 in the peasants' revolt. Second, John Leland states categorically that Lavenham died at Winchester in 1383. (No other source associates Lavenham with Winchester.) Third, Bale also records that view that Lavenham died at Bristol, and gives the date 1383 in agreement with Leland. All three early traditions are contradicted, however, by the evidence of Braybrooke's register, and by Lavenham's collection of Purvey's heresies, which cannot have been written as early as that.

If the details of Lavenham's life are uncertain, somewhat more is known about his writings. Over sixty works have been attributed to him, many of which can still be identified. In theology, his list of Purvey's heresies is preserved in the *Fasciculi zizaniorum*. All but the last section of it was translated by John Foxe and published in the 1570 edition of his *Actes and Monumentes*. Lavenham is also said to have written a separate tract against the Lollards, a work concerning the controversy over evangelical poverty (*Defensorium pauperum* or *Clypeus paupertatis*), a commentary on Peter Lombard's *Sentences*, commentaries and notes on various books of the Bible (Isaiah, the epistle to Titus, Tobit), and a *Dictionary of the Scriptures*. Several early biographical reports note that Lavenham was an accomplished preacher and attribute to him one or more collections of sermons. On the other hand, despite his work against Purvey, there is no evidence that before John Bale's account in the sixteenth century Lavenham had any special reputation as a dedicated opponent of the Wycliffites or as an exceptionally skilled public debater.

Lavenham wrote an account of the founding of the Carmelite order and *A Litil Tretys*, in Middle English, on the seven deadly sins. Other religious works are attributed to him too.

In philosophy Lavenham produced commentaries on Aristotle's *Physics* and *Ethics*, a compendium of the *De caelo et mundo*, treatises on the soul and its powers, on the division of the continuum, and other topics. In logic in particular, Lavenham's writings have been preserved in two known collective manuscripts (BL, Sloane MS 3899, and Venice, San Marco, MS Zanetti lat. 300). In this area at least, he appears to have been an unoriginal and derivative author. Nevertheless his writings are valuable indicators of academic currents of thought in his day. His logical works include several of a quite summary nature that appear to be intended as handbooks for teaching. Among them is a *Summulae logicales*, containing standard logical doctrine drawn from Aristotle, Porphyry, and others. There are also short works on the semantic theory of supposition and on the theory of inference. His treatise on the logical behaviour of the words 'differ' and 'other' (*Tractatus qui differt et aliud nuncupatur*) seems to be the same as a work included in one version of the *Logica Oxoniensis*, a loose collection of logical writings that circulated in manuscript form during the fifteenth century. Again, his short study of syncategorematic words (*De syncategorematibus*—referring to words which cannot be used on their own, such as prepositions and conjunctions) is a version of a work that appeared in printed form in the *Libellus sophistarum ad usum Cantabrigiensium*.

In his *Tractatus de eventu futurorum*, on contingent propositions about the future, Lavenham presents a concise statement of William Ockham's view. His *Insolubilia*, on semantic paradoxes, is based in part on the work of Thomas Bradwardine (*d.* 1349), but its main interest lies in its extensive use of the Parisian Master Albert von Sachsen's work, whom he cites by name. The influence of continental authors is not often found so explicitly in Oxford logical writings of this period. Lavenham's discussion of the disputation-form known as *obligationes* is curious for adopting outright Roger Swineshead's theory, which most other authors both before and after Lavenham acknowledged but rejected out of hand. Lavenham's short work 'On the proofs of propositions' (*De probationibus propositionum*) is derived at least in part from Wyclif's treatment in the latter's *Logicae continuatio*. Lavenham's *De relativis*, a discussion of the semantics of relative pronouns, is an abbreviation of chapter 3 of William Heytesbury's *Regulae solvendi sophismata*. Many of Lavenham's other surviving writings have not yet been carefully studied by late twentieth-century scholars.

PAUL VINCENT SPADE

James Laver (1899–1975), by Karl Pollak, *c.*1948

Sources A. Hudson, 'John Purvey: a reconsideration of the evidence for his life and writings', *Lollards and their books* (1985), 85–110 [first pubd in *Viator*, 12 (1981), 355–80; crucial article for the dating of John Purvey, and so for dating Lavenham] · E. J. Ashworth and P. V. Spade, 'Logic in late medieval Oxford', *Hist. U. Oxf. 2: Late med. Oxf.*, 35–64 · P. V. Spade, 'The treatises *On modal propositions* and *On hypothetical propositions* by Richard Lavenham', *Mediaeval Studies*, 35 (1973), 49–59 [incl. analysis of the contents of BL, MS Sloane 3899] · P. V. Spade, 'Notes on some manuscripts of logical and physical works by Richard Lavenham', *Manuscripta* [St Louis], 19 (1975), 139–46 [analysis of Venice, San Marco, MS Zanetti lat. 300 (1872), incl. 30 treatises by Lavenham] · Bale, *Cat.* · P. Vergil, *Anglicae historiae* (Basel, 1546) · *Commentarii de scriptoribus Britannicis, auctore Joanne Lelando*, ed. A. Hall, 2 vols. (1709) · L. M. De Rijk, '*Logica Oxoniensis*: an attempt to reconstruct a fifteenth century Oxford manual of logic', *Medioevo*, 3 (1977), 121–64 · P. V. Spade, 'Richard Lavenham and the Cambridge logic', *Studies in medieval linguistic thought dedicated to Geoffrey L. Bursill-Hall*, ed. K. Koerner, H. -J. Niederehe, and R. H. Robins (1980), 241–7 [vol. appeared as two issues of *Historiographia Linguistica*, 7, nos. 1/2] · *Libellus sophistarum ad usum Cantabrigien[sis]* [1510] [1510 and 1524] · [T. Netter], *Fasciculi zizaniorum magistri Johannis Wyclif cum tritico*, ed. W. W. Shirley, Rolls Series, 5 (1858) [incl. Lavenham's collection of Purvey's heresies pp. 383–99] · J. Foxe, *The first volume of the ecclesiasticall history contayning the actes and monumentes of thynges passed*, new edn (1570) [incl. (649–53) an Eng. trans. of all but the last section of Lavenham's collection of Purvey's heresies]

Archives BL, Sloane MS 3899 · San Marco, Venice, MS Zanetti lat. 300

Laver, James (1899–1975), expert on fashion and writer, was born in Liverpool on 14 March 1899, the second child and only son of Arthur James Laver, maritime printer and stationer, and his wife, Florence Mary Barker. The family were strict Congregationalists. He was educated at the Liverpool Institute and at New College, Oxford, his college fees and the expenses of many English and foreign travels being subsidized by a rich shipping magnate, Lawrence D. Holt. His war service as a second lieutenant caused his residence at New College to be deferred until 1919, but by 1921 he had taken his BA degree, gaining a second class in modern history, and by 1922 had added a BLitt in theology, for a thesis on John Wesley. In 1921 he won the Newdigate prize with a poem on Cervantes, and began moving in literary, instead of 'hearty', circles, becoming a regular contributor to *Isis*. In the long vacations he climbed mountains in Switzerland, travelled in Germany, and developed his keen visual faculties at every opportunity. In 1922 Laver entered the department of engraving, illustration, design, and painting at the Victoria and Albert Museum, where he was eventually keeper (1938–59). While there he used his leisure to write contributions to magazines, and much light verse. What he described as 'my first real piece of luck as a literary man' was the publication of a verse narrative, an open pastiche of Alexander Pope called *A Stitch in Time* (1927). Being in exactly the right key for the period, it sold rapidly, and he was soon in demand at the fashionable parties for which the decade was notable. No social activities, however, were allowed to interfere with his voluntary classes for the Working Men's College at Camden Town. At first he ran an English literature course but after two years—about 1926—with the aid of Percy Horton he reorganized the art class, which until then had never had living models.

Although his puritanical upbringing had prevented his going to a theatre until he was adult, Laver now became an enthusiast. This may partly have been due to his having in his charge a vast accumulation of theatre material (he produced a book on theatre design with George Sheringham in 1927), but it was enhanced by his attachment to a gifted Irish actress, (Bridget) Veronica Turleigh (d. 1971), daughter of Martin Turley of the Royal Irish Constabulary. He married her in 1928; they had a son and a daughter. The couple spent their first years in a flat in Piccadilly, where their theatrical friends formed a habit of 'dropping in for drinks after the show'. Laver engaged in any literary work for which he could receive payment—dramatic criticism, book reviews, and translations of plays, all done after a full day at the museum.

It was after moving to Chelsea that Laver found time to write Nymph Errant (1932), a novel about the adventures of a girl on her way back to her finishing school. Not only was this a bestseller, but in 1933 it was turned into a musical by the leading impresario C. B. Cochran, with songs by Cole Porter and Gertrude Lawrence as leading lady. Its success was immense and the film rights were competed for. Laver confessed to having been made 'a little dizzy' by this heady experience. He continued to write fiction, however, and to do theatrical and film work on a less ambitious scale, but renounced the transient idea of living by his pen.

Laver also wrote on J. A. McN. Whistler (1930), James Tissot (1936), French nineteenth-century painting (1937), and several works on costume for museum publication. His interest in costume had grown out of his need to know the details of dress in order to date pictures. He formed a philosophy of costume, expounded in Taste and Fashion (1937), an important work on which he elaborated in several later books. Not all his theories were unquestionable (for example, the idea that the feminine waistline is raised or lowered in times of war or civil strife can only be upheld by very selective glimpses of the mode), but he brought a much more knowledgeable eye to his study of the sources and cycles of fashion than most of his predecessors in this field. The outbreak of war in 1939 engendered many problems in connection with dispersing the treasures of the Victoria and Albert Museum to places of safety. Laver urged that almost the greatest treasures of all were the catalogues. 'To replace a hundred years of cataloguing', he said, 'would take a hundred years.' His A Complete Catalogue of the Etchings and Drypoints of Arthur Briscoe (1930) demonstrates Laver's scholarship within his own department at the museum.

During its closure Laver was transferred for a brief period to the Treasury, but it was soon decided that so good a public speaker would be put to better use promoting the national savings campaign. He addressed innumerable speeches to munition workers, miners, shipbuilders, labourers constructing airfields, and had the knack of holding the attention of tired or even reluctant audiences. During long train journeys he studied the London Library's holdings under the rubric 'occultism', and he published a book on the sixteenth-century prophet Nostradamus in 1942.

On returning to the museum after the war, Laver resumed his writing on costume and allied subjects, and also wrote a biography of J. K. Huysmans, The First Decadent (1954). He became well known for his part in radio programmes, especially The Brains Trust and The Critics, and was probably the first to demonstrate through television the workings of fashion, using genuine costumes. He was also a frequent and valued contributor to the Dictionary of National Biography. He retired from the museum in 1959 and later moved to Blackheath, London. He was equable and adaptable to an uncommon degree, he was learned without being pedantic, and convivial without becoming intemperate, a quietly genial man. He is now remembered for his analysis of fashion trends and his books on art and artists.

Laver was appointed CBE in 1951, and was also a fellow of the Royal Society of Arts and of the Royal Society of Literature and honorary member of the Royal Society of Painter-Printmakers. An honorary doctorate was conferred on him by Manchester University. His wife died in 1971 as the result of an accident and Laver's own death occurred in a fire at 10 The Glebe, his Blackheath home, on 3 June 1975. 							DORIS LANGLEY MOORE, rev.

Sources J. Laver, Museum piece (1963) [autobiography] · personal knowledge (1986) · private information (1986) · CGPLA Eng. & Wales (1975) · The Times (4 June 1975) · R. Martin, 'Brave new wardrobe, or James Laver's speculations on the prospects for fashion in A letter to a girl on the future of clothes', Arts Magazine, 62 (Nov 1987), 60–61

Archives Ransom HRC, corresp. and literary papers · U. Glas. L., corresp.

Likenesses H. Coster, two photographs, 1933–6, NPG · K. Pollak, photograph, c.1948, NPG [see illus.]

Wealth at death £15,160: probate, 24 Oct 1975, CGPLA Eng. & Wales

Laverty [née Kelly], **Maura** (1907–1966), journalist and writer, was born on 15 May 1907 in Rathangan, co. Kildare, Ireland, the second eldest of thirteen children of Michael Kelly, variously a farmer, draper, and merchant, and his wife, Maryanne Tracey, a dressmaker. The family lived on an estate of 200 acres but her father's gambling ruined the family financially. On his death Kelly's mother turned to dressmaking to support herself and nine surviving children. Kelly's grandmother, who is idealized in one of her novels, also had a dressmaking business in Kildare. Kelly boarded at the Brigidine convent in Tullow, co. Carlow, with the intention of being a teacher, but she appears to have been an unwilling pupil.

At the age of nineteen Kelly went to Bilbao in Spain as a governess. She was treated badly and had a couple of unhappy love affairs, including a short engagement to a Hungarian called Peter, which was soon broken off. She later acted as secretary to the writer Princess Bibesco and also earned a living as a 'foreign correspondent', at the Banco Calamarte and as a freelance journalist in Madrid working on the daily El debate. In 1928 she returned to Dublin and worked as a journalist and broadcaster with the newly established national broadcasting station Radio Éireann. In Dublin, on 3 November 1928, she married the journalist Seamus (James) Laverty, with whom she had corresponded while in Spain; they had a son and two daughters. The family's finances were precarious (her husband lost money through a business venture with the

Irish sweepstake), and Maura Laverty began to write in the 1940s to support her family. The marriage ended in separation. Laverty remained with Radio Éireann; she was in charge of women and children's programmes and hosted the electricity supply board's radio programme for eleven years, discussing books, poetry, and matters of interest to women.

Laverty's first book, *Flour Economy* (1941), was a popular self-help book on how to overcome wartime shortages. Her first novel *Never No More* (1942) was based on her own life growing up in Kildare and inspired by her grandmother's cooking. It was enormously successful and well received by such critics as Sean O'Faoláin. The *New York Times* noted that it was a 'book written as only one of Irish blood could write it, breathing a civilisation that has never succumbed to industrial strain or to overexigencies of modernity' (Binchy, xvii). Two of her novels were banned in Ireland for their sexual and political content: *Alone we Embark* (1943; published as *Touched by the Thorn* in the USA), with a central character who undertakes two unhappy marriages, which received the Irish women writers' award in 1944, and *No More than Human* (1944), a sequel to *Never No More*, the story of a Kildare girl working as a governess in Spain. In 1945 she published a children's story, *The Cottage in the Bog* (*Gold of Glanaree* in the USA), and in 1946 she brought out *Lift up your Gates* (1946), a study of slum life in Dublin which was later republished as *Liffey Lane* in 1947. In the same year she published another cookery book *Kind Cooking* illustrated by Louis le Brocquy which was the Irish non-fiction book of the month in America. In 1948 she scripted an election campaign film for Clann na Poblachta entitled *Our Country* and directed by Liam O'Leary. This highlighted the problems of Ireland in the 1940s. The narration is interspersed with footage of dole queues and dirty tenements contrasted with shop windows stocked with imported luxury goods. In 1949 she produced another children's book, *Green Orchard*.

In the 1950s Laverty adapted *Liffey Lane* as a series of plays including *Tolka Row*, subtitled *A Play of Dublin Life*, which was an exploration of the day-to-day life of the Nolan family set on the fringes of Dublin city. Her cookbook *Full and Plenty* (1960) made her a much loved national figure. In 1964 Laverty adapted *Tolka Row* for television with the script editor Carolyn Swift. It became a long-running, popular weekly serial for Radio Telefís Éireann and was its first soap opera. In the 1960s Laverty also presented her own radio programme featuring 'agony aunt' advice, listeners' letters, and recipes.

Laverty had suffered some ill health early in 1966 and had been hospitalized with a broken hip in March of that year. She died of a heart attack at 30 Butterfield Drive, Rathfarnham, Dublin, in July 1966, having left hospital in June. In 1995 her fairy tales were collected in *The Queen of Aran's Daughter* with illustrations by her daughter Barry Castle. She is fondly remembered for her cookbooks, and *Never No More* and *No More than Human* appeared as Virago Classics in the 1980s.   MARIA LUDDY

Sources M. Binchy, introduction, in M. Laverty, *Never no more* (1985), xi–xix · *Irish Times* (28 July 1966) · S. J. Brown and D. J. Clarke, *Ireland in fiction*, 2 (1985) · www.pgil-eirdata.org/html/az-datasets/authors/1/Laverty_Maura/life.htm · Blain, Clements & Grundy, *Feminist comp.* · P. Parker and F. Kermode, eds., *The reader's companion to twentieth-century writers* (1995) · b. cert. · m. cert. · d. cert. · C. Clear, '"I can talk about it, can't I?": the Ireland Maura Laverty desired, 1942–46', *Women's Studies*, 30/6 (2001), 819–35
Archives U. Reading, Longman Group archives, corresp.
Likenesses photograph, repro. in *The Bell*, 11/4 (1946)

Lavery, Hazel Jenner, Lady Lavery (1880–1935). *See under* Lavery, Sir John (1856–1941).

Lavery, Sir John (1856–1941), painter, was born in Belfast, the second son of Henry Lavery (*d.* 1859), a publican, and his wife, Mary Donnelly (*d.* 1859). His exact date of birth is unknown, but he was baptized in St Patrick's Roman Catholic Church, Donegal Street, Belfast, on 26 March 1856. His father died in the sinking of the *Pomona*, *en route* for New York, on 29 April 1859; three months later his mother died, apparently of grief. Lavery then lived with his father's brother and his wife, aunt Rose, on their farm until, at the age of ten, he was sent to live in Saltcoats, Ayrshire, with a cousin of Rose, a pawnbroker. When he was seventeen he was apprenticed to a photographer in Glasgow and resolved to become a painter. He was a successful and diligent employee and saved enough from his salary to pay his fees at the Haldane Academy of Art in Glasgow, a predecessor of the Glasgow School of Art, which followed the South Kensington curriculum.

In his earliest paintings Lavery was influenced by the work of various minor but financially successful Glasgow artists, usually historical genre painters, whose pictures were derided by the group of painters with whom Lavery was later associated, the *Glasgow Boys. This admiration of an ability to earn a substantial living by painting popular but aesthetically inferior work is indicative of an ambitious and calculating streak in Lavery's character which perhaps prevented him from making the best intellectual and artistic use of his undoubted facility as a painter. Two incidents give evidence of his ruthlessness. His sister, who lived in his Glasgow flat as his housekeeper, became pregnant, and Lavery encouraged her to follow her lover to America, thus concealing her plight from his social circle. She soon returned, however, pregnant again, and Lavery refused to take her in. Two days later she committed suicide, drowning in the River Clyde. When, in his eighties, he wrote his autobiography, secure in his knighthood and social position, Lavery was able to express his remorse, but in 1876 she was a social embarrassment to an aspiring young painter. From the late 1870s he began to exhibit his genre paintings in and around Glasgow and with the proceeds bought and insured a studio in the city. Very shortly afterwards it succumbed to a mysterious fire, and with the £300 insurance money Lavery financed his departure in 1880 for the Heatherley School of Fine Art in London and then Paris.

Lavery enrolled at the Atelier Julian in Paris in 1881 and began to associate with the young British and American artists who followed the *plein-air* creed of Jules Bastien-Lepage. The latter's impact on these young artists, including James Guthrie and Stanhope Forbes, was crucial in the

Sir John Lavery (1856–1941), by Walter Stoneman, 1918

development of British painting in the 1880s. Lavery sought him out and eventually followed his example of painting contemporary life by settling in Grez-sur-Loing, where he painted the life of the village and its inhabitants *en plein air*. He was joined at Grez by two other Glasgow artists, William Kennedy and Thomas Millie Dow, and together they formed one of the three distinct factions of the group that was to become known as the Glasgow Boys. Throughout the early 1880s Lavery often returned to Glasgow and was a frequent exhibitor at the Royal Glasgow Institute of the Fine Arts, where he would have seen the works of James *Guthrie, E. A. *Walton, George Henry, and William York Macgregor. They were also responding to the naturalism of Bastien-Lepage, and from 1885 they joined with Lavery and other Glasgow artists of similar interests in forming a loose association of painters who were to exhibit together in Glasgow, London, and across Europe and North America. Despite Lavery's adherence to Bastien-Lepage's teaching and example, his paintings of this period retain an anecdotal or narrative element, as he realized that this was vital in ensuring sales to an unsophisticated Scottish clientele. Even in his masterpiece of this period, *On the Loing, an Afternoon Chat* (1884; Ulster Museum, Belfast), there is a strong element of genre that is missing in the work of James Guthrie and E. A. Walton, his main Glasgow rivals. Further, on his return to Scotland in 1885, Lavery realized that to sell to the middle classes he needed to change his subject matter from the rural poor to something more socially acceptable. This resulted in *The Tennis Party* (1885; Aberdeen Art

Gallery), a key work in the development of British painting, both in its artistic complexity and subject matter and in its translation of naturalistic painting from rural subjects to a more sophisticated urban setting.

In addition this picture owed much to photography, in which Lavery was a skilled practitioner, although he concealed its use as it was not considered a valid artistic tool. It was also of vital assistance to him in the completion of the work which was a foundation of his career as one of the leading portrait painters of his age. In 1888 Glasgow staged a major international exhibition in Kelvingrove Park. Its aim was to raise funds for a new municipal art gallery, and the Glasgow Boys played a considerable part in the organization of its artistic events. Lavery painted a series of small pictures, sometimes little more than vignettes, of the events, buildings, and colourful figures which characterized the success of the exhibition. The exhibition was visited by Queen Victoria, and Glasgow corporation offered a commission of £600 for an artist to record the formal ceremony of her visit. The fee did not attract many artists, as the successful artist would be expected to record all of the 253 persons present. Lavery realized that the commission would be a milestone in his career and accepted the enormous task, not without some trepidation. He had surreptitiously photographed the ceremony from a vantage point above the queen's dais, and this photograph became the basis for his composition. He had some difficulty persuading the various participants to sit for him but eventually settled for a formula of making a quick sketch and taking a portrait photograph in his studio. Many of these sketches, like the exhibition pictures themselves, confirm his gifts as reporter, and once the queen had been persuaded to give him a twenty-minute sitting he found that the other participants in the event were unable to refuse his requests for sittings. The result, *The State Visit of Queen Victoria to the International Exhibition, Glasgow, 1888* (1888; Glasgow Museums and Art Galleries), although somewhat stiff and unnatural compared to Lavery's contemporary work, formed the basis of his subsequent career.

In 1889 Lavery met Kathleen McDermott (*née* Annie Evans; *c*.1872–1891), whom he married in 1890 and who died a year later after giving birth to their daughter, Eileen. He painted many of the leading industrialists and society figures of the period, including Miss Mary Burrell (1895; Glasgow Museums and Art Galleries), the daughter of the shipowner and art collector Sir William Burrell; and also, in 1893, R. B. Cunninghame Graham (Glasgow Museums and Art Galleries), who became a close friend and introduced him to Morocco, where a number of the Glasgow Boys, among them Joseph Crawhall, Arthur Melville, William Kennedy, and Thomas Millie Dow, were also to live and paint. He was elected a member of the Royal Scottish Academy in 1896 and began to exhibit at the Royal Academy in London. Lavery's career was by this time well established, and as the Glasgow Boys achieved national and international renown he moved to London in 1896. In 1897 he helped establish the International Society of Painters, Gravers, and Sculptors in London, with

J. A. M. Whistler as president and himself as vice-president. Whistler became a close friend and inspiration for many of his finest later portraits, but his reputation was made by his success as a more prosaic portrait painter than Whistler had ever been.

Although Lavery continued to paint a wide variety of subjects, often drawn from his life in Morocco, where he had a house in Tangier, he was best-known for formal portraits of the royal family (*The King, the Queen, the Prince of Wales, the Princess Mary*, 1911; NPG) and those of major social and political figures of his day, notably *La dame aux perles* (*Baroness von Hölriggl*) (1901) and *Winston S. Churchill, MP* (1915) (both Hugh Lane Municipal Art Gallery, Dublin). He was also accomplished in the rendering of complex interior studies, which reflected his interest, among other things, in contemporary politics and racing—such as the trial of Roger Casement in *The Court of Criminal Appeal* (1916; Hugh Lane Municipal Art Gallery, Dublin) and *The Jockey's Dressing Room at Ascot* (1923; Tate collection). As a war artist he produced the memorable *First Wounded at London Hospital* (1914; Dundee Museums and Galleries) and *A Convoy, North Sea, 1918, from NS7* (IWM).

Lavery's own family life, particularly after his marriage to Hazel Martyn Trudeau [**Hazel Jenner Lavery**, Lady Lavery (1880–1935)], provided material for many of his finest later works (such as *The Studio Window, 7 July 1917*; Hugh Lane Municipal Art Gallery, Dublin). Lavery met Hazel, who was born in Chicago on 14 March 1880, the daughter of the industrialist Edward Jenner Martyn, in Brittany in 1903, shortly before her marriage, on 28 December 1903, to Dr Edward Livingstone Trudeau junior (1863?–1904), with whom she had a daughter, Alice, born after Trudeau's death in May 1904. Lavery married her, with Cunninghame Graham as best man, on 22 July 1909. Hazel Lavery became one of the great society hostesses of her day—the friend, confidante, and occasionally lover to many powerful social and political figures. Her close friendship with Michael Collins was crucial in his negotiations with the British government over the future of the Irish Free State in 1920–21.

Lavery and his wife were supporters of Irish home rule, and after the establishment of the Irish Free State they spent much time in Dublin, although Lavery never denied or neglected his roots in Belfast; he presented large groups of his paintings to both cities. Such was his involvement with Irish politics and politicians of the 1920s and 1930s—he painted Eamon de Valera and a posthumous portrait of Michael Collins—that his portrait of Hazel as the personification of Ireland, Cathleen ni Houlihann (*Killarney*; Central Bank, Dublin), was incorporated on the free state banknotes, in use from 1928 to 1975. Hazel died on 1 January 1935, and Lavery's daughter, Eileen, also died in the same year. A grieving Lavery moved to the USA and established another career as a portrait painter of America's aristocracy, the stars of Hollywood, painting, among others, Maureen O'Sullivan, Loretta Young, and Shirley Temple.

Lavery was honoured by academies and institutes around the world. He was knighted in 1918, and was a member of the orders of the Crown of Italy and of Leopold of Belgium. In 1906 he became a member of the Royal Hibernian Academy and in 1921 of the Royal Academy; he was also a member of the academies of Rome, Antwerp, Milan, Brussels, and Stockholm. He was a freeman of both Belfast and Dublin and received honorary doctorates from the Queen's University of Belfast and Trinity College, Dublin.

Lavery died on 10 January 1941 at Rossenarra House, Kilkenny, Ireland, and was buried at Putney Vale cemetery, London. After his death his reputation began to wane, as social and financial ambition had set him apart from the other Glasgow Boys, who similarly aimed for recognition and security as painters but who did not compromise their work as frequently as Lavery did. By the end of the twentieth century, however, with the critical reassessment of the advances made both by the Glasgow Boys and by other naturalist painters of the period, his early paintings were recognized by a steep rise in their price. The few guineas achieved by Christies for major late works at the end of the 1940s have been eclipsed by the hundreds of thousands of pounds regularly paid for his early works some fifty years after his death.   ROGER BILLCLIFFE

Sources W. S. Sparrow, *John Lavery and his work* (1911) · J. Lavery, *Life of a painter* (1940) · K. McConkey, *Sir John Lavery* (1993) · S. McCoole, *Hazel: life of Lady Lavery, 1880–1935* (1996) · m. cert.
Archives Tate collection, corresp., papers, picture registers | NL Scot., letters to R. B. Cunninghame Graham
Likenesses J. Lavery, self-portrait, oils, 1896–7, Musée National d'Art Moderne, Paris · J. Lavery, self-portrait, oils, 1906–11, Uffizi Gallery, Florence; related portrait, 1928, Ulster Museum, Belfast · photograph, 1909, NPG · W. Stoneman, photograph, 1918, NPG [*see illus.*] · J. Gunn, chalk drawing, *c.*1924, Art Gallery and Museum, Glasgow · G. H. Paulin, bronze head, exh. RA 1935, Art Gallery and Museum, Glasgow · H. Mann, oils, 1936, Art Gallery and Museum, Glasgow · GAL, ink and wash caricature, NPG · J. Kerr-Lawson, oils, Ferens Art Gallery, Kingston upon Hull · J. Kerr-Lawson, pencil drawing, Scot. NPG · J. Lavery, self-portrait, oils, Musée d'Orsay, Paris · Lady Hazel Lavery, oils, Hugh Lane Municipal Gallery of Modern Art, Dublin · B. Partridge, pencil and chalk caricature, NPG; repro. in *Punch* (30 March 1927) · A. P. Ritchie, caricature, mechanical reproduction, NPG; repro. in *VF* (7 May 1913) · D. Wilson, caricature drawing, Hugh Lane Municipal Gallery of Modern Art, Dublin · double portrait, oils (with Shirley Temple), priv. coll. · photographs, repro. in McConkey, *Sir John Lavery*

Lavington. For this title name *see* Payne, Ralph, Baron Lavington (1739–1807).

Lavington, Frederick (1881–1927), economist, was born on 19 November 1881 at Broad Hinton, Wiltshire, son of Henry Lavington, farmer, and his wife, Katherine Ann Chandler (*d.* in or after 1927). He was educated at Marlborough College, Wiltshire, and, after eleven years' service in the Capital and Counties Bank, he went into residence in 1908 at Emmanuel College, Cambridge. Together with D. H. Robertson, H. Henderson, G. F. Shove, C. W. Guillebaud, P. Sargant Florence, P. Noel-Baker, and H. Dalton, he was among J. M. Keynes's first students at Cambridge. After taking his degree in 1911 (a first class in economics) he received a research scholarship from his college, and in the following year he won the Adam Smith prize for his dissertation, 'The agencies by which capital is associated with business power'. In 1912 he published his maiden scientific article in the *Economic Journal*, 'Uncertainty in relation to the rate of interest'.

Though fully qualified for an academic career, Lavington returned to administrative work, this time in the civil service. In 1912 he obtained a post in the newly created labour exchanges department of the Board of Trade. During this six-year spell in government he became seriously ill, and though he never recovered fully he returned to Cambridge in 1918 for the most active intellectual years of his life. Elected in 1920 to the Girdlers' lectureship in economics in succession to Keynes, he published in the following year his *magnum opus*, *The English Capital Market*, in which he cleverly blended new insights in monetary theory with his banking experience. In 1922 he was elected a fellow of Emmanuel College and published a textbook, *The Trade Cycle*.

Despite ill health, Lavington's services were very valuable in the life of Cambridge University and his college. He helped in drafting the new statutes that the royal commission on Oxford and Cambridge demanded, he took part in the administrative work of the college, and he presided over the college hockey club and a lively Emmanuel economics society. Little is known about his personality. C. R. Fay described him as an excellent and tough supervisor. Harold Wright quipped about Lavington's 'firm and peculiar standards of conduct and personal relationships': if 'by some happy chance one had passed his obscure tests and qualified for his friendship', Lavington would be the best of friends (Wright, *Economic Journal*). Eventually his modesty and his self-effacing personality explain in part why his influence on Cambridge economics was less than it might otherwise have been. Having lived so long in the presence of death he died, without descendants, on 8 July 1927 in the Evelyn Nursing Home, Cambridge, leaving his property to his mother.

During his decade as an academic economist Lavington was the most orthodox of Cambridge economists. The whole Cambridge school was at the time dominated by the teaching of Alfred Marshall (1842–1924). But Lavington went much further than simply acknowledging the still living master's towering influence. He seemed almost to believe in the literal inspiration of Marshall's writings. This reverence for his master was reflected in his favourite saying (as reported by Wright): 'It's all in Marshall, if you'll only take the trouble to dig it out' (Wright, 504). If Keynes—another Marshallian—has often been accused of 'unnecessary originality' (Myrdal, 8), Lavington probably suffered from the opposite vice, an excess of modesty as to the novelty of his theoretical contribution. His own work in monetary theory and on the capital market was designed to fill in the details left out by Marshall. For him, only the application of Marshall's analysis to practical problems remained to be done; he did not consider improving on an economic analysis that he considered as practically completed. However, he developed Marshall's

monetary theory in an original direction much earlier than Keynes did.

Lavington's central contribution to monetary economics appears in his *English Capital Market* (1921, 29–33). Basically, and for the first time in the literature, he extends the analysis of the demand for money beyond money in the form of income deposits (transactions demand for money) to take account of the influence on this demand of the rate of interest and of the general state of expectations. His discussion of the 'general principles on which [people] allocate their resources among competing uses' is one of the clearest attempts at the time in England of reintegrating money into the general theory of choice. Most importantly, the individual demand for money is no longer exclusively determined by the level of income, or the 'volume of payments'. To the traditional Marshallian transactions motive (Marshall's k in the famous cash balance equation) is added a 'security motive', according to which part of the total demand for cash is held against 'the uncertain events of the future', or, alternatively, 'on the degree of uncertainty in [the] business situation'. Despite adding the 'general level of confidence' as the second determinant of the demand for money, Lavington fails to make an explicit mention of the individual's wealth as yet another determinant of the demand for cash. The 'wealth motive' being still missing, he cannot formally relate variations of the demand for money either to the price of securities that can be held as alternative assets or indeed to the rate of interest.

A decade later, in his *Treatise on Money* (1930), Keynes eventually provided the missing link (without, however, referring to Lavington's earlier attempt): the liquidity preference analysis of the demand for money implies that there is a direct influence of this demand on the rate of interest. To the long-recognized wealth effect of money changes is added a portfolio adjustment substitution effect: changes in the composition of portfolio assets can alter the rate of interest without any money change having to take place. During later debates on the theory of interest, J. R. Hicks (1935) and D. H. Robertson (1937) eventually rescued from oblivion Lavington's prescient elaboration of the Cambridge cash balance theory.

PASCAL BRIDEL

Sources H. Wright, *Economic Journal*, 37 (1927), 503–4 · C. R. Fay, *Economic Journal*, 37 (1927), 504–5 · *Emmanuel College Magazine*, 27 (1928), 67–8 · b. cert. · G. Myrdal, *Monetary equilibrium* (1939) · P. Bridel, *Cambridge monetary thought* (1987) · P. Bridel, 'Lavington, F.', *The new Palgrave: a dictionary of economics*, ed. J. Eatwell, M. Milgate, and P. Newman, 4 vols. (1987) · D. Patinkin, 'Keynesian monetary theory and the Cambridge school', *Issues in monetary economics*, ed. H. G. Johnson and A. R. Nobay (1974) · Emmanuel College archives, Cambridge

Wealth at death £2,249 0s. 7d.: probate, 11 Oct 1927, CGPLA Eng. & Wales

Lavington, George (1684–1762), bishop of Exeter, was born and baptized on 18 January 1684 at Mildenhall, near Marlborough, Wiltshire, the son of Joseph Lavington, a Church of England clergyman, and his wife, Elizabeth. He

George Lavington (1684–1762), by Thomas Gainsborough, c.1760

was educated at Winchester College, which he entered as a scholar in 1698, and was admitted as probationer at New College, Oxford, in 1706, where he became a full fellow in 1708. He was ordained priest in 1712, and took the degrees of BCL and DCL in 1713 and 1732 respectively. Appointed rector of Upper Heyford, Oxfordshire, in 1717, he resigned his fellowship at New College the following year and held the living until 1730. In 1719 he obtained a stall at Worcester, where he was to become prebendary treasurer. In 1730 he was made rector of St Michael Bassishaw, London, and, in 1731, a canon residentiary of St Paul's Cathedral. He was appointed chaplain-in-ordinary to the king, and from 1742 to 1747 he held the rectory of St Mary Aldermary in London, which was annexed to the parish of St Thomas the Apostle. He was nominated to the bishopric of Exeter in December 1746 and was consecrated in February 1747; he held the see, while holding other livings in plurality, until his death.

Lavington is chiefly remembered for his attack on the early Methodists, *The Enthusiasm of Methodists and Papists, Compar'd*. His anger was initially aroused when a paper, purporting to be part of his primary visitation charge, was circulated in manuscript and then printed; it represented him as a supporter of Methodism. In September 1748 he stated in the press that the paper was no part of his charge and declared his hostility to the Methodists. The matter did not die and Selina, countess of Huntingdon, later obliged him to own that John Wesley and George Whitefield were utterly unconnected with the fabrication.

Goaded by these events Lavington anonymously published parts one and two of *The Enthusiasm of Methodists* in 1749; a third part followed in 1751. The work was learned

and wide ranging but also rambling, crude, and sometimes caustic. Its form was simple: it detailed the Methodists' behaviour, often substantiating its claims with quotations from Wesley's *Journal* or from Whitefield's *God's Dealings with the Rev. George Whitefield*, and made comparison with various 'Antichristian Saints' of the Roman Catholic church (pt 1, 32). Thus the Methodists' personal mortifications, ecstatic raptures, vainglory, and other perceived characteristics were ridiculed and castigated. So was their undutiful behaviour towards the civil powers. Enthusiasm was '*Religion run mad*' (ibid., 81), the Methodists 'rambling, warm-headed, *itinerant Teachers*' (pt 2, 63). In addition Lavington detailed case histories of those who had become frenzied or had suffered convulsions through their contact with the Methodists: '[s]ome of their wild Tenets, and horrid Doctrines, have so harrow'd the Souls of the poor People, and caused such a vehement Distraction, as to drive them into *Despair, Madness*, and *Bedlam*' (pt 3, 3).

Lavington's *Enthusiasm* can be dismissed as a brutal diatribe but it should be remembered that Methodism was attacked from many quarters in its early years. Nor were all the charges contained in the *Enthusiasm*, or its central premise, far from the mark. Lavington also made earnest efforts to discover the truth about Methodist activity in his diocese. He (now openly) and Wesley continued the debate in pamphlets. On 29 August 1762 Wesley recorded in his *Journal*: 'I was well pleased to partake of the Lord's Supper with my old opponent, Bishop Lavington' (pt 4, 527). Lavington died on 13 September 1762. His monument in Exeter Cathedral records that he was a 'successfull Exposer of Pretence & Enthusiasm'.

Lavington was also deeply hostile to the Moravians. There are swipes at them in *The Enthusiasm of Methodists* but in 1755 he published *The Moravians Compared and Detected*. Lavington made his intention clear at the start of the work: 'to draw a *Comparison* between *Count Zinzendorf and his Society*, and the *Ringleaders and Disciples* of the most *Infamous Antient Heretics*' (p. 1). This he did, treating not only theological issues but also various sexual charges brought against the Moravians. Comparisons were also made between the Moravians and the papists. Although erudite the book's form is clumsy (with its sections on Moravians and Parallels); it is crude and rambling. Again the work must be viewed in context. There was much antagonism to the Moravians in the mid-1750s, and nearly all the bishops, who, with the exception of Lavington, had been their supporters a few years before, were now hostile—a change largely wrought by the efforts of Henry Rimius, to whom Lavington's work owed much.

Respecting politics Lavington was a whig; his monument at Exeter notes that he 'early distinguished himself By a conscientious & disinterested attachment To the cause of Liberty and the Reformation'. A leading member of the whig Constitution Club in tory Oxford he ostentatiously celebrated George I's birthday in 1715 (members of the club were subsequently summoned before the vice-chancellor's court). He was long promised a bishopric by the duke of Newcastle and Lord Hardwicke before he was given Exeter. He denounced the Jacobite rising in a sermon delivered at Bath in October 1745; he argued that George II's *'interest and our own are evidently the same, inseparably united*; and the present dispute is, not only who shall be the *King*, but who the *People of Britain*; whether *Protestants and Freemen*, or *Papists and Slaves'* (G. Lavington, *A Sermon Preach'd in the Abbey Church at Bath*, 26). Preferring to reside in his diocese his attendance in the Lords was irregular. It is revealing that he did not attend the debates on the legislation of 1749, which recognized the Moravians as an 'antient Protestant Episcopal Church', despite his view of them.

In addition to his attacks on the Methodists and the Moravians Lavington published nine of his sermons (though two of these were only epitomes). His sermon *The Influence of Church-Music* was preached at the meeting of the choirs of Worcester, Hereford, and Gloucester in 1725, and in 1753 it reached its third edition.

Lavington's pluralism and *The Enthusiasm of Methodists* have tarnished his reputation. A portrait, painted in his later years, shows him as a sour-looking man. Chesterfield called him 'the Baudy Bishop' (Podmore, *The Moravian Church in England*, 279–80), and certainly his writings sometimes appear to display prurient interests. His wife, Frances Maria, was apparently the maid of the daughter of Lord Coningsby, to whom Lavington had been chaplain (*Portland MSS*, 7.367). Two of his children died tragically young: poignantly one of them was buried precisely two years after her baptism. The attendance at the theatre of his wife and his surviving daughter, Ann, resulted in a stinging letter from an outraged Methodist. None the less despite his contemporary and posthumous critics Lavington was a conscientious bishop. He conducted his visitations until his last six years, when he was in his seventies, and ordained regularly. He was fiercely anti-Catholic, describing popery as 'that *scandal and scourge of the Christian world'* (*Sermon Preached before the House of Lords*, 23) but, as with his opposition to Methodism, this was the corollary of his traditional Anglicanism. His monument noted that his absences from his diocese were short and rare, and that his clergy found him accessible and hospitable. It is therefore important to judge him in the round rather than, overwhelmingly, on specific aspects of his career.

Colin Haydon

Sources parish register, Mildenhall, Wiltshire, Wilts. & Swindon RO, 1532/2 · G. Lavington, will, 1762, PRO, PROB 11/880, 417 · Oxford diocesan registers, 1699–1736, Oxfordshire Archives, MS Oxf. Dioc. papers, c. 266 · *GM*, 1st ser., 1 (1731) · *GM*, 1st ser., 17 (1747) · *The manuscripts of his grace the duke of Portland*, 10 vols., HMC, 29 (1891–1931) · *Worcestershire parish register society: the register of Worcester cathedral, 1693–1811*, ed. E. O. Browne, J. W. W. Bund, and F. S. Colman (1913) · *The journal of the Rev. John Wesley*, ed. N. Curnock and others, 8 vols. (1909–16); repr. (1938) · monument, Exeter Cathedral · F. Baker, 'Bishop Lavington and the Methodists', *Proceedings of the Wesley Historical Society*, 34 (1963–4), 37–42 · C. J. Podmore, 'The bishops and the brethren: Anglican attitudes to the Moravians in the mid-eighteenth century', *Journal of Ecclesiastical History*, 41 (1990), 622–46 · C. J. Podmore, *The Moravian church in England, 1728–1760* (1998) · S. Taylor, 'The bishops at Westminster in the mid-eighteenth century', *A pillar of the constitution: the House of Lords in British politics, 1640–1784*, ed. C. Jones (1989), 137–63 · S. Taylor, '"The fac totum in ecclesiastic affairs"? The duke of Newcastle and the crown's ecclesiastical patronage', *Albion*, 24 (1992), 409–33 · W. R. Ward, *Georgian Oxford: university politics in the eighteenth century* (1958) · A. Warne, *Church and society in eighteenth century Devon* (1969) · Foster, *Alum. Oxon.* · E. B. Fryde and others, eds., *Handbook of British chronology*, 3rd edn, Royal Historical Society Guides and Handbooks, 2 (1986) · G. Hennessy, *Novum repertorium ecclesiasticum parochiale Londinense, or, London diocesan clergy succession from the earliest time to the year 1898* (1898) · T. F. Kirby, *Winchester scholars: a list of the wardens, fellows, and scholars of … Winchester College* (1888) · J. E. Sewell, unpublished first register, Library of New College, Oxford

Archives BL, corresp. with Lord Hardwicke, Add. MSS 35590–35597, *passim* · Devon RO, Exeter diocesan MSS · LPL, corresp. concerning Methodists and Moravians

Likenesses T. Gainsborough, oils, c.1760, Auckland Art Gallery [*see illus.*] · oils, bishop's palace, Exeter

Lavington, John (c.1690–1759), Presbyterian minister, was the son of an Exeter merchant. He was probably educated for the ministry in London. In 1709, while still a student, he accompanied Edmund Calamy on his tour of Scotland, and was awarded an honorary MA degree by Edinburgh University on 21 April, the day before Calamy received his. Lavington was first recorded at the Exeter assembly in May 1711 as a candidate for the ministry. With the death of Benjamin Hooper in May 1715 Lavington's family, who had been prominent supporters of the three United Congregations in Exeter, put him forward for the vacancy. He was chosen on a majority vote to be the second minister of the Bow Meeting with John Withers, and he was ordained on 28 September 1715. He defended in Latin the question 'An Foedus gratiae sit conditionatum?' He and Withers also preached at Little Meeting in rotation with Joseph Hallett and James Peirce, the ministers of James's Meeting. Of the four, Lavington alone remained strictly orthodox.

Though a young man, Lavington took a prominent part in the Exeter controversy that destroyed the doctrinal accord of old dissent. The controversy began in November 1716, when the Arian opinions of a small group of younger ministers became public after Hubert Stogdon expressed his opinions freely in private conversation with Lavington. Lavington chose to publish the conversation 'and the town presently rang of it' (Peirce, 13). A period of comparative calm followed Stogdon's removal to Somerset until in 1717 Peirce, in his Christmas week lectures, aroused Lavington's alarm by appearing to reflect on the true nature of Christ. Concern at the apparent growth of Arian opinions led to demands for a public declaration of belief in the Trinity at the Exeter assembly of dissenting ministers in September 1718. Lavington dictated to the clerk the orthodox formula adopted by the majority. When, in November 1718, the Committee of Thirteen, the lay managers of Exeter dissent, sought assurances from the city's four ministers on the disputed doctrine they received satisfaction only from Lavington. On 5 March the committee asked the Exeter ministers to subscribe to the Trinity. Lavington agreed; Peirce and Hallett refused; Withers subsequently subscribed and escaped ejection.

Lavington became a major defender of orthodoxy in

Exeter and the south-west, yet he lived to see his Trinitarian formula overturned at the Exeter assembly in May 1753 by a majority of fourteen ministers to ten. He headed the list of those who opposed the change. He published nothing under his name but had a hand in several anonymous pamphlets issued during the Exeter controversy (1719–20).

On 15 March 1713 Lavington married Bridget (*bap.* 1690), the daughter of John Ball, minister of Honiton. They had four sons: the eldest, John, is noticed below; William (*b.* 1723) had a medical practice in Exeter; and Andrew died, aged eighteen, while a student at his eldest brother's academy. Samuel (1726–1807), after a classical education under John Churley, Presbyterian minister at Uffculme, was sent first to John Moore's academy in Bridgwater but, on the latter's growing heterodoxy, he was removed to Plasterers' Hall Academy in London. From 1752 until his death he was minister at Bideford, Devon.

John Lavington died in 1759. His eldest son, **John Lavington** (*c.*1715–1764), Presbyterian minister and tutor, was educated for the ministry under John Eames and Thomas Ridgley at their academy in Moorfields, London; in January 1736 he passed his trials in London to qualify him to preach as a candidate for the ministry. He was the first minister of the Broadway Meeting, Somerset, which was established by his father in 1739, following divisions at Ilminster chapel between the Trinitarians and the heterodox, and he was ordained at Exeter on 27 August 1739. It is not known how long he remained at Broadway but he subsequently served the Presbyterian meeting at Luppitt, Devon; he also supplied Bridport, in Dorset, although he did not settle there. He was called to the Presbyterian congregation at Ottery St Mary, Devon, in 1751, where he remained until his death. Following his marriage to Susanna in 1757 he appears to have gained the friendship of George Whitefield.

In response to concerns over the supply of orthodox candidates for the ministry the Congregational Fund board in London resolved in December 1751 that Lavington 'be encourag'd & assisted … as a Tutor' in the west of England (Congregational Fund board, minute book, DWL, OD 405, p. 32). In February 1752 the board sent four students to Lavington, with a grant of £12 each, and in total supported eighteen students under him. The full course appears to have lasted four years. A former student, Joseph Wilkins, described Lavington as 'a very good linguist, especially in the three learned languages … and well skilled in the various branches of theology' (Wilkins, 225). Little survives concerning his teaching but his theological lectures, based on Joannes Marckius's *Christianae theologiae medulla*, were used by his successor. He published *An Humble Enquiry into the Nature of the Gospel-Offer, Faith, and Assurance* (1759) and a couple of funeral sermons; a volume of discourses, *The Case of Desertion and Affliction Considered*, was published posthumously in 1789. Following his death on 20 December 1764 the academy, later known as the Western Academy, was continued under the Revd James Rooker at Bridport.   DAVID L. WYKES

Sources A. Brockett, *Nonconformity in Exeter, 1650–1875* (1962), 71, 80, 87, 92–3, 108, 206–7 · A. Brockett, ed., *The Exeter assembly: the minutes of the assemblies of the United Brethren of Devon and Cornwall, 1691–1717*, Devon and Cornwall RS, new ser., 6 (1963) · J. Murch, *A history of the Presbyterian and General Baptist churches in the west of England* (1835), 320n., 399, 405–6, 412 · J. Peirce, *The western inquisition, or, A relation of the controversy … among the dissenters in the west of England* (1720), 11–12 · E. Calamy, *An historical account of my own life, with some reflections on the times I have lived in, 1671–1731*, ed. J. T. Rutt, 2nd edn, 2 (1830), 145 · 'Memoir of the Rev. Samuel Lavington, of Bideford, Devon', *London Christian Instructor, or, Congregational Magazine*, 1 (1818), 57–64, 113–16, 192 · Exeter assembly, minute book B, 1721/2, 1744–53, Devon RO, 3542D M1/2 · Congregational Fund board, minute book, 4 Jan 1748–5 Dec 1757, DWL, OD 405, pp. 32, 34 · Congregational Fund board, book of memoranda, DWL, OD 455, p. 14 · list of students, Ottery St Mary, DWL, New College collection, L54/4/72 · DWL, Walter Wilson MS, vol. D', p. 64 · copy of part of the Rev. John Lavington's theological lectures from Marckius's *Medulla* in 3 vols., transcribed & studied over again (especially after the 12th Lecture), by Thomas Reader (*d.* 1795), tutor of the academy, DWL, New College collection, WES 5–7 · J. Wilkins, 'Lavington's observations on the Epistle to the Hebrews', *Protestant Dissenter's Magazine*, 2 (1795), 225 · G. M. Tucker, *Ottery St Mary Congregational Church* (*c.*1962), 12–13 · J. C. Johnstone, 'The story of the Western College', *Transactions of the Congregational Historical Society*, 7 (1916–18), 98–9 · A. W. Sims, *The Western College, Bristol* (1952) · [J. W. Standerwick], 'Broadway Meeting, Somerset', *Transactions of the Congregational Historical Society*, 3 (1907–8), 357 · W. Densham and J. Ogle, *The story of the Congregational churches of Dorset* (1899), 52 · L. Tyerman, *The life of the Rev. George Whitefield*, 2 (1877), 2.402–3 · parish register, Warpford, Devon [marriage]
Archives DWL, lecture notes

Lavington, John (*c.*1715–1764). *See under* Lavington, John (*c.*1690–1759).

Lavino, William Edward (1846–1908), journalist, was born on 10 March 1846 at Lower Broughton, Lancashire, the son of Joseph George Lavino (*b.* 1810), a Dutch protestant businessman naturalized as a British subject in 1850, and Elizabeth Matilda Lavino (*née* Reiss). Lavino was educated in England before being sent, aged fifteen, to study civil engineering in Hanover. About 1861 his parents moved to Paris; Lavino later joined them and spent two years at the École Supérieure du Commerce. He was engaged in commerce in Antwerp between about 1865 and 1867, before becoming secretary to Bertrand Fourquet, a Parisian merchant commissioned to supply material for the modernizing efforts of the Ecuadorian dictator, General Gabriel Garcia Moreno (1821–1875). Lavino soon became private secretary to General Francisco Javier Salazar (1824–1891), the Ecuadorian minister to France, and held the post until 1874, when Salazar left Paris.

In 1874 he was offered the post of secretary to the San Salvador legation but Lavino's career lay not in South American diplomacy but in assisting the formation of European opinion, especially in the troublesome arena of Anglo-French relations. His cosmopolitanism, intelligence, tact, and sensitivity gained the widest possible scope for their exhibition in journalism. He began with a scoop for the *New York Herald* when he persuaded the exiled Marshal Bazaine to publish a self-justification for the paper. He then became editor of the London-based *Continental Herald*, before his career began in earnest as assistant to the Paris correspondent of the *Daily Telegraph* in 1874. In 1878 he moved to Vienna as that paper's representative, a position he held until 1892 when he was appointed, on Lord Rosebery's recommendation, to *The Times*. Over the next sixteen years he garnered increasing recognition as one of the paper's most influential correspondents. Since he was positioned at the diplomatic crossroads of Europe, Lavino's letters and columns reveal both an absorption in contemporary crises, and a growing fear of the international issues of the future, notably the future of Anglo-German relations.

In 1903 Lavino replaced Henri de Blowitz as Paris correspondent for *The Times*. As early as 1896 Lavino had written of the need for a *rapprochement* with France, and he is best known for his association with the Anglo-French *entente cordiale* of 1904. There seems little reason to accept uncritically the judgement of contemporaries that Lavino was of primary importance in sealing the *rapprochement*. However, inasmuch as good personal relations between British and French politicians were crucial corollaries of the entente, Lavino's close contacts with Théophile Delcassé and Eugène Étienne, his dispatches and the avowedly diplomatic agenda which informed—if it did not propel—his journalism, must have influenced public and private *rapprochements*. Over the years he developed a strong belief in the deep-rootedness of German antipathy to Britain, its inexorable evolution into hostile action, and the concomitant need for the security of an equally innovative Anglo-Russian agreement to supplement the entente. This assessment of the European diplomatic situation was shared by Sir Donald Mackenzie Wallace, and Valentine Chirol at Printing House Square. It formed an agenda that was given a great deal of publicity, and which was difficult for politicians to avoid. The influence of *The Times* on diplomacy before the First World War, if difficult to locate precisely, can never be ignored, and Lavino was one of its vital correspondents.

Lavino was, for his contemporaries, a solitary figure. He never married, and in both Vienna and Paris he forsook society for the diplomatic world. He died suddenly at 7 rue de la Chaise, Paris, on 4 August 1908, from complications arising from diabetes and an operation for a strangulated hernia; he was buried in Poissy.   ROBERT BICKERS

Sources J. Walters, *The Times* (6 Aug 1908), 8 · [S. Morison and others], *The history of The Times*, 3 (1947) · A. J. A. Morris, *The scaremongers: the advocacy of war and rearmament, 1896–1914* (1984) · News Int. RO, *The Times* archive, W. E. Lavino MSS · b. cert. · denization cert. of Joseph George Lavino, PRO, HO/1/32, no. 1090 · *Almanach National 1874* (published in Paris, 1874)
Archives News Int. RO, papers
Likenesses E. Walker, portrait (after a photograph in *History of the Times*), NPG · photograph, repro. in *History of the Times*, facing p. 376
Wealth at death £761 2s. 2d.: probate, 21 Aug 1908, *CGPLA Eng. & Wales*

Law, Andrew Bonar

Law, Andrew Bonar (1858–1923), businessman and prime minister, was born on 16 September 1858 in Kingston, New Brunswick, Canada. His father, the Revd James Law (1822–1882), was an Ulsterman of Scottish descent who served as Presbyterian minister of the Free Church of Scotland for the parishes of Kingston and Richibucto. His

Andrew Bonar Law (1858–1923), by Sir James Guthrie, c.1919–21

mother, Elizabeth Annie, *née* Kidston (d. 1860), was born in Scotland but had also migrated to Canada. Andrew Bonar Law was his parents' fourth son and fourth child—a fifth child, a daughter, was born two years after him.

Family and early life Bonar Law, as he was generally known, spent the first twelve years of his life in New Brunswick, and surviving recordings of his voice indicate that he never completely lost the Canadian accent acquired in his youth. He was brought up in an austere Calvinist environment dominated by the brooding presence of his father, a man who, from all reports, would in the late twentieth century have been diagnosed as a depressive. Throughout his life Bonar Law was described as having a tendency to melancholy, and it is difficult to avoid the conclusion that this stemmed from childhood influences. The family's financial position was by no means comfortable. Bonar Law's mother was related to the wealthy Kidston family of Glasgow and Helensburgh, but the Laws were dependent on James's modest stipend. On the death of Bonar Law's mother, when he was two, Janet Kidston, Bonar Law's aunt, came out from Glasgow to keep house for the Revd Law and to look after his children. In 1870 Bonar Law's father remarried; his new wife was Sophia Wood, a New Brunswick schoolmistress. As Janet Kidston's services as housekeeper and surrogate mother were no longer required she decided to return to Scotland, and suggested that Bonar Law go with her on the grounds that her wealthy relatives could provide for his education and launch him on a career in the family banking business. In 1870 Bonar Law left for Scotland, never to return to New Brunswick.

Business, marriage, and parliament Initially Bonar Law was sent to Gilbertfield boarding-school at Hamilton, and from there he went on to Glasgow high school. He showed some academic promise, but his formal education ended in 1874 at the age of sixteen, when he was offered a position in the Kidstons' banking business. In 1885 the Kidstons decided to merge their firm with the Clydesdale Bank. With this development imminent Bonar Law was offered a partnership in a company that had close connections with Kidstons, the iron merchants William Jacks & Co. The founder of the company, William Jacks, had been adopted as Liberal candidate for the Leith district (for which he was elected MP in November 1885) and was seeking a partner to whom he could delegate most of his business responsibilities. Bonar Law himself did not have the financial resources to buy into the partnership, but his Kidston cousins provided him with the necessary funding. Thus at the age of twenty-seven Bonar Law became a substantial businessman in his own right.

Although a newcomer to the sector Bonar Law proved to be a competent and hard-working entrepreneur: the business expanded during his time at the helm, with new branches being opened in Middlesbrough in 1888 (managed by Bonar Law's elder brother Jack) and in London in 1894. One of William Jacks's most important business links was with the Nova Scotia Steel and Coal Company. The German firm Krupps was also a major customer, purchasing large quantities of iron ore through Jacks. As a businessman Bonar Law gained a reputation, in Lord Blake's words, for being 'quick, efficient, hardworking, straightforward, a trifle dictatorial' (Blake, 35). Certainly by the late 1890s he was well known and well respected by the Glasgow business community, and he had seats on the boards of a number of companies.

Although his formal schooling ended relatively early Bonar Law appears to have been something of an autodidact thereafter. In later life he claimed to have read Gibbon's *Decline and Fall of the Roman Empire* three times by the age of twenty-one, and developed an 'encyclopaedic knowledge' of the works of Thomas Carlyle. He attended lectures at Glasgow University, and was a member of numerous essay and debating societies. A teetotaller, his social life was not based upon parties or revelry. He disliked music, and therefore dancing, and regarded eating as a utilitarian rather than an epicurean or social occasion. His only vice was tobacco, which he indulged throughout his life through pipe smoking and ample supplies of cigars. He was not, however, unsocial. He helped found a tennis club at Helensburgh, and played golf whenever he had the time. Indoor games also proved somewhat of a passion: he was a keen and talented chess player, and was equally enthusiastic and skilful at cards, especially bridge, which became an almost fanatical pastime (in later years political colleagues seeking to tempt Bonar Law to attend weekend political gatherings saw the promise of a good bridge game as vital bait).

If Bonar Law's business career did not preclude recreation neither did it prevent romance. In 1890 he met Annie Pitcairn Robley (d. 1909), the daughter of a shipbroker who lived in Helensburgh. She evidently made a profound impression upon him, for he was induced to attend dances and fancy-dress balls in her company. They became engaged towards the end of the year, and on 24 March 1891 were married at the West Free Church of Helensburgh. After a honeymoon in Paris they returned to live in Helensburgh. From the outset the marriage was a source of happiness and security for both partners. They were to have seven children, although the eldest was stillborn. Their second son was Richard Kidston *Law, first Baron Coleraine (1901–1980). Initially they lived in a house called Seabank, which was given to them by Bonar Law's aunt as a wedding present. With a growing family they required larger accommodation, provided by Annie's childhood home, Kintillo, which they inherited on the death of Mr Robley. This was to be their main residence until 1909, when the family moved to Pembroke Lodge in Kensington.

Bonar Law had been introduced to politics in the 1870s. The Kidstons were ardent Conservatives and their house provided a meeting point for local Conservative notables, and Bonar Law adhered to the Kidston political faith. As a young man he became a member of the Glasgow Parliamentary Debating Association, where he gained the kind of oratorical training that the Oxford and Cambridge unions provided for many of his future colleagues. His devotion to business and family life circumscribed his political activities, and he was not particularly active in local politics. By the late 1890s both his business and family were secure, and in April 1897 he mentioned to one correspondent the possibility of becoming a parliamentary candidate. Early in 1898 he was named the prospective Conservative candidate for the Blackfriars and Hutchesontown division of Glasgow, hitherto a safe Liberal seat held by the Gladstonian A. D. Provand against the Conservatives' general election landslide of 1895. However, Bonar Law was fortunate enough to contest the seat at the election of September 1900, when the so-called 'jingo hurricane' whipped up by the Second South African War saw the Conservatives achieve an even greater victory than in 1895. Bonar Law rode the 'khaki' wave into parliament with a majority of 1000—his national political career was thus launched when he was forty-two.

Tariff reform On entering parliament Bonar Law relinquished his active partnership in Jacks, but he retained shareholdings in the company, as well as his holdings in the Clydesdale Bank and his other directorships. Together these brought him an annual income of £6000. He also benefited from Kidston family legacies. The combination of his investments, director's fees, and legacies ensured that Bonar Law had the financial independence and security for a full-time political career. By no means a traditional tory, he was however typical of the new breed of urban Conservative politician who had emerged in increasing numbers from the pineries and vineries of Britain's affluent suburbs in the late nineteenth century, and who had been so crucial in extending the party's social constituency in Britain's still fast-growing urban centres.

Bonar Law made his maiden speech in the House of

Commons during the debate on the address in February 1901, defending the government against an attack by David Lloyd George on the British army's treatment of Boer families. His speech gained little notice, largely because another new MP, Winston Churchill, made his maiden speech on the same day, and, as the son of a famous father, Churchill's speech received more attention. He soon became discontented with parliamentary life. In a mood of depression he told Austen Chamberlain, 'Austen, this is no place for me. It's all very well for men like you who came into it [politics] young; but if I had known then what I know now, I would never have stood for Parliament' (J. A. Chamberlain, *Down the Years*, 1935, 224). He made little impression in the 1901 parliamentary session, but on 22 April 1902 he made an effective intervention in a debate over the decision by the chancellor of the exchequer, Sir Michael Hicks Beach, to introduce a 1 s. per quarter tariff on imported wheat. The Liberal opposition denounced the duty as the thin end of a protectionist wedge, a threat to Britain's established free-trade policy, and an indication that the Conservatives were attempting, covertly, to reintroduce the reviled corn laws that had led to 'dear food' in the era before their repeal in 1846. Rather than flatly denying the Liberal argument he counter-attacked, accusing the Liberals of treating free trade as a theological creed rather than an economic policy; he acknowledged that free trade was probably at that juncture the best policy for Britain, but that did not mean it would always be the case. Speaking without notes Bonar Law buttressed his case with trade statistics and used his reputation as a successful businessman to press home his case with an air of authority, which marked him out as an 'expert'.

In July 1902 Bonar Law was appointed by the new prime minister, Arthur Balfour, as parliamentary secretary to the Board of Trade under Gerald Balfour, the prime minister's brother. His parliamentary duties were relatively minor, for Gerald Balfour was also in the Commons and took most of the responsibility. He made one important speech in November 1902 on the Brussels sugar convention, but otherwise his duties were quite mundane. The most significant development in terms of his future came in the shape of events quite beyond his control. On 15 May 1903 Joseph Chamberlain made his famous speech in Birmingham that launched what came to be known as the tariff reform campaign.

At the core of Chamberlain's campaign was a proposal to link the British and colonial economies through reciprocal tariff arrangements: the colonies were to give British manufactured goods preferential tariff treatment, and the British were to do the same for colonial agricultural goods, which necessarily entailed imposing tariffs on imported foodstuffs, which came to be known as 'food taxes'. Chamberlain's initiative divided the Conservative Party and transformed the British political scene. From 1903 to the outbreak of the First World War it was impossible for a British politician not to have a view on the tariff question. Bonar Law certainly had a view—he was committed to the tariff reform cause. As his speech in April 1902 had indicated, he did not see free trade as an inviolable principle; he saw it as a policy which was either good or bad depending on the circumstances, and in his view circumstances had shifted to the point where Britain's adherence to free trade was no longer tenable. Here he was in tune with much Conservative back-bench and grass-roots opinion. Many in the Conservative Party were either increasingly hostile to or sceptical about adhering to free trade in a competitive international economy in which Britain's main rivals were protectionist. For Bonar Law, familiar as he was with the increasing pressure that British industry, especially the iron trade, was facing from foreign competition and import penetration, scepticism about free trade was understandable and logical.

Tariff reform was a dominant issue in Bonar Law's political life from 1903 to 1914. The great majority of his most important speeches from 1904 to 1912 (when the Irish question began to occupy equal amounts of his time) were devoted to the fallacies of free trade and the need for imperial preference and industrial protection. Determined that the case for tariffs should be properly researched and rigorously presented, he sought advice from sympathetic economists, most notably W. J. Ashley, the professor of commerce at Birmingham University, to whom he commented in December 1904 that 'There is nothing ... which tells more against us than the idea that *scientific* authority is against us' (A. Ashley, *William James Ashley*, 1932, 135).

Conservative front-bencher Tariff reform was the vehicle which took Bonar Law to the centre, and ultimately to the top, of the Conservative Party. Chamberlain regarded him as one of the ablest members of the tariff reform ranks. Perhaps equally important, Bonar Law was never openly critical of Arthur Balfour's leadership. As a consequence he enjoyed the best of both worlds. After he lost his seat in the Liberal landslide of January 1906, he was soon (May 1906) offered a safe seat in the Camberwell (Dulwich) constituency. With the Conservatives' Commons contingent reduced to 157, Balfour the subject of both open and covert criticism, and Chamberlain rendered *hors de combat* by a stroke, there was a vacuum waiting to be filled. Opportunity beckoned for any able parliamentary performers in the much-thinned Conservative ranks, and men such as F. E. Smith, Arthur Steel-Maitland, and Bonar Law were able to take advantage of this situation. Although he continued to be, along with Austen Chamberlain, the most prominent spokesman for the tariff cause, he also broadened his portfolio. In 1908 he made a major intervention in the Commons debate on the Liberal government's licensing legislation, defending the liquor trade against what he saw as a politically motivated attack. He followed up his parliamentary efforts with an acerbic correspondence with the Liberal president of the Board of Trade, the renegade tory Winston Churchill. At a time when the Conservatives could do little in the face of the Liberals' overwhelming Commons majority, such aggressive action buoyed Conservative spirits and enhanced the reputation of the actor.

Bonar Law was also prominent in attempts to construct a positive response to the Liberal government's social reforms. Along with a group of younger Conservative MPs and publicists, including Edward Goulding, J. W. Hills, Leo Amery, and Fabian Ware, Bonar Law played a major role in developing an 'unauthorized programme' of Conservative social reform proposals, published in the *Morning Post* in October 1908. Included in the programme were ideas for an extension of the pensions system (through making it contributory), a national insurance scheme, regulation of so-called 'sweated trades', and land reform to create a substantial class of small-holding owner-occupiers. Crucially, these reforms were to be underpinned and financed by tariffs to protect employment and raise revenue. In the 1909 parliamentary session, as the leading Conservative respondent to the Liberal government's legislation on labour exchanges and the Trade Boards Act (which regulated the sweated trades), he struck a positive note, welcoming both initiatives while adding that tariffs were essential if either mechanism was to fulfil its function effectively.

For Bonar Law the run-up to the general election of January 1910 was marked not only by arduous political and parliamentary activity but also by personal tragedy. In the summer of 1909 his wife had become ill, and specialists advised an operation on her gall bladder, which was carried out at the end of October. At first the operation appeared to have been a success, but three days after the operation, on 31 October, she collapsed and died. Bonar Law was overwhelmed with grief, and the melancholy to which he was always prone temporarily paralysed him. Briefly he considered retirement from public life, but, partly at the urging of his colleagues, but perhaps more importantly because it provided him with a distraction from his loss, he chose to throw himself into the political fray with even greater vigour.

The January 1910 election was taken as a mandate for the Liberals to pass the 'people's budget', but the Liberal government also announced its intention to reduce the powers of the House of Lords. Edward VII, who died in May 1910, had indicated that he would wish a further election to test public opinion on this issue, and his successor, George V, was of a similar view. Inter-party negotiations designed to produce a compromise on the constitutional question broke up without result in early November 1910, and another general election was called as the Liberals sought a mandate for constitutional change.

The Conservatives faced two key questions: first, whether 'one more heave' would turn the Liberals out, and, second, whether they could achieve this while still committed to a tariff reform platform that included proposals for duties on imported foodstuffs. Opinion in the party was divided as to whether the food tax was an electoral incubus. Arthur Balfour inclined to the view that it was, and in April 1910 he attempted to dilute the food tax problem by announcing that under any new tariff regime colonial wheat would not have to pay even a preferential tariff but would enter the UK duty free. Even committed tariff advocates, including Bonar Law, were willing to accept this as a reasonable course of action, but the question still remained as to whether this would be sufficient

to reassure the electorate, especially in the key electoral battleground of Lancashire. The dominant figure in Lancashire Conservatism was the seventeenth earl of Derby, who suggested to Balfour in October 1910 that a leading tariff reformer contest a Lancashire constituency in order to carry the fight to the Liberals, and proposed Bonar Law as the ideal candidate. Bonar Law agreed to leave his Dulwich constituency and contest the seat of North West Manchester, and at the same time secured the candidacy of his new friend Max Aitken, another tariff reformer and product of New Brunswick, for the Lancashire seat of Ashton under Lyne.

In the December 1910 general election both Bonar Law and Aitken fought their campaigns exclusively on the tariff issue, but whereas Aitken was successful Bonar Law failed to make the hoped-for breakthrough. In spite of his defeat in the Manchester contest, his tenacious and much-publicized campaign made him a genuinely national figure and a Conservative hero, while he developed a close relationship with Lord Derby. Derby and other Conservative notables in Lancashire put pressure on him to play down the food tax aspect of the tariff case in his campaign, and suggested that the Conservatives promise a referendum on food taxes if elected. He was persuaded by this argument, and in turn his views influenced Balfour, who announced at the Albert Hall in early December that a Conservative government would hold such a referendum if the Liberals pledged to do likewise on the question of Irish home rule. The announcement made Balfour unpopular with committed tariff reformers, though Bonar Law, who only publicly supported it after the announcement had been made, escaped direct association with this 'betrayal'.

Shortly after his defeat at North West Manchester Bonar Law returned to parliament as MP for another Lancashire constituency, Bootle, after a by-election in March 1911. In June 1911 he was made a privy councillor in the coronation honours. The political agenda in the spring and summer of 1911 was dominated by Liberal plans to remove the veto powers of the House of Lords. At the end of June the Liberal premier, H. H. Asquith, made it known that the king had promised to create enough Liberal peers to give them a majority in the Lords if the upper chamber rejected the government's constitutional reforms. The Conservative Party was divided over how to respond to this development. At a meeting of the shadow cabinet on 21 July Balfour advocated a policy of non-resistance to the Parliament Bill. Bonar Law supported this position and thereby found himself opposed to some of his closest colleagues in the tariff reform campaign, notably Austen Chamberlain and F. E. Smith. Bonar Law's stance was based on pragmatism. The Parliament Bill still left the upper chamber a two-year delaying power, and in the circumstances he felt this was better than forcing the monarch to create a Liberal majority in the House of Lords. If that were to happen, he explained in a letter to *The Times* on 26 July, then the Liberals would be able to carry 'in a single session Bills to establish Home Rule [for Ireland], to disestablish the Church in Wales, and to gerrymander the constituencies'.

The Parliament Bill was passed by the House of Lords on 11 August, to a howl of protest from the 'diehard' faction in the Conservative Party that had advocated all-out resistance. Criticism of Arthur Balfour reached new peaks of intensity, and on 8 November 1911 he announced his decision to resign the party leadership.

Conservative leader The Conservative hierarchy, especially the chief whip, Lord Balcarres, wanted to settle the leadership question quickly. Three candidates, Austen Chamberlain, Walter Long, and Bonar Law, were put forward at the meeting of the parliamentary party held at the Carlton Club on 13 November. After Chamberlain, the favoured candidate of the Conservative whips and Conservative central office, and Long, a Wiltshire landowner more in keeping with the specifically tory tradition, both withdrew their candidacies, Bonar Law was elected unopposed by a unanimous vote. Two factors worked to Bonar Law's advantage. The first was that the party wished to avoid a contest and the likely legacy of bitterness between Chamberlain and Long and their respective supporters; Bonar Law's position as a compromise candidate had a great deal to offer. The second was Bonar Law's political trajectory over the previous year. He had retained his credibility as a tariff reformer, but had distanced himself from the more extreme positions with which Chamberlain was associated.

On hearing of Bonar Law's election Lloyd George is rumoured to have remarked 'the fools have stumbled on the right man by accident'. However, in the first three years of Bonar Law's leadership the Welsh Wizard's judgement seemed deeply misplaced. On the food tax question Bonar Law faced a major internal party crisis. After the 1910 defeats there was a growing body of opinion within the party, led by the Lancashire Conservatives, which saw the food taxes as a severe handicap. Under increasing pressure from this faction Bonar Law sought to modify the Conservative position. Speaking in Max Aitken's constituency of Ashton under Lyne in December 1912 Bonar Law announced that under a future Conservative government any initiative for food taxes would have to come from the colonies. This statement outraged the still numerous and vocal section of the party that was committed to what they called 'the full tariff programme'. Through December 1912 and into the new year tensions within the party ran dangerously high. Bonar Law himself and his leader in the upper chamber, Lord Lansdowne, were the subject of much criticism, and threatened to resign together. A hasty but intensive round of negotiations between Bonar Law and Lansdowne and other leading figures resulted in the parliamentary party sending a memorial to Bonar Law on 10 January 1913, signed by 231 of the 280 Conservative MPs, expressing confidence in his leadership, and accepting his Ashton under Lyne formula on the tariff question. Emboldened by this vote of confidence Bonar Law went a stage further in a speech at Edinburgh later in January, declaring that if the Conservatives won a general election they would not introduce food taxes without holding another election. His 'triumph', though, was more apparent than real. Rather than peace breaking out in the Conservative Party there was more of an armed truce. In March 1913 the party's new chief whip, Edmund Talbot, reported that Bonar Law was 'hankering after his bridge and golf' and complaining that 'the glory of his position is much diminished … by reason of the discordant cries of his followers and the difficulty of satisfying his adherents' (J. S. Sandars to A. Balfour, 23 March 1913, BL, Add. MS 49768, fols. 42–5).

Ulster crisis Bonar Law also had difficulties in uniting his party behind his stance on the Irish question, following the Liberal promise of home rule for Ireland announced in the spring of 1912. From the outset he saw the exclusion of Ulster from Irish home rule as the critical issue, a perspective shaped by his family ties and the politics of Glasgow protestantism. From mid-1912 he also developed close relations with Edward Carson, who emerged as the great champion of Ulster during the home-rule debates. With the Lords veto gone there was little the Conservatives could do to prevent home rule passing in some form, and Ulster was acknowledged as the weakest link in the home-rule case. Carson's argument that exclusion of Ulster was 'the best settlement if Home Rule is inevitable' (Lansdowne to Bonar Law, 26 Sept 1913, HLRO, 30/2/27) thus carried some force. But not all Conservatives agreed with Bonar Law's 'Ulsterization' of the Irish question. Southern Irish unionists were appalled that the Conservative leadership appeared willing to surrender their interests. A significant number of mainland Conservatives, who found a voice in Walter Long's Union Defence League, which distanced itself from Bonar Law's leadership, also stressed that the party's *raison d'être* was defence of the union, and not just Ulster.

Bonar Law's Ulsterization of the Irish issue was a high-risk strategy. It led him to support the activities of the paramilitary Ulster Volunteer Force (UVF) and to declare that, no matter what form it took, he would back Ulster's resistance to home rule. This was tantamount to offering support for armed resistance to the legal authority of an elected government. He may have apologized to Asquith in advance for the fact that he was to be 'a little vicious' in debate, but the tone of his speeches in 1913–14 and the disruptive behaviour of his followers in the Commons ran counter to established norms of parliamentary behaviour. He even endorsed a proposal that the Lords amend the annual Army Act to the effect that troops could not be deployed to subdue resistance to home rule in Ulster. His party chairman warned that if the Conservatives appeared to be responsible for fomenting civil disorder in Ulster then they would be condemned by public opinion. He himself recognized this, and in negotiations with Asquith in July 1914 he showed himself more willing to compromise than his public statements indicated. But the UVF and other militants on the ground in Ulster were not under his control and, having helped to whip up their militancy, it would have been difficult for him to advocate a compromise solution without risking a violent outburst in Ulster and a backlash against his leadership.

In the period from November 1911 to the outbreak of the First World War it is difficult to see Bonar Law's leadership of the Conservative Party as a great success. In the face of continuing criticism from within his own party he threatened to resign on average about once every six months, and there was a sense of desperation in his behaviour over Ireland. The party's landed grandees made snide remarks about the poor quality of the catering provided at his house in Kensington on the 'wrong side of the park', and, apart from Max Aitken, he had few friends with whom to share his burdens. In short, Bonar Law looked like what he was: an inexperienced, often isolated, second-choice leader struggling to overcome a series of severe crises which, in truth, were probably beyond the capacity of any individual to solve.

War and coalition Bonar Law's situation, and that of his party, were transformed by the First World War. Initially the war proved awkward; it was difficult to criticize the government for fear of being labelled unpatriotic. Scandals over shell shortages, reversals at sea, stalemate on the western front, and disaster in the Dardanelles ensured that by the early summer of 1915 unease in the Conservative ranks over the war was becoming uncontrollable. Following bad news from the Dardanelles, swiftly followed by the resignation of Admiral Fisher as first sea lord, Bonar Law held a meeting with Lloyd George on 17 May. When Bonar Law made it clear that he could no longer hold back from publicly criticizing the government, Lloyd George responded that 'we must have a coalition' (Blake, 243), and he immediately took Bonar Law to see Asquith. After the meeting at 10 Downing Street Bonar Law consulted Lord Lansdowne and Austen Chamberlain, and they sent Asquith what was tantamount to an ultimatum, indicating that unless the government was reconstructed the Conservatives would press for a critical debate on the conduct of the war. Asquith had little option but to comply, and on 18 May informed Bonar Law that he had accepted the resignation of the entire cabinet in order to reconstruct the government.

Few Conservatives gained high office in the Asquith coalition, the formation of which was announced on 19 May 1915, and Bonar Law himself merely became colonial secretary. He and his followers were more interested in which Liberals to exclude, and made it a condition of joining the government that Churchill be asked to leave the Admiralty. The 'pro-German' Haldane was also targeted for removal. It is possible that Bonar Law did not press his own claims more strongly as a result of being embroiled in a somewhat embarrassing scandal. On becoming leader of the Conservative Party Bonar Law had resigned his company directorships and his partnership in William Jacks, but he still used the banking facilities of Jacks & Co. as a deposit for surplus sums at his disposal. He thus had no direct connection with the firm, but he still had a connection, and his brother Jack remained a partner. Early in May 1915 the company was accused of trading with the enemy, having delivered a cargo of iron ore from Canada to the German steel and arms manufacturer Krupps in August 1914. There was never any serious suggestion that Bonar Law would be accused of involvement, but his brother narrowly escaped prosecution, and two other partners in the firm, both friends of the Conservative leader, were imprisoned as a result of the case. The scandal hardly provided the best background for him to conduct delicate negotiations about the form of the coalition.

On the formation of the coalition Bonar Law was made a member of the war committee, a large group of senior cabinet members who discussed overall war strategy. He emerged the strongest advocate of evacuation from the Dardanelles. The war committee decided in early November to postpone any decision until Lord Kitchener, the war minister, had visited and reported on the Gallipoli front. Bonar Law initially supported this action, but then changed his mind and demanded an immediate evacuation, offering his resignation on the issue. Fortunately for Bonar Law, Asquith prevailed upon him to wait, for Kitchener's report supported the evacuation proposal, and on 23 November the decision was taken to abandon the Gallipoli campaign. The outcome strengthened Bonar Law's position. When, in November, Asquith moved to reduce the unwieldy war committee's size he initially proposed five members: himself, Balfour, Lloyd George, Reginald McKenna, and Kitchener. But he could no longer afford to ignore or dismiss the Conservative leader's views or sensibilities, and reluctantly felt constrained to add Bonar Law's name to the list.

During 1916 Bonar Law became increasingly critical of Asquith personally and disillusioned with his conduct of the war, while events at home and continued problems with the war effort served to widen the political gulf between them. In April the cabinet's decision to introduce conscription saw Asquith struggling to appease Liberal opponents of the measure. Bonar Law acknowledged Asquith's party difficulties, but was impatient with the premier's indecisiveness. Lloyd George, facing the same party constraints as Asquith, had advocated compulsory service as essential to the war effort, and not for the first time Bonar Law found himself closer to Lloyd George than to Asquith on questions of war policy. During the conscription debates the Easter rising in Ireland took place. The government was united in suppressing the rising and disposing of its leaders in the aftermath. But divisions emerged over possible longer-term arrangements for the governance of Ireland. He supported the agreement brokered by Lloyd George between Edward Carson and the moderate Irish nationalist leader John Redmond, which would have seen a temporary introduction of home rule, excluding Ulster, with a permanent solution to be decided by an Imperial Conference on the cessation of the war. In some respects Bonar Law was fortunate that the scheme failed, in that his security as Conservative leader may well have been threatened if he had continued to support a measure that attracted so much Conservative opposition. One lesson he drew from the Irish situation was that he could not afford to be too 'coalitionist' in his outlook.

Lord Kitchener's death early in June 1916 required the

appointment of a new war minister. Bonar Law favoured Lloyd George as his successor, on the strength of the latter's excellent work at the Ministry of Munitions. He met Lloyd George at Max Aitken's house on 11 June and agreed to support his claims to the post. After finding Asquith absent from London, he drove to the prime minister's country house and, after being kept waiting, found Asquith willing to offer Bonar Law the post. Feeling honour-bound by his agreement with Lloyd George, Bonar Law declined, at which point Asquith agreed to Lloyd George's succession and returned to his guests. Bonar Law considered that Asquith had handled the question with unpardonable levity, and was further alienated from the prime minister.

Conscription and Ireland had provoked Conservative criticisms of their Liberal partners, with some of the critics, including powerful figures such as Lord Milner and Carson, advocating a reconstructed government led by Lloyd George. With the British offensive on the Somme, launched on 1 July 1916, proving ineffective and costly the government faced increasingly hostile Conservative views in both parliament and the press. In early November Bonar Law felt the strength of Conservative opinion when, as colonial secretary, he had to defend the government's decision to sell captured German businesses in west Africa to the highest non-German bidder. On the Conservative benches there was a call for only British firms to be considered, and sixty-five Conservative MPs voted against the policy defended by their leader. He later highlighted the importance of this rebellion as indicating that his party's hostility to the government was reaching such a point that neither he nor other Conservative ministers could remain in the cabinet.

Manoeuvres within the cabinet itself, in which Bonar Law played a leading role, finally brought about Asquith's replacement as prime minister by Lloyd George. He strongly supported Lloyd George's proposal of November 1916 to streamline the governmental war machinery through the creation of a small war council with authority over all departments. He and other senior Conservatives saw Lloyd George as the only person to chair this new body, even though Asquith would be reduced to a cipher. When, on 4 December, Asquith demanded that Lloyd George issue a statement publicly affirming the prime minister's continued overall authority, the war minister resigned. Bonar Law then informed Asquith that if Lloyd George felt obliged to resign, he and the other Conservative members of the cabinet would do likewise. Asquith had no real option but to tender his own resignation on 5 December, for without Conservative support his government was unsustainable.

On the evening of 5 December 1916 the king invited Bonar Law, as the leader of the largest party in the House of Commons, to form a government. When Asquith declined to serve under him, he advised the king to invite Lloyd George instead, for only he could attract enough Liberal support to head an effective coalition. The new government under Lloyd George, formed on 7–8 December, still contained a large number of Liberal ministers, but the senior posts were dominated by Conservatives, and Bonar Law himself became chancellor of the exchequer, leader of the House of Commons, and the effective deputy premier. Every morning he would meet Lloyd George and discuss policy for perhaps two hours, with the prime minister using him as a sounding-board for ideas and proposals—if they survived Bonar Law's scrutiny Lloyd George was confident they would survive cabinet and the Commons.

Bonar Law's main task as chancellor of the exchequer was to finance the war effort. As a former businessman he possessed enough financial and economic knowledge to develop his own ideas, and was capable of pursuing his own line of policy. In January 1917 he overruled his officials and (successfully) floated a new war loan at an interest rate of 5 per cent, as opposed to the 6 per cent level advised by the Treasury and the bank, a reversal of the earlier policy of high money rates. The national war bonds which he launched in October 1917 proved a remarkably successful device for ensuring a steady flow of money to pay for the war. In the fifth and sixth war budgets over which he presided, in May 1917 and April 1918 respectively, he sought to achieve two aims: to raise as much money for the 'war chest' as possible at as little long-term cost as could be achieved. In 1918 he budgeted for a revenue income of £842 million and an expenditure of £2972 million. The borrowings of over £2000 million in that year alone were three times the pre-war national debt, but nevertheless Bonar Law as chancellor sustained Britain's record, unrivalled among the other belligerents, of funding 26 per cent of wartime expenditure from revenue. He was in this respect as orthodox a chancellor as circumstances permitted, and thereby helped sustain the government's credit-worthiness in the last two years of the war.

Bonar Law had little direct input into war strategy in the Lloyd George coalition. He was less inclined than Lloyd George to criticize the high command, although during the Passchendaele offensive of 1917 he was privately sceptical of the military establishment's strategy. As leader of the House of Commons he had to keep the coalition's parliamentary cohorts in order. Lloyd George's unilateral decision to bring Churchill back into the cabinet in mid-July 1917 did not go down well with either Bonar Law or his party, but Bonar Law's insistence that Churchill be excluded from strategic decision making soothed Conservative tempers. In April 1918 criticisms of the government's conduct of the war by General F. D. Maurice briefly threatened the coalition's stability. But Bonar Law, personally attacked by Maurice, stood by Lloyd George as the prime minister demolished Maurice's and Asquith's arguments in the Commons, and no Conservatives voted with Asquith's censure motion. Conservative loyalty was less assured when the issue of home rule came to the fore again in the wake of the decision to introduce conscription in Ireland in the spring of 1918. There was strong Conservative opposition to any suggestion that home rule be enacted as a quid pro quo for Irish conscription, and Bonar Law faced some difficult moments until the discovery of Sinn Féin contacts with Germany effectively sidelined the issue. With the military tide turning in the summer the coalition's political problems evaporated.

Bonar Law suffered heavy personal losses during the war through the deaths of his second eldest son, Charles, killed in action at the battle of Gaza in April 1917, and of his eldest son, James, a pilot in the Royal Flying Corps, who was shot down and killed in France six months later. Work provided a distraction, but in future years friends and colleagues claimed that he never fully recovered from these bereavements. In political terms, though, he had a 'good war'. By taking the Conservatives into the Asquith coalition he had got his party into the corridors of power through the back door, and ended the Conservatives' longest period in opposition since the mid-nineteenth century. In November 1918 he had become, if not 'the man that won the war', then at least the man who had stood by the man who won the war. The day after the armistice he chaired a meeting of Conservative MPs, and they decided to fight the forthcoming general election as supporters of the coalition. In his view Lloyd George's popularity was so great that there was no option but to continue to serve under him, but he was also clear that his party would continue to be an independent political entity. At the December 1918 general election the vast majority of candidates who received the so-called 'coupon'—a joint letter of endorsement from Lloyd George and Bonar Law which was sent to all coalition candidates—were Conservatives. Thus although the election produced a coalition victory, the Conservatives were dominant—holding 333 seats to the Coalition Liberals' 136. Bonar Law himself decided to leave Bootle and return to Glasgow, where he was elected for the Central division.

Post-war administration In the new cabinet Bonar Law relinquished the exchequer, but to the chagrin of the new chancellor, Austen Chamberlain, he continued to live at 11 Downing Street in order to be close to Lloyd George. Bonar Law's official positions were leader of the house and lord privy seal, but in effect he was deputy prime minister. In the early part of 1919 he spent long periods in Paris with Lloyd George and the British delegation to the Versailles conference. He was not predisposed to a 'Carthaginian' peace, and the moderation of many of his pronouncements, both public and private, placed him closer to critics of Versailles such as his one-time Treasury secretary J. M. Keynes. But Lloyd George was the dominant British voice at Versailles, and increasingly Bonar Law remained in Britain to manage domestic affairs. The most pressing problem during the spring and summer of 1919 was labour unrest, particularly on the railways and in the mines. With the government benches dominated by Conservative MPs, many of them 'hard-faced' businessmen who had 'done well out of the war', there was not a great deal of sympathy for the workers' demands. Bonar Law was not as hard-faced as many of his supporters, and hoped for conciliation rather than confrontation. But he was also clear that, as the mines and the railways were still under government control, strikes in these industries were strikes against the state, and that the state had to defend itself to the utmost. This stance—a mixture of

publicly liberal, conciliatory words backed up with, if necessary, aggressive anti-union actions—set the tone not only for the coalition's approach to industrial relations over the next three years but also for the Conservatives' strategy in the mid- to late 1920s. In the short term Bonar Law's insistence on resistance informed the Emergency Powers Act passed in 1920, but it also informed the future industrial relations strategy of the man who was eventually to become Bonar Law's successor as Conservative leader, Stanley Baldwin.

Not surprisingly the Irish question returned to dog British politics. Here Bonar Law seemed to achieve what had been his chief objective since 1912. He agreed with Lloyd George's stance that, with a Home Rule Bill already on the statute book, the Union could no longer be preserved, but Lloyd George also agreed with Bonar Law's view that Ulster was not to be coerced. A cabinet committee worked throughout 1919 to draw up amendments to the existing home-rule legislation, and concluded that separate parliaments for Ulster and the south was the best solution. On 30 March 1920 Bonar Law made what was generally regarded as his finest parliamentary speech, defending these proposals against an attack by Asquith, and the Government of Ireland Act became law in December 1920. The following year the scheme was rejected by the Irish nationalists in the south, but Bonar Law's beloved Ulster was apparently secure.

In early 1920 by-elections began to go against the government, and relations between local coalition Conservative and Liberal associations were deteriorating. One proposed solution was for a fusion of the two parties, an idea actively canvassed by Arthur Balfour and endorsed by other Conservative luminaries such as Austen Chamberlain and F. E. Smith. Bonar Law was not so enthusiastic about fusion, though coalitionism remained his creed. Rumblings of protest in the Conservative ranks against the coalition continued, but they were controllable and his own leadership was not threatened. Personal matters were a deeper concern. In the summer of 1920 his daughter Isabel married Sir Frederick *Sykes, the controller of civil aviation and a friend of Max Aitken (now Lord Beaverbrook). The event was an upheaval for Bonar Law. In the years immediately after his wife's death his sister, Mary, had supervised his domestic affairs, but towards the end of the war Isabel Law had become the main source of both practical assistance and close family affection. Her leaving home came as a shock to her father—his immediate reaction to her engagement was to tell Beaverbrook, 'Max, a dreadful thing has happened' (Blake, 419). The initial concern soon passed and Bonar Law developed close ties with his son-in-law, but he returned to living as a single man.

Bonar Law's own health was not good in the last half of 1920. In March 1921, when he made his rectorial address to the University of Glasgow (he had been elected rector in late 1919), some observers noted that his hesitant speech marked a contrast to his normally fluent style. He was suffering from dangerously high blood pressure, and his doctors advised complete rest. The announcement in the Commons of his resignation, on 17 March 1921, came as a shock to the political world. He left for a holiday in Cannes, remaining in France, apart from two brief visits to England, until the end of September 1921. By the late summer his health and spirits had recovered to the point where there was no physical obstacle to his return. What was required, however, was an incentive.

Ireland was the issue which saw Bonar Law re-enter political life. During his absence in France the government negotiated a treaty with Sinn Féin which appeared to compromise the security guaranteed to Ulster by the legislation of 1920. A large body of Conservative opinion was critical of the treaty's implications for Ulster, and Bonar Law's successor as Conservative leader, Austen Chamberlain, was attacked by his own back-benchers. Bonar Law initially intervened through the press, letting it be known to the editor of *The Scotsman* that he defended Ulster's right to be excluded from an all-Ireland parliament and that he opposed any move to coerce Ulster. Having satisfied himself that Ulster would retain the right to its own assembly he returned to the Commons to speak in favour of the Irish treaty in mid-December 1921. He also spoke out on economic and foreign affairs in early 1922, and though both in private and in public he denied that personal ambition motivated his interventions, a growing number of Conservatives, disillusioned with Austen Chamberlain's seeming subservience to Lloyd George, regarded him as 'the king over the water'.

By early October 1922 many Conservatives, both in parliament and in the constituencies, had become irreconcilably hostile to the coalition. They were alarmed by Lloyd George's aggressive stance on Graeco-Turkish relations—the so-called Chanak crisis—which created the possibility that Britain could be dragged into another conflict. Bonar Law signalled opposition to the government's stance in a letter published in both *The Times* and Beaverbrook's *Daily Express* on 7 October, arguing that no British interests were at stake in the Near East and that Britain could not 'act alone as the policeman of the world' (A. B. Law, *Daily Express*, 7 Oct 1922). His intervention drew a direct, sympathetic response from a number of Conservative MPs, who wrote asking him to reassume the party leadership, though he remained hesitant about openly challenging the government and his successor. The issue at stake in the autumn of 1922 was whether the Conservatives should reassert their political independence. By-election reversals, particularly those occasioned by the intervention of Anti-Waste League candidates in late 1921 and 1922, indicated that grass-roots Conservative activists were disillusioned with government economic policy, and Ireland and Chanak only served to increase discontent.

At a meeting of Conservative ministers and MPs held at the Carlton Club on 19 October 1922 Austen Chamberlain, wishing to confirm his authority and to end Conservative criticism of the coalition, argued that the interests of the party were best served by continuing the coalition, if necessary by fusion. Against him, many Conservatives felt that the government's policies and the very existence of the coalition were alienating Conservatives in the constituencies. Bonar Law was undecided as to his own course

of action until the eve of the meeting, when he made it clear to both Lord Curzon, the foreign secretary, and Archibald Salvidge, the Conservatives' Liverpool party boss, that he would speak against the coalition. His decision was based on a conviction that the Conservative Party would be united behind the idea of 'independence'. He was proved right. His speech against the coalition was greeted with enthusiasm by the meeting, and the party voted to end the coalition. Lloyd George was thereby placed in a hopeless parliamentary position, and he resigned the premiership immediately. Austen Chamberlain, having lost the confidence of his party, tendered his resignation of the Conservative leadership.

Prime minister On the evening of 19 October 1922 Bonar Law was asked to go to Buckingham Palace, the clear indication being that the king wished him to form a government. Bonar Law demurred on the grounds that he could not take the premiership without being leader of his party. A further meeting of the party was convened on 23 October at which he was unanimously elected Conservative leader. He immediately went to the palace and was appointed prime minister, and the following day named his cabinet, sometimes referred to as the 'second eleven', since Chamberlain and other senior Conservative supporters of the coalition refused to serve under him. Two days later parliament was dissolved, and a general election was called for 15 November. Facing divided opposition at the polls, the Conservatives won their first solo election victory since 1900, with a comfortable majority of 77 over all other parties.

Bonar Law's first major task was to pilot the Irish treaty through parliament, which was successfully accomplished by early December 1922. At the same time his government had to face an assault on its conduct of foreign policy, launched by disgruntled Conservative coalitionists. This, too, was dealt with quickly and effectively. His first parliamentary session was thus a success. The second session, in the new year, was more problematic. Negotiations with the French over German war reparations saw him attempt, unsuccessfully, to persuade the French to take a less aggressive stance. Meetings with the French government in Paris in late December and early January proved frustrating, and at one stage he wanted to break off discussions. This abrupt course of action was averted, but the French occupation of the Ruhr on 11 January marked an important breach in Anglo-French relations. Further foreign affairs complications arose in terms of Anglo-Turkish relations, which had been poor since the Chanak crisis. He was determined to avoid war, and advocated arbitration by the League of Nations. In late January 1923 a conference at Lausanne, held under the aegis of the league, ended with the Turks refusing to sign a proposed Anglo-Turkish treaty dealing with all grievances. But Bonar Law had achieved his main objective of defusing a potential conflict, and within five months the Turks signed a slightly modified treaty.

Britain's war debt to the United States represented Bonar Law's most awkward problem. His view was that Britain's debt had to be considered in relation to debts owed to Britain by other allied powers, especially France, and that this in turn was connected to the issue of German reparations. The United States, however, had been pressing for action on the British debt alone since the summer of 1922, and in January 1923 Bonar Law's chancellor, Stanley Baldwin, sailed to America to discuss a settlement. Initially the loans to Britain had been made at an interest rate of 5 per cent, which was generally agreed to be too high. Bonar Law wished to get this reduced to 2.5 per cent, but the best American offer was for 3 per cent, rising to 3.5 per cent after ten years. In money terms the difference was between annual repayments of £25 million and £36 million, rising to £40 million. Baldwin, acting on his own initiative, accepted the American offer and announced to the British press that they were the best terms available. Bonar Law was appalled, and on 30 January announced at cabinet that he would resign rather than accept the settlement. In cabinet he was isolated, with only one minister supporting his position. At a further meeting of the cabinet on 31 January, with Bonar Law absent, all but one again supported the settlement negotiated by Baldwin. However, the cabinet also sent a deputation to Bonar Law to ask him to reconsider his resignation threat. Bonar Law agreed, for he also knew that his resignation, as the only figure who enjoyed the full confidence of the Conservative Party, would have been a disaster for the government and the party. He therefore swallowed his objections and agreed to the terms of the American settlement.

The American settlement meant a 4 per cent increase in public expenditure at a time when a priority of the Conservatives' core constituency was a reduction in expenditure and taxes. In this respect it threatened to undermine a key *raison d'être* of Bonar Law's government. In mid-January 1923, addressing a TUC deputation on unemployment, a growing problem following the downturn of 1921, he stressed that the government's priority was to balance the budget and return the country to 'normal' economic conditions through fiscal and monetary orthodoxy. Specifically he pointed to conditions in Germany as an example of the problems that followed on from high levels of government expenditure and borrowing. In the post-war fiscal and economic climate, with its pressing implications for the extended number of taxpayers and small savers created by wartime finance, he saw retrenchment and a reduced role for government as essential to his government's survival. In other respects the government faced few problems. Bonar Law's inexperienced team began to find their feet in office, and some of his cabinet, notably Baldwin and Neville Chamberlain, made strong impressions in parliament and in their departments. The prospects for Bonar Law's regime thus looked healthy when parliament reassembled on 10 April.

Bonar Law's own health was not as good as his government's. During the general election campaign of November 1922 he had suffered from pains in his throat, which had rendered him unable to speak at one point. The problem seemed to pass, but by early April 1923 his throat was bothering him again, and in the first debates of the new parliamentary session his speeches were occasionally inaudible. On the advice of his doctor, Sir Thomas Horder, he took a month's break from work, leaving Lord Curzon to preside over the cabinet and Baldwin to lead in the Commons. But the break saw a deterioration in his condition. On arrival at Aix les Bains after a cruise he met his old friend Rudyard Kipling, who was so alarmed by his appearance that he telephoned Beaverbrook, who in turn contacted Horder. Horder examined Bonar Law in Paris on 17 May, diagnosed him to be suffering from an incurable cancer of the throat, and gave him six months to live. It seems likely that Bonar Law's one vice, tobacco, had caught up with him.

Resignation and death Bonar Law returned to London on 19 May and immediately wrote to the king to tender his resignation—he was already too unwell to visit the palace in person, and could barely speak. In France Bonar Law had been agitated by the question of who was to succeed him, but had been informed that this decision lay with the king and that he need not offer advice. However, a memorandum ostensibly representing his views was presented to the king, which favoured Stanley Baldwin and presented Curzon, the only other candidate, in an unfavourable light. This memorandum was in fact written by Bonar Law's parliamentary secretary, J. C. C. Davidson, and did not, it seems, express Bonar Law's personal views with total accuracy. Nevertheless, if Bonar Law had not had profound political and personal reservations about Curzon he could easily have intervened more strongly on the foreign secretary's behalf, and, likewise, could have placed more obstacles in Baldwin's path.

Following his departure from office Bonar Law took no further active part in politics—he did not resign his seat, but neither did he attend the Commons. He went to Brighton for specialist treatment and paid a brief visit to Le Touquet, where he felt well enough to play golf. But this rally was short-lived, and through September his condition deteriorated. He was nursed during his final weeks by his daughter Isabel, and Beaverbrook virtually abandoned business and politics to spend time with his friend. After a further round of treatment in Brighton, Bonar Law returned to his London home, 24 Onslow Gardens, where he died in the early hours of 30 October 1923. In his will he expressed a wish to be buried beside his wife in the cemetery at Helensburgh. But the dean and chapter of Westminster offered to hold his funeral in the abbey, and the cabinet too favoured an abbey ceremony. Bonar Law's family thus set aside his wishes and agreed to a state occasion, held on 5 November.

Reputation and assessment Bonar Law's burial in Westminster Abbey prompted his old adversary Asquith to remark that 'we have buried the Unknown Prime Minister by the side of the Unknown Soldier' (Blake, 531), an uncomplimentary remark that has served as Bonar Law's epitaph. Given that Bonar Law was prime minister for only 209 days, the shortest tenure of any prime minister since Viscount Goderich, this seems at first glance not unjustified. But Bonar Law's political importance cannot be measured solely by the length of his period in the highest office. Had it not been for the accident of his fatal illness he could have served a full term and more in the premiership. Moreover, his period as leader of the Conservative Party, twelve years, places him behind only Margaret Thatcher, Winston Churchill, and Stanley Baldwin in the twentieth century in terms of political longevity.

The achievement of which Bonar Law was most proud, and which has proved to be his most lasting legacy, was keeping Ulster in the United Kingdom. This, however, was hardly an unmixed blessing for subsequent generations of politicians, or indeed for the populations of mainland Britain and Ulster itself. Of course he was not solely responsible for the partition of Ireland and the difficulties which it subsequently caused, but his insistence that it was the only acceptable solution narrowed the range of options available to policy makers including himself. Apart from the Irish treaty there are no major pieces of legislation which can be attributed to his influence.

It was as a party leader, rather than as a legislator, that Bonar Law achieved most. Here he was fortunate, in that he was rescued from obvious difficulties and personal failings by the First World War. But when placed in a position of strength by wartime developments he made the most of his and his party's opportunities, and helped reconstruct the Conservatives as a viable governing party. He was by no means a charismatic leader, but in the post-1918 period, especially in 1922, his lack of charisma was a positive asset. His reputation for straightforwardness, his modest lifestyle, and his no-nonsense manner of debate were welcomed by the Conservative rank and file, who had had a surfeit of charisma in the shape of Lloyd George. The events of 1922 illustrated Bonar Law's ability to read and manage back-bench opinion, and underlined his devotion to the fortunes of his party. He was, above all else, a good party man.

Part of Bonar Law's success as leader was that he was genuinely representative of a new kind of Conservative Party. He was the first leader of the Conservatives not to be drawn from the ranks of the aristocracy (leaving aside the peculiar case of Disraeli, who spent his life imitating them), and he presided over a rapid urbanization of the party in terms of its social make-up, the geography of its support, and its policy priorities. The party he left was very different from the one that he had joined, and his own background enabled him to manage and indeed welcome this development. He was, in this respect, the first clearly modern leader of the Conservative Party.

E. H. H. GREEN

Sources R. Blake, *The unknown prime minister: the life and times of Andrew Bonar Law* (1955) · J. Turner, *British politics and the Great War: coalition and conflict, 1915–1918* (1992) · J. Ramsden, *The age of Balfour and Baldwin, 1902–1940* (1978) · C. Hazlehurst, *Politicians at war, July 1914 to May 1915* (1971) · E. H. H. Green, *The crisis of conservatism: the politics, economics and ideology of the Conservative Party, 1880–1914* (1995) · K. O. Morgan, *Consensus and disunity: the Lloyd George coalition government, 1918–1922* (1979) · BL, Balfour MSS · HLRO, Bonar Law papers

Archives HLRO, corresp. and papers | BL, corresp. with Sir W. J. Ashley, Add. MS 42256 · BL, corresp. with Arthur James Balfour,

Add. MSS 49693 *passim* · BL, corresp. with Lord Long, Add. MS 62404 · BL, corresp. with Lord Northcliffe, Add. MS 62158 · BLPES, corresp. with Tariff Commission · Bodl. Oxf., corresp. with Viscount Addison · Bodl. Oxf., corresp. with Herbert Asquith · Bodl. Oxf., letters to H. A. Gwynne · Bodl. Oxf., letters to Lord Selborne · CAC Cam., letters to Sir H. Page Croft · Glos. RO, corresp. with Sir Michael Hicks Beach · HLRO, corresp. with Lord Beaverbrook · HLRO, letters to R. D. Blumenfeld · HLRO, corresp. with David Lloyd George · HLRO, letters to Herbert Samuel · HLRO, corresp. with John St Loe Strachey · L. Cong., letters to Moreton Frewen · Lpool RO, corresp. with Lord Derby · Mitchell L., Glas., Glasgow City Archives, letters to Arthur Jamieson · NA Scot., Steel-Maitland MSS · NL Aus., corresp. with Viscount Novar · PRO, corresp. with Lord Kitchener, PRO 30/57; WO 159 · U. Birm. L., Austen Chamberlain MSS · U. Newcastle, Robinson L., corresp. with Walter Runciman · University of New Brunswick Library, letters to Sir Robert Borden and others · University of Sheffield Library, corresp. with W. A. S. Henins · Wilts. & Swindon RO, corresp. with Viscount Long | SOUND BFI NFTVA, documentary footage · BFI NFTVA, news footage · BFI NFTVA, propaganda footage (Hepworth Manufacturing Company) · Thorn-EMI archive, catalogue reference 01007

Likenesses M. A. Cohen, pencil drawing, 1890, NPG · J. Guthrie, group portrait, oils, *c.*1919–1921, Scot. NPG [*see illus.*] · M. Beerbohm, caricature, 1923 (*The Glasgow School*), Columbus Gallery of Fine Arts, New York · W. Stoneman, photograph, 1923, NPG · J. B. Anderson, oils, Conservative Club, Glasgow · F. Carruthers, caricature, NPG · J. Guthrie and J. B. Anderson, oils, Constitutional Club, London · R. de L'Hôpital, oils, Carlton Club, London · W. Orpen, group portrait, oils (*A peace conference at the Quai D'Orsay*), IWM · W. Orpen, group portrait, oils (*The signing of the peace in the Hall of Mirrors, Versailles, 28 June 1919*), IWM · B. Partridge, pen-and-ink caricature, NPG; repro. in *Punch* (18 Sept 1912) · B. Partridge, pen-and-ink caricature, NPG; repro. in *Punch* (9 Feb 1921) · Spy [L. Ward], chromolithograph, NPG; repro. in *VF* (2 March 1905) · Strickland, chromolithograph caricature, NPG; repro. in *VF* (10 April 1912)

Wealth at death £35,736 2s.: confirmation, 11 Dec 1923, *CCI* · £24,223 13s. 3d.: eik additional estate, 12 June 1924, *CCI*

Law, Augustus Henry (1833–1880). *See under* Law, Edward, first Baron Ellenborough (1750–1818).

Law, Charles Ewan (1792–1850), judge, was born on 14 June 1792, the second son of Edward *Law, first Baron Ellenborough (1750–1818), and his wife, Anne, daughter of George Phillips Towry of the Royal Navy. His elder brother was Edward *Law, first earl of Ellenborough, politician and governor-general of India. His brothers included William Towry *Law, chancellor of the diocese of Bath and Wells, and Augustus Henry *Law [*see under* Law, Edward, first Baron Ellenborough]. He was educated at Winchester College and at St John's College, Cambridge, matriculating in 1810. He graduated MA in 1812 and LLD in 1847.

First at Gretna Green on 8 March, and subsequently on 22 May 1811, Law married Elizabeth Sophia (1789–1864), third daughter of Sir Edward Nightingale, bt, of Kneesworth, Cambridgeshire; they had three sons and seven daughters.

Admitted a member of the Inner Temple on 16 January 1813, Law was called to the bar on 7 February 1817, and subsequently took up practice as a barrister in London. He had earlier been appointed by his father clerk of the *nisi prius* in London and Middlesex in the court of king's bench, and shortly after his call to the bar he became a commissioner of bankruptcy. On 30 January 1823 he was elected by the court of common council one of the four common pleaders of the city of London, and in 1828 he was appointed a judge of the sheriff's court. In 1829 he became a king's counsel, and in the same year was elected to the bench of the Inner Temple, of which he was treasurer in 1839. In November 1830 he was appointed to the office of common serjeant. On the resignation of Newman Knowlys in 1833 Law was elected to the post of recorder, which he continued to hold until his death.

At a by-election in March 1835, Law was returned unopposed to the House of Commons for the University of Cambridge as the colleague of Henry Goulburn, with whom he continued to represent the constituency until his death. The only occasion on which his seat was contested was at the general election of 1847, when he was returned at the head of the poll as a protectionist, while Goulburn only narrowly escaped being defeated by Viscount Feilding. Law was a staunch tory, but did not take any prominent part in the debates of the House of Commons: he was a man of moderate abilities (*Law Magazine*, 44, 1850 291). He died at his home, 72 Eaton Place, Belgrave Square, London, on 13 August 1850, aged fifty-eight, and was buried at St John's Church, Paddington. His remains were later moved to Wargrave, Berkshire. His second son, Charles Edmund Towry Law, succeeded his uncle, Edward, earl of Ellenborough, as third baron in December 1871.

G. F. R. BARKER, *rev.* ERIC METCALFE

Sources *Law Magazine*, 44 (1850), 291 · *GM*, 2nd ser., 34 (1850), 433–4 · *GM*, 3rd ser., 16 (1864), 402 · *Annual Register* (1850), 122 · *Law Times* (17 Aug 1850) · *ILN* (17 Aug 1850) · Burke, *Peerage* · J. Foster, *The peerage, baronetage, and knightage of the British Empire for 1883*, 1 [1883], 264 · Venn, *Alum. Cant.*
Likenesses G. Hayter, pencil drawing, BM · H. W. Pickersgill, oils, St John Cam.

Law, David (1831–1901), etcher and landscape painter, was born in Edinburgh on 25 April 1831 and baptized there on 12 November, the son of John Law and his wife, Charlotte. Having been apprenticed at an early age to the steel-engraver George Aikman, he was admitted in 1845 on his master's recommendation to the Trustees' Academy, where he studied until 1850 under the painters Alexander Christie and Elmslie Dallas. On the termination of his apprenticeship he was appointed a 'hill' engraver in the Ordnance Survey office, Southampton, a post he held until he resigned in 1870. Although the start of his career as an artist was postponed he quickly achieved success, and between 1873 and 1899 showed fifty-two works at the Royal Academy. He later exhibited at the Royal Watercolour Society and the Society (later Royal Society) of British Artists, to which he was elected in 1882 and 1884 respectively. Law painted in oils, but the majority of his exhibited works were in watercolour and were predominantly views in Scotland, Wales, and southern England, produced in a fluent and attractive manner.

Law was best known, however, for the role he played in the revival of etching, and he was one of the founders of the Society of Painter-Etchers in 1880; he showed forty-

David Law (1831–1901), by George Paul Chalmers, 1878

two works there. Since he employed etching as a reproductive medium, and since his style was somewhat mechanical and laboured in a manner reminiscent of the steel-engraver, however, he cannot be classed with the innovators of the movement. None the less, his skill as a draughtsman and his sensitivity to light effects resulted in a series of highly attractive plates after Turner, Corot, and contemporary British landscape painters, and during the time (1875–90) that reproductive etching was fashionable he was in great demand with publishers. His best and most vital work was executed after his own watercolours. The most popular series include the twenty etchings published in 1882 as *The Thames, Oxford to London* and sets of views of *The English Castle*, *The Trossachs*, and *Historic Edifices Along the Banks of the River Wye*. Law also produced etchings after his own works for periodicals such as *The Etcher* and *The Portfolio* and made some lithographs.

Law, who settled in London in 1876, died, unmarried, at Worthing, Sussex, on 28 December 1901, after some years of declining health. A portrait by Seymour Lucas was reproduced in 1902 in the *Art Journal*, for which magazine Law had occasionally etched a plate. Examples of his work are in the print rooms of the British Museum and the Victoria and Albert Museum, London.

J. L. CAW, *rev.* GREG SMITH

Sources R. K. Engen, *Dictionary of Victorian engravers, print publishers and their works* (1979) · M. H. Grant, *A dictionary of British etchers* (1952), 126 · Graves, *RA exhibitors* · IGI · *CGPLA Eng. & Wales* (1902)
Likenesses G. P. Chalmers, oils, 1878, Scot. NPG [*see illus.*] · S. Lucas, oils, repro. in *Art Journal* (1902)

Wealth at death £7155 os. 8d.: probate, 3 Feb 1902, *CGPLA Eng. & Wales*

Law, Edmund (1703–1787), bishop of Carlisle and theologian, the only son of Edmund Law and Patience Langbaine, was born in the parish of Cartmel in Lancashire on 6 June 1703, where he was baptized at the priory church on 17 June. His father, who was descended from a family of yeomen long settled at Askham in Westmorland, was curate of Staveley-in-Cartmel and master of a small school there from 1693 to 1742. He and his wife, who was from the parish of Kirkby-Kendal, married at Kendal on 29 November 1701, and Edmund was born on the property at Buck Crag which his father gained on his marriage. Law was educated first at Cartmel School, and then at the free grammar school at Kendal, from where he went to St John's College, Cambridge, graduating BA in 1723. He was elected a fellow of Christ's College and took his MA in 1727. At Cambridge his close friends were Daniel Waterland, master of Magdalene College, John Jortin, the historian and classical scholar, and John Taylor, the editor of Demosthenes. In 1737 he was presented to the living of Greystoke in Cumberland, the gift of which had devolved on Cambridge University, and he married in the same year Mary Christian (1722–1762), the daughter of John Christian of Unerigg in Cumberland, who was related to Fletcher Christian, the *Bounty* mutineer. In 1743 he was made archdeacon of the diocese of Carlisle, and in 1746 he left Greystoke for Great Salkeld, the rectory of which was annexed to the archdeaconry.

Law's first literary work was a translation of Archbishop William King's theodicy, *De origine mali*, which he published in 1731 as an *Essay on the Origin of Evil*. This appeared with copious notes, and it had a great influence on the way in which the problem of theodicy—the attempt to reconcile God's omnipotence and goodness with the all too manifest presence of evil in the world—was to be treated in eighteenth-century England, from Pope through to Malthus. It became the major treatment of the subject in English. Not all were convinced by its argument; George Horne, the Hutchinsonian divine, was suspicious of its orthodoxy, and remained critical of Law's entire approach to theology: Horne proved typical of many orthodox divines in suspecting heterodoxy in Law's theology. Natural religion was a matter of great suspicion to Law's high-church opponents, who viewed it as a fatal compromise with deism, as Horne made plain in his vituperative remarks concerning Law's notes to King:

> That such kind of *learning* as that book is filled with, and the present age is much given to admire, has done no service to the cause of *truth* but on the contrary, that it has done infinite disservice to it, and almost reduced us from the *unity* of *Christian faith*, to the *wrangling* of *philosophic scepticism*, is the opinion of many, besides ourselves; and too surely founded on fatal *experience*. (G. Horne, *An Apology for Certain Gentlemen in the University of Oxford, Aspersed in a Late Anonymous Pamphlet*, 1756, 17)

Despite such opposition, Law's edition of King went through many editions, and quickly established itself as a major piece of latitudinarian apologetic. It was particularly influential in Cambridge. The work also contained

Edmund Law (1703–1787), by George Romney, 1781

an important short essay in Lockean moral theory, 'Preliminary dissertation concerning the fundamental principle of virtue or morality', which had been provided for Law by John Gay, a fellow of Sidney Sussex College.

In 1734 Law prepared, along with John Taylor, T. Johnson, and Sandys Hutchinson, an edition of Robert Stephens's classic *Thesaurus linguae Latinae*. Also in 1734, Law produced a major critique of a priori proofs of the existence of God, his *Enquiry into the Ideas of Space and Time*. This took the form of a reply to *The Existence and Unity of God Proved from his Nature and Attributes*, a work by John Jackson (1686–1763), a close follower of Samuel Clarke's Newtonian physico-theology. Law's attack on Jackson's Newtonianism was fundamentally Lockean in inspiration. It was accompanied, anonymously, by Daniel Waterland's critique of Clarke's physico-theology, his 'Dissertation upon the argument a priori for proving the existence of a first cause'. Law was the major figure in a group of Cambridge divines, extending back to Phillips Gretton of Trinity College, and on to Waterland and Joseph Clarke of Magdalene, who were extremely critical of Newtonian natural theology.

Law's most influential work was *Considerations on the State of the World with Regard to the Theory of Religion*, which originated in lectures in Cambridge, where it was published in 1745. This stated the progressive case for God's gradual education of humanity over time. The main idea of the book is that the human race has been, and is, through a process of divine education, gradually and continuously progressing in religion, both natural and revealed, at the same rate as it progresses in all other knowledge, the one confirming the other as a deeper knowledge of the world created by God was attained. This theory built on the ideas of earlier Anglican divines, and Law's was a particularly succinct statement of the argument. He also argued that religion would be purified of all the corruptions it had acquired over previous centuries as this knowledge progressed. This work had a profound influence on Lessing, as can be seen in his own version of the argument, *Die Enziehung des Menschensgeschlechts* (1771). A German translation of Law's work was printed in Leipzig in 1771. Later enlarged editions also contained a sermon originally preached in Durham Cathedral, 'Reflections on the life and character of Christ', and an 'Appendix concerning the use of the words soul and spirit in the holy scripture'.

The appendix to the *Considerations* developed Law's scripturally grounded defence of mortalism, or 'soul-sleeping', the heterodox view that the soul, which was not naturally immortal but was only made so by Christ, passed into a state of sleep between death and the resurrection into eternal life. He had kept his public exercise for the DD with a defence of this notion, which had caused great controversy, with several heads of houses refusing to support his advocacy of a heretical belief. Mortalism was also ably defended by Law's long-standing friend from Cambridge, Archdeacon Francis Blackburne, and it provoked a good deal of pamphlet literature in the 1750s and 1760s, with several extensive replies to Law having been penned by Peter Stephen Goddard, a Cambridge divine, alongside John Steffe, John Bristed, and Thomas Morton. In 1756 Law became master of Peterhouse, thus instituting a notable period of political and theological liberalism in the college; he resigned his archdeaconry at the same time. In 1760 he was appointed librarian (proto-bibliothecarius) of the university, and in 1764 was made Knightbridge professor of moral philosophy. In 1763 he was appointed to the archdeaconry of Staffordshire and a prebend in the church of Lichfield by his old pupil Frederick Cornwallis, the bishop of Coventry and Lichfield; he received a prebend in the church in Lincoln in 1764, and in 1767 a prebendal stall in the church of Durham through the influence of the duke of Newcastle. In 1768 Law was recommended by the duke of Grafton, a former Peterhouse undergraduate, then chancellor of the university, to the bishopric of Carlisle. Law's friend and biographer, William Paley, declared that he had regarded his elevation as satisfactory proof that decent freedom of inquiry was not discouraged.

In 1774 Law published anonymously an outspoken declaration in favour of religious toleration in a pamphlet entitled *Considerations on the Propriety of Requiring Subscription to Articles of Faith*. This was his belated contribution to the debate inspired by a petition against subscription to the Thirty-Nine Articles presented to parliament in 1772 by Blackburne and a group of young Cambridge dons, many of whom were connected with Peterhouse. For Law, creeds represented a corruption of Christianity's primitive plainness and practicality. He called for revision of the liturgy, making a case for a firmly scripture-based

faith in which biblical exegesis was to be made by 'our reason on the whole'. He felt that enforced subscription led to a careerist abuse of the ministry, which corrupted Reformation ideals. A clergyman's beliefs, he argued, could not and ought not to be imposed on him by the church. Dr Thomas Randolph, archdeacon of Oxford, attacked the publication, but it was defended by William Paley in his first published tract, which he wrote under the alias of 'A Friend to Religious Liberty'. In 1777 Law published the major eighteenth-century edition of Locke's *Works* in four volumes, with a laudatory preface and a life of the author. Law was the most convinced and actively engaged Lockean divine at work in the eighteenth-century church. His interleaved Bible, with many manuscript notes, is preserved in the British Museum.

Law died at Rose Castle, Carlisle, on 14 August 1787, in the eighty-fifth year of his age, his wife having predeceased him in 1762, leaving eight sons and four daughters. He was buried in the cathedral at Carlisle, where the inscription on his monument commemorates his zeal alike for Christian truth and Christian liberty, adding 'religionem simplicem et incorruptam nisi salva libertate stare non posse arbitratus' ('he deemed religion to be simple and incorrupt, unless it was unable to exist in secure liberty'). Paley praised his delicate manners, and his mild and tranquil disposition. He was described as being small but perfectly formed. His eldest son, Edmund, died a young man; four younger sons, John *Law, bishop of Elphin, Edward *Law, later first Baron Ellenborough, George Henry *Law (1761–1845), bishop of Bath and Wells, and Thomas *Law, are noticed separately.

B. W. YOUNG

Sources W. Paley, *A short memoir of the life of Edmund Law* (1800) · W. Jackson, 'Laws of Buck Crag', *Transactions of the Cumberland and Westmorland Antiquarian and Archaeological Society*, 2 (1875–6), 264–76 · O. Chadwick, *From Bossuet to Newman*, 2nd edn (1987) · L. Stephen, *History of English thought in the eighteenth century*, 2 vols. (1876) · D. Spadafora, *The idea of progress in eighteenth-century Britain* (1990) · B. W. Young, *Religion and Enlightenment in eighteenth-century England: theological debate from Locke to Burke* (1998) · G. Dening, *Mr Bligh's bad language: passion, power and theatre on the Bounty* (1992) · *DNB* · *IGI*

Archives BL, corresp. with duke of Newcastle, Add. MSS 32860–32990

Likenesses G. Romney, portrait, 1781, National Gallery of Victoria, Melbourne [*see illus.*] · W. Dickinson, mezzotint (after G. Romney), BM · oils (after G. Romney), Peterhouse, Cambridge

Law, Edward, first Baron Ellenborough (1750–1818),

judge, was born on 16 November 1750 at Great Salkeld, Cumberland, the sixth child of Edmund *Law (1703–1787), later bishop of Carlisle, and his wife, Mary (1722–1762), the daughter of John Christian, of Unerigg, Cumberland. George Henry *Law, John *Law, and Thomas *Law were his brothers. At the age of eight he went to live with his uncle, the Revd Humphrey Christian, at Docking, Norfolk, and attended school at Bury St Edmunds before becoming a scholar at Charterhouse School in January 1761. In 1767 he matriculated at Peterhouse, Cambridge, where his father was master, and where he first came under the influence of his brother's friend William Paley.

Edward Law, first Baron Ellenborough (1750–1818), by Charles
Turner, pubd 1809 (after Sir Thomas Lawrence, 1806)

He was disappointed to be only third wrangler when he
graduated BA in 1771. Though his father wanted him to
enter the church Edward preferred the law, and was
admitted to Lincoln's Inn in June 1769. Having obtained a
fellowship at Peterhouse in 1771 he commenced his legal
studies, becoming a pupil of the eminent special pleader
George Wood. After two years in Wood's office Law began
to practise as a special pleader himself, and soon attracted
much business, as well as numerous pupils. He was called
to the bar in June 1780 and immediately obtained a large
number of retainers on the northern circuit, from his old
clients and from his family's connections.

At the bar, 1787–1802 It was only after Law was made a
king's counsel in June 1787 that he made his fame and fortune at the bar in London. In that year he became counsel
to Warren Hastings in his impeachment, on the recommendation of his brother-in-law, Sir Thomas Rumbold,
whom he had assisted when Rumbold faced a bill of pains
and penalties in 1783. His legalistic insistence on following the rules of evidence and procedures of a court, which
so frustrated the eloquent managers from the Commons,
landed an early blow when the Lords agreed that the managers would have to go through the whole of their case,
before calling on the defence to present theirs, rather
than proceeding to judgment item by item. There were
many sharp exchanges during the hearings between Law
and Edmund Burke and R. B. Sheridan, who wasted no
opportunity to deride Law as a special pleader playing for
a technical acquittal. For his part Law felt that Burke was
attempting to smear Hastings with stories of atrocities
which were unconnected with his client, and condemned

'the harshness and brutality of their personal invective'
(PRO 30/12/17/3, fol. 187). Law's oratorical powers were no
match either for those of his adversaries, nor even for
those of his juniors, and his opening of the defence case in
February 1792 was rather nervous. However, his defence
of Hastings showed close forensic reasoning and a great
mastery of the evidence, which secured an acquittal for
Hastings in 1795.

As a young man Law followed his family's whig politics,
joining the Whig Club in 1785. However, he became alienated from the whigs as a result of the French Revolution.
In November 1792 he became attorney-general for the
county palatine of Durham, and in 1793 king's attorney
and serjeant for the county palatine of Lancaster. He
intended to enter parliament once Hastings's impeachment had ended and, with that in mind, Lord Abingdon's
Westbury seat was held for him from 1790 onwards by his
brother Ewan. However, as an opponent of the war with
France, Law came to regard his connection with Abingdon
as 'very embarrassing and disagreeable' (PRO 30/12/17/3,
fol. 297) and he requested his patron in 1795 to allow Ewan
to vacate the seat in favour of someone else.

During the 1790s Law was counsel for the crown in a
number of state prosecutions, having already appeared
for the crown in 1787 in the trial of Lord George Gordon
for libel. In 1794 he prosecuted Thomas Walker in Manchester for a conspiracy to overthrow the constitution,
but withdrew the charges during the trial, when it
became apparent that one of the main witnesses was a
perjurer. In the same year he was one of the crown counsel in the treason trial of John Horne Tooke, and in the following year successfully prosecuted Henry Redhead Yorke
for a seditious conspiracy. In 1796 he appeared in the treason trials of William Stone and Robert Crossfield, and in
the trial of John Reeves for a seditious libel. In 1799 he was
counsel for the prosecution against the earl of Thanet,
Robert Fergusson, and others, tried for a riot during the
trial of Arthur O'Connor for treason at Maidstone. In this
trial his insistent cross-examination of Sheridan made his
old adversary seem evasive and effectively secured a conviction. In 1800 Law was one of the counsel for the crown
in the treason trial of the insane James Hadfield.

On the fall of Pitt's ministry, in February 1801, Law was
asked by Henry Addington to become attorney-general in
the new government. Having some difficulties in forming
a ministry, Addington gave Law some time to reflect on
the offer; but he needed none. Accepting at once, he
replied 'I am yours, and let the storm blow from what
quarter of the hemisphere it may, you shall always find
me at your side' (Campbell, 3.143). He was to prove as good
as his word, remaining a close and loyal friend of Addington's until his death. Paley noted that his promotion was
'in consequence neither of parliamentary service, nor political connection, but solely of professional practice and
reputation' (PRO 30/12/17/4, fol. 49). Law was knighted at
the same time. As attorney-general he prosecuted in only
one state trial: that of Joseph Wall in 1802, for the death of
a soldier who had been sentenced by Wall, as governor of
Senegal, to 800 lashes. Although the events had happened

twenty years previously Law, spurred on by a popular cry for vengeance, urged a conviction, which he obtained, and Wall was executed with no delay.

Lord chief justice In April 1802 Law was appointed chief justice of the king's bench, and was raised to the peerage at the same time. Law took the name of the ancient residence of his maternal ancestors, Ellenborough, as his title, rejecting that of his birthplace, Salkeld, since he felt that the latter's association with the name of a dull law reporter would degrade rather than decorate him. While at the bar Ellenborough—Francis Buller's protégé—had suffered from his predecessor Kenyon's constant attempts to belittle him, and he was therefore determined, on assuming office, to avoid Kenyon's practice of mixing favouritism to some with peevish incivility to others. In the event, however, Ellenborough proved himself often to be irascible and impatient with everyone. He particularly rebuked barristers he felt were wasting his time, and often sought to expedite cases by taking them into his own hands. He was especially hostile to abuses. He sought to humiliate and shame untruthful witnesses, and on one occasion flung the record at the head of an attorney found guilty of some chicanery. However, he was popular with the bar, even gaining the respect of those, like H. Brougham and John Campbell (1779–1861), who suffered from his rough treatment. He had a sharp, ironic wit which deflated many a pompous or pedantic barrister but delighted the bar in general.

Ellenborough was chief justice at a time when the commercial business of the king's bench had increased vastly, in part thanks to the economic conditions caused by the Napoleonic wars. Before being raised to the bench Ellenborough had acquired a strong reputation as a mercantile lawyer, and his decisions on commercial law helped build on the foundations laid by Lord Mansfield, particularly in the fields of bills of exchange and insurance. His decision in *Bilbie* v. *Lumley* (1802), which stated that money paid under a mistake of law in an insurance policy could not be recovered since 'every man must be cognisant of the law' (472), was strongly criticized by later legal authorities, but remains a leading authority. He also presided in several important cases in the law of contract, such as *Adams* v. *Lindsell* (1818), which established the postal rule in the formation of contracts, or *Stilk* v. *Myrick* (1809), which ruled that a promise by a ship's captain to pay his crew more money to work harder after some sailors had deserted was void for failing to provide fresh consideration money. Some of his decisions in tort had lasting, if controversial, effect. For instance, in *Baker* v. *Bolton* (1808) he ruled that in fatal accident cases there could be no compensation for emotional damage or loss of income, since in a civil court 'the death of a human being could not be complained of as an injury'.

Ellenborough presided in the king's bench at a time when the role of the jury was being gradually diminished, as more questions of fact were turned into questions of law, and the chief justice contributed to this with many decisions on the law of evidence and damages. He was particularly keen to reduce the level of damages in cases of criminal conversation, which he felt Kenyon had allowed to escalate. He also presided in two important constitutional cases. In *Burdett* v. *Abbott* (1812) he ruled that the speaker of the House of Commons did have the power to imprison for contempt, while in *R.* v. *Creevey* (1813) he held that a member of parliament who printed a report outside parliament of libellous matters spoken in the house could not be protected by parliamentary privilege.

Among lawyers Ellenborough had a reputation for being impartial. In Brougham's view, 'his honest and manly nature ever disdained as much to trample overbearingly on the humble, as to crouch meanly before the powerful' (Brougham, 12). On one occasion he directed a jury to give exemplary damages against magistrates who had put a young man on a prison ship for seven days for an offence carrying only a 10s. fine, observing that magistrates had to guard against playing with the liberties of the subject. In a number of cases he also showed himself in favour of free speech, as in the case of *Carr* v. *Hood* in 1808, when he ruled that it was no libel to parody a work to make it look ridiculous and render it unsaleable. Similarly, his even-handed direction of the jury in the *ex officio* prosecution of the *Morning Chronicle* proprietors, John Lambert and James Perry, in 1810 was widely praised. Nevertheless, in other political cases, where the interests of the state were affected, he showed himself much more executive-minded, and appeared much less even-handed. This was seen, for instance, in the conviction of Jean Peltier for a libel on Napoleon, during the period of peace with France.

In public life Ellenborough had acquired a fortune at the bar which exceeded £60,000 even before his elevation to the bench. As a young man he had been told by his father that all he could expect was 'a good education, and afterwards half a crown to begin the world with—and then you must shift for yourselves' (*Lord Eldon's Anecdote Book*, 1960, 70). In fact, in 1785 he turned down the only patronage in his father's gift—the chancellorship of Carlisle—in favour of Paley. In his political life he abhorred what he saw as jobbery, robustly attacking in 1805 the bill which gave additional compensation to the duke of Atholl for rights lost in the Isle of Man, and voting to convict Viscount Melville on six out of the ten articles of impeachment he faced in 1806. Nevertheless, he valued his own patronage, and used his political influence to secure ecclesiastical preferments for his brothers. When he was appointed chief justice he observed that 'The great patronage of the office affords me, if I live, a fair prospect of providing for the boy upon whom this honour may descend' (PRO 30/12/17/3, fol. 368). This he achieved in 1804 when the highly lucrative clerkship of the king's bench fell vacant: Ellenborough rode hard to London to fill it at once, executing the deed as soon as he dismounted from his horse. It was money which motivated the libel committed on Ellenborough in 1817 by R. G. Butt, one of the defendants in the trial of Thomas *Cochrane in 1814 for conspiracy to defraud the public funds. Butt became so obsessed with the idea that Ellenborough and his family had pocketed the large fine he had paid, that he posted placards all over London denouncing the judge for corruption. As a result he was prosecuted for libel and sentenced to six months in the king's bench prison, or Ellenborough Castle, as it was popularly known.

In 1806 Ellenborough joined the 'ministry of all the talents'. He had initially turned down the post of lord chancellor, on the ground that he had no knowledge of chancery, and the great seal went instead to Thomas, Baron Erskine, whom Ellenborough believed to be wholly unfit for the job. Ellenborough had not sought office—the idea had initially been suggested by George Grenville, aware that Addington, now first Viscount Sidmouth, would not join without an ally—and was at first reluctant to join. However, he concluded that he could not refuse 'without materially disturbing an arrangement which I think is necessary to the public interests at the present moment' (PRO 30/12/15/1, fol. 6). His appointment caused a furore, however, since many felt it unconstitutional to have the chief criminal judge present at deliberations regarding public prosecutions. Although he received entreaties from numerous friends not to accept, Ellenborough was convinced that there was no impropriety, since he saw no constitutional distinction between being a privy councillor and a member of the cabinet, and dismissed any opposition to his appointment as being motivated by mere party bias. Defended by the whigs in parliament and *The Times* outside, Ellenborough easily survived parliamentary motions against his position. Nevertheless, he later regretted joining the ministry, and was the last chief justice to sit in the cabinet.

If the fact of Ellenborough's being in the cabinet was controversial, he was well placed within it to act as a mediator between factions. Some Pittites in opposition, such as Charles Yorke, regarded him as the most valuable man in the cabinet, one who could be trusted to prevent mischief; and after the death of Charles James Fox (whom Ellenborough grew to admire while in cabinet), he was used by Grenville as an intermediary in an attempt to woo Spencer Perceval into the cabinet. Equally, after the fall of the ministry the Grenvillites, despairing of Sidmouth's support in opposition, nevertheless felt it worthwhile to court Ellenborough.

Perhaps Ellenborough's most important contribution in government was his participation in 1806, with Erskine, George Spencer, and Grenville, in the 'delicate investigation' into the conduct of the princess of Wales. This inquiry exonerated the princess of marital infidelity, but was critical of her conduct. Convinced of her moral guilt, Ellenborough resisted any attempt to declare the princess unequivocally innocent, fearing this might result in her becoming regent, were her daughter to become queen during her minority. The princess's advisers attacked the procedure taken by the investigating lords, and the conduct of the investigation was questioned again in parliament in 1813, when Ellenborough robustly rejected the accusation as being 'as false as hell' (*Hansard 1*, 25.209). In the event, most agreed that the privy councillors had acted properly. The ministry of all the talents fell in March 1807 when Ellenborough, Sidmouth,

and Erskine, siding with the king, opposed reforms to the Mutiny Act which would open senior ranks to Roman Catholics. Ellenborough never again held political office, although he remained on close terms with both the prince of Wales and those in office, and continued to give advice on such matters as who should be appointed law officers. He was also, in 1811, appointed to the queen's council to look after the king, during the Regency.

Ellenborough's politics Ellenborough continued to play an active role in parliament, where he lived up to the younger Boswell's characterization of him as 'the worst tempered man living' (*Farington Diary*, ed. Greig, 7.29). After hearing Ellenborough's maiden speech William Woodfall observed to Lord Auckland that 'lawyers so rapidly raised to high station cannot on the sudden forget their nisi prius manners' (*Journal and Correspondence of … Auckland*, 158). Never one to shy away from a confrontation, he tended to be sarcastic, bullying, and rude, and was known to dismiss his opponents as incapable or ignorant men. For Lord Glenbervie, Ellenborough in debate was like 'a strong and active but clumsy cart-horse galloping down a miry lane and scattering mud and dirt as he moved along' (*Diaries of Sylvester Douglas*, 2.17). He caused particular offence in 1811, when attacking Lord Holland's motion for a return of *ex officio* prosecutions for libel with 'the coarse violence of a demagogue' (*Memoirs of … Sir James Mackintosh*, 2.117). Resort to temper rather than eloquence generally failed to carry the house, however, and on this occasion Ellenborough was left floundering by the eloquent put-down given by the dignified Holland.

Ellenborough's political creed was fundamentally conservative, seeking to maintain the Church of England and all the ancient rights of the crown, and to resist any hasty changes in the laws and institutions of the state. His maiden speech in the Commons had supported the continuation of martial law in Ireland, and he also supported the suspension of habeas corpus while in the lower house. In later years he consistently supported measures designed to facilitate the suppression of popular tumults. In the Lords, in 1804, during debates on the Volunteer Consolidation Bill, he strongly defended the prerogative power of invoking the assistance of all subjects in an emergency, declaring that, should it be necessary, even he would not hesitate to 'cast this gown from my back, and … grapple with the enemy' (*Hansard 1*, 1.1028–9). This came ill from a man who had been turned out of the Lincoln's Inn Volunteers—the awkward squad—for awkwardness. Resolutely hostile to Catholic emancipation, he argued against the petition for Catholic relief in 1805, holding that Catholics could not be given full civil rights until they renounced their allegiance to a foreign sovereign, the pope.

Most significant was Ellenborough's sustained opposition to Sir Samuel Romilly's attempts to reform the criminal code. In 1810 he spoke against Romilly's bill to abolish capital punishment for privately stealing goods in a shop, dismissing the reformers' 'speculative mode of legislating upon humanity' (*Hansard 1*, 19, appendix, lxxxvii). Ellenborough's arguments were largely borrowed from his friend Paley, whom he regarded as 'by far the most powerful instructor in the art of thinking' he had ever met (PRO 30/12/17/3, fol. 422). He believed that it was impossible to create a system of graduated punishments, and that the imposition of punishment should always be left to the discretion of the judge. He saw Romilly's initiative as the thin end of a wedge, which would end in the property of the poorest cottager being rendered utterly insecure; and he maintained that the terror of the gallows was the only way to prevent crime, since hardened criminals saw punishments such as transportation as 'a summer's excursion, in an easy migration, to a happier and a better climate' (*Hansard 1*, 19, appendix, cxx). It was thanks to Ellenborough's authority that Romilly's bills were repeatedly rejected, and the latter became convinced (despite Ellenborough's protestations to the contrary) that the chief justice was in effect encouraging his fellow judges to enforce the law more rigorously, in the manner encouraged by Martin Madan.

Ellenborough himself contributed to the swelling bloody code in 1803, when he introduced a statute (43 Geo. III c. 58) creating ten new capital offences against the person. His traditionalist attitudes on crime were shown in *R. v. Fletcher* in 1803, when he took the view that the body of a felon convicted of murder could be dissected without the sentence of dissection having been pronounced: for the body was now the king's, to deal with as he pleased. Similarly, in 1814, Ellenborough (with John Scott, Lord Eldon) insisted on amending a bill of Romilly's to ensure that dissection would remain part of the punishment for treason. Nor was he always keen to recommend mercy. When Colonel Despard, convicted of high treason in 1803, was recommended to mercy by the jury after hearing evidence of his past high character, the chief justice was 'perfectly at a loss to comprehend upon what reasonable principle this recommendation can have proceeded' (BL, Add. MS 37538, fol. 8), since for him, his previous good character made the crime so much the worse. Despard was duly executed. Similarly, he once sentenced to death a man convicted for stealing in a shop after he had 'lolled out his tongue and acted the part of an idiot' (*Memoirs of … Romilly*, 3.331).

In the 1810s Ellenborough was increasingly perceived by the radicals as the willing instrument of a repressive government. After Daniel Isaac Eaton had received a lengthy prison sentence and the pillory for blasphemy in 1812, Shelley wrote *A Letter to Lord Ellenborough*, in which he portrayed the chief justice as the reincarnation of the Marian persecutors. Ellenborough's courtroom manner did not help his reputation, particularly when, in the same year, he accused Henry Brougham, the counsel for the Hunt brothers in a case for libelling the prince of Wales, of being inoculated with all the poison of the libel. These comments were widely condemned as unseemly by politicians and lawyers alike. In 1814 his sentencing of the radical naval hero Thomas, Lord Cochrane, to a fine, imprisonment, and the pillory on his conviction for a fraudulent conspiracy was generally seen as being unduly degrading

for a man of his station, and led to the abolition of the pillory in all cases save forgery. In the following year Ellenborough's house was attacked by a mob during debates on the corn law, and Cochrane charged him in parliament with gross partiality in the handling of the case. Although many whigs felt a personal dislike of the judge they rallied behind the chief judge, and Cochrane's motion was unanimously defeated and expunged from the parliamentary record.

In the popular mind Ellenborough's greatest defeat came in 1817, with the prosecution of William Hone for blasphemous libel. After Hone had been acquitted in a first trial, Ellenborough took over as presiding judge from Charles Abbott, so determined was he to secure a conviction. However, Hone proved more than a match for the chief justice, portraying himself as the victim of a court which was biased against him, and quoting a raft of historical examples of biblical parodies which had gone unpunished. When he sought to invoke the testimony of Ellenborough's father, who had doubted the authenticity of Anathasius' creed (which Hone had parodied), the weary judge interrupted: 'For common delicacy, forbear'. Hone was acquitted twice more, and Ellenborough and the court were mercilessly caricatured by his friend George Cruikshank. Ever defiant, the judge remarked to Bishop Turner on his way home that he was more afraid of the saliva of the mob following his carriage than of their bite, and even stopped to buy some kippers. However, the image of the court being baffled and defeated by Hone was widely seen to have degraded the law, and on the following day Ellenborough wrote to Sidmouth that he owed it to himself and the public to resign. Though persuaded to remain in office, he was never able to hold his head up in public again.

Family life In his early life Ellenborough had been a renowned womanizer, with a number of mistresses, and in 1782 his natural daughter, Elizabeth Thornton, was born. In 1789 he began to court Ann Towry (*d.* 1843), the daughter of George Phillips Towry, a commissioner of the navy victualling office, and his wife, Elizabeth. She was a great beauty, and was initially reluctant to marry the ungainly and unrefined barrister; indeed, it was only on the fourth proposal that she accepted. They were married on 17 October 1789. On his marriage Ellenborough moved to a house in Bloomsbury Square, and in 1808 bought a large house in St James's Square, to be nearer to Westminster Hall. An entertaining companion, full of anecdote and information, he acquired a reputation for being a great voluptuary, indulging heartily in huge dishes of rich food, notably turtle. His fondness for drinking also contributed to his periodic severe attacks of gout.

Well versed in the classics thanks to his upbringing, Ellenborough found the time to read Euclid with his sons while not on circuit, and was a conscientious governor of Charterhouse. He was said to speak in the strong and nervous manner of Dr Johnson, but without any pedantry or affectation, and always in the broad Cumberland accent of his childhood. Physically he was an ungainly man, with a large forehead, dark eyes, and shaggy eyebrows, and a habit of entering court walking like a crab, while puffing out his cheeks like a war horse preparing for battle. When in 1812 the actor Charles Mathews imitated his mannerisms on the stage of Covent Garden it caused such merriment that the prince regent insisted on the actor's performing it for him at Carlton House. Ellenborough, however, was not amused and requested the lord chamberlain to have the scene cut from the play. Indeed, he never lost a sense of his own importance, expecting obsequious deference even at Serjeant's Inn and berating officials in assize towns if they failed to attend him with due pomp on his ceremonial approach.

Ellenborough's rich lifestyle began to take its toll on his health, and by 1816 his appearances in court became less frequent. In 1817, he was so fatigued in the treason trial of James Watson that he had to call on Justice Bayley to sum up the evidence for him. As his health and spirits softened, so he became more civilized, if less witty. With his eyesight fading, he decided in September 1818 to resign from the king's bench, to the sincere regret of both his friend Eldon and the prince regent. His condition rapidly deteriorated, and after suffering a stroke in November he died at his home, 13 St James's Square, London, on 13 December 1818. He was buried at Charterhouse, London, on 22 December.

Ellenborough was survived by five sons, including the politician Edward *Law and the judge Charles Ewan *Law, and five daughters from his marriage. His youngest son, **William Towry Law** (1809–1886), was born on 16 June 1809 and educated at Middlesex School and Eton College. He entered the army in 1826, serving first in the Ionian Islands, and subsequently with the Grenadier Guards in London. On leaving the army in 1831 he entered Peterhouse as a fellow commoner, and on 15 March that year married the Hon. Augusta Graves (*bap.* 1812), daughter of the second Lord Graves. He subsequently took orders and became chancellor of the diocese of Bath and Wells. In 1845 he became vicar of Harborne, near Birmingham, having previously been vicar of East Brent. His first wife died on 16 October 1844, and on 25 January 1846 he married Matilda (*bap.* 1813), the second daughter of Sir Henry Montgomery of Donegal. In 1850 he published *A Sermon Preached in the Parish Church of Harborne*, in which he attacked the pope's attempts to reassert his authority in England, and bemoaned the 'unfaithful defection and secession of some who have once ministered at our altars, men of unstable minds, wanting Christian courage' (p. 9). However, he was already having his own doubts, and was very shaken by Henry Manning's decision to defect to Rome. In September 1851 he converted to Catholicism and in 1852, in another pamphlet, *A Letter to his Late Parishioners*, explained that he never had any authority as a priest in the Church of England, as there was only one indivisible church. He died on 31 October 1886 at Hampton Court Palace, Middlesex, survived by his second wife and by children from both marriages.

His eldest son, **Augustus Henry Law** (1833–1880), was born on 21 October 1833 at Trumpington, near Cambridge. Although he wanted to become a churchman he joined the navy at the age of twelve, at his uncle Ellenborough's suggestion, after attending Somerton School, Somerset. However, he continued to be pious, and after his father's conversion was also received into the Catholic church in May 1852. Quitting the navy the following year, he determined on pursuing a religious life, and became a Jesuit novice. After a period of teaching in a Jesuit college in Glasgow he was ordained a priest in 1865. Law had a particular desire to be a foreign missionary in India, but in 1866 he was sent to the West Indies, where he worked in Demerara and British Guiana, returning in 1871 to teach in Edinburgh and Galashiels. In 1875 he was sent to Grahamstown in the eastern Cape, where he taught at St Aidan's College. In April 1879 he set out from Grahamstown to establish a mission on the Zambezi, reaching Lobengula's kraal at Bulawayo in September. After eight months there he set off eastwards aiming for the kraal of the Shona king, Umzila. The journey proved difficult, with the missionaries taking their wagons through open country with often hostile local populations; and eventually they were forced to abandon their wagons and continue on foot. Reaching the kraal, short of food and weakened by the journey, they were received by a largely indifferent Umzila. Worn out by hunger and fatigue, Law contracted yellow fever and died on 25 November 1880 at Umzila's kraal, Mashonaland.   MICHAEL LOBBAN

Sources John, Lord Campbell, *The lives of the chief justices of England*, 3rd edn, 4 vols. (1874), vol. 3, p. 143; vol. 4, pp. 148–308 · W. C. Townsend, *The lives of twelve eminent judges*, 2 (1846), 299–397 · H. Brougham, *Historical sketches of statesmen who flourished in the time of George III*, 3rd ser., 2 (1845) · PRO, Ellenborough MSS, PRO 30/12 · Holdsworth, *Eng. law*, 13.499–516 · R. G. Thorne, 'Law, Edward', HoP, *Commons, 1790–1820*, 4.389–91 · W. H. Bennet, *Select biographical sketches from the note-books of a law reporter* (1867), 7–17 · [I. Espinasse], 'My contemporaries: from the notes of a retired barrister', *Fraser's Magazine*, 6 (1832), 419–20 · [I. Espinasse], 'My contemporaries: from the notes of a retired barrister', *Fraser's Magazine*, 7 (1833), 44–8 · S. Romilly, *Memoirs of the life of Sir Samuel Romilly*, 3 vols. (1840) · *The Farington diary*, ed. J. Greig, 8 vols. (1922–8) · *The diaries of Sylvester Douglas (Lord Glenbervie)*, ed. F. Bickley, 2 vols. (1928) · *The manuscripts of J. B. Fortescue*, 10 vols., HMC, 30 (1892–1927), vols. 7, 9 · *The correspondence of George, prince of Wales, 1770–1812*, ed. A. Aspinall, 8 vols. (1963–71), vols. 5–8 · P. Ziegler, *Addington: a life of Henry Addington, first Viscount Sidmouth* (1965) · D. Gray, *Spencer Perceval: the evangelical prime minister, 1762–1812* (1963) · L. Radzinowicz, *A history of English criminal law and its administration from 1750, 1: The movement for reform* (1948) · Hansard 1 · State trials · Venn, *Alum. Cant.*, 2/4.107 · R. L. Patten, *George Cruikshank's life, times, and art*, 1 (1992), 129–38 · *Memoirs of the life of the Right Honourable Sir James Mackintosh*, ed. R. J. Mackintosh, 2 vols. (1835) · *The journal and correspondence of William, Lord Auckland*, ed. [G. Hogge], 4 vols. (1861–2) · *The Times* (2 Nov 1886) [obit. of W. T. Law] · Gillow, *Lit. biog. hist.*, 4.154–7 · Boase, *Mod. Eng. biog.*, 2.323 · *Catholic Times and Catholic Opinion* (5 Nov 1886), 2 · *The Tablet* (6 Nov 1886), 744 · *Augustus Law SJ: notes in remembrance* (1886) · W. T. Law, ed., *A memoir of the life and death of the Rev. Father Augustus Henry Law SJ*, 3 vols. (1882–3) · W. T. Law, *A sermon preached in the parish church of Harborne* (1850), 9

Archives Harvard U., law school, legal notebook [microfilm] · PRO, corresp. and papers, PRO 30/12 | BL, corresp. with Lord Grenville, Add. MS 58954 · BL, speeches on trial of Warren Hastings, Add. MSS 24235, 24239, 24246 · BL, corresp. with first and second earls of Liverpool, Add. MSS 38248–38328, 38450, 38473, 38571–38573, *passim* · Harrowby Manuscript Trust, Sandon Hall,

Staffordshire, corresp. with Richard Ryder • NRA, priv. coll., letters to Sir John Bayley • U. Durham L., corresp. with second Earl Grey **Likenesses** C. Turner, engraving, pubd 1809 (after T. Lawrence), BM [*see illus.*] • T. Rowlandson, caricature, *c.*1815 (with Gibbs and Thomson), Laing Art Gallery, Newcastle upon Tyne • F. L. Chantrey, sculpture, 1819–22, Charterhouse Chapel, London • B. F. Hardenberg, marble bust, 1820, Royal Collection • G. Cruikshank, caricatures, repro. in F. G. Stephens and M. D. George, *Catalogue of prints and drawings in the British Museum*, 11 vols. (1870–1954) • S. Drummond, oils, NPG; on loan to Royal Courts of Justice • oils (after T. Lawrence, *c.*1806), Lincoln's Inn, London • photograph (Augustus Henry Law; as a young man), repro. in W. T. Law, ed., *A memoir of the life and death of the Rev. Father Augustus Henry Law SJ* • photograph (Augustus Henry Law), repro. in W. T. Law, ed., *A memoir of the life and death of the Rev. Father Augustus Henry Law SJ*
Wealth at death £240,000: Thorne, 'Edward Law', 4.389; *The Times* (25 Dec 1818), 3a

Law, Edward, first earl of Ellenborough (1790–1871), politician and governor-general of India, was born on 8 September 1790, the eldest son of Edward *Law (1750–1818), who made his name at the bar as counsel for the defence at Warren Hastings's impeachment, and his wife, Anne Towry (*d.* 1843), daughter of Captain George Phillips Towry RN. Created a peer in 1802 on becoming lord chief justice of the king's bench, the first baron was a Foxite whig turned Pittite, and a politically reactionary judge. The younger Edward Law passed from his private school to Eton College (1802–5), where he was captain of the Oppidans, and St John's College, Cambridge. Having matriculated in Michaelmas term 1807, he won a university prize for a Latin ode, and proceeded to his MA in 1809. 'From what I saw of them at Cambridge', he wrote many years afterwards, 'the persons I least respect are Fellows of Colleges' (E. Law, 1.341). The sweeping comment was typical. As able as he was ambitious, handsome, charming, and self-confident, he was thought of as a possible MP for the university when only nineteen and too young to stand.

The road to the cabinet, 1809–1828 Law's heart was set on going into the army, compatible then with a seat in parliament; he was a lifelong and passionate amateur of war. His redoubtable father kept him out of the contemporary conflict, but an abbreviated Mediterranean tour took him to Malta and Sicily, where he applied himself to acquiring fluent French and Italian and to filling his diary with detailed accounts of government, defences, and mores. He sat in the Commons between 1813 and 1818 as one of the members for the Cornish pocket borough of St Michael's, returned on Lord Falmouth's interest. From 1812 he enjoyed a lucrative sinecure, always his main source of income, the chief clerkship of the pleas in his father's court, worth nearly £8000 a year and a political embarrassment until commuted for a life pension in 1838. The political career on which he embarked was affected by his two marriages. The first, in 1813 (11 December), to Lady Octavia (1792–1819), daughter of Robert Stewart, the first marquess of Londonderry, and sister of Lord Castlereagh, the foreign secretary, was a very happy one, though childless. The admiration he felt for his brother-in-law probably prevented him from being drawn into the emergent Canningite group in tory politics. Although he

Edward Law, first earl of Ellenborough (1790–1871), by Frederick Richard Say, *c.*1845

nursed a personal dislike for Canning, Castlereagh's rival, Law was distinctly liberal in his views. He spoke and voted against the Vienna treaties of 1814–15, which Castlereagh had helped to negotiate. The offence of the peace settlement, in his eyes, was its treatment of Italy: the failure to revive the ancient Genoese republic and the subjection of Lombardy and Venetia to Austria. At home he was a supporter of Catholic emancipation and the abolition of slavery. The efficiency of the army and freer trade were among his other topics. By conscious effort he was making himself an effective speaker.

Shortly after Law gave up his seat to care for his ailing wife, who died in 1819, he succeeded to his father's peerage as second Baron Ellenborough. On the death of Castlereagh in 1822 he gave his allegiance to Lord Grey, the future whig premier, but in January 1828 joined Wellington's cabinet as lord privy seal. He hoped to see Grey and his political friends included before long. Yet he did not resign with Huskisson and other liberal tories in May 1828, staying to become president of the India board in September. Wellington had recruited Ellenborough on advice that 'maturing talent and ready eloquence' made him potentially dangerous (Aspinall, xii): his unpopularity was exposed by the end of his second marriage in a resounding scandal. A celebrated beauty, Jane Elizabeth (1807–1881) [*see* Digby, Jane Elizabeth], daughter of Admiral Sir Michael Digby and his wife, Lady Andover, had little in common with her serious husband. Married in 1824 (15 September), she followed her lover, Prince Schwarzenberg, to Paris in 1829. Ellenborough fought a duel with the prince, got £25,000 damages from him in the courts, and obtained his divorce by a private bill in 1830. The parliamentary proceedings gave the radicals and the press an opportunity to pillory a minister in a government about to be submerged by the tide of reform. Nor were the circles in which Ellenborough moved inclined to spare him: from an early stage in his political life arrogance verging on insolence had made him many enemies. Some members of both houses took their revenge. This humiliating experience, and the death of his only child, a son, in the same year, almost extinguished his consuming ambition. A confident performance as a minister hid 'the dreadful distress of mind I have endured' (ibid., 92).

The India board, 1828–1830 Responsibility for India provided scope for Ellenborough's ability and an imperial vision; he swiftly mastered the routine of his office and relished policy making. He favoured substituting the crown for the rule of the East India Company in the subcontinent. The company's directors in London, a powerful vested interest, did not impress him: 'They think to humbug and bully me. They will find both difficult' (E. Law, 2.102). After the contemporary fashion, he was strong for economy through administrative reform: Indians were cheaper than Europeans at the lower levels of a government that was running a considerable deficit. 'I will not sit here to sacrifice India to England', he said in his discussions with the company. It was, he reflected, an unguarded remark, but one which 'I feel to be correct, not only socially but politically' (ibid., 2.13). He approved of a Westernizing education for selected Indians to whom, in time, even the covenanted civil service should be open, and disapproved of European settlement. He could not share the Canningite governor-general's rather indistinct idea of an India led towards Christian civilization and self-government by British businessmen and planters. India's real masters in Whitehall and Westminster had a duty to create wider prosperity—'There can be no profitable commerce with … a pauper people' (Imlah, 45)—but Indians could never be admitted to the higher ranks in the company's armies. 'No man in his senses', he said, 'would propose to place political and military power … in the hands of natives' (*Hansard 3*, 19, 191).

Ellenborough envisaged a more efficient and economical, and a stronger, British administration in India, divested of its residual character as a trading corporation. The whigs' India Act of 1833 incorporated much of his thinking. Lord William Bentinck, the governor-general he once thought of having recalled, soon agreed on the continuing expansion of Britain in the subcontinent. She ruled by the sword: and her conquests would not be secure until British influence was dominant in the Punjab, Sind, Afghanistan—and beyond. The policy Ellenborough wanted to make was, above all, foreign policy, with which he had helped the first of Wellington's foreign secretaries, Lord Dudley. He put India at the centre of a grandiose imperial project. Anti-Russian in his sympathies during the war of 1828–30 between the tsar and the Ottoman sultan, he believed British policy had failed to take account of the Russian threat to India. 'We have been made the tools of

Russia', he exclaimed. On arriving at the board he was ready to mount a challenge in central Asia: 'I would, in Persia and everywhere, endeavour to create the means of throwing the whole world in arms upon Russia at the first convenient time' (E. Law, 2.25; 1.238). His first term at the board initiated the 'great game' of vying with Russia for influence in those regions (Ingram, x). While Wellington and Dudley's successor restrained their colleague over Persia and Turkestan, Ellenborough prepared for a British advance to the Indus; subsequent treaties with Sind and the Punjab opened the river to trade. 'Asia is *mine*', he said to himself, and dreamed of taking Egypt by an expedition from India (E. Law, 2.88; *Greville Memoirs*, 2.350). In two years he had asserted the home government's authority over the company and the governor-general, supervised India's restoration to solvency, and mapped out the historic expansion to the north-west.

The Great Reform Bill and the practice of opposition, 1830–1841 The fall of the Wellington ministry in November 1830 turned Ellenborough's attention to parliamentary reform. One of the twenty-two peers who voted against the third reading of the Great Reform Bill, he was not, in fact, uncompromising in his resistance. Believing that both whig ministers and the tory leadership had underestimated popular agitation, he supported, at one moment, the idea of a scot and lot franchise—in effect a household suffrage—in the boroughs. Otherwise, he wrote, 'we shall have a servile war, or universal suffrage' (Aspinall, 237). In the bill's last stages, when Wellington and others had withdrawn from the Lords, he moved an unsuccessful amendment to increase the number of industrial towns enfranchised. He upset many tories and, by organizing opposition to the bill in the constituencies, reformers too. Throughout he was concerned to improve his political position: 'The Party may some day or other place me at their head' (ibid., 268).

Ellenborough returned to the India board in Peel's brief administration of 1834–5: his offer to stand aside because of persistent unpopularity with the tories was rejected. No one on either side doubted his ability: he was 'laborious, accurate and practical' in scrutinizing legislation, besides being among the best debaters of his generation. But Greville also recorded his 'extreme contempt' for less gifted mortals, including the young Queen Victoria (*Greville Memoirs*, 4.236). Power went to his head when, after Peel had sent him to the India board for the third time, in September 1841, he accepted the governor-generalship of India a month later, as the obvious choice. 'It seemed to me like a dream', he noted as he sailed for the East and the distinction he craved (Imlah, 78).

Governing India, 1842–1844: war in Afghanistan, Sind, and Gwalior Notwithstanding his desire to see British influence extended, Ellenborough deplored the invasion of Afghanistan under his whig predecessor, Lord Auckland. It strained the available military resources; left the occupying forces far from their bases, exposed to attack by Afghans, Persians, and the warlike Sikh state; and diverted Indian revenues from irrigation, better administration, and police: 'We draw the last rupee from the people and do little or nothing for it'. He feared '*a general outbreak*' against British rule (A. Law, 3–4). His intention to evacuate Afghanistan was well known: but before he reached India the Afghans had risen and wiped out the retreating Kabul garrison (January 1842). Ellenborough's numerous critics recognized, eventually, the magnitude of his achievement in restoring Britain's prestige after a disaster unprecedented in her Indian history. After landing at Madras in February 1842, he intervened personally to calm mutinous sepoys under orders for service in the war being waged with China. Despite the rising in the north-west he reinforced the Chinese expedition to reduce the risk of another imperial failure. He used the authority vested in him by the cabinet to change the plan of attack, ensuring the speedy success of a limited operation that induced the Chinese to come to terms in the treaty of Nanking (Nanjing). From Calcutta he directed the regrouping of the remaining British garrisons in Afghanistan. Moving up country to Allahabad, he was able to order an advance on Kabul in July. His generals received instructions that emphasized political as well as military realities, and were accordingly criticized for excessive caution. It was vital for the sepoys' morale to re-establish and maintain 'the feeling of superiority' over their Afghan foes. Successful actions at several points were a necessary prelude to the advance (Colchester, 258).

The governor-general's regular letters to Wellington display a sure understanding of war, of Asiatic politics, and of the divisions in his own camp. He insisted that political officers on the frontier wedded to Auckland's policy should be subordinated to the military commanders. There could be no question of permanently occupying Afghanistan. Kabul fell to the British in September 1842; its splendid bazaar was burnt and a handful of prisoners in the hills liberated. The victorious army withdrew, bringing with it a trophy, the gates of the famous Hindu temple of Somnath, carried off by a medieval Muslim invader. Like Wellington, Ellenborough was convinced that the Muslim minority in India, her former rulers, sympathized with the Afghans. His prize, the authenticity of which was disputed, served to advertise their disappointment and remind the Hindu majority of 'the security of *their* religion under British rule' (A. Law, 55). Ellenborough's proclamation of 1 October 1842 combined fulsome praise of the army with a statement of policy. Abandoning the Afghans to 'the anarchy which is the consequence of their crimes', the government of India would be content with the frontier to the north-west as it was. 'Pacific and conservative' in its foreign policy, it intended to devote the expenditure saved by retiring from 'a false military position' to 'the improvement of the country and the people' (*Parl. papers*, 1843, 35.71). British and Indian soldiers had demonstrated their superiority to potential enemies.

As Ellenborough was well aware, this proclamation, and a second on 4 October announcing the return of the gates of Somnath, invited attack in Britain. In his defence, he dwelt on the isolation of the British in India, the 'painfully evident' indifference of the masses to their rulers, the unwise treatment of Indian princes and of Hindu susceptibilities, and the neglect of public works 'indicating greatness, and liberality'. The language of the proclamation was meant, he told the East India directors, to 'give … our Government a national character … to make the people feel … it exists not for the English only, but for them'. The Peel ministry, and Wellington in particular, stood by him in the face of derision and the unfeigned anger of the whigs, furious at the aspersions on their policy and governor-general. There was even talk of impeachment: but a reaction set in on the publication of the blue book containing his dispatches, and he received the thanks of parliament for his services. Politicians and newspapers recognized the force of his contention that 'British power in India … is in a state of constant peril'. The situation had compelled him to rebuild the morale of 'a defeated army' that was always a latent menace to its employers by exaggerating its successes, and by giving returning troops an elaborately staged reception that excited fresh mockery (A. Law, 63–4, 54).

In the midst of this passing storm, Ellenborough did not conceal from friends his intention of ruling India 'as if I were its sovereign, having nothing to look to but India'. A British governor-general was the successor of the Mughal emperors, and he consciously emulated them: 'I must act like Akbar and not like Auckland' (A. Law, 64). The annexation of Sind in 1843 seemed in Britain to be the act of an oriental despot, and inconsistent with his undertaking in the proclamation of 1 October 1842. It was Auckland, however, who had stationed troops in Sind and forced a protectorate on the ruling family whose princes divided the territory between them. The amirs saw in the British retreat from Afghanistan the chance to throw off their tutelage. Ellenborough, who had contemplated liquidating the British position in Sind, countered with a demand for strengthened control. In the circumstances, leaving Sind would be interpreted as an admission of weakness, particularly by the Sikhs. Sir Charles Napier, the soldier whom Ellenborough invested with political as well as military responsibility, was eager to annex. He easily persuaded the governor-general that the step was justified after fighting broke out and the amirs were overcome. 'Any half measure would have failed', argued Ellenborough in reply to criticism of his prompt decision in Britain and India. The safety of the Indian empire, 'which I did not desire to extend', and the good of the amirs' subjects dictated an action which the East India directors formally condemned. They, like Peel's government, had not been consulted, and were alarmed at the implications for relations with other Indian states. The faith of princely treaties with Britain was in question. In the event, Ellenborough and Napier were right: Sind had been terribly misgoverned; British administration was so successful that the Sindis remained quiet during the Indian mutiny. But an abrupt and unauthorized reversal of policy was held against its author (A. Law, 78, 76).

The extinction of princely India did not form part of

Ellenborough's plans. He enjoined upon the British residents at Indian courts a greater respect for the rights and dignities of rulers, and enforced it. On the other hand, his intervention in Gwalior, occasioned by a quarrel in the reigning house, produced an enduring doctrine: as the paramount power Britain had a duty to maintain order in and among Indian states. It was imperative, moreover, that no state, or states, should pose a threat to 'our military preponderance, by which alone all we have won, was, and is, preserved' (A. Law, 92). An alliance between Gwalior, with the martial traditions of the Marathas and a large army, and the independent Sikhs of the Punjab was a real danger. Ellenborough accompanied his invading troops and came under fire at the battle of Maharajpur, accused of exposing himself needlessly. A new treaty left Gwalior's reduced army outnumbered by a British-officered contingent supported by the revenue from districts placed under British civil administration. The disarming of Gwalior was an essential precaution in the context of the Sikhs' changed attitude, again the result of Britain's diminished prestige after Afghanistan. Sooner or later, Ellenborough was certain, Sikh disunity must deliver the Punjab into British hands. A 'pacific and conservative' policy was hardly possible for the heirs of the Mughals: Hardinge and Dalhousie, the governors-general who followed him, continued the process of expansion.

Ellenborough and 'the Indian nation' If Ellenborough had renounced Afghanistan, he still thought of taking Egypt, and 'Perhaps I may have seen in a vision something beyond this' (Imlah, 164). War and conquest were inseparable from his conception of empire in India. 'It is maintained', he repeatedly said of British rule, 'wholly by the fidelity of the [Indian] army'. He described the army, rewarded and flattered after redeeming itself in Afghanistan, as 'the spoilt child of victory' (A. Law, 64; Imlah, 118): its loyalty needed to be reinforced by making sure of the leaders of Indian society. While he would not consider admitting them and their sons to the army on an equal footing with British officers, he was anxious to court them by means short of that: a college, and a troop in the governor-general's bodyguard reserved for young men of high birth and caste. Those selected for the latter should be treated as gentlemen, taught English, and employed as aides-de-camp rather than troopers. 'I want', he explained to the president of the India board, 'to work downwards from the highest classes to the lowest … Auckland began at the other end.' Educating a middle class, as the British had started to do, was 'just the worst thing'. His scheme, 'silly and ridiculous' though it might seem to liberals at home, was the only way 'to identify the Indian nation with their English rulers'. The experiment of a 'noble troop' in the bodyguard was not tried, but more than one 'noble college' was subsequently founded (Ellenborough to Lord Fitzgerald, 22 April 1843, BL, Add. MS 40864). Ellenborough made an important contribution to the argument about the future of India that went on for decades. The British ignored traditional India at their peril: and the mutiny vindicated him. But in the long run Westernization imposed other values.

Ellenborough's objection to the indiscriminate diffusion of those values, from which he predicted 'ruin' (Ellenborough to Lord Fitzgerald, 22 April 1843, BL, Add. MS 40864) for Britain in India, was developed in an attack on the post of legal member in his council, which had been Macaulay's. Legislation, Ellenborough contended, was everywhere an evil, and especially in India, unless absolutely necessary. Legal members of council, 'having hardly anything to do', busied themselves with drafting measures quite unsuited to Indian conditions. These strictures were aimed at Macaulay and his law commission: they had been 'a sort of standing committee of change' in a vast country with a rich and complex history. Indians ought to be able to feel that 'under the British government something can be permanent' (Ellenborough to court of directors, 22 April 1843, BL, Add. MS 40472). It should be remembered that the widespread unease arising from insensitive legislation was a cause of the rebellion in 1857. Change that promoted prosperity was another matter. With nearly two-thirds of the revenue committed to military expenditure and to servicing debt Ellenborough could do little to realize his hopes for large-scale public works, but he made considerable progress towards his aim of making India 'one great empire' commercially by attacking the imposts on internal trade. He complained bitterly of the lack of financial controls in the struggle to reduce an inherited deficit (Imlah, 194).

Ellenborough ascribed his frustrations across the whole range of government and policy to the company and its civil service in India. The tory minister was outspoken in condemning the network of interest and patronage centred on the East India House in London. Every civilian, he reminded Peel, had his patron among the company's directors. As governor-general he was reproached, to his face, with ignoring a man's interest at home. Individual directors and their disappointed clients, he alleged, had stirred up 'a spirit of mutiny' throughout the service. He made no secret of his own preference for soldiers wherever, outside the old regulation provinces, he was free to put them into administrative appointments instead of civilians. Experienced army officers, unlike civilians, tended to like and trust Indians seen at their best, 'altogether changed and ennobled by military service' (Ellenborough to Peel, 18 April 1844, BL, Add. MS 40472; Ellenborough to the court of directors, 15 June 1844, ibid.). That was his answer to the directors when they rebuked him for installing soldiers in the place of civilians whose mismanagement was deemed to have provoked a local uprising in central India.

This episode in 1843, and Ellenborough's assumption of independence in annexing Sind, almost brought the directors to exercise their statutory power of recalling a governor-general, which had never been used. Ellenborough made it plain that they had no real authority, and ought not to retain their patronage. When he excluded the legal member from meetings of his council, the directors acted. Ellenborough had the support of Peel and his cabinet: but the company had the letter of the law, and evidence of the governor-general's disregard for it, on its side. He had gone so far as to taunt the directors with their reluctance to deploy 'the only weapon you possess without control' and recall him (Imlah, 224). Cabinet ministers owned that his behaviour had been impossible. From the end of 1842 Ellenborough himself believed that he might be dismissed at any time. His council in India was no check on him: when he spent long periods away from Calcutta he took with him the officials whom he considered 'much more efficient' than its members (Colchester, 189).

Hubris was Ellenborough's undoing; there is, perhaps, no clearer instance of this in British imperial history. On reaching India, he told an astonished Auckland that he proposed to 'come the Aurangzebe' over his subjects (*Greville Memoirs*, 5.72–4). He was contemptuous of the European 'public' in India, and its newspapers, which vented the civil servants' discontent (A. Law, 143). At his desk for up to sixteen hours a day, he entertained less than was expected of him. Of the memsahibs of Calcutta he remarked: 'one never sees the native ladies, and one never wishes to see the English ladies' (Imlah, 198, n. 5). His distaste did not go unnoticed. None of this mattered very much: his true offence was to let it be known that his ideal for the Indian services was a meritocracy. As usual with him, the offence was aggravated by scathing references to mediocrity and jobbery. Cabinet colleagues wrote to tell him that the tone of his dispatches had alienated the directors: he declined 'to compress my soul within the limits of that of a mere clerk' (A. Law, 64). The bonds of party were not strong enough to contain the resentment he excited. Whigs and tories on the court of directors united in taking the extraordinary decision (April 1844) to recall a proconsul with his record of success.

In his correspondence Ellenborough often referred to 'the Indian nation'. He saw that 'we have created the elements of Revolution'. The British had weakened—typically, he wrote 'destroyed'—native political institutions. By unifying the subcontinent they were fostering a new national consciousness: his sympathy with nationalism in continental Europe, in Italy, and also Poland showed him what was likely to happen in India. He nevertheless hoped that with the acquisition of 'modes of thinking resembling our own', Indian princes and nobles would one day be capable of 'zealous co-operation' in the improvement of the people, the civilizing mission which he took for granted (A. Law, 56, 115). They, and the army, were to be partners rather than allies. Ellenborough had taken over Charles Metcalfe's ideas for a semi-military form of government. In that setting, Christianizing India, even in the very long term, was out of the question: 'The black races', he felt, 'had better be left to a religion which makes them safe and not unhappy subjects of a foreign power' (*Letters of … Hardinge*, 84). Such robust views—or his candour in expressing them—set him apart from those who observed the conventional pieties.

Tory politics and Indian statesmanship, 1844–1871 Peel and his colleagues chose one of their number, Sir Henry Hardinge, to succeed Ellenborough. Hardinge's wife was the sister of Octavia Stewart, and the two brothers-in-law were friends. The new governor-general, who promised to adhere to Ellenborough's policies, had to be forced upon the East India directors. In October 1844 Peel marked the return of the deposed proconsul with an earldom, the GCB, and the offer of a seat in the cabinet as postmaster-general. Ellenborough refused the last as an office without real responsibility, but took the Admiralty in January 1846 when the protectionists seceded from the ministry. At a time of Anglo-American tension he suggested himself as governor-in-chief of British North America: Peel joked about the consequences for peace, and sent another member of the cabinet, Lord Elgin. After the corn laws were repealed in 1846, Ellenborough sided with the protectionist majority of the Conservative Party until he considered, in 1851, that protectionism was dead. The Peelites saw to it that he was not included in Aberdeen's coalition. During the Crimean War Derby had him in mind for the War Office in January 1855, while calling him 'very able … but … very unmanageable'. 'Almost mad', commented the queen (*Letters of Queen Victoria*, 1st ser., 3.81). Although he was rated a formidable critic of any government, his carefully prepared assault on the Palmerston ministry's conduct of the Crimean War was surprisingly ineffectual.

Ellenborough's hour appeared to have come when the Indian mutiny broke out in May 1857. He had played a constructive part in discussions of a new India Act in 1853, which increased the control of ministers and parliament over the company. But the political and administrative trends in India were away from the model he favoured. He had read the warning signs and pointed to them in letters to Lord Canning, then governor-general, before the mutiny. Indian religions, princes, and soldiers all had reason to be disaffected. He urged Canning not to reduce the strength of European troops in India, depleted for the Crimea, 'by one man' (Steele, 348). Afterwards he was quick to see that the reconquest of the huge areas lost to the rebels in northern and central India must be tempered with mercy: 'a blood feud between the natives and ourselves … will make it impracticable to re-establish civil government' (*Hansard 3*, 148, 1362). As president of the India board for the fourth time in February 1858, he had the congenial task of legislating the company out of existence, begun by the outgoing Palmerston ministry. The distinctive feature of his India Bill in March, fatal to a minority government's hopes of passing it, was the popular election of five out of the eighteen members of the council in London to advise the minister in undivided charge of India. Ellenborough wanted the elective element to represent the commercial centres of India, not those of the British Isles. The cabinet ruled that out: and the Commons objected to the principle of election in any form.

The conviction that a historic opportunity was being thrown away in India helps to explain the behaviour that brought Ellenborough down three months later. Canning's proclamation confiscating the proprietary rights of the *talukdars*, or barons, of Oudh was, on the face of it, a draconian measure. Ellenborough censured him in a dispatch published at home before it could have reached Canning. The continuing resistance in Oudh, where the population had witnessed the dispossession of their king and nobility, had, he declared, 'rather the character of legitimate war than that of rebellion' (*Parl. papers*, 1857–8, 43.411). The adverse reaction to this attack on a governor-general trying to restore order compelled Ellenborough to resign as the price of the government's survival. 'I could almost pity the poor Peacock. He is so miserably crestfallen', wrote Canning's friend Lord Granville, referring to the fallen minister by one of his nicknames (Fitzmaurice, 1.306). But in resigning (10 May 1858) Ellenborough had saved his policy, leaving behind him a cabinet that reaffirmed it. The royal proclamation of November 1858, with its offer of a wide-ranging amnesty and promises to respect the rights and beliefs of Indians, was the outcome at which he had aimed, impatient of political restraints. In a notable resignation speech he claimed that the offending dispatch was 'a message of peace to the people of India' which no one else could have addressed, at the same time, to his countrymen there, engaged in the work of repression (*Hansard 3*, 150, 410–12).

When finally out of office Ellenborough indulged his undoubted liberalism by supporting Italian unification and the Polish rising of 1863. The queen was outraged by his 'malignant and unmanly' criticism of her German leanings in the war of 1864 that deprived Denmark of Schleswig and Holstein (*Letters of Queen Victoria*, 2nd ser., 1.199). On that occasion he lived up to another nickname, the Elephant, an allusion to his uncontrollable propensity for trampling underfoot those who opposed him. The contemporary consensus set him down as a brilliant failure. In a sense, this was justified: he excelled as a parliamentary orator, his vision and courage in India were acknowledged, but he was a bad politician, like his hero Wellington. Lord Stanley, who succeeded Ellenborough at the India board in 1858 and carried out the transfer of India to the crown, thought there was 'more about him of the Roman of classical times than … seems to suit … our peaceable and commercial community' (*Diaries of E. H. Stanley*, 54). To the end, he wished the British to rule India 'like the old Emperors … as active as Akbar'. Yet in dealing with Indians he never lost sight of 'whatever they may have of national feeling' (Imlah, 252; *Parl. papers*, 1857–8, 43.410).

Ellenborough died at his Gloucestershire seat, Southam House, Southam Delabere, on 22 December 1871, and was buried at nearby Oxenton church on 29 December. He left three illegitimate children from a liaison that followed his divorce. There was no heir to the earldom, but his nephew Charles Law succeeded as the third baron.

DAVID STEELE

Sources A. H. Imlah, *Lord Ellenborough* (1939) · E. Law, Lord Ellenborough, *A political diary, 1828–1830*, ed. Lord Colchester, 2 vols. (1881) · A. Law, ed., *India under Lord Ellenborough, 1842–1844* (1926) [documents] · *History of the Indian administration of Lord Ellenborough: in his correspondence with the duke of Wellington*, ed. Lord Colchester (1874) · A. Aspinall, ed., *Three early nineteenth-century diaries* (1952) [extracts from Le Marchant, E. J. Littleton, Baron Hatherton, and E. Law, earl of Ellenborough] · E. Ingram, *The beginning of the great game in Asia, 1828–1834* (1979) · J. Rosselli, *Lord William Bentinck: the making of a liberal imperialist, 1774–1839* (1974) · C. S. Parker, ed., *Sir Robert Peel: from his private papers*, 3 vols. (1891–9) · BL, Peel MSS · BL, Ripon MSS · *The letters of Queen Victoria*, ed. A. C. Benson, Lord Esher [R. B. Brett], and G. E. Buckle, 9 vols. (1907–32) · *The Greville memoirs, 1814–1860*, ed. L. Strachey and R. Fulford, 8 vols. (1938) · *The letters of the first Viscount Hardinge of Lahore … 1844–1847*, ed. B. S. Singh, CS, 4th ser., 32 (1986) · *The diaries of E. H. Stanley, 15th earl of Derby, 1869–1878*, CS, 5th series, 4 (1994) · *Disraeli, Derby and the conservative party: journals and memoirs of Edward Henry, Lord Stanley, 1849–1869*, ed. J. R. Vincent (1978) · E. D. Steele, *Palmerston and liberalism, 1855–1865* (1991) · H. T. Lambrick, *Sir Charles Napier and Sind* (1952) · E. G. Petty-Fitzmaurice, *The life of Granville George Leveson Gower, second Earl Granville*, 2nd edn, 2 vols. (1905) · *Hansard 3* · *Parl. papers* · GEC, *Peerage* · *The Times* (23 Dec 1871) · *The Times* (30 Dec 1871) · BL, Fitzgerald MSS, Add. MSS 40863–40865 · *Dod's Parliamentary Companion*

Archives PRO | BL, Aberdeen MSS · BL, F. R. Bonham MSS, Add. MS 40617 · BL, G. Broadfoot MSS, Add. MS 40127 · BL, Fitzgerald MSS, Add. MSS 40863–40865 · BL, J. C. Herries MSS, Add. MS 57410 · BL, Holland MSS, Add. MS 51596 · BL, Peel MSS · BL, Ripon MSS · BL OIOC, Clerk MSS, MSS Eur. D 538 · BL OIOC, Elphinstone MSS, MSS Eur. F 87–89 · BL OIOC, Hay MSS, MSS Eur. F 96 · Bodl. Oxf., Disraeli MSS · Bodl. Oxf., Napier MSS · Bodl. Oxf., Phillipps-Robinson MSS · Borth. Inst., Halifax MSS · CKS, Stanhope MSS · Durham RO, Vane-Tempest-Stuart MSS · Lpool RO, Stanley MSS · NA Scot., Ramsay MSS · NAM, Jasper Nicolls MSS · NRA Scotland, priv. coll., Campbell MSS · priv. coll., S. H. Walpole MSS · PRO, Granville MSS, 30/29 · U. Durham, Grey of Howick MSS · U. Lond., University College Manuscripts Room, Chadwick MSS · U. Newcastle, Pelham MSS · U. Nott., Cavendish-Bentinck MSS · U. Southampton L., Wellesley MSS · W. Yorks. AS, Canning MSS

Likenesses F. R. Say, oils, c.1845, NPG [*see illus.*] · attrib. I. Cruickshank, group portrait, pen and wash (*Members of the House of Lords c.1835*), NPG · J. Doyle, caricatures, BM · G. Hayter, group portrait, oils (*The trial of Queen Caroline, 1820*), NPG · G. Hayter, pen-and-pencil drawing, BM · wood-engraving, NPG; repro. in *ILN* (1872), 37

Wealth at death under £60,000: probate, 5 Feb 1872, *CGPLA Eng. & Wales*

Law, Sir Edward Fitzgerald (1846–1908), diplomatist, was born at Rostrevor House, co. Down, on 2 November 1846, the third son of the nine children of Michael Law, senior partner of Law and Finlay's Bank, Dublin, and afterwards director of the Bank of Ireland, and his wife, Sarah Anne, daughter of Crofton Fitz-Gerald. His eldest brother, Robert, lived on his Irish estates. His second brother, Michael, was an early member of the international courts in Egypt. Law went to schools at Brighton and St Andrews, and thence to the Royal Military Academy at Woolwich. He was gazetted to the Royal Artillery in July 1868, and served in India. There he became known as a sportsman and a fine steeplechaser, while his instinct for topography and linguistic aptitude in French, German, and Russian promised well for a military career. But, invalided home, he retired from the army for private reasons in October 1872, keeping his name on the reserve of officers. He next went to Russia, where he started a business as an agent for agricultural machinery; after mastering many difficulties, he prospered there until he was ruined by the conduct of his partners, against whom he brought legal proceedings. Thereupon he joined Messrs Hubbard, the English firm of Russian merchants, and on their behalf travelled widely in the Russian empire. His intimate knowledge of the country and the people was turned to account in a long series of magazine articles on Russian ambitions in central Asia.

From December 1880 to March 1881, and from August to

September 1881, Law acted as consul at St Petersburg. In 1883 he declined the offer of a post in the Belgian service in central Africa, which the War Office had been asked by Leopold II to fill, and he accepted the managership of the Globe Telephone Company in London. That company was then in fierce competition with the United Telephone Company. Law pushed through a scheme of amalgamation in the interests of the shareholders in 1884, and thereby abolished his own post. Having volunteered for duty in the Sudan in 1885, he served with the commissariat and transport staff of the guards brigade. He received the medal and clasp and the khedive's bronze star, was mentioned in dispatches, and promoted to the rank of major (June 1886). He was meanwhile recalled to England for work in the army intelligence department in connection with troubles with Russia over the Panjdeh incident on the Afghan frontier.

After visiting Manchuria to develop the services of the Amur River Navigation Company, Law was associated with Colonel E. J. Saunderson in the anti-home rule campaign of the Irish Loyal and Political Union. Of inventive mind, he also patented a machine for setting up type at a distance by the transmission of electric impulses, and a flying machine, the precursor of the aeroplane.

In January 1888 Law was posted to St Petersburg as commercial and financial attaché for Russia, Persia, and the Asiatic provinces of Turkey. He rendered valuable service to the British ambassador, Sir Robert Morier. After visiting Persia in the course of 1888, he was attached the following summer to Nasir al-Din, shah of Persia, on his visit to England. In 1890 he acted as British delegate for the negotiation of a commercial treaty with Turkey. In 1892 he went to Greece to make an exhaustive inquiry into the financial situation there, his report appearing early in 1893. While in Greece he married, on 18 October 1893, Catherine, only daughter of Nicholas Hatsopoulo, of an old Byzantine family, settled in Athens. They had no children.

In March 1894 Law was promoted to a commercial secretaryship in the diplomatic service. After a riding tour all through Asiatic Turkey he reported on railway development there in October 1895, and was the first to suggest British association with Germany in the Baghdad railway and British control of the section from Baghdad to the Persian Gulf; that policy he advocated to the end of his life.

In December 1896 Law was transferred as commercial secretary to Vienna with supervision of Austria–Hungary, Russia, Italy, Greece, and the Balkan states. In that capacity he, with Francis Elliot, British minister at Sofia, negotiated a commercial treaty with Bulgaria in the winter of 1896-7. He represented Great Britain at Constantinople on the international committee for determining the indemnity payable by Greece after its war with Turkey in 1897. His influence helped to keep the amount within reasonable limits, and in the autumn he served at Athens on the international commission for the due payment of the indemnity and the regulation of Greek finance. Law was president of the international financial commission on Greek finance in 1898, devising an ingenious system of consolidation of revenues, which rendered the international commission acceptable and useful to Greece. While engaged in this business he was created a KCMG in May 1898, and given the rank of resident minister in the diplomatic service. He declined the grand cross of the Grecian order of the Saviour and other foreign decorations. At the close of 1898 he went to Constantinople to represent British, Belgian, and Dutch bondholders on the council of the Ottoman debt.

In March 1900 Law went out to India as finance member of the government and took a wide view of his responsibilities. He lost no time in completing the currency reform begun in 1893, setting aside the large profits from rupee coinage to form a gold-standard reserve fund as a guarantee for stability of exchange. A great famine was afflicting the country when he took office, but a period of prosperity followed and, notwithstanding the cost of the many administrative improvements which Lord Curzon effected, Law was able to write off heavy arrears of land revenue and to make the first serious reduction of taxation for twenty years. The limit of income-tax exemption was raised from Rs 500 to Rs 1000 per annum, and the salt tax—a burden on the masses which had been a subject of perennial criticism of government—was significantly reduced. In the budget of 1905-6, promulgated after Law left office but which he was mainly responsible for framing, the salt tax underwent a further reduction, and the district boards received a material annual subvention. One of Law's useful reforms was to give the local governments a larger interest in the revenue and expenditure under their control—a principle which was permanently adopted and later extended. As Lord Curzon testified, Law came into closer touch with the commercial community than any predecessor. To projects like the Tata iron and steel works at Sakchi, Bengal, he gave earnest encouragement, and he eagerly advocated the new system initiated in 1904 of co-operative rural credit under government supervision.

Law, who was made CSI on 1 January 1903, and KCSI in 1906, resigned his membership of the council on 9 January 1905, some three months before the completion of his term. He dissented from Curzon's views in his controversy with Lord Kitchener over army administration, and on coming home served on the committee appointed by the secretary of state in May 1905 to make recommendations on the subject. This report advised changes, which led to Curzon's resignation ('Correspondence regarding the administration of the army in India', *Parl. papers*, 1906, 81, Cd 2718).

On his return home, Law became a vice-president of the Tariff Reform League, and actively championed its policy. He represented Great Britain on the Cretan reform commission in January 1906, and on the committee which sat in Paris under the provisions of the Act of Algeciras (April 1906) to found the Bank of Morocco. Appointed English censor of the bank, he paid thenceforth a fortnightly visit to Paris. Law, who was also connected with many financial enterprises in the City of London, died at the Hôtel Bellevue, in the avenue de l'Opéra, Paris, on 2 November 1908, and was buried at Athens on 21 November with the public and military honours due to a grand cross of the Grecian order of the Saviour (notwithstanding his having refused the award itself). His wife survived him.

F. H. BROWN, *rev.* H. C. G. MATTHEW

Sources T. Morison and G. P. Hutchinson, *The life of Sir Edward Fitzgerald Law* (1911) • *The Times* (4 Nov 1908)

Wealth at death £7751 18s.: probate, 12 Feb 1909, CGPLA Eng. & Wales

Law, George Henry (1761–1845), bishop of Bath and Wells, was the thirteenth child and seventh son of Edmund *Law (1703–1787), bishop of Carlisle, and his wife, Mary (*b*. 1722), daughter of John Christian. He was born at Peterhouse lodge, Cambridge, on 12 September 1761. His mother died when he was six months old. He was educated at Ipswich and at Charterhouse before going up to Queens' College, Cambridge, in October 1777, where his tutor was Isaac Milner. On 23 January 1779 he was elected scholar, and in 1781 he graduated BA as second wrangler and senior chancellor's medallist, thereby emulating the achievements of his two elder brothers, John *Law, afterwards bishop of Elphin, and Edward *Law, later Lord Chief Justice Ellenborough. Another brother was the financial writer Thomas *Law. Elected fellow of Queens' College in 1781, he proceeded MA in 1784, DD in 1804, and was incorporated *ad eundem* at Oxford in 1834. He was also a fellow of the Royal Society and of the Society of Antiquaries.

In July 1784 Law vacated his fellowship on his marriage to Jane (*d*. 1826), eldest daughter of General J. W. Adeane (1740–1802), MP for Cambridgeshire. In 1785 he was collated to a prebendal stall in Carlisle Cathedral by his father, who also, a few days before his death in 1787, presented him to the vicarage of Torpenhow, Cumberland. On the presentation of Bishop Yorke of Ely he became rector of Kelshall, Hertfordshire, in 1791, and of Willingham, Cambridgeshire, in 1804. In July 1812, upon the translation of Bishop Sparke to Ely, he was consecrated bishop of Chester. Although this elevation was thought to owe as much to the powerful influence of his brother, the lord chief justice, as it did to the personal favour of the prince regent, Law proved to be an excellent pastor for this large and difficult diocese during a period of great industrial and social change. Personal experience, gained from frequent visitations, convinced him of the need for far-reaching initiatives in church extension, factory reform, and the provision of education, and in 1817 his establishment and partial endowment of a theological training college at St Bees conferred great benefit on an impoverished diocese. Moved by observation of children's conditions in the cotton mills of Stockport, he was the only bishop to give active parliamentary support to Sir Robert Peel's attempts in 1818–19 to amend the hours of factory working, and he readily promoted church building schemes and the provision of extra evening services and lectures in an attempt to meet the spiritual needs of rapidly growing centres such as Manchester and Preston. However, such support was not uncritically given. As a high-churchman of the old orthodox school Law believed that reform was acceptable only as long as it did not erode the principles

and privileges of the church. Distrustful in equal measure of heresy, schism, and political agitation, he condemned what he termed 'morbid liberality' as 'the evil of this day' in 1816; he justified the decision to prosecute John Wright of Liverpool, a unitarian preacher, for blasphemy in 1817, and devoted much of his 1820 charge to warning against the spread of Calvinist doctrines.

A good man of business, Law immediately played a key role in putting the finances of Chester Cathedral back on a sound footing. From 1822–4 he served on a committee appointed to advise Queen Anne's Bounty on the augmentation of poor livings, and in this short period helped to bring nearly 400 livings up to a minimum value of £50 a year. Between 1821 and 1825 he spoke frequently in the House of Lords against measures to promote the interests of Roman Catholic and other dissenters, and his effectiveness attracted the favour of lords Liverpool and Eldon. In 1824, on the death of Richard Beadon, he was translated to the see of Bath and Wells, which he held until his death. Although his opposition to the repeal of the Test and Corporation Acts in 1828 was ultimately, and reluctantly, abandoned, his unyielding refusal to accept proposals for Roman Catholic emancipation in 1829 was described by his biographer, S. H. Cassan, as 'Eldon-like'. Law argued that the admission of Roman Catholics to a share in political power would tend, inevitably, 'to subvert the Protestant establishments of the country', and he justified the torrent of petitions in February and March 1829 against the bill (several of which he presented, including one from 700 Cambridge undergraduates) on the grounds that they reflected the true opinion of the people of England.

By contrast, Law did not speak in the dramatic debates of 1831–2 over the question of reform, a measure for which he eventually voted with reluctance, having been intimidated into taking a house at Torquay during the intervening winter following threats of violence at Wells. In a similar spirit he consented to vote for the Church Temporalities (Ireland) Bill on its second reading in July 1833, deeming it pointless to continue in opposition to a measure that had the support of the House of Commons. However, by this stage his interests had moved beyond politics. Ever since his days as a parson in Cambridgeshire he had been deeply concerned about the condition of the rural poor, and he had become convinced that it was the clear duty of the higher orders to relieve their hardships by means of small land grants, lower rents, and tax concessions. These theories, which he expressed with particular clarity and dignity in *Remarks on the Present Distresses of the Poor* (1830), were reiterated in two speeches made in the House of Lords during the same year, as well as in his *Pastoral Letter, on the Present Aspect of the Times* (1831) and his *Reflections upon Tithes, with a Plan for a General Commutation* (1832). Convinced that the principles of political economy threatened the fabric of a society that depended upon 'benefits mutually conferred and received', Law also deplored the working of the new poor laws (which he saw would weaken family ties and create dependence), just as he had previously condemned the Speenhamland system for promoting wages depression and pauperism.

Declining health after 1836 precluded Law from the active discharge of his duties, although he gave passive support to the establishment of the Wells Theological College, which opened in 1840. He died at Banwell on 22 September 1845 and was buried at Wells. He left five daughters and four sons, three of whom were in holy orders: James Thomas *Law, chancellor of Lichfield; Henry *Law, dean of Gloucester; and Robert Vanbrugh Law, canon of Chester and treasurer of Wells.   RICHARD SHARP

Sources GM, 2nd ser., 24 (1845), 529–31 [incl. full bibliography] · S. H. Cassan, *The lives of the bishops of Bath and Wells*, 2 (1829), 189–227 · *Hansard 1* (1812), vol. 5 · R. A. Soloway, *Prelates and people: ecclesiastical social thought in England, 1783–1852* (1969) · Venn, *Alum. Cant.*

Archives BL, letters to third earl of Hardwicke, Add. MSS 35677, 35687, 35689 · BL, corresp. with third earl of Liverpool, Add. MSS 38248–38328 *passim* · BL, letters to Revd W. Phelps, Add. MSS 33836 · St Deiniol's Library, Hawarden, corresp. with Sir John Gladstone

Likenesses W. Beechey, portrait, 1814, bishop's palace, Chester · attrib. G. Hayter, portrait, *c.*1815, bishop's palace, Wells · W. Say, mezzotint, pubd 1820 (after H. W. Pickersgill), BM, NPG · attrib. W. Beechey, oils, *c.*1828, bishop's palace, Wells · R. C. Lucas, bust, 1832 · G. Hayter, group portrait, oils (*The trial of Queen Caroline*, 1820), NPG · R. C. Lucas, wax model, possibly priv. coll. · attrib. H. W. Pickersgill, oils, bishop's palace, Wells

Law [née Frost], **Harriet Teresa** (1831–1897), secularist, was born in Ongar, Essex, on 5 November 1831, the daughter of Henry Frost, a butcher, farmer, and contractor. She was reared as a Strict Baptist in the severe Calvinist tradition. When her family moved to London she taught in a Sunday school and started her own school to assist the family's finances. In east London she came in contact with secularists, initially speaking against them but gradually being won over to their point of view.

On 11 January 1855 Harriet married Edward Law, a dealer in property and the son of William Law of Newton Abbot; they had a son and three daughters. Law was a Christian undergoing a crisis of faith similar to her own. They soon both became secularists, and their house at 38 Boyson Road, Walworth, London, became a centre for secularist social occasions, especially from the mid-1870s. From 1860 Harriet Law was established as the leading female secularist platform speaker, working in the mould of Emma Martin. Edward Royle notes of her: 'as a young woman she was remembered as having a low, pleasant voice, but her later efforts in large halls and out-of-doors gave her a harsher tone' (Royle, 5.135). She took the view that women were the equals of men, and had a hostility towards doctors. Though associated with Charles Bradlaugh she did not join the National Secular Society; in 1869 she was president of the Freethought League and was one of the founders in 1877 of the British Secular Union (both organizations being independent of Bradlaugh). In 1876 she took over the *Secular Chronicle* and edited it for three years, losing heavily on it while promoting secularism, republicanism, and the emancipation of women. She also published *An Hour with Harriet Martineau* (1877).

Harriet Law was a rough advocate of secularist views which, though the obverse of her earlier Calvinism, she advanced with the same uncompromising dogmatism.

She lacked the social graces of Annie Besant, who eclipsed her in her later years. In 1867 she was elected a member of the general council of the First International. On 7 July 1878 she wrote a biographical article on Karl Marx in her *Secular Chronicle* and on 4 August that year published his reply to George Howell. Her socialist opinions made her much more cautious than most secularists about associating with the Liberal Party. Ill with bronchitis, she retired from public life and died from a heart attack at 24 Somerville Road, Peckham, London, on 19 July 1897, being buried at Forest Hill cemetery on 23 July. Her husband survived her.   H. C. G. MATTHEW

Sources DLB · *The Freethinker* (1 Aug 1897) · *The Freethinker* (8 Aug 1897) · *Agnostic Journal* (11 Sept 1897) · *Agnostic Journal* (16 Oct 1897) · E. Royle, *Radicals, secularists and republicans: popular freethought in Britain, 1866–1915* (1980) · H. Collins and C. Abramsky, *Karl Marx and the British labour movement* (1965) · S. Budd, *Varieties of unbelief* (1976) · B. Taylor, *Eve and the new Jerusalem: socialism and feminism in the nineteenth century* (1983) · m. cert. · d. cert.

Wealth at death £238 1s. 6d.: administration, 24 Aug 1897, CGPLA Eng. & Wales

Law, Henry (1797–1884), dean of Gloucester, was born on 29 September 1797 at Kelshall rectory, Hertfordshire, where his father was rector. He was the third son of George Henry *Law (1761–1845), bishop successively of Chester and of Bath and Wells, and his wife, Jane, the eldest daughter of General James Whorwood Adeane of Babraham, Cambridgeshire, a politician. James Thomas *Law was his brother. The natural theologian William Paley was his godfather.

Law was educated first at a private school in Greenwich kept by the classical critic and bibliophile Charles Burney, and from 1812 at Eton College. He matriculated at St John's College, Cambridge, in 1816, graduating BA (1820) as fourth wrangler and MA (1823). In 1821 he was ordained deacon and priest by his father and became a fellow and tutor of St John's College, Cambridge, where he helped to establish the classical tripos and was one of the first examiners (1824–5).

Between 1822 and 1826 Law briefly held various livings before being appointed archdeacon (1826) and residentiary canon (1828) of Wells, offices he retained until his move to Gloucester. As a residentiary canon he took an active part in, and contributed generously to, the restoration of Wells Cathedral. From 1830 to 1834 he was also rector of Yeovilton, and from 1834 to 1838 of Weston-super-Mare, then still a small fishing village. In 1838 he accepted from the Simeon trustees the rectory of Bath, but became ill and resigned in 1839. After being vicar of East Brent for a few months, in 1840 he was again appointed to Weston-super-Mare, where he remained for the next twenty-two years. As the little village grew into a fashionable health resort he took an active part in promoting the religious, educational, and social facilities of the town. The parish church was enlarged on three occasions and excellent schools were established; three other churches were built and endowed, largely at his private expense. When disagreements arose between local people over the purchase of a town hall, Law bought the building at a cost of £4000 and presented it to the town.

In 1862 Law was nominated dean of Gloucester by Lord Palmerston. Characteristically Law's first project was to improve the cathedral buildings. The deanery was also restored at considerable cost. George Gilbert Scott was engaged to construct a suitably elegant neo-Gothic choir and several side chapels; a reredos was added, and attention given to the standard of music in the services. In addition to helping to pay for architects of Scott's calibre, Law also contributed—both publicly and anonymously—to many charitable organizations.

Despite his taste for the neo-Gothic, Law was a firmly evangelical Anglican throughout his life. While at Weston he organized frequent meetings of evangelical clergy in the west of England and enjoyed an influence among them second only to that of his friend Francis Close of Cheltenham. Among his other close friends were Hugh McCalmont, first Earl Cairns, leader of the Conservative Party in the House of Lords, and the politician and evangelical social reformer Anthony Ashley Cooper, seventh earl of Shaftesbury. Since Palmerston invariably asked Shaftesbury's advice in appointing bishops, and he in turn took Law's advice on the subject, he had a great deal of influence in episcopal appointments, though he refused the offer to be made bishop himself.

Law was an accomplished mathematician and classical scholar as well as being well read in English. Several of his own writings, mainly sermons and modest works of biblical exegesis, were published in his lifetime; one popular scholarly work, *The Gospel in the Pentateuch* (1854–8), sold over 100,000 copies. He died, unmarried, at the deanery, Gloucester, on 25 November 1884, and was buried four days later in Gloucester cemetery.

J. R. WASHBOURN, *rev.* STEPHEN GREGORY

Sources *The Record* (28 Nov 1884) • *The Record* (5 Dec 1884) • *Gloucester Journal* (29 Nov 1884) • *The Eagle*, 13 (1885), 213–14 • Boase, *Mod. Eng. biog.* • Venn, *Alum. Cant.* • personal knowledge (1892) • D. R. Leader, *A history of the University of Cambridge*, 1: *The university to 1546*, ed. C. N. L. Brooke and others (1988)
Likenesses portrait, repro. in H. Law, *Christ is all: the gospel in Genesis* (1960), back cover
Wealth at death £15,583 14s. 2d.: probate, 31 Dec 1884, CGPLA *Eng. & Wales*

Law, Hugh (1818–1883), judge, was born on 19 June 1818 at Woodlawn, co. Down, Ireland, the only son of John Law and his wife, Margaret, the youngest daughter of Christopher Crawley of Cullaville, co. Armagh. He was educated at the Royal School at Dungannon until 1834 and then at Trinity College, Dublin, where he matriculated on 17 October 1834, became a scholar in 1837, gained a first in classics in moderations, and graduated BA in 1839. In 1840 he was called to the bar and joined the north-eastern circuit, but he mainly practised in the courts of equity in Dublin and in Irish appeals in the House of Lords. In 1860 he took silk and in 1863 he married Ellen Maria White (d. 1875).

Law took little part in politics until the disestablishment of the Irish church was proposed. Though generally believed to be a Conservative, he took the Liberal side in

that debate and drafted the Irish Church Act. He was appointed legal adviser to the lord lieutenant at Dublin in 1868; and in 1870 he drafted the Irish Land Act under Gladstone. In the same year he became a bencher of the King's Inns, and in 1872 he succeeded Christopher Palles as solicitor-general. In December 1873 Law was sworn of the Irish privy council, and was appointed attorney-general. When the Gladstone ministry fell a few weeks later, however, he lost the office. In 1874 he entered parliament for Londonderry, was re-elected in 1880, and became Irish attorney-general in Gladstone's second administration in April 1880.

Law conducted the Land League prosecution against Charles Parnell and others in December 1880. In committee on the Land Bill of 1881 he was Gladstone's primary assistant; he proved himself conciliatory, accepting Timothy Healy's amendment which proposed that no rent should be payable on improvements made by tenants. This was important, as it gave more power to tenants. Law succeeded Lord O'Hagan as lord chancellor for Ireland in 1881, and resigned his seat in parliament. As chancellor he was widely respected. After a very brief illness Law died of lung disease at Rathmullen House, co. Donegal, on 10 September 1883. J. A. HAMILTON, *rev.* SINÉAD AGNEW

Sources Boase, *Mod. Eng. biog.* • F. E. Ball, *The judges in Ireland, 1221–1921*, 2 (1926), 312, 327, 373–4 • *Law Times* (15 Sept 1883), 339, 349 • *Law Journal* (15 Sept 1883), 500 • *Solicitors' Journal*, 27 (1882–3), 738 • Burtchaell & Sadleir, *Alum. Dubl.* • Gladstone, *Diaries* • Ward, *Men of the reign*, 522 • J. S. Crone, *A concise dictionary of Irish biography*, rev. edn (1937), 121 • T. P. O'Connor, *Gladstone's House of Commons* (1885), 212 • T. P. O'Connor, *The Parnell movement*, 2nd edn (1886), 330, 372, 379, 428 • *Irish Law Times and Solicitors' Journal*, 17 (1883), 489
Archives BL, corresp. with W. E. Gladstone and memoranda, Add. MSS 44309–44783
Wealth at death £70,447 11s. 6d.: probate, 7 Nov 1883, CGPLA *Ire.* • £19,717 18s. in England: Irish probate resealed in England, 8 Dec 1883, CGPLA *Eng. & Wales*

Law, Jacques Alexandre Bernard, of Lauriston, marquess of Lauriston in the French nobility (1768–1828), army officer, was born on 1 February 1768 in Pondicherry, India, the son of Jean Law de Lauriston (b. 1719), *maréchal de camp* and governor of Pondicherry, and his wife, Jeanne Carvalho. Of partly Scottish descent, he was a great-nephew of John Law (1671–1729) of Lauriston, the financier. An artillery officer (lieutenant, September 1785), he married on 5 December 1789 Antoinette Claudine Julie Le Duc. He fought in the republican army, which relied much on the expertise of *ancien régime* officers, and was *chef de brigade* of the 4th regiment of light artillery (February 1795). From 1796 to 1800 he was inactive, reportedly because of ill health. In 1800 he was aide-de-camp to Bonaparte, the first consul. In 1801 he went on a diplomatic mission to Copenhagen, and in October took to England the ratification of the preliminaries of the treaty of Amiens. Promoted *général de brigade* (September 1802) and *général de division* (February 1805), in 1805 he commanded the troops accompanying Villeneuve's fleet, intended in Bonaparte's grand design to enable the French invasion of Britain, and was at the naval battles of Ferrol (22 July 1805) and Trafalgar (21 October 1805). He rejoined the *grande* *armée* and commanded divisions and later corps in Bonaparte's campaigns in the wars of the third, fourth, fifth, and sixth coalitions. In 1807 he was governor of Venice. In June 1808 he was made a count of the French empire, and later that year he served in Spain. He served on Bonaparte's campaigns in central and eastern Europe, and at Wagram (July 1809) commanded the massed artillery (112 guns). From 1811 to 1812 he was ambassador to Russia. During the invasion of Russia in 1812 he was Bonaparte's aide-de-camp, then in October his envoy to Marshal Mikhail Kutuzov, the Russian commander-in-chief. He fought in the 1812–13 campaigns, at Wachau (October 1813) leading several cavalry charges. At the French defeat at Leipzig (October 1813) he was separated from the French army by the premature blowing of a bridge, and taken prisoner.

Returned from captivity in May 1815, Law rallied to the restored Louis XVIII, who rewarded him with honours and appointments: he was made a chevalier de Saint Louis and commandant of the 1st company of grey musketeers. During the 'hundred days' (1815) he did not support Bonaparte, and the re-restored Louis further rewarded him. He held various senior commands and appointments, was made a marquess (August 1817) and marshal of France (June 1823), and commanded a corps during the 1823 French intervention in Spain. He died on 11 June 1828 in Paris, survived by his wife, after a career as a brave and competent commander, whose success depended on his decisions when and whether to change sides in France. Like Sieyès, he survived.   ROGER T. STEARN

Sources S. Bradley, ed., *Archives biographiques françaises* (1998) · *DNB* · D. Chandler, *The campaigns of Napoleon* (1967) · P. W. Schroeder, *The transformation of European politics 1763–1848* (1996) · C. J. Esdaile, *The wars of Napoleon* (1995) · D. Gates, *The Napoleonic wars 1803–1815* (1997) · G. Ellis, *Napoleon* (1997) · P. Griffith, *The art of war in revolutionary France, 1789–1802* (1998)

Law, James (d. 1632), archbishop of Glasgow, was the son of James Law of Spittal, a portioner of Lathrisk, Fife, and Agnes Strang of the family of Balcaskie, Fife, and brother of Andrew Law, later minister of Neilston parish church, Renfrewshire. He graduated MA from the University of St Andrews in 1581 and was ordained and admitted minister of Kirkliston within the newly erected administrative bounds of the Linlithgow presbytery in 1585. In July 1587 he married Marion, daughter of James Dundas of Newliston; they had a daughter, Margaret, who in January 1612 married Patrick Turner, minister of Dalkeith. His second marriage, to Grizel Boswell (d. July 1618), produced four sons and two daughters: James of Brunton, Thomas (later minister of Inchinnan), George, John, Jean, and Isabella.

It is clear from the extant synod of Lothian records that Law was a regular participant in the affairs of the higher church courts. Unlike many of his contemporaries he was no strict sabbatarian and along with the future Scottish metropolitan, John Spottiswoode, was censured by the synod of Lothian for playing football on a Sunday. By the turn of the century he was a conspicuous adherent of the king's party within the church. In 1600 he was chosen as a standing commissioner at King James's bidding, and was made a royal chaplain the following year. On 28 February

1605 he was appointed titular bishop of Orkney in the king's newly reconstituted episcopal Church of Scotland, and in July 1608 acted as moderator in the Linlithgow assembly. After the restoration of ecclesiastical jurisdiction to bishops by the Glasgow assembly of 1610, in which Law himself had played a significant part, he used his new found authority to striking effect in Orkney and Shetland. He was made a commissioner of the peace for Orkney and Shetland in November 1610. To this office was added that of chamberlain and commissioner of justiciary and sheriff principal shortly after. During Law's relatively short but efficacious tenure at Orkney, Scots law replaced Norse, the oppression of Patrick, earl of Orkney, was suppressed, and the earldom and crown lands were permanently annexed to the crown. Moreover, the bishopric was re-established on a sure financial and legal basis.

Law's loyalty and service to the church and crown were rewarded in the summer of 1615 when he was elevated to the archiepiscopal see of Glasgow, left vacant by John Spottiswoode's transference to St Andrews. In 1616 he was chosen to compile a book of canon law for the church at the king's prompting. As archbishop of Glasgow he played a pivotal role in the court of high commission, which was the main instrument used in the enforcement of the highly controversial five articles of Perth from 1618. He remained in Glasgow for the rest of his life. He died there on 12 November 1632 and was buried in the chancel of Glasgow Cathedral. He was survived by his third wife, Marion, daughter of John Boyle of Kelburne and widow of Matthew Ross of Haning Ross.   A. S. WAYNE PEARCE

Sources *Fasti Scot.*, new edn, 7.322 · D. Calderwood, *The history of the Kirk of Scotland*, ed. T. Thomson and D. Laing, 8 vols., Wodrow Society, 7 (1842–9), vols. 5–7 · D. G. Mullan, *Episcopacy in Scotland: the history of an idea, 1560–1608* (1986) · P. D. Anderson, *Black Patie: the life and times of Patrick Stewart, earl of Orkney, lord of Shetland* (1992) · P. D. Anderson, *Robert Stewart, earl of Orkney, lord of Shetland, 1533–1593* (1982), 140 · J. Kirk, ed., *The records of the synod of Lothian and Tweeddale, 1589–1596, 1640–1649*, Stair Society, 30 (1977) · *Original letters relating to the ecclesiastical affairs of Scotland: chiefly written by … King James the Sixth*, ed. D. Laing, 2 vols., Bannatyne Club, 92 (1851) · *State papers and miscellaneous correspondence of Thomas, earl of Melros*, ed. J. Maidment, 2 vols., Abbotsford Club, 9 (1837)
Archives NL Scot., Advocates MSS

Law, James Thomas (1790–1876), Church of England clergyman, born in Carlisle on 8 December 1790, was the eldest son of George Henry *Law (1761–1845), bishop of Bath and Wells, and his wife, Jane (d. 1826), daughter of James Whorwood Adeane MP, of Brabaham, Cambridgeshire. Henry *Law was his brother. He was educated at Carlisle grammar school and then at Charles Burney's school at Greenwich before entering Christ's College, Cambridge, where he was elected to a scholarship in 1808. He graduated BA in 1812 as second senior optime, proceeded MA in 1815, and held a fellowship of his college from 1814 to 1817. After taking orders in 1814 he became rector of Tattenhall, Cheshire, in 1816 and vicar of Childwall, Lancashire, in 1818, two livings in the gift of his father as bishop of Chester. He was prebendary of Chester from 1818 to 1825 and of Lichfield from 1818. He married on 16 December 1820 Lady Henrietta Charlotte Grey (d. 1866), eldest daughter of

George Harry, sixth earl of Stamford and Warrington. In 1821 he was appointed chancellor of the diocese of Lichfield, a position which he held until 1873, and was appointed in 1824 commissary of the archdeaconry of Richmond (where his brother, Edmund, was archdeacon). In 1840 he became special commissary of the diocese of Bath and Wells, owing to the prolonged illness of his father, who was bishop, though he resigned the office before his father's death. In both Richmond and Bath and Wells he was active in improving schools and church buildings. He was vicar of Harborne, Staffordshire, in the gift of the dean and chapter of Lichfield, from 1825 to 1845, when William Towry *Law [see under Law, Edward, first Baron Ellenborough], a relative, succeeded him to the living. He was also master of St John's Hospital, Lichfield.

Along with H. E. Manning, Law persuaded his father of the need for a theological college in Wells (which opened in 1840). In 1844 Law published a call for literates (intending clergy who were not university graduates), schoolmasters, and others to be ordained as deacons in order to assist in the many urban parishes where there was a shortage of clergy. Like his father, who had founded St Bees College for Literates in 1816, he believed it a mistake to restrict ordinands to graduates. In order to maintain standards he proposed a strictly administered certificate of suitability be required before ordination. He looked forward to the proliferation of diocesan colleges in cathedral cities, away from the party atmospheres of Oxford and Cambridge, where the bishop would appoint the staff and become 'well acquainted with the life and conversation of each Divinity student'. Law took a particular interest in the development of Queen's College, Birmingham, of which he was elected honorary warden in 1846. In 1848 Law himself purchased property to help institute a theological department attached to the Birmingham School of Medicine and Surgery. A seven-year course of education from the age of sixteen was proposed; Law himself was to have oversight of the final two years' education. A chair of pastoral divinity was established in 1849. He also took a close interest in the theological college which opened at Lichfield in 1857. In addition to a number of publications on theological education and ecclesiastical law he published in 1830 *The poor man's garden, or, A few brief rules for regulating allotments of land to the poor for potatoe gardens*, which reached a fourth edition in 1831. Law died at Lichfield on 22 February 1876, leaving a son, James Adeane Law. J. R. GARRARD

Sources *Guardian* (1 March 1876), 280 · Boase, *Mod. Eng. biog.* · Venn, *Alum. Cant.* · F. W. B. Bullock, *A history of training for the ministry of the Church of England* (1955) · E. C. Inman, *History of Lichfield Diocesan Training College* (1928) · W. M. Jacob, 'The diffusion of Tractarianism: Wells Theological College, 1840–49', *Southern History*, 5 (1983), 189–209

Wealth at death under £450: administration, 9 March 1876, *CGPLA Eng. & Wales*

Law, John (*bap.* 1671, *d.* 1729), finance minister in France, was born in Edinburgh and baptized on 21 April 1671. His father, William Law (*d.* 1683), a successful goldsmith and banker, acquired the estate of Lauriston, a few miles from

John Law (*bap.* 1671, *d.* 1729), attrib. Alexis-Simon Belle, *c*.1715–20

Edinburgh. William was one of the leading Edinburgh merchants of his time, but his fortune at his death was largely in outstanding loans (some £25,000 out of a total of £29,000). At school in Edinburgh, John Law was proficient in arithmetic and algebra. He was thus well placed to give practical application to his interest in probability theory, and he went to England to make his fortune, where he spent his time 'gaming and sharping' in the early 1690s. He was forced to sell his rights of inheritance to Lauriston to his mother in 1692. In April 1694 he killed Edward (Beau) Wilson in a duel. Convicted of murder at the Old Bailey in London on 20 April and sentenced to death, he escaped from prison and took refuge on the continent. It was not until 1719 that he was pardoned. (He pleaded in person for this retrospectively in the court of king's bench in 1721.)

The death of Wilson in 1694 confirmed Law in his career as an adventurer who had to earn his livelihood either from gambling or the attempt to sell his speculative ideas to interested governments. This period of wandering did not formally end until the issue of naturalization papers for him as a Frenchman on 26 May 1716. During this time he visited several countries, including France in 1702 (when he proposed a privately owned Banque de France to Madame de Maintenon, the morganatic wife of Louis XIV), Scotland in 1704–5, France again in 1706, Venice (where he observed the activities of the Banca di Rialto), Turin in 1711–12, the Netherlands in 1712, and France for the last time in 1713. The precise details of his itinerary are obscure, but it is known that by April 1714 he was considered one of the most able speculators on the French–Dutch exchange rates. He had contracted a permanent liaison with Katherine Knollys before 1715; but it seems unlikely that they were married in Scotland in 1708 (as has been claimed), since the naturalization papers of 1717 make no mention of his wife. Two children, John and Mary Katherine, were born illegitimately, but neither the places nor the dates of birth are known with certainty. (Both were subsequently excluded from any rights of succession because of the 'vice of their birth'.)

France and finance The best-studied period of Law's career is the seven years he spent in France between December 1713 and December 1720. There, he proposed a scheme for a royal bank to Louis XIV and his finance minister, Nicolas Desmarets, which came close to acceptance but was rejected shortly before the king's death in September 1715. The advent of the Régence enhanced Law's prospects almost overnight. The régent, Philippe d'Orléans, was an unconventional figure for whom Law's ideas had great appeal, not least because it seemed that they would help alleviate the burden of debt left on the royal finances by Louis XIV. A general bank was established in May 1716 at Law's prompting. This was followed on 21 August 1717 by the Company of the West (Compagnie d'Occident) which had exclusive rights to exploit the French colony in Louisiana (hence the title Mississippi Company and, later, Mississippi System or, simply, the system for Law's whole enterprise). On 4 December 1718 the General Bank (Banque Générale) was renamed a royal bank (banque royale). Gradually, from August to October 1719, the Banque Royale came to assume control of the entire revenue-raising system of the French crown, for both direct and indirect taxes. The driving force behind these changes was none other than Law, though each measure depended on the favour of the régent.

Law abjured his native protestant faith at Melun on 17 September 1719. Although he was criticized for this in the House of Lords in 1721 (criticism which was linked to the claim that he had consorted with Jacobites), in reality conversion to Catholicism was a prerequisite for his assumption of ministerial office in France. On 5 January 1720 he was appointed controller-general of finance and in April received the more prestigious title of superintendent (surintendant des finances, a title not used since 1661 and never again to be used in France). In the course of April and May 1720 he was effectively chief minister and minister of finance, a sort of latter-day Cardinal Mazarin and Nicolas Fouquet combined; but on 27 May, the first crisis of his 'financial system', he was temporarily dismissed from office and threatened with imprisonment in the Bastille in Paris. Yet the eclipse was only brief: he returned to office on 2 June with the additional responsibilities of the superintendence of French commerce, the director-generalship of the Banque Royale, and a councillorship of state with a seat in the council of regency. With the collapse of his system Law was forced to offer his resignation on 9 December 1720, and he went into exile abroad, first to the Austrian Netherlands on 17 or 18 December. He returned to England, though his time there was not untroubled. The death of the régent in 1723 wrecked his hopes for a restoration in France and he moved on to Italy two years later with a commission from the king of England to any other prince or state 'not for use but for protection' (*DNB*). He died from pneumonia at Venice in comparative poverty on 21 March 1729, having received the Catholic last rites. The collapse of his system had brought down his own personal finances, which though very considerable in 1720 (a letter from Law to the régent, dated 1 March 1721, talked of his shareholdings at that time being worth nearly 100 millions) had been inflated by paper assets which in the end proved worthless.

The precise ways in which Law gained power, and hung on to it for a few months in 1719–20, have never been described in detail, partly because the king's council in France kept only formal minutes of decrees and not detailed records of debates. What can be stated with confidence is that the Mississippi System was a unique creation which 'involved a giant holding company controlling [almost the entire revenue-raising system], the national debt, the overseas companies, the mint, as well as the note issuing bank' (Murphy, 'John Law's theories', 1110). A central question in Law's career is whether he had a 'grand design', or whether the system at its apogee in 1719–20 merely represented a collection of piecemeal creations which were unified as opportunities arose. This raises the related issue of the evolution of his ideas between his earliest known writings about 1704, and the creation of the Company of the West in 1717 which marked the beginning of the non-banking side of the system. He certainly referred in February 1720 to 'a sequence of ideas which are interlinked and which reveal more and more the principle on which they are based', which suggests a grand design (Law, *Œuvres complètes*, 3.98–9).

Law's land bank According to Gray, Law's first biographer in 1721, the projector 'offer'd his paper credit scheme to the Lord Godolphin [lord treasurer] before he carry'd it down to the Parliament of Scotland'. Godolphin did not lightly dismiss the 'fine and nice calculation' but argued that it 'could never be put into execution under a limited Government; that it would want the authority of an absolute prince to carry it through'. (Interestingly, Law met the opposite argument in France with regard to his later, more developed, proposals; namely, that they could not be implemented under an absolute monarchy but only a limited one.) The central idea in Law's 'Essay on a land bank' (*c*.1704), which remained unpublished until 1994, was to create a land bank which would issue money based on a careful evaluation of the land in England:

> land may be brought to a standard and … a land money may be established either so as to rise and fall with the land or to be liable to no changes in its quality, in its quantity, or in the demand for it. (*John Law's Essay on a Land Bank*, 63–4)

Law contended that, unlike silver, the value of land was not eroded by increases in bullion imports or debasement of the coinage.

The idea itself was not original: Hugh Chamberlen, John Briscoe, John Asgill, and Nicholas Barbon had all proposed a land bank scheme of sorts in the 1690s, and Law sought to differentiate his proposals from theirs. He contended that Chamberlen's land bank had failed because it over-valued land, while Briscoe's proposal would have created a new type of money less valuable than silver money. Law's central objectives were to arrive at low interest rates and a stable value for money. Whereas the Bank of England promised to pay silver money on demand, the land bank promised 'a payment of land when demanded' (*John Law's Essay on a Land Bank*, 49). The Bank of England's silver reserves were clearly finite, whereas the credit of the land bank could 'be extended equal to the value of the whole lands in the nation' (ibid., 89). This argument raised the possibility of a substantial expansion in the money supply, which was the central idea of Law's system in France by 1720.

Scotland appeared to offer better prospects for Law than England, since in 1704–5 there was agreement that the services supplied by the Bank of Scotland were inadequate and that the money supply needed to be expanded. In 1705 he unsuccessfully presented the idea of a land bank to parliament in Scotland, and in the same year his seminal work *Money and Trade Consider'd with a Proposal for Supplying the Nation with Money* was published in Edinburgh. (By 'trade' Law meant economic activity in general.) The central thrust in his argument was that an expansion in the money supply would produce an expansion in output, which he considered erroneously would lead to an export surplus: 'more money, by employing more people, will make an overplus to export' (Law, *Œuvres complètes*, 1.16). A similar theme recurred in his *Mémoire touchant les monoies et le commerce* presented to the French government in November 1706, in which he argued that effective labour was dependent upon money. Money, in other words, is required to facilitate the circular flow of income: Antoin Murphy argued in 1993 that it was Law, not Richard Cantillon or François Quesnay, who formulated the so-called 'circular flow of income' model (Murphy, 'John Law and Richard Cantillon', 55). In *Mémoire pour prouver qu'une nouvelle espèce de monnaie peut être meilleure que l'or et l'argent* (1707) Law recognized that financial innovation had led to the existence of 'new' forms of money. Thus, for example, the shares of the English East India Company were 'not promises of payment in specie' but 'a new type of money' (Law, *Œuvres complètes*, 1.205); money was thus defined as any financial instrument that could be used as a medium of exchange. Instead of linking money to land alone, Law wanted his monetary system to be linked to the entirety of the 'real' economy.

Influences on Law, 1707–1712 Not much is known of Law's activities between 1707 and 1711. In 1712 he proposed the establishment of a bank and a company of commerce to Victor Amadeus II, duke of Savoy-Piedmont. By this date the primary influence on his thought was the experience of the Bank of England and the East India Company, while he made fundamental criticisms of the French experience of *billets de monnaie*, which had been issued during the War of Spanish Succession. It was not that an 'absolute' monarchy could not produce a satisfactory system which could only succeed under a representative system. Rather, the solution adopted in France had been a bad one: the *billets de monnaie* had been issued in excessively high denominations, not backed by adequate reserves of specie, refused by the government in certain exchange transactions, and yet forced on an unwilling merchant community. In contrast, Law calculated (erroneously) that England had benefited in effect from an expansion of the money supply of some £4.4 million. The British model was therefore the one to follow, and it was a British-inspired system that he sought to introduce in France over the next five years.

Further activities in France, 1713–1719 The duke of Savoy-Piedmont rejected Law's scheme allegedly with the remark that he was not rich enough to take the risk of ruining himself. By 1713 Law was back in France. It was the scale of the public debt incurred in France during the reign of Louis XIV, especially in the War of Spanish Succession, which encouraged Law to persist in his lobbying of the French authorities, rather than the relatively small (and effectively administered) state of Savoy-Piedmont. If the central government could be converted to his viewpoint in an absolute monarchy, then his career was assured. If the governing principles of a great kingdom such as France could be adapted to his ideas, then the prospects for European hegemony, at least in economic and financial respects, were great indeed. Thus, first Desmarets, the controller-general of finance in the last years of Louis XIV's reign, and then the régent were lobbied. Whereas the old king and his experienced minister were extremely cautious, Philippe d'Orléans was less conventional and was a gambler by instinct. The eighteenth-century mania for gambling is at least a partial explanation for the initial success of Law's system and perhaps for its subsequent overextension. Law rapidly expanded the market capital of his company from 34 million livres to over 5 billion livres between August 1717 and October 1719. While at first the rapid rise in the share price increased confidence in the system, capital gains rather than dividends occupied the minds of most 'investors', including the shrewd Richard Cantillon who later implicitly denounced Law's system in his 'Essai sur la nature du commerce en général' (written in 1728–30 though not published until 1755). Fevered share-dealing led to a speculative bubble, and the speculation was transferred abroad: the English South Sea Bubble was in part at least a response to the initial success of Law's system.

Such international competition was also a consequence of Law's ideas, for he had stressed that the establishment of a bank on the lines of the Bank of England would not only 'furnish 500 million [livres] which would cost the public nothing'; it would also increase the national income from 1200 million to 1500 or even 1800 million, some three times the British figure (Law, *Œuvres complètes*, 2.51–2). Thus, true French national greatness would return in the aftermath of a long and bloody war which had resulted, if not in a national defeat, at least in a settlement which had favoured British interests. Law's bank would 'surprise Europe by the changes' it would generate in France's favour greater than those from the discovery of the Indies or the introduction of credit (ibid., 2.266). The attraction of such a scheme was great given the enormous problems posed in servicing a public debt which was in the region of 1739 million (or 1977 million, if non-interest-bearing debts are included). The precise figure is of some importance, because Law's critics sought to reduce the figure for the total debt to strengthen their argument that his system had worsened, rather than alleviated, the debt problem. On balance, it would seem that his system did increase the debt, but by much less than his critics claimed, and had the predicted growth in national income occurred simultaneously royal revenues would have been so increased that the problem of the national debt would have faded into insignificance. Instead, it was subsequently said of Law's system by a writer close to its author that the whole edifice had been sacrificed to 'the extinction of all the debt', which was seen as 'the greatest obstacle to affluence' (ibid., 3.373).

Compagnie des Indes From being a simple trading company, Law's Compagnie des Indes took over the collection of indirect taxes and redemption of the debt on 27 August 1719. In return for lending the crown 1200 million at 3 per cent p.a., the company assumed the lease of the general revenue farms. Direct taxes followed in mid-October, when the company assumed administration of the *recettes générales* and *pays d'impositions*. Only the administration of taxation within the *pays d'états* remained firmly outside the newly integrated revenue-raising process. These changes were of considerable potential significance in the long term. In the short term, the reality was that the expansion of Law's system had greatly outstripped the growth of the real economy and tax revenues. The consolidated debt represented by office-holding, estimated at perhaps 0.75 billion livres, or four times the annual revenue of the crown, enjoyed a higher rate of interest than that intended by Law (5 per cent as against 2 per cent). The elimination of this unproductive capital would eventually have freed a substantial amount of investment for economic growth. In March 1720 Law launched a rumour that he was contemplating the complete abolition of venality of office. In the end, nothing came of the idea, which most regarded as impracticable: in any case, it would have consumed resources because of the need to compensate office-holders for the loss of their property rights. On 21 May 1720 shares were reduced by four-ninths and banknotes were to be reduced by a half between May and December. The decree was revoked on 27 May due to popular pressure, but confidence in the system never recovered from this moment. It was the excessive expansion of the scheme, rather than the resistance of vested interest groups, which brought about the final collapse of the system on 17 July 1720.

Law's significance as an economist The economist Eli Filip Heckscher called Law an exponent of 'paper money Mercantilism'. He argued that his views did not differ from earlier exponents of paper money; 'all he did was to express the doctrines of the new school with particular clarity, and he becomes of special interest because he later was able to translate his ideas into action' (Bonney, 206). This view minimizes Law's originality. In contrast, Joseph

A. Schumpeter considered Law to be 'in the front rank of monetary theorists of all times' (ibid., 206n., 285). The importance of Law rests less with his unsuccessful and short period in office in France ('the fatal bankruptcy in 1720', as Sir James Steuart termed it) than in his 'splendid, but visionary ideas' (as Adam Smith termed them). Smith commented that 'the idea of … multiplying paper money to almost any extent, was the real foundation of what is called the Mississippi scheme, the most extravagant project both of banking and stock-jobbing that, perhaps, the world ever saw' (ibid., 470–71). Subsequent epochs of hyperinflation in France during the 1790s and in the Weimar Republic in the late 1920s have served only to demonstrate the dangers inherent in Law's ideas. On the more positive side, the abandonment by most Western states of convertibility against a fixed monetary exchange such as the gold standard has shown that modern states cannot manage without that recourse to fiduciary issues of which Law was the earliest exponent. The difference was that at no stage in his career did he suggest that the new paper money would be valueless and issued merely at the whim of the ruler.

The study of Law was revitalized in the twentieth century, first, by the publication of his works by Paul Harsin in 1934, though this collection included two works, the *Restablissement du commerce* and the *Histoire des finances pendant la Régence*, which are no longer considered to be by Law. The great economic historian Earl J. Hamilton stressed Law's importance and intended a study of his career which remained unwritten at the time of his death. Biographies by Montgomery Hyde (1948) and Edgar Faure (1978) contain numerous errors. J. P. Poisson (1985) enumerated the number of notarial acts passed by Law between October 1713 and April 1721; as might be expected, these reached a peak in 1719–20. A second period of renewed scholarly study has subsequently been undertaken by Antoin Murphy. His study of Richard Cantillon (1986) contains an important discussion of Law's system; and in his writings on Law, culminating in his biography (1997), Murphy has contended that he was an economist of the highest calibre. Murphy has also discovered and published some of Law's early writings which were hitherto entirely unknown. A satirical engraving of Law stoking a cookpot of inflationary shares in his system has been reproduced in several studies.

RICHARD BONNEY

Sources R. J. Bonney, *Economic systems and state finance* (1995) · E. Faure, *La banqueroute de Law: 17 juillet 1720* (1978) · J. M. Félix, 'Les dettes de l'état à la mort de Louis XIV', *Comité pour l'histoire économique et financière de la France: études et documents*, 6 (1994), 603–8 · E. J. Hamilton, 'John Law', *International encyclopaedia of the social sciences*, ed. D. L. Sills, 9 (1968), 78–82 · E. J. Hamilton, 'The political economy of France at the time of John Law', *History of Political Economy*, 1 (1969), 123–49 · H. Montgomery Hyde, *John Law: the history of an honest adventurer* (1948) · T. E. Kaiser, 'Money, despotism and public opinion in early eighteenth-century France: John Law and the debate on royal credit', *Journal of Modern History*, 63 (1991), 1–28 · T. M. Kavanagh, *Enlightenment and the shadows of chance: the novel and the culture of gambling in eighteenth-century France* (1993) · J. Law, *Œuvres complètes*, ed. P. Harsin, 3 vols. (1934); repr. (1980) · C. F. Lévy,

La monarchie buissonnière, 1718–23 (1980), vol. 3 of *Capitalistes et pouvoir au siècle des lumières* • A. E. Murphy, *Richard Cantillon: entrepreneur and economist* (1986) • A. E. Murphy, 'John Law and the assignats', *La pensée économique pendant la Révolution française*, ed. G. Faccarello and P. Steiner (1990), 431–48 • A. E. Murphy, 'John Law: aspects of his monetary and debt management policies', *Perspectives on the history of economic thought*, ed. W. J. Barber (1991), vol. 5 of *Themes in pre-classical and Marxian economics*, 49–60 • A. E. Murphy, 'The evolution of John Law's theories and policies, 1707–1715', *European Economic Review*, 34 (1991), 1109–25 • A. E. Murphy, 'John Law's proposal for a bank of Turin, 1712', *Économies et Sociétés, Série Oeonomia*, 15 (1991), 3–29 • A. E. Murphy, 'John Law and Richard Cantillon on the circular flow of income', *European Journal of the History of Economic Thought*, 1 (1993), 47–62 • *John Law's essay on a land bank*, ed. A. E. Murphy (1994) • A. E. Murphy, *John Law: economic theorist and policy-maker* (1997) • J. P. Poisson, 'Introduction à une étude quantitative des effets socio-économiques du système de Law', *Notaires et société: travaux d'histoire et de sociologie notariales* (1985), 309–56 • *DNB* • A. E. Murphy, *John Law: economic theorist and policy-maker* (1997)

Archives Hants. RO • NRA, priv. coll., corresp. and papers • University of Chicago Library, financial papers

Likenesses attrib. A.-S. Belle, oils, *c*.1715–1720, NPG [*see illus.*] • line engraving, pubd 1720 (after a portrait), NPG • E. Desrochers, line engraving, BM, NPG • L. Schenk, line engraving, BM, NPG • G. F. Schmidt, line engraving (after H. Rigaud), BM • C. Wermuth, silver and pewter medal, BM • engraving, repro. in Murphy, *Richard Cantillon* • medals, BM

Law, John (1745–1810), Church of Ireland bishop of Elphin, was born on 6 May 1745 at Greystoke, Cumberland, the second of seven sons of Edmund *Law (1703–1787), bishop of Carlisle, and Mary Christian (1722–1762). Law's brothers included Edward *Law, Lord Ellenborough, George Henry *Law, bishop of Bath and Wells, and Thomas *Law, financial writer. John was educated at Charterhouse School and at Christ's College, Cambridge, where he graduated BA (1766), MA (1769), and DD (1782). He was a fellow of his college from 1770 to 1774 and took holy orders. He was appointed prebendary of Carlisle in 1773 and archdeacon four years later.

In April 1782 Law went to Ireland as chaplain to the lord lieutenant, William Henry Cavendish Cavendish-Bentinck, third duke of Portland. In August of the same year he was appointed to the see of Clonfert, co. Galway; he was translated to that of Killala, co. Mayo, in 1787, and to that of Elphin, co. Roscommon, in 1795. William Paley, his friend and successor in the archdeaconry, accompanied him to Ireland and preached his consecration sermon. Law married Anne, widow of John Thomlinson of Carlisle, and of Blencogo Hall, Cumberland; they had no children.

Law published *A Sermon Preached at Christ Church, Dublin* (1796) and *A Sermon Preached in St Paul's Cathedral at the Meeting of the Charity School Children* (1797). Among other philanthropic acts was his founding of prizes for the study of mathematics at Dublin University. Law died at Dublin on 18 or 19 March 1810 and was buried at St Patrick's Cathedral, Dublin.   WILLIAM REYNELL, *rev.* PHILIP CARTER

Sources Venn, *Alum. Cant.* • H. Cotton, *Fasti ecclesiae Hibernicae*, 1–2 (1845–8)

Archives Yale U., Beinecke L., corresp. with Thomas Percy and others

Law, Jonathan (1674–1750), colonial governor and lawyer in America, was born on 6 August 1674 in Milford, Connecticut, the only child of Jonathan Law (1637–1712), farmer and local office-holder, and his wife, Sarah (1644–1706), daughter of Deacon George Clark of Milford and his wife, Sarah. When he entered Harvard College in 1691 Law's social class ranking, twelfth of twenty-three, indicates that his family enjoyed substantial local prominence.

After receiving his BA degree in 1695 Law returned to Milford, studied theology, and preached occasionally, but was never ordained. Partly because he did not like speaking in public, he decided not to pursue a career as a minister but, instead, opened a law practice in 1698. The only lawyer in Milford, Law was also the only college graduate, with the exception of the Revd Samuel Andrew. Thus he had opportunities for leadership thrust upon him. He served on a multitude of local committees and as clerk of the proprietors of the new settlement of New Milford, and in 1706 was elected a deputy to the general assembly. Remarkably, the assembly elected him clerk in his first session, and in 1714 he became speaker of the house. Three years later he was elected to the governor's council, in 1725 he was elected deputy governor, and, after serving in that capacity for seventeen years, he assumed the governorship in 1741 on the death of Governor Joseph Talcott. The following year the freemen elected him governor, and he was re-elected annually until his death in 1750. He also served as chief justice of the superior court of Connecticut from 1725 to 1750, during his tenure as both deputy governor and governor.

Throughout his life Law was known for being pious, conservative, and studious. For better and for worse, he brought these traits to bear on the issues he faced. He served on six boundary commissions that tried to sort out tangled legal issues with Connecticut's three neighbouring colonies, he successfully fought British attempts to impose primogeniture laws on Connecticut, and he laboured hard to maintain the integrity of Connecticut's currency in an era of inflation. In relations with Britain and with other colonies, Governor Law's legal abilities and cautious nature served Connecticut well. He is remembered more, however, for his implacable opposition to the evangelical 'New Lights' who, during the Great Awakening of the 1740s, challenged the established church. As governor, Law led the forces that tried to stamp out religious dissent in Connecticut with harsh, restrictive measures that outlawed itinerant preaching and even placed limits on the speech of orthodox ministers. To call Law a tyrant for these actions, as some scholars have, is probably excessive, but he did have a commitment to government support of religion that was more consistent with seventeenth-century attitudes than with those of the eighteenth century. He told the general assembly in 1743 that 'kings indeed should be nurturing fathers to the church of God … proper measures, therefore should be consulted by civil powers for that part of religious affairs which are of a civil nature' (Shipton, 239).

Law remained firmly attached to Milford during all his

years as chief justice, deputy governor, and governor. He designed the Milford First Society Meeting-House in 1727 and took an active role in local church business. Despite being a Harvard graduate, he was an ardent supporter of Yale College. Additionally, Law conducted agricultural experiments on silk husbandry, and produced the raw material for the first silk waistcoat made in Connecticut.

Law married five times and was widowed on four occasions. On 20 December 1698 he married Ann Eliot (1677–1703) of Guilford, with whom he had three children; his second wife, whom he married on 14 February 1705, was Abigail Arnold (1685–1705) of Providence, Rhode Island (one child); his third (1 August 1706) Abigail Andrew (1686–1724) of Milford (four children); his fourth (1 June 1726) Sarah Burr (1673–1727) of Fairfield; lastly in 1730 he married Eunice Hall (1700–1774) of Wallingford, with whom he had four children and who survived him. Law died on 6 November 1750 after a three-day illness and was buried in Milford cemetery two days later. His attachment to the place of civil power in church affairs meant that New Lights and other dissenting thinkers tended to blame his intransigence for the divisiveness that beset Connecticut at mid-century. Supporters and opponents alike, however, agreed that he had been the dominant political leader in the colony for the second quarter of the century, and that his personal integrity was beyond reproach. A sombre, steadfast leader, Law combined the qualities of piety, intellectuality, and devotion to duty that were embedded in New England's puritan past.   BRUCE C. DANIELS

Sources A. C. Bates, ed., *The Law papers: correspondence and documents during Jonathan Law's governorship of the colony of Connecticut*, 3 vols. (1907–14) · C. K. Shipton, 'Law, Jonathan', *Sibley's Harvard graduates: biographical sketches of those who attended Harvard College*, 4 (1933), 237–42 · M. L. Greene, *Development of religious liberty in Connecticut* (1905) · B. Trumbull, *A complete history of Connecticut* (1818) · L. W. Labaree, 'Law, Jonathan', *DAB* · S. W. Abbott, *Families of early Milford, Connecticut* (1979) · N. Stowe, *Sixty-years' recollections of Milford* (1917) · B. Church, *A poem occasioned by the death of the Honorable John Law, Esq. late governor of Connecticut* (1751) · *World family tree*, 3, pedigree SS13, 1
Archives Connecticut Historical Society, letters · Connecticut State Library, Hartford, letters
Likenesses J. Werlaud, portrait, Museum of Connecticut History, Hartford, Connecticut; repro. in Shipton, 'Law, Jonathan'
Wealth at death very wealthy; two slaves; also lands in seven towns (six in Connecticut and one in Rhode Island): will, probate records, New Haven division, file 6337; inventory

Law, Richard Kidston, first Baron Coleraine (1901–1980), politician, was born on 27 February 1901 at Helensburgh, Dunbartonshire, the second son in the family of four sons and two daughters of Andrew Bonar *Law (1858–1923), Conservative prime minister from October 1922 to May 1923, and his wife, Annie Pitcairn, daughter of Harrington Robley of Glasgow. She died in 1909. While Bonar Law was a Canadian by birth, the son of an Ulster Presbyterian minister in humble circumstances, and reared in Scotland by well-to-do relatives (Richard's second name, Kidston, was the surname of one of them), Richard was brought up in affluence and received an English education at Shrewsbury School and St John's College, Oxford, where he

received a third class in modern history in 1923. He was never distinctively Scottish, Canadian, or Ulster.

After experience as a journalist on the *Daily Express* and the *Morning Post* and in the United States, Law entered parliament as the unionist member for Hull South-West at the landslide election of 1931, and sat there until the reverse landslide of 1945. He had married, on 26 January 1929, an American, Mary Virginia, daughter of Abram Fox Nellis of Rochester, New York, to whom he remained conspicuously devoted down to her final years of infirmity, which ended in her death in 1978. They had two sons.

In the large Conservative majorities of the 1931 and 1935 parliaments, Law attracted attention less by any striking speeches or actions than as the son of a respected former party leader. His most remembered contribution was his speech in June 1933 relating that, but for sickness, he believed his father would have broken up the new Conservative administration rather than accept the harsh terms agreed in January 1923 for repayment of the American war debt. Luckily escaping office—he was among those who opposed 'appeasement' and did not vote to approve the Munich agreement—Law was included in Winston Churchill's 1940 war coalition and served successively as financial secretary to the War Office (1940–41), parliamentary under-secretary of state at the Foreign Office (1941–3), and minister of state at the Foreign Office, with cabinet rank (1943–5). In 1943 he was sworn of the privy council. In his last office he was principally concerned with inter-allied arrangements for food, raw materials, and post-war relief.

When Churchill scraped the ministerial barrel to form a 'caretaker government' after the coalition was dissolved in May 1945, Law became minister of education; but after six weeks he lost both office and seat, though returning in the spate of contrived by-elections to the opposition front bench as member for South Kensington before 1945 was out. He showed little taste or talent for the work of opposition, and his disastrous performance in debating the National Health Service Bill against Aneurin Bevan may well have been the deciding factor in excluding him from Churchill's government in October 1951. By then he had already, to his credit, migrated back to Hull, winning there Haltemprice, a new seat formed by redistribution; but the back benches in government were no more congenial than the front bench in opposition, and in 1954 he took his peerage and went to the Lords. The title, Coleraine, alluded to the co. Londonderry origins of his grandfather.

Coleraine was now on the list of 'the great and the good' from whom the chairmen and members of respectable public bodies are recruited. He was chairman of the National Youth Employment Council (1955–62), the central transport consultative committee (1955–8), the British Sailors' Society, the Marshall scholarship commission (1956–65), the Standing Advisory Committee on the Pay of the Higher Civil Service (1957–61), and the Royal Postgraduate Medical School of London (1958–71), of which he became a fellow in 1972; and these occupied him along with numerous business directorships, including the chairmanship of Horlicks. He received an honorary LLD degree from New Brunswick University in 1951.

Meanwhile, something else had been happening: Coleraine had found the detachment to think his politics through and discovered, in the process, first that he was a Conservative and second, more significantly, that he was a tory. He concluded an article contributed to *The Times* in mid-1974 with the words: 'Probably it is time that we began to think about the unthinkable.' That was what he did himself during his thirty years out of political office. The beginning and the end of the process were marked by two polemic works. These were *Return from Utopia* (1950), published as Attlee's Labour government was nearing its close, and *For Conservatives Only* (1970), published at the corresponding stage of that of Harold Wilson and on the eve of the accession to office of Edward Heath, an event which Coleraine deeply mistrusted. It was through these two books that a political generation which had never known him in office or in the House of Commons found him influential in formulating its own changing perceptions.

Somewhat to their surprise, readers discovered that Coleraine commanded a remarkably pure and perspicuous English prose. Two sentences which strike the keynote of the respective books are fair specimens of the style:

> I know of no cure for living, and society is a living thing, bound to the trials and pains of life. A perfect society is no more to be realised than a perfect human being, and the search for Utopia has always ended in disillusionment. (*Return from Utopia*)

> The dangerous and demeaning delusion that man can properly be regarded as raw material for the sociologist to mould as he thinks fit has implications as absurd as they are terrifying. No one can say what will be the effect of the most carefully considered system of education upon a child. How then can it be possible to predict with any assurance at all the consequences of this kind of social engineering upon that infinitely more complex and baffling organism, human society? (*For Conservatives Only*)

Right at the end, in the presence of bereavement and infirmity, Coleraine made the last discovery. He was not only a Conservative and not only a tory; he was also, and therefore, an Anglican. In his last two or three years Coleraine became a regular communicant and valued member of the congregation of the Thames-side parish church of Battersea. It was there that his friends took leave of him when he died in London on 15 November 1980. His elder son, (James) Martin Bonar Law, born in 1931, succeeded him in the barony.   J. ENOCH POWELL, *rev.*

Sources *The Times* (17 Nov 1980) · personal knowledge (1986) · *CGPLA Eng. & Wales* (1981)

Archives PRO, private office papers, FO 800/430 | BL, corresp. with P. V. Emrys-Evans, Add. MS 58239 · JRL, *Manchester Guardian* archives, letters to *Manchester Guardian* · U. Birm. L., corresp. with Lord Avon | FILM BFI NFTVA, news footage · IWM FVA, news footage

Wealth at death £54,954: administration with will, 14 Jan 1981, *CGPLA Eng. & Wales*

Law, Robert (d. *c*.1686), field preacher, was the eldest son of Thomas Law (d. 1649), minister of Inchinnan, Renfrewshire, and Jean, daughter of Sir Robert Hamilton of Silvertonhill, and the grandson of James *Law (d. 1632), archbishop of Glasgow. He studied at the University of Glasgow, graduating MA in 1646. He married Jean, or Anna, Colquhoun of Easter Kilpatrick, Dunbartonshire, and the couple had a son, John.

As an expectant minister in 1650–51 Law joined the widespread protest against the decision to rescind the Act of Classes of 1649. He was proposed for the vacant ministry of Easter Kilpatrick in 1652, but—the presbytery being composed mainly of the opposing party of resolutioners—his induction was refused. On the appeal of the heritors of the parish to the synod (which group included the family of his wife, Jean), a committee of that court 'put the young man to some new tryall' and he was admitted (*Letters and Journals of Robert Baillie*, 3.186). The issue left the presbytery in a 'pitifull confusion' that was not resolved until August 1654. At that date, and despite his uncompromising presbyterianism, Law was received into the latter court. He declined to conform to episcopacy at the Restoration and was deprived of his benefice on 11 June 1662.

Following his deprivation Law offered sermons at 'privy meetings' and 'field conventicles' throughout lowland Scotland. By 1672 his activities had come to the attention of the privy council, and he was ordered to 'repair to and be confined in' the parish of Cambusnethen, near Hamilton (*Reg. PCS*, 4.104–5). Despite the order Law continued to preach at conventicles, and (on several occasions) in the vacant church of Kilsyth, in Glasgow. For these offences he was arrested on 9 July 1674 and spent some months in ward at the tolbooths of Glasgow and Edinburgh. In September 1679 the privy council ('upone the petition of [certain of the] heritours and people' of Easter Kilpatrick) permitted Law to return to his parish, granting him liberty to preach on a caution of £2000 Scots. He ministered to his supporters at the parish for some months, but their gatherings were prohibited in June 1680, because the 'meeting house [was] within a myle of [the] parish kirk where the regular incumbent serves' (ibid., 6.327, 470–71).

Thereafter Law avoided the attention of the authorities, ministering to sympathetic parishioners in private and perfecting his *Memorialls, or, The memorable things that fell out within this island of Brittain from 1638 to 1684*. The work, which contains little biographical detail, was published in 1818. Law inherited the lands of Balernok and others from his father in 1657, together with his library, valued at approximately £360 Scots. He died about 1686 of causes unknown and was buried at St Mungo's Church, Glasgow.   VAUGHAN T. WELLS

Sources *Reg. PCS*, 3rd ser., vols. 3–6 · *The letters and journals of Robert Baillie*, ed. D. Laing, 3 vols. (1841–2) · R. Wodrow, *The history of the sufferings of the Church of Scotland from the Restoration to the revolution*, ed. R. Burns (1856) · *Fasti Scot.*, new edn, vols. 3, 7 · [C. K. Sharpe], *Letters from and to Charles Kirkpatrick Sharpe*, ed. A. Allardyce, 2 vols. (1888) · R. Law, *Memorialls, or, The memorable things that fell out within this island of Brittain from 1638 to 1684*, ed. C. K. Sharpe (1818) · *DNB*

Law, Samuel (*fl.* 1772–1783), poet and weaver, is of unknown origins. The title-page to his single publication, *A domestic winter-piece: a poem, exhibiting a full view of the author's dwelling place in the winter-season. In two parts. Interspersed with a great variety of entertaining reflections* (1772), tells that the author lived in the village of Barewise, near Todmorden, Yorkshire, near the border with Lancashire. Archival records held in Halifax of contracts to enter into a cotton manufacturing business indicate that later on Law may also have lived in Toad Carr and then in Hundersfield, and that he supplemented his work as a weaver with work as a clog maker.

In the preface to his poem Law claims to have been illiterate until the age of twenty-one, and to have suffered many 'grievous calamities' in the years subsequent. Like many other eighteenth-century labouring-class poets, Law published his poem by subscription. In the autobiographical preface to *A Domestic Winter-Piece*, Law appeals to his readers' charity, reminding them that he undertook the composition of his poem without thought of publication, and dedicated himself to his studies only in hours stolen from sleep. He claims to have sought solace in poetical musings while at his loom to distract himself from the torments of the winter season. The overtly pious and self-deprecating tone of the poem and its prefatory material suggest that Law was a humble man with no great literary aspirations. None the less the poem is directly modelled upon James Thomson's *Seasons*, and Law attempts many of the same poetic techniques, including similar panoramic sweeps and eagle's eye views of his native region. The numerous classical allusions (particularly in the first part of the poem), all of which are carefully documented by the author's footnotes, contradict Law's claim to a total lack of poetic education. The poem perhaps outdoes Thomson's in its vivid presentation of the ghastly horrors caused by the winter weather and approaches an almost Gothic representation of the sublime horror inspired by the season. In his preface Law explains that he chose to describe his native region because:

> It is more like a dreadful wilderness of stony promontories, and direful sinking vales, where roaring lions, savage bears, ravenous wolves, hissing snakes, and horrid birds of prey resort, than an inheritance from any of the human race. And the singularity whereof, was the very first motive that induced me to write a poetical essay on Winter; giving a display of Nature's face, even as it, in this strange, sequestered, solitary desert, appears, when terrible storms and tempests roar, and binding frosts intensely freeze.

The second part of the poem relies upon biblical rather than classical allusions and focuses particularly on the figure of Wisdom as a source of solace to poets and other rural dwellers enduring the hardships of the season.

The religious themes of the poem and Law's emphasis on the morally beneficial effects of his self-improvement, as well as the absence of historical records pertaining to baptism or marriage for Law, would indicate that he may have been Methodist. His work is significant in so far as it bespeaks the variety of poetic production by labouring-class poets. The poem's direct relationship to Thomson's masterpiece reveals not only Thomson's widespread and enduring popularity throughout the eighteenth century but also the self-conscious erudition of labouring-class writers.   BRIDGET KEEGAN

Sources S. Law, *A domestic winter-piece* (1772) · Langfield title deeds and related MSS, 1603–1943, W. Yorks. AS, Calderdale, Fielden papers
Archives W. Yorks. AS, Calderdale, Fielden papers

Law, Thomas (1756–1834), financial writer, was born on 23 October 1756, probably in Cambridge, where his father, Edmund *Law (1703–1787), later bishop of Carlisle, was master of Peterhouse. His mother was Mary Christian (1722–1762), from Unerigg in Cumberland. One of Law's seven brothers, George Henry *Law, became bishop of Bath and Wells, another, John *Law, became bishop of Elphin, and a third, Edward *Law, became lord chief justice and was created Baron Ellenborough. He also had four sisters.

Through Sir Eyre Coote, Law gained an appointment in 1773 in the East India Company's service in Bengal. Not much is known of his private life in India, but he had three sons, John, George, and Edmund, with an Indian wife or mistress. He was appointed to the important post of a district collector in Bihar, with his headquarters at Gaya. (An elder brother, Ewan or Evan, also held a company appointment in Bihar.) While this position gave Law, like the rest of the company's servants, the opportunity to make money through private trading, it was here that he developed an interest in the system of land revenue collection, the crucial aspect of the East India Company's administration that became the foundation of British rule. As he struggled to understand the system of revenue collection that had been in effect under the Mughal empire, and which the British had inherited, he became one of the most knowledgeable of the company's officials, and, as his reports indicate, one of the most concerned to have a system established that would benefit both the peasants and the company. He became an early and persuasive advocate for the view that sound government depended upon private property owned, either by inheritance or purchase, by Indian landlords. Furthermore, he argued that what was needed to make the owners of the land into energetic entrepreneurs was a system that fixed the rate of taxation in perpetuity. He wanted to do away with the system of tax farming instituted by Warren Hastings which gave the right to collect land taxes to the highest bidder, who then paid a specified amount to the company and kept the rest. Later he wrote that, as a young man, he had come to the conclusion that under the farming system the peasant always ended the year in debt, often forcing him to sell his plough and his cattle. Law experimented with the '*mukarari* system' in a few districts of Bihar, giving the owners fixed tenure and a permanent rate of taxation. Against the view that there was no private ownership of land in India, that all the land was the property of the ruler, with *zamindars* or landlords being merely appointed tax collectors, Law argued that his researches proved that the *zamindars* were actually landowners and should be treated as such by the company.

When Lord Cornwallis was governor-general (1786–93) he was so impressed by Law that he made him a member of the board of revenue. Law's arguments were fully stated in two lengthy pamphlets: in *Upon Internal Taxation* (1790) he argued that all internal taxes, except the land tax, should be abolished as they were a hindrance to the commerce of Bengal; in the other, *A Sketch of some Late Arrangements, and a View of the Rising Resources of Bengal* (1792), with a persuasive show of comparative data, he argued that a permanent settlement would increase the prosperity of the Bengal peasantry as well as that of the company. Law later claimed that he, more than anyone else, had been responsible for the arguments that convinced Cornwallis to adopt the permanent settlement in Bengal in 1793. This claim seems justified by Cornwallis's private correspondence, and modern research agrees that, as some contemporaries in Bengal claimed, Law was indeed 'the brain behind the Permanent Settlement' (Guha, 175). In his old age he looked back on his work in India, writing in *Correspondence Respecting the Permanent Settlement of the Land Revenue* (1825) that, because of it, 'commercial capital and enterprise have been turned towards the land'.

Law returned to England in 1791, but he left for the United States in 1793, accompanied by his three young sons. His own explanation for this action was his disapproval of England's war with France, and his anger with the East India Company for having sequestered £10,000 of the £50,000 he had brought back from India. The company held him responsible for its claim for this amount against one of its officials in India to whom Law had given surety. He sued the company, and the money was restored to him in 1799. Law saw prospects for business in America, and was an admirer of George Washington, with whom he soon became acquainted. This relationship became closer when, on 21 March 1796, he married Elizabeth Parke Custis (1779–1832), the granddaughter of Washington's wife, Martha. Seventeen at the time of the marriage, she is described as having great talent and beauty, but the marriage did not last. They separated in 1804, Law gaining custody of their only child, Elizabeth, and divorced in 1811, when Law settled £1500 a year on her. His three 'Indian' sons all predeceased him, as did his daughter Elizabeth. In his will, he left £1000 each to two other children 'who bear my name', one the son of Margaret Jones, the other of Mary Robinson.

American sources describe Law as an 'extremely wealthy but eccentric Englishman' (Decatur, 293). He became very active as an entrepreneur and commentator on public issues. He invested his money in land in the new capital city, but was disappointed at its slow growth. His concern is shown in a letter written to George Washington in 1798, urging him to build a house there as this would 'ensure the rapid rise of the city by doing away with doubts' as to its future (Ritter, 230). Washington took his advice and built two houses, while Law built a large one for himself. He worked out an elaborate scheme for building a canal to bring trade to the city, but there was little capital available to invest in the project. Drawing upon his experience in Bihar, he established a sugar refinery in Washington. His investments as a land speculator were not successful, and he lost much of his fortune in the last years of his life. After the British burnt Washington during the 1812 Anglo-American War there was a move to relocate the capital elsewhere, and Law was a leading opponent, arguing that such a move would be a breach of public faith which would ruin himself and other property owners who had invested their money in the new city. He died in Washington in the autumn of 1834, after some years of ill health. He was buried in Washington.

Law wrote a number of works, some financial, others attempting to reconcile Christian doctrine with eighteenth-century rationalism. In *Letters on a National Currency* (1817) he promoted the idea of a national paper currency to replace the use of specie controlled by the different states, a view he shared with Thomas Jefferson, with whom he had become friendly. Law was famous in his time, as a friendly commentator put it, for his eccentricities, his lavish hospitality, his brilliant talk, his good works, and his aristocratic English connections, but he has found little place in American historiography. His work on the land revenue system in Bengal, however, and the fact that his career directly linked the intellectual life of late eighteenth-century England with the new British empire being built in India and with the new nation emerging in America, deserve lasting recognition.

AINSLIE T. EMBREE

Sources *DNB* · R. Guha, *A rule of property for Bengal: an essay on the idea of permanent settlement* (Paris, 1963) · A. C. Clark, *Greenleaf and Law in the federal city* (1901) · J. A. Imlah, *Lord Ellenborough* (1939) · G. W. P. Custis, *Recollections and memoirs of Washington* (1860) · list of the company's covenanted servants, 1773, BL OIOC · writers' petitions, BL OIOC · *Correspondence of Charles, first Marquis Cornwallis*, ed. C. Ross, 3 vols. (1859) · *GM*, 2nd ser., 2 (1834), 437 · S. Decatur, *Private affairs of George Washington* (1933) · H. Ritter, *Washington as a business man* (1931)
Archives BL OIOC, proceedings of the board of revenue and letters to the court of directors
Likenesses portrait (as young man), repro. in Clark, *Greenleaf and Law*, 217
Wealth at death very straitened circumstances: Guha, *Rule of property*; Custis, *Recollections*; Decatur, *Private affairs*

Law, Thomas Graves (1836–1904), historian, was great-grandson of Edmund *Law, bishop of Carlisle, and grandson of Edward *Law, first Baron Ellenborough. Born on 4 December 1836 at Yeovilton in Somerset, Law was third son and fourth of eight surviving children of William Towry Law (1809–1886), Lord Ellenborough's youngest son [see under Law, Edward, first Baron Ellenborough], and his first wife, Augusta Champagné (d. 1844), fourth daughter of Thomas North Graves, second Baron Graves. His father originally served in the 51st regiment and the Grenadier Guards, but in 1831 entered Peterhouse, Cambridge, and subsequently took orders in the Church of England. At the time of his son's birth, he was rector of Yeovilton and chancellor of the diocese of Bath and Wells.

On the death of his mother in 1844, Law was sent to

Thomas Graves Law (1836–1904), by William Crooke

zeal. Law was married on 15 April 1880 to Wilhelmina Frederica (*d.* in or after 1904), youngest daughter of Captain Allen of Errol, Perthshire, and his wife, Lady Henrietta Dundas; they had one son, Duncan, and five daughters. After a long and painful illness Law died at his home, Woodlands, Duddingston, Edinburgh, on 12 March 1904.

Law's main historical interests lay in the sixteenth century, and especially in its religious and ecclesiastical aspects. In his treatment of contending religious forces he showed remarkable freedom from partisanship, and everything that he wrote was based on all the accessible sources relative to his subject. His most important historical work was *The Conflicts between Jesuits and Seculars in the Reign of Queen Elizabeth* (1889); but he also wrote many reviews and articles (the most important of which will be found in *Collected Essays and Reviews of Thomas Graves Law, LLD*, 1904), and sixteen memoirs for the *Dictionary of National Biography*. For the Camden Society he edited *The Archpriest Controversy* (2 vols., 1896–8); and for the Scottish Text Society, *Catholik Tractates of the Sixteenth Century* (1901), and *The New Testament in Scots* (3 vols., 1901–3). Of special note among Law's contributions to Scottish history are his edition of *Archbishop Hamilton's Catechism*, with preface by W. E. Gladstone (1884), and a chapter on Mary Stewart in volume 3 of the *Cambridge Modern History*.

P. H. BROWN, *rev.* H. C. G. MATTHEW

Sources *Collected essays and reviews of Thomas Graves Law*, ed. P. H. Brown (1904) [incl. bibliography] · Gladstone, *Diaries* · *CGPLA Eng. & Wales* (1904)
Archives BL, letters to W. E. Gladstone, Add. MSS 44458–44524 · CUL, letters to Lord Acton
Likenesses W. Crooke, photograph, repro. in Brown, ed., *Collected essays … of … Law* [see illus.]
Wealth at death £9826 4s. 1d.: confirmation, 14 April 1904, *CCI* · £1319: additional estate, 22 Sept 1904, *CCI*

school at Somerton, but in the following year, on his father's removal to the living of Harborne in Staffordshire, he was successively sent to St Edmund's School, Birmingham, and (as founder's kin) to Winchester College, then under the charge of Dr George Moberly. In 1851 his father joined the Roman Catholic church, a step which necessitated his son's leaving Winchester. In 1852 he studied at University College, London, where he had Augustus De Morgan, the mathematician, and Francis Newman among his teachers, and in 1853 he entered the Roman Catholic college at Stonyhurst. For a time he hesitated between the church and the army as a profession, and his father actually obtained for him a cadetship in the military service of the East India Company. In 1855, however, under the influence of his father's friend, Frederick Faber, he entered the Brompton Oratory, London, where he was ordained priest in 1860. He remained in the Oratory until 1878, when, owing to the loss of his faith in the teaching of the church, he left its communion.

In 1879 Law, who had long devoted himself to historical and literary study, was appointed keeper of the Signet Library in Edinburgh, partly through the recommendation of W. E. Gladstone, who had befriended him; in that post he passed the remainder of his life and was active in promoting the study of Scottish history. He was one of the founders, in 1886, of the Scottish History Society, and acted as its honorary secretary. In 1898 the University of Edinburgh made him an honorary LLD 'in recognition of his learned labours and indefatigable industry'; and in the last year of his life the Scottish History Society presented him with a valuable gift in recognition of his disinterested

Law, William (1686–1761), devotional writer and nonjuror, was born in the village of King's Cliffe, Northamptonshire, near Stamford, Lincolnshire, and baptized on 3 February 1687 in the parish church, All Saints'. He was the fifth among the eleven children of Thomas Law (*bap.* 1657, *d.* 1714), a grocer and chandler of King's Cliffe, and his wife, Margaret Farmery (*d.* 1718). Nothing certain is known of his early education. At the time of his mother's death six of his siblings were still living, and one died shortly afterwards. Three of his brothers settled in King's Cliffe and brought up their numerous children there, and William remained on close terms with his family. He was to become an important beneficiary of the village later in life and its most famous inhabitant.

Cambridge and early career, 1705–1716 Law was admitted a sizar of Emmanuel College, Cambridge, on 7 June 1705; he graduated BA in 1708, was ordained deacon at Peterborough on 23 September 1710, was elected to a fellowship in 1711, and graduated MA in 1712. At the age of eighteen he was a keen reader of classical literature, but 'this *Ardour* soon went off' (*Some Animadversions*, in *Works*, 6.2.318); he turned instead to a life of religious devotion, set out in the characteristically demanding 'Rules for the good conduct of my life' (printed by Overton, 6–7, based on Walton, 345–

6n., slightly altered from the MS in Dr Williams's Library). He told his friend John Byrom in 1729 of the strong impression made by his chance discovery of the seventeenth-century French philosopher Malebranche, as a result of which he kept his act (i.e. read his thesis in public) on 'Omnia videmus in Deo' ('we see all things in God'). He did not conceal his Jacobite sympathies, and after giving an injudicious tripos speech on 19 March 1713, in which he asked thinly veiled questions referring favourably to the Pretender, James Stuart, on 17 April 1713 he was temporarily degraded from his degrees. Byrom, who did not know Law at this time, said in a letter home of 27 April 1713 describing the affair that he had 'the character of a vain, conceited fellow' (*Private Journal*, 1.1.20–21). Law's MA status was restored by 15 June 1713, after his second appearance in the vice-chancellor's court and his promise not to offend in like manner in the future.

On 13 July 1711 Law was licensed as curate at Haslingfield, near Cambridge, where John Heylin was vicar from 1714 to 1719, and on 7 July 1713, the day appointed by Queen Anne for the celebration of the peace of Utrecht, he preached a highly political sermon, subsequently published (but not included in the *Works*), on the tory themes of the duty of submission and the wickedness of resistance to lawful rulers. A manuscript Ascension day sermon on 1 Corinthians 15: 55, perhaps written for Haslingfield, survives in Dr Williams's Library. On 5 July 1714 Law was respondent in the philosophy act and distributed verses on the anti-Hobbesian and anti-freethinking topics of 'Status naturae non est status belli' ('the state of nature is not a state of war') and 'Materia non potest cogitare' ('matter cannot think'). Copies survive in the Bodleian Library, Oxford, and Cambridge University Library. He was appointed moderator for 1714–15 and Barnaby lecturer in rhetoric for 1715. After the accession of George I his brief academic and ecclesiastical career came to an end in January 1716, when he refused the abjuration oath, requiring allegiance to the new king and abjuration of the Pretender, and as a result lost his fellowship. He wrote an explanatory letter to his eldest brother, George, regretting the hurt he was causing his mother but insisting that he could not go against his conscience: 'I expected to have had a greater share of worldly advantages than what I am now likely to enjoy; but am fully persuaded, that if I am not happier for this trial it will be my own fault' (Overton, 14).

Nonjuror and tutor, 1716–1740 No firm information has come to light about where Law lived or how he supported himself from 1716 to 1723. He and his siblings received £115 each on his mother's death in 1718. He began to be noticed as a participant in the Bangorian controversy, publishing two letters in 1717 and a third in 1719 from a strongly high-church perspective in response to Benjamin Hoadly's notorious sermon *The Nature of the Kingdom, or Church, of Christ* (1717) and his answer to convocation (1719). Shortly before his death Law mentioned to the Moravian Francis Okely that he had been a curate in London, presumably to a nonjuring congregation. From 1723 to 1737 he was a member of the household of the wealthy tory

stockjobber Edward Gibbon at Putney in Surrey, acting as private tutor to his son Edward (father of the historian Edward Gibbon) and accompanying him to his own former Cambridge college, Emmanuel, during his two periods of residence (1723–4 and 1727–34). Edward was an idle student, and when he went on his grand tour Law stayed at Putney, 'the much-honoured friend and spiritual director of the whole family' (*Autobiographies*, 17). He conducted Edward's marriage service on 3 June 1736 at St Christopher-le-Stocks, Cheapside. Though he failed to mould Edward he exercised a profound influence on Hester Gibbon, his pupil's sister, who was later to join him in his religious retirement. Some time after the death of Gibbon senior in 1737 he moved to lodgings in London; in 1739–40 he was living in Arundel Street, near Somerset Gardens.

There are glimpses of Law's activities in the quarrelsome nonjuring church during the Putney period. He was eventually ordained priest on 27 January 1728 by the nonjuring bishop Henry Gandy, after considerable pressure had been put on him by his superior. He made himself unpopular in 1731–2 for twice changing sides in the dispute between the two parties among the nonjurors about 'usages' in the eucharist, which particularly concerned the reintroduction of the 'mixed chalice' of water and wine, and prayers for the dead. He was described at this time by the nonjuring bishop George Smith as 'one of the proudest men living' and 'a very weak or a very insincere man' (Broxap, 159, 167). As a result of his increasing interest in mysticism he was to move away from the ecclesiastical and ceremonial concerns of the nonjurors, though he retained his Jacobite allegiance. Smith complained in 1742 that he was 'heartily sorry to find so much difference between the Mr Law who wrote so judiciously against the Bishop of Bangor twenty years ago and the Mr Law that writes now' (ibid., 217).

Law's fame as the author of *A Practical Treatise upon Christian Perfection* (1726) and *A Serious Call to a Devout and Holy Life* (1729) brought would-be disciples to Putney. John Byrom, who was to remain a lifelong friend and admirer, visited him regularly from 1729 to 1739 at Putney, Cambridge, and London, keeping an invaluable record in his journal of Law's conversation and of the critical observations on his hero made by his own acquaintance. The bookseller Charles Rivington (the source of the information that Law was Heylin's curate) told Byrom on 31 December 1734 of Heylin's view that 'his book would have been better if he had travelled that way himself' (*Private Journal*, 1.2.542). One of Byrom's coffee-house companions told him on 18 April 1737 that Law 'was terribly perplexed with scruples, always uneasy, wearing a pair of stockings that a ploughman would not have picked off a dunghill' (ibid., 2.1.114). John Wesley first visited him on 31 July 1732 and became a correspondent, earnestly following his advice about reading and self-regulation. Both Charles and John Wesley began to turn against Law in 1737, and in an intemperate letter of 14 May 1738 John Wesley told Law that it was impossible to live by following his two practical treatises and that Law did not know and had not taught him true justifying faith. After a swift exchange of letters Law concluded the dispute by asking 'Who made me your teacher?' (*Letters of … John Wesley*, 1.244). He told the countess of Huntingdon in a defensive letter of 16 February 1756, after Wesley had attacked him in print, 'I was once a kind of oracle with Mr. *Wesley*' (*Works*, 9.3.123). It is clear that Law was very willing to give advice about spiritual and ecclesiastical matters. He wrote three warning letters in 1731–2, probably to Elizabeth Dodwell, the daughter of the nonjuror Henry Dodwell and the sister of his namesake the freethinker, which were published posthumously through the medium of John Payne as *Letters to a Lady Inclined to Enter into the Communion of the Church of Rome* (1779). At Byrom's request he wrote several letters in November and December 1736 to the latter's friend Fanny Henshaw (first published by Hobhouse, 1927), warning her unsuccessfully against joining the Quakers.

Earlier writings, 1717–1740 Law's principal publications in his lifetime fall into three chronological groups: 1717–31, 1737–40, and 1749–61. The works in the first group are partly controversial and partly practical. The former consist of replies to Hoadly (1717–19); to Bernard Mandeville, in *Remarks upon a Late Book, Entituled, The Fable of the Bees* (1724); and to Matthew Tindal, in *The Case of Reason, or, Natural Religion, Fairly and Fully Stated: in Answer to a Book, Entitul'd, Christianity as Old as the Creation* (1731). The most brilliant of the polemical works is the attack on Tindal, in which Law ridicules contemporary assumptions about the efficacy of reason as a source of knowledge and as a means of regulating human affairs. His fame has always rested on the practical works of this period—*A Practical Treatise upon Christian Perfection* (1726) (which incorporates the earlier pamphlet *The Absolute Unlawfulness of the Stage-Entertainment Fully Demonstrated* of 1726) and *A Serious Call to a Devout and Holy Life* (1729). Both are addressed primarily to wealthy and cultivated readers, who must learn to renounce the world, submit themselves to the demands of the gospel in all their rigour, and devote themselves totally in intention and action to God. This uncompromising message is conveyed in *A Serious Call* by means of characters who exemplify on the one hand the favourite sins of the leisured, such as Classicus, Negotius, and Flatus, and on the other the holy and useful lives they ought to lead, such as Paternus the Christian educator, Ouranius the country priest, and Miranda the charitable gentlewoman. Despite the moral rigour of these works, which made them theologically suspect to Calvinists and which oppressed John Wesley and Samuel Johnson in different ways, they were very widely read and played a significant role in the evangelical revival. Law's characters became a kind of shorthand for self-definition. For example George Whitefield, acting as temporary curate in Dummer, Hampshire, in 1736, reconciled himself to ministering to a poor and illiterate flock by reading the character of Ouranius.

Law had long been a reader of mystical writers, but at some point in the mid-1730s his understanding of Christianity was profoundly altered by his reading of the German protestant mystic Jacob Boehme. He discussed mystics with Byrom several times in the mid-1730s. On 17 April 1737 he recommended Tauler, Rusbrochius (Ruysbroeck), and Thomas à Kempis, criticized Antoinette Bourignon and Madame Guyon, and first mentioned Boehme approvingly. He told Byrom in May 1743 and Okely in 1760 that he had first come across a reference to Boehme in a book recommended to him by George Cheyne, entitled *Fides et ratio*; this was an anti-Lockian mystical work edited by Pierre Poiret (1708) and written in part by Baron von Metternich. Shortly thereafter Law found a complete edition of Boehme (in the seventeenth-century translation by John Sparrow and John Ellistone). He told Okely that reading Boehme put him 'into a *perfect Sweat*', but he found himself prompted 'to *dig* in these Writings; … till at length I found what a Treasure there was hid in this Field' (Okely, 105n.).

Law's publications from 1737 onwards all reflect the influence of Boehme. In the second period (1737–40) these consist of *A Demonstration of the Gross and Fundamental Errors of … 'A Plain Account of … the Lord's Supper'* (1737), a lengthy attack on an anonymous work by Hoadly; *The Grounds and Reasons of Christian Regeneration* (1739), a pithy summary of his position; *An Earnest and Serious Answer to Dr Trapp's Discourse* (1740), a short attack on Joseph Trapp's anti-enthusiastic and anti-Methodist sermons *The Nature, Folly, Sin, and Danger of being Righteous over-much* (1739); and the substantial treatise *An Appeal to All that Doubt or Disbelieve the Truths of the Gospel* (1740), published with *Some Animadversions upon Dr Trapp's Reply to An Earnest and Serious Answer*. In *Some Animadversions* Law told Trapp that he had been a diligent reader of mystical divines of all ages of the church, and that, 'If a man has no Desire but to be of the Spirit of the Gospel, … it is a great Unhappiness to him … to pass a Day without reading something of what they wrote'. He explained that Boehme 'was no Messenger from God of any thing *new* in Religion, but the Mystery of all that was *old* and *true* both in Religion and Nature was *opened* in him' (*Works*, 6.2.321, 323). Law believed, as summarized in *Christian Regeneration*, that the aim of the religious life is the return to the light of paradise and the love of God and the recovery of the image of the Trinity in human nature, all of which have been lost through Adam's freely chosen fall into the darkness and imprisonment of worldly life. The unregenerate state is one of self-tormenting fire, the four hellish elements of selfishness, envy, pride, and wrath; regeneration is a progressive state, the recovering of the birth of Christ in the soul, and the total separation of the inward from the outward. 'This inward Man is alone the *Subject* of Religion and divine Grace' (ibid., 5.2.69). This was to be Law's concern in all his later work.

Retirement at King's Cliffe, 1740–1761 Law left London in 1740 for his native village of King's Cliffe, where he owned a house in Hall Yard, next to the church, the only property he had inherited from his father. Here for the rest of his life he put his precepts into practice by living a life of charity, celibacy, prayer, study, and writing. Despite his non-juring status he was always a regular attender at church. He was soon joined by two companions, Hester Gibbon and Elizabeth Hutcheson, the latter a wealthy widow whose second husband, Archibald Hutcheson, MP for Hastings, had been a friend of Law at Putney. Hutcheson died on 15 August 1740, having recommended his wife to live a retired life with Law's help. In 1743 Law took a house for her and Hester Gibbon at Thrapston, about 10 miles from King's Cliffe, but as this proved inconvenient they joined him in Hall Yard the following year. Elizabeth Hutcheson had an annual income of about £2000 and Hester Gibbon one of between £500 and £700, most of which they devoted to charity on the model of Law's character Miranda in *A Serious Call*. Law also had substantial sums for charitable purposes. After the publication of *Christian Perfection* he received from an unknown person a banknote for £1000, and in 1753 a Dr Stratford left him £100. His *Short Account of the Two Charitable Foundations at King's Cliffe in the County of Northampton* (1755) provides details, dated 6 May 1754, of the trusts established by himself and Mrs Hutcheson. In 1727 he founded a school for poor girls (presumably with the £1000 gift), and in 1745 she founded one for poor boys; they also provided school buildings and built almshouses for elderly women. Strict instructions were laid down for the conduct of the master and mistress and the beneficiaries of the charities. In 1752 Law founded a library of pious books for public use, to be kept in the schoolhouse under the care of the schoolmaster; above the door can still be seen the inscription, in capitals, 'Books of piety are here lent to any persons of this or ye neighbouring towns'. There was also a small library for the benefit of neighbouring clergy, consisting of Hebrew, Greek, and Latin bibles and 'a choice collection of the most spiritual Christian writers in the learned and foreign languages' (Law, *Short Account*, 22). In addition to these highly prescriptive charitable foundations, Law and his companions regularly gave food, clothes, and money indiscriminately to all beggars who came to the house, to the disgust of the villagers and the rector, Wilfrid Piemont, who regularly preached against this practice. In a letter of 21 February 1753, addressed to those who had objected to the local justices, Law and his companions threatened to leave the village and take all their charities elsewhere, after which there were no further complaints. The document of 6 May 1754 stated that the rector of King's Cliffe was always to be a trustee.

Law continued his detailed study of spiritual writers. He taught himself German in order to read Boehme in the original and considered undertaking a new translation, though he never did so. He borrowed and transcribed manuscripts by the Behmenists Dionysius Andreas Freher and Francis Lee, and, alongside his favourite Catholic mystics such as Rusbrochius, he read the Quaker Isaac Penington with approval. He had a large private library in addition to those he established for public use, containing Hebrew, Greek, Latin, French, German, and Dutch religious books; after Hester Gibbon's death 'boxes upon boxes' were sold about 1800 by her heirs (Walton, 501–2n.). Yet none of these books really mattered to him except for the Bible and Boehme, as he explained in a letter of 3 November 1759. What was opened in Boehme enabled him to understand what was hidden in himself: 'And therefore in reading of him I am always at home, and kept close to the kingdom of God that is within me' (*Works*, 9.196).

Law was not a recluse in King's Cliffe. Old and new friends visited him. Byrom first came in May 1743, when they discussed among other matters his poem 'Enthusiasm', based on a passage from *Some Animadversions*; they continued to correspond irregularly but warmly, and Law took pleasure in Byrom's further attempts at versifying his prose. Other visitors and correspondents included Thomas Hartley, rector of Winwick, and two Londoners, Thomas Langcake, a clerk in the Bank of England, to whom Law became much attached, and George Ward, who between them acted as his literary agents, and who later brought out an edition of Boehme (1764–81) based on the old translation.

Later writings, 1749–1761 Law's nine-year silence can be accounted for by his continuing attempt to master Boehme and his immersion in the manuscripts of Freher and Lee. In the last eleven years of his life he published a number of works, the most important of which are *The Spirit of Prayer, or, The Soul Rising out of the Vanity of Time into the Riches of Eternity* (part 1, 1749, part 2, 1750), the longer second part in the form of dialogues between Academicus, Rusticus, and Theophilus; *The Way to Divine Knowledge* (1752), intended as an introduction to a new edition of Boehme, in which the former characters are joined in discussion by the convert Humanus, who was silent earlier; and *The Spirit of Love* (part 1, 1752, part 2, 1754), the first part in the form of a brief letter to a friend, the second in the form of dialogues between Theophilus and two new characters, Theogenes and Eusebius. Theophilus is Law's spokesman; Academicus and Humanus may represent aspects of his early life. Through a retelling of the narrative of the fall and redemption that more conventional or orthodox contemporaries found at best fanciful and at worst blasphemous, Law developed his fundamental idea that the spirit of God is within and can be regained by all who are willing to learn how to find it. One of the functions of the dialogues is to show the irrelevance of contemporary arguments about the reasonableness and evidences of Christianity and to wean the academic reader from books to the spirit within, a point that Law repeated in advice to his correspondents about how to read his own books: 'For they mean nothing else but to lead you from me, and from yourself, … to expect and find all that you want, in God alone, in the immediate operation of his *living Word* and Spirit in your soul' (Walton, 573n.).

Despite Law's avowed distaste for theological debate, he continued to engage in controversy. He attacked William Warburton's *Divine Legation of Moses* in *A Short but Sufficient Confutation* (1757), and made Warburton's sermons his central target in the last work he wrote, *An Humble, Earnest, and Affectionate Address to the Clergy* (published posthumously,

1761). In 1756 John Wesley published his critical *A Letter to the Reverend Mr. Law*, appalled by what he saw as Law's unscriptural, philosophical religion in *The Spirit of Prayer* and *The Spirit of Love*. Law did not reply directly, but in *A Collection of Letters* (1760), edited by Ward and Langcake in consultation with him, he described his *Letter* as 'a juvenile composition of emptiness and pertness' (*Works*, 9.3.181–2). In *Of Justification by Faith and Works: a Dialogue between a Methodist and a Churchman* (1760), he criticized the Calvinist views of the evangelical John Berridge.

Death and reputation Law was writing his *Address to the Clergy* up to a few days before his death, at Hall Yard, King's Cliffe, on 9 April 1761. He suffered from rheumatism for some months, and towards the end he had severe pain in his kidneys. On his deathbed he spoke rapturously of 'the fire of love within, which has burned up everything contrary to itself' (*Private Journal*, 2.2.649). His tombstone in All Saints' churchyard, where he was buried, erected by Hester Gibbon, carried a long inscription by Langcake and Ward (now illegible, but transcribed in Overton, 447). In appearance and character, according to his first biographer, Richard Tighe, who spoke to those who had known him, Law was stout with broad shoulders and a ruddy complexion, cheerful and warm-hearted, but not remarkable for meekness. He made Hester Gibbon executor and beneficiary of his will, but in a codicil he asked her to give such part of the property as she chose to the descendants of his brother George.

Two years after his death Warburton had his revenge, comparing Law's 'incredible appetite' for 'the trash dropt from every species of Mysticism' with that of a fanatic who has sworn only to taste food that 'has passed through the entrails of some impure or Savage Animal' (W. Warburton, *The Doctrine of Grace*, 3rd edn, 1763, 223). Several of Law's admirers came to his defence: Payne added a 250-page letter in answer to Warburton, essentially an anthology of Law's works, to his *Evangelical Discourses* (1763); Hartley added 'A short defence of the mystical writers' to *Paradise Restored* (1764); and Langcake recommended Law in *A Serious and Affectionate Address* (1781). The early Law was given respectability by the 200 or so quotations from *A Serious Call* in the revised fourth edition of Johnson's *Dictionary* (1773).

Law has been regarded by some as an isolated writer who was entirely at odds with the dominant religious culture of his time and by others, more accurately, as an important conduit through which a particular stream of seventeenth-century devotion was transmitted to the later eighteenth century and beyond. Paradoxically, one of the principal means by which knowledge of Law was spread was through Wesley's abridgements and recommendations; he included much of Law's Behmenist writing in *An Extract from the Rev. Mr. Law's Later Works* (1768), and there were several Methodists among Law's later followers, such as Henry Brooke the younger and Ralph Mather. The Methodist Christopher Walton discovered Law in 1831 through Wesley's 1768 edition, and went on to rescue many of his papers and letters (now in the Walton collection in Dr Williams's Library), quoting from them at

length in his biography (1854), which in turn was much used by Overton (1881). The nine-volume 1762 edition of Law's *Works* (essentially a collection of existing editions) was reissued by G. B. Morgan in 1892–3, but over a century after that date no complete scholarly edition has been undertaken. Despite attempts to awaken interest in his later writings, particularly by his principal twentieth-century biographer and interpreter, the Quaker Stephen Hobhouse, Law has remained known as the author of *A Serious Call*.   ISABEL RIVERS

Sources [C. Walton], *Notes and materials for an adequate biography of the celebrated divine and theosopher, William Law* (1854) • J. H. Overton, *William Law, nonjuror and mystic* (1881) • *The works of the Reverend William Law*, 9 vols. (1762) • *The private journal and literary remains of John Byrom*, ed. R. Parkinson, 2 vols. in 4 pts, Chetham Society, 32, 34, 40, 44 (1854–7) • *The letters of the Rev. John Wesley*, ed. J. Telford, 8 vols. (1931), vols. 1, 3 • S. Hobhouse, *Selected mystical writings of William Law, edited with notes and twenty-four studies in the mystical theology of William Law and Jacob Boehme*, 2nd edn (1948) [incl. new biographical material in appx 1] • W. Law, *A short account of the two charitable foundations at King's Cliffe in the county of Northampton* (1755) • S. Hobhouse, *William Law and eighteenth century Quakerism, including some unpublished letters and fragments of William Law and John Byrom* (1927) • *The autobiographies of Edward Gibbon*, ed. J. Murray (1896) • R. Tighe, *A short account of the life and writings of the late Rev. William Law* (1813) • H. Broxap, *The later non-jurors* (1924) • S. Hobhouse, '*Fides et ratio*: the book which introduced Jacob Boehme to William Law', *Journal of Theological Studies*, 37 (1936), 350–68 • *A catalogue of the library at King's Cliffe Northamptonshire, founded by William Law, M.A. 1752* (1927) • A. von Frankenberg and C. Weissner, *Memoirs of the life, death, burial, and wonderful writings, of Jacob Behmen … with an introductory preface of the translator*, ed. and trans. F. Okely (1780) • A. Starkie, 'William Law and Cambridge Jacobitism, 1713-16', *Historical Research*, 75 (2002), 448–67 • P. Malekin, 'William Law's career, 1711–23', *N&Q*, 212 (1967), 405–6 • T. Underhill, 'William Law's suspension at Cambridge, 1713', *N&Q*, 237 (1992), 42–4 • E. S. Shuckburgh, *Emmanuel College* (1904), 123 • P. Malekin, 'Jacob Boehme's influence on William Law', *Studia Neophilologica*, 36 (1964), 245–60 • D. Hirst, *Hidden riches: traditional symbolism from the Renaissance to Blake* (1964), chaps. 7 and 9 • C. F. E. Spurgeon, 'William Law and the mystics', *The Cambridge history of English literature*, ed. A. W. Ward and A. R. Waller, vol. 9: *From Steele and Addison to Pope and Swift* (1912), 305–28 • J. Hoyles, *The edges of Augustanism: the aesthetics of spirituality in Thomas Ken, John Byrom and William Law* (1972) • B. W. Young, *Religion and Enlightenment in eighteenth-century England: theological debate from Locke to Burke* (1998), chap. 4

Archives Northants. RO, his library from King's Cliffe • Northants. RO, records of Law and Hutcheson charities | BL, letter to George Law, Add. MS 34486 • Bodl. Oxf., letters to Elizabeth Dodwell • DWL, Walton collection, corresp. and papers

Wealth at death estate (house at King's Cliffe, books, etc.) left to Hester Gibbon, then through her to collateral descendants: will, 13 Sept 1753

Law, William John (1786–1869), judge, was born on 6 December 1786, the eldest son of Ewan Law (*d.* 1829), and his wife, Henrietta Sarah (1763/4–1844), eldest daughter of William *Markham, archbishop of York. Law's father, the second son of Edmund *Law, bishop of Carlisle, was member of parliament for Westbury, Wiltshire, from 1790 to 1795, and for Newtown, Isle of Wight, in 1802. Law was educated at Westminster School before matriculating on 16 May 1804 from Christ Church, Oxford, where he held a studentship until 1814. He graduated BA in 1808, and MA in 1810. On 11 February 1813 he was called to the bar at Lincoln's Inn. On 1 January 1817 he married Charlotte Elizabeth, daughter of Robert Simpson of Middlethorpe Hall, Yorkshire. In 1825, on the passing of Lord Eldon's act, he became one of the commissioners of bankruptcy. Subsequently he was appointed a commissioner of the court for the relief of insolvent debtors, and on 1 August 1853 promoted to be the chief commissioner. This court was abolished in 1861. Law was a hard-working and intelligent lawyer. He published several works relating to bankruptcy.

Law was a keen follower of racing; he knew the *Racing Calendar* by heart, and never missed seeing the Derby. His other great fondness was for the classics. Between 1854 and 1856 he was engaged in controversy with Robert Ellis whose views respecting Hannibal's route over the Alps he sharply attacked in three pamphlets (1855–6). In 1866 he published a two-volume treatise, *On the Passage of Hannibal over the Alps*, which he had worked on for many years. He died at 5 Sussex Square, Brighton, on 5 October 1869.

G. C. BOASE, rev. ERIC METCALFE

Sources *The Times* (13 Oct 1869), 8 · *Register and Magazine of Biography* (Nov 1869), 255 · J. Foster, *The peerage, baronetage, and knightage of the British empire for 1883*, 1 [1883], 264 · *Law Journal* (15 Oct 1869), 560 · Foster, *Alum. Oxon.* · W. P. Baildon, ed., *The records of the Honorable Society of Lincoln's Inn: the black books*, 4 (1902)
Archives BL, corresp. with Sir Robert Peel, Add. MSS 40225–40522
Wealth at death under £45,000: probate, 16 Nov 1869, *CGPLA Eng. & Wales*

Law, William Towry (1809–1886). *See under* Law, Edward, first Baron Ellenborough (1750–1818).

Lawerne, John (*d.* 1481/2), Benedictine monk, was admitted to Worcester Cathedral priory in 1427 or 1428, ordained deacon in 1432, and sent to study at Gloucester College in Oxford that same year. For the next sixteen years he pursued his theological studies there, on a part-time basis, obtaining his BTh in 1445, followed by his DTh in 1448.

Lawerne held several obedientiary offices in the priory: he was almoner (1448–56), sacrist (1458–69), and sub-prior (1474–8). On at least four occasions he represented the Worcester community at the triennial black monk chapters in Northampton. There are several references to his preaching and lecturing assignments, the earliest of the former being in 1437 when he was recalled from Oxford to give the sermon in Worcester Cathedral on the eve of the feast of the Assumption. In October 1445, following a precedent set at least a century earlier, he began to lecture on the *Sentences* of Peter Lombard before the bishop of Worcester, members of his monastic community, and others, in the Worcester chapter house. Three years later he delivered similar lectures in Oxford. In August 1469 he was presented to the bishop, who had the right of final selection, as one of the seven most suitable candidates for the priorate.

Lawerne's name occurs in five Worcester Cathedral manuscripts—F.13, F.19, Q.22, Q.27, and Q.89—all of which were at one time in his possession. Of these MS Q.27 contains a list, in his hand, of thirty volumes that were probably used at Oxford by him and his fellow Worcester monk–students. His notebook (Bodl. Oxf., MS Bodley 692) contains theological lectures, sermons, and a miscellaneous collection of letters; some of these last were copied from an earlier source or sources, others relate to Gloucester College and university affairs, and some are copies of his correspondence with the bishop concerning his obligations as sacrist, whose appointment at Worcester was the bishop's prerogative. His death is recorded on the almoner's account for 1481/2 where the customary 'corrody' of a deceased monk in the form of a daily distribution to the poor was entered in his name.

JOAN GREATREX

Sources Worcester Cathedral, Muniments [Register A.6(i) and ibid. obedientiary and manorial accounts, class C] · Worcester Cathedral, MSS F.13, F.19, Q.22, Q.27, Q.89 · Bodl. Oxf., MS Bodley 692 · T. Polton and J. Carpenter, bishops' registers, Worcs. RO · J. W. Willis Bund, *The register of the diocese of Worcester during the vacancy of the see, usually called 'registrum sede vacante', 1301–1435*, Worcestershire Historical Society, 8 (1897) · W. A. Pantin, ed., *Documents illustrating the activities of … the English black monks, 1215–1540*, 3 vols., CS, 3rd ser., 45, 47, 54 (1931–7), vol. 3 · Emden, *Oxf.* · J. Greatrex, *Monastic or episcopal obedience: the problem of the sacrists of Worcester*, Worcester Historical Society: Occasional Publications, 3 (1980) · J. Greatrex, 'Benedictine monk scholars as teachers and preachers in the later middle ages: evidence from the Worcester Cathedral priory', *Monastic Studies*, 2 (1991) · J. Greatrex, *Biographical register of the English cathedral priories of the province of Canterbury* (1997)
Archives Bodl. Oxf., MS Bodley 692 · Worcester Cathedral, F.13, F.19, Q.22, Q.27, Q.89

Lawes, Sir Charles Bennet. *See* Wittewronge, Sir Charles Bennet Lawes-, second baronet (1843–1911).

Lawes, Henry (*bap.* 1596, *d.* 1662), singer and composer, was born at Dinton, near Wilton, Wiltshire, and baptized there on 5 January 1596, the eldest son of Thomas Lawes (*d.* 1640), a church musician, and his wife, Lucris (or Lucrece or Lucretia) Shepherd (*d.* 1661), and elder brother of William *Lawes (*bap.* 1602, *d.* 1645), Elizabeth (*b.* 1605), Thomas (1608–1666), and John (*d.* 1655), the last two of whom also became church musicians. On his father's appointment as a lay vicar in 1602, the family moved to the cathedral close at Salisbury, and although no direct evidence exists it is likely that Henry was a chorister at the cathedral and educated at its school.

Court and patrons, 1615–1638 As a young man it is possible that Lawes enjoyed the patronage of William Herbert, earl of Pembroke, whose seat was at Wilton; alternatively, Edward Seymour, earl of Hertford, who resided at Amesbury, may have taken an interest in him, as he later did with his brother William. From about 1615 he must have been in London and perhaps on the fringes of the court, for many years later (in a poem by John Berkenhead which prefaced Lawes's *Ayres*, 1655) it was said that he had:

liv'd forty Summers, where
What the best Wits have writ or spoke didst hear.

His long connection with the Egerton family may also have begun then, although his engagement as music master for the daughters of the earl and countess of Bridgewater cannot positively be set earlier than 1627. By then he

Henry Lawes (*bap.* 1596, *d.* 1662), by unknown artist, *c.*1648

was a member of the Chapel Royal, having been appointed 'pistoler' on 1 January 1626 and gentleman on 3 November following, with a stipend of £40 per annum. Five years later, on 6 January 1631, he was appointed to the king's musick as one of the 'lutes and voices' with a further £20 per annum and livery of £16 2s. 6d.

Already Lawes must have come into contact with the poets whose verse he set—the so-called cavalier poets such as Thomas Carew, whose lyrics he put to music more than any other's (at least forty, including doubtful attributions). He must also have taken part in some of the court masques of this time, not only singing and playing in them, but very likely composing music for them. Although the evidence is ambiguous, one such masque was probably Carew's *Coelum Britannicum* (performed 18 February 1634); unfortunately, even where Lawes is known to have been involved, as in Davenant's *The Triumphs of the Prince d'Amour* (23 February 1636), very little of his music survives.

Beyond the court Lawes's association with the Egerton family continued. Presumably it was he who approached Milton to write *Arcades* for the earl of Bridgewater's children to perform at Harefield in honour of their grandmother, Alice, the dowager countess of Derby. The date is not known for certain, but it was probably in May 1634, to celebrate her seventy-fifth birthday. Later that year, on 29 September, yet another entertainment was put on by the earl's children, this time before their parents at Ludlow to mark the earl's appointment as lord president of the Council of Wales. Milton, again at Lawes's behest, wrote *Comus* for the occasion, and it was Lawes who published the first edition in 1637 (as *A Mask Presented at Ludlow Castle 1634*), dedicating it to Viscount Brackley, the earl's son. In

this case all Lawes's songs survive, although they are rather different in style from the sort of thing usually written for a court masque—just as *Comus* itself is very different. Four of the five songs were written for himself, playing the part of the Guardian Spirit (also the shepherd Thyrsis), but Lady Alice Egerton (as the Lady) sang 'Sweet Echo', which, overheard by Comus, excites his passion and leads to her abduction and the rest of the action.

Later in the decade Lawes wrote songs for plays put on at Oxford to entertain the king and queen (and their nephews the elector palatine and Prince Rupert) during their visit to the university in August 1636. The most important of these was William Cartwright's *The Royal Slave* (30 August), which was so successful that it was repeated at Hampton Court the following winter (12 January 1637).

Publications, performance, and teaching, 1638–1660 So far, none of Lawes's songs had appeared in print (and did not do so until 1652), but 1638 saw the publication of the first of two collections of psalm settings from the metrical version of George Sandys. *A Paraphrase upon the Psalmes of David … Set to New Tunes for Private Devotion* consisted of twenty-four tunes, treble and bass, capable between them of being fitted to all the psalms of Sandys's version. The second came out in 1648 with the title *Choice Psalmes Put into Musick for Three Voices*. Manuscripts show that many had been written at least ten years earlier, but the impetus for publication was supplied by the desire to commemorate the death of Lawes's brother William in 1645 at the siege of Chester. The memorial volume, dedicated to the king, contains thirty of Henry's psalm settings, another thirty by his brother (also ten canons), and a number of elegies by Henry and others (among them John Wilson, John Jenkins, and John Hilton) bewailing William's untimely death. Milton, though he seems to have been unaware of the exact nature of the volume, contributed a commendatory poem; his sonnet 'To my friend Mr Henry Lawes' begins:

> *Harry*, whose tunefull and well measur'd song
> First taught our English Music how to span
> Words with just note and accent, not to scan
> With *Midas* eares, committing short and long …

With the disbandment of the Chapel Royal and the breakup of the king's musick, Lawes was thrown on his own devices. Throughout the Commonwealth period he maintained his Egerton connection. He may have been the Henry Lawes who married at St James's, Clerkenwell (where his patron Viscount Brackley himself married in 1641), first, on 22 September 1644, Elizabeth Dally (*d.* 1648) and second, on 23 January 1650, Elizabeth Miles. He also developed a fashionable teaching practice. His name heads a list of teachers 'for the Voyce and Viole' in John Playford's *A Musicall Banquet* (1651), and among his pupils were Mary Harvey and the singer Mary Knight. He also held concerts at his house: Margaret, duchess of Newcastle, recalled that while in London between 1651 and 1653 she went 'with my Lord's brother [Sir Charles Cavendish] to hear music in one Mr. Lawes house, three or four times' (Ashbee and Lasocki, 708), and other frequenters undoubtedly would have included members of the coterie surrounding Katherine Philips ('the Matchless Orinda'), among them Sir Edward Dering (husband of Mary Harvey, who had been at school with Mrs Philips), Francis Finch, and John Berkenhead. A concert of his church music was given on 22 November 1655 (St Cecilia's day), when, according to the published programme, 'Select Psalmes of a new Translation, To be sung in Verse and Chorus of five Parts, with Symphonies of Violins, Organ and other Instruments' were performed.

Lawes brought out three books of *Ayres and Dialogues*, the first (1653) dedicated to his erstwhile pupils Lady Alice, now countess of Carbery, and Lady Mary Herbert—'most of them being Composed when I was employed by Your ever Honour'd Parents to attend Your *Ladishipp's* Education in Musick'. The oft-quoted preface takes his fellow countrymen to task for their uncritical admiration of Italian music and recounts the story of his setting the table of contents from an Italian songbook (Cifra's *Scherzi et arie*, 1614) 'which read together made a strange medley of Nonsense … whereby it hath passed for a rare *Italian* Song'. In dedicating the second book of *Ayres and Dialogues* (1655) to his pupil Lady Dering, he claimed that they had 'receiv'd much lustre by your excellent performance of them', adding that 'some which I esteem the best of these *Ayres*, were of your own *Composition*, after your Noble Husband was pleased to give the *Words*'. The third book of *Ayres and Dialogues* (1658) was dedicated to Lord Coleraine (Hugh Hare), and contains mostly settings of lyrics by the little-known poet Dr Henry Hughes. Previous books had contained settings of Carew, Robert Herrick, Aurelian Townshend, Edmund Waller, as well as poets from Mrs Philips's circle and others.

Lawes was one of the composers involved in Davenant's operatic experiments—*The First Dayes Entertainment at Rutland House* (23 May 1656) and, more significantly, *The Siege of Rhodes* ('a Representation by the Art of Prospective in Scenes … the Story sung in *Recitative* Musick') later the same year (on or after 3 September). For the latter he composed the vocal music for the first and last acts ('entries'); Henry Cooke and Matthew Locke were the other composers employed for the vocal music, but unfortunately all the music is lost.

Restoration career and reputation At the Restoration, Lawes was reinstated in all his court posts and was made in addition 'Composer in the Private Musick for Lutes & Voices'. He was also elected clerk of the cheque to the Chapel Royal. He composed the anthem 'Zadok the priest' for the coronation of Charles II (23 April 1661), but by the end of the year Pepys reported that he 'lies very sick' (30 December). He died on 21 October 1662, at the Little Almonry, Westminster, and was buried in the cloisters of Westminster Abbey four days later. In his will he made provision for presumably his third wife, Elianor, and for his brother John's daughter, Margaret Crispe, and her three children; evidently he had no surviving children of his own. He also left £10 to the poor of the parish of Dinton, and his chest of viols and his brother's scores to Francis Sambrooke, an old friend and Salisbury attorney.

Without doubt Lawes was the most famous songwriter of his age; the testimony of numerous poets including Herrick and Milton shows this. His work links the period of Dowland to that of Purcell. Although more than 430 songs are extant, others have been lost, as have all but 6 of 22 known anthems. (Almost no instrumental music survives.) Apart from the three books of *Ayres and Dialogues* that he published, Playford included many of his more popular songs in miscellanies such as *Select [Musical] Ayres and Dialogues* (1652, 1653, 1659, etc.) and brought out thirty-seven more songs posthumously in book two of a collection entitled *The Treasury of Musick* (1669)—'transcribed from his Originals, a short time before his Death, and with his free consent for me to Publish them, if occasion offer'd'. But the most important source of his songs is undoubtedly a large autograph manuscript (BL, Add. MS 53723) containing 325 songs, which was probably compiled between the mid-1630s and 1650. Other sources, in some cases preserving earlier versions, are widely distributed in contemporary manuscripts preserved in libraries in London (British Library), Oxford (Bodleian Library), and New York (Public Library, Drexel collection).

Lawes's solo songs are of two basic types, tuneful and declamatory. The first is usually in triple time, based on dance rhythms such as the saraband and treated strophically. These were popular at the time and have remained so over the centuries; his setting of Herrick's 'Bid me but live, and I shall live' is a good example. Many of these tuneful songs were also arranged for three voices and published as glees. The second type is usually in common time, and allows the vocal line to be shaped by the rhetorical aspects of the verse—the rhythm, phrasing, and rise and fall of the spoken or declaimed text. It is less likely to be strophic, for the reason that not every stanza will reproduce the rhetorical or expressive features of the first. At one extreme this results in 'recitative music', which is what, in effect, the setting of Cartwright's 'Theseus! O Theseus! Hark, but yet in vain' is; at the other, a mildly declamatory style that nevertheless retains tuneful elements, such as is found in the setting of Donne's 'Sweet stay awhile! Why do you rise?'. Between them comes the subtle, sophisticated, sensitive word treatment—now veering towards melody, now towards recitative—characteristic of the Carew settings; for example, 'Go thou gentle whispering wind' and 'When thou, poor excommunicate'. Another category of song is the dialogue, usually of a pastoral nature, which employs the declamatory style to set an amatory exchange between two shepherds, alternating with each other but singing together in chorus at the end; for example, Carew's 'When Celia rested in the shade'.

Lawes's sacred music makes less appeal today, though some of the 1638 psalm tunes are found in modern hymnbooks. The *Choice Psalmes* (1648), written for three voices and continuo, represents a species of sacred chamber music aimed at domestic performance rather than church use. On the other hand, the anthems were written for the Chapel Royal. The few that survive are in themselves technically and aesthetically disappointing, though no doubt at the time they served their purpose. Lawes's reputation certainly does not depend on them.

IAN SPINK

Sources I. Spink, *Henry Lawes: cavalier songwriter* (2000) · W. M. Evans, *Henry Lawes, musician and friend of poets* (1941) · A. Ashbee and D. Lasocki, eds., *A biographical dictionary of English court musicians, 1485–1714*, 2 (1998), 706–9 · P. J. Willetts, *The Henry Lawes manuscript* (1969) · D. H. Robertson, *Sarum Close: a history of the life and education of the cathedral choristers for 700 years* (1938) · I. Spink, ed., *English songs, 1625–1660*, Musica Britannica, 33 (1971); 2nd edn (1977)
Archives BL, Add. MSS 32343, fol. 14; 53723
Likenesses portrait, 1622, South Canonry, Salisbury · oils, *c.*1648, U. Oxf., faculty of music [*see illus.*] · W. Faithorne, line engraving, BM, NPG; repro. in H. Lawes, *Ayres and dialogues* (1653)

Lawes, Sir John Bennet, first baronet (1814–1900), agriculturist, was born at Rothamsted, near St Albans, Hertfordshire, on 28 December 1814, the only son of John Bennet Lawes (*d.* 1822), owner of the Rothamsted estate of somewhat more than 1000 acres and lord of the manor of Rothamsted, and his wife, Marianne, daughter of John Sherman of Drayton, Oxfordshire. He was educated at Eton College and at Brasenose College, Oxford, where he matriculated on 14 March 1833.

Lawes later recalled that in his days 'Eton and Oxford were not of much assistance to those whose tastes were scientific rather than classical', and that consequently his early pursuits 'were of a most desultory character', by which he meant that his interests did not extend much beyond shooting and fishing (*Agricultural Gazette*, 3 Jan 1888).

Experiments with herbs Lawes left Oxford without a degree in 1834, when the tenant to whom Rothamsted had been let went bankrupt; Lawes and his mother returned to take charge of the house and the home farm. From an early age, he later recalled, he had 'had a taste for chemistry', and he at once had 'one of the best bedrooms in the house fitted up with stoves, retorts, and all the apparatus necessary for chemical research', much to his mother's dismay (*DNB*). Within a year or two, however, this apparatus had been banished to an old barn, which was to serve as the Rothamsted laboratory for nearly twenty years. Lawes's first experiments had nothing to do with agriculture: he was intrigued by the composition of drugs, and he amused himself by growing various medicinal plants such as poppies, hemlock, henbane, belladonna, and colchicum, in a corner of one of his fields, and by trying to isolate their active ingredients in his bedroom. He also cultivated the acquaintance of Anthony Todd Thomson (1778–1849), professor of materia medica at the new University College, London. Thomson was the author of *The Conspectus Pharmacopoeia* (1810), a standard work which ran through many editions, and he became Lawes's instructor and adviser.

Experiments with bones While dabbling in drugs and retorts, Lawes was influenced by a chance remark of Lord Dacre of the Hoo, who farmed near him, who pointed out that in one farm bones were invaluable for the turnip crop, and on another they were useless. This experience

Sir John Bennet Lawes, first baronet (1814–1900), by Sir Hubert von Herkomer, 1893

had perplexed other farmers, who were making increasing use of bones and bonemeal as manures after 1815, and in 1829 a published report had stated that bones were most effective in raising the yield of turnips on dry sands, limestone, and chalk soils, but were utterly ineffective on clays and strong loams. Lawes set out to solve this puzzle in a series of field experiments which ran for six years from 1836. In these he established by trial and error that both bones and mineral phosphates would, when treated with sulphuric acid, produce striking results on turnip growth, while untreated bones in whatever quantity would have no effect at all. The theoretical explanation, which came much later and not from Lawes, was that bones contained calcium phosphate, which was inert and only released by contact with acid; and that this made the phosphate soluble and available for plant growth. While some soils were naturally acidic and made this conversion spontaneously, many others were not.

It was the practical result which mattered to Lawes, just as it was the practical proof he provided—that superphosphate of lime, as he named the product of the treated bones or phosphates, increased the yield of turnips—which mattered to farmers. In May 1842 Lawes applied for a patent for 'chemically decomposing for purposes of manure by means of sulphuric acid of Bones, or Bone Ash or Apatite or Phosphorite or any other substances containing phosphoric acid' (patent no. 9353). He was fortunate to obtain a patent for a chemical reaction which had been known to chemists for some years, and whose fertilizing properties had been explicitly described by the great German agricultural chemist, Baron Justus von Liebig, FRS (1803–1873), in his *Organic Chemistry in its Application to Agriculture and Physiology*, published in 1840 (simultaneously in English and German editions).

Marketing fertilizers, and marriage Liebig was a laboratory scientist who did not make field trials; Lawes was an entrepreneur with a taste for applied science. Having secured the patent and with the prospect of monopolizing the market for the new fertilizer, Lawes single-mindedly put business interests before domestic and family concerns. On 28 December 1842 he married Caroline (d. 1895), daughter of Andrew Fountaine of Narford Hall, Norfolk; and it was to the latter, the owner of the Narford estate, that six months previously, Lawes had sold the first big consignment of superphosphate. (It had proved to be hugely successful.) Instead of taking his bride on a promised continental honeymoon, Lawes hired a boat on the Thames and took her on a river cruise to its less appealing reaches, prospecting for a suitable site for a manure factory. Caroline Lawes never forgot the disappointment, though the search laid the foundations of her husband's fortune. They had one son, Charles Bennet (1843–1911), a sculptor, and one daughter, Caroline (1844–1946).

The site chosen for Lawes's factory was on Deptford Creek, on the south bank of the Thames. It had the added advantage of proximity to sugar refineries, whose waste product, spent bone charcoal, Lawes found was a rich source of phosphate for his acid treatment. The factory was ready by the summer of 1843, when Lawes made his first commercial sales of superphosphate. The new fertilizer sold readily to market gardeners and turnip-growing farmers, but the first half dozen years or so were still a lean time for Lawes as he strained to expand his business, temporarily giving up residence in the big house at Rothamsted to save money and thus adding to Caroline's disenchantment with her unexpected role as a manure manufacturer's wife.

The chance discovery of coprolites in Suffolk in 1843 by the Cambridge professor of botany J. S. Henslow (1796–1861), while on holiday in Felixstowe visiting his living, attracted Lawes into the business of excavating and opencast mining for these phosphatic nodules. His ownership and control of what was, until the 1870s, the most important raw material for making superphosphate was an important factor in assuring his prosperity. Another factor, paradoxically, was the effort of imitators and competitors to upset his patent, for two lawsuits brought by them in 1848 and 1853 ended by upholding Lawes's sole right to make superphosphate out of minerals (and holding that coprolites were a mineral substance), while he surrendered any claim to monopolize the use of bones. Crucially, the judgment confirmed a lucrative agreement that all other superphosphate manufacturers would pay Lawes a royalty of 10s. per ton on their output for the remaining currency of the patent.

With business flourishing Lawes set up a second, much larger, factory in 1857, on the north bank of the Thames, at Barking Creek, and this became internationally renowned, and visited, as the model of a well laid out, technologically advanced, and efficiently run fertilizer factory. In the 1860s he was drawing an income of about £50,000 a year from his fertilizers; and in 1872, at the peak of his prosperity, Lawes sold the two factories at Deptford and Barking to a public company for £300,000, retaining possession of a quite separate plant making tartaric and citric acid. In the 1880s he inherited a sugar plantation in Queensland, from a nephew of his wife, but this does not seem to have been very successful as a business. After 1872, however, Lawes ceased to be directly involved in commerce and business management.

The Rothamsted Experimental Station Lawes was unusual among successful industrialists in that he did not wait until his retirement from business before energetically, and expensively, pursuing his chief hobby. In 1843, while busy setting up the Deptford plant, Lawes invited Joseph Henry *Gilbert (1817–1901) to join him at Rothamsted as chemist, and in practice to be director in charge of the day-to-day management of agricultural experiments. This began a lifelong association, and virtually all the results of the Rothamsted experiments, certainly from the mid-1850s onwards, were published under the joint names of Lawes and Gilbert. The establishment of the Rothamsted Experimental Station also effectively dates from 1843, when the previous superphosphate trials ceased and the continuous recording of the wheat yields from Broadbalk Field began. This was—and continues to be—a 'control' plot on which wheat was grown continuously without any manure, and it became the most famous field in the world. At the same time on other plots different manurial applications and rotations were applied. Similar very long-running trials were conducted with barley and mangolds and, over shorter runs of years, with oats, clover, beans, turnips, and potatoes, on Broadbalk, Barnfield, Geescroft, Hoos Field, and Park Grass, using the same technique of one plot or strip receiving no manure and others receiving measured doses of different fertilizers. The hallmarks of this work were the meticulous control and measurement of every step in the cultivations, the weighing and composition analysis of the crops, and the publication of the results as soon as it was felt that the evidence of a meaningful run of years had been gathered, in the agricultural and scientific journals.

Personally responsible for deciding the main lines of the work at Rothamsted, Lawes also provided all the finance. The claim of a one-time Rothamsted research chemist that 'all the time he was accumulating a fortune by business in London, he was at home spending a fortune in laborious scientific agricultural investigations' had an element of truth (*Agricultural Gazette*, 17 Sept 1900, 180). The fortune was large enough to support both the investigations and an increasingly comfortable gentry lifestyle. The farming community appreciated the generous way in which he freely publicized the results and thus provided extremely valuable guidance on which fertilizers, or farmyard manure, and in what amounts, to use on which crops. His growing reputation for liberality and support of objective and disinterested agricultural research helped him to win the patent cases; it moved the farmers, initially of Hertfordshire and then of the country at large, to raise a public testimonial to him in 1853 in recognition of his contributions to the improvement of agriculture. The money was used to build the Testimonial Laboratory at Rothamsted, which replaced the original barn. This was a pretentious and poorly constructed building, which collapsed in 1912; when (Alfred) Daniel Hall (1864–1942) took over Rothamsted in 1902 he found it much more like a museum than a laboratory, though it had served Gilbert well enough for the rather restricted range of laboratory work that he undertook.

The Lawes Agricultural Trust While Lawes's disinterestedness was recognized by most people, there was a strand of opinion, intermittently vocal, which held that Lawes was first and foremost a manure manufacturer and merchant, and that his agricultural investigations were primarily designed to further his business interests. This excited vehement denials from his supporters, who pointed out that many of the Rothamsted results, widely publicized, tended to establish the restricted range of beneficial and profitable applications of superphosphate and to demonstrate the crops which thrived without it or on which it was a waste of money to apply it. Nevertheless, it was not until after Lawes had withdrawn from the fertilizer industry in 1872 that he became universally recognized as the world's leading authority on agricultural science. Rothamsted became so frequently and intensively visited that a marquee with beer and other refreshments for visiting groups was almost permanently in use. This reputation was further enhanced by Lawes's announcement that he would give £100,000 from the proceeds of selling his factories to provide for the long-term future of the Rothamsted station. He redeemed this promise in 1889 by establishing the Lawes Agricultural Trust with that endowment, to which the laboratory, and the several fields of the home farm which were used for the experiments, were assigned on long lease.

These efforts to continue and perpetuate his life's work were institutionally successful, and when some ten years after his death the Rothamsted Experimental Station received its first government grant, as a research institute for soil and plant nutrition, its future was assured. By that time Rothamsted was badly in need of rejuvenation. Lawes's attempt to inject new ideas by recruiting the young chemist Robert Warington (1838–1907) were frustrated by Gilbert's conservatism and refusal to let Rothamsted venture beyond the well-tried routines of analysing the ash residues of crops and the chemical composition of land drainage water. Hence the last twenty years or so of the Lawes–Gilbert association were largely unproductive. However, the jubilee was celebrated in style in 1893, with a public ceremony at which Lawes was presented with his portrait by Hubert von Herkomer and a large granite boulder from Shap, inscribed 'to commemorate the completion of fifty years of continuous experiments (the first of their kind) in agriculture conducted at Rothamsted by Sir John Bennet Lawes and Joseph Henry Gilbert, A.D. MDCCCXCIII'; this was erected in front of the laboratory. By then the pioneering days of the experiments were long past. Lawes and Gilbert published a 354-page summary of their fifty years of experiments with crops and the feeding of animals in the *Transactions of the Highland and Agricultural Society of Scotland* (fifth ser., 7, 1895); but the most lucid account is by A. D. Hall, in *The Book of the Rothamsted Experiments* (1905).

Experiments with farm animals In essence the work of Lawes and Gilbert laid the foundations for the systematic study of the effects of fertilizers and nutrients on soils and plant growth. Their less well-known experiments with farm animals, mainly conducted between 1848 and 1864, initiated controlled research into the effects of different diets on weight-gain in cattle, sheep, and pigs, and, crucially, into measuring the chemical composition and manurial value of the excreta produced by the different diets. This last was of immediate practical use to farmers and valuers as a guide to the objective valuation of the amount of compensation for 'unexhausted improvements' which might be left behind on or in the soil of a farm by an outgoing tenant. Indeed, all the work was intended to be of direct practical utility in farming. The essentially chemical approach of both Lawes and Gilbert did, however, mean that they had a somewhat restricted view of the scope of agricultural research and a tendency to regard chemical properties, notably fertilizers, as the most important and interesting variables. It is significant that there is no record that Lawes ever made contact with Eleanor Ormerod (1828–1901), the leading entomologist of the day and an authority on insects which are injurious to crops, though she lived only 3 miles away in St Albans. The enormous prestige and authority of Lawes and Gilbert, and their success in their own line of research, may have served to discourage the vigorous pursuit of other lines of agricultural research in Britain in the late nineteenth century. Lawes was nevertheless sufficiently flexible to abandon his dogmatic assertion, often repeated, that plants were unable to fix free nitrogen from the atmosphere, when it was demonstrated in 1891 that certain plants— the legumes—did precisely that.

Other activities, habits, and death Lawes joined the Royal Agricultural Society of England in 1846, and became a member of its governing body in 1848 and a vice-president in 1878; he was not offered the presidency until 1893, when he declined on grounds of age. He was elected FRS in 1854, and was awarded (with Gilbert) the society's royal medal in 1867. In 1894 he was awarded (with Gilbert) the Albert gold medal of the Society of Arts. He received honorary doctorates from Edinburgh (1877), Oxford (1892), and Cambridge (1894). He was created a baronet in 1882. He served on the royal commission on the sewage of towns between 1857 and 1865, and he conducted trials at Rugby from which he concluded, egregiously, that the best way of dealing with it was to use untreated raw sewage to irrigate grassland at a rate of 9000 tons per acre per year—equivalent to a depth of about 2 metres.

Lawes was below middle height, careless in matters of dress, and very fond of salmon fishing and deer stalking. He invariably spent several months every summer and autumn in Scotland with his family—his wife painting while he shot—in the early years at Dalmally and later on at Loch Etive, where he kept a steam yacht. He was a benevolent squire of Harpenden; he started an allotment scheme in 1852, and in 1857 he built a clubhouse for the allotment-holders, who elected the management committee. Providing cheap beer, the clubhouse was a popular meeting place (it lasted until demolished in the 1950s); it was described by Charles Dickens, after a visit, in 'The Poor Man and his Beer', *All the Year Round*, in April 1859. A savings bank which he started in 1856 was also successful; but a pig club, a flour club, and the Harpenden Labourers' Store Society failed to attract support.

Lawes died on 31 August 1900 from dysentery, at Rothamsted, and was buried at St Nicholas's Church, Harpenden, on 4 September. His wife, Caroline, had died in 1895, and his son, Sir Charles Bennet Lawes-*Wittewronge, succeeded as second baronet.

F. M. L. THOMPSON

Sources E. J. Russell, *A history of agricultural science in Great Britain, 1620–1954* (1966), 88–107, 143–75, 232–4 · R. W. [R. Warington], *PRS*, 75 (1905), 228–36 · *Agricultural Gazette* (3 Jan 1888), 13 · A. D. Hall, *The book of the Rothamsted experiments* (1905) · J. B. Lawes and J. H. Gilbert, 'The Rothamsted experiments … over a period of fifty years', *Transactions of the Highland and Agricultural Society of Scotland*, 5th ser., 7 (1895), 11–354 · *The Times* (1 Sept 1900) · *Agricultural Gazette* (17 Sept 1900) · *Journal of the Royal Agricultural Society of England*, 3rd ser., 11 (1900) · G. V. Dyke, *John Lawes of Rothamsted* (1993)
Archives Herts. ALS, personal papers · Rothamsted Experimental Station, Harpenden, Hertfordshire, corresp. and papers | Rothamsted Experimental Station, Harpenden, Hertfordshire, corresp. with Sir Joseph Gilbert
Likenesses H. von Herkomer, oils, 1893, Rothamsted Experimental Station, Harpenden, Hertfordshire [*see illus.*] · Verheyden, marble bust, 1901, Rothamsted · T [T. Chartran], caricature, watercolour study, NPG; repro. in *VF* (8 July 1882) · cartoon, repro. in *Punch* (1882) · engraving, repro. in *Agricultural Gazette* (1882) [reprinted from 1871] · memorial, St Nicholas's Church, Harpenden · wood-engraving, NPG; repro. in *ILN* (10 July 1882)
Wealth at death £583,115 2s. 10d.: probate, 1 Nov 1900, CGPLA Eng. & Wales

Lawes, William (*bap.* 1602, *d.* 1645), instrumentalist and composer, was baptized in Salisbury Cathedral on 1 May 1602, son of the singing man Thomas Lawes (*d.* 1640), native of Dinder by Wells, Somerset, and his wife, Lucretia (or Lucris or Lucrece) Shepherd of Dinton, near Salisbury, and younger brother of Henry *Lawes (*bap.* 1596, *d.* 1662). The family moved to Sarum Close when Thomas became a lay vicar at Salisbury Cathedral in 1602, not seemingly through any blood relation to another William Lawes, alias Coldbeck (*c.*1553–1624), a predecessor at Salisbury for more than two years before August 1596 who then moved to Chichester and in 1602 to the Chapel Royal. Possibly Thomas's sons became cathedral choristers and received an education at the free school in the close. According to Thomas Fuller, a friend of the eldest son, Henry, William's

youthful promise became known to Edward Seymour, earl of Hertford (*d.* 1621), who at his Amesbury estate nearby on Salisbury Plain sometimes played host to the court composers Alfonso Ferrabosco the younger and John Coprario. Seymour sponsored William's indenture to Coprario in an apprenticeship that could have lasted until Coprario died in 1626. The claim of the Wiltshire antiquarians Robert Benson and Henry Hatcher (*Old and New Sarum*) that William was accepted when under the age of twenty-three into the private musick of Charles, prince of Wales, and retained with increased favour after his accession, is unsubstantiated. His post is in fact documented only from 25 March 1635, when he replaced the dead lutenist John Laurence at the basic annual rate of £40. However, the appointment may imply previous deputizing in the day-to-day supply of court music, no doubt under the wing of his brother Henry, who had entered the Chapel Royal in 1626 and the 'lutes and voices' of the king's musick in 1631. The influence of William Herbert, third earl of Pembroke, or his brother and successor, Philip Herbert, may be detectable. The Herberts, resident at Wilton, had a local interest in the Lawes family and influence as court office-holders. Backed by King Charles himself, Philip intervened to secure Thomas Lawes a vicar-choralship at Salisbury in 1632.

Before and even after royal appointment, William Lawes's activities have to be inferred mainly from musical sources. The principal hand in one partbook set (BL, Add. MSS 40657–40661), which is uncontentiously his, was copied largely before 1632 for a Northamptonshire branch of the Shirley family, the later earls Ferrers. The novice here followed others' works with some trial casts of his own, embodying novel features. It may have been the success of his brothers (another, John, was a singing man at Westminster Abbey) that gave Lawes his opening in London, but he soon established himself as a tenor voice and player on lute and viol, skills commemorated by Robert Herrick and other elegists. Mildmay Fane, earl of Westmorland, mentioned him in the same breath as older lutenists Nicholas Lanier and Jacques 'English' Gaultier as having a touch he considered to 'excell the dying swan' (*Otia sacra*, 1648). One friendship with John Tomkins (*d.* 1638) of St Paul's Cathedral, whom Lawes praised in a memorial lament, brought him into the stylistic orbit of two other mannerist composers employed there, William Cranford and Martin Peerson.

Lawes's first attestable public activity as a composer appears to have been the vocal music for Ben Jonson's *The King's Entertainment at Welbeck*, performed for the earl of Newcastle on 21 May 1633. On meagre evidence, he may have assisted his brother Henry in the private entertainments by John Milton, *Arcades* (*c.*1634?) and *Comus* (1634). In 1633 Lawes was promising enough for Bulstrode Whitelocke to select him as joint composer with Simon Ives for *The Triumph of Peace* (1634), James Shirley's inns of court masque which defended the impugned integrity of the king and queen. He took payment of £5 for a performance in this masque by 'my Lord Chamberlains boy', a servant of Philip Herbert assigned or possibly apprenticed to him.

Possibly as early as 1634, and certainly from 1636, when theatres reopened after a year of plague, he became chief provider of songs for the royal troupes and 'Beeston's Boys' at the Cockpit-in-Court of Whitehall and Black-friars, though the music survives in isolation from the often part-extemporized context. By 1636 Lawes had also graduated to full collaborator with his brother Henry in William Davenant's masque *The Triumphs of the Prince d'Amour* and William Cartwright's play *The Royal Slave*, during the royal summer progress to Oxford. For private as for public song-settings his spirit was attuned less to Thomas Carew and the suave Edmund Waller, favoured by Henry, and more to brisker cavalier writers such as Davenant, Richard Lovelace, Shirley, Sir John Suckling, and John Tatham, although both William and Henry had a phase of association about 1640 with Robert Herrick, then lodging in the Little Almonry by Westminster Abbey. Little survives of William's secular partsongs, but until 1678 John Playford and others kept in print a valid selection of his solo songs, dialogues, glees arranged from solo form, and catches. He had no post in the Chapel Royal, but two non-extant verse anthems by him are listed for its use. Another, unrecorded at court, the starkly declamatory 'The Lord is my light', survived in the cathedral repertory to merit a place in William Boyce's *Cathedral Music* (1760–78). Lawes's one recorded pastime from this period is tavern-crawling, with Henry and also John Wilson, a boisterous playhouse musician notorious for his 'buffoonery' who won a royal post soon after William. Wilson figures as their ringleader in one unamusing street prank, bearding suspected Catholic passers-by, in Sir Nicholas L'Estrange's 'Jestbook' (BL, Harleian MS 6395, item 361). This suggests ready candidates for the 'three merry boys' in one of William's own rounds.

After 1641 Lawes's employment in London theatres ended, and in the autumn of 1642 he may have accompanied the court to Oxford. While there is no direct evidence of his presence in the city, Edward Lowe, the organist at Christ Church, copied Lawes's novel and unique 'Psalmes … to Common Tunes' (Christ Church MSS), which may plausibly date from this period and a time of war. Its marriage of Genevan tunes and early English protestant texts by Thomas Sternhold, John Hopkins, and others, with a declamatory style favoured by the Laudians and sections set for only three trained singers, indicates unusual circumstances, such as the conjunction of a reduced choir with the need to foster congregational morale through participation. Normally such practice was considered too undignified for cathedral services, but, according to Thomas Mace (*Musick's Monument*, 1676), such psalm-singing by both choir and congregation was tolerated during the siege of York between April and June 1644. Lawes, who had evidently enlisted in the royalist army at an early stage (his salary, like those of other musicians, years in arrears), was certainly present there: he devised a round for the garrison at nearby Cawood Castle. Royal service was also, according to Henry Lawes, the context for the

thirty three-part biblical texts, mainly psalms, set to a figured bass, which appear in his posthumous edition of his brother's *Choice Psalmes* (1648).

The post in the king's service which Lawes may have accepted was the relatively safe one of commissary in Charles Gerard's regiment of foot, based first in Oxford and then active in Wales from May 1644. In September 1645 he was in Chester, possibly arriving on the 23rd in attendance on the king. In the late afternoon of 24 September he joined a sortie north of the besieged city led by Gerard. Halted by a counter-attack at Rowton Heath, the party were caught in crossfire. Lawes was among many killed. Although he had also lost his cousin Bernard Stuart in the action, the king still felt impelled to instigate special mourning for a close musical servant. Royalists sharpened their quills, adding to a brimming quiver outrage for mutilation of this harmless Orpheus. 'Will. *Lawes* was slain by such whose *wills* were *laws*', the climax of an elegiac quatrain by Thomas Jordan in *The Muses Melodie in a Consort of Poetrie* (n.d.), had venom durable enough for reuse in prefatory verse to John Playford's *The Musical Companion* (1673). A sense of deprivation was handled less pugnaciously by Robert Herrick in *Hesperides* (1647–8), Robert Heath in *Clarastella*, and John Tatham in *Ostella* (both 1650).

Choice Psalmes (1648), William's chief memorial, enshrined his non-liturgical sacred vocal music with an equal quantity of his brother Henry's, and the latter pointedly rededicated the authors' joint service in life and death to their royal patron, then facing final defeat. Alongside the commendatory verse of sympathizers (Francis Sambrooke, James Harington, Aurelian Townshend), John Milton's tribute of a sonnet to Henry Lawes shows esteem for artistry tactfully circumventing partisanship. Eight musical elegies were included by a circle of friends—Henry himself, John Cob, Captain Edmond Foster, John Hilton, Simon Ives, John Jenkins, John Taylor, and John Wilson, most of whom had plainly written their own verse. The most elaborate, a pastoral dialogue by Jenkins, has affinities to Herrick's briefer dirge on Bernard Stuart. In it, an informant figure (Henry) is portrayed under the sobriquet of Cleon, and William is dubbed Medoro, the young Moorish soldier left for dead at the fanciful siege of Paris in Ariosto's *Orlando Furioso*. Henry's Arcadian lament can be lineated in urn form, and coincidentally mentions the same 'silent urne' for which Jordan's epitaph was purportedly designed. However, no burial site is known, nor any proof that William was accorded cremation. He is presumed without wife or children.

Music by Lawes circulated solely in manuscript during his life; none can be shown to precede 1630 or thereabouts. Writing in an idiosyncratic but persuasive idiom beholden partly to the Italian early baroque, he took melodic and harmonic liberties in attempting exalted emotional states. In the mature chamber works this project won a peerless authority. Even the traditionalist Jenkins admitted the bracing effect of his innovations: a sophisticated grasp of continuo and string technique, and a fresh ear for sonorities that blossomed amid the permutations of violins, viols, theorbos, harp, and chamber organ available in the private musick. He was at the forefront in establishing the basic international form of baroque dance suite: alman, corant, saraband, jig. Varied types of dance suite form the matrix for his suites for violins and viols in which elaborate fantasy movements are embedded; for these, the best sources are those autograph playing parts and working scores that survive. Manuscript copies, good or indifferent, show immediate acceptance of those works beyond the court, but a need for independent organ continuo, and above average musicianship, may have limited circulation. Towards the end of a working life which probably was increasingly devoted to these chamber works in the period 1638–42 he expanded some dance suites, first written without fantasies, for a court 'harpe consort'. Most acclaimed was his similar treatment of a brilliant collection of over sixty dances for paired violins, viols, and theorbos, in a flexible scoring capable of broadening into six real parts. At some undefined point it acquired the title 'The Royall Consort', probably not a coinage of the innermost circle: a variant found in one major copy is 'The Great Consort'. It had wide impact, from initial copying at some time in the 1630s right up to 1680, the final turn against Caroline music. The verve that made William pre-eminent in dance kept him in chief place for these 'aires' when anthologized in a series of popular publications by John Playford: A Musicall Banquet (1651), expanded in the nostalgically titled Court-Ayres (1655), and Courtly Masquing Ayres (1662). Now somewhat fragmentary, his writing for the viol played 'lyra-way', chordally in groups of up to three, was copious. His only surviving lute suite adds a contrepartie for a second lute to a solo alman by René Mesangeau (d. 1638), unacknowledged. Elsewhere, resettings of attributed works by the senior generation (Coprario, Cormacke MacDermott, the harpist, and Ferrabosco) evoke the feeling of a fast-maturing court tradition robbed of clear identity by cultural discontinuity.

Few tributes besides those published in 1648 survive to the decided magnetism exerted by Lawes, or the 'depth of music' that he sounded, in Townshend's words (Lawes and Lawes, commendatory verse); in distracted times this neglect held nothing personal. Fuller mentions the king's accolade to William in his lifetime of an uncommon title, 'Father of Musick'. Sir Peter Leycester, the knowledgeable Cheshire antiquarian, ranked William the head of England's musicians, even above Henry, for the year 1640. The music kept its charm long into the reign of Charles II: 'The Royall Consort', the printed psalm-settings, rounds, and lighter songs were longest in domestic use. By 1670 older memories of what, pre-war, had cut a dash were fading before recent French dance, Italian sonata, and a part-archaizing tradition concocted to re-establish the Anglican liturgy: by 1680 no composer would have admitted debts to Lawes. Even so, traits palpably his survived into the practice of Purcell and his contemporaries, so long as 'English' dissonance was employed. One amateur opinion

voiced by Anthony Wood timidly deprecated Lawes's wilfulness: 'to indulge the ear—he broke sometimes the rules of mathematicall composition' (MS Wood D. 19 (4) no. 106, fol. 83). In mind here was probably 'The Royall Consort', where Lawes threw counterpoint most wantonly to the breeze in chase of luxuriant textures; but the remark occurs in notes compiled at a time (after 1675) when canons of art were already veering to high-baroque classicism. It was a trend complete by the time of Charles Burney's General History of Music (1776–89), which, through a disparaging notice of 'The Royall Consort' in particular, did most to inhibit responses to the breadth of achievements by Lawes and his generation: the depth too had by that time been lost to view. Attention to the music and times lapsed until the 1890s, when the newly sympathetic advocacy of Arnold Dolmetsch and his circle of friends and disciples (principally Percy Grainger and Gerald Hayes) began to win increased respect.   DAVID PINTO

Sources Fuller, Worthies (1662) • H. Lawes and W. Lawes, Choice psalmes (1648) • M. Lefkowitz, William Lawes (1960) • W. M. Evans, Henry Lawes, musician and friend of poets (1941) • R. Benson and H. Hatcher, The history of modern Wiltshire, ed. R. C. Hoare, 6 (1843) • A. Ashbee, ed., Records of English court music, 1 (1986); 3–5 (1988–91); 8 (1995) • A. Ashbee and D. Lasocki, eds., A biographical dictionary of English court musicians, 1485–1714, 2 vols. (1998) • [B. Whitelocke], 'Whitelocke's labour remembered', BL, Add. MS 53726 • L. Ring, 'Wednesday, 24 September 1645—the death of William Lawes', William Lawes (1602–1645): essays on his life, times and work, ed. A. Ashbee (1998) • D. Pinto, 'William Lawes at the siege of York', MT, 127 (1986), 579–83 • [N. L'Estrange], 'Jestbook', BL, Harleian MS 6395 • 'Prolegomena historica de musica', Ches. & Chester ALSS, Tabley House MSS, MS DLT/B31 • A. Wood, Bodl. Oxf., MS Wood D 19 (4), fol. 83 [no. 106]

Archives BL, Add. MSS 17798 (ensemble part, remnant), 31432 (songbook), 40657–40661 (ensemble instrumental parts) • Bodl. Oxf., Music School collection, MSS B.2, B.3 (scores: drafts of instrumental suites incl. The Royall Consort, masque music, part-songs, and catches), D.229, D.238–240 (keyboard and string parts for suites, variously for viols, violins, harp, theorbo lute) • Christ Church Oxf., Mus MSS 725–727 (lyra-viol ensemble parts), 754–759 (The Royall Consort, non-autograph) • Harvard U., Houghton Library, Mus 70 (lyra-viol ensemble part, remnant)

Likenesses oils, c.1628, U. Oxf., faculty of music; repro. in Lefkowitz, William Lawes • W. Dobson, portrait, 1645, Ferens Art Gallery, Kingston upon Hull; repro. in D. Pinto, ed., Musica Britannica, 60 (1991) • portrait, Royal Academy of Music, London

Wealth at death unknown except that musical possessions were left to, or acquired by, his brother Henry, whose will (made 1662) specifies some manuscripts

Lawes, William George

Lawes, William George (1839–1907), missionary, son of Richard Lawes and his wife, Mary, daughter of Joseph Pickover of Reading, was born at Aldermaston, Berkshire, on 1 July 1839. After education at the village school in Mortimer West End, he was apprenticed to a business in Reading for six years. In 1858 his thoughts turned towards missionary work. He was accepted by the London Missionary Society, and after training at Bedford was ordained to the Congregational ministry on 8 November 1860. Just before ordination he was married to Fanny, née Wickham; they had four sons and one daughter. Fanny Lawes was an active partner in her husband's missionary work.

On 23 November 1860 the Laweses sailed for the island of Niue (known in Victorian times as Savage Island) in the south Pacific Ocean. They arrived in August 1861 and worked there, joined by Fanny's brother Frank in 1868, until 1872. Besides general work in the mission and the industrial training of the people, Lawes learned the local language and in 1886 completed the task begun by others of rendering the New Testament into Niue. In 1872 he came home on furlough, taking with him corrected versions of Exodus, the Psalms, and the New Testament in the vernacular. While in Britain he was appointed to the New Guinea mission, for which he sailed in April 1874. The Laweses were the first settled European residents on the island, living initially at Port Moresby. Lawes became fluent in the Motuan language, wrote it down, prepared simple books in the language (including a grammar and vocabulary of Motu, published in 1885), set himself to the translation of the New Testament, and founded a training institution for people in New Guinea.

When the British protectorate over New Guinea was proclaimed in 1884, Lawes, with James Chalmers, who had arrived in 1877, gave much help to the British authorities, acting as interpreter at the time of the proclamation. For twenty years his home was at Port Moresby; then, when the training institution was moved to Vatorata, Lawes made that his centre. His position among both the settlers and the Papuans enabled him to give much help to the British administration, but he was also active in protesting against aspects of the labour trade, his reports and letters being discussed in the House of Commons. His help was gratefully acknowledged by Sir William Macgregor, the first governor. By the influence of Sir William, Lawes received the degree of DD from Glasgow University in April 1895. In the following year he visited Australia, and during his stay in Sydney he saw through the press several works in Motu—selections from Old Testament history, a collection of 204 hymns, a catechism, forms of service, and a manual of geography and arithmetic. In 1901 he took to England a revised Motu version of the New Testament.

In 1898 Lawes explored the mountainous region at the back of Vatorata. In 1905 he marked on a map ninety-six villages with the inhabitants of which he had been friendly. On the other hand the murder and consumption by cannibals of his colleague Chalmers was a severe setback, and Lawes determined to retire. When he left New Guinea in March 1906, an address signed by the acting lieutenant-governor and the chief commercial representatives in the island noted his services to geographical and philological science, as well as to the missionary cause.

Lawes settled in retirement at Sydney and died there from pneumonia on 6 August 1907, his wife surviving him. Chalmers's reputation and spectacular death to an extent obscured the undoubted role of Lawes in the origins of modern New Guinea.

A. R. BUCKLAND, rev. H. C. G. MATTHEW

Sources J. King, *W. G. Lawes of Savage Island and New Guinea* (1909) · *James Chalmers: his autobiography and letters*, ed. R. Lovett (1902) · R. Lovett, *The history of the London Missionary Society, 1795–1895*, 2 vols. (1899) · W. Canton, *A history of the British and Foreign Bible Society*, 5 vols. (1904–10) · J. W. Lindt, *Picturesque New Guinea* (1888) · *AusDB*

Archives Mitchell L., NSW

Lawler [*née* Corben; *other married name* Bagshawe], **Sylvia Dorothy** (1922–1996), human geneticist, was born on 15 January 1922 at 33 St Clement's Road, Bournemouth, the only child of Frederick Norman Corben, owner of a furniture business, and his wife, Dorothy Agnes Gwendolyn, *née* Cole (*b*. 1898), a schoolteacher who survived her daughter to become a centenarian. Educated locally at Wentworth School, Bournemouth, she became the school's first pupil to study medicine and entered University College, London, in 1939. There she distinguished herself as the gold medallist of her year and qualified in 1945. On 14 July the same year she married Lawrence John Lawler (*b*. 1919/20), son of John Lawler, a motor mechanic. Laurie Lawler was then a captain in the Royal Electrical and Mechanical Engineers (REME); he later became a schoolteacher. They had one son, Anthony John (*b*. 1955).

After junior hospital appointments Sylvia Lawler joined the laboratory of Dr R. R. Race at the Lister Institute, working mainly on the rhesus blood-group system whose complexity had recently been decoded by Race and R. A. Fisher. Her MD thesis, 'Blood groups and human genetics' (London, 1949), gained a distinction. In 1949 she was invited by Professor L. S. Penrose to join the Galton Laboratory at University College, London, the world's first department for the study of human genetics. There, together with Dr J. H. Renwick, she described one of the earliest linkages between blood groups and a human disease in a paper published in 1955 in *Annals of Human Genetics*. This was the first study to exploit the use of likelihoods in large families. Their collaboration uncovered several linkages and set new standards in both documentation and analysis. The Galton Laboratory was then the leading centre for the typing of both red cells and serum for genetic purposes and, through their combined use in families with inherited disorders, established its world leadership in human linkage analysis. While still a young researcher Lawler attended an international meeting in Montreal in 1956, when the distinguished American geneticist Sewall Wright sought her clarification on some detail of the rhesus blood groups. For twenty minutes those present were privileged to hear a discussion pursued by two scientists who achieved perfection in both manners and clarity of thought.

Lawler was appointed as research scientist at the Institute of Cancer Research in London in 1960 and became the institute's first female professor in 1980. There she developed a broad interest in the genetics of malignancy and established close links with the Royal Marsden Hospital in London, working at the interface between genetic research and patient care. At the time it was appreciated that white blood cells could be typed by difficult techniques, revealing a degree of variability unknown in red cells, and she made major contributions to the development of these tissue-typing techniques. She was fascinated by the significance of acquired chromosome abnormalities in malignancy and exploited the advent of chromosome analysis in the late 1950s as a means to characterize leukaemias. As head of the department of

Sylvia Dorothy Lawler (1922–1996), by unknown photographer

Sources 'Sylvia Lawler', *Bulletin of the Royal College of Pathologists*, 96 (Sept 1996) · *The Times* (26 Jan 1996) · Archives of the Royal College of Pathologists, London · private information (2004) · personal knowledge (2004) · m. cert. · d. cert.
Archives Royal College of Pathologists, London, archives
Likenesses photograph, News International Syndication, London [*see illus.*]
Wealth at death £820,854: administration, 1996

immunogenetics and cytogenetics Lawler laid the scientific foundation for the Royal Marsden Hospital's pioneering work in bone-marrow transplantation and became chairman of the transplantation immunology subcommittee of the National Organ-Matching Service. She was a founder member of the International Workshops on Chromosomes in Leukaemia, and also established the first national fetal tissue bank in the UK, with support from the Medical Research Council.

A principal interest was in the genetic basis of trophoblastic disease, which encompasses molar pregnancies (hydatidiform moles) and choriocarcinoma, and in efforts to improve the diagnosis and treatment of this disease. Lawler's work on histocompatibility leukocyte antigens (HLA antibodies) provided evidence that choriocarcinomas may arise from an earlier rather than simply the antecedent pregnancy. She went on to use genetic polymorphisms to determine the origins of complete and partial hydatidiform moles. Lawler was also a pioneer in the analysis of the human genome. The department she established exerted a profound influence through the staff she trained and encouraged from both the UK and abroad, and did much to establish the concept of a genetic basis to human disease. She was remarkable for the way she supported her staff and maintained a personal interest in the careers and research of former colleagues. She was a foundation member and fellow of the Royal College of Pathologists and an honorary fellow of the Royal College of Physicians.

Lawler's first marriage was dissolved in 1976, and on 28 January 1977 she married Kenneth Dawson Bagshawe (*b.* 1925), professor of medical oncology in the University of London, and son of Harry Bagshawe. Lawler became an emeritus professor in 1987, and despite two cardiac operations continued to be involved in the research on leukaemia and trophoblastic disease which she had established. Retirement allowed her, though, to indulge her love of the visual arts and opera to the full. She died suddenly in London at her home, 115 George Street, Westminster, on 17 January 1996. She was survived by her husband and the son of her first marriage.

J. H. Edwards and Veronica J. Buckle

Lawless, Emily (1845–1913), novelist, was born on 17 June 1845 at Lyons Castle, co. Kildare, Ireland, the fourth child and eldest daughter of Edward Lawless, third Baron Cloncurry (1816–1869), and his wife, Elizabeth (1812–1895), the daughter of John Kirwan of Castle Hackett in co. Galway and a famous society beauty and sportswoman. Her paternal grandfather, Valentine Browne *Lawless, the second baron, was, in his youth, an Irish patriot who was imprisoned for a short time because of his sympathies with the United Irishmen in 1798 and his opposition to the union of the parliaments in 1800. Privately educated, Lawless herself had an intense, apparently lifelong, interest in Irish history and politics, although she was never a supporter of home rule, and so was seen by many of her more patriotic contemporaries as being insufficiently devoted to her country's cause. She spent what seems to have been a contented childhood at the family seat in Kildare; an autobiographical story in her collection *Traits and Confidences* (1897) presents her as a confident, indulged ten-year-old, taking full advantage of the freedom available to a child on a country estate and, in doing so, laying the groundwork for both her intellectual development and her love of Ireland. In her biography of Maria Edgeworth (1904), Lawless indirectly reinforces this sense of the importance of her own privileged Irish childhood to her future career as she disputes an earlier biographer's argument that Edgeworth was fortunate to be raised in England. Sharply disagreeing, Lawless contends that for an Irish novelist '[t]o have had the right, so to speak, to a childhood in an Irish country home, and to have been … defrauded of that right' is 'a state of affairs almost too regrettable to contemplate' (Lawless, *Edgeworth*, 48–9). Following the death of her father by suicide Lawless divided her time between England, Dublin, and her mother's home in Galway. Two sisters also committed suicide.

Galway was the setting of Lawless's first successful novel, *Hurrish* (1886), which takes place during the days of the Land League. (She had written two novels before that, but they made so little impact that the authors of her obituaries in both *The Times* and *The Athenaeum* were apparently unaware of them.) She was encouraged, in the early stages of her literary career, by her friend Margaret Oliphant, to whom she dedicated *Hurrish*, 'with a great deal of admiration and more affection'. Lawless continued to explore Ireland's troubled past: *With Essex in Ireland* (1890) and *Maelcho* (1894) are about Elizabethan expeditions against the country. In *Grania: the Story of an Island* (1892), a novel about peasant life on the Aran Islands in the 1860s, Lawless paid as much attention to landscape and natural history as she did to culture and society (she also published monographs on entomology). She was praised especially for 'her familiarity with [the islands'] geology, their flora and fauna, [which] lends completeness to the framework of her drama' (*The Athenaeum*, 16 April 1892, 496). Her short stories included works set during the potato famine, during the uprising of 1798, and during the campaigns of Richard II against Ireland. Lawless also wrote poetry, and in the most successful of her collections of poems, *With the Wild Geese* (1902), she focused on the exiled Irish soldiers serving in the French army in the continental wars of the late seventeenth and early eighteenth centuries.

At her best, Lawless was not just historically thorough, but also stylistically experimental. For example, she passed off *With Essex in Ireland* as an authentic first-person journal with such success that Gladstone, an admirer of her work, friend, and occasional correspondent, was said to be 'deceive[d] … into believing it reprinted from a genuine journal kept by a follower of Essex in 1599' (*The Times*, 23 Oct 1913). In *Grania*, Lawless developed a formal, deliberately poetic style to represent the speech of her unilingual Gaelic characters, thereby avoiding what she referred to in her dedication as 'the tiresome necessity' of brogue. Despite what *The Athenaeum* described as her preoccupation with 'the tragedy and pathos of the distressful past' (25 Oct 1913, 457), Lawless also conveyed in her writing a sardonic sense of humour. A single-volume history of Ireland, published in the series The Story of the Nations in 1887 (reissued and expanded in 1912), makes sharp judgments about both events and individuals and does not shy away from political commentary. (She notes drily and concisely, for example, of the events following 1800, that 'the Union had not brought union'; p. 376.)

Lawless's judgments admittedly do not always stand up to hindsight. She concluded a generally positive assessment of the state of Irish literature in 1912, for example, with a reluctant confession that Ireland could not match the literary achievements of other small European countries: 'To encourage the explorer to look for an Ibsen or a Björnson, even for a Georg Brandes … in Ireland would be, an austere critic will perhaps say, to mislead him', she writes (Lawless, *Ireland*, 434). Yet if not aware of the full extent of the early twentieth-century Irish literary renaissance, she was an ardent defender of the value of Irish writing, as she demonstrated in her biography of Maria Edgeworth, a work that also revealed Lawless's sardonic bent. Early in the book she calmly and wittily shredded Richard Lovell Edgeworth's rather self-serving account of his ancestors, and she later dismissed Edgeworth's English *Fashionable Tales*—so that she could turn her attention back to the Irish work—by quoting R. L. Edgeworth's dauntingly moralistic praise of his daughter's work: 'After so judicious and so thoroughly exhaustive a summary', she observed blandly, 'the reader will perhaps hardly feel that it is requisite for his peace of mind to know very much more' (Lawless, *Edgeworth*, 131). Such comments bear out the rather carefully phrased comment in her *Times* obituary that 'she was a lady of decided opinions and speech' (23 Oct 1913, 11). Her non-fiction was not as well received as the novels, however. *The Times* reports merely that her history 'presents the point of view of the native Irish without lapsing into extravagance or injustice', and

that the book on Edgeworth, while 'full of good things', was 'lacking in the chief qualities of literary biography' (ibid.).

Lawless's fiction attracted the interest of Gladstone and Oliphant, and her other admirers included W. E. H. Lecky, George Meredith, and Algernon Swinburne. She also received more official recognition with an honorary DLitt degree from the University of Dublin in 1905. But not all contemporaries were impressed by her writing. Yeats included *Hurrish* and *With Essex in Ireland* in two separate lists of what he considered to be the best of Irish fiction, both published in 1895, but he was dubious about the value of much of her work. While praising her 'manifest sincerity and her agile intellect', he regretted her 'imperfect sympathy with the Celtic nature' and her acceptance of 'the commonplace conception of Irish character as a something charming, irresponsible, poetic, dreamy, untrustworthy, voluble, and rather despicable' (Yeats, Aug 1895, 134). Nor has Lawless's fiction survived as part of the main canon of British literature, although it has continued to attract the attention of readers such as Terry Eagleton, who, in a study of ascendancy fiction, praised *Hurrish* for its 'perceptive portrait of the harassed landlord' (Eagleton, 157).

Despite her passionate attachment to Ireland, Lawless became disillusioned with Irish politics and moved near Gomshall, Surrey, where she pursued her literary and non-literary interests, the latter of which, according to her characteristically eccentric *Who's Who* entry, included 'dredging, mothing, gardening, geologising'. During her final years she was in poor mental and physical health, and she died, unmarried, at her home, Hazelhatch, Gomshall, on 19 October 1913.   PAM PERKINS

Sources E. Lawless, *Hurrish: a study* (1886); facs. edn with introduction by R. L. Wolff (1979) · E. Lawless, *Traits and confidences* (1897); facs. edn with introduction by R. L. Wolff (1979) · E. Lawless, *Maelcho: a sixteenth century narrative* (1894); facs. edn with introduction by R. L. Wolff (1979) · E. Lawless, *Grania: the story of an island*, 2 vols. (1892); facs. edn with introduction by R. L. Wolff (1979) · E. Lawless, *With Essex in Ireland* (1890); facs. edn with introduction by R. L. Wolff (1979) · E. Lawless, *Maria Edgeworth* (1904) · E. Lawless, *Ireland*, rev. edn (1912) · *The Times* (23 Oct 1913) · 'Novels of the week', *The Athenaeum* (16 April 1892) · W. B. Yeats, 'Irish national literature', *The Bookman* (Aug 1895) · W. B. Yeats, 'Irish national literature', *The Bookman* (Oct 1895) · *The Athenaeum* (25 Oct 1913), 457 · T. Eagleton, *Heathcliff and the great hunger* (1995) · Burke, *Peerage* (1917) · d. cert. · *CGPLA Eng. & Wales* (1914) · R. Hogan, ed., *Dictionary of Irish literature* (1979)

Archives BL, corresp. with Macmillans, Add. MS 54966 · Hove Central Library, Sussex, letters to Lady Wolseley

Wealth at death £2000 0s. 7d. in England: probate, 3 Feb 1914, *CGPLA* Eng. & Wales

Lawless, John [called Honest Jack Lawless] (*c*.1773–1837), Irish nationalist, born at Warrenmount, Dublin, was the eldest son of Philip Lawless, a brewer, and Bridget Savage. He was a distant cousin of Valentine Browne Lawless, second Baron Cloncurry. His education is somewhat obscure; a John Lawless entered Trinity College, Dublin, in July 1794 but took no degree. Lord Clare was said to have refused Lawless admission to the bar because of his association with the United Irishmen.

For some time Lawless worked for his father in the brewery, but finding the business less congenial to his tastes than literature, he took shares in the *Ulster Record*, published at Newry, and afterwards went to Belfast, where he became editor of the *Ulster Register*, a political and literary magazine, and subsequently of the *Belfast Magazine*. He was soon known as an ardent politician, and was one of the most energetic members of the committee of the Catholic Association. He was a leading opponent of the proposed 'veto' on the appointment of Catholic bishops, and in 1825 he opposed Daniel O'Connell in the debate on 'the wings', as the proposal to accompany Catholic emancipation with a state endowment of the Catholic clergy and the disfranchisement of the forty-shilling freeholders was called. In 1828 he campaigned in co. Clare, and was sent by the association to address meetings in the north, where he spoke at Kells and Dundalk. However, when he attempted to hold a monster demonstration at Ballybay, it was prevented by the determined opposition of the Orangemen. Lawless, realizing that if he persisted the meeting would certainly end in bloodshed, wisely, and at some personal risk to himself, withdrew with his followers. His moderate conduct on this occasion was referred to by the duke of Wellington in 1829 in support of the move to grant Catholic emancipation.

In later years Lawless became particularly obnoxious to O'Connell, who spoke of him as Mad Lawless and even opposed his candidature for County Meath. For a short period in 1831 he was held under arrest. He died on 8 August 1837, at his home, 19 Cecil Street, Strand, London, after an operation to relieve a hernia, and was buried on 17 August in the Roman Catholic chapel, Moorfields; his illness was thought to have been aggravated by overexcitement due to frequent speaking at political meetings during the general election. He left a widow and four children.

Lawless was regarded as open, honest, and enthusiastic, but with little grasp of political reality. As well as articles for newspapers and periodicals, he wrote *A Compendium of the History of Ireland from the Earliest Period to the Reign of George I* (1814), which was condemned by O'Connell. He also wrote in 1818 an account of Belfast politics, which was thought to be so offensive that the government ordered it to be burnt; copies of it are consequently rare.

ROBERT DUNLOP, *rev.* MARIE-LOUISE LEGG

Sources Burtchaell & Sadleir, *Alum. Dubl.* · E. Keane, P. Beryl Phair, and T. U. Sadleir, eds., *King's Inns admission papers, 1607–1867*, IMC (1982) · *Belfast News-Letter* (18 Aug 1837) · *The Times* (11 Aug 1837) · *GM*, 2nd ser., 8 (1837), 317–18 · *The correspondence of Daniel O'Connell*, ed. M. R. O'Connell, 1–6, IMC (1972–80)
Likenesses R. Rothwell, oils, *c*.1820, Ulster Museum, Belfast · Harding, silhouette, NPG · group portrait, lithograph (with Irish politicians), BM

Lawless, Matthew James (1837–1864), painter and illustrator, was born in Dublin, the son of Barry Edward Lawless, a solicitor, of 13 Harcourt Street. His family moved to London in 1845. He was educated at Prior Park School, Bath, but his studies were constantly interrupted by poor health. On leaving he moved to London, intending to make a career as an artist. He studied at various art institutions including the Langham, Heatherley's, Cary's, and Leigh's and also under the painter Henry O'Neil. He became a member of the Junior Sketching Club and sent his first pictures to the Royal Academy in 1858, continuing to exhibit there yearly until 1863; he also exhibited at the Suffolk Street Gallery. His subjects were almost invariably historical or literary (especially Shakespearian) and his work was noted for its finish and accuracy. Probably his best-known oil is *The Sick Call* (exh. RA, 1863, National Gallery of Ireland, Dublin), which reveals profound knowledge of Dutch seventeenth-century painting.

It is as an illustrator in black and white that Lawless should be especially noted. It seems that at the Langham he met Charles Keene and Frederick Walker, and the influence of the former in particular is apparent in his illustrations. His sharp line and clean draughtsmanship owe much to Keene, as well as to Adolf Menzel, a German Romantic illustrator who was a master of the vignette. The influence of Menzel on English illustrators such as Keene, George Du Maurier, John Tenniel, and Lawless was clearly linked to their fascination with the subject matter and fine draughtsmanship of German Renaissance artists such as Dürer and Hans Sebald Beham. Many of Lawless's finest wood-engraved designs appeared in periodicals, especially *Once a Week* (1859–64), *Churchman's Family Magazine* (1863), and *London Society* (1862–70). His book illustrations are far fewer in number but among the most distinguished are a single design of a woman weeping in *Lyra Germanica* (1861) and a little-known group of drawings in Henry Formby's *Pictorial Bible and Church History* (1862). Drawings and wood-engravings by him are in the collections of the British Museum and the Victoria and Albert Museum, London.

Lawless died of consumption on 6 August 1864 at his father's home in Pembridge Crescent, Notting Hill, London, and was buried in Kensal Green Roman Catholic cemetery, London. He was an ardent Roman Catholic and it is believed that his obituary in *The Tablet* was written by the future cardinal Henry Manning. A talented musician who enjoyed composition, Lawless also found time for skating and angling. The respect which his art held for contemporaries can be gauged by Edmund Gosse's comments in 1876 that he felt:

> quite absurd affection for all the few relics of this gifted lad whose early death seems to have deprived his great genius of all hope of fame … No doubt in M. J. Lawless English Art sustained one of the sharpest losses it ever had to mourn. (*The Academy*, 177)

PAUL GOLDMAN

Sources G. White, 'In memoriam: Matthew James Lawless', *The Quarto*, 4 (1898), 45–59 · Thieme & Becker, *Allgemeines Lexikon*, vol. 22 · W. G. Strickland, *A dictionary of Irish artists*, 2 vols. (1913) · P. Butler, *Irish watercolours and drawings* (1990) · F. Reid, *Illustrators of the eighteen sixties* (1928) · R. K. Engen, *Dictionary of Victorian wood engravers* (1985) · P. Goldman, *Victorian illustrated books, 1850–1870: the heyday of wood-engraving, the Robin de Beaumont collection* (1994) · P. Goldman, *Victorian illustration* (1996) · Mallalieu, *Watercolour artists*, vol. 1 · E. Gosse, 'Illustrations to *Historical and legendary ballads and songs*', *The Academy* (19 Feb 1876), 177–8 · *DNB*
Likenesses carte-de-visite, NPG

Lawless, Valentine Browne, second Baron Cloncurry (1773–1853), politician and landowner, only surviving son of Nicholas, first Baron Cloncurry (1733–1799), and Margaret (1748–1798), only child and heir of Valentine Browne of Mount Browne, co. Limerick, a wealthy Roman Catholic brewer of Dublin, was born in Merrion Square, Dublin, on 19 August 1773. He was educated successively at a boarding-school at Portarlington in Queen's county, where he contracted a scrofulous complaint which left a permanent mark upon his face; at Prospect School, in the neighbourhood of Maretimo, Blackrock, co. Dublin, his father's residence, where he remained for two years; and at the King's School at Chester. He subsequently entered Trinity College, Dublin, where he graduated BA in 1792. The two following years were spent on the continent, chiefly in Switzerland.

After returning to Ireland in 1795, at the moment of Lord Fitzwilliam's recall, Lawless threw himself with enthusiasm into Irish politics, and in the summer of that year he was sworn a United Irishman, just at the time when the society was being reconstructed on a new basis with distinctly republican aims, though, according to his own account, the oath he took was the original one, unaccompanied by any obligation to secrecy. At the same time he became an officer in the yeomanry, and an active promoter of a voluntary police organization known as the Rathdown Association. He was destined for the bar, and in 1795 he entered the Middle Temple; during the next two years he spent a considerable part of his time in London. Dining in company with Pitt in 1797, he first learned of the government's intention to form a union between the two countries. Acting on this information, he immediately wrote and published his *Thoughts on the Projected Union between Great Britain and Ireland* (1797), the first of a long succession of pamphlets on the subject. He was also a regular contributor to *The Press* newspaper, at that time the accredited organ of Irish independence.

In July 1797 Lawless presided at the aggregate meeting held in the Royal Exchange to protest against the union. In October he attended for the first and only time a meeting of the executive directory of the United Irish Society. It is difficult entirely to credit his own statement that it was without his wish, and even knowledge, that he was elected a member of the Directory. Of this fact the government soon became cognizant and, a friendly warning having reached his father, Lawless was obliged to return to his studies at the Middle Temple, where he was kept under strict government surveillance. His conduct in London, the society he kept, his acquaintance with Arthur O'Connor and O'Coigly, and the fact that he furnished funds for the defence of the latter, increased suspicion, and on 31 May 1798 he was arrested at his lodgings, 31 St Albans Street, Pall Mall, on suspicion of high treason. His detention on this occasion lasted about six weeks, during which time he was more than once examined before the privy council. He was discharged on bail, and, being forbidden by his father to return to Ireland, he spent the summer in making a tour through England on horseback. At Scarborough he made the acquaintance of Mary, daughter of

Valentine Browne Lawless, second Baron Cloncurry (1773–1853), by John Hogan, 1841

Phineas Ryal, of Clonmel, whom he received his father's consent to marry on condition that he was first called to the bar.

Lawless returned to London in December. On 14 April 1799 he was again arrested on suspicion of treason and on 8 May he was committed to the Tower. It is difficult to determine how far he was really guilty of the offences with which he was charged. He claimed that he had taken no part in politics since his first arrest, and the government lacked direct evidence of his complicity in any United Irish conspiracy. During his imprisonment in the Tower his father, grandfather, and fiancée all died. Many efforts were made to obtain his release, but without success; his father, who died in 1799, fearing the consequences of his prosecution might extend to a confiscation of his property, altered his will and left away from him a sum of between £60,000 and £70,000. He was released when the Habeas Corpus Suspension Act expired in March 1801, but spent the rest of the year in England in order to recover his health. He returned to Ireland on 31 January 1802, and went in the autumn to the continent in company with his sisters Charlotte and Valentina.

At Nice, Lord Cloncurry met Elizabeth Georgiana, youngest daughter of Lieutenant-General Charles Morgan, whom he married at Rome on 16 April 1803. At Rome, where he resided for more than two years in the Palazzo Acciaioli, close to the Quirinal, he went much into society, and occupied himself in forming a collection of antiquities, the more valuable part of which was lost at sea in transportation to Ireland. He left Rome in the summer of

1805, and, proceeding through Austria and Germany, returned to Ireland at the close of the year, to find that during his absence his house at Lyons, co. Kildare, had been ransacked by one of his tenants, who was also a magistrate, during the disturbances that attended the suppression of Emmet's rebellion, and that some family plate and papers, including letters from the geologist Richard Kirwan, had been removed or destroyed. During the rest of his life Lord Cloncurry resided almost constantly either at Lyons or Maretimo.

On 26 June 1811 Lord Cloncurry divorced his wife by act of parliament, having obtained in 1807 £20,000 in damages from Sir John Piers for adultery with Lady Cloncurry. Four days after the divorce was finalized he married on 30 June 1811 Emily (d. 1841), third daughter of Archibald Douglas of Dornock and widow of the Hon. Joseph Leeson. The first marriage produced a son (d. 1825) and a daughter. With his second wife, Cloncurry had two sons and a daughter.

For several years Cloncurry took no active part in politics, but devoted himself to the duties of his position as a magistrate and landed proprietor. He inaugurated the system of petty sessions, which was afterwards extended by parliament with good effect throughout the kingdom and he took an active part in 1814 in founding the County Kildare Farming Society, for the promotion of a better system of agriculture. He strongly urged the reclamation of bogs and wastelands, was a director of the Grand Canal between Dublin and Ballinasloe, a friend of Robert Owen and Father Theobald Mathew, and projector of various abortive schemes, such as a ship canal between Dublin and Galway, and the establishment of a transatlantic packet station at Galway. He supported Catholic emancipation, but he was convinced of the futility of arguing the question in the Westminster parliament; in 1824 he urged O'Connell, in a celebrated letter to the Catholic Association, to make the repeal of the union the main plank in his programme.

During the first viceroyalty of Henry William Paget, marquess of Anglesey, in 1828, Cloncurry grew intimate with the Dublin Castle administration. He knew that Lord Anglesey's intentions were favourable to Ireland, and, unwilling to hamper his administration during his second viceroyalty (1830–34), he declined to join O'Connell in his repeal campaign. His attitude exposed him to the misconstruction of his friends and the bitter reproaches of O'Connell. 'The three years', he wrote, 'that followed Lord Anglesey's return to Ireland, though full of excitement and action, was to me the most unhappy I had passed since my release from the Tower' (*Personal Recollections*, 415). Nevertheless he took an active part in the anti-tithe agitation, and having been created an English peer and an Irish privy councillor in September 1831, he spoke for the first time in the House of Lords on 7 December on that subject. In 1836 a temporary reconciliation was effected between him and O'Connell, but in 1840 a further estrangement took place owing to an attack made by O'Connell on Cloncurry's nephew Lord Dunsany, a noted Orangeman.

After the death of his second wife in 1841 Cloncurry ceased gradually to take any active interest in politics. The two following years he passed on the continent, but in 1843 he exerted his influence as a privy councillor to avert what he afterwards described as 'a projected massacre' by the government of Lord de Grey on the occasion of O'Connell's intended repeal demonstration at Clontarf. At the first appearance of the great famine in 1846 he urged upon the government the necessity of taking extraordinary preventive measures, but when his advice was rejected he indignantly declined to attend any further meetings of the council. Nevertheless, as a member of the famine committee and a trustee of the central relief committee, he spared neither time nor money in endeavouring to relieve the general distress. He disapproved of the Young Ireland movement, believing that it would only retard the repeal of the union, but he testified his personal sympathy with John Mitchel, the editor of the *United Irishman*, by subscribing £100 for the support of his wife. In 1849 his *Personal Recollections* were published: in Ireland the work was well received, but in England it was severely criticized, especially by J. W. Croker in the *Quarterly Review* (86.126), and by persons mentioned in the text. It is likely that Cloncurry was not himself the author of the work published under his name.

In 1851 Cloncurry showed signs of failing health, but he lived to see the great Irish Industrial Exhibition of 1853. On 24 October that year he caught a cold, on Friday 28 October he died at Maretimo, and on 1 November his remains were moved from there to the family vault at Lyons.

Cloncurry was noted for his hospitality; he was a generous landlord, a lover of the fine arts, and he did his best to cultivate and reward Irish talent. He was, to quote O'Connell, 'the poor man's justice of the peace, the friend of reform, in private society—in the bosom of his family—the model of virtue, in public life worthy of the admiration and affection of the people'.

ROBERT DUNLOP, rev. GERARD MCCOY

Sources V. B. L. Cloncurry, *Personal recollections of the life and times: with extracts from the correspondence of Valentine, Lord Cloncurry* (1849) · W. J. Fitzpatrick, *The life, times and contemporaries of Lord Cloncurry* (1855) · *Memoirs and correspondence of Viscount Castlereagh, second marquess of Londonderry*, ed. C. Vane, marquess of Londonderry, 12 vols. (1848–53) · GEC, *Peerage*

Archives NL Ire. | BL, corresp. with Lord Holland, Add. MS 51573 · Lpool RO, letters to E. G. Stanley · PRO NIre., corresp. with marquess of Anglesey

Likenesses J. Hogan, plaster bust, 1841, NG Ire. [see illus.]

Lawless, William (1772–1824), army officer in the French service, was born at Dublin on 20 April 1772. He joined the United Irishmen, participated in the 1798 uprising, and was outlawed by the Attainder Act of 1798 (known as the Fugitive Act); he took refuge in France and entered the army. He was placed on half pay in 1800, but in 1803 was appointed captain of the Irish legion. In July 1806 he was ordered to Flushing, then threatened by the British, to command the Irish troops. To reach his post he had to pass in a small, open boat through the British fleet. He was dangerously wounded in a sortie. When General Monet capitulated, without stipulating that the Irish should be treated as prisoners of war, Lawless escaped from the town with the eagle of his regiment. After concealing himself for two months in a doctor's house, he eventually fled to Antwerp one night in a fishing boat. Marshal Bernadotte welcomed him, praised him in general orders, and reported him to Napoleon, who summoned him to Paris, decorated him with the Légion d'honneur, and promoted him lieutenant-colonel. In 1812 he gained a colonelcy, and in August 1813 was wounded at Löwenberg, and his leg was amputated. On the restoration of the Bourbons, the Irish troops were looked on with little favour, and in October 1814 Lawless was placed on half pay with the rank of brigadier-general. He died at Paris on 25 December 1824.

J. G. ALGER, rev. DAVID GATES

Sources R. R. Madden, The United Irishmen: their lives and times, 2nd ser., 2 (1843), 525 • E. Fieffe, Histoire des troupes étrangères au service de France, 2 vols. (1854) • N. J. Curtin, The United Irishmen: popular politics in Ulster and Dublin, 1791–1798 (1994) • R. B. McDowell, Ireland in the age of imperialism and revolution, 1760–1801 (1979) • T. Pakenham, The year of liberty: the story of the great Irish rebellion of 1798 (1969)

Lawley, Francis Charles (1825–1901), journalist, born on 24 May 1825, was the fourth and youngest son of Paul Beilby Lawley-Thompson, first Baron Wenlock, and his wife, Catherine, daughter of Richard Neville, second Lord Braybrooke. After attending a school at Hatfield, Frank Lawley entered Rugby on 24 May 1837; he matriculated from Balliol College, Oxford, on 21 March 1844. In 1848 he won a second class in literae humaniores, graduated BA, and was elected a fellow of All Souls. In 1847 he entered the Inner Temple as a student, but was not called to the bar. He proceeded BCL in 1851. In July 1852 he was elected MP for Beverley as an advanced Liberal.

From an early age Lawley was fascinated by horse-racing—although while a fellow of All Souls he could not (he said) run horses in his own name—and he soon involved himself disastrously in gambling and speculation. The colt Clincher, which he bought in 1849 with the earl of Airlie, started favourite for the Derby of 1850, but ran third to Voltigeur and Pitsford, with the result that Lawley lost many thousands of pounds. In 1851 he was to some extent interested in the fortunes of Teddington, which won the Derby. Subsequently he was owner of Gemma di Vergy, which won thirteen races as a two-year-old. Debts, and his innate enthusiasm for risk, caused his political downfall.

In December 1852, when Gladstone became chancellor of the exchequer, he made Lawley one of his private secretaries (Mrs Gladstone was his relative). Lawley resigned his fellowship at All Souls and on 8 June 1854, after earlier soundings by the duke of Newcastle, he was appointed governor-general of South Australia by Sir George Grey, the duke's successor as colonial secretary. Unbeknown to Gladstone, Lawley had been using inside knowledge to gamble in government stocks; the scandal was exposed and Lawley's appointment cancelled. Despite this, Gladstone defended him in the Commons, remained his

friend, and subsequently often turned to him for information, and sometimes even advice. He helped informally in the secretariat several times in Gladstone's later career.

Following his exposure, Lawley left England for the United States, and worked for a time in the legation in Washington. From 1862 he was special correspondent of The Times with the Confederate army during the civil war, and played a part in Gladstone's ill-judged support for the south. His dispatches were admirable, both as to style and matter, and his useful Account of the Battle of Fredericksburg was published separately. A man of handsome presence and courtly demeanour, he gained easy access to the Confederate leaders and generals.

On his return to England in May 1865, Lawley settled in London as a sporting writer and journalist, and quickly acquired a literary reputation. On 18 December 1869 he married Henrietta Louisa Amelia, daughter of Frederick Augustus Zaiser, chaplain to the king of Saxony; they had no children. Lawley was a frequent contributor to the Daily Telegraph, and its correspondent during the Franco-Prussian War (1870); he retained the connection until his death. He also published much in Baily's Magazine. An accurate and polished style, a retentive memory, and a vast fund of first-hand knowledge and anecdote, gave value to his work. His range of topics in newspaper and magazine was wide, extending over 'Trainers, new and old', 'Sport in the southern states', 'Napoleon's chargers', 'Decline of Irish humour', 'A word for pugilism', and 'Mr Gladstone's coaching days'. He contributed a memoir of Admiral Rous to the Dictionary of National Biography. In 1889 he intervened in the bitter controversy over the conduct of Charles Wood, the jockey, with a pamphlet in Wood's defence, entitled The Bench and the Jockey Club. As a writer of books Lawley's most successful effort was a biography of the sporting writer Henry Hall Dixon, The Life and Times of 'The Druid' (1895). In conjunction with John Kent he published in 1892 The Racing of Lord George Bentinck, an important work in the history of the turf.

Lawley died of an internal haemorrhage on 18 September 1901, in King's College Hospital, London, having been taken ill that day in the street; his wife survived him.

H. C. G. MATTHEW

Sources The Times (21 Sept 1901) • Daily Telegraph (21 Sept 1901) • The Sportsman (20 Sept 1901) • Gladstone, Diaries • W. S. Hoole, Lawley covers the Confederacy (1964) • DNB
Archives U. Hull, Brynmor Jones L., corresp. | BL, corresp. with W. E. Gladstone, Add. MSS 44373–44520 • Bodl. Oxf., corresp. with Lord Kimberley • Flintshire RO, Hawarden, Gladstone–Glynne MSS • NL Scot., corresp. with Blackwoods • NL Scot., corresp. with Lord Rosebery
Likenesses portrait, repro. in Baily's Magazine (Feb 1902)
Wealth at death £70 3s. 9d.: probate, 1 Jan 1902, CGPLA Eng. & Wales

Lawrance, Hannah (1795–1875), historian and journalist, was born in 1795. She can be identified with Hannah, daughter of Thomas Lawrance, baptized at New Broad Street Independent Chapel, London, on 1 September 1795. Her mother, who had married Thomas Lawrance in 1793, was Hannah, daughter of John Stafford, minister of the New Broad Street Chapel. These family connections are confirmed by Hannah Lawrance's will, in which she left a large diamond ring to William Warlow Harry, minister of Knutsford, 'in remembrance of New Broad Street where my grandfather wore it for forty two years'. It is probable that John Stafford Lawrance (baptized on 21 August 1794), Thomas George Lawrance (baptized on 22 November 1797), and Catherine Lawrance (baptized on 2 October 1812) were her siblings, but it seems likely that they died young, as her will only mentions cousins. The will suggests that she remained a lifelong Congregationalist, since she bequeathed £50 to the Congregational Fund Board for the Relief of Poor Ministers, as well as leaving legacies to the London Missionary Society and the Home Missionary Society. Her other bequests included her books: a copy of Edward Blore's *Monumental Remains of Noble and Eminent Persons* is specifically mentioned, reflecting her historical interests, as is a stereoscope and slides, as well as a great deal of jewellery.

The early stages of Hannah Lawrance's writing career are not easy to trace. She has been tentatively identified as the author of *London in olden time, or, Tales intended to illustrate the manners and superstitions of its inhabitants, from the twelfth to the sixteenth century* (1825, 1827). Certainly it reflects her later historical interests and tendency to illustrate morals and manners through short historical tales. Two articles on 'The Anglo-Norman trouvères' in *Blackwood's Magazine* of 1836 have also been attributed to her, as have two articles on medieval French literature in *Fraser's Magazine* in 1844 and 1847. In 1838 she published the *Historical Memoirs of the Queens of England*, a predecessor of Agnes and Elizabeth Strickland's more sustained *Lives of the Queens of England* (1840–48): indeed, the publication of Lawrance's *Memoirs* temporarily persuaded Agnes to abandon her work, and forced a revision of the proposed title of their publication. Lawrance's biographies of the English queens, though they dealt in much less detail than the Stricklands' *Lives* with each individual, were scholarly in approach and championed several maligned figures, including Eleanor of Aquitaine and Isabella of France. Christian Johnstone's review in *Tait's Magazine* (April 1838) praised them as superior in depth of research to other historical memoirs by women writers, adding that Lawrance had 'dug deeper in the tumulus of antiquity, than more accredited excavators of the other sex' (Johnstone, 263). In 1843 Lawrance published *The History of Woman in England, and her Influence on Society and Literature*, which was intended to be the first volume of a series. In this knowledgeable work she dwelt on a theme which she had already announced in the *Memoirs*: the significant role of women in cultural developments, if only as patrons and facilitators. She also argued convincingly that Anglo-Saxon women had enjoyed greater social, political, and legal liberties than their later medieval and early modern successors.

Lawrance's lack of further publications on the history of women can be attributed to her commitment as a major contributor to the *British Quarterly Review*. Between 1847 and 1870 she contributed more than sixty articles to this periodical, a heavyweight vehicle for the nonconformist

intelligentsia. Often highly readable and intelligent, they exhibit the width of her knowledge of English literature, art, and history, including topics as diverse as the education and employment of women, the Crystal Palace exhibitions, Elizabethan and Jacobean social life, Anglo-Norman poets, and African explorations. She was the regular art critic for the journal, producing workmanlike if uninspired accounts of the exhibitions (though an admirer of Ruskin, she usually found the works of the Pre-Raphaelites incomprehensible). More pioneering was her steady and well argued support for better education and wider employment opportunities for her own sex.

Hannah Lawrance also contributed several articles to *Macmillan's Magazine*, and was a reviewer for *The Athenaeum*: possibly she wrote the rather critical 1840 review of the first volume of the Stricklands' *Lives of the Queens of England*, in which Lawrance herself is staunchly defended against the charge of stealing a march on her rivals. In 1844 she wrote two historical tales and one book review for *Hood's Magazine*. In 1852 she published a full-length historical novel, *The Treasure-Seeker's Daughter*. Set in London in 1620, it has a puritan heroine whose religious beliefs reflected Lawrance's own dissenting beliefs as a Congregationalist (the villain being, needless to say, a Catholic). It also reflected her fascination with court intrigues, seventeenth-century superstitions, and everyday life in Jacobean London. In 1854–5 Lawrance contributed five articles to Charles Dickens's *Household Words*, depicting seventeenth- and eighteenth-century social life, again through the medium of short stories. She seems not to have mixed in London literary circles; from her works Elizabeth Barrett surmised that she was a 'deeper-minded woman' than her rival Agnes Strickland and 'qualified to take, in literature, the higher place' (*Letters of Elizabeth Barrett Browning … to Richard Hengist Horne*, ed. S. R. Townsend Mayer, 1877, 1.210). Lawrance died, unmarried, on 20 November 1875 at her home, 22 Albion Grove, Barnsbury Park, Middlesex. ROSEMARY MITCHELL

Sources A. Lohrli, ed., *Household Words: a weekly journal conducted by Charles Dickens* (1973), 338–9 · *Wellesley index* · Boase, *Mod. Eng. biog.* · F. Korn, 'An unpublished letter by Thomas Hood: Hannah Lawrance and *Hood's Magazine*', *English Language Notes*, 18 (March 1981), 192–4 · R. A. Mitchell, *Picturing the past: English history in text and image, 1830–1870* (2000) · R. A. Maitzen, *Gender, genre and Victorian history writing* (1998) · U. Pope-Hennessey, *Agnes Strickland: biographer of the queens of England, 1796–1874* (1940) · C. Johnstone, 'Hannah Lawrance's *Historical memoirs of the queens of England*', *Tait's Magazine*, new ser., 5 (April 1838), 257–63 · 'Lives of the queens of England … by Agnes Strickland, vol. 1', *The Athenaeum*, 642 (15 Feb 1840), 123–5 · *The letters of Charles Dickens*, ed. M. House, G. Storey, and others, 7 (1993), 318–19, 323 · will · IGI · CGPLA Eng. & Wales (1876)

Wealth at death under £2000: probate, 1 March 1876, *CGPLA Eng. & Wales*

Lawrance [*married name* Kearse], **Mary** (*fl.* 1794–1830), flower painter, of whose parents little is known, first exhibited, a flower piece, at the Royal Academy in 1795. During the years 1796–9 Mary Lawrance published a monograph entitled *A Collection of Roses from Nature*, which included a series of coloured plates from her own drawings. Her *Sketches of Flowers from Nature* was published in

1801, followed by *Collection of Passion Flowers Coloured from Nature* in 1802. In 1804 she was living with her parents and sister in Queen Anne Street East, London, where she gave lessons in 'drawing Botany at ½ a guinea a lesson & a guinea entrance' (Farington, *Diary*, 6.2301, 19 April 1804). Farington responded to her request, supported by Charles Greville, brother of the earl of Warwick, to place her works well in the Royal Academy exhibition that year (ibid., 2361). She married Thomas Kearse in 1813, and their son William Lawrance Kearse was baptized on 22 June 1815 at St Mary Street, Marylebone Road, St Marylebone, Middlesex. Up to 1830 she continued, under her married name, to exhibit studies of flowers, which were finely executed. She was a friend of the horticulturist Robert Sweet, who named the *Rosa lawranceana* after her.

ANNETTE PEACH

Sources Desmond, *Botanists* · Farington, *Diary*, 6.2301, 2361; 7.2535–6 · *IGI* · Mallalieu, *Watercolour artists*

Lawranson, Thomas (*d.* in or after **1777**), painter, is said to have been born in Ireland. In January 1742 he advertised two large prints of Greenwich Hospital that he had drawn and published some time previously. They were too big to glaze, so Lawranson also advertised his 'Method of varnishing them, that they look as clear and much more beautiful than through any Glass, and may be cleaned at any Time with a Spung and fair Water if they are dirty'd by Flies' (*London Evening-Post*). He contributed a self-portrait to the first exhibition of the Society of Artists in 1760 and was a regular contributor to their exhibitions until 1777, sending portraits, miniatures, and the occasional landscape. He was a fellow of the Incorporated Society and a director in 1772. In 1774 he exhibited a portrait which he claimed to have executed in 1733. Lawranson's own portrait, or what Bromley took to be his portrait, was scraped in mezzotint by his son. In 1771 he was elected a fellow of the Society of Antiquaries. He lived at 1 Great Russell Street, Bloomsbury, London, and may have died there soon after he stopped exhibiting in 1777. Examples of his work may be found in the National Portrait Gallery, London (portraits of the dramatist John O'Keefe and the comedian John Quick) and in the British Museum.

William Lawranson (*bap.* 1742, *d.* in or after 1783), painter and engraver, was baptized on 20 April 1742 at St Andrew's, Holborn, London, the son of Thomas Lawranson and his wife, Mary. He won regular premiums for drawings from the Society of Arts between 1760 and 1766. Those awarded in 1760 and 1761 were for drawings by an artist under twenty years old. He first exhibited with the Society of Artists in 1762, continued to exhibit with the Free Society at the Society of Arts in 1763 and 1764, but joined the Incorporated Society in 1765, with which he exhibited until 1773; he then switched his allegiance to the Royal Academy, having entered its school in 1769, and exhibited there until 1780. For the most part he exhibited portraits, often in crayons. He specialized in theatrical portraiture and several of his portraits of actors in character were published. These included John Dixon's mezzotint *William Powell* (1769), his own mezzotint *Mr Smith in the*

Character of Iachimo (1772), and Robert Dunkarton's *Miss Catley in the Character of Euphrosyne* (1777). A few 'fancy pictures' and literary subjects were also engraved, notably by John Raphael Smith, who published *Palemon and Lavinia*, *A Lady at Haymaking*, and *Cymon and Iphigenia* in 1780. He was elected a fellow of the Society of Antiquaries in 1771. A portrait of the engraver John Hall, attributed to William Lawranson, is in the National Portrait Gallery, London. William Lawranson may have gone to Ireland in the mid-1780s and there painted some theatrical portraits that have sometimes been attributed to his father, but there is considerable confusion between the work of the two Lawransons and it is not known when either of them died.

TIMOTHY CLAYTON

Sources J. C. Smith, *British mezzotinto portraits*, 4 vols. in 5 (1878–84) · W. G. Strickland, *A dictionary of Irish artists*, 2 vols. (1913); repr. with introduction by T. J. Snoddy (1989) · R. Walker, *National Portrait Gallery: Regency portraits*, 1 (1985), 375–6 · *London Evening-Post* (23–6 Jan 1742) · Waterhouse, *18c painters* · *Neue Bibliothek der Schönen Wissenschaften und der freyen Künste*, 22 (1778); 179; 26 (1781), 360; 30 (1785), 152; 31 (1785–6), 318 [contemporary reviews of prints] · H. Bromley, *A catalogue of engraved British portraits* (1793) · *IGI* · B. Stewart and M. Cutten, *The dictionary of portrait painters in Britain up to 1920* (1997) · K. K. Yung, *National Portrait Gallery: complete illustrated catalogue, 1856–1979*, ed. M. Pettman (1981) · Graves, *Soc. Artists*

Likenesses W. Lawranson, mezzotint, *c.*1770, BM, NPG

Lawranson, William (*bap.* **1742**, *d.* in or after **1783**). *See under* Lawranson, Thomas (*d.* in or after 1777).

Lawraunce, Ane (*fl.* **1610**), gentlewoman, is known only for a letter she wrote in May 1610 to Thomas Sutton, a businessman and moneylender, proposing that he name her as a beneficiary in his will. The letter is currently lodged with the other Sutton documents (LMA, ACC 1876 F3 351) and, transcribed by Joseph Crowley, is reproduced in '*The Muses Females Are': Martha Moulsworth and other Women Writers of the English Renaissance*, edited by Robert Evans and Anne Little (1995). Lawraunce describes herself as 'a poore gentlewoman and a maide', 'youndge', living in Battersea, Surrey. Her father could not provide for her, while her own 'infirmyties in my heade and eyes' prevent her employment. The manner of her argument and its intertextual references to biblical and classical sources suggest that Lawraunce was both intelligent and very well educated.

Lawraunce had previously sought to borrow £200 from Sutton, renowned for lending credit, meeting him twice. Despite her undoubted eloquence, which can be gauged in the letter itself, Sutton stuck to sound business principles and refused to lend the money without security. Her commentary on his decision displays her personal determination and perspective on their potential business arrangement, which provides a counterbalance to Sutton's business and worldly ethics:

> I coulde not give yow sitch security wich worldly wise men to mutche staundes upon; yet by godes healpe I woulde with all possible speade as justly have paide that mony againe and interest for it as if the Excheacor of Einglaunde had bin my Seaurety. ('"A sutor for my selfe"', 271)

This binary opposition, between his worldly ethics and

her view of charity, informs the tenor and rationale of Lawraunce's letter to Sutton: her beneficiary request is postponed until the last two paragraphs of the letter, while the main part is a sermon-like exhortation on the need for charity and repentance before death. Her letter displays a sophisticated use of literary and rhetorical tools. Its structure clearly follows the seven-part Ciceronian oratory model and she includes classical, Christian, and native English literary modes and sources within this rhetorical structure. She frames her argument within a Christian *memento mori* tradition; she interweaves quotations and language from Proverbs and the gospels, and includes secular stories. The interlinking of the secular and the Christian both promises Sutton that redemption is possible and argues that this will be through charity to her. The whole argument is an intellectual *tour de force*, which unfortunately did not convince Sutton to name her as a beneficiary. KATE AUGHTERSON

Sources '"A suter for my selfe": a letter, 1610, from Ane Lawraunce to Thomas Sutton', ed. J. Crowley, '*The muses females are*': *Martha Moulsworth and other women writers of the English Renaissance*, ed. R. C. Evans and A. C. Little (1995), 267–79 **Archives** LMA, Sutton papers, ACC 1876 F3 351

Lawrence. See Laurence (*d.* 619); Durham, Lawrence of (*c.*1110–1154). *See also* Laurence, Lawrance.

Lawrence (*d.* 1173), abbot of Westminster, came from the north of England. As a young man he studied at the abbey of St Victor, near Paris, where he attended the lectures of Hugh of St Victor (*d.* 1141) and was reputed himself to have taught theology. In 1143 he returned to England, bringing to Prior Roger and the convent of Durham a letter from Bernard of Clairvaux on the subject of Durham's current election dispute, in which Bernard commended Master Lawrence as someone who had worked faithfully and effectively on behalf of the prior and chapter. In 1153 he took part in the proceedings leading up to that year's disputed election to the bishopric. When a Durham delegation set out for Rome, however, Lawrence turned aside from the party and joined the monastic community of St Albans. He is said to have found favour with Henry II, and this is likely, in view of his subsequent election as abbot of Westminster, *c.*1158. Royal support perhaps contributed to Lawrence's programme of repairs to the fire-damaged abbey, as well as to his recovery of those lands in the west midlands which had been harried by Robert, earl of Gloucester (*d.* 1147). It is likely that Lawrence instigated the denigration of the previous abbot, Gervase, so that his own administration should appear by contrast to be more successful. He obtained much material support from Robert de Gorham, abbot of St Albans, but while some of this contributed to improvements in the monks' conditions, it is likely that certain items were utilized as gifts to foster the king's goodwill. However, disagreements later arose between him and St Albans, in part over disputed franchisal rights in Aldenham, Hertfordshire. A second source of contention concerned the deposed Prior Alquin of St Albans, who fled to Westminster, where he was well received and where in due course he became prior.

Lawrence successfully petitioned for the canonization of King Edward (*d.* 1066). Made with the unanimous support of the Westminster monks, the new petition was based upon the procedures outlined by Pope Innocent II (*r.* 1130–43) when rejecting an earlier petition made in 1139. Care was also taken to secure the support of the king and the diocesan bishops. The bulls concerning the canonization were issued on 7 February 1161, and Lawrence then commissioned his kinsman, the Cistercian abbot Ailred of Rievaulx, to rewrite and update the earlier life of King Edward. In preparation for the translation of the new saint's relics, Lawrence, with a few carefully chosen monks, investigated King Edward's tomb and found his corpse in good condition. Lawrence removed a ring, believed to be that which was returned to Edward by St John the Evangelist, and preserved it as a memorial of the saint and as a token of his own devotion to him. Three cloths were also taken from the tomb and were made into copes. Thomas Becket presided at the translation, despite his worsening relations with the king, who was also present. Lawrence subsequently encouraged the cult of St Edward at Hurley Priory, Berkshire, by granting it the church of Easthampstead, Berkshire, so that its revenues would provide the monks with extra food, in return for which it was anticipated that they would show themselves more devout and prompt in celebrating this feast.

Lawrence visited Durham some time between July 1163 and October 1164. One of his monks was instructed by the hermit Godric of Finchale (*d.* 1170) to tell Thomas Becket that he would suffer exile but would eventually triumph. Lawrence himself conveyed the message to the archbishop. However, once Becket was in exile, Lawrence was more cautious. He wrote to Pope Alexander III (*r.* 1159–81) in 1169 in support of Gilbert Foliot, but otherwise seems to have played no real part in the dispute. He had earlier, probably in 1161, obtained a papal grant that entitled him and his successors to wear mitre and ring on Sundays and other solemn festivals. Other papal bulls obtained by Lawrence included one confirming Westminster's jurisdiction over its dependent cells of Great Malvern (Worcestershire), Hurley, and Sudbury (Suffolk). Another, of December 1171, confirmed the exemption of Westminster from the jurisdiction of the bishop of London. This was obtained while the bishop, Gilbert Foliot, was under sentence of excommunication, and Henry II was estranged from the pope as the result of Becket's murder. But, despite occasional differences over matters of jurisdiction, Lawrence appears to have been on generally good terms personally with Gilbert Foliot.

Relations with Henry II were variable as the reign progressed, and at Michaelmas 1165 Lawrence was recorded as having been amerced £100 for some unspecified offence. The influence of the king and queen ensured that royal nominees were occasionally appointed to Westminster's parish churches. Thus the rectory of Datchworth, Hertfordshire, was granted to the powerful royal minister Richard of Ilchester (*d.* 1188), whose relations with Lawrence appear to have varied between co-operation and its reverse, since Richard on occasion misappropriated land belonging to the abbey. The last of the surviving abbatial writs regarding Westminster's right to offer sanctuary dates from the time of Abbot Lawrence.

Lawrence was reputed to be an eloquent preacher, posthumously famed for his sermons. He kept up his early contacts with the abbey of St Victor. In a letter to his kinsman, Abbot Hervey (r. 1162–72), he commended its bearer, John, who was himself a member of the abbot's *familia* as well as a kinsman of the current prior of Westminster. A second letter, dated 1166, commended a second John, who was Lawrence's own nephew. It was intended that these young men should study at St Victor, as Lawrence himself had done. However, Westminster's confraternity agreement with St Victor apparently dates from shortly after Lawrence's death, which occurred on 10 or 11 April 1173. He was buried on the south side of the cloister, under a white marble stone, with his image superimposed. He had assigned income to the monastic infirmary from the churches of Wandsworth and Battersea, together with rents in Battersea, for the commemoration of the anniversary of his death.   EMMA MASON

Sources E. Mason, J. Bray, and D. J. Murphy, eds., *Westminster Abbey charters, 1066–c.1214*, London RS, 25 (1988) · J. Flete, *The history of Westminster Abbey*, ed. J. A. Robinson (1909) · R. W. Southern, 'St Anselm and his English pupils', *Medieval and Renaissance Studies*, 1 (1941), 3–34, 169–71 · *Gesta abbatum monasterii Sancti Albani, a Thoma Walsingham*, ed. H. T. Riley, 3 vols., pt 4 of *Chronica monasterii S. Albani*, Rolls Series, 28 (1867–9) · *Materials for the history of Thomas Becket, archbishop of Canterbury*, 6, ed. J. C. Robertson, Rolls Series, 67 (1882) · F. Barlow, *Edward the Confessor* (1970) · Reginald of Durham, *Libellus de vita et miraculis S. Godrici, heremitae de Finchale*, ed. J. Stevenson, SurtS, 20 (1847) · F. Anderson, 'Three Westminster abbots: a problem of identity', *Church Monuments*, 4 (1989), 3–15
Archives COXE, Catalog. codicum, MSS i. 70, Balliol 223, fol. 255, sec. xii

Lawrence of Arabia. *See* Lawrence, Thomas Edward (1888–1935).

Lawrence, Alfred Kingsley (1893–1975), portrait and figure painter, was born on 4 October 1893 at 24 Grange Road, Southover, Lewes, in Sussex, the son of Herbert Lawrence (b. 1858/9), solicitor and at that time clerk to the clerk of the peace, and his wife, Fanny Beatrice (b. 1863/4), daughter of John Williams, solicitor, of Lewes. A. K. (as he became known to his friends) seldom spoke of his youth but it seems that he had a brother (who died in his early teens as the result of an accident), that the father died when they were still boys, and that the mother was then remarried; her husband was a Mr Giffin, with whom she had two more sons.

Lawrence's art training began at Armstrong College, Newcastle upon Tyne, where he met his future wife, Margaret Crawford Younger (1886/7–1960) (daughter of Robert Younger of that city, gentleman, and his wife, Catherine), whom he married on 26 June 1915. It was, however, interrupted by service in the Northumberland Fusiliers throughout the First World War and, on demobilization, he continued his studentship at the Royal College of Art in London, whence he won a travelling scholarship in 1922 and the prix de Rome in 1923. The consequent period of study in Italy greatly influenced his aims and he became devoted to the works of Piero della Francesca, particularly the mural paintings at Arezzo. Thereafter he was for ever attempting to achieve in his own compositions the simple structure of form, the clarity of colour, and the statuesque quality of the figures which he so much admired in the masterpieces of the quattrocento.

Lawrence's first opportunity to emulate such works came immediately when, in 1924, he painted *The Altruists* for the basilica in the international exhibition at Wembley, quickly followed by *Building Pons Aelii* for the Laing Art Gallery, Newcastle, and, in 1926, *Queen Elizabeth Commissions Sir Walter Raleigh to Discover Unknown Lands, AD 1584*, one of the cycle of mural paintings in St Stephen's Hall at the houses of parliament. He was then asked to carry out, in the early 1930s, a group of large paintings, including *The Committee of the Treasury* (1928) for the new Bank of England and, subsequently, *Queen Elizabeth Visits her Armies at Tilbury, AD 1588* which was installed in the county hall at Chelmsford, Essex, in 1939. There were no opportunities for such work throughout the Second World War and, except for *The Resurrection*, an altar-piece for the church of St James, Beckenham, Kent, in 1954, thereafter no further commissions of comparable nature seemed to come his way. He still, however, retained his interests in the British School at Rome, being a member of its faculty of painting from 1926 to 1950, and in the encouragement of mural painting, having been a founder member of the Incorporated Edwin Austin Abbey memorial scholarships and serving on the council from 1926 to 1953.

Lawrence had been elected an associate of the Royal Academy, where he exhibited regularly from 1929, in 1930 and Royal Academician in 1938, and a member of the Royal Society of Portrait Painters in 1947. His easel paintings included various classical subjects, particularly depictions of the female nude, such as Venus, Leda, and Persephone (for example, his diploma work deposited in the Royal Academy), as well as theatrical themes, such as scenes from *Romeo and Juliet* and *Miss Vivien Leigh as Cleopatra* (1952), and presentation portraits such as *Mrs Eveline M. Lowe, Chairman of the London County Council* (1941) and *Sir Robert Robinson, President of the Royal Society* (1950). Many portraits by him, particularly in the latter part of his career, were in pencil, pastel, charcoal, or pen and wash, as for example *Sir Malcolm Sargent* (1954), *The Countess of Dundee* (1961), and most members of the royal family.

Lawrence had a great interest in the theatre and, had he turned professional actor instead of painter, he might well have been equally successful, especially in heroic roles. He was a tall, dignified man with a resounding voice, a stalwart in debate, forthright in his adherence to traditions, and rather grand in his renderings of Shakespeare. He was, however, prone to be too lengthy both in speech and in his frequent letters, self-typed and with innumerable amendments and insertions. Just as he hated anything unfinished or ephemeral, so was he a stickler for the correct use of words. He affirmed that all art was abstract and therefore considered that word's modern connotation in regard to painting to be a nonsense. He was also strongly against the use of photography as an aid or substitution for good draughtsmanship.

Margaret Lawrence died in 1960 and, apart from their daughter, Margaret, and son, Julius, who settled in New Zealand, Lawrence seemed to be rather a solitary figure in his last years. He still continued with his art but withdrew himself from aesthetic arguments. He died suddenly, from a heart attack, at his home, 30 Holland Park Road, London, on 5 April 1975.   S. C. HUTCHISON, *rev.*

Sources *Daily Telegraph* (7 April 1975) · *The Times* (9 April 1975) · *The Times* (11 April 1975) · records, RA · personal knowledge (1986) · b. cert. · m. cert. [H. Lawrence] · m. cert. [A. K. Lawrence]
Wealth at death £16,525: probate, 15 Sept 1975, *CGPLA Eng. & Wales*

Lawrence, Alfred Tristram, first Baron Trevethin (1843–1936), judge, was born at Pontypool on 24 November 1843, the eldest son of David Lawrence, surgeon, and his wife, Elizabeth, daughter of Charles Morgan Williams. Intending to study medicine, Lawrence left Mill Hill School early. At nineteen, however, having watched Hardinge Giffard and Henry Matthews in a case in which some property of his father's was involved, his interest turned towards the bar. He entered Trinity Hall, Cambridge (of which he was elected an honorary fellow in 1908), and was placed second in the first class in the law tripos of 1866. In 1869 he was called to the bar by the Middle Temple (of which he became a bencher in 1904 and treasurer in 1914). On 25 August 1875 he married his cousin Jessie Elizabeth (*d.* 1931), daughter of George Lawrence, of Moreton Court, near Hereford, and sister of Sir Walter Roper Lawrence; they had four sons and a daughter.

Lawrence joined the Oxford circuit and soon acquired a practice on circuit and in London. In 1882 he was made junior counsel to the Admiralty and in 1885 recorder of the royal borough of Windsor. In this office he became the friend and unofficial adviser of the dean of Windsor, Randall Davidson; and the future archbishop consulted him on many problems arising in the court of Queen Victoria. He did not take silk until 1897, at the late age of fifty-four, and there is disagreement about his success at the bar, although his practice has been described as 'substantial' (Heuston, 61). His appointment to be a Queen's Bench judge in 1904, at the age of sixty-one, caused some surprise. It should not have done.

Lord Halsbury, the lord chancellor, had a policy of appointing Conservatives to the bench, and, while Lawrence was not an MP, he had powerful political support. Arthur Balfour, the prime minister, wrote to Halsbury urging his case because of his good political work on behalf of the Conservative cause. So did Alfred Lyttelton, the colonial secretary. Lawrence proved to be an adequate rather than distinguished judge and he might well have passed into history without note, but for another political event. In 1921, as the Lloyd George coalition government was entering its final phase, Sir Gordon Hewart, the attorney-general, had set his heart on becoming lord chief justice—at that time thought to be the attorney-general's

Alfred Tristram Lawrence, first Baron Trevethin (1843–1936), by Walter Stoneman, 1925

as of right if a vacancy occurred. A vacancy did occur in 1921, when Lloyd George needed Lord Reading (Rufus Isaacs), the incumbent lord chief justice, to become viceroy of India. Hewart, who had turned down the posts both of Irish secretary and of home secretary to keep his right of reverter to the chief justiceship alive, struck a deal with the prime minister.

It was agreed that an elderly judge would be appointed to keep the lord chief justice's seat warm, while Hewart remained attorney-general. The tiresome Lord Darling and the then 77-year-old Mr Justice A. T. Lawrence competed for the dubious honour. Lawrence was chosen, taking office on 15 April 1921, and was required to give an undated letter of resignation. Although the rumour was put about that the king had blessed the arrangement, the judges were, not unnaturally, offended. They refused to attend the farewell for Lord Reading. Even Lord Birkenhead, no stranger to intrigue, in a letter to Lloyd George of 9 February 1921, called the plan illegal: it 'would make the Lord Chief Justice a transient figure subject to removal at the will of the government of the day and the creature of political exigency' (Jackson, 141). The result was foregone, as the Lloyd George administration collapsed early in 1922, and Lawrence, who had been raised to the peerage as Baron Trevethin of Blaengawney (24 August 1921), read of his own resignation in *The Times* (3 March 1922). Hewart duly became chief justice.

By the time of his resignation, Trevethin was too deaf to hear cases effectively and so did not sit as a law lord in the House of Lords as would then have been the norm. Rather, he retired to his house, Aber-nant, Builth Wells, Brecknockshire, and lived the country life for fourteen more years. As a young man he was a fine horseman, not only in the hunting field but also as a successful rider in point-to-point races and steeplechasing; in middle age he was a well-known and popular figure on the golf links, particularly at Nairn and Woking; and in retirement he was a keen angler. On 3 August 1936, while fishing in the Wye at Builth Wells, he accidentally fell into the river and died from heart failure. He was cremated at Golders Green on 7 August.

Trevethin's eldest son, Alfred Clive Lawrence (1876–1926), who was Treasury solicitor and king's proctor, having predeceased him, the barony passed to his second son, Charles Trevor Lawrence (1879–1959). The third son, Geoffrey *Lawrence, had a distinguished judicial career and was raised to the peerage as Baron Oaksey.

N. G. DAVIDSON, rev. ROBERT STEVENS

Sources Venn, *Alum. Cant.* · R. F. V. Heuston, *Lives of the lord chancellors, 1885–1940* (1964) · R. Jackson, *The chief: the biography of Gordon Hewart, lord chief justice of England, 1922–40* (1959) · R. Stevens, *The independence of the judiciary: the view from the lord chancellor's office* (1993) · d. cert.
Likenesses R. G. Eves, oils, 1922, Middle Temple, London · W. Stoneman, photograph, 1925, NPG [*see illus.*] · A. Cluysenaar, oils, priv. coll. · W. Orpen, oils, priv. coll. · Spy [L. Ward], caricature, NPG; repro. in *VF* (16 Oct 1907) · J. H. Walker, oils, priv. coll.
Wealth at death £38,935 13s. 8d.: probate, 2 Oct 1936, *CGPLA Eng. & Wales*

Lawrence, Arnold Walter (1900–1991), archaeologist, was born at 2 Polstead Road, Oxford, on 2 May 1900, the fifth of five illegitimate sons of Thomas Robert Lawrence and Sarah Lawrence, the names adopted for purposes of parentage by Sir Thomas Robert Tighe Chapman (1846–1919), bt, and Sarah Junner (b. 1861?). Thomas Edward *Lawrence (1888–1935) was one of his brothers. He was educated at the City of Oxford School and New College, Oxford, and graduated with a third in *literae humaniores* in 1921, having acquired the diploma in classical archaeology the year before. Blessed with private means, he was a student at the British Schools at Rome and Athens from 1921 to 1926, the last two years as Craven fellow of Oxford University, and travelled widely to examine Greek and especially Hellenistic sculpture. A season at Ur in 1923 under Leonard Woolley convinced him that excavation was not his line. In 1925 he married Barbara Innes (1902–1986), daughter of the Revd Edgar Wesley Thompson, and a fellow student. They settled at Hermitage in Berkshire. Their daughter, registered as Helen Thera, but soon renamed Jane, was born in 1926. At Hermitage, Lawrence put together the results of his studies and *Later Greek Sculpture*, the principal subject of his research, appeared in 1927. It was followed two years later by *Classical Sculpture*, a wider survey. In 1930 he was elected to the Laurence readership in classical archaeology at Cambridge, where he built a then very modern house on Madingley Road, the architect being his friend Marshall Sisson. Lawrence's interest had now turned away from sculpture and his next book, published in 1935, was *Herodotus*, a revision of George Rawlinson's translation with copious new notes.

Lawrence had always been close to his brother T. E. Lawrence—the eldest brother had become a missionary and the two others were killed in the First World War—and T. E. Lawrence's death in 1935 saddled him with a literary executorship which he performed long and faithfully, and with an embarrassing exposure to the devotees and denigrators of his famous brother. During the Second World War he was employed in generally futile jobs. In 1944 he succeeded A. J. B. Wace as Laurence professor of classical archaeology at Cambridge and as such was elected to a fellowship at Jesus College. In 1951 he obtained a Leverhulme research fellowship for the study of ancient fortifications, a subject inherited from T. E. Lawrence. The same year he resigned his Cambridge post to go to the Gold Coast (later Ghana) to be what was in effect archaeological supremo—professor of archaeology at the University College, director of the National Museum, and secretary and conservator of the monuments and relics committee. He resigned these posts in 1957 and soon after settled at Pateley Bridge in Yorkshire, later moving up the dale to Bouthwaite. His *Greek Architecture* had appeared in 1957 and in retirement he wrote *Trade Castles and Forts of West Africa* (1960), *Greek and Roman Sculpture* (1972), a much revised version of his earlier book, and *Greek Aims in Fortification* (1979), which was followed by a long paper on Byzantine fortifications in the *Annual of the British School at Athens*, 1983. Eventually, when neither he nor his wife could any longer drive, they moved to Langford, near Biggleswade, where soon—in 1986—his wife died unexpectedly (his daughter having already died in 1978). Without her Lawrence lost interest and was quietly pining away, until Peggy Guido, an old friend, took him off to her house at 44 Long Street, Devizes, Wiltshire. There he revived and started working again on Herodotus. He died suddenly at Peggy's home on 11 March 1991.

Lawrence—he did not like to be called by either of his forenames—was a good-looking and active man, in character conscientious, hard-working, modest, and basically shy. In company, though, he liked to shock, and indulged an impish humour so that casual acquaintances tended to consider him shallow or frivolous. In contrast or reaction to his mother's doctrinal fervour Lawrence was conscientiously anti-religious. He did not seem troubled by his illegitimacy, which indeed few knew of before Richard Aldington's *Lawrence of Arabia* appeared in 1955. His marriage was a happy one. Barbara was an intelligent and attractive woman, with—fortunately—a less insistent conscience: she regularly accompanied him on his many travels. As a teacher, Lawrence was for long handicapped by his shyness and it was not until he went to Ghana that he became a confident lecturer. He was, though, a good judge of students and a helpful adviser. He was also, when he had the opportunity, a capable and energetic organizer, as he showed at Cambridge in the Museum of Classical Archaeology (of which as professor he was curator) and on a grander scale in Ghana. Lawrence's writings were on subjects unfashionable in Britain and he did not advertise himself by lecturing in other institutions or attending conferences, and his often unorthodox views made him suspect to some elder scholars, so that he was for long undervalued and his fellowship of the British Academy was disgracefully belated. But he was one of the more original classical archaeologists of his time, with an exceptional knowledge of other cultures, which he used with disconcerting effect. Deservedly, his later books became standard works. R. M. COOK

Sources personal knowledge (2004) · private information (2004) · R. Aldington, *Lawrence of Arabia* (1955) · university and college records, U. Oxf. · *The Times* (6 April 1991) · *The Independent* (4 April 1991) · b. cert.
Likenesses photograph, *c.*1950, U. Cam., Museum of Classcial Archaeology · bronze statue, Scott Polar RI
Wealth at death £435,536: probate, 5 July 1991, *CGPLA Eng. & Wales*

Lawrence, Charles (*c.*1709–1760), army officer and colonial governor, was born in England, the son of Herbert Lawrence; his origins and early life are obscure. Apparently commissioned in the 11th regiment of foot (Montagu's) in 1727, he served in the West Indies and the war office before promotion to lieutenant in 1741 and captain in 1742. With the 54th regiment, he was wounded at Fontenoy, one of 7000 British casualties on a single sanguinary day in May 1745. In 1747, as a major in the 45th regiment (Warburton's), he was at occupied Louisbourg. After the British withdrawal from Cape Breton pursuant to the treaty of Aix-la-Chapelle, Lawrence in late 1749 joined the 40th regiment (Philipps's) in newly founded Halifax, Nova Scotia. Without private means, Lawrence had probably secured his original commission by kinship with the Montagu family; he now enjoyed the patronage of George Montagu Dunk, second earl of Halifax, president of the Board of Trade, for whom the new settlement was named.

The governor, Colonel Edward Cornwallis (who had also been in the thick of the fight at Fontenoy), appreciating the energetic, assiduous, and aggressive qualities of his new subordinate, made Lawrence a member of the council. In April 1750 he marched with a large company to the isthmus of Chignecto to warn off the French, who were erecting a fort, ironically named Beauséjour, on the north bank of the Missaguash River, later the Nova Scotia–New Brunswick border, then the disputed frontier between New France and British Nova Scotia. French colonial troops and Mi'kmaqs had made numerous destructive incursions on the south bank intended to force the Acadians to flee to French protection. Fort Beauséjour was the first and easternmost strongpoint of a new French *cordon sanitaire* from the St Lawrence to Fort Duquesne on the Ohio erected to assert their borders and inhibit British colonists' penetration. Rebuffed, Lawrence withdrew. Promoted lieutenant-colonel, he returned to Chignecto a few months later. With great *élan* and personal courage he routed from the south bank a force under the Spiritan missionary to the Mi'kmaqs, Abbé Jean-Louis Le Loutre. On the site of an Acadian village destroyed by the Mi'kmaq,

he erected Fort Lawrence facing Fort Beauséjour a cannon shot away.

Lawrence stood guard there for almost two years, until a new governor, Peregrine Thomas Hopson, confided to him the settling of Rhineland immigrants, in a mutinous state after two years in Halifax in poverty and some servitude. This he did at Lunenburg with energy and military precision, winning the trust of the settlers. When Hopson, in ill health, went home to Britain in late 1753, Lawrence took executive power as president of the council.

Lawrence's less than pleasant sojourn at Chignecto—his commissary shot under a white flag, possibly by a Mi'kmaq warrior, continuous alarums of skirmishers, and threats from hostile Acadians who had deserted to the French—left him with three convictions: that a final and climactic decision by arms between the two imperial powers was already in train; that Nova Scotia was defensible only by the most vigorous military effort; and that despite having been under British rule since 1710 the Acadian inhabitants were unreliable and potentially treasonous when subjected to French menaces and religious blandishments. The first put him in the van of those colonial governors ready to press belligerently against the French *cordon* for strategic positioning preparatory to a declared war. The second confirmed his soldierly predilection for a military over a political solution. Thus he joined with William Shirley of Massachusetts in 1754 to obtain grudging authority from Whitehall to maintain pressure in Chignecto, which let them raise two Massachusetts battalions for Nova Scotia service paid for by Lawrence's skimming the colony's parliamentary subvention. Once Whitehall decided to challenge the French threat and dispatched Major-General Edward Braddock to command all forces in North America, Lawrence was unleashed. Fort Beauséjour fell on 16 June 1755. Three other thrusts—Shirley's against Fort Niagara, Sir William Johnson's against Fort St Frédéric (Crown Point, New York), and Braddock's that ended in ambush, rout, and his death near Fort Duquesne (Pittsburgh, Pennsylvania) in July—failed of their objectives. Everywhere save at Chignecto, New France's borders remained secure.

Lawrence's military strengths and corresponding political frailties were most evident in his treatment of the Acadians. He was largely ignorant of them, as was the entire Halifax regime. Newcomers to the colony, they had no opportunity to learn—as their predecessors of the old military government at Annapolis Royal had learned between 1710 and 1749—that serious Acadian collaboration with the French was a manageable peril. Lawrence saw the Acadians' refusal to take an unqualified oath of allegiance as an offence *per se*, sufficient to deprive them of the protection accorded the king's subjects. Admittedly his Chignecto sojourn had meant contact with the most hostile and bitter Acadians, those closest to the French, who had removed themselves furthest from the British. His conventional anti-Catholic sentiments barred his understanding the peculiar apoliticalness of Acadian fidelity. His gruff directness made him unbelieving of the subtle shifts by which the majority of Acadians maintained an unarmed neutrality even while facing possible Mi'kmaq hostility. While governors had considered expelling the Acadians from the outset, Lawrence was the first to sustain the necessary determination to do so and to find in military necessity the efficient cause for it. The decision was taken, with the support of his council but without Whitehall's explicit approval, in July 1755. The arrival of news of Braddock's defeat added urgency. In August the expulsion began. Its horrors were unintended and incidental, and by twentieth-century criteria for diasporas *le grand dérangement* was a modest atrocity. Since Whitehall subsequently distanced itself from his act, the obloquy has been all Lawrence's.

Lawrence became governor in July 1756. He strived with mixed results to settle New England planters on Acadian lands. Impatient of popular government, he resisted demands from the large New England contingent to establish a legislative assembly until 1758. In that same year, with temporary rank of brigadier-in-America, he played a major role in conquering Louisbourg. Though denied a command under General James Wolfe at the plains of Abraham in 1759, he had been instrumental in the logistical preparation for that campaign. Hale and hardy, none the less he succumbed in Halifax to a chill caught after a strenuous evening dancing and died, unmarried, in Government House on 19 October 1760. He was buried on 23 October in the nave of St Paul's Church, Halifax. He amassed no fortune, though his many political adversaries accused him, unsuccessfully, of peculation. Many whom he had offended by his arrogance praised him in death. He had been always an exemplary soldier.

THOMAS G. BARNES

Sources PRO, CO 5/13–19, 21, 46–7, 52, 212, CO 217/10, 14–18, CO 218/2–6, CO 324/12–15, CO 325/1–2 · extracts, copies, Public Archives of Nova Scotia, Halifax, RG 1/4A–4B · minutes of council, Public Archives of Nova Scotia, Halifax, RG 3 · 'Journals and letters of Colonel Charles Lawrence', *Public Archives of Nova Scotia Bulletin*, 10 (1953) · T. B. Atkins, ed., *Selections from the public documents of Nova Scotia* (1869) · *Collection de documents inédits sur le Canada et l'Amérique, publiés par 'Le Canada-français'*, 1–2 (1888–9) · G. Du Boscq de Beaumont, *Les derniers jours de l'Acadie (1748–1758) … de M. Le Courtois de Surlaville* (1899) · B. Murdoch, *A history of Nova Scotia or Acadie*, 3 vols. (1866) · G. A. Rawlyk, *Nova Scotia's Massachusetts: a study of Massachusetts–Nova Scotia relations, 1630 to 1784* (1973) · N. E. S. Griffiths, *The Acadian deportation: deliberate perfidy or cruel necessity?* (1969) · N. E. S. Griffiths, *The Acadians: creation of a people* (1973) · P. Gaudet, *Le grand dérangement: sur qui retombe la responsabilité de l'expulsion des Acadiens* (1922) · A. W. Savary, 'The seizure and dispersion of the Acadians reviewed and considered', in A. W. Savary, *A history of the county of Annapolis* (1897) · D. Graham, 'Lawrence, Charles', *DCB*, vol. 3 · T. G. Barnes, 'Historiography of the Acadians' *grand dérangement*, 1755', *Quebec Studies*, 7 (1988), 74–86 · private information (2004) [A. C. McKay]

Archives Public Archives of Nova Scotia, Halifax, journal | Hunt. L., letters to James Abercromby · NA Canada, letters to Robert Monckton [copies]

Lawrence, Charles (1794–1881), agriculturist, born on 21 March 1794, was the son of William Lawrence (1753–1837), surgeon of Cirencester, Gloucestershire, and Judith, second daughter of William Wood of Tetbury, Gloucestershire. Sir William *Lawrence the surgeon, was his eldest

brother. In 1812 he attended chemistry lectures given by Dr Hugh. This helped to encourage the development of what was to become a lifelong interest in the application of science to agriculture. On 26 May 1818 Lawrence married Lydia, youngest daughter of Devereux Bowly of Chesterton House, Cirencester.

Lawrence took a leading part in founding and organizing the Royal Agricultural College at Cirencester between 1842 and 1845. For many years he owned an adjoining farm, where his experiments, resulted in several improvements in agricultural machinery. Many visitors, among others Baron Liebig, came to inspect the farm. His main aim was to devise an efficient way of maximizing the fertility of the land. His farm was always open for inspection to students from the agricultural college.

By the standards of his contemporaries, Lawrence was a prolific writer on a wide variety of topics dealing with improved methods of farming. Nine papers of significance were published in the *Transactions of the Royal Agricultural Society*, on diverse subjects: 'On diminishing the quantity of roots used in fattening cattle' (*Trans.*, 15.488); 'Swedes, mangold and the steam plough' (ibid., 25.248); and 'On the Royal Agricultural College of Cirencester' (ibid., 2nd series, i.1).

In addition Lawrence also compiled a number of more general tracts offering advice to both farm workers and aspiring farmers. These encompassed *Practical Directions for the Cultivation of Cottage Gardens* (1831), and *A Letter to a Youth who has Resolved on Farming as an Occupation* (1851). His most famous text was *Handy Book for Young Farmers* (1860), which was a compendium, in the form of a monthly calendar, covering advice on farming methods. This practical and popular text played a key role in enhancing Lawrence's reputation as an agriculturist. In 1860 he published a text, *On the Economy of Food*, for agricultural workers. Lawrence's reputation stems from his role in popularizing a more scientific approach to agricultural practice, and from his contribution in developing the Royal Agricultural College at Cirencester. Lawrence died at his house, Querns, Cirencester, on 5 July 1881.

M. G. WATKINS, rev. JOHN MARTIN

Sources *The Times* (19 July 1881), 8a · *The Times* (10 July 1881) · Burke, *Peerage* · N. Goddard, *Harvests of change: the Royal Agricultural Society of England, 1838–1988* (1988) · C. Lawrence, 'The Royal Agricultural College of Cirencester', *Journal of the Royal Agricultural Society of England*, 2nd ser., 1 (1865), 1–9 · d. cert.

Wealth at death £44,219 11s. 7d.: probate, 30 Sept 1881, CGPLA Eng. & Wales

Lawrence, David Herbert (1885–1930), writer, was born on 11 September 1885 at what is now 8A Victoria Street, Eastwood, near Nottingham, the fourth of the five children of Arthur John Lawrence (1846–1924) and his wife, Lydia Beardsall (1851–1910). Arthur Lawrence, like his three brothers, was a coalminer who worked from the age of ten until he was sixty-six, was very much at home in the small mining town, and was widely regarded as an excellent workman and cheerful companion. Lawrence's mother Lydia was the second daughter of Robert Beardsall and his wife, Lydia Newton of Sneinton; originally lower

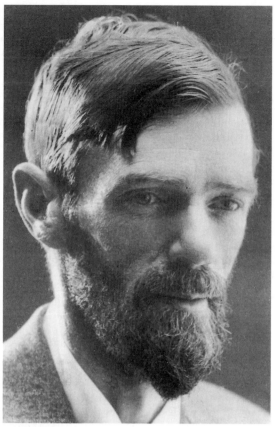

David Herbert Lawrence (1885–1930), by Ernesto Guardia, 1920s [copy by Peter A. Juley]

middle-class, the Beardsalls had suffered financial disaster in the 1860s and Lydia, in spite of attempts to work as a pupil teacher, had, like her sisters, been forced into employment as a sweated home worker in the lace industry. But she had had more education than her husband, and passed on to her children an enduring love of books, a religious faith, and a commitment to self-improvement, as well as a profound desire to move out of the working class in which she felt herself trapped. The resulting differences between her and her husband left their children permanently divided in loyalty, and played a considerable role in Lawrence's subsequent writing.

Early years Growing up in Eastwood, which depended almost completely on the mining industry (ten pits lay within walking distance), was difficult for a boy like Bert Lawrence, often in poor health and obviously frail. He was bullied at school, failed to join in games with the other boys, and—still worse—clearly preferred the company of girls, who talked rather than fought. School reinforced in him a sense of isolation and difference: 'When I go down pit you'll see what — sums I'll do' (Worthen, *Early Years*, 85) was the constant refrain of his contemporaries, and Lawrence knew from very early on that, in spite of his father's expectations, he would not be a miner. It took him some time to do well at school: he felt the pressure of being unlike the other boys, and he was following his elder

brother William Ernest, who had excelled in everything he did, whether schoolwork or playing games. By the age of twelve, however, Lawrence was a success; he became the first boy from Eastwood to win one of the recently established county council scholarships, and went to Nottingham high school.

At the high school, however, Lawrence did not distinguish himself. The scholarship boys were a class apart; Lawrence made few friends, and after an excellent start his performance fell away (not helped by the notoriety necessarily brought on his family by the arrest of his father's brother Walter in 1900 for killing his fifteen-year-old son). Lawrence left school in summer 1901 with little to show for the experience, and started work as a factory clerk for the Nottingham surgical appliances manufacturer Haywoods. That autumn, however, a catastrophe overtook the Lawrence family: William Ernest, by now a successful clerk in London, fell ill and died. Lydia Lawrence was distraught (she needed her children to make up for the disappointments of her life), and when Lawrence himself went down with pneumonia that winter, her affections turned significantly towards him. When he recovered he started work as a pupil teacher at the British School in Eastwood, where he spent the next three years.

Another important development during this period was Lawrence's acquaintance with the Chambers family, who had recently moved from Eastwood into the country. He and his mother visited the Haggs Farm in summer 1900, and Lawrence began regular visits there after his illness, becoming a particular friend of the eldest son, Alan. The second daughter, Jessie, however, made herself his intellectual companion; they read books together and endlessly discussed authors and writing. It was under Jessie's influence that in 1905 Lawrence started to write poetry: 'A collier's son a poet!' he remarked sardonically (Worthen, *Early Years*, 130), but his mother had written poetry in her time too. In 1906 he started his first novel, which eventually became *The White Peacock*. Jessie Chambers saw all his early writing, and her encouragement and admiration were crucial.

In 1904 Lawrence achieved the first division of the first class in the king's scholarship examination, and his mother was determined that he should study for his teacher's certificate at the University College of Nottingham. After a year's full-time teaching in Eastwood, he went to Nottingham in 1906 to follow the normal course. He completed its demands without difficulty, acquiring a considerable contempt for academic life while doing so; he also completed a second draft of his novel, as well as entering three stories in the *Nottinghamshire Guardian* Christmas story competition in 1907: 'A Prelude' won, under the name of Jessie Chambers.

Schoolteacher Lawrence qualified as a teacher in 1908 and took a post in Davidson Road elementary school in Croydon. He found the demands of teaching in a large school in a poor area very different from those at Eastwood under a protective headmaster. Nevertheless he established himself as an energetic teacher, ready to use new teaching methods (Shakespeare lessons became practical drama classes, for example). The contacts he made through school were probably more important than his job: Agnes Mason, rather older than Lawrence, tended to mother him, but a younger friend of hers, Helen Corke, at another school, caught his interest; Arthur McLeod, on the Davidson staff, read Lawrence's work and lent him books. He was now reading significantly modern authors such as William James, Baudelaire, and Nietzsche (whom he discovered while in London), and during these years he lost his religious faith. Above all Lawrence was trying to develop his writing career by working in the evenings and holidays; he was engaged on yet another draft of his novel and writing a great deal of poetry. In the summer of 1909 came the breakthrough. Jessie Chambers had sent some of his poems to Ford Madox Hueffer (later Ford), at the *English Review*, and Hueffer not only printed them, but saw Lawrence and, after reading the manuscript of *The White Peacock*, wrote to the publisher William Heinemann recommending it. By now the novel was an extraordinary mixture of the literary, the pastoral, the romantic, and the tragic; Lawrence referred to it as 'a kind of exquisite scented soap' (*Letters*, 1.158). Hueffer also got Lawrence to write about his mining background, which resulted in a short story, 'Odour of Chrysanthemums', and his first play, *A Collier's Friday Night* (in 1910 he wrote a second play, *The Widowing of Mrs. Holroyd*). Hueffer's successor at the *English Review*, Austin Harrison, continued to publish Lawrence's stories and poems.

Lawrence was finding Croydon fruitful for other reasons, too. He was attracted to yet another Croydon teacher, Agnes Holt; and discovered that Helen Corke had recently had an affair with a married man who killed himself. She told Lawrence the whole story, and he re-created it in the first draft of another novel, *The Trespasser*, falling in love with her as he did so. In winter 1909–10, however, he started a new relationship with Jessie Chambers and they had a rather unhappy affair through spring and summer 1910. In August he broke off their relationship, just before his mother was taken fatally ill. He spent as much time at her side in Eastwood as he could that autumn, and in October started the first draft of his autobiographical novel *Paul Morel*, with its vivid picture of Mrs Morel. Lydia Lawrence died in December 1910 shortly after Lawrence had got engaged to his old college friend Louie Burrows.

The year 1911 was, in spite of Heinemann's publication of *The White Peacock* in January, a desperate year for Lawrence. He was mourning his mother, unhappy in his engagement, missing Jessie Chambers's support, and desperate to get out of a job which took him away from writing (he could make only limited progress with *Paul Morel*, for example). He was fortunate in making contact with Edward Garnett, reader for the publishers Duckworth, who helped him place his work; but in November he fell seriously ill with double pneumonia and nearly died. His career as a teacher was now over. After convalescence in Bournemouth, where characteristically he rewrote *The Trespasser* in a month (Garnett had got it accepted by Duckworth, and had given him good advice for its revision), Lawrence broke off his engagement to Louie Burrows, returned to the midlands, and worked to complete the book on which he felt his future as a writer really depended, *Paul Morel*.

A new life   Having decided to visit his cousins in north Germany, Lawrence called on his Nottingham professor Ernest Weekley for advice. At Weekley's house, on 3 March 1912 Lawrence met and fell in love with Weekley's wife Frieda Emma Maria Johanna, *née* von Richthofen (1879–1956), six years older than himself. The whole direction of his life changed; he broke off for the last time with Jessie Chambers and set himself to earn his living as a professional writer. When Frieda visited her family in Germany in May, Lawrence travelled with her, and worked to persuade her to leave her husband, which meant leaving her three young children too. The situation was unresolved for months. Frieda's desire to be free of her marriage was not consistent with Lawrence's insistence that she become his partner, and she suffered agonies from the loss of her children (Weekley was determined to keep them away from her). Some of the vicissitudes of this time are recreated in Lawrence's poetry collection *Look! We have Come Through!* (1917). In Germany, Lawrence finished *Paul Morel*, and worked hard at essays and short stories. He and Frieda ended up living in a flat in Icking, near Munich, rented by Alfred Weber, lover of Frieda's sister Else Jaffe. Heinemann turned down *Paul Morel* on grounds of indecency, but Duckworth took it over and Garnett persuaded Lawrence to give it a final revision, doubtless feeling (as with *The Trespasser*) that the book needed to be made 'more actual' and more focused on its theme. Lawrence and Frieda travelled down to Italy, walking wherever they could (over the Pfitscher Joch, for example), and in September settled in Villa, near Gargnano, beside Lake Garda. Lawrence completed the revisions of *Paul Morel* and turned it into *Sons and Lovers* (it was published the following May). What supported them financially was *The Trespasser*; and to add to his happiness, during their months in Italy, Frieda finally resolved to stay with him. He was a man exhilarated by the new experience of Italy, by creative achievement, and by a very strenuous kind of love. Frieda was 'the one possible woman for me, for I must have opposition—something to fight'; marrying Jessie Chambers 'would have been a fatal step, I should have had too easy a life, nearly everything my own way' (Nehls, 1.71). He cooked, cleaned, wrote, argued; Frieda attended little to housekeeping (though washing became her speciality), but she could always hold her own against his theorizing, and maintained her independence of outlook as well as of sexual inclination (she slept with a number of other men during her time with Lawrence).

During winter 1912–13 Lawrence wrote two plays (including his best, *The Daughter-in-Law*) and more poetry (his first volume, *Love Poems and Others*, was published in February 1913), and started a number of new novel projects. He wrote 200 pages of a book he called 'The Insurrection of Miss Houghton'; but it was 'The Sisters', originally 'for the "jeunes filles"' (*Letters*, 1.546), which determined his course as a novelist for the next three years. Back in Germany by early summer 1913 he wrote some of his finest short stories, including the story published as 'The Prussian Officer'. He returned to England and with Garnett's help took care of the publication of short stories new and old; his meeting with Edward Marsh and immediate fellow feeling with Katherine Mansfield and John Middleton Murry established friendships which were long and significant. The reviews of *Sons and Lovers* were also very encouraging: 'an achievement of the first quality', wrote the poet Lascelles Abercrombie, for example (introduction, *Sons and Lovers*, lxv), and although its sales remained fairly low the book and its author had gathered a significant reputation.

The period from August 1913 to June 1914 saw Lawrence revising *The Widowing of Mrs. Holroyd* (published 1914) and working through many drafts of 'The Sisters'; the book had turned into a huge saga of midlands life and marriage, 'written in another language almost' from *Sons and Lovers*; 'I have no longer the joy in creating vivid scenes, that I had in *Sons and Lovers*' (*Letters*, 2.132, 142). It had now come to deal with the Brangwen ancestors as well as the two sisters' experiences with men, in a style which Lawrence referred to as 'exhaustive'. In an attempt to write the inner lives of his characters, he was starting to experiment with language and metaphor in a way that disconcerted his contemporaries; his writing did not concentrate on people's psychological make-up so much as on their embodied emotions and needs. *The Wedding Ring*, the novel Lawrence ended up with in the spring of 1914, however, sounded an attractive prospect to publishers who had been impressed by *Sons and Lovers*; Lawrence acquired an agent, J. B. Pinker, and a three-volume novel contract with Methuen. Back in England and living in London, he and Frieda married on 13 July 1914. Lawrence also compiled his short-story collection *The Prussian Officer and other Stories*, and met Catherine Carswell, Richard Aldington, and S. S. Koteliansky, all of whom remained his friends for life.

The Lawrences had intended to return to Italy, but the outbreak of war saw *The Wedding Ring* returned by Methuen and travel abroad impossible. For the rest of the year they lived in Buckinghamshire, near Murry and Katherine Mansfield, and here Lawrence first fantasized a community (Rananim) which he would occupy with friends like the Murrys and Koteliansky; a fantasy which would constantly recur, shift focus, and be remade over the next ten years. In Buckinghamshire, too, he wrote his *Study of Thomas Hardy* before starting yet another revision of his novel, this time turning its first half into *The Rainbow* and leaving the rest of the material (Ursula's and Gudrun's marriages) on one side. Lawrence was now starting to move in circles centred on Garsington Manor and Lady Ottoline Morrell; he met (and thoroughly impressed) Bertrand Russell and E. M. Forster, and later befriended Philip Heseltine (Peter Warlock), the young Aldous Huxley, and the painters Mark Gertler and Dorothy Brett. In March 1915 he finished *The Rainbow*, and remarked 'Now off and away to find the pots of gold at its feet' (*Letters*, 2.299). He planned a lecture course with Bertrand Russell, and in the autumn started a magazine, *The Signature*, with Murry and Katherine Mansfield.

But all these developments came to nothing. *The Signature* folded; he quarrelled with Russell; Methuen published *The Rainbow* in September 1915, but it got savage reviews, most of which attacked what was understood as the book's overt sexuality, and it was withdrawn from sale. At Bow Street magistrates' court on 13 November it was banned as obscene (Lawrence having no opportunity to defend it). Its religious language, emotional and sexual explorations of experience, and sheer length had given its readers problems, but it was Ursula's lesbian encounter with a schoolteacher in the chapter 'Shame' which had finally condemned it in the eyes of the law and of a country now focused on conflict: 'A thing like *The Rainbow* has no right to exist in the wind of war', one review had said (Kinkead-Weekes, 277). Lawrence's career as a writer was catastrophically damaged; he had already thought of going to America to start again there, though at this stage he elected to stay in England. But after the *Rainbow* disaster he left London to live in Cornwall: 'a temporary refuge until they could get out of England altogether' (ibid., 296). The idea of leaving his country marked the first stage of his major disillusionment with what England offered him, and with what he could do for it as a writer. He felt profoundly rejected; he responded with anger and a retreat into a world as much his own as he could make it.

War Lawrence had declared in January 1915 that 'The War finished me: it was the spear through the side of all sorrows and hopes' (*Letters*, 2.268), and not just of his hopes of returning to Italy, or of living happily with Frieda, or working as a writer, though all these things were affected by changes in the world between 1914 and 1918. Rather, the war also seems to have killed his belief in the potential goodness and progress of his own civilization. Lawrence had formulated such a response to the war long before there was much fighting (he was never a pacifist like Bertrand Russell); it was a reaction to the very idea of the war rather than to anything which happened in it. His disillusion with what he saw as the mob spirit and the authoritarian rule of his own country affected the rest of his life and writing career, but the war's main effect at this stage was to sharpen his own sense of isolation.

Lawrence was ill when first in Cornwall, and the problem of earning enough to keep Frieda and himself preoccupied him. He remained resourceful, and Pinker did what he could to help; Lawrence published his first travel book, *Twilight in Italy*, in June 1916, and between 1916 and 1919 brought out four books of poetry, including *Amores* and his verse narrative of love and marriage, *Look! We have Come Through!* In spite of what he feared would be the fate of his fiction after *The Rainbow*, in spring 1916 he started again on the 'Sisters' material; after an enormous creative effort in which he wrote the whole book twice he had finished the first version of *Women in Love* by November 1916. But it was rejected by every publisher who saw it; the fact that it contained recognizable re-creations of several people (including Russell, Heseltine, and the Morrells) did not help; nor did its vivid portrayal of what one publisher's reader called 'the writer's expressions of antipathy to England and the forms of English civilisation' (introduction, *Women in Love*, xxxiv). To Lawrence it was a novel in which 'I have knocked the first loop-hole in the prison where we are all shut up' (*Letters*, 2.663), but it would not be published for another four years.

Lawrence and Frieda stayed on in Cornwall, living as cheaply as they could. Early in 1917 they made another, more serious attempt to be allowed to go to America, but they could not obtain passports. To make matters worse, in October 1917 they were expelled from Cornwall; the military authorities objected to a suspect writer and an enemy alien living near shipping lanes where German submarines were inflicting heavy losses on allied ships. This confirmed Lawrence's sense of alienation from his country; what role could he now play, except that of an outsider? All the Lawrences could now afford to do was to live precariously in friends' flats and country cottages. In the summer of 1917 Lawrence had completed a major revision of *Women in Love*; it was the novel which represented his last comprehensive attempt to write for his country, as it examined and characterized contemporary anxiety and conflict.

By 1918 Lawrence was back in the midlands, at Middleton by Wirksworth, living in a cottage paid for by his sister Ada, and the *English Review* published the first versions of what became *Studies of Classic American Literature*, his pioneering study of the great eighteenth- and nineteenth-century American writers. Lawrence also wrote essays, the play *Touch and Go*, and poems; his new publisher, Martin Secker, also published *New Poems*, and he wrote the first version of his short novel *The Fox*. The death of his old friend and neighbour Frankie Cooper in Eastwood, however, brought back poignantly his hatred of the midlands. He was himself desperately ill again in the influenza outbreak of February 1919, and only just pulled through; he was reduced to writing a school history book for money. Only in the summer of 1919 did he start to regain what he felt was his freedom. In the autumn Frieda returned to Germany to see her surviving family (her father had died in 1915), while Lawrence finally scraped together what money he had, and left England for Italy. It was the real end of his life rooted in England. Italy in 1912 had been a radical new experience; it was now a place to go when his relationship with England was finished.

Farewell to Europe The first four months of Lawrence's return to Europe saw him going steadily further south. After a brief return visit to Fiascherino, he went on to Florence, making contact with the writer Norman Douglas and the latter's friend the American writer Maurice Magnus; he joined Frieda and then together they tried Picinisco, in the Abruzzi Mountains, where an English friend, Rosalind Baynes, had thought of living. But although it provided a wonderful setting for the last part of *The Lost Girl*, it proved impossibly cold and remote; they went further south still, to Capri, where the English writing colony, including Compton Mackenzie and Francis Brett Young, made them welcome; and finally, in February

1920, they went down to Sicily, to the Fontana Vecchia on the outskirts of Taormina. Here Lawrence and Frieda lived for almost two years, and he got down to some serious work. He had been writing the essays of *Psychoanalysis and the Unconscious*, a sustained attack on Freud; he now wrote *The Lost Girl* (which drew on the 'Insurrection' novel from 1913), and arranged for the publication of *Women in Love* in America with a new publisher, Thomas Seltzer, and in England with Secker. He also worked at a novel unfinished since 1917, *Aaron's Rod*, and started a new book, *Mr Noon*, but did not finish that either. He was clearly full of ideas for novels after the lean years of the war. In its fragmentary state *Mr Noon* constitutes a sardonic critique of the contemporary novel-reading public's supposed sensitivities and frailties, as well as providing a vivid recreation of his first months of passionate attraction to Frieda back in 1912, seen from the perspective of a writer who no longer believed in love. In the late summer of 1920 he had a very brief affair with Rosalind Baynes, now living near Florence, but such a relationship made no difference to his commitment to marriage; nor would it have had anything, he hoped, to do with love. A number of his poems in *Birds, Beasts and Flowers*, especially in the section 'Tortoises', drew on the affair, and his continuing sense of apartness. Although about this time he added some new friends, Earl and Achsah Brewster, to those whose company he enjoyed (and who would remain important for the rest of his life), his separateness as man and writer grew steadily more marked.

In January 1921 Lawrence and Frieda visited Sardinia and he wrote the second of his travel books, *Sea and Sardinia*, an acute and often very funny diary of the journey. He also found himself able that spring to complete *Aaron's Rod*, the novel he had been struggling with, in which a working-class musician manages to leave his wife, family, and England, and to live by his art. In this and subsequent novels Lawrence's voice often, quite consciously, came from the sidelines; in them he would stage guerrilla attacks as well as full-frontal assaults; his writing would be goading, insistent, revelatory. In *Aaron's Rod* he went closer than ever before to writing directly about sexual experience (Seltzer and Secker heavily censored the passages describing Aaron's affair with the marchesa). Like *Women in Love* it received a mixture of enthusiastic and bewildered reviews: Middleton Murry had declared that *Women in Love* showed Lawrence 'far gone in the maelstrom of his sexual obsession' but called the new book 'the most important thing that has happened to English literature since the war' (introduction, *Aaron's Rod*, xlii). To most reviewers, however, it was simply another interesting book made rather unpleasant by Lawrence's obsession with sex.

In the autumn of 1921 Lawrence wrote *Fantasia of the Unconscious*, a more light-hearted successor to *Psychoanalysis and the Unconscious*. At the end of 1921 his thorough revision of the short novels *The Fox*, *The Captain's Doll*, and *The Ladybird* showed him working in a new form and with extreme intensity. He also revised all his stories of the war years to create the collection *England, my England and other*

Stories: a way of coming to terms with the past, and putting it behind him. After Maurice Magnus's suicide Lawrence wrote an introduction to Magnus's book about the foreign legion. One of Lawrence's finest pieces of writing, it concentrates on a writer who struggled to articulate what he experienced, and who lived by his wits on the outskirts of conventional society (Magnus was clearly someone in whom Lawrence saw reflections of himself and his own career).

Lawrence found Sicily wonderful, perhaps because it represented a final toe-hold on Europe: the Fontana Vecchia, the garden, the sun, the prospect out over the Mediterranean made it the place where he had been happier to live than anywhere since Cornwall. But by the end of 1921 he was determined to move on and go to America, his ambition for eight years now. In the event, the contact he had with the American hostess Mabel Dodge Sterne and her friends in the artists' colony of Taos in New Mexico made him decide to go first to Ceylon, to visit the Brewsters, before approaching America from the west coast. In February 1922 he and Frieda set out for Ceylon.

Round the world and back again Ceylon was too hot for Lawrence and in most ways a disappointment; he wrote little, which was unusual for him, except letters and his translation of Giovanni Verga; but a previously unconsidered diversion to Australia, provoked by contacts made on the voyage to Colombo, led to an unexpected and (in terms of writing) immensely worthwhile visit. After a brief stay in Western Australia, where they met the writer Mollie Skinner, the Lawrences settled on the coast south of Sydney, at Thirroul; and here, in six weeks, Lawrence wrote his novel *Kangaroo*, drawing upon his experience of Europe in the new context of Australia; the long chapter 'The Nightmare' was a retrospective on what had happened to him during the war, and how his character Richard Somers—in many ways an *alter ego*—now felt 'Without a people, without a land. So be it. He was broken apart, apart he would remain' (*Kangaroo*, 1994, 259). In this novel he questioned the very nature of the novel form, with one chapter reprinting pieces of newspaper in collage fashion, another laconically starting 'Chapter follows chapter, and nothing doing' (ibid., 284).

In Australia the Lawrences saw almost nobody; in America they were plunged into activity after activity. After meeting the poet Witter Bynner and his companion Willard (Spud) Johnson in Santa Fe, in New Mexico, Mabel Sterne and her Indian lover Tony took them around by car from Taos; they visited an Apache reservation and Taos pueblo and saw Indian dances, and Mabel did her best to persuade Lawrence to write both about her and about the American south-west (part of her mission in bringing him there had been to have him re-create the place in his writing). Lawrence and Frieda both reacted strongly against her, however, and spent the winter of 1922–3 at the Del Monte ranch on Lobo Mountain, out of the orbit of Mabel so far as they could manage it; two Danish painter friends (Knud Merrild and Kai Götzsche) lived with them. While up at the ranch Lawrence managed a final reworking of the much revised *Studies*, shortening and Americanizing

the studies in accordance with his new experience. He also finished his poetry collection *Birds, Beasts and Flowers*, which represents the best and most innovative of his poetry writing.

In the spring of 1923 the Lawrences went down to Mexico with Bynner and Johnson; they visited historical sites, ending up living beside Lake Chapala; and here Lawrence began 'Quetzalcoatl', the novel of the American continent which he had not managed to write in Taos. This first draft of what became *The Plumed Serpent* occupied him until he and Frieda decided they should go to New York to see Seltzer (currently publishing book after book by Lawrence), and in order to go back to Europe. Frieda was especially anxious to see her children, as two of them were now aged twenty-one or over, and she could see them freely for the first time since 1912. Lawrence, however, could not face Europe and stayed behind in America, after one of their most serious quarrels. After a few months wandering down the west coast in the company of Götzsche (and turning a novel by Mollie Skinner into one for which he was equally responsible, *The Boy in the Bush*), he resolved to return briefly to Europe. He was in England only for a couple of months; but in a traumatic and significant move, having invited his London friends to dinner at the Café Royal, he invited them to come back to New Mexico with him and Frieda. He felt committed, as has been pointed out, to 'establishing a new life on earth' (Ellis, 151); the final version of his idea for communal living, however, came to nothing. Dorothy Brett was the only one to accept (Middleton Murry said yes, but had decided not to come). After Lawrence and Frieda had been to Germany to see Frieda's mother (of whom Lawrence was increasingly fond), Brett accompanied the Lawrences back to America in March 1924.

This time they resolved to live the life of the ranch from the start, and on a small and partly derelict property given to Frieda by Mabel (Lawrence insisted on paying for it with the manuscript of *Sons and Lovers*) they spent a busy time getting the cabins ready; and then, with the hard physical work done, Lawrence devoted himself to writing. In an amazingly short time he produced three of his greatest works of the American continent: *St. Mawr*, 'The Woman who Rode Away', and 'The Princess'. His work was, however, succeeded in August by his first bronchial haemorrhage, perhaps aggravated by the altitude of over 7000 feet. When he felt better, all three of them went down to Mexico in October, where Lawrence wanted to finish *The Plumed Serpent*. They settled in Oaxaca, Lawrence deliberately choosing a far less Europeanized town than Chapala.

Lawrence wrote the whole novel again, composing his *Mornings in Mexico* essays in the interim, as a kind of light relief. In many ways this was his most ambitious novel since *Women in Love*; it attempted to create the sense of a whole society, and of how religion could bring change to society—but it was achieved at a dreadful cost of health and spirits, and perhaps in disregard of his own disillusion with both society and Mexico. No sooner had he completed the novel than he went down with a combination of typhoid and pneumonia, and nearly died. After they had struggled back to Mexico City, Lawrence relapsed, and a doctor diagnosed tuberculosis. Lawrence and Frieda had planned to return to England, but the doctor advised altitude, and they made their way back up to the ranch.

Amazingly, over the summer of 1925 Lawrence recovered much of his health, though he was never so well again as during the strenuous spring and summer of 1924; he compiled the essays in *Reflections on the Death of a Porcupine*, and also wrote his last play, *David*. On the ranch, well away from civilization, the Lawrences and Brett lived close to the wildness of nature, although such a life was necessarily always a struggle, and physically demanding. Lawrence wrote in an essay of 1928 how 'New Mexico was the greatest experience from the outside world that I have ever had' (*Phoenix*, 142), but it was also too much for him. His and Frieda's visas limited how long they could stay in the USA, and in September they travelled back to Europe, Lawrence always hoping he would one day be able to return.

Struggle It was not long before Lawrence and Frieda were back in Italy, this time in Spotorno, where Lawrence wrote the first version of his short novel *Sun*, drawing on memories of the Fontana Vecchia. Their landlord at Spotorno was Angelo Ravagli, to whom Frieda was soon attracted, and with whom she lived after Lawrence's death. (Ravagli and Frieda were married in 1950.) To Spotorno came Frieda's daughters too (she could now see her youngest, Barby, as well as Elsa); and Lawrence put their experiences to good use in his short novel *The Virgin and the Gipsy* which, however, he resolved not to publish (it was too satirical of Ernest Weekley in its portrayal of the Revd Arthur Saywell). A visit from his own sister Ada in the spring of 1926 precipitated another dreadful quarrel with Frieda; he left for a month, to visit the Brewsters and to see Brett, who was back from America for a European holiday. He probably had some kind of brief sexual relationship with Brett at this point before returning to Frieda. They settled down again in a new place, the Villa Mirenda near Florence, in a new mood of reconciliation.

Lawrence's tuberculosis was now a real problem, but he was convinced that he should neither go to a sanatorium nor submit to surgery. He gave good advice to Gertie Cooper, who lived with his sister Ada and her husband, and who was also tubercular, but privately resolved that he himself would stay independent for as long as he could. He had always been good at taking care of himself in sickness and health, and nowhere is this clearer than in his determination during the last years of his life. The word 'tuberculosis' was, indeed, not permitted; he suffered, he insisted, from dreadful bronchials, remarking irritably that 'I have had bronchitis since I was a fortnight old' (Worthen, *Early Years*, 6). A visit to England during the coal strike of 1926 brought his last opportunity to see his old haunts, and it was probably this experience which prompted the first version of *Lady Chatterley's Lover*, one of several works revisiting the themes and places of his youth, and the problems of his own early life. His sympathy was now far more with his father (who had died in 1924) than

with his mother, and the novel's central character was thoroughly working-class. The second version, started in November 1926, made the novel sexually explicit; it became a hymn to the love-making of the couple, to the body of the man and the woman, for sexuality as it could potentially be between an independent working-class man and an independent upper-class woman. It was a final fictional reworking of a theme which he had always written about for the chance it gave him to concentrate on sexual attraction (and to some extent had enacted in his own life and relationships), but which he now returned to both polemically and nostalgically.

A revived friendship with Aldous and Maria Huxley turned out to be one of the sustaining elements in these difficult years. Lawrence also started to paint, and found it a compensation for much. Early in 1927 he finished the second version of *Lady Chatterley's Lover* and visited the Etruscan sites of central Italy with Earl Brewster; the trip gave rise to one of the most attractive books of his last years, *Sketches of Etruscan Places*, which developed the Lawrentian myth of the fulfilled body in the context of a beautifully imagined and recreated civilization. A rather similar work was *The Escaped Cock*, the first half of which showed Jesus, after the resurrection, valuing above all else the natural, phenomenal world about which Lawrence had always written so compellingly, and which was becoming increasingly important to him as he endured the progressive deteriorations of illness.

The publication (for subscribers) of the final version of *Lady Chatterley's Lover*—written in the astonishing time of just five weeks, in one of Lawrence's last great bursts of creative energy—also sustained him, as he overcame the difficulties lying in the way of an individual publishing and distributing his own book. With the help of the Florentine bookseller Pino Orioli, the handsome volume was printed in and distributed from Florence, and made Lawrence more money than he had ever imagined. In June he wrote the second part of *The Escaped Cock*, in which Jesus experiences sexual desire again, after the resurrection; another work of intense nostalgia for the body. Lawrence had, however, suffered more than one haemorrhage at the Mirenda, and always tended to distrust places where he had been seriously ill; he left Florence in the summer of 1928, just at the time when *Lady Chatterley's Lover* was making it possible for him to pay doctors' bills and live more comfortably (often in hotels) than his previously careful existence had allowed.

Dying game Lawrence and Frieda tried living first at altitude in Switzerland, at Gsteig, and then went down to the Mediterranean island of Port Cros, but a small hotel in Bandol, in the south of France, by the sea, as in Fiascherino, Taormina, Thirroul, and Spotorno, suited Lawrence better than anywhere. He was now no longer writing fiction, but he created many of the poems in *Pansies* during winter 1928–9; he also wrote short personal articles for newspaper publication, as he targeted yet another audience with his writing. As a friend commented, 'he challenged everything' (Nehls, 2.318). The fact of his writing itself was rooted in opposition; he remarked to another friend that 'If there weren't so many lies in the world ... I wouldn't write at all' (ibid., 3.293). In 1925 he had described his role as a writer as not to sit aloft or detached but increasingly to be 'in among the crowd, kicking their shins or cheering them on to some mischief or merriment' (*Letters*, 5.201); of all his books, *Lady Chatterley's Lover* most mischievously both attacked and cheered on its readers.

It turned out that *Lady Chatterley's Lover* was being extensively pirated in Europe and the USA. The theft irritated Lawrence, who had always meant to make the novel available in a cheap edition; in the spring of 1929, accordingly, he went to Paris to organize it. He was further stirred to action by the police seizure in England of the unexpurgated typescript of his volume of poems *Pansies*; meanwhile the exhibition of his paintings in London in summer 1929 (which he was too ill to attend) was raided by the police, and court hearings were necessary before the paintings could be returned to their owner. These irritations both provoked and stimulated Lawrence, as in his poem 'Innocent England':

Virginal, pure, policemen came
And hid their faces for very shame.

But in an increasingly desperate desire to find a place where his health would improve, he and Frieda visited Majorca, France, and Bavaria before they returned to Bandol for the winter. Beside the Mediterranean once again, he wrote *Apocalypse*, his last book about the European psyche and its needs, which had started as an introduction to a book by Frederick Carter; he also wrote the poems published posthumously as *Last Poems* (1932). He saw a good deal of the Huxleys and the Brewsters, who rallied round him and Frieda as his health failed.

In a final attempt to stave off his illness Lawrence agreed with an English doctor to spend a month doing nothing (after he had finished his poems and *Apocalypse*), but felt the action had had no result; consequently, at the start of February 1930, he went into the ominously named Ad Astra sanatorium in Vence. It was too late; he was terrifyingly thin, almost ethereal, virtually incapable of walking, and the doctors could do nothing for him. Determined, as he put it to Gertie Cooper, to 'die game' (*Letters*, 5.632), he discharged himself from the sanatorium on 1 March 1930, and Frieda helped him move into the Villa Robermond, a rented house in Vence. He was not going to die where he did not choose to live: it was his last independent act. He died on the evening of the following day, Sunday 2 March, and was buried in Vence cemetery on 4 March. In 1935, following cremation, his ashes were reportedly either taken to New Mexico, where they were mixed into concrete and kept in a 'chapel' at the Kiowa ranch, or scattered into the Mediterranean.

After life When very young Lawrence was almost white-haired (Billy the White-Nob was one of his names at home); before the war, when first becoming known as a writer, he was red-moustached, pale-complexioned, with thick brown hair and bright eyes. He was a person of immense charm and strikingly attractive, not so much for his features as for his uncanny sympathy with and marvellously quick understanding of others. Someone as normally shrewd as Bertrand Russell was overwhelmed by his first encounter with Lawrence; 'he is amazing; he sees through and through one ... He is infallible. He is like Ezekiel or some other Old Testament prophet' (Kinkead-Weekes, 190). Lawrence grew his famous red beard only in autumn 1914 and it quickly became the mark of his difference. In 1928 a vicious attack on *Lady Chatterley's Lover* referred to its author as 'this bearded satyr' (Nehls, 3.262), and the beard remains the characteristic identifying feature of Lawrence's posthumous self.

In spite of the notoriety of *Lady Chatterley's Lover*, Lawrence became really famous only after his death; and at first only briefly. The editor of the relevant *Dictionary of National Biography* supplement, J. R. H. Weaver, was squeezed rather reluctantly up to a longer word allowance in 1933 by the secretary to the Oxford University Press, who feared 'howls of execration' unless Lawrence received his due. 'I was full of doubt (and, I suppose, of prejudice—though I try not to be)', Weaver replied; 'I wondered what would be thought about him—even 20 years hence. However, a great deal is said about him now, and no doubt we ought to reflect that'. His reputation lapsed in the late 1930s: he had written too unconventionally and had made too many enemies, and numerous memoirs (mostly by women who had known him) published between 1930 and 1935 combined to make him appear an absurd rather than important figure. Penguin Books began to republish his work after the Second World War, and by the late 1950s he was widely seen as one of the great writers of the twentieth century; F. R. Leavis's *D. H. Lawrence: Novelist* (1956) had confirmed his new reputation. The prosecution of the Penguin edition of *Lady Chatterley's Lover* in 1960 led to a trial in which both academics and senior figures of the British establishment spoke on Lawrence's behalf; E. M. Forster, too, stood up for him. Films were made of his work; Jack Cardiff's *Sons and Lovers* of 1960 and Ken Russell's *Women in Love* of 1970 typified his new standing, with its use of leading contemporary actors such as Alan Bates and Glenda Jackson, and a script designed to shock and surprise; the filming of the naked wrestling of Birkin (Bates) and Gerald (Oliver Reed) was a landmark in what was publicly acceptable. Films of *The Virgin and the Gipsy* (1970) and a soft-porn version of *Lady Chatterley's Lover* (1980) confirmed, however, that it was Lawrence's standing as a supposed sexual specialist (to which he had objected in his own lifetime) which was primarily being exploited. By the mid-1970s Lawrence's reputation was in something of a decline. Feminist writing, such as Kate Millett's *Sexual Politics* (1970), denounced him for chauvinism, and while neither a modernist revolutionary like Joyce, nor—like Virginia Woolf—reacting as a woman against the social and literary world which confined her, Lawrence occupied a problematic position in the writing history of the century. He came to be unthinkingly branded both sexist and (because of his denunciations of democracy and mob-rule) fascist.

The republication of Lawrence's work in a scholarly edition by Cambridge University Press, and in particular the publication in full of his letters—one of his greatest achievements—suggest that he may be seen differently in future. He turns out to have been a writer far more concerned with the careful revision and linguistic precision of his work than his early reputation as an uneducated, spontaneous, and unthinking genius suggested; he was ahead of his time in many of his attitudes to the individual and society; he had an extraordinary range as a writer in many genres (novels, stories, travel books, poems, plays, and essays); he was also a writer who explored an extremely wide range of subjects, in particular the need for a language of relationship which involves the experience of the body, rather than any idea of love. He was precise about what he saw as the malign influence of Freud, never allied himself with the excesses of Nietzsche, and was strikingly modern in his expression of a need to be ecologically aware. He never believed in right-wing governments and hated the fascism he saw in the early and middle twenties in Italy and Germany, though he always believed in human beings' need for government and authority; his writing certainly concentrated on female sexuality, but that was his particular, and in his period a strikingly original, focus. What the feminism of the 1970s saw as an effort at phallic supremacy in his writing can also be seen as a strikingly 'female' account of sexuality, with its constant stress on the feelings rather than on observed sexual activity, and on intimacy and necessary opposition rather than on the superiority of one gender over the other. He was a writer who constantly struggled to find and to articulate the experience, not of a body or mind or spirit, but of the whole person. This was what he wrote about most magically and most tellingly, and what he attempted to remain true to in his own life. The last page of his last book, *Apocalypse*, written when he was confronting death, ended: 'the magnificent here and now of life in the flesh is ours, and ours alone, and ours only for a time. We ought to dance with rapture that we should be alive and in the flesh' (p. 149).   JOHN WORTHEN

Sources *The Cambridge edition of the letters of D. H. Lawrence*, ed. J. T. Boulton and others, 8 vols. (1979–2000) · Introduction, D. H. Lawrence, *Sons and lovers*, ed. H. Baron and C. Baron (1992) · Introduction, D. H. Lawrence, *Women in love*, ed. D. Farmer, L. Vasey, and J. Worthen (1987) · Introduction, D. H. Lawrence, *Aaron's rod*, ed. M. Kalnins (1988) · Introduction, D. H. Lawrence, *Kangaroo*, ed. B. Steele (1994) · D. H. Lawrence, *Phoenix* (1936) · J. Worthen, *The early years, 1885–1912* (1991), vol. 1 of *The Cambridge biography: D. H. Lawrence, 1885–1930*, ed. D. Ellis, M. Kinkead-Weekes, and J. Worthen (1991–8) · M. Kinkead-Weekes, *Triumph to exile, 1912–1922* (1996), vol. 2 of *The Cambridge biography: D. H. Lawrence, 1885–1930*, ed. D. Ellis, M. Kinkead-Weekes, and J. Worthen (1991–8) · D. Ellis, *Dying game, 1922–1930* (1998), vol. 3 of *The Cambridge biography: D. H. Lawrence, 1885–1930*, ed. D. Ellis, M. Kinkead-Weekes, and J. Worthen (1991–8) · E. Nehls, ed., *D. H. Lawrence: a composite biography*, 3 vols. (1957–9) · F. W. Roberts, *A bibliography of D. H. Lawrence*, rev. 2nd edn (1981) · private information (2004) · D. Brett, *Lawrence and Brett: a friendship*, ed. J. Manchester, rev. 2nd edn (1974) · E. Brewster and A. Brewster, *D. H. Lawrence: reminiscences and correspondence* (1934) · W. Bynner, *Journey with genius: recollections and reflections concerning the D. H. Lawrences* (1951) · C. Carswell, *The savage pilgrimage* (1932) · E. T. [J. Chambers], *D. H. Lawrence: a personal record* (1935) · H. Corke, *D. H. Lawrence: the Croydon years* (1965) · M. Green, *The von Richthofen sisters: the triumphant and tragic modes of love* (1974) · F. Lawrence, *Not I, but the wind* (1934) · F. Lawrence, *The memoirs and correspondence*, ed. E. W. Tedlock, American edn (1964) · M. Luhan, *Lorenzo in Taos* (1933) · H. T. Moore, *The priest of love: a life of D. H. Lawrence* (1974) · J. M. Murry, *Reminiscences of D. H. Lawrence* (1933) · R. Parmenter, *Lawrence in Oaxaca: a quest for the novelist in Mexico* (1984) · P. Preston, *A D. H. Lawrence chronology* (1994) · K. Sagar, *D. H. Lawrence: a calendar of his works* (1979) · R. Spencer, *D. H. Lawrence country* (1980) · J. Worthen, *D. H. Lawrence: a literary life* (1989)

Archives Bucknell University Library, Lewisburg, Pennsylvania, corresp., notebooks, and MSS · Col. U., Rare Book and Manuscript Library, corresp. and literary MSS · Harvard U., Houghton L., corresp. and literary MSS · Nottingham Central Library, literary MSS, papers, and corresp. · Notts. Arch., corresp. · Ransom HRC, corresp. and papers · Stanford University, California, corresp., literary MSS, and papers · U. Cal., Berkeley, corresp., literary MSS, and papers · U. Cal., Los Angeles, papers · U. Nott. L., literary MSS, corresp., and papers · University of New Mexico Library, literary MSS and papers · Yale U., Beinecke L., corresp., literary MSS, and notebooks · University of Cincinnati Libraries, papers | BL, corresp. with Society of Authors · BL, letters to S. S. Koteliansky · Harvard U., Houghton L., corresp. with A. Lowell · Iowa State Education Association · King's AC Cam., letters to E. M. Forster · Morgan L. · NYPL, Berg collection · Philip H. & S. W. Rosenbach Foundation · Princeton University Library, Dora Marsden Collection, corresp. · Princeton University Library, Sylvia Beach Papers, corresp. · Tate collection, letters to A. Brackenbury · U. Birm., letters to F. Brett Young and J. Brett Young · U. Lpool, letters to B. Jennings and MSS · U. Nott. L., letters from him and F. Lawrence to C. Carswell · University of Toronto Library

Likenesses photograph, 1906, U. Nott. · W. G. Parker, photograph, 1913, U. Nott. · Bassano & Vandyk, photograph, 1915, NPG · J. Juta, oils, 1920, NPG; charcoal study, 1920, U. Texas · M. Hubrecht, chalk drawing, *c.*1920–1921, NPG · E. Guardia, photograph, 1920–29 (copy by P. A. Juley), NPG [*see illus.*] · K. Götzsche, oils, 1923, Ransom HRC · N. Murray, silver print, 1923, NPG · E. Weston, photograph, 1924, Yale U., Beinecke L. · D. Brett, oils, 1925, NPG · D. Brett, oils, 1925, Ransom HRC · E. Guardia, photograph, 1929, U. Nott. · K. Merrild, oils (posthumous?), Philadelphia Museum of Art

Wealth at death £2438 16s. 5d.: administration, 5 June 1930, *CGPLA Eng. & Wales*

Lawrence, Dorothy (1860–1933). *See under* Lawrence, Penelope (1856–1932).

Lawrence, Dorothy (*b.* 1896), sexual impostor and soldier, was born on 4 October 1896 at Polesworth, Warwickshire, the second daughter of Thomas Hartshorn Lawrence, a drainage contractor, and his wife, Mary Jane Beddall. Nothing is known of her childhood.

In 1914, at the start of the First World War, Lawrence was living in Paris. She contacted several British newspapers, offering to work as a war correspondent from the front line in France, but all the editors she contacted refused to employ a woman to cover such dangerous work. The military veto on civilians at the front line made it almost impossible to get even male reporters to the front, although one editor did respond with the comment, 'Of course if you could get to the front' (Lawrence, 41).

Lawrence later recorded her thoughts at this time in her autobiography: 'I'll see what an ordinary English girl, without credentials or money can accomplish' (Lawrence, 41–2). After being turned down several times in her attempt to get to the front, including a request for a first-

Dorothy Lawrence (b. 1896), by unknown photographer, 1915

aid posting by the British War Office, she finally joined the voluntary aid detachment. However, no one would send her anywhere because she was too young, so she reverted to journalism. She befriended two English soldiers in a Parisian café, and they agreed to provide her with a uniform which they smuggled into her flat in small parcels under the guise of washing. Lawrence bound her chest, and padded her back with sacking and cotton, struggling with her unfamiliarity with masculine clothing. Her friends taught her to drill and march. She managed to persuade two Scottish military policemen to cut her hair and then dyed her skin using a diluted furniture polish to give it a bronzed hue. After obtaining identification as Private Denis Smith of the 1st Leicestershire regiment, and with a real identification disc and a forged pass, which she wrote herself, and a safe-conduct pass from the mayor, she headed for the front lines. She cycled towards Bethune, and eventually arrived in Albert.

A Lancashire coalminer named Tom Dunn befriended Lawrence and found her a place in the British expeditionary force tunnelling company, a mine-laying company within 400 yards of the front line, where she was constantly under fire. He found her an abandoned cottage in Senlis Forest to live in, and she returned to it each night after laying mines by day. After working hard at her job and harder at hiding her gender, she was assaulted by the daily hardships of a front-line soldier. Suffering from chills and rheumatism, she also became increasingly aware of the physical danger she was in. Lawrence worried about what would happen to the men who had helped her if she were wounded and her gender discovered. After ten days the worry and discomfort became too much and she requested an interview with her commanding sergeant. After revealing her true gender to him, she was hauled from the trench and placed under military

arrest. She escaped her arresting officers, but shortly afterwards gave herself up.

Dorothy Lawrence was taken to the British expeditionary force headquarters and interrogated as a possible spy and was made a prisoner of war. She explained that the reason for her masquerade was to obtain a byline as a journalist. Since the army did not know what to do with her she was taken cross-country on a horse to Calais. There, her interrogation occupied the time of six generals and approximately twenty other officers, and her ignorance about the term 'camp follower' caused problems for her. Lawrence recalled later, 'We talked steadily at cross purposes. On my side I had not been informed what the term meant, and on their side they continued unaware that I remained ignorant! So I often appeared to be telling lies' (Lawrence, 161).

After her interrogation Lawrence was taken back to the Third Army headquarters in St Omer, where she was re-examined. She was thrown into a guard room policed by eight soldiers who were under strict instructions to refuse her all visitors. The army was embarrassed because of the serious breach in its security system and because of growing fears about women taking on male roles during the war. She was then detained in the Convent de Bon Pasteur, which kept her for two weeks until she agreed to swear an affidavit promising that she would not write for the newspapers and reveal to the British public how she had fooled the British army. Escorted back to Boulogne, she was then sent back to England.

In Folkestone, Dorothy Lawrence was made to promise not to divulge anything of her experiences until she received permission. This completely destroyed her original purpose of writing articles regarding the front lines: 'In making that promise I sacrificed the chance of earning by newspaper articles written on this escapade, as a girl compelled to earn her livelihood' (Lawrence, 189). Upon arrival in London she was taken to Scotland Yard but was released on the proviso she could guarantee her address for ten days. Unable, apparently, to do so, she was released onto the Embankment with a guinea-pig as a gift of covenant under her arm, and with nowhere to go.

Lawrence published her account of her experiences in 1919. Nothing more is known of the remainder of her life.   EMMA MILLIKEN

Sources D. Lawrence, *Sapper Dorothy Lawrence: the only English woman soldier, late royal engineers, 51st division, 179th tunnelling company, BEF* (1919) • J. Wheelwright, *Amazons and military maids* (1989) • b. cert. • census returns, 1881, 1901

Likenesses photograph, 1915, repro. in Wheelwright, *Amazons and military maids* [*see illus.*] • four photographs, repro. in Lawrence, *Sapper Dorothy Lawrence* • photograph, BL

Lawrence, Edith (1890–1973). *See under* Flight, (Walter) Claude (1881–1955).

Lawrence [Laurence], **Edward** (d. 1695), ejected minister and religious writer, was born in Moston in Hawkstone, Shropshire, the son of William Laurence of Shrewsbury and his wife (d. 1653); although Edmund Calamy gives 1623 as his date of birth his matriculation record suggests 1627/8. Having attended Whitchurch School, Shropshire, he was admitted as a sizar to Magdalene College, Cambridge, on 8 June 1645, aged seventeen. He graduated BA early in 1648. On 11 September that year he became vicar of Baschurch, Shropshire, having been ordained by the fourth Shropshire presbyterian classis, centred on Whitchurch. He probably married about the same time. With his wife, Deborah, he had at least nine children, of whom the eldest, Deborah, was baptized at Baschurch on 9 December 1649.

For most of his ministry there Lawrence was a member of the second Shropshire presbyterian classis. He proceeded MA in 1654. In 1655 commissioners reporting on the provision of preaching in his county gave him their approval. Two years later he was probably among the Shropshire ministers who attempted to practise the ministerial strategies outlined in Richard Baxter's *The Reformed Pastor* (1656). On 20 January 1657 he wrote to Baxter thanking him for his publications but questioning the latter's affirmation that 'noe unregenerate men are truly & really … in the covenant of grace' (Keeble and Nuttall, no. 352, 1.241); Baxter responded three days later offering further explanation.

In November 1661 Lawrence's friend Philip Henry noted that he was one of ten lecturers present at a lecture at Wem, Shropshire, and that he delivered an address on Psalm 62: 5, 'My soul, wait thou only upon God; for my expectation is from him'. His *Christ's Power over Bodily Diseases* (1662), based on several sermons on Matthew 8: 5–15, appeared with a recommendatory preface by Baxter dated 1 August 1661. By 26 November 1662, when his successor was installed, Lawrence had been ejected from his living. He and his family remained in the parish, lodging with a gentleman, until March 1666 when the provisions of the Five Mile Act forced him to move away. He settled in the village of Tilstock in Whitchurch parish, where he had many friends.

In February 1668 Lawrence and Henry were invited to Betley, Staffordshire, where they preached in the church. This event was reported, with exaggerations, in the House of Commons. The following year an episcopal survey of nonconformists in Shropshire discovered a congregation of eighty persons at Whitchurch, ministered to by seven ejected ministers, including Lawrence and Henry. While he was preaching one Sunday afternoon in a private house in May 1670, Lawrence was arrested by the vicar, Dr Fowler, under the terms of the second Conventicle Act, and prosecuted. His conviction led to the confiscation of his goods and then to a lengthy and unsuccessful lawsuit for their recovery. As a consequence, in May 1671 Lawrence moved to London.

On 8 May 1672 Lawrence, then living in Spitalfields, was licensed as a presbyterian minister under the declaration of indulgence. He became pastor of a congregation meeting near the Royal Exchange and continued to preach there and elsewhere, despite fines. His 'There is no transubstantiation in the Lord's Supper' was published as sermon 21 of Nathaniel Vincent's *The Morning Exercise Against Popery* (1675), while his *Parents' Groans over their Wicked Children* (1681) is composed of sermons on Proverbs 17: 25.

In the dedication, addressed to his children Deborah, Samuel, Edward, John, Thomas, Elizabeth, Mary, Benjamin, and Nathaniel, he commented bitterly that 'I had never been the Author of a Book of this title, had not two of you, but especially one, made me the Father of fools'. He was living in Moorfields when on 18 January 1685 he was bound over at Middlesex assizes for attending a conventicle. After the Act of Toleration of 1689 Lawrence was licensed as a preacher at his house in Moorfields. He died there in November 1695. His funeral sermon was preached by Nathaniel Vincent, whose *The Perfect Man Described* (1696) is an important source for Lawrence's life. Lawrence had been troubled by the divisions in the church, and Vincent considered him 'for no party, very moderate towards all' (p. 19). Baxter, who admired this moderation, called Lawrence 'solid, calm, peaceable and godly man and a good Preacher' (*Reliquiae Baxterianae*, 3.94). Lawrence's son Nathaniel (1670–1708) also became a nonconformist minister, serving in Banbury.

C. D. GILBERT

Sources *Diaries and letters of Philip Henry*, ed. M. H. Lee (1882) · *Calamy rev.* · B. Coulton, 'The fourth Shropshire presbyterian classis, 1647–62', *Shropshire History and Archaeology*, 73 (1998), 33–43 · N. Vincent, *The perfect man described* (1696) · *IGI* · Venn, *Alum. Cant.* · *Reliquiae Baxterianae, or, Mr Richard Baxter's narrative of the most memorable passages of his life and times*, ed. M. Sylvester, 1 vol. in 3 pts (1696) · *Calendar of the correspondence of Richard Baxter*, ed. N. H. Keeble and G. F. Nuttall, 2 vols. (1991) · E. Calamy, *A continuation of the account of the ministers … who were ejected and silenced after the Restoration in 1660*, 2 vols. (1727), vol. 2, pp. 557, 722 · *JHC*, 9 (1667–87), 61

Lawrence, Emmeline Pethick-, Lady Pethick-Lawrence (1867–1954), suffragette, was born on 21 October 1867 in Clifton, Bristol, the second and eldest surviving child in the family of thirteen children (five of whom died in infancy) of Henry Pethick, a nonconformist businessman of Cornish farming stock, and his wife, whose maiden name was Collen, and to whom he was happily married. Emmeline Pethick's early years in Clifton and at the boarding-school in Devizes which she briefly attended from the age of eight were not happy—beset as she was by fear of the unknown, ignorance about sexuality, remorse at committing unintended solecisms, and resentment at perceived injustice. In later life she had no children of her own, yet her lifelong instinctive sympathy with children was striking, and a misunderstood childhood was one experience she shared with her future husband. She portrayed herself later as a truthful and rational child, but to adults she must have seemed wilful and stubborn. Things improved with the family's move to Weston-super-Mare, where she attended a day school and at fifteen a nearby finishing school, and her relationship with her father burgeoned, the first of her three close father–daughter relationships with men. He was courageous but also good fun, and his staunch defence of liberty and justice was a lifelong influence. Many years later she recalled her pride when he defended the Salvation Army against local hooligans: 'in my dumb, childish fashion I simply worshipped him for it, and it forged our relationship for ever' (*Votes for Women*, 2 May 1913, 439). Her Pethick relations remained

Emmeline Pethick-Lawrence, Lady Pethick-Lawrence (1867–1954), by Bassano, 1910

central to Emmeline Pethick's social life, but her mother, more conventional in her views, was also affectionately recalled.

Shy, immature, and not pretty, Emmeline Pethick now experienced the twin pressures of socialism and a yearning for independence, and diverged from what was then the young woman's conventional course of marriage and motherhood. Her father eventually shed his Methodism and drifted through other Christian allegiances into unbelief, but it was through going to the Methodist West London Mission in 1890 that Emmeline Pethick realized her potential. Walter Besant's *The Children of Gibeon* (1886) had inspired her to mix with other social classes in the big city, and here was her opportunity. While philanthropy for women was then often a substitute for a career, it could also sometimes offer an escape from convention—in her case from 'the petty life of a second-rate seaside resort' (Pethick-Lawrence, 95). She delivered her first public speech in a large hall at the mission's anniversary meeting on 21 October 1891. At the mission she met Mary Neal, and in jointly running its working girls' club they discovered their complementary qualities, from which stemmed a lifelong friendship. In 1895 she and Mary Neal planned to leave the mission to found the Espérance Working Girls' Club. Influenced by William Morris, Edward Carpenter, and Walt Whitman, Emmeline Pethick's evangelical background was waning concurrently with the advance of her social concern. But her loss of faith, unlike her father's, was masked through the

transfer of her religious emotions to other causes, and during the transition she needed help from her second father–daughter relationship, for 'the strongest influence upon the first half of my life' (ibid., 97) was the evangelical Christian socialist Mark Guy Pearse. Reluctant at first, he eventually gave full backing to her breakaway movement. The club was reinforced in 1897 by the Maison Espérance, a co-operative dressmaking business set up in Wigmore Street, and in 1900 by a hostel at Littlehampton for working girls' holidays.

Emmeline Pethick was active in the late 1890s at Percy Alden's Mansfield House settlement in Canning Town, and there she met Frederick Lawrence [*see* Lawrence, Frederick William Pethick- (1871–1961)]. The son of Alfred Lawrence, carpenter and later owner of a building firm, he was living at the settlement as a prospective Liberal Unionist MP. In a highly emotional courtship, replete with exchanges of flowery and high-toned letters, Emmeline Pethick edged him away from Unionism towards the more internationalist, ethical, and egalitarian outlook to be found among Liberals, and thereby built up the third among her father–daughter relationships. They married at the Town Hall, Canning Town, on 2 October 1901. It was the start of an unusual lifelong partnership in which each annexed the surname of the other, while each retained separate bank accounts and considerable autonomy within a marriage whose harmony was much advertised and celebrated. Commemorative social functions and exchanges of curiously mannered and formal correspondence henceforth annually recalled the key moments of their courtship.

At first their life was taken up with several causes, including Chinese labour and working-class representation in parliament, but in 1906 James Keir Hardie introduced Emmeline Pethick-Lawrence to the Pankhursts. There followed what she recalled as 'a very extraordinary sequence of incidents' whereby a person 'not of a revolutionary temperament, was drawn into a revolutionary movement' (Pethick-Lawrence, 148). Annie Kenney's artless entreaties drew her into becoming treasurer to the Women's Social and Political Union (WSPU), and with her husband's support she became central to the women's suffrage movement's militant wing. She brought three major skills to it. Her vague but elevated and enthusiastic eloquence, enhanced in timing and attire by a sense of drama—even of melodrama—inspired many. Her shrewd eye for dramatic propaganda, allied with uncritical acceptance of Christabel Pankhurst's ruthlessly sectarian strategic sense, greatly boosted the union's funds, to which she and her husband alone contributed more than £6000. And, as she later recalled, 'it became my business to give their genius a solid foundation' (ibid., 152); the Pethick-Lawrences' organizational skills provided offices and staff, as well as the mass-circulation periodical *Votes for Women*, which they co-edited. They worked informally but closely with Christabel Pankhurst until 1912, the contrasting temperaments of the trio providing firm, imaginative, and efficient leadership. Nor did Emmeline Pethick-Lawrence shrink from personal sacrifice at more than one level. In 1906 when she was first imprisoned for militancy her claustrophobia produced breakdown and she capitulated. But by braving five further imprisonments she thereafter led by example, also enduring forcefeeding at Holloway gaol on one occasion in June 1912. When suffragette violence escalated in 1912, the Pethick-Lawrences and Mrs Pankhurst were tried for conspiracy, and after their conviction the courts sequestered the contents of the Pethick-Lawrences' country home.

There had always been a latent divergence between the charismatic loner Emmeline Pankhurst and the Pethick-Lawrences as brilliant organizers. When Christabel Pankhurst changed horses and backed her mother, the divergence opened out. In a ruthless break with the past, the two Pankhursts in 1912 launched a more extreme form of militancy, and ousted the Pethick-Lawrences from the WSPU. Emmeline Pethick-Lawrence later realized that her husband's wealth, hitherto an asset to the union, might at that point have become a liability, but she rightly questioned Pankhurstian tactics. Privately bitter and shocked at how they had been treated, the Pethick-Lawrences behaved during this crisis with some dignity, and were keen to avoid dividing the movement, but in later life they were more sympathetic to Sylvia Pankhurst than to her mother and elder sister. In 1913–14 they continued to edit *Votes for Women*, and gradually formed a group of moderate militants round it: the Votes for Women Fellowship. Emmeline Pethick-Lawrence's moralistic and libertarian mentors, from Mazzini to her father, were at one with Olive Schreiner (another major influence upon her at this time) in envisaging freedom as a cause which could unite both sexes. The fellowship in 1914 evolved into a new structure, the United Suffragists, which she saw as a vehicle of 'militancy without violence' (*Votes for Women*, 7 Feb 1913, 273), a bridge between militants and non-militants, and between men and women.

The First World War introduced violence of quite another order, and for Emmeline Pethick-Lawrence, as for many pre-war feminists, the promotion of international peace and of rights for women abroad seemed linked causes that flowed naturally out of British suffragism. Given her worldwide travels, her opposition to the Second South African War, and her Liberal nonconformist background, she naturally sought to bring about the worldwide family of men and women that had long been present within her mind, and from 1915 until 1922 was treasurer of the Women's International League for Peace and Freedom. For her the war was 'the final demonstration of the unfitness of men to have the whole control of the human family in their hands' (*Votes for Women*, 16 Oct 1914, 21). She participated in 1915 in the international women's peace conference at The Hague, and deplored the terms of the Versailles peace settlement. Here, in her view, lay the roots of the Second World War: on 14 October 1939 she told Sylvia Pankhurst that Britain's earlier injustice towards Germany made it impossible for her to support another war (Sylvia Pankhurst collection, Institute of Social History, Amsterdam).

Emmeline Pethick-Lawrence never retreated from her feminist ideals, but her public career suffered almost immediately from the way political party cut across interwar feminist loyalties. In 1918 she stood as Labour candidate for Rusholme, championing nationalization, a capital levy, equal pay, and an equal moral standard, but she came bottom of the poll with only a sixth of the votes cast. She publicly campaigned against black-and-tan British policy in Ireland, and from 1926 to 1935 was president of the Women's Freedom League. She backed the Open Door Council and the Six Point Group, fiercely feminist bodies, but within the National Union of Societies for Equal Citizenship she tried in the mid-1920s to straddle the divide between 'old' (libertarian) and 'new' (interventionist) feminists, and more than once publicly asserted the need for economic equality between the sexes.

As her husband's inter-war political career advanced, however, Emmeline Pethick-Lawrence's public career went into decline. She accompanied him on overseas tours, backed him in his election campaigns, and ran the Surrey homes and gardens that they both loved so much. Nobody reading the letters they exchanged when parted during his cabinet mission to India in 1946 will doubt the intensity of their affection. But this was no Webb or even Cole partnership: politics were not central to Emmeline's life, she had her own circle of friends, and she put more effort into gardening than into public commitments, paradoxically displaying many of the traits associated with the unemancipated woman. Though four years older than her husband, she elicited from him the same paternal and chivalrous response that she had evoked in her father and Pearse. Moody, impulsive, self-indulgent, and frequently taking to her bed, she was in later life careless with money, untidy, and absent-minded. Yet she could deploy her charm, in alliance with her wealth and classless outlook, to win devotion from a semi-commune of servants and secretaries: substitute children who benefited socially and educationally thereby. Her public life contracted further after the 1930s because of growing deafness, her unconcealed deaf-aid constituting more of a distraction for her audiences than a help. Prolonged disability and ultimately demoralizing illness preceded her death at home at Fourways, Gomshall, Surrey, on 11 March 1954.

It is for her central role in the militant suffrage movement that Emmeline Pethick-Lawrence is remembered. Her autobiographical *My Part in a Changing World* (1938), which she enjoyed writing, is dedicated to her husband, 'my unchanging comrade and my best friend'. It is reticent about her married life, but valuably documents in its first eight chapters the influences moulding her life as child and young woman. Appropriately it devotes its largest section, eleven chapters, to the WSPU—and only two jejune chapters to the years after 1914. Though impressively fair-minded and at times perceptive, her account of the suffragettes is essentially an uncritical and largely impersonal chronology. Nowhere did she convincingly justify the contradiction between her humanitarian and democratic instincts on the one hand, and her promotion of violent tactics and authoritarian suffrage structures on the other.

Her prose and oratory could be embarrassingly sentimental and stagey; as she once told a young admirer, 'my dear, it doesn't matter a bit as long as you *feel* what you're saying' (Lutyens). Virginia Woolf cast a cold eye over the performance at a suffrage rally in 1918: 'I watched Mrs Pethick Lawrence [*sic*] rising & falling on her toes, as if half her legs were made of rubber, throwing out her arms, opening her hands, & thought very badly of this form of art' (*Diary*, 125).

Emmeline Pethick-Lawrence's personal contribution to winning the vote for women, if she had focused on describing it, would have been difficult to disentangle from that of her husband. The Pethick-Lawrences' wealth, their courage, their vague and highly emotional idealism, and the example they set as a married couple who combined liberty with harmony—all helped to ward off any British feminist tendency towards sex war, and made a national movement out of what might otherwise have remained a Labour Party sect. In later life her career was eclipsed and in some ways cramped by that of her husband, as well as by disability, and the *Dictionary of National Biography* felt no need to commemorate her in its volume for the 1950s. The joint Pethick-Lawrence archive was once very large, but wartime salvage and deliberate destruction after her death impoverished it. None the less, ample materials exist for the full-blown biography that would be fully justified, but remains as yet unwritten.

BRIAN HARRISON

Sources E. Pethick-Lawrence, *My part in a changing world* (1938) · B. Harrison, 'The politics of a marriage: Emmeline and Fred Pethick-Lawrence', *Prudent revolutionaries: portraits of British feminists between the wars* (1987), 242–72 · *Votes for Women* (7 Feb 1913) · *Votes for Women* (2 May 1913) · *Votes for Women* (16 Oct 1914) · *The diary of Virginia Woolf*, ed. A. O. Bell and A. McNeillie, 1 (1977) · Internationaal Instituut voor Sociale Geschiedenis, Amsterdam, Sylvia Pankhurst collection · N. Lutyens, interview with B. Harrison, 28 March 1975, Women's Library, London
Archives Internationaal Instituut voor Sociale Geschiedenis, Amsterdam, letters to Sylvia Pankhurst · Trinity Cam., corresp. with her husband | FILM BFI NFTVA, news footage
Likenesses Bassano, photograph, 1910, NPG [*see illus.*] · Mrs A. Broom, group photograph, 1910, NPG; *see illus. in* Davison, Emily Wilding (1872–1913) · J. Baker, double portrait, oils (posthumous; with Lord Pethick-Lawrence), Peaslake Village Hall, Surrey · photographs, Women's Library, London
Wealth at death £4208 4s. 6d.: probate, 1954, *CGPLA Eng. & Wales*

Lawrence, Esther Ella (1862–1944), educationist, was born in 1862 in New York, the second daughter and third of the nine children of John M. Lawrence (*b. c.*1827), a merchant, and his wife, Emily (*b. c.*1833). Her father was English and her mother came from Spanish Town, Jamaica. The family moved from New York to London while Esther was a child and settled at 37 Belsize Lane, St John's Wood. From 1878 to 1880 she attended South Hampstead high school, which was strongly supported by the Jewish community to which she belonged. In 1880 she entered Bedford College, London, at the beginning of the Michaelmas term and remained for two terms, studying mathematics, English literature, French, German, Latin, and botany. Esther Lawrence continued her studies in 1881 at the Tavistock Place Training College, opened under the auspices of the Froebel Society in 1879, where she trained as a kindergarten teacher and gained a second-class certificate in 1883. The principal at this point in the college's short-lived history was Penelope Lawrence, who became headmistress of Roedean School in 1885. After completing her studies Esther opened a kindergarten in Gower Street, London. In 1884 she was invited to take charge of the preparatory department of the Chiswick high school by the headmistress, Alice Woods, who was herself a keen Froebelian; this collaboration initiated a friendship which lasted until Woods's death in 1941.

Esther Lawrence left Chiswick high school in 1893 to take up the post of kindergarten mistress of the kindergarten and transition classes held at Glazbury Road, West Kensington, in conjunction with the Froebel Training School of Primary Instruction run by Emilie Michaelis in Norland Place, Notting Hill. This school became the Froebel Educational Institute in 1894 and the classes formed the Colet Gardens demonstration school, moving to a wing of the new institute buildings in 1895. The institute was founded after extensive fund-raising efforts by Julia Salis Schwabe, who persuaded Sir William Mather to become chairman with Claude Goldsmid Montefiore as the first treasurer. The link between these figures was the Froebel Society and, in the case of Esther Lawrence and Claude Montefiore, their shared adherence to the liberal wing of British Judaism. Froebel's spiritual view of education and his belief in the unity of God, man, and the natural world held a particular appeal for her.

After serving for four years as head of the demonstration school Esther Lawrence resigned and went to visit Adele du Portugall, head of the Froebel Institute in Naples. When she returned to England in 1899 she was appointed mistress of method in the institute. On the retirement of Emilie Michaelis in 1901, Esther succeeded her as principal and remained in this post until her own retirement thirty years later in 1931. During this long period of office the institute underwent great change, moving from the increasingly cramped Talgarth Road site to the spacious grounds at Grove House, Roehampton, where it developed as a residential college and the training was extended to three years.

Esther Lawrence set out her educational ideas in a number of articles, notably 'The application of Froebel's principles' (*Child Life*, 6/23, 1904, 136–41) and 'The training of Froebelian teachers' (*Child Life*, 7/27, 1905, 128–37), and in her powerful address to the Froebel Society in 1914, 'Nations and nurseries' (*Child Life*, 16/91, suppl., 1914, 1–16). She made her own contribution to Froebelian practice in *The Circular Tablet: a Connecting Link in the Froebel Series of Gifts* (1896). Her cousin Samuel Alexander was reported to be so impressed with the book's mathematical conceptions that he read part of it to his philosophy class at Manchester University (Jebb, 2). In her presidential address to the Froebel Society in 1926, 'The education of the spirit', she argued that

A child considers that he is the centre of the universe, and so, indeed, he is. From the place where he stands in time and space he has the power, crude and undeveloped, of viewing the whole of life … We often say, 'I must put that child in his place,' meaning that we must suppress him. But if we put him *properly in*, or into, his place, we should make him feel the importance and the responsibility of the place which is actually his, and no other's. (*Child Life*, 1927, 49)

Her affection for and friendship with children was described as the key to much of her life: 'there was a natural affinity between them, and intuitive understanding, a close sympathy with the mistakes, experiments and efforts of immaturity, a secret bond with the rebel' (*The Link*, 1945, 13).

As a member and later president of the Froebel Society, Esther Lawrence sought to make a Froebelian education available to all children. Hitherto kindergarten education had been the province of the middle class but she was deeply concerned for slum children whose squalid lives held little prospect of joy, with a stunted capacity for physical, creative, and intellectual growth. She was responsible for opening nursery schools in two of the most deprived areas of London, the Michaelis Free Kindergarten in Notting Dale (1908) and the Somers Town nursery school, Crowndale Road, St Pancras (1910). Both schools were supported by students of the Froebel Institute and the Michaelis Guild and, as well as education, offered health care and activities for parents. Lawrence encouraged mothers in these areas of London, many of them initially unwilling and suspicious, to send their children to the schools. They and others like them in London and Edinburgh, 'were the first example of separate free nursery schools in Britain' (Whitbread, 56).

Esther Lawrence gave many gifts to the Froebel Educational Institute over the years, most notably the Lawrence family's country home, Hill House, at Inworth, Kelvedon, Essex, given in trust to the Froebel Institute in 1944 for educational or social welfare use. The house was subsequently administered by the Save the Children Fund, in which she had been interested since its foundation in 1919. The Esther Lawrence Association, originally formed in 1939 to manage the assets of Somers Town nursery school during its evacuation, and the Esther Lawrence Research Fellowship Fund, established in 1948, provided a continuing focus for the work which she held to be so important.

A wealth of reminiscences attest Esther Lawrence's inspiration of a wide range of people—colleagues, students, parents, and the children to whom she dedicated her life's work. On her retirement from the Froebel Educational Institute in 1931 Michael Sadler, a colleague and friend of many years, and Maude Royden were among those who paid tribute to her work. To mark her retirement the Lawrence scholarship was established in 1932. After her death students who had studied at Froebel during her long principalship, wrote of her spiritual as well as intellectual vision for the college, and of her power to draw out the best in those around her (*The Link*, 1945, 20–21). She died, unmarried, on 23 July 1944 at 43 Park Road, Radlett, Aldenham, Hertfordshire, after a short illness.

JANE READ

Sources E. M. Jebb, 'Esther E. Lawrence, 1862–1944', *National Froebel Foundation Bulletin* (Sept 1944) · *The Link* (1945) [Lawrence memorial number] · University of Surrey, Roehampton, London, Froebel College, Froebel Educational Institute archives · University of Surrey, Roehampton, London, Froebel archive for childhood studies, Lawrence MSS · census returns, 1881, 1901 · d. cert. · *The Link* (1910–44) [annual letters of E. E. Lawrence] · University of Surrey, Roehampton, London, Froebel College, National Froebel Foundation archives · N. Whitbread, *The evolution of the nursery-infant school* (1972) · E. M. Lawrence, ed., *Friedrich Froebel and English education* (1952)

Archives University of Surrey, Roehampton, London, Froebel Institute, Froebel archive for childhood studies, MSS | University of Surrey, Roehampton, London, Froebel Institute, National Froebel Foundation archives, Froebel Society minute books · University of Surrey, Roehampton, London, Froebel Institute, Froebel Educational Institute archives

Likenesses G. Kelly, oils, Froebel College, London

Wealth at death £146,189 9s. 10d.: probate, 3 May 1945, *CGPLA Eng. & Wales*

Lawrence, Frederick (1821–1867), barrister and journalist, was born at Bisham, Berkshire, the eldest son of John Lawrence, a substantial farmer at Bisham, and his wife, Mary, daughter of John Jennings of Windsor. After education in a private school at St John's Wood, London, he found employment with Simpkin and Marshall, publishers. In December 1846 he entered the printed book department of the British Museum where he worked on the compilation of the general catalogue, remaining there until May 1849, when he resigned in order to qualify for the bar. He was called at the Middle Temple on 23 November 1849, joined the Oxford circuit, and attended the Berkshire sessions, but subsequently practised with some success at the Middlesex sessions and the Old Bailey. Lawrence frequently contributed to the periodical press, especially to the *Weekly Dispatch* and *Sharpe's London Journal*, to the last of which he contributed a series of articles on 'literary impostures' and on eminent English authors. In 1841 he edited three numbers of *The Iris, a Journal of Literature and Science*. He also edited the *Lawyers Companion* from 1864 to 1868 and published at least two other legal works. His most significant publication was *The Life of Henry Fielding* (1855).

Social and political questions always interested Lawrence, and he acted as chairman of the Garibaldian Committee. While at Boulogne in the autumn of 1867 he was attacked by dropsy, which compelled him to return to London, and on 25 October 1867 he died suddenly at his chambers, 1 Essex Court, Temple. He was buried at Kensal Green cemetery. He was unmarried.

W. P. COURTNEY, rev. ERIC METCALFE

Sources *Law Times* (16 Nov 1867), 46 · R. Cotwan, *Memories of the British Museum* (1872), 363 · O. Hamst, *Anonymous literature*, 205 · S. Halkett and J. Laing, *A dictionary of the anonymous and pseudonymous literature of Great Britain*, 4 vols. (1882–8), vol. 1, p. 548; vol. 2, p. 1251 · *CGPLA Eng. & Wales* (1867)

Wealth at death under £3000: administration, 4 Dec 1867, *CGPLA Eng. & Wales*

Lawrence, Frederick William Pethick-, Baron Pethick-Lawrence (1871–1961), politician, was born on 28 December 1871 in London, the youngest in the family of two boys and three girls of Alfred Lawrence, carpenter and later

Frederick William Pethick-Lawrence, Baron Pethick-Lawrence (1871–1961), by Karl Pollak, c.1948

owner of a building firm, and his wife, Mary Elizabeth, daughter of Henry Ridge of Upper Clapton, Middlesex. His father died when he was three. Frederick Lawrence was a restless, difficult child who in his own words 'objected to the whole status of childhood' (Pethick-Lawrence, 15). He attended a day school in London, then at eleven boarded at Wixenford, a prep school in Wokingham, moving on in 1885 to Eton College, where he stayed until 1891. There he was bullied, bored with the classics, and 'remained … something of an outsider and a critic' (ibid., 22).

Early career From his youngest days, however, Lawrence had been fond of figures and games, and for much of his life was keen on and skilled at tennis and billiards. Happy at last at Trinity College, Cambridge, he gained first classes in mathematics (part one, 1891) and natural sciences (part one, 1895), won several prizes, became president of the Union, played billiards for the university, and was inspired by Alfred Marshall's lectures on economics. His social conscience was roused at Cambridge by meeting Percy Alden, warden of Mansfield House university settlement in Canning Town. As he recalled, 'Marshall stimulated my brain to ascertain the facts. Alden forced me to face them and, if I could, to justify them' (Pethick-Lawrence, 48). Trinity College elected him a fellow (1897–1903) but he decided against an academic career and left on a world tour, visiting India, Australasia, the Far East, and the United States.

Lawrence's Unitarian upbringing exposed him to Hindu influence, and at this time he began creating his personal amalgam of Christian and oriental religion. In his autobiographical chapter on 'my philosophy' he described 'the enlargement of personality' as life's main objective (Pethick-Lawrence, 204); the individual must through open-mindedness and self-control ensure that good comes out of ill, and cultivate a sense of proportion which will transcend the many divisions between human beings. Pethick-Lawrence's ideas seem imprecise, and their flowery expression was for Hugh Dalton 'quite blush-making' (War Diary, 556). Nor are they clarified in what Pethick-Lawrence once described as 'my favourite book' (Pethick-Lawrence, 149): Mabel Collins's Light on the Path (1885), a highly abstract theosophical booklet consisting of a set of mystical and often paradoxical injunctions. Two years before he died he told Lord Layton that he was an agnostic, adding half-seriously, 'I am the most religious-minded agnostic I know' (Hansard 5L, 17 Oct 1961, 327). Yet his beliefs sufficed to bear him up through a lifetime of ideals challenged, pain endured, and career setbacks surmounted.

On returning to London, Lawrence went to live in Canning Town, intending to extend Charles Booth's social survey work. But university settlement business absorbed him, and he became its treasurer; he studied law, and was called to the bar by the Inner Temple in 1899. The death of his elder brother in 1900 made him wealthy, and in the following year he was selected Liberal Unionist candidate for North Lambeth. Meanwhile, what he recalled as 'love at first sight' (Pethick-Lawrence, 51) for Emmeline [see Lawrence, Emmeline Pethick- (1867–1954)]—daughter of Henry Pethick, of Weston-super-Mare—edged him politically leftwards. Her progressive views, together with his strong opposition to the Second South African War, made him abandon North Lambeth, and when the serious-minded couple married at the Town Hall, Canning Town, on 2 October 1901, disapproval from the relatively conservative Lawrence family was made apparent and hit his pocket. Lawrence, who quickly grew fond of his wife's family, prefixed his wife's name to his own. Their marriage was childless, and the Pethick-Lawrences now collaborated in trying to improve East End conditions. He gave the Dunkin lectures at Manchester College, Oxford, on economic issues, in 1900–01, and in 1902 published an article on the need for town planning in the symposium The Heart of the Empire, edited by C. F. G. Masterman. To assist organized labour he bought The Echo, a radical evening halfpenny newspaper; in 1902 he became its editor when Percy Alden resigned. Its contributors included H. N. Brailsford and J. Ramsay MacDonald, but although Pethick-Lawrence increased the paper's circulation and invested a fortune in it, he could not make it pay and in 1905 closed it down. From 1905 to 1907 he edited the Labour Record and Review.

Women's suffrage leader Pethick-Lawrence welcomed the Liberal landslide at the general election of 1906, but increasingly diverged from the Liberal government when sucked into the Pankhursts' militant Women's Social and Political Union (WSPU). His unobtrusive but full-time commitment to the union from 1907 to 1912 reflected his paradoxical combination of new-found feminist conviction with old-fashioned chivalry and personal devotion to Christabel Pankhurst, who christened him 'Godfather'. She and the Pethick-Lawrences pushed aside the union's democrats, who seceded into the Women's Freedom League in 1907; thereafter the trio gave the WSPU firm and efficient direction until 1912. He provided much needed level-headed financial, organizational, and legal expertise, and published extensively for the cause. Already in 1906 he was supporting suffragettes in the law courts, guiding them in self-defence, and standing bail for more than 100 of them. In 1907 the Pethick-Lawrences founded and became joint editors of the periodical *Votes for Women*. In 1909, when his wife was in prison, he became joint treasurer, his first official post in the union. The man at the heart of the WSPU warded off sex conflict just as the rich man within the labour movement had earlier warded off class conflict.

In 1912, however, the Pethick-Lawrences were convicted of conspiracy to incite members of the WSPU to cause damage in the West End of London, and despite the jury's recommendation to clemency they were sentenced to nine months' imprisonment; Pethick-Lawrence and Mrs Pankhurst were ordered to pay the costs of the trial. All three went on hunger strike, but only Pethick-Lawrence had to face the full rigours of forcible feeding twice a day for several days; his wife was forcibly fed only once and Mrs Pankhurst not at all. After five weeks the Pethick-Lawrences were released. As Pethick-Lawrence refused to pay the costs he was declared bankrupt, a declaration rescinded a year later. Disagreements about militant strategy now caused the Pankhursts to expel the Pethick-Lawrences from the WSPU. The Pethick-Lawrences, concealing their private bitterness at how they had been treated, continued to edit *Votes for Women*, gathered the Votes for Women Fellowship around it, and in 1914 eventually merged it with the United Suffragists, a bridge-building body aiming to draw together suffragists of both sexes, and to unite militants with non-militants.

Labour politician The First World War changed everything, but it gave Pethick-Lawrence another sphere in which to pursue conciliation—this time between conflicting or potentially conflicting nations, for he opposed coercive imperialism and pressed for an early peace settlement. He told John Maynard Keynes in 1920 that his *Economic Consequences of the Peace* (1919), condemning the Versailles peace settlement, was 'of epoch making importance' (Pethick-Lawrence to Keynes, 23 Jan 1920, Marshall Library, Cambridge, Keynes papers EC1/2)—hence Lawrence's support for 'appeasement' in the 1930s. He became treasurer of the Union of Democratic Control, but standing in 1917 at the by-election for South Aberdeen as a 'peace by negotiation' candidate he won only 7 per cent of the votes cast. In 1918 he became liable for conscription, but because he favoured a negotiated peace he refused to serve, and was assigned to work on the land. This made him enemies among supporters at Hastings, where he had been adopted as Labour candidate, and at

the general election of 1918 he withdrew. His reflections on war finance led to his book *A Levy on Capital* (1918) on the need for such a levy, followed by his *Why Prices Rise and Fall* (1920).

By 1922 Pethick-Lawrence, as a seasoned author on economic policy, was of value to the Labour Party. Standing at South Islington he was disappointed to win only 30 per cent of the votes cast, coming bottom of the poll in a three-cornered contest. In 1923, however, with 45 per cent of the votes cast in another three-cornered contest at West Leicester, he defeated Winston Churchill—more than preserving the Labour majority in a seat he retained until 1931. He set about mastering parliamentary procedure, grew to love the House of Commons, and took a genuine pride in its traditions. His maiden speech advocated pensions for widowed mothers, but he specialized in finance. He spoke in favour of a capital levy, and opposed the return to the gold standard in 1925. In the second Labour government he enjoyed his role as financial secretary to the Treasury, and got on well with his civil servants, usually sharing the Treasury view. In 1931, however, he strongly opposed the financial policy of the National Government, rejected Ramsay MacDonald's suggestion that he might be prepared to join it, and rapidly published his lucid and wide-ranging book *This Gold Crisis* (1931). For him, the crisis had arisen from the mistakenly punitive policy the allies had adopted towards Germany in the 1920s; there was, he said, no question of British national bankruptcy, and his remedy was to restore confidence and peg the exchange rate by announcing that the government would mobilize British-owned foreign investments, as occurred in both world wars. Nor did he shrink in the early 1920s or the late 1930s from the capital levy or wealth tax as an egalitarian device for curbing the national debt.

At the general election of 1931, in a straight fight with a Liberal, Pethick-Lawrence won only a third of the votes cast and was soundly defeated. This freed the Pethick-Lawrences to resume their frequent worldwide travels. In his visit to Russia in 1932 he acknowledged its totalitarian structure, but 'saw much to admire' (Pethick-Lawrence, 178), and like many in the Labour Party until the 1960s 'formed a very high opinion of the way in which planning was being carried out' (ibid., 177); nor is it surprising that the preface to an autobiography written in December 1942 should refer to 'the heroic Soviet Union' (ibid., 5). His concern at Fascist advance forced him in the 1930s to reject pacifism in favour of collective security through the League of Nations. As Labour candidate for Edinburgh East at the general election of 1935 he won 43 per cent of the votes cast in a three-cornered contest. He immediately attacked the Hoare–Laval pact in parliament, but his main role was now to act as principal financial spokesman for Labour, and in 1937 he was proud to be appointed privy councillor. He claimed in 1959 to have been a lifelong 'unrepentant Keynes-ite' (*Hansard 5L*, 15 April 1959, 645). Certainly he repeatedly contested in the 1930s the analogy between individual and public finance, denying that the budget must be balanced every year. He also cited Sweden and New Zealand as exemplars for getting out of depression by expanding purchasing power, but later in the decade he regretted that the National Government chose a time of boom rather than slump for expanding the economy, and with the aim of rearmament rather than to boost national wealth. Throughout his career he saw the budget not as a narrowly fiscal measure, but as the occasion for monitoring the progress of the economy as a whole. In his later career, as the Treasury gained increasing control over the economy, his two major interests—taxation and banking—came together.

All-party government in 1940 separated the roles of Labour Party leader and leader of the opposition, a role assumed by H. B. Lees-Smith with Pethick-Lawrence as his unofficial deputy and chairman of the public accounts committee. Then, on Lees-Smith's death, Labour unanimously elected Pethick-Lawrence as his successor until departure from the cabinet soon freed Arthur Greenwood to assume the role. Pethick-Lawrence was now an experienced and much-respected member of the party, of which he became vice-chairman. He had long looked older than he really was, and evoked impatience from younger zealots like Aneurin Bevan, who once referred to him as 'a crusted old Tory'. Such critics underestimated Pethick-Lawrence's continuing capacity for pushing nineteenth-century Liberal ideals in ever more radical directions: fruitfully combining statism with respect for the individual, applying reason and a faith in human progress to emotive issues such as penal reform and capital punishment, and keeping the free-trade flag flying amid protectionist reaction.

Elder statesman Pethick-Lawrence had long believed that the British empire could rest secure only on a basis of goodwill, and with his wife built up over many years a network of Indian contacts. For some years until 1923 he had contributed a weekly letter to Mrs Besant's *New India*, and as a Labour MP in the 1920s he championed Indian self-government. His one burst of fury as parliamentary orator was on 18 April 1944 when L. S. Amery showed himself insensitive to Indian nationalist opinion. British wartime set-backs rendered Pethick-Lawrence's ideas practicable, and after he had been re-elected at Edinburgh East by an even larger majority in 1945, independence for India became government policy. He was appointed secretary of state for India, with a seat in the House of Lords. In 1946, accompanied by Stafford Cripps and A. V. Alexander, he led the cabinet mission to Delhi which aimed to demonstrate the sincerity of Britain's commitment to Indian independence. He did not enjoy the experience: unhappy at being parted from his wife, frustrated by Indian negotiators whose language was subtler than his own, oppressed at the age of seventy-four by the heat and by the failure in long-drawn-out negotiations of goodwill alone to prevail, he could not bridge the gulf between Hindu and Muslim, and at one point privately told his wife that he had 'nearly reached the limit of human endurance' (Brittain, 175). Still, his fairness and sincerity held the mission together and demonstrated the British government's goodwill, nor would the subsequent settlement have been possible if the mission had not first exposed the difficulties without undue rancour. Before agreeing to go as viceroy to India, however, Earl Mountbatten pressed for Pethick-Lawrence's removal, and in April 1947 Pethick-Lawrence resigned as secretary of state, though in the House of Lords he supported the government's Indian policy thereafter.

As an elder statesman Pethick-Lawrence was influential throughout the 1950s in the House of Lords, a more congenial forum than the Commons for his approach to politics, and one which reciprocated his obvious affection for it. The house respected his technical expertise, his long experience, and his consistent courtesy when voicing views that were controversial there. His intellect remained alert to the end, and he was capable of long synoptic speeches on large policy issues. His contributions became if anything more numerous after his wife died in 1954, nor did their quality decline. In 1956 he deplored the Suez venture's threat to Britain's moral authority, but his debating year was by then oriented round three major economic events: his speeches at the start of the new session, in the annual debate on the economic situation, and on the Finance Bill—all informed by much leisure reading on economics and banking. He consistently deprecated what he saw as the government's clumsy and short-term fiscal controls by comparison with the more closely targeted and longer-term physical controls that Labour favoured, and urged close collaboration between government and the TUC. He disliked the general direction of government economic policy, as well as what was in his view an increasingly self-indulgent mood within the nation as a whole.

Concluding assessment Behind all this activity was a powerful secretarial machine, driven by a punctilious and demanding master. With the day's engagements carefully listed for him, the appropriate documents attached, Pethick-Lawrence began the day by going through the agony column in the newspapers, sending condolences punctiliously. Not a moment was wasted, filing and the keeping of accounts were meticulous, newspaper clippings were systematically marked up for his attention, internal memoranda were frequently exchanged, unexpected interruptions (especially from the telephone) were discouraged and could well evoke rudeness. None the less, Pethick-Lawrence won loyalty from staff through his classless outlook; he publicly expressed pride in his secretaries, who worked as a team, and the Pethick-Lawrences drew them into their private life. His mind combined opposites: on the one hand rationalistic and in many respects radical, he was at the same time highly sentimental (especially in religion and personal relations) and also traditionalist—proud of British institutions, eager to keep up with old friends, and an enthusiast for commemorating anniversaries. His mathematical mind might have led him to take black and white views in politics, and yet he was a lifelong enthusiast for compromise and for the British institutions which encouraged it.

Attractive to intimates was Pethick-Lawrence's almost

childlike personality. Carefully graduated lists of charities supported and Christmas cards sent and received were prepared, and he took a childlike pleasure in opening presents and anticipating birthdays—hence his close rapport with children. Spartan in personal comforts, hating waste of food or time, walking and exercising regularly to keep fit, he was a fanatic for routine and punctuality. Visiting Kew Gardens annually to look at the magnolias, holidaying from year to year with the same friends, stringent about the unchanging timing and content of meals, he took some pleasure in shopping, cooking, and jam-making at weekends. The contrast with his wife's habits could hardly have been greater, and she too was caught up in his bureaucratic routine, with notes regularly shuttling between them about day-to-day matters as well as formal letters on special occasions. Somehow this famous Fred and Emmeline partnership survived for more than half a century. Fred needed company, and Emmeline when ill in later life made it clear that she expected him to remarry. Some friends were surprised that after she died on 11 March 1954 he sought a replacement. On 14 February 1957 he married Helen Millar, widow of Duncan McCombie and daughter of Sir John George Craggs, chartered accountant. She was not the first to be approached, but they had been friends since the time when Helen had herself been a militant suffragette, and the inevitable difficulties in mutual adjustment were somehow surmounted. Pethick-Lawrence died in the Manor House Hospital, London, on 10 September 1961, whereupon the barony became extinct.

In 1943 Pethick-Lawrence published his autobiography, *Fate has been Kind*, dedicated to 'my wife by whose constant inspiration my life has been enriched'. It was revealing and reflective on his childhood, and provided a description of the suffragette movement more vivid and personal than appears in his wife's autobiography. But his view of Pankhurstian tactics up to 1912 remained uncritical, and he did not adequately justify the contradiction between, on the one hand, the militancy and authoritarian control which he had endorsed in the WSPU, and on the other the humanitarian and democratic ideals which so patently inspired the rest of his career. Nor was the detailed case for militancy that he presented to G. M. Trevelyan in 1949 at all convincing (see Brittain, appx 1, 215–18). His account of the inter-war years contained penetrating insights, but in discussing the 1930s it degenerated into a mere narrative; it was written too close to the events under discussion for the Labour Party and his role within it to receive the close analytical attention they deserved. Vera Brittain's *Pethick-Lawrence: a Portrait* (1963) took the story to the end of his life, drew on unpublished material, and furnished useful context, but was in important respects less penetrating than the autobiography, giving 'causes' too much attention by comparison with his role in parliament and party. Although feminism retained his support to the end, for example, far more important in his career was his role as a leading Labour spokesman on economic matters. Full justice to him will probably never be done because his personal papers, once so ample and so efficiently organized, were mostly lost through wartime salvage and through deliberate destruction at the end of his career.

Pethick-Lawrence had every facility for rising to the top in politics: a fine brain, wealth, industriousness, and a bevy of able secretaries and helpers. Vera Brittain explained his failure to reach the peak by noting that he was 'disinclined to be pushful' (Brittain, 75), but this will not suffice. Pethick-Lawrence's somewhat quietist personal philosophy may have held him back, but it is his personality that provides the key. His speeches read well in *Hansard*, and he was as capable of the broad-sweep survey as of well-informed detailed contributions on technical issues. The latter were often economic, but his policy range was wide. He took great trouble in preparing his speeches, circulated them widely, and expressed himself lucidly. Yet he lacked the essential ingredient: rapport with his audience. Nicknamed in the press gallery Pathetic Lawrence, he had 'no charm, no imaginative background' (Johnston, 200), and no amount of professional guidance could remedy the defect. 'Very sound', said Attlee, 'but never really came over in the House of Commons' (*Yorkshire Post*, 27 June 1963, 4). Pethick-Lawrence was a clubbable parliamentarian, with a ready fund of anecdote, but he developed no close trade-union or local-government links. Nor was he ever prominent at the party conference; besides, so coldly rational and humourless a speaker could never have won the Labour Party's heart, and he lacked the prestige of working-class status. He was unlucky, too, in his timing—rarely within the control of politicians but often integral to their success—for he had arrived late on the parliamentary scene, and always looked his age. When he and other potential leaders were out of parliament from 1931 to 1935, Attlee was getting entrenched. Add to this Pethick-Lawrence's personal foibles, which to many made him seem eccentric, even a crank: 'funny old Pethick' is Dalton's phrase (*War Diary*, 556). Yet none of this should detract from his career's considerable significance. Few politicians more conventionally successful were as far-sighted as he on international, social class, and feminist issues—few as resolutely decent in their values or as selfless in their personal and political integrity.

BRIAN HARRISON

Sources V. Brittain, *Pethick-Lawrence: a portrait* (1963) · F. Pethick-Lawrence, *Fate has been kind* (1943) · B. Harrison, 'The politics of a marriage: Emmeline and Fred Pethick-Lawrence', *Prudent revolutionaries: portraits of British feminists between the wars* (1987), 242–72 · *The Second World War diary of Hugh Dalton, 1940–1945*, ed. B. Pimlott (1986) · J. Johnston, *A hundred commoners* (1931) · *CGPLA Eng. & Wales* (1961) · *Yorkshire Post* (27 June 1963)
Archives BL OIOC, corresp. and papers relating to India and Burma, MS Eur. D 540 · Trinity Cam., corresp. and papers | BL, corresp. with the Society of Authors, Add. MS 56777 · BL, corresp. with Marie Stopes, Add. MS 58555 · BL OIOC, corresp. with R. H. Dorman-Smith, MS Eur. F 169 · BL OIOC, corresp. with Sir Hubert Rance, MS Eur. E 215 · BLPES, corresp. with the independent labour party · Bodl. Oxf., letters to Evelyn Sharp Nevinson · Internationaal Instituut voor Sociale Geschiedenis, Amsterdam, letters to Sylvia Pankhurst · NA Scot., corresp. with Lord Lothian | FILM

BFI NFTVA, news footage · BFI NFTVA, recorded talk |SOUND BL NSA, documentary recording

Likenesses H. Coller, oils, 1933, NPG · W. Stoneman, photograph, 1945, NPG · K. Pollak, photograph, c.1948, NPG [see illus.] · A. Moroder, carved wooden head, 1949, NPG · J. Baker, oils, Pethick-Lawrence House, Dorking; repro. in Brittain, *Pethick-Lawrence*, frontispiece · photograph, repro. in Pethick-Lawrence, *Fate has been kind*, frontispiece · photographs, repro. in Brittain, *Pethick-Lawrence* · postcards, Women's Library, London

Wealth at death £75,739 9s. 1d.: probate, 23 Nov 1961, *CGPLA Eng. & Wales*

Lawrence, Geoffrey, third Baron Trevethin and first Baron Oaksey (1880–1971), lawyer, was born in London on 2 December 1880, the youngest in the family of three sons and one daughter of Sir Alfred Tristram *Lawrence (later first Baron Trevethin) (1843–1936), lord chief justice of England in 1921–2, and his first cousin Jessie Elizabeth (d. 1931), daughter of George Lawrence.

After Haileybury College where he was senior to C. R. Attlee, Lawrence went to New College, Oxford. He received a third class in *literae humaniores* in 1903. Lawrence was called to the bar at the Inner Temple in 1906 (bencher 1932, treasurer 1955), and had a steady unspectacular career with such positions as counsel to the Jockey Club, chairman of Wiltshire quarter sessions, and recorder of Oxford. From 1928 to 1932 he was attorney-general to the prince of Wales. In 1925 he took silk, and in April 1932 he was appointed a judge of the King's Bench Division, being appointed a lord justice of appeal in 1944. He was sworn of the privy council in 1944, and was elected an honorary fellow of New College in the same year. In April 1947 he was appointed a lord of appeal in ordinary, having already been granted in January a hereditary peerage in recognition of his work at the international tribunal at Nuremberg (1945–6). In 1947 Oxford awarded him the honorary degree of DCL.

Lawrence's work at Nuremberg was of an international significance which surpassed anything he had done as a puisne judge or was to do as a law lord. The twenty-one defendants were accused of enormous wrongdoing before and during the Second World War in an indictment which took two days to read and 218 days to try before a tribunal composed of two judges from each of the four victorious countries. The documentation was vast, and the prosecuting teams of unequal strength, the British under Sir David Maxwell Fyfe being the strongest. Lawrence was elected British president, and discharged his difficult task with a calmness, courtesy, and firmness which won universal approval, even from the defendants, the soldiers among whom thought that their problems were appreciated by one who had been made DSO as a gunner officer in the First World War. Praise was also given by the British alternate judge, Sir Norman Birkett, who was secretly resentful that he had not been chosen for the post. He was passed over not because of Attlee's undisguised preference for products of Haileybury, but because the Foreign Office insisted on a more senior judge. After Nuremberg, Oaksey, as he became, found it difficult to adjust to the work of a law lord. His brief judgments were conscientiously prepared, but his heart did not seem to be in the job.

In appearance Oaksey was a sturdy figure, slightly below middle height, prematurely bald, with the fresh complexion and unhurried manner of an English gentleman who was interested in country life. He could sometimes be induced to talk about his presidency of the Guernsey Cattle Society, but never about his presidency of the international tribunal. After exactly twenty-five years on the bench, Oaksey retired in April 1957. In June 1959 he inherited from a brother his father's barony of Trevethin, but he continued to be styled Oaksey.

On 22 December 1921 Lawrence married Marjorie Frances Alice (d. 1984), youngest daughter of Commander Charles Napier Robinson RN; they had one son and three daughters. Oaksey died in Oaksey, Malmesbury, Wiltshire, on 28 August 1971 and was succeeded in both baronies by his son, John Geoffrey Tristram (b. 1929).

R. F. V. HEUSTON, *rev.*

Sources personal knowledge (1993) · private information (1993) · Burke, *Peerage* (1967) · *The Times* (30 Aug 1971)

Archives FILM BFI NFTVA, news footage · BFI NFTVA, documentary footage

Likenesses J. M. Crealock, oils, Inner Temple, London · D. Fowler, oils, Haileybury College, Hertfordshire

Wealth at death £46,708: probate, 8 Dec 1971, *CGPLA Eng. & Wales*

Lawrence, Sir (Frederick) Geoffrey (1902–1967), judge, was born at 152 Clapham Road, London, on 5 April 1902, the eldest of three sons of a master butcher, Frederick James Lawrence, and his wife, Lilian Kate Burden, a teacher of singing. Educated at the City of London School, he won an open scholarship to New College, Oxford, where he obtained a first class in classical honour moderations (1923), and seconds in *literae humaniores* (1925) and jurisprudence (1926). When he left university he tutored for a time the two sons, then hoping to enter Oxford, of Jan Masaryk, the Czech diplomat who was later murdered after the communist *coup d'état* in February 1948. He travelled with them to America and Prague and they remained close friends.

Eventually settling on a career in law, Lawrence was awarded a Harmsworth law scholarship and became a pupil of Eric Neve, who was then in chambers with Norman Birkett and who had a strong junior practice in Sussex. In 1930 he was called to the bar (Middle Temple). Conducting his practice on the south-eastern circuit during those early days from Brighton, he devilled opinions for busier colleagues; as a result, it was said that clients of at least one very senior barrister noted a remarkable improvement in that experienced practitioner's opinions. He soon acquired a reasonable general practice and by the outbreak of the war had secured the best junior practice on the circuit, entailing frequent appearances in the High Court, where his eloquence was marked. In 1941 Lawrence married Marjorie Avice, daughter of Charles Angelo Jones; they had no children.

One of Lawrence's more unusual appearances during the Second World War was when he was junior to Sir Walter Monckton in late 1944. On that occasion they persuaded a 'parliament' of nineteen Middle Temple benchers, including senior judges, in its capacity as a professional disciplinary body dealing with errant barristers, effectively to retry and then to reject (rather than, in the absence of the original witnesses, to limit itself to a judicial review of) the findings of a court martial earlier that year. The military tribunal had convicted former Flight Lieutenant Pensotti, a Royal Air Force judge advocate (and himself a barrister from Brighton), of tampering with court martial papers the previous year. No pardon was forthcoming, however, and as part of Pensotti's post-war parliamentary campaign for redress, the London evening papers in September 1946 referred to the previous involvement of Lawrence, among the cast of legal luminaries, in the affair.

After the war Lawrence was recorder of Tenterden (1948–51) and took silk in 1950, and while continuing to undertake a wide range of work, including crime, divorce, and Chancery cases, he later began to specialize in parliamentary and planning work. He was a member of the royal commission on marriage and divorce chaired by Lord Morton of Henryton from 1951, which reported in 1956. The report rejected (as did the Denning report of 1946) the proposal to grant divorce jurisdiction in undefended cases to the county courts on the ground that the sanctity of marriages was such that only High Court judges could end them (which led to the absurd solution that county court judges should be appointed 'special divorce commissioners' for the purpose and wear the same robes as a judge of the Divorce Division of the High Court). He became recorder of Canterbury (1952–62) and was chairman of west Sussex quarter sessions.

In 1957 Lawrence achieved national fame as a result of his successful defence of Dr John Bodkin Adams, the Eastbourne doctor prosecuted at the Old Bailey for the murder, seven years earlier, of his patient and benefactress Mrs Morrell. Among many possible examples, Mrs Morrell's case was selected by the prosecution as the most likely to sustain the case that Adams had been administering overdoses of morphine and heroin in order to shorten the life of one of his patients and to benefit under her will (it was irrelevant whether she would have died of natural causes within a short time). In the belief that notebooks kept by nurses at the time, which had recorded the injections administered and Mrs Morrell's condition, had been destroyed, the prosecution relied on the nurses' testimony. But Lawrence pulled a rabbit out of the hat by producing the notebooks, whose entries were inconsistent with the prosecution witnesses' evidence. Moreover, as a master of the medical details, he was able, by a 'virtuoso performance of the art of cross-examination' (Simpson, 809), to demolish the theory of an expert medical witness for the crown which still suggested Adams's guilt. In the end, following the judge's direction that a doctor is 'entitled to do all that is proper and necessary to relieve pain and suffering even if the measure he takes may incidentally shorten life' (Devlin, 171), the jury were persuaded that the so-called overdoses were in fact the only treatment the doctor could give to alleviate pain and distress.

The case remains a *cause célèbre*, with interest maintained partly as a result of the conviction in 1999 of Dr Harold Shipman for the murder by lethal injection of at least fifteen of his patients, and partly as a result of the publication in 1985 of the account of the case by the trial judge, Lord Devlin. *Easing the Passing* revealed Lawrence's deep (and in the event unwarranted) pessimism after the nine-day committal hearing before the Eastbourne magistrates at which the press and public were present (under the rules then obtaining). For as Devlin revealed, the 'quiet and conscientious' (Devlin, 42) Lawrence had expressed concern to the judge about whether his client would receive a fair trial. Prosecution information emerging from the committal hearing, as well as disclosed evidence from a coroner's inquest and from a previous committal hearing on charges (eventually upheld) alleging that Adams had falsified cremation and other documents, had been widely reported in the press, creating an impression of his guilt. Lawrence had also been concerned that the committing magistrates had admitted, probably wrongly, evidence of 'system'—that is, the suggestion that Adams had also killed two other patients, Mr and Mrs Hullett, even though he had not been charged with their unlawful killing. It is a tribute to Lawrence's advocacy skills that he was able to deflect the jury from concluding that Adams (who did not go into the witness box) was either a grasping killer or even a practitioner of (unlawful) euthanasia. Yet it was possible to infer that latter conclusion from Adams's own explanation of his actions, as it was, indeed, from a less charitable interpretation of Devlin's direction regarding the 'double effect'. An unexpected acquittal was secured and Lawrence's reputation as a legal celebrity was established.

In the following year Lawrence built on this 'star' quality when he successfully defended Charles Ridge, the chief constable of Brighton who, with other officers, had been prosecuted for conspiracy to obstruct the course of public justice. The allegations involved payments of 'hush' money by burglars, club owners, and others to the officers in exchange for the latter turning a blind eye to criminal activities or warning of raids on the clubs. At the Old Bailey on 27 February 1958 Ridge (who since 1925 had risen through the ranks of the local police), together with the proprietor of a drinking club, was acquitted while a detective inspector, a detective sergeant, and a commission agent were convicted. After Ridge had been discharged, the trial judge, Mr Justice Donovan, observed that the local force required a new leader who would be a fresh influence and set a better example. The Brighton watch committee met almost immediately after the trial and dismissed Ridge. However five years later Ridge succeeded in the House of Lords in overturning the dismissal on the ground that the procedure adopted was a breach of the principles of natural justice in that the committee had failed to accord him a fair opportunity to be heard in his own defence (see *Ridge v. Baldwin* [1964] A. C. 40). The case was a major landmark in public law and laid down that the right to a fair hearing in respect to the decisions of public bodies embraces administrative as well as judicial or quasi-judicial decisions.

Lawrence was now at the height of his career as a barrister. Without dominating the profession in the manner of, say, Gerald Gardiner with his reforming zeal, Lawrence none the less became chairman of the general council of the bar (1960–62), and in that capacity he visited the United States to address the American Bar Association in New York. The visit was a resounding success and tributes from his listeners flowed in abundance. In 1963 he was knighted for services to the profession.

In 1962 Lawrence assumed a new responsibility when he was appointed by the government to chair the newly created National Incomes Commission (NIC). The original idea, following a pay 'pause' in 1961 and the creation of a tripartite National Economic Development Council (NEDC), was that in furtherance of a government policy designed to prevent wage increases from outstripping production and leading to inflation, the commission would examine any proposed wage increase and pronounce accordingly. Wage disputes would be subject to compulsory arbitration. However, the unions were predictably hostile to what they saw as a policy of wage restraint while dividends and profits were unregulated, and the idea of compulsory powers for the commission was replaced by the more limited power to make recommendations. But the circumstances were unpropitious. The NEDC was far more important, and neither trade unionists nor industrialists were members of the NIC, whose credentials in the industrial relations community were consequently limited. None the less Lawrence threw himself enthusiastically into this new venture and four reports, including one favourable to improvements in university teachers' pay, were issued over a period of eighteen months. A change of government led to the demise of the commission despite the hopes for the scheme which Lawrence had harboured (the successor Labour government's National Board for Prices and Incomes, as the name suggested, moved beyond the confines of wages). In the end Lawrence's commission was 'unable to make any effective contribution towards the development of an agreed wages policy' (Guillebaud, 42).

A similar responsibility was Lawrence's chairmanship of an independent inquiry into parliamentary remuneration. The report, published in November 1964, recommended large increases in the pay of ministers of all grades, members of parliament, the lord chancellor, the speaker, and the English and Scottish law officers. Lawrence then returned to practice and after a few months was appointed in 1965 to the High Court, where he was quiet, courteous, and fair, with no hint of flamboyance. But serious illness soon struck him before he had any opportunity to make his mark on the bench.

Lawrence was small, slight in build, with good features and an attractive and well modulated voice. Though lacking the physique of an athlete, he enjoyed yachting, swimming, cricket, and games in general. Time spent on his farm in Sussex gave him tremendous pleasure, but his passion was for music. He was already an accomplished violinist and capable pianist when he arrived at Oxford. President of the university musical club, he formed the Magi string quartet with his brother, a cellist and fellow student at Oxford. The viola player was Mrs Joseph, the daughter of Robert Bridges, the poet laureate, and the wife of H. W. B. Joseph. Lawrence also played first violin in the orchestra of the Oxford Bach Choir under Sir Hugh Allen and gave violin recitals, often accompanied by the pianist Jean Hamilton, the future Lady Redcliffe-Maud. In his later years he regretted that he hardly ever had time to take his fiddle out of its case.

Lawrence is somewhat difficult to categorize. As an advocate he was neither especially cerebral nor spectacular although he was undoubtedly sound, determined, and systematic. The impression that his reputation rested on his good fortune in representing Bodkin Adams and then Chief Constable Ridge is a little unfair, though his forensic and cross-examining skills were well demonstrated in those cases. His specialism usually lay, not in high-profile crime nor in fashionable libel proceedings, but in planning law which covered 'every sort of dreary dispute in which local authorities and their natural opponents engage' (Devlin, 42), where sustained advocacy at the highest levels would normally have only a limited audience to appreciate it. His elevation to the bench was thus deserved in professional terms (and achieved, arguably, despite rather than because of his exploits in 1957 and 1958 at the Old Bailey). His subsequent service on public bodies weakened his already less than robust constitution. Once he was on the bench, unremitting work in court and late nights reading briefs probably took their toll on his health, prematurely ending his judicial career. He died at Cuckfield Hospital, Sussex, on 3 February 1967. He was survived by his wife.   G. R. RUBIN

Sources The Times (6 Feb 1967) · The Times (10 Feb 1967) · DNB · b. cert. · P. Devlin, *Easing the passing: the trial of Dr John Bodkin Adams* (1985) · A. W. B. Simpson, 'Euthanasia for sale?', *Michigan Law Review*, 84 (1986), 807–18 · J. Morton, *Bent coppers* (1993), 36–41 · G. R. Rubin, 'The Pensotti Royal Air Force court martial controversy, 1944–1965', *New Zealand Armed Forces Law Review*, 1 (2001), 36–41 · H. A. Clegg, *The system of industrial relations in Great Britain* (1970) · C. W. Guillebaud, *Wage determination and wage policy* (1967) · B. Abel-Smith and R. Stevens, *Lawyers and the courts* (1967)

Likenesses photograph, 1957, repro. in Devlin, *Easing the passing*, 118 · photograph, repro. in *The Times* (6 Feb 1967)

Wealth at death £55,567: probate, 27 Sept 1967, CGPLA Eng. & Wales

Lawrence, George (*bap.* 1613, *d.* 1691x8), clergyman and ejected minister, was baptized on 30 January 1613 at St Dunstan and All Saints, Stepney, Middlesex, the son of George Lawrence. He was a poor scholar at St Paul's School, London, under Alexander Gill and received a gratuity from the school on 7 February 1632 and was elected an exhibitioner on 5 February 1633. He went up to Oxford and matriculated at the notoriously puritan college of

New Inn Hall on 27 June 1634. He graduated BA on 2 July 1636 and proceeded MA on 2 May 1639. At New Inn Hall he befriended the later presbyterian martyr Christopher Love. There is some debate as to whether Lawrence took holy orders (Wood, *Ath. Oxon.*, 4.873) but he was probably ordained by bishop Curle of Winchester.

In 1640 Lawrence was chosen as lecturer at the London church of St George's, Botolph Lane, but the churchwardens' accounts suggest that his preaching may have been too political for the parish leaders. On 19 November 1641 the churchwarden asked Lawrence to stop his lectures but promised to pay him until Christmas if he remained quiet. Lawrence was an early supporter of the parliamentarian cause and in 1642 preached a controversial series of sermons at St Michael Cornhill, supporting parliament's protestation. In early 1642 he co-operated with Christopher Love to write a tract entitled *The Debauched Cavalleer, or, The English Midianite*. This work urged parliament to prepare for a bloody war with the royalists. As a result, Anthony Wood remembered Lawrence as 'a most violent puritan and a great admirer of the Scotch covenant' (Wood, *Ath. Oxon.*, 4.783).

It is likely that Lawrence spent the civil war as an army chaplain; he records that he was with Oliver Cromwell at army headquarters at Berkhamsted in 1647. In 1651 he tried unsuccessfully to use his former influence with Cromwell and the army to save the life of Christopher Love. Writing as G. L. he entitled his tract *Love's Advocate* and was probably among the Presbyterian and Independent clergy who 'weekly [met] to seek God for a happy reconciliation of the difference between them' to save Love's life (G. L., *Love's Advocate*, 7). By 1651 he had married his wife, Susannah (*d.* 1692/3); two of their children died in that year.

About 1650 Lawrence was chosen as chaplain to the hospital of St Cross, near Winchester. He was not officially appointed, however, until January 1654 and was formally admitted by John Cooke on 22 July following. Like many other presbyterians he was a supporter of the Cromwellian protectorate. On 13 October 1658 he preached a sermon to commemorate the death of Oliver Cromwell, published the same year as *Peplum Olivarii, or, A Good Prince Bewailed by a Good People*. Lawrence chose 2 Chronicles 35: 24 as the topic of his sermon and expounded the doctrine that 'the deaths of publick persons, are to be attended with the publick lamentations of the people'. *Peplum Olivarii* was dedicated to Cromwell's son Richard, showing the hope that Lawrence, like many other presbyterians, had in the new lord protector.

Lawrence remained at St Cross Hospital until the restoration of Charles II. In June 1660 the master, Dr William Lewis, petitioned the House of Lords for his removal. Although Lawrence attempted to resist, he was expelled later that year and joined the ranks of the ejected nonconformists. He initially continued in Winchester as a nonconformist preacher and eventually returned to London, where he held conventicles. A government agent noted in 1676 that Lawrence was both preaching and teaching at Mr Mead's meeting-house in Stepney. He described himself as a gentleman of St Giles Cripplegate, London, upon making his will on 25 April 1691 and died some time between then and 23 March 1698 when the document was proved. His wife was buried in Bunhill Fields on 10 January 1693. They had a number of children but only two sons, Noah and Daniel, and a daughter, Deborah, appear to have been alive in April 1691; both Noah and Deborah were still alive in March 1698.　　　　E. C. VERNON

Sources G. Lawrence, *Peplum Olivarii* (1658) · G. Lawrence, *Laurentius Lutherizans* (1642) · GL, MS 951/1 · G. L. [G. Lawrence] and C. L. [C. Love], *The debauched cavalleer* (1642) · G. L. [G. Lawrence], *Love's advocate* (1651) · M. McDonnell, ed., *The register of St Paul's School, 1509–1748* (1977) · *CSP dom.*, 1661 · *The manuscripts of the duke of Leeds*, HMC, 22 (1888) · Wood, *Ath. Oxon.*, new edn, 4.783–4 · *Calamy rev.*, 318 · *The nonconformist's memorial … originally written by … Edmund Calamy*, ed. S. Palmer, 2nd edn, 2 vols. (1777) · *IGI* · Foster, *Alum. Oxon.* · *DNB* · will, PRO, PROB 11/444, fols. 250v–251r
Wealth at death left real property: will, PRO, PROB 11/444, fols. 250v–251r

Lawrence, George Alfred (1827–1876), novelist, was born on 25 March 1827 at the rectory, Buxted, Sussex, the eldest of the four sons of the Revd Alfred Charnley Lawrence (1791–1874), from 1831 rector of Sandhurst, Kent, and his wife, Emily Mary Finch-Hatton (1797–1868), third daughter of George Finch-Hatton (1747–1823), of Eastwell Park, Kent, landowner, and his wife, Lady Elizabeth Mary Murray (*d.* 1825), and sister of George William Finch-*Hatton, tenth earl of Winchilsea (1791–1858). In 1838 G. A. Lawrence was briefly at his father's old school, Harrow School, but later went to Rugby School (1841–1845) where he had some success, winning a prize for his poem on the marriage of Marie Antoinette and gaining a leaving exhibition to Balliol College, Oxford. However, perhaps for reasons of economy, he graduated not from Balliol but from New Inn Hall, taking a second-class degree in classics in 1850. He studied law, and was called to the bar at the Inner Temple in November 1852, but he does not seem to have practised long or successfully; Ernest Baker says he gave up after the success of his first novel. On 4 February 1851 at St Mary's Church, Bathwick, near Bath, he had married Mary Anne Georgiana Kirwan (1823/4–1893), fourth daughter of Patrick Kirwan (1787–1847) of Cregg, Galway, landowner, and his wife, Louisa Margaret Browne (*d.* 1826), sister of the first Lord Oranmore.

Lawrence's *Songs of Feast, Field and Fray* appeared in 1853 under the pseudonym Δ, and was not much noticed. In June 1857 his best-known work, *Guy Livingstone, or, Thorough*, was published anonymously in one volume, and according to a commentator in *The Spectator* after Lawrence's death, 'storms of applause, ridicule, and censure arose on all sides' (*Spectator*, 1345–7, 1346). It was parodied by Bret Harte as *Guy Heavystone*. The novel follows the hero's career through school, university, love affairs, and an early death on the hunting field. Gossip reported that an episode in which the schoolboy Livingstone infuriates the headmaster by fascinating his wife was based on Lawrence's own relations with Archibald Campbell Tait (1811–1882), headmaster of Rugby from 1842 to 1850, and subsequently archbishop of Canterbury, and the latter's wife,

George Alfred Lawrence (1827–1876), by unknown photographer

Catherine Spooner (1819–1878). Livingstone is irresistibly attractive to women: his engagement to the pure and religious Constance Brandon is broken off when she finds him kissing the predatory and vicious Flora Bellasys in a conservatory. He then becomes a passive victim as the two of them play out the struggle between his higher and lower selves. Constance, now consumptive, summons him to see her; Flora diverts the letter; she is discovered; he flies to Constance's deathbed, resolves to lead a better life, and dies nobly having begged her brother's forgiveness. *Sword and Gown* (1859) is set in a French resort, and structured, as the title suggests, as a conflict between a soldier, Royston Keene, and the English clergyman Mr Fullarton, as they struggle for the soul of the beautiful Cecil Tresilyan. Although Fullarton is shown as cowardly, boring, pretentious, and malicious, he turns out to have been right to suspect Keene's designs on Cecil, because, although Keene is brave and brilliant, he has been concealing the existence of a wife, and nearly succeeds in getting Cecil to elope with him. Foiled by one of her previous admirers, he dies nobly during the charge of the light brigade. It was followed by *Barren Honour: a Tale* (2 vols., 1862), whose hero has wasted a fortune, and so is prevented from marrying the woman he loves, partly as a result of her worldly mother's Machiavellian plots.

During the American Civil War, Lawrence made an unsuccessful attempt to join the Confederate army; he subsequently published a lively account of his journey, which ended ignominiously with six weeks in gaol. This book, *Border and Bastille* (1863), was published by William Tinsley, who later wrote that Lawrence had been sent out as a war correspondent by the *Daily Telegraph*; Lawrence himself, however, stated categorically that he had intended to fight, and had only promised some freelance articles to the *Morning Post*. Tinsley described Lawrence as a reckless gambler who used his advances to finance jaunts to foreign casinos, but testified that 'although he had often a good portion of the thousand pounds in advance that I used to pay him for each of his new books, he never failed to complete any contract he made with me' (Tinsley, 1.80). Tinsley published *Maurice Dering, or, The Quadrilateral* (2 vols., 1864), whose four heroes are intended as mid-Victorian versions of the heroes of *The Three Musketeers* (1844–5) by Alexandre Dumas, *Sans merci, or, Kestrels and Falcons* (3 vols., 1866), in which Flora Bellasys reappears as the villainous Lady Dorrillon, and *Brakespeare, or, The Fortunes of a Free Lance* (3 vols., 1868), Lawrence's only historical novel, set during the Hundred Years' War. A sequel to *Sans merci, Breaking a Butterfly, or, Blanche Ellerslie's Ending* (3 vols., 1869), was serialized in *Tinsley's Magazine*, but then published by Routledge. By 1871 Lawrence was already suffering from terminal cancer, and his last novels, *Anteros* (3 vols., 1873) and *Hagarene* (3 vols., 1874) are much his weakest. A second travel book, *Silverland* (1873), an account of a visit to Utah and California, was called by *The Athenaeum* 'not only the worst book about America that we have read but also one of the most reprehensible productions that ever came from the pen of a known writer' (*Athenaeum*, 436).

There is a laudatory reference to the fiction of Charles Kingsley (1819–1875) in *Sword and Gown*, and from the 1850s to the present it has been usual to discuss Lawrence's fiction in the context of the 'muscular' school of novelists, such as Kingsley, Tom Hughes (1822–1896), Frank Smedley (1818–1864), and G. J. Whyte-Melville (1821–1878), whose work appealed to a male readership because of its emphasis on sport and its concern with manliness. However Lawrence's glamorous depiction of fast social life among the upper classes also had a strong influence on romantic novelists who wrote mainly for women, such as Ouida (1839–1908) or Mrs Margaret Hungerford (1855–1897). Like Kingsley in *Two Years Ago* (1857) and Hughes in *The Scouring of the White Horse* (1859) he celebrates physical prowess, and sees aristocratic masculinity at risk from the feminizing ethos of a sedentary middle class. The novels are marked by what the *Spectator* obituarist reasonably described as 'the sneering disparagement of city and professional men' (p. 1347) and equally by a worship of aristocracy, extravagance, personal violence, and physical courage. Anthony Powell plausibly suggests that Lawrence's attitudes may have been shaped by the contrast between his mother's family and his father's: his thuggish and reactionary uncle Lord Winchilsea representing a more congenial model to him than his clergyman father. This point of view is reflected in several scenes in his novels in which the class struggle is literally enacted in battle, and the valour of the upper-class characters leads them to victory. The first of these is a bloody and rather irrelevant episode in *Guy Livingstone* involving the siege of an Irish house by peasants who are fought off by the gentry inside; later examples include the occasion in *Sword and Gown* where Royston Keene beats up an impertinent French peasant; and the hideous revenge exacted by Maurice Dering for the rape and murder of his fiancée in the Indian mutiny. For all Lawrence's admiration for Kingsley, his novels are entirely free from the interest in social reform and the welfare of the working class which were defining features of the muscular Christian school. His own not infrequent references to Christianity often involve the narrator's expressing a belief that one of his characters who has outraged conventional morality is in fact a better Christian than many a hypocritical bourgeois. Like much fiction of the 1860s his novels explore the question of unsuccessful marriages; they express with a good deal of venom the view that society is unfair to both men and women who are trapped with partners who are cruel, or adulterous. A feature of the books to which contemporary critics particularly objected is the tendency to sentimentalize the adulterous wives (who endure society's scorn having escaped from violent husbands) and fallen women (seduced by the hero and others) who litter Lawrence's pages. One reason so many of these women appear in his books is the fact that he conceives of male desire as literally irresistible—the volcanic passions of his heroes are such that they cannot control them, and the women they want are equally incapable of resisting temptation. But his heroines are virtuous, because his conception of female value is essentially conventional. The novels are written in a world-weary and sophisticated tone, their language larded with foreign phrases and quotations, and with archaic and poetic diction, an affectation amusingly parodied by Bret Harte in *Sensation Novels Condensed* (1871). Another of his tricks is to have a character drop down dead from a heart attack brought on by emotion. For all that the books are entertaining and fast moving.

Lawrence was an officer in a militia regiment, and to some extent the vogue for his fiction can be seen, like the volunteer movement, as a response to the war fever of the 1850s. He shared his heroes' enthusiasm for hunting and shooting, and also writes about gambling in Homburg and rock climbing in the Alps. He lived at Gressenhall, near Old Buckenham, Norfolk, and in London at 86a Portland Place. According to Henry Vizetelly he had a pronounced squint. His character was implicitly disparaged by many reviewers; there is also the testimony of a school contemporary, the Hon. Percy Feilding, quoted by Ellis (p. 202), who called him 'a scoundrel … devoid of honour or feeling', and of R. D. Blackmore, who was at Oxford with him, who wrote that 'his delight was in working wickedness' (R. D. Blackmore to Paul H. Hayne, 16 Aug 1884, cited in Burris, 178). However when he died his friend the journalist George Augustus Sala commented on the harshness of his obituaries, and wrote of his own desire to 'express sorrow for the loss of the bright genius and the kind gentleman' (*ILN*, 339). He died on 23 September 1876 in a nursing home at 134 George Street, Edinburgh, where he had undergone an operation for the removal of a cancer of the tongue at the hands of the well-known surgeon Thomas Annandale (1838–1907). He and his wife had one son, George Patrick Charles Lawrence (1859–1908), a barrister and a member of the Liberal Party.

CHARLOTTE MITCHELL

Sources S. M. Ellis, *Wilkie Collins, Le Fanu, and others* (1931) • W. Tinsley, *Random recollections of an old publisher*, 2 vols. (1900) • A. C. Fox-Davies, ed., *A genealogical and heraldic history of the landed gentry of Ireland* (1912) • Venn, *Alum. Cant.* • Foster, *Alum. Oxon.* • A. T. Michell, ed., *Rugby School register*, 3 vols. (1901–4) • M. G. Dauglish, ed., *The Harrow School register, 1801–1900*, 2nd edn (1901) • H. Vizetelly, *Glances back through seventy years: autobiographical and other reminiscences*, 2 vols. (1893) • [G. A. Lawrence], *Guy Livingstone*, ed. E. A. Baker (1903) • [G. A. Lawrence], 'Guy Livingstone', *Novels of high society from the Victorian age*, ed. A. Powell (1947) • *The Spectator* (28 Oct 1876), 1345–7 • *The Times* (2 Oct 1876), 10 • *The Times* (25 Oct 1893), 1 • *The Times* (25 April 1908), 12 • *ILN* (7 Oct 1876), 339 • d. cert. • m. cert. • Q. G. Burris, *Richard Doddridge Blackmore* (1930) • *The Athenaeum* (5 April 1873) • *GM*, 1st ser., 97/1 (1827) • *IGI*

Likenesses photograph, repro. in Ellis, *Wilkie Collins*, facing p. 202 [*see illus.*]

Lawrence, Sir George St Patrick (1804–1884), army officer, was the third son of Lieutenant-Colonel Alexander Lawrence (1762x7–1835) and his wife, Catherine Letitia (1774–1846), daughter of the Revd George Knox, rector of Lifford. He was elder brother of Sir Henry Montgomery *Lawrence and of John Laird Mair *Lawrence, Lord Lawrence. His father, an Indian army officer, led, with three other lieutenants, the forlorn hope at the storming of Seringapatam on 4 May 1799, and returned to England in 1809 after fifteen years' tough service. George was born at Trincomalee, Ceylon, on 17 March 1804, and educated at Foyle College, Londonderry, and at the East India Company's military seminary, Addiscombe College (1819–21). In 1820 he was appointed a cavalry cadet, and in September 1821 arrived in India. On 15 January 1822 he joined the 2nd light cavalry in Bengal (cornet 1821, lieutenant 1824), and was its adjutant from 5 September 1825 until 22 March 1834. On 3 April 1830 Lawrence married, at Karnal, Charlotte Isabella, daughter of Benjamin Browne MD of the Bengal medical board. She died on 12 May 1878, having had three sons and six daughters.

With his regiment Lawrence took part in the Anglo-Afghan War of 1838, and was present at the storming of Ghazni on 23 July 1839 and in the attempt to capture Dost Muhammad Khan, the amir of Afghanistan, in his flight in August through the Bamian Pass. On returning to Kabul, Lawrence became political assistant to Sir William Hay Macnaghten, the British envoy in Afghanistan, and subsequently his military secretary, a post which he kept from September 1839 until Macnaghten's death. On the surrender of Dost Muhammad Khan on 3 November 1840 he was placed in the charge of Lawrence until he was sent to Calcutta. During the rising at Kabul, in November 1841, Lawrence had many narrow escapes, and on the surrender was one of the four officers delivered up on 11 December as hostages for the compliance of the treaty with the Afghans. On 23 December when Macnaghten and others

Sir George St Patrick Lawrence (1804–1884), by A. Murano

were murdered by Akbar Khan, he was saved by Muhammad Shah Khan.

In the retreat from Kabul on 6 January 1842 Lawrence had charge of the women and children, with whom he remained until 8 January, when he was again given up to Akbar Khan as a hostage. With the women and children he was imprisoned, and remained with them until their release on 17 September. He apparently owed his safety to Akbar Khan's high opinion of his character, and to his keeping his promises. Ill health obliged Lawrence to return to England in August 1843, and shortly afterwards the East India Company awarded him £600 for his services in Afghanistan. He was promoted captain on 5 January 1844. On his return to India in October 1846 he was appointed an assistant political agent in the Punjab, having charge over the important Peshawar district. In the autumn of 1847 Lawrence, with only 2000 troops, engaged and defeated on two occasions large numbers of the hill men of the Swat border. At the beginning of the Second Anglo-Sikh War in 1848, Lawrence's great personal influence at Peshawar for some time kept his regiments loyal, but at last they went over to the enemy, and on 25 October 1848 he was a prisoner in the hands of Chuttur Singh; but such was his character for probity and his personal influence over the Sikhs, that Lawrence was three times permitted to leave his captivity on parole. With his wife and children he was released after the peace following the battle of Gujrat, on 22 February 1849, and received the thanks of both houses of parliament and of the governor-general. On 7 June 1849 he was promoted brevet lieutenant-colonel, and appointed deputy commissioner of Peshawar. In the capacity of political officer he, in the following November, accompanied the forces sent under General

Bradshaw into the Yusufzai country, and was present at the capture of Pullee on the Swat border. Again in February 1850, in command of militia, he went with Sir Charles Napier to the forcing of the Kohat Pass, and guided him through that defile. In July 1850 he became political agent in Marwar, one of the Rajputana states, where he remained until 13 March 1857, when he succeeded his brother Henry Lawrence as resident or chief agent for the governor-general in the Rajputana states, and in April took up his residence in Mount Abu.

On the outbreak of the 1857 mutiny Lawrence was appointed brigadier-general of all the forces in Rajputana, and on the death of Colonel Dixon, on 12 June, had to take the chief military command. By his vigorous action the arsenal of Ajmer was retained; a proclamation addressed on 23 May confirmed the Indian princes in their loyalty, and the Rajputana states were prevented from joining the revolt. Such outbreaks as did take place were successfully quelled, first by himself, and afterwards by Major-General Roberts.

On 18 May 1860 Lawrence was created a civil CB and on 25 May 1861 he was promoted major-general. In December 1864 he resigned his post in Rajputana, and ended his Indian career after forty-three years. Both Sir Charles Napier and Lord Dalhousie praised his character and achievements. On 11 January 1865 he received a good-service pension of £100 a year, and on 24 May 1866 was created a KCSI. He also held the third class of the Afghan order of the 'Durani empire'. He retired on full pay on 29 October 1866, and was advanced to honorary lieutenant-general on 11 January 1867. He took a warm interest in the officers' and soldiers' daughters' homes, and was on the managing committees of both these charities. He wrote *Forty-Three Years in India*, which, edited by W. Edwards, was published in 1874. Lawrence died at his home, 20 Kensington Park Gardens, London, on 16 November 1884. The *Annual Register* commented that he was 'the eldest member of a famous brotherhood, the names of which will be handed down to the remotest posterity of Englishmen' (*Annual Register*, 1884, 162).

G. C. BOASE, *rev.* JAMES LUNT

Sources G. St P. Lawrence, *Forty-three years in India*, ed. W. Edwards (1874) · J. W. Kaye, *History of the war in Afghanistan*, 3rd edn, 3 vols. (1874) · J. W. Kaye and G. B. Malleson, *Kaye's and Malleson's History of the Indian mutiny of 1857–8*, 6 vols. (1888–9) · H. B. Edwardes and H. Merivale, *Life of Sir Henry Lawrence*, 2 vols. (1872) · V. C. P. Hodson, *List of officers of the Bengal army, 1758–1834*, 3 (1946) · P. Macrory, *Signal catastrophe: the story of a disastrous retreat from Kabul, 1842* (1966) · W. Broadfoot, *The career of Major George Broadfoot … in Afghanistan and the Punjab* (1888) · *The Times* (18 Nov 1884) · *ILN* (29 Nov 1884) · E. J. Thackwell, *Narrative of the Second Seikh War, in 1848–49* (1851) · V. Eyre, *The military operations at Cabul, which ended in the retreat and destruction of the British army, January 1842* (1843); repr. with an introduction by J. Lunt as *Journal of an Afghanistan prisoner* (1976) · G. Pottinger, *The Afghan connection* (1983) · H. C. B. Cook, *The Sikh wars: the British army in the Punjab, 1845–1849* (1975) · *Annual Register* (1884)
Archives BL OIOC, corresp., MSS Eur. D 830 | BL OIOC, corresp. with Henry Lawrence, MSS Eur. F 85 · NA Scot., letters to Dalhousie
Likenesses F. C. Lewis, group portrait, oils (*A Durbar at Udaipur, 1855*), BL OIOC · A. Murano, cabinet photograph, NPG [*see illus.*] ·

portrait, repro. in C. R. Low, *Golden hours* (1869), 314–29 · wood-engraving, NPG; repro. in *ILN* (29 Nov 1884), 533, 542
Wealth at death £41,322 2*s.* 11*d.*: resworn probate, Nov 1885, *CGPLA Eng. & Wales*

Lawrence, Gertrude [*real name* Gertrud Alexandra Dagma Lawrence Klasen] (1898–1952), actress, was born in London on 4 July 1898. Her father, Arthur Lawrence Klasen, a music-hall singer, was Danish; her mother, Alice Louise Banks, was English. The child's parents were divorced while she was still in infancy and she lived first with her mother, a small-part actress, then later with her father. She was thus brought up in a theatrical atmosphere from her earliest years. She made her first stage appearance in a pantomime at Brixton, London, in 1910. In his autobiography Noël Coward tells how he met her as a child performer in the year 1913:

> Her face was far from pretty, but tremendously alive. She was very *mondaine*, carried a handbag with a powder-puff and frequently dabbed her generously turned-up nose. She confided to me that her name was Gertrude Lawrence, but that I was to call her Gert because everybody did … She then gave me an orange and told me a few mildly dirty stories, and I loved her from then onwards.   (Morley, *Talent to Amuse*, 20)

She became the foremost of all of Coward's leading ladies, a perennial feather in his brilliant cap.

In her early days Gertrude Lawrence was solely a revue and cabaret artist. Her first manager was André Charlot and her first really big success was in *London Calling* in 1923, a revue written by Noël Coward. The best of his musical plays, *Bitter Sweet* (1929), was written with her in mind, but it was finally decided that her voice was too light for so heavy a singing part as that of Sari, so he wrote *Private Lives* (1930) in which they played together. The play's success was immediate in both London and New York. Thereafter New York would never willingly allow Gertrude Lawrence to return to her native London. James Agate, seeing her in a musical comedy, had already called her a very considerable artist who could neither dance nor sing but had an astonishing power of mimicry and sense of fun, adding that she gave a brilliant edge to everything she said and did. George Jean Nathan in New York—another critic with few favourites—spent the subsequent twenty-five years praising her glitter and effervescence in plays that included *Lady in the Dark* and Shaw's *Pygmalion*, and finally in the excellent and evocative Rodgers and Hammerstein musical *The King and I*, in which Gertrude Lawrence was triumphantly appearing on Broadway when her fatal illness overtook her.

Noël Coward knew and understood her better than her critics or her public. In the last pages of his *Present Indicative* he records her personal qualities of 'quick humour, insane generosity, and a loving heart', and recalls her performance in *Private Lives*: 'the witty quick-silver delivery of lines; the romantic quality, tender and alluring; the swift, brittle rages; even the white Molyneux dress'. She was an actress of high vitality, keen wit, and undoubted style—a fine flaunting player—with a strange gift of mutability, of altering her appearance for each part she played or even within the same part.

Gertrude Lawrence was twice married: first, in 1917, to

Gertrude Lawrence (1898–1952), by Paul Tanqueray, 1932

Francis Xavier Howley, playwright and producer, with whom she had a daughter. The marriage was dissolved. In 1940 she married Richard Stoddard Aldrich, an American. She published her own racy but unreliable reminiscences, *A Star Danced*, in 1945 (they were ghosted by her agent Fanny Holtzmann). But Lawrence comes more vividly and touchingly to life in Noël Coward's *Present Indicative* (1937) and *Future Indefinite* (1954); her art, charm, and elegance are best epitomized in the recording she made with him of scenes from his *Private Lives*, culminating in the haunting song 'Some day I'll find you'. Gertrude Lawrence died in New York on 6 September 1952 and was buried in Park View cemetery, Upton, Massachusetts. A largely inaccurate film of her life entitled *Star!*, was made in 1968, with Julie Andrews playing Gertrude Lawrence, and she also featured in Sheridan Morley's musical play *Noel and Gertie*.   ALAN DENT, *rev.* K. D. REYNOLDS

Sources G. Lawrence, *A star danced* (1945) · R. S. Aldrich, *Gertrude Lawrence as Mrs A* (1957) · private information (1971) · S. Morley, *Gertrude Lawrence* (1981) · S. Morley, *A talent to amuse: a biography of Noel Coward* (1969) · *The Times* (8 Sept 1952) · www.findagrave.com, Aug 1999

Archives Theatre Museum, London, letters | University of Virginia, Charlottesville, letters to Daniel Nye

Likenesses C. Beaton, photograph, 1930–39, NPG · Yevonde, photographs, 1930–39, NPG · B. A. Haggin, pastel drawing, 1931, Museum of the City of New York · P. Tanqueray, photographs, 1932–7, NPG [*see illus.*] · D. Wilding, photographs, 1940–49, NPG · R. S. Sherriffs, ink and wash caricature, NPG

Lawrence, Giles (1522–1584/5), Greek scholar, was admitted to Corpus Christi College, Oxford, on 19 August 1539, aged seventeen and six months, as a native of Gloucester. His origins are otherwise unknown. He proceeded bachelor of civil law, probably after his admission to a legist fellowship at All Souls in 1542. In 1551 he was appointed regius professor of Greek, replacing George Etheridge, who had held the chair since 1547. On Queen Mary's accession Etheridge resumed the chair by order of the privy council of 27 August 1553, Etheridge taking the full stipend for the first year, sharing it equally with Lawrence the next year, and allowing Lawrence £6 13s. 4d. out of the £40 stipend in 1555. Lawrence clearly remained *persona grata* in Oxford as he supplicated for the DCL on 13 March 1556. For part at least of Mary's reign, however, he was acting as tutor to the children of Sir Arthur Darcy, who had served briefly as lieutenant of the Tower under Edward VI and was still living in that vicinity. It was when Lawrence was thus employed, in 1554, that he assisted the flight overseas of his friend John Jewel whose funeral sermon he was later to preach. Shortly after Mary's death, in April 1559 Lawrence resumed the regius chair. His ecclesiastical career was no less disjointed. He was appointed archdeacon of Wiltshire on 18 September 1564, on the deprivation of one John Lawrence, whom Anthony Wood surmised to have been either his father or his uncle. This post he held until 19 October 1577; the reason for his leaving it is not known. He had subscribed to the articles of faith at the convocation in London in 1572. On 3 January 1581 he was collated to the archdeaconry of St Albans, and, on the same day, to the vicarage of Rickmansworth; he soon resigned both positions.

Highly praised for his scholarship, along with Bartholomew Dodington, regius professor of Greek at Cambridge, by Edward Grant in the prefatory letter to his *Graecae linguae spicilegium* (a book which he doubtless hoped would find a ready sale at the universities), Lawrence's only known surviving manuscript, 'De significatione verbi *prosphero* et *prospheromai*' ('On the meaning of the words prosphero and prospheromai'), is to be found among Matthew Parker's papers at Corpus Christi College, Cambridge. Strype, however, in appendix 85 to his life of Parker gives a substantial sample, from manuscripts now apparently lost, of criticisms made by Lawrence of the translation of the New Testament in the Bishops' Bible, and it was apparently in response to these criticisms that many revisions were made for the 1572 edition. It is not clear whether Lawrence's role was that of reviser or adviser. The Corpus manuscript may represent an aid to Parker in his revision of Hebrews. Strype also records that Lawrence 'read Greek to the Lady [Mildred] Cecil … of whom the said Laurence testified, that she equalled, if not overmatched, any of the same profession in that language' (Strype, 404). Of his skill in the composition of Greek verse there is an example in the seven elegiac couplets he contributed to Thomas Wilson's *The Three Orations of Demosthenes* (1570). The precise date of Lawrence's death is not known, but it was presumably shortly before the appointment of his successor to the regius chair on 25 March 1585.   Elisabeth Leedham-Green

Sources *Reg. Oxf.*, 1.231 · *APC*, 1552–4, 333 · G. D. Duncan, 'Public lectures and professorial chairs', *Hist. U. Oxf.* 3: *Colleg. univ.*, 335–61 · E. G. [E. Grant], *Tēs Hellēnikēs glōssēs stachyologia: Graecae linguae spicilegium* (1575) · *The works of John Jewel*, ed. J. Ayre, 4 vols., Parker Society, 24 (1845–50), vol. 4 · *Fasti Angl., 1541–1857*, [St Paul's, London] · *Fasti Angl., 1541–1857*, [Salisbury] · J. Strype, *The life and acts of Matthew Parker*, new edn, 3 vols. (1821) · B. F. Westcott, *A general view of the history of the English Bible*, 3rd edn, rev. W. A. Wright (1905) · T. Wilson, *The three orations of Demosthenes* (1570) · Wood, *Ath. Oxon.*: *Fasti* (1815) · Emden, *Oxf.*, 4.343–4
Archives CCC Cam., papers | BL, Lansdowne MS 682

Lawrence, Harry Lawrence Bradfer- (1887–1965), antiquary and collector of manuscripts, was born on 1 April 1887 at 8 Paynes Court, Church Street, King's Lynn, the son of Charles Bradfer (d. 1886/7), a draper's assistant, and his wife, Elizabeth Lawrence. He was educated initially at home because of poor health, and then at secondary school in King's Lynn. He married Violet Evelyn, daughter of William Charles Bradfield, a draper, on 23 July 1913. They had a daughter, Bridget Evelyn (d. 1997) and a son, Philip Leslie (who shared his father's love of book collecting and became a member of the Roxburghe Club in his own right). Bradfer-Lawrence became a land agent and worked in Norfolk until 1935 when he was appointed managing director of Hammond's brewery in Yorkshire, a firm which greatly expanded under his administration. When it merged in 1960 to become United Breweries he became the first chairman.

Bradfer-Lawrence was an enthusiastic antiquary. He made occasional contributions to the *Antiquaries Journal* and was elected fellow of the Society of Antiquaries in 1924; he exhibited items from his collections for the society. He became its treasurer in 1944 and did much to set the society's affairs in order. He gave collections of manuscript materials to the Yorkshire Archaeological Society and the Norfolk and Norwich Archaeological Society.

Bradfer-Lawrence published a number of volumes chiefly connected with the history and archaeology of Norfolk. He edited *The account of Edmund Carvell and Humfrey Bedyngfelde as the executors of the will of Thomas Karvell of Wiggenhall* (1916) for the Norfolk Record Society, and *The Muster Returns for Divers Hundreds in the County of Norfolk* (1935) for the Norfolk and Norwich Archaeological Society. In addition he wrote *The Merchants of Lynn* (1927) and a history of Castle Rising (1929). He was also a distinguished book collector, particularly of medieval manuscripts, of which he owned nearly sixty. After his death his collection of manuscripts was deposited for a number of years in the Fitzwilliam Museum, Cambridge, before being sold to Quaritch, who dispersed them by private sale and auction. He also collected printed books from the fifteenth to the twentieth centuries, many of which were sold at Sothebys after his death. In addition, he had a substantial collection of manuscripts and printed books relating to Richard Jefferies. His achievements as a book collector were acknowledged by his election to the Roxburghe Club in 1954.

Bradfer-Lawrence died on 19 October 1965 at Ashby Hall, Ashby St Mary, Norwich.   A. S. G. Edwards

Sources *Antiquaries Journal*, 46 (1966), 172 · P. M. Giles, 'A handlist of the Bradfer-Lawrence manuscripts deposited on loan at the Fitzwilliam Museum', *Transactions of the Cambridge Bibliographical Society*, 6 (1973), 86–99 · b. cert. · m. cert. · d. cert. · *CGPLA Eng. & Wales* (1966)
Archives Norfolk RO, corresp., research notes, papers | W. Yorks. AS, Leeds, calendars, notes, and papers relating to Lister family archives
Wealth at death £342,938: probate, 1966, *CGPLA Eng. & Wales* · new grant, 1967

Lawrence, Henry, appointed Lord Lawrence under the protectorate (1600–1664), politician, was born late in 1600, the eldest son of Sir John Lawrence (d. 1604) of St Ives, Huntingdonshire, and Elizabeth, daughter and heir of Ralph Waller of Beaconsfield, Buckinghamshire. Sir John died when Lawrence was three and his widow married Robert Bathurst of Gloucestershire. Lawrence entered Gray's Inn on 7 August 1617, and joined Queens' College, Cambridge, at Easter 1621 but migrated to Emmanuel College in October 1622 on the appointment of John Preston, possibly his tutor, as president; he proceeded MA in 1627. Preston probably played a crucial role in developing his strong puritan sympathies, but an early influence appears to have been his mother, who had theological interests. In the satirical *Narrative of the Late Parliament* (1657) Lawrence is called a Baptist. He married on 21 October 1628 Amy, daughter of Sir Edward Peyton of Iselham, Cambridgeshire, a noted puritan and future parliamentarian; her piety was later ridiculed by royalists.

Residing at St Ives, Lawrence let Slepe Hall and its adjoining farm to his impoverished relative Oliver Cromwell from 1631 to 1636. He retired to the Netherlands in the late 1630s, apparently to escape the danger of prosecution for his religion, and was abroad when the civil war broke out. In the Netherlands until late in the conflict, he was in Guelderland in December 1645 and at Altona in January 1646. An elder in the English congregation at Arnhem ministered to by Thomas Goodwin, he took advantage of Dutch licensing laws to publish *Of Baptisme* (1646), a lengthy defence of believer's baptism republished as *A Pious and Learned Treatise of Baptism* (1649). He appears to have continued his association with Goodwin's independent congregation following the return of both men to London. A work on the influence of good and evil angels, *Of our Communion and Warre with Angels*, followed later in 1646, dedicated to his mother.

Lawrence entered English politics with the parliamentarian victory, being chosen as recruiter MP for Westmorland on 1 January 1646. He joined the parliamentary committee appointed to investigate offences (not listed in earlier legislation) for which individuals would be excluded from the sacrament of the Lord's supper, and in July was nominated one of the commissioners for maintaining peace between England and Scotland. He is said to have strongly disapproved of the proceedings against Charles I, and regarded it as his duty to speak out for moderation while boycotting parliament. In his uncompromising *A Plea for the Use of Gospel Ordinances* (1649) he attacked the anarchism of 'spiritual Levellers' and 'holders of extravagant opinions' who rejected established places of worship. Respected for his integrity and godliness, Lawrence was eulogized by Milton in his *Second Defence of the People of England* as of the highest ability and accomplishments, and as an ally of Cromwell he denounced the ungodly present leadership of parliament in February 1652 in the second edition of *A Plea*. Following the expulsion of the Rump Parliament, on 14 July 1653 he was added to the council of state, sharing former Lord President Bradshaw's lodgings at Whitehall with Edward Montagu. His main role was reporting the council's decisions to the Barebone's Parliament, in which he sat for Hertfordshire, where he now lived. He also sat on the council's foreign affairs committee, used his Dutch knowledge in negotiations with their ambassadors, and helped to arrange Bulstrode Whitelocke's embassy to Sweden.

On Cromwell's assumption of power, Lawrence was named first in the list of the new councillors of state on 16 December 1653. On 19 December he was chosen as lord president, titular head of the council, for a month, and proved so suitable that his post was made permanent on 16 January 1654 at a salary of £300 per quarter. He was responsible for drawing up the lists of council decisions made when Cromwell was absent and presenting them for his approval, as well as signing official letters such as those announcing the new government to the American colonies and General Venables's commission for the 'Western Design'. He was one of the councillors chosen to negotiate the Dutch treaty on 13 March, and to negotiate with the French ambassadors and arrange foreign treaties. Inclined towards an even-handed approach to the Swedish–Dutch conflict for the Baltic, he was one of those Cromwell consulted privately about mediation in November 1655. His diligence was such that he attended an unmatched 163 of 164 council meetings in 1654, all but two in January–October 1655, and 126 of 129 in November 1655–June 1656. He also represented Hertfordshire in parliament in 1654, and in 1656 was chosen for both Colchester (once the corporation had been remodelled) and, probably through the influence of Lord Chief Justice Glyn, Caernarvonshire; he chose the latter. A commissioner for the ejection of scandalous ministers in Cambridgeshire, Huntingdonshire, Hertfordshire, and Norfolk in 1654, he joined that autumn's visitation of Cambridge University. On a more personal level he took charge of the library at St James's House in London while its keeper, Whitelocke, was in Sweden, and agreed to the Queen of Bohemia's request that he help the royalist Lord Craven to recover his property.

Lawrence was ably assisted by his talented eldest son, Edward (1633–1657), the addressee of Milton's twentieth sonnet as 'of virtuous father virtuous son' and a correspondent of Henry Oldenburg. Edward served as his father's amanuensis until his untimely death from smallpox. Lawrence occasionally spoke in Cromwell's second parliament, though eclipsed on government business by Thurloe, and was raised to the upper chamber or 'other house' as Henry, Lord Lawrence. When Cromwell died he administered the oath of office to his son and successor Richard, but took no part in the resulting factional struggles. His council role ceased late in July 1659, but the general council of officers considered him reliable enough to be selected for the committee of safety they established, on 26 October. At the Restoration he withdrew to his house at Theale, in the parish of Stanstead St Margaret's, Hertfordshire, which Edward Lawrence had purchased in 1651 and bequeathed to him. He died there, intestate so probably unexpectedly, on 8 August 1664 and was buried in the parish church. He left seven sons and six daughters; his second son, Henry, administered the estate for the younger children. A son, John, may have emigrated to Barbados, and a daughter, Martha, probably married Richard, second earl of Barrymore. A man of integrity and forceful political moderation, respected by intellectual heavyweights such as Milton and Oldenburg, Lawrence was both a serious theologian and a capable administrator who bore much of the weight of day-to-day government business under the protectorate. His input on policy was limited, but his reliability valued.

TIMOTHY VENNING

Sources council books, 1853–6, PRO, SP 25/47–60 · council order books, 1654–8, PRO, SP 25/75–78a · council committee books, 1653–6, PRO, SP 25/121–2 · Dutch papers, PRO, SP 84/160 · J. E. Bailey, 'President Henry Lawrence and his writings', *N&Q*, 5th ser., 11 (1879), 501–3 · J. Lawrence, 'History of the antient family of Lawrence', *GM*, 1st ser., 85/2 (1815), 12–17 · *CSP dom.*, 1653–60 · *The diary of Bulstrode Whitelocke, 1605–1675*, ed. R. Spalding, British Academy, Records of Social and Economic History, new ser., 13 (1990) · B. Whitelocke, *A journal of the Swedish embassy*, ed. C. Morton, rev. H. Reeve, new edn, 2 vols. (1855) · *CSP col.*, vol. 1 · *The correspondence of Henry Oldenburg*, ed. and trans. A. R. Hall and M. B. Hall, 1 (1965) · *VCH Huntingdonshire*, vol. 2 · *VCH Hertfordshire*, vol. 3 · J. W. Clay, ed., *The visitation of Cambridge ... 1575 ... 1619*, Harleian Society, 41 (1897) · W. H. Rylands, ed., *The visitation of the county of Buckingham made in 1634*, Harleian Society, 58 (1909) · Venn, *Alum. Cant.* · J. Foster, *The register of admissions to Gray's Inn, 1521–1889, together with the register of marriages in Gray's Inn chapel, 1695–1754* (privately printed, London, 1889) · C. H. Firth and R. S. Rait, eds., *Acts and ordinances of the interregnum, 1642–1660*, 3 vols. (1911) · GEC, *Baronetage* · warrants for Lawrence's pay, 1654, Bodl. Oxf., MS Rawl. A. 328, fols. 113, 151 · M. Tolmie, *The triumph of the saints: the separate churches of London, 1616–1649* (1977)

Likenesses R. Cooper, stipple, NPG · portrait, repro. in Clarendon, *Hist. rebellion*

Wealth at death estate at Theale, Stanstead St Margaret's, Hertfordshire, had been purchased thirteen years earlier by son for £1090: *VCH Hertfordshire*, vol. 3, p. 474

Lawrence, Sir Henry Montgomery (1806–1857), army officer in the East India Company, was born on 28 June 1806 at Matura, Ceylon, the fourth son of Colonel Alexander William Lawrence (1762x7–1835), an officer serving in the 19th foot, and his wife, Catherine Letitia (1774–1846), daughter of the Revd George Knox of Lifford, co. Donegal, Ireland. In 1808 the family returned to England and Lawrence was educated with his brothers Alexander and George St Patrick *Lawrence, after 1815 at Foyle College, Londonderry, where his maternal uncle, the Revd James Knox, was headmaster. In 1819 Lawrence was sent to the Revd James Gough's school, College Green, Bristol, with his younger brother John Laird Mair *Lawrence after his

Sir Henry Montgomery Lawrence (1806–1857), by Ahmed Ali Khan, 1857

family moved to Clifton, Bristol. He and his brothers were much influenced by their beloved eldest sister, Letitia Catherine (1802–1865), later Mrs Henry Horace Hayes. Through a family connection Lawrence was nominated by John Huddleston MP, an East India Company director, for a cadetship in its army. In August 1820 Lawrence joined his brother George at the company's Addiscombe College, near Croydon, where he worked hard but was not a particularly distinguished student. On one occasion he was rescued by Robert Guthrie MacGregor from drowning in the nearby canal.

Early career and marriage On 10 May 1822 Lawrence was commissioned second lieutenant, Bengal artillery, and he sailed for India in September, aged sixteen. He landed at Calcutta on 21 February 1823 and joined the headquarters of the Bengal artillery. While serving at Dum-Dum he was strongly influenced by the Revd George Crauford, the chaplain, and joined his small band of devout Christian officers that lived at Fairy Hall. Following Lord Amherst's declaration of war with Burma on 17 March 1824 Lawrence sailed with his battery to Chittagong early in June. He took part in the capture of the Arakan and on 18 November was appointed adjutant of the artillery, south-east division. On 25 April 1826 he was appointed deputy commissary of ordnance at Akyab, but after contracting malaria and dysentery was sent to Calcutta. While recovering Lawrence was nursed by George Crauford until he sailed, via the China route, for England on sick leave on 2 August. In May 1827 he arrived in England, where he remained for two and a half years to recover. During this time he met his future wife and joined the trigonometrical survey in the north of Ireland, where he gained valuable experience and training.

In September 1829 Lawrence sailed for India, accompanied by his sister Honoria and younger brother John, who had just joined the East India Company's civil service. On 9 February 1830 they landed at Calcutta and Lawrence was posted to a foot artillery battery at Karnal on the northwest frontier, where his recently married brother George was adjutant of a cavalry regiment. For eighteen months Lawrence lived with his brother and intensively studied his profession and Indian languages with the intention of obtaining civil employment. During the autumn of 1830 he travelled to Simla, and on his return trip visited his friend Captain Proby Thomas Cautley to see the large irrigation works he was constructing. On 27 September 1831 Lawrence was gazetted to a horse artillery troop at Meerut and then on 29 November was posted to the 1st horse artillery brigade at Cawnpore. During this time Lawrence lived abstemiously, spending his time studying for staff employment and saving for the 'Lawrence fund' which he and his siblings had started to provide for their mother when their old and ill father died. On 12 September 1832 he qualified in Urdu, Persian, and Hindi, and was specially recommended for the duties of an interpreter. During the cold weather his troop was sent to Dum-Dum and Lawrence passed the examination at the college, Fort William, further qualifying in Indian languages. On 13 January 1833 he was appointed interpreter and quartermaster to the 7th battery of artillery, but later that month he resigned and was reappointed to the horse artillery at Cawnpore.

Lawrence obtained lucrative civil employment when he was appointed, with his brother George's assistance, on 22 February 1833 an assistant revenue surveyor in the North-Western Provinces, in the newly instituted revenue survey of India. He assumed his duties at Moradabad where he was soon occupied in collecting information from the surrounding countryside to enable the government periodically to assess land taxation fairly. On 2 June 1835 Lawrence was promoted to the rank of full surveyor and became a captain on 10 May 1837. Following a long engagement Lawrence married, at Calcutta on 21 August 1837, his cousin Honoria [see Lawrence, Honoria, Lady Lawrence], daughter of the Revd George Marshall, rector of Cardonagh, Fahan, co. Donegal, Ireland. They had two sons, Alexander Hutchinson (1838–1864) and Henry Waldemar (1845–1908), and two daughters, Letitia Catherine (1840–1841) and Honoria Letitia (1850–1923). His wife accompanied him to Gorakhpur and then during his field journeys in Allahabad district, which he surveyed shortly afterwards. In 1838 Lawrence became involved in a dispute with a Captain McNaughton over a memoir of Sir John Adams he had adversely reviewed, and was dissuaded by his friends from fighting a duel.

The First Anglo-Afghan War and civil service Lawrence requested that he be placed at the disposal of the commander-in-chief (on 29 September) during the summer of 1838, as preparations began for the First Anglo-Afghan War, and rejoined his battery. When the Persians abandoned the siege of Herat, however, the army of the Indus was reduced in size and his services were surplus to requirements. Through the influence, however, of Frederick Currie, on 14 January 1839 Lawrence was appointed officiating assistant to George Clerk, the governor-general's agent for the affairs of the Punjab and the northwest frontier, to take over the civil administration of Ferozepore district. His friend Frederick Currie, who had recommended him, later wrote: 'I have helped to put your foot in the stirrup. It rests with you to put yourself in the saddle' (Lawrence, 73–4). Although financially less rewarding than working in the revenue survey, this political appointment as an assistant to the frontier agency while a military campaign was in progress offered Lawrence considerably improved career prospects.

On 31 March 1840 Lawrence was confirmed assistant to the governor-general's agent for the affairs of the Punjab and the north-west frontier. While Lawrence administered Ferozepore district he oversaw the rebuilding of the town with a wall and fort, widened roads and improved drainage, settled boundaries, and found time to write a series of articles for the Delhi Gazette. Following news of the disaster at Kabul in November 1841 Lawrence was busily employed preparing help for Jalalabad and maintaining good relations with the Sikh inhabitants of Peshawar, where he had been sent in December 1841 to assist Major Frederick Mackeson, the senior political officer. When Pollock finally advanced in April 1842 through the Khyber Pass into Afghanistan, accompanied by Mackeson, Lawrence was left behind at Peshawar to carry out his important duties.

When the British advanced on Kabul, Lawrence changed places with Mackeson and, in addition to his duties as political officer with Pollock's force, he was given command of the Sikh contingent, which had been sent by the durbar to co-operate with the British. He joined the expedition at Jalalabad, where he met Henry Havelock and attended several religious meetings this officer had organized for his men. At this time Lawrence also received news that his brother George, who was among those detained by Muhammad Akbar Khan as hostages, was safe and had been sent on parole to make terms for their surrender. On 20 August Pollock advanced on Kabul, and Lawrence, commanding the Sikhs, took part in the battles of Tezin and Haft Kotal. On 16 September 1842 he entered Kabul with Pollock's troops, two days before Nott's force arrived from Ghazni. A few days later his brother George and other captives arrived at the city unharmed. On 12 October Lawrence returned with Pollock's, Nott's, and Sale's combined forces to India.

Lawrence was promoted brevet major on 23 December 1842 for his services during the campaign, although he was bitterly disappointed at not being made a CB. On 31 December he was presented with a sword by the maharaja of Lahore and the same day was appointed superintendent of Dehra Dun and Mussooree by the governor-general. In January 1843 he arrived at Mussooree, but soon afterwards it was discovered that according to regulations this post could only be held by a covenanted civil servant. As a result on 17 February he was transferred to Ambala as assistant to the envoy at Lahore. Two months later the raja of Kaithal died without a successor, causing his territory to lapse to the British government. Lawrence was appointed at Lord Ellenborough's suggestion as political agent, and quickly completed the settlement of this new territory.

Nepal and the First Anglo-Sikh War Lawrence was promoted by the governor-general on 1 December 1843 to the important post of resident at the court of Nepal. While proceeding to Katmandu Lawrence met at Karnal his recently married brother John, who had just returned from England, and wrote a defence of Sir William Macnaghten. Lawrence and his wife resided at Katmandu for two years, but he had comparatively little to do as he had been instructed to interfere as little as possible with the Nepalese government and to offer advice only when it was sought or thought likely to be acceptable. His free time was occupied contributing articles on military and political affairs regularly to the *Calcutta Review*, recently founded by J. W. Kaye, and other periodicals. Lawrence also suggested the founding of a school in the hills for the children of European soldiers, which eventually led to the construction of the Lawrence Asylum at Sanawar. This was supported at considerable self-sacrifice by Lawrence throughout his life, and by other donors.

Lawrence accompanied his wife to Calcutta at the end of 1845, when it became clear that for her health and that of their two children they needed to return to England. On 6 January 1846 while *en route* Lawrence received orders to join the army of the Sutlej following the battles of Mudki on 18 December and Ferozeshahr on 21 December during the opening phase of the First Anglo-Sikh War. When he arrived Lawrence replaced Major George Broadfoot, who had been killed in action, and found that Lord Ellenborough, the governor-general, had appointed him on 3 January 1846 the governor-general's agent for foreign affairs and for the affairs of the Punjab. Later, on 1 April, the appointment of governor-general's agent for the affairs of the north-west frontier was also added to his responsibilities. Lawrence was present at the battle of Sobraon on 10 February 1846, the later occupation of Lahore after which Lawrence assisted Currie in negotiating the treaties of Kasuri and Amritsar. He was in complete agreement with the governor-general, who opposed annexation, preferring instead to leave the Sikh state intact as a potential source of support for British India. In June 1846 he was promoted brevet lieutenant-colonel for his services at Sobraon.

Lawrence remained at Lahore, supported by a force of British troops, to provide advice and guidance to and bolster the Sikh government in accordance with the peace settlement. However, Lal Singh and the Sikh durbar remained a hotbed of intrigue. Lawrence displayed firmness and energy, compelling the reticent Sikh government to deal with the rebellious governor of the hill fort of Kot Kangra and then to send troops to force Sheikh Imam ud din to hand over Kashmir as agreed to Gulab

Singh, the raja of Jammu, according to treaty. Following a brief campaign Imam ud din personally surrendered to Lawrence. When he returned to Lahore, Lawrence deposed Lal Singh from the vizarat and pensioned him off. A council of regency was formed in his place 'acting under the control and guidance' of the British resident, and under the treaty of Bhyrowal, signed on 22 December 1846, it was agreed that British troops should remain in Lahore. The resident was given virtually unlimited authority to 'direct and control' in all matters of internal administration and external relations during the minority of the maharaja. Lawrence, now appointed resident at Lahore, effectively ruled the Punjab through his hand-picked band of young, able, and energetic British assistants, who included his younger brother John, Herbert Edwardes, John Nicholson, George Macgregor, James Abbott, and Henry Coxe. Despite this change intrigues continued at Lahore, and Lawrence ordered that the young maharaja Duleep Singh should be separated from Maharani Jindan, who was removed from Lahore. Lawrence's arduous duties, however, as resident caused his health to fail and in November 1847 he proceeded on sick leave to England, handing over his post to Frederick Currie. On his homeward journey he accompanied Lord Hardinge aboard the *Mozuffer*. Following arrival in England in March 1848 Lawrence was fêted and on Hardinge's recommendation he was made a KCB on 28 April 1848, in recognition of his services.

The Second Anglo-Sikh War and the administration of the Punjab Lawrence divided his holiday between England and Ireland, spending time with his family and friends. When news of the murder of P. A. Vans Agnew and Lieutenant Anderson at Multan and of the outbreak in the Punjab reached England, however, he was soon occupied in lengthy consultations with the Indian authorities in London. In November 1848 Lawrence and his wife left England, and landed at Bombay a month later. He at once went to the Punjab, joining the army in the field early in 1849. Lawrence was present during the final phase of the siege of Multan, and witnessed the bloody battle of Chilianwala on 13 January 1849. After this indecisive engagement Lawrence successfully persuaded Sir Hugh Gough to remain on the battlefield and thereby demonstrate that the battle had been a draw at worst. After the decisive battle of Gujrat on 21 February and the effective pursuit of the remaining organized troops the Sikhs were finally compelled to surrender. On 1 February Lawrence resumed his duties as resident at Lahore, but he was soon frequently in dispute with Lord Dalhousie, the new governor-general, whose strong views were often opposed to his own. Despite Lawrence's strong opposition the Punjab was annexed to British India, and accordingly he resigned. However, Dalhousie persuaded him to withdraw his resignation and on 14 April 1849 Lawrence was appointed president of the new board of administration for the affairs of the Punjab, with his brother John and Charles Greville Mansel, and he was also made agent to the governor-general. Lawrence took responsibility for political work such as the disarmament of the country, negotiating with the local chiefs, raising and organizing new regiments, and educating the young maharaja, while John took responsibility for the civil administration and settlement of the land revenue, and Mansel the judicial management of the province. While Lawrence headed the board each commissioner had a voice in the general council and was responsible for the acts of the other two. Although this organization worked well for four years, the administration of the Punjab became a subject of increasing friction between the members of the board. While Lawrence toured the Punjab his two colleagues opened direct communications with Lord Dalhousie and secured decisions that differed from the views of their absent president. As a result considerable personal animosity developed between Lawrence and his brother, particularly over the land settlement. The end result was that Lawrence tendered his resignation, which was accepted by Lord Dalhousie who, after abolishing the board of administration, retained John in charge of the Punjab. In recompense Henry Lawrence was offered the governor-general's agency in Rajputana, with the same salary as in the Punjab. Henry was mortified that he had not been selected to govern the Punjab, but early in 1853 took up the important political post at Ajmer. In July 1853 he declined Dalhousie's offer of the residency of Hyderabad. His wife, who had been in bad health for some time, died on the night of 14–15 January 1854 at Mount Abu, Rajputana. On 19 June 1854 Lawrence was made aide-de-camp to the queen and promoted colonel in the army.

When Lord Dalhousie resigned from office on 29 February 1856 Lawrence at once wrote to Lord Canning, the new governor-general, to set himself right on points on which he believed that he had been misjudged. On 18 May 1856 he was promoted a regimental lieutenant-colonel. On 19 January 1857, shortly before he was to depart for England with his daughter to restore his health, Lord Canning offered Lawrence the post of chief commissioner and agent to the governor-general in Oudh. Despite continued ill health Lawrence immediately accepted this job, which he regarded as compensation for the loss of the Punjab and as public recognition of his services.

The Indian mutiny Lawrence immediately sent his daughter home and succeeded Coverley Jackson as chief commissioner and agent to the governor-general in Oudh at Lucknow in March 1857. When he arrived at the residency on 20 March Lawrence found widespread discontent among the local population largely due to the failure to observe instructions laid down by the government when the kingdom of Oudh had been annexed, and to his predecessor's violent temper and hasty judgement. Pensions had not been paid, country chiefs had been deprived of their estates, and many old officials and three-quarters of the former army were unemployed. Lawrence immediately tackled these problems, by holding frequent durbars to announce his new policy and energetically redressing the real grievances held by sections of the local population. His success was reflected when revenue was collected with greater ease than before.

When news of the outbreak of the Indian mutiny in Meerut and at Delhi in May 1857 reached Lucknow, Lawrence at once began organizing the defence of the unfortified city and surrounding area. With a force of 700 British troops (from the 32nd foot) and a large number of Indian soldiers of questionable loyalty Lawrence faced a difficult problem. He finally took the questionable decision to defend both the residency and the Machhi Bhawan (a large dilapidated fort) located 4 miles apart in the city. At his request he was also promoted major-general late in May 1857, and given command of all troops stationed in Oudh. Initially the mutiny did not touch Lucknow, however, and with an outward display of confidence Lawrence ordered the collection of treasure from the city and outlying stations, bought up and stored grain and other supplies, arranged for a water supply, built outworks, strengthened the defences of the residency and Machhi Bhawan, cleared fields of fire, and brought in guns and ammunition to the residency where they were emplaced.

The mutiny did not seriously affect Lucknow until 30 May, when several British officers were killed by disaffected Indian sepoys in the cantonment north of the city. These mutineers were quickly checked and a general insurrection averted by British troops, who pursued the rebels 10 miles from the city and inflicted heavy losses upon them. Elsewhere in Oudh during June, however, the situation rapidly deteriorated. Most Europeans living in outlying cantonments had to escape hurriedly from the bands of marauding sepoys. Lawrence's earlier policy of reconciliation paid off, however, and with only one exception the local chiefs and peasantry helped or ignored fugitives heading for the safety of the city. Similarly the majority of the Hindu population of Lucknow held themselves aloof from the rebellion, and, again with only one exception, the local *talukdars* more or less actively helped protect the European population.

The news of various defeats elsewhere in India caused Lawrence growing fears about the loyalty of his remaining Indian troops upon whom the defence of the city depended. Under the immense strain of organizing the defence his health temporarily failed and between 9 and 12 June Lucknow was ruled by a council presided over by the revenue commissioner. Throughout June the ranks were carefully weeded of unreliable elements, the reliable Sikh troops were formed into separate companies, and further efforts were made to strengthen the city and construct a defensive position around the residency. Lawrence refused urgent appeals from General Hugh Wheeler at Cawnpore to send him aid, as his own position at Lucknow was not secure. When Cawnpore fell on 26 June the mutineers moved on Lucknow. Three days later the rebel advance guard reached Chinhat, 8 miles from the residency. Lawrence, acting upon the advice of Martin Gubbins (the revenue commissioner), made the serious error of deciding to check their advance, and to do so assembled a force of 300 European and 220 Indian infantry, 36 European and 80 Sikh cavalry, and 11 guns, leaving only the Machhi Bhawan and the residency garrisoned. Lawrence led this column when it marched towards Nawabganj at dawn the following day. When it attacked the rebels at

Chinhat it was quickly discovered that they were in greatly superior numbers, and many of his Indian gunners from the Oudh irregular artillery and cavalrymen deserted. Under heavy attack the surviving British troops retreated in disorder into Lucknow. Lawrence helped cover the rout by arranging artillery support, but by the time the disorganized survivors reached safety 118 European officers and men had been lost, which greatly weakened the defence of Lucknow.

The disaster at Chinhat on 30 June 1857 precipitated the occupation of the city overnight by the rebels, who opened fire on the Machhi Bhawan and the residency the following morning. Without sufficient troops the Machhi Bhawan was now clearly indefensible and it was abandoned without loss by Lawrence that night after its guns were spiked and the magazines and defences blown up. The exposed residency, now packed with large numbers of unarmed men, women, and children, was quickly surrounded by more than 7000 mutineers with heavy guns. Lawrence, with only 927 European and 768 Indian troops, faced a difficult problem as the residency was seriously exposed to enemy artillery batteries. To co-ordinate the defence Lawrence occupied a room at the top of the building with a commanding view of the surrounding area, but which was vulnerable to enemy artillery fire. On the first day of the siege an 8 inch shell exploded in the room without causing any injury, and Lawrence was entreated by his subordinates to move to a less exposed position, which he agreed to do the following day. Lawrence rose early on the morning of 2 July, however, to organize the defences and then at 8 a.m. returned exhausted from the heat to rest. While he recuperated on his bed another shell burst in the room, and a small fragment wounded him severely in his upper left thigh and abdomen. Lawrence was immediately removed to Dr Fayrer's house for treatment, but this too came under heavy artillery fire and he was moved once again to a less vulnerable position within the residency. However, Lawrence's case was hopeless and the surgeons could only try to alleviate his suffering. Despite his wounds he remained lucid and handed over the chief commissionership to Major John Sherbrook Banks, commander of the Lucknow division, and placed Colonel John Inglis in command of the garrison. Lawrence also gave detailed instructions about the conduct of the defence of the residency and ordered them never to surrender. He was in extreme pain. Mrs James Harris, who nursed him, stated 'his screams were so terrible that I think the sound will never leave my ears' (Lawrence, 255). He said he wanted his epitaph to be only 'Here lies Henry Lawrence who tried to do his duty. May the Lord have mercy on his soul' (Hibbert, 237). He received the holy communion and finally died from his wounds at about 8 a.m. on 4 July 1857. He was buried the same day in the residency churchyard, attended only by the chaplain, as all the defenders had to remain at their posts. Canning wrote: 'there is not a man in India could have been less well spared at the present moment' (Maclagan, 113).

Henry Lawrence was a bold, energetic, and skilled administrator who rose to high position by dint of sheer ability and hard work. He had a sympathetic and kind-hearted nature, and his disregard for money or personal luxury was partly responsible for the influence he established over his subordinates. However, he possessed a fiery temper, which he struggled to control, and often had a brusque manner with subordinates, often mistaking disagreement for personal antagonism. Throughout his career he showed considerable literary ability in a series of articles and books on Indian political and military affairs. The esteem in which he was held was shown when, before news of his death reached England, the directors of the East India Company appointed him on 22 July 1857 provisionally to succeed as governor-general, should an accident befall Lord Canning, and until his successor arrived. Although his military judgement was at times questionable, it was due to his foresight and preparations that the residency held out until relieved. Following the relief of Lucknow, Colonel Sir John Inglis wrote:

> Few men have ever possessed to the same extent the power which he enjoyed of winning the hearts of all those with whom he came in contact, and thus insuring the warmest and most zealous devotion for himself and for the government which he served. The successful defence of the position has been, under Providence, solely attributable to the foresight which he evinced in the timely commencement of the necessary operations, and the great skill and untiring personal activity which he exhibited in carrying them into effect.   (*DNB*)

Lawrence's earlier work in pacifying the Punjab was also instrumental in reconciling the population to British rule to the extent that many flocked to the British colours during the mutiny. In recognition of his services his eldest son, Alexander Hutchinson, was created a baronet. Lawrence was commemorated by a memorial in St Paul's Cathedral, and in the church in Lucknow. Perhaps his most important legacy was the military asylums set up for European children, which still bear his name, and which were taken over and expanded by the government of India after his death.   T. R. MOREMAN

Sources J. L. Morison, *Lawrence of Lucknow, 1806–1857: being the life of Sir Henry Lawrence retold from his private and public papers* (1934) · J. Lawrence, *Lawrence of Lucknow: a story of love*, ed. A. Woodiwiss (1990) · H. B. Edwardes and H. Merivale, *Life of Sir Henry Lawrence*, 3rd edn (1873) · J. J. Innes, *Sir Henry Lawrence, the pacificator* (1898) · C. Hibbert, *The great mutiny, India, 1857* (1978) · J. W. Kaye, *Lives of Indian officers*, new edn, 2 vols. (1904) · H. M. Vibart, *Addiscombe: its heroes and men of note* (1894) · V. C. P. Hodson, *List of officers of the Bengal army, 1758–1834*, 4 vols. (1927–47) · M. E. Yapp, *Strategies of British India: Britain, Iran and Afghanistan, 1798–1850* (1980) · J. S. Grewal, *The new Cambridge history of India, 2/3: The Sikhs of the Punjab* (1990) · R. H. Phillimore, ed., *Historical records of the survey of India*, 4 (1958) · C. J. Radcliffe, *Sir Henry Lawrence: centennial address delivered in Magee University College, Londonderry, 8 November 1957* (1958) · S. B. Singh, ed., *Letters of Sir Henry Montgomery Lawrence: selections from the correspondence of Sir Henry Montgomery Lawrence (1806–1857) during the siege of Lucknow from March to July 1857* (1978) · C. E. Buckland, *Dictionary of Indian biography* (1906) · T. A. Heathcote, *The military in British India: the development of British land forces in south Asia, 1600–1947* (1995) · F. W. Stubbs, ed., *History of the organization, equipment, and war services of the regiment of Bengal artillery*, 3 (1895) · BL OIOC, Cadet MSS · *DNB* · R. Young, *Reminiscences of the great and good Sir Henry Lawrence KCB, also of the Indian sepoy mutiny of 1857, including the siege and capture of Delhi, being extracts from the story of my chequered life by Y* (1893) ·

The journals of Honoria Lawrence: India observed, 1837–1854, ed. J. Lawrence and A. Woodiwiss (1980) · M. Maclagan, *'Clemency' Canning* (1962) · b. cert.

Archives BL OIOC, corresp. and papers, MSS Eur F 85 | NA Scot., Dalhousie MSS, corresp. with Lord Dalhousie, GD45 · NAM, letter-book · NAM, letters (11) to W. S. R. Hodson, Acc. 6404–6474 · W. Yorks. AS, Chapeltown Road, Sheepscar, Leeds, Canning MSS, letters (20) to Lord Canning

Likenesses oils, *c*.1827, NPG · miniature, *c*.1847, BL OIOC; version, NPG · T. Campbell, marble bust, 1849, NPG · Chotay Meah [A. A. Khan], photograph, 1857, NPG · A. A. Khan, photograph, 1857, NPG [*see illus.*] · lithograph, *c*.1857, V&A · C. Baugniet, lithograph, 1858 · J. G. Lough, marble statue, 1862, St Paul's Cathedral, London · H. W. Phillips, oils, exh. RA 1862, Lawrence Asylum, India · C. G. Lewis, group portrait, mixed engraving, pubd 1864 (*The intellect and valour of Great Britain*; after T. J. Barker), NPG · J. R. Dicksee, mezzotint, 1866 · W. Theed, plaster sculpture, 1874 (after E. Campbell, 1849) · J. R. Dicksee, oils, NG Ire. · W. J. Edwards, stipple (after photograph), NPG · J. H. Foley, medallion, St Paul's Cathedral, Calcutta · M. & N. Hanhart, two lithographs, BL OIOC · A. A. Khan, group photograph (Sir Henry Lawrence with George Lawrence and Sir Herbert Edwardes), NPG · F. C. Lewis, group portrait, oils (*A durbar at Udaipur, 1855*), BL OIOC · J. G. Lough, statue, Lahore Art Gallery, India · J. G. Lough, statue, exterior of old India office building · bust, BL OIOC · engraving, repro. in H. B. Edwardes, *A year on the Punjab frontier, 1848–49*, 1 (1851), frontispiece · engraving, repro. in Lord Roberts, *Years in India*, 1 (1897), 348 · engraving, repro. in F. P. Gibbon, *The Lawrences of the Punjab* (1908), frontispiece · group portrait (*The second Lahore durbar, 26 Dec 1846*), BM · miniature, Lahore Art Gallery, India

Lawrence, Sir Herbert Alexander (1861–1943), army officer and banker, was born on 8 August 1861 at Southgate, London, the fourth son of Sir John Laird Mair *Lawrence, later first Baron Lawrence (1811–1879), viceroy of India, 1864–9, and his wife, Harriette Katherine (1820–1917), daughter of the Revd Richard Hamilton of Donegal. Dame Maude Agnes *Lawrence was his sister. Lawrence was brought up in England and educated at Harrow School (1875–9) and the Royal Military College, Sandhurst. He was commissioned into the 17th lancers on 10 May 1882. His early military career was little more than a round of sports, at which he excelled, but appointment as regimental adjutant offered some inkling of administrative ability and professional ambition. This was confirmed by his passage into the Staff College at Camberley (1894–6). His first appointment after graduating was the fateful one of staff captain (intelligence) at the War Office. In the Second South African War he served on the intelligence staff of Sir John French's cavalry division. Here he came into close contact with one of the cavalry division's operations staff, Douglas Haig, who was to have a profound influence on Lawrence's military career. Haig's initial effect on Lawrence's career, however, was to terminate it.

Lawrence ended the Second South African War with a brevet lieutenant-colonelcy. He was an able and ambitious officer, still only 41, and with great expectations. But within little more than a year he had resigned his commission and returned to England to embark on a career in banking. The cause of this dramatic change was Lawrence's being overlooked as commanding officer of the 17th lancers. In an army where regimental loyalties were paramount, command of one's own regiment was especially esteemed. Lawrence believed himself qualified for the post and refused to play second fiddle to an outsider who was his junior. The outsider was Douglas Haig. Lawrence built his later reputation, both as a banker and a soldier, on the measured quality of his judgement, but it is difficult to see his decision to resign from the army in May 1903 as anything more than a fit of pique.

That he was able to contemplate a change of career was in large part because of the connections Lawrence had made as a result of his marriage on 26 April 1892 to Isabel Mary (*d*. 1941), second and eldest surviving daughter of Charles William *Mills, second Baron Hillingdon (1855–1919) [*see under* Mills family (*per*. 1773–1939)], senior partner in Glyn, Mills, Currie & Co. Lawrence's success, however, was not simply the result of his wife's and his own connections. He did not join the Mills's family bank until 1907, by which time he had already established the reputation for financial judgement which made him sought after as a director. Lawrence did not entirely sever his military links. He joined King Edward's Horse (King's Colonials) and commanded the regiment from 1904 to 1909. But it took the outbreak of the First World War in August 1914 to bring him back into the regular army fold.

Trained staff officers were at a premium in the autumn of 1914. Lawrence was recalled in September and made general staff officer, grade 1 (GSO1) of the 2nd yeomanry division. He went with this unit to Egypt and then to Gallipoli. The commander-in-chief on Gallipoli, Sir Ian Hamilton, was painfully aware of his lack of able commanders. In June 1915 he gave Lawrence command of the 127th (Manchester) brigade, part of the 42nd (East Lancashire) territorial division. Within eleven months of the outbreak of war, Lawrence had risen from retired major to brigadier-general. The speed of his rise was resented by some, a resentment which Lawrence's rather superior manner at this period did little to allay. He later commanded the 53rd (Welsh) and 52nd (Lowland) divisions on Gallipoli. But it was Lawrence's other appointments during that muddled and ill-fated campaign which gave the clue to his real abilities. In July 1915 he was made deputy inspector-general of communications and sent to the island of Lemnos where he averted a complete breakdown in the Mediterranean expeditionary force's logistical arrangements. During the successful evacuation of the Gallipoli peninsula (December 1915 – January 1916), the only part of the campaign from which military planners could derive any credit, he was in command of the beach at Cape Helles, from which he was one of the last to leave. After Gallipoli he returned to Egypt, where in the summer of 1916 he achieved a conspicuous success by defeating a German–Turkish force at Romani (4–12 August 1916), a victory which returned the Sinai Desert to British control. But then his career suffered a reverse. Unconvinced of the wisdom of invading Palestine, Lawrence asked to be relieved of his command and was banished to the backwater of the 71st home service division in England. He did not receive another fighting command until February 1917 when he was given a second-line territorial division, the 66th (2nd east Lancashire).

Lawrence did not become properly acquainted with the war's greatest battlefield until 9 October 1917 when the 66th division was 'blooded' at Poelcappelle, the last and least successful of General Sir Herbert Plumer's set-piece attacks during the third battle of Ypres (or Passchendaele). Although one of the 66th division's brigades fought its way into the ruins of Passchendaele village, it was compelled to retreat through a mixture of inexperience, German enfilade fire, and inadequate artillery support. A German counter-attack had to be repulsed by the firing of an SOS barrage which inflicted considerable casualties on its own infantry. Lawrence's baptism of fire on the western front was, therefore, hardly propitious, but as an omen for his personal future it was also irrelevant.

During the winter of 1917–18 Field Marshal Haig's command underwent sweeping changes. Within the space of a few weeks, his chief engineer, quartermaster-general, director-general of transportation, director of military intelligence (DMI), and chief of staff were all replaced. Lawrence's military career took a final sharp turn. In January 1918 he was selected to replace the discredited Brigadier-General John Charteris as chief intelligence officer. The choice of Lawrence was not so much surprising as astonishing and has never been satisfactorily explained, especially as Haig claimed the decision to be his own. Haig had given up the trusted Charteris reluctantly. He and Lawrence were hardly close and perhaps antipathetic. Lawrence had been Haig's senior in the service, but now found himself a major-general while Haig was a field marshal. This disparity might have been expected to tell on a relationship previously strained by such considerations. Although Lawrence had a background in intelligence, he had had no intelligence experience since his resignation from the army in 1903 and precious little experience of any kind on the western front. If their collaboration had ended in failure and acrimony there would have been no cause for surprise. The surprise, however, was that it worked so well. In the event Lawrence was DMI for only a few weeks. At the end of January he was promoted to the more important post of chief of the general staff, in succession to Sir Lancelot Kiggell. He retained this post through the vicissitudes of the spring and the triumphs of the autumn of 1918.

The 'improvement' in Haig's generalship in 1918 is sometimes attributed to the benign influence of his new team of more independent-minded senior advisers, among whom Lawrence was paramount. John Terraine described Lawrence as the 'right arm' which Haig had always lacked (Terraine, 386). But Lawrence's precise influence is difficult to delineate. He does not appear to have radically influenced operational doctrine. Generally he was in accord with Haig's view of the war and how it should be fought. His dealings with the general officer commanding, Fifth Army, General Hubert Gough, were no more helpful to that beleaguered commander on the eve of the German offensive than were Haig's. There is no doubt, however, that Lawrence provided Haig with unfailing moral support and was a source of cool reassurance

and sensible advice. On those occasions when Haig was absent in London, Lawrence made swift, confident, and correct decisions. This was particularly true in July 1918 when Marshal Foch demanded the transfer of four British divisions and a corps headquarters to the Champagne. Lawrence reassured Foch with the transfer of one division and the promise of another, while holding back the other two. In doing so, entirely on his own judgement, he showed a fine sense of the importance of Anglo-French solidarity without dangerously weakening the British line. Although a man who was not frightened of confrontation, his particular contribution was perhaps in smoothing the often rough path of Anglo-French relations.

Lawrence, who was appointed KCB in 1917 and GCB in 1926, returned to the City of London after the war and became one of its most senior figures. He was appointed chairman of Vickers in 1926 and of Glyn's Bank in 1934, a position he retained until his death. He was a member of the royal commission on the coal industry in 1925. His reputation for circumspection and wisdom made his advice sought beyond the organizations to which he was formally attached and he was a close friend and confidant of Montagu Norman, governor of the Bank of England.

Herbert Lawrence was a highly intelligent man of cool judgement and clear insight. But he was also intense and driven. In the famous photograph of Haig and his senior commanders taken on the steps of the *mairie* (town hall) at Cambrai on 11 November 1918 it is possible to read in his face the personal costs of the war. His sons, Lieutenant Oliver John Lawrence (1893–1915) and Temporary Captain Michael Charles Lawrence (1894–1916), were both killed on the western front. Lawrence himself died on 17 January 1943 at Woodcock, Little Berkhamsted, Hertfordshire, and was buried at Seal, near Sevenoaks in Kent.

J. M. BOURNE

Sources G. MacMunn and C. Falls, *Military operations: Egypt and Palestine*, 3 vols., History of the Great War (1928–30), vol. 1 · J. E. Edmonds, ed., *Military operations, France and Belgium, 1917*, 2, History of the Great War (1948) · J. E. Edmonds, ed., *Military operations, France and Belgium, 1918*, 5 vols., History of the Great War (1935–47) · *The private papers of Douglas Haig, 1914–1919*, ed. R. Blake (1952) · H. Gough, *Fifth Army* (1931) · J. Davidson, *Haig: master of the field* (1953) · J. Marshall-Cornwall, *Haig as military commander* (1973) · J. Terraine, *Douglas Haig: the educated soldier* (1963) · T. Travers, *How the war was won: command and technology in the British army on the western front, 1917–1918* (1992) · *The Times* (18 Jan 1943) · *CGPLA Eng. & Wales* (1943) · *Army List* · *The Harrow School register* · Burke, *Peerage*
Archives NL Scot. |FILM BFI NFTVA, news footage · IWM FVA, record footage
Likenesses O. Birley, oils, 1842, William and Glyn's Bank Ltd, London · W. Stoneman, photograph, 1918, NPG · group photograph, 11 Nov 1918, IWM · O. Birley, portrait, Cavalry Club, London · photograph, repro. in *The Times history of the war*, 22 vols. (1914–21), 17.105 · photograph, repro. in *The Times*, 8
Wealth at death £107,207 8s. 10d.: probate, 22 Feb 1943, *CGPLA Eng. & Wales*

Lawrence [née Marshall], **Honoria**, Lady Lawrence (1808–1854), writer, was born on 25 December 1808 at Cardonagh, Donegal, the twelfth of fifteen children of the Revd George Marshall and his wife, Elizabeth. She was brought

Honoria Lawrence, Lady Lawrence (1808–1854), by unknown artist, in or before 1837

up by her uncle Admiral Heath, who lived nearby, and was educated in a devoutly protestant environment; her literary tastes and love of nature were both encouraged. She first met her future husband, Henry Montgomery *Lawrence (1806–1857), who was a cousin, on his return from India in 1827. Despite their mutual attraction, he was deterred from proposing by his lack of prospects; they finally married in Calcutta on 21 August 1837. She bore four children, of whom two sons and one daughter survived. She was slight and lithe, with fair hair and blue eyes, but her attraction lay in more than her looks: 'She was not beautiful in the ordinary sense of the term; but harmony, fervour and intelligence breathed in her expression, emanating from a loving heart and cultured mind' (Diver, 78).

Honoria Lawrence's maturity, independence, flexibility, and sense of humour helped her face the demands of her husband's career as a soldier–administrator. She was always on the move in north-western India, and was the first European woman to live in several areas, including Kashmir and the independent state of Nepal. The difficulties of life in these remote areas were considerable, particularly with regard to the birth and upbringing of children. She recorded her life with perception and enthusiasm in voluminous letters and journals, including those written for her two young sons at school in England, selections from which were subsequently published. In these she also reflects her ever-deepening appreciation and love of India.

However, while Honoria Lawrence later became known as a writer, contemporaries singled out her invaluable role in supporting her husband in his career and other activities. Her view of marriage and of the role of women marked her life in India. She was deeply romantic, quoting Coleridge's view that an individual found his or her completion only in another being. Nevertheless, as she wrote in an article in the Calcutta Review in 1845, she believed that a husband played the dominant role: 'a wife is useful and happy just in proportion as she can … identify herself with her husband … He has a profession as

well as a family; her profession is that of being a wife' (Lawrence, 'English women in Hindustan', 100–01). She carried out her precepts with dedication and enthusiasm. In the early months of their marriage she revelled in Henry Lawrence's camp life as a surveyor, and assisted in his work. When he was placed in civil charge of Ferozepore, she spent long hours helping run the post office, while in 1849–50 she threw herself wholeheartedly into the professional demands of his life in Lahore, where he was president of the board of administration for the Punjab. The Lawrences shared a deep commitment to philanthropy, and Mrs Lawrence played a valuable part in helping establish near Simla the Lawrence Asylum for the children of soldiers, to provide a boarding education in a healthy hill climate.

Writing became an important medium for the expression of Henry Lawrence's views on Indian affairs, and here, too, Honoria Lawrence played an essential collaborative role. She edited many of his articles on military and political matters for the Delhi Gazette, which paper also published in instalments The Adventurer in the Punjaub, a novel which she helped write, composing some of the romantic sections, including poetry. More influential were the articles Henry Lawrence contributed from 1844 to the newly formed Calcutta Review; these his wife edited, and in some cases co-authored. Though she published little independently, several of her own articles dealing with the female 'profession' of marriage and motherhood appeared anonymously in the Calcutta Review and the Friend of India. She was sceptical about the performance of British women in India, and was critical of their lack of concern for Indians and the wives and children of British soldiers. Her success in fulfilling her own role was attested by many. Her friend Lady Login commented:

> I have never met a woman quite like Honoria, never a wife who more entirely shared in, and helped, her husband in his work, yet without in any way bringing that fact to the knowledge of the world at large. (Login, 63)

She became Lady Lawrence when her husband was knighted in 1848, following the First Anglo-Sikh War. She died at Mount Abu in Rajputana on 15 January 1854, and was buried there two days later.

ROSEMARY CARGILL RAZA

Sources M. Diver, Honoria Lawrence: a fragment of Indian history (1936) · The journals of Honoria Lawrence: India observed, 1837–1854, ed. J. Lawrence and A. Woodiwiss (1980) · J. Lawrence, Lawrence of Lucknow: a story of love, ed. A. Woodiwiss (1990) · H. B. Edwardes and H. Merivale, Life of Sir Henry Lawrence, 2 vols. (1872) · J. W. Kaye, 'Sir Henry Lawrence', Lives of Indian officers, new edn, 2 (1904), 387–496 · E. D. Login, Lady Login's recollections: court life and camp life, 1820–1904 (1916) · [H. Lawrence], 'English women in Hindustan', Calcutta Review, 4 (1845), 96–127 · G. F. L. Marshall, Marshall of Manor Cunningham (1931)

Archives BL OIOC, Henry Lawrence collection, MS Eur. F 85

Likenesses miniature, in or before 1837, priv. coll. [see illus.] · J. Fisher, portrait, c.1847, priv. coll.; repro. in Lawrence and Woodwiss, eds., The journals, following p. 128 · portrait, c.1850, priv. coll.; repro. in Lawrence, Lawrence of Lucknow, pp. 76–7 · K. Hill, silhouette, c.1852, priv. coll.; repro. in Lawrence and Woodwiss, eds., The journals, following p. 128 · K. Hill, daguerreotype, 1853, priv.

coll.; repro. in Lawrence and Woodwiss, eds., *The journals*, following p. 128 · miniature (aged twenty-one), priv. coll.; repro. in Lawrence and Woodwiss, eds., *The journals*, following p. 128
Wealth at death few small personal legacies, incl. large Kashmiri shawl for daughter: Diver, *Honoraria Lawrence*, 444

Lawrence, James Henry [*known as* Chevalier Lawrence] (1773–1840), writer, was the son of Richard James Lawrence of Fairfield, Jamaica, whose ancestor, John, younger son of Henry Lawrence (1600–1664), had settled in that island in 1676. His mother was Mary Hall, also of a Creole family, with roots in Worcestershire. Lawrence was educated at Eton College, where he was Montem poet in 1790, and afterwards at the University of Göttingen in Germany. A precocious author, he produced in 1791 a poem entitled 'The Bosom Friend', 'which', said the *Monthly Review* of April 1792, 'instead of being a panegyric on friendship, is written in praise of a modern article of a lady's dress'. In 1793 his essay on the heterodox customs of the Nairs of Malabar with respect to marriage and inheritance was inserted by Wieland in his *Der Teutsche Merkur* and in 1800 Lawrence, who seems in the interim to have lived entirely on the continent, at Schiller's behest completed a romance on the subject, also in German, which was published in the *Journal der Romane* for the following year, under the title of 'Das Paradies der Liebe', and reprinted as *Das Reich der Nairen*. The book was subsequently translated into French and English by the author himself, and published in both languages; the English version, entitled *The Empire of the Nairs*, was published in four volumes in 1811 by Thomas Hookham. It is considerably altered from the original, and is preceded by an introduction seriously advocating the introduction of the customs of the Nairs into Europe. The novel's attack on the institution of marriage and its advocacy of matrilineal inheritance was influenced by William Godwin, Mary Wollstonecraft, and the French *philosophes*. Its idealized portrait of Nair society, in part derived from Francis Buchanan's *Journey from Madras through the Countries of Madras, Canara, and Malabar* (1807), in part represents the Nair Queen Samora's struggle against 'Mahommedan despotism and polygamy', but little attempt is made to flesh out the Indian setting. On 17 August 1812 Percy Shelley wrote to Lawrence 'Your "Empire of the Nairs", which I read this Spring, succeeded in making me a perfect convert to its doctrines', and he met with Lawrence in London the following year (*Letters*, 1.322–3). The novel exerted an important influence on Shelley's poem *Queen Mab* (1813) and other works.

In 1801 Lawrence's poem 'Love: an Allegory' appeared in a German version in a German magazine entitled *Irene*, and the original was published in London in the following year. It was attacked in 1803 by the *Anti-Jacobin Review*, which dismissed it as 'a dull and licentious publication'. In 1803 Lawrence, happening to be in France with his father, was arrested, along with the other English residents and tourists, and detained for several years at Verdun. Having eventually effected his escape by passing himself off as a German, he published in London a prose account of his captivity entitled *A Picture of Verdun, or, The English Detained in France* (2 vols., 1810), and in 1813 a drama in five acts

entitled *The Englishman at Versailles, or, The Prisoner of Peace*. Also in 1813 Lawrence published an article in volume 2 of *The Pamphleteer* entitled 'Dramatic emancipation, or, Strictures on the state of the theatres, and the consequent degeneration of the drama'.

Subsequently Lawrence led a roving life, chiefly in Europe, and was apparently never at a loss for money. Having been made, as he asserted, a knight of Malta, he assumed the title of Sir James Lawrence, and was frequently known as the Chevalier Lawrence. In 1824 he published *On the Nobility of the British Gentry*, intended to establish the proposition that an English gentleman, in the sense in which the author employed the term, is the equal of a foreign nobleman, and protesting against its employment in any other. In 1828 he brought together most of his early writings, with others of a similar description, in a collection entitled *The Etonian Out of Bounds*. He died unmarried on 26 September 1840, and was interred with his father in the burial-ground of St John's Wood Chapel. By the time of his death his *Nobility of the British Gentry* had reached four editions, and it was republished posthumously in 1842, under the title *British and Continental Titles of Honour*.

RICHARD GARNETT, *rev.* NIGEL LEASK

Sources *GM*, 2nd ser., 15 (1841), 205 · *GM*, 1st ser., 85/2 (1815), 16–17 [genealogy on father's side] · J. Lawrence, *The empire of the Nairs, or, The rights of women*, 2nd edn, 4 vols. (1811); facs. edn with introduction by J. Todd (1976) · Watt, *Bibl. Brit.* · *The letters of Percy Bysshe Shelley*, ed. F. L. Jones, 2 vols. (1964), vol. 1, pp. 322–3 · T. J. Hogg, *The life of Percy Bysshe Shelley* (1906), 446–7 · W. Graham, 'Shelley and *The empire of the Nairs*', *Proceedings of the Modern Language Association of America*, 40 (1925), 881–91 · *A new biographical dictionary of 3000 cotemporary* [*sic*] *public characters, British and foreign, of all ranks and professions*, 2nd edn, 3 vols. in 6 pts (1825)

Lawrence, John (1753–1839), writer on horses and animal welfare, was born in or near Colchester on 22 January 1753, the son of John (1707–1763) and Anne Lawrence (1722–1810). Both his father and grandfather were brewers. He married Anne Barton at about the age of thirty, and the couple had one son and five daughters. Lawrence claimed that his concern with the welfare of animals began early, and that he first wrote a pamphlet on the subject when he was fifteen. He did not begin to publish, however, until he was in his forties. Lawrence's early works were anonymous and political. He contributed to *The Patriot's Calendar* (1794, 1795, 1796), a miscellaneous collection of documents supporting the French Revolution. He is also thought to have contributed to *Right and Remedies* (1795), which is a staunch defence of French Revolutionary principles and an attack upon the hostilities between Britain and France. In the early 1790s Lawrence had been living in Lambeth Marsh in London, but by the time of his earlier publications he was resident in Bury St Edmunds. It seems likely that he had purchased a small farm in this area some years before with money inherited on the death of his father.

In 1796 Lawrence published the first volume of what has become his most significant work, *A Philosophical and Practical Treatise on Horses and the Moral Duties of Man towards Brute Creation* (the second volume was published in 1798). Lawrence gives an encyclopaedic account of the horse, considering such topics as the merits of previous writers on horses and horsemanship; the varieties of horse; the breed, shape, and size of an animal suitable for a given task; the art of equestrianism; effective training methods; various kinds of carriages to be pulled; and the illnesses to which horses are prone and their most appropriate treatments. The most strikingly controversial and enduring aspect of the work, however, is its third section on the welfare of animals, 'On the right of beasts'. In line with Christian charitable views in this period, Lawrence argues that animals clearly have both rational and sensible attributes, and should be regarded as possessing souls in some limited sense. On this basis alone, he contends, animals deserve to be treated with kindness and consideration. The most innovative aspect of his discussion, however, is that he does not allow his case for animal welfare to rest on appeals to charity, but forcefully applies a doctrine of rights. 'The rights of beasts', he insists, 'should be formally acknowledged by the state, and that the law be formed on that principle, to guard and protect them from acts of flagrant and wanton cruelty, whether committed by their owners or others' (Lawrence, *Treatise*, 123). Lawrence argues crucially that legislation with respect to the treatment of animals should be detached from property rights, and that animals should enjoy (irrespective of ownership) a basic right of care. The state should outlaw vivisection and wilful cruelty to animals and implement statutory regulations for the handling, transportation, and slaughter of livestock.

Lawrence later suggested that the initial reception of the *Philosophical and Practical Treatise* was mixed. The *Monthly Review*, however, wrote favourably of the work at the time, remarking 'on its spirit, good sense, and humanity', and glossing over its political and social implications. The *Treatise* was sufficiently successful to have run to three editions by 1810. Lawrence produced two more works specifically on horses in the nineteenth century. These were a glossy quarto volume with engravings, *The History and Delineation of the Horse, in All his Varieties* (1809), and a small volume, *The Horse in All its Varieties and Uses* (1829). The latter was intended (in one of Lawrence's infelicitous but representative equestrian metaphors) 'to form a convenient manual for the use of the hitherto initiated, who may neither have the inclination nor leisure to ride the great horse in larger volumes' (Lawrence, *History and Delineation*, iii).

Though best known for his work on horses, Lawrence's contemporary literary success was achieved mainly through his writings on practical agrarian matters. He produced three substantial works in this area at the beginning of the nineteenth century: *The New Farmer's Calendar* (1800), *The Modern Land Steward* (1801), and *A General Treatise on Cattle, the Ox and Swine* (1805). All sold sufficiently well to warrant further editions. The most successful of these, *The New Farmer's Calendar*, sold out within months of publication, and was in its fifth edition by 1829. He also published a short treatise on the care of poultry in 1822 (under the pseudonym Bennington Moubray), which ran to eight editions in his lifetime.

Lawrence wrote two books on field sports in the later part of his career; again, both were published pseudonymously, this time under the name G. H. Scott. In these works Lawrence surveys the various practices of sports in Britain (such as shooting, fishing, and horse-racing), as well as including lengthy polemics against the game laws. In both works he reiterates his concern for the welfare of animals and declares his detestation of animal baiting of any kind. He does, however, argue that animals can be killed for sport, as long as those animals are subsequently used for food. He more surprisingly, and rather speciously, argues in favour of fox-hunting, justifying his position on the basis of a kind of *lex talionis*: the fox is vermin and a hunter himself, and so deserves, in turn, to be hunted and killed. Lawrence also wrote for a number of periodicals on equestrian, agrarian, and sporting matters, contributing regularly to the *Gentleman's Magazine* and the *Sporting Magazine* from 1799.

Not much is known of Lawrence's life outside his writings. He was advertising for a position as a landlord's agent on a preliminary sheet of his *Modern Land Steward* (1801), but it is unknown whether he was successful in securing this place. He relates in his final work on horses how he was consulted by Richard Martin, MP for Galway, prior to the second introduction and passing of Martin's Ill Treatment of Cattle Bill in July 1822. Lawrence wrote a biographical sketch of another philanthropic MP in 1821, *A Memoir of the Late Sir T. C. Bunbury*. Charles Bunbury had managed the first unsuccessful attempt to introduce animal welfare legislation into the Commons in 1809. Lawrence recalls in this sketch his conviviality, his benevolence, his implacable opposition to the slave trade, his radical whig politics, and his love both of horses and horse-racing. It is reasonable to suggest that if these were not qualities that Lawrence possessed himself, then they were certainly those to which he aspired. Lawrence's obituary in the *Sporting Magazine* mentions that he lived toward the end of his life at Peckham, Surrey. He died of influenza at Peckham on 17 January 1839, and was buried at Norwood cemetery. The *Sporting Magazine*'s epitaph was that Lawrence 'was certainly an eccentric, but if the shell was husky, the kernel was sound' (*Sporting Magazine*, 19, 1839, 63).

Victorian commentators gleaned similar signs of eccentricity in Lawrence's writings, noting with some justification both his lack of literary organization and his prolixity. Lawrence's important discussions on the issues of animal rights and welfare are mostly contained in the early book on horses. The expression of such concerns would become more emotive and less consistently argued in his later work. He remains, however, a highly significant figure for the development of theories of animal rights in the nineteenth and twentieth centuries. The Bodleian librarian E. W. B. Nicholson included a reprint of 'On the rights of beasts' in his *The Rights of an Animal* (1879), and the leading exponent of animal rights at the beginning of the twentieth century, Henry S. Salt, wrote favourably of Lawrence. Late twentieth-century proponents of the rights of animals have acknowledged an intellectual debt to their predecessors, but have also accused them of not pressing their arguments to their logical conclusion by advocating vegetarianism. Nevertheless, Lawrence's argument that the state should accord animals basic rights of care and treatment and that deliberate cruelty should be illegal has been widely influential. SEBASTIAN MITCHELL

Sources *DNB* · J. Lawrence, *A philosophical and practical treatise on horses*, 2nd edn, 2 vols. (1802) · *Sporting Magazine*, 2nd ser., 19 (1839), 63 · J. Lawrence, *The history and delineation of the horse, in all his varieties* (1809) · E. W. B. Nicholson, *The rights of an animal* (1879) · J. Donaldson, *Agricultural biography* (1854) · A.-H. Maehle, 'Cruelty and kindness to the "brute creation": stability and change in the ethics of man-animal relationships', *Animals and human society: changing perspectives*, ed. A. Manning and J. Serpell (1994) · H. Ritvo, *The animal estate: the English and other creatures in the Victorian age* (1987) · H. S. Salt, *Animal rights considered in relation to social progress*, rev. edn (1922) · J. Turner, *Reckoning with the beast: animals, pain and humanity in the Victorian mind* (1980)
Archives Bodl. Oxf., Nicholson MSS
Likenesses Holl, engraving (after Wivell)

Lawrence, John Laird Mair, first Baron Lawrence (1811–1879), viceroy of India, was born at Richmond, Yorkshire, on 4 March 1811, the sixth son of Major Alexander Lawrence (1762×7–1835) of the 19th foot, a much wounded veteran of Ulster protestant stock, and his wife, Catherine Letitia (1774–1846), daughter of George Knox, rector of Lifford. Sir Henry Montgomery *Lawrence and Sir George St Patrick *Lawrence were his elder brothers. In 1823 John went from a day school at Bristol to the free grammar school at Londonderry, where his maternal uncle was headmaster, and in 1825 to Wraxall Hall, Wiltshire, an unexacting proprietary school. Through a family friend, he received in 1827 a nomination to East India College, Haileybury; his indifferent education was enough to carry him through the qualifying examination. Tall, strong, and physically adventurous, he had hoped to follow his brothers into the East India Company's army; the influence of an elder sister, Letitia, reconciled him to a civilian career. To her he owed, in large part, the evangelical faith, deeply held though undemonstrative and unintellectual, with which he was content within his inherited churchmanship.

An Indian apprenticeship, 1827–1840 Lawrence always felt that he had neglected his educational opportunities. Nevertheless, he passed out third from Haileybury (1829) among those destined for the Bengal presidency. He described himself as quite widely read, 'in a desultory fashion', for someone of his age. A Haileybury contemporary remembered him for 'a good deal of the Irish element' in his behaviour. He went out to India with his brother Henry, to whom he was particularly close, but was ill and depressed during a year spent learning languages at Calcutta. Neither the Bengal climate nor the social life of the Indian capital suited him. At his own request he obtained a posting to the Delhi territory, where he was to spend most of his service until transferred to the Punjab. These first years made an indelible impression on him. Charles Metcalfe had pioneered in the Delhi territory the methods

John Laird Mair Lawrence, first Baron Lawrence (1811–1879), by George Frederic Watts, 1862

of administration later associated with Lawrence and his disciples—the 'Punjab school': the head of a district combined in his person the functions of government, administrative and judicial, separated elsewhere in British India. The region was, moreover, home to those 'village republics' in which Metcalfe saw the eternal India of the peasantry, whose well-being it was the duty of government to safeguard and enhance. Rural society was under Metcalfe's regime protected from disruption by Western influences operating through an imported legal system. When engaged in settling the record of rights on which taxation was based the young Lawrence found 'no districts … where the practice of our civil courts has … done so little harm' (Stokes, *The Peasant Armed*, 128–9). He absorbed, too, the official bias against the Indian aristocracy, characteristic of Metcalfe and of Robert Merttins Bird, the directing intelligence of settlement work in the surrounding North-Western Provinces.

After four years as assistant judge, magistrate, and collector of Delhi, Lawrence was given temporary charge of the Panipat district to the north, with the additional responsibility of surveying its lands and assessing their taxation. Without a European assistant, to begin with, for a population of several hundred thousand, he displayed the qualities that were to become a legend and a model. Riding armed through a district with a turbulent history, attired for comfort in a mixture of Western and Indian dress, he made himself accessible to its people, in patriarchal fashion, and acquired a local reputation for omniscience. He excelled in settlement work, spending the greater part of the year under canvas. Reverting briefly to his assistant's post at Delhi in 1837, he was promoted deputy collector, and acted as collector of the city before taking over the Gurgaon district to the south. The next year Bird picked him to be settlement officer in the drought-stricken Etawah district of the North-Western Provinces. In 'that hole Etawah' Lawrence experienced the reality of an Indian famine. There, too, this evangelical learned that it was worse than useless to challenge Indian religions—'the miserable superstition of the people'—directly. Only education could very gradually diffuse 'truer and more enlightened ideas' (Smith, 1.111, 121–2). His authoritarian temperament, hardened by India, went with an openness that impressed the Quaker diarist Barclay Fox when they met after Lawrence had returned to Europe on extended sick leave (1840–42), following a near fatal attack of jungle fever.

From Delhi to the Punjab, 1840–1849 So far Lawrence had not been singled out as anything more than a promising settlement officer. He returned to India against medical advice, after marrying, on 26 August 1841, Harriette Katherine (1820–1917), daughter of Richard Hamilton, rector of Culdaff, co. Donegal, with whom he had ten children, the youngest of whom was the civil servant Dame Maude Agnes *Lawrence. An able woman, Harriette often combined the duties of secretary with those of a wife and mother. She received the Order of the Crown of India in 1878.

Temporary posts preceded Lawrence's appointment as collector of Delhi and Panipat, concurrently, in 1844. He had come to know the city and its inhabitants very well, and expressed a marked sympathy with the underpaid Indian officials who usually represented the British: 'People are fond of remarking that the natives are great rogues, but who makes them so, in great measure?' he asked the small European community in the *Delhi Gazette*. British administrators had taken bribes as a matter of course before their salaries were raised by Lord Cornwallis and Lord William Bentinck (Smith, 1.179). On the eve of the First Anglo-Sikh War, Lawrence made a lasting impression upon the visiting military governor-general, Sir Henry Hardinge, who shortly afterwards appealed to him for help in getting supplies to an army which had come close to disaster at Ferozeshahr in December 1845. By the use of traditional methods of requisitioning which he thought unjust, Lawrence assembled within days some 4000 cartloads which arrived in time for the decisive engagement of the campaign at Sobraon.

Lawrence's reward in March 1846 was the commissionership of the Trans-Sutlej States, the fertile Jullundur Doab taken from the Sikhs. Later that year, and again in 1847–8, he deputized for his brother Henry as resident at Lahore, the Sikh capital. On the assassination of two British officers at Multan in April 1848, John Lawrence urged the immediate intervention that might have prevented the Second Anglo-Sikh War. When full-scale hostilities began in the autumn, he and his subordinates held the Jullundur Doab with small forces by practising the doctrine of mobility which, then and subsequently, he preached to soldiers, and by employing locally raised

Sikhs against their co-religionists. The final British victory found the Lawrence brothers at odds with each other. In contrast with Henry, who pleaded with the governor-general, Lord Dalhousie, for the defeated Sikhs, John favoured their total subjection to direct rule. He was not inclined to pity the fallen dynasty and its nobles. Henry's outlook reflected his years as a political officer at Indian courts, and a naturally chivalrous disposition; he saw what was best in his protégés: 'all your politicals look more to politics than to statistics and the internal economy of the country', John had written to him in 1846. It was a mistake to rely on princes and nobles in trying to win over the conquered. Lower taxation and greater security for the peasantry was a better policy: 'Introduce our laws, our system, our energy and our forethought, and you will do real good' (Smith, 1.199, 205).

The Punjab after annexation, 1849–1856 The board now set up to administer the former Sikh territories had Henry at its head, with his brother and a third member who from 1850 was Robert Montgomery, John's contemporary at Londonderry and Wraxall Hall and intimate friend. Differences of temperament and opinion made it increasingly hard for the brothers to work together; by 1852 both had applied for a transfer. They would not agree, wrote John to Henry, on 'organic changes', meaning the treatment of the Sikh *sirdars* and *jagirdars*, nobles and grantees of broad lands under the old order. Dalhousie, who once stigmatized the Indian aristocracy as 'false, oppressive and corrupt', backed John, whose views on the point were, however, less radical than those of the governor-general. In 1853 the board was dissolved, Henry posted away, and his brother named chief commissioner of the Punjab.

The removal of Henry confirmed John as the dominant figure in the Punjab school, gathering round him, on Dalhousie's instructions, a selection of the best men to be had. They were the instruments of paternal government. Simplicity and fairness were the official priorities of this administration, in accordance with Lawrence's conviction, given practical expression in the Jullundur Doab, that to involve illiterate peasants in legal forms and proceedings was 'the very devil'. From another angle the Punjab system was one of rigid control, through 'an almost military chain of command'; each British official had to answer for his actions, in writing, to those above him. Lawrence personified both aspects of the system; his ideal of personal contact with Indians yielded to the reality of long hours at a desk and interminable correspondence (Stokes, *The English Utilitarians*, 244–5). Nevertheless, the achievements of the Punjab bureaucracy in its formative period were considerable. After a warlike population, predominantly Sikh and Muslim, had been disarmed to secure British rule, a police force of over 20,000 men, half paramilitary and half a civil constabulary, set a standard of public order unequalled in the subcontinent. Within three years of annexation the scourges of thuggee and dacoity—the clandestine activity of a sinister criminal brotherhood, and undisguised banditry—had been eradicated. Curbing the power of the Punjab's baronage was a controversial move. When acting resident at Lahore, Lawrence's efforts to recover alienated lands for the Sikh state, then under British tutelage, had contributed to the renewal of war in 1848. As the member of the Punjab board responsible for fiscal policy, he proceeded with greater caution, restrained by Henry's concern for the class affected. Over one-fifth of the land revenue remained in the hands of those who qualified 'in virtue of prescriptive possession, or … on special considerations of family influence and antiquity, or of individual character and services' ('General report on the administration of the Punjab, 1849–51', *Parl. papers*, 1854, 69, para. 320). This was the outcome of protracted argument between the brothers.

For John Lawrence the Punjab system centred on the interests of the cultivator, pictured as 'the hardy yeoman, the strong-handed peasant'. 'Assess low' was his refrain to juniors fixing the demands on land that furnished three-quarters of the province's taxation. His object was to make the Punjab the granary of northern India: 'Let means of export, the grand desideratum, be once supplied, the rest will follow' (Thorburn, 184). The 'enterprising trader, the thrifty capitalist', were to flourish with the peasant. A market economy needed a network of roads usable in the rainy season, bridged and policed, whose construction the board pressed forward. In this context, irrigation had great importance: planning started in 1849; the Bari Doab Canal to the Sikh heartland, the Manjha, was begun two years later. The ambitious programme of improvement embraced schools—over 3000 existed by 1856, providing education described as 'of course most primitive'—as well as prisons that incorporated progressive thinking, and the telegraph. The north-west frontier acquired with the Punjab posed a special problem. There the policy was one of containment rather than improvement; Lawrence, like Dalhousie, would have preferred to halt British expansion on the Indus. The inhospitable territory beyond, with its unruly Muslim tribes, was a financial drain on the rest of the Punjab; it required 12,000 regulars in the Peshawar valley and a provincial contingent of similar strength, the famous Punjab irregular frontier force. These constructive labours embodied John Lawrence's vision and drive, although the policies were, in a real sense, the governor-general's. Dalhousie obtained the honour of KCB (5 February 1856) for his favourite lieutenant, and strongly recommended him for appointment as the Punjab's first lieutenant-governor, 'the man whom universal acclamation would select', a status delayed until 1859.

The Indian mutiny, 1857–1859 The mutiny made a forceful Indian administrator into a national hero in Britain: but Lawrence was surprised by events at Meerut and Delhi in May 1857. 'I cannot conceive', he wrote on hearing the news, 'what has misled the sepoys'. He was, however, quick to understand the nature of the outbreak. Realizing that the entire Bengal army was suspect, he set about disarming its regiments stationed in the Punjab, in which he was anticipated by his friend and subordinate Robert Montgomery at Lahore. To replace them, he raised over

40,000 Punjab horse and foot, trebling the existing provincial forces, all organized on the irregular model with very few British officers. His hold on the Punjab and his leadership in this crisis rescued the British in northern India. He counted on the Sikhs' traditional antagonism towards the Mughal emperors, whose lineal representative, the king of Delhi, the mutineers acknowledged as their sovereign, on the Punjab Muslims' indifference, for good historical reasons, to the residual prestige of the Delhi dynasty, and on the undoubted popularity of the British administration in the Punjab, helped by good harvests which brought home the benefits of moderate assessments. Nevertheless, he believed that the Punjab's loyalty to its very recent conquerors would crumble unless the British moved decisively to retake Delhi, the political and military centre of the rising. He put unremitting pressure on the generals, Anson, Barnard, and Archdale Wilson, who were slow to grasp 'the whole political bearings' of the situation.

To find reinforcements, British and Indian, for the troops encamped outside Delhi from early June, Lawrence wanted to evacuate the territory beyond the Indus, leaving it to the relatively friendly Afghanistan of Dost Muhammad. A withdrawal, vetoed by the governor-general, would almost certainly have been interpreted as a sign of desperate weakness. Otherwise the ruler of the Punjab enjoyed the freedom of action he requested from Canning, Dalhousie's successor, a freedom enlarged by the interruption of communications between northern India and Calcutta. Admirers of Henry Lawrence, dead of his wounds at Lucknow in July 1857, held that the response of the Punjab was determined by those elements whom the elder Lawrence had befriended. John lost no time in appealing to the Sikh *sirdars*, the natural leaders of their people, urging them to show their loyalty by raising a specified number of men in each case: 'a step … which really saved upper india', recalled one of his staff. As recruits came in—34,000 between May and August—they were enrolled in the new Punjab formations. The Sikhs—about a third of the 60,000 strong Punjab force at its peak—and the frontier tribesmen were excellent fighting material; the remainder guarded disarmed regulars, found escorts, and kept open the road to Delhi. 'I am no advocate of trusting John Sing[h] a bit more than I can help', remarked Lawrence, 'we had no option but to trust him, and other Punjabees, or have our throats cut.' Pressed by those around him not to jeopardize the Punjab, he held back British regiments at first; the initial reinforcements he sent to Delhi were all Indian. He badly underestimated the likely performance of the rebels in the field without their British officers, and predicted that Delhi would offer 'no real resistance' to a swift counter-stroke (Lord Lawrence MS F90/12, 1 Nov 1857).

When the British arrived before the city, after hard fought engagements along the way, its garrison was being strengthened by mutineers converging upon the Mughal capital. Despite aid from the Punjab, the besiegers were heavily outnumbered. In the circumstances, Lawrence authorized a negotiation with the king of Delhi, Bahadur

Shah, who sought the forgiveness of the British as the price of admitting them to his fortified palace on the walls to take the city from within. Defending himself against later criticism of this abortive transaction in early July, Lawrence pointed to the 'great political results' that had flowed from the capture of Delhi. Had the negotiation succeeded, it would have foreshortened the rising, which spread in the two months that elapsed before the successful, and costly, assault in September. Sickness and casualties from constant skirmishing depleted the European core of the besieging force. From his Punjab base, Lawrence opposed suggestions of retreat as fatal to the British cause, and the signal for Indian princes to side with the rebels, the Bombay army to mutiny, and his Punjabis to emerge as 'Pretorian bands to destroy us'. Yet the risks incurred by delaying the assault did not clearly outweigh those of failing in the attempt. Lawrence's men at Delhi, Henry Norman, Henry Daly, Neville Chamberlain, and above all John Nicholson, worked to stiffen the resolve of their superiors. 'His mantle … fell on me', said Lawrence of the distant governor-general. Without the men and supplies he forwarded the British could not have recovered Delhi. There is some evidence from Indians inside the city to support his contention that it might have fallen three months earlier to a less deliberate and conventional attack in June, before the rebel garrison had built up its strength.

Lawrence argued from the outset that 'in war time, time is everything'. To speed and mobility he added calculated ruthlessness: 120 men in one Bengal regiment were too many to execute—'I do not think … we shall be justified in the eyes of the Almighty in doing so'—a quarter or a third of their number should die. In the case of some Muslim tribesmen in southern Punjab who rose in September, his instructions were to hang not more than 10 per cent, fewer if the example did its work (Smith, 2.72, 235). He set his face against indiscriminate reprisals such as those at Delhi, and the accompanying 'systematic spoliation' of a wealthy city. Behind the scenes his was the most influential voice in favour of an early amnesty that would exclude only those rebels directly implicated in the killings of Europeans and their families which were a feature of the mutinies. The revenge exacted at Delhi and elsewhere had the appearance of racial war: 'we may excite terror, but it will be terror mixed with undying hatred', he warned.

Victory at Delhi dispersed the largest concentration of rebel troops and deprived the uprising of its natural centre and nominal head. The strain on British manpower, both white and Indian, was matched by that on the finances of the Punjab: Lawrence levied what were in effect forced loans on Indian bankers and traders, and borrowed from princes. It was soon clear that the struggle had entered a new phase of guerrilla warfare as the remnants of the uniformed rebels were driven into the countryside. It was a kind of warfare for which the British regulars now reaching India in large numbers, and their commanders, were not well fitted. Their commander-in-chief, Sir Colin Campbell, joined in pressing for the amnesty

eventually conceded late in 1858. Prolongation of the conflict by what Lawrence termed 'an exterminating policy' involved serious danger, in his judgement, from the conclusions which too numerous Sikh and Punjabi soldiers and hitherto friendly princes might draw from British inability to finish the war quickly. At the start Lawrence viewed the uprising as 'essentially … military', then as 'a religious and political affair', attributable to Muslim agency in particular. Finally, he recognized in it a spontaneous revulsion that had spread deep into central India and eastwards to Bihar against the domination of 'a stranger race alien in religion, colour … and sympathies' (Lord Lawrence MS F90/12, 4 Dec 1857, 7 Jan 1858, 23 April 1858). The collapse of British administration in the North-Western Provinces and Oudh exposed the shallowness of its foundations, notwithstanding the benefits enjoyed by the peasantry. Only the rebels' failure to throw up a leader of even 'ordinary ability' and, time and again, to exploit their advantages had saved the British.

Lawrence thought pacification and reconstruction needed a governor-general 'who can see what is to be done in the twinkling of an eye, and … will have his own way'; others, too, felt that he was the man to succeed Canning. His British officers in the Punjab had distinguished themselves because the incompetent were weeded out early in their service, and because an active sympathy with Indians was integral to his brand of paternalism. He wanted civil administration throughout India and the reorganized Indian army to emulate the Punjab spirit and methods. The evangelical Christianity that inspired him and some of his school led Lawrence to see the mutiny as a combat between Christian and heathen. He rejected the charge that the growing religiosity of the British in India, as at home, had undermined their position. The presence of 'more really God-fearing men' among them would have given the British greater influence over the Indian mind: 'natives think that most of us have no religion'. However, he distanced himself from his friend H. B. Edwardes's programme of Christianizing measures. Principle and expediency required government to be even-handed between religions; there was room enough for Christian example. Like Canning, but more effectively, he reminded frightened and angry fellow countrymen that Indians were not a different order of creation: 'Justice, mercy, consideration, and kindness have an effect *even on them*' (Lord Lawrence MS F90/12, 1 Nov 1857, 10 June 1858). In the event, Canning weathered the storm of criticism directed at him for indecision and weakness, and stayed until 1861, when Lawrence was not chosen to succeed him.

Viceroy of India, 1864–1869 Promoted GCB (11 November 1857), sworn of the privy council (13 May 1859), and awarded a pension of £2000 a year by the East India Company directors which enabled him to accept a baronetcy (16 August 1858) he had previously declined, Lawrence went back to England in February 1859 to a seat on the council that advised the secretary of state under the India Act of 1858. On the inception of the order, the new Star of India was conferred upon him (KSI 1861, GCSI 1866). An advisory role did not suit him, but he made his opinions known on the important questions discussed at that period. His evangelical bent and the offence given by his views on the deficiencies of the British military and on army reform in India counted against him when Canning's replacement, Lord Elgin, lay dying in November 1863. Press and public did not share ministerial doubts; the choice of Lawrence was popular. As viceroy, he was to prove a disappointment to himself, if not to those who knew little of bureaucratic politics in the East. Well aware that he could not rule India as he had ruled the Punjab, he assumed that 'the element of despotism' at the centre would be stronger than the changed character of Indian government permitted. His council, chosen in London, was encouraged by the Indian Councils Act of 1861 to strike parliamentary attitudes. Its members attacked and frustrated his policies, supported by newspapers that spoke for the European official and business community. Rapidly growing investment since the 1857 uprising had enhanced the influence of British business, to which Lawrence saw his councillors defer: 'How can we be strong under such circumstances?' he inquired (BL, Iddesleigh MSS, Add. MS 50024, 2 Sept 1867).

Lawrence appealed for help to successive secretaries of state until in 1868 Sir Stafford Northcote gave him two of his old Punjab officers, Richard Temple and John Strachey, 'a great accession of strength' in council. It was hard for a cabinet minister to know what to do with a viceroy who lamented, 'I have not the authority to resist. At every turn one is met with opposition' (Lord Lawrence MS F90/30, 1 Aug 1865). Lawrence explored the possibility of acquiring or subsidizing a Calcutta European newspaper, but, not surprisingly, his council was divided over the idea. The autocrat of the Punjab lacked the political skills with which British political experience equipped most holders of his office. Moreover, neither he nor the Punjab school was universally liked in official India; his preference for them aroused considerable jealousy. Calcutta society compared him unfavourably with his aristocratic predecessors: the biographer selected by his family and friends went to the trouble of countering allegations of bad manners and parsimony in his viceregal hospitality. On his side, Lawrence was critical of the civil service in Bengal proper, and by implication elsewhere, for knowing and seeing too little of the people it administered. Solicitude for the governed characterized his five years as viceroy with all their frustrations.

Contingency planning in the event of another uprising on the same scale, and the necessity for a white garrison larger than that surprised in 1857 were two lessons that Lawrence drew from the mutiny. A great deal of latent discontent remained, and trust between British and Indians had to be carefully rebuilt. The new Bengal army, recruited from peoples who had fought with the British, was 'a superior … also a more dangerous animal' (Lord Lawrence MS F90/30, 15 April 1865). Lawrence strenuously opposed arming it with the latest weapons, not needed for its internal security role or for fighting the tribes on the north-west frontier. It was equally important to attend to the army's 'moral feelings'; he successfully advocated

officering the Bengal, Bombay, and Madras armies on the irregular system, which gave Indians more responsibility under a small, carefully chosen British cadre. Sir Charles Wood at the India Office defended the viceroy's patriarchal ideal of an Indian regiment against military objections. Narrowing the divide between European and Asian in the service overrode all other considerations.

Next to security, and inseparable from it to Lawrence's mind, came finance. He was soon urging some reduction in the British garrison as safer than adding to fiscal burdens: 'the poor cannot afford to be further taxed, and the rich will kick up a row' (Lord Lawrence MS F90/30, 18 Sept 1865). Recurrent deficits in 1866–8 were preferred to higher taxes, partly because the viceroy failed to retain a low income tax, finding himself isolated in council, but averted an increase in the remunerative salt duties which bore heavily on the poorest. A licence tax on traders and professions was passed, to loud protests organized by the British community. The drawbacks of that measure, together with the advent of Temple, as finance member, and of Strachey, finally allowed Lawrence to reintroduce an income tax on the eve of his departure. He condemned the British in India for their unwillingness to pay anything like their share of rising government expenditure: 'they desire that all taxation should fall on the natives and especially on the lower class' (BL, Iddesleigh MSS, Add. MS 50023, 28 March 1867). He wanted money for canals and railways, giving canals priority, and argued against the employment of private capital in carrying out plans that led to the appointment of Richard Strachey as the first inspector-general of irrigation in 1867. The irrigation companies were not to be trusted with the interests of the cultivator, and in Indian conditions the state could do the work more efficiently. Similarly with the expansion of the railway network after the mutiny, his strictures on the practice of guaranteed returns for railway companies, at the Indian taxpayer's expense, eventually resulted in London's consent to the construction of new lines by government.

British business was too powerful for the viceroy on several occasions. 'Everybody', he commented, 'is more or less afraid of the planter interest' (Lord Lawrence MS F90/30, 19 July 1865). Legislation to protect coolie labour on Assam tea plantations had a limited impact in view of official sympathies at district level and above. In the long drawn out dispute between indigo planters and cultivators in Bengal and Bihar, Lawrence received Wood's backing; they prevented changes in the law of contract and in legal procedure that would have diminished the peasants' resistance to what the viceroy called 'a system of pressure and terror'. While he did not suggest that his councillors approved of the planters' methods, he suspected that they were reluctant to brave the reproaches of the Calcutta European world. Conventional notions of *laissez-faire*, invoked by the planters, were also utilized by administrators who opposed Lawrence in the 'aristocratic reaction' after the rising. That movement of official opinion revived the issue which had divided Henry and John Lawrence: the justice, and the prudence, of discriminating against large

Indian landholders in the settlement of rights. Henry's legacy had helped keep the Sikh *sirdars* loyal: the resentment of their counterparts in the North-Western Provinces and Oudh had worked the other way. Subsequently, in Oudh and part of the Punjab, new instructions divested many thousands of peasants of rights only recently decided, reducing them to the status of tenants-at-will. So marked was the shift in official thinking that Lawrence had to 'deny absolutely that the Punjab school deserves the title of "a levelling school"' (ibid., 8 March 1865). Everywhere in India, he believed, there was evidence that the cultivators held land in descent from the ancient village communities.

The judgment of the Calcutta high court in the *Great Rent case* (1865) defeated the indigo planters' legal offensive against the statutory tenant-right reinforced a few years earlier by the famous Bengal Act X of 1859. Lawrence greeted the decision with relief. He had warned Wood of his weakness in council on agrarian questions in the existing climate of British Indian opinion. This weakness was demonstrated by the terms of the one-sided compromise in the Oudh Rent Act (1868), by which the great majority of Oudh tenants did not regain their lost rights. Lawrence was more successful with the Punjab Tenancy Act (1868), steered through council by Richard Temple. But his endeavours are not to be measured by enactments. Without Lawrence the tide might have run more strongly against that care for 'ancient tenures' which he considered was the most important single factor in reconciling Indians to British rule. He hoped to extend beyond Lord Cornwallis's Bengal the permanent settlement of the land revenue, so as to give the peasant a greater incentive to create the prosperity that would carry forward the whole of India. Wood agreed in principle, but financial considerations prevailed. A threat to rural contentment that Lawrence and his school tried to contain was the sale of land for debt. They succeeded in their province until the restrictions they had enforced were eroded by the assimilation of the Punjab's legal machinery from 1866 to that established in the older regulation provinces. Paternalism commenced a long retreat before lawyers and moneylenders. Like others, the viceroy could not see clearly how commercial pressures must affect his ideal of a proprietary peasantry.

The failure that Lawrence felt more than any other was his responsibility for the Orissa famine of 1866, shared with his executive council and with Bengal officials from the lieutenant-governor, Sir Cecil Beadon, downwards. More than a year later the councillors who had been present declined to confirm the viceroy's recollection, his 'very firm conviction', that he had wished to overrule the Bengal authorities' crude political economy and order the import of rice into Orissa before it was too late. He attributed his acquiescence in the opposition of his colleagues to the assumption that relief could still reach the area in the monsoon season that closed in after the delay. Both viceroy and councillors hesitated to challenge Bengal's rigid adherence to the laws of the market, an intellectual servitude which angered Lord Cranborne as secretary of

state. 'I shall never cease to blame myself', Lawrence confessed, faced with a mortality estimated at, perhaps, a million. The man of action who attained the height of his fame in the mutiny was now a careworn figure, owing to a disinclination to act against his council in this emergency. While decades of Indian service had taken their physical toll, it is evident that he never really adjusted to heading something resembling a cabinet, one divided over policy and by resentment of 'Punjabization' in the distribution of patronage. The impression is often of a man out of his element. Lawrence's persistent opponent in council H. M. Durand remembered the discussion of intervening in Orissa as being 'of the most vague and intangible kind' (BL, Iddesleigh MSS, Add. MS 50024, 2 Sept, 2 Oct 1867).

This episode should not overshadow the contemporary extension of government's functions. As in Britain, improvement was the order of the day and the state its promoter, although the scale of India's problems and the cost of addressing them were daunting. The development of a system of public education envisaged by Wood's dispatch of 1854 continued within narrow budgetary limits. On the other hand, the desire to husband central funds influenced the government of India's declaration in April 1864 that 'The people of this country are perfectly capable of administering their own local affairs', an allusion to the traditions of the village community, 'the most abiding of Indian institutions'. Municipal committees, generally nominated bodies, existed in every major Indian town by the late 1860s, levying the allotted taxes and spending them on roads, water supply, and police charges, with the power to lay out the surplus on other local purposes. In rural districts the government proceeded more cautiously; there the committees had little to spend, or to do (Tinker, 36–40). Lawrence resisted larger proposals for financial decentralization until he left India. In his view, the centre was already too weak, and growing weaker, in its dealings with subordinate governments. He tried hard, but with indifferent success, to control expenditure in the strongest of them, Bombay and Madras. It was imperative to keep taxation low—'the panacea for foreign rule in India' (Smith, 2.497)—and to allocate scarce resources to irrigation and railways. Only central direction would ensure that these aims were balanced; security, too, demanded that the centre's powers should not be reduced. He repelled an attempt, well supported in council, to give Bengal the status enjoyed by the other presidencies, but could not persuade his colleagues to endorse his proposed abolition of Bengal's separate legislative council.

Lawrence observed, as far as possible, a rule of non-intervention towards both India's neighbours and the princely states within her borders. Dalhousie's policy of absorbing the latter whenever an opportunity arose did not survive the mutiny, in which their activity, or inactivity, had materially assisted the victors. Lawrence objected, however, to the prospective and conditional restoration to Indian rule of the large state of Mysore, after many years of British administration: 'a retrograde step, which would inevitably lead to the undoing of all the improvements ... effected' (Lord Lawrence MS F90/32a, 28 March 1867). He instituted inquiries into the comparative merits of British and princely dominion, sure that the real interests of Indians were best served by the former. Despite his language at the spectacular Lahore durbar in October 1864, he did not trust the princes' loyalty should it again be severely tested. Their reliability was an aspect of the internal situation which, taken as a whole, shaped his conduct of India's foreign policy. He had negotiated for Dalhousie and Canning the treaties of 1855 and 1857 with Afghanistan that exchanged guarantees of territorial integrity and provided her with a British subsidy. The agreements, and Britain's military intervention in the Persian Gulf (1856–7) to secure a Persian withdrawal from Herat, kept Afghanistan from helping the mutineers in 1857. In the war of succession on Dost Muhammad's death in 1863, the government of India under Lawrence switched diplomatic recognition between claimants until one was strong enough to be rewarded with British arms and money. Ever mindful of the Afghans' destruction of a British occupying force in 1842, he ascribed the desire for expansion on the north-western frontier to restless administrators and soldiers far from headquarters, who, 'having little on their hands, must do something, if ... only to show that they are necessary' (Lord Lawrence MS F90/31, 4 Oct 1866). With the support of his secretaries of state he was able to deny advocates of moving the frontier forward, notably Sir Henry Rawlinson, a change of policy. To counter the publicity given to his opponents, Lawrence's case was expounded, at his instance, by J. W. S. Wyllie in the *Edinburgh Review* (January 1867) and the *Fortnightly Review* (December 1869; March 1870).

'Masterly inactivity', as Wyllie famously termed Lawrence's policy, signified a flexible defence of the frontier against incursions by tribes on the Afghan side, and a refusal to be alarmed by Russian progress through central Asia towards Afghanistan and India. Russia's conquests would 'absorb her energies and waste her resources', to Britain's advantage. There was nothing she could do to stop Russia: why 'irritate and annoy' her by protests, and by schemes to dispute the control of territory militarily inaccessible from India? (Lord Lawrence MS F90/30, 27 May 1865). Lawrence dismissed fears that Russia's approach, and her seduction of the frontier tribes, would stir up renewed unrest in India, whose millions had no love for Russians, or for the savage allies they might recruit. It was British expansion in that quarter, or deeper into Burma on the north-eastern frontier, that would increase discontent by making exorbitant fiscal demands upon the Indian population. Lawrence's preoccupation with the peasantry did not blind him to the emergence of an Indian élite, better educated and often richer than many of the Europeans whose overbearing attitude antagonized them. They would provide the political leadership of mass unrest generated by the higher taxation that a different foreign policy would impose. The princes and nobles added to the legislative council in 1861 seldom took much interest in its work: he wanted to improve the limited prospects of employment that government service offered to the Indians 'we are educating ... in wholesale fashion', and to do so without raising taxes, aims impossible to realize if the Indian empire expanded into 'distant, difficult and hostile regions' (Lord Lawrence MS F90/31, 4 Oct 1866).

A changing reputation The first Indian entered the covenanted civil service in 1864, but Lawrence was cautious about modifying the regulations in order to encourage more Indians to compete; a few scholarships enabling them to study for the examinations in Britain sufficed for the time being. This hesitancy was noticeable throughout his viceroyalty. While his private papers, first used by Bosworth Smith in the Victorian life, show him to have been an authentic liberal, it was not easy to be a liberal in India, especially in the aftermath of rebellion. His confessions of weakness contrast strangely with his previous record. In the Punjab he had implemented rather than made policy; Dalhousie believed, with some reason, that his lieutenant got too much of the credit for their work. An Indian historian has compared Lawrence the viceroy to 'a senior foreman awaiting orders' from London, and summed up his years of rule as 'a period of tired authority with little perspective or hint of the future' (Gopal, 62). It is a harsh judgement, mitigated by recognition of his devotion to the peasant. Another recent historian nevertheless put Lawrence beside Lord Ripon as an 'outspoken reformer' (Metcalf, 326). Bosworth Smith concealed his hero's shortcomings, but the compensating virtues are not less real for that. Some contemporary critics, it should be remembered, had suffered at the hands of the Punjab school. John Beames, deemed 'far too insolent' for continued service in the Punjab, left an unflattering portrait of Lawrence: 'a rough, coarse man ... more like a "navvy" than a gentleman', who treated civil servants as 'governing machines' (J. Beames, *Memoirs of a Bengal Civilian*, 1961, 102–3).

A weightier critic of Lawrence and 'his Punjab friends' complained that the viceroy had 'clogged' the machinery of government by circulating far more than Canning to the council and so widening the scope of its discussions (H. M. Durand, *Life of Maj.-Gen. Sir Henry Marion Durand*, 1883, 1.312, 333). That was not in itself a failing but a development in line with the expansion of the state in India. Harassed by councillors like Durand himself, Lawrence worried over a loss of viceregal authority. He did not seek to reduce their involvement in decision making; a collegiate administration was a necessity at the top. After the shock of the mutiny, his regime resumed the deliberate modernization of Lord William Bentinck and Dalhousie, with the greater sensitivity to Indian feeling dictated by a chastening experience. Yet, for all his good intentions and knowledge of Indians, he was divided from them by the narrowness of his belief in the superiority of Christianity and of his own national culture. It was that same certainty which bore him up in the summer of 1857 and earned him a place in the Victorian pantheon. A soldier *manqué* from childhood, he checked the mutiny in northern India by his promptness in disarming the Bengal regulars in the Punjab, and was the organizer of victory at Delhi. His ability to deliver the resources of the Punjab was vital for many months afterwards. The military respected and resented this formidable civilian, who was a powerful advocate of army reform from the first weeks of the conflict. The doubts and difficulties of the viceroy were lost in the legend of the man who made the Punjab prosperous and loyal, and who in May 1857 asked a slow-moving commander-in-chief to reflect that since Clive at Plassey the British had not won India by being prudent: 'Where have we failed when we acted vigorously?' (Smith, 2.30).

Peerage and death John Lawrence came home to a peerage as Baron Lawrence of the Punjaub and of Grateley (3 April 1869), Grateley being a small estate on Salisbury Plain left to him by his favourite sister. Parliament extended for the life of his son the pension voted by the East India directors. Settling in London, he served for three years as the first chairman of the London school board, and supported Gladstone's Irish church and land bills in the Lords. At the end of his life, though in poor health, he attacked the Conservatives' 'forward policy' on the north-western frontier in letters to *The Times* (September–November 1878), and chaired the national committee that protested against the impending war with Afghanistan. His last speech in parliament deplored the consequent increase of Indian taxation, a week before his death on 27 June 1879 at his London house, 23 Queen's Gate Gardens. Despite Lord Beaconsfield's partisan objections, he was buried in Westminster Abbey. In retirement and earlier he had been generous with time and money to relatives, friends, and good causes; a shrewd investor, he died a comparatively wealthy man. The eldest of his four sons, John (1846–1913), succeeded to the peerage; the third, Charles (d. 1927), a businessman and railway chairman, became Baron Lawrence of Kingsgate in 1923; and the fourth was General Sir Herbert *Lawrence.   DAVID STEELE

Sources R. B. Smith, *Life of Lord Lawrence*, 2 vols. (1883) · E. Stokes, *The English utilitarians and India* (1959) · S. S. Thorburn, *The Punjab in peace and war* (1904) · P. H. M. van den Dungen, *The Punjab tradition: influence and authority in nineteenth-century India* (1972) · M. Naidis, 'John Lawrence, mutiny hero', *Bengal Past and Present*, 82 (1963), 1–11 · E. Stokes, *The peasant armed: the Indian revolt of 1857* (1986) · R. J. Moore, *Sir Charles Wood's Indian policy, 1853–1866* [1966] · T. R. Metcalf, *The aftermath of revolt: India, 1857–1870* (1965) · S. Gopal, *British policy in India, 1858–1905* (1965) · D. Pal, *Administration of Sir John Lawrence in India, 1864–1869* (1952) · H. Tinker, *The foundations of local self-government in India, Pakistan and Burma* (1954) · *Barclay Fox's journal*, ed. R. L. Brett (1979), 229–30 · BL OIOC, Lord Lawrence MSS · BL, Iddesleigh MSS, Add. MSS 50023, 50024 · *CGPLA Eng. & Wales* (1879) · GEC, *Peerage*

Archives BL OIOC, papers, MSS Eur. F 90 · Bodl. Oxf., letters | BL, Iddesleigh MSS · BL, corresp. with Florence Nightingale, Add. MS 45777 · BL, corresp. with Sir Stafford Northcote, Add. MSS 50023–50026 · BL OIOC, Henry Lawrence MSS · BL OIOC, letters to John Nicholson, MSS Eur. E 211 · BL OIOC, corresp. with Sir Richard Temple, MSS Eur. F 86 · BL OIOC, Wood MSS · CUL, corresp. with Lord Mayo · Lpool RO, corresp. with fifteenth earl of Derby · NA Scot., corresp. with Lord Dalhousie · NAM, letters to W. S. R. Hodson · NRA, priv. coll., letter to duke of Argyll and duchess of Argyll · U. Newcastle, Robinson L., letters to Sir Charles Trevelyan · W. Yorks. AS, Leeds, letters to Lord Canning

Likenesses R. Theed, marble bust, 1861, Grocers' Company, London · G. F. Watts, oils, 1862, NPG [*see illus.*] · C. G. Lewis, group portrait, mixed engraving, pubd 1864 (*The intellect and valour of Great Britain*; after T. J. Barker), NPG · J. R. Dicksee, oils, *c*.1865, City of London School · H. Weekes, bust, 1867, St Bartholomew's Hospital, London · T. Woolner, bronze bust, *c*.1871, Commonwealth Relations Office · E. G. Lewis, chalk drawing, 1872, NPG · T. Woolner, bronze statue, 1875, Government House, Calcutta · V. Prinsep, oils, 1876, Government House, Calcutta · J. E. Boehm, bronze statue, *c*.1882, Waterloo Place, London; related plaster bust, NPG · J. Collier, portraits, 1911–14, Oriental Club, London · Ape [C. Pellegrini], chromolithograph, caricature, NPG; repro. in *VF* (21 Jan 1871) · Elliott & Fry, cabinet photograph, NPG · T. W. Knight, stipple (after Mayall), NPG · Maull & Polyblank, photograph, NPG · D. J. Pound, stipple and line engraving (after Mayall), NPG · T. Woolner, marble bust, Westminster Abbey; replica, 1882, NPG · cartes-de-visite, NPG

Wealth at death under £140,000: probate, 17 July 1879, *CGPLA Eng. & Wales*

Lawrence, Dame Maude Agnes (1864–1933), civil servant, was born on 16 April 1864 at Southgate House, Southgate, Edmonton, Middlesex, the tenth surviving and youngest child of John Laird Mair *Lawrence, first Baron Lawrence (1811–1879), and his wife, Harriette Katherine Hamilton (1820–1917). Sir Herbert Alexander *Lawrence was her brother. Her father was appointed viceroy of India in the year of her birth, and, with her sisters, she was taken to India later that year, arriving in December. Lady Lawrence and her daughters remained in India until early in 1868, when they returned to England. They lived at 26 Queen's Gate, London, where Lord Lawrence joined them in March 1869. The daughters were educated at home; their companion, Miss Gaster, recalled that 'Lord Lawrence was very anxious about the education of his two youngest children'. However, his views on women and their education were conservative. He thought that girls were 'naturally better [than boys] … more painstaking, more amiable' and that women's most valuable qualities were 'gentleness, implicit obedience, and good looks' (Smith, 2.618).

Apart from two terms at Bedford College in 1881, where she followed a course of lectures in English literature, Maude Lawrence seems to have had no formal education. After the marriages of her sisters she remained at home as her mother's companion. She was a school manager and, like her father, a member of the London school board. In 1900 she was co-opted on to the Westminster school board and subsequently elected to it at the last school board election in 1901. She was a co-opted member of the London county council (LCC) education committee between 1904 and 1905, and vice-chairman of the special schools committee, in which capacity she gave evidence to the royal commission into the care and control of the feeble-minded. Her evidence to the commission suggests that she had taken seriously her responsibilities on the special schools committee. She provided a history of London special schools, an account of the results they had obtained, and made recommendations for their future development. She supported voluntary and philanthropic effort in special education, but believed that the provision of special schools should be compulsory on local authorities.

She stressed the importance of aftercare for the children who left such schools, and revealed that she had undertaken studies of the careers of about fifty children while she was a member of the LCC committee. She believed that permanent care was necessary for certain children who would never be able to support themselves unaided, and she subscribed to the view that feeble-mindedness could be passed on to the next generation and that some sufferers would need to be confined for their own protection, even though they 'may not now be certifiable cases under existing laws' (*Parl. papers*, 1908, 35.422).

Maude Lawrence was appointed chief woman inspector of the Board of Education on 21 January 1905. Apart from her school board service, she had no direct qualifications for the post. Her appointment seemed to owe more to her family connections and to her conventional views on women's nature and on the education of working-class children. Robert Morant, permanent secretary at the Board of Education, who had created the new body of women inspectors separate from the rest of the inspectorate, made it clear that he was not looking for a specialist. He sought an outsider 'whose name stands high in the world of women's work and of general estimation' (PRO, ED23/152B). Her duty was to give 'prestige to the work of Women Inspectors as such … to inspire a new and proper sense of the real importance and possibilities of their work' (ibid.). The appointee was constantly to bear in mind, and ensure that the women inspectors did also, the fact that most of the girls would be mothers and needed 'to be looked at from the maternal and physical aspect—not merely from what is called the intellectual and book-learning aspect' (ibid.).

Although one historian of the education inspectorate claimed that Maude Lawrence, 'strongly supported by Sir Robert Morant, created the Women Inspectorate' (Boothroyd, 76), she was perhaps less instrumental than her successor, Anna Wark, in ensuring that it was recognized as a professional service. In the view of some contemporaries the ethos for the women's inspectorate ensured that it remained inferior to and separate from the men's service. In 1906 a former inspector, Edith Marvin, who proposed to campaign for the appointment of more women inspectors, was warned by one of the existing women inspectors that it was important to stress that such appointments should go to 'properly qualified women as highly qualified in every respect as the men, instead of Society "Jobs"'. Maude Lawrence, Marvin was told, was completely unqualified, and was the 'laughing stock' of the male inspectors, who nicknamed her department the 'washtub women'; appointments such as hers had harmed the cause of women inspectors (R. A. Munday to Edith Marvin, 18 Oct 1906, Bodl. Oxf., MS Eng. lett. c. 257, fols. 150–52). These views were later echoed by Susan Platt who, on her appointment in 1896 as one of the first women inspectors of schools, was told by Sir John Gorst, vice-president of the board, that 'women inspectors were to begin as assistants, and reach step by step (he hoped) the highest positions in the service, on equal terms with men'. She attributed to Morant the idea of placing women inspectors under a woman chief and assigning them to particular subjects (S. Platt, letter to the *Times Educational Supplement*, 10 May 1930, included as part of the evidence submitted to the royal commission on the civil service, on 15 Oct 1930, by the London and National Society for Women's Service).

One of Maude Lawrence's first tasks was to serve as one of the official representatives on the interdepartmental committee to inquire into the medical inspection and feeding of children attending public elementary schools, set up in February 1905 in response to the growing campaign for state provision for free school meals. The problems of poor health and malnutrition had been highlighted during the recruitment of soldiers for the Second South African War, and various inquiries had been held. However, the provision of free meals was controversial, seen by many as incipient socialism, and the committee's personnel and terms of reference were carefully chosen so as to ensure that its recommendations were not 'such as would result in, or tend towards, universal provision, from the rates, of free meals for school children generally' (Board of Education, internal memo, 10 Feb 1905, PRO, ED24/106). Among the committee's seventeen recommendations was the establishment of cookery centres for instruction in cookery; the teaching of cookery formed the subject of one of Miss Lawrence's investigations for the inspectorate. She also produced reports on the schooling of under-fives (1905) and the teaching of needlework (1907). Those reports are apparently her only published work.

Maude Lawrence took a limited part in the campaign, after the First World War, to overhaul the salary system of the inspectorate, possibly because of some antagonism from her male colleagues, who noted that women's promotion prospects in the service were better than those of men with superior academic qualifications. Women inspectors were, none the less, paid at a lower rate than the men, a practice that she seemed to have supported, although she did argue for an increase in the women's rate in order to maintain suitable recruits, basing her argument on a comparison with the salaries of headmistresses, from whom most of the women inspectors were recruited (PRO, ED23/608).

The women inspectors seem to have stepped up their part in the campaign after Maude Lawrence left in October 1920 to become director of women's establishments at the Treasury. Her Treasury post was created at the recommendation of the committee on the machinery of government, chaired by Lord Haldane, which recommended that

one or more women of special qualifications and experience should regularly be included in responsible posts as part of the staff of that separate branch of the Treasury which the Committee suggested should be set up to specialise in establishment work, and to study all questions of staff, recruitment, classification etc. in their application to the several Departments of State.   (*Parl. papers*, 1918, 12, pt 1, para. 47, Cd 9230)

She was appointed DBE in 1926. Her employment was

extended for five years in 1929, when she reached the normal civil service retirement age, so valuable were her services regarded, and she continued in her post until her death.

Dame Maude Lawrence's work at the Treasury was remembered in domestic terms. She was described as the 'Mother of the Civil Service'.

> If chairs were of the wrong shape, or aprons of the wrong material; if there should have been a lift where there was not one, or a half-day holiday where it had been forbidden, the trouble was referred to Dame Maude.   (*Daily Telegraph*, 13 Jan 1933, 8)

It was also noted that 'If a girl clerk in the War Office was uncertain whether to sacrifice her official career for matrimony, Dame Maude helped her to decide' (ibid.). She supported the marriage bar for women in the civil service, to which she referred in her evidence to the royal commission into the civil service in October 1930. She told the commissioners that there was little prejudice against women in the service. She favoured the retention of unequal pay, the marriage bar, and the exclusion of women from certain posts, stating her belief that women's long-term value to the service was not as great as men's. She also told the commission that she did not think that lower pay for women adversely affected their status, noting that the public service should not be seen to be going ahead of private businesses: 'We have to remember that the economic value of women, rightly or wrongly, outside is not the same as yet as that of men' (Royal Commission on the Civil Service, Evidence, p. 950, 15 Oct 1930). Such views were not shared by many of her female colleagues, who fought against the marriage bar and pay differentials in the civil service and whose evidence to the commission gave a more realistic picture of women's status. Other women witnesses expressed some criticism of Dame Maude's post: Miss Sanday of the Council of Women Civil Servants told the commission that women's establishment posts were useful as an interim measure to ensure wide representation of women in the service, but that there should be enough women at higher grades who would serve on appointment boards for men and women (ibid., 943).

In the early 1920s Dame Maude moved from London to Ickenham Hall, Ickenham, Middlesex, where she became a member, and a vice-chairman, of the parochial church council, and served as a rector's warden. She was an active sportswoman and took a keen interest in the Civil Service Sports Council for which she organized women's golf, hockey, and swimming. She died at her home at Ickenham on 11 January 1933 after a severe cold which had developed into influenza and bronchitis, and was buried three days later at All Saints' Church, Banstead, Surrey.

ELAINE HARRISON

Sources *The Times* (13 Jan 1933) · *The Times* (18 Jan 1933) · *Daily Telegraph* (13 Jan 1933) · *Middlesex Advertiser and County Gazette* (20 Jan 1933) · R. B. Smith, *Life of Lord Lawrence*, 2 vols. (1883) · H. E. Boothroyd, *A history of the inspectorate* (1923) · PRO, ED23/152B, 608, 648 · M. Zimmeck, 'The "new woman" in the machinery of government: a spanner in the works?', *Government and expertise: specialists, administrators and professionals, 1860–1919*, ed. R. Macleod (1988) · WW · WWW · R. Aldrich and P. Gordon, *Dictionary of British educationists* (1989) · M. Zimmeck, 'We are all professionals now: professionalisation, education and gender in the civil service, 1873–1939', *Women, education and the professions*, ed. P. Summerfield (1987) · b. cert. · d. cert.
Likenesses photograph, repro. in *The Times* (13 Jan 1933)
Wealth at death £172,407 8s. 9d.: resworn probate, 25 Feb 1933, CGPLA Eng. & Wales

Lawrence, Millicent (1863–1925). *See under* Lawrence, Penelope (1856–1932).

Lawrence, Sir Paul Ogden (1861–1952), judge, was born in Wimbledon on 8 September 1861, the second son of Philip Henry Lawrence (1822–1895), solicitor and later barrister, and his wife, Margaret Davies (d. 1903). He was educated at Malvern College and abroad and never went to university. He was called to the bar (Lincoln's Inn) in 1882 and joined the northern circuit where he entered the chambers of Ralph Neville, later a Chancery judge. In 1887 he married Maude Mary (d. 1947), daughter of John Turner of Wimbledon Park. They had no children. He practised in the palatine court (a locally administered court equivalent to the High Court) until 1896 when, having taken silk, he commenced a Chancery practice in London. This grew considerably and by the time of the First World War he was acknowledged as one of the leading practitioners in his field. He appeared often in the House of Lords and before the judicial committee of the privy council. He acted frequently in Indian appeals and in 1918 represented the elected members of the (white-only) legislative council in Southern Rhodesia in respect to claims to ownership of unalienated lands (see *In re Southern Rhodesia*, 1919).

Nearer home Lawrence represented private businesses during the First World War in some of the most celebrated cases which had arisen out of the extensive requisitioning by the state of private property for war purposes. The major cases included the Shoreham Aerodrome case of *In re a Petition of Right* (1916); *Cannon Brewery Co. Ltd.* v. *Central Control Board* (*Liquor Traffic*) (1918); and (at first instance and for much of the Court of Appeal hearing before his elevation to the bench) the great 'case of requisition', *De Keyser's Royal Hotel Ltd* v. *R.* (1918) whose House of Lords ruling (1920) is familiar to generations of law students. The issues raised by the cases were compared to the constitutional struggles between the common law and the prerogative in the early seventeenth century. Whether Lawrence identified ideologically with individual property owners against the claims of the collectivist wartime state cannot of course be determined by his court advocacy but the approach of the two post-war committees of inquiry into legal aid for the poor which he chaired rejected any solutions which entailed state funding of legal services for the poor.

In 1918 Lawrence was appointed a Chancery judge to succeed Ralph Neville, and was knighted in 1919. The first Lawrence committee on legal aid, controversially containing only lawyers (two solicitors, two barristers, and Lawrence), was set up in 1919 against a background of huge increases in the number of divorce petitions following the social dislocations of the war. In its report published in the same year, it readily acknowledged that many petitioners were unable through poverty to cover the expense (usually about £10) of presenting divorce petitions and that only a fund would assist them to secure their decrees. Yet the idea of such state funding was unacceptable to the committee as being, among other things, inconsistent with the principles of the autonomy of the lawyer–client relationship and likely to encourage a small group of speculative solicitors to hunt up cases and make a business out of pocketing office expenses (a regrettable development which the committee had claimed to detect). Instead, the committee recommended that poor petitioners, to cover office expenses, should be required to deposit a sum of £5 (and £10 in nullity petitions) notwithstanding that it was already conceded by the committee that this sum was beyond the reach of many petitioners and would further deter applications from the poor. Charity, not state funding, was the recommended solution, with further exhortations to respectable solicitors to work merely for limited expenses, not for profit, and for barristers to undertake the work without payment (even the proposal to give the county courts jurisdiction over divorce was rejected on Lawrence's casting vote when the members of the committee divided on predictable lines over the issue of solicitors' rights of audience before the county courts). Such appeals fell on deaf ears within the profession. Sir Claud Schuster at the Lord Chancellor's Office hinted darkly at a state take-over of the system unless the Law Society acted to improve the situation. Yet delays and inefficiency continued. Eventually he approached Lawrence again. 'The Poor Persons' business is once again in desperate straits', he pleaded, and so the judge agreed to chair another inquiry into 'this thorny subject' (PRO, LCO2/644).

A second Lawrence committee was therefore set up in July 1923, though with terms of reference limited to High Court cases (prompting the government to establish the Finlay committee in 1925 to cover the remaining ground). It reported in February 1925. While again rejecting a publicly funded scheme, it recommended that instead of the scheme continuing to be administered through the High Court, the Law Society should administer the scheme through local committees. By that means it was hoped to recruit more solicitors to the scheme. The committee explained that the profession owed a moral obligation to provide legal services for the poor in return for its professional monopoly (so long as the burden was not unevenly distributed among solicitors). It also proposed helping with the cost of administration by means of a Treasury grant to the Law Society. It was a small shift. While the provision of a state grant (initially only £3000) offered the merest hint of a corporatist solution (which was none the less a pointer to central government funding in the future), the proposal remained primarily for an in-house voluntary scheme detached from the state. Indeed the bottom line of the committee's approach was that where the Law Society approved an application for assistance (and as the income limit was only £2, many of the poor fell outside its scope), a £5 deposit was still required. Thus while

the problem of recruiting solicitors to the scheme was temporarily overcome, the £2 income limit no doubt continued to exclude many of the poor from legal representation. Lawrence's record on the committees therefore suggests a failure to address fundamental problems in the provision of legal services for the poor and a, perhaps explicable, preoccupation with the autonomy of both branches of the legal profession.

From 1913 until his elevation to the bench in 1918 Lawrence was chairman of the general council of the bar. He was also chairman of the Incorporated Council of Law Reporting from 1917 to 1919 and in 1925 became treasurer of his inn. In 1926 he was promoted to the Court of Appeal and made a privy councillor. The appointment caused some surprise within the bar as other names had circulated in Lincoln's Inn as more likely candidates for promotion. He retired in December 1933 but, preferring to cultivate his garden, he declined Lord Sankey's invitation to take up more legal work thereafter (it was thought that he had been offered a peerage if he were willing to sit in House of Lords appeals or in the judicial committee). His judicial record was not especially memorable and tended to reflect his cautious and shrewd approach as a barrister. Though he is often listed in printed sources as a KC, he reminded the Lord Chancellor's Office at the time of Sankey's approach, that is, during the reign of a male monarch, that he was in fact a QC (as shown, for example, in his Who's Who entry for 1949).

Lawrence should be acknowledged for his activities in two rather unanticipated spheres. First, in 1885 he provided his three sisters, Penelope *Lawrence, Dorothy *Lawrence, and Millicent *Lawrence [see under Lawrence, Penelope], with financial support for the establishment of the famous girls' school Roedean in Sussex. He remained chairman of the board of governors for many years and generations of pupils knew him as 'Uncle Paul'. Second, many children brought up in the 1970s and beyond (and their parents) will be grateful, without necessarily knowing why, both to Lawrence's father and to Lawrence himself. For it was the former's litigation efforts as a solicitor (he later became a barrister) which secured the public enjoyment of Wimbledon Common, and it was Lawrence himself in his capacity as conservator of the common in 1901 who helped to maintain that enjoyment. As a consequence the most famous occupants of the green expanse, the 'Wombles of Wimbledon Common', were enabled to thrive and to entertain generations of youngsters in the last quarter of the twentieth century. Lawrence died at Radley Lodge, Inner Park Road, Wimbledon, on 26 December 1952.   G. R. RUBIN

Sources The Times (29 Dec 1952) · G. R. Rubin, Private property, government requisition and the constitution, 1914–1927 (1994) · R. I. Morgan, 'The introduction of civil legal aid in England and Wales, 1914–1939', Twentieth Century British History, 5 (1994), 38–76 · R. Egerton, Legal aid (1945) · PRO, LCO2/644 · PRO, LCO6/1213 · P. Polden, A history of the county court, 1846–1971 (1999) · L. Scott and A. Hildesley, The case of requisition (1920) · DNB
Likenesses H. Rivière, oils, Roedean School, Sussex
Wealth at death £66,374 19s. 6d.: probate, 21 Feb 1953, CGPLA Eng. & Wales

Lawrence, Penelope (1856–1932), a founder of Roedean School, Brighton, with her sisters **Dorothy Lawrence** (1860–1933) and **Millicent Lawrence** (1863–1925), was the only child of Philip Henry Lawrence (1822–1895), a solicitor and descendant of the nonconformist minister Philip Henry, and his first wife, Charlotte Augusta, daughter of Edward and Charlotte Augusta Bailey; Charlotte Lawrence was related to the Unitarian Chamberlain, Kenrick, and Martineau families. Penelope (called Nelly by the family, P.L. at Roedean) was born in London on 10 November 1856 at 1 Devonport Street, Hyde Park; her mother died in 1857, less than three months after the birth. In 1858 Philip Lawrence married secondly Margaret (d. 1903), daughter of John Davies, an architect practising in London. They were to have thirteen children, seven girls and six boys, of whom Dorothy (Dolly), born on 7 August 1860, was the second, and Millicent (Milly), born on 26 February 1863, was the fourth. Both were born at Copse Hill, Wimbledon, where the Lawrences were living.

In 1864 Philip Lawrence's health broke down because of overwork, and he carried off his family to Freiberg in Saxony. Returning to work in the autumn, he installed the family at Versailles so that they might learn French. It was here that Penelope learned to swim—it was to become a lifelong passion, and early Roedeanians were to watch her bulky form with awe as she swam between the two piers at Brighton. In 1865 the family returned to England, where Philip Lawrence became a founder member of the Commons Preservation Society (1865), translated a work by the German mineralogist Bernhard von Cotta on the classification of rocks (1866), and was appointed in 1868 solicitor to the board of works. In 1869 (by which time there were nine children), he took two ill-judged decisions which were indirectly to lead to the foundation of Roedean. One was to give up his profession as a solicitor and read for the bar, the other to build a grandiose mansion for his family. In 1869 he was admitted as a student of Lincoln's Inn (he was called to the bar in 1872), and in 1870 he bought a large field in Wimbledon Park and began building Fearegg House. Meanwhile he settled the family in Dresden, and then later in Gotha in Thuringia. Penelope, whose education so far had included attendance at four different schools in England, France, and Germany, attended the seminary of Dr Köhler, a follower of Froebel, and began working for the Froebel diploma. After attending private day schools in Dresden and Gotha, her sisters had lessons at home under the supervision of a German governess.

In 1873 Fearegg House was ready and the family (there were twelve children now) came back to England, where the two last sons were born in 1874 and 1876. With her father's encouragement, Penelope Lawrence went to Newnham College, Cambridge, in 1874, where she became a friend of Alix von Cotta, daughter of the German scientist. Dorothy Lawrence, a pupil at Mrs Edwardes's private school, Lansdowne Road, Wimbledon, went to Bedford College, London (which then took school-age pupils) in 1875. Philip Lawrence's finances were by then hopelessly overstretched, and he was not as successful at the bar as he had hoped. The new house had to be

Penelope Lawrence (1856–1932), by Sir William Orpen, 1926

mortgaged, and he could not afford to send Dorothy and Millicent to Newnham. Penelope, who had studied botany, physiology, and zoology, and in 1878 gained a second class in the Cambridge natural sciences tripos, to which women candidates were informally admitted, was appointed as a demonstrator to women students in the physiological laboratory under Michael Foster. From her salary she paid for Millicent, though still very young, to take a year's teacher training course at the Maria Grey College, where she was taught by Agnes Ward. Penelope herself was principal, in succession to Caroline Garrison Bishop, of the Froebel Society's Kindergarten Training College in Tavistock Place from 1881 until it closed in 1883, and then taught part time at Wimbledon high school.

In 1881 the financial crisis became even more serious. Philip Lawrence, climbing a rock in Cumberland, fell and fractured his pelvis—an injury from which he never properly recovered and which virtually ended his legal career. Mrs Lawrence was a gifted woman of great resource as well as charm and energy, and with Dorothy and Millicent she began to teach neighbours' children and to take in boarding pupils. But after four strenuous years the sisters realized that they could not run a school in the same house as an invalid father and boisterous young siblings. Accordingly, on 14 February 1885 Dorothy wrote to Penelope, then in Madeira, outlining her and Millicent's scheme to start a separate school and begging her to join them. It was settled that Brighton would be a promising locality, and here they rented a house in Lewes Crescent. The school opened in October with ten pupils, 'six paying and four for show', as Penelope used to say—two of the latter being her young sisters Christabel (1869–1952) and

Theresa (1870–1950). (In 1902 Theresa went out to South Africa to found another Roedean near Johannesburg.) The emphasis in those early years was on pupils' health, and the first prospectus stressed that 'two or three hours daily will be allotted to out-door exercise and games'.

The new school was successful from the start. Not only were the three founders able to move to larger premises in Sussex Square, where all their five sisters helped with the teaching, but they could also provide for their parents and young brothers, who came down to live in Brighton with them, Fearegg House having long since been abandoned. (The school now was given the name of Wimbledon House.) There was always great family affection and solidarity, and when the decision was taken in 1895 to build new premises high on the cliffs above Rottingdean, the second brother, Paul Ogden *Lawrence (1861–1952)—later a judge but known as Uncle Paul by the school—helped them with a gift of £50 from his first earnings at the bar.

The sisters' energy, public relations skills, and business acumen in raising the necessary money were astonishing, as was their determination (in spite of the disaster of Fearegg House) to build on such a grand scale. The foundation-stone for what was now to be known as Roedean was laid on 26 July 1897, and the impressive buildings in free Jacobean style were ready for occupation in January 1899. The change from an easy-going family establishment, where pupils had been allowed much freedom, to a highly organized entity, divided into houses and run on boys' public school lines, was considerable, and at this stage formality, not to say regimentation, crept in.

The sisters each took over one of the four houses: Dorothy Number One, Millicent Number Two, and Penelope Number Three. Throughout their reign they operated as a triumvirate—they were known collectively to Roedenians as 'the Firm'—but in practice it was Penelope who took the lead; she was the dominant personality who organized the academic side (described in her memorandum to the royal commission on secondary education in 1895) and though not athletic herself enthusiastically promoted team games. Her paper, 'Games and athletics in secondary schools for girls', was published in the Board of Education's Special Reports on Educational Subjects (vol. 2, 1898). She urged the value of games for girls as a means of training character, teaching obedience to law, and acting together to a common end. Hockey was played in winter and cricket in summer; she also became president of the Women's Lacrosse Association. Christabel, a founder of the All-England Women's Hockey Association (1895), supervised games during the mid-1890s. Dorothy, who had first taken the initiative over starting a school and who was lovingly remembered as the most accessible of the three principals, was dogged by ill health and recurrent bouts of severe depression; she was white-haired even in her thirties. The Lawrence family had been brought up as Unitarians, but Dorothy joined the Church of England, and the school chapel was her great interest. Millicent, who had remarkable business skills, was concerned with finance and administration. She also ran the school Girl Guide company and interested herself in

women's suffrage, a cause which she promoted among both the pupils and the teaching staff. Penelope, who retained the family's Unitarianism, was, to the disappointment of some of her friends, an opponent of the suffrage cause, following the line of her kinsman Joseph Chamberlain.

The school became a public company in 1920 and in 1924 all three sisters retired, Penelope to her house, Widgeon's Rest, in Boxmoor, near Hemel Hempstead, Hertfordshire, where she royally entertained family, friends, and old members of the school, as well as working women from London. (She was now wealthy, having been left a substantial inheritance by her mother's sister Fanny Martineau, who died in 1921.) Millicent, who also lived in Boxmoor, died there at her home, Roefield, Felden Lane, on 5 November 1925; Penelope died at her home on 3 July 1932, after a short illness, and was cremated at Golders Green crematorium on 7 July; and Dorothy—who had lived first in Gravesend and then in St Albans—died there at her home, Highclere, Avenue Road, on 2 May 1933.

GILLIAN AVERY

Sources The founders of Roedean (1935) · D. E. de Zouche, Roedean School, 1885–1955 (privately printed, Brighton, 1955) · C. S. Gaskell and J. Sharpe, Newnham College Roll Letter (1933), 44–50 · d. cert. · CGPLA Eng. & Wales (1926) · CGPLA Eng. & Wales (1932) · CGPLA Eng. & Wales (1933) · The Times (8 July 1932)
Likenesses photographs, 1863–1932, repro. in The founders of Roedean, pp. 34–43 · photographs, 1865–1921 (Dorothy Lawrence), repro. in The founders of Roedean · photographs, 1887–1922 (Millicent Lawrence), repro. in The founders of Roedean, facing pp. 20, 22, 23 · C. F. T. Blyth, photograph, 1909 (Millicent Lawrence) · W. Orpen, oils, 1926, Roedean School, Brighton [see illus.] · H. Rivière, oils (Dorothy Lawrence), Roedean School, Brighton · H. Rivière, oils (posthumous Millicent Lawrence), Roedean School, Brighton
Wealth at death £12,472 1s. 4d.: probate, 31 Aug 1932, CGPLA Eng. & Wales · £5971 16s. 8d.—Dorothy Lawrence: probate, 1933, CGPLA Eng. & Wales · £27,689 15s. 0d.—Millicent Lawrence: probate, 1926, CGPLA Eng. & Wales

Lawrence, Philip Ambrose (1947–1995), headmaster, was born on 21 August 1947 at 78 Harcourt Street, Dublin, the son of John Lawrence, a retired colonel in the Indian army living in co. Wicklow, and his wife, Carmel Smyth. He was educated at Ampleforth College, Yorkshire, from where he won an entrance exhibition to read English at Queens' College, Cambridge (BA, 1969; MA, 1980). He was an entertaining and gregarious undergraduate with a strong interest in politics and economics; he sat on the committee of the University Liberal Club. After Cambridge he taught English during the early 1970s at St Benedict's, Ealing, an independent school attached to a Roman Catholic monastery. He was an unconventional, provocative, and eager teacher who won the affection of his pupils. His flamboyant clothes, angular handwriting, quick smile, and sprightly walk were all distinctive. On 10 February 1973 he married a fellow teacher at St Benedict's, Frances Kathryn Huntley, daughter of David Huntley, a chartered accountant. They had three daughters and one son.

Subsequently Lawrence worked as head of the English department at Gunnersbury Boys' School at Brentford, and then taught in a Lambeth comprehensive school where he rose to become headmaster. He was a man of vitality, charm, and *joie de vivre* who was keenly attuned to the needs and feelings of other people. Politics, the arts, sciences, and religion all interested him.

In January 1993 he became headmaster of a voluntary-aided Roman Catholic comprehensive school, St Joseph's, in Maida Vale, London. The school had a reputation for unruliness and poor examination results. He recruited younger and fresher staff, and produced a new prospectus stressing the school's commitment to homework, good behaviour, and an improving atmosphere. He provided determined leadership, clear vision, and dedicated purpose to both staff and pupils. During his headmastership he expelled over sixty pupils, a national record at the time. Although the academic achievements of his pupils improved, he was bedevilled by problems with playground violence and street gangs in the surrounding area. School buildings had barred windows and other security precautions. Both parents and pupils responded to his efforts with gratitude and respect. Lawrence declared his credo in an interview given to a journalist on 8 December 1995: 'I am giving parents what they want, Christian values in their children. We believe there is a difference between right and wrong. There is no relativist position. There is forgiveness but there is wrong' (*Sunday Times*, 10 Dec 1995). These were rules needed, he felt sure, by all children. A few hours after speaking to this journalist Lawrence ran from St Joseph's to prevent a thirteen-year-old pupil from being beaten with a bat by a gang. The gang, which postured as a juvenile version of Chinese triads, was led by Learco Chindamo, an aggressive youth aged fifteen. After a brief altercation Chindamo slapped Philip Lawrence in the face and then stabbed him in the chest. Following emergency treatment Lawrence died, on 8 December 1995, at St Mary's Hospital, Paddington. He was survived by his wife and their four children.

Philip Lawrence's murder grieved and shocked all who had known him. It also prompted a national outcry, of which his election as BBC personality of the year for 1995 was only one sign. His murderer was convicted in October 1996 and sentenced to indefinite detention. The Philip Lawrence awards to recognize outstanding achievements of good citizenship by young people were launched in 1997 under the aegis of the Home Office.

RICHARD DAVENPORT-HINES

Sources *Queens' College Record* (1996) · *The Times* (9 Dec 1995) · *The Times* (11 Dec 1995) · *The Times* (15 Dec 1995) · *The Times* (27 Dec 1995) · *The Times* (24 Sept 1996) · *The Times* (18 Oct 1996) · *Sunday Times* (10 Dec 1995) · b. cert. · m. cert. · d. cert.

Lawrence, Richard (*b.* 1618). See under Lawrence, Richard (*d.* 1684).

Lawrence, Richard (*d.* 1684), army officer and author, first emerged into prominence as commissary of provisions in Lord Manchester's army in September 1643. He served in a similar capacity in the New Model Army and accompanied Cromwell's expeditionary force to Ireland in August 1649 as marshal-general of horse. In 1647 two pamphlets, *The*

Wolf Stript and *The Anti-Christian Presbyter*, showed Lawrence to be a champion of the gathered churches. He opposed the efforts of parliament to restrict the freedom of the sectaries to worship according to their chosen forms. He regarded the pretensions of the presbyterians as tantamount to the sacerdotalism of the Laudian clergy in the 1630s.

Once in Ireland, Lawrence gravitated to the Baptists, remaining one of their highest-ranking adherents for the rest of his life. There he was also entrusted with important commands as the island was first reconquered and then resettled. In 1651, when governor of Waterford, he was authorized to settle 1200 protestant newcomers in and around the port. He was one of the senior officers who, in October 1654, was given oversight of the arrangements for removing the bulk of the surviving Irish Catholics to the inhospitable western province of Connaught. This policy originated with earlier decisions of the English parliament. It adopted a traditional tactic of expropriating the property of the defeated to pay for the reconquest of Ireland. It also aimed to punish those thought responsible for the uprising of 1641 and subsequent 'atrocities'. Lawrence's zeal for the work of transplantation, conceived as vital to uphold the English interest in Ireland, led him into paper warfare. In two pamphlets he answered Vincent Gookin, who had argued that prudence and humanity should moderate the intended severity. Lawrence repeated in *The Interest of England in the Irish Transplantation Stated* (1655) and *England's Great Interest in the Well Planting of Ireland with English People Discussed* (1656) the widely held view that the Irish Catholics, responsible for the bloodshed in and after 1641, not only remained a danger but deserved punishment. In the resulting controversy, he spoke for the radical officers associated with the lord deputy, Fleetwood. This group felt it was losing ground, especially once Fleetwood had been effectively superseded as chief governor of Ireland by Henry Cromwell in August 1655. Lawrence suspected that Henry Cromwell was moving closer to the longer-established protestant settlers, such as Gookin, who counselled moderation. The wholesale removal of Irish Catholics to Connaught was soon quietly dropped. In time, as Lawrence engaged more closely with the problems of Ireland, he too tempered his original hostility, and accepted the need to retain Catholics as tenants and artisans. His influence diminished under Henry Cromwell's regime between 1655 and 1659. Having acquired Irish property, mainly in recompense for his military service, he attended to its exploitation. He quarrelled with Cromwell's secretary and confidant William Petty, who had overseen the allocation of confiscated lands to the soldiery.

The hopes of the radicals and sectaries revived as the protectorate collapsed in 1659. Lawrence regained some of his former importance. He was employed as one of three agents dispatched from Ireland to the restored Rump Parliament in the dog days of Henry Cromwell's rule in May 1659. He kept the command of his regiment in Ireland, but by December 1659 was being shouldered aside by more conservative officers. The return of Charles

II faced Lawrence not just with eclipse but the possible loss of property and perhaps even punishment. He was not elected either to the Irish Convention in the spring of 1660 or to the Irish House of Commons in the following year. But, thanks to collusive trusts, he retained part of his newly acquired estates scattered across the island. He was watched warily at times of possible trouble, such as 1663 and 1683, and was known still to frequent religious conventicles in Dublin. Yet, his evident good affection to the restored monarchy and his skills recommended him for public duties. In good odour with the lord lieutenant, Ormond, Lawrence was appointed to the newly formed council of trade in 1664. In this capacity, he was active in schemes to improve the textile industries and agriculture. In particular, he discerned the potential of Ireland to support a successful linen manufacture. Ownership of lands in co. Down, where flax was being cultivated, strengthened this belief. Later in the 1660s Lawrence was entrusted by the state with the management of the textile works outside Dublin at Chapelizod, intended as a model of what private projectors might also achieve. Lawrence took seriously this responsibility, securing skilled artificers from abroad and dispatching an agent to study methods in the Low Countries and England. Despite a state subsidy and contracts to clothe the Irish army, the venture did not answer Lawrence's high expectations. Indeed he claimed he had lost £2000 of his own, and was obliged throughout the 1670s to engage in a variety of trading activities, none of which seems to have prospered.

These disappointments obliged Lawrence to curtail his hitherto expansive style of living in central Dublin, as did the costs of a large family. They also stimulated him to analyse the more general causes of the apparent economic underdevelopment of Ireland. This enquiry was published in 1682 as *The Interest of Ireland*. The title echoed but inverted that of his earlier contribution to the fight with Gookin. *The Interest of Ireland* showed how Lawrence had deepened his knowledge of the country and softened some of his earlier hostility to the indigenes. He appreciated that lack of credit facilities and the parlous state of the coinage inhibited investment. Accordingly, he urged the establishment of a bank and a mint in Ireland. He also lamented how many of the promising initiatives of the council of trade had been abandoned. Similarly, private efforts to create industry had mostly foundered by 1682, paralleling his own unhappy experiences at Chapelizod. He subscribed to the opinion that Ireland was impoverished owing to the discriminatory policies adopted by England towards its neighbour. He was an early critic of the habit of numerous owners of Irish land of absenting themselves from the country. Indeed he made a precocious but not altogether convincing attempt to quantify the attendant losses.

Lawrence incorporated the detail of problems and solutions into a framework which reminded of his strong religious convictions. He traced many shortcomings to the moral failings of the population. However, where, in 1655, he had castigated the Catholic majority, he now censured the ascendant protestant minority. He attacked luxury and immorality for their dire financial consequences, and called for both sumptuary regulations and a reformation of manners which prefigured the more organized campaign of the 1690s. At the same time he feared that the sinfulness of the protestant nation might again provoke divine wrath, as seemingly it had in 1641. He contended that Antichrist was still at work in the 1680s, no less than in the 1640s. Earlier he had identified the episcopal and Presbyterian clergy as the villains. By 1682, somewhat tactlessly, he viewed the main threat as Catholicism. His analysis of Irish society and economy lacked the rigour or originality of that by his sparring partner Petty. Nevertheless it offered a valuable, if sometimes idiosyncratic, guide to the state of the country, and continued to be read throughout the next century. Then some of his recommendations, for developing a bank, the linen industry, and Irish fisheries, were taken seriously.

Although he had chosen to settle permanently in Dublin, Lawrence retained links with former comrades and other sectaries throughout Britain and protestant Europe. Contacts outside Ireland may have been exploited as he engaged in making textiles. These links made him suspect during the Popish Plot and attempts to exclude James, duke of York, from the succession. However, he suffered no serious harassment, probably because of the trust that he had established with Ormond and his family. In addition, while Lawrence remained a principal prop of the small Baptist community in Ireland, he was not irreconcilably opposed to the re-established episcopal Church of Ireland. His will, made on 26 June 1684 shortly before he died, in either late June or early July of that year, indicated continuing nonconformist links and comfortable material circumstances. He was probably buried in Dublin, as requested in his will. It is suggested that he married three times, although nothing is known about any earlier relationships. However, his wife at the time of his death (probably Agnes Hewson) was still alive in 1698. He is not to be confused with **Richard Lawrence** (*b.* 1618), son of George Lawrence of Stepleton in Dorset, who entered Magdalen Hall, Oxford, in 1636 and was last heard of as the author of *Gospel Separation Separated from its Abuses* in 1657.

TOBY BARNARD

Sources R. L. [R. Lawrence], *England's great interest in the well planting of Ireland with English people discussed* (1656) • R. Lawrence, *The interest of England in the Irish transplantation stated* (1655) • R. Lawrence, *The interest of Ireland in its trade and wealth stated* (1682) • will, 26 June 1684, priv. coll. [Waringstown, co. Down] • *A memoir of Mistress Ann Fowkes (née Geale) … with some recollections of her family* (1892) • R. Dunlop, ed., *Ireland under the Commonwealth*, 2 vols. (1913) • BL, Lansdowne MS 821, fols. 7, 276, 823 • BL, Egerton MS 542, fol. 370 • *The Clarke Papers*, ed. C. H. Firth, 4, CS, new ser., 62 (1901), 11 • Bodl. Oxf., MSS Carte 35, fol. 861; 36, fols. 330, 332–3, 347–8, 497–8, 521, 523–5, 609; 37, fol. 553; 45, fols. 10, 437, 458; 49, fol. 643; 50, fol. 38; 66, fol. 40; 154, fols. 303, 323; 160, fols. 36–7 • Surrey County RO, 84/49/1-4 • K. Herlihy, 'The Irish Baptists, 1650–1780', PhD diss., TCD, 1992 • W. Petty, *The history of the survey of Ireland: commonly called the down survey, AD 1655-6*, ed. T. A. Larcom (1851) • T. C. Barnard, 'Crises of identity among Irish protestants, 1641–1685', *Past and Present*, 127 (1990), 39–83 • T. C. Barnard, *Cromwellian Ireland: English government and reform in Ireland, 1649–1660* (1975) • A. Clarke, *Prelude to Restoration in Ireland* (1999) • *Calendar of the manuscripts of the marquess of Ormonde*, new ser., 8 vols., HMC, 36

(1902–20), vol. 3, pp. 97, 332–7, 346–51; vol. 4, p. 86; vol. 5, pp. 19, 434, 450–1; vol. 7, pp. 14, 27, 53–4, 63–5, 70–1, 76, 97 • *CSP Ire.*, 1647–60, 857; 1666–9, 711; 1669–70, 126, 635–6 • *Propositions approved and granted by the deputy-general of Ireland to Colonel Richard Laurence* (1651) • E. MacLysaght, ed., *Calendar of the Orrery papers*, IMC (1941) • [W. Penn], *My Irish journal, 1669–70*, ed. I. Grubb (1952)
Archives priv. coll. | Bodl. Oxf., Carte MSS
Wealth at death suggestion of straitened condition: *A memoir of Mistress Ann Fowkes*, 26–7

Lawrence, Robert Daniel [Robin] (**1892–1968**), physician, was born on 18 November 1892 in Aberdeen, the second son of Thomas Lawrence, brush manufacturer, and Margaret Lawrence. He was educated at Aberdeen grammar school and at the university, and graduated MB in 1916. He joined the Royal Army Medical Corps and served in India until being invalided home in 1919. He intended a career in ear, nose, and throat surgery and took a junior appointment at King's College Hospital, London. While practising a mastoid operation on a corpse a bone chip flew in his eye. Because the injury was slow to heal he was admitted to hospital where it was found that he had diabetes, a diagnosis which at that time and at his age was fatal. Determining not to be a burden on his family and to eke out his remaining time as pleasantly as possible he moved to Florence to practise among the British colony there. Then came a dramatic telegram from his friend G. A. Harrison, biochemist at King's College Hospital: 'I have got some insulin. It works. Come back quick.' Lawrence arrived on 29 May 1923 and had his first injection of insulin the next day. His life was saved.

Lawrence rapidly learnt how to manage diabetes and he acquired a large practice in the specialism. From the beginning he realized how important it was that doctors, nurses, and above all patients learned how to manage the disease. He published his famous and well-named book, *The Diabetic Life*, in 1925, and in 1929 he produced a practical guide, especially to his 'line' diet, *The Diabetic ABC*. Both works ran to numerous editions. Lawrence married Doreen Nancy (Anna) Batson (*d.* 1964), daughter of Thomas Batson, schoolmaster, on 7 September 1928. They had three sons.

Lawrence's professional achievements came quickly—membership (1927) and fellowship (1932) of the Royal College of Physicians, and appointment as physician in charge of the diabetic department at King's College Hospital in 1939, a department he had himself created with the help of friends and well-wishers and which became the largest in Britain. Doctors and patients came from all over the world to see 'RDL'. He made special contributions to the treatment of diabetic coma and of pregnancy in the diabetic (with his colleague W. G. Oakley)—previously nearly half the babies born to diabetic mothers had died. In 1934 with the public support of his friend and patient H. G. Wells he founded the Diabetic Association (later the British Diabetic Association); he was chairman of its executive council from 1934 to 1961. In 1950 he helped found the International Diabetic Federation and was its president until 1958. In that year he had a stroke and retired from hospital practice, though he continued in private work.

Lawrence was awarded the Banting medal of the American Diabetes Association in 1946 and was its Lilly lecturer in 1955. He was Banting lecturer of the British Diabetic Association in 1949, and honorary life president from 1962 to 1968. He was Oliver Sharpey lecturer of the Royal College of Physicians in 1946. In 1964 he was awarded an honorary LLD from Toronto University.

Lawrence was a highly individual, even flamboyant figure as a consultant physician, but few doctors have made a greater contribution to the care of patients. He dominated the diabetic scene in Britain to a unique extent from the mid-1920s until the 1950s. He was an enthusiastic golfer, a keen player of hockey and tennis (real and lawn), and a fisherman; and he loved music. He was Presbyterian by upbringing but lost his religious faith in early adult life. He died peacefully at his home, 7 Sheffield Terrace, London, on 27 August 1968.　　　　　　　　DAVID PYKE

Sources *BMJ* (7 Sept 1968), 621–2 • Munk, *Roll* • J. G. L. Jackson, *Diabetic Medicine*, 13 (1996), 9–22 • private information (2004) • personal knowledge (2004)
Archives British Diabetic Association, London
Wealth at death £35,902: probate, 10 Dec 1968, *CGPLA Eng. & Wales*

Lawrence, Samuel (*bap.* **1661**, *d.* **1712**), dissenting minister, was born at Wem, Shropshire, and baptized there on 5 November 1661, the only son of William Lawrence (*d.* 1695), dyer, and his wife, Sarah. He was the nephew of Edward *Lawrence (*d.* 1695), ejected minister. He was educated at the grammar schools at Wem and Newport before receiving religious instruction from local ministers including Francis Tallents at Shrewsbury and Philip Henry at Broadoak. He completed his ministerial training at Charles Morton's Newington Green academy, which he entered in 1681. When Morton disbanded his academy in 1685 Lawrence became an assistant to Thomas Singleton at the grammar school in Bartholomew Close, and in or about 1687 became domestic chaplain to Lady Irby, widow of Sir Anthony Irby, at Dean's Yard, Westminster. While there he occasionally preached for Vincent Alsop at Tothill Street, Westminster.

In 1688 Lawrence accepted the invitation to become minister to the dissenting congregation at Nantwich, Cheshire, and settled there in September of that year. In early November he was ordained at Warrington. He remained as minister at Nantwich for the remainder of his life, proving to be a popular, industrious, and much respected preacher and a scholar of some distinction. He was a prominent member and four times moderator of the Cheshire classis, which he joined at its fourth meeting on 30 June 1691. On more than one occasion he was offered a lucrative position in the established church, but his conscience would not allow him to conform. In later years he began training gratis young men for the dissenting ministry, a vocation in which he demonstrated a considerable talent. Until the last few days of his life Lawrence had enjoyed good health, but he was then 'seized with a fever' (Henry, 48), which within nine days had caused his death in Nantwich on 24 April 1712. He was buried in the chancel of Nantwich church on 28 April, when the funeral sermon was preached by his close friend since childhood, Matthew Henry. He was twice married: his first wife died in April 1700. He was survived by his second wife, who died in November 1712, and by three sons from his first marriage and two daughters from his second. His second son, Samuel (1693–1760), became a distinguished dissenting minister at Newcastle and later in London.

C. W. SUTTON, rev. M. J. MERCER

Sources M. Henry, *A sermon preached at the funeral of Mr. Samuel Lawrence* (1712), 33–48 · A. Gordon, ed., *Cheshire classis: minutes, 1691–1745* (1919), 6–8, 17–19, 22–4, 26–8, 30–42, 44, 48–50, 187–8 · W. Urwick, ed., *Historical sketches of nonconformity in the county palatine of Cheshire, by various ministers and laymen* (1864), 125–9 · W. Wilson, *The history and antiquities of the dissenting churches and meeting houses in London, Westminster and Southwark*, 4 vols. (1808–14), vol. 4, pp. 67–8 · A. Gordon, ed., *Freedom after ejection: a review (1690–1692) of presbyterian and congregational nonconformity in England and Wales* (1917), 300 · J. Toulmin, *An historical view of the state of the protestant dissenters in England* (1814), 570–71 · H. McLachlan, *English education under the Test Acts: being the history of the nonconformist academies, 1662–1820* (1931), 76–80
Archives BL, letter to D. Williams, Add. MS 4291, fol. 159

Lawrence, Sir Soulden (1751–1814), judge, was the son of Thomas *Lawrence MD (1711–1783), president of the Royal College of Physicians, and his wife, Frances (d. 1780), daughter of Charles Chauncey MD, of Derby. He was educated at St Paul's School and at St John's College, Cambridge, where he graduated BA in 1771 as seventh wrangler, and proceeded MA and was elected fellow in 1774. At Cambridge he was a contemporary of Edward Law, afterwards Lord Ellenborough, Vicary Gibbs, who would later take Lawrence's place on the court of common pleas upon Lawrence's resignation, and Simon Le Blanc, who would later join Lawrence on the court of king's bench. He was called to the bar at the Inner Temple in June 1784, and quickly established himself as a leader on the western circuit. He was raised to the degree of serjeant-at-law on 9 February 1787. He was described by Lord Campbell as one of 'the best lawyers that have appeared at Westminster Hall in my time' (Campbell, 3.155). In March 1794 Lawrence was knighted and succeeded Sir Henry Gould as a puisne justice of common pleas. Three months later, on the resignation of Sir Francis Buller, he transferred to king's bench, where he served for fourteen years. Reportedly because of a disagreement with Lord Ellenborough he returned in March 1808 to common pleas, where he remained until Easter term 1812 when poor health brought on his retirement.

Campbell called Lawrence 'a most learned judge' (Hardcastle, 1.250), one whose visage 'denoted great acuteness and discrimination' (Campbell, 3.58). Soon after his appointment he acted as a member of the special commission that tried Thomas Hardy, John Horne Tooke, and others for high treason in 1794–6. As a judge he showed great ability and independence of mind, occasionally differing in opinion while on king's bench from his chief, Lord Kenyon. In the case of *Haycraft* v. *Creasy* (1801), all three puisne justices (Lawrence, Nash Grose, and Simon Le Blanc) disagreed with Kenyon and rejected a plaintiff's

claim for injury caused by the defendant's false representation of another's credit, and the rebuff was said to have hastened Kenyon's death. Lawrence was known for his courtesy and civility, and has been described, toward the bar, as 'a model of judicial suavity', except that 'he could never bring himself to be barely civil to advocates known to be "upon the press"' by providing reports for newspapers (Jeaffreson, 2.371). His extreme scrupulousness is shown by a codicil to his will that directed his executors to pay damages, with interest, to the plaintiff in an action tried before him against a defendant for allegedly diverting a watercourse. The jury, as directed, had found for the defendant, but Lawrence learned from a later action that the plaintiff's claim had been sound.

In addition to his published opinions Lawrence's legacy to legal history lies in manuscripts that survive in Lincoln's Inn library and the Middle Temple Library. The Dampier manuscripts at Lincoln's Inn Library comprise an extensive collection of pleadings and documents involved in cases heard by the court of king's bench from 1770 to 1816. The manuscripts are the personal case papers and notes of four puisne judges—William Ashurst, Francis Buller, Soulden Lawrence, and Henry Dampier. At the Middle Temple Library a further eleven notebooks contain summaries of both reported and unreported cases decided by king's bench, plus indexes. These notebooks are largely from Lawrence's collection, although they were passed on to and continued by Henry Dampier.

Lawrence died unmarried on 8 July 1814 and was buried in the church of St Giles-in-the-Fields, London, where there is a monument to him. He was a connoisseur of art, and during his lifetime assembled a collection of works by ancient and modern masters including Franz Hals, Sir Joshua Reynolds, Pannini, and Spagnoletto.

JAMES OLDHAM

Sources John, Lord Campbell, *The lives of the chief justices of England*, 3 (1857) · *Life of John, Lord Campbell, lord high chancellor of Great Britain*, ed. Mrs Hardcastle, 2 vols. (1881) · J. C. Jeaffreson, *A book about lawyers*, 2 vols. (1867) · J. Haydn, *The book of dignities: containing lists of the official personages of the British empire*, ed. H. Ockerby, 3rd edn (1894) · Foss, *Judges* · R. B. Gardiner, ed., *The admission registers of St Paul's School, from 1748 to 1876* (1884) · Munk, *Roll* · Holdsworth, *Eng. law* · *LondG* (6–10 Feb 1787) · *GM*, 1st ser., 64 (1794) · *GM*, 1st ser., 70 (1800) · *GM*, 1st ser., 84/2 (1814), 92 · *GM*, 1st ser., 85/2 (1815) · T. Baker, *History of the college of St John the Evangelist, Cambridge*, ed. J. E. B. Mayor, 2 vols. (1869) · [I. Espinasse], 'My contemporaries: from the notebooks of a retired barrister', *Fraser's Magazine*, 6 (1832), 316–19
Archives Lincoln's Inn, London, Dampier MSS · Middle Temple, London, 11 Dampier notebooks
Likenesses C. Turner, mezzotint, pubd 1808 (after J. Hoppner), BM, NPG

Lawrence, Stephen Adrian (1974–1993), murder victim, was born on 13 September 1974 at Greenwich District Hospital, the son of Neville George Lawrence (b. 1942), a jobbing tailor, builder's labourer, plasterer, and decorator, and his wife, Doreen Delcitia Graham (b. 1952), a bank clerk, part-time care assistant, office cleaner, and guide for schoolchildren with special needs. He had one younger brother and one younger sister. His parents, who had been born in Jamaica, moved to Britain during the

Stephen Adrian Lawrence (1974–1993), by unknown
photographer

early 1960s. They were self-reliant, hardworking, and
unselfishly ambitious; their elder son followed their good
example.

There was nothing exceptional about Stephen Lawrence, but much to like or admire. He was an amiable,
steady, alert, and thoughtful child. At school he was calm,
diligent, and popular. From early childhood he had
enjoyed sketching and drawing: his ambition was to
become an architect, and he made a notable success during his work experience in an architectural practice. In
appearance he was lean and handsome. He had athletic
prowess and competed as a sprinter with the Cambridge
Harriers club. Throughout his short, promising life he
lived in Plumstead, south London.

Racism was endemic among the bored, ill-educated
white adolescents of nearby Eltham. It was pronounced in
a gang of 'hard cases' led by two brothers, James and Neil
Acourt, and by David Norris. The Acourts were nephews of
a convicted south London criminal, Terry Stuart, while
their friend was the son of Clifford Norris, who between
1988 and 1994 was 'on the run' from the police in connection with major drug-dealing offences. This trio collected
two adherents, Gary Dobson and Luke Knight. The
Acourts became locally notorious as 'real nutters' after
allegedly stabbing other youths (Cathcart, 65). Although

some of their targets were white, the Acourts and their
associates were later described as 'infected and invaded by
gross and revolting racism' (Macpherson, paragraph 7.31).
Neil Acourt once proposed writing a letter beginning,
'Enoch Powell, mate, you are the greatest. You are the don
of dons' (Macpherson, appx 10, sequence 11; Cathcart,
234)—the reference being to (John) Enoch Powell, Conservative politician, whose 'rivers of blood' speech of 1968
had predicted violent conflict between white and black
people in Britain.

Stephen Lawrence spent the evening of 22 April 1993
with his closest friend, Duwayne Brooks, playing
Nintendo games at the home of his uncle. While waiting
for a bus in Well Hall Road, Eltham, he was abruptly
engulfed by a group of white youths who yelled the word
'nigger'. During the incident, which lasted only a few
seconds, he was stabbed twice. He ran 200 yards before
collapsing, and died in Well Hall Road some minutes later
of a haemorrhage caused by stab wounds to the chest and
arms. He was buried on either 3 or 4 July at his mother's
birthplace, Clarendon, near Kingston, Jamaica.

The early investigation of this brutal murder was characterized, in the words of the subsequent inquiry, by 'disarray and uncertainty' (Macpherson, paragraph 11.16).
Within a few hours several informants had directed police
attention to the Acourt group. Officers were slow to
respond to these leads, delayed their cursory searches of
the suspects' houses, bungled their surveillance, and
made a calamitous mistake in waiting a fortnight before
making arrests. These arrests and subsequent identity
parades were disorganized and flawed. Throughout, the
investigation 'was marred by a combination of professional incompetence, institutional racism and a failure of
leadership by senior officers' (Macpherson, paragraph
46.1). A 'substantial number of officers of junior rank
would not accept that the murder of Stephen Lawrence
was simply and solely "racially motivated"' (Macpherson,
paragraph 6.21). As a result investigation of the suspects'
racist notoriety was neglected. The Acourt group swiftly
began to threaten those who might be indiscreet about
them, and the police could not quell this intimidation.
The reputation and influence of David Norris's father
were especially frightening. Stephen Lawrence's parents
meanwhile felt patronized by the police. There is no doubt
that some officers (while not consciously racist) were so
steeped in racial stereotyping, and so committed to preju-
diced assumptions, that their treatment of the Lawrence
family and the crucial eyewitness Duwayne Brooks was
obtuse (Macpherson, paragraphs 5.12 and 26.37). Relations
between the Lawrences and the detectives deteriorated.
The police resented the activities of anti-racist campaigners and the initiatives of the Lawrences' solicitor,
Imran Khan.

On 7 May the suspects were arrested, and later Neil
Acourt and Knight were charged with murder. Subsequently, a disputed conversation between Brooks and a
detective sergeant after an identity parade convinced
police that his identifications were unsafe. Consequently,

on 28 July the prosecution was abandoned. Shortly afterwards an internal police review of the handling of the case was undertaken. However, its report was 'flawed and indefensible' (Macpherson, paragraph 46.21).

During 1994 the police, under a new senior investigating officer, redoubled their efforts to catch the murderers, but without avail. They therefore co-operated when the Lawrences, supported by an exasperated black community, brought a private prosecution for murder against the alleged killers in 1995. Ultimately Neil Acourt, Dobson, and Knight went for trial (17–25 April 1996), but it was a hopeless effort. Brooks's evidence of identification was considered unreliable by the judge, who instructed the jury to acquit.

A second police review (1997–8) concluded that the early months of the murder investigation had been mismanaged and uninspired. Additionally, the incoming Labour government of 1997 appointed a judicial inquiry chaired by a former High Court judge, Sir William Macpherson of Cluny. Its public hearings (opening on 16 March 1998) attracted huge publicity, especially when police witnesses suffered robust questioning by the Lawrences' legal representatives. The tenacity, controlled anger, and measured dignity of the grieving parents won widespread praise. Macpherson's report (issued in February 1999) vindicated the family's complaints about police conduct, and upheld the dissatisfaction of minority ethnic communities at their treatment by officers. He indicted the Metropolitan Police for 'institutional racism', mainly 'unconscious' or 'unintentional', including 'well intentioned but patronizing words or actions', the 'canteen culture' of police stations, and 'racist stereotyping of black people as potential criminals or troublemakers' (Macpherson, paragraphs 6.6, 6.13, 6.17, 6.28). Macpherson confirmed the Acourt group as 'prime suspects' (Macpherson, paragraph 7.7). His recommendations on police reform and social policy were bold, imaginative, and practical.

The Stephen Lawrence Charitable Trust was established in 1998 to commemorate Lawrence. It prepared a scheme to provide architectural and design courses for young people from black and other ethnic minorities at the Stephen Lawrence Technocentre in Deptford. The Millennium Commission and other public bodies agreed in 2001 to contribute towards the £9.2 million capital cost. Neville and Doreen Lawrence, co-founders of the Stephen Lawrence Charitable Trust, were both appointed OBE in the 2003 new year's honours list.

Stephen Lawrence's murder was a waste that nothing could mitigate; but its consequences for police methods and for social policy were extensive. His parents' gruelling struggle for fair treatment ensured that he became British anti-racism's equivalent of Rosa Parkes, whose refusal to give up her seat on a bus in Montgomery, Alabama, in 1955 was the start of the American civil rights movement.

RICHARD DAVENPORT-HINES

Sources B. Cathcart, *The case of Stephen Lawrence* (1999) · W. Macpherson, *The Stephen Lawrence inquiry*, 2 vols. (1999) · b. cert. · d. cert.
Archives priv. coll., family MSS

Likenesses photograph, 1993, repro. in Cathcart, *The case of Stephen Lawrence*, facing p. 210 · photograph, Rex Features Ltd, London [*see illus.*]

Lawrence, Stringer (1697–1775), army officer in the East India Company, was born in Hereford on 24 February 1697 and baptized on 27 February at All Saints' Church, Hereford, son of John Lawrence and his wife, Mary. His military career began at the rather late age of thirty as an ensign in Clayton's regiment (later the 14th foot) at Gibraltar on 22 December 1727. After twenty years, including service in Spain and Flanders, and in the Jacobite rising of 1745 where he fought at Culloden, Lawrence resigned the king's service as captain (perhaps for financial reasons) and was given a major's commission by the East India Company in 1746 to command its forces at Madras and to infuse them with greater regularity and a more professional spirit. His success in this role led to him later being dubbed 'the father of the Indian Army', since he transformed the company's Madras soldiers (European and Indian) from mere garrison guards into a small army which within a few years had performed very creditably in the field.

For nearly twenty years (1748–66), with two home leave breaks (1750–52 and 1759–61), Lawrence served with distinction in the field, and less successfully in helping to manage the East India Company's political affairs at Madras. During this time the company moved from being merely a large intercontinental trading concern to the threshold of hegemonical political power in India. Lawrence contributed significantly to making this choice possible, though his own ambitions for the British were much more limited, saying in 1754 (before Clive's victory at Plassey in 1757 gave the company the virtual control of Bengal and Bihar), 'all the Rights that we [should] demand or any Europeans ought to have, are a few Settlements with a little country for their Bounds allotted to them, and a Liberty for a free Trade' (Lawrence to Madras council, 17 March 1754, *Diary and Consultation Book, Military Dept, 1754*, 1912, 67–8).

Early Indian career Lawrence, robustly corpulent and fifty years old, arrived in India on 13 January 1748 at the tail-end of the War of Austrian Succession to find the company's fortunes at a low ebb with the French capture of Madras over a year earlier. This left them with Fort St David, a few miles south of Pondicherry, as the only remaining British foothold on the Coromandel Coast. However, reinforcements soon arrived (26 July 1748) under Admiral Boscawen which gave the British temporary naval and military superiority. Boscawen was under orders to capture Pondicherry but did not have much idea how to go about it. The subsequent expedition was described by Clive, who was a junior participant, as a fiasco, and Lawrence, commanding the company's troops under Boscawen, was captured defending an entrenchment with another officer after all their men had fled.

News of peace in Europe soon brought Lawrence's release to resume his command at Fort St David (Madras had been returned but was deemed uninhabitable for several years). The company hoped that with the peace it

Stringer Lawrence (1697–1775), by Thomas Gainsborough,
c.1774–5

could resume its previously lucrative trade, unencumbered by political complications. But the presence at Pondicherry of an imperialist adventurer, Governor Joseph Dupleix, and the current disarray of local Mughal politics with two claimants to the governorship of the Carnatic, determined otherwise, as Dupleix backed one of the rivals with French military power left over from the war. Fearing that if his candidate, Chanda Sahib, succeeded, Dupleix would be able to shut the company out of the Carnatic, the Fort St David council (including Lawrence) decided reluctantly to support his rival, a son of the former nawab, Muhammad Ali Khan.

Already, a clique of four senior men at Fort St David (Boscawen, the civilian president and his deputy, and Lawrence) had in June 1749, against the spirit of company instructions but probably to rescue their reputations after the débâcle at Pondicherry, indulged in their own little essay in post-war 'country' (Indian) politics, by supporting a claimant to the throne of Tanjore, a small but rich Hindu kingdom to the south. Although the bid failed for lack of local support, the company still received its price, the strategically placed port of Devakottai at the mouth of the River Coleroon which upstream flowed through the large fortified town of Trichinopoly, which controlled routes in all directions and was soon to be a vital asset in the struggle for the Carnatic. Lawrence commanded the force which captured Devakottai and Lieutenant Clive was one of his subordinate officers. Clive greatly impressed Lawrence in this operation and a bond of mutual professional esteem formed between the two men which deepened over the next few years as the company's forces entered the wider scene of extended field operations in the Carnatic.

The struggle for the Carnatic, 1749–1756 Officially, the British and French companies acted as auxiliaries to the contending Mughal princes, but militarily their armed forces were the principals, and this promoted them to aspirant unofficial controllers of the province in a war which continued long after Chanda Sahib had been killed (1752). The contest was finally resolved in 1761 when the British took Pondicherry and Muhammad Ali, 'their' nawab, was recognized in the treaty of Paris at the end of the Seven Years' War in 1763. Though Colonel Eyre Coote, in command of crown and company forces supported by a Royal Navy squadron, consummated the British success at the battle of Wandiwash in 1760 and at the subsequent fall of Pondicherry, this was only made possible by Lawrence's desperate efforts in the early 1750s to defend Muhammad Ali's position against the often superior numbers of the French and their Indian allies, when defeat could well have seen the extirpation of the company from the Carnatic.

In the proxy war the British and French fought in the Carnatic between 1749 and 1756, neither could attack the other's settlements on the coast since their governments were at peace, so operations largely focused on the British defence of Trichinopoly (100 miles inland and 120 miles south-west of Fort St David and Pondicherry), where Muhammad Ali had sought refuge. The armies which fought around the town were a hotchpotch of contingents contributed by the French and British East India companies and their Indian allies, in which the European commanding officer was supposedly in overall control but in fact had little authority over the allied 'country' forces. The European units themselves were a mixture of European and Indian troops, very small scale forces compared with contemporary armies in north India or Europe. They usually consisted of a weak European battalion (500–600 men), plus increasing numbers of sepoys (Indian troops trained to fight in the European manner)—rising in the British case from 2000 in 1751 to 7000 in 1758—to which were added up to 20,000 'country' cavalry and infantry (irregulars in European eyes).

The opening phase of the war (1749–51) was largely taken up with armed diplomacy. The British (commanded by Lawrence) and French forces manoeuvred around one another in an attempt to catch the attention and support of Nasir Jang, the *subahdar* or viceroy of the Deccan, who had entered the Carnatic with a large army in March 1750 to settle the dispute. Dupleix plunged into a court intrigue which resulted in Nasir Jang's assassination; his successor, Muzaffar Jang, with French support, withdrew his army to Hyderabad to establish his power, leaving the rival nawabs and their European allies to fight it out in the Carnatic.

Commander-in-chief Lawrence had gone home two months before these momentous events to dispute his pay with the directors; he returned in April 1752 with his pay doubled (£500 plus expenses) and with a new grandiloquent title of commander-in-chief of the company's forces in India, but still only with the rank of major. In Lawrence's absence, the British and French had largely spent their time skirmishing around Trichinopoly; the only military operation of note had been Clive's daring campaign 150 miles to the north, with a vastly outnumbered scratch force from Madras, to take and defend Arcot, the capital of the Carnatic, held formerly by Chanda Sahib.

The years 1752–3 marked the apogee of Lawrence's military career; his account of the period was incorporated into R. O. Cambridge's *Account of the War in India between the English and the French*, published in 1762. In April 1752, exploiting a temporary superiority of numbers, Lawrence, ably assisted by Clive, marched to Trichinopoly and counter-blockaded Chanda Sahib and the timidly led French force on the island of Srirangam in the River Cauvery outside the city walls. After two months, with the British tightening the ring and firing into the allied camp, Chanda Sahib unwisely surrendered to his Tanjorean enemies and was beheaded; the French (on 14 June 1752) were treated more gently by Lawrence in accordance with European protocols. Although this defeat had temporarily deprived the French of most of their troops and had raised the prestige of Muhammad Ali and his British sponsors in the Carnatic, it did not end the war. Pondicherry was inviolate and Dupleix soon received substantial reinforcements, while it turned out, unbeknown to Lawrence, that Muhammad Ali had promised to cede Trichinopoly to his Mysorean allies (whose contribution to operations had been minimal) in the event of its liberation. The nawab 'forgot' his promise. This was fertile ground for Dupleix to exploit and he had soon got the Mysoreans over to the French side and bought out the Marathas as well. The blockade of Trichinopoly therefore continued while Lawrence sat down with most of his force in front of Pondicherry to watch the French.

Lawrence in the field On 26 August 1752 Lawrence managed, by feigning a retreat, to entice the French out of their sanctuary and attacked them at Bahur, between Pondicherry and Fort St David. It was a battle between roughly equal forces which revealed Lawrence's nerve, celerity, and tactical inventiveness; it also illustrates the scale of field actions in this war. Lawrence approached his enemy before dawn in two lines, 1700 sepoys in the first to reconnoitre the French positions; they were followed by 450 of the company's European infantry, grenadiers in the centre flanked by four field guns on either side; 500 of Muhammad Ali's cavalry kept pace with this force on the other side of a bank along the line of the march. Skirmishing between the opposing forces began just after dawn. The British line then advanced on the French, who were formed up between the bank and a tank (pool), accompanied by an exchange of artillery and small arms fire. This was one of those rare occasions when the outcome was decided by hand-to-hand bayonet fighting as the French stood their ground. Eventually they broke and fled as the British grenadiers in the centre cut through their line. The nawab's horse should have completed the rout, but as was

often the case, these troops, with months of back pay owing, preferred to plunder the enemy baggage. The French commander and fifteen of his officers surrendered with all their artillery.

Strategically, matters continued in their inconclusive way for eight months, with neither side strong enough to assert general control over the Carnatic. In April 1753 Lawrence had to rush down to Trichinopoly by forced marches, losing men on the way through heat exhaustion, on news of its imminent surrender through starvation. This precipitated a series of actions over the summer of 1753 and into 1754 which enhanced Lawrence's reputation as a field commander and demonstrated that he had created a small, integrated army of Europeans and Indians whose high morale under good leadership made them equal to often much bigger armies.

On 26 June 1753 the French stormed an under-manned British outpost on a rocky eminence (Golden Rock) 3 miles south of Trichinopoly dominating the main supply route into the town. Lawrence, with a large detachment (400 Europeans, 2000 sepoys, field artillery, and 3000 of the nawab's horse), arrived too late to defend it and found himself out on the plain facing the whole enemy allied army (300 Europeans, 500 sepoys, and over 20,000 Mysorean and Maratha cavalry and infantry) and enfiladed by the guns of the French post on Golden Rock. To retreat would have been to invite a massacre, so without hesitation Lawrence sent the grenadiers to retake Golden Rock, which they did with such *élan* that the enemy did not stop to fight. Now aided by their covering fire, Lawrence, with one end of his line anchored on Golden Rock, routed the French line with fire and a bayonet charge at 20 yards. On the march back to camp Lawrence's diminutive force had to repel repeated and very costly attacks by large numbers of Indian cavalry by forming a square and with discharges of grape.

The supply situation at Trichinopoly remained critical and Lawrence, returning from the country to the south with a large, cumbersome convoy, on 9 August 1753 found his way blocked by the enemy lying between two rocky hills (Sugarloaf Rock and Golden Rock). Giving priority to his convoy, Lawrence sought to evade the enemy by feinting to his right, leading the French commander to redeploy forces to his left, before marching round the French right flank. But the French still sent a detachment to intercept the convoy, and Lawrence responded by personally leading his whole force against it and putting it to flight, thereby breaking through to Trichinopoly. Actions such as these around the town continued into 1754, the British suffering reverses as well as successes. Towards the end, Lawrence, still in command, retired sick into Trichinopoly; in Clive's absence he had found in Captain Caillaud (later commander-in-chief of the Bengal army) a very able second.

Lawrence and the governing council of Madras This effectively marked the end of Lawrence's military career in the field. His achievements earned him a royal commission of lieutenant-colonel from 26 February 1754 and the gift of a jewelled sword from the grateful company. The same year saw two other developments which changed his situation: a truce between the two exhausted companies became a provisional peace in the Carnatic which lasted until the outbreak of the Seven Years' War (1756), and Lawrence was superseded by the arrival of the inexperienced Colonel Adlercron, in command of the 39th (1st Royal) regiment to see service in India. Lawrence's last military service, after the unhappy Adlercron had gone home, was to assist the civilian governor, George Pigot, in 1758 in the successful defence of Madras when it was again besieged by the French. Lawrence, feeling his years, went home in 1759. Clive, up in Bengal, had remarked to a director of the East India Company two years earlier that Lawrence had 'grown old and his intellect begins to fail' (Clive to William Mabbott, 21 Aug 1757, NL Wales, Clive MS 200, fols. 73–6); but the directors apparently disagreed and in 1761 persuaded Lawrence, now with a major-general's rank in the East Indies only, to return to Madras on £1500 plus expenses a year.

Lawrence had always been a member ('perpetual Third') of the governing council at Madras, even acting as governor during a brief interregnum between two civilian heads in 1750, but had otherwise rarely attended in the early years. Political, even less commercial, business was not to his taste. From the field, he constantly rowed with the very able but exasperated governor, Thomas Saunders, over civil–military demarcations and over his role as a member of a select committee of the council charged with formulating grand strategy. Lawrence had a very narrow strategic vision: it extended only to hammering the French, and he objected to Saunders's diversion of military resources into handling the complex and volatile 'country' political situation in the Carnatic, refusing to see how the policies of the Indian powers might impinge on his own strategy since he disdained their military strength. Both men, the one a former captain, the other recruited as a merchant, were under-experienced to play in the high-rolling political game the company was now enmeshed in in India, and they did remarkably well in the circumstances.

There are few references in the records to Lawrence's individual contributions at the council table other than as a military administrator, where he was on firmer ground. On his arrival in 1748 he had organized the independent European infantry companies into a battalion which lay at the heart of his subsequent field operations. Ten years later he similarly organized the sepoys into battalions and fatefully placed European officers in command of them. Undoubtedly this improved their military effectiveness, but the permanent slight to the Indian officers festered to become one of the causes of the mutiny of 1857. Another Lawrence plan, in 1766, to brigade the Madras forces to create two field armies, one at the frontier and one near Madras, was stillborn for lack of money.

Retirement and reputation Lawrence left India for the last time in 1766. His record was of a brave officer who relished combat and who could take quick and effective decisions in perilous tactical situations. He was a far less certain strategist, often trying to shuffle off responsibility for difficult decisions, reacting irascibly to reasonable requests from civilian colleagues to help in devising a plan of operations. Another weakness, at least according to the civilians, was his susceptibility to the importuning of officers for preferment, even though he was constantly reminded that promotion in the company's army was by seniority. That said, Lawrence himself never sought the great riches which fell to most of his senior contemporaries in India. In 1759, a royal officer said of him, he 'has saved his Country, yet is not worth a Groat, whilst Clive for one or two trifling Affairs has got half a million' (Colonel William Draper to Pierson?, 18 Feb 1759, BL OIOC, MS Eur. D667). Clive did give Lawrence, when he retired, an annuity of £500 from his own fabled wealth, and the company and the nawab granted him further pensions worth £2000. There is no evidence that he ever married.

Lawrence died at his London residence in Bruton Street on 10 January 1775 and was buried in the village church of Dunchideock, near Exeter. He had been living with Sir Robert Palk and his family at Haldon House, near Exeter. Palk erected a column in Lawrence's memory on nearby Haldon Hill. Sir Joshua Reynolds painted Lawrence's portrait, and the directors of the East India Company placed a monument, with a bust, to him in Westminster Abbey, inscribed: 'For Discipline established, Fortresses protected, Settlements extended, French and Indian armies defeated, and Peace restored in the Carnatic.'

G. J. BRYANT

Sources R. O. Cambridge, *An account of the war in India between the English and the French*, 2nd edn (1762) • *DNB* • J. Biddulph, *Stringer Lawrence: the father of the Indian army* (1901) • Fortescue, *Brit. army*, vol. 2 • secret military and political consultations of the president and council, BL OIOC, range 240, vol. 9; range C, vols. 48, 50–52; range D, vols. 41–4; range 251, vols. 47–56 • BL OIOC, Home misc., vol. 84 • court book, 1746–8, BL OIOC, vol. 62 • G. Forrest, *The life of Lord Clive*, 2 vols. (1918) • [R. Orme], *A history of the military transactions of the British nation in Indostan*, 4th edn, 3 vols. (1803) • W. J. Wilson, ed., *History of the Madras army*, 5 vols. (1882–9) • M. Wilks, *Historical sketches of the south of India, in an attempt to trace the history of Mysoor*, 3 vols. (1810–17) • NL Wales, Clive papers • *Report on the Palk manuscripts*, HMC, 74 (1922) • parish register, All Saints, Hereford, 27 Feb 1697, Herefs. RO, BC63/40 [birth]
Archives BL OIOC, corresp. and MSS, MSS Eur Orme • Duke U., narrative of affairs on the coast of Coromandel • Royal Artillery Institution, London, journal and MSS | BL OIOC, letters to John Carnac, MS Eur F128 • Lewis Walpole Library, Farmington, Connecticut, journal • NL Wales, Clive MSS
Likenesses J. Reynolds, oils, c.1760, BL OIOC • P. Scheemakers, marble statue, 1764, BL OIOC • oils, c.1767 (after J. Reynolds), Oriental Club, London • T. Gainsborough, oils, c.1774–1775, NPG [*see illus.*] • W. Tyler, bust on monument, 1775, Westminster Abbey • attrib. J. Reynolds, oils, Victoria Memorial Museum, Calcutta, India • J. Reynolds, portrait, repro. in Biddulph, *Stringer Lawrence*
Wealth at death not a rich man; pensions of £2000 p.a. from East India Company, Clive, and Nawab Muhammed Ali: Biddulph, *Stringer Lawrence*; Forrest, *The life of Lord Clive*

Lawrence, (Arabella) Susan (1871–1947), politician, was born in London on 12 August 1871. Her family were prosperous; her father, Nathaniel Tertius Lawrence (1823/4–1898), was a prominent solicitor, and her mother, Laura

(Arabella) Susan Lawrence (1871–1947), by Walter Stoneman, 1930

Bacon, was the daughter of a judge. Susan Lawrence as she was known, was educated at home and then at the Francis Holland School in Baker Street, London. Subsequently she attended University College, London, and in 1895 entered Newnham College, Cambridge. She was placed among the senior optimes in part one of the mathematical tripos in 1898; she then left Newnham following the death of her father.

As an undergraduate Lawrence was a committed Conservative, a supporter of empire and the Church of England. Her concern with education incorporated a strong emphasis on provision for church schools, which was evident in her subsequent activities as a school manager and a member of the London school board. She had a deep commitment to philanthropy and a thorough appreciation of the principles underlying the work of the Charity Organization Society. In March 1910 she was elected to the London county council (LCC) as a Municipal Reform (Conservative) councillor for affluent West Marylebone.

This success was followed rapidly by a political conversion; early in 1912 Lawrence announced her resignation from the LCC. The accepted explanation is that she had become disenchanted with her party on account of the low rates of pay for school cleaners employed by the LCC. Her letter of resignation indicated other issues—poor-law reform and a change in her position on religious schools. The latter emphasis might well have been associated with a personal shift from high Anglicanism to a

more secularist position. Above all, the change in her politics involved an acknowledgement that social improvement could not depend on voluntary initiatives; state action was essential. She joined the Fabian Society, serving on its executive from 1913 to 1945, and developed close friendships with Sidney and Beatrice Webb.

Lawrence's commitment to collectivism was paralleled by a strong involvement in women's trade unionism. Her outrage at the treatment of LCC school cleaners brought her into contact with Mary Macarthur, the inspirational secretary of the Women's Trade Union League (WTUL). Her friendship with Macarthur was central to her activities until the latter died in 1921. For a decade this educated, affluent rentier worked to organize working-class women, overcoming social barriers as well as that of her forbidding appearance—she wore a monocle—to earn the sobriquet 'Our Susan'.

Lawrence's induction into working-class culture was aided by her return to the LCC as a Labour councillor for Poplar in 1913. She presented herself as 'the only Socialist member elected by a socialist organisation' (*The Times*, 14 March 1913). Unlike other Labour councillors, she was not elected under the Progressive label in alliance with the Liberals; in Poplar local Labour strength was such that the Progressives stood only one candidate for the two seats, leaving Lawrence a free run against her former party. Following her mother's death she moved house to the East End, off the East India Dock Road. Her political metamorphosis was complete.

During the First World War, Lawrence's work for the WTUL was complemented by attempts to extend state collectivism in ways that would protect and advance working-class interests. She was a Fabian representative on the War Emergency Workers' National Committee, a grand coalition of Labour and socialists that avoided divisive debate over the legitimacy of the war and concentrated on practical proposals for working-class amelioration. Similarly Lawrence became a member of the Central Committee on Women's Employment and served on a Ministry of Reconstruction committee on relations between employers and employed. Her politics epitomized progressive optimism about post-war reconstruction and the advance of collectivism. One manifestation of this mood was the organizational reform of the Labour Party; its new constitution in the context of an expanded franchise gave notice of heightened electoral ambitions. In 1918 Lawrence was elected to the new women's section of the party's national executive; she had established herself after just six years as one of Labour's leading women.

The Poplar connection further strengthened Lawrence's reputation on the left. In 1919 the Labour Party won an overwhelming majority on the Poplar borough council and Lawrence was chosen to fill one of the aldermanic vacancies. In 1921 under George Lansbury's leadership the council majority responded to rising unemployment with a radical strategy. Rejecting the view that impoverished Poplar should deal with the burden of its own unemployed, the councillors decided to withhold required payments to the LCC and other bodies. The local support for the policy was impressive, but in September 1921 all the defaulting councillors were gaoled for contempt. Lawrence with four women colleagues entered Holloway prison on 5 September. During her incarceration she read Russian novels and *The Future of Local Taxation*; she complained about being unable to smoke. Legal contrivance produced the release of the councillors on 12 October without any effective purging of their contempt. Although Poplar's principal demand for a London-wide fund to deal with unemployment was subsequently met, the strategy became marginalized within the Labour Party. Its deliberate illegality was objectionable to party strategists dedicated to the use of existing constitutional procedures. Within London its prime critic was Herbert Morrison, secretary of the London Labour Party and subsequently leader of the LCC Labour group. Possibly it was as a legacy of the Poplar controversy that Lawrence unsuccessfully opposed Morrison for the group leadership in 1926.

This opposition was effectively as the candidate of the left; yet in other respects Lawrence's politics in the 1920s were very much those of the party loyalist. She became increasingly focused on a parliamentary career; her membership of Poplar borough council ended in 1924, and of the LCC in 1928. Her first parliamentary contest was a by-election in North West Camberwell in March 1920; unsuccessful there and then at East Ham North in the general election of 1922, she was elected for the latter constituency in December 1923. This meant that she became one of the first three Labour women MPs. During the Labour government of 1924 she was parliamentary private secretary to Charles Trevelyan at the Board of Education, but lost her seat in October 1924 at the general election. However, she regained it at a by-election in April 1926, and strengthened her parliamentary reputation with impressive and erudite opposition to Neville Chamberlain's de-rating legislation. Another success at East Ham in the general election of 1929 was the prelude to her appointment as parliamentary secretary at the Ministry of Health in the second Labour government under Arthur Greenwood. Yet this parliamentary achievement rested on an insecure electoral base. Her constituency was socially mixed, her victories were by narrow margins, and they depended on a divided opposition.

This advancement as the dedicated, loyal party figure was perhaps not without its personal tensions. Beatrice Webb offered nuanced portraits of Lawrence in the 1920s, aided by the fact that Lawrence had become tenant of the Webbs' Millbank house. Alongside the cerebral, widely read product of Newnham, Webb also claimed a more emotional side to Lawrence evident in her speeches to East Ham workers during the general strike of 1926—'the somewhat wild woman of demagogic speech … abasing herself and her class before the *real* wealth producers' (*Diary*, ed. Mackenzie, 4.80).

If class identities generated problems for Lawrence, it appears that gender identities posed fewer difficulties. Like others among her generation of Labour women, such as Ethel Bentham and Margaret Bondfield, and in contrast

to Lady Astor and some of the younger Labour women like Jennie Lee and Ellen Wilkinson, Lawrence was completely indifferent to pressure to present a 'feminine' image. It was noted how, as a minister, she took no interest in her choice of clothes, sending round to a department store for half a dozen inexpensive dresses to be sent to her office, and briefly raising her head from her papers to select one by pointing with a pencil. In 1927 Beatrice Webb commented on the celibacy of the three woman Labour MPs (*Diaries, 1924–1932*, ed. Cole, 150) and later described Lawrence as a person who 'belongs to the old order of irreproachable female celibates, which used to be an important caste in Victorian days, and which has no votaries among the young generation—a fact, by the way, which she denies' (*Diary*, ed. Mackenzie, 4.357).

Before 1914 Lawrence seems to have been at best unsympathetic to demands for women's suffrage; the antisuffragist Lord George Hamilton addressed a Marylebone election meeting for her in 1910. In the post-war Labour Party she resolutely opposed any development of woman's identity that risked dividing the party. What mattered for her, as for several other leading women in the party, was the strengthening of a Labour identity to which all other identities should be subordinated. This commitment informed two interventions by her in 1929. The first at the National Women's Conference dismissed a proposal to ban male speakers as 'degrading to women' (*Labour National Women's Conference*, 1929, 33). The second, at the party conference, disingenuously ignored the realities of women's position in the party to claim that no rule prevented the national executive from being an all-woman body.

Lawrence was a ministerial success; her command of detail secured her authority both in her department and at the dispatch box. In October 1930 she became the first woman to chair the Labour Party conference. Her opening address called for unity behind an increasingly embattled government. Public loyalty masked private doubts about the administration's timidity. As early as July 1929 Beatrice Webb chronicled Lawrence contemplating resignation (*Diaries, 1924–1932*, ed. Cole, 229). The government's collapse in August 1931 produced an unambiguous response from Lawrence. She had not been close to MacDonald and she became a vigorous opponent of the National Government. Her loyalty to the party was expressed through a more thorough espousal of socialist solutions to economic crisis. When the new party leader, Arthur Henderson, responded to the National Government's abandonment of the gold standard with a mild speech in the Commons, Lawrence attacked him at a meeting of the Parliamentary Labour Party. She articulated the robust sentiments that were increasingly characteristic of the party. But her decisive defeat at East Ham in the general election in October 1931 ended her parliamentary career.

Although Lawrence remained on the party's national executive, the initiative after 1931 lay with a new and younger leadership group. Beatrice Webb observed her eagerness to re-enter parliament; her increasing alienation was no doubt deepened by her failure to do so at the general election held in November 1935. She left familiar territory to fight Stockton-on-Tees in the depressed northeast. Her principal opponent was a Conservative critic of the National Government, Harold Macmillan. Her orthodox Labour campaign encountered not so much the National Government's programme as Macmillan's middle way, and he held the seat comfortably. Frustrated by British politics, she was excited by the turbulence and radicalism of the early new deal and responded positively to Jewish communes in Palestine constructed on Tolstoyan lines. Unlike many contemporaries she did not see the Soviet Union as a worthwhile exemplar for socialists. Yet her last significant intervention within the party's national executive in March 1940 was to oppose the expulsion from the party of the pro-Soviet lawyer D. N. Pritt for his position on the Russo-Finnish war. Perhaps such opposition indicated her disenchantment. Having lost her seat on the executive in 1941, not before time, as Hugh Dalton rather uncharitably recorded, she spent much time transcribing books into Braille. After her Millbank home was bombed in the blitz she lived in a property on Buscot Park, Berkshire, owned by the Labour peer Lord Faringdon. At the end of the war she returned to London, where she died, at her home, 28 Bramham Gardens, South Kensington, on 24 October 1947. She was cremated at Golders Green on the 29th. 'Tall and gaunt of figure in her later years', an obituarist wrote, 'with rather close-cropped grey hair, piercing eyes, and an engaging habit of darting a finger at one in conversation, speaking in a rather sibilant, husky voice, she was the most transparently honest and unegotistical of politically minded women' (*The Times*, 25 Oct 1947, 6).

Susan Lawrence was an impressive politician, painstaking rather than original, and both cerebral and passionate. Her career as a national figure was limited by the electoral uncertainties of the 1920s and effectively terminated by the trauma of 1931. Its trajectory illuminates two themes fundamental to the growth of the Labour Party. One concerns upper- and middle-class recruits often from a declining Liberalism, but as Susan Lawrence's case demonstrates also from the Conservative Party. Second, her politics demonstrated the incorporation of women into the Labour Party through an emphasis on the Labour identity that they claimed in common with their male comrades. The forceful public figure had a rich hinterland concerned with literature, foreign travel, and not least conversation. She regularly mislaid her possessions, and was a chain smoker. As with other late-Victorian educated upper-class women, spinsterdom became an identity and a resource for public life. At a moment of transition from voluntarism to collectivism this identity and commitment brought Susan Lawrence into the Labour Party.

DAVID HOWELL

Sources D. Martin, 'Lawrence, Arabella Susan', *DLB*, 3.128–32 · B. Harrison, *Prudent revolutionaries: portraits of British feminists between the wars* (1987) · J. Hannam and K. Hunt, *Socialist women: Britain, 1880s to 1920s* (2001) · P. Graves, *Labour women: women in British*

working class politics, 1918–39 (1994) · C. Rackham, *Newnham College Roll Letter* (1948) · C. Rackham, *Fabian Quarterly* (March 1948) · H. Laski, 'Susan Lawrence: our best woman MP', *Daily Herald* (16 Aug 1930) · J. Johnston, *A hundred commoners* (1931) · *Beatrice Webb's diaries, 1912–1924*, ed. M. I. Cole (1952) · *Beatrice Webb's diaries, 1924–1932*, ed. M. Cole (1956) · *The diary of Beatrice Webb*, ed. N. MacKenzie and J. MacKenzie, 4 vols. (1982–5) · P. Thompson, *Socialists, liberals and labour: the struggle for London, 1885–1914* (1967) · N. Branson, *Poplarism, 1919–25: George Lansbury and the councillors' revolt* (1979) · J. Schneer, *George Lansbury* (1942) · S. K. Bracker, *The 'Herald' book of labour members [with supplement]* (1924)

Archives Labour History Archive and Study Centre, Manchester, corresp. and papers

Likenesses W. Stoneman, photograph, 1930, NPG [*see illus.*]

Wealth at death £10,471 11s. 10d.: probate, 6 Dec 1947, CGPLA Eng. & Wales

Lawrence, Thomas (1711–1783), physician, born in the parish of St Margaret, Westminster, on 25 May 1711, was the second son of Captain Thomas Lawrence RN and his wife, Elizabeth (d. 1724), daughter of Gabriel Soulden, merchant, of Kinsale, Ireland, and widow of a Colonel Piers. He was the grandson of Thomas Lawrence (d. 1714), first physician to Queen Anne, and physician-general to the army, who in turn was nephew of Henry Lawrence (1600–1664), Cromwell's lord president of the council of state.

Lawrence attended school in Dublin for a while, when his father was appointed to the Irish station about 1715. Following the death of his mother, his father left the navy and settled with his family at Southampton. The son finished his preliminary education at the local grammar school, and in October 1727 was entered as a commoner of Trinity College, Oxford. After graduating BA in 1730, and MA in 1733, he chose medicine as his profession, and moved to London, where he attended the anatomical lectures of Frank Nicholls, and the practice of St Thomas's Hospital. He graduated MB at Oxford in 1736 and MD in 1740, and succeeded Nicholls as anatomical reader in the university, but continued to live in London, where he also delivered anatomical lectures.

Lawrence was admitted as a candidate of the Royal College of Physicians in 1743, and as a fellow in 1744. After filling various college offices he was elected president in 1767, and was re-elected for seven consecutive years. On 25 May 1744 Lawrence married Frances (d. 2 Jan 1780), daughter of Charles Chauncy, physician, of Derby. They had six sons, one of whom was Sir Soulden *Lawrence, and three daughters.

After 1750, the popularity of Lawrence's anatomical lectures was diminished by the increasing celebrity of William Hunter. He decided to abandon them, and devote himself solely to medical practice, but achieved less success than he deserved, due to his occasional fits of deafness, as well as 'a vacuity of countenance very unfavourable to an opinion of his learning and sagacity, and certain convulsive motions of the head and shoulders that gave pain to the beholder and drew attention from all that he said' (Munk, 2.152).

Lawrence is chiefly remembered as the friend of Samuel Johnson, who was one of his patients. He was introduced to Johnson by Richard Bathurst. Johnson, who corresponded with him in London about his own ailments, said that Lawrence was 'one of the best men whom he had known' (19 March 1782). Mrs Thrale gives a poignant account of a visit which she and Johnson paid Lawrence when he had only partially recovered from a paralytic stroke. When one of Lawrence's sons went to the East Indies, Johnson wrote an alcaic ode about him, 'Ad Thomam Laurence, medicum doctissimum, cum filium peregre agentem desiderio nimis tristi prosequeretur'.

Lawrence's works were all written in Latin, which he regarded as the only fitting medium for medical treatises. They include *Hydrops, disputatio medica* (1756), in the form of a dialogue between William Harvey, Sir George Ent, and Baldwin Hamey, grounded on the doctrines of Stahl, and *Praelectiones medicae duodecim de calvariae et capitis morbis* (1757). An analysis of this work and of *De natura musculorum* (1759) was given by Albrecht von Haller in his *Bibliotheca Anatomica* (2, 1774–7, 537–8). He also wrote lives of Harvey (1766) and Frank Nicholls (1780).

About 1773, Lawrence's health began to fail, and he noticed symptoms of angina pectoris, which he suffered from for many years. In 1782 he had an attack of paralysis, and moved from London to Canterbury, where he died on 6 June 1783. He was buried in St Margaret's Church, and a tablet was placed in the cathedral.

W. A. GREENHILL, *rev.* CLAIRE L. NUTT

Sources Munk, *Roll* · R. Brain, 'Thomas Lawrence, 1711–83', *Medical History*, 1 (1957), 293–306 · *GM*, 1st ser., 57 (1787), 191 · A. Chalmers, ed., *The general biographical dictionary*, new edn, 20 (1815) · *The works of Samuel Johnson, together with his life*, ed. J. Hawkins, 11 vols. (1787) · J. Boswell, *The life of Samuel Johnson*, ed. [E. Malone], 8th edn, 4 vols. (1816)

Archives RCP Lond., papers · Wellcome L., account of continental travels

Likenesses J. Flaxman, marble tablet on memorial, Canterbury Cathedral

Lawrence, Sir Thomas (1769–1830), painter and draughtsman, chiefly of portraits, was born on 13 April 1769 at 6 Redcross Street, Bristol, the youngest of the five surviving children of Thomas Lawrence (1725–1797), then a supervisor of excise, and Lucy (1731?–1797), younger daughter of the Revd William Read and his wife, Sarah, *née* Hill. Through her father Lucy Lawrence was related to the Read family of Brocket Hall, Hertfordshire, and she had connections through her mother with other county families. As many as perhaps eleven other children were born to her between 1754 and 1772, but all died in infancy.

Childhood and early activity To a most unusual degree, childhood and early activity were synonymous in the life of Lawrence. His father moved from Bristol to Devizes in 1773, becoming landlord of the Black Bear, a well-known coaching inn of the London–Bath road. Within two or three years the very young Lawrence had revealed his talent for drawing, being capable particularly of sketching, in pencil, likenesses of people.

Visitors to Lawrence's father's inn included numerous social and cultural personalities, and the boy was much noticed by them—for his own sake and through the efforts of his proud, pretentious, and probably over-persistent father. Profile portraits in pencil of Lord and

Sir Thomas Lawrence (1769–1830), self-portrait, *c.*1825

Lady Kenyon, who stayed at the Black Bear in 1779, document Lawrence's ability at that date (1779; priv. coll.). He would remain continuously at work as an artist for the subsequent fifty years, until the day before he died.

The boy Lawrence was early noticed, additionally, because of his handsome appearance and his gift for reciting verse, from Shakespeare and Milton. Fanny Burney recorded in April 1780 that she had found at the inn 'a most lovely boy of ten years of age' (*Diary and Letters*, 1.304), who possessed an astonishing skill in drawing. Mrs Lawrence informed her that he had already visited London and been pronounced a genius by Sir Joshua Reynolds. Another, more frequent visitor, David Garrick, seems to have seriously considered that the future career of the boy (not quite ten at Garrick's death) lay between painting and the stage.

Although early and usefully conditioned in social behaviour, with manners that were to be commented on later by contemporaries as extremely, if not excessively, polished, Lawrence received little formal general education. In adulthood, he wrote of his regret that his parents, for all their love, had not provided their son with 'two or three parts in education of the utmost importance to the future happiness of the man' (Williams, 2.43). He referred specifically to practical grasp on money matters, but must have intended a wider application.

Lawrence's father was naturally improvident, though naturally optimistic. In 1779 he was declared a bankrupt, and thenceforward his youngest son became the chief financial mainstay of the family. Some sort of promotional tour for him was conceived by Lawrence senior in or about 1780, beginning at Oxford, where his earliest biographer states that he took 'the likenesses of the most eminent people' (Williams, 1.67). The episode is obscure, however, since no such portraits have been identified, and the tour may in reality have been something of a failure.

After a short stay at Weymouth, the Lawrence family settled in Alfred Street at Bath. By 1783 Lawrence was practising mainly as a painter of small portraits in pastel, receiving for half-lengths 3 guineas, 'at that time and for Bath a very extraordinary sum' (Williams, 1.73). The medium of pastel was one Lawrence ceased to use after approximately 1790, and the majority of surviving pastel portraits from his years at Bath are no more than competent. But the lively, fashionable cultural milieu of the city was to be of great significance in his development, both artistically and emotionally.

Still only in his teens, Lawrence was yet able at Bath to emancipate himself—to some degree—from his father. Among collectors and connoisseurs he found several friendly patrons and admirers who allowed him access to drawings, prints, and other works of art they owned— thus firing him with a passion to collect himself, as well as giving him some contact with the greatest Italian old masters, supremely Michelangelo. Writing to Charles Eastlake in 1822, he described how he had used to copy, 'Night after Night', prints after the prophets and sybils of the Sistine Chapel ceiling, and he characterized his mind at that period as being 'however fettered, strongly and singularly excited' (Layard, 170). One potential patron offered to finance his journey to Italy, though obtuseness or self-interest led his father to refuse. But Lawrence was also made welcome socially, especially in the sympathetic family circle of a local physician, Dr William Falconer; he was probably the first of those older male figures who would become father-surrogates throughout Lawrence's life. And at Bath, Lawrence's enthusiasm for the theatre resulted in his seeing and being fascinated by Mrs Siddons, with whose two elder daughters, Sally and Maria, he was later to be romantically entangled.

Lawrence's artistic education seems to have been no more firmly grounded than was his general education. He passed as self-taught, though at Bath he most probably had some lessons in handling of oil paint from the fashionable elderly portrait painter William Hoare, whose son Prince Hoare remained a supportive friend. It was apparently in 1786 that he painted in oils a large composition of Christ bearing the cross (lost), which is likely to have been copied or derived from William Hoare's painting of the same subject (St Michael with St Paul Church, Bath). A copy made by Lawrence in crayons of Raphael's *Transfiguration* (ex Sothebys, London, 12 March 1987, lot 29) gained him the award in 1784 of a silver palette and 5 guineas from the Royal Society of Arts in London. All the evidence suggests that in these years he aspired to a future not merely as a painter of portraits but as an artist in the grand manner. However fruitful Bath had been in his development, it could not compete with all the advantages of London. In 1787 Lawrence left Bath for London and was admitted to the Royal Academy Schools there.

First years in London In going to London, Lawrence had taken a decisive step. He remained based there for the rest of his life. He moved from a first address at 4 Leicester Square to 41 Jermyn Street, then to 24 Old Bond Street, and next to Greek Street, Soho, where his parents lived with him. He retained the house until he finally settled in a large house at 65 Russell Square (des.), where he lived by himself from 1813 until his death.

Lawrence soon ceased to attend the Academy Schools. His proficiency in drawing was recognized at once as outstripping all his fellow students. He sent several works, in pastel, to the Royal Academy exhibition in 1787, and in 1789 he exhibited a full-length portrait in oils, *Lady Cremorne* (1788–9; Tate collection) which, despite some stiffness in the pose and face, is remarkable for its bravura passages of paint, especially in the sky and landscape. In a letter written to his mother in Bath, dating from either 1787 or 1788, he made the characteristically hedged yet extraordinarily confident declaration, 'To any but my own family I certainly should not say this; but excepting Sir Joshua, for the painting of a head, I would risk my reputation with any painter in London' (Layard, 7–8).

The year 1790 marked full public recognition of Lawrence's achievements, in terms of prestige as well as of art. In that year he exhibited at the Royal Academy twelve portraits, among them two full lengths, the actress *Elizabeth Farren* (1789–90; Metropolitan Museum of Art, New York) and *Queen Charlotte* (1789–90; National Gallery, London). Reviews of the exhibition warmly praised both paintings, which rank among his finest achievements. Paint is handled with a richness, crispness, and confident pleasure seldom seen in British art, while the likenesses and costumes are seized with equally pleasurable confidence. And complementing the freshness of portrayal is a vivid, fresh response to differing aspects of English landscape.

Lawrence had been bidden to Windsor in September 1789, to paint the queen and also Princess Amelia (1789; Royal Collection). Although the queen's portrait was not acquired by the king, Lawrence at twenty had received his first important royal patronage. Gainsborough was dead, and Lawrence was widely recognized as the successor to Reynolds, whose health and art were in decline. George III pressed the Royal Academy to elect him an associate in 1790, but it refused because of the regulation against election of associates aged under twenty-four. However, it elected him the following year. When Reynolds died in 1792, the king appointed him painter-in-ordinary. In 1794, at the earliest permitted age of twenty-five, he was elected a full academician.

During the 1790s Lawrence seems to have believed that he could combine activity as a portrait painter with producing occasional history paintings. At the Royal Academy in 1791 he exhibited, as well as several portraits, a small history painting, *Homer Reciting his Poems* (1790; Tate collection), a composition commissioned by the antiquarian scholar and connoisseur Richard Payne Knight. The effect is of a pastoral landscape, attractive but hardly ambitious, nor particularly classical in mood. More interesting may have been the Shakespearian subject *Prospero Raising the Storm* (exh. RA, 1793), a large canvas he is said to have later utilized for the portrait of John Philip Kemble as Rolla (1800; Nelson-Atkins Museum of Art, Kansas City, USA).

In 1797 Lawrence exhibited his most ambitious attempt at a history picture, turning back for inspiration to Milton's *Paradise Lost*, the poem which had been a source for recitation and delineation by him from his boyhood. The huge canvas of *Satan Summoning his Legions* (1796–7; RA) was his final effort to create a grand historical composition. It was very unfavourably received, but Lawrence himself defiantly continued to esteem it. After seeing it again in 1811, he wrote despondently of experiencing a sense of 'the past dreadful waste of time and improvidence of my Life and Talent' (Layard, 84). Darkened though the painting now is, and extremely difficult to assess, it is by no means unimpressive, for all the old master echoes and its debt to the style of Fuseli.

The 1790s proved testing for Lawrence in numerous ways. In 1797 first his mother and then his father died, and between the two deaths he reflected ruefully on the differences of character and disposition separating himself from his 'essentially worthy' father, concluding, 'To be the entire happiness of his children is perhaps the lot of no parent' (Williams, 1.186). Later in the same decade he conducted a highly charged, frustrated love affair involving both Sally and Maria Siddons, and profoundly perturbing Mrs Siddons. Maria died in 1798, and Sally in 1803. Like his two brothers, Lawrence was never to marry.

From very early on in his London years Lawrence established links of unfailing friendship with the interrelated families of William Lock, of Norbury Park, Surrey, and John Julius Angerstein, of Woodlands, Blackheath, Kent. Both were collectors and became his patrons, and through Angerstein's stepdaughter, the wife of Ayscoghe Boucherett MP, he became friendly also with the Boucherett family of North Willingham, Lincolnshire. As well as painting portraits of various members of these families, he made several tender and charmingly informal drawings of the children and of the mothers, for example, Amelia Angerstein, *née* Lock, nursing a baby (inscribed 'Willingham 1810'; priv. coll.). The most important of all friendships was the one that he early established with the much older fellow artist Joseph Farington, who advised and guided him until the latter's death in 1821. Farington's now fully published *Diary* provides a mass of information about Lawrence's personal, financial, and artistic affairs but attempts no overall view of the man.

The opening years of the nineteenth century The first years of the new century were probably the most difficult and stressful in Lawrence's life and career. In 1801 he wrote privately to Mrs Boucherett of feeling 'shackled into this dry mill-horse business' of painting portraits, which must yet be gone through, 'with steady industry' (Williams, 1.222). A sense of being thus 'shackled' seems to have continued to haunt him. And in the same letter, with accidental accuracy, he assumed that half his life was already over.

Lawrence's debts became a crippling burden from which he never escaped. He had been generous with financial help to his family, and would always be so to other, often younger, artists. He spent large sums on artistic materials, as well as on adding drawings to his collection. Contemporary rumours of his gambling, or even of being blackmailed, appear groundless; and it seems much more likely that his temperament and upbringing united to leave him bewildered or bored by the demands of prosaic daily existence.

By 1807 Lawrence's affairs had fallen into the gravest confusion. He owed more than £20,000. For Farington he drew up a detailed estimate of work to be done and moneys to be earned, with highly optimistic totals inserted, implying almost unceasing labour. Farington responded prudently by advising him to consult the well-disposed banker Thomas Coutts, providing him with an explicit statement of all debts, and warning him against presuming on too large an income until 'you have worked off much of the heavy load of unfinished pictures' (Layard, 54–5). Work though he did, that was a goal Lawrence would never achieve.

During these years Lawrence's art revealed virtually nothing of his private difficulties. He continued to exhibit regularly at the Royal Academy, with portraits which were often rightly hailed as remarkable for their originality as well as for their sheer accomplishment. It seems clear that the prospect of public exhibition, with the concomitant requirement to meet a fixed date, acted upon him as a necessary and almost essential spur.

Many commissions remained unfinished, and patrons complained bitterly. But Lawrence could produce portraits which ranged from agreeable presentation of well-bred children and fashionable women to such a tough, characterful depiction as *Lord Thurlow* (1802–3; Royal Collection), exhibited at the Royal Academy in 1803 to a chorus of praise. In 1806 he contributed a bravura variation of the mother and child theme in a large, richly coloured portrait, in tondo format, of the duke of Abercorn's mistress, with her son, tactfully entitled *A Fancy Group* (1805; priv. coll.). In the following year his chief exhibit was a group portrait, at once dignified yet animated, of the financier Sir Francis Baring with his brother, John, and son-in-law, Charles Wall (1806–7; priv. coll.). It too was well received, though Lawrence was piqued by comments in the *Morning Chronicle*, whose editor, James Perry, championed the rival portraitist John Hoppner.

Hoppner was patronized by the most fashionable and influential figure in society, the prince of Wales, who did not employ Lawrence at that period. The prince's near-ostracism of Lawrence probably arose not only from opposition to those favoured by his father but because Lawrence had been patronized by the princess of Wales, Caroline of Brunswick. At the Royal Academy in 1802 he showed a somewhat hectic full length of her with her daughter, Princess Charlotte, (1801–2; Royal Collection), and his own conduct in connection with the princess came under review in the 'delicate investigation' of 1806. While entirely cleared of any impropriety, he is likely to have appeared tainted in the prince's eyes simply by association with his estranged wife.

The not unexpected death of Hoppner in January 1810 removed Lawrence's chief competitor, leaving him conscious that their long, acrimonious rivalry had ended without any reconciliation. It must be more than coincidence that in the same year he raised the prices of his portraits, from 200 guineas to 400 guineas for a full length.

The pattern of Lawrence's existence was apparently set. He painted unremittingly, seldom entertained, and tended to prefer a modest social life spent in the company of ungrand, sometimes unmarried female friends. Some kind of *amitié amoureuse* seems to have developed between him and Mrs Isabella Wolff, *née* Hutchinson, who separated from her husband, Jens Wolff, the Danish consul in London, about 1810. Lawrence had begun a beautiful, profoundly meditated portrait of her in pensive mood several years before, but finished it only years later, for the Royal Academy exhibition of 1815 (*c*.1803–1814/15; Art Institute of Chicago). Until her death in 1829 she was probably the most important person in his emotional life.

The regent's patronage and travel abroad In or about 1810 Major-General the Hon. Charles Stewart, Lord Castlereagh's half-brother and later third marquess of Londonderry, sat to Lawrence for the first time. The resulting portrait (not certainly identifiable) was exhibited at the Royal Academy in the following year. More important than the painting was the unexpected friendship which quickly sprang up between the painter and the aristocratic soldier-cum-diplomat, nine years his junior. Lawrence would greatly benefit from being under Stewart's aegis abroad, and characterized him later as 'one of the most zealous friends that ever man had' (Williams, 2.463).

Almost certainly it was Stewart who stimulated the prince regent's interest in Lawrence's work, persuading him in 1814 to sit for a first full-length portrait, in field marshal's uniform, commissioned by Stewart himself (1814–15; priv. coll.). The timing and tone were especially happy, since Napoleon had been defeated and banished to Elba, and the regent had become convinced of his own prominent part in Napoleon's overthrow.

In the same year, two of the allied sovereigns, King Friedrich Wilhelm of Prussia and Tsar Alexander I of Russia, with their leading generals, respectively Blücher and Platov, arrived in London. In an atmosphere of victorious celebration the regent commissioned from Lawrence full-length portraits of all four personalities, and of the duke of Wellington, as well as a half-length of Metternich (all Royal Collection). The portraits of Blücher, Platov, Wellington, and Metternich were worked on with notable speed and shown at the Royal Academy exhibition in 1815, where Mrs Wolff's portrait was the sole example by Lawrence of a female sitter.

The instigation for what eventually became the complete series of portraits by Lawrence in the Waterloo Chamber at Windsor Castle can be traced back to the poet Lady Anne Barnard. According to Farington, she wrote in April 1814 to the prince regent, proposing that a composition of himself with the tsar and the king of Prussia should be painted, by Lawrence, 'to commemorate the great events' (Farington, *Diary*, 13.4496). And she had proposals for at least one other composition.

With collective good sense, all those involved preferred to avoid group portraits, or high-flown subjects, and single portraits of individuals were settled on. *Pace* the usual assumption, however, the tsar (who took every opportunity to disoblige the regent) seems to have given Lawrence no sittings on his visit to London later in 1814. And a major set-back to proceeding with the scheme, in both triumphalist and in practical terms, was caused by Napoleon's return from Elba in 1815. Nevertheless, partly as preparation for his proceeding to the continent to paint the allied sovereigns, Lawrence was knighted by the regent in April of that year.

Lawrence's first visit abroad was to Paris in September 1815. There, following the battle of Waterloo and Napoleon's final exile, most of the treasures looted for the Musée Napoléon were being returned to their respective countries. Lawrence saw for the first time the original of Raphael's *Transfiguration* (Vatican Gallery, Rome), which he had copied as a boy. And in Paris, Lord Stewart (as he had become) was there to welcome him. Lawrence painted no portraits but clearly hoped to have some of his work shown in the city. He also met and became very friendly with the sculptor Antonio Canova, who sat to him a month or two later in London for a fiery, Byronic portrayal (1815–16; Gipsoteca Canoviana, Possagno).

In 1816 Lawrence was called to give evidence to a House of Commons committee on whether the nation should acquire the Elgin marbles (British Museum) and strongly argued for acquisition. In the same year Stewart responded to Lawrence's expression of 'still anxious desire' to paint the tsar by suggesting 'a tremendous journey', to St Petersburg, after a preliminary stay in Vienna, where he might paint the emperor and empress and Napoleon's son (Layard, 100–01). Nothing came immediately from this bold proposal, but Lawrence received fresh royal favour when Princess Charlotte, recently married to Prince Leopold of Saxe-Coburg-Saalfeld, chose him to paint her portrait, intended as a birthday present for her husband. It was in tragic circumstances that Lawrence eventually took the finished painting (1817; Belgian Royal Collection) to Claremont to show Prince Leopold. The princess had died in November 1817, after giving birth to a stillborn son. Because of her pregnancy, she had been painted at home, giving Lawrence the opportunity to observe the royal couple closely. In his letters he wrote of their life together, and he described in touching and acute detail, worthy of any diarist of the period, his interview with the bereaved prince.

Lawrence himself suffered in 1818 the deaths first of his brother, Major William Lawrence, and then of his young niece, Susan Bloxam, daughter of his sister Ann. He heard of her death while at Aix-la-Chapelle in the autumn of that year, having resumed his mission of painting the allied sovereigns, gathered there for the peace negotiations. He completed his portrait of Friedrich Wilhelm of Prussia (1814–18; Royal Collection) and began a seated full length of the Austrian emperor (1818–19; Royal Collection), but seems to have found most inspiration—and challenge—in working on the full-length portrait of the tsar (1818; Royal Collection). Reporting minutely on the first sitting, he recorded the tsar's opening words, in English: 'I am glad to see you. I am very glad in forming my acquaintance with you' (Layard, 136). While pleased and relieved by the portrait's subsequent enthusiastic reception within the tsar's circle, he confessed privately that he had 'less and less confidence as I grow old' (Layard, 139).

From Aix, Lawrence travelled on to Vienna, where he remained for some months, until May 1819. He was received everywhere and enjoyed much social as well as artistic success. Although busy professionally, he was able, thanks to Lord Stewart, to witness imperial occasions of the greatest magnificence. He undertook several private commissions, for both paintings and drawings, and among his sitters was the young duke of Reichstadt, Napoleon's son (1818–19; Harvard U., Fogg Art Museum).

Before leaving Aix, Lawrence had learned of the prince regent's wish that he should proceed from Vienna to Rome to paint full lengths of the pope, Pius VII, and his chief minister, Cardinal Consalvi, to complete the Waterloo Chamber series. The news was not entirely palatable, and he arrived in Rome in May 1819 'with many apprehensions, indeed, of failure' (Williams, 2.193).

But Lawrence was at once welcomed warmly by both the cardinal and the pope, treated as a guest distinguished in his own right and as the emissary of the regent. Accommodation was provided for him in the pope's own palace of the Quirinale. And he found himself befriended by artists such as Canova and by distinguished foreign visitors like the Austrian foreign minister, Prince Metternich, in addition to such admiring English residents as Elizabeth, the duchess of Devonshire.

In Rome, Lawrence was much less active artistically than he had been in Vienna, concentrating his energies on the two important commissions. He produced a brilliant, swift-seeming study in scarlet of the alert, benevolent cardinal, but approached the subject of the aged pope in, as it were, a slower tempo, with respectful rapport and greater subtlety. The pope gave him nine sittings, and he created a masterpiece. He sincerely admired his subject, who had survived so much, and conceived of him as an enlightened patron of the arts, and a symbol, too, of Europe restored to calm, with some of the most famous, restituted treasures of Vatican sculpture visible at the left of the composition. Lawrence exhibited the portrait in Rome to much, probably genuine, praise, though it was never seen publicly in England during his lifetime.

In December 1819 Lawrence turned north from Rome, hastily visiting Florence, Parma, and Venice, impressed most perhaps by what he saw of the work of Correggio and Parmigianino at Parma. He was back in England at the end of March 1820, to find that the regent had succeeded George III.

The final decade Comparable elevation in his own sphere awaited Lawrence. Shortly before he returned to England,

Benjamin West had died, and with the news Lawrence received an intimation that the Royal Academy proposed to elect him president in West's place. He was elected almost unanimously and set off for Brighton, to seek a first audience in his new capacity with the new king. George IV marked his appreciation of the Royal Academy's action, and of Lawrence's distinction, by presenting him (and his successors) with a gold chain and medal bearing the king's likeness. Close artistic and human affinity united monarch and painter in a way unknown in England since the time of Charles I and Van Dyck.

Personally without vanity, Lawrence urged that as president, and as an artist honoured by a successful major royal mission abroad, he should be assigned a position in the splendid coronation procession of 1821. Some of his finest and most subtle late portraits, like that of Princess Sophia (1825; Royal Collection), were commissioned by George IV. And it is apt that the last painting ever touched by Lawrence, shortly before his death, should have been yet one more version of his official portrait of the king.

As regent, George IV had posed for Lawrence for a swagger full-length portrait in Garter robes and had at once recognized it as the best likeness painted of himself (1818; Hugh Lane Municipal Gallery of Modern Art, Dublin). As king, with or without further sittings, he established the composition as his standard image, the Garter robes replaced by coronation robes (1821; Royal Collection). Numerous versions were worked on in Lawrence's studio. The king also sat for a much more sober portrait in 'his private dress' (1822; Wallace Collection, London), mildly ridiculed by some contemporaries but which Lawrence perceptively thought 'perhaps my most successful resemblance [of him] … and the most interesting' because of its domestic nature (Williams, 2.319). It became familiar through being engraved.

George IV sent Lawrence on one last mission abroad, to Paris in August 1825, with the not very inspiring task of painting Charles X and the dauphin, the duc d'Aumale (1825; Royal Collection). The French king had earlier in 1825 appointed him a chevalier of the Légion d'honneur, and he received him with marked graciousness, presenting him with—among other gifts—a set of Sèvres porcelain. Lawrence rose to his task adroitly and wrote letters home describing his reception and the charming informality of the king's grandchildren playing around boisterously during the first sitting.

Lawrence's international reputation was recognized by a succession of honours from foreign academies of art, including those of Rome (1816), Florence (1820), Venice (1823), Denmark (1823), and New York (1818). From his status and official position flowed numerous obligations, many performed, it seems, more dutifully than eagerly, and as printed his annual addresses to the Royal Academy students can only be termed insipid. But he made a point of being accessible and helpful to younger, sometimes foreign, artists, and would thus be gratefully remembered by, for instance, Eugène Delacroix. On the death of John Julius Angerstein in 1823 he actively urged the retention of his collection in Britain, for the nation, and was appointed one of the superintending body (later trustees) when the government purchased the collection and the National Gallery was founded in 1824.

Despite the pressures upon him, Lawrence's art preserved all its vitality, while gaining in empathy and depth. To the annual Royal Academy exhibitions he regularly managed to send some six or more new portraits, and the range of his sitters was matched by the range of his interpretation. With absolute assurance he captured the bright-eyed vivacity of the two very young Calmady girls (1823–4; Metropolitan Museum of Art, New York) and the stony, quasi-judicial severity of an octogenarian in *Lady Robert Manners* (1825–6; National Gallery of Scotland, Edinburgh). Simplicity and directness characterize his *Lady Blessington* (c.1821; Wallace Collection, London). A quite unusually serious, Wordsworthian blending of sublime natural setting and reflective child gives resonance to the deservedly famous portrait *Charles William Lambton*, 'The red boy', (1824–5; priv. coll.).

In this artistically fruitful autumnal period, Lawrence acquired a new and distinguished patron in Robert Peel, the most discerning perhaps of all his patrons. For Peel he painted several family portraits—notably that of his wife (1826–7; Frick Collection, New York), conceived in pictorial homage to Rubens's *Chapeau de paille* (National Gallery, London), then owned by Peel, but a tribute also to Lawrence's personal response to the sitter. In addition, Peel had him paint portraits of political associates, destined for Drayton Manor, his Staffordshire country house. The less elaborately composed of those are the more impressive, and among the best is the simple portrait *The Earl of Aberdeen* (1829; priv. coll.). Peel mentioned it approvingly in a letter of October 1829 to his wife, 'a most beautiful head' (*Private Letters of Sir Robert Peel*, 116), and it was praised in the press when exhibited at the Royal Academy in 1830, following Lawrence's death.

Lawrence died very suddenly on 7 January 1830 at home in London. He had become increasingly susceptible to the chill winter weather and to physical languor. Yet in his last few days he dined with Peel, who commissioned from him a self-portrait, and had earlier been concerned to send his sister Ann, Mrs Bloxam, a print after his drawing of a new young actress who fascinated him, Mrs Siddons's niece, Fanny Kemble. A detailed account of the last, fluctuating week of his life was drawn up by a devoted female friend, Miss Elizabeth Croft. She was in the house but not present when he fainted and died while being attended by his faithful valet, Jean Duts.

Lawrence was slightly under average height and seems to have retained a trim figure all his life. His appearance in middle age in documented by a rare self-portrait (c.1825; RA), unfinished but in its cool, discreet, impersonal air suggestive of a temperament kept under tight rein. He shows his head bald and his face pale yet barely marked by signs of age.

Lawrence's true character remains largely opaque. But a salient trait of it was kindness and consideration to his servants. Reluctant to paint himself, he seems to have been comparably reluctant to reveal himself unreservedly in his usually rather stilted letters. Contemporaries tended to find him suavely polite, though notably reticent. Thomas Moore concurred with a friend's hostile opinion that the man was 'oily' (*Journal*, 3.973). In 1821 Byron recalled having met Lawrence at Earl Grey's in 1814, when he 'talked delightfully' (*Byron's Letters and Journals*, 8.28). Miss Croft wrote down some recollections of their nearly thirty-year acquaintance which provide many welcome human details but lack focus and coherence.

Posthumous events and reputation The suddenness of Lawrence's death shocked society. He had long been established as the leading portrait painter in England and was a familiar social figure. Almost every prominent person of the day—with the exception of Byron—had been painted by him. And his lifetime had remarkably spanned the generations in two centuries. As a boy he had been acquainted with Garrick, and he himself, painting Princess Mary, the duchess of Gloucester (1824; Royal Collection), was mentioned by Queen Victoria as one of her earliest recollections (Princess Marie Louise, 156).

Lawrence's funeral, held at St Paul's Cathedral on 21 January 1830, was an elaborate and public occasion, with Peel and Lord Aberdeen among the pallbearers. Although *The Times* had, the previous day, announced that a private carriage of the king's would follow immediately behind the coffin, the king was not represented amid the numerous carriages sent by the nobility and others, often Lawrence's sitters, who did not bother to attend. Among the Royal Academicians present was J. M. W. Turner, who made a watercolour sketch of the scene, 'from memory' (1830; Tate collection). Lawrence was buried in the cathedral.

Despite the public tributes, Lawrence's reputation was already starting to dwindle, and even the intentions in his will failed to be accomplished. In that document of 1828 his bequests had included one to the Royal Academy of the set of Sèvres porcelain given him by Charles X of France. He had also desired that his superb collection of old master drawings should be offered successively to George IV, the British Museum, Peel, and the earl of Dudley, for the sum of £18,000, which was far below his expenditure on it or its total value. But all those approached declined the offer.

Lawrence had died so deeply in debt that even the bequest to the Royal Academy could not be fulfilled. His possessions, including his collection of drawings, were dispersed in a series of sales. The impressive scope of his collection, with chronology of the various sales, is set out concisely in F. Lugt's *Les marques de collections de dessins & d'estampes*. Eventually, most of the drawings by Raphael and Michelangelo entered the Ashmolean Museum, Oxford.

To Lawrence's executor, Archibald Keightley, fell the task of dealing not only with his tangled affairs but also with the contents of his studio, in which remained over a hundred unfinished portraits, several begun many years before, in addition to some sitters' personal property.

Keightley scrupulously sifted every claim and drew up a detailed list of 430 items (V&A).

Beyond Keightley's care was the reputation of Lawrence. By the mid-nineteenth century, reaction against the world represented by the regency and by George IV was as much moral as aesthetic. 'Tawdry and beautiful' were Thackeray's words, denigrating Lawrence's portraits in *Vanity Fair* (Thackeray, chap. 49), though that ambivalent verdict shows a consciousness of their appeal unlikely to have been shared by most of Thackeray's contemporaries. Not until the beginning of the twentieth century were any serious attempts made in England to assess Lawrence's achievements as an artist. But he recovered neither popularity nor critical favour. His untraditional, un-English virtuosity, especially in handling oil paint, probably helped to make his work suspect, and it seems significant that some of his greatest paintings (such as *Elizabeth Farren*) left England for the United States. There his work has been far more warmly and widely appreciated. Yet the shrewdest summing-up of his gifts came from Roger Fry, who emphasized his unerring eye and hand: 'he showed a consummate mastery over the means of artistic expression' (Fry, 91).

For delicacy and precision, Lawrence is rivalled as a draughtsman in his own period only by Ingres. As a painter of portraits in oil, he had an uncanny ability to create not merely accurate, if often flattering, likenesses, but eyes, flesh, and clothing invested with an astonishing, disturbing illusion of actuality. In that achievement he has subsequently been approached only—and to a lesser degree—by John Singer Sargent.

Major, pioneering scholarship on Lawrence during the second half of the twentieth century was carried out single-mindedly by Kenneth Garlick. He championed the artist, clarified many questions, and produced exemplary catalogues of his work in all media. But at the end of that century Lawrence had still to receive just and general appreciation in Britain.   MICHAEL LEVEY

Sources D. E. Williams, *The life and correspondence of Sir Thomas Lawrence*, 2 vols. (1831) · Farington, *Diary* · K. Garlick, 'A catalogue of the paintings, drawings and pastels of Sir Thomas Lawrence', *Walpole Society*, 39 (1962–4) [whole issue] · K. Garlick, ed., *Sir Thomas Lawrence: a complete catalogue of the oil paintings* (1989) · M. Levey, *Sir Thomas Lawrence, 1769–1830* (1979) [exhibition catalogue, NPG, 9 Nov 1979 – 16 March 1980] · *GM*, 1st ser., 100/1 (1830), 174–82 · O. Millar, *The later Georgian pictures in the collection of her majesty the queen*, 1 (1969), 59–80, nn. 871–928 · G. S. Layard, *Sir Thomas Lawrence's letter bag* (1906) · *An artist's love story: told in the letters of Sir Thomas Lawrence, Mrs Siddons and her daughters*, ed. O. G. Knapp, 2nd edn (1905) · K. Garlick, *Sir Thomas Lawrence: portraits of an age, 1790–1830* (1993) [exhibition catalogue, New Haven, Ct, Fort Worth, Tx, and Richmond, Va, 1993] · A. Cunningham, *The lives of the most eminent British painters, sculptors, and architects*, 6 (1833), 155–271 · R. S. Gower, *Sir Thomas Lawrence* (1900) · K. Garlick, *Sir Thomas Lawrence* (1954) · *Sir Thomas Lawrence PRA* (1961) [exhibition catalogue, RA] · D. Goldring, *Regency portrait painter* (1951) · Graves, *RA exhibitors*, vol. 5 · F. Lugt, *Les marques de collections de dessins et d'estampes* (Amsterdam, 1921) · R. Fry, *Reflections on British painting* (1934) · *Diary and letters of Madame D'Arblay*, ed. [C. Barrett], 7 vols. (1842–6) · *The private letters of Sir Robert Peel*, ed. G. Peel (1920) · *The journal of Thomas Moore*, ed. W. S. Dowden, 6 vols. (1983–91) · *Byron's letters and journals*, ed. L. A. Marchand, 12 vols. (1973–82) · *The Times* (20 Jan

1830) · Princess Marie Louise, *My memories of six reigns* (1956) · W. M. Thackeray, *Vanity Fair: a novel without a hero* (1848)

Archives BL, letters, Add. MS 24425 · CUL, corresp. · Harvard U., Houghton L., corresp. and papers · Hunt. L., letters · RA, corresp. and papers | BL, corresp. with Lord Aberdeen, Add. MSS 43229–43234 · BL, letters to John Angerstein, microfilm M/554 · BL, letters to Prince Lieven, Add. MSS 47290–47293 · BL, corresp. with Sir Robert Peel, Add. MSS 40364–40607 · Croft Castle, Herefordshire, corresp. with Miss Croft–Lawrence · FM Cam., corresp., mainly relating to sittings · Lambton Park, Chester-le-Street, co. Durham, letters to earl of Durham · NL Scot., letters to Thomas Coutts · NL Scot., corresp. mainly with Sir David Wilkie · Staffs. RO, letters to duke of Sutherland · U. Leeds, Brotherton L., letters to Benjamin Gott · V&A NAL, scrapbook of items relating to Lawrence compiled by his sister · V&A NAL, letters to Francis Robertson and Laura Robertson (*née* Ross)

Likenesses T. Lawrence, self-portrait, drawing, 1786, Burghley, Northamptonshire · J. Trumbull, drawing, 1789, Boston Athenaeum · T. Lawrence, drawing, c.1789–1791, AM Oxf. · W. Daniell, engraving, c.1800 (after a drawing by G. Dance), BM · L. Gahagan, bronze sculpture, 1812, NG Ire. · W. Brockedon, pencil drawing, 1820–30, NPG · T. Lawrence, self-portrait, oils, c.1825, RA [*see illus.*] · R. W. Sievier, marble bust, c.1830, Sir John Soane's Museum, London · C. Turner, mezzotint, pubd 1830, BM, NPG · G. G. Adams, medal sculpture, 1860, NPG · E. H. Baily, marble bust, NPG · G. Dance, drawing, RA · R. E. Evans, oils (after T. Lawrence, c.1825), NPG · W. Giller, mezzotint (after T. Lawrence), BM, NPG · R. J. Lane, lithograph (after a drawing by T. Lawrence, 1812), NPG · T. Lawrence, engraving (after a drawing by J. Worthington, c.1804), repro. in Williams, *The life and correspondence of Sir Thomas Lawrence*, frontispiece · T. Lawrence, self-portrait, stipple (aged thirty-five; after chalk drawing, c.1804), NG Ire. · H. Singleton, group portrait, oils (*The Royal Academicians, 1793*), RA · plaster cast of death mask, NPG

Wealth at death died in debt; £15,444 17s. 6d. from immediate posthumous sales of collections of works of art at auction: Garlick, ed., *Sir Thomas*, 29; Williams, *The life*, vol. 2, p. 568

Lawrence, Thomas Edward [*known as* Lawrence of Arabia] (1888–1935), intelligence officer and author, was born on 16 August 1888 at Woodlands, Tremadoc, Caernarvonshire, the second of the five sons of Thomas Robert Tighe Chapman (1846–1919), an Anglo-Irish landowner, and his mistress, Sarah Junner (1861–1959). The couple had assumed the name Lawrence after the birth of their first child, Robert, in 1885 and were known as Mr and Mrs Lawrence for the rest of their lives.

Background and upbringing, 1888–1914 Thomas Chapman of South Hill, near Delvin, co. Westmeath, was already married when he began his liaison with Sarah Junner, who was governess to his four daughters. After making a financial settlement on his first family he and Sarah began a peripatetic existence, living successively at Tremadoc, Kirkcudbright, Dinard in Brittany, Langley in Hampshire, and Oxford, where they settled at 2 Polstead Road in 1896. In 1914 Chapman inherited the family baronetcy, but never used the title, which became extinct on his death.

In later years Lawrence liked to present himself as a child brought up in straitened circumstances and engaged in intermittent tussles with his mother. These rows reached such a pitch that he ran away and enlisted in 1905, or so he claimed. No record of his army service or of his father's buying him out has been discovered. Mr Lawrence had sufficient income to provide his family with domestic servants and all the comforts commonly

Thomas Edward Lawrence [Lawrence of Arabia] (1888–1935), by Augustus John, 1919

enjoyed by the Edwardian bourgeoisie. He and Mrs Lawrence were deeply pious, she with strong evangelical inclinations which made her hope that her sons might follow vocations in the service of God and mankind. She was a strong-minded woman and Thomas (Ned to the family) was a wilful child who, at the age of about ten, had uncovered the truth of his parents' liaison and his own and his brothers' illegitimacy. He kept this knowledge to himself although, as he matured, it may well have coloured his attitude towards his parents' religious enthusiasms and severe moral code.

The tension was in part resolved by the Lawrences' agreeing to build Ned a well-provided bungalow at the bottom of the garden in 1908. Here he could study and follow his idiosyncratic daily regime undisturbed. By this date it was clear that Ned was a scholar: he had passed successfully through Oxford high school (1896–1907) and gained a Meyricke exhibition to read modern history at Jesus College. The young Lawrence had developed a taste for archaeology and chivalry. He was an enthusiastic and accomplished brass rubber, knowledgeable in arcane matters of armour, costume, and heraldry, and an avid reader of medieval romances. Just over 5 feet 5 inches tall and small-boned, Ned undertook rigorous exercise which, he liked to boast, turned him into a pocket Hercules. He was a good distance runner, but disliked team games.

His parents indulged his passions. In the summers of 1907 and 1908 they provided the wherewithal for him to undertake extended bicycle tours of France in search of castles which he measured and photographed. His interest in medieval military architecture impelled him towards the crusades and in summer 1909 he proceeded through Lebanon and Syria recording the still little known castles there. His findings formed the basis of a BA dissertation which substantially contributed to his first in July 1910. During all his excursions he wrote home regularly with vivid impressions of what he had seen. These letters are not only evidence of his powers of description, but of the warm affection which existed within his family. Past tensions had evaporated, not least because Lawrence had secured the freedom to live on his own terms and pursue his own interests.

Before graduating Lawrence came to the attention of Dr D. G. Hogarth, keeper of the Ashmolean Museum, who had encouraged his antiquarian pursuits. Through Hogarth's patronage Lawrence secured an award from Magdalen College and a position on the British Museum's excavations at Carchemish in Syria. He worked there between 1911 and early 1914. As well as supervising the uncovering and cataloguing of Hittite artefacts Lawrence became immersed in the life of a turbulent region. According to his letters home he acted as a sort of consul, arbitrating disputes among Arabs and Kurds and threw himself into their intermittent squabbles with German engineers, then supervising the construction of the Berlin to Baghdad railway. As well as playing the Hentyesque Englishman, Lawrence cultivated an intimate friendship with an Arab youth, Dahoum, whose natural intelligence impressed him and qualified him for tutelage. Lawrence's enchantment with Dahoum helped convince him of the Arabs' capacity for regeneration, but on their own terms and without repudiating their traditions and culture. What he had seen in Lebanon made Lawrence hostile towards those Arabs who looked to the West for salvation and absorbed European, particularly French, values. Likewise, he despised the far-reaching modernizing projects of the Young Turks, who then controlled the Ottoman empire, a contempt which developed into a passionate loathing during the war. For him, Dahoum represented the simple purity of the Arab at ease with his surroundings and culture.

In 1912 Lawrence had told his family: 'I don't think anyone who tasted the East as I have would give it up half-way, for a seat at high table and a chair in the Bodleian' (M. R. Lawrence, 232). Not that he would have either the chance of a conventional academic career or of fulfilling his wish to continue digging at Carcemish in 1914. He did return in December, but to Cairo as a subaltern attached to the military intelligence department of the Egyptian expeditionary force.

Military service, 1914–1919 Lawrence brought with him a knowledge of the Arab language and world based upon experience. It had also shaped his political outlook which was deeply conservative: he wanted the Arabs to secure independence without losing their historic identity and traditions. From December 1914 to October 1918 Lawrence was intimately involved in collecting and assessing intelligence and in shaping strategy and policy in the Middle

East. His academic training fitted him for tasks which he performed diligently and well. As an intellectual he had opportunities to promote his private convictions, particularly on the post-war political future of the Middle East. His sympathies made him susceptible to a Francophobic circle in Cairo, which included his own commanding officer, Colonel Gilbert Clayton, Sir Henry McMahon, and Sir Reginald Wingate, whose objective was to limit as far possible the extension of French power in the region.

Lawrence hoped that his and his colleagues' intrigues would 'biff the French out of all hope of Syria', where they expected post-war territorial and political concessions (*Letters of T. E. Lawrence*, 1938, 196). This urge to frustrate French ambitions animated Lawrence from November 1916 onwards when he was attached to Hejazi forces and co-operating with the Arab bureau. This section, created in January 1916, was suspected of manipulating Arab nationalism to frustrate French imperial ambitions. Like his associates Lawrence tended to take a myopic, Middle East focused view of the war and was willing to pursue policies at odds with those of the British government, which was obliged to accommodate the wishes of its ally.

Before the spring of 1916 Lawrence undertook routine, largely desk-bound duties. He was an apt and hardworking officer, untidy in appearance but noted for his quick-wittedness and Puckish charm. Like him, his colleagues were amateur soldiers, in khaki because of their specialized knowledge of local conditions and languages. The two MPs George Lloyd and Aubrey Herbert, and also Ronald Storrs, became his friends. Herbert accompanied Lawrence on a mission to Mesopotamia in April 1916 to assist in negotiations to deliver and possibly ransom the army besieged in Kut. Both were appalled by the incompetence of the Anglo-Indian army staff and Lawrence compiled a disparaging assessment of its intelligence section which was forwarded to the War Office, adding no doubt to the general impression of a campaign which was being grossly mishandled. While in Mesopotamia, Lawrence also discovered the extent of the Indian government's opposition to British backing for Arab nationalism. Cairo's schemes ran counter to Delhi's proposals for planting Indian colonists in Mesopotamia. None the less, there was some satisfaction in India when Sharif Hussein of Hejaz rebelled in June 1916. He had, as it were, drawn Mecca into the allied orbit and his stature as a religious figurehead weakened the force of Turco-German pan-Islamic propaganda.

Lawrence had taken part in the preliminary planning of the Arab uprising and, in October 1916, was ordered to Jiddah to assess the military situation. What followed is recorded in *The Seven Pillars of Wisdom*, a personal, emotional narrative of the Arab revolt in which Lawrence reveals how by sheer willpower he made history. It was a testimony to his vision and persistence and a fulfilment of his desire to write an epic which might stand comparison in scale and linguistic elegance with his beloved *Morte d'Arthur* and C. M. Doughty's *Arabia deserta*. Subtitled 'A triumph', its climax is the Arab liberation of Damascus, a victory which successfully concludes a gruelling campaign

and vindicates Lawrence's faith in the Arabs. In a way *The Seven Pillars* is a sort of *Pilgrim's Progress*, with Lawrence as Christian, a figure sustained by his faith in the Arabs, successively overcoming physical and moral obstacles.

Whether style mattered more to Lawrence than content is still a matter of contention; what is not is that the book endowed the Arab revolt and its mentor with heroic qualities. As a record of war and politics it is neither a distortion nor a repository of dispassionate historical truth. Much of what Lawrence set down has been upheld by contemporary documents. Nevertheless there are areas, most notably his version of the fall of Damascus, in which Lawrence the creative artist prevails over Lawrence the chronicler. Sir Cyril Falls, who possessed a detailed overview of the Middle Eastern front and admired Lawrence as a 'genius' warned that his version of events needed to be 'treated with caution, since he occasionally exaggerated without shame or scruple' (Falls, 8).

In October 1916 the Arab insurgents were wobbling. The Turks still occupied Medina, had the strategic initiative and superior troops and weaponry, and Arab morale was flagging. Lawrence met their leaders, of whom the emir Feisal impressed him most; according to *The Seven Pillars* he injected them with hope and an ambitious goal, Damascus. His official report was thorough, well argued, and optimistic, in so far as Lawrence suggested that the Arab movement had enormous potential. He ruled out the landing of British troops, which pleased the chief of general staff, Sir William Robertson, who feared 'a most costly and useless expedition' which would divert manpower needed in France (PRO, CAB 45/80, Robertson to Sir James Edmonds, 29 Dec 1925). Lawrence had the knack of saying what his superiors wanted to hear and at the same time was able to demonstrate how Arab forces might be used to the best effect and in support of the overall British regional strategy. In 1917 this centred on an advance across Sinai towards the Holy Land with Jerusalem as the final goal. From November 1916 onwards Lawrence was permanently attached to Feisal's forces as a liaison officer, advising on strategy and supervising among other things the procurement of arms and delivery of Treasury subsidies. At times he was a prickly subordinate who disliked contradiction. What mattered was that his patience and sensitivity to Arab feelings won him respect and affection. 'He found himself in a new environment, among people not accustomed to certain systems and procedures', Feisal observed, 'and he adapted himself, assisted by his intellect. Many other Europeans were not so' (Mousa, 'Arab sources', 167).

The turning point in both the revolt and Lawrence's career was his *coup de main* against 'Aqabah on 17 June 1917. It came at the close of an arduous and dangerous reconnaissance trip in which Lawrence had proceeded northwards, possibly as far as Damascus, to discover whether various tribal chiefs would throw in their lot with the allies. Then, and in subsequent discussions with potential defectors, Lawrence may have promised more than his government could deliver. During the final advance in September 1918 some Syrians said they had expected to see British troops the previous year (PRO, CAB 45/80, Major G. White to Sir James Edmonds). Lawrence was, however, able to persuade his superiors that they had been wrong to underrate the Arab fighting spirit. Between 23 and 24 June he co-ordinated and led a series of attacks by tribal irregulars which overran ʿAqabah's outposts and compelled the garrison to surrender. It was a masterstroke which solved several strategic and political problems: the French had been contemplating occupying the port independently, the navy wanted it eliminated as a base for minelaying, and it provided the Arabs with a convenient base for raids against a Damascus–Medina railway, 100 miles away.

What Robertson called 'an adventurous and successful' foray made Lawrence's reputation as a resourceful and daring commander. The new commander-in-chief of the expeditionary force, Sir Edmund Allenby, judged Lawrence as 'a very fine soldier' and the 'best man for the job' (Durham University Library, Sudan Archive, Wingate papers, 146/1, p. 7). Allenby was impressed by his plans for the future of Arab revolt. Feisal's tribal forces and units of the growing Hejazi regular army, supported by allied specialist and technical units, including British aircraft, armoured cars, and a French mountain battery, would tie down local Turkish forces through sorties against the Damascus–Medina railway. Allenby's South African experience had taught him the corrosive effect of guerrilla warfare and he welcomed an operation that required tiny numbers of British troops and provided an invaluable diversion for his forthcoming offensive.

Lawrence established a warm personal and professional rapport with the volatile Bull Allenby based upon shared interests in archaeology and natural history. A practical soldier, Allenby appreciated a clear-headed officer who delivered what was needed. Lawrence's intrigues at Damascus in October 1918 and his post-war career made the general revise his opinions. He once remarked: 'I had a dozen chaps who could have done the job better' (King's Lond., Liddell Hart C., Edmonds papers, III, 2, 15; Barrow, 215). After Lawrence's death Allenby did, however, deliver a glowing tribute on the BBC.

Between the summer of 1917 and the occupation of Damascus, Lawrence was preoccupied with the planning and conduct of Arab–allied operations based on ʿAqabah, largely against the Hejaz railway and Turkish units based on Maʾan and Amman. His energy was as enormous as his forbearance. Each was needed handling the tribesmen, who tended to flinch whenever they faced Turkish regulars, and British and French officers who undervalued the tribal forces and wanted irregular operations to be undertaken according to the rule book. Tempers were sometimes frayed and afterwards Lawrence frequently condemned the inflexibility of the regular officer's mind. He also—and this made him enemies, particularly among the Australians—underplayed the part played by British, dominion, and Indian forces in the campaigns of 1917–18.

In November 1917 Lawrence led a raiding party in southern Syria to harry Turkish communications and, he confided to George Lloyd, to stir up local opposition to France. Disguised as a Circassian and in search of topographical intelligence, he was captured in Deraa and identified by a Turkish officer. Lawrence then suffered homosexual rape and a flogging before making his escape. His story, first related in 1919, has been accepted by some biographers and rejected by others on extensive circumstantial grounds. Whatever did or did not happen, Lawrence lost none of his rashness: in April 1918 he disguised himself as a woman during a brief reconnaissance into the garrison town of Amman (*Seven Pillars*, 527).

During the first half of 1918 forces based on ʿAqabah maintained pressure on the Damascus–Medina railway through demolition raids which hindered Turkish communications by derailing trains and damaging track, but did not fracture the line permanently. Nor did the Turkish force in Medina suffer unduly; it surrendered only in January 1919. In January 1918 Lawrence was awarded the DSO for his masterful direction and command of Arab forces in an encounter at Tafilah. In September a substantial Arab column—well supported by Arab, British, and Egyptian regular units—was earmarked for a diversionary role on the eastern flank of Allenby's offensive against Damascus. With the assistance of RAF aircraft summoned by Lawrence, the Arabs created considerable mischief. As the Turkish army fell back in disorder, tribal detachments snatched at the opportunity for random plunder and to revenge themselves on their old rulers by murdering prisoners of war. Lawrence would later excuse their crimes as vengeance, but, aware of the harm that their atrocities would do to the Arab cause, he endeavoured to restore discipline.

Arab outrages were a tiresome distraction for Lawrence, who knew that the moment was right for an Arab *coup de main* in Damascus. If the city fell to Arab forces he imagined its possession might immeasurably help their post-war political pretensions in Syria. He therefore did all in his power to steal a march on the British and dominion units that were converging on the city, which he finally reached, driven in a Rolls-Royce and escorted by Indian lancers, on 1 October (PRO, CAB 45/80, Major G. White to Sir James Edmonds).

Damascus had fallen to Australian cavalry a few hours before. The hastily formed makeshift Arab administration was unable to prevent the anarchy which Lawrence vividly described in *The Seven Pillars*. On 2 October the city was occupied by allied units who swiftly restored order. When Allenby arrived, he made it plain that for the moment the terms of the Sykes–Picot agreement would hold, and that Feisal would have to accept French administrative supervision. Lawrence vainly protested that the Arabs had never been made aware of these arrangements. He was overruled and at Allenby's suggestion went home for some leave with the rank of full colonel.

Lawrence had not misled the Arabs, although he later wrote in *The Seven Pillars* that he had worn a 'mantle of fraud' throughout the campaign. He had never been a plenipotentiary. The Arab leadership knew from the Anglophobe Egyptian press and Soviet Russia's revelations of secret allied diplomacy in December 1917 that the allies had agreed to partition the Turkish empire. None the less Lawrence continued to feel a burden of shame in having been an accomplice to what he believed to have been a cynical betrayal of the Arabs.

This largely self-induced conviction that he had acted dishonestly added to the immense physical strain Lawrence had suffered during two years of almost uninterrupted campaigning in extremes of heat and cold and often in considerable danger. His appearance and actions before, during, and after the taking of Damascus indicated severe battle fatigue. In a sense, Lawrence had been engaged in a war on two fronts: one as a commander in the field against the Turks and the other as the advocate of the Arabs in Cairo. The first contest had ended in victory, in so far as the Turkish empire had been defeated. The second had yet to be concluded, nor could it be, so long as the Arabs were denied what Lawrence believed to be their just reward: self-determination. This would not, it must be added, pose any threat to British strategic and imperial interests, for he was certain the new Arab states would flourish only within the imperial orbit.

Diplomat, 1919–1922 Two concerns exercised Lawrence's mind and energies during the immediate post-war years: his struggle to secure justice for the Arabs and writing a book about his and their war. In both he was greatly assisted by the fact that he became a public celebrity who gained entry to and circulated among the élites which dominated British politics and literature. Details of his exploits, withheld for security reasons during the war, became general knowledge during 1919 and aroused considerable interest and admiration. For the rest of his life he was a figure who exerted a powerful hold over the public imagination, a condition he often found uncongenial.

Lawrence's apotheosis and the genesis of what became his 'legend' began in August 1919, when the American journalist Lowell Thomas presented 'With Allenby in Palestine and Lawrence in Arabia' at the Royal Opera House, London, where it ran for six months. It was a spectacular and compelling *mélange* of Thomas's colourful narrative, music, slides, and film of scenes at ʿAqabah. Thomas had picked up the outline of Lawrence's story when he had briefly covered operations at ʿAqabah at the suggestion of John Buchan of the Ministry of Information. The upshot was the romantic and exciting tale of 'The Uncrowned King of Arabia' (Thomas's phrase) and an upsurge of public interest in the man who would become the most interesting figure to emerge from the war. Lawrence was embarrassed by Thomas's hyperbole, but the publicity it generated was useful at a time when Lawrence was lobbying for the Arab cause.

In 1919 and at the suggestion of the Foreign Office, Lawrence had attended the Versailles Conference as Feisal's adviser and translator. The Middle East was of secondary importance and Arab claims to Syria were stiffly opposed by Clemenceau. In May, Lawrence was flown back to Cairo to take command of an armoured unit which was in readiness to help Hussein resist an invasion of Hejaz by Ibn Saʿud. Lawrence was injured in a plane crash and did not carry out the mission. By August he was back in England where he was demobilized and was soon afterwards elected to a fellowship of All Souls. For the rest of the year and most of the next he concentrated on his writing.

The years 1919–20 witnessed an imperial crisis with nationalist uprisings in Ireland, Egypt, India, and Iraq. Feisal was evicted from Syria by a French army. Lawrence blamed the Middle East's instability on the government which had frustrated the legitimate ambitions of the Arabs, and he conducted a vigorous press campaign on their behalf. In a letter to *The Times* of 12 August 1920 he pertinently asked whether those Arabs who had fought alongside the allies had merely done so to exchange one unloved imperial government for another. He added that the Anglo-Indian regime in Iraq enjoyed a worse reputation than its Ottoman predecessor.

In December, Winston Churchill, then colonial secretary, invited Lawrence to join the new Middle East department and use his knowledge and local contacts to prepare the ground for a permanent settlement in the area. It was achieved in March 1922 at the Cairo conference which Lawrence attended: Feisal was offered the throne of Iraq and his brother, Abdullah, that of the Transjordan. Both were mandates and, rather like Indian princes, both rulers had British-officered armies. Palestine was also administered under a League of Nations mandate and, his early reservations withdrawn, Lawrence warmly supported Jewish immigration. A liberal imperialist, Lawrence believed that the Arab states were bound to follow India's path towards self-government, perhaps becoming Britain's first 'brown dominion'.

Lawrence endorsed the scheme to use RAF bomber and armoured car squadrons as a substitute for the customary army garrisons. Together with Sir Hugh Trenchard, Lawrence was a godfather of the controversial system of aerial policing which was employed across the Middle East until the 1950s. Looking back Lawrence believed that he had settled a debt of honour and had achieved an equitable dispensation of power that was in the best interests of the empire and his former brothers-in-arms. His spent the next fourteen months negotiating with the increasingly cantankerous Hussein in Hejaz and advising Abdullah in the Transjordan. He found both tasks tedious.

Ranker and author, 1922–1935 In July 1922 Lawrence resigned from the Colonial Office and the following month enlisted in the RAF as John Hume Ross. According to the recruiting officer, W. E. Johns, his acceptance had been sanctioned at the highest level. In December, while attached to the RAF School of Photography at Farnborough, his subterfuge was uncovered by the press. He was discharged and re-enlisted in another technical unit, the tank corps, in March 1923 as T. E. Shaw. Just over two years later and after threatening suicide he was permitted to transfer to his preferred service, the RAF, where he remained until February 1935. At each stage in these proceedings, he was helped by well-placed connections including friends and admirers, John Buchan and George Bernard Shaw, who exerted pressure on the prime minister, Stanley Baldwin.

Lawrence's motives for enlistment were complex. He

had a genuine interest in machinery—this was the period which saw his love affair with Brough Superior motorcycles—and between 1929 and 1935 he worked on the development of seaplane tenders and air–sea rescue craft. Lawrence also once expressed the hope that, having led from above, he could lead from below in a service which had captured his imagination during the war. The RAF also provided him with a relatively secure refuge from the intrusions of the press. These in the form of a bogus story about his involvement in covert intelligence gathering on the north-west frontier triggered his recall from Miramshah in 1929. The incident later formed the scenario for a Soviet propaganda film.

Since at least 1923 Lawrence had submitted to a bizarre and potentially scandalous regime of ritual beatings, undertaken by various men and at the instructions of an invented uncle who demanded his nephew's chastisement for various peccadilloes. There was a sexual element in these proceedings, although Lawrence's younger brother, Arnold *Lawrence, claimed that they were therapeutic and the equivalent of the disciplinary beatings undergone by medieval ascetics. There were homoerotic passages in The Seven Pillars and, soon after the war, at least one of his brother officers accused him of being a homosexual (James, 255). Rumours of this nature were so persistent that Lowell Thomas took the extraordinary step of denouncing them in a posthumous volume of tributes compiled by Lawrence's friends. Lawrence himself denied any such inclinations to E. M. Forster.

Service life, and his Dorset cottage retreat, Clouds Hill (purchased in 1924), gave Lawrence the time to write. By November 1919 he had completed the first draft of The Seven Pillars, which he lost on Reading Station. A second was finished during 1922 which, with amendments and alterations, appeared as a private edition in 1926. Elegantly printed and richly illustrated by artists chosen by Lawrence, it was a reflection of his delight in fine printing. An abridged version, Revolt in the Desert, was published in 1927. Observations of life among his fellow aircraftmen formed the raw material for The Mint, a brutal but faithful record which Lawrence completed in 1927 and which appeared in a bowdlerized version in 1955. In 1932 Lawrence's translation of Homer's Odyssey was published.

At every stage of his writing career Lawrence was anxious about his felicity of expression and sought his friends' advice; his lack of confidence was utterly groundless. His friends were aware of and, by and large, tolerated his ambivalent attitude towards his own celebrity, neatly summed up by Trenchard: 'He was the sort of man who, on entering a roomful of people, would have contrived to be sick … had not everyone stood up to applaud him'. If recognition had not been immediately forthcoming, 'Lawrence might well react by standing on his head' (Boyle, 428). A charming, agreeable, though occasionally acerbic, manner compensated for the egotism.

Lawrence was deeply concerned with posterity. His revelatory letters, particularly to Mrs Charlotte Shaw, were certainly the raw material for future biographers. He also wrote to his living biographers, Robert Graves and Basil Liddell Hart, and through them became an accessory in the making of his own legend. Both augmented the heroics of Lowell Thomas's With Lawrence in Arabia (1924) and its sequel, The Boys' Life of Colonel Lawrence (1927). All these biographies sold well, evidence of the extent and endurance of Lawrence's appeal to the inter-war generation.

Lawrence fulfilled a special need: he was a hero in the pre-war mould (there were comparisons with General Gordon) and a brave man who, like so many other veterans, had been inwardly and outwardly scarred by their experiences. He was an amateur who did well in a conflict in which the professionals had blundered and his war had a romance and glamour which were lacking in the mass struggle of men against machines, chemicals, and mud. Lawrence was photogenic, an ideal icon of a lost generation, but also very much a modern man, as his passion for flight proved. Intellectuals could admire an unconventional man of their stamp and, in the early thirties, looked to him for some kind of leadership in the imminent struggle of political ideologies, as briefly did Auden and Isherwood. That they, along with Thomas Hardy, Winston Churchill, Lady Astor, and George Bernard Shaw were among his admirers is some indication of the universality of Lawrence's appeal. 'Such men win friends—such also find critics and detractors' observed Allenby in his obituary broadcast (The Listener, 22 May 1935). Among the latter were soldiers who objected to Lawrence's cocksure and sometimes insubordinate manner and to the way in which he had underplayed the part by the regular forces which had won the decisive victories.

There were also those, including his friends, who raised their eyebrows at some of Lawrence's tales. Among these was an account of how he had interrogated Mustapha Kamal (Kamal Atatürk) after he had been taken by Arabs in the closing days of the Damascus campaign. Sensing from his conversation that Kamal might prove a friend to the Arabs, Lawrence let him go. No one, including Kamal, ever referred to this encounter and, given Lawrence's observations on the Arabs' vengeful mood, it passed belief that a Turkish general could have survived capture (Wilson, 558, 1104–5). Nor could anyone corroborate Lawrence's undergraduate tales of exchanging shots with a Turkish brigand or his account of his capture and imprisonment by Turks near Urfa, where, disguised as an Arab, he had been seeking antiquities in 1912. This yarn was circulating in 1917 and was related by Lawrence to Liddell Hart (T. E. Lawrence to his Biographers Robert Graves and Liddell Hart, 2.141).

Lawrence's unsubstantiated and far-fetched tales were hostages to fortune, in so far that they threw into question his attitude to the truth. For him it was an artist's raw material which he could embellish for effect in the manner of his beloved troubadours. An undergraduate who once expressed a disdain for historical facts did not allow them to constrain his creativity; Lawrence's ornamentation of the truth was the exercise of artistic licence. He perplexed rather then deceived and, as his distant kinsman, Lord Vansittart, commented, he may have been a 'show-off', but 'he had something to show' (*Daily Telegraph*, 12 Feb 1955).

Lawrence could never distance himself from the alluring persona of Lawrence of Arabia (which put him on a par with Clive of India) although he often hoped he might, once expressing sympathy with that other celebrity who sought privacy, Greta Garbo. In 1935 he left the RAF and turned to a life of reading, writing, and printing fine books. On 13 May, swerving on his powerful motor cycle to avoid two boys cycling abreast, he was violently thrown, and after lingering unconscious for five days, Lawrence died in Bovington Camp Hospital on 19 May 1935. The obituaries were fulsome and reflected a sense of national loss which was genuine. The word 'enigma' was widely used. There were rumours that Lawrence had not died, but had withdrawn into an Arthurian limbo from which he would emerge to assist an imperilled nation. There had been similar tales after Kitchener's death.

Reputation The private Lawrence was buried on 21 May 1935 in St Nicholas's churchyard, Moreton, Dorset; the public was commemorated by a bronze bust by Eric Kennington in the crypt of St Paul's, where Nelson was buried. The juxtaposition seemed appropriate: both were heroes who were adulated in life and death as exemplars of peculiar national virtues. And each was extraordinarily vain. No equivalent of Southey's *Life of Nelson* appeared after Lawrence's death to lend permanence to his legend and teach his countrymen how they ought to behave. Such a biography was unnecessary: the unabridged *Seven Pillars* was published within a few months. It soon became an international best-seller and has rarely been out of print in the English speaking world.

What turned out to be the custodianship of the 'Lawrence legend' was given to his youngest brother and literary executor, Arnold Lawrence, an archaeologist. It was a hard task: he had to balance the almost obsessive interest in his brother with a natural desire to keep secret details of his birth (their mother died in 1959 aged ninety-eight).

What became the prolific Lawrentian literary heritage began with various short inspirational biographies, the publication of a series of often sharply drawn and candid portraits by his friends and brothers-in-arms (*T. E. Lawrence by his Friends*, ed. A. W. Lawrence, 1937, and a selection of his correspondence, *The Letters of T. E. Lawrence*, ed. D. Garnett, 1938). Plans by Alexander Korda to produce a film based on Lawrence's desert exploits had been made shortly before his death, although he was uneasy about the enterprise. The project proceeded, but was scuppered by the Foreign Office, which was nervous about the film's effect on Anglo-Turkish relations. Korda persisted and in its final wartime version the scenario revealingly concentrated on Lawrence's work with the RAF and portrayed him as one of the progenitors of the force that would win the battle of Britain. The film was never made.

The favourable public image of Lawrence was radically transformed by Richard Aldington's *Lawrence of Arabia: a Biographical Enquiry*, which was published early in 1955. Aldington began his researches with an open mind, but as he trawled through the available sources he found abundant evidence of contradictions, inconsistencies, and fabrications. This convinced him that his subject was a consummate deceiver who had fabricated his own legend with Lowell Thomas, Robert Graves, and Basil Liddell Hart as his chief accomplices. The result was an excoriating biography which treated Lawrence as a boastful charlatan. Forewarned, and aware that his own as well as Lawrence's reputation was on the line, Liddell Hart mounted a distasteful campaign of vilification against Aldington in an attempt to rebut his charges (Crawford, esp. 66–90).

In a bad-tempered debate, Lawrence's defenders insisted that Aldington was not only traducing a national hero, but the values he and his generation had stood for. These soon came under a more sustained barrage as Britain dismantled its empire and, in the process, repudiated its architects and their beliefs. Aldington was a step ahead of his times when he dismissed Lawrence as a hero of his class and age.

The literary offensive against Aldington proved self-defeating because Liddell Hart and his supporters cavilled over Aldington's errors, rather than concentrating on his shaky thesis that because Lawrence sometimes told lies he did so always. During the altercation Aldington received the public endorsement of some of Lawrence's wartime colleagues who recalled his presumptuousness and how he exaggerated his own and the Arabs' achievements (James, 442–3).

Aldington's unrelenting waspishness distorted his picture of Lawrence, who, despite his self-promotion, had been a fundamentally decent man. By debunking Lawrence, Aldington prepared the way for his being given the same treatment as any other prominent historical figure who had left behind an extensive record of his part in great events. Aldington's iconoclasm also replaced the hitherto one-dimensional paladin with an infinitely more intriguing creature who was flawed and driven by complex motives. These were evident in Terence Rattigan's *Ross* (1960), which Arnold Lawrence tried to ban, and David Lean's film *Lawrence of Arabia* (1962). Immensely popular, this magnificent epic was the apotheosis of the legend of Lawrence the heroic adventurer, brave, flamboyant, and disturbed by spasms of self-doubt. The inner frailties of the screen Lawrence added to his attractiveness without diminishing his accomplishments. Lean had done for Lawrence what Shakespeare had for Henry V. The film revived the Lawrence legend and guaranteed future interest in him as an individual.

The historical Lawrence underwent fresh dissection. His role as an agent of British imperial expansion was examined in S. Mousa's *T. E. Lawrence: an Arab View* (1966), which rejected some of the claims made in *The Seven Pillars*. The opening of Foreign and War Office files in the 1960s and the exposure by the *Sunday Times* of Lawrence's masochistic beatings in 1968 kept him in the public eye and opened up a new field for conjecture, his sexuality. This was among the subjects examined by J. E. Mack. A psychiatrist, he approached Lawrence from a new angle by endeavouring to unravel the strands of his neuroses. Analysed in absentia, Lawrence revealed interior struggles which Mack believed were common to twentieth-century man (*A Prince of our Disorder: the Life of T. E. Lawrence*, 1976).

Lawrence's subsequent biographers (there have been five since 1979, and two respectful television documentaries) have been split into two factions. One has upheld his integrity and attempted to rescue him from allegations of egotistic misrepresentation. The other has followed Aldington and treated whatever Lawrence said with varying degrees of scepticism. Both approaches rest on the fragile premise that public figures were models of rectitude, objectivity, and accuracy whenever they wrote about themselves and assessed their achievements.

The sixty or more years after Lawrence's death witnessed the fulfilment of his ambition to fascinate and bewilder posterity. How far this conditioned his behaviour during his lifetime cannot be known. What is beyond doubt is that even after his flaws had been exposed, his capacity to grip the public imagination remained as strong as ever.   LAWRENCE JAMES

Sources correspondence for the official history of the E. E. F.'s 1917–18 campaigns, PRO, CAB 45/80 • R. Aldington, *Lawrence of Arabia: a biographical enquiry* (1955) • R. C. Busch, *Britain, India and the Arabs, 1914–21* (Berkeley, California, 1971) • A. J. Hill, *Chauvel of the light horse* (Melbourne, 1978) • T. E. Lawrence, *The seven pillars of wisdom* (1986) • *The letters of T. E. Lawrence*, ed. M. Brown (1988) • S. Mousa, *T. E. Lawrence and the Arabs* (1967) • L. James, *The golden warrior: the life and legend of Lawrence of Arabia*, rev. edn (1995) • J. Wilson, *Lawrence of Arabia* (1989) • M. R. Lawrence, ed., *The home letters of T. E. Lawrence and his brothers* (1954) • Bodl. Oxf., MSS Milner 53–54, 452 • *Selected letters of T. E. Lawrence*, ed. D. Garnett (1938) • C. Falls, *Armageddon, 1918* (1964) • S. Mousa, 'Arab sources on Lawrence of Arabia: new evidence', *Army Quarterly and Defence Journal*, 116 (1986), 167 • Wingate papers, U. Durham L., department of palaeography and diplomatic, Sudan archive • King's Lond., Liddell Hart C., Edmonds MSS • G. W. Barrow, *The fire of life* (1941) • A. Boyle, *Trenchard: man of vision* (1962), 428 • *The Listener* (22 May 1935) • *T. E. Lawrence to his biographers Robert Graves and Liddell Hart* (1963) • *Daily Telegraph* (12 Feb 1955) • A. W. Lawrence, ed., *T. E. Lawrence by his friends* (1937) • F. D. Crawford, *A cautionary tale: Richard Aldington and Lawrence of Arabia* (1998) • J. E. Mack, *A prince of our disorder: the life of T. E. Lawrence* (1976) • *CGPLA Eng. & Wales* (1935)

Archives BL, annotated and corrected copy of *Seven pillars of wisdom* • BL, diaries and literary papers, Add. MSS 45912–45917, 45930, 45983, 46355 • BL, corresp. and papers, Add. MSS 63549–63550 • Bodl. Oxf., commonplace book • Bodl. Oxf., corresp., literary MSS, papers, and personal papers • Bodl. Oxf., papers, MS RES.C.54 • Bodl. Oxf., letters to his mother [copies] • Bodl. Oxf., letters • Harvard U., Houghton L., corresp., literary MSS, and papers • IWM, notes relating to campaign in Hedjaz • Jesus College, Oxford, corresp. and papers • Ransom HRC, corresp. and papers | All Souls Oxf., letters to Lionel Curtis • BL, letters to C. F. Bell, Add. MSS 63549–63550 • BL, corresp. with Charlotte Shaw, Add. MSS 56495–56499 [copies] • BL, corresp. with George Bernard Shaw, Add. MSS 45903–45904, 45916, 45922 • Bodl. Oxf., letters to A. E. Chambers • Bodl. Oxf., corresp. with Lionel Curtis • Bodl. Oxf., corresp. with Geoffrey Dawson • Bodl. Oxf., letters to E. T. Leeds • CAC Cam., corresp. with George Lloyd • CAC Cam., corresp. with Lady Spencer-Churchill • CUL, letters to Lady Kennet • Gon. & Caius Cam., letters to Charles Doughty • Jesus College, Oxford, letters to R. V. Buxton • Kettle's Yard, Cambridge, corresp. with H. S. Ede • King's AC Cam., corresp. with E. M. Forster • Mitchell L., NSW, letters to Frederic Manning • NA Scot., corresp. with marquess of Lothian • NL Scot., letters to John Buchan [copies] • Palestine Exploration Fund, London, corresp. with Palestine Exploration Fund • PRO, intelligence reports/summaries (Middle East),

WO • PRO, Jidda consulate/Arab bureau, FO 686, FO 882 • Royal Air Force Museum, Hendon, department of research and information services, letters to A. S. Frere-Reeves • U. Durham L., Clayton papers • U. Durham L., Wingate papers • U. Lond., Allenby papers • U. Reading L., corresp. with Nancy Astor • University of Essex, letters to Harold Stanley Ede | FILM BFI NFTVA, 'T. E. Lawrence, 1880–1935', BBC, 1962 • BFI NFTVA, *True stories*, Channel 4, 29 July 1997 • BFI NFTVA, documentary footage • BFI NFTVA, news footage • BFI NFTVA, record footage • IWM, news footage, [Allenby's entry into Jerusalem, Dec 1917] | SOUND BL NSA, 'Personal recollections of T. E. Lawrence in the Near East during the 1914–1918 war', 19 May 1935, 1CLD067793 S1 • BL NSA, 'T. E. Lawrence and the media', 6 Nov 1985, C125/49 BD1

Likenesses B. E. Leeson, bromide print, 1917, NPG • photograph, *c*.1917, IWM • R. G. Goslett, photograph, *c*.1917–1918, IWM • photograph, *c*.1917–1918, NPG • J. McBey, oils, 1918, IWM • A. John, drawing, 1919, All Souls Oxf. • A. John, oils, 1919, Tate collection [*see illus.*] • A. John, oils, 1919, Yale CBA • A. John, pencil drawing, *c*.1919, NPG • W. Rothenstein, portrait, 1919, National Museum, Belgrade • F. D. Wood, plaster head, 1919, IWM; bronze cast, Tate collection • W. Roberts, oils, 1922–3, AM Oxf. • photograph, 1925–6, Bodl. Oxf. • E. Kennington, bronze head, 1926, NPG; also in Clouds Hill, Dorset • E. Kennington, pastel drawing, *c*.1926, U. Texas • three photographs, *c*.1926–1928, NPG • A. John, chalk drawing, *c*.1929, NPG • A. John, oils, 1929, AM Oxf. • A. John, pencil drawing, *c*.1929, NPG • C. Wheeler, marble head, 1929, NPG • photograph, 1929, NPG • H. Coster, photographs, 1931, NPG • A. John, drawing, chalk, 1935, AM Oxf. • A. John, portrait, 1935, National Gallery of Canada, Ottawa • E. Kennington, stone effigy, 1939, St Martin's Church, Wareham, Dorset • H. Gurschner, oils (posthumous), NG Ire. • H. S. Tuke, oils, Clouds Hill, Dorset • photograph, NPG • photographs, Hult. Arch.

Wealth at death £7441 9*s*.: probate, 26 Aug 1935, *CGPLA Eng. & Wales*

Lawrence, Sir Walter Roper, first baronet (1857–1940), administrator in India, son of George Lawrence JP of Monmouthshire and his second wife, Catharine, daughter of Edward Lewis of Wenvoe, Glamorgan, was born at Moreton Court, near Hereford, on 9 February 1857. He was educated at Cheltenham College and in 1877 came first in the open competition for the Indian Civil Service. In 1879, after two years' probation at Balliol College, Oxford, he joined the Bengal civil service, serving initially in the Punjab, the Kurram valley of Afghanistan, and Rajputana. In 1885 he was appointed revenue under-secretary to the Punjab government, and in 1886 under-secretary to the government of India in the revenue and agriculture department.

In 1889, well-versed in both the political service and the principles of revenue assessment, Lawrence was appointed settlement commissioner of Kashmir. The post suited him perfectly. He was always happiest working in the relatively backward princely states, partly because he disliked the cumbersome bureaucracy of Calcutta and Simla, but also because it was here that he could best entertain visions of an unspoiled, traditional India. A conservative, who even in the late 1920s expected India to need British guidance for generations to come, he was nevertheless often uncomfortable with Britain's role in India, especially when in the presence of articulate and educated Indians; princely India, unheedful of Westernizing reforms, often seemed to him a simpler, happier place.

In 1896, perhaps loath to return to a post in a regulation province, Lawrence resigned the service and became

Sir Walter Roper Lawrence, first baronet (1857–1940), by Elliott & Fry

agent-in-chief to Herbrand Arthur Russell, eleventh duke of Bedford. In 1898, however, he willingly accepted the invitation to return to India as private secretary to Lord Curzon. This proved to be an exhilarating but exhausting post for Lawrence as he attempted to mediate between the reforming zeal of his tactless chief and the lumbering proceduralism of an increasingly resentful civil service. In 1903, thinking it foolhardy of Curzon to stay on for a second term, Lawrence resigned. Back in England he wrote weekly columns on Indian affairs for *The Times* until December 1904, when the prince of Wales commandeered him to organize a royal tour of India in the cold season of 1905–6. Lawrence's exacting but delicate management of the tour, which was widely regarded as a success, initiated a lifelong friendship with the future George V, and he later wrote a number of speeches for the king.

In 1907 Lawrence became a member of the Council of India but a conflict of interest with his business affairs prompted his resignation in early 1909. At the outbreak of the First World War he became commissioner for the Indian sick and wounded in France and England; he subsequently conducted extensive enquiries for the War Office into the rehabilitation of war-disabled soldiers. In 1917–18 he toured the United States on a recruiting and propaganda mission and in 1919 travelled to Palestine to report for Lord Curzon, now foreign secretary, on currency problems in the administration of the Occupied Enemy Territories.

Lawrence counted many literary figures, including Rudyard Kipling, among his friends and was himself an accomplished writer. In 1895 he published *The Valley of Kashmir* and in retirement wrote a witty, often self-deprecating memoir of his years in India, *The India we Served* (1928). The 'we' of the title was a gracious acknowledgement of the companionship of his wife, Lilian Gertrude (*d.* 1929), daughter of John Gwynne James of Ayleston Hill, Hereford, whom he had married on 18 March 1885 and who had accompanied him around India for almost twenty years.

He was appointed KCIE in 1903 and GCIE in 1906, in which year he was also created a baronet for his services during the royal tour. In 1917 he was appointed CB and in 1918 GCVO. He died at Gorse Hill, Hook Heath, Woking, Surrey, on 25 May 1940, survived by his two sons. The elder son, Roland, born in 1886, succeeded as second baronet.

KATHERINE PRIOR

Sources J. R. Dunlop-Smith, *List of the private secretaries to the governors-general and viceroys from 1774 to 1908* (1908) · B. Allen, introduction to Lawrence MSS handlist, 1979, BL OIOC · *WWW* · E. Hilliard, ed., *The Balliol College register, 1832–1914* (privately printed, Oxford, 1914) · E. S. Skirving, ed., *Cheltenham College register, 1841–1927* (1928) · W. R. Lawrence, *The India we served* (1928) · Burke, *Peerage* (1959) · *CGPLA Eng. & Wales* (1940)
Archives BL OIOC, corresp. and papers, MSS Eur. F 143 | BL OIOC, letters to Curzon · BL OIOC, letters to Lord Reading, MSS Eur. 238, F 118 · CUL, corresp. with Lord Hardinge
Likenesses D. Dayal & Sons, group portrait, photograph, 1902, BL OIOC · Herzog & Higgins, group portrait, photograph, 1902, BL OIOC · W. Stoneman, photograph, 1918, NPG · Elliott & Fry, photograph, NPG [*see illus.*] · Spy [L. Ward], caricature, chromolithograph, NPG; repro. in *VF* (15 June 1905)
Wealth at death £112,963 14*s.* 8*d.*: probate, 8 July 1940, *CGPLA Eng. & Wales*

Lawrence, William (*c.*1613–1682), lawyer, was the elder son in a family of eight—two sons and six daughters—born to William Lawrence (1579–1640) of Wraxall, Dorset, and Elizabeth (*d.* 1672), daughter of William Gibbs, bencher of the Middle Temple, of South Perrott, Dorset. Though Lawrence's father, like others of the family, was merely a tenant on the Stawell estates and formally denied gentry status by the heralds, he took the lead in exposing foul abuses in the county gaol to the privy council. Lawrence matriculated as a gentleman commoner from Trinity College, Oxford, in 1631, spending three years 'under a careful tutor' (Wood, *Ath. Oxon.*, 62). He was admitted to his grandfather's inn in 1634, and under his father's will he was to complete his studies in the common law on a generous allowance of £60 a year.

Lawrence was called to the bar in 1641 and remained in London during the civil war, his mother retaining control of Wraxall until he was thirty-one. She contributed supplies and money to the parliamentary cause, with which Lawrence identified himself by his marriage in 1649 to Martha (*b.* 1622), daughter of William Sydenham, from a local branch of the Somerset magnate family. Her five brothers had all been in arms for parliament. Lawrence's landlord, Sir John Stawell, on the other hand, was a sufficiently obstinate cavalier to incur the forfeiture of his entire estate, and Lawrence bought the Stawell moiety of Wraxall from the Rump. As a safe man he was appointed to the county bench under the Commonwealth, and to a Dorset commission for the relief of poor prisoners. His brother-in-law Colonel William *Sydenham, reporting from the council of state on 24 October 1653, recommended him as a replacement for one of the English judges who introduced an unprecedented degree of efficiency into the Scottish judicial system. From Edinburgh he conducted a pamphlet war with Stawell over the validity of his purchase. Sydenham had Lawrence elected for the Isle of Wight in 1656 and for one of the boroughs in 1658, but he made no mark in either parliament.

Compromised by Sydenham's collusion with the military junto in 1659, at the Restoration Lawrence quietly resumed his practice at the English bar as 'a counsellor of note' (Wood, *Ath. Oxon.*, 62), though he did not return to chambers and never became a bencher. As bailiff of Wraxall he attended Stawell's grandiose funeral in 1662. Lawrence's marriage broke up in 1669 'upon a discontent arising from his wife, … whom he esteemed disloyal to him' (ibid., 62). 'Mrs Lawrence', wrote a local magistrate, 'seems confident that her husband will not be brought to anything but a starving allowance' (Alnwick Castle MS 533, fol. 51). The episode inspired in him an interest in the marriage laws, which the collapse of episcopal censorship eventually allowed him to pursue in print in three substantial volumes. A believer in hereditary succession as against the inconveniences of an elective monarchy, he took up a strictly constitutional attitude towards the succession. The duke of York had forfeited his right to the throne by his conversion to Roman Catholicism. In these circumstances Charles II would have been justified in divorcing his blameless but barren queen, leaving him free to produce an unchallengeable heir. But Lawrence took account of the king's obstinacy over this issue, and adopted the unorthodox position that 'carnal knowledge and not ceremonies make marriage' (W. Lawrence, *Marriage by the Law of God Vindicated*, 1680, 113). This was very acceptable to those inclined to support the claims of the duke of Monmouth, the king's eldest bastard.

Lawrence signed his will on 6 March 1682, and died at Bedfont, Middlesex, on the road to London twelve days later; he was buried in Bedfont. The will was proved on 17 March 1683. A memorial, bearing some verses of his own composition, but with an impossible date of death, was erected in the chancel at Wraxall. His only child, William, went bankrupt about 1712 and died in a debtors' gaol.

'A man of parts and considerable reading' (Wood, *Ath. Oxon.*, 62), Lawrence was able to dismiss most of the arguments against his position as the work of papists or bishops, whom he disliked just as much. It cannot be said that he tackled the practical difficulties, and interest in his work lapsed when it lost topical relevance with the execution of Monmouth in 1685. JOHN FERRIS

Sources J. Hutchins, *The history and antiquities of the county of Dorset*, 3rd edn, ed. W. Shipp and J. W. Hodson, 2 (1863), 201–3 · Wood, *Ath. Oxon.*, new edn, 4.62–3 · letter-book of Sir John Fitzjames, 1668–70, Alnwick Castle, Northumberland, Alnwick Castle MS 533, fols. 44–51 · F. A. Crisp, *Fragmenta genealogica*, 13 (1909), 135 · G. Donaldson, *Scotland: James V to James VII* (1965), vol. 3 of *The Edinburgh history of Scotland* (1965–75), 348 · G. K. Fortescue and others, eds., *Catalogue of the pamphlets, books, newspapers, and manuscripts relating to the civil war, the Commonwealth, and Restoration, collected by George Thomason, 1640–1661*, 2 (1908), 91, 101, 114 · will, PRO, PROB 11/184, fol. 277 [William Lawrence, father, 1638] · C. T. Martin, ed., *Minutes of parliament of the Middle Temple*, 4 vols. (1904–5), vol. 2, p. 894 · G. E. Aylmer, *The state's servants: the civil service of the English republic, 1649–1660* (1973), 135 · will, PRO, PROB 11/372, fol. 279 · quarter sessions order and minute book, 1625–37, Dorset RO, QSM 1/1 [Sherborne, April 1637; Bridport, October, 1637] · C. H. Mayo, ed., *The minute books of the Dorset standing committee* (1902), 518 · H. Nenner, *The right to be king* (1995)

Archives Alnwick Castle, Northumberland, papers | Dorset RO, QSM 1/1

Wealth at death see will, PRO, PROB 11/372, fol. 279

Lawrence, Sir William, first baronet (1783–1867), surgeon, was born on 16 July 1783 in Cirencester, the eldest of the four sons (there were also four daughters) of William Lawrence (1753–1837), a prominent surgeon, and his wife, Judith (d. 1839), second daughter of William Wood of Tetbury, Gloucestershire. Charles *Lawrence (1794–1881), the agriculturist, was his brother. Lawrence was educated at a school at Elmore, near Gloucester, then in March 1799 was apprenticed to John Abernethy, assistant surgeon to St Bartholomew's Hospital in London. As was the custom Lawrence lived in his master's house during his early years in London. Abernethy also lectured on anatomy at the hospital, and in 1800 he appointed Lawrence as his demonstrator. Lawrence held this position for twelve years with notable success; he was remarkable for his skill as a dissector and was a popular and gifted teacher. Among his early publications was his *Description of the Arteries of the Human Body* (1801), a translation from the Latin of Adolphus Murray. Lawrence also published *Comparative Anatomy* (1807), translated from the German of Johann Friedrich Blumenbach. In the same year he published *A Treatise on Hernia*, a prize essay at the Royal College of Surgeons. In addition he made numerous technical contributions to professional journals.

In 1805 Lawrence became a member of the Royal College of Surgeons, and in 1813 he became an assistant surgeon at St Bartholomew's. In the same year he was elected a fellow of the Royal Society. As well as his work at Bart's, Lawrence obtained posts in some of the more specialized medical establishments: he was from 1814 surgeon to the London Infirmary for Diseases of the Eye and from 1815 to the royal hospitals of Bridewell and Bethlem. The former post is of particular significance since the London Infirmary was an early example of a hospital specializing in the diseases of a single organ. Lawrence subsequently sought to place the treatment of ophthalmic disorders on a sound footing by publishing his *Treatise on Diseases of the Eye* (1833).

Bart's remained, however, Lawrence's most important affiliation; in 1824 he became a full surgeon there, a post he was to hold for more than forty years. In parallel with developing his private and hospital practice, Lawrence sought to strengthen his credentials as a teacher. After a disagreement with the other medical staff at Bart's he was instrumental in the establishment of the private school of medicine at Aldersgate Street in London. But in 1829 he

Sir William Lawrence, first baronet (1783–1867), by Henry William Pickersgill, exh. RA 1841

returned to hospital teaching when he succeeded Abernethy as lecturer on surgery at Bart's. Some of Lawrence's lectures were published in 1863.

In 1815 Lawrence was appointed professor of anatomy and surgery at the Royal College of Surgeons. His first series of lectures was published as *An Introduction to Comparative Anatomy and Physiology* in the following year. In these lectures Lawrence made a point of praising French science and drawing unfavourable comparisons between the facilities available for research in that country and the severely limited provisions for serious study that existed in Britain. He drew particular attention to 'those liberal institutions for the advancement of natural knowledge, and that uniform encouragement of talent, for which science will ever be indebted to the late French government' (Lawrence, *Introduction*, 75). In the political atmosphere obtaining in the immediate aftermath of the revolutionary and Napoleonic wars, this was a daring view to espouse.

Lawrence's lectures were also controversial because he chose to take issue with the views of those who 'suppose the structure of the body to contain an invisible matter or principle, by which it is put in motion' (Lawrence, *Introduction*, 166). This was a reference to John Hunter's theory of vitality, which had recently been expounded in the college by Lawrence's former mentor, John Abernethy. Lawrence maintained that all such powers superadded to the material organization of the body were superfluous to scientific explanation and merely imaginary constructs. Abernethy made a somewhat peevish response to these

criticisms in his own 1817 lectures at the college. While not mentioning Lawrence by name he denounced the party of 'Modern Sceptics' who espoused French materialism without regard to the risks such ideas posed to social stability.

Lawrence took up this challenge in his second series of lectures at the college. He scoffed at Abernethy's allegation that 'there is a party of modern sceptics, co-operating in the diffusion of these noxious opinions with a no less terrible band of French physiologists, for the purposes of demoralizing mankind!' (Lawrence, *Lectures*, 4). He reiterated his earlier position that life was immediately dependent on organization: there was, for instance, 'no thought without a brain' (ibid., 61). Lawrence maintained, however, that this was a purely physiological doctrine with no implications for theology or ethics. Lawrence also made a strong plea for the freedom of scientific discourse from all attempts to trammel its scope and competence.

In his later lectures Lawrence continued to propound provocative political opinions. He was particularly scathing about the influence that the restored monarchy in France was likely to exert upon the pursuit of science in that country. The United States was, in contrast, a nation:

> sacred to civil liberty; where man may walk erect in the conscious dignity of independence … and enjoy full freedom of word and action; without the permission of those combinations or conspiracies of the mighty, which threaten to convert Europe into one great state prison. (Lawrence, *Lectures*, 37)

Lawrence was equally reckless in his discussion of the natural history of man. He argued that this was a subject to be pursued according to the same canons of scientific method as any other branch of general physiology. He recognized that any enquiry into human origins might seem superfluous to those who had unquestioning faith in the account provided by the 'Hebrew Scriptures'. Lawrence ventured to cast doubt upon the direct divine inspiration of the Old Testament adding that 'The account of the creation and subsequent events, has the allegorical figurative character common to eastern compositions' (Lawrence, *Lectures*, 248).

Lawrence was widely condemned for publishing such allegedly inflammatory views at a time of social disorder and political tension, and eventually withdrew the lectures from sale. When the copyright of these lectures came before the courts after two pirate editions had appeared in 1822, Lord Eldon, the lord chancellor, refused to protect the author's rights on the grounds that the book was blasphemous. Conversely radical agitators reproduced Lawrence's arguments seeing them as a weapon against priestcraft and despotism. Because of the furore his lectures had provoked he had been suspended from his post at Bridewell and Bethlem; he was obliged to provide a written retraction of his previous views before reinstatement.

Lawrence was chastened by this experience and never again published such dangerous opinions. Throughout the nineteenth century, however, he was often regarded as a martyr for the cause of science and of intellectual liberty. His lectures were even cited as precursors for such later works of scientific naturalism as Charles Darwin's *Descent of Man* (1871) and Thomas Huxley's *Man's Place in Nature* (1863).

Despite this experience Lawrence did not entirely eschew controversy in his later career. He became associated with the reformist party within the London medical community that championed the rights of general practitioners and challenged the prerogatives of the oligarchy that controlled the council of the Royal College of Surgeons. In 1824 the college had enacted new regulations aimed at limiting the number of medical schools at which candidates for its certificate could study. Lawrence chaired two meetings of members of the college at the Freemasons' Tavern at which he roundly denounced this measure as a particularly flagrant example of the members of the council abusing their position for personal profit. The true intention of 'the framers of so contemptible a production' was to oblige candidates to study only at London's hospital medical schools, in which most of the council members had a vested interest, and to force the private medical schools out of business.

The council's response to this outspoken challenge was in 1828 to appoint Lawrence to their number. He also received various other distinctions, such as the privilege of delivering the Hunterian oration in 1834 and 1846 and a place on the board of examiners. In December 1843 Lawrence became one of the original 300 fellows of the college. In 1846 and 1855 he also served as its president. As soon as he was admitted to the college's ruling élite Lawrence's earlier radicalism evaporated; he became a staunch defender of the privileges of the council. This volte-face was neither forgiven nor forgotten by his erstwhile allies. As late as 1867 *The Lancet's* obituarist could not forbear to remark that after the council had bought his loyalty, 'from that moment Mr Lawrence became a conservative and an obstructionist. He not only deserted his former friends, but lost no opportunity of reviling them.'. The writer concluded that Lawrence had 'advocated reform merely for the purpose of obtaining place' (*The Lancet*, 45). While this judgement may appear harsh, Lawrence's actions did invite such condemnation.

As a member of the medical establishment Lawrence received many honours. He was appointed sergeant-surgeon to Queen Victoria in 1857. Ten years later he received a baronetcy. He served as president of the Medical and Chirurgical Society and was also a member of several foreign scientific academies. On 14 August 1828 Lawrence married Louisa (d. 1855), daughter of James Trevor Senior of Aylesbury; they had two sons and three daughters.

Lawrence resigned the office of surgeon at Bart's in 1865. He continued to act as an examiner at the Royal College of Surgeons until he suffered a stroke in May 1867. This left him partially paralysed and unable to speak. He died on 5 July 1867 at his home, 18 Whitehall Place, London. L. S. JACYNA

Sources W. Lawrence, *An introduction to comparative anatomy and physiology* (1816) • W. Lawrence, *Lectures on physiology, zoology, and the natural history of man* (1819) • W. Lawrence, *A corrected report of the speeches delivered by Mr Lawrence, as chairman, at two meetings of members of the Royal College of Surgeons ... held at the Freemasons' Tavern* (1826) • *The Lancet*, 2 (1867), 44–6 • V. G. Plarr, *Plarr's Lives of the fellows of the Royal College of Surgeons of England*, rev. D'A. Power, 1 (1930) • P. J. Wallis and R. V. Wallis, *Eighteenth century medics*, 2nd edn (1988) • A. Desmond, *The politics of evolution: morphology, medicine and reform in radical London* (1989) • Burke, *Peerage* • *IGI* • *GM*, 1st ser., 98/2 (1828), 269

Likenesses F. C. Lewis, sen., stipple, 1835 (after F. C. Lewis, jun.), Wellcome L. • C. Turner, mezzotint, pubd 1839, BM, Wellcome L. • C. Turner, portrait, 1839, repro. in Desmond, *Politics of evolution* • H. W. Pickersgill, oils, exh. RA 1841, St Bartholomew's Hospital, London [*see illus.*] • E. R. Whitfield, line engraving, 1842 (after H. W. Pickersgill), Wellcome L. • G. B. Black, group portrait, lithograph, pubd 1851 (*English physicians*; after daguerreotypes by Mayall), BM • J. Cochran, stipple (after H. Wyatt), NPG, Wellcome L. • Maull & Co., photograph, Wellcome L. • H. Weekes, marble bust, RCS Eng. • wood-engraving, BM, NPG; repro. in *ILN* (1867)

Wealth at death under £40,000: probate, 1 Aug 1867, *CGPLA Eng. & Wales*

Lawrenson [*née* Molyneux], **Mary Ann** (1850–1943), co-operative movement activist and educationist, was born on 23 March 1850 at 49 Castle Street East, Marylebone, Middlesex, the eldest of eleven children of John Molyneux, printer, trade unionist, and co-operative movement activist, and his wife, Ellen, *née* Keys. After moving to Woolwich in 1862, Molyneux did printing work for local organizations including the Royal Arsenal Co-operative Society (RACS). This contact with working-class initiatives shaped his daughter's social and intellectual development. She also inherited from her father a faith in the somewhat unusual combination of Roman Catholicism and Christian socialism. From 1869 she taught English in several schools, including a spell in Paris. On returning to Woolwich in 1876 she married John Marcus Lawrenson, a government clerk and auditor for the RACS, with whom she had one son.

In February 1883 Mary Lawrenson responded to Alice Acland's suggestion in the *Co-operative News* that a women's co-operative league be formed. Lawrenson advocated a national organization to co-ordinate local branches which would themselves assist co-operative extension and promote female educational and social development. For this, and her role in framing its constitution, she deserves recognition with Acland as a co-founder of the Women's Co-operative Guild.

Lawrenson established a guild branch in Woolwich, the second of three founded nationally during 1883, and joined the first national guild central committee in 1884. She was also elected to the education committee of the RACS in 1884, when female participation in co-operative management remained rare. She organized classes for women and a juvenile guild for children. However, her educational and charitable agenda and her advocacy of productive workshops were at odds with 'progressive' elements in Woolwich, who sought links with the labour movement and campaigners for women's suffrage. Hence she resigned as Woolwich Guild secretary in 1885 and from the education committee in 1888. Her subsequent involvement with the RACS was limited, although she returned to the education committee in 1895–8 and 1902–5.

Lawrenson assumed national office as guild general secretary in 1885–9. An accomplished speaker, she travelled widely, promoting new and established guild branches. The increase in guild branches to fifty-one by 1889 prompted Lawrenson's suggestion of regional co-ordination, a system implemented after her departure as secretary. Lawrenson resented the termination of her office in that year. The secretaryship passed to Margaret Llewelyn Davies, ostensibly because she was thought better placed to carry the administrative burden created by the expanding guild; but Lawrenson was also seen as too independent in her Christian socialism, particularly her enthusiasm for co-operative workshops and labour co-partnerships. She lost her place on the guild's central committee in 1893, but her service on the southern sectional board of the Co-operative Union in 1893–4 and 1896–8 breached another male bastion. She was also the first female member of a national co-operative committee, through her place on the union's central board.

In 1905 Lawrenson moved to Bournemouth, where she was active in the local guild. After her husband's death during the First World War she withdrew from co-operative work. Latterly she lived quietly in Brighton with her son. The guild leadership still regarded her as a maverick, and initially resisted her nomination for the freedom of the guild in 1931. She was, however, fêted at the guild's jubilee celebrations in 1933, and both the guild and the RACS supported Lawrenson financially in old age. Bedridden in her final years, Lawrenson died at the Brighton Municipal Hospital on 1 January 1943. Her funeral on 7 January at St Joseph's Roman Catholic Church, Brighton, and burial in the borough cemetery were attended by numerous guild representatives.

Mary Lawrenson was somewhat isolated in the co-operative movement, both as a woman in a male-dominated movement and in her faith in co-operative production amid advocates of consumers' interests. She was a determined champion of education, Christian socialism, and improvements in women's daily lives. The women's guild which she helped establish was a pioneer among organizations to give a public role and voice to working-class women.   MARTIN PURVIS

Sources Co-operative News (9 Jan 1943) · Co-operative News (16 Jan 1943) · J. Gaffin and D. Thoms, Caring and sharing: the centenary history of the Co-operative Women's Guild (1983) · W. T. Davis, The history of the Royal Arsenal Co-operative Society Ltd, 1868–1918 (1922) · J. Attfield, With light of knowledge: a hundred years of education in the Royal Arsenal Co-operative Society, 1877–1977 (1981) · National Co-operative Archive, Rochdale, Mary Lawrenson MSS · Proceedings of the 75th Annual Co-operative Congress [Co-operative Union] (1943) · Women's Outlook (30 Jan 1943) · M. L. Davies, The Women's Co-operative Guild, 1883–1904 (1904) · Kentish Independent (2 April 1942) · b. cert. · d. cert.
Archives Co-operative College, Manchester, National Co-operative Archive
Likenesses photograph, c.1905–1915, repro. in E. Sharp, Buyers and builders: the jubilee sketch of the Women's Co-operative Guild, 1883–1933 (1933), 5 · photograph, 1941, repro. in Women's Outlook, 130–31

Lawrenson, Thomas. See Lawranson, Thomas (d. in or after 1777).

Lawrie, Sir Archibald Campbell (1837–1914), lawyer and antiquary, was born on 8 September 1837 in West Nile Street, Glasgow, the eldest son of John Adair Lawrie (1801–1859), surgeon and professor of surgery at the University of Glasgow, and his wife, Janet Finlay, of The Moss, Stirlingshire. He was educated at the University of Glasgow, where he graduated BA in 1856, and was admitted a member of the Faculty of Advocates in December 1860. At about this time he moved to Edinburgh. Lawrie was active in the Speculative Society at Edinburgh University, holding the offices of secretary and president in the early 1860s.

Lawrie was introduced through family connections to Cosmo Innes (1798–1874), an antiquary of medieval Scotland, and was therefore brought into contact with the movement—particularly associated with publishing clubs such as the Bannatyne and Maitland clubs—responsible for gathering, editing, and publishing early Scottish records. As Lawrie put it later, he did not know if he had been attracted to record scholarship and antiquities by Innes or the reverse. The fruit of his close working relationship with Innes was their compilation, with another advocate, Archibald Anderson, of the great index to the eleven volumes of The Acts of the Parliaments of Scotland. This appeared in 1875 and crowned an enterprise begun in the early part of the century by the pioneering record scholar Thomas Thomson and completed by Cosmo Innes.

While in practice at the bar Lawrie acted on several occasions as interim sheriff-substitute at Glasgow, Greenock, and Peebles. In 1873, shortly before the completion of the index, Lawrie was appointed, on the recommendation of Lord Advocate George Young, as district judge of Kandy, Ceylon. The ingrained sceptical turn of his nature, which was held to be a mark of his historical work, was also reportedly a feature of Lawrie's judicial practice, together with a patient approach to investigation and unfailing good humour. The latter could sometimes run to 'playful' sarcasm. Residence in Ceylon did not mean, however, an abandonment of his work as a compiler. A Gazetteer of the Central Province of Ceylon (1896), a descriptive miscellany with translations of source material about his jurisdiction, marks Lawrie's continuing interest in such work even while overseas. In 1880 he married Constance, daughter of John Dennistoun and widow of John W. Hamilton. She died in 1890.

Lawrie remained in Kandy until his appointment as senior puisne judge of the supreme court of Ceylon in 1892, at which time he moved to Colombo. During his time there he met and entertained many of the dignitaries of empire, including Edward, prince of Wales, and Prince George. From this position he retired in 1901 and was knighted in the same year.

During the last part of his life Lawrie earned a leading reputation in his own right as a collector, editor, and critic of early Scottish records. He chose on his return to Scotland to settle at The Moss, Dumgoyne, Stirlingshire, the ancient home of the Buchanan family, from whom he claimed descent. The house, which he had inherited from his uncle William Finlay, was a good setting for work on his plan to make a critical study of the early reigns in Scottish history, beginning with David I. In 1906 Lawrie played host to the 'pilgrimage' made to The Moss to mark the quatercentenary of George Buchanan, tutor to James VI. He did not, however, contribute to the accompanying volume and was generally reported to be averse to speech making, essay writing, and reviewing.

In 1905 Lawrie, in accordance with his scheme, published *Early Scottish Charters Prior to AD 1153*. He used annals, charters, and cartularies, and the result was less a narrative than a collection of texts with extensive annotation of each document. Although not always accurately transcribed, the documents in this work became essential for historians of Scotland because of the void in pre-fourteenth century Scottish records caused by Edward I's removal of documents to England in 1291. Lawrie's zeal for caution was a hallmark of his work. George Neilson commented that he was 'a constitutional doubter, but generous enough in his admission of his own occasional error' (Neilson, 247). Even this description may have been too lenient, as is suggested by Lawrie's refusal to believe new documentary evidence in support of the authenticity of the Scone foundation charter of 1120, which he had denied. This aside, he avoided generalizations and ethnological inferences, and concentrated his interest on chronology, genealogy, and cross-examination of individual sources. In the same year (1905) as this work was published, Lawrie received recognition from his alma mater in the form of an LLD from Glasgow University.

A change in his plan was revealed by the publication in 1910 of his second major work, *Annals of the reigns of Malcolm and William, kings of Scotland, AD 1153–1214*. In this the annals appeared and were edited separately, and were intended to be followed by the charters. This intention was not to be fulfilled, but after his death Lawrie's material was put in the hands of John Maitland Thomson, who had given him valuable help and to whom the volume of 1910 had been dedicated. It was later deposited in the Advocates' Library in Edinburgh. Lawrie died at The Moss on 11 May 1914 of a heart-related illness and was buried on 15 May in the parish church graveyard at nearby Killearn.

GORDON F. MILLAR

Sources G. Neilson, 'Sir Archibald Lawrie's charter collections', *SHR*, 19 (1921–2), 241–53 · *Glasgow Herald* (12 May 1914) · *The Times* (13 May 1914) · *The Scotsman* (12 May 1914) · *The Scotsman* (13 May 1914) · *Glasgow Herald* (13 May 1914) · *Glasgow Herald* (16 May 1914) · *SHR*, 12 (1914–15), 113–14 · *Scots Law Times: News* (16 May 1914) · *WWW* · S. P. Walker, *The Faculty of Advocates, 1800–1986* (1987), 96 · F. J. Grant, ed., *The Faculty of Advocates in Scotland, 1532–1943*, Scottish RS, 145 (1944), 121 · G. Donaldson, *The sources of Scottish history* (privately printed, Edinburgh, 1978), 11 · W. I. Addison, *A roll of graduates of the University of Glasgow from 31st December 1727 to 31st December 1897* (1898), 325 · W. I. Addison, ed., *The matriculation albums of the University of Glasgow from 1728 to 1858* (1913), 274, 495 · *SHR*, 2–12 (1904–16) [reviews and articles] · *SHR*, 19 (1923) [reviews and articles] · R. G. Cant, *The writing of Scottish history in the time of Andrew Lang* (1978), 9, 17 · IGI

Archives NL Scot., Advocates' Library, 'Notes on early Scottish history' · NL Scot., corresp. and papers | NL Scot., Advocates' Library, collection of charter transcripts incl. some in connection with his *Early Scottish charters*
Likenesses photograph, repro. in *SHR*, 12 (1914–15), facing p. 113

Lawrie, George (1727–1799), Church of Scotland minister and patron of Scottish poetry, was born on 21 September 1727 at Kirkmichael manse, Ayrshire, the youngest of three sons of James Lawrie (d. 1764), minister of Kirkmichael from 1711 until his death, and Ann (d. 1747), daughter of George Ord, attorney in Owley, Wooler, Northumberland. He entered the University of Edinburgh in 1743 and was licensed to preach by the presbytery of Edinburgh on 25 November 1756. Early in the spring of 1763 he was presented by the commissioners for John, earl of Loudoun, to the parish of Loudoun, Newmilns, east of Kilmarnock, Ayrshire, where he was ordained on 28 September and remained for the rest of his life. On 21 November 1764 Lawrie married Mary (1730–1818), daughter of Archibald Campbell, professor of divinity at the University of St Andrews. They had seven children, including a son, Archibald (1768–1837), who succeeded his father as the minister of Loudoun.

Lawrie is significant as an exemplar of the enlightened clergy of the moderate party in the Church of Scotland, and as a friend of leading Scottish writers and intellectuals. He is best known for his influence on the careers of James Macpherson and Robert Burns. Lawrie was in the spa town of Moffat, Dumfriesshire, in October 1759 when James Macpherson intimated that he possessed translations of ancient Celtic poetry. Recognizing that such fragments might serve to authenticate the existence of a native literary culture of some antiquity, Lawrie and John Home, moderate clergyman and dramatist, referred the translations to Hugh Blair. Four letters from Macpherson indicate that Lawrie initially acted as intermediary between him and Blair and, through his encouragement, played an important role in the genesis of the project. The third letter, dated 24 March 1760, ends: 'if [the fragments] will be published you will have enough of them; but if they won't take, their blood be upon their head' (Yale MS C 1871). In 1789 Lawrie sought Macpherson's help in advancing the career of his brother, Colonel James Lawrie, governor of the Mosquito Coast. When Macpherson failed to remember him, Lawrie sent him a memorial of their meeting and the events to which it gave rise.

Lawrie subscribed, on the recommendation of Gavin Hamilton, to the Kilmarnock edition of Burns's *Poems, Chiefly in the Scottish Dialect*, published on 31 July 1786. Lawrie sent a copy of the book to Thomas Blacklock who, in a reply of 4 September 1786, advised publication of a second edition and promised to bring the poems to the notice of Blair. The content of Blacklock's encouraging letter was conveyed from Lawrie to Burns by Hamilton, and it had the effect of 'rousing my poetic ambition', as Burns wrote to John Moore on 2 August 1787 (*Letters*, 1.145), and of helping to persuade Burns to abandon his plan to take up a post as bookkeeper on a Jamaica estate. About October 1786 Burns visited Lawrie and his family at the manse of Loudoun, overlooking the River Irvine, and was warmly received by the minister, his wife, four daughters, and son. Hearing young Christina Lawrie play on the spinet Burns 'told her that she knew the magic way to a poet's heart' (Life and Works, 1.412), and during the evening's dancing—a pastime indicative of Lawrie's liberal manners—his daughter Louisa noted that Burns 'kept time admirably' (ibid., 413). Burns retired 'deeply touched by the simple refinement, good-nature, and mutual affection of the family, as well as by the kindness ... shown to himself' (ibid.) and the poem 'O thou dread power' was the immediate outcome. The visit also promoted the song 'The Night was Still', which Burns gave to Louisa Lawrie, and a window-inscription, 'Lovely Mrs. Lawrie, she is all charms'. Early in November Burns again visited the Lawries, and in discussion of a local scandal made a remark to which Mrs Lawrie took exception. By way of apology, he sent, along with a volume of songs and a copy of the Poems of Ossian, the poem 'Rusticity's Ungainly Form'; in the accompanying letter to Archibald he alludes to the Lawrie family as offering 'one of the sweetest scenes of domestic Peace and kindred Love that ever I saw' (Letters, 61). Learning that Burns had been some time in Edinburgh (he arrived on 28 November 1786), Blacklock regretted, in a letter to Lawrie of 11–12 December, that the poet had not visited him. On 22 December Lawrie advised Burns to 'lose no time in waiting upon [Blacklock]' (Life and Works, 2.42). Alert to the reproof and conscious of his delay in replying, Burns wrote to Lawrie on 5 February 1787: 'I feel, and ever shall feel for you the mingled sentiments of esteem for a friend & reverence for a father' (Letters, 1.88). In 1791 Lawrie received a doctor of divinity degree from the University of Glasgow. He contributed the account of Loudoun in Sir John Sinclair's Statistical Account of Scotland (1791–9), his only known publication. He died on 17 October 1799 at Loudoun manse, Newmilns, Ayrshire, and was buried in the local kirkyard. Lawrie was survived by his wife, who died on 23 January 1818.   KENNETH SIMPSON

Sources The poems and songs of Robert Burns, ed. J. Kinsley, 3 vols. (1968) · The letters of Robert Burns, ed. J. de Lancey Ferguson, 2nd edn, ed. G. Ross Roy, 2 vols. (1985), vol. 1 · The life and works of Robert Burns, ed. R. Chambers, rev. W. Wallace, [new edn], 4 vols. (1896), vols. 1–2 · C. Rogers, The book of Robert Burns: genealogical and historical memoirs of the poet, his associates and those celebrated in his writings, 3 vols. (1889–91), vol. 2 · Fasti Scot., new edn, vol. 3 · parish register, Kirkmichael [birth, baptism] · parish register, Loudoun · H. G. Graham, Scottish men of letters in the eighteenth century (1908) · F. B. Snyder, The life of Robert Burns (1932) · C. Carswell, The life of Robert Burns (1930) · M. Lindsay, The Burns encyclopedia, 2nd edn (1970) · A. M. Boyle, The Ayrshire book of Burns-lore, 2nd edn (1996) · [J. Walker], Account of the life and character of Robert Burns (1811) · J. A. Mackay, R. B.: a biography of Robert Burns (1992) · matriculation albums, U. Edin. L., special collections division, university archives · Yale U., Yale MSS C 1869–72

Lawrie, William (fl. 1645–1699), estate steward, appears to have belonged to the family of Lawrie of Auchinheath, in Lesmahagow parish, Lanarkshire. By 1645 he had married Marion Weir, heiress of Blackwood, and the couple had a son called George, who became heir to the Blackwood estate on the death of his cousin, while he was still an infant. Lawrie therefore became tutor or guardian to his son, managing his estate until he attained his majority in 1666. When the son died in March 1680, leaving a minor son himself, Lawrie was tutor to this boy as well. Because of this, he was generally known as the Tutor, or, inaccurately, the Laird, of Blackwood.

Lawrie was a member of the committee for war for Lanarkshire in 1648 and 1649. After the Restoration he was for some reason excluded from the Act of Indemnity of 1662 until he had paid a fine of £600 Scots. In 1666, Lawrie, who apparently had covenanting sympathies, was involved in the abortive Pentland rising. He took a letter explaining the views and wishes of the covenanters to the privy council in Edinburgh, which, unimpressed either by the letter or its bearer, had Lawrie imprisoned in Edinburgh Castle. He was, however, released in 1667.

On 14 March 1670 Lawrie was appointed chamberlain on the estates of James Douglas, second marquess of Douglas, over whom he soon acquired a powerful influence. He may have been involved in the estrangement of the marquess from his wife, Lady Barbara Erskine, and appears in the Scottish ballad 'The Marchioness of Douglas' as 'fause Blackwood', who causes trouble between the marchioness and her husband (Mackay, 191). In the ballad, Lawrie is hanged for his wickedness and the marquess reconciled to his wife, but this is unhistorical.

In the 1680s Lawrie again fell foul of the law. On 22 November 1682 he was charged before the council for allowing covenanting tenants, who may have been involved in the Bothwell Brig uprising of 1679, to live on the Blackwood lands without reporting them to the authorities. On 31 January 1683 his case came to the criminal court, and on 7 February 1683 he was sentenced to be beheaded at the market cross in Edinburgh. He was spared death as a result of a petition by the marquess of Douglas, who based his appeal on the grounds that he needed Lawrie's services, as only Lawrie understood the affairs of his estates. Lawrie was reprieved on 12 January 1684, but remained in prison until the revolution of 1688. After his release he was included in a general act rescinding all fines and forfeitures imposed since 1685. In addition, a special act was passed, declaring his conviction in 1683 null and void. In 1690 he was named a commissioner of militia and supply.

Lawrie ended his life in trouble due to his mismanagement of the Douglas estates. By 1681 he had already reduced them to such a state that he suggested the marquess sell lands at Abernethy and Forfarshire to repair the damage. At one time he allowed the marquess's coach horses to be seized and publicly sold rather than pay an Edinburgh tradesman. Even Charles II became worried about the condition of the Douglas estates, and repeatedly asked for information about them. Lawrie's influence over the marquess was so strong, however, that the marquess refused to listen to any advice about better management from friends or family. In the late 1690s Douglas's second wife, Lady Mary Ker, appealed to her father the earl of Lothian for help, and the marquess was pressurized into allowing a commission including the duke of Queensberry and the earl of Argyll to supervise his affairs.

When this commission saw the full extent of the ruin Lawrie had caused, they dismissed him as chamberlain. In 1699 the marquess, having turned against Lawrie, requested that he be prosecuted. Lawrie, by this time an old man, probably died soon afterwards. ALEXANDER DU TOIT

Sources W. Fraser, ed., *The Douglas book*, 4 vols. (1885), vol. 2, pp. 450–51, 455–8; vol. 4, pp. 273–88 · J. B. Greenshields, *Annals of the parish of Lesmahagow* (1864), 85–90 · R. Wodrow, *The history of the sufferings of the Church of Scotland from the Restoration to the revolution*, ed. R. Burns, 2 (1829), 26, 29, 271–2; 3 (1829), 449–52 · G. V. Irving and A. Murray, *The upper ward of Lanarkshire described and delineated*, 2 (1864), 208–9 · J. Kirkton, *The secret and true history of the Church of Scotland*, ed. C. K. Sharpe (1817), 239 · J. Lauder, *The decisions of lords of council and session, from June 6th, 1678 to July 30th, 1712* (1759), 196, 213–15 · C. Mackay, ed., *The legendary and romantic ballads of Scotland* (1861), 189–94
Archives NL Scot., Douglas papers

Laws, John (1765–1844). *See under* Bewick, Thomas, apprentices (*act.* 1777–1828).

Laws, Robert (1851–1934), missionary, was born on 28 May 1851 in Mannofield, Aberdeen, the only son of Robert Laws (1818–1898), a cabinet-maker, and his first wife, Christian (1829–1853), daughter of Alexander Cruikshank, a small farmer of Kidshill in Buchan. Laws went to live with his maternal grandparents after his mother's death in 1853. He returned home in 1856, to 48 Summer Street, Aberdeen, where his father was by then remarried; his new wife was Isabella Cormack. At the age of twelve Laws left school and trained as a cabinet-maker. His family were devout members of St Nicholas Lane United Presbyterian Church, and it was there that Laws first met his future wife, Margaret Troup Gray (1849–1921).

Laws was fifteen when he felt called to be a missionary, and he decided to train as both a minister and a doctor. He studied at night to gain university entrance and began his arts course at Aberdeen in 1868. This qualified him to begin, in 1872, both the medical and theological courses simultaneously. Like many poor students he had to support himself, and he worked part-time with the Glasgow city mission to the fever hospital (he felt free to take the risk since he had already had smallpox). This long, arduous experience marked his character, teaching him that utter dedication in pursuing a goal which appeared in the eyes of those who disagreed with him as autocratic ruthlessness.

It was at this busy time that Laws heard of the two projected missions in honour of David Livingstone to eastern central Africa (later Nyasaland and then Malawi), one by the Free Church of Scotland and the other by the Church of Scotland. Laws's denomination, the third largest of the three main presbyterian churches in Scotland, was not involved. After some negotiation he found that the Free Church was willing to take him, and that his family would let him go. Thus 1875 was an *annus mirabilis* for Laws: he graduated in medicine, was licensed and ordained by the United Presbyterian church, was appointed second in command of the Livingstonia Mission, and became engaged to Margaret Gray, whom he eventually married at Blantyre, Nyasa, on 28 August 1879. The mission which he

was to lead from 1877 until his retirement left for Africa with a small steamboat, which arrived at Lake Nyasa on 12 October 1875. The missionaries' first base was at Cape Maclear at the south end of the lake, but they finally settled at Bandawe, 160 miles to the north. There they began contacting the various peoples of what became Northern Rhodesia and Nyasaland through a growing network of mission stations and village schools. It was there in 1886 that Robert and Margaret's only child, Amelia Nyasa, was baptized in 1886.

In Laws's view, education was central to the task of creating an African Christian church, because Africa was being drawn into the modern world and African Christians had to be prepared to play their part in it. This led Laws to create the Overtoun Institution on Khondowe Mountain, overtowering the lake shore at Florence Bay, where he developed a technical college, a teacher training college, a theological school, and a hospital. This complex, lit by its electricity generator and having its own piped water supply, was very much Laws's own creation and some other missionaries saw it as a threat to the general outreach of the mission because it drew so many resources of money and talent to itself. Under Laws's leadership the mission helped to bring into being an African church which joined with the congregations produced by the Church of Scotland mission in the south, to form the Church of Central Africa Presbyterian in 1901. Also under his leadership, and often his personal tutoring as well, a series of distinguished local people emerged to play a leading role in the development of Christianity in Nyasaland and Northern Rhodesia as well as the development of nationalism in both countries. The careers of Levi Mumba (first vice-president of the Nyasaland African National Congress), Charles Chinula, Clement Kadalie (president of the first effective black trade union in South Africa), Yesaya Chibambo, Y. Z. Mwasi, David Kaunda (father of Kenneth, the first president of Zambia), and many others, highlighted Laws's weaknesses as well as his strengths. He cultivated men with enquiring minds and leadership qualities, yet he was slow to promote them and so a number of his most brilliant protégés left to lead independent Christian movements. British patriot that he was, he was made CMG in 1923. But it was also Laws who encouraged the development of the native associations which were to form the Nyasaland African National Congress in 1944, and who used his influence with the governor to prevent them being proscribed in 1920. Although Laws did not possess any deep empathy for African traditional culture, he nevertheless supported the initiative of others which produced in northern Nyasaland the richest indigenous African Christian hymnody of the twentieth century.

With many honours, including the degrees of DD from Aberdeen (1891) and LLD from Cape Town (1925), as well as being made a freeman of his native city, Laws retired in 1927 very much against his will. He returned to Edinburgh, where he lived with his daughter, and continued to serve the now United Free Church of Scotland, the moderator of whose general assembly he had been in 1908, by speaking and writing about mission. He died on a visit to London on 6 August 1934 and was buried, on 10 August, in St Machar's churchyard, Aberdeen.

ANDREW C. ROSS

Sources *Aurora* [magazine of the Livingstonia Mission] (1897–1902) · *Livingstonia News* [magazine published by the Livingstonia Mission] (1903–12) · R. Laws, *Reminiscences of Livingstonia* (1934) · J. McCracken, *Politics and Christianity in Malawi, 1875–1940* (1977) · J. McCracken, 'Livingstonia in the development of Malawi: a reassessment', *Bulletin of the Scottish Institute of Missionary Studies*, 10 (1994), 3–13 · W. P. Livingstone, *Laws of Livingstonia* (1921) · H. McIntosh, *Robert Laws: servant of Africa* (1993) · D. Fraser, 'Dr Robert Laws of Livingstonia: a tribute and an appreciation', *Bulletin of the Scottish Institute of Missionary Studies*, 10 (1994), 56–8 · m. cert. · J. A. Lamb, ed., *The fasti of the United Free Church of Scotland, 1900–1929* (1956), 562

Archives NL Scot., letters to Alexander Gill · U. Aberdeen, Special Libraries and Archives, papers · U. Edin. L., journal and material relating to the mission at Livingstonia · U. Edin. L., notebooks and papers relating to Livingstonia mission · Wellcome L., list of medical stores at Livingstonia mission | NL Scot., letter-books of the secretaries of the foreign missions committee of the Free Church of Scotland · NL Scot., letters to Alexander Gill · NL Scot., letter-book of the secretary of Livingstonia committee · U. Edin. L., Macalpine MSS

Likenesses W. B. Fagan, bronze plaque, c.1936, Overtoun Institution, Khondowe, Malawi · plaster cast, 1936 (after bronze plaque by W. B. Fagan, c.1936), Christ's College, Aberdeen

Lawson, Adam Mansfeldt de Cardonnel- [*formerly* Adam Cardonnel] (1746/7–1820), antiquary, was born Adam Cardonnel; he was a great-nephew of Adam de Cardonnel, secretary to the duke of Marlborough, and the sole surviving son of Mansfeldt de Cardonnel (1696/7–1780), of Musselburgh, a commissioner of the customs and salt duties in Scotland, and his wife, Anne, the daughter and heir of Thomas Hilton of Low Ford, co. Durham. After being educated for the medical profession he practised for a while in Edinburgh as a surgeon, but his easy circumstances left him leisure to indulge his interest in the study of antiquities and numismatics. Upon the institution of the Society of Antiquaries of Scotland, under the presidency of the earl of Bute, in December 1780, Cardonnel was elected a fellow; he also served as curator from 1782 to 1784, and contributed to the second volume of the *Archaeologia Scotica* (1.159–67), 'A description of certain Roman ruins discovered at Inveresk'. He also produced *Numismata Scotiae, or, A Series of Scottish Coinage* (1786), which he illustrated himself. Although it was largely derived from Thomas Snelling's *View of the Silver Coin and Coinage of Scotland* (1774), it contained some interesting historical material and was regarded as generally accurate. Cardonnel also published, in four parts, *Picturesque Antiquities of Scotland* (1788–93), etched by himself; a second edition in one volume was published in 1802.

When Francis Grose visited Scotland, Cardonnel, who then resided at Edinburgh, assisted his brother antiquary with notes from his extensive collections, besides accompanying him on various archaeological expeditions, attentions that Grose acknowledged in the introduction to his *Antiquities of Scotland*. In the autumn of 1789 Burns addressed a letter to Grose, under cover to Cardonnel at Edinburgh. While in the act of folding it up the quaint old song of 'Sir John Malcolm' ran through his mind, and he inscribed within the wrapper his well-known impromptu 'Ken ye ought o' Captain Grose?' (J. Kinsley, ed., *Poems and Songs*, 1968, 564).

Soon after this Cardonnel left Scotland, having in 1791 succeeded (it was said, though entirely without foundation, by the failure of fourteen families whimsically listed in the entail) to the estates of his second cousin Hilton Lawson (d. 1768) at Chirton and West Cramlington in Northumberland. He assumed additional names and in 1798 served as sheriff for the county. In 1811, on the opening of Burdon Main mine on the estate, Chirton House was demolished, and he went to live at Cramlington. His latter days were chiefly spent at Bath.

Cardonnel had married Mary (d. 1830), daughter of General James Kidd, and had two sons and two daughters. He died in June 1820, aged seventy-three, and was buried at Cramlington on 14 June. His elder son, bearing the same names, was an officer of the 21st light dragoons; by his death on 21 November 1838 at Acton House, Acklington, Northumberland, without children, the family became extinct in the male line.

GORDON GOODWIN, *rev.* ALAN BELL

Sources *A history of Northumberland*, Northumberland County History Committee, 15 vols. (1893–1940), vol. 8. p. 323 [incl. genealogical tree], vol. 13, pp. 388–9 · R. W. Cochran-Patrick, *Records of the coinage of Scotland*, 2 vols. (1876) · *Autobiography of the Rev. Dr. Alexander Carlyle … containing memorials of the men and events of his time*, ed. J. H. Burton (1860); repr. as *Anecdotes and characters of the times*, ed. J. Kinsley (1973), 112–13, 212

Archives Museum of Scotland, Edinburgh, Society of Antiquaries of Scotland MSS

Lawson, Cecil Gordon (1851–1882), landscape painter, fifth and younger son of the Scottish portrait painter William Lawson (*fl.* 1819–1864), was born at Wellington, Shropshire, on 3 December 1851. Among his siblings were Malcolm Lawson, who became a composer and musician; Francis Wilfrid Lawson (1842–1935), who was an illustrator working for *Cornhill Magazine* and *Once a Week* and an occasional painter; and Kate, a person of artistic sympathy to whom Cecil was especially attached. When Cecil Lawson was ten years old his family settled in London, because his father sought to establish a professional practice in the capital. The Lawsons lived first in Doughty Street, Holborn, later moving to Oakley Street, Chelsea, and finally settling in Carlton House, an eighteenth-century mansion overlooking the river on Cheyne Walk.

Cecil Gordon Lawson learned to paint at home, following the example of his father and brother. Record survives of his making a copy of Clarkson Stanfield's *Dutch Mill* and of painting portraits of neighbours. He also painted stage sets for operas and plays devised for home production by his brother Malcolm; one of these shows was apparently attended by the artist and illustrator George John Pinwell. Landscape and nature were, however, the principal sources of his inspiration, as Edmund Gosse recalled:

> When he was twelve years old he had taken his education into his own hands, and had already adopted a style of training which was justified by its success. He would steal quietly away, with his palette and his colour-box, in the early

morning, march up to Hampstead, and spend the whole day making studies. He would come home in the evening with half-a-dozen scraps, effects of cloud, foliage against the sky, six inches square of vegetation under the hollow of the hedge, [or] two or three stones with the moss creeping over them. (Gosse, 10)

The painter and illustrator Fred Walker encouraged Lawson to make 'minute and careful studies of fruit and flowers, bits of landscape—foreground highly finished, and portraits of special clouds and leaves and blossoms' (ibid., 11). In 1866 Lawson made a painting tour of Kent, Surrey, and Sussex in the company of his brother Malcolm. In 1869 he devoted himself to the study of Dutch seventeenth-century landscape, copying paintings in the National Gallery. Lawson was familiar with the work of contemporary illustrators, notable among which group were Pinwell and Walker, but also J. E. Millais, A. B. Houghton, and William Small. Between 1870 and 1873 he himself made designs for illustrations, for example for the magazine *Dark Blue*, a design entitled *Spring*.

In 1869 two paintings by Lawson were rejected by the Royal Academy, but in 1870 his *Cheyne Walk, Chelsea* (ex Christies, London, 1 June 1984)—an autumnal view of the river from Carlton House with figures including that of Thomas Carlyle—was admitted. Two further Chelsea riverfront subjects appeared at the academy in 1871, and were displayed to advantage, discussed and admired, and sold. *The River in Rain* was latched upon by Fred Walker, who expounded its merits to fellow members of the academy. The following year Lawson was less fortunate: his large upright composition *A Hymn to Spring* (Santa Barbara Museum of Art, California), which was a reworking of his previous design for *Dark Blue*, was rejected, while *A Lament*, a painting which expressed regret 'for the old order of things. In this the piles of the new works [connected with the embankment of the Thames] are being driven in; a steamer passes out in the river' (Gosse, 16), was skied and ignored. This was notwithstanding the fact that Millais had applied a dab of red to the smoke emerging from the steamer's funnel. Lawson must have looked for alternative exhibition spaces, and his works did appear in both the displays of watercolour and cabinet pictures at the New British Institution, which was established in 1870.

In 1874 two further pictures—*The Bell Inn* and *The Foundry*—were rejected by the academy, despite being painted in a deliberately unchallenging style after the furore associated with *The Hymn to Spring*, and described later by Gosse as 'elegant and accomplished works' (Gosse, 22). In 1876 Lawson's *The Hop Gardens of England* (ex Christies, London, 19 May 1978), for which he had great hopes and which had in fact been submitted to the academy the previous year and rejected, was accepted (on the recommendation it was said of Frederic Leighton), finding a place on the walls of the Great Room at Burlington House in uncomfortable proximity to Charles West Cope's group portrait of the academy council.

Lawson was clearly dissatisfied with the Royal Academy as an outlet for his works. In 1876–7 three of his paintings, including *A Pastoral—Trafalgar Square, Chelsea*, appeared in an exhibition at Deschamps' Gallery, London. Although he was not represented in the opening summer exhibition at the Grosvenor Gallery in 1877, the following year three works of his—including *In the Minister's Garden* (Manchester City Galleries)—were shown in pride of place in the west gallery and caused a sensation. In 1879 Sir Coutts Lindsay ignored the usual restriction on works that had already been seen at (or rejected by) the Royal Academy, and accepted *The Hop Gardens of England* (retitled *Kent* for the occasion), one of no fewer than seven Lawson paintings at the Grosvenor that year. In the 1880 Grosvenor exhibition he showed his masterpiece *The August Moon* (Tate collection), described by Gosse as 'the most audacious composition which he has attempted' and in which the artist sought (in his own words) 'to produce the effect of the autumn golden moon rising over an English landscape before the daylight has quite disappeared and the moon has asserted her full power' (Gosse, 34). Between 1878 and 1882, the year of his death, Lawson showed eighteen works at the Grosvenor, while in the winter of 1882–3 a memorial exhibition of 108 of his works was shown there. It was Joseph Comyns Carr, a director of the Grosvenor Gallery, who took up Lawson's cause, and who drew Coutts Lindsay's attention to his landscapes. Carr later wrote fondly of Lawson in a postscript to Gosse's memoir, and in his own reminiscences, *Some Eminent Victorians* (1908). It was as a result of the annual exhibitions of the Grosvenor Gallery that Lawson came to public notice and gained a circle of patrons and admirers.

Lawson made occasional painting expeditions. In 1873 he went to Ireland where he painted a work entitled *Twilight Grey* in which is reflected the contemporary landscape work of Whistler and the influence of Japanese art. The following year he explored the Low Countries and France, staying for a while in Paris. In 1874 he settled in the countryside at Wrotham in Kent, the landscape of which was the inspiration for *The Hop Gardens of England*. Of this painting the *Art Journal* recorded, 'we look over miles of lovely hop country, the red-tiled farmhouses on the hillside foreground being almost embowered in the yellow greenery of the abounding plant. The treatment is at once original and truthful' (*Art Journal*, 1876, 231). In 1879 Lawson married Constance (*fl.* 1874–1892), daughter of the sculptor John Birnie Philip and sister of Beatrice, the wife of first E. W. Godwin and later James Whistler. Constance Lawson was a specialist flower painter who exhibited at the Royal Academy between 1874 and 1892 and at the Grosvenor Gallery between 1882 and 1889. After a honeymoon in Switzerland, the couple settled at Haslemere in Surrey. *The August Moon*, of 1880, was painted at Blackdown Hill near by, while *The Voice of the Cuckoo*, its pendant at the 1880 Grosvenor, was likewise completed in the Surrey countryside. In the autumn of 1880 he stayed in Yorkshire with his patron Henry Mason, and among his exhibits the following year were a number of Yorkshire views—*In the Valley of Desolation, Yorkshire* and *Wharfedale* (ex Christies, 7 May 1982)—at the Grosvenor, and another—*Barden Moor*—at the Royal Academy.

From about 1880 Lawson's health began to break down.

In 1881–2 he travelled to the Mediterranean in search of a beneficial climate. *On the Road to Monaco from Mentone, January 1882*, shown at the 1882 Grosvenor, resulted from the trip. Back in England, however, Lawson suffered a relapse. He stayed for a while at Eastbourne and then sought medical attention in London. He died on 10 June 1882 at 9 Redcliffe Street, South Kensington, aged thirty, of infection of the windpipe and inflammation of the lungs. He was buried at Haslemere. Shortly before his death a son was born to Constance and Cecil Lawson.

Later in 1883 Edmund Gosse's memoir of the artist, illustrated with etchings after Lawson's paintings by Herkomer and Whistler, was published by the Fine Art Society. In a notice in the *Art Journal* it was stated that 'Lawson's pictures may not be popular yet, but this is because they are comparatively little known. As time goes on his power will assuredly be more widely acknowledged' (*Art Journal*, 1884, 132). Carr, in his valedictory essay on his friend's art, concluded:

> There was in all his work from first to last the essential secret of beauty in landscape—the sense of a certain poetry imprisoned in nature which it was the artist's business to set free … He brought to every scene the eager faith of a poet, and he knew how to bring the facts it contained into subjection to a poet's vision.　(Gosse, 37)

The view that Lawson was one of the most original and progressive landscape painters of the day, and that his tragic early death represented a great loss to English art, was repeated by critics and fellow artists in the years up to the turn of the century.　　　　　　　　CHRISTOPHER NEWALL

Sources E. W. Gosse, *Cecil Lawson: a memoir* (1883) · H. Owen, 'In memoriam: Cecil Gordon Lawson', *Magazine of Art*, 17 (1893–4), 1–6, 64–70 · Bryan, *Painters* (1903–5), 3.189 · *Art Journal*, new ser., 2 (1882), 223–4 · *Art Journal*, new ser., 29 (1909), 102 · *DNB* · *The Times* (13 June 1882), 10 · *The Athenaeum* (17 June 1882), 770–71 · J. C. Carr, *Some eminent Victorians: personal recollections in the world of art and letters* (1908), 143–5 · A. Staley, 'Art is upon the town!', *The Grosvenor Gallery: a palace of art in Victorian England* (1996), 59–74 [exhibition catalogue, Yale U. CBA] · d. cert.

Archives Chelsea Library, London, scrapbooks of drawings, sketches, newpapers cuttings, etc.

Likenesses H. von Herkomer, pencil drawing, 1877, NPG · H. von Herkomer, watercolour drawing, 1877, NPG · H. von Herkomer, photogravure photograph, NPG · F. Lawson, pencil drawing, NPG

Wealth at death £2576 0s. 6d.: probate, 22 July 1882, *CGPLA Eng. & Wales*

Lawson [*née* Constable], **Dorothy** (1580–1632), recusant and priest harbourer, was born at Wing, Buckinghamshire, the second daughter of Sir Henry Constable (*d.* 1607) of Burton Constable, Holderness, Yorkshire, and his wife, Margaret, daughter of Sir Robert Dormer of Wing, Buckinghamshire. She was raised as a pious Roman Catholic by her mother, who had spent time in prison for her recusancy. In 1597, aged seventeen, Dorothy married Roger (1570/71–1613/14), eldest son of Sir Ralph Lawson of Brough in Yorkshire. Initially they lived with Roger's parents at Brough, but in 1605 their increasing family necessitated the establishment of their own household at Heaton Hall, Northumberland. The exact number of children they had is unknown. There were at least fourteen: Ralph (*d.* 1612), Dorothy (1600–1628), Henry (*c.*1601–1636), George

(baptized 1605), Margaret (*fl.* 1607–1650), John (baptized 1608), Mary (*fl.* 1609–1672), Roger, Thomas, Edmund (*d.* 1642/3), James, Catherine (*d.* 1637), Anne, and Elizabeth. The Lawsons remained at Heaton until the untimely death of Roger in 1613 or 1614. In 1616 Sir Ralph sold the manor and Dorothy moved her household to St Antony's, overlooking the Tyne, where she built a house more suited to her domestic and religious requirements.

When Dorothy and Roger were married the Lawsons of Brough conformed to the Church of England, although Roger's mother, Elizabeth, had been listed as a recusant in 1592–3 and imprisoned for her nonconformity. Raised in a household with a resident chaplain, Dorothy was determined to have access to the Catholic sacraments in her new home. Within a few weeks of her arrival at Brough she had contacted Richard Holtby, a Jesuit working in northern England, and secured monthly visits by a priest. Within a short time Lady Lawson and all her children, with the exception of Roger, had returned to recusancy. Roger, the heir, apparently joked that 'his family was become Papists ere he perceived it' (Palmes, 17). He spent considerable time away from home practising law in London, and did not succumb to his wife's missionary influence until upon his deathbed. Dorothy did not restrict her proselytizing to her relations. According to her chaplain and biographer William Palmes she had converted the entire neighbourhood bordering Heaton and St Antony's by her death, and was renowned throughout the district for her charity, religious zeal, and the physical and spiritual comfort she offered women in childbirth.

Dorothy Lawson's uncompromising support for the Society of Jesus led her to devote her household at St Antony's to their needs. She supported a succession of Jesuit chaplains, including Palmes. Yet despite her overt recusancy and her patronage of the Jesuits, Dorothy apparently escaped official censure. Her name is absent from recusancy lists, her house was never searched, and she was neither imprisoned nor fined. Moreover, her biographer claimed that her nocturnal Catholic burial, held on 27 March 1632, the day after her death of consumption at St Antony's, was conducted at All Saints' Church, Newcastle, under the eyes of the town's civic officers, who did nothing to prevent it. Her remarkable immunity is most likely attributable to the sympathy of local officials who, if they did not have recusant kin themselves, were of the close-knit circle of Northumberland gentry. She also had powerful relatives who might have intervened on her behalf. Her uncle was created Baron Dormer in 1615, and her brother Henry *Constable (*d.* 1645) curried favour at court after purchasing his peerage in 1620. These circumstances, and her independent status as a widow, allowed Dorothy the freedom to pursue her religious activities without fear of endangering a husband's career or property.

Dorothy Lawson offers an excellent example of the way women were well suited to preserving and extending nonconformity in the sixteenth and seventeenth centuries. They were expected to be pious and to uphold religious practices within the domestic realm, but the further expectation of charitable assistance to their neighbours enabled them to proselytize. Lawson baptized infants in danger of miscarrying at their birth, and provided catechism for local children on feast days. Her healing skills offered a further medium through which she could persuade people of the veracity of Catholicism. As a mother she raised her children in her faith. Some of them entered religious institutions abroad. Ralph, the heir, died at school in Douai. Her daughter Dorothy was professed an Augustinian canoness at Louvain in 1618. Margaret (Dame Gertrude) and Mary (Dame Benedicta) became Benedictines at Ghent in 1626 and 1631. Others married into Catholic families and imparted the same religious principles to their offspring. Several generations of Lawsons were indicted for recusancy and became nuns and priests. Moreover, Dorothy's life, which was immortalized in the annals of her children's religious communities and in William Palmes's biography, provided subsequent generations with an exemplary model of female piety and missionary zeal. CLAIRE WALKER

Sources W. Palmes, *Life of Mrs Dorothy Lawson of St Antony's near Newcastle-upon-Tyne in Northumberland*, ed. G. B. Richardson (1851) · *A history of Northumberland*, Northumberland County History Committee, 15 vols. (1893–1940), vol. 13, pp. 392–5 · A. Hamilton, ed., *The chronicle of the English Augustinian canonesses regular of the Lateran*, 1 (1904), 175–9, 189–90, 205–6 · A. Hamilton, ed., *The chronicle of the English Augustinian canonesses regular of the Lateran*, 2 (1906), 65 · *Annals of the English Benedictines at Ghent, now at St Mary's Abbey, Oulton in Staffordshire* (privately printed, [1894]) · J. D. Hanlon, 'These be but women', *From the Renaissance to the Counter-Reformation*, ed. C. C. M. Carter (1976), 371–400 · Gillow, *Lit. biog. hist.*, 4.161–5 · P. Caraman, *Henry Morse: priest of the plague* (1957), 32–53 · M. M. C. Calthrop, ed., *Recusant roll no. 1, 1592–3*, Catholic RS, 18 (1916), 98–9 · R. Connelly, *The women of the Catholic resistance in England, 1540–1680* (1997), 184–90 · GEC, *Peerage*
Wealth at death see Palmes, *Life*, 9, 16–17; Hanlon, 'These be but women', 376

Lawson, Edward Frederick, fourth Baron Burnham (1890–1963), newspaper manager and army officer, was born on 16 June 1890 at 9 Upper Grosvenor Street, Mayfair, London, the elder son of William Arnold Webster Levy-Lawson, third Baron Burnham (1864–1943), soldier, and his wife, Sybil Mary (d. 1933), daughter of Lieutenant-General Sir Frederick Marshall. He was educated at Eton College and Balliol College, Oxford, where he obtained a third-class degree in modern history in 1913 and played polo for the university.

His two careers ran in parallel. On leaving Oxford he joined the family business, the *Daily Telegraph*, first as a reporter in Paris, then in New York. But he returned from New York on the outbreak of war in 1914 and joined his father's former regiment, the Royal Buckinghamshire hussars, into which he had already been commissioned. In 1915 the regiment was sent to the Middle East, where he acted as landing officer at Gallipoli and took part in the Palestine campaigns and Lord Allenby's entry into Jerusalem. At the age of twenty-six he was appointed commander of the Middlesex yeomanry. He was awarded the DSO and the MC and mentioned three times in dispatches. In 1920 he married Marie Enid (d. 1979), daughter of Hugh

Scott Robson, of London and Buenos Aires. They had two sons and a daughter.

After the war Lawson rejoined the *Daily Telegraph*, under the proprietorship of his uncle Harry Lawson Webster Levy-*Lawson, Viscount Burnham (1862–1933). Popularly known in the office as 'the Colonel' (Hartwell, 154), he became in effect his uncle's second in command. This was one of the least successful periods in the paper's history, with sales dropping from 180,000 in 1920 to 84,000 at the end of 1927 as it failed to compete effectively with the *Daily Mail* and *The Times*. Lord Burnham lacked the financial resources and, given weighty public service commitments, the time and energy to be an effective proprietor in a highly competitive market and in 1927 decided to sell the *Telegraph* to the Berry brothers and Sir Edward Illiffe. Lawson was angered and disappointed by the sale: 'he felt strongly that, given the chance, he could have raised the necessary funds through friends and given the paper new life himself' (Hart-Davis, 55). That opinion was shared by Sir William Berry, who believed that 'If he had succeeded to control instead of his uncle, I doubt very much if the *Telegraph* would have reached the position where a sale was desirable or necessary' (Griffiths, 362). Camrose appointed him general manager. Lawson joked that this was because he was reputed to be the only person capable of finding his way around the labyrinthine *Telegraph* offices (Hart-Davis, 59). Camrose's son recalled that he was so impressed by Lawson's grasp of the business that he made the appointment a condition of the sale going through (Hartwell, 155).

Lawson's tasks during the succeeding decade, as sales of the *Telegraph* grew spectacularly—particularly after the November 1930 price cut from 2*d*. to 1*d*., a move Lawson had been advocating for some time—included supervising the installation of new production plant in 1929 and acting as go-between in the negotiations which led to the takeover by the *Telegraph* of the *Morning Post* in 1937.

Colin Coote, editor of the *Telegraph* from 1950, recalled Lawson's 'compound of wisdom, kindness and courage' (Coote, 228), while the paper's obituarist noted his 'diffident, almost self-effacing demeanour' and described him as a 'tactful negotiator of the front rank' (*Daily Telegraph*). Lawson displayed these qualities in twenty-five years (1934–59) as chair of the Newspaper Publishers' Association's labour committee, although his conciliatory attitude to trade unions was not universally popular. Cecil King of the *Daily Mirror* felt that 'though a pleasant social figure he was a major disaster for the industry' and accused him of being supine in the face of union general secretaries (Wintour, 38).

Lawson maintained his interest in the army during peacetime, helping to transform the Royal Buckinghamshire hussars from cavalry to artillery and then to merge them with the Berkshire yeomanry to become the 99th (Buckinghamshire and Berkshire) field brigade Royal Artillery, which he commanded from 1929 to 1933. In 1938, unusually for a non-regular officer in peacetime, he was appointed commander of the Royal Artillery 48th (South Midland) division with the rank of brigadier. In this capacity he was sent to France with the British forces after the outbreak of the war and was created CB for his work as the perimeter officer at Dunkirk. He was promoted to major-general in 1941, but in the following year was appointed simultaneously to two posts that made use of his military and journalistic expertise—senior military representative at the Ministry of Information and director of public relations at the War Office.

Lawson held these posts until the end of the war in 1945, when he returned to the *Telegraph*, where he was appointed managing director. As Lord Burnham—he had succeeded his father as fourth baron in 1943—he remained in the post until his retirement in 1961. In 1955 he wrote the paper's centenary history, *Peterborough Court*. He was an expert crossword solver and a senior freemason: he became provincial grandmaster of the Buckinghamshire masons in 1946. Many of his other outside interests reflected his role after 1943 as the owner of a 6000 acre Buckinghamshire estate. A racehorse owner, he hunted with the Whaddon chase and shot over his own estates. His wife was president of the Girl Guides' Association of England (1961–70) and of the Buckinghamshire Red Cross. She was appointed CBE in 1957.

Lord Burnham died in the Middlesex Hospital, London, on 4 July 1963 and was succeeded as the fifth baron by his son William Edward Harry Lawson.   HUW RICHARDS

Edward Levy-Lawson, first Baron Burnham (1833–1916), by Elliott & Fry

Sources D. Hart-Davis, *The house the Berrys built: inside the 'Telegraph', 1928–1986* (1990) · Lord Burnham [E. F. L. Burnham], *Peterborough Court: the story of the Daily Telegraph* (1955) · Lord Hartwell, *William Camrose: giant of Fleet Street* (1992) · *The Times* (5 July 1963) · *Daily Telegraph* (5 July 1963) · C. Coote, *Editorial* (1965) · C. Wintour, *The rise and fall of Fleet Street* (1989) · S. E. Koss, *The rise and fall of the political press in Britain*, 2 (1984) · *Newspaper World* (27 Nov 1930) · *WWW, 1961–70* · Burke, *Peerage* (1980) · *CGPLA Eng. & Wales* (1963) · *DNB* · b. cert. · D. Griffiths, ed., *The encyclopedia of the British press, 1422–1992* (1992)

Archives NRA, priv. coll., corresp. and papers

Wealth at death £458,120 16s. 11d.: probate, 29 July 1963, *CGPLA Eng. & Wales*

Lawson, Edward Levy-, first Baron Burnham (1833–1916), newspaper proprietor, was born in London on 28 December 1833, the eldest of the eight children of Joseph Moses *Levy (1812–1888), manager of a printing establishment in Shoe Lane, Fleet Street, and his wife, Esther (d. 1883), second daughter of Godfrey Alexander Cohen. Edward Levy assumed the additional surname of Lawson by royal licence in 1875, in consideration of a deed of gift by his father's brother, Lionel Lawson. He was educated at University College School, Gower Street, London, and, on leaving, joined as drama critic the staff of the *Sunday Times*, at that time owned by his father. 'It was in the back office on the ground floor at the corner of Bridge Street,' he told an audience many years later. 'I sometimes, in the intervals of providing copy, had visions of a future, which, with the help of many kind friends, has been happily realized.' In 1855 Joseph Levy acquired the *Daily Telegraph and Courier*, after three months' precarious existence, from its original founder, Colonel Arthur Burrows Sleigh, to pay off a printing debt. The new owner put fresh capital and energy into the business, dropped the second half of the

cumbrous title, gathered round him a vigorous staff (including his son), and turned a losing into a paying property.

In 1860 the *Telegraph* absorbed the *Morning Chronicle*. The moment was exceptionally favourable for new developments in journalism. The possibilities of the electric telegraph, then still a novelty and a wonder, were just beginning to be understood, although it was not until later that the London press made extensive use of the opportunities it provided for the rapid transmission of news. Gladstone's abolition of the last of the paper duties in 1861 cleared the way for the development of the penny press, of which the *Daily Telegraph* was the pioneer in London. Edward Levy undertook his first public work in connection with these paper duties, serving with Richard Cobden and John Bright on the committee whose report finally led to their abolition. He had personal knowledge of almost every department of a newspaper: he could set type; he had 'handled copy'; he could turn a neat paragraph, and dictate a telling leader. His main interest soon focused on politics, and he was much in the lobby of the House of Commons, where he shared with John Thadeus Delane, editor of *The Times*, the special privilege, rarely granted, of standing at the bar of the House of Lords with members of the House of Commons.

On 20 February 1862, in a Church of England ceremony at the parish church, Kennington, Levy married Harriette Georgiana, daughter of the actor Benjamin Nottingham *Webster (1798–1882), and his wife, Elizabeth (d. 1897). They had two sons, Harry Lawson Webster Levy-*Lawson and William Arnold Webster Levy-Lawson, and a daughter, Edith Maude. Levy converted to the Church of England at an unknown date, and died an Anglican.

The dominant idea of those who conducted the *Daily Telegraph* was to break away from the ponderous stiffness of the older journalism, to brighten the paper by a more lively presentation of the news, and to appeal to the sentiment of the reader as well as to chronicle facts. By 1871 the circulation of the *Daily Telegraph* had risen to the then unprecedented figure of 200,000 copies a day, easily replacing *The Times* as the best-selling newspaper in the capital, and by 1888 circulation was 300,000 a day. Edwin Arnold, George Augustus Henry Sala, Edward Litt Laman Blanchard, Thornton Leigh Hunt, Frederick Greenwood, William Beatty Kingston, Campbell Clarke, Joseph Bennett, James Macdonnell, Francis Charles Lawley, and Clement William Scott were among the best-known of those who helped Levy-Lawson to achieve and maintain 'the largest circulation', but none did more than John Merry Le Sage, managing editor for thirty years.

Long before his father's death in 1888 the principal direction of the paper had been in Levy-Lawson's hands; he had indeed been managing proprietor and sole controller since 1885. He was never formally its editor, but he directed the day-to-day content of the paper. A good judge of men, he knew also how to get the best work out of them. His instructions never left a doubt of his meaning; a few sentences scribbled in pencil in a large, round hand on the back of a used envelope would often serve to convey his wishes. For many years he read and passed the proofs of all the principal articles that were to appear in the next morning's issue.

Throughout the 1860s and 1870s the *Daily Telegraph* consistently supported William Ewart Gladstone, whose nickname, 'the People's William', was coined by Lawson. Thornton Leigh Hunt acted as a day-to-day contact. But Lawson was estranged by Gladstone's lack of attention in 1874–5, despite the *Daily Telegraph's* loyal support in the 1874 general election. The paper supported Disraeli's purchase of the Suez Canal shares in 1875, and in 1876 publicly split from Gladstonian Liberalism on the Eastern question on which, like many prominent British Jews, Levy-Lawson supported the Conservative government's attempts to shore up the Turkish empire. Gladstone and Levy-Lawson had an ill-tempered and festering row over the 'Negropontis' affair in 1877 (Gladstone, *Diaries*, vol. 9), and Levy-Lawson was libelled by the radical Henry Labouchere in 1879 over his holdings of Turkish bonds (an episode which even led to fisticuffs in the street between Levy-Lawson and Labouchere). By 1876 Levy-Lawson saw the *Daily Telegraph* as an 'imperial' newspaper (Koss, 1.203). In the 1880 election, he kept lines open to Gladstone, but was strongly unionist in 1886 and subsequently, and by the late 1880s, the *Daily Telegraph* was in effect lost to the Liberals. Gladstone gave Levy-Lawson a baronetcy in October 1892, but it was not enough to win him back.

Levy-Lawson introduced regular theatre criticism and excellent coverage of sport. He used the telegraph system to give a regular service of national as well as metropolitan news. The *Daily Telegraph* became known for its lurid crime reporting; Levy-Lawson's son, Lord Burnham,

thought the paper 'thrived on crime' and 'sometimes overdid it' (Koss, 1.345). Though it made mistakes, the paper avoided the sloppiness that brought *The Times* into disgrace with the Pigott forgery affair in the late 1880s. Levy-Lawson saw the value of associating the *Daily Telegraph* with national charitable appeals and he raised considerable sums of money for charity by this means, especially during the Lancashire cotton 'famine' in the winter of 1862–3, and during the Second South African War, when the paper's fund for widows and orphans of the troops raised and distributed £255,275. Lawson also sponsored exotic expeditions, such as George Smith's archaeological expedition to Assyria in 1873, H. M. Stanley's exploration of the Congo in 1874 (jointly sponsored with the *New York Herald*), and Sir Harry Johnston's journey to Mount Kilimanjaro in 1884.

A gregarious member of the Beefsteak Club and a trustee of the Garrick Club, Levy-Lawson was a well-known Londoner. He was 'a good talker and a good speaker—the utterance large, the style rotund' (*DNB*). He spoke well as president of the Royal Institute of Journalists in 1892–3, and of the Empire Press Union from 1909. But he rarely spoke on public platforms and never in the House of Lords after his peerage. Levy-Lawson retired from day-to-day involvement with his paper in 1903, his son Harry, much more liberal than his father, succeeding him as managing proprietor. A. J. Balfour raised Levy-Lawson to the peerage as the first Baron Burnham, the title being derived from the hundred in which stood his house, Hall Barn, bought in 1881. He made Hall Barn a centre of country pursuits, the prince of Wales (later Edward VII) staying there every year from 1892 to 1910. Burnham was justice of the peace and deputy lieutenant of Buckinghamshire, of which he had been high sheriff in 1886. Burnham died from heart failure at his home, 20 Norfolk Street, London, on 9 January 1916, and was buried next to his wife at Beaconsfield.   H. C. G. MATTHEW

Sources *Daily Telegraph* (10 Jan 1916) · *DNB* · Lord Burnham [E. F. L. Burnham], *Peterborough Court: the story of the Daily Telegraph* (1955) · S. E. Koss, *The rise and fall of the political press in Britain*, 1 (1981) · A. J. Lee, *The origins of the popular press in England, 1855–1914* (1976) · Viscount Camrose [W. E. Berry], *British newspapers and their controllers* (1947) · *Men and women of the time* (1899) · d. cert.
Archives NRA, priv. coll., papers | BL, corresp. with W. E. Gladstone, Add. MSS 44421–44513 · BL, corresp. with Lord Northcliffe, Add. MS 62172
Likenesses M. Beerbohm, caricature, watercolour, ink, and crayon drawing, 1903, NPG · M. Beerbohm, caricature, 1908, Art Institute of Chicago, Illinois · H. von Herkomer, oils, *c*.1910 · M. Beerbohm, caricature, fresco, 1922, U. Texas · M. Beerbohm, caricature, sketch, Merton Oxf. · Elliott & Fry, sepia photograph, NPG [*see illus.*] · H. Furniss, pen-and-ink caricature, NPG · photographs, repro. in Lord Burnham, *Peterborough Court* (1955)
Wealth at death £267,871 4s. 10d.: probate, 2 Dec 1916, *CGPLA Eng. & Wales*

Lawson, Frederick Henry [Harry] (1897–1983), jurist, was born in Leeds on 14 July 1897, the only child of Frederick Henry Lawson, a woollens merchant, and his wife, Mary Louisa Austerberry. Harry (as he was always called) was educated at Leeds grammar school and the Queen's College, Oxford, where he won a Hastings exhibition in classics in 1915. He had always, however, wanted to be a historian and, after commissioned service in an anti-aircraft regiment from 1916 to 1918, he switched to the school of modern history, obtaining first-class honours in 1921. He then took the law school in one year, again with a first (1922), and went on to be called to the bar by Gray's Inn in 1923. He was determined, however, on an academic career and subsisted for some time as a lecturer at various colleges. Merton gave him a junior research fellowship in 1925 and he was encouraged to take up Byzantine law, the study of which took him for a year to Göttingen and in 1929 led to his appointment as university lecturer in the subject (a post he held until 1931). The lasting result of his year in Germany, however, was the turning of his interests towards foreign law and the comparative approach.

In 1930 Lawson finally became established, as a tutorial fellow of Merton. He was a tutor in the old style, teaching almost every subject in the syllabus and concerned with the whole intellectual formation of his pupils. He retained to the end of his life a zest for new ideas and an eagerness to impart them which, coupled with a remarkable range of intellectual interests, made him, for those who could and would keep up with him, a fascinating teacher. In 1933 he married Elspeth (d. 2000?), younger daughter of Alexander Webster, of Kilmarnock, a ship's captain with the Ben Line. They had a son and two daughters.

The principal directions of Lawson's interests reflected his classical and historical backgrounds. While he was a lecturer at University College he had met David Lindsay Keir and their *Cases in Constitutional Law* began its long and influential career in 1928. From 1931 to 1948 he was All Souls reader in Roman law and though, as he himself said, he was never a real Roman law specialist, the subject coloured all his work in private law. What mainly interested him in law was not the detail, but the conceptual structure of the systems of continental civil law and his gift for inspired generalization illuminated not only those systems, as in *A Common Lawyer Looks at the Civil Law* (1955), but also the English common law itself, as in *The Rational Strength of English Law* (1951). Perhaps his best book was *Introduction to the Law of Property* (1958), which, though not ostensibly a work of comparative law, could hardly have been written without his wide reading in other systems. In it he broke away from the traditional historical approach and treated the subject from the point of view of its function in modern life. He gained an Oxford DCL in 1947.

In 1948 Lawson became the first occupant of the chair of comparative law and moved from Merton to Brasenose. He now became a figure on the international stage, his gregarious nature and his unusual gift for foreign languages helping him to establish contact with foreign lawyers. Their high opinion of him was reflected in honorary doctorates from Louvain, Paris, Ghent, and Frankfurt (as well as Glasgow and Lancaster) and membership of the Accademia dei Lincei. He became a fellow of the British Academy in 1956.

Lawson was quite without false pride or any sense of distinctions of age or position. He excelled in the self-effacing task of editing other men's works (some of his most interesting *aperçus* are to be found in his edition of *Roman Law and Common Law* (1952) by W. W. Buckland and A. D. McNair. His definitive history of the Oxford law school, 1850–1965, appeared in 1968.

Lawson retired from his Oxford chair in 1964 and immediately began a fresh life in the new University of Lancaster where, before the creation of the law school, he taught a variety of legal subjects to a wide range of non-lawyers and once again created for himself a devoted following. He finally retired to his native Yorkshire in 1977 at the age of eighty, and died in Middlesbrough on 15 May 1983.

J. K. BARRY M. NICHOLAS, *rev.*

Sources *The Times* (17 May 1983) · *The Times* (28 May 1983) · *Oxford Journal of Legal Studies*, 4 (1984), 153–6 · P. Wallington and R. M. Merkin, eds., *Essays in memory of Professor F. H. Lawson* (1986) [incl. list of works] · private information (1990) · *CGPLA Eng. & Wales* (1983) · B. Nicholas, 'Frederick Henry Lawson, 1897–1983', *PBA*, 76 (1990), 473–85 · F. H. Lawson, *The Oxford law school, 1850–1965* (1968)
Likenesses portrait, repro. in Wallington and Merkin, eds., *Essays in memory of Professor F. H. Lawson*
Wealth at death £26,585: probate, 20 Sept 1983, *CGPLA Eng. & Wales*

Lawson, George (*bap.* 1598?, *d.* 1678), Church of England clergyman and political writer, was most probably baptized at Langcliffe, in the parish of Giggleswick, West Riding of Yorkshire, on 25 May 1598, the eldest son of Thomas Lawson (*b.* 1564), of Langcliffe, and his wife, Ellen Watkinson (1569/70–1610). They had married on 4 December 1597. For a short time Lawson had a younger sister, Margaret (*bap.* 1603, *d.* 1610). There is no record of Lawson's education at the local grammar school at Giggleswick, which lists a number of the Lawson clan as attending before going on to Cambridge, but in 1615 his signature in the records of Emmanuel College, Cambridge, confirms that he entered as a sizar and matriculated. Lawson later claimed to have proceeded MA from Emmanuel, but the college records give no evidence of this.

Lawson was ordained as a priest by the bishop of Chester in 1619 and reordained on 12 October 1624. In 1632 he was licensed to serve and in 1637 licensed to preach by Archbishop Laud. By 1635 he was a stipendiary curate for Mainstone, a poor living in southern Shropshire. There he recorded in his neatest Latin (his preferred language for church registers) the birth of 'Jeremiah' on 3 April of that year to George Lawson and his wife, Anne. A concerted effort was made, possibly by Sir Humphrey Macworth, to foist Lawson onto the parishioners of the important church of St Chads, Shrewsbury. Sir Paul Harris had complained that 'by colour of popular election' a pluralist, Richard Poole, had thrust himself into the parish, while he and Archbishop Laud wanted to appoint Lawson, reputedly a man of considerable learning and allegedly an outspoken defender of the archbishop (*CSP dom.*, 1637, 55). The bishop of Lichfield and Coventry was directed to remove Poole but the electoral colour stayed fast. Instead

Harris's brother-in-law Richard More, patron of the parish of More, Shropshire, appointed Lawson to the living following the death of the rector, William Biggs, in March 1637. Lawson would have been known to More as he was already living in the village and may have made himself useful in Richard More's *A True Relation* (1641), a defensive account of the notorious Clun murders of 1633 by Enoch ap Evan against the anti-puritan polemic of Peter Studley. Lawson would remain closely associated with the More family, probably educating some of Richard's grandchildren with his own son. During the interregnum he worked through all changes of ecclesiastical government in association with Richard's father, Colonel Samuel More, and in 1655 had responsibility for the neighbouring parish of Lydham. At the restoration of the Church of England he accommodated himself to a regime of episcopacy as Samuel settled for a monarchy. The Hereford visitation book does not record Lawson's swearing acceptance of the Act of Uniformity in 1662 but he did sign the subscription rolls on 21 August: his name, in two inks and shakily written, is obscured by the stitching. He may have been ill at the time: two months earlier he had buried his patron, Samuel More, signing the register in an uncertain hand. He may also have been extremely reluctant to conform.

Lawson's known associates, to say nothing of the egregiously parliamentarian Mores, and his own writings would all suggest a suspicion of episcopacy. Lawson was a long-term friend and critic of Richard Baxter and of the Independent oriental scholar Francis Tallents; a good proportion of other men with whom he had worked were unable to take the oath of uniformity, and although he was a member of the Church of England his work looked unfashionably outwards to maximal comprehension within a national settlement.

Early extensive theological writings by Lawson were unpublished, some remaining in manuscript among the Baxter treatises in the Dr Williams's Library, London. It has been claimed that he wrote the 'engagement tract' *Conscience Puzzled* (1651), though there is no evidence to support this. His first certain publication was *An Examination of the Political Part of Mr. Hobbs, his 'Leviathan'* (1657), one of the more balanced and perceptive of contemporary critiques of Hobbes. *Theo-politica* (1659), a theological treatise on the offices of Christianity, was much admired by Baxter. *Politica sacra et civilis* (1660) is the first part of a planned treatise in the 'politica' genre of European public law, of which *Leviathan* had been the most glowing example. *Politica*, published with a national settlement of church and state in mind, had probably been germinating for some time, carrying the residue of the engagement controversy of 1649–51 and being in some ways closer to *Leviathan* than the more *ad hoc Examination* might suggest. *Politica* is Lawson's most important work. Although informally written for a general audience it displays its learning to impress. It blends an incisive and ameliorating account of Britain's troubles with a theoretically assured and linguistically acute analysis of formal relationships in church and state. Its reception was not sufficiently encouraging for Lawson to bring out the second volume,

but it may well have had an impact on John Locke, who certainly owned all Lawson's published works. It was reprinted in 1689, possibly with the support of Richard More the younger, who was active in the Convention Parliament. Its vocabulary is noticeable and familiarity with its seems assumed in public debate until the early eighteenth century, when like its author it fell into obscurity. In 1662 Lawson had helped obscure himself with an impenetrably dark commentary on Hebrews, but in 1665 he briefly came up for air with *Magna charta universalis*, a simplified restatement of *Theo-politica*. These works both did sufficiently well to warrant republishing, but Lawson himself seems to have remained a figure of learned and respected marginality except for peripheral figures such as the indefatigable John Humfrey, who, as something of a disciple, proclaimed the importance of *Politica*, and for Richard Baxter, whose *Reliquiae Baxterianae* (1696) would pay his friend the most remarkable valedictory testimony. Lawson was buried at More on 12 July 1678, his wife, Anne, two years later in August 1680, his son 'Jeremy' as a pauper in 1705. The letters of administration for his estate suggest that Lawson had a materially comfortable living and a large library, and itemize a hair shirt. After Anne Lawson died the library was sold but can be partially reconstructed; the donation of a substantial teaching library to the village of More by Richard More in 1680 was possibly a memorial gift.

CONAL CONDREN

Sources parish register, Mainstone, 1603–41, Shrops. RRC · subscription books, rolls, visitation books, and register of titles, Herefs. RO, Hereford diocese · Sir Jasper More family papers relating to the seventeenth century, Shrops. RRC, 1037 · G. Lawson, letters of administration, July 1679, Herefs. RO · archives, Emmanuel College, Cambridge · *CSP dom.*, 1637 · C. Condren, *George Lawson's 'Politica' and the English revolution* (1989) · C. Condren, 'More Parish Library, Salop', *Library History*, 7/5 (1987), 141–61 · R. W. Hoyle, ed., *Parish register of Giggleswick*, vol. 1: *1558–1668*; *parish register section*, Yorkshire Archaeological Society, 147 (1984) · E. M. Cockell, ed., *The register of More, Shropshire, 1569–1812* (1900) · G. Lawson, *Politica sacra et civilis*, ed. C. Condren (1992)
Archives DWL, The Baxter treatises, notes, unpublished treatise, corresp.
Wealth at death moderate

Lawson, George (1749–1820), university professor, was born at Boghouse Farm in the parish of West Linton, Peeblesshire, on 13 March 1749. He was the second son of Charles Lawson and his wife, Margaret Noble. His father was a carpenter as well as a farmer, and was able to provide a good education for George, the only one of his six sons to survive childhood. George was studious and disinclined to manual labour, and his parents, intending him for the ministry, sent him to the University of Edinburgh in 1764. In 1766 he moved to the Associate Synod Divinity Hall where he studied divinity under John Swanston of Kinross and John Brown of Haddington. He was licensed as a preacher in 1769, and on 17 April 1771 he became pastor of the Associate Synod congregation in Selkirk.

Lawson knew the Bible by heart, and much of it in Hebrew and Greek. He left at his death some eighty large volumes in manuscript, forming a commentary on the Bible. He frequently preached extempore in a simple popular

George Lawson (1749–1820), by James Tassie, 1794

style, which belied his vast learning in philosophy, history, and science. On the death of John Brown, Lawson was chosen his successor as professor of theology (2 May 1787) in the Associate Synod Divinity Hall, which was henceforth situated at Selkirk to enable Lawson to continue as pastor there. He was active as the synod's theology professor until his death. In 1806 the University of Aberdeen conferred upon him the degree of DD.

Lawson was loved by all who knew him for his evident goodness: Thomas Carlyle dubbed him 'the Scottish Socrates', declaring that 'no simple-minded more perfect lover of wisdom do I know of in that generation' (quoted in A. Thomson, *Life of Principal Harper*, 1881 16). Many notable clergymen were trained by him, including the congregationalist Ralph Wardlaw and the Church of Scotland minister John Lee, who achieved distinction in other denominations. Lawson is said to have been the model for Josiah Cargill in Sir Walter Scott's *St Ronan's Well*.

Lawson's chief writings were commentaries on the books of the Bible, including *Lectures on the Book of Ruth* (1805); *Lectures on the History of Joseph* (2 vols., 1807); *Discourses on the Book of Esther* (1804); *Exposition of the Book of Proverbs* (2 vols., 1821); and *Discourses on the History of David* (1833). These were widely read and appreciated in nineteenth-century Britain and America. His *Considerations on the overture … concerning the power of the civil magistrate in matters of religion* (1797) advocated religious toleration and was regarded as a masterpiece of argument. Lawson also had a reputation for absentmindedness and

was alleged to have forgotten the day fixed for his marriage.

Lawson was married twice. His first wife was Miss Roger, the daughter of a Selkirk banker, who died within a year of the marriage. He then married the daughter of a Mr Moir, his predecessor in Selkirk, widow of the Revd Mr Dickson of Berwick. They had five daughters and three sons; two of the latter, George and Andrew, were in turn their father's successors in Selkirk. Lawson died at Selkirk on 21 February 1820 and was buried there.

HENRY PATON, *rev.* N. R. NEEDHAM

Sources J. MacFarlane, *The life and times of George Lawson* (1862) · R. Small, *History of the congregations of the United Presbyterian church from 1733 to 1900*, 2 vols. (1904) · H. Belfrage, 'Memoir', in G. Lawson, *Discourses on the history of David* (1833) · N. R. Needham, 'Lawson, George', *DSCHT*
Archives NL Scot., sermons · U. Aberdeen L., notes
Likenesses J. Tassie, wax medallion, 1794, Scot. NPG [*see illus.*] · J. Horsburgh, line engraving (after J. Pairman), BM; repro. in G. Lawson, *Exposition of the Book of Proverbs*, 2 vols. (1821)

Lawson, George (1831–1903), ophthalmic surgeon, was born at 39 St Mary-at-Hill, Eastcheap, London, on 23 August 1831, the second son of William Lawson, partner in a firm of wine merchants, and his wife, Anne Norton. About 1835 the family moved to Blackheath, where Lawson went to the new proprietary school. He entered King's College Hospital, London, in 1848. Admitted MRCS in 1852, he served for a year as house surgeon to Sir William Fergusson. In 1852 he became a licentiate in midwifery of the Royal College of Surgeons and a licentiate of the Society of Apothecaries.

Early in 1854 Lawson volunteered for military service as an assistant surgeon, and in March of that year he left England with the first draft of troops, bound for Gallipoli. On the outbreak of the Crimean War he was sent to Varna, from where he went to the Crimea; he was present at the battles of Alma and Inkerman, and was sent to Balaklava about the middle of January 1855. He had a severe attack of typhus fever in May 1855, and for several months could not use his legs. He was invalided home and arrived at Portsmouth in August, and at the end of the war he resigned his commission.

Lawson then decided to practise in London. Elected FRCS in 1857, he settled at 63 Park Street, Grosvenor Square, and turned his attention more especially to ophthalmic surgery, probably at the suggestion of Sir William Bowman, with whom he had worked at King's College Hospital. He married, on 5 March 1863, Mary Louisa, daughter of William Thomson, of the Indian Medical Service (IMS); they had seven sons. Lawson became clinical assistant to Bowman at the Royal London Ophthalmic Hospital, Moorfields, and in 1862 was elected surgeon to the hospital on the retirement of Alfred Poland (1822–1872); he was appointed full surgeon in 1867 and consulting surgeon in 1891. He held the post of surgeon to the Great Northern Hospital, London, for a short time. To the Middlesex Hospital, London, he was elected assistant surgeon in 1863, surgeon in 1871, lecturer on surgery in 1878, and consulting surgeon in 1896. He served as a member of the council of the Royal College of Surgeons from 1884 to 1892, and in 1886 he was appointed surgeon-oculist to Queen Victoria.

Lawson practised ophthalmic surgery as a part of general surgery and was little affected by the growing tendency towards specialism in these subjects. He died at his home, 12 Harley Street, Cavendish Square, London, on 12 October 1903, and was buried at Hildenborough, Kent. His wife survived him.

D'A. POWER, rev. ANITA MCCONNELL

Sources V. Bonham-Carter, ed., *Surgeon in the Crimea: the experiences of George Lawson recorded in letters to his family, 1854–1855* (1968) • D. M. Albert and D. D. Edwards, eds., *The history of ophthalmology* (1996) • *The Lancet* (24 Oct 1903), 1184 • *BMJ* (17 Oct 1903), 1019–21 • private information (1912)
Likenesses photograph, repro. in Bonham-Carter, ed., *Surgeon in the Crimea*, frontispiece • portrait, repro. in *The Lancet* • portrait, repro. in *BMJ*
Wealth at death £24,968 5s. 6d.: probate, 28 Nov 1903, *CGPLA Eng. & Wales*

Lawson, George Anderson (1832–1904), sculptor, was born in Edinburgh on 3 May 1832, the son of David Lawson and Anne Campbell. He received his early education at George Heriot's Hospital in Edinburgh and his instruction then followed the usual pattern of apprenticeship in a local studio while enrolled part-time at the local art school. He worked in the studio of Alexander Handyside Ritchie as a fellow student of John Rhind, and at the Trustees' School of Design in Edinburgh he was, along with John Hutchison, a pupil of Robert Scott Lauder. On the completion of his training Lawson moved to Glasgow, where he worked from 36 St Georges Place in 1860 and 1861; this was followed by a brief sojourn in Rome, where he saw the work of John Gibson. He probably visited Paris while on this journey. On his return to Britain he married Jane, daughter of Matthew Frier, on 28 August 1862 at Blythswood, Glasgow, and settled in Liverpool at 40 Norton Street. This move was influenced by the commission he won in limited competition in 1861 for the Liverpool monument to the duke of Wellington. The statue of the duke was his first major award and was followed by commissions for monuments to Lord Cochrane (1874, Valparaiso, Chile), John Pease (1875, Darlington, co. Durham), Robert Burns (versions 1891, Ayr, and 1893, Belfast), and James Arthur (1893, Glasgow). In 1904 a replica of the Ayr statue was commissioned for Melbourne, Australia.

Such portrait works were not, however, the mainstay of Lawson's *œuvre*. He specialized in imaginative figures and groups, often illustrative of literary subjects and usually in marble or terracotta. Subject matter from Scottish history and the writings of Sir Walter Scott figures strongly among these: he won commissions for three of the sixty-four statues on the Scott monument, the national memorial to Sir Walter Scott in Edinburgh. In addition, he also worked in the area of architectural decoration: for example, the pediment for Glasgow city chambers (1883) and the façade of the Aberdeen Art Gallery (completed, after his death, in 1905). Overall his work is characterized by technical competence and variety in style and composition. It encompasses an early affiliation to neo-classicism,

the more naturalistic portraiture evident in his bust of David Tod of Aytoun (1860, Glasgow Art Gallery and Museum), the quaint and comical character study of bailie Nicol Jarvie (1873, Scott monument, Edinburgh), and the languid sensuality of *Summer* (George Watson's School, Edinburgh).

From 1866 Lawson lived in London but he remained in close contact with artists and patrons in Scotland. His work was shown in Dundee as well as at the Royal Glasgow Institute of the Fine Arts, and he exhibited regularly at the Royal Academy and the Royal Scottish Academy between 1860 and 1892. His group *Motherless* (1901, Glasgow Art Gallery and Museum) was shown at the 1901 Glasgow International Exhibition at Kelvingrove Park. He was elected an honorary member of the Royal Scottish Academy in 1884. On three occasions he was unsuccessfully nominated an associate of the Royal Academy. He died at his home, 21 Church Road, Richmond, Surrey, on 23 September 1904.

S. E. FRYER, rev. ROBIN L. WOODWARD

Sources R. L. Woodward, 'Nineteenth century Scottish sculpture', PhD diss., U. Edin., 1979 • *IGI* • *CGPLA Eng. & Wales* (1905)
Likenesses T. Graham, oils, 1882, Aberdeen Art Gallery • Brown, Barnes & Bell, cabinet, c.1890, NPG • J. Archer, oils, Scot. NPG • woodcut (after T. B. Wirgman), BM; repro. in *Century Magazine* (1883)
Wealth at death £163 7s. 8d.: administration, 7 June 1905, *CGPLA Eng. & Wales*

Lawson, Harry Lawson Webster Levy-, Viscount Burnham (1862–1933), newspaper proprietor and chairman of public bodies, was born on 18 December 1862 in London, the elder son of Edward Levy-*Lawson, first Baron Burnham (1833–1916), newspaper proprietor, and his wife, Harriette Georgiana (d. 1897), only daughter of the actor-manager Benjamin Nottingham Webster. He was educated at Eton College and at Balliol College, Oxford, where he was awarded a first-class degree in modern history in 1884 and was elected secretary of the union. In 1884, while still an undergraduate, he married Olive (d. 1939), eldest daughter of General Sir Henry Percival de Bathe. They had one daughter.

Levy-Lawson's life was divided between the family business, the *Daily Telegraph*, and politics. Benjamin Jowett, master of Balliol College, told him: 'Your father owns a great newspaper. There is nothing to beat the job at hand. You must go to it' (Burnham, 180). His own personal inclinations, and those of his mother, who saw in him a future prime minister, were more towards politics. At twenty-two he was the youngest member of the House of Commons when returned for West St Pancras as a Liberal at the 1885 general election. However, his Commons service was to be punctuated by electoral misfortune and a change of party. He lost West St Pancras at the 1892 general election. He was rapidly offered the candidature at the East Gloucestershire by-election in the same year. The first count showed that he had lost by three votes, and the recount produced a dead heat, necessitating a fresh election. He won this in early 1893, only to lose the seat when the Liberals were heavily defeated at the 1895 general election. He was not to return for another ten years, in which time he had left the Liberal Party in opposition to its policy of home rule for Ireland. In 1905 he won the Mile End by-election for the Liberal Unionists, only to be swept away in the Liberal landslide of the following year. After regaining Mile End in 1910 he held the seat until he succeeded to his father's baronetcy and barony in 1916. He was also a member of the first London county council, elected in 1889, representing West St Pancras until 1892. He later represented Whitechapel from 1897 to 1904 and was mayor of Stepney from 1907 to 1909.

In 1903 he became proprietor of the *Daily Telegraph*, the then prime minister, Lord Salisbury, ruling that his father's elevation to the peerage was incompatible with continuing to run a national newspaper. He was not wholly successful in the role. The *Telegraph*, the highest-selling paper in Britain for most of the second half of the nineteenth century, struggled to retain its sales against the competition of the *Daily Mail*, which had been launched in 1896, and *The Times*, particularly when the latter was revitalized under Lord Northcliffe after 1908.

Other duties meant that Levy-Lawson was rarely able to give the paper his undivided attention, and he lacked the business and journalistic talents that had made his father so spectacularly successful. His nephew Edward Frederick *Lawson, later fourth Baron Burnham (1890–1963), recorded that he had the 'défauts de ses qualités' in that he was too serious-minded to preside over lively news coverage and was 'absent when cunning was doled out' (Burnham, 165–9). The journalist Bernard Falk credited him with only limited journalistic talent and 'almost childlike trustfulness in the integrity of human nature' (Falk, 230).

The obituary notice that mentioned his 'pervasive urbanity, sense of humour and conciliatory moderation' pointed also to 'a positive and, on occasion, somewhat obstinate opinion of his own' (*The Times*). This obstinacy was in evidence in 1922 when, against all advice, he insisted on retaining the *Telegraph's* traditional paper size, an unwieldy 3 inches larger than its competitors, when the necessity of ordering new printing presses offered the chance to change.

The *Telegraph* struggled badly in the 1920s, its daily sale dropping by more than half to the end of 1927 when Burnham sold it to the Berry brothers, Sir William and Sir Gomer, and Sir William Iliffe. The editor of the time, Arthur Watson, recalled that 'control had been too parsimonious', with too little editorial matter and too many advertisements (Hart-Davis, 65). Even so, Levy-Lawson was an influential, hugely respected figure in the newspaper business, its 'accredited spokesman' in parliament. He was variously president of the Newspaper Press Fund, chairman of the Newspaper Publishers' Association, and president (1909–10) of the Institute of Journalists and (1916–29) of the Empire Press Union. He was also president of the Imperial Press conferences held in Ottawa in 1920 and Melbourne in 1925.

It was as a chair of public bodies, both nationally and internationally, that Levy-Lawson's talents found their truest outlet. The Liberal politician Walter Runciman labelled him 'an unofficial servant of empire' (Burnham,

167) for his formidable record of service, starting with membership of the 1889–94 royal commission on civil establishments. He also, as a member of the 1916 speaker's conference on electoral reform, moved the resolution which led to the enfranchisement of women in 1918. He was longest remembered for his chairmanship of the standing joint committee on teachers' pay, which in 1920 established scales of pay for all state school teachers. These rapidly became known as the 'Burnham scales', prompting an obituarist to assert that 'his name will always be associated with education affairs' (*The Times*). The negotiating body for teachers' pay was known as the Burnham committee until its abolition in 1987. He was also president of Birkbeck College, London, from 1929 until his death, and was awarded honorary degrees by the universities of Athens, Cambridge, Durham, Ghent, Oxford, and Perth.

Levy-Lawson won an international reputation by chairing the third, fourth, and ninth international labour conferences at Geneva in 1921, 1922, and 1926, the public health conferences at Bordeaux in 1924 and Ghent in 1927, and the first World Press Conference at Geneva in 1927. His last years were devoted to India. In 1927 he was appointed to the Simon commission on the government of India. This appointment, involving three years of work and two long trips to India, was the cause of his finally giving up the *Telegraph*. In 1933 he was one of eight peers appointed to the joint select committee on Indian government reform, attending a meeting only two days before his death. His numerous honours included Companion of Honour (1917), a viscountcy conferred in 1919 in part in recognition of his work for the Territorial Army, and being made GCMG (1927). He was also decorated by the governments of France, Belgium, Italy, Romania, Greece, and Sweden. Levy-Lawson died in his sleep at his London house, 13 Bryanston Square, on 20 July 1933. The viscountcy became extinct as he had no son, and he was succeeded in the baronetcy and barony by his brother William Lawson (1864–1943).   HUW RICHARDS

Sources D. Hart-Davis, *The house the Berrys built: inside the 'Telegraph', 1928–1986* (1990) · *Daily Telegraph* (21 July 1933) · *The Times* (21 July 1933) · *Newspaper World* (22 July 1933) · *Times Educational Supplement* (22 July 1933) · *World's Press News* (27 July 1933) · *WWW* · B. Falk, *Five years dead* (1938) · Lord Burnham [E. F. L. Burnham], *Peterborough Court: the story of the Daily Telegraph* (1955) · Lord Hartwell, *William Camrose, giant of Fleet Street* (1992) · Burke, *Peerage* (1980) · D. Griffiths, ed., *The encyclopedia of the British press, 1422–1992* (1992) · *DNB* · S. E. Koss, *The rise and fall of the political press in Britain*, 2 (1984) · *CGPLA Eng. & Wales* (1933)

Archives NRA, priv. coll., corresp. and papers | BL, corresp. with Lord Northcliffe, Add. MS 62172 · Bodl. Oxf., corresp. with Lord Simm · HLRO, corresp. with David Lloyd George

Likenesses J. Russell & Sons, photograph, *c*.1915, NPG · W. Stoneman, photograph, 1932, NPG

Wealth at death £229,558 12*s*. 6*d*.: probate, 1 Nov 1933, *CGPLA Eng. & Wales*

Lawson, Henry (1774–1855), astronomer, was born at Greenwich, Kent, on 23 March 1774, the second son of Johnson Lawson (*d*. 1778), dean of Battle in Sussex, and his wife, Elizabeth (*d*. 1823), the daughter of Henry Wright of Bath. She married in 1788 Edward *Nairne (1726–1806), an optician, of Cornhill, London. Lawson attended Dr Burney's school in Greenwich, then in 1788 was apprenticed to Nairne in the Spectaclemakers' Company. He was twice master of the company, in 1803–5 and 1822–4, although he was only briefly in the optical business, preferring to devote himself to private scientific study. He lived in Chelsea with his mother until her death in 1823, when he married Amelia (d. 1855), the daughter of Thomas Jennings, vicar of St Peter's, Hereford.

In Hereford Lawson equipped an observatory in 1826 with a 5 foot refractor and in 1834 with an 11 foot refractor, considered by Dollond the finest telescope he had ever made. His observations of an occultation of Saturn on 8 May 1832, Galle's first comet in December 1839 and January 1840, and the falling stars of 12–13 November 1841 were published by the Royal Astronomical Society, to which he was elected in 1833. In 1840 he was elected FRS by virtue of his contributions to meteorology and astronomy. He became a member of the British Meteorological Society in 1850.

A relative having left him a fortune, in 1841 Lawson moved to 71 Lansdowne Crescent, Bath, and mounted his instruments on the roof of his house. He published in 1844 a paper 'On the arrangement of an observatory for practical astronomy and meteorology' and in 1847 a brief *History of the New Planets*. The Society of Arts, of which he had been a member since 1803, voted him a silver medal in 1844 for the invention of a reclining medical and observing chair, called 'Reclina', and awarded him a prize for a thermometer stand, the first of its kind and intended to standardize shade temperature readings. Lawson also described it to the British Association in 1845. He made communications to the same body in 1846 and 1847 on solar telescopic work, and published in 1853 accounts of a 'lifting apparatus' for invalids and of a 'surgical transferrer', both contrived by himself.

Lawson offered in December 1851 his entire astronomical apparatus, with 1000 guineas, to the town of Nottingham, conditional on an observatory being built, and endowed with £200 a year, but the plan failed through disputes about the valuation of the instruments. His 11 foot telescope was later presented to the Royal Naval College at Greenwich, the smaller instrument to William Snow Lettsom, a retired diplomat, and his meteorological appliances to E. J. Lowe of Beeston, Nottinghamshire. Lawson devoted much time to promoting the scientific pursuits of young people, and dispensed liberal and unostentatious charity. He was a member of the Askesian and numerous local societies. He died at his home in Bath on 22 August 1855, a few weeks after his wife, and was buried at Weston. The last of his family, he bequeathed to Agnes Strickland several relics of his probable ancestor Katherine Parr, which had been handed down as heirlooms for nearly two centuries, and left £200 each to the Royal Astronomical Society, the Royal Society, and the British Meteorological Society. His large fortune was divided by will among 139 persons, in addition to bequests to hospitals and charitable institutions in Bath.

A. M. CLERKE, *rev.* ANITA McCONNELL

Sources *Monthly Notices of the Royal Astronomical Society*, 16 (1855–6), 86–90 · *Annual Register* (1856), 226 · minutes of committees, 1844–5, RSA, 264–8 · minutes of committees, 1843–6, RSA, 671–683 · minutes, 1803–4, RSA, 33 · *GM*, 1st ser., 58 (1788), 836 · Boase, *Mod. Eng. biog.*

Lawson, Henry John (1852–1925), bicycle designer and company promoter, was born at 1 Nevills Court in the City of London on 23 February 1852, the son of Thomas Lawson, brass turner and Methodist preacher, and his wife, Ann Lucy, *née* Kent. Little is known about Lawson's early life, but he appears to have gained experience in the bicycle trade in Brighton as a young man. His adult life falls into three distinct phases, of which the first was active and inventive involvement in the cycle trade and industry, when Lawson contributed to the complex and gradual evolution of the safety bicycle. In the second phase he turned to company finance, initially in the related areas of cycles and pneumatic tyres, but culminating in the motor industry, which in its early years was closely related to them. After the collapse of his profiteering and monopolistic schemes, the last years of Lawson's life seem to have been spent in obscurity and poverty.

In 1873–4 Lawson designed a safety bicycle, described as the 'first authentic design of safety bicycle employing chain-drive to the rear wheel which was actually made' (Caunter, 34). In 1876 the Likeman and Lawson low bicycle was patented, with a large rear wheel and powered by pedals and levers. It superficially resembled a back to front Ordinary or penny-farthing machine, but with an easier riding position; a few were made by Haynes and Jefferis of Coventry. The Bicyclette, Lawson's third design, appeared in 1879. This more closely resembled the Ordinary machine in having a larger front wheel, but its smaller size, improved distribution of the rider's weight, and chain drive permit Lawson to be classed with others, above all John Kemp Starley, as a progenitor of the modern safety bicycle which was central to the boom of the mid-1890s. Lawson had become manager of the Tangent and Coventry Tricycle Company, but appears not to have had plans to manufacture his own design, approaching BSA, who produced two prototypes only.

In 1884 Lawson patented a lady's safety bicycle, but then entered the second phase of his life, for which he was to become notorious, that of company promotion. In 1887 the Haynes and Jefferis concern was transformed into the Rudge Cycle Company, Lawson acting with the Coventry solicitor George Woodcock. The latter died in 1891, but by then Lawson's role in company promotion was linked to those of E. T. *Hooley and his associate, Martin Rucker. Their activities stemmed from a desire to benefit from the exceptionally favourable market conditions by obtaining capital gains in cash through company flotations. However, Lawson went on into new fields with a scheme 'to create a motor car industry in this country and to control it himself' (Richardson, 17).

Lawson floated the British Motor Syndicate Ltd in 1895 (this subsequently became the British Motor Company Ltd, then the British Motor Traction Company Ltd), followed in 1896 by the Great Horseless Carriage Company

Ltd (subsequently the Motor Manufacturing Company Ltd). The reality failed to match these grandiose titles or Lawson's greedy ambition, with one exception: the Daimler Motor Company (re-formed in 1904) proved to be an enduring outcome of Lawson's schemes. The Daimler patent rights had been bought from F. R. Simms's Daimler Motor Syndicate by the British Motor Syndicate in 1895 and sold in 1896 to the Daimler Motor Company which was based in Coventry.

For the embryonic automotive industry, there were no profits records to assess and scarcely any measure of current demand. In such a situation, a showman–promoter like Lawson could flourish, at least temporarily. The Motor Car Club, which Lawson founded in late 1895, may be regarded as part of his publicity machine, and the more responsible element in the motor world, including F. R. Simms, found it desirable to create the independent Automobile Club of Great Britain and Ireland (later the RAC) in mid-1897.

Meanwhile Lawson continued his scheme of monopoly. To the Daimler rights he added those of the American inventor E. J. Pennington (1858–1911), which were of doubtful value. Their joint Anglo-American Rapid Vehicle Company, organized in the United States in 1899, collapsed. In July 1901 the death blow to Lawson's schemes was delivered by Mr Justice Farwell in a High Court decision; he dismissed an action by the British Motor Traction Company for alleged infringement of Maybach's carburettor patent, on the grounds that Maybach's method had been anticipated by both Edward Butler and George Wilkinson.

A receiver was appointed to the Traction Company in February 1903 and in the following year Lawson was indicted with Hooley for conspiring to defraud a speculator, Alfred Paine, and also shareholders and creditors of the Electric Tramways Construction and Maintenance Company Ltd. Hooley, defended by Rufus Isaacs, was acquitted, but Lawson, who conducted his own case, was sentenced to one year's hard labour. By then in his fifties, Lawson, who was married, with two sons, thereafter seems to have faded from the motor world and the public scene, until the Blériot affair of 1915–16. In this Lawson again played the syndicate card, acquiring the Blériot Manufacturing Aircraft Company Ltd on 17 June 1915, a few days before the issue of a prospectus which gave no indication that control had in effect passed into Lawson's hands. The company was wound up in 1916 following an extraordinary general meeting marked by some disorder. Lawson died at his home, 25 Roxborough Avenue, Harrow, on 12 July 1925, summed up by the *Motor* as 'poor' Harry J. Lawson, although it charitably commented that his chief fault was that 'his optimism was twenty-five years before the times' (cited in *DBB*).   RICHARD A. STOREY

Sources K. Richardson and C. N. O'Gallagher, *The British motor industry, 1896–1939* (1977) • C. F. Caunter, *The history and development of cycles as illustrated by the collection in the Science Museum* (1955), pt 1 • R. Storey, 'Lawson, Henry John', *DBB* • A. E. Harrison, 'Joint-stock company flotation in the cycle, motor vehicle and related industries, 1882–1914', *Business History*, 23 (1981), 165–90 • St J. C. Nixon, 'H. J. Lawson, the would-be dictator of the British motor industry', *Veteran and Vintage Magazine* (Jan 1957), 167–8 • J. B. Rae, *The American automobile: a brief history* (1965) • Marquess of Reading [G. R. Isaacs], *Rufus Isaacs, first marquess of Reading*, 2 vols. (1942–5) • A. Ritchie, *King of the road* (1975) • G. Williamson, *Wheels within wheels: the story of the Starleys of Coventry* (1966) • *The Times* (19–20 Jan 1916) • b. cert. • *CGPLA Eng. & Wales* (1926) • D. Burgess-Wise, 'The secret history of the British motor car', *Daily Telegraph Motoring* (20 Jan 1996), C1 [pt 1] • Lord Montagu and D. Burgess-Wise, *Daimler century* (1995) • T. R. Nicholson, *The birth of the British motor car, 1769–1897*, 3 (1982) • d. cert.

Archives Veteran Car Club of Great Britain, Ashwell, Hertfordshire, Simms MSS

Wealth at death £99: administration, 8 June 1926, *CGPLA Eng. & Wales*

Lawson, Isaac (d. 1747), physician, was born in Scotland, and became a student of Leiden University on 17 May 1730. He studied medicine and botany under Herman Boerhaave and Adrianus van Royen, and became a good friend of Linnaeus, whom he assisted several times with gifts of money. Together with J. F. Gronovius he shared the expense of the printing of Linnaeus's *Systema naturae* in 1735. Lawson graduated at Leiden as MD in 1737, his thesis being entitled *Dissertatio academica sistens nihil*. He afterwards became a physician to the British army. Linnaeus dedicated to him the genus *Lawsonia*, the henna of the East. In W. G. Maton's edition of Linnaeus's *Diary*, included in his reprint of Richard Pulteney's *A General View of the Writings of Linnaeus*, Lawson is inaccurately spoken of as John Lawson (p. 530). Another Isaac Lawson, possibly a son, entered Leiden University on 13 March 1747, and is described in the register as Britanno-Edinburgensis. Lawson died at Oosterhaut in the Netherlands in 1747.

G. S. BOULGER, *rev.* MICHAEL BEVAN

Sources Desmond, *Botanists*, rev. edn • *A selection of the correspondence of Linnaeus, and other naturalists, from the original manuscripts*, ed. J. E. Smith, 2 vols. (1821), vol. 1, p. 18; vol. 2, pp. 173, 175 • R. Pulteney, *A general view of the Writings of Linnaeus*, ed. W. G. Maton (1781), 15, 530 • *Extracts from the literary and scientific correspondence of Richard Richardson*, ed. D. Turner (1835), 343–5

Archives NHM, plants

Lawson, James (1538–1584), Church of Scotland minister, was born in Perth to unknown parents and educated at the grammar school there before proceeding to St Andrews University, where he entered the class of 1559–60 in St Mary's College along with Andrew Melville. Although the graduation rolls for the eleven students in this class have not survived, Lawson, like Melville, made for the continent on completing his course; by 1567 he was tutor at Paris University to the three sons of the countess of Crawford. It may have been now that he acquired his knowledge of Hebrew. The onset of fresh religious strife in France led to his returning to London and then to Cambridge for further study in 1569. On arriving home in February 1569 he was appointed second master in St Mary's College in St Andrews, where he taught Hebrew until his appointment in July 1569 as sub-principal of King's College, Aberdeen, following the reforms initiated at Aberdeen University by Regent Moray.

In September 1572 John Knox confided in Lawson that he felt in 'nature so decayed, and daylie to decay, that I looke not for a long continuance of my battell' and urged him 'to visite me that we may confere together of heavenlie things' (Calderwood, 3.224). The outcome was Lawson's appointment as Knox's colleague and, from November 1572, his successor as minister of St Giles's. Inaugurated to his charge by the reformer himself, Lawson soon gained the stature of 'chief minister' in Edinburgh. A strong supporter of efforts to found a college of arts in Edinburgh, he secured the services of Robert Rollock from St Andrews as the college's first principal in 1583. In all this he plainly seized the initiative by sending Rollock 'a most courteous letter, entreating him to undertake the duty'; and when Rollock accepted he approached the town council, 'where his influence was very great, and informed them that there was no person better qualified for the charge of the university than Rollock' (*Select Works of Robert Rollock*, 1.lxiii).

In the debate on episcopacy in the general assembly in 1575 Lawson sided with Melville, and he participated in drafting the second Book of Discipline of 1578 with its presbyterian programme for the church. Elected moderator of the assembly held at Dundee in July 1580, which condemned episcopacy, he was summoned before the privy council in 1582 and again in 1583 for his persistent criticism of the duke of Lennox and Captain James Stewart, who headed King James's government. After praising Melville's defiance in declining to acknowledge the king's authority in doctrinal matters, he proceeded to condemn the 'black acts' passed by parliament in May 1584 and followed Melville's example by seeking safety in England. Leaving behind his wife, Janet Guthrie (with whom he had three children), to conduct a spirited defence of her husband against attack from Archbishop Patrick Adamson, he escaped on 27 May to Berwick and made his way to London in June. He visited Oxford and Cambridge universities in July before returning to London, where he died, on 12 October 1584, in the home of Anthony Martin in Honey Lane, Cheapside. His funeral was the occasion of a gathering of English and Scottish presbyterians 'not only more impressive than any other recorded in the sixteenth century, but far more representative of Scots than even the Westminster assembly was to be' (Donaldson, 184).

To his younger contemporary John Spottiswoode, later archbishop of St Andrews, Lawson was a man 'of good learning and judgment, of a pious and peaceable disposition, but carried too much with the idle rumours of the people' (Spottiswoode, 2.318). James Melville's recollection of him was of 'a godlie lernit man, of a wounderfull moving utterance in doctrine whom I delyted mickle to heir and whom I never hard bot with teares bathe of remors and joy' (*Autobiography and Diary*, 52).

JAMES KIRK

Sources J. M. Anderson, ed., *Early records of the University of St Andrews*, Scottish History Society, 3rd ser., 8 (1926) · R. Bannatyne, *Memoriales of transactions in Scotland, 1569–1573*, ed. [R. Pitcairn], Bannatyne Club, 51 (1836) · D. Calderwood, *The history of the Kirk of Scotland*, ed. T. Thomson and D. Laing, 8 vols., Wodrow Society, 7 (1842–9) · J. Spottiswoode, *History of the Church of Scotland*, ed. M. Napier and M. Russell, 3 vols., Spottiswoode Society, 6 (1847–51) · *The autobiography and diary of Mr James Melvill*, ed. R. Pitcairn, Wodrow Society (1842) · J. Kirk, *The Second Book of Discipline* (1980) ·

T. Thomson, ed., *Acts and proceedings of the general assemblies of the Kirk of Scotland*, 3 pts, Bannatyne Club, 81 (1839–45) · J. D. Marwick, ed., *Extracts from the records of the burgh of Edinburgh, AD 1573–1589*, [4], Scottish Burgh RS, 5 (1882) · *CSP Scot.*, 1574–85 · *Select works of Robert Rollock*, ed. W. M. Gunn, 2 vols., Wodrow Society, 8 (1844–9) · Lord Lindsay [A. W. C. Lindsay, earl of Crawford], *Lives of the Lindsays*, [new edn], 1 (1849) · J. Kirk, *Patterns of reform: continuity and change in the Reformation kirk* (1989) · G. Donaldson, *Scottish church history* (1985) · J. Kirk, "Melvillian" reform in the Scottish universities', *The Renaissance in Scotland: studies in literature, religion, history, and culture offered to John Durkan*, ed. A. A. MacDonald and others (1994), 276–300

Lawson, James Anthony (1817–1887), judge, was born in Waterford, Ireland, the eldest son of James Lawson, procollector, and Mary, daughter of Joseph Anthony. Lawson was educated at the endowed school in Waterford, and entered Trinity College, Dublin, on 21 October 1833. Elected a scholar in 1836, he obtained a senior moderatorship in 1837 and was a gold medallist, with a first class in ethics and logic. He graduated BA 1838, LLB 1841, and was awarded the honorary degree of LLD in 1850. From 1840 to 1845 he was Whately professor of political economy at Trinity; *Five Lectures on Political Economy* was published in 1844.

Lawson entered Gray's Inn in 1838, was called to the Irish bar in 1840, and soon obtained a good practice, especially in the chancery courts. In 1842 he married Jane *née* Merrick, the eldest daughter of Samuel Merrick of Cork, and on 29 January 1857 he took silk. He was elected bencher of King's Inns, Dublin, in 1861, and he acted as legal adviser to the crown in Ireland from 1858 to 1859, having already published *Duties and Obligations Involved in Mercantile Relations: a Lecture* (1855). He was appointed solicitor-general for Ireland in February 1861, and attorney-general in 1865, when he was also sworn of the Irish privy council. As attorney-general he dealt with the 'Fenian conspiracy', when he suppressed the *Irish People* newspaper and prosecuted its leaders.

On 4 April 1857 Lawson contested the seat for Dublin University; he was unsuccessful, despite publishing *A Speech at the Election for Members to Serve in Parliament for the University of Dublin* (1857). On 15 July 1865 he was elected for Portarlington, the same year in which he and H. Connor brought out *Reports of Cases in High Court of Chancery of Ireland during the Time of Chancellor Sugden*. Lawson continued to represent his constituency until defeated in the general election of December 1868. He was then appointed fourth justice of the common pleas, Ireland, and held the post until his transfer to the Queen's Bench Division in June 1882. During the Land League agitation he presided at several important political trials and an attempt was made on his life on 11 November 1882 by Patrick Delaney, who was afterwards tried for the Phoenix Park murders.

A distinguished classical scholar, political economist, and statesman, Lawson was considered never to have received the recognition due to his abilities. He was made an Irish church commissioner in July 1869 and became a privy councillor in England on 18 May 1870. He acted as a commissioner for the great seal from March to December 1874, was a vice-president of the Dublin Statistical Society, and was granted the honorary degree of DCL by the University of Oxford in 1884. He died at his home, Clontra, Shankhill, co. Dublin, on 10 August 1887, and was buried at Dean's Grange cemetery, Dublin.

G. C. BOASE, *rev.* SINÉAD AGNEW

Sources F. E. Ball, *The judges in Ireland, 1221–1921*, 2 (1926), 304, 306, 314, 317, 329–30, 367–8 · *Debrett's Illustrated House of Commons and the Judicial Bench* (1885), 349 · Boase, *Mod. Eng. biog.* · J. S. Crone, *A concise dictionary of Irish biography*, rev. edn (1937), 122 · *Solicitors' Journal*, 31 (1886–7), 694 · Burtchaell & Sadleir, *Alum. Dubl.* · *Men of the time* (1875), 629 · A. Law, 'Lawson, James Anthony', *Dictionary of political economy*, ed. H. R. I. Palgrave (1894–9) · Allibone, *Dict.* · D. J. O'Donoghue, *The poets of Ireland: a biographical and bibliographical dictionary* (1912), 276 · *Irish Law Times and Solicitors' Journal*, 11 (1887), 464 · *The Times* (11 Aug 1887) · *CGPLA Ire.* (1887)

Archives BL, letters to W. E. Gladstone, Add. MSS 44414–44660 · Bodl. Oxf., corresp. with Lord Kimberley

Wealth at death £30,673 19*s.* 4*d.*: probate, 22 Oct 1887, *CGPLA Ire.* · £994—effects in England: probate, 22 Oct 1887, *CGPLA Ire.*

Lawson, Sir John (*c.*1615–1665), naval officer, was born in Scarborough, Yorkshire, where he spent the greater part of his life. Though he adopted the arms of the Lawsons of Longhirst in Northumberland, no evidence to link him with that family has been found. Of his mother nothing is known, but his father may have been William Lawson, a master mariner and leading member of Scarborough's mercantile community. In January 1640 he married Isabel (*b.* 1615/16), daughter of William Jefferson, master mariner of Lythe. By that time he was already master of the *Adventurer*, carrying coals from Sunderland.

Civil wars When civil war broke out in the autumn of 1642 Lawson immediately offered his services to parliament. For the next three years he was master of the *Covenant* of Hull, an armed merchantman of 140 tons in which he had a part share. After Sir Hugh Cholmley, governor of Scarborough, went over to the king in March 1643, Lawson was one of the few townspeople who refused to live under a royalist regime. He took his wife and their eldest daughter, Isabella, into exile in Hull. For a hired civilian his contribution to parliament's cause was extraordinary. Besides conveying vital supplies into beleaguered Hull, under his command the *Covenant* played a key role in the blockade of royalist Scarborough, during which he captured ten guns from an enemy vessel and chased off a man-of-war. Moreover, in his own words, 'it pleased God' to make him 'an instrument in discovering and (in some measure) preventing the intended treacherie of Sir Jo: Hotham' (PRO, SP 18/47/63). After Cholmley's surrender in July 1645 he brought his family back to Scarborough where he bought a substantial house and several valuable leases. He was elected to the town's ruling body, the First Twelve of the Common Hall, and made journeys to London on behalf of the corporation. In April 1646 he was commissioned captain of the 100 soldiers ordered to serve as Scarborough's garrison, a post that he held for almost five years. Two years later, in the *Covenant*, he located and seized his former comrade, the notorious privateer Browne Bushell, who was operating off Tynemouth. Soon afterwards parliament's governor of Scarborough, Colonel Boynton, defected to the king and for a second time

Sir John Lawson (*c.*1615–1665), by Sir Peter Lely, *c.*1665

Lawson withdrew his family to Hull. In December 1648 he was a signatory to the articles of Boynton's surrender and his company of infantry occupied the castle after its fall.

State service Lawson kept his seat in Scarborough's First Twelve until 1653, but for the last three years he never occupied it. In 1650 he was recruited into the Commonwealth navy where he soon increased his reputation for audacity and vigour. From under the guns of the Danish fort at Glückstadt he retrieved a stolen collier and restored it to its Scarborough owners. Later that year he was reported to have scattered a large fleet of French fishing vessels off Newfoundland. As captain of the newly built *Centurion*, a warship of 500 tons and 40 guns, he provided support for Cromwell's Scottish campaign. Early in 1651 he followed Vice-Admiral Penn, who had been ordered to seek out Rupert, to the Azores. During the next fourteen months they sailed from the Azores as far east as Malta and took many prizes. When Lawson returned home in the summer of 1652 his intention was to retire from 'sea employment' but at the outbreak of the First Anglo-Dutch War he could not 'satisfy [his] conscience' to leave the nation's service at such a critical time (Gardiner and Atkinson, 4.46). It may have been Lawson's connection with his fellow north-easterner Sir Henry Vane, a religious radical and strong republican, which kept him in naval service at this time.

When the first war against the Dutch began Lawson was only one of dozens of ships' captains; when it ended he had become vice-admiral of the fleet, the fourth most senior officer in the navy. Of the major engagements fought between the two battle fleets he had a crucial part in at least four. In May 1652 off Dover, both Dutch losses, the *Santa Maria* and the *St Laurens*, were surrendered to Lawson, now commander of the *Fairfax*. The following September the *Fairfax* was still undergoing storm repairs at Chatham when Blake and Penn missed an opportunity off the Kentish Knock to inflict a crushing defeat on the Dutch. When the battle fleet was reorganized into three divisions in the spring of 1653, Lawson was appointed vice-admiral of the red, led by generals-at-sea Blake and Deane. At the battle of Portland on 18–20 February 1653 Lawson saved the day by rapid and daring manoeuvres. 'For the first time in war, an English flag officer was showing something more than fighting spirit' (Baumber, 174). He lost a hundred men killed or wounded and the *Fairfax* was so badly shattered that it had to be docked for major repairs. In his new ship, the *George*, he was promoted to rear-admiral of the fleet and admiral of the blue. Lawson again took the initiative when next the two met off the Gabbard on 2–3 June 1653. Closing first with the Dutch, ahead of the others, the *George* endured the brunt of the battle. The Dutch were routed and driven back to their home ports. Finally, at Scheveningen on 29–31 July 1653, the English won a decisive victory and Lawson had the satisfaction of disabling the ship of his old enemy, De Ruyter. For their conspicuous bravery and success gold medals and chains were awarded to Blake, Monck, Penn, and Lawson. Soon afterwards Lawson was given command of the North Sea Fleet blockading the Dutch coast, and he retained this post with the rank of vice-admiral throughout 1654 and 1655.

Political intrigue Whether Lawson deliberately sought the overthrow of Cromwell's protectorate seems unlikely, but his political innocence and inexperience led him into the dangerous waters of conspiracy. He helped to secure the election of John Wildman as member of parliament for Scarborough, though Wildman was an outspoken critic of Cromwell's government, and he had meetings with disaffected army colonels. Charles II thought he might even come over to the royalists. Most serious of all, Lawson promoted and endorsed a seamen's petition which threatened to undermine Cromwell's plans for a war with Spain. Finally, in January 1656, when Montagu, a much younger man without naval experience, was made general-at-sea over Lawson, he resigned his commission on the specious grounds that the projected attack on Spain was ill prepared. If Lawson had hoped to prompt a naval mutiny he was badly misinformed; several officers resigned but the fleet sailed. As a tribute to Lawson's popularity with captains and crews, he was not arrested and continued to receive full pay. Nevertheless, he still associated with militant Fifth Monarchists, rebellious army officers, and radical parliamentarians. Cromwell lost patience and ordered his imprisonment, and after a short spell in the Tower he was banished permanently to his home in Scarborough. In 1657, at the age of forty-two, it seemed that his naval career was finished.

'Finest hour' Within two years, however, following the downfall of Richard Cromwell, Lawson was reinstated as vice-admiral in command of the Channel Fleet. His loyalty to the parliamentary republic was thought to be absolute, and so it seemed. After the military junta of Lambert and Fleetwood had seized power, with the full support of all his captains, Lawson brought the fleet of twenty-two warships up to Gravesend to blockade the capital. In midwinter he had the means to starve and freeze London into submission. On Christmas day 1659 Fleetwood abdicated and thereby opened the way not only to the return of the Rump but eventually to the restoration of the monarchy. In January 1660 Lawson was elected to the new council of state, summoned to the Commons to receive its 'hearty thanks' and a pension of £500 a year (*JHC*, 7.799, 801, 806, 818). As the historian of the Commonwealth navy has written: 'The second restoration of the Rump was Lawson's finest hour … His control over the navy was complete' (Capp, 350). Nevertheless, he was soon deceived and outmanoeuvred by Monck and Montagu; in March they were named generals-at-sea over him and he was dropped from the council of state. By April Lawson at last realized that the republic was bankrupt and that of the choices facing the country—anarchy, military dictatorship, or monarchy—the last was the least worst. Still, his reluctant acceptance of the Restoration was a necessary condition of its smooth achievement; he alone commanded the loyalty of the Channel Fleet. In May 1660 the duke of York came ashore at Dover from Lawson's flagship, the *London*. The revengeful cavaliers in the Convention Parliament wanted to dismiss him and take away his pension, but Charles and James understood how much they owed to Lawson. He was knighted and awarded a free gift of £1000 and a pension of £500 per annum. In June 1661, as second to Montagu, now earl of Sandwich, he was sent to the straits to subdue the Barbary corsairs and secure England's new acquisition, Tangier. During the next four summers he was commander of a powerful Mediterranean squadron. According to Pepys his success in compelling Algiers, Tunis, and Tripoli to sign treaties respecting English shipping won him 'great renown among all men' (Pepys, 4.4). Less successful was his involvement in the construction of a great mole at Tangier, 'the greatest engineering work as yet undertaken by Englishmen' (E. Routh, 'The English occupation of Tangier, 1661–1683', *TRHS*, 2nd ser., 19, 1905, 66). When the Second Anglo-Dutch War seemed imminent in the autumn of 1664 Lawson was summoned back to England. The duke of York, now lord high admiral, made him second in his Red division. However, at the first encounter off Lowestoft, on 3 June 1665, Lawson's luck deserted him. After he and the duke had pounded their way through the Dutch centre and destroyed their admiral's flagship, in the ensuing chase Lawson was struck in the knee by a musket ball. The wound was not considered dangerous but gangrene set in and he died at Greenwich on 29 June and was buried on 1 July in St Dunstan-in-the-East, next to his daughter Abigail. He was survived by his widow and their three daughters, Isabella, Elizabeth, and Anna. In addition to the bequests to his own family, the admiral left £100 to the poor of Scarborough which was eventually used to buy a site for a hospital for superannuated seamen and the widows of seamen.

Great sea captain Lawson owed his exceptional success to good fortune, radicalism in religion and politics, and seamanship. At any time between 1642 and 1664 he might have been killed or maimed in battle, struck down by sickness, or drowned. Generals-at-sea Deane and Sandwich were killed in battle, Admiral Penn survived Lowestoft only because he wore a full suit of armour, and wounds and prolonged service at sea finished off Blake. But 'luck' was not a word in Lawson's limited vocabulary; his deliverance he attributed to 'godes great favour and providence' (PRO, SP 46/115/89). The longer he survived the stronger his conviction that he was God's weapon against His enemies, whether they were English royalists, Scottish presbyterians, north African pirates, or the Dutch. Religious devotion and patriotic duty went hand in hand, and when promoted to flag officer he vowed 'to secure the designs of God ... and the honest interest of England' (PRO, SP 18/48/57). It was this supreme self-assurance that so demoralized his opponents and inspired his fellow officers and seamen. Lawson is often described as a Baptist, though he does not appear to have belonged to any congregation. His puritanism was tolerant and undogmatic, his only serious objection to the established church was its collection of tithes. Lawson's courage, seamanship, and natural affinity with the lower deck won him a unique devotion from his officers and sailors. With the exception of Penn, all the most senior admirals were gentlemen soldiers before they became naval officers. Lawson was a 'tarpaulin' who had learned his profession in the demanding school of North Sea navigation. His lowly origins, rough manners, and bare literacy disqualified him from the highest rank and greatest rewards, but they found favour with common sailors. Unlike most contemporary captains he was genuinely concerned for the welfare of ordinary seamen—their pay, food, clothing, and conditions of service, as well as their morals. Even their dependants mattered to him. For one of his crew killed on the *Fairfax* at Portland he signed a note certifying the death and added in his own clumsy hand: 'The father of the above named is an Inpotent Aged man and in great want' (PRO, SP 46/119/321). Lawson might have been politically naive but he had an unrivalled grasp of naval strategy as well as battle tactics. He was one of the first to appreciate the need for a permanent, protected harbour in the Mediterranean. At the outbreak of the Second Anglo-Dutch War the duke of York, Sandwich, and Rupert all had to concede from experience that Lawson had been right to counsel against a fruitless and exhausting blockade of the Dutch coast. Clarendon, a good judge of men, had only the highest praise for Lawson, 'incomparably the modestest and the wisest man' whose loss to the country and the navy was 'almost irreparable' (Capp, 377). If he was not a great man, John Lawson was certainly one of England's greatest sea captains.   JACK BINNS

Sources B. Capp, *Cromwell's navy: the fleet and the English revolution, 1648–1660* (1989) • Scarborough corporation records, N. Yorks. CRO, DC/SCB • *CSP dom., 1643–65* • state papers 18, domestic, interregnum; SP 46, admiralty, 1644–73, PRO • S. R. Gardiner and C. T. Atkinson, eds., *Letters and papers relating to the First Dutch War, 1652–1654*, 6 vols., Navy RS, 13, 17, 30, 37, 41, 66 (1898–1930) • Pepys, *Diary* • Thomason tracts [BL] • *Sixth report*, HMC, 5 (1877–8) • *The manuscripts of J. Eliot Hodgkin ... of Richmond, Surrey*, HMC, 39 (1897) • *The manuscripts of J. M. Heathcote*, HMC, 50 (1899) • *Report on the manuscripts of F. W. Leyborne-Popham*, HMC, 51 (1899) • *Report on the Pepys manuscripts*, HMC, 70 (1911) • R. C. Anderson, 'English fleet lists in the First Dutch War', *Mariner's Mirror*, 24 (1938), 429–50 • *Mariner's Mirror*, 37 (1951), 251 [correspondence concerning the origin of the maxim of the navy and politics]; 38 (1952), 70, 242–3; 39 (1953), 232 • A. H. Taylor, 'Galleon into ship of the line [pt 1]', *Mariner's Mirror*, 44 (1958), 267–85 • A. H. Taylor, 'Galleon into ship of the line [pt 2]', *Mariner's Mirror*, 45 (1959), 14–24 • *Mariner's Mirror*, 55 (1969), 100–01 [contributions by R. C. Anderson, J. R. Powell, and M. L. Baumber on Lawson's naval career] • T. Hinderwell, *The history and antiquities of Scarborough* (1832) • M. Baumber, *General-at-sea: Robert Blake and the seventeenth century revolution in naval warfare* (1989) • *The journal of Edward Mountagu, first earl of Sandwich, admiral and general at sea, 1659–1665*, ed. R. C. Anderson, Navy RS, 64 (1929) • J. Binns, 'Sir John Lawson: Scarborough's admiral of the red', *Northern History*, 32 (1996), 90–110 • will, 19 April 1665, PRO, PROB 11/317

Archives NMM, letters | BL, letters to Captain Baynes, Add. MSS 21418–21423 • Bodl. Oxf., MSS Clarendon • N. Yorks. CRO, Scarborough corporation records, DC/SCB • PRO, state papers, domestic, interregnum SP 18; admiralty SP 46

Likenesses P. Lely, oils, *c.*1665, Royal Collection [*see illus.*] • P. Lely, oils, second version, NMM, Admiral's Gallery

Wealth at death houses at Alresford, Essex, and Scarborough, Yorkshire, and three closes in the latter; pension of £500 p.a.; £100 for the poor of Scarborough; two gold chains; £15 in money to relatives: will, 19 April 1665, PRO, PROB 11/317

Lawson, John (*d.* 1711), surveyor, may have been the son of Andrew Lawson, citizen and salter of London who on 1 February 1676 apprenticed a son, John, for eight years to the London apothecary John Chandler and, after Chandler's death the following year, to James Hayes. Early in 1700, being persuaded by 'a Gentleman, who had been Abroad, and was very well acquainted with the Ways of Living in both Indies' (Lawson, 7), he left London, reaching Charles Town, Carolina, in late August.

On 28 December Lawson, commissioned to investigate the virtually unexplored interior of Carolina, began a journey covering 550 miles in eight weeks. He followed the Santee and Wateree rivers inland, moved north and east on the trading path to the region of latter-day Hillsborough, North Carolina, thence to Pamlico Sound. Living off the country or being royally entertained by friendly American Indians, he kept a detailed record of his travels, noting the fauna and flora, and compiling an Indian vocabulary. He settled on the Pamlico river, and was soon profitably engaged in surveying, at first on his own account and afterwards as a deputy for Edward Moseley, the colony's surveyor-general. On 15 March 1701 he applied for his first land grant, and on 12 April wrote to England offering to send specimens of the local fauna and flora and a copy of his travel journal. When Bath was incorporated on 8 March 1705, Lawson was named one of the town's first commissioners, and almost certainly laid it out. The first recorded sale of town lots on 26 September 1706 included two bought by Lawson. From January 1707 until August 1708 he was clerk of the court and public register of Pamlico precinct, an office he surrendered on his departure for England. At that time he also made his will, leaving his property at Bath to his common-law wife, Hannah Smith, his daughter Isabella, and the child Hannah was then carrying.

If Lawson took his manuscript journal with him, he must have reached London by December 1708, when John Stevens began publication of *A New Collection of Voyages and Travels*, the first number including Lawson's *A New Voyage to Carolina*. He was certainly in London by 12 April 1709. On 21 July he was appointed with Edward Moseley to survey Carolina's disputed northern boundary with Virginia, and by September his journal was independently published, the title-page styling him 'John Lawson Gent. Surveyor-General of North-Carolina'. After giving an account of his winter journey in 1700–01 and briefly describing Carolina's geography and history, he gave a much longer natural history of the region, followed by a lengthy and sympathetic account of the Indians of North Carolina. The work ended with 'The second charter granted by King Charles II to the proprietors' and an abstract of the colony's constitution. In the final paragraph of this last he referred to 'a very large and exact Map' he had drawn, which

> begins at Cape *Henry* in *Virginia* … and contains all the coasts of *Carolina*, or *Florida*, with the *Bahama* Islands, great part of the Bay of *Mexico*, and the Island of *Cuba*, to the Southward, and several Degrees to the Westward of the *Messiasippi* River, with all the *Indian* Nations and Villages, and their Numbers.

The map actually printed, however, was a mere reworking of a map already a generation old. Though Lawson's manuscript is not known to survive, it is clearly the source for another virtually contemporary map providing almost identical information (Cumming, no. 157, plate 46A).

In London, Lawson met James Petiver, a botanist with whom he corresponded until his death, and Baron Christoph von Graffenried, a Swiss promoter intent on founding a colony in Virginia. Lawson persuaded him to settle in Carolina, where he bought 18,750 acres, 1250 of them from Lawson. Lawson also took charge of some 650 refugees from the Palatinate, whose passage to America the British government would pay, and by 9 November 1709 he was at Portsmouth, where some of the youngest were already dying. Only half the Palatines survived the voyage. Lawson took them overland to the confluence of the Trent and Neuse rivers and there laid out for them the town of New Bern, where they were joined by von Graffenried and his Swiss in September 1710.

Lawson, meanwhile, had gone to Virginia to survey the disputed border. Nothing was then agreed, and in October 1710 the Virginia commissioners accused Moseley and Lawson of delaying a decision for personal gain; but when the dispute was settled in 1728, the final line 'agreed to half a minute with the observations made formerly by Mr Lawson' (Lawson, xxii).

These events took place against a background of turmoil associated with Cary's rebellion. With the colonists divided, the Tuscarora Indians were able to express their violent resentment at the incursions of the growing numbers of settlers. The first victim of their wrath was Lawson: having set out with von Graffenried to explore the headwaters of the Neuse, he was intercepted at Catechna by the Tuscaroras in September 1711 and killed. A year later Hannah Smith sought the appraisal of his estate.

DAVID R. RANSOME

Sources J. Lawson, *A new voyage to Carolina*, ed. H. T. Lefler (1967) · BL, Sloane MSS 3337, 4063, 4064, 4067 · R. P. Stearns, 'James Petiver promoter of natural science, c.1663–1718', *Proceedings of the American Antiquarian Society*, 62 (1953), 243–365 · D. L. Rights, 'The trading path to the Indians', *North Carolina Historical Review*, 8 (1931), 403–26 · W. P. Cumming, *The southeast in early maps*, 3rd edn, ed. L. De Vorsey (1998) · A. Dill, *Governor Tryon and his palace* (1955) · H. T. Lefler and A. R. Newsome, *North Carolina: the history of a southern state* (1963) · *The writings of 'Colonel William Byrd of Westover in Virginia'*, ed. J. S. Bassett (1901) · *William Byrd's histories of the dividing line*, ed. W. K. Boyd (1929) · A. L. V. Briceland, 'Lawson, John', *ANB*
Archives BL, Sloane MSS 3337, 4063, 4064, 4067

Lawson, John (1708/9–1759), writer on oratory, was born in Magherafelt, co. Londonderry, the son of Alexander Lawson (d. 1718), Church of Ireland clergyman, and his wife, Katherine. After being tutored by a Mr McMahon in Monaghan, Lawson entered Trinity College, Dublin, as a sizar, on 1 June 1727, aged eighteen, and won a scholarship in 1729. He graduated BA (1731), MA (1734), and DD (1745), and became a fellow in 1735. He held a succession of university posts before being elected Erasmus Smith professor of oratory and history in 1750. Unlike some of his predecessors Lawson took his teaching duties seriously and delivered a course of lectures each term as well as coaching students in the art of declamation. He rejected a mechanical approach to oratory, whereby the stresses and cadences were marked with a form of musical notation, and argued that the speaker should be guided by a proper understanding of the text to be read. Lawson accepted that genius played a part in creating the most eloquent orators and believed that the ancient Greek orators were superior to their Roman counterparts. His *Lectures Concerning Oratory* were published in Dublin in 1758 to lukewarm reviews; subsequent editions appeared in 1759 and 1760.

Lawson lived up to his teaching, for he excelled as a preacher. Appointed Archbishop King's lecturer in 1746 and professor of divinity in 1752, he delivered hundreds of sermons, many of which were charity sermons on behalf of schools and hospitals. A selection was published posthumously in 1764, together with a Latin oration delivered by him at the funeral of Richard Baldwin, provost of Trinity College, on 4 October 1758.

Lawson suffered poor health in the 1750s, and died at Trinity College on 9 January 1759; he was buried in the college chapel three days later. He had not married, and in his will left bequests to his sister, stepmother, three half-sisters, and one half-brother.

GORDON GOODWIN, *rev.* S. J. SKEDD

Sources preface, J. Lawson, *Occasional sermons … written by a late eminent divine of the Church of England*, 3rd edn (1776) · E. N. Claussen and K. R. Wallace, 'Introduction', in J. Lawson, *Lectures concerning oratory*, new edn (1972) · Nichols, *Lit. anecdotes*, 2.311 · Burtchaell &

Sadleir, *Alum. Dubl.*, 2nd edn · R. B. McDowell and D. A. Webb, *Trinity College, Dublin, 1592–1952: an academic history* (1982) · will, PRO, PROB 11/848, fols. 291r–292r

Lawson, John (1723/4–1779), geometer, was the eldest son of Thomas Lawson, vicar of East Kirkby, Lincolnshire, where he was born; another mathematical son, Charles (1728–1807), became head of Manchester grammar school. From Boston grammar school Lawson was admitted to Sidney Sussex College, Cambridge, in 1741, becoming BA 1746, fellow in 1747, and MA and mathematical lecturer in 1749. Three years after his attaining BD in 1756 the college presented him to the rectory of Swanscombe, Kent.

Lawson remained a bachelor, and pursued his main interest, classical geometry. In 1774 he described himself as 'a man of leisure, and living … remote from … [other] mathematicians' (Wilkinson, 526). His first publication, in 1764, was a translation from Latin: *The Two Books of Apollonius Pergaeus, Concerning Tangencies*; another similar one, … *Concerning Determinate Section*, followed in 1772. In the next year appeared *A Synopsis of All the Data for the Construction of Triangles*, containing much information in coded form condensed into twenty pages. It was notable for its citations from a dozen mathematical periodicals, to some of which Lawson also contributed. It was reprinted by Thomas Leybourn (1770–1840) in 1802, and by John Bonnycastle (1750–1821) as an appendix to the sixth edition (1818) of his *Elements of Geometry*.

Lawson's most substantial work, even so of less than sixty pages, appeared anonymously in 1774: *A Dissertation on the Geometrical Analysis of the Ancients, with … Theorems and Problems*. He laments that 'this noble science seems of late to have met with less regard than it's dignity and usefulness demand', having been eclipsed by algebra. In some copies an extra leaf appealed for interested readers to communicate, resulting in correspondence with Jeremiah Ainsworth (1743–1784), Henry Clarke (1743–1818), and others. Lawson collected solutions to some of the problems, but the manuscripts are lost. The *Dissertation* was reprinted by Leybourn in his *Mathematical Repository*, with the problems later set for correspondents to answer.

Lawson died in Chislehurst on 13 November 1779. He was 'remarkable for his knowledge in antient and modern geometry, and was admired … by those who had a true taste for that sublime science' (GM).   RUTH WALLIS

Sources Venn, *Alum. Cant.* · T. T. Wilkinson, 'The Rev. John Lawson and his mathematical manuscripts', *N&Q*, 7 (1853), 526–7 · *GM*, 1st ser., 50 (1780), 50 · *Mathematical and Philosophical Repository*, 1 (1798), 1–14 [ed. T. Leybourn]
Archives Chetham's Library, Manchester, corresp. | Chetham's Library, Manchester, corresp. with Charles Wildbore and mathematical papers

Lawson, John James [Jack], **Baron Lawson** (1881–1965), coalminer and politician, was born on 16 October 1881 at Dobson's Buildings, Whitehaven, one of ten children of John James Lawson (d. 1930?), a merchant seaman turned miner, and his wife, Elizabeth, *née* Savage (d. 1929?). Although he knew material hardship in his early years, Lawson's childhood experiences in the small Cumberland

John James Lawson, Baron Lawson (1881–1965), by Howard Coster, 1945

villages of Kells and Flimby gave him an abiding love of the countryside and the seashore, while his elementary schooling at the Glass House national school, Whitehaven, opened the door to a lifelong enjoyment of books. When Lawson was nine, his family moved to Boldon colliery, in co. Durham; and on leaving the Boldon colliery school in 1893 he joined his father and older brothers down the pit, at a starting wage of 10d. a day. He progressed steadily through the hierarchy of pit work to reach the élite grade of hewer in 1904; and on 22 February 1906 he married Isabella Graham (1882–1968), a domestic servant, daughter of Robert Scott, a machinist. They had three daughters.

As a young miner, Jack Lawson was torn between two conflicting interests, gambling and self-improvement. However, at about the age of twenty he underwent a religious conversion and joined the Wesleyan Methodists; he was an active lay preacher for the rest of his life. At the same time his pursuit of knowledge through a mixture of private reading and public debate led to a growing interest in social problems and socialist solutions. By 1905 he had joined the Independent Labour Party and taken the first step towards a possible trade union career on being elected an assistant checkweighman by his fellow hewers. All this made him obvious material for Ruskin College, the recently established trade union college at Oxford. He was offered a scholarship there in 1906, and his wife went back into service to help support him. 'Thrilled and inspired beyond words' in 1937 by reading H. A. L. Fisher's *History of Europe*, Lawson recalled these early years when 'you kindly took me, with other obscure ones, into a special class ... shall I ever forget those days of spiritual exaltation when I sat at your feet?' (Lawson to Fisher, 10 Jan 1937, Bodl. Oxf., MS Fisher 73, fol. 1). On completing his studies, Lawson rejected the possibility of making a new career in teaching or the ministry, and took the deliberate decision to resume his work as a miner.

After returning to co. Durham, Lawson threw himself into local Labour politics. He acted as agent for the socialist Pete Curran at Jarrow in the general election of January 1910, and in 1913 he was elected to Durham county council, on which he sat for the next ten years. Following war service as a driver in the Royal Artillery, he was chosen to fight Seaham Harbour for Labour in the 'coupon' election of 1918, but lost to the sitting Liberal. However, in the turbulent post-war world the political tide in the British coalfields was running strongly in Labour's favour; and in 1919 Lawson entered the Commons in a by-election for Chester-le-Street. He held the seat continuously, rarely polling less than seventy per cent of the popular vote, until he retired in 1949.

During thirty years as a member of parliament, Lawson's first loyalty was always to 'his own people', the pitmen of the north-east and their families. He dealt assiduously with his constituents' personal problems, especially in matters of pensions and benefits, and he was vociferous in demanding government action to deal with the wider regional issues of poverty and unemployment. Given his background, he was a strong contender for junior office in Ramsay MacDonald's two minority administrations. In the first Labour government of 1924 he became MacDonald's parliamentary private secretary along with Clement Attlee, and also served as financial secretary to the War Office; while in 1929–31 he was parliamentary secretary at the Ministry of Labour under Margaret Bondfield. As the jobless total rose inexorably in the aftermath of the 1929 Wall Street crash, Lawson's department came in for serious criticism from Labour's trade union allies for its unsympathetic handling of unemployment problems; but his personal reputation seems to have suffered little as a result.

As one of the few survivors of Labour's electoral débâcle in 1931, Lawson's future looked uncertain. Gradually, however, his career recovered. He joined the opposition front bench in 1937; and on the outbreak of the Second World War he was appointed deputy commissioner for civil defence in the northern region. This was a demanding job, both physically and emotionally, especially in the early years of the war, when the industrial north-east suffered heavy German bombing raids; and the accidental death of a young grandson, whom the Lawsons had brought up as their own, in the aftermath of one such raid was a personal tragedy from which perhaps he never fully recovered.

Following Labour's landslide victory in 1945, Attlee—

with whom Lawson enjoyed a warm personal friendship—offered him the cabinet post of secretary of state for war, charged with the urgent task of ensuring a swift, orderly, and equitable demobilization of the wartime armed forces. His duties included a 35,000 mile round trip to India and the Far East, during which he justified his policy at sixty mass meetings of troops eagerly awaiting their discharge. Within little more than a year of his appointment ill health forced his reluctant resignation from the government; but by then he had completed the immediate task to his own satisfaction. After three years on the back benches he retired from the Commons to become vice-president of the National Parks Commission; and in March 1950 he went to the House of Lords as Baron Lawson of Beamish.

For much of his time in the Commons Lawson supplemented his salary by journalism and occasional broadcasting, dispensing homespun philosophy and personal observations in accessible, and often poetic, language. Among his more substantial writings were full-length character sketches of two older miners' leaders whom he had known personally: Durham's Peter Lee and the phlegmatic Yorkshireman Herbert Smith. However, his best-known and best-loved work was his autobiography, *A Man's Life* (1932), which had sold over 30,000 copies by the time Lawson retired from the Commons. Its insights into working-class life, its individual style, and its author's patent modesty and sincerity marked it out as a classic of its kind. Not only does it provide the essential key to understanding Lawson's own beliefs and achievements: it was also influential in creating the enduring image of the Durham miners as the backbone of the British labour movement in the twentieth century. James Callaghan in 1977 gave 'the book I had admired for many years' to President Carter on his visit to Durham, and claims that Carter read it on his flight home (J. Callaghan, *Time and Change*, 1977, 482).

Jack Lawson's socialism was always more sentimental than scientific. Pragmatic and patriotic, his good sense, moderation, and reliability won him friends and admirers in all walks of life and all political parties; for example, he kept up an amicable correspondence with the high tory historian Arthur Bryant. Once it had been realized that figures such as Lawson posed no real threat to the established order, his personal qualities made him a worthy candidate for public honours and non-partisan appointments. He was awarded an honorary DCL by Durham University in 1947, and the freedom of Sunderland in 1950; but he took particular pride in becoming, in 1949, the first pitman to be lord lieutenant of co. Durham. He filled the post with an easy grace for nine years, during which he claimed to have attended over 1500 functions and meetings. Yet if he enjoyed the recognition which came his way, he also remained unambitious and unspoilt. He never became a rich man, and for the last forty years of his life he lived in the same small cottage in Beamish, among the 'ordinary folk' whom he had sought to serve.

Lord Lawson died in Chester-le-Street General Hospital

on 3 August 1965, and was buried at West Pelton churchyard, co. Durham. A memorial service in Durham Cathedral on 13 September made an appropriate end to a career which epitomized the almost painless incorporation of the Labour Party into British public life during the first half of the twentieth century. DUNCAN BYTHELL

Sources J. Lawson, *A man's life* (1932) • U. Durham L., archives and special collections, Lawson MSS • J. Bellamy and D. E. Martin, 'Lawson, John James', *DLB*, vol. 2 • J. Lawson, *Who goes home? Broadcasts and sketches* (1945) • H. Beynon and T. Austrin, *Masters and servants: class and patronage in the making of a labour organisation* (1994) • Burke, *Peerage* (1963) • b. cert. • m. cert. • *CGPLA Eng. & Wales* (1965)
Archives U. Durham L., additional papers • U. Durham L., journals, diaries, corresp. | BL, letters to Albert Mansbridge, Add. MS 65253
Likenesses H. Coster, photograph, 1945, NPG [*see illus.*]
Wealth at death £3461: probate, 15 Sept 1965, *CGPLA Eng. & Wales*

Lawson, John Parker (*d.* 1852), ecclesiastical historian, was also a deacon or a minister in the Scottish Episcopal church. He was for some time a chaplain in the army, but afterwards lived in Edinburgh, earning his living by writing for the booksellers. He died in 1852 at his home, 6 Rose Street, Edinburgh, and was buried in Edinburgh.

Lawson wrote many works of which the most enduring and important was his *History of the Scottish Episcopal Church from the Revolution to the Present Time* (1843). Evidently an apologetic, it nevertheless attempted a more critical approach to Scottish episcopalian history than most previous works, and remains a valuable historical source. Historiographically the work is significant for containing the earliest interpretation of the Oxford Movement as entirely beneficial to the Episcopal church. Writing during the movement itself, Lawson is concerned to refute contemporary accusations of Romanism levelled at Tractarians in Scotland by emphasizing the Tractarian similarities to the nonjurors. Entirely nonjuring and high church for most of the eighteenth century, the Scottish Episcopal church was therefore traditionally antagonistic to Roman Catholicism and consequently suspicious of later Tractarianism. Lawson was attempting to enlist Scottish episcopalian sympathies for Tractarianism, as well as those of English Anglicans for the Episcopal church. As expected from a literary hack, Lawson wrote a number of other works, primarily on English and Scottish history and chiefly from the usual high-church episcopalian perspective. Among these were his editions of 1844 of the first two volumes of Bishop Robert Keith's *History of the Affairs of Church and State in Scotland* for the Spottiswoode Society. ROWAN STRONG

Sources Allibone, *Dict.* • Boase, *Mod. Eng. biog.* • NA Scot., SC 70/1/78, p. 326
Wealth at death £139 18s. 1d.: inventory, 4 Feb 1853, NA Scot., SC 70/1/78, p. 326

Lawson [*née* Albury], **Louisa** (1848–1920), newspaper proprietor and suffragist in Australia, was born on 17 February 1848 on Guntawang station, near Mudgee, New South Wales, Australia, the second of the twelve children of Henry Albury (1825–1908), a station hand, and his wife, Harriet Elizabeth, *née* Winn (1826–1895), a needlewoman, both English-born immigrants. Henry moved his family to Mudgee and later to New Pipeclay goldfield nearby, where he ran a bar. Louisa was educated at Mudgee national school. On 7 July 1866, at the Wesleyan parsonage, Mudgee, she married Niels Hertzberg Larsen (known as Peter Lawson), a Norwegian-born master mariner and goldminer. They went to the Grenfell goldfield, where their first son, Henry Archibald, was born on 17 June 1867. Living in harsh circumstances, with Peter often absent on contract work or fossicking, Louisa bore two other sons and twin daughters, one of whom died in infancy. She learned dressmaking, sold produce from Peter's small farm at Eurunderee, and became postmistress.

In 1883 Louisa Lawson and her younger children moved to Sydney. Earlier her second son, Charles, had run away to his grandmother after being savagely punished by his father. Mrs Albury ran a boarding-house in Sydney, where Charles was shortly to appear on a stealing charge. Louisa took boarders, resumed dressmaking, and brought her son Henry to Sydney to work as a carriage painter. Peter Lawson occasionally sent money and on his death in 1888 left her £1103. Louisa encouraged Henry's literary ambitions. A brief flirtation with spiritualism brought them radical friends and together, under the name Archie Lawson, they edited *The Republican* (1887–8). When it failed Louisa Lawson bought its press to publish *Dawn* (1888–1905), a monthly newspaper for women. *Dawn* survived a boycott initiated by the all-male Typographical Union, which refused membership to Louisa's women typographers. It became the longest running and most successful early feminist journal in Australia, offering a lively mix of news, commentary, and service items. Louisa wrote most of the copy. She challenged the male monopoly of law and the conventions which disadvantaged women: her criticism of the behaviour of husbands to wives was as pungent as her reporting of laws which failed to protect women and of women's exclusion from public office. She condemned drunkenness, blamed prostitution on bad law, and called for appointment of women warders in gaols. She had a vision of women's coming role, which required they abandon frivolousness, dress sensibly, lead healthy lives, and become informed on public affairs.

There was a practical, even entrepreneurial, side to Louisa's preaching. To educate women she founded the Dawn Club, where 'bright clever papers', written by women in the interests of women, would be heard. She persuaded the Sydney Mechanics' School of Arts debating clubs to admit women, and encouraged women to join for experience in public speaking and also to attend its night classes. She was the first woman elected to its board of management. She took out a miner's right which carried entitlement to vote. She also ran a mail-order paper pattern and ready-made clothing business.

When the Womanhood Suffrage League was formed in 1891, Mrs Lawson brought her Dawn Club members into it. She printed its publicity material free of charge, gathered signatures for its suffrage petition, joined its delegation to the premier, Sir George Dibbs, and became one of its most valued public speakers. When the women of New

South Wales were enfranchised in 1902, tribute was paid to Mrs Lawson. She joined the executive of the Women's Progressive Association, but physical and financial difficulties hampered her. Neither her novel *Dert and do* (1904) nor *The Lonely Crossing* (1905), a collection of poems, was a financial success. She closed *Dawn* in 1905 and became dependent on the sale of short stories.

In 1900 Louisa Lawson was thrown from a tram and seriously injured. She anticipated economic independence from a patent she held on a mailbag fastener but after protracted legal action alleging conspiracy to defraud won meagre compensation. Her son Charles lived with her, but was unstable and sometimes absent; she was estranged from Henry whose writing she had originally promoted. As alcoholism gripped him and his marriage failed, his embittered relations with his wife reverberated in his writing. Misogyny fuelled a literary tradition which labelled Louisa an uncaring, self-absorbed mother, a blight on a talented son.

With age Louisa Lawson's mind deteriorated and she refused food. She died on 12 August 1920 in Gladesville Hospital for the Insane and was buried on 14 August in Rookwood cemetery. Feminist historians in recent years have proclaimed her vigour in reform; Brian Matthews, in his prize-winning *Louisa* (1987), rescued her from the obloquy of literary critics and acknowledged the 'power and inventiveness' of her poems.   HEATHER RADI

Sources *Dawn* (1888–1905) · H. Radi, ed., *200 Australian women* (1988) · *AusDB* · B. Matthews, *Louisa* (1987) · C. Roderick, *The real Henry Lawson* (1982) · *Henry Lawson letters, 1890–1920*, ed. C. Roderick (1970) · B. Matthews, 'Dawn crusade Louisa Lawson', *Rebels and radicals*, ed. E. Fry (1983) · *Womans Budget* (28 Aug 1920)
Archives Mitchell L., NSW | Mitchell L., NSW, Miles Franklin MSS · Mitchell L., NSW, Gertrude O'Connor MSS · Mitchell L., NSW, Scott MSS
Likenesses photographs, *c.*1866, repro. in *RANS Journal*, 18 (1932), 285, 311
Wealth at death £545 0s. 8d.

Lawson, Robert (1741/2–1816), army officer, of whose parents nothing is known, entered the Royal Military Academy, Woolwich, on 17 July 1758 and passed out as a lieutenant fireworker in the Royal Artillery on 25 December 1759. He served at the siege of Belle Île in 1761, and from 1763 was stationed at Gibraltar; while there he was promoted second lieutenant (1766) and first lieutenant (1771). After returning to England, he sailed for America in 1776. In 1779 he was promoted captain-lieutenant and appointed bridgemaster to the army in New York (he had previously acted as deputy bridgemaster under Sir William Howe). With his promotion to captain on 11 March 1782, Lawson received command of the 40th company, Royal Artillery, which he took to the West Indies at the end of 1783. For the next three years he commanded the artillery on Jamaica.

In January 1793, on the creation of the Royal Horse Artillery, Lawson, now back in England, was chosen to take command of its first troop. Once four troops had been raised, the training of the entire corps fell to him, to ensure that it could act in concert with cavalry. He was promoted major (5 December 1793) and lieutenant-

colonel (30 August 1794), then commanded the artillery in the north-east district, based at Newcastle upon Tyne.

Following promotion to colonel in January 1800, Lawson was selected to command the artillery in General Sir Ralph Abercromby's expedition to the Mediterranean; an appointment as brigadier-general resulted (6 June 1800). Abercromby's army having arrived in Egypt, Lawson displayed considerable ingenuity in transporting his guns across the soft sands, introducing horse barrows or litters and modifying carriages to make lighter-weight naval 24-pounder carronades available for siege operations. Wounded at the battle of Alexandria (21 March 1801), Lawson nevertheless saw the campaign through to its successful conclusion and was highly commended by General Hutchinson, Abercromby's successor.

During the 1803 invasion scare Lawson sited batteries for the defence of London; he afterwards moved to the Chatham lines. On 1 February 1808 he was appointed colonel commandant of the 10th battalion, Royal Artillery, and was promoted major-general on 25 April. His posting to Chatham continued until 1813, when he was promoted lieutenant-general.

Lawson's marital status is uncertain, but he had a son, Captain Robert Lawson, Royal Artillery (*c.*1777–1819), who served in the Peninsula, and another son, George Robert (*b.* 1806), whose mother was called Ann, and to whose upbringing by guardians Lawson left £6000 in his will. Captain Robert Lawson made provision for Jane (*b.* 1794x1800), his father's illegitimate daughter by Sophia Harrison. Lawson died at Woolwich, Kent, where he was then living, on 25 February 1816 aged seventy-four, and was buried on 2 March at St Nicholas's Church, Plumstead, Kent.

H. M. CHICHESTER, rev. ALASTAIR W. MASSIE

Sources J. Philippart, ed., *The royal military calendar*, 3 vols. (1815–16) · R. Lawson, 'Memorandums of artillery arrangements … on the expedition to Egypt, 1801', *Minutes of the Proceedings of the Royal Artillery Institution*, 12 (1884), 207–20 · J. Kane, *List of officers of the royal regiment of artillery from the year 1716 to the year 1899*, rev. W. H. Askwith, 4th edn (1900) · F. Duncan, ed., *History of the royal regiment of artillery*, 2nd edn, 2 vols. (1874) · PRO, PROB 11/1578 (149) · PRO, PROB 11/1620 (431) [Captain Robert Lawson (son)'s will] · parish register, Plumstead, St Nicholas, LMA, 2/3/1816 [burials] · parish register, St James, Piccadilly, City Westm. AC, 1806 [baptism] · M. E. S. Laws, ed., *Battery records of the royal artillery, 1716–1859* (1952) · P. Mackesy, *British victory in Egypt, 1801: the end of Napoleon's conquest* (1995)
Archives Royal Artillery Institution, Woolwich, MD 3054/1, MD 3054/2
Wealth at death £6000—bequests made to two sons: will, 1807, PRO, PROB 11/1578

Lawson, Thomas (1619/20–1695), Independent minister, was admitted to St Catharine's College, Cambridge, in 1633; he graduated BA in 1637, proceeded MA in 1640, and was elected a fellow of St John's College in 1644. The following year, on 13 May, he was appointed rector of Langenhoe, Essex. On 20 June 1646 he was admitted to the vicarage of Fingringhoe, Essex, following the sequestration of Joseph Long and the rejection of Owen Reeve by the committee for plundered ministers. On 4 May 1647, on the presentation of Henry Tunstall, he was instituted by the

House of Lords as rector of the neighbouring parish of East Doniland, by then united with Fingringhoe. About April 1648 he signed the *Testimony of the ministers of the province of Essex, to the trueth of Jesus Christ, and to the solemn league and covenant*. On 28 October 1649 Lawson joined the Independent church at Norwich, but continued in his official livings. Admitted to the rectory of Denton, Norfolk, on the presentation of Robert Wilton in late 1650 or early 1651, Lawson compounded for the first fruits on 5 May 1653. On 29 April 1655 the Norwich Independent church dismissed 'brother Thomas Lawson' to join with 'the Christians at Denton' and on 3 June an Independent church there was received into fellowship with that of Norwich. Lawson probably acted as minister at Denton.

Lawson later moved to Suffolk. Admitted rector of Market Weston on 12 October 1658, he was presented formally to the living under the great seal on 27 June 1659, but after the Restoration ceded it before the induction of Maurice Moseley on 24 August 1660. During his tenure of Market Weston, Lawson was a member of the Independent church centred on the parish, but he then moved to Bury St Edmunds, married, and baptized a son, Jabez, at the Bury St Edmunds Independent church on 26 July 1661. Another son, Deodate went to New England, where he became minister at Scituate, but was dismissed for absence about 1698 and appears to have found it hard to rebuild his reputation in Independent circles. In 1669 Lawson was reported to be preaching at Rattlesden, Wattisfield, and Bury St Edmunds. On 17 April 1672 he was licensed as a teacher at his own house at Norton, Suffolk, and at Mary Cook's house, Southgate Street, Bury St Edmunds. On 20 October 1689 he joined Bury's Independent church. According to Calamy he was 'a man of parts, but had no good utterance' (Calamy, *Continuation*, 629). He died in 1695, probably at Bury St Edmunds, aged seventy-five. ALEXANDER GORDON, *rev.* STEPHEN WRIGHT

Sources Calamy rev. · J. Browne, *A history of Congregationalism and memorials of the churches in Norfolk and Suffolk* (1877) · T. W. Davids, *Annals of evangelical nonconformity in Essex* (1863) · *Walker rev.* · *JHL*, 9–10 (1646–8) · E. Calamy, *A continuation of the account of the ministers … who were ejected and silenced after the Restoration in 1660*, 2 vols. (1727) · *CSP dom.*, 1671–2, 327, 388

Lawson, Thomas (*bap.* 1630, *d.* 1691), Quaker minister and botanist, was baptized on 10 October 1630 at Lawkland in the parish of Clapham, Yorkshire, the son of Thomas Lawson (*d.* 1649), a yeoman or peasant farmer, and his wife, Elizabeth (*d.* 1636). He had at least two siblings, Margaret (*bap.* 28 Feb 1620) and Elizabeth (*bap.* 1 April 1626), and probably a third, Hugh, who graduated BA from Christ's College, Cambridge, in 1657. After attending grammar school at Giggleswick, Lawson was admitted as a sizar at Christ's College on 25 July 1650, but left after a year or two without earning a degree. He became the minister at Rampside, Lancashire, probably as an assistant to the vicar of Dalton, for Rampside was a chapel in that parish. When Lawson learned that George Fox was at Aldingham in 1652, he welcomed him to his church and encouraged his congregation to hear Fox preach. As Lawson's

'notionary knowledge begun to fade away' he became a Quaker and resigned his position at Rampside (Swarthmore MSS, 1.246). After he conferred with Fox, James Nayler, and Richard Farnworth at Swarthmoor, he testified at Clapham, where the minister, Christopher Place, and some of his parishioners physically assaulted him. He was accused of inappropriate sexual conduct with a young Quaker woman who witnessed with him at Clapham, but he professed his innocence in a letter to Margaret Fell.

Lawson became one of the more than sixty 'valiant' ministers who spread the Friends' message in the north. In 'Of the false ministry', published in Thomas Aldam, Benjamin Nicholson, and John Harwood's *A Brief Discovery* (1653), Lawson castigated professional clergy as thieves, witches, and blasphemers. He was briefly incarcerated in York Castle, and in October 1653 he and Richard Hubberthorne won converts from a gathered church established by Walter Cradock at Wrexham in Denbighshire. With John Slee he left in May 1655 for Sussex, where Thomas Laycock joined them, and they subsequently witnessed in Surrey as well. On this trip Lawson confronted apparent Ranters, and at Crawley, Sussex, he and Slee were challenged by the General Baptist Matthew Caffyn. In Lawson's account of the debate, *An Untaught Teacher* (1655), he argued that the word of God is 'the incorruptible seed', not the Bible (p. 2), and that salvation is through the light within rather than external means. Caffyn retorted in *The Deceived, and Deceiving Quakers* (1656), to which Nayler replied in *The Light of Christ* (1656). Lawson was also attacked by Magnus Byne, vicar of Clayton, Sussex, in *The Scornfull Quaker Answered* (1656), to which he responded in *The Lip of Truth Opened* (1656). On 4 March 1656 he, Alexander Parker, Anthony Pearson, and others engaged in a debate with non-Quakers at Preston, Lancashire, with Major-General Charles Worsley presiding.

Some time after his southern trip Lawson settled at Newby, near Great Strickland, Westmorland. It was likely during the winter of 1655–6 that he went to Newcastle to obtain a Hebrew lexicon, finally purchasing one—probably that of Johannes Buxtorfius—from a distant relative. He travelled in Yorkshire in 1657 with Thomas Killam and Gervase Benson. On 24 May 1659 he married Frances Wilkinson (*bap.* 1637, *d.* 1693), daughter of William Wilkinson (*d.* 1647) of Great Strickland, where Lawson would live the rest of his life; they had four children. By his marriage he acquired customary tenancies, and he subsequently increased his holdings; from 1667 until his death he was described as a gentleman. In June or July 1659 he established a school, where an early pupil was Francis Howgill's son. With other schoolmasters and parish clergy he attended a meeting at Appleby on 27 April 1664.

In 1660 Lawson published *An Appeal to the Parliament*, exhorting it to require each parish to provide relief for the elderly, the physically incapacitated, and orphans, and to establish 'a Poor mans Office' to assist the able-bodied to find jobs and apprentices to locate masters. He was repeatedly cited for refusing to pay tithes, excommunicated in

1664, and imprisoned at Durham in 1666. When John Joachim Zentgraff linked Quakers to Seekers in *Colluvies quackerorum* (1666), Lawson repudiated the charge in *Eine Antwort auf ein Buch* (1668). Cited for teaching without a licence, he appeared before the bishop of Carlisle on 12 July 1671, subscribed to the Thirty-Nine Articles, took the oaths, was absolved from excommunication, and received a licence. He soon returned to his Quaker beliefs, lost his licence, was cited in July 1673 for recusancy and teaching illegally, and was briefly imprisoned. Threatened with the loss of two-thirds of his estate as an alleged popish recusant, he sought refuge in Lancashire. By the summer of 1674 he was at Swarthmoor, instructing Thomas Lower and the Fell sisters in botany, the earliest firm evidence of his interest in this subject, which had probably been sparked by John Ray's *Catalogus plantarum Angliae* (1670). Aware of Lawson's pedagogical skills, Fox wrote to William Penn on 10 October 1674 proposing a garden-school near London in which Lawson and Richard Richardson would use plants as well as books to teach children. Ralph Cudworth thought it was an excellent idea, though the school never materialized.

Lawson now prepared for a walking tour of England, extracting botanical data from works by Ray, John Parkinson, and others and recording it county by county. Starting in the spring of 1677 he travelled south, through Manchester, Stafford, and Worcester to Bristol and Bath, and then to Oxford, Bedford, and London, collecting specimens and recording his observations. Using London as a base he visited Kent and Essex, but he also found time for Quaker activities, obtaining the morning meeting's approval on 6 August for publication of his *Baptismalogia, or, A Treatise Concerning Baptisms* (1678), which espoused the Friends' doctrine of spirit-baptism and their opposition to a physical celebration of the Lord's supper. After finishing his tour by returning home via Cambridge, Lincoln, York, and Scarborough, he continued to collect botanical material in later years, mostly in Yorkshire and Durham. He contributed material to Robert Morison's *Plantarum historiae universalis Oxoniensis pars secunda* (1680) and corresponded with Ray, for whom he collected fossils to facilitate the study of insects.

Taking advantage of the lapse of book licensing in the final years of Charles II's reign, Lawson published four more books, beginning with *Dagon's Fall* (1679), in which he denounced heathen philosophy and literature, lascivious verse, and wanton comedies, citing Augustine, Tertullian, Gregory the Great, and Luther for support. He continued the attack in *A Mite into the Treasury* (1680), condemning academic degrees and dress, clerical garb, obscene books, and astrology, and calling for the study of utilitarian subjects. In *A Treatise Relating to the Call, Work & Wages of the Ministers of Christ* (1680) he rejected compulsory tithes as the wages of Antichrist's clergy. The fourth book, *A Serious Remembrancer* (1684), was occasioned by the death of his son Jonah on 23 February 1684 of smallpox and pneumonia, and stressed the necessity for believers to eschew wickedness.

Lawson reopened his school, probably about 1686, admitting non-Quakers as well as Friends. Among the former was Christopher Yates (Yeats), curate of Thrimby, Westmorland, who secretly married Ruth Lawson in the spring of 1687 despite her father's objections, though Lawson eventually accepted his son-in-law, sparking criticism from some Friends. On 20 April 1689 Lawson told Fox he had manuscripts on many subjects 'relateing to the primitive order, & how it came to be lost', as well as the continuation of pagan, idolatrous, and Jewish elements in supposedly reformed churches (Barclay MS 42). Yet his circle of friends included not only such Quaker stalwarts as Penn (from whom he apparently purchased 250 acres in Pennsylvania in 1684), Parker, and George Whitehead but also the Anglican cleric William Nicolson, a fellow botanist. In early 1691 he revived the proposal for a garden-school, but failed to obtain patronage from John Rodes of Barlbrough Hall, Derbyshire.

Following his death at Great Strickland on 12 November 1691, Lawson was interred that same month in the Quaker burial-ground at Newby Head, Westmorland. His widow died in 1693 and was buried on 3 February. Although Fox exaggerated when he described Lawson as 'one of the greatest simplers in England' (*Narrative Papers*, 16), he was the first botanist to provide detailed data about Cumbrian flora. In 1786 his name was given to a plant—*Hieracium lawsonii*—found in the Pyrenees, the south-western Alps, and the mountains of southern France.

RICHARD L. GREAVES

Sources E. J. Whittaker, *Thomas Lawson, 1630–1691: north country botanist, Quaker and schoolmaster* (1986) • RS Friends, Lond., Swarthmore MS 1.241-6 • RS Friends, Lond., Barclay MSS 42, 139, 169 • Venn, *Alum. Cant.* • *The journal of George Fox*, ed. N. Penney, 2 vols. (1911), vol. 1, pp. 49, 408; vol. 2, p. 332 • *The papers of William Penn*, ed. M. M. Dunn and R. S. Dunn, 1 (1981), 295; 2 (1982), 647 • *Narrative papers of George Fox*, ed. H. J. Cadbury (1972), 16 • Mrs G. Locker-Lampson, ed., *A Quaker post-bag: letters to Sir John Rodes of Barlbrough Hall, in the county of Derby, baronet, and to John Gratton of Monyash, 1693–1742* (1910), 20–23 • W. C. Braithwaite, *The beginnings of Quakerism*, ed. H. J. Cadbury, 2nd edn (1955), 448–9 • J. Besse, *A collection of the sufferings of the people called Quakers*, 2 vols. (1753), vol. 2, pp. 24, 35 • T. L. Underwood, *Primitivism, radicalism, and the lamb's war: the Baptist–Quaker conflict in seventeenth-century England* (1997)
Archives Cumbria AS, Kendal, will and minute book • Linn. Soc., botanical notebook • priv. coll., minute book • RS Friends, Lond., letters and MSS | RS Friends, Lond., letters to Margaret Fell and papers
Wealth at death land in Westmorland; 250 acres in Pennsylvania (later contested); daughter Hannah received £38; daughter Deborah £37 14s.; grandchildren got £5; 10s. for poor; two books and MSS to son-in-law; all remaining possessions to wife and daughters, Deborah and Hannah: MS P.1691/2, Cumbria AS, Carlisle; summarized in Whittaker, *Thomas Lawson*, 163, 188

Lawson, Thomas George (1814–1891), colonial official and Baptist leader, was born in October 1814 in the town of New London, Anecho, in west Africa, the second son of George Acquatay Lawson (*c*.1778–1856), political leader and merchant, and his wife, Adólèvi Apé, a sister of the king of Anloga (Awuna in British documents). George A. Lawson, born Akuété Zankli, was the son of Laté Awoku (*c*.1739–1795) and the grandson of Laté Bewu, who came from Accra to the kingdom of Glidji about 1730. A few years after his arrival Laté Bewu married Adaku, a daughter of Assiongbon Dandjé, king of Glidji.

The coastal region near Glidji was one centre of European trade with which local African rulers were closely involved. In the 1750s, as a means of becoming better informed, Laté Bewu entrusted Laté Awoku to the British captain of a merchant ship for education in commerce and the English language. In family documents the captain's name is given as Law or Lawson, and a Captain William Lawson was active along the coast during this period. Laté Awoku returned well versed in commerce and was granted land by the ruler of Anecho about 1767. In turn Laté Awoku sent Akuété Zankli 'to Britain' to study, but it is likely that he settled for a time in the Sierra Leone colony and may have had a son there who remained in Freetown when Akuété Zankli returned to Anecho in 1812 or before. There he succeeded his father as an adviser to the king and built a town called Badji, later renamed New London. It was he, or possibly his father, who assumed the family name Lawson.

By 1825 New London was closely allied with the United Kingdom, and following family tradition Thomas George Lawson was entrusted to Captain Isaac Spence from London for further education. Whether or not he was meant to study in London, Lawson disembarked at Freetown and was taken in by John McCormack, a wealthy timber merchant and a chief adviser to the colonial government. He lived in McCormack's large house on Rawdon Street and was educated in colonial schools. He often travelled with McCormack on business and fact-finding tours into the interior north and east of the colony. For several years he was employed by McCormack's timber company as a trading agent in the interior and as an interpreter. Through his extensive contacts he learned several African languages and gained substantial knowledge of Arabic. By about 1840 he was married to a woman from one of the royal houses of Koya kingdom, located about 30 miles east of Freetown. It appears that at least three children came from this liaison: William Thomas George Lawson, who was born about 1840; Thomas George Lawson, who died in 1897; and a daughter, who died in 1878.

McCormack was so favourably impressed by Lawson's knowledge of African cultures and languages and by his skill as an intermediary that he recommended him for the position of the governor's personal messenger to African rulers in the interior. Between 1846 and 1851 Lawson ably fulfilled his mission, and Governor Norman William Macdonald recommended to the Colonial Office that he be appointed as the first official colony messenger and interpreter with an annual salary of £100. He became the principal colonial official responsible for representing British interests in the interior and for receiving African notables who travelled to Freetown.

From Lawson's official appointment on 1 May 1852 until January 1889 he was the director of 'native affairs' for the British administration, and was deeply involved in the expansion of the coastal settlement into the colony and protectorate of Sierra Leone which occurred in 1896.

Under government auspices he went on dozens of missions to various African kingdoms and towns, he arranged the housing and interpreted for African rulers or their representatives when they came to Freetown, and he presented thousands of pages of reports and memoranda to senior colonial officers. His writings and personal advice to several governors and administrators-in-chief provided the data and analytical basis for colonial policy.

Lawson was a devoted Christian and an outspoken supporter of Queen Victoria and British administration in Africa. His religious proclivities are attested to by his active role in the West African Methodist church between 1840 and 1850. In 1850 he became a Baptist, and in 1853 he assisted John McCormack in founding the Church of God Chapel, an independent Baptist church for which he acted as manager. He married his second wife, Sarian (Sarah Anne in its Anglicized form), in St George's Cathedral in January 1863. They had at least two children. Moses Thomas George and Catherine Sarah Anne, like their older siblings, were educated in colonial schools and married into prominent Sierra Leone families. All Lawson's children and at least one grandson, James Glynn Lawson, became important members of Sierra Leone society.

As a devout Christian and firm exponent of British colonial expansion Lawson took every opportunity to pursue his mission and to exhort African rulers to accept British values and administration. From his experiences with African notables he had developed a strong respect for Islam which he considered to be a 'civilizing' influence, and he had good relations with many important Muslim leaders whom he successfully brought into the British colonial administration.

The Colonial Office in London recognized Lawson's essential role in representing British interests and in providing information and analysis that led to a network of treaties with African rulers by granting him British citizenship in 1860, by rewarding him with regular increases in his salary, and by authorizing a grand retirement ceremony for him in 1886. Governor Rowe wrote to the secretary of state in the Colonial Office on 18 May 1886: 'I do hope that Your Lordship may be pleased to show some special mark of appreciation of the services rendered by Mr. Lawson. They stand, I believe, alone and without equal in the history of Her Majesty's Settlements on this Coast' (PRO, CO 267/363, Dispatch 160). Hundreds of colonial officials and African notables from Freetown and the interior attended the ceremony in September 1886. He did not officially retire until January 1889, as his services were so essential for the smooth running of the administration.

Lawson's salary at retirement was £350, with substantial additional income as a landlord in Freetown and owner of valuable farm lands in the interior. He continued to reside in his large house on Charlotte Street until his death, in Freetown, in June 1891. His funeral was held on 14 June 1891 in Freetown, and services were conducted by the Revd C. Marke at the Church of God Chapel on Regent Street. More than four thousand persons attended the funeral. Among them were all the chief colonial officials, political and professional leaders, merchants, and Muslim and Christian clerics. Lawson was the most significant African officer in the British colonial service during the nineteenth century. DAVID E. SKINNER

Sources D. E. Skinner, *Thomas George Lawson* (1980) · D. E. Skinner, 'Thomas George Lawson: colonial civil servant in Sierra Leone, 1846–89', *West African colonial civil servants in the nineteenth century*, ed. K. Arhin (1985), 21–43 · C. Fyfe, *A history of Sierra Leone* (1962) · J. Hargreaves, 'The evolution of the native affairs department', *Sierra Leone Studies*, 3 (1954), 168–84 · N. Gayibor, *Récueil des sources orales de la région d'Aneho* (1977) · N. Gayibor, *Le Genyi (Royaume de Glidji), 1680–1884* (1978) · D. E. Skinner, 'The Arabic letter books as a source for Sierra Leone history', *Africana Research Bulletin*, 3 (1973), 51–9 · governor's letter-books, Sierra Leone Archives · *Sierra Leone Weekly News* (20 June 1891) · PRO, CO 267/363, Dispatch 153

Archives PRO, Granville MSS, CO 267 · University of Sierra Leone, Freetown, Sierra Leone Archives, government interpreter's memoranda and letter-books, Aborigine minutes, governor's letter-books

Likenesses group portrait, photograph (with colonial administrators in Freetown, Sierra Leone), repro. in C. Fyfe, 'The administration in 1885', *Sierra Leone Studies*, 4 (1955), 226–8

Lawson, Sir Wilfrid, second baronet

Lawson, Sir Wilfrid, second baronet (1829–1906), politician and temperance campaigner, born on 4 September 1829 at his father's house, Brayton, near Carlisle, was the eldest son in a family of four sons and four daughters of Sir Wilfrid Lawson, first baronet (1795–1867), and his wife, Caroline (*d.* 1870), daughter of Sir James Graham, first baronet, of Netherby, and sister to Sir James Robert George Graham, the Peelite statesman.

The family surname was originally Wybergh. The politician's father was the younger son of Thomas Wybergh of Clifton Hall, Westmorland, whose family had settled there in the fourteenth century. Thomas Wybergh's wife, Elizabeth, was the daughter of John Hartley of Whitehaven, and the sister of Anne, wife of Sir Wilfrid Lawson, tenth and last baronet, of Isel Hall, Cockermouth, who died childless on 14 June 1806; this Sir Wilfrid's property passed by his will to the eldest son of his wife's sister, another Thomas Wybergh, who assumed the surname of Lawson; when he died unmarried on 2 May 1812 he was succeeded in his estates by his next brother, Wilfrid Wybergh, who also took the name of Lawson and was made a baronet on 30 September 1831.

Young Lawson was brought up at home. His father, an advanced Liberal, was devoted to the causes of temperance, peace, and free trade. He held dissenting opinions, and he chose as tutor for his boys a young man, J. Oswald Jackson, who had just left the dissenting college at Homerton, and later became a Congregationalist minister. Lawson later declared that he 'had never had any education', and that Adam Smith's *Wealth of Nations* was the book that taught him all he knew, but in fact he acquired a good knowledge of Greek and Latin. At an early age he was initiated into the sports of hunting, shooting, and fishing, and was a good shot and a hard rider. In 1854 he bought the hounds that had belonged to John Peel, of the hunting song, amalgamated them with a small pack that he already possessed, and became master of the Cumberland foxhounds. He took a keen interest in agriculture, woodcraft, and all rural pursuits. He was made JP at an early age, and was active in the social and public life of the county;

Sir Wilfrid Lawson, second baronet (1829–1906), by Lock & Whitfield, pubd 1882

he limited his travels abroad, however, so attached was he to his daily newspaper.

Lawson's father, whose political convictions he shared, wished him to enter parliament at the earliest opportunity. On 21 March 1857 he stood as a Liberal for West Cumberland, which had always been represented by two tory members. During the contest Lawson first gave proof of his faculty for public speaking, in which humour and sarcasm played a chief part. But he was at the bottom of the poll, with 1554 votes against 1825 recorded for the second tory. The new parliament was dissolved in 1859, and Lawson, standing for Carlisle with his uncle Sir James Graham, was returned to the House of Commons, in which he sat with few intervals until his death, forty-seven years later. He married (on 12 November 1860) Mary (*d.* 23 Jan 1910), daughter of Joseph Pocklington-Senhouse of Netherhall, Cumberland, with whom he had four sons and four daughters.

Lawson's maiden speech in 1860 was made amid tumult as he unwittingly began at the dinner hour, but he showed unusual self-possession. He soon made a reputation as, in his own words, 'a fanatic, a faddist, and an extreme man'. He joined the radical section of his party, which was out of sympathy with the Liberal prime minister, Lord Palmerston, and doggedly voted for the principles of 'peace, retrenchment, and reform', for abstention from interference in foreign affairs, and for the promotion of religious equality. Lawson was already committed to the furtherance of temperance reform although he was not yet a professed abstainer, and with this cause he chiefly identified himself in the House of Commons and the country. In the session of 1863 he supported a motion in favour of Sunday closing, and the home secretary, Sir George Grey, who opposed it, said that Lawson's argument was equally good for total prohibition. 'That' wrote Lawson 'was just where I wanted my argument to tend'. He produced on 8 June 1864 his 'Permissive Bill', which provided that drink-shops should be suppressed in any locality where a two-thirds majority of the inhabitants voted against their continuance. The bill was rejected by 294 to 37.

On the dissolution of parliament in July 1865 Lawson stood again for Carlisle, and was defeated by fifteen votes. His radicalism had offended moderate Liberals; and the 'Permissive Bill' had angered the liquor trade. Excluded from parliament, Lawson spoke elsewhere in favour of extension of the suffrage, abolition of church rates, Irish disestablishment, and, above all, liquor-law reform. He became closely associated with the United Kingdom Alliance (founded in 1853 for the total suppression of the liquor traffic), and he was elected its president in 1879. He sought every opportunity of pleading for legislation on the lines of his 'Permissive Bill' of 1864. The policy acquired the new name of 'local option' or 'local control', and later it was known as 'local veto' or 'direct local veto'. Lawson's lifelong principle was: 'No forcing of liquor shops into unwilling areas'.

In 1867 Lawson's father died, and he succeeded to the baronetcy and estates. After the dissolution of 1868 Lawson, who was an enthusiastic champion of Gladstone's policy of Irish disestablishment, was returned for Carlisle at the top of the poll. In the new parliament he identified himself with many unpopular causes: women's rights, suppression of the opium traffic, and opposition to enlargement of the army and to treaties that bound Britain to fight foreign powers. However, he still concentrated his main energies on his 'Permissive Bill'. He reintroduced it on 12 May 1869, 17 May 1871, 8 May 1872, 7 May 1873, and 17 June 1874. The adverse majorities fluctuated from 257 in 1864 to 72 in 1871, but Lawson's enthusiasm never slackened. During the recess of 1871–2 he was busy throughout the country speaking in favour of his measure. Accompanied by George Trevelyan, he met in some large towns a furiously hostile reception. He did not take part in the republican agitation of Sir Charles Dilke and others, but on 19 March 1872 he voted in the minority of two for Dilke's motion of inquiry into Queen Victoria's expenditure, which Auberon Herbert seconded.

In the next parliament (1874–80), for which he was again returned for Carlisle, but in the second place, Lawson continued his fight for temperance, introducing his proposals in each of four sessions, and incurring heavy defeats. In 1875 the bill was rejected by a majority of 285. He advocated in 1875–6 Sunday closing in Ireland, a measure that was carried in 1879. In 1877 he supported with some misgivings Joseph Chamberlain's 'Göteborg system' for municipal control of liquor traffic, which eliminated the element of private profit. In 1879 he changed his 'Permissive Bill' for a local option resolution, which avoided controversy over details. It was rejected by a majority of eighty-eight.

Despite his love of sport and horses, Lawson opposed in 1874 the traditional adjournment of parliament on the day of the Derby race. For many years he annually waged war on the proposal to make the day a holiday, and in 1892 he carried his point, with the result that the motion for adjournment was not renewed.

To the parliament of 1880–85 Lawson was again returned for Carlisle in the second place. He argued for religious freedom when Charles Bradlaugh, an avowed atheist, was excluded from the house. He voted against Forster's Irish Coercion Bill in 1881, and with the Irish nationalists. He persistently resisted the Liberal government's policy in Egypt in 1882–3. To his proposed reform of the liquor traffic a majority of the new house was favourable, and in June 1880 he for the first time carried his resolution in favour of local option, by twenty-six votes. In the following year he carried it by forty-two, and in 1883, when Gladstone voted with him, by eighty-seven. In 1884 he supported an amendment for women's suffrage. He later protested that he had 'never been able to understand the terrible fear of women which men entertain' (Russell, *Lawson*, 86).

At the general election of November 1885, which followed the extension of the suffrage to the agricultural labourers, Lawson was defeated in the Cockermouth division of Cumberland by ten votes. Five hundred Irish constituents voted against him. There was a paradox in his defeat by the labourers and the Irish, in both of whose interests he had consistently worked hard during the last parliament. He watched from the Riviera the subsequent struggle in parliament over Gladstone's Home Rule Bill, with which he was in complete sympathy. In June 1886 he stood as home-rule candidate for the Cockermouth division, and won by 1004 votes. He told Sir William Harcourt: 'I shall be glad to get back to the House to fight publicans, parsons, and peers' (Lawson to Harcourt, 20 July 1886; Bodl. Oxf., MS Harcourt 13, fol. 116). In the new parliament he supported the Irish cause, and resisted Balfour's policy of coercion. In 1888 he successfully opposed the clauses in the local government bill which would have provided compensation for publicans whose licences were not renewed.

Lawson was re-elected for the Cockermouth division in 1892 and 1895, but took a less conspicuous part in the parliament, although he was steadfast to all the causes that he had earlier espoused. A reduction in his majority at Cockermouth in 1895 he attributed to the unpopularity of the local veto bill, on which Harcourt (though not the prime minister, Lord Rosebery) had appealed to the country. To the Second South African War, which broke out in October 1899, he was absolutely opposed, and as a pro-Boer he was defeated at Cockermouth by 209 votes. He found comfort in polling over 4000 votes, but the popularity of the Second South African War shook his old confidence in the political common sense of the people.

During the autumn and winter of 1901 Lawson returned to political activity outside parliament. In April 1903 he was returned at a by-election for the Camborne division of Cornwall, on the understanding that, at the expiration of the parliament, he should be free to contest his old constituency. The controversy in 1903 over tariff reform gave him the opportunity to restate his passionate belief in free trade. At the general election of January 1906 he was again returned for the Cockermouth division, though he declined the offer by the Liberal prime minister, Sir Henry Campbell-Bannerman, of a privy councillorship.

Lawson was elated by the Liberal triumph of 1906, but his health showed signs of failure. He had long given up hunting, and latterly did not ride, but he went on shooting to the end. On 29 June 1906 he voted in the house for the last time in a division on the Education Bill. Lawson died at his London house, 18 Ovington Square, on 1 July 1906, and was buried in the churchyard of Aspatria, the parish in which his Cumberland estate was situated. His eldest son, Sir Wilfrid Lawson, third baronet (1862–1937), held the Cockermouth seat as a Liberal from 1910 to 1916. After the death of his nephew in 1959, the baronetcy became extinct.

Lawson, despite his strong and unchanging convictions, was absolutely just to friend and foe alike, and his justice was tempered by a singularly humane disposition. He always claimed for others the same freedom of opinion and expression that he claimed for himself. His power of speech was well adapted to great popular audiences: published selections from his speeches included *Wisdom, Grave and Gay*, edited by R. A. Jameson (1889). His humour was spontaneous and unforced; his jokes, like those of Sydney Smith, were rich and various, and always served the purposes of his serious argument. He had a vein of sarcasm which, though never personal, was extremely keen, and he wrote light verse with quickness and ease, and often combined in it humour and sarcasm with great pungency. His verses on political themes were collected by Sir F. Carruthers Gould in *Cartoons in Rhyme and Line* (1905). His main political aim was as simple and sincere as his character. He saw in the liquor traffic the great moral and material curse of Britain, and he devoted all his energies to the attempt to destroy it. Lawson won some symbolic victories, such as the inclusion of prohibition by local veto in the Newcastle programme of 1891, but by the time of his death his version of temperance reform had lost much of its support. Even advanced reformers doubted that parliament could be persuaded to enact 'local veto' of the retail drink trade.   G. W. E. RUSSELL, *rev.* DAVID M. FAHEY

Sources G. W. E. Russell, ed., *Sir Wilfrid Lawson: a memoir* (1909) · B. Harrison, *Drink and the Victorians: the temperance question in England, 1815–1872*, 2nd edn (1994) · D. A. Hamer, *The politics of electoral pressure: a study in the history of Victorian reform agitations* (1977) · A. E. Dingle, *The campaign for prohibition in Victorian England: the United Kingdom Alliance, 1872–1895* (1980) · G. W. E. Russell, *Portraits of the seventies* (1916) · letter to Harcourt, 20 July 1886, Bodl. Oxf., MS Harcourt 13, fol. 116 · D. M. Fahey, 'Lawson, Sir Wilfrid', *BDMBR*, vol. 3, pt 2 · *CGPLA Eng. & Wales* (1906)

Archives BL, letters to W. E. Gladstone, Add. MSS 44456–44526, *passim* · BL OIOC, letters to Lord Curzon, MSS Eur. F 111–112 · BLPES, letters to Henry Broadhurst · Bodl. Oxf., letters to Sir William Harcourt and Lewis Harcourt · Bodl. Oxf., corresp. with Lord Kimberley · Castle Howard, North Yorkshire, letters to earl of Carlisle · U. Newcastle, Robinson L., letters to Sir W. Trevelyan · United Kingdom Temperance Alliance and Institute of Alcohol Studies, London, UK Alliance executive committee minute books

Likenesses daguerreotype, 1858, repro. in Russell, ed., *Sir Wilfrid Lawson*, facing p. 26 · Bassano, photograph, 1884, repro. in Russell, ed., *Sir Wilfrid Lawson*, frontispiece · B. Stone, photograph, 1897, Birmingham Reference Library, NPG · Lafayette, photograph, 1906, NPG; repro. in Russell, ed., *Sir Wilfrid Lawson*, facing p. 274 · A. Bryan, pen-and-ink drawing, NPG · C. L. Burns, oils; known to be at Brayton, 1912 · M. Klinkicht, wood-engraving (after a photograph), BM, NPG; repro. in *ILN* (23 March 1889) · Lock & Whitfield, woodburytype photograph, NPG; repro. in T. Cooper, *Men of mark: a gallery of contemporary portraits* (1882) [*see illus.*] · D. McGill, bronze statue, Embankment Gardens, London · Roselieb, medallion; known to be at Aspatria, Cumbria, 1912 · T. Wast, caricature, watercolour study, NPG; repro. in *VF* (11 May 1872) · lithographs, NPG

Wealth at death £227,114 4s. 10d.: probate, 31 Aug 1906, *CGPLA Eng. & Wales*

Lawson, William (1553/4–1635), writer on gardening and Church of England clergyman, was probably a member of the extensive northern English gentry family of Lawson, but his parents' names are not known. He was ordained deacon in 1580, and became vicar of Ormesby, near Teesmouth, in the North Riding of Yorkshire, in 1583. He spent the rest of his life there. His first wife, Sibille, with whom he had two children, was buried at Ormesby in 1618; on 28 April 1619 he married Emme Tailer, who survived him. His only book, *A new orchard and garden, or, The best way for planting, grafting, and to make any ground good for a rich orchard; particularly in the north parts of England*, was published by Roger Jackson in 1618, with a dedication to a connection of one branch of the Lawsons, Sir Henry Belasyse. It was the first published work on gardening in the north of England, and its second section, *The Countrie Housewifes Garden*, was the first horticultural work written specifically for women (there would not be another in English for a century). The 'sound, clear, natural wit' manifested in it was praised by John Beale forty years later (Beale, 14), and it continued to be reprinted, often in a collection called *A Way to Get Wealth*, with works by Gervase Markham and others, until 1683. Lawson also wrote practical annotations, at Roger Jackson's request, to the second edition (1620) of John Dennys's verse treatise *The Secrets of Angling*. He was buried on 16 August 1635 at Ormesby, where he was remembered as a good man.   JOHN CONSIDINE

Sources J. Harvey, 'William Lawson and his orchard: a 17th-century gardening writer identified', *Country Life*, 172 (1982), 1338–40 · J. Beale, *Herefordshire orchards* (1657) · J. Taboroff, '"Wife, unto thy garden": the first gardening books for women', *Garden History*, 11/1 (1983), 1–5 · parish registers of Ormesby, Yorkshire: unpubd transcript, Society of Genealogists, London · B. Henrey, *British botanical and horticultural literature before 1800*, 1 (1975) · F. N. L. Poynter, *Bibliography of Gervase Markham, 1568?–1637* (1962)

Lawther, Sir William (1889–1976), trade unionist, was born on 20 May 1889 at Choppington, Northumberland, the eldest son of Edward Lawther, a coalminer of Choppington, and his wife, Catherine Phillips. It was a family of radical traditions: a grandfather had been an active Chartist, and Edward became politically sympathetic to the Independent Labour Party. After attending colliery school,

Will Lawther began to work in the mines soon after he was twelve, and in 1907 the family—there were fifteen children, of whom eleven survived—moved to the new colliery of Chopwell in co. Durham. The village was already developing a militant tradition—it was known later as Little Moscow—and Will Lawther became a political and industrial activist from his late teens.

Lawther continued his education at night school, read widely in socialist literature—*Merrie England* (1893) by R. P. G. Blatchford was especially influential—and the Durham Miners' Association sent him to study at the Central Labour College in London from September 1911 for nearly two years. When he returned to Durham he joined Ebenezer Edwards in establishing Plebs League classes, and in 1914 helped found the Socialist Sunday school in Chopwell, known locally as the 'anarchist school'. He married on 29 December 1915 Lottie (d. 1962), the daughter of Joseph Laws, a coalminer, and she was active in his support during the whole of his career. The marriage was childless.

During the First World War Lawther adopted a strong anti-militarist position and was one of a small number who refused to subscribe to the Red Cross. In these years he began to occupy official positions in the union hierarchy and attended his first Trades Union Congress in 1918. In the aftermath of the war, as checkweighman at Victoria Garsfield colliery, co. Durham, he consolidated his reputation as a left-wing militant, although by this time he had shed his earlier version of anarchist syndicalism and had become very active within the Labour Party: probably through the influence of Peter Lee. By 1923 he was a member of the national executive, upon which he served until 1926. From 1925 to 1929 he was on the Durham county council. During the 1926 general strike he was a leading figure in his own region, and spent two months in gaol on charges of intimidation and interference with food distribution.

Lawther stood unsuccessfully on three occasions (1922, 1923, and 1924) as parliamentary candidate for South Shields before he was elected for Barnard Castle in 1929. He proved an effective back-bencher with an abrasive speaking manner but lost his seat in the Labour débâcle of 1931. For the next eighteen months he was unemployed, but came back into union affairs when he was appointed an agent for the Durham miners in 1933, moving to the full-time treasurer's position in December of the same year. From then on he was always a full-time official. He was elected vice-president of the Mineworkers' Federation of Great Britain (MFGB) in 1934 and president in 1939, and when the National Union of Mineworkers replaced the federation Lawther became its first president, retiring under the age-limit rule when he was sixty-five. He had been on the general council of the TUC since 1935.

Throughout the 1930s Lawther had remained on the left of the labour movement. He was pro-Soviet, a supporter of the communist-led hunger marches, vigorous in defence of republican Spain—his brother Clifford was killed in February 1937 while serving with the International Brigades—and a trenchant critic of the policy of appeasement. Within the Labour Party he advocated both the United Front and the Popular Front of Sir R. Stafford Cripps, and only the threat of expulsion made him withdraw his support from the latter. As late as 1943, on behalf of the MFGB, he moved an amendment at the Labour Party conference in favour of accepting the affiliation of the Communist Party. But the later war years were a period of marked change in Lawther's political views and with the Labour victory in the summer of 1945 he emerged as one of the triumvirate who dominated the TUC and who used the large votes of their respective unions to defeat the left. Together with Arthur Deakin of the transport workers' and Tom Williamson of the municipal workers' unions, Lawther played a major part in first containing the Communist Party and their allies in the TUC, and then the Bevanites within the Labour Party. In these post-war years Lawther became as paranoid about the left as Deakin; and it was the consistent use of their block votes that kept the right–centre in political control of both the TUC and the Labour Party. Not all members of the Lawther family were sympathetic with his shift to the political right.

Lawther was knighted in 1949 and had also been awarded the decoration of chevalier of the Légion d'honneur. He retired in 1954 and went to live in Whitley Bay, where he was a magistrate. He died in hospital at Newcastle upon Tyne on 1 February 1976.

JOHN SAVILLE, rev.

Sources corresp., press cuttings, and other papers, County Archives Department, Newcastle upon Tyne · U. Hull, Brynmor Jones L., *Dictionary of labour biography* collection, DLB · 'An interview with Sir William Lawther', *Bulletin of the Society for the Study of Labour History*, 19 (1969), 14–21 · *Bulletin* [North East Group for the Study of Labour History], 10 (Oct 1976), 27–33 · *The Times* (3 Feb 1976) · private information (1986) · *The Labour who's who* (1927) · CGPLA Eng. & Wales (1976)
Archives Northern Film and Television Archive, Gateshead, personal and family papers · NRA, corresp., reports, and papers · Tyne and Wear Archives Service, Newcastle upon Tyne, papers | FILM BFI NFTVA, news footage | SOUND IWM SA, oral history interview
Wealth at death £14,044: probate, 1 March 1976, CGPLA Eng. & Wales

Lawton, Charlwood (1660–1721), writer, was the son of Ralf Lawton of Egham in Surrey, surgeon-general in the army. He entered Wadham College, Oxford, as a fellow commoner on 23 August 1677, matriculated on 7 December, but left without taking a degree. In 1688 he was called to the bar from the Middle Temple, though he did not practise. Lawton became acquainted with the Quaker and founder of Pennsylvania, William Penn, through a chance meeting on a coach in the summer of 1686, and the two remained friends for life. On 6 September 1690 Lawton's only son, Henry, was baptized at Egham, though details of his marriage are unknown. In 1700 Lawton acted as Penn's agent in London. In addition to Penn he was intimate with many notable people of the time, including John, Lord Somers; John Trenchard, whose pardon he procured by Penn's agency in 1686; and Lord Chief Justice Sir George

Treby. For a long time he lived near Windsor but at the time of his death, from an apoplectic fit, on 13 June 1721 he was described as 'of Northampton'.

Lawton had intended to publish a volume of memoirs and left a large quantity of papers relating to the affairs of the time. One such document, dealing with the life of Penn, was printed in *Memoirs of the Historical Society of Pennsylvania* (vol. 3, 1834). Lawton's other published pamphlets included *A Letter Concerning Civil Comprehension* (1705), a second letter on the same subject (1706), *A Letter Formerly Sent to Dr. Tillotson*, and *The Jacobite Principles Vindicated*. All these were later republished in the Somers Tracts (1748–52).

W. A. J. ARCHBOLD, *rev.* PHILIP CARTER

Sources R. B. Gardiner, ed., *The registers of Wadham College, Oxford*, 1 (1889) · *N&Q*, 3rd ser., 9 (1866), 511

Lawton, George (1779–1869), antiquary, was born at York on 6 May 1779. He was educated at a school in York and articled to a proctor in the ecclesiastical courts there; he was admitted a proctor on 3 November 1808. He was also a solicitor, notary public, and was appointed registrar of the archdeaconry of the East Riding of Yorkshire by Archdeacon Wilberforce. He served in the ecclesiastical courts under five archbishops of York. His legal experience led to publications on aspects of the law of marriage and on inheritance, but his most important work was *Collectio rerum ecclesiasticarum* (2 vols., 1840). This comprised a study, arranged topographically, of the parochial institutions of the diocese of York based on the manuscripts of James Torre (1649–1699), and remains a standard authority.

Lawton married Ellen Robinson at York on 10 June 1810. He ceased to practise as a solicitor in 1863, and died a widower at his residence, Nunthorpe, near York, on 1 December 1869, leaving at least one son and one daughter.

W. A. J. ARCHBOLD, *rev.* WILLIAM JOSEPH SHEILS

Sources *Yorkshire Gazette* (11 Dec 1869) · private information (1892, 2004) · C. R. J. Currie and C. P. Lewis, eds., *English county histories: a guide* (1994), 447–55 · *CGPLA Eng. & Wales* (1869) · parish register (marriage), St Michael le Belfrey, York, 10 June 1810
Archives Bodl. Oxf., collection of letters on antiquarian matters · York Minster Library, York Minster archives, Yorshire collections | Bodl. Oxf., letters to Sir Thomas Phillipps
Wealth at death under £5000: probate, 24 Dec 1869, *CGPLA Eng. & Wales*

Lawton, Thomas [Tommy] (1919–1996), footballer, was born at 43 Macdonald Street, Farnworth, near Bolton, on 6 October 1919, the son of Thomas Lawton, a signalman on the Lancashire and Yorkshire railway, and his wife, Elizabeth Riley, a weaver at the Harrowby mill. His parents separated when Thomas was eighteen months old and he went with his mother to live with his grandfather James Hugh Riley, in a two-up and two-down terrace house off the Folds Road, near the centre of Bolton. Lawton's uncles were all keen recreational footballers and introduced their nephew to the pleasures of both street football and, later, Sunday games for side stakes. Lawton's mother and grandfather were probably most influential in shaping his early career.

Thomas Lawton (1919–1996), by unknown photographer, 1953

Tommy Lawton was an outstanding schoolboy footballer at Tonge Moor council school and Castle Hill and Folds Road central school (he scored an astonishing 570 goals in three seasons for the latter) and for Hayes Athletic, a Bolton league side for whom he played on Saturday afternoons. He played for Lancashire schools in 1933 and 1934 but strangely never for England at schoolboy level. As a fifteen-year-old Lawton played for Rossendale United in the semi-professional Lancashire combination, by which time he was working in a Bolton tannery, although Football League clubs queued up to take him out of it. Sheffield Wednesday almost signed him but his mother thought Sheffield was too far away from their Bolton home. Instead Lawton signed amateur forms for Burnley, who gave him a job in their office at £2 10s. a week—good money for a sixteen-year-old in 1935. The club also had to find a place for Granddad Riley, who became an assistant groundsman at £3 10s. a week. Soon the Riley family were given a rent-free house in Brunshaw Road, Burnley. Lawton made his début in the first team, at sixteen and a half, and signed as a professional in October 1936 on wages of £7 a week, with bonuses of £2 for a win and £1 for a draw. Granddad Riley had tried, but failed, to secure a signing-on fee of £500. Four days later Lawton scored three goals in a second-division match against Tottenham Hotspur. If this was a nice return on a modest investment, an even more satisfying one quickly followed when in January 1937 Everton paid Burnley £5400 for his transfer.

Everton clearly saw Lawton as a replacement for Dixie Dean, and he did not disappoint. In 1937–8 he was the leading goal-scorer in the first division with twenty-eight goals and the following season, 1938–9, his thirty-five goals were crucial in the winning of the league championship. A well-built 5 feet 11 inches, Lawton was muscular and sharp. He shot well with both feet, but it was his heading ability which was really exceptional. The timing and height of his leaps were unsurpassed. From his boots to the heavily slicked centre-parted hair he was a menacing handful for any defence. Lawton's presence on away grounds would put thousands on the 'gate'. He was as much of a star as either Stanley Matthews or later, Tom Finney, but his twenty-year career in professional football was not the complete triumph it ought to have been. Like many other players of his generation, he had six years wrenched out of his prime by the Second World War. He also had a knack of falling out with his employers, and his half a dozen transfers, particularly in an era of the maximum wage, look eccentric and suggest a restless streak which he was unable to control. On the field Lawton was never booked or sent off, but off the field his character was an odd mixture of shyness and assertiveness. Only at Everton was he at the right club at the right time, and the disruption of war meant that he had little time to fulfil his potential.

In 1938 Lawton was selected for England while still in his teens, and in 1939 he headed the winning goal in a famous victory over Scotland. When, in 1940, the army asked the Football Association to provide a list of players to be trained as physical training instructors, Lawton was one of those selected. Based in Aldershot, he played a lot of wartime football, including twenty-three games for England. On 15 January 1941 he married Rosaleen May Kavanagh (b. 1920/21), daughter of Thomas Kavanagh. The marriage ended in divorce in 1951. After being demobilized in 1945 Lawton moved again, after arranging his own transfer from Everton to Chelsea for £11,500. The main purpose of the change appears to have been to improve the state of his marriage. Looking back thirty years later, Lawton thought that he should have stayed with Everton and transferred his wife. He arrived at Chelsea just in time to play in their spectacular match against Moscow Dynamo. He liked London but stayed for only one full season with a team who were notorious under-achievers, even though his twenty-six goals that season were a club record. Instead Lawton surprised the football world by joining Notts County in 1947 for a fee of £20,000, a new British record. They were an unexceptional team which for several years before the war had been embedded in the middle of the southern section of the third division of the league. However, the club had potential, and Lawton began to realize some of it. Crowds rose from an average of 9,000 to 35,000, and in 1949–50 the championship was won and with it promotion to the second division. The success did not last.

In the meantime Lawton had become the first post-war player from the third division to be selected for England, for whom he appeared three times in 1948. But he was never picked again, even though he was only twenty-nine and remained a regular goal scorer with Notts County with ninety goals in 151 matches. The rest of his career was sombrely anti-climactic. In 1952 he moved to second-division Brentford, where he became player–manager in the new year. Results were poor, the crowd critical, and he soon resigned as manager while continuing as a player. He had also been cited as co-respondent in a divorce case. On 23 September 1952 he married the woman, Gladys May Rose (b. 1919/20), daughter of Wilfred Ruebin Seabrooke, master decorator, whom he later called the love of his life. There was an even more surprising twist to his football career. In September 1953, at thirty-four, he was bought by Arsenal, whose young side had made a disappointing start to the season. Although he failed to score until March and was not a regular member of the first team, he did act as a catalyst in the improvement of the team. In 1956 he left Highbury to become player–manager of Kettering Town. He led them to the southern league championship in 1956–7, a success which led back to Notts County and the manager's office. The club suffered relegation from the second division at the end of the season and Lawton left, to spend the next four years as landlord of the Magna Carta pub in Lowdham, a village near Nottingham.

It has often been said that great players do not necessarily make good managers. Most players made little preparation for the end of their careers and there were certainly no training courses for management. Lawton later said that his mistake had been to leave the first division for Notts County and in self-critical mood reflected that perhaps great playing success had made him over-confident. It may not have helped that he was opposed to modern coaching. Lawton had another managerial stint at Kettering in 1963–4 and was coach and chief scout at Notts County between 1968 and 1970. His 231 goals in 390 league games and his 22 in 23 matches for England did not insure him against a difficult middle age. Lawton found it hard to keep jobs for long and was involved in several failed business enterprises. He worked as a salesman for a firm making grandstand seats but he suffered a heart attack in 1970 and by 1972 was unemployed and in debt. It was a sad decline from his three seasons as a star player at Notts County, when he may have earned as much as £3000 a year, drove a grey Sunbeam Talbot sports car, and was probably the first surtax-paying footballer. Old footballing friends Andy Beattie, Matt Busby, and Joe Mercer persuaded Everton to arrange a testimonial match in 1972 which raised £6300, but Lawton continued to find it difficult to make ends meet. Two court appearances for minor fraud led to three years' probation in 1972 and 200 hours of community service in 1974. In 1984, at sixty-five, he was 'rediscovered' by the *Nottingham Evening Post* and his conversations with journalists were turned into a weekly football column. His wife died in 1988, after which declining health forced Lawton into sheltered accommodation. He died on 6 November 1996 at his home, Abbeyfield, 49 Rosedale Road, Bakersfield, Nottingham, leaving a daughter, Amanda, by his first wife and a stepdaughter, Carol, and a son, Tommy, by his second.   TONY MASON

Sources T. Lawton, *Football is my business* (1949) · D. McVay and A. Smith, *Tommy Lawton: the complete centre forward: the authorised biography* (2000) · T. Lawton, *When the cheering stopped* (1973) · *The Times* (7 Nov 1996) · *Daily Telegraph* (7 Nov 1996) · *The Guardian* (7 Nov

1996) • *The Independent* (7 Nov 1996) • *Nottingham Evening Post* (12 Nov 1996); (14 Nov 1996) • b. cert. • m. certs. • d. cert.
Likenesses photograph, 1953, NPG [*see illus.*]

Lax, William (1761–1836), astronomer, was the son of William Lax of Ravensworth, North Riding of Yorkshire. He was educated at Kirkby on the Hill, North Riding of Yorkshire, and was admitted as a sizar in 1780 to Trinity College, Cambridge. He graduated in 1785 as senior wrangler and first Smith's prizeman, was elected a fellow of his college, and proceeded MA in 1788. In 1795 he succeeded Dr Smith as Lowndes's professor of astronomy and geometry in the University of Cambridge, and after some years spent in tuition was presented by Trinity College to the livings of Marsworth, Buckinghamshire, and of St Ippollitts, near Stevenage, Hertfordshire, where he built a small observatory.

Lax published in 1807 *Remarks on a Supposed Error in the Elements of Euclid*; his *Tables to be Used with the Nautical Almanac* were printed by the board of longitude in 1821, and a new edition was issued in 1834. The Royal Society, of which he was elected a fellow in 1796, published his papers on 'A method of finding the latitude of a place by means of two altitudes of the sun' (1799) and 'On a method of examining the divisions of astromical instruments' (1808). Lax died at his house at St Ippollitts on 29 October 1836.   A. M. CLERKE, *rev.* ANITA McCONNELL

Sources *Annual Register* (1836), 218 • *Abstracts of the Papers Printed in the Philosophical Transactions of the Royal Society of London*, 3 (1830–37), 438 • W. W. Rouse Ball and J. A. Venn, eds., *Admissions to Trinity College, Cambridge*, 3 (1911), 273 • *Fasti Angl.* (Hardy), 3.645, 665

Laxfield, Eadric of. *See* Eadric of Laxfield (*d.* in or after 1066?).

Laxton, Sir William (*d.* 1556), mayor of London, was the son of John Laxton of Oundle, Northamptonshire. His date and place of birth are unknown. William and his brother John became members of the Grocers' Company of London, the former being admitted to the freedom during the year 1518–19. He married Joan Luddington (*d.* 1576), daughter and heir of William Kirkeby (*d.* 1531), gentleman, of London, and widow of Henry Luddington (*d.* 1531), citizen and grocer of London and gentleman of Gainsborough, Lincolnshire. Laxton was warden of his company in 1534, and master in 1536, 1539, 1541, and 1543. He was elected alderman of Lime Street ward in 1536 and sheriff in 1540. While lord mayor in 1544–5 Laxton conducted the examination of the protestant martyr Anne Askew, and oversaw the city's guarantee of Henry VIII's Antwerp loan of 1545. The non-parliamentary royal taxation, termed 'the benevolence', proved to be the most controversial event of Laxton's term in office. He acquiesced when Henry, in an unprecedented action, silenced opposition by conscripting Alderman Richard Rede to serve in the army. Laxton was knighted by the king in 1545.

Laxton became one of the wealthiest London merchants of his time. He purchased extensive property in Essex, Suffolk, Hertfordshire, and London. His apprentices included John Rivers, lord mayor in 1573–4, and he numbered among his close friends Sir Thomas White, lord mayor in

1553–4, Sir Robert Broke, chief justice of common pleas, and the royal justices John Southcote and Robert Catlyn. Laxton died on the night of 29 July 1556 at his house in St Mary Aldermary. His funeral on 9 August 1556, in the parish church, was a notable event, followed by a great dinner hosted by the Grocers and a mass conducted by John Harpsfield, archdeacon of London. John Stow, however, criticized the removal of the bones of the church's benefactor, the grocer Henry Keble (*d.* 1518) who paid £1000 towards the rebuilding, so that Laxton's remains could occupy his vault.

By the terms of Laxton's will of 17 July 1556, his estate after the death of his widow was to be divided among his own right heir, his niece Joan Wanton, and the three children of his wife, Joan, from her marriage to Henry Luddington: Nicholas, Joan, and Anne. By a codicil dated 22 July 1556 Laxton surrendered to the Grocers' Company substantial property in London with the intent that the company would purchase from the crown the property of the dissolved religious guild at Oundle, Northamptonshire, in order to erect a free grammar school and almshouse. This charitable bequest was enacted only after long delay. The Wanton family did not relinquish its claim to the London property until after an expensive suit in chancery in 1572, and Dame Joan Laxton only relinquished her life interest on 6 May 1573. The school was established for forty-eight scholars in June, with the school room located in the former brotherhood house, at that time 'with high tables round about more like a Tavern than a school house' (Guildhall Library, MS 11625/1, 15). Sir William's stipulation that seven poor and honest male parishioners of Oundle be accommodated in the almshouse forced the removal of the five poor women lodged on the premises by Lady Laxton. The school, established by a pious Catholic lord mayor, speedily fell under the control of the Northamptonshire notable, the Calvinist Sir Walter Mildmay. Laxton's widow, one of the wealthiest inhabitants of London, a substantial purchaser of real estate, and a powerful matriarch, died in August 1576.   J. D. ALSOP

Sources will, PRO, PROB 11/38, fols. 79–80*v* • will of Dame Joan Laxton, PRO, PROB 11/58, fols. 163–164*v* • orders of the Company of Grocers for the free grammar school at Oundle, Northamptonshire, GL, MS 11625/1 • membership lists of Company of Grocers, GL, MS 11592A • R. Cooke, *Visitation of London, 1568*, ed. H. Stanford London and S. W. Rawlins, [new edn], 2 vols. in one, Harleian Society, 109–10 (1963), 85, 117 • BL, Harley MS 897, fol. 24 • *The survey of London*, ed. H. B. Wheatley (1956), 103, 226–7 • *The diary of Henry Machyn, citizen and merchant-taylor of London, from AD 1550 to AD 1563*, ed. J. G. Nichols, CS, 42 (1848), 111, 113, 167, 198, 351, 375 • W. A. Shaw, *The knights of England*, 2 (1906), 57
Wealth at death see will, PRO, PROB 11/38, fols. 79–80*v*

Laxton, William (1802–1854), surveyor and author, was born in London on 30 March 1802, one of at least three boys and one girl born to William Robert Laxton (*b. c.*1776), surveyor and architect, and his wife, Phoebe Laxton, and was educated at Christ's Hospital. He was a citizen of London, was made a liveryman of the Haberdashers' Company in 1823, and in his youth was an active member of the City Philosophical Society. Brought up as a surveyor, he mastered all aspects of a profession which he enjoyed.

He surveyed and laid down several lines of railway and, although he did not obtain the contract to construct any line, he was connected with several. Hydraulic engineering was his favourite pursuit, but he died before completing his work on this subject. He constructed waterworks at Falmouth and Stonehouse, in which he introduced many improvements, and with Robert Stephenson was engineer of the Watford water company for supplying London with water from the chalk formation. In October 1837 he founded the *Civil Engineer and Architect's Journal*, a monthly periodical, which he edited and which was only the second such professional journal to be established. He soon after bought the rival weekly, the *Architect and Building Gazette*, which he later joined to the journal. His father began the *Builder's Price Book*, a standard work in the profession and in the courts of law, which William and his younger brother Henry continued for thirty years. Laxton was the surveyor to Sir Isaac Lion Goldsmid, baron of Palmeira, the first Victorian builder at Hove where Laxton laid out a large part of the new town and designed and built many pleasant but not particularly distinguished houses. He died of epilepsy at 19 Arundel Street, Strand, on 31 May 1854, and was interred in the family vault in St Andrew's burying-ground, Gray's Inn Road. His only son, William Frederick Laxton, was called to the bar at the Middle Temple on 26 January 1854, and died in 1891. Henry Laxton succeeded to his brother's surveying business and his most notable work was the laying out of the Castelnau estate in Barnes for the Boileau family, a project which has been misattributed to William.

G. C. BOASE, *rev.* ELIZABETH BAIGENT

Sources P. Bandon, *The Sussex landscape* (1974) · *The Builder*, 12 (1854), 361 · H. M. Colvin, *A biographical dictionary of British architects, 1600–1840*, 3rd edn (1995) · J. Orbach, *Victorian architecture in Britain* (1987) · *Sussex*, Pevsner (1965) · 'Memoir of William Laxton', *Civil Engineer and Architect's Journal*, 17 (1854), 270–71 · d. cert. · *GM*, 2nd ser., 42 (1854), 199–200

Lay, Benjamin (1681–1759), opponent of slavery, was born of Quaker parents, William Lay and Mary Dennis, at Colchester on 26 November 1681. After a rudimentary education he was apprenticed to a glove maker, and later worked on his brother's farm before going to sea at the age of twenty-one. He returned home in 1710, married Sarah (*d.* 1735) the same year, and settled in London. He seems to have busied himself in public affairs, and is said to have presented to George I a copy of Milton's tract on removing hirelings from the church. He annoyed his fellow Quakers by his opposition to the practice of allowing ministers to speak when they had not been directly prompted by God, and in 1720 was disowned by Devonshire House monthly meeting. That same year Lay moved to Colchester, where he opened a shop, probably as a draper. He continued to disrupt Quaker meetings and in 1723 received what amounted to a second disownment. In 1731 he left England, and after a year in Barbados finally settled outside Philadelphia.

It seems likely that Lay's concern with slavery dates from his time in Barbados. He quickly became well known for his demonstrative protests against slaveholding among American Quakers. His most famous exploit took place in Burlington, New Jersey, when he entered a meeting-house in military uniform, complete with a sword. After a lengthy tirade, he thrust the sword into a bladder of red juice hidden between the covers of a Bible, warning those present that holding a slave was no better than stabbing a man to death. Besides speaking out against slavery on every possible occasion, Lay wrote a tract on the subject, *All Slave-Keepers that Keep the Innocent in Bondage, Apostates*, which was printed in 1737 by his close friend Benjamin Franklin. He also 'had a testimony' against tobacco and tea, and on one occasion carried a set of expensive china to the market place in Philadelphia and destroyed part of it as a public protest. A more dangerous fancy induced him to try to fast for forty days in imitation of Christ, and brought him to the verge of death. It was not only on the subject of slavery that Lay was ahead of his times. In 1737 he published a pamphlet on criminal code reform, which advocated the abolition of capital punishment. He was also an early supporter of temperance.

Lay was of small stature, being only 4 feet 7 inches, and almost certainly suffered from a congenital growth disorder. A strict vegetarian, he made his own clothes and refused to wear boots or anything else made of leather. His wife, Sarah, who also suffered from a deformity, died in 1735. He died in Philadelphia on 3 February 1759, and was buried at the Quaker burial-ground in Abington, near Philadelphia. Lay's eccentric behaviour undoubtedly alienated many Quakers, but he played an important role in persuading the Society of Friends to renounce slavery. A year before his death, in 1758, the Philadelphia monthly meeting decided that slave holders should henceforth be excluded from all business meetings. When this news reached Lay he is reported to have risen from his chair and exclaimed, 'I can now die in peace'. J. R. OLDFIELD

Sources C. B. Rowntree, 'Benjamin Lay (1681–1759) of Colchester, London, Barbadoes, Philadelphia', *Journal of the Friends' Historical Society*, 33 (1936), 2–19 · D. B. Davis, *The problem of slavery in western culture* (1966) · R. Vaux, *Memoirs of the lives of Benjamin Lay and Ralph Sandiford: two of the earliest of public advocates of the emancipation of the enslaved Africans* (1815) · *The papers of Benjamin Franklin*, 1, ed. L. W. Labaree and W. J. Bell (1959) · *The papers of Benjamin Franklin*, 2, ed. L. W. Labaree and W. J. Bell (1960) · J. E. Illick, *Colonial Pennsylvania: a history* (1976) · G. B. Nash, *Forging freedom: the formation of Philadelphia's black community, 1720–1840* (1988) · C. Bridenbaugh and J. Bridenbaugh, *Rebels and gentlemen: Philadelphia in the age of Franklin* (1962) · IGI

Likenesses portrait, RS Friends, Lond. · portrait, London Friends' Institute, Devonshire House, London · print, repro. in Vaux, *Memoirs of the lives of Benjamin Lay and Ralph Sandiford*, frontispiece

Wealth at death £518 10s. 6d.—personal property: Vaux, *Memoirs of the lives*

Layamon (*fl.* 13th cent.), poet, is known only from one early Middle English poem, *Laȝamon's 'Brut'*, of which two versions are extant in manuscripts in the British Library: Cotton MS Caligula A.ix, and, damaged in the fire of 1731, Cotton MS Otho C.xiii, both dated palaeographically as of the later thirteenth century. The usual Middle English forms of his name, Laȝamon and Laweman (or Loweman), are often modernized as Layamon and Lawman respectively.

In the proem some biographical facts about Layamon are given. He is referred to in the third person singular, as often when medieval writers speak of themselves; the proem is regarded as autobiographical. Layamon says that he was a priest (in the past tense, which need not mean that he is so no longer). In the opening initial in Caligula a priest is seen writing within a frame formed by capital A, though presumably not, in fact, Layamon's likeness. It is unusual for an early Middle English poet to give his name, which is not an uncommon one in England. Laȝamon is an occupational surname, ultimately of Scandinavian origin: 'one learned in the laws, a lawyer'; more specifically, 'one whose duty it was to declare the law', in the only Old English use referring to legal process near the Welsh border, where the law had to be declared in Welsh and in English. His father's name was Leovenath; in Otho, Levca. Leovenath is from the common Old English name Leofnoth; Levca is from Leofeca, recorded only as Leoveca by John of Worcester. Levca is perhaps to be respected as the *difficilior lectio*; it is, however, not known if variant readings in Otho have any authority. Both versions say that Layamon dwelt at Areley Kings, on the Severn near Redstone Rock. At line 3 Caligula has 'dwelt … at a noble church' (a church with undistinguished Norman traces survives), whereas Otho reads 'dwelt … with a good knight' which, if authoritative, may indicate Layamon's place as a priest attached to a knight's household. There 'he read books', either fulfilling his clerical duties, or in scholarship as he wished to trace the excellence of the English. The proximity of Areley to Wales is likely to have given Layamon access to Welsh sources; a theory of oral sources, both English and Welsh, has been canvassed, but is inevitably undemonstrable.

The *Brut* is essentially a pseudo-history of Britain from its legendary Trojan foundation to the seventh century. The account of events in the seventh century, with confusion going back to Geoffrey of Monmouth's *Historia regum Britanniae*, mentions King Cadwaladr's journey to Pope Sergius I in Rome: the journey of Ceadwalla or Cædwalla, king of the West Saxons, is recorded in the Anglo-Saxon Chronicle entry for 688, but Layamon's Cadwaladr is king of Britain, that is, Bede's Caedualla, king of the Britons, identical with Cadwallon, king of Gwynedd, who died in 634. After the Romans in Britain, the story of the Anglo-Saxon perfidy of Hengist and Horsa is told; then King Arthur is the centre of the *Brut*, and, as a hope in troublous times, Merlin's prophecy is recalled (Laȝamon, ed. Brook and Leslie, l. 14297), that 'an Arthur must come back to help the English'. At greater length than in the ultimate source, Geoffrey of Monmouth, or the immediate source, Wace's *Roman de Brut*, pagan myth (the deities known from the names of the days of the week (Laȝamon, ed. Brook and Leslie, ll. 6935–69)) and the foundation myths of English cities are related, including Leicester with King Leir and his daughters (ibid., ll. 1450–888); the renaming of Trinovant by King Lud as Kaer Lud now London (ibid., ll. 3524–55), with a vigorous criticism of the Normans who

did harm to the nation as is symbolized by their wilful renaming of the country's ancient towns; the building of Stonehenge (ibid., ll. 8465–732, cf. ll. 9888–92), and the construction of the Arthurian table (ibid., ll. 11345–464). Later events are referred to incidentally, including: King Alfred as lawgiver (ibid., ll. 3147–53), and the renewal of the payment of 'Peter's pence' under King Æthelstan (ibid., ll. 15947–64).

The poem is over 16,095 lines long as printed in recent editions, 32,241 short lines in Frederic Madden's great *editio princeps* of 1847. The verse is alliterative, and seems to recall Old English heroic verse, both in prosody and in diction including the use of kennings and poetic nominal compounds, many not found elsewhere in Old or Middle English. Many speeches are introduced. Unlike Old English verse, rhyme is used frequently, but it is often inexact, and is very often on unstressed inflexional syllables. In a section of the *Brut*, the source of which is not known, Layamon uses several epic similes.

The antique flavour is much stronger in the Caligula version than in Otho. The vocabulary of the former contains very few words of Norman origin, highly unusual for Middle English; the vocabulary of the Otho version is normal for Middle English. The Otho version is about 3000 lines shorter than Caligula, and in the abridgement many poeticisms have been excluded; it has somewhat less alliteration. Scholars are agreed that the Caligula version is closer to Layamon's original; but some lines in only the Otho version look authentic, and it is possible, at least theoretically, that Layamon wrote both versions. The spellings of the Caligula version are archaic for a manuscript of the later thirteenth century, and, since the spellings accord with Layamon's retrospective Englishry, they may be archaistic rather than genuinely twelfth-century.

Layamon says that he gathered sources which were to be a model to him, namely, three works: first, Bede; secondly, Albin (perhaps Albinus of Canterbury, one of Bede's informants, or Alcuin who is sometimes called Albin in the middle ages) and Augustine of Canterbury; and thirdly, Wace (d. 1180), Layamon's principal source. No likely book by Albin and Augustine (however that combination is interpreted) is known, and it may never have existed. The only trace in the *Brut* of Bede's *Historia ecclesiastica gentis Anglorum* is the account (Laȝamon, ed. Brook and Leslie, ll. 14695–728) of Gregory the Great, moved to pity by the English slaves near Rome, sending forth Augustine to convert the English; and that is not close to Bede, and probably not derived from him directly. It leads on to the story, in Wace, not in Bede, of the shaming with fishtails of the missionaries at Dorchester (Dorchester in Wace, but Rochester in Otho) and the resulting, similar shaming as *cued* (a very rare word of Norman origin, meaning 'tailed') of all Englishmen ever after (ibid., ll. 14756–72); it goes back to Wace's elaborate account ('Roman de Brut', ll. 13731–48).

Wace, Layamon says, presented his *Roman de Brut* to Eleanor 'who was Henry's queen'. This provides a *terminus a quo* for Layamon's *Brut*, namely, after the death of Henry II in 1189. No *terminus ad quem* has met with general acceptance, and the poem could have been composed at any time until the date of the manuscripts in the later thirteenth century.

More than other vernacular poets of the age, Layamon makes no secret of his opinions: he is pro-English and anti-Norman to the extent that, in the Caligula version, it colours his poetic language and his choice of verse form as he recreates a lost world. He shows a vigorous interest in Wales, in Ireland too, and especially in the ancient Britain before Hengist and Horsa arrived: the English and the British merge in his poem, and, though not blind to individual faults, he loves all the peoples of the British Isles before the Normans came.　　　　　　　　E. G. STANLEY

Sources *Laȝamons Brut, or, Chronicle of Britain*, ed. and trans. F. Madden (1847); repr. (1967) · *Laȝamon: Brut*, ed. G. L. Brook and R. F. Leslie, 2 vols., EETS, 250, 277 (1963–78) · *Layamon's Brut: a history of the Britons*, trans. D. G. Bzdyl (1989) · *Lawman: Brut*, trans. R. Allen (1992) · Laȝamon, *Brut, or, Hystoria Brutonum*, ed. and trans. W. R. J. Barron and S. C. Weinberg (1995) · *Le 'Roman de Brut' de Wace*, ed. I. Arnold, 2 vols. (Paris, 1938–40) · E. D. Kennedy, *A manual of the writings in Middle English, 1050–1500*, 8 (1989), 2611–17, 2781–98 · F. H. M. Le Saux, *Laȝamon's Brut: the poem and its sources* (1989) · J. S. P. Tatlock, *The legendary history of Britain: Geoffrey of Monmouth's Historia regum Britanniae and its early vernacular versions* (1950); repr. (1974) · J. A. W. Bennett, *Middle English literature*, ed. D. Gray (1986), vol. 1, pt 2 of *The Oxford history of English literature*, 68–89 · *VCH Worcestershire*, 4.277–30 · John of Worcester, *Chron.*

Archives BL, Cotton MS Caligula A.ix · BL, Cotton MS Otho C.xiii
Likenesses portrait, BL, Cotton MS Caligula A.ix, fol. 3[ra]

Layard, Sir Austen Henry (1817–1894), archaeologist and politician, was born in a Paris hotel on 5 March 1817, the eldest of four children of Henry Peter John Layard, formerly of the Ceylon civil service, and Marianne, daughter of Nathaniel Austen, banker, of Ramsgate. The Layards were of Huguenot descent. His father was asthmatic, and the family travelled much in Europe in search of a benign climate. They settled in Florence and enjoyed a cultured existence, entertaining visiting poets, painters, and writers. An altarpiece by Filippino Lippi hung over the young Layard's bed—it later formed part of his bequest to the National Gallery. He was briefly at school in Putney, Moulins (France), and Florence; then at the age of twelve he was sent to England to live with his uncle and aunt, Benjamin and Sara Austen, in search of a more formal education, which he received in Richmond, Surrey. In January 1834 he entered Austen's solicitors' office in London. His original forenames, Henry Austen, were reversed at the request of his uncle, whose partner and heir Layard hoped to become. However, he skimped and disliked the work of an articled clerk; the partnership, unsurprisingly, was not forthcoming; relations with his uncle deteriorated (he continued through life to use the name Henry). He was more interested in the literary men whom he met at his aunt's salon, not least her protégé Benjamin Disraeli. Like Disraeli, Layard grew up a Romantic, desperate for fame and exotic experiences, and contemptuous of English professional mores. A paternal uncle, living in Ceylon, suggested that he emigrate there to practise as a barrister, and introduced him to Edward Mitford, a young man bound for the same destination. Deciding to journey

Sir Austen Henry Layard (1817–1894), by George Frederic Watts, 1848

overland, the pair left England in July 1839. The Royal Geographical Society commissioned Layard to research the terrain.

Travel and excavations, 1839–1851 Layard and Mitford travelled through the Ottoman lands, visiting Constantinople (where Layard nearly died of malaria, which recurred in following years) and Jerusalem. He also made a reckless journey alone to see Petra and other ancient sites east of the Dead Sea; he was robbed and nearly killed by tribesmen. They stayed in Mosul and Baghdad; then in August 1840, in Persia, the two parted company, as Layard, who had become enamoured of the simplicity and independence of local life, preferred to stay in the region. He travelled, read widely in local history, learned Arabic and Persian, and spent time in the Bakhtiari Mountains with a tribe which was resisting the oppression of the shah. He returned to Baghdad and Mosul, where he had become fascinated by mounds opposite Mosul which the French consul, Emil Botta, was tentatively exploring. His funds depleted, Layard regained Constantinople in the summer of 1842, expecting to have to return to England. However, he made himself known to Stratford Canning, British ambassador to the Ottoman empire, who admired his spirit and his knowledge of the Turkish–Persian border, which was then in dispute. Layard agreed to stay in Turkey and work for Canning, believing that this was a place of promise for an enterprising and ambitious man. Canning paid him himself, since the Foreign Office under Lord Aberdeen refused to make him a paid attaché. He went on two information-gathering missions in European Turkey. In 1845, fearing that the French would otherwise get the honour, he persuaded Canning to support excavation work on the mounds near Mosul.

Layard left Constantinople in October and began to dig the mound of Nimrud. His earlier experience of living among local tribes paid off handsomely: he managed what became a workforce of 130 men with generosity and firmness, entertained visiting Arab sheikhs hospitably and patiently, dealt diplomatically with the local rulers, and so progressed with speed and economy. Guided by intuition founded on his discursive reading, his archaeological achievement was remarkable. He uncovered three palaces, most importantly that of Ashurnasirpal II, and many notable objects including the Black Obelisk of Shalmaneser III and several pairs of human-headed winged lions and bulls. In May 1846 Canning received authorization for the export of some of these to England, and then applied successfully to the trustees of the British Museum for further funding, which lasted until June 1847. In the last few weeks of this period Layard began excavations at Kuyunjik, nearer Mosul, and quickly discovered the largest Assyrian palace, that of Sennacherib. Forced to end excavations and return to Constantinople, Layard, encouraged by Henry Rawlinson (the scholar and British consul at Baghdad), claimed that Nimrud was Nineveh. Only after the publication of his first book did he realize that it was not, and that Kuyunjik was. In July 1847 Canning finally secured (from Palmerston) Layard's appointment to the embassy staff to work on the Turkish–Persian boundary question, though in fact illness prevented him from carrying out his duties.

Suffering from exhaustion and the recurrence of malaria, Layard returned to London in December 1847 for the first time in eight and a half years. In 1848 he worked hard to publicize his discoveries. He was made DCL at Oxford in July 1848, and in May 1849 received the gold medal of the Royal Geographical Society. When his book *Nineveh and its Remains* was published early in 1849 it had an enthusiastic reception. So did the arrival of the Assyrian sculptures at the British Museum. Layard was admired as a type of the fearless, independently minded English explorer. Moreover, men who were anxious to rebut recent criticisms of the authenticity of holy scripture were excited by Assyrian references to biblical names and events and proclaimed that he had 'made the Bible true'. When he was presented with the freedom of the City of London in 1853, it was for demonstrating 'the accuracy of Sacred History'. His cynical Constantinople friend Charles Alison had told him: 'if you can by any means humbug people into the belief that you have established any points in the Bible, you are a made man' (Waterfield, 171). So it proved.

Layard was appointed a paid attaché at Constantinople in April 1849, but between October 1849 and April 1851 conducted major excavations at Kuyunjik, funded by the British Museum and described in a second book, *Nineveh and Babylon* (1853). These yielded further important trophies and discoveries, including the cuneiform library of Sennacherib's grandson Ashurbanipal, on which most modern knowledge of Assyrian culture is founded. At the new Crystal Palace, opened in 1854, there was an Assyrian court, on which Layard advised.

Political career, 1851–1869 From 1851 Layard abandoned archaeology and sought to use his fame to launch a political career. Lord Cowley, whom he had known in 1844 at Constantinople, offered him a post at the Paris embassy, but he preferred to take the under-secretaryship of foreign affairs which the new foreign secretary, Lord Granville, gave him (through Cowley's influence) in February 1852. Rocked by the sacking of Granville's predecessor, Palmerston, the Liberal government needed to demonstrate its openness to talent. Layard seemed a man of the people, though in fact it was as Lord Carrington's candidate that he became Liberal MP for Aylesbury in July 1852.

Layard held office for only three months, because Lord John Russell's government fell and (after blandishments and considerable hesitation) he declined to continue under the incoming Conservatives. His hopes for future employment depended on Russell, but the latter had few bargaining counters on the formation of the Aberdeen coalition of December 1852, and Layard was one of the many Liberals who were excluded from office in order to make way for Peelites. Russell offered him the consul-generalship in Egypt in 1853, but he wished to stay in British politics. Thereafter he was critical of whig haughtiness but much more angry at Peelite principles of government, particularly in Eastern policy. From his time in Constantinople he had been suspicious of Aberdeen's friendliness to Russia, which he regarded as a sinister influence in the East. Britain, he argued, must support the Ottoman empire in order to thwart Russia, and must ignore Russian-inspired complaints about Turkish misbehaviour towards the Balkan Christians. He believed that the Turkish people had as much right to live in the Balkans as the Christians and suffered as much from the internecine conflicts there, while the Greek hierarchy in particular was venal and oppressive. If the Turkish sultan's prestige were undermined, Ottoman control over the Asian peoples would be lost, creating anarchy which would damage British interests in the area. Pressure from energetic, trustworthy British ambassadors at the Porte was the best way to promote administrative reforms in the Ottoman empire, and these, together with Western capital investment, would help the Christians to acquire the talents which would eventually see the government of the Balkans pass relatively painlessly into their hands. With these views (afforced by a visit to Constantinople in 1853) he became a vigorous and expert parliamentary critic of government policy towards Russia. The descent into war early in 1854 seemed to validate his criticisms, and he journeyed to the Crimea in the autumn to witness the battles, forming a low opinion of British military strategy and administration.

In 1854–5 Layard mounted an outspoken crusade against the incompetence of Aberdeen's government and the war effort. Aberdeen fell early in 1855 and his successor, Palmerston, saw the merit of bringing Layard into government as under-secretary at the War Office. But

Queen Victoria refused to consider him for this post on account of his open abuse of the Crimean military commanders Lord Raglan and Admiral Dundas. Palmerston then offered him the under-secretaryship of the Colonial Office, but he refused, regarding this as an unsuitable post and preferring to launch an extra-parliamentary campaign against 'family and party influence' in government, on the motto 'Fitness not favour'. This was genuinely subversive, and at first it caught the public mood. *Punch* supported him, representing him digging out the British (John) Bull buried beneath a great weight of official incompetence. He was elected lord rector of Marischal College, Aberdeen, and in his inaugural address explained how Britain, like Nineveh and Babylon, might lose her empire if she preferred vested interests and tired routine to virtue and individual responsibility. In May the campaign culminated in the establishment of a much-publicized pressure group, the Administrative Reform Association. However, Layard's star waned with the improvement in the war effort, the growth of confidence in Palmerston, and the capture of the Administrative Reform Association by moderates. By the end of the session he realized the need to turn his energies elsewhere. In 1856 he showed his personal commitment to the cause of reform and capitalism in Turkey by establishing the Ottoman Bank, which was intended to channel loans to the government and to commercial developers and so underpin the promises for Ottoman regeneration which the sultan made at the end of the Crimean War. He remained chairman until 1861.

Layard was unable to regain political standing after the war, disliking the spirit of chauvinism on which Palmerston had to rely to stay in office. His sympathy for, and confidence that he could manage, the peoples of the Near East made him hostile to the harsh treatment meted out by Sir John Bowring to the Chinese at Canton (Guangzhou) in 1856 and by the British troops suppressing the Indian mutiny in 1857. Having opposed Palmerston's government on the former issue, he lost his seat at the 1857 election, and went to India on a fact-finding tour. His disdain for British chauvinism was also evident in his revived interest in the land of his childhood. With few roots in England, and alienated from government, he found in Italy two causes which gave him emotional fulfilment and a political *raison d'être*. One was the Risorgimento, which had stimulated him when an ardent youth and which also worked on his ingrained hostility to the papacy. Sympathy for Italian self-government, together with memories of his wartime patriotism, explained his attraction to the working-class constituency of Southwark, which elected him in 1860 to succeed the radical war hero Sir Charles Napier. (Layard had been defeated at York at the 1859 election.) It also kept him close to Russell, whose under-secretary at the Foreign Office he became in 1861. Layard held this post until the government fell in 1866.

The second of his causes was art. Layard had an artist's eye, as can be seen from the many invaluable drawings that he made during the Assyrian excavations. He was among the pioneer enthusiasts for early Italian Renaissance painting, seeing it as expressing truthful religious ideas with simple piety. Contrasting this with the formulaic or sensuous art of more materialistic and decadent regimes, he warned that in modern Britain there was too much of the latter, and that there was an urgent need to elevate public taste by state and private encouragement. He was part of a circle which took several initiatives to this end. In 1856 his chromolithography edition of Perugino's fresco of St Sebastian revitalized the struggling Arundel Society, founded in 1848 to make reproductions of early Renaissance artworks widely available; he subsequently produced monographs on four other painters. He made annual visits to Italy to buy paintings for himself and the National Gallery. Russell (now prime minister) wanted him to succeed Sir Charles Eastlake as director of the gallery in 1865, while continuing at the Foreign Office. The obstacles to this were insuperable, and he became a trustee instead, in February 1866. He secured a parliamentary grant to help fund trips by artisans to the Universal Exhibition of 1867 at Paris and the publication of their reports on the displays in their trades; eighty were produced and Layard personally took two thousand of his Southwark constituents to the exhibition.

At first sight Layard's appointment as first commissioner of works (and a privy councillor) in Gladstone's government of 1868 marked a gesture of support for this policy of state-supported aesthetic education. At this time the office of works was responsible for an unprecedented number of major metropolitan public building schemes, and Layard and his supporters hoped that his influence could place London, which he called 'the ugliest capital in the civilized world' (*The Times*, 10 Nov 1869), on a footing with the rest of Europe. He appointed the eminent historian of Indian architecture James Fergusson as an architectural adviser. Unfortunately for them the office of works had since 1851 been clearly subordinate to Treasury control, and all the Treasury ministers involved—Gladstone, Robert Lowe, and A. S. Ayrton—were anxious to trim expenditure. So was a reformed House of Commons, in a tax-cutting, utilitarian, and somewhat anti-metropolitan mood. Layard encountered insuperable opposition from a number of quarters to his grand scheme of placing the new law courts and the Natural History Museum (to be followed by other public buildings) on a magnificent Thames Embankment. Bridling at Treasury demands, unpopular in the Commons, and accusing Gladstone of failing to support him, he hinted that he would prefer a diplomatic appointment. In October 1869, in an unusual move that ruffled career diplomats' feathers, he was appointed ambassador to Madrid.

Ambassadorship and retirement Layard's parliamentary career marks him out as an old-school radical. In the early 1850s he complained that aristocratic exclusiveness prevented inadequately connected individuals of energy and talent from serving the state. But as time went on he found the constraints increasingly imposed by party and by ignorant constituents equally offensive. Though a parliamentary reformer in the 1850s, he blamed the effects of the 1867 Reform Act for lessening the independently minded politician's scope to act out a vision for the nation. Angry that men like him were not promoted to cabinet in the tawdry age of Gladstone, he hoped that the international stage would be more congenial than insular Britain. This hope was only partially borne out. Holding the Palmerston–Russell line that Britain must play a leading part in world diplomacy with a view to developing liberty and trade, and deriving his conception of an ambassador's role from the forceful behaviour of Stratford Canning, he was bound to be disappointed by life at Madrid at a time when the home government was anxious to keep a low profile in Europe. He complained that Britain did not do more to find and support a good king for Spain in the early 1870s. But he did good work in trying to defuse Franco-German tension over Spain in 1870 and—with more permanent results—in 1873-4. He laboured hard to keep tariffs between Britain and Spain low. His personal sympathies for the Spanish liberals were well known: in 1873 the Layards gave asylum to one of them, Serrano, and smuggled him to the coast, and he was critical of the restrictions on protestant liberties brought in by the Bourbons after 1875. He was a professional, hard-working, able, and hospitable ambassador. He was helped greatly by his young wife, Mary Enid Evelyn (1843–1912), eighth child of Sir John Guest and his wife, Lady Charlotte Guest [see Schreiber, Lady Charlotte Elizabeth] (with whom Layard was said to have been romantically linked in the late 1840s), whom he married on 9 March 1869 at St George's, Hanover Square, London.

In March 1877, seeking an ambassador for Constantinople who would revive British influence in Turkey while persuading the sultan to reform, Disraeli chose Layard. He was happy there, but plunged into intense controversy. He regarded the agitation of 1876–7 in Britain against the Turkish massacre of Bulgarians as naïvely sentimental; by paralysing the British government's Eastern policy, it had directly inspired the Russians to invade Turkey. His dispatches constantly urged a more aggressive anti-Russian policy, and converted the queen to his side. In 1878 government policy was more congenial to him, and he played a valuable part in persuading the sultan to agree to the concession of Cyprus to Britain. Foreign Secretary Salisbury held that he had greatly increased British influence at Constantinople, and he was awarded the GCB in June 1878. Soon after the Congress of Berlin, however, the sultan began to suspect the British of plotting against him, and this affected his relations with Layard, which had previously been exceptionally good. Layard attributed this suspicion to a developing neurosis, but the sultan may have felt, rationally, that the reforms which the British wished to impose on Asiatic Turkey would undermine his authority. In 1880 Layard wrote an overheated dispatch which was pessimistic about the prospects for reform and labelled the sultan a hypocrite. This coincided with the return to power of Gladstone, with whom Layard's relations were passionately hostile as a result of the former's role in the Bulgarian agitation. Gladstone had publicly accused Layard of exaggerating reports of Christian massacres of Turks, and of conniving with a journalist against him, abusing the status of an ambassador. Gladstone now published Layard's dispatch, exposing his change of mind about the sultan (to considerable ridicule) and his heated language (for which the queen never forgave the writer). In Layard's view the publication did immense damage to Anglo-Ottoman relations. Layard was recalled from Constantinople, at first on leave of absence, but then permanently. He hoped for another diplomatic post, especially at Rome, but was kept waiting until 1883 before being told that he would not get one.

Disappointed at not receiving a peerage Layard retired to Venice, where he had bought a Renaissance house, Ca' Capello, in 1874. Here the Layards, free at last of English snobberies and ingratitude, lived in seigneurial style, running an unofficial embassy-cum-gallery; nearly a hundred of his paintings elegantly displayed there were later bequeathed to the National Gallery. A stream of political and artist friends came from England and abroad, including the Empress Frederick of Germany. Layard led the campaign to establish an Anglican church in Venice, St George's, which was consecrated in 1892; he was the first elected churchwarden. From 1868 he was involved with a local glass and mosaic company, which undertook a number of important commissions in England at his instigation. He published his *Early Adventures in Persia, Susiana, and Babylonia* in 1887 and in the same year comprehensively revised Kügler's *Handbook of Painting*, basing the revision on his prolonged observation of Italian painting and his admiration for the views of the art critic Giovanni Morelli. He was *membre de l'institut* of the Académie Française, honorary foreign secretary of the Royal Academy of Arts, and president of the Huguenot Society. Suffering from cancer, he went back to London, where he died on 5 July 1894, at 1 Queen Anne Street. His funeral was held at St Margaret's, Westminster; he disliked the 'odious practice of interment', and was cremated on 9 July at Woking.

Layard was stocky, of medium height with a large head and, from about 1850, a luxuriant beard. In congenial company he was amiable, humorous, and engaging. In public, however, he could not govern his temper or emotions, and this, together with his propensity for blunt criticism, made him a large number of enemies, some of whom blackened his reputation. He had indomitable self-belief, but his hatred of subordinate place bordered on the pathological. He carried to extremes the Romantic myth of the self-made, self-reliant man of insight and talent. He hated humbug and casuistry, and had a genuine and intense sympathy with the oppressed, especially those suffering under clerical rule. In that sense he was a man of the people. He was too hasty, single-minded, and unworldly to be successful in politics. But his zest, imagination, creativity, and idealism made him an important figure in a dazzling variety of fields, an unusually cultivated and vigorous all-rounder even by the high standards of his age.

JONATHAN PARRY

Sources G. Waterfield, *Layard of Nineveh* (1963) · A. H. Layard, *Autobiography and letters from his childhood until his appointment as H. M.*

ambassador in Madrid, ed. W. N. Bruce, 2 vols. (1903) • F. M. Fales and B. J. Hickey, eds., *Austen Henry Layard: tra l'Oriente e Venezia* (1987) • A. H. Layard, *Early adventures in Persia, Susiana, and Babylonia* (1887) • M. H. Port, 'A contrast in styles at the office of works: Layard and Ayrton, aesthete and economist', *HJ*, 27 (1984), 151–76 • Gladstone, *Diaries* • *The political correspondence of Mr Gladstone and Lord Granville, 1868–1876*, ed. A. Ramm, 2 vols., CS, 3rd ser., 81–2 (1952) • *The Times* (10 July 1894)

Archives BL

Likenesses G. F. Watts, chalk, 1848, NPG [*see illus.*] • S. W. Reynolds, jun., mezzotint, pubd 1850 (after H. W. Phillips), BM, NPG • G. F. Watts, pencil, *c*.1851, NPG • P. Park, marble bust, 1855, BM • cartoon, 1855, repro. in Waterfield, *Layard of Nineveh*, 268 • portrait, *c*.1890, Gov. Art Coll. • J. E. Boehm, marble bust, *c*.1891, BM • L. Passini, watercolour, 1891, NPG; repro. in Waterfield, *Layard of Nineveh* • Ape [C. Pellegrini], chromolithograph, NPG; repro. in *VF* (28 Aug 1869) • W. Brockedon, pencil and chalk, NPG; repro. in Waterfield, *Layard of Nineveh* • J. Brown, stipple (after H. W. Phillips), BM, NPG • E. Layard, bronze plaque, Gov. Art Coll. • lithograph, NPG; repro. in *The Whitehall Review* (27 July 1878) • photographs, NPG

Wealth at death £92,464 16*s*. 4*d*.: resworn probate, Dec 1894, CGPLA Eng. & Wales

Layard, Daniel Peter (1721–1802), man-midwife and physician, was the son of Major Layard. On 9 March 1742 he graduated MD at Rheims. In April 1747 he was appointed man-midwife-in-ordinary to the Middlesex Hospital, London, but resigned in 1749 over a dispute concerning the enlargement of the lying-in ward, which caused a split among the hospital's governors. Layard and the other man-midwife at the Middlesex, Francis Sandys, who were in favour of increasing the size of the ward, left and founded the British Lying-in Hospital at Brownlow Street. In 1750 Layard settled at Huntingdon, and he practised there for twelve years. On 3 July 1752 he was admitted a licentiate of the Royal College of Physicians and by the same year had retired as man-midwife from the Brownlow Street Hospital. He did, however, become physician to the hospital in 1752 and served until his retirement in 1755.

About 1762 Layard returned to London and soon obtained an extensive practice as an accoucheur. He was physician to the princess dowager of Wales, and fellow of the royal societies of London (1746) and Göttingen. On 20 June 1792 he had the honorary degree of DCL conferred upon him at Oxford.

Layard contributed some papers to the *Philosophical Transactions*, and published *An Essay on the Nature, Causes, and Cure of the Contagious Distemper among the Horned Cattle in these Kingdoms* (1757); *An Essay on the Bite of a Mad Dog* (1762); *An Account of the Somersham Water in the County of Huntingdon* (1767); and *Pharmacopoeia in usum gravidarum puerperarum* (1776).

Layard died at Greenwich in February 1802. His son Charles Peter Layard (1750–1803), successively prebendary of Bangor, prebendary of Worcester (1793), and dean of Bristol (1800), was grandfather of Sir Austen Henry Layard. GORDON GOODWIN, *rev.* MICHAEL BEVAN

Sources Munk, *Roll* • A. Wilson, *The making of man-midwifery: childbirth in England, 1660–1770* (1995) • *GM*, 1st ser., 72 (1802), 281 • Foster, *Alum. Oxon.* • Venn, *Alum. Cant.* [Charles Peter Layard]

Archives U. Nott. L., Cavendish-Bentinck MSS

Layard, John Willoughby (1891–1974), anthropologist and psychologist, was born on 27 November 1891 at 68 Palace Garden Terrace, Kensington, London, the second child and first son of George Somes Layard (1857–1925), a barrister and author, and his wife, Eleanor Gribble Layard. He was educated at the Priory School, Malvern, and Bedales, spent a year abroad improving his French and German (1908–9), and graduated in 1912 from King's College, Cambridge, with a degree in modern languages. Through friends he met W. H. R. Rivers, a doctor with a great interest in psychology and also the leading anthropologist of his day, who persuaded Layard to spend a fourth year in Cambridge to study anthropology.

In 1914 Rivers and Layard journeyed to Australia to attend the meetings of the British Association being held there. While they were on board, war was declared. Since Rivers thought Cambridge would be disrupted by mobilization, he decided to mount an expedition to Vanuatu (then the New Hebrides) and invited Layard to accompany him. On advice they chose to work on Atchin, an islet off the island of Malekula (now Malakula). But Rivers departed within ten days of arriving, leaving a surprised Layard on his own. He stayed on Atchin for a year to study the local way of life and so became one of the earliest intensive fieldworkers in British anthropology.

Layard always remembered his stay on Atchin as one of the happiest periods of his life, enormously enjoying his time participating with the locals in both their rituals and their everyday tasks. He also found life there very tiring and on return to England suffered severe mental distress. Over the next decades of his life he worked with a series of therapists achieving, in the process, a hybrid intellectual style.

His first therapist was Rivers, who was then working with shell-shocked soldiers. But the main consequence of this encounter was a disagreement which finally concluded their association. In the mid-1920s Layard was treated with some success by Homer Lane, the unorthodox American psychologist. During the later part of this decade he lived in Berlin for three years, where it appears that he became involved in the city's thriving expatriate homosexual scene and became mentor to W. H. Auden, who was almost twenty years his junior. According to Christopher Isherwood, Layard held both him and Auden spellbound with his Lane-influenced talk about the psychosomatic origin of all disease and his belief that every external effect had an internal cause. But Layard's own personal problems continued; he survived a suicide attempt, which left him with a gunshot wound in the head.

In 1936, while in London, Layard was introduced to Carl Jung, who first treated and then collaborated with him in the years before and just after the Second World War. Jung was a major intellectual stimulus to Layard, and his influence can be discerned throughout Layard's main contribution to anthropology: his monumental ethnography, *Stone Men of Malekula* (1942). Layard stated that his return to anthropology was due largely to the encouragement of and the attentions paid to him by Doris Dingwall (*née* Dunn) (*d.* 1973), then the moving spirit of the human anatomy department of University College, London, whose seminars he attended. They later married and had one child, Richard (who became professor of labour economics, London School of Economics, and was made a life peer in 1996). In the post-war decades Layard practised as a Jungian psychologist in London and Oxford, and published a series of papers in which he reanalysed his Malakulan material in Jungian terms. He died at the Cowley Road Hospital, Oxford, on 26 November 1974.

Layard's intellectual approach was distinctive for its synthesis of diffusionism and structural functionalism—two trends usually thought of as competing for attention in the anthropology of the 1930s—together with Jungian psychology. According to Layard's 'structural Jungianism', social function was to be interpreted in terms of Jungian archetypes. Transposing Jung's psychology from the level of the individual to that of society, he saw kinship as an externalized form of the self, and the ritual passage of a Malakulan male from initiation to final rest, after death, in a nearby volcano as but a local version of the universal striving towards wholeness.

Layard's original and imaginative interpretations failed to sway his anthropological contemporaries, who promoted other approaches and regarded psychological explanations as over(ly) speculative. Since Layard himself never held an academic post, he had no students to further his work and thus his unique, if somewhat eccentric, contribution to the history of British anthropology has not won the attention it deserves. However, his indirect contribution to English literature has been much more clearly demonstrated. Layard had a profound effect on Auden's development during his Berlin period, especially in his long poem *The Orators*; Isherwood based one of the key characters of *The Memorial* (1932) on Layard; T. S. Eliot acknowledged his debt to Layard's ideas about his Malakulan material in his essay on 'Cultural forces in the human order' (1952) while the influence of *Stone Men of Malekula* on Eliot's *The Cocktail Party* has been discerned.

JEREMY MACCLANCY

Sources J. Layard, *Stone men of Malekula* (1942) · I. Langham, *The building of British social anthropology, 1898–1931* (1981) · J. MacClancy, 'Unconventional character and disciplinary convention: John Layard, Jungian and anthropologist', *History of Anthropology*, 4 (1986), 50–71 · E. Mendelson, *Early Auden* (1981) · J. Layard, 'Study of a failure', unpublished autobiography, U. Cal., San Diego, Layard MSS · W. Harmon, 'T. S. Eliot, anthropologist and primitive', *American Anthropologist*, 78 (1976), 797–811 · R. Crawford, *The savage and the city in the work of T. S. Eliot* (1987) · orpheus.ucsd.edu/speccoll/findaids/social_sci/layard, 21 March 2002 · private information (2004) · b. cert. · d. cert.

Archives U. Cal., San Diego

Wealth at death £14,394: probate, 1975, *CGPLA Eng. & Wales*

Layard, Nina Frances (1853–1935), poet and archaeologist, was born on 20 August 1853 at Stratford Green, Essex, fourth child of Charles Clement Layard (1817–1895), Church of England clergyman, and his wife, Sarah, *née*

Somes (1817–1886). In childhood an avid egg and shell collector, she lived at Wembley and Harrow rectories 1858–73, and attended a dame-school in Willesden, Middlesex. Of distinguished Huguenot ancestry, her father's cousins Sir A. H. Layard, E. L. Layard, and Lady Charlotte Guest were inspirational examples, and Matthew Arnold encouraged her earliest poetry. The family moving to Combe-Hay rectory, Bath, in 1873, she spent many solitary hours collecting, and despite having a weak constitution travelled round the world via New Zealand in 1878–9. She became aware of the fossil kingdom in 1882, and began serious collecting and reading under the guidance of Leonard Jenyns and John Ellor Taylor.

Having published minor critiques of the theory of rudiments in evolution, Layard moved permanently, with private means, to Ipswich in 1889, presented the first paper by a woman to the Victoria Institute, and from 1890 to 1895 broke similar ground with the British Association. In this period, with Andrew Lang's help, her poetry was published to brief acclaim, and she met Mary Frances Outram (1862–1935), eldest daughter of Sir Francis Outram, of Pitlochry, from 1894 her constant companion. She commenced systematic archaeological work on Ipswich monastic sites (1898), winning honourable recognition. In 1902–5 she discovered and excavated a palaeolithic site in Ipswich analogous to Hoxne and Hitchin, advised by Sir John Evans and Boyd Dawkins, and was elected fellow of the Anthropological Institute (1902) and Linnean Society (1906). Her methodical rescue excavation of an Anglo-Saxon cemetery at Ipswich in 1906–7 received publication by the Society of Antiquaries (London), though at this time she was excluded (being a woman) despite Evans's attempted intervention.

In 1907 Sir Ray Lankester established Layard as honorary curator of a room in Christchurch Mansion, Ipswich, where until 1920 she developed substantial prehistoric collections (which she popularized through press notices) by excavations in East Anglia and elsewhere, receiving encouragement from distinguished archaeologists, and inspiring several future prehistorians, including James Reid Moir and her anthropologist nephew John Willoughby Layard (1891–1974). A founder member of the Prehistoric Society of East Anglia (1908) and president (1921), Layard deliberated on the putative Tertiary implements in 1910–11, and was also an active officer of the Suffolk Institute of Archaeology in 1912–20. She was one of the first group of women to be made fellow of the Society of Antiquaries, *honoris causa* (1921), and throughout the 1920s continued excavation and publication, studying continental sites, and developing international academic contacts. In her work she rebuffed anti-feminine prejudice by courtesy, thoroughness, excellence, and perseverance. Her excavations, publications, collections, and academic connections helped shape a rising generation of prehistoric discourse, bridging nineteenth- and twentieth-century outlook and method. Her early religious views, which prompted several initiatives in temperance and social reform, broadened through her studies towards a synthetic Christian spirituality. She worked until her last year, and died shortly after Miss Outram, in Ipswich Nursing Home, 57 Fonnereau Road, Ipswich, on 12 August 1935. They were buried in a shared grave in Kelvedon churchyard, Essex, on 15 August.　　　STEVEN J. PLUNKETT

Sources　Suffolk RO, Layard MSS, S.2/3/1–5 · *East Anglian Daily Times* (14 Aug 1935) · '"Silly Suffolk", Miss Layard's poems', *East Anglian Daily Times* (12 Jan 1924) · S. J. Plunkett, 'Nina Layard, Hadleigh Road and Ipswich Museum, 1905–1908', *Proceedings of the Suffolk Institute of Archaeology and History*, 38 (1993–6), 164–92 · S. J. Plunkett, 'Nina Layard and the sub-crag committee of 1910', *East Anglian studies: essays presented to J. C. Barringer on his retirement*, ed. A. Longcroft and R. Joby (1995), 211–22 · M. Outram, 'Mary Frances Outram, 1862–1935', Ipswich Museum · H. Wagner, 'Pedigree of Layard', *Proceedings of the Huguenot Society*, 9 (1909–11), facing p. 254 · *Proceedings of the Suffolk Institute of Archaeology and Natural History* (1899–1935) · *Proceedings of the Prehistoric Society of East Anglia* (1908–35) · b. cert. · d. cert. · *CGPLA Eng. & Wales* (1935)
Archives　BM, corresp. · Christchuch Mansion, Ipswich, papers relating to her collections · PRO NIre., corresp., journals, press cuttings, sketchbooks · Suffolk RO, Ipswich, articles, corresp., lectures, notebooks, and other papers | priv. coll., Layard-Whytehead family albums · U. Nott. L., letters to H. S. Sutton
Likenesses　photograph, 1906, repro. in S. J. Plunkett, *Guardians of the Gipping* (1994), 10 · J. S. Corder, cartoon, 1906–7, repro. in S. J. Plunkett, *Guardians of the Gipping* (1994), 47 · portrait, *c.*1924, repro. in Plunkett, 'Nina Layard, Hadleigh Road and Ipswich Museum', 164 · E. Gribble, pastel drawing, 1935, Ipswich Borough Museums · photographs, Suffolk RO, Layard MSS · photographs (in youth), priv. coll.
Wealth at death　£3475 17s. 11d.: probate, 3 Oct 1935, *CGPLA Eng. & Wales*

Layborn, Thomas Alec Edwin (1898–1984), life-assurance and pensions consultant, was born on 30 November 1898 at 57 St Mary's Grove, Chiswick, Middlesex, the son of William Edwin Layborn, a wine merchant, and his wife, Mary Ellen, *née* Stevens. He was educated at Latymer Upper School, which he left upon the death of his father in 1914. He then went to work for the Car and General Insurance Company, but in 1915 he became a junior clerk with Liverpool, London, and Globe Insurance. In the First World War, aged seventeen, he volunteered for the Artists' Rifles, and later was commissioned in the Royal Flying Corps. In 1920 he married a teacher, Helen Field, daughter of John Field, a paymaster. They had a son, John (*d.* 1948), and a daughter, June.

After demobilization Layborn rejoined Liverpool, London, and Globe, but he moved some months later to Legal and General as a junior inspector. He rose rapidly to become general inspector of insurance agents in the East End, chief City inspector in the firm's new fire and accident departments, City accident manager (1925), and West End manager (1926). In 1931 he was sent to southern Africa to arrange a pension scheme for the Victoria Falls Power Company, and it was in this line of business that Layborn was to make his mark. In 1933 he became group pensions manager and in 1937 agency manager, one of the company's most senior positions. His impatience to succeed, unremitting energy, and brilliance in marketing helped to transform Legal and General from a venerable but ordinary life office to the dynamic leader in the field of group life assurance and pensions.

Layborn's forte proved to be the selling of life-assurance schemes to large commercial organizations. When in 1930 the company sold its first large scheme, for the 6000 employees of the Gramophone Company (later EMI), Layborn persuaded his golf partner, then editor of the *Sunday Express*, to run a lead story, 'Killing the dread of old age'. Other papers followed suit, and for a decade a favourable press helped to boost demand for group pensions. In 1933 the purchase of the UK pensions business of Metropolitan Life of New York left Legal and General as the dominant force in the British market. Layborn was personally involved in selling some of the largest life and pension schemes, notably to United Steel, the tobacco manufacturers Gallaghers, and the Austin Motor Company, as well as to the Rhodesian copper mining companies. By 1938 190,000 workers were covered by Legal and General's schemes. Between 1933 and 1945 the company's life-assurance fund rose threefold, with group schemes rising the most rapidly. During his career Layborn helped to set the long-run growth pattern for the whole British life-assurance industry. By 1978 total UK premium income from group business exceeded that from ordinary life assurance.

Layborn's connections with corporate bodies led to invitations to join several boards, and his field of activities widened considerably. He became a director of Chessington Zoo, Standard Industrial Trust, Rhodesian Housing Estates, Austin Motors, British Motor Corporation, and British Leyland. During the Second World War he was a member of the Mitchison committee which dealt with the reorganization of pensions, for which service he was appointed CBE in 1944. In 1947 he joined the Industrial Injuries Advisory Council, and in 1960 he was on the committee established by the Ministry of Agriculture to advise on the problem of fowl pest.

In 1945 severe exhaustion from overwork led to Layborn's retirement from Legal and General. On his recovery, he established in 1946 his own life and pensions consultancy, Layborn & Son Ltd. The firm was bought by C. T. Bowring in 1953, and Layborn became deputy chairman of C. T. Bowring and Layborn Ltd, for whom he continued to work up to the time of his death. He delivered several lectures, some of which were published, to various institutes. From 1958 to 1960 he was founding president of the new Corporation of Insurance Brokers' Society of Pension Consultants, and in 1961–2 he was president of the Insurance Institute of London, the first broker to hold that office since the foundation of the institute in 1907. Layborn died from heart disease on 17 December 1984, at Holmesdale Park, Nutfield, Surrey.

ROBIN PEARSON

Sources　H. Cockerell, 'Layborn, Thomas Alec Edwin', *DBB* · T. A. E. Layborn, autobiography, (typescript), 1977, priv. coll. · *The Times* (8 Jan 1985) · L. Hannah, *Inventing retirement: the development of occupational pensions in Britain* (1986) · 'President for 1961–2 — T. A. E. Layborn', *Journal of the Insurance Institute of London*, 50 (1962), 5 · T. A. E. Layborn, 'Presidential Address', *Journal of the Insurance Institute of London*, 50 (1962), 1–8 · d. cert.
Likenesses　photograph, 1961, repro. in 'President for 1961–2', *Journal of the Insurance Institute of London* · photograph, repro. in Cockerell, 'Layborn, Thomas Alec Edwin'

Laycock, Sir Robert Edward (1907–1968), army officer, was born in London on 18 April 1907, the eldest surviving son of Sir Joseph Frederick Laycock (1867–1952) and his wife, Katherine Mary (*d.* 1959), daughter of Hugh Henry Hare and formerly marchioness of Downshire. His father, who had been appointed DSO in 1900, was in 1918 commander of a brigade of the Royal Artillery, and was one of the very few Territorial officers to be appointed KCMG (1919) for services in the field. Laycock was devoted to his father, and probably inherited a soldierly disposition from him.

Robert Laycock, known as Bob, was educated at Eton College and at the Royal Military College, Sandhurst, where he became senior under-officer. He was commissioned an officer of the Royal Horse Guards in 1927. In 1935 he married Angela Clare Louise, daughter of William Dudley Ward, a privy councillor, and Liberal member of parliament for Southampton (1906–22); they had two sons and three daughters.

Laycock's wide interests included scientific ones, and he took every professional opportunity to enlarge his knowledge of these; as a result on the outbreak of war in 1939 he found himself GSO2, chemical warfare, at the British expeditionary force (BEF) headquarters in France. From this unrewarding post he was transferred to England to attend the first wartime course at Staff College, Camberley. He thus took no part in the first battle of France.

In the period succeeding the fall of France, Admiral Sir Roger Keyes was founding the commandos, and requested Laycock's services which he had in fact already volunteered. He was thus saved from the threat of another chemical warfare appointment. An ideal officer for special service employment, Laycock was promoted lieutenant-colonel, and early in 1941 he sailed for the Middle East in command of 'Layforce', an enlarged battalion of five commandos.

The little force carried out several minor but hazardous tasks with varying success until it was allotted the daunting mission of rearguard action in the British defence of Crete. Throughout this action (May–June 1941) Laycock's personal assistant was Captain Evelyn Waugh. The experience of the British disaster in Crete is reflected in Waugh's novel *Officers and Gentlemen* (1955). Laycock and Waugh were in the last British ship to leave the island.

Later in 1941 Laycock took part in the unsuccessful raid led by Lieutenant-Colonel Keyes (the admiral's son) on Rommel's supposed headquarters, and after the action he escaped into the Libyan desert and lived for nearly two months behind the enemy lines. He afterwards declared that he owed his survival to his knowledge of the habits of foxes, and in gratitude he never went hunting again.

Early in 1942 Laycock was ordered back to England from Egypt to command the Special Service brigade, his main duties being its training, organization, and planning in concert with the combined operations command of Lord

Sir Robert Edward Laycock (1907–1968), by Howard Coster, 1944

Louis Mountbatten. Various raids on the continent resulted; it was rightly said that 'Laycock made the commandos what they were.'

In 1943 Laycock was again in the front line when he led an assault in the Sicily landings, and faced a harder military task at Salerno where, against a more numerous and heavily armed enemy, and for the loss of half his small force, he successfully held bridgehead positions for eleven crucial days. For his action in Sicily he was appointed DSO, and for his action at Salerno he was awarded the medal of the United States Legion of Merit.

In October 1943 Laycock was promoted major-general, as the inevitable successor to Mountbatten when the latter was transferred to the south-east Asia command. Laycock's later war service, in which he was chief of combined operations, was less spectacular, but remained as valuable and highly valued. He was appointed CB in 1945. In the same year he stood for parliament in the general election, as Conservative candidate for Bassetlaw, where his chance of victory was slender since the sitting member was Frederick John Bellenger who had made a name in parliament as 'the soldier's friend'.

After his defeat Laycock was reappointed chief of combined operations and remained in the post until 1947. He then retired to the family house at Wiseton, Nottinghamshire, near Doncaster, and the management of his property. In 1954, on the advice of the secretary of state for war, his friend and contemporary Antony Head, Laycock was appointed governor and commander-in-chief of Malta.

Laycock entered on his new duties at a critical time. Dominic Mintoff was rising to political mastery, and represented the popular desire for independence and for the abolition of the British position on the island. To add to Laycock's difficulties some in authority deliberately gave him misleading advice for interested reasons. Negotiations with the independence party broke down at the end of 1958, and the British government suspended the constitution. During that time of conflict Laycock remained none the less a much esteemed and effective governor. His term of office was twice extended, and when he retired in 1959 he had successfully initiated a five-year development plan.

Laycock was appointed KCMG in 1954; he held the posts of high sheriff (1954–5) and lord lieutenant (from 1962) of Nottinghamshire, and in 1960 he was appointed colonel commandant of the Special Air Service and the Sherwood Rangers yeomanry. An enthusiastic horseman and yachtsman, he also maintained many intellectual and other interests; he was an inveterate reader and collector of books, and his versatility included such minor accomplishments as Bond Street barbering. His acquaintance and friendships were among a very wide variety of people, and his gaiety and modesty placed him among those rare beings who seem to have no enemies.

In the last years of his life Laycock was troubled by an arterial disorder which gave him continual pain in one leg. An operation failed to cure it, and he was threatened by the need for amputation. Typical of his impetuous spirit, he at once called at a hospital to make an immediate appointment for this purpose, and was somewhat indignant on being told that preliminary discussion must involve delay. On 10 March 1968 he collapsed from a heart attack while walking from church at Wiseton and died instantly.　　　　　　　　　　　　　　C. H. Sykes, rev.

Sources *The Times* (11 March 1968) · personal knowledge (1981) · private information (1981) · *WWW* · *CGPLA Eng. & Wales* (1968) · Burke, *Peerage* (1980) · C. Sykes, *Evelyn Waugh: a biography*, rev. edn (1977)
Archives King's Lond., Liddell Hart C., personal and military papers | FILM BFI NFTVA, news footage · IWM FVA, actuality footage · IWM FVA, news footage | SOUND IWM SA, oral history interview
Likenesses H. Coster, photograph, 1944, NPG [*see illus.*]
Wealth at death £153,999: probate, 7 June 1968, *CGPLA Eng. & Wales* · £279,910: further grant, 31 Oct 1968, *CGPLA Eng. & Wales*

Laycock, Samuel (1826–1893), dialect poet, was born on 17 January 1826 at Intake Head, Pule Hill, Marsden, Yorkshire, the third of the four children of John Laycock (1791–1861), a hand-loom weaver, and his wife, Sarah, née France (1791–1860). The family worshipped at Buckley Hill Independent Chapel, Marsden, and Laycock's only formal education was at the Sunday school and a few months at the minister's school. He started work, aged nine, in a woollen mill. In 1837 the family moved to Stalybridge, Cheshire, where Laycock worked as a cotton weaver, then as a foreman cut-looker. He married Martha Broadbent (b. 1828), a cotton weaver, on 9 December 1850, but she died two

years later, and he remarried on 30 October 1858; his new wife was Hannah Woolley (1837–1863).

Laycock began to write poetry while working in the mill, his first published work being a broadsheet in 1855. The cotton famine (1861–5) left him unemployed and gave him the time and incentive to write while providing a market for his broadsheet poems. Other unemployed cotton workers set them to music and sang in the streets for spare coppers. This success encouraged Laycock to publish two books, *Lancashire Rhymes* (1864) and *Lancashire Songs* (1866). These poems, recording the everyday life of cotton workers, are his best.

The death of Hannah in 1863 left Laycock with several young children, including John Edward (b. 1859) and Hannah, later Mrs Schofield (1863–1939), and he became unsettled, taking a range of different, unsuccessful, jobs while his already poor health further declined. His fortunes changed with his third marriage in June 1864 to Eliza Pontefract (1836–1917), as she took an important role in supporting the family. Laycock then became the librarian at Stalybridge Mechanics' Institute in 1865, and at Whitworth Institute, Fleetwood, in 1867. After a year the family moved to Blackpool, eventually settling in Foxhall Road where Eliza ran a lodging-house and confectioner's shop while Laycock worked as a photographer (retired by 1881). They had at least two more children, Bertha, later Mrs Bowness (b. 1870) and Arthur (1869–1957) who became a Labour councillor and novelist. Laycock published a collection of poems, *Warblin's fro' an Owd Songster*, just before his death from bronchitis on 15 December 1893 at his home, 48 Foxhall Road, Blackpool. He was buried in Layton cemetery, Blackpool, on 18 December. His *Collected Writings* was edited by George Milner and published in 1908.　　　　　　　　　　　　　　　　　ALICE LOCK

Sources D. King and J. Raven, *Another look at Laycock* (1993) · G. Milner, introduction, *Collected writings of Samuel Laycock*, ed. G. Milner, 2nd edn (1908) · S. Laycock, *Warblin's fro' an owd songster* (1893) · G. Hughes, introduction, in *Selected poems: Samuel Laycock* (1981) · M. Vicinus, *The industrial muse: a study of 19th-century British working class literature* (1974) · B. Hollingworth, ed., *Songs of the people* (1977) · B. Maidment, ed., *The poorhouse fugitives: self-taught poets and poetry in Victorian Britain* (1987) · L. M. Angus-Butterworth, *Lancashire literary worthies* (1980) · M. Nevell, *People who made Tameside* (1994) · S. Hill, *Old Lancashire songs and their singers* (1898) · G. H. Whittaker, *Some Stalybridge songs and their singers* (1944) · T. Middleton, *Poets, poems, and rhymes of east Cheshire* (1908) · Tameside Local Studies Library, Laycock MSS, DD312
Likenesses S. Lawson Booth, oils, 1910, Blackpool Art Gallery and Lytham Reading Room · photograph, 1922, Tameside Local Studies Library · Shackleton, drawing, Tameside Local Studies Library
Wealth at death £405 13s. 3d.: administration with will, 13 March 1894, *CGPLA Eng. & Wales*

Laycock, Thomas (1812–1876), physician, was born on 12 August 1812 at Wetherby, near York, the second of the four children of Thomas Laycock (c.1770–1833), a Wesleyan preacher, and his wife, the daughter of Mr Cattle, a landed Cheshire gentleman. Educated at the Methodist Woodhouse Grove School until the age of fifteen, he was then apprenticed to John and William Spence, surgeons at Bedale in the North Riding of Yorkshire. In 1833 Laycock attended the medical school of London University (later

Thomas Laycock (1812–1876), by Charles Martin

University College), and after a short period of study at Paris, he qualified MRCS on 7 May 1835. Six months later he took the LSA, and in the following year was appointed house apothecary at York County Hospital. In 1839 he resigned his post in order to graduate MD at Göttingen, after which he became a general practitioner in York. In 1842 he was appointed a licentiate *extra urbem* of the Royal College of Physicians, and became physician to the York Dispensary in the same year. Subsequently he became secretary to the local Health of Towns Association (1843), and a lecturer at York medical school (1846–55).

In 1848 Laycock married Anne Lockwood (1822–1869), the daughter of William Lockwood, a prosperous attorney from Easingwold, York; they had two surviving children, George Lockwood Laycock (1855–1926), a medical graduate who practised in Melbourne, Australia, and Beatrice Rachel (*b.* 1857). Laycock became professor of the practice of physic at the University of Edinburgh in 1855. Already an *ex officio* FRCP (Edinburgh) by virtue of his professorship, he became a fellow of the Royal Society of Edinburgh in 1856. In 1857 he commenced annual extramural classes in medical psychology and mental disease. In 1869 he was appointed physician-in-ordinary to the queen in Scotland and president of the Medico-Psychological Association.

Laycock was small, wore glasses, and dressed impeccably. His manner was described as formal if not cold, and he was widely feared as an adversary in public controversies, such as the dispute in 1857 over the rota of attending clinical professors in the university teaching wards at the Royal Infirmary of Edinburgh. Nevertheless, friends and former students recalled his kindly disposition and generosity. Throughout his life Laycock suffered periodic bouts of ill health, which were probably due to the complications of tuberculous disease. He underwent an amputation of his left leg in 1866.

Laycock's success as a professorial consulting physician was said to be unremarkable, notwithstanding his teaching practice at the clinical wards of the Royal Infirmary of Edinburgh. Nevertheless, he produced over 250 publications, including three books. *A Treatise on the Nervous Diseases of Women* (1841) gained him a European reputation in this area, which he consolidated by a paper, 'On the reflex function of the brain', originally presented in 1844 to the British Association for the Advancement of Science, and subsequently published (1845) in the *British and Foreign Medical Review*. Laycock argued on analogical grounds that the concept of reflex function, formerly confined to the spinal column, should be extended to the cerebral hemispheres. This conceptual leap, and the methodology of psycho-physical parallelism which grew out of it, helped to lay the foundations of modern physiological psychology and neuropsychiatry.

Laycock also made other historically important contributions to medicine. In medical ethics he adapted Johann Gottlieb Fichte's *Einige Vorlesungen über die Bestimmung des Gelehrten* to the duties of the physician. In public health he reported on the sanitary condition of York for the Health of Towns Commission. He also strove for a better understanding of mental disease by applying ideas of the evolution and regression of the higher nervous centres to explain symptoms of insanity. While at Edinburgh, he published *Lectures on the Principles of Medical Observation and Research* (1856), and *Mind and Brain, or, The Correlations of Consciousness and Organisation* (1860). In the latter he explored the correlations between consciousness and biological organization from the viewpoint of a physiological psychology which attempted to take into account the evolution of nervous centres in animals and man. Laycock died at his house, 13 Walker Street, Edinburgh, on 21 September 1876, as a result of pulmonary consumption.

Laycock was regarded by his contemporaries as an able reviewer and translator, and enjoyed a posthumous reputation as a medical thinker considerably in advance of his time. Little of his correspondence has survived; but as a young man he kept a journal and wrote an autobiographical account of the contest for the Edinburgh chair. Both these sources provide insights into his private character and motivation. His motto, *Robore labore spe*, succinctly captures those personal qualities he set most store by in his single-minded pursuit of a successful career in medicine without the aid of wealth or patronage. Laycock's long professional journey from surgeon's apprentice to professorial physician was certainly one in which the pen was mightier than the pleximeter.

MICHAEL BARFOOT

Sources M. Barfoot, ed., *'To ask the suffrages of the patrons': Thomas Laycock and the Edinburgh chair of medicine, 1855* (1995) · F. E. James, 'The life and work of Thomas Laycock, 1812–76', PhD diss., U. Lond., 1996 · 'A journal kept by Thomas Laycock from 1833 including the time spent in London when a medical student', U. Edin. L., MS Gen., 1813 · *The Scotsman* (22 Sept 1876) · *CCI* (1876) · *DNB*
Archives Royal College of Physicians of Edinburgh, diary, lecture notes, and papers · U. Edin. L., journal | NL Scot., corresp. with George Combe · U. Edin. L., corresp. with David Ramsey Hay · UCL, corresp. with Sir Edwin Chadwick
Likenesses C. Martin, oils, Royal College of Physicians of Edinburgh [*see illus.*] · bas-relief, Royal College of Physicians of Edinburgh · photograph, U. Edin.
Wealth at death £14,276 12s. 8d.: confirmation, 8 Nov 1876, *CCI*

Layden, Sir John [Jack] (1926–1996), miner and local politician, was born at 7 Millicent Square, Maltby, Rotherham, Yorkshire, on 16 January 1926, the second of three sons of Thomas Henry Layden, miner, of Maltby, and his wife, Annie, *née* Peach. Jack, as he was always known, received his elementary education at Maltby Crags School and his secondary education at Maltby Hall School, leaving school at fourteen to work at the Maltby Main colliery. He would remain a working miner until he became, in effect, a full-time local government figure in the 1970s, and technically left the pit only when offered redundancy in 1986. He managed to extend his education by taking day-release courses at Sheffield University and Doncaster Technical College in the early 1940s, gaining in the process skills which would advance his later work both in the trade union movement and in local government. In 1944 he joined the Labour Party. Support for Labour was, of course, routine in the mining towns of south Yorkshire, but in Layden's case it was reinforced by his own family poverty and by the childhood memory of 'men queuing to draw the "dole" in the early 1930s' (*Rotherham Advertiser*, 5 April 1974). Similar concerns lay behind his involvement in mining unionism—he would eventually become a local branch president and a member of the Yorkshire executive of the National Union of Mineworkers—and in local government. He was first elected to Maltby urban district council in 1953 and would represent the same ward (Maltby West) for 43 years. He served as Maltby council leader in 1959–60 and 1970–71 and became the first leader of Rotherham council when Maltby was incorporated into the new metropolitan borough under the 1974 local government reorganization. The 1974 reorganization also led to the formation of the Association of Metropolitan Authorities, which became the principal lobby group for urban local government. Layden served on the policy committee of the new association from the start, and became deputy chairman of the association in 1980 and chairman in 1984. He married Dorothy Brenda McLean on 26 March 1949.

Layden believed throughout his public career that local authorities were the agencies best equipped to respond to the particular problems of individual communities—'to channel energies and enterprise, to try new approaches on a local scale' (Layden). Like most local government leaders of his generation he faced the difficulty of reconciling this belief in localism with the post-war reality of local authority amalgamations and growing dependence upon central government. Even in 1974 he had worried that reorganization had produced a *de facto* regionalism: 'any one who still regards it as local government is pretty wide of the mark' (*Rotherham Advertiser*, 5 April 1974). He believed that any dilution of localism increased the vulnerability of local authorities to Whitehall empire building: celebrating in 1985 the 150th anniversary of the formation of the British municipal system, he chose to stress that the 1835 Municipal Corporations Act 'was not about creating agents of central government' (Layden). It was Layden's misfortune that his arrival upon the national stage occurred when the most centralizing government of the modern age was at the height of its power. Though he opposed most of the Conservative initiatives—bus deregulation, compulsory tendering, the removal of further education powers from local government—in themselves, his consistent objection was to the extension of central control. He had pioneered the sale of council houses to sitting tenants in Rotherham before it became national policy, but he objected to a statutory right to buy forcing councils to dispose of their assets. He particularly opposed Whitehall's growing control over local finance in the 1980s, exemplified by the restructuring of the grant system, the statutory capping of local expenditure, and the replacement of local rates by the poll tax—'a tax on existence', as Layden called it (*Municipal Review and AMA News*, June 1985). He would enjoy the satisfaction of seeing off both Margaret Thatcher and the poll tax before retiring as association chairman in 1991, but he was little happier with the council tax, or 'Whitehall (1991) Tax', as he called it (*Rotherham Advertiser*, 3 May 1991), and he resented the continuation of the capping system, by which his own authority of Rotherham had been shackled in 1990.

Layden's long period as leader of Rotherham council was overshadowed by the contraction of the coal industry. The critical episode of the 1984–5 miners' strike posed enormous problems for him. He accepted the claim of Arthur Scargill, National Union of Mineworkers' leader, that the government envisaged an extensive closure programme and believed that 'pit closures will destroy [Rotherham]' (*Rotherham Advertiser*, 20 April 1984). Rotherham council donated more than £750,000 from the rates to support the families of men on strike, as Maltby became a militant outpost in the generally moderate south Yorkshire coalfield. Nevertheless, Layden stood some distance to the right of Scargill on Labour's ideological continuum, and had stood against him when Scargill was first elected leader of the Yorkshire miners in 1973. He had considerable misgivings about the union's tactics: as chairman of the Association of Metropolitan Authorities he had to urge local authorities to remain within laws of which he thoroughly disapproved, and he remained convinced that Scargill's confrontational stance and his disregard of the legal obligation to ballot his members would prove unsuccessful.

After the miners' defeat Layden accepted that Rotherham could no longer depend upon the coal industry, and his policies as council leader reflected an eagerness to modernize the local economy. Through the work of Rotherham's enterprise zone subcommittee and through his involvement on the Dearne Valley Partnership Board, Layden explored the potential of public–private partnerships to revitalize the area. He succeeded in enticing a superstore to Rotherham, on the site of a rolling mill, which he hoped would stem the loss of commerce to Doncaster and Sheffield. In his competitive promotion of his area—'I'll use every legitimate means to get industry into Rotherham', he declared in 1984 (*Municipal Review and AMA News*, May 1984)—he anticipated standard local authority practice of the 1990s. His departures from traditional municipal socialism reflected both his faith in the flexibility of local government and his long held doctrine that 'Socialism is all about bringing people up, not dragging people down' (private information). In the 1990s Layden—socially and culturally as pure an example of 'old labour' as could be found—would become an enthusiastic supporter of Tony Blair's modernization of the Labour Party. His rejection of the politics of confrontation exacerbated tensions with the left wing of the Rotherham Labour group, but he was able to choose his own moment to step down in May 1996. He enjoyed only the briefest of retirements, dying of a heart attack on holiday with his family in Blackpool on 28 May 1996; he was buried at Grange Lane cemetery, Maltby, on 6 June. His wife and their two children, John (*b.* 1956) and Keith (*b.* 1959), survived him.

Layden was an unassuming man who never sought celebrity from his national position. He was knighted for services to local government in 1988. He took pride in the fact that a man who had walked barefoot to school as a child had been able to meet a reigning monarch, a pope, and every British prime minister from Churchill to Major. His recreational pursuits were similarly unaffected, notably music—he played cornet in the Maltby miners' brass band—and football. He was a director and subsequently president of Rotherham United Football Club, and was said to mention this passion in virtually every speech. A life of seventy years proved just long enough to enable him to see Rotherham play at Wembley to win the Autoglass Windscreen Shield in April 1996.

JOHN DAVIS

Sources *Municipal Review and AMA News* (May–Oct 1984); (May–June 1985); (April 1991); (May–June 1996) · *Rotherham [and South Yorkshire] Advertiser* (5 April 1974) · *Rotherham [and South Yorkshire] Advertiser* (20 April 1984) · *Rotherham [and South Yorkshire] Advertiser* (26 Oct 1984) · *Rotherham [and South Yorkshire] Advertiser* (6 April 1990) · *Rotherham [and South Yorkshire] Advertiser* (3 May 1991) · *Rotherham [and South Yorkshire] Advertiser* (31 May 1996) · private information (2004) [K. Layden] · *The Times* (7 June 1996) · *The Guardian* (30 May 1996) · WWW · J. Layden, 'Local people have the right to set their own priorities', *Municipal Review and AMA News* (Aug–Sept 1985) [suppl. on 150th anniversary of Municipal Corporations Act] · D. Butler, A. Adonis, and T. Travers, *Failure in British government* (1994) · P. Routledge, *Scargill: the unauthorised biography* (1993) · J. Winterton and R. Winterton, *Coal, crisis and conflict* (1989)
Likenesses photograph, repro. in *Municipal Review and AMA News* (June 1996), 65 · photograph (receiving knighthood), repro. in *Municipal Review and AMA News* (Aug 1988), 113 · photograph, repro. in *The Guardian* · photograph, repro. in *The Times* · portraits, repro. in *Municipal Review and AMA News* (1984–91)

Wealth at death under £180,000: probate, 4 Sept 1996, *CGPLA Eng. & Wales*

Laye, Evelyn [*real name* Elsie Evelyn Lay] (**1900–1996**), actress and singer, was born on 10 July 1900 at 8 Bloomsbury Place, London, the daughter of Gilbert James Lay (stage name Gilbert Laye), actor and theatrical manager, and his wife, Evelyn Stuart, *née* Froud (stage name Evelyn Stuart), actress. Her father ran a concert party, The Fascinators, before the First World War, and her mother was an acclaimed principal boy in regional pantomimes. She was educated in Folkestone and Brighton and made her stage début at the Theatre Royal, Brighton (where her father was briefly manager of the pier), in 1915, playing a mute Chinese servant in *Mr Wu*. When her father's concert party disbanded she became the family's main source of income and went into several revues and pantomimes before joining the celebrated troupe of Gaiety Girls established by George Edwardes.

Laye first made her name as *The Merry Widow* at Daly's Theatre in 1923, and was then to stay at Daly's for two subsequent hits, *Madame Pompadour* (1923) and *The Dollar Princess* (1925), which made her the highest-paid star in the West End for most of the 1920s. On 10 April 1926 she married John Robert Hale Monro (stage name Sonnie Hale; 1902–1959), actor and son of John Robert Hale Monro, actor. In 1928, however, her husband left her for her great and only rival, Jessie Matthews, and for several months Laye went into a decline both privately and professionally, even rejecting the first London production of Noël Coward's *Bitter Sweet* (1929) because it was to be presented by Charles B. Cochran, who had first brought her husband and Jessie Matthews together in the revue for which they sang Coward's 'A Room with a View'. Rapidly realizing her mistake, however, Laye reclaimed the role of Sari Linden for the Broadway *Bitter Sweet* (1929) and progressed from there to Hollywood to film *One Heavenly Night* in 1933.

Having divorced her first husband in 1931, in 1934 Laye married the actor Frank Lawton (1904–1969), who had made his name as *Young Woodley* and to whom she was to remain happily married until his death. In the 1930s Laye enjoyed a string of hits on stage, including *Helen!* (1932), *Give me a Ring* (1933), and *Sweet Aloes* (1936), and on screen, including *Waltz Time* (1933), *Princess Charming* (1934), and *Evensong* (1934). During the Second World War she continued to enchant London audiences with *The Belle of New York* (1942) and *Three Waltzes* (1945), while making regular Christmas appearances as the principal boy in Palladium pantomimes.

With the coming of a new, American post-war musical world, it was clear that Laye's middle-European brand of nostalgia and chandeliers was going rapidly out of fashion; in considerable career trouble, she reinvented herself as a straight actress in *The School for Scandal* (1948) and (replacing Gertrude Lawrence) Daphne Du Maurier's *September Tide* (1950), but she never entirely recovered from being passed over in favour of Valerie Hobson for the first London production of *The King and I*, by Rodgers and Hammerstein, in 1953. There were still a few hit musicals left for her, however, including *Wedding in Paris* (1954), *Charlie*

Girl (1969), in which long-running production she replaced Anna Neagle, and *Phil the Fluter* (1969), in which she sang 'They Don't Make them Like that any More', written by the composer as a tribute to her longevity on stage.

As late as 1978 Laye was touring as the Countess in Sondheim's *A Little Night Music*, while spending most of the rest of the 1970s opposite Michael Crawford in a long and lucrative run of the West End farce *No Sex Please—we're British*. She made a number of television appearances, including in *The Gay Lord Quex* (1983) and *My Family and other Animals* (1987). In 1990 she made a remarkable return to New York, singing at Carnegie Hall for its centenary celebration the 'I'll See you Again' she had first sung in *Bitter Sweet* on Broadway all of sixty years earlier. By 1992 she was Britain's oldest working musical star, touring in an anthology of her old hits, *A Glamorous Night with Evelyn Laye and Friends*. She was appointed CBE in 1973. A bright, particular star, she remained throughout a long working lifetime professionally dedicated to her work and, as Max Reinhardt once noted, she was 'that rare and holy trinity of the stage, a great singer, a great actress and a great beauty' (*The Independent*). She died at St George's Nursing Home, 61 St George's Square, Westminster, of heart failure on 17 February 1996. There were no children from either of her marriages. Her body was cremated and a memorial service was later held, at St Paul's, Covent Garden, on 2 July 1996; she is commemorated by an Evelyn Laye award for musical performance at the London Academy of Music and Dramatic Art.　　　SHERIDAN MORLEY

Sources E. Laye, *Boo, to my friends* (1958) · *The Times* (19 Feb 1996) · *The Times* (3 July 1996) · *The Independent* (19 Feb 1996) · *WWW* · b. cert. · m. cert. · d. cert.
Likenesses H. Leslie, silhouette drawing, 1923, NPG · photograph, repro. in *The Times* (19 Feb 1996) · photograph, repro. in *The Independent*
Wealth at death under £145,000: probate, 5 July 1996, *CGPLA Eng. & Wales*

Layer, Christopher (1683–1723), lawyer and Jacobite conspirator, was born on 12 November 1683 in Henrietta Street, Covent Garden, London, the son of John Layer, a dealer in lace, and his wife, Mary, daughter of Valentine Browne, treasurer of Berwick. He was brought up by his uncle, also Christopher Layer, of Booton, in Norfolk, a man of high tory and Jacobite principles, and one of those whose arrest had been ordered in March 1696 on suspicion of being disaffected to the government (*Lothian MSS*, 141–2). Upon leaving Norwich grammar school in 1701, Layer was articled to Henry Rippingall, a leading attorney and tory of Aylsham, in Norfolk. In 1709 Layer married Elizabeth (*d.* in or after 1723), daughter of Peter Elwin of Tuttington, in Norfolk. Admitted to Gray's Inn on 13 July 1715, Layer was called to the bar on 4 July 1720. After his call to the bar he built up a large practice with Lord North and Grey, a professional soldier who had distinguished himself at the battle of Blenheim, as his principal client.

The principles which Layer had absorbed from his uncle led to his involvement in the plot of 1722, a scheme which

Arthur Onslow thought had been intended to take advantage of the disaffection felt against George I and his ministers after the failure of the South Sea Company in 1720. Although inspired by Francis Atterbury, bishop of Rochester, the scheme's chief planner was Layer's client, Lord North and Grey. Layer's own function was twofold: to enlist supporters from those among the English aristocracy and gentry whom he judged would be sympathetic to the Stuart cause in the event of a rising, and to recruit NCOs to discipline the troops. The Pretender (James III in the Stuart succession) was told of the plot in May 1721 when Layer visited him in Rome, having travelled there with another conspirator, John Plunkett. Layer's purpose in visiting James was not only to tell him of the intended rising but also to acquire credibility in the eyes of prospective supporters of the insurrection by obtaining from Queen Clementina, the Pretender's wife, what he described as a token. The token was that the queen should be godmother to Layer's newly born daughter. It was agreed that the queen should stand as godmother and James himself as godfather, and that arrangements would be made for their representation at the ceremony by proxies.

Armed with these credentials, Layer returned to England to help recruit forces for the rising. The rising had originally been planned to coincide with the general election of 1722, but lack of funds led to its postponement to the autumn. The plotters intended to seize the Tower, the Bank of England, and the Royal Mint, and to take George I into protective custody if he had not by the autumn left England for Hanover. Once London had been taken, the general commanding the forces would send messengers to those who had agreed to rise in their respective districts outside London.

Before starting to recruit supporters, a task which he began in June 1722, Layer made arrangements for his daughter's baptism. She was baptized Mary Clementina in April 1722 at a ceremony conducted in a china shop in Chelsea by Aaron Thompson, a friend of Layer's and domestic chaplain to the earl of Burlington. Lord North and Grey and the duchess of Ormond stood as proxies for James and Queen Clementina. How the authorities came to know of the plot is uncertain, but it was said that it was first revealed to the government ministers Robert Walpole and Viscount Townshend by Philippe, duc d'Orléans, regent of France, whose political interests had drawn him close to the English court. When they heard of the scheme, Walpole and Townshend issued orders for the mustering of troops in Hyde Park. This did not deter the conspirators from recruiting, for they even tried to enlist support from troops in the encampment.

By whatever means the plot had been revealed, Layer was arrested on 18 September 1722 and Lord North and Grey on 28 September. Layer was confined in the house of William Squire, a king's messenger, but escaped out of a second-floor window on 19 September. However, he was retaken on the same day in St George's Fields. Layer's involvement in the plot was conclusively proved by documents given to a Mrs Elizabeth Mason for safe keeping.

Among those documents was a description in Layer's own handwriting of how the scheme was to be implemented. While Layer admitted communicating some heads of the scheme to Lord North and Grey when he was questioned on 19 January and 4 February 1723 by the secret committee of the House of Commons set up to investigate the plot, he did not name him as a conspirator, taking entire responsibility for the enterprise upon himself.

Layer was tried and convicted of high treason before the court of king's bench on 21 November 1722. On 27 November 1722 he was sentenced to be hanged, drawn, and quartered. Execution of the sentence was frequently respited in the hope that Layer would give information about his co-conspirators. He refused to implicate others and the sentence was carried out at Tyburn on 17 May 1723.

There is a story that John Pearce, a nonjuring attorney, picked up Layer's head after it had been blown from Temple Bar and sold it to Richard Rawlinson, the antiquary and nonjuring bishop, who directed that he should be buried with the relic in his right hand (Nichols, 5.497-8).

ROGER TURNER

Sources *The whole proceeding upon the arraignment, tryal, conviction and attainder of Christopher Layer, esq.* (1722) · 'The report from the committee appointed by order of the House of Commons to examine Christopher Layer, and others', *Reports from Committees of the House of Commons*, 1 (1722-3), 99-350 [incl. appxs] · *State trials*, 16.93-322 · J. Foster, *The register of admissions to Gray's Inn, 1521-1889, together with the register of marriages in Gray's Inn chapel, 1695-1754* (privately printed, London, 1889), 360 · R. J. Fletcher, ed., *The pension book of Gray's Inn*, 2 (1910), 177 · W. Harvey, *The visitation of Norfolk in the year 1563*, ed. G. H. Dashwood and others, 1 (1878), 26 · 'MS extracts from a diary of Peter Le Neve', ed. G. A. Carthew, *Norfolk Archaeology*, 2 (1849), esp. 379-80, 385 · F. Rye and A. Rye, *Calendar of correspondence and documents relating to the family of Olive Le Neve, of Witchingham, Norfolk, 1675-1743*, ed. W. Rye (1895), 155, 159 · Nichols, *Lit. anecdotes* · *Report on the manuscripts of the marquess of Lothian*, HMC, 62 (1905), 141-2 · *The manuscripts of the Marquess Townshend*, HMC, 19 (1887), 140-42 · PRO, SP 35/43/51 · *The manuscripts of the earl of Buckinghamshire, the earl of Lindsey ... and James Round*, HMC, 38 (1895), 512-14

Archives BL, Egerton MS 2719, fol. 312; 2721, fols. 192, 204 · PRO, SP 35/39; 35/33/39; 35/33/61; 35/43/51

Likenesses line engraving, pubd 1740, BM · engraving, priv. coll. · portrait, repro. in Caulfield, *Remarkable persons* (1819) · woodcut, BM

Wealth at death in attainder proceedings during trial for high treason, jury found he had no goods, chattels, lands, or tenements when he committed high treason or since: *The whole proceeding*, 139

Layer, John (*bap.* 1585, *d.* 1641), antiquary, was baptized on 12 September 1585 at St Mary-le-Bow, London, the youngest child of William Layer (*d.* 1596), merchant of Cheapside, and his wife, Martha, daughter of Thomas Wanton, grocer. His education included legal training, and he was admitted to Gray's Inn in 1606. Layer's elder brother, William (1573-1649), succeeded to the family's estates in Norfolk. John was sole heir to his three maternal uncles, from whom he received the manor and rectory of Shepreth, Cambridgeshire, where he built himself a substantial residence of ten hearths. In 1611 he married Frances (*b.* 1586), daughter of Robert Sterne (*d.* 1616), gentleman of Malton, Cambridgeshire, and his wife, Beatrice (*d.* 1609). They had

seven children, of whom three sons and two daughters survived infancy.

Layer was a justice of the peace for Cambridgeshire. In the 1620s he compiled a lengthy manual of statutes for use at quarter sessions, entitled 'The reformed justice'; the manuscript, dedicated to his friend Sir John Cutts, was licensed for publication in 1633 but was never printed. His shorter work *The Office and Duties of Constables, Churchwardens, and other the Overseers of the Poore* was published posthumously in 1641.

Layer's principal occupation was his unpublished 'Description of Cambridgeshire'. The surviving manuscripts, mostly in finished narrative form, record manorial descents from Domesday to the 1630s. The work is remarkable for its thorough organization, as it intended to proceed from a general account of county government and topography to a full history of every parish and town in the style later established by William Dugdale. Layer exchanged material with the antiquary Roger Dodsworth, but his work was largely unknown until the eighteenth century when William Cole had it transcribed. In 1932 his notes on the heraldry and monumental inscriptions in seventy-two Cambridgeshire churches were printed, recognizing the value of transcriptions taken immediately before the civil wars with their accompanying iconoclasm.

Layer exemplified the dutiful gentleman typical of early seventeenth-century society, combining legal training and topographical and genealogical research with an active role in local government: some of his antiquarian notes are written on the back of depositions taken on the Cambridge circuits in the 1630s (Bodl. Oxf., MS Rawl. Essex 2). His official and social status, and his connections by birth and marriage to many Cambridge gentry, enabled him to make collections from private archives since destroyed.

Layer made his will on 23 January 1641, died in Shepreth, and was buried on 29 January in the chancel of Shepreth church, which he had rebuilt. His will included payments of debt and bequests amounting to £620, funded by the sale of property in Yorkshire and one third of his plate. Shepreth remained in his descendants' possession at the end of the twentieth century. His son Benjamin was vicar from 1649 until his death in 1659, succeeded by his grandson in 1672. Layer's manuscripts passed to his eldest son, William, then by descent to John Eyre (1718-1772), who was transported to Virginia in 1772, causing the sale, dispersal, and loss of much of the collection.

PETER SHERLOCK

Sources W. M. Palmer, *John Layer (1586-1640) of Shepreth, Cambridgeshire: a seventeenth-century local historian* (1935) · W. M. Palmer, *Monumental inscriptions and coats of arms from Cambridgeshire* (1932) · W. Cole, 'Cambridgeshire collections', BL, Add. MS 5823, vol. 22 · *VCH Cambridgeshire and the Isle of Ely*, 5.251-62 · parish register, London, St Mary-le-Bow, 12 Sept 1585 [baptism] · parish register, Orwell, 1611 [marriage] · *The visitation of London, anno Domini 1633, 1634, and 1635, made by Sir Henry St George*, 2, ed. J. J. Howard, Harleian Society, 17 (1883) · J. Foster, *The register of admissions to Gray's Inn, 1521-1889, together with the register of marriages in Gray's Inn chapel, 1695-1754* (privately printed, London, 1889) · Ely marriage licences · will, 12 Feb 1641, PRO, PROB 11/185, sig. 22 · inquisition post mortem, PRO, C 142/612, fol. 24

Archives BL, Cambridge collections, Add. MSS 5954, 5808, 5812, 5819–5823, 5847–5849 · Bodl. Oxf., notes and transcripts taken from his collections · Bodl. Oxf., MS Rawlinson B 275 · Bodl. Oxf., MS Rawlinson B 278 · Bodl. Oxf., MS Rawlinson Essex 2 · Bodl. Oxf., MS Gough Camb. 19

Wealth at death bequests and debts totalling £620, funded by sale of property in Yorkshire and one third of his plate, suggesting at least £2000 total estate: will, PRO, PROB 11/185, sig. 22

Layfield, John (1562/3–1617), Church of England clergyman, was the son of Edward Layfield (d. 1583), rector of Fulham and prebendary of Holbourn in St Paul's Cathedral, and his wife, Elizabeth. John was admitted a pensioner of Trinity College, Cambridge, on 18 April 1578, and graduated BA in 1582. Elected a minor fellow on 2 October 1583 and a major fellow on 29 April 1585, he proceeded MA in 1585 and BTh in 1592. He was also lector in Greek in 1593 and examiner in grammar in 1599. Rector of Aldwincle St Peter's, Northamptonshire, on the presentation of Thomas Cecil, second Baron Burghley, from 1598 to 1602, in 1598 he accompanied George Clifford, third earl of Cumberland, as chaplain to the earl during his expedition against the West Indies; his 'A large relation of the Porto Ricco voiage … very much abbreviated', wrongly attributed by Wood to Edmund Layfield, was printed in 1625 in *Purchas his Pilgrimes* by the elder Samuel Purchas. For Cumberland's biographer Layfield's 'detailed description of the whole voyage is the most reliable as well as the most complete of the extant accounts' (Spence, 144). On 23 March 1602 Layfield was instituted rector of St Clement Danes, London, again on Cecil's presentation, and resigned his fellowship at Trinity in 1603.

On 22 January 1603, now aged forty, Layfield obtained a licence from the bishop of London to marry Bridget (*née* Robinson) (d. 1628/9), widow of John Brickett, merchant, of the parish of St Ethelburga, Bishopsgate. They married at St Mary, Whitechapel, two days later, and had two sons and a daughter. In 1605 Layfield was also rector of Graveley, Hertfordshire. In 1606 he was one of the Greek and Hebrew scholars appointed by James I to produce what became the Authorized Version of the Bible. Several books of the Bible were allocated to each of six groups of scholars. Layfield was one of ten who met at Westminster to work on the Old Testament, Genesis to 2 Kings inclusive. In the list quoted by Jeremy Collier, beside Layfield's name it is stated: 'Being skilled in architecture, his judgment was much relied on for the fabric of the Tabernacle and Temple' (Collier, 7.337).

Layfield was admitted at the Inner Temple in 1606, and in 1610 became one of the first fellows of Chelsea College, newly founded as a centre for the production of anti-Catholic polemic by spokesmen for the Church of England. In 1613 he contributed laudatory verses to the preface of Sir William Leighton's *Tears or Lamentations of a Sorrowful Soul*. He died, probably in London, in 1617. In his will, drawn up on 20 May that year and proved on 16 December following, he left land in Old Cleeve, Somerset,

and Royston, Hertfordshire, to his wife for her lifetime, with remainder to their eldest son, Edward. Bridget Layfield died in 1628 or 1629.

RONALD BAYNE, *rev.* MARGOT JOHNSON

Sources Venn, *Alum. Cant.* · J. Collier, *An ecclesiastical history of Great Britain*, 7 (1840), 337, 350 · J. B. Whitmore, 'J. Layfield', *N&Q*, 147 (1924), 30–32 · Wood, *Ath. Oxon.: Fasti* (1815), 427 · R. T. Spence, *The privateering earl* (1995) · G. Hennessy, *Novum repertorium ecclesiasticum parochiale Londinense, or, London diocesan clergy succession from the earliest time to the year 1898* (1898)

Archives Trinity Cam.

Layman, William (1768–1826), naval officer, entered the navy in 1782 on the *Portland*, served for four years (1782–6) in the *Myrmidon* on the home station, and a year and a half (1786–8) in the *Amphion* in the West Indies. He seems then to have gone into the merchant service, and was principally employed in the East India and China trade. In late 1796 he was on the *Isis* in the North Sea, and is known to have returned to the navy in 1800 under the patronage of Lord St Vincent. He passed his examination on 5 June 1800, at the age of thirty-two. He served for a few weeks in the *Royal George*, St Vincent's flagship, in the blockade of Brest, and was promoted lieutenant of the *Formidable* with Captain Thornbrough on 12 September. In December, at Lord Nelson's wish, he was appointed to the *San Josef*, and in February 1801 to the *St George*. At the battle of Copenhagen he served with distinction aboard the *Isis* in command of a party of men sent from the *St George*. In April 1803 he again joined Nelson's flag in the *Victory*, remaining in her when Nelson went to the Mediterranean in the *Amphion*. When the *Victory* followed she recaptured the *Ambuscade*, which had been taken by the *Bayonnaise* in 1798. Layman, with a prize crew, was sent on board to take her to Gibraltar, where she arrived with a French merchant ship which she had captured on the way. This merchant ship was, in the first instance, condemned as a prize of the *Victory*, but the judgment was reversed, and Layman received no prize money.

In October 1803 Layman was appointed to command the *Weasel*, a small vessel employed for the protection of trade in the Strait of Gibraltar. In the following March the *Weasel* was lost on Cabrita Point in a fog. Mainly as a consequence of the representations of the merchants of Gibraltar, warmly backed up by Nelson, Layman was nevertheless promoted to the rank of commander on 8 May 1804, and a few months later was appointed to the sloop *Raven*, in which he sailed on 21 January 1805, with dispatches for Sir John Orde and Nelson. On the evening of the 28th he arrived at Orde's rendezvous off Cadiz, and, not seeing the squadron, lay to for the night, during which the ship was allowed to drift inside the Spanish squadron in the outer road of Cadiz. This can only be attributed to carelessness, and as captain, Layman was responsible. His position thus became almost hopeless, and the next morning, in trying to escape, the ship was driven ashore near Fort Santa Catalina; the men escaped to the shore with very little loss. Layman, in his report to Nelson, attributed the disaster to neglect on the part of the officer of the watch. Nelson had a high opinion of Layman's abilities, but not of his discretion; on a former occasion he had written: 'His tongue runs too fast; I often tell him neither to talk nor write so much' (Marshall, 327), and he now seems to have repeated the caution, warning him against making serious charges without certain proof. Layman, however, understood Nelson to advise the suppression of his account of the accident, or rather the rewriting of it, particularly omitting 'that part relative to the misbehaviour of the officer of the watch, who will be sentenced to death if the narrative, worded as it is at present, is laid before the court' (ibid., p. 330). The court martial found Layman guilty of want of care in approaching the land, and sentenced him to be severely reprimanded and to be put to the bottom of the list, with seniority 9 March 1805, the date of the trial.

Nelson afterwards wrote very strongly in Layman's favour, both to the first lord of the Admiralty and to the secretary. It is probable that if Nelson had lived, or Lord Melville had continued in office, Layman might have had further employment. The remainder of his life seems to have been chiefly devoted to offering suggestions to the Admiralty, and to publishing pamphlets on nautical and naval subjects.

Layman's publications included *Outline of a plan for the better cultivation … of the British West Indies, being the original suggestion for providing an effectual substitute for the African slave trade* (1807), proposing the importation of Chinese instead of African slaves; and *The Pioneer, or, Strictures on Maritime Strength and Economy* (1821), in three parts: the first a sensible essay on the condition of British seamen and impressment; the second a proposed method for preserving timber from dry rot; and the third the syllabus of a contemplated maritime history from the earliest times (including the building, plans, and navigation of the ark, with notes on the weather experienced) to the termination of the second Anglo-American War. Layman committed suicide on 22 May 1826.

Layman's career demonstrated that although the navy was open to all talents, there were limits. Despite his humble origins, his skill earned him the support of two great admirals, and while Nelson lived his chances of reaching the rank of captain were excellent. He might have done so earlier had he not allowed his tongue to run away with his discretion, notably when being interviewed by the Admiralty. His later efforts to interest the Admiralty in schemes for timber treatment were unlikely to bear any fruit at a time when every species of crank was writing on the subject, and the final decision lay with the surveyors of the navy. He was an able man who was the author of his successes and his failures.

J. K. LAUGHTON, rev. ANDREW LAMBERT

Sources J. Marshall, *Royal naval biography*, 3/2 (1832) • *The dispatches and letters of Vice-Admiral Lord Viscount Nelson*, ed. N. H. Nicolas, 7 vols. (1844–6) • W. P. Gosset, *The lost ships of the Royal Navy, 1793–1900* (1986) • D. Syrett and R. L. DiNardo, *The commissioned sea officers of the Royal Navy, 1660–1815*, rev. edn, Occasional Publications of the Navy RS, 1 (1994)
Archives BL, letters to Lord Nelson and others, Add. MSS 34914–34930

Layton [*née* Osmaston]**, Eleanor Dorothea** [Dorothy], **Lady Layton** (1887–1959), suffragist and politician, was born on 4 October 1887 at 18 Church Row, Hampstead, London, the only daughter and eldest of the three children of Francis Plumptre Beresford Osmaston (*b.* 1857), a barrister, of Stoneshill, Limpsfield, Surrey, and his wife, Eleanor Margaret, daughter of Canon Thomas Field. Her mother was often ill, and she spent much of a somewhat lonely childhood in the care of relatives. Dorothy, as she was always known, received her early education at home from governesses and later attended boarding-schools at Denmark Hill and Bexhill. After her father inherited money, in 1901, she was sent to Julia Huxley's newly opened Prior's Field School at Godalming. Under Huxley's influence she broadened intellectually, learned to play the piano, and developed a passion for cricket and other games. She also became friendly with the Huxley children, Aldous and Julian.

Dorothy Osmaston arrived at Newnham College, Cambridge, in October 1906, politically and socially aware. Her mother had been an active suffragist, and at the general election in January Dorothy had canvassed the voters at Limpsfield to sign a petition in favour of votes for women. She joined the National Union of Women's Suffrage Societies in her first year at Cambridge and in her second year attended meetings of the university Fabian Society. Contemporaries at Newnham remembered her as a vital and exuberant young woman with 'gloriously blue eyes in a fairytale pink and white complexion and a halo of really blonde hair' (Hubback, 24). She captained the college at cricket, played the piano, pursued a busy social life, and graduated second class in part one of the historical tripos (1908) and part two of the economics tripos (1909).

In 1909 Dorothy attended the economics lectures of a brilliant young don Walter Thomas *Layton (1884–1966), whom she thought 'the best looking young man in Cambridge after Rupert Brooke' (Hubback, 14). They soon became friends, finding common ground in a love of music, the outdoors, and the advocacy of women's suffrage, and were married at Limpsfield on 2 April 1910. In March 1911 their first child was born, a daughter, and another three daughters and three sons followed, the last, Christopher, born in 1929. Having three children in little more than three years, 1911–14, did not stop Dorothy Layton's political activities. Once a week she sold the *Common Cause*, the journal of the National Union of Women's Suffrage Societies, outside the post office in Cambridge. And in 1913, with her husband's support, she participated in the movement's march on London. It was then that she first ventured into public speaking, 'standing on a tub in the various villages and towns' along the route (Layton, 50).

Dorothy Layton's warmth and colour provided the perfect foil to her husband, 'who normally concealed his feelings and was famous for his silences' (Hubback, 244). His work with the Liberal Party, and later the League of Nations, meant that he spent long periods away from home, but the marriage endured and proved one of the great partnerships in British public life. Although Liberal divisions on the suffrage question prevented her from joining the party, Dorothy Layton zealously supported her husband's political work. He trusted her judgement and sought her advice; Lloyd George was fond of observing that she was 'much the best radical of the two' (Layton, 52). She had strong views on drink, which Walter Layton did not altogether share, and none was served at their home. And while she was accommodating in discussion, she also possessed intense moral conviction and crusaded passionately for her ideals.

During the war the Laytons gave over their Cambridge home to Belgian refugees and began a peripatetic lifestyle that ended with a move to Weybridge, close to London, in 1921. Dorothy Layton was as active in war work as the demands of her young family would allow: then, as later, the home was 'first in affection, first in her sense of responsibility and first in inclination' (Layton, 68). After the passage of suffrage legislation in 1918 she joined the Liberal Party. She helped to rejuvenate the local Weybridge branch and was involved in the annual Liberal summer schools from 1922. She was also active in the National Union of Societies for Equal Citizenship, whose policies she pressed on the Liberal Party. She campaigned in particular for family allowances, with the support of Eleanor Rathbone, an independent ally in a number of causes. Partly as a result of Layton's efforts the Women's Liberal Federation adopted family allowances in 1937, and the full party organization later followed. Layton regarded this as one of her greatest political achievements.

At the end of 1925 the Laytons moved to Wimbledon. In that year Dorothy was elected to the executive of the League of Nations Union, having joined her local branch at Weybridge. This work became increasingly important to her and complemented her husband's role in the league's international organization. The high point of her involvement came with the 'peace ballot' of 1935, which made clear the terms on which a substantial section of the British public was prepared to support war. It was 'the most important educational job' that she ever undertook for the league, and a ringing public endorsement of the principle of collective security (Layton, 96).

Somewhat ironically, given her large family, Lady Layton (her husband was knighted in 1930) became one of the keenest advocates of birth control in Britain between the wars, and associated herself vigorously with the same cause in India. In 1929 she travelled on the subcontinent with her husband, who was financial assessor to the statutory commission, and for the next six years she hardly spoke at a public meeting without mentioning India. She joined Eleanor Rathbone's British Committee for Indian Women's Franchise and gave evidence on its behalf to the parliamentary joint select committee on Indian franchise reform. In 1931 she became chairman of the British Women's Advisory Council on Indian Affairs (she retired in 1951). Her 'humorous impatience at over-caution and her clever turns of phrase' made her an invaluable member of the many committees on which she sat (Layton, 109). Her interests extended to Basque refugee children from the Spanish Civil War; Chinese refugees from the

Sino-Japanese War; and later, European refugees from totalitarianism. In February 1937 she joined the duchess of Atholl and Eleanor Rathbone on a tour of Yugoslavia, Romania, and Czechoslovakia, to promote mutual solidarity in the face of Nazi aggression. The three women, 'physically tough as well as mentally alert campaigners', met a barrage of propaganda from all sides, but also 'an unappeased hunger for British friendship and British understanding' (Stocks, 238, 239).

During the Second World War the Laytons lent their London home to a Czech refugee committee and divided their time between Twittens, a family home in Sussex, and a London flat. A lung complaint in 1941–2 left Dorothy Layton weakened, and she afterwards struggled to remain active in public life. Her presidency of the Women's Liberal Federation (1947–9) was a fitting finale to her political career. In this capacity she chaired a committee of inquiry into 'women's place in the community'. The findings were published in a Liberal Party report, *The Great Partnership* (1949), which identified the obstacles to women's equality, and suggested also remedies. The title was a statement of Layton's own personal philosophy. She believed that a successful marriage showed the way forward for society as a whole, with the greatest benefits being delivered by a full partnership between the sexes based on equality.

As president of the Women's Liberal Federation, Dorothy Layton attended the congress at The Hague in May 1948, and she became a strong supporter of a united Europe. She tried to mobilize support for this cause in her capacity as a member of the executive of the United Nations Association, the practical successor to the League of Nations Union. After a long illness she died on 18 March 1959. In 1961 Walter Layton published an intensely emotional biography, *Dorothy*, in which he suggested that his wife's triumph was to have combined the role of a mother with that of a public figure: 'many young women of to-day feel that they have to choose between a career and founding a home. Yet this woman had contrived to do both and to do them both extremely well' (Layton, 9).

MARK POTTLE

Sources *The Times* (19 March 1959); (11 April 1959) · 'Layton, Walter Thomas, first Baron Layton', *DNB* · W. Layton, *Dorothy* (1961) · D. Hubback, *No ordinary press baron: a life of Walter Layton* (1985) · *The great partnership*, Women's Liberal Federation (1949) · M. Stocks, *Eleanor Rathbone* (1949) · Burke, *Gen. GB* (1914) [Osmaston of Stoneshill] · b. cert. · *CGPLA Eng. & Wales* (1959)
Likenesses H. J. Stocks, portrait, *c.*1903, repro. in Layton, *Dorothy*, 20 · photograph, repro. in *The Times* (19 March 1959) · photographs, repro. in Layton, *Dorothy*, facing pp. 81, 140, frontispiece
Wealth at death £18,515 16*s.* 7*d.*: probate, 4 June 1959, *CGPLA Eng. & Wales*

Layton, Sir Geoffrey (1884–1964), naval officer, was born on 20 April 1884 at Glendale, Leyfield Road, West Derby, Lancashire, the son of George Layton, a Liverpool solicitor, and his wife, Sarah Greene. He received his early education at Eastman's School, Winchester, then on the naval cadet ship *Britannia*, from which he passed out as sublieutenant in 1903. Progress through the ranks at a typical pace saw him begin the First World War as a lieutenant. Wartime service brought out the best in Layton, who

Sir Geoffrey Layton (1884–1964), by Walter Stoneman, 1936

made a name for himself as one of the navy's most successful submarine commanders. Such an independent command in such an experimental arm called for drive, determination, even ruthlessness, as well as the ability to make fast decisions and see them through. Layton had all these qualities in abundance. On the negative side he was firm sometimes to the point of bullying with subordinates, and often coarse and blunt. He was a good judge of character, however, and those who gained his trust had a firm backer as they pursued their own ideas. On 17 December 1908 he married Eleanor Gwladys (b. 1881/2), daughter of Frederick Theobald Langley, a solicitor.

Layton ended the war a commander, and was promoted captain in 1922—an important vote of confidence in the downsizing environment of naval limitation agreements. Peacetime service led him in 1934 to the appointment of commodore naval barracks, Portsmouth, and in 1935 to promotion to rear-admiral. From 1936 to 1938 Layton put his talent as a judge of men to work as director of personnel services at the Admiralty. That was followed by a much more congenial appointment as commander of the battle-cruiser squadron in 1938. The outbreak of the Second World War brought for Layton promotion to vice-admiral and appointment as commander 1st battle squadron, second in command, Home Fleet. This further mark of confidence found Layton at the heart of the nation's maritime struggle, which for him reached a personal climax with heavy action in the Norwegian campaign of the spring of 1940. Following a knighthood and promotion later that

year, Layton was sent to the Far East as commander-in-chief, China station.

For Layton this was not exactly fortunate timing. China station had been reduced by imperial overstretch to a marginal holding operation, as the navy concentrated nearly all its strength on the fight for survival closer to home. A motley collection of warships keeping watch on the Japanese menace operated from Singapore, the hub of the extensive network of British colonies in Asia. There the now completed naval base awaited the battle fleet that the navy could no longer afford to send. But the approach of war in 1941 produced the controversial decision to send the ill-fated battle squadron known as force Z. Amounting in the end to HMS *Prince of Wales* and HMS *Repulse*, force Z was intended by Prime Minister Winston Churchill to help deter the Japanese from attacking the British empire. Many assumed that the Japanese were gearing up for just such an attack and the squadron therefore faced the imminent threat of war when it arrived. Critics such as Andrew Cunningham reacted with surprise and concern when Layton, an experienced combat commander on the spot—Cunningham rated him highly enough to suggest him as a possible successor as commander-in-chief, Mediterranean Fleet—was passed over for command of this new Eastern Fleet in favour of a man with much less experience at sea, Vice-Admiral Sir Tom Phillips. Layton busied himself by readying his motley fleet for war and preparing to hand over to his successor, Phillips, whose arrival in early December made his appointment redundant.

Fate and the Japanese had other ideas. Phillips and his two capital ships were sunk off the coast of Malaya on 10 December 1941, barely sixty hours after the outbreak of war. The Admiralty immediately ordered Layton to stay in Singapore and take command of what was left of the Eastern Fleet. With a fleet in name only Layton could do little or nothing to delay the fall of Singapore and the loss of the naval base; but his experience there left its mark on him and others. Many in the service considered his blunt pressure to prod survivors of the lost capital ships back to immediate duty as insensitive at best. Personalities naturally influenced judgements of behaviour, and Layton was always a man to rub some people the wrong way without caring about it. As he had no responsibility for the local defence of the base, the Admiralty authorized him to shift his command from Singapore. He left when the situation demanded, on 5 January 1942. But his farewell message left a sour taste with many: 'With your heads held high and your hearts beating proudly, I leave the defence of Singapore in your strong and capable hands. I am off to Colombo to collect a new fleet' (Marder, Jacobsen, and Horsfield, 19–20). Layton gave as well as he received. His reports and comments on the loss of force Z, the Malayan campaign, and the traumatic fall of Singapore were so vitriolic in their criticism of senior commanders that the official records were closed for fifty rather than the usual thirty years, and his personal wartime papers were also sealed at the British Library for fifty years.

Although Singapore might have been an unhappy time

for Layton, what proved to be his final wartime posting was the exact opposite. Layton went to Ceylon on 13 January to prepare to collect the fleet that the navy was now striving to assemble to cover the Indian Ocean. Yet sea command passed him by once again, going instead to James Somerville. But Layton found his niche when another grave emergency, with the Japanese threatening to run wild in the Indian Ocean and cut the lifeline of the eastern empire, led the British government to give him an extraordinary command in Ceylon. On 5 March Layton was appointed commander-in-chief, Ceylon, with full powers over all civil and military authorities on the island, including the governor. The effect of this concentration of authority, which came in response to Layton's own suggestion, was bracing. Layton found a colonial élite in torpor and three services divided over almost everything. Running roughshod over any and all concerns and sensitivities, Layton forced the island to prepare seriously for war and invasion. Red tape was cut, emergency restrictions were imposed, defences were prepared, and everyone was prodded and pummelled onto a war footing. Sensation peaked when Layton requisitioned the property of the Turf Club and the residence of a senior judge in order to build an emergency airstrip! The governor helped drive the message home when he answered indignant officials who complained about being bullied and insulted by the new supremo, one to the point of being called a 'black bastard', by the simple remark, 'My dear fellow that is nothing to what he calls me' (Roskill, *Churchill and the Admirals*, 203). Although Layton's efforts were not decisive in dealing with the Japanese naval–air attacks that hit Ceylon hard in April, they nevertheless helped create a sense of purpose and control which to that point had been sorely lacking. Henceforth Ceylon was alert and in the war, gripped by a firm and sure hand.

From that position Layton co-operated effectively with Somerville in the latter's necessarily patient effort to build up a force that could protect the Indian Ocean and take the war back to the Japanese. The line was thin but it was capably held. Layton later hosted the new south-east Asia command which set up its headquarters in Ceylon, testimony to its security as the base for preparing the counter-offensive. Success in Ceylon redounded to Layton's credit with his appointment in 1945 as commander-in-chief, Portsmouth, a traditional final command for a successful flag officer. Layton retired in 1947 as a full admiral to a quiet life pursuing his gardening hobby in rural Hampshire—interrupted by occasional exchanges, all forthright, with those preparing various official histories of the war. The very personification of the gruff sailor, basking in the satisfaction of duty done, Layton died on 4 September 1964 in the Royal Naval Hospital, Haslar, Gosport, and was buried with full service honours.

BRIAN P. FARRELL

Sources A. J. Marder, M. Jacobsen, and J. Horsfield, *Old friends, new enemies: the Royal Navy and the imperial Japanese navy*, 2 vols. (1981–90), vol. 2 · C. Barnett, *Engage the enemy more closely: the Royal Navy in the Second World War* (1991) · S. Roskill, *Churchill and the admirals* (1977) · S. W. Roskill, *The war at sea, 1939–1945*, 3 vols. in 4 (1954–61) · war history cases and papers, PRO, ADM 199 · M. Simpson, ed., *The Somerville papers* (1995) · M. Tomlinson, ed., *The most dangerous moment* (1976) · P. Elphick, *Singapore, the pregnable fortress: a study in deception, discord and desertion* (1995) · E. F. C. Ludowyk, *The modern history of Ceylon* (1966) · M. Stephen, *The fighting admirals: British admirals of the Second World War* (1991) · *The Times* (7 Sept 1964) · b. cert. · m. cert. · d. cert. · WWW

Archives BL, corresp. and papers · Royal Naval Museum, Portsmouth, war diary in command of the 18th cruiser squadron | PRO, admiralty MSS, ADM 1, ADM 116, ADM 199, ADM 205 | FILM IWM FVA, actuality footage · IWM FVA, news footage

Likenesses W. Stoneman, photographs, 1936–45, NPG [*see illus.*] · M. Bone, oils, 1945, IWM · photographs, IWM · photographs, NMM

Wealth at death £40,453: probate, 21 Dec 1964, *CGPLA Eng. & Wales*

Layton, Henry (1622–1705), writer on theology, was born at Rawdon, in the West Riding of Yorkshire, the eldest of the six sons of Francis Layton (1576/7–1661), master of the jewel-house to Charles I and Charles II, and Margaret, daughter of the well-known benefactor Sir Hugh Brown of London. The Laytons were an ancient and well-to-do family, and in pursuance of his father's will, Henry built a chapel at Rawdon. It is said that he:

> was educated at *Oxford*, and afterwards at *Grays-Inn*, in the study of the Law, and was called to the Bar; but made no other use of his profession … than to do good offices, among his neighbours without fee or reward. (Blackburne, 75)

Yet there is no evidence either that he studied at Oxford or that he was a barrister. He married Elizabeth (1646/7–1702), daughter of Sir Nicholas Yarborough. They had no surviving children.

Layton is mainly known as a theological controversialist but he was also 'a good historian', the author of 'many tracts against pluralities' and of *Observations Concerning Money and Coin* (1697) dealing especially with English coins (*Diary of Ralph Thoresby*). Late in life he started devoting himself to the question of the nature of the human soul, on which he published twelve tracts from 1694 to 1705, all but one without title-page, author's name, and date. It is likely that they were not printed for general distribution and 'the few copies now to be met with, were originally presents to his friends' (Blackburne, 76). His thoughts had been directed to this subject about 1684. 'In summer 1690', he says, 'I practised my monastick discipline, reading within doors, and labouring the ground abroad … what I read within I ruminated without.' But it was only after Candlemas 1691 that he started writing a treatise in which he explicitly denied the commonly accepted doctrine of a soul as an independent thinking substance surviving the body after death. At this stage of his life Layton had come to the conclusion that between body and soul there is 'a Close and Natural Contexture', that they are 'both of one same Nature' (*A Second Part of a Treatise* [1698?]), that the soul dies with the body, and that they both finally will gain immortality at the last judgment. After midsummer 1691 the manuscript treatise, with its fifteen pages, was partially finished, but very few were willing to read it and only 'a Neighbour-Minister' undertook to argue with the author. Their exchange of letters lasted until 21 November

1693 when the minister, rather tired than satisfied, warned Layton not to publish his 'dangerous and false' opinions (ibid.).

In the meantime Layton had been attracted by the publication of Richard Bentley's *Matter and Motion cannot Think* (1692), a stalwart defence of the immateriality and immortality of the soul against the Lockian doctrine of thinking matter. He then set aside his treatise and decided to reply to Bentley in his *Observations upon a Sermon Intituled 'A Confutation of Atheism'*, a tract stressing the pagan origin of the concept of the natural immortality of the soul which the author claimed to be rather 'a material Spirit generated, growing and falling with the Body' (*Observations* [1694?]). This work, probably published at the beginning of 1694 and criticized in print only in 1697, was Layton's first publication. Later on another 'Neighbour-Minister' referred him to John Flavell's *Pneumatologia* (1685), which contained a summary of arguments on behalf of the immortality of the soul. Layton thought it worthwhile to rebut it in his original manuscript treatise, which in the meantime had swelled to fifty sheets. He then resumed, finished, and sent the manuscript to London for printing, but nobody would undertake the charge and the hazard of such a publication without a fitting reward. The author refused to pay out a 'considerable Summ of Money' and ordered his correspondent to pack the manuscript away in a box labelling it 'The Treatise of such a Man concerning the Humane Soul' (*Observations upon a Short Treatise* [1697?]).

In 1697 Timothy Manlove, a presbyterian minister from Leeds, published a refutation to Layton's criticism of Bentley, arguing that Layton's materialistic view of man undermined personal identity and hence moral responsibility. This charge drove Layton to publish a reply to Manlove, under the title of *Observations upon a Short Treatise, Written by Timothy Manlove* (1697?), and finally to print his manuscript treatise, in two parts, under the titles *A Search after Souls* (1698?) and *A Second Part of a Treatise Intituled A Search after Souls* (1698?). By this time his eyesight had failed and therefore he needed the help of Timothy Jackson, his amanuensis. Yet his production of pamphlets continued and from about 1699 to the year of his death he published seven criticisms of immortalist tracts by Wadsworth, Nicholls, Turner, Broughton, Sherlock, and others, whose attacks were directed mainly against William Coward, the mortalist physician with whom Layton was often confused. Besides these works of controversy he published *Arguments and Replies* (1703), consisting of a collection of letters between himself and an anonymous correspondent (probably Henry Dodwell) on the connection between matter and mind.

From a vitalistic point of view, Layton criticized rigid Cartesian mechanism and dualism arguing that our 'Spirit of Life' springs from the combination of breath and blood, the animal body being living matter and the mind a sort of material spirit. The animal organism was for him a mortal 'Compositum' that wholly perishes and will rise at the final resurrection after the last judgment. Layton's argumentations were similar to those of the many Christian mortalists who lived in seventeenth-century England, although he was indebted more to the Lockian speculation on thinking matter and to medical theories on the soul than to the reasoning of those mortalists whose biblical suggestions were the result of a heterodox criticism against the Catholic and Anglican notions of soul, immortality, and the afterlife. Yet despite his dangerous statements Layton, in fact, professed to be a member of the Church of England, which he thought to be 'the purest Church … in the World', claiming that only 'Scripture' and 'Reason' were his proper guides (*Arguments and Replies*, 1703).

Layton died on 18 October 1705, aged eighty-three. He left in his cousin's custody a number of manuscripts on different subjects, among which are his memoirs and the five large treatises on practical divinity mentioned in *A Second Part of a Treatise Intituled A Search after Souls*. Unfortunately these works were probably mislaid or even suppressed. His literary executor was his nephew, William Smith, rector of Melsonby in the North Riding. A two-volume collection of his tracts was issued a year after his death under the title of *A Search after Souls … by a Lover of Truth*. It is hard to know how influential Layton's works were, although Locke, whom he occasionally mentioned, had eight of his pamphlets in his library. Layton's *Search* was first discussed in 1758 by the dissenting polemist Caleb Fleming, who wrongly thought it had been written by William Coward. DARIO PFANNER

Sources R. Thoresby, *Ducatus Leodiensis, or, The topography of … Leedes*, ed. T. D. Whitaker, 2nd edn (1816), 260 · *The diary of Ralph Thoresby*, ed. J. Hunter, 2 vols. (1830), 1.398 · *DNB* · H. Layton, *A search after souls*, 2 vols. (1706) · G. Carabelli, 'Un pio Anglicano alla ricerca dell'anima materiale: Henry Layton', *Materiali Filosofici*, 1 (1975), 36–47 · J. W. Yolton, *Thinking matter: materialism in eighteenth-century Britain* (1983) · F. Blackburne, *A short historical view of the controversy* (1765), 74–80 · [J. Hunter], ed., *Letters of eminent men, addressed to Ralph Thoresby*, 2 (1832), 193–5 · D. Berman, 'Layton, Henry', *The dictionary of eighteenth-century British philosophers*, ed. J. W. Yolton, J. V. Price, and J. Stephens (1999) · D. Berman, 'Die Debatte über die Seele', *Die Philosophie des 17. Jahrhunderts*, ed. J. P. Schobinger (Basel, 1988), 759–81 · L. E. Froom, *The conditionalist faith of our fathers*, 2 vols. (1966), 2.199–203 · D. Bank and A. Esposito, eds., *British biographical index*, 4 vols. (1990) · [H. Layton], *Arguments and replies, in a dispute concerning the nature of the human soul* (1703)
Archives BL, family MSS, MSS 45131–45133, 46354 | BL, Stowe MSS 746, fol. 107; 747, fols. 25, 47, 49

Layton, Richard (c.1498–1544), dean of York and agent in the suppression of the monasteries, was probably born in the late 1490s at Dalemain in Cumberland, and is said to have been one of thirty-three children of William Layton. He was related to Robert Aske and Cuthbert Tunstall and boasted to Cromwell in 1535 that he had 'friends and kinsfolk' everywhere in the north (*LP Henry VIII*, vol. 8, no. 822). Little is known of his early life but he was admitted BCL at Oxford on 25 June 1522 and was DCL by 1531. Cambridge also claims him as an alumnus but there is no evidence of his ever having studied there. Layton was ordained subdeacon on 19 September 1523 and deacon on 26 March

1524 in London, and may have entered the service of Cardinal Wolsey soon after leaving Oxford. He was admitted to the rectory of Stepney in Middlesex on 23 December 1522 and soon after was made a canon of St Paul's Cathedral, being collated to the prebend of Kentish Town on 9 May 1523.

It is not clear what services (if any) Layton performed for Wolsey, but it must have been during the 1520s that he made the acquaintance of Thomas Cromwell, for by the mid-1530s he considered Cromwell to be his chief patron. Layton was already living comfortably as a clerical pluralist when Cromwell commissioned him to be one of the visitors to the monasteries in the second half of 1535. He had been appointed dean of Chester-le-Street and rector of Wolsingham in co. Durham on 1 September 1533, rector of St Peter ad Vincula in the Tower of London on 15 March 1534, and archdeacon of Buckingham on 14 October 1534. He also prospered within the legal profession during the 1530s, being appointed a clerk in chancery and clerk of the privy council in 1534 and a master in chancery in 1538. Layton was one of the crown agents who interrogated Bishop John Fisher and Sir Thomas More in June 1535. It was at this time that he wrote to Cromwell suggesting a visitation of the diocese of York in order to root out the 'frantic fantasies and ceremonies' of the superstitious northerners. His challenge that 'You will never know what I can do until you try me' (*LP Henry VIII*, vol. 8, no. 955) was taken up by Cromwell and Layton was appointed to make a formal visitation of Oxford University in July 1535. The injunctions which he and Dr John Tregonwell issued to the university in September were scornfully dismissive of scholasticism and aimed at firmly establishing the 'new learning' at Oxford. The study of canon law was abolished and replaced with lectures in civil law. Daily public lectures in Greek and Latin were also established and they forbade the use of the *Sentences*. Moreover they appear to have encouraged the pillaging of college libraries for scholastic texts. Layton proudly wrote to Cromwell that he and Tregonwell left New College with the leaves of Duns Scotus blowing across the quadrangle.

The reform of Oxford occurred halfway through Layton's visitation of the monasteries in the south of England which had been under way since late July 1535. Beginning at Cirencester he spent six weeks making his way through Gloucestershire, Worcestershire, Somerset, and Wiltshire before arriving in Oxford. At first he was reprimanded for his leniency in imposing Cromwell's injunctions on the unwilling religious communities but he soon warmed to the task as he uncovered various abuses in the monastic houses on his itinerary. By mid-October he was bullying the prior and sub-prior of Lewes into admitting both treason and moral corruption. At Langdon in Kent he broke a door down to gain entry to the monastery and pursued the abbot and his mistress with a pole-axe. A few days later he was at Canterbury Cathedral priory, where on 23 October he was awoken in the night by a fire which destroyed part of the king's lodging. It was Layton who took control of the situation during the emergency, securing the shrine and jewels and preparing the monks for an evacuation. He

continued on his way through Kent towards London where Cromwell employed him in a vain attempt to secure the submission of Syon Abbey to the royal supremacy.

From London, Layton set out for Yorkshire with Dr Thomas Legh. During the first two months of 1536 they covered over 1000 miles and visited 121 religious houses in the north. Their report on this visitation, the *Compendium compertorum*, was a document full of allegations of gross moral misconduct among the religious and was used in parliament to secure the passing of the act dissolving the lesser monasteries. Layton made many enemies during his visitation of the northern counties, including Archbishop Lee of York, but his services to Cromwell secured for him a place as one of the crown's most useful servants. Layton's administrative skill and loyalty were continually called upon by Cromwell between 1535 and 1540. Layton took part in the trial of Anne Boleyn in May 1536, was one of the commissioners who took confessions after the Pilgrimage of Grace, and from December 1536 until April 1537 was involved in the trial of prisoners taken after the northern rising. On 24 March 1537 he was called to attend the bishops in their discussions about the saints, purgatory, and other doctrinal matters. Towards the end of 1537 he was a commissioner for the surrender of religious houses, and during 1538 he spent most of the year taking such surrenders, including that of the London Charterhouse. Throughout 1539 he continued the work of dissolving monasteries, and in September he was one of the commissioners who presided over the arraignment of the abbots of Reading and Glastonbury. From Glastonbury he turned north and between 20 November 1539 and 14 January 1540 he was present at the surrender of at least fourteen houses.

By early 1540 Layton had become a very wealthy man through Cromwell's patronage. His preferments included the rectories of London St Faith's, Brington, in Northamptonshire, and Sedgefield in co. Durham, to which he was appointed in 1535, and in 1537 he was collated to the rectories of Harrow on the Hill, Middlesex, and Lyth, Yorkshire. Layton had his heart set on greater promotions, however, and petitioned Cromwell for the chancellorship of Salisbury in 1537–8. As a reward for his services he was ultimately made a canon of York and prebendary of Ulleskelf on 20 June 1539, and finally became dean of York a month later, on 26 July. Two years later he was admitted to the rectory of Eccleston, Lancashire, on 19 May 1541. These numerous preferments brought him an enormous income of around £800 per annum, but by 1540 he was anxious for further promotion in the king's service and began to petition Cromwell for a diplomatic post abroad. It was now, however, that Cromwell fell from power and Layton's career stalled. He was also troubled at this time by the arrest in the Low Countries of his brother William Layton on suspicion of treason. It was not until 18 January 1543 that William Layton was finally pardoned.

Layton himself was relatively unscathed by both his brother's suspected treason and Cromwell's fall from grace, but his hopes for a commission in Henry VIII's diplomatic service had to be put on hold. He was in London to take part in the convocation which annulled the king's marriage with Anne of Cleves in July 1540, but from then until late 1543 he probably spent most of his time in the north. In February 1543 Henry finally appointed Layton ambassador to the French king but later in the year Layton was sent to Brussels to replace Dr Nicholas Wotton as ambassador to Mary of Hungary, regent of the Netherlands. Layton arrived in Brussels on 10 December 1543 and immediately threw himself into negotiations for the transport and victualling of the English army which was then being assembled for an attack on France. In mid-February 1544 Layton's business with the regent took him on a journey to Ghent where he caught a severe chill and flux. This illness gradually became more serious during the following months as he struggled to complete preparations for the projected landing of the English army on 15 May. By late May he was suffering from 'the worst kind of a dropsy' (*LP Henry VIII*, vol. 19/1, no. 566) and he eventually died some time between 8 and 11 June 1544. His brother William, who had acted as his secretary in Brussels, was left to complete the arrangements for the army and was later rewarded with Layton's prebend of Kentish Town in October 1544, followed by a canonry at York in January 1545. A sale of Layton's goods and chattels in August 1544 raised £231.

Richard Layton's place in the history of the dissolution rests partly upon his prominence as a crown commissioner during the visitation and dissolution of the monasteries, but equally upon his reputation as a salacious scandalmonger and mean-spirited bully. This assessment of his character has had little revision since Cardinal Gasquet judged him to be of 'a thoroughly brutal and depraved nature' (Gasquet, 1.437). Knowles felt that Layton was 'active and enterprising, with a gift for swift action' and the most energetic and resourceful of all the royal visitors, but his unswerving desire to serve Cromwell made him no better than the other 'adulatory, pliant, time-serving' and 'wholly materialistic' servants of Henry VIII (Knowles, 270–71). Layton's seventy-odd surviving letters, most of them calendared in the *Letters and Papers of Henry VIII*, are at once both racy and informative. They have been used widely by historians of the dissolution, and together with the *Compendium compertorum* of 1535 are responsible for much of the fierce debate which has surrounded the events which led to the end of medieval English monasticism.   PETER CUNICH

Sources D. Knowles [M. C. Knowles], *The religious orders in England*, 3 (1959), 268–72, 279–90, 300, 322, 329, 380–81 • Emden, *Oxf.*, 4.346, 349 • *LP Henry VIII*, vols. 7–19 • T. Wright, ed., *Three chapters of letters relating to the suppression of monasteries*, CS, 26 (1843) • F. A. Gasquet, *Henry VIII and the English monasteries*, 1 (1888), 252–7, 268, 286, 336, 349, 400, 412, 437–40, 443, 452 • G. Baskerville, *English monks and the suppression of the monasteries* (1940), 89, 103, 124–32, 141, 145, 165, 219 • C. Cross, 'Oxford and the Tudor state', *Hist. U. Oxf.* 3: *Colleg. univ.*, 117–49, esp. 128 • J. Caley and J. Hunter, eds., *Valor ecclesiasticus temp. Henrici VIII*, 6 vols., RC (1810–34), vol. 1, pp. 364, 375, 433, 434; vol. 4, pp. 28, 323; vol. 5, pp. 1, 90, 231, 312, 316 • A. N. Shaw, 'The northern visitation of 1535/6: some new observations', *Downside Review*, 116 (1998), 279–99 • C. B. Norcliffe, ed., *The visitation of Yorkshire in the years 1563 and 1564*, Harleian Society, 16 (1881), 262 • *DNB*
Archives BL, Cotton MSS • PRO, state papers
Wealth at death £231 goods and chattels; £800 livings p.a.: *LP Henry VIII*, 19/2, 328; Caley and Hunter, eds., *Valor ecclesiasticus*

Layton, Walter Thomas, first Baron Layton (1884–1966), economist and newspaper proprietor, was born in Chelsea, London, on 15 March 1884, the second son and third of the four children of Alfred John Layton (1849–1934), of The Chalet, Fulham Park Road, London, and his wife, Mary, née Johnson (1849–1929). Layton's father was a professional singer and his mother, also a musician, was the first woman to become a fellow of the Royal College of Organists. He had a younger brother, Gilbert, and an elder sister and brother, Margaret and Wilfred.

Layton continued the family's musical tradition when he was sent to St George's Chapel choir school in Windsor in 1891. Though this school usually recruited from Anglican families, Layton was brought up as a Congregationalist, both sides of his family being nonconformists. A sickly child, he suffered from rickets at an early age. After a period of ill health and homesickness in Windsor, he spent six months in Hastings convalescing with a family friend, prior to moving to King's College School, London, in 1894. While a member of the Temple Church choir, he sang at the diamond jubilee of Queen Victoria from the steps of St Paul's, and at the funeral of W. E. Gladstone in Westminster Abbey.

Having won a scholarship to Westminster City School in 1899, Layton moved to University College, London, in 1901, graduating with a third in history in October 1903. His performance suffered from his being sidetracked by statistical work on wages which he undertook for the Board of Trade in summer 1903; he had proved his ability by winning academic prizes in both economics and history. Taking a further economics course at University College, London, in 1903–4, he went to Cambridge in 1904, to Trinity College, to read for the new economics tripos, gaining firsts in both parts (1906, 1907). He continued to earn money from the Board of Trade for his flair for statistics.

Academic career and the First World War Layton moved to Gonville and Caius College, Cambridge, in 1907 as a postgraduate, and became a university lecturer in economics at Cambridge in 1908. In 1909 he became a fellow at Caius (remaining until 1914), and combined this with the Newmarch lectureship at University College, London (1909–12). In 1908 he also began giving lectures to the Workers' Educational Association, in London, Leicester, and Portsmouth, and began writing for *The Economist*, as well as being one of its assistant editors. During this time he carried out research into the history of wages and prices, which led him to publish several articles and his first and best-known book, *An Introduction to the Study of Prices* (1912).

When war broke out in 1914, Layton was one of countless academics who joined the civil service. Simultaneously, he parted company with *The Economist*, disagreeing with the anti-war views of its editor, F. W. Hirst. He began at the Local Government Board under Seebohm Rowntree, looking at employment issues, but soon moved to the Board of Trade, carrying out a weekly census of employment as part of the government's measures to tackle labour shortages.

When the Ministry of Munitions was set up in May 1915, Layton transferred there as director of requirements and programmes. He was also a member of the Milner mission to Russia in February 1917, the Balfour mission to America in April and May 1917, and the negotiations of the military and economic clauses of the treaty of Versailles in 1919. On the Milner mission Layton was particularly involved in negotiating the delivery of British artillery to the eastern front, and played an important role in relaying to Lloyd George the view that Russia was on the edge of revolution. Meanwhile, as part of the Balfour mission, Layton negotiated details of the allied arms programme with the Americans and the French military. He also made important contacts with crucial figures such as J. P. Morgan. His work on both missions was a major reason for his becoming a Companion of Honour in 1919.

Layton's involvement in the First World War contrasted interestingly with that of both J. M. Keynes and William Beveridge—though in all three cases the roots of their post-1919 interests can partly be seen in their wartime work. For Keynes Treasury matters and the eventual peace settlement loomed large both before and after 1919. Beveridge was primarily involved in domestic issues during the war, and this set the tone for his life's work. Layton, on the other hand, had gained experience in the negotiation of deals between nations on a wide range of issues, with the close involvement of banks, and this helped to set the tone for some of his post-war work in the League of Nations and other bodies.

The League of Nations and journalism During the war Layton acquired an international reputation as an economist and statistician, and worked closely with Jean Monnet and Arthur Salter among others. After a brief spell as director of the Iron and Steel Federation from summer 1919 to March 1920, he found that a range of options was open to him. He decided to develop his interest in international economic matters by becoming the director of the economic and financial section of the League of Nations. He had been released for this post for a year by the Iron and Steel Federation, and when his year was up, he returned to the federation. However, he soon found that he was out of sympathy with his employer's attitudes to trade unions, on which Layton took a liberal view, believing that the unions should have a greater say in the running of industry.

At the end of 1921 Layton moved back into the world of journalism, in which he had been involved before 1914. This move encompassed not only the editorship of *The Economist* in 1922–38 (followed by its chairmanship from 1944 to 1963), but also, in 1930–40 and 1944–50, chairmanship of the *News Chronicle* and *The Star*. Under Layton's guidance *The Economist* was transformed, acquiring a reputation for authority on international economic issues. One

achievement was to secure the independence of the editor from the proprietors, and Layton played a major part in negotiating the sale of the magazine from the trustees of the Bagehot daughters to the Financial Newspapers Group in which Brendan Bracken was prominent. A key part of the new editorial charter at the time of the sale in 1928 was that the editor had complete control of editorial policy. Layton was very much a hands-on editor of *The Economist*. As Graham Hutton commented,

> Sir Walter Layton
> Has a passion for alterat'on
> Would to God someone could alter
> Sir Walter.
> (Hubback, 91)

This approach ensured the highest standards in journalism, and circulation rose steadily from 6,000 to 10,000 in 1938. Layton was knighted in 1930.

The Economist was Layton's most enduring journalistic interest, but not his only one. In 1927 he joined the board of the *Daily News*, and in 1930 negotiated the merger of that paper with the *Westminster Gazette* and the *Daily Chronicle*, to form the *News Chronicle*. As chairman he played a large part in the paper's positioning as a mass circulation Liberal publication, with a strong emphasis on international issues. He spent four to five hours each day in the editorial offices, and often wrote the 'Notes of the day' column himself. He was also closely involved in the newspaper's leader columns—for example, during the Munich crisis. On this occasion, though Layton and the *News Chronicle* were broadly anti-appeasement, the newspaper's editor, Gerald Barry, believed that Layton was insufficiently critical of the government's dealings with Hitler.

Layton's writing as a journalist was austere and often cautious, but at both *The Economist* and the *News Chronicle* he showed an ability to bring together writers of talent and win their loyalty. In the 1930s the *News Chronicle* office became a haven for many political refugees from the rising tide of fascism and a beacon of liberal thinking in a Europe heading back to war.

Layton's creative financial skills were also keys to the founding of the *News Chronicle* and the restructuring of *The Economist*. But he did not have a controlling financial interest in the *News Chronicle* and in the post-war world differences over strategy between him and Lawrence Cadbury, the major shareholder, inhibited a single-minded response to the paper's competitive decline and eventual demise in 1960.

Liberal politics During the 1920s and 1930s Layton became heavily involved in politics. He stood unsuccessfully for parliament three times as a Liberal for Burnley (1922), Cardiff South (1923), and London University (1929). But his importance as a Liberal had little to do with elections. Rather, his work at the *News Chronicle* and *The Economist* put him at the heart of Liberal politics. He was a leading member of a group of Liberals with a major influence on public opinion. They moved in Whitehall and Westminster circles, Fleet Street, the City, and Oxford and Cambridge. Among the number were Keynes, Beveridge, Gilbert Murray, and Seebohm Rowntree. They were at the heart of the political, business, and journalistic establishments, and sought, with some success, to place Liberal ideas firmly on the political agenda, even though the parliamentary Liberal parties of various guises were bent on splitting and self-destruction. But they were also listened to by politicians of other parties. Layton advised the Conservatives on India in 1927–9, and gave advice on reparations both to Labour in 1929–31 and to the National Government in the early 1930s. He was also closely involved in the creation of the Basel Bank for International Settlements (BIS) and an abortive plan to create a European customs union under the wing of the League of Nations. His involvement in the BIS was a particular reflection of widespread respect for his expertise. The governor of the Bank of England, Montagu Norman, believed that central banks should be free from political control, and Layton had been highly critical of this view, but it was at Norman's personal request that Layton joined the BIS committee.

Layton's highest-profile role in developing Liberal policy was as chairman of the executive committee of the Liberal Industrial Inquiry (as opposed to 'Enquiry', carefully chosen to avoid the acronym LIE), which produced the *Yellow Book* of 1928. This put forward ideas on more widespread economic planning, and plans to use public works schemes to tackle unemployment. After a decade of struggling to define new economic ideas in response to more polarized politics, the Liberals had developed a clear agenda. Layton's contacts and drive had provided much of the stimulus underpinning the project.

International economic affairs Layton's influence on the political direction of Liberalism reached its peak in the late 1920s and the 1930s as a result of his understanding of international affairs. As a regular speaker at meetings of both the Liberal summer school, and the National Liberal Federation, he closely linked international economic issues to international politics in its broadest sense. His particular contribution to Liberal international thought was to develop the idea of 'interdependency'. He developed the traditional Liberal belief in free trade, in which his thought was rooted, by arguing that free trade was effective because the world was 'interdependent'. The first clear statement of interdependency came in a leader article written by Layton in *The Economist*, which became a valuable platform for his views, in April 1929. He was responding to recent criticisms of free trade, which had claimed that it was a political shibboleth, possibly relevant to the nineteenth century, but no longer valid. Layton said:

> Circumstances, it is true, have changed since the nineteenth century. But the main trend of change is in the direction of the enormously greater interdependence of nations; and the trend has served, not to destroy, but to re-inforce every argument against trade restriction. (*The Economist*, 13 April 1929, 783)

It was not new to see *The Economist* arguing the free trade case, but it was uncommon for anybody to justify it on the basis of an 'interdependence of nations' that went beyond economics. The implications of this for foreign policy were twofold in the eyes of Layton and *The Economist*: first,

governments must maintain a tariff-free economic policy; second, the League of Nations must be developed to ensure that political interdependence was recognized. This was summarized in a special free trade supplement, in which *The Economist* claimed:

> It is only possible to develop a policy of political co-operation between nations if there is some degree of economic co-operation. Free Trade in economic affairs is the counterpart of the work of the League of Nations in political matters. They stand as a joint policy against the alternatives of Protection, competition in armaments and aggressive nationalism. (*The Economist*, 13 April 1929, suppl., 2)

Through the pages of *The Economist* Layton showed how political and economic issues were related, and how the emergence of a global economic system had implications for the political organization of the world. But equally, he defined clearly how far the political and economic aspects of interdependence differed, with the spread of free trade not being complemented by the political structures that could provide rules for dealing with the shocks and jolts of national competition. This thread ran through much of Liberal international policy in the 1930s, and particularly through its alternative to appeasement. Layton had been crucial to putting it forward.

When the depression struck, however, and governments around the world sought salvation through tariffs, Layton's response was pragmatic: he told the 1932 Liberal summer school that it would be impractical to sweep away all tariffs immediately, but that there should be an attempt to work with other nations to define a 'standard of reasonableness' (*News Chronicle*, 2 Aug 1932, 2). This never became formal Liberal policy, but it provided a valuable stimulus to thought at a time when many Liberals were all too willing to sit back on old orthodoxies, knowing that they were far from being in a position to form a government.

The Second World War and after During the Second World War Layton was again a civil servant, as director-general of programmes in the Ministry of Supply in 1940–42, chairman of the executive committee at the same ministry in 1941–2, chief adviser on programmes on planning in the Ministry of Production in 1941–3, and head of joint war production staff in 1942–3, in effect a resumption of his role in the First World War.

Layton was, however, much less comfortable in the larger bureaucracy of 1940 than in 1914–18 when, as one of the handful of bright young men in Lloyd George's 'Kindergarten' of advisers, he had brought his keen analytical mind to the novel challenges of wartime economic government and the planning of arms production. In February 1943 he resigned from the civil service. He had three reasons for doing so. First, he had set up planning systems which were now operating. Second, he wanted to speak publicly about war aims and the peace settlement, articulating in particular his vision of a united Europe. Third, he had been ill, and needed to rest. When he did return to *The Economist* and the *News Chronicle* in 1944, he again applied his ideas on building up international post-war co-operation. The creation of new international bodies with real power was the direction advocated by many Liberals, and Layton was at the fore in supporting both the United Nations and European unity. He was also a keen advocate of Anglo-American understanding, but the focal points of his activities were work for the European movement from 1946, and his post as vice-president of the Council of Europe Consultative Assembly in 1949–57. There his bent for bridge-building found expression in the joint meetings set up by himself and Jean Monnet between members of the assembly and the new assembly of the Coal and Steel Community. He also initiated joint meetings between members of the assembly and the US congress. Having been created Baron Layton in January 1947, he found the House of Lords a valuable platform. He became Liberal spokesman on economic affairs and the Council of Europe and in 1952–5 was deputy Liberal leader in the Lords.

Layton was generally seen to be a reserved man, who kept his feelings to himself, and eschewed the high life: Violet Bonham Carter described him as 'the handsomest little grey mind in Europe' (Hubback, 62), despite her high regard for him. Yet close friends found him much warmer and appreciated his wit.

At university Layton had told his sister that his philosophy of life could be summed up in the phrase 'how can I help?' (Hubback, 15). His varied career reflected that idealism, leavened by ambition and a passion for work. Yet beneath the natural authority which he brought to both public and family life was great sensitivity and, in his own words, shyness. It was an attractive combination, but it meant that he was less effective as a public speaker than as a chairman of committee or as a patient negotiator, seeking a common view.

Layton's main support was his wife, Eleanor Dorothea Osmaston (1887–1959), known as Dorothy [see Layton, Eleanor Dorothea], whom he married on 2 April 1910. She had been a Cambridge student when they met, and described Layton as the next best-looking man in Cambridge after Rupert Brooke. She was politically active in her own right, attending Fabian meetings and taking part in suffragette campaigns. They had seven children (three sons and four daughters) and twenty-three grandchildren.

Layton's densely-packed work schedule and perhaps his shyness often left him little time for family or holidays, yet he could respond with dramatic effect to family needs. Layton's youngest son, Christopher, was a wartime evacuee in the USA. One day in 1942 Layton, in America to negotiate Lend-Lease of armaments, paid a surprise visit to the boy of twelve. 'The war's turned the corner. We shall win in a couple of years. Would you like to come home?' he asked. The homesick boy fell into his arms and within a month both were on a troopship convoy heading back to Europe.

Layton was devastated when his wife died from cancer in 1959, and wrote an account of her life in 1961 entitled *Dorothy*. Layton himself died on 14 February 1966, at Putney Hospital, London, and his ashes were buried at Putney Vale cemetery near those of his wife. He was succeeded as baron by Michael John Layton (1912–1989), his eldest son.

David Hubback's biography *No Ordinary Press Baron* (1985) sees Layton's principal importance as resting upon his role in inter-war journalism. But Layton is also representative of those academics who played important roles as civil servants in both world wars. More recent work emphasizes his status as an influential thinker in inter-war Liberalism, whose thinking on 'interdependency' has continued relevance in the twenty-first century's globalized economy.   RICHARD S. GRAYSON

Sources D. Hubback, *No ordinary press baron: a life of Walter Layton* (1985) · C. Layton, 'Walter Layton', *Dictionary of liberal biography*, ed. D. Brack and others (1998), 217–19 · *DNB* · private information (2004) [Christopher Layton, son] · *The Times* (15–16 Feb 1966); (18 Feb 1966); (23 Feb 1966) · R. S. Grayson, 'Liberals, international relations and appeasement', *The liberal party, 1919–1939* (2001) · R. D. Edwards, *The pursuit of reason: The Economist, 1843–1993* (1993) · Lord Layton [W. T. Layton], *Dorothy* (1961)
Archives Trinity Cam., corresp. and papers | Bodl. Oxf., report on the work of department of munitions, requirements and statistics · HLRO, corresp. with Lord Beaverbrook; letters to Lloyd George · Joseph Rowntree Foundation, York, library, corresp. with B. Seebohm Rowntree and others relating to the general strike · JRL, letters to the *Manchester Guardian* · NA Scot., corresp. with Lord Lothian
Likenesses W. Stoneman, photographs, 1935–53, NPG
Wealth at death £45,388: probate, 29 June 1966, *CGPLA Eng. & Wales*

Lazarus, Harris Meyer (1878–1962), rabbi, was born in Riga, Latvia, on 11 June 1878, the eldest son of nine children of Julius Lazarus (Yudel Leiser or Leizera) (1852–1940) and his wife, Esther Golda Itzikovitz (1858–1928). Julius Lazarus emigrated to England about February 1895, and his eldest son, aged nineteen, followed in June 1897, Anglicizing his name Hirsch as Harris. He was naturalized on 18 January 1904. He had received a traditional Jewish education in Riga and had qualified as a *shochet* (Jewish ritual slaughterman). In January 1898 he entered Jews' College, the training ground for the 'native' Anglo-Jewish ministry. He at first studied *hazanut* (Jewish cantoral music) and then turned to rabbinics, gaining *semicha* (rabbinical ordination) in 1910. He was also a student at University College, London, graduating BA in 1904 and MA in 1913. Between 1904 and 1906 he taught in the East End at the Toynbee Hall Hebrew training classes. In 1905 Lazarus was appointed minister of the newly built Brondesbury synagogue in north-west London, where he remained until 1938, the only congregational post which he ever held.

In the same year, on 15 June 1905, Lazarus married Ada (1884–1950), the youngest daughter of Rabbi Susman Cohen of Manchester and his wife, Bertha, a daughter of Dayan Jacob Reinovitz (1818–1893). The couple made their home in the Willesden and Brondesbury neighbourhood and had one son and two daughters. Lazarus's father-in-law had served as a *dayan* or judge on the *bet din* (ecclesiastical court) of Chief Rabbi Hermann Adler between 1893 and 1906. Lazarus followed in his footsteps. In 1914 he was appointed an assistant *dayan* and combined his work at the court with his synagogal duties until he retired from

Brondesbury at the age of sixty. He then served as a full-time *dayan* until 1945.

From 1946 to 1948 Lazarus was recalled from retirement to the post of deputy chief rabbi, after the death of J. H. Hertz. He stood firm against recognition of the legitimacy of Liberal Judaism that was then seeking the right of its synagogues to appoint marriage secretaries and conduct weddings approved by the registrar-general. Under civil law such rights were conferred following certification by the president of the Board of Deputies of British Jews in consultation with his (exclusively Orthodox) 'ecclesiastical authorities', namely the *haham* (chief rabbi) of the Spanish and Portuguese Jews' Congregation and the chief rabbi of the United Hebrew Congregations, on whose *bet din* Lazarus served. No compromise was possible, even after Lazarus's departure from office, and in 1949 the Liberals left the board. They eventually (in 1958) had recourse to parliament in order to redress their grievances.

Lazarus collaborated on the Soncino Press translation of the Talmud and translated some previously unpublished poems by the medieval Spanish Hebrew poet Solomon Ibn Gabirol (1906). His most widely read work was a traditionalist handbook for Jewish women entitled *The Ways of her Household* (1923). He died at his home, 33 Cholmley Gardens, West Hampstead, on 25 February 1962 and was buried the following day at Willesden Jewish (United) cemetery, next to his wife, who had predeceased him by a dozen years.   SHARMAN KADISH

Sources *The Times* (27 Feb 1962) · *Jewish Chronicle* (12 Jan 1940) · *Jewish Chronicle* (10 Feb 1950) · *Jewish Chronicle* (2 March 1962) · *Jewish Chronicle* (18 May 1928) · *Jewish Chronicle* (12 Jan 1963) · *Jewish Year Book* (1963) · G. Alderman, *Modern British Jewry* (1992) · private information [M. Musai, *née* Lazarus, granddaughter] · *CGPLA Eng. & Wales* (1962) · burial records, Willesden Jewish (United) cemetery
Archives U. Southampton, MS 130 | LMA, London Beth Din archives
Likenesses oils, priv. coll.
Wealth at death £3501 17s. 1d.: probate, 30 April 1962, *CGPLA Eng. & Wales*

Lazell, (Henry George) Leslie (1903–1982), pharmaceutical industrialist, was born at 9 Canal Terrace, Camden Town, London, on 23 May 1903, the elder son (there were no daughters) of Henry William Lazell, a wine merchant's manager, who died prematurely, and his wife, Ada Louisa King. Leslie Lazell (as he was known) was educated at a London county council elementary school until he was thirteen and a half, when he became an office boy in the solicitor's department of the Inland Revenue at Somerset House. After the end of the First World War Lazell sat and failed the examination for a permanent civil service post. For a time he worked as a bookmaker's clerk and then joined the wholesale druggists Allen and Hanburys as a ledger keeper. Determined to succeed in life, he attended evening classes for his professional examinations, including those of the Association of Certified and Corporate Accountants and the Chartered Institute of Secretaries, which bodies later gave him fellowships. On 17 November 1928 he married Doris Beatrice, daughter of Edwin Try, an engineer; they had one son.

Lazell's first opportunity to show his worth came in 1930

when he was recruited as an accountant by Alexander Maclean, an enthusiastic marketing man who had founded the Macleans toothpaste and stomach powder firm. Maclean needed an up-to-date budgeting system; Lazell, having set this up, was made company secretary, and a director in 1936. His managerial horizons were widened when he became Macleans' representative on certain trade associations. Contact with his opposite numbers in international corporations such as Colgate and Sterling Drug persuaded him that unless British companies paid more attention to research, they would fall badly behind these giants.

In 1938 Philip Ernest Hill, chairman of Beechams, acquired Macleans. Almost immediately he made Lazell secretary of Beechams, in 1940 promoting him to the board and to its inner committee. Lazell then went back to take charge of the profitable Macleans. In wartime conditions of shortages and disruptions, he quickly learned how to improvise within the framework of a clear business strategy. Before Hill died in 1944, Lazell secured the board's authority to create a central research organization for the parent company, and in the following year the Beecham Group—as it had become—set up the Beecham Research Laboratories. Lazell's ultimate goal was to achieve some major pharmaceutical discovery. However, Hill's successor at Beechams, Sir Stanley Holmes (later first Baron Dovercourt) planned to diversify into wholesale groceries, and had little time for pharmaceutical research. Lazell therefore volunteered to take control of research, and meet its running costs out of the buoyant profits of Lucozade, a Macleans' glucose drink. Group profits, however, remained disappointing: groceries proved to be poor earners, and a widespread corporate malaise was exacerbated by infighting among senior executives. As a result Beechams earned a mediocre reputation in investment circles. Finally, in 1951, institutional investors forced Lazell's appointment as group managing director, mandated to give the company once again a sense of direction.

Lazell's initial task was to reorganize the group along more logical, and hence more profitable, lines. This involved amalgamating and restructuring more than a hundred subsidiary companies and their shareholdings, thus allowing Beechams to raise money on more advantageous terms. Not until 1962 was he able finally to create an organization of three—later four—divisions in product, and later regional, groupings. That step both rationalized production and marketing and permitted more effective head office control. On the sales side, he made the group into one of the largest advertisers in Britain; he adopted American publicity methods and improved on them by requiring top management personally to lead marketing teams.

Once the first phase of Lazell's corporate plan was satisfactorily launched, he arranged in 1954 for his researchers to begin investigations of antibiotics. The group's consultant, Sir Charles Edward Dodds, worked closely with Ernst Chain, the leading scientist in the field. Existing types of penicillin needed improvement, which they hoped to achieve by a chemical rather than by the existing biological process. Eventually the basic penicillin molecule, 6-APA (amino-penicillanic acid), was isolated. By 1959 Beechams had developed its first semi-synthetic penicillin, Broxil, obtaining some help from the American company Bristol–Myers, with which a licensing agreement was concluded.

According to Lazell, it was in the early 1960s that the balance of the group's affairs shifted from proprietary goods towards pharmaceuticals, that decade being probably the most hectic for the group as a whole as well as for his research activities. As managing director, and then as chairman from 1958 onwards, he was the driving force in the conversion of Beechams into an international science-based and marketing orientated enterprise. To become truly international, the group needed above all to build up a strong presence in both the United States and Europe. While some products had little success in the American market, Brylcreem, the hair preparation, and Macleans' toothpaste both did well after some years of intensive marketing effort.

The considerable financial and management resources required for development in the United States delayed the group's entry into Europe on a large scale. Even so, by the time Lazell stepped down as chairman in 1968, the western hemisphere—which included Australia and New Zealand—accounted for almost a quarter of Beechams' sales and nearly a third of its profits, while continental Europe contributed one-seventh of sales and over a fifth of profits. In 1951–2, the year of his appointment as managing director, group turnover had been £25 million and profits £2½ million; in 1968–9 turnover was £134 million and profits £25 million, the ratio having nearly doubled. Lazell was then made president of the Beecham group, and until 1972 retained the chairmanship of Beecham Inc. in the United States.

Like the company's founder, Thomas Beecham (1820–1907), Lazell was essentially a self-educated man, almost uniquely so among those then at the head of a major UK manufacturing enterprise. He had a healthy disrespect for snobbery and nepotism, and never became assimilated into the British establishment; Lord Dovercourt is said to have dubbed him 'not one of us' (Lazell, *Pills*, 2). Possessing an incisive and analytical mind, he was quick to learn from both mentors and trusted lieutenants. As a layman he was able to pick up a working knowledge of the scientific technicalities of pharmaceutical research. He was a great reader, especially of autobiographies; as a young man he played cricket and squash, and later enjoyed yachting.

Lazell's outside professional interests were necessarily limited, and chosen very much to harmonize with his philosophy of life. A tireless and uncompromising free-market advocate, he was one of the original subscribers to the Institute of Economic Affairs, founded in 1957. Although in his outlook he was ahead of his time, he was granted no honours from the state or any university. He was chairman of the board of governors of Ashridge Management College and a council member of the Institute of

Directors. He also acted as appeal president of the British Heart Foundation. He was hostile to bureaucracy in all its forms; as a non-executive director of ICI from 1966 to 1968, he regularly voiced his criticism of that company's top-heavy structure. In retirement he spent much of each year in Bermuda, but he was in London when he died of heart failure at his home, 3 Whaddon House, Williams Mews, Westminster, on 17 November 1982. As no will seems to have been proved in England, the value of his estate is unknown.   T. A. B. CORLEY

Sources H. G. Lazell, *From pills to penicillin: the Beecham story* (1975) · T. A. B. Corley, 'Lazell, Henry George Leslie', *DBB* · T. A. B. Corley, 'The Beecham Group in the world's pharmaceutical industry, 1914–70', *Zeitschrift für Unternehmensgeschichte*, 39/heft 1 (1994), 18–30 · H. G. Lazell, 'Development and organisation of the Beecham Group Ltd', *Edwards Seminar Papers, London School of Economics*, 252 (Feb 1960) · H. G. Lazell, 'The years with Beechams', *Management Today* (Nov 1968) · E. Chain, 'Thirty years of penicillin therapy', *PRS*, 179B (1971), 293–319 · R. W. Clark, *The life of Ernst Chain: penicillin and beyond* (1985) · *Chemist and Druggist* (27 Nov 1982) · *Pharmaceutical Journal*, 229 (1982), 692 · *The Times* (19 Nov 1982) · b. cert. · m. cert. · d. cert.
Archives Glaxo Smithkline, Brentford, Middlesex
Likenesses D. Wilding, photograph, *c*.1960, priv. coll.

Lea, Sir George Harris (1912–1990), army officer, was born on 28 December 1912 at Franche, Kidderminster, Worcestershire, the eldest in the family of two sons and three daughters of George Percy Lea, chairman of the family textile business, and his wife, Jocelyn Clare, *née* Lea (his mother and father were distant cousins). Educated at Charterhouse School and at the Royal Military College, Sandhurst, he was commissioned into the Lancashire Fusiliers in 1933. Lea was handsome, broad, and tall—well over 6 feet—a robust and skilful games player, but a gentle and considerate man. He served in Britain, China, and India before the Second World War.

In India in 1941, Lea was among the first to join airborne forces, becoming in 1943 brigade-major of 4th Parachute brigade during operations with the 1st airborne division in Italy. Within this organization, he commanded the 11th battalion of the Parachute regiment at Arnhem in September 1944. In the battle his force was overwhelmed by enemy armour. Wounded and captured with his soldiers, he mistakenly but characteristically blamed himself for this outcome. He spent the rest of the war in a German prison camp.

In 1948 Lea married Pamela Elizabeth, daughter of Brigadier Guy Lovett-Tayleur. His wife accompanied him wherever possible and contributed notably to his accomplishments. They had a son and two daughters.

In the immediate post-war years Lea continued his service with airborne forces in India and at home, and in staff posts with the Royal Marine commando brigade and NATO, as a lieutenant-colonel, prior to taking command of the Special Air Service regiment in 1955. Revived for the emergency in Malaya, the unit lacked direction. Within ten days of his arrival, a sergeant remarked: 'the whole outfit came to life. He stretched us—and himself—to the limit, but we could see it was leading to an operational future.' During the next two years of his command, he developed the exacting standards and extraordinary skills for which the regiment became renowned.

As a consequence, Lea was promoted directly to a brigade command in England in 1957. He was then competing with peers in the favoured armoured warfare environment in Germany. Appointment to command the 42nd Lancashire territorial division and north-west district in 1962 appeared to limit his further employment. But he was selected in 1963 to the politically sensitive command of the armed forces of Northern Rhodesia and Nyasaland, colonies moving imminently to self-government. His political tact and decisive containment of dissident groups were judged exemplary. As this task concluded, he was chosen to succeed General Walter Walker as director of Borneo operations early in 1965.

Responsibility for the civil government of the former British Borneo territories had passed to Malaysia, whose authority was disputed by neighbouring Indonesia and Chinese communists in Sarawak. Lea was required to secure a mountainous border 1000 miles in length amid dense jungle, and to pacify the communist faction. He served three authorities: the British commander-in-chief in Singapore, the Malaysian government in Kuala Lumpur, and, to an extent, the sultan of Brunei.

Lea possessed only a proportion of the powers necessary to ensure the co-operation of civil government, the Malaysian police and armed services, and the Australian and New Zealand sea, land, and air elements which reinforced his British forces from time to time. The rest depended upon goodwill, which he won by his open manner, humour, and modesty. Nothing ruffled him. Even when his wooden house caught fire and he lost in minutes the greater part of his personal possessions, he continued as if it were a matter of the least importance.

Making adroit use of air and sea resources, Lea developed the policy of pre-emptive cross-border attacks by his troops, while containing the Chinese communists with police backed by military units. The success of these methods contributed to the change of political leadership in Jakarta and the emergence of an accord between Indonesia and Malaysia in 1966.

Promoted to lieutenant-general, Lea was posted in 1967 to Washington, DC, as head of the British services joint mission, the link between the British and American joint chiefs of staff. Maintaining the close alliance in a period of British economic difficulty and defence retrenchment was not easy. But the Americans opened their offices and confidences to him more fully than protocol demanded, because they liked and respected him, as the chairman of the American joint chiefs observed on his retirement in 1970. He had evoked similar responses through the greater part of his professional life.

Colonel of the Lancashire Fusiliers from 1965 to 1968, Lea was deputy colonel and then colonel (1974–7) of the Royal Regiment of Fusiliers into which it was drawn. He was appointed MBE (1950), CB (1964), KCB (1967), and to the DSO (1957). For his services in Borneo, he was made Dato Seri Setia, order of Paduka Stia Negara, Brunei (1965).

He retired to live in Jersey and was on the board of several commercial companies. Lea died at home in St Brelade, Jersey, on 27 December 1990.

ANTHONY FARRAR-HOCKLEY, *rev.*

Sources WW · *The Times* (28 Dec 1990) · *The Times* (25 Feb 1991) · personal knowledge (1996) · private information (1996)

Leach. *See also* Leech.

Leach, Arthur Francis (1851–1915), historian of education, the third son of Thomas Leach, barrister, of Seaford Lodge, Ryde, Isle of Wight, and his wife, Sarah Green, was born in London on 16 March 1851. He was educated at Winchester College, and gained a scholarship at New College, Oxford, in 1869. In 1872 he won the Stanhope historical essay prize—with his pro-Cromwell, anti-royalist 'The protectorate'—and in 1873 obtained a first class in *literae humaniores*. He was a fellow of All Souls College from 1874 until his marriage, in 1881, to Emily Archer, daughter of Silas Kemball Cook, secretary of the Seamen's Hospital, Greenwich, and sister of Sir Edward Tyas Cook; they had four sons and two daughters.

In 1876 Leach was called to the bar by the Middle Temple, and in 1884 he was appointed an assistant charity commissioner (endowed schools department). From 1901 to 1903 he was administrative examiner at the Board of Education, from April to December 1903 senior examiner, and from 1904 to 1906 assistant secretary. He was second charity commissioner from 1906 until his death in 1915. His work as an assistant charity commissioner was largely writing reports determining from historical evidence schools' legal status relative to the 1869 Endowed Schools Act. From this developed the historical studies which became his main purpose and achievement. He encouraged the allocation of endowments to girls' schools, and favoured technical education for girls.

Leach was associated with the endowed schools department at an interesting period, that following the Public Schools Act of 1868 (based on the recommendations of the royal commission of 1861–4 on the public schools) and the Endowed Schools Act of 1869 (which embodied the recommendations of the schools inquiry commission of 1864–8). The latter commission had dealt with 782 grammar schools and 2175 endowed elementary schools, and the provision of new schemes for these was transferred to an augmented Charity Commission, of which Leach was a member. Appendix 5 of the report of the schools inquiry commission contained a list of endowed schools, in chronological order of foundation. Leach worked over this material de novo, and in 1896 published *English Schools at the Reformation (1546–1548)*, in which he claimed the attribution of fifty-one new foundations to Edward VI's reign was false. His study of the Chantry Acts of 1546–8 (edited in the same book) alleged that the government of Edward VI was the spoiler rather than the founder of schools, and that in his reign 200 grammar schools were abolished or crippled, and that other schools were apparently swept away without record. However, he too readily identified schools with chantries, and exaggerated his case. Leach investigated the provision of pre-Reformation schools connected with cathedral churches, monasteries, collegiate churches, hospitals, guilds, chantries, and independent institutions, and published the results in *Schools of Medieval England* (1915), the first connected history of English schools to the accession of Edward VI. He asserted the extensive provision of schools in medieval England, and their continuity with later grammar schools. He emphasized secular collegiate churches as educational centres, and virtually excluded monastic educational provision, which he considered of minimal importance. He associated monasticism with superstition, believing it to be one of the harmful results of the Norman conquest, and Henry VIII's dissolution of the monasteries to be a deserved retribution. He also challenged the received interpretation of the effect of the Renaissance on English education, claiming, 'The very term Renaissance is misleading. There was no new birth of learning wanted, because learning had never died—in schools at all events' (Miner, 97). He claimed (as he had first proposed in *The Times*, 12 September 1896) that the King's School, Canterbury, is the oldest English school; earlier he had preferred the claim of St Peter's School, York (*Fortnightly Review*, Nov 1892). His book was influential in creating a sense of the continuity in development of English grammar schools from the time of the conversion of England to Christianity, but its ambitious hypothesis has not found favour with subsequent writers.

Leach supplied, almost single-handed, the history of schools in nineteen counties for the early volumes of the Victoria History of the Counties of England. His summaries of county school history at the head of each of his contributions are of interest for social as well as educational history. His opinions were sometimes hasty and unsafe, but his comprehensive collection of facts gave the articles lasting value.

Leach also wrote histories of Winchester College (1899) and Bradfield College (1900), *Early Yorkshire Schools* (for the Yorkshire Archaeological Society, 1899 and 1903), a *History of Warwick School* (1906), and *Early Education in Worcester* (1913). He produced a document collection, *Educational Charters and Documents, 598 to 1909 A.D.* (1911); in this, he aimed to do for educational history what Stubbs's *Select Charters* did for constitutional history, but failed. His work, however, placed the history of schools and education in England on a high level of research and called attention to the question of continuity of their development. Leach also pronounced, in 1896 *National Observer* articles and elsewhere, on the controversial question of the meaning of 'free schools', arguing they were free of fees, and so disagreeing with Benjamin Hall Kennedy (of Shrewsbury School and the *Latin Primer*) and others with vested interests in the Victorian public schools.

Leach's pioneer unearthing and editing of documents was considered laudable, but his interpretations and criticism were controversial. His main themes—that monasteries contributed minimally to medieval education, and that the Reformation and Edward VI's government

harmed education—challenged strongly held orthodoxies and the then dominant protestant 'whig interpretation'. He considered himself a revisionist: he claimed in 1913, 'My researches have led me first to doubt, then to deny, and finally to disprove the authorized version, and to revise, recast, or perhaps rather to create *de novo* the history of English education' (Miner, 228). His interpretations were criticized: F. W. Maitland wrote that he gave 'the rashest judgment about the most disputable matters' (ibid., 12), and monastic historians alleged he was ignorant of monastic history. He was a 'furious controversialist' whose tone was 'generally ungracious, and sometimes violent' (ibid., 236). Yet, despite his historical iconoclasm and his view of the 'Norman yoke' largely similar to that of Thomas Paine and other radicals, Leach remained within the establishment. He was an active member of the Society of Antiquaries. In recent years educational historians, while recognizing Leach's limitations and disagreeing with some of his conclusions, have acknowledged the importance of his pioneering contribution to educational history. Nicholas Orme has written that Leach 'created the modern study of the subject' (Orme, 4), and John N. Miner considers that his work on documents and his local studies 'place all modern students of the subject heavily in his debt' (Miner, 266).

Leach died at the Bolingbroke Hospital, Wandsworth, London, after an operation, on 28 September 1915. He was survived by his wife. His second son, Lieutenant G. K. Leach, had been killed at Gallipoli the previous week.

FOSTER WATSON, *rev.* ROGER T. STEARN

Sources *The Times* (29 Sept 1915) · *The Times* (1 Oct 1915) · J. N. Miner, *The grammar schools of medieval England: A. F. Leach in historiographical perspective* (1990) · *Times Educational Supplement* (5 Oct 1915) · N. Orme, *English schools in the middle ages* (1973), 3–7 · P. Gordon, *Selection for secondary education* (1980) · S. Fletcher, *Feminists and bureaucrats* (1980) · *CGPLA Eng. & Wales* (1915) · *WWW* · private information (1927)
Archives PRO, ED 27
Wealth at death £1983 1s. 1d.: probate, 30 Nov 1915, *CGPLA Eng. & Wales*

Leach, Bernard Howell (1887–1979), potter and writer, was born on 5 January 1887 in Hong Kong, the only child of Andrew John Leach (1852–1904), barrister and puisne judge, and his wife, Eleanor (known as Nellie; 1862–1887), daughter of Hamilton Sharp of Manchester, headmaster, and his wife.

Early years and education Three months after the death of his mother, who died while giving birth to Bernard, Leach was taken from Hong Kong to Japan by his maternal grandparents who were travelling to Kyoto to work as missionary teachers. About 1891 his father married a distant cousin of his mother, Jessie Sharp, a devout Catholic, and he came to Japan to take the four-year-old child back to Hong Kong and then to Singapore where Andrew Leach was appointed to the bench in 1894. While devoted to his father, Bernard Leach remembered his childhood as lonely, his only friend being his half-Irish, half-Chinese amah. Relations with his stepmother were difficult, and his father seemed distant and undemonstrative. Although

Bernard Howell Leach (1887–1979), self-portrait, 1914

there are no records of any early education Bernard discovered the joys of drawing as a child, spending hours sketching the boats in the harbour.

In 1897, at the age of ten, Leach was taken to England by a great-uncle, travelling across the United States by train, to attend Beaumont Jesuit College on the edge of Windsor Great Park, generally regarded as the 'Catholic Eton'. Again he was lonely and isolated, and formed no lasting friendships within the school, an environment he found needlessly severe. While he made little impact academically he did excel in drawing and elocution, for which he was awarded prizes, and made the first eleven at cricket, a sport he continued to enjoy throughout his life. Religious ceremony and sacred music also offered some consolation for his continuing unhappiness.

Since Leach showed no inclination for an academic career in business or law his father reluctantly agreed to allow him at the age of sixteen to enter the Slade School of Fine Art at the University of London. Under the watchful if highly critical eye of Henry Tonks, who was in charge of drawing at the Slade, Leach's graphic skills blossomed, though his ability to handle paint proved elusive. After only three terms his father was diagnosed as having advanced cancer and Leach was forced to leave the Slade and to spend the final few months with his father at his home in Bournemouth. In a desperate bid to please him, Leach made a deathbed promise to enter the Hongkong and Shanghai Bank and embark on a respectable and secure career. For a time he studied for his bank examinations in Manchester, staying with his uncle, William

Evans Hoyle, director of the Manchester Museum, his aunt Edith (his mother's sister), and their daughter his cousin Edith Muriel (1885–1955), with whom he fell in love. Her parents, however, did not approve of the relationship.

After returning to London Leach found work as a junior bank clerk intolerable. In complete despair he lost his belief and never returned to the Roman Catholic faith. Despite the promise made to his father, he resigned from the bank and at the age of twenty-one used his modest inheritance to attend the London School of Art where he came under the powerful influence of Frank Brangwyn who taught him etching. Brangwyn, who had worked for several years in William Morris's workshop, was a keen Japanophile, and may have impressed Bernard with ideas about the relationship between art and craft and with his fascination with Far Eastern culture. The return of his grandparents from Japan and the vivid images of old Japan described in the accounts of the travels of Lafcadio Hearn, rekindled childhood memories and Leach decided to move to Japan, and try to make a living by teaching etching. His love for his first cousin Muriel had never wavered and eventually family objections were overcome and they made plans to marry in Kyoto. Leach moved to Japan in 1909, and lived in Tokyo; and he and Muriel married there later the same year.

Move to Japan Much to his surprise Bernard Leach found it hard to adapt to Japanese life; tall, thin, with a mass of hair and a bushy moustache, he found the rooms were too small for his large frame and sitting cross-legged on the hard floor proved to be a trial. Despite this he had a traditional Japanese house built, although he sought to retain some Western customs by having a central well in the living room fitted with a table so he could avoid sitting cross-legged. He also designed furniture in a mixture of oriental, Western, and arts and crafts styles. Although critical of many aspects of Japanese culture, he was enthralled by the craftwork and the use of traditional techniques, but he felt that in the urge to Westernize many old and valuable customs were being lost or forgotten. His first child, David, was born in 1911, eventually followed by another boy and three girls.

Unfortunately few Japanese responded to the etching process, and far from finding himself continuing in the role of teacher Leach became a student, eager to learn about a culture that seemed so fundamentally different from anything he had encountered in the West. Through an involvement with a group of progressive young intellectuals known as the Shirekaba (White Birch), he became friends with Soetsu Yanagi who later established and became director of the Folk Art Museum or Mingei Kan. In an attempt to escape the limits of traditional Japanese life the Shirekaba investigated the spiritual aspects of Western literature, poetry, and painting, and published their ideas in a journal of the same name. Like Leach they were concerned with the impact of industrial modernization, fearing that the values of new Japan would eliminate rather than free the spirit of man. Leach's involvement with the group was largely to introduce the work of European artists and writers such as William Blake and Augustus John.

It was through the Shirekaba that Leach was introduced to the magic of pottery for the first time. Invited to a raku party, he painted a biscuit-fired pot that was then covered with glaze and fired quickly in a small portable charcoal kiln. Enraptured, Leach decided to learn the craft and found an old potter Urano Shigekichi (then living in the slum area of Tokyo) who held the title Ogata Kenzan VI, for he claimed descent from the poet, painter, and potter the first Kenzan. From Shigekichi, Leach learned the rudiments of pottery, the art of painting on pots, and the techniques of raku and high-fired stoneware and porcelain. Although the convention was to employ a skilled thrower who threw under direction, he acquired limited throwing skills working on a wheel that revolved clockwise, the opposite of Western wheels, a method that he would retain throughout his life. In 1914, prior to a move to Peking (Beijing) in China, Leach held his first one-person show of pots, paintings, fabrics, and furniture in Tokyo and published a book *A Review, 1909–1914*. This contained poems, prose pieces, his credo and his belief in the unity of East and West, as well as illustrations of pots and reproductions of etchings. This was the first of a series of books in which he propounded his personal philosophy and aesthetic concepts, most notably in *A Potter's Outlook* (1928).

In China, under the influence of the mysterious and rather sinister German Dr Westharp, Leach sought to revive aspects of traditional Chinese teaching methods following the ideas of Maria Montessori. In 1917, realizing the futility of his quest, he and his family returned to Japan, thoroughly disillusioned with the search for social, philosophical, and educational fulfilment, accepting Yanagi's advice that his true vocation was to be a potter. Encouraged by friends he set up a workshop on Yanagi's land at Abiko, Chiba Province. When this was totally destroyed by fire Viscount Koroda, a patron of the arts, came to the rescue by building a workshop and kiln for his use and supplying two skilled potters to work under his direction. For his final exhibition before returning to England, Leach published another small book with essays by Yanagi and his friend and fellow potter Kenkichi Tomimoto among others.

Return to England To enable his children to have an English education, and assuming that his work would find as enthusiastic a response as it had in Japan, Leach returned to England in 1920 bringing with him Shoji Hamada, a potter who had studied at a technical school in Tokyo. With financial help from a local philanthropist, Frances Horne, Leach set up the Leach Pottery on the outskirts of St Ives, Cornwall, building a large, oriental-type climbing kiln fired with wood, the first of its kind to be built in the West. Despite great technical problems local materials were found and they produced stoneware and porcelain that reflected oriental influence. In a smaller round kiln he fired earthenwares drawing on more Western styles, and also raku. In organizing a workshop and in the sort of pots that were produced the pottery played a pioneering role in establishing an identity for studio potters in the twentieth century.

Early exhibitions of both individual pots and tablewares in London attracted favourable reviews but limited sales, and until the standard range of tableware was introduced the pottery struggled financially. Fortunately regular shipments of pots and drawings to Japan were a continuing success and helped supplement the finances of the pottery at St Ives. Much to Leach's surprise the Japanese preferred earthenware pots with slip-trailed decoration, described by Yanagi as 'born not made', rather than the individual stoneware pieces that more closely emulated oriental wares.

Early students at the pottery included Michael Cardew, Katharine Pleydell-Bouverie, and Norah Braden, and contact with contemporary stoneware potters, who included William Staite Murray, proved useful in discussing technical and aesthetic problems. Several times the pottery teetered on the verge of bankruptcy and was eventually rescued by Leonard and Dorothy Elmhirst at Dartington who invited Leach to move the pottery to their estate in south Devon. In 1932 a combination of the breakdown of his marriage and worsening financial situation led Bernard to accept the offer and he settled in Dartington where he set up a small pottery making earthenware, while continuing to operate the Leach Pottery at St Ives. At Dartington, Bernard was introduced to the Baha'i faith by the American painter Mark Tobey and in 1940 he proclaimed himself a believer in Bahá'u'lláh, a faith that strengthened to become more central in his life. On 7 July 1944 he married Laurie Gladys Annie Cookes (1895–1976), who had worked as secretary and helper at the Leach Pottery.

In 1930 Leach's eldest son, David, joined the Leach Pottery but recognizing his own technical ignorance spent two years studying ceramics at Stoke-on-Trent, much to his father's disapproval who referred to it as 'the industrial devil'. From 1937 David Leach introduced a series of innovations that put the Leach Pottery at St Ives on a more stable footing, converting the kiln from the laborious process of firing with wood to oil, and introducing a range of repetition wheel-thrown tablewares that became known as standard ware. This was fired to high temperature with a white or black glaze on the inside only so that it contrasted pleasantly with the rich, toasted colour of the body. Leach standard ware was made by assistants like Bill Marshall, many of whom remained for many years. Production of standard ware continued until Leach's death, and was regarded by many as setting the classic standard for handmade high-fired pottery, and in time was widely emulated.

Beyond East and West In 1934 Leach returned to Japan for a fifteen-month visit where he toured country potteries and collected material for *A Potter's Book* (1940), by far his most influential text. With its blend of philosophical thoughts on 'standards' for studio pottery and sound practical advice on clay bodies, techniques, glazing, and kilns, the book became regarded as the 'potter's bible' and is still in print.

Following the Second World War Leach felt confident enough to want to talk about his ideas, successfully touring Scandinavia in 1949, the United States and Canada in 1950, 1952 (with Yanagi and Hamada), and 1961, and later Australia and New Zealand, always accompanied by exhibitions of his pots. In talks, lectures, slide and film shows he advocated the need for work that involved the 'head, hand and heart', that was anti-materialistic and that looked to but did not seek to emulate tradition. An engaging speaker, Leach quickly got the feel of his audience. His manner tended to be conversational rather than declamatory and often involved much waving of arms. He could be generous in his praise though always wary of anything that might be construed as imitative or superficial. Favourite topics in his talks and lectures were based on his personal experience such as his impressions of Japan and his early training. In the alternative society of the 1960s Leach and 'life-style' pottery had a great vogue.

Leach continued to make regular visits to Japan, often travelling round the country, making sketches of the landscape, and decorating with lively brushwork pots made to his design at country potteries. On 26 March 1956 he married his third wife, Janet Darnell (1918–1997) [see Leach, Janet], an American potter he had first met in the States, who, following David Leach's departure in 1955 to set up his own workshop, took over the running of the Leach Pottery. His pots still received a muted reception in England but in Japan exhibitions of his work sold out almost instantly; in 1967 he was awarded the order of the sacred treasure, second class, the highest accolade the country could give to a non-Japanese person. In 1974 the Japanese Foundation awarded him the equivalent of the Nobel prize for services to East–West understanding. Although there was an Arts Council retrospective exhibition 'Fifty years a potter' in the council's London gallery in 1961, he was given no further major exhibitions in the UK until 1977 when a large retrospective at the Victoria and Albert Museum finally brought the full range of his achievements to wide public acclaim. Public honours included freeman of St Ives in 1968, the appointment as a CBE in 1966 and CH in 1974. With failing sight Bernard Leach stopped making and decorating pots in 1973–4, when glaucoma was diagnosed, and he concentrated on writing. A book of his poems, *Drawings, Verse and Belief*, published in 1973, expounds the importance of his commitment to the Baha'i faith, and it was followed in 1978 by a book of memoirs *Beyond East and West: Memoirs, Portraits and Essays*, a series of autobiographical writings about his life and his views on pottery and religion. Other books included a translation of Yanagi's writings, *The Unknown Craftsman: a Japanese Insight into Beauty* (1972), a study of Hamada, *Hamada: Potter* (1975), and *Kenzan and his Tradition* (1966). Leach died on 6 May 1979 in St Ives, and was buried there in Longstone cemetery.

Reputation In his work as a potter Bernard Leach sought to unite the high-firing processes of oriental wares with a Western understanding, producing bottles, bowls, lidded boxes, and vases in stoneware or porcelain mostly thrown on the wheel. At their best the pots have a powerful sense of form enhanced with minimal decoration, many freely but surely painted or incised. Few pots over 12 inches were produced; most were smaller, so ensuring that their scale was essentially domestic. Preferred colours were muted creams, pale blues and greens, or dark intense glowing blacks and browns, intended to be objects of contemplation and quiet reflection. Some jug forms were based on medieval forms. Leach came closest to traditional English country wares in the range of large earthenware dishes in terracotta that he made in the 1920s and 1930s and again briefly in the early 1950s. Many were decorated with slip patterns, carried out with great freedom and assurance, which included the Mermaid of Zennor, reflecting Cornish folklore, while others offered powerful interpretations of Japanese landscape.

The influence of Bernard Leach, both nationally and internationally, lies in both his writing and his practice as a potter. As an author he attempted to 'set standards', whether in the quality of work made, or in discussing concepts of beauty. Pots were often imbued with human characteristics and references were made to the neck, belly, shoulder, and foot. 'The pot is the man' was an oft-repeated maxim used when seeking to assess quality. Following William Morris's ideas, Leach believed that the nature of work affected the person who made it and should be a 'joy to the maker and to the user'. Yanagi, who inclined towards Buddhism, introduced Leach to Zen Buddhist concepts and their intimate relationship with aesthetics. Leach attempted to look at the fundamental basis of the religion and how this related to the idea of beauty in pots. As a Western artist he often found the concept of rejecting self in favour of a wider and more anonymous creativity a great challenge.

For the form of his pots, Leach drew heavily on the classic bottle shapes of Korea rather than China or Japan, having seen them at first hand during visits to the country in 1918 and 1935, though always softened and muted rather than austere and sharp. He was a great initiator, more famous and influential than contemporaries such as Charles Vyse or William Staite Murray, partly because he courted publicity and partly because of the widespread success of *A Potter's Book* that combined theory and practice with personal experience. Leach saw himself as having a mission in bringing together the cultures of East and West, and to propound the value of hand as opposed to machine work. Following his death in 1979 Leach's reputation went into severe decline. After dominating the world of studio pottery for over fifty years there was a strong reaction against his oriental-inspired aesthetic of sombre tones and eastern forms in favour of more colour and a lighter mood. Leach's own pots also suffered from a series of fakes made in the early 1980s. More recently a large retrospective at the Crafts Council Gallery, London (1997) and a monograph (1999) have begun to offer a more balanced view of Leach and his undoubted position as the most influential figure of twentieth-century studio pottery.

EMMANUEL COOPER

Sources B. Leach, *Beyond east and west: memoirs, portraits and essays* (1998) · Surrey Institute of Art and Design, Farnham, Crafts Study

Centre, Leach archive · O. Watson and others, *Bernard Leach, potter and artist* (1997) [exhibition catalogue, Odakyu Museum & elsewhere, Japan, 26 Feb – 26 Oct 1997] · E. de Waal, *Bernard Leach* (1999) · *CGPLA Eng. & Wales* (1979) · *The Times* (19 Nov 1979) · *Daily Telegraph* (7 May 1979) · m. certs.

Archives Holburne Museum of Art, Bath, papers · Surrey Institute of Art and Design, Farnham, Crafts Study Centre, collection and archive | Tate collection | Aberystwyth Arts Centre/University, Craft Potters Association archive | SOUND BL NSA

Likenesses R. Kishida, oils, 1913, National Museum of Modern Art, Tokyo · B. H. Leach, self-portrait, etching, 1914, NPG [*see illus.*] · J. S. Lewinski, photograph, 1970, NPG · photographs, Leach Pottery, St Ives, Cornwall

Wealth at death £95,686: probate, 4 Oct 1979, *CGPLA Eng. & Wales*

Leach, Sir Edmund Ronald (1910–1989), social anthropologist, was born in Sidmouth, Devon, on 7 November 1910, the second son and youngest of three children of William Edmund Leach, part owner and sometime chairman of sugar plantations and a factory in northern Argentina, and his wife, Mildred Brierley. His parents were already related at the time of their wedding, being descended from closely intermarried families of Rochdale mill owners. He was educated at Marlborough College ('a foretaste of hell on earth'; Hugh-Jones and Laidlaw, 2.301) and at Clare College, Cambridge ('a glorious experience'; ibid., 1.7), where he graduated with a first in mechanical sciences in 1932.

Business, anthropology, and war On leaving Cambridge with as yet unfocused ambitions Leach followed his father in seeking opportunity overseas. A position with the trading firm Butterfield and Swire took him to China. He found he was more interested by his surroundings than by his work, and in his spare time he travelled extensively and collected jade and pottery. But when he resigned, in Peking (Beijing) in 1936, it was with no definite plan beyond travelling home overland through Russia. The outbreak of Stalin's purges delayed his visa, and an alternative plan emerged from a chance meeting at an embassy party. He agreed to join an amateur ethnographic expedition to the Yami, the aboriginal inhabitants of the island of Botel Tobego (now called Lanyü), off the coast of Taiwan.

This expedition was formative. It gave Leach his first direct experience of psychoanalysis when the expedition's leader, the American former Mormon missionary Kilton Stewart, analysed his dreams. It also led him to consider an anthropological career. Although, as he later remarked, 'I had no idea what I was up to' (Hugh-Jones and Laidlaw), he made conscientious notes of what he observed, and his engineer's training is evident in his drawings of Yami boats, houses, and technology. When he returned to England he contacted his childhood friend Rosemary Upcott, who had recently married the anthropologist Raymond Firth. As Leach wrote at the time, 'I feel that only then could the Hermit, the Wanderer, and the pseudo-Philosopher within me, find mutual satisfaction' (*DNB*). Firth introduced him to Bronisław Malinowski, and he soon joined Malinowski's now legendary seminar at the London School of Economics (LSE). He was at first an

Sir Edmund Ronald Leach (1910–1989), by David Hockney, 1971

impassioned convert to Malinowski's functionalist theory, and although he later rejected many of his first teacher's ideas he remained in general a fierce defender when anyone else presumed to attack him.

Fieldwork for a doctoral dissertation began in 1938. The chosen site, in Iraqi Kurdistan, was 'inspired by a love affair with an archaeologist' (Hugh-Jones and Laidlaw, 1.7). But the affair fell apart, and with it the projected doctoral dissertation, although Leach did write a short monograph, *Social and Economic Organisation of the Rowanduz Kurds*. By the time this was published he had a new romance and also a new research project. In London Kilton Stewart introduced him to Celia Buckmaster, a novelist and painter, and under Firth's supervision (Malinowski having departed for Yale) he was preparing for a study of domestic organization and trading networks among the Kachin of north-east Burma. War was declared just after he arrived in Burma, but he carried on to the Kachin hills area and established himself in the village of Hpalang. He also volunteered for the Burma army. It became clear that he would not be able to return to England in summer 1940 as planned. So Celia joined him, and they were married in Rangoon in February 1940. They were able to spend some time together in the hills, but in 1942, after the Japanese had arrived, Celia, nursing their infant daughter, Louisa, was evacuated. Leach remained in Burma almost continuously until 1945, and deployed his local and linguistic knowledge in recruiting for the Kachin levies behind enemy lines, and then in administering liberated areas. So in place of the anthropological fieldwork practice that was then customary of living in one local community, he travelled widely in the region (including an escape on foot to China in 1942), and saw at first hand how 'the Kachin' included peoples with very different political and social arrangements. If this war experience did not lead to military career success (he quarrelled with his superior who, at one stage, 'more or less had me court-martialled' (Kuper, 377)) it decisively influenced his anthropology.

Leach returned to London on compassionate leave in 1945, and a son, Alexander, was born the following year. Following his demobilization Leach completed his PhD in 1947. There followed a period of fieldwork in Sarawak, Firth having persuaded the Colonial Office to commission an assessment of the prospects for social research there. He then joined Firth and Audrey Richards on the teaching staff at the LSE. But he was unhappy with the 'practical anthropology' then practised in the department, and felt frustrated by what he saw as his own lack of intellectual development. He resigned and retired to his house in the country to work full time on his book. Many of his field notes had been lost during the war, but he read deeply within the historical sources on the area, as well as more widely in philosophy and other fields. His attempts to make sense of his data were influenced by the appearance in 1949 of Claude Lévi-Strauss's *Les structures élémentaires de la parenté*. Leach regarded the analysis of Kachin social structure included there, though factually mistaken, as brilliantly insightful. Aspects of Lévi-Strauss's structuralist method struck a chord with his mathematical and engineering training, and helped him build on his own earlier analyses (such as 'Jinghpaw kinship terminology', 1945). The influence is evident in his essays from this period as well as his book on the Kachin.

Political Systems of Highland Burma: a Study in Kachin Social Structure (1954) showed how the great variety of apparently separate political and cultural forms in the Kachin area—ranging from highly decentralized egalitarian polities to hierarchical centralized states—were part of a dynamic system. It differed from conventional analyses of the time in taking a large and varied cultural area rather than a single, putatively bounded society or tribe as the unit of analysis, and in showing historical change and the transformation of social and political structures to be part of the overall system. It became an instant classic, and has remained a landmark study in the discipline. It stands out for its proto-structuralist interest in the logical relations between cultural categories, its pragmatist interest in the effects on social structure of the pursuit by individuals of their perceived self-interest, and its attempt to describe, as a constitutive part of the social structure, a culturally distinctive pattern of historical change. Leach insisted that the explicit standards of good conduct in a society are necessarily ambiguous and always leave individuals room for manoeuvre; therefore ideals stated by members of a society cannot be equated with reality, or what he sometimes called the 'statistical norm'. In this, which remained a theme throughout his anthropology, he was developing lessons learned from Malinowski and Firth.

Cambridge maverick With the final text of the book submitted Leach returned to work, now as a reader, at the LSE. But almost immediately, in 1953, he took a demotion and a cut in salary to become a lecturer at Cambridge, where Meyer Fortes was head of department. If this was intended to be an institutional homecoming there was initial disappointment. He was not elected to a fellowship at his old college, Clare, nor indeed anywhere else until 1960, when he joined Fortes in the fellowship of King's. The intervening years were nevertheless productive and he was promoted reader in 1957. A sceptical interest in psychoanalysis is evident in his work from this period. There were also disagreements with his Cambridge colleagues and others, especially with regard to the study of kinship. These were most dramatically expressed when he delivered the first Malinowski memorial lecture in December 1959, later published as the title essay in his 1961 collection, *Rethinking Anthropology*. The disagreements were also pursued during another period of field research, this time in Ceylon. His 1961 monograph, *Pul Eliya—a Village in Ceylon: a Study of Land Tenure and Kinship*, made up for the deficiencies in field data that some critics had perceived in *Highland Burma*. He argued that for a society dependent on irrigated agricultural land the apparently all important rules of kinship and descent were really a cultural idiom for the expression of relations based on property ownership. The argument was stated in somewhat exaggerated terms and added to his growing reputation as an enthusiastic controversialist.

In the 1960s Leach came into his own as a teacher, writer, intellectual, and public figure. He was a gifted and dedicated teacher, and used undergraduate lectures and seminars to try out ideas for his forthcoming papers and books. He encouraged a generation of graduate students to explore new anthropological ideas in places as diverse as Africa, Amazonia, India, Ladakh, Mongolia, Panama, and Thailand. In 1960–61 he spent a year at the Center for Advanced Study in the Behavioral Sciences at Palo Alto, where he met the structural linguist Roman Jakobson, who had already influenced Lévi-Strauss. Communication theory and cybernetics were rapidly expanding and fashionable fields, and Leach was an early proponent of their relevance to anthropology, for instance in his essays on ritual. Many of these interests ran in parallel with those of Lévi-Strauss, and Leach published early expositions of the latter's ideas for anthropologists.

Throughout his career Leach was noted for the vivid directness of his writing. As structuralism became an intellectual fashion beyond anthropology he became a popular commentator and reviewer in the press. In his academic writings he became progressively more critical of Lévi-Strauss (see, for example, his *Lévi-Strauss*, 1970), and he accorded the latter an increasingly marginal position in his general expositions of structuralism (in, for example, *Culture and Communication*, 1976). He was also an enthusiastic public speaker and broadcaster, and relished explaining abstract or technical ideas to non-specialist audiences. From the late 1950s he lectured, published, and broadcast on a wide range of topics: radio broadcasts on Churchill's funeral and political violence in Ceylon; public lectures on terrorism, urban planning, and education; articles on children's books, the family, make-up, racism, sociobiology, and the wedding of the prince of Wales. He gained notoriety as a progressive don when he delivered the BBC Reith lectures in 1967 under the title 'A runaway world?'. The public controversy these lectures caused was mostly provoked by his saying in passing that older people in positions of power were often behind the times, and that families are often not the supportive environments they are generally cried up as being. The main theme, however, was that in a world of very rapid technological change we need consciously to create new moral values and rules of behaviour to deal with new social realities.

Leach was elected provost of King's in 1966 and was an effective chairman and a genial and gregarious administrator, though he could be irascible when frustrated or crossed. His personal ambivalence about formality and ceremony, and his sense of the mood of the times, led to the 'modernization' of a number of college rituals, but student radicals who listened to his Reith lectures were surprised by his evident impatience with some of their methods and aims. Nevertheless he steered the college through a number of changes which he regarded as desirable and necessary. Student members were added to the council and governing body, and membership of the college was opened to women. The latter was felt to be a momentous change at the time, and was co-ordinated with Clare and Churchill, so that these three formerly all male colleges became, simultaneously, the first in Cambridge to make the change. Leach was proud that in King's the governing body eventually approved the vote overwhelmingly. He later exaggerated this in his memory to a vote *nem. con.*, and commented that 'if I had not already begun to acquire the reputation of being much more conservative than my erratic predecessor, I doubt if we would have made it at all' (Kuper, 382). His provostship in many ways exemplified the description he gave of his character back in the 1930s: he was, he said, 'Rebel and High Tory' at the same time (Hugh-Jones, 6).

Honours, religion, final years Leach remained in Cambridge and at King's for the rest of his life, and steadily accumulated honours and distinctions. The American Academy of Arts and Sciences elected him foreign honorary member in 1968. A personal professorship at Cambridge and election to the British Academy in 1972 were followed by a knighthood in 1975. He laughed off complaints from radicals among colleagues and family when he accepted the knighthood, and wrote an entertaining anthropological analysis of the ceremony, which he gave repeatedly as a public lecture, comparing it to a pig sacrifice he had witnessed in Sarawak in 1947. He was active in the Royal Anthropological Institute, serving as its president from 1971 to 1974 and helping to steer it through difficult times. He set up and funded its Esperanza Trust for Anthropological Research, using money inherited from the sale of La Esperanza, a sugar factory in Argentina. He also served as trustee of the British Museum and president of the Humanist Association.

A declared atheist Leach's upbringing was 'hard-boiled Christian', his mother, to whom he was close as a child,

being a devout Anglican (Firth, 10). His rejection of Christianity while an undergraduate was bound up with his growing independence from her, but as he later remarked, 'mud sticks if you throw enough' (ibid.). He spent much of his working life studying religion and increasingly in the latter half of his career his interest was absorbed by the Bible and Christian iconography. Partly this was to do with his insistence that anthropology is not just about exotic or 'primitive' societies but has important things to say about the human condition in general and about how 'we' live and think. So he applied structuralist analysis to Western cultural artefacts such as the Sistine Chapel paintings, the windows of King's College Chapel and, especially and increasingly in later years, the Bible (*Genesis as Myth*, 1969; *Structuralist Interpretations of Biblical Myth*, 1983). But these were not just any Western cultural artefacts. Myth and religious thought is preoccupied, he believed, 'with the ambiguous borderline between what is animal and what is human, what is natural and what is cultural' and his own anthropology was a sustained and wide-ranging engagement with just these questions (Hugh-Jones and Laidlaw, 1.316). In his work on classification and taboo he drew on psychoanalysis as well as structuralism to help address them. And he maintained an informed interest in the biological sciences, and watched with interest the development of sociobiology. As provost he sponsored a conference for the fledgeling discipline in King's, though he was a fiercely hostile critic of what he regarded as popularizing abuses of the ideas, and published coruscating reviews of offending books in the most prominent places he could find. But he was equally critical of the bland insistence on cultural relativism that was common in American anthropology.

Leach combined these concerns about the big questions of anthropology with an insatiable interest in ethnographic detail, and had an unsurpassed knowledge in particular of Malinowski's works on the Trobriand Islands. Several of his best essays turned on re-analyses of Malinowski's ethnography. Towards the end of his life, as his own powers were failing, he encouraged a new generation of scholars to undertake fresh research in the region, and he co-edited a volume on their work (*The Kula*, 1983). His idea of appropriate homage to his teacher was to challenge his ideas, and his own students report that he was never more critical and challenging than when they thought they were agreeing with him. So it is unsurprising that he left no Leachian school of anthropology, although it is probably true that his teaching and encouragement of junior colleagues were almost as influential as his published works on what was still a young discipline.

Leach retired from his university professorship in 1978 and from the provostship of King's in 1979, though he remained active as a fellow and elder statesman. In his last years he suffered first from disfiguring skin cancer on the head and then from an inoperable brain tumour, which caused neurological problems and impaired his communication. He died in a hospice in Cambridge on 6 January 1989, and his funeral was held in King's College Chapel.

JAMES LAIDLAW

Sources S. Hugh-Jones and J. Laidlaw, eds., *The essential Edmund Leach* (2000) · S. Hugh-Jones, *Edmund Leach* (privately printed for King's College, Cambridge, 1989) · C. Fuller and J. Parry, 'Petulant inconsistency?', *Anthropology Today* (5 March 1989) · *Edmund Leach: a bibliography*, Royal Anthropological Institute occasional papers, no. 42 (1990) · A. Kuper, 'An interview with Edmund Leach', *Current Anthropology*, 27 (1986) · R. Firth, 'A Cambridge undergraduate', *Cambridge Anthropology*, 13 (1990) · *DNB*

Archives King's AC Cam., corresp. and papers; further papers | BLPES, corresp. with B. Z. Seligman · CUL, corresp. with Meyer Fortes

Likenesses D. Hockney, drawing, 1971, King's Cam. [*see illus.*] · photographs, Royal Anthropological Institute, London

Wealth at death £315,174: probate, 8 May 1989, *CGPLA Eng. & Wales*

Leach, Henry (1836–1879), physician, was born at Wisbech, Cambridgeshire, into 'a family long known and esteemed in that borough' (Cook, 133). He was educated at St Albans School and became a pupil of Dr Thomas Walker, a Peterborough medical practitioner. In 1853 he entered St Bartholomew's Hospital medical school in London, and qualified MRCS LSA five years later. For a brief time he was a house surgeon at the Peterborough Infirmary; he then undertook voyages to India and back. In 1862 he was appointed resident physician to the Seamen's Hospital Society (SHS) at Greenwich; most of his professional career was spent on the *Dreadnought* hospital ship (the third consecutive hulk anchored on the River Thames off Greenwich) and, after 1870, the land-based Dreadnought (Seamen's) Hospital, part of the Royal Naval Hospital, Greenwich. When his colleague Henry T. L. Rooke died in September 1870, Leach was appointed chief medical officer to the *Dreadnought*. However, some three years later he resigned from the SHS and on 24 July 1873 was appointed first port medical officer for the City of London; in that capacity he occupied an office in the foreign cattle market at Deptford. Also in 1873 he qualified MRCP. In 1876 his association with the SHS was renewed and he was appointed visiting physician to this institution. Another appointment was as medical inspector of the Turkish railways.

Leach achieved an enormous amount for the health of the mercantile marine, upon which Britain was heavily dependent throughout his lifetime. In 1867 he wrote (anonymously) five articles in the *British Medical Journal* entitled: 'Report on the hygienic condition of the Mercantile Marine, and on the preventable diseases of merchant seamen'. This series was based largely on Leach's personal experience at the SHS, and was published in book format later in the same year. In it Leach dealt with health problems associated with ocean-going ships, coasters, barges, and training ships, and also the sanitary control of the Port of London; for example, he considered that all ships arriving in the Thames should be fully inspected. The timing of this publication was admirable, because there was at that time much public (and parliamentary) concern about the appalling health conditions in the merchant navy; in fact mercantile marine reform was a dominant theme in Queen Victoria's speech at the opening of parliament in 1867. Later, the *British Medical Journal* considered that Leach had 'been the means of conferring an inestimable boon upon the mercantile marine' (*BMJ*).

Arguably of even greater importance was Leach's campaign against scurvy. Mindful of his experience of treating the disease at the SHS, he contributed a series of eight letters to the editor of *The Times* on this topic; this began with a reply to an anonymous leading article in that newspaper for 10 January 1866. Very importantly, Leach stressed the importance of adulterated lime juice in the causation of the disease, and advocated lime juice inspection by an authorized officer (which he was subsequently to become). He also insisted that there should be a full official inquiry into every case of scurvy occurring on board ship. Largely as a result of his efforts, the Merchant Shipping Act of 1854 was amended in 1867; as a result, some three years later, the number of scorbutic cases on the *Dreadnought* hospital ship was reduced by 84 per cent of its former total. Leach's obituary in the *Medical Press and Circular* later summarized his contribution to scurvy control in the merchant navy: '[Leach] did excellent service in directing attention to the prevalence of scurvy among sailors, and his untiring efforts resulted in such amendment of the Merchant Shipping Act [of 1867] as has been followed by the most beneficial results' (Cook, 135).

Leach also undertook (under the auspices of the SHS) exacting duties during an anticipated cholera epidemic of 1866; he took charge of the *Belle Isle* (a ship reserved for cholera cases), and organized with his colleague (Rooke) an extensive ship-to-ship visitation on the River Thames. For a period of three months, every vessel between London Bridge and Woolwich was visited daily. Owing to a growing suspicion that the last of the hospital ships was far from sanitary (in the light of Florence Nightingale's experiences at Scutari during the Crimean War in 1854–6) moves were made to shift the clinical facilities to dry land; Leach and his colleagues were in favour of the transfer, which took place on 13 April 1870, to the infirmary of the Royal Naval Hospital.

As first port medical officer for the City of London, Leach was able to deploy his unique experience with the SHS to the full. His efforts prevented a threatened epidemic of cholera (he was a strong believer in the efficacy of quarantine) and he was fully aware of the serious pollution of the docks and River Thames by sewage and industrial effluent. He also dealt with outbreaks among the seafarers of scarlatina (scarlet fever), smallpox, and typhoid, and fears at that time of the import of yellow fever and plague never materialized.

Leach was a prolific author; his *Ship Captain's Medical Guide* (1868) went to seven editions during his life and, in modified form, remains in use to this day. Other books were *Brief Notes on the Last Epidemic of Cholera in Turkey* (1866), *Pocket Doctor for the Traveller and Colonist* (1875), and *A Bit of Bulgaria* (1877).

In 1875 Leach had a haemoptysis which heralded pulmonary phthisis (tuberculosis). He then made two voyages with his wife, Susannah Elizabeth, to South Africa—generally considered to be beneficial to tuberculosis sufferers—but the course of his disease was progressive and relentless. In the early phase of his illness he consulted Dr Wilson Fox, and throughout the latter days he was cared for by his brother Mathew Leach, Dr James Andrew, and Dr Stephen Ward (a former colleague from his SHS days). Leach died on 26 November 1879 at his home, 12 Albert Mansions, Victoria Street, Westminster, London, and was buried at Norwood cemetery. He was survived by his wife.

A man of boundless energy, Leach was described by one obituarist as 'the most genial of companions, hospitable, kindly, considerate, and possessed of the happy faculty of adapting himself in personal intercourse to every variety of social and mental demand' (Cook, 138).

G. C. COOK

Sources *BMJ* (29 Nov 1879), 870 · *ILN* (6 Dec 1879), 539 · *The Lancet*, 2 (1879), 842, 855–6 · G. C. Cook, 'Harry Leach MRCP (1836–1879): control of scurvy in the British mercantile marine, and first port medical officer for the City of London', *Journal of Medical Biography*, 8 (2000), 133–9 · W. G. Swann, 'The work of Dr H. Leach, the first M.O.H. of the port', *London Port Health Authority Centenary* (28 June 1972), 9 · *CGPLA Eng. & Wales* (1879)

Wealth at death under £3000: probate, 24 Dec 1879, *CGPLA Eng. & Wales*

Leach, James (*bap.* 1761, *d.* 1798), composer, was stated to have been born at Wardle, near Rochdale, in 1762. Circumstantial evidence, however, suggests that he was probably the son of James Leach and Betty Clegg of Townhead, Rochdale, and that he was baptized there on 25 December 1761. He was a handloom weaver like his father, and studied music in his spare time before teaching and directing choirs professionally. Earlier biographers, beginning with Hirst, also state that he sang countertenor at a Westminster Abbey musical festival and was an instrumentalist in the king's band, though no supporting evidence now exists. It seems likely that Leach married Esther Grindrod on 7 August 1786, and they moved to Salford about 1795. He was killed on 8 February 1798 when the Leeds to Manchester stagecoach overturned at Blackley, near Manchester, and was buried at Union Street Wesleyan Chapel, Rochdale, where his headstone was engraved with his tune 'Egypt'. When this became illegible a new monument was erected in July 1904.

Although nearly forgotten today, Leach was one of the most famous eighteenth-century composers of nonconformist church music. He published *A New Sett of Hymns and Psalm Tunes* (1789), containing twenty-two hymn tunes and two set pieces (metrical anthems), with instrumental accompaniment, and *A Second Sett of Hymns and Psalm Tunes* (1794?), containing forty-eight tunes and three set pieces. A second edition of the first set was produced during his lifetime, and after his death a committee was formed to republish his music for the benefit of his widow and four young children. New editions of both sets were printed from the original plates, without the prefaces, and a notice was added to the *Second Sett* asking for subscribers to a volume of Leach's previously unpublished compositions, to be issued in periodical numbers: *A Collection of Hymn Tunes and Anthems* (1798–) contains eight hymn tunes, five anthems, seventeen set pieces, and one secular song. It has been suggested that Leach also composed

string trios, but this is probably a reference to *Six Sonatas* (*c.*1775) by the unrelated Samuel Leach.

Leach's music was condemned in the *Dictionary of National Biography* for its 'erratic rhythmic form', but according to a more recent critic he produced some of the best examples of the elaborate Methodist style 'frankly based on the livelier secular and operatic music of the time' (Temperley). It was reprinted in many nineteenth-century psalmody books, especially in America: *David's Companion, or, The Methodist Standard* by James Evans (1810) includes forty-eight of his tunes. In 1884 his work was still sufficiently popular for all of his hymn tunes, edited by James Butterworth, to be reissued, with a sketch of his life by Thomas Newbigging. Butterworth had no qualms about improving the harmony despite the preface to the *Second Sett*, in which Leach remarked that anyone who altered another's compositions should be made to wear a hat labelled 'Assassin'.

SALLY DRAGE

Sources J. Leach, *A new sett of hymns and psalm tunes* (1789) · J. Leach, *A second sett of hymns and psalm tunes* (1794?) · J. Leach, *A collection of hymn tunes and anthems* [1798] · T. Newbigging, *James Leach, the Lancashire composer* (1884) · J. Butterworth, ed., *Psalmody by James Leach* (1884) · T. Hirst, *The music of the church* (1841) · N. Temperley, 'Leach, James', *New Grove* · J. T. Clegg, 'Th' owd weighver "James Leach"', *Sketches and rhymes in the Rochdale dialect* (1895) · *DNB* · J. T. Lightwood, *Hymn-tunes and their story* (1905) · G. A. C., 'James Leach of Rochdale', *MT*, 19 (1878), 226–7 [letter] · Brown & Stratton, *Brit. mus.* · records, St Chad's, Rochdale

Wealth at death seemingly very little as committee formed after death to republish his music and support wife and children

Leach, James (*c.*1806–1869), Chartist, was born in Wigan, Lancashire. His family origins and early years are entirely unknown, although it may be that he was an Anglican and that he had worked as a hand-loom weaver. He moved to Manchester in 1826; and in 1839, when he led the resistance to a cut in wages, he was sacked as a power-loom weaver after twelve years in the same employment. According to Friedrich Engels, however, who described him as 'my good friend', Leach had 'worked in various branches of industry both in factories and coalmines' (Engels, 151–2, 342).

Leach was to claim in 1851 that he had been politically active for twenty years. By 1836 he was chairing meetings of the Manchester Radical Association, in 1838 he was elected to the council of the Manchester Political Union, and during the following year he began to represent Manchester at regional Chartist meetings. Given this local radical prominence, it made excellent sense for him, on losing his job, to set up as a bookseller and printer in Oak Street, Manchester. It was at this time, however, that his Chartist career moved on to the national level. In July 1840 he chaired the delegate conference in Manchester at which the key organization of Chartism, the National Charter Association, was established. He was subsequently appointed provisional president and in both 1841 and 1842 came second only to Peter Murray M'Douall in the national elections to the executive. He sat as a delegate in the 1842 convention, of which he acted as vice-chairman.

According to Gammage, the Chartist activist and historian, Leach

> never attempted to play the orator. In addressing a public meeting he was just as free and easy as in a private conversation; but for fact and argument there were but few of the speakers at that period who excelled him. (Gammage, 211)

His reputation was as a 'terror, not only to the cotton lords, but every other humbug' (Pickering, 199). To O'Connor he was a 'plain blunt man' (ibid.); and Engels considered him 'upright, trustworthy and capable' (Engels, 152) and drew extensively upon his 84-page pamphlet *Stubborn Facts from the Factories by a Manchester Operative* (1844) in *The Condition of the Working Class in England*.

Leach played a prominent part in bringing Chartism and the trade unions together, notably in support for the general strike movement of August 1842, and was one of the fifty-nine defendants in the mass trial at Lancaster in March 1843, although, like the others found guilty of conspiracy, he was not sentenced. He continued as a leading Chartist throughout the 1840s, but was also active in the co-operative movement (while not an Owenite) and in the agitation for a ten-hour limit on the working day. It had been in a series of open letters to Leach that O'Connor had, during his imprisonment of 1840–41, begun to develop his ideas about the centrality of land ownership to the emancipation of the working class, and in due course Leach too became an enthusiastic advocate of the Chartist Land Company, serving from 1845 as one of seven trustees. In 1848 he was a member of both the national convention of April and the national assembly of May, and the latter appointed him to the militant provisional executive. A committed supporter of collaboration between English Chartists and Irish confederates, he had represented the Chartists in Dublin on 12 January at the first meeting between the two movements. From July 1848 he was printer, publisher, and co-editor of the *English Patriot and Irish Repealer*, which was terminated by his prosecution in December on another charge of conspiracy, for which he was sentenced to nine months' imprisonment in Kirkdale gaol.

After his release, from late 1851 Leach came to favour an alliance with the middle-class radicals, a startling volteface for one who had displayed unremitting personal and ideological hostility towards the Anti-Corn Law League. This phase was short-lived as he soon retired from politics and returned to the obscurity from which Chartism had lifted him. His wife, Hannah, who died on 17 August 1865, may have been the Hannah Hurst who married a James Leach in Burnley, Lancashire, on 4 September 1826. It is known that they had five children, of whom the first son was named Alexander. Leach gave up his printing and bookselling business to manufacture soft drinks, and on his death at Eagle Street, Hulme, Manchester, on 4 July 1869 his occupation was given as ginger beer maker.

DAVID GOODWAY

Sources P. A. Pickering, *Chartism and the chartists in Manchester and Salford* (1995) • E. Frow, R. Frow, and J. Saville, 'Leach, James', *DLB*, vol. 9 • F. Engels, *The condition of the working class in England*, ed. and trans. W. O. Henderson and W. H. Chaloner, 2nd edn (1971) • R. G. Gammage, *History of the Chartist movement, 1837–1854*, new edn (1894) • J. West, *A history of the Chartist movement* (1920) • D. Goodway, *London Chartism, 1838–1848* (1982) • S. Roberts, *Radical politicians and poets in early Victorian Britain: the voices of six chartist leaders* (1993) • IGI • private information (2004) [P. P. Pickering]

Leach, Janet Darnell (1918–1997), potter, was born on 15 March 1918 in Grand Saline, Texas, USA, the only child of Charles Walter Darnell, a salesman. She inherited much of her gritty, pioneering spirit from her ancestors, of part-Spanish descent, who had travelled to Texas by horse and wagon. Showing an early aptitude for art, especially sculpture, as a child she carved wood and stone with a pocket knife. Determined to become an artist, she arrived in New York at the age of eighteen, speaking with an accent so broad she felt almost as much a foreigner as she was to do later when living in Japan. After working with the sculptor Robert Cronbach she became involved in the Federal Works Art Project. Following the entry of the United States into the war in 1941 she became a skilled welder in a shipyard, a job traditionally carried out by men, and rode an ex-army 32cc motorcycle she named Dude. Two unsuccessful marriages were short-lived, one to Joseph Turino (Joe), a fellow shipyard worker. Politically aware and strongly anti-fascist, for a time she supported the communist cause but like many others she was disillusioned by the 1939 Nazi–Soviet pact.

Janet was introduced to clay in the late 1940s at the Inwood Pottery run by two elderly sisters, and found her ideal medium. Largely self-taught and feeling dissatisfied with her pots, she came into contact with a more oriental approach to potting through the ideas of Bernard *Leach (1887–1979) in his 1940 groundbreaking technical and philosophical text *A Potter's Book*, and a lecture he gave in New York in 1950; both made a tremendous impact on her thinking. In Spring valley, 25 miles from New York, she became involved with a community of Rudolph Steiner followers that had established an experiment in group living, which emphasized creative intuition, myth, and the balance of creative powers. At Threefold Farm she built a house and pottery workshop, embracing the threefold concept of anthroposophy, which can be interpreted as head, heart, and hand, and thereafter used a seal on her pots in the shape of a triangle.

A major turning point came at a workshop at Black Mountain College, North Carolina, in 1952 where she encountered at first hand Eastern ideas from Bernard Leach, the Japanese potter Shoji Hamada, and the writer and critic Soetsu Yanagi. Although attending in order to meet Leach, her attention was riveted by watching Hamada sitting cross-legged on a table making pots while someone else turned the wheel. Working with soft clay and a relatively slow wheel speed, he seemed to create his pots organically, patting and squeezing the clay with almost childlike ease. The forms had a sense of growth that she found lacking in her own, more mechanical work. In the evenings she talked to the visitors about Japan, discovering that Leach had not only learned the craft there but was regarded as one of their finest potters. In search of a harmony of living and working, she moved in 1954 to Japan, where she stayed with a traditional pottery family in the village of Tamba, in the central mountains. Here she absorbed the mysteries of clays and firing, learning how to retain the natural qualities of the material. With Bernard Leach, then on an extended visit to Japan, she travelled around the country, typing the manuscript for his book *A Potter in Japan*, meeting potters, and seeing traditional potteries.

Their friendship deepened and they agreed to marry, planning to remain in Japan. Marrying the most important and influential studio potter of the twentieth century, who was over thirty years her senior, proved difficult, as they soon discovered. Yanagi and others disapproved, and reluctantly they decided to live in St Ives, Cornwall, and travel to Japan as visitors. Following their marriage in 1956 Janet took over the management of the Leach Pottery from David Leach, Bernard's eldest son, but as a foreigner and without any experience of working with a team of potters she was viewed with suspicion. Yet in addition to successfully running the pottery and overseeing the production of the Leach standard range of tablewares, she made her own pots, agreeing under pressure from Bernard Leach to take the family name. While Janet's manner could be intimidating, she also inspired deep devotion in both men and women. The marriage was never easy but both loved Japan and they enjoyed their frequent visits, Janet mounting several highly successful exhibitions of her pots. With Bernard Leach's death in 1979 production of Leach standard ware ended, and Janet continued to share the pottery with Trevor Corser, a former apprentice, until her death at St Ives on 12 September 1997. She was buried in St Ives.

Although Bernard Leach initially hoped that Janet would be inspired by his work, she was resolute in following her own ideas, and he acknowledged that her pots showed no direct influence from him. Nevertheless he was surprised and pleased when the Japanese saw her ceramics as an important part of the modern movement in calling on traditional work but interpreting it in a modern idiom. Her freely rendered thrown and hand-built pots, often irregular in shape, incorporate the texture of clay, embodying many characteristics of traditional Tamba and Bizen wares, some making use of Japanese forms associated with the tea ceremony. She developed a highly distinctive, relaxed style that allowed the soft, plastic qualities of clay to be paramount. Surfaces are often covered with rich runny ash-type glazes, and a range of black pots are enlivened with a dramatic white slash that animates and defines their form. In their strength and clarity her pots carry an unmistakable style, combining both austerity and sensuality.

Janet Leach was a major post-war potter who, although married to an eminent potter, evolved her own methods of making or decorating. In addition to her commitment to the Leach Pottery at St Ives she established an international reputation in the 1970s and 1980s for powerful, often monumental pots that reflect the strength and determination of her character. Important pieces are in the Victoria and Albert Museum in the Crafts Council collection, London. Exhibitions in London at major venues such as the British Crafts Centre, Craft Potters' Shop, Primavera, Marjorie Parr Gallery, and Anshels Gallery were complemented by ten important one-woman shows in Japan.

EMMANUEL COOPER

Sources personal knowledge (2004) · J. P. Hodin, 'Janet Darnell Leach', *Pottery Quarterly*, 9 (1967), 7–13 · 'Janet Leach: American foreigner', *Studio Potter* [USA], 11 (1983), 76–93 · E. Cooper, 'Janet Leach: sculptural potter', *Ceramic Review*, 120 (1989), 8–11 · *CGPLA Eng. & Wales* (1998)
Likenesses photograph, 1955, repro. in *The Independent* (13 Sept 1997) · H. Schneebeli, photograph, repro. in *The Guardian* (18 Sept 1997) · photograph, repro. in *The Times* (17 Sept 1997)
Wealth at death £788,569: probate, 1 July 1998, *CGPLA Eng. & Wales*

Leach, Sir John (1760–1834), politician and lawyer, was born on 28 August 1760 in Bedford, the second son of Richard Leach, a coppersmith there, and his wife, Frances *née* Green. After studying at Bedford grammar school, Leach became a pupil of the architect Sir Robert Taylor. Encouraged by his friend Samuel Pepys Cockerell, he opted for a career in law. He was admitted to the Middle Temple on 26 January 1785, and became the pupil of the equity draftsman William (later Baron) Alexander. After being called to the bar on 12 February 1790, he practised on the home circuit and at the Surrey sessions, building up a considerable practice over ten years, before giving up common law for equity in 1800.

Leach's first important case came in 1792, when he was counsel for the ministerial sitting members of parliament for Seaford when a bid was made to unseat them on petition. He settled in Seaford, becoming recorder in 1795, and sought to use it as a base for his political career. He unsuccessfully contested the borough in 1796, but a combination of political intrigue and purchase of property enabled him to be returned as its member of parliament in 1806, and to control the borough by 1807. Leach was a whig in politics, having been introduced early in his career to Fox and Sheridan. His support for the 'ministry of all the talents' was rewarded with the silk gown of a king's counsel in 1807, conferred thanks to the recommendation of Grenville. In the Commons, where he was not a frequent speaker, he made a name for himself in 1809 with a powerful defence of the duke of York in the debate on Colonel Wardle's motion. The duke was so impressed that he begged Leach's acquaintance the following day, and introduced him to the prince of Wales. Leach also distinguished himself in the Regency debates in 1810, when he argued that it was both inexpedient and unconstitutional to restrict the powers of the regent.

As his relations with the prince became closer, so those with his own party became weaker. Though loyalty to the whigs led him in 1813 to decline the offer of the solicitor-generalship, in February 1816 he accepted the post of chancellor of the duchy of Cornwall. While his whig friends sensed a betrayal, he said that he regarded it as a personal office which need not interfere with his political conduct. However, at the same time, he gave up his seat in parliament, and brought in Sir Charles Cockerell, a supporter of the ministry, in his place. He apparently sold his interest in Seaford by 1823.

As the prince regent's first legal officer, Leach was asked in the autumn of 1817 to look at all the information which had been received concerning the conduct of the princess of Wales. He recommended that a public commission be sent to Italy, to collect more evidence. The more cautious Liverpool agreed to fund an informal commission, without giving any pledge to act on its findings. The evidence collected by the three members of the Milan commission chosen by Leach formed the backbone of the case against Caroline in the bill of pains and penalties against her in 1820, when Leach urged the new king to insist on a divorce. Facing a government keen to avoid a confrontation, Leach sounded out moderate whigs to see if they would take office while securing the divorce, while telling the king that his ministers were not standing by him. Liverpool, for his part, told the king that both the king and the government had been 'grossly deceived' by Leach (*Letters of George IV*, 2.361). As a result of the proceedings against the queen, Leach attracted much opprobrium, 'the leech' appearing in Shelley's *Oedipus tyrannus*, as well as in a host of caricatures and prints. At the hearings in parliament he was damned by Thomas Denman's quotation from *Othello* that the slander against the queen must have been devised by 'some cogging, cozening slave, to get some office' (W. Shakespeare, *Othello*, IV.ii).

Leach had indeed a burning ambition to become lord chancellor, but he never fulfilled it. His name was mentioned as a possible candidate in 1819 and 1826, and as late as 1830 he felt 'exceedingly disappointed' (*Greville Memoirs*, 2.70) to be overlooked in favour of Brougham. However, he never commanded sufficient political support to be a strong candidate, while the king's backing wavered. Similarly, he coveted a peerage, but never obtained one. He was knighted on 17 January 1818, on his appointment as vice-chancellor of England, having in the previous year been made chief justice of Chester. There was an irony in the former appointment, for Leach had been one of the strongest parliamentary opponents in 1813 of the measure creating the vice-chancellorship, which he argued would diminish the higher office. In April 1827 he declined the post of lord chancellor of Ireland, becoming master of the rolls in England the following month, after William Conyngham Plunket had reluctantly refused it in face of loud protests from the English bar at the promotion of an Irishman. At the same time he turned down Canning's offer of a seat in the Commons. Leach's name had been mentioned as early as 1823 as a possible assistant to the lord chancellor in reducing the backlog of appeals cases in the Lords, but his promotion was strongly resisted by Liverpool, and by Eldon, who despised him. However, in May 1827 he was made a deputy speaker of the House of Lords, to assist with Scottish appeals.

Leach was a member of the chancery commission appointed in 1824. In the absence of Eldon, he exercised a considerable influence over the commission, both by regularly chairing the meetings of the commissioners and by bringing before them a plan of largely minor reforms (agreed with Eldon), which formed the basis of much of the discussion. In fact he was not an enthusiastic reformer, opposing Lyndhurst's plans for a fourth equity judge in 1830, and telling Lord Chancellor Brougham in 1831 that 'the delays of the Court of Chancery have been the result not of the constitution of the Court but of the constitution of the Judge' (Brougham MSS, UCL, MS 6015). He also opposed the setting up of the judicial committee of the privy council, though the statute creating it made him an *ex officio* member.

In court, Leach's style was the opposite of Eldon's. Where Eldon was the master of the broad principles of equity, Leach was (in Romilly's view) 'extremely deficient in knowledge as a lawyer', while in judgment he was 'more deficient than any man possessed of so clear an understanding that I ever met with' (*Memoirs of … Romilly*, 3.216). What he lacked in finesse he made up in speed, and in an age where the chancery was fabled for its chronic delays, many eminent counsel, such as John Bell, chose to confine their practice to his court. However, it was felt that Leach's haste was excessive. Lawyers soon began to quip that suitors in equity had a choice between Eldon's court of 'oyer sans terminer' and Leach's court of 'terminer sans oyer'. In fact, Leach's success in clearing his cause paper was derived from his practice of constantly referring cases to the masters or to a jury. He thereby managed progressively to reduce the arrears in his court, at least until he fell ill in 1826, but without actually settling cases, or assisting the suitor. At the same time, the lack of confidence that was widely felt in his legal learning led to many cases being appealed to the lord chancellor.

Leach's courtroom manner was intemperate and dictatorial, which made him very unpopular among his own profession. Once he had made up his mind on a case, he was impatient of arguments to the contrary, and as a result he was prone to argue with counsel in a way considered unbecoming in a judge. This became so obnoxious to the senior barristers in his court that a deputation of them presented him with a formal remonstrance on his behaviour towards them. However, after he became master of the rolls his manner softened, and relations with the bar improved. In 1829 he changed the sittings of the court, so that the rolls would sit in the mornings instead of the evenings.

In private life Leach aspired to be a man of fashion. Spurning the company of lawyers, he would hurry from his court to be seen at the theatre or in the salons of fashionable aristocratic society. Seeking to be an elegant host, with a cellar stocked with fine wines and a French chef ready to serve the finest cuisine, he felt snubbed when Eldon once requested simple liver and bacon. His pride in his aristocratic intimacies was sometimes felt to be presumptuous; his manner of speaking, which to some sounded like a man singing out of tune, was regarded as affected. Leach, who had never married, died at Simpson's

Hotel, Edinburgh, on 14 September 1834, while on his way from a visit to the duchess of Sutherland. He was buried in Greyfriars churchyard, Edinburgh, on 22 September.

MICHAEL LOBBAN

Sources B. Murphy and D. R. Fisher, 'John Leach', HoP, *Commons, 1790–1820* · B. Murphy and D. R. Fisher, 'Seaford', HoP, *Commons, 1790–1820*, 2.475–80 · Foss, *Judges*, 9.92–5 · 'Judicial characters, no. XIV: Sir John Leach', *Legal Observer*, 8 (1834), 449–52 · 'The judicial character of Sir John Leach', *Law Magazine*, 12 (1834), 427–34 · S. Romilly, *Memoirs of the life of Sir Samuel Romilly*, 3 vols. (1840) · J. Campbell, *Lives of the lord chancellors*, 8 vols. (1845–69), vols. 5–8 · *The letters of King George IV, 1812–1830*, ed. A. Aspinall, 3 vols. (1938) · *The later correspondence of George III*, ed. A. Aspinall, 5 vols. (1962–70), vol. 5 · A. Aspinall, ed., *The formation of Canning's ministry, February to August 1827*, CS, 3rd ser., 59 (1937) · A. Mitchell, *The whigs in opposition, 1815–30* (1967) · *The correspondence of Charles Arbuthnot*, ed. A. Aspinall, CS, 3rd ser., 65 (1941), 57 · *The manuscripts of J. B. Fortescue*, 10 vols., HMC, 30 (1892–1927), vol. 10, p. 444 · *The Greville memoirs, 1814–1860*, ed. L. Strachey and R. Fulford, 8 vols. (1938), vol. 2 · *GM*, 2nd ser., 2 (1834), 647–50 · PRO, PROB 11/1837, fol. 231 · H. A. C. Sturgess, ed., *Register of admissions to the Honourable Society of the Middle Temple, from the fifteenth century to the year 1944*, 2 (1949), 398
Archives BL, corresp. with second earl of Liverpool, Add. MSS 38281–38288, 38565 · UCL, Brougham MSS
Likenesses caricatures, *c.*1820, repro. in F. G. Stephens and M. D. George, *Catalogue of prints and drawings in the British Museum*, 11 vols. (1870–1954) · T. Wright, stipple, pubd 1821 (after A. Wivell), BM, NPG · H. Dawe, mezzotint, pubd 1825 (after C. Penny), BM, NPG · G. R. Lewis, watercolour stipple drawing, BM
Wealth at death quite substantial; £7000 p.a. salary · £5000 legacy to niece; property in trust for brother: will, PRO, PROB 11/1837, fol. 231 · not said to have died rich: *GM*

Leach, Thomas (1746–1818), barrister and legal writer, was the eldest son of Stephen Leach of Rochdale, Lancashire. He was called to the bar from the Middle Temple on 25 June 1784. In 1790 he was appointed police magistrate at Hatton Garden, London, and was also chairman of the county court of requests in Fulwood's Rents, Holborn. An able lawyer, his career was undermined by ill health, and he sent in his resignation in November 1818.

In 1791, in advance of the bill by Charles James Fox advocating amendments, Leach published a treatise on the law of libel. He also produced a number of editions of reports of pioneering legal cases heard in the courts of king's bench, chancery, common pleas, and exchequer, from the restoration of Charles II down to the reign of George II. These included *Modern Reports*, which ran to twelve volumes (1793–6). He also produced editions of reports of cases made by Sir Bartholomew Shower and William Hawkins. For some years he served as editor of the *Whitehall Evening Post*. On 30 December 1818 Leach was taken seriously ill while returning by coach to his home in Muswell Hill; he died at the Kentish Town assembly rooms the following day.

GORDON GOODWIN, rev. ROBERT BROWN

Sources J. Hutchinson, ed., *A catalogue of notable Middle Templars: with brief biographical notices* (1902) · *GM*, 1st ser., 88/2 (1818), 647 · [J. Watkins and F. Shoberl], *A biographical dictionary of the living authors of Great Britain and Ireland* (1816)
Likenesses Audinet, line engraving (after Drummond), NPG; repro. in *European Magazine* (1793)

Leach, William (*fl.* 1631–1655), attorney and pamphleteer, was the son and heir of John Leach of Felmersham, Bedfordshire, gentleman. Little else is known of his personal background except that he resided for most of his adult life with his wife in a ground chamber of the Middle Temple on the side leading out of Pump Court, which he was granted for life in 1655.

Leach entered the Middle Temple in June 1631 and was specially admitted on 25 January 1632. By the summer of 1635 he had established himself as a 'common attorney', rather than advancing to the bar. Although almost nothing is known of his professional life in the London area, court records indicate that he and his wife were frequently in debt in the latter half of the 1640s. Nevertheless he acceded to the honorary office of tipstaff to the high court of justice in 1650.

Leach brought his experience as a common attorney, as well as a defendant, to the public discussion of legal reform that followed the execution of Charles I in 1649. Over the next four years he published sixteen pamphlets consisting of 'queries and proposals' which together outlined a programme for the reform of the entire English legal system. His concern throughout was to spur debate on the institutional corruption and nuisance cases that he believed cost the English people 'millions of money' yearly and to offer viable remedies.

Leach's primary focus was the corruption and inadequacies of local legal jurisdiction. He devoted several pamphlets to the need for the complete overhaul of debtor's law, which, he thought, contributed to the rise of begging, vagabondage, and crime. He estimated that there were some 20,000 people imprisoned for debt in England in 1650. Most of these, he argued, either did not have the immediate means to pay their creditors or chose to remain in prison to defraud them. As a remedy, he proposed that a creditor be granted a court writ authorizing the seizure of a debtor's possessions in lieu of imprisonment. He also advocated stringent regulation of the jury system. In *The Bribe-Takers of Jury-Men* (1652) he complained that the fall in money values allowed such disreputable types as 'needy alehouse-keepers', who were subject to pressure from their bailiff customers, to sit on lower court juries. He also charged that sheriffs failed to summon knights, esquires, gentlemen, and the 'better sort' in general to jury service, in return for gain or patronage. Leach's proposals for juries included a property qualification of at least 40s. annual taxable value, a sobriety test, a secret ballot system for verdicts, laws to punish jury tampering by men of influence, and the right to attaint individual jurors.

Leach was fully aware of the rising tide of litigation inundating the Westminster courts. Unlike radical reformers who called for the abolition of the common law courts, he instead focused on procedural reforms to cut waste and increase efficiency, since he believed that decentralization of the courts would inevitably lead to excessive variation in the interpretation of law. To reduce litigation, Leach recommended that plaintiffs offer a security in the amount for which they were suing, and that the decisions of courts at every level be final. He also highlighted the widespread abuse of writs issued by the chancery court by those attempting to impede or expedite the judgments of lower courts, and by the chancery clerks who trafficked in the sale of writs and precedents. As a palliative he proposed that disputed judgments be returned to their court of origin for amendment and that all writs and precedents be published so that the common litigant would have free access to them.

In *A New Parliament* (1651) Leach applied his understanding of the corruption of local jurisdictions to the election and sitting of parliament. He recommended annual sittings with fixed election dates, a franchise limited to all ratepayers, secret ballots, the use of election scrutineers, and an end to the representation of depopulated boroughs. He also believed that the presence of 'learned lawyers' among the MPs was necessary for the enactment of good laws and the avoidance of confusion. Yet despite his high estimation of the legal profession, he elsewhere advocated the abolition of its monopoly on pleading in the lower courts, a set schedule of fees, and the establishment of a central registry of all legal documents open to the people in the name of cost-efficiency.

Leach's work bears witness to the marked upsurge of litigation in the first half of the seventeenth century, and the resulting popular frustration with the justice system at all levels. On the whole, his views were in line with most contemporary moderate reformers, whose work he supported in Barebone's Parliament and the Hale commission. MARY S. REDD MAGNOTTA

Sources J. H. Baker, *An introduction to English legal history*, 3rd edn (1990) · C. W. Brooks, *Petty-foggers and vipers of the Commonwealth: the lower branch of the legal profession in early modern England* (1986) · Greaves & Zaller, *BDBR*, vol. 2 · D. Veall, *The popular movement for law reform, 1640–1660* (1970) · C. H. Hopwood, ed., *Middle Temple records*, 4 vols. (1904–5)

Leach, William Elford (1791–1836), naturalist, was born at Hoe Gate, Plymouth, on 2 February 1791, the third and youngest son in the family of four children of George Leach (1748–1823), a solicitor and well-known naturalist, and his wife, Jenny Elford. Both parents were from well-established Devon families and had private fortunes which later gave Leach independent financial means.

From the age of twelve Leach was at a school in Exeter attached to the Devon and Exeter Hospital, where he began to learn anatomy and chemistry, but by the time he was seventeen he was in London at St Bartholomew's; in 1810 he moved to Edinburgh medical school, where he completed his MD, and he finally graduated from St Andrews University Hospital in 1812. Despite his qualification, Leach never practised medicine. He instead took up a post as assistant at the British Museum in 1813 with a view to a career in natural history. His interest and enthusiasm for the subject had been nurtured by his father, who had taken him on collecting forays as a boy, passing on his knowledge of insects and natural history in general. Although Leach's interests ranged over many groups of animals, he soon developed a passion for entomology and malacology. He was an enthusiastic collector of British insects who greatly enriched the entomological collections at the British Museum, and whose knowledge of the Crustacea was regarded as superior to that of any other

naturalist of his time. The naturalist William Swainson, a great personal friend, regarded Leach as a man of warm and generous disposition. He later described him (in *Taxidermy: with Biography of Zoologists*) as a remarkably active man, who was seen vaulting over stuffed zebras and leaping up stairs three or four at a time, and as a witty and animated conversationalist.

Despite his generous nature, Leach proved unsympathetic to the curatorial achievements of the past, and tidied up the British Museum collections by holding bonfires (cremations as they were known) in the gardens of Montague House, some of which even disposed of specimens once in the collections of the museum's august founder, Sir Hans Sloane. On the other hand, Leach greatly admired Sir Joseph Banks, to whom he dedicated his *Zoological Miscellany* of 1814, and Cuvier, visiting him in Paris and championing Cuvier's system of nomenclature over that of Linnaeus. Leach quickly developed a high reputation for his zoological studies and was elected to fellowship of the Royal Society (1817), the Linnean Society of London, and the Entomological and Zoological societies of London. He was a fellow of the Royal College of Surgeons, the Wernerian Society of Edinburgh, and various societies in America and France.

His total dedication to clearing the muddles of the British Museum, together with his collecting and writing and not least his absorption with his interests in entomology and malacology led his colleagues to believe overwork was the cause of the mental illness that Leach now began to show. The problems grew steadily worse and his periods of necessary absence from the museum became longer. The trustees of the museum were tolerant but ultimately decided that Leach must leave their employment. None the less, appreciative of the high calibre of his work, they bought his collections and in 1822 awarded him an annuity of £100 per annum.

His service to the museum at an end, Leach wrote to Alexander Macleay, then secretary of the Linnean Society, stating categorically that he had signed his will, leaving various articles and drawings to the Linnean Society, and named his brother George (a solicitor) as his executor. He revealed to Macleay that he was taking large doses of mercury under medical supervision and that it was unlikely that his illness would be totally eradicated. It seems likely, therefore, that he was suffering from venereal disease, and the tone of this letter suggests the nature of his illness was not entirely unrecognized.

Leach left England for Italy in 1822, accompanied by his sister, Jenny. They settled in Genoa and there Leach continued with his collecting, sending many insects to the British Museum and corresponding with his colleagues. In 1836 there was an outbreak of cholera in the region, and Leach and his sister moved to the small town of S. Sebastiano Curone near Tortona. However, the move was too late and Leach died there of cholera on 25 August of that year. His religion precluded his interment in the local cemetery but his sister obtained permission from the owner of the Palazzo de Ferraris, where they had both lived, for a burial site to be set up in the courtyard of the house. Remnants of the grave and monument were discovered in later years by enthusiastic Italian naturalists, and his remains were then interred against the perimeter wall of the cemetery, marked by his sister's original monument.

Despite his short life Leach's publishing record was phenomenal—the Royal Society *Catalogue of Scientific Papers* lists thirty-two publications. Major works include catalogues of mammals and birds of the British Isles (1816), three volumes of the *Zoological Miscellany* (1814–17), and *A Monograph of the British Crabs, Lobsters, Prawns and other Crustacea* (1815–16). His *Synopsis of the Mollusca of Great Britain* was completed by J. E. Gray in 1852, sixteen years after Leach's death. He was an artist of some skill who illustrated many of his own works.   Pamela Gilbert

Sources E. Zavattari, 'La tomba di William Elford Leach in S. Sebastiano Curone', *Natura, Milano*, 50/2, 33–42 • W. Swainson, *Taxidermy: bibliography and biography* (1840), 237–40 • A. E. Gunther and E. Smith, corresp., 1968–87, NHM • A. E. Gunther, *A century of zoology at the British Museum through the lives of two keepers, 1815–1914* (1975) • A. E. Gunther, *The founders of science at the British Museum, 1753–1900* (1980) • R. W. Ingle, 'Carcinology in the Natural History Museum, London; the brachyuran crab collections and their curation from 1813–1904 (Leach to Calman)', *Bulletin of the British Museum (Natural History)* [Historical Series], 19 (1991), 161–224 • *Bulletin Société entomologique de France*, 6 (1837), xxxiv–xxxv • *Magazine of Natural History*, 1 (1837), 390 • J. N. Eiselt, *Geschichte, Systematik und Literatur der Insectenkunde* (Leipzig, 1836), 86–8 • E. Edwards, *Lives of the founders of the British Museum* (1870)

Archives Linn. Soc., papers • NHM, specimens | BL, corresp. with Macvey Napier, Add. MSS 34611–34612 • Linn. Soc., corresp. with MacKeay • Maison d'Auguste Comte, Paris, letters to Henri Ducrotay De Blainville • NHM, letters to members of the Sowerby family • U. Edin. L., corresp. with Du Fresne

Likenesses Cruikshank, cartoon, BM

Leachman, Gerard Evelyn (1880–1920), army officer and traveller, was born in Petersfield, Hampshire, on 27 July 1880. Known to his friends as Gerald, he was the sixth child and only surviving son of Dr Albert Leachman, a medical practitioner, and his wife, Louise Caroline Singer. After four years at Charterhouse School (1893–7) he attended the Royal Military College, Sandhurst, passing out in the summer of 1899. He embarked for service in the Second South African War early in 1900 as a second lieutenant in the 1st battalion of the Royal Sussex regiment, and after two years' service in South Africa he was posted to India.

Leachman's first postings in India were near the border with Nepal, and in June 1905 he made a daring (and unauthorized) journey into Tibet for several weeks, the first of many adventurous travels into the mountains and deserts of Kashmir, Persia, Iraq, and Turkey. Early in 1907 he left India for leave in England, travelling from Bombay to Muscat, up the gulf to Basrah, on by paddle steamer to Baghdad and Abu Kemal, and then by land to Aleppo.

On his return to India Leachman was assigned to military intelligence in Simla. The Anglo-Russian convention of August 1907, setting out spheres of influence in Afghanistan and Persia, effectively marked the end of the 'great game', the struggle between Russia and Britain for influence over central Asia which had lasted for most of

the nineteenth century. Russia had extended its borders and indirect influence hundreds of miles south, in a seemingly inexorable advance towards British India. By 1907 it had become clear to Britain, Russia, and France that a more imminent threat was the growing naval power and imperial ambition of Germany.

In the early twentieth century the intelligence agencies of Britain and Germany were attempting to establish footholds within the Ottoman empire (and, to a lesser extent, in Persia), by such apparently innocent means as archaeology, mapping, exploration, the telegraph, and commercial activity, since—apart from Britain's unequal treaties with the gulf sheikhdoms and her occupation of Egypt—more direct forms of colonial rule could not be employed. In Simla, Leachman learned Arabic and German and studied intelligence reports from Arabia. He arrived in southern Iraq late in 1909 to begin his career in the field, one of a cohort of colourful contemporaries including Douglas Carruthers, T. E. Lawrence, Alois Musil, S. F. Newcombe, Conrad Preusser, Barclay Raunkiaer, William Shakespear, E. B. Soane, and Wilhelm Wassmuss.

Like many of them Leachman took to wearing Arab dress. In 1910 he undertook a journey into the desert south of Baghdad, apparently in an effort to persuade the Rashids of Haʾil not to attack Ibn Saʿud. In March 1911 the Royal Geographical Society awarded him its Gill memorial medal for his account of these travels (published in the *Geographical Journal*, 38, 1911, 265–74), and also offered to fund a modest expedition to central Arabia. He set off from Damascus at the end of 1912, probably with the connivance of ʿAbd al-ʿAziz ibn Saʿud (who was anxious to secure British protection against the Rashids, and subsequently, recognition of his independence *vis-à-vis* the Ottomans), visiting Qasim and Riyadh and bringing back the first photographs of members of the Saʿudi royal family.

Early in March 1915 Leachman was posted to Basrah to work among the tribes of southern Iraq as the Mesopotamia campaign moved northwards to Baghdad, competing for their allegiance with the German archaeologist Preusser on the Ottoman side. What appeared to be an unopposed advance was firmly halted at Kut, where the Indian expeditionary force was besieged by fresh Ottoman troops. In an act of extraordinary heroism Leachman entered the city and enabled some 5000 troops to escape in the first days of December 1915, before the Turkish troops were fully organized.

At the same time as the defeated army of Kut was being marched to prison camps in Turkey, the Arab revolt was beginning on the west of the Arabian peninsula. Once Baghdad had been captured in March 1917, and the situation had become more stable, it was important that someone from Mesopotamia should be sent to Cairo to be briefed on London's plans for the post-war Arab world. The authorities in Iraq had not been informed either of the Sykes–Picot agreement or of the McMahon–Husayn correspondence. Leachman, who shared his Mesopotamian superiors' mistrust of the Arab revolt, went first to Cairo and then to Hejaz, where he met Faysal and T. E. Lawrence at Wajh in May. Captain Bray has described the meeting, with Lawrence in sumptuous Arab clothing, and Leachman in his army khakis: Faysal's aristocratic charm, Leachman's straightforwardness, Lawrence's condescending superiority.

On his return to Mesopotamia in 1917 Leachman, gazetted brevet lieutenant-colonel, was posted to the Shiʿi shrine city of Karbalaʾ. Two of his contemporaries, Captain I. Chalmers and Edmund Candler, described him in *Blackwood's Magazine* and *The Long Road to Baghdad* (1919) as 'O.C. (Officer Commanding) Desert'; this description, which was later used in the title of a biography, referred to his 'parish' of some 20,000 square miles. He was awarded the DSO in November 1918.

In April 1920 the treaty of San Remo awarded the Middle Eastern mandates to Britain and France. Arnold Wilson, together with many of his colleagues in the Mesopotamia administration, was unable to accept even the limited independence that this implied. Pent-up nationalist feelings, nourished partly by British support of the Hashemites over the previous years and partly by Shiʿa seeking independence, combined to cause a major insurrection in Iraq in June 1920. Leachman, whom Wilson had asked to return to Iraq early in 1920, was killed in the course of the revolt, at Khan Nuqta near Baghdad on 12 August 1920, by Khamis, son of Dhari al-Mahmud of the Zubaʾ tribe. Leachman's body was subsequently reinterred at the British cemetery in Baghdad on 1 March 1921. He never married.

Along with many of his contemporaries Leachman was largely unsympathetic towards aspirations for Arab independence (both from Ottoman rule and more generally) which were gathering momentum before and during the First World War. He was imbued with many of the stock attitudes of his generation towards 'inferior peoples' though he evidently respected many individual Arabs with whom he came into contact. Upright, cantankerous, and ascetic, he was a courageous and devoted servant of empire. PETER SLUGLETT

Sources N. N. E. Bray, *A paladin of Arabia: the biography of Brevet Lieut-Colonel G. E. Leachman, C.I.E., D.S.O., of the royal Sussex regiment* (1936) · D. Gillard, *The struggle for Asia, 1828–1914* (1977) · P. Sluglett, *Britain in Iraq, 1914–1932* (1976) · A. T. Wilson, *Loyalties: Mesopotamia, 1914–1917* (1930) · A. T. Wilson, *Mesopotamia, 1917–1920: a clash of loyalties* (1931) · H. V. F. Winstone, *Leachman: 'O.C. Desert': the life of Lieutenant-Colonel Gerard Leachman D.S.O.* (1982) · Colonial Office Records · BL OIOC
Archives St Ant. Oxf., Middle East Centre, diaries and press cuttings
Likenesses photographs, repro. in Winstone, *Leachman*
Wealth at death £6343 13s. 5d.: administration, 29 June 1921, *CGPLA Eng. & Wales*

Leacock, Stephen Butler (1869–1944), university teacher and humorist, was born on 30 December 1869 in Swanmore, near Winchester, Hampshire, the third of the eleven children of (Walter) Peter Leacock (1848–1940), asphalt contractor, and Agnes Emma (1844–1934), daughter of the Revd Stephen Butler. Both sides of the family were well-to-do. Leacock's great-grandfather, John Leacock, had made a fortune in the wine trade in Madeira. Peter squandered much of the family's money by general mismanagement and by failed attempts at farming in South Africa and Kansas. In 1876 the Leacocks emigrated to Canada and settled on a farm in Sutton, Ontario, near Lake Simcoe in the township of Georgina. In 1887, after repeated incidents of domestic brutality and drunkenness, Peter abandoned his family forever.

Between 1882 and 1887 Leacock attended Upper Canada College, Toronto, graduating as head boy. He studied modern languages for a year at the University of Toronto, went to Strathroy Collegiate Institute where he acquired his teacher's certificate, taught for half a year at Uxbridge high school, and returned to Upper Canada College in the autumn of 1889 as a junior master. Leacock completed his undergraduate degree in 1891. Disenchanted by the low pay, the lack of recognition, and the general lack of interest among his pupils in the learning of languages, he left schoolteaching and went to the University of Chicago in 1899 as a graduate student in political economy. He obtained his doctoral degree in 1903 with a dissertation entitled 'The doctrine of laissez faire'. In 1900 Leacock was appointed as a lecturer in political science and history at McGill University in Montreal. He remained at McGill until his forced retirement in 1936, having become the William Dow professor of political economy and chair of the department of economics and political science in 1908. At McGill Leacock was renowned as a legend on campus, recognizable by his threadbare academic gown, his ragged racoon coat, and crushed fedora. Many testimonials from his colleagues and students attest to his magnanimity, wit, erudition, and tolerance.

Between 1894 and 1899, while at Upper Canada College, Leacock wrote more than thirty humorous articles for magazines such as *Grip*, *Life*, and *Truth*. In 1910, at his own expense, he arranged for the publication of many of these early pieces under the title *Literary Lapses*. This book came to the attention of John Lane who published an enlarged edition. Leacock's next book, *Nonsense Novels* (1911), was a parody of literary genres. His most enduring books of humour, *Sunshine Sketches of a Little Town* (1912) and *Arcadian Adventures with the Idle Rich* (1914), established his reputation internationally as the 'Canadian Mark Twain'. Leacock believed that the essence of humour is human kindliness. To a great extent this point of view is reflected in his sketches. However, he was also quite capable of biting satire when his targets were self-serving politicians, ill-educated plutocrats, and gullible socialites.

Leacock's canon is immense and varied. Until the onset of the depression, he enjoyed large royalties from his humorous books; his income was also supplemented by lecture tours. From 1910 onwards, he usually wrote at least one book a year in addition to numerous articles in magazines such as *Collier's*, *Vanity Fair*, and *Harper's*. In the 1920s he was a weekly syndicated columnist for the Metropolitan Newspaper Service. In the year before his death he wrote or revised every article in the *Encyclopaedia Britannica* pertaining to Canada.

Known primarily as a humorist, Leacock was also a historian, biographer, political economist, and social critic.

Some of his serious works include *Elements of Political Science* (1906), *Baldwin, Lafontaine, Hincks: Responsible Government* (1907), three books in the Chronicles of Canada series (1914), *The Unsolved Riddle of Social Justice* (1920), biographies of Twain (1932), Dickens (1933), and Lincoln (1934), *Our British Empire* (1940), and *Canada: the Foundations of its Future* (1942). The latter book was published by the Distillers Corporation–Seagrams Ltd as a 'limited edition', but in fact, more than 165,000 copies were distributed up to 1967 to anyone who wrote and asked for a copy.

In politics Leacock was a radical tory, who wanted reform without revolution. He was equally sceptical of socialism and untrammelled capitalism. He opposed women's liberation, spoke out against the immigration to Canada of Asians and non-Anglo-Saxon Europeans, and campaigned against prohibition. His overriding political interest lay in maintaining and strengthening the ties of Canada to Great Britain. In 1907–8 he made a tour of the British empire for the Rhodes Trust, lecturing on imperial organization. During the First World War, he gave readings from his humorous work in aid of the Belgian Relief Fund.

On 7 August 1900 in New York, Leacock married Beatrix Hamilton (1879?–1925), an actress and the daughter of Colonel Robert B. Hamilton and granddaughter of Sir Henry Pellatt. They had one son, Stephen Lushington (1915–1974). Leacock received several honorary degrees: LittD from Brown University in 1917, from Dartmouth College in 1920, from the University of Toronto in 1927, and from the University of Michigan in 1936; LLD from Queen's University in 1919 and from McGill in 1936; and doctor of civil laws from Bishop's College in 1934. In 1935 Leacock was awarded the Mark Twain medal by the International Mark Twain Society. In 1937 the Royal Society of Canada honoured him with the Lorne Pierce medal for his contribution to Canadian letters. In 1938 he received the governor-general's prize for *My Discovery of the West* (1937) in the non-fiction category. Leacock died at Toronto's Western Hospital from cancer of the throat on 28 March 1944. He was cremated in Toronto on 31 March and his ashes were interred in the Leacock family plot at St George's Church in Sibbald Point, Ontario.

In private life Leacock was a charming and companionable man whose superlative gifts as a talker and raconteur made him shine in any company. During the summer at the end of the academic year, he normally resided in his country home at Old Brewery Bay in Orillia, Ontario. He found diversion there from his literary labours in entertaining family and friends, gardening, fishing, and sailing. His country estate was declared to be a national historic site by the Canadian government in 1958, and now serves as a museum dedicated to his memory and humorous writing. Since 1947 the Stephen Leacock medal for humour has been awarded annually for the best book of humour written by a Canadian.   CARL SPADONI

Sources S. Leacock, *The boy I left behind me* (1946) • G. R. Lomer, *Stephen Leacock: a check-list and index of his writings* (1954) • R. L. Curry, *Stephen Leacock: humorist and humanist* (1959) • D. M. Legate, *Stephen Leacock: a biography* (1970) • A. Moritz and T. Moritz, *Leacock: a biography* (1985) • A. Anderson, *Remembering Leacock: an oral history* (1983) • P. McArthur, *Stephen Leacock* (1923) • H. J. Morgan, ed., *The Canadian men and women of the time*, 2nd edn (1912) • McGill University, Montreal, Leacock Building • NA Canada • E. A. Collard, ed., *The McGill you knew: an anthology of memories, 1920–1960* (1975) • E. Kimball, *The man in the panama hat: reminiscences of my uncle, Stephen Leacock* (1970) • C. Spadoni, *A bibliography of Stephen Leacock* (1998)

Archives McGill University, Montreal, rare books and special collections division • McGill University, Montreal, archives • NA Canada • Orillia Public Library, Ontario, Canada • Stephen Leacock Museum, Orillia, Ontario, Canada • U. Reading, papers and contracts | Harvard U., Houghton Mifflin collection • McMaster University, Hamilton, Ontario, Macmillan Company of Canada collection and Dodd Mead collection • Ransom HRC, John Lane The Bodley Head collection | SOUND BL NSA, 'Stephen Leacock: a portrait', recorded talk

Likenesses E. Holgate, oils, National Gallery of Canada, Ottawa • R. Jack, oils, Montreal University Club • F. Taylor, oils, McGill University, Montreal, rare books and special collections division • photographs, McGill University, Montreal, Leacock Building • photographs, NA Canada

Lead [*née* Ward], **Jane** (1624–1704), mystic and author, was born in March 1624 in Norfolk, one of nine children of Hamond Ward (d. 1651), squire and magistrate, and his wife, Mary (b. c.1582), daughter of Sir James Calthorpe of Cockthorpe. Her parents were affluent members of the landed gentry who ensured that Jane was given a good Anglican upbringing and education at home. During Christmas festivities, when she was about fifteen, a voice told her to cease the vanity of music and dancing, whereupon she fell into a religious melancholia that lasted three years. She began to retire into herself, to study the Bible, and to search for a more pious way of life. She told no one of her spiritual enquiries except, finally, the chaplain of the house, who caught her surreptitiously reading in his study. In 1642 she was allowed a six-month visit to her brother Hamond's house in London that enabled her to frequent religious meetings, to listen to diverse preachers, notably the antinomian Tobias Crisp, and to come into direct contact with radical millenarianism. After rejecting several suitors she was obliged, at the age of twenty, to marry William Lead (1621?–1670), a distant relative and wealthy merchant from King's Lynn, a royalist borough. During their marriage they lived in London and had four daughters, two of whom survived to adulthood.

Although her husband was a godly man Lead longed to live a contemplative life and saw her duties to her husband as an obstacle to her true vocation. After her husband's death, on 5 February 1670, she wrote of their time together: 'My Spirit ever failed within me, as desponding ever to get rid of my First Husband; without which no Marriage with the Lord from Heaven can be' (Lead, 1.69). Unfortunately she was left destitute, her husband having entrusted his affairs to an overseas executor who swindled Lead out of her inheritance. Nevertheless, in 1676, when one of her brothers promised to alleviate her financial cares if she would come to live under his roof, she refused the offer despite her daughter's 'laying much to my Charge, for slighting such Providences' (ibid., 1.327). By then Lead had made a spiritual pact to live as 'fellow labourers' in the 'Paradisical Husbandry' with John Por-dage, sometime rector of Bradfield, and a leading expo-nent of the theosophy of the German mystic Jakob Boehme (ibid., 1.143). During the early 1650s Pordage and his spiritually gifted wife, Mary, had set up a small Behmenist commune in their Bradfield household. In 1654 Pordage was prosecuted by Cromwell's officials for his spiritual experiments and lost his living, which was returned to him only after the Restoration. Lead met Por-dage in 1663, but it was not until 1674 or 1675 that she and Pordage joined together in the same household as co-seekers after Divine Wisdom, a figure that looms large in the sapiential books of the Bible as well as in Boehme's writings.

In 1681, the year of Pordage's death, Lead published her first book, *Heavenly Cloud now Breaking*, in which she intro-duces her readers to Boehme's cosmology and reveals that Divine Wisdom is, even now, operating intrinsically in some souls in order to restore that 'Virgin Nature, and Godlike Simplicity, that have been defloured through the subtilty of Reason' (p. 22). Two years later she not only helped to bring to press Pordage's *Theologica mystica*, she also wrote its preface, 'To the impartial and well-disposed Reader' (p. 1). In the same year she published *Revelation of Revelations*, which presents a significant rereading of scrip-ture, especially Revelation, in order to authorize her prophecies regarding the Virgin Wisdom's re-entry into history. Aside from the information given on the title-page of *Revelation of Revelations* that she was selling her book from an address at 'the Carpenters in Bartholomew Close', not much is known of Lead's life during the 1680s. Possibly she was associated with a small Behmenist circle which met in Baldwins Gardens at the home of Ann Bath-urst, the mystical writer of the two-volume diary, *Rhap-sodical Meditations and Visions*, who later joined with Lead to found the Philadelphian Society. In 1694 Francis Lee, one-time fellow of St John's College, Oxford, and nonjuror, came searching for Lead after hearing about her writings while he was in the Netherlands. He found her living in a cell at Lady Mico's College, a home for impoverished gentlewomen, next to the Stepney church. At the time he was thirty-four and she was seventy years old, going blind from cataracts, yet charismatic enough to attract Lee and others to her vision of a new age. Although her first two books had been largely ignored in England, Lead was beginning to attract a devoted following on the continent. A German benefactor named Baron Kniphausen commis-sioned Loth Fischer of Utrecht to translate Lead's manu-scripts; accordingly, by 1696, six of her tracts and an auto-biography appeared in German editions. Kniphausen also granted Lead a pension and set her up in a house in Hoxton (Hogsdon) Square, probably in 1695, so that she could carry out her work more conveniently. By then Lee considered himself Lead's spiritual son, and, despite the objections of friends and his brother, decided to marry Lead's widowed daughter Barbara Walton, and to move into the Lead household at Hoxton Square. They were soon afterwards joined by Lee's former classmate at St John's College, the Revd Richard Roach. This spiritual

household became the nerve centre of the international theosophical movement known as the Philadelphian Society, an ecumenical and millenarian movement whose main aim was to work together to build a culture of peace, receptive to the coming of Virgin Wisdom.

All of Jane Lead's writings bear testimony to the immi-nent entry into history of an androgyne God, so full of sympathy and love for creation that the groans of the fallen earth can no longer be ignored. At the same time Lead offers her readers a method, authenticated by her own long course of trials, for reclaiming the imagination as the one faculty capable of overcoming the narrow and materialistic perspective of reason and achieving vision-ary access to true nature. The most influential of Lead's books is her three-volume spiritual diary, *Fountain of Gar-dens*, which presents the daily prophecies given to Lead, along with their interpretations, for the period April 1670 to August 1686. Even with its missing entries the printed diary is some 2500 pages long; it was published in four stages: volume one in 1697; volume two later the same year; volume three, part one, in 1700; and volume three, part two in 1701. Lead's diary begins two months after her husband's death when she had her first vision of the Virgin-hidden-in-God and of the coming restoration of all creation to its original luminosity. Lead was invited to enter into a new covenant with Divine Wisdom: 'She would be my Mother … For if I would apply myself to her Doctrine, and draw my Life's Food from no other Breast, I should then know the recovery of a lost kingdom' (Lead, 1.25–6). The composition of the diary is remarkable because Lead was in the habit of writing down her visions as private memorandums on loose cards, and then giving them away 'day by day' to friends who needed aid in their own spiritual exercises (ibid., vol. 2, sig. A3v). During the period of their collaboration Pordage copied out her notes to guide his own meditation practice. Her 'loose slips of paper' and the copy made by Pordage were used by Francis Lee to edit the published version, but for the period after Pordage's death there are large gaps in the diary (Walton, 203). Even as the final volume was going to press in 1701 every effort was being made to retrieve these diary notes for publication.

During the decade of Philadelphian activism, between 1694 and 1704, fifteen books by Lead, as well as new edi-tions of *Heavenly Cloud* (2nd edn 1701) and *Revelation of Rev-elations* (2nd edn 1701), were published in England. The publication of Lead's third book, *Enochian Walks with God* (1694), marked a pivotal point in her work because she went beyond what had been revealed by Boehme to declare the doctrine of apocatastasis, the universal restor-ation of all creation to its original harmony; this was to include the apostatized angels, once their term of punish-ment was up. This provocative revelation about the revol-utionary power of divine compassion was reiterated three years later in *A Revelation of the Everlasting Gospel-Message*. Some affinity between the Philadelphians and the Quak-ers was indicated in 1695 when Lead's *The Laws of Paradise* and *The Wonders of God's Creation Manifested in the Variety of Eight Worlds* were published by Tace Sowle, the daughter of

Andrew Sowle, who had published Lead's *Revelation of Revelations* in 1683. In order to prepare the way for their public phase the Philadelphians explained their mission in a series of publications: *Theosophical Transactions*, a five-volume periodical edited by Lee and Roach (1697); Francis Lee's *The State of the Philadelphian Society* (1697); and Jane Lead's three messages to the society (1696–8), the last of which, *The Messenger of an Universal Peace, or, A Third Message to the Philadelphian Society*, was the most important. In it Lead praised the English king for the recent advancements in religious liberty that allowed the Philadelphian movement to flourish even as she called for all monarchs to abandon repressive laws against the spirit: 'Go on in this great Latitude, Universality of Love, under the great and Mighty Shepherd Christ Jesus, to bring in all the scatter'd and divided Flocks into one Fold to feed upon … the sweet scented Flowers of Love' (pp. 48–9). *The Messenger* went on to define the true Philadelphian, also called the androgyne or 'Virgin spirit', as one who repudiates the 'contracted spirit' of the world with its narrow distinctions of gender, class, and wealth to become a most obliging, kind, and public spirited person, always seeking 'the Good of the Whole' (p. 61). As the first issue of *Theosophical Transactions* announces, the guiding adage of the Philadelphians was 'Blessed are the Peace-makers' (*Theosophical Transactions*, 1, 1697, 5).

In a contemporary manuscript account Roach claims that before it was known by that name the Philadelphian Society had existed for about fifty years, since the days of the Pordage Behmenist household which had followed the holy model of the early Christians. When the society first undertook its public work in 1697 it continued to meet at Mrs Bathurst's house in Baldwins Gardens until so many people came that the society was forced to divide and to open two more commodious sites. The first site in Hungerford market was greeted with such rudeness that it was forced to close within a year, but the second site, led by Lead and her household at Westmoreland House, met with a more 'favourable and civilized' reception (Bodl. Oxf., MS Rawl. D. 833, fol. 82). Even so, before long increased tumult led to the necessity of changing locations, first to Twisters Alley in Bunhill Fields and then to Loriners' Hall, where the Philadelphians read their *Declaration of the Philadelphian Society* to a large crowd on Easter Sunday 1699. They were calling on all Christians to abandon divisive interests and to unite in mutual charity, as mystics from all denominations, including Catholics, were beginning to do. Finally, amid malicious rumours and persecutions, the Philadelphians were driven to home ground in Hoxton Square, where they held their final public meeting in June 1703. Questions about the credibility of the prophecies and the sustainability of the movement, given Lead's advanced age, were addressed in a number of tracts, notably: the editor's preface to Lead's *The Wars of David, and the Peaceable Reign of Solomon* (1700); Lead's own *A Living Funeral Testimony* (1702), and Francis Lee's *Der Seelig und aber Seeligen Jane Leade letztere Lebens-Stunden* (*The most Blessed Jane Lead's Last Hours of Life*, Amsterdam, 1705), the English version of which has been lost. On

19 August 1704 Jane Lead died at Hoxton Square, aged eighty, of stomach cancer, and was buried three days later in a modest grave at Bunhill Fields cemetery. After Lead appeared to him in a dream authorizing his leadership the movement was taken over by Roach but eventually petered out. Traces of the distinctive ideas of Jane Lead and the Philadelphians can be found in certain pietistic traditions of Germany and America, as well as in the writings of Joanna Southcott and Ann Lee, and in the practice of the Shaker commune.   SYLVIA BOWERBANK

Sources J. Lead, *A fountain of gardens: watered by the rivers of divine pleasure*, 2 (1697), esp. sig. a1r–a4v • J. Lead, *The wars of David, and the peaceable reign of Solomon* (Amsterdam, 1700), preface • C. Walton, ed., *Notes and materials for an adequate biography of the celebrated divine and theosopher, William Law* (1854), 188–232 • R. Roach, miscellaneous papers, Bodl. Oxf., MSS Rawlinson D. 832–833, esp. D. 833, 80–82 • N. Thune, *The Behmenists and the Philadelphians: a contribution to the study of English mysticism in the 17th and 18th centuries* (1948) • J. M. Sperle, 'God's healing angel: a biography of Jane Lead', PhD diss., Kent State University, 1985 • J. L. [J. Lead], 'To the impartial and well-disposed reader', in J. P. M. D. [J. Pordage], *Theologica mystica, or, The mystic divinitie of the aeternal invisibles* (1683), 1–9 • A. Bathurst, 'Rhapsodical meditations and visions', 1679–93, Bodl. Oxf., MSS Rawlinson D. 1262–1263 • C. F. Smith, 'Jane Lead's wisdom: women and prophecy in seventeenth-century England', *Poetic prophecy in Western literature*, ed. J. Wojcik and R. J. Frontain (1984), 55–63 • P. McDowell, *The women of Grub Street: press, politics and gender in the London literary marketplace, 1678–1730* (1998) • *Theosophical Transactions*, 1 (1697)

Archives Bodl. Oxf., papers of Richard Roach, MSS Rawlinson D. 832–833; MS Rawlinson D. 1318 • DWL, Francis Lee papers, MS 186.18(1) a, b • LPL, Philadelphia Society MSS; Richard Roach MSS, MSS 942/129, 942/130, 942/141, 1559

Leadbeater [*née* Shackleton], **Mary** (1758–1826), author, was born on 1 December 1758 at Ballitore, co. Kildare, the second child of the three daughters and one son of Richard *Shackleton (1726–1792) [*see under* Shackleton, Abraham (1696–1771)] and his second wife, Elizabeth Carleton (1726–1766). Her parents were Quakers. As the only female student she was educated at the famous Quaker school in Ballitore where her father was the master. Mary in her youth worked closely with her aunt, who was the local herbal healer, and from 1787 she took on that role within the local community. In 1784 she travelled to London with her father and paid several visits to Edmund Burke's house, where she met Sir Joshua Reynolds and George Crabbe. She corresponded with Burke for many years. While in England she also visited some Primitive Quakers at Selby in Yorkshire, a community that she described in her journal.

On 6 January 1791 Mary married William Leadbeater (1763–1827), a farmer and businessman. The couple lived in Ballitore where Mary kept the village post office and directed a bonnet making enterprise. In 1794 she published, anonymously, her first book of poetry, *Extracts and Original Anecdotes for the Improvement of Youth*, which contains poems on secular and religious subjects. Mary Leadbeater kept a journal from 1766 to 1824 which noted the daily events of Ballitore. In this journal she recorded the frightening events of the Irish uprising of 1798. Ballitore was occupied first by the yeomanry and soldiers and then by insurgents. The government took revenge on the inhabitants of Ballitore once the village had been vacated by the insurgents. Many homes were burned and a number of individuals were summarily executed. Leadbeater and her husband narrowly escaped death. She thought her food tasted of blood and had nightmares of massacre for years afterwards.

In 1808 Mary Leadbeater published *Poems*, with a metrical version of her husband's prose translation of Maffaeus Vegio's *Thirteenth Book of the Aeneid*. A number of the poems concern Burke, while the remainder are on domestic and local subjects. In 1811 she published *Cottage Dialogues among the Irish Peasantry*; the London edition had an introduction and notes written by Maria Edgeworth, and four editions, with some alterations, had appeared by 1813. The *Dialogues* was intended to give advice on household management and family organization. Leadbeater proposed the virtues of thrift, good management, and industry for the peasantry. Recipes for nourishing meals, and information on the medicinal qualities of herbs are provided through the use of conversations between friends. She later published a second series of *Dialogues* (1813) devoted to working men and intended to 'perform the same service to the Men of the Cottage that was in the first Part designed for their consorts'. Leadbeater also gave advice to the gentry in another set of dialogues called *The Landlord's Friend* (1813). *Tales for Cottagers*, written with Elizabeth Shackleton, appeared in 1814. These tales illustrate the virtues of perseverance, frugality, and temperance, and the volume also contains a play entitled 'Honesty is the Best Policy'. In 1822 she concluded this series with the publication of *Cottage Biography, being a Collection of Lives of the Irish Peasantry*. She based these stories on the lives of real individuals she knew in Ballitore. *Memoirs and Letters of Richard and Elizabeth Shackleton … Compiled by their Daughter*, was issued in 1822 (new edn, 1849, ed. Lydia Ann Barclay). Her *Biographical Notices of Members of the Society of Friends, who were Resident in Ireland* appeared in 1823, and is a summary of their spiritual lives. Her last work, *The Pedlars: a Tale*, was published in 1824.

Leadbeater corresponded with Burke, and among others, Maria Edgeworth, George Crabbe, and Melusina Trench (Mrs Richard Trench). Leadbeater's best work is acknowledged to be *The Annals of Ballitore* which was not published until 1862 when it was brought out under the title *The Leadbeater Papers* (2 vols.) by Richard Davis Webb, a Quaker printer. It tells of the inhabitants and events of Ballitore from 1766 to 1823, and provides an excellent social history of the period. The second volume includes unpublished letters of Burke and correspondence with Mrs Richard Trench and with Crabbe.

Leadbeater died at Ballitore on 27 June 1826, and was buried in the Quaker burial-ground there. She had six children, and one of her daughters, Mrs Lydia Fisher, was a close friend of the poet and novelist Gerald Griffin.

MARIA LUDDY

Sources DNB • M. Leadbeater, *The Leadbeater papers*, 2nd edn, 2 vols. (1862); repr. with new introduction by M. Luddy (1998) • K. O'Neill, '"Almost a gentlewoman": gender and adolescence in the diary of Mary Shackleton', *Chattel, servant or citizen: women's status in church, state and society*, ed. M. O'Dowd and S. Wichert (1995) • R. S. Harrison, *A biographical dictionary of Irish Quakers* (1997)
Archives NL Ire., diaries and correspondence • TCD, correspondence with family • U. Cal., Santa Barbara, correspondence • Yale U., correspondence and MSS | BL, correspondence with George Crabbe, Eg. MS 3709 • Kildare County Library, Newbridge, corresp. • Religious Society of Friends, Dublin, Leadbeater Shackleton collection • Yale U., letters to her cousin Anne Shannon; holograph MS of 'The annals of Ballitore'

Leadbetter, Charles (1681–1744), writer on astronomy and practical mathematics, was born on 26 September 1681 in the village of Cronton, Lancashire. An early interest in practical astronomy is presumed from his *Mechanick Dialling* (1737), which includes a vertical sundial for a wall facing exactly 21°10′ west of south, for the latitude of Cronton. In November 1707 Leadbetter was accepted into the Excise Office for instruction by the officer at nearby Prescot. He was appointed supernumerary in the Worcester collection in June 1708, and later was promoted gauger for the Bromsgrove area. A bond and allegation of intent to marry Dorothy Hollington of Tardebigge, near Bromsgrove, was recorded in April 1711. Confirmation of the marriage has not been located, but Leadbetter was described as 'widower' when he married Sarah Hall at St Benet Paul's Wharf, London, in June 1742. After refusing to accept a posting to Henley in Arden, Leadbetter was discharged from the excise in August 1713.

The *Ladies Diary* for 1711 records Leadbetter as a respondent to a mathematical question posed in 1710. The editor, John Tipper, printed an arithmetical conundrum by Leadbetter in the January 1711 number of his short-lived monthly *Delights for the Ingenious*. From 1721 the *Ladies Diary* regularly included Leadbetter's eclipse predictions for London, drawing on his first separate publication, *A Treatise of Eclipses for 26 Years, Commencing anno 1715* (1717). Leadbetter had moved to London by April 1715, where he observed the total solar eclipse. By 1717 he was established at the Hand and Pen in Cock Lane, Shoreditch, where until mid-1742 he taught:

> Vulgar and Decimal Arithmetick, Geometry apply'd to the Mensuration of Superficies and Solids, by Pen and Sliding-Rule; Projection of the sphere on any circle, Trigonometry, plain and spherical; Surveying of Land by any Instrument now in use; Gauging of all sorts of vessels, with all the practical methods used by the Officers of the Excise; Astronomy in all its branches; navigation by the Plain and Mercator's Chart, and by the Arch of a great Circle; Geography and the Use of the Globes; with all other Mathematical Instruments whatsoever. Dialling upon any plane for any Latitude. (C. Leadbetter, *Astronomy of the Satellites of the Earth, Jupiter and Saturn*, 1729, sig. A1v)

A broadsheet computational diagram of a complex planetary conjunction was published in 1722, followed by books dealing with positional astronomy aimed at the general reader willing and able to undertake some arithmetical computation. *Astronomy of the True System of the Planets* (1727) includes plates intended to be cut out and mounted on boards to provide instrumental means of determining planetary positions with minimal calculation. Leadbetter edited reprinted texts, such as William

Leybourn on the Gunter quadrant (1721 and 1731). *The Young Mathematicians Companion* (1739) encapsulates his teaching style. For some years he silently edited the annual almanac begun by John Partridge in 1678, inserting particularly full eclipse prediction data 'as they are very exactly computed by my very ingenious Friend Mr *Charles Leadbetter*, whose skill in these matters few can parallel' (J. Partridge, *Merlinus Libertus … for 1733*, 1733, sig. C3v). In 1739 shameless praise of books written by his 'close friend' Mr Leadbetter led competitors to blow his cover.

Leadbetter drew on earlier professional experience to edit the ninth (1727) and tenth (1738) editions of Thomas Everard's *Stereometry*, which since 1684 had become a standard work on gauging. His expanded sequel, *The Royal Gauger*, appeared in 1739 and rapidly became the best guide to the practice of gauging for the levying of excise duty across the broad spectrum of trades subject to tax. Illustrative examples are drawn from his Bromsgrove duties; the final (seventh) edition appeared in 1776. Leadbetter championed the use of the slide-rule to undertake gauging computations; his 1727 improvement on the Everard rule was rapidly accepted by the London rule makers. He appears to have withdrawn from business on his second marriage in 1742 and moved to the parish of St Katharine by the Tower, where he died on 21 November 1744 and where he was buried. An obituary described him as 'greatly esteem'd for his comprehensive Knowledge in the Mathematical Sciences' (*Penny London Post*, 28 Nov 1744).   D. J. BRYDEN

Sources E. R. Wood, 'Charles Leadbetter, teacher of the mathematics', 1967, U. Newcastle, Robinson L., Wallis collection · B. S. Capp, *Astrology and the popular press: English almanacs, 1500–1800* (1979), 239 · C. Leadbetter, *The royal gauger* (1739) · R. V. Wallis and P. J. Wallis, eds., *Biobibliography of British mathematics and its applications*, 2 (1986), 86 · *Penny London Post* (28 Nov 1744) · will, proved, Nov 1744, PRO, PROB 11/736, sig. 288
Archives MHS Oxf., letters
Likenesses H. Roberts, engraving, 1734, repro. in C. Leadbetter, *Uranoscopia* (1734), frontispiece

Leadbetter, Stiff (*c*.1705–1766), architect and builder, was possibly the eldest son of William Leadbetter (*fl.* 1705–1715), a tailor at Aylesbury, Buckinghamshire. He rose from humble origins to be one of the most successful architect–builders of the 1750s and 1760s, working for many leading aristocratic families. Apprenticed in 1719 as a carpenter for the modest sum of £5 to Henry Leadbetter of Sherfield-on-Loddon, Hampshire, Leadbetter worked as a journeyman carpenter in the 1720s and 1730s. By the 1740s he was employed as a builder in his own right; in the 1750s and 1760s he was responsible for a steady stream of new country houses, hospitals, and speculative urban development, along with alterations and mundane surveying work. He was so busy at the peak of his career in 1759 that he had to turn work away.

Although in the 1750s and 1760s Leadbetter designed most of the buildings for which he was responsible, his principal activity was as a builder. He also carried out the designs of other architects, including Robert Adam and James Stuart, principally decorative work in shells which

he had designed and built. He was an innovative and possibly influential planner at a time when the design of the British country house was undergoing rapid change. His country houses, though plain in their interior and external detail, are imaginative, varied, and above all practical in their planning. Although he was not a leader in stylistic development, Elvills, Surrey (1758–63), was the first completely new house of the Georgian Gothic revival.

Most of Leadbetter's commissions were either centred around Eton or can be explained through a network of closely allied aristocratic families. Leadbetter had settled at Eton by 1731; he acted as carpenter to Eton College from 1740 and leased the Eton College wharf, his principal home and workshop, from 1744. Many of his buildings can be found within 5 miles of Eton, an area popular for suburban villas. Others can be traced through family links, particularly to his patron Francis Godolphin, second earl of Godolphin. Through Godolphin, Leadbetter gained work from the dukes of Portland, Marlborough, and Bedford, the countesses of Essex and Pomfret, Lord Foley, Admiral Boscawen, Sir John Elvill, and others. Leadbetter also had a network of ecclesiastical patrons thanks to his position (from 1756) as surveyor of St Paul's Cathedral, to which he was appointed by the dean, Thomas Secker, later Archbishop of Canterbury.

In 1731 Leadbetter married Elizabeth Hill (*b. c.*1709), daughter of a London timber merchant; she predeceased him in 1737, as did four of their five children, leaving only their eldest son, Henry. Leadbetter died at his house at Eton College wharf on 18 August 1766. He had raised himself to a position of respectability, being described at the time of his death as 'Stiff Leadbetter, gent'. A trustee of the Eton parish almshouses and treasurer of the Colnbrook turnpike trust, he died worth over £3000, with leases of four houses in Eton, a house and workshop in Berwick Street, Soho, London, and Spencer's Farm, near Cookham in Berkshire, which he appears to have used as an occasional retreat.   GILES WORSLEY

Sources G. Worsley, 'Stiff but not dull', *Country Life* (25 July 1991), 90–93 · Hoares Bank Archives, London · Colvin, *Archs.* · 'Index to apprenticeship registers', GL · will, PRO, PROB 11/921, sig. 311 · U. Nott. L., Portland London MSS · Eton, archives · Sir John Soane's Museum, London, Robert Adam MSS · LPL, Archbishops of Canterbury MSS · LPL, Faculty Office records · Bodl. Oxf., Harcourt MSS · Bucks. RLSS, Drake of Shardeloes MSS · LMA, Middlesex Deeds Register · G. Worsley, *Classical architecture in Britain: the heroic age* (1994) · Aylesbury parish register
Archives Bodl. Oxf., MSS Harcourt · Bucks. RLSS, Drake of Shardeloes MSS · LPL, Archbishops of Canterbury MSS · Sir John Soane's Museum, London, Robert Adam MSS · U. Nott. L., Portland London MSS
Wealth at death over £3000: will, PRO, PROB 11/921, sig. 311

Leader, Benjamin Williams [*formerly* Benjamin Williams] (**1831–1923**), landscape painter, was born on 12 March 1831 in Worcester, the second son and the third of eleven children of Edward Leader Williams (1802–1879) and his wife, Sarah Whiting (1801–1888). Although Benjamin's birth was recorded in the Quaker birth register, his parents are recorded as non-members of the Society of Friends, having been disowned following their

Anglican marriage at St Giles's, Reading, in 1827. His father, himself an amateur landscape painter, was a prosperous ironmonger and engineer in Worcester. Williams senior took a keen interest in Worcester Athenaeum, a scientific and literary institute which also held significant art exhibitions.

Benjamin Williams attended Worcester Royal Grammar School and the Silver Street Academy, Worcester, whence he moved on to an informal apprenticeship in his father's firm. He is also recorded as having worked as a clerk in a bank in Worcester. His desire to become an artist manifested itself early, however, and he pursued this ambition at the Worcester School of Design, where he attended evening classes. On 24 December 1853, when he was twenty-two, a study from the antique completed at Worcester won him admission to the Royal Academy Schools in London, but he seems not to have taken up his place there. The academy offered little to the landscape painter, and Williams seems to have favoured this branch of art from the beginning. His earliest surviving works, dating from the mid-1850s, are, however, not pure landscapes but, rather, brightly lit rural narrative paintings in landscape settings, influenced by Pre-Raphaelitism. One of these appeared in each Royal Academy exhibition from 1854 to 1856.

These works had been exhibited under the name 'B. Williams', and sent to London from the family's home address, Diglis House, Worcester. The name Williams, however, presented a problem for a young artist seeking renown, since a large family of landscape painters of this name was already well established. Indeed, three of the six sons of the painter Edward Williams (1782–1855), not related to Benjamin's family, had begun to adopt their wives' maiden names in order to establish an independent identity. From 1857 Benjamin adopted his father's second name, Leader, using 'Williams' as his middle name from 1858. Under this final form—Benjamin Williams Leader—from which he never deviated, he built a rising reputation as a painter of highly finished landscapes close in style to those of his friend George Vicat Cole, with whom he sketched at Albury, in Surrey, in 1858. He was to continue to paint in this region for the rest of his life and was eventually to abandon his native Worcestershire to move there permanently in 1889.

However, it was as a painter of Welsh scenery, notably the mountains of north Wales, that Leader secured a high reputation and considerable prosperity. His works of the 1860s—carefully crafted, replete with detail, and often highly coloured—became popular with dealers and middle-class patrons. In *A Welsh Churchyard* (1863; London, Guildhall Art Gallery), for example, a meticulous rendering of foreground detail and some more distant yew trees is complemented by an effect of brilliant sunshine in the background, with figures of local women and children providing picturesque staffage.

A trip to Paris in 1865, where *Autumn's Last Gleam* was displayed prominently at the Universal Exhibition, allowed Leader to see work by painters of the Barbizon school and while there he copied a landscape by Jean-Baptiste-Camille Corot. From about this time (and perhaps as a result of this French influence), he began to broaden his style, adopting freer and more visible brushwork and often aiming for more dramatic effects of lighting. This tendency culminated in *February Fill Dyke* (1881; Birmingham City Museums), Leader's most celebrated work, in which a golden sunset is strikingly reflected in standing water. Although the scene was actually sketched in November, the painting's title, drawn from an old country rhyme, 'February fill the dyke / Be it black or be it white …', added to the painting's popular appeal. Leader's work continued to be admired in Paris, and following his success at the 1889 Universal Exhibition, he was awarded the decoration of the Légion d'honneur.

From the 1850s Leader had aspired to membership of the Royal Academy, where he was a regular and prolific exhibitor: 216 of his paintings appeared there over a period of sixty-nine years from 1854, including three oil sketches exhibited posthumously in the exhibition of 1923. His name was first put forward as a candidate for membership in 1867; it was not until 1883, following the exhibition of *'In the evening shall there be light'* (priv. coll. Greenwich, Connecticut, USA) that he secured election as an associate of the academy. This painting was another dramatic landscape in which the sunset beyond a deserted graveyard seems to offer the promise of redemption. Leader had to wait until 1898 for full membership of the Royal Academy, depositing as his diploma work *The Sand Pit, Burrows Cross* (1899; RA), which pays homage to the work of John Constable. Leader's later work, from 1890, tends to repetitiousness, though the industrial landscape *The Manchester Ship Canal: Works in Progress at Eastham, Sept. 1890* (National Trust), unique in his œuvre, shows the artist at his most vigorous. The painting was commissioned by Lord Egerton, the chairman of the canal company, on the suggestion of the artist's elder brother, Sir Edward Leader Williams, who was chief engineer of the canal. Although Leader continued to paint until 1920, there was a gradual decline in the quality of his work in his last years.

There is little to note of Leader's uneventful personal life. He was married on 29 August 1876, at the age of forty-five, to Mary Eastlake (1853–1938), whom he always called Fluff, at Buckland Monachorum in Devon. The destination of their honeymoon is recorded in *Unterseen, Interlaken: Autumn in Switzerland* (1878; Royal Holloway Collection). They had two sons (of whom the elder, Benjamin Eastlake Leader, was killed in action in 1916) and four daughters. In 1889 the family moved from the Lodge at Whittington in Worcestershire to Burrows Cross House, south of Gomshall in Surrey, which had been designed by Norman Shaw for the artist Frank Holl. Leader died there on 22 March 1923 and was buried in Shere churchyard. Leader's work, highly regarded in its own day, has been unjustly neglected since. Although the sheer quantity of his output inevitably resulted in many mundane canvases, the best of his works, from before 1890, achieve an attractive synthesis of Pre-Raphaelite rigour and Francophile freedom of gesture. The popularity of Leader's paintings can perhaps be attributed to their accessible presentation of ideal English and Welsh landscapes, much in demand among urban Victorian patrons.   TIM BARRINGER

Sources R. Wood, *Benjamin Williams Leader RA, 1831–1923* (1998) · F. Lewis, *B. W. Leader RA* (1971) · J. Dafforne, 'British artists, their style and character, no. XCVII: Benjamin Williams Leader', *Art Journal*, 33 (1871), 45–7 · A. Chester, 'The art of Mr B. W. Leader, RA', *Windsor Magazine* (Jan 1910), 211–24 · A. Chester, 'The art of Mr B. W. Leader, RA', *Windsor Magazine* (March 1911), 451–63 · A. Chester, 'The art of Mr B. W. Leader, RA', *Windsor Magazine* (May 1912), 693–704 · L. Lusk, 'B. W. Leader RA', *Art Annual*, 3 (1901), 1–31
Archives priv. coll., account books · priv. coll., diaries · priv. coll., records of paintings sold
Likenesses B. W. Leader, self-portrait, oils, 1884, Aberdeen Art Gallery · mechanical process postcard, *c*.1898, repro. in J. Maas, *The Victorian art world in photographs* (1984) · H. von Herkomer, group portrait, oils, 1908 (*The Council of the Royal Academy*), Tate collection · B. W. Leader, self-portrait, oils, priv. coll. · R. Taylor, woodcut (after photographs), BM · photograph, NPG
Wealth at death £86,185 15*s*.: probate, 25 May 1923, *CGPLA Eng. & Wales*

Leader, John Temple (1810–1903), politician and connoisseur of the arts, born at his father's country house, Putney Hill Villa, sometimes called Lower House, on 7 May 1810, was the younger son (in a family of two sons and four daughters) of William Leader (1767–1828), a wealthy London merchant, and his wife, Mary (1762–1838).

The father, son of a coach maker of the same names, who was coach maker to the prince of Wales, was in turn coach builder, distiller, and glass manufacturer; he sat in the House of Commons from 1812 to 1818 as whig member for Camelford, a pocket borough that he bought from Lord Holland. From 1820 to 1826 he represented Winchelsea, also a pocket borough, where his colleague as MP was Henry Brougham, who became a friend. A patron of art, he commissioned George Henry Harlow to paint several portrait groups of his children, in one of which (formally at Holmwood, Putney Heath) John figures as a boy.

After education at private schools, John Leader entered Charterhouse in 1823, and won a gold medal there, but he soon left to study under a private tutor, the Revd Patrick Smyth of Menzies, with whom he visited Ireland, Norway, and France. The accidental death at Oxford of his elder brother, William, in February 1826 made him heir to the main part of his father's large fortune, which he inherited on his father's death on 13 January 1828. For the rest of his life he had no financial worries. On 12 February 1828 he matriculated as a gentleman commoner from Christ Church, Oxford. Although he was an idle and spendthrift undergraduate, he was friendly with some notable contemporaries, including James Robert Hope Scott, W. E. Gladstone, and Sir Stephen Glynne. With the last he made archaeological expeditions which stimulated a lifelong taste. His favourite recreation in youth was swimming, which he practised to extreme old age. In his Oxford vacations he continued his foreign travels. He was in Paris during the revolution of 1830, and there, through the introduction of his father's friend Henry, Lord Brougham, he came to know many liberal politicians. He went down from Oxford without a degree and entered radical politics.

John Temple Leader (1810–1903), by William Henry Mote, pubd 1840 (after Bryan Edward Duppa)

He was elected MP for Bridgwater in January 1835. He at once made a mark in political circles. In the Commons he generally acted with George Grote, Sir William Molesworth, and the philosophic radicals, and was a prominent supporter of the Chartists. In his first session he seconded Grote's resolution in favour of the ballot. John Arthur Roebuck regarded him as a useful politician, but was apprehensive about his profligate social life. In the 1830s he shared a house in Eaton Square with Molesworth. Some of his political friends complained that his political speeches were too violent and bitter. In 1836 he joined the Reform Club, of which he remained a member until his death. In February 1837, as a disciple of Brougham and Grote, he was admitted to the first council of the new London University and in the same month he presided at a dinner for Thomas Wakley, which was attended by Daniel O'Connell, Joseph Hume, and most of the forward radicals.

In May 1837 Leader adventurously resigned his seat in order to contest the constituency of Westminster at a by-election against Sir Francis Burdett. Having abandoned his radical principles, Burdett had resigned the seat and challenged his constituents to return him anew as a Conservative. Leader was defeated, polling 3052 votes against 3567, but he stood again for Westminster at the general election in August and topped the poll. He held the seat until 1847, when he did not stand. He continued to advocate Chartism and radicalism with unabated energy. On 2 May 1842 he seconded Thomas Duncombe's motion 'that the petitioners for the national charter be heard at the bar of the house'. In the same session (18 February) he supported C. P. Villiers's motion for the total repeal of the corn laws. On 13 February 1844 he spoke on behalf of the liberties of Canada, which he joined Roebuck in championing. This was his last speech in the Commons.

While in the Commons Leader was a prominent figure in London society. His friendship with Brougham grew and he was with him when Brougham had, on 21 October 1839, a dangerous but not fatal carriage accident at Brougham Hall; Leader was a party to the practical joke by which a report of Brougham's death was published in *The Times*.

Leader entertained generously at his residence at Putney and at a house that he rented in Stratton Street. His friend Edward John Trelawny long lived with him at Putney. Others of his guests there included Richard Monckton Milnes, Charles Austin, and French, Italian, and American visitors to the country (for list see R. E. Leader, *Autobiography of J. A. Roebuck*, 1897, 106–7). He was a friend in London of Louis Napoleon, who, when planning his landing at Boulogne in 1840, requested Leader's help with his French friends. He moved in literary and artistic as well as in political circles, and showed an interest in Gabriele Rossetti, the father of Dante Gabriel Rossetti (W. M. Rossetti, *Reminiscences*, 1906, 366–7). His archives include the only known copy of his *An Italian Ghost Story* (1896).

In 1844 Leader's career underwent, without explanation, a sudden change. Abandoning his promising political prospects and his wide-ranging interests at home, he left England for the continent (traditionally an exit signifying a scandal to be quickly avoided, though none has been traced), and, although he lived for nearly half a century more, he thenceforth rarely visited Britain. At first he spent much time at Cannes with his friend Brougham, and here Richard Cobden met them both in 1846. Like Brougham, Leader bought property at Cannes, and played a part in its development as a favourite resort of the British. He built a house there, known as Château Leader, and the municipality named a thoroughfare boulevard Leader. But he sold his property in Cannes some time before his death.

It was with Florence that Leader's self-imposed exile was mainly identified. In that city and its near neighbourhood he bought many old buildings of historic interest, elaborately restoring them at considerable cost and filling them with works of art and antiquities. On 16 February 1850 he bought the ancient Villa Pazzi, in the village of Maiano, near Florence. On 5 March 1855 he purchased the ruined medieval castle of Vincigliata, in 1857 no. 14 in the piazza dei Pitti in Florence itself, and on 8 April 1862 the Villa Catanzaro, also at Maiano. All these buildings were practically rebuilt under his supervision. The two houses at Maiano were each renamed Villa Temple Leader (*La parrocchia di S Martino e Majano: cenni storici*, 1875; G. Marcotti, *Simpatie di Majano: lettere dalla Villa Temple Leader*, 1883). In the restoration of the gigantic castle of Vincigliata Leader took immense interest. The exhaustive reconstruction was the work of Giuseppi Fancelli, son of

the *fattore* or steward of Leader's Florentine estates, whom he had had trained as an architect. At his villas at Maiano and at Vincigliata Leader built spacious swimming pools in the grounds, in which he swam round the year until his death. Although he lived part of each year in the restored castle, he freely opened it to the public. His pride in it increased with his years, and he delighted in conducting distinguished visitors round it, including, on 15 April 1888, Queen Victoria. He commemorated many of these visits by inscriptions on marble slabs fixed to the castle walls. Some of his Florentine guests renewed old associations. In January 1888 he acted as cicerone to Gladstone and his family, and he began a correspondence with the statesman that continued until the end of Gladstone's life. Gladstone thought Vincigliata 'a curious fabric with interesting and one or two very beautiful objects' (Gladstone, *Diaries*, 13 Jan 1888, 12.91). Leader surprised Gladstone by his vitality, and interested him in a collection that he formed of English words derived from the Italian (see J. T. Leader, *Philological Pastimes of an Englishman in Tuscany, with some Letters of Gladstone to J. T. Leader*, 1898).

Leader's practical interest in Florentine archaeology, which extended beyond his own possessions, was rewarded by the bestowal on him of the knight commandership of the Crown of Italy by King Victor Emmanuel. He sponsored the compilation and publication of many archaeological treatises on Vincigliata and Maiano and several Italian manuscripts of literary, historical, or genealogical interest were printed at his expense. He was an enthusiastic biographer, and published with Giuseppe Marcotti a life of Sir John Hawkwood, as *Giovanni Acuto* (1889) and in English translation, and a *Life of Sir Robert Dudley, Duke of Northumberland* (1895). In both works he was assisted by Lucy *Baxter (writing as Leader Scott).

On 19 August 1867 Leader married, on one of his few visits to London, by special licence, Maria Louisa di Leoni, widow of Count Antonio di Leoni and daughter of Constantine Raimondi. She died at Florence on 5 February 1906. The marriage was childless. Leader himself died, active to the last, at piazza dei Pitti 14, Florence, on 1 March 1903. Late in life he adopted the Roman Catholic faith, and in accordance with a codicil to his will he was buried with Roman Catholic rites.

Leader left over £279,000. He made several bequests to educational and charitable institutions in Florence, including the sum of £7000 for the restoration of the central bronze door of the duomo. The rest of his property in England and Italy, including Vincigliata, was bequeathed to his grandnephew Richard Luttrell Pilkington Bethell, third Lord Westbury (1852–1930), whose maternal grandfather, the Revd Alexander Fownes-Luttrell, had married Leader's sister Anne Jane. Leader still owned at his death the family residence on Putney Hill. He proved his lifelong interest in the district by giving £2000 in 1887 for the restoration of St John's Church there.

SIDNEY LEE, *rev.* H. C. G. MATTHEW

Sources *The Times* (3 March 1903) · *The Times* (11 May 1903) · *The Tablet* (16 May 1903) · J. T. Leader, *Rough and rambling notes, chiefly of my early life* (1899) · R. E. Leader, *Life and letters of John Arthur Roebuck*

(1897) • Gladstone, *Diaries* • W. Thomas, *The philosophic radicals: nine studies in theory and practice, 1817–1841* (1979) • G. Marcotti, *Vincigliata* (1870) • A. Papini, *Majano Vincigliata Settignano* (1876) • Leader Scott [L. Baxter], *Vincigliata and Maiano* (1891) • A. Adburgham, *A radical aristocrat … Sir William Molesworth … and his wife Andalusia* (1990)

Archives HLRO, personal and family corresp. and papers | BL, letters to W. E. Gladstone, Add. MSS 44503–44525 • BL, letters to Sir A. H. Layard, Add. MSS 39045–39048, 39098–39099 • NL Scot., letters to J. R. Hope-Scott

Likenesses J. Doyle, caricature, pen-and-pencil drawing, 1839, BM • J. Doyle, caricature, pen-and-pencil drawing, 1842, BM • bronze medallion, 1895, Reform Club, London • G. H. Harlow, group portrait (as a boy); formerly Holmwood, Putney Heath • D. Lucas, aquatint print (after B. E. Duppa), NPG • W. H. Mote, stipple (after B. E. Duppa), BM, NPG; repro. in J. Saunders, *Political reformers* (1840) [*see illus.*] • portraits (with his wife), Piazza dei Pitti, Florence • portraits (with his wife), Villa Temple Leader, Maiano • stipple, NPG

Wealth at death £282,401 0s. 2d.: resworn double probate, June 1903, *CGPLA Eng. & Wales*

Leaf, Walter (1852–1927), banker and classical scholar, was born at Gibson's Hill, Norwood, Surrey, on 26 November 1852. Small, short-sighted, and frail as a child, Leaf's education, friends, and work in the City transformed him into a curious, sceptical, and bold man of affairs. His father, Charles John Leaf, was a partner in a firm of silk and ribbon dealers. His mother, Isabella Ellen, was the daughter of John Tyas, a classical scholar who was for twenty years on the staff of *The Times*.

Sickly, Leaf was tutored at home as a boy, but his cleverness was quickly recognized and he won an entrance scholarship at Winchester College. His parents, however, felt him too frail to be a boarder and moved so that he could become a day boy at Harrow School. He found his feet at Harrow after being taken up by two schoolmasters there, Edward Ernest Bowen and Edward Mallet Young, both members of the Apostles, the secret discussion society at Cambridge. They took him off to Rome and Naples, where he smoked his first cigar and was charged with the vitality of classical letters by contact with the actual scenes of antiquity. Back at Harrow he came under the personal teaching of the headmaster, Henry Montagu Butler. In 1869 an event which changed Leaf's life occurred. Park House at Harrow had fallen under the control of a group of roughs who established the kind of tyranny for which the public schools were infamous. The housemaster, Frederick William Farrar, brought in Leaf as head to establish order. With terror and trembling Leaf stepped to the task. He gave the ringleader ten of the best and, in so doing, discovered his own self-reliance and self-confidence. In 1870, having won a classical scholarship, Leaf went up to Trinity College, Cambridge, where he became senior classic (1874) and was elected to a fellowship (1875). More importantly the Apostles elected him, and he became a part of a generation of literary luminaries that helped forge his intellectual character and outlook on life as he set forth into the wider world.

Leaf contemplated a career at the bar, but family circumstances—the deaths of his grandfather and uncle, and his father's illness—called him home to the firm at Old Change. He had to contend with his father's meddling and the weakening position of the firm. So, driven by anxiety and by a stern sense of duty, Leaf moved with great effectiveness and consolidated the firm's financial position, converting it to a limited liability company in 1888 and amalgamating it with another company in 1892 to form Pawsons and Law Ltd. Although he had a seat on the board of the new company, he ceased to take an active part in its management. In 1891 he was elected a director of the London and Westminster Bank, to which he brought to bear his experience as a partner in a mercantile firm. During his period on the board the London and Westminster amalgamated with the London and County Bank and, in 1918, with Parr's Bank. By 1923 the Westminster Bank Ltd, as the amalgamation was named, was securely among the five largest banks in Britain. Leaf had been effectively chairman since 1914, and was formally elected to the chair in 1918, becoming chairman also of the Institute of Bankers in 1919. He published in 1926 a well-regarded handbook, *Banking*, for the Home University Library.

Leaf took a keen interest in economic questions that ranged outside the world of Old Change, and was one of the founders of the London chamber of commerce (1882). After the First World War, as president of the International chamber of commerce (1920), he went to Germany to promote economic reconciliation. He was a staunch free-trader and supported a return to the gold standard in 1925. Yet Leaf recognized the emotional and intellectual dangers of the business world. Although he rose to become a power in the City, he was not intellectually taxed by banking and its problems: he felt he was dealing with trivial matters of little usefulness, going on from day to day without ambition or aim.

Therefore, from the time he went down from Cambridge Leaf's literary work consoled him with a sense of permanence and meaning. Macmillan had contracted Leaf and John Henry Pratt, another friend from the Apostles, to produce an edition of the *Iliad*, but Pratt's death by drowning in Lake Como in 1878 left Leaf to do it alone. Leaf produced *The Iliad* with introduction and notes (2 vols., 1886–8), which remained for decades the best edition in English. It was followed by *Troy: a Study in Homeric Geography* (1912), *Homer and History* (1915), and *Strabo on the Troad* (1923), among other works. Leaf's keen geographical and topographical sensitivity, which he first grasped at Pompeii as a boy, combined with his life in the active world of business, led him always to combine scholarship with a sense of physical reality. It was vital for him to know that there actually had been a Troy and a Trojan war, an attitude which set him apart from Jane Harrison and the Cambridge Ritualists and Gilbert Murray, and gave his prose a thoroughness, a common sense, and simplicity. Leaf passionately believed in classical work as the best preparation for the active life and he urged reforms of the study of the ancient world in universities so that it would meet the standards of modern disciplines. A person of wide learning Leaf had, in addition to the classical languages, a firm knowledge of French, German, Russian, Italian, and

Persian. The degrees of LittD and honorary DLitt were conferred upon him by Cambridge (1889) and Oxford (1904) respectively.

Alpine climbing, along with his youthful visit to Naples, gave Leaf an acute visual understanding of intellectual problems. An enthusiastic member of the Alpine Club, Leaf ascended the Breithorn with his brother, Herbert Leaf, in 1871, and made an assault on the Aletschhorn from the north with Frederick Pollock and Pratt in 1872. He climbed Mont Blanc in 1873 and the Matterhorn with Pratt in 1875. Leaf climbed Piz Tschierva in 1880, and made the first ascents of Becca di Ciardonnay in 1890 and the Fluela Schwarzhorn with G. W. Prothero in 1893. Like many of his contemporaries at Cambridge, Leaf was seized by the new world of scientific, literary, and emotional possibilities which mountaineering, with its freedom and comradeship, opened to them. Leaf gave accounts of his adventures in papers to the Alpine Club: 'Climbing with a hand camera' and 'In the land of bears'. Leaf sealed his association with that band of literary alpinists—Pratt, Horatio Brown, Roden Noel, the Sidgwicks—who had gathered for summers for climbing and talk at Davos Plaz, when he married, on 22 May 1894, Charlotte Mary, the daughter of John Addington *Symonds. Henry Montagu Butler presided over the wedding in the parish church at Lyme Regis in Dorset.

Such a man could only be a Liberal, but Leaf separated himself from Gladstone over Irish nationalism, and with his friends James Parker Smith, Bowen, and J. E. C. Welldon left the Liberal Eighty Club. Leaf was chairman of the Liberal Unionists in Marylebone and might have contested a parliamentary seat if he had not had to stand against his friend James Bryce. Leaf, however, was a long-time member of the London county council where his directness and speaking power made him an influential figure. And Leaf's religion was of a piece with his politics. As a young man at Cambridge, as soon as he felt he could think and speak freely on questions of religion, the moderate evangelicalism in which he had been raised fell away effortlessly. Without anguish he simply realized literal dogmatism had no meaning for him. He refused to take communion with his parents, but continued his attendance at church. Leaf became, as he said, a theoretical agnostic but with a strong tendency toward an intimate theism; he was a member of the Society for Psychical Research. Walter Leaf died at the Imperial Hotel, Torquay, on 8 March 1927.   WILLIAM C. LUBENOW

Sources W. Leaf, *Walter Leaf, 1852–1927: some chapters of autobiography, with a memoir by Charlotte Leaf* (1932) · D. W. F. and F. P., 'In memoriam: Walter Leaf', *Alpine Journal*, 39 (1927), 123–4 · Venn, *Alum. Cant.* · Y. Cassis, 'Leaf, Walter', *DBB* · J. Oppenheim, *The other world: spiritualism and psychical research in England, 1850–1914* (1985) · b. cert. · m. cert. · d. cert.

Archives BL, corresp. with the Macmillans, Add. MS 55126 · Bodl. Oxf., letters to Gilbert Murray

Likenesses W. Rothenstein, crayon drawing, 1910, NPG; repro. in W. Rothenstein, *Portrait drawings of William Rothenstein, 1889–1925* (1926) · R. Schwabe, pencil drawing, 1927, Trinity Cam. · photograph, repro. in *Alpine Journal*, 122

Wealth at death £125,740 12s. 11d.: resworn probate, 17 May 1927, *CGPLA Eng. & Wales*

Leahy, Arthur (1830–1878), army officer, seventh son of John Leahy (1770–1846), JP, of South Hill, Killarney, was born on 5 August 1830, and educated at Corpus Christi Hall, Maidstone, and the Royal Military Academy, Woolwich. He was commissioned lieutenant, Royal Engineers, on 27 June 1848, and, after the Chatham course, was quartered in Ireland until 1853, and after that at Corfu.

On the outbreak of the war with Russia in 1854, Leahy joined the army at Varna and went with it to the Crimea. He was at the battles of the Alma and Inkerman. During the early part of the siege of Sevastopol he was acting adjutant, and in charge of the engineer park of the left attack under Major Frederick Chapman. In managing the park and the engineer transport train he showed his characteristic energy and industry. As the winter set in Leahy was appointed deputy assistant quartermaster-general for the Royal Engineers. In the official *Journal of the Siege Operations* Leahy is credited with invaluable services in providing for the comfort and maintenance of the engineer troops. He received the Mejidiye (fifth class).

From the Crimea, Leahy returned to Corfu in 1856, and became a second-captain on 2 December 1857. His brevet majority for service in the Crimea, which he received some time after, was antedated to 3 December 1857. He returned home early in 1858, was stationed for a short time at Woolwich, and in June was appointed to the staff of the inspector-general of fortifications at the War Office. In 1864 he became assistant director of works in the fortification branch of the War Office. The defence of the home arsenals and dockyards was then considered a matter of urgency, and the defence loan, the result of the 1859 royal commission on the defences of the United Kingdom, provided the necessary funds. The work required of the fortification branch was enormous, and Leahy's share of it large. In addition to his regular work he was a member of many committees, and in 1870 was secretary of that presided over by Lord Lansdowne on the employment of Royal Engineers officers in the civil departments of the state.

Leahy was employed at the Paris Exhibition of 1867 and made three reports, which were published, on military hospitals and barrack buildings, on field hospital equipment, and on military telegraphy and signalling. He became brevet lieutenant-colonel on 29 November 1868. In July 1871 he was appointed instructor of field works at the School of Military Engineering at Chatham, and owing to his efforts the instruction in fieldworks and related subjects was made available not only for the whole regular army but also for the militia and volunteers. Due to his initiative classes for pioneer sergeants of infantry were introduced, and he himself prepared the official manual for their instruction. He brought the field park and its workshops to a high state of efficiency. He was promoted regimental lieutenant-colonel on 10 December 1873, and in March 1876 was sent to Gibraltar as second in command of the Royal Engineers. He was promoted brevet colonel on 1 October 1877.

Leahy was twice married, first in 1857 to Miss Tabuteau, with whom he had two children, and secondly to Miss E. J.

Poynter, with whom he had five children. He was the author of a pamphlet on army reorganization (1868). In 1878 Leahy was attacked by Rock fever, was taken home, and died on 13 July 1878 at the Royal Victoria Military Hospital, Netley, near Southampton.

R. H. VETCH, *rev.* ROGER T. STEARN

Sources Royal Engineers Institute, Chatham, royal engineers records · *Royal Engineers Journal*, 9 (1878) · A. D. Lambert, *The Crimean War: British grand strategy, 1853–56* (1990) · I. V. Hogg, *Coast defences of England and Wales, 1856–1956* (1974) · Boase, *Mod. Eng. biog.*
Likenesses Disderi, photograph, *c.*1863, NPG
Wealth at death under £2000: resworn probate, Jan 1879, *CGPLA Eng. & Wales* (1878)

Leahy, Edward Daniel (1797–1875), painter, was born in London, the son of David Leahy of Dublin, afterwards of London (who was from a Cork family). He was a student at the Dublin Society's Schools, where he won several prizes between 1811 and 1814. He exhibited at the Hibernian Society of Artists and the Dublin Society's house in Hawkins Street in 1815. In the following year he sent four portraits to the exhibition in Hawkins Street and was awarded a premium by the Irish Institute. In 1817 he exhibited three works; shortly afterwards he moved to London and established himself there as a portrait and subject painter. In 1820 he sent a *Portrait of Mrs. Yates of Covent Garden in the Character of Meg Merrilies* to the Royal Academy, and became a frequent exhibitor, both there and at the British Institution.

Both the duke of Sussex and the marquess of Bristol sat to Leahy; his sitters also included, among other prominent Irishmen, the earl of Rosse, R. L. Sheil MP, Sir John M. Tierney MD, and Father Theobald Mathew the 'Apostle of Temperance' (exh. RA, 1847; NPG). He exhibited mostly portraits at the Royal Academy, but also historical subjects, for example, *Mary Stuart's Farewell to France* (exh. RA, 1825 and Royal Hibernian Academy, 1842), engraved by J. Goodyear in 1828. He painted marine subjects in both Ireland and England. In 1826 he sent two paintings to the first exhibition of the Royal Hibernian Academy, *Recovery of the Intercepted Letter* (exh. RA, 1824) and *The Fortune Teller* (exh. RA, 1821). He continued to exhibit in Dublin at intervals until 1846; that year he exhibited *Portrait of William Cumming, ex-President of the Academy* (exh. RA, 1832; Royal Hibernian Academy). Between 1837 and 1843 Leahy lived in Italy, and in Rome he painted a portrait of the sculptor John Gibson RA (exh. RA, 1843). After his return he exhibited a few Italian subjects, and showed at the Royal Academy for the last time in 1853. He died at Brighton on 10 January 1875, leaving a widow, Eliza.

F. M. O'DONOGHUE, *rev.* RUTH STEWART

Sources W. G. Strickland, *A dictionary of Irish artists*, 2 (1913); facs. edn with introduction by T. J. Snoddy (1969) · Wood, *Vic. painters* · *CGPLA Eng. & Wales* (1875)
Likenesses portrait, repro. in Strickland, *Dictionary*
Wealth at death under £200: administration, 1 April 1875, *CGPLA Eng. & Wales*

Leahy, Patrick (1806–1875), Roman Catholic archbishop of Cashel, was born at Fennor, in the parish of Gortnahoe, co. Tipperary, on 31 May 1806, the son of Patrick Leahy (*d.*

1850), civil engineer and surveyor of Cork, and Mary Margaret *née* Cormack (*d.* 1845), a native of Gortnahoe. He received his early education in the classical day school in Thurles, co. Tipperary. In August 1826 he entered St Patrick's College, Maynooth, the Irish national seminary, where he studied philosophy and theology for the next seven years. He was ordained priest on 19 June 1833.

Leahy's first appointment was to the parish of Knocklong, co. Limerick, where he served as curate from 1833 to 1835; he then transferred to Thurles as curate from 1835 to 1837. In 1837 he was appointed professor in the newly established St Patrick's College, Thurles, and in 1842, when the college opened an ecclesiastical department catering for candidates for the foreign missions, he taught sacred scripture. In 1847 he became president of St Patrick's College, Thurles. When the Irish Roman Catholic church met for its national synod in August 1850 in Thurles, Leahy acted as one of the secretaries. Among the recommendations of this synod was the establishment of a Catholic university, which was eventually opened in Dublin in 1854. Leahy was selected for the office of vice-rector by Dr John Henry (later Cardinal) Newman, and filled the chair of exegetics. In 1855 Leahy severed his connection with St Patrick's College, Thurles, following his appointment as parish priest of Cashel, co. Tipperary. He received a special indult from Rome, allowing him to reside for most of the year in Dublin, in order to fulfil his university commitments.

On 3 May 1857 Leahy was appointed to the vacant see of Cashel, and was consecrated on 29 June 1857. As archbishop of Cashel, he showed himself to be a leader, especially in the field of education. In 1866 and 1867 he was deputed by the Irish Catholic bishops to conduct negotiations with Lord Mayo, the chief secretary for Ireland, in regard to the proposed endowment of the Catholic university. A strong advocate of the cause of temperance, he enforced the Sunday closing of the public houses in his diocese. His term of office coincided with the beginnings of the Fenian (Irish Republican Brotherhood) movement in Ireland. He advised the Roman authorities against condemning the Fenians, hoping that 'the Fenian bubble would burst of its own accord'.

Thanks to Leahy's energy, the fine cathedral at Thurles was built at the cost of £30,000. He died of heart disease at his episcopal residence in Thurles on 26 January 1875 and was buried in Thurles Cathedral on 3 February. According to many of his contemporaries, he was remarkable for his dignified bearing and uniform courtesy.

G. C. BOASE, *rev.* D. MARK TIERNEY

Sources C. O'Dwyer, 'The life of Dr Leahy, 1806–1875', MA diss, St Patrick's College, Maynooth, 1970 · parish register, Gortnahoe, co. Tipperary, 3/6/1806 [baptism] · *Freeman's Journal* [Dublin] (4 Feb 1875)
Archives archbishop's house, Thurles, co. Tipperary · Cashel and Emly Diocesan Archives, corresp. and papers | archbishop's house, Drumcondra, Dublin, Cullen MSS · Oratory, Birmingham, Newman MSS · Sacra Congregazione di Propaganda Fide, Rome, papers relating to congresses in Ireland
Likenesses oils, archbishop's house, Thurles, co. Tipperary · oils, St Patrick's College, Maynooth, co. Kildare

Leake. *See also* Leeke.

Leake, Sir Andrew (d. 1704), naval officer, was the eldest son of Andrew Leake (d. 1675), merchant, of Lowestoft and his wife, Deborah Soaps (d. 1704). His sister Margaret married the future admiral Sir John Ashby and it was Ashby who started Leake's career in the navy. He served as a midshipman with Ashby on the *Mordaunt* in 1688 and on the *Defiance*, from 11 September to 1 December 1688, when he was re-entered as master's mate. He was present at the battle of Bantry Bay on 1 May 1689. He was appointed second lieutenant of Ashby's *Berwick* on 16 June 1689, and on 1 May 1690 first lieutenant of the *Sandwich*, Ashby's flagship at the battle of Beachy Head on 30 June. On 7 August 1690 he was promoted to commander of the fireship *Roebuck*, and he commanded the fireship *Fox* in the spring and summer of 1691. Around this time Admiral Edward Russell, in his list of captains, noted concerning him 'a young man but good, know little of him', adding 'a good seaman but query whether well affected to the government', though it is not clear on what grounds he raised the question of Leake's possible political leanings (Folger Shakespeare Library, Rich MS xd 451 (98)).

Leake was not employed as a captain in 1692 but served with Ashby on board his flagship, the *Victory*, and commanded one of the boats which burnt the French ships at La Hogue on 23 May 1692. It was probably as a result of this action that in April 1693 the Admiralty recommended Leake to the three admirals who appointed him captain of the *James Galley* on 25 June 1693, followed by command of the *Greenwich* (July 1693 to May 1694), the *Lancaster* (29 May 1694 to 9 June 1695), and the *Canterbury* (9 June 1695 to January 1698). During ten months without employment in 1698 he collected funds for rebuilding the church at Lowestoft. On 18 November 1698 Leake was appointed captain of the *Hampshire* and given the rank of commodore and command of a squadron at Newfoundland. He returned to England in January 1701 but on arrival in the Downs found that his crew had dispatched a round robin to the Admiralty alleging his ill usage of them. He protested that 'I always took care to do the sailors justice' and argued that the accusations were lodged because his crew wanted to cheat their landladies of large bills (PRO, ADM 1/2033). Should the accusations result in their being 'turned over' to another ship the crew would not be paid off in the Downs, leaving open the possibility that they might eventually be paid off elsewhere and manage to keep their wages. The Admiralty accepted his explanation and in January 1702 he was appointed flag captain to Vice-Admiral Sir Thomas Hopsonn in the *Torbay*. As such he was present at the abortive attempt on Cadiz on 12 August and the attack on the Franco-Spanish fleet at Vigo Bay on 12 October, being knighted by Queen Anne for his conduct in the latter engagement.

From February 1703 Leake commanded the *Ranelagh* at the Nore, then the *Lancaster*, and on 3 May was appointed to the *Grafton*. He served in the Mediterranean under Sir Cloudesley Shovell in 1703 and under Sir George Rooke in 1704, when he was sent to conclude a peace treaty with the emperor of Morocco. The *Grafton* was one of the ships, under Sir George Byng, that attacked and captured Gibraltar on 22 July 1704. The *Grafton* used up a great deal of ammunition in bombarding Gibraltar, which may have affected it at the battle of Malaga on 13 August. There the *Grafton* engaged as the leading ship of the Red squadron and, shortly after 10 a.m., Leake was mortally wounded. After his wound had been dressed he was carried up on to the quarter-deck and placed in an armchair, where he died. It is not known if he had ever married; by his will, of March 1703, he left his estate to his mother, who had remarried, and various amounts of money to his brothers and sisters. 'From the grace and comeliness of his person', he was sometimes known as 'Queen Anne's handsome captain' (*Calendar of Treasury Books, 1704–5*, 228).

J. K. LAUGHTON, rev. PETER LE FEVRE

Sources Mutford and Lethingland pedigrees, Lowestoft Public Library and RO · paybook *Mordaunt*, PRO, ADM 33/123 · paybook *Defiance*, PRO, ADM 33/109 · paybooks *Sandwich* and *Roebuck*, PRO, ADM 33/122 · admiralty minute book, PRO, ADM 3/8 · letter of the three admirals, 1693, PRO, ADM 7/694 · half pay registers, PRO, ADM 25/2 · captain's letters, PRO, ADM 1/2033, 2034 · PRO, PROB 11/478, fols. 213v–214v · captain's journal *Grafton* (ends 13 Aug 1704), PRO, ADM 51/407, pt 3 · E. Russell, 'Characters of captains, Nov. 1691', Folger, Rich MS xd 451 (98) · *LondG* (14–18 Sept 1704) · J. Charnock, ed., *Biographia navalis*, 2 (1795), 331 · W. A. Shaw, ed., *Calendar of treasury books*, 19, PRO (1938), 228 · captain's journal *Victory* (23 May 1692), PRO, ADM 51/4384, pt 2
Archives Folger, Rich MSS · PRO, admiralty MSS
Wealth at death over £1000: will, PRO, PROB 11/478, fols. 213v–214v

Leake, Arthur Martin- (1874–1953), surgeon, was born at Marshalls, High Cross, Hertfordshire, on 4 April 1874, the seventh of eight children (two daughters and six sons) of Stephen Martin *Leake (1826–1893), a well-known barrister and legal writer, and his wife, Isabel Plunkett (1835–1913). The family originated in southern Ireland but had played a prominent part in English life since the seventeenth century. One of his ancestors, Sir John Leake (1656–1720), was commander-in-chief of Queen Anne's fleet and his son, Stephen (1702–1773), became the Garter king of arms. The family continued to serve with distinction in the army and navy, and three of Arthur's brothers made careers in the armed services. The family was imbued with a strong pride in their country and its empire.

Arthur Martin-Leake attended Westminster School and University College, London, where he studied medicine, qualifying MRCS and LRCP in 1898. Shortly afterwards war broke out in South Africa and he joined the imperial yeomanry as a trooper, unable to find employment immediately as a medical officer. The following year he transferred to the South African constabulary and was appointed surgeon-captain.

Like many other civilian surgeons working in South Africa, Martin-Leake was critical of the British army and its medical department. He felt that medical officers were more interested in correct military procedure than in the welfare of their patients. He was particularly scathing about the failure of the Royal Army Medical Corps (RAMC) to prepare for the epidemic of typhoid fever that ravaged the army in 1900. Typhoid was endemic to the region and a serious outbreak was predicted well in advance. In his letters home he praised the maverick Conservative MP William Burdett-Coutts for disclosing the breakdown of medical arrangements in South Africa. 'I am sure Burdett-Coutts has done a very great work in exposing the matter', he wrote, 'for I know what a hopeless set of idiots most of the RAMC men are and I am quite sure they are not capable of organising anything' (Hertfordshire Archives, acc. 599, 86794).

Unlike his brothers Arthur Martin-Leake found military life distasteful; his sense of duty nevertheless compelled him to take extraordinary risks in the service of his country. On 8 February 1902, at Vlakfontein, he went out under heavy fire to attend a badly wounded officer, receiving three bullet wounds in the process. He gave up only when absolutely exhausted and refused water until other wounded men had been served. For his great bravery he was awarded the Victoria Cross on 13 May 1902.

It was some time before Martin-Leake was able to resume professional duties, but he was fit enough to study for the fellowship examinations of the Royal College of Surgeons and was admitted FRCS in June 1903. A few months later he left for India to take up an appointment with the Bengal–Nagpur railway. As the railway's chief medical officer he was in charge of an excellent hospital, in which he was able to hone his surgical skills. He was also in medical charge of two battalions of infantry volunteers formed from among staff at the railway. Very content with his position in India, he retained his post with the railway for thirty-four years.

When Montenegro declared war on Turkey in 1912, Martin-Leake was on leave in England and was given permission by the British Red Cross to form a medical unit for service with the Montenegrin army. Though grateful to the Red Cross for this opportunity, he became very critical of the organization. He found that there was plenty of medical equipment but very few drugs; medical staff and equipment were also poorly distributed and there was a great deal of waste.

The First World War did little to change Martin-Leake's opinion of the Red Cross. Despite his earlier aversion to the RAMC he took leave of absence from his railway post to join the corps on a temporary commission as a lieutenant, and was subsequently posted to 5th field ambulance in Belgium. On joining his unit he found that the army and the Red Cross were 'having a constant feud' and he described the Red Cross as 'an impossible organisation' (Hertfordshire Archives, acc. 599, 86959).

The life of a medical officer at the front was hazardous, and military doctors were often forced to work under heavy fire. Martin-Leake showed conspicuous bravery on several occasions by treating wounded men close to the German trenches at Zonnebeke during the first battle of Ypres, between 29 October and 8 November 1914. His selfless acts gained him the distinction of being the first man to win a bar to his Victoria Cross, which was awarded on 15 February 1915. Later in the same year he was also awarded the British Medical Association's gold medal for those who had 'conspicuously raised the character of the medical profession'.

Martin-Leake's previous experience in the Balkans led to his being attached, in 1915, to the 'Adriatic mission', dispatched to assist the Serbian army. The mission, however, arrived too late to be of much assistance, and after spending a short time in Corfu and Italy he returned to England in March 1916. Shortly afterwards he was dispatched to the western front, where his brother Theodore was also serving, in the Royal Engineers. A year later Arthur was given command of a field ambulance and promoted to the rank of lieutenant-colonel.

After the war ended Martin-Leake resumed his post with the Bengal–Nagpur railway. On 1 October 1930 he married Winifred Frances (c.1884–1932), the widow of C. W. A. Carroll, agent of the Bengal–Nagpur railway, and second daughter of William Alfred Nedham of the central provinces commission, India. Until that time he had shown little interest in the company of women and was something of a misogynist, disliking nurses, 'railway wives', and suffragettes. Winifred was clearly an exception, and the two had much in common: both loved India and enjoyed hunting and the outdoor life. She died only two years later and there were no children from their marriage.

Martin-Leake returned to Hertfordshire in 1937, his retirement being interrupted by the outbreak of war in 1939. From 1939 to 1945 he commanded a mobile air raid precaution unit at Puckeridge, which was often praised for its efficiency. Arthur Martin-Leake was a keen motorist and motorcyclist and, for a short time, held a pilot's licence. In later life he also became a passionate gardener and was famed for his vegetables. He was widely admired and respected as a man of simple tastes and good character. He died at the family home, Marshalls, on 22 June 1953 and was buried at St Mary's churchyard, High Cross, Hertfordshire. MARK HARRISON

Sources Herts. ALS, Martin-Leake papers, acc. 599 · A. Clayton, *Martin-Leake—double VC* (1994) · *BMJ* (4 July 1953) · *The Lancet* (4 July 1953) · *The Times* (24 June 1953) · *The register of the Victoria cross*, 3rd edn (1997) · www.chapter-one.com/vc/award, 25 Oct 2001 · www2. prestel.co.uk/stewart/hertford.htm, 25 Oct 2001 · Burke, *Gen. GB* (1937) [Martin-Leake, late of Thorpe Hall]
Archives Herts. ALS, family corresp. | Royal Army Medical Corps, Camberley, Surrey, muniments room, VCs
Likenesses photograph, VC record · photograph, repro. in www. chapter-one.com/vc/award, accessed 25 Oct 2001; originally appeared on Gallaher cigarette cards
Wealth at death £110,320 12s.: probate, 19 May 1954, *CGPLA Eng. & Wales*

Leake, George (1856–1902), lawyer and politician in Australia, was born on 3 December 1856 in Perth, Western Australia, the eldest son of the eight children of George Walpole Leake (1825–1895), a barrister and later attorney-general, and his first wife, Rose Ellen *née* Gliddon (d. 1888). His father and an uncle, Sir Luke Samuel Leake, had both achieved success in Western Australia, the former as a lawyer, the latter as a merchant. George Leake was educated at Bishop Hale's School, Perth, and St Peter's College, Adelaide, before being articled in his father's law firm. In 1880 he was admitted to the bar and partnership in the firm but in 1882 became acting crown solicitor; in 1883 he was confirmed in that post, which he retained until 1894. The regular income which went with a government appointment was important to Leake, for on 15 September 1881 he had married Louisa Emily (*b*. 1856), the daughter of Sir Archibald Burt, a former chief justice of Western Australia. Leake was an affable and popular man but an effective courtroom advocate, especially in criminal cases, with a gift for witty repartee. In 1898 he was appointed QC.

In 1890 Leake was elected to the first Western Australian legislative assembly, expecting to become attorney-general in the ministry formed by Sir John Forrest, but when this did not eventuate he resigned after only three weeks as, without a ministerial salary, he could not afford to give up the crown solicitorship. In 1894, however, he entered parliament for Albany and became an active member of the emergent opposition to the Forrest government and eventually opposition leader.

The 1890s was a decade of change in Western Australia, the colony experiencing a major gold rush which brought rapid population growth, an insatiable demand for public works, and social and political upheaval. The burgeoning goldfields community was critical of government policy, which favoured agricultural interests, and Leake found himself a parliamentary spokesman for some of their views. He also enthusiastically advocated Western Australia's becoming an original member of the Australian commonwealth. He was a delegate to the Australasian Federal Convention of 1897–8 and subsequently became president of the Western Australian Federal League and pressed the government to allow a referendum on the draft Commonwealth Bill. This eventually came in 1900 and was a triumph for the federalists.

Leake declined an invitation to stand for the first federal parliament, but took on an even more prominent role in the local parliament following Forrest's entry into the federal cabinet. He became premier of Western Australia in May 1901, but even with the cautious support of the eight Labor Party members he lacked a majority, and in October 1901 his government lost a no-confidence motion moved by one of Forrest's erstwhile supporters. Governor Sir Arthur Lawley refused a dissolution but two of Leake's opponents failed in their attempts to form a ministry, and eventually Leake returned to office in December 1901 in a stronger position, at the price of including a rural representative in his predominantly urban and goldfields-based team. This initiated a political realignment, which by 1905 saw the coalescence of the groups led in the 1890s by Forrest and Leake and the emergence of a two-party system on Labor versus non-Labor lines.

Leake's own contribution was over by this time, however, since he unexpectedly collapsed and died on 24 June 1902, at the age of forty-five, survived by his wife, a daughter, and four sons. He was buried in the East Perth cemetery on the 26th. Leake was one of the first generation of the colonial born to take a lead in Western Australian public life and was noteworthy among his contemporaries for

his broadly liberal sympathies. Although his two administrations totalled little more than twelve months he had, with the aid of his friend, law partner, and cabinet colleague Walter James, been responsible for significant legislation. The most notable measures were his Trades Unions Act, Workers' Compensation Act, and Industrial Conciliation and Arbitration Act. A keen cricketer in his youth, he was later a committee member of the Western Australian Turf Club. A CMG was gazetted posthumously.

B. K. DE GARIS

Sources B. K. de Garis, 'Leake, George', *AusDB*, vol. 10 • *Morning Herald* (25 June 1902) • *West Australian* (25 June 1902) • G. S. Reid and M. R. Oliver, *The premiers of Western Australia, 1890–1982* (1982) • *Cyclopaedia of Western Australia*, ed. J. S. Battye (1912) • *The Inquirer* (21 Jan 1874) • E. Russell, *A history of the law in Western Australia and its development from 1829 to 1879* (1980) • L. Hunt, 'A political biography of Walter Hartwell James, 1894–1904', MA diss., University of Western Australia, 1974 • C. T. Stannage, ed., *A new history of Western Australia* (1981) • D. Black, ed., *The house on the hill: a history of the parliament of Western Australia, 1832–1990* (1991)
Archives Battye Library of West Australian History, Perth | NL Aus., Deakin MSS

Leake, James (1686–1764), bookseller, was born on 4 April 1686 in the parish of St Botolph, Aldersgate, London, the second of the eleven children of John Leake (*c*.1660–1720), printer, and his wife, Elizabeth (*d*. 1721), probably the daughter of Richard and Amey Hurst of the parish of St Michael-le-Querne, London. There is no evidence to connect him with the family of booksellers named Leake who had been active since Elizabethan times: his father, who was apprenticed to John Macock and set up business in the parish of St Botolph about the time of his marriage in May 1684, was the son of a yeoman of 'Blemill' (probably Blymhill), Staffordshire.

Leake was brought up in the Jewen Street premises in which his father was established by 1687, and entered the Merchant Taylors' School in January 1699. He is listed in the register for September 1701, but had left by March 1702. He was apprenticed in October 1702 to the bookseller William Freeman, made free of the Stationers' Company in November 1709, and admitted to the livery in September 1720. By 1717 he was a bookseller in Stationer's Court in the parish of St Martin Ludgate in partnership with Joseph Hazard, but he moved from London some time after his marriage on 23 April 1721 to Hannah Hammond (*bap*. 1699, *d*. 1751), daughter of the Bath bookseller Henry Hammond (*d*. 1724), to whose business he succeeded. 'H. Hammond and J. Leake in Bath' are on the imprint of Matthew Hole's *Gamaliel's Advice in the Case of the Apostles* (1721), but Leake may for a while have kept up his business in Ludgate, where his short-lived first child, though buried in Bath in October 1722, had been born the previous August, and where he continued to vote until December 1724.

In the month of his marriage Leake inherited half his mother's estate, including her 'Printing Presses and Letter Utensils of trade' (Eaves and Kimpel, 'Samuel Richardson and his family circle', 268). These (together with three of the family's apprentices and the premises in Blue Ball Court which Leake appears to have been renting for his mother's business) were taken over by his future brother-in-law Samuel *Richardson, in whose business Leake retained an investment for several years. The two maintained close relations personally and professionally thereafter. Richardson married Elizabeth Leake in 1733 (the year in which Leake published the first substantial work of Richardson's own pen, *The Apprentice's Vade Mecum*), and was probably responsible for the puff which, in the 1738 edition of Defoe's *Tour*, identified Leake's establishment on Terrace Walk as 'one of the finest Bookseller's Shops in *Europe*' (Defoe, 2.241). A key institution in the social and literary life of Bath as the town approached its heyday, and the source of most of the important books published there over four decades, Leake's shop (which also operated from 1731 as a circulating library) brought him familiarity with such luminaries of the resort as Allen, Chesterfield, Pope, and Warburton, and made him a wealthy and celebrated man.

A blow to Leake's reputation came in 1741 when his name appeared on the false imprints of two pornographic Curll publications, *A New Description of Merryland* and *Merryland Displayed* (to the printing of which an otherwise shadowy John Leake of Angell Street, St Martin's-le-Grand, London, confessed in 1745). His keen sense of his own eminence earned him detraction of a more personal kind. George Cheyne thought him 'honest intentioned but surely the worst judging, wrongheaded, insolent Fellow living whom none can oblige but by Flattery and a Junket' (*Letters*, 46–7). To the earl of Orrery he was 'the Prince of all the coxcomical Fraternity of Booksellers', an unlearned master of literary ceremonies who 'disposes of his Favours and Regards as methodically as Nash takes out the Ladies to dance' (Orrery, 1.99).

From the mid-1740s Leake regularly published in partnership with William Frederick, the other leading Bath bookseller of the period. Leake died in Bath on 26 December 1764 (where he was buried on the 28th), and was succeeded in the trade by his sons James (1724–1791), Samuel (*b.* 1739), and Henry (*b.* 1741), who was also a portraitist.

THOMAS KEYMER

Sources T. C. D. Eaves and B. D. Kimpel, 'Samuel Richardson and his family circle, II: the Leakes', *N&Q*, 209 (1964), 264–70 • A. L. Reade, 'Samuel Richardson and his family circle [pts 2–3]', *N&Q*, 12th ser., 11 (1922), 224–6, 263–4 • A. L. Reade, 'Samuel Richardson and his family circle [pt 23]', *N&Q*, 12th ser., 12 (1923), 504–6 • T. C. D. Eaves and B. D. Kimpel, *Samuel Richardson: a biography* (1971) • T. C. D. Eaves and B. D. Kimpel, 'Samuel Richardson's London houses', *Studies in Bibliography*, 15 (1962), 135–48 • K. Maslen, *Samuel Richardson of London, printer* (Dunedin, New Zealand, 2001) • H. R. Plomer and others, *A dictionary of the printers and booksellers who were at work in England, Scotland, and Ireland from 1726 to 1775* (1932) • H. R. Plomer and others, *A dictionary of the printers and booksellers who were at work in England, Scotland, and Ireland from 1668 to 1725* (1922) • G. Lamoine, *La vie littéraire de Bath et de Bristol, 1750–1800*, 2 vols. (1978) • T. Fawcett, *Bath entertain'd: amusements, recreations and gambling at the eighteenth-century spa* (1998) • D. Foxon, *Libertine literature in England, 1660–1745* (1965) • A. D. McKillop, *Samuel Richardson: printer and novelist* (1936) • R. Straus, *The unspeakable Curll* (1927) • parish registers of St Botolph Aldersgate; St Martin Ludgate, St George the Martyr, Southwark • A. J. Jewers, ed., *The registers of the abbey church of SS Peter and Paul, Bath*, 2 vols., Harleian Society, Register Section, 27–8 (1900–01) • will of James Leake, PRO, PROB 11/908, sig. 148 • depositions of John Leake, PRO, SP 36/65, SP 44/83 • D. F. McKenzie, ed., *Stationers' Company apprentices*, 3 vols. (1961–78), vols. 2–3 • *The letters of Doctor George Cheyne to Samuel Richardson (1733–1743)*, ed. C. F. Mullett • countess of Cork and Orrery [E. C. Boyle], ed., *The Orrery papers*, 2 vols. (1903) • [D. Defoe], *A tour thro' the whole island of Great Britain*, 2nd edn, 3 vols. (1738) • private information [Michael Treadwell, Keith Maslen, John Dussinger] • *London Magazine*, 33 (1764), appx, 690

Wealth at death wealthy: will, PRO, PROB 11/908, sig. 148

Leake, Sir John (1656–1720), naval officer, was born in June 1656 at Rotherhithe, Surrey, the son of Richard *Leake (1629–1696), a master gunner, and his wife, Elizabeth (1631–1695). Instructed in mathematics and gunnery by his father he entered the navy at a young age and served with his father, who from about 1669 was master gunner in *Royal Prince*. By 1673 John Leake had joined his father in her when she was flagship of Admiral Sir Edward Spragge during the battle of the Texel, 10 August 1673. Among the casualties in the action was John's elder brother, Henry Leake.

At the end of the Third Anglo-Dutch War, in 1674, John Leake left the navy and served in merchant vessels, eventually becoming master on several voyages to the Mediterranean. He was reputed to have returned to the navy by 1677, when his father became master gunner of England. About 1681 he married Christian (*bap.* 1669, *d.* 1709), daughter of Captain Richard Hill of Great Yarmouth, Norfolk, who was among those who died the following year in the wreck of *Gloucester*, accompanying James, duke of York to Leith. In April 1682 Leake became mate to the master gunner of England, and also served, through his father's influence, as the master gunner of the 90-gun *Neptune* after she was commissioned in 1683.

In 1687–8 Richard Leake was arming a newly invented type of vessel, the bomb, supplied with a mortar on a turntable. Late in September 1688 John Leake was appointed to command the second of these new vessels, *Firedrake*. While fitting out the new mortar (or cushee piece, as it was then called) an explosion occurred, killing Leake's younger brother Edward. Once fitted out the vessel was immediately assigned to Lord Dartmouth's fleet and remained under his command until the end of 1688.

In April 1689 *Firedrake* joined the fleet under Admiral Herbert and on 1 May engaged the French under Châteaurenault in Bantry Bay. Leake was able to use the mortar his father had devised to set fire to and damage *Le Diamante*, commanded by the Chevalier de Coëtlogon. During the battle *Firedrake* had three men wounded, her foretopmast and topgallant mast shot away, with her mainstay shot and other rigging disabled. On the following day Herbert promoted Leake to command the 32-gun *Dartmouth*. Remaining in her as post captain for the following six months Leake first sailed for Liverpool, where he joined the escort for the forces under Major-General Percy Kirke to relieve Londonderry. For this purpose she joined the squadron commanded by Sir George Rooke on 8 June. Ordered to enter Lough Foyle and to reconnoitre the boom blocking the river Leake brought back information that led a council of war to decide, on 15 June, against risking the attempt. Then, operating under Rooke, Leake cruised

Sir John Leake (1656–1720), by Sir Godfrey Kneller, 1712

the Irish coast in an attempt to intercept several French warships that had been reported there.

Irish campaigns Over the following weeks the situation of the defending forces in Londonderry grew increasingly desperate. In mid-July Kirke sent a request to Rooke, asking that Leake be sent back to Lough Foyle. Rooke and Leake returned together on 28 July and Kirke ordered Leake to engage Culmore Castle and to take under his protection the victualling ships that also entered Lough Foyle with *Dartmouth*. An armed party of seamen went ashore from *Swallow*'s longboat and cut the boom to make a passage for Leake. Under heavy attack Leake held his fire until close under the castle. He opened fire with his heavy guns only when within musket shot range, creating a diversion that allowed two victuallers to pass into the river. With the wind falling *Mountjoy* and *Phoenix* passed slowly up the river to the Londonderry quay on the tide and under tow from *Swallow*'s longboat. With their successful arrival Leake's operation forced the enemy to raise the siege of Londonderry. Having observed Leake during all this Kirke reported to the duke of Hamilton that he 'behaved himself so bravely and discretely in this action, that I must beg your Grace to desire his Majesty to give him particular thanks for at his going up to the Castle' (Powley, 248).

In October 1689 Leake took command of the two-deck, 42-gun *Oxford* and joined Vice-Admiral Henry Killigrew's squadron, sailing first with the main fleet under Russell to convoy the queen of Spain to Corunna, then as an independent squadron to the Mediterranean. *En route* a storm heavily damaged the fleet, but after repairs in Cadiz Leake convoyed trade from Cadiz to Malaga and Alicante. On

news that the French Toulon squadron had put to sea Killigrew gathered his ships at Gibraltar to prepare for battle. There, on 11 May 1690—after only seven months in command of *Oxford*—the admiral ordered Leake to command the 70-gun *Eagle*. Killigrew and his squadron immediately searched for the French, and found and chased them, but they could not bring them to battle. Killigrew's squadron returned to England in July, just two weeks after the battle of Beachy Head.

In September 1690 Leake sailed from Portsmouth to join the convoy escort taking the earl of Marlborough's troops to Cork and Kinsale, returning to Chatham in late October. On 10 December Leake was one of the twenty-seven naval officers who sat on the court-martial board at Chatham and acquitted Lord Torrington of the charges brought against him in connection with the battle of Beachy Head. Returning to sea in March 1691 Leake in *Eagle* joined Admiral Russell's fleet operating in the channel. In May 1692, after reports were circulated that there were traitors in the fleet, Leake joined all the flag officers and captains in an address to the queen swearing their loyalty. A few days later the fleet was off the coast of France, where it encountered the French fleet off Point Barfleur on the Cotentin peninsula on 19 May 1692. In the line of battle Leake was three ships ahead of Russell's flagship in the centre squadron, where the heaviest fighting occurred. In the action *Eagle* had seventy men killed, more than a hundred wounded, lost her mizzenmast and foretopmast, and damaged her bowsprit and rigging. Leake was part of the squadron that attempted to pursue the French in the calm and fog that followed. On 23 May Vice-Admiral George Rooke, under orders to attack the French ships that had sought shelter close inshore near St Vaast-la-Hougue, shifted his flag to *Eagle*. Leake sailed *Eagle* as close inshore as possible, firing at the French ships while armed parties in *Eagle*'s boats rowed in to set them afire. After the action the fleet returned to Portsmouth for repairs, and in mid-June Leake sailed under Rooke to cruise off the French coast between St Malo and Brest. Between September and November *Eagle* cruised off Ushant carrying the flag of Admiral Sir John Ashby. At the end of December 1692 Leake left *Eagle*, having commanded her for 32 months, and immediately took command of the 60-gun *Plymouth* for the next seven months. In her he cruised the channel against enemy trade and provided convoy protection, then joined the main fleet under the joint admirals, when it convoyed the Smyrna convoy on only the first portion of the passage in which the French later destroyed it.

In July 1693 Leake took command of the three-deck, 90-gun *Ossory* and remained in her for the next four and a half years. After cruising in the channel for six weeks in summer 1693 *Ossory* entered Chatham Dockyard for repairs. Remaining there until March 1694 she joined Russell's fleet preparing for service in the Mediterranean. Arriving there in May they were joined by a Dutch squadron and cruised off Barcelona and Alicante for the French fleet. Wintering in Cadiz, Russell's squadron again cruised in the western Mediterranean without French opposition, returning to England in November 1695. After refitting *Ossory* at Chatham, Leake rejoined the fleet at the Downs in April 1696, sailing with it the following month for duty off Brest and in the Bay of Biscay, where during the summer he operated under the command of Admiral Lord John Berkeley raiding the French coast. Leake returned to Blackstakes in October, remaining there for the winter. In 1696 his father, Richard Leake, the master gunner of England, had died and Admiral Russell had attempted to procure that position for the son, but John Leake declined the nomination. Returning to sea in April 1697 Leake joined the Anglo-Dutch fleet under Sir George Rooke, cruising in the western channel. On the conclusion of peace at Rijswick, Leake was ordered to lay up his ship at Chatham. He left command in December 1697, having been continuously in command of six ships over nine and half years.

Leake was on half pay for nearly a year and a half and sought appointment as a Navy Board commissioner, but no vacancies were available. In May 1699 Leake accepted command of the just rebuilt 70-gun *Kent*. Immediately on taking command he embarked troops for Ireland in the squadron under Rear-Admiral Thomas Hopsonn, and then returned to Spithead. After ten months in *Kent*, Leake went ashore on half pay for a year in February 1700. In June of that year he retired from the post of mate to the master gunner of England and his only son, Richard Leake (1682–1720), succeeded him. Apparently through the personal patronage of Admiralty commissioner Captain George Churchill, Leake returned to sea in February 1701 in command of the newly rebuilt 70-gun *Berwick*, but found her in such unsatisfactory condition that he was unable to join Rooke's fleet in the channel until July, remaining with it until October.

In January 1702 William III dissolved the Admiralty commission and appointed the earl of Pembroke as lord high admiral. Employing his prerogative Pembroke planned to command personally a proposed expedition to Cadiz. Since he was not an experienced fleet commander he chose Leake to advise him, appointing him first captain of the 100-gun fleet flagship *Britannia*, a post that Leake held for five months until Prince George of Denmark succeeded Pembroke.

In Iberian waters On 1 June 1702 Leake temporarily took command of the 90-gun *Association* for three weeks until Churchill, now promoted to admiral and member of the newly formed prince's council, arranged Leake's appointment as commander-in-chief of the Newfoundland squadron on 24 June. While making preparations for this duty Leake was one of the members of the court martial that acquitted Sir John Munden at Spithead on 13 July 1702. On 25 July Commodore Leake sailed with his squadron for Newfoundland, flying his pennant in *Exeter* (Captain T. Swanton), convoying trade to New England. Arriving on 26 August, Leake's ships captured or destroyed fifty-one French vessels and attacked French settlements at Trepassy, St Mary's, Collonet, Greta, Little St Lawrence, and St Peters. After returning to Spithead on 9 November 1702

Leake was appointed to serve as one of the advisers for the new ordnance establishment on 7 December, and two days later was promoted to rear-admiral of the blue.

In January 1703 Leake chose as his first flag captain Stephen Martin, the husband of Leake's wife's sister. Martin repeatedly served with Leake from this point forward and eventually became his heir. In his first assignment as a flag officer Leake served as commander-in-chief at Spithead and Portsmouth. Then, after only three months as a rear-admiral, Leake was promoted to vice-admiral of the blue in March 1703. He served under Rooke in the channel, then joined the Anglo-Dutch fleet under Sir Cloudesley Shovell at Lisbon in late July, remaining with him in the western Mediterranean until September. After returning to England in November, Leake's flagship, *Prince George*, lay anchored in the Downs during the great storm of 26–7 November. As she was one of the few ships not seriously damaged, Leake and his flag captain were able to help others less fortunate and less skilled in seamanship. In December 1703 Leake came ashore temporarily and served on Admiralty boards to examine the recruitment of seamen and to establish regulations for marines serving in the fleet.

When Rooke sailed with the main fleet to deliver the Archduke Charles to Lisbon in early February 1704, Leake waited in England for the remainder of the Dutch forces to arrive. When calling on the lord high admiral to receive his final instructions before leaving the prince presented him to the queen, who knighted him, although he had apparently declined the honour following his operations in Newfoundland in 1702. Sailing on 21 February 1704, Leake reached Lisbon on 1 March and remained there until April, when he accompanied Rooke and the fleet, entering the Mediterranean. As second in command of the fleet Leake was present when Rooke took Gibraltar for the allies on 23 July.

In the battle of Velez Málaga on 13 August, Leake's squadron led the van into action. At one point he and six of his ships faced thirteen of the enemy and forced the French van to withdraw to leeward. Shovell denied Leake's request to pursue the enemy van to leeward, presumably to support the ships in Rooke's centre, but this left Leake out of the remainder of the action. Nevertheless, Leake's squadron lost eighty-nine men killed and 227 wounded. The seven wounded officers included both Leake and his flag captain, Martin, injured by splinters.

In September 1704 Rooke returned to England with the majority of the allied fleet, leaving Leake to command the remaining vessels at Lisbon. Shortly after Rooke's departure Leake learned that the French naval forces under de Pontis were off Gibraltar and that General Villadarís was attempting to bring 8000 troops to take Gibraltar before the allies could return to reinforce it. Facing logistical difficulties at Lisbon Leake had to wait until the Dutch ships under van der Dussen returned from convoying in order to gather thirteen English and six Dutch warships that could sail for Gibraltar on 24 October. Arriving there five days later the sudden appearance of Leake's force led the

French to drive some of their smaller ships ashore and burn them, while Leake relieved the garrison.

French and Spanish forces continued to threaten Gibraltar until March and Leake was closely involved in supporting the garrison from Lisbon and obtaining reinforcements. In January 1705 Leake was promoted to vice-admiral of the white and appointed commander-in-chief Mediterranean. Shortly after learning of this promotion Leake was at sea and sighted de Pontis's squadron on 10 March off Marbella. Chasing the French, Leake's force exchanged shots with them, but the French declined an engagement. After seven months of siege French sea and Spanish land forces withdrew, unable to break down the prince of Hesse's defence of Gibraltar ashore or interrupt Leake's allied reinforcement of it by sea.

Returning to Lisbon in April 1705 Leake remained there awaiting Sir Cloudesley Shovell and the earl of Peterborough, who jointly took over the overall command of the Anglo-Dutch fleet in the Mediterranean. Coming under their command Leake sailed with them and participated in the siege of Barcelona in August–September and was present at its capitulation to the allies on 3 October 1705, and the subsequent entry of Charles III into the city. During this period a violent gale struck, producing a rarely seen waterspout, while lightning struck Leake's flagship, *Prince George*, 'with seamen struck senseless not only upon the deck but in the hold' (Martin-Leake, *Life of Sir John Leake*, 1.294).

Immediately afterwards Peterborough went ashore and Shovell returned to England with the majority of the fleet, while Leake remained as senior naval officer in the Mediterranean with fifteen English and ten Dutch ships. Leaving four English and two Dutch ships at Barcelona, Leake left Barcelona on 14 October and sailed for Lisbon for the winter. In need of water and provisions, and heavily damaged by bad weather *en route*, Leake's squadron took thirteen weeks to make the passage to Lisbon, arriving on 16 January 1706. During the following months Leake and the English envoy, John Methuen, were involved in difficult negotiations over the conflicting demands of the Portuguese court, including their demand for allied naval protection of the Brazil trade, and in dealing with what appeared to Leake as the counter-productive diplomatic representations of the Dutch envoy, Francis Schonenberg. Although the Brazil trade was key to the Portuguese war economy Leake's priorities lay with supporting the army in Spain and in trying to capture Spanish ships carrying silver from America to Cadiz. In March 1706 a compromise was worked out so that Leake could use some ships to attack the approaching Spanish ships heading for Cadiz as well as protect the Portuguese Brazil trade. Difficulties arose over signalling with the Brazil fleet and, at Leake's request, an embargo closed the Tagus to shipping to maintain the secrecy of naval movements. However, when Leake tried to leave, Lisbon's Fort St Julian fired on Leake with the allied ships and forced them to stop. Delayed by this misunderstanding for 24 hours, Leake left on 9 March and missed the opportunity to take the Spanish galleons. Sailing on to Gibraltar, Leake learned there that Marshal Tessé was besieging Barcelona, and Toulouse had blockaded the port with twenty-eight ships of the line. Misinformed that the French fleet was larger than his own Leake awaited Byng's approaching squadron from England. When it arrived he proceeded with an Anglo-Dutch fleet of forty-eight ships of the line and 5000 troops. *En route* Peterborough sent him directives to land forces in Valencia instead of bringing them to Barcelona. Aware of this, King Charles III wrote to Leake, explicitly asking that he come to relieve Barcelona without stopping *en route*. With this request in hand Leake chose to disobey Peterborough, his commander-in-chief.

Ten miles from Barcelona on the morning of 17 April, and expecting a major action with Toulouse, Leake deployed his ships for battle. Shortly afterwards some local ships carrying about 1300 troops joined Leake. As they joined, the earl of Peterborough with an aide appeared in a small boat alongside *Prince George*. Peterborough came on board and, although he broke his union flag as commander-in-chief at the mainmast, Leake refused to argue with him and Peterborough did not interfere with Leake's command of the fleet in relieving Barcelona. On arrival in Barcelona they found that the French fleet had weighed during the night, having intelligence of Leake's approach. With Leake controlling the sea approaches Tessé gave up the siege on 12 May. Contemporaries made much of the coincidence that Tessé had withdrawn on the same day that Barcelona was plunged in darkness during a total eclipse of the sun, the symbol of Louis XIV.

During the remainder of the summer Leake supported operations that resulted in the capture of Cartagena in May, Alicante in July, and Ibiza and Majorca in September. In early October Leake passed command in the Mediterranean to Sir George Byng and, in company with the Dutch ships under Wassenaer, sailed for England. He arrived there on 18 October 1706, having been abroad for two years and eight months. After his return, Admiral George Churchill presented Leake to Prince George of Denmark, who received him in his bedchamber and presented Leake with a diamond ring worth £400 and a gold sword. Queen Anne also rewarded him with £1000.

Leake returned to sea on 28 April 1707 in command of a squadron in the channel, convoying British trade. He came ashore in June, remaining until October when he broke his flag as commander-in-chief Spithead and Portsmouth to preside over the court martial that acquitted Captain Sir Thomas Hardy of failing to chase the enemy; the verdict was later challenged by members of parliament, but not overturned. Following this Leake returned to trade protection duties until December.

On 15 January 1708 Prince George promoted Leake to be admiral of the white, succeeding Sir Cloudesley Shovell, who had died the previous October, and also to be commander-in-chief of the fleet with the right to wear the union flag at the mainmast in any ship in which he was present—a right usually reserved to the admiral of the red. As Leake's first captain, the Admiralty appointed Sir Thomas Hardy, the controversial officer over whose court martial Leake had recently presided. On 6 February Leake sailed with the fleet intending to reach Lisbon, but bad weather prevented the fleet from getting out of the channel. Meanwhile, believing that Leake and the main fleet were no longer in home waters the French launched their attempt to land the Pretender in Scotland. Due to the fortunate delay Leake was able to provide a timely reinforcement for Sir George Byng's squadron and helped frustrate the French plan.

Proceeding to Lisbon, where he arrived on 27 March, Leake continued to Barcelona. As they approached that city Leake's fleet intercepted a French convoy of supplies intended for their army to besiege Tortosa.

MP and Admiralty councillor While these events were occurring in the Mediterranean, at home in London Prince George appointed Leake a member of the lord high admiral's council on 19 June 1708. In July Leake was elected MP for both the borough of Harwich and for Rochester. Preferring to represent Rochester, Leake retained that seat until 1715.

Meanwhile Leake stayed only briefly at Barcelona and proceeded to Vado in Italy, where he embarked Austrian troops and Charles III's future queen, then sailed with her for their marriage at Barcelona, along with the troops. Shortly after his arrival Leake embarked troops and sailed to Cagliari, Sardinia, which capitulated to him on 1 August, providing a valuable source of supply for the allied army in Spain. From there Leake intended to sail for Italy to transport more Austrian troops to Spain and to carry out the queen's instructions to bombard the Papal States if the pope did not pay 400,000 crowns to Britain for his affront in supporting the Pretender. Before this action could be carried out Charles III and General James Stanhope both requested Leake's immediate support in taking Menorca in the hope of establishing Mahon as a winter base for the allied fleet. Leake responded so quickly that he arrived off Menorca more than a week ahead of Stanhope. Waiting offshore Leake blockaded the island, cut off supplies and made preparations for the troops that could take the forts. On Stanhope's arrival Leake's war council considered the situation. Faced with prior orders to protect the Portuguese coast, Leake detached Rear-Admiral Sir Edward Whitaker with English and Dutch ships and 500 marines to remain in the Mediterranean to capture Menorca for Charles III and carry out the remaining orders. After fully supporting Stanhope's preparations and arranging for various other winter operations Leake sailed with fifteen ships on 19 September for England, where he arrived with the Dutch off Portland on 15 October.

A few days after Leake's arrival Prince George died and the lord high admiral's council was dissolved. On Christmas day 1708 Lord Pembroke, the newly appointed lord high admiral, renewed Leake's appointment as admiral and commander-in-chief of the fleet for an expedition to the Baltic. This plan was soon set aside and a smaller expedition under a more junior flag officer, Sir John Norris, sailed instead for the Baltic.

On 24 May 1709 the queen appointed Leake rear-admiral of Great Britain, a post vacant since Sir Cloudesley Shovell's death in 1707. Until October 1709 Leake cruised with the fleet for the protection of trade in the channel. In November Lord Pembroke left office as lord high admiral and Leake was appointed one of the five commissioners for executing the office with Lord Orford recalled as first lord. As this occurred Leake relinquished his sea post as admiral of the fleet to Mathew Aylmer. On 9 December 1709 Leake's wife, Christian, died at Mile End and was buried at Stepney church.

On Orford's departure from the Admiralty Leake was named senior member in November 1710, but declined the role of first lord, as he did again when a new commission was appointed in December 1712. In January 1711, while remaining an Admiralty commissioner, Leake was again appointed commander-in-chief of the fleet for an expedition. Leake's fleet cruised the channel for the protection of trade, but missed intercepting the squadron under Duguay-Trouin, when it slipped out of Brest in May. Much pressure was placed on Leake to take up actively the role of first lord at the Admiralty. The duke of Buckingham proposed making him a peer, but Leake declined both suggestions, desiring either that the government appoint a first commissioner or that he be released from active service and be retired on half pay. The queen personally requested that he continue in office at the Admiralty until a successor could be found. In April 1712 Leake was again appointed admiral and commander-in-chief of the fleet for the expedition that was preparing to take possession of Dunkirk, in accordance with the arrangements that were under negotiation at Utrecht. On 8–9 July Leake landed troops from the fleet and the forts of Dunkirk surrendered to him. Leake struck his flag and returned to London on 31 July, where he learned to his satisfaction that the earl of Strafford, who was just about to return from Utrecht, would replace him at the Admiralty. On 30 September a new Admiralty commission was made with Leake as the second member, but Strafford's continuing absence at Utrecht left Leake in charge. On 17 March 1713, Leake was again appointed admiral and commander-in-chief of the fleet and remained in full pay until August. Leake remained an Admiralty commissioner for another year and a half until 14 October 1714. On the death of Queen Anne in August 1714 his appointment as rear-admiral of Great Britain expired and the honorary post remained vacant for some years.

On 30 July 1715 George I granted Leake a pension of £600 per year. Declining re-election to parliament Leake retired dividing his time between a house in Beddington, Surrey, and another at North Hill in East Greenwich, Kent, where he died on 21 August 1720. He was buried in Stepney church nine days later. Sir John Leake left an estate valued at £25,195, including a mansion house and 16 acres at Beddington with other lands at Oxted, houses at Mile End, and his house at Greenwich. His only child, Captain Richard Leake, having died in March 1720 the bulk of Leake's estate passed to his brother-in-law and former flag captain, Stephen Martin (1666–1740), who from that point took the additional surname of Leake. His eldest son and

Leake's biographer, Stephen Martin-Leake (1702–1773), described his uncle as

> of a middle stature, well set and strong, a little inclining to the corpulent, but not so as to incommode him in the least. His complexion was florid, his countenance open, his eye sharp and piercing, and his address both graceful and manly denoting both a military man and a gentleman. As he had a good person he also had a good constitution, hardly ever knowing what it was to be sick. And though he took his bottle freely, as was the custom in his time in the fleet, yet he was never disguised, or impaired his health by it. (Martin-Leake, *Life of Sir John Leake*, 2.427)

JOHN B. HATTENDORF

Sources commissions and warrants, PRO, ADM 6/3, 5, 6, 7, 9, 10, 11 · Pitcairn-Jones, 'Ship histories', NMM [card file] · *CSP dom.*, 1693, 103, 269; 1702–3, 43, 137–9, 177, 292, 678; 1703–4, 2, 37, 89, 559, 668 · S. Martin-Leake, *The life of Sir John Leake*, ed. G. Callender, 2 vols., Navy RS, 52, 53 (1920) · S. Martin-Leake, *The life of Captain Stephen Martin*, Navy Records Society, 5 (1895) · A. D. Francis, *The Methuens and Portugal* (1966) · J. C. Sainty, ed., *Admiralty officials, 1660–1870* (1975) · J. A. C. Hugill, *No peace without Spain* (1991) · P. Aubrey, *The defeat of James Stuart's armada* (1979) · E. B. Powley, *The naval side of King William's war* (1972) · P. Le Fevre, 'The battle of Bantry Bay, 1 May 1689', *Irish Sword*, 18 (1990–91), 1–16 · H. T. Dickinson, 'The capture of Minorca, 1708', *Mariner's Mirror*, 51 (1965), 195–204 · *Report on the manuscripts of Allan George Finch*, 5 vols., HMC, 71 (1913–2003), vol. 2, pp. 234, 438 · will, PRO, PROB 11/575, fols. 249–53 · parish register, London, St Giles Cripplegate, 31 Oct 1669, GL [baptism, Christian Hill]

Archives BL, corresp., journals, and papers, Add. MSS 5431–5443, 9326, 47968–47978 | CKS, corresp. with J. Stanhope, U1590/O136–38

Likenesses G. Kneller, oils, 1712, NMM [*see illus.*] · J. Faber, mezzotint, 1722 (after G. Kneller), NMM · M. Dahl, oils, NMM

Wealth at death £25,195 incl. prints, inventory, and valuation of estate: will, PRO, PROB 11/575 fols. 249–53; Martin-Leake, *Captain Stephen Martin*, 142–3

Leake, John (1729–1792), man-midwife, was born on 8 June 1729 at Ainstable in Cumberland, the son of Revd William Leake, curate at Ainstable. He attended schools at Croglin, Cumberland, and the grammar school, Bishop Auckland, Durham, before being apprenticed to George Starkin, a surgeon of Wapping, London, on 9 March 1748. Leake travelled to Lisbon and Italy to further his medical education, and was awarded an MD at Rheims on 9 August 1763. He became a licentiate of the Royal College of Physicians of London on 25 June 1766. This licence was then necessary for anyone who wished to practise as a physician in London. Leake turned to midwifery perhaps because medical London at this time was full of new and interesting ideas about the subject and its practice, largely brought about because of recent public knowledge of the obstetric forceps described by Edmund Chapman in his *Treatise on the Improvement of Midwifery* (1733). William Smellie, also in London, had an extensive teaching practice out of which came his seminal work, *A Treatise on the Theory and Practice of Midwifery* (1752), which became the foundation of modern midwifery and obstetrics.

John Maubray had mooted the idea of founding a hospital for lying-in women about 1725, and a few were opened from 1749 to 1757, north of the Thames. John Leake took up the idea and called a meeting of sponsors to Appleby's Tavern in Parliament Street in 1765. The intention was to build a lying-in hospital on the Lambeth (southern) side of Westminster Bridge, which had been opened in 1750. Leake bought the land there and a hospital was built. In 1767 he assigned the leases of the land and building, without payment, to the governors of the New Westminster Lying-in Hospital. The hospital was intended:

> for the Relief of those Childbearing Women who are the wives of poor Industrious Tradesmen or distressed Housekeepers, and who either from unavoidable Misfortunes or the Expences of maintaining large Families are reduced to real Want. Also for the Reception and immediate Relief of indigent Soldiers and Sailors Wives, the former in particular being very numerous in and about the City of Westminster. (New Westminster Lying-in Hospital minutes, LMA)

Single women were accepted for admission to the hospital, if vouched for by a sponsor, which was a most unusual and compassionate dispensation for the time. The governors later amended this ordinance to make sure that such women were not admitted for a second time. To be admitted all women had to obtain a certificate from a sponsor, often a layman, saying that she was 'an Object worthy of the Charity'.

Leake taught midwifery in a course of lectures at his house in Craven Street, off the Strand, and at the new hospital, where he had been appointed physician. He wrote extensively. His main work was the wide-ranging *Introduction to the Theory and Practice of Midwifery* (1777, 1787). He taught that puerperal fever was not due to corrupted milk, in opposition to the then prevalent belief, but correctly attributed it to inflammation in the uterus. He recommended treatment by ventilation, clean linen, and disinfection of wards with brimstone. The woman herself was to be treated by therapeutic bleeding from an arm vein, which was then a widely accepted practice. The dangers of puerperal fever are shown by the fact that in the six months to May 1770 nineteen women in the hospital were infected of whom fourteen died.

Leake's students, both medical men and midwives (who lived in), were able to practise midwifery on patients both within the hospital and in the surrounding district. The courses had to be paid for at a rate of 4 guineas for the first lecture course, 2 guineas for the second, and 10 guineas if the pupil wished to be able to attend the practice of the hospital and district as well (Leake's *Syllabus of Lectures*). After instruction and practice the students were issued with a certificate of completion of the course. This was an early instance of such an award in midwifery and the general idea has persisted in many fields since.

Leake invented a three-bladed obstetric forceps, the intention of the third blade being to keep the head flexed during extraction. The notion was good in theory but quite impractical. His contemporaries scorned them and they were never in vogue. Criticism of them by Thomas Denman was answered by Leake in his *Vindication of the Forceps* (1774).

A useless nostrum was described by Leake in *A dissertation on the properties and efficacy of the Lisbon diet drink in the venereal, scurvy, gout &c.* (1767). The new Westminster Lying-in Hospital became the General Lying-in Hospital, York Road, Lambeth and remained in being for over 200 years, training hundreds of midwives during that time. Leake died in Parliament Street, London, on 8 August 1792 and was buried on 16 August in the north cloister of Westminster Abbey. Leake's obituarist in the *Gentleman's Magazine* described him as being:

> somewhat below the middle size, temperate in diet, active in business, acute in his perceptions, voluble and very entertaining in his discourse; polite, but somewhat precise, in his manners; and, from a too great irritability of temper, sometimes disgusted both his pupils and patients, to whom he was, nevertheless, ever anxious to be serviceable. He was, what every man of taste and reflection must necessarily be, a warm admirer of Shakespeare. (*GM*, 864)

PHILIP RHODES

Sources P. Rhodes, *Dr. John Leake's Hospital: a history of the General Lying-in Hospital, York Road, Lambeth, 1765–1971* (1977) · H. R. Spencer, *The history of British midwifery from 1650 to 1800* (1927) · H. Graham, *Eternal Eve* (1950) · L. T. Morton, *A medical bibliography* (1983) · *Library catalogue of the Royal College of Obstetricians and Gynaecologists*, 2nd edn (1968) · Munk, *Roll* · *GM*, 1st ser., 62 (1792), 773, 863–4 · IGI · A. Wilson, *The making of man-midwifery: childbirth in England, 1660–1770* (1995) · P. J. Wallis and R. V. Wallis, *Eighteenth century medics*, 2nd edn (1988) · New Westminster Lying-in Hospital minutes, LMA
Archives LMA, New Westminster Lying-in Hospital minutes
Likenesses F. Bartolozzi, stipple (after D. Gardner), BM, NPG; repro. in J. Leake, *Medical instructions* (1781) · portrait, repro. in Rhodes, *Dr. John Leake's Hospital*, frontispiece · print, Royal Society of Medicine, London

Leake, Richard (1629–1696), master gunner, was born in Harwich, the son of Richard Leake, naval gunner. His father took him to sea at a very young age to learn the trade of a seaman. Sir William Penn, a clerk of the cheque or muster master, is said to have taught Leake to write, and as he grew older he learned mathematics. The elder Richard Leake served as a naval gunner in the parliamentarian navy during the civil wars and in the 1650s, and was charged with embezzling gunpowder on more than one occasion. The younger Richard Leake appears to have served under his father but to have deserted to the king's service and crossed to the Netherlands. He may have served with Prince Rupert's royalist fleet or with royalist privateers before joining the Dutch army as an artillery officer. By 1656 he had returned to England where he is said to have commanded a merchant ship in several voyages to the Mediterranean. In that year a second son, Admiral Sir John *Leake, was born to Leake and his wife, Elizabeth (1631–1695).

Leake served as gunner of the *Speedwell* in 1661 and 1662 and then as gunner of the *Princess*, participating in various actions in the Second Anglo-Dutch War. In the North Sea on 20 April 1667 the *Princess* was engaged with seventeen Rotterdam privateers and succeeded in beating them off. The *Princess* then sailed to Göteborg and, returning to England, was attacked by two Danish ships on 17 May off the coast of Norway. After an hour's fighting the captain had his left thigh blown off by a cannon shot and died; the master was also killed and the ship's lieutenant badly wounded. Command devolved on Leake who fought for three hours, beat off the Danes, and brought the *Princess* safely back to the Nore. He was given £30 and was appointed, on 13 August 1667, 'one of his majesty's gunners within the Tower of London, in consideration of his good and faithful service to his majesty during the war with the French, Danes, and Dutch' (Martin-Leake, 1.5).

In May 1669 Leake was promoted to be gunner of the *Royal Prince*, Sir Edward Spagge's flagship at the battle of the Texel (11 August 1673), during the Third Anglo-Dutch War. His son's biographer recounts that Leake refused to allow George Rooke, first lieutenant and commander of the heavily damaged *Royal Prince*, to surrender, but countermanded the order and, with his sons John and Henry, inspired the crew to keep fighting, Henry Leake being killed in the action (Martin-Leake, 1.6–9). The story does not appear to stand up to investigation. Though Leake was serving as ship's gunner and John Leake as midshipman, his eldest son, Henry, was not serving on the *Royal Prince*, whose captain in the battle was Thomas Fowler. Leake was discharged from the *Royal Prince* on 12 May 1675.

By 1677 Leake had been given command of the Ordnance office yacht and was appointed master gunner of Whitehall. On 21 May 1677 he was appointed master gunner of England and storekeeper of his majesty's ordnance and stores of war at Woolwich. He was on board the *Gloucester* in 1682 and because he was awake raised the alarm and prevented the duke of York and his entourage from drowning. In 1683 he accompanied the earl of Dartmouth to Tangier to demolish the fortifications there. Though described as skilful and ingenious in his art, he did not impress Samuel Pepys who expressed amazement at the failure of an attempt to blow up the mole at Tangier because the master gunner did not know what he was doing. Pepys was even more disgusted when Leake failed to hit the butt while carrying out 'a public proof and practise' at Woolwich before Dartmouth and Laurence Hyde, earl of Rochester. But Leake's 'particular genius' for gunnery and engineering was shown in a variety of experiments with fireshot and mortars which were tested before Charles II and his brother James at Woolwich. He was the originator of a new method of igniting the fuses of shells by firing the mortar and was the contriver of the 'infernals' used at St Malo in 1693. He also invented what appears to have been a type of howitzer, called a cushee-piece, to fire shell and carcases; in theory it seemed a formidable arm, but in practice it could prove more dangerous to its friends than to its enemies. While loading the shells for the cushee-piece his youngest son, Edward, was killed in September 1688. It was used successfully against the French at the battle of Bantry Bay on 1 May 1689 and Leake demonstrated it to William III in Hyde Park. But he was not impressed and the piece was not adopted for general service. On 23 February 1694 Leake was one of five men appointed to look into the question of fixing mortars on ships so they could be more serviceable. He drew up his will on 23 September 1695 leaving 'one double brass mortar piece and one single brass mortar piece and also my brass gauges' to his son John (PRO, PROB 11/433, fol. 245). He was buried at Woolwich on 26 July 1696 alongside his wife, Elizabeth, and son Edward.

J. K. LAUGHTON, *rev.* PETER LE FEVRE

Sources S. Martin-Leake, *The life of Sir John Leake*, ed. G. Callender, 1, Navy RS, 52 (1920), 1–11 · S. Pepys, *Naval minutes*, ed. J. R. Tanner, Navy RS, 60 (1926), 150, 315 · *The Tangier papers of Samuel Pepys*, ed. E. Chappell, Navy RS, 73 (1935), 45, 149, 315 · Chatham dockyard ordinary, 1660–80, PRO, ADM 42/1 · Woolwich dockyard ordinary, 1660–80, PRO, ADM 42/1723 · PRO, ADM 33/110 · PRO, W.47/10–14 · original letters and papers of Sir John Leake, 1703–5, BL, Add. MS 5440, fol. 13 · A. B. Caruana, *The history of English sea ordnance, 1523–1715* (1994), 113–14 · C. Ware, *The bomb vessel: shore bombardment ships of the age of sail* (1994), 88 · PRO, PROB 11/433, fols. 244v–245
Archives PRO, Admiralty and Ordnance Office MSS

Leake, Stephen Martin (1702–1773), herald and numismatist, was born Stephen Martin on 5 April 1702 and baptized at St Dunstan's, Stepney, on 20 April, the only surviving son of Captain Stephen Martin (1666–1736), naval officer, and his wife, Elizabeth (1665/6–1723), younger daughter of Captain Richard Hill RN of Yarmouth, who had died as a result of the wreck of HMS *Gloucester* in 1682. Captain Hill's elder daughter, Christian, was the wife of Admiral Sir John *Leake (1656–1720), who left almost his whole estate, including property in Stepney, Mile End, and Beddington in Surrey, to Captain Martin on condition that he and his family adopt the additional name and arms of Leake. This was accomplished by royal licence in 1721. As soon as the bequest was received, however, it was almost cancelled out by losses of more than £20,000 in the South Sea crash, and it became imperative for the son, who had been educated at the school at Mile End run by Michael Maittaire (from 1711) and was then holding a clerkship in the Navy Office, to find a more gainful position. An attempt to buy a post in the Treasury ended in disaster, his father losing both the asking price of £840 and several hundred more in legal fees. Leake returned to the Navy Office, being admitted to Middle Temple and sworn a younger brother of Trinity House (of which his father was an elder brother) in 1723. In 1724 he became a deputy lieutenant for Tower Hamlets.

On the 'revival' of the Order of the Bath in 1725, Sir John Anstis, who as Garter king of arms had met Leake concerning the royal licence four years earlier, arranged for him to become esquire to one of the knights, the earl of Sussex, deputy earl marshal. In March 1726 he was elected to the Society of Antiquaries, and in the same year he published his *Nummi Britannici historia*, a concise essay on the entire series of English coinage which, though not without errors, was well written and well received; an enlarged second edition appeared in 1745 as *An Historical Account of English Money*, and was reissued with a supplement in 1793.

Still looking for a lucrative appointment, Leake now tried the College of Arms. Here he immediately fell into the clutches of Anstis, who according to Leake's account

Stephen Martin Leake (1702–1773), by Thomas Milton, pubd 1803 (after Robert Edge Pine)

was trying to get a re-grant of the Gartership with remainder to his son: it served his purposes to have a rival candidate, and he offered the Gartership itself to the 25-year-old Leake for £4000, only to withdraw the offer on obtaining his true aim. Leake, risking a repeat of the Treasury débâcle, correctly predicted that being so cruelly used by Anstis would win him sympathy in other quarters, and in May 1727 a place was found for him in the college as Lancaster herald. He was promoted Norroy king of arms in December 1729 and resigned his position in the Navy Office.

As a herald and king of arms, Leake chiefly directed his considerable energies and abilities towards reviving the fortunes of the College of Arms, and though almost all his projects were defeated his activities did enhance the institution's reputation. In 1729 he unsuccessfully applied to the attorney-general for the prosecution of a painter-stainer who (like others of his trade) offered not only to paint arms but to research them, and sought a new charter for the college that would have confirmed its monopoly of these activities. His attempts in 1731 and 1744 to resuscitate the visitations, which the kings of arms had carried out in the sixteenth and seventeenth centuries, were impeded first by Anstis (since Garter traditionally had no part in the enterprise) and then by the administration, which considered the regulation of heraldry 'inconsistent in a trading country, and unpopular' (S. Martin Leake, 'Heraldo-memoriale', 2.135). His *Reasons for Granting Commissions to the Provincial Kings of Arms for Visiting their Provinces* was printed in 1744.

In 1732 Leake was engaged in the attempted revival of the high court of chivalry, bringing three causes 'of office' for the use of unauthorized arms. But the end of the visitations had curtailed the easiest way people had to authorize their arms and the civilian defence advocates were able to argue that the court was oppressive. After five years nothing had been achieved, and the court closed, not to sit again until 1954.

In 1735 Leake married Anne (1714–1802), daughter and coheir of Fletcher Powell, a partner in the Anchor Brew House in Mile End, later the headquarters of Charringtons, the brewers. They had six sons and three daughters, who all survived their father. Powell's estate of Marshalls in Hertfordshire later passed to Leake's descendants. Leake himself dwelt both in Mile End, where he was active in vestry affairs and helped raise volunteer units during the Jacobite rising of 1745, and at Thorpe-le-Soken in Essex, where his father had acquired an estate in 1720.

Promoted Clarenceux king of arms in 1741, Leake negotiated with Cromwell Mortimer in 1748 to set up at the College of Arms a central registry for births among the dissenting and Jewish communities. This scheme met with little support among the dissenters—whose various subdivisions Mortimer had omitted to consult fully—and only slightly more among the Jews, who continued to use it sporadically until 1793, when it ceased.

Leake became Garter principal king of arms in 1754, and immediately concerned himself with his role in the Order of the Garter, arranging with the dean of Windsor to borrow the official registers for the twin purpose of bringing them up to date (not done since Queen Anne's reign) and making an abridgement. He also compiled a highly useful collection of drawings of knights' stall-plates from St George's Chapel, and twice travelled abroad to invest foreign princes with the Garter: Prince Ferdinand of Brunswick in 1759 and the duke of Mecklenburg-Strelitz in 1764. In 1767 he was the first Garter to introduce inheriting peers to the House of Lords (under a scheme which lasted until 1802). By 1770 he was suffering badly from gout and rheumatism and he died at Mile End on 24 March 1773. In accordance with his will (addressed 'to all and singular', like heraldic letters patent) he was buried in Thorpe-le-Soken church.

A strong critic of the patronage and purchase by which heralds (like others) were then appointed, Leake none the less forced through the oddest appointment of his or any other age, namely that of his thirteen-year-old son, John Martin Leake, who became Chester herald in 1752. His uncompromisingly low opinion of his brother officers convinced him that the boy could be no worse. He also worked hard to place his other sons, public schools or universities having no esteem for him. For his own part he applied himself diligently to his career, as defined by its rights, appurtenances, and privileges: these he excelled at identifying and defending, using considerable antiquarian skill in the process. The meticulous notes he made as a result are still valuable. But he appears to have had little independent interest in coats of arms or family trees, and his private studies were directed towards the history of his profession, numismatics, and detailed biographies of his uncle Admiral Leake and his father, the former of which was published in 1750, the latter not until 1895. His lean, serious features are preserved in an oil portrait by Robert Edge Pine, formerly at Marshalls and now in the College of Arms.   C. E. A. CHEESMAN

Sources S. Martin Leake, 'Memorandum: an epitome of my life', 1770–72, BL, Add. MS 47989, fols. 121–8 · S. Martin Leake, 'Heraldick annals of my own time', c.1726–1770, Coll. Arms, SML 44–6 · S. Martin Leake, 'Heraldo-memoriale, or, Memoirs of the College of Arms', 1765–71, Coll. Arms, SML 64–6 · S. Martin Leake, 'Life of Captain Stephen Martin', c.1740, BL, Add. MS 47978 · S. Martin Leake, *The life of Sir John Leake* (1750), 456–8 · S. Martin Leake, letter-book, from 1726, Coll. Arms, SML 75 · M. Noble, *A history of the College of Arms* (1804), 408–14 · D. B. Morris, 'Mile End old town and the East India Company', *East London Record*, 9 (1986), 20–28 · will, proved, 7 April 1773, Coll. Arms, MS SML 64 · will of Fletcher Powell, proved, 12 Aug 1773 · parish register (marriage), Middlesex, St Lawrence Jewry, 23 Jan 1735 · parish register (marriage), 23 Feb 1692, Stepney, St Dunstan · parish register (baptism), 20 April 1702, Stepney, St Dunstan · *GM*, 1st ser., 5 (1735), 52 · D. B. Morris, *Mile End old town, 1740–1780* (2002)

Archives BL, corresp. and papers, Add. MSS 47978–47999 · Coll. Arms, collections relating to court of chivalry, order of the Garter, etc. · Herts. ALS, corresp. and papers

Likenesses R. E. Pine, oils, in or after 1754, Coll. Arms · T. Milton, line engraving (after R. E. Pine), BM, NPG; repro. in Noble, *College of Arms* (1803) [*see illus.*]

Wealth at death £6100 total unsettled wealth; also settled estate, incl. manor and estate of Thorpe-le-Soken, Essex: letter from son John to son Thomas, 9 April 1773, BL, Add. MS 47998B, fols. 7–8

Leake, Stephen Martin (1826–1893), legal writer, was born in London on 19 March 1826, the eldest son of Stephen Ralph Martin Leake (1782–1865), assistant secretary to the Treasury, and his wife, Georgiana, daughter of Captain George Stevens. The family was seated at Thorpe Hall, near Colchester, Essex, and at Marshalls in High Cross, Ware, Hertfordshire. Leake's grandfather John Leake was a bencher of the Middle Temple, and was said at the time of his death in 1862 to be the senior barrister in England by date of call. John was a grandson of Stephen Martin *Leake (1702–1773), Garter king of arms.

Stephen Leake attended King's College School, and went on to Cambridge in 1844 as a pensioner at St John's College. He was placed as twentieth wrangler in the mathematical tripos in 1848, when he took his BA degree. On graduation he was admitted to the Middle Temple, and he was called to the bar five years later in 1853, reading as a pupil in the chambers of the eminent special pleader, Edward Bullen. He became a member of the home circuit, and attended the Hertfordshire and Essex sessions. On 24 September 1859 he married Isabella (or Isabel; d. 1924), daughter of William Plunkett, a conveyancing counsel.

Leake (or Martin(-)Leake, as he was sometimes called) practised for about ten years from various sets of chambers in the Temple, but his reputation was chiefly built on his legal writing. His first work, for which he is still best remembered, was *Precedents of Pleadings in Common Law*; it was compiled in collaboration with Bullen and published in 1860. Bullen and Leake, whose work reached a twelfth edition by 1975, were household names for all barristers for well over a century.

However, Leake's literary career was to be longer and more distinguished than Bullen's. Belying the image of crabbed pedantry which had traditionally attached to experts on pleading, he was a prominent member of the Juridical Society, founded in the 1850s to promote the scientific study of law. In a paper which he delivered to the society in 1857 he explored the possibility of identifying universal fundamental principles of property law, comparing English and Roman law. Three years later he presented a paper to the Social Science Association on 'The formal science of law'. His inclinations were therefore already turning to legal scholarship when in 1863, worried by increasing deafness, he made the decision to leave practice and retire to his father's seat in Hertfordshire. There he became a county magistrate and made use of the comparative leisure of country life to compose lucid and methodical treatises on the law. His *Principles of the Law of Contracts* (1867) was the first scientific treatise on what was soon to become a core subject in the legal curriculum; it was also the first treatise to identify and analyse some recently developed doctrines, such as vitiation by mistake. The book was to exercise a beneficial effect on the academic legal literature of the next generation; it was the basis of an American textbook by W. A. Keener, published in 1891, and its influence in English universities was acknowledged by Sir William Anson.

Leake was inspired by the codification movement, and in 1868 he responded to the general invitation from Lord Cranworth's commission of 1866 by producing *A Scheme of a Digest of Law, with a Specimen Digest of the Law of Bills of Exchange*. The guiding principle of his scheme was that 'the contents might be recognized intuitively as standing in their proper relations, so that the inquirer might be guided to any point by his sense of order only'. He described the construction of a digest as 'a translation of the law from an historical to a systematic or scientific form', though (in contrast with a code) the cases from which it was derived would be cited. The method was essentially that adopted by Pollock and Chalmers in their respective digests of the law of partnership, bills of exchange, and the sale of goods, each of which resulted in codifying legislation.

Leake spent his remaining years preparing digests of the common law according to his scheme, beginning with the land law. His *Elementary Digest of the Law of Property in Land* (1874) was followed by *A Digest of the Law of Uses and Profits of Land* (1888), which (according to the half-title) was conceived as the third part of his *Digest of the Law of Property*. This last part was not concerned with uses and trusts, but with 'uses of land' in the lay sense; two further parts were planned but did not materialize. His *Elementary Digest of the Law of Contracts*, which appeared in 1878, was a revised edition of *Principles* and was designed to fit into the same scheme. The uncompleted works on real property, though revised in a posthumous second edition of 1909, made no particular impact; the solution to the problem of the land law was to be fundamental reform rather than

codification. On the other hand, the treatise on contracts reached an eighth edition in 1931 and was still sometimes consulted throughout the twentieth century.

Leake died at Ware, Hertfordshire, on 7 March 1893, and was buried at Thorpe-le-Soken, Essex. He was survived by his wife, six sons, and two daughters. The eldest son, Stephen (1861–1940), was a co-editor of two editions of *Precedents of Pleadings in the Common Law*, and a Hertfordshire magistrate. The fifth son, Lieutenant-Colonel Arthur Martin-*Leake (1874–1953), was twice awarded the Victoria Cross.   J. H. BAKER

Sources W. R. A., 'Stephen Martin Leake', *Law Quarterly Review*, 10 (1894), 2–4 · *Law Times* (18 March 1893), 470 · *Solicitors' Journal*, 37 (1892–3), 359 · Burke, *Gen. GB* · Venn, *Alum. Cant.*

Wealth at death £9099 10s. 7d.: probate, 28 April 1893, CGPLA Eng. & Wales

Leake, William Martin [*known as* Colonel Leake] (1777–1860), topographer and numismatist

Leake, William Martin [*known as* Colonel Leake] (**1777–1860**), topographer and numismatist, was born on 14 January 1777 in Bolton Row, Piccadilly, London, the second son and third child of John Martin Leake (1739–1836) and his wife, Mary (d. 1821), daughter of Peter Calvert of Great Hadham, Hertfordshire. At the time John Martin Leake was Chester herald (1753–91), as well as in the Treasury (1763–83). He became a commissioner on the board for auditing the public accounts (1783–93) and comptroller of army accounts (1793–1811).

After training at the Royal Military Academy, Woolwich (21 February 1792–1 January 1794), Leake served in the garrison on Antigua from 1795 to 1798. Membership of the British military mission to the Ottoman empire allowed him to travel in Anatolia (18 January – 9 February 1800), Cyprus (11 February – 7 March 1800), the Holy Land (September 1800 – February 1801), Egypt (February 1801 – March 1802), and Syria (April–June 1802), as well as to see action at the battle of al-Khanka (16 May 1801) and the siege of Alexandria (July–August 1801). On his way home he spent time in Athens (30 June – 9 July and August 1802) and on excursions into central Greece (9 July – 7 August 1802) and the eastern Peloponnese (September 1802). Most of the materials collected on these journeys, however, were lost when the *Mentor*, on which Leake was travelling to Malta with a consignment of Lord Elgin's marbles, foundered off the coast of Kithera on 16 September 1802. Leake continued back to Britain by way of Zante, Cefalonia and Corfu, Trieste, the Mount Cenis Pass, and Paris.

At the end of August 1804 Leake set out for Greece on a special mission to liaise with the Ottoman authorities about defence arrangements in the event of an expected French invasion and to collect information which would be useful in the event of military operations. He travelled extensively in central Greece and the Peloponnese (December 1804 – April 1806) investigating likely landing places on the west coast and possible lines of advance towards Constantinople, before sailing round the south coast of Greece and through the Aegean Islands to Mount Athos (8 September – 23 October 1806). From there he travelled to Salonika and then southwards as far as Larissa (September–December 1806). In February 1807 Leake was put under house arrest in Salonika following news that the Ottoman empire had allied itself with France. He remained under restraint until 24 October 1807.

On his release Leake was ordered to sail to north-western Greece, to make contact with Ali Pasha (the most powerful Ottoman governor in the southern Balkans, to whom Leake was already known) and to discover whether he would support the French alliance or side with the British. At a secret meeting on a beach near Prevesa, Ali indicated that he was inclined to favour the British. Leake returned home via Sicily, where he was able to explore for at least three weeks in November and December 1807.

In 1808 Leake was again sent to Ali Pasha: this time the objectives were to encourage the vizier to support British operations against the French forces occupying the Ionian Islands and to deliver a cargo of munitions to him. Leake travelled in Sicily once more (30 December 1808 – 29 January 1809) before reaching Greece in February 1809. Much of the next year was spent negotiating with Ali Pasha, but some short excursions were made in Epirus and Leake completed his explorations in central Greece from November 1809 to January 1810. Byron arrived during Leake's residency and found him 'taciturn', ill-dressed and quite unlike 'an (English)man of this world' (Marchand, 2.102). The mission was not a complete success: increasingly, Leake felt his life was threatened by Ali Pasha and eventually he left, probably before 1 May 1810.

Back in London and based at 26 Nottingham Place, Marylebone, or sometimes on the family properties at Marshalls, near Hertford, and Thorpe-le-Soken in Essex, Leake was elected to the African Association (9 June 1813), the Society of the Dilettanti (6 February 1814), and the Royal Society (13 April 1815). His first book appeared in 1814. However, scholarly activity was interrupted by the return of Napoleon from exile, and Leake was sent to liaise with the army of the Swiss cantons in anticipation that French operations would begin on the upper Rhine (28 May – 4 December 1815).

Leake remained in the army, and eventually became a lieutenant-colonel in the artillery (1820), as well as in the army (brevet rank, 1813). He retired in 1823, as part of the slimming-down of the peacetime army, though his prospects for further promotion were low and his health was 'impaired'. Subsequently regretting his decision, Leake applied unsuccessfully to be reinstated. On 18 September 1838 he married Elizabeth Wray, eldest daughter of one orientalist, Sir Charles *Wilkins (bap. 1749, d. 1836), and widow of another, William Marsden (1754–1836). They lived at 50 (now 9) Queen Anne Street, Cavendish Square, London.

Leake wrote thirty-three articles for learned journals: eight appeared in the Classical Journal between 1814 and 1822, and twenty in the Transactions of the Royal Society of Literature between 1829 and 1851. He also published nine books, excluding second editions. Most of his publications were concerned with the topography of ancient Greece and they are still of considerable importance in that field, though Travels in the Morea (3 vols., 1830) and Travels in Northern Greece (4 vols., 1835) also incorporate firsthand observations of socio-economic conditions under Ottoman rule. His published inscriptions in ancient Greek soon entered the standard corpora. Leake edited some of the papers left by the traveller Jean-Louis Burckhardt (1819, 1822), produced the first background study to the Greek War of Independence (1825), and prepared an influential catalogue of his own extensive coin collection (1856; 2nd edn, 1859). Through his letters to such newspapers as the Morning Chronicle and the Daily News and ten pamphlets (1847–58, several published under pseudonyms) he showed himself a steady supporter of Greek independence and a severe critic of British policy towards Greece and Russia, especially during the Crimean War.

Colonel Leake (as he was universally known) was a well-respected member of the unseen college of intellectuals, politicians, and wealthy individuals which flourished in early nineteenth-century London. Despite a 'singular modesty' which endeared him to close friends but appeared to other people as 'incommunicative reserve' (Marsden, 42), Leake frequently attended the convivial dinners of the Dilettanti and was an active member of the dining clubs associated with the African Association (from 13 June 1815) and the Royal Society (from 27 January 1831). He was, in addition, a founder member not only of the Raleigh Club (1826), but also of the Travellers' Club (1819) and the Athenaeum (1824), and he helped to establish the Royal Society of Literature (1821) and the Royal Geographical Society (1830). He was a member of the Numismatic Society from its beginnings in 1836.

Leake died on 6 January 1860 at 57 Upper Brunswick Place, Hove, from 'paralysis—three days' (d. cert.). He was survived by his wife and was buried in Kensal Green cemetery. Leake's collections of coins and vases, now in the Fitzwilliam Museum in Cambridge, were not remarkable, but his principles of numismatic organization—by region and city—were influential for his contemporaries. His small collection of sculptures went to the British Museum, where one item from it—a marble bust of a man (Aeschines)—is on display.   J. M. WAGSTAFF

Sources MS notebooks, U. Cam., Museum of Classical Archaeology · J. H. Marsden, A brief memoir of the life and writings of the late Lieutenant-Colonel William Martin Leake (1864) · W. M. Leake, Journal of a tour in Asia Minor (1824) · W. M. Leake, Travels in the Morea (1830) · W. M. Leake, Travels in northern Greece (1835) · Herts. ALS, Martin Leake MSS · PRO, FO 42/5–12; FO 74/40–43; FO 78/28–72; FO 352/4A–5 · Byron's letters and journals, ed. L. A. Marchand, 2 (1973) · Society of Dilettanti, minute books 5–7, 1798–1860, Society of Antiquaries · Society of Dilettanti, D.MSS, 3–7, 1831–60, Society of Antiquaries · minutes of the Association for Promoting the Discovery of the Interior Parts of Africa, 1788–1831, CUL · The journals and letters of George Finlay, ed. J. M. Hussey, 2 (1995) · R. Hallett, ed., Records of the African Association, 1788–1831 (1964) · CGPLA Eng. & Wales (1860) · d. cert.

Archives Herts. ALS, corresp. and papers · U. Cam., faculty of classics, notebooks | BL, letters to Lord Aberdeen and others · BM, sculptures · Bodl. Oxf., corresp. with Sir J. G. Wilkinson · British School of Athens, corresp. with George Finlay · Cornwall RO, letters to John Hawkins · FM Cam., coins and vases · W. Sussex RO, letters to John Hawkins

Likenesses C. A. Jensen, oils, 1838, priv. coll. · W. Behnes, marble bust, 1840, FM Cam.

Wealth at death under £25,000: probate, 23 Feb 1860, CGPLA Eng. & Wales

Leakey, Caroline Woolmer (1827–1881), author, was born on 8 March 1827 in Exeter, the fourth daughter and sixth child of the eleven children of James *Leakey (1775–1865), a painter, and his wife, Eliza Hubbard Woolmer (d. 1855). Her delicate health restricted her early education, although she read voraciously; she spent most of her childhood as the close companion of her extremely pious mother and as a readily available model for her father. At the age of eighteen her health improved and she began charitable work, collecting for the Jews' Society, the Christian Missionary Society, and the Seamen's Society, and joining the newly formed Patagonian Society. With her mother she also visited the workhouse and the local poor.

At the age of twenty Caroline Leakey embarked for Van Diemen's Land, with the intention of assisting a married sister there who was reluctant to entrust her children to convict nurses. She arrived in January 1848 and lived mainly in Hobart, although she spent a year with friends in Port Arthur, a secondary punishment centre. Less than a year after her arrival in Van Diemen's Land fever and a hip complaint rendered her an invalid for the next five years. As a child she had literary ambitions, and she now turned to the writing of poetry for solace. Friends—including Bishop Nixon of Tasmania and his wife, with whom she lived for some time—encouraged her to publish her poems; unknown to her, her doctor, J. W. Agnew, sent some of them to the local newspaper.

In 1853 Caroline Leakey returned to England, on the advice of her doctors. A recovery followed, but she never enjoyed prolonged good health: in 1854, 1858, 1863, 1867–9, and 1875 she was seriously ill, with a variety of complaints including acute bronchitis, typhoid fever, and suspected consumption. Nevertheless, she pursued a literary career, publishing her poetry soon after her return as *Lyra Australis, or, Attempts to Sing in a Strange Land* (1854) under her own name. She also began to write short pieces for magazines, such as *Sunday at Home* and (later) the *Girl's Own Paper*, and short tracts for the Religious Tract Society: these pietistical homilies, only very thinly disguised as short stories, are notably unappealing. Her poetry, although unoriginal in content and style, still retains a modest lyrical charm.

From October 1854 Caroline Leakey ran a deceased sister's London school for a year and a half, returning to Exeter after the death of her mother in 1855 to look after her father. Here, between March 1857 and March 1858, she wrote *The Broad Arrow, being Passages from the History of Maida Gwynnham, a Lifer*. This two-volume novel, based on her experiences in Van Diemen's Land and appearing under the name of Oliné Keese, was published in London in 1859 and in Hobart in 1860. *The Broad Arrow* was one of the earliest novels to portray a convict as the central character; an important precursor of Marcus Clarke's *His Natural Life* (1874), it was one of a group of novels which argued that convicts were more sinned against than sinning. Leakey's observation of both the convict system and the social life of Hobart—through the eyes of a lively new arrival in the colony, Bridget—is shrewd and convincing,

while her portrait of the secondary punishment centre at Port Arthur towards the end of the novel is genuinely harrowing. However, the novel is marred by lengthy and pious interventions by the author and generally poor characterization. Mrs Evelyn, as the complacent and insensitive mistress of convict servants, is entirely convincing; the character of the proud and resistant Maida, although unoriginal, is forcefully drawn, but other figures, such as the pious invalid Emmeline, are stereotypical and lifeless. Questions also arise over the choice of such an atypical convict—Maida is innocent of the crimes for which she is transported and separated by her superior class from her convict associates—as the vehicle of criticism of the convict system. Leakey's attempt to combine a travel book, a social novel, and a pious tract seems to have been rather too ambitious, but it met with a favourable reception: the reviewer in *The Athenaeum* praised its 'life-like interest and graphic reality', comparing it hyperbolically with the works of Daniel Defoe (*The Athenaeum*, 580). One recent critic, exploring its stylistic conservatism, has seen it as an Australian *Uncle Tom's Cabin*, and has emphasized its attempt to deal with 'the awful disjunctions between Victorian personal morality and Victorian public ideas' (Scheckter). Attempts to portray it as an implicitly feminist work are much less convincing.

Caroline Leakey combined her literary work with charitable activities; in 1861 she helped to raise funds for and to establish a home in Exeter for 'fallen women' (the heroine of *The Broad Arrow* was one such). According to her devoted sister and memorialist, Emily, she gave the proceeds of her poetry to the needy and distributed apples, flowers, and tracts to the working-class passers-by; she also stinted her own expenditure on clothes to fund an annuity of £14 for an old servant. For the last sixteen years of her life she was housebound and concentrated on her writing. She died after a painful illness on 12 July 1881 in Exeter.

ROSEMARY MITCHELL

Sources E. P. Leakey, *Clear shining light: a memoir of Caroline W. Leakey* (1882) · J. C. Horner, 'Leakey, Caroline Woolmer', *AusDB*, vol. 5 · W. H. Wilde, J. Hooton, and B. Andrews, *The Oxford companion to Australian literature*, 2nd edn (1994), 120, 458 · J. Scheckter, 'The broad arrow': conventions, convictions, and convicts', *Antipodes*, 1/2 (1987), 89–91 · L. T. Hergenham, 'The broad arrow': an early novel of the convict system', *Southerly*, 36/2 (1976), 141–59 · J. E. Poole, 'The broad arrow: a re-appraisal', *Southerly*, 26/2 (1966), 117–24 · A. Rutherford, 'The wages of sin: Caroline Leakey's The broad arrow', *The Commonwealth writer overseas*, ed. A. Niven (1976), 245–54 · *The Athenaeum* (30 April 1859), 580

Leakey, Henrietta Wilfrida (1902–1993). *See under* Leakey, Louis Seymour Bazett (1903–1972).

Leakey, James (1775–1865), miniature painter, was born on 20 September 1775 at Exeter, the son of John Leakey who was engaged in the wool trade as a wool-stapler. Little is known of James Leakey's early life and training but it is recorded that he was about to become Sir Joshua Reynolds's pupil at the time of Reynolds's death. He became established at Exeter, where he painted oil portraits, landscapes, and genre scenes in the Dutch manner, as well as miniatures in the unusual medium of oil on ivory. Joseph

Farington reported that by January 1808 Leakey had already 'met with much success in the west of England' (Farington, *Diary*, 9.3203) and by November 1810 he was making a living of 'abt. £800 a year' from his profession (ibid., 10.3799). Leakey remained in Exeter, with the exception of a spell in Bath in 1813 and residence in London from 1821 to 1825. There he made the acquaintance of John Constable, Sir Thomas Lawrence, Sir David Wilkie, and other leading painters, perhaps through his connection with Farington.

Leakey exhibited at the Royal Academy between 1821 and 1846 but, a devout Calvinist, retired to become a preacher some years before he died at his home, in Southernhay, Exeter, on 16 February 1865. He had married Eliza Hubbard Woolmer (*d.* 1855) on 28 August 1815, and at least three of their eleven children also became church ministers. Caroline Woolmer *Leakey (1827–1881), their daughter, became a religious writer. The Royal Albert Memorial Museum and Art Gallery, Exeter, and the Guildhall, Exeter, both have paintings by Leakey in their collections.   F. M. O'DONOGHUE, *rev.* V. REMINGTON

Sources Farington, *Diary* · G. Pycroft, *Art in Devonshire: with the biographies of artists born in that county* (1883), 82–5 · *Exeter and Plymouth Gazette* (16 Feb 1865) · *Art Journal*, 27 (1865), 125 · D. Foskett, *Miniatures: dictionary and guide* (1987), 320, 586 · B. S. Long, *British miniaturists* (1929), 261–2 · L. R. Schidlof, *The miniature in Europe in the 16th, 17th, 18th, and 19th centuries*, 1 (1964), 473 · S. Edwards, *Miniatures at Kenwood: the Draper gift* (1997), 222 · G. C. Williamson, *The history of portrait miniatures*, 1 (1904), 189–90; 2 (1904), 135 · Graves, *RA exhibitors* · private information, 1892 [family, friends] · *CGPLA Eng. & Wales* (1865) · parish register (marriage), 28 Aug 1815, Exeter, St Sidwells · J. Frankau, *An eighteenth century artist and engraver: John Raphael Smith, his life and works* (1902)

Wealth at death under £800: resworn probate, April 1866, *CGPLA Eng. & Wales* (1865)

Leakey, Louis Seymour Bazett (1903–1972), archaeologist and palaeoanthropologist, was born on 7 August 1903 at Kabete mission station, near Nairobi, Kenya, the third of the four children of Canon Henry (Harry) Leakey (*d.* 1940) and his wife, Mary (known as May) Bazett (*d.* 1948), one of thirteen children of Colonel Bazett, who had retired to Reading after serving in the Indian army. Both his parents were missionaries with the Church Missionary Society working among the Kikuyu people in the Kenyan highlands.

Upbringing and early fossil-hunting Louis (pronounced Lewis) Leakey spent most of the first sixteen years of his life at Kabete, and was educated initially by governesses and later by his father. His playmates were Kikuyu boys and he was initiated into the Kikuyu tribe along with his Kikuyu peer group. He spoke Kikuyu fluently and in the first volume of his autobiography, *White African* (1937), wrote that 'in language and in mental outlook I was more Kikuyu than English, and it never occurred to me to act other than as a Kikuyu' (p. 32), also commenting that all his life he was to 'think and even dream' in Kikuyu (*National Geographic*, Feb 1965, 200).

During these early years Leakey developed a passion for

Louis Seymour Bazett Leakey (1903–1972), by unknown photographer, *c.*1955

everything to do with Africa, which was to last all his life. He was also inspired by a gift of an adventure story about Stone Age Britain and in 1916 decided to become an archaeologist. In 1919 he was sent to school at Weymouth College, and in 1922 was admitted to St John's College, Cambridge. He initially read for the modern language tripos, and achieved a first in French and Kikuyu. In 1923 kicks to his head during a rugby game left him with post-traumatic epilepsy. The advised rest period enabled him to initiate his fossil-hunting career by joining the British Museum east African expedition to Tanganyika to collect dinosaur fossils in 1924. In 1925 he returned to Cambridge to read the archaeology and anthropology tripos, with encouragement from his archaeology tutor, M. C. Burkitt, and, particularly, his anthropology tutor, A. C. Haddon. He gained a first in 1926 and was awarded grants which enabled him to organize his first east African archaeological expedition.

Cambridge don and first African expeditions Between 1926 and 1935 Leakey led four such expeditions to east Africa, which established the sequence of early cultures in Kenya and northern Tanganyika and laid the foundations for subsequent archaeological and palaeontological research in the region. In 1930 he was awarded a PhD degree by Cambridge University. From 1929 to 1934 he held a fellowship at St John's College, Cambridge, and in 1936 was Munroe lecturer at Edinburgh University. During this time he revealed himself as an enthusiastic and inspiring teacher and learned to knap flint.

Contrary to the beliefs of most other contemporary scientists, Leakey was convinced, and determined to show, that human beings originated in Africa rather than in Asia. He claimed that hominid fossils he had found in 1932 at Kanam and Kanjera, on the north-east shore of Lake Victoria, were the remains of ancient creatures that would prove the antiquity of human beings in Africa. However, reports to the Royal Society and the journal *Nature* by Professor P. G. H. Boswell in 1935 showed that Leakey had made serious errors in his fieldwork and interpretation. Even if some were due to circumstances beyond his control, the ensuing scandal dealt his credibility and scientific career a severe blow. Leakey's claims for the age of the Kanam fossil were later widely accepted, but the Kanjera remains are thought to be considerably younger than he proposed.

Marriages At this time Leakey was also the subject of censure in his personal life. In 1928 he had married Henrietta Wilfrida [**Henrietta Wilfrida Leakey** (1902–1993)], known as Frida, the third daughter of Henry Avern, a cork merchant from Reigate, Surrey. She attended the Sorbonne in Paris and, from 1921 to 1924, Newnham College, Cambridge, after which she was employed as a French teacher at Benenden School. A daughter, Priscilla Muthoni, was born in 1931, and a son, Colin Avern, in 1933. She assisted Leakey in his fieldwork, in sketching stone tools found during his expeditions, and at Olduvai Gorge in northern Tanganyika discovered a side gorge named FLK (for 'Frida Leakey Korongo' or Gorge), where important fossil discoveries would later be made.

Frida Leakey was granted a divorce on the grounds of adultery in 1936, and did not remarry. She settled with their children in Girton, near Cambridge, and became involved in BBC broadcasts and community activities, founding in 1936 an infant welfare centre in Girton, and acting as chief billeting officer for London refugees in Girton during the Second World War. During the 1960s she was chairman of the Women's Institute in Cambridgeshire and occupied a seat on the county council as an independent. She died on 19 August 1993.

Shortly after the divorce from Frida, Leakey, whose conduct was disapproved by family and colleagues, married, on 24 December 1936, Mary Douglas Nicol (1913–1996) [*see* Leakey, Mary Douglas], daughter of Erskine Nicol, artist, and his wife, Cecilia. Mary was to become closely involved in his work and recognized as an archaeologist in her own right. There were three sons of this second marriage, Jonathan Harry Erskine (*b.* 1940), Richard Erskine (*b.* 1944), and Philip (*b.* 1949). A daughter, Deborah, was born and died in 1943 when three months old. Richard was to follow in his father's footsteps and make many spectacular fossil hominid discoveries, as well as to serve as a member of the Kenyan parliament and director of Kenya wildlife services. Although often challenged by Richard, just four days before his death Leakey was delighted to see a roughly 2 million-year-old hominid fossil found by Richard, which vindicated his belief that large-brained human ancestors lived in Africa some 2 million years ago.

African origin of humans: Olduvai Gorge discoveries From 1941 Leakey served as honorary curator, and from 1945 to 1961 as curator, of the Coryndon Memorial Museum (now the National Museums of Kenya) in Nairobi. In 1962 he established the Centre for Prehistory and Palaeontology under the trustees of the National Museums of Kenya, and served as its honorary director until 1972, when it was transferred to the National Museums of Kenya. Leakey's

work was conducted with the support of many foundations, of which the National Geographical Society of Washington became the most important.

Important discoveries during the 1940s included a remarkable scatter of handaxes at Olorgesailie, and remains of *Proconsul*, a Miocene ape considered a key to understanding the evolutionary split between monkeys and apes. During this period Leakey founded the Pan-African Congress on Prehistory and Quaternary Studies, of which he was secretary-general from 1947 to 1951 and president from 1955 to 1959. The first of its four-yearly meetings was held in Nairobi in 1947.

But the work that will forever be associated with Leakey is that at Olduvai Gorge. In 1959, at a site in the Frida Leakey Korongo (FLK), Mary found the skull of a 1.8 million-year-old australopithecine, which Leakey named *Zinjanthropus boisei*, affectionately called Dear Boy. A film of the excavation of 'Zinj' reached a wide television audience, and the Leakeys became celebrities. Although Leakey was initially disappointed that the skull was of an australopithecine rather than an early human or *Homo*, in her autobiography *Disclosing the Past* (1984) Mary notes that 'There was probably no one in the world better able than Louis to exploit the publicity value, and hence the fundraising potential, of a find like Zinj' (p. 122), welcome news to the ever cash-strapped Leakeys.

Important discoveries of hominid and animal fossils as well as early stone tools continued to be made at Olduvai throughout the following years at such a rate that colleagues referred to 'Leakey's luck'. In 1960, at Olduvai, the Leakeys' son Jonathan discovered the 1.75 million-year-old remains of a creature later named *Homo habilis*. At the time, this creature was the oldest known fossil of the human genus, *Homo*, and is presumed to have used the first known stone tool technology, which Leakey named the Oldowan culture.

While Mary directed excavations at Olduvai, Leakey was responsible for fund-raising and was a popular public speaker, described by a contemporary, Mary Smith, as a 'bear of a man' (Morell, 210), with a shock of white hair, a spring in his walk, and a gleam in his eye.

Although Leakey was not the first to find early hominids in Africa, and was often criticized for being a headline-seeker rather than a cautious scientist, it was the discoveries at Olduvai Gorge and the publicity orchestrated by Leakey that firmly established Africa as the place where humans originated. It also led to the development of palaeoanthropology as a science, as well as an enormous ongoing research effort in east Africa, on which a great deal of current knowledge of human evolution is based.

Phillip Tobias noted that 'Three abiding impressions of Dr Leakey are of his singular energy, his immense enthusiasm and his vision … He sparkled with an effervescent enthusiasm with which he was able to infect others' (p. 6). He became fascinated with primate evolution and launched the careers of Jane Goodall, Dian Fossey, and Biruté Galdikas, who respectively undertook ground-breaking studies of chimpanzees, gorillas, and orang-utans.

However, sometimes Leakey expressed his views violently, was intolerant of criticism, and was carried to extremes by his convictions. In the late 1960s his unfounded belief that there was evidence for early human beings at Calico hills in California was regarded by many as his ultimate folly. It resulted in serious disagreement with and virtual separation from Mary, who was also greatly upset by his womanizing and retinue of young female protégées.

Kenyan citizen Leakey's talents and pursuits were wide-ranging. From 1937 to 1939 he undertook a detailed investigation of Kikuyu customs (*The Southern Kikuyu*, published posthumously, 1977). During the Second World War he was an intelligence officer and handwriting expert in charge of a special branch of the Nairobi criminal investigation department. He also loved animals and served the Kenya national parks, the East Africa Wildlife Society, and the East Africa and Uganda Natural History Society; he was a dog judge and president of the East Africa Kennel Club, and an authority on birds and tropical fish.

Leakey took a keen interest in Kenyan politics, and after Kenyan independence in 1963 became a Kenyan citizen. In 1949 his warnings to the Kenyan governor about a secret Kikuyu society, known as the Mau Mau, which allegedly aimed at the violent overthrow of the colonial government, initially went unheeded. Although he considered that 'I am in so many ways a Kikuyu myself' (Leakey, *Mau Mau and the Kikuyu*, viii), and sympathized with their land grievances and distrust of the government, he regarded Mau Mau as an 'evil campaign' rather than a nationalistic movement. The ensuing period of terror brought Leakey death threats and fears for the safety of his family. Leakey was the court interpreter at the trial which convicted Jomo Kenyatta (elected the first president of an independent Kenya in 1964) and five others of organizing Mau Mau.

During the last four years of his life he continued exhausting fund-raising lecture tours in America, despite his failing health. He suffered a fatal heart attack and died at St Stephen's Hospital, London, on 1 October 1972. He was buried on 4 October 1972 at Limuru in Kikuyu country near Nairobi.

Leakey's contributions did not go unrecognized. Among the awards and honours showered upon him were the Viking Fund medal of the Wenner-Gren Foundation for Anthropological Research (1961–5), the Hubbard medal of the National Geographic Society, Washington (jointly with Mary Leakey, 1962), the Royal medal of the Royal Geographical Society of London (1964, an award he particularly valued), and the Haile Selassie award (1968), as well as honorary doctorates from the universities of Oxford (1953), California (1963), East Africa (1965), and Guelph (1969).

The Louis Leakey Memorial Institute for African Prehistory (TILLMIAP) established in Nairobi after his death merged with the National Museums of Kenya in 1980. The L. S. B. Leakey Foundation for Research Related to Man's Origin, which was founded by Leakey's supporters in California in 1968 to fund his work, now known as the Leakey Foundation, solicits funds and awards grants for new research in all fields investigating human evolution.

ANNE I. THACKERAY

Sources DNB · L. S. B. Leakey, *White African* (1937) · L. S. B. Leakey, *By the evidence: memoirs, 1932–1951* (1974) · P. V. Tobias, 'Louis Seymour Bazett Leakey 1903–1972', *South African Archaeological Bulletin*, 28 (1973), 2–12 [with bibliography excluding posthumous publications] · M. Leakey, *Disclosing the past* (1984) · V. Morell, *Ancestral passions: the Leakey family and the quest for humankind's beginnings* (1995) [with extensive but incomplete bibliography incl. posthumous pubns] · S. Cole, *Leakey's luck: the life of Louis Seymour Bazett Leakey, 1903–1972* (1975) · L. S. B. Leakey, *Mau Mau and the Kikuyu* (1952) · L. S. B. Leakey, *Defeating Mau Mau* (1954) · L. S. B. Leakey, *Kenya: contrasts and problems* (1937) · Leakey Foundation, San Francisco · J. D. Clark, *PBA*, 59 (1973), 456 · J. A. J. Gowlett, 'Archaeological studies of human origins and early prehistory in Africa', *A history of African archaeology*, ed. P. Robertshaw (1990), 13–38 · personal knowledge (2004) · private information (2004) · *The Times* (2 Oct 1972) · *The Times* (1 Sept 1993)

Archives Leakey Foundation, San Francisco · London Royal Anthropological Institute, corresp. and papers · Nairobi Museum, stone artefacts, animal and hominid fossils · Olduvai Gorge Museum, Tanzania, stone artefacts, animal and hominid fossils · U. Cam., Museum of Archaeology and Anthropology, notes, papers, photographs relating to work in east Africa | Bodl. Oxf., corresp. with J. L. Myres · Bodl. RH, corresp. with Lord Lugard · Rice University, Houston, Texas, Woodson Research Center, corresp. with Sir J. Huxley · U. Cam., Museum of Archaeology and Anthropology, letters to M. C. Burkitt · W. Yorks. AS, Leeds, letters to Bernhard Verdcourt | FILM National Geographic Society, Washington, DC [incl. National Geographic Society video entitled 'Dr Leakey and the dawn of man']

Likenesses photographs, c.1955–1972, Hult. Arch. [*see illus.*] · D. Bartlett, photograph, 1959 (with Mary Leakey), repro. in Leakey, *Disclosing the past* · A. Brower, photograph, 1959, Hult. Arch. · photograph, 1965, National Geographic Society, Washington, DC · B. Campbell, photograph, 1966–1969?, repro. in Tobias, 'Louis Seymour Bazett Leakey', 2

Leakey [*née* Nicol], **Mary Douglas** (1913–1996), archaeologist and palaeoanthropologist, was born on 6 February 1913 at Trevor Square, Knightsbridge, London, the only child of Erskine Edward Nicol (*d.* 1926), landscape artist, and his wife, Cecilia Marion Frere (*d.* 1946), an amateur painter. After spending the First World War years in London, the Nicol family travelled regularly to south-west France, where Mary experienced her first encounters with archaeology. Father and daughter visited cave-art sites and collected artefacts from excavators' spoil heaps, an acceptable practice at the time, which she recalled in her autobiography, *Disclosing the Past* (1984), as 'powerfully and magically exciting' (p. 25). At about ten years old, she began drawing without any formal instruction, taking to it 'naturally and with pleasure on my own initiative' (p. 14). When she was thirteen her father died in France after a short illness. She and her mother returned to London, where she was expelled from two Roman Catholic convent schools in quick succession, on the second occasion for deliberately causing an explosion in a chemistry class. Thereafter the rebellious young lady was educated by private tutors and took up gliding as a hobby.

Mary Nicol decided to pursue a career in archaeology,

but as her lack of formal education precluded admission to university, she attended lectures in geology at University College, London University, and in archaeology given by Mortimer Wheeler at the London Museum, and wrote to archaeologists offering her services at their excavations. Her first published drawings of stone tools from Dorothy Liddell's excavations at Hembury Fort in Devon brought her to the notice of the archaeologist Gertrude Caton-Thompson. In 1933 Caton-Thompson introduced her to the archaeologist and palaeoanthropologist Louis Seymour Bazett *Leakey (1903–1972), who asked Mary to illustrate his book *Adam's Ancestors* (1934). He was ten years older than Mary and at the time married to Henrietta Wilfrida (Frida) Leakey (1902–1993), who was expecting their second child. Shortly after his son Colin was born on 13 December 1933, to the intense disapproval of both his and Mary's families and colleagues, Louis left Frida, whom he later divorced to marry Mary in the register office at Ware on 24 December 1936. A successful personal and professional partnership of some thirty years followed, until Mary experienced the anguish of Louis's physical and mental decline in the years preceding his death in 1972.

Louis and Mary Leakey settled in Kenya, and three sons were born, all of whom have had notable careers: Jonathan Harry Erskine (*b.* 1940), Richard Erskine (*b.* 1944), and Philip (*b.* 1949). A daughter, Deborah, was born in 1943 and died from dysentery at the age of three months. On the birth of her first child, Mary wrote that 'I quite liked having a baby—I think I won't put it more strongly than that—but I had no intention of allowing motherhood to disrupt my work as an archaeologist' (*Disclosing the Past*, 79–80). In 1952 the Leakeys built a permanent home at Langata, an outer suburb of Nairobi. In the 1950s Louis's involvement in Kenyan politics against the Mau Mau movement for Kenyan independence brought fears for the family's safety. An attempt was made to sabotage Mary's car and she wore a pistol on her belt at night.

Mary Leakey quickly established a reputation as a competent excavator of Stone Age sites. In 1951 she recorded some 1600 Stone Age rock paintings in the Kondoa-Irangi region of central Tanzania, a task she regarded as one of the highlights of her life and work, which were published many years later in *Africa's Vanishing Art: the Rock Paintings of Tanzania* (1983). On 6 October 1948, on Rusinga Island near the west coast of Lake Victoria, Mary discovered part of a skull of *Proconsul africanus*, an 18 million-year-old Miocene ape, in which there was tremendous public interest. Some of her favourite finds—a collection of Miocene fossil insects, fruits, and seeds which she and Louis stumbled upon during a cigarette break—were also made at Rusinga Island.

The site that will always be associated with Mary Leakey is Olduvai Gorge, a canyon in northern Tanzania containing rich collections of fossils and artefacts spanning about the last 2 million years. This became her second home, where she enjoyed fieldwork and research, accompanied by her pack of beloved dalmatian dogs, of which she was a well-known breeder. At Olduvai on 17 July 1959 she made one of the most famous fossil discoveries of all time, the

skull of a 1.8 million-year-old early human relative whom Louis named *Zinjanthropus* (now *Australopithecus* or *Paranthropus*) *boisei*. Television coverage of the find made the Leakeys household names all over the world and brought them desperately needed funding from the National Geographic Society. Mary laboured under the hot sun, meticulously recording scatters of early stone tools and fossil bones, setting new standards for archaeological fieldwork, while Louis concentrated on fundraising and lecturing. The technical details of her work are published in volumes 3 (1971) and 5 (1994) of the *Olduvai Gorge* series of Cambridge University Press and a popular account is given in *Olduvai Gorge: my Search for Early Man* (1979).

Perhaps the crowning triumph of Mary Leakey's remarkable career was the discovery and excavation at her dig at Laetoli in northern Tanzania during 1978–1979 of 3.7 million-year-old trails of early hominid footprints, which proved that hominids walked on two legs more than a million years before the earliest known stone tools.

Mary Leakey was a hard-working, modest, retiring person who disliked the limelight, deferring publicity to her husband. Her son Richard however noted that 'Her commitment to detail and perfection made my father's career. He would not have been famous without her. She was much more organized and structured and much more of a technician. He was much more excitable, a magician' (Holloway, 1994). She was known for her short answers, toughness, and for insisting on correct behaviour, as well as for her fondness for cigars and whisky. Although she famously refused to theorize about human evolution, arguing that 'I never felt interpretation was my job. What I came to do was to dig things up and take them out as well as I could' (Holloway, 1994), she did not escape controversies with colleagues.

Mary's awards include the gold Hubbard medal of the National Geographic Society (jointly with Louis, 1962), honorary doctorates from the universities of the Witwatersrand (1968), Yale (1976), Western Michigan (1980), Chicago (1981), Oxford (1981), Cambridge (1987), Emory (1988), Massachusetts (1988), Brown (1990), and Columbia (1991), the Linnaeus medal of the Royal Swedish Academy of Sciences (1978), and the gold medal of the Society of Women Geographers (Washington, 1978). She was elected a fellow of the British Academy (1973), a foreign honorary member of the American Academy of Arts and Sciences (1979) and a foreign associate of the United States National Academy of Sciences (1987).

Despite blindness in her left eye caused by a thrombosis in 1982, Mary Leakey spent the last years of her life lecturing and fund raising and died peacefully in Nairobi on 9 December 1996, 'one of the last of a remarkable array of scholars who first exposed humanity's African past to the light of research' (Tobias). In accordance with her wishes, her ashes were scattered over Lake Natron in Tanzania.

ANNE I. THACKERAY

Sources M. Leakey, *Disclosing the past* (1984) · M. Leakey, *Olduvai Gorge: my search for early man* (1979) · V. Morell, *Ancestral passions: the*

Leakey family and the quest for humankind's beginnings (1995) [with extensive but incomplete bibliography] · P. V. Tobias, 'Salute to Mary Douglas Leakey, 1913–1996', *South African Journal of Science*, 93 (1997), 153–4 · A. Hunsinger, 'Remembering Mary Leakey', *Anthroquest: the Newsletter of the L. S. B. Leakey Foundation*, 3 (spring 1997), 1–5 [with F. Brown, R. Hay, F. C. Howell, M. Kleindienst and A. Walker] · J. D. Clark, 'Mary Leakey's legacy to Palaeolithic archaeology', *Anthroquest: the Newsletter of the L. S. B. Leakey Foundation*, 3 (spring 1997), 1–6 · K. H. Woods, 'President's message: in tribute to Mary Leakey', *Anthroquest: the Newsletter of the L. S. B. Leakey Foundation*, 3 (spring 1997), 2 · M. Holloway, 'Unearthing history: profile: Mary Leakey', *Scientific American*, 27/4 (Oct 1994), 20–21 · *Daily Telegraph* (11 Dec 1996) · *The Independent* (11 Dec 1996) · *Daily Mail* (17 Dec 1996) · *The Times* (10 Dec 1996) · *The Guardian* (17 Dec 1996) · private information (2004) · J. D. Clark, *PBA*, 111 (2001), 595–64 · D. Roe, *The year of the ghost: an Olduvai diary* (2002)

Archives Leakey Foundation, San Francisco · Nairobi, Kenya, files and papers, family papers | National Museum, Dar es Salaam, material artefacts: collections of stone artefacts, animal and hominid fossils from East African sites · National Museum of Kenya, Nairobi, material artefacts: collections of stone artefacts, animal and hominid fossils from East African sites · Olduvai Gorge Museum, Tanzania, material artefacts: collections of stone artefacts, animal and hominid fossils from East African sites | FILM BFI NFTVA, documentary footage · National Geographic Society, Washington, DC | SOUND BL NSA, performance recording

Likenesses D. Bartlett, photographs, 1959, repro. in Tobias, *Disclosing the past* · photograph, repro. in Tobias, 'Salute to Mary Leakey', 154 · photograph (in later years), repro. in Hunsinger and others, 'Remembering Mary Leakey', 1 · photograph, repro. in *Daily Mail* · photographs, repro. in Morell, *Ancestral passions*

Sir David Lean (1908–1991), by Baron, *c.*1940

Lean, Sir David (1908–1991), film director, was born at 38 Blenheim Crescent, Croydon, on 25 March 1908, the elder of the two sons of Francis William Le Blount Lean (*d*. 1973) and his wife, Helena Annie Tangye (*d*. 1962). The Tangyes and the Leans were both old-established Quaker families, and after attending a preparatory school in Croydon David was sent to Leighton Park, a Quaker school in Reading. He was an undistinguished scholar, but the school's liberal regime allowed him to pursue his enthusiasm for photography and overlooked his illicit visits to the local cinemas. At the age of nineteen he began work as a ledger clerk at Viney, Price, and Goodyear, where his father worked as a chartered accountant. It was obvious, however, that he had no aptitude for figures, and his father arranged for him to be taken on at the Shepherd's Bush studios of the Gaumont-British Picture Corporation.

Entry into the film world Protected by the Cinematograph Films Act of 1927, British film production was expanding rapidly, and Lean grasped the opportunity to gain experience as an assistant cameraman, assistant director, and—after being demoted for accidentally exposing a series of close-ups of Madeleine Carroll to white light—wardrobe assistant. It was as an editor, however, that he established his reputation. He adjusted more easily than many of his older colleagues to the coming of sound and the problems of synchronization it entailed, and was made editor of Gaumont Sound News in 1930. On 28 June 1930 he married his cousin Isabel Mayo Lean (*b*. 1907/8), daughter of Edmund Wylde Lean, chartered accountant; their son, Peter, was born in October.

Lean's career progressed rapidly. Early in 1931 he moved to British Movietone News, the most prestigious of the

newsreel companies, and while there he supplemented his income by editing low-budget feature films, most notably *Money for Speed* (1933) and *The Ghost Camera* (1933), both of which were directed by Bernard Vorhaus. His marriage progressed less happily, and in August 1932 Lean left his wife and son.

Lean's speed in decision-making and his comprehensive memory for visual images made him an extremely good newsreel editor, but he was increasingly in demand as an editor of feature films. When Dr Paul Czinner was invited to Britain to make prestige films starring his wife, Elizabeth Bergner, Lean was recruited as editor. From a starting salary of 10s. a week at Gaumont-British he was able to command an unprecedented £60 a week for cutting *As You Like It* (1936). After editing the last of the Czinner–Bergner films, *Dreaming Lips* (1937), however, Lean, like many others, was thrown out of work by the disastrous slump which hit the industry. He had saved nothing during his years of plenty and was in a perilous financial situation.

Lean was helped through this crisis by his younger brother, Edward, then a reporter on the *News Chronicle*, and the actress and dancer Kay (Kathleen) Walsh (*b*. 1910/11), daughter of James Walsh, an engineer, with whom he began a relationship in 1936. Lean edited *The Last Adventurers* (1937), a low-budget film about Grimsby trawlermen in which Walsh had a part, but his big break came when he was recommended to Gabriel Pascal, an expatriate Hungarian who had persuaded George Bernard Shaw to let him make a film adaptation of *Pygmalion*. The film was a big success, and Lean went on to work with the director,

Anthony Asquith, on *French without Tears* (1939) and with the producer, Pascal, on *Major Barbara* (1940).

Director Lean, a dedicated and reliable craftsman whose advice was often sought when a film seemed to be in trouble, had been offered the chance to direct several times. However, he was wary of directing low-budget films where there was little opportunity for creative expression and the danger of being blamed for the shortcomings of a poorly developed script, skimpy sets, and miscast actors. On *Major Barbara* Pascal's inexperience led Lean and the 'dialogue director' Harold French to direct much of the film themselves. With this experience behind him, Lean felt able to accept Noel Coward's offer to help in the direction of *In which we Serve* (1942), a prestigious naval drama based on the experiences of Earl Mountbatten as the commander of a destroyer, and to insist on being credited as co-director.

Coward and Lean worked well together, and Coward (who had written the script and was playing the leading role) was increasingly content to leave directorial duties to Lean. *In which we Serve* went on to become a critical success and the most popular British film of the war years. Coward encouraged Lean to form a production company, Cineguild, with the film's producer, Anthony Havelock-Allan, and cinematographer, Ronald Neame. Three very different Coward adaptations followed: *This Happy Breed* (1944), *Blithe Spirit* (1945), and *Brief Encounter* (1945). *This Happy Breed*, which follows the fortunes of a typical English lower-middle-class family between the wars, was another huge commercial success; but it was the much smaller-scale *Brief Encounter*, a success only in what the film trade termed 'the better-class halls', which established Lean's international reputation as a director. At the time, critics praised it for its realism, and for the emotional honesty of its portrayal of an unconsummated love affair between two married, middle-class, middle-aged people. But in retrospect its expressive use of Rachmaninov's second piano concerto, its *noir*-ish lighting, and its convoluted use of flashbacks look typical of a romantic stylization which became characteristic of Lean's films.

The ending of *Brief Encounter* sees the triumph of duty and conformity over romantic self-expression, but for both Lean and Coward the film was fuelled by creative empathy rather than personal experience. Unlike Laura and Alex, Lean repeatedly broke out of his commitments to begin a new life with a new love. According to Ronald Neame, 'David always had a girl on any film he worked on' (Brownlow, 213). In August 1936 Lean had been divorced by his wife, Isabel, and on 23 November 1940 he married Kay Walsh, but this marriage survived only because she was prepared to overlook his persistent infidelity. In 1946 he left her for the costume designer Margaret Furse, although they continued to have a fruitful working relationship, Walsh writing the conciliatory ending of *Great Expectations* (1946) and the dramatic opening of *Oliver Twist* (1947).

Great Expectations, the first film Lean made without Noel Coward, was rapturously received: Richard Winnington

in the *News Chronicle* asked his readers 'to pay attention to the first big British film to have been made, a film that confidently sweeps our cloistered virtues into the open'. There was a degree of disappointment, however, when Lean chose to follow up his success with another Dickens adaptation, and although *Oliver Twist* was popular in Britain, in the USA it became caught up in the political wrangles over Britain's handling of the Palestine mandate and was boycotted by Jewish groups objecting to Alec Guinness's portrayal of Fagin.

Cineguild shared in the declining fortunes of the British film industry in the late 1940s, and Lean's next two films, *The Passionate Friends* (1949) and *Madeleine* (1950), were both commercial failures. Both films starred Ann *Todd (1907–1993), who, following international success in a modestly budgeted melodrama, *The Seventh Veil* (1945), had been invited to Hollywood to star in Alfred Hitchcock's *The Paradine Case* (1948). Lean, who had taken over the directing of *The Passionate Friends* from Ronald Neame, found it difficult to work with an actress who regarded herself as a star, but during location shooting at Lake Annecy they fell in love. After Lean was divorced by Kay Walsh and Todd by her husband, Nigel Tangye (Lean's second cousin), they married on 21 May 1949.

Apart from *Ryan's Daughter*, *The Passionate Friends* and *Madeleine* are Lean's most under-rated films probably because they are unabashed melodramas which concentrate on the psychology and dilemmas of their heroine in a way which was untypical of British cinema at the time. Celia Johnson's Laura Jessop in *Brief Encounter* could be seen as an ordinary woman (if only by upper-middle-class film critics); Mary Justin and Madeleine Smith are disturbingly unusual women and manifestations of Ann Todd's star persona. A third film with Todd followed, *The Sound Barrier* (1952), but this is much less of a melodrama, and her role, important though it is, is as part of an ensemble rather than as a star. The film's setting in the brave new world of British aviation helped to make it a commercial success, but Lean's relationship with his third wife was severely strained. Henceforth they pursued their careers separately.

Cineguild's films had all been made for J. Arthur Rank, but when Rank cut back on production budgets in response to the adverse financial conditions at the end of the 1940s, Cineguild was dissolved, and Lean made *The Sound Barrier* and his next film, *Hobson's Choice* (1953), for Alexander Korda. It was Korda who initiated the next phase in Lean's career by sending him to India to research for a film about the Taj Mahal. Lean was enchanted by India, stayed a month, and began a romance with an unhappily married Indian woman, Leila Matkar (d. 1998). The Taj Mahal film never materialized, and instead Lean went to Venice to make *Summer Madness* (1954), an Anglo-American co-production between Korda and United Artists starring Katharine Hepburn. Ann Todd stayed in London playing Lady Macbeth at the Old Vic.

Summer Madness, Lean's favourite film, marked a shift in his style of film-making. It was his first film aimed at an international audience and his first film shot on location.

Hitherto, apart from excursions for exterior shots (such as Carnforth station in *Brief Encounter* and Lake Annecy in *The Passionate Friends*), Lean's films, with their chiaroscuro lighting and meticulously prepared sets, were very much a product of the studio system in which he had served his apprenticeship. With *Summer Madness*, Lean discovered that, given a big enough budget and a dedicated camera and set design team, he could mould the external world to his vision. Quintessentially English though he was, he also found that he enjoyed living abroad. His wanderlust was enhanced when, after separating from Ann Todd, he was told that he would be liable for the tax debts of her company, Glendorgal, were he to stay in England. After the première of *Summer Madness* in May 1955 he began an exile from Britain which lasted for thirty years.

Lean returned to India, where he was reunited with Leila Matkar, and worked with Richard Mason on an adaptation of his novel *The Wind Cannot Read*, a wartime romance between an RAF officer and a Japanese woman set in India and Burma. Unfortunately, Korda thought the script unacceptably sentimental and refused to finance the film. The script then passed to Betty Box and Ralph Thomas, who made the film for the Rank organization in 1958. By this time Lean had made an adaptation of Pierre Boule's best-selling novel *The Bridge on the River Kwai* for the American producer Sam Spiegel. Boule's critique of the British military ethos was very different from the subdued, respectful heroism of British war films like *The Cruel Sea* and *The Dam Busters*, and Lean quickly fell out with Carl Foreman, the exiled American writer whom Spiegel had commissioned to write the script. As Lean told Spiegel:

> The subject is pretty tricky at the best of times. If it misses it will be a bad miss. To put it over, one has to have a real understanding of the British mentality or it will be offensive. Mr Foreman hasn't got the first glimmer and he is offensive. (Brownlow, 350)

Foreman was replaced with another blacklisted American writer, Michael Wilson, with whom Lean forged a much better relationship. Nevertheless, in the harsh conditions of location filming in the jungles of Ceylon, Lean encountered a degree of hostility from his cast and crew, who assumed he was making an anti-British film. In fact, with the sympathetic performance of Alec Guinness and the clever use of the popular band tune 'Colonel Bogey' Lean maintained a delicate balance between criticizing and celebrating British courage and intransigence. The film was internationally successful, and in 1958 won several American academy awards, including that for best director. Lean was inundated with offers to make films in Hollywood, but he preferred to maintain his independence, and began a collaboration with Emeric Pressburger on a film about Gandhi, which was to star Alec Guinness. The resulting script, however, was a disappointment, and Lean and Spiegel switched to a film about T. E. Lawrence.

Lawrence of Arabia and after Attempts to make a film about Lawrence's exploits in Arabia went back to the 1930s, when Korda had attempted to persuade Lawrence to allow Leslie Howard to play him in a film to be directed by Lewis Milestone. Lawrence was killed in a motorcycle crash in 1935, and all subsequent attempts to make a film about him had been thwarted by his brother and literary executor, Professor A. W. Lawrence. Spiegel's charm and money, Lean's impressive record of film-making, and a thoughtful analytical treatment written by Michael Wilson now persuaded the professor to allow a film to go ahead. The film's gestation period was a troubled one, with the playwright Robert Bolt eventually replacing Wilson as writer and Peter O'Toole playing the role for which actors as various as Marlon Brando and Albert Finney had been proposed. After four months' shooting in the Jordanian desert, Spiegel forced Lean to suspend production, and the remaining sequences were shot in Spain and Morocco, Seville standing in for Cairo, Jerusalem, and Damascus. Lean shared Lawrence's passion for the desert, and his experience of shooting the film was enriched by his harmonious relationship with the cinematographer, Freddie Young, and his romantic involvement with the New Zealand-born Barbara Cole, who handled continuity on the film. Ann Todd had divorced Lean in July 1957, and in July 1960 he married Leila Matkar. But it was with Barbara Cole that he spent most of the next seven years.

Though *Lawrence of Arabia* (1962) had gone considerably over budget, its intelligent approach to a far-from-conventional hero and the visual splendour of the desert imagery made it a genuine modern epic; the film was awarded seven American academy awards in 1962. The partnership between Lean and Spiegel had been severely strained by tensions over the shooting schedule for *Lawrence of Arabia*, and for his next film, an adaptation of Boris Pasternak's Nobel prize-winning novel *Doctor Zhivago*, Lean turned to a less intrusive producer, Carlo Ponti. The commercial success of his last two films had given Lean considerable power, and he was allowed to make a hugely expensive film (production lasted 232 days) with the two main parts filled by relatively unknown actors. Lean and his scriptwriter Robert Bolt resisted pressure from Ponti to cast his wife (Sophia Loren) in the part of Lara and instead chose Julie Christie. After considering Paul Newman, Max von Sydow, Burt Lancaster, and Peter O'Toole, Lean took a chance on Omar Sharif, the Egyptian actor who had made a strong impression as Sherif Ali in *Lawrence of Arabia*. When *Doctor Zhivago* opened in New York in December 1965 press reviews were mixed, some critics objecting to it as a shallow and sentimental rendering of Pasternak's novel. But after the first few days public reaction shifted decisively in the film's favour. It was nominated for ten American academy awards, winning five, and became an international box-office success. *Doctor Zhivago* made Lean rich and allowed him virtual carte blanche to make what he wanted. He had also decided to make a permanent break with Leila and settle down with Barbara Cole, but in November 1966, while he was in India for the release of *Doctor Zhivago*, he met and fell in love with Sandra Hotz, a twenty-year-old Swiss South African whose family owned the Laurie Hotel in Agra, which Lean had patronized regularly since his first visit to India in 1954. They lived together for the next nineteen years, though for twelve of them Lean remained married to Leila.

Rejecting Bolt's attempt at the Gandhi project and his idea of adapting *Madame Bovary*, Lean encouraged him to write an original story which would transpose Flaubert's account of a woman's tragic search for sexual self-expression in a repressive society from nineteenth-century France to somewhere with more dramatic potential. Bolt responded with *Ryan's Daughter*, set in a remote Irish village shortly after the Easter rising of 1916. Lean had been angered by the accusations that he had lost the ability to make small-scale, intimate films, and planned to shoot it in ten weeks. With the production plagued by the weather on the Dingle peninsula in the far south-west of Ireland, the costs escalated rapidly, and when the film was finally completed it was dismissed by most critics as an overblown and old-fashioned melodrama. Lean, unused to such critical mauling, was bitterly upset, and it was fourteen years before he made another film. The film's length (over three hours), the seeming flimsiness of the story, and the odd casting of Robert Mitchum as the gentle, flower-loving cuckolded husband combined with the film's poor critical reception to alienate audiences. With hindsight, *Ryan's Daughter*, with its beautifully judged performances, spectacular imagery, and boldly sympathetic focus on female sexuality, can be judged less harshly, but it was out of time with a new mood in film-making which stressed fast pace, urban environments, and a much cheaper and more improvisatory style of film-making.

Final years Lean's absence from film-making was not something he intended, and over the next fourteen years he was involved in a number of interesting projects—most notably a lavish two-part dramatization of the events surrounding the mutiny on the *Bounty*—which failed to come to fruition. After a long sojourn on the South Sea islands of Tahiti and Bora Bora, he returned to London in June 1981 and was approached by Lord Brabourne to direct *A Passage to India*. Lean agreed but insisted on writing his own script, which departed significantly from E. M. Forster's novel in the more sympathetic role allotted to its female protagonist, Miss Quested. Though Lean faced the usual accusations of extravagance during the shooting of the film, it was generally well received both in Britain and in the USA when it was released in December 1984.

In 1983 Lean had received one of the first British Film Institute fellowships. In June 1984 he was knighted. In 1990 he received an American Film Institute lifetime achievement award. Amid these honours, however, Lean's personal life remained turbulent. In August 1978 he was finally divorced from Leila, and in October 1981 he married Sandra Hotz. In November 1985 the couple were divorced, and in December 1990 Lean married Sandra Cooke, an art dealer, with whom he had been living since 1985. Shortly after the wedding Lean was diagnosed with throat cancer. He responded well to radiotherapy, but in February 1991 he developed pneumonia, and he died at his home at Sun Wharf, 30 Narrow Street, Limehouse, London, on 16 April. He was buried at Putney Vale crematorium on 22 April. A memorial service was held at St Paul's Cathedral on 3 October 1991.

Lean's thorough apprenticeship gave him a confidence in his own abilities which made it possible for him to handle large-scale productions without being panicked into rushed decisions. He was prepared to accept the embarrassment of having large numbers of people standing idle while he made his mind up because he was convinced that there was only one way to film a sequence and that even the most rigorous pre-planning could not always predict what that best way was.

Lean's Quaker background, though it failed to implant in him deep religious beliefs, gave him an austere seriousness which made him impatient of the sybaritic lifestyle favoured by many people in the film industry. Though his early success accustomed him to wealth and luxury and he was always immaculately and expensively dressed, he seemed happiest among the hardships of location filming. He was a handsome man who liked and was liked by women, and he regarded a satisfying sexual relationship as a priority.

Though there is still a tendency to judge Lean's modest English black and white films as superior to his lavish epics, the intelligence, flair, and visual splendour of the latter were what made him an internationally renowned director, and their achievements have proved difficult to emulate. ROBERT MURPHY

Sources K. Brownlow, *David Lean* (1997) • G. Fuller and N. Kent, 'Return of the native', *Stills* (March 1985), 29–36 • H. Hudson, 'Dreaming in the light', *Sight and Sound* (Sept 1991), 18–21 • H. Kennedy, 'I'm a picture chap', *Film Comment* (Jan–Feb 1985), 28–32 • G. Pratley, *The cinema of David Lean* (1974) • D. McVay, 'Lean—lover of life', *Films and Filming* (Aug 1959), 9–10 • A. Silver and J. Ursini, *David Lean and his films* (1974) • M. Sragow, 'David Lean's right of passage', *Film Comment* (Jan–Feb 1985), 20–27 • A. Turner, *The making of David Lean's 'Lawrence of Arabia'* (1994) • R. Winnington, *Film criticism and caricatures, 1943–53* (1975) • 'David Lean: a life in film', London Weekend Television, *The South Bank show*, 1986 • b. cert. • m. certs. [Isabel Mayo Lean; Kathleen Walsh; Dorothy Ann Tangye] • d. cert.

Archives FILM NF and TUA, films

Likenesses Baron, photograph, *c*.1940, Hult. Arch. [*see illus.*] • photographs, Hult. Arch.

Leander a Sancto Martino. *See* Jones, John (1575–1635).

Leanerd, John (*fl.* 1677–1679), playwright, of whose life the details are almost totally obscure, is credited with the authorship of three plays, but was manifestly a plagiarist. Gerald Langbaine aptly described him as a 'confident Plagiary ... One, who tho' he would be esteemed the Father, is at best but the Midwife to the Labour of others' (Langbaine, 319). The first of these plays, *The country innocence, or, The chambermaid turned Quaker, a comedy with alterations and amendments. As it is now acted at the Theatre Royal. Written by John Leanerd* (1677), was largely borrowed from a certain T. B.'s *The Country Girl* (1647), and only the last two acts reveal any substantial alterations. Leanerd printed the verse of his source as prose and shortened it considerably. Staged at Drury Lane by the King's Company, it was probably first performed to scant applause by an undistinguished cast, and without scenery to judge by the epilogue, in Lent 1677. It was licensed on 6 April of that year. T. B. has been variously identified as Thomas or Anthony

Brewer. Leanerd asserts that he had avoided writing a play of the modern kind, 'compos'd of Noise and Ornament', preferring the 'Antient way of Writing' (sig. A2v of the printed edition).

The second play, *The Rambling Justice, or, The Jealous Husbands. With the Humours of Sir John Twiford*, was certainly performed at Drury Lane in late February 1678, though it may have been staged earlier. The prologue speaks of a 'Lenten Play'. It was licensed on 13 March 1678. Published in the same year (two printings), it was reprinted in 1680 and 1694, which suggests that it was revived about the latter date. *The Rambling Justice* is in part blatantly indecent, but the obscenities are mixed with moralistic sentimentalism. A substantial part of the plot is borrowed from Thomas Middleton's *More Dissemblers besides Women* (written *c*.1615, published London, 1657), which had been assigned by the lord chamberlain to Killigrew's Company at the Restoration. Whole passages coincide word for word with Middleton's text, of which there is no recorded production on the Restoration stage. Leanerd transferred the setting from Italy to London, indulged in a good deal of slapstick and pantomine and titillating bed scenes, and provided the characters with the usual Restoration ticket names. Some sections of the play, not to be found in Middleton, may well have been adapted from sources that have not been identified to date.

Leanerd's third play, *The Counterfeits*, printed in London in 1679 after being performed at the Dorset Garden Theatre by the Duke's Company in May 1678, has been rated by Montague Summers as a 'capital comedy', and listed among 'comedies of great merit' (Summers, 415, 447). However, not only is the attribution to Leanerd questionable, but Langbaine already noted: ''Tis founded on a translated *Spanish* novel, call'd *The Trapanner Trapann'd*, octavo *Lond.* 1655, and I presume the Author may have seen a *French* Comedy, writ by *Tho. Corneille*, on the same Subject, call'd *D. Caesar d'Avalos*'. Ironically, this proved to be the only one of the three plays that survived on the stage, for Colley Cibber probably adapted it in his own comedy *She Would and She Would Not, or, The Kind Imposter*, produced at Drury Lane in 1702, which was revived as late as 1884 at Toole's Theatre in London, though Cibber may, of course, have used the Spanish original rather than *The Counterfeits*. JAMES HOGG

Sources G. Langbaine, *An account of the English dramatick poets* (1691), 319 · D. E. Baker, *Biographia dramatica, or, A companion to the playhouse*, rev. I. Reed, rev. S. Jones, 3 vols. in 4 (1812), vol. 3, p. 192 · Genest, *Eng. stage*, 200, 226, 246–47 · M. B. Stevens, 'The dramatic legacy of Thomas Middleton: a study of the use of his plays, from 1627–1800', PhD diss., Harvard U., 1930, 530–48 · P. H. Gray, 'Lenten casts and the nursery: evidence for the dating of certain Restoration plays', *Publications of the Modern Language Association of America*, 53 (1938), 781–94 · A. Nicoll, *A history of the English drama, 1660–1900*, 1: *Restoration drama, 1660–1700* (1955), 23, 43, 57, 269 · G. E. Bentley, *The Jacobean and Caroline stage*, 7 vols. (1941–68), vol. 3, pp. 5–8; vol. 4, pp. 888–9 · M. Summers, *The playhouse of Pepys* (London, 1935); repr. (New York, 1964), 412–17, 447 · W. Van Lennep and others, eds., *The London stage, 1660–1800*, pt 1: *1660–1700* (1965), 255, 270, 418–19 · G. Sorelius, 'The giant race before the flood: pre-Restoration drama on the stage and in the criticism of the Restoration', *Studia Anglistica Upsaliensia*, 4 (1966), 57–8, 160, 176–7 · W. W. Greg, *A bibliography of English printed drama to the Restoration*, 1: *Stationers' records plays to 1616: nos. 1–349*, Bibliographical Society (1970), 61 · C. J. Strathman CSV, D. Spencer, and M. E. Devine, *Restoration and eighteenth-century theatre research: a bibliographical guide, 1900–1968* (1971) · C. Leech, T. W. Craik, L. Potter, and others, eds., *The Revels history of drama in English*, 8 vols. (1975–83), vol. 5 · J. Hogg, 'John Leanerd's *The rambling justice, or, The jealous husbands*: a Restoration plagiarism of Thomas Middleton's *More dissemblers besides women*', Salzburg Studies in English Literature, Elizabethan and Renaissance Studies, 70 (1978), 111–24

Leapor, Mary (1722–1746), poet, was born on 26 February 1722 at Marston St Lawrence, Northamptonshire, the only child of Philip Leapor (1693–1771), gardener, and his wife, Anne Sharman (*d*. 1741). Most of her childhood was spent in the nearby market town of Brackley, where in 1726–7 her father ran his nursery and worked in the gardens of the local gentry. Leapor would probably have attended the free school in Brackley, but if so this constituted her only formal education. She was said by her father to have begun writing verse at about ten or eleven years old, a habit her parents tried unsuccessfully to discourage.

At some point in her adolescence Leapor went into service, first as a kitchen maid at Weston Hall, 6 miles from Brackley. Here she was employed by Susanna Jennens, the Parthenissa of Leapor's poetry, and probably had access to the house's small library. She next took up a similar position in a gentleman's family apparently at Edgcote House, a few miles away, which she described under the name Crumble Hall in her poem of that title. According to a later account 'her fondness for writing verses there displayed itself by her sometimes taking up her pen while the jack was standing still, and the meat scorching'. The same writer describes her employer's recollections of her as 'extremely swarthy, and quite emaciated … much resembling, in shape, a bass-viol' (*GM*, 807).

In 1745 Leapor was dismissed from this position and returned to Brackley to keep house for her widowed father. Here she met Bridget Freemantle (1698–1779), an educated local lady whose friendship and encouragement were a turning point in her life. Freemantle suggested a subscription edition of Leapor's unpublished verse and tried to interest the London stage in a tragedy she had composed. Neither plan had come to fruition before Leapor's death at Brackley from measles at the age of twenty-four. She was buried at Brackley on 14 November 1746.

Leapor's renown beyond Brackley was solely posthumous. 'Proposals for printing by subscription the poetical works, serious and humorous, of Mrs. Leapor', apparently penned by David Garrick, appeared on 1 January 1747, and nearly 600 subscribers received the first volume in April 1748. The less successful second volume of 1751 was printed by Samuel Richardson.

Leapor's verse, largely in the style of Pope, achieves a considerable range of feeling and forcefully displays an individual voice. After renewed interest in her work she is counted one of the leading women poets of her century. STUART GILLESPIE

Sources R. Greene, *Mary Leapor: a study in eighteenth-century women's poetry* (1993) · M. Leapor, *Poems on several occasions*, 2 vols.

(1748–51) • parish register, Brackley, Northants. RO • *GM*, 1st ser., 54 (1784) • B. W. Rizzo, 'Christopher Smart, the "C.S." poems, and Molly Leapor's epitaph', *The Library*, 6th ser., 5 (1983), 22–31 • G. Sitwell, *A brief history of Weston Hall, Northamptonshire* (1927)

Lear, Edward (1812–1888), landscape painter and writer, was born on 12 (or possibly 13) May 1812 at Bowman's Lodge, Upper Holloway, London, the twentieth of the twenty-one children of Jeremiah Lear (1757–1833) and Ann (1769–1844), daughter of Edward Skerrett and his wife, Florence. Until 1799 Jeremiah Lear worked as a sugar refiner, but in that year he became a stockbroker. In 1790 he was elected a member of the Fruiterers' Company and a freeman of the City of London, and in 1799 was appointed master. Early biographical writing on Edward Lear's family was based on much misinformation. He himself claimed that his grandfather was Danish: 'My own [name], as I think you know is really … LÖR, but my Danish grandfather picked off the two dots and pulled out the diagonal line and made the word Lear' (*Later Letters*, 18–19). In fact, his father was of English descent; his mother's maternal grandmother was Scottish, and moved to London at some time in the mid-eighteenth century.

Early years and education According to later family tradition, recorded about 1907, Jeremiah Lear became a bankrupt and was committed to king's bench prison where he remained for four years. No date is given for this, and what evidence there is suggests that there is no truth in it. Jeremiah's name is not found in any surviving record of debtors' prisons, nor is it listed in the *London Gazette*; indeed he remained a member of the livery of the Fruiterers' Company until his death, which would not have been possible had he been bankrupt. However, there is evidence that at some time in Edward's early childhood his father served a short prison sentence for fraud and debt. Probably at this time, but possibly from his birth, Edward was entrusted to his eldest sister, Ann, twenty-one years older than him, and responsible for his upbringing.

When he was eleven Lear was sent to school for a short period, but apart from this he was educated at home by Ann and his second sister, Sarah. This may have been because of his ill health, for he suffered from short sight, asthma, bronchitis, and, from the age of about five, epilepsy. All his life he was aware of his lack of formal education, although he came to see its possible advantage, writing in 1859:

> I am almost thanking God that I was never educated, for it seems to me that 999 of those who are so, expensively and laboriously, have lost all before they arrive at my age—& remain like Swift's Stulbruggs—cut and dry for life, making no use of their earlier=gained treasures:—whereas, I seem to be on the threshold of knowledge. (Noakes, *Edward Lear: Life of a Wanderer*, 17)

This image of life as a voyage of discovery informs much of his later 'nonsense'.

An important part of Lear's otherwise inadequate education was his sisters' tuition in drawing and painting, and at fifteen he began to earn his living as an artist. To begin with he relied on teaching, on decorating screens

Edward Lear (1812–1888), by William Holman Hunt, 1857

and fans, and on making morbid anatomy drawings. None of his medical work survives, but a commonplace book which he gave to a pupil about 1830 contains some of his decorative work. By 1829, however, he had become an ornithological draughtsman.

Lear as an ornithological draughtsman Lear served an unofficial apprenticeship with the ornithologist Prideaux Selby who, between 1821 and 1834, published *Illustrations of British Ornithology*. One engraving in this work, the *Great Auk*, is known to be based on Lear's drawings. The early part of the nineteenth century was a period of excellence in natural history illustration, encouraged by zoological voyages and the need to identify and classify newly discovered species. The gardens of the Zoological Society of London were opened in 1829, and in June 1830 Lear applied to make drawings of the parrots there. Permission was given at a meeting chaired by the president, Lord Stanley, and Lear devoted the next two years to a publication of his own entitled *Illustrations of the Family of Psittacidae, or Parrots*. This book, published for 175 subscribers in twelve parts between 1830 and 1832, was new in three ways: it was the first devoted to a single family of bird, the first in a large format (imperial folio) in which the illustrations were reproduced by lithography, and the first in which the artist worked direct from nature, using living birds rather than stuffed skins. Lear prepared the lithographic stones himself, and the prints were then hand-coloured. The work received immediate acclaim, the *Red and Yellow Maccaw* being compared by the naturalist William Swainson to John James Audubon's work. The day after the publication of the first two folios, he was recommended for associate membership of the Linnean Society.

In total Lear produced forty-two lithographs of parrots, but after the appearance of the twelfth part in April 1832 he was forced to abandon the project because his subscribers were so slow in paying that he could no longer afford his printer or colourer. He now had to seek employment, and during the next five years he contributed plates to further works by Prideaux Selby, to Sir William Jardine's series The Naturalist's Library (1825–39), and to works by T. C. Eyton, Thomas Bell, and John Gould, in particular Gould's *Birds of Europe* (1832–7) and *A Monograph of the Ramphastidae, or Family of Toucans* (1834). As in the *Parrots*, he combined precise anatomical accuracy with bold, rhythmic designs and an understanding of the individual personalities of the birds. His work was so fine that he is now considered by many to be England's leading ornithological draughtsman.

One of those who admired Lear's work was Lord Stanley, one of the foremost natural historians of his day, who in 1834 became the thirteenth earl of Derby. He had built a private menagerie at his home at Knowsley, near Liverpool, and was looking for an artist who could make an accurate record of his collection. Lear was invited to take on the project, and between 1831 and 1837 spent long periods at Knowsley, making drawings and watercolours of both animals and birds. A small selection of more than 100 highly finished watercolours was published in 1846 in *Gleanings from the Menagerie and Aviary at Knowsley Hall*.

For Lear, however, the time at Knowsley produced more than his zoological work, for it was here that he was introduced to one of the earliest published book of limericks, *Anecdotes and Adventures of Fifteen Gentlemen* (1821?). He had been writing absurd verse since his childhood, but finding himself

> in a Country House, where children and mirth abounded … the greater part of the original drawings and verses for the first 'Book of Nonsense' were struck off with a pen, no assistance ever having been given me in any way but that of uproarious delight and welcome at the appearance of every new absurdity.   (Lear, introduction to *More Nonsense*, 1871)

By the mid-1830s Lear was finding that the minutely detailed work required in natural history draughtsmanship was straining his already weak eyesight, and that the damp climate of the north-west was exacerbating his bronchitis and asthma. In these years his interest was turning increasingly to landscape. In 1835 he visited Ireland with Edward Stanley, bishop of Norwich, and his son, Arthur Penrhyn Stanley, later dean of Westminster; he returned with a folio of pencil drawings, to which he added during the following year while touring the Lake District. Many of these drawings are characterized by sweeping, chunky lines drawn in soft pencil, demonstrating a release from the close discipline required in his ornithological work. In 1837 Lord Derby and his cousin Robert Hornby offered to send Lear to Rome where he could recover his health and paint landscape. As he left England in July he was turning his back on natural history work; during the rest of his life he produced no more than two or three drawings of birds and animals, although he was later to draw on his knowledge of them in the illustrations to his nonsense.

Roman years From 1837 to 1848—apart from two extended visits to England—Lear lived in Rome, finding there an international community of artists with whom he spent the happiest period of his life. Among his friends were the Danish painter Wilhelm Marstrand, the English sculptors John Gibson and William Theed, the painters Penry Williams, Thomas Uwins, and Samuel Palmer, and the architect Thomas Wyatt. His routine was to breakfast and dine with others in the artistic community, spending his days drawing in the city or on the Campagna, or working in his studio, experimenting with different media and ways of handling paint. In the summer months he and his friends would explore other parts of Italy, going south to Naples in 1838 and north to Florence the following year, spending the summer months of 1840 closer to Rome, in Subiaco.

In summer 1841 Lear returned to England to publish his first landscape book, *Views in Rome and its Environs*, with twenty-five lithographic plates and a brief descriptive text. As with the *Parrots*, this was published for subscribers, a method he used for all his subsequent travel books. His income from painting and teaching was used for day-by-day expenses, but the money he earned from writing was invested in Government bonds so that he could one day buy a house of his own.

Lear was back in Rome in December 1841, spending the following summer in Sicily and the Abruzzi. He returned to the Abruzzi the next year, collecting drawings and keeping a detailed journal of his travels. At the end of 1845 he was once more in England, this time staying for more than a year preparing two volumes of his *Illustrated Excursions in Italy*. The first, published in April 1846, containing thirty lithographic plates and forty vignettes, described his journeys in the Abruzzi; the second, which appeared the following August, contained fifteen lithographic plates and thirteen vignettes, with brief topographical and historical notes. One of his travel companions, Charles Church, nephew of Sir Richard Church, described how Lear believed that it was the combination of words and pictures, rather than pictures alone, that best re-created an image of the places he had visited, an interdependence also characteristic of his limericks. Queen Victoria, one of the subscribers, was so impressed with the work that she invited Lear to give her a series of twelve drawing lessons; two examples of her work done under his tutelage are in the Royal Library at Windsor Castle.

In that same year, 1846, Lear also published *A Book of Nonsense*, a two-volume collection of seventy-two limerick verses and drawings. Lear himself did not use the word limerick: the first occurrence dates from 1898 in the *Oxford English Dictionary* and its origins are obscure; he called the verses his 'Nonsenses' or his 'Old Persons'. The first edition did not received much attention; it was not until the third, single-volume edition, published in 1861 and containing 112 verses and drawings, that the limerick swept to popularity. Its appeal to a nineteenth-century children's audience came partly from its simplicity and partly from the benignly anarchic exploits of the characters; Lear's men and women display human foibles and excesses which are accepted without criticism. In other writers' hands the limerick has become sophisticated and often bawdy, almost ceasing to be a verse-form for children, so that some contemporary audiences now find Lear's verses tame. In their time, however, and within the context of children's literature, they were revolutionary and liberating, while his line-drawings, confident and bold, have had a lasting influence on illustration, particularly in the development of the cartoon. Lear published the book himself, selling the rights to Routledge in November 1862 for £125. *A Book of Nonsense* went through twenty-four editions in Lear's lifetime, and has never been out of print.

In December 1846 Lear returned to Rome. He was now working increasingly in oils, the earliest of which date from 1838 and are freely handled *plein-air* sketches on paper; his first commissioned oil painting is dated 1840. The paintings of this period measure typically 10 by 15 inches, but in 1847 he began work on the painting *Civitella di Subiaco*, measuring 50 by 76 inches (Clothworkers' Hall, the City of London). As he turned increasingly to oil painting, the purpose of Lear's watercolours and drawings changed. He now saw them less as works of art in their own right, but rather as the basis for later studio oils and finished watercolours. In works of the mid-1840s we can see the gradual development of his mature watercolour style, which was established by 1847. His method was to make an accurate pencil drawing on the spot, annotating the drawing with descriptive notes which could relate to content ('rox', 'sheep', 'fig trees'), to colour ('dove grey', 'dim purple', 'bloo ski'), or to form ('wider apart', 'this set of lines is the real proportion'). A friend described him at work:

> When we came to a good subject, Lear ... would lift his spectacles, and gaze for several minutes at the scene through a monocular glass he always carried; then, laying down the glass, and adjusting his spectacles, he would put on paper the view before us, mountain range, villages and foreground, with a rapidity and accuracy that inspired me with awestruck admiration. (*Later Letters*, 23)

Later, following his colour notes, he would spend winter evenings in his studio laying in watercolour washes, and then go over the pencil lines and annotations in sepia ink.

In 1847 Lear paid two visits to Naples and Sicily, collecting material for a projected book, *Journals of a Landscape Painter in Southern Calabria, &c.* (1852). In these as in others of his journeys he would travel on foot, or on horseback, from first light until it grew dark, stopping to draw wherever he saw suitable scenery and settling down each night to write up his journal. Many of the places he visited were uncharted and scarcely known beyond their own communities, and people who travelled with him have described the discomfort and hardship of the conditions, the primitive food and often disagreeable sleeping places, and how he pushed himself physically so that he could not only cover large distances but also produce the work which was one purpose of his journeys. It was thus that he hoped

to reach the more remote and most beautiful places which he wanted to see; for a person who had endured a sickly childhood and who continued to suffer from short sight, from chest infections, and from epilepsy, it was an extraordinary achievement.

As Lear went through Calabria he sensed the growing political unrest there, and in April 1848 he decided he must leave Italy. However, before returning to England he decided to spend fifteen months gathering material from which he could later work. He went first via Malta to Corfu, and then on to Greece, where he visited Athens, Marathon, Thermopylae, and Thebes. Prevented from continuing his Greek travels by an outbreak of cholera, he went to Constantinople before returning to Greece, and then on to Albania, journeys described in *Journals of a Landscape Painter in Albania, &c.* (1851). By December he was back in Malta, and from there, at the beginning of 1849, he set out for Egypt and Sinai. In February, in Malta once more, he met Franklin Lushington, who was to become his closest friend, and with whom he now explored southern Greece. By July 1849 he was in England, where he planned to settle down and build a reputation as a landscape painter, particularly of remote and unusual places.

The middle years Until now Lear had been largely self-taught, and he believed that his lack of knowledge, especially of human anatomy, would hamper his artistic ambitions. When in autumn 1849 he received a legacy of £500, he decided to fulfil a long-standing ambition and apply as a student to the Royal Academy Schools. He was now thirty-seven. He had first to pass a qualifying exam: he enrolled at Sass's School of Art, where he prepared drawings for the examiners, and in January 1850 he was accepted. Almost nothing has survived from this period of Lear's life, and we do not know how long he stayed at the academy, nor why he left. It seems that he was there for only a few months, although he later looked back on this brief interlude as a valuable time. Then, in 1852, came the most significant meeting of his painting career, when he was introduced to William Holman Hunt, a leading member of the Pre-Raphaelite Brotherhood.

In his days as a natural history draughtsman Lear had known the importance of working direct from nature, and in this he shared something of the Pre-Raphaelites' approach to painting; he now asked for Hunt's help in overcoming the technical problems he encountered as he worked on large oils. In summer 1852 they rented a farmhouse together at Fairlight, Sussex. Here he was able to watch Hunt painting and to make notes about his methods in 'Ye booke of Hunte'. Hunt's influence can be most clearly seen in Lear's use of colour as the browns and ochres of his Roman work were replaced by warmer pinks and mauves, and clear greens. That summer he painted *Reggio* (Tate collection), *The Mountains of Thermopylae* (Bristol City Art Gallery), and *The Quarries of Syracuse* (priv. coll.).

The Mountains of Thermopylae was exhibited at the British Institution in spring 1853, and *The Quarries of Syracuse* at the Royal Academy in 1853, where it was chosen by Frederick Lygon, later sixth Earl Beauchamp, as his Art Union prize. In March that year Lord Derby commissioned Lear to paint *Windsor Castle from St Leonards*, one of only three oil paintings he did of English scenes. The weather was bad and the light unpredictable, and Lear grumbled about the problems this caused, writing to Holman Hunt: 'supposing a tree is black one minute—the next it's yellow, and the 3^d green: so that were I to finish any one part the whole 8 feet would be all spots—a sort of Leopard Landscape' (Noakes, *Edward Lear: Life of a Wanderer*, 93). Indeed, he was finding the English climate increasingly difficult, for his asthma and bronchitis had returned. In December 1853, to escape the English winter, he sailed for Egypt. By the late spring he was back in London, but in August he left for a walking holiday in Switzerland, a country to whose landscape he did not respond. Back in London, he faced another winter of rain and semi-darkness. His lungs were now so bad that he could scarcely go out, and he realized that he could not settle permanently in England. Franklin Lushington had recently been appointed judge at the supreme court of justice in the Ionian Islands, and so Lear decided to join him and make a winter home in Corfu. They sailed from Dover in November 1854.

The issue of Lear's supposed homosexuality has been much discussed. He never married, but evidence suggests that this was because of his epilepsy; he believed it to be inherited, and that he might pass it on to his own children. However, he longed for children of his own, and in 1867 he contemplated proposing to Augusta (Gussie) Bethell, daughter of the lord chancellor, who almost certainly would have accepted him. But at the last minute he drew back, probably believing that once she knew of his illness she would refuse to marry him. Although his childhood companions were aware of his illness, no adult friend ever realized that he was an epileptic. The loneliness which maintaining this secret forced upon him is an important key to Lear's personality, the source both of his lonely unhappiness and of much of his nonsense. His closest friendships were with men, and for a time he had a powerful, but unreciprocated, emotional involvement with Franklin Lushington, but beyond this there is no evidence to suggest that he was a homosexual. Despite his loneliness, and his frequent bouts of debilitating depression, until the last and loneliest years of his life when he became irritable and cantankerous, more especially to strangers, Lear was a sought-after and convivial companion, with a wide circle of acquaintance and many real friends who remained trusted and supportive even in the final years of his life. Children responded to his tall, shambling, bearded, bespectacled figure with warmth and happiness, and he treated them with humorous understanding and respect.

In August 1856 Lear crossed over from Corfu to Greece and went on to Mount Athos, but while he was there his servant, Giorgio Kokali, was taken ill with malaria. Lear had to stay close to the monastery where Kokali was being looked after, which meant that he could spend more time than usual on individual drawings, and on 9 and 10 September 1856 he drew one of his finest watercolours, *The Monastery of St Paul* (priv. coll.). After a second winter in Corfu he returned via Venice to London. In that year, 1857, *The Quarries of Syracuse* was exhibited in the International Exhibition in Manchester. The following March he went from Corfu to revisit Egypt and Palestine, travelling on to Petra and Lebanon. Lushington had now resigned his post, and so Lear decided that the following winter he would return to Rome. Within days he realized that it was a mistake: both he and the city had changed. He had taken rooms for three years, but after a second winter he decided not to return. Instead he spent the winter of 1860–61 in England; his sister Ann was unwell and he wanted to be near her, and he planned to work on a large painting of the cedars of Lebanon.

Although he had made a number of studies of the cedars during his trip to Lebanon in 1858, Lear wanted to work from living trees: these he found at Oatlands Park Hotel in Weybridge. In March Ann died, and his sense of loneliness deepened, but work on the 9 foot painting progressed well, and it was completed in May 1861. *The Cedars of Lebanon* was his largest and most important painting, and he awaited the critical response to it anxiously. In August it was exhibited in Liverpool, where it was highly praised, but in the following May, when it was shown in the Great International Exhibition in South Kensington, it was hung so high that it could scarcely be seen. The influential Tom Taylor, reviewing the exhibition in *The Times*, dismissed the painter as being no more than a mirror of the scene where he should have recreated what he saw and set upon it the seal of his own mind, a charge of lack of poetic feeling frequently levelled against topographical painting at that time. This was something to which Lear was particularly sensitive, delighting in Arthur Stanley's description of him as 'the Painter of Topographical Poetry' (Noakes, *Edward Lear, 1812–1888*, 132), and he was both mortified and angered by what he saw as uninformed and unjust criticism.

Lear had priced *The Cedars* at 700 guineas, but after its dismissal by the critics it failed to sell. 'What I do with the Cedars I do not know', he wrote a year later:

> probably make a great coat of them. To a philosopher, the fate of a picture so well thought of & containing such high qualities, is funny enough:—for the act of two Royal Academicians in hanging it high, condemn it first,—& 2ndly the cold blooded criticism of Tom Taylor in the Times, quasi=approving of its position, stamps the poor canvass into oblivion still more & I fear, without remedy. (Noakes, *The Painter Edward Lear*, 77)

Five years later it was still unsold, and he wrote in despair:

> sometimes I consider as to the wit of taking my Cedars out of its frame & putting round it a border of rose colored velvet,—embellished with a fringe of yellow worsted with black spots, to protypify the possible proximate propinquity of predatorial panthers,—& then selling the whole for floorcloth by auction. (Noakes, *Edward Lear: Life of a Wanderer*, 178)

It was eventually bought in 1867 for 200 guineas; its present whereabouts is unknown. From the time of Lear's return to England in 1849 his paintings had been commanding increasing prices and finding ready buyers. The failure of this work was the turning point of his career, and he was to live the rest of his life in professional isolation, disappointment, and financial insecurity.

In summer 1861 Lear travelled to Florence to make a painting for one of his most consistent patrons, Frances, Lady Waldegrave, later the wife of his close friend Chichester Fortescue. Lear spent the two following winters in Corfu, and it was here in November 1862 that he began the first of a series of watercolours which lastingly damaged his reputation, but which brought in a steady but undramatic income: he called these his Tyrants. First, he sorted through the drawings he had done on his travels, selecting sixty on which to base studio watercolours. Then he prepared sixty sheets of paper and, working on them in two groups, he drew pencil outlines of thirty views, which he spread out around his studio. He then moved from one to the next, laying in blue washes, then red, then yellow, and so on, until he had thirty completed works. He then repeated this process with the second group. 'For the present I have done with oil painting, & have collapsed into degradation & small 10 & 12 Guinea drawings calculated to attract the attention of small Capitalists' (Noakes, *Edward Lear: Life of a Wanderer*, 156). When they were finished he ordered sixty frames, and by mid-February he was ready to exhibit them. The small capitalists responded, for within days many had sold and he could once more pay his bills. Between 1862 and 1884, Lear produced nearly one thousand Tyrants. The income from their sale was essential, but they did his reputation little good. As a friend later remarked: 'if he had exercised a judicious selection of his exhibition pieces, instead of hanging good, bad and indifferent pictures together … his value at the time would have been considerably enhanced' (Malcolm, 118).

With the first set of Tyrants finished, Lear turned his mind to other possible sources of income. The Ionian Islands had been ceded to the Greeks in 1863, and before leaving he toured the islands in preparation for *Views in the Seven Ionian Islands*, which he published in December 1863. In this he returned to the format of the earlier books; there were twenty lithographic plates, each with a short descriptive text, but no personal account of his journey. In April 1864 he left Corfu, and set out to explore Crete. By June he was back in England. With the failure of his artistic ambition, he began to consider living permanently abroad. The savings from his publications, and a small legacy from Ann, meant that he could afford to build a house where he would live quietly and paint. He needed now to find a suitable place: in winter 1864–5 he was in Nice, and after spending a month working on a group of 240 Tyrants, he set out with Giorgio Kokali to walk along the corniche. In blustery winter weather he crossed into Italy, passing through San Remo, his first visit to the place where he spent the last seventeen years of his life.

In the following winter Lear went via Venice to Malta, but he found it a dull, unstimulating place to winter. A year later he was in Egypt, keeping a detailed diary of his voyage down the Nile, one of several which he planned, but failed, to publish. In 1867–8 he wintered in Cannes, wondering if France might be the best place to settle, and

from there he visited Corsica, the subject of his last, and least successful, travel book, *Journal of a Landscape Painter in Corsica*, which was published in 1870.

In many ways these were rootless and dispiriting years, and yet it was during the latter half of the 1850s and throughout the 1860s, when Lear had given up hope of becoming a sought-after painter, that he produced his finest watercolours. He had achieved a masterly control of his medium, combining powerful composition with strong line and a fluid freedom in the handling of paint which would establish him as one of the great English watercolour painters. But—living in a time when an artist's reputation was made in mixed exhibitions of large oils—he regarded these small masterpieces as no more than the basis of his studio work. Then, in the late 1860s, Lear discovered a new means of expression. The success of the third edition of *A Book of Nonsense* (1861) had made his a household name. In February 1865 he wrote a prose story, the 'History of the Seven Families of the Lake Pipple-Popple', for the children of Lord and Lady Fitzwilliam, who were wintering close to him in Cannes. Two years later he composed 'The Story of the Four Little Children who Went Round the World' for Gussie Bethell's nephews and nieces. Then, in December 1867, when Janet, the six-year-old daughter of his friend John Addington Symonds, was ill in bed, Lear wrote and illustrated for her a poem called 'The Owl and the Pussycat': this was the first of his nonsense songs which can be positively dated.

It is interesting to speculate whether, if Lear had achieved his ambition as a painter, he would have written the songs which were composed over the next nine years, between December 1867 and August 1876, and which are the most enduring of his nonsense creations. Some are simple nursery songs; some are tales of misfits who travel together to places where their oddities no longer matter and where they can dance and sing joyously together. Others are poems of risk and adventure, loneliness and rejection. Be bold, he is saying to the children, and dare to leave behind the safe world you know, for as you go in search of distant places you may discover majestic beauties and new freedoms which the faint-hearted cannot even imagine. But in the songs of the later 1870s he speaks also of the loneliness which can await those who find themselves abandoned on some distant shore. He published two nonsense books in quick succession, *Nonsense Songs, Stories, Botany and Alphabets* (1871), which contained among others 'The Owl and the Pussy-cat', 'The Duck and the Kangaroo', 'The Daddy Long-Legs and the Fly', and 'The Jumblies', and *More Nonsense* (1872), a book of 100 new limericks.

Later nonsense writing, and the return to Italy Meanwhile, Lear decided that southern France was too fashionable and too expensive, and instead he began to search for land across the border in Italy. At the end of 1869 he found a plot in San Remo, a place 'Neither too much *in*, nor altogether *out* of the world' (Noakes, *Edward Lear: Life of a Wanderer*, 204). He designed the house, which he called Villa Emily, so that he would have a large first-floor studio looking out over olive groves towards the sea, and a ground-floor exhibition room where he could have a permanent exhibition of his work to which people could come on open days. He moved in during March 1871 and, once he was settled, his thoughts turned to a project he had had in mind since 1851, a series of drawings for Alfred Tennyson's poems. He had met Tennyson that year, and shortly after their meeting had sent Alfred and his new wife, Emily, a copy of his Albania journal as a wedding present; in response to this, Tennyson had written the poem 'To E.L. on his Travels in Greece'. Later, as Lear found Alfred increasingly overbearing, the friendship between them cooled, but he remained devoted to Emily, who understood perhaps more than anyone the loneliness and sadness of his life. He set a number of Tennyson's poems to music, publishing some of them between 1853 and 1860. These settings are no more than pleasant Victorian ballads, but Alfred was delighted by them, saying that 'they seem to throw a diaphanous veil over the words—nothing more' (C. Tennyson, *Alfred Tennyson*, 1949, 441). Lear knew that Tennyson disliked his work being illustrated, and he cautiously disclaimed his drawings as illustrations, suggesting that '"Painting=sympathizations" would be better if there were such a phrase' (Noakes, *Edward Lear, 1812–1888*, 132). His plan was to prepare 250 drawings based on drawings chosen from the estimated 10,000 watercolours he had made on his travels, and which he would publish as the summation of his life's work, modelled on Turner's *Liber Studiorum*. From the beginning he had difficulty finding a suitable method of reproduction, and over a number of years he experimented with one possibility after another, none of which satisfied him. As the years went on his eyesight deteriorated and the experiments became more crude and unsatisfactory, until he finally abandoned the project in autumn 1887. It was not until after his death, in 1889, that a small selection of the drawings was published in *Poems of Alfred, Lord Tennyson, Illustrated by Edward Lear*, a publication limited to an edition of 100 copies, each signed by the poet.

After settling in San Remo, Lear had planned to make no more extended journeys, but in 1872 his friend Lord Northbrook was appointed viceroy of India; he now wrote inviting Lear to visit the subcontinent. Lear was uncertain whether to accept, but that summer he visited England and was given nearly £1000 worth of work painting Indian landscape. Such commissions were now rare, and with this encouragement he decided to go. Back in San Remo he closed Villa Emily and set out for Alexandria, where he would pick up the boat for India. Some weeks earlier he had fallen and knocked his temple, an accident which left him unsteady and anxious. When he arrived in Egypt there were delays, and this and the heat made him suddenly decide he could not go on, and within days he was back in San Remo. In the quiet of his home he worried about his sudden, irrational change of mind. He wondered if the fall might be to blame, but all his life he had feared that the epilepsy might one day damage his brain and he wondered if this was the real cause of his impulsiveness. However, he settled down to a winter of hard work, completing a fine painting, *The Pyramids Roads at Ghizeh* (priv. coll.), a work of bold and audacious composition. For companionship he bought a tailless cat whom he called Foss, immortalised in Lear's nonsense drawings.

In October 1873 Lear and Giorgio Kokali left once more for India. This time the journey was uneventful, and they docked in Bombay in late November. It was the start of a fifteen-month journey in which they travelled from the west to the east, and from the north to the south of the subcontinent, fulfilling a rigorous itinerary for a man who was now in his sixties. When they reached Ceylon in November 1874, Kokali became ill with dysentery, and Lear realized that they had had enough; they sailed from Bombay in January 1875. Back in San Remo, Lear settled down to work on his Indian commissions, painting a powerful oil, *Kinchinjunga* (Kangchenjunga), for Lord Northbrook (priv. coll.). However, in autumn 1878 he realized that there was building activity on the olive grove which separated his house from the sea. He had been given first refusal should the land ever be sold, and he was shocked to discover that this had not been honoured and that a large hotel was to be built on the site. Gradually, as the building progressed, it blocked his view to the sea, and when it was painted white its reflected brilliance destroyed his studio light. Had he been less alone, what he saw as the treachery of his neighbours might have acquired less overwhelming proportions in his mind, but as it was he became obsessed with 'the Enemy' as he called them. He began to search for another site, and found one, still in San Remo, telling Emily Tennyson: 'unless the Fishes begin to build, or Noah's Ark comes to an Anchor below the site, the new Villa Oduardo cannot be spoiled' (Noakes, *Edward Lear: Life of a Wanderer*, 236). Villa Emily was put on the market, and work began on the new house, to be called Villa Tennyson. By June 1881 it was completed, but Villa Emily remained unsold. His few years of financial security were over, for the house did not sell, and he was not free of debt until February 1884.

In 1877 Lear published his last book of nonsense, *Laughable Lyrics*, which contained some of his finest, but also his saddest songs, including 'The Pelican Chorus', 'The Yonghy-bonghy-bò', and 'The Dong with a Luminous Nose'. He was still to write 'How pleasant to know Mr Lear!' (1879), and 'Incidents in the Life of my Uncle Arly' (1886), though his other late attempts at nonsense were flat and uninspired. But in February 1886 came praise which lit up his bleak and lonely life, for John Ruskin wrote: 'I really don't know any author to whom I am half so grateful, for my idle self, as Edward Lear. I shall place him first of *my* hundred authors' (*Pall Mall Gazette*, 43, 1886, 2). His young San Remo neighbour, Hubert Congreve, later wrote: 'I never knew him repeat any story telling against his Nonsense, and Ruskin's praise was very dear to him' (*Later Letters*, 22).

Giorgio Kokali, his servant for twenty-five years, had

died in August 1883, and in September 1887 Foss, his last faithful companion, also died. Lear survived him by only four months, dying at home in San Remo on 29 January 1888. Of his funeral a San Remo friend wrote:

> I have never forgotten it, it was all so sad, so lonely. After such a life as Mr Lear's had been and the immense number of friends he had, there was not one of them able to be with him at the end.   (*Later Letters*, 361)

He was buried in San Remo, and lines from Tennyson's poem to him are inscribed on his headstone:

> all things fair,
> With such a pencil, such a pen,
> You shadow'd forth to distant men,
> I read and felt that I was there.

Posthumous reputation Lear's achievements as a painter were obscured for many years by his reputation as a nonsense writer, and by his need to exhibit only his studio works. The first time that the general public saw his travel watercolours was in 1930. Most of these he bequeathed to Franklin Lushington, and they began to come onto the market in 1929. In summer 1930 Martin Hardie wrote a pioneering study of these previously little-known drawings in *Artwork* (no. 22, pp. 280–81). Angus Davidson's biography in 1938 discussed for the first time all aspects of his work. However, Lear's reputation was slow to develop, and a sustained scholarly interest in his work did not begin until the late 1960s. He benefited from the general reassessment of Victorian painters, but the most important step towards a wider recognition of his contribution was the major exhibition of his work at the Royal Academy of Arts in 1985. Covering every area of his output, it demonstrated his versatility as a pioneering natural history draughtsman, as a powerful landscape painter whose limpid watercolours are characterized by strong, rhythmic line and a free handling of colour, and as a nonsense illustrator whose simplicity and boldness have had a profound effect on subsequent illustration and caricature. The first complete and scholarly edition of his poetry and nonsense appeared in November 2001. The most important collections of Lear's works are the Houghton Library at Harvard which has more than 3000 of his watercolour drawings, the Paul Mellon Center for British Art at New Haven, the Walker Art Gallery and Liverpool Public Library, the British Museum and Tate collection. There is an important collection of his ornithological work in the Blacker-Wood Library, McGill University, Montreal.

VIVIEN NOAKES

Sources T. Byron, *Nonsense and wonder: the poems and cartoons of Edward Lear* (New York, 1977) · A. C. Colley, *Edward Lear and the critics* (Columbia, SC, 1993) · A. Davidson, *Edward Lear: landscape painter and nonsense poet (1812–1888)* (1938) · V. Dehejia, *Impossible picturesqueness: Edward Lear's Indian watercolours, 1873–1875* (New York, 1989) · *Edward Lear: the Cretan journal*, ed. R. Fowler (Athens, 1984) · P. Hofer, *Edward Lear as a landscape draughtsman* (1967) · S. Hyman, *Edward Lear's birds* (1980) · *Edward Lear in the Levant: travels in Albania, Greece and Turkey in Europe, 1848–1849*, ed. S. Hyman (1988) · P. Levi, *Edward Lear: a biography* (1995) · I. Malcolm, *The pursuits of leisure and other essays* (1929) · *Edward Lear's Indian journal*, ed. R. Murphy (1953) · V. Noakes, ed., *Edward Lear: the life of a wanderer*, 3rd edn (1985) · V. Noakes, *Edward Lear, 1812–1888* (1985) [exhibition catalogue, RA] · V. Noakes, *The painter Edward Lear* (1991) · *Selected letters*, ed. V. Noakes (1988) · *Edward Lear: the complete verse and other nonsense*, ed. V. Noakes (2001) · R. Pitman, *Edward Lear's Tennyson* (1988) · B. Reade, *Edward Lear's parrots* (1949) · *Edward Lear: the Corfu years*, ed. P. Sherrard (Athens, 1988) · W. B. O. Field [B. C. Slade], *Edward Lear on my shelves* (New York, 1933) · *The letters of Edward Lear*, ed. Lady Strachey (1907) · *The later letters of Edward Lear*, ed. Lady Strachey (1911) · S. Wilcox, *Edward Lear and the art of travel* (New Haven, 2000)

Archives FM Cam. · Harvard U., Houghton L., corresp., papers and drawings · Liverpool Central Library, annotated copy of *A book of nonsense* · Morgan L. · Ransom HRC · Yale U., Beinecke L. | Balliol Oxf., letters to David Morier · BL, letters to Lord Avebury, Add. MSS 49647–49649 · BL, letters to W. Holman Hunt, RP800, 3731 (ii) · BL, letters to F. T. Underhill, RP 1752 (ii) [microfilm] · Glamorgan RO, Cardiff, letters to Lord Aberdare and Lady Aberdare · Hunt. L., letters, mainly to W. Holman Hunt · Lincoln Central Library, letters to Emily, Lady Tennyson and Hallam Tennyson · Lpool RO, letters to the fourteenth earl of Derby · Museum of Scotland, letters to W. Jardine · NRA, priv. coll., letters to his sister · NYPL, Berg Collection · Som. ARS, corresp. with Chichester Fortescue · Som. ARS, letters to E. Strachey and Lady Strachey · Somerville College, Oxford, letters to Amelia Edwards and Marianne North · Syracuse University, New York, corresp. with John Simeon · V&A NAL, letters and papers relating to the Newsome family

Likenesses W. Marstrand, pencil drawing, 1840, NPG · W. H. Hunt, chalk drawing, 1857, Walker Art Gallery, Liverpool [*see illus.*] · E. Lear, self-portrait, pen-and-ink caricature, 1862–3, NPG · Schier & Schoefft, carte-de-visite, *c.*1863, NPG · E. Lear, self-portraits, caricature drawings, Harvard TC · McLean, Melhuish & Haes, carte-de-visite, NPG · silhouette, NPG

Wealth at death £2820 14*s.* 2*d.*: probate, Nov 1888, *CGPLA Eng. & Wales*

PICTURE CREDITS

Knox, Alexander (1757–1831)—© National Portrait Gallery, London

Knox, Edmund Arbuthnott (1847–1937)—© National Portrait Gallery, London

Knox, Henry (1750–1806)—Copyright 2004 Museum of Fine Arts, Boston; Deposited by the City of Boston

Knox, Robert (1791–1862)—Scottish National Portrait Gallery

Knox, Ronald Arbuthnott (1888–1957)—© National Portrait Gallery, London

Knox, Vicesimus (1752–1821)—© National Portrait Gallery, London

Knox, Wilfred Lawrence (1886–1950)—photograph reproduced by courtesy of The British Academy

Knyvett, Charles (1752–1822)—© National Portrait Gallery, London

Koch, Ludwig Karl (1881–1974)—© reserved; unknown collection; photograph National Portrait Gallery, London

Koenig, Ghisha (1921–1993)—Graves Art Gallery, Sheffield; photograph National Portrait Gallery, London

Kokoschka, Oskar (1886–1980)—© DACS, 2004; private collection, on loan to the Scottish National Gallery of Modern Art, Edinburgh; photograph National Portrait Gallery, London

Korda, Sir Alexander (1893–1956)—Getty Images - Hulton Archive

Kosterlitz, Hans Walter (1903–1996)—Godfrey Argent Studios

Kotzé, Sir John Gilbert (1849–1940)—© National Portrait Gallery, London

Kratzer, Nicolaus (b. 1486/7, d. 1550)—© Photo RMN - Hervé Lewandowski

Kray brothers (act. 1926–2000)—Getty Images - William Lovelace

Krebs, Sir Hans Adolf (1900–1981)—© National Portrait Gallery, London

Kronberger, Hans (1920–1970)—Godfrey Argent Studios / Royal Society

Kropotkin, Peter (1842–1921)—© National Portrait Gallery, London

Kruger, Stephanus Johannes Paulus (1825–1904)—© National Portrait Gallery, London

Kubrick, Stanley (1928–1999)—Getty Images - Hulton Archive

Kuhn, Heinrich Gerhard (1904–1994)—© National Portrait Gallery, London

Kurti, Nicholas (1908–1998)—© reserved; News International Syndication; photograph National Portrait Gallery, London

Kyd, Robert (1746–1793)—© The Natural History Museum, London

Kyle, James Francis (1788–1869)—© National Portrait Gallery, London

Kynaston, Edward (bap. 1643, d. 1712?)—unknown collection / Christie's; photograph National Portrait Gallery, London

Kynynmound, Gilbert Elliot Murray, first earl of Minto (1751–1814)—in the collection of Scottish Borders Council; photograph courtesy the Scottish National Portrait Gallery

Kynynmound, Gilbert Elliot Murray, second earl of Minto (1782–1859)—© National Portrait Gallery, London

Kynynmound, Gilbert John Elliot Murray, fourth earl of Minto (1845–1914)—© The de László Foundation; The British Library

Labouchere, Henry, Baron Taunton (1798–1869)—© National Portrait Gallery, London

Labouchere, Henry Du Pré (1831–1912)—© National Portrait Gallery, London

Lacaita, Sir James Philip (1813–1895)—© National Portrait Gallery, London

Lacey, James Harry (1917–1989)—The Imperial War Museum, London

Lack, David Lambert (1910–1973)—© National Portrait Gallery, London

Lackington, James (1746–1815)—© National Portrait Gallery, London

Lacy, John (c.1615–1681)—The Royal Collection © 2004 HM Queen Elizabeth II

Lacy, Peter (c.1310–1375)—reproduced by courtesy of H. M. Stutchfield, F.S.A., Hon. Secretary of the Monumental Brass Society

Lacy, Thomas Hailes (1809–1873)—V&A Images, The Victoria and Albert Museum

Laidlaw, Sir Patrick Playfair (1881–1940)—© National Portrait Gallery, London

Laidlaw, William (bap. 1779, d. 1845)—Scottish National Portrait Gallery

Laing, Alexander Gordon (1794–1826)—© National Portrait Gallery, London

Laing, David (1793–1878)—Scottish National Portrait Gallery

Laing, Sir John William (1879–1978)—© reserved; private collection

Laing, Ronald David (1927–1989)—HAG; collection National Portrait Gallery, London

Laing, Samuel (1812–1897)—© National Portrait Gallery, London

Lake, Arthur (bap. 1567, d. 1626)—by permission of the Warden and Scholars of Winchester College

Lake, Gerard, first Viscount Lake of Delhi (1744–1808)—© National Portrait Gallery, London

Lake, Sir Henry Atwell (1808–1881)—© National Portrait Gallery, London

Lake, John (bap. 1624, d. 1689)—by permission of the Master and Fellows of St John's College, Cambridge

Laker, James Charles [Jim] (1922–1986)—Getty Images - Hulton Archive

Lamb, Lady Caroline (1785–1828)—Devonshire Collection, Chatsworth. By permission of the Duke of Devonshire and the Chatsworth Settlement Trustees

Lamb, Charles (1775–1834)—© National Portrait Gallery, London

Lamb, Edward Buckton (bap. 1805, d. 1869)—RIBA Library Photographs Collection

Lamb, Elizabeth, Viscountess Melbourne (bap. 1751, d. 1818)—reproduced by kind permission of Lord Ralph Kerr, Melbourne Hall

Lamb, George (1784–1834)—© National Portrait Gallery, London

Lamb, Hubert Horace (1913–1997)—School of Environmental Sciences UEA, Norwich

Lamb, Mary Anne (1764–1847)—© National Portrait Gallery, London

Lamb, William, second Viscount Melbourne (1779–1848)—© National Portrait Gallery, London

Lambarde, William (1536–1601)—© reserved

Lambert, (Leonard) Constant (1905–1951)—© National Portrait Gallery, London

Lambert, Daniel (1770–1809)—Leicestershire Museums and Art Galleries / Bridgeman Art Library

Lambert, George (1699/1700–1765)—© National Portrait Gallery, London

Lambert, James (bap. 1725, d. 1788)—The British Library

Lambert, John (bap. 1619, d. 1684)—private collection

Lambton, John George, first earl of Durham (1792–1840)—© National Portrait Gallery, London

Lamburn, Richmal Crompton (1890–1969)—© National Portrait Gallery, London

La Motte, John (1577–1655)—© National Portrait Gallery, London

Lampe, Geoffrey William Hugo (1912–1980)—photograph reproduced by courtesy of The British Academy

Lampe, John Frederick (1702/3–1751)—© Copyright The British Museum

Lampson, Frederick Locker- (1821–1895)—© National Portrait Gallery, London

Lampson, Miles Wedderburn, first Baron Killearn (1880–1964)—© National Portrait Gallery, London

Lancaster, Joseph (1778–1838)—© National Portrait Gallery, London

Lancaster, Nancy Keene (1897–1994)—© reserved; News International Syndication; photograph National Portrait Gallery, London

Lancaster, Sir Osbert (1908–1986)—© National Portrait Gallery, London

Lancaster, William (1649/50–1717)—© National Portrait Gallery, London

Lancastre Saldanha, Adeline Louisa Maria de, Countess de Lancastre (1824–1915)—The Women's Library, London Metropolitan University

Lanchester, Elsa Sullivan (1902–1986)—© Estate of Doris Clare Zinkeisen; collection National Portrait Gallery, London

Lanchester, George Herbert (1874–1970)—© reserved; photograph National Portrait Gallery, London

Lander, Richard Lemon (1804–1834)—© National Portrait Gallery, London

Landon, Letitia Elizabeth (1802–1838)—© National Portrait Gallery, London

Landor, Walter Savage (1775–1864)—© National Portrait Gallery, London

Landseer, Sir Edwin Henry (1802–1873)—© National Portrait Gallery, London

Landseer, Jessica (1807–1880)—Mackenzie Collection; photograph © National Portrait Gallery, London

Landseer, John George (1763/9–1852)—© National Portrait Gallery, London

Lane, Sir Allen (1902–1970)—© Science & Society Picture Library; photograph National Portrait Gallery, London

Lane, Edward William (1801–1876)—© National Portrait Gallery, London

Lane, Sir Hugh Percy (1875–1915)—courtesy the Hugh Lane Municipal Gallery of Modern Art, Dublin

Lane, Jane, Lady Fisher (d. 1689)—© National Portrait Gallery, London

Lane, Lupino (1892–1959)—© National Portrait Gallery, London

Lanfranc (c.1010–1089)—© The Bodleian Library, University of Oxford

Lang, Andrew (1844–1912)—Scottish National Portrait Gallery

Lang, (William) Cosmo Gordon, Baron Lang of Lambeth (1864–1945)—© National Portrait Gallery, London

Lang, William Henry (1874–1960)—© reserved

Langdale, Marmaduke, first Baron Langdale (bap. 1598, d. 1661)—© National Portrait Gallery, London

Langley, John Newport (1852–1925)—by kind permission of the Department of Physiology, University of Cambridge

Langton, Stephen (c.1150–1228)—Master and Fellows of Corpus Christi College, Cambridge

Langtry, Lillie (1853–1929)—courtesy of The Jersey Heritage Trust

Lanier, Nicholas (bap. 1588, d. 1666)—Kunsthistorisches Museum, Vienna

Lankester, Edwin (1814–1874)—© National Portrait Gallery, London

Lankester, Phebe (1825–1900)—Ipswich Borough Council Museums and Galleries

Lankester, Sir (Edwin) Ray (1847–1929)—© National Portrait Gallery, London

Lansbury, George (1859–1940)—© Estate of Felix H. Man / National Portrait Gallery, London

Lant, Thomas (1554/5–1600/01)—© National Portrait Gallery, London

Lany, Benjamin (1591–1675)—with permission of the Bishop of Lincoln

Larcom, Sir Thomas Aiskew, first baronet (1801–1879)—© National Portrait Gallery, London

Lardner, Dionysius (1793–1859)—private collection; photograph © National Portrait Gallery, London

Lardner, Nathaniel (1684–1768)—© National Portrait Gallery, London